HANDBOOK
OF
INDUSTRIAL
AND
ORGANIZATIONAL
PSYCHOLOGY

CONTRIBUTORS

George W. England, *The University of Minnesota* • Robert Dubin, *University of California, Irvine* • F. Kenneth Berrien, late, *Rutgers University* • John P. Campbell, *The University of Minnesota* • Robert D. Pritchard, *Purdue University* • Russell W. Burris, *The University of Minnesota* • Chris Argyris, *Harvard University* • Thomas D. Cook, *Northwestern University* • Donald T. Campbell, *Northwestern University* • David J. Weiss, *The University of Minnesota* • Thomas J. Bouchard Jr., *The University of Minnesota* • Howard L. Fromkin, *Purdue University* • Siegfried Streufert, *Purdue University* • Marvin D. Dunnette, *The University of Minnesota* • John L. Holland, *The Johns Hopkins University* • Harrison Gough, *University of California, Berkeley* • William A. Owens, *The University of Georgia* • Ernest J. McCormick, *Purdue University* • Alphonse Chapanis, *The Johns Hopkins University* • Patricia C. Smith, *Bowling Green State University* • Robert M. Guion, *Bowling Green State University* • John R. Hinrichs, *International Business Machines Corp.* • Robert D. Finkle, *The Standard Oil Company (Ohio)* • Kenneth Thomas, *University of California, Los Angeles* • Michael Beer, *Harvard University* • John B. Miner, *Georgia State University* • J. Frank Brewer, *University of Maryland* • Jacob Jacoby, *Purdue University* • J. Richard Hackman, *Yale University* • William H. Starbuck, *University of Wisconsin, Milwaukee* • Roy Payne, *University of Sheffield* • Derek S. Pugh, *London Graduate School of Business Studies* • J. Stacy Adams, *University of North Carolina* • George Graen, *University of Illinois* • Edward E. Lawler III, *University of Michigan* • Edwin A. Locke, *University of Maryland* • Joseph E. McGrath, *University of Illinois* • Kenneth R. MacCrimmon, *University of British Columbia* • Ronald N. Taylor, *University of British Columbia* • Victor H. Vroom, *Yale University* • Lyman W. Porter, *University of California, Irvine* • Karlene H. Roberts, *University of California, Berkeley* • Clayton P. Alderfer, *Yale University* • Gerald V. Barrett, *University of Akron* • Bernard M. Bass, *University of Rochester*

HANDBOOK
OF
INDUSTRIAL
AND
ORGANIZATIONAL
PSYCHOLOGY

Marvin D. Dunnette
EDITOR
The University of Minnesota

RAND McNALLY COLLEGE PUBLISHING COMPANY

Chicago

Current printing (last digit)
15 14 13 12 11 10 9 8 7 6 5 4 3

Copyright © 1976 by Rand McNally College Publishing Company
All Rights Reserved
Printed in U.S.A.
Library of Congress Catalog Card Number: 74-18664

PREFACE

According to Ferguson,[1] Industrial Psychology had its beginning on December 20, 1901, when Walter Dill Scott gave a short talk before a group of Chicago businessmen about psychology's potential uses in advertising. Over the next year, Scott expanded on his theme by writing a dozen magazine articles. The articles were combined in 1903 to form the first book in applied psychology, *The Theory of Advertising.*

Industrial and organizational psychology has expanded startlingly over the nearly seventy-five years since then. As I prepared to write these comments, I glanced at the contents of the most recent issues of thirteen of the most significant journals relevant to research and practice in industrial and organizational psychology. Here is a sampling of the titles contained in those particular issues:

- Relationship Between Consumers' Category Width and Trial of New Products: A Reappraisal
- Functional Job Analysis: An Approach to a Technology for Manpower Planning
- The Small Company, EEOC, and Test Validation Alternatives: Do You Know Your Options?
- Some Correlates of Organization Effectiveness

- Basic Strategy and Expectation in Casino Blackjack
- Life Style, Organization Structure, Congruity, and Job Satisfaction
- Attitudes of College Men Toward Working Wives
- Decision Processes of Baseball Batters
- Building Organizational Commitment: The Socialization of Managers in Work Organizations
- Organizational Development: Some Problems and Proposals
- Further Studies of the Human Observer as a Statistical Decision Maker
- Designing Preemployment Training for the Hard to Employ: A Cross-Cultural Psychological Approach
- Behavior Modification and Absenteeism: Intervention in One Industrial Setting
- Employing the Disadvantaged: Lessons from the Last Decade
- Sensitivity Training: An Established Management Development Tool?
- Epidemiology of Ski Injuries: The Effect of Method of Skill Acquisition and Release Binding on Accident Rates
- A Factor Analytic Test of the Porter-Lawler Expectancy Model of Work Motivation
- Employee Assistance Program for Alcoholism and Drug Abuse: An Industry Approach
- Sex Roles and Leadership: Perceptions of the Leaders and the Led

[1] Ferguson, L. W. The development of industrial psychology. In B. von Haller Gilmer (Ed.), *Industrial Psychology.* New York: McGraw-Hill, 1961.

• Sleep Deprivation Effects on the Vestibular Habituation Process
• Effectiveness of Paraprofessionals: The Evidence
• The Bases and Use of Power in Organizational Decision Making: The Case of a University
• Executives' Guide to Computer Based Planning

The above titles show how broad the field has become. They show, too, that industrial and organizational psychology has broadened its concern to include many highly relevant social issues and questions, ranging from such matters as equal employment opportunity, alcoholism and drug abuse, work motivation, and organizational effectiveness to such intriguing problems as basic strategies in Casino Blackjack, decision processes by baseball batters, and the epidemiology of ski injuries. In addition, the above titles show the degree to which industrial and organizational psychology has become a blend of practice, theory, and research rather than being simply a technology or trade as it was for so many years.

Such a breadth of subject matter presented a serious challenge to successfully represent the entire domain of industrial and organizational psychology within the covers of a single handbook. I did not believe in 1970, when this all began, that any one person could properly select the subjects to be included in the *Handbook* without seriously distorting the sampling plan to fit his own particular areas of knowledge and bias. Fortunately, the distinguished panel of industrial and organizational psychologists[2] who served as associate editors did much to help me keep the coverage broad enough to represent the entire field. Any sampling deficiencies which remain are, of course, my own responsibility. Nonetheless,

I greatly appreciate my colleagues' counsel and advice during the early planning phases of this project; and, even more, their persuasiveness in "lining up" the very best psychologists to participate in this enterprise.

As should be apparent from a perusal of the names of the forty-five authors of the thirty-seven chapters of this *Handbook,* we made every effort to obtain scholars of diverse training and institutional affiliations. Thus, institutions from all areas of this country are represented as well as two in England and one in Canada. Moreover, these contributors represent twenty-eight different academic and industrial organizations. The table below shows also that authors' affiliations reflect quite well the increasingly varied loci of Industrial/Organizational psychology within academia:

	Number of Authors
Academic Locus	
Psychology Department	22
Business School Department	15
Other Behavioral Science Department	2
Business Firm Locus	5

One of the most gratifying aspects of this five-year effort has been that our original chapter plan survived almost intact. In only four instances did invited contributors withdraw after having initially agreed to do a chapter. In two of these four cases, we were able to secure the participation of equally qualified replacements on quite short notice. In the other two cases, we were able to incorporate their subject matter into other chapters, thereby avoiding any serious loss of subject matter representation.

In our first letters to selected contributors, we described our hopes for the *Handbook* as follows:

As you can see, the plan is to produce a *Handbook* that is broad in scope, giving strong emphases to both conceptual and methodo-

[2] The Associate Editors include George W. England of The University of Minnesota, John P. Campbell of The University of Minnesota, Robert M. Guion of Bowling Green State University, and J. Richard Hackman of Yale University.

logical issues relevant to the study of industrial and organizational behavior. Moreover, we hope the outline reflects accurately our desire to cover substantive issues at both individual and organizational levels and to reflect both theory and practice. Most important, it is our most fervent hope that the *Handbook,* when it appears, will not only be up to date, but ahead of its time, and that it will be pacesetting and guide the development of industrial and organizational psychology in the remaining years of this century.

Only time will determine how well these lofty ambitions have been realized.

Truly, the task could not have been completed without much good help from many fine persons. My associate editors were instrumental in helping to plan the *Handbook's* content, suggesting and contacting authors, and keeping in touch with them to help keep things moving.

The many contributing authors came through magnificently. Not only did they meet their commitments by writing excellent, original chapters in their special areas of expertise, but they also showed constant enthusiasm and continuing willing cooperation even in the face occasionally of editorial criticism from. me that now and then suffered from a degree of brusqueness not usual among peers. Each author worked hard and long with little additional compensation to supplement the "honor" of doing a chapter. I thank them all very warmly for agreeing so willingly to create this *Handbook* with me.

I have had the good fortune over the last three years to enjoy indispensable assistance from Mary Towner. She has typed and re-typed manuscripts, handled all correspondence with authors and editors, arranged to obtain all required permissions, sent galleys here and there, and otherwise relieved me of all sorts of the most vexing chores.

I have had the privilege, too, of working with two absolutely first-rate editorial assistants, Gay Perkins and Leaetta Hough.

I express my special gratitude to them for editing and shortening some of the longer chapters in order to meet space constraints imposed by production requirements of our publisher—and for being able to do such a task without eliciting so much as a murmur of protest from the authors whose chapters they edited.

Finally, I express special thanks to Mrs. Ann Jablin, our Rand McNally editor, who so conscientiously shepherded this entire project through all phases of production, from manuscript to bound book.

This task has taken far too long, nearly twice the time I originally anticipated. As a result, hardly a place I've been over these last five years does not carry with it an association related to some particular chapter of this *Handbook.* I've read and edited various drafts of chapters and other materials in Bogota, Colombia, Seoul, Korea, Paradise Island, Vancouver, Toronto, Washington, D.C., Berkeley, New York City, Snowmass, Colorado, and my hometown of Austin, Minnesota. Manuscripts, or portions of them, have been with me during all sorts of circumstances while doing all sorts of things— at conventions, symposia, and professional gatherings; on skiing, shelling, sunning, and camping vacations; while consulting, partying, mingling, loving, cavorting, and traipsing.

Tomorrow is a Monday, the beginning of a new work week. This will be the first Monday of nearly the last 250 that sees no new writing, editing, or reading requirements for the *Handbook of Industrial and Organizational Psychology.* I rather like the feeling. It's nice to contemplate what those places and those activities may be like when no manuscripts are there lying all around me.

Marvin D. Dunnette
Minneapolis, Minnesota
February, 1975

CONTENTS

LIST OF FIGURES

Chapter 7

Chapter 16

LIST OF TABLES

Toward Fusion

MARVIN D. DUNNETTE
The University of Minnesota

An introductory chapter to a *Handbook* such as this should provide some structure for the reader. He needs to gain both a sense of the scope of the subject matter and the underlying dimensions which carve up that subject matter into more readily digestible subunits.

Industrial and Organizational Psychology's scope is so broad and so diverse that I've been frustrated in my efforts to develop a conceptually satisfying or dimensionally clean structure. The six section headings[1] chosen initially by my associate editors and me seem at least to divide the domain into relatively homogeneous groupings, but now that they're completed, the sections have obviously turned out to be indiscreetly non-discrete. Theories relevant to Industrial and Organizational Psychology are discussed in Section I, but theories and models are presented in all the other sections too. Similarly, methodology, clearly the major subject mat-

ter of Section II, appears in most other sections also. No firm boundaries exist among the six sections. And the boundaries between chapters are even more indistinct. Authors apparently were only moderately constrained by the chapter titles assigned to them.

The eclecticism implied by such fusion is one sign of a maturing discipline, an indication that the knowledge base for solving practical problems, theorizing, or doing research extends over the entire field. No longer is it possible for an Industrial Organizational Psychologist to do a completely effective job if he only knows about individual differences or knows only about psychometrics, or psychological tests, or social and group processes, or structural differences between organizations. The overlapping content in many of the sections and chapters of this *Handbook* is testimony to the melding of fields called for by Leavitt and Bass (1964) in their *Annual Review* chapter of 1964 and to the "marriage" between personnel-differential and social-organizational hoped for by Porter (1966) in his *Annual Review* statement of 1966.

Though gratifying as an indication of increasing maturity for the field as a whole, the wide range of content, overlapping as it does among various chapters, yields no simplifying guidelines to help the reader organize his journey through the *Handbook*.

---

[1] The headings are:

Section I: Conceptual Foundations of Industrial and Organizational Psychology

Section II: Methodological Foundations of Industrial and Organizational Psychology

Section III: Basic Attributes of Individuals in Relation to Behavior in Organizations

Section IV: The Practice of Industrial and Organizational Psychology

Section V: Attributes of Organizations and Their Effects on Organization Members

Section VI: Behavioral Processes in Organizations

A ROADMAP

Instead of trying to create a structure where either none or many may exist, I have used a different approach. I have conducted a crude theme analysis of all thirty-seven chapters of this *Handbook*. The results of this analysis have been converted into the subject matter $\times$ chapter matrix shown in Figure 1. I hope that reference to this matrix may help the reader choose many potentially satisfying routes through the *Handbook*. Figure 1 shows the particular chapters which cover the many areas of industrial and organizational psychology's subject matter. The lightly shaded areas of intersection designate some amount of coverage for a particular subject matter; the blackened areas of intersection designate major or in-depth coverage of a particular subject matter. Thus, Berrien has discussed General Systems theory in depth in Chapter 2, but systems theory concepts also form important features of the authors' formulations in Chapters 19, 25, 27, 28, 35, and 36. Similarly, concepts related to measuring effectiveness and developing criteria are the central theme of Smith's Chapter 17, but many others (Chapters 11, 15, 23, 26, 29, 30, 31, 33, 34) also discuss issues related to the measurement of individual and group performance but with lesser depth and breadth of coverage. In a word, then, the matrix of Figure 1 provides the reader with a crude map to guide him toward gaining a reasonably complete coverage of any area of particular interest to him or her. In addition, by examining the columns of the matrix of Figure 1, the reader will gain a quick overview of the major themes covered in each of the chapters. For example, Beer's Chapter 22, titled "The Technology of Organization Development" is shown in Figure 1 to contain not only an in-depth coverage of various strategies for organizational change but also some coverage of subjects such as organizational diagnosis, models of organization change, organization structure and climate, communication in organizations, and role and boundary influences on members of organizations.

INDUSTRIAL/ORGANIZATIONAL PSYCHOLOGY: PAST AND PRESENT

Figure 1 serves another useful purpose. It represents a rough content analysis of the subjects and themes seen as important by the forty-three authors of these thirty-seven chapters. As such, the subject matter areas emerging from the content analysis constitute a kind of empirically derived listing of what these scholars view as *the* important theories, methods, and practices of Industrial and Organizational Psychology. How does this listing compare with what was contained in Fryer's and Henry's *Handbook of Applied Psychology* (Fryer & Henry, 1950)? Moreover, how does the listing of the present *Handbook*'s subject matter areas compare with the chapter and section headings of current textbooks and books of readings in industrial and organizational psychology?[2] Answers to these two questions may be gleaned from Table 1.

Changes in the field of industrial organizational psychology over the last quarter century are startlingly evident by comparing the contents of the two handbooks. The 1950 *Handbook* was almost exclusively a handbook of *practice,* emphasizing techniques and applications and giving little attention to research or research methodology and no attention at all to theories of individual or organizational behavior. In contrast, the current *Handbook* gives heavy emphasis to strategies of research and re-

[2] The following books were examined to form the listing of contents of current texts and books of readings which appear in Table 1: Bass and Barrett, 1972; Bass and Deep, 1972; Blum and Naylor, 1968; Deci, Gilmer and Korn, 1972; Fleishman and Bass, 1974; French and French, 1973; Fryer and Henry, 1950; Gilmer, 1971; Hamner and Schmidt, 1974; Korman, 1971; Leavitt, Dill, and Eyring, 1973; McCormick and Tiffin, 1974; Perrow, 1972; Scott and Cummings, 1973; Siegel and Lane, 1974; Tosi and Hamner, 1974; Yoder and Heneman, 1974–1975; and Zedeck and Blood, 1974.

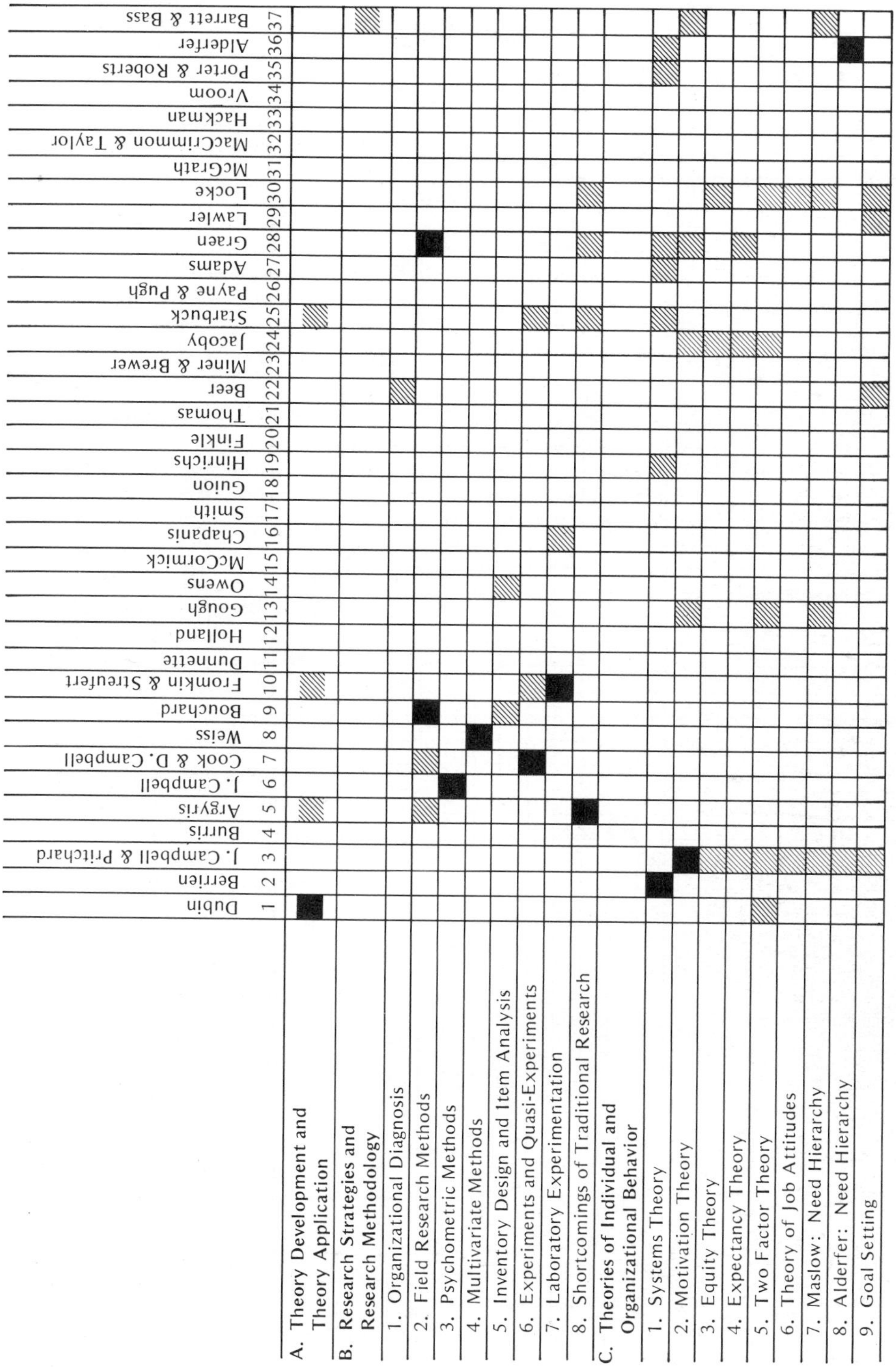

Authors (columns 1–37):

1. Dubin
2. Berrien
3. J. Campbell & Pritchard
4. Burris
5. Argyris
6. J. Campbell
7. Cook & D. Campbell
8. Weiss
9. Bouchard
10. Fromkin & Streufert
11. Dunnette
12. Holland
13. Gough
14. Owens
15. McCormick
16. Chapanis
17. Smith
18. Guion
19. Hinrichs
20. Finkle
21. Thomas
22. Beer
23. Miner & Brewer
24. Jacoby
25. Starbuck
26. Payne & Pugh
27. Adams
28. Graen
29. Lawler
30. Locke
31. McGrath
32. MacCrimmon & Taylor
33. Hackman
34. Vroom
35. Porter & Roberts
36. Alderfer
37. Barrett & Bass

Subject matters (rows):

A. Theory Development and Theory Application

B. Research Strategies and Research Methodology
1. Organizational Diagnosis
2. Field Research Methods
3. Psychometric Methods
4. Multivariate Methods
5. Inventory Design and Item Analysis
6. Experiments and Quasi-Experiments
7. Laboratory Experimentation
8. Shortcomings of Traditional Research

C. Theories of Individual and Organizational Behavior
1. Systems Theory
2. Motivation Theory
3. Equity Theory
4. Expectancy Theory
5. Two Factor Theory
6. Theory of Job Attitudes
7. Maslow: Need Hierarchy
8. Alderfer: Need Hierarchy
9. Goal Setting

Figure 1.   Subject matters covered by various chapters of the *Handbook of Industrial and Organizational Psychology*.

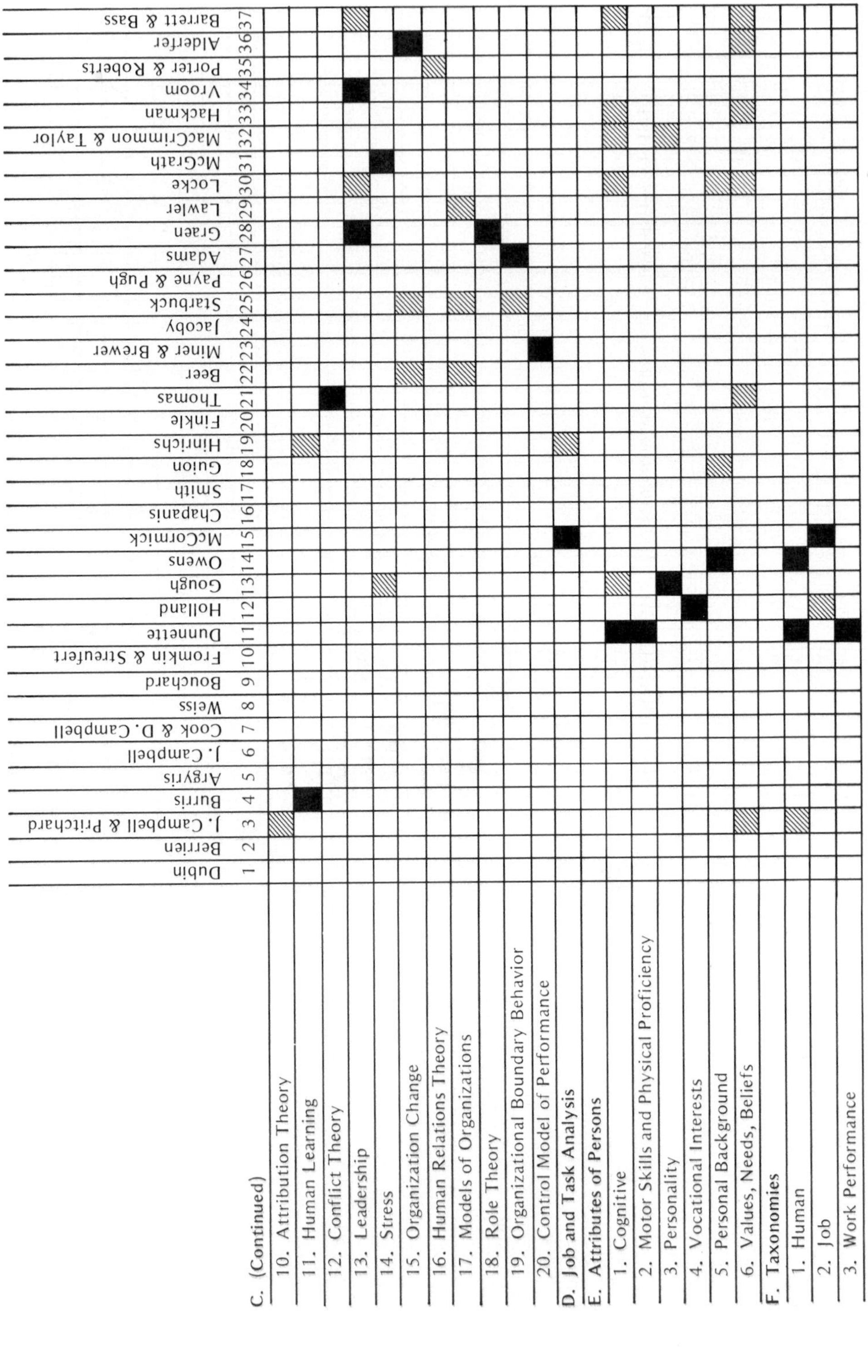

Columns (authors), left to right:

1. Dubin
2. Berrien
3. J. Campbell & Pritchard
4. Burns
5. Argyris
6. J. Campbell
7. Cook & D. Campbell
8. Weiss
9. Bouchard
10. Fromkin & Streufert
11. Dunnette
12. Holland
13. Gough
14. Owens
15. McCormick
16. Chapanis
17. Smith
18. Guion
19. Hinrichs
20. Finkle
21. Thomas
22. Beer
23. Miner & Brewer
24. Jacoby
25. Starbuck
26. Payne & Pugh
27. Adams
28. Graen
29. Lawler
30. Locke
31. McGrath
32. MacCrimmon & Taylor
33. Hackman
34. Vroom
35. Porter & Roberts
36. Alderfer
37. Barrett & Bass

Rows (topics):

C. (Continued)
10. Attribution Theory
11. Human Learning
12. Conflict Theory
13. Leadership
14. Stress
15. Organization Change
16. Human Relations Theory
17. Models of Organizations
18. Role Theory
19. Organizational Boundary Behavior
20. Control Model of Performance

D. Job and Task Analysis

E. Attributes of Persons
1. Cognitive
2. Motor Skills and Physical Proficiency
3. Personality
4. Vocational Interests
5. Personal Background
6. Values, Needs, Beliefs

F. Taxonomies
1. Human
2. Job
3. Work Performance

Figure 1 (continued)

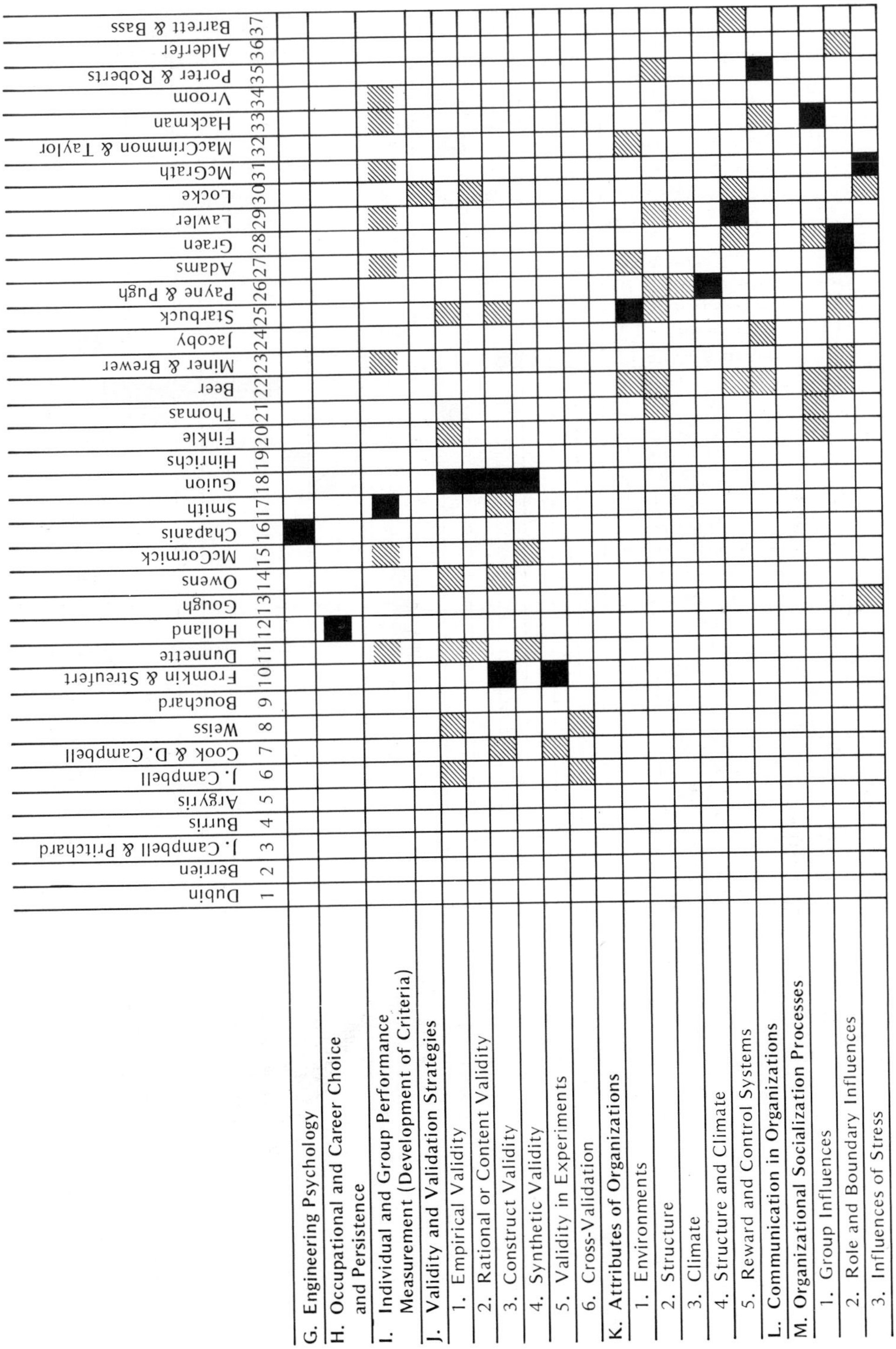

Dubin — 1
Berrien — 2
J. Campbell & Pritchard — 3
Burris — 4
Argyris — 5
J. Campbell — 6
Cook & D. Campbell — 7
Weiss — 8
Bouchard — 9
Fromkin & Streufert — 10
Dunnette — 11
Holland — 12
Gough — 13
Owens — 14
McCormick — 15
Chapanis — 16
Smith — 17
Guion — 18
Hinrichs — 19
Finkle — 20
Thomas — 21
Beer — 22
Miner & Brewer — 23
Jacoby — 24
Starbuck — 25
Payne & Pugh — 26
Adams — 27
Graen — 28
Lawler — 29
Locke — 30
McGrath — 31
MacCrimmon & Taylor — 32
Hackman — 33
Vroom — 34
Porter & Roberts — 35
Alderfer — 36
Barrett & Bass — 37

G. Engineering Psychology
H. Occupational and Career Choice and Persistence
I. Individual and Group Performance Measurement (Development of Criteria)
J. Validity and Validation Strategies
1. Empirical Validity
2. Rational or Content Validity
3. Construct Validity
4. Synthetic Validity
5. Validity in Experiments
6. Cross-Validation
K. Attributes of Organizations
1. Environments
2. Structure
3. Climate
4. Structure and Climate
5. Reward and Control Systems
L. Communication in Organizations
M. Organizational Socialization Processes
1. Group Influences
2. Role and Boundary Influences
3. Influences of Stress

Figure 1 (continued)

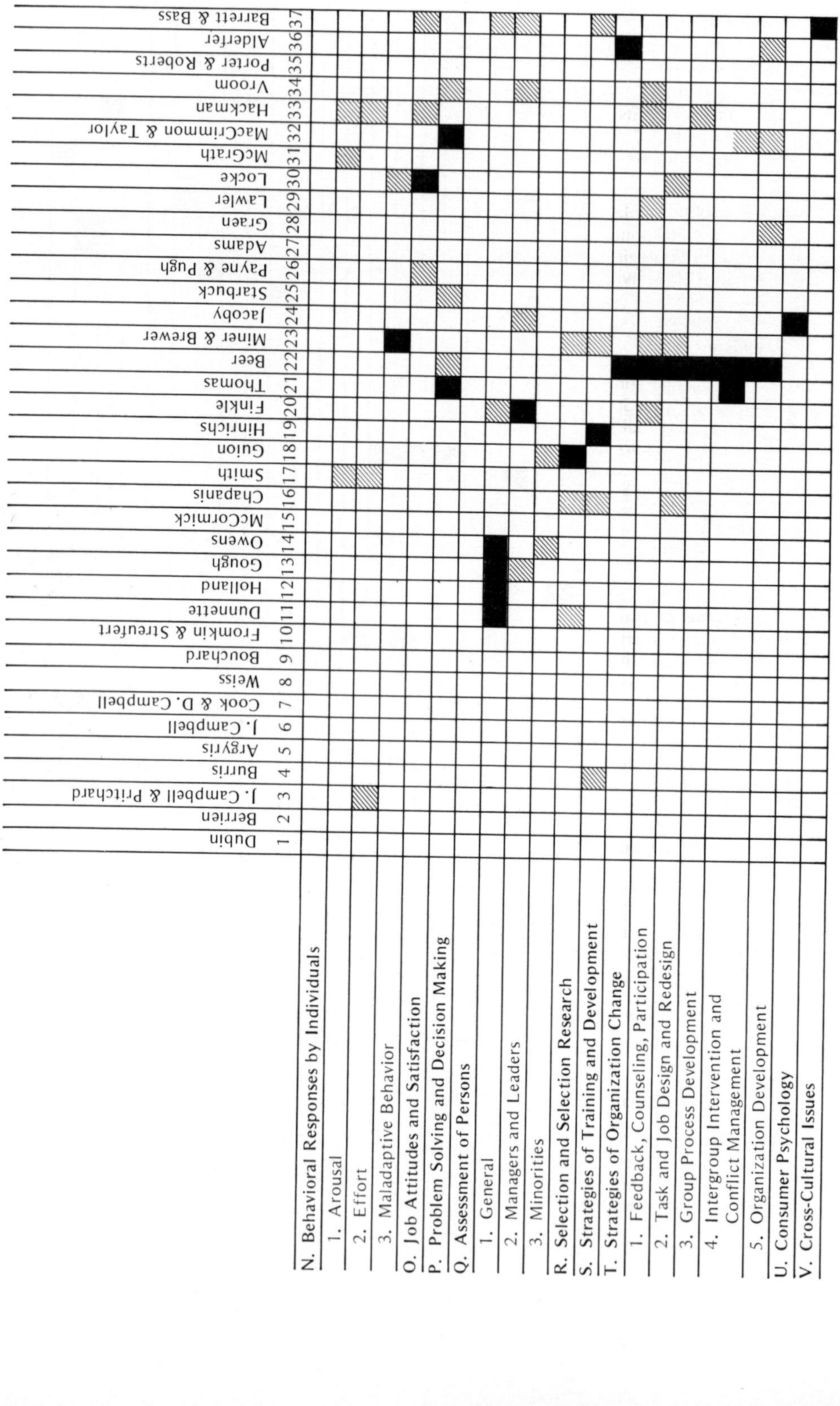

Authors (columns, numbered 1–37):

1. Dubin
2. Berrien
3. J. Campbell & Pritchard
4. Burris
5. Argyris
6. J. Campbell
7. Cook & D. Campbell
8. Weiss
9. Bouchard
10. Fromkin & Streufert
11. Dunnette
12. Holland
13. Gough
14. Owens
15. McCormick
16. Chapanis
17. Smith
18. Guion
19. Hinrichs
20. Finkle
21. Thomas
22. Beer
23. Miner & Brewer
24. Jacoby
25. Starbuck
26. Payne & Pugh
27. Adams
28. Graen
29. Lawler
30. Locke
31. McGrath
32. MacCrimmon & Taylor
33. Hackman
34. Vroom
35. Porter & Roberts
36. Alderfer
37. Barrett & Bass

Topics (rows):

N. Behavioral Responses by Individuals
  1. Arousal
  2. Effort
  3. Maladaptive Behavior
O. Job Attitudes and Satisfaction
P. Problem Solving and Decision Making
Q. Assessment of Persons
  1. General
  2. Managers and Leaders
  3. Minorities
R. Selection and Selection Research
S. Strategies of Training and Development
T. Strategies of Organization Change
  1. Feedback, Counseling, Participation
  2. Task and Job Design and Redesign
  3. Group Process Development
  4. Intergroup Intervention and Conflict Management
  5. Organization Development
U. Consumer Psychology
V. Cross-Cultural Issues

Figure 1 (continued)

TABLE 1
COMPARISON OF MAJOR AREAS OF COVERAGE
IN THE "HANDBOOK OF INDUSTRIAL AND ORGANIZATIONAL PSYCHOLOGY" (1976),
THE "HANDBOOK OF APPLIED PSYCHOLOGY" (1950),
AND TYPICAL CHAPTER AND SECTION TITLES
IN CURRENT INDUSTRIAL
AND ORGANIZATIONAL PSYCHOLOGY TEXTBOOKS
AND BOOKS OF READINGS

I. **Handbook of Industrial and Organizational Psychology (1976)**
   A. Theory Development and Theory Application
   B. Research Strategies and Research Methodology
   C. Theories of Individual and Organizational Behavior
   D. Job and Task Analysis
   E. Attributes of Persons
   F. Taxonomies
   G. Engineering Psychology
   H. Occupational and Career Choice and Persistence
   I. Individual and Group Performance Measurement (Development of Criteria)
   J. Validity and Validation Strategies
   K. Attributes of Organizations
   L. Communication in Organizations
   M. Organizational Socialization Processes
   N. Behavioral Responses by Individuals
   O. Job Attitudes and Satisfaction
   P. Problem Solving and Decision Making
   Q. Assessment of Persons
   R. Selection and Selection Research
   S. Strategies of Training and Development
   T. Strategies of Organization Change
   U. Consumer Psychology
   V. Cross-Cultural Issues

II. **Handbook of Applied Psychology (1950)**
   A. Group Living
   B. Individual Efficiency
   C. The Individual Adjusting to His Environment
   D. Techniques of Personnel Psychology
   E. Selection and Training
   F. Industrial Psychology
   G. Transportation
   H. Business Psychology
   I. Educational Adjustment
   J. Fields of Educational Psychology
   K. Clinical Psychology
   L. Fields of Clinical Psychology
   M. Penology
   N. Consulting Psychology
   O. Contributions of Psychology to the Professions
   P. Contributions of Psychology to the Arts
   Q. Administration of Psychological Services
   R. The Professional Psychologist

III. **Content of Current Textbooks and Books of Readings in Industrial and Organizational Psychology**
   A. Research Methodology
   B. Theories of Behavior
   C. Job Analysis
   D. Psychological Testing
   E. Training

TABLE 1 (continued)

F. Motivation
G. Job Satisfaction
H. Performance Criteria
I. Leadership
J. Human Relations
K. Selection Techniques
L. Special Groups (Executives, Minorities, Females, etc.)
M. Organizational Attributes
N. Individual Adjustment
O. Labor-Management Relations
P. Effecting Organization Change
Q. Work Environment (Safety, Accidents, etc.)
R. Consumer Research
S. Organization Development
T. Social-Psychological Processes
U. Reward and Control Systems

search methodology, theories of behavior, and very strong emphasis to organizational characteristics and the impact of social psychological forces and influences involving interaction processes between organizations and persons. Research and theory are highlighted in the current volume. Practice, though strongly present too, is presented in a much different context than it was in the 1950 volume. Today, we see practice emerging from the knowledge base developed out of research and theory. In 1950, practice was technique-oriented and cookbookish. Practice is still carried out in an atmosphere of behavioral applications in response to individual and organizational problems, but today it is much less apt to be merely an end in itself. A major thrust of what the forty-three authors of the present *Handbook* are saying is that research, practice, and theory in industrial organizational psychology are interdependent and that they will become more so in the years ahead. Practices and techniques are derived from research and theory and they also contribute further data to fuel the enterprises of research and theory development. Research methodology in industrial organizational psychology is well advanced. Theorizing is at an earlier stage of development, but its presence in industrial organizational psychology is expansive and its emerging maturity in the form of increasing rigor is reassuring. Perhaps the

most significant and most hopeful trend apparent from this comparison between the two handbooks, therefore, is the discovery of the healthy state of symbiosis which is seen to have emerged between our practices, our research, and our theories.

Also of interest is the additional indication—gained from comparing current contents of I/O textbooks with the *Handbook's* subject matter—that this state of symbiosis is probably reflected better in the *Handbook* than in most currently available textbooks or readers. Research methodology and strategies of research are given much deeper attention and greatly increased breadth of coverage in the *Handbook*. Various theories are covered in detail, and many of the authors are presenting new conceptualizations for the first time. In addition, most topical areas covered by various current texts or books of readings also receive good coverage. The major spots where gaps occur involve either special groups, particular techniques or instruments, or topics so specialized as to require fuller coverage than seemed feasible for this *Handbook*. The following "gaps" illustrate the points made in the immediately preceding statement:

• No extensive coverage is given to groups such as women, minorities, the disadvantaged, or to particular occupational subgroups.

- No separate attention is given to such practices as employment interviewing, the use of particular tests or inventories, or a variety of other personnel management procedures and techniques. Readers will find personnel management procedures dealt with in detail in the eight volumes of the *ASPA Handbook of Personnel and Industrial Relations* (Yoder & Heneman, 1974–1975).
- Although implicit to the content of the chapter on Engineering Psychology (Chapter 16), no explicit attention is given to questions involving work fatigue, safety, or accident behavior.
- Finally, labor-management relations are not the central subject of any chapter, though, of course, several chapters include important sections (such as conflict management, problem solving and decision making, leadership theory, etc.) which have obvious implications for the type of group process and negotiation issues which are involved in management-labor interrelationships.

INDUSTRIAL/ORGANIZATIONAL PSYCHOLOGY: SCIENTIFIC INQUIRY

The subject matter analysis shown in Figure 1 proves useful in still another way. If we think of industrial organizational psychology as a field of scientific inquiry (as I prefer), we may examine its subject matter according to the problem-solving processes of discovery, justification, and application common to sciences. Figure 2 portrays a simplified model of problem detection and problem-solving processes and shows how different areas of this *Handbook*'s industrial organizational subject matter apply to each. The figure illustrates six steps of scientific problem solving. The six steps are connected in a circular way in order to denote the never ending feature of scientific discovery and application. Applied to industrial and organizational settings, the six steps involve the following:

I. *OBSERVE*. Behavioral observations are made of individuals and organizations in natural settings. Presumably, some standard exists of expected behavioral consequences, and the behavior is monitored in order to detect deviations from standard or to audit the effects, if any, of changes which may have been introduced. At this stage, observation may be systematic or haphazard, but it is not typically experimental or explicitly oriented toward hypothesis testing. The areas related to this sort of observation are dealt with best under B1: Organization Diagnosis; B2: Field Research Methods; and B6: Experiments and Quasi-Experiments, of this *Handbook*.

II. *DETECT AND MEASURE*. The presence of a standard or criterion against which behavior may be evaluated during the observational process obviously implies measurement of some type, sufficient, at least, to indicate whether deviations are great enough to be defined as problems in need of correction or changes of interest to the investigator. Issues related to the methodology of developing measurement and questions related to dependent variables which might be of greatest interest are dealt with under I: Development of Criteria; L: Communication in Organizations; N: Behavioral Responses by Individuals; O: Job Attitudes and Satisfaction; and P: Problem Solving and Decision Making, of this *Handbook*.

III. *SPECULATE AND SPECIFY*. The usual next step in the process of scientific problem solving is to develop hypotheses about areas which may involve causal agents related to the problems under investigation. This is the point at which the investigator's familiarity with existing theory and knowledge is crucial. Obviously, not much other than shotgun problem-solving efforts can be brought to bear unless the scientist-investigator has at his disposal a useful repertoire of existing theory and accumulated knowledge. As a result of his speculation, the investigator typically will specify areas in which additional information will need to be gathered or developed. Issues related to hypothesis and theory development, theory, knowledge, and specifying what is needed are dealt with under A: Theory Development and Theory Applica-

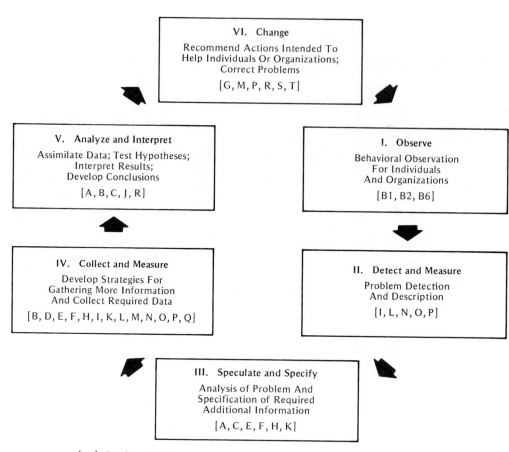

[   ] Brackets indicate relevant subject matter areas; refer to Figure 1 for titles.

Figure 2.   Processes of observation, detection, justification, and application in Industrial/Organizational Psychology.

tion; C: Theories of Individual and Organizational Behavior; E: Attributes of Persons; F: Taxonomies; H: Occupational and Career Choice and Persistence; and K: Attributes of Organizations, of this *Handbook*.

IV. *COLLECT AND MEASURE.* Once the information required for illuminating the problem has been specified, strategies must be devised for collecting the information in a form which will lend itself readily to careful analysis and interpretation during Step V. The investigator, at Step IV, must, therefore, have an excellent grasp not only of research methodology and data gathering methods, but must also be well equipped substantively to handle special data collection problems within particular areas and sub-domains. Methodological matters related to gathering information in industrial organizational psychology are covered in many subject areas of this *Handbook* including at least the following: B: Research Strategies and Research Methodology; D: Job and Task Analysis; E: Attributes of Persons; F: Taxonomies; H: Occupational and Career Choice and Persistence; I: Development of Criteria; K: Attributes of Organizations; L: Communication in Organizations; M: Organizational Socialization Processes; N: Behavioral Responses by Individuals; O: Job Attitudes and Satisfaction; P: Problem Solving and Decision Making; and Q: Assessment of Persons.

V. *ANALYZE AND INTERPRET*. Next, the investigator uses the best means at his disposal to interpret his data. Here, he is guided by methodology and by theory and he may, in the process of "working" his data, develop and test new hypotheses, models, or theories. The industrial organizational psychologist should find the *Handbook* methodological subject areas of B: Research Strategies and Research Methodology; J: Validity and Validation Strategies; and R: Selection and Selection Research especially helpful, as well as the two theory subject matter areas of C: Theories of Individual and Organizational Behavior; and A: Theory Development and Theory Application helpful in this stage of problem solving and discovery.

VI. *CHANGE*. The processes of problem detection, information gathering, information analysis, testing and interpretation lead inevitably to conclusions of some sort. It is the hope of scientists, investigators, and practitioners alike that such conclusions may then yield recommendations for actions to be taken to ameliorate the initial problem or, at least, to change the field in such a way as to suggest the utility of further observation and research. Strategies involving change technology relevant to industrial organizational psychology are dealt with in this *Handbook* in the following subject areas: G: Engineering Psychology; M: Organizational Socialization Processes; P: Problem Solving and Decision Making; R: Selection and Selection Research; S: Strategies of Training and Development; and T: Strategies of Organization Change.

Figure 2 shows, of course, that once efforts have been made to implement recommended changes, the entire process begins anew with observation, monitoring, an orientation toward the detection and measurement of changes in dependent variables, and so on—creating, in effect, an upwardly extending spiral of increased knowledge, bet-

ter theory, and more rigorous methodology, leading to more fully informed and more certain change recommendations as a particular discipline advances.

Obviously, the scheme shown in Figure 2 should not be regarded as invariant. A point of entry may be made at any stage in the process, and in many instances, the steps may be short circuited. For example, action or change recommendations may frequently be made on the basis of existing theory or knowledge as soon as a problem has been defined instead of carrying out the data collection and analysis steps of III, IV, and V. The usefulness of the schema shown in Figure 2 is merely that it portrays the broad activities engaged in by an industrial organizational psychologist in his professional and scientific endeavors. As such, Figure 2 may help readers of this *Handbook* cast the *Handbook*'s subject matter into the contexts provided by their own professional and scientific activities.

INDUSTRIAL ORGANIZATIONAL PSYCHOLOGY: AN ACADEMIC DISCIPLINE

Exactly a decade ago, Guion (1965) expressed his concern that academic industrial psychology too often was simply a mirror of current professional practice. He saw, then, that the pressure was great for narrowing the teaching of industrial psychology to become merely a professional education consisting of telling and showing students how it's done in industry. Guion saw such an emphasis as inappropriate to the academic function, and he argued that:

...the success or failure of industrial psychology must be measured in terms of the degree to which it contributes to repeatable generalizations, well integrated into some reasonably systematic framework, about behavior. (Guion, 1965, p. 817)

Now, a decade later, with publication of this *Handbook of Industrial and Organiza-*

tional Psychology, I believe that success for the field, as envisioned by Guion, is just around the corner. Industrial and Organizational Psychology *is* today an academic discipline, an emerging blend of research, theory, and practice. The blend offers great promise, in the years ahead, for further developing and extending our knowledge of those behavioral processes which are critical to an understanding of interactions between persons and the institutions and organizations of society.

REFERENCES

Bass, B. M., & Barrett, G. V. *Man, work, and organizations.* Boston: Allyn and Bacon, 1972.

Bass, B. M., & Deep, S. D. *Studies in organizational psychology.* Boston: Allyn and Bacon, 1972.

Blum, M. L., & Naylor, J. C. *Industrial psychology: Its theoretical and social foundations.* New York: Harper and Row, 1968.

Deci, E. L., Gilmer, B. von H., & Korn, H. W. *Readings in industrial and organizational psychology.* New York: McGraw-Hill, 1972.

Fleishman, E. A., & Bass, A. R. *Studies in personnel and industrial psychology.* Homewood, Ill.: Dorsey Press, 1974.

French, C. H. Jr., & French, W. L. *Organization development: Behavioral science interventions for organization improvement.* Englewood Cliffs, N.J.: Prentice-Hall, 1973.

Fryer, D. H., & Henry, E. R. *Handbook of applied psychology,* Vols. I & II. New York: Rinehart, 1950.

Gilmer, B. von H. *Industrial and organizational psychology.* New York: McGraw-Hill, 1971.

Guion, R. M. Industrial psychology as an academic discipline. *American Psychologist,* 1965, 20, 815–821.

Hamner, W. C., & Schmidt, F. L. *Contemporary problems in personnel.* Chicago: St. Clair Press, 1974.

Korman, A. K. *Industrial and organizational psychology.* Englewood Cliffs, N.J.: Prentice-Hall, 1971.

Leavitt, H. J., & Bass, B. M. Organizational psychology. In P. H. Mussen & M. R. Rosenzweig (Eds.), *Annual Review of Psychology,* Vol. 15. Palo Alto, Calif.: Annual Reviews, 1964.

Leavitt, H. J., Dill, W. R., & Eyring, H. B. *The organizational world.* New York: Harcourt Brace Jovanovich, 1973.

McCormick, E. J., & Tiffin, J. *Industrial psychology.* (6th ed.) Englewood Cliffs, N.J.: Prentice-Hall, 1974.

Perrow, C. *Complex organizations: A critical essay.* Glenview, Ill.: Scott, Foresman, 1972.

Porter, L. W. Personnel management. In P. R. Farnsworth, O. McNemar, & Q. McNemar (Eds.), *Annual Review of Psychology,* Vol. 17. Palo Alto, Calif.: Annual Reviews, 1966.

Scott, W. E., & Cummings, L. L. *Readings in organizational behavior and human performance.* Homewood, Ill.: Irwin, 1973.

Siegel, L., & Lane, I. M. *Psychology in industrial organizations.* Homewood, Ill.: Irwin, 1974.

Tosi, H. L., & Hamner, W. C. *Organizational behavior and management: A contingency approach.* Chicago: St. Clair Press, 1974.

Yoder, D., & Heneman, H. G. Jr. *ASPA Handbook of personnel and industrial relations.* (8 Vols.) Washington, D.C.: Bureau of National Affairs, 1974–1975.

Zedeck, S., & Blood, M. R. *Foundations of behavioral science research in organizations.* Monterey, Calif.: Brooks/Cole, 1974.

PART ONE

Theoretical and Methodological Foundations of Industrial and Organizational Psychology

SECTION I.

Conceptual Foundations of Industrial and Organizational Psychology

GEORGE W. ENGLAND
The University of Minnesota

INDUSTRIAL AND ORGANIZATIONAL PSYCHOL-
OGY possess no unified and generally accepted theoretical or conceptual base. While
the chapters of the *Handbook* bear eloquent
testimony to this observation, they also suggest a young field composed of many specialties working on diverse and complex
problems. Thus it seems small wonder that
we lack what Kuhn (1962) calls a *scientific
paradigm* which provides a set of rules and
examples specifying of what reality is composed, identifying legitimate problems in
the field, outlining acceptable rules of interpretation and explanation, and setting
forth those puzzles that can be potentially
solved within the framework.

While it seems premature to expect any
general paradigm, the authors in Section I
are treating topics that are essentially conceptual in nature. Dubin in Chapter 1 very
directly confronts the topic of theory building in applied areas. He identifies and illustrates the essential elements of a theoretical
model as consisting of: (a) units or variables of concern, (b) the laws by which
these units interact, (c) the boundaries of
the theory, and (d) the system states within
which the theoretical model is operative.
Within a framework of these essential elements of a theoretical model he focuses on
problems of theory development, prediction
and understanding, theory testing, theory
improvement, and the differing roles of the

theorist and the practical user of theory.
Dubin uses the Herzberg two-factor theory
of job satisfaction to illustrate the elements
of a theoretical model and provides the most
explicit theoretical analysis of the two-factor
theory yet in print.

The late Kenneth Berrien in Chapter 2
illustrates how the approaches of general
systems theorists can be utilized in observing and studying organizations. Defining a
system as a set of components interacting
with each other which are enclosed by a
boundary which selects both the kind and
rate of flow of inputs and outputs to and
from the system, Berrien examines such diverse notions as formal achievement of the
organization; group need satisfaction; organizational stability, adaptability, survival,
and growth. A general systems theory approach to organizations emphasizes an
holistic view of organizations and places
primary importance on exchange processes
within and across system boundaries. The
heuristic value of such thinking is readily
appreciated and its near term impact upon
research, theory, and practice in industrial
and organizational psychology is apt to be
considerable.

In Chapter 3, Campbell and Pritchard
provide a compilation and synthesis of current motivation theory applicable to individual behavior in organizations. They suggest that it is most meaningful to view mo-

15

tivation as a label for the determinants of the *choice to* (a) initiate effort, (b) expend a certain amount of effort, and (c) persist in expending effort over a period of time. Viewed in this way, the impact of aptitude, skill, task understanding, and environmental constraints on performance must be clearly distinguished from that of motivational constructs. The authors distinguish between *process* and *content* theories of motivation and show the historical roots of each type of theory.

The Campbell and Pritchard analysis of available motivation theory leads them to conclude that the main virtue of available models is their heuristic value for suggesting how we allocate our limited research resources. Their list of suggested areas of research concentration include: (a) more knowledge about the outcomes people really want from work, (b) better description and empirical analysis of the process by which individuals choose to expend effort, (c) the development of better measures of the independent and dependent variables utilized by various motivational models, (d) a systematic program of research devoted to the criterion problem in motivational studies, (e) more knowledge about how people orient themselves toward tasks, both in terms of the parameters they use to define them and the processes they use to assign values to them, and (f) greater use of available theoretical tools to examine systematically the processes by which specific practi-

cal procedures work or don't work in practice.

The Burris chapter (4) on Human Learning focuses on defining and discovering how to account for the nature of *productive performance*. Burris identifies the critical learning issues in complex behavior by treating the general areas of performance criteria, learning sequences, learning strategies, instructional modes and media, motivation and individual differences. Burris's approach to human learning is grounded in the practical problems of instruction, training, and personnel development and provides suggestions to many of these problems.

The topics of theory building, general systems theory, human motivation and human learning have been examined as major elements in the conceptual foundations of industrial and organizational psychology. In toto, the chapters suggest considerable progress has been made in the last twenty years. As long as conceptual and empirical efforts in industrial and organizational psychology continue to interact, prospects for the future seem bright.

REFERENCES

Kuhn, T. A. *The structure of scientific revolutions.* Chicago: University of Chicago Press, 1962.

CHAPTER 1

Theory Building in Applied Areas

ROBERT DUBIN

University of California, Irvine

THE PURPOSE OF this chapter is to set forth some guidelines for the construction of theoretical models that have considerable likelihood of being applied to, and utilized in, real-life situations. While the general structure of theory is independent of the practical utility of the model, there are some special contributions that users of theoretical models make to the development of the theory itself. The special roles of users in the theory building processes are emphasized in this summary analysis of the manner in which theories are constructed. The analysis concludes with a description of some of the differences in orientations and purposes of theorists-researchers, on the one hand, and practitioners, on the other hand, together with a statement of some of the dilemmas that develop in the relationships between the two groups.

This chapter will set forth some guidelines for the construction of theories that have immediate and direct application. Industrial psychology is preeminently an applied field and this concern with application changes somewhat the emphasis among the various aspects of theory building. The general structure of theory, however, is the same regardless of whether the theory is intended for immediate application or as an intellectual tool of the scientist.

Of special concern in building applied theory is that practitioners who expect to use some outcomes of the theory can often play a critical role in defining the content of the theoretical model to be developed. The present discussion starts with this consideration, and then moves to a summary analysis of the manner in which theories are built and the characteristics of their components. Particular attention will be given to the way in which contributions to theory building operations may be made by experienced men of affairs.

REAL WORLD ORIGIN

In any applied field, the theory or theories utilized have to confront reality when they are put to the applied test. This issue, a central one, will be discussed in detail below.

Another issue, however, is equally important. That is, the theory's point of origin. It is exceedingly difficult to say something meaningful about the real world without starting in the real world. Observation and description of the real world are the essential points of origin for theories in applied areas like industrial psychology, if not in all areas. Industrial psychology has been especially fortunate since it has, from its earliest development, placed considerable emphasis on good description and observation to provide the data base for the sub-discipline. It is perhaps only in the more recent periods with the tremendous emphasis placed on attitude measurement, that we have been losing touch with the behavioral world in pursuit of the mind-life of men at work.

Work is a human activity and any student of working behavior is simply forced to start with reality. Consequently, there is little need to reinforce the dependence on observation and description among theorists whose intellectual focus is behavior and activity.

A somewhat greater intellectual demand is placed on the researcher to understand the process of induction. Theories, after all, represent levels of generalization beyond a statistical summary of data points. Any generalization that starts from the data points generated by observation and description is arrived at through an inductive process. To report that the amount of autonomy measured in jobs is possibly correlated with workers' measured job satisfaction, is to report the descriptive statement about the data points. What further conclusions the researcher chooses to draw from the correlation depends upon his skill and cleverness in reaching an inductive generalization at a level higher than the correlational conclu-

sion. He may, for example, fancy the notion that requires options in choosing behaviors and if too many options are foreclosed by environmental demands the individual expends energies in defending his remaining options for action. This high expenditure in defensive actions in turn lowers his sense of satisfaction about being in the situation demanding his defensive behavior. Now we have reached an inductive conclusion that is already removed from the data base from which it originates. We have clearly not measured the total options the individual has available to him nor have we measured any aspect of defensive behavior. Nevertheless, having started from sound observation and description, we could be well on the road to developing new theory.

Once the inductive conclusion has been set forth, the next step involves explorations of its implications. We may, for example, formulate the option-defense model in a manner that suggests there is some threshold of number of options below which the reactions of defense come to dominate the orientation of an individual. From such formulation, we can make deductions regarding when that threshold is reached, and the probable shape of the relationship of defensive behavior to the individual's feeling of satisfaction. This deductive process, then, provides us with hypotheses which become the basis for further empirical testing founded in description and observation. There is the possibility that the theory from which the deductions were drawn will not hold up and, therefore, new inductions are necessary to develop a substitute theoretical model.

It is largely in the social sciences that we seem to value *deductive* theorizing much more than *inductive* theorizing. In the natural sciences, inductive theorizing is more highly valued, perhaps because of a strong observational and experimental bias. In the applied field of industrial and organizational psychology, we are forced to do no less than give equal honor to the induction of theory from good observation and description, forced to do so because the applied character of the disciplines involves a consumer group—men of affairs—who usually possess a good descriptive knowledge of their affairs and can test our theorizing against the real world they know. This makes inductive theorists of us regardless of our own preferences in the matter.

THE APPLIED BIAS

The demand that theory be useful clearly characterizes a field like industrial psychology. Executives in organizations are particularly concerned that they make their managerial decisions affecting people on sensible grounds, and even prefer that these be theoretically respectable grounds, if the theory makes sense. There is a strong desire to be "scientific" in fulfilling the managerial responsibilities, providing the science is useful.

The demands of management "science" place an interesting burden on the scientist to respond. The effective response is to address the scientific theories to the analytical problems characterizing managerial decision making. Thus, an immediate limitation is imposed on the scientist who is concerned with making his science useful to practitioners. There has to be a market orientation for the theory, and only then will there be some reason to believe that the theory will be applied, and hopefully found useful in guiding affairs of men. This does not mean, however, that industrial psychologists are not capable of, or even interested in, pursuing theoretical concerns that do not converge with the practical interests of consumers of their work. Indeed, so-called basic research and "fundamental" theory may have the highest priority for a substantial proportion of those who practice industrial psychology. Nevertheless, as an examination of the contents of this volume clearly reveals, most of the research and theorizing done in the field of industrial psychology is with the intent that the good results be used in affecting and improving work organizations.

Having said that the theorist is limited by the kind of problems to which an executive is willing to address himself does not mean that the industrial psychologist has "sold out" to the Establishment. This is a common charge made by certain critics of modern social science, usually from a leftist political position. This is patent nonsense and one has only to review the history of applied sciences (especially industrial psychology) in socialist countries to realize that the ideological orientation of the Establishment officialdom does not determine the contribution of the applied scientist. For example, all the standard problems that work organizations encounter in capitalist societies are also encountered in socialist societies where technology is comparable. It turns out that the industrial psychologists in both economies deal with essentially the same problems and, interestingly enough, use very comparable theoretical models to make analytical sense of these problems. We may conclude that the applied scientist has to make sense to the practitioners who consume his results. But making sense, and being committed to the same ideological position, are not identical.

More interesting in the relationship between a scientist and a practitioner using the product of science is the issue of how the analytical problem gets defined. This is the central issue around which the distinction between scientist and practitioner may be drawn. If the practitioner was acutely capable of analyzing his own problem, then his logical analysis and broad experience should have provided him with a wide range of alternative solutions. But it does not quite work that way, and for very good reasons. The practitioner defines the world he experiences in terms of his deep but narrow range of knowledge about it. Very often he may diagnose a problem from its symptom by reference to a model from which he may make a prediction concerning how to correct the undesirable symptom. For example, absenteeism as a symptom can suggest an underlying model that says explicit behavioral rules, reinforced by appropriate sanctions, amplify compliant behavior. A practitioner might, therefore, tighten up the rules governing absence from work and predict that that would lead to the lowering of absenteeism. The scientist who is alerted to the problem of absenteeism may formulate it analytically in different terms as, for example, an aspect of the processes linking individual with organization, with absenteeism being a voluntary break in the linkage by the individual. The scientist would then analyze the circumstances generating such a condition by focusing on the processes involved. The practitioner has limited his attention to symptoms, and usually employs a preexisting model to indicate how the symptoms should be treated. It is precisely this difference of constructing a model, rather than using a preexisting model that distinguishes the industrial psychologist, or any applied scientist, from the practitioner. Indeed, the field of operations research developed on the premise that the scientist was better off being ignorant about what practitioners thought about a problem since such ignorance permitted the scientist to adopt a very distinctive perspective on presenting symptoms of a practical problem to be solved (Morse & Kimball, 1951).

The point of initial congruence between the practitioner and the theorist lies in their sharing of a common body of symptoms defined by the practitioner as revealing an undesirable situation. The practitioner is concerned with improving the situation. The scientist is concerned, from that point on, with building a model of how the situation that produced the undesirable symptoms came into being. The scientist joins with the practitioner in their mutual appreciation that the symptoms indicate something is wrong. The practitioner is ready to do something about it. The scientist's task is to make sense out of the situation producing the symptoms in a manner that is respectable from his own standpoint and convincing to the practitioner as well.

Thus, after the initial point of contact where characteristics of the situation are shared between practitioner and scientist, a wide divergence may occur between the two, until such time as the scientist is in a position to present to the practitioner a model of the situation or behavior that provides evidence of possible improvement of the symptoms. As we will emphasize later, there are points of continuing contact in which significant contributions can be made by the practitioner to the scientific enterprise. These contributions, however, are of a very special sort and constitute resources utilized by the scientist rather than a direct collaboration in doing the scientific thing.

The definition of a problem confronted by a practitioner is in itself an interesting process. The essential nature of a practitioner's "problem" is that he made a prediction, embodied in a particular decision, that was not fulfilled. The consequence is that something else needs to be done in order that the same or related prediction will, indeed, be fulfilled in a succeeding repetition of the event. Problem, in this sense, says that the prediction has gone awry. This is hardly an analytical problem. It simply says that the decision maker does not know enough about a situation, and does not have an alternative capable of coping with an undesirable outcome.

From the standpoint of the scientist, the notion of problem has a totally different meaning. He sees the analytical problem in terms of his concern about the relationship between two or more interacting things about which his curiosity is aroused. The scientist's concern is to model this relationship in some sensible way so that if, in the empirical world, he can measure the characteristics of the relationship, a prediction made about the interaction will have a reasonable probability of being accurate. Thus, for the scientist, the analytical problem is to make sense of the unknown.

At still another crucial point the scientist parts company with the man of affairs. Scientists are interested in understanding as well as predicting about the real world. Understanding for the scientist focuses attention on *processes* of interaction among the variables or units he chooses to consider. For him, understanding processes may be as crucial as his ability to predict outcomes. Indeed, the philosopher of science, Bergmann, has made "process knowledge" the center of science (Bergmann, 1957). Thus, for the industrial psychologist, the learning of norms of work behavior may center his analytical attention on learning and socialization processes (e.g., rote learning of task elements, or "internalization" of work norms) that contribute to an understanding of what is going on in the real world for which these processes are models. For the practitioner, this process knowledge is not relevant. He wants to be able to predict that a given teaching method will result in employees learning norms of work behavior with a minimum of time involved and error in outcome.

The scientist's and practitioner's views of what constitutes a "problem" clearly differ. The practitioner operates with a finite world and continually grounds his decisions and predictions about how that finite world will be ordered. Problems occur when the predictions go wrong and decisions deriving from the predictions become inaccurate. The scientist looks at the same world as an interesting, disordered array of interacting things and zeroes in only when his interest is captured by the relationships he thinks might exist among these things. Absenteeism is a problem to a business executive because he would like to make decisions based on a prediction that would mean low absenteeism for his organization. For the scientist, the nature of an individual's attachment to an organization may be his analytical problem and he views absenteeism as a form of temporary disengagement, the reasons for which is one of his analytical tasks to discover.

In the very process of pursuing an analytical problem, the scientist may have little concern with whether, in the end, a better decision will be produced for the practitioner. Whether the practitioner will benefit may

indeed be problematical. On the other hand, there is no reason for the scientist to be surprised if his findings turn out to have high utility in the real world of decision. In the convergence between the practitioner's interest and the scientist's concern, it is more likely that the practitioner will be in hot pursuit of the scientist, rather than the other way around. The benefits of their cooperation are clearly one-sided, since the scientist could probably do his science without the practitioner, but the practitioner is more likely to be a better one if he grounds his decisions in good scientific models. It is perhaps for this reason that, given the growth of a scientific management in both capitalist and socialist economies, there has come a broadening recognition that scientists, including social scientists, have utility in providing a knowledge base for the better management of work and other organizations.

There is an obvious additional issue of the scientist as consultant to the practitioner. Since many industrial psychologists are also consultants, it may be worthwhile simply to mention the fact that, typically, a consultant is a substitute decision maker rather than a scientist. The occasion for hiring a consultant is that the man of affairs believes the consultant knows something that he does not. The consultant is hired whose expertise has resulted from his professional knowledge (including his scientific knowledge). In the role of substitute decision maker, the scientist-turned-consultant may indeed have more knowledge, better knowledge, or different knowledge than the practitioner. But the consultant's role is fundamentally a substitute decision-making role and, in this capacity, the scientist as consultant claims his fee on the basis that his knowledge about alternative decisions is better than the knowledge of those who receive his advice. When the scientist becomes a consultant, he transforms an analytical problem of science into an operating problem of management. The roles of scientist and consultant are not antithetical. They are simply different. There is no point in confusing or trying to disguise the difference by saying that when the scientist consults he is being scientific. He is not.

BEHAVIORAL SCIENCE AS MORALITY

Behavioral science theories have a special audience far broader than that of the behavioral science fraternity. The very subject matter of such theories makes them of interest to men of affairs and especially the executives and managers of organizations. Their most immediate interest is grounded in the possibility that the theories developed by social scientists will be useful in the management of organizations. Insofar as the models developed are understood by laymen, and, insofar as the models are incorporated into the thinking of laymen, they become the basis for decision and thereby directly influence the operations of organizations. Indeed, in a broader sense, the comprehension of scientific models by rank-and-file members of work organizations as well as by management may also influence the decisions taken by the rank and file with respect to their own working behavior. Of course, efforts are being made by industrial psychologists, acting as consultants, to maximize the opportunity for practical people to understand industrial psychology models and to learn to apply them in the conduct of daily affairs.

There is another use that practitioners make of theoretical models that is often disguised and not clearly understood, yet has a very real function in linking the intellectual with the practical man. I refer to the role of theoretical models in providing a moral justification for decision making and managerial behavior. We live in a highly secular world. The morality of the Judeo-Christian tradition is no longer the consensual boundary within which practical decisions are taken in the operation and management of work organizations. Secular man, even though he is an executive and decision maker, is very much in need of

moral guidelines within which to make his decisions. In the modern world there is a clear-cut preference for knowledge and, hopefully, scientific knowledge as an important ingredient in decision making. Scientists in the modern urban-industrial world have been elevated to the role of philosophers to the kings. The doctrines they propound, of the virtues of truth as revealed by scientific inquiry, become the moral justification by which anything labeled "scientific" may be used as the grounds for decisions.

Put another way, the scientist is the lay theologian for a secular world that has forsaken the "impractical" traditional morality. Today's rational organizational decision makers avidly seek moral justification for their actions and are only too ready to see the new morals in the scientific theories of the applied behavioral scientists. Could there be a more lofty moral purpose for a businessman than to provide his employees with opportunities for self-actualization? Never mind that if some employees achieve self-actualization in organizationally appropriate ways they might be more productive. Both the boss and his minions can bask in the moral sunshine of having "done good" in providing opportunities for and in realizing self-actualization.

Once this phenomenon is recognized, it becomes easier to understand how simple theories can often be widely accepted by practitioners at the very moment that they come under questioning and dispute among scientists. Likert, for example, is more honored among practitioners than he is among fellow scientists for his contributions to the understanding of industrial behavior. Maslow is honored among practitioners for having set forth a very simple model of motivation that has peculiarly attractive features when utilized in the industrial setting, although very little scientific inquiry has been directed at testing this model.

The question that needs answering is why do these large models of working behavior gain such ready currency among practitioners? The answer lies in the fact that there is as much morality as science in these models. Or rather, there is morality as well as science in these models. For example, the model of job enlargement is offered as a way of expanding the range of incentives available to encourage working input on the part of the individual. Job enlargement is attractive from a managerial standpoint because it permits a more complete delegation to individuals of responsibilities for work, may promote higher morale and commitment, and may even induce greater effort. Job enlargement is equally attractive to managers because it implies that there is already a kind of moral imperative in working men to seek enlarged jobs and to accept the increased responsibilities accompanying the enlarged positions. Thus, the manager can see this model as morally justified because in applying it he is serving the larger expectations of basic man. It is not out of the goodness of his heart or his Christian charity that he does this. He is willing to enlarge jobs because he is doing good works by making "fulfilled" men of the job holders, a morally satisfying outcome. That this is generally a latent function of applied social science for the practitioner does not make it any less an operative function for him (Merton, 1949).

These conclusions are not reached with derogatory intent. Indeed, it is interesting that the scientist has become the lay theologian of the secular world, by combining knowledge with morality and achieving more than ever before the idealized role of Plato's philosopher-king (or at least the near-miss position of brain-truster and moralist).

EXAMPLE OF A THEORETICAL MODEL

Let us briefly outline the features of a theoretical model before we look at an example of one that is widely recognized among industrial psychologists. A theoretical model starts with things or variables, or

(1) *units* whose interactions constitute the subject matter of attention. The model then specifies the manner in which these units interact with each other, or (2) the *laws of interaction* among the units of the model. Since theoretical models are generally of limited portions of the world, the limits, or (3) *boundaries* must be set forth within which the theory is expected to hold. Most theoretical models are presumed to represent a complex portion of the real world, part of whose complexity is revealed by the fact that there are various (4) *system states* in each of which the units interact differently. Once these four basic features of a theoretical model are set forth, the theorist is in a position to derive conclusions that represent logical and true deductions about the model in operation, or the (5) *propositions* of the model. So far, we see only the theoretical side of the theory-research cycle. Should there be any desire to determine whether the model does, in fact, represent the real world, then each term in each proposition whose test is sought needs to be converted into (6) *an empirical indicator* of the term. The next operation is to substitute the appropriate empirical indicators in the propositional statement to generate a testable (7) *hypothesis*. The research operation consists of measuring the values on the empirical indicators of the hypothesis to determine whether the theoretically predicted values are achieved or approximated in the research test.

It is useful to analyze an example to illustrate the elements of a theoretical model. We choose the Herzberg two-factor theory of job satisfaction since it is widely known among industrial psychologists and is readily explicated.

Herzberg suggests that a situation of behavior is divided into two fundamental components from the standpoint of the actor: (1) extrinsic factors and (2) intrinsic factors. He also suggests that the reaction of the actor to a situation of behavior can be described as "satisfaction" or "dissatisfaction." The elements, or "units," composing the model are, therefore, intrinsic factors, extrinsic factors, satisfaction, and dissatisfaction. It is the relations among these that constitute the Herzberg theory.

The system modeled by the theory consists of individuals interacting with their perceived situation of behavior. More particularly, the situations of behavior that are routinely recurrent are focused upon.

There are two fundamental laws of interaction among the variables, or units of the model: (1) there is an inverse relationship between the levels of an individual's dissatisfaction and the perceived adequacy of the extrinsic factors of his situation of behavior; and (2) there is a positive relationship between the individual's satisfaction and the perceived adequacy in the intrinsic factors of a behavioral situation.

Herzberg focuses his two-factor theory on the situations of employment in an organization. There is, therefore, an implicit or "benign" boundary of the model limiting its anticipated application to a social situation in which an individual is a member of, or employed by, an organization. (A "benign" boundary is one beyond which the model is alleged not to hold, but where the characteristics of the boundary are not themselves relevant to the manner in which the model operates.) In Herzberg's view, incidentally, this is not restricted as to kind of organization or kind of economic system within which the organization operates.

There is also another benign boundary of this model, namely, that it does not apply to collectivities of individuals. It is not, therefore, a model of morale of organization members (morale being viewed as a collective phenomenon). Furthermore, the model is not a model of *behavior* in organizations, and, therefore, does not include within its scope a concern with predicting behavior.

The limiting values (and, therefore, boundaries) of the law of interaction are also clearly built into the model. The dissatisfaction variable has a zero value and may increase to a level where the system is destroyed (the system being the attitudinal reaction of the individual toward his environment), namely, where the individual either leaves the organization, or is removed from it on the initiative of organizational functionaries (i.e., is fired). These two boundaries are clearly limits on the law of relationship between the individual's perceived payoff from the extrinsic factors, and his level of dissatisfaction. In a parallel way, the relation between intrinsic factors and satisfaction has comparable limits. The lower limit of satisfaction is zero, and the upper limit is presumably high but unspecified, since, for example, a personality evaluating intrinsic factors may have an untested limit of expectation with respect to the level of payoff.

Having set forth the units of the theory, the laws by which they interact, and the boundaries of the theory, we need one additional element before we put the model to use: the system states within which the theoretical model is operative. We think of a system state as being a condition of the system being modeled in which the units of that system take on characteristic values that have a persistence through time, regardless of the length of the time interval. The system state is defined by the values taken by all the variables or units in the system. For example, in the Herzberg system we might characterize the individual as being in a state of equal dissatisfaction and satisfaction. We might further build into the system, therefore, a description of what this means in terms of his attitudes toward the employing organization and toward himself. We might characterize another state of the system in which the satisfaction level is far higher than the dissatisfaction level and build further notions about the impact of this on the individual's attitudes. A third system state might be the one in which the balance of dissatisfaction and satisfaction is outweighed on the dissatisfaction side. Thus, we might think of three system states in the relations between satisfaction and dissatisfaction levels of the individual and, on the assumption that these might be persistent states for the individual, to then have a basis for predicting for the model (1) the consequences of persistence of the state and (2) the state to which the individual is likely to go if he moves from that state to another.

Having established the essential features of the Herzberg model or theory (the terms are used interchangeably), we are now in a position to examine the propositions derivable from the model. Propositions are truth statements about a model. (These are not necessarily truth statements about the real world that the model represents.)

Propositions of a theory must be true because they are logical statements about the theoretical system. A large number of truth statements can be made about Herzberg's model, but we will focus on a small number for illustrative purposes. Illustrative propositions are simply listed without explications. These truth statements derivable from the model are the kinds of propositional statements that can be made from any model that has had its units, laws of interaction, boundaries and system states specified. (1) An individual's attitudinal orientation toward his work is a sum of a level of satisfaction and a level of dissatisfaction. (This is not unusual, since poets and philosophers have for centuries emphasized the possibility of love-hate characterizing an individual's orientation toward others.) (2) An individual may feel no dissatisfaction and no satisfaction in the organizational situation, that is, be genuinely indifferent. (This is a perfectly logical truth statement about the model, and a very important one, for it may be a significant characterization of a large body of industrial workers, singularly ignored by the Herzberg theorists.) (3) The level of dissatisfaction and the level of satisfaction felt by an individual are independent of each other.

We now come to the problem of matching the model with the real world it is intended to characterize. At this point it becomes necessary to convert the propositional statements into hypotheses. The hypotheses are statements of predictions of what will be true in the real world if the evidence from the real world is marshaled. For example, Herzberg has specified among the extrinsic factors of the work situation, or what he has called the hygiene factors, pay, technical supervision, the human relations quality of supervision, company policies and administration, working conditions, and job security. Any one of these factors either is itself an empirical indicator of extrinsic factors or can be converted into one. Obviously, pay is in itself a metric and can be measured directly. Working conditions, on the other hand, have to be further specified in terms of such elements as physical surroundings—facilities like toilets and washrooms available—or physiological conditions like rest periods. In the same way, the intrinsic factors of the work situation which Herzberg defines as achievement, recognition, responsibility, and advancement, also have the potential for being made operational (Herzberg, 1959, 1966).

What is now necessary is to substitute operational terms into the statement of the propositions so that a parallel statement, called an hypothesis, becomes empirically testable. In the Herzberg model, we not only have to specify the extrinsic and intrinsic factors, but in each case we have to further specify that it is the perception by the individual of these factors that is being measured. Thus, we would not simply take pay level as the measure of extrinsic factors, but we would have to go to the individual to get his attitude about his pay level, which would presumably be expressed in terms of his comparison with what he thinks he ought to get, or expects to get, in the way of pay. Thus, the operationalizing of the terms of a proposition in order to make an hypothesis is a very critical stage in the theory-research cycle. It is here, of course, that notions of validity have been widely employed in psychological research. While this is not the place to engage in professional controversy, it should be pointed out that the empirical indicators chosen by scientists are in the end a matter of consensus and not validation. What is perhaps much more crucial from the standpoint of the theory building, research testing cycle is that the empirical indicators employed in testing theories have a reasonable level of reliability (Dubin, 1969, Chap. 8).

If the given piece of research produces data that conform to the hypothesized outcome, we would conclude that the model is unchallenged at that stage. Either the tested proposition should be subject to a replicative test in order to be certain that it is accurate or, assuming it is accurate, we may then test other propositions of the model. Where the hypothesis is disconfirmed by the data, the theorist-researcher is then required to examine immediately the possibility of revising the model so that it generates propositional statements, or truth statements, about itself, which will conform post hoc to the empirical findings that have disconfirmed a previous proposition. This, in turn, will result in new empirical tests of the model, and so on in an endless cycle.

This has been a very brief examination of an illustration to help keep in mind several very critical elements about the theory-research linkage.

1. A theoretical model is limited only by the imagination of the theorist in what he may use as elements in building the model, or laws of interaction among the elements or boundaries that he chooses to set on the model. It is, therefore, perfectly legitimate to build a theory of ESP, or "primal scream," or psychic healing that conforms to all the canons of theory building.

2. A theoretical model is not simply a statement of hypothesis; nor is it a catalogue of the units or variables employed and their definitions; nor is it a descriptive statement of a world of the scientific imagination.

3. The argument about the *adequacy* of the theoretical model is always and only an argument about the logic employed in constructing it.

4. The argument about the *reality* of a theoretical model, that is, whether or not it indeed models the empirical world, is a scientific issue that is resolved by research tests.

5. A theoretical model is a scientific model if, and only if, its creator is willing to subject it to an empirical test. Otherwise, it falls into the realm of philosophy or theology which, incidentally, not only give us the logic by which to test the adequacy of scientific models, but subject their own creations to the same logical test.

Theorists and researchers may be distinguished from each other at the point where they enter into the theory-research cycle. However, it is improbable that theorists, if they are scientists, will be disinterested or unable to carry out research to test theories, or that researchers may be so insensitive that they are unaware of the theories which they subject to tests.

THEORY

My published volume, *Theory Building* (Dubin, 1969) sets forth the components and structure of theories, their sources, and their empirical tests through research. I will summarize here some of the more important considerations, letting those readers interested in more details peruse the volume itself. This summary follows closely a chapter in a more recent publication (Dubin, 1971) than my book.

A theory is the attempt of man to model some aspect of the empirical world. The underlying motive for this modeling is either (1) that the real world is so complex it needs to be conceptually simplified in order to understand it, or (2) that observation by itself does not reveal ordered relationships among empirically detected entities. A theory tries to make sense out of the observable world by ordering the relationships among elements that constitute the theorist's focus of attention in the real world. The process of building a theory requires hard work and ingenuity.

Involved, at first, is a focus of attention concerned essentially with choosing the elements or "things" whose relationships with each other are of interest. These "things," out of which theories are built, are usually called variables, although I prefer the more neutral term, "unit." It should be emphasized that these "things" or units out of which theories are built constitute an arbitrary list selected by the theorist as of particular interest to him (Ashby, 1952). The theorist may, if his imagination is vigorous enough, invent imaginary units, or units that have not yet been apprehended empirically, and build them into his model. Freud did this, for example, with the unconscious mind and the Id.

It may seem strange that, if a theory is supposed to model some portion of the empirical world, the theorist would consider thinking of using units in his model that themselves are not empirically apprehended. This apparent idiocy is less difficult to comprehend when it is recognized that the predictions made on the basis of a theoretical model need not be tested in research. More about this point later. The theorist starts with a selection of things or units which he is curious about how they interrelate in the real world.

The next step in building a theory is to determine conceptually how the selected units are related to each other. It is at this point that two considerations emerge that are essential features of a theory. (1) A mode of relationship among the units needs to be specified in detail. (2) A simple test is necessary for determining the domain of the theory that will include within its scope only those units that are conceptually linked to at least one other unit within the model. The specification of modes of interaction among the units is, therefore, one important step in determining the boundaries of the model.

The modes of interaction among the units of a theory are what I call its "laws of interaction." The lawful statement in any theory is how two or more of its units are related. While the statement of the law must, of course, specify the units interacting,

the lawful part of the statement is the specification of the mode of interaction. Thus, for example, in occupational choice, one may build a theory of the individual's behavior of choosing in at least two alternative, and mutually exclusive, forms. The first law of interaction would be: an individual ranks known occupations on a preference scale from high to low and then proceeds to choose from the top, or most preferred, occupation, downward. The alternative law of interaction would be: an individual ranks known occupations on a preference scale from high to low and then proceeds to make his choice by progressive elimination of the least preferred occupations. These two laws of interaction have identical units: (1) a choosing individual, (2) an individual preference scale, and (3) occupations known to him. They differ in the manner in which individuals go through the process of choosing a preferred occupation. Most decision theorists prefer the first law of interaction, that people choose from the most to the least preferred alternative. The empirical research of the choice process among children (Tyler, 1955) and the occupational aspirations of working class parents (Chinoy, 1955) suggests that the second law of interaction is viable and may actually be the more prevalent method of choosing. According to Tyler, children make choices by eliminating least desirable ones, and Chinoy (among many others) found assembly line workers reporting that they did not want their children to follow Daddy's occupation, a choosing process that must surely be communicated to their children.

The process of putting things or units together in lawful relation to each other establishes the fundamental building blocks out of which a theory is constructed. However, there are additional features of a model that need to be specified if the model is to be completed.

Theories have a domain over which they are expected to mirror the empirical world. Beyond that domain it may be problematic as to whether the theory holds. What separates the domain of a theory from the "beyond" is a boundary. Every theoretical model, if it is complete, must specify the boundary within which the units interact lawfully. Beyond that boundary it may not be at all clear that the units will continue ιo interact by the specified law, or that all units will remain in the system, or even that the system will remain intact. Thus, for example, if occupational choice is one area of decision making, the units involved are obviously not the same and the law of interaction in choice behavior may be quite different from what would be true in the domain of mate selection; both decision domains, then, might be modeled quite differently from the decisional process of picking a winner in the sixth race at Hollywood Park. There are clear-cut boundaries that distinguish the occupational choice decision from the mate selection and the winning horse decision, although all three are forms of decision making. We, therefore, expect theorists dealing with these respective areas of personal choice to develop separate theories of occupational choice, mate selection, and race horse handicapping. Whether there is an underlying commonality among these three domains of decision, giving rise to a grand decision theory, is an issue that needs to be explored independently.

In the social sciences particularly, there is a strange incapacity to recognize that a theoretical model must have a boundary. This is partly true because in dealing with human behavior we are prone to think there is a commonality among the units involved and the laws by which they interact. We also operate with simplistic laws of interaction that are viewed as universal for all situations of human interaction. Finally, social theorists have an almost religious belief in the unity of the human personality and psyche, leading to the assumption that any individual actor will behave the same, in keeping with the imperatives of personality, regardless of the situation of action. For these three reasons we often assume we can safely ignore the boundary conditions surrounding a given

theoretical model, or even apply the model indiscriminately to all realms of human interaction. This is an unfortunate intellectual habit we employ as theorists and practitioners. The sooner we recognize that the human actor may be different in different action situations, the more realistic will be the boundaries of the theoretical models we create.

We now come to the final feature of a theoretical model involved in its construction. This is the specification of the states in which the model or theoretical system operates. A system state is a condition of the system as a whole. When the integrity of the system is maintained, but its condition is markedly different from what it was previously, we describe the alteration as a change of system state. A steady state, or a change of state of a system, is important to specify, for it calls attention to the fact that while the integrity of the system is maintained, the system may change from one state to another.

It will be noted that I have changed terms from "theoretical model" or "theory" to "system." These three terms are used interchangeably. The terms serve to designate that unity representing man's picture of some segment of the real world.

It is perfectly simple to illustrate the idea of a system state, and, through the example, to suggest the importance of the notion. We can think, for instance, of an audience in a theatre as constituting a focused crowd, a group that can be moved to a state of panic with the shout of "Fire." We have no difficulty in understanding, for example, the theoretical model that an individual in a state of "frustration" presumably can be moved to a new state called "aggression." Indeed, it is one of the common features of social science models, as used in guiding practice, that we have focused attention almost exclusively on system states whose persistence, or the oscillation among which, are the prime subject matters of theoretical predictions. This is particularly true in the area of industrial psychology where much theorizing involves a concern with the same individuals changing from one state to another: for instance, from vocational indecision to vocational commitment; or at the group level, from a low morale to a high morale condition. Much of social science theory is concerned with changes within persons and groups through time. The theoretical models we build to mirror these longitudinal changes are typically models describing successions of system states, whether the system is an individual or a social group.

Given the units, their laws of interaction, the boundaries within which the units interact lawfully, and the states through which the system may move, we have the necessary and sufficient components from which to build a complete theoretical model. When these features are exhibited, we may properly say we have a theory, a model, or a theoretical system. A warning, however, is necessary as many theorist-labeled products falsely bear the title "theory." Omissions may include a set of laws relating the units within the system or necessary to connect some units to the system, a failure to specify the boundaries within which the system operates, or an author who may not have envisioned states through which the system moves. Any of these omissions requires correction before we may properly acknowledge the existence of a theoretical model.

It is obvious at this point that only the components of a theoretical model have been set forth. Attention now turns to consideration of the utilization of such a model.

The first operation is a logical elucidation of the model itself. This consists of making as many truth statements that derive from the model as suit the tastes or interests of the theorist. These are the propositions of the theory. The sole test of propositions is that they are logically consistent with the model. If the theorist can specify his system of logic, then he can follow its rules in determining the propositions he can make about his theory. A fair amount of theory building, and extension of the existing theory, involves discovery of new propositions, or truth statements, about the model that had previously escaped notice.

Strategic propositions and trivial propositions always emerge from a theory. Strategic propositions are those that hold true where something significant is happening in the relationship among units of the theory. For example, in psychophysics, the propositions about thresholds are strategic, as it is at those points that something really happens in the phenomena under consideration. On the other hand, many propositions can be made about a theory that are trivial because they distinguish only very narrowly from other propositions. One of the beauties of building a theory is the fact that strategic propositions focus upon the exciting points in the world being modeled, and the theorist is able to segregate such strategic propositions for special attention.

After the propositions of a theory have been set forth the theorist becomes concerned with determining whether the model has any connection with the empirical world. The linkage with reality is made by testing one or more of the propositions. This involves a conversion process. Each proposition has to be converted to an hypothesis by substituting for each named unit in the proposition an empirical indicator of it. We have already seen in the Herzberg example how this substitution is accomplished. While the general process of going from proposition to hypothesis is straightforward, there are details beyond the scope of this discussion that need further elaboration (cf., Dubin, 1969, Chaps. 8, 9).

In order to make predictions from a theoretical model, it is necessary to operationalize the appropriate components of the model. We start with the propositions or truth statements about the model. Such propositions declare that the units of the model should take on characteristic values. Thus, for example, in a model of a love relationship, one proposition might be that "the amount of love felt by each partner in the relationship is equal to the amount received." For this proposition to be tested, it is necessary to establish an empirical indicator for "the amount of love felt" and "the amount of love received." We might ask an individual in a relationship with another individual to tick off on a Likert-type (summated rating) scale the amount of "felt love for the other." We might then measure the amount of love received by having the same individual indicate his "perceived love received" on a similar Likert-type question. We can now convert the proposition into an hypothesis by substituting the operational measures for the generalized subjects of the proposition as follows: The amount of love felt by each partner, as measured by Likert question "felt," is equal to the amount received, as measured by Likert question "perceived love received." We can now use the two measures in the field and determine whether the data collected (i.e., the "scores" on the questions) produce values on the units that accord with the propositional prediction that has been converted into our hypothesis. That is what "operationalism" is all about.

Note, however, that we have another ball game if we decide to use different empirical indicators to test the same proposition. Suppose we now measure "amount of love felt" by a behavioral measure of "loving actions toward" as observed and recorded by an observer, and measure "amount of love received" by a Likert-type question to the other partner on the "amount of love he gives." These new empirical indicators establish an entirely new hypothesis, testing the same proposition. In fact, of course, there is an infinite number of hypotheses that can be tested for every proposition of a model, for each time a new empirical indicator is utilized, a new hypothesis is generated.

This abbreviated description of a theoretical model has laid out its components and suggested the derivations from a theory that link it with research. Before turning to the research test of a theory we shall examine the twin scientific goals of prediction and understanding to set forth some of their properties relevant to theorizing.

PREDICTION

We may now turn to a general consideration of what we do with a proper theoretical model. It is a schoolboy maxim that science predicts. We may, therefore, assume that one function of a theoretical model is to predict something.

In the social sciences particularly it is generally believed that a scientific model will also provide opportunity for developing understanding and insight about some empirical phenomenon. We will examine this second product of building a theory after an analysis of prediction and its consequences.

Prediction from a scientific model is a simple and straightforward operation. What is *always* and *only* predicted is the value that may be taken by one or more units in the theoretical model, measured on some metric. This conclusion is simple and often ignored or misunderstood and, therefore, bears repeating. The only thing that is ever predicted from a scientific model is a *value* or *magnitude* of one or more units in that model.

The empirical test of a scientific model is never a test of its laws directly, but only a test of the values taken by one or more of the units that may be predicted from the lawful relationships among the units of the system. This conclusion should not prove surprising as one can never test a relationship, the possible test being only the consequences of a relationship. Putting this into the context of common experience, if we said, for example, that two people are linked together by a relationship of love, we would then predict that each would behave toward the other in certain ways, would not behave in other ways, and would act in concert in particular ways in relation to third parties in their environment. Thus, we do *not* test the lawful relationship by which two people interact when we declare that "they are in love." We *do* test the consequences of this law of interaction by measuring the behaviors between the individuals, and together in relation to other individuals. In short, we measure values on some scales of behavior for the two people connected by a love relationship.

It is common usage to speak of the "laws of science" and to view their construction as the important element in scientific thinking. The central importance of the laws of inter-action in all scientific models is not to be gainsaid. Nevertheless, we must fully understand that we never test these laws directly, but only through their consequences for the values of the units in the models that are related by the laws.

The task of empirical testing of a prediction is made easy precisely because the scientist is required to develop empirical indicators of only the units built into his scientific model, and not of the laws of interaction. Thus, in our previous example, I would have to develop empirical indicators only of the behaviors of a person in relation to one other individual, and empirical indicators of the behaviors of such pairs in relation to other people. It seems obvious that it is much easier to develop empirical indicators of such behaviors than it would be to construct an empirical indicator of "being in a love relationship."

Prediction is a major goal of science. Scientific models should, if they are complete and adequate, result in reasonably accurate predictions. We should now clearly recognize that what we are predicting is always the value of some characteristic of the units interacting, and not characteristics of the laws by which they interact.

A special case of prediction is one in which the boundary of the model is involved. A general prediction is that the value taken by two or more units in a model are determinant up to some limiting set of values, but beyond that are not any longer determinant by the laws relating those units. Thus, the boundary of a model may come to be defined in terms of critical values of the units composing the model. There are technical features of system boundaries and

boundary determining criteria that need not concern us here since they have been elaborated elsewhere (Dubin, 1969, Chap. 5).

Another class of predictions made from a scientific model is about the change among the states of the system. The condition of no change of state in the system is what is normally called a "steady state." That is to say, the system remains in the same condition throughout a period of time. This steady state may be characterized by a fixed set of values or a fixed range of values for all the units composing the system.

When a system changes from one state to another, this will be signaled by changes in the values of all the units composing the system. The prediction problem with respect to system states is: (1) to predict the length of time a steady state will endure, and/or (2) to predict the succeeding state to which the system will move, knowing the present state in which it operates. Simple systems having only two or three system states in which they can exist make possible oscillation predictions with a high level of certainty. For example, if a system can exist in only two states, then there is a 100 percent certainty in the prediction that, knowing its present state, one can absolutely predict that it will move to its other state, whenever it changes state. This, of course, is a beguiling feature of social science theory for the theorist wins the game before he starts if he specifies only a two-state system and then predicts to which state the system will go, knowing its present state. The prediction of the inevitability of individual aggression following frustration is a forecast of this order. Even in a system having three possible states, there is a 50 percent chance of predicting correctly on the basis of guessing that a system will move from its present state to one or the other of its remaining possible states.

From the standpoint of sheer utility, a theoretical model is best judged by the accuracy of the predictions generated by it. These are always predictions of the values taken by single units, combinations of units, or the units composing the system. For the practitioner, these are the features of a scientific model that turn out to be the usable outcome of theoretical models.

UNDERSTANDING

If accurate prediction is the practical outcome of utilizing scientific models, then the intellectual outcome is the understanding they provide of the characteristics of the empirical domain they model. What is gained in understanding through the use of a scientific model to portray a portion of the real world is achieved by comprehending the law or laws of interaction built into the model. The locus of understanding in the scientific model is to be found in its laws of interaction. To say that two things (units) are inversely related is to provide us with an understanding of the nature of their relationship. The prediction we would make from such a statement is: As the values of "thing A" increase, the values of "thing B" decrease. But the lawful part of the statement—that there is an inverse relationship—is the heart of our understanding of how "thing A" and "thing B" interact over the full range of their lawful relationship.

In a more elaborate exposition of the difference between understanding and prediction I have suggested that the former is knowledge of *process* while the latter is knowledge of *outcomes* (Dubin, 1969, Chap. 1). The statement of the inverse relationship in the preceding example is a statement of the process of interaction. The statement of outcomes holds that if the values of "thing A" are large, the values of "thing B" are small. The first is our understanding of the relationship; the second is the prediction of the values of the "things" related when they are linked in a single system.

Understanding is an intellectual and/or aesthetic product of a theoretical model. Accurate prediction is the practical product of the theory. From the standpoint of the practitioner, what is important about a theoretical model is the accuracy of its predictions, and not the understanding that it may contribute. Thus, the structural engineer may forego the joys of intellectual comprehension of the laws of stress of materials if he is given formulas that are accurate in predicting the reaction of structural material to given kinds and levels of stress. He can design structures on the basis of the latter knowledge without partaking of the understanding knowledge. In exactly the same way, the practitioner in any discipline can forego the understanding knowledge (not that it is desirable, only that it is possible) if the theory with which he operates provides accurate or reasonably accurate predictions.

This is not the "raw empiricism" issue in another guise. The "raw empiricism" approach is one in which the values measured on two or more units are related or correlated. Beyond some chance level, it is discovered that these measured values are systematically related. It is then possible to predict that given a value on one unit, there is a greater than chance likelihood that the value on a related unit will be of a given magnitude. This approach may give rise to accurate predictions.

When a theoretical model is utilized for its predictions, the user may forego wanting or trying to understand the theory itself. He may find its content too demanding or too "theoretical" or may only want to know whether the theory works, that is, whether it generates accurate predictions. For example, "expectancy theory" has been widely developed as a theory of managerial motivation, but it is complex and not likely to be understood, although it is utilized by practitioners (Atkinson, 1964; Vroom, 1964; Porter & Lawler, 1968). The great advantage of depending upon theories for only their predictive accuracy lies in the fact that the practitioner need not be committed to any given theory if an alternative one is more accurate in its predictions. The practitioner can operate with a simple pragmatic test that he makes of any theory in his practice: Is it more or less accurate in its predictions than an alternative theory? A scientist, on the other hand, may relish a particular theory because of the understanding it contributes to his knowledge. The scientist may also value his theory because he is its intellectual parent, and be only mildly disturbed that its predictions may be untested or inaccurate. This is obviously no credit to the scientist, but it is recognition of human frailty.

RESEARCH

From this point on, I will use the term "theory-research" or "theorist-researcher" to indicate what seems to me to be the proper designation of theory building. Research, except when it is confined to pure description, is concerned with testing theory, just as theory, when it is differentiated from theology, is concerned with being tested through research. It is literally impossible to separate theory and research since the function of each is dependent upon the realization of the other.

I have made a strong case for description as providing the stuff from which the theorist-researcher builds models (Dubin, 1969, pp. 85, 226–228). Good description is essentially good reporting of what may be apprehended and observed systematically in the empirical world. The habits and skills involved in accurate reporting are not confined to those functionaries carrying the designation of "researcher." Indeed, it is often true that practitioners are more knowledgeable about, and more capable of, accurately describing the domain of their practice than are researchers. There may, however, be important instances when the trained observer can see what the man on the job overlooks, partly because of the latter's habituation to the experience. Thus, it is not possible to draw a strict line between the ability of practitioners and theorist-researchers to perform the functions of descriptive

analysis. This is one of the important areas in which there is a significant joint contribution to the scientific enterprise by the practitioner and the theorist-researcher.

In contrast to their joint contribution of descriptive accuracy in the domain being modeled by theory, there is a real disjunction between theorist-researcher and practitioner regarding the purposes of research. As indicated above, research is performed to test a theory. The practitioner may be interested in knowing if a theory has been tested in order to determine the degree of confidence he will accord its predictions. Beyond that, the practitioner has little, if any, interest in the theory-testing operations. The theorist-researcher has a much different orientation which needs to be examined in order to appreciate a significant source of non-overlap in outlook between theorist-researchers and practitioners.

There are two possible research stances toward a theoretical model.

1. The researcher may set as his task the *proof* of the adequacy of his theoretical model.

2. The researcher may set as his task to *improve* the starting theoretical model.

If the purpose is to prove the adequacy of the theoretical model, then important limitations are placed upon the research operations. If, on the other hand, the purpose is to improve the theoretical model, then some of these limitations are removed.

The limitations of the proof orientation are the following:

1. Data are likely to be collected for values on only those units incorporated in the theoretical model. This usually means that, either experimentally or by discarding data, attention in the empirical research is focused solely upon values measured on units incorporated in the theory.

2. In very much the same fashion, either experimentally or by discarding data, values on any given unit incorporated in the study beyond the predicted range may also be excluded from attention. In this manner, im-

portant data on the units that have been incorporated in the theoretical model are ignored because the model does not predict values in the empirical range of values.

We may conclude that the orientation of seeking to prove the empirical relevance of a theoretical model is wholly legitimate and important in establishing the initial linkage between a theoretical model and its empirical domain. Furthermore, it is psychologically important to the theorist to establish some certitude that his theoretical model does, indeed, link up with the empirical world.

At the same time, it should be recognized that the knowledge added by an empirical test to prove the viability of a model is limited only to the fact that the model does link in some useful way with an empirical domain. The knowledge of the phenomenon being modeled is contained in the theory, not in the empirical world. The empirical test to "prove" a model adds nothing to an understanding of the domain being modeled, for all the understanding is contained in the model itself. Furthermore, so long as subsequent tests continue to prove the theory, the theory remains static and unchanged. This is another simple, but often ignored, feature of the theory-research enterprise.

The alternative approach to improving a theory is one that does not have the limitations of the proof orientation (Popper, 1961). Consequently, it is likely to give rise to a constant reevaluation and reformulation of the theoretical models of a discipline as the empirical knowledge requires such modifications. The essential operations involved in a research approach oriented toward improving a theory is to give particular attention and prominence to deviant cases and non-fitting data. The result feeds back immediately to the theory building process, resulting in theory modifications. The theory is forced to be modified to incorporate the previously non-fitting or non-conforming empirical results. None of the advantages of the theory proving orientation are lost. However, the opportunities exist for theory modification and, therefore, for growth and improvement in the theoretical structure of a discipline.

PRACTICE

The practitioner in the field of human enterprise is concerned with making something work. He may be an industrialist trying to make a work organization effective; he may be a government official concerned with adequate performance of civic functions; he may be a school executive trying to maintain an adequate educational environment; or he may be a social worker concerned with improving the adjustment of individuals to their environment. The emphasis upon doing something that has observable consequences has important implications for the distinction between a practitioner and a theorist-researcher. This distinction can be appreciated by examining the concerns of the practitioners.

1. The practitioner has to know the present conditions with which he is dealing and which he is intent upon either preserving or changing.

2. The practitioner has to have a purpose or goal for preserving or changing the present situation.

3. Where change is the decision, the practitioner has to have some preferred direction in which the change should go.

4. Normally, the practitioner wants to evaluate whether the subsequent state of affairs achieves the goal set for it.

It is evident that the scientist building a theory and testing it and the practitioner directing or intervening in the practical affairs of men share only one of these four concerns, namely, an interest in the accurate knowledge of the conditions of the situation. The scientist is interested in good description of present conditions because this provides the stuff from which he builds his theories. The practitioner is interested in the same kind of descriptive knowledge because accurate knowledge permits him to make changes.

Beyond this commonality, however, their interests diverge. The theorist-researcher is interested in testing and improving his models. The predictions that he makes from the models are intensely practical from the standpoint of the practitioner. The theorist-researcher normally is not interested in the normative decisions as to whether the present state of affairs is to be continued or changed, nor the direction in which the change is to be oriented, nor the evaluation of whether the change has been attained successfully. However, prominent theorists in the field of industrial psychology have engaged themselves in the normative problems. As a result, they have become the lay theologians of the world of practical affairs, as indicated earlier. In the usual circumstances, the practitioner is left to his own resources to solve these three problems and to share with the theorist-researcher a concern with an accurate description of the present state of the domain of his interest.

This limited articulation between theory and practice has its obvious consequences for the functions of, and relations between, the two spheres of intellectual activity. The theorist-researcher presents the practitioner with models of an empirical domain and then says: "If my model accurately reflects the characteristics of this domain, then I predict the following things will happen should any of the elements of this domain change their values." If the model is a reasonably accurate depiction of the real world, these predictions may be very useful in suggesting to the practitioner what the most probable outcomes are if he changes the values of one or more units in the system. Such a prediction is useful, however, only if the practitioner is willing to accept the theorist-researcher's modeling of the empirical domain.

Suppose, however, the practitioner is confronted with two or more models that together purport to represent the same empirical domain. The fact that they are different models means that they may generate different predictions about the system being modeled, should the values of its units be changed. The practitioner now has to ask: "Which of these models do I want to utilize?" The answer may be grounded in some normative consideration that can vary widely among practitioners. This is by no means an easy choice, and I shall point out presently that there is a dilemma relating to the education of practitioners that leads them to become attached to certain models and to prefer them over others.

The theorist-researcher is in no position to be more knowledgeable than the practitioner about the desirability of change, the goals of change, or the successful achievement of a chosen change. It is at precisely this point that we find one of the major structural reasons for failure of theorist-researchers and practitioners to become effective cooperators in problems of social policies and their realization.

The theorist-researcher is normatively neutral, not because this makes his product more "objective," but is normatively neutral because what he is doing does not require normative considerations in formulating or carrying out his scientific functions. The situation is reversed for the practitioner for he is centrally concerned with normative issues in deciding if a system should be changed, the direction change should take, and the success with which it may be attained.

Furthermore, the goals of research in the theory-research realm, as we have already seen, are not the goals of the practitioner, and, indeed, are in important ways antithetical to what the practitioner is doing. The practitioner needs a fixed and stable theoretical model whose predictions guide his normative conclusions at least with regard to the desirability of change and its goals. The scientist is almost literally bored with a fixed theory and has no interest in it precisely because it is fixed or "established."

Thus, on the grounds of orientation toward theory the theorist-researcher has a very distinctive point of view with little in common with the equally distinctive point of view of the practitioner.

SOME DILEMMAS

One of the important dilemmas with which practitioners are faced when confronted with theorist-researchers is the disjunction between contemporary theory, on the one hand, and the kind of theory the practitioner is likely to have learned through his formal or informal education, on the other hand. If it is true that social theorists are working constantly to improve their theory, and, if it is true that they are sometimes successful, then there is a high probability that the kind of theory about human behavior that practitioners have learned in their own schooling is likely to be supplanted during the period of their active practice. To the extent that practitioners use theory in their work, they are likely to be using an outmoded theory, or one that has been significantly modified since they learned it. There is thereby created a further disjunction between the work of the theorist-researcher and his contemporary colleagues in practice. This phenomenon is characteristic in the field of medicine; as a result medical practitioners have learned the desirability of insisting upon regular in-service training for doctors in the field to bring them up to date about medical theory. In addition, doctors use closed circuit television to bring experts from medical centers to the local practitioners. Professional conventions also serve this same function by bringing the practitioners into contact with theorists, thereby disseminating the newest theories to the field.

The practice of in-service training has been less developed in the applied areas of social science with the result that a high proportion of practitioners using social science theory may be significantly behind current theoretical developments in the social science disciplines. There is probably a lag of five to ten years between the time a theoretical model becomes fashionable in a discipline and its utilization by practitioners in areas of social behavior. In this connection, journals have been established solely to provide liaison between theory and practice, as with *Psychology Today* and *Trans-Action–Social Science and Modern Society* in the United States and *New Society* in Great Britain.

Another dilemma in linking theory with practice rests on the messianic stance sometimes adopted by theorist-researchers. There is the tendency to assume that the skills of the theorist-researcher automatically, and perhaps uniquely, qualify him to solve the problems of the practitioner, regardless of the theorist's competence or knowledge in the areas of practice in question. There is a very unfortunate tendency for social science theorist-researchers to lack the modesty essential to a scientific community. This is made easier if the scientist can trade upon a general reputation in his discipline to provide entree as an "expert" into an area of practical concern about which he does not possess any scientific knowledge. Needless to add, it is a responsibility of the practitioner to guard himself and his colleagues against being influenced by incompetent theorist-researchers.

THEORY, RESEARCH, AND PRACTICE

So far I have indicated that there is significant discontinuity between theory-research and practice. This disjunction is the product of the manner in which theory is developed and research tested on the one hand and the purposes of practice, on the other. Theorists and practitioners alike would be comforted if they knew a magical way to link interests in order to achieve a higher level of accomplishment on each side. Having said that there are good reasons why theory and practice do not readily articulate, I will now point out that cooperation is nevertheless possible.

As already indicated, the contribution of theory to practice is to provide reliable predictions about what will happen to the system on which the practitioner is working. There is surely a significant contribution from theory to practice that requires no further amplification.

The practitioner makes a significant contribution to the theorist-researcher by providing the knowledge of the real world that comes from constant experience with it. This knowledge, based upon experience, has two important ways in which it influences the theorist-researcher.

1. Knowledge of the "real" situation may lead to the selection of the units built into a model different from what would have been chosen had the theorist simply thought about the problem by contemplating his navel.

2. Knowledge of the "real" situation may influence the choice of empirical indicators utilized in testing a theoretical model.

In the domain of human behavior the varieties of possible actions far exceed the ability of any individual to derive them logically. For example, I have shown that there are 1,048,586 distinctive ways in which two persons can interact if we employ Parsons's model of social behavior (Dubin, 1960). As theorists we have a much greater chance of dealing with real actions in their many guises if we listen to the practitioners whose daily work is focused upon human interaction. I can, perhaps, best illustrate this by calling your attention to the theory and research in the field of social power. You will recall that the theory of what is popularly called "power structures" derives from an analysis of the reputations of individuals in a community as to their ability to determine, or influence, social decisions. This reputational approach is based upon a belief that if knowledgeable individuals in a community are asked to specify those who exercise social influence, these respondents will give accurate answers that will reflect the real world of social power. The theory of how large or small, how homogeneous or mixed,

how old or young is the population of the power elite is inductively derived from the knowledgeable responses of the practitioners wielding power. It took Hunter, with his interest in developing a "realistic" model of community power structure, to turn to those who lived with and in local power structures in order to find their composition (Hunter, 1953). The contribution made by Hunter was due to his wisdom in turning to the practitioners to learn more about the subject of his attention.

In a similar fashion, the practitioner in a field may contribute to the development of better empirical indicators for measuring the values on the units employed in theoretical models. To cite a personal example, I once had a lengthy conversation with a knowledgeable industrial relations executive who described an interesting member of his company work force. The man, in his late thirties, was a good worker but lacked commitment to his job or the company. The executive declared that he was puzzled by this apparent incongruity until he accidentally learned that the man was a lay preacher in a minor religious denomination of working-class members. This one case immediately set me thinking about measuring what I had long since incorporated into my own models of industrial behavior, namely, the compartmentalization of actions into separate institutional realms. I saw in that one example the suggestion of how I might measure compartmentalization; as a result I developed the Central Life Interest instrument. Although unwittingly, the practitioner made a very important contribution to my research by pointing out a solution to a vexing problem of measurement.

You will note that in the examples cited, the practitioner is not conscious of the contribution he is making to the theorist-researcher. Although the contribution is real enough, it is not self-consciously made. This raises the problem of what is it that the practitioner can do that will deliberately contribute to the scientific enterprise.

The starting point of a self-conscious

contribution is to overcome a feeling of awe in the presence of theory. There is some tendency for the theorist to be accorded unwarranted respect by the practitioner. To the extent that this overrides the objective judgment of the utility of the predictions derivable from theoretical models, the respect is misplaced and can be positively dysfunctional, for it may suppress the practitioner's critical evaluation of the efficacy of the model.

The practitioner has a genuine responsibility to maintain a skepticism about theoretical models, which has as its affirmative outcome a willingness to improve upon them. The skills of a theorist are not so esoteric that they remain beyond the reach of practitioners. At least in the two ways I have suggested above the practitioner can become a working member of the theory-research team.

It has already been indicated that the theorist-researcher and the practitioner have differing goals that lead to differing viewpoints about a theoretical model. It is precisely the difference in viewpoints that makes it difficult for the two roles to be combined in one person. Should this happen, the theoretical models are likely to become nothing more than ad hoc collections of variables whose values are most likely to predict values on variables of special interest. Thus, if one is interested in predicting movements of the business cycle, some of the best predictors are statistical series whose upward or downward movement signal the more general movement of business activity. In the same way, the prediction of success on parole depended solely upon finding some demographic or personality indicators that correlated highly with actual success of parole, and then using these indicators to make predictions about future parole applicants. In a comparable fashion the profile of interests of successful men in an occupation or profession is used as a basis for matching the interests of persons being given vocational guidance when the Strong Vocational Interest test is uti-

lized as a tool for prediction. Trade tests employed in rehabilitation counseling use the same technique of extrapolating past correlations to future situations. In every instance, there may be good predictions without any model or theory upon which it is based. The simple analytical tool employed is to extrapolate from existing relations, future conditions that are believed to have high probability of obtaining.

Most theorists would recoil from such predictions as being essentially atheoretical. However accurate the predictions may be in given instances, there exists no model within which the lawful relationship among the variables correlated can be found. The practitioner can accept the adequacy of the predictions without knowing how they obtain. The theorist will feel compelled to build a model that tells him how the predicted outcome results from the interaction among the variables incorporated in the model. In the process of doing so, he may generate predictions different from those obtained by extrapolation, and perhaps not as good. Nevertheless, the theorist will hold to his theory because it provides him with some understanding of how variables are related to each other while the extrapolation may not yield such understanding.

It is unlikely that good theorists make good practitioners, or vice versa. The practitioner can contribute most to the theory building enterprise by maintaining the critical appraisal that his contact with the real world entitles him to make. If the theoretical model does not correspond with its purported empirical domain it should be the practitioner who is first to note and announce this. If the predictions made from a theoretical model are imprecise, then the practitioner, who has to live with such predictions, should be firm in proclaiming this inadequacy. Constant pressure should be exerted by the practitioner upon the theorist to do better. Certainly the theorist should be expected to do better than the folk wisdom of the average practitioner. But the practitioner's folk wisdom should not be abandoned either, simply because some theorist has declared his product to be better. The utility of the theory must ultimately meet the test of application by the practitioner. When it does, we have the fruitful interplay between practitioner and theorist.

REFERENCES

Ashby, W. R. *Design for a brain*. London: Chapman and Hall, 1952.

Atkinson, J. W. *An introduction to motivation*. Princeton: Van Nostrand, 1964.

Bergmann, G. *Philosophy of science*. Madison: University of Wisconsin Press, 1957.

Chinoy, E. *Automobile workers and the American dream*. Garden City, N.Y.: Doubleday, 1955.

Dubin, R. Parsons' actor: Continuities in social theory. *American Sociological Review*, 1960, 13, 501–518.

Dubin, R. *Theory building*. New York: The Free Press, 1969.

Dubin, R. Theory and research. Chapter 3 in R. O'Toole (Ed.), *The organization management and tactics of social research*. Cambridge: Schenkman Publishing, 1971.

Herzberg, F. *Work and the nature of man*. Cleveland: World Publishing, 1966.

Herzberg, F. et al. *The motivation to work*. (2nd ed.) New York: Wiley, 1959.

Hunter, F. *Community power structure*. Chapel Hill: University of North Carolina Press, 1953.

Merton, R. K. *Social theory and social structure*. New York: The Free Press, 1949.

Morse, P. M., & Kimball, G. E. *Methods of operations research*. New York: Technology Press of M.I.T. and Wiley, 1951.

Popper, K. R. *The logic of scientific discovery*. New York: Science Editions, 1961.

Porter, L. W., & Lawler, E. E. III. *Managerial attitudes and performance*. Homewood, Ill.: Irwin, 1968.

Tyler, L. The development of vocational interest. 1: The organization of likes and dislikes in ten-year-old children. *Journal of Genetic Psychology*, 1955, 86, 33–44.

Vroom, V. H. *Work and motivation*. New York: Wiley, 1964.

CHAPTER 2

A General Systems Approach to Organizations

F. KENNETH BERRIEN
Late, Rutgers University

THE AUTHOR REVIEWS the basic elements of General Systems Theory (GST), and discusses its application to the study of organizations. Systems are sets of interacting subsystems, distinguished by boundaries which select the kind and rate of flow of inputs from, and outputs to, the environment. Constructs of system boundaries, inputs and outputs of various types, adaptation, growth, and resource storage are defined, and their impact on system viability discussed. The author's social system model of organizations is compared with other organizational models, and some criticisms of GST are reviewed. Currently, hierarchical open systems models of organizations appear promising in explaining human behavior within and across organizations. Both the explanatory and the predictive power of GST for organizations may be enhanced if more rigorous operationalizations can be developed for such constructs as social needs satisfaction, system inputs, and other relatively intangible transactions within and between organizational systems.

Perhaps the earliest recorded formal organization was established by Moses in the flight from Egypt. Exodus, Chapter 18, describes how the children of Israel, having crossed the Red Sea, wandered about in the wilderness before Moses's father-in-law—left behind in the dash from Egypt—caught up with the multitude and saw with perhaps fresh eyes the need for some organization.

And it came to pass on the morrow that Moses sat to judge the people: and the people stood by Moses from morning until evening. And when Moses's father-in-law saw all that he did to the people, he said, "What is this thing that thou doest to the people? Why sittest thou thyself alone and all the people stand by thee from morning until evening?" And Moses said, "Because the people come unto me to inquire of God. When they have a matter they come to me and I judge between one and another...." And Moses's father-in-law said unto him, "The thing thou doest is not good. Thou wilt surely wear away, both thou and this people...for this thing is too heavy for thee; thou art not able to perform it thyself alone. Harken now unto my voice, I will give thee counsel...." (This is the first recorded instance of a management consultant.)

"Thou shalt teach them ordinances and laws (the manual of standard operations), and shalt show them the way they must walk and the work they must do (give them a training program). Moreover, thou shalt provide out of all the people able men such as fear God, men of truth, hating covetousness (select according to personnel specifications), and place such over them to be rulers of thousands, rulers of hundreds, rulers of fifties, and rulers of tens (table of organization). And let them judge the people at all seasons and it shall be that every great matter they shall bring to thee, but every small matter they shall judge; so shall it be easier for thyself (assign responsibilities; chain of command), and they shall bear the burden with thee."

The main features of this organization have since characterized governments, armies, corporations, volunteer fire companies, and churches. Perhaps no social invention has persisted unchanged and unexamined so long nor pervaded our lives so extensively as the pyramidal shape of social systems. Moreover, only within the short span of the last fifty years—especially within the post-World War II years—have we become self-conscious of organizational dynamics. Modern society is a network of social systems growing increasingly complex, overlapping, competitive, combative, sometimes cooperative, in which as individuals we find ourselves enmeshed. The very complexity of organizations and their less than perfect operations have no doubt been a major reason for recent efforts to conceptualize the social processes and events that for centuries have been going on within and around organizations.

General Systems Theory (GST) is one attempt to understand not only social organizations but organizations running from molecular to astronomical levels. Such a brash, audacious task is not only controversial but perhaps unfruitful. At the moment it is certainly incomplete, yet some fundamental propositions have been laid down and their applications have found root in ecology, communications theory, weapons development, urban planning, international relations, meteorology, and physiology. Moreover, the development of GST has been a system itself, having drawn from concurrent conceptions in cybernetics, information theory, game theory, and network theory in mathematics to each of which it has returned its own contributions.

Bertalanffy, a theoretical biologist, is generally credited with having first formulated the general outline of General Systems Theory (1950) that attracted the attention of Boulding, an economist (1956), who was joined by a growing list of persons representing a diversity of specialties and professional affiliations, including Miller, a psychiatrist and psychologist (1955); Ashby, a bacteriologist (1958); Rapoport, a mathematician (1956); Buckley, a sociologist (1968), to name only a sampling.

The conception of society as a system of interdependent components, however, has been floating through the writings of a long list of philosophers and social theorists from Thomas Hobbes (1588–1679), Auguste Comte (1798–1857), Karl Marx (1818–1883), Herbert Spencer (1820–1903), down to Parsons (1951), Roethlisberger (1944), and Mayo (1933) of more recent times. These formulations, which space prevents us from examining, though provocative, stood mostly on their own assumptions largely but not completely disconnected conceptually from assumptions that could with equal justification undergird biological and nonliving systems. It is the boast of GST that such assumptions can be made explicit and on such a foundation a structure of definitions and propositions can be erected having meaning for a wide range of systems.

Perhaps an illustration will provide some tentative credibility to the claims of GST before presenting its formal assumptions and logical structure. Andre Lwoff of the Pasteur Institute, Paris, and Nobel laureate in physiology, began his Nobel lecture with these words (1966): "An organism is an integrated system of interdependent structures and functions. An organism is constituted of cells and a cell consists of molecules which must work in harmony. Each molecule must know what the others are doing. Each one must be capable of receiving messages and must be sufficiently disciplined to obey. You are familiar with the laws that control regulation. You know how our ideas have developed and how the most harmonious and sound of them have been fused into a conceptual whole which is the very foundation of biology and confers on it its unity."

If one were to reread this statement, substituting for *organism,* organization; for *cell,* group; and for *molecule,* person, the statement would still have the ring of truth. Moreover, the parallel which Professor Lwoff draws between the harmony of biological units and conceptual integrations again points to the potentials which lie in the general systems approach for spanning the natural and social sciences.

SOME BASIC ASSUMPTIONS[1]

As the above illustration suggests, one basic assumption of GST is that systems exist within systems: for example, molecules within cells; cells within tissues; tissues within organs; organs within organisms; organisms within colonies; colonies within nutrient cultures; cultures within some larger set of cultures, etc.

A second assumption flowing from the first asserts that all such systems are open. That is, each system one examines at any level, except the smallest and largest, receives and discharges something from and to other systems—usually those that are contiguous. Open systems are characterized by a never-ending[2] exchange process with their surroundings—which are other systems. It is possible to conceive of closed systems and sometimes it may be convenient to do so as, for example, a clock work energized by a spring mechanism. One may study such a system as if it were closed. But such a system requires periodic new inputs of energy as the spring dissipates its tension. Genuinely closed systems "die"—cease to function—after a period of time.

A third important assumption, perhaps more questionable than those above, is that the functions of a system are dependent upon its structure. For biological and mechanical systems the assumption has intuitive validity. Muscle tissue contracts because it is built in a certain way. The eye responds to light waves and not sound waves because it has a certain structure, and vice versa for the ear. The structure of a small informal human group, however, is less easily specified, yet the structure of a legislative body or any formal organization can be described. We shall have more to say about social structures later.

SOME DEFINITIONS

One is reminded of the old negro spiritual: "Ever-abody talk about heaven ain't gonna heaven." So many people who talk about systems rarely define what they mean by a system. Definitions, however, are arbitrary conveniences—neither true nor false. It is the privilege of any theorist to establish his own definitions hopeful that his readers will find them not discordant with their own thinking and of equal convenience. A system, for our purposes, is a set of components (also systems) interacting with each other, "enclosed" by a boundary which selects both the kind and rate of flow of inputs and outputs to and from the system.

---

[1] These assumptions and most of the remaining portions of this chapter are developed more fully in F. K. Berrien, *General and Social Systems* (New Brunswick, N.J.: Rutgers University Press, 1968).

[2] Once the exchanges cease, the system disintegrates; that is, it loses its boundary.

The terms of this definition also require explanation. When we say the components are "enclosed" by a boundary, we do not mean necessarily a physical barrier. An organization (athletic team, corporation, church) includes certain persons and excludes others. Membership in any organization requires certain qualifications and to remain a member requires further specifiable behavior. These requirements constitute the boundary of a social system. It is selective in two ways: (1) in filtering people who are admitted to or rejected from membership (recruitment and employment procedures for a commercial organization); and (2) in limiting the behavior of members to only those actions (role behaviors) which the organization establishes as appropriate for itself. Any one of us may hold membership in several organizations (Democratic party, university faculty, hunting club, shade tree commission), but each organization permits the expression of only certain actions within its boundaries out of the total behaviors of which the individual is capable. Organization *A* permits and expects certain roles of its members that would be inappropriate in Organization *B*. For example, the faculty member who used his classroom for promoting the candidacy of his party's nominee would be violating the role expectations within the university, and to "trade" on his university connection while running for public office would at least raise some ethical questions. The usual conflict of interest controversies are conflicts of role expectations when the individual is a member of more than one organization.

The boundary also selects or controls the flow of inputs and outputs. What does this mean? Apart from the employment (input) and discharge or retirement of persons (output), an organization has other kinds of exchanges. To understand these it is necessary to move to a biological level of system analysis for a moment. It is quite clear that any living system (the basic proposition that follows is also true of nonliving systems but we must pass over these in the interest of

conserving space) must first live before it can "do anything." Living requires for animals the digestion and assimilation of nutrients and oxygen; wastes of the metabolic processes are discharged into the surrounding system. These nutrients are what we call *maintenance* inputs: they merely keep the organism alive. In addition, animals as well as plants are irritable: responsive to energies having nothing *directly* to do with maintaining life. These inputs, we claim, can be identified in all systems and serve to *signal* the system to function in ways beyond mere living: locomote, explore, make contact with like systems. Deprived of signal inputs, living systems degenerate; the sensory mechanisms atrophy in higher animals even if kept alive by the usual methods; sensory deprivation in humans even before atrophy sets in produces marked cognitive and emotional distortions. To maintain a fully functioning system both kinds of inputs, maintenance and signal, are necessary but in some balanced relationship.

Applying the broad definitions of GST to particular classes of systems requires the use of terms appropriate to those systems. For a *social* (not an economic) organization signal inputs are the orders, directives, and information it accepts as relevant to its own functioning. A small work group within a larger corporation receives orders (Fleishman, Harris, & Burtt, 1955, called it *structure*) from its foreman or supervisor; the total corporation receives its social directives via the larger society's laws governing policies and practices having some possible impact on that society. This supra-system "signals" the corporation certain proscriptions and prescriptions.

Where are the maintenance inputs for a social system? What keeps it alive? Since any social system is composed of people performing specified roles, their interactions generate either positive or negative affect. We set it as a proposition that individual Homo sapiens require positive social affect as a condition for their effective functioning within any micro-social system; indeed one's distinctive humanness in any circumstance is a consequence of the warmth and persistence of his commerce with his fellowman. Hence a social system is maintained by what we have called the Group Need Satisfactions (GNS) arising out of social interactions.[3] The primary maintenance of a social system thus arises out of the interactions among the components, although we shall see later other sources of maintenance that also exist.

The *outputs* of a system are those energies, products, services, information that are discharged from a system. They are, in some identifiable way, different from the inputs. Systems, we have said, not only exist; they function, do something with the inputs. Systems add, subtract, combine, compare, and/or choose inputs in some fashion to expel outputs. These outputs, in principle, must be different from the inputs given the definition of a functioning system. This is an extremely important feature of systems because it leads to a host of consequences. Moreover, the outputs of a system may be classified as useful to some other system, or useless. The latter, if they are not acceptable to any other system, eventually become additions to entropy—waste. For example, this would include unrecoverable heat in the operation of an electro-mechanical system, or, for a social system, those role behaviors which prove to be unacceptable to all other social systems. One may think of the extremely mentally retarded—the helpless idiots—as having no acceptable social role, and in fact as consumers of the energies of social subsystems that in turn are maintained by resources drawn from the larger society. To the extent that such humanitarian subsystems consume resources which might otherwise be employed in the production of useful outputs for the total society, these energies represent a diversion of energies if not an outright addition to entropy.[4] It is,

of course, conceivable but highly improbable that in time some useful roles may be found for these and similarly handicapped persons. This is merely one out of many instances of entropy at the social system level.

Let us return to useful outputs. We shall argue that every surviving system must provide some output acceptable usually to a collateral or supra-system. A manufacturing enterprise conceived as an economic system must provide a product acceptable in sufficient numbers and rate to the consumer system which returns to the enterprise those resources necessary for its survival. Every social system likewise produces something in addition to Group Need Satisfactions. Two or more people are brought together to produce a report, a product, make a decision, build and maintain a recreation center, form a family, play a game, or create a musical composition. What the group does in these terms we have called its Formal Achievement (FA). Moreover, this FA output is variable on some dimension of quality (kind) and/or quantity. This fact is, of course, only a specific instance of the general assumption that all structures may perform several functions. It is the finite variability of outputs which makes it possible for the "producing" system to provide outputs which are acceptable as inputs to some other system. Systems can only be linked by such means, and the hierarchy of systems, each level dependent upon the others, would be impossible if this were not so.

Let us summarize to this point. A system is a set of interacting components surrounded by a filtering and transforming boundary, accepting inputs of two kinds, maintenance and signal. The components process these inputs, transforming them into useful and useless outputs. For a social system, the components are role behaviors, interacting with other role behaviors gen-

---

[3] This is by no means a new idea although the terms may differ from Hobbes (1651), Comte (1896), or Spencer (1898).

[4] Custodial institutions exist (a) in societies with surplus resources to support them and (b) provide surro-

gate affection and care otherwise expressed directly within the family. The fact that individuals are lodged in such institutions is evidence in itself that the invalids are unacceptable and unproductive burdens on the usual family system.

erating GNS that provides a major but not exclusive source[5] of maintenance. The boundary is the set of social norms characteristic of the group. Signal inputs are mostly related to the FA output of the group, and that FA must be acceptable to some other system if the system is to survive. Whatever the group produces that is not acceptable to other systems are wastes.

Another definition is basic to an understanding of the propositions which follow. The *state* of a system is the particular pattern of relationships existing among the components and the particular filtering condition of the boundary at any given moment in time. The state concept is perhaps only a convenience for purposes of analysis, for without it we would be forced to speak of a never-ending sequence of systems each time the relationships among the components changed. On the other hand, the Roman Catholic Church has an identity extending over nearly two thousand years even though dogma, role incumbents, and internal structure have undergone major modifications during its history. Individuals change from birth to death and yet in another sense are the same. However, it is obvious that the state of the system influences not only what it will accept as inputs (e.g., hungry versus satiated), but the manner in which it processes inputs as well as some aspects of the outputs.

The number of possible states a relatively simple system may assume turns out to be very large. Consider a system of eight input channels and one output—a rough approximation to a neuron of multiple dendrites and a single axion. Let us assume that on both sides the channels may merely "fire" or "not fire." On the *input* side there would be 2^8 input states possible. With only two possible *output* states, the number of possible internal connecting, or not connecting input-output states is 2^n where n is the number of input states. That number is 2^{2^8} or 2^{256}! Clearly, one cannot meaningfully describe

or experimentally test the consequences of each of these states (Beers, 1959). Furthermore, the states are not equally probable, hence their investigation would be of only temporary interest.

This simple calculation is presented not to discourage experimentation, but rather as an example of how a systems analysis may account for non-consistent findings in the study of much more complex social systems. One of the persistent complaints about organizational studies is their failure in many cases to agree even when experimental treatments have apparently been identical. One should rather be amazed at the small degree of agreement that has been attained rather than at the differences in outcomes.

It would be helpful to remember that the variability of a system's outputs is limited by a finite number of functions which a given component may perform and a limited number of states which the total system may assume. Although these numbers may be large they nevertheless begin to provide us with an understanding of the possible parameters inherent in the outputs of systems.

Up to this point we have, with difficulty, avoided the *feedback* concept central to cybernetics and an understanding of surviving systems. Boulding (1956) has suggested that feedback appears in those systems which he places at level three in a hierarchy of nine levels of complexity; therefore, feedback is not a necessary feature of *all* systems. Basically feedback means that some portion of output is returned to the input side and reprocessed through the system. This is illustrated in a microphone-amplified-speaker system when the basic amplifier oscillations (the "hum") emitted by the speaker are picked up by the microphone, re-amplified, re-emitted at a louder level and so on until a loud howl occurs. In more sophisticated systems the output itself is not feedback. Instead, a sensor of some kind "monitors" the output and returns signals to a control device in the input channel. It is convenient to speak of positive

---

[5] Other sources will be specified later.

and negative feedback. Positive feedback signals the control device to provide greater input flow; negative feedback, just the reverse, less input flow. The conventional thermostat-furnace system is typical in which the room thermostat permits a small variation in room temperature, but if the temperature exceeds a given level the signals to the furnace are negative—shutting off the fuel supply—or, contrariwise, if the temperature drops below a given point, the signals are positive and open some kind of valve to allow fuel to flow again. Although this is an engineered system, many examples can be found in nature—physiology, ecology, chemistry.

The great importance of the signal feedback concept and mechanism lies in the fact that its function is self-regulatory and permits systems so equipped to maintain a steady internal state in the midst of great variations in surrounding systems either on the input or output side. In a real sense feedback is the key mechanism that permits systems to live and retain their identity in a changing environment that would otherwise destroy them. To state the idea differently, it is the central but not the sole means of adaptation.

In presenting these definitions it has been necessary not only to illustrate the essential features of systems but to introduce closely related implications of each definition. The meaning of these basic concepts takes on richness as we proceed to examine their application to social organizations and especially to commercial and industrial enterprises. In the following pages, we want to emphasize the adaptive features of organizations, the conditions that lead to survival, as well as the balancing of dependence and independence among systems which must have commerce with each other.

ADAPTATION TO CHANGE

No problem is more important to organizational theory than the management of change, both internal and external. The pace of change within western twentieth century society has reached such a point that serious attention is being directed toward temporary systems, especially in the business world. Miles (1964), Warren Bennis (1966), L. E. Greiner (1967) are but a sample of those who have examined the trend described by Greiner as follows: "Whereas only a few years ago the target of organizational change was limited to a small group or a single department...the focus is now converging on the organization as a whole, reaching out to include many divisions and levels at once and even to top managers themselves." This phenomenon requires that we examine the propositions derived from our definitions that pertain to both internal adaptations and external relationships, discovering how they help in understanding the flux and flow of organizational changes. We shall argue that both kinds of change have some common characteristics although clothed in different operational language. Yet to understand the dynamics of change, we must first come to grips with dynamic stability.

We may start by considering a subsystem within a larger organization—a work group operating under the supervision of a foreman, or perhaps some standing committee of middle managers. Earlier we defined such a group as a set of role incumbents interacting with each other surrounded by a boundary and producing something—service or a product—we labeled Formal Achievement. The evidence for a boundary rests on two characteristics: (1) clear criteria exist indicating who is in or out of the group; (2) the exchanges, verbal and otherwise, among the group members have a different character from the exchanges between the group and other groups, either at the same or different level in the organizational hierarchy. Some features of the discussions among the middle managers are not likely to be reported either up or down the organization. At the very least they will be condensed, filtering out some confidences, irrelevances, or other details which may prove embarrassing. Members of the base level work group likewise interact with each other, passing materials or tools to each other in a pattern unique to that system. Roethlisberger and Dickson (1939) were perhaps the first to emphasize in their report on the Relay Assembly and Bank Wiring Rooms that in addition to these gross physical patterns the internal social exchanges and conversation networks formed relatively stable identifiable patterns. Both supervision and the work groups filtered information in both directions. In these respects the groups satisfied the system's criteria.

The formal achievement of work groups is typically measured with a fair degree of precision, although the particular units employed in various organizations may show great variation.[6] Bowers (1970) suggests three reasonably general indicators of what he calls "effectiveness" but which fit our concept of FA: "1. Volume as a percent of capacity, or alternatively as a percent of schedule. 2. Cost per product unit. 3. Quality $\times$ Volume, divided by total cost." Notice an unspoken assumption in these measures. The cutoff levels are to be established by some agency or system outside the one being measured. The acceptable output must meet the standards of the supra- or subsystem to which the output is delivered. Such measures of FA are especially applicable to base level working groups or for a commercial organization in toto.

In the case of a middle management standing committee, FA is less precisely recorded and may be defined as recommendations to a higher level, better coordination among their respective staffs, decisions pertaining to budgets, safety practices, or other operating routines. Whatever their raison d'être they produce something that is passed on to or evaluated by some other person or group. Moreover, the impact of their FA may often be felt at levels above *and* below them. Barnard (1938) was among the first

to emphasize the "zone of acceptability" for directives coming down the organizational hierarchy. If the committee establishes new safety procedures, tightens the budget, or fails to promote a deserving subordinate, the negative repercussions bounce back. If its recommendations to higher management are frequently unacceptable, the committee may be reorganized. Middle level people always keep a weather eye out for the prevailing winds of opinion and policy above their heads making judicious estimates of when to tack into those winds and when to run with them.

Two points arise out of these considerations. First, groups at every level are under a continuing requirement to deliver FA that is acceptable elsewhere and are capable (under usual circumstances) of modifying their output in accord with these requirements. *A system must first be variable if it is to be adaptable.* The second point is perhaps only a logical corollary of the first. Systems which fail to produce FA acceptable to some other system are doomed, after a time, to extinction.

Earlier we proposed that every system must have a maintenance input and for social systems this can be called Group Need Satisfactions (GNS), arising out of the interactions of the role incumbents themselves. In spite of the fact that something like this has been recognized as essential to the continued life of social systems since Auguste Comte (1896), our technology has fallen far behind in measuring this input-output with the precision that we measure FA. Public opinion polling techniques have been adapted to morale surveys within organizations, yet their sensitivity even to major adverse changes in employment conditions has been questioned (Berrien & Angoff, 1960). However, granting that GNS may not be adequately reflected in any available metric[7] does not invalidate the importance of the concept or its relevance

---

[6] See Seashore, Indik, and Georgopoulos (1960) for evidence of low correlations among several possible measures of FA—accidents, errors, productivity.

[7] Absenteeism, grievances, or labor turnover are imprecise and crude measures but what is required is some metric that can be "tracked" as accurately as FA.

to the continued survival of social systems. It seems a reasonable hypothesis to suppose that *no group will voluntarily continue to function unless its members experience a net positive affect from their interactions.* This does not assume that no negative affect is experienced—only that the balance of negative and positive affect will be in favor of the latter over time.

This hypothesis is rooted at a more fundamental level in the evidence that humans as well as many lower species seek contacts with their like. In another place (Berrien, 1968, pp. 102–104), empirical and theoretical support has been provided for the proposition that an individual must, in principle, interact with others who modify or confirm the individual's evaluations and cognitions, especially those concerning himself. We need not assume some misty instinct for affiliation or gregariousness.

Social exchanges are simply required for the development of one's knowledge of himself. Private experience can only be validated by the slippery media of public communication with others. The stability of the "person system" depends on net positive reinforcements from others.

Finally, the FA of a social system has the potential of contributing to system maintenance. It is not unusual to find people who genuinely enjoy making widgets. In a former era, management often operated on the assumption that work in itself was obnoxious and, therefore, required inducements—mainly wages—to entice men into the organization. We now know this is only a partial truth. The pro football team that wins (this is its FA) has a higher esprit de corps than the losing team. The great joy expressed by NASA personnel when a rocket is successfully launched is another example. A group completing a particularly difficult assignment takes satisfaction from a job well done.

Figure 1 is an effort to portray the relationships just described.

But not all the sources of maintenance reside in the interactions of the role incumbents themselves. The nature of the supervisory climate has a bearing as well (see Taguiri & Litwin, 1968). Fleishman, Harris, and Burtt (1955) made a distinction in the supervisor's behavior between giving structure (directions, orders, or what we have called signals), and giving "considerations." A brief period earlier, Katz, Maccoby, and Morse (1950) had suggested that supervisors could be classified as primarily "person" or "production" centered. Supervisory styles that gave due emphasis to "considerations"—providing encouragement, promoting harmonious interpersonal relations, keeping open channels of communications, mediating quarrels—appear to have a positive impact on productivity or FA.

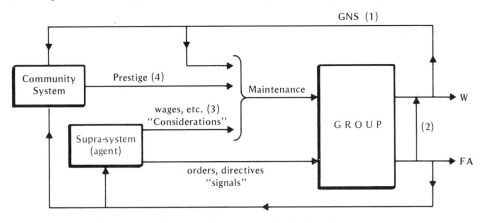

Figure 1. Flow of inputs to and outputs from an organizational work group.

deCharms and Bridgeman (1961) found in an experiment that both FA and satisfactions increased when supervisors deliberately complied with (rather than denied) requests from their subordinates. Wages and salary when influenced by supervisory judgments are, of course, an element in the "considerations." Supervisors are, therefore, a source of both signal and maintenance inputs.

The organization as a whole is embedded in a community which may also be a source of maintenance. Every company has a public image generated by various means—partly by the nature of the work in which it is engaged, partly by its employment and personnel management policies, and partly by the physical appearance and location of its plants. It is a mark of some prestige to be employed or associated with Organization A instead of Organization B because it has a good address, or for reasons just enumerated. Youngberg, Hedberg, and Baxter (1962), for example, found great dissatisfaction with their system of compensation among more than 1,000 salesmen. Yet they also felt that the public prestige of their occupation was the most important factor in their job satisfaction.

In what ways are these features of a social system related—GNS and FA? By definition, dynamically stable systems are those characterized by minimal variation on one or more dimensions in a less stable environment. A stable social system, we propose, is one in which the levels of GNS and FA are *controlled, interdependent* and so operate as to dampen the variability of the supra-system. Let us take as a case a base level work group within an industrial organization. Their upper level productivity limit is a function of physiological skill, and work method factors. It is well known that such groups rarely approach these limits but instead settle upon a production rate defined more by the group norms. On the other hand the lower limit of FA is within the control of the supervision—the supra-system —which may bring to bear various sanctions

for intolerably low FA levels. Individuals or the group as a whole may be dismissed, disciplined, or reprimanded. Thus the FA level at a point in time is the result of balanced forces in opposite directions.

A similar but reverse set of conditions apply with respect to GNS. The lower level of GNS is established by the group itself— the subsystem. Should satisfactions fall below a certain level, people will leave the group. Bickering, discord, hostility, or merely failure to find one's work associates congenial tends toward physical or psychological resignation from the group. On the opposite side, too much socialization, excessively long coffee breaks or lunch hours, and other similar behaviors having no visible relation to FA activities are suppressed by the supra-system.

The situation can be diagrammed as in Figure 2.

To summarize, the supra-system controls the upper limit of GNS and the lower limit of FA. On the other hand the subsystem exercises control over the lower limit of GNS and the upper limit of FA. The system taken as a whole shows a balance of interdependent opposing forces.

From this model it is possible to derive a number of propositions. These have little empirical support at the moment, but they may be tested. Since the supra-system and subsystems are conceived as controlling each other, it would seem reasonable to suppose

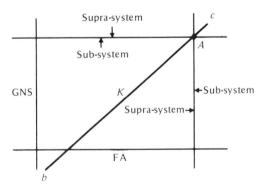

Figure 2.   Countervailing supra-system forces on levels of FA and GNS in an organizational setting.

that the optimal condition would be one in which they are approximately balanced. It follows that if one or other system loses control of its respective variables the balance or ratio of GNS to FA will depart from that optimal condition.

Simon (1947) and, later, March and Simon (1958, Chap. 4) advanced an organizational equilibrium theory which held that a surviving organization is one in which a certain balance is struck between inducements and contributions. This was framed mostly in individual terms, the central proposition being that "each participant and each group of participants receives *from* the organization *inducements* in return for which he makes *to* the organization *contributions*" (March & Simon, 1958, p. 84). The meaning of this statement would not be significantly altered if we substituted GNS for inducements and FA for contributions. We seem, therefore, to be in good company in proposing a variant on a basic concept of balance between production and satisfaction that has been around for some time (cf., Parsons, 1949).

Perhaps we can now see how the system "works." Let us assume a task group which takes pride in its FA, is supervised by a "considerate" foreman, is generally congenial toward each other and works for a company with a satisfactory reputation in its community. Its GNS maintenance from all sources is appropriate and, furthermore, it is producing an FA that meets the standards of the management. In other words, we have a well-balanced system. Let us now assume that for a variety of reasons some increase in FA is required, the GNS feedback from increased FA would, according to Figure 1, add an increment to maintenance even if all other sources of maintenance remained constant. Up to a point the system adjusts itself for the increased FA load. On the other hand, assuming that the system is operating at some point along line *K* in Figure 2, the group takes little or no pride in its FA. Then any increase in FA must be compensated by additions to

maintenance from other sources—possibly "considerations" from the foremen, wages or promises of subsequent time off, etc. (GNS from the community is relatively constant, but may change slowly.)

In a similar manner one may trace the effects of alterations in any of the inputs to discover what compensating adjustments are required to bring the system back to a point somewhere close to line *K*.

The resolution of forces at point *A* cannot be considered a consequence which comes about quickly. For those groups which have existed for some time, point *A* is "norm-determined." That is, the norms of both the sub- and supra-systems play an important part in bringing about the resolution of their respective needs. It should be clear from our earlier discussion of norms that these, in turn, may vary from one group or organization to another. Within one firm having a given reputation, kind of work, and personnel policy, the resolution at point *A* may be quite different from that in another kind of firm. The Michigan studies, for example, of a large insurance company revealed that work groups having "employee-centered" supervisors were more productive than groups with "production-centered" supervisors. The norms were such as to lead employees to expect a moderately high degree of personal consideration. This finding was not confirmed by the same team of investigators when studying railroad section gangs (Katz, Maccoby, Gurin, & Floor, 1951). The railroad workers, whether in high- or low-productivity gangs, evidently were operating within norms that did not require supervisors to give them as much consideration as was true of the office workers.

One of the major empirical problems associated with these formulations to which we have referred earlier resides in the difficulties of discovering the GNS metric. A virtue of any conceptual model is the extent to which it directs attention to hypotheses that require verification. In this case, we have postulated a plausible relationship between one measurable variable (FA) and another

(GNS) that is poorly or crudely measurable and cries out for empirical attention. Until we find the technology appropriate to the problems, we must rest with informed speculations. (This formulation, incidentally, is at variance with a number of organizational theorists including Price [1968], who sets FA as the only criterion of "effectiveness," and "morale" being an intervening variable, although at points productivity is also included as an intervening variable.)

In the presentation so far we have dealt with the conditions which appear to account for the dynamic stability of a social system, especially those systems engaged in doing the world's work. Lying behind all that has preceded is a more basic assumption that stability is desirable or necessary. We had better take a look at this assumption before going forward. For example, is not the growth of an organization also desirable?

It must be emphasized again that the kind of stability so far described is dynamic —the consequence of a continuous flow of events holding the levels of GNS and FA within narrow limits of variability. Such stability has its counterpart in a spinning gyroscope rather than a flat stone on a flat surface. It is the stability similar to the relatively constant room temperature maintained by the furnace-thermostat system which operates in an ambient environment of much greater temperature variations. When one looks into biological systems so linked and interdependent as to function in an "effective" manner, one is impressed with the fact that most if not all of them maintain some feature within narrow limits in the face of surrounding conditions that would radically alter their functioning. For instance, the chemical composition of the blood remains relatively constant whether one is exercising and "in shape," or asleep. Body temperature is another example of variation within narrow limits regardless of wide variations in ambient temperatures. Of course, fevers occur when the organism is invaded by noxious viruses or microbes,

but the rise in temperature is itself one of several automatic means for combating the invasion.

These "natural" examples suggest that if the complex interlocked processes of biological systems are characterized by nodes of stability we might also discover similar stability centers or features of effective social systems which, though man-made, are essential for their survival, and even perhaps their growth.

Computer programming advanced by patterning itself after the logic of humans; but, in so doing, we also learned much about the cognitive processes of men. In similar manner, the functioning and structure of biological systems may provide suggestions for improving or just understanding existing social systems. The processes that operate to maintain a dynamic stability (in our case a relatively constant GNS/FA ratio) can be thought of as processes of adaptation adjusting to non-routine fluctuations in input or output requirements.

ADAPTATIONS TO GROWTH

We define the *growth* of a social system as role additions—an increase in the number of people interacting within the system boundary which also requires some adaptation. Now, one of the interesting features of growth is that a mere increment in size brings with it (1) modification in role specialization and (2) changes in the interactions among the components. Let us illustrate:

A foreign car agency began with the proprietor, his wife as a bookkeeper, and one assistant who was both stockroom clerk and mechanic. Fifteen years later these three persons were still in the organization but the staff had grown to approximately thirty-five. The proprietor who first handled all sales, scheduled repair jobs, ordered cars and parts, negotiated with finance companies, and performed numerous other functions (he would occasionally pick up a paint spray gun or make minor engine adjustments), came to assume more directly personnel functions—hiring, promoting—and retained mostly the financial functions. The stockroom clerk-mechanic became service manager. A staff of five were salesmen; the rest were bookkeepers, stockroom clerks, mechanics (some specialized on electrical systems, others on body repairs, or on the engine itself). The proprietor rarely interacted in the expanded organization with any customer and never picked up a wrench or spray gun. This anecdote illustrates the changing role functions people take on as a system expands—not because they wish but because they must. And new, more highly specialized roles were of necessity introduced into the system.

Haire (1959) has provided a number of ingenious analyses of several business concerns which bear out the square-cube law.[8] He assumed that the employees of a firm assigned to purchasing, shipping, selling, reception, and the like were "surface" employees. They met and dealt with systems outside the firm. The remainder were those who made up the internal portion of the system. Each of four rapidly growing firms was followed over a number of years—as many as thirty-five—and the respective numbers of inside versus surface employees were tabulated at regular intervals. Taking the square root of the second and the cube root of the first and plotting these values gave a scatter plot that was virtually a straight line. If the relationship had been perfectly in accord with the geometric law, the slope of the line would have been 1. The plots for each of the four firms had slopes of .72, .51, .50, and .97, which argues in favor of the view that social organizations appear to grow in accord with a general principle applicable to other systems as well. No measure of the effectiveness of these firms was reported. Had there been such a measure, it would have been possible to determine whether or not those firms most closely approximating a slope of 1 were the most effective.

Furthermore, as our example of the auto agency illustrated, new and much more restricted roles emerged. In larger organizations, individuals are added whose function is largely that of promoting communication among all others. According to Haire's data, another organizational invention—the specialized personnel officer—was established in those firms when they grew to a size of 177, 152, 138, and 248 employees. The remarkable similarity in the size, except for the last, suggests that the accumulation of special kinds of issues pertaining to the recruitment, hiring, promotion, and morale of people reaches a critical point where the full-time attention of a specialized person is required. In three sets of organizations Indik (1965) found that increased size was associated with increasing task specialization. It is one of the lamented features of large organizations that too many specialties have evolved. Too few persons are available who possess the global view which holds the specialists in their proper perspective.

It should be clear that organizational growth beyond a given point not only requires role specialization but also additions of several persons discharging identical or similar roles; for example, several, rather than a single, body-repairman in the auto agency. Now these individuals begin to form social subsystems with their own interactions and boundaries, their own GNS/FA ratios. The internal adaptations required for growth essentially reside in these subsystems making provision for the proper balance of maintenance and productivity. We have then come full circle in the analysis. When one examines organizations that have fallen into difficulties because they have grown too fast, the problems can usually be found in (1) a breakdown in exchanges among the subsystems that would otherwise sustain their mutual supports and (2) inadequate maintenance inputs or some other condition unbalancing the GNS/FA ratio within a

---

[8] A simple geometric principle that as volume increases by a cube function, the surface enclosing it increases by a square.

few critical subsystems or throughout the organization.

Yet there is another phenomenon implicit in the growth of subsystems—in fact in every system—and that is the tendency, once it has some history of effective operation, to persist. Each social system develops its own identity—its pattern of interactions, privacies, and internal hierarchy based on subtle personal differences beyond those of skill or performance.[9] Resistance to measures (signals) that would disrupt these features is particularly strong as they become increasingly satisfying to the members of the system. The members protect their boundary and uniqueness. In this sense they seem to move toward greater independence. Yet holding to the fundamental assumption that all social systems are open requires that they also be dependent on other systems partly for maintenance sources (see Figure 1) and partly for the acceptance of FA. The labor union would have no raison d'être if it were not for the corporation, and the corporation (conceived as all levels of management) would be powerless without a labor force. Many conflicts within the industrial scene can be viewed as efforts on the part of the contending parties to preserve or enhance their independence under conditions which require some mutual dependence.

Shapiro (1964) has given a fascinating analysis of the operation and reorganization of the Ontario Hog Producers Marketing Board in terms not far different from those just presented. This Board provided a marketing mechanism standing between hog producers and packing houses but was subject to the legislative regulations of the Ontario Farm Products Marketing Act, administered by the Farm Products Marketing Board. Essentially, the Hog Producers Mar-

keting Board accepted telephone offering prices from packing houses and allocated shipments to the highest bidders, although identical offers were often received. In such cases, the "Hog Board" arbitrarily assigned shipments, and thus exposed themselves to charges of discrimination among the packers. (Large packers believed they were not getting their share of the crop.) The Farm Products Board tried unsuccessfully for two-and-a-half years to persuade the Hog Board to devise practices beyond reproach. Finally, and with considerable reluctance, harsh disciplinary measures were imposed by the Farm Products Board and an electronic auction system was established. A majority of the Hog Board members shortly thereafter declined reelection.

This capsule account does not do justice to the emotional and political struggle that transpired during the period. Shapiro highlights the dependence-independence issue and the adamant stand of the Hog Board to discharge its functions (FA) as it saw fit, believing that it had the support (maintenance) of the vast majority of hog producers, even though the Board was under a supra-system's legal control in the shape of the Farm Products Board.

This example drawn from marketing illustrates how a subsystem attempts to sustain itself in the face of threats to its existence, especially when its procedures had the support of the input community (hog farmers who in the showdown did not deliver the political clout anticipated). On the other side, it is obvious that the receiving system was dissatisfied with the Hog Board's performance and was effective via the supra-system Farm Products Board to bring about a change more to its liking. The supra-system in this case had the overall responsibility for integrating the exchanges between producers and packers and, therefore, had to recognize complaints from the latter.

Shapiro struggles with the question of whether the Hog Board in fact survived because the membership changed. If one holds

---

[9] A sadly neglected study of "restricters" and "rate busters" is especially relevant here. Dalton found markedly different rates of production were related to family background (rural vs. urban), political affiliation, and religious ideology. See W. F. Whyte, *Money and Motivation* (New York: Harper Bros., 1955), Chapter 6.

to the definition of a social system as composed of roles having specified functions, then the question is easily answered in the affirmative. The major function of the Hog Board continued to be discharged but in a modified way, just as a local or national government or a corporation may survive as an identifiable entity even though the role incumbents change and with these changes modification in the discharging of functions may also occur. The important fact is that a subsystem may develop so much auxiliary maintenance from sources outside its "parent" system that it may operate with increasing independence of the latter. The Hog Board evidently overestimated its auxiliary support and consequently was brought to heel by the supra-system which had created it.

Numerous parallels can be found to the Ontario case, where subsystems grow to the point of generating maintenance sources and acceptable receivers of their FA so that they can become relatively independent. One may recall instances in the academic world where institutes within a university apply on their own initiative for, and receive, grants or funds from foundations or governmental funding agencies and subsequently develop practices and policies independent of the university itself. In some instances, such institutes have separated themselves from their former shelter. Although the recent corporate history has been marked by mergers of firms that were formerly independent, it is also true that some "spin-offs" have occurred where a subsidiary has found it more advantageous to operate without the control of its former corporate management. In either case, a close examination of the transition period will reveal that important and painful adjustments were necessary in redefining the roles of the system's components and in establishing appropriate levels of maintenance.

The important principle to be remembered is that in virtually any large social system composed of social subsystems a source of tension is built in. The subsystems must, if they are to discharge their specialized function, retain an element of uniqueness and autonomy. At the same time, as the behavior of the Farm Products Board illustrates, the supra-system must, in discharging its functions, impose restraints and limits on its own subsystems yet it cannot afford to dominate them completely. Should the latter occur, their boundaries and hence their uniqueness would disappear. The dynamic adjustment requires balancing the control by supra-system against the requirement for some autonomy and independence among the subsystems.

The account so far has emphasized adaptations within a system embedded within some larger supra-system and the necessity of all systems to protect their boundaries and thus ensure survival. Yuchtman and Seashore (1967) and Seashore and Yuchtman (1968) have argued for a somewhat different mode of survival emphasizing the system's "ability to exploit its environment in the acquisition of scarce and valued resources to sustain its own functioning" (1968, p. 186). They hasten to qualify this statement by pointing out, first, that some organizations exist in relatively rich environments (little competition for "valued resources"). Second, "the *ability* to exploit the organization's environment cannot be equated with maximum *use* of this ability in the short run, for an organization might then destroy its environment and reduce its longer-run potential for favorable transactions. We must invoke an optimization concept" (1968, p. 186).

Looking into the records of seventy-five independently owned and managed life insurance sales agencies, they were able to select seventy-six performance variables which were analyzed into ten factors most of which in our framework could be classified as FA —business volume, production cost, new member productivity, youthfulness of members (a state variable), business mix, manpower growth (another state variable), manager's personal commissions, maintenance costs (maintenance of accounts as opposed to selling new policies), member productivity, and market penetration. It is of interest that nowhere in this list is any measure of what we have labeled maintenance or GNS. However, a survey study of management practices in these agencies showed that measures of the managers' supportiveness (presumably a GNS source) correlated with seven performance measures with coefficients running from .20 to .50 *in the year following the survey*. The three performance measures correlating less than .20 were production costs, business mix, and managers' personal commissions.

From the standpoint of the general systems model presented herein, it is significant that Seashore and Yuchtman have not made much of the correlations that provide some indirect empirical support for the proposition that FA and GNS are positively related. However, these investigators view as one of the organization's environments the individual members' personalities which by appropriate managerial policies (supportiveness) are more completely "exploited"—that is, engaged in the system's production of FA.

Looking at these same data from the assumption of "nested" open systems, one would see the individual members not as environments but as system components performing roles (mainly selling) whose maintenance was enhanced by appropriate "consideration" inputs.[10] Such a shift in orientation from the conceiving of individuals as environment to subsystem components results in a somewhat different interpretation of the data. For example, youthfulness correlated .50 with managerial supportiveness. Clearly, youthfulness was not the

---

[10] The published account is not sufficiently detailed to permit a firm conclusion that business mix and production costs were under direct control of the manager, but the manager's personal commissions surely were. If the other two reflected more managerial decisions than performances of the direct salesmen, then this condition might explain the low correlations of business mix and production costs with managerial supportiveness.

consequence of supportiveness but just the other way around—supportiveness was required because of the agents' youthfulness—in our terms, a feature of the system's state. At the same time supportiveness correlated $-.49$ with member productivity, that is, average *new* business volume per agent, young as well as old, although total volume correlated .37. One might hazard the hypothesis in the absence of the partial correlations that great supportiveness is counterindicated in those agencies having a high proportion of experienced salesmen, where a large volume of policies are in force. Without pursuing the details further, if one models such organizations as systems within systems and makes the distinction between state and output, with the manager providing both signal and maintenance inputs (see Figure 1), the data from this study take on meanings somewhat at variance with the "exploitive" feature offered by Seashore and Yuchtman.

The issue, moreover, goes somewhat deeper. The question at stake is whether commercial organizations survive best *even when* they optimize rather than maximize their exploitation of valued resources. The emphasis in the Seashore-Yuchtman model (but not the data) is on the input side and explicitly rejects the Parsonian notion that an organization is effective (survives and adapts) to the degree that it supplies a service or product to some superordinate system (Parsons 1960; Yuchtman & Seashore 1967, pp. 895–896). They argue that Parsons's view places the assessment of organizational effectiveness not in the organization itself but rather in the superordinate system. This they claim only moves the standards of assessment from one level to another without being specific about the standards themselves. Moreover, they assert:

Now there is no argument that the organization, as a system, must produce some important output for the total system in order to receive in return some vital input. However, taking the organization itself as the frame of reference, its contribution to the larger system must be regarded as *an unavoidable and costly requirement* rather than a sign of success. While for Parsons the crucial question is "How well is the organization doing for the superordinate system?", from the organizational point of view, the question must be "How well is the organization doing for itself?" (Yuchtman & Seashore, 1967, p. 896; italics added)

The systems model proposed herein would lead one to conclude that neither question is irrelevant to the other. If one holds clearly and steadfastly to the assumption that such systems are open and, therefore, dependent for maintenance and signals upon some other system and must also produce acceptable outputs, the Yuchtman-Seashore-Parsons issue vanishes. "How well is the organization doing for itself; that is, optimizing resource inputs?" can only be answered by also asking "How well is the organization doing for the superordinate system; that is, delivering acceptable FA?" The survival of supra- and subsystems is interlocked. Rather than an exploitive relationship, the systems model presented earlier requires a mutually supportive relationship between one system and its collateral and/or supra-systems. In making this assertion we are not ruling out the possibility that the mutually supportive relationships may be mediated by intervening third or fourth systems in some chainlike fashion, so that the "vital input" in the question above may come "third, fourth—Nth hand" from the system's output.

It is of some relevance that Katz and Kahn (1966) viewed organizational effectiveness as "the maximization of return to the organization by all means" (p. 170), which Yuchtman and Seashore subsequently modified by invoking optimization but without providing a criterion for optimization. How does one know when the system has or has not reached a point of optimal resource input or exploitation, or is it possible

that some feedback mechanism operates to inhibit total exploitation of resources?

Of course, every scientist knows that if you pose the wrong questions the answers will be misleading—and that is the trouble with the questions just presented. A prior issue must be faced. The questions assume a system input capacity in excess of that which is used and also ignore the fact that many but not all systems have a characteristic we have so far not discussed—storage. Let us deal with the storage feature first, without developing the storage concept as it is found in other than social systems.

We start with the assumption that systems are "nested" and second, that social systems are imperfect inventions of mankind. The Constitution of the United States, though perhaps the greatest instrument struck off by the brains of men, is still imperfect and subject to amendment. At a more prosaic level informal family social structures are in many cases imperfect systems (one out of three end in divorce). At both extremes the systems were created by people. The imperfections of these systems extend to their inadequate articulation with each other. That is, the exchanges among systems either in the supra- or subsystem cycle or between collateral systems are imperfectly matched. Mismatching is the "primitive" condition; improved matching evolves. "Primitive" matching means that one or another of the systems produces too much, too little, or an unacceptable kind of output for another system.

If the subsystem produces too much, storage of the excess may be a possible adjustment. The finished products of a factory not immediately sold are warehoused. The reservoirs of a city's water system is another example of excess output from the meteorological system that is stored for future use. Given mismatching in this sense, those systems that will most likely survive will have the capacity to store resources when the demands of other systems are light, and draw upon those stores when the requirements are heavy. Yet excessive storage capacity can be a handicap: large unused and unprocessed inventories of raw materials on the input side, or finished goods on the output side, are an economic cost. "Stockpiled" personnel not employed to their capacities are not just an economic drain, they are a source of maladaptation. Such groups would be operating perhaps with an overbalance of GNS (Figure 2 in the upper left quadrant) and might be described as fat and happy, prone to resist changes in routines or to deal effectively with emergencies.

If on the other hand a system is called upon to deliver its FA to another system at a rate that exceeds its capacity, "draining" away its stored reserves, it approaches and may reach the point of dissolution. Stated purely in social-psychological as opposed to economic or material terms, a system which is called upon to operate at an extreme level of FA (in the leftish portion of Figure 2) "exhausting" reserves of GNS is in grave danger of personnel defections and resignations. Corrective measures would involve increasing maintenance inputs or reducing the demands for excessive FA (see Figure 2).

An analysis from this point of view does not require the notion of optimizing the system's exploitation of its environment solely for itself, but instead joins the demands for acceptable output to the requirements for adequate input maintenance. Whatever optimizing is involved is not with respect to preserving the environment's total resources but with respect to the maintenance-achievement ratio, internally.

This rather extended reinterpretation of the Seashore-Yuchtman data and model was not presented to attack that model but rather to illustrate how the general systems model may be usefully applied. In particular, the reinterpretation leads to the resolution of some issues separating Parsons from the Michigan investigators and changes the system's environmental relationship from one that could be characterized as relatively self-centered independence to one of interdependence on both the input and output

sides. At the same time, it provides a means for answering the question posed by Yuchtman and Seashore, "How well is the organization doing for itself?"

SOME COMPARISONS WITH OTHER MODELS

A group of social scientists associated with London's Tavistock Institute, especially Trist (1963) and Rice (1963), have developed a systems model of organization not far different from what has just been presented. The chief difference lies in their conceiving of organizations as socio-technical systems thus mixing the economic, material, or machinery features with psychosocial phenomena. One must, of course, recognize that the various systems intermesh in the real world. Moreover, in the preceding account it has been necessary to allude to familiar events in nonsocial systems to make clear the subtle and less evident social transactions or consequences. However, our effort has been to design a *social* model without regard to technological or material exchanges. Whatever transfer of money may be involved, for instance, is only a medium whose psychological meaning is the significant feature. FA, as another example, may be a material product, but its *acceptance* is the important aspect in the proposed model.

The way in which one approaches the task of designing a systems model will be largely determined by the issue or problem he addresses.[11] The Trist and Rice contributions are not, therefore, in necessary conflict with our model, but instead are attempting to deal with matters we have set aside.

The same may be said of Homans's (1950) model that specifies physical, cultural, and technological environments, each having its inputs to and constraining the outputs from the human group. In Homans's terms these are givens and are not conceived as systems themselves, as we do,

---

[11] I am indebted to one of my students, Richard Butsch, for this idea.

each operating with maintenance and signal inputs. Admittedly, this account does not address the culture as a system because as noted above that was not our issue. Nevertheless, it appears that the GST framework could provide the appropriate starting points for such an analysis. Homans in fact makes much of the interdependence between the human group and the environments in which it is embedded and in this respect is consonant with the GST approach.

The linking pin model provided by Likert (1967) emphasizes the fact that key individuals in one system performing specified roles may also be members of other sub- or supra- or collateral systems who serve to link the various systems together somewhat in the fashion of an elaborate mobile. The focus is on these individuals as leaders and carriers of information whose measure of success is essentially the organization's productivity. The performance of the total organization, according to Likert, depends on three basic concepts: "(1) the use by the manager of the principle of supportive relationships; (2) his use of group decision making and group methods of supervision; and (3) his high performance goals for the organization" (Likert, 1967, p. 47).

Although these concepts imply exchange relationships among sub- and supra-systems, the emphasis is on the manager-leader role rather than more broadly on the total system. Again, it is evident that conceptualization of organizations cannot be ranked in some order of good-bad but represent different issues of major concern to the conceptualizer.

LIMITATIONS OF GENERAL SYSTEMS THEORY

This account has not developed in detail the conceptual connections between the GST model of organizations and the more general systems theory as it applies to non-living as well as living systems. The emphasis has been on describing a model within a broader framework just as chess or poker are models within the broad theory of games.[12] One of the criticisms directed at General Systems Theory has been its reliance on analogies. General Systems Theory is no theory at all, say its critics; it is only a collection of interesting similarities between one level of analysis and another. Arguing from analogies is not a respectable logical method.

On the other hand the long view of scientific advance teaches us that progress is made by efforts to unite what at first blush may seem to be different. Bronowski (1959) has observed that "all science is the search for unity in hidden likenesses.... The scientist looks for order in the appearances of nature by exploring such likenesses.... The scientist or the artist takes two facts or experiences which are separate; he finds in them [a] likeness which had not been there before, and he creates a unity by showing the likeness." Moreover, the perception of analogies among systems has been a powerful means for stimulating a search for additional similarities and the formulation of wider and more abstract generalizations. Nagel (1961) observes that "the history of theoretical science supplies plentiful examples of the influence of analogies upon the formation of theoretical ideas; and a number of outstanding scientists have been quite explicit about the important role models play in the construction of new theories. For example, Huygens developed his wave theory of light with the help of suggestions borrowed from the already familiar view of sound as a wave phenomenon; Black's experimental discoveries concerning heat were suggested by his conception of heat as a fluid, and Fourier's theory of heat conduction was constructed on the analogy of the known laws of the flow of liquids; the kinetic theory of gases was modeled on the behavior of an immense number of elastic particles, whose motions conform to the established laws of mechanics.... In each of these examples, as in many others that could

---

[12] For those who may wish to pursue these connections, see in addition to Berrien (1968), Miller (1965) and Bertalanffy, (1968), as well as the various issues of *General Systems Yearbook*.

be mentioned, the model served both as a guide for setting up the fundamental assumptions of a theory as well as a source of suggestions for extending the range of their application." Consequently, while analogies cannot be employed as proof of any theory, they can be, and have been useful ways of reaching an understanding of complex phenomena.

A second criticism directed at General Systems Theory has been that it rarely provides a basis for prediction. It is well to bear in mind that theories like systems *evolve* starting with relatively primitive statements and moving toward more precise, mathematical formulations. For example, it was one of Lewin's hopes (Marrow, 1969) that his formulations concerning life space could be ultimately expressed understandably in topological terms; and, had he lived, this might have been his ultimate triumph. Psychology today is about at the "leaning tower of Pisa stage" through which physics has long since passed. The propositions of GST are mainly descriptive, providing an orienting framework for inspecting events and conditions for the initial purpose of making these understandable to the imperfect intelligence of mankind. Dewey, in his later years, came to believe that the main business of theory building was not to find a copy of nature but instead to reconstruct nature in terms that made human sense.

Hopefully, the abstractions generated by GST may become increasingly precise to the point where they can be reduced to mathematical meta language, and some progress has been made in this direction. However, such progress will probably occur by first developing mathematical statements applicable to models within the theory, and testing these against empirical data. It was pointed out earlier that the social model herein requires measures of GNS and FA. A variety of FA measures are typically available in most organizations or can be obtained readily. On the other hand, only very crude and indirect measures exist for GNS—grievances, absences, turnover—but very little of a positive sort. FA is often recorded by

weeks, months, or even days, but no such close tracking exists for GNS. If the model has any plausibility, then it would seem highly appropriate to develop a better technology to measure more carefully the GNS variables and test the model empirically. Pending this, the model may be useful largely as an heuristic device or as an aid in suggesting post hoc explanations which can be intellectually satisfying. It is often comforting to "understand" what has occurred even in the absence of sufficient knowledge to predict future events.

Although in this account we have concentrated on relatively small groups, the model has some possibilities of being applied to much larger social systems. Among others, Gross (1966) and Bauer (1966) have been exploring the possibilities of developing social indicators at the national level which might be classified according to our scheme. For instance, opportunities for leisure and recreational activities may be conceived as contributing to GNS. Records of paid holidays, reductions in working hours, expenditures on sports, entertainment, and other leisure-time pursuits combined in some rational way might serve to give gross indices of maintenance over a large population. Economic data—gross national product, employment, percentages, corporation earnings, expenditures for hospitals, schools, roads, transport, housing, and food—could provide measures of FA. When one gets down to the operational level to deal with these data there are formidable statistical problems that, however, are solvable, before the indices can be properly designed and interpreted. For instance, as Figure 1 indicates, FA under some circumstances may contribute to GNS, but how much? If one takes employment percentages as one element in the measure of FA, what portion of this is going to be fed into the maintenance channel? Estimates of this sort run through the empirical test of this or any other model of a society (cf., Watt, 1970). Nevertheless, it is only by erecting conceptual frameworks that we discover where ignorance lies, and take appropriate steps to fill the gaps.

The general systems approach to organization is clearly somewhat more complex than the stimulus-response mode which has characterized a great deal of psychological theorizing including theories of organization. John Dewey (1896) more than half a century ago criticized the simplified reflex arc concept as a building block unit for psychology emphasizing that the organism was not a mere receiver of stimuli that reacted. He insisted that the organism influenced what stimuli would be responded to—and how. The systems theory presented here sees the organization not as a pyramid of ascending questions and descending orders as portrayed in *Exodus,* but as interlocking exchange processes within and across system boundaries such that the systems play a great part in determining what they will receive, and searching for what other systems will accept as a requirement for their own survival. Stimulus and response give way to a cycle of activities in which any portion of the cycle may be labeled stimulus or response—which means the distinction so dear to the hearts of many becomes hopelessly blurred.

Moreover, general systems with its emphasis on "nesting" and interdependent exchanges among systems leads to an holistic view of organizations. The component on which one may temporarily focus is understandable only in relation to other components and the total system's functions or operations. The behavior of one piece of an organization is, of course, partly determined by its constituent parts, but it is also partly determined by the larger system in which it is embedded. An enriched understanding of organizations requires orientations in both directions—and sidewise.

REFERENCES

Ashby, W. R. *General systems theory as a new discipline.* Ann Arbor: University of Michigan, *General Systems Yearbook,* 1958, 3, 3ff.

Barnard, C. I. *The functions of the executive.* Cambridge: Harvard University Press, 1938, Chapter 12.

Bauer, R. A. *Social indicators.* Cambridge: M.I.T. Press, 1966.

Beers, S. *Cybernetics of management.* London: English Universities Press, 1959, Chapter VI.

Bennis, W. G. *Changing organizations.* New York: McGraw-Hill, 1966.

Berrien, F. K. *General and social systems.* New Brunswick, N.J.: Rutgers University Press, 1968.

Berrien, F. K., & Angoff, W. H. The sensitivity of employee attitude questionnaires. *Personnel Psychology,* 1960, 13, 317–327.

Bertalanffy, L. von. An outline of general systems theory. *British Journal of Philosophical Science,* 1950, 1, 134–165.

Bertalanffy, L. von. *General systems theory.* New York: George Brazillier, 1968.

Boulding, K. E. *General systems theory: The skeleton of science.* Ann Arbor: University of Michigan, *General Systems Yearbook,* 1956, 11–17.

Bowers, D. *Perspectives in organizational development.* Ann Arbor: University of Michigan, Institute of Social Research, Technical Report Contract #170-719/7-29-68, September, 1970.

Bronowski, J. *Science and human values.* New York: Harper and Row, 1959, 22ff.

Buckley, W., Ed. *Modern systems research for the behavioral scientist.* Chicago: Aldine, 1968.

Comte, A. *The positive philosophy,* Vol. II, Book VI. Trans. Harriet Martinson. London: George Bell and Sons, 1896.

deCharms, R., & Bridgeman, W. *Leadership compliance and group behavior.* St. Louis, Mo.: Washington University, Technical Report 9, Contract Nonr-816(11), 1961.

Dewey, J. The reflex arc concept in psychology. *Psychological Review,* 1896, 3, 357–370.

Fleishman, E. J., Harris, E. F., & Burtt, H. E. *Leadership and supervision in industry.* Columbus: Bureau of Educational Research, Ohio State University, 1955.

Greiner, L. E. Patterns of organizational change. *Harvard Business Review,* May-June, 1967, 119–120.

Gross, B. M. The state of the nation: Social systems accounting. In R. A. Bauer, *Social indicators.* Cambridge: M.I.T. Press, 1966.

Haire, M. Biological models and empirical histories of the growth of organizations. In

M. Haire (Ed.), *Modern organization theory*. New York: Wiley, 1959, 272–306.

Hobbes, T. *Leviathan*. Oxford: James Thornton, 1881; original publication, 1651.

Homans, D. C. *The human group*. New York: Harcourt, Brace and World, 1950.

Indik, B. P. Organization size and member participation: Some empirical tests of alternative explanations. *Human Relations*, 1965, 18, 339–350.

Katz, D., & Kahn, R. L. *The social psychology of organizations*. New York: Wiley, 1966.

Katz, D., Maccoby, N., Gurin, G., & Floor, L. G. *Productivity, supervision, and morale among railroad workers*. Ann Arbor: Survey Research Center, University of Michigan, 1951.

Katz, D., Maccoby, N., & Morse, N. *Productivity, supervision, and morale in an office situation*. Ann Arbor: Institute for Social Research, 1950.

Likert, R. *The human organization: Its management and value*. New York: McGraw-Hill, 1967.

Lwoff, A. Interaction among virus, cell, and organization. *Science*, 1966, 152, 1216.

March, J. G., & Simon, H. A. *Organizations*. New York: Wiley, 1958.

Marrow, A. J. *The practical theorist*. New York: Basic Books, 1969, Chapter 11.

Marx, K. *A contribution to the critique of political economy*. Trans. N. J. Stone from 2nd German ed. New York: International Library Publishing Co., 1904.

Mayo, E. *The human problems of an industrial civilization*. New York: Macmillan, 1933.

Miles, M. B. On temporary systems. In M. B. Miles (Ed.), *Innovation in education*. New York: Bureau of Publications, Teachers College, Columbia University, 1964, Chapter 19.

Miller, J. G. Toward a general theory for the behavioral sciences. *American Psychologist*, 1955, 10, 513–553.

Miller, J. G. Living systems. *Behavioral Science*, July, 1965, 10, 193–237, 337–411.

Nagel, E. *The structure of science*. New York: Harcourt, Brace and World, 1961, 108–109.

Parsons, T. *Essays in sociological theory, pure and applied*. Glencoe, Ill.: The Free Press, 1949, 35f.

Parsons, T. *The social system*. Glencoe, Ill.: The Free Press, 1951.

Parsons, T. *Structure and processes in modern societies*. New York: The Free Press, 1960, 16–96.

Price, J. L. *Organizational effectiveness: An inventory of propositions*. Homewood, Ill.: Irwin, 1968.

Rapoport, A. *The diffusion problem in mass behavior*. Ann Arbor: University of Michigan, *General Systems Yearbook*, 1956, 1, 6.

Rice, A. K. *The enterprise and its environment*. London: Tavistock, 1963.

Roethlisberger, F. J. *Management and morale*. Cambridge: Harvard University Press, 1944.

Roethlisberger, F. J., & Dickson, W. J. *Management and the worker*. Cambridge: Harvard University Press, 1939.

Seashore, S. E., Indik, B. P., & Georgopoulos, B. Relationships among criteria of job performance. *Journal of Applied Psychology*, 1960, 44, 195–202.

Seashore, S. E., & Yuchtman, E. The elements of organizational performance. In B. P. Indik & F. K. Berrien, *People, groups, and organizations*. New York: Teachers College Press, 1968, 186.

Shapiro, S. J. The survival concept and the nonprofit behavior system. In R. Cox, W. Anderson, & S. J. Shapiro, *Theories in marketing*, Series II. Homewood, Ill.: Irwin, 1964, 109–124.

Simon, H. A. *Administrative behavior*. New York: Macmillan, 1947.

Spencer, H. *The principles of sociology*, Vol. II, Book II. New York: Appleton, 1898.

Taguiri, R., & Litwin, G. H., Eds. *Organizational climate*. Cambridge: Harvard University Graduate School of Business Administration, 1968.

Trist, E. L. et al. *Organizational choice*. London: Tavistock, 1963.

Watt, K. A model of society. *Simulation*, 1970, 14, 153–163.

Whyte, W. F. *Money and motivation*. New York: Harper Bros., 1955, Chapter 6.

Youngberg, L. F. X., Hedberg, R., & Baxter, B. Recommendations based on one one-vs.-two dimensions of a job satisfaction questionnaire. *Personnel Psychology*, 1962, 15, 145–150.

Yuchtman, E., & Seashore, S. E. A system resource approach to organizational effectiveness. *American Sociological Review*, 1967, 32, 891–903.

CHAPTER 3

Motivation Theory in Industrial and Organizational Psychology[1]

JOHN P. CAMPBELL
The University of Minnesota

ROBERT D. PRITCHARD
Purdue University

AFTER ATTEMPTING TO DEFINE motivation and motivation theory as they pertain to the study of individual behavior in organizations, the historical roots of current motivational concepts are traced. A distinction is then made between the treatment of motivation in the organizational literature and in traditional experimental psychology, and the research and theoretical issues prevalent in the experimental literature are discussed. Motivation theory pertaining to organizational behavior is then discussed in terms of a process versus content distinction. Within the process theory category, several variants of cognitive expectancy theory and the research they have generated are reviewed. The research data are found to be inconclusive and a large number of problems facing expectancy theory research are cataloged. Content theories are discussed primarily in terms of attempts to develop taxonomies of job related rewards and taxonomies of more basic human needs. Empirical taxonomic work is amazingly sparse. Equity theory, goal setting, the theory of need achievement, and attribution theory are then discussed in terms of how they supplement or contradict the broader expectancy model. Finally, conclusions are drawn concerning (a) the state of the motivation theory art in organizational psychology, (b) the disparity between the experimental and organizational literature, and (c) some new directions for future research in organizational settings.

---

[1] Preparation of this chapter was supported in part by the Office of Naval Research, Contract N00014-68-A-0141-0003, awarded to The University of Minnesota.

INTRODUCTION

This chapter is meant to be a discussion of current motivation theory applicable to individual behavior in organizations. In the best of all possible worlds we might hope that such an examination would produce a set of critical questions, the answers to which would allow us to choose between directly competing theories and ultimately explain considerable variance in organizational behavior. Even the most naive realize that such an aim is presently out of reach. For several reasons, the various theories or models actually conflict at very few points. Motivational theories are not theories in any rigorous sense, and it is difficult to derive directly competing hypotheses that can't be transformed into identical predictions by some parametric manipulation which is not prohibited by the antecedent model. Also, no pair of models deals with precisely the same domain of behavior, although some overlap more than others. This condition has been forced on us by the complexity of the behavior domain we have chosen to study. It simply is not possible to make one theory or model do the job and still keep it within comprehensible bounds. We wish to argue that the various models presented in the literature tend to be complimentary rather than competing and most of them have their own particular utility. Viewed in this way, the organizational motivation literature, while it still tends to be piecemeal and lacking in common terminology, is anything but depressing. Instead, we feel that the conceptual gains made during the past twenty years have been substantial and it is a worthwhile endeavor to examine them.

The period 1960–1975 has seen a large exponential growth in the theoretical and empirical literature concerned with behavior in organizations. In general, as the number of individual contributions to a research domain increase, the pressure for summarization, integration, and codification grows. The individual bits and pieces become too much to handle. This pressure has produced a number of recent reviews of organizational motivation literature (Heneman & Schwab, 1972; House & Wahba, 1972; Lawler, 1973; Lawler & Suttle, 1973; Mitchell & Biglan, 1971). The recent book by Lawler is an especially valuable source.

Our intent is not to go over all this same ground again. Rather, we will try to view motivation in a somewhat broader context than most of the above sources, almost all of which were written with more specific objectives in mind, and fill in the gaps around them.

What Is Motivation?

There is a frequently appearing expression in industrial and organizational psychology which reads, performance $= f$ (ability $\times$ motivation). Many people experience severe stomachaches over the meaning attributed to the term motivation. The primary reason for such pain seems to be the felt need to equate "motivation" with a particular behavior or physical state. For example, the term sometimes is used synonymously with deprivation level, effort expended, general activity level, or degree of satisfaction. Following such a path can quickly produce frustration and a desire to reject the concept altogether. This would be an unfortunate choice. Motivation does have meaning if we take it merely as a summary label that identifies a class of independent variable/dependent variable relationships. That is, the term does identify a certain body of theory which can be distinguished from other theoretical domains, and we shall try to characterize its parameters.

It would help if we expanded the performance $= f$ (ability $\times$ motivation) function a bit. Performance can be regarded as almost any behavior which is directed toward task or goal accomplishment. It may involve the production of a certain number of pieces, resolving a conflict with a co-worker, getting a project done by a certain date, or being seen as a satisfactory performer by one's boss. We will worry about the discrete versus continuous properties of performance goals later. Based on what seems to organize the prevailing literature best, the expression can be rewritten as follows:

$$
\begin{aligned}
\text{Performance} = f\,(&\text{aptitude} \times \text{skill} \\
&\text{level} \qquad \text{level} \\
\times\; &\text{understanding} \times \text{choice to} \\
&\text{of the task} \qquad \text{expend} \\
&\qquad\qquad\qquad\; \text{effort} \\
\times\; &\text{choice of degree} \times \text{choice to} \\
&\text{of effort} \qquad\quad\; \text{persist} \\
&\text{to expend} \\
\times\; &\text{facilitating and} \\
&\text{inhibiting conditions} \\
&\text{not under the control} \\
&\text{of the individual})
\end{aligned}
$$

It is intended to illustrate some obvious points. Performance is not synonymous with effort, ability, or a combination of the two. The choice to work on the task, the understanding of what is to be done, the choice to persist, and the environmental constraints all play an important role. It seems most meaningful to view motivation as a label for the determinants of (a) the choice to initiate effort on a certain task, (b) the choice to expend a certain amount of effort, and (c) the choice to persist in expending effort over a period of time. That is, motivation has to do with a set of independent/dependent variable relationships that explain the direction, amplitude, and persistence of an individual's behavior, holding constant the effects of aptitude, skill, and understanding of the task, and the constraints operating in the environment.

What Are Motivational Theories?

This question is necessary because there are several major classes of theory which operate in different parts of the motivational domain. To imply that all the available theories or models address themselves to the same set of questions is misleading. To compare and contrast them, a certain amount of pigeonholing is necessary.

A major distinction pointed out by Campbell, Dunnette, Lawler, and Weick (1970) is between *mechanical* or *process* theories and *substantive* or *content* theories. The former attempt to provide a generalized explanation of the processes involved which lead to choices among alternative courses of action, varying degrees of effort expenditure, and persistence over time. Process theories first try to define the major variables which are necessary for explaining choice, effort, and persistence. For example, incentive, drive, reinforcement, and expectancy are major variables appearing in various models. Such theories then attempt to specify how the major variables interact to influence particular dependent variables. A simple example might be the assertion that an individual will choose the course of action that leads to outcomes with the greatest total utility to him. Drive theory, reinforcement theory, expectancy theory, and equity theory are all process theories.

Content theories are more concerned with trying to specify the substantive identity of the variables that influence behavior and less so with the process by which they do it. That is, what are the specific rewards people want? What are the basic needs which they try to satisfy? What incentives are the most powerful? Thus a content theory may try to identify the specific entities within a more general class. For example, it may assert that promotions, salary increases, job security, recognition, and friendly co-workers make up the general variable we call job performance outcomes. Another theory may suggest a substantially different list. Although there are usually additional statements which imply how these variables influence the individual, a content theory is not centrally concerned with specifying the precise form of the interactions among variables.

Besides being different in form, these two kinds of theory spring from essentially different traditions in psychology (e.g., see

Madsen, 1965). Process models such as those articulated by Thorndike, Hull, Spence, Hebb, Tolman, and Atkinson have been generated almost exclusively by the experimental side of the science; while the content theorists such as Freud, McDougall, Murray, McClelland, and Maslow have been in the clinical-differential mold. It is of some note that industrial and organizational psychology is one of the few domains in which these two orientations are being used jointly.

Unfortunate though it may be, motivational theorists can also be dichotomized relative to whether their empirical developmental work has been carried out on human or infrahuman subjects. To a certain extent, this phenomenon has pushed the respective theories farther apart than the original intent and the theoretical issues which developed in one set tended to lose relevance for the other.

PROCESS THEORY

To understand many of the issues centered in current process theories it would be helpful to consider briefly their conceptual predecessors. We need not go back to the Greeks even though a number of motivational issues had their intellectual beginnings there (e.g., see Cofer & Appley, 1964).

A Bit of History

As noted by Birch and Veroff (1968) and Madsen (1965), attempts to postulate a formal explanation for the direction, amplitude, and persistence of behavior are of relatively recent vintage. Before the eighteenth century any notion of determinism was largely absent from discussions of behavior. Rationality and free will were the dominant antecedents and concepts, such as motives, needs, desires, etc., were given little credence. However, simple observation of human and animal behavior gave rise to an increasing realization that there were forces beyond rational will that seemed to exert control, especially with regard to animal behavior (Bolles, 1967).

Descartes (1911) attempted to reconcile these observations with prevailing philosophy and theology by invoking a duality of mind and matter. Rationality was retained as an explanation of human behavior, but animal behavior was given over completely to mechanical responding set in motion by instincts. In many respects Descartes's concept of rational choice is very similar to cognitive expectancy as it appears in the models of Edwards (1961), Peak (1955), Vroom (1964), and others. Man makes choices among behavioral alternatives on the basis of his knowledge. For Descartes, the crucial knowledges concerned what was optimal for enhancement of man's God-given nature. Contemporary cognitive theorists are content with notions such as perceived utility and instrumentality for need satisfaction.

Much of the duality was wiped away and motivational concerns took on a more modern form when the English associationists and utilitarians articulated their hedonistic model (Cofer & Appley, 1964). Bentham's "Hedonic Calculus" postulated that individuals consciously calculated the relative pleasures and pains of various outcomes provided by alternative actions and sought to maximize their total pleasure. It's not all that long a jump from hedonic calculus to subjective expected utility (e.g., Edwards, 1961), and the foundations for a cognitive-incentive type theory of motivation had clearly been laid.

Two additional developments created a number of theoretical issues that still prevail in the motivation domain. The English associationists introduced the idea that at birth the mind is a clean slate and knowledge, desires, preferences, etc. are built up through associations of contiguous events. Such a notion was the forerunner of the learning, or associative component, of later models. This learning element was incorporated in a hedonistic framework by the associationists and was used to explain why particular outcomes came to be evaluated as pleasurable or painful.

A second major development was Herbert Spencer's transformation of Darwin's model of biological evolution into a theory of psychological determinism. At the species level he postulated that since organisms indulged in pleasurable activities and avoided painful ones, a correlation developed between behaviors yielding pleasure and behaviors facilitating survival. The same model was applied on the individual level. Since individual behaviors which lead to pleasure are treated favorably by the environment, Spencer hypothesized that the organism's nervous system would evolve in such a way as to make that behavior more likely to occur in the future. Please note that Spencer's theory marks the first articulate conceptualization of the principle of reinforcement and shifts the pleasure principle from a goal or incentive orientation, in which the cognitive *expectation* is critical, to a focus on an individual's reinforcement history. Hedonism has been transformed from a pull theory to a push theory and the battle lines between the two were drawn.

The major component of twentieth century process theory that remains to be identified in earlier work is some conceptualization of how behavior is energized or set in motion. An explanation of behavior virtually requires some parameter representing the force that makes it go. The contemporary labels are *need* and *drive* and they are taken up in the various models discussed below. Their antecedents relative to animal behavior are relatively clear since the energizing force of *instincts* was frequently postulated, even before Descartes (Bolles, 1967). On the human side, various thinkers talked vaguely of impulses and desires but it was not until Darwin's evolutionary model introduced biological explanations into behavioral analyses that instincts were used to explain human behavior. McDougall (1908) gave the term instinct its greatest refinement but also stimulated an overuse of the concept and lists of instincts proliferated beyond reason during the early part of this century. Partly as a result of this sheer promiscuity and partly because it was difficult to deal experimentally with innate behavior patterns, a new concept was needed and Woodworth (1918) coined the term *drive*. He defined the variable as neither innate nor specific to particular behaviors but as a unitary concept which represented an organism's overall activity level, and it was in this form that drive supplanted instincts in experimental psychology.

What this historical analysis is meant to illustrate is that most of the ingredients of contemporary process theories of motivation had been formulated before the twentieth century and before the migration of psychology to America. What remained was for these concepts to be refined and cast in theoretical models that were amenable to the empirical investigations of twentieth century science. For better or for worse this usually meant bringing them into the animal laboratory.

Some Contemporary Issues

Most, but not all, of the theoretical and empirical development of process theory before 1960 took place at the infrahuman level. Some of the issues considered and principles developed have relevance for organizational behavior and some do not. It would be instructive to consider such issues relative to their possible contribution to our understanding of human behavior in organizations.

Determinants of Action: Three Major Theoretical Positions

Reinforcement, drive (or need), and incentives constitute three motivational determinants of behavior that have been used either singly or in combination to form the major motivational models of the twentieth century developed before 1960. The names which loom largest as spokesmen for the various combinations are Clark Hull, B. F. Skinner, and Kurt Lewin.

Hull's theoretical life spanned two major phases and recapitulated a major portion of motivational phylogeny. Sometime before 1937, Hull explained behavior primarily on associative or reinforcement grounds (Bolles, 1967). That is, one could account for an organism's actions on the basis of its prior history of reinforced S-R connections. Hull was thus almost completely dependent on the Law of Effect as articulated by E. L. Thorndike. However, Hull eventually came to the position that S-R associations were not an adequate explanation of how behavior was energized and his model was expanded to include the drive component. Behavior or reaction potential (sE_R) was viewed as a function of two principal components which combined in a multiplicative fashion. The associative component which gives behavior its direction was represented by sH_R, or habit strength, which was a function of the magnitude, frequency, and latency of the amount of reinforcements an organism had been given in the past for emitting a particular response. The motivational, or energizer, component was represented by drive (D) which indicated the general level of pressure for activity. The resulting equation, $sE_R = f(sH_R \times D)$ became a psychological household word. For Hull, sH_R represented learning and D represented motivation. Difficulties in defining these two components still persist and will be briefly enumerated below.

In what was perhaps a third phase of Hullian thought the basic model was altered to accommodate subsequent experimental results that the original algorithm could not handle (Hull, 1952). The discrepant data pertained to the abrupt shifts in behavior produced by changes in reinforcement magnitude (e.g., Crespi, 1942). The original $sE_R = f(sH_R \times D)$ formulation incorporated reinforcement magnitude as one determinant of habit strength (i.e., learning). Thus changes in reinforcement magnitude should produce only gradual changes in behavior as the associative bonds gradually become stronger or weaker. To accommodate the more sudden shifts the model was changed to $sE_R = f(sH_R \times D \times K)$ where K represented the incentive value of the reward and changes in K would be reflected immediately by changes in sE_R. In yet a later modification of the Hullian model, Spence (1956) postulated that $sE_R = f[(D + K) \times sH_R]$. Within this model, behavior can be activated either by a significant drive state or the pressure of an incentive. These different versions of what explains behavior have stimulated a great deal of research within the experimental side of psychology and have created some of their own measurement and explanatory problems. We will touch on some of them later on.

Lewin (1951) was perhaps the only major process theorist who built his model around human behavior rather than the animal laboratory. In bare outline, his theory postulated that individuals have, at any point in time, certain physiological and psychological needs. Two consequences flow from the existence of an individual need structure. Needs create a state of tension which the individual attempts to relieve through appropriate action. They also influence the perceived attractiveness of various actions or outcomes in terms of their ability to relieve tensions. The perceived attractiveness of an activity was referred to as its *valence*. Lewin's concept of need was not too distant from Hullian drive in terms of its tension producing and energizing properties, even though Lewin spoke of an individual structure of specific needs while Hull viewed D as a generalized energizer. However, instead of combining tensions with associative strength to account for behavior, Lewin viewed the force on an individual to be a combination of the push of need tensions and the pull of highly valent outcomes. Lewin explicitly rejected reinforcement history as a predictor of behavior and preferred to know what value the individual *expected* from certain actions.

Thus an individual could take action directly counter to his reinforcement history if some new influence (e.g., new information) led him to assign a higher valence to it. This view was the first major twentieth century step toward incorporating human thoughts and expectations within a process model of motivation. It is the principal foundation underlying the bulk of current theory pertaining to work motivation.

The third major dominant force is Skinner who rejected theory building as a legitimate endeavor and preferred to base his explanation of individual actions on one overriding engineering principle, reinforcement. For Skinner, needs, drives, tensions, or other internal states are anathema and predicting behavior on the basis of perceived incentive value or valence is an indirect way to proceed and potentially misleading. To understand behavior and to control it, what we need to know are the reinforcement contingencies to which an individual or class of individuals has been responsive in the past. Upon this knowledge entire cultures can be built, changed, or destroyed (Skinner, 1948, 1971).

The Skinnerian position should be distinguished from a more theory oriented "pure associationism" view of motivation which retains certain parts of the drive concept. For example, as noted by Weiner (1972) association theorists such as Postman and Estes distinguish between the stimulus properties of a drive and the energizing properties. The internal stimuli produced by a drive state can be incorporated in a learning, or associationist, framework in the form of discriminative stimuli that influence response selection. The concept of drive as a generalized pressure on the organism to act is thus exorcised.

Thus our three major theoretical positions have been laid out. Hull combined reinforcement history and drive, or need state. Lewin combined need state and the incentive value (valence) of outcomes which were expected to occur if action were taken. Skinner focused exclusively on the organism's reinforcement history. What kinds of empirical questions have these theoretical positions generated? Since the Lewinian position underlies so much of the study of motivation in organizations, the issues and questions associated with need-expectancy-valence concepts will unfold in subsequent sections of this chapter. What we would like to do now is consider a brief list of research questions generated by the experimental and infrahuman literature. Such a list may help us delineate relevant issues that are pertinent to human behavior in organizations.

Recurring Experimental Questions

What follows leans heavily on the review work by Atkinson (1965), Berlyne (1967), Bindra (1969), Birch and Veroff (1968), Black (1969), Bolles (1967), Cofer and Appley (1964), Kendler (1965), Madsen (1965), Weiner (1972), and Wike (1969).

1. How should the concept of drive, or need, be defined? Historically, drive was referenced to level of deprivation in physiological needs. The physiological referent soon proved untenable and for some (e.g., Miller, 1948) drive became synonymous with the need to reduce any strong stimulus, regardless of whether it was acquired (learned) or physiological. However, it did not take long to show that both animals and men will act to increase the intensity of certain stimuli, and constructs such as the curiosity drive were invoked. Current thinking seems to center on an optimal or homeostatic level of stimulation which may be influenced by many parameters associated with (a) the individual, (b) the situation, and (c) the particular drive at issue. A state of high drive is then the discrepancy between the current level of stimulation and the optimal level. Thus an individual in an employment role may have a drive or need for security, but his objective is to optimize, not minimize or maximize, the level of stimulation created by the need.

2. Is drive a undimensional or multidimensional construct? Hull was clearly on

the side of a generalized activator of behavior. Regardless of whether drive level was increased by food, water, or sex deprivation, the effect on behavior should be the same. This position has been relatively well devastated (Atkinson, 1965; Bindra, 1969), but the alternative of postulating many specific drives is uncomfortable to contemplate theoretically. It is interesting to note that Bolles (1967) and Berlyne (1967), both hard core experimentalists, have called for what amounts to a factor analytic approach to obtaining a drive taxonomy.

3. By what mechanisms does drive influence behavior? Hull's original formulation stated that D was supposed to energize any and all behavior. It interacted with associative history (learning) to determine the *strength* of the dominant response, which had already been *selected* via learning. However, there are really two major alternative roles that drive could play. One focuses on the reinforcement properties of changes in drive. The other involves the effect of drive level on the incentive value of a stimulus, or valence of outcomes. This distinction is one of the major differences between a Hullian and an associationist type model, as mentioned in the previous section. The distinction is synonymous with the backward working or "push" characteristic of reinforcement and the forward working or "pull" characteristic of incentives (Weiner, 1972). To oversimplify, the question being asked is whether both D and K are necessary in the Hullian formula $sE_R = f(sH_R \times D \times K)$. If we concentrate on the reinforcing properties of drive, we again come up against the question of what kind of manipulation is reinforcing. Is it (a) drive reduction, (b) an increase in drive, or (c) a change in the direction of some optimal level that is reinforcing? The experimental literature suggests that it can be all three. The incentive view creates questions about how particular needs or drives ascribe values to specific stimuli, which is certainly a popular question in the organi-

zational literature. Running through both arguments is the question of whether the relationship between change in need state and change in incentive or reinforcement value is a continuous function or is discontinuous at one or more points.

4. Is the influence or reinforcement primarily a "learning" or "motivational" phenomenon? That is, did Hull (1952) and Spence (1956) make the right move when they factored K out of sH_R and made it a separate "motivational" component? In the experimental domain this question appears as a consideration of whether reinforcement acts to facilitate the gradual building up of associative connections or whether it operates on response strength independently of associative strength. Kendler (1965) argues that it is not possible to separate the two issues either conceptually or experimentally. However, the issue is important because if traditional learning concepts can explain all the relevant features of response then there is no need for a body of theory labeled motivation. In spite of the experimental difficulties involved both Bindra (1969) and Black (1969) argue strongly that learning or association cannot explain a number of experimental findings and that reinforcement indeed has a large motivational component. The most frequently mentioned datum is that a change in reinforcement magnitude produces abrupt shifts in behavior that cannot be accounted for by a gradual building up of associative bonds.

5. Consideration of the reinforcement literature also forces a confrontation between the Skinnerian and Hullian models. Do we really need concepts such as drive and incentives or can reinforcement explain it all? Attempts to demonstrate the independent effects of reinforcement and D have been singularly unsuccessful, except in the instance of food deprivation. Most of the experimental effects produced by variations in drive level have also been produced by changes in reinforcement magnitude or reinforcement latency. In sum, demonstrating

the independent effects of $_sH_R$ (learning), K (incentives), and D (drive or needs) has been experimentally slippery and scientifically frustrating. Perhaps it would be better to follow Skinner's dictum—reject all constructs involving surplus meaning, and stick to the observable effects of reinforcement, where a reinforcer is completely defined by the operations involved.

6. The Skinnerian point of view is perhaps not so simple as it first appears. For example, suppose we consider the following question a bit more closely. What is a reinforcement? It is very difficult, even in principle, to define reinforcement. Black (1969) notes at least two different uses of the term. First, it can refer to the empirical principle that certain stimuli or events can apparently alter the probability of a response if they follow that response closely in time. Such stimuli are called reinforcers. Second, reinforcement is often used to describe a set of operations performed by the experimenter as in the statement, "the subject was reinforced for every fifth response." Black (1969) notes that it is now the behavior of the experimenter, not the subject, that defines a reinforcement. The distinction creates certain difficulties. For example, how do we know that every fifth response, as perceived by the experimenter (or his recording device), is always the same response, or that there indeed were four, and not three or six, responses in-between each reinforcement? Such questioning exposes the fact that within experimental psychology there is also no conceptual formulation of what is a response. This may not be a problem in a highly controlled laboratory setting but when the behavior under consideration is more complex, the question of what responses are being reinforced is paramount. Also, the distinction between defining reinforcement in terms of subject versus experimenter actions leads to situations such as E offering a reward but S refusing to take (consume) it. Has a response been reinforced or not? If so, what is the real rein-

forcer? Parallel problems in the organizational situation are obvious.

In an attempt to get out of this bind, Black (1969) prefers to talk about "reinforcers" as stimuli which have in the past changed the probability of some response and "reinforcement" as the act of presenting reinforcers to subjects.

7. A number of heavily researched questions have revolved around reinforcement parameters. For example, what governs how secondary reinforcers develop? That is, under what conditions can a previously neutral stimulus become reinforcing? What are the asymmetries in behavioral effects between presentation of a positive reinforcer and removal of an aversive or negative one? What are the effects of punishment (presentation of a negative reinforcement after a response is not the same as removal of an aversive one after the response has been made)? What's the optimal reinforcement schedule? What is the effect of delayed reinforcement? How do variations in reinforcement magnitude affect the response?

The experimental evidence is relatively clear on a number of points. The powerful effects of variable ratio reinforcement are well known. It is also clear that the magnitude of reinforcement is associated with the strength and latency of a response. Unfortunately, the asymmetry between positive conditioning and aversive conditioning is not well known and there are no generalizations to offer. Punishment does weaken a specific response if an alternative response is permitted. However, by necessity in most instances, the response which is reinforced is that elicited by the punishment itself. Since this is almost always some sort of fear or withdrawal response the societal or organizational value of punishment can legitimately be questioned. Evidently, it is not possible to produce competing behavior via punishment such that the new response can be positively reinforced (Bolles, 1967).

From the standpoint of organizational psychology, perhaps the most serious gap in the experimental literature is the lack of any definition for a response. In the laboratory, the question may be moot but in the organization it is the touchstone of the entire enterprise.

8. What is the locus or mechanism of reinforcement? That is, what makes a reinforcer reinforcing? Such a question would not concern a Skinnerian, but it has concerned others. As noted by Berlyne (1967), most of the experimental work has revolved around three possibilities. The first involves the change in stimulus conditions, originally stimulus reduction. Following this route leads directly to a search for the crucial stimuli. Is it stomach contractions (altered by eating), the sight of an onrushing car (altered by running), or the fluid pressure in the cells (altered by drinking)? The second alternative suggests that consummatory behavior itself is reinforcing. The experiments comparing the reinforcing properties of saccharin versus sugar (e.g., Sheffield & Roby, 1950) and those where food is allowed to reach the stomach normally versus being injected through a fistula (e.g., Berkun, Kessen, & Miller, 1952) have been attempts to determine the reinforcing properties of the consummatory act itself. A third alternative involves changes in the central nervous system. That is, considerable recent research (e.g., Miller, 1957; Olds, 1956, 1962; Olds & Milner, 1954; Roberts, 1958) has centered around trying to find specific locations in the brain whose chemical or electrical stimulation will reinforce behavior.

Premack (1965) has recently offered yet another conceptualization for what makes a reinforcer reinforcing. His explanation is centered in the response and says that if the situation is such that a low probability response is followed by a high probability response, the latter will reinforce the former. For example, turning left in a T-maze is a low probability response for a rat and eating at the goal box is a high probability response. Thus, any response can serve as a reinforcement if the situation can be arranged properly. A rat may operate an activity wheel for a chance to lick water from a cup or vice versa. Similarly, an individual may work hard to be able to spend money or he may spend money for a chance to work hard. It depends.

In sum, research in this area has produced a number of interesting hypotheses but there is as yet no definitive answer as to what makes a reinforcer reinforcing. Future work may or may not produce unifying concepts which will tie together consummatory acts, response probabilities, and changes in the central nervous system (CNS).

9. Berlyne (1967) argues that the concept of drive has indeed foundered on our inability to give it a reasonable definition and would agree that reinforcement can assume most of its functions. However, it may yet be possible to preserve its role as a general behavioral energizer if we root it firmly in an organism's physiological functioning. In this form, drive level has been defined as *arousal* or *activation* level and has spawned a very recent but large and growing literature. We can thus ask questions concerning the locus of arousal and how it interacts with rewards and incentives to influence behavior.

The precise definition of arousal is an active issue and the arguments are analogous to those centering around intelligence. Berlyne wishes to deal with a general factor derived from the first principal component. Others (e.g., Lacey, 1967) believe the low intercorrelations among some measures suggest a number of common factors which have different behavioral effects. The issue is not resolved. Variables frequently used to measure arousal are such things as heart rate, galvanic skin response (GSR), certain derivations of EEG recordings, and the level of stimulation in certain areas of the reticular formation and hypothalamus.

When viewed in this physiological framework, it seems permissible to make a few generalizations from the empirical evidence. For example, arousal can be made experimentally independent of reinforcement and it does enhance the effects of reinforcement under certain conditions. Changes in arousal may also serve as positive or aversive reinforcements in their own right. Whether a change in arousal is positive or aversive depends to a large extent on the magnitude of the change in relation to the existing arousal level. Larger and larger departures from the base level have increasingly positive effects until a peak is reached. The curve then drops and further increases eventually become aversive. This curvilinear relationship also seems to hold for the interaction of arousal and incentives. Individuals prefer the difficult instead of the easy, and novel instead of routine tasks under conditions of moderate, rather than high or low arousal.

10. By what mechanisms is an organism's behavior sustained or stopped? Even a cursory reading of the motivation literature shows that to a great extent theorists have been concerned with explaining behavior over a relatively short run of responses. The Skinnerian model, as well as most reinforcement theories, is strangely silent on the matter. By implication, reinforcement theories tend to fall back on some notion of satiation or homeostasis which tends to limit them to reinforcers operating on tissue needs, which in turn severely limits their applicability to behavior in organizations. Premack (1965) offers a non-tissue hypothesis when he suggests that behavior will stop in a given situation when the probability of the reinforced response begins to approach the probability of the reinforcing response. Helson's (1959) notion of adaptation level suggests that for every stimulus (physiological, social, or whatever) there is a region or level of adaptation (AL) at which the organism will no longer respond. The adaptation level is a function of three components: (a) the current stimulus magnitude, (b) the context in which it occurs, including the magnitude of stimuli recently presented, and (c) some parameter associated with the individual. Thus, other things being equal, continued presentation of the same reinforcing stimulus will even-

tually raise AL and render the reinforcer ineffective. Few data are available to suggest what this function might look like in an organizational situation. Thus the general experimental literature is not much help to use in explaining how behavior is motivated over a long period of time.

SUMMARY COMMENT. Infrahuman though it is, we think there are a few provocative suggestions that can be drawn from the experimental literature. For example, the concept of drive has not proven useful in explaining experimental results and the preponderance of opinion is that it should be discarded. Bolles (1967) feels reinforcement can do it all. Berlyne (1967) opts for an interaction of arousal, as he defines it, and reinforcement. A possible moral for organizational psychologists is that we should stop talking about need theories and start putting together lists of reinforcements while at the same time trying to get some handle on the assessment of arousal. The power of variable ratio reinforcement and the impotence of punishment in laboratory settings also begs for consideration in the organizational situation. However, lest we get too enamored with a Skinnerian view of reinforcement, the literature reviewed by Bindra (1969) and Black (1969) reminds us that it would be worthwhile to worry about the incentive properties of reinforcement. It might also pay dividends to explore the adaptation level phenomenon with regard to rewards and incentives under the control of the organization.

Unfortunately, the experimental literature provides few guides as to how to identify reinforcers and how to define a response. Skinner (1971) passes over these problems much too glibly. Perhaps the most unfortunate by-product of infrahuman research is that the nature of the species precluded intensive investigations of cognitive type models, even though Black (1969) would argue that a concept such as "assumed reward value" is useful for explaining nonhuman behavior. Thus a large chunk of the theoretical domain for which these were ample historical antecedents went virtually unexplored, until recently. It is to these recent developments in cognitive models that we now turn.

Cognitive Process Theories

Although we cannot verify the state of affairs for infrahuman species, we can be reasonably certain that women and men have thoughts about things that have happened to them, have expectations about what might happen in the future if they follow a particular course of action, and will most likely state their intentions if asked what they intend to do vis-à-vis some goal. In short, people think; and motivation theories which take account of this fact can be labeled cognitive theories. Most of these models are of relatively recent origin and they are being developed in the context of organizational, or at least adult, task behavior.

Most of the current cognitive theories owe their immediate ancestry to Lewin (1938) and Tolman (1932). Both held that individuals have cognitive expectancies concerning the outcomes that are likely to occur as a result of what they do, and they have preferences among outcomes. That is, an individual has an idea about the possible consequences of his or her acts and conscious choices are made among consequences according to the perceived probability of their occurrence and their perceived value to the individual. Tolman and Lewin's theoretical notions gave rise to at least three important models which have relevance for organizational behavior: (a) a model of human decision making (e.g., Edwards, 1961), (b) the theory of need achievement, and (c) Vroom's expectancy-valence theory of work motivation.

Another body of cognitive theory, but stemming from somewhat different origins, is that having to do with cognitive consistency or cognitive valence as an internal state toward which individuals strive. The

dominant model in this category is Festinger's (1957) theory of cognitive dissonance. The organizational manifestation of this theoretical theme is in the form of equity theory (Adams, 1963a) which will be discussed later in this chapter.

Since Vroom's expectancy-valence model soon became, rightly or wrongly, the dominant motivational theory in organizational psychology (Lawler, 1973), we would like to discuss briefly its basic parameters and their subsequent modifications. More detailed treatments of these topics can be found in Lawler (1973) and Mitchell (1974). Following a brief look at the expectancy-valence theory, we will examine the other major theoretical forces in terms of how they compliment or contradict the expectancy-valence model.

Vroom's Theory of Work Motivation

The Vroom model attempts to predict (a) choices among tasks or (b) choices among effort levels within tasks. In brief, he sees the force on a person to choose a particular task or effort level as a function of two variables: the valence, or perceived value of outcomes stemming from the action, and the expectancy, or belief, that the behavior will result in attaining these outcomes. Thus, the Vroom formulation in its simplest terms is Force = (Expectancy that effort results in attaining outcomes) × (the valence of the outcomes). The complete model is a bit more complicated than this and contains three basic constructs: valence, instrumentality, and expectancy.

Valence refers to the perceived positive or negative value ascribed by the individual to the possible outcomes of action on the job. In the case of the effort model there are really two kinds of outcomes. The first is simply the level of performance achieved. Different levels can take on different valences. The second type are those outcomes which might be contingent on performance. These can include pay, promotion, transfer, peer acceptance, working irregular hours, recognition, supportive supervision, etc. These outcomes are also ascribed a valence.

Instrumentality refers to the perceived contingency that one outcome has for another. That is, given any "index" outcome the model implies we should ask questions about the extent to which possessing the index outcome is instrumental for obtaining other outcomes. One very important index outcome is the level of performance an individual achieves. For example, high performance by an hourly paid carpenter on a construction job will probably not result in a pay raise. Thus, the instrumentality of high performance for pay is low. However, the instrumentality of high performance for supervisory recognition may be quite high. Instrumentality is seen by Vroom as a correlation coefficient varying from $+1.0$ through 0 to -1.0. That is, high performance could mean avoidance of certain outcomes as well as their attainment.

Valence and instrumentality combine to determine the valence of a given performance level. More specifically, the valence of a given performance level is obtained by multiplying the instrumentality of that performance level for obtaining each outcome times the valence of that outcome, and these products are summed over all outcomes.

Recall that the basic Vroom model was given above as Force = Expectancy × Valence. The last term of this equation has now been specified. *Expectancy* refers to the perceived relationship between a given degree of effort expenditure and a given level of performance. Its metric value is viewed as a perceived probability varying between .00 and 1.00. An example of a low effort-performance expectancy situation would be an assembly line where the number of units produced is determined largely by the speed of the line. In this situation the probability is very low that increased effort would result in producing more units.

At this point we have specified the model's three basic ingredients. The *Force* on a person to choose to expend a given level of effort is a function of these three

variables and is determined by the sum of the products of expectancy × valence, or, as Vroom puts it:

The force on a person to exert a given amount of effort in performance of his job is a monotonically increasing function of the algebraic sum of the products of the valences of different levels of performance and his expectancies that this amount of effort will be followed by their attainment. (p. 284)

Finally, the level of effort a person will choose to expend is that for which force is a maximum.

Please note that Vroom's theory is stated in terms of expectations and perceptions of *future* consequences. The individual's previous reinforcement history plays no role. Neither does the concept of drive or need; however, Vroom notes that if the perceived valences of a number of outcomes are highly correlated and the individual seems to have a high or low preference for the entire class of outcomes, we could think of the class as representing a "need." But in no sense is the concept of need basic to the theory. What the model says we need to know are: (a) the value an individual anticipates for each outcome in an exhaustive list of outcomes, (b) the degree to which each outcome is perceived as being contingent on various levels of performance, and (c) the perceived probability that the individual can attain each of those levels of performance.

We would now like to discuss a number of elaborations and modifications of Vroom's original statement. Again, the reason for this approach is that the expectancy-valence formulation is currently the dominant theme in work motivation.

Graen

The extension proposed by Graen (1969) is an attempt to broaden the conceptual base of the expectancy-valence model by incorporating theoretical notions from attitude theory, role theory, and the interpersonal influence process. The resulting increase in the number of parameters that must be considered may seem to give his model considerable additional complexity; however, his purpose is to make explicit at the outset variables that must be faced sooner or later anyway. These can be grouped under two major headings.

First, the task of a motivational model is not seen as merely to explain effort or choice as they are directed toward greater performance on some specific task, but to consider the full spectrum of job behavior in a system of multiple employment roles. Some examples of different roles are effective performer, friendly co-worker, leader, manager, and dependable employee. The set of roles which best describe the domain of organizational behavior is an empirical question. However, after making an argument for the importance of the multiple role orientation, Graen concludes that the roles of effective versus standard performer are the central roles in his model. A crucial point is that for any particular role there are a set of implicit or explicit standards which indicate whether an individual has or has not met the role expectations.

The second major modification is to consider all the possible outcomes of meeting or not meeting the standards for specific work roles and break them into three major classes. First, there is a class of intrinsic, or internally generated, consequences that individuals grant or do not grant to themselves as a result of meeting the standards for a particular role. Externally mediated outcomes are in turn broken down into the second and third sub-categories: One has to do with pressures to comply with the role expectations that emanate from some person(s) in power (e.g., the supervisor); the second, although not explicitly stated, has to do with role outcomes that are specified by the organization or the culture as being attached to that role. For example, meeting the requirements for "executive" may mean a high salary, neighborhood respect, but perhaps your undergraduate son's disdain.

Being a friendly co-worker may lead to interesting conversations and/or wasting time.

These three classes of outcomes are combined in a multiplicative way with the instrumentality of a particular role for achieving them to yield the overall attraction of a particular role for the individual. The effort an individual exerts to achieve the role (e.g., none, "standard amount," "superior amount") is then a function of the attraction of the role and the expectancy that a particular amount of effort will lead to meeting the role expectations. A more formalized, but abridged, schematic representation of the Graen model is given in Figure 1 for the two seminal roles of effective versus standard performer.

Basically, Graen is attempting to predict the probability of superior effort expenditure. As the bottom of Figure 1 indicates, the Probability of Superior Effort equals Path-Goal Utility plus External Pressures toward Superior Effort plus Internal Pressures toward Superior Effort. The first component, Path-Goal Utility, is similar to Force in the Vroom model. It is composed of what Graen terms Goal Attraction and Path Efficacy. Goal Attraction is similar to Vroom's Valence of Performance. It is the sum of the products of the valence of outcomes multiplied by the instrumentality of a given performance level for attaining these outcomes. The other component of Path-Goal Utility is Path Efficacy which is the perceived degree of relationship between a given effort level and attaining a given performance level, similar to Vroom's Expectancy.

The second component is External Pressures toward a given effort level. This component is composed of the individual's perceptions of effort levels others expect him to exert (a kind of valence index) multiplied by the amount of pressure these other persons would apply to influence his compliance (a kind of instrumentality).

Internal Pressures toward a given effort level constitutes the third component. It consists of the individual's preferences (va-

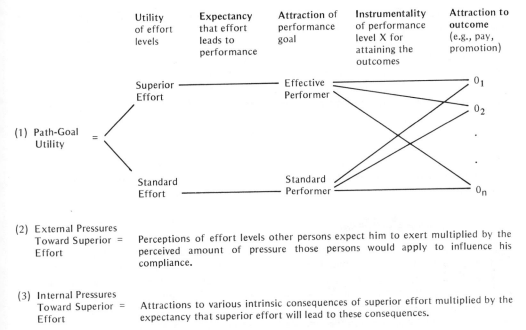

Figure 1.   Schematic representation of simplified Graen model.

lences) for various intrinsic consequences of a given effort level multiplied by the expectancy that that effort level will result in these consequences. The total amount of internal pressures toward a given effort level is the sum of these products.

Graen postulates that the three components of this model—Path-Goal Utility, External Pressures, and Internal Pressures—combine additively to produce the overall probability of superior effort. Further, each of the three major components is weighted via a multiple regression beta weights. This implies that research is needed to determine the relative contribution of each to the weighted linear sum.

While this is the basic idea of the Graen model, the actual operationalization of the model quickly becomes more complex. This complexity results from Graen considering

the probability of superior effort, his ultimate criterion of motivation, as a function of the resolution of pressures toward or against superior effort applied through path-goal utility, external pressures, and internal pressures. He speaks of utility of superior effort versus the utility of standard effort; the goal attraction of the role of effective performer versus the goal attraction of not attaining the role of effective performer; external pressures toward superior effort versus external pressures against superior effort, etc.

Much of the real complexity of the Graen model, as well as the Vroom model, stems from using discrete effort levels such as high versus low, superior versus standard. Both models deal with the anticipated value of each of the effort levels to the individual. But how many effort levels are needed? Graen talks about two, Vroom doesn't really say. The use of discrete effort levels makes operationalizing either of the models difficult. Even if one were to arbitrarily specify two effort levels as all that need be considered, someone interested in testing the Vroom model is forced to measure expectancies for *each* effort level and performance level combination. The problem is larger for the Graen model when external pressures and internal pressures, each composed of two sets of values, must be measured twice.

Porter and Lawler

The model proposed by Porter and Lawler (1968) attempts to avoid the problem of dealing with discrete effort levels and differs somewhat from the Vroom and Graen models. It is the least complex of any of the expectancy-valence models we have so far discussed and the basic variables in their model are as follows.

Value of rewards is similar to the corresponding concept in the other models in that it refers to the perceived attractiveness of possible extrinsic and intrinsic outcomes to the individual.

The dependent variable to be explained is individual effort as it is directed toward performance. The usual distinction is made between effort and performance (i.e., performance has a number of other determinants besides effort and these are not the concern of the model). Performance refers to the sum total of successful role achievement and is not limited to productivity or physical output.

As the result of performing, an individual receives certain rewards, either from the organization or from himself. Thus Porter and Lawler make a distinction between intrinsic rewards, such as feeling of accomplishment that the individual grants to himself as a result of his performance and extrinsic rewards that are granted by other people, such as pay, recognition, or an opportunity to attend a T-group. Reward is

virtually synonymous with the term outcome as used by Vroom and Graen. One of the major determinants of effort is the individual's perceived *value of reward* (i.e., valence).

A second major determinant is *effort-reward probability* or the perceived contingency between effort expenditure and obtaining certain specific rewards. This overall relationship is composed of two component relationships. One has to do with the perceived contingency between effort and performance. Porter and Lawler state it in terms of the perceived probability that performance depends on effort. The second component is the perceived contingency between performance and obtaining rewards, or as they state it, the probability that rewards depend upon performance. They are not explicit about the nature of the function between effort and performance and between performance and reward. Does the individual carry a correlation around in his head, which implies a continuous function, or does he estimate probabilities only in terms of specific performance goals and/or specific effort levels (à la Vroom and Graen)? In subsequent research using their model, Porter and Lawler used questionnaire items asking the subject to estimate the overall relationship between effort and reward, which implies they are thinking of continuous functions.

In sum, the amount of effort an individual will expend toward performing is hypothesized to be a multiplicative function of the perceived value of rewards and the perceived contingency between expending effort and obtaining rewards, which in turn is a multiplicative function of the two components described above.

The model also incorporates two feedback notions. One straightforward hypothesis is that over time the perceived effort-reward contingency will change as a result of the actual reward practices that are followed by the organization (extrinsic) and the individual (intrinsic). This is merely saying that reinforcement history affects cognitions. The second feedback loop involves the effect of felt satisfaction with a reward on subsequent anticipated value or satisfaction. Felt satisfaction results from the degree to which an individual perceives the rewards he receives to be equitable. Equity or inequity is derived by comparing the level of rewards actually received with the level an individual feels he should receive for a particular level of performance or for occupying a particular organizational role. The implication is that rewards can vary from fair to deficient. That is, Porter and Lawler do not deal with the consequences of over-reward. In any event, the question immediately arises as to whether satisfaction with a reward increases or decreases its perceived value in the future. Porter and Lawler enter a plea (legitimately so) of "no data" and surmise that it may have either effect, depending on the reward involved. At the extremes it is reasonable to hypothesize that satisfaction with food may decrease its perceived value as a reward but satisfaction with a feeling of accomplishment may increase the value of such a reward. Again it's a distinction between a "homeostatic" view and a "growth" model. It is unfortunate that motivation theory, especially in the human domain, has been so silent on the dynamics of this situation. Porter and Lawler at least acknowledge the issue.

Lawler Modifications

The basic Porter and Lawler portrayal of expectancy theory subsequently has been modified, or rather elaborated, somewhat by Lawler (1971, 1973). The modifications are also discussed in Lawler and Suttle (1973). Basically, the elaborations entail a more formal specification of the parameters that determine an individual's expectancy that effort will lead to task accomplishment and an inclusion of a third feedback loop.

The individual's subjective probability that effort will lead to goal accomplishment is seen as being determined by (a) the task information specific to the particular stimulus situation under consideration, (b) the individual's fund of information concerning how he or she has done on similar tasks in the past, and (c) the individual's self-esteem, or a relatively permanent characteristic of the individual's personality that reflects the generalized perception of competence across almost all task situations. Lawler does not specify how these components might combine to determine the expectancy judgment or whether "sub" expectancies defined by these various components might relate differentially to behavior.

The additional feedback loop concerns the effect of task success or failure on the individual's general self-esteem and on the specific expectancies which become characteristic of specific kinds of tasks. Lawler does not speculate further on what some of the dynamics of these feedback loops might be. For example, one might expect generalized self-esteem to change more slowly as the result of feedback than the specific expectancies of task success which are attached to specific tasks.

A Composite Picture of VIE Theory

Expectancy-instrumentality-valence theory (VIE) represents the dominant theme in motivational explanations of human behavior in organizations and we have just reviewed three major versions. They differ somewhat in the terminology they use, the variables they deem as important, and the kinds of relationships they postulate. The distinctions are not great but they are sufficient to require a very careful reading before the similarities and differences are apparent. It would be desirable if we had some composite picture which combined the contributions of Vroom, Graen, and Porter and Lawler, seriously contradicted none of them, and provided a framework with which to integrate additional theoretical notions and research data. What follows is meant to be such a composite.

Again, our justification of trying to combine the above ideas and present yet another picture is that we do believe that an expectancy-valence model adds clarity to our thinking about motivation, even though it very quickly becomes operationally complex. Human beings have thoughts and intentions which influence their behavior. Expectancy-valence theory takes account of these phenomena, reinforcement and drive theory do not. Also, we will see that such a model can profitably incorporate a number of additional theoretical notions, as well as a lot of research data.

The schematic shown in Figure 2 is meant to point out the relevant variables and their juxtaposition. In our opinion, a precise statement of how they interact is still beyond the power of our science and we will come back to that problem later. However, knowing the precise nature of the interactions, perhaps it is not necessary for the model to be useful in guiding research and practice. We will proceed sequentially through the diagram and try to indicate where the same variable or relationship was present or absent in previous models.

Basic Components

The *dependent variable* to be explained is either (a) the *choice* which is made among alternatives, (b) the amount of *effort* which is directed toward some goal, or (c) the *change* in effort or choice which results from what actually happens to the individual over time. Vroom's Force and Graen's probability of an act are consistent with all three while Porter and Lawler's discussion of effort as a dependent variable makes no mention of choice behavior. For purposes of brevity, most of what follows deals with amount of effort as a dependent variable. Again, as was stated earlier in this chapter, performance is not the dependent variable the model is trying to explain, since performance is a function of many other antecedents besides the "motivational" ones.

Choice or effort is directed toward something. For our own purposes, we wish to talk about choices directed toward alternative tasks and effort directed at performance levels within tasks, and we would like to refer to a specific performance level for a specific task as a *task goal*. Porter and Lawler talk only of effort directed at total performance, Vroom's Force to act is directed at choices among tasks or choices among specific performance levels. For Graen, the probability of an action governs a choice between performance levels within a particular organizational role. Our use of the term task is not meant to conflict with the term role. First, a role is simply a very

Force to expend specific level of effort	Expectancy that specific level of effort will/will not accomplish task	Valence of task goal accomplishment/failure	Instrumentality of task accomplishment/ failure for job outcomes	Valence of job outcomes	Instrumentality of job outcomes for need satisfaction	Valence of "basic" needs

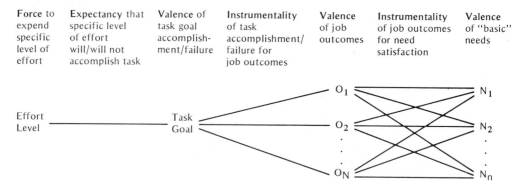

a For purposes of simplicity this schematic portrays only one level of effort and one level of success on one task goal. A similar set of relationships exists for alternative levels of effort and alternative tasks or alternative levels of success.

Figure 2.   Composite expectancy-valence model[a].

general kind of task. Obviously, task goals incorporate several parameters that might have important implications for behavior. For example, tasks vary in terms of their *content,* or simply the kinds of behaviors that are required to perform them. Second, another related parameter would be the *dimensionality* (e.g., unifactor versus multifactor) of the task's content. In most job situations Graen's "effective" performer goal would be multidimensional. Third, given a certain content structure, tasks vary in terms of their level of difficulty. Fourth, task goals can vary in terms of their relative clarity or ambiguity. At one extreme both the methods to be used to accomplish the task and the criteria for judging when the goal is met may be readily apparent to all observers. At the other end, there may be very little agreement. Fifth, task goals can vary in terms of who determines them. That is, who specifies their content and difficulty? Is it the organization, the experimenter, or some other external agent, or is it the individual? Thus, it becomes relevant to ask whether task goals are *externally* or *internally* mediated, and sometimes it may not be so obvious. The supervisor or experimenter may think the individual is behaving in accordance with an externally formulated goal when in fact the individual has redefined the situation quite differently and has a quite different goal in mind. All this is a somewhat roundabout way of saying that task content, difficulty, goal clarity, and locus of goal definition are important parameters of tasks to consider when using an expectancy type model.

At this point, we should also keep in mind the distinction between behaviors, or actions, and the outcomes produced by the behaviors or actions. As Lawler (1973, p. 46) notes, this is not always an easy distinction to make when dealing with expectancy theory. Parenthetically, we should also note that it is not an easy distinction to make when evaluating any kind of performance, and it has plagued the "criterion" problem for decades (Campbell, Dunnette, Lawler,

& Weick, 1970). In the present context the observable behaviors taken in pursuit of a goal are actions, in the Vroom sense, while the *decision* as to whether the actions, or products produced by the actions, meet the criteria for goal accomplishment is an outcome.

As the result of achieving or failing to achieve a particular task goal, certain other outcomes may result. That is, a number of other outcomes may be directly contingent on achieving or not achieving the goal (performance) outcome. This array is composed of outcomes which are the direct result of task performance. Following Graen's discussion of internal versus external pressures and Porter and Lawler's intrinsic versus extrinsic rewards, we think it makes sense to talk about two major classes of goal contingent outcomes. *External* outcomes are those provided by the organization or other people (e.g., recognition, money, promotion, harassment, or freedom from harassment) and *internal* outcomes are those mediated within the individual and which the individual grants to himself or herself (e.g., a feeling of having used abilities to the fullest or disgust at having to do something considered reprehensible). Making this distinction in a specific organizational context does not argue against the notion that internal outcomes originally came to be established via external mediators. That is, an individual's previous learning history produced the association of feelings of disgust with certain kinds of tasks. The distinction is really meant to differentiate between those outcomes which are under the direct control of the individual and those which are not.

Although not included in any previous model, we would like to distinguish between outcomes which are directly contingent on task accomplishment and another class of outcomes which are at least one step removed from the direct consequences of task performance. These more "distant" outcomes have to do with the satisfaction or somewhat more basic individual needs. For example, a salary increase (first level or performance contingent outcome) might be used to finance the purchase of a new home (second level outcome). To the extent that a number of such outcomes are highly interrelated we might say that their principal component represents an underlying *need*. Vroom speaks of needs in much the same manner but he does not distinguish between first and second level outcomes. Within his framework, needs are seen simply as clusters of interrelated outcomes. Admittedly, adding this third class of outcomes to the picture introduces more complexity and it may indeed be empirically superfluous since using an expectancy model does not require these outcomes to be identified. However, what must be identified are the outcomes which are directly contingent on performance and to mix up these two kinds of outcomes in a measuring instrument would cloud the use of the model.

As it is in all expectancy models, a basic determinant of action is the *valence* of outcomes, that is, their perceived or anticipated value to the individual. The valence of an outcome may vary from extremely positive to extremely negative (aversive).

The outcomes contingent on task accomplishment acquire their valence through their ability to satisfy the more basic needs people have. Dependent on the need in question, positive valence may accrue from maximizing need satisfaction, minimizing it, or moving it toward some optimum level. It's sticky business and reminiscent of the arguments over the reinforcing properties of drive. The weight of the experimental infrahuman literature says the need concept is not required, but as we shall see, the organizational literature persists in talking empirically and theoretically about specific needs. The valence for the directly contingent outcomes is the same concept as Vroom's valence of outcomes, Graen's attraction of role outcomes, and Porter and Lawler's value of rewards.

As pointed out by Campbell, Dunnette, Lawler, and Weick (1970), there is difficulty regarding the association between acquiring performance contingent outcomes and need satisfaction. As the magnitude or amount of the outcome increases, the needs on which it operates may change. For example, Cofer (1967) speaks of the sign versus consummatory value of money in that at lower pay levels a wage increase represents more of life's necessities, but at higher levels it is *symbolic* of greater achievement, more status, etc. Thus the function may be discontinuous at a number of points.

Following Vroom and Graen, it also makes sense to posit a *valence for performance* or task accomplishment itself which is in turn a function of the valence of the goal contingent outcomes and the *instrumentality* of performance (i.e., task success or failure) for obtaining these outcomes. For example, salary increases might be positively contingent on performance, unrelated to performance, or even negatively contingent (e.g., the boss is threatened by high performers and rewards them less).

Different types of metrics have been assumed for the instrumentality variable. Some people think of it as a correlation (e.g., Vroom) that varies from $+1.0$ to -1.0. Others think of it in terms of a subjective probability statement that varies from 0.0 to 1.0. Regardless of what metric is used, the instrumentality measure is fundamentally a conditional probability. That is, the model says to ask people to estimate the degree to which an outcome is dependent on performance, given that the performance goal is achieved or given that it is not achieved. For example, given that a project is finished satisfactorily, what are the chances that a bonus will be received? Or given that an individual meets the standards for "satisfactory performer," what are the chances that he or she will not be fired? It is also true that any correlation coefficient can be represented as an array of conditional probabilities. Thus the distinction between the operational uses of the two is still whether we want people to make the transformation from conditional probabilities to a correlation in their heads or whether the measurement method used to assess instrumentality should make the probability judgments explicit. Asking for conditional probability estimates requires asking a larger number of questions, but it does allow use of something other than the bivariate normal distribution to represent the relationship between the level of performance which is reached and the amount of the outcome that is received.

The remaining link in the picture is an individual's expectancy that the task in question can be accomplished; that is, the subjective probability or degree of belief that the task goal(s) can be met. Again, there are two general ways we could query someone about their expectancies, regardless of the specific methodology that is used. First, the individual could simply be asked the question, "What is the probability that you can meet this task goal?" Second, the judgment could again be made a conditional one and the individual could be asked, "What is the probability that you can meet this task goal, *if* you expend X amount of effort?" As was the case with instrumentality, the first question can be transformed to the second if a representative sample of effort levels is chosen.

How should the issue of a conditional versus nonconditional mode of estimating expectancy and instrumentality be resolved? As we noted before, if estimates of expectancy and instrumentality must be obtained for several levels of effort and several levels of task accomplishment then using the model becomes quite expensive. Nonconditional estimates are cheaper but the distinction between linearity and nonlinearity is lost.

In general, if we wish to use the model to interpret what's going on in a field setting or make predictions about the *general* level of effort in a particular situation then overall estimates of the relationship between effort and performance and between performance and outcomes seem appropriate, given that we satisfy the conditions which make an overall estimate (i.e., the correlation coefficient) meaningful. However, if

we are motivation theorists interested in testing various aspects of the model itself then it is more informative to deal with effort as directed toward specific task goals or performance levels. For example, what level of expectancy generates the most effort? On its face, the model says the higher the expectancy the greater the effort, but perhaps that's not so. We could ask the same thing about instrumentality. The usual expectancy model says one thing, Skinner says another. To test such questions, a linear estimate of instrumentality will not do; we need to portray the distribution. In this situation we aren't required to deal with a large number of goal or performance levels but can choose those which suit our experimental purposes.

Feedback Loops

Although they are not shown in Figure 2, recall that Porter and Lawler were the only previous expectancy theorists to include feedback loops in their model. Satisfaction, or the degree of perceived equity generated by the obtained rewards, most surely influences the perceived value of rewards in the future; but the direction of influence most likely depends on the kind of need for which the reward has instrumentality. For example, for needs such as achievement, the more rewards that are piled on the *more* the individual may want. It's unfortunate that this kind of feedback relationship has received so little empirical or conceptual attention. Besides a feedback loop for valence of outcomes, similar loops should be considered for expectancy and instrumentality. For example, what is the effect on expectancy of continued success or failure? What are the long term effects of a .50 probability for receiving certain valued outcomes? Answers to these questions are fundamental to our understanding of behavior over significant intervals of organizational life. They also take the expectancy theory out of its ahistorical context, which has both advantages and disadvantages.

Summary of Composite Picture

In summary, within the organization itself, effort is a function of three determinants: (a) the expectancy that effort will lead to task accomplishment, (b) the instrumentality of task accomplishment for obtaining or avoiding task contingent outcomes, and (c) the valence of the outcomes. The joint function of instrumentality and task contingent outcome valences yields a valence for a specific standard of performance. Effort is then a joint function of expectancy and the valence of performance. The corresponding functions are:

Effort $= f$(Expectancy
$\times$ Valence of Performance)
or
Effort $= f$(Expectancy $\times$ Instrumentality
$\times$ Valence of Task
Contingent Outcomes)

While most expectancy theorists subscribe to a multiplicative function for combining the effects of these three major determinants, we feel uneasy about such a formulation and would prefer to leave the question open.

Certain predictions flow from the above picture, most of them relatively obvious, but worth listing, if only to call them into question.

1. The greater the individual's expectancy that effort will accomplish task goals, the greater the effort expended, other things being equal. Under certain conditions, other models make opposing predictions and we shall review some conflicting data.

2. The greater the instrumentality, or the perceived probability that reward is contingent on performance, the greater the effort expended, other things being equal. However, on their face the laboratory data on reinforcement schedules do not support this assertion and any garden variety Skinnerian would opt for a probability considerably less than 1.0.

3. The greater the valence of a performance contingent outcome, the greater the effort expended, other things being equal. This prediction is general enough that there are few conceptual or empirical conflicts with it. It is well established in the laboratory at least that increasing the size of the reward increases the magnitude of the response. For the organizational situation there are problems like how to combine internal versus external outcomes when they have similar instrumentalities, but opposite valence (e.g., you get a lot of money for performing tasks that really disgust you). However, this seems to be a measurement problem rather than a theoretical one.

4. If expectancy, instrumentality, or valence is zero then effort in the direction of performance is zero. This makes reasonable sense and is one of the strongest arguments for a multiplicative rather than an additive model.

5. The model also predicts that if we think of job satisfaction as the extent to which important needs are satisfied by rewards, then satisfaction is a resultant of performance (that leads to rewards), but not vice versa. There will exist a correlation between performance and satisfaction if and only if the relevant instrumentalities are not zero.

Research Evidence Pertaining to Expectancy-Instrumentality-Valence Theory

Before going on to consider the content side of organizational motivation theory and the more specialized models that supplement or contradict the general expectancy model at various points, we would like to consider briefly the present state of empirical research relative to expectancy-valence theory. This is in no sense meant to be a comprehensive literature review, but is intended to give, in rather Spartan fashion, a representative sample of the prevailing empirical winds and the methods by which the theory has been operationalized. More detailed treatments can be found in Vroom (1964, 1965), Campbell, Dunnette, Lawler, and Weick

(1970), Lawler (1971, 1973), Heneman and Schwab (1972), Dachler and Mobley (1973), Mitchell and Biglan (1971), House and Wahba (1972), Miner and Dachler (1973), and Mitchell (1974).

Kinds of Studies

Before discussing specific findings we would like to outline two basic parameters that we think are important for distinguishing among studies. The first has to do with the research setting in which the study was done and whether it was experimental or correlational in nature. A cross-classification of setting and methodology yields five principal varieties.

1. A few investigators have conducted laboratory experiments using students as subjects (e.g., Arvey, 1972; Motowidlo, Loehr, & Dunnette, 1972; Pritchard & DeLeo, 1973). Keep in mind that VIE theory deals with perceptions as determinants of behavior and even though expectancy, instrumentality, valence, or some combination thereof might be manipulated experimentally, the model says that the subject's perceptions of the manipulated situation must then be obtained and related to behavior. Not all experimental studies purporting to "test" VIE theory have done that.

2. There have been at least two attempts to manipulate VIE components experimentally in simulated organizations (e.g., Graen, 1969; Jorgenson, Dunnette, & Pritchard, 1973). Both of these set up temporary "employer overload" type organizations and "hired" subjects to work on a very short term basis. Such studies preserve the controls necessary for a true experiment but also add a great deal of realism to the task content.

3. There has been only one study (Pritchard, DeLeo, & VonBergen, 1974) to date that has approached the nature of a true field experiment in which VIE variables were experimentally manipulated in an ongoing organizational setting.

4. Perhaps the bulk of the studies pertaining to the VIE model are correlational field studies in which existing perceptions of expectancy, instrumentality, and valence are assessed via a questionnaire instrument and the resulting scores and combinations of scores are correlated with the dependent variable (e.g., Arvey & Neil, 1972; Dachler & Mobley, 1973; Gavin, 1970; Hackman & Porter, 1968; Lawler, 1968a; Lawler & Porter, 1967; Mitchell & Albright, 1972; Mitchell & Nebeker, 1973; Schuster, Clark, & Rogers, 1971).

5. A subset of the above would be a correlational field study which attempts to measure the independent and dependent variables at two points in time and then employs a panel design or path analysis in an attempt to gain some insights into the causal relationship. The Lawler and Suttle (1973) study is an example of such a design.

The second major parameter pertains to the way in which the dependent variable has been operationalized. Consider the following list:

1. A few studies have used occupational or job preference as a dependent variable (e.g., Holmstrom & Beach, 1973; Mitchell & Knudsen, 1973; Sheard, 1970; Vroom, 1966; Wanous, 1972). However, this is analogous to using the valence of specific task goal or performance level as a dependent variable and only one study (Sheridan, Richards, & Slocum, 1974) has attempted to predict an individual's actual choice of a job.

2. A number of studies have used "rated" effort as a dependent variable (e.g., Hackman & Porter, 1968; Lawler & Porter, 1967; Mitchell & Albright, 1972; Mitchell & Nebeker, 1973; Pritchard & Sanders, 1973; Schuster, Clark, & Rogers, 1971). Almost all of these studies have been carried out in a field setting, but there is a major distinction between studies that have employed self-ratings of effort versus those that have used supervisor or peer ratings.

3. Several experimental laboratory or simulation studies used measures of task performance (e.g., Arvey, 1972; Cartledge, 1972; Graen, 1969; Jorgenson, Dunnette, &

Pritchard, 1973; Motowidlo, Loehr, & Dunnette, 1972). Strictly speaking, the expectancy model does not try to explain performance, since there are many other determinants of performance besides motivational ones. However, for the most part, the laboratory and simulation studies have chosen very simple and repetitive tasks for which the explicit or implicit assumption has been that individual differences in performance should reflect primarily effort differences and not differences in skill, aptitude, or task understanding. Everyone should have more than enough skill to perform well. For example, Graen (1969) and Jorgenson et al. (1973) had subjects search for simple errors in computer printouts, and Arvey (1972) and Motowidlo et al. (1972) asked subjects to add two digit numbers. The field study reported by Dachler and Mobley (1973) also focused on simple production tasks, but for real jobs in two different manufacturing operations.

4. Finally, other studies have used the VIE model to predict performance or job satisfaction in relatively complex jobs. Again, these dependent variables are outside the confines of the VIE model, but a number of investigators have used them anyway.

Valence and Behavior

While a few data do exist pertaining to the relation between valence and effort and between valence and performance, the results are quite mixed. In several managerial samples Porter and Lawler (1968) found in general that the greater the importance attributed to pay, the higher were the individual's performance evaluations and ratings of effort. In a study by Pritchard and Sanders (1973), 148 employees in a government agency who were learning a new job completed a questionnaire that included measures of valence of job outcomes and performance-outcome instrumentalities. The criteria consisted of self and supervisors' ratings of effort for different aspects of the training program. The sum of the valence

ratings correlated .54 with self-reported effort and .21 with supervisors' ratings of effort.

There are also some negative findings. Hackman and Porter (1968), in a survey of telephone operators found that the median correlation between measures of performance and valence of outcomes was only .16. However, when valence was multiplied by instrumentality to get an overall prediction, significant correlations with performance were obtained even though correlations of instrumentality with performance were also low. Further negative evidence comes from an experimental study by Jorgenson, Dunnette, and Pritchard (1973). Although the design was complex, the essential elements consisted of hiring subjects for what they felt was a real job and paying them on a high performance-outcome instrumentality pay system (a semi-piece rate) for six days. The valence of outcomes portion of the model would predict that for subjects on such a pay system, there should be positive correlation between the valence of pay and performance. However, this was not the case. Correlations between rated importance of pay and job performance ranged from −.18 to .15 for the six days, with a median of .05.

The predominant impression generated by these data is that no definite conclusions can be drawn regarding the predictive utility of the valence of outcomes portion of the model. However, three conditions must hold for the valence of outcomes to be related to effort or performance. Performance-outcome instrumentalities must be greater than zero, effort-performance expectancy must be greater than zero, and there must be some variability in the valence of outcomes.

Low correlations between valence of outcomes and effort or performance cannot in themselves be taken as negative evidence for the influence of valence of outcomes, if the research effort was not specifically designed to control for these factors. It is also apparent that methods used to measure valence have been of the crudest sort. In spite of the fact that the measurement of the utility of an outcome to an individual has consistently been shown to be one of the most difficult problems in the investigation of human choice behavior (e.g., Becker & McClintock, 1967), organizational psychologists have exhibited little sense of urgency about the matter. The difficulty is illustrated by asking simply, "What is the utility to an individual of a $500 salary increase?" The analogous question for other outcomes presents even more problems. Assuming they can put them all on a common dimension, asking subjects to rate the importance or desirability of various outcomes produces a weak ordering at best, yet the model requires a utility scale with substantial interval or perhaps even ratio properties. All of which argues that we should spend more time developing better measures of valence.

It would seem unwise to conclude that valences don't affect behavior since the literature in experimental psychology is quite clear in showing the significant influence of reward magnitude on subsequent behavior.

Performance/Outcome Contingency (Instrumentality)

The literature on this component of the model is fairly extensive and offers consistent support for the effects of the component on effort and performance. The crucial question concerns the form of the relationship.

The classic study by Georgopoulos, Mahoney, and Jones (1957) surveyed 621 production employees on an incentive system in a unionized household appliance factory. Via questionnaire they measured both the instrumentality of high *and* low performance for the attainment of the three outcomes of making more money in the long run, getting along well with the work group, and promotion to a higher salary rate. The results indicated that subjects who reported high instrumentalities tended to be higher producers.

A number of other correlational studies have supported the link between instrumentality and behavior. Lawler and Porter

(1967) used a three-item composite measure of instrumentality which included two items dealing with performance-outcome instrumentality and one item dealing with effort-outcome instrumentality and found low positive relationships between this composite instrumentality measure and ratings of effort (median $r = .18$), but little relationship between the instrumentality measure and ratings of performance (median $r = .11$). In a more extensive study (Porter & Lawler, 1968), using a similar instrumentality measure, they found instrumentality generally related to ratings of performance, and even more strongly related to ratings of effort. Using the Lawler and Porter questionnaire with male and female managerial candidates, Gavin (1970) found that instrumentality was positively and significantly related to supervisors' ratings of performance for both males and females (median $r = .27$). Schuster, Clark, and Rogers (1971) also used the Lawler and Porter measures in a survey of professional workers. They found that subjects who saw work quality and productivity as very important determinants of pay were rated as higher performers. Spitzer (1964) obtained uncross-validated multiple correlations of .40–.50 when the perceived instrumentalities for nine outcomes were used to predict five different productivity criteria. However, there were only ninety-six subjects (production foremen) and the lack of cross-validation is critical. Wofford (1971) found a correlation of .43 between the performance-outcome instrumentality averaged across outcomes and supervisory ratings of performance. However, the carefully done field study by Dachler and Mobley (1973) could find only small correlations between average instrumentality and performance, even when the research site was one using an incentive pay system.

In addition to these correlational studies, several experimental investigation studies of performance-outcome instrumentality have been reported. Jorgenson, Dunnette, and Pritchard (1973) manipulated performance-outcome instrumentality by paying employees in a temporary organization created for purposes of the experiment on either an hourly basis (low instrumentality) or a type of piece rate (high instrumentality). After individuals had worked for three four-hour days under their respective pay systems, each group switched to the other system and worked for three more days. The data indicated that people under the high instrumentality pay system performed higher than those under the low instrumentality pay system for the first three days. Furthermore, immediately following the shift in pay systems, and for all three subsequent days, the performance of subjects who were shifted to the high instrumentality system was higher than their own performance under the low instrumentality system and higher than the performance of those subjects who were shifted to the low instrumentality system. Results similar to Jorgenson et al. were obtained previously by Graen (1969) who also hired subjects to work in a temporary organization. In Graen's study the subjects were females hired to find errors in batches of computer output. Changes in outcomes produced changes in performance only if outcomes were contingent on performance. Similar results in a laboratory simulation study were obtained by Pritchard and DeLeo (1973) who compared an hourly and incentive pay system.

An experimental study by Arvey (1972) manipulated performance-outcome instrumentality by giving subjects who worked on an arithmetic task differing chances to "win" extra subject participation points for their introductory psychology course. In the high instrumentality condition, subjects who were high performers had a .75 probability of getting the extra points while in the low instrumentality condition subjects had a .25 probability. The results did *not* support the hypothesis since there was no difference in performance between the two levels of performance-outcome instrumentality.

One unfortunate characteristic of almost all the experimental studies that have manipulated the performance-outcome instrumentality is that only two levels of instrumentality have been used. A good Skinnerian should be furious, since with only two data points we cannot distinguish a linear from a nonlinear relationship between performance and instrumentality, and it very well may be the latter.

In a laboratory study where female undergraduates were first paid an hourly wage for scoring test answer sheets and then were switched to an incentive condition, Yukl, Wexley, and Seymore (1972) were able to show that performance was higher when subjects were paid 25¢ per sheet on the basis of a coin flip (i.e., expected value of payoff probability = .50) than when they were paid 25¢ for every sheet completed. On the surface this appears to argue that effort is not maximized when instrumentality = 1.0.

Another source of data on performance-outcome instrumentality comes from the literature on the effects of incentive pay, since an incentive pay system is one where the instrumentality of performance for a financial outcome should be perceived as high.

Several reviews of this literature were made some time ago (Marriott, 1957; Viteles, 1953) and the general conclusion seems to be that incentive plans tend to increase performance for non-salaried personnel but "may not realize their full potential in increasing performance because of the 'rate restriction' phenomenon ..." (Campbell et al., 1970, p. 366). These results are very much in line with the model since increases in performance-outcome instrumentality should result in increases in performance but high instrumentalities for peer sanctions and for lowered piece rate wage would tend to decrease effort and performance.

Effort/Performance Contingency (Expectancy)

While there is not a great deal of literature on the perceived degree of relationship between effort and performance, the bulk of the evidence seems to support it as a useful component. Schuster, Clark, and Rogers (1971) compared the performance ratings of those subjects who were higher in perceived effort-performance expectancy to the performance of subjects lower in effort-performance expectancy. While the difference was not statistically significant, it was in the predicted direction. In the experimental study by Arvey (1972) described above, subjects working on the arithmetic task were told they were in competition with other members of their group and that only a certain proportion of them would be designated as "top performers." Expectancy was manipulated by varying the proportion of subjects who would be designated as top performers from one fifth (low expectancy), to one half (medium expectancy), to three-quarters (high expectancy). The results of the study offered support for the expectancy model in that subjects in the low expectancy condition performed lower than subjects in the high expectancy condition. This finding was supported in a similar study reported by Motowidlo, Loehr, and Dunnette (1972).

Somewhat less direct evidence comes from studies which do not explicitly measure effort-performance expectancy, but rather measure the perceived degree of relationship between effort and outcomes. Such a measure combines effort-performance expectancy and performance-outcome instrumentality. All the studies using such a measure (Hackman & Porter, 1968; Lawler & Porter, 1967; Porter & Lawler, 1968) reported positive relationships between this expectancy-instrumentality composite and measures of performance, but the confounding of these two variables does not permit any direct assessment of the effects of perceived effort-performance expectancy.

Rather negative evidence comes from the study described above of government workers learning a new task (Pritchard & Sanders, 1973). Measuring effort-performance expectancy by questionnaire, it was found that expectancy correlated .14 with self-reports of effort, and this correlation dropped to .02 when expectancy was compared with supervisory ratings of effort.

In sum, while the effort-performance expectancy variable shows consistently significant results (at least in a statistical sense), there is still considerable inconsistency in how this variable should be conceptualized and measured. While the question is most often posed in terms of asking the subject for a subjective probability estimate, the object of the question (i.e., what's meant by performance) varies considerably.

Multiplicative Composites of VIE Components

The literature we have reviewed so far seems to indicate that each component separately shows at least some moderate relationship to effort or performance, but another question is whether their combination increases the level of prediction over and above what each one does separately.

Considering first the combination of the valence of outcomes and the performance-outcome instrumentality, Lawler and Porter (1967) found in their sample of managers from five different organizations that predictions of performance and effort using instrumentality alone resulted in correlations from .17 to .32 with a median of .23. When outcome valences were multiplied by instrumentalities the correlations ranged from .18 to .44 with a median of .29. Correlational studies by Spitzer (1964) and Evans (1970) also showed only a small increment in correlations as a result of multiplying performance-outcome instrumentalities by the importance or desirability of outcomes. Similar, but generally stronger, differences were obtained by Hackman and Porter (1968), Porter and Lawler (1968), Galbraith and Cummings (1967), and Mitchell and Pollard (1973). In contrast, two other studies (Gavin, 1970; Pritchard & Sanders, 1973) found no increase in the accuracy of prediction when the two elements were combined. However, the Gavin (1970) study found a correlation of .91 between measures of instrumentality and measures of valence and thus it would be highly unlikely for any combination of the two elements to increase prediction over each used alone. This correlation raises the issue of whether instrumentality and valence are independent events. The multiplicative VIE model implicitly assumes they are independent, but it also seems reasonable that they are not. Moreover, it is not unreasonable that for some people there is a positive relationship (i.e., the higher the instrumentality the higher the anticipated value of the reward) and for others the correlation may be negative.

There have been a number of studies which have combined all three major components in an attempt to predict individual effort, or performance on repetitive tasks. One of the most elaborate studies to date is reported by Dachler and Mobley (1973). It was a correlational field study carried out in each of two research sites using semiskilled operatives as subjects. Both sites were manufacturing operations but individuals were on an hourly pay plan in one plant and an incentive system in the other. The researchers took considerable care to identify as many of the relevant outcomes in the two situations as they could. Through interviews and questionnaires they eventually assembled a list of forty-five relevant outcomes. Rather than asking subjects to estimate correlations between effort and performance and between performance and outcomes they broke performance and valence into specific levels and asked the subjects to estimate the appropriate conditional properties. Their overall finding was that the multiplicative combination of expectancies, instrumentalities, and valences was the single best predictor of performance, but the correlation was only significant for the plant which used the incentive system; that is, where at least some outcomes were directly contingent on performance level. The correlation of .30 is in line with the previously cited research. The most important single component in the Dachler and Mobley study was

the expectancy variable and combining expectancy with the valence of performance levels, which in turn was a function of outcome valences and the instrumentality of that performance level, did not increase the correlations much. This finding is also consistent with previous findings.

An exceptionally thorough correlational field study utilizing a panel design is reported by Lawler and Suttle (1973). The subjects were sixty-nine retail managers each of whom was measured twice. Half the sample was remeasured after a six-month interval and the remainder after a twelve-month interval, which unfortunately resulted in a rather small N for the cross-lagged correlations. The questionnaire focused on eighteen outcomes and obtained data on their valences, the rated instrumentality of "good job performance" for each of the eighteen outcomes, the rated expectancy that "working hard" would lead to each of the eighteen outcomes, and the expectancy that "working hard" would lead to "good job performance." The dependent variables consisted of peer, superior, and self-ratings of effort and performance, and an objective performance measure consisting of sales data for the manager's department adjusted to correct for certain obvious biases. In an attempt to account for additional determinants of performance, data were also obtained on the subjects' role perceptions. In addition, the verbal, quantitative, and total scores from the *Thurstone Test of Mental Alertness* were available from company files. The analysis was thorough and consisted of calculating the static and cross-lagged correlations (for both six- and twelve-month intervals) of every VIE component, and combination of components, with each dependent variable. For our current purposes, the correlations with effort ratings are the crucial ones. For the static analysis, the correlations of the VIE components and component combinations range from approximately .30–.40 for self-rated effort, from .20–.30 for superior ratings of effort, and from .10–.20 for peer ratings of effort, and there is little advantage to one combination over the other. Weighting instrumentalities and/or expectancies by valence did not increase the correlations. The correlations for the "full" model are .39, .27, and .15 respectively. The results of the cross-lagged correlations gave only slight support to a causal analysis.

A number of other studies (e.g., Arvey & Neil, 1972; Galbraith & Cummings, 1967; Mitchell & Albright, 1972; Mitchell & Nebeker, 1973; Pritchard & Sanders, 1973) also attempted to determine via correlational field studies the correlation between a multiplicative combination of the components in the complete VIE model and ratings of effort and performance. Although their instrumentation was generally less elaborate than either Dachler and Mobley or Lawler and Suttle the obtained results are quite consistent with these two studies.

Summary of Expectancy Theory Research

As of this date there have been approximately thirty-five published studies that have some relevance as "a test" of expectancy theory predictions. What summary statements can be made about the data themselves? We offer the following:

1. Almost all of the studies purporting to test the full model have been correlational field studies and the correlational "ceiling" seems to be approximately .30 when independent ratings of effort are used as the criterion. The mode seems to be closer to .25. Virtually the only time the r's exceed this ceiling is when self-rated effort is used as a dependent variable. However, this introduces so much method variance into the correlation that interpretation of such a coefficient would be quite risky.

2. While a multiplicative combination of expectancy, instrumentality, and outcome valence typically yields a higher correlation than that for the individual components or simpler combinations of components, the differences are usually not very great. Expectancy or instrumentality usually accounts

for most of the variance that is to be accounted for and multiplying by valence seldom makes much difference. To date, it does not seem possible to choose sides between effort-performance expectancy and performance-outcome instrumentality as the more potent variable.

3. The results from the experimental studies do not seriously contradict the correlational investigations. That is, the variance in the dependent variable accounted for by the experimental treatment does not exceed $.30^2$. One additional characteristic of the experimental studies is that significant interactions were not typically found (e.g., Arvey, 1972; Pritchard & DeLeo, 1973) which further supports the lack of advantage attributed to the multiplicative combinations. However, we should also point out that most of the experimental studies did not deal with *perceptions* of the VIE components as independent variables, as an expectancy theory says should be the case, but focused on the experimenters' manipulation. The Arvey (1972) and Motowidlo et al. (1972) experiments are exceptions, but their results do not change the overall conclusion.

4. In those experimental studies which used performance on a simple repetitive task as a dependent variable and which also obtained measures of ability, a brief aptitude or general intelligence test almost always accounted for much more variance in performance than did the motivational variables (Dunnette, 1972). However, keep in mind that this was not the case in the Lawler and Suttle (1973) correlational field study which used rated effort and performance on a managerial job as dependent variables.

5. The attempts to account for additional variance in performance by some multiplicative combination of motivational and ability variables have been singularly unsuccessful. However, the performance = ability × motivation formulation is a muddled one at best and perhaps little else could have been expected.

6. There is a slight hint in the literature that performance-outcome relationships attached to internally mediated outcomes are more potent than those attached to externally mediated outcomes (e.g., Lawler & Suttle, 1973).

7. Although we did not review any of the evidence on this question, the available research comparing a multiplicative versus additive combination of the VIE components (e.g., Hackman & Porter, 1968; Porter & Lawler, 1968; Pritchard & Sanders, 1973) tends to show a slight advantage for the multiplicative formulation, but the differences are neither startling nor easy to interpret (Mitchell, 1974).

In sum, the available data do not portray the VIE model as a very powerful explainer of behavior. However, the above conclusion begs a number of questions and we would like now to turn to a discussion of various problems that plague both conceptual and research activity in this area. When all is said and done, we think the heuristic value of the expectancy framework will remain as a powerful force in organizational psychology even though its empirical house is certainly not in order.

Difficulties with VIE Theory and Research

The expectancy point of view has not been without its critics and a number of conceptual, measurement, and inferential problems have been pointed out (e.g., see Behling & Starke, 1973; Heneman & Schwab, 1972; Mitchell, 1974; Schmidt, 1973; Wahba & House, in press). Perhaps it would be wise to briefly list the problems that confront anyone who wishes to use the full VIE model as an explanation of effort or choice behavior in organizations. In total, we think these problems constitute a strong indictment of the full multiplicative model, but we also think they point the way to more fruitful avenues of research on motivational issues.

1. One major problem is with the dependent variable itself. The model attempts to predict choice or effort and most of the research activity has been directed at the latter. However, organizational psychology is without any clear specification of the meaning of effort and consequently there is no operationalization of the variable that possesses even a modicum of construct validity. The most frequently used measures are self, peer, or supervisor ratings of overall effort after some attempt has been made to distinguish between performance and effort in the instructions for the rater. Most often this consists of reminding the rater that the amount of energy, concentration, and perhaps time, that an individual puts into a task is not synonymous with the performance outcome that results and that the latter is also a product of skills, task understanding, and whatever constraints may be operating. On the basis of this reminder, it is hoped that the rater will use these two factors in some fashion approximating their arrangement in the "true" factor space, even though we, as yet, do not have even the beginnings of a theory that would suggest what such a factor space might look like. Obviously, or perhaps not so obviously, the problem can be better handled in a laboratory setting where the dependent variable can be "sanitized" in various ways. However, a careful experimental operationalization of effort may destroy the ecological validity of the variable for translation to field settings. It is in the measurement of effort in situ where we are really hurting and it would be well worth our while to start an in depth look at the meaning and measurement of just this variable.

Aside from the overall conceptual vacuum, or perhaps because of it, the use of self and superior ratings of effort are each beset by a number of problems. For example, the supervisor simply may not know how the individual spends time; and even if the individual were observed constantly, by what indicator does an individual signal a high effort or a low effort input? Hand in hand with some intelligent conceptual analyses as to what effort might mean, it would also be worthwhile to employ some policy capturing techniques in an attempt to "recover" the indicators that lead various kinds of raters to judgments of high effort or low effort.

Self-ratings of effort present special problems since the same individual provides ratings of the independent variables (i.e., expectancy, valence, and instrumentality) and the dependent variable. The method variance door is wide open and the two measures are not experimentally independent. It's no wonder the "model" correlates higher with self-rated effort than with independent ratings. In our opinion, self-ratings of effort should not be used in motivation research until we know more about them.

Practically the only systematic investigation of effort measures in a field setting is a multi-trait-multimethod study by Williams and Seiler (1973) who obtained self and superior ratings of both effort and performance for a sample of engineers. Two measures of each were used, a global rating and a dimensionalized set of scales constructed via the method of scaled expectations. The correlations among these variables suggested that (a) effort ratings obtained from independent observers correlated hardly at all (i.e., .24 and .33), (b) performance ratings show more convergent and discriminate validity than effort ratings, (c) effort ratings don't show any discriminate validity at all, and (d) superior ratings of effort exhibit more halo than self-ratings. This study and previous literature suggest that self-ratings of effort and performance correlate about .40–.50 while superior ratings of the same two correlate about .55–.65. Obviously, there are many explanations for why these correlations are not 1.00 besides the fact that there are real differences between the two factors.

2. An allied problem concerns the methods that have been used to measure the independent variables. Most often these have been questionnaire items using summated ratings (i.e., Likert) response formats and almost no effort (*sic*) has been devoted to testing (via some kind of process analysis or scaling technology) whether the subjects are using the variable the way the researcher has in mind. A few studies (e.g., Sheridan, Richards, & Slocum, 1974) have used paired comparison methods, which at least permit a transitivity test, but that's about as far as we have progressed.

Someone must get busy and try to find out what subjects are really doing when they generate "scores" on these variables. For example, data gathered by the decision theorists in gambling situations (Slovic & Lichtenstein, 1968) suggests that when subjective probabilities are compared to objective probabilities, people tend to underestimate the probability of almost certain events and overestimate the probability of rare events. Does the same thing happen in an employment setting?

3. Mitchell (1974) points out that Vroom's theory was originally designed to make *within* individual not *between* individual predictions. That is, the basic question is what task or effort level would an individual choose from among a range of alternatives? As Mitchell also points out, almost all the research designed to test VIE theory has used *between* individuals comparisons. We have already alluded to the trade-offs involved. If a study is meant to be a within subjects analysis, as the Dachler and Mobley (1973) study was in part, then estimates of expectancy and instrumentality must be obtained for several effort levels and several performance outcomes and the number of questions the subject must be asked quickly escalates. If a between subjects analysis is to be used, then the meaning of a variable must be the same across subjects. Serious response biases (e.g., tendency to use extremes) or differing underlying utility functions would confuse the between people comparisons and confuse the observed relationships.

4. Without citing chapter and verse (see Mitchell, 1974, for a partial review), the available data concerning the reliability with which VIE components are measured sug-

gests that while internal consistency estimates are reasonably high, any estimate obtained by measuring the variable at two different times is usually quite low (i.e., .30–.50). We do not wish to get into a long argument as to what kind of reliability should be demanded of VIE variables, but it seems to us that the theory requires the true score to be relatively stable across at least relatively short time periods. This is not to say that the true scores could not change drastically as the result of some new informational input. After all, accommodating such an event is one of the virtues of a cognitive theory. However, in an ongoing work setting which is relatively stable in character, we might expect the expectancy and instrumentality estimates to be relatively stable. In general, they have not been and this does present problems for the model. It suggests that the high internal consistency estimates may be partially the result of common method variance rather than common substantive variance.

5. Another issue concerns the precise nature of the predictions to be made. The major focus of the model is really on the *change* in the dependent variable as a function of changes in the independent variables. However, to test the model, researchers have relied primarily on relating predicted effort to ratings of effort and performance via static correlations.

6. The available studies have also relied primarily on subjects from a single organization, who were all doing the same job. It would seem quite possible that data collection from one job in one organization could result in a serious restriction in range in expectancies and instrumentalities.

7. Yet another issue concerns the specific first level outcomes for which valence measurements should be obtained. The VIE model is a process theory and it does not specify which outcomes are relevant for particular people in a particular situation. Such specifications are left to the ingenuity of the individual researcher. As a conse-

quence, negative results or unsupported predictions can almost always be explained on the grounds that all the relevant outcomes operating on the subjects were not included in the study. Mitchell (1974) argues that the problem of outcomes breaks down into three sub-questions. How many should be used? How specific should they be? What is their content? There are as yet no systematic answers to these questions.

8. Most versions of the full VIE model contain sums of cross-products between valences and expectancies and between valences and instrumentalities. Computing such cross-products makes several assumptions. First, for the multiplication to make sense, the two terms being multiplied must be independent. That is, the model assumes no interaction between valence and expectancy or between valence and instrumentality, or between instrumentality and expectancy. This may or may not be the case but it seems hardly likely that such zero interactions are always true. For example, as Atkinson (1965) suggests, the outcome of, "I will feel a high sense of achievement if I accomplish task X" may be dependent on the individual's estimate of his/her probability of success on task X. Also, a drastic increase in the instrumentality of performance for obtaining some outcome may influence its perceived value. For example, outcomes that have a very low contingency on performance may be devalued. Recall the previous study by Gavin (1970) which obtained a correlation of .91 between instrumentality and valence.

9. Strictly speaking, variables must also be measured on a ratio scale if the scores are subsequently to be multiplied together. In a pointed discussion of this matter, Schmidt (1973) shows that the correlations of sums of cross-products generated by VIE type operations with other variables can be changed drastically by transformations that would be invariant if the scales possessed ratio properties. This problem is an old one in psychology, and it remains to be seen

whether the use of a scaling technology that is consistent with the multiplicative requirements of the theory will appreciably change the results it generates. Schmidt suspects that it will and worries that using "weak" measures with a very demanding theory may be very misleading.

10. Most versions of the model also carry the assumption that outcome valences are additive in some sense. However, perhaps individuals at work do not really sum valences, but combine them in some other fashion, such as focusing on a dominant outcome under certain conditions and forgetting about the rest.

11. There is inherent in the model a general notion that the world is built in a linear or at least monotonic fashion. The higher the expectancy the greater the force, the greater the instrumentality the greater the force, and the greater the valence the greater the force. All these linearity assumptions are grounds for debate, and to the extent they do not mirror reality, the predictions of the model are weakened. Atkinson (1965) and reinforcement theorists (e.g., Bolles, 1967) would challenge such an assumption for expectancy and instrumentality respectively. Certain "need" theorists (e.g., Maslow, 1954), to be discussed in the next section, might also challenge the assumption as it pertains to valence. For example, the valence of pay might change as we go up the pay scale because the need outcomes for which it is instrumental change as a function of amount. The valence of a salary increase at a high salary level may be much higher or much lower than a salary increase at a lower pay level because some people might see it as instrumental for status or some other powerful need, while for others pay is instrumental for nothing besides food, clothing, and shelter.

12. Finally, in the tradition of Spearman, the research using expectancy models has tended to adopt a general factor plus specifics as its view of the "structure" of expectancy, instrumentality, and valence. That is, instrumentality is a general factor that is made up of a number of specific instrumentalities, expectancy is a general factor made up of a number of specific expectancies, and so on. However, it may be the case, for example, that the components of an individual's expectancy estimate attributable to general self-esteem versus that attributable to specific task characteristics may relate to behavior in different functional ways and some tasks may elicit more of the self-esteem component than others.

Some versions of the model do speak to a distinction between internally and externally mediated outcomes (rewards) and some studies have analyzed results separately for these two sub-general factors. However, what about positive versus negative outcomes (e.g., Reitz, 1971) and the nature of the instrumentalities attached to internal versus external or positive versus negative outcomes? Since internally mediated outcomes are under the control of the individual, perhaps the instrumentality of task accomplishment for obtaining these outcomes is nearly always 1.00.

A Summary Comment

In general what message does this list of problems seem to convey? We think it says quite clearly that the VIE model is a simple appearing formulation that encompasses a highly complex and poorly understood set of variables and variable dynamics. Rather than strive for large scale studies that provide a complete test of the "full" model with superficial measures of poorly understood variables, we think researchers could better spend their time studying the individual components in depth. For example, a host of questions surround the expectancy variable. We shall talk about a few of these later on. We think it would be far better to ask what is expectancy and how does it relate to well defined variables than to ask what is the correlation between $E \cdot \Sigma(V \times I)$ and a global rating of effort.

SUBSTANTIVE, OR CONTENT THEORIES

The models described below attempt to suggest the specific identity of variables discussed in general terms by the process models outlined earlier. As such, the theorizing is mainly of a taxonomic sort, although considerations of dynamic relationships are not completely absent.

Need Theory

Much of the history of this class of theory is rooted in theories of instincts which, as we have noted, fell into disrepute soon after the turn of the century because of the propensity to postulate a specific need for almost every human act. Relative to human behavior, instincts were again made respectable when they were transformed to the concept of needs acquired through learning. Needs were firmly rooted in contemporary motivational theory by Murray (1938).

Murray hypothesized the existence of a relatively large number of specific needs which human beings attempt to satisfy. The exact number in the list varies according to the particular stage in Murray's career, but about twenty basic needs were usually included. The following list and abbreviated definitions are abstracted from Hall and Lindzey's (1957) presentation of Murray's theory.

1. *Abasement*. To submit passively to external force. To accept injury, blame, criticism, punishment. To surrender. To become resigned to fate.

2. *Achievement*. To accomplish something difficult. To master, manipulate, or organize physical objects, human beings, or ideas. To do this as rapidly and as independently as possible.

3. *Affiliation*. To draw near and enjoyably cooperate or reciprocate with an allied other (an other who resembles the subject or who likes the subject).

4. *Aggression*. To overcome opposition forcefully. To fight.

5. *Autonomy*. To avoid or quit activities prescribed by domineering authorities. To be independent and free to act according to impulse.

6. *Counteraction*. To master or make up for a failure by re-striving. To overcome weaknesses, to repress fear.

7. *Defendance*. To defend the self against assault, criticism, and blame.

8. *Deference*. To admire and support a superior. To praise, honor, or eulogize.

9. *Dominance*. To influence or direct the behavior of others by suggestion, seduction, persuasion, or command.

10. *Exhibition*. To make an impression. To be seen and heard.

11. *Harmavoidance*. To avoid pain, physical injury, illness, and death.

12. *Infavoidance*. To quit embarrassing situations or to avoid conditions which may lead to belittlement: the scorn, derision, or indifference of others.

13. *Nurturance*. To give sympathy and gratify the needs of a helpless object.

14. *Order*. To achieve cleanliness, arrangement, organization, balance, neatness, tidiness, and precision.

15. *Play*. To act for "fun" without further purpose.

16. *Rejection*. To separate oneself from a negatively cathected object.

17. *Sentience*. To seek and enjoy sensuous impressions.

18. *Sex*. To form and enjoy sensuous impressions.

19. *Succorance*. To have one's needs gratified by the sympathetic aid of an allied object.

20. *Understanding*. To ask or answer general questions. To be interested in theory.

Murray's list and his accompanying definitions were not based on empirical research. Rather, they represented his conceptualization of what internal states govern human behavior and were generated from his clinical experience and observation. Notice also that almost every "need" appearing in twentieth century literature of organizational psychology appears on this list.

Maslow's Hierarchy

As everyone knows, Maslow (1954) postulated a *hierarchy* of human needs incorporating several levels. Basic to Maslow's theory is the notion that needs at a particular level of the hierarchy must be "largely" satiated before the needs at the next higher level become operative. This is not to say that two levels cannot be operative at the same time, but the needs at the lower level take precedence. It follows that if lower level needs are substantially satisfied in our society, they may never actually be very important for energizing and directing behavior.

The basic outline of Maslow's hierarchy from the lowest level to the highest level is as follows:

1. *Physiological needs.* As one might expect, these include such things as hunger and thirst. Maslow also goes on to talk about a number of specific hungers.

2. *Safety needs.* These refer primarily to freedom from bodily threat and in our culture are probably most active for young children.

3. *Belongingness or social needs.* These include the need for friendship, affection, love, and perhaps something akin to affiliation as that term is used by Murray and McClelland.

4. *Esteem needs.* These represent an individual's need for self-respect, for the respect of others, and for a stable, positive evaluation of himself.

5. *Self-actualization.* At the top of the hierarchy is the need level most existential in nature and most difficult to define. A succinct definition is simply that an individual's need to self-actualize is the need to be what one wants to be, to achieve fulfillment of one's life goals, and to realize the potential of one's personality.

Self-actualization is similar to the construct of need achievement except that *n* Ach is a more normative concept and is intended to have a similar meaning across a wide range of people, situations, and cultures. Self-actualization must be defined individually. As noted by Lawler (1973) many different personality theorists have given a self-actualization type variable a prominent place in their theories. If the consensus of "experts" is any guide then outcomes which are instrumental for self-actualization are a pervasive influence in the lives of most people.

As was true of Murray's theory, Maslow's characterization of human needs is not based on any empirical foundation, but was derived primarily from Maslow's clinical experience.

Alderfer's ERG Model

Alderfer (1969, 1972) has attempted to reformulate the Maslow hierarchy into a more meaningful set of three basic needs labeled *existence* needs, *relatedness* needs, and *growth* needs.

Existence needs consist of desires for material substances that are in finite supply. That is, one person's gain is another person's loss. Food, shelter, and money would fall in this category. Luckily there is a way out of the zero sum dilemma. Existence needs are not insatiable and individuals have a certain degree of satisfaction they regard as "enough" and in time of plenty no one need be a loser.

Relatedness needs have as their object the mutual sharing of thoughts and feelings with other people. That is, the theory says that people desire to tell other people their thoughts and feelings and to have the other person(s) reciprocate. That is not a zero sum situation but one in which the satisfactions of the parties are highly correlated. Notice also that no positive or negative connotations are given to the exchange. The open and accurate nature of the communication is what's important, not the pleasantness or unpleasantness involved.

The definition of growth needs is as slippery as ever and Alderfer presents no major conceptual breakthrough. Such needs are said to involve the interaction of the individual with the environment in such a way as to develop whatever abilities and capacities the individual feels are most important for him or her. Thus, satisfying growth needs involves a fairly fundamental change in individual capacities.

Although one important thrust of the theory is the taxonomic one, the theory speaks to certain processes. However, it is not intended to explain dependent variables such as the direction or amplitude of behavioral responses. Rather, the process side of the theory concerns the dynamics of two subjective states labeled *satisfaction/frustration* and *desire*.

Alderfer (1972) lists a number of propositions dealing with interrelationships between the desire for the objects incorporated by a certain need and the satisfaction/frustration with those objects. In general, these propositions suggest that: (a) the less a need is satisfied the more it is desired; (b) the less a "higher order" need is satisfied the more lower order needs are desired; and (c) the more a need is satisfied the more higher order needs are desired. The term higher order is not used in the Maslow sense but refers to the level of concreteness in the need objects. Existence needs simply have more concrete referents than relatedness needs and relatedness need objects are less ambiguous than growth need objects.

A rationale for (a) above is older than psychology. The explanation for (b) is not quite so self-evident and is based on the notion that if one type of need desire is frustrated, the individual will seek to satisfy desires with more concrete referents. The progression up the hierarchy, as in (c), occurs because satisfaction of existence or relatedness desires frees the individual from the effort required to satisfy and he or she can then turn to relatedness or growth.

Thus, contrary to Maslow's notion of prepotency, the need is always there and consciously recognized. It is the means to pursue it that is at issue here.

Data Relevant for Need Theories

There are perhaps three major kinds of available data that have been generated by content theories of needs.

1. Descriptive and correlational studies pertaining to which needs are strongest for which people.
2. "Tests" of the hierarchical or prepotency elements of need structures.
3. Tests of the taxonomic adequacy of a proposed model using multivariate psychometric methods.

We do not wish to discuss the available findings in detail but would like to highlight the basic issues.

Correlates of Need Satisfaction

Although not a lot of data exist in this category, Vroom (1965) and Campbell et al. (1970) review studies pertaining to the relationship between job performance, job duties, organizational level, and need satisfaction. The now classic study in this area is the national survey by Porter (1964) of 2,000 managers drawn at random from the membership of the American Management Association (AMA). A thirteen-item questionnaire based on Maslow's need hierarchy asked the respondent to assess the manifestation of each need relative to (a) how much there is now, (b) how much should there be, and (c) how important is it.

In general, higher level managers placed greater emphasis on self-actualization and autonomy needs, but there were no differences across levels for the other three need categories. In terms of specific item content, the higher level managers rated as more important the opportunity for personal growth and development, the opportunity for independent thought and action, the opportunity for participation in the setting of goals, and the authority connected with their management position. Using the same questionnaire, similar small but significant hierarchical differences have been found in a military organization (Porter & Mitchell, 1967). It is interesting to note that within Porter's AMA sample, neither the size of the company nor the distinction between line and staff had any appreciable effect on the importance ratings for various needs.

Tests of the Hierarchical or Prepotency Mechanism

There are at least three possible explanations for the Porter-type findings. First, some mechanism such as Maslow's prepotency notion could be operating and for lower level jobs at lower levels in the organization the lower order needs may not yet be satisfied. Second, the differential results could be due to individual self-selection. That is, people with certain kinds of needs wind up in certain kinds of jobs. Third, certain jobs might provide certain kinds of outcomes that both stimulate and satisfy a particular kind of need, and a hierarchical or prepotency mechanism is not necessarily involved.

A few studies have tried to test the prepotency notion empirically. Alderfer (1969) used questionnaires and interviews to measure both the importance and satisfaction of existence, relatedness, and growth in a sample of managers. The study was cross-sectional in nature and the crucial statistic is the correlation between the reported satisfaction of a particular need and the reported importance of the next higher need. This correlation should be positive while the correlation of satisfaction with importance reported for the *same* need should be negative. That is, as Maslow's model would predict, as a lower level need is satisfied the importance of that need decreases while the importance of the next higher need increases. The correlations did not support the prepotency predictions, but were in the opposite direction.

Hall and Nougaim (1968) examined the same kind of relationships in a longitudinal study. They were able to secure five yearly follow-up interview protocols from each of fifty participants in A.T.&T.'s Management Progress Study. The interviews covered numerous aspects of both work and nonwork related experiences and a panel of judges was used to infer the satisfaction and potency of Maslow's needs. The correlation of satisfaction with potency for the same need and with potency for the next higher need confirmed the Alderfer findings and again disconfirmed the Maslow-type predictions. Further, changes in satisfactions over a year period were correlated with changes in potency of the next higher need and the coefficients were zero or negative rather than positive.

While the above studies cast doubt on the prepotency notion, they do not permit a choice between the self-selection explanation and the job itself explanation.

A longitudinal study by Festinger (1964) bears on this issue and points up the complexity of the relationships that are encountered when such a global variable as management level is used as a correlate of need satisfaction. Festinger and his associates interviewed 175 "promotable" managers and then followed them for approximately four years, at which time about half had been promoted and the entire sample was reinterviewed. In general, the motive and value orientations seemed to be unchanged by promotion. However, the varying nature of the promotions suggested an interactive effect. If it was not perceived by the individual as a dead end job and in fact raised his level of aspiration, then work achievement tended to take on more importance. However, if the promotion attenuated the individual's level of aspiration, then family and other outside considerations took on greater importance.

Further support for the self-selection hypotheses is provided in a study by Vroom (1966), which suggested that MBA students tend to select jobs that will complement their expressed need preferences. In sum, the major thrust of what little data there are is that expressed motives do not seem to change a great deal as an individual rises in the organization. However, we should not forget that the data are scanty and the ability of certain jobs to "teach" people that self-actualization or growth needs are important has not really been closely examined.

Tests of the Taxonomy

A number of studies have attempted to determine if questionnaire items written to reflect the importance of or satisfaction with various needs intercorrelate the way they should when administered to samples of job-holders. In general, the items generated by the Maslow classification have not been able to reproduce the expected factors or clusters with any degree of clarity (Herman & Hulin, 1973; Payne, 1970; Roberts, Walter, & Miles, 1971). In contrast, Alderfer (1972) has been able to write items on the basis of his ERG model that do apparently exhibit significant convergent and discriminant validity. In the same series of studies, a set of items designed to tap the Maslow categories did not exhibit as much psychometric clarity.

We should keep in mind that there could be a number of alternative explanations of the above results and the correctness or incorrectness of the underlying taxonomy is only one. Nevertheless, what data there are suggest that the Maslow hierarchy is not as powerful and robust a notion as some people assume.

Content Models of Performance Outcomes (Rewards)

The second major class of content models is comprised of attempts to specify taxonomies of the job outcomes, or rewards, that are important for explaining job behavior.

Since the content of most multifaceted job satisfaction scales deals with outcomes that are the direct result of task (job) performance, the primary source of such taxonomies

is the job satisfaction measurement literature. Therefore, it seems reasonable to examine the available job satisfaction measures with an eye toward their adequacy as taxonomic models of job outcomes.

After looking at the available information it was surprising to realize that there have been relatively few comprehensive programs of research that have tried to define and sample systematically the overall domain of possible job outcomes; and that most of what is available has used some variant of the factor analytic procedure. One exception is the original study of satisfiers and dissatisfiers by Herzberg, Mausner, and Snyderman (1959).

Herzberg's Two-Factor Theory

On the basis of an extensive review of the earlier literature on job attitudes (Herzberg, Mausner, Peterson, & Capwell, 1957) and their well-known study involving a series of interviews with engineers and accountants (Herzberg, Mausner, & Snyderman, 1959), Herzberg and his colleagues have postulated the existence of two classes of work motivators—extrinsic and intrinsic factors which are in effect a taxonomy of first level outcomes (rewards). They are listed below.

Extrinsic Factors

1. *Pay,* or salary increase
2. *Technical supervision,* or having a competent supervisor
3. The *human relations* quality of supervision
4. *Company policy* and *administration*
5. *Working conditions,* or physical surrounding
6. *Job security*

Intrinsic Factors

1. *Achievement,* or completing an important task successfully
2. *Recognition,* or being singled out for praise

3. *Responsibility* for one's own or other's work
4. *Advancement,* or changing status through promotion

The intrinsic factors are viewed as being derived from the individual's relation to the job itself. Alternative labels are job *content* factors or motivators. Extrinsic factors are rewards or sources of need satisfaction that stem from the organizational *context* and are thus somewhat divorced from the direct influence of the individual. In later versions of the theory they are called hygiene factors. Since the behavioral implications of the theory are not stated in terms of energizing, sustaining, or directing effort, but are concerned with changes in job satisfaction, we will have no further concern with that aspect of the two-factor theory. It is the taxonomic question that is of interest here.

Note that Herzberg's use of extrinsic and intrinsic rewards does *not* conform to our previous distinction between internal and external outcomes. For example, recognition could be granted by the individual to himself or more formally by someone else in the organization. Similarly, either the individual or someone else could label something he or she did as an "achievement." This confusion of the event and the agent mediating the event has the effect of reducing the clarity of the content analysis of the interview protocols (Schneider & Locke, 1971).

To its credit the Herzberg taxonomy was not produced by generating an item pool, casting the items in a summated ratings (Likert) format, administering the items to a sample, and factoring or clustering the resultant correlation matrix. Unfortunately, rather than going on to explore systematically the potential of the free response procedure, the same procedure has been repeated over and over. For taxonomic purposes, it would have been more fruitful to explore the effects of systematic changes in certain parameters, such as the nature of the episode to be described, the time frame

of the recollection, the mode of data collection (e.g., oral versus written), type of job, alternative procedures for the content analysis, etc. If this had been done, we would now have a much more complete picture of what people consider to be the important outcomes of work.

Vroom's Summary of Factor Analytic Studies

Vroom (1964) reviewed much of the factor analytic work on measures of job satisfaction and outlined the following seven factors as seeming to be those which have appeared consistently across a number of studies.

1. Company policies and management
2. Promotional opportunities
3. The job content
4. Supervision
5. Financial rewards
6. Working conditions
7. Co-workers

Interestingly enough, most of the studies which Vroom reviewed used the Science Research Associates job satisfaction questionnaire (e.g., Baehr, 1954).

On the basis of much of this same literature, Smith, Kendall, and Hulin (1969) decided to pursue a job satisfaction measure comprised of four factors: supervision, the work itself, pay and promotions, and co-workers. Subsequent correlational analyses indicated that the pay and promotions factor should be split into two separate factors. The result was the five job satisfaction factors currently measured by the *Job Description Index* (Smith et al., 1969).

ISR Survey of Working Conditions

If a factor analytic type procedure is used to determine the facets that people see as the "basic" outcomes of work, a distinction can be drawn between the individual's satisfaction with an outcome and the importance attributed to an outcome. We do not wish to jump into the question of whether weighting an individual's satisfaction of an outcome with the rated importance of the outcome will yield a "better" overall measure of job satisfaction. That is again a matter for theories of job satisfaction, not motivation. Our interest here is in whether ratings of importance will yield a different factor structure than ratings of satisfaction.

One example of such a study using importance data is reported by Quinn and Cobb (1971). Importance ratings for a list of twenty-three outcomes included in the 1969/1970 *Survey of Working Conditions* administered by the Institute for Social Research (ISR) were factored. Data were collected from a national random sample of employed adults ($N = 1,500$) and the resulting five factor solution is shown in Table 1.

Table 1 illustrates one of the obvious pitfalls of the empirical factor analytic procedure. What comes out must go in, and it would be possible to quibble with the content of the Table 1 list. For example, where are outcomes having to do with opportunities for promotion?

Minnesota Studies On Work Adjustment

Imbedded in another theory of job satisfaction (Dawis, Lofquist, & Weiss, 1968) is another taxonomy of outcomes which is the culmination of an attempt to be extremely thorough in the sampling of the population of job outcomes. A series of factor analyses across several different occupational groups produced twenty relatively homogeneous factors, each measured by five items, which constitute perhaps the longest list of outcomes generated by this method. The factor labels and the highest loading item in each factor are given below.

1. *Ability utilization.* The chance to do something that makes use of my abilities.

2. *Achievement.* The feeling of accomplishment I get from the job.

3. *Activity.* Being able to keep busy all the time.

4. *Advancement.* The chances for advancement on this job.

TABLE 1

FACTOR ANALYSIS OF IMPORTANT RATINGS FOR 25 JOB FACETS INCLUDED IN 1969/1970 ISR SURVEY OF WORKING CONDITIONS

Factor I: *Resources*
I receive enough help and equipment to get the job done
I have enough information to get the job done
My responsibilities are clearly defined
My supervisor is competent in doing his job

Factor II: *Financial Rewards*
The pay is good
The job security is good
My fringe benefits are good

Factor III: *Challenge*
The work is interesting
I have enough authority to do my job
I have an opportunity to develop my special abilities
I can see the results of my work
I am given a chance to do the things I do best
I am given a lot of freedom to decide how I do my work
The problems I am asked to solve are hard enough

Factor IV: *Relations With Co-Workers*
My co-workers are friendly and helpful
I am given a lot of chances to make friends

Factor V: *Comfort*
I have enough time to get the job done
The hours are good
Travel to and from work is convenient
Physical surroundings are pleasant
I am free from conflicting demands that other people make of me
I can forget about my personal problems
I am not asked to do excessive amounts of work

5. *Authority.* The chance to tell other people what to do.

6. *Company policies and practices.* The way company policies are put into practice.

7. *Compensation.* My pay and the amount of work I do.

8. *Co-workers.* The way my co-workers get along with each other.

9. *Creativity.* The chance to try my own methods of doing the job.

10. *Independence.* The chance to work alone on the job.

11. *Moral values.* Being able to do things that don't go against my conscience.

12. *Recognition.* The praise I get for doing a good job.

13. *Responsibility.* The freedom to use my own judgment.

14. *Security.* The way my job provides for steady employment.

15. *Social service.* The chance to do things for other people.

16. *Social status.* The chance to be "somebody" in the community.

17. *Supervision—human relations.* The way my boss handles his men.

18. *Supervision—technical.* The competence of my supervisor in making decisions.

19. *Variety.* The chance to do different things from time to time.

20. *Working conditions.* The working conditions.

Interestingly enough, second order factor analyses of these twenty scales tend to produce two higher order factors which look very much like Herzberg's intrinsic versus extrinsic dichotomy (Weiss, Dawis, England, & Lofquist, 1967). Regardless of the outcome of the arguments surrounding the specifics of the two-factor theory it is apparent that the notion of two higher order factors has considerable meaning, even though its precise nature has not been specified.

An Emerging Structure

In view of the large number of studies in which measures of job satisfaction have played an important part, it is surprising to find that so little attention has been devoted to its basic structure. The information that is available suggests that a hierarchical picture might fit the current data best. That is, the overall judgment about the "job" is made up of two sub-general factors corresponding roughly to the intrinsic versus extrinsic breakdown originally identified by Herzberg. Each of the two sub-general factors can be broken down further into more specific factors, such as those measured by the Minnesota Satisfaction Questionnaire (MSQ).

Obviously, labeling such a structure begs several questions. One concerns whether the taxonomic structure should be pursued to more specific levels still. Certainly it should make sense to break the compensation or pay factor into the major components of pay. The same may or may not be true for other factors. For the purpose of providing a taxonomy of potential outcomes to use in motivational theories, we do not think that lists of outcomes, such as those provided by the MSQ, are specific enough. It is an empirical question whether more specific facets that still possess significant discriminability can be defined and measured, but we think it is a useful avenue to pursue.

The above point is related to the question of whether the job outcome domain has been representatively and comprehensively sampled as yet. Recall that by means of interviews with a sample of jobholders, Dachler and Mobley (1973) were able to generate a list of forty-five outcomes thought to be important for people on relatively simple production jobs. Perusal of their list suggests that the existing multifacet measures of job satisfaction may not be as comprehensive as we think they are. One disturbing element of this literature is the tendency for everyone to borrow everyone else's items. The content is thus rather self-perpetuating.

If a full definition and more complete sampling of the job outcome domain is actively pursued, then questions surrounding how to stratify the population of such outcomes become extremely important. Possible strata (i.e., facets, parameters, etc.) to consider are those having to do with the *job* (e.g., job level, job function, "prestige" rating, etc.), and those having to do with the *individual* (e.g., age, education, career expectations, etc.). A useful definition of facets or parameters with which to stratify the sample would greatly facilitate sampling operations. So far, such questions concerning the job outcome population have suffered from considerable benign neglect.

Intrinsic/Extrinsic Interactions

So far, we have discussed intrinsic and extrinsic job outcomes as two major taxonomic classes. Additional questions could be asked concerning the differential effects of these two classes of rewards on behavior and whether they interact in some form other than simple summation. As already noted, the Herzberg two-factor theory is a theory about job satisfaction not job behavior. The processes spelled out by the expectancy model imply that the total effect of all rewards is derived by simple summation.

However, deCharms (1968) has postulated that intrinsic and extrinsic outcomes may interact in non-additive ways. For example, if intrinsic rewards are being obtained for an activity, the introduction of additional extrinsic rewards may lower the value of the overall package, rather than enhance it. Deci has tested these notions in a series of laboratory studies (Deci, 1971, 1972; Deci & Cascio, 1972) designed to determine the interaction between extrinsic rewards and the intrinsic rewards associated with "doing" the task. Typically, subjects were asked to work on interesting puzzle games for specific time periods and then were given rest periods during which they could do anything they liked. The experimental treatment had to do with whether or not external rewards (e.g., money, verbal reinforcement, punishment) were also provided and whether or not they were contingent on performance.

The general conclusion derived from this series of studies is that extrinsic rewards which are contingent on performance decrease the valence of the intrinsic rewards. This is inferred from the fact that extrinsically rewarded subjects tended to spend less time working on the puzzles during their free time than subjects who were not extrinsically rewarded. Unfortunately, as noted by Calder and Staw (in press) no actual performance data are reported and we do not know how the two kinds of rewards interacted to influence performance itself.

Deci's explanation as to why introducing an extrinsic reward decreases the valence of an intrinsic reward is that it "teaches" the subject that performance should be motivated by the extrinsic reward and when that reward isn't present, performance should cease. In effect, the organization is disagreeing with the subject that the task is interesting in its own right. However, Calder and Staw (in press) also point out that the perception of *why* the reward is being offered is important. For example, if a financial reward is perceived as a bonus for good work rather than as an inducement to keep people on the job, it may not have a deleterious effect on the valence of intrinsic outcomes.

In sum, the available research on the differential effects of intrinsic versus extrinsic rewards is still sparse and full of loopholes. However, it is a step in the right direction. We need to know much more about how the available job outcomes combine to influence behavior.

SUPPLEMENTARY MODELS

Relative to adult individual behavior in organizations, it is no secret that there is more to motivation theory than the process and content models that we have just outlined. We will discuss briefly four additional theoretical notions: equity theory, the influence of goals and intentions, the theory of need achievement, and attribution processes. These four topics vary considerably in breadth and theoretical scope; however, all of them seem narrower in focus than the valence-instrumentality-expectancy model. Consequently, we will treat them as subtheories which appear to either supplement or contradict the basic expectancy notions at various points.

Equity Theory

Equity theory is also a cognitive theory concerning individual perceptions. It is based on cognitive dissonance and social comparison processes. It deals with exchange relationships and the fairness or equity of these exchange relationships. Of the models dealing with equity concepts (Homans, 1961; Jaques, 1961; Patchen, 1961) the formulation presented by Adams (1963a, 1965) is the most explicit and has stimulated by far the greatest amount of research. In his most complete statement, Adams (1965) considers (a) the nature of a person's inputs and outcomes in an exchange relationship, (b) the social comparison process that is used by the individual, (c) conditions leading to perceptions of equity or inequity, (d) possible effects of inequity, and (e) behavioral and cognitive actions a person may take to reduce feelings of inequity. The exchange process under consideration is that which takes place between the organization and the individual within the relevant organizational role.

Inputs include any and all factors (e.g., effort, education, age, beauty, etc.) perceived by a person as relevant for getting some return. In contrast, outcomes include any and all factors perceived to be returns on the individual's job investments. The net "value" of the exchange to the individual may then be expressed as a ratio of inputs to outcomes, in which the specific outcomes and inputs are each weighted according to their perceived importance.

Perceived equity or inequity results when a person compares his or her outcome/input ratio, either consciously or unconsciously, to what is perceived to be the ratio of another person or persons. This comparison object need not necessarily be any one individual; it may be an abstraction based on a broad class of others seen to be relevant for comparison purposes. Adams refers to this generalized comparison as "Other," and to the one who compares as "Person."

Perceived equity results when Person perceives the two ratios to be equal. This is true regardless of the absolute level of inputs and outcomes for either party. For example, equity is said to exist in a situation where Person's inputs do not match his outcomes but Other is perceived to be in an identical situation. Perceived inequity arises whenever Person's ratio differs from Other's ratio.

Adams postulates that the consequence of inequity is an induced tension (drive?) with motivating properties impelling Person to reduce or eliminate this tension. Moreover, the magnitude of the tension should be proportional to the magnitude of the inequity. Thus, the strength of the behavioral tendency (effort, choice, etc.) toward reducing inequity is determined by the magnitude of the perceived difference between the two ratios.

Adams lists several things Person can do to reduce or avoid inequity. One or both of the two ratios can be changed by (a) cognitively distorting inputs or outcomes, (b) acting on Other to get him or her to change inputs or outcomes, (c) actually changing Person's own inputs or outcomes, (d) changing the comparison Other, or (e) leaving the particular exchange relationship. Adams notes, of course, that all these modes of inequity reduction are not equally available to Person either behaviorally or cognitively, and he offers tentative hypotheses about the most likely modes for Person to choose in seeking to reduce inequity. Adams suggests that Person will seek to maximize positive outcomes, will seek to minimize effortful or costly inputs, and will resist both behavioral and cognitive changes in those inputs and outcomes which are most central to his or her self-esteem or perceived self-concept. In addition, Person will be more resistant to altering cognitions about his or her own inputs and outcomes than to altering cognitions about the inputs and outcomes of Other. Leaving the field or retreating from the exchange relationship is viewed as a last resort, occurring only when inequity is great and other means of reducing it seem to be unavailable. Finally, if comparisons with a particular Other have stabilized over time, Person will be highly resistant to changing comparison persons.

Relevant Data

Equity theory literature has dealt primarily with financial compensation as an outcome. The majority of studies have dealt with the effects of overpayment and underpayment on job performance and, to a lesser extent, on job satisfaction. Since the data have been reviewed extensively elsewhere (Goodman & Friedman, 1971; Lawler, 1968c; Opsahl & Dunnette, 1966; Pritchard, 1969), we will attempt only to summarize the highlights.

The major research hypotheses have been those directed at quantity and quality of performance as a function of over- and underpayment within both incentive and hourly pay systems. The job or task at hand is usually simple enough to permit the assumption that performance, defined as either quantity or quality of output, is largely a function of effort. Under these conditions, equity theory would make the following predictions, *if* other means of equity resolution are controlled:

A. For the overpayment condition
  1. Under an hourly system either quantity or quality should increase depending on the "set" given the individual since either one would increase Person's inputs.
  2. Under an incentive system where the payoff is contingent on the quantity of items produced, quantity should stay the same or decrease. Producing more simply increases the financial outcome and increases inequity even more; however, quality should increase since this would allow an increase in inputs to redress the inequity.
B. For the underpayment condition
  1. Under an hourly system quantity and quality should both decrease depending on which would reduce the individual's input the most.
  2. Under an incentive system quality should go down and quantity may

or may not increase depending on the cost versus benefit (input/outcome) ratio for each additional unit of production.

Predictions of equity theory concerning the effects of *underpayment* have consistently been supported. From studies by Clark (1958), Homans (1953), Lawler and O'Gara (1967), Andrews (1967), and Pritchard, Dunnette, and Jorgenson (1972) one can conclude that when discrepancies in outcome/input ratios exist, inequity is felt and thus inequity leads to behavioral attempts to balance outcome/input ratios. In the case of hourly payment, this inequity reduction takes the form of decreased productivity, and under piece rate payment, increases in productivity are accompanied by decreases in quality.

At first glance, the research on the effects of *overpayment* on productivity seem to support equity predictions. Studies by Arrowood (1961), Adams and Rosenbaum (1962), Adams (1963b), Adams and Jacobsen (1964), Andrews (1967), Friedman and Goodman (1967), Lawler, Koplin, Young, and Fadem (1968), Lawler (1968b), Moore (1968), Goodman and Friedman (1968, 1969), Weiner (1970), Wood and Lawler (1970), and Pritchard et al. (1972) have generally supported the prediction that hourly overpayment leads to increases in productivity and piece rate overpayment leads to decreases in quantity of production and increases in quality.

However, three problems have plagued efforts to study overpayment. First, as Lawler (1968c) and Pritchard (1969) have pointed out, it has been difficult to manipulate perceived inputs and outcomes without at the same time threatening Person's self-esteem. The typical overpayment manipulation has consisted of informing the subjects, usually in a rather gruff fashion, that they are not qualified to do the task and thus are to receive more money than they are worth. Such an initial contact with the "employer" may not only have induced conditions of overpayment inequity in the subject, but also to threaten self-esteem. If these were indeed the feelings aroused by this type of manipulation, it seems quite plausible that the subjects would attempt to do an especially good job to convince both experimenter and themselves that they were not as poor as they were made out to be.

The second problem in the overpayment literature is that some studies appear to have induced a set toward increased quality. Subjects made to feel over paid by the "typical" method (attacking the subjects' qualifications) are told to "pay close attention," etc. Thus, as Opsahl and Dunnette (1966) point out, they may tend to concentrate on doing high quality work at the expense of quantity.

A third problem, noted by Lawler (1968c), is that subjects made to feel overpaid due to their poor qualifications may also believe they are in danger of being fired, and thus seek to do especially good work to assure their job security. Lawler points out that this could take the form of increased quantity under an hourly pay system, and increased quality under piece rate, since quantity and quality may be more salient under hourly and piece rate systems, respectively.

Probably the most serious of the three is the self-esteem problem and several studies have dealt with it directly. Andrews and Valenzi (1970) had eighty subjects role play an overpayment manipulation which threatened the "employees'" qualifications and express what their reaction would be in that situation. They found that none of their subjects responded to open-ended questions about how they would feel in the situation in terms of wage inequity. However, fifty-nine of their subjects responded in terms of self-image as a worker. Subjects were also asked to rank order several possible reactions to the "employment interview" in terms of how plausible each reaction would be. Wage inequity reactions were chosen as least plausible while self-image reactions

were chosen as most plausible. Studies by Evans and Molinari (1970) and Weiner (1970) also offer data supporting the contaminating effects of threats to qualifications in overpayment research. The latter study also demonstrated that the effect due to threats to self-esteem was greater when the task seemed to involve highly valued abilities than when it was portrayed as not involving skills that were central to the individual's self-concept.

If one considers only those studies which do not manipulate overpayment by threats to qualifications, a somewhat different picture emerges. The data produced by Andrews (1967), Lawler (1968b), Moore (1968), Weiner (1970), and Pritchard, Dunnette, and Jorgenson (1972) suggest that overpayment has a small effect in the predicted direction, but it frequently falls short of statistical significance.

One explanation for the asymmetry between over- and underpayment deals with the type of exchange relationship present in most organizational settings and in the experiments on overpayment. Exchange relationships can be ordered on the basis of the amount of psychological contact in the relationship (Pritchard, 1969). At one extreme is an intimate emotional relationship between two people. Less intimate would be two partners working in cooperation with each other; then two co-workers (friends) in an exchange relationship with a third party, their employer; and finally, a worker and an unknown generalized comparison group (e.g., lathe operators in general) who are both in exchange relationships with employers. An important characteristic of this intimate-impersonal continuum is that differences in inputs or in outcomes are much easier to perceive and may be more salient at the intimate end than at the impersonal end. It should be less likely that Person will experience inequity relative to Other the closer the relationship is to the impersonal end of the continuum and vice versa. Aside from these direct determinants of inequity, it would also seem easier to distort cognitively one's inputs and outcomes at the impersonal end, and thus decrease the chances that inequity would persist for very long.

In addition to the argument that inequity will be less likely to occur and easier to eliminate in an impersonal exchange relationship (e.g., an organizational compensation setting), there is another reason for not expecting over-reward effects in real world employment roles. The basic assumption of equity theory is that if someone perceives a situation of inequitable treatment, forces are generated within the person to alleviate the situation. It is proper to speculate on whether or not these forces are the same for over- and under-reward.

In the organizational situation, Person may react to underpayment with decreased effort, demands for more pay, or by generally addressing attempts to achieve equity directly toward the company. In the case of over-reward, however, Person may indeed feel too highly paid relative to Other, but the cognitive and behavioral effects of this inequity may occur only if Person somehow comes to believe that he or she is treating someone else *unfairly*. However, it may appear that the organization does not feel it is being taken advantage of or it would lower Person's pay, fire the individual, or take some other action to increase its own outcomes, increase Person's inputs, etc. Thus, it seems likely that even if feelings of over-payment could be generated in Person, he or she would not behave in a way that could be construed as reducing feelings of over-payment, if indeed no one else seemed to think Person was being overpaid.

In sum, there are a number of reasons why overpayment might produce less behavioral change than underpayment. The identity of the comparison Other, the mode of inequity resolution, and the nature of the "feeling" of inequity are all items of interest. As was the case with the VIE model, we again see a dearth of research dealing with these component questions in favor of "tests" of the overall model. Again, we would argue that the enterprise would derive more benefit if a greater proportion of our resources were devoted to finding out more about the model's components. For example, the process of inequity resolution seems so complex in its own right that to bypass it seems self-defeating.

A study of Tornow (1971) indicates another area of concern that is virtually ignored by equity theory and research. Reasoning that individual differences may indeed play a part in the intensity of feelings of over- and underpayment, Tornow constructed a questionnaire designed to measure whether an individual was typically input or outcome oriented. For example, some people view "responsibility" or "hard work" as something they must put into a job. Others view these as outcomes that the job provides for them. Tornow began by generating a large list of such items and then asked samples of subjects (students) to indicate whether they considered each item to be an input or outcome relative to working at a job. The items for the final scale were those which yielded the most ambiguous splits (i.e., 60/40 to 40/60), but which still possessed internal consistency reliability.

The Pritchard et al. (1972) study yielded somewhat uneven support for equity theory predictions. The original study ran for six days, involved the creation of a simulated organization in several different cities, hired students on vacation to work, and used two different manipulations for over- and under-payment. Tornow tracked down virtually all the subjects who had participated in the experiment and gave them his input/outcome checklist. The subjects within each of the original experimental treatments were then classified further into input oriented versus outcome oriented individuals. Supposedly, a manipulation of overpayment should have more of an effect on someone who is outcome oriented than input oriented since such individuals should feel even more over-rewarded. For each of the eight cells defined by type of payment (hourly versus incentive), type of inequity (over- versus under-reward), and type of manipulation (experimental versus natural), the difference in performance on a simple repetitive task between the input oriented and outcome oriented subjects was in the predicted direction. Individual differences were having an effect. One person's input is another person's outcome. Tornow's study is well worth emulating.

The Relation of Equity Theory to Expectancy Theory

A final issue concerns how equity theory relates to the VIE model. Is it in direct opposition? Is it completely consistent? Where does it fit? One feature of equity theory that narrows its focus is that it has come to be used almost exclusively as a theory of financial payment rather than dealing with the complete spectrum of outcomes. One advantage of this restriction in range is that in the context of financial payment it is possible to make predictions about the quantity and quality of performance under the four conditions specified by crossing overpayment versus underpayment with incentive versus hourly payment; and we have tried to summarize the evidence in each of these four cells. Would similar predictions be made by the VIE model or are the two models in conflict? A comparison of the two models within each of the four cells might look something like the following below.

	UNDERPAYMENT	OVERPAYMENT
INCENTIVE	• Equity theory predicts more quantity and lower quality. • The VIE model predicts the same thing depending on the costs associated with a minimal increase in effort balanced against the increased financial reward. Equity theory must take the same trade off into consideration.	• Equity theory predicts higher quality and lower quantity. • Presumably the VIE model would predict higher quantity and similar quality, depending on what was really perceived as being rewarded; and thus, the VIE prediction would conflict with equity theory. However, this assumes the valence of money doesn't change, and that other outcomes don't become salient.
HOURLY	• Equity theory predicts a decrease in quality and/or quantity depending on which is the "cheapest." • The VIE model (assuming we are trying to explain a change in payment on a difference between two groups) would predict the same if the individual was trying to avoid the outcome of being fired. Presumably, the performance required to avoid firing would be less for a lower-paid situation.	• Equity theory predicts higher quality and/or quantity depending on which reduces the imbalance more efficiently. • The VIE model might predict the same thing if the individual perceives that a higher level of performance is required to "keep the job."

Based on these comparisons, and a similar analysis by Lawler (1968c), several generalizations seem appropriate. The two models are not really in conflict. In part this is due to the looseness of the two theories. It is almost always possible to conjure up previously unrecognized outcomes that will reconcile conflicts in predictions. In addition, it seems reasonable to hypothesize that individuals have a concept of fair payment (Jaques, 1961) and departures from "fairness" changes the perceived value (valence) of money. Thus we agree with Lawler (1973) that equity theory can be subsumed under the general umbrella of the VIE model as an explanation and definition of the need for equity which in turn influences the valence of outcomes.

Goals and Intentions

Without being very explicit, expectancy models of the motivational process point to the task to be performed as an important intervening link between effort or choice behavior and the outcomes desired by the individual. For a cognitive model it is virtually axiomatic that individuals have intentions about what they will do in the face of certain task requirements and these intentions (goals) have an influence on the choices they make among task content and the effort they expend toward specific performance goals within tasks.

Locke and his associates (e.g., Locke, 1968; Locke, Cartledge, & Knerr, 1970) have suggested a cognitive model which tries to make more explicit how goals and intentions govern effort and choice. Their basic notions are quite consistent with an expectancy model and can best be viewed as an elaboration of the performance component. As it turns out, the evidence which has been subsequently gathered appears at first glance not to support one of the implicit hypotheses of the expectancy valence theory.

In brief, the Locke formulation, which is referred to as a "partial model of task motivation," has the following basic ingredients: First, the most immediate motivational determinant of effort or choice is the individual's goal or intention vis-à-vis some task. By implication, such a conscious intention, or goal, is defined as a goal the individual *has consciously decided to pursue*. That is, the individual has already made certain conscious decisions about the goal in question and this is an extremely important boundary condition in terms of a comparison of this model with other models. In terms of

their behavioral influence, such goals have two important properties. One has to do with the fact that stating a goal or intention is synonymous with giving behavior a direction. This is really a non-motivational consideration in that the existence of a goal reflects knowledge of what is to be done rather than reflecting which goal is the more attractive. The second property is a motivational consideration and has to do with the energizing function in that effort is concentrated on particular goals and some goals require more effort expenditure than others. Thus, research should be concerned with finding goals that elicit the most effort once they become conscious intentions; that is, once the individual makes a commitment to the goal.

The second major ingredient of the model is that changes in the value of incentives (i.e., valence of first level outcomes) can only have effects on behavior insofar as a change in valence is coupled with a change in the individual's goals. This is quite consistent with saying, as does expectancy theory, that changing the availability (instrumentality) and/or magnitude (valence) of incentives changes the valence of specific task goals, such that a particular performance goal now has a high enough valence to elicit effort in that direction.

Third, an individual is satisfied or dissatisfied with performance to the extent that actual performance matches the individual's performance goals. If it does not, a condition analogous to Adams's (1963a, 1963b) inequity results and the individual tries to reduce his or her dissatisfaction. However, Locke et al. (1970) speak only of the case where actual performance falls below the previously accepted goal and the method used to reduce the resulting dissatisfaction is to set a goal to increase output by the necessary amount. Other methods of reducing dissatisfaction, à la equity theory, such as refusing to accept the original performance goal and adopting a lower one, are not really considered. In any event, if we stick to their circumstances, Locke et al. (1970) predict that dissatisfaction will be significantly correlated with changes in performance via the setting of improvement goals.

Locke and his associates are careful to point out that their model is meant to concentrate on the goals component and is not overly concerned with what influences the establishment and acceptance of goals in the first place. Vroom and Porter and Lawler are criticized for their lack of attention to the controlling properties of goal setting. However, to the extent that Locke et al. do discuss goal instrumentalities and the value of ensuing rewards their discussion is consistent with an expectancy model.

Research by Locke and his associates has tended to support their basic notions. Virtually all their data has been generated in the laboratory, with undergraduates as subjects, and using simple tasks such as reaction time, addition, unscrambling letters in scrambled words, and building windmills from tinker toys as the experimental vehicle. Subjects typically work on several blocks of trials during a session, and, depending on the objective of the experiment, may either be assigned goals (external), be asked to state their goal (internal) before working on a block, or be asked to verbalize their goals after a block is finished. The rewards investigated to date have been money and knowledge of results.

Based on a large number of individual studies, several conclusions seem warranted.

1. The effects of rewards do seem to be mediated by changes in goals. If offering an individual an opportunity for higher pay does not commensurately increase performance goals then most likely behavior will not change. By implication, assessing goal changes should be one way of predicting the effects of newly instituted incentives.

2. Specific performance goals (above a certain critical magnitude) elicit higher performance on the above type of tasks than do instructions to "do your best."

3. In general, the more difficult the per-

formance goal, so long as it is accepted by the individual, the higher the performance. This is true no matter if the goal becomes so difficult that virtually no one can achieve it.

4. In this restricted kind of laboratory situation, the anticipated satisfaction attached to a changed performance goal (i.e., the valence of a specific performance level in our composite model) does correlate significantly with future performance.

Support for the second or third conclusions also can be found in at least four field studies. Meyer, Kay, and French (1965) compared a traditional kind of superior-subordinate performance review with a mutual goal setting approach and found that the crucial aspect was not whether goal setting was mutual or superior initiated, but whether specific goals were set at all. Looking at goal difficulty, Stedry and Kay (1966) asked production foremen to achieve either the 50th or 75th percentile of their work groups' distribution of weekly quantity and quality scores over the previous twenty-six weeks. Over a thirteen-week test period the results showed that work groups whose foremen perceived the higher goal as "challenging" produced 28 percent fewer defective parts while groups whose foremen saw the goal as impossible experienced a 35 percent increase in defective units. Similar, but less pronounced results were produced for the quantity criterion. If a perception of "challenging" is taken as goal acceptance, then Locke's results are supported. The prediction that difficult specific goals lead to higher performance, other things being equal, than do the best goals has also been supported in field studies by Latham and Kinne (1974) and Latham and Baldes (in press).

A study which tends not to support the first conclusion in the above list is reported by Pritchard and Curtis (1973). Student subjects worked on a card sorting task in the laboratory. After a base trial subjects were assigned to one of six conditions defined by performance goal versus no goal and three financial incentive levels (i.e., none, low, and high). The results suggest that not all the effect of a change in incentives is mediated by a change in goals. However, sample sizes were small and the determination of the actual operating goals used by the subjects was difficult.

Comparisons with Composite Expectancy Model

As we noted above, there is little in the arguments of Locke and his associates that is inconsistent with the composite expectancy model. The Locke model could be best viewed as an elaboration of the task goal component. However, at first glance one might interpret the above results as contradicting the composite model's prediction that the *higher* the perceived relationship between effort and task accomplishment (expectancy) the greater the expenditure of effort. Their data suggest that the harder the goal and thus the *lower* the probability of success, the greater the effort (given the assumption that performance on the task was almost entirely a function of effort). Unfortunately, it is not possible to know precisely what the subjects in the laboratory studies regarded as the performance goal. Was it actually the task goal specified by the experimenter, in which case the contradiction is real; or was it "demonstrating to the experimenter an ability to work very hard?" In the latter case, the relationship between effort and demonstrating hard work to the experimenter would be greater for the more difficult goal condition and there is no contradiction. In general, perhaps the act of choosing to commit effort to a particular goal changes the definition of the goal. Also, the act of commitment might serve to introduce a new set of highly valent outcomes that have an influence on behavior. If nothing else, this "confrontation" between the Locke formulation and the expectancy model points up the ambiguous nature of the task goal component and the rather

abysmal looseness with which it has been treated by most motivational models, including expectancy theory. We need much more investigation into the motivational properties of tasks and the way in which tasks are defined and redefined by people under various conditions.

The Theory of Need Achievement

McClelland, Atkinson, and their associates (Atkinson, 1957, 1964; Atkinson & Cartwright, 1964; McClelland, 1951; McClelland, Atkinson, Clark, & Lowell, 1953) have proposed a very tightly constructed expectancy/valence theory of task behavior which is firmly grounded in two specific but pervasive motives—the need for achievement and the fear of failure. Their basic model has gone through several revisions since the early fifties and we will try to portray the flavor of its evolution.

A motive is regarded as a label for a class of incentives (outcomes in our terminology), all of which have much the same effect. Motives are viewed as relatively stable behavior dispositions, or learned tendencies, which are not presumed to operate until aroused by the presence of one or more of the relevant incentives, or situational cues that have become associated with the incentive. Need achievement is defined as a predisposition to strive for success. The fear of failure is defined as a predisposition toward the minimization of failure and pain. The strength of the achievement need is typically measured via a prescribed method of content analysis for responses to the Thematic Apperception Test (TAT). The scoring method was empirically constructed by comparing the responses of people under benign conditions with those in situations where the need was presumed to be operating. Other methods have sometimes been used (Aronson, 1958; French, 1958; O'Connor, 1962) and very recently paper and pencil test *n* Ach has been developed by Hermans (1970). According to Weiner (1970), the strength of the motive to avoid failure is usually measured by the Mandler-Sarason Test Anxiety Questionnaire (Mandler & Sarason, 1952).

In addition to the strength of the achievement need (M_s) and the need to avoid failure (M_{AF}), the theory includes four other independent variables: $P_s =$ the subjective probability of success, or the expectancy that action will result in accomplishing the goal; $P_f =$ the subjective probability of failing to accomplish the goal; $I_s =$ the incentive value of success or goal accomplishment; and $I_f =$ the incentive value (negative) of not accomplishing the goal. The dependent variable is the strength of the tendency to approach the task (T_A), which is similar to the notions of force and effort as they appear in other expectancy/valence models.

T_A represents the resultant of the approach and avoidance vectors and is specified by the following equation:

$$T_A = (M_s \times P_s \times I_s) - (M_f \times P_f \times I_f)$$

Unlike the composite picture of expectancy theory presented earlier, this expression contains some important dependencies. According to the theory, the incentive values of success and failure have no operational meaning themselves. Rather, $I_s = 1 - P_s$ and $I_f = 1 - P_f$. The rationale is that for I_s the satisfaction or pride in successfully accomplishing a task is inversely related to its perceived difficulty. The more difficult the goal the greater the sense of pride in accomplishment if it is reached. Note that this conceptualization of incentive restricts the theory to one particular first level outcome of an internal nature. Note also that the product of $P_s \times I_s$ is at a maximum when $P_s = .50$. Relative to I_s, the feeling of failure or shame generated by not reaching the goal should be inversely related to the subjective probability of failure. That is, the greater the probability of failure the less shame or guilt the individual should feel if she or he does indeed fail.

By definition, it is further stipulated that $P_s + P_f = 1.0$. As pointed out by Weiner (1970), this reduces the degrees of freedom in the basic formula to one and the expression can be transformed to the following:

$$T_A = (M_s - M_{AF}) [P_s \times (1 - P_s)]$$

This form of the model indicates that it is only the relative strength of the two motives that determines the direction of behavior toward the task (i.e., approach or avoidance); and given a particular motive level, the tendency to approach or avoid is greatest when $P_s = .50$.

The above expression is really the second stage in the overall evolution of the model. The beginnings of the theory did not deal with the motive to avoid failure but it is made necessary by subsequent research findings. A third stage can be identified in Atkinson's (1964) later inclusion of extrinsic, or what he calls non-achievement oriented, outcomes. They were included because of the assumption that any response is overdetermined; that is, it most likely is controlled by a number of incentives besides achievement oriented ones. In any experiment designed to test the model these motivational determinants are regarded as error and the basic expression becomes:

$$T_A = \text{Resultant achievement tendency} + \text{extrinsic motivation}$$

Thus if for one individual $M_{AF} > M_s$ but he still approaches rather than avoids the task, the explanation is that the individual has a high valence for money, grades, or whatever.

The need for still further modification of the model resulted from its inability to handle phenomenon such as the Zeigarnik effect and other data which indicated that behavior persisted even when the incentives thought to be necessary for its support were absent (Atkinson & Cartwright, 1964). Atkinson and Cartwright postulated the concept of inertial tendency (T_{Gi}) to account for the persistence of goal-directed behavior and defined it as the strength of the previously aroused but unsatisfied motivation to strive for an achievement related goal. Thus, the full need achievement algorithm became:

$$T_A = \text{Resultant of time specific achievement motivation} + \text{inertial tendency} + \text{extrinsic motivation}$$

However, the original definition of the inertial tendency could not account for the experimental finding obtained in several studies (summarized in Weiner, 1970) that when the expectancies are unknown high need achievement subjects who experienced failure tended to persist in achievement oriented responses and low need achievement subjects who experienced failure tended to be inhibited even further. Without going through the mechanisms of it all, the above expression will predict the former but not the latter result. To account for this interaction, Weiner (1972) has proposed that the inertial tendency also be thought of as a *resultant* force. Thus, for individuals with high need achievement, greater approach than avoidance is aroused in an achievement-task situation and this persists after failure and supplements the resultant achievement motivation in the next situation. However, for people low in need achievement, greater avoidance than approach is aroused and if failure is experienced the result will be to inhibit behavior in the next similar situation. The strength of the inertial tendency is a function of the magnitude of the difference between M_S and M_{AF} and the original task difficulty. However, the direction of the carry-over effect is the same, regardless of the original expectancy. The original model which did not incorporate T_{Gi} would have predicted this result for low n Ach—high fear of failure people only if they failed at an easy task. If they experienced failure at

a difficult task the original model would predict an increase in performance.

Thus the full-blown model sees the tendency to approach or avoid a task as being a function of:

1. $(M_S \times P_S \times I_S) - (M_{AF} \times P_f \times I_f)$ = the resultant achievement motivation stemming from current stimulus conditions.
2. T_{Gi} = the result inertial tendency.
3. Extrinsic incentives.

Comparisons with Expectancy Theory

Please note that this model of achievement motivation is consistent with the composite expectancy model except for one important discrepancy. It is confined to one particular first level outcome defined in a very specific way (i.e., $I = 1 - P$). That is, by definition the valence of a performance goal is completely dependent on the perceived probability of being able to achieve it. For this particular kind of outcome, this may indeed be a more reasonable assumption than the composite expectancy model's blanket assumption that all outcome valences are independent of expectancy. For externally mediated outcomes, Atkinson and his colleagues use assumptions consistent with the composite model.

The trade-off for the restriction in focus to one outcome is that more specific and finely differentiated behavioral predictions can be made and the persistence of behavior can be accounted for, given that we stay within the boundaries of the model.

Many examples of such predictions can be found in the excellent monograph by Weiner (1970). To mention just one, consider the effects of programmed instruction in which 100 percent reinforcement schedules are created. Under the condition of repeated *successes* the tendency of low achievement oriented people to engage in further achievement oriented activity is maximized; however, the converse is true for people high in achievement orientation and the PI technique will suffer. According to the model, high need achievers should receive reinforcement only 50 percent of the time.

Although Locke (1968) sees his experimental results as being contradictory to the need achievement notion that the behavioral tendency is maximized when $P_s = .50$, the two formulations seem to be quite different in operational terms. Again, the crucial element is the commitment of the individual to the goal. Almost by definition, if an Atkinson subject accepts a goal, he or she has interpreted it as one which provides achievement oriented outcomes, and would, if asked, describe the goal as "challenging" or some other adjective signifying "moderate" difficulty. In sum, the two models seem to operate on opposite sides of the commitment point and the subject's own definition of the task is again crucial.

Attribution Processes and Motivational Dynamics

The notion of expectancy, or the subjective probability that effort will lead to goal accomplishment, pervades contemporary human motivation theory. However, as we pointed out at the beginning of this chapter, the actual level of performance on a task or in an organizational role can be a function of a number of things besides effort. Thus, it is reasonable to view an individual's expectancy estimate as being influenced by his or her explanation of how the various components influence performance in a given situation. If we could describe an individual's "theory of performance" it would do at least two things for us: First, on a priori grounds it would simply be a good thing to understand the antecedents of the expectancy variable, and other variables as well. Second, it would also provide a means for hypothesizing what happens to behavior (e.g., effort) over the long run as an individual experiences successes and failures under various conditions. So far, motivation theories pertaining to employment behavior have been woefully silent as to what happens to behavior over time.

One body of theory that provides such leverage has been labeled attributional analysis, or the processes by which individuals attribute characteristics or causal relations to various objects as explanations for their appearance or behavior.

As pointed out by Kelley (1967) and Weiner and Kukla (1970), two general kinds of attributional processes have been brought under consideration. The first can be attributed to Heider (1958) and Jones and Davis (1965), and emphasizes the environmental factors or stimulus conditions that affect attribution. The second is most closely identified with Rotter (1966), and focuses on an individual differences variable labeled "internal versus external" control. That is, there seems to be stable individual differences in the degree to which people feel they control or are controlled by their environment.

The first way of looking at attribution has implications for the justifications used by the organization to reinforce success or failure and the resulting alteration of the individual's instrumentalities. For example, an individual's task success or failure might be attributed either to ability or to effort (Heider, 1958). Suppose someone fails, and the people in the organization who control the external rewards attribute the failure to a lack of ability rather than effort. In organizations such as schools, or other training institutions, this may result in greater reinforcement ("that was a really nice try") for failure rather than for success, if task success were in turn attributed to high ability with little effort. Conversely, in a business organization, when failure is attributed to a lack of ability rather than effort it may result in a dismissal, whereas failure due to a lack of effort (in the presence of high ability) may put the responsibility on the organization's back and set management to wondering where it went wrong and how it could improve the "motivation" of capable employees. The individual himself can affect his internal outcomes in much the same way by attributing his performance to skill, effort, or external factors. In the case of goal achievement, attribution via effort may not lead to as great a feeling of accomplishment as attributions of the form, "I succeeded because I had a great deal of ability to bring to bear on this task." If failure is experienced, it might be much less negatively rewarding if the individual can attribute it to environmental factors or the fact that he or she just didn't feel like trying. Considerable data support this kind of defensive attribution (e.g., see Weiner & Kukla, 1970).

Weiner and Kukla (1970) also report the results of several of their own experiments, albeit with elementary school children, that show how differential rewards are produced by experimentally induced differences in attributions of effort versus ability. Their data also suggest that self-generated attributions and internally mediated negative outcomes have a much more severe effect than externally mediated negative outcomes. Thus, while punishment administered by an independent party may have little effect on behavior, as argued by many reinforcement theorists, it may be quite potent when self-administered.

Given the importance of self-generated attributions, it might be wise for the motivational models to consider the possibility of stable individual differences in these processes. For example, Rotter (1966) suggests that individuals vary in the degree to which they believe they control events (internal control) or events control them (external control) and he has developed a paper and pencil inventory to assess this characteristic. Within our valence-instrumentality-expectancy model, such a variable has important implications for the expectancy component. Someone scoring toward the external end of the continuum may seldom see a connection between either ability or effort and task accomplishment. It is possible that such attributions are associated with being at the very bottom of the socioeconomic ladder

and, therefore, has a very deleterious effect on both academic and employment behavior. Conversely, someone scoring toward the internal control extreme may always interpret the attainment of outcomes as dependent on the individual's own behavior. However, if the situation is really such that no matter what the individual does rewards cannot be brought under self-control there would surely be long-term behavorial effects. For example, self-esteem could steadily erode.

Looking at the same phenomenon in a somewhat different way, Weiner and Kukla (1970) hypothesized that individuals high in resultant achievement motivation (i.e., $M_S > M_{AF}$) are more likely to attribute success in achievement oriented situations to themselves than people low in resultant achievement motivation (i.e., $M_S < M_{AF}$), which would in turn enhance the valence of first level outcomes and result in a higher probability of greater effort. They present a number of experiments on grade school children to support this hypothesis.

The data relative to attributions of failure are not quite so clear. However, a provocative suggestion from their studies is that both individuals who are high and low on resultant achievement motivation tend to attribute failure to themselves, but high scorers attribute their failure to a lack of effort while low scorers attribute theirs to a lack of ability. A practitioner attempting to use an expectancy/valence framework to deal with organizational behavior would do well to take these suggestions into account.

In subsequent statements concerning the interaction of need achievement and attribution theory concepts, Weiner (1972, 1974) introduced another major parameter pertaining to the perceived causal agents of success and failure. The four major causal factors considered are effort, ability, luck, and task difficulty; and a distinction is made between stable and unstable agents. Ability and task difficulty are viewed as stable causal agents, while luck and effort are causal elements that can vary a great deal from time to time. What results is a 2×2 classification of causal factors where the two major parameters are internal versus external control and stable versus unstable factors. The fourfold table is as follows:

	Stable	Unstable
Internal	Ability	Effort
External	Task Difficulty	Luck

Weiner (1974) is critical of the Rotter-type distinction between internal and external control because it is confounded with the stability dimension. Attribution in each of the four cells may have different antecedents and different behavioral consequences.

For example, Weiner and his colleagues have conducted a number of laboratory-type studies (e.g., Weiner, Heckhausen, Meyer, & Cook, 1972) which suggest that attribution of causality to stable factors results in a much greater change in subsequent expectancy judgments than attributing causality to unstable factors.

If we were to consider the full range of interactions posed by the above conceptual and empirical analysis, the situation would appear as in Figure 3. Given that an individual is high or low on need achievement we can ask whether task success or task failure is experienced. For either success or failure we must next ask whether the individual attributes the cause of the performance outcome to internal or external con-

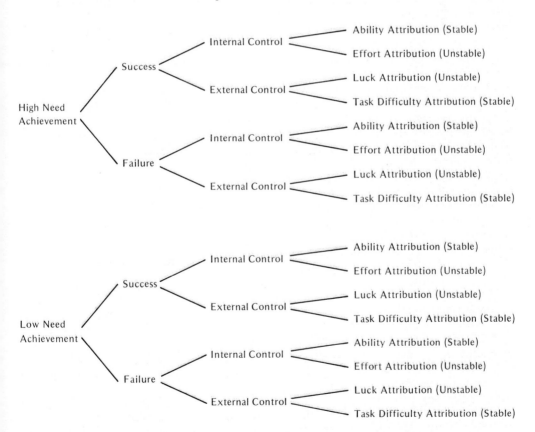

Figure 3.   Possible interactions among IDs (n Ach), performance outcomes, and attributions of causes for success and failure.

trolling agents. If the outcome is seen as being under internal control then the final question is whether the outcome is perceived as resulting from ability or effort. If the performance outcome is perceived as under external control then the final question is whether the cause is attributed to luck or task difficulty.

Such an analysis has several major implications for any attempt to develop a more precise expectancy model of individual motivation in organizations. First, the cell an individual is in has implications for how the perceived value (valence) of accomplishing or not accomplishing a goal might change over subsequent periods. Previous research (e.g., Osipow, 1972) suggests that, in general, people who experience success on a task tend to value future accomplishment of the task more highly than people who experience failure. However, Figure 3 suggests that such a finding masks some important interactions. For example, data summarized by Weiner (1974) suggest that attributions of internal causes increase the subsequent variability in the valence assigned to task success and task failure. External attributions should decrease it. The change in the variance of valence should be further increased if only the "stable" causal elements are considered. Other things being equal, attribution of unstable factors should decrease the difference in the valences of success and failure. For example, high need achievers who experience success but attribute it to their effort rather than their ability may devalue such task accomplishment in the future.

The second major implication pertains to how attributions affect future expectancies. One obvious example is that task failure may influence future expectancies differently depending on whether failure is attributed to internal or external causes.

Third, the above discussion deals only with attributions pertaining to one event, task success or task failure. It would be profitable if we also had an attributional analysis for how individuals explain why they were granted or not granted rewards by the organization or why someone else was granted or not granted the same rewards. In general, the need achievement model does not make a distinction between expectancy and instrumentality as discussed previously. However, in the organizational situation, it may be profitable to explore how individual differences in causal attribution affect subsequent judgments of instrumentality, as well as expectancy.

The above touches only on some of the implications of the attribution process and our discussion only in a somewhat ahistorical sense. That is, we have not dealt with how attributions develop or can be altered. It is beyond the scope of this chapter to do so. However, Kelley (1967) and Weiner (1972) present an excellent summary of these considerations and the reader is enthusiastically referred to these sources. A deeper understanding of these processes and further research on the issues they suggest seem mandatory. This domain of research and theory is one of the few that speaks directly to how the motivational antecedents of organizational behavior might change over time. Perhaps the best summary statement of how this causal attribution model for performance relates to expectancy theory is to say that it provides part of the missing link that explains how expectancies, instrumentalities, and valences change from time 1 to time 2.

Some Conclusions

This chapter has spanned a broad range of motivational theory and research. Based on this brief examination, what can be concluded? Is motivation theory alive and well in organizational psychology? Or should we again decide that whatever ails motivation, it's incurable, and while the patient should be kept comfortable, its life should not be prolonged unnecessarily? Neither extreme seems palatable, and as an assessment of where we are and where we ought to go we would like to: (a) offer some general conclusions about the state of the art in I/O (Industrial-Organizational) psychology; (b) ask whether issues raised by the experimentalist, but ignored by the organizational literature, might profitably be re-examined; and (c) suggest some directions that future research on adult motivation in organizations might take.

The State of the I/O Art

1. Conceptually, motivation theory in organizational psychology has come a long way since 1960. Previous to that time there was very little for the practitioner or scientist to fall back on when a systematic set of questions was needed to analyze a real situation or a potential research domain. Of course, there was the soon-to-be-shot-down notion that satisfied people are productive people, and a certain amount of attention was devoted to the notion of fatigue and its determinants as well as to the benefits of incentive payment. However, it was not until the 1960s that a much more systematic set of models evolved to provide more comprehensive specifications for the practitioner or researcher who wishes to make a "motivational" analysis of a situation. During the last fifteen years motivational models have come of age, or at least have moved through the pubescent years. Whether optimum use is being made of the available theory is another story. We think not.

2. In spite of the potential usefulness of the available models, there is a strong suggestion that industrial and organizational psychology is repeating a historical mistake in its quest for an overall, all encompassing model such as valence-instrumentality-expectance. Previously, Hull attempted to formulate a general model of behavior, and failed. As a result, the experimentalists seem to have given up the objective of a motivational "grand design." Whether the proposed function is $sE_R = sH_R \times D \times K$ or $F = E(\Sigma V \times I)$, the behavior domain involved is too complex and its bits and pieces are too poorly understood to permit one

algorithm to do the job. To make such an algorithm serve this purpose, either the right side of the equation will have to be made impossibly complex or the left side (i.e., the dependent variable) must be defined so narrowly that all resemblance to organizationally meaningful behavior is lost. Also, we have already discussed the more specific problems created by invoking multiplicative relationships among poorly understood variables. These compound the overall problem.

For these reasons we suggest that I/O psychology abandon attempts to predict behavior using the quantity $F = E(\Sigma V \times I)$. This is not to argue that the function can't serve as a useful heuristic for identifying specific variables or relationships of interest and for guiding future research. What we are counseling against is seeking one overall grand design that will produce one summary index that has a high correlation with a highly important dependent variable.

3. Another aspect of the grand design syndrome is the expectation that a relatively simple operationalization of the function, "performance = ability × motivation" will yield meaningful and significant correlations. Again, this equation may have a certain amount of heuristic value but to take it literally and multiply an aptitude test score by some composite of expectancy, instrumentality, and valence for the purpose of predicting performance is to come very close to jousting at windmills. We could better spend our time asking less cosmic and more useful research questions.

By outlining the schematic representation of task performance attributions in Figure 3 we certainly were *not* trying to offer up a grand design of attributional processes that should be "tested" by one overall study. Such studies would meet a predictable fate, the results would be confusing and inconclusive. Rather, it should function as a heuristic device for trying to sort through a wide range of potential research questions which would yield the most useful information about performance attributions.

4. By implication, the above arguments

also point an accusing finger at the dependent variables used by motivation theory and research. There is almost universal agreement that what we are trying to predict is choice behavior, effort expenditure, or the persistence of behavior. Effort expenditure is probably the most popular. However, we know virtually nothing, in a measurement or construct validity sense, about the dependent variables we are trying to explain. The "criterion problem" is no less important here than in personnel selection. Why has it been so largely ignored? For example, how should effort be defined? How should it be measured? How should the construct validity of an effort measure be established? Even if we could successfully predict self-ratings of overall effort, we do not at this time know what we would be predicting. Research on performance measurement took a step forward when it backed away from an ill-defined global rating measure and began to look at performance in terms of multiple factors defined by concrete observables. Perhaps research on effort should do the same thing.

5. The measurement of motivational independent variables is also in a very primitive state. We have been much too content with one-item measures couched in Likert formats. We share Guion's (1973) strong misgivings about this procedure as well as his advice that many of the criteria for judging the usefulness of psychological tests should be applied to these variables as well. There is virtually no research that has attempted to develop measures of instrumentality or expectancy such that they possess demonstrated construct validity. Items are simply written down and the investigator goes on to test a series of "hypotheses."

6. In spite of the above problems of execution, we think that motivation theory has exhibited a great deal of progress on the conceptual level. There is considerably more clarity in the motivational domain vis-à-vis industrial and organizational psychology than there was before 1960. One qualifica-

tion to this point is that the taxonomic models described in the section on content theory do not yet seem to provide very much guidance concerning the potential outcomes that should be considered in a particular situation. In terms of desired job outcomes, or rewards, we still have very fragmentary knowledge about why people work.

Issues from the Experimentalists

If we go back to our listing of motivational issues taken from the experimental literature and compare them to the issues prevalent in the organizational literature there are some obvious discrepancies that deserve mention.

1. By and large the experimentalists have backed away from the concept of need or drive while need theories are still a viable topic in the organizational literature. Given the difficulties experienced in the infrahuman laboratory, perhaps it would be wise to seriously consider concentrating on taxonomies of observable outcomes rather than underlying need structures. Sticking with observables would obviate many of the problems created by need theories.

To the extent that experimentalists have been concerned with the drive concept, the organizational literature has tended to parallel the experimental literature. That is, questions concerning the definition of needs, their dimensionality, and the dynamics by which they influence their effects have been prominent in the organizational literature. The frustrations involved in answering these questions have also been parallel.

2. In contrast, the notion of arousal level which became an important variable in the experimental literature has been largely ignored in the organizational setting, except for the work by Scott (1966). However, Scott and his colleagues have not anchored arousal in physiological measures, which is how Berlyne (1967) and others think it should be operationalized.

3. Experimentalists have been quite con-

cerned with the question of what mechanisms make a reinforcer reinforcing. While cognitive models pay lip service to the notion that job outcomes take on value because of their instrumentality for obtaining other valued outcomes, such data have not really been systematically collected. For example, we really do not have a systematic body of data pertaining to why money is or is not valent for some people.

4. The notion of adaptation level, and other mechanisms by which the "value" of an outcome might change have also been largely ignored in the organizational sphere. Equity theory addresses itself to this problem, but only in a very limited domain.

5. Some experimental issues have no real analog in the organizational setting. Primary versus secondary reinforcement and the consequent issues surrounding the parameters of secondary reinforcement is one such area. This one, as well as others, seem to be issues that arise almost as the result of the organism under study.

6. A number of experimentalists have worried a lot about whether the behavioral effects of a particular variable are of a motivational or learning sort. That is, to what extent is the acquisition of new responses involved, rather than the selection or implementation of already available responses? For the experimentalist this question occurs in the context of reinforcement and animal behavior, and thus appears to lack relevance for human behavior in organizations. However, the basic issue is quite real when the effects of goal setting or causal attributions are being considered. We would do well to pay much more attention to the distinction.

7. One glaring discrepancy in the organizational literature is the lack of a systematic concern for the Skinnerian or pure reinforcement point of view. Cognitive models have tended to overwhelm noncognitive ones. Unfortunately, it would be difficult to make any systematic comparison between the two in an organizational setting since each of them incorporates quite different

variables. A Skinnerian model makes no use of variables that pertain to internal states or otherwise involve surplus meaning, while such variables are the very foundation of an expectancy model. Thus, it is difficult to construct situations in which the two "models" would make contradictory predictions.

If we take Skinner at his word and think of the reinforcement orientation as a technology rather than a theory, the general principles that positive reinforcement is more effective than negative reinforcement and shorter latencies are better than long ones would not really be disputed by a cognitive model. What might be disputed are the notions that an outcome's incentive value is best inferred from an individual's past reinforcement history and that variable ratio reinforcement is a more powerful influence on behavior than other reinforcement schedules.

Any attempt to resolve the latter question must deal with the twin questions of what is a response and what is a reinforcement. In the employment situation, these are extremely difficult questions to answer and we have devoted little attention to them. Without any information concerning what the individual defines as a response and a reinforcement, it is always possible to explain away discrepancies between the expectancy and reinforcement models on the grounds that the subjects were defining responses or reinforcers differently from what we thought. For example, in the Yukl, Wexley, and Seymore (1972) lab experiment cited earlier we really do not know whether or not the subjects perceived the situation in the same way as the experimenters. They may have defined a response (i.e., task achievement) as, "whatever number of completed units it takes to get paid."

To put it bluntly, there is simply a fundamental difference between the reinforcement and cognitive models that gives them a qualitatively different approach to the explanation of behavior, and rather than try to pit them against each other it might be a wise strategy to make intelligent use of what each has to offer. Thus, if we are expectancy theorists, there is really no reason why we should not carefully review the past history of individuals, attempt to document the outcomes that controlled their behavior, and use this information in conjunction with individual judgments about future preferences to account for effort or choice behavior. There is no denying that using proven reinforcers to provide immediate reinforcement for clearly defined responses is a powerful technology with which to affect behavior. When the reinforcers are known, can be manipulated (by the individual or some designated change agent), and the responses are clearly identifiable, the potential of the Skinnerian approach, for good or evil, is awesome. However, we must at the same time take into account the individual's perceptions of the situation or serious trouble can result. The rate restriction phenomena is one object lesson to keep in mind. Others are making the news almost daily.

Future Research Directions

Again, it is our belief that the available theory is too lacking in precision to make specific predictions about behavior that can be confirmed or disconfirmed by some overall "test." The principal virtue of the available models is their heuristic value for suggesting where we might better put our limited research resources. The following list constitutes our suggestions:

1. We still do not have much systematic data pertaining to the precise nature of job outcomes that people value. The taxonomic work is sparse and we need much more of it. For example, when we ask someone to rate the degree to which their job provides friendly co-worker relationships, what do they think about before answering? The outcomes incorporated in job satisfaction questionnaires have typically not been defined in terms of observables. As yet we can not really describe in concrete terms the

outcomes for which people work. We also do not have a great deal of faith that the outcomes used in laboratory and field research have been the most relevant set of such outcomes. For example, assuming that the financial piece rates used in laboratory studies in any way represent a sample of the real world outcome domain is a risky procedure in itself.

Determining the nature of relevant job outcomes is much in need of a multimethod approach. As noted earlier, Herzberg and his colleagues took one tentative step and then stopped. Why doesn't someone also ask subjects to think of a time when they felt like changing jobs or to think of the time when they did change a job, accept an offer, work overtime, etc., and then describe what led to that feeling or decision? We could also spend much more time trying to document the reinforcement histories of individuals as per the reinforcement view.

Since the available outcomes play such an important role in all the models we have discussed it is a bit startling that so little hard-nosed attention has been devoted to their description and definition. We are badly in need of both substantive and methodological innovation in this area.

2. In general, we think the entire spectrum of motivational concerns is in need of more descriptive or process type research. That is, besides attempting to predict effort or choice behavior with an a priori set of independent variables, we should also devote some of our resources to empirically analyzing the process by which individuals choose to expend a certain level of effort. An analog is the history of research on the employment interview. One frequent type of interview study was the investigation of the reliability and validity of interviewer judgments for predicting later job performance. That line of research was really something of a dead end. Subsequently, the understanding of the employment interview took a giant step forward when the actual processes by which interviewers arrived at a de-

cision began to be studied. We think similar benefits would accrue to an understanding of effort or choice behavior if we used a variety of methods to "recover" the processes by which individuals came to choose one task over another or change their level of effort expenditure.

3. We have already spoken to the need to develop better measures of the independent and dependent variables incorporated by the various models. For example, expectancy and instrumentality are constructs deemed to be important, and developing measures for them requires a substantial construct validity effort. Trying to build an understanding of motivation on unresearched measures of one item is a bad gamble. For example, we really don't know if subjects interpret the expectancy and instrumentality questionnaire items in ways that are consistent with the theoretical notions of the investigator.

4. In a similar vein, our science would benefit a great deal if a systematic program of research (or researches) could be devoted just to the criterion problem. As noted in the introduction to this chapter, what we should be trying to explain are effort and choice behavior and the dynamics thereof. These dependent variables must be defined in such a way that they are not confounded with ability, task understanding (i.e., learning), and the constraining influences of the situation. The experimentalists worry a lot about learning versus motivational effects; and we should share some of their anxiety. For example, much of the research on goal setting seems to confound learning and motivational considerations.

In pursuit of this line of research, we think it would be a mistake to seek a continuous criterion variable representing a "pure" measure of effort. Rather, it would be better to think of the dependent variable in terms of discrete decisions that individuals make. Thus, we should develop methods to assess whether individuals decide to work harder, adopt a certain goal, or stop

trying for a particular goal. This argument is based primarily on technological grounds. Development of a continuous pure measure of effort does not look all that feasible. Please note that we are not advocating predicting self-reports of decisions. The intent is to deal with observable behavior, but the developmental research for such an indicator must show that it measures observed behaviors that are consistent with individual intentions.

5. Atkinson, Locke, and others have produced enough evidence to convince us that the task goal and the way it is perceived are important determinants of the volitional side of behavior. Much more work on tasks and their important parameters is needed. Again, a certain amount of process research is called for. One important component of this research should be the separation of learning and motivational effects. For example, to what extent does increasing the specificity of goals result in "knowing what to do" versus "deciding to expend greater effort"?

6. Finally, it is surely obvious to all readers that there are now available a large number of practical motivational techniques designed to alter the effort or choice behavior of individuals. Incentive payment, flexible hours, employee counseling, management by objectives, supervisory consideration, participation in decision making, and job enrichment are but a few. In our opinion we really have very little systematic knowledge about the actual motivational processes involved in each of these. For example, why does participation work? A frequent answer is that participation increases commitment to the implementation of a decision. But what does that mean? Such an answer is still much too coarse to be very informative, and we need much more systematic information about the processes involved. For example, what valued outcomes are created and provided by participation? Does it influence expectancy and/or instrumentality? Does it involve equity considerations in any

way? A similar set of questions could be asked about job enrichment. Lawler (1973) posed a few of them but the list of process questions he suggested could be expanded considerably.

In sum, unless we use our available theoretical tools to examine systematically the processes by which a specific practical procedure works or does not work, we are not using motivation theory in industrial/organizational psychology to its best advantage.

REFERENCES

Adams, J. S. Toward an understanding of inequity. *Journal of Abnormal and Social Psychology,* 1963, 67, 422–436. (a)

Adams, J. S. Wage inequities, productivity, and work quality. *Industrial Relations,* 1963, 3, 9–16. (b)

Adams, J. S. Inequity in social exchange. In L. Berkowitz (Ed.), *Advances in experimental social psychology,* 2. New York: Academic Press, 1965.

Adams, J. S., & Jacobsen, P. R. Effects of wage inequities on work quality. *Journal of Abnormal and Social Psychology,* 1964, 69, 19–25.

Adams, J. S., & Rosenbaum, W. B. The relationship of worker productivity to cognitive dissonance about wage inequities. *Journal of Applied Psychology,* 1962, 46, 161–164.

Alderfer, C. P. An empirical test of a new theory of human needs. *Organizational Behavior and Human Performance,* 1969, 4, 142–175.

Alderfer, C. P. *Existence, relatedness, and growth: Human needs in organizational settings.* New York: The Free Press, 1972.

Andrews, I. R. Wage inequity and job performance: An experimental study. *Journal of Applied Psychology,* 1967, 51, 39–45.

Andrews, I. R., & Valenzi, E. Overpay inequity or self-image as a worker: A critical examination of an experimental induction procedure. *Organizational Behavior and Human Performance,* 1970, 53, 22–27.

Aronson, E. A need for achievement as measured by graphic expression. In J. W. Atkinson (Ed.), *Motives in fantasy, action, and society.* Princeton: Van Nostrand, 1958.

Arrowood, A. J. Some effects on productivity of justified and unjustified levels of reward under public and private conditions. Unpublished doctoral dissertation, University of Minnesota, Minneapolis, 1961.

Arvey, R. D. Task performance as a function of perceived effort-performance and performance-reward contingencies. *Organizational Behavior and Human Performance,* 1972, 8, 423–433.

Arvey, R. D., & Neil, C. W. Testing expectancy theory predictions using behaviorally based measures of motivational effort for engineers. Mimeograph, University of Tennessee, Knoxville, 1972.

Atkinson, J. W. Motivational determinants of risk-taking behavior. *Psychological Review,* 1957, 64, 359–372.

Atkinson, J. W. *An introduction to motivation.* Princeton: Van Nostrand, 1964.

Atkinson, J. W. Some general implications of conceptual developments in the study of achievement oriented behavior. In M. R. Jones (Ed.), *Human motivation: A symposium.* Lincoln: University of Nebraska Press, 1965.

Atkinson, J. W., & Cartwright, D. Some neglected variables in contemporary conceptions of decision and performance. *Psychological Reports,* 1964, 14, 575–590.

Baehr, M. E. A factorial study of the SRA employee inventory. *Personnel Psychology,* 1954, 7, 319–336.

Becker, G. M., & McClintock, C. G. Value: Behavioral decision theory. In P. R. Farnsworth (Ed.), *Annual review of psychology,* Vol. 18. Palo Alto, Calif.: Annual Reviews, 1967.

Behling, O., & Starke, F. A. Some limits on expectancy theories of work effort. Proceedings, Midwest Meeting, American Institute of Decision Sciences, 1973.

Berkun, M. M., Kessen, M. L., & Miller, N. E. Hunger-reducing effects of food by stomach fistula versus food by mouth measured by consummatory response. *Journal of Comparative and Physiological Psychology,* 1952, 45, 550–564.

Berlyne, D. E. Arousal and reinforcement. In D. Levine (Ed.), *Nebraska symposium on motivation.* Lincoln: University of Nebraska Press, 1967.

Bindra, D. The interrelated mechanisms of reinforcement and motivation, and the nature of their influence on response. In W. J. Arnold & D. Levine (Eds.), *Nebraska symposium on motivation*. Lincoln: University of Nebraska Press, 1969.

Birch, D., & Veroff, J. *Motivation: A study of action*. Belmont, Calif.: Brooks/Cole, 1968.

Black, R. W. Incentive motivation and the parameters of reward in instrumental conditioning. In W. J. Arnold & D. Levine (Eds.), *Nebraska symposium on motivation*. Lincoln: University of Nebraska Press, 1969.

Bolles, R. C. *Theory of motivation*. New York: Harper and Row, 1967.

Calder, B. J., & Staw, B. M. The interaction of intrinsic and extrinsic motivation: Some methodological issues. *Journal of Personality and Social Psychology*, in press.

Campbell, J. P., Dunnette, M. D., Lawler, E. E. III, & Weick, K. E. Jr. *Managerial behavior, performance, and effectiveness*. New York: McGraw-Hill, 1970.

Cartledge, N. D. An experimental study of the relationship between expectancies, goal utility, goals and task performance. Unpublished doctoral dissertation, University of Maryland, College Park, 1972.

Clark, J. V. A preliminary investigation of some unconscious assumptions affecting labor efficiency in eight supermarkets. Unpublished doctoral dissertation, Harvard University, Cambridge, 1958.

Cofer, C. N. Motivating effects of money: Theoretical approaches. Paper presented at the McKinsey Foundation Conference on Managerial Compensation, Tarrytown, New York, March, 1967.

Cofer, C. N., & Appley, M. H. *Motivation: Theory and research*. New York: Wiley, 1964.

Crespi, L. P. Quantitative variation of incentive and performance in the white rat. *American Journal of Psychology*, 1942, 55, 467–517.

Dachler, H. P., & Mobley, W. H. Construct validation of an instrumentality-expectancy-task-goal model of work motivation: Some theoretical boundary conditions. *Journal of Applied Psychology*, 1973, 58, 397–418.

Dawis, R. V., Lofquist, L. H., & Weiss, D. J. A theory of work adjustment. (A revision.) *Minnesota Studies in Vocational Rehabilitation*, XXIII. Minneapolis: University of Minnesota, 1968.

deCharms, R. *Personal causation: The internal affective determinants of behavior*. New York: Academic Press, 1968.

Deci, E. L. The effects of externally mediated rewards on intrinsic motivation. *Journal of Personality and Social Psychology*, 1971, 18, 105–115.

Deci, E. L. The effects of contingent and non-contingent rewards and controls on intrinsic motivation. *Organizational Behavior and Human Performance*, 1972, 8, 217–229.

Deci, E. L., & Cascio, W. F. Changes in intrinsic motivation as a function of negative feedback and threats. Paper presented at the Eastern Psychological Association Conference, April, 1972.

Descartes, R. (1649) Passions of the soul. In E. S. Haldane & G. R. T. Ross (Eds.), *Philosophical works of Descartes*. Cambridge: University Press, 1911. (Reprinted by Dover, 1955.)

Dunnette, M. D. Performance equals ability and what? Mimeographed paper, University of Minnesota, Minneapolis, 1972.

Edwards, W. Behavioral decision theory. In P. R. Farnsworth (Ed.), *Annual review of psychology*, Vol. 12. Palo Alto, Calif.: Annual Reviews, 1961.

Evans, M. G. The effects of supervisory behavior on the path-goal relationship. *Organizational Behavior and Human Performance*, 1970, 5, 277–298.

Evans, M. G., & Molinari, L. Equity, piece-rate overpayment, and job security: Some effects on performance. *Journal of Applied Psychology*, 1970, 54, 105–114.

Festinger, L. *A theory of cognitive dissonance*. Evanston, Ill.: Row, Peterson, 1957.

Festinger, L. *A technical study of some changes in attitudes and values following promotion in General Electric*. Crotonville, N.Y.: Behavioral Research Service, 1964.

French, E. G. Development of a measure of complex motivation. In J. W. Atkinson (Ed.), *Motives in fantasy, action, and society*. Princeton: Van Nostrand, 1958.

Friedman, A., & Goodman, P. S. Wage inequity, self-qualifications, and productivity. *Organizational Behavior and Human Performance*, 1967, 2, 406–417.

Galbraith, J., & Cummings, L. L. An empirical investigation of the motivational determinants of task performance: Interactive effects between instrumentality-valence and motivation-ability. *Organizational Behavior and Human Performance,* 1967, 2, 237–257.

Gavin, J. F. Ability, effort, and role perception as antecedents of job performance. *Experimental Publication System,* 1970, 5, Ms. No. 190A, 1–26.

Georgopoulos, B. S., Mahoney, G. M., & Jones, N. W. A path-goal approach to productivity. *Journal of Applied Psychology,* 1957, 41, 345–353.

Goodman, P. S., & Friedman, A. An examination of the effect of wage inequity in the hourly condition. *Organizational Behavior and Human Performance,* 1968, 3, 340–352.

Goodman, P. S., & Friedman, A. An examination of quantity and quality of performance under conditions of overpayment in piece rate. *Organizational Behavior and ·Human Performance,* 1969, 4, 365–374.

Goodman, P. S., & Friedman, A. Adams's theory of inequity. *Administrative Science Quarterly,* 1971, 16, 271–288.

Graen, G. Instrumentality theory of work motivation: Some experimental results and suggested modifications. *Journal of Applied Psychology Monograph,* 1969, 53, 1–25.

Guion, R. M. A note on organizational climate. *Organizational Behavior and Human Performance,* 1973, 9, 120–125.

Hackman, J. R., & Porter, L. W. Expectancy theory predictions of work effectiveness. *Organizational Behavior and Human Performance,* 1968, 3, 417–426.

Hall, C. S., & Lindzey, G. *Theories of personality.* New York: Wiley, 1957.

Hall, D. T., & Nougaim, K. E. An examination of Maslow's need hierarchy in an organizational setting. *Organizational Behavior and Human Performance,* 1968, 3, 12–35.

Heider, F. *The psychology of interpersonal relations.* New York: Wiley, 1958.

Helson, H. Adaptation level theory. In S. Koch (Ed.), *Psychology: A study of a science,* Vol. 1. New York: McGraw-Hill, 1959.

Heneman, H. G. III, & Schwab, D. P. An evaluation of research on expectancy theory predictions of employee performance. *Psychological Bulletin,* 1972, 78, 1–9.

Herman, J. B., & Hulin, C. L. Managerial satisfactions and organizational roles: An investigation of Porter's need deficiency scales. *Journal of Applied Psychology,* 1973, 57, 118–124.

Hermans, H. J. M. A questionnaire measure of achievement motivation. *Journal of Applied Psychology,* 1970, 54, 353–363.

Herzberg, F., Mausner, B., Peterson, R. O., & Capwell, D. F. *Job attitudes: A review of research and opinion.* Pittsburgh: Psychological Service of Pittsburgh, 1957.

Herzberg, F., Mausner, B., & Snyderman, B. *The motivation to work.* (2nd ed.) New York: Wiley, 1959.

Holmstrom, V. L., & Beach, L. R. Subjective expected utility and career preferences. *Organizational Behavior and Human Performance,* 1973, 10, 201–207.

Homans, G. C. Status among clerical workers. *Human Organizations,* 1953, 12, 5–10.

Homans, G. C. *Social behavior: Its elementary forms.* New York: Harcourt, Brace, and World, 1961.

House, R. J., & Wahba, M. A. Expectancy theory in industrial and organizational psycology: An integrative model and a review of literature. Paper presented at the meetings of the American Psychological Association, Honolulu, Hawaii, 1972.

Hull, C. L. *A behavior system.* New Haven: Yale University Press, 1952.

Jaques, E. *Equitable payment.* New York: Wiley, 1961.

Jones, E. E., & Davis, K. E. From acts to dispositions: The attribution process in person perception. In L. Berkowitz (Ed.), *Advances in experimental social psychology,* Vol. 2. New York: Academic Press, 1965.

Jorgenson, D. O., Dunnette, M. D., & Pritchard, R. D. Effects of the manipulation of a performance-reward contingency on behavior in a simulated work setting. *Journal of Applied Psychology,* 1973, 57, 271–280.

Kelley, H. H. Attribution theory in social psychology. In D. Levine (Ed.), *Nebraska symposium on motivation.* Lincoln: University of Nebraska Press, 1967.

Kendler, H. H. Motivation and behavior. In D. Levine (Ed.), *Nebraska symposium on motivation.* Lincoln: University of Nebraska Press, 1965.

Lacey, J. I. Somatic response patterning and stress: Some revisions of activation theory. In M. H. Appley & R. Turnbull (Eds.), *Psychological stress: Some issues in research.* New York: Appleton-Century-Crofts, 1967.

Latham, G. P., & Baldes, J. J. The "practical significance" of Locke's theory of goal setting. *Journal of Applied Psychology,* in press.

Latham, G. P., & Kinne, S. B. Improving job performance through training in goal setting. *Journal of Applied Psychology,* 1974, 59, 187–191.

Lawler, E. E. A causal correlation analysis of the relationship between expectancy attitudes and job performance. *Journal of Applied Psychology,* 1968, 52, 462–468. (a)

Lawler, E. E. Effects of hourly overpayment on productivity and work quality. *Journal of Personality and Social Psychology,* 1968, 10, 306–313. (b)

Lawler, E. E. Equity theory as a predictor of productivity and work quality. *Psychological Bulletin,* 1968, 70, 596–610. (c)

Lawler, E. E. *Pay and organizational effectiveness: A psychological view.* New York: McGraw-Hill, 1971.

Lawler, E. E. *Motivation in work organizations.* Belmont, Calif.: Brooks/Cole, 1973.

Lawler, E. E., & O'Gara, P. W. Effects of inequity produced by underpayment on work output, work quality, and attitudes toward work. *Journal of Applied Psychology,* 1967, 51, 403–410.

Lawler, E. E., & Porter, L. W. Antecedent attitudes of effective managerial performance. *Organizational Behavior and Human Performance,* 1967, 2, 122–142.

Lawler, E. E., & Suttle, J. L. Expectancy theory and job behavior. *Organizational Behavior and Human Performance,* 1973, 9, 482–503.

Lawler, E. E., Koplin, C. A., Young, T. F., & Fadem, J. A. Inequity reduction over time in an induced overpayment situation. *Organizational Behavior and Human Performance,* 1968, 3, 253–268.

Lewin, K. *The conceptual representation and the measurement of psychological forces.* Durham, N.C.: Duke University Press, 1938.

Lewin, K. *Field theory in social science.* New York: Harper and Row, 1951.

Locke, E. A. Toward a theory of task motivation and incentives. *Organizational Behavior and Human Performance,* 1968, 3, 157–189.

Locke, E. A., Cartledge, N., & Knerr, C. S. Studies of the relationship between satisfaction, goal-setting, and performance. *Organizational Behavior and Human Performance,* 1970, 5, 135–158.

McClelland, D. C. *Personality.* New York: Dryden Press, 1951.

McClelland, D. C., Atkinson, J. W., Clark, R. A., & Lowell, E. L. *The achievement motive.* New York: Appleton-Century-Crofts, 1953.

McDougall, W. *An introduction to social psychology.* London: Methuen and Co., 1908.

Madsen, K. B. Theories of motivation: An overview and a synthesis. In M. R. Jones (Ed.), *Human motivation: A symposium.* Lincoln: University of Nebraska Press, 1965.

Mandler, G., & Sarason, S. B. A study of anxiety and learning. *Journal of Abnormal and Social Psychology,* 1952, 47, 166–173.

Marriott, R. *Incentive payment systems: A review of research and opinion.* London: Stapler Press, 1957.

Maslow, A. H. *Motivation and personality.* New York: Harper and Row, 1954.

Meyer, H. H., Kay, E., & French, J. R. P. Jr. Split roles in performance appraisal. *Harvard Business Review,* 1965, 43 (1), 123–129.

Miller, N. E. Studies of fear as an acquirable drive: I. Fear as motivation and fear-reduction as reinforcement in the learning of new responses. *Journal of Experimental Psychology,* 1948, 38, 89–101.

Miller, N. E. Experiments on motivation: Studies combining psychological, physiological, and pharmacological techniques. *Science,* 1957, 126, 1271–1278.

Miner, J. B., & Dachler, H. P. Personnel attitudes and motivation. In P. H. Mussen & M. R. Rosenzweig (Eds.), *Annual review of psychology,* Vol. 24. Palo Alto, Calif.: Annual Reviews, 1973.

Mitchell, T. R. Expectancy models of satisfaction, occupational preference, and effort: A theoretical, methodological, and empirical appraisal. Unpublished paper, University of Washington, Seattle, 1974.

Mitchell, T. R., & Albright, D. W. Expectancy theory predictions of the satisfaction, effort, performance and retention of naval aviation officers. *Organizational Behavior and Human Performance,* 1972, 8, 1–20.

Mitchell, T. R., & Biglan, A. Instrumentality theories: Current uses in psychology. *Psychological Bulletin,* 1971, 76, 432–454.

Mitchell, T. R., & Knudsen, B. W. Instrumentality theory predictions of students' attitudes towards business and their choice of business as an occupation. *Academy of Management Journal,* 1973, 16, 41–51.

Mitchell, T. R., & Nebeker, D. M. Expectancy theory predictions of academic effort and performance. *Journal of Applied Psychology,* 1973, 57, 61–67.

Mitchell, T. R., & Pollard, W. E. Instrumentality theory predictions of academic behavior. *Journal of Social Psychology,* 1973, 89, 34–45.

Moore, L. M. Effects of wage inequities on work attitudes and performance. Unpublished master's thesis, Wayne State University, Detroit, 1968.

Motowidlo, S. J., Loehr, V., & Dunnette, M. D. The effect of goal specificity on the relationship between expectancy and task performance. Minneapolis: University of Minnesota, Technical Report No. 4008, 1972.

Murray, H. A. *Explorations in personality.* New York: Oxford University Press, 1938.

O'Connor, P. An achievement risk preference scale: A preliminary report. *American Psychologist,* 1962, 17, 317 (Abstract).

Olds, J. Runway and maze behavior controlled by basomedial forebrain stimulation in the rat. *Journal of Comparative and Physiological Psychology,* 1956, 49, 507–512.

Olds, J. Hypothalamic substrates of reward. *Physiological Review,* 1962, 42, 554–604.

Olds, J., & Milner, P. Positive reinforcement produced by electrical stimulation of septal area and other regions of rat brain. *Journal of Comparative and Physiological Psychology,* 1954, 47, 419–427.

Opsahl, R. L., & Dunnette, M. D. The role of financial compensation in industrial motivation. *Psychological Bulletin,* 1966, 66, 94–118.

Osipow, S. H. Success and preference: A replication and extension. *Journal of Applied Psychology,* 1972, 56, 179–180.

Patchen, M. *The choice of wage comparisons.* Englewood Cliffs, N.J.: Prentice-Hall, 1961.

Payne, R. Factor analysis of a Maslow type need satisfaction questionnaire. *Personnel Psychology,* 1970, 23, 251–268.

Peak, H. Attitude and motivation. In M. R. Jones (Ed.), *Nebraska symposium on motivation.* Lincoln: University of Nebraska Press, 1955.

Porter, L. W. *Organizational patterns of managerial job attitudes.* New York: American Foundation for Management Research, 1964.

Porter, L. W., & Lawler, E. E. *Managerial attitudes and performance.* Homewood, Ill.: Dorsey Press, 1968.

Porter, L. W., & Mitchell, V. F. Comparative study of need satisfactions in military and business hierarchies. *Journal of Applied Psychology,* 1967, 51, 139–144.

Premack, D. Reinforcement theory. In D. Levine (Ed.), *Nebraska symposium on motivation.* Lincoln: University of Nebraska Press, 1965.

Pritchard, R. D. Equity theory: A review and critique. *Organizational Behavior and Human Performance,* 1969, 4, 176–211.

Pritchard, R. D., & Curtis, M. I. The influence of goal setting and financial incentives on task performance. *Organizational Behavior and Human Performance,* 1973, 10, 175–183.

Pritchard, R. D., & DeLeo, P. J. Experimental test of the valence-instrumentality relationship in job performance. *Journal of Applied Psychology,* 1973, 57, 264–270.

Pritchard, R. D., & Sanders, M. S. The influence of valence, instrumentality, and expectancy on effort and performance. *Journal of Applied Psychology,* 1973, 57, 55–60.

Pritchard, R. D., DeLeo, P. J., & VonBergen, C. W. An evaluation of incentive motivation techniques in Air Force technical training. Air Force Human Resources Laboratory Technical Report, Purdue University, Lafayette, Ind., 1974.

Pritchard, R. D., Dunnette, M. D., & Jorgenson, D. O. Effects of perceptions of equity and inequity on worker performance and satisfaction. *Journal of Applied Psychology,* 1972, 56, Monograph No. 1, 75–94.

Quinn, R., & Cobb, W. *What workers want: Factor analysis of importance ratings of job facets.* Ann Arbor, Mich.: Institute for Social Research, 1971.

Reitz, H. J. Managerial attitudes and perceived contingencies between performance and organizational responses. Proceedings of the 31st Annual Meeting of the Academy of Management, 1971, 227–238.

Roberts, K. H., Walter, G. A., & Miles, R. E. A factor analytic study of job satisfaction items designed to measure Maslow need categories. *Personnel Psychology,* 1971, 24, 205–220.

Roberts, W. W. Both rewarding and punishing effects from stimulation of posterior hypothalamus of cat with same electrode at same intensity. *Journal of Comparative and Physiological Psychology,* 1958, 51, 400–407.

Rotter, J. B. Generalized expectancies for internal versus external control of reinforcement. *Psychological Monographs,* 1966, 80.

Schmidt, F. L. Implications of a measurement problem for expectancy theory research. *Organizational Behavior and Human Performance,* 1973, 10, 243–251.

Schneider, J., & Locke, E. A. A critique of Herzberg's incident classification system and a suggested revision. *Organizational Behavior and Human Performance,* 1971, 6, 441–457.

Schuster, J. R., Clark, B., & Rogers, M. Testing portions of the Porter and Lawler model regarding the motivational role of pay. *Journal of Applied Psychology,* 1971, 55, 187–195.

Scott, W. E. Activation theory and task design. *Organizational Behavior and Human Performance,* 1966, 1, 3–30.

Sheard, J. L. Intrasubject prediction of preferences for organizational types. *Journal of Applied Psychology,* 1970, 54, No. 3, 248–252.

Sheffield, F. C., & Roby, T. B. Reward value of a non-nutritive sweet taste. *Journal of Comparative and Physiological Psychology,* 1950, 43, 471–481.

Sheridan, J. E., Richards, M. D., & Slocum, J. W. A longitudinal test of expectancy and heuristic models of job selection. Unpublished manuscript, Wayne State University, Detroit, 1974.

Skinner, B. F. *Walden II.* New York: Macmillan, 1948.

Skinner, B. F. *Beyond freedom and dignity.* New York: Knopf, 1971.

Slovic, P., & Lichtenstein, S. C. The relative importance of probabilities and payoffs in risk taking. *Journal of Experimental Psychology Monograph Supplement,* 1968, 78 (3, Part 2).

Smith, P. C., Kendall, L. M., & Hulin, C. L. *The measurement of satisfaction in work and retirement.* Chicago: Rand McNally, 1969.

Spence, K. W. *Behavior theory and conditioning.* New Haven: Yale University Press, 1956.

Spitzer, M. E. Goal attainment, job satisfaction, and behavior. Unpublished doctoral dissertation, New York University, New York City, 1964.

Stedry, A. C., & Kay, E. *The effects of goal difficulty on performance.* General Electric, Behavioral Research Service, 1966.

Tolman, E. C. *Purposive behavior in animals and men.* New York: Century. (By permission of the University of California Press, 1932.)

Tornow, W. W. The development and application of an input/outcome moderator test on the perception and reduction of inequity. *Organizational Behavior and Human Performance,* 1971, 6, 614–638.

Viteles, M. S. *Motivation and morale in industry.* New York: W. W. Norton, 1953.

Vroom, V. H. *Work and motivation.* New York: Wiley, 1964.

Vroom, V. H. *Motivation in management.* New York: American Foundation for Management Research, 1965.

Vroom, V. H. Organizational choice: A study of pre- and post-decision processes. *Organizational Behavior and Human Performance,* 1966, 1, 212–225.

Wahba, M. A., & House, R. J. Expectancy theory in work and motivation: Some logical and methodological issues. *Human Relations,* in press.

Wanous, J. P., & Lawler, E. E. Measurement and meaning of job satisfaction. *Journal of Applied Psychology,* 1972, 56, 95–105.

Weiner, B. New conceptions in the study of achievement motivation. In B. A. Maher (Ed.), *Progress in experimental personality research,* Vol. 5. New York: Academic Press, 1970.

Weiner, B. *Theories of motivation: From mechanism to cognition.* Chicago: Markham, 1972.

Weiner, B. An attributional interpretation of expectancy-value theory. Paper presented at the American Association for the Advancement of Science, San Francisco, February, 1974.

Weiner, B., Heckhausen, H., Meyer, W. U., & Cook, R. E. Causal ascriptions and achievement motivation: A conceptual analysis of effort and reanalysis of locus of control. *Journal of Personality and Social Psychology,* 1972, 21, 239–248.

Weiner, B., & Kukla, A. An attributional analysis of achievement motivation. *Journal of Personality and Social Psychology,* 1970, 15, 1–20.

Weiss, D. J., Dawis, R. V., England, G. W., & Lofquist, L. H. Manual for the Minnesota

Satisfaction Questionnaire. *Minnesota studies in vocational rehabilitation,* Vol. 22. Minneapolis: University of Minnesota, 1967.

Wike, E. L. Secondary reinforcement: Some research and theoretical issues. In W. J. Arnold & D. Levine (Eds.), *Nebraska symposium on motivation.* Lincoln: University of Nebraska Press, 1969.

Williams, W. E., & Seiler, D. A. Relationship between measures of effort and job performance. *Journal of Applied Psychology,* 1973, 57, 49–54.

Wofford, J. C. The motivational bases of job satisfaction and job performance. *Personnel Psychology,* 1971, 24, 501–518.

Wood, I., & Lawler, E. E. Effects of piece-rate overpayment on productivity. *Journal of Applied Psychology,* 1970, 54, 234–238.

Woodworth, R. S. *Dynamic psychology.* New York: Columbia University Press, 1918.

Yukl, G., Wexley, K. N., & Seymore, J. D. Effectiveness of pay incentives under variable ratio and continuous reinforcement schedules. *Journal of Applied Psychology,* 1972, 56, 19–23.

CHAPTER 4

Human Learning[1]

RUSSELL W. BURRIS
The University of Minnesota

A Frame of Reference

Performance Criteria—Competence and
    Assessment

Summary

References

THE OBJECTIVE of this chapter is to describe what is known and theorized about human knowledge and skills in a way which is useful in accounting for effective and productive performance. A frame of reference is suggested as an approach for relating applied problems of instruction and training to the basic principles of the human learning process.

The frame of reference and an illustrative question for each topic are:

1. *Performance criteria:* What does an individual "know" when we say he "knows"?

2. *Learning sequence:* What sequence or sequences of material to be learned optimizes learning effectiveness?

3. *Learning strategies:* What must be learned and what must the learner do to learn?

4. *Instructional modes and media:* What characterizes the selection of appropriate instructional techniques and technologies so that they relate optimally to learning strategies?

5. *Motivation:* What considerations of affective variables optimize learning?

6. *Individual differences:* In what ways are individual differences in learning relevant to effective learning situations?

The discussion attempts to identify the critical issues of learning, competency, and pedagogy in terms meaningful to both the science and engineering of teaching and learning.

---

[1] Work associated with the development of this chapter was supported in part by the Center for Research in Human Learning, University of Minnesota, through grants from the National Institute of Child Health and Human Development (HD-01136), the National Science Foundation (GS 1761), and the Graduate School of the University of Minnesota. Special acknowledgment is given also to the contributions made by students, faculty members and others from a variety of subject matter areas and professions who have been associated with projects in the Programmed Learning Center, University of Minnesota, and in the Instructional Resources Center, State University of New York at Stony Brook. They greatly aided the author's considerations of this chapter's issues.

The major objective of this chapter is to describe what is known and theorized about how humans develop knowledge and skills to the level necessary for their performances to be effective and productive. As reasonable as this objective appears on the surface, the difficulties are several. First, the learning literature is so extensive that some kind of organized categorization of issues and topics must be made if we are to avoid the pitfalls of including literature that has questionable relevance to an understanding of the complexities characteristic of productive performance. Second, the current controversies over what questions and issues are most critical to an understanding and interpretation of the learning processes involved cannot be ignored. Also, the apparently limitless number of different situations and contexts out of which such questions and issues arise obliges an assiduous, but practical, fixing of this chapter's objectives.

Anyone who has searched the literature for authoritative advice relevant to instructional and training problems is surely aware of these and related difficulties. In an attempt to meet the above objective, this chapter will focus primarily on defining the nature of "productive performance" and discovering how to account for it. Relevance to instructional and training situations within the context of industrial and organizational psychology is an overriding criterion in the selection of topics and arguments presented here.

Recognizing the performance of "expert" individuals is not too difficult; most people know various individuals—administrators, foremen, physicians, researchers, engineers, musicians, artists, teachers, mechanics, and parents—who are "expert" in a particular field or role. Usually, different observers agree about the level of expertise exhibited in these individuals' performances. But as expertness is studied in depth, more difficult questions appear. What distinguishes expert performance? What characterizes the performance of outstanding individuals from different fields? How can the characteristics

that distinguish the "expert" from the "non-expert" be described? What are the similarities in the performances of several "expert" individuals? An even more difficult question than being able to describe "expertness" is to account for what it is and how it was acquired. A maximally useful chapter on human learning must, therefore, identify and address the issues involved in these difficult questions.

Anyone familiar with the psychological and educational literature describing the processes of learning in complex situations realizes the difficulty of such an undertaking. Although there is lack of agreement about defining critical issues and making parsimonious interpretations of observed phenomena, the science of human learning can still contribute to an understanding of "expertness" and how it is attained.

Over the past few years more and more experimental psychologists interested in learning have gone outside the laboratory to study problems within applied and complex situations. Glaser and Resnick (1972, p. 207) note this trend and an accompanying feeling shared by many psychologists "that the interaction between task-oriented and discipline-oriented research will be mutually beneficial for society and for psychological science."

To review the objectives of this chapter then, we can examine the kinds of questions appropriate for such mutually beneficial interaction and the approaches which relate present-day interpretations of learning processes to these questions. First, the issues and questions addressed in this chapter will be referenced in the engineering context, and then a discussion of the learning processes appropriate to those questions will follow. To anyone unfamiliar with the psychological literature from the learning laboratory, the reasons for this approach may not be immediately apparent. Straightforward extrapolations from laboratory interpretations will not be meaningful for most applied situations involving complex behavior. Most of the topical categories found in the literature, while certainly appropriate to the experimentalist and theoretician, are not directly relevant to the design of training and educational environments. Melton (1964, p. 337f.) makes this point in summarizing a conference specifically directed to the issue of what is known and not known about learning and the usefulness of contemporary taxonomies and categories of this knowledge to both psychologists and other users of the knowledge.

A more important reason for questioning the usefulness of such direct extrapolation procedure is the recognition that the learning psychologist's focus has been on the micro-level, non-ecological analyses of the associations between stimulus and response events. The dominance of behaviorism, associationism, and positivism in American and western psychology has directed the laboratory effort toward the prediction and control of responses by stimuli. The emphasis on explaining the associations between stimulus and response events at a micro-level has omitted many complex and higher-order behaviors common to human activity. Too often the wide gap between the behavior studied in the laboratory and the more ecologically valid complex behavior has been neither recognized nor acknowledged. Extrapolations across this gap have limited benefit, and there have been many examples of rather violent misuses of laboratory observations applied to training and educational environments.

Much of the experimental literature of the past decade has noted the weaknesses of the stimulus-response paradigm as an experimental approach to the description of the complex features of cognitive behavior such as language, perception, and memory. Broadbent (1971) and Jenkins (1968) provide detailed arguments for this expanded concern. Jenkins (1968) stresses the importance of using questions which emphasize "the nature of the organism that behaves" to guide the experimental and theoretical efforts in human learning. Thus, the descriptions of complex higher-order and ecologically valid human learning behavior must go beyond the mere consideration of stimuli, responses, and their associations.

In what way, then, is the consideration of the "organism's nature" relevant to bridging the gap between the experimentalist in the laboratory and the user of the knowledge produced? If the major concerns are the characteristics of the stimuli, responses, and the associations between them, attention gets diverted from questions of (1) what internal processing operates within the competent individual, (2) what makes up that competence, and (3) how that competence is structured and organized. Indeed, the behaviorist in the laboratory has excluded just these kinds of questions which stress the importance of the individual's internal rules of processing and manipulation. However, to describe higher-order and complex behavior common to everyday activity one must account for both the encoding of environmental information and its processing along with past knowledge.

Even a rather superficial examination of human complex behavior yields a number of ecological features of learning necessary for understanding the nature of that behavior within the framework of this volume. Stimuli and responses are important to such considerations, but not in isolation. The nature of the input, encoding, storage, and output within the context of the total learning situations becomes the emphasis for this chapter. We establish a framework for questions appropriate to ecologically valid complex behavior and necessary for discussion about productive performance. No attempt will be made to review or evaluate various theoretical positions in fashion today. Furthermore, we do not even try to include everything known about the learning processes which are valuable to the individual concerned with problems of instruction or training. The objectives of this chapter are to help the reader develop a frame of reference useful for the analysis of a variety of learning situations with emphasis on what is learned and how it might have been acquired.

At a more general, yet fundamental, level, we need to be able to say what an individual "knows" when we say he "knows." To be able to do this means describing what distinguishes the expert from the non-expert across different areas of expertise. Also, we must describe how a learner progresses from a state of "not knowing" to a state of "knowing." In order to construct development and training programs and to evaluate their effectiveness, we must recognize the difficulties in distinguishing expert performance. To understand productive behavior, we must address questions relevant to constructs, such as competency, mastery, comprehension, performance, individual differences, and pedagogy as well as analyze the learning processes involved. The complexities inherent in these questions, and the inadequacy of the present theory to handle them, should cause us to be extra cautious in extrapolating a description of what and how individuals learn in the process of acquiring skill or of reaching a high level of expertise.

Illustrations of these points come from many areas of skill and knowledge noted earlier in the chapter. An example from medical diagnosis demonstrates the difficulties in accounting for the acquisition of expertise.

Although each patient's laboratory and personal history is unique, the medical internist must generate an appropriate diagnosis and treatment plan for a particular disease. He anticipates a transfer of principles from his prior education and experience with physiology, biochemistry, and medicine, to an appropriate performance in an infinite number of possible cases. For the purpose of describing *what* is transferred and *how* it takes place, it is almost useless to write an extensive list of exhibited behaviors because of the size of such a list and, it will be argued, because of its prescriptive rather than descriptive nature. *What* does the internist "know" from which appropriate behavior is generated, and *how* might the internal processing necessary to account

for such behavior be explained? It seems reasonable to suggest that the competent internist has a body of knowledge with some structure or logical organization which he manipulates or transforms according to the rules of his knowledge domain and which he then applies to a patient's normal and pathological biological functioning. The internal processing referred to earlier becomes the "grammar" or rules for manipulating or transforming a body of knowledge. Much of the recent work of psycholinguistics and cognitive psychology suggests the view which this chapter presents. Such an approach to description and explanation of complex behavior is hopefully more fruitful than accounting for the complexity through lists of stimulus discriminations and stimulus generalizations, and associated response differentiations and response generalizations.

While it may be necessary for the psychological scientist to study hierarchies of behavior complexities independently of their contexts, it is difficult to imagine how such hierarchies can presently be used to adequately describe the differences among experts from diverse areas. Skilled managers, engineers, lawyers, physicians, and carpenters are different from each other, and hierarchies which attempt to generalize behavioral similarities across areas of expertise tend to obscure these distinctive differences. Although the behavioral scientist must continue the search for parsimony in his description of human learning, the issue of ecological validity cannot be ignored at present if we want to apply knowledge about the processes of learning to problems of training and the development of competence. Much work in learning and educational research makes this point, either explicitly or implicitly; for a fuller analysis, human behavior must be considered within the context of its occurrence.

In summary, then, this chapter's objective is to identify the issues and questions relevant to behavior in particular contexts and critical to a description and explanation of that behavior. Assuming that the users of this handbook are interested in applying the learning researchers' results and techniques to productive performance, the focus will be on accounting for the attainment of complex levels of competency and relating this to training and educational programs.

A FRAME OF REFERENCE

This chapter establishes the general areas of performance criteria, learning sequences, learning strategies, instructional modes and media, motivation, and individual differences as a frame of reference to help relate problems of an applied nature to present levels of understanding of the learning processes. These particular area labels are merely constructs to group the application-oriented questions, but they also provide a frame of reference for the analysis and design of training and educational programs. While these are not the usual constructs for organizing a survey of learning literature, they are used here to provide a useful frame of reference in directing attention toward the critical learning issues in complex behavior.

Performance Criteria

Under the topic of performance criteria occur the two most fundamental and far-reaching questions: What does an individual "know" when we say he "knows," and how can we determine that the learner has reached an appropriate level of achievement? Such questions are fundamental to both the basic researcher and the applied manager of teaching and learning situations. Instructional or developmental programs can be designed and evaluated in a systematic manner only after we have carefully investigated the issues relevant to these questions. A later section on performance criteria in this chapter examines the issues necessary for developing a description of what has been or is to be learned. Such a description underlies both the design of training and educational programs and the evaluation of performance.

Learning Sequence

After describing what is to be learned, we may start to develop a sequence for learning. While such a relationship between the *what* and *how* of learning may seem obvious, learning sequences are often developed with only a superficial consideration of what is to be learned. Any individual experienced in training and instructional programs recognizes that some sequences of material are more effective for learning than others. This chapter identifies those issues and questions which relate instructional sequences to learning effectiveness. The issues associated with learning sequences are related not only to what is to be learned, but are concerned also with the processes involved in progressing from a state of "not knowing" to a state of "knowing."

Learning Strategies

Designing strategies for learning follows the development of learning sequences. The issues involved in designing strategies concern optimizing the environmental conditions so that effective learning can take place. Here, focus is on what the learner must do in order to learn. Again, the experienced trainer and teacher recognize the superior effectiveness of some learning activities. But what characterizes these activities to make them effective? More importantly, for our purposes here, what issues and questions direct attention to the characteristics of effective learning strategies?

Instructional Modes and Media

This section on instructional modes and media discusses the operationalization of particular learning strategies. As an applied learning concern it is only indirectly related to the more basic and theoretical questions of learning. Although the relationship is remote, the selection of instructional modes and media depends on the more basic questions of what is learned and how it takes place. The optimal design of learning situations and materials is firmly intertwined with what the learner must do in order to learn. Too often tradition rather than a careful study of this fundamental relationship between teaching and learning dictates the selection of instructional modes and media.

Motivation

Motivation, attitudes, and other questions of affect have a clearly recognizable impact on learning. Although these constructs make explanations of learning processes at a basic level difficult, their impact on learning in applied situations cannot be ignored. This chapter focuses on those issues and questions of motivation relevant to learning effectiveness.

Individual Differences

The final topic for consideration in this chapter is individual differences. Again, while a good deal of research has been directed at the issues involved with individual differences, very little systematic work has been done relating individual differences to the processes of learning to provide a better understanding of how individuals learn. Questions of individual differences need to be related to effective learning situations.

Summary

Building an effective program of training, instruction, or skill development generates many difficult problems. Use of today's knowledge about the learning processes for training and instructional situations raises more questions than can be answered. The present state of learning theory development provides only intriguing variations to the questions of how and why such programs are or might be effective. Because people must and do construct educational and training programs, many complex questions must be addressed if effectiveness is a concern. If knowledge and theory of human learning are to be meaningfully applied to assess learning effectiveness in practical situations, a frame of reference is necessary to help raise the right kinds of questions and to direct attention toward the critical issues.

This frame of reference, then, organizes most of the complex dimensions of various learning situations as well as focuses on the question of how and why effectiveness is achieved. The topics of the frame of reference, used as the major headings for the remaining discussion of the chapter, are summarized below.

1. *Performance criteria:* What does an individual "know" when we say he "knows"? What occurs in his performance on which we make the judgment that he knows? What distinguishes his performance from that of the individual who does not know?

2. *Learning sequence:* What sequence or sequences of material to be learned optimizes learning effectiveness? What structure or structures of the knowledge is observed, and what relationships exist with sequences for learning?

3. *Learning strategies:* What must be learned and what must the learner do to learn?

4. *Instructional modes and media:* What characterizes the selection of appropriate instructional techniques and technologies so that they relate optimally to learning strategies?

5. *Motivation:* What considerations of affective variables optimize learning?

6. *Individual differences:* In what ways are individual differences in learning relevant to effective learning situations? What kind of different learning situations are needed to optimize effective learning among different individuals?

The rest of the chapter will relate knowledge about the processes of learning to these topics and issues.

PERFORMANCE CRITERIA— COMPETENCE AND ASSESSMENT

For some time educators have stressed the importance of specifying the objectives of training programs. Furthermore, these objectives are to be stated in terms of the learner's directly observable responses to clearly identifiable stimuli. Testimony and other evidence suggest that instructional programs using these procedures have significant benefits. Several writers have described methods for developing behavioral objectives in training and instructional programs. Among these, Mager (1962) and Briggs (1970) present perhaps the most straightforward procedures for writing objectives, and Gagné (1970) provides a thorough discussion relating behavioral objectives, task analysis and hierarchies of learning. Briggs and especially Gagné clearly recognize the difficulties in establishing objectives for the more complex levels of behavior. Gagné (1970, p. 237f.) discusses a task taxonomy which distinguishes seven levels of learning from simple stimulus-response connections through higher-order rule learning and problem solving including the combining of novel combinations. This higher-order behavior at a complex level is most relevant to this chapter's purpose.

Volumes edited by Popham (1971) and Block (1971) contain these three writers' and others' behavioral objectives used to establish criteria for evaluating learner performance and program effectiveness. Again, difficulties occur at the more complex levels of behavior in establishing criteria and developing adequate tests and situations for observing achievement. Carroll and Bloom writing in Block (1971) analyze the difficulties and illustrate many of the errors and weaknesses involved in assessing attainment.

Listing such objectives may aid in the description of the structure of a particular body of knowledge and may even help establish the criteria for successful knowledge attainment. However, making lists of responses should not be confused with describing how particular knowledges and skills might be structured and how the individual who has gained mastery or competency manipulates or processes that structure. If listing objectives diverts attention from the questions of what the structure of knowledge is and what the individual does to process that structure, inappropriate or weak evaluation techniques may be utilized.

The two questions fundamental to the considerations of learning are what an individual "knows" when we say he "knows" and how we assess his attainment of that knowledge or skill at some appropriate level. Any further application of learning principles needs relatively confident answers to these questions. In order to design an educational program or to assess productive behavior one must be able to describe what that behavior is. To adequately describe complex levels of behavior, we must look beyond merely identifying the responses and their associated stimuli.

This distinction implies the importance of being able to say something about what happens in the "black box"; making a list of behavioral outcomes is different from describing how a competent individual manipulates a particular knowledge structure. Because the expert shows the ability to generate appropriate responses for a potentially infinite number of novel situations, a system of rules for manipulating this knowledge becomes not only more parsimonious than a lengthy list of responses but also becomes necessary for an adequate description of complex behavior.

Much of the work in language behavior and psycholinguistics makes this distinction necessary. For example, Morton (1971) suggests that processing "extracts the meaning and structure and ignore(s) the precise form of the stimulus." He gives the following interaction from Labov, Cohen, Robins, and Lewis (1968) to illustrate a kind of extraction that occurs in the processing:

Interviewer:	I asked Boot whether he knew how to play basketball.
Subject:	I asked Boot did he know how to play basketball.
Interviewer:	I said, "I asked Boot *whether* he knew how to play basketball," but you said, "I asked Boot *did* he know." Try again. I asked Boot whether he knew how to play basketball.
Subject:	I asked Boot... *whether* ...did he know how to play basketball.

Morton (1971) reports work of his own and others which give further "positive evidence that the unit of processing has an internal (i.e., linguistic-cognitive) rather than an external (stimulus-response) definition."

Jenkins (1968) uses different classes of sentences to show the necessity of the linguist's psychological distinction between deep structure and surface or derived sentence structure. For example, the "growling of lions" has a similar surface structure to the "raising of flowers," but they differ at a deeper structure level from which the phrases are generated, that is, "Lions growl" but "Flowers do not raise." Further, active and passive sentences, while differing in surface structure, apparently are generated from the same deep structure, for instance, "The boy hit the ball," and "The ball was hit by the boy." Ambiguous sentences are used to illustrate that the identical sentences can be derived from quite different deeper structures, for example, "The shooting of the hunters was dreadful," "Flying planes may be dangerous," and "They are cooking apples." Again, as stated by Morton (1971), the adequate description of both the operation and comprehension of such sentences require more than a surface-level description of the stimuli and responses. Thus, we must consider some sort of organization of knowledge at a deep structure level along with rules for processing and manipulating that knowledge to account for the complex behavior which distinguishes expertise and competence.

Similarly, much of the work of Gibson (1966) and others in ecological optics suggests we must consider the deep structure of perceptual events to explain perceptual learning. Shaw (in press) argues that an individual's ability to perceive an object or event as an identity or to perceive the equivalence among similar objects or events comes from logical invariants present at a level of deep structure. In spite of the transformations due to time, movement, orientations, and other changes, the invariances allow the individual to perceive similar or identical objects or events. Such an explanation of logical invariance helps to describe what highly competent individuals do that distinguishes them from the less able or novices.

What, then, is required to describe what an expert "knows" and to assess his achievement in ways which distinguish "knowing" from "not knowing"? The recent work in psycholinguistics, cognition, and perception argues for an analysis of a deep structure of the knowledge beyond the derived or surface structure and of the rules or "grammar" for manipulating and processing that structure. Thus, both the recognition or recall of data or lexemic items in a knowledge field and the ability to appropriately manipulate, transform, and assimilate new information distinguish the expert as he solves problems. It is this ability to manipulate, transform, and assimilate data relevant to a structure of a knowledge field which seems to characterize "expertness" in any field. The "expert" radiologist, hematologist, design engineer, business manager, administrator, teacher, or mechanic solves problems involving new and different data in ways appropriate to "thinking as an expert" in a special area of knowledge.

In a section on task analysis of their chapter on "Instructional Psychology" in the *Annual Review,* Glaser and Resnick (1972, p. 219) make an observation which seems to support the argument.

The studies we have chosen to define the field come from a variety of sources and only some of them have an explicit instructional orientation. What is especially striking, however, is their convergence on the analysis of performance in terms of the interaction between task structure variables and the learning and information processing capacities of the individual. Such an emphasis seems to us to be crucial for an instructional psychology which seeks to explicate the conditions under which educationally relevant learning takes place.

What Glaser and Resnick have referred to as "the interaction between task structure variables and the learning and information processing capacities" appears to be essentially similar to this chapter's discussion of knowledge structure and the rules for manipulating that structure. To address the complexities inherent in nearly all instructional situations, an adequate learning theory must thus consider both the structure of what is to be learned and the processing and manipulation of the structure.

Those distinct elements which have shared meaning among those knowledgeable in an area compose knowledge or task structures. In nearly all areas these elements have symbols which comprise the common "vocabulary." This "vocabulary" has many stimuli elements which have distinctive meanings to those who "know." For example, verbal, literary, and mathematical symbols identify auditory and visual elements.

However, merely knowing the identifying symbols does not make the expert. Knowing how these elements relate to each other and fit together (i.e., are structured) as a body of knowledge is also a necessary skill. Part of learning an area of knowledge or a skill consists of making the discriminations and generalizations necessary for "knowing." Distinguishing and symbolizing the perceptual features of the elements and relating the various elements mean not only knowing the vocabulary but also knowing the structure. Yet, knowing the vocabulary and structure of an area of knowledge does not explain what an expert knows.

An adequate description of what is learned must also account for how the structure is manipulated and how new data and information are processed for solving problems and performing appropriately in a particular field of knowledge. The work of Klahr and Wallace (1970), Newell and Simon (1971), and Burris, McIntyre, Shaw, and Mast (1971) suggests that there are rules learned for this processing and manipulation. If we think of different areas of knowledge or skill as different "languages," we can speak of the vocabulary and "grammar" (i.e., rules of manipulation and processing) of particular areas of expertise. This grammar which experts seem to share distinguishes them from the amateurs and novices of an area. An adequate description of what an individual "knows" before attaining "expertise" in a field includes not only the vocabulary and structure relevant to that knowledge area, but also, and more importantly, the rules or grammar by which he processes, manipulates, and transforms information and data within the structure. For example, the ability to solve new and different problems involving unusually combined or additional data differentiates the expert radiologist, design engineer, business manager, lawyer, or mechanic; the ability to recall or recognize vocabulary items does not distinguish expertness.

Summarizing a "grammar" which adequately explains how to generate all possible meaningful performances in a "language" is a very difficult task. Linguists and psycholinguists have not reached universal agreements in their descriptions or interpretations. However, attention to questions of the structure, organization, and internal processing necessary to generate appropriate and meaningful responses results in a more adequate treatment of complex levels of behavior. Recent educational and training efforts in course development and curriculum planning which emphasize cases or problems suggest the importance of considering the manipulation and processing of information, rather than the recognition or recall of data.

In solving problems or working with cases, the learner practices the rules or "grammar" appropriate to that field. We have known for a long, long time that people learn by "doing"; however, we have not been sure of what they have "done" or what they have learned.

Although this chapter does not argue for a radically new learning paradigm, we want to emphasize the importance of internal processing and manipulation for complex behavior. Such emphasis helps to describe the critical features of higher-order behavior found in most educational and training programs. To achieve adequate descriptions of these critical features, we must go beyond most behavioral taxonomies of hierarchy. The invariants, grammar, or rules for manipulating data and information vary from one area of knowledge to another; physicians "think" differently from lawyers who, in turn, "think" differently from business administrators. The scientist must have faith in the fundamental commonality of the "thinking" processes across all human activities. However, present science cannot yet make a generalization about what the expert learns. We must seek rules of manipulation or grammar within the context of particular areas of expertise. By observing what various experts do in particular situations and across different situations, as well as what differentiates them from nonexperts, we can build a description of the distinctive manipulations. As crude as this line of action appears, there is no available alternative for basing a description of what is to be learned.

Finally, the performance criteria for describing what an individual "knows" when we say he "knows" must account for vocabulary, structure, and rules of manipulation and processing. Such descriptions begin to specify not only the criteria for learning assessment, but also how to make that assessment. This is especially true in specifying the situation which requires the application of manipulation and processing rules necessary for "knowing." Thorough considerations of relating human learning processes to educational and training programs depend on describing such features.

Learning Sequence

After the applied scientist or practitioner has developed criteria to distinguish the performance of individuals who "know," "understand," or "have a skill" from those who do not, he must establish a learning sequence optimally effective for his human subjects. Common sense suggests proceeding from the "easy" to the "difficult" aspects of the knowledge or skill to be learned. Anyone who has attempted to teach something to another individual recognizes the superior effectiveness of some sequences. In most teaching or training situations, such judgments are usually made on the basis of intuition and tradition. Certainly, the use of learning theory aids experience very little in outlining the most effective learning sequences.

The issue of sequencing concerns identifying the progressions of steps through which the novice must proceed to attain competence. The instructor's choice of "routing" for the student must be both effective and efficient. What questions aid an instructor in making such choices? How can the learning literature help the teacher?

There is very little in the literature about sequencing per se. Briggs (1968) and Gagné (1970) both identify sequencing as a condition crucial to the development of an effective instructional program. Gagné (1970, p. 237f.) argues that the use of his learning hierarchy maps out an instructional sequence or "learning route." Learning subordinate skills must precede learning higher order skills to provide a hierarchy or "a basis for finding a suitable route for every student" (p. 241). By "working backwards" from the instructional objectives, we can determine necessary skills and their prerequisite learnings which generate the "map" and the alternative "routes" (p. 242). Working out such a sequence becomes necessary "to avoid the mistakes that arise from omitting essential steps in the acquisition of knowledge of a content area" (p. 243). Gagné then illustrates the use of his hierarchy for subjects such as mathematics, science, foreign language, and English.

Certainly, an experienced instructor can agree with Gagné's emphasis on working out instructional sequences before starting instruction. If his suggested hierarchy approach helps determine what distinguishes the expert from the novice, it becomes extremely useful for working out instructional sequences. However, there are many areas of expertise in which the structure of knowledge and the rules for processing and manipulating that knowledge are so complex or so little understood that using such a hierarchy may have little value. Clearly, when the structure of knowledge and the rules for manipulating that knowledge are not understood well enough to distinguish competence and mastery, an instructional sequence must rely on tradition and experience.

Learning theory must account for what is acquired and how it is acquired to be useful for sequencing instruction. This chapter suggests that the individual who "knows" learns both knowledge structure and the rules for processing and manipulating that structure. Because present theory cannot make adequate generalizations about structure and rules across different areas of knowledge and thus generate pedagogical sequences, we must rely on careful observations of the performances distinguishing the expert and novice, empirical testing, and revisions of sequences. Thus, common sense and experience become the major resources for the initial development of sequences.

Several questions and issues in addition to those Gagné (1970) presents, however, are useful and important when acquiring knowledge and various skills are considered analogous to learning a language. For example, knowing the "grammar" or rules for processing and manipulating is fundamental to learning any "language." Sufficient drill and practice must be started as early as possible and continued throughout the sequence. The amount of vocabulary should be limited although adequate for "meaningful" drill and practice. The learner needs practice in generating "utterances" or responses which require transformations or manipulations of the "vocabulary" or data in meaningful ways. Although we presently have no adequate theory of language learning, the experience of second language teaching offers some suggestions. The "grammar" or rules of manipulation must be carefully identified and sequenced. The size of the vocabulary is expanded most easily and rapidly after the learner has shown some ease in manipulating a limited vocabulary; the "utterances" or responses which the learner generates as a result of this manipulation must be meaningful to him. Although these suggestions seem reasonable and sensible, many instructional and training programs do not carefully identify such rules for processing and manipulating structures of knowledge within an area and fail to provide questions, problems, or other practice to help learn the rules. Clearly, these sequencing issues crucial to effective human learning should not be ignored in designing instructional programs.

Learning Strategies

Next, our frame of reference generates a set of questions concerned with what the learner does in order to learn. Issues under performance criteria and learning sequence logically generate problems about the types of information to be distributed and displayed, the kinds of tasks designed for and asked of the learner, and the environmental arrangements made to support learning. In the absence of a well-formulated and generally accepted learning theory to account for these considerations, we must form a notion about what and how the learner should practice to attain the knowledge structures and the processing rules of complex skills.

Glaser and Resnick (1972, pp. 207–208) point out that several writers distinguish between the problem of describing the processes and mechanisms of learning and that of prescribing the characteristics and procedures for optimizing learning. Pedagogical theory, as distinguished from learning theory, specifies the procedures for making instruction effective. The problem of relating performance criteria, or our best notions of what must be learned in order to "know," to learning strategies, or our best notions of what the learner does in order to learn, characterizes this third dimension of our frame of reference.

To specify the learning strategies and procedures truly optimal for acquiring a particular knowledge or skill, we need an adequate description of what is to be learned. As noted earlier in the discussion of performance criteria, our present learning theory cannot generate such descriptions of complex behavior. However, when the criteria established for "knowing" and "performing" closely approximate an adequate description of a knowledge area or skill, the task of specifying the strategies and procedures for learning is simpler. The strategies and procedures established for acquiring knowledge and skill in a particular area must provide the learner an opportunity to practice processing and manipulating the information, data, and structure in ways similar to what the experts do. A focus on the learning strategy dimension raises questions about optimal learning of both the structure as well as the rules for processing and manipulating that structure. Although consideration of the "manner of learning" certainly necessitates reference to the matter, or structure, information and data of learning, exercises or other events designed for the learner often stop there, and pay little, if any, attention to the rules for processing and manipulating those data. Recent revisions of medical school curricula show recognition of the importance of processing and manipulating information. For example, the structure, information, and data of anatomy, physiology, and biochemistry are no longer isolated from the clinical problems which require practice in processing and manipulating these structures. Similarly, many teachers and students in law schools and business schools are pressing for increased clinical experiences and case studies in the curricula. Although most arguments about curriculum design do not refer to theories of learning and pedagogy, the inclusion of more clinical experiences in new curricula designs parallels the cognitive and instructional psychologists' learning rules of processing and manipulation to "knowing" and "understanding."

Outstanding teachers and other training and development people have long been at least intuitively aware of many of the "truths" of effective learning strategies. More recently, the efforts in the development of programmed instruction and educational technology have resulted in specific procedures for optimal learning. Active participation in learning, self-pacing, immediate feedback on performance, and meaningfulness have become important variables.

Research and experience suggest overwhelmingly that learning is more effective when the learner is active rather than passive. The literature is unclear, however, in describing the characteristics of the learner's activities. Learning the vocabulary and structure of a field's knowledge without manipulating and processing new data and information in a problem-solving situation may be minimally effective. On the other hand, solving problems without attending to the relevant knowledge structure at a more abstract level seems inefficient also. As noted earlier, a problem basic to sequencing is arranging activities between learning the structure and learning rules for manipulating and processing data in relation to that structure. Defining the nature of those activities is a question for the learning strategy problem. One can "know" Ohm's Law without "knowing" how to solve a circuit design problem. Similarly, one can "know" how to solve circuit design problems at some level without "knowing" Ohm's Law. Analogous statements can be made about most areas of knowledge. The strategy issue addresses the question of how to distribute practice between learning structure and learning rules of manipulation and processing. The learning literature does not explain whether such a distribution should be 20-80 or 50-50 between the former and latter, especially when we are considering complex areas of knowledge and skill which take a long time to learn. Probably, the percentage varies from one area of knowledge to another, at different points of acquisition, and from one learner to another.

The nature of the learner's exercises must consider the subset of practiced manipulations and processing within its universe of all possible activities. For example, limited practice in manipulating and processing his native language teaches a child grammatical rules sufficient for generating and processing a language unique to him at one point in time. This is similar to the internist's diagnostic problem-solving situation in which the patient's data present a singular pattern never previously observed. What different manipulations from a universe of all possible manipulations will teach the learner rules for generating appropriate responses in new situations? Such a question considers not only traditional response differentiation and generalization but also the manipulation and processing of rules necessary for generating many responses. We do not know the rules for manipulating at a deep structure, although this is a basic question of describing how man thinks. But clearly something is learned which is essentially rulelike, and this something apparently is learned through practicing the manipulations and processing necessary to generate responses appropriate to "knowing." Thus, learning activities should include or at least infer the manipulations critical to "knowing," and present a variety of activities to somehow help "internalize" the rules underlying the manipulations.

The relationship of response error to learning is controversial. The negative motivational effect of many errors is obvious in both everyday experience and laboratory data. However, should we seek errorless performance in designing activities for the learner? Do we "learn from our mistakes"?

All theoretical orientations agree that the *possibility* of error should exist. However, it seems unreasonable to arbitrarily set some percentage of error to judge the effectiveness of activities designed to teach different knowledge areas and skills. If learning a rule at a deep structure level requires active manipulations, making errors may be as necessary as making correct responses.

The importance of immediate feedback to the learner becomes obvious. Although errors should not be practiced, many positive and negative instances of a rule may be necessary for its "internalization." Delay of feedback diminishes these effects on learning.

A recent renewal of attention to the problem of comprehension seems to bear intriguing relationships to learning strategy. Bransford and Johnson (1974) demonstrate the effectiveness of establishing context before training. They suggest the use of analogy as a technique for pre-establishing the learning context. Many writers have noted the similarity of processes between analogy (and metaphor) and what might be called a "creative thinking ability." The processing involved in analogy and metaphor may be similar to the manipulation abilities characteristic of "knowing."

In summary, learning theory provides no direct guide to the design of activities for the learner. The use of our frame of reference principles along with sensitive observation gathered through experience should help develop effective learning activities. Although there is no general agreement about its greater efficiency, any systematic approach for building effective learning strategies must consider the issues involved.

Instructional Modes and Media

This section relates the previously discussed issues critical to learning effectiveness to the selection of media through which the learner receives instruction. New and developing technology adds variety to the more traditional forms of lecture, discussion, and textbooks in constructing appropriate activities. As the placement of this section implies, form follows function. We must consider performance criteria and sequencing strategy before the selection of particular devices and techniques for designing learning activities. The effective use of television, slides, audio-tape, and textbooks depends less on the characteristics of the medium than on how the particular medium achieves the objectives of the strategy at a particular point in the sequence. The relative effectiveness of a medium must be gauged within the context of its purpose.

Gagné (1970, p. 345f.), McKeachie (1963, p. 1118f.), and MacKenzie (1970, p. 53f.) describe major features of the many modes and media for instruction and learning activities, and discuss those characteristics important in establishing the form of instruction. No attempt is made here to repeat or expand on their efforts. We present a brief discussion of the major characteristics of selected modes and media to illustrate the kinds of questions to ask in relating this aspect of design to the other aspects of the learning process.

There are many ways to display information, data, illustrations, simulations, and problems. If display-only is appropriate for one part of the instructional objectives, many different techniques, such as lectures, textbooks, slides, audio-tapes, television, movies, and field demonstrations may be used. Display-only components have limited appropriateness, however, if the learner's active manipulation and processing of information and data are concerns. Furthermore, such components provide restricted feedback as the learner progresses.

Other techniques and devices, such as discussions, tutorials, laboratory projects, programmed instruction, and computer-assisted instruction require activity on the part of the learner. However, this does not guarantee practice of those aspects critical to learning. The choice of design components must allow the learner training in those features of the learning task which are necessary for knowledge and skill acquisition.

Thus, "form must follow function" in the design of teaching-learning programs.

Consideration of each dimension of our frame of reference should generate issues, analyses, and finally a selection of information, media, and participative activities necessary for the learner to acquire the desired knowledge and skill. If an analysis of competent performance can provide an adequate vocabulary, list of "facts," or other description of a knowledge or skill's structural components, the problem of display becomes choosing the form or variety of forms necessary to assure the learner appropriate practice and use in learning activities. Lectures, texts, still pictures, movies, or other means of display may be used either alone or in combination. Since different media seem to be equally effective, the adequacy and meaningfulness of the described "vocabulary" become more important considerations.

The major difficulty in selecting instructional media and modes, however, is to relate these appropriately to the practice needed to learn complex and poorly understood rules for manipulating a knowledge structure. Passively watching a movie of an expert diagnostician is not sufficient to learn these complex rules—not all of which are understood. It is necessary to manipulate the structure against new and different data from many actual or simulated cases. Because the manipulation rules appear to be complex, the number of cases should be large enough to assure an adequate sample of the rule application and practice of it. Not all practice can be carried out in real environmental situations; other media, such as computers, texts, discussions, and lectures can be used in various combinations to provide enough practice for learning. The critical issues are what is practiced and whether what is practiced is sufficient to learn the rules; the medium or media used may or may not be appropriate to these issues.

Finally, we must consider costs in terms of educational and economic efficiency. To design optimal instructional and training programs, some value must be attached to each of the dimensions considered in this chapter. No simple algorithms are available to insure optimal decisions among various trade-offs in instructional design.

Motivation

No one doubts the importance of learner motivation in assessing the effectiveness of a teaching and learning program. However, present motivational theory cannot precisely predict how various affect variables interact with the learning process to vary learning effectiveness. Several factors have empirically demonstrated facilitative or inhibitory effects on learning; thus, an effective instructional program includes as many of the former factors as possible. This chapter presents representative questions from general areas of concern in constructing instructional programs, rather than trying to provide an extensive review of the motivation theory and research.

The first such area involves why and how the learner has become involved in a program. To what degree does the learner feel some need to participate, or is his participation from some externally imposed requirement? Will the activities during the course of instruction have some long-term value to the learner? Important considerations are not only the nature of the learner's need and desire, but also the maturity and realism of his expectations. For example, what is the similarity between the course objectives and the learner's expectations, and to what degree are the learning activities meaningful within those expectations? The learner must understand not only the purpose of the course and the learning activities, but also why certain responses may be correct or incorrect and how to assess his progress toward "knowing." Although grades and other forms of evaluative feedback have some apparent motivational effect, this varies among individuals. It is unclear if this variability stems from change in other factors critical to learning effectiveness or from individual differences.

Similarly, the effectiveness of different modes of instruction varies among different individuals. The data suggest that the observed differences are a function of individual "learning style" rather than motivation. The motivational effect may be essentially a "Hawthorne effect."

Individual Differences

Two major fields of psychological research are the measurement of individual differences and the experimental psychology of learning. Glaser and Resnick (1972, p. 242) state that many of the fundamental problems in instructional psychology "revolve around the issues inherent in adapting educational alternatives (learning conditions or learning activities) to individual differences...." Although several areas with intriguing relationships have been observed and identified, there has been little interpretation of the relationships between the two fields. Glaser and Resnick (1972, pp. 242–253) have reported most of the research suggesting such possible relationships. We point out the issues important for consideration in constructing educational and training programs.

Individuals vary in their stated preferences among different modes and media of instruction. Do these preferences reflect more fundamental differences in learning style? Are attitudinal differences indicative of capacity, skill, or some other fundamental difference? Do differences in learning rate have an interactive effect with learning strategies?

Clearly, the issue of individual differences is a consideration important to effective instruction. Although the means for interpreting this importance is not clear, we can suggest some reasonable practices. Activities which allow more individualized approaches seem sensible. More fundamentally, varying the design of activities to require a different kind of manipulation and processing may help to avoid mistakes from inadequate recognition and understanding of possible individual dimensions.

SUMMARY

Only the research of the past decade or so has recognized the complex difficulties inherent in understanding principles of the human learning process and applying them to instructional and training programs. Although this chapter offers no easy ways for dealing with such complexities, a frame of reference has been suggested as a useful approach for relating problems to the basic issues of learning. The frame of reference attempts to identify the critical issues of learning, competency, and pedagogy from the perspective of the practical problems of instruction, training, and personnel development. This chapter's objectives have been met if the questions relevant to theories of learning, perception, evaluation, and pedagogy seem overlapping and are meaningful to both the science and engineering of teaching and learning.

REFERENCES

Block, J. H. *Mastery learning: Theory and practice*. New York: Holt, Rinehart and Winston, 1971.

Bloom, B. S. Mastery learning. In J. H. Block (Ed.), *Mastery learning: Theory and practice*. New York: Holt, Rinehart and Winston, 1971.

Bransford, J. D., & Johnson, M. K. Contextual prerequisites for understanding: Some investigations of comprehension and recall. *Journal of Verbal Learning and Verbal Behavior*, 1974.

Briggs, L. J. *Sequencing of instruction in relation to hierarchies of competence*. Pittsburgh: American Institutes for Research, 1968.

Briggs, L. J. *Handbook of procedures for the design of instruction*. Pittsburgh: American Institutes for Research, 1970.

Broadbent, D. E. Cognitive psychology: Introduction. *British Medical Bulletin*, 1971, 27, 191–194.

Burris, R. W., McIntyre, M., Shaw, R. E., & Mast, T. *Coordinating resources for a systematic approach to instructional research and development: An illustration in art*

history. A symposium presented at the annual meeting of the American Psychological Association, Washington, D.C., 1971.

Gagné, R. M. *The conditions of learning*. (2nd ed.) New York: Holt, Rinehart and Winston, 1970.

Gibson, J. J. *The senses considered as perceptual systems*. New York: Houghton Mifflin, 1966.

Glaser, R., & Resnick, L. G. Instructional psychology. *Annual Review of Psychology*, 1972, 23, 181–276.

Jenkins, J. J. The nature of psychological theory. *Psychological Scene*, 1968, 2, 55–60.

Klahr, D., & Wallace, J. G. An information processing analysis of some Piagetian experimental tasks. *Cognitive Psychology*, 1970, 1, 358–387.

Labov, W., Cohen, P., Robins, C., & Lewis, J. A study of the nonstandard English of Negro and Puerto Rican speakers in New York (Cooperative Research Project No. 3288), Vol. 1, *Phonological and grammatical analysis*. Office of Education, U.S. Department of Health, Education and Welfare. Washington, D.C.: Government Printing Office, 1968.

McKeachie, W. J. Research on teaching at the college and university level. In N. W. Gage (Ed.), *Handbook of research on teaching*. Chicago: Rand McNally, 1963.

MacKenzie, H., Eraut, M., & Jones, H. *Teaching and learning: An introduction to new methods and resources in higher education*. Paris: United Nations Educational, Scientific, and Cultural Organization, 1970.

Mager, R. F. *Preparing objectives for programmed instruction*. San Francisco: Fearon Publishers, 1962.

Melton, A. W., Ed. *Categories of human learning*. New York: Academic Press, 1964.

Morton, J. Psycholinguistics. *British Medical Bulletin*, 1971, 27, 195–199.

Newell, A., & Simon, H. A. *Human problem solving*. Englewood Cliffs, N.J.: Prentice-Hall, 1971.

Popham, J. W. *Criterion-referenced measurement*. Englewood Cliffs, N.J.: Educational Technology, 1971.

Shaw, R. E., McIntyre, M., & Mace, W. The role of symmetry in event perception. In H. Pick et al. (Eds.), *Essays in honor of James J. Gibson*. Ithaca, N.Y.: Cornell University Press, in press.

Methodological Foundations of Industrial and Organizational Psychology

JOHN P. CAMPBELL
The University of Minnesota

THE BIGGEST PROBLEM encountered in assembling this section was preventing the creation of a handbook of behavioral science methodology. Since industrial and organizational psychology is such a broad domain and brings almost all of psychology to bear on the understanding of organizational behavior, a consideration of its methodology is necessarily broad also. However, the goal here is not to summarize and comment upon every facet of psychological research methodology. There obviously isn't space; and even if there were, it would duplicate too much of what is already published. Rather, the intent of this section is to present in some coherent fashion a reasonably brief explanation of the state of the art in the major "core" areas. These core topics resulted from our qualitative hierarchical factor analysis of the reliable variance exhibited by research in I/O psychology. Further, the individual "items" in each chapter are meant to represent the primary definers of that core factor. Factors accounting for very small proportions of the common variance in industrial and organizational psychology were omitted altogether.

In our view there are two second order factors that organize this section and they might be labeled research *models* and research *methods*. The former includes the chapters on psychometric theory, multivariate procedures, and experimental design. The latter includes the chapters on field research and laboratory experimentation. Within each of these second order factors there are first order factors corresponding roughly to the differential versus experimental tradition in psychology. Within the "models" category the psychometric theory and multivariate procedures chapters are intended to include the highest loading items from the differential side and the experimental design chapter lives up to its namesake. The dichotomy among the methods chapters (i.e., field research and laboratory strategies) should become apparent when you read them. They represent the differential versus experimental points of view quite nicely.

Argyris's Chapter 5 on *Problems and New Directions for Industrial Psychology* defied integration into this kind of factor space, but it stands as a sobering reminder that an exclusive concern with methodological models and rigorous techniques can blind us to larger issues and concerns. Unlike the little boy who acquired a hammer and suddenly discovered that everything in the world needed pounding, industrial and organizational psychology should not get so engrossed in research methodology that it loses sight of the questions it is trying to answer. Perhaps it is fitting that Argyris's statement should lead off this section and that he should take us to task for any number of assumptions, values, and research questions by which we appear to operate. Research and practice in industrial and organizational psychology has a number of soft spots and one gets the impression that for Professor Argyris none of them are sacred. However, I/O psychology is a secular area of research and practice, and rather than protest in outrage or nod agreement we might better ask how Argyris's probes can help us see our own approach more clearly.

Because of our belief that certain basic notions of reliability and validity theory are virtual prerequisites for discussing the topics in the remaining chapters, the next offering is J. Campbell's Chapter 6 on *Psychometric Theory*. Only a few basic topics are covered but the intent is to place them in a clear historical and logical perspective that emphasizes the similarity of the underlying models rather than the discreteness of alternative reliability and validity conceptualizations. If this chapter does not present a more unified Gestalt of both historical and recent developments in psychometric theory then it has failed to achieve one of its major goals.

The Weiss chapter (8) on *Multivariate Procedures* follows logically on the discussion of psychometric theory and tries to organize in a coherent fashion the multitude of available techniques in terms of their primary objectives, underlying models, and advantages and limitations for meeting those objectives. The discussion is firmly within the domain of the differential approach to psychology with regard to principal problem areas. One concerns the methodology for examining the underlying structure that best explains the pattern of relationships among a set of variables (e.g., factor analysis). The other pertains to alternative methods of using multiple pieces of information to predict a dependent variable (e.g., discriminant function). One overriding aim of the chapter is to pull together a lot of discrete information and present a systematic plan for the intelligent use of these methods and models. It is our hope that a careful

reading of this chapter will prevent the overuse as well as the inappropriate use of things like principal factors factor analysis.

The Cook and D. Campbell chapter (7) on *Experimental Design* is not a chapter on statistical inference. It is a chapter on *substantive* inference, and as such, performs what we think is a much more important service for the readership. It is also devoted to the "art of the possible" vis-à-vis conducting experimental research in organizational settings and is a significant extension of the classic Campbell and Stanley (1963) monograph on quasi-experimental design. After an extended treatment of the factors that support statements of causality within an experimental paradigm, they discuss in detail a variety of quasi-experimental designs that should be of considerable use to I/O psychology research. The authors also wittingly reveal their excellent scholarship by reaching back for many lovely examples from our own past. Although it was not an explicit goal of the chapter, the reader should come away with a somewhat better sense of his or her own history. Finally, the authors refuse to give up the belief that experimental research in organizations is (a) eminently possible, (b) capable of preserving significant "rigor," and (c) both politically feasible and personally rewarding. They support this belief with very strong arguments.

Bouchard's Chapter 9 on *Field Research* represents the shift from a discussion of analytic models to a consideration of substantive research techniques. The intent of this chapter was to survey the available literature in depth and to organize both the frequently and infrequently used methods in some kind of meaningful catalogue. The chapter takes a divergent approach to the topic but questions of feasibility are not ignored. Industrial and organizational psychology is sometimes accused of being in a methodological rut (e.g., tests and questionnaires) and Bouchard's chapter is an attempt to encourage us to think of other alternatives. Since he springs from the differential tradition in psychology it is not surprising that Bouchard takes a differential approach to field research. His emphasis is on measurement and description.

In Chapter 10, Fromkin and Streufert consider very carefully the costs and benefits associated with studying organizational behavior via *Laboratory Experimentation*. They are painstaking and thorough, but they also take the role of advocates and argue vociferously that laboratory experimentation need not produce a psychology of college sophomores (my apologies to college sophomores, most of us were there once) based on dependent variables of trivial interest. In a word, they come out fighting and the overall effect should be to raise the level of the laboratory versus field argument to a much more sophisticated level. At the same time they deal straightforwardly with the limitations of laboratory research. Topics such as demand characteristics, experimenter effects, and the available means for dealing with them are summarized in quite useful fashion.

In sum, the intent of these chapters is to cover the principal methodological domains closest to the hearts and minds of those of us who wish to study individual behavior in organizations. However, no one should forget that methodology is methodology is methodology, and not psychology. Good psychology entails good methodology, but good methodology does not necessarily entail good psychology. If this section raises significantly the level of discourse surrounding research methods in industrial and organizational psychology then it has achieved its major aim. If it raises our consciousness level as psychologists, so much the better.

REFERENCES

Campbell, D. T., & Stanley, J. C. Experimental and quasi-experimental designs for research on teaching. In N. L. Gage (Ed.), *Handbook of research on teaching*. Chicago: Rand McNally, 1963.

CHAPTER 5

Problems and New Directions for Industrial Psychology[1]

CHRIS ARGYRIS
Harvard University

SEVERAL SHORTCOMINGS limit traditional industrial psychology, including: (1) a focus on description of and prediction from individual differences, with no attempt to understand the *processes* of human behavior in organizations; (2) a mechanistic selection-placement process, using a limited range of once-valid criteria, and aimed at maintaining a steady state despite a dynamic environment; (3) a focus on selection and placement without regard for education and development at either organizational or individual levels; (4) research methods characterized by dominance over subjects, resulting in the alienation of subjects, and a hindrance of information flow.

The author recommends: (1) pursuit of theoretical understanding of behavior, derived from interventions within organizations; (2) a search for optimal levels of behavioral variability within organizations, permitting control without inhibiting the creativity of organization members; (3) member participation in research to obtain maximum subject cooperation and information flow; and (4) combining selection and placement with feedback of results and education to permit maximum development of the potential of organization members.

In the past several years important reviews have been written about the state of research and knowledge in industrial psychology (Dunnette, 1962; Gilmer, 1960; Hinrichs, 1970; Owens & Jewell, 1969; Porter, 1966). These reviews have emphasized the importance of the development of more rigorous research methods, models to cope with complex situations, dynamic criteria, the eventual integration of industrial

[1] The writer wishes to express his appreciation to Professors Clayton Alderfer, Robert Cooper, Douglas Hall, Edward Lawler, Benjamin Schneider, and Gerrit Wolfe for their helpful comments.

and organizational psychology, etc. Their suggestions make sense.

This chapter looks at other steps that may be taken to deepen the scientific validity of industrial psychology and enlarge the generalizability of its findings to the world of action.

The chapter is divided into two sections. In the first section some of the foundations of industrial psychology (such as selection, placement, job analysis and design, wage-system design, safety, and training) are explored. These foundations have produced much that is useful. However, they may have produced some unintended forces which constrain industrial psychology from enlarging its scope of scientific interests and applicability.

In the second section some possible courses of action are explored that may help industrial psychology enlarge its scientific domain, deepen its usefulness to the practitioner and hasten the day when it can integrate itself conceptually and empirically with sister areas of psychology.

INDIVIDUAL DIFFERENCES: A FOUNDATION OF INDUSTRIAL PSYCHOLOGY

Nearly all industrial psychology textbooks leave little doubt that the study of individual differences is a major foundation of the field. They all begin with the fact that people differ greatly, that these differences are important, and that they "... provide the basis of psychology, the science of human behavior" (Dunnette, 1966, p. 1). Indeed, if anyone were to question this foundation "... it would seriously weaken the net effectiveness of psychological research in industry, and it should be strenuously avoided" (Dunnette & Kirchner, 1965, p. 7).

How did individual differences become so important?

There are several reasons that are generally accepted. First is the pressure placed on psychologists (especially during the two world wars and the post-World War II industrial boom) to select, place, and train soldiers and personnel for the new plants, a pressure that continues today. The second reason follows from the technology needed to select, place, and train individuals. Effective personnel selection and placement requires that differences be measurable. Measurement is a "... fundamental assumption when we set out to make sense of the chaos of variation present in the world around us" (Dunnette, 1966, p. 14). Measurement permits the psychologist to be precise.

How does the industrial psychologist use measurement? First he measures attributes characterizing people and uses them as predictor variables. Examples are IQ, social class, cognitive or motor abilities, attitudes, etc. Obviously, the attributes he chooses must show some degree of reliable variance in order that they be capable of being correlated with the criterion variables. Thus his task is to relate statistically the variance in the predictor variable(s) to that in the criterion variable(s).

What are criterion variables? Again this is a difficult question to answer. Schneider[2] (1969) suggests that industrial psychologists went from situation to situation always asking what was adaptive behavior; that is, what was effective in that situation. In each situation, the operational definition for effective behavior was the criterion variable.

Several important consequences flow from this strategy.

1. The primary focus of industrial psychologists becomes the documentation of the nature and variance of individual differences (Anastasi, 1965, pp. 1–2).

2. The major methodological strategy becomes measurement. "Unless it can be measured it does not hold the attention of the industrial psychologist," a senior scholar recently told the writer. Guion (1965, p. 5) suggests that this set remains predominant in the thinking processes of industrial psy-

---

[2] Personal communication.

chologists. They tend to ignore phenomena that are not quantifiable.

3. The primary index of success becomes prediction. If one can accurately predict the criterion, the industrial psychologist has fulfilled his scientific and professional obligations.

The Consequence Upon Industrial Psychology as a Scientific Discipline

Are these three foci adequate to develop a scholarly field? Anastasi (1965, pp. 1–2) responds that they are not enough. In addition to measuring the nature and extent of individual differences and predicting criterion variables one needs to focus on (1) discovering causal relationships, (2) modifying individual differences, and (3) discovering relationships between variables.[3] Measurement, prediction, control, and understanding are equally important.

Prediction is possible without understanding. It is possible to predict accurately that there will be a traffic jam in New York City about 5 P.M. or that aspirin relieves headaches, etc. But accurate predictions tell us little about causes or how the variables can be altered.

When prediction is separated from explanation it is assumed that facts, such as individual differences, can exist "independent of theory" (Ghiselli & Brown, 1955, p. 5). The separation of facts from theory, supported by many industrial psychologists (Guion, 1965; Tiffin, 1946), is rejected by most philosophers of science (Braithwaite, 1956; Hanson, 1958; Kaplan, 1964) as well as by many psychologists. These people maintain that facts get their meaning from theory, that to separate facts from theory implies a theory, and that to separate facts from theory is to separate explanation from description.

[3] Recently, Dunnette has raised similar questions. See Marvin D. Dunnette, "Research needs of the future in industrial and organizational psychology," *Personnel Psychology*, 1972, 25, 31–40.

Unfortunately, causal explanations and the processes by which these phenomena may be altered tend to be the central focus of scientists outside of industrial psychology. Industrial psychologists have not focused heavily on conducting research that explains their phenomena or shows how they can be altered because of the kind of pressures that have been applied; namely, fulfilling practical demands for effective selection, placement, and training. If they show that individual differences exist, if they measure their variance, and if they correlate the variance in the predictors with the variance in the criterion variables, then their objective is accomplished. These pressures are both real and heavy. It may be that individuals preoccupied with applications in specific situations may become so focused on the concreteness and complexity of these situations that it is difficult to generate interest in generalizing (Hinrichs, 1970).

Industrial psychologists have the right to define their field any way they wish. However, with that right may come an obligation to make explicit the unintended consequences of defining the field in the manner that they choose. Two unintended consequences are (1) it places the field primarily in what Lewin (1935) called the Aristotelian mode of thought; and (2) the field becomes focused upon stability, upon steady state processes, and upon the status quo. First a word about Aristotelian logic and industrial psychology.

ARISTOTELIAN LOGIC AND INDUSTRIAL PSYCHOLOGY

In the Aristotelian mode of thought, explanation resides "in" the properties of the phenomena under study and not in the relationships among the phenomena (which would be Galilean mode of thought).

If the variables under study are attributes "in" people, or "in" situations, and if relationships are not sought, the natural consequence is to explain by finding the "cause" in the individual or the situation. Thus individual *A* is successful because he has certain attributes and because these attributes correlate with something in the situation. This is Aristotelian logic.

The folly of focusing on describing individual differences and then correlating those differences with some other phenomena that manifest variance is exemplified by looking at other fields and pondering where they would be if they had pursued such an avenue of investigation. If physicists, as they sought to understand the laws of falling bodies, had concentrated only upon describing differences in sizes and weights of falling objects and correlating such variables with whether the objects fall directly to the ground, roll down a hill, or fall down a ravine, the laws of physics relevant to falling bodies probably would have been quite different. If the biologist had used the industrial psychologist's paradigm he might have asked about the effectiveness of leaf sizes in, for example, creating shade (a very important practical question in farming). He might then have correlated the different sizes of leaves with the different amounts of shade (criterion variables). As a result, he might have been able to select with a respectable degree of precision, which leaves would give the greatest amount of shade. But, historically, biological scientists did not make these types of questions central to their discipline. The size of a leaf was much less important than understanding the processes by which leaves grew, turned green, turned yellow, etc. This type of knowledge is more explanatory. But initially, the knowledge was much more difficult to derive and the field was much less "practical." Eventually, however, answers about shade effectiveness were provided. Moreover, it led to knowledge about how to grow the leaves larger, how to hasten the trees getting leaves, and how to delay the loss of leaves. Thus the explanatory route can provide the basis for a wide range of applications regarding shade.

The Emphasis Upon Steady State and Status Quo

In Aristotelian thought there is little emphasis upon understanding causal relationships by explaining the interaction or transaction processes between the individual and his environment. Thus as Forehand and Gilmer (1964), Pugh (1966), and Vale and Vale (1969) have pointed out, industrial psychology has not focused adequately on the interactions that exist in the environment. Instead, industrial psychologists emphasize the steady state.

Organizational Processes as a Black Box

What is the primary environment within which the individual interacts or within which the individuals are embedded? The organization. Where is the environment—the organization—in the model used by industrial psychologists who select, place, and train individuals for organizations? The answer is, I believe, in a black box between the predictor variables and the criterion variables. Why? Because given the emphasis on prediction, the paradigm used in selection and placement must assume that the organizational environment is relatively static and benign and, therefore, need not be known. The paradigm assumes (1) that minimal or unimportant changes occur in the black box or (2) if important changes do occur they are random and cancel out each other (although importance and randomness may be contradictory), (3) that whatever changes occur they are benign to the interests of the industrial psychologists' activities, or more ironically (because the assumption is anti-individual differences) the contents of the black box have equal impact on all individuals.

The latter assumption was questioned early by Fleishman's study of supervisory training (1953) and later by Meyer, Kay, and French (1965) in their study of management performance evaluation activities.

Forehand and Gilmer (1964) have also written a systematic exploration of the importance of studying "organizational climate" which includes variables that have been relegated to a black box status.

As an example of the dangers in ignoring organizational processes there are the recent social psychological experimental studies which have suggested that organizational structure can influence leadership selection in hitherto unnoticed ways. Lowen, Hrapchak, and Kavanagh (1969) suggested that the leadership studies based on the concepts of Initiation of Structure and Consideration may have suffered by not taking into account the nature of the organizational structure, the nature of the task requirements, and the expertise of the superior or subordinate. First, they noted that Initiation of Structure and Consideration may not be orthogonal, as was once assumed. A high use of Initiation of Structure can influence a subordinate's view of the superior's sense of consideration. This high use of Initiation of Structure, in turn, could be caused by the demands the organizational structure imposes on the participants. Moreover, Initiation of Structure did not show the predicted relationship with productivity. To explain these results the authors hypothesized that the very nature of organizational structure and the way information was handled in the system had to be understood. "It is perfectly reasonable that the productivity of a subordinate (an index of organizational effectiveness) will sometimes vary directly with the extent of imposed intelligent structuring of his activities by experts" (Lowen et al., 1969, p. 248). If their findings are replicated and their theorizing found valid then the correlations reported between Initiation of Structure and indices of effectiveness "...must be understood as statements generalizable only to organizations in similar settings (Schneider & Bartlett, 1968). The data will not replicate in settings where the level of subordinate-anticipated structuring is markedly different, or where the new task

and environment allow a greater or lesser contribution of imposed instructions to subordinate proficiency" (Lowin et al., 1969, p. 249).

Implicit Use of Traditional Management Theory

When one uses the paradigm described above, the major contact with organizational factors comes primarily when industrial psychologists attempt to relate their predictor variables to criterion variables such as production, quality of output, absenteeism, volume of sales, and turnover. The implicit assumption is that these factors are valid indices of effective organization. This assumption is based on principles of "scientific management" such as chain of command, unity of direction, and span of control and the concept of effectiveness embedded in these principles. However, they have been shown to be less principles and more rules of thumb (Argyris, 1957; March & Simon, 1958).

Industrial psychologists, then, actually do depend upon a theory. Unfortunately, the theory has been subject to little systematic test, indeed much less than the behavioral organizational theory that many industrial psychologists view with skepticism. Until recently, industrial psychologists have chosen to use this traditional management theory in spite of the increasing theoretical and empirical research regarding its dysfunctionality. The early works of Argyris (1957, 1964), McGregor (1960), and Likert (1967) were seen as too theoretical, overly anecdotal, or empirically primitive (Dunnette, 1962). Likert's (1967) empirical work was more acceptable although the theorizing was equally doubted.

Consequences of Using an Implicit Organizational Theory

Organizational research increasingly supports the notion that the effectiveness of the whole organization cannot be understood by limiting the criterion variables to those that management would tend to see as relevant since most of those focus primarily on the formal aspects of the organization. Criterion variables tend to be those which management sees as signs of effectiveness. Few studies focus on criteria that go beyond management's perceptions and fewer still focus on how the organization can become more effective by going beyond the present conception of effectiveness.

Where we need to improve

Yet such information is important, especially in light of recent research which suggests that organizations may have built-in forces that cause slow deterioration (organizational entropy) and make it difficult to produce valid information about important issues (Argyris, 1964; Likert, 1967). Gardner (1968) has predicted that our organizations will end slowly from the dry rot that permeates their makeup. Elsewhere, the writer has listed examples of organizational turmoil in organizations that have been considered to have exemplary personnel programs, for example, telephone and oil companies (Argyris, 1970).

Recently, Andrews (1967) contrasted an aggressive, expanding, efficient company with a sluggish one. He found that the first company was more likely to advance executives high in achievement and not to reward those high on power. The second company rewarded those who were high on power and low on achievement. Each company rewarded those leaders who were useful in its *present* makeup. The industrial psychologist may see this as an example of a fit between organizational demands and individual traits. The organizational theorist would agree, but also ask questions, about the long range dysfunctional consequences of such an equilibrium state.

In another study, it was concluded that a bank favored what its officers called a "right type" for promotion. Three of the more important qualities of the "right type" were passivity, non-confrontation of, or withdrawal from, conflict, and a lack of

awareness of their impact upon the organization. The organizational theorist noted that a large number of such officers had dysfunctional consequences on internal problem solving, the growth of the bank, and the development of officers to meet the challenges of the next decades (Argyris, 1958). The result of the study created some argument and conflict within the top group. In a few years, because of normal retirement, officers who wanted to make changes came into power. One change they instituted was a new selection program that would identify men who were "non-right-typers." The first few "non-right-typers" had great difficulty; some even resigned in frustration (Argyris, 1958). However, as the number enlarged *and* as the bank changed its rewards to support the new behavior, the newer men began to be integrated into the organization. Thus organizational change and selection were integrated, resulting in a program that was, overall, better than either approach if used alone.

A recent study of the same bank by Alderfer (1971) suggests the need for even further organizational change and development. For example, there has developed a schism between the "right-typers" and the "non-right-typers." This schism is not being dealt with effectively. The "non-right-typers" have found themselves in the middle with "right-typers" at the highest and lowest levels. These findings emphasize the incompleteness of any organizational change that is not designed to monitor and correct itself. Unless an organization is able to develop competence in generating valid information, free choice, and internal commitment to decision, it may be unable to correct its own dysfunctional consequences (Argyris, 1970).

Some industrial psychologists would deny that many organizational environments produce conformity via the effects of individuals desiring promotion. Ambitious young men observe the behavior of executives and they learn much from observing. They emulate the successful executives and make that behavior their own. They conform to the organization's present standards and thereby perpetuate the status quo. It is these persons that the organization, its management, and its industrial psychologists reward with promotions.

The writer has interviewed executives and has twenty-five tape recordings of executive meetings in a particular organization (Argyris, 1965). The executives, during the interviews, emphasized that they promoted men who did not conform, who were open, and who took risks. Yet, the inferences made from the behavioral observations were quite different. The forces toward conformity were some of the strongest measured in any organization. Strong norms were found against open confrontation of important but threatening substantive or business issues and against risk taking. Another relevant finding was that the individuals showed less conformity outside the business settings and that they were able to behave in many more ways than they exhibited during the meetings. Moreover, they tended to be unaware of how much they actually conformed. These comments are not included as proof of anything. They are included to legitimize the suggestion that industrial psychologists working on the identification and selection of executives have to focus more on specifics of on-the-job-behavior.

To summarize, given the industrial psychologist's basic assumptions and his lack of interest in organizational processes, there may develop an unintended but powerful thrust toward the development of a point of view that supports the steady state. This, in turn, leads to the reinforcement of the status quo in organizations. I would question the position of Ryan and Smith (1954, pp. 5–6) that industrial psychologists have been captured by management because they are paid by management. Pay has little to do with the issue. Organizational theorists (McGregor, Likert, Bennis, Schein, etc.) probably have received as high or higher rates of pay from management than many industrial psychologists, and yet, they have been un-

willing to accept the problems as defined by management.

There is another way in which industrial psychologists ignore the environment. They ignore the environment of the testing situation. Industrial psychologists have conducted little empirical research on the interpersonal relationships, group dynamics (in the case of large groups taking tests), and the organizational norms that may develop during the testing activities.[4] Indeed, when the industrial psychologist does talk about the tester-testee relationship he may become as much, and perhaps more, imprecise and anecdotal than the organizational behaviorists, whom he has ignored because of the imprecision and anecdotal nature of their data.

To select from one of the more recent books, Blum and Naylor (1968) devote less than a page to the interpersonal dynamics of the testing situation. It is instructive to read carefully their message to the tester. They begin by stating, "Chances are that the inexperienced examiner underestimates his interference to the same extent that the subject overestimates it; the happy medium is somewhere in between. The experienced examiner takes pains to develop rapport. He is frank and interested and explains the purpose of the tests within the limits of the directions. He attempts to encourage relaxation or at least reduce the applicant's tension" (Blum & Naylor, 1968, p. 97).

Blum and Naylor (1968, p. 97) indicate that fear of tests (on the part of the person being tested) may be caused by the feeling that the test is unfair, that it may keep him from getting the job, that he may feel he is unable to estimate if he is doing well or poorly, and that the test may be experienced as an imposition. Their answer to these critical feelings is, "For all these reasons the atti-

---

[4] Recently, because of race issues, the impact of white and black testers has been studied. However, even in these studies the interpersonal dynamics have been only minimally explored (Sattler, 1970). For a recent study that focuses on interpersonal factors, see Alderfer and McCord, 1970.

tudes of the person taking the test must be taken into consideration." There is nothing else that they say.

Several pages later Blum and Naylor (1968, pp. 99–100) quote the major parts of the American Psychological Association's ethical code for psychological tests. None of the eight items mentioned deal with the interpersonal relationships created between the psychologist and the subject.

The reader might infer that the testing situation has little impact in the area in which a code of ethics might apply. Yet, later on Blum and Naylor cite impressive evidence of how an interviewer or interviewee can distort reality in an interview situation, such as a selection interview. Why is it that industrial psychologists have conducted impressive research on the unreliability of the selection interview, yet have not manifested the same intensity of research interest in the interpersonal relationships of the situations their technology creates? One reason may be that interpersonal relationships are difficult to measure. But this difficulty should also be true for the interpersonal relationships in the selection interviews. Another possibility is that the industrial psychologists have genuinely mistrusted the interview situation because of the potential for bias. Perhaps this has caused some industrial psychologists to unwittingly assume that one way to reduce bias in the testing situation is to de-emphasize the dynamics of that situation and emphasize the objectivity and rigorousness of the test. But how can they do this with so little intellectual discomfort? One hypothesis suggested by Storrs (1963) is that people design their interpersonal life around the fear of being overwhelmed or the fear of being rejected. Those who have the former fear as the primary one, tend to develop vocational interests where it is possible to deal with people at a distance (psychological testing, job analysis, etc.). Such individuals would prefer to collect data quickly from subjects and get their deepest kicks out of poring over the statistical analysis. Those

whose primary concern is the fear of being rejected would spend more time on research techniques that emphasize interpersonal relationships (interviews, T-groups, etc.). The experimental and industrial psychologists would tend to be in the former category; the field researchers and clinicians would tend to be in the latter category.

JOB ANALYSIS, JOB SATISFACTION, AND JOB ENLARGEMENT STUDIED WITHIN CONSTRAINTS OF TRADITIONAL MANAGEMENT THEORY

Conceptualizing their field in a way that relegates the internal organizational processes to a black box status and that accepts the traditional managerial assumptions (since they are the basis for the criterion variables) may lead industrial psychologists to conduct research without ever questioning its basis in traditional management theory.

For example, the industrial psychologist's focus on motion and time study, job analysis, and certain aspects of human engineering is very much in the tradition of scientific management and Taylorism. Job analysis is an accurate study of various components of a job. It concerns itself with fitting individuals to the jobs and with "testing" the fit through performance and reported employee satisfaction. The former is usually defined in terms of some organizational output, preferably objective, such as the number of pieces produced, the quality of the product, etc. The latter is usually measured by asking the individual to report his satisfaction.

One difficulty with using employee satisfaction as a test for the degree of fit between the individual and the job is that employees can be satisfied for many different reasons. They can be satisfied if the job is monotonous or complex and varied, because the work is involving or noninvolving. Information is, therefore, needed to help us understand what makes the individual satisfied. For example, Korman (1971) has shown that it is possible for individuals performing repetitive work to have high job satisfaction because their self-acceptance is low while others have low job satisfaction with the same job because their self-acceptance tends to be high.

On the other hand, Hulin and Blood (1968) suggest and Blood (1969) presents evidence that the individuals' degree of commitment to the Protestant Ethic may influence their job satisfaction, and that the Protestant Ethic is high in the rural areas and low in the urban areas. If the Protestant Ethic has the impact that the authors suggest, how would they account for the attitude and performance changes *among city workers* reported in the literature when their work has been enlarged? For example, Banks notes that 33 percent of the employees reported higher fulfillment after they were assigned to jobs of greater interest, variety, or responsibility (Banks, 1960, pp. 24–25). Mann and Williams (1962) took two populations of employees for whom matched data existed before and after the introduction of new equipment. They reported that the employees with the more enlarged jobs reported greater fulfillment with the increased amount of responsibility, more variety, and change as well as greater tension and more job risk. These experiences, therefore, could lead some employees to feel satisfied with their jobs and others to become frustrated, tense, and dissatisfied, and still others to go through a change from dissatisfaction to satisfaction (Mann & Williams, 1962; Banks, 1960). The first condition could lead to increasing job involvement which, in turn, could feed back to strengthen satisfaction. The second condition could lead to decreasing job involvement, which, in turn, could feed back to strengthen the frustration, tension, and, thus, dissatisfaction. The third condition would lead to ambivalence or sequential dissatisfaction to satisfaction.

The point is that in both studies cited above many workers "changed" their values. There appears to be little room for such changes in the views of many industrial psychologists, including Hulin and Blood. People seem to adhere to the Protestant Ethic or they do not. The word "changed" above was placed in quotes because there is the possibility that no change occurred in the workers' value system. It is possible for workers to value the Protestant Ethic but not adhere to it in a particular situation. Workers may become more oriented toward the Protestant Ethic once work becomes meaningful. If one reads the early studies of workers on assembly lines (Argyris, 1957), or the more recent work by Goldthorpe, Lockwood, Bechhofer, and Platt (1968), it should be clear that many workers value challenging work and being involved *if* the work is worth becoming involved with. When it is not, they do not value that particular work nor do they become involved in it, even though they may prefer a work world where this were possible. This is not to imply that all workers will seek enlarged jobs. It is to imply that we have offered such opportunities only to a very small fraction of workers who do prefer more meaningful work (as long as they aren't being forced to risk unfavorable economic conditions by accepting such work).

Another possibility apparently overlooked by the critics of job enlargement is the possibility that if it failed it may be a function of alienation from management. If the employees believe that the job enlargement is a trick or a gimmick created by management, they will mistrust the entire process. In some recent research Meyer and his associates have shown that job enlargement can lead to increased sense of "stewardship" and productivity (Sorcher, 1969). However, Sorcher also cautions that job enlargement programs cannot be based on a few mechanically applied gimmicks. They need to be based on genuine trust; otherwise, the programs will fail (Sorcher, 1969, pp. 9–10).

Finally, job enlargement may not be immediately and positively related to satisfaction. Indeed, Argyris (1964) predicted an initial decrease in satisfaction for apathetic, instrumentally and deficiency oriented employees, if they were offered enlarged jobs. Some would resist job enlargement for years (Argyris, 1960). Job enlargement was hypothesized to be related positively to increasing experience of psychological success or increasing the employee's control over his work or the use of more abilities. Job satisfaction may or may *not* follow. Thus, for Hulin and Blood to attempt to relate enriched or enlarged jobs to questionnaire items of job satisfaction may be a misreading of the complexity of the theory related to job enlargement.[5]

Returning to the concepts appropriate for understanding employee satisfaction, it may be that the more appropriate ones are those suggested by the works of Lodahl (1964) on job-involvement, Koch (1956) and McReynolds (1971) on intrinsic and extrinsic orientation, and the concept of psychological involvement by Argyris (1960).

For those scholars who prefer the concept of the Protestant Ethic, they could contribute more to the field if they would (1) be more explicit as to why they selected the Protestant Ethic as a concept, (2) define

conceptually the meaning of the concept, and (3) relate it to other concepts because the acceptance of a concept is partially a function of is relationship to a set of interrelated concepts, which, in turn, are evaluated by their ability to explain comprehensively, commensurate with greatest simplicity.

Valid Instruments Reinforcing the Status Quo

If a field tends to be atheoretical, if it tends not to be primarily concerned about causal explanations and the development of knowledge about altering its variables, the very processes of developing valid instruments can also come to support the status quo and lead to the use of hidden or implicit theory.

To explore this consequence, let us focus on some aspects of the Ohio State Leadership studies because they had an important impact on the field and because much research has been generated about them. (For some reviews see Blum & Naylor, 1968, pp. 421–424; Korman, 1966.) In order to develop their leadership questionnaire, an original pool of 1,800 items was selected and studied empirically. Several factor analyses were made. The responses to the 150 items indicated two distinct groupings of supervisory behavior. They were labeled "Consideration" and "Initiation of Structure."

This inventory, like any other similar instrument, tells us where the individual "is" on these two dimensions. He could be high on one and low on the other, low on both, or high on both. So far, we have an accurate description of the status quo.

But what would happen if a supervisor wished to alter his behavior? Could he utilize the questionnaire to help him change? Recently, it has been suggested that, in order for the information to be helpful for change, it must, in addition to being valid, be given in terms of *directly observable* behavior. The more concrete and operational is the feedback, the more helpful it can be (Argyris, 1968). These suggestions

---

[5] One way to judge the defensiveness of an article is to note if the writers utilize logic and argument that they condemn others for using. Hulin and Blood's article is full of such examples. They condemn the use of anecdotal evidence to make points, yet they state, with no evidence, that the experience of an assembly line worker is significantly different from the experimental settings where vigilance decrements were reliably obtained. They decry the use of generalizations that ignore individual differences, yet they make generalizations about the influence the grandfathers and fathers have upon the present employees which ignore individual differences and which are not supported with empirical evidence. They hypothesize that workers may feel hesitant to admit that they are *not* dissatisfied with their work to interviewers when the overwhelming evidence is that workers freely make such statements (Argyris, 1960; Blauner, 1960; Goldthorpe et al., 1968). They make inferences that interviewers can bias the results when the evidence for such biases come from selection interviews or marketing and public opinion studies. Even these studies recently suggest that verbal reinforcement does alter the responses *and* the responses turn out to be more accurate (Cannell, 1969).

should not be new to industrial psychologists. DuBois (1960, p. 232) has pointed out that, "the greatest achievements of psychological measurement have been reached where the behavior of interest has been actually worked into the testing situation." This is what is meant by directly observable behavior. The writer is aware of the situational leaderless group tests by Bass (1959) and the in-basket technique (Frederiksen, 1966). These do go in the direction that is being suggested and that may be one reason why they show (especially the in-basket) a relatively high degree of predictive validity (Bray & Grant, 1966). Both are situational exercises which attempt to simulate conditions of actual on-the-job behavior.

Returning to the supervisor, to be told he is high or low on Consideration and/or Initiation of Structure is to give feedback that is typically not based on observable behavior. Even the Leadership Behavior Description Questionnaire (LBDQ) which is filled in by subordinates or others who have observed the supervisor is made up of statements that are inferences from behavior.

Let us assume the supervisor is able to obtain a copy of the Leadership Behavior Description Questionnaire and he examines the items with the highest loadings on Consideration. The items are:

1. He expresses appreciation when one of us does a good job.

2. He is easy to understand.

3. He stresses the importance of high morale among those under him.

4. He makes those under him feel at ease when talking with him.

5. He is friendly and can be easily approached (Blum & Naylor, 1968, p. 422).

These items are not directly observable behavior. They are inferences. Thus, the category, Consideration, is not composed of directly observable behavior. There is no feedback about how to change behavior from such categories. For example, no cues are given regarding the actual behavior involved in "expresses appreciation," "is easy to understand," "makes those under him

feel at ease." The variance of behavior that could be perceived to accomplish these may be very great. In one study, "friendly and easily approachable foremen" (upon observation) turned out to be foremen "who left the men alone and rarely pressured them" (Argyris, 1960). In another study "friendly foremen" were men who took the initiative to discuss "difficult issues" with the men (Argyris, 1965).[6]

Lowin et al. (1969, pp. 246–247) have raised similar questions. In an attempt to prepare scripts related to Consideration and Initiation of Structure they found it difficult to understand precisely the behavioral content of these categories, especially Initiation of Structure. They wondered about the applicability of the concepts in the evaluation and education of supervisors.

Recently, Dunnette and Campbell (1969) have conducted some thorough research in order to develop a new career index for a particular organization. After a systematic series of research studies, nine dimensions were chosen to describe the relative effectiveness of managers. The items are primarily of the inferred category variety. There are no items that the writer could find that described behavior in directly observable categories. For example:

"Maintains harmonious relationship with sales associates";

"Avoids and counteracts harmful turnover among sales associates";

"Exercises tact and consideration in working with sales associates."

The question arises, how (in actual behavior) does an individual "maintain harmonious relationships"? Dunnette and Campbell are aware of these questions. They have attempted to make the instru-

---

[6] Another problem with leadership inventories (and many other instruments that depend upon variance for their validity) is that the dimensions used are those that differentiate among respondents and not those that are common to all the respondents. Perhaps these results should be included because many insights may reside in the qualities or attributes in which there is little variance.

ment more operational by developing scales that have actual critical incidents defining the levels of effectiveness. For example, one such scale is reproduced in Table I. The questions raised above, however, still seem to remain unanswered. How does a manager behave so that he impresses a customer to buy more than she would ordinarily buy? How does he "smooth things over beautifully"? How is he "friendly and tactful"?

Does he smooth things over by withdrawal or compromise? These can be significantly different behaviors. Thus, it would be difficult to use the Dunnette and Campbell instrument directly for purposes of behavioral change and individual development. Moreover, could not one raise questions about the effectiveness of compromise or withdrawal? Blake and Mouton (1969) would answer affirmitively. Moreover, they would contend that the strategies for being a successful salesman (as identified by Dunnette and Campbell) may lead to long run difficulties. For example, maintaining harmonious relations could be done at the expense of quality of the openness; being tactful and diplomatic could lead to a lowering of the salespeople's levels of aspiration.

The time may be appropriate for industrial psychologists to explore these issues. As they integrate individual diagnosis with development and as they provide maps of possible new designs for organizational and customer relationships their work may become even more relevant and applicable.

The industrial psychologists may respond that they do not typically design such instruments for education; they design them for selection. But this is the issue that is being raised. Why is this the case? Must it continue to be the case? Isn't there some value to designing instruments that integrate selection and education, which would lead to change? Would not such instruments provide more valid knowledge about our understanding of human behavior, in addition to being of more practical value? Could not helping supervisors alter their leadership behavior also provide excellent field oppor-

tunities for predictive tests regarding Consideration and Initiation of Structure? In medicine, cancer will be understood when the analysis developed explains the processes that cause cancer, can be used to create cancer, and can lead directly to a cure for cancer. Medicine does have some tests that identify illness but give no insight into cures (e.g., the Pap test for cancer). But these are seen as incomplete and temporary tests to be outdated as quickly as possible. Medical researchers are, therefore, not content to relegate the processes of cancer to a black box status. They place their heaviest emphasis on conducting research that will explain the processes within the black box. The predictor and criterion variables are seen as phenotypic; the black box processes are seen as genotypic.

Why should not this be the case in the study of human behavior? Why cannot instruments be developed that diagnose leadership styles and provide the basis for change? The argument often made that the instruments would be too cumbersome and not acceptable to management can hardly square with experience. The managerial grid, for example, is a program that permits diagnostic and educational functions. The diagnosis is followed by exploration of behavior in a group setting where directly observable feedback is possible. It has generated wide acceptance on the part of administrators of many different kinds of organizations throughout the world (Blake & Mouton, 1969). This is not to suggest that the instrument is perfect, indeed much more empirical research is needed. The point being made is that diagnosis and change are complementary. However, in order to integrate the two applications, one needs to develop knowledge about conflict, the nature of organizations, and the management of conflict in systems. Blake and Mouton have presented a theoretical framework about these issues and some empirical research. Some may wish to fault them on either or both counts but that would not be relevant to the point that they have shown it is pos-

TABLE 1
A JOB PERFORMANCE SCALE FROM THE PENNEY CAREER INDEX
(Dunnette & Campbell, 1969)

HANDLING CUSTOMER COMPLAINTS AND MAKING ADJUSTMENTS

In his job as department manager, how well does this man handle customer adjustments? Consider not only his day-to-day or **typical** job behavior but also how he does when he's at his **best**.

Write BEST on the scale opposite the action that seems to fit him most closely when he's doing his best in handling customer adjustments.

Write TYPICAL on the scale opposite the action that seems to fit him most closely when he's doing his usual or typical job of handling customer adjustments.

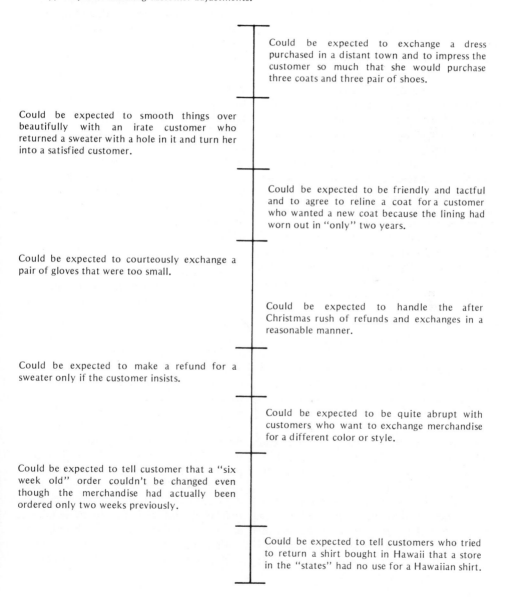

Could be expected to exchange a dress purchased in a distant town and to impress the customer so much that she would purchase three coats and three pair of shoes.

Could be expected to smooth things over beautifully with an irate customer who returned a sweater with a hole in it and turn her into a satisfied customer.

Could be expected to be friendly and tactful and to agree to reline a coat for a customer who wanted a new coat because the lining had worn out in "only" two years.

Could be expected to courteously exchange a pair of gloves that were too small.

Could be expected to handle the after Christmas rush of refunds and exchanges in a reasonable manner.

Could be expected to make a refund for a sweater only if the customer insists.

Could be expected to be quite abrupt with customers who want to exchange merchandise for a different color or style.

Could be expected to tell customer that a "six week old" order couldn't be changed even though the merchandise had actually been ordered only two weeks previously.

Could be expected to tell customers who tried to return a shirt bought in Hawaii that a store in the "states" had no use for a Hawaiian shirt.

sible to work on understanding these processes.

If more systematic knowledge can be developed from instruments that integrate selection and education, we may be able to shed light on why supervisors do not tend to be effective selectors. Based on data from assessment centers, supervisors tend to come off second best in their ability to predict who will be an effective supervisor (Bray & Grant, 1966; DeNelsky & McKee, 1969). Why is this so? One reason may be that the supervisor may not know about the actual behavior of his subordinates on-the-job. Such a situation may be the result of supervisors not creating a climate where the subordinate exposes his behavior. For example, subordinates may tend to suppress their leadership styles in a meeting. Consequently, during an assessment center, or any evaluation situation, when the supervisor does observe non-distorted behavior he has had little previous experience with such behavior and lacks a basis for making a prediction about its effectiveness.

If one decides to design questionnaires that individuals can use as a basis for their personal development, then another alteration of practice may become necessary. Given the criteria of analytic simplicity and comprehensiveness, it is routine to conduct factor analyses to reduce a larger set of factors to a smaller set which are relatively independent of each other. Thus, in the Ohio State Leadership studies nearly ten factors were reduced to two. However, if the questionnaire were to be used to facilitate individual learning it may be helpful for the learner to have all the factors that were collapsed into Consideration and Initiation of Structure. This may help him become more aware of the behavioral requirements of each factor.

To put the issue another way, redundancy and overlap may be qualities of "poor" research; but they may be helpful as a basis for education and learning, *and* they may gain higher status as we realize

that redundancy and overlap may be key processes in man's rational activities. This is not to ignore the scientific canon of parsimony. Parsimony means that, other things equal, the simplest explanation is the best. The question arises as to when one has an explanation and when one has a description. The writer would argue that psychologists who develop such instruments as the leadership questionnaire have been primarily interested in describing what the respondents say rather than why they say what they do or do what they do. An accurate description would include the original items and not the categories of higher level of abstraction. It is when one attempts to develop an explanation for the data that the law of parsimony applies.

A field that tends to ignore theory, but uses it implicitly, may unwittingly become tied to this implicit theory. Thus, those who utilize the leadership inventories may become tied to implicit theories that contribute little to validating, or correcting, or adding to existing explicit theory (Korman, 1966).

Rigorous Research Methods Compound the Focus on the Steady State

Our intention to this point has been to suggest that industrial psychology, as an academic discipline, was greatly influenced in its development by the applied problems of developing selection, placement, and training activities. This tended to lead to minimum interest in theory building and to explanations in terms of the Aristotelian mode of thought. The consequences of this were (1) to relegate the organizational processes (or the environment in which the individual was embedded) to the status of a black box, (2) to use implicit theories that were untested, (3) to undertake such actions as job analysis and job enlargement under unnecessarily extreme constraint, and (4) to develop valid instruments that tend not to be helpful in testing or developing new theory or in providing a basis for reeducation of individuals.

To these consequences we may now add another. It may be that the concepts of rigorous research accepted by industrial psychologists (and most other behavioral scientists) may actually compound the difficulties just described above. Recently, the writer has argued that rigorous research may not be achieved as fully as possible unless the concepts of what constitutes empirical methodology is altered (Argyris, 1968).

Rigorous research has two characteristics. One is related to the output, the other to the process. The output is usually viewed as empirically validated, publicly verifiable generalizations hopefully stated in quantitative terms. The process is usually conceived to be empirical research following the rules of the scientific method.

The process. The procedures of rigorous research and the methods of traditional scientific management are similar. For example, rigorous research and the pyramidal organization assume that rigor is obtained (1) by unambiguous operational definition and measurement of the relevant variables and (2) through control by the researcher (or manager) of the design of the research situation (production situation) in which data are collected (products produced). Control is obtained by the researcher (management) defining the subject's (worker's) role as rationally and clearly as possible (to minimize error) and as simply as possible (to assure understanding and performance). The researcher (manager) also provides as little information as possible beyond the tasks he wants the subject to perform (thereby creating a relationship of dependence and minimal time perspective). Finally, the researcher attempts to standardize the inducements for participation, the methods for scoring, and interpreting the data (Argyris, 1968).

The output. In testing, selection, and job analysis, the industrial psychologist strives to produce products that are (1) objective (minimal subjective influence in arriving at scores), (2) reliable and valid, (3) uniform in the method for interpretation of results, and (4) standardized. Moreover, there is an emphasis on techniques that reduce "error." Ryan and Smith (1954), Dunnette (1966), and Guion (1965) suggest that errors may be minimized by (1) obtaining adequate samples, (2) utilizing appropriate statistical techniques, (3) minimizing chance response tendencies, and (4) minimizing changes in environment and in persons taking the tests.

All these requirements characterize the essence of the management activity in pyramidal organizations. They strive to define jobs, to develop measures that are objective, reliably evaluated, standardized, etc. They strive to minimize system error through continual quality control which is based on adequate samples and appropriate statistical procedures. The industrial psychologist also strives to maintain control, to define the tasks clearly and to standardize them, to provide minimal opportunity for the subject to contaminate the results through conscious or unconscious distortion, and to score and evaluate the performance of the subject with little or no participation by the subject, etc. The subject, be he in a testing, placement, or job analysis situation, is being largely controlled by the professional. He is, therefore, in a dependent, subordinate situation to the professional and has a short time perspective.

To compound the problem the subject (employee) is usually told that he is being placed in such a situation for his own good. That is, if he is to be helped to find the best possible job for his talents, then he must accept these conditions. The same is true when he is being asked to complete a morale or satisfaction questionnaire. He is asked to fill out a questionnaire designed by the experts whose results could influence his work life, but whose makeup and rationale must be kept secret from him. Thus the subject is being asked to be open, manifest a spirit of inquiry, and take risks, when he is placed in a (testing or questionnaire) situation that has many of the repressive characteristics of formal organizations, which he has long ago learned to adapt to by not being open or taking risks (Argyris, 1968, pp. 190–192).

From previous research on organizational settings, it is possible to predict some of the probable consequences that the subjects will manifest. They can refuse to take the tests or keep putting them off. They can withdraw psychologically and thus give answers that may not be representative of their true feelings or views. They can express different types of covert hostility by knowingly, but carefully, giving false data. They can also resist overtly. These types of reactions are not new to industrial psychologists. Indeed, it is safe to state that our society has reached the point where the resistance is active and overt. The recent congressional hearings and the new constraints placed over the use of psychological tests may be an example.

RESULTANT STATUS OF INDUSTRIAL PSYCHOLOGY IN THE EYES OF PRACTITIONERS

The use of models which relegate most of the living system to a black box status; the emphasis of static analysis over process; the acceptance of management values, pyramidal organizational structure, and administrative controls as given; the use of research methods and measuring instruments that place subjects in temporary systems that can be as constrictive as the formal aspects of organizations; the separation of selection from development; the apparent disdain of industrial psychology for raising basic questions about, or seeking to redesign crucial aspects of the working world—all these factors have important consequences for industrial psychology as an academic, scientific, and professional enterprise. Here are some of those consequences:

1. There is an increased probability that

workers' perceptions of the industrial psychologist may tend to become similar to their perceptions of the earlier industrial engineers and time-study men. Employees may see industrial psychologists (the testers, the designers of performance appraisal programs, inventors of different wage schemes and incentive programs, the authors of job descriptions) as part of management's human control system (more diplomatically entitled personnel activities).

A second major perception of industrial psychologists may be that they are the measurers of employee morale in order to keep management informed of employee attitudes and concerns. The reaction to the morale surveys may vary with the quality of the relationship between employee and company and the union (when that exists). In some cases, the industrial psychologists may be seen as a genuine link to the top. In other cases, they are seen as the gestapo. In both examples, industrial psychologists are seen as playing a linkage role; yet, industrial psychologists are rarely seen as having a significant influence in their areas.

2. Unions may fear and tend to mistrust industrial psychologists. They may be seen as being in the pay of management to use research technology to make management policies and practice "scientifically" valid. They may especially mistrust the wage and salary schemes and the incentive programs. The latter are seen as insidious attempts to place employees in competition with each other thereby pitting worker against worker. Such competition could have negative effects upon the union because its members would begin to compete and mistrust each other.

Given that the industrial psychologist is perceived as supporting the status quo, one may hypothesize that the people who will tend to support their services are those who themselves are oriented toward the status quo (e.g., "old time" top executives, *less* innovative and progressive supervisors, and personnel administrators). One would expect to find, as does Thornton (1969), that personnel administrators see industrial psychology as being useful. It is still the field from which they draw much of their technology. Some supervisors may seek the technology that the industrial psychologists develop for selection, testing, wages, etc. because, if the workers feel unfairly treated, the supervisors can blame "personnel." In short, the role of "personnel" as the keeper of the status quo may suit the less innovative supervisors, because they can transfer their problems to the personnel specialists. The old time executives may like the industrial psychologists because they help to make their management more "concerned" about people; yet, they rarely want studies which ask questions about the way jobs are designed, the organization is structured, the use of administrative controls (such as budget and production bogeys), and the interpersonal relationships among top executives. Such studies may threaten persons at the top.

This may seem like a harsh judgment but I believe it is an accurate one. The writer is acquainted with several key top executives in three organizations in the United States that have supported the largest, most systematic, and thorough top management identification and selection studies. Although these projects have made, and will continue to make, contributions to the firms and important copy for textbooks, the boards of directors and the top executive committees have relatively vague knowledge about them. Where the top line executives are enthusiastic, it tends to occur where the evaluation programs are not used to assess their behavior.

There is another consequence that deserves special attention.

3. During the past two decades a revolution has been going on in schools of business. With the impetus of the Ford report (Gordon & Howell, 1959), the schools redesigned and upgraded themselves. The changes were well timed because the schools became the largest producers of future top line executives. No longer were law and engineering the major sources of top executives. For reasons which will be discussed below, the schools of business tended to shun the traditional industrial psychologists and vice versa. Instead, they focused increasingly in the areas of organizational behavior, industrial sociology and psychology, and the research aspects of the human relations emphasis. The result was that several new generations of executives were fed into the system, many of whom are now in key positions.

These young executives are not as doctrinaire as their older predecessors. They tend to see less sacredness in maintaining the present technology, organizational structure, administrative controls, and in their own behavior. Indeed, many believe that these variables may represent the new leverage points for instituting changes. Thus, when they look into their organizations for help in the "people area" they are neither attracted to selection, testing, job analysis, etc., nor to the methods of study and analysis that industrial psychologists tend to use. Those methods may be more rigorous but, in the eyes of these young top executives, they are neither relevant for, nor applicable to, the problems that interest them. Unfortunately, the result may be that industrial psychologists could become, unintentionally, to the field of human behavior, what the shiny-pants, green-shade bookkeeper is to finance.

THE INDUSTRIAL PSYCHOLOGIST REACTS

If these descriptions are accurate portrayals of trends, how are industrial psychologists reacting to them? There are two major reactions that the writer has been able to identify. One is to continue, with even more deliberate speed and conviction, the processes of developing more sophisticated methodologies. The other is to enlarge the interests to take on some of the activities traditionally developed outside of the field. Concerning the latter, those who have enlarged their interests and skills *and* integrated them with the previously learned ones bring to their job a unique combination of rigor and vigor that will probably make them extremely useful to their organizations. It is hoped that they will write conceptually about their achievements because by doing so, they can make important contributions to their field.

The larger number have reacted to the above by returning to their field to rework it and to develop more sophisticated empirical technology. Several years ago, the writer asked two of the highest ranking industrial psychologists in the Civil Service to identify a major innovation in industrial psychology produced by professional psychologists in the Civil Service. They immediately identified Primoff's J-coefficient approach to job analysis as an important breakthrough. Yet, that approach questions no basic tenets of job design. Indeed, one could argue that the time study engineers, when they establish standard times for new operations primarily on an a priori basis through the use of synthetic times for the various elements of the job in question, were doing what Primoff did for industrial psychology.

The point is that better empirical methods may actually compound some of the problems. If it is technically possible to track down multivariate relationships with bigger computers, moderator models with multiple discriminant analyses, etc., then the researcher may increase his investment in pursuing blind, atheoretical leads, which may reduce his openness to use theory to guide his activities. Another way to innovate with dynamic criteria and moderator variables is to develop a theory from which they may be derived. Likert (1967) is an example of a scholar who has succeeded in this way.

An excellent example of a more advanced selection model has been developed by Dunnette (1966, pp. 104–112). He asks industrial psychologists to look into the black box and begin to note the variance and dynamics of its variables. The model is too new to say with certainty what its impact will be. However, if Dunnette's own

work is illustrative, the most effective use has been to differentiate populations within the organization. Ironically, the biggest barrier to the Dunnette model may be its complexity. The number of combinations possible among individuals, job behaviors, and situations may be too large for developing meaningful generalizations or for applicable results. As shall be argued below, the next step may not be to make the analysis more complex and dynamic.

IMPORTANT RESEARCH QUESTIONS

The second objective of this chapter is to explore some possible courses of action that may be taken to reduce the unintended consequences. One major suggestion that flows from the previous analysis is that more emphasis should be placed on the construction of explicit theories that attempt to explain phenomena; more attention should be given to the interaction between the individual and the environment in which he exists; more research should be done on systematically changing or altering the variables to study their impact in other relevant variables; more concern should be held for studies about other states of individual-environmental interaction that do not exist in the present world; a greater integration should be made between systematic diagnosis (on the individual, group, or organizational levels) and the reeducation, development, or growth of these systems.

More specifically, there are five research questions that deserve increasing attention in the future. They are:

1. How do individuals and organizations optimally reduce individual differences in predictor, moderator, and criterion variables?

One fruitful next step for some part of industrial psychology to take may be to ask how are individual differences "optimally suppressed" so that individuals and the organizations gain? In asking this question, we do not want to be understood as asking how can individuals give themselves up for the sake of the organizations. Such an over-socialized view of man is as incomplete and inaccurate as an over-individualized view (Wrong, 1961). The emphasis will be on the integration of man with system.

Tyler (1959) has raised a similar question. She concluded that the traditional way of dealing with individual differences, "...shows signs of becoming completely unworkable because of the proliferation of dimensions" (p. 76). She had hoped that factor analytic methods might resolve the problems but she now doubts this possibility. Tyler then suggested that perhaps we need to accept the evidence indicating that no individual is able to actualize all his potential. The individual, through choice, selects the potential he wishes to express and organizes it into a meaningful pattern so that its expression becomes possible (Tyler, 1959, p. 77).

The work in psychological ecology by Barker and Wright (1955) makes it clear that there are almost unlimited possibilities to determine individuality. However, people have to choose or they become immobilized. Indeed, one of the criteria of mature development may be whether the individual makes valid choices and develops patterns that encourage competence in life. This process of the conscious and (unconscious) narrowing down of individual differences to a meaningful pattern is part of the process to which I refer when I speak of "optimal suppression" of individual differences.

The second part of "optimal suppression" of individual differences is based upon the assumptions of reciprocity (Gouldner, 1960) and constructive intent (Buhler, 1962, pp. 36–39). Individuals manifest a willingness to be just in reciprocal relationships and intend to be constructive even if they do not succeed in many instances. Thus individuals coming to an organization may be willing to give of (but not give up) themselves if they believe that the returns are equitable and just (Adams, 1963; Homans, 1961).

The employees may be aware of the dysfunctional aspects of formal organization. They may have learned to adapt by creating informal systems, unions, and attitudes toward work involvement that sanction psychological withdrawal (Argyris, 1968).

To be sure, these informal activities can have dysfunctional effects upon individuals. Psychological withdrawal may create internal forces within individuals to smother their own individual differences and to worry more about how much they are worth than who they are as human beings (Fromm, 1941). This could lead to functional smothering (Argyris, 1964). What we are seeking is that optimal relationship where the individual gives up aspects of self that would not harm him and that might, in fact, facilitate the growth of other aspects. The choice would be made out of responsibility for himself *and* the organization. Research is needed to specify the processes by which this could occur. One may hypothesize that if such choices are to be free and informed, individuals may need much more awareness of themselves, more knowledge of the needs of the organization, and more information about the benefits and costs.

Presently, individual differences are smothered in organizations but little attention is given to whether it is an optimal suppression of individual differences. In a series of observational studies of twenty-eight different types of groups, ranging in duration from two to fifteen months some strong similarities among groups were found. In a total of nearly 46,000 units of behavior, the "typical" interpersonal relationships formed a pattern called *A*. Pattern *A* could be described as individuals tending to express their ideas in ways that supported the norm of conformity. Individuals did not, nor did group norms, support their owning up to their feelings, being open to their own and others' feelings. There was almost no experimenting with ideas and feelings, and also no trust observed in the groups. Rarely did individuals help others to own up, to be open with, and experiment with ideas and feelings (Argyris, 1969, pp. 894–895).

The result of such a world was to tend to make people "diplomatic," "careful," "not make waves," to credit conformity. Again individual differences, at the upper levels, tended to be smothered. As was reported in many of these studies, the executives learned to suppress many of their feelings and abilities in order not to upset the systematic equilibrium. Their individual differences did not dissipate; they could report them in a psychological test. They simply did not use them in their everyday working life.

These findings underline the importance of studying individual differences in such a way that we come "...to grips meaningfully with the problem of the *interaction* of organisms and environments" (Vale & Vale, 1969, p. 1093). More knowledge is needed about what happens to individual differences under differing environmental settings.

To raise the question in another way, the more sophisticated selection model by Dunnette described previously assumes that if researchers had a more differentiated view of predictors, job behaviors, and situations, prediction of criterion variables would be more effective. Another possibility is to study how individuals create work worlds that reduce the variance of all these factors, including the criterion variables. How do individuals decide to conform to systematic demands? How do they get to the point where "don't rock the boat" becomes expected, and, indeed, is seen as competent behavior? How many organizations are designed so that the individual differences the individual gives up are those that are functional to his continued development and to the organization's effectiveness?

Another related issue is generated by the fact that the overwhelming number of executives report that they *do* express feelings; that they *do* behave in trusting manners, they *are* very open, etc., and they select executives who behave in similar ways. Yet, in every study reported above, almost none

of that behavior was observed. That the researchers could be perceiving reality inaccurately was unlikely because the researchers were able to make more accurate predictions based on their view of the world than were the executives based on their view (Argyris, 1969). Thus the organizational world may be populated with executives who tend to be genuinely unaware of their own impact, unaware about what the factors may be that affect their own personnel selection strategies, and unaware that their subordinates and peers act to maintain the blindness. What is the impact of these consequences on selection research?

Finally, perhaps the attitudinal or behavioral variance being reported by psychologists represents variance "within" individuals which they do not tend or expect to use.

Is it possible that when attitudinal or behavioral variance is found to be great, the variables being studied may not be, organizationally speaking, the potent ones and that is why the variance exists? Perhaps organizations limit the variance in the potent variables.

Research is also needed to understand the causes and the content of performance variance in actual settings. Some hypothesize that there are at least two organizational forces that inveigh against the exposure of as wide a variance as is possible. First are the wage systems which provide the highest rewards for moderate performance (Argyris, 1964; Lawler, 1971; McGregor, 1960), and second is the design of organizational control mechanisms by the principle of "management by exception." This is one of the most central principles of scientific management. It defines as an acceptable level of performance the maintenance of performance that is close to an externally set standard. The performing individuals are checked only when their performance goes significantly above or significantly below the standard. If it goes below, they may be warned or punished. If it goes above, they may be rewarded and their peers or that individual punished (by a re-timing or redesign of the job to make it "tighter"). The consequence may be for individuals to play it safe. Indeed, the "rate busters" may be ostracized (Whyte, 1969). What is the meaning of the performance variance reported on criterion variables under these conditions?

2. How may organizations be designed to reduce the dysfunctional suppression of individual differences in human capacities and performance?

Another task that industrial psychologists may find fruitful to consider is the redesign of organizations that encourages optimal use of individual potentialities. This is the position taken by Argyris (1964), Bennis (1966), and by Hackman and Lawler (1971).

The suggestion to encourage the optimal use of individual differences may seem contradictory to the previous discussion in which we argue that reduction of individual differences may be a necessary activity of life. I believe that the contradiction is. more accurately a dilemma and that the dilemma provides a basis for problem solving and individual development. One might say that human self-expression or actualization would have little impetus or only vague meaning without the dilemma.

How do we arrive at this conclusion? First consider the work of Barker and Wright (1955), Tyler (1959), and Simon (1969). The first two document the proposition that man's social environment is extremely rich and complex. Simon's research supports this proposition and adds another important one about the nature of human problem-solving capacity. He suggests that man's apparatus for problem solving is really quite simple compared to the richness of the environment. In order for man to use his simple capacities effectively he has to conceptualize and organize reality into more simple and more manageable units. As man does this he necessarily chooses aspects of his environment to organize. As he con-

tinues this process of simplification and organization, he stores up the successful attempts and throws out or represses the unsuccessful attempts. The strategies that he stores up become parts of himself. Indeed, they may be what we call individual identity and uniqueness. Man develops his identity by these sequential decision-making processes.

Implicit in this model is that the environment must be rich and complex (relative to man) *and* permit man to do the searching, choosing, and integrating. But, as we have seen, most formal organizations are designed and/or result in living systems that reduce the complexity and restrict greatly the processes of search and choice.

The organizations of the future, therefore, may require designs where complexity and richness can be increased. This will probably be encouraged by the computer science technology introducing much more complex information systems *and* the increasing interdependence among organizations in our society. As richness and complexity are returned to the internal makeup of organization, the processes of search, choice, and organization become paramount.

Research is needed to identify the conditions under which these processes are effective. One may hypothesize that the probability of effective search and free choice increases as individuals experience psychological success and feelings of essentiality. The opportunity for psychological success necessarily means less unilateral dependence, submissiveness, and more opportunity to express one's important abilities. The more these conditions exist, the higher the probability that individuals will experience increased sense of competence and confidence. These would, in turn, increase their need for new experiences of psychological success and essentiality.

On the organization side, one may hypothesize that as the above processes are set in motion the amount of energy for work and internal commitment to a decision would tend to increase. As internal commitment increases, the willingness to monitor one's own effectiveness in the decisions increases. This means that the individual is more open to being corrected and more motivated to work and perform.

If the above logic can be confirmed by empirical research, then organizations may find it useful to design for their employees experiences that provide the maximum possible opportunity for psychological success (individuals significantly influencing the definition of their goals, the paths to these goals, the degree of challenge, etc.) and feelings of essentiality. This does *not* mean that all employees will strive to reach the maximum possible. Some may find it too great a challenge. What we are suggesting is that the organization design itself in ways where the range of individual differences can be expressed.

I should like to take a moment to emphasize that the logic developed stems from a concept of man and his environment that is evolving from research in child development, personality, cognitive processes, clinical and social psychology. As such, it is not a middle-class concept as suggested by Strauss (1963). Argyris (1964) has cited several large studies while Herzberg (1966), and more recently Tannenbaum (1968), have presented evidence that lower level employees prefer more control over their working world which would lead to their being less dependent upon management and more able to utilize their abilities (e.g., those involved in self-control). If the design of organizations is based on conclusions about man that he exists in impoverished environments, the organizations will create impoverished men, impoverished organizations, and impoverished societies.

If research is to be conducted on these questions of redesign, the descriptively oriented researcher is faced with the following dilemma: Studies that require the testing of new designs that are contrary to existing norms will tend to be perceived as deviant ideas by the potential subjects. Such changes will rarely be permitted by subjects unless

they have some degree of assurance that the change will be for the "better." To make such assurances (even very modestly) requires a cognitive map, or theory, of the new world and why it may be more effective. Such a map would be a prescriptive one and the development of such normative maps has hitherto been looked upon with disfavor. One of the reasons for this negative attitude has been the fear that to study normative questions and to develop maps with prescriptive implications necessarily means that the researcher must take a normative position about what the organization should look like. This is not necessarily the case. There are several strategies that researchers may take to understand these normative states of affairs. They are:

The first strategy is to conduct research that increases knowledge about the alternatives open to the client and that provides him with an increasing opportunity for informed and free choice.

An example of such research may be the study of job enlargement under differently enlarged or enriched conditions. Such research may well provide insights into employee motivation, performance, and job satisfaction (Goodman, 1969; Hackman & Lawler, 1971; Scott, 1966). Moreover, such research may help industrial psychologists to preserve the importance and relevance of individual differences which tend to be suppressed in the highly specialized jobs designed by job simplification experts. As Cronbach and Gleser (1965, p. 143) have pointed out, the psychologist is competing with job simplification experts who are, in effect, treatment simplifiers. They are trying to make the job requirements so simple that selection would not be necessary. Their method is the more economical, for their changes may be more permanent while the tester must evaluate new employees forever.

Job enlargement may also provide a research setting where the alteration of individual differences may be studied. Tiffin has concluded that training "... tends to increase individual differences in proportion to the complexity of the task in question" (1946, p. 17). And later, "Whenever the effect of training has been to increase the magnitude of individual differences, a study of the task involved usually reveals it to be fairly complicated (i.e., it requires a fairly long learning period for the average individual to reach maximum level of performance)" (Tiffin, 1946, p. 17). In other words, if psychologists had a genuine scholarly interest in studying the alteration of individual differences, which could also lead to insights into their causal processes, the study of job enlargement would provide such an opportunity.

Such research may also have consequences for raising the ability levels in the total society. Apparently, the Russians have concentrated less on testing and differentiating students and more on developing the most efficient means of raising the total educational level of society. There is evidence that they are succeeding (Goslin, 1963, p. 37). Interestingly, Goslin suggests that such a program tends to generate high enthusiasm and motivation on the part of the students and faculty because it focuses on growth and development opportunities.

The second strategy is to conduct studies that identify inconsistencies between what the clients want for their system and what they are getting. The researcher does *not* decide what they should want; he helps them to see if they are accomplishing their goals. Part of the study may focus on discrepancies among individuals' goals or between individuals' and the systems' goals.

For example, the clients may say that they want employees who are committed to the organization, who take risks, and who are productive. The researcher may show them that the pyramidal structure, the administrative controls, and the style of leadership all tend to cause employee apathy, indifference, lower productivity, and to reduce risk taking.

The third strategy is for the researcher to examine the validity of the criteria the client system used for defining success. For example, it may be that low turnover and absenteeism could be signs of system illness as well as health. In some cases it may be that the organization has minimal turnover and absenteeism because the people are not required to be responsible for being productive. In other cases, high absenteeism may be necessary because it provides the involved and committed people a periodic respite from extreme pressure. Without absenteeism they might quit or become less involved.

A fourth strategy is to conduct research which helps people to explore more meaningfully what they want their norms and criteria to be. For example, research on the nature of human self-acceptance could suggest criteria for designing work which have hitherto been unexplored. Studies of the source of human energy and its variability could shed important light on employee productivity.

In none of these strategies is the researcher telling the client what he ought to desire, what criteria of system success he should use, or what values he should accept or reject. This is the domain of the client.

There is one way in which such research could become normative; it could focus on the study of the many informal activities that exist in organizations as well as the interpenetration of the formal and informal activities creating the "living system." These factors, we have suggested, have been part of the industrial psychologists' black box. Moreover, to study the "living system" of organization is difficult and would require the organizing and guiding power of theory (an activity shunned by industrial psychologists) and the temporary emphasis on naturalistic observation (a focus not valued by industrial psychologists).

There is another sense in which the systematic study of job enlargement (whether it is successful or not in the practical sense) may be instructive for industrial psychologists to consider. If one examines the Blum and Naylor (1968) book, and we have selected a book that is more supportive of expanding the interests of industrial psychologists, one will find that they discuss job enlargement for only half a page. Job analysis, on the other hand, is given an entire chapter. Sadly, detailed descriptions of job analysis, the activity that describes the world of work as it is, receives a much more thorough treatment than job enlargement, the activity that describes the world of work as it might become or, perhaps, should be.

However, there is one area in which the researcher may have to become more normative in his relationships with the client. This is the area of how the information will be obtained, how a valid diagnosis can be made, how the client can be helped to make informed choices, and how clients can monitor their own decisions once implemented. Thus the processes of diagnosis and intervention will require a normative position.

Formidable as these challenges may be, I should like to suggest that we have no— or should not seek any other—alternative. Such research is necessary if the original, academic goal of understanding human behavior is to be achieved. Studies of this type are needed, for example, to develop valid knowledge about the interaction of individuals (and their individual differences) in environments (that are also different).

The second reason why such research is necessary is that the universe of social sciences is an "ought"-oriented, normative universe. It is composed of what mankind considers how people ought and ought not to behave. This universe, unlike the universe of the physical sciences, is continually subject to change. The changes, until now, have been made by individuals and groups who are not utilizing social scientific knowledge. Therefore, the changes represent what the groups in a particular generation wish to alter.

Perhaps it is time that social scientists take more initiative to conduct descriptive research that sheds light on normative issues such as the design of more effective human relationships and the quality of life within complex systems. For example, it seems that experiential learning theory and technology could help to produce a pattern *B* world where openness, trust, and expression of feelings are high. Under these conditions dissonance reduction, attribution, and social evaluation could be so reduced that they would no longer play a central role in social psychological theory (Argyris, 1969).

To the extent that changes are created by non-social scientists, the social scientist relegates himself (and has been by society, gladly relegated) to a passive position of observing and documenting changes. In the course of human events, the social scientist becomes the keeper of the minutes, a scribe, a role which he would probably resist in most groups to which he belongs.

If one realizes that change is going on all the time, he should also realize that the issue becomes one of how much one wishes to influence such changes. I believe social scientists should wish to influence such changes, *not* by telling people what to do, but by providing relevant valid information and by creating conditions for open interchange, free choice, and the likelihood of internal commitment to the choices made (Argyris, 1971). They can help create a process of change that will help to increase the probability that the new behavioral requirements are as effective as was possible to design. They could also help to design monitoring systems to evaluate the changes made, and to continue designing changes.

Two other reasons why social scientists may wish to include themselves in the activity of redesigning the universe may be inferred from the research on interpersonal relations described previously (Argyris, 1969). People who live in a pattern *A* world do not tend to generate valid information about threatening issues. One example of a threatening issue is basic change in the system. Consequently, there is little monitoring of the system and much prohibition against change. The result is that those who are disaffected tend to withdraw or to become angry and aggressive. People who have psychologically withdrawn will rarely effect change. People who are angry and aggressive may effect change but in ways that reduce free choice and internal commitment to the people.

Moreover, under conditions of festering frustration, pent up hostility, and eventually open aggression, there is every reason to question whether or not the agents for change will seek or even recognize valid information. If they do not, the prognosis for any long-range effectiveness of the change cannot be an optimistic one. Indeed, the prognosis for even descriptive research is not encouraging if the subjects have difficulties in generating valid information.

3. How can research technology be designed that does not unintentionally require the acceptance of the status quo in the universe?

A third area for exploration is how to design research methods whose nature is less congruent with the mechanistic pyramidal relationships and more congruent with organic relationships.

This will not be an easy objective to achieve. There is need for more emphasis on combining clinical and measurement approaches (Alderfer, 1967; Kahn, Wolfe, Quinn, & Snoek, 1964; Porter, 1966) and longitudinal research and time series design (Argyris, 1965; Alderfer & Lodahl, 1971; Lawler & Hackman, 1969; Scheflen, Lawler, & Hackman, 1970). It may also be necessary to overcome the mistrust that people have begun to develop about empirical research (Argyris, 1968; Kelman, 1968). There may be some individuals who cannot be involved even if the research is designed correctly. For example, people with poor mental health may reject participating in research (Westley & Epstein, 1969).

Some dimensions that describe differences between mechanistic and organic research and may be worth empirical study are below (and on the following page):

In a mechanistically oriented research	*In an organically oriented research*
1. The interventionist takes the most prominent role in defining the goals of the program.	1. The subjects participate in defining goals, confirming and disconfirming, and modifying or adding to those goals defined by the professionals.
2. The interventionist assumes that his relationship of being strictly professional is not influenceable by the clients. He maintains his power of expertise and, therefore, a psychological distance from the clients.	2. The interventionist realizes that, in addition to being a professional, he is also a stranger in the institution. Subjects should be encouraged to confront and test relationships. His power over the subjects, due to his professional competence, is equalized by his encouragement to them to question him and the entire program.
3. The interventionist controls the amount of client participation in the project.	3. Both client and interventionist determine the amount of client participation.
4. Interventionist depends upon the client's need for help or need to cooperate to be the basis for their involvement. Expects clients to be used as information givers.	4. Interventionist depends upon the client's need for help to encourage internal involvement in the control and definition of the program. The client feels as responsible as the interventionist.
5. If participation is encouraged, it tends to be only skin-deep, designed to keep subjects "happy."	5. Participation is encouraged in terms of designing instruments, research methods, and change strategy.

6. The costs and rewards of the change program are defined primarily by the interventionist.

6. The costs and rewards of the change program are defined by the clients and the interventionist.

7. Feedback to subjects is designed to inform them how much the diagnostician learned about the system, as well as how professionally competent was the diagnosis.

7. Feedback to subjects is designed to unfreeze them, as well as to help them develop more effective interpersonal relations and group processes.

It should be noted that the organic dimensions involve providing the subjects a greater opportunity for free choice internal involvement with the research so that they will help the researchers produce valid information. Organic research does *not* alter the value of such activities as constructing theory, developing operational definition, stating hypotheses, using control groups, or making statistical analyses.

The second challenge is to strive to collect data by the use of instruments that integrate diagnosis and change, analysis and development (individual or organizational). If instruments are designed to create temporary systems or settings for the subject which produces information in terms of directly observable categories, attributions and evaluations can then be made by the researcher or the subject. Each is then required to show explicitly how he progressed from the directly observable behavior to the inferences that he made. One example is in the use of tape recordings. A group meeting can be studied, individual behavior observed, and inferences made by the researcher. When he gives the feedback of his results, he presents the inferred categories (e.g., how much openness, trust, and risk taking was observed) and connects these inferred categories to actual portions of the tapes. This permits the subjects to see unambiguously how the inferences were made by the professional. Dependency on the professional and the mystery-mastery relationship (Bakan, 1968) may be reduced. The subject is less likely to feel, as Blum and Naylor (1968, p. 97) have suggested, that the tests are unfair, that they are imposed, and that he is unable to estimate whether he is doing poorly or well. It may also help to reduce

some of the "seven deadly sins" (Gellerman, 1958) of selection, such as overdependence upon expert opinion, careless treatment of candidates, and poor estimates of job requirements.

Some readers may wonder why these problems cannot be overcome by the use of unobstrusive measures. Have not Webb, Campbell, Schwartz, and Sechrest (1966) shown that instruments can be designed that do not interfere with on-going life and, therefore, can generate accurate data?

Unfortunately, there are at least two difficulties with the accounts of unobstrusive measures published to date. First, they do not provide a direct basis for change. Thus, the observation of where the floor tiles were worn tells us much about the most popular paintings in a gallery, but they provide little insight into why this is so. A more damaging criticism is that unobtrusive measures raise serious ethical issues. Should people be aware that they are being studied? Should their consent be genuinely sought? If not, social scientists could create the same ethical problems created by those (especially in law enforcement agencies) who wish to "bug" rooms, telephones, etc. in order to obtain data. It is our hypothesis that subjects will be most highly involved in providing valid data about issues important to them *if* they are active participants in the research and have consented to the study.

A final point that needs to be made is related to the ethical issue involved in using the generalizations obtained from rigorous (mechanistically oriented) experimental research. Generalizations obtained from research ought to "work" (in the sense that they account for substantial portions of the nonrandom variance) only in life situations which are analogous to the experimental situations in which the original data were collected. In industry, the analogous situation to the mechanistically oriented experimental research is one that contains authoritarian relationships and provides for social isolation of the participants (Argyris, 1968). The ethical difficulties arise when individuals utilize generalizations obtained through mechanistically oriented research to change people's needs and to coerce them into making choices that reflect the researcher's choices.

An example is the recent work of Varela who utilizes generalizations and methods derived from mechanistically oriented experimental learning theories. If one analyzes his strategy, Varela treats his subjects exactly the way learning theorists treat their animal subjects (Zimbardo & Ebbesen, 1969). For example, Varela is continuously in control of the situation. He openly states that he is responsible for planning the "powerful manipulations" in order to make people buy (curtains) during a time period that they have never done so before, even though the country is in a depression and curtains are not urgently needed by the population. Varela keeps his tactics secret; if he succeeds he will do so whether the subject likes it or not—indeed the subject may even be manipulated into liking it. The subject has little opportunity for free choice to develop internal commitment to "his" decision. By using the theory of reactance (the view that a communication that is seen as attempting to influence will tend also to be seen as a threat to one's freedom to decide for one's self) and by continued reinforcement, Varela manipulates people into buying curtains in hitherto unheard-of quantites. For example, Varela manipulates the customer to expand "his latitude of acceptance" of buying. He then manipulates the customer into systematically altering his views of a rival company. Much of this is done in accordance with those experimental learning theories in which attitudes are changed by manipulating the individual to justify his behavior (because he put the salesman to the trouble of getting out the samples, an act Varela aimed at from the beginning).

Perhaps this is enough to make two points that are relevant to our analysis. Varela's paradigm may be neutral but his way of putting it into effect is theory X—indeed X^3. Varela gets into difficulty because he uses the experimental setting as his model for interpersonal relationships between the influencer and the influencee. He uses the model because this is the type of setting in which the generalizations were developed (Argyris, 1966, pp. 189–190). The experimental setting is, as we have noted, based upon theory X. It is ironic that Miller (1969, p. 1070) recently cited Varela's work as an excellent example of applied research.

4. How can systematic knowledge be produced that enhances the competence of the systems being studied?

Theoretically, a sophisticated selection system could reduce many management problems. If there were effective selection and proper job placement, presumably the organization difficulties might be reduced. But so may some of the challenges that face executives today. Moreover, individuals who believe that selection can be an ultimate solution could unintentionally lead to a psychological set that influences the individual to see fewer problems and less need for radical changes (Alderfer, 1972). Also, if the match between people and system is so perfect, there is a strong tendency for the system to resist, indeed to be unaware of the necessity for, change (Argyris, 1965; Culbert, 1969).

Another alternative that may be profitably explored is the extension of the applicability of knowledge. This will not be an easy task to accomplish.

The applicability of behavioral science knowledge has traditionally been based on identifying the relevant variables, studying them systematically, verifying them publicly, and incorporating them into increasingly comprehensive and logically consistent theories. Although all fields can improve on these activities, we have suggested that industrial psychology may have to focus especially on identifying the relevant variables and on producing theories that are empirically verified.

The applicability of behavioral science knowledge also depends on two other activities that to date may not have received the attention they deserve. The first is the development of rigorous research methods that take into account the nature of man (his needs, his defenses, the social mores, and cultural norms that he has internalized). As we have noted, such methods should probably fall toward the organic ends of the continua described above. The second factor is related to the usability of knowledge.

Usability of knowledge is partly a function of semantic clarity. Although this can be a difficult barrier because all groups (including practitioners) have their "jargonese," let us assume that the problem is solvable if the parties find it worthwhile to learn each other's language.

The more difficult and relatively unexplored aspect of usability is related to the form knowledge must be in if man is to be able to use it (even though he may understand it). The very nature of man may create constraints on the form and kind of knowledge that is usable. Man, as the applier, may need knowledge that is in somewhat different form than that which behavioral scientists tend to produce when they aspire to being rigorous.

Some behavioral scientists may argue that their responsibility is simply to generate valid knowledge. It is someone else's responsibility to put it in usable form. This position may make sense if the behavioral scientist takes on responsibility to train the "someone" else to do it and does it well. Unless knowledge does become more applicable, man may become so disenchanted with behavioral science that he may fight the development of further knowledge or he may become so disinterested that he may withdraw from its development. In either case, the behavioral scientist would be in difficulty because the motivations associated

with either stance would not, as a minimum, encourage people to give (consciously or unconsciously) valid data.

There is another argument, that presently may be less visible, but is worthy of consideration. If the researcher decides to separate himself from the problem of application, the resulting stance may create internal processes within the researcher that may tend to distort or constrain the kind of knowledge that he may think of producing, the kind of knowledge that he may obtain, and the kind of theories that he may create. For example, having separated the development of knowledge from its applicability, many behavioral scientists have stated that the objective of research should be primarily the development of descriptive knowledge. They have ignored, and in some cases openly condemned, normative research. There are at least two unintended consequences of such a stance. The first is a result of testing the theory by creating the variables being studied and then changing them systematically. But, if one is going to change variables systematically, society will probably permit the change only if it is in a "good" direction. What is a good direction? Who will define what is good? One possible answer is to leave that to the man on the street or to the politicians. Another possibility is for behavioral scientists to take normative positions based upon the existing descriptive research (as has been done with the issue of integration). The separation between research on "is" and on "ought" may be an artificial one if we keep in mind that the "ought" in human behavior comes from what "is." People behave at time t_1 or $t_2, \ldots,$ t_n like they behaved at time t_o because they believe that the behavior at t_o is good for them.

A second problem with separating descriptive and normative questions may be illustrated by a recent analysis of consistency and attribution theories currently popular in social psychology (Argyris, 1969). The theories were confirmed by the empirical data collected by the writer. However, certain data collected from normative research showed that if human beings behaved in accordance with these theories, they would tend to create and maintain ineffective, interpersonal relationships.

When asking how systematic knowledge can be produced which enhances the competence of the system, it is profitable to examine the constraints on the use of that knowledge. Two very important constraints are related to man's mechanisms for thinking and problem solving (Simon, 1969) and his mechanisms for seeking to enhance his sense of competence (White, 1956).

Beginning with the sense of competence, recent preliminary research suggests that man as an activist may tend to feel successful when he makes self-fulfilling prophecies (i.e., make things come true). In striving to make these self-fulfilling prophecies he marshals all the resources available to him. Also he may make his behavior redundant and overdetermined in order to increase the probability that he will succeed. He will be especially conscious that ambiguity will tend to be high while the time available to solve the problem will tend to be little.

To make matters more difficult, Simon's recent work on thinking suggests that man's machinery for thought is finite and relatively simple. It is the environment that is complex. Man may need much time to work out a problem because he has to go through a laborious process of examining his memory (which is in the form of lists) and matching the problem as he conceives it with the knowledge stored up in his mind. The relevance of this knowledge to our problem is that under conditions of ambiguity and complexity the time available is frequently inadequate. Under these conditions man's thinking capacities are most taxed. Given these constraints, how can knowledge be "packaged" so that it is most useful to man as an activist?

1. Knowledge should be stated in the form of units that are usable by man. Research needs to be conducted concerning the size of unit with which man can deal. It is the writer's experience that much research is stated in units that are much more molecular than the human mind can use effectively. It is as if man is capable of thinking primarily in feet while much research is defined (in order to be rigorous) in inches.

2. If we were to take seriously the aspirations to develop generalizations such as X varies monotonically with Y, then the number of such generalizations needed to accurately describe the complexity of the non-contrived world would probably lead to generalizations which would become as difficult to utilize and manage as (at least) a complex chess game. The reaction of the user will be, according to Simon, to develop heuristics which greatly simplify the generalizations without losing too much of their usability. If so, perhaps we should take more interest in developing the heuristics for the practitioner to assure their proper translation of the rigorous generalization. Developing these heuristics will be no easy task. However, as Simon indicates, it is possible to do so and can be systematically studied.

One may conjecture that such heuristics would be statements that take into account man's apparent capacity to overdetermine, and to be redundant, and to use variables that stand up under conditions of noise or ambiguity. The calculus of heuristics may turn out to be sloppy (compared to precise mathematical formulations). This conjecture may not be too unreal. As Von Neumann has suggested, the capacity to use sloppy categories and yet make accurate predictions may be a basic characteristic that distinguishes the human being from other problem-solving unities, be they animal or computer (Von Neumann, 1958).

3. Scientific generalizations may have to be stated in a form in which man can utilize his capacity and need to make self-fulfilling prophecies. This means that man may prefer generalizations that specify the variables that are relevant more than the systematic empirical generalizations about relationships among the variables (e.g., X varies monotonically with Y). He may prefer a theory that specifies the possible relevant variables more than knowledge about the potency of

the variables. For example, a group of executives preferred the following theoretical but untested generalization (i.e., an hypothesis):

The higher up one goes in the organizational hierarchy, the more potent are the interpersonal relationships and the less the individuals tend to trust each other, to the generalization that was inferred from empirical research that specifying a quantifiable relationship between trust, on the one hand, and position in the hierarchy and length of time on the job on the other (Alderfer, 1967; Hall & Lawler, 1968).

The reasons for the preference for the less rigorously tested generalizations are that it apparently provided the executives with the knowledge that they needed in order to create their own self-fulfilling prophecies. The more they used generalizations that spelled out rigorously the relationships among the variables, the less they felt that they could attribute success to their efforts; therefore, the less the possibility of psychological success and of feeling competent.

Moreover, given the necessary incompleteness of most generalizations, the executives expect that most behavioral sciences generalizations will tend to be inadequate. Consequently, they may prefer decision-making processes where they design the sequence of steps and then elicit corrective feedback, and where they define the relationships among the variable so that they can create a self-fulfilling prophecy. Thus a variable may be shown by research to account for 10 percent of the nonrandom variance; however, the executive may wish to structure the world so he can make the same variable (under the same conditions) account for 80 percent of the nonrandom variance. To say this another way, scientifically rigorous generalizations that systematically explain the world could deprive the users of the very activities (e.g., making self-fulfilling prophecies, setting own level of aspiration, exploring ambiguity) that could lead to their experiencing psychological success and a sense of competence.

Cronbach and Gleser (1965, pp. 145ff.)

have differentiated between wide-band and narrow-band methods of information gathering. The wide-band methods (which tend to be more qualitative and rich) transmit more information but the clarity and dependability of the information may be less than for the narrow-band method. The authors suggest that the wide-band methods may be especially suited for early research and diagnosis where exploration is a primary objective and sequential decisions are possible (where feedback and correction are possible). The narrow-band method may be more relevant when the objective is to arrive at a terminal decision.

The distinction made by Cronbach and Gleser is relevant to my argument in the following way. If the conclusions from the management information systems studies are replicated, they suggest that executives, in order to survive, may prefer sequential decision making and resist both terminal decisions and narrow-band methods. They would prefer to keep their options as open and flexible as possible and to receive as much feedback as possible in order to correct for errors. If so, one way to make social science information more applicable is to develop models and generalizations that utilize, or are congruent with, wide-band methods and sequential decision making. It may be that the best executives will prefer the wide-band to the narrow-band methods while the reverse may be the case for the less effective executives. The latter may prefer terminal decisions made by psychological technology in order to reduce their sense of responsibility and accountability.

5. How can industrial and organizational psychologies be effectively integrated?

One of the most important challenges facing industrial and organizational psychologists is the conceptual integration of their work into a unified systematic intellectual discipline. This will not be an easy task.

Perhaps the problem can be illustrated by examining the win-lose, intergroup dynamics that have been created by two sub-groups in the field: industrial psychologists centrally involved in testing, selection, job evaluation, etc. and organizational psychologists involved in individual change and organizational change. Alderfer (1972) has suggested that the latter has come from an intellectual tradition that might be characterized by adjectives such as clinical, holistic, organic, and humanistic. The former group's tradition might be characterized by adjectives like experimental, precise, and objective. The industrial psychologists have focused more on matching individuals with existing jobs and on being uninterested in change. The organizational change researchers have focused on modifying job, interpersonal, and organizational conditions; have been uninterested in matching individuals to jobs; and have been willing to use less rigorous methods in order to obtain valid data.

The challenge is for both sides to learn from each other. For example, the less rigorous methods may actually obtain more valid, publicly certifiable data than the presently accepted rigorous methods. The reason is that the presently accepted methods may create resistance to being placed in a dependent, submissive situation or being asked to fill out instruments that they perceive as full of concepts that are not clearly relatable to their needs. This does not mean that rigor should be dropped, but that, in order for it to be increased, the concept may need to be modified (Kelman, 1968).

On the other hand, subjects may not resist questionnaires or tests if they are effectively designed; a subject may accept a certain degree of submissiveness and dependence if he knows that the statistical analyses to be made (that require his passivity) are sophisticated enough to protect his interests and to increase the chances that he can rely on the results.

The task will not be an easy one. Alderfer (1972) has suggested that Dunnette, Campbell, and Argyris got into a debate which had some of the characteristics of an intergroup rivalry. The result was that each side played down its own innovative contributions, suppressed the many times each had encouraged its professional brethren to consider the views of the other side, and probably created "calls of support" from loyal members of each group (which would, of course, act to further polarize the situation). Although neither Argyris nor Dunnette agreed completely with Alderfer's analysis, they did meet in an attempt to explore the issues openly and to generate more valid understanding. The writer found the confrontation very helpful and informative. He learned, for example, that he had misread some of Dunnette's motives; that Dunnette and he were much closer on key issues than he (Argyris) was with many professional change agents; that Dunnette enjoyed the process of analyzing quantitative data while he enjoyed theorizing and collecting data; that both unintentionally created conditions of win-lose dynamics; that until the confrontation session, each was bewildered by the behavior of the other; and that somehow Argyris wanted to help create more opportunities to work with Dunnette.

In addition to the development of an integrated systematic field, there is another reason why we need to reduce the win-lose dynamics among us. An observer can identify such dynamics and, as a result, may tend to instruct both sides (Blake & Mouton, 1969). If the observers are practitioners who seek help, they may reject both houses and turn to others less competent but more overtly diplomatic in the way they handle their intragroup conflict. No one will gain if this happens.

REFERENCES

Adams, J. S. Toward an understanding of inequity. *Journal of Abnormal and Social Psychology,* 1963, 67, 422–436.

Alderfer, C. The organizational syndrome. *Administrative Science Quarterly,* 1967, 12 (3), 440–460.

Alderfer, C. The effect of individual, group, and intergroup relations on attitudes toward a management development program. *Journal of Applied Psychology,* 1971, 55, 302–311.

Alderfer, C. Conflict resolution among behavioral scientists. *Professional Psychology,* 1972, 3, 41–47.

Alderfer, C., & Lodahl, T. A quasi-experiment on the use of experiential methods in the classroom. *Journal of Applied Behavioral Science,* 1971, 7 (1), 43–70.

Alderfer, C., & McCord, C. G. Personal and situational factors in the recruitment interview. *Journal of Applied Psychology,* 1970, 54, No. 4, 377–385.

Anastasi, A. *Differential psychology.* New York: Macmillan, 1965.

Andrews, J. D. The achievement motive and advancement in two types of organizations. *Journal of Personality and Social Psychology,* 1967, 6, 163–168.

Argyris, C. *Personality and organization.* New York: Harper and Row, 1957.

Argyris, C. Some problems in conceptualizing organizational climate: A case study of a bank. *Administrative Science Quarterly,* 1958, 2 (4), 501–520.

Argyris, C. *Understanding organizational behavior.* Homewood, Ill.: Dorsey Press, 1960.

Argyris, C. *Integrating the individual and the organization.* New York: Wiley, 1964.

Argyris, C. *Organization and innovation.* Homewood, Ill.: Irwin, 1965.

Argyris, C. Some causes of organizational ineffectiveness within the Department of State. Center for International Systems Research, Department of State, November, 1966.

Argyris, C. Some unintended consequences of rigorous research. *Psychological Bulletin,* 1968, 70 (3), 185–197.

Argyris, C. The incompleteness of social-psychological theory. *American Psychologist,* 1969, 24 (10), 893–908.

Argyris, C. *Intervention theory and method.* Reading, Mass.: Addison-Wesley, 1970.

Argyris, C. Management information systems: The challenge to rationality and emotionality. *Management Science,* February, 1971, 17, 275–292.

Bakan, D. *Disease, pain, and sacrifice.* Chicago: University of Chicago Press, 1968.

Banks, O. *The attitude of steelworkers to technological change.* England: University Press of Liverpool, 1960.

Barker, R. G., & Wright, H. F. *Midwest and its children.* Evanston, Ill.: Row, Peterson, 1955.

Bass, B. M. An approach to the objective assessment of successful leadership. In B. M. Bass & I. A. Berg (Eds.), *Objective approaches to personality assessment.* New York: Van Nostrand, 1959, Chapter 8.

Bennis, W. G. *Changing organizations.* New York: McGraw-Hill, 1966.

Blake, R. R., & Mouton, J. S. *Building a dynamic corporation through grid organization development.* Reading, Mass.: Addison-Wesley, 1969.

Blauner, R. Work satisfaction and industrial trends in modern society. In W. Galenson & S. M. Lipset (Eds.), *Labor and trade unionism: An interdisciplinary reader.* New York: Wiley, 1960, 339–360.

Blood, M. R. Work values and job satisfaction. *Journal of Applied Psychology,* 1969, 53 (6), 456–459.

Blum, M. L., & Naylor, J. C. *Industrial psychology.* New York: Harper and Row, 1968.

Braithwaite, R. B. *Scientific explanation.* Cambridge, England: University of Trinity College, 1956.

Bray, D. W., & Grant, D. L. The assessment center in the measurement of potential for business management. *Psychological Monographs,* 1966, 80 (17), Whole No. 625.

Buhler, C. *Values in psychology.* New York: Free Press of Glencoe, 1962, 36–39.

Cannell, C. Interactions of respondent interviews examined. *ISR Newsletter,* Institute for Social Research, University of Michigan, Ann Arbor, 1969, 1 (4), 5–7.

Cronbach, L. J., & Gleser, G. C. *Psychological tests and personnel decisions.* Urbana: University of Illinois Press, 1965.

Culbert, S. A. Organization renewal using internal conflicts to solve external problems. Mimeographed. Paper presented, Annual IRRA conference, December 29, 1969, Graduate School of Business, University of California at Los Angeles.

DeNelsky, G. Y., & McKee, M. G. Prediction of job performance from assessment reports: Use of a modified Q-sort technique to expand predictor and criterion variance. *Journal of Applied Psychology,* 1969, 53 (6), 439–445.

DuBois, P. H. Individual differences. *Annual Review of Psychology,* 1960, 2, 225–254.

Dunnette, M. Personnel management. *Annual Review of Psychology,* 1962, 13, 285–314.

Dunnette, M. *Personnel, selection, and placement.* Belmont, Calif.: Wadsworth Publishing, 1966.

Dunnette, M. D., & Campbell, J. P. *Development of the Penney Career Index: Final technical report.* Mimeographed. Minneapolis: University of Minnesota, 1969, 79 pages.

Dunnette, M., & Kirchner, W. K. *Psychology applied to industry.* New York: Appleton-Century-Crofts, 1965.

Fleishman, E. A. Leadership climate, human relations training, and supervisory behavior. *Personnel Psychology,* 1953, 6, 205–222.

Forehand, G. A., & Gilmer, B. von H. Environment variation in studies of organizational behavior. *Psychological Bulletin,* 1964, 6 (2), 361–382.

Frederiksen, N. In-basket tests and factors in administrative performance. In A. Anastasi (Ed.), *Testing problems in perspective.* Washington, D.C.: American Council on Education, 1966, 208–221.

Fromm, E. *Escape from freedom.* New York: Rinehart, 1941.

Gardner, J. America in the twenty-third century. *New York Times,* July 27, 1968.

Gellerman, S. W. Seven deadly sins of executive placement. *Management Review,* 1958, 47, 4–9.

Ghiselli, E. E., & Brown, C. W. *Personnel and industrial psychology.* New York: McGraw-Hill, 1955.

Gilmer, B. von H. Industrial psychology. *Annual Review of Psychology,* 1960, 11, 323–350.

Goldthorpe, H., Lockwood, D., Bechhofer, F., & Platt, J. *The affluent worker: Industrial attitudes and behavior.* England: Cambridge University Press, 1968.

Goodman, R. Job content and motivation: A hypothesis. *Industrial Engineering,* May, 1969, 40–46.

Gordon, R. A., & Howell, J. E. *Higher education for business.* New York: Columbia University Press, 1959.

Goslin, D. A. *The search for ability.* New York: Russell Sage Foundation, 1963.

Gouldner, A. W. The norm of reciprocity: A preliminary statement. *American Sociological Review,* 1960, 25, 161–179.

Guion, R. M. *Personnel testing.* New York: McGraw-Hill, 1965.

Hackman, J. R., & Lawler, E. E. III. Employee reactions to job characteristics. *Journal of Applied Psychology Monographs,* 1971, 55 (3), 259–286.

Hall, D. R., & Lawler, E. *Attitude and behavior patterns in research and development organizations.* New Haven: Sponsored by Connecticut Research Commission and Department of Administrative Sciences, Yale University, May, 1968.

Hanson, N. R. *Patterns of discovery.* England: Cambridge University Press, 1958.

Herzberg, F. *Work and the nature of man.* Cleveland: World Publishing, 1966.

Hinrichs, J. R. Psychology of men at work. *Annual Review,* 1970, 21, 519–554.

Homans, G. *Social behavior: Its elementary form.* New York: Harcourt, Brace, 1961.

Hulin, C. L., & Blood, M. R. Job enlargement, individual differences, and workers resources. *Psychological Bulletin,* 1968, 69 (1), 41–55.

Kahn, R. L., Wolfe, D. M., Quinn, R. P., Snoek, J. D., & Rosenthal, R. A. *Organizational stress: Studies in role conflict and ambiguity.* New York: Wiley, 1964.

Kaplan, A. *The conduct of inquiry.* San Francisco: Chandler Publishing, 1964.

Kelman, H. C. *A time to speak.* San Francisco: Jossey-Bass, 1968.

Koch, S. Behavior as "intrinsically" regulated: Work notes toward a pre-theory of phenomenon called motivation. In R. Jones, (Ed.), *Nebraska symposium on motivation.* Lincoln: University of Nebraska Press, 1956.

Korman, A. K. Consideration, initiation structure, and organizational criteria: A review. *Personnel Psychology,* 1966, 19 (4), 349–361.

Korman, A. K. *Industrial and organizational psychology.* Englewood Cliffs, N.J.: Prentice-Hall, 1971.

Lawler, E. *Pay and organizational effectiveness: A psychological view.* New York: McGraw-Hill, 1971.

Lawler, E. E. III, & Hackman, J. R. Impact of employee participation in the development of incentive plans. *Journal of Applied Psychology,* 1969, 53 (6), 467–471.

Lewin, K. *A dynamic theory of personality.* New York: McGraw-Hill, 1935, 1–42.

Likert, R. *The human organization: Its management and values.* New York: McGraw-Hill, 1967.

Lodahl, R. M. Patterns of job attitudes in two

assembly technologies. *Administrative Science Quarterly*, 1964, 8 (4), 482–519.

Lowin, A., Hrapchak, W. J., & Kavanagh, M. J. Consideration and initiating structure: An experimental investigation of leadership traits. *Administrative Science Quarterly*, 1969, 14 (2), 238–253.

McGregor, D. *The human side of enterprise*. New York: McGraw-Hill, 1960.

McReynolds, P. The nature and assessment of intrinsic motivation. In P. McReynolds (Ed.), *Advances in psychological assessment*, Vol. 2. Palo Alto, Calif.: Science and Behavior Books, 1971.

Mann, F. C., & Williams, L. K. Some effects of the changing work environment in the office. In S. Lundstedt (Ed.), *Mental health and the work environment*. Foundation for Research on Human Behavior, 1962, 16–30.

March, J. G., & Simon, H. A. *Organizations*. New York: Wiley, 1958.

Meyer, H. H., Kay, E., & French, J. R. P. Split roles in performance appraisal. *Harvard Business Review*, 1965, 43, 123–129.

Miller, G. A. Psychology as a means of promoting human welfare. *American Psychologist*, 1969, 24 (12), 1063–1075.

Owens, W. A., & Jewell, D. O. Personnel selection. *Annual Review of Psychology*, 1969, 20, 413–446.

Porter, L. W. Personnel management. *Annual Review of Psychology*, 1966, 17, 395–422.

Pugh, D. S. Modern organization theory: A psychological and sociological study. *Psychological Bulletin*, 1966, 66 (4), 235–251.

Ryan, T. A., & Smith, P. C. *Principles of industrial psychology*. New York: Ronald Press, 1954.

Sattler, J. Racial "experimenter effects" in experimentation, testing, interviewing, and psychotherapy. *Psychological Bulletin*, 1970, 73 (2), 137–160.

Scheflen, K. G., Lawler, E. E. III, & Hackman, J. R. The long-term impact of employee participation in the development of pay incentive plans: A field experiment revisited. *Journal of Applied Psychology*, 1970.

Schneider, B. Some differences between students about to study industrial organizational psychology in psychology and non-psychology departments. Mimeographed. Symposium, American Psychological Association, August 31, 1969, Department of Administrative Sciences, Yale University.

Schneider, B., & Bartlett, C. J. Individual differences and organizational climate: I. The research plan and questionnaire development. *Personnel Psychology*, 1968, 21, 323–333.

Scott, W. E. Jr. Activation theory and task design. *Organizational behavior and human performance*, 1966, 1 (1), 3–30.

Simon, H. *The science of the artificial*. Cambridge: M.I.T. Press, 1969.

Sorcher, M. *The effects of employee involvement on work performance*. New York: Personnel Research Planning and Practices, General Electric Company, 1969.

Storrs, A. *The integrity of personality*. Baltimore: Penguin Books, 1963.

Strauss, G. Some notes on power-equalization. In H. J. Leavitt (Ed.), *The social science of organizations: Four perspectives*. Englewood Cliffs, N.J.: Prentice-Hall, 1963.

Tannenbaum, A. S. *Control in organizations*. New York: McGraw-Hill, 1968.

Thornton, G. C. Image of industrial psychology among personnel administrators. *Journal of Applied Psychology*, 1969, 53 (5), 436–438.

Tiffin, J. *Industrial psychology*. Englewood Cliffs, N.J.: Prentice-Hall, 1946.

Tyler, L. E. Toward a workable psychology of individuality. *American Psychologist*, 1959, 14, 75–85.

Vale, J. R., & Vale, C. A. Individual differences and general laws in psychology: A reconciliation. *American Psychologist*, 1969, 24 (12), 1093–1108.

Von Neumann, J. *The computer and the brain*. New Haven: Yale University Press, 1958.

Webb, E. J., Campbell, D. T., Schwartz, R. D., & Sechrest, L. *Unobstrusive measures: Nonreactive research in the social sciences*. Chicago: Rand McNally, 1966.

Westley, W. A., & Epstein, M. B. *Silent majority*. San Francisco: Jossey-Bass, 1969.

White, R. Motivation reconsidered: The concept of competence. *Psychological Review*, 1956, 66, 297–334.

Whyte, W. F. *Organizational behavior*. Homewood, Ill.: Irwin, 1969.

Wrong, D. The over-socialized conception of man in modern sociology. *American Sociological Review*, 1961, 26, 183–193.

Zimbardo, P., & Ebbesen, B. *Influencing attitudes and changing behavior*. Reading, Mass.: Addison-Wesley, 1969.

CHAPTER 6

Pyschometric Theory[1]

JOHN P. CAMPBELL
The University of Minnesota

THE OVERALL OBJECTIVE of this chapter is to review a selected number of basic topics in psychometric theory that are of most interest to industrial and organizational psychology. Problems and issues in scaling and test theory (e.g., the latent trait models) are not considered. Reliability theory is treated at length from the point of view of the overlap between its theoretical foundations and practical applications. Beginning with Spearman, alternative conceptualizations of measurement error are first placed in a historical perspective. Cronbach's generalizability model is then used to integrate alternative reliability models and alternative estimation methods into what is essentially a stratified domain sampling point of view. This model makes it possible to discuss validity models as a logical extension of reliability theory. An important special case pertains to the prediction of discrete criterion outcomes and validity in the context of decision theory is treated at some length. Special reference is made to the effects of both explicit and implicit utility judgments. Finally, some special problems of inference relevant for generalizing reliability and validity estimates to populations are mentioned.

What is psychometric theory? It could include such topics as reliability theory, validity models, prediction strategies, utility theory, scaling theory, test construction, item response and latent trait models, response sets and response styles, models to correct for guessing, and the like. Covering all these would quickly get out of bounds

and, therefore, some selectivity is required. Also, many of these topics are included within the appropriate substantive chapters elsewhere in this volume. What follows is intended to be the basic core of psychometric theory as it pertains to the problems of the industrial and organizational psychologist. The core topics would be somewhat different for some other area of application, such as educational measurement.

The reason for psychometric theory's existence is the obvious fact that measure-

[1] Preparation of this paper was supported in part by Office of Naval Research contract number N00014-68-A-0141-0003.

ments of many important human characteristics are not error free and the relationships between these characteristics and other variables deemed important by society are not perfect. To deal with these problems, some theory or model is required to help specify the amount or kind of uncertainty that is present and the level of explanation and prediction that is still possible. Even in measurement, Lewin's dictum holds. There is nothing quite so practical as a good theory.

Since every story of measurement must begin there, alternative conceptualizations of an observed score are considered first. This leads quite naturally into a discussion of measurement error and alternative reliability models for dealing with such error. Under certain conditions the concept of reliability becomes indistinguishable from that of validity. After these conditions have been identified, the notion of validity will be pursued within the framework of both practical decision making and scientific investigation. Lastly, the peculiar problems associated with estimating measurement and predictive accuracy in the population will be explored.

After a period of relative quiescence, a small revolution has begun to take shape in psychometric theory. It was stimulated first by questioning some of the assumptions of the classic true score model and attempting to develop models that are at the same time less restrictive and closer to our measurement realities. A second influence has been the increased emphasis on the individual item rather than the total score as the basic unit of measurement (Bock & Wood, 1971). These changes in orientation have in turn led to the gradual development of a more integrated item, or individual component, oriented approach to reliability and validity models.

It is the aim of this chapter to reflect some of these newer developments in garden variety language as well as to recapitulate the more established developments in psychometric theory that bear repeating. For a much broader, more detailed, and more sophisticated treatment the reader is referred to three recent books which have become classics in their own time. They are *Statistical Theories of Mental Test Scores* by Lord and Novick (1968), *Psychological Tests and Personnel Decisions* (2nd ed.) by Cronbach and Gleser (1965), and *The Dependability of Behavioral Measurements* by Cronbach, Gleser, Nanda, and Rajaratnam (1972).

Concurrent with the changes in reliability and validity models the increased emphasis on the item as a unit of measurement has produced new developments in psychological test theory and test technology. The Lord and Novick (1968) volume summarizes a number of different models that purport to describe how individual item responses are related to the underlying trait being measured. Latent trait theory and the logistics models, of which the Rasch model (Rasch, 1966) is a special case, are two examples. The basic hope behind the development of these models is that they will eventually permit much more efficient and accurate methods for constructing tests with which to make specific decisions for specific groups of people. However, as pointed out by Bock and Wood (1971) we are not at the point yet, except perhaps where decisions using well-known measures (e.g., vocabulary or arithmetic reasoning items) are being made for very large numbers of people (e.g., in educational or military organizations). Because of their limited applicability and because they are more in the domain of educational measurement than psychometric theory, they will not be discussed further. For much the same reason the newer developments in test technology, such as individually tailored testing via a computer mode, will not be discussed in any detail. However, it will be interesting to note a bit later that some of the more recent conceptualizations of the reliability problems present a reasonable way for handling the reliability estimation problems generated by individualized or tailored testing.

MODELS OF A SCORE

The first model of an observed score which attempted to deal with the uncertainty inherent in any measurement is Spearman's brilliant statement of true and error scores, which is still the most influential model in psychological research. Briefly, any observed score is a function of two components: a true score (or the *real* magnitude) and an error score.

$$X = T + e$$

Three assumptions make the theory a practical way to interpret the uncertainty involved in interpreting observed scores (i.e., measurement error):

1. Across many measurements of one person with the "same" instrument, error scores comprise a random normal deviate and the only reason an individual's score differs from one measurement to the next is because the error score is different. This implies that for the model to be useful we must apply it to a situation where the true score is stable.

2. Error scores are independent of true scores ($r_{TE} = 0$). For example, being high or low on an ability continuum should have no influence on the magnitude of the error component in the observed score.

3. True and error scores combine in a simple sum.

For a number of people, the assumptions entailed by Spearman's version of a score are a bit too forceful. A statement of so-called "weak" true score theory is given by Cureton (1971). If we consider what might actually happen when an individual is measured on several parallel measures the observed raw score on any one measure can perhaps be expressed in terms of three components.

$$X = T + e_s + e_c$$

where:

$T =$ the true score

$e_s =$ the error in the observed score associated with situational and time factors, such as level of fatigue, anxiety, motivation, haphazard fluctuations in the memory trace, etc. Cureton calls these instability errors.

$e_c =$ the error in the observed score associated with the fact that repeated measurements may not be taken with the same operations. Cureton calls these inconsistency errors and they are associated with differences in content, not differences in people. He also makes the cogent argument that the test-retest method does not hold this source of error constant since the very act of testing may change the stimuli for the subject the second time around. Using parallel forms allows these errors to operate but in a way that can be estimated. The test-retest method builds in the kinds of errors whose relative variance cannot easily be estimated and it should be avoided in most instances.

In this version of a weak true score theory the true scores are assumed to be independent of both kinds of error scores and instability errors are assumed to be independent of inconsistency errors. However, the instability errors are not assumed to be uncorrelated across repeated measurements. No matter what the time interval some portion of the extraneous factors affecting scores at time 1 may still be present at time 2.

Further modifications of the classic model have come from two additional directions. First, a number of people (e.g., Maxwell, 1968; Williams & Zimmerman, 1968) have suggested that the error component(s) may not be independent of the true score, and thus may be neither random nor normally distributed. An observed score might then be represented simply as:

$$X = T + e_b + e_r$$

where:

e_b = biased error score
e_r = residual error which is a random normal deviate
$r_{Te_b} \neq 0$
$r_{Te_r} = 0$

Such a biased error component could arise in an aptitude testing situation in which the error variance produced by guessing is greater the lower the true score. An analogous situation seems reasonable for the measurement of typical performance. Individuals with extreme true scores may indeed exhibit more stable observable behavior because of a more limited adaptation capability than people in the middle of the score range. As always, the crucial consideration is how to estimate the relative variability due to each of these components.

A more generalized attack on the classic model flows from adapting an analysis of variance framework and segregating the error score into a number of specific variance components each attributable to a verifiable source. Quite naturally, the ANOVA applications were first developed at the University of London by Jackson and his collaborators (Burt, 1945; Hoyt, 1941; Jackson & Ferguson, 1941). If we think of repeated measures $(1, 2, \ldots i \ldots)$ as columns and individuals $(1, 2, \ldots j \ldots)$ as rows, then the basic two-way ANOVA model can be written as follows:

$$X_{ij} = M + (M_i - M) + (M_j - M) + e_{ij}$$

where:

M = grand mean
$(M_i - M)$ = column effect, or a deviation score about the grand mean attributable to variation in test scores averaged over people
$(M_j - M)$ = row effect, or a deviation score about the grand mean attributable to variation in people averaged over tests
e_{ij} = residual, independent of main effects and randomly distributed

Further, the model can be thought of as completely fixed, completely random, or mixed. A completely fixed model implies that individuals are not sampled from a larger population and inferences about the column (i.e., content) differences are not meant to generalize to a larger domain of content. A random model implies that individuals are randomly sampled from a population and the substantive content in each column (e.g., test items) was obtained by taking random samples of content from a larger population of content.

Cronbach, Rajaratnam, and Gleser (1963) used an ANOVA model originally developed by Cornfield and Tukey (1956) to expand on the above conceptualization of a score. In effect the model becomes:

$$X_{ijk} = M + (M_i - M) + (M_j - M) + (M_{ij} - M_i - M_j + M) + e_{ijk}$$

where:

The first three terms are defined as before.

$(M_{ij} - M_i - M_j)$ = a cell effect which results from taking the mean of repeated observations (measurements) occurring at the intersection of each row and column; that is, the mean for a specific person when the same item or element is administered a number of times.

e_{ijk} = a residual associated with each cell. It is tied to the particular row and column which define it and may differ in nonrandom ways from cell to cell. Within each cell, however, it is a random variable which is normally distributed.

As will be noted below, Cronbach et al. (1963) and others have attempted to derive some generalized notions of reliability and validity from this conceptualization of an observed score.

Given a particular view of an observed score, the next step is to specify a model and procedure for assessing the relative importance of each component; and in its traditional form, this has been the task of reliability theory. Historically, attempts to assess reliability have been attempts to construct situations (real or conceptual) in which the true score is assumed to be a constant and the only reason for variation in observed scores is variation in the error component(s). As an index of the relative amount of error that's present, attention has focused almost exclusively on the product moment correlation between two sets of scores for which the true score is assumed constant. As Cronbach et al. (1963) and others have argued, this is an overly narrow view of the reliability problem and has led to considerable confusion, frustration, and disappointment. Broader models are now

available and one objective of the present chapter is to trace the development of the reliability problem from Spearman to the present, so that the important issues, theoretical choice points, and alternative means of estimation are illustrated.

MODELS OF MEASUREMENT RELIABILITY

Theory of True and Error Scores

The classic theory (Gulliksen, 1950; Spearman, 1904) views reliability as the relative stability of one individual's observed scores over *parallel* measures of the same attribute. Parallel measures are defined as measures which are *constructed,* such that the true score component is constant across measures for any one individual (Novick & Lewis, 1967). The basic picture is as shown in Figure 1.

If parallel measures are defined in this way, a number of very important algebraic relationships are easily obtainable.

1. Since the mean of a simple sum composite is the sum of the component score means (e.g., $\bar{X}_{.1} = \bar{T}_{.1} + \bar{e}_{.1}$) and $\bar{e}_{ij} = 0$, the mean of the observed scores equals the

		MEASURES				
		1	2	• • •	k	
INDIVIDUALS	1	$X_{11}=T_1+e_{11}$	$X_{21}=T_1+e_{21}$	• • •	$X_{k1}=T_1+e_{k1}$	$\bar{X}_{.1} = \bar{T}_1 + \bar{e}_{.1}$
	2	$X_{12}=T_2+e_{12}$	$X_{22}=T_2+e_{22}$	• • •	$X_{k2}=T_2+e_{k2}$	$\bar{X}_{.2} = \bar{T}_2 + \bar{e}_{.2}$
	•	•	•		•	•
	•	•	•		•	•
	•	•	•		•	•
	n	$X_{1n}=T_n+e_{1n}$	$X_{2n}=T_n+e_{2n}$		$X_{kn}=T_n+e_{kn}$	$\bar{X}_{.n} = \bar{T}_n + \bar{e}_{.n}$
		$\bar{X}_1 = \bar{T} + \bar{e}_1.$	$\bar{X}_{2.} = \bar{T} + \bar{e}_2.$		$\bar{X}_{k.} = \bar{T} + \bar{e}_{k.}$	

Figure 1.   Scores of n individuals on k parallel measures.

true score for each row. Thus the average of his observed scores is an estimate of an individual's true score.

2. Since the mean of the true scores is the same for each *column* and $\bar{e}._j = 0$, the means of the observed scores must also be the same for each column.

3. By considering the variance of the observed scores in each column as the variance of the simple sum $(T + e)$, it can quickly be shown (cf., Ghiselli, 1963) that $\sigma_x^2 = \sigma_T^2 + \sigma_e^2$ and since σ_T^2 and σ_e^2 are the same for each column, the variance of the observed scores must be the same for each column.

4. It can also be shown via the algebra of additive composite scores that the correlation between any pair of parallel measures is equal to the correlation between any other pair and this intercorrelation is equal to the ratio of the true score variance to the observed score variance. That is, if the correlation between two parallel tests is defined as:

$$r_{x_1 x_2} = \frac{\Sigma x_1 x_2}{N \sigma_{x_1} \sigma_{x_2}}$$
$$= \frac{\Sigma (t_1 + e_1)(t_2 + e_2)}{N \sigma_{x_1} \sigma_{x_2}}$$
$$= \frac{\Sigma (t + e_1)(t + e_2)}{N \sigma_x^2}$$

This form of the equation can quickly be shown to reduce to:

$$r_{xx} = \frac{\sigma_T^2}{\sigma_x^2}$$

which is the same value for any pair of parallel tests and is precisely the most important index to estimate under the classic model.

Thus, if we wish to estimate the proportion of true score variance in any set of scores all we need do is compute the correlation between any two parallel tests. For identification purposes, parallel tests have equal means, equal variances, equal intercorrelations, and equal correlations with independent variables.

5. Besides estimating the reliability coefficient, we might also want to estimate the variance of error scores in one individual's scores across many parallel tests. The standard deviation of these errors is labeled the standard error of measurement. Since e is assumed to be a random normal deviate, its variability across several parallel measures for one individual should be the same as its variance across many people for one measure. Therefore, we can very quickly move from the reliability coefficient defined as the ratio of true score variance to observed variance (for any one column) to the standard error of measurement as:

$$\sigma_e = \sigma_x \sqrt{1 - r_{xx}}$$

Again, all we need to estimate the standard deviation of scores across a large number of measures is the standard deviation of the observed scores on one and the correlation between any two.

6. Lastly, the algebra of composite scores can also be used to derive the correlation between the observed scores on any measure and the true scores. To make a long story shorter:

$$r_{XT} = \frac{\Sigma (x - e_1) x}{N \sigma_t \sigma_x} = \sqrt{r_{xx}}$$

This coefficient is most often referred to as the *reliability index*.

The Eclectic Parallel Test Model

A very similar formulation, which Ghiselli (1963) refers to as the eclectic model, was developed in the early work of Brown (1910) and Kelly (1924). Rather than beginning with a model of a single score and proceeding to a derivation of the true score in terms of observables, the eclectic model *begins* by defining the true score as the mean of the observable scores. Although it may seem to require weaker assumptions at the outset, this particular alternative arrives at the same formulae for the reliability coefficient and standard error of measurement and eventually incorporates the same assumptions explicitly or implicitly used by the classic theory. In the historical scheme of things it does not represent a significant departure from classic reliability concepts. The task is still to estimate the correlation between any two parallel measures under conditions of true score stability.

Estimation Methods Based on True Score Model

Nothing in Spearman's formal model stipulates whether parallel measures are the same measure repeated at different points in time or are different sets of operations. Neither does it mention the temporal relations among parallel measures or the necessity for similar formats, similar situational conditions, and the like. Besides the problem of the appropriateness of the basic assumptions, these additional loopholes have in turn created added difficulties when the actual task of estimating the reliability coefficient is confronted. There are many real world sources of error variance and different kinds are included in the reliability coefficient depending on the research design used to gather the data. The classic theory does not deal with these distinctions. Given the blindness of the model, the use of either test-retest or equivalent forms as designs for estimating r_{xx} flow naturally from the classic

theory. Early in the century Spearman (1910) and Brown (1910) independently developed a third technique for estimating r_{xx} using data from only one administration of a measure, given that it was composed of individual components that could be divided into two parallel subsets.

The resulting Spearman-Brown prophecy formula can be derived in a number of ways. One of the simplest is to consider r_{xx} as the correlation between two composites, each composed of several components or part scores, say k and m. Then:

$$r_{xx} = \frac{1}{N\sigma_{c_x}\sigma_{c_n}} \cdot \Sigma[(x_1 + x_2 + \dots x_k)$$
$$\cdot (y_1 + y_2 + \dots y_m)]$$

which is simply the deviation score form of the Pearsonian r with the corresponding component scores substituted for the two total scores. The denominator is the product of the standard deviations of the two composite scores and the number of observations (N).

The numerator can be multiplied by considering a k x m matrix of cross products as shown in Figure 2.

After multiplication, the parentheses in the numerator includes all the entries in the

	x_1	x_2	x_3			x_k
y_1	x_1y_1	x_2y_1	x_3y_1	•	• •	x_ky_1
y_2	x_1y_2	x_2y_2	x_3y_2	•	• •	x_ky_2
y_3	x_1y_3	x_2y_3	x_3y_3	•	• •	x_ky_3
•	•	•	•	•	• •	•
•	•	•	•	•	• •	•
•	•	•	•	•	• •	•
y_m	x_1y_m	x_2y_m	x_3y_m	•	• •	x_ky_m

Figure 2. Matrix of deviation score cross-products when the scores in each pair represent component scores from different composites.

matrix, km of them. If the summation sign is brought inside the parentheses and numerator and denominator are divided by N, each term in the numerator becomes a covariance (e.g., $\Sigma x_1 y_1 / N = \sigma_{x_1} \sigma_{y_1} r_{x_1 y_1}$). The product of the two total score standard deviations is left in the denominator. If the numerator is written in terms of the average covariance the expression becomes:

$$r_{xx} = \frac{km \overline{\sigma_{x_i} \sigma_{y_j} r_{x_i y_j}}}{\sigma_{c_x} \sigma_{c_y}}$$

Now the expression for the standard deviation of a composite score in terms of its components is (for X_c and Y_c):

$$\sigma_{c_x} = \sqrt{k \bar{\sigma}_i^2 + (k^2 - k) \overline{\sigma_{x_i} \sigma_{x_{i'}} r_{x_i x_{i'}}}}$$
$$\sigma_{c_y} = \sqrt{m \bar{\sigma}_j^2 + (m^2 - m) \overline{\sigma_{y_j} \sigma_{y_{j'}} r_{y_j y_{j'}}}}$$

The terms under the radical are the average component variance and the average covariance between components within a composite. The quantities under the radical are equal to the sum of the component variances and all the intercomponent covariances for a particular composite. This sum is equal to the variance of the total score. Since the components are assumed to be parallel (i.e., equal means and variances) it is legitimate to get rid of the variance terms altogether by transforming to standard scores; the correlation thus becomes:

$$r_{xx} = km \bar{r}_{x_i y_j} / (\sqrt{k + k (k - 1) \bar{r}_{x_i x_{i'}}}$$
$$\cdot \sqrt{m + m (m - 1) \bar{r}_{y_j y_{j'}}}$$

Further, if $k = m$ and if the components in each measure are parallel, all the intercorrelations and cross-correlations are equal and all the average correlations can be replaced by a single value, $r_{ii'}$. The expression now becomes:

$$r_{xx} = \frac{k^2 r_{ii'}}{k + k (k - 1) r_{ii'}}$$

Dividing both numerator and denominator by k yields the general form of the Spearman-Brown formula:

$$r_{xx} = \frac{k r_{ii'}}{1 + (k - 1) r_{ii'}}$$

When $k = 2$, as when the half scores constitute the components and we wish the correlation between two measures composed of two such half tests (i.e., a test twice as long), the formula becomes:

$$r_{xx} = \frac{2 r_{\frac{1}{2}\frac{1}{2}}}{1 + 2 r_{\frac{1}{2}\frac{1}{2}}}$$

Derived in this manner and based on the accompanying assumptions the above formula specifies the prophesized correlation between the measure or test in hand and one precisely equivalent to it (i.e., which measures exactly the same things to the same degree) *if* the two measures could be taken at the same point in time. That is, there is no opportunity for the true score to change or for the intrusion of additional sources of error associated with the passage of time.

An important decision is how to split the available components or items into two subsets. The optimal solution is a split that divides each common factor precisely in half and thereby *maximizes* the correlation between the two subsets. If the test material is arranged in a logical sequence with areas of content arranged in blocks rather than randomly, then the odd-even split is an inexpensive way to approximate the optimal. A random split under these conditions would most likely underestimate r_{xx} to a greater degree.

An expression equivalent to the Spearman-Brown which uses variances instead of the half score intercorrelation was derived by Rulon (1939) who showed that the variance of the differences between half scores was an estimate of the error variance, given the assumption of parallel halves. Therefore:

$$r_{xx} = 1 - \frac{\sigma^2_{(A-B)}}{\sigma_x^2} = 2\left(1 - \frac{\sigma_A^2 + \sigma_B^2}{\sigma_x^2}\right)$$

where the two halves are designed as A and B.

It is a relatively short step from entering the correlation between half scores in the Spearman-Brown to using the correlation between fourths, eighths, or finally the inter-correlation between any pair of individual components, again under the assumption that the individual components satisfy the criteria for parallel measures.

Kuder and Richardson (1937) used the Spearman-Brown to develop several expressions for estimating r_{xx} in terms of individual component or item statistics. The most well known are KR-20 and KR-21.

$$r_{xx} = \frac{k}{k-1}\left(1 - \frac{\Sigma\sigma_i^2}{\sigma_x^2}\right) \qquad KR\text{-}20$$

$$r_{xx} = \frac{k}{k-1}\left(1 - \frac{\Sigma pq}{\sigma_x^2}\right) \qquad KR\text{-}21$$

The number of items or components is equal to k. The numerator in both is the sum of the item variances, the only difference being that KR-21 is appropriate for dichotomously scored items and thus each item variance is equal to pq where p is equal to the proportion choosing a particular alternative and $q = 1 - p$. To derive these formulae all the item intercorrelations are not required to be precisely equal, but the assumption was made that the inter item correlation matrix was of unit rank; that is, all items must be measuring only one common factor. In addition, the individual components are assumed to have equal means and equal variances. Under these assumptions KR-20 and KR-21 are equivalent to entering the average item intercorrelation in the Spearman-Brown.

The Kuder-Richardson formulae were developed with discrete or dichotomously scored components in mind. A generalized expression, appropriate for continuous part scores and any desired division of the total

score into separately scored part scores is Cronbach's coefficient alpha (Cronbach, 1951) shown below:

$$r_{xx} = \frac{k}{k-1}\left(\frac{V_x - \Sigma V_i}{V_x}\right)$$

$$= \frac{k}{k-1}\left(\frac{\Sigma\Sigma CV_{ii'}}{V_x}\right)$$

where $\Sigma\Sigma CV_{ii'} =$ sum of the inter "part" covariances, or in its more familiar form:

$$r_{xx} = \frac{k}{k-1}\left(1 - \frac{\Sigma V_i}{V_x}\right)$$

Again the denominator is the variance of the total score, ΣV_i is the sum of the part variances, and k equals the number of parts. If the number of parts $= 2$ (e.g., split half) coefficient alpha reduces to the Rulon formula.

One can see from the above expressions that the magnitude of coefficient alpha is a function of the ratio of the sum of the inter item, or inter part, covariances to the variance of the total score. The sum of the covariances in turn is largely a function of the intercorrelations among the parts.

Using similar equivalence assumptions and the ANOVA score model proposed by Jackson (1939), Hoyt (1941) developed an analysis of variance technique for estimating the reliability coefficient. If items are columns and individuals are rows, we have a two-way ANOVA with one case per cell. To the extent that items are equivalent, each item should order individuals in the same manner and there should be no interaction between items and people. Under this assumption, which is the same as that for KR and alpha, the residual or interaction sum of squares is an estimate of error variance and the Hoyt coefficient works out to be:

$$r_{xx} = \frac{MS_p - MS_r}{MS_p}$$

where:

MS_p = mean square for people

MS_r = mean square residual (interaction)

This expression was later shown to be algebraically equivalent to *KR*-20 and Coefficient Alpha.

The *KR* formula, Coefficient Alpha, and the Hoyt formula all represent the correlation to be expected between the measure, or test, in hand and a hypothetical parallel measure obtained at exactly the same point in time. It has become the custom to use the term internal consistency to identify this class of reliability coefficients. However, the term is a misnomer in the sense that the magnitude of the coefficient is a function of the number of components (k) as well as the degree to which they all measure one factor. Given *some* common variance, the coefficient is always asymptotic to 1.0 as k increases without bound. Thus, if we want an index of internal consistency rather than reliability there must be a correction for the number of components.

Another confusion arises when the above coefficients, Rulon's formula, and the split half coefficient corrected by the Spearman-Brown are all lumped under the internal consistency label. If the intercomponent correlation matrix departs from unit rank then it is always possible to obtain a split half or Rulon coefficient that is higher than coefficient alpha computed on the individual components. For example, consider a test composed of items tapping two common factors, verbal fluency and number facility. This departure from unit rank would reduce coefficient alpha a commensurate amount but to the extent that each factor could be equally represented in the two half scores the Spearman-Brown coefficient need not suffer.

The above points lead to certain generalizations about the appropriate method for estimating r_{xx}, within the framework of true score theory. The principal considerations are the static versus dynamic properties of the true score and its dimensionality. Nothing in the true score model says that the true score component must be unidimensional. To the extent that it is not and to the extent that the total score is composed of component scores varying in factor content, reliability estimates based on component characteristics (e.g., *KR,* Coefficient Alpha, Hoyt ANOVA) will be relatively low, but equivalent forms and split half estimates could still be high, other things being equal. Recognizing multidimensionality when we see it is not always an easy task. For example, rules for when to stop extracting factors are always arbitrary in some sense. Perhaps the wisest course is to always make the comparison between the split half and internal consistency estimates after first splitting the components into two halves on a priori grounds. That is, every effort should be made to balance the factor content of each half *before* looking at the component intercorrelations.

By contrast, the choice between the split half and equivalent forms estimate of reliability is a function of the dynamics of the true score. If the true score is relatively stable over a particular time period then an equivalent forms estimate is appropriate. There are many obvious examples of when it is not. The correlation between a mathematics achievement test administered before and after a course in mathematics would not be a reliability coefficient. Hopefully, the class members are increasing their knowledge of mathematics, most likely at different rates. Likewise, the correlation between two forms of a job satisfaction questionnaire or organizational climate questionnaire may not be a reliability coefficient if events have occurred to change an individual's perceptions.

It also seems reasonable that during the interval between the administration of two equivalent forms, or at the time of the second administration, a number of events can operate to lower the inter-form correlations which should be attributed to error variance rather than bona fide changes in the true score. Poor testing conditions, motivational differences, and situational anxiety are examples. Since it is not possible to distinguish these kinds of extraneous sources of error variance from real changes in the true score on the basis of the observed correlation, we must always live with the confounding.

Because of this confounding, it is unwise to rely on only one equivalent forms estimate as an index of reliability. Comparison of an equivalent forms estimate with an internal consistency or split half estimate should yield valuable information about the "dynamic" nature of the characteristic being measured. Cureton (1971) has considered a more formal method for making this comparison and presents the derivation of a "stability coefficient" which is essentially an equivalent forms reliability coefficient corrected for attenuation due to a lack of internal consistency in the individual forms. If we make the assumption that at a specific time and place the unreliability in a measure is due to errors associated with *inconsistency* in content, then this source of error variance should be controlled if we want to accurately reflect the *instability* of the characteristics over time

The expression for correcting the equivalent forms coefficient for a lack of content consistency is as follows:

$$r_s = \frac{r_{x_1 x_2}}{\sqrt{r_{x_1 x_1} r_{x_2 x_2}}}$$

where:

$r_{x_1 x_2}$ = equivalent forms coefficient

$r_{x_1 x_1}$ & $r_{x_2 x_2}$ = internal consistency or split half (Spearman-Brown corrected) estimates for each form

The resulting stability coefficient (r_s) should more accurately reflect the degree of unreliability associated with non-content sources of error. Although Cureton does not deal with the question, our previous discussion of the multidimensionality question is also relevant. If the measure is unidimen-

sional it would be appropriate to use *KR*, Hoyt, Coefficient Alpha, or some other internal consistency measure in the denominator. However, if the test or measure is multidimensional the appropriate split half coefficient should be used in the denominator.

The Effect of Correlated Errors on Reliability Estimation

At the beginning of this chapter modifications of the classic model of an observed score were made on the basis of error components that were correlated with either the true score or other error components. Derivations by Maxwell (1968) and Williams and Zimmerman (1968) have shown that if errors across items or across test administrations are positively correlated then the reliability coefficient, regardless of the variety, will be an overestimate of the percentage of true score variance. This could happen if the instability errors (à la Cureton) persevered across administrations or if the true scores and the error scores were *negatively* correlated. This might occur with a multiple choice aptitude or achievement test when there is no correction for guessing.

Since it is not possible to make a statistical correction in the reliability coefficient for correlated errors, the problem must be handled experimentally, if at all. Thus the burden falls on the investigator to anticipate possible sources of non-independent errors and control for them if he or she can.

THEORY OF DOMAIN SAMPLING

The above formulation constitutes the core of the classic model of reliability or the "parallel by construction" approach, which has dominated psychometric theory throughout most of its history. It is the model of choice in such outstanding texts as Guilford's *Psychometric Methods* (1954), and Gulliksen's *Theory of Mental Tests* (1950). The major criticisms of this model are contained in Tryon (1957), Cronbach et al.

(1963), Cronbach, Gleser, Nanda, and Rajaratnam (1972), Nunnally (1967), and the monumental work of Lord and Novick (1968). What follows is intended to be a brief summary of the major issues that have been raised.

One of the first to articulate a break with classic concepts was Tryon (1935, 1957) who rejected the true versus error dichotomy and preferred to think of reliability as the stability of an individual's scores across several independent measures when these measures are obtained by randomly sampling successive subsets of components from a much larger domain, or population, of such content. The basic tenets of what has become the *domain sampling* theory of reliability are as follows:

The notion of a true score is replaced by a domain or universe score which is an individual's standing if he could be measured on all the components in the universe. Besides their universe score, the components have population parameters corresponding to their average variance, average inter-component covariance, and average covariance with some external variable. The task of measurement is to estimate the universe score via a score on a sample. Measurement error is the extent to which the sample value differs from the population value. If samples are random, then smaller sampling errors lead to greater stability in observed scores across samples and the correlation between samples is an index of both their stability and the degree of sampling error involved.

If components are sampled randomly, then obtaining the correlation between samples of components is rather easy. Consider two samples, each made up of the same number of components (k). In definitional form the correlation between them is the ratio of their covariance to the product of their standard deviations.

$$r_{x_I x_{II}} = \frac{\frac{1}{N}\Sigma x_I x_{II}}{S_{x_I} S_{x_{II}}}$$

If we substitute the components scores for the total scores on each sample, the correlation becomes:

$$\frac{1}{N S_{x_1} S_{x_{11}}} \Sigma (x_{I_1} + x_{I_2} + \ldots + x_{I_k})$$

$$(x_{II_1} + x_{II_2} + \ldots + x_{II_k})$$

Multiplying out the numerator, bringing the summation sign inside the parentheses, and dividing each term by N yields $k \times k$ covariance terms, which can be found in the following matrix (Figure 3) in either quadrant B or quadrant C.

We can now substitute k^2 (the number of terms) times the average cross-covariance for the sum of the cross-covariances. The correlation between the two samples then becomes:

$$r_{x_I x_{II}} = \frac{k^2 S_{x_{I_i}} S_{x_{II_i}} \overline{r_{x_{I_i} x_{II_i}}}}{S_{x_I} S_{x_{II}}}$$

The next step is the crucial one for the sampling model. Since the two measures are random samples from the same universe, covariances between components within a particular sample should differ from covariances between components coming from different samples, only because of sampling error; and on the average, they should be the same. Thus the average covariance in quadrants A and D in the matrix should be the same as average covariance in quadrants B and C. Further, there is no reason to expect any systematic difference between product of the standard deviations of any two sample scores and the square of their individual standard deviations. Therefore, the correlation can be rewritten as follows:

$$r_{x_I x_{II}} = \frac{k^2 \overline{S_{x_i} S_{x_i}' r_{x_i x_{i'}}}}{S_x^{\,2}}$$

where the x_i and $x_{i'}$ refer to pairs of variables within a particular sample. The impor-

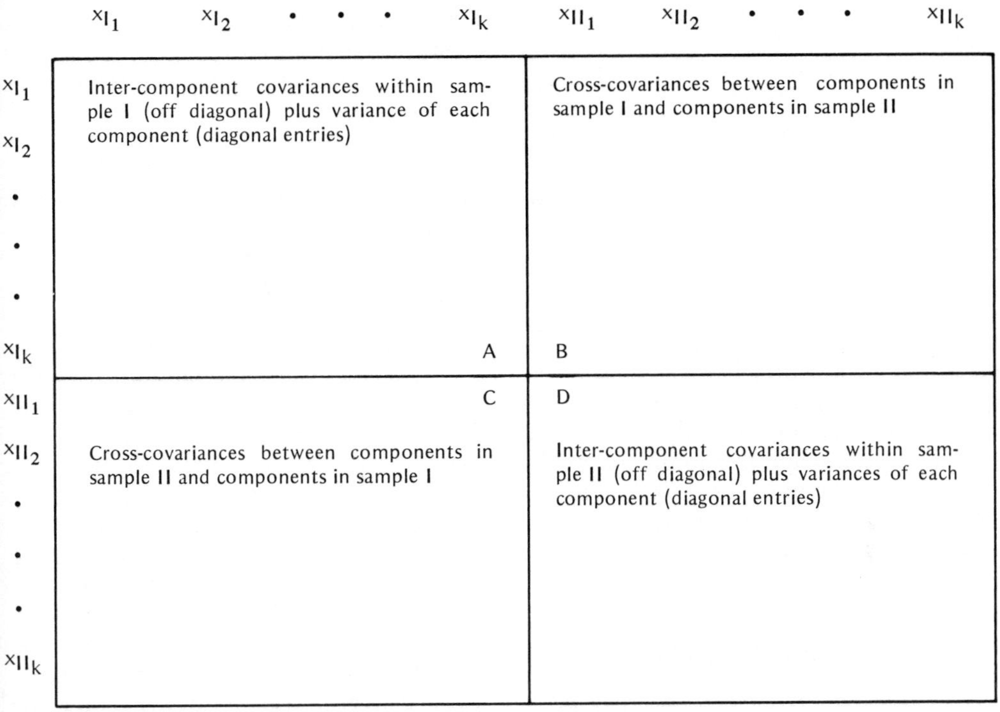

	x_{I_1}	x_{I_2}	$\bullet$ $\bullet$ $\bullet$	x_{I_k}	x_{II_1}	x_{II_2}	$\bullet$ $\bullet$ $\bullet$	x_{II_k}
x_{I_1} x_{I_2} $\bullet$ $\bullet$ $\bullet$ x_{I_k}	Inter-component covariances within sample I (off diagonal) plus variance of each component (diagonal entries) A				Cross-covariances between components in sample I and components in sample II B			
x_{II_1} x_{II_2} $\bullet$ $\bullet$ $\bullet$ x_{II_k}	Cross-covariances between components in sample II and components in sample I C				Inter-component covariances within sample II (off diagonal) plus variances of each component (diagonal entries) D			

Figure 3.   Portrayal of within composite and cross-composite covariances when two composites are being considered.

tant point is that we now have an estimate for the correlation between any two samples expressed in terms of the data from just one administration of just one sample and this correlation has been derived without formal assumptions of equivalence (parallelism) or unit rank. It is the basic reliability formula given by Tryon (1957) and is algebraically equivalent to KR-20, Coefficient Alpha, the Hoyt coefficient, and the average of all possible split half coefficients. Only its interpretation is different.

The standard error of measurement can also be derived via sampling considerations and its estimation formula is the same as for the classic theory. However, without equivalence assumptions it is no longer a constant for each individual, but is an average across people. Further, if the universe (true) score is seen as the limit of the average sample score as the number of samples increases without bound, then it can also be shown that:

$$r_{x_I x_{II}} = \frac{S_T^2}{S_x^2}$$

Under the sampling model, test-retest and equivalent forms correlations are not reliability coefficients since they include sources of variation that cannot be accounted for and they do not give the correlation of the sample with the universe score.

Stratified Domain Sampling

The basic reliability coefficient under the sampling model is given a different interpretation if it is conceptually possible to *stratify* the universe of content in some manner.

Stratification implies that the population proportions for different types of content (e.g., verbal fluency versus number facility) or different levels of difficulty are knowable. If items could be sampled to match these proportions, content sampling error should be less and reliability would be higher. However, since basic coefficient is based on non-stratified random sampling it must necessarily be a lower bound for what could be obtained if stratification were possible. Under stratified sampling the correct method of estimation would be some form of the split half coefficient which permits each strata to be represented equally in each sample. Thus, although the sampling model does not assume unidimensionality to derive its basic equation, the estimate is a lower bound to reliability if the domain is indeed not of unit rank.

Is There a Population?

But what of the obvious fact that strict random sampling of components or items is not possible? Loevinger (1965) has argued that it makes little sense to think of a population of content since one has never been shown to exist; and researchers do not sample items or components, they create them. Responses to this criticism have come from several directions. Cronbach et al. (1963) argue that it is not necessary to enumerate the population. All we need do is to conceptualize it and be able to identify individual components as either belonging or not belonging to it. Following this notion, Nunnally (1967) argues that even though components are *composed,* not sampled, once we have constructed a measure, it is permissible to think of it as a sample from a population that it resembles. Hopefully, this would be the population of interest. Finally, a number of investigators (Bormuth, 1970; Guttman & Schlesinger, 1967; Hively, Patterson, & Page, 1968; Osburn, 1968) have devised rules for constructing test items in particular content areas, which in effect define a universe of such items.

The argument over whether it is possible to conceptualize a universe of content is hazy at best, but certainly no worse than arguments about populations in other areas of statistical inference. Conceptually it seems quite reasonable to define a population in terms of the sample that was randomly drawn from it.

THE GENERALIZABILITY MODEL

The next step beyond sampling theory has been the generalizability model first systemized by Cronbach, Rajaratnam, and Gleser (1963) and since amplified (Cronbach, Gleser, Nanda, & Rajaratnam, 1972). The notion of randomly sampling components from a universe remains central to the theory but the conceptualization of what's meant by "universe" is given a much broader interpretation. Instead of talking about items, or components of *content,* the generalizability model speaks of sampling "conditions of measurement" which include additional sources of variation besides substantive content.

For example, suppose the job performance of a group of individuals is rated on a number of tasks by a number of raters at several different times. The traditional view of a content domain would focus on the task items as samples from the universe of all such performance tasks. However, there are most likely systematic differences among raters of how they assign scores on each of the items; and there are probably systematic differences among scores obtained on a task at different times. Thus task items, raters, and different times all could produce variation in the total rating score and all qualify as potential elements of the universe. In Cronbach et al. terminology tasks, raters, and time are *facets* of the universe. Individual task items, individual raters, and specific times are all *conditions* of measurement. If the individuals in the sample perform a task (e.g., typing) in the context of different jobs (e.g., stenographer versus executive secretary) then "jobs" would constitute still another facet of the universe. Likewise, if a factor analyst groups the tasks into relatively independent clusters the result is several content facets where before there had been only one.

Cronbach et al. and others have suggested that it is easier to think of the make-up of the universe if we adopt an analysis of variance framework. The ANOVA framework for reliability which evolved at the University of London during the late 1940s included only one facet (content items) which was completely crossed with subjects (i.e., people) yielding a two-way ANOVA with one case per cell. It should come naturally to think of more complex universes in terms of more complex ANOVA designs.

Suppose each individual in the above example was rated on each of ten performance tasks by three raters at the same point in time. Since time does not vary, it is not a facet, but both tasks and raters are. Moreover, they are completely crossed. We thus have a completely crossed three-way ANOVA with one case per cell. If ratings of each person were made by each rater at several points in time in counterbalanced order the result would be a completely crossed four-way.

Rather than measure each individual on each combination of facet conditions some facets could be "nested" within others. For example, each individual could be rated by three *different raters,* in which case raters would be nested within individuals. Likewise each individual could be rated on a different sample of tasks from the same universe of tasks. Tasks would then be nested within people. In the testing area this is analogous to giving each subject a different sample of test items, supposedly from the same population of test items. Cronbach et al. (1963) originally referred to the case of everyone being measured on the same items as a *matched design* and contrasted it with the *unmatched design* in which each subject responded to a different sample of items. More recently (Cronbach et al., 1972) they use the crossed versus nested terminology, which is more in keeping with ANOVA jargon.

Obviously, if the ANOVA framework is followed we can also make a distinction between fixed and random effects (i.e., facets). In the above example people are supposedly random and perhaps tasks are too, but what about raters? If we are only concerned about the reliability of performance scores when these same three raters are used then raters can be considered as a fixed effect. If we wish to generalize to a population of such raters then a random model makes more sense.

The nice thing about an ANOVA formulation is that it guides us into thinking about each facet as a source of variation in the total score; and, if things don't get too complex and we have sufficient degrees of freedom, we may even be able to estimate empirically the variance attributable to each source.

At this point we should not lose sight of the basic aim which is to determine the "generalizability" of the observed scores we have in hand. Generalizable to what? Well, to the universe, of course. One index of the degree of generalizability is the correlation between scores on the observed sample of conditions and scores on the universe of conditions. If conditions are sampled randomly, then it can easily be shown that the correlation between any two random samples is, on the average, equal to the square of the correlation between the sample and universe score. The reasoning is identical to that used when Tryon's theory of domain sampling was discussed.

Given the way the generalizability model defines a universe, it should be obvious that a particular "test" (i.e., set of items or measurement operations) can have more than one generalizability coefficient, depending on which facets are fixed and which are allowed to vary. In the previous example of rating performance tasks the generalizability coefficient would be different if one rater were used for all individuals or if several raters were used and the mean differences among raters were allowed to become part of "measurement error." Also, the value for generalizability would be different if all the ratings were obtained at one point in time rather than at different points in time. Again, any number of generalizability coefficients are possible, depending on which facets are held constant and which are allowed to vary when data are collected.

Computing several coefficients instead of just one should provide a great deal of information in most studies. This comparison is not unlike our previous discussion of the different things to be learned from computing the various types of reliability coefficients. The major benefits of the Cronbach et al. (1972) treatment are that everything is integrated within an ANOVA framework and many of the previous gaps are filled in.

Two additional features of the Cronbach et al. model distinguish it from previous views of reliability. First, the possibility is allowed that various kinds of measurement errors are not independent of various individual characteristics and thus result in different standard errors of measurement for different people. Second, a distinction is made between the research used to determine the reliability or generalizability of a measure (G study) and the later activity of actually making predictions or decisions with the same measure (D study). The information of real interest is the reliability of the sample of measurement conditions to be used in the D study; however, we may have available either a larger or smaller sample of conditions for the G study. Ideally, the G study should include variation on a larger number of facets with sufficient degrees of freedom such that generalizability (reliability) could be estimated for a number of different situations that might prevail in the D study.

To handle these kinds of contingencies, Cronbach et al. (1963, 1972) use a generalized ANOVA treatment and seek to estimate generalizability or reliability via the *intraclass correlation* that's appropriate for a given set of circumstances. The basic model on which they build is the Cornfield and Tukey (1956) two-way analysis mentioned earlier. The composition of expected mean squares is shown below for the completely random two-way ANOVA with one observation per cell, as would be the case if rows correspond to persons and columns to items (or measurement "conditions"), and both were sampled (at least conceptually) from a much larger population.

$$EMS \text{ rows}$$
$$\text{(people)} = \sigma_{error}^2 + \sigma_{res}^2 + n_c\sigma_p^2$$
$$EMS \text{ columns}$$
$$\text{(conditions)} = \sigma_{error}^2 + \sigma_{res}^2 + n_p\sigma_c^2$$
$$EMS \text{ residual } = \sigma_{error}^2 + \sigma_{res}^2$$

If the data are gathered via a matched (crossed) design, then the different components, or measurement conditions, serve as columns and individuals as rows (e.g., each column could correspond to each item on paper and pencil test). An unbiased estimate of the intra-class correlation, or the ratio of the variance due to individuals to the total variance, is given by:

$$r_{xx} = \frac{MS_p - MS_r}{MS_p + \dfrac{(k_i - k_{i'})\, MS_r}{k_{i'}}}$$

where:

$MS_p =$ mean square for people (rows)

$MS_r =$ mean square for the residual

$k_i \ \ =$ number of components in G study

$k_{i'} \ =$ number of components in D study

In the Cronbach et al. formulation this intra-class correlation is the ratio of the estimated universe score variance to the estimated observed (sample) score variance. It is also the correlation between two random samples from the defined universe, if all other conditions are held constant.

If $k_i = k_{i'}$ as when the same number of conditions are used in the reliability study as in the predictability study, the above expression reduces to the Hoyt coefficient discussed earlier and is numerically equivalent to the Kuder-Richardson and Coefficient Alpha as well.

If data are unmatched but each person is observed on the same number of variables, the two-way ANOVA must necessarily reduce to a one-way in which columns correspond to people, items are nested within people, and there are an equal number of observations (conditions) per column. The estimate of the intra-class correlation thus becomes:

$$r_{xx} = \frac{MS_p - MS_{wp}}{MS_p + \dfrac{(k_i - k_{i'})MS_{wp}}{k_{i'}}}$$

The only difference between this estimate of r_{xx} and the previous one is that the mean square for the residual is replaced by the mean square within columns (people). If the data were in fact crossed, but we still wanted to use the above estimate, then MS_{wp} could be obtained from a two-way analysis by pooling the residual and between persons sums of squares. This would be counterproductive since the residual is the appropriate error term. The moral is that some information is lost by resorting to an unmatched or nested design, if it's not really necessary.

An occasion may arise when data in the reliability or G study are crossed but will be nested in the D study. For example, in the reliability study all subjects might be rated by the same raters, but when real predictions are made different people will be rated by different raters. If k_i conditions are used in the crossed G study but $k_{i'}$ conditions will be used in the nested D study then r_{xx} may be estimated by:

$$r_{xx} = k_{i'}(MS_p - MS_r) \, / \, [k_{i'}MS_p \\ + (k_i/n_p)MS_c \\ + (k_i n_p - n_i' n_i - n_p/n_p)MS_r]$$

where n_p equals the number of people in the G study sample and MS_c equals the mean square for columns (conditions). If the same three raters were used for each person in the G study but a different set of three raters were used for each person in the D study, this expression would estimate the reliability of the average of the three raters, if they were randomly drawn from the same population that provided the raters used in the G study.

These are three basic intra-class correlations presented by Cronbach et al. (1963). The 1972 treatment extends the ANOVA framework to a number of more complex situations. In each situation the aim is to compute the variance attributable to each source. From these variance components the intra-class correlation representing the ratio of estimated universe score variance to estimated observed score variance can be computed. The variations are too numerous and complex to be presented here but they are there for the taking in the 1972 volume. Again, one of the beauties of the ANOVA design is that once the data are collected in a G study the pooling of appropriate variance components permits a kind of simulation of what might be the situation in a D study and the appropriate intra-class correlation can be computed.

The Generalizability Model Summarized

To summarize, the touchstone of their argument is to restate the problem of reliability as the extent to which scores on a sample of observations can generalize to the class (population) of observations to which they belong. This forces the investigator to define the universe he or she has in mind. If the universe of interest includes observations made at different points in time, as when averaging ratings obtained from different raters on different days, then the sample must be representative of the time points comprising the population. If the universe includes several content factors then each of them must be represented in the sample. If the universe includes several item formats then the different formats must be represented in the sample.

This kind of model removes the somewhat arbitrary distinctions among coefficients of "stability," "equivalence," and "internal consistency" and replaces them with a general continuum of representativeness. It also makes the concepts of convergent and discriminate validity (Campbell & Fiske, 1959) more flexible. If we *define* our universe to include different methods for measuring the same factor then high convergent validity, in the Campbell and Fiske sense, would be desirable. However, our model of say "garden variety anxiety" may specify that anxiety as measured by paper and pencil inventory and anxiety as measured by interviewer observation are not to be included in the same universe. That is, they do not represent the same construct. Under these circumstances, convergent validity is to be avoided.

By a similar argument, the correction for attenuation is placed in a clearer perspective. The coefficient used to make the correction must be based on precisely the same universe as the score being corrected. If the investigator can't argue convincingly that this is so, then he or she has no business making corrections for attenuation.

The overall moral is that any interpretation of a "reliability" coefficient must be based on a definition of the universe to which we want to generalize.

VALIDITY

Prior to 1954 the notion of validity was in considerable disarray, and as everyone knows, a special APA committee on test validity and reliability was constituted to assist in instilling a modicum of order. The ensuing technical recommendations (American Psychological Association, 1954) collapsed the competing taxonomies into the now classic formulations of content, concurrent, predictive, and construct validity. There is little need to redefine them here.

What is of some interest is to consider briefly the differences between the original technical recommendations and their first revision published some twelve years later (American Psychological Association, 1966). Most of the debate during these twelve years centered around the meaning and usefulness of construct validity and is also so well known that it need not be repeated. The reader is referred to Cronbach and Meehl (1955), Bechtoldt (1959), and Campbell (1960).

One major confusion regarding construct validity concerns the breadth of its interpretation. In its widest sense one could think of construct validity as pertinent to any theory of behavior. That is, understanding the construct, or knowing the theory, permits a host of predictions about behavior using the construct as the independent variable. In this sense, construct validity is a deductive notion. By contrast, an investigator could be concerned with giving substantive meaning to a particular set of measurement operations (e.g., a specific paper and pencil inventory) for which he was not yet ready to predict empirical relationships. Thus the process becomes inductive and what's being validated is not a theory about some characteristic of individual differences but the content of a particular score. The original technical recommendations made construct validity sound almost synonymous with the standard ingredients of deductive theory building which detracted somewhat from its uniqueness in the validity taxonomy. The 1966 statement of test standards moved away from this position a bit but remained committed to the deductive view. Taking either extreme is not in the best interests of psychometric theory. Viewing construct validity as purely deductive theory building gives it no distinctive reason for being. Also, the psychological study of individual differences is still at a primitive enough level that many promising avenues of research could be dried up prematurely if a deductive approach were required and the first few hypotheses went down the drain. It would seem more productive for a validity model to give investigators some guidance for a certain amount of inductive "fishing" before moving to substantive hypothesis testing. At the other extreme, adopting a strictly inductive view throws away the power of hypothesis testing. If an investigator never sticks his neck out with regard to what he thinks his instrument is measuring, he will never establish surplus meaning or rule out competing explanations as to why his measure acts the way it does in the empirical world.

A second important distinction regarding construct validity is whether the theory being validated concerns the construct as it is represented by a specific set of measurement operations or whether it is independent of any specific measuring instrument. The latter option again makes construct validity synonymous with the validity of almost any psychological theory and detracts from its unique character. The power of the construct validity notion is derived from its function as means for assessing the validity of a specific measuring instrument intended to measure a human characteristic for which there is no naturally occurring criterion. Thus in a multi-trait multimethod matrix we indeed may not want convergent validity of the usual kind.

At this writing, a second revision of the standards is being prepared but the publication date is as yet uncertain. However, it is interesting to note in a recent draft of the proposed guidelines (Joint Committee on the Revision of Standards, 1973) the locus of construct validity was more firmly rooted in the specific set of operations used to measure it; and by implication, construct validity has both inductive and deductive properties.

In sum, construct validity applies when the investigator wants a measure of a characteristic which is deemed important by somebody but for which there is no already available indicator. The entity being validated is a set of measurement operations and the process should include both an inductive and deductive component. The following kinds of studies make useful contributions to construct validity:

1. Factor or cluster analyses of the components making up the total measure.

2. A wide range of reliability estimates.

3. Correlations with other variables theorized to measure the same thing.

4. Correlations with other variables which might account for or rule out potential sources of variance in the instrument being validated. Such sources of variance might be associated with substantive content (e.g., verbal fluency) or methodological elements (e.g., item format, social desirability).

5. If deemed appropriate, a formal use of the multi-trait multimethod matrix.

6. Experimental studies using the measure being validated either as the dependent variable or as a blocking variable.

7. Establishment of content validity via the judged appropriateness of the sampling plan and method used to obtain the measurement operations.

8. Process analysis. This would entail the detailed questioning of subjects as to why they responded a certain way to a test item or the questioning of raters as to how and why they actually chose a rating for an individual. The Ss or raters should be using a process reasonably close to that which the researcher had in mind when he developed the instrument. Such process data is often an eye opener.

Almost all of these different lines of evidence can be used in both an inductive and deductive manner. At some point, however, the investigator must get serious and stick his neck out with predictions about how the instrument will act in empirical studies. Two principal characteristics make one series of hypotheses better than another. First, more construct validity can be attributed to the instrument to the extent that the hypotheses being tested are non-overlapping. That is, much less is gained from confirming the same hypothesis ten times than from confirming ten hypotheses of very different kinds. For example, if we are validating a measure of "garden variety anxiety" we could predict its correlation with grade point average in ten different random samples from the same population or we could make ten very different predictions, such as the responsiveness of the anxiety scores to threats of low grades, the kinds of reliability which would be high and low, the correlation of the anxiety test with intelligence, etc. Second, more construct validity is accumulated to the extent that hypotheses are more "stringent" and are easier to negate. For example, it is not very stringent and we don't learn very much if we support the hypothesis that under conditions X, Y, and Z, garden variety anxiety correlates with job performance somewhere between $-.60$ and $+.60$. It would mean a great deal more to confirm a prediction that these two variables are correlated between $+.30$ and $+.40$.

If construct validity is viewed in the above fashion it does have a unique place in psychometric theory. However, we should keep in mind that it does not come cheaply, is a never ending process, and is not an easy out for organizations which must make equitable and valid predictions about specific criterion outcomes that in fact do exist.

Validity and the Generalizability Model

At the risk of being simple minded, we might further collapse the validity taxonomy into criterion versus non-citerion related validation. One is almost tempted to label it practical versus scientific validity or validity for understanding versus validity for decision making. That is, content and construct validity are geared toward the production of generalizable knowledge and "surplus" meaning while criterion centered validities have to do with the accuracy of practical decision making.

Cronbach et al. (1963) made an attempt to integrate certain aspects of reliability and non-criterion centered validity within their concepts of generalizability. Although their logic is not spelled out in detail, the connection proceeds something like this: Generalizability refers to the degree to which behavior on a sample of measurement conditions can be generalized to a particular population of conditions. Again, the term condition is more inclusive than the term item and a sample of conditions might include variation in the times at which various items are administered, and/or different test administrators at different times. As another example, suppose each individual were rated on each of ten rating scales and each scale were used by a different rater. This procedure includes rater variations as well as scale content variations. Having a different sample of raters for each person (unmatched design) adds yet another source of variation in measurement conditions. Since it is possible to estimate generalizability from the data generated by only one sample, a priori predictions can be made about the magnitude of the generalizability coefficient as systematic changes are made in the conditions or facets making up the sample. For example, we might predict that the generalizability coefficient should increase from .50 to .70 if a ten-item inventory measuring "garden variety anxiety" were administered by using a different administrator for every person in the sample because the differential reaction to authority figures is one thing we want to include in our construct and this procedure builds in differences across people for all items.

The conclusion reached by Cronbach et al. (1963) was that generalizability is synonymous with much of the construct validity notion. Also, if all the different sources of variation in measurement conditions are held constant *except* content (strictly defined) then the generalizability coefficient reduces to an empirical indication of content validity, as internal consistency reliability indices always have been.

Decision Centered Validity

During recent years considerable discussion has also centered around the appropriate models for assessing criterion centered validity. The villain has been the so-called classic validity model in the form of the normal bivariate distribution. The model implies (a) there is one normally distributed criterion or criterion composite; (b) there is one normally distributed predictor or predictor composite; (c) the relationship between them is linear and homoscedastic; and (d) the index of validity is some form of the product moment correlation coefficient.

Numerous alternatives to the one predictor-one criterion configuration have been proposed and these are discussed elsewhere in this volume. What concerns us here is the role of the correlation coefficient itself. Specifically, alternatives to the *PM* coefficient as an index of accuracy and alternatives to the linear view of association are discussed.

As an index of the level of practical predictive accuracy the *PM* coefficient is difficult to translate into meaningful terms. How useful is a value of .55? Most practical men of prediction have a vague feeling that .55 is reasonably good but they would be hard pressed to say why explicitly. Falling back on statistical significance and the probability of a Type I error is no solution (Bakan, 1967; Lykken, 1968; Rozeboom, 1960), although people still submit manuscripts to journals in which statistical significance is implicitly equated to practical or scientific significance.

One alternative is to think of the prediction problem as a task in predicting discrete outcomes. Almost all practical situations can be translated into the problem of predicting "criterion categories" of various kinds, the most frequent being success and failure. Once the problem is recast in these terms it becomes meaningful to talk about validity, or accuracy, as the proportion of correct predictions.

If the variable to be predicted is a dichotomy, the bivariate distribution reduces to a four-fold table and four different outcomes are possible: (a) correctly predict hi-criterion category; (b) correctly predict low-criterion category; (c) overpredict (false positive); and (d) underpredict (false negative). This simple arrangement is shown in Figure 4. Certain things become obvious from looking at the figure. The proportion of correct predictions is a function of the criterion split (base rate), the predictor split (cutting score), and the degree of association between the predictor and the criterion.

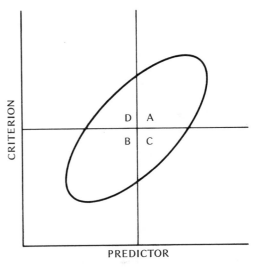

Figure 4. The continuous bivariate distribution between predictor and criterion reduced to a dichotomous prediction decision.

The two different kinds of errors are affected differentially by changes in the cutting score and base rates. For example, moving the cutting score to the right reduces the proportion of false positives at the expense of more false negatives. The Taylor-Russell tables (1939) take advantage of this fact and portray the increase in the percent of correct predictions as the cutting score is raised, given a particular base rate and correlation coefficient. However, the tables deal with only one kind of error—false positives—and one kind of correct prediction—hi hits. Thus, in the Taylor-Russell sense the percent of correct predictions is $A/(A + C)$. What is often forgotten is that this choice of an accuracy statistic is very much a value judgment by somebody. Traditionally, the false positive (section C in Figure 3) may have been the prediction mistake to avoid in personnel or educational selection. However, the weight of public policy seemed to swing, at least for awhile, in favor of minimizing the false negative, especially with regard to minority and disadvantaged groups. It seems safe to predict that we will endure considerable conflict and soul searching before the issue of who bears the implicit and explicit costs of both false positives and false negatives is decided. Nevertheless, it must be considered, and the issue is obscured by looking only at the correlation coefficient as an index of accuracy.

Relative to the base rate, maximum gain in decision accuracy from a specific validity coefficient is obtained when the base rate equals .50. As the base rate becomes more extreme in either direction, achieving large increases in the number of correct decisions becomes progressively more difficult (i.e., takes greater validity and/or smaller selection ratios). At some point, when the increase in correct decisions is compared to the cost of prediction, the prediction system may not seem worth it. If the proportion of people who fail is very small it may make more sense to use the base rate and predict "success" for everyone. In a selection situation we might select on the basis of first come first served, random assignment, or some other strategy deemed as equitable by prevailing community standards. If the proportion of people who succeed is very small the situation is a bit different. In a selection situation nobody would be hired if we used the base rate to predict. It would make more sense to restructure the applicant pool to make the base rate less extreme. To take an obvious example, accept as applicants only those individuals who have successfully performed the job in the past in some other organization. More subtle examples should come to mind.

Ignoring expense for the moment, we should remember that ,if the predictor has greater than zero validity there will almost always be *some* improvement in predictive accuracy in excess of the base rate, although it may not be great. The "almost" will be examined below. It is also true that under certain conditions the base rate can be beaten even when a predictor has *zero* validity (in the correlational sense), but let's ignore these unnamed conditions for the moment.

If, as in the Taylor-Russell tables, the primary concern is with the false positives, the base rate can be beaten by setting a higher and higher predictor cutting score. If the total number of errors is important then the base rate can still be beaten if the cutting score is set at the point where the predictor distributions for the high and low criterion groups intersect (Cureton, 1957), as in Figure 5–a. As shown in Blum and Naylor (1968) this rule holds even for peculiar distributions, as when there are two points of intersection (Figure 5–b). In this instance, applicants would be accepted if they scored between the two cutting scores (CS_1 and CS_2) and rejected otherwise. The classic example concerns aptitude measures as a predictor and a criterion that individuals below CS_1 are not capable of meeting and people above CS_2 are too disinterested to meet. However, we should keep in mind that if the cutting scores are not set properly even a valid predictor can yield less accuracy than the base rate (Meehl & Rosen, 1955).

Notice that focusing empirically on the proportion of correct predictions rather than the correlation coefficient and making no assumptions about the form of the distribution takes advantage of the non-linear as well as linear components of association between the two variables. If the twisted pear phenomenon holds (Fisher, 1959), then predictions will be better at the bottom of the predictor distribution and it will be much easier to avoid false negatives than false positives. As always, we are faced with the question of whether departures from the normal bivariate distribution are real or merely re-

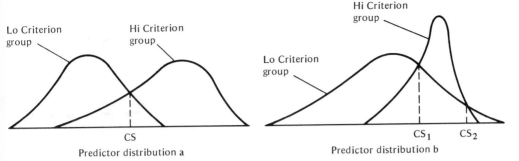

Figure 5. Optimal cutting scores when the objective is to minimize the total number of prediction errors (i.e., false positives + false negatives).

flect sampling error. If we opt for the latter then it might be more advantageous in the long run to "smooth out" the frequencies in the four-fold table by computing the product moment correlation and converting the coefficient to the corresponding proportions of hits and misses via the Taylor-Russell tables, if both predictor and criterion are dichotomous; or with the Tiffin and Mc-Cormick (1965) theoretical expectancy charts if we wish to look at five categories on the predictor.

However, Curtis (1971) has quite insightfully pointed out that even though the correlation coefficient may underestimate the degree of association in a curvilinear relationship, if the variables are continuous, the phi coefficient will overestimate the relative number of correct predictions when the variables are dichotomous and the splits depart very much from 50-50. Thus, entering a phi coefficient in the Taylor-Russell tables would be inappropriate if the splits suggested nonlinearity. Curtis suggests using Goodman and Kruskal's (1963) lambda statistic when the association between two dichotomous variables is being examined. The value for lambda is directly interpretable as the percent of reduction in total errors made by using the predictor rather than the base rate.

$$\lambda = \frac{\text{decrease in error frequency}}{\text{error frequency without } X} = \frac{\Sigma f_e - f_r}{N - f_r}$$

where:

Σf_e = sum of largest cell frequencies in the columns

f_r = largest row total

We in industrial and organizational psychology would do well to get more familiar with lambda.

At this point it might be informative to ask how the correlation coefficient is related to the proportion of correct predictions if the bivariate distribution is indeed linear and homoscedastic. One aspect of the conventional wisdom interprets the correlation coefficient in terms of the coefficient of determination, or r^2. The implication is that the goodness of a predictor is a linear function of r^2, or the "proportion of variance explained." However, Curtis and Alf (1969) have shown that the proportion of total correct predictions (i.e., considering both kinds) is a near linear function of r, not r^2. Thus, an increase in predictability from $r = .20$ to $r = .40$ is as valuable as an increase from .50 to .70, providing we accept the proportion of correct predictions as the appropriate index. Further, Brogden (1946) has shown that the increase in the criterion mean resulting from selection is also a linear function of r.

The correlation coefficient can be transformed to its equivalent increase in the criterion mean via the Naylor-Shine tables (Blum & Naylor, 1968). The existing criterion distribution in the organization is assumed to be unit normal and the validity coefficient is taken as a concurrent validity computed on the existing organizational population which was previously selected by whatever procedures have been in use. Then for a particular selection ratio the increase in the criterion mean (in standard score units) which would be obtained by employing the new selection method can be read from the table. Keep in mind that using the Naylor-Shine tables, or for that matter the Taylor-Russell tables, to convert r to a more meaningful index is dependent on the degree of *linear* association.

Curtis (1966) has also argued that since there is a strong possibility that many of our prediction situations resemble the twisted pear (Fisher, 1959), it might be fruitful to think of the bivariate distribution in discrete chunks rather than as a continuous function. If, as in the twisted pear, good criterion predictions can be made for the lower part of the prediction continuum but not for the upper part, it might be useful to select a cutting score below which the predictor score is used and above which a blanket prediction corresponding to the larger criterion category is used (i.e., the base rate information). There are sampling problems associated with setting the cutting score, but the idea has considerable appeal.

Important Parameters Frequently Forgotten

The above discussion of cutting scores and errors of prediction has been fairly simple minded in terms of all the relevant parameters that might possibly be involved. Again, the appropriate portrayal of the cutting score(s) and the prediction errors which it yields is a plot of the predictor distributions for both criterion groups, as in Figure 5. Consider a list of all the parameters contained in this picture. They are:

1. The difference between the means of the two distributions (validity).

2. The number of observations in the two distributions (base rate).

3. The cutting score(s).

4. The shape of each distribution.

5. The difference between the variances of each distribution.

So far we have discussed some of the implications of differences in validity, base rate, and cutting score, as well as touching on the problem of the shape of the distribution. We have said nothing about what happens when the variability of the two distributions is different and have been implicitly assuming they are the same. It follows that we also have not considered the interactive effects of variance differences with the other parameters.

Fortunately, Rorer, Hoffman, LaForge, and Hsieh (1966) provide a clear statement of some of the implications of these additional considerations and their paper deserves careful consideration. They present a series of tables to facilitate the selection of cutting scores in various situations; however, the development of their tables is dependent on the assumption that the predictor distributions are normally distributed (Taylor-Russell and Naylor-Shine assume the same thing), and differential values are not assigned to different types of errors. To enter the tables one must estimate the difference between the two means in standard score form (i.e., the predictor validity), the base rate, and the ratio of the two standard deviations. The tables then provide the cutting score, or scores (if there are two), the proportion of false positives, the proportion of false negatives, and the proportion of the total group that will be misclassified. The usual cautions about sampling error apply.

We observed previously that if the base rates depart very far from 50/50, relatively small changes in the cutting score can lead to relatively large changes in the number of prediction errors. The Rorer, Hoffman, LaForge, and Hsieh (1966) analysis illustrates how the same danger arises when the variances of the two distributions begin to depart from each other. When the base rate departs from 50/50 *and* the variances depart from equality, the going really gets sticky, and incorrect cutting scores create even more trouble and precise cutting scores become even more crucial. One useful feature of the tables is that they permit an investigator to work backwards from a given validity and estimate how far base rates can depart from 50/50 before even the optimal cutting score(s) will not improve predictions over the base rate.

The tables also illustrate several other interesting points. For example, it is possible for no cutting scores to exist (as in Figure 6-*a*). Here one distribution is completely contained in the other. Also, even though the predictor means for the two criterion groups may be identical (as in Figure 6-*b*) and validity is zero, the proper cutting scores may still be able to improve the accuracy of prediction over and above the base rate. The leverage is provided by the difference in variances. Finally the tables show how changes in cutting scores may differentially affect false positives, false negatives, and total errors as the base rate varies and the ratio of the two standard deviations varies.

From Accuracy to Utility

We have now moved from a notion of predictive validity in the form of a correlation coefficient to predictive accuracy in the form of the proportion of correct predictions in excess of the base rate. One could still wonder about how to interpret the value of a particular increase in predictive accuracy. Given a specific base rate, is the value of a 15 percent increase in predictive accuracy always the same?

Among others, Cronbach and Gleser (1965) have reminded us that it is not. The value of an increase in predictive accuracy is dependent upon the costs associated with obtaining it versus the payoffs to the organization from each additional correct prediction. In most situations the cost of increasing predictive accuracy for managerial positions may be considerable but they pale beside the payoff from making even one more correct selection decision. In short, Cronbach and Gleser moved us from a concern with predictive validity and predictive accuracy to a concern for predictive usefulness.

The Cronbach and Gleser volume has become a classic in spite of the fact that the prescriptions for how to judge validity make such demands on our scaling technology that they are not possible to implement in any strict sense. The utility of the formulations lies instead in posing the very central issues that always must be considered in any validity judgment situation, however imperfectly, and deserve at least a brief summarization here.

Cronbach and Gleser's basic definitional algorithm is as follows:

$$\Delta u = \sigma_y r_{xy} E(x') - C_x$$

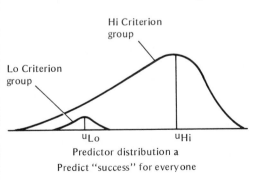

Predictor distribution a

Predict "success" for everyone

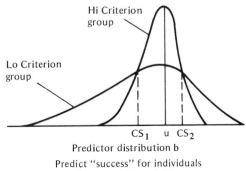

Predictor distribution b

Predict "success" for individuals between CS_1 and CS_2

Figure 6. Portrayal of the effects of extreme differences in base rates and predictor variances on dichotomous prediction decisions.

where:

Δu = net gain in utility

r_{xy} = validity coefficient obtained concurrently on the *present* organizational population

σ_y = standard deviation of the payoff (criterion) distribution

$E(x')$ = the ordinate of the unit normal distribution at the point on the base line corresponding to the cutting score (selection ratio) on the predictor distribution

C_x = the cost of obtaining the predictor information

To use this algorithm effectively, it should be computed for a variety of alternative predictors, including the one currently in use. If this could be done the interaction of the validity and costs of prediction for different predictors would be made quite clear.

The problem, of course, is the metric for the payoff distribution. It must reflect the differential payoffs to the organization associated with different jobs and different organizational needs. It seems obvious that the value for σ_y would vary tremendously across situations. If only it could be measured! Also, since the basic algorithm involves the correlation coefficient, another problem is the implication that payoff is linearly associated with the predictor continuum, and that false positives and false negatives are given equal weight.

A number of interpretive principles flow from the utility theory view. Some of the major ones are as follows:

1. The predictor with the highest validity coefficient may not have the highest utility, compared to alternatives, if:

    a) It is proportionately more costly than it is more valid.

    b) It predicts a criterion that is proportionately less important.

2. If adaptive treatments are possible, then the gain in utility given a gain in validity is no longer linear but becomes posi-

tively accelerated. For example, a validity increase of .40 to .60 is worth greater and greater payoff to the extent that the sample can be partitioned on the basis of the predictor score and different training or different task assignments provided for the people in each category.

3. Relative to the choice among using two tests as a battery (i.e., weighted sum), sequentially (e.g., successive hurdles), or singly (i.e., just one of them), the model replies:

    a) As the selection ratio moves from .50 to the extremes, the strategy of choice goes from using both tests as a battery to using them sequentially, to using just one test. This progression is speeded up to the extent that the tests are intercorrelated and have different costs associated with them. Obviously, if the costs are quite different and the predictors are highly intercorrelated, it literally "pays" to use the cheapest one.

    b) A similar progression of choices exists as the difference between the two validity coefficients becomes greater and greater, other things, such as inter-*r*'s and costs, being equal.

4. In sequential testing, the predictor given first is the one with the greatest difference between cost and benefit. This is in contrast to the more conventional wisdom, which says to use the most "valid" predictor first.

In sum, the Cronbach and Gleser treatment highlights a number of considerations that people interested in practical decision making should keep in mind. Without indulging in a prolonged argument and lengthy documentation, I would be willing to stipulate that (a) few organizations consider the relative size of the payoff matrix, except for jobs that are extremely different; (b) that few organizations make even rough comparisons of alternative selection systems;

and, (c) that few organizations really consider the full costs of researching (if research is done), implementing, and maintaining various selection and prediction systems.

Further Utility Considerations

Lest we try to ignore utility considerations on the grounds of scaling difficulty, Darlington and Stauffer (1966), and Rorer, Hoffman, and Hsieh (1966) have convincingly argued that we cannot hide from the real world so easily. It may, indeed, be a difficult task to measure utility but it is there nevertheless and no matter what type of prediction model is used, utilities play an important role even if unrecognized. For example, if we act as if the value of all kinds of errors are equal, we have made an implicit value judgment about utilities that may be so far from the "truth" (as judged by "reasonable" men) that the organization is seriously hurt because of it. The two papers cited above make the case that if we drop back from thinking about utility in terms of continua, ignore costs for the time being, and again adopt a decision-making framework (e.g., prediction of a dichotomous outcome) much ground can be regained if the *ratio* of the utilities for false positives and false negatives or the *ratio* of utilities for correct predictions of success and correct predictions of failure can be reasonably estimated.

In some prediction situations the cutting scores may be a "given," as when the predictor is a single test item that is scored right/wrong. For this situation Darlington and Stauffer (1966) present a very simple method for trying out different utility ratios, such that the relative utility of using the predictor versus using the base rate can be determined. Their example concerns the case when a dichotomous prediction is made and one of two treatments (drugs versus counseling) is available. If instead of drugs versus counseling we prescribe hire versus not hire

the example is transformed to the personnel selection situation. To complete the transformation to a personnel selection example, we should also use different utilities than did Darlington and Stauffer. In their example, all outcomes are assigned positive utilities which is analogous to saying that not hiring someone who would have succeeded has positive utility for the organization. It's possible but not probable.

Consider then the situation portrayed in Table 1. The first matrix shows the proportions of people at each possible outcome. The second matrix shows a hypothetical set of relative utilities for each outcome. Matrix three contains the cross products for each cell.

The relative utility of using the predictor is the sum of the cell entries in matrix 3 in Table 1 or $+2.8$. If we do not use the predictor, we can either predict success for everybody or predict failure for everybody. Our estimate of the base rate is that 40 percent of the population will succeed and 60 percent will fail. If we predict failure for everybody, the relative utility is $(.60 \times 10) + (.40 \times -5) = 4.0$. If we predict success for everybody the relative utility is $(.60 \times -30) + (.40 \times 10) = -14.0$. Obviously, predicting success for everybody is not the thing to do and predicting failure for everybody is somewhat better than using the predictor. However, if the *costs* of not filling the job outweigh the *gain* in overall utility from hiring no one, the predictor should be used. The thing that produced this result is the relatively small utility assigned to someone who succeeds. However, if these relative utilities are deemed reasonable, the moral is that a rough but reasonable assignment of relative utilities can give a more detailed picture of what's going on in a selection situation than we have without an assignment of relative utilities.

It should be noted that the computations in the Darlington and Stauffer paper do not look precisely like the above because they also considered the situation analogous to

TABLE 1
ILLUSTRATIVE EXAMPLE OF RELATIVE UTILITIES APPLIED TO A
DICHOTOMOUS PREDICTION DECISION WITH A FIXED CUTTING
SCORE (i.e., PROPORTION ABOVE CS = .36)

1.	Proportion of total for each outcome state			2.	Relative utilities of each outcome		3.	Products of relative frequencies and relative utilities	
Success	.16	.24	.40	Success	−5	10	Success	−.80	2.40
Failure	.48	.12	.60	Failure	10	−30	Failure	4.80	−3.60
	Predict Failure	Predict Success			Predict Failure	Predict Success		Predict Failure	Predict Success

hiring everyone who scores high and not hiring everyone who scores low, which doesn't seem reasonable in our case.

If the predictor is continuous and we can choose a cutting score, or scores, to maximize utility, then the Rorer, Hoffman, and Hsieh (1966) modification of the Rorer, Hoffman, LaForge, and Hsieh (1966) tables mentioned earlier are appropriate. Again, the tables provide cutting scores for different combinations of: (a) predictor validity; (b) base rate; and (c) the ratio of the predictor score standard deviations for each criterion group. The values in the tables were generated algorithmically given the assumption that the distributions for both criterion groups were unit normal. If relative utilities can be estimated, then Rorer, Hoffman, and Hsieh (1966) provide the following function, which may be used to "adjust" the non-utility weighted base rate.

$$\frac{B'}{1 - B'} =$$

$$\frac{B}{1 - B} \cdot \frac{\text{Utility of true positive} - \text{Utility of false negative}}{\text{Utility of true negative} - \text{Utility of false positive}}$$

where B equals the original base rate and B' is the adjusted base rate with which to enter

the table so as to provide optimum cutting scores with utilities taken into account. The investigator can then "play around" with various utility patterns and note the effects on his situation.

In an insightful application of the Rorer, Hoffman, and Hsieh formulation, Schmidt (in press) has worked backwards from the base rates to recover the utilities for false positive versus false negative prediction errors which Strong unknowingly used when he scored the SVIB by treating the men-in-general and an occupational group as if they were of equal size. In fact, they are quite unequal in the population (e.g., physicians versus MIG) and treating them as equal produces a marked shift in the operative utilities. For example, suppose we assume that a reasonable base rate for physicians in the population of occupations included in the SVIB is .02, that the validity of the scale is as reported by Strong, that optimal cutting scores are used, and that the two types of correct predictions are of equal value. Under these conditions the "recovered" utility for avoiding the error of predicting entry into the men-in-general group when the actual outcome is "physician" is forty-nine times as great as avoiding predicting physician when the individual will actually fall within men-in-general. Schmidt's results are startling and carry the clear message that if we do not use estimates of utilities, they might very well use us in ways we do not understand and of which we are not aware.

ESTIMATING POPULATION PARAMETERS

So far we have not considered the issues related to estimating population values for reliability and validity indices when the entities being sampled are individuals, as distinguished from test items or other measurement conditions. This is the usual kind of statistical estimation and a fair question is why consider it in a chapter on psychometric theory. Unfortunately, certain of the techniques used in the measurement of individual differences and the prediction of criterion outcomes create their own special problems with regard to estimating population parameters. The estimation problem is especially crucial for applied psychology because the population parameter is of immediate practical importance. We are making real decisions that have economic, legal, and humanitarian implications for people and it would be good to know how well we will actually do in the population of interest.

Three different considerations bearing on the estimation problem are discussed below. The first has to do with the conflict between using sample data to *develop* decision rules versus using sample data to *estimate* the worth of the decision rules in the population. The second pertains to the problem of range restriction. The third considers an almost universal constraint forced upon applied psychologists which is that we must estimate population parameters on the basis of data sampled from specific cohorts of the population rather than randomly from the entire population.

Developing Decision Rules Versus Estimation

Consider the following activities in which a differentially oriented applied psychologist might indulge:
- Higher reliability for an inventory is obtained by selecting the most homogeneous or the most stable items from a pool of items.
- Items are selected for a test on the basis of their correlation with a criterion.
- A stepwise multiple regression procedure is used to select and weight predictors in a selection battery.
- A cutting score for a predictor is set by comparing the distribution of predictor scores for high and low criterion groups.
- A moderator variable is developed by selecting items which discriminate between predictable and nonpredictable subgroups.

All of these examples involved looking at sample data and devising empirical rules for how to use the potential sources of information. It is well known that such procedures run the risk of capitalizing on fortuitous errors in the direction of higher reliability, higher validity, or whatever we are trying to maximize. Some of the measures, or predictors, will act the way we would like by chance, but an empirical search technique cannot distinguish between real reliability and fortuitous error or real validity and fortuitous error. If we then determine the reliability, validity, or cutting score of the final scale or battery on the same data on which it was developed, the estimate of the population parameter will be an overestimate. To be more specific, the classic examples of Cureton (1950) and Kurtz (1948) illustrated how quite respectable validity coefficients can be obtained from what are essentially random data. All we need are a large enough pool of components, such that some of them will be valid by chance and an opportunity to be very selective in choosing components for the final measure and/or an opportunity to differentially weight components on the basis of sample data. The reader should keep firmly in mind that the applied psychologist's real interest is the population parameter and that the estimation problem is paramount.

One way to correct for this kind of "error fitting" is to use the derived rules to compute the parameter estimate on an independent sample from the same population. For example, if the most homogeneous or stable items are selected for a test or inventory on the basis of a specific sample then an independent sample must be used to compute the reliability of the total score. If a predictor cutting score is set on the basis of data from one sample then the "hit rate" must be computed on a second sample, using the original cutting score. If multiple regression weights for a set of predictors are computed on one sample then the weights must be applied to the data from a second sample. This is, of course, the classic cross-validation procedure. A second parameter estimate can be obtained by developing the decision rules on the second sample and applying them to the first, in which case the procedure is known as double cross-validation. The flow of double cross-validation is diagrammed in Figure 7.

Cross-validation must be distinguished from mere replication. For example, computing a multiple correlation coefficient again in a second sample increases the N on which the R is based, but it is not cross-validation. The second computation also takes advantage of fortuitous error. The defining characteristic of cross-validation is that prediction rules are derived on one sample and then used on another.

Cross-validation is designed to yield an unbiased estimate of the population value. Unfortunately, it does not. Rather, it trades off one kind of bias for another. Also, the difference between the biased estimate and the cross-validated estimate is often referred to as "shrinkage" and is thought of as an index of the amount of fortuitous error that was fitted in the developmental sample. However, things are not quite so clear here either. To make the discussion easier, suppose we focus on a particular problem, the differential weighting of components to maximize the correlation of the weighted sum with a criterion variable, as in multiple regression or the selection of test items on the basis of their criterion correlations. The issues are the same for the other previously

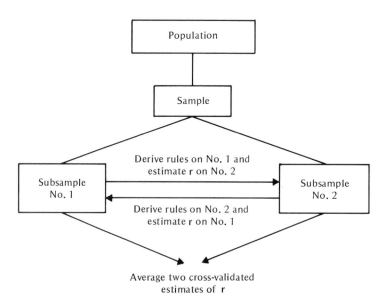

Figure 7.   The classic double cross-validation design.

mentioned examples of using sample data to derive empirical rules for maximizing some function.

We must first get clear as to what's meant by population parameter. In this instance, it is when the very best sample weights we can get are applied to all the data in the population and the weighted total score is correlated with the criterion in the population. That coefficient is the true indicator of how effective our prediction rules will be when applied to all future individuals that walk through the door. The best weights we can get are those derived from all the available *sample* data, assuming that it is a representative sample from the population. Notice that the population parameter of real interest is not the multiple correlation coefficient computed on the entire population or the correlation of the criterion with a test composed of items selected on the basis of data from the entire population. By definition, we can never get those weights or items and will never make predictions with them; consequently, why worry about how accurate they are?

Since the best weights are those computed on the total sample we should use them for decision making, but if all the data are consumed for computing the prediction rules how then can we get an unbiased estimate of the population parameter? The answer is that we can't. Every possible obtainable estimate is biased in some respect. Consider the following alternatives yielded by the double cross-validation procedure portrayed in Figure 7:

1. The estimate obtained by using the weights derived on the full sample to compute predictive efficiency on the same sample is biased upward for reasons already discussed.

2. The estimate obtained by using weights computed on the developmental subsample to compute predictive efficiency in the same subsample also is biased upward for the same reasons but to an even greater extent than for the total sample.

Fewer degrees of freedom make it easier for the scoring system to capitalize on error.

3. Taken as estimates for the population parameter as defined above, the cross-validated values are biased downward since they are each computed from less than full sample weights.

4. Any average of the two cross-validated values will also be biased downward, for the same reasons as in 3; however, the sampling error in the estimate should be considerably reduced.

5. If multiple regression is being used, so called "shrinkage" or correction formulae can be applied to the full sample estimate. The Wherry (1931) formula is perhaps the most popular. Lord (1950) gives another which reduces the original estimate even more. Unfortunately, as Darlington (1968) has reminded us, neither value was derived to estimate the population parameter obtained by applying full sample weights to all the data in the population. The Wherry formula is meant to be an estimate of the parameter obtained by using weights computed in the population. Lord's formula is meant to yield an estimate of the average cross-validated value. At present it is not possible to derive an unbiased estimate of the population parameter of real interest and thus none exists.

Besides the question of systematic bias there is also the problem of relative dispersion (statistical efficiency) to consider when comparing alternative means of estimating the population value. If our aim is to use the estimate that comes closest to the parameter, on the average, then perhaps we would be willing to trade off a bit more systematic bias for a lot less variability. Thus in a particular situation (i.e., specific values for *df*, reliability, etc.), the full sample estimate may be systematically biased upward to a greater extent than the cross-validated coefficient is biased downward. However, the cross-validated value is computed on a much smaller sample and the much greater dispersion in its sampling distribution may far outweigh its smaller systematic bias. Averaging the two cross-validated values may handle part of the problem, but it can never be resolved precisely.

It would be desirable to be able to specify the estimate yielding the smallest absolute error under various measurement conditions (e.g., df, reliability, zero order validity, predictor intercorrelations, etc.). Unfortunately, this is presently beyond the capability of statistical theory and there are as yet few empirical guidelines to fall back on. Studies by Schmidt (1970) and Claudy (1969) are two examples of empirical studies but they are limited in scope. Nevertheless they do suggest that it is unwise to use multiple regression at all when N is less than approximately 150. The full scope of the problem is probably much more complex. For example, it might very well be possible that there are conditions under which the predictive strategy used to make predictions in the population would not be the best strategy to use in estimating the level of accuracy in the population. To take an extreme example, multiple regression weights from the complete sample might yield the most accurate predictions in the population, but the best *estimate* of that population parameter might come from using unit weights on the sample data. We can only hope that when a firm set of guidelines is finally mapped out they are not so complex as to be unusable.

For now, appropriate behavior on the part of an applied psychologist would be to avoid developing empirical prediction rules on anything but very large samples and to double cross-validate in those instances. A single cross-validated estimate is never appropriate.

There remains one further complication in all of this. In some situations, empirical rules are used to construct a predictor composite. On the basis of sample data a predictor cutting score is then chosen for the purpose of making a practical decision about individuals. For example, we might use sample data to choose and differentially weight tests for a selection battery. Data

are also used to set a cutting score for the predictor composite, such that only people above the cutting score are hired. Within the conventional wisdom of cross-validation this strategy would require *three* random samples from the same population. However, as was argued above, trying to estimate the population parameters involves multiple trade-offs of different kinds of biases and an unbiased estimate is not possible. By using data both to develop a predictor composite and to set a cutting score we have severely escalated the complexity of the trade-offs involved. We are badly in need of empirical studies in this area.

Restriction of Range

It is often the case in industrial and organizational psychology that the reliability and validity of measures must be computed on samples that differ from the population in terms of the range or variability of the relevant variables. If the sample exhibits systematically less variance than the population to which we really want to generalize, then the reliability and/or validity in the population will be consistently underestimated.

What's to be done about it? The prototype statistical techniques, as distinct from an experimental or other more substantive approach (e.g., finding an unrestricted sample in a similar organizational setting), have been presented in quite systematic fashion by Gulliksen (1950) and the basic algorithms have not been substantially changed or supplanted in the intervening time period. As Lord and Novick (1968) point out, there also has been relatively little empirical study of the appropriateness of the techniques under actual operating conditions. However, the empirical studies that do exist suggest some precautions that ought to be observed. More about these later.

With regard to the correlation of one variable with another, as in predictive validity, there are several variants of the range restriction problem and each has its corresponding correction formula. The formulae are different depending on what information is available concerning the restricted and unrestricted variances and on whether we are interested in the correlation between two variables (say X and Y) with range restriction on one of the pair (say X) or whether the restriction is on a third variable (Z) that is correlated with X or Y.

Two primary assumptions are needed to derive the correction formulae. First, the regression of Y on X or the regressions of Y on X and Y on Z must be linear; and second, the bivariate distributions must be homoscedastic. That is, for all specific values of X or Z the expected values for the variance of Y (i.e., the variation of Y about the regression line for specific values of X or Z) must be equal for all X or for all Z. These are reasonable but perhaps not always appropriate assumptions.

An enumeration of the major range restriction situations with which it's possible to deal are as follows:

1. Formulae are available for the so-called two variable case where we are interested in correcting the correlation between X (a predictor) and Y (a criterion) and selection has been on either X or Y. Suppose entry into an organization is restricted to individuals scoring above the median on X and the research sample consists of people who have already been selected. Gulliksen (1950) and others refer to X as the *explicit* selection variable. If there is a significant correlation between X and Y, then to some degree the range of Y (the criterion) will also be restricted. Gulliksen refers to Y as the *implicit* selection variable. The nomenclature would be reversed if there were no restrictions on hiring but everybody scoring below the 50th percentile on the criterion was asked to leave the organization.

The formula for estimating the correlation in an unselected population is somewhat different depending on:

  a) If the variances in the selected and unselected groups are known for the explicit selection variable but not for the implicit variable.

  b) Vice versa.

2. Similar formulae are available for the three variable case in which the explicit selection, or restriction, is on a third variable Z that is significantly correlated with X and/or Y. Our problem is still that we have available the predictor/criterion correlation r_{xy} in a sample restricted by selection on Z, but we really want to be able to compute R_{xy} or the estimate of the correlation in the unrestricted population. For example, suppose applicants were originally selected on the basis of a general intelligence test, but we would like to know the correlation between a mechanical aptitude test and the criterion in an unselected group. If we can obtain data only on current employees, the variances of the mechanical aptitude test (X) and the criterion (Y) will be implicitly restricted if they are correlated with the intelligence measure (Z).

There are really six different variants of this situation. For all of them we have to know r_{xy}, r_{zy}, and r_{xz}; that is, the intercorrelations of the three variables in the *selected* sample. The six different formulae then correspond to whether we wish to estimate R_{xy} or R_{zy} in the population and to whether we know both the restricted and unrestricted variances only for Z, X, or Y.

3. Things get more complex, but it is still possible to arrive at workable correction

TABLE 2
SIX POSSIBLE SITUATIONS IN WHICH METHODS FOR CORRECTING FOR RESTRICTION OF RANGE ARE AVAILABLE

Variance in both a restricted and an unrestricted sample is known only for:

	Z	X	Y
Interest is in estimating R_{xy} in unrestricted population	1	2	3
Interest is in estimating R_{zy} in unrestricted population	4	5	6

formulae under certain conditions when there is explicit selection or restriction on several predictor variables and the aim is to estimate the *multiple* correlation in the unrestricted population. One limitation on the solution (as given by Gulliksen) is that the number of criteria must equal the number of predictors. If such is the case and we can compute all the variance and covariance matrices among and between the two sets of variables (i.e., c_{xx}, c_{yy}, c_{xy}) in the restricted sample and we know the covariance matrix (C_{xx}) for the predictors in the unrestricted sample, then we can estimate a multiple correlation for each of the criteria in the unselected population. The computing formulae are given in Gulliksen (1950).

Restriction of range is often a serious problem for the applied psychologist attempting to estimate reliabilities and validities in the appropriate population and the various correction formulae sound appealing. However, a number of cautions are in order. Linn (1968) and Lord and Novick (1968) argue that the assumptions of linearity and homoscedasticity which are needed to derive the correction formulae may not be all that appropriate in real life. They observe that many bivariate distributions tend to exhibit much less variability at the extremes than in the middle and that rather than being linear the standard score regression line tends to be steeper at the ends than it is in the middle. The violation of the homoscedasticity assumption tends to inflate the correction while the departure from linearity toward a sigmoid curve tends to deflate it. How these two biases might interact in a particular situation cannot be readily known.

A second major difficulty arises because corrections are made on the basis of what is assumed to be explicit selection on a particular variable (X) but significant selection is also being made on one or more other variables (e.g., Z). For example, an organization may claim it is selecting on the basis of a test score but what really happens, as the application progresses through the employ-

ment process, is that people are selected on the basis of educational level (Z).

By plugging in a wide range of values and plowing through the formulae for the case when there is one unknown predictor (Z), Linn (1968) has shown that correcting the correlation coefficient as if X were the explicit selection variable results in the following:

1. The formula overcorrects when the correlation between the available and unavailable predictor variables (R_{xz}) is low.

2. The formula undercorrects when the correlation between X and Z is in the middle range but moves back toward an appropriate correction when the correlation between the two variables is near unity. The relationship appears as in Figure 8 where the dashed line is the actual correlation between X and Y in the unselected population. The ordinate refers to the corrected value for r_{xy}, or R_{xy}.

3. The under- and overcorrection phenomena become more severe as the degree of actual selection on Z (The unavailable predictor) becomes more severe. (Not shown in the figure.)

These kinds of considerations make using the correction formulae rather risky business. In almost every real situation their estimate of the population parameter will most likely be biased in some respect, except in very clear and straightforward situations. The safest recourse is not to use them and to fall back on the collection of more data

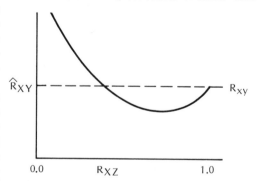

Figure 8.   Effects of corrections for restriction of range as a function of the correlation between the available and unavailable predictors.

in hopes of accounting for the selection factor by more substantive means.

Nonrandom or Cohort Sampling

For any specific research study that has appeared in the industrial and organizational psychology literature it would be a difficult task to demonstrate that the sample data are a random selection from the population of real interest. It is a problem common to most of social and behavioral science. However, it takes on much greater and more concrete importance when the research sample data are going to be used to make real life decisions about additional people from the population. The question of randomness is then no longer "academic."

Unfortunately, the populations of interest to many industrial and organizational psychologists are not static over time. For example, in personnel selection there may be systematic changes in the nature of the available labor supply for specific positions, such as an increasing level of education or a greater percentage of people with specific skills. However, most research studies aimed at determining the validity of a selection instrument are based on applicants or current jobholders from a particular span of time. Sampling from one particular time period is not random sampling from the population to which we want to generalize. It is sampling from one cohort of the population. The phenomenon is even more clear in educational and training settings. Prediction rules are derived and validity estimated by sampling current undergraduates or current enrollees in a training program. During X number of future years prediction rules derived during year one are used to make predictions for individuals who subsequently wish to enter the institution. In this case, classes are cohorts and the memberships of successive classes are most likely not random samples from the same population.

What is the effect of sampling (and perhaps not randomly even then) from a spe-

cific cohort rather than from the entire population in which decision making will be carried out? Almost by definition the amount of sampling error in our estimates will increase, but we have no way of knowing how much. Besides an increase in the variability of the estimate, cohort sampling may also introduce systematic biases of one sort or another. Again there is no algorithmic way to account for this kind of "population drift."

There are a number of partial solutions to the problem, none of them very satisfactory. Since it is not possible to know very well the population's characteristics that are changing or that distinguish one cohort from another, an alternative would be to simulate a number of population drift situations with real data pools and use Monte Carlo techniques to describe the variance of the sampling distribution. These new estimates of the sampling error could be used to "correct" the probability of a Type I error. Unfortunately, this would require that an investigator could accurately fit his situation to the appropriate simulation. Accounting for systematic bias in the estimate rather than the dispersion is even more difficult. One might be able to get an indication of whether it is up or down by correctly anticipating the major ways a population is going to change (e.g., becoming younger and better educated) and conducting a series of pilot studies in another, but similar, organization which has already experienced those kinds of changes. The practical difficulties are obvious.

We might expect the above difficulties to become worse to the extent that prediction rules are empirically derived and to the extent that they use up more and more degrees of freedom in their computation. The more a prediction model makes use of the sample data the farther out on a limb it will be when the population drifts. For example, sampling distributions of predictive validity estimates may become increasingly more variable and systematically biased as the prediction strategy moves from unit weights to using zero order validity coefficients as weights to using multiple regression. If estimation under nonrandom sampling conditions is a cause for worry, one possible strategy is to retreat to simpler prediction strategies.

A CONCLUDING STATEMENT

This has been a very brief look at a few basic concepts in psychometric theory that are of general importance for the work of industrial and organizational psychologists. It was not intended to be a review of new developments in scaling theory or testing technology. These are specialized topics in their own right and are deserving of their own treatment elsewhere. Rather, the intent of the present chapter was to take a look at the current state of some basic problems in psychometric theory in light of their historical background. Nobody needs to be reminded that there is no such thing as *a* reliability or *a* validity for a psychological measure. However, we now have in hand, in the form of generalizability theory and decision theory, the means for a much more systematic treatment of reliability and validity concepts and these concepts go far beyond any taxonomy of "kinds of reliability" or "types of validity." We should take advantage of them.

REFERENCES

American Psychological Association. *Technical recommendations for psychological tests and diagnostic techniques.* Washington, D.C.: American Psychological Association, 1954.

American Psychological Association. *Standards for educational and psychological tests and manuals.* Washington, D.C.: American Psychological Association, 1966.

Bakan, D. *On method: Toward a reconstruction of psychological investigation.* San Francisco: Jossey-Bass, 1967.

Bechtoldt, H. P. Construct validity: A critique. *American Psychologist,* 1959, 14, 619–629.

Blum, M. L., & Naylor, J. C. *Industrial psychology: Its theoretical and social foundations.* (Rev. ed.) New York: Harper and Row, 1968.

Bock, R. D., & Wood, R. Test theory. In P. H. Mussen & M. R. Rosenzweig (Eds.), *Annual review of psychology,* Vol. 22. Palo Alto: Annual Reviews, 1971.

Bormuth, J. R. *A theory of achievement test items.* Chicago: University of Chicago Press, 1970.

Brogden, H. E. On the interpretation of the correlation coefficient as a measure of predictive efficiency. *Journal of Educational Psychology,* 1946, 37, 65–76.

Brown, W. Some experimental results in the correlation of mental abilities. *British Journal of Psychology,* 1910, 3, 296–322.

Burt, C. The reliability of teachers' assessments of their pupils. *British Journal of Educational Psychology,* 1945, 15, 8–92.

Campbell, D. T. Recommendations for APA test standards regarding construct, trait, and discriminant validity. *American Psychologist,* 1960, 15, 546–553.

Campbell, D. T., & Fiske, D. W. Convergent and discriminant validation by the multitrait-multimethod matrix. *Psychological Bulletin,* 1959, 56, 81–105.

Claudy, J. G. An empirical investigation of small sample multiple regression and crossvalidation. Doctoral dissertation, University of Tennessee. Ann Arbor: University Microfilms, 1969, No. 70-7553.

Cornfield, J., & Tukey, J. W. Average values of mean squares in factorials. *Annals of Mathematical Statistics,* 1956, 27, 907–949.

Cronbach, L. J. Coefficient alpha and the internal structure of tests. *Psychometrika,* 1951, 16, 297–334.

Cronbach, L. J., & Gleser, G. *Psychological tests and personnel decisions.* (2nd. ed.) Urbana: University of Illinois Press, 1965.

Cronbach, L. J., Gleser, G., Nanda, H., & Rajaratnam, N. *The dependability of behavioral measurements: Theory of generalizability for scores and profiles.* New York: Wiley, 1972.

Cronbach, L. J., & Meehl, P. E. Construct validity in psychological tests. *Psychological Bulletin,* 1955, 52, 281–302.

Cronbach, L. J., Rajaratnam, N., & Gleser, G. Theory of generalizability: A liberalization of reliability theory. *British Journal of Statistical Psychology,* 1963, 16, Part 2, 137–163.

Cureton, E. E. Validity, reliability, and baloney. *Educational and Psychological Measurement,* 1950, 10, 94–96.

Cureton, E. E. A recipe for a cookbook. *Psychological Bulletin,* 1957, 54, 494–497.

Cureton, E. E. The stability coefficient. *Educational and Psychological Measurement,* 1971, 31, 45–55.

Curtis, E. W. Necessity/sufficiency as a conceptual model. *Technical Bulletin* (STD 66-30). San Diego: U. S. Naval Research Activity, April, 1966.

Curtis, E. W. Predictive value compared to predictive validity. *American Psychologist,* 1971, 26, 908–914.

Curtis, E. W., & Alf, E. F. Validity, predictive efficiency, and practical significance of selection tests. *Journal of Applied Psychology,* 1969, 53, 327–337.

Darlington, R. B. Multiple regression in psychological research and practice. *Psychological Bulletin,* 1968, 69, 161–182.

Darlington, R. B., & Stauffer, G. F. Use and evaluation of discrete test information in decision making. *Journal of Applied Psychology,* 1966, 50, 125–129.

Fisher, J. The twisted pear and the prediction of behavior. *Journal of Consulting Psychology,* 1959, 23, 400–405.

Ghiselli, E. E. *Theory of psychological measurement.* New York: McGraw-Hill, 1963.

Goodman, L. A., & Kruskal, W. H. Measures of association for cross classification: III. Approximate sampling theory. *Journal of the American Statistical Association,* 1963, 58, 310–364.

Guilford, J. P. *Psychometric methods.* New York: McGraw-Hill, 1954.

Gulliksen, H. *Theory of mental tests.* New York: Wiley, 1950.

Guttman, L., & Schlesinger, I. M. Systematic construction of distractors for ability and achievement testing. *Educational and Psychological Measurement,* 1967, 27, 569–580.

Hively, W. II, Patterson, H. L., & Page, S. H. A "universe defined" system of arithmetic achievement tests. *Journal of Educational Measurement,* 1968, 5, 275–290.

Hoyt, C. Test reliability estimated by analysis of variance. *Psychometrika,* 1941, 6, 153–160.

Jackson, R. W. B. Reliability of mental tests. *British Journal of Psychology,* 1939, 29, 267–287.

Jackson, R. W. B., & Ferguson, G. A. *Studies on the reliability of tests.* Bulletin #12, Department of Educational Research, University of Toronto, Toronto, Canada, 1941.

Joint Committee on Revision of Standards. Standards for development and use of educational and psychological measurement. (3rd draft) *APA Monitor,* 1973, 4 (2), I–XV.

Kelly, T. L. Note on the reliability of a test: A reply to Crum's criticism. *Journal of Educational Psychology,* 1924, 15, 193–204.

Kuder, G. F., & Richardson, M. W. The theory of the estimation of test reliability. *Psychometrika,* 1937, 2, 151–160.

Kurtz, A. K. A research test of the Rorschach test. *Personnel Psychology,* 1948, 1, 41–51.

Linn, R. L. Range restriction problems in the use of self-selection groups for test validation. *Psychological Bulletin,* 1968, 69, 69–73.

Loevinger, J. Person and population as psychometric concepts. *Psychological Review,* 1965, 72, 143–155.

Lord, F. M. Efficiency of prediction when a regression equation from one sample is used in a new sample. *Research Bulletin* (50-40). Princeton: Educational Testing Service, 1950.

Lord, F. M., & Novick, M. R. *Statistical theories of mental test scores.* Reading, Mass.: Addison-Wesley, 1968.

Lykken, D. T. Statistical significance in psychological research. *Psychological Bulletin,* 1968, 70, 151–159.

Maxwell, A. E. The effect of correlated errors on estimates of reliability coefficients. *Educational and Psychological Measurement,* 1968, 28, 803–811.

Meehl, P. E., & Rosen, A. Antecedent probability and the efficiency of psychometric signs, patterns, or cutting score. *Psychological Bulletin,* 1955, 52, 194–216.

Novick, M. R., & Lewis, C. Coefficient alpha and the reliability of composite measurements. *Psychometrika,* 1967, 32, 1–3.

Nunnally, J. C. *Psychometric theory.* New York: McGraw-Hill, 1967.

Osburn, H. G. Item sampling for achievement testing. *Educational and Psychological Measurement,* 1968, 28, 95–104.

Rasch, G. An item analysis which takes individual differences into account. *British Journal of Mathematical and Statistical Psychology,* 1966, 19, 49–57.

Rorer, L. G., Hoffman, P. J., & Hsieh, Kuo-Cheng. Utilities as base rate multipliers in the determination of optimum cutting scores for the discrimination of groups of unequal size and variance. *Journal of Applied Psychology,* 1966, 50, 364–368.

Rorer, L. G., Hoffman, P. J., LaForge, G. E., & Hsieh, Kuo-Cheng. Optimum cutting scores to discriminate groups of unequal size and variance. *Journal of Applied Psychology,* 1966, 50, 153–164.

Rozeboom, W. W. The fallacy of the null hypothesis significance test. *Psychological Bulletin,* 1960, 57, 416–428.

Rulon, P. J. A simplified procedure for determining the reliability of a test by split halves. *Harvard Educational Review,* 1939, 9, 99–103.

Schmidt, F. L. The relative efficiency of regression weight and simple unit predictor weights in applied differential psychology. Doctoral dissertation, Department of Psychology, Purdue University, Lafayette, Ind., 1970.

Schmidt, F. L. Probability and utility assumptions underlying use of the Strong Vocational Interest Blank. *Journal of Applied Psychology,* in press.

Spearman, C. The proof and measurement of the association between two things. *American Journal of Psychology,* 1904, 15, 72–101.

Spearman, C. Correlation calculated from faulty data. *British Journal of Psychology,* 1910, 3, 271–295.

Taylor, H. C., & Russell, J. T. The relationship of validity coefficients to the practical validity of tests in selection: Discussion and tables. *Journal of Applied Psychology,* 1939, 23, 565–578.

Tiffin, J., & McCormick, E. J. *Industrial psychology.* (5th ed.) Englewood Cliffs, N.J.: Prentice-Hall, 1965.

Tryon, R. C. A theory of psychological components. *Psychological Review,* 1935, 42, 425–454.

Tryon, R. C. Reliability and behavior domain validity: Reformulation and historical critique. *Psychological Bulletin,* 1957, 54, 229–249.

Wherry, R. J. A new formula for predicting shrinkage of the coefficient of multiple correlation. *Annals of Mathematical Statistics,* 1931, 2, 440–457.

Williams, R. H., & Zimmerman, D. W. An extension of the Rulon formula for test reliability: The case of correlated true and error score components of scores. *Journal of Experimental Education,* 1968, 36, 94–96.

The Design and Conduct of Quasi-Experiments and True Experiments in Field Settings[1]

THOMAS D. COOK
DONALD T. CAMPBELL
Northwestern University

THIS CHAPTER has three purposes. The first is to explicate four kinds of validity. Statistical conclusion validity refers to the validity of conclusions we draw on the basis of statistical evidence about whether a presumed cause and effect co-vary; internal validity refers to the validity of any conclusions we draw about whether a demonstrated statistical relationship implies cause; construct validity refers to the validity with which cause and effect operations are labeled in theory-relevant or generalizable terms; and external validity refers to the validity with which a causal relationship can be generalized across persons, settings, and times.

The second, and major, purpose of the chapter is to outline a number of quasi-experimental designs that have been previously used in industrial and organizational psychology or could be so used. These designs are grouped as non-equivalent control group designs, cohort designs, regression-discontinuity designs, time-series designs, and correlational designs. The specific designs under each of these headings are critically examined with respect to each kind of validity, and each design's typical strengths and weaknesses are pointed out.

The last purpose of the chapter is to examine why true experiments (involving random assignment to treatment groups) are not more common in field research on organizations since true experiments permit stronger causal inferences than quasi-experiments. The practical problems besetting field experiments are outlined, and ways of overcoming these are mentioned as are the contexts that are particularly appropriate for successful randomization. Our discussion points out several past examples of true experiments that were successfully implemented and maintained in field settings.

[1] Cook's contribution was supported by a grant from the Russell Sage Foundation, and Campbell's by NSF Grant number GSOC-7103704.

INTRODUCTION

In reading back numbers of the major journals devoted to industrial and organizational psychology we have been struck by the relative paucity of field experiments. By "experiment" we understand any experimenter-controlled or naturally occurring event (a "treatment") which intervenes in the lives of respondents and whose probable consequences can be empirically assessed. By "field" we understand any setting which respondents do not perceive to have been set up for the primary purpose of conducting research. Our hope is that this chapter might contribute to increasing the number of field experiments in future research.

Experiments can be divided into two major categories depending on whether the various treatment groups were formed by assigning respondents to treatments in random or nonrandom fashion. The former designs are called *"true" experimental* and the latter *quasi-experimental*. Most of this chapter will be spent outlining and discussing quasi-experimental designs because there is probably less knowledge about them than about true experiments, because quasi-experiments are sometimes more feasible in field settings than are true experiments, and because planned true experiments sometimes break down and have to be analyzed in quasi-experimental fashion.

The major survey of quasi-experimental designs is by Campbell and Stanley (1966). The present chapter inevitably goes over some of the same ground, although the emphasis is upon extension and elaboration. We want, in particular, to explicate two kinds of validity other than the internal and external validity of Campbell and Stanley and to outline some designs that were not in the earlier work. The present chapter contains fewer quasi-experimental designs than Campbell and Stanley, and readers who want the most comprehensive coverage should consult both the present chapter and the earlier book.

The stress on quasi-experiments should not be understood as a preference for quasi-experiments over true experiments. Quite the opposite! As will become clear later, the results of quasi-experiments are less interpretable than the results of true experiments, and this alone should embolden us to ask why random assignment has not taken place more often in organizational research and why, even after taking place, it has sometimes not been maintained for the whole course of an experiment. Hence, the chapter will close with an analysis of the major obstacles to forming and maintaining randomly constituted treatment groups in field settings. Moreover, some strategies will be outlined for overcoming these obstacles, and some field situations will be mentioned that are particularly conducive to carrying out true experiments of relevance to organizations.

A broad definition of industrial and organizational psychology is implicit in the present chapter. This is because most human behavior is relevant to formal and informal organizations in some way. The broad definition is advantageous for our purposes since it justifies the presentation of quasi-experimental designs which have been reported in, say, educational or legal journals and which have not yet been reported in journals that are more narrowly labeled as "industrial" or "organizational." We shall also be concerned with the usefulness of field experiments for building and testing theory as well as for assessing the effectiveness of changes that are made for reasons unrelated to formal theory. We feel close to Pugh's (1966) conception of organizational research in adopting both the broad definition of the field and the joint concern for theory and for what might be called the evaluation of techniques designed to increase performance and/or work satisfaction.

FOUR KINDS OF VALIDITY

Testing Causal Relationships

Experiments are vehicles for testing causal hypotheses. It is traditionally assumed that there are three necessary conditions for assuming with any confidence that the relationship between two variables is causal and that the direction of causation is from A to B. The first relates to temporal antecedence and states that a cause must precede an effect in time. It is normally simple to meet this condition if the investigator knows when respondents experienced a treatment. In quasi-experiments, the investigator can combine such knowledge with his knowledge of respondents' pretest and posttest performance, and he can associate the introduction of a treatment with some measure of change in the dependent variable. The investigator who conducts a true experiment knows that a proper randomization procedure will ensure, probabilistically, the pretest equivalence of his various experimental groups. Hence, if there are posttest differences related to the treatments, he knows that these probably took place after the treatments were introduced.

A second necessary condition for confidently inferring a causal relationship from A to B is that the treatment or treatments have to co-vary with the effect, for if the potential cause and effect are not related, the one could not have been a cause of the other. Statistics are used for testing whether there is covariation, and arbitrary criteria have been developed for deciding whether there is or is not "real" covariation in the data (e.g., $p < .05$). Thus, statistics function as gatekeepers. Unfortunately, they are fallible gatekeepers even when they are properly used, and they fail to detect both true and false patterns of covariation. Since statistics lead to such important decisions, it would seem wise to explicate the threats that lead to false conclusions about covariation. These will be called threats to *statistical conclusion validity*.

The third necessary condition for causal inference is that there must be no plausible alternative explanations of B other than A. This condition is the most difficult to meet in two distinct senses. The first, which is particularly a problem with quasi-experiments, concerns the viability of alternative interpretations which imply that an

apparent causal relationship from A to B may, in fact, be due to third variables which caused the change in B. For instance, one might introduce a new machine into a factory and note whether it was associated with an increase in productivity. If it were, one might want to attribute the increase to the machine. However, it is always possible that the increase might have nothing to do with the machine itself and might be due to a seasonal increase in productivity that occurs at that time every year. This is only one example of such third variables, and we shall later present a systematic list of third variables under the heading of threats to *internal validity*.

Threats to internal validity suggest that a hypothesized causal relationship might be spurious. This is different from a second meaning of "alternative interpretation" which assumes that A-as-manipulated and B-as-measured are indeed causally related but which casts doubt on whether the empirical operations represent the A and B constructs which the investigator has tried to designate by his names for A and B. Most of the theoretical controversies in psychology are of this nature—controversies, for example, about whether a relationship between being paid more money and higher productivity should be explained as a consequence of the high payment creating feelings of inequity, or violating expectations, or threatening one's self-concept, or whatever. The issue in such studies is *not* about the internal validity issue of whether the payment manipulation caused a change in the index of productivity. Rather, it is about how the payment should be labeled in theory-relevant and generalizable terms. To give another example, for some persons the interpretative problem in the famous Roethlisberger and Dickson (1939) experiments at the Hawthorne plant is one of labeling what caused the women to increase productivity and is not one of determining whether the treatment increased productivity. Was the causal variable the fact of change irrespective of its nature, or the feedback about one's behavior given by the new changes, or improved work-group cohesiveness, or a new perception of management interest, or whatever? We shall later discuss threats to *construct validity,* and these should be understood as threats to the correct labeling of the cause and effect operations in abstract terms that come from common linguistic usage or from formal theory. Actually, the problem of construct validity is broader than this and obviously applies to attempts to label any aspect of an experiment including the nature of the setting, the nature of the persons participating, and so forth.

It is worth noting that "internal validity" has been misused in the past to refer both to doubts about whether a causal relationship from *A* to *B* can be reasonably inferred and to doubts about how the cause and effect should be labeled. This confusion may arise because alternative interpretations have to be ruled out in establishing both internal and construct validity. However, internal validity involves ruling out alternative interpretations of the presumed causal *relationship* between *A*-as-manipulated and *B*-as-measured, and construct validity involves ruling out alternative interpretations of how *A* and *B* are referred to in hypothetical terms. Since the very rationale for experiments is to test whether the relationship of two variables is causal, the alternative interpretations that have to be ruled out as a *necessary* condition for inferring cause are alternative interpretations of the relationship (i.e., threats to internal validity) and not alternative interpretations of the cause and effect operations (i.e., threats to construct validity).

The good experiment (a) makes temporal antecedence clear; (b) is sensitive and powerful enough to demonstrate that a potential cause and effect could have covaried; (c) rules out all third variables which might alternatively explain the relationship between the cause and effect; and also (d) eliminates alternative hypotheses about the constructs involved in the relationship. At least one further step is use-ful. To infer a causal relationship at one moment in time, using one research setting, and with one sample of respondents, would give us little confidence that a demonstrated causal relationship is robust. A concern with the generalizability of findings across times, settings, and persons will be called a concern for *external validity* and we shall shortly list the major threats to this kind of validity.

The preceding discussion should not be taken to imply that, as a means of inferring cause, experiments are unique. A science like astronomy has progressed without experimentation, in part because it has been blessed with reliable observational methods and quantitative theories that have predicted precise locations in space, precise orbits, and precise time intervals for crossing space. The numerical precision of predictions has meant, first, that predictions could be tested with a high degree of accuracy, and second, that different theories making different numerical predictions could be pitted against each other. This is not to say that all the validity problems are answered in astronomy or that the investigator can give up the required task of trenchantly thinking through as many alternative hypotheses as possible, and consciously pitting each of them against the data to see if they can be ruled out. Our point should only be taken to mean that there will typically be fewer validity threats where measurement is as reliable as in astronomy and theories are as precise.

Unfortunately, the social sciences are not yet blessed with such powerfully precise theories, such reliable measurement, or such recurrent cyclical orders in the observational data. Imagine observing a difference in a worker's performance between a pretest which he takes before beginning a special course and a posttest which he takes after completing the course. What are the chances of predicting how much of this difference can be explained in terms of the course itself, spontaneous maturation by the worker, gains in test-taking skill between the pretest and posttest, unique historical events which affected the dependent variable between the pretest and posttest, or any combination of these forces? Moreover, even if we could predict specific numbers to be associated with each of the explanations above, how confident would we be that we could measure the relevant performance reliably enough to discriminate between the theories? The answer to this would depend, of course, on the size of the predicted differences in gain and on the particular kind of performance test. We believe, however, that there are few non-experimental settings in the social sciences where precise predictions can be successfully used to test competing hypotheses about cause.

Though the preceding discussion implies that experiments are better than non-experiments for testing causal propositions, it should not be taken to imply that experiments are infallible means of testing all the questions associated with causal hypothesis-testing. The following list of threats to internal, statistical conclusion, external, and construct validity, and the discussion of the interrelationship of these kinds of validity should make patently obvious the fallibility of experimentation. Improvements in design need to be made, can be made, and should be made in order to facilitate better causal inferences. But we would delude ourselves if we believed that a single experiment, or even a research program of several years' duration, would definitely answer the major questions associated with confidently inferring a causal relationship, naming its parts, and specifying its generalizability.

Internal Validity

The threats to internal validity are:

History. "History" is a threat when an observed effect might be due to some event which took place between the pretest and posttest and when this event is not the treatment of research interest.

Maturation. This is a threat when an observed effect might be due to the respon-

dent's growing older, wiser, stronger, etc. between pretest and posttest and when this maturation is not the treatment of research interest.

Testing. This is a threat when an effect might be due to effects associated with taking a test different numbers of times.

Instrumentation. This is a threat when an effect might be due to a change in the measuring instrument between pretest and posttest and is not due to the treatment's differential impact at each time interval.

Statistical Regression. This is a threat when an effect might be due to respondents being classified into experimental groups at, say, the pretest on the basis of pretest scores or correlates of pretest scores. When this happens, and measures are unreliable, high pretest scorers will score relatively lower at the posttest and low pretest scorers will score higher at the posttest. It would be wrong to attribute such differential "change" to a treatment. It is due to statistical regression.

Selection. This is a threat when an effect may be due to the difference between the kinds of persons in experimental groups rather than to the different treatments each group has received.

Mortality. This is a threat when an effect may be due to the different kinds of persons who dropped out of particular treatment groups during the course of an experiment. This results in a selection artifact, since the experimental groups are composed of different kinds of persons at the posttest.

Interactions with Selection. Many of the foregoing threats to internal validity can interact with selection to produce forces that might spuriously appear as treatment effects. Perhaps the most common such force is the *selection-maturation* interaction which results when experimental groups are composed of different kinds of persons who are maturing at different speeds. Such group differences in growth rates typically occur, for example, when middle-class and lower-class children are compared at two different time intervals on some test of cognitive knowledge.

Ambiguity About the Direction of Causal Influence. It is possible to imagine a situation in which all plausible third variable explanations of an *A-B* relationship have been ruled out and where it is not clear whether *A* causes *B* or *B* causes *A*. This is an especially salient threat to internal validity in simple correlational studies where it will often not be clear whether, for example, less foreman supervision causes higher productivity or whether higher productivity causes less supervision. This particular threat is not salient in most experiments since the order of temporal precedence is clear. Nor is it a problem in those correlational studies where one direction of causal influence is relatively implausible (e.g., it is more plausible to infer that a decrease in the environmental temperature causes an increase in fuel consumption than it is to infer that an increase in fuel consumption causes a decrease in outside temperature). But it is a problem in all other correlational studies.

The use of randomized experiments provides an appropriate safeguard against all the foregoing threats to internal validity. But the five following threats may jeopardize the validity of randomized experiments as well as quasi-experiments. They represent additions to the list of threats provided by Campbell and Stanley (1963, 1966). The first three of them have the effect of equalizing the experimental and control group, while the last two may create a spurious difference.

Diffusion or Imitation of the Treatment. If the treatments involve widely diffused informational programs or if the experimental and control groups can communicate with each other, the controls may learn the information and, thereby, receive the treatment. The experiment thus becomes invalid because there is no functional difference between the treatment and the control groups in the treatments that they have experienced. In many quasi-experiments it is desirable to have units that are as similar as possible in all aspects except for the treatment. One way of doing this is to sample physically adjacent units. But this very propinquity can lead to the treatment being experienced by all the units. For example, if one of the New England states were used as a control group to study the effects of changes in the New York abortion law, any true effects of the new law would be obscured if New Englanders went freely to New York for abortions.

Compensatory Equalization of Treatment. When the experimental treatment provides goods generally believed to be desirable, there may emerge administrative and constituency reluctance to tolerate the focused inequality that results. Thus in nationwide educational experiments, such as Follow Through, the control schools, particularly if equally needy, tended to be given Title 1 funds in amounts equivalent to those coming to the experimental schools. Several other experimental evaluations of compensatory education have met the same problem. It exemplifies a problem of administrative equity that must certainly occur among units of an industrial organization, and it explains some administrators' reluctance to employ random assignment to treatments which their constituencies consider valuable.

Compensatory Rivalry. Where the assignment of persons or organizational units to experimental and control conditions is made public (as it usually must be in experiments in industrial and organizational psychology), conditions of social competition are generated. The control group, as the natural underdog, is motivated to a rivalrous effort to reduce or reverse the expected difference. This result is particularly likely where intact units (such as departments, plants, work crews, etc.) are assigned to treatments, or if members of the control group stand to lose if a treatment were successful. For instance, Saretsky (1972) has pointed out that performance contracting would threaten the job security of schoolteachers and has reviewed evidence suggesting that the academic performance of children taught by teachers in the control groups of the OEO Performance Contracting Experiment was better during the experiment than it had been in past years. The net effect of atypically high learning gains by controls would be to diminish the difference in learning between control students taught by their regular teachers and experimental children taught by outside contractors who were paid according to the gains made by children. Saretsky describes this special effort by the controls as a "John Henry effect" in honor of the John Henry who, when he knew his work as a railroad steel driver was to be compared with that of a steam drill, worked so hard that he outperformed the drill but then died of overexertion. Compensatory rivalry is in many ways like compensatory equalization. However, the latter results from administrators anticipating problems from the groups that receive less desirable treatments, while the former results from the way that members of these groups react to their treatments or non-treatments.

Resentful Demoralization of Respondents Receiving Less Desirable Treatments. When an experiment is obtrusive, the reaction of a no-treatment control group can be associated with resentment and demoralization, as well as with compensatory rivalry. This is because controls are often relatively deprived when compared to experimentals. In an industrial setting the controls might retaliate by lowering productivity and company profits. This situation is likely to lead to a posttest difference between treatment and no-treatment groups and it might be quite wrong to attribute the difference to the treatment. It would be more apt to label the no-treatment as the "resentment" treatment. (Of course, this phenomenon is not restricted to control groups. It can occur whenever treatments differ in desirability and respondents are aware of the difference.)

Local History. Random assignment to treatments controls for the contemporaneous irrelevant sources of change that are listed under "history." But this only holds under two conditions: first, that these irrelevant events are shared by experimentals and controls alike, and second, that these events do not occur in individual data-collection sessions which are unique to experimentals or controls. Where one collects data by groups, for example, randomly assigning all experimental persons to one group session will mean that any idiosyncratic events that took place in the session are confounded with the experimental treatment and may be responsible for effects. The cure for this, where feasible, is to administer the treatment to individuals or to many small groups, randomizing experimental and control sessions as to special location and time. In this latter procedure, the appropriate degrees of freedom are based on the number of groups, not persons. The likelihood of a local history explanation is often higher in quasi-experiments than in true experiments because in the former case the treatments are likely to be confounded with differences in the universe of respondents. Thus, the different treatments will be associated with all the unique historical experiences that each group has. Local history is equivalent to the interaction of selection and history in that the same events happen in different settings at different times, or in that some events happen in one kind of setting but not in others.

Estimating the internal validity of a relationship is a deductive process in which the investigator has to be his own most trenchant critic and has to systematically think through how each of the above factors may have influenced his data. Then, he has to examine the data to test which relevant threats can be ruled out. When all of them can be, it will be possible to make confident conclusions about whether a relationship is causal. When all of them cannot, perhaps because the appropriate data are not available or because the data indicate that a particular threat may indeed have operated, then the investigator has to conclude that a demonstrated relationship between two variables may or may not be causal. Sometimes, he will have to *act as if* the relationship were causal because practical decisions have to be made and it is possible that the relationship might be causal. At other times, the alternative interpretations may seem implausible enough to be ignored and the investigator will be inclined to dismiss them. He can dismiss them with a great deal of confidence when the alternative interpretation seems unlikely on the basis of findings from a research tradition with a large number of relevant and replicated findings. Often, however, it will be difficult to obtain higher inter-judge agreement about the plausibility of a particular alternative interpretation. Moreover, theory-testers place great emphasis on testing theoretical predictions that seem so implausible that neither common sense nor other theories would make the same prediction. There is in this an implied confession that the "implausible" is sometimes true and that "implausible" alternative interpretations should reduce but not eliminate our doubt about whether a relationship is causal.

The major difference between true experiments and quasi-experiments has to do with internal validity. When respondents are randomly assigned to treatment groups, each group is similarly constituted (no selection, maturation, or selection-maturation problems); each experiences the same testing conditions and research instruments (no testing or instrumentation problems); there is no deliberate selection of high and low scorers on any tests except under conditions where respondents are first matched according to, say, pretest scores and are then randomly assigned to treatment conditions (no statistical regression problem); each group experiences the same global pattern of history (no history problem); and if there are treatment-related differences in who drops out of the experiment, this is interpretable as a consequence of the treatment and is not due to selection. Thus, randomization takes

care of most, but not all, the threats to internal validity.

With quasi-experimental groups, the situation is quite different. Instead of relying on randomization to rule out most internal validity threats, the investigator has to make them all explicit and then rule them out one by one. His task is, therefore, more laborious. It is also less enviable since his final causal inference will not be as strong as if he had conducted a true experiment.

Statistical Conclusion Validity

Experiments are conducted to make decisions. The investigator wants to decide whether his treatment has had some effect, has had no effect, or whether a decision cannot be made on the basis of the information on hand. Sometimes, effects are specified as points (e.g., the treatment is effective if productivity increases by 10 percent or if absenteeism is less than 2 percent of all working days per employee), and such point specifications reflect a concern with the magnitude of an effect as opposed to its mere existence.

Typically, however, we are interested in the mere existence of effects, which we infer from statistically significant differences either between specific statistics in a treatment group or between specific statistics in a treatment group relative to other treatment groups or to a no-treatment control group. We shall deal in this chapter with the threats that preclude valid conclusions about the existence of treatment effects, and this should not be taken to imply that we consider it unimportant to estimate the magnitude of effects. Rather, we consider this important once an effect can be reasonably inferred.

Arbitrary statistical traditions have developed for drawing conclusions about covariation from sample data. The most widely known of these is probably the cutting point $p < .05$. Relationships below the 5 percent level are treated as though they were "true" while those above it are treated as though they were "false." However, we can be wrong in concluding that the population means of various treatment groups truly differ even when the probability level is less than .05 and we can be wrong in concluding that they do not differ when the probability level is above that level. Drawing false positive or false negative conclusions about causal hypotheses is the essence of internal validity, and this was a major justification for Campbell (1969) adding "instability" to his list of threats to internal validity. "Instability" was defined as "unreliability of measures, fluctuations in sampling persons or components, autonomous instability of repeated or equivalent measures," and these are obviously threats to drawing correct conclusions about a treatment's effect. What precipitated the need for this addition was the viewpoint of some sociologists who had argued against using tests of significance unless the comparison followed random assignment to treatments (see Winch & Campbell, 1969, for further details).

The status of statistical conclusion validity as a special case of internal validity can be further illustrated by considering the distinction between bias and error. Bias refers to factors which systematically affect the value of means; error refers to factors which increase variability and decrease the chance of obtaining statistically significant effects. If we erroneously conclude from a quasi-experiment that A causes B, this might either be because threats to internal validity bias the relevant means or because, for a specifiable percentage of possible comparisons, differences as large as those found in a study would be obtained by chance. If we erroneously conclude that A does not affect B (or cannot be demonstrated to affect B), this can either be because threats to internal validity bias means and obscure true differences or because the uncontrolled variability obscures true differences. Statistical conclusion validity is concerned, not with

sources of systematic bias, but with sources of error variance and with the appropriate use of statistics and statistical tests.

Before proceeding to a taxonomy of threats to statistical conclusion validity, we should perhaps briefly mention four points. The first concerns the logical impossibility, but practical necessity, of concluding that a treatment has had no measured effects. It is a standard statement in the literature on experimental design that the null hypothesis cannot be proven. This is because there is always the possibility, however remote, that statistics have failed to detect a true difference, and because we cannot know what would have resulted in an experiment if the treatment had been more powerful, or sources of random error had been controlled, or suppressor variables had been measured, or an analysis with greater statistical power had been used. However, in many practical situations failure to reject the null hypothesis can be taken as sufficient for believing that the treatment-as-implemented makes so small a difference that it would not be worth worrying about even if it had made a statistically significant difference. Notwithstanding this, there are other more theory-relevant situations where we can consider accepting the null hypothesis only if the experimental design was demonstrably sensitive enough in the ways described below that it maximized the chances of obtaining a true difference, and only if we can also be assured that all the theory-derived conditions that facilitate a particular effect were present in the experimental design that resulted in no differences.

The second point concerns the problem that one can falsely conclude that there is covariation just as one can falsely conclude that there is no covariation. Our discussion has thus far focused on the latter problem since field settings do not permit as much control over error variance as the laboratory, and so true differences are more likely to be obscured in the field. However, elementary statistics textbooks teach us that the control possibilities of the laboratory are of no help in avoiding Type I errors, concluding that there is covariation when there is not.

Third, a special problem of statistical conclusion validity arises in designs where there are two (or more) experimental groups and when there are pretest-posttest differences within each group, but there are no differences between these differences. At first glance, it would seem that there is and is not statistical covariation at the same time. However, the within-group comparisons test whether any change at all has taken place but fail to specify the locus of such change— it might be due to the treatment or to testing or to maturation or to history. The between-group comparison tests whether there is any more change in one experimental group than another. This specifies the locus of cause more adequately (since randomization rules out the possibility of maturation, etc.), but risks the underestimation of treatment effects if different treatments have an impact of comparable magnitude or if performance in the control group is raised by a John Henry effect (Saretsky, 1972). The within-group and between-group comparisons are thus tests of different things, and it is only an apparent contradiction if one of them indicates an effect but the other does not. Unfortunately, though, neither of them inevitably measures a treatment's effects alone: the one measures the effects of a treatment plus other factors, while the other measures only those treatment effects that are over and above what is found in other treatment or control groups. For purposes of making confident conclusions about cause, the between-group comparisons are obviously much stronger than the within-group comparisons.

Finally, much of this chapter deals with quasi-experiments but none of it deals in detail with how to conduct inferential statistical tests of the null hypothesis. Sometimes, we give references to sources in which appropriate tests can be found, and at other times we give references to the best approximate tests that, to our knowledge, are available. But it is a sad fact that research on the statistical evaluation of quasi-experiments has not reached the stage of definitiveness that currently characterizes the state of the statistical art for randomized experiments. In particular, no adequate statistical tests yet exist for the most frequently used quasi-experimental design in which non-equivalent groups, whose pretest performance levels vary, receive different treatments. Even with time-series analyses (in which observations are made at multiple times before and after a treatment), there is no definitiveness yet despite much vigorous and enlightened research that we shall mention later which promises well for the not-so-distant future.

However, it should not be forgotten that inferential statistics are useful for testing only one of many threats to valid inference—that of chance. If they loom larger than this in the minds of many research workers, we suspect that this is because the researchers received their statistical training in such a way that they concentrated on true experiments in which randomization takes care of most other threats to validity. It may also be because we learn to value criteria that reduce uncertainty, and statistical tests do this because they determine the "eyeball" differences that do and do not require interpretation. In any event, we shall provide references about appropriate and approximate statistical tests, but shall not examine the tests in any detail.

Here, now, is our taxonomy of threats to statistical conclusion validity.

Statistical Power. The likelihood of making an incorrect no-difference conclusion (Type II error) increases when sample sizes are small, α is set low, one-sided hypotheses are incorrectly chosen and tested and most kinds of distribution-free statistics are used for hypothesis-testing. The likelihood of making incorrect difference conclusions (Type I error) increases if α is set high.

Fishing and the Error Rate Problem. Type I errors will result when multiple comparisons of mean differences are possible and no cognizance is taken of the fact that a certain proportion of the comparisons will be different by chance. Ryan (1959) has distinguished between the error rate per comparison ("the probability that any one of the comparisons will be incorrectly considered to be significant"), the error rate per experiment ("the expected number of errors per experiment"), and the error rate experiment-wise ("the probability that one or more erroneous conclusions will be drawn in a particular experiment"). The last two are the most important, and Ryan has illustrated one method of adjusting for the error rate per experiment. This involves computing a new t value which has to be reached before significance at a given α level can be claimed. The new t is obtained by taking the desired α (e.g., .05) and dividing it by the number of possible comparisons so as to give a proportion (p) that will be lower than .05. Then, the t value corresponding to this adjusted p is looked up in the appropriate tables, and it will, of course, be higher than the t values normally associated with $\alpha = .05$. This higher value reflects the stringency required for obtaining a true level of statistical significance when multiple tests are made. A second method for dealing with the error rate problem involves using the conservative multiple comparison tests of Tukey or Scheffé which are discussed in most moderately advanced statistics texts. And when there are multiple dependent variables in a factorial experiment, a multivariate analysis of variance strategy can be used for determining whether any of the significant univariate F tests within a particular main or interaction effect are due to chance rather than to the manipulations.

The Reliability of Measures. Measures of low reliability (conceptualized either as "stability" or "test-retest") cannot be depended upon to register true changes because they will inflate error terms. Some ways of controlling for this, *where possible,* are to use longer tests for which items have been carefully selected for their high intercorrelation,

and to decrease the interval between tests and retests. Or, large units of analysis can be used (e.g., groups instead of individuals), though the reliability gain will be partly offset by fewer degrees of freedom. Or, standard corrections for unreliability can be used.

The Reliability of Treatment Implementation. The way a treatment is implemented may differ from one person to another if different persons are responsible for implementing the treatment. There may also be differences from occasion to occasion when the same person implements the treatment. This lack of standardization within and between persons will inflate error variance and decrease the chance of obtaining true differences. The threat can be most obviously controlled by making the treatment and its implementation as standard as possible across occasions of implementation.

Random Irrelevancies in the Experimental Setting. Some features of an experimental setting other than the treatment will undoubtedly affect scores on the dependent variable and will inflate error variance. This threat can be most obviously controlled by choosing settings free of extraneous sources of variation, or by choosing experimental procedures which force respondents' attention on the treatment and lower the saliency of environmental variables, or by measuring sources of extraneous setting variance that are common to the various treatment groups and using them in the statistical analysis.

Random Heterogeneity of Respondents. The respondents in an experiment can differ with respect to the major dependent variables. Sometimes, certain kinds of respondents will be more affected by a treatment than others, and this—as we shall soon see—is a matter of external validity. But irrespective of whether this happens, the error term for testing treatment effects, including interactions, will be inflated the more respondents are heterogeneous with respect to variables that affect the dependent variable. This threat can obviously be controlled by selecting homogeneous respondent populations (at some cost in external validity), or by blocking on these respondent characteristics, or by choosing within-subject error terms as in pretest-posttest designs. The extent to which within-subject error terms reduce the error terms depends on the correlation between each subject's scores: the higher the correlation, the greater the reduction in the error term.

External Validity

Some of the concerns that Campbell and Stanley mentioned under external validity are here treated under the separate heading of construct validity. Those aspects that focus on generalizing to, or across, times, settings, and persons are retained under external validity, while those that have to do with interpreting operationalized treatments and measures in generalized terms (i.e., as abstract concepts) are grouped under construct validity. In the last analysis, as Bracht and Glass (1968) pointed out, external validity has to do with the correspondence between available samples, the populations they represent, and the populations to which generalization is required.

We have chosen to include under construct validity issues having to do with generalization to, or across, effect constructs. This is because in much research we want to know whether we can generalize from, say, a relationship between a new educational program and learning the alphabet to a relationship between the program and reading; or we might want to know whether a guaranteed annual income affects family stability as well as motivation to remain in the work force. The issue of whether the construct A causally affects the constructs B, C, D, and E involves an attempt to specify how far the effects of A can be generalized, and as such it seems both conceptually related to external validity and conceptually distinct from the construct validity question of whether A affects multiple measures of B alone. However, the distinction becomes clouded since it is not

unknown to discover empirically that the various planned measures of B are differently related to A, though it was originally thought that they would be similarly related. Such an unexpected data pattern suggests that more than one outcome construct was involved in the research. Moreover, another way of extending construct validity requires multiple outcome constructs, some of which should be affected by a treatment if the outcome is B and others of which should not be affected if the outcome is not C. For instance, a theory might predict an increase in the quantity of task performance but not its quality; or a theory of specific belief change might predict a change in belief measures but no change in overt behavioral measures that would at first sight seem related to the beliefs. The difficulty of classifying multiple outcome constructs under traditional validity headings might have prompted Snow (1974) to list it separately under "referent generality." But in the last analysis it is more important to note the multiple outcome issue and to know how to deal with it than it is to be able to classify it neatly under one of our validity labels.

Interaction of Treatments and Treatments. This threat occurs if respondents experience more than one treatment. We do not know in such an instance whether we could generalize any findings to the situation where respondents received only a single treatment. The solution to this problem is either to give only one treatment to respondents, or, wherever possible, to conduct separate analyses of the treatments which respondents received first and those which they received later.

Interaction of Testing and Treatment. To which kind of testing situations can a cause-effect relationship be generalized? In particular, can it be generalized beyond the testing conditions that were originally used to probe the hypothesized cause-effect relationship? This is an especially important question when the pretesting of respondents is involved and might condition the reception of the experimental stimulus. We would want to know whether the same result would have been obtained without a pretest, and a posttest-only control group is necessary for this. Similarly, if repeated posttest measurements are made, we would want to know whether the same results would be obtained if respondents were posttested once rather than at each delay interval. The recommended solution to this problem is to have independent experimental groups at each delayed test session.

Interaction of Selection and Treatment. To which categories of persons can a cause-effect relationship be generalized? Can it be generalized beyond the groups used to establish the initial relationship—to various racial, social, geographical, age, sex, or personality groups? In particular, whenever the conditions of recruiting respondents are systematically selective, we are apt to have findings that are only applicable to volunteers, exhibitionists, hypochondriacs, scientific do-gooders, those with nothing else to do with their time, etc. One feasible way of reducing this bias is to make cooperation in the experiment as convenient as possible. For example, volunteers in a TV studio audience experiment, who have to come downtown to participate, are much more likely to be atypical than are volunteers in an experiment carried door-to-door. Or, an experiment involving executives is more likely to be ungeneralizable if it takes a day's time than if it takes only ten minutes, for only the latter experiment is likely to include busy persons who have little free time.

Interaction of Setting and Treatment. Can a causal relationship obtained in a factory be obtained in a bureaucracy, in a military camp, on a university campus? The solution here is to vary settings and to analyze for a causal relationship within each. This threat is of particular relevance to organizational psychology since its settings are at such disparate levels as the organization, the small group, and the individual. When can we generalize from any one of these units to the others? The threat is also rele-

vant because of the volunteer bias as to which organizations cooperate. The refusal rate in getting the cooperation of industrial organizations, school systems, etc. must be nearer 75 percent than 25 percent, especially if we include those that were never contacted because it was considered certain they would refuse. The volunteering organizations will often be the most progressive, proud, and institutionally exhibitionist. For example, Campbell (1956), although working with Office of Naval Research funds, could not get access to destroyer crews and had to settle for high-morale submarine crews. Can we extrapolate from such situations to those where morale, exhibitionism, pride, or self-improvement needs are lower?

Interaction of History and Treatment. To which periods in the past and future can a particular causal relationship be generalized? Sometimes, an experiment takes place on a very special day (e.g., when a president dies), and the researcher is left wondering whether he would have obtained the same cause-effect relationship under more mundane circumstances. But even when circumstances are relatively more mundane, we still cannot logically extrapolate findings from the present to the future. Yet, while logic can never be satisfied "common-sense" solutions for short-term historical effects lie either in replicating the experiment at different times (for other advantages of consecutive replication see Cook, 1974a), or in conducting a literature review to see if there is prior evidence which does not refute the causal relationship.

Generalizing Across Effect Constructs. One very often hears the comment: "I wonder what would have happened if we had measured such and such a variable? Would the treatment have affected it, I wonder?" This issue is perhaps most critical when considering the unanticipated negative side effects that a treatment might have. For instance, does this new popular television program for children both teach *and* decrease reading? Does the new technological innovation increase productivity *but* decrease job satisfaction and so threaten turnover in the long run? Does a guaranteed annual income in an experiment lead to reduced labor force participation *and* patterns of conspicuous consumption by the poor that make it difficult for politicians to vote for such an income because they think that their constituencies will think it wasteful? The issue is not restricted to such negative side effects, however. Someone studying how a persuasion campaign affects beliefs might also wonder how it affects overt behaviors, while someone studying how an open floor arrangement affects communication patterns in a bureaucracy might also wonder how it differentially affects the promotion prospects of the gregarious and the shy. Of course, there is no end to the list of variables that a treatment might influence. The problem is to anticipate in advance as many secondary effects as are useful for theory building (by helping to elucidate the range of variables that are and are not affected by a treatment) or are useful for policy-guidance. In this respect, it is useful for experimenters to share their research question with a heterogeneous sample of persons before beginning the actual experiment. The more different the implications of the research from person to person or from interest group to interest group, the more useful will be the net of dependent variables that is collected (Cook, 1974b; Rossi, Boeckmann, & Berk, 1974).

Assessing external validity, unlike internal validity, is an inductive process. We cannot extrapolate with any logical certainty from the persons, settings, and times of a study to *all* persons, settings, and times, or even to specified limited future settings, persons, and times.

However, this is not to say that we have no techniques for increasing external validity. One infrequently used way involves *random sampling* from designated universes in order to obtain representative samples, a procedure that takes advantage of the outstanding achievements of survey research. But in quasi-experiments one has different

populations of respondents in the various treatment conditions, none of which are randomly representative of any specifiable population other than themselves. Even with true experiments, randomization for assuring experimental-control group equivalence is usually much easier than randomization for achieving the representativeness of each sample from some universe of interest. This is because the persons or organizations that agree to be randomly assigned to experimental conditions, or that for political reasons can be so assigned, are typically a biased sample of all the persons or organizations in a particular universe of interest. Unfortunately, universes of convenience are much more likely than universes of interest.

A more practical model of external validity involves the deliberate creation within the research design of *heterogeneous groups* of persons, settings, and times. It would thereby be possible to estimate whether a particular cause-effect relationship holds over a wide range of the units in question, although one would not know whether the units were representative of anything in particular. One would merely attempt to test the range of variables across which a causal relationship could be inferred. Thus, generalizing *across* would replace generalizing *to*; and "quasi-representativeness" would replace the more "formal representativeness" of the random sampling model.

Another practical model requires *generalization to modal instances*. This occurs whenever groups of respondents, work settings, and conditions of testing can be specified that are modal for a given problem area. Imagine, for example, someone who wanted to develop a theory of piecework. External validity would be low if this person studied piecework on a sample of psychotherapists who were paid according to the quality of their therapy—with quality being perhaps assessed by supervisors from therapists' notes. We actually know of such a work setting, and it is obviously very different from the industrial settings where most piecework in the United States presumably goes on. That is, the kinds of persons who take on factory work are very different from those who become therapists; the quantity of output is more easily and objectively assessed in industrial settings than in therapy; and continuous feedback about his performance is typically accessible to the industrial worker in a way that it is not to the therapist. A theory of piecework which has been tested in the settings where most piecework takes place will apply to more persons and settings than a theory which has been tested on the few psychotherapists in the nation who are paid on a piecework basis.

A final model is really a special case of the preceding and it involves impressionistically *generalizing to target instances* even if these are not modal in the sense discussed above. For example, there may be investigators interested in psychotherapists who are paid on a piecework basis, and they may have no aspirations beyond generalizing to such a small and particular body of persons. Much consulting work has this narrower focus and the major concern has to be to make sure that the research respondents, settings, and testings are comparable (on an impressionistic basis at least) to the target respondents, settings, and testings. (Of course, generalization to target instances would be more accurate with randomly drawn samples of instances than with purposive samples. But it is often not practical to draw random samples of persons from meaningful universes, and it is difficult in most situations to conceive of populations of settings and times.)

The relative feasibility of these four models of external validity can be gained by examining the piecework example in more detail. The random sampling model would require developing a list of the universe of pieceworkers. While this would be possible within a firm or agency, it would be very difficult to accomplish across all the pieceworkers in the United States or beyond. Hence, while client-focused research may sometimes permit use of the random sample model, theory-focused research will

not because there is no reason why theories should be limited to certain firms or agencies. The heterogeneity model requires that the investigator think through the range of settings, times, tests, and persons across which piecework is practiced. Then, he has to sample as diverse units as possible. The difficulties here, of course, are that it is expensive to track down heterogeneous samples (especially when geography is one element of heterogeneity), and that it is difficult to gain access to multiple settings. The specific target model is easy to follow in client-focused work, where generalization to local instances is required. But if the investigator wants to explore how widespread a theory-relevant relationship is, then the model requires him to explicate the impressionistically modal instances—the kinds of persons most likely to be on piecework, the settings where this most typically occurs, the ways output or satisfaction are most typically measured, etc. Then, he has to find one or several research sites where the local conditions correspond with his analysis of the most typical conditions. Major difficulties here involve knowing what is typical and knowing where the typical can be found without laborious pilot-testing. Mostly, there will have to be a reliance on what experience says is typical.

The random sampling model is the most powerful for inferential purposes, and the heterogeneity and the modal target models are probably the next most powerful in that order. However, feasibility seems to us to be negatively correlated with inferential power, and it is this—together with the basically inductive nature of external validity—that makes external validity the Achilles heel of the behavioral sciences. These are not the only reasons. In any single experiment there are many subgroups of persons, settings, times, and effect constructs across which we could potentially generalize, but typically few of them can be examined. For instance, if we restrict ourselves just to generalizing across persons, they can differ by sex, age, SES, place of residence, intelligence, extroversion, anxiety, and so on. Even if we could sample to include considerable heterogeneity on all these dimensions—which we mostly cannot—it would still be difficult to take account of all of them in the data analysis so as to specify in which particular subgroups a causal relationship can be inferred. While this will be possible for some groups, it will not be possible for all of them, and for the person variables that cannot be separately examined the most that we could do would be to test whether a relationship holds *despite* such person-related sources of heterogeneity. That is, we would relegate the heterogeneity to the error-term instead of examining each of its sources as a factor in the experimental design. This difficulty is compounded, of course, once one realizes that settings may be as multidimensional as persons.

The difficulties associated with external validity should not blind experimenters to the very real steps they can make toward increasing generalizability. For instance, one can often deliberately choose to perform an experiment at three or more sites in each of which different kinds of persons live or work. Or, if one can randomly sample, it is useful to do this even if the population involved is not meaningful, for random sampling insures heterogeneity. Thus, in their experiment on the relationship between beliefs and behavior about open housing, Brannon et al. (1973) choose a random sample of all white households in the metropolitan Detroit area. While few of us are interested in generalizing to such a population, the sample was nonetheless considerably more heterogeneous than that used in most research, even despite the homogeneity on the attributes of race and geographical residence. It is especially worth remembering that our four methods of increasing external validity can be used in combination in the experiment, as has been achieved in some survey research experiments on improving survey research procedures (Schuman & Duncan, 1974). Usually, random samples of respondents are chosen in such experiments, but the interviewers are

not randomly chosen—they are merely impressionistically modal of all experienced interviewers. Moreover, the physical setting of the research is limited to one target setting that is of little interest to anyone who is not a survey researcher—the respondent's living room—and the range of outcome variables is usually limited to those that survey researchers typically study—that is, those that can be assessed using paper and pencil. However, great care is normally taken that these questions cover a wide range of possible effects, thereby insuring considerable heterogeneity in the effect constructs studied.

Our pessimism about external validity should not be overgeneralized, for a consciousness of targets of generalization, of the kinds of settings in which a target class of behaviors most frequently occurs, and of the kinds of persons who most often experience particular kinds of natural treatments, will, at the very least, prevent the designing of experiments that many persons shrug off willy-nilly as "irrelevant." And it is sometimes possible to conduct multiple replications of an experiment at different times, in different settings, and with different kinds of experimenters and respondents.

Construct Validity

Construct validity is what experimental psychologists mean by "confounding"—the possibility that the operational definition of a cause or effect can be construed in terms of more than one construct, all of which are stated at the same level of reduction. Confounding means that what one investigator interprets as a causal relationship between A and B another investigator might interpret as a causal relationship between A and Y or between X and B or even between X and Y, and later experiments might support one or the other of these reinterpretations. The reference to the level of reduction is important because it is always possible to "translate" sociological terms into psychological terms, or psychological terms into biological terms. For example, participative decision making could become conformity to membership group norms on the one level, or some correlate of, say, the ascending reticular activating system on the other. Each of these levels of reduction is useful in different ways and none is more legitimate than any other. But such "translations" from one level to another do not involve the confounding of rival explanation that is at issue here.

Before we continue our abstract characterization, some well-known, concrete examples of construct validity problems may help. In medical experiments on the effects of drugs, the psychotherapeutic effect of the doctor's helpful concern was confounded with the chemical action of the pill. Also, the doctor's and the patient's belief that the pill should have helped were confounded with the chemical action as potential causes of patients' later reports of improvement. The placebo control group and the double-blind experimental design were introduced to unconfound these. In industrial relations research, the Hawthorne effect is another such confound; if we assume for the moment that productivity was increased, was this due to an increase in illumination or to the demonstrated administrative concern over improved working conditions or to feedback to the women about how well they were doing in their work?

High construct validity requires rigorous definition of potential causes and effects so that manipulations or measures can be tailored to the constructs they are meant to represent. But since single exemplars of constructs never give a perfect fit, researchers should use multiple exemplars of each construct wherever possible. These should demonstrably share common variance attributable to the target construct and should also differ from each other in unique ways that are irrelevant to the target construct. Such "multiple operationalism" allows tests of whether a particular cause-effect relationship holds even though a variety of different theoretical irrelevancies are present in each operation. One need not, therefore, be in the situation where a particular irrelevancy is associated with every exemplar of a construct, thereby confounding the construct and the irrelevancy.

Four other points are worth making about assessing construct validity. First, the proposed independent variables should demonstrably vary what they are meant to vary, and measuring this is usually called "assessing the 'take' of the independent variable." Second, the independent variables should not co-vary *with measures of related but different constructs*. For instance, a manipulation of "communicator expertise" should be correlated with reports from respondents about the communicator's level of knowledge but should not be correlated with attributions about his trustworthiness, likability, or power. Third, the proposed dependent variables should tap into the factors that they are meant to measure. Normally, some form of inter-item correlation can demonstrate this. And fourth, the dependent variables should not be dominated by irrelevant factors that make them measures of more or less than was intended. Without all or some of these data-bound processes, the interpretation of manipulations and measures can appear somewhat arbitrary.

The similarity and difference between external and construct validity can be seen at this point. External validity involves drawing samples that represent populations, and construct validity also seems to involve selecting a sample of measures or manipulations that represent the abstract construct (the "population," as it were). But while it is sometimes possible to conceptualize populations for external validity purposes and to draw up a list of all the instances in the population, it is often not possible to get high agreement among persons about the conceptualization of abstract constructs like, say, "aggression," and it is never possible to draw up a list of all possible instances of aggression from which a random sample of measures could be drawn. Moreover, when we decide on a measure or manipulation there will inevitably be some sources of equivocality concerning their fit with their referent construct, and we always have to settle for imperfect representations of constructs. The researcher's task is to minimize the imperfection, which he does by the processes listed in the previous paragraph and by insuring that he has multiply operationalized manipulations and measures so that he can test whether different versions of the same construct—each of which hopefully has different imperfections—are similarly related.

We can illustrate these points by considering a possible experiment on the effects of supervisory distance. Suppose we operationalized "close supervision by a foreman" as standing within comfortable speaking distance of workers. This would exclude longer distances where speaking was not possible but from which workers might nonetheless perceive they were being supervised. Hence, the treatment might be more exactly characterized as "supervision from speaking distances" as opposed to "close supervision" or "supervision" in general. Indeed, it might be dangerous to generalize from the treatment to the construct, especially if supervision has different consequences if it comes from speaking rather than from seeing but not speaking distances. It would be much more useful for construct validity, therefore, if supervisory distance were systematically varied by means of planned manipulations, or if it inadvertently varied across a wide range because each foreman differed in his behavior from day to day. The systematic variation of distance would allow us to test whether we can generalize from one supervisory distance to another (and hence to the general construct), while the naturally occurring heterogeneity in the treatment implementation would allow us to conclude whether supervisory distance affects outcomes despite the error-inflating heterogeneity that is attributable to variation in the theoretical irrelevancy of actual physical distance.

The foremen might also differ from each other, or might themselves differ from day to day, in whether they supervise with a smile, in an officious manner, or inad-vertently during some other task. Neither the smile, the officiousness, nor the inadvertence would seem to be necessary components of "supervision," and a researcher would hope that such behaviors were equally frequent across instances where supervisory distance was manipulated or that they could be measured and used in analyses to ascertain whether the closeness of supervision had similar effects despite the heterogeneity introduced by the theoretical irrelevancy of a foreman's smile, officiousness, or inadvertence. If effects could not be generalized across all of these irrelevancies, important contingencies would be specified that determine the particular type of supervision that causes a particular effect, thereby implying a restriction in generality. But the restriction would add accuracy and better specify the causal construct as, say, "close supervision with a smile" rather than "close supervision."

The kind of specification we have just been discussing concerns variables that are manipulated contemporaneously with the intended treatment. It is more difficult to spell out the implications for construct validity of "developmental sequences," which are the processes that causally follow from the treatment and mediate its consequences. For example, close supervision by a foreman might mean that workers can ask for, and receive, task-relevant feedback that increases the quality or quantity of their performance. Alternatively, workers might feel resentment that their freedom is being curtailed by the supervision, and so might work less. The feedback and resentment process are consequences that presumably depend on who the foreman or worker is, how past relations have been in the particular work environment, etc. The researcher is, therefore, faced with the dilemma: Should the treatment be specified as, say, "closeness of supervision and task-relevant feedback," for this is the construct that led to the observed effects even though it was not the planned cause and is less general than the original construct? We are presently inclined not to include developmental sequences under the heading of construct validity since they do not have to do with the correspondence between referent constructs and either a treatment or a measure. Instead, they have to do with treatment consequences that are often situation or person-bound and that often lead to theoretical reformulations (i.e., one might rephrase research questions in terms of the determinants and consequences of resentment rather than closeness of supervision, for resentment would seem to be a more reliable determinant of productivity than supervisory style). However, the elucidation of "developmental sequences," is well worth while in its own right.

It is a mistake to think that construct validity should only be a concern of the theoretician. Many treatments in applied research are complex packages of variables rather than indicators of apparently unidimensional constructs. Hence, it will sometimes be difficult to reproduce the total package, and some effects might not be as easy to replicate as they would be if the causal components of a treatment could be specified. A concern with construct validity can also indicate whether the most policy-relevant questions have been asked in a research project. For intance, "Sesame Street" was evaluated in an experiment where children were visited on a weekly or monthly basis in the home and were encouraged to view the show by research staff members who left behind toys, books, and balloons which advertised the series (Ball & Bogatz, 1970; Bogatz & Ball, 1971). Such face-to-face encouragement probably cost between $100 and $200 per child per six-month viewing season over and above the costs of developing and distributing the program, and it probably is not a process that is, to the extent we understand it, as widespread nationally as viewing without encouragement from a research staff (Cook, Appleton, Conner, Shafer, Tamkin, & Weber, 1975). Since viewing the show without encouragement costs only between $1 and $2 per child per season, and since most children in the United States view the show this way, viewing would

seem to be a more policy-relevant construct than encouragement. It would, therefore, be useful to know whether the effects of viewing without encouragement are similar to those attributable to viewing with encouragement. While it is true that the applied researcher's major goal is, *and should be,* to make an impact on some neatly labeled outcome, it is nonetheless possible and desirable for him or her to conduct internal analyses of the experimental data which might help specify a causal construct more adequately. It is even better, of course, if the research is designed so that there is a high initial correspondence between the treatment and the policy-relevant variable to which generalization is desired.

Here, then, is a list of threats to construct validity. They all have to do either with the operations failing to incorporate all the dimensions of the construct, which we might call "construct underrepresentation," or with the operations containing dimensions that are irrelevant to the target constructs, which we might call "surplus construct irrelevancies." The list concentrates on the fit between operations and their referent constructs rather than on the fit between constructs and the way that the research problem is conceptualized. Getting the initial question "right" is not the same as the construct validity issue of getting one's operations to reflect one's research constructs. The list that follows is about the latter:

Inadequate Pre-Operational Explication of Constructs. The choice of operations should depend on the result of a conceptual analysis of the essential features of a construct. By consulting dictionaries (social science or otherwise) and the past literature on a topic, one would find, for example, that "attitude" is usually defined as a stable predisposition to respond, and that this stability is understood either as consistency across response modes (affective, cognitive, and behavioral) and/or as stability across time (responses to the same attitude measure taken at different times should correlate positively). Such an analysis immediately suggests that it would not be adequate to measure preferences or beliefs at a single session and to label this as "attitude," which is unfortunately done all too often. To give another example, many definitions of aggression include both the intent to harm others and the fact that harm results from actions. This is to distinguish between (a) the black eye one boy gives another as they collide coming round a blind bend; (b) the black eye that one boy gives another to get his candy (instrumental aggression) or to harm him (non-instrumental); and (c) the verbal threat by one child to another that he will give him a black eye unless the other boy gives him some candy. Since intent and physical harm are stressed in the definition, only (b) above is adequate as an example of the construct "aggression," though it will not be adequate for the minority of persons who prefer a more idiosyncratic definition of the term. A precise explication of constructs is vital for high construct validity since it permits tailoring the manipulations and measures to whichever definitions emerge from the explication.

Mono-Operation Bias. Many experiments are designed to have only one exemplar of a particular possible cause, and some have just one measure to represent some of the possible effect constructs. Since single operations both underrepresent constructs and contain irrelevancies, construct validity will be lower in single exemplar research than in research where each construct is multiply operationalized in order to triangulate on the referent. There is usually no excuse for single operations of effect constructs, since it is not costly to gather additional data from alternative measures of the targets. There is more excuse for having only one manipulation of a possible causal construct since increasing the total number of treatments in a factorial design. This can lead either to very large sample research or to small sizes within each cell of the design should it not be possible to increase the total sample size. Moreover, if one lets irrelevancies in

the treatment presentation vary spontaneously from occasion to occasion, this threatens statistical conclusion validity, even though any treatment effects that emerge *despite* the inflated error are presumably not due to those irrelevancies that differed from occasion to occasion. There is really no substitute, where possible, for deliberately varying two or three exemplars of a treatment. Thus, if one were interested in the expertise of a communicator, one might have one distinguished male professor from a distinguished university, one distinguished female research scientist from a prestigious research center, and the most famous science journalist in Western Germany. Then, the variance due to the difference between these sources can be examined to test whether the different combinations of irrelevancies (sex, affiliation, nationality, affiliation, or academic standing) differently affected responses and whether each expert—or the three combined —caused the expected outcome. If sample size did not permit analyzing separately by source, the data could be combined from all three and the investigator could then test whether expertise was effective despite the irrelevant sources of heterogeneity.

Mono-Method Bias. To have more than one operational representation of a construct does not necessarily imply that all irrelevancies have been made heterogeneous, and this is never the case when all the manipulations or measures use the same means of presenting treatments or recording responses. Thus, if all the experts in the previous hypothetical example had been presented to respondents in writing, it would not logically be possible to generalize to experts who are seen or heard and it would be more accurate to label the treatment as "experts presented in writing." Attitude scales are often presented to respondents without apparent thought (a) to using methods of recording other than paper-and-pencil; (b) to varying whether the attitude statements are positively or negatively worded; (c) to varying whether the positive or negative end of the response scale appears on the right or the left of the page. On these three points depends whether one can rule out if the measure has been of "personal private attitude" or "paper-and-pencil non-accountable responses" or "acquiescence" or "response bias."

Hypothesis-Guessing within Experimental Conditions. The internal validity threats called "resentful demoralization" and "compensation rivalry" were assumed to result because persons receiving no treatment, or less desirable treatments, compared themselves to persons receiving the most desired treatments, making it unclear whether there were any treatment effects of any kind. It is also possible for reactive research to result in real but uninterpretable treatment effects, especially when persons in these groups compare themselves to others and guess how they are supposed to behave (in many situations it is not difficult to guess what is desired, especially perhaps in education, or in industrial organizations). Furthermore, a hypothesis can be guessed without social comparison processes operating so that, informing respondents only of their own treatment and isolating them from others, does not by itself get around the problem of hypothesis-guessing. The problem can best be avoided by making hypotheses hard to guess (if there are any), by decreasing the general level of reactivity in the experiment, or by deliberately giving different hypotheses to different respondents. But these solutions are at best partial since respondents are not passive and may generate their own treatment-related hypotheses that are independent of experimenters' attempts to dampen hypothesis-guessing. However, having a hypothesis does not necessarily imply either the motivation to comply with it (or to "sabotage" it) or the ability to alter one's behavior in the direction indicated by the hypothesis. Despite the widespread discussion of treatment confounds that are presumed to result from wanting to give data that will please the researcher—which we suspect is a result of discussions of the Hawthorne effect—there is neither widespread evidence of the Hawthorne effect in field experiments (see reviews by D. Cook, 1967, and Diamond, 1974) nor is there evidence of an analogue orientation in laboratory contexts (Weber & Cook, 1972). However, we still lack a sophisticated and empirically corroborated theory of the conditions under which (a) hypothesis-guessing occurs, (b) is treatment-specific, and (c) is translated into behavior that (d) could lead to erroneous conclusions about the nature of a treatment construct.

Evaluation Apprehension. Weber and Cook (1972) reviewed considerable data from laboratory experiments in social psychology which indicated that subjects behaved in the manner attributed to them by Rosenberg (1969). That is, they were apprehensive about being evaluated by experimenters who were experts in personality adjustment and task performance, and so the respondents attempted to present themselves as both competent and psychologically healthy. It is not clear how widespread such an orientation is in social science experiments (as opposed to psychology experiments) in field settings, with treatments that last a long time, and with populations that that do not especially value the way that social scientists or their sponsors evaluate them. Nonetheless, it is entirely plausible to assume that some past treatment effects may be due to respondents in the most desirable treatment groups presenting themselves to experimenters so as to be evaluated favorably. Yet this is rarely the target construct around which experiments are designed. It is a confound.

Experimenter Expectancies. There is some literature (Rosenthal, 1972) which indicates that an experimenter's expectancies can bias the data that he obtains. When this happens, it will not be clear whether the causal treatment is the treatment-as-labeled or the experimenter's expectations. This threat can be decreased by having experimenters who have no expectations or false expectations, or by analyzing the data separately for experimenters with different kinds or levels of expectancy. Experimenter expectancies are thus a special case of treatment-correlated irrelevancy.

Confounding Levels of Constructs and Constructs. Experiments typically involve the manipulation of several discrete levels of an independent variable that is continuous. Thus, one might conclude from an experiment that A does not affect B when in fact A-at-level-1 does not affect B, or A-at-level-4 does not affect B, whereas A-at-level-2 might affect B, as might A-at-level-3. Obviously, this threat is a problem when A and B are not linearly related, and it is especially prevalent, we assume, when treatments have only a weak impact. Thus, low levels of A are manipulated but conclusions may be drawn about A without qualification about the strength of the manipulation. The best control for this threat is to conduct parametric research in which many levels of A are varied and many levels of B are measured.

Generalizing Across Time. We often do not know how long a treatment would affect a cause. If the effect were short-lived, it would be less useful to state that A caused B than it would to state that A caused B and effects persisted for n weeks, or that A did not seem to cause B at first but after n weeks a "sleeper effect" was observed. Generalizing across time is particularly important with constructs like attitude that are sometimes defined in terms of "consistency in responding" to specific attitude objects. If we conducted an experiment, observed posttest differences that were related to a treatment, but had no delayed follow-up measures, we could not be certain of having obtained any consistency in responding over time because we would not have measured attitude often enough to test this. Generalizing across time can also be a problem with the treatment, of course. Would a guaranteed income lasting for three years be similar to one lasting ten years or for life?

Interaction of Procedure and Treatment. Sometimes the respondents in the treatment and control groups will learn new information or undergo new experiences as part of the context in which treatments are embedded, and this may influence how treatments are reacted to. For example, respondents in the New Jersey Income Maintenance Experiment were guaranteed a fixed minimum income of various levels for three years. Thus, each respondent may have been reacting, not just to the payment but to the knowledge that this payment would only last three years. Was the manipulated cause a specified level of income maintenance payments or the provision of these payments for three years?

Construct validity is like external validity both in its inferential character and in the means necessary for reducing validity threats. If one wants to generalize across settings, persons, etc., one has to take heterogeneous instances of settings and persons. Similarly, if one wants to corroborate a generalization from one operational exemplification of a treatment or effect to the referent construct, one needs multiple operationalizations. Or, to switch to another model of external validity, if one has a target setting or target population of persons to whom one wants to generalize, one can carefully think through these settings and populations and can try to obtain as representative a sample as possible. In a similar vein, by a careful explication of constructs and reliable measures of the "take" of the independent variable, one can isolate some single operational definitions that are better approximations of the target construct than are others.

Field research affords poor prospects for achieving high construct validity of the cause. This is because it is costly to implement multiple operationalizations of a single causal concept and because multiple operationalization is a better means of enhancing construct validity than is the careful tailoring of a single operation to a referent construct. The prospects are brighter for the high construct validity of outcomes, because investigators typically have a much greater latitude for multiple measurement than for multiple manipulation. This means that they can measure using multiple methods (observation, interviews, questionnaires, etc.) and that within each method, they can have multiple items or observational categories. In many respects it is only the ingenuity and conceptual skill of investigators that stand between research operations and a high degree of construct validity of outcomes.

Some Relationships Among the Four Kinds of Validity

We have previously noted how internal and statistical conclusion validity are more like each other than they are like external and construct validity. We have also noted how these last two are, in their turn, like each other in several distinct ways. We want now to mention three other relationships among the different kinds of validity.

First, some ways of increasing one kind of validity will decrease another kind. For instance, internal validity is best served by carrying out true experiments, but the organizations willing to tolerate this are probably less representative than organizations willing to tolerate passive measurement; statistical conclusion validity is increased if the experimenter can rigidly control the stimuli impinging on respondents, but this procedure can decrease both external and construct validity; increasing the construct validity of effects by multiple operationalizing each of them is likely to increase the tedium of measurement and cause attrition from the experiment or a decrease in measurement reliability for individual tests. These countervailing relationships suggest that crucial parts of planning any experiment have to be an explication of the priority-ordering among the four kinds of validity, a search for ways of avoiding all unnecessary trade-offs between one kind of validity and another, and a search for ways of minimizing the loss entailed by the necessary trade-offs. However, since some trade-offs are inevitable, we think it unrealistic to expect that a single piece of research will

effectively answer all of the validity questions surrounding even the simplest causal relationship.

Second, the general primacy of internal validity should be noted. Since experiments are conducted to make causal statements, internal validity assumes a particular importance because it relates to whether a relationship—of whatever strength—is unambiguously causal or not. The primacy of internal validity does not stand out where true experiments are concerned because the random allocation procedure rules out almost all the pertinent threats. But there is no randomized assignment of treatments in quasi-experiments, and the investigator's major task is to rule out the internal validity threats one by one. It is for these reasons that the next section on quasi-experiments will deal more with threats to internal validity than to any other kind of validity.

Third, the priority-ordering of the other threats varies with the kind of research being conducted. For persons interested in theory-testing it is almost as important to show that A causes B (a problem of construct validity) as it is to show that something *causes* something (a problem of internal validity). Moreover, most theories do not specify target settings, populations, times, or the like, so that external validity is of relatively little importance. In particular, it can be sacrificed for the statistical power that comes through having isolated settings, standardized procedures, and homogeneous respondent populations. Thus, for investigators with theoretical interests the rank-ordering of types of validity, in order of importance, is probably internal, construct, statistical conclusion, and external validity. (It is our impression that the construct validity of causes is more important for practitioners of such research than is the construct validity of effects. Think, for example, of how oversimply "attitude" is operationalized in many persuasion experiments, or "cooperation" in bargaining studies, or "aggression" in studies of interpersonal violence, and think how much care goes into demonstrating that the manipulation varied cognitive dissonance and not reactance. Might not the construct validity of effects come after statistical conclusion validity for most theory-testing researchers? If it does, it would be ironic in the sense that it is easier to achieve high construct validity of effects than of causes because multiple operationalization is easier with the former than the latter.)

Much applied research has a different set of priorities. It is often concerned with testing whether a particular specific problem has been alleviated (high construct validity of the effect), and it is critical that this demonstration be made in a setting and with persons that permit either wide generalization or generalization to specific targets (high interest in external validity). The research is relatively less concerned with whether the causal treatment is, for example, better lighting or a Hawthorne effect (low interest in construct validity of the cause). Thus, the priority-ordering for such researchers is something like internal validity, external validity, construct validity of the effect, statistical conclusion validity, and construct validity of the cause.

Though experiments are designed to test causal hypotheses, and though internal validity is the sine qua non of causal inference, there are nonetheless contexts where it would not be advisable to subordinate too much to internal validity. Someone commissioning research to improve the efficiency of his own organization might not take kindly to the idea of testing a proposed improvement in a laboratory setting with sophomore respondents. A necessary condition for meeting a client's needs is that the client could generalize any findings to his own organization and to the indicators of efficiency that he regularly uses for monitoring performance. Indeed, his need in this respect may be so great that he is prepared to sacrifice some gains in internal validity for a necessary minimum of external validity. However, he runs the risk because of this that he will not be able to answer his preliminary causal question with any

confidence. Hence, while the sociology of doing research might sometimes incline one to rate external validity higher than internal validity, the logic of testing causal propositions suggests tempering this inclination lest the very hypothesis-testing rationale for conducting experiments be vitiated. "Common sense" is obviously called for in trading off internal and external validity in any research project, which is why we mentioned the general primacy of internal validity rather than its absolute primacy.

Disciplines like industrial and organizational research that have members with each of these different orientations would appear to have special difficulties of communication in that members share different systems of priorities. But at the same time such disciplines have a special advantage in that all four kinds of validity are represented at a high priority level in some persons. This may provide the potential for a fruitful integration of ideas and findings from both the theory-relevant and applied areas. Disciplines with no such mixture of persons with different validity priorities are likely never to know much about, say, external validity on the one hand or the construct validity of causes on the other hand.

QUASI-EXPERIMENTAL DESIGNS

Notational System

This section will be devoted to an exposition of some quasi-experimental designs. In outlining them we shall use a notational system in which X stands for a treatment; O stands for an observation; subscripts 1 through n refer to the sequential order of implementing treatments $(X_1 \ldots X_n)$ or of recording observations $(O_1 \ldots O_n)$; and a dashed line between experimental groups indicates that the groups were not randomly formed.

Three Generally Uninterpretable Designs

The designs below are frequently used in industrial and organizational research.

While they are often useful for suggesting new hypotheses, they are normally not sufficient for permitting a strong test of hypotheses. The reasons for this should become clear from the discussions below.

a. The One Group Posttest-Only Design

This design is sometimes called the "case study" and involves making observations on persons who have undergone a treatment. The diagram below illustrates the design and highlights its two basic deficiencies. There are no pretest observations of persons receiving the treatment, nor is there a control group of persons who did not receive the treatment. As a consequence, no threats to internal validity can be ruled out and so

$$X \quad O_1$$

there is little point in worrying about the other kinds of validity. Hence, while the case study may be useful for suggesting causal hypotheses, it is inadequate for testing them.

b. The One Group Pretest-Posttest Design

This design is one of the more frequently used designs in organizational research and it is diagrammed below:

$$O_1 \quad X \quad O_2$$

It can be seen that pretest observations are recorded on a single group of persons (O_1), who later receive a treatment (X), after which posttest observations are made (O_2). Since the use of this design is so widespread, we would like to illustrate its weaknesses using a hypothetical example.

Imagine the case where the supervisory style of foremen is altered in a work setting and where the change is expected to increase productivity. Imagine, further, that the posttest level of productivity is reliably higher than the pretest level. One might want to attribute such an increase to the change in supervisory style. However, the change might alternatively be due to *history* in the sense that other events could have happened between the pretest and posttest that affected productivity. Some of these could have occurred within the work setting (e.g., a new salary scale might have been implemented; union policies might have changed; or a new training program might have been introduced). Other events could have taken place outside of the work setting (e.g., a new export drive might have been started nationally; or the weather might have become warmer, allowing workers to feel better or become better acquainted). Any of these events, or others, *could* have affected productivity, and it is incumbent upon the researcher to demonstrate that they did not operate or are not plausible. Otherwise, no confident conclusion can be drawn about cause.

Consider, next, *statistical regression*. Why should supervisory styles be changed? One reason might be that productivity is low and needs to be increased. Now, productivity in any one year can be low because of a genuinely stable decline in productivity or because productivity has been consistently low for some time. But it might also be *low in any one year* because of random factors, including measurement error. In this last case, the impetus for change will be negatively correlated with productivity, and this is tantamount to deliberately choosing an extreme year for conducting one's experiment. What will happen in such a case is that productivity will probably increase in the next year as it regresses towards the grand mean of the productivity trend. In other words, by choosing to change one's work practices when productivity is low, one can capitalize upon random fluctuations in productivity.

A more common form of regression artifact for this design arises when a special program is given only to those with extreme scores on the pretest. For example, a compensatory program that is given only to low scorers will seem to produce improvement if the pretest-posttest correlation is less than 1.00 (McNemar, 1940). Similarly, if an advanced training program is given to the best salesmen of one year, and is in fact totally ineffective, it will nonetheless appear to reduce the sales volume of its graduates when they are compared to other salesmen. (The magnitude of such a regression phenomenon would depend on how highly each salesman's sales volume is correlated from year to year.)

Even when the pretest-posttest correlation is high, a posttest increase in productivity could be accounted for in terms of maturation. Typically, productivity levels do not stay constant from year to year, being subject to both random and systematic fluctuations. Whenever productivity is systematically rising over the years or when it is subject to cyclical fluctuations within any one year, a posttest increase over pretest levels will appear in the design under discussion. This increase would not be unambiguously attributable to the supervisory change. It could alternatively be attributed to workers becoming more experienced, or to machinery becoming more and more sophisticated, or to the average height and weight of males in the United States being on the increase, or whatever. This threat is particularly relevant because many of the factories that allow outside investigators to conduct research may be proud of the fact they are getting better and better.

In some contexts there are ways of estimating whether maturation could plausibly account for any pretest-posttest difference in productivity. Imagine that the pretest and posttest are separated by a year and that the mean level of experience (years worked in an organization) increases by a year between pretest and posttest. If the pool of *pretest scores were sufficiently large,* one could regress productivity onto years worked. If the resulting correlation were zero, the maturation hypothesis would be rendered implausible. If there were a corre-

lation, one could use the regression equation to predict what scores would have been at the posttest in the absence of any treatment. Then this expected mean performance could be compared with the obtained performance. However, care must be taken with this estimation procedure because of the problems of under-adjustment or regression artifacts (see p. 297ff.) and of multiple testing. That is, the mean expected posttest performance is obtained from a pool of pretest scores where measurement has only taken place once. But the obtained mean comes from a second, posttest measurement of respondents. Thus, the contrast is of expected and obtained scores that differ (a) on the basis of coming from a first or second test as well as (b) on the basis of the presence or absence of a treatment. (Of course, this testing problem will be less if measurement is unobtrusive and based on regular administrative records of productivity.)

Sometimes, there will be specific settings where the threats of history, maturation, and regression are implausible and in those settings the one group pretest-posttest design will be interpretable. Unfortunately, these settings are likely to be rare. To rule out effects of history, the respondents would have to be *physically isolated* from historical forces that affect productivity. To rule out statistical regression and maturation we would need a *series of pretest observations* which demonstrated, first, that the single posttest observation could not be easily fitted to the pretest trend and, second, that the introduction of the treatment was not associated with extreme values of the pretest. However, the one group pretest-posttest design is defined as having only one pretest observation, and so we know nothing of the pretest trend. Occasionally, it might seem plausible to accept the assumptions of physical isolation and a stable pretest trend (e.g., in some anthropological work on tribes in remote settings), but this is not likely to be the case in research on organizations, especially those that are open systems.

c. Posttest-Only Design with Non-Equivalent Groups

Often a treatment is implemented before the researcher can prepare for it and the research design worked out after the treatment has begun. In this sense, the research is ex post facto. Such research does not necessarily imply that there will be no pretest observations, since archival records can often be used to establish what the pretest scores of the various experimental units were. We shall understand ex post facto here in the restricted sense that no pretest observations are available on the same or equivalent scales for which posttest observations are available.

If we add to the case study a non-equivalent control group which does not receive the treatment, the design under discussion results. Its most obvious flaw is the absence of pretests, and the fact that any posttest differences between the groups can be attributed either to a treatment effect or to *selection* differences between the non-equivalent groups. This renders the design uninterpretable.

$$X \quad O$$
$$\overline{\quad\quad O \quad}$$

It would be incorrect to infer from our preceding remarks that all posttest-only designs are uninterpretable. There are at least three contexts where posttest-only designs are interpretable, and we shall detail each of them in the following pages. One context is when there are multiple control groups that can be ordered along some quantitative continuum and when the group or groups receiving a treatment deviate from the overall trend which relates the quantified group classification variable to the outcome measure. In addition, there may be some correlational designs of the path analytic type where no pretests are involved and causal

inferences are possible. Finally, higher-order interaction hypotheses can sometimes be predicted which, if corroborated by the data, cannot be easily reinterpreted. We shall mention each of these cases later. At this stage it is sufficient to note that, while posttest-only designs with a single no-treatment control group are not interpretable, there are other posttest-only designs which may permit causal inferences.

Some Generally Interpretable Non-Equivalent Control Group Designs

In this section we shall distinguish among seven kinds of generally interpretable non-equivalent control group designs. These are: (a) the no-treatment control group design; (b) the reversed-treatment control group design; (c) the removed-treatment control group design; (d) the repeated treatment design; (e) the non-equivalent dependent variables design; (f) selection cohorts designs; and (g) predicted higher-order interaction designs with intact groups.

Our separate discussion of the designs should not blind the reader to the importance of incorporating more than one of them into the work he or she does. The designs have different strengths and weaknesses, and their creative mixture within a single study can significantly increase our confidence in making causal attributions. Several of the studies we shall be dealing with in detail (e.g., Broadbent & Little, 1960; Lawler & Hackman, 1969; Lieberman, 1956) were significantly improved by mixing the designs that we shall treat separately for pedagogic convenience.

a. The Untreated Control Group Design with Pretest and Posttest

This is a frequently used design, is often interpretable, and can be recommended in situations where nothing better is available. It can be diagrammed in the fashion below, and its interpretability depends, in part, on the particular empirical outcomes obtained in a particular study.

$$O_1 \quad X \quad O_2$$
$$O_1 \qquad O_2$$

Hence, we shall discuss five different outcomes of this basic design.

Outcome 1: The design above often controls for all but three threats to internal validity. One uncontrolled threat is that of selection-maturation due to the respondents in one group growing more experienced, more tired, or more bored than the respondents in another group. Imagine the situation where a new practice is introduced into one of two settings in which identical tasks are being performed and where the treatment group outperforms the controls at the pretest. If the treatment increased productivity, we would expect a posttest difference between groups that was larger than the pretest difference, as Figure 1 illustrates. But we would also expect this pattern of data if the treatment and control groups differed because the former were, on the average, younger or more fit or more intelligent and so were performing better on a particular task.

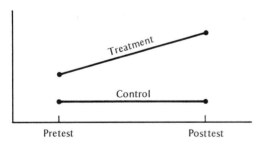

Figure 1. First outcome of the no-treatment control group design with pretest and posttest.

It is sometimes erroneously believed that a selection-maturation threat can be controlled by matching. In the example we have just discussed, matching would involve taking some control respondents who produced more than their group average at the pretest and some treatment respondents who produced less than their group average. This procedure can be carried out so as to result in treatment and control means that are identical at the pretest. It is then assumed that any posttest differences must be due to the treatment, and not to group differences, because there were no group differences at the pretest. Unfortunately, matching will result in a spurious treatment effect in the above instance, for the control respondents would regress to a lower posttest mean and the treatment respondents would regress to a higher posttest mean (Thorndike, 1942).

Let us take a concrete example of this. In a quasi-experiment with many otherwise excellent design features we shall later comment upon, Lieberman (1956) used a number of demographic, attitudinal, and motivational variables to match persons who were not foremen with persons who had just become foremen. He then studied the effects of changing work roles (i.e., becoming a foreman) on attitudes towards management and unions. Not surprisingly, Lieberman found that foremen came to adopt more managerial and less union attitudes than did non-foremen. However, this might be due to regression, for if we assume that workers with more managerial and less union attitudes are likely to be chosen as foremen in the first place, then it follows that the matched non-foremen will have higher managerial and lower union attitudes relative to the pool of laborers they were selected from. Since the attitude scores will include a component of measurement error, the controls should regress to the mean of all non-foremen. This would be towards less managerial and more union attitudes, thereby creating a spurious posttest difference between foremen and their matched controls that was not present at the pretest. In the absence of further analyses it would be wrong to attribute this difference to the adoption of role-relevant attitudes by foremen. (The same regression phenomenon can also explain why new shop stewards and their matched controls differed at the posttest but not at the pretest.)

A second, also erroneous, practice is to use regression techniques (covariance analysis, partial r, stepwise multiple regression) in an attempt to equate the pretest groups statistically. As Lord (1960, 1967, 1969) and Cronbach and Furby (1970) have pointed out, there is no way of equating non-equivalent groups via statistical procedures unless measurement is error-free. While these adjustments will reduce pretest group differences, they will not eliminate them. Consequently, any adjusted posttest differences in a covariance analysis will reflect an unknown combination of possible treatment effects and pretest differences that have not been adjusted away.

It might be thought that a better analysis strategy would be to leave the groups non-equivalent, to plot the pretest and posttest means, and to compute a two-way analysis of variance with experimental groups as a between-subjects factor and time of testing as a within-subjects factor. A treatment effect would be indicated by the interaction of groups and time of testing. However, this test would not control for selection-maturation and would also be subject to a *scaling* alternative interpretation that arises because, with many scales, it is not clear that the intervals are equal and because, in many instances, change is easier at some points on a scale than others. Scaling problems are presumably more acute the greater the non-equivalence of experimental groups and the farther apart they are on the scale, especially if any of the group means approaches one end of the scale. Obviously, there is less room for change when a group pretest mean is high (the so-called ceiling effect), and change may also be difficult when a pretest mean is low (the so-called basement effect). Sometimes, a logarithmic transformation will reduce the problem, as will careful

choice of intact and unmatched groups that score in the middle of a scale and close to each other.

A third problem relates to *local history*, events other than the treatment which affect the experimental group but not the control group, or vice versa. Imagine introducing some participative decision-making procedure to a group of day workers while leaving decision making as it was among night workers. Imagine, further, that the investigator was interested in seeing whether participative decision making induced higher work morale. Now, if the experiment started in the early spring and ended by midsummer we might expect the work morale of day workers to be more affected by the increasingly warm weather than the work morale of night workers. The plausibility of a local history explanation has to be examined within the particular context of specific research settings, but it is a general class of threat that the investigator has to consider.

The threat of local history has to be clearly differentiated from the threat to construct validity that arises when it is not clear whether the causal variable is the treatment alone or the treatment and some local history force. For example, suppose in the experiment by Lieberman (1956) that the newly promoted foremen had been given large bonuses as part of a profit-sharing scheme that only operated among supervisory personnel (and thus did not affect the non-equivalent control group of rank-and-file workmen). It would not be clear whether any increase in pro-management attitudes by foremen was due to a change in reference groups or to identification with persons who were instrumental in giving them large rewards. The latter is not an inevitable consequence of becoming a foreman since bonuses are contingent on profits, but it is nonetheless a result that would not have happened to the men if they had not become foremen. Thus, the local history effect of the bonus is part of the global treatment "becoming a foreman" and is not a threat to internal validity. The researcher would have to seek out foremen who had and had not received bonuses in order to test whether the causal construct in the hypothetical example above was receiving a bonus or some other feature of becoming a foreman.

Outcome 2: There is a type of selection-maturation interaction which is both more common and more lawful than the one depicted in Figure 1. This occurs in growth situations where pretest group differences can be explained by differences in average growth rate. These differential growth rates might be expected to continue, producing still larger differences on the posttest that would not be at all due to the intervention of different treatments. Figure 2 shows such a case, and it differs from Figure 1 in two respects:

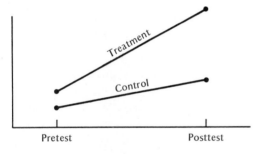

Figure 2. Second outcome of the no-treatment control group design with pretest and posttest.

(a) both groups are growing; and (b) if the group mean differences are a result of biased social aggregation or selection only, then the differential growth between groups should also be occurring within groups, producing increased variance for each group on the posttest. If such a differential growth process were homogeneous within and between groups, a rescaling of the measures (e.g., through substituting I.Q.s for mental ages or through standardizing pretest and posttest scores around their pooled means and variances) should remove the appearance of a treatment effect. Even in a situation such as Figure 1, an inspection of variances for each group at each point in time

will help judge the plausibility of a selection-maturation interaction versus a treatment effect.

Outcome 3: Our discussion of the non-equivalent no-treatment control group design has thus far focused on the outcome where the treatment group is superior to the controls at the pretest and appears to be even more superior at the posttest. Let us now look at the related outcome where the pretest superiority is diminished or eliminated by the posttest. (See Figure 3.)

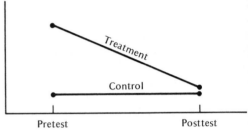

Figure 3. Third outcome of the no-treatment control group design with pretest and posttest.

This particular outcome was obtained from a sample of black third, fourth, and fifth graders in a study of the effects of school integration on academic self-concept (Weber, Cook, & Campbell, 1971). At the pretest, black children who attended all-black schools had a higher academic self-concept mean than black children who attended integrated schools in the same school district. But after formal school integration had taken place, the initially segregated and initially integrated black children did not differ. While the basic logic of experimental design with control groups involves starting with equality between groups and finishing with differences between them, we should be alert to "catch up" designs in which the "control group" already has the treatment which the experimental group receives between pretest and posttest. Of course, all of the problems described for Figure 1 are still relevant, especially the possibility of a selection-maturation interaction.

Outcome 4: A fourth possible outcome

of the no-treatment control group design with pretest and posttest is depicted in Figure 4.

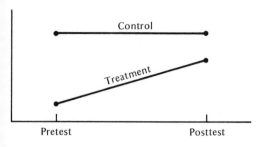

Figure 4. Fourth outcome of the no-treatment control group design with pretest and posttest.

This is a particularly interesting outcome since it is the one desired when organizations introduce compensatory inputs to increase the performance of groups who have started out at a disadvantage (as in some educational contexts) or where performance did not seem up to par for other reasons (as happens in industry where change attempts are intended to improve poor performance).

This outcome is subject to the typical ceiling and local history threats that were discussed earlier. But two special aspects stand out. First, regression is more of a threat than it is when the outcome is as depicted in Figure 1. When there is no matching, regression is normally not a threat in Figure 1 because we would expect respondents in the treatment condition to regress downwards from their higher pretest scores and we would also expect the low-scoring controls to regress upwards. But in the case depicted in Figure 4 the treatment is sometimes deliberately given to the experimental group because their scores are low. This will lead to regression upwards by the posttest and to the data pattern in Figure 4. Such a regression threat is especially likely when treatments are given to groups that perform badly *and where this poor performance is unexpected*. This is because there is likely to be an especially large error component determining the low pretest mean. Regression is less likely, however, in the case of

reforms or new programs aimed at groups where a stable pattern of poorer performance can be assumed. Stable and low pretest means presumably reflect more true score variance than is the case with means that have shifted unexpectedly downwards.

Second, despite the above problems of interpretation, the outcome in Figure 4 is particularly useful in many organizational contexts because it rules out the most probable selection-maturation interactions. This is because some maturational processes are cumulative (the rich get richer and the poor get poorer), and persons scoring lower at the pretest could be expected to be further behind at the posttest than the pretest. When such a maturational pattern operates (e.g., in educational contexts where the gap in academic achievement between social classes widens over the school years), the data from Figure 4 would imply that the treatment has had an effect *despite* the expected lower growth rate among respondents in the treatment group. Of course, it should not be assumed willy-nilly that all maturational trends follow the pattern of the higher scoring group spontaneously changing faster than the lower scoring group. This has to be checked against the growth patterns reflected in the pretest scores or against any general laws that might be applicable to a given area of organizational research.

Outcome 5. Bracht and Glass (1968) have noted the desirability of basing causal inferences on interaction patterns like that in Figure 5, where the trend lines cross over and the means are significantly different from each other in one direction at the pretest but in the opposite direction at the posttest. The important point is not the cross-over per se, since any interaction tells us that trends differ. The important point concerns the pattern of switching mean differences, for this tells us that the low scoring pretest group (the "experimentals") has overtaken the high scoring control group. None of the other interaction patterns that we have presented thus far do this; nor is it done if the trend lines cross but the two posttest means do not differ.

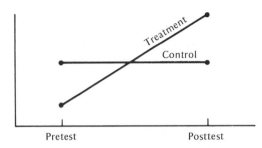

Figure 5. Fifth outcome of the no-treatment control group design with pretest and posttest.

There are several other reasons why Figure 5 is usually more interpretable than other outcomes of the non-equivalent control group design. First, the plausibility of an alternative scaling interpretation is reduced, for no logarithmic or other transform will remove the interaction. Moreover, any reference to a "ceiling" effect mediating the cross-over is inappropriate. While this effect might explain why a lower-scoring pretest group comes to score as high as a higher-scoring group, it would not explain how the lower-scoring group then drew ahead. A more convincing scaling artifact would have to be based on the notion that there is some true change in the lower-scoring group, but that it is inflated because the scale intervals are such that change is easier for both low and high scoring units than for units scoring closer to the grand mean. Note, though, that this entails postulating the exacerbation of a true effect and not the mediation of an artifactual effect.

Second, the Figure 5 outcome renders a regression alternative explanation less likely. While there is reason to suspect, when groups are selected on the basis of pretest scores or variables related to pretest scores, that a low treatment mean might be regressing to a higher grand mean, there is very rarely reason to expect that this grand mean will be higher than that of the higher-scoring control group. It would have to be, however, if statistical regression were to explain why the experimental group comes to overtake the control group and significantly differs from it at the posttest.

Third, Cook et al. (1975) have commented on the interpretability of Figure 5 when a selection-maturation threat is feared. They reanalyzed some of the Educational Testing Service (ETS) data on the effectiveness of Sesame Street and found that children in Winston-Salem who had been randomly assigned to being encouraged to view the show knew reliably less at the pretest than children who had not been assigned to such encouragement. However, the encouraged children knew reliably more at the posttest, so that the obtained data pattern resembled Figure 5. The selection-maturation problem is reduced in this case because so few documented maturation patterns can be described in terms of trends that cross over. It is more usual to find that groups which start at a higher position on some scale grow faster rather than slower, and only the latter would fit Figure 5. But selection-maturation cannot be ruled out willy-nilly if the data turn out as in Figure 5. For instance, analyses had to be carried out in the Sesame Street case to examine whether the encouraged children were younger and brighter than their controls, for they might have scored lower at the pretest because they were younger and might have developed faster over time because they were brighter. Fortunately, the encouraged and non-encouraged groups did not differ in either of these ways.

Though the Figure 5 pattern is usually interpretable, any attempt to set up a design so as to achieve it is a high risk endeavor that should not be undertaken lightly. This is especially true in growth situations where a true treatment effect would have to countervail against a lower expected growth rate in the lower-scoring experimental group. As a consequence, a no-difference finding would be hard to interpret—since it would not be clear whether there really is no difference or whether two countervailing forces have canceled each other out. Even if there were a difference, this would much more readily take the form of Figure 4 than Figure 5, and on other grounds also, Figure 4 is much less interpretable than

Figure 5. Even if one were lucky enough to obtain the Figure 5 data pattern, there would be difficulties in estimating the true size of the effect. It is one thing to comment on the advantages of a cross-over interaction with reliable and switching pretest and posttest differences, and quite another thing to obtain the data pattern. Indeed, in growth situations everything is against being so lucky.

We have discussed these five outcomes of the no-treatment control group design because the basic design is widely used and its interpretability depends, in part, on the particular outcomes obtained in a research project. The investigator who employs this design would do well to ponder the anticipated patterns of outcome, for these will be a guide to the validity threats that are most likely to operate in his study. Such an examination may even convince him that his anticipated outcomes will be too equivocal to justify the study. (Equivocality is especially a problem with Outcome 4.)

A very special version of the no-treatment control group design is sometimes used when there are non-equivalent groups and non-equivalent measurement instruments at the pretest and posttest. Typically, the design is the response to an ex post facto situation where the investigator feels he has to find some kind of pretest data that correlate (within groups) with posttest scores. In other words, he is looking for proxies of the pretest. Such a "pretest-proxy" design is illustrated below, where A and B refer to non-equivalent but, hopefully, correlated measures:

O_{A1}	X	O_{B2}
O_{A1}		O_{B2}

A fundamental problem which makes this design usually uninterpretable is that the pretest observations (O_{A1}) will correlate less highly with O_{B2} than the missing O_{B1} observation would have done. The lower $O_{A1} - O_{B2}$ correlation will exacerbate the normal difficulty of statistically removing group pretest differences from the crucial posttest scores since the efficacy of procedures like covariance analysis depends on the correlation of the covariate and the dependent variable and this will be lower with proxy pretests than with standard pretests. As a result, less of the group non-equivalence will be removed from the posttest and erroneous conclusions are all the more likely. Moreover, attempts to control for initial group differences by matching on O_{A1} will only lead to a regression artifact which makes a difference between the O_{B2} means inevitable. Proxy pretest designs of the kind we are discussing are difficult to interpret.

Let us consider a concrete example. Imagine a large firm that offers a year-long business leadership evening course to all of its first-year executives. Some thirty of the new junior executives take it, another fifty cannot fit it in, are not interested, etc. At the end of the year, they are given a test of Business Leadership Skills (O_{B2}) which should have been developed independently of the curriculum materials. As a control, all of the other first-year junior executives are given the same test, and significant differences are found favoring the alumni of the course. Now, skeptics might allege that the alumni would have had better leadership skills even without the course. So, an effort might be made to control for this probability by using personnel selection test scores in each man's file. Imagine, further, that within each group, tests of General Ability, Social Intelligence, and Interpersonal Dominance are found to correlate substantially with the scores on Business Leadership Skills, and so an equally weighted composite of standard scores is formed which correlates .70 within each group. This composite is O_{A1}.

If the course alumni and their controls turn out not to have differed on O_{A1} (or any of its components), this provides reasonable assurance that the groups did not differ on the shared components producing the correlation between O_{A1} and O_{B2}. In such a case, the use of the proxy pretest would increase the interpretability of the quasi-experiment, although the possibility of pretreatment differences on unmeasured components of O_{B2} remains. If, however, a group difference is found on O_{A1}, the usual procedures of matching, covariance, partial r, or multiple regression will *under-adjust*, and the practitioner of these procedures will misleadingly package this under-adjustment as a treatment effect. Indeed, when the correlation between O_{A1} and O_{B2} is .00, no adjustment will take place, and all of the pretest differences will remain in the posttest. When the correlation is substantial and less than 1.00, some of the pretest differences will be removed but not all. Hence, we would erroneously conclude from posttest group differences in leadership skills that the course was effective when, in fact, the posttest difference might be due to selection. It is only when the correlation of O_{A1} and O_{B2} is 1.00 (when corrected for unreliability in O_{B2}) that the adjustment will be adequate and all the group pretest differences will be removed from the posttest. Such a high correlation is unlikely between a posttest and a proxy pretest, and it is this fact that makes the proxy pretest design so difficult to interpret.

The hypothetical example we have just discussed refers to the situation where there is a reliable posttest difference between non-equivalent groups. Sometimes, when there is no such difference, the ex post facto design under discussion can be used to infer that there is no treatment effect. Here, too, one can be in error. The figure below gives the hypothetical pretest and posttest means for two non-equivalent groups measured on the same scale at each time interval. The group scoring the lowest at the pretest should be considered the treatment group. If we only had posttest information we would conclude from Figure 6 that the posttest means did not differ. Now, if we had pretest scores that correlated highly with posttest scores, a statistical adjustment like covariance analysis would reveal a difference between the adjusted posttest scores, with the treatment mean being higher. But if the pretest scores did not correlate highly with

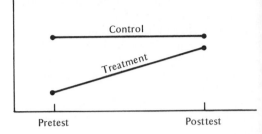

Figure 6.   Hypothetical pretest and posttest means of a treatment and non-equivalent control group.

the posttest, which is more likely with proxy variables, there will be little adjustment of the posttest means and no reliable differences would be obtained. However, such differences might have been found with the same posttest data if we had better pretest measures. What this implies is that any no-difference conclusion based on the use of proxy pretest variables might be false, reflecting the inadequacies of the design rather than the ineffectiveness of the treatment. (Campbell & Erlebacher, 1970, have discussed this special case of the ex post facto design in greater detail, and the interested reader should consult that reference.)

b. The Reversed-Treatment Non-Equivalent Control Group Design with Pretest and Posttest

This design can be diagrammed:

O_1	$X+$	O_2
O_1	$X-$	O_2

where $X+$ represents a treatment that is supposed to influence an effect in one direction and $X-$ represents the conceptually opposite treatment that should reverse the pattern of findings in the $X+$ group.

Morse and Reimer (1956) probably used this design to investigate how decision-making procedures that were either "democratic" (i.e., participative) or "hierarchically controlled" affected productivity and job satisfaction. Their design involved the use of four divisions in an organization, two of which were assigned to each experimental condition. However, it is not clear from the report whether the assignment of treatments to the four divisions was done on a random basis. But even if the assignment was random, the low number of experimental units makes it difficult to believe that the treatment and control groups were comparable at the pretest. Indeed, at one point in their report Morse and Reimer commented that the two experimental groups tended to differ in satisfaction at the pretest, and tables in the research report also indicate a possible group pretest difference in respondents' perception of the locus of decision making. Thus, we shall consider the Morse and Reimer study as a quasi-experiment for our present illustrative purposes, a quasi-experiment which indicated that satisfaction increased between pretest and posttest in the "democratic" decision-making group and decreased in the "hierarchically controlled" group.

Respondents in the Morse and Reimer study probably did not select themselves into work divisions and these work divisions probably did not select themselves into being in one experimental group or the other. If these suppositions are correct, selection-maturation would not be a threat to internal validity since we would have no reason to suspect that the two groups were spontaneously maturing in different directions. What makes a selection-maturation interaction less likely in this design than in many others is that we would have to postulate a specific pattern of maturational processes which operated in *different directions* in each group rather than the more typical processes which operate *at different rates in the same direction* in each group. Furthermore, if the two groups started out comparably at the pretest, there is less danger of scaling artifact, and matching would not be a problem if the divisions in the "democratic" and "hierarchically controlled" groups came

from similar populations and were not equated at the pretest by matching. In general, the reversed-treatment control group design is strong with respect to internal validity.

It is also stronger than the no-treatment control with respect to external validity. This is because the effects of the treatment construct can be replicated across two different settings (in the Morse and Reimer case, across more divisions).

The reversed-treatment design is even stronger with respect to construct validity. This is because the causal variable has to be rigorously specified if it is to affect one group one way and another group the other way and because many of the irrelevancies associated with one treatment will be different from those associated with the reversed treatment. Consider what would have happened if Morse and Reimer's design had involved only a "democratic" decision-making group and a no-treatment control group. A steeper pretest-posttest satisfaction slope in the "democratic" group could have been attributed to the new locus of decision making or to a Hawthorne effect. But the plausibility of a Hawthorne effect is lessened when we note the pretest-posttest decrease in satisfaction in the "hierarchically controlled" group. This is because awareness of being in a research study is typically considered to elicit socially desirable responses (higher productivity or greater satisfaction) rather than less desirable responses such as decreased satisfaction. It is the high construct validity of the cause which makes the reversed-treatment design potentially more appropriate for theory-testing research than the no-treatment control group design.

The last statement should not be taken to mean that the reversed-treatment design is flawless with regard to specifying the causal construct. For instance, Morse and Reimer found that productivity was greater at the posttest than at the pretest in both the "democratic" and "hierarchical" decision-making groups. If we accept for the moment that these data indicate an increase in productivity (which is not clear in the absence of a no-treatment control group), the possibility arises that a Hawthorne effect may have caused the productivity outcomes. A Hawthorne effect is more plausible for the productivity than the satisfaction data because the productivity outcomes did not result in the expected pattern of changes in opposite directions in the two experimental conditions. In other words, the potentially high construct validity of the reversed-treatment design depends on the research revealing changes in opposite directions. When change is in the same direction in both groups, we are left in the same position as with the relatively uninterpretable One Group Pretest-Posttest design. What are needed as adjuncts to the reversed-treatment design would be both a placebo control group which received a treatment not expected to influence productivity or satisfaction except through a Hawthorne effect, and also a no-treatment control group which would provide a no-cause base line.

Moreover, in many organizational contexts treatments are intended to increase productivity and satisfaction. Hence, reversed treatments, if they are implemented (despite their ethical and practical drawbacks), might well be unpopular with respondents who would not give the treatment a strong chance to manifest its potential. In other words, any causal influences that seem to be due to a reversed treatment may be due to affective components rather than to instrumental components which affect work processes.

There is also a real problem of statistical conclusion validity with the reversed-treatment design. If we were to obtain an interaction of experimental groups and time of testing, and if the posttest differences were greater than the pretest ones, we would not know from this whether the effect was due (a) to sampling error; (b) to one treatment causing its expected effect; (c) to the reverse treatment causing its expected effect; or (d) to both treatments causing effects in opposite directions. Significant pretest-posttest differences in each group would decrease the

chances of (a) above, but would be ambiguous with respect to (b), (c), and (d), since it would be reasonable to assume that at least one of the differences was due to group-specific maturation. This problem of interpreting the direction of change would be exacerbated if only one of the two pretest-posttest differences were significant. While it would seem at first glance that the significant difference represents directional change, this need not be so, for the difference might be due to maturation, and the nonsignificant difference in the other condition might be due to maturation suppressing a real difference. What is needed to remove ambiguity about the direction of change is a no-treatment control group added to the reversed-treatment groups. Researchers who are particularly interested in the direction of change should ponder hard before using a reversed-treatment design without a no-treatment control group. But with a mixed design of three groups (treatment, reversed treatment, and no-treatment), they would be in a very strong position. And they would be even better off if they could add a fourth group of placebo controls.

c. The Removed-Treatments Design with Pretest and Posttest

It is sometimes not feasible to obtain even a non-equivalent control group. In such a situation one is forced to create conditions that meet the conceptual requirements of a no-treatment control group, and the design that we outline below does this in many instances.

$$O_1 \quad X \quad O_2 \quad \vdots \quad O_3 \quad \bar{X} \quad O_4$$

In essence, the design calls for a simple one group pretest-posttest design plus the collection of a third wave of data before the treatment is removed from the treatment group ($\bar{X}$ symbolizes the removed treatment). A final measure is then taken after the treatment has been removed, and the experimental sequence from O_3 to O_4 serves as a no-treatment control for the sequence from O_1 to O_2. Though the same group is involved throughout the whole design, the dotted line indicates that the respondents will have changed from the first experimental sequence to the second removed-treatment sequence, in part because they have experienced the treatment. Thus, the two sequences are non-equivalent.

If a treatment were effective we would expect it to cause a difference between O_1 and O_2 that is opposite in direction to the difference between O_3 and O_4. However, since it is possible that the initial effects of the treatment might dissipate between O_2 and O_3, it is important to add that there has to be a noticeable discontinuity after $\bar{X}$ (as in Figure 7). If there is not, and if there is a smooth trend from O_2 to O_4, then any difference between O_3 and O_4 that was different from the $O_1 - O_2$ difference might be due to the treatment having no long-term effects rather than to the treatment effects dissipating because of the removal of the treatment.

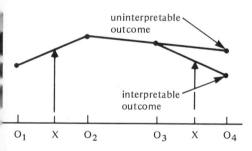

Figure 7. Generally interpretable outcome of the removed-treatment design.

The problems with the interpretable outcome in Figure 7 would seem to be only four in number. First, it might be difficult to obtain the pattern of statistical effects necessary for conclusion validity, since this would require both that $(O_1 - O_2) \neq (O_3 - O_4)$ and that $(O_2 - O_3) \neq (O_3 - O_4)$.

A second problem concerns construct validity when the treatment is removed.

Many treatments are ameliorative in nature, and removing an ameliorative treatment might be not only hard to defend ethically but also conducive to arousing a frustration in respondents that should be correlated with indices of aggression, satisfaction, and perhaps performance. This will be a major restriction to using this design if a deliberate choice has to be made by research personnel to remove the treatment.

The design is utilizable, however, even when subjects self-select themselves out of the treatment group, though special care has to be taken in such a case. Imagine someone who becomes a foreman (X), develops pro-managerial attitudes between O_1 and O_2, dislikes his new contact with managers, and becomes less pro-managerial by O_3. This person would be a likely candidate for resigning from his position or for being relieved of it $(\bar{X})$. Any continuation of his less pro-managerial attitudes after changing from a foreman back to a factory worker would result in an $O_3 - O_4$ difference that differed from the $O_1 - O_2$ difference, and the researcher has to decide whether the $O_3 - O_4$ difference reflects spontaneous maturation or the change of jobs. The maturation explanation would be more likely if the $O_3 - O_4$ difference were similar to the $O_2 - O_3$ difference (see the outcome marked "uninterpretable" in Figure 7), but would be less likely if the $O_3 - O_4$ difference were greater than the $O_2 - O_3$ difference (see the "interpretable" outcome in Figure 7). A rise in pro-managerial attitudes between O_1 and O_2, and a decline in pro-managerial attitudes between O_3 and O_4 that was greater than the $O_2 - O_3$ decline would strongly suggest that entering a new role causes one to adopt the attitudes appropriate to that role.

It is advantageous with this design that the observations be made at equal time intervals. This permits a control for any spontaneous linear changes that take place over a given time period. A simple comparison of the differences between $O_2 - O_3$ and $O_3 - O_4$ would be meaningless if the $O_3 - O_4$ time interval were longer than the $O_2 - O_3$ interval because a constant rate of decay would reveal larger $O_3 - O_4$ differences than $O_2 - O_3$ differences. It is more meaningful either to keep the time intervals equivalent or to examine linear slopes rather than differences between any two means.

Lieberman (1956) used a simpler version of the removed-treatment design in his examination of the attitude change that follows role change. He obtained samples of foremen who lost their new position and reverted to being workers again. Lieberman had three waves of measurement: before becoming a foreman, after becoming a foreman, and after reverting back to worker. The part of his design under discussion differed, therefore, from the one we have outlined in that there was only one measure between the treatment and the removal of the treatment. Hence, we are unable to attribute any differences between the $O_2 - O_3$ and the $O_1 - O_2$ measures as due to the attitude of former foremen reverting to that of workers or to the fact that foremen with attitudes that were becoming less managerial were selected for demotion. In addition, the statistical analysis of the three-wave design could involve contrasting the $O_1 - O_2$ difference with the $O_2 - O_3$ difference, a procedure that makes the O_2 observations appear twice. If, through sampling error, the O_2 mean were raised, this would necessarily be reflected in an $O_1 - O_2$ difference of different sign from the $O_2 - O_3$ difference. This would occur even if nothing had happened as a result of the treatment! Having two observations between the treatment and removed treatment rules out these possibilities in the design we have advocated.

d. Repeated Treatment Design

When the investigator has access to only a single research population it will sometimes be possible to introduce the treatment, fade it out, and then reintroduce it at a later date. Obviously, this design is most viable in contexts where the initial effects of the treatment are transient or do not prevent the treatment from having an even stronger effect when it is reintroduced. The design is diagrammed below.

$$O_1 \quad X \quad O_2 \qquad O_3 \quad X \quad O_4$$

The only interpretable outcome of this design is when O_1 differs from O_2, O_3 differs from O_4, and the $O_3 - O_4$ difference is in the same direction as the $O_1 - O_2$ difference. The design is of the general type associated with Skinnerians, and the basic logic behind it was used in the original Hawthorne studies (Roethlisberger & Dickson, 1939). It may be remembered that in some of those studies female factory workers were separated from their larger work groups and at different times were given different rest periods so that the experimenters could investigate the effects of rest on productivity. In some cases, the same rest period was introduced at two different times, and if we were only to regard these repeated rest periods we would have the basic design under discussion here.

One threat to internal validity comes from the possibility of cyclical maturation—that is, productivity is affected by regularly occurring systematic factors. For example, if O_2 and O_4 were recorded on Tuesday morning, and O_1 and O_4 on Friday afternoon, any differences in productivity might be related to differences in daily performance rather than to a treatment. It would be preferable, therefore, if such cyclical factors could be ruled out. A second threat to internal validity can arise if there is resentment when the treatment is removed between O_2 and O_3. If this were to happen, O_3 would be decreased and an $O_3 - O_4$ difference might be erroneously attributed to a replication of the treatment's effect when it was in fact due to removing a source of frustration by reinstating the treatment.

When the basic design is used as it was in the Hawthorne studies, it is particularly vulnerable on grounds of external and statistical conclusion validity. For example, many of the performance graphs in Roethlisberger and Dickson (1939) are of individual women workers; and in the Relay Assembly Row Experiment there was a grand total of only six women! Moreover, there appears to be considerable variability in how the women reacted to treatments (particularly the Mica Splitting Room Experiment), and we cannot be sure to what extent results would be statistically significant if the analyses were based on summing across all the women. (We cannot help but note in passing how closely the Hawthorne studies parallel the design of Skinnerian experiments. There is the same preference for few subjects and repeated reintroduction of the treatment, and there is the same disdain for statistical tests.) Of course, the repeated treatment design does not *require* that there be a small population or an absence of statistical tests. These are merely correlates of the use of this design in the past.

Construct validity is a major threat because respondents may well notice the introduction, removal, and reintroduction of the treatment with the consequence that they can guess and respond to a hypothesis. It is worth noting that this can occur even when there is none of the obtrusive observation or special group status that was involved in the original Hawthorne experiments. When respondents are reacting to their special status in an experiment or to a hypothesis they might have guessed, we cannot be sure about how the treatment should be labeled. This design is better, therefore, when there are unobtrusive treatments and a long delay between the treatment and its reintroduction. It is also necessary that there be no confounding of cycles and reintroductions of the treatment, and the design is best of all when the reintroductions are frequent and randomly distributed across time blocks. (This last point will be discussed later in the context of Equivalent Time Samples Designs.)

e. The Non-Equivalent Dependent Variables Design

This is one of the weakest interpretable quasi-experiments and it can only be convincingly used in restrictive contexts. This is why it is probably best used as part of a quasi-experiment that has design features which control for its weaknesses rather than as a complete design in its own right. It can be diagrammed:

$$O_{1A} \quad X \quad O_{2A} \left.\right\} \quad \text{A and B represent}$$
$$O_{1B} \qquad\quad O_{2B} \left.\right\} \quad \begin{array}{l}\text{different measures}\\ \text{from a single group}\end{array}$$

The essence of the design is that a single group of persons is pretested on two scales, one of which is expected to change because of the treatment (O_A) and the other is not (O_B). Hence, its use is restricted to theoretical contexts where differential change is predicted. If the research is conducted without hypotheses, the design reduces to being a simple One Group Pretest-Posttest design with multiple dependent variables, and any pattern of differential change might be due to chance or to ceiling/basement effects, or to differences in reliability between the measures. These last points are important, for even when change and no-change are predicted (as opposed to change in opposite directions), it is imperative to demonstrate that the predicted no-change variable is capable of registering effects.

Furthermore, the design is only interpretable when the two outcome variables are conceptually similar and each would be expected to be affected by most plausible alternative interpretations other than the treatment. To take an exaggerated example, it would be trivial to demonstrate that a new machine was related to a pretest-posttest difference in productivity (O_A) but to no difference in hair styles (O_B). Rather, one would want to show that the machine caused a difference in, say, the quantity of production during its hours of operation but not during the hours when it was broken down and different machines were used. The importance of the two related but different dependent variables comes from the fact that alternative interpretations like history would be expected to affect productivity whether the machine were operating or not.

Let us illustrate by an actual example how the convincingness of this design depends on initial expectations that both variables A and B might be affected by the treatment. Broadbent and Little (1960) surveyed the literature from laboratory experiments on the effects of noise on industrial productivity. They concluded that "the effect of noise is to increase the frequency of momentary lapses in efficiency rather than to produce decline in rate of work, gross failures of coordination, or similar inefficiency." They set out to test this in an industrial setting where personnel have the job of perforating the edge of film. This was a particularly fortunate work setting since, for payment reasons, measures of the rate of work and the number of broken films were routinely collected and archived. The number of broken films was one of the operational definitions of "momentary lapse," a variable that should be affected by noise, and the amount of work performed while machines were working was one measure of "rate of work," a variable that should not be affected by noise. Moreover, it was possible to obtain the relevant archival data both before and after a workroom was experimentally treated and the noise level was reduced. A comparison of before-after changes showed that there were fewer "momentary lapses" after the noise was reduced—this held for two measures of lapse—and that neither rate of work nor absenteeism was affected when noise was reduced. Without the literature review and the hypotheses it generated, it would probably not have been possible to predict that noise should affect the number of momentary lapses but not the rate of work.

Actually, we have distorted the Broad-

bent and Little quasi-experiment to make our point. The investigators found that the rate of work increased in the room where the noise had been experimentally reduced, and they attributed this to historical factors. They were able to do this because their design very wisely also included a non-equivalent control group work area where the noise had not been experimentally reduced. Thus, the investigators were able to demonstrate that the noisy and less noisy rooms did not differ in the rate of work but did differ in the number of momentary lapses. Without this control for the effects of history, Broadbent and Little would have had some difficulty in explaining why the rate of work increased and lapses decreased in the less noisy work areas. This was, after all, the very outcome that they did not want because it would not have supported the propositions about the *differential* effects of noise that were derived from laboratory experiments.

The non-equivalent dependent variables design is entirely dependent on contrasting patterns of change and no-change, and it cannot handle the pattern of general change that Broadbent and Little obtained in their reduced noise condition alone. The design is elegant in theory-relevant ways, but it is probably better used as part of a larger design rather than as a complete design in and of itself. (Useful applications of this control concept occur below in the context of Selection Cohort Designs and Time-Series Designs.)

f. Selection Cohort Designs

Organizations often have regular turnover as one group of persons graduates to another level of the organization. An obvious example of this is schools, but the process also takes place when trainees graduate from some technical program, or when a different group of persons is brought in each month for month-long sensitivity training classes, or when there is regular rotation around the various tasks that have to be completed in an organization, or when an older child from some family is compared with his or her siblings. Two factors make such a rotational system useful for experimental design. First, groups which precede treatment groups in undergoing some work or growth experience can often be assumed to have had the same organizational experience as treatment groups except that they never received the treatment. And second, the persons in the non-treatment cohort groups can sometimes be assumed to be similar on many background variables to the persons in the treatment cohort groups. To illustrate further, siblings typically share a common family background, making them similar environmentally. They differ only randomly on the genetic components of ability, etc., further increasing their comparability. Thus, siblings would provide a better non-equivalent control group for most treatments than would a group of non-related children. The logic of cohort analysis is to seek out cohorts who differ in as few ways as possible except for receiving the treatment. This should reduce the likelihood of selection artifacts in particular.

1. SELECTION COHORT DESIGNS WITHOUT A PRETEST. Let us make the point about selection clearer by taking a concrete example. One of the least interpretable of designs is the posttest-only design with non-equivalent groups $\left(\begin{array}{cc} X & O \\ \hline & O \end{array} \right)$. A major reason for this is that the groups may differ for reasons that have nothing to do with the treatment. Minton (1975) wanted to examine the effects of viewing Sesame Street on a socially heterogeneous sample of kindergarten children, and she only had data from the Metropolitan Readiness Test that were collected at the end of Sesame Street's first season. But she also had access to the scores of the children's older siblings when they had been the same age. Thus, she was able to compare the post-kindergarten scores of children who were potential Sesame Street viewers with the post-kindergarten scores of their siblings who could not have watched the show because it was not being broadcast then. The design can be diagrammed below, with the wavy line indicating a restricted degree of selection non-equivalence:

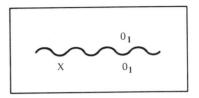

The design as it stands is not strong. First of all, the older siblings are more likely to be first-born children, and any group differences might be due to being first- or later-born. It would be desirable, therefore, if effects of ordinal birth condition could be reduced (but not eliminated) by analyzing the data separately for second-born older children and their third-born siblings, for third-born children and their fourth-born siblings, etc.

The design is also weak with respect to history, for the older and younger siblings in Minton's design might well have experienced different events other than Sesame Street that could affect the level of knowledge in one condition but not in the other. An indirect way of partially examining this threat would be to break down the cohorts into those whose kindergarten experience was separated by one, two, three, or more years to see if the greater learning of the younger group held over these particular sets of unique historical events. This procedure would be less than optimal, of course, because there would be no control for the historical events other than Sesame Street that took place in the same year that Sesame Street was introduced.

Another control for history would have been to split the children into viewers and non-viewers or, if this were not possible, into heavy and light viewers. We would then expect larger knowledge differences between the heavy and light viewers than among their respective siblings. In the absence of a treatment there would be no reason to assume that the difference between children who became heavy viewers of Sesame Street and their siblings should be different from the difference between children who became light viewers and their siblings. Moreover, both the heavy and light viewers experience the same history. It is for these reasons that partitioning respondents into treatment groups greatly strengthens the internal validity of this particular design, and Figure 8 represents an interpretable outcome of the expanded and recommended design.

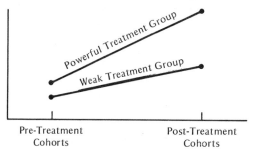

Figure 8. Interpretable outcome of a posttest-only cohort design with two treatment levels.

Actually, even though Minton had none of the controls for history listed above, her design was slightly more complicated than previously portrayed in ways that increase interpretability and that once more suggest the utility of implementing research with several of the various design features that control for particular threats to internal validity. Minton found that the mean of the younger Sesame Street cohorts only differed from their siblings' mean on a sub-test that measured knowledge of letters. There were no differences on five other sub-tests. As we have seen, there are dangers to interpreting a non-equivalent dependent variables design when a differential pattern of findings was not predicted. Nonetheless, it is clear from content analyses of the first year programming of Sesame Street (Ball & Bogatz, 1970) that more time was spent teaching letters

than anything else. Hence, it might be assumed that a letters test would be more likely to pick up effects of the program than would the other tests.

2. SELECTION COHORT DESIGNS WITH A PRETEST. The posttest-only selection cohorts design can obviously be transformed and strengthened by including pretest scores. Let us explain. Imagine a situation in which maturation or selection-maturation was a problem. It would be desirable to have a pretest cohort group that was at exactly the same maturational stage as their posttest cohorts, be the maturational stage indexed by age, years of work experience, or whatever. Given such maturational equivalence, it would be impossible to attribute any pretest-posttest difference to maturation and, to the extent that the cohorts were comparable on background features, it would also be difficult to attribute differences to selection. The design can be diagrammed:

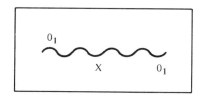

The essential features of this design were used by Ball and Bogatz (1970) in part of their evaluation of Sesame Street. They took all the children in their sample who watched Sesame Street at home and split them into (a) a pretest cohort of children who were between 53 and 58 months of age at the pretest, and (b) a posttest cohort whose age fell within the same range at the posttest and had obviously been 47–52 months at the pretest. Maturation could not explain any outcome difference between these pretest and posttest cohorts since they were of equivalent age and at a comparable maturational stage. Moreover, a selection effect would not be likely if all the available children had entered into the age group appropriate to their cohort. This was in fact the case, and the cohorts did not differ from each other on any of the measured background variables.

The above design is far from perfect, but fortunately can be strengthened. Its major weaknesses are three-fold. First, there is the problem of history; second, there is the difficulty of definitively demonstrating that the pretest and posttest cohorts are equivalent with respect to selection (everything depends on this); and third, there is a testing problem that occurs since the scores of the pretest cohort come from a first measurement and the scores of the posttest cohort from a second measurement. Any differences might be due to the treatment or to differences in the frequency of measurement.

The problems of history, selection, and testing can be reduced by following the procedure that Ball and Bogatz actually used. They partitioned their samples into eight groups: pretest and posttest cohorts being cross-cut by four levels of reported viewing of Sesame Street.

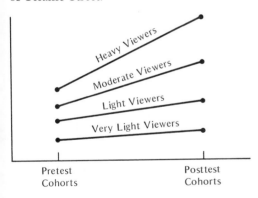

Figure 9. Interpretable outcome of a selection cohorts design with pretest and posttest cohorts.

An analysis of variance resulted in an interaction of cohorts and viewing such that the differences in learning between the viewing groups were greater among the posttest than the pretest cohort. Figure 9 presents an idealized portrait of the most interpretable pattern of outcomes for this design, and the Ball and Bogatz results were similar. Since the cohorts were of the same mean age, since they were of comparable social background within the heavy and light viewing groups, and since the heavy and light viewers experienced the same history and testing sequences (all posttest cohorts were pretested), an interaction outcome like the one that Ball and Bogatz obtained can account for all the threats to internal validity.

The selection cohorts design is very useful whenever it is feared that age or experience can alternatively account for results in a pretest-posttest design. It is especially interpretable when there are different levels of a treatment and when it is found that the different levels of the treatment statistically interact with the cohort groups.

g. Posttest-Only Designs with Predicted Higher Order Interactions

There are circumstances where no pretest information is available and it is desirable to establish a causal relationship. Unfortunately, there are few quasi-experimental designs which permit this, and pretests are an absolute necessity for most designs unless some form of a cohorts strategy or interaction strategy is used. (It is a different matter with true experiments, of course, and pretests can be dispensed with since randomization probabilistically ensures the pretest equivalence of the different treatment groups. However, it is advisable to collect pretest data nonetheless, for without it there may be difficulties in designing an interpretable quasi-experiment to fall back on if the comparability of treatment groups is not maintained over the course of an experiment, as would be the case if there were higher attrition from the experiment in some treatments than in others.)

Let us illustrate the use of interaction predictions with intact groups for providing relatively strong inferences about cause in the absence of pretest data. Nisbett and Kanouse (1969) were interested in testing the idea that overweight persons lack the ability to discriminate the internal body cues that indicate hunger. Hence, the authors hypothesized that there would be no relationship between the time of last eating and the amount of grocery purchases among the overweight and that there would be a positive correlation among persons of normal weight. Hence, they asked customers who entered a supermarket when they had last eaten, and they also observed the customers' weights and the size of their grocery bills. Body weight (overweight *versus* normal weight) and the reported number of hours since last eating (six levels) interacted to determine the size of the grocery bill. As predicted, there was a positive correlation between purchases and time since last eating among normals but, unlike the prediction, there was a *negative* correlation of these variables among the overweight.

A major difficulty with this design is selection. Assume for the moment that persons of normal weight who wait the longest time between meals are more likely to have jobs. (After all, it is more difficult for social and practical reasons to eat at work than at home.) If this were the case, normal persons who had gone longer without eating might well be more affluent and have more money to spend on food. This would explain the pattern of discrimination that Nisbett and Kanouse predicted for normals. But it would not explain the pattern among the overweight. However, if we further assume that the overweight persons who go longer without eating may do so because they are less affluent, then they should have less to spend on groceries than their overweight counterparts who have recently eaten. This would explain the negative relationship among the overweight. Alternatively, the overweight persons who have not eaten for a comparatively long time might be abstaining in order to diet, and this might also be related to lower grocery purchases. The point is that various selection mechanisms *could* explain the interaction of body weight and time since last eating, though a different

selection mechanism has to be invoked for each weight group.

A second potential problem with this design relates to the specificity of the predicted outcomes and the difficulty of obtaining such specific patterns of data. Nisbett and Kanouse predicted that there would be no relationship between purchases and the time since last eating among the overweight who are relatively insensitive to internal cues. But they unexpectedly obtained a negative relationship among the overweight. The authors needed, therefore, to explain this unexpected pattern. Since they had creatively collected estimates of intended purchases from shoppers as they entered the supermarket, they were able to show that the overweight persons who had gone longer since last eating both intended to buy less and actually did buy less. This was interpreted as demonstrating that the purchasing behavior of overweight persons was probably determined by their expectations about purchasing rather than by their internal hunger cues. The corollary of this is that normal persons' behavior should be determined more by their internal hunger cues than by their expected purchasing. However, the evidence for this was ambiguous. While the difference between what normals expected to buy and what they actually bought increased over five levels of time-since-last-food, it deviated markedly from this pattern among normals who had not eaten for more than five-and-a-quarter hours. Persons in this last group actually bought less than they intended, even though the theory predicted that they should have been more sensitive to their internal hunger cues than others and that they should have been the most prone of all to buy on impulse, thereby buying more than they intended.

The moral is clear: causal interpretation tends to be facilitated the more complex is the predicted interaction between nonequivalent groups. But the chance of obtaining so many data points in the predicted order decreases with the number of data points predicted. There are many reasons for this, including chance, selection differences in intact groups that influence data patterns but that are irrelevant to theory, and theories that are partially or totally incorrect.

The importance of the relative complexity of the interaction prediction can be further illustrated from an archival quasi-experiment by Seaver (1973), who was interested in examining the effects of a teacher's performance expectancies on students' academic achievement. To do this, Seaver located from school records a group of children whose older siblings had obtained high or low achievement scores and grades in school. Then, he split the two groups of younger children into those who had had the same teacher as their sibling and those who had had a different teacher. This resulted in a 2 x 2 design (same or different teacher crossed with high- or low-performing sibling). Seaver predicted that children with high-performing siblings and the same teacher would do better than comparable children with a different teacher, and that children with low-performing siblings and the same teacher would do less well than comparable children with a different teacher.

Seaver obtained the predicted interaction of same/different teacher with low/high-performing sibling on several sub-tests of the Stanford Achievement Test, and the means indicated support for the teacher expectancy hypothesis. Moreover, it is not easy to invoke a selection alternative interpretation. The one that springs most readily to mind is that children who had low-performing siblings might be assigned to teachers with a reputation for "teaching difficult children" by keeping strict discipline and teaching little. Alternatively, children with high-performing siblings might be assigned to teachers with a reputation for stimulating potential "stars." But this simple selection explanation cannot be correct since children in the different teacher condition were also labeled as low or high performers and so should have

also been sent to a particular kind of teacher. The only selection interpretation which can be invoked is rather complicated and will not strike some readers as very plausible. It is that the children in the different teacher condition were those who would have gone to teachers with reputations for dealing with high or low performers if this had been possible but that they did not go because it was not possible. The best ways to examine this last threat in detail would be to have definite information that the assignment of teachers to children was haphazard or to have teachers equally represented in all cells of the design.

Two questions about the construct validity of the treatment in the Seaver study can be raised. First, it is assumed that it was the teacher's expectancy about the child's performance that influenced the child's performance. It is also possible, though probably less plausible, that it was the child's expectancy about the teacher's skill or about her liking him and his family that influenced the child's learning. It would not be easy to dissociate these two interpretations without an experimenter-controlled manipulation of the child's and the teacher's expectancy or without convincing evidence from questionnaire or interview data that some children who showed an expectancy effect did not expect the teacher to teach them differently because he or she had taught their sibling. Second, there is no evidence from the study of why expectancy influenced performance. Was the apparent effect due to teachers calling less on children with poor-performing siblings, or to teachers reinforcing them differently, or to teachers publicly attributing lesser ability or motivation to them, or whatever? Of course, the Seaver study was designed to answer questions about whether an expectancy effect could be demonstrated at all in a nonreactive archival quasi-experiment, and an examination of process variables was not intended. This was probably just as well, for archival experiments tend to be weak on process. This is because archives are typically set up to record performance outcomes and not the processes mediating performance.

The investigator who has only posttest data is indeed fortunate if he can translate his research hypothesis into an interaction in which one group of respondents is superior to some other group in one experimental condition and is inferior in another. Nisbett and Kanouse succeeded in doing this, as did Seaver. The major threat to the single-interaction design is that of selection, and the basic design's interpretability depends in large measure on the extent to which selection artifacts are explicitly ruled out or are rendered less plausible. One technique for reducing the plausibility of selection is to make the interaction hypothesis involve a second- or third-order interaction. However, it is ironical that, on the one hand, interpretability increases with the *specificity* of predictions about particular statistics or particular interaction patterns and that, on the other hand, the *probability of obtaining* specific and expected data outcomes decreases with the very specificity of the predictions! Nonetheless the interaction prediction designs we have just outlined are very useful if carefully interpreted.

Regression-Discontinuity Designs

There are many situations in industrial and organizational contexts where persons or groups are given awards and where persons in special need are given extra help. If one would like to discover the consequences of these provisions, a regression-discontinuity design is appropriate. The logic behind the design is simple. If respondents can be classified along some quantified continuum of merit, there will be a cutting point such that persons who score above it will gain the award and those who score below it will not. Now, if the new provisions had any influence, we would expect a discontinuity at the cutting point when regression lines relating the quantitative classification variable to an outcome measure are fitted to the

groups above and below the cutting point. This is because the persons above the cutting point should have had their outcome scores increased by the provision while those below the point should not have.

Let us now attempt to make this basic point more explicit by considering two different contexts of a regression-discontinuity design. The first is discussed in greater detail in Thistlethwaite and Campbell (1960) and in Campbell (1969), while the second is mentioned in Riecken, Boruch, Campbell, Caplan, Glennan, Pratt, Rees, and Williams (1974).

a. Regression-Discontinuity with Pretest and Posttest Measures

Imagine the situation in which one has a continuous interval-scale measure of pretest organizational performance, be it output level, grades, or whatever. One gives a bonus —financial or symbolic—to persons with a given output or school grade level, and one wants to know how this bonus affects subsequent performance. A graph could be constructed with pretest output level along the horizontal and posttest output level along the vertical as in Figure 10, and a scatterplot results when each person's posttest score is graphed as a function of his pretest score. If the award were effective, there should be a discontinuity when fitting separate regression lines to the individuals above and below the pretest performance cutting point. Such a hypothetical case is portrayed in Figure 10.

(Actually, the discontinuity is nothing more than a special case of how most treatment effects would appear when posttest scores are plotted as a function of pretest scores in a true experiment covering the full range of pretest scores. A main effect of the treatment would make the regression line of the treated group higher than that of the control group. If there were no interaction of treatment and pretest, this would hold for all values of the pretest. In the regression-discontinuity case where awards are dispensed and the treatment is successful, the

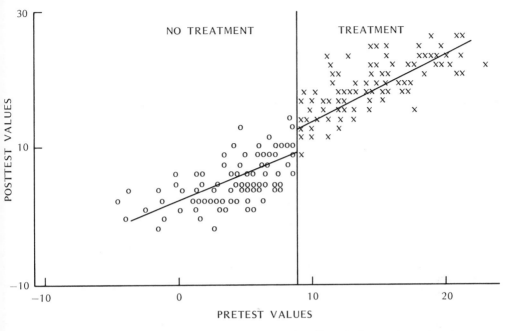

Figure 10. Hypothetical outcome of a pretest-posttest regression-discontinuity quasi-experiment.

outcome would be the same except that all the control cases above the cutting point, and all the experimental cases below it, are missing.)

Seaver and Quarton (1973) have used the design to examine the effects on students of being assigned to the Dean's List in college. (Assignment to the list came as a result of the previous quarter's grades.) The investigators obtained grades for 1,002 students from the school archives for the quarters before and after going on the list, and the sample included persons who did and did not gain the award. We would expect students who get on the list to do better than others for a variety of reasons. The issue with regression-discontinuity analysis is whether the rewarded students do better than others by a factor over and above what would be expected because they would have done better anyway. Seaver and Quarton's data for the regression of grade point average in one term on grade point average in the previous term are displayed in Figure 11. It can be seen that there is a discontinuity

in the regression lines at the cutting point. This seemed to be corroborated by their statistical analysis in which the differences between the two predicted cutting point scores derived from each regression equation were compared. As an added precautionary measure to test whether the students who entered the Dean's List were spontaneously maturing at a rate which was discontinuous with that of other students, all the grade scores from the pretest quarter in Figure 11 were used as the pretest and the grades from the quarter before that were used as the posttest. Fortunately, there was no evidence of a discontinuity in this auxiliary analysis.

The regression-discontinuity design can result in some outcomes that are difficult to interpret. What would one conclude, for example, if there were no discontinuity between slopes at the cutting point but there was a change in slope with the slope after the cutting point being steeper than that before it? This could be interpreted as an interaction of treatment and pretest, and it

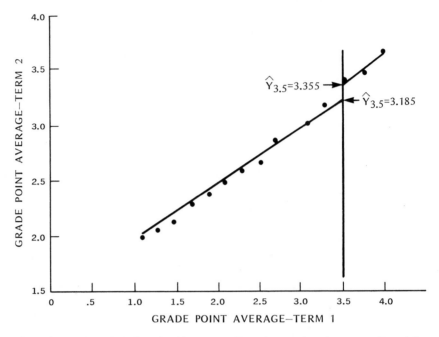

Figure 11.   Regression of grade point average Term 2 on grade point average Term 1 for the non-Dean's list and Dean's list groups.

might be claimed that persons with higher scores particularly benefit from rewards or from extra provisions if they are in need. But such an interpretation would be based on the implicit and untested assumption that the regression of the pretest on the post-test would not have been curvilinear in the absence of any special provisions. We cannot know this definitively, and—in general—we think it plausible that curvilinear regression of the kind implied by different slopes above and below the cutting point is more likely in nature than are sharp discontinuities at the cutting point.

The way to rule out such a selection-maturation alternative interpretation would be to obtain independent data on comparable persons and to see whether, in the absence of awards, the regression is curvilinear.

As a matter of record there is a difference in both slopes and cutting points in the Seaver and Quarton data, and this raises the possibility that the regression of grades in one quarter on grades in an earlier quar-

ter might not be linear in the absence of a Dean's List. If the underlying relationship were not linear, fitting trends to the data on each side of the cutting point would make for an artifactual discontinuity in instances where the relationship between grades in different quarters was more strongly positive at higher grade levels. Thus, the Seaver and Quarton data still need to be displayed in scatterplot form and to be fitted to more complicated regression models. Or, the full scatterplot of scores from persons in the experiment should be presented and appropriate statistical tests conducted to check whether there is any evidence of curvilinearity among the control cases who have not received special awards. If there is, a tentative extrapolation of the regression line should suggest how the experimental scores on the other side of the cutting point might have been related to each other in the absence of a treatment, and the regression line among experimentals can be examined to see how well it fits the extrapolation.

The major threat to regression-discontinuity designs comes from confounding patterns of nonlinear regression that would have been obtained from all the cases if there had not been any special awards or provisions with the particular pattern of nonlinear regression from which a treatment effect could be inferred. Data from comparable persons and from the controls provide the only approximate and tentative ways we have of estimating what the regression might have been in the absence of a treatment. But whatever is done, there can be no substitute for presenting the data from all the persons above and below the cutting point in scatterplot form and for attempting to fit the data to more complicated regression models before proceeding on the assumption that the linear model is appropriate.

A second problem with many regression-discontinuity designs is that awards or special provisions are often given to the especially gifted or the especially needy. This means that there will be a restricted range of scores on one side of the cutting point. It is difficult to obtain sensitive estimates of the regression of the posttest on the pretest when the range of scores is restricted, and such estimates are vital both for the kind of statistical test that Seaver and Quarton conducted and for assessing whether the trend among persons obtaining the award or special provision might simply be a nonlinear continuation of the trend obtained among the controls. (The often very narrow range of award winners and persons in dire need means that the regression-discontinuity design will frequently be associated with low external validity because results cannot be generalized beyond the most meritorious or the most needy.)

A third problem with the design is that the cutting point is sometimes not so clear-cut. In particular, there are instances where some individuals are given special provisions for reasons that are irrelevant to merit or need. They might be especially eager, or friends of friends, or persons to whom a special debt is owed, etc. This makes the cutting point more "fuzzy" than it should be. The solution to this problem is to explicate all possible causes of such special assignment, to find out who these specially treated persons are, and to remove them from the data analysis if not from access to the new provisions. A special problem of fuzziness occurs when a cutting point is well known, for this may give rise to pressures to help some persons achieve the cutting point score. For example, the Irish government publishes the passing score on various national examinations. A frequency distribution of the number of children obtaining the possible scores on the physics exam shows a less than expected number of students scoring just below the passing score and a higher than expected frequency above it (Greaney, Kellaghan, Takata, & Campbell, in preparation). It seems likely, therefore, that examiners gave students scoring just below the cutting point "an extra helping hand."

b. Quantified Multiple Control Groups Posttest-Only Design

Actually using the pretest to classify units on a merit or need basis is merely a special case of the more general principle that regression-discontinuity designs are possible wherever units can be ordered along some quantifiable dimension which is systematically related to assignment of treatment. Let us illustrate this with reference to a study by Lohr (1972; Wilder, 1972), who was interested in exploring the effects of Medicaid. The program was designed to make medical care available to the very poor (income under $3,000 per family per year) by means of Federal government payments, and one question of importance was whether the poor would indeed avail themselves of the new opportunity to obtain medical help.

Lohr's data can be displayed so as to plot the mean visits to the doctor per family per year as a function of annual family income (each measure was based on interviews done in connection with the Current Population Reports). The relationship of the two variables is portrayed in Figure 12, where it can be seen that the number of visits per year systematically decreases as income decreases. The one discontinuity from this trend is for families with an income under $3,000, where the number of medical visits sharply increases and even tends to exceed the number of visits made by the more affluent families. Since these data indicate that Medicaid might have increased medical visits by the poor, we have to ask ourselves the perennial question: Are there any plausible alternative interpretations of the relationship?

The chronically sick aside, visits to the doctor are presumably highest among the aged. Income is also lower among the aged. Thus, if the aged fell disproportionately into the lowest income category, the relationship

in Figure 12 might reflect a special selection phenomenon. But against this we have to consider that there is no reason why the aged should be so discontinuously represented in the lowest income group as opposed to being systematically more frequently represented in each lower income group. Fortunately, the relationship of age to income is ultimately an empirical issue and national demographic data exist for checking it. It is perhaps more important to note that persons over sixty-five are eligible for Medicare as well as Medicaid, and that there are indications that many older persons use both programs. Hence, an evaluation of Medicaid by itself should be restricted to persons below sixty-five years of age, though an evaluation of it in its social context should also include separate analyses of persons over sixty-five. Thus, there is good reason for wanting to see the Figure 12 data separately

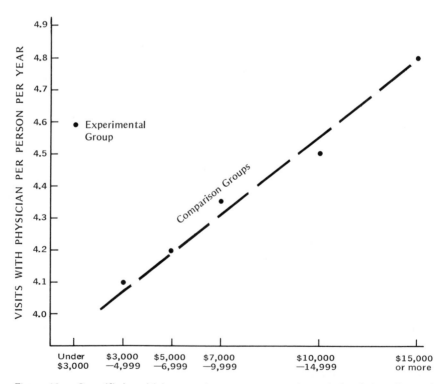

Figure 12.   Quantified multiple control group posttest-only analysis of the effects of medicaid. (After Lohr, 1972; Wilder, 1972.)

presented for families where no one is eligible for Medicare and for families where someone is so eligible.

A different age explanation is based on the possibility that medical visits are most needed by the pregnant and by young children. Hence, we have to consider whether the lowest income group was disproportionately composed of persons prone to pregnancy and large families. If so, they might have had more frequent visits to doctors even before Medicaid, though such visits were presumably to state hospitals on a non-fee-paying basis. There is every need, therefore, to disaggregate the data even further so as to examine the relationship of income to medical visits among persons of different family sizes as well as at different age levels.

A different kind of possible selection bias cannot be ruled out merely by disaggregating on the basis of demographic factors that are routinely measured in surveys, and that can be easily used in archival studies. Some families in the lowest income group were eligible for assistance from many programs, some of which mandated (and paid for) medical visits by recipients and their children as a precondition for receiving aid or for continuing to receive it. The issue, therefore, arises: Were the disproportionately frequent visits to doctors by the poor the result of Medicaid meeting a need or a response to the pre-Medicaid requirement of other programs that a doctor be consulted? If it were the latter, no effect of Medicaid would need be invoked. This problem would be easy to solve if we knew something about the programs in which family members were enrolled, especially those requiring work-related and welfare-related physical checkups. Only if data on mandated checkups were collected at the time of the survey could disaggregation on this variable take place, and without foresight the required information would probably not be collected. The best one could do if it were not collected would be to consult the best available data on the number of persons eligible for mandated medical visits and see if such eligibility related to income in the discontinuous manner suggested by Figure 12 and was of a magnitude that could plausibly account for the pattern in that figure.

Another possible alternative interpretation is based on selection-maturation, and it suggests that the demand for medical care was greatest among the poor, that the supply of doctors was increasing year by year, and that the new supply could only find outlets among those sections of the population whose prior demands had not been met and whose physical state required urgent, even if not munificently rewarded, care. Against this, however, is the fact reported to us by Lohr that, though the number of doctors per capita was increasing between 1960 and 1970, the number *in medical practice* was not increasing. Presumably, some doctors were going into medical research or into non-medical careers.

A final threat to internal validity arises because the direction of causality is not clear from Figure 12. Did Medicaid cause an increase in medical visits, or did the desire for medical visits by the sick and hypochondriac lead these persons to underreport their true income both to doctors and to interviewers in order to continue the pretense that they were eligible for programs for which they were not in fact eligible? An indirect check of this might be possible by using non-medical surveys to estimate the proportion of persons in each of the outcome categories in Figure 12. The opposite-direction-of-causality explanation would not be ruled out if more persons reported poverty-level incomes in medical than non-medical surveys, but it would be ruled out if equal proportions fell into each category. (However, this test is only approximate, for sick persons might generalize their underreporting of true income to all surveys, be they oriented to medical services or not.)

What is perhaps worth stressing about most of the threats to internal validity that we have just listed is that their plausibility can be assessed without undue effort by consulting available archives in order to disaggregate the data from Figure 12 or to collect additional data that rule out specific alternative explanations. Thus, our list of threats should not discourage; like other lists for other projects, it should spur those persons into action whose interest lies in strengthening a particular causal inference.

It should be noted that the Lohr-Wilder data actually cover three waves, one coming before Medicaid. As displayed in Riecken et al. (1974, Fig. 4.18), data indicated that the lowest level of pre-Medicaid attention was devoted by doctors to the least financially advantaged group. This invalidates many of the alternative interpretations listed here which were presented for pedagogical reasons since two waves of measurement is unfortunately more typical than three.

Some important problems of construct validity should also be mentioned with respect to Lohr's quasi-experiment. Given the stimulation of demand by Medicaid and the apparent inelasticity of supply, does an increase in the quantity of care for the poor entail a decrease in the quality of their care and that of others? Furthermore, is the dependent variable appropriately labeled as "an increase in physician visits" or as "a temporary increase in physician visits," for the frequency of chronic and ill-monitored disease is presumably higher among the poor and might well be decreased by Medicaid, thereby leading to a later decrease in visits as more and more chronic problems are cured or detected before they become worse.

Interrupted Time-Series Designs

Interrupted time-series designs involve repeated measurement of an effect both before and after a treatment is abruptly introduced and "interrupts" previous data patterns. These designs are particularly appropriate when measurement is unobtrusive and respondents are not reacting to multiple testings. The basic design has been extensively

commented on in Campbell and Stanley (1966, pp. 37–43), in Campbell (1969, pp. 412–417), and in Riecken, Boruch et al. (1974). The present discussion will employ different illustrations and will introduce a new variant of the basic time-series design.

It is fitting to begin the discussion of this design with examples from those classic studies of the British Industrial Fatigue Research Board in the early 1920s which introduced our present period of experimental quantitative management science. These were the studies which inspired, and were eclipsed by, the Hawthorne studies. While their methodology leaves much to be desired by present standards, it was a great forward leap in the direction here advocated and was probably stronger than the methodology used in the Hawthorne studies.

Figure 13 comes from Farmer (1924). He concluded that shortening the work day from ten to eight hours improved hourly productivity. With modern methodological concerns, we cannot be so sure. First, there is the possibility of an interaction of selection and maturation since there is an upward self-improvement trend which we assume would have continued even without the change to an eight-hour day. Second, there may be a seasonal trend, and we do not have enough data to take it out statistically. (The change in the number of hours worked was introduced in August 1919. Note that in 1918 August was a low month followed by an upward trend, as it was in 1919 when the change was introduced. But in 1920, this summer slump is absent—perhaps due to the change?)

The typical statistical analysis of such data includes fitting regression lines before and after the change and then looking for changes in slope and intercept. But this should not be done by ordinary least-squares methods since the error in time-series is of an auto-regressive or moving-average sort. This means that adjacent points in the series are more highly correlated with each other than are remote ones, and that too many Type I errors are produced since the as-

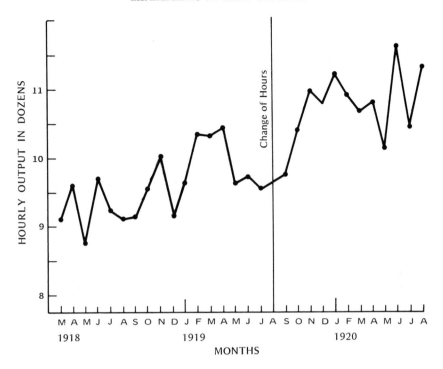

Figure 13.   Change in hourly productivity as a result of shifting from a ten-hour to an eight-hour work day. (After Farmer, 1924.)

sumption of independent error for each point is violated. Using a Bayesian, moving-average model (Glass, Willson, & Gottman, 1975; Glass, Tiao, & Maguire, 1971; Box & Jenkins, 1970; Box & Tiao, 1965) on these data fails to indicate a change in either slope or intercept, although it must be pointed out that many more data points are required for a sensitive statistical test. Indeed, Glass, Willson, and Gottman (1975, p. 143) recommend a minimum of fifty data points for estimating the underlying model.

There are many situations in which it is not possible to collect data for so many time points or where examination of the autocorrelations and partial autocorrelations indicates that the Bayesian test of Glass, Willson, and Gottman is not appropriate. We want to advocate the use of time-series designs even when no statistical test of the hypothesis can be carried out. In such a case, we consider it useful to plot the data and to

"eye-ball" whether there is a discontinuity in the time trend that cannot be readily explained in terms of the continuation of trends that are observable in the pretest time series, or in terms of statistical regression following from a deviantly low score just before the treatment is introduced. The most important feature of time-series designs is that there be a sufficient number of pretest data points covering a sufficiently extended time period so that all plausible patterns of variation can be ascertained. While it is undoubtedly advantageous also to be able to test whether an observed discontinuity at the time of the treatment can or cannot be plausibly attributed to chance, it should not be forgotten that chance is only one of many alternative interpretations that has to be ruled out. It would be a shame if time-series designs were not used because of "too few observations for sensitive statistical analysis." Even without tests of significance, they represent a powerful gain over designs with only one pretreatment observation.

Figure 14 gives time-series data from a quasi-experiment by Lawler and Hackman (1969) where the threats to validity are somewhat different from those in the previous example. The treatment was the introduction of a participative decision-making scheme to three groups of men doing janitorial work at night, and the dependent variable was absenteeism (the proportion of possible work hours actually worked). A noteworthy feature of Figure 14 is that a false picture would have been given if there had been only a single pretest and a single posttest. The total pretest data reveal that the last pretest measure is atypically low and, as a consequence, statistical regression will almost certainly be inflating the difference between the last pretest and the first posttest measure. A major strength of time-series designs is that they allow assessment of the pretest time trend, thereby permitting a

check on the plausibility of a regression alternative explanation of findings.

The major threat to internal validity with most single time-series designs is a main effect of history. There are several controls for this, the best being to add a no-treatment control group. But this is sometimes not necessary. For instance, Lawler and Hackman's unobtrusive measure of absenteeism was calibrated into weekly intervals, and the historical events that can explain an apparent treatment effect are fewer with weekly intervals than with monthly or yearly ones. Moreover, if records are kept of all plausible effect-causing events that could influence respondents during a quasi-experiment, it should be possible to ascertain whether some unique force operated during the period between the last pretest and the first posttest.

Another threat concerns the fact that time-series are subject to many influences of a cyclical nature, including seasonal variation in performance, attitudes, communica-

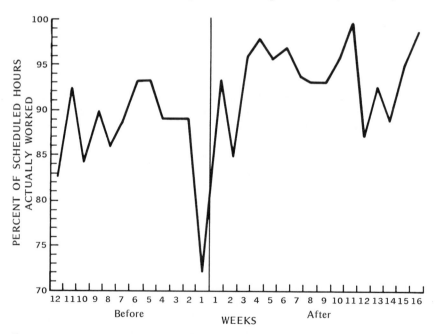

Figure 14. Mean attendance of the participative groups for the twelve weeks before the incentive plan and the sixteen weeks after the plan. Attendance is expressed in terms of the percentage of hours scheduled to be worked that were actually worked. (From Lawler & Hackman, 1969.)

tion patterns, or whatever. It is important to analyze the data in a way that removes such variation, for it can sometimes masquerade as a treatment effect. For example, it is not clear from the Lawler and Hackman quasi-experiment when the study was conducted or how performance is normally related to temporal cycles among the particular groups of janitors studied. Just suppose, however, that the study began in December when the weather is cold, illness more prevalent, and absenteeism higher. Twelve weeks later, when the treatment was implemented, it would be March or April when the weather is better, health improved, and absenteeism lower. If the treatment were indeed introduced in December (and we have no evidence that it was), the decrease in absenteeism could be alternatively attributed to seasonal variation rather than to the new decision-making scheme. Removing cyclical variation is not easy because it requires establishing what the cyclical pattern is, and this requires information about a long time-series.

Another threat is that of instrumentation; sometimes a change in administrative procedures will lead to a change in the way records are kept. In particular, persons who want to make their performance look good can simply change bookkeeping procedures to redefine performance or satisfaction, and persons with a mandate to change things may interpret this to include changes in the way that records are kept or in the way that criteria of success and failure are defined. (Though instrumentation can be a threat in the single time-series, there is no indication that it was in the Lawler and Hackman study.)

As far as statistical conclusion validity is concerned, Lawler and Hackman analyzed their data by tests in which they compared the collapsed pretest percentage of hours worked with the collapsed posttest percentage. But in doing this, first, they used a test that is only appropriate for comparing two independent groups and not the same group at two times, and second, they did not use the full data from the pretest and posttest trends. They would have done better to use some sort of a moving-average model, perhaps the one advocated by Glass, Willson, and Gottman (1975). When we in fact used their test, it showed that the changes in intercept and slope were not statistically significant, although once again the limitation has to be mentioned that the Bayesian test is more sensitive when there are many more data points than Lawler and Hackman could collect.

As far as construct validity is concerned, the single time-series design will typically not have limitations imposed by reactivity, but there will typically be only a single operationalization of the treatment and sometimes of the effect. Concerning external validity, evidence of temporal persistence of effects can sometimes be convincing, but only at the cost of strong assumptions about what the trend would have been without the treatment. (These assumptions get more tenuous the further one has to extrapolate.) Typically, there will be only one population. Of course, efforts can be made to make the population as heterogeneous as possible and, when this happens, social units should be blocked into groups which are internally homogeneous and which maximize the heterogeneity between groups. Time-series should then be separately examined for each group.

Interrupted Time-Series with a Non-Equivalent No-Treatment Control Group Time-Series

Consider the addition to the simple time-series design of a time-series from a nonequivalent no-treatment control group. The resulting design is diagrammed below.

$$O_1 \ O_2 \ O_3 \ O_4 \ O_5 \ X \ O_6 \ O_7 \ O_8 \ O_9 \ O_{10}$$
$$O_1 \ O_2 \ O_3 \ O_4 \ O_5 \ \ \ O_6 \ O_7 \ O_8 \ O_9 \ O_{10}$$

Lawler and Hackman (1969) actually incorporated this control into their experiment because one set of work groups made the decision to award themselves a bonus while a control group was given the same bonus at the same time without any participative decision making. The control group considerably strengthened the Lawler and Hackman quasi-experiment, and the relevant data from the group are in Figure 15, which should be compared with the time-series from the treatment group in Figure 14 on page 276.

It can be seen that there is little evidence of a decrease in absenteeism among the controls and our particular Bayesian analysis showed no difference in slope or intercept. However, the analysis of the difference between the experimental and control series also showed no differences, thereby casting some doubt on whether the treatment had any effects. (Remember, though, that there was some indication that the data did not fit the Bayesian model very well, so the statistical analysis of trend differences cannot be considered definitive.)

Since the groups worked over the same time period, it is unlikely that a treatment-correlated historical event caused the apparent decrease in absenteeism in the treatment group. The ability to test for the threat of history is the major strength of the control group time-series design. However, it normally also allows tests of the other threats to internal validity that operate on the single time-series. There is no reason, for example, why the measurement instrument should have differed between the treatment and control groups, and no reason why each group should be experiencing different cyclical patterns of absenteeism.

The threats to external validity that apply to the simple time-series also apply to the control group time-series. Consider the interaction of populations and treatments. The data of Lawler and Hackman (1969) suggest relatively flat pretest slopes with considerable "noise" (the immediate pretreatment pretest value in the experimental

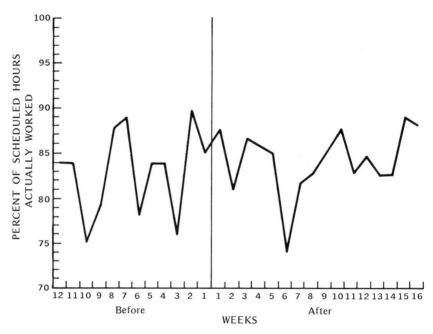

Figure 15. Mean attendance of the imposed groups for the twelve weeks before the incentive plan and the sixteen weeks after the plan. Attendance is expressed in terms of the percentage of hours scheduled to be worked that were actually worked. (From Lawler & Hackman, 1969.)

group being a salient example). Let us assume, therefore, that the pretest trends are flat for the sake of exposition. If so, work attendance during the pretest was higher in the treatment groups (average of twelve weeks = 88 percent) than among controls (average over twelve weeks = 83 percent), and this difference would have been even more marked if the one deviant pretest value had been removed from the experimental time-series. Hence, the effect in the treatment group may reflect the restriction that participative decision making is more effective with conscientious persons who attend work regularly than with others. The probability of an interaction of treatment and population would have been reduced if the intact groups of janitors had been matched on pretest averages and then randomly assigned to the different conditions. While the number of groups in Lawler and Hackman's study was so low that matching plus randomization would not have ensured pretest equivalence, it might well have reduced pretest differences between conditions.

Lawler and Hackman's study also illustrates that the frequency of posttest measures should not be confused with their temporal duration. The dangers of such confounding are well illustrated by the followup study by Scheflen, Lawler, and Hackman (1971). The latter investigators used the same groups as Lawler and Hackman but assessed absenteeism from 53 to 64 weeks after the treatment. The major finding was that the bonus scheme developed through participative decision making had been removed from two of the three treatment groups by disgruntled managers. More importantly for the present discussion, they also found that in the one group where the bonus scheme was retained, the average attendance for the 53rd to the 64th weeks after the treatment (93 percent) did not differ from the immediate post-treatment average

and was 5 percent higher than during the pretest. But in the control groups where the bonus scheme was imposed by management, the average attendance between the 53rd and 64th weeks was 87 percent, which was a rise of 4 percent over the 83 percent average from the pretest phase. Thus, assuming that the 5 percent and 4 percent rises were not different from each other, the 53–64 week data support the conservative conclusion that participative decision making was not demonstrably more effective than was imposed decision making over the long term, though this conclusion has to be tempered by the knowledge that change may not have been as easy from the 88 percent pretest level in the treatment group as from the 83 percent level in the no-treatment controls. Without the control group it would have been much more difficult to assess the temporal persistence of treatment effects since, with a single experimental time-series, persistence is confounded with both history and maturation.

Interrupted Time-Series with Non-Equivalent Dependent Variables

We have previously mentioned how history is the main threat to internal validity in a single time-series and how the effect of history can sometimes be examined by minimizing the time interval between measures or by including a no-treatment control group in the design. History can also be examined, and the construct validity of the effect enhanced, by collecting time-series data for some dependent variables that should be affected by a treatment and for others that should not. Of course, the restriction holds—as it did in examining the non-equivalent dependent variables design earlier—that the dependent variables must be conceptually related. The design in question is diagrammed as:

$$O_{1A} \quad O_{2A} \quad O_{3A} \quad O_{4A} \quad O_{5A} \quad X \quad O_{6A} \quad O_{7A} \quad O_{8A} \quad O_{9A} \quad O_{10A}$$
$$O_{1B} \quad O_{2B} \quad O_{3B} \quad O_{4B} \quad O_{5B} \quad X \quad O_{6B} \quad O_{7B} \quad O_{8B} \quad O_{9B} \quad O_{10B}$$

An example of the use of this design comes from a study of the effectiveness of the British Breathalyser Crackdown (Ross, Campbell, & Glass, 1970). The project involved evaluating whether this effort in determining drunken driving reduced serious traffic accidents in Great Britain by keeping intoxicated drivers off the road or by making them drive more safely. One feature of British drinking laws is that pubs can only be open during certain hours. Thus, if we are prepared to assume that a considerable proportion of British drinking takes place in pubs rather than at home, we might predict, if the Breathalyser were effective, that the number of serious traffic accidents should decrease during the hours pubs are open, particularly during weekend nights, and should be less affected during commuting hours when pubs are closed. The importance of the distinction between serious accidents when pubs are open or closed derives from the fact that most history alternative interpretations of a decrease in serious accidents are interpretations that should affect *all* serious accidents *irrespective of the time of day.* Such alternative interpretations might include weather changes, the introduction of safer cars, a police crackdown on speeding, contemporaneous newspaper reports of high accident rates or particularly gory accidents, etc.

It is obvious from visual inspection of Figure 16 that there is a marked drop in the accident rate at weekends but there is much less of a drop during non-drinking hours in the week. Statistical analysis using the advocated Bayesian procedure corroborated the

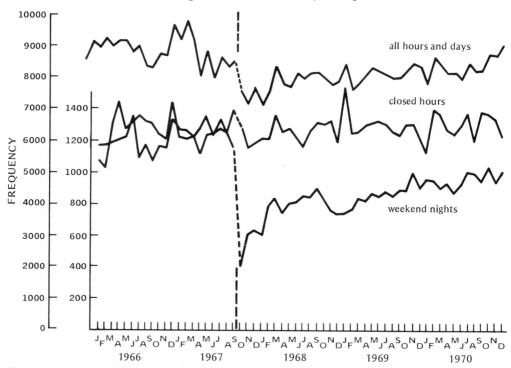

Figure 16. British traffic casualties (fatalities plus serious injuries) before and after the British Breathalyser crackdown of October 1967, seasonally adjusted. (Modified from Figure 1: Ross, H. L., Campbell, D. T., & Glass, G. V. Determining the social effects of a legal reform: The British "breathalyser" crackdown of 1967. *American Behavioral Scientist*, March/April, 1970, 13, No. 4, 493-509. By permission of the publisher, Sage Publications, Inc.)

decrease in 1967 in the weekend nights time-series (and also in the all-hours-and-days series). It is very difficult to fault either the internal or statistical conclusion validity of these data.

But questions can be raised about both construct and external validity. An obvious external validity question is: Would the same results be obtained in the United States? Another concerns possible unanticipated side effects of the Breathalyser. How did it affect accident insurance rates, sales of liquor, public confidence in the role of technological innovations for solving social problems, the sale of technical gadgetry to the police, the way the courts handled drunken driving cases? Many such issues are examined in Ross (1973).

If we consider Figure 16 more carefully, it is apparent that not all of the initial decrease in serious accidents during the weekend is maintained. That is, the accident rate drops at first but then continually rises toward the level in the control time-series, though the two trends still do not meet by the last measure. Thus, it is possible that something inflated the effects of the Breathalyser at the time it was introduced or deflated its effects after it was introduced.

The Breathalyser was introduced into Britain with much nationwide publicity, and the publicity may have made the general public especially mindful of the desirability of not drinking and driving. Or it may have made the police especially vigilant in controlling the speed of traffic, especially during and immediately after pub hours. Ross (1973) also suggested that the Act may have reduced the overall number of hours driven, or may have cut down on drinking, or may have led drunken drivers to drive more carefully. He very ingeniously ruled out some of these explanations. He took the regular surveys by the British Road Research Laboratory of miles driven, converted the number of serious accidents and fatalities to the number of accidents per mile driven, and showed that the introduction of

the Breathalyser was still associated with a decrease in accidents when the estimate of accidents per mile driven was used. Hence, to the extent the estimate is valid, we can rule out the explanation that the Breathalyser's effect is due to a reduction in the number of miles driven. Ross also examined the sale of beer and spirits before and after the Breathalyser and could find no evidence of a discontinuity in sales when the instrument was introduced. This ruled out the interpretation that the Breathalyser had reduced drinking. He was also able to show for ten months after the Breathalyser that more persons reported walking home after drinking than had been the case in the equivalent ten months preceding the Breathalyser. Finally, he also showed that fewer of the post-Breathalyser traffic fatalities had high alcohol levels in their blood than had the corpses of the pre-Breathalyser fatalities. These last data indirectly supported the explanation that the causal construct was a reduction in drunken driving; rather than a significant reduction in either drinking or driving.

Though Ross's analysis is ingenious and innovative as an attempt to establish construct validity for a non-manipulated cause, it still leaves some alternative interpretations open. For example, we do not know whether the Breathalyser led to no change in drinking but rather to an increase in careful driving. Nor do we know whether the effect was due to enhanced police vigilance during and after pub hours. Nor do we know whether the cause was the deterrent power of the Breathalyser alone, or was it the deterrence plus either increased police vigilance, or national publicity, or more careful driving by persons who had not reduced their drinking, or—as Ross prefers—the deterrent power allied to rigorous legal enforcement of drink-related traffic violations? The attempts by Ross to use data to rule out alternative explanations of the causal construct should alert us to the importance and difficulty of this endeavor as well as to the number of irrelevancies that are often associated with the introduction of new practices.

Interrupted Time-Series with Switching Replications

Imagine two non-equivalent samples, each of which receives the treatment at different times so that, when one group receives the treatment the other serves as a control, and when the control group later receives the treatment the original treatment group serves as the control. The design can be diagrammed as at bottom of page.

The power of the design derives from its control for most threats to internal validity and from its potential in extending external and construct validity. External validity is enhanced because an effect can be demonstrated with two populations in at least two settings at different moments in history. Moreover, there are likely to be different irrelevancies associated with the application of each treatment and, if measures are unobtrusive, there need be no fear of the treatment's interacting with testing.

Figure 17 gives previously unpublished data from a study which used the replicated time-series design (Parker, Campbell, Cook, Katzman, & Butler-Paisley, 1971). The treatment was the introduction of television into various Illinois communities, and the hypothesis was that television would cause a decrease in library circulation (Parker, 1963) because it would serve as a substitute for reading. Thus, the dependent variable was the annual per capita circulation of library books. The unique feature of this particular quasi-experiment is the sharp differentiation of the treatment groups. This occurred because the Federal Communications Commission stopped issuing new licenses for television stations in 1951. This split Illinois communities into two groups: an urban,

wealthy group with growing population that had television before the freeze (the so-called Early TV communities) and a rural, poor group with static population growth that received television only after the freeze was lifted in 1953 (the so-called Late TV communities). It can be seen from Figure 17 that library circulation declined about 1948 for the Early TV group and during 1953 for the Late TV group. The Glass, Taio, and Maguire (1971) statistic confirmed that each of these decreases was statistically significant. This corroborated the hypothesis, and it is noteworthy that the design involved archival measures, distinctly different populations, different historical moments for introducing the treatment (in nonreactive fashion), different irrelevancies associated with how the treatment was introduced, and repeated measures to ascertain if an initial effect can be generalized over time.

But even the replicated time-series design can have problems of internal validity. Paperback books may have been introduced earlier into the rich Early TV communities than into the poor Late TV communities. If so, the declines in library circulation in 1948 and 1953 might have been due to historical differences in the availability of paperbacks—an interaction of history and selection. This alternative interpretation could be ruled out by collecting data on the circulation of paperbacks in each set of communities. This would be a laborious but worthwhile operation for someone with a vested interest in knowing that the introduction of television *caused* a decrease in library circulation, albeit a temporary one as Figure 17 shows. A different strategy, following the example of Parker (1963), would be to split the library circulation into fiction and nonfiction books. Television, as a predominantly fictional medium, would be expected to have a greater effect on the circulation of

$$O_1 \quad O_2 \quad O_3 \qquad O_4 \quad O_5 \quad O_6 \quad O_7 \quad O_8 \quad X \quad O_9 \quad O_{10} \quad O_{11}$$
$$O_1 \quad O_2 \quad O_3 \quad X \quad O_4 \quad O_5 \quad O_6 \quad O_7 \quad O_8 \qquad O_9 \quad O_{10} \quad O_{11}$$

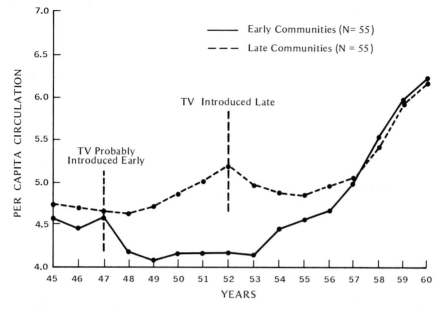

Figure 17. Per capita library circulation in two sets of Illinois communities as a function of the introduction of television. (From Parker et al., 1971.)

fiction than of fact books. Using non-equivalent dependent variables in this way would render the paperback explanation less plausible because we would have to postulate that fiction books were introduced into the different communities at different times, but that nonfiction books were not. This is not impossible—only relatively implausible.

The replicated time-series design is clearly a powerful one. But is it practical? We think it is wherever a time-series design with a no-treatment control group is feasible. If treatments of an ameliorative nature have been successful, then it is likely that their utilization will be of benefit to the groups or organizations which served as no-treatment controls. Representatives of these groups can be approached to see if they will agree to an experiment that has once before produced desirable consequences. Consider the consequences if Lawler and Hackman (1969) had been able to persuade the persons who authorized their participative decision-making study that the resulting bonus scheme had reduced costly absenteeism and

that it might do the same for the control groups where there was no participation. Then, a participative decision-making scheme might have been introduced into the control groups at a later date, and Lawler and Hackman would not have had the problem of a threat to external validity based on the interaction of populations and treatments. Nor would they have had as many other problems of external validity. Their final design would have had a replicated time-series with each condition receiving the treatment *at its own level of pretest absenteeism*.

Interrupted time-series are among the most powerful quasi-experimental designs. Their use is rapidly increasing. This being the case, it seems well to take time to make clear the pseudo-dynamic patterns which matching can produce.

Imagine in the Parker et al. (1971) study that the experimental and control communities had differed in per capita library circulation in the manner indicated in Figure 18, where State *A* represents the experimentals

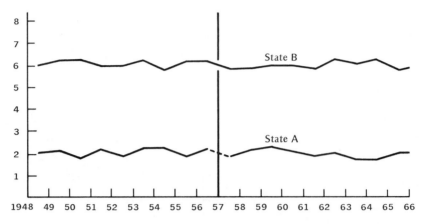

Figure 18. Hypothetical library circulation data pre-matching.

and State *B* the controls. Imagine, further, an attempt to make the series more comparable by matching low-circulation communities in State *B* with high-circulation communities in State *A* so that the states are equivalent in library circulation just before the treatment is introduced. If the measures are errorful, the pretest trends will converge to the point of matching and will diverge after the matching to produce the pattern in Figure 19. This looks like a dramatic effect of the treatment with the State *B* time-series reversing a downward trend and the State *A* series reversing an upward trend. Yet this apparent effect could alter-

natively be interpreted as a regression effect due to matching.

Correlational Designs

Causal Modeling, Path Analysis, and Structural Equation Techniques

In the last decade techniques for causal inference from correlational data have emerged within sociology under such names as causal models, path analysis, and structural models (e.g., Blalock, 1971). These are highly related to well-established regression methods in economics (Goldberger & Dun-

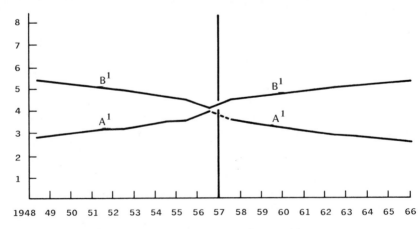

Figure 19. Hypothetical library circulation data after matching just before a treatment is introduced.

can, 1973), and are dominant among theory-related quantitative empirical studies in sociology as well as in methodological journals such as *Sociological Methods and Research* and *Social Science Research*. Indications are that this dominance will increase rather than decrease in the next few years. Thus, if only to be able to communicate with important social science research literature, industrial and organizational psychologists should acquire competence in the methods. This chapter is not the place to begin such an education, nor are we appropriate teachers. (Blalock, 1971, is a good starting point; Goldberger & Duncan, 1973, is more advanced.) Nonetheless, a few comments are appropriate here, for our concern is with causal inference, and these methods can be viewed as at the very least weak forms of quasi-experimental designs. The reader must be warned, however, that we approach the topic with a negative bias akin to the experimentalist's traditional distrust of purely correlational evidence.

Path analysis is most commonly applied to several different variables produced by a single cross-sectional measurement effort. Forced into the schema of this chapter, such uses of path analysis would have to be classified as a sub-type of the "Posttest-Only Design with Non-equivalent Groups," although differing in several ways. First and most important, the temporal priority of X to O would be only conjectural in such path analysis since X and O would usually have been measured at the same time and on the same measuring instrument (e.g., interview or questionnaire). While it would often be conceivable that O caused X, the analysis would provide no way of choosing between the $O \rightarrow X$ model and the $X \rightarrow O$ model (to say nothing of more complex ones such as $O \rightleftarrows X$ or $O \leftarrow Z \rightarrow X$, where Z is an unmeasured variable). Only one of these models could be chosen for testing, and the others would have to be ruled out on a priori grounds such as background information or theories currently believed to be true. Once a model has been assumed,

then the strength of the causal relationship can be estimated for the data. If one were to apply to this type of path analysis the set of threats to internal validity used here, the failure to independently ascertain the time relationship between X and O makes it even weaker than the general Posttest-Only Design with Non-Equivalent Groups as we have described it.

Another major difference between path analysis and the non-equivalent posttest-only design is that path analysts never analyze as simple a model as the two-variable one we have used for illustration. Three variables and two causal paths are a minimum, and more complex models are commoner. In these multivariate models, some variables will play double roles, being assumed causes (independent variables) in one relation and assumed effects (dependent variables) in another. When n variables are measured and many of the possible causal paths can be ruled out on a priori grounds, the model may be "over-identified" (rather than "just-identified" [as our $X \rightarrow O$ model] or "under-identified"), thus making possible tests of the fit of the model, or multiple estimates of certain causal paths.

Suppose one had the causal model $A \rightarrow B \rightarrow C$ (eliminating from consideration $C \rightarrow A$, $C \rightarrow B$, and $B \rightarrow A$, and withholding judgment on the need for $A \rightarrow C$). If the correlation pattern turned out to be $r_{AB} = .80$, $r_{BC} = .80$, $r_{AC} = .64$, then the two-path model $A \rightarrow B \rightarrow C$ is not disconfirmed by the data. r_{AC} has just the value expected from r_{AB} and r_{BC}, and no direct path $A \rightarrow C$ needs to be hypothesized. (It should be noted that this outcome is equally confirmatory of a $C \rightarrow B \rightarrow A$ model, but presumably this has been ruled out on the basis of other prior considerations, other facts, accepted theory, or common sense.) Had r_{AC} been higher than .64, a positive path coefficient for $A \rightarrow C$ would have been required; if lower, a negative path.

Such simple, three variable causal models are rarely used. More complex models, with larger proportions of ruled-out paths, are more common. Because of this, advocates of path analysis might well reject the primitive "Posttest-Only with Non-Equivalent Groups" classification here suggested, and also the accompanying pessimistic inference about validity status. Decisions on this issue are probably best made in the settings of specific uses of path analysis, noting the threats to validity that seem plausible in these settings. Third variable causation (appearing in our list as selection bias) and ambiguity about the direction of causality are probably the most frequently relevant. Among third variables, shared method factors (Campbell & Fiske, 1959; Heise, 1969; Schnaiberg & Armer, 1972) are a frequently neglected causally irrelevant source of correlation. These are commonalities introduced by measuring assumed cause and effect variables on the same instrument.

In support of path analysis, as of other correlational designs, we recognize that while correlation does not *prove* causation, causal theories imply correlations, and thus checking for their presence can be a useful *probe* of causal hypotheses. But this is a weak probe compared to true experiments or most of the other quasi-experiments here discussed. Even where the temporal sequence of X and O seems clear because each is measured at different times, correlations can be misleading if one does not have a complete causal model. In particular, one should beware of *imperfect compensatory mechanisms* that actually *reverse* the direction of a causal correlation. For example, if one experimentally introduced high-quality tutoring into a large competitive introductory course in an old-fashioned grade-giving university, one would no doubt find that, in general, the more tutoring the higher the grade received in the subsequent final examination. However, if one used non-experimental correlational data, one would find that the direction of the relationship is reversed—the more tutoring, the lower the subsequent grade. This would be because the valid popular belief in the value of tutoring leads to investment in it by those who

validly anticipate that they need it most. But, while tutoring is effective, it is usually not effective enough, or is not purchased in sufficient amounts, to completely compensate for the original need. Thus, some degree of negative correlation between grades and need for tutoring persists to dominate the correlation of grades and actual tutoring even though tutoring has been partially effective!

Neglect of the problem of error and unique variance in causal variables is another problem in much of the published literature, although not for some of the more advanced models. If we use the old-fashioned diagrams once used to explain correlation in terms of overlap of shared components of variance, the simple path model under discussion assumes the model of Figure 20-1. For $A \rightarrow B \rightarrow C$, all of the variance in A is contained in B, and all of the variance in B is contained in C. Considering the causal variables a social scientist is apt to use makes this an unreasonable model. For example, A might be father's occupation, education, social class, or income; B the respondent's education, I.Q., or hours of tutoring; C the respondent's income or grades. The As and Bs, as well as the Cs, have to be measured by fallible means, and as measured will contain both error and systematic irrelevance not contributing to the effect. Take, for example, education. Its measurement is affected by haphazard and biased reporting errors, even when reports are verified from school records. In addition, ten years of verified education has a wide range of meanings for genuine causal effects on later career opportunities since it does not reflect the amount learned for any given grade received, grading standards within curricula, curriculum differences within schools, and school-to-school differences. Thus, even if one had course-specific grades, there would be irrelevant but reliable variance not contributing to adequacy of preparedness for earning a living, etc. Another example: When one looks at how social class is estimated, one can see that even if rater-to-rater agreement were .99 rather than .70, much of this reliable variance would be irrelevant to the causal impact of social class on other variables. I.Q. measures might seem better, but they are not since they contain systematic irrelevancy for the purported causal theory if examined in detail. Moreover, there is age-specific irrelevance in that two I.Q. tests typically correlate .90 one year apart and only .50 five years apart, an auto-regressive moving average true-score process being, therefore, required to fit the data and the causal effects.

Figure 20–2 is a more realistic $A \rightarrow B \rightarrow$

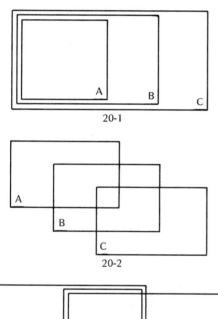

20-1

20-2

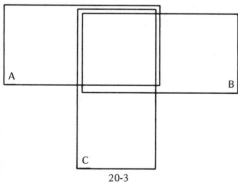

20-3

Figure 20. Overlap diagrams of three $A \rightarrow B \rightarrow C$ models.

C model. All variables have unique variance, including the "causes" or "independent" variables. However, Figure 20–3 shows a neglected model which most psychologists will want to rule out before considering either Figure 20–1 or 20–2. It implies that A, B, and C are different measures of a common underlying construct, and it is probably best eliminated by first rejecting the hypothesis of single-factoredness (Brewer, Campbell, & Crano, 1970). Only if there is evidence for more than one factor, may Figure 20–2 be plausible.

Another and perhaps more compelling reason for relegating these models to a low place among quasi-experimental designs is their passivity. Essential to the idea of an experiment is a deliberate, arbitrary human intervention—a planned intrusion or disruption of things-as-usual. Probably the psychological roots of the concept of cause are similar. Causes are preeminently things we can manipulate deliberately to change other things. Evidence of cause best comes as a result of such manipulation. Such evidence is perhaps "correlational" at root, but it is a very special sub-type of correlation; namely, that sub-type which we can use for changing one thing by changing another. Of all the correlations we can observe in nature, few are tools for easy manipulation, and those that are probably best tested by deliberate intrusive interventions via experimentation. There are more powerful analytic designs for such interventions than those associated with passive correlational analysis.

Though we are not optimistic about the prospects of path analysis for hypothesis-testing in most situations, we do think that it is useful in several ways. First, the more complex path models embody systems-theorizing in which the stress is placed on trying to understand relationships between variables that can affect and be affected by each other both directly and through the mediation of other variables. Once such complex models have been set up, path analysts are likely to pose research questions in terms of reciprocal causation, secondary or tertiary effects, and in terms of the multivariate determination of effects. Nature is presumably at least as complex as path analysts' models suggest, so that their work often appears to have a descriptive fidelity that seems to be missing in tests of simple hypotheses such as: Does A cause B, C, and D?, and even in tests of contingency hypotheses such as: Does A have similar effects on B for persons of types 1, 2, 3, etc.? Second, the path analysts' stress on passive measurement points to their perception of the desirability of testing hypotheses without the possible special disturbances that might result from the *experimental* introduction of a new practice. Third, posing questions in systematic fashion can often lead to new insights about possible relationships between variables that would have gone unimagined had there not been the discipline imposed by needing to think through a wide variety of possible relationships between a large number of variables. Fourth, while the basic data usually remain synchronous correlations, these are not worthless for testing causal hypotheses since nearly all such hypotheses imply correlations between variables. Thus, checking for correlations probes hypotheses, even though, working the other way, correlation does not imply causation. Fifth, current complex path analysis models provide a convenient way of making explicit the very assumptions of path analysis to which the critics point: assumptions about error in variables, completeness of the specification of the model, unidirectional causal path between two observed variables, etc.

Cross-Lagged Panel Correlations

Like path analysis, this method takes a passive rather than deliberately experimental approach to the diagnosis of causal relationships. Lazarsfeld (e.g., 1947, 1948; Lipset, Lazarsfeld, Barton, & Linz, 1954) has long argued that repeated measurement of the same two variables potentially provides information about the direction of any causal asymmetries between them. His "16-Fold Table" (two dichotomous variables at two times generating 16 cells) probably finds its best modern descendant in Goodman (1973). Campbell (1963; Campbell & Stanley, 1966) in an effort to convert the 16-fold table for use with continuous variables (in a manner still not convincing to Lazarsfeld) and to relate it to the use of lagged correlations in economics, came up with the cross-lagged panel correlation method. Working independently, and with more impressive illustrations, Pelz and Andrews (1964) developed essentially the same model, and have continued with important explorations of it which are so far only available as research reports. While Campbell has been inconsistent in his presentation of the model, his is nonetheless the tradition we find most convenient to present. Insofar as any model is recommended, it is the version developed by Kenny (1973; Crano, Kenny, & Campbell, 1972).

Figure 21 presents the set of terms and images we will reuse in this presentation. A and B represent two variables each measured at two times, 1 and 2, on the same persons (i.e., a "longitudinal" study or, in social survey terms, a "panel study"). The question at issue is whether A is a stronger cause of B than B is of A. The synchronous correlations, $r_{A_1B_1}$ and $r_{A_2B_2}$, and the test-retest correlations, $r_{A_1A_2}$ and $r_{B_1B_2}$, provide the interpretative framework for the two cross-lagged correlations $r_{A_1B_2}$ and $r_{B_1A_2}$. If A is the stronger cause, not vice versa, and if there are real storage processes (such as bank accounts and memories) spreading out the causation in time, then it might be expected that $r_{A_1B_2}$ would be larger than $r_{B_1A_2}$, as is illustrated in Figure 21, where a clear-cut $A \rightarrow B$ causation of a positive nature is indicated (i.e., increases in A cause B_2). Because $r_{A_1B_2}$ is also larger than $r_{A_1B_1}$ or $r_{A_2B_2}$, and because the latter two are equal, this illustration avoids many of the sources of equivocality that will be discussed below.

Built into the presumptions of the method is a bias against discovering specific

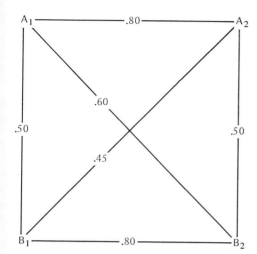

Figure 21. Hypothetical cross-lagged and background correlations between two variables (A and B) measured at two successive time periods (1 and 2) on the same sample.

causes and in favor of regarding A and B as both symptoms of a common or third variable. Thus the synchronous correlations, $r_{A_1B_1}$ and $r_{A_2B_2}$, .50 in Figure 21, are regarded as evidence of shared variance between A and B, but not as evidence of $A \rightarrow B$ or $B \rightarrow A$. "Instantaneous" causation is ruled out by fiat. (This differs from much of path analysis practice, although path models can be designed using the cross-lagged panel assumptions [Duncan, 1969].)

The cross-lagged panel method looks for causal asymmetries in an open causal model in which none of the variables involved is expected to have all of its variance represented in the causal paths under examination. It is assumed that each measure has unique factors, as well as error, that are unshared with the others. Thus if both $r_{A_1B_2}$ and $r_{B_1A_2}$ had been equal to .45, both hypotheses $A \rightarrow B$ and $B \rightarrow A$ would have been rejected in favor of the cosymptom model: $A \leftarrow Z \rightarrow B$. However, common forms of path analysis would find a positive value for the $A_1 \rightarrow B_2$ path even with $r_{A_1B_2} = r_{B_1A_2}$, for the partial correlation $r_{A_1B_2 \cdot B_1}$ would differ from zero.

Initially, Campbell (1963) was only willing to infer causation where the synchronous correlation was increasing, that is, $r_{A_1B_1} < r_{A_2B_2}$, but subsequently it has seemed that interpretability is maximum when a condition of "stationarity" exists; that is, when the componential or causal model remains the same at each time period. One symptom of stationarity is that the synchronous correlations be stable, although with only two waves of measurement, the assumption of stationarity is poorly tested. Another consideration in the present model is "temporal erosion" (Kenny, 1973). It is ubiquitously observed that relationships are lower over longer lapses of time. For example, an intelligence test might correlate .90 over a one-year lapse but only .50 over a five-year gap, with intermediate periods having intermediate values. Cross-trait correlations show a comparable diminution over time. Figure 22 shows an extension of the hypothetical case of Figure 21, illustrating both stationarity and a homogeneous temporal erosion process. It also illustrates an $A \rightarrow B$ causal effect that persists over longer lags but in diminished degree. Thus over one interval, the lagged correlations are .60 and .45, while over two intervals they are .54 and .40. In the "correllograms" of time-series statistics and in the unpublished work of Pelz, attention is given to determining the optimal lag; that is, the lag at which the lagged cross-trait correlation is maximum. Social feedback cycles, pay periods, seasonal factors, construction time between the decision to expand production capacity and increased production—all may work to put this maximum beyond the shortest lag. However, with test-retest intervals of months or years, the commonest pattern is probably the one shown in Figure 22, in which the dissipation of effect begins immediately.

The rate and pattern of temporal erosion are matters to be determined empirically. In the simple case of Figure 22, A and B are equally reliable and have the same rate of temporal erosion. In the hypothetical case, each has an "instantaneous" reliability of .89

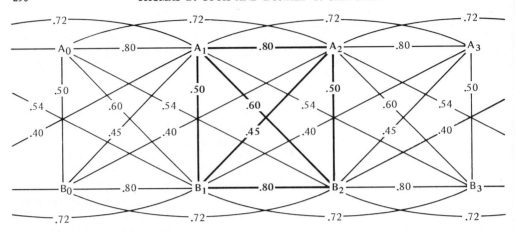

Figure 22. The hypothetical cross-lagged panel correlations from Figure 21 extended as a stationary process in repeated measures. (To avoid confusion, lags beyond two time periods have not been included in the diagram.)

(not shown in Figure 22) and a temporal erosion rate of .90 per unit of time. Thus $r_{A_1 A_2} = .89 \times .90 = .80$, $r_{A_1 A_3} = .80 \times .90 = .72$, $r_{A_1 A_4} = .72 \times .90 = .65$, etc. This conforms to the auto-regressive model known as a first-order Markov process, which is probably the most reasonable model for most time-series data in economics and the other social sciences. The rates of temporal erosion are expected to vary for the differing components of systematic variance making up each variable. The erosion rate for the components generating the A-B correlation are of special importance since they provide the basis for estimating what the lagged cross-correlations would be in the absence of any $A \rightarrow B$ or $B \rightarrow A$ causation. In the simple case of Figures 21 and 22, where the overall erosion rates of A and B are the same, it may seem reasonable to assume that the erosion rate of their shared component is the same as the two overall rates. On this basis, the values $r_{B_1 A_2} = .45$, $r_{B_1 A_3} = .41$, $r_{B_1 A_4} = .36$, etc., represent no causation, just temporally attenuated cosymptomicity.

Making such estimates in practice turns out to be a difficult problem. However, if the assumptions of stationarity are appropriate, the expected values for $r_{A_1 B_2}$ and $r_{B_1 A_2}$ are the same if there is no specific $A \rightarrow B$ or $B \rightarrow A$ causation, and it would be appropriate to compare these two values directly,

without estimation of erosion rates. Whereas in Figures 21 and 22, one of the cross-lagged values is higher than the synchronous values, causal inference is supported no matter what estimate of temporal erosion is used. And when the synchronous values are zero (as in a true experiment and occasionally in cross-lagged panel correlations), no further erosion is possible, clarifying cross-causational inference.

But stationarity is not always the case, and the assumption is not met when variables change in reliability, as happens in longitudinal studies with children where reliability increases over time. When such changes are uniform across all variables, they may not bias the comparison of cross-lagged values. If, however, one variable is changing at a different rate from the others, mistaken inferences can result. Other things being equal, a variable that is increasing in reliability will be mistakenly judged to be an effect rather than a cause. (For example, if A_2 is more reliable than A_1, all correlations involving A_2 will tend to be higher than those involving A_1, including $r_{B_1 A_2} > r_{A_1 B_2}$.) If appropriate reliability estimates are available (it is not clear that internal consistency reliability estimates are appropriate), correction for attenuation may restore stationarity. Kenny (1973) has developed a "correction for communality" for use where many variables are involved. Using factor-analytic logic, though not performing a factor analysis, estimates of reliability ratios are based on the inter-trait correlations. The best application and exposition of Kenny's approach is found in Crano, Kenny, and Campbell (1972). Figure 23 illustrates the best of their many cross-lagged panel correlations, showing that vocabulary "causes" spelling, to some degree at least. (Since in this case the correction for communality did not change the picture, the original correlations are presented.)

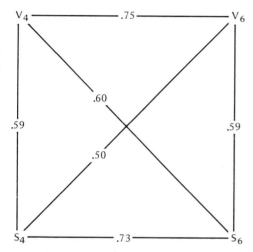

Figure 23. Cross-lagged correlation pattern between vocabulary and spelling scores from the Iowa tests of basic skills, Milwaukee Public Schools, grades 4 and 6, n = 5,495. The t for the comparison $r_{V_4S_6} > r_{S_4V_6}$ = 9.32. (After Crano, Kenny, & Campbell, 1972.)

The presentation so far, and the original presentations of Pelz and Andrews (1964) and Campbell (1963), have implied that only two causal hypotheses are in competition: $A \rightarrow B$ and $B \rightarrow A$. But a causal relation between two variables can be either negative or positive. Increases in A can result in increases in B, or in decreases in B. Expanding our symbolism, there are at least four hypotheses: $A \overset{+}{\rightarrow} B$, $A \overset{-}{\Rightarrow} B$, $B \overset{+}{\rightarrow} A$, and $B \overset{-}{\Rightarrow} A$. Some examples will help clarify this. Rozelle and Campbell (1969) set out to probe the method by confirming that in an

achievement-oriented suburban high school, high attendance caused high grades, testing this against the unlikely alternative (for this population) that high grades caused high attendance. They surprised themselves by also concluding that high grades in one semester caused lower attendance in the following, which made sense in terms of high grades giving a student freedom to join his parents on a winter vacation or to cut one class to study for another. (All correlations were very low. The synchronous correlations were essentially zero, making noticeable the sign difference between $r_{A_1G_2} = .08$ and $r_{G_1A_2} = -.06$. With an n of 1,000, this difference is highly significant.) Thus their significant difference between $r_{A_1G_2} > r_{G_1A_2}$ was best interpreted as a pooled effect of two causal processes. Inspecting Pelz and Andrews's (1964) wide range of illustrations provides other examples. In the analysis of data from the Survey Research Center panel on economic trends, intentions-to-purchase at one time no doubt "caused" purchases a later year. For television sets, $r_{I_1P_2} = .75$, $r_{P_1I_2} = -.57$. But certainly some of this 132-point difference in correlation is due to a negative component: purchases one year reduce subsequent intentions. (In their results on intentions to purchase pooled over a wide range of household durables, $r_{I_1P_2} = .33 > r_{P_1I_2} = .09$, the negative component $P \Rightarrow I$ is less noticeable because both signs are positive, but it is no doubt still there.)

Rozelle and Campbell (1969) attempted to solve the problem of confounding negative and positive causation by computing a "no-cause comparison base" against which each of the cross-lagged values could be separately compared. Thus in the case of Figure 22, using the lagged auto-correlations (test-retest correlations) and the synchronous cross-correlations, one would estimate what each of the cross-lagged correlations would be in the absence of an $A \rightarrow B$, $B \rightarrow A$ causation. The obtained cross-lagged correlations would each be separately compared with this value, rather than directly with each other. One could confirm two separate causal hypotheses at one time, and each of these could be one of two types, positive or negative. In Figure 21 (and 22), had both $r_{A_1B_2}$ and $r_{B_1A_2}$ been .60, with the no-cause comparison base .45, the two conclusions would have been $A \nrightarrow B$ and $B \nrightarrow A$. Had each been .30, the two conclusions would have been $A \Rightarrow B$ and $B \Rightarrow A$. Had $r_{A_1B_2}$ been .60 and $r_{B_1A_2}$ .30, the conclusions would have been $A \nrightarrow B$ and $B \Rightarrow A$, etc. (Some outcomes will turn out to be incompatible with the requirement of stationarity.) The use of a "no-cause comparison base" would be appropriate if there were reasonable grounds for estimating it. Rickard (1972) and Kenny (1973) have, however, persuasively rejected Rozelle and Campbell's estimation procedure, which involved treating temporal erosion as though it were a characteristic of a variable as a whole. When A and B differed in erosion rate, Rozelle and Campbell recommended using the geometric mean of the two as the rate at which the synchronous correlations would erode to become the lagged cross-correlations under no-cause conditions. Rickard and Kenny correctly point out that the relevant temporal erosion is that of the shared latent factors producing the synchronous correlation, and that there is no logical reason why that should be an average. (In Rozelle and Campbell's data, since the synchronous correlations were essentially zero, the niceties of estimating erosion rates and no-cause comparison bases did not affect their substantive conclusions.)

As a result, Kenny advocates a less ambitious version of cross-lagged panel analysis, in which the two cross-lagged correlations are compared directly with each other. In many instances some of the four causal hypotheses will be so implausible that (à la path analysis) they can be ruled out on a priori grounds. In Crano et al. (1972) it seemed a real question whether the preponderant causal direction was from intelligence to achievement or from achievement to intelligence—Piaget's theories being invoked for the latter. But it was inconceivable that either had a negative effect on the other, thus in Figure 23, $V \Rightarrow S$ and $S \Rightarrow V$ could be disregarded. Where this is not so, the cross-lag differences reflect on the preponderance of two composite effects. Had Rozelle and Campbell (1969) found a substantial synchronous correlation between grades and achievement (as would have been expected from a general conscientiousness factor) then the finding that $r_{A_1G_2} > r_{G_1A_2}$ would have had to be interpreted as merely showing that the composite effect of $A \nrightarrow G$ and $G \Rightarrow A$ was greater than the composite $G \nrightarrow A$ and $A \Rightarrow G$. Of these four only the last is inconceivable (and this perhaps inconceivable only to us educators). In such a case, a rather frustrating degree of equivocality would remain even if a striking cross-lag differential were found.

Variations on the same general model may produce interpretable causal inferences. Figure 24 shows an "interspersed" lag pattern, interpretable as an $A \nrightarrow B$ causation if only positive causation is plausible. (There are no synchronous correlations to tempt the "no-cause comparison base" approach.) A single triangle from this might be interpreted with caution, and a replicated pattern of

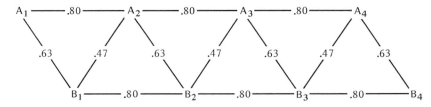

Figure 24.　Interspersed lagged design. (If the B measures are not evenly spaced between the As, the different amounts of lapsed time could explain a correlational difference in the direction of higher values for shorter time periods. Longer lags should also be computed.)

results across several time periods with some confidence. A triangular fragment from a synchronous cross-lag pattern (Figure 25) provides some evidence, even if not totally compelling, that viewing violence on television as measured in the third grade is causally related to violence when children are in the thirteenth grade (Eron, Huesmann, Lefkowitz, & Walder, 1972, as interpreted by Kenny, 1972). Here the argument comes from a synchronous versus single-lag comparison, rather than from comparing the two lags of opposite direction. The synchronous value is usually not

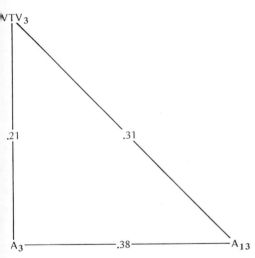

Figure 25. Fragmentary cross-lagged analysis of the effects of preference for violent television (VTV) on aggression (A). Based on 211 boys measured 10 years apart, at grades 3 and 13. (After Eron et al., 1972, as interpreted by Kenny, 1972.)

a good general comparison base for the lagged values since it tends to be inflated by shared time-specific measurement errors and by absence of temporal erosion. If, however, the lagged value (.31 in Figure 25) is higher than the synchronous value (.21) despite these factors, then it can be presumed that the causal effect must have been strong enough to more than overcome these disadvantages.

In summary, cross-lagged correlational analysis is certainly worth exploring where

the data being collected make it possible. (If one is planning such a study, three waves provide much more power than do two, and still more are desirable.) It has some advantages over ordinary path analysis, through using an incomplete causal model and through better handling of the error and the unique variance that every social science measure almost certainly has. It also has more of the orientation of putting causal models into competition rather than assuming a single causal model and estimating its parameters. But the cross-lagged panel method is still a passive correlational approach in contrast to the active, intrusive, experimental approaches generally advocated in this review. Moreover, it is addressed to the question: Is A a stronger cause of B than B is of A? It is not, therefore, addressed to the traditional causal question: Does a change in A cause a change in B?

Treatment-Effect Correlations

Campbell (1971) has advocated the use of treatment-effect correlations in a number of circumstances for answering whether A can reasonably be assumed to be a cause of B. The logic behind the design can perhaps best be understood by conceptualizing the true experiment in correlational terms. If we took the simplest treatment *versus* no-treatment design, we could assign the treatment a "dummy" value of 1 and the control experience a "dummy" value of 0. Then if we correlated the treatment with pretest scores, the resulting biserial correlation should not differ from zero. After all, randomization insures that the average score in the treatment group should not differ from the average score in the control group. However, if the treatment were effective, we would expect more of the higher posttest scores to come from the treatment group so that the biserial correlation of the treatment and posttest should be greater than zero and should be different from the correlation of the treatment and pretest. Unlike true experiments, quasi-experiments have non-comparable groups, and the pretest-treatment correlation will usually differ from zero. Thus a treatment effect would only be suggested if the posttest-treatment correlation differed from the pretest-treatment correlation.

It is not inevitable that treatment-effect correlations involve biserial correlations. Sometimes, though rarely, an experimenter will be able to vary multiple levels of a quantitative independent variable. More often, one will be able to measure a naturally occurring continuous variable whose effects are to be assessed (e.g., the number of hours worked, the percentage of work time spent on the job, etc.), or one will be able to measure differences in the extent to which units in a single treatment group have actually received the intended treatment. For instance, it is one thing to assign all the persons in an experimenter-designated group as, say, the "job counseling group" and it is quite another thing to get the persons so designated to go for counseling as often as the experimenter would hope. Instead, it is only realistic to expect that there will be considerable heterogeneity within the group, and this could be measured on a continuous scale as an index of "the number of counseling visits during 1974." Then, this measure could be related to both pretest and posttest outcome variables using the statistically more powerful Pearson product moment correlation.

Treatment-effect correlations have another important characteristic. When selection-maturation is a problem, they are probably less prone to bias than are other quasi-experimental designs, especially those where an attempt is made to adjust statistically for pretest differences. The reason for this can be perhaps understood by considering one version of the formula for a Pearson product moment correlation:

$$r = \frac{\Sigma xy}{NS_x S_y}$$

At the pretest, the covariation factor in the numerator would often be positive since higher scores on a test would be from per-

sons who were to go on and get some potential benefit (e.g., the more efficient young executives get selected out for more advanced training). Now, if these executives were becoming increasingly more efficient anyway when compared to those who were not assigned to the training course, we would expect the covariation of posttest efficiency and attendance at the advanced training course to be even higher than the pretest level of covariation. Thus, selection-maturation would inflate the numerator. But since the overall variability in efficiency would be increasing over time if there were selection-maturation, we should also expect higher variability across all executives at the posttest than at the pretest. Since variability in efficiency is a feature of the denominator, selection-maturation should inflate the denominator as well as the numerator. Since both the numerator and denominator of the formula would be inflated, their combined effect should reduce this source of bias. The crucial issue is whether the increase in the numerator due to selection-maturation would be exactly proportional to the increase in the denominator, for only if this were so would a selection-maturation threat be entirely ruled out. Unfortunately, we do not yet know the answer to this question, and on it depends a sensitive understanding of when the reduction in bias entails an elimination of bias.

But several other sources of bias are well known, and they are similar to those mentioned above for the cross-lagged correlation. First, the treatment will be more highly correlated with measures that are more reliable. Thus, in the normal situation where the number of testings increases reliability, the treatment-posttest correlation will tend to be inflated relative to the treatment-pretest correlation. This can masquerade as a treatment effect in some situations.

Second, there is the problem that the factor structure of complex variables can shift over time, making the pretest and posttest similarly named measures of somewhat different constructs. Shifts in correlation can result because of such changes, and this then involves the threat of stationarity that we mentioned earlier. It is perhaps most acute as a threat in situations where a third variable is differently correlated with the pretest and posttest, which is especially likely when discontinuities in growth patterns are found. For instance, if Piaget's theory of cognitive development were true, we might expect to find SES correlated with some measures of pretest achievement (perhaps because more lower SES children were still preoperational than higher SES children). But if all the children had become concrete operationalist by the posttest, the correlation with SES might disappear on some measures. More importantly, those test items that had depended on SES at the pretest would presumably be differently related by the posttest to the items that had never depended on SES. Thus, the factor structure of the pretest and posttest would differ and each measure would reflect somewhat different variables. Fortunately, Kenny (in press) has developed some adjustment procedures for use when the stationarity assumption is violated.

The third problem is of temporal erosion. Variables which are measured at further distances in time from each other tend to have lower correlations. Thus, a treatment measured simultaneously with a pretest would tend to be more highly correlated with the pretest than the posttest, thereby masquerading as a harmful treatment effect for most programs and as an erroneously successful treatment for programs with "compensatory" goals (i.e., the program's purpose is to reduce an existing negative correlation rather than to cause or increase one). Conversely, if a treatment was measured at the same time as the posttest, it would masquerade as an effect with most programs and as a falsely harmful effect with "compensatory" programs. The problem of temporal erosion is likely to be exacerbated where the treatment is measured both at the same time as the posttest and on a similar scale to the posttest. This would be the case, for example, if job satisfaction and social integration at a work setting were measured in the same "posttest" interview, for commonalities in the testing session will inflate the correlation of the two variables at the posttest and also presumably increase the problem of differential erosion. The solution to this problem is to measure the treatment at a point (or, preferably, at a series of points) equally distant from both the pretest and posttest, so as to have approximately equal erosion for the treatment to the posttest and from the treatment to the pretest. In addition, the treatment should be measured on a different scale from the pretest and posttest by persons who have had no association with pretest or posttest interviews.

The pitfalls and advantages of treatment-effect correlation can be quickly illustrated with reference to the evaluation of "Sesame Street" (Bogatz & Ball, 1971; Cook et al., 1975; Kenny, in press). Four measures were taken by ETS of the extent to which children reportedly viewed "Sesame Street." One required children to recognize characters from the series and was collected at the posttest. Thus, the test was a recognition test of knowledge—as were the learning tests—and was collected at the posttest. Both test similarity and time of testing should, therefore, be expected to inflate posttest-treatment correlations over pretest-treatment correlations. A second measure was also collected at the posttest, but mothers were asked to estimate their child's average viewing. Thus, any erosion should have relatively inflated posttest correlations, but there was little likelihood of common testing features inflating correlations because mothers provided the data and not the children. The other two viewing measures were continuously collected from parents during the six-month viewing season, and so they avoided each of the problems just analyzed. Unfortunately, however, they were inferior to the posttest viewing measures on a number of psychometric grounds (especially reliability). Hence, the best single measure was probably the mother's posttest estimate of her child's viewing.

TABLE 1
RESULTS OF THE TREATMENT-OUTCOME CORRELATIONAL ANALYSES
OF SESAME STREET'S EFFECTS ON EIGHT LEARNING TESTS

Learning Test	Nonencouraged Children (N = 130)						Encouraged Children (N = 330)					
	Analysis with Partialing			Partialing plus Communality Correction			Analysis with Partialing			Partialing plus Communality Correction		
	Pretest r	Posttest r	t	Pretest r	Posttest r	t	Pretest r	Posttest r	t	Pretest r	Posttest r	t
Body Parts	.226	.234	.08	.226	.234	.09	.102	.149	.83	.102	.149	.82
Forms	.217	.353	1.19	.232	.331	.87	.144	.206	.98	.147	.201	.85
Letters	.071	.296	2.41*	.076	.277	2.14*	.116	.287	2.79*	.139	.239	1.56
Numbers	.099	.300	2.34*	.098	.303	2.38*	.150	.257	2.15*	.154	.252	1.97*
Relations	.103	.275	1.59	.102	.278	1.62	.036	.172	2.05*	.037	.165	1.92
Classification	.110	.221	1.05	.114	.214	.94	.133	.199	1.01	.141	.188	.70
Sorting	.064	.139	.64	.087	.103	.12	.015	.180	2.23*	.018	.152	1.75
Puzzles	.077	.246	1.55	.061	.314	2.15*	.135	.075	−.89	.128	.079	−.72

* p. < .05.

Table 1 displays data relating this estimate of viewing to pretest and posttest scores among children who had or had not received the complex encouragement treatment that we mentioned earlier. All the correlations are displayed after partialing on a number of background characteristics of the children, and two versions of each correlation are given: one with and one without Kenny's previously mentioned "correction for communality," a correction for the lack of stationarity due to reliability shifts over time (see p. 290 of this chapter). It can be seen that posttest-viewing correlations tended to be higher than pretest-viewing correlations; that statistically significant differences were obtained for two of eight tests among the non-encouraged and for four of eight tests among the encouraged; that the adjustments for non-stationarity did not radically affect the direction or magnitude of differences in correlation, so that three of eight tests reached conventional levels of statistical significance among the non-encouraged and only one did among the encouraged. (These analyses were conducted by Kenny and reported in Cook et al. The statistical test can be found in Van Voorhis and Peters, 1940, and is a test of the difference between correlations that share an array. Since then Kenny has reanalyzed these same data using a more powerful statistical test, and it increases the t values in Table 1 by up to .10. Thus, the more powerful test makes no major difference.)

Treatment-effect correlations are particularly useful to fall back upon should a true experiment not be successfully implemented or maintained. But such a correlational analysis can only be computed if there are both pretest measures and *valid* measures of the intended treatment that are collected at an equal time removed from both the pretest and posttest. Hence, though true experiments do not logically require either pretests or measures of the "take" of the independent variable, the field experimentalist who decides to forego such measures runs the great risk that if his true experiment breaks down, he will not be able to classify units along the intended treatment dimension and will not be able to conduct sensitive quasi-experimental tests of his major research question. Sometimes it will be useful to conduct treatment-effect analyses in the unfortunate situation of an aborted true experiment.

Regression Adjustments for Biased Assignment to Treatments

Perhaps the most common mode of analysis for experimental designs using casual, rather than random, assignment to treatments is some form of regression adjustment in which, by use of covariates or pretests, the posttest means of experimental and control groups are adjusted in an effort to remove pretreatment differences. Such methods share the same chronic under-adjustment ("regression artifacts") produced by matching or covariance adjustment (Campbell & Erlebacher, 1970). However, this realization has not spread to most practitioners of multiple regression techniques.

Table 2 presents a set of correlations based upon a simple single-factored model, a setting in which regression adjustments would commonly be expected to work, if

TABLE 2
HYPOTHETICAL INTERCORRELATIONS AMONG VARIABLES FOR REGRESSION ADJUSTMENT DEMONSTRATION

	Pr	Po	T	C_1	C_2	C_3
Pr						
Po	.800					
T	.505	.505				
C_1	.632	.632	.399			
C_2	.632	.632	.399	.500		
C_3	.632	.632	.399	.500	.500	

anywhere. In this hypothetical simulation, the population is from middle management and the pretest (*Pr*) and posttest (*Po*), which might be similar measures of executive and managerial aptitude, have 80 percent of their variance determined by some common social advantage factor. The experimental treatment (T) might be a year at a graduate school of management, awarded somewhat haphazardly but on the average given to the most socially advantaged so that 50 percent of its variance comes from this factor. (Since it is a dichotomous variable, its correlations are lower than if it were continuous.) The covariates might be father's income (C_1), mother's educational level (C_2), and socioeconomic level of residence (C_3). Each of these hypothetical covariates has 50 percent of its variance from the social advantage factor, and 50 percent from unique determinants, including error. This is a simulation of a null case in that the correlation of treatment with posttest, like that of treatment with pretest, reflects the social advantage factor but no true treatment effect. Thus $r_{TPr} = r_{TPo} = .505$. Rather than adjusted means, let us use partial correlation coefficients, which will be zero when the difference between adjusted means is zero. Our focus is on r_{TPo}, that is, on the correlation between the treatment and the posttest.

Let us first consider ex post facto analyses, in which the pretest is not available but in which three good covariates are: r_{TPo} starts out at .505 before adjustment. Using one covariate, the partial $r_{TPo \cdot c_1} = .355$, somewhat smaller but still far from the zero it should be if one covariate were providing adequate adjustment for pretreatment differences or for the biased assignment to treatment. Using two and three covariates makes the partial smaller, $r_{TPo \cdot c_1 c_2} = .277$, $r_{TPo \cdot c_1 c_2 c_3} = .229$, but these are still of a magnitude that would be mistakenly reported as impressive results for the graduate management training. Even if we had ten such marvelously good covariates, with a large number of cases an impressive difference between adjusted means would remain: $r_{TPo \cdot c_1 c_2 c_3 c_4 c_5 c_6 c_7 c_8 c_9 c_{10}} = .104$. The only way such covariates can provide adequate adjustment is for one or more of them to be a perfect measure of the common factor (i.e., social advantage). Such covariates simply do not exist, and in the ordinary situation few, if any, of the covariates are as good as the ones in Table 1.

What if we do have a pretest, and adjust on it? $r_{TPo \cdot Pr} = .195$. What if we use both pretest and covariates? $r_{TPo \cdot Pr c_1 c_2 c_3} = .136$. Though reduced, these adjusted correlations are still of a magnitude frequently packaged as treatment effects in the form of adjusted mean differences. If the factorial pattern is more complex, multiple and partial correlation are even less relevant. All in all, multiple regression adjustments are nearly always inadequate to the task assigned them in quasi-experimental research.

THE CONDUCT OF TRUE EXPERIMENTS IN FIELD SETTINGS

The Need for True Experiments

The foregoing list of quasi-experiments is not exhaustive. In particular, there is no discussion of "patched-up" designs which can be evolved by determining the particular threats to validity that operate in a specific instance and by using one control after another until as many threats as possible have been ruled out. However, it was in this spirit of "patching up" that we advised readers not to treat the designs we outlined as fixed and, instead, to follow the practice of Lieberman (1956), Broadbent and Little (1960), and Lawler and Hackman (1969) inasmuch as each of these studies incorporated more than one of the design features that we outlined earlier.

But when all is said and done most quasi-experiments, including even the stronger ones, leave some doubt about internal validity, and true experiments are much stronger in this regard. True experiments have another advantage, albeit of lesser importance. There are quasi-experimental designs for which no compelling statistical test yet exists, the non-equivalent no-treatment control group design being a salient case in point. But there are appropriate and powerful statistical tests available for most true experiments, largely because inferential statistics were developed with true experiments in mind.

It would be wrong to see true experiments as having any necessary advantage over quasi-experiments with respect to external validity. Each type of research is likely to be restricted to a few sites, a homogeneous population, and a few times in history. Nor is it clear whether one type of research enjoys any advantage of construct validity over the other. It might be thought, at first glance, that true experiments have had an edge because they are more likely to be planned in advance and to involve experimenter-developed treatments rather than spontaneously occurring treatments. But we shall later see how experimenter-developed treatments are not necessarily the treatments that get implemented in field settings, and we might also note that experimenter-developed treatments are more likely—in general—to deviate from the natural variability in "treatments" that spontaneously occurs within an organization. Experimenter-controlled treatments are also more potentially reactive than spontaneously occurring treatments or treatments that are planned and implemented by the organization itself as part of its change plans. Thus, the reader would be mistaken if he were to believe that true experiments mean unimpeachable external or construct validity.

In the sections that follow we shall spend little time outlining research designs. The ones that are appropriate are contained in classical texts on experimental design that were originally intended for agricultural or laboratory researchers (e.g., Walker & Lev, 1953; Edwards, 1963; Winer, 1961; Hays, 1963; Kirk, 1968; McNemar, 1971). Instead, we shall concern ourselves with (1) obstacles to random assignment in field research, (2) strategies for overcoming these obstacles, and (3) developing a list of situations that are most conducive to randomization. Our stress is, therefore, on some *problems of implementing true experiments* in field settings rather than on the *interpretation of true experimental designs.*

Major Obstacles to Conducting True Experiments in Field Settings

It is difficult to gain and maintain access to research populations in field settings, irrespective of whether true experiments or quasi-experiments are contemplated. The problem of access can probably best be conceptualized in terms of social power. Access is more likely if one has power over the persons determining access. This can be a power based on the ability to reward or punish, on being personally respected or being sponsored by respected research institutions, on belonging to the same membership groups as persons determining access, on promising research that might benefit an organization, or on being the kind of person who can successfully badger, cajole, or charm others into compliance with one's wishes. This is not to say that negotiations about access should only be conducted with persons responsible for authorizing immediate entry into an organization. Obtaining access and maintaining good field relationships over time may well depend on a study being explicitly or implicitly endorsed by the persons from whom data are collected or by representatives of such persons. Endorsement of this kind would probably decrease the problems that arise when respondents think they are being studied without their consent and for a nebulous reason that may not necessarily be to their immediate or long-term advantage.

Since access is a problem in all field experimentation, we shall not especially concern ourselves with it in the present discussion of true experiments. Rather, we shall concentrate on the special problems of access and implementation that face investigators because they plan to use random assignment.

a. Withholding the Treatment from No-Treatment Control Groups

Self-selection into treatment and no-treatment groups is less likely in true experiments than in quasi-experiments since true experiments require randomization and this is usually done by the experimenter or his accomplices rather than the respondents themselves. In many designs the investigator's request for randomization will be accompanied by a request that the treatment be deliberately withheld from some respondents. Such requests may seem particularly questionable ethically if potentially ameliorative treatments are to be withheld from persons who might need or deserve them. Indeed, many of the problems of implementing true experiments arise because valuable resources are allocated by chance instead of by the more accepted criteria of need or merit.

The failure to provide the treatment to controls can lead to problems of public relations and construct validity as well as ethics. Both Bishop and Hill (1971) and Hand and Slocum (1972) have attributed unexpected decrements in performance and attitude in no-treatment control groups to the control respondents becoming resentful when they compared their own lack of a treatment with the treatment received by others. The persons who authorize access may well anticipate such resentment and, if they do, the work cited above suggests that they may have some justification. It also suggests that, even where the apprehensions of decision makers have been overcome, an experiment would be hard to interpret if the no-treatment control group was, in fact, a "resentful-of-no-treatment" group. Using such a group as a no-cause base line might be misleading under some circumstances, for one might attribute a causal difference between treatment and no-treatment groups as due to the treatment causing an increase in the dependent variable when in fact the

apparent "no-treatment" might have caused a decrease.

Withholding the treatment is not a problem in designs where multiple treatments are implemented in order to assess how well they solve a unique problem or test a theory. Atkinson (1968) provides an ingenious example of this strategy in a study of computer-assisted instruction where pupils were randomly assigned to receiving computer-assisted mathematics or computer-assisted English. Both groups took tests of both mathematics and English, with the groups "switching" as to which was the experimental and which the control group. This design is available where one has multiple problems for ameliorative action, and where these are relatively independent in content.

Withholding a treatment is also less of a problem when each respondent receives one of several treatments that are approximately equal in desirability and that are aimed at solving the same problem, a strategy that also puts the investigator in a position to contrast the relative efficacy of the various treatments so that the most powerful can be ascertained. The only real drawback when multiple treatments are targeted on a common problem is that there may be no group to provide a no-cause base line. All the comparisons will be between different treatment groups.

The problem of withholding a treatment is also partially solved in designs like that of Bishop and Hill (1971) where a change is given to the control group that is not expected to affect the performance being examined. A placebo control group of this nature is useful because it differentiates the effects of any change at all from the effects of a specific change that was introduced for experimental reasons. For example, Bishop and Hill used the control in their experiment on job enlargement so that the construct "job enlargement" could be distinguished from the construct "change in the job," the latter being an inevitable but irrelevant correlate of job enlargement.

The problem of withholding treatments

is also reduced when resources are scarce and it is simply not possible to provide everyone with the treatment. In this case, the investigator knows that there will have to be no-treatment controls. But he has no guarantee that these controls will be equivalent to the treatment group since in many organizations there will be pressure to distribute the treatment to those who are thought to merit it most rather than to a randomly selected group. This means that the investigator has to use all of his persuasive powers to inform persons controlling access that we *hope* a treatment will have ameliorative consequences but we *do not know* it will; that, if we did know, there would be no need to conduct an experiment; and that, since we do not know, to conduct any study other than a true experiment would decrease the likelihood of eventually learning whether the treatment had solved the practical or theoretical problem to which it was addressed. The investigator might further add that he would like to provide the treatment, or a refinement of it, to the no-treatment controls if it were established that the treatment was successful. This information should help the persons who control access because it ensures that everyone would finally receive a definitely ameliorative treatment. However, it would also benefit investigators who would have a chance to replicate previous findings or even, if the appropriate permission were obtained, to add to already existing knowledge by modifying the replication.

The problems associated with withholding treatments are grave and not easy to solve. In the last analysis, persuasion has to be the weapon (perhaps even when other sources of power are available). However, we might presume that persuasion is more likely to be successful with persons who are genuinely concerned about the ethical and practical problems associated with withholding treatments than with persons who use the problems as justification for their reluctance to randomize or to conduct any kind of research.

b. Faulty Randomization Procedures

Randomization is a process of selecting a sample so that each unit in the population has an equal chance of appearing in the sample. It has two principal functions in the behavioral sciences. The first is to provide samples that are representative of specified populations and the second is to provide samples that are comparable to each other so that different treatments can be assigned to each. The first function relates to external validity and the second to internal validity. Both are, of course, important, but the function of establishing comparable experimental groups is more important in the context of experimentation.

The most commonly used method of drawing random samples is to use a book of edited random numbers like the one published by Rand (1955). The book can be used in the following way. After a population of units has been designated, each unit is then numbered so that there is no duplication of numbers. Then the tables can be used to assign each unit to a treatment condition according to the order in which its number is encountered in proceeding through the listed random numbers. This procedure is hardly likely to be biased since the tables of random numbers have been edited to take out nonrandom number sequences that occurred by chance (*sic!*). Mechanical procedures are generally less effective. For example, Fienberg (1971) and Notz, Staw, and Cook (1971) have commented upon the bias in the 1969 draft lottery in which slips of paper bearing different birth dates were drawn out of an urn with the order in which dates were drawn deciding the order in which men would be called up for service in the armed forces. This bias arose because the urn was not sufficiently shaken, with the result that the numbers put into it last (those of December, November, October, etc.) lay on the top and were more likely to be drawn out early. Care must be taken in examining all randomization procedures lest biases creep in and prevent the pretest equivalence of treatment groups.

c. Sampling Variability and the Number of Units for Randomization

It is often the case that units larger than individuals have to be randomly assigned to conditions. This need arises because of the fear that if different individuals receive different treatments in a common setting they will talk about these treatments and will "contaminate" them (diffusion and imitation of the treatment). Thus, Lawler and Hackman (1969) assigned small groups to conditions; Broadbent and Little (1960) assigned workrooms; and Morse and Reimer (1956) assigned whole divisions. While the use of groups entails more reliable measurement than the use of individuals, it, typically, also entails a smaller sample size. Indeed, if we look at the Lawler and Hackman study, only nine groups were involved in four experimental conditions, while for Broadbent and Little it was nine work areas in two experimental conditions, and for Morse and Reimer it was four work divisions in two experimental groups.

When there is a significantly different variability between experimental units, it is not likely—for reasons of sampling variability—that randomly assigning so few units to conditions will result in conditions that are equivalent. If there is no equivalence there can be no true experiment even if randomization has been correctly carried out. It is our distinct impression that experiments in organizational behavior run a greater risk than experiments in other disciplines of pretest non-equivalence because experiments are more likely to involve units larger than the individual.

The problem can be reduced by matching the units before randomization. Indeed, given the high variability associated with field research, such pre-randomization matching is advisable in most instances. It will have the incidental advantage of per-mitting strong tests of the interaction of the treatments and matching variables, thereby giving information about external validity. Alternatively, the number of units could be increased, or, as with the experiment by Worchel and Mitchell (1972) to test the effectiveness of the culture assimilator, a small sample experiment can be replicated in a different setting.

It is perhaps worth noting in this regard that a persistent error of data analysis runs through many of the field experiments we have read. The error results from assigning units larger than individuals to conditions and then analyzing the data with the degrees of freedom based on the number of respondents rather than on the number of assigned units. This error is sometimes made deliberately on the grounds that the low number of degrees of freedom precludes a sensitive statistical analysis. (Just think for the moment of the t value required for statistical significance at the .05 level with 5, 10, 25, and 50 degrees of freedom.) When there are few units it will occasionally be possible to reconceptualize the design and either transform it into a time-series (by adding additional pretest and posttest observations) or into an experiment where the treatment is faded in and out at different times. Alternatively, repeated measures will sometimes be possible between the pretest and the final posttest. This then bases a test of the treatment's main effect on scores that are especially reliable: first, because the scores are formed by summing across individuals within units, and second, because each unit's score is the sum of all the repeated posttest observations. But the advantage of repeated measurement between the pretest and final posttest is most clear where it is expected that the treatment's effects will increase with time, as is normally the case. Then, it makes sense to examine the interaction of the treatment and the time of testing to see if the difference between experimental and control means is progressively increasing (at least until asymptote is reached). Fortunately, the degrees of freedom for testing this interaction will be higher than for testing the main effect of the treatment. Thus, in a design with nine units, five of which are randomly assigned to one condition and four to the other, and with seven times of testing, there would be seven degrees of freedom for the between-units error term that tests the main effect of the treatment, six for the main effect of time of testing, six for the interaction of treatments and time of testing, and forty-two for the error term to test this last crucial interaction. Unfortunately, the test will be positively biased because of the correlated error problem associated with repeated measurement on the same units. However, Greenhouse and Geisser (1959) have demonstrated that the true effect of treatments and times of testing will lie between that resulting from a statistical test with six and forty-two degrees of freedom and a test with one and seven degrees of freedom. Thus, it will be possible to bracket the true effect in separate conservative and positively biased tests, even though the true effect cannot be exactly determined. (This strategy of bracketing is very important and useful, especially when analyzing quasi-experimental designs for which no single adequate statistical test exists, but for which different tests with different directions of bias can be specified. Then, multiple tests can be conducted and the true effect bracketed, even though the true effect can never be estimated in anything approaching point fashion.)

d. Treatment-Related Refusals to Participate in the Planned Experiment

Sometimes, experimental units will be randomly assigned to treatments, and some individuals will refuse to receive the treatment that was scheduled for them. For instance, Ball and Bogatz (1970) randomly assigned preschool classes to either be encouraged or to not be encouraged to view Sesame Street. However, some teachers assigned to the non-encouraged group insisted on receiving television sets and having their children view the show while others in the encouraged group insisted on their children not being encouraged to view. Hence, some teachers self-selected themselves into treatments and vitiated that part of the design which dealt with at-school children. Alternatively, there may be personal or political pressures on investigators to ensure that certain individuals or groups receive the treatment or are excluded from it, and it may not always be possible to withstand such pressure.

One strategy for avoiding this general class of problem is to refine the population by randomly assigning units from those with an equal chance of being in the various treatment groups and by ignoring those cases that had to be included in, or excluded from, particular treatments for political reasons. By so doing the experimenter would create two populations: those receiving a particular treatment for political reasons who are not part of the experiment and those who are not affected by political considerations and who might or might not receive a particular treatment depending on the outcome of the randomization procedure. In effect, the experimenter would be ensuring higher internal validity at the cost of lower external validity.

It is sometimes desirable to refine the population even further as when respondents know there is more than one treatment. The population in this case should be restricted to persons who agree *before random assignment* to be in any treatment to which they might be assigned. This would increase the chances that the various treatment groups would be equivalent after the treatment, though it would also restrict external validity and would make a reactive experiment even more reactive. Hence, the strategy is perhaps most useful of all in any programmatic research where a quasi-experiment can also be conducted that is perhaps less strong with respect to internal validity but more strong in external validity. Then, the correspondences between the studies form the basis for decision making.

e. Treatment-Related Attrition from the Experiment

Experimental treatments differ in their attractiveness to respondents so that the number and nature of persons remaining in an experiment may differ between conditions if the experiment lasts any period of time. To give an obvious example, respondents in the New Jersey Negative Income Tax Experiment were given guaranteed incomes of different amounts, and it was not surprising that persons who received the higher guarantees were less likely to drop out of the experiment (Kershaw, 1972). In addition, Rosen and Turner (1971) compared two training programs for the hard-core unemployed and found that one of them led to less turnover than the other. This result is entirely attributable to the treatment and is an important finding in its own right. But it also means that the two groups would not be comparable for any other kinds of comparisons. This illustrates the major restriction to inference when treatment-related attrition takes place in a true experiment: while the attrition is interpretable as a treatment effect, no other data from non-comparable groups are.

One obvious, but difficult and rare, way of controlling for this threat is to consult archives that are kept on both those who stayed in an experiment and those who dropped out. For example, national Internal Revenue Service records could be consulted in the case of the New Jersey Income experiment to see if reported income varied with treatments. This is possible because—with adequate safeguards against an invasion of privacy—there are some national archives that contain data on most adults in the United States. While such use of archives would help, it would not be perfect. This is because not all earnings involve FICA deductions or withholding taxes, and not all persons file returns. However, such underrepresentation is a datum in its own right, and the bias it involves is presumably less systematic than that due to dropping out of an experiment for treatment-related purposes.

Another partial solution to the attrition problem is to be determined in following up those who had dropped out so that their data can be included with those of persons who completed the experiment. This should decrease statistical conclusion validity, because the treatment condition would be "watered-down" by the inclusion of some persons who never received the treatment. But including such persons would increase internal validity, and large effects would be detected in an analysis of the original assigned treatment groups.

A third solution is to disaggregate the data as much as possible in order to isolate those particular sites, or kinds of respondents, or occasions of treatment implementation, where the proportion of respondents in each treatment condition is the same at the end of the experiment as at the beginning and where the various treatment groups have comparable pretest means and standard deviations when only those respondents are considered who remained in the experiment until its end. (The need for pretests is particularly acute in true experiments in field settings since error variance tends to be high and can be reduced by using pretest scores as covariates and since the pretest data provide one indirect way of testing for group comparability.) Care has to be taken when disaggregating. First, there is the danger of picking out those instances of group pretest comparability that are due to chance and of thereby obtaining posttest differences that are caused by statistical regression rather than treatment differences; and then there is the threat to statistical conclusion validity that arises because disaggregating entails smaller sample sizes. The latter is a potential problem, not only because true posttest differences can be obscured, but also because true pretest differences can be obscured and it can be erroneously concluded that the various treatment groups probably did not differ at the pretest. As a consequence, disaggregating the data is an important tool in the repertoire of any data analyst who fears that a true experiment may have broken down and who wants to preserve the true experiment for at least some of the original research sample. But it is a tool to be used with care, and stress should be placed on finding more than one setting, or kind of person, or time of treatment implementation that appears to meet the conditions of being a successful true experiment.

A final, and easier, solution is to explicate the differences in attractiveness between conditions and to try to increase the attractiveness of the less desirable. For example, Hudson (1969) wanted to test the effectiveness of an autotelic teaching machine on economically disadvantaged children, but he was faced with the problem that the children and their parents had to travel many miles to use the machine. It seemed, therefore, that more of the experimental children would drop out of the experiment than the controls who were tested closer to home. So, Hudson arranged for the experimental children to be transported by bus to the teaching machine—a simple, but effective, move that reduced treatment-correlated attrition, though it may also have affected construct validity.

There will be many contexts, particularly those involving social ameliorative experiments, where it will not be easy to make the treatments equal in attractiveness or cost since the essence of such experiments is to assess the differential effect of resources that vary in value. Thus, while it will be possible to explicate and control for many extraneous sources of attractiveness, it will not be possible, and it is not desirable, that all differences in attractiveness be controlled. Because it is reasonable to expect that persons who are not coerced will drop out of experiments in greater numbers if their treatment is less desirable, then it is also reasonable to expect that treatment-related attrition will be a frequent problem. Indeed, once agreements have been made that randomization should take place, we might anticipate that this will be the most serious threat to the internal validity of implemented true experiments. It is, therefore, imperative that fall-back quasi-experimental designs be built into social-ameliorative experiments and, that, where possible, subsidiary true experiments be conducted that are restricted to the population of persons who agree before randomization to be in any treatment condition to which they might be assigned.

f. Heterogeneity in the Extent of Treatment Implementation

Mullen, Chazin, and Feldstein (1972) tested whether a demonstration program of counseling for the newly dependent who had just gone on welfare was more effective than the traditional program that was available to them. The authors found that, over fourteen months, the number of face-to-face interviews with the counselor in the demonstration group varied from one to 129 with a median of fifteen and that the number of telephone and letter contacts varied from none to eighty-one with a median of 9.5. It is obvious in such a case that there was considerable variability in the extent to which the treatment was received, and it would be unrealistic to expect counseling effects from individuals who had hardly received any counseling. Similarly, in situations where managers, foremen, or teachers are expected to implement treatments we might expect them to differ in the extent to which they comply; such differences might result from dependence on old habits or the extent of approval for the new treatment or its sponsors, or the effort that the treatment requires, etc. (Analyses of effects by number of sessions attended immediately becomes quasi-experimental, and with very plausible selection or selection-maturation hypotheses to explain posttest differences, without invoking treatment effects.)

The problem of treatment heterogeneity is of less importance when treatments are standardized and delivered by machines or by research personnel (as opposed to organization personnel). Otherwise, the problem can presumably be reduced by soliciting respondents for services (in the case of the new welfare program) or by the extensive training of experimenters, whether they be from the "research team" or the indigenous organization being studied. But training, even with behavioral simulation of treatment implementation, is not enough, and efforts have to be made to conduct periodic checks on those responsible for the treatment to make sure the treatment is getting across. In addition, the investigator or his staff should be available to answer questions from experimenters so that motivation can be kept high. In some cases, a newsletter for experimenters will be useful in which information about treatment implementation can be presented and experimenters can exchange experiences about difficulties they have met in implementing the treatment and procedures they have adopted for attacking these problems.

g. The Treatment in the No-Treatment Control Group

We have previously commented on the fact that a no-treatment control group should, under some circumstances, be conceptualized as a "resentment" treatment group—that is, respondents resent not having a treatment. The point here is that it is naive to consider groups without an experimenter-planned treatment or theory-relevant natural treatment as being groups that experience nothing between a pretest and posttest. Numerous things can happen to the controls over and above spontaneous maturation. For instance, Rosen and Turner (1971) had planned to use a company-controlled orientation program for the hard-core jobless as a control for a university-developed quasi-therapeutic package designed to help the hard-core adjust to work by finding group-based solutions to common problems. But the authors discovered that the company-sponsored program was not a

passive, information-centered approach as was thought. Instead, it had become a program with individual counseling and concrete behavioral support for the employee in his on-the-job difficulties with others. Thus, the control group became a treatment group, and this may have been a response by the company to the knowledge that the other treatment existed (compensatory rivalry). In a similar vein, Ball and Bogatz (1970) randomly assigned children to being encouraged or non-encouraged to view Sesame Street in the hope that encouraged children would view more than non-encouraged children. But the success of Sesame Street was so great that the non-encouraged children viewed the show quite heavily, thereby becoming more than the planned no-treatment control group (diffusion of treatment). Also, Feshbach and Singer (1971) attempted to assess the effects of a high-violence television diet on the aggressiveness of children by randomly assigning institutionalized children to receiving either a high- or a reduced-violence diet. They found that the high-violence groups were reported as less aggressive. But this difference may have been due to the low violence controls being frustrated because they were taken off their regular diet of televised violence. Thus, they were probably not an appropriate no-violence control group and they may have received a violence-causing frustration treatment.

When there are grounds for suspecting that the control group fails to serve its no-cause base line function, it is nonetheless important at first to analyze the data as though it came from a true experiment. For example, Ball and Bogatz (1970) believed that they were forced to use quasi-experimental methods in evaluating Sesame Street because some of the control group children viewed the show. Cook et al. (1975) took the same data, preserved the original distinction between the randomly formed encouraged and non-encouraged groups and demonstrated that, though some of the non-encouraged did view Sesame Street, the average amount of viewing was less than in the encouraged group. This meant that the true experimental distinction could be maintained, though the difference in viewing was less than planned, and it fortunately transpired that the encouraged knew more than the non-encouraged at the posttest. Rosen and Turner (1971) also treated their data as coming from a true experiment and were able to show that the intended controls out-performed the experimental group by the posttest! The problems the authors then faced were deciding how they should label the treatment in the control group and determining whether any effects had occurred in the experimental group.

h. Treatment Contamination

We have previously commented upon the possibility of control subjects comparing themselves to experimental subjects and thereby reacting differently because they know they are being treated differently from others. This problem also exists when persons receiving different treatments observe these differences and can communicate freely with each other. This is most likely to happen in industrial contexts where the nature of the work requires communication between different sections producing parts of a total product or where the industry's personnel come from a single town where people mix freely. For instance, in the experiment by Bishop and Hill (1971) on the effects of job change and job enlargement, the manipulations were administered to persons within work groups and all the work groups came from the same employment center for the handicapped. It is conceivable, therefore, that the respondents discussed why some persons' jobs were not changed, others were changed but not enlarged, while others were both changed and enlarged. The effects of such treatment contamination are difficult to assess, but it is at least possible that respondents in the job enlargement condition were led by the comparison with the job change condition to define their new work

as a job change rather than as a job enlargement. This would then explain the data pattern that Bishop and Hill interpreted as indicating that job change and job enlargement do not have noteworthy differences for employees' performance.

We shall deal in detail with strategies for avoiding the contamination problem in parts of the section that follows, particularly in dealing with equivalent time samples designs and spatially separated units. The section is devoted to an explication of the situations most conducive to true experiments in field settings.

i. Unobtrusive Treatment Implementation

Most of the previously cited experiments were obtrusive because respondents knew that a treatment was being implemented even if they did not always know which outcome measures were being collected. It is technically desirable that treatments be unobtrusive, for this rules out many reactivity-based threats to both internal and construct validity. However, from ethical, and perhaps legal, perspectives, much technically feasible unobtrusive experimentation is not desirable since it violates the ethical requirement of "informed consent" and since it may sometimes violate United States laws, though the issues are not yet clear on this last point (Silverman, in press). There are, though, some innocuous but valuable field experiments where little time or effort is demanded of potential respondents and where respondents run no danger that could reasonably be foreseen. Campbell (1969) has commented favorably on such experiments. But other experiments clearly involve potential cost and risk to respondents, and there is a grey area where many reasonable persons would disagree as to whether the potential benefits outweigh the anticipated costs. In general, the innocuous experiments are those that last only a few minutes for any one respondent and where the treatment falls within the range of the respondent's "normal" experience. Hence, a major problem with unobtrusive field experiments is that they are likely to be restricted in scope —that is, they are likely to be based on fleeting encounters between persons in organizations or on the street or to be based on mail or telephone experiments. They are not likely to deal with significant changes in respondents' lives or with unusual experiences, the reactions to which might be damaging. Though there are some published field experiments that do involve unusual acts (e.g., falling down in a subway car with blood coming from one's mouth), many people may find it hard to justify them and easier to justify more innocuous treatments.

Silverman (in press) has commented on the legal problems that unobtrusive field experiments might run into. He presented two lawyers with the details of ten published experiments and asked them if they found any possible legal violations. A defense lawyer found few problems, but the other, an expert in prosecuting medical liability cases, consistently found possible legal infringements, particularly with respect to trespass, harassment, disorderly conduct, and criminal negligence. Though the determination of courts on such issues is not yet known, the general question is a grave one worth more study. But these are not the only legal issues. Consider one experiment from an excellent series by Feldman (1968). He had compatriots or foreigners in Boston, Athens, and Paris give too much money to taxi-drivers, and he was interested in determining how the city and the passenger's nationality affected the taxi-drivers' honesty. Most of the drivers took more money than they were entitled to, and if individual drivers had been identified they could have had problems with employers or with the law. If so, they might have been able to argue that they had been "trapped" by the experimenter and they could have used the "entrapment" issue to fight an indictment. Of course, Feldman did not report the identity of individual drivers, and it would have been desirable if he had not collected such data. However, if cab numbers had been recorded he could have been subpoenaed for them, and since social scientists do not yet enjoy the "testimonial privilege" of doctors and lawyers, he would have had to produce his records or go to jail. There are, therefore, three legal issues: experimenters' violations of the law during an experiment, their protecting records from subpoena after an experiment, and their discovery of illegal acts by respondents during an experiment.

(Perhaps the most famous example of the last two problems comes from an obtrusive study, the New Jersey Negative Income Tax Experiment, where a Mercer County Grand Jury, suspecting that some respondents were fraudulently receiving both experimental payments and welfare, subpoenaed the experimenters' records in order to identify respondents. This placed the experimenters in a difficult dilemma: in order to protect possible lawbreakers who had been promised that their responses would be kept confidential, the experimenters would have had to break the law. However, the dilemma never reached the point of concrete decision making, for a legal settlement was made by the experimenters out of court. Though we have only just begun to scratch the surface of the relationship between the social sciences and the law, it is clear that unobtrusive treatments and measures lead to special legal problems, the ramifications of which we are not yet well aware of. But notwithstanding this, any experimenter would do well not to keep records that identify individuals or institutions in easily understandable form or for any longer time period than he has to.)

Restricting the range of unobtrusive field experiments to the innocuous and the unquestionably ethical and legal often leads to a problem of reduced treatment salience. This would occur, for example, if we varied the nature of signs in a factory, or sent out letters with different kinds of appeals for some pro-social end like blood donating, or varied the physical layout of offices, or arranged for different kinds of seat-belt appeals to be televised to different communities. In most experiments of this type one runs the risk that some respondents will not even see the treatment and that others will pay scant attention to it even if they do see it. After all, one characteristic of the "mundane" treatments that are unquestionably permissible is that they are mundane—they do not stand out. Consequently, there will be a problem of statistical conclusion validity.

One example of the problem that we think typifies it comes from Bryan and Test's (1967) experiment on modeling and helping that was conducted on a Los Angeles freeway. The dependent variable was whether motorists stopped to help a female whose tire was flat, and the independent variable was whether the motorist could or could not have seen someone helping a second stranded motorist about one-quarter of a mile before they came upon the stranded test car. We wonder how many persons in the modeling condition were concentrating on the road ahead of them and failed to notice the first stranded car, especially motorists in the outside lanes or at busier times of the day. Or, if they noticed it, how many paid enough attention that the first car was still salient one-quarter of a mile later? In mail experiments, how many target persons do not even receive the letter if other members of the family get the mail first, open it, and consign it to the "junk and wastebasket" category. Or, if the target person receives it, how likely is it that he will read it closely rather than briefly getting the gist of it? One answer to the problem of low treatment salience is to conduct large sample research, and the feasibility of this depends on the financial cost of additional observations. (Bryan & Test, 1967, actually followed this strategy and found that of about 2,000 motorists in the model condition 58 stopped, whereas 35 of 2,000 stopped in the non-modeling condition— $.01 < p < .05$.) Another answer is to enhance the salience of the treatment. For instance, Bryan and Test might alternatively

have conducted their experiment on a one- or two-lane road and could have positioned their first stranded car at a bend where it is harder not to see it. And in the mail experiments one does better to have individually addressed and personally signed letters sent by first class mail that tie into the interests of the addressee. (In some cases even special delivery letters or telegrams might be called for.) The problem of low treatment salience is widespread in ethical unobtrusive experiments, but it can frequently be reduced as a problem even though it cannot always be eliminated.

Situations Conducive to Field Experiments

a. When Lotteries Are Expected

True experiments are lotteries in which each unit has an equal chance of being in a particular treatment condition. Occasionally, but all too rarely, lotteries are used as a socially accepted means of distributing scarce resources. When they occur, a true experiment is created and it is up to the investigator's ingenuity to decide how he will exploit the opportunity. For example, Siegel and Siegel (1957) noted that a lottery was used to assign female students at Stanford to a dormitory for their last three college years. They also noted that some dormitories were associated with higher levels of authoritarianism and that these were in greater demand than the others. Siegel and Siegel used the Stanford housing lottery to examine how joining a living group led to the adoption of the "personality style" of that group. To do this, they obtained measures of authoritarianism both before the women entered their dormitories and after they had been there for a year. As expected, the level of reported authoritarianism varied with the level of authoritarianism in the dormitory to which random assignment had been made.

Staw (1974) used the 1970 draft lottery to examine the effects of a randomly allocated reward (freedom from the draft) on organizational performance and on attitudes towards the organization. He did this by selecting ROTC programs where some students had already committed themselves to military service before learning their draft number while other students had not. Staw reasoned that persons without any legal commitment would leave ROTC in greater numbers (and would be less inclined to join in the first place) if their draft number exempted them from military service. These effects were indeed obtained among students without a legal commitment. But Staw also reasoned that, if the theory of cognitive dissonance were correct, students who were legally bound to military service would have a stronger need to justify their being in ROTC if their lottery number exempted them from service than if it did not. He also reasoned that being in ROTC could be justified if students generated liking for the program and performed well in it. Hence, he related draft numbers to ROTC grades and to satisfaction with ROTC and, among the legally bound students, he found positive relationships which indicated that persons whose numbers exempted them from military service liked ROTC more and performed better. Moreover, attrition from ROTC among the committed was not related to draft number, thereby increasing our confidence in the comparability of students with different draft numbers.

Sechrest (1970) has been attempting to use public lotteries as experiments on the long-term effects of income supplements, using small prize winners as randomly equivalent controls for large prize winners whose incomes are greatly supplemented either as a single large sum or as a series of regular payments. Hafeez Zaidi and Lee Sechrest (personal communication) are attempting to use Pakistan's land lotteries in a similar way.

Here, then, are examples of the creative use of natural randomization to test hypotheses of distinct relevance to industrial and organizational psychology. But, since

lotteries do not occur frequently in the United States, they cannot be relied upon as a frequent laboratory. This does not mean, however, that we should ignore them when they do occur.

b. When Demand Outstrips Supply

One signpost that indicates the potential for randomization is when there is greater demand than supply for some resource. When this happens, there will be arguments to the effect that certain groups of persons need the resource more than others and should have priority, or that a different group cannot under any circumstances benefit from the resource. These arguments may sometimes be specious. Even when they are not, it may be possible to create two populations: persons getting the resource or excluded from it on a systematic basis, and those who might or might not get it on a random basis. What is so advantageous about scarce resources for experimental purposes (if for no other reason) is that they can be used to create a credible justification for randomization, both to those wanting and those dispensing the resource. (When there is no scarcity, persons dispensing resources will typically be reluctant to create a no-treatment control group because they know that there are in fact resources and they will want to see them used.)

In organizational settings, true experiments could be conducted on who gets to go to training programs outside the firm, or which classes get additional teachers' aides, or which economically disadvantaged parents get job training or job vacancies, or which applicants for early retirement can be allowed to retire, or which factory work areas should have videophones, or the like. We know, for instance, of two school districts with special laboratory schools that have local reputations for academic excellence and where the demand for places by parents exceeds the supply. In fact, lotteries are held to determine who is offered a place at the schools, and the only restriction is that a specified racial quota be maintained. As Diamond (1974) has suggested to us, would these not be useful settings for studying how racial integration affects children in "optimal" school environments, even though generalization could only be made to children whose parents volunteered for them? Such a study would be largely (or totally) archival and would require comparing the performance and attitudes of children who did or did not get assigned to the laboratory school of their choice.

c. When an Innovation Cannot Be Delivered to All Units at Once

When a firm has decided upon an innovation (e.g., computerizing its accounting procedures, introducing a new form of inventory control, giving all of its executives or foremen a specialized training program), it often happens that it is physically impossible to introduce the innovation simultaneously in all parts at once. This creates the possibilities of deliberately planning an *experimentally staged introduction,* using matching followed by randomization, so that the units modernized first and those modernized last are as equivalent as possible. These first and last units can then provide an experimental and control comparison until all are finally modernized.

This type of opportunity regularly goes unused, the spacing out of introduction being done on the basis of convenience and favoritism. It seems to go against managerial thinking and the psychology of dissonance reduction to take an experimental orientation in this situation. This is probably because, once a particular decision has been made, the need to make decisions seems to be sated and it is perhaps assumed that the change will be beneficial after so much effort has gone into making it. There may also be the fear that the experiment might show too late that the innovation was not beneficial or was less beneficial than the decision makers believed it would be.

Yet from a hard-headed reality-oriented point of view, the information from an experiment might be very valuable. It could reflect on the validity of the decision-making process just used and which the firm will be using again and again. In addition, the specific issues involved in the innovation will arise again since in many cases, as in decisions to decentralize management, a new broom a decade later will reverse the direction of change. Finally, and from a larger perspective, society and our collective applied social science (and the firm's competitors) need the information from an experiment even if the innovating firm feels no immediate need for it.

d. When Experimental Units Can Be Temporally Isolated: The Equivalent Time Samples Design

The art of designing nonreactive true experiments is to capitalize upon the natural variation in a potential cause or causes so as to schedule when a group of respondents receives a treatment, or to schedule which treatment they receive, or to schedule what modifications they receive. We shall now discuss several contexts in which natural variation in time can be capitalized upon.

One of the easiest situations for conducting true experiments is when there are multiple rotations. That is, when one group of persons undergoes an experience and goes away; another group comes and goes; a third group comes and goes, etc. Each of these groups is isolated from the others in time and perhaps in space (if they come from different areas), and each group can be given a different treatment. For example, Mase (1971) was fortunate enough to be able to randomly assign one of two kinds of sensitivity training to twenty-four groups of persons who came for separate two-week stays at a center for pastoral counseling. Thus, twelve groups received each treatment in a design where each treatment was twice represented in each block of four groups and there were six such blocks.

Kerr (1945) used time in a different way

to make one set of time periods during which a single group of respondents received one treatment and an equivalent set of times during which they received a second. The treatments involved the presence or absence of music in a factory which was related to productivity. Campbell and Stanley (1966) called the Kerr experiment an "Equivalent Time Samples Design" in order to highlight that the time periods when the treatment was present were made equivalent via randomization to the time periods when it was absent. The design is altogether useful when the effect is not expected to be of long duration or is presumed to be modifiable by continued exposure to the treatment. When these last conditions do not hold, Kerr's design would be uninterpretable because there would be no decrease in the level of the effect at times when the treatment was absent and there would be no increase in the effect after the treatment was received for the first time.

The equivalent time samples design is useful because it can be employed when the investigator has access to only a single institution. Consider the problem that Doob, Carlsmith, Freedman, Landauer, and Tom (1969) tackled. They hypothesized that discounting an article would increase initial sales but would decrease long-term sales of various products. Their hypothesis was based on customers thinking they bought the discounted product because of the favorable price and not because they liked the product. So, very creatively, the authors went to twelve discount houses, matched them for sales volume, and then randomly assigned them to discount or not discount various items. As hypothesized, discounting led to lower long-term sales. Imagine, for the moment, that Doob et al. had only had access to one store. They might then have arranged that, for a given period, one random set of items would be discounted and another random set not discounted. After sufficient time had elapsed so that both the initial increase and the long-term drop were evident, they could then have replicated the study by having the previously non-discounted items discounted and the previously discounted items sold at the regular price.

In much the same way, persons with a social reform intention could establish whether or not agencies were doing their duty. For instance, some organizations send white and nonwhite couples to real estate agents to see if they are given the same lists of houses for sale or rent. If there is a target real estate operator in mind, it would be possible to send in white and nonwhite couples on the same or adjacent days. This procedure could then be repeated at a later date with different samples of couples until a series of equivalent time samples is obtained. Or, if someone wanted to test whether police discriminated against certain classes of persons, he might drive his car on some days with, say, a Black Panther bumper sticker and on other equivalent days with a Support Your Local Police sticker (Heussenstamm, 1971). The dependent variable in this experiment would be the number of stoppings by police, and it would be imperative that the sticker be affixed without the driver knowing which sticker is on the car (Gordon & Myers, 1970). (If he knew, this might bias how he drives so that the number of stoppings might be a response to his driving rather than to the nature of the bumper sticker.)

Perfect internal validity results when treatments are randomly assigned to time samples, providing, of course, that there is an adequate number of time samples. Moreover, if random assignment takes place in an ordered sequence so that the different treatments or the presence and absence of the treatment are randomized within blocks of, say, four time samples, the data can be analyzed as coming from as many different replications of the experiment as there are blocks. Such an analysis would increase external validity. However, external validity is low in those instances where the design is used because of its feasibility with a single sample of persons in a single setting. (Of course, the design is not restricted to such contexts; it is merely most useful in them.) Finally, the design is vulnerable to threats of construct validity if respondents were to notice that the presence and absence of a particular treatment were related to time. For this reason, it is probably best to use the design when treatments are non-obtrusive or when the scheduling of treatments is random within larger time blocks so that no simple pattern of presence/absence can be ascertained by respondents.

e. When Experimental Units Are Spatially Separated or Inter-Unit Communication Is Low

The actual experiment by Doob et al. (1969) on the effects of discounting on subsequent sales was made possible because discount houses are geographically separated from each other and the personnel may have minimal contact with each other. This makes it relatively easy to match discount houses and then randomly assign them to the various conditions. Lawler and Hackman (1969) were helped in their study of participative decision making among groups of janitors because the different groups never met. Rather, each group received a new job assignment when it was already on a job and then the members reported to the new job without having to check back to some common headquarters where the different groups might have met and discussed the different treatments. Robertson, Kelley, O'Neill, Wixom, Eiswirth, and Haddon (1972) were able to conduct a true experiment on the effects of a televised seat-belt campaign because homes in mountainous Pennsylvania towns receive television by cable, and because advertising researchers had used two cables (A and B) to divide the towns into two essentially random samples. This made it possible to assign the televised seat-belt wearing commercials to half of the people. Observers were then posted at stop signs, and they noted seat-belt wearing and license plate numbers. Through state records, the licenses were identified with house numbers, and thus to Cable A or Cable B. (It is not reported whether neighbors were ever aware that they were getting different commercials.) In their true experiment on Sesame Street, Bogatz and Ball (1971) provided either television cables or a UHF adapter to a randomly selected group of neighborhood blocks in areas where Sesame Street could not otherwise be picked up. Their reason for using blocks was that treatment contamination would be less likely than if assignment were by, say, homes within individual streets.

It is worthwhile pointing out a second strength of some of the above experiments besides the spatial isolation of experimental units. We expect there to be variability in which items in a store are discounted, or in which public service ads are on TV, and part of the experimenter's skill lies in tempering the naturalness of these features to deliver interpretable treatments in unobtrusive fashion. Contrast this with introducing participative decision making or providing homes with special TV cables or UHF adapters. The last treatments are more likely to be obtrusive because we do not normally expect changes in our lives relating to participative decision making or obtaining a TV cable. Such one-time changes need to be explained to respondents and in many cases the explanation will have to be research-related. A change in TV ads or in the items discounted is less obtrusive because we expect these things to vary.

There are, of course, instances where the treatment is deliberately designed to stand out from what respondents expect, and in these instances construct validity is not threatened as it is where unexpectedness is not part of the intended treatment. For example, Ivancevich and Donnelly (1971) conducted a true experiment to determine if telephoning persons who had just accepted jobs would decrease the rate of acceptees who later failed to appear for their new job. Hence, the researchers had cooperating firms call a random half of the new hirings to answer any questions the latter might have had about the job and firm. The no-treatment control group was not telephoned, and more of the controls failed to show up for the job than the experimentals. What is worth noting here is, first, that the job acceptees were socially isolated from each other, and second, that the experimental manipulation was deliberately designed to make respondents feel that they were being treated in an out-of-the-ordinary way.

Spatially isolated treatment units are potentially available when organizations have multiple branches. This occurs with supermarkets, industries whose specialized units produce a common product, units in the armed forces, university alumni, schools within school districts, wards within hospitals, residential units of religious orders, branches of health clubs in large cities, dealerships that sell automobiles, appliances, etc. What counts is that there be spatially isolated units and little communication between units. Of course, spatial isolation does not guarantee low levels of communication and care should be taken to ensure this, for the special advantage of isolated units is that they reduce treatment contamination.

f. When Change Is Mandated and Solutions Are Acknowledged to Be Unknown

A mandate for change can be issued when a situation is generally acknowledged to be less desirable than it should be. Often, it is not clear which changes should be made despite passionate advocacy of certain alternatives by interested parties. From the perspective of someone in charge of an organization it might not be at all clear how things should be changed and so he might want to try out several alternatives so as not "to have all his eggs in one basket." Formal experimentation is especially likely when change is required and several alternative kinds of change are possible.

The 1960s witnessed a powerful mandate for change in some aspects of the educational system in the United States, though much of the change took the form of haphazard non-experimental program changes or unevaluatable quasi-experiments. However, some of the changes took the form of systematically planned variations. For example, Head Start was a response to the problem that, even before they enter school, middle-class children out-perform lower-class children on standardized achievement tests. Hence, some of the Head Start programs were primarily aimed at teaching lower-class children basic cognitive skills, and some of these programs were evaluated by means of true experiments (Bereiter & Engelmann, 1966; Weikart, 1972). At the level of school children, Performance Contracting experiments were conducted to see if outside contractors could enter schools with prepackaged learning programs that would lead to a year's cognitive growth in a year's schooling. Unfortunately, though the intention was to set up the performance contracting experiments as true experiments, they were in fact implemented as quasi-experiments and the report on these quasi-experiments (Ray, 1972) does not allow one to infer without reasonable doubt which programs met their learning goals and which programs were more successful than others. Nonetheless, the strategy of planned variations was evolved and proposed as a response to a problem whose solution was not clear. This was also the case with the New Jersey Income Maintenance Experiment.

g. When a Tie Can Be Broken

We previously advocated the regression-discontinuity design when "awards" are distributed to the meritorious or the needy. Some scale of merit or need is obviously required to implement the design. It is realistic, we think, to assume that the scale will be unreliable and to postulate that there will be some persons above the cutting point whose true score lies below it, that there will be some persons below the point whose true score lies above it, and that, in addition, there will be cases of tied scores at the cutting point where the true scores are different—some above and some below the point. In other words, there is a kind of region of uncertainty in which one does not know if certain individuals or groups fall above or below the cutting point. This is a prime situation for implementing a randomized design.

The University of Illinois decided in 1967 to admit students on a random basis which would have permitted an assessment of the effects of attending that University if it had been possible to follow the controls to whichever university the students attended or whichever job they took. A public outcry ensued when the random allocation procedure became known to the public due to feelings that some meritorious students would be denied entry and that an inequitable criterion based on chance had been substituted for an equitable criterion based on merit. How different would the public reaction have been, we wonder, if University of Illinois authorities had (1) ranked students according to their criteria of merit, (2) admitted as many of the highest scorers as were required to fill, say, 75 percent of the places at the University, (3) honestly pointed out the fallibility of the merit measures, (4) designated an equal number of merit scores on each side of the obtained cutting point as ambiguous, and (5) randomly chosen the remaining 25 percent of the students to attend the University from the sample around the obtained (and hence unreliable) cutting point. We suspect that, with careful public statements about this procedure, University of Illinois officials would have been able to randomize, to test how their University affected students, and also to educate the public about unreliability and the justice of randomly assigning individuals to social opportunities where no clear merit or need criteria exist.

h. When Some Persons Express No Preference Among Alternatives

Many organizations that would like to monitor how various parts of their system "work" have an opportunity to do this even if considerations of ethics or public relations require that assignment to the various parts of the system be by choice rather than by lottery. This is because some persons will not want to express a preference as to whether they should work in building A or B, or whether they will receive curriculum X or Y. The assignment of these persons can then be done by chance. For example, Valins and Baum (1973) wanted to study some effects of "crowding." Freshmen enter one of two kinds of living quarters at Stony Brook. These quarters do not differ in terms of the immediate living space per person, but do differ in terms of the number of persons whom one is likely to meet in everyday interactions because of the building layout (more than 30 *versus* 6). The authors restricted their study to a population of 30 percent of the freshmen who had indicated to University authorities before coming that they had no preference for the kind of housing they lived in, and whom the authorities had assigned to living units on a haphazard (but not formally random) basis. It would presumably have been easy to have had the assignment done absolutely randomly, which would then permit strong inferences about the different ways the living units affected students. Whenever surveys are conducted in organizations to elicit preferences, it is advisable to include a "No Preference" option so that later experimental evaluations can be made of the effects of the various resources about which no preference was stated. But any conclusions about cause from such an experiment could not be generalized beyond the kinds of persons who have no preference on the issue. Thus, if it were especially important to know how the "keen" and "decisive" use resources, the technique cannot be used on its own, for these kinds of persons are not likely to express no initial preference. If the "keen" and "decisive" are of special interest, an inferentially powerful true experiment of limited generalizability should be conducted together with the best possible quasi-experiment that utilizes a wider range of respondents. Then, the results of the studies can be impressionistically compared, for the weakness of the one is the strength of the other. Where the results coincide, a global overall inference will be easy. Where they do not, a final uncertainty will be engendered about the quasi-experiment, but not about the limited causal relationship corroborated in the true experiment.

i. When You Can Create Your Own Organization

Many experiments on equity theory have involved investigators creating their own organization (e.g., Adams, 1965; Pritchard, Dunnette, & Jorgenson, 1972). Respondents in Adams's experiments came to work in response to newspaper advertisements and had no idea they were involved in research. Having his own organization enabled Adams to control many of the respondents' experiences—the particular treatment received, the isolated room in which the respondent could work without error-inflating distractions, and the measures of the quantity and quality of work that were unobtrusively collected. Adams had this much control because the organization was tailored to meet his research needs. It was not the normal case where research has to be tailored to realistic organizational constraints about what can be manipulated and measured, and how the research is introduced to respondents.

Despite these last-mentioned constraints, there are some other contexts where organizations can be created to facilitate true experimentation. For example, it is difficult to evaluate the relative effectiveness of different drug-abuse programs. There are many reasons for the difficulty—for instance, different programs often have different goals, different attrition rates, little chance to create appropriate control groups, a hostility to being evaluated and especially to being evaluated in terms of the researcher's criteria of success rather than their own (see Cook, 1974b). Moreover, different kinds of persons are attracted to different programs for reasons of program philosophy, friendship, and convenience. Some of these problems, especially the last one, could be reduced by setting up city-wide clearinghouses so that all new referrals had to be via the city or state-controlled clearinghouse. (And if there were special reasons for assigning certain persons to specific programs, this could and should be done. But the remaining persons would be assigned to programs on a random basis and would form the population of experimental respondents who, with sufficient tact, perseverance, and luck, could be used to assess the relative efficacy of different programs.) The establishment of such a clearinghouse would be similar to the establishment of a new organization. It could be used in some contexts for assigning elderly persons to nursing homes, children to day-care centers, or soldiers to units. It must be repeated that this assignment need not be coerced. Selection could come from a pool of persons who do not mind where they are assigned. Restricting the population to volunteers (but volunteers to be in *any* program) would decrease external validity. But it would not restrict personal freedom and it would enhance internal validity over quasi-experimental alternatives for honestly assessing the relative efficacy of various solutions to a problem.

j. When You Have Control Over Experimental Units

Being able to establish one's own organization is an extreme in control, and it confers many of the advantages of the laboratory. (The laboratory is, after all, a special case of establishing one's own organization in order to schedule events and treatments to suit research goals.) But most field researchers do not have the same control opportunities as their laboratory counterparts or the founders of organizations. They are more likely to be guests than hosts, and they may derive many of their possibilities for control from being associated with their powerful hosts. Strong links to the host or to the host's benefactors increase the chance of randomization. We might, therefore, expect randomization whenever major funders of organizations insist that a true experiment has to be conducted, and this makes institutions like the Office of Education (OE), the Department of Defense, and the large foundations major potential catalysts of true experiments. (However, the organizational separation of the implementing branch from the evaluation branch in OE, though justified as leading to unbiased evaluation [Williams & Evans, 1969], makes experimental implementation all the more difficult to achieve.) The major officials in industrial and other organizations can also be potential catalysts, especially if vice-presidents for Research and Development (R&D) are convinced enough of the benefits of randomization that they will endorse it, to their superiors if necessary.

Control is "the name of the game" in most organizations where subordinates expect to receive and carry out orders. The demands of experimentation fit neatly into this pattern, for control over treatments, measures, time schedules, aspects of the physical environment, and the like are part of the stock in trade of experimenting. This aspect of experimentation has recently come under attack (for a review see Kelman, 1972) because it involves the manipulation of people for ends that may benefit the researcher and his sponsors more than the respondent, and because manipulation may take place without the respondent's consent and in a way that will make him feel like a pawn in the investigator's elaborate game.

Because control is of the essence in most organizations, research in this area may be expected to continue for some time in spite of social trends against such arbitrary control, provided, of course, that the research control was gained in the first place through a coalition with top officials. Nonetheless, the day may come when unions, representatives of respondents, and even individual respondents will have to be fully informed about a study and consent to take part in it. When and if that day comes, experiments will be more reactive, and random assignment may have to be from populations of research volunteers. But until that day, true experiments are more likely to take place in field settings where investigators have control or have it conferred on them by their sponsors. It is especially likely where respondents have little obvious counter-power, and field experiments will probably continue to take place with children in schools, with the handicapped, aged, and infirm in institutions, with soldiers of low rank in the army, with factory workers who have weak unions or none at all, and with economically disadvantaged children and adults.

The relationship between experimentation, control, and the absence of effective counter-power is a sobering one that should indicate the long-term danger of abusing the control opportunities that are afforded to investigators who come as guests into host organizations. Even if we leave aside the important ethical problems and look only to pragmatic issues, it may be self-defeating to conduct one's true experiment in a way that directly or indirectly demeans respondents. In the future, we shall need volunteers —and the motivation to volunteer tomorrow may well be related to how we treat respondents in experiments today. To have absolute control in an organization one has founded; to have a large measure of control in organizations managed by friends or acquaintances or in organizations on whom one has been gently, or not-so-gently, forced by outside agencies that dispense funds; to have some, albeit circumscribed, measure of control as a guest in organizations to which one was invited—all of these relationships imply, to different degrees, that one will be able to conduct a true experiment. All of them also imply that one should control how one uses this control.

True experiments are feasible, as is indicated by those cited here and elsewhere (see especially the appendix to Riecken et al., 1974). However, they are not easy to conduct, and we hope that this brief section on true experiments will help investigators recognize and avoid some of the pitfalls that prevent sound work. We also hope that we have helped investigators recognize research situations where true experiments are especially likely. These are not the only situations where true experiments are feasible. They are merely some of the more convenient ones. In the last analysis, and without wanting to be facetious, field experiments are possible wherever they can be done, and we have not yet fully explored the limits of where they can be done.

SUMMARY

We explicated four kinds of validity—internal, external, statistical conclusion, and construct—and illustrated the relevance of each of these to the full interpretation of experiments in basic and applied organizational research. The priority of each kind of validity depends on whether the research is "basic" or "applied." Nonetheless, the information yield is enhanced the more we know about those kinds of validity that appear to be of relatively low importance in a particular study, and research should be designed with all four types of validity in mind. However, it is unrealistic to expect to control for all the validity threats we mentioned in a single experiment or in a single set of experiments. So, improving validity should not be confused with naive expectations of creating "a valid experiment."

Next, we discussed a series of quasi-experimental designs that involve non-equivalent groups. These designs involved no-treatment controls, reversed-treatment controls, removed-treatment controls, repeated-treatment controls, non-equivalent dependent variable controls, selection-maturation or cohort controls, and the regression-discontinuity design. After this, designs involving time-series were presented: the single time-series, the no-treatment control time-series, the non-equivalent dependent variable time-series, and the time-series with switching replications. A final quasi-experimental section dealt with correlational designs: path analysis, cross-lagged panel correlations, treatment-effect correlations, and regression adjustments.

Because of the difficulties of internal validity with quasi-experiments, we went on to stress the advisability of conducting true experiments. We also discussed some difficulties in implementing randomization and some possible solutions to these difficulties. Special attention was given to the types of setting that are conducive to randomized comparisons. Both the requirements of control and the dangers of abusing control were discussed, and the feasibility of using informed volunteers was stressed.

The general tone of this chapter was meant to be guardedly optimistic. It was meant to be guarded because quasi-experiments are often hard to interpret; because true experiments are often hard to set up and maintain; and because all the threats to internal, external, statistical conclusion, and construct validity cannot be ruled out within a single study. However, the tone was also meant to be optimistic because, as the examples in the chapter illustrated again and again, good quasi-experiments and true experiments have been conducted in the past. They have reduced all or most of the threats to internal and statistical conclusion validity, many of the threats to the construct validity of effects, and they have even reduced some of the threats to external validity and the construct validity of causes. The task of the field experimenter is not easy. But it is an important and exciting task, and it can bring valid knowledge to the careful and self-critical investigator.

APPENDIX: SOME NOTES ON UNOBTRUSIVE RESEARCH

We were originally asked to discuss unobtrusive research in this chapter. Because of the issue's importance and complexity we wanted to devote a special section to it. But since unobtrusive research does not necessarily involve the same kind of design considerations that were highlighted in the main body of the chapter, we decided to put the discussion of unobtrusiveness into a separate appendix.

It was clear to the women in the four work divisions studied by Morse and Reimer (1956) that they were in an experiment, that the experiment was about decision making, that different divisions received different treatments, and that various measures of satisfaction were being made. Reactivity of this magnitude typically leads to problems of testing and to the viability of a Hawthorne effect as an alternative interpretation of findings. In contrast, the Seaver (1973) quasi-experiment was unobtrusive in that the treatments (same *versus* different teacher and high- *versus* low-scoring sibling) were defined from available school records, as were the achievement outcome measures. Thus, as in the work of Parker (1963) on television and library circulation, the totally archival nature of the project meant that there was no problem associated with subjects thinking they were in a research study.

Organizational research is perhaps more fortunate than many other areas of the social sciences in that organizations exist, or claim to exist, for the purpose of influencing performance. Hence, performance measures are regularly kept as part of an organization's self-monitoring, as are such variables as hours worked, salaries earned, pensions contributed to, unions joined, etc. Turnover, absenteeism, and lateness are also typically measured and can serve as indirect indexes

of satisfaction. Moreover, there is no serious hindrance to organizations increasing the scope of their current self-evaluation procedures and instituting annual attitudinal inventories dealing with the satisfaction that is experienced in the various aspects of work. Such a recurring survey would be useful for management and union officials among others, both as feedback about how their constituencies feel and as an unobtrusive base line against which to assess the results of planned and unplanned changes in the organization's future.

Unobtrusive measures need not be restricted to *archives* or, as we have briefly hinted, to *regularly collected surveys* which, though obtrusive at the time of testing, are not seen as linked to a true or quasi-experiment. As Webb, Campbell, Schwartz, and Sechrest (1966) have pointed out, *physical traces* can also serve as unobtrusive measures. These are the traces left behind after usage, and one might go to the wastebasket after work is finished to count the number of false starts that a typist made in typing letters, and one might use this as one index of efficiency. Alternatively, one might count the number of pages she has typed (assessed from carbon copies or the number of pages used) as an index of productivity. Or, one might count the number of suggestions in a suggestions box as an index of cooperation with the organization. Or, one might count the number of cigarette butts in ashtrays as an index of the tension level of a meeting.

Besides physical traces, one might use *unobtrusive recording devices*. A counter will register the number of local and long-distance phone calls to check, for example, on the degree to which an organization is cosmopolitan, and a slight improvement to the counter would give the range of different exchanges called. Or, a counter could be attached to machines to register how often an operation is carried out. Or, a counter might be attached to a door to see how often a particular room is visited, etc.

Finally, *observation* can sometimes be

utilized to record unobtrusively. Webb et al. (1966) discuss situations where the observer is hidden from view or is one of many in a crowd. But it is also possible to imagine situations where an observer is expected to be present as part of the routine. Thus, at certain meetings a secretary is expected to attend and take notes, and instead of recording what is said he or she could record details of the communication flow or of the habits of the participants. Alternatively, time and motion engineers are expected to make notes and could be trained to observe some human factors other than those they are expected to monitor.

Outcome measures are not the only part of an experiment that would benefit from unobtrusiveness. Treatments can sometimes be implemented in non-obtrusive manners with the result that respondents are not aware of being in an experiment. Seaver's study is a case in point. In addition, if a union wanted to find out which of several appeals was more effective in increasing contributions to, say, a pension fund, they could mail out letters with different appeals to different members, or they could exhibit different notices in different places, or they could ask different shop stewards to say different things. Alternatively, if personnel officials were not satisfied they were getting truthful responses about the reasons why people were leaving a company, they might experiment with different questionnaire or interview formats to see which one gives results that most closely reflect what someone leaving an organization has said to co-workers or to his family.

Despite its obvious utility and our strong advocacy, unobtrusive research is no panacea. It involves at least five major weaknesses. For one, there is probably only a restricted range of measures that can be obtained, particularly with archival data. Investigators are often restricted to what is in the archives, and that may not always be what one wants to measure. Indeed, if one's interest is in the cognitive or "process" consequence of treatments, it is unlikely that archives will help,

for archives tend to be repositories for records of behavior rather than cognitions, and for records of the outcomes caused by behavior rather than the means used to achieve the outcomes. This is why an annual attitude inventory would fill a real gap that exists in current data archives.

Second, unobtrusive measures are often subject to modifications in that there may be changes in the definition of important variables like lateness, or performance, or retirement age, or whatever. When such changes take place, there will be a discontinuity in the level of lateness, performance, etc., and this can masquerade as a treatment effect. Often, such definitional change may be the honest response to new environmental contingencies, but it can also be more politically motivated—deliberately designed to make a person or organization "look good." Obviously, the definitional fixity of records, traces, and observations is vital if unobtrusive measures are to be useful.

Third, unobtrusive experiments can run into considerable and complex ethical problems. They can involve invasions of privacy; they can be conducted without the consent of respondents; they can be used to affect hiring and firing decisions in a way that smells of entrapment; they are more likely to be used with the authorization of management rather than other levels in an organization; and they could be used for the benefit of narrow rather than broad interests. Some of these ethical problems slide over into the public relations sphere in the sense that a loud outcry might ensue if some parties were to think they were being experimented upon in a "sneaky" and unauthorized way. Indeed, some of the problems even slide into the legal sphere, and Silverman (in press) has reported receiving legal opinion to the effect that some unobtrusive experiments may violate some laws. There is obviously a great need for legal clarification of specific issues that arise with unobtrusive research.

Fourth, there is a question concerning access to unobtrusive measures, particularly archived ones. Since these archives belong to organizations and many contain sensitive or potentially sensitive records, they are not likely to be made accessible to all who would be interested. Rather, their use is likely to be limited to research personnel who are guests of the organization and whose research aims are either commensurate with organizational goals or are, at the very least, commensurate with being a guest and respecting the norms that are expected of guests. These include not embarrassing the host. Even when the guest researcher and host organization have saliently overlapping aims, it is not certain that the researcher will have equal access to all records, for some will be more sensitive than others.

Finally, a problem of construct validity is associated with unobtrusive measures. Archival data are typically not collected with academic research needs in mind, and there is likely to be more than the usual slippage between operationalizations and their referent constructs. To some extent, organizational research is better off than other disciplines in this regard, for the interests of on-going organizations, efficiency and satisfaction have also come to be defined as major target variables of organizational research, although they by no means exhaust the scope of the field's enquiry. But there is still a lack of archives relevant to, say, problems of communication or goal-setting or the like. Also, archival and trace measures can have a distinct disadvantage unless there are several of them that are related. This is because most single measures can be conceptualized in several different ways. For example, the number of false starts to typed letters may be an index of an employee's efficiency. But it may also be an index of the number of letters someone is asked to type, or the difficulty of the content, or the state of repair of the machine, or the standards of an immediate supervisor, or the standards of the typist, or many other factors. Some of these can be empirically examined, but others not. Clearly, one would do better to operationalize efficiency *in multiple ways* so that one could construct an

index composed of the number of false starts, the number of letters completed, the number of telephones answered, the number of spontaneous favorable comments from supervisors and others, annual ratings by supervisors, etc. This multiple operationalist perspective would decrease reliance on a single measure which might not exhaustively complement the construct being defined and which might have unique dimensions that are irrelevant to the construct of interest.

Unobtrusive research has many advantages of interpretation, and organizational research should be one of the disciplines using it most widely. But while we need more vigorous attempts to plan and implement unobtrusive research, we also need honest criticism in evaluating the designs that result. And this honest criticism should consider both methodological and ethical perspectives.

REFERENCES

Adams, J. S. Inequity in social exchange. In L. Berkowitz (Ed.), *Advances in experimental social psychology,* Vol. 2. New York: Academic Press, 1965.

Atkinson, R. C. Computerized instruction and the learning process. *American Psychologist,* 1968, 23, 225–239.

Ball, S., & Bogatz, G. A. *The first year of Sesame Street: An evaluation.* Princeton: Educational Testing Service, 1970.

Bereiter, C., & Engelmann, S. *Teaching disadvantaged children in the preschool.* Englewood Cliffs, N.J.: Prentice-Hall, 1966.

Bishop, R. C., & Hill, J. W. Effects of job enlargement and job change on contiguous but non-manipulated jobs as a function of workers' status. *Journal of Applied Psychology,* 1971, 55, 175–181.

Blalock, H. M. Jr., Ed. *Causal models in the social sciences.* Chicago: Aldine, Atherton, 1971.

Bogatz, G. A., & Ball, S. *The second year of Sesame Street: A continuing evaluation.* Princeton: Educational Testing Service, 1971, two vols.

Box, G. E. P., & Jenkins, G. M. *Time-series analysis: Forecasting and control.* San Francisco: Holden Day, 1970.

Box, G. E. P., & Tiao, G. C. A change in level of nonstationary time series. *Biometrika,* 1965, 52, 181–192.

Bracht, G. H., & Glass, G. V. The external validity of experiments. *American Educational Research Journal,* 1968, 5, 437–474.

Brannon, R., Cyphers, G., Hesse, S., Hesselbart, S., Keane, R., Schuman, H., Viccaro, T., & Wright, D. Attitude and action: A field experiment joined to a general population survey. *American Sociological Review,* 1973, 38, 625–634.

Brewer, M. B., Campbell, D. T., & Crano, W. D. Testing a single-factor model as an alternative to the misuse of partial correlations in hypothesis-testing research. *Sociometry,* 1970, 33, 1–11.

Broadbent, D. E., & Little, E. A. J. Effects of noise reduction in a work situation. *Occupational Psychology,* 1960, 34, 133–140.

Bryan, J. H., & Test, M. A. Models and helping: Naturalistic studies in aiding behavior. *Journal of Personality and Social Psychology,* 1967, 6, 400–407.

Campbell, D. T. Leadership and its effects upon the group. In *Ohio Studies in Personnel.* Columbus: Ohio State University, Bureau of Business Research Monographs, 1956, No. 83.

Campbell, D. T. From description to experimentation: Interpreting trends as quasi-experiments. In C. W. Harris (Ed.), *Problems in measuring change.* Madison: University of Wisconsin Press, 1963, 212–254.

Campbell, D. T. Reforms as experiments. *American Psychologist,* 1969, 24, 409–429.

Campbell, D. T. Temporal changes in treatment-effect correlations: A quasi-experimental model for institutional records and longitudinal studies. In G. V. Glass (Ed.), *The promise and perils of educational information systems.* Princeton: Educational Testing Service, 1971, 93–110. (Proceedings of the 1970 Invitational Conference on Testing Problems.)

Campbell, D. T., & Erlebacher, A. E. How regression artifacts in quasi-experimental evaluations can mistakenly make compensatory education look harmful. In J. Hellmuth (Ed.), *Compensatory education: A national debate,* Vol. 3, *Disadvantaged Child.* New York: Brunner/Mazel, 1970.

Campbell, D. T., & Fiske, D. W. Convergent and discriminant validation by the multitrait-multimethod matrix. *Psychological Bulletin,* 1959, 56, 81–105. (Also, Bobbs-Merrill Reprint series in the social sciences, S-354.)

Campbell, D. T., & Stanley, J. C. Experimental and quasi-experimental designs for research on teaching. In N. L. Gage (Ed.), *Handbook of research on teaching.* Chicago: Rand McNally, 1963. (Also published as *Experimental and quasi-experimental designs for research.* Chicago: Rand McNally, 1966.)

Cook, D. *The impact of the Hawthorne effect in experimental designs in educational research.* Washington, D.C.: U.S. Office of Education, No. 0726, June, 1967.

Cook, T. D. The potential and limitations of secondary evaluations. In M. W. Apple, M. J. Subkoviak, & H. S. Lufler Jr. (Eds.), *Educational evaluation: Analysis and responsibility.* Berkeley, Calif.: McCutchan, 1974a.

Cook, T. D. The medical and tailored models of evaluation research. In J. G. Abert & M. Kamrass (Eds.), *Social experiments and social program evaluation.* Cambridge: Ballinger, 1974b.

Cook, T. D., Appleton, H., Conner, R., Shaffer, A., Tamkin, G., & Weber, S. J. *Sesame Street revisited: A case study in evaluation research.* New York: Russell Sage Foundation, 1975.

Crano, W. D., Kenny, D. A., & Campbell, D. T. Does intelligence cause achievement? A cross-lagged panel analysis. *Journal of Educational Psychology,* 1972, 63, 258–275.

Cronbach, L. J., & Furby, L. How we should measure "change"—or should we? *Psychological Bulletin,* 1970, 74, 68–80.

Diamond, S. S. Hawthorne effects: Another look. Unpublished manuscript, University of Illinois at Chicago, 1974.

Doob, A. N., Carlsmith, J. M., Freedman, J. L., Landauer, T. K., & Tom, S. Jr. Effect of initial selling price on subsequent sales. *Journal of Personality and Social Psychology,* 1969, 11, 345–350.

Duncan, O. D. Some linear models for two-wave, two-variable panel analysis. *Psychological Bulletin,* 1969, 72, 177–182.

Edwards, A. L. *Experimental design in psychological research*. New York: Holt, Rinehart and Winston, 1963.

Eron, L. D., Huesmann, L. R., Lefkowitz, M. M., & Walder, L. O. Does television violence cause aggression? *American Psychologist*, 1972, 27, 253–263.

Farmer, E. *A comparison of different shift systems in the glass trade*. London: His Majesty's Stationery Office, 1924. (Report No. 24, Medical Research Council, Industrial Fatigue Research Board.)

Feldman, R. Response to compatriot and foreigner who seek assistance. *Journal of Personality and Social Psychology*, 1968, 10, 202–214.

Feshbach, S., & Singer, R. D. *Television and aggression*. San Francisco: Jossey-Bass, 1971.

Fienberg, S. E. Randomization and social affairs: The 1970 draft lottery. *Science*, 1971, 171, 255–261.

Glass, G. V., Tiao, G. C., & Maguire, T. O. Analysis of data on the 1900 revision of German divorce laws as a time-series quasi-experiment. *Law and Society Review*, 1971, 4, 539–562.

Glass, G. V., Willson, V. L., & Gottman, J. M. *Design and analysis of time-series experiments*. Boulder: Colorado Associated University Press, 1975.

Goldberger, A. S., & Duncan, O. D. *Structural equation models in the social sciences*. New York: Seminar Press, 1973.

Goodman, L. A. Causal analysis of data from panel studies and other kinds of surveys. *American Journal of Sociology*, 1973, 78, 1135–1191.

Gordon, A. C., & Myers, J. R. Methodological recommendations for extensions of the Heussenstamm bumper sticker study. Duplicated report, Northwestern University, Center for Urban Affairs, Evanston, Ill., September, 1970.

Greaney, V., Kellaghan, T., Takata, G., & Campbell, D. T. Regression-discontinuities in the Irish "Leaving Certificate." In preparation.

Greenhouse, S. W., & Geisser, S. On methods in the analysis of profile data. *Psychometrika*, 1959, 24, 95–112.

Hand, H. H., & Slocum, J. W. Jr. A longitudinal study of the effects of a human relations training program on managerial effective-ness. *Journal of Applied Psychology*, 1972, 56, 412–417.

Hays, W. L. *Statistics for psychologists*. New York: Holt, Rinehart and Winston, 1963.

Heise, D. R. Separating reliability and stability in test-retest correlation. *American Sociological Review*, 1969, 34, 93–101.

Heussenstamm, F. Bumper stickers and the cops. *Transaction*, 1971, 8, 32–33.

Hudson, W. W. *Project breakthrough: A responsive environment field experiment with preschool children from public assistance families*. Chicago: Cook County Department of Public Aid, 1969.

Ivancevich, J. M., & Donnelly, J. H. Job offer acceptance behavior and reinforcement. *Journal of Applied Psychology*, 1971, 55, 119–122.

Kelman, H. C. The rights of the subject in social research: An analysis in terms of relative power and legitimacy. *American Psychologist*, 1972, 27, 989–1016.

Kenny, D. A. Threats to the internal validity of a cross-lagged panel inference, as related to "Television violence and child aggression: A follow-up study." In G. A. Comstock & E. A. Rubinstein (Eds.), *Television and social behavior: Reports and papers*, Vol. 3. Washington, D.C.: HEW, Health Services and Mental Health Administration, 1972, 136–140. (A technical report to the Surgeon General's Scientific Advisory Committee on Television and Social Behavior. Washington, D.C.: Superintendent of Documents, U.S. Government Printing Office.)

Kenny, D. A. Cross-lagged and synchronous common factors in panel data. In A. S. Goldberger & O. D. Duncan (Eds.), *Structural equation models in the social sciences*. New York: Seminar Press, 1973, 153–156.

Kenny, D. A. A quasi-experimental approach to assessing treatment effects in the nonequivalent control group design. *Psychological Bulletin*, in press.

Kerr, W. A. Experiments on the effect of music on factory production. *Applied Psychology Monographs*, 1945, No. 5 Whole Vol.

Kershaw, D. N. A negative income tax experiment. *Scientific American*, 1972, 227, 19–25.

Kirk, R. E. *Experimental design procedures for the behavioral sciences*. Belmont, Calif.: Brooks/Cole, 1968.

Lawler, E. E. III, & Hackman, J. R. Impact of

employee participation in the development of pay incentive plans: A field experiment. *Journal of Applied Psychology,* 1969, 53, 467–471.

Lazarsfeld, P. F. The mutual effects of statistical variables. Duplicated report, Bureau of Applied Social Research, Columbia University, New York, 1947.

Lazarsfeld, P. F. The use of panels in social research. *Proceedings of the American Philosophical Society,* 1948, 92, 405–410.

Lieberman, S. The effects of changes in roles on the attitudes of role occupants. *Human Relations,* 1956, 9, 385–402.

Lipset, S. M., Lazarsfeld, P. F., Barton, A. H., & Linz, J. The psychology of voting: An analysis of political behavior. In G. Lindzey (Ed.), *Handbook of social psychology,* Vol. II. Reading, Mass.: Addison-Wesley, 1954, 1124–1175.

Lohr, B. W. An historical view of the research on the factors related to the utilization of health services. Duplicated Research Report, Bureau for Health Services Research and Evaluation, Social and Economic Analysis Division, Rockville, Md., January, 1972, 34 pp.; U.S. Government Printing Office, in press.

Lord, F. M. Large-scale covariance analysis when the control variable is fallible. *Journal of the American Statistical Association,* 1960, 55, 307–321.

Lord, F. M. A paradox in the interpretation of group comparisons. *Psychological Bulletin,* 1967, 68, 304–305.

Lord, F. M. Statistical adjustments when comparing preexisting groups. *Psychological Bulletin,* 1969, 72, 336–337.

McNemar, Q. A critical examination of the University of Iowa studies of environmental influences upon the I.Q. *Psychological Bulletin,* 1940, 37, 63–92.

McNemar, Q. *Psychological statistics.* (4th ed.) New York: Wiley, 1971.

Mase, B. F. Changes in self-actualization as a result of two types of residential group experience. Unpublished doctoral dissertation, Northwestern University, Evanston, Ill., 1971.

Minton, J. The impact of Sesame Street on reading readiness of kindergarten children. *Journal of Sociology of Education,* 1975.

Morse, N. C., & Reimer, E. The experimental change of a major organizational variable.

Journal of Abnormal and Social Psychology, 1956, 52, 120–129.

Mullen, E. J., Chazin, R. M., & Feldstein, D. M. Services for the newly dependent: An assessment. *The Social Service Review,* 1972, 46, 309–322.

Nisbett, R. E., & Kanouse, D. E. Obesity, food deprivation, and supermarket shopping behavior. *Journal of Personality and Social Psychology,* 1969, 12, 289–294.

Notz, W. W., Staw, B. M., & Cook, T. D. Attitude toward troop withdrawal from Indochina as a function of draft number: Dissonance or self-interest? *Journal of Personality and Social Psychology,* 1971, 20, 118–126.

Parker, E. B. The effects of television on public library circulation. *Public Opinion Quarterly,* 1963, 27, 578–589.

Parker, E. B., Campbell, D. T., Cook, T. D., Katzman, N., & Butler-Paisley, M. Time-series analyses of effects of television on library circulation in Illinois. Unpublished paper, Northwestern University, Evanston, Ill., 1971.

Pelz, D. C., & Andrews, F. M. Detecting causal priorities in panel study data. *American Sociological Review,* 1964, 29, 836–848.

Pritchard, R. D., Dunnette, M. D., & Jorgenson, D. O. Effects of perceptions of equity and inequity on worker performance and satisfaction. *Journal of Applied Psychology,* 1972, 56, 75–94.

Pugh, D. S. Modern organization theory: A psychological and sociological study. *Psychological Bulletin,* 1966, 66, 233–251.

Rand. *A million random digits.* Santa Monica, Calif.: Rand Corporation, 1955.

Ray, H. W. *Final report on the Office of Economic Opportunity experiment in educational performance contracting.* Columbus, Ohio: Battelle Columbus Laboratories, 1972.

Rickard, S. The assumptions of causal analyses for incomplete sets of two multilevel variables. *Multivariate Behavioral Research,* 1972, 7, 317–359.

Riecken, H. W., Boruch, R. F., Campbell, D. T., Caplan, N., Glennan, T. K., Pratt, J., Rees, A., & Williams, W. *Social experimentation: A method for planning and evaluating social innovations.* New York: Academic Press, 1974.

Robertson, L. S., Kelley, A. B., O'Neill, B., Wixom, C. W., Eiswirth, R. S., & Haddon,

W. *A controlled study of the effect of tele-vision messages on safety belt use.* Washington, D.C.: Insurance Institute for Highway Safety, 1972.

Roethlisberger, F. J., & Dickson, W. J. *Management and the worker.* Cambridge: Harvard University Press, 1939.

Rosen, H., & Turner, J. Effectiveness of two orientation approaches in hard-core unemployed turnover and absenteeism. *Journal of Applied Psychology,* 1971, 55, 296–301.

Rosenberg, M. J. The conditions and consequences of evaluation apprehension. In R. Rosenthal & R. L. Rosnow (Eds.), *Artifact in behavioral research.* New York: Academic Press, 1969.

Rosenthal, R. On the social psychology of the self-fulfilling prophecy: Further evidence for Pygmalion effects and their mediating mechanisms. Unpublished manuscript, Harvard University, Cambridge, 1972.

Ross, H. L. Law, science, and accidents: The British Road Safety Act of 1967. *Journal of Legal Studies,* 1973, 2, 1–75.

Ross, H. L., Campbell, D. T., & Glass, G. V. Determining the social effects of a legal reform: The British "breathalyser" crackdown of 1967. *American Behavioral Scientist,* 1970, 13, 493–509.

Rossi, P. H., Boeckmann, M., & Berk, R. A. Some ethical implications of the New Jersey-Pennsylvania income maintenance experiment. Unpublished manuscript, University of Massachusetts, Amherst, 1974.

Rozelle, R. M., & Campbell, D. T. More plausible rival hypotheses in the cross-lagged panel correlation technique. *Psychological Bulletin,* 1969, 71, 74–80.

Ryan, T. A. Multiple comparisons in psychological research. *Psychological Bulletin,* 1959, 56, 26–47.

Saretsky, G. The OEO P.C. experiment and the John Henry effect. *Phi Delta Kappan,* 1972, 53, 579–581.

Scheflen, K. C., Lawler, E. E. III, & Hackman, J. R. Long-term impact of employee participation in the development of pay incentive plans: A field experiment revisited. *Journal of Applied Psychology,* 1971, 55, 182–186.

Schnaiberg, A., & Armer, M. Measurement evaluation obstacles in sociological surveys: A grounded reassessment. Paper presented to American Sociological Association meetings, August, 1972.

Schuman, H., & Duncan, O. D. Questions about attitude survey questions. In H. L. Costner (Ed.), *Sociological methodology, 1973–1974.* San Francisco: Jossey-Bass, 1974.

Seaver, W. B. Effects of naturally induced teacher expectancies. *Journal of Personality and Social Psychology,* 1973, 28, 333–342.

Seaver, W. B., & Quarton, R. J. Social reinforcement of excellence: Dean's List and academic achievement. Paper presented at the 44th annual meeting of the Eastern Psychological Association, Washington, D.C., May, 1973.

Sechrest, L. Dissipating and snowballing effects in social amelioration: Lotteries as true experiments. Northwestern University, Evanston, Ill., duplicated memorandum, 1970, 11 pp.

Siegel, A. E., & Siegel, S. Reference groups, membership groups, and attitude change. *Journal of Abnormal and Social Psychology,* 1957, 55, 360–364.

Silverman, I. Inobtrusive methods and the law. *American Psychologist,* in press.

Snow, R. E. Representative and quasi-representative designs for research on teaching. *Review of Educational Research,* 1974, 44, 265–291.

Staw, B. M. Attitudinal and behavioral consequences of changing a major organizational reward: A natural field experiment. *Journal of Personality and Social Psychology,* 1974, 29, 742–751.

Thistlethwaite, D. L., & Campbell, D. T. Regression-discontinuity analysis: An alternative to the ex post facto experiment. *Journal of Educational Psychology,* 1960, 51, 309–317.

Thorndike, R. L. Regression fallacies in the matched groups experiment. *Psychometrika* 1942, 7, 85–102.

Valins, S., & Baum, A. Residential group size, social interaction, and crowding. *Environment and Behavior,* 1973, 5, 421–439.

Van Voorhis, W. R., & Peters, C. C. *Statistical procedures and their mathematical bases.* New York: McGraw-Hill, 1940.

Walker, H., & Lev, J. *Statistical inference.* New York: Holt, Rinehart and Winston, 1953.

Webb, E. J., Campbell, D. T., Schwartz, R. D., & Sechrest, L. *Unobtrusive measures: Nonreactive research in the social sciences.* Chicago: Rand McNally, 1966.

Weber, S. J., & Cook, T. D. Subject effects in laboratory research: An examination of subject roles, demand characteristics, and valid inference. *Psychological Bulletin,* 1972, 77, 273–295.

Weber, S. J., Cook, T. D., & Campbell, D. T. The effects of school integration on the academic self-concept of public school children. Paper presented at the meeting of the Midwestern Psychological Association, Detroit, 1971.

Weikart, D. P. Relationship of curriculum, teaching, and learning in preschool education. In J. C. Stanley (Ed.), *Preschool programs for the disadvantaged.* Baltimore: Johns Hopkins University Press, 1972.

Wilder, C. S. Physician visits, volume, and interval since last visit, U.S., 1969. Rockville, Md.: National Center for Health Statistics, Series 10, No. 75, July, 1972, DHEW Pub. No. (HSM) 72-1064.

Williams, W., & Evans, J. W. The politics of evaluation: The case of Head Start. *The Annals,* 1969, 385, 118–132.

Winch, R. F., & Campbell, D. T. Proof? No! Evidence? Yes! The significance of tests of significance. *American Sociologist,* 1969, 4, 140–143.

Winer, B. J. *Statistical principles in experimental design.* New York: McGraw-Hill, 1961.

Worchel, S., & Mitchell, R. R. An evaluation of the effectiveness of the culture assimilator in Thailand and Greece. *Journal of Applied Psychology,* 1972, 56, 472–479.

CHAPTER 8

Multivariate Procedures

DAVID J. WEISS

The University of Minnesota

Multivariate Prediction	References
Multivariate Covariation Analysis	

METHODS OF MULTIVARIATE PREDICTION and multivariate covariation analysis (factor analysis, cluster analysis) are classified and explained in non-mathematical terms, within the context of research in industrial-organizational psychology. Classification schemes used are designed to assist the researcher in choosing methods most appropriate for a given applied problem. Decision criteria used in choosing among multivariate prediction models are based on whether the criterion variable is single or multiple and whether it is continuous or categorical, and whether the researcher is willing to assume linear relationships between the set of multiple predictors and the criterion variable(s). Each method is discussed in terms of its rationale, interpretations, and limitations. Methods for analyzing matrices of multivariate correlational data are divided into those methods that analyze total variance (components analysis and cluster analysis) and methods for analyzing common variance (factor analysis). Within each of these major classifications additional distinctions are made among available techniques to help researchers identify the methods most appropriate for a given problem and to assist in the interpretation of the results of analyses using the methods.

Industrial-organizational psychologists typically obtain multivariate information from their observations of individuals and organizations. In the classical problem of personnel selection and placement, the psychologist is likely to view the prospective employee in terms of not just one score on one variable, such as a verbal ability test score, but the individual is viewed as an organism on whom a variety of observations can be made. That is, the psychologist may obtain information on such additional variables as the individual's typing speed, typing accuracy, educational level, type of education, sex, and age.

In measuring job satisfaction or job performance, the psychologist also frequently encounters multivariate information. Rather than treat job satisfaction as a global variable, more information is made available for practical use if job satisfaction can be seen in terms of an individual's satisfaction with his pay, his supervisors, working conditions, or the amount of variety his job provides. Likewise, job performance, part of the more global criterion of satisfactoriness, includes in its multivariate representation such aspects as the amount of work an individual does, the quality of his work, his dependability, and his willingness to conform to the rules and regulations of his work environment.

While observing individuals or organizations on multiple variables can provide the researcher or practitioner with considerably more information than simply observing a single variable, it does raise problems which dealing with a single variable does not. Just the mass of information that multivariate observations create can cause problems for many observers. It is reasonably easy for a psychologist to help the organization evaluate an individual's job performance if only a global, univariate measurement is made. In this case, the individual with the highest score on the measure is the most satisfactory. If, however, individuals are measured on a multivariate job performance scale, decisions as to who is the best employee might become more complex. For example, one individual might be highest of a group on quantity of work performed, lowest on quality of work, and average on three other scales; another individual might be highest on the last three scales and lowest on the first two. The question of who is "most satisfactory" then becomes difficult to answer since the multivariate nature of the observations makes it too complex for the observer to comprehend.

Multivariate procedures can be helpful in this case since they can provide an *organizing* function. The methods of *multivariate covariation analysis* can help the observer to organize his observations in at least two ways. First, procedures of factor analysis are designed to reduce a large number of variables into a smaller number which are more easily comprehendible to the observer. By these procedures, the researcher can take observations on, say, twenty variables and reduce them to as few as two or three variables which best summarize the common information in the twenty variables. Patterns of individual differences in

the two or three basic variables are then more easily perceived than are patterns of differences in the original twenty variables.

Multivariate covariation analysis procedures can help to organize observations in another way. Sometimes the psychologist hypothesizes that certain *kinds* of people exhibit certain behaviors more frequently than other kinds of people. To continue the job performance example, it might be observed that employees who have certain patterns of job performance scores are likely to be stable employees, while those who do not exhibit these characteristics are more likely to quit a job within three months. To determine whether this observation is in fact true, the psychologist must somehow organize the profiles of his employees on the multivariate job performance measure to determine if different *types* of individuals exist, that is, different subsets of individuals who have different patterns of job performance scores. If this is in fact the case, then it would be possible to examine the differential quit rates of the various types of employees, as determined from their job performance ratings. This taxonomic question can be approached by procedures of cluster analysis, another type of multivariate covariation analysis.

In addition to helping the researcher organize data to permit better understanding, multivariate procedures are also important in *prediction* in industrial-organizational psychology. One of the most important functions of the industrial-organizational psychologist is to be able to predict which individuals will exhibit certain behaviors which are deemed desirable by the organization. Management frequently needs to know which individuals are likely to be good workers, which will cost the company extra money in training or disciplinary costs, or which will stay on the job long enough to repay the initial investment in hiring or training. When dealing with univariate predictor information, such as the single global job performance score, prediction of the single criterion is relatively simple. The problem gets more difficult to understand in the situation where multiple predictor measures are used to predict a single criterion, and more complex yet where the criterion itself is multivariate. In both these situations, the sheer amount of information available requires the use of statistical techniques of multivariate prediction rather than the simple experience tables or correlation coefficients that are usable when predictor information and criterion information are measured by only one variable each.

MULTIVARIATE PREDICTION

Selection of an appropriate technique for multivariate prediction rests on three considerations: (1) whether the criterion variable is a single variable (univariate) or consists of measurements on many variables (multivariate), (2) whether the criterion variable or variables are measured as continuous or categorical variables, and (3) whether the researcher is willing to assume that his predictor variables are linearly related to the criterion or criteria.

Whether the criterion variable is single or multiple, and whether it is continuous or categorical are usually predetermined by the nature of the data. However, some apparently univariate criterion variables can be also measured as a multivariate set of variables. This is the case, as indicated above, where such typical criterion variables as job satisfactoriness or satisfaction are each measured by a set of relatively independent sub-scales rather than one univariate composite. In some cases, there is information to be gained in prediction by analyzing an apparently univariate measure into its multivariate components. Likewise, the apparently single continuous variable can sometimes be classified into a dichotomous or polychotomous categorical variable for making certain kinds of predictions. This would be the case where a variable, such as job performance measured on a continuous scale, can be divided at some point into those individuals whose performance is "inade-

quate," "adequate," or "superior." In each case, different multivariate prediction techniques are appropriate for the data.

The question of linear versus nonlinear relationships is somewhat more difficult to resolve in some cases. Where the *predictor* variables are categorical, nonlinear techniques are preferred over the linear techniques if there are more than two categories in any of the predictor variables. For two category predictors the linear methods will be appropriate since curvilinear relationships with a criterion variable are not possible with only two categories on the predictor. For polychotomous predictors the assumption of linearity will generally be inappropriate unless the categories are orderable or the investigator has prior knowledge of the relationship between the predictor categories and the criterion variables so that he can order the relationship in a linear fashion.

When the predictors are continuous, however, the researcher has the opportunity to choose between the assumption of linear predictor-criterion relationships and nonlinear relationships. Usually this choice should be made on the basis of the hypothesized relationships between the predictors and the criterion. When the researcher is willing to assume that equal increments on the predictor are related to equal increments on the criterion variable, linear methods are appropriate. An example would be the familiar relationship between measured ability and job performance. If it can be assumed that each "unit" of measured ability at every point on the ability scale is related to an equal unit increase in job performance, then linear methods of prediction will suffice. On the other hand, it might be assumed that after a certain point on the ability continuum increases in ability do not relate to increases in performance. This would be the case where job performance has a built-in maximum or plateau that cannot be exceeded. In such a situation, linear models of prediction would not be appropriate, and nonlinear models would give more accurate predictions.

Decisions about the nature of the criterion or criteria as univariate or multivariate, or continuous or categorical, must be carefully considered by the researcher. The linearity decision is, in a sense, the most crucial of the three. While wrong decisions about the nature of the criterion will affect the utility of the information obtained, erroneous choice of a linear technique where a nonlinear one is more appropriate will result in decreased accuracy of prediction.

Figure 1 summarizes and classifies the most common multivariate prediction methods; it is designed to assist researchers in choosing the technique most appropriate to their data based on the above considerations. It should be noted in using Figure 1 that a categorical criterion is classified as "single" if it has only two categories, and multiple if it is comprised of more than two categories.

As Figure 1 shows, when linearity can be assumed the choices are quite clear—there is only one technique generally appropriate for each of the four situations; these techniques are all closely related to each other, and have similar rationale and interpretation. When linearity cannot be assumed, however, a variety of choices are available for the single criterion situation,

whether it is continuous or categorical. For the nonlinear situation with multiple continuous criteria, no appropriate technique is available. Each of the nonlinear methods is based on a different set of assumptions, which should be carefully considered by the researcher in making his choice of a prediction method.

Linear Multiple Regression

Rationale

Linear multiple regression is the most commonly used multivariate prediction technique in the behavioral sciences; it is designed to predict one continuous criterion variable from a set of continuous predictor variables.

The development of a linear multiple regression equation is a complex mathematical procedure which has been treated in many statistics texts (e.g., Guilford, 1965; McNemar, 1969; Cooley & Lohnes, 1971; for a basic introduction see Tatsuoka, 1969). In essence, the mathematical procedure is designed to find a set of weights which are applied to scores on the predictor variables to define a weighted linear composite (or weighted sum) for each individual. Since

	MULTIPLE PREDICTORS			
	Single Criterion		Multiple Criteria	
Assumption	Continuous	Categorical	Continuous	Categorical
Linear relationships	Linear Multiple Regression	Discriminant Function	Canonical Correlation	Multiple Discriminant Function
Nonlinear relationships (including categorical predictors with three or more categories)	Curvilinear Multiple Regression Reciprocal Averages Prediction Configural Methods (Actuarial Pattern Analysis)	Configural Methods Multiple Cut-off Methods Weighted Application Blank Methods		Dual Pattern Analysis

Figure 1.   Classification of multivariate prediction methods.

there are an endless variety of ways in which such weights may be chosen, the weights chosen by the mathematical solution are those which *maximize* the product-moment correlation between the predictor variate (the predicted score, or the weighted linear composite) and the actual continuous criterion score. At the same time that the weights to be applied to the predictor variables maximize this correlation, they *minimize* the sum of the squared differences between predicted criterion scores and the actual criterion scores.

This latter characteristic puts linear multiple regression procedures in the class of mathematical procedures called *least squares solutions,* since the solution yields errors of prediction (sometimes called residuals) which are the least (minimal) of those possible by other weighting procedures.

The weights applied to the predictor variables in developing the least squares solution are called *partial regression weights,* or simply *regression weights.* These weights usually occur in two forms: raw score regression weights, commonly called *b*-weights; and standard score regression weights, or beta weights. The *b*-weights are multiplied by raw scores on the predictors to obtain a predicted raw score on the criterion variable; beta weights are applied to standard scores or *z*-scores on the predictors to obtain predicted *z*-scores on the criterion.

Interpretations

The multiple correlation coefficient (R), resulting from the use of linear multiple regression procedures, reflects the accuracy with which actual criterion scores can be predicted from the predictor variate. R is the product-moment correlation between actual and predicted scores; therefore, R-squared represents the proportion of variance of the criterion variable that is explainable or predictable from the predictor variate. When R^2 is zero no differential prediction of the criterion is possible.

The beta weights (*not* the *b*-weights) indicate which of the predictors best predict the criterion; the variable with the highest beta weight contributes most to the predictor variate and is, therefore, the best predictor. Beta weights can also be tested for statistical significance to determine which are the significant predictors.

Limitations

While the mathematical procedures for linear multiple regression yield a prediction equation that is usually considered "maximal," it should be clearly understood that this technique maximizes prediction of the criterion only within its assumptions. In using linear multiple regression techniques, the researcher assumes that all relationships between predictors and the criterion do not deviate significantly from a linear relationship. To the extent that nonlinearity does not exist the predictions will be "maximal." If significant nonlinearity exists, however, alternative techniques will provide better prediction. The method further assumes that all predictors relate linearly to all other predictors. If the relationships among predictors deviate from a straight line relationship, that nonlinearity will also lower the accuracy of the predictions.

Since linear multiple regression techniques are optimization procedures they are subject to "shrinkage." This means that multiple correlation coefficients obtained on a group of individuals are artificially inflated because they capitalize on sample-specific group characteristics. In other words, results obtained on a similar group of individuals are likely to be somewhat different. When regression weights developed on one group are applied to data from another group (this process is called "cross-validation"), the multiple correlation usually "shrinks," in some cases to nonsignificant values. To reduce the possibility of shrinkage, researchers should (1) sample individuals using a deliberate random sampling scheme from a well-defined population, (2) use large numbers of individuals in relation to the number of predictor variables, and (3) cross-validate regression equations on a "hold-out" group before applying regression equations for any purpose.

Stepwise Multiple Regression Procedures

RATIONALE. On occasion the researcher enters a prediction problem with a large number of predictor variables which he wishes to reduce to a smaller set for some later purpose. For example, an investigator may be attempting to predict job success using a series of ability tests. In order to assure that he includes all likely predictors of job success, he begins with ten ability tests, for which sixty minutes of testing time is required. His objective is to arrive at the smallest number of predictor variables with maximal prediction of the criterion, so that testing time in the employment screening situation will be minimized. Note that this is a two-stage procedure in that the initial set of ten predictors is to be reduced to a smaller number, and the smaller number is to be used in the second stage of actually selecting employees.

Stepwise regression procedures (Efroymson, 1960) are designed for this two-stage situation. Three general varieties of stepwise procedures are in general use: decremental, incremental, and mixed approaches. In the decremental approach, the total multiple regression equation is first calculated. Variables are then dropped from the equation if they do not contribute significantly to the prediction of the criterion, based on the magnitude of their beta weights. In this procedure, the multiple correlation coefficient is usually reduced slightly as each variable is removed. When enough variables are removed, a significant drop occurs in the magnitude of R; at this point the stepwise procedure (i.e., dropping a variable at each step and recomputing R) is terminated. The result (not including the last step) is a smaller subset of predictor variables that predict the criterion almost as well as the total set.

The incremental stepwise procedure works from the "bottom up." Beginning with no predictor variables in the regression equation, variables are added which have the highest relationship with the criterion, as indicated by their partial correlations with the criterion. As variables are added, the multiple correlation is recomputed at each step until increments in R become no longer significant. At that point the prediction equation includes only those variables that are significantly predictive of the criterion.

The "mixed" approach simultaneously combines both the incremental and decremental approach. In this procedure, a variable added or dropped at one step may be dropped or added at another step if its relationship with the criterion changes significantly, as reflected in its partial correlation or partial regression coefficient.

LIMITATIONS. Stepwise regression procedures obviously have all the limitations of non-stepwise linear multiple regression procedures. That is, deviations from linearity will reduce the predictability of the criterion from the chosen subset of predictors. Stepwise procedures are, however, considerably more susceptible to sample-specific error than are the regular multiple regression procedures, because of the larger number of decisions made in the stepwise procedure. Since many of these decisions in selecting variables are based on sometimes small differences in values of regression weights or partial correlations, stepwise procedures applied to two different samples from the same population are likely to identify different subsets of predictors as the "best." Therefore, cross-validation of the final regression equation resulting from stepwise procedures is mandatory before firm conclusions can be drawn about the accuracy of prediction resulting from their application.

Use of stepwise regression procedures is further complicated by the fact that incremental, decremental, and mixed procedures do not, in general, arrive at the same choice of variables on the same data. Thus, if the investigator wants to identify the "best" subset of predictors for use in a subsequent prediction problem he is likely to identify one "best" subset from the incremental approach, another "best" subset from the decremental approach, and still a third "best" subset from the mixed approach. While the subsets sometimes overlap, the question of which is "best" still remains unresolved.

Because of these limitations of stepwise regression procedures they should not be used in simple "one-stage" research procedures. The one-stage procedure is where the researcher has a fixed set of predictor variables and simply wants to know how well they predict the criterion and which are the best predictors. In this case, the full multiple regression equation will give the highest R, and the magnitude of the beta weights indicates which predictors are most highly related to the criterion. If the predictor pool does not have to be reduced for a subsequent practical application, stepwise regression procedures are inappropriate since they (1) likely reduce (but cannot increase) predictive accuracy and (2) capitalize heavily on sample-specific error to reduce the cross-sample stability of the results.

Canonical Correlation

Rationale

Canonical correlation is the extension of linear multiple regression to the case of multiple criterion variables. As a result, it is appropriate for the situation in which a set of continuous predictor variables is to be related to a set of continuous criterion variables. When there is only one continuous criterion variable, the multiple correlation coefficient and the canonical correlation coefficient are identical.

Canonical correlation might be used by the industrial-organizational psychologist if he were interested in predicting a multivariate criterion measure, such as job performance measured in terms of number of units produced, number of errors made, and judged quality of the product, from a set of four ability tests. Had the criterion been only a single variable, linear multiple regression would have been sufficient. However, with the multivariate criterion, some way of weighting the criterion must be found in order to combine the three criterion scores into a predictable composite.

The method of canonical correlation accomplishes this by developing the "most predictable criterion" (Hotelling, 1936). In essence, the criterion variables and the predictor variables are weighted simultaneously, by means of two sets of regression weights, to arrive at two variates which correlate as highly as possible with each other. In this way, the weights applied to the criterion variables define a variate, or a weighted linear combination of the criterion variables, which is "most predictable" from a weighted linear composite of the predictor variables. The canonical correlation is the product-moment correlation between the variate of the predictor variables and the variate of the criterion variable, when both variates are derived from beta weights chosen to maximize that correlation.

Since canonical correlation is simply an extension of the rationale of linear multiple regression (or, more precisely, linear multiple regression is a special case of canonical correlation), canonical correlation procedures are least squares procedures. In canonical correlation, however, the quantity minimized is the sum of the squared differences between the predictor variate and the criterion *variate*.

Because each variable in the predictor set and each variable in the criterion set of the canonical equation is multiplied by a usually fractional beta weight to arrive at variate scores, some of the variance of the full set of predictors and some of the criterion variance will not be accounted for by a specific canonical correlation. As a result, there will be some "residual" or remaining predictor and criterion variance left over from any canonical correlation. The procedure, therefore, allows the researcher to derive additional canonical correlations from the residual variance. These additional canonical correlations then represent different ways of weighting the predictors and criterion variables to see if variates of the two sets are related to each other. Usually the researcher is interested in the maximal predictive relationship between two sets of variables; in that case, the first or maximum canonical correlation is appropriate. Frequently, however, second or succeeding canonical correlations are almost as large as the first and represent a better weighting of the criterion for some applied purpose; in that case, assuming that succeeding canonicals are statistically significant, the researcher is justified in using them for practical predictions.

Interpretations

Canonical correlations represent the product-moment correlation between two variates. In interpreting this predictive relationship, it should be kept in mind that the squared canonical correlation represents the proportion of variance of each *variate* that is predictable from the *variate* of the other set. Since each variate is derived from the application of fractional regression weights, as indicated above, the variate does *not* account for all the variance of the variables in a set. Hence, a canonical correlation of .80 derived from the 4×3 problem of predicting job performance from ability test scores does *not* indicate that 64 percent ($.80^2$) of the variance of job performance is predictable from ability test scores. Rather, it means that 64 percent of the variance of a specified *weighted linear combination* of job performance sub-scores is predictable from a *weighted linear combination* of ability tests. Only by considering the proportions of variate variance from *all* possible canonical correlations derivable from the 4×3 prediction problem (the number of these being 3, in this case, or in general, the smaller number of the two sets) can the researcher determine the "redundancy" of the two sets of

variables, or how much variance of one *set* is predictable from the other *set*. Further discussion of this concept can be found in Weiss (1972); procedures for calculating redundancies are outlined by Stewart and Love (1968), and Cooley and Lohnes (1971).

Canonical correlation analysis yields two sets of regression weights—one to be applied to predictor variables and the other to the criterion variables. These regression weights are usually standard regression weights which, when multiplied by standard scores on the appropriate variables of the data set, yield variate scores in standard score form. Since the weights are analogous to standard partial regression weights they can, of course, be compared to each other. Thus, the magnitudes of the regression weights indicate which variables are contributing the most to the variate scores. Both predictor and criterion variates can then be interpreted as being composed primarily of the variables with high regression weights, and in this way the researcher can determine which aspects of the criterion are "most predictable" from a given predictor variable. Canonical variates can also be interpreted in terms of the correlations of the original variables with the variates. A discussion of this approach can be found in Cooley and Lohnes (1971), who also provide computer programs and computational formulas.

Since the distinction between predictors and criteria is arbitrary in canonical correlation, the technique indicates, in general, which aspects of one set of variables are predictable from which parts of the other set. This can assist the researcher in predicting specific *kinds* of criterion performance, as indicated by specific variables in the criterion set which have large regression weights or high variable-variate correlations.

Limitations

Because of its close relationships with linear multiple regression, canonical correlation has essentially the same limitations.

That is, it is appropriate only for data that do not violate the assumption of linearity. Note that not only must all relationships between each predictor and each criterion variable be linear, but also all relationships within the predictor set and within the criterion set must also be linear.

Like linear multiple regression, canonical correlation is a maximization procedure. That is, it tends to capitalize on sample-specific covariation to give results that are artificially inflated due to unique characteristics of the sample. As a result, if canonical correlations are to be used for prediction purposes, the regression weights should be applied to data of a holdout group for cross-validation purposes; the cross-validated canonical correlation is then a more realistic indication of the level of prediction possible for that set of data (see Thorndike, Weiss, & Dawis, 1968, for an example of cross-validating canonical correlations).

Discriminant— and Multiple Discriminant— Function

Rationale

Linear discriminant functions (Tatsuoka, 1970; Cooley & Lohnes, 1971) are designed to predict to a categorical criterion from a continuous set of predictor variables, when relationships among predictor variables are assumed to be linear. When the criterion is dichotomous (i.e., is composed of two categories), linear discriminant function has certain similarities to linear multiple regression. When the criterion is polychotomous (i.e., three or more categories), it is referred to as linear *multiple* discriminant function, and it has certain similarities to canonical correlation (Tatsuoka, 1971).

A typical discriminant function problem in industrial-organizational psychology might be the prediction of job termination from measured job satisfaction, where job satisfaction is measured by a multivariable instrument (e.g., Taylor & Weiss, 1972).

The criterion in this case was dichotomous —whether or not an individual quit a given job; the predictor variables were measured job satisfaction on a number of components of job satisfaction (e.g., satisfaction with pay, supervisor, variety) measured a year prior to obtaining the criterion information.

This problem could be approached by considering the criterion as an artificial dichotomous (or 0, 1) variable, with "staying on the job" given a value of 1, and "quitting" a value of 0. The researcher might then use linear multiple regression to develop a prediction equation for predicting the artificially numeralized criterion from the continuous predictor variables. The regression equation would yield a "predicted score" (or variate score) which would then be correlated with the artificial 0, 1 dichotomy, to assess the accuracy of prediction. But this index of prediction, the multiple correlation coefficient, would not present the data in usable form.

To be of use in a dichotomous prediction situation, the data must tell the researcher how many people who were predicted to "stay" on the job actually "stayed," and how many who were predicted to "quit" the job actually "quit." In general, in the categorical prediction situation, the prediction equation must yield categorical predictions in the same terms as the original criterion.

Discriminant function analysis derives from the logic of multiple regression and canonical correlation to permit categorical predictions for categorical criteria. In essence, each individual's "predicted score," derived from a weighted linear composite of the predictor variables, is similar to that of the variate score in multiple regression. To obtain categorical predictions, the beta weights used to develop the weighted linear composite are applied to the *mean* predictor scores of each of the criterion groups. This procedure yields a weighted linear composite of means for a group, or a group variate score, which is referred to as a "centroid." Each criterion group's centroid is calculated, and they can be plotted on a straight line which can be referred to as the "discriminant." Each individual's discriminant score (variate score) is then calculated and compared to the centroids of the criterion groups. An individual is then classified as a predicted member of that criterion group whose centroid is closest to his discriminant (variate) score.

Predicted classifications, from the above procedure, are related to actual group memberships to obtain a "hit-miss" table. The overall "hit" rate is the proportion of actual members of each criterion group who are predicted, on the basis of the discriminant equation, to be in that criterion group. The discriminant weights are chosen by the mathematical procedure to maximize the number of "hits," or the number of correct classifications.

Interpretations

The beta weights associated with the predictor variables in a linear discriminant function equation are analogous to the standard score regression weights in linear regression. Larger beta weights indicate those variables which differentiate most highly on the categorical criterion. Those variables with the largest discriminant weights will also likely have the largest mean differences (corrected for pooled variance) between criterion groups on the predictor variables; occasional violations occur when two predictor variables are highly intercorrelated with each other, and one predictor with an apparent large mean difference receives a low beta weight.

In multiple discriminant function, that is, a discriminant problem with three or more criterion categories, the analogy is to canonical correlation analysis with arbitrarily coded multivariate criterion variables, where the number of "dummy variables" is the number of categories minus one (Tatsuoka, 1971). Because of this similarity, multiple discriminant function problems yield more than one discriminant equation, with the number of equations (sets of beta weights) equal to the number of criterion categories minus one, or number of predictor variables, whichever is smaller. Thus, with a five-category criterion and ten predictor variables, four discriminant equations would result; with five categories on the criterion and three predictor variables, only two discriminant equations are possible.

In multiple discriminant function, as in canonical correlation, the first set of beta weights represents the discriminant equation with the greatest discriminating power, or the highest hit rate. Successive discriminant functions may or may not be statistically significant. When they are, they represent different ways of weighting the predictor variables to classify individuals on the criterion. In some cases, the researcher may be interested in these successive discriminant functions since, while not providing as high a degree of prediction as the first, they may represent a predictor weighting approach which has more practical or theoretical utility. Since successive discriminants are independent of each other, use of two or more significant discriminants in combination can increase accuracy of prediction over what would be possible using only one (see Rulon, Tiedeman, Tatsuoka, & Langmuir, 1967).

Interpretations of hit rates resulting from linear discriminant functions should take into account the "base rates" existing in the sample (Meehl & Rosen, 1955). Thus, a discriminant equation which predicts that 80 percent of a group of individuals is likely not to quit a specified job adds little information for prediction purposes if 80 percent of the group did not quit over a specified period of time.

However, base rates such as these should be interpreted differentially for each prediction being made. For example, while the base rate of 80 percent indicates that only 20 percent of the individuals actually left the job, the discriminant equation might differentially predict the criterion categories well beyond the base rate. While the 80 percent total base rate is appropriate for the "total" prediction and the prediction of "stay," the prediction of "leave" has a base rate of 20 percent, since 20 percent of the group actually left the job. The discriminant equation might yield a hit rate of about 80 percent for the "total" prediction, 80 percent for "stay," but its real value would be in its ability to accurately predict "leaving" well beyond the 20 percent base rate. In a specific study concerned with this problem (Taylor & Weiss, 1972), the hit rate for the discriminant function prediction of "leave" was 67 percent compared to a 20 percent base rate, while both other predictions were close to the base rates of 80 percent. By examination of the *differential* base rates, the real value of the discriminant equation was illustrated.

Limitations

Since the logic and mathematics of discriminant function and multiple discriminant function are closely related to that of linear multiple regression and canonical correlation, they suffer from many of the same problems. That is, deviations of relationships among predictors from linearity will reduce the accuracy of predictions. Discriminant equations are also highly susceptible to sample-specific covariation, since it is a maximization procedure. Therefore, it is very important that discriminant equations be cross-validated on a hold-out sample to determine the predictive efficiency of the equations when the sample-specific covariation of the development group is eliminated.

Curvilinear Multiple Regression

Rationale

Curvilinear multiple regression methods are designed for the prediction problem with a continuous criterion variable and two or more continuous predictor variables. The technique differs from linear multiple regression in that a linear or straight-line

function is not assumed to exist between every predictor variable and the criterion variable. Rather, curvilinear multiple regression techniques require that the researcher determine the form of the relationship between a predictor and the criterion, or that he assume that relationship to be of a specified nonlinear form.

While a linear relationship is reflected in the fact that the increase (or decrease) in the criterion score is proportional to increases in predictor scores throughout the range of scores, a curvilinear relationship occurs where the same increase in predictor score is related to different amounts of increase in the criterion. That is, the relationship between predictor and criterion differs at different points in the predictor distribution. The figures below illustrate (a) a linear relationship, (b) one common type of curvilinear relationship, and (c) and (d) two other forms of curvilinear relationships:

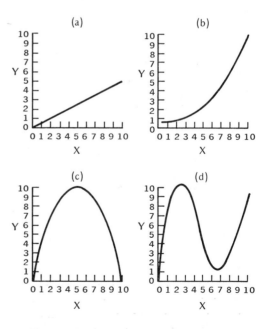

In figure (a), every increase in *x*, from score values of 0 to 9, is accompanied by an equal increase in *y*. In figure (b) increases in *x* from values of 0 to 3 are accompanied by relatively small increases in y; however, at about $x = 4$ the increase in y associated with increases in x begins to become larger until at $x = 7$ through $x = 9$, increases in x are accompanied by very large increases in y. Figure (c) shows increases in y associated with increases in x for values of x from about 0 through 4, but *decreases* in y with increasing values of x are evident for $x = 6$ through 9. In figure (d), each unit increase on x from $x = 0$ through 2 and 7 through 9 is accompanied by an increase in y while values of x from 3 to 6 are accompanied by decreases in y.

There are an endless variety of curvilinear relationships possible between two variables. To use curvilinear multiple regression techniques, the researcher must identify the type of curve involved in each bivariate predictor-criterion relationship by one of three methods: (1) estimate the type of curve involved; (2) use procedures for curve fitting, which are available on most scientific computers; or (3) use the method of orthogonal variance components. Once the type of curve is identified, an equation describing the curve is written. The equation for the linear relationship in (a) is $y = bx$, or each value of y is proportional (by a constant b) to each value of x. The equation describing (b) is $y = bx^2$, or each value of y is equal to the *square* of x times some constant. In similar fashion, the equation describing (c) is $y = bx + cx^2$ and that for (d) $y = bx + cx^2 + dx^3$.

Given the form of the relationship between each predictor and the criterion, the multiple curvilinear regression equation combines all predictor variables into one large equation and solves for the regression weights (Ezekiel & Fox, 1965; Cooley & Lohnes, 1971, pp. 76–94). The procedure is similar to that in linear multiple regression, with the exception that there is likely to be more than one regression weight for each predictor variable. However, the procedure derives a set of regression weights for all predictor variables designed to maximize the product-moment (linear) correlation between the continuous criterion score and the weighted composite of the predictor variables. It should be noted, however, that the weighted composite includes variables which are weighted to reflect their curvilinear relationships with the criterion variable. The linear multiple regression equation is of the form:

$$y = b_1 x_2 + b_2 x_2 + b_3 x_3$$

Where curvilinear relationships are found, the equation would look like:

$$y = f_1(x_1) + f_2(x_2) + f_3(x_3)$$

where f represents some curvilinear relationship, such as,

$$f_1 = b_1 x_1 + b_2 x_1{}^2$$
$$f_2 = c_1 x_2{}^2 + c_2 x_2{}^3$$
$$f_3 = d_1 x_3 + d_2 x_3{}^3 + d_3\left(\frac{1}{x_3}\right)$$

so that the total curvilinear regression equation for the three variables would be:

$$y = b_1 x_1 + b_2 x_1{}^2 + c_1 x_2{}^2 + c_2 x_2{}^3$$
$$+ d_1 x_3 + d_2 x_3{}^3 + d_3\left(\frac{1}{x_3}\right)$$

Rather than having only three regression weights for three predictor variables, as in the linear equation, the above curvilinear equation has seven weights:

two for variable x_1 (b_1 & b_2), two for x_2 (c_1 & c_2), and three for x_3 (i.e., d_1, d_2, d_3).

Interpretations

The results of fitting curvilinear multiple regression equations can be interpreted in a similar fashion to those of linear multiple regression. The correlation of observed and predicted scores still represents the maximum relationship possible between the weighted composite and the criterion variable; it is a least squares solution which minimizes the sum of squared differences between the criterion variable and the predictor variate. The essential difference is that the variate derived from the predictor variables is designed to take into account the curvilinear relationships known to exist between predictors and the criterion. All other interpretations of linear multiple regression equations apply to the curvilinear equations.

Limitations

Curvilinear multiple regression equations will, of course, give better accuracy of prediction than linear multiple regression if there are in fact nonlinear relationships between predictors and the criterion. While many curvilinear relationships are "true" curvilinear relationships, that is, they reflect a stable nonlinear relationship between predictor and criterion, curvilinear relationships tend to be somewhat unstable from sample to sample from the same population. Thus, the form of a specific nonlinear relationship might vary slightly from sample to sample, as measured by the same two variables, leading to instability of curvilinear multiple regression equations. Because this instability leads to predictive "shrinkage" on cross-validation, it is essential that curvilinear regression equations be cross-validated on a hold out group.

Reciprocal Averages Prediction

Rationale

The method of reciprocal averages prediction (Weiss, 1963; Weiss & Dawis, 1968) is designed for use with a continuous criterion variable and can intermix either continuous or categorical (dichotomous or polychotomous) predictors. This method does not require the user to make any assumptions about the specific nature of predictor-criterion relationships, nor does it require that the form of the predictor-criterion relationships be known in advance,

as do curvilinear regression techniques. Rather, reciprocal averages prediction fits a prediction equation to whatever predictor-criterion relationships exist, and the resulting weights reflect the form of those relationships.

In the first step of the procedure, if there are continuous predictor variables, all continuous predictors are divided into categories. This division can be made so that there are approximately equal numbers of subjects in each category of the predictor (preferably a minimum of twenty-five or thirty subjects in a category). Categories can also be developed on the basis of relevant theory or other characteristics of the predictor distribution. No special procedure is followed for categorical variables, unless the number of subjects in a category is very small; it then would be appropriate to combine that category with a logically related category.

Following the division of all predictor variables into categories, the mean score on the criterion is obtained for all individuals in each category of each predictor. Thus, if there were five predictors with six categories each, there would be thirty mean criterion scores. One mean criterion score represents the average criterion score for all individuals whose predictor score occurs in a given predictor score category. Each individual's criterion score is used once for each predictor variable in the computation of mean criterion scores.

Once all mean criterion scores are available, they are listed in descending order of magnitude. At this point the researcher must decide what range of integer weights he wishes to apply to predictor variables to obtain variate scores. While using the mean criterion scores themselves as weights will give highest predictive accuracy, little accuracy is lost by using integer weights, and application of the prediction equation is simplified. The usual range of weights chosen (i.e., the range of scores to be applied to each predictor variable in computing a variate score) is from five to nine. Assuming that seven weights were to be assigned, the distribution of mean criterion scores is divided into seven approximately equal sections. These sections are then assigned weights from one to seven, giving the lowest weight to the section containing the lowest means. In this way, integer weights corresponding roughly to the magnitude of the mean criterion scores are available for use in the prediction equation.

The integer weights thus derived are then associated with the predictor categories from which each mean criterion score was derived. This yields an integer weight for each category of each predictor. An individual's predicted score or variate score is determined by summing the integer weights for those categories of the predictors that contain his predictor scores. The variate score thus obtained is then correlated with the continuous criterion score, using the Pearson product-moment correlation, to obtain an index of predictive accuracy.

Interpretations

The correlation of the variate scores which is derived from the reciprocal averages prediction equation and the criterion scores is analogous to the multiple correlation coefficient from multiple regression procedures. It represents the degree to which criterion scores can be predicted from the weighted linear composite, and its square can be interpreted as the proportion of variance in the criterion variable predictable from the predictor variate. However, it should be noted that there are important differences in the nature of the reciprocal averages predictor variate and the regression variate. First, in reciprocal averages prediction all continuous predictors are divided into categories, thus reducing the effects on total variate scores of extreme predictor scores. Second, and more important, the reciprocal averages procedure, yielding different weights for different levels of a continuous predictor, can fit a curvilinear relationship between predictor and criterion while the regression methods require the

form of that relationship to be known in advance.

The integer weights of the reciprocal averages prediction technique, being roughly proportional to the mean criterion scores, reflect the form of predictor-criterion relationships. A set of integer weights, for a given predictor, of the form 1, 3, 5, 7, 5, 3, 1, would indicate a predictor-criterion relationship resembling an inverted-U; weights of 8, 6, 4, 1, 3, 5, 7 reflect an approximate U-shaped relationship. If the predictor-criterion relationship were linear and positive, the resulting integer weights would approximate a 1, 2, 3, 4, 5, 6 relationship, while no predictor-criterion relationship would appear as 4, 4, 4, 4, 4, 4. Computer programs for the method also provide the user with predictor-criterion relationships described by product-moment correlations, eta coefficients, and tests for curvilinearity of each bivariate relationship.

Limitations

The technique has no mathematical rationale and no generality to other prediction models. Because the weights are derived taking into account bivariate relationships as they appear in a given group of subjects, there is a tendency to capitalize somewhat on artifactual relationships specific to a given sample of subjects. This tendency is counteracted to some extent, however, by the categorizing process for continuous predictors which would tend to lower the influence of random deviations in predictor scores, except for those individuals near the category boundaries.

To the extent that this method is not an explicit maximization procedure it is somewhat less susceptible to shrinkage on cross-validation than those techniques that do maximize or minimize a mathematical criterion. The method is also relatively easy to compute with only the assistance of a calculating machine, and offers statistical tests of both bivariate relationships and the significance of the correlation of actual and predicted scores.

Configural Methods

Rationale

All methods of prediction considered thus far are based on the additive model. In that model, a weighted linear composite or variate score is derived by adding an individual's weighted score on one variable to his weighted scores on other variables. A major limitation of that procedure is that a given total score on the variate may be obtained in a variety of ways. If total variate scores are considered as predictor "categories," then it is possible for two individuals to be in the same "category" as the result of different configurations of predictor variables, defined by different profiles of predictor scores.

Configural prediction approaches reject the additive model in favor of an interactive model. In the configural approaches to prediction, an individual falls into a predictor "category" *only* on the basis of the same set of observations as every other individual in that category.

The interactive model of configural prediction can be simply illustrated by considering two dichotomous predictors, for example, sex and having high or low scores on a typing test, with a dichotomous criterion, for example, satisfactory or unsatisfactory job performance. Tabulating the relationship between one predictor (sex), and job performance, might yield the following results:

PREDICTOR 1		JOB PERFORMANCE		
		Sy	Usy	N
SEX	M	50	50	100
	F	50	50	100
	N	100	100	200

Thus, for 200 employees, 100 of whom are male and 100 female, it is found that 50 of each are satisfactory (*Sy*) employees and 50 are unsatisfactory (*Usy*). Tabulation of the second predictor (test performance) for the same 200 employees, yields the same result, as follows:

PREDICTOR 2		JOB PERFORMANCE		
		Sy	Usy	N
TEST PER- FORMANCE	High	50	50	100
	Low	50	50	100
	N	100	100	200

Since an equal number of those who are high on the predictor test and those who are low on it are satisfactory or unsatisfactory employees, no differential prediction of the criterion is possible from test performance, or from sex. Moreover, since neither predictor separately predicts the criterion, treating them in linear combination cannot increase predictability.

Treating the predictors as configurations, or interactively, can in some cases increase predictability. The configural approach, with two predictors, classifies an individual into a predictor category based on *both* predictor variables treated simultaneously. Tabulation of the above data for configural prediction might be as follows:

PREDICTOR 1		PREDICTOR 2 TEST PERFORMANCE		
		High	Low	N
SEX	Male	50 Sy 0 Usy	0 Sy 50 Usy	100
	Female	0 Sy 50 Usy	50 Sy 0 Usy	100
	N	100	100	200

Tabulating the data in the following way then shows the relationship that exists:

PREDICTOR CONFIGURATION	JOB PERFORMANCE		
	Sy	Usy	
1. Female low or male high	100	0	100
2. Female high or male low	0	100	100
N	100	100	200

Thus, by considering the predictors in interaction or configuration, prediction of the criterion is perfect since all people in predictor configuration 1 (female low or male high) are observed to be satisfactory workers, while those in either of the other two combinations of predictor categories are unsatisfactory.

Interpretations

Configural methods of prediction from two dichotomous variables to a dichotomous criterion were first developed by Meehl (1950). McQuitty (1957b) extended the development to more than two predictors, showing that while single predictors can have zero validity and second order configurations can have zero validity (i.e., the interaction or cross-classification of predictors taken two at a time), it is possible that higher order configurations (i.e., the intersection of three or more predictors taken at a time) can have high predictive validity (see Dual Pattern Analysis on p. 347).

In interpreting configural predictions of dichotomous criteria, the proportion of individuals in one or the other criterion category is of interest. Thus, differential prediction of the criterion is possible if the proportions in a criterion category differ for different predictor configurations. In the above example, a proportion of 1.00 (or 100 percent) of those in predictor configuration 1 were predicted to be satisfactory employees, while 0 percent of those in configuration 2 were so predicted.

Lykken (1956) extended the logic of configural prediction to include the single continuous criterion variable. Rather than using the proportion of individuals in a criterion category, this application uses the mean or average criterion score for individuals in a predictor configuration. Thus, if the criterion in the above example was number of units produced, configural predictive accuracy might be indicated if the data showed that those in configuration 1 produced 1,000 units per day while those in

configuration 2 produced only 250 units per day. For the continuous criterion, evidence of significant mean criterion score differences for the predictor configurations is an indication of differential predictability.

Lykken's "actuarial pattern analysis" can also be extended to the case of continuous predictor variables with a continuous criterion variable, simply by dividing the predictor variables into appropriate categories. In this way, both continuous and categorical predictors can be mixed in the same prediction problem.

Limitations

Configural prediction techniques, or actuarial pattern analysis, are simply the extension of the idea of expectancy tables to interactions of predictor variables. As such, the techniques are essentially applications of the methods used by insurance companies. Their basic limitation, then, is the necessity for very large sample sizes in order to obtain stable predictions. More so than linear additive techniques, configural techniques capitalize on chance fluctuations in the development sample; thus, cross-validation is mandatory.

The necessity for large samples becomes greater as the number of predictors and/or predictor categories increases. For example, with eight dichotomous predictor variables, 2^8 or 256 combinations or configurations of predictors are possible. If all predictors were completely unrelated and it was desired to have thirty individuals per cell to achieve minimally stable predictions, a development group of 7,680 individuals would be minimal. To the extent that predictors are related to each other (correlated) a much larger group would be required.

A related problem of configural prediction is the frequent appearance of "empty cells" in a development group that is not very large. An "empty cell" is a case where no individuals in the development group exhibit a specified combination of predictor characteristics; hence, no criterion proportion or mean criterion score is available. If, on applying the configural prediction system to a cross-validation group or a new sample of individuals for whom predictions are required, one or more individuals exhibit that particular combination of predictor characteristics, it is impossible to make a differential prediction of the criterion score for those individuals.

Configural prediction techniques, therefore, are best used when there are a small number of predictors which are dividable or divided into a small number of categories, for a large group of subjects. In this situation, they frequently improve on predictability beyond the linear additive techniques. As the ratio of subjects to number of predictor-category interactions decreases, however, the predictions become more unstable to the point where linear additive techniques hold up better on cross-validation. Configural techniques are more appropriate, however, when typological theory is more relevant to prediction than dimensional theory; that is, when it can be assumed that certain "types" of people will exhibit certain criterion scores rather than only those with a given score on a weighted linear composite.

Multiple Cutoff Methods

Rationale

The multiple cutoff method, sometimes referred to as the method of "successive hurdles," is one of several prediction methods (including configural methods, weighted application blank methods, and reciprocal averages prediction) which are noncompensatory. Compensatory prediction methods are those in which an extremely high score on one predictor variable can compensate for a low score on another; all regression-based prediction methods are compensatory since scores on the weighted linear composite are derived by multiplying predictor weights by scores on the predictors. In the noncompensatory models, variate scores, where they are used, may be additive, but the components of the variate scores representing each predictor are not a multiplicative function of the original predictor scores. Thus, extremely high scores on one predictor cannot compensate for low scores on another predictor.

Multiple cutoff methods are designed to predict to a dichotomous criterion from a set of initially continuous variables; the predictor set may also include some categorical predictors. Proponents of the method (e.g., Dvorak, 1956) suggest that the method does not assume linear relationships between each predictor and the criterion variable. But, since the method uses a dichotomized criterion variable, the assumption of linearity or nonlinearity is irrelevant.

In developing a multiple cutoff equation, the researcher first examines the relationship between each predictor and the criterion to identify statistically significant predictor-criterion relationships. The index of relationship used at this stage should be appropriate to the form of the data (e.g., phi coefficient for dichotomous predictor and dichotomous criterion; point biserial correlation for continuous predictor and dichotomous criterion). Next, from the bivariate relationships calculated at the first stage, a subset of predictors is chosen which are significantly related to the criterion. Third, for each significant predictor variable, the relationship between the continuous predictor and the dichotomous criterion is examined to obtain a cutoff score on the predictor which maximizes the number of correct predictions on the criterion. This is accomplished by plotting the continuous predictor score on the horizontal axis and the dichotomous criterion on the vertical axis of a two-dimensional plot (e.g., Guion, 1965, p. 151). The number of "successful" and "unsuccessful" individuals at each predictor score is then plotted, and a vertical line is shifted along the horizontal axis until a point is located that maximizes the number of "hits" (i.e., correct predictions). The cutting score is then set at that point.

The process of setting the cutting score is repeated separately for each predictor variable. The result is a set of cutting scores —one for each predictor variable—each of which is determined separately to maximally classify individuals on the criterion dichotomy.

Interpretations

Applications of multiple cutoff methods require that any individual's predictor scores equal or exceed the minimum cutoff scores on *all* relevant predictors before he can be predicted to be a member of the criterion group. If a given prediction problem identifies six significant predictors, with six different minimum cutoff scores, an individual whose scores on five of the predictors, but not the sixth, exceed the minimum scores is predicted *not* to be a member of the "successful" criterion group. The method bears a similarity to configural methods in the sense that an individual becomes a member of a given predictor category (someone who "passes" all the predictor cutoffs) only by exhibiting exactly the same kinds of predictor behaviors as all others in that category. The method is, on the other hand, similar to regression methods to the extent that "predicted" scores from each predictor are additive rather than treated interactively as in configural methods. It differs from multiple regression, however, in that the "predicted score" across all predictors must be equal to a given number (the number of predictors, using 0, 1 for individual predictor scores) in order for an individual to be predicted to be a member of the criterion group.

When data on the predictor variables are not available at the same point in time, the multiple cutoff method becomes the method of successive hurdles. In this application of multiple cutoffs, the researcher identifies from the subset of significant predictor variables that predictor which has the highest hit rate for the criterion. Data for a group of individuals for whom predictions are to be made are then obtained only on that predictor variable. Those individuals who obtain the minimum score or above are identified. For those individuals, data are then obtained on the second predictor variable, which had been selected to be the one predictor out of the remaining pool which had the highest hit rate. The procedure is repeated for each succeeding predictor, at each stage eliminating those individuals whose score on *any* predictor is below the cutoff score for that predictor. The result is a group of individuals who meet all minimum cutting scores (i.e., have "jumped all the hurdles"), but time and money are saved in some cases because it is necessary to obtain all predictor data on only a small proportion of the initial pool of subjects.

Limitations

Multiple cutoff methods are limited primarily to the case of continuous predictor variables and a dichotomous criterion. Where the criterion is initially continuous, but the researcher is willing to dichotomize it, the procedure is applicable, but varying degrees of loss of information occur from the dichotomization procedure on the criterion, unless the criterion is clearly distributed bimodally.

The major limitation of the method is that it tends to ignore errors of measurement in the predictor variables by specifying exact cutoff points on the predictor variable distribution. This is evident by the case of a cutoff score of 100 applied to the individual who gets a score of 99 and does not qualify, but on repeated measurement might have gotten a score of 103 and would have qualified. This deficiency is somewhat alleviated by considering predictor scores to include errors of measurement, and using the observed score plus the error of measurement to make the prediction (e.g., U.S. Department of Labor, 1970). However, this is somewhat of a pseudosolution since it simply shifts the level of the arbitrary decision to the newly defined upper limit of the observed score.

As with all other methods that maximize

or minimize some function (in this case, the hit rate for each predictor variable taken separately), multiple cutoff methods tend to capitalize on specific relationships in a sample. Since the maximization procedure occurs separately for each predictor variable, and is used to set somewhat arbitrary cutoff scores, results of multiple cutoff procedures are likely to be more susceptible to shrinkage or mis-prediction on cross-validation. It is, therefore, important that the cutoff scores be applied to a new group to determine the accuracy of prediction separately for each predictor and for the entire set of predictors in combination.

While the method yields a high degree of accuracy in terms of identifying "successful" individuals who are in fact successful, it does so at the expense of identifying a large number of false negatives, that is, predicting a large proportion of people to be "unsuccessful" who might otherwise be "successful." It is, therefore, most appropriate when there is a large number of individuals for whom predictions are to be made, and where a false negative is not a serious occurrence. In addition, results of multiple cutoff predictions should be considered in relation to total base rates and differential base rates which occur in the sample for which predictions are being made.

Weighted Application Blank Methods

Rationale

Weighted application blank types of prediction techniques (England, 1971) are designed for use with dichotomous or dichotomized criterion variables and polychotomous predictor variables. These methods do not require an assumption of linear relationships between the predictors and the criterion. They can, of course, be used with continuous predictor variables if the continuous predictors are divided into categories. Because they require all predictors to be categorical or categorized, these methods are partially noncompensatory and, therefore,

have the same advantages and disadvantages as the multiple cutoff and configural prediction methods.

The first step in applying the method is to determine separately for each category of each predictor variable the percent (or proportion) of each criterion group that falls in each category. For example, if the predictor were marital status and the criterion groups were "quits" and "remains" on a given job, the following results might be obtained:

PREDICTOR 1	CRITERION GROUP	
Marital Status	Quit	Remained
Single	50%	20%
Married	20%	40%
Divorced	20%	20%
Widowed	10%	20%
	100%	100%

The next step is to determine the percent differences in each category of each predictor variable. For the above data, percent differences are 50% — 20% or 30% for the "single" category, —20% for "married," 0% for "divorced," and —10% for "widowed." Third, the percent differences are converted to integer weights, simply for the sake of convenience in use. Thus, the 30% difference might be given a weight of +3 and the —10% difference a weight of —1. A variety of weighting schemes are possible at this point, but available evidence shows little difference in predictive efficiency as the result of different weighting procedures; the integer weights need only be roughly proportional to the differences in percents.

Next, a predicted score or variate score is obtained for each individual using the integer weights assigned to the categories of each predictor variable. This is accomplished by determining which category the individual falls in (e.g., he is "single") and assigning the weight determined for that predictor category (e.g., +3, in the above example). This process is repeated for each predictor variable separately, and the integer weights identified for an individual are algebraically summed to obtain his variate score.

The variate scores obtained in this fashion are then related to the individual's actual status on the criterion. This is accomplished by developing a two-dimensional plot with variate scores on the horizontal axis and criterion classification on the vertical axis. Individuals are plotted in this diagram, using a horizontal line to represent criterion classification. A vertical line is then moved along the variate axis to determine the point at which the number of "hits" is maximized. This line can be so located to maximize either total number of "hits" or to minimize the number of false positives or false negatives (England, 1971, p. 35).

Interpretations

The weighted application blank procedures were developed originally, as the name suggests, to predict relevant industrial criteria from information available on application blanks. They are, however, quite similar in conceptualization to the empirical weighting techniques used to develop scales for such well-known instruments as the Strong Vocational Interest Blanks, the Minnesota Multiphasic Personality Inventory, and the California Psychological Inventory. In the case of these three instruments, however, item responses are used as the predictor variables and group membership of one sort or another as the criterion variable. The variate score in all cases is essentially the same. It is a linear composite (linear because weights on one variable are added to weights on other variables) of weights which represent the degree of difference between criterion groups on the predictor variables. As the variate score becomes larger in positive or negative value (if negative weights are retained in the weighting procedure) the probability increases that the individual is more like one or the other criterion group. A high variate score indicates that the individual is very probably a member of one

criterion group; this probability, however, must be considered in relation to the probability of mis-classification derived from the hit-miss table.

The method can be extended to include configurations of predictor variables as well as single predictor variables (see Sorenson, 1964, for an example). Such configurations represent two or more predictors considered in combination, as in configural analysis. For example, combining sex as a predictor with marital status would yield eight categories: (1) single-male, (2) single-female, (3) married-male, (4) married-female, (5) divorced-male, (6) divorced-female, (7) widowed-male, (8) widowed-female. This "configural" predictor would then be treated as a single eight-category predictor variable and could be used in an equation with other configural (or non-configural) predictors. Higher-order configurations are, of course, possible. However, if configurations are used, larger sample sizes are required.

Weighted application blank methods are advantageous, in comparison to some prediction methods (e.g., discriminant function) in that they are easily computed by hand. In addition, they are likely to be more stable in cross-validation than the regression-based approaches because they do not consider the interactions among predictor variables, thus utilizing less information about the sample. As a result, they are less likely to capitalize on characteristics of the data that are unique to a particular sample. These methods also are advantageous in that they are about the only readily available technique for predicting from categorical predictors to a categorical criterion, with the exception of the configural techniques which require very large samples.

Limitations

Because hit rates are maximized on the predictor score variate, weighted application blank approaches must be cross-validated on an independent sample. Moderately large samples (100 or more subjects in each criterion group) are desirable in order to obtain stable percentages and, therefore, meaningful percentage differences for deriving weights.

An occasional problem that arises is that of empty cells, although the problem is not as serious as in configural techniques. Where empty cells do occur in the development group (i.e., a predictor category with no observations in it for that subject group), no prediction is possible for individuals who do exhibit that characteristic. The problem can be circumvented by combining the empty category with another non-empty one, but such loss of information may decrease predictive accuracy.

Usual applications of these approaches do not include statistical tests in deriving the weights. A more precise weighting procedure would assign weights only if the differences in percentages were both statistically significant and substantial, with the magnitude of the weights reflecting the magnitude of the difference. This approach has not generally been followed, and weights are usually assigned on an arbitrary percentage difference basis.

Perhaps the major limitation of these prediction approaches is that they represent simply "blind" empirical prediction, yielding no interpretability concerning which variables are the best predictors of the set. The researcher can simply look at the relative spread of weights for various predictor variables to get a "feel" for which is the best predictor, but proponents of the method have come forth with no relational-type statements or indices to help the user eliminate those variables with low contributions to the variate score. Such lack of interpretability somewhat limits the usefulness of an otherwise utilitarian technique.

Dual Pattern Analysis

Rationale

Dual pattern analysis, as developed by McQuitty (1957b), is designed to predict from a set of polychotomous predictors to a criterion set composed of categorical or polychotomous variables. Although it is designed for use with categorical variables, it can also be applied to categorized variables —variables which are initially continuous, but which are divided into a number of categories.

This method of prediction is a typological method rather than a dimensional one. It is an extension of the configural prediction techniques and actuarial pattern analysis, and bears no similarities to the regression-based techniques. It is, therefore, more useful when the researcher is concerned with predicting from identified types of individuals, defined by a unique configuration or pattern of predictor scores, rather than simply the additive model characteristic of the non-pattern analytic approach.

McQuitty's development of the method begins with analysis of the criterion data. In analyzing that set of data he uses a method based on "agreement analysis," which simply tabulates the number of subjects that have exactly the same pattern of criterion information. For example, if the criterion were three scales measuring job performance and each was trichotomized, all individuals scoring "high" on all three scales would constitute a pattern. He extends the analysis further to classify all unique lower order configurations (e.g., sets of two scales) that are not determined by higher order configurations. Each unique configuration in the criterion data is identified and those that include some minimum number of subjects are retained for analysis.

The next step in applying the method is to identify predictor variables associated with the criterion types. This is done by analyzing each predictor separately as the data relate to individuals in the criterion category, and retaining those predictors which are associated with different distributions of criterion types. This procedure is repeated for all predictors, and the subset of predictors which are found to differentially relate to criterion categories is identified. These tentative subsets of predictors are then compared across all criterion category types, and those predictors with similar patterns across criterion types are eliminated, on the assumption that they are not differentially predictable. The final step of this method is to determine accuracy of prediction, preferably on a cross-validation sample, by predicting an individual's criterion category from his configuration of responses on the predictors.

Interpretations

The method of dual pattern analysis relates predictor types of behavior to criterion types of behavior. As such, it implies that individuals with a specific configuration or pattern of responses on the predictor set have a specified probability of exhibiting a specified pattern of responses on the criterion. The method is designed to take into account the interactions among variables that exist in the data, in contrast to the dimensional methods of prediction that do not consider these interactions. It is, therefore, a non-compensatory method of prediction in which individuals can obtain a given "predicted score" (or category configuration, in the case of this method) only by obtaining a unique configuration of responses on the predictor subset. Because the method categorizes continuous data, extremely high scores on one predictor cannot compensate for very low scores on another.

This method makes categorical assignments of subjects. Therefore, validity of the predictions should be evaluated in terms of "hit rates," as with other methods of predicting categorical criteria. Interpretation of the "hit rates," therefore, should take into account the base rates existing in the sample if no predictions were made at all.

Limitations

The major limitation of this method is that common to other pattern-analytic methods—namely, that in order to predict for all possible new individuals, the method requires extremely large samples, even when the number of predictors and criterion variables is small. In applications of his method, McQuitty eliminates non-frequently occurring patterns in the analysis. By this approach, he is essentially unable to make predictions for persons having nonstandard or atypical patterns of either predictors or criteria. Since patterns are examined on both the predictor and criterion sets in this method, the number of subjects for whom predictions can be made will likely be considerably smaller than for other configural methods. These "empty" cells on either predictors or the criterion set can be filled only by using extremely large numbers of subjects. Even with large numbers, however, some patterns may not appear, while others might simply be the result of unreliable observations on predictors and/or criterion variables. The method, therefore, is best applied to (1) very large groups of subjects, in relation to the number of variables, with (2) highly reliable variables in both the predictor and criterion sets and (3) cross-validated predictions derived from an independent sample.

MULTIVARIATE COVARIATION ANALYSIS

Observations or measurements on a number of individuals, using a number of different variables, is the beginning step in multivariate covariation analysis. The objectives of the covariation analysis determine the second step.

Covariation analysis may be done in order to obtain new independent or uncorrelated variables from a set of variables for use in certain prediction techniques. These prediction methods, all based on the linear regression model, are those in which maximal levels of prediction are possible when all predictors are uncorrelated with (independent of) each other (see Guilford, 1965, p. 407). These methods include linear multiple regression, discriminant function and canonical correlation.

Secondly, multivariate covariation procedures can be used to reduce the number of variables in a given set to a smaller number of variables, or to identify important "underlying" variables in a larger set. In this use of covariation analysis, the number of new variables, or "factors," underlying a set of variables is always smaller than the number in the original set. The reduced number of variables usually represents a major portion of the variance of the original variables, and scores on the original variables are used to obtain scores on the new variables.

A third important use of covariation analysis is to group variables into subsets. This application is that of classification; multivariate covariation analysis is used to develop a taxonomy of the variables. The objective is to determine which variables "go with" other variables or which variables fall into groups with other variables.

Multivariate covariation analysis is also used for formulating hypotheses about the structure of a domain. For example, the industrial psychologist might wish to develop hypotheses about the important components underlying performance on a certain job. Likewise, these techniques might be used to

support or refute specific hypotheses about structure. In this case, covariation analysis would be concerned with whether given variables group themselves as hypothesized, or whether certain underlying variables appear in a larger set of variables, in accordance with previous expectations.

Methods Available for Multivariate Covariation Analysis

Techniques of multivariate covariation analysis fall into three general categories, depending on the purposes of the analysis: factor analysis, components analysis, and cluster analysis. Appropriate techniques are diagrammed in Figure 2.

Factor Analysis

Methods of common variance analysis are those usually referred to as factor analysis techniques. These methods do not use all the covariation between variables; rather, they analyze only that portion of the total variability of each variable which is common

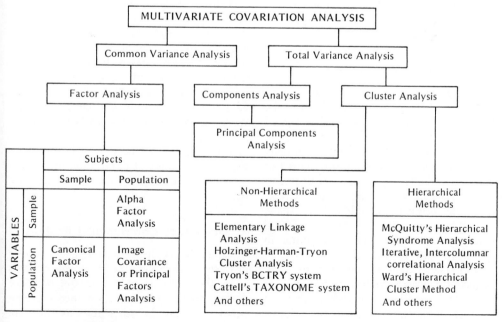

Figure 2.   Classification of methods for multivariate covariation analysis.

with, or related to, the variability of the other variables to be analyzed. If some portion of the variability of a variable is uncorrelated with all other variables to be analyzed at that time, techniques of factor analysis ignore that unique variance.

Factor analysis is the appropriate method for multivariate covariation analysis if the objective is to study the *structure* of a set of variables or to generate or refute hypotheses about structure. In using factor analysis, the investigator is concerned with determining whether there are "underlying" variables (or factors) which account for the observed covariation among variables. Factor analysis may also be used to reduce a larger set of variables to a smaller set which accounts for a major portion of the observed covariation among the original variables.

The distinguishing characteristic of a factor analysis is that the variance of each variable is broken up into its "underlying" sources and distributed among a new set of variables, which are the factors. By fractionating variables in this manner, factor analysis helps the researcher understand the structure of the original variables in terms of the underlying factors, or helps describe the structure of the factors in terms of parts of the original variables.

Components Analysis

Components analysis differs from factor analysis in that it is concerned with the structure of the *total* variance of the original variables, rather than only their common variance. Components analysis is usually done in order to transform an original set of correlated variables into a new set of uncorrelated variables, which are linear composites of the original variables. These new, uncorrelated, variables can then be used in the regression-based prediction techniques in order to increase predictability.

Components analysis can also be used, like factor analysis, to reduce an initial set of variables to a smaller subset, which accounts for much of the covariation in the original

set, or to study the structure of a set of variables in terms of underlying factors or sources of covariation. However, in these uses of components analysis, the researcher must be aware that he is likely analyzing some unreliable variance of his variables and results of the components analysis are likely to capitalize on that unreliability. In general, components analysis should not be used for most research problems.

Cluster Analysis

Techniques of cluster analysis differ from those of components analysis in one important way, although both techniques analyze the total variance of a variable. The primary distinction is in their treatment of that total variance: in components analysis (and in factor analysis, using only common variance) the variance of each variable is fractionated or broken up and distributed among the underlying factors; in the majority of cluster analysis techniques, the variance of a variable is usually treated as a unit, and variables are grouped together or assigned to a subgroup, as whole variables.

Cluster analysis, therefore, is the appropriate technique to be used when the objective is to *classify* variables (or objects) in relationship to each other. These methods serve best to assist researchers in developing taxonomies or classification schemes to be used for theoretical or applied purposes. Cluster analysis should also be used for covariation analysis, in place of factor or components analysis, when characteristics of the data violate the assumptions of factor analysis, or if the index of covariation to be used is not appropriate for the factor analytic model.

Factor (and Components) Analysis

The primary distinguishing characteristic of factor analysis versus components analysis is in their use of only common variance (factor analysis) or total variance (components analysis). In other respects they are quite similar. Both techniques are concerned with fractionating the variance of a variable (total or common variance) and distributing it among a new set of variates, or "factors." Each factor (or component, in the case of components analysis) can be considered as an "underlying" variable which represents the common parts of those variables loading highly on (correlating with) the factor. Components analysis differs from factor analysis in that frequently many of the components are defined by the unique variance of a single variable, rather than variance common to two or more variables.

In most uses of factor analysis, the number of new variates (i.e., factors) is substantially less than the total number of original variables, thus permitting the researcher to describe a large portion of the common or total variance of the original variables by a smaller number of variates. In this way, the researcher achieves an economy of description or some understanding of the "basic" factors or sources of covariation underlying a set of variables. In addition, factor analysis and components analysis can help the investigator determine for a given variable how its variance "breaks up" and distributes itself in relation to other variables. Also, the researcher can differentiate the less complex variables—those that remain unitary even in the presence of other variables—from the more complex variables which essentially decompose themselves into variance components associated with other variables in the matrix.

Decisions in Factor Analysis

There are a number of ways of doing a factor analysis (see Weiss, 1970, 1971; Rummel, 1970; Harman, 1967). The decisions made from the choices available are likely to importantly affect the interpretation of the obtained results. It is important, therefore, that the researcher carefully review his rationale for each decision, record it carefully, and interpret the results in accordance with those decisions.

ARE THE DATA WORTH FACTOR-ANALYZING? The first step in doing a factor analysis is the computation of the matrix of intercorrelations among the variables. Most frequently, the researcher simply assumes that the intercorrelation matrix reflects something other than the intercorrelations of random data. That is, he assumes that the deviations of his correlations from zero (no relationship) are significant or meaningful, or, in other words, that his data are worth factor-analyzing. Usually this decision is made simply on the basis of the fact that the results of the factor analysis are "meaningful" or interpretable, since the factor analysis yields factors which "make sense."

This question was recently confronted by Armstrong and Soelberg (1968) who factor-analyzed the intercorrelations of *random* data and found what appeared to be "meaningful" factors. Their results imply that the appearance of meaningfulness in the results of a factor analysis has no implication for the worth of the original data.

To avoid factor-analyzing worthless (random, or nonsignificant) data, the researcher should first test his intercorrelation matrix for statistical significance and proceed to factor analysis *only if* he can conclude that his data represent significant deviations from a random intercorrelation matrix. Correlation matrices can be tested for statistical significance using Bartlett's test (Weiss, 1970) which determines whether a given correlation matrix represents significant deviation from an essentially random correlation matrix. The formula for Bartlett's test is easily adaptable to computer analysis; Bartlett's test should, therefore, be used on all intercorrelation matrices prior to factor analysis, with factor analysis to follow only when the correlation matrix is statistically significant at some appropriate level.

PORTION OF VARIANCE AND METHOD OF EXTRACTION. Whether the researcher wishes to analyze the total variance of his variables (components analysis) or only common variance (factor analysis) will determine the range of choices for methods of extraction.

Total variance. Components analysis utilizes the raw intercorrelation matrix of the variables. This matrix has values other than zero in some of the off-diagonal elements, but always has values of 1.0 in the principal diagonal, representing the correlation of a variable with itself. When total variance is to be analyzed, the most commonly used method is the method of principal components.

The method of principal components is designed to rescale the total variance of a set of variables into a new set of variates (factors) which account for all the variance in the original variables. The primary aim of principal components analysis is to develop from a set of variables a new set of variates, equal in number to the original set, which are uncorrelated with each other. The new variates can then be used in prediction, or for other purposes for which uncorrelated variates are desirable. On occasion, principal components analysis may also be used to identify a smaller number of variates that account for a major portion of the total variance of the original variables. This use of components analysis requires a further decision, discussed below under "number of factors."

Common variance. Most covariation analyses fall under the class of "factor analysis" problems in that they are concerned with the analysis of common variance of a set of variables. Factor analysis does not consider the unique portion of the variance of a variable, which is that portion of the variance uncorrelated with other variables, but is concerned only with discovering underlying variates responsible for the common parts of a set of variables.

Techniques of factor analysis deal with some form of a *reduced* correlation matrix. Such a matrix has something other than 1.0 in the principal diagonal, with the diagonal value representing some estimate of the amount of variance that variable has in common with the other variables in the matrix. In a reduced correlation matrix the diagonal element is usually referred to as the *"estimated communality."*

Communality estimates are generally of three types: (1) reliability estimates, (2) highest correlation of a variable with others, and (3) the squared multiple correlation. Reliability estimates are generally the highest of the three, since a reliability coefficient usually includes some specific reliable variance in addition to the common (reliable) variance of the variable. Highest correlation of a variable with other variables in the matrix is based on the assumption that a variable cannot correlate higher with any other variable than its reliability, and it usually correlates lower. The "highest correlation" estimate, therefore, usually gives a conservative communality estimate lower than that of the reliability coefficient. The most conservative estimate of communality of a variable is the squared multiple correlation of a given variable with all other variables in the matrix. The squared multiple correlation gives the best initial estimate of communality of the three approaches and should be used wherever possible. However, in some cases, it is impossible to calculate the squared multiple correlation. Such would be the case if the correlation matrix were made up of elements derived from different groups of individuals, if the correlations were not all Pearson product-moment correlations, or if the data were completely ipsative (Hicks, 1970). In these cases, it is appropriate to use one of the other initial estimates of communality, but the difference should be kept in mind in determining the "number of factors."

Figure 2 shows the methods of factor analysis available under given assumptions as to whether subjects or variables represent samples or populations. If both subjects and variables are assumed to represent populations (i.e., no attempt is to be made to generalize beyond those variables or that group of subjects), the appropriate method of factor analysis is Principal Factors Analysis, or Image Covariance Analysis. Principal Factor Analysis is a principal axis solution on a reduced correlation matrix, that is, a matrix with estimated communalities (usually squared multiple correlations) in the diagonal. Image Covariance Analysis accomplishes about the same result, but it involves rescaling of the correlation matrix as an initial step. Rescaling involves adjusting the correlation matrix so that the diagonal elements are 1.0, with the off-diagonal elements adjusted accordingly. Such rescaling results in an "image" of the correlation matrix, with variables rescaled in terms of communalities, which is then used in principal components analysis.

If the researcher is concerned with generalizing the results of his factor analysis to the structure of a population of variables, he should select a sample of variables to represent that population. The sample of variables is then measured on a large group of individuals who can be assumed to be a population. Under these circumstances—subjects as a population and a sample of variables—the appropriate method of factor analysis is Kaiser's Alpha Factor Analysis. Like Image Covariance Analysis, Alpha Factor Analysis involves rescaling of a reduced correlation matrix; the matrix is also rescaled in terms of the communalities. However, Alpha Factor Analysis differs in that the initial communalities are not assumed to be exact. Rather, an iterative or repetitive computational process is followed adjusting the original communality estimates until a "true" communality estimate is reached. Once the communality estimates stabilize, the matrix is rescaled and followed by principal components analysis.

The objective of Alpha Factor Analysis is to arrive at a set of factors, derived from the sample of variables, that best represent the factors that exist in the population of variables. Thus, the factors derived from Alpha analysis are said to have maximum "generalizability" to the factors in the total domain of variables. From a sample of variables, then, the researcher can make statements about the underlying factors in the larger set (population) of variables.

Canonical Factor Analysis makes the reverse assumptions of Alpha Factor Analysis. The Canonical method assumes that variables are a population and that subjects represent a sample from that population. The method is designed to yield a set of factor scores for individuals which have maximum predictability, in terms of the canonical correlation of factor scores and scores on the original variables. Canonical Factor Analysis assumes that the communalities in the reduced correlation matrix are exact and rescales the correlation matrix in terms of the uniqueness of the variables, giving higher weights to those variables with low uniqueness. The method requires that the number of factors be known in advance, and it derives, by an iterative procedure, a set of factor loadings which is a "best estimate" of the loadings for that number of factors, for a sample of individuals of that given number. In doing so it gives a set of factor scores which correlate highest with the original variable scores. Canonical Factor Analysis should, therefore, be used where the objective of factor analysis is to obtain measurements on the factors (factor scores) for individuals.

NUMBER OF FACTORS. In extracting factors by means of factor analysis, it is usually possible to extract a number of factors equal to the number of original variables entering into the correlation matrix. Since, however, one objective of factor analysis is to *reduce* the number of variables into a smaller number of dimensions that explain what is common among the original set of variables, there is a need to determine when it is appropriate to stop extracting factors.

For some methods of factor analysis the answer to this question is reasonably clear. If the researcher is using principal components analysis and the objective is to rescale the total variance of all the variables into a new set of uncorrelated variates, the number of new factors is equal to the number of original variables. If principal components analysis is used and the objective is to obtain a minimal set of factors that best accounts for the common variance of the original variables, the "Kaiser criterion" should be used. This specifies that all factors with "eigenvalues" or "factor contributions" (the sum of the squared factor loadings) of 1.00 or greater should be retained. The Kaiser criterion is also appropriate for use in Alpha Factor Analysis.

Canonical Factor Analysis requires that the researcher specify the number of factors in advance. The decision as to the number of factors for this method of factor analysis is usually based on theoretical considerations, or data from previous empirical studies.

In Principal Factors Analysis, or Image Covariance Analysis, the decision rule for the number of factors is less clear. A variety of solutions has been proposed (Weiss, 1971), each based on a different definition of what is an "error" or "residual" factor. The method with the most logical appeal is that proposed by Humphreys and Ilgen (1969), referred to as "parallel analysis." In this method the researcher carries out *two* factor analyses—one with real data and a "parallel analysis" using randomly generated data for a sample of individuals and variables of the same size. The factor contributions derived from the analysis of the random data are compared with those derived from the real data. A factor of the real data is designated as "residual" if its factor contribution is of the same magnitude as that of the random data.

ROTATION. *Why rotate?* Factors resulting from principal components or principal factors solutions are usually rotated for one or both of two reasons. The primary reason for rotation is to achieve interpretability of the results. Factors resulting from principal axes analysis (i.e., principal factors or principal components) tend to have little inter-

pretability since the principal axes solutions are mathematical rather than psychological solutions. That is, the principal axes solutions are designed to meet the mathematical criterion of extracting as much as possible of common variance with each successive factor, rather than extracting factors in some way that could be considered intuitively "meaningful."

The difficulty in interpreting principal axes factors results partly from their mathematically determined characteristics. The first factor resulting from principal axes analyses is almost always a general factor, with most variables loading high on it. Succeeding factors are generally artifactually bipolar, with both positive and negative high loadings. These factors are difficult to interpret in a psychological sense since factor interpretation involves making hypotheses concerning the common elements underlying variables which load high on a given factor. Where most or all variables load highly, because of the mathematical characteristics of the extraction method, a differential hypothesis about underlying common elements is most difficult to make.

The second reason for rotation of factor matrices is that rotated solutions are more reliable, replicable, or reproducible than are the unrotated solutions. This derives from the fact that the unrotated solutions are complex mathematical maximization solutions, designed to extract the maximum amount of variance with each factor. Such maximization procedures tend to capitalize on chance characteristics of a given sample and, therefore, are less replicable from one sample to another.

Thus, by rotating his factor solution, the researcher arrives at a solution which gives him interpretable factors—that is, factors that he can "name," which are likely to have both theoretical and practical utility—and, at the same time he arrives at a factor solution which is more likely to appear in another sample of variables and/or subjects from the same population.

How to rotate. If the objective of factor

alysis is to locate variables with reference other variables whose function is to serve "marker" or "reference" variables, the searcher should use Eysenck's (1950) "crierion analysis" as the method of rotation.

this method, one variable is defined as e "criterion" and all other variables are nsidered to be rotated with reference to is criterion, by running one of the rotated es through the criterion variable. This ethod then locates all other variables with erence to the criterion, indicating which rtions of each variable are related to the terion. Criterion analysis is also sometimes own as rotation to "psychological meangfulness."

The more desired general objective of :ation is that of "simple structure." Thurne's simple structure doctrine states that ation should be done in order to achieve scriptive simplicity of the factors, or a most rsimonious description or definition of h factor. According to Thurstone (1947), scriptive simplicity of a factor is achieved en each factor is described by the smallest mber of variables and, at the same time, h variable correlates highly with (loads) the smallest number of factors. When se simultaneous conditions are achieved ., the number of zero factor loadings is ximized), the rotated simple structure trix is of minimal complexity, resulting a parsimonious and interpretable set of tors.

Attempts to operationalize the simple ucture concept have led to two general es of solutions: oblique rotations and hogonal rotations.

Orthogonal factor rotations require that rotated factors retain a 90° angle been them, or that the factors remain unrelated, as are the factors resulting from principal axes solutions. Oblique solus, on the other hand, permit the factors become somewhat correlated with each er in order to arrive at a clearer definition simple structure. Whether a researcher s oblique or orthogonal rotations depends his willingness to deal with complexity.

Orthogonal factors lead to easier interpretations since it is not necessary to take into account the relationships among factors in generating descriptive hypotheses for the factors. Oblique factors require that the intercorrelations among the factors themselves be taken into account in understanding the factor analytic results, as well as the loadings of the variables on the factors. Proponents of the orthogonal approach argue that the simplicity of the factors is in keeping with the scientific doctrine of parsimony; oblique factorists counter that constructs in nature are rarely independent of each other.

Given the decision to use orthogonal or oblique rotations, the researcher is confronted with further choices, since simple structure is a theoretical concept which can be operationalized in a variety of ways. Among the orthogonal solutions two methods have achieved prominence in their attempts to achieve simple structure. Quartimax rotational procedures operationalize simple structure by simplifying the description of each variable (or row) in the factor matrix. Quartimax rotation should, therefore, be used if the researcher is interested in studying the variance composition of his variables, as each variable is distributed among the underlying factors. On the other hand, Varimax rotations yield orthogonal factors which approximate simple structure but do so by simplifying the description of each factor (or column) of the factor matrix. Varimax, therefore, should be used if the objective is to interpret the underlying factors, or to understand the factor composition of the set of variables. Thus, in their operationalization of simple structure, Quartimax will maximize the number of zero loadings for each variable in the matrix (i.e., across the rows of the factor matrix), while Varimax maximizes the number of zero loadings for the factors (i.e., down the columns of the factor matrix).

Among the oblique factor solutions, two closely parallel Varimax and Quartimax, while allowing factors to become correlated. The Quartimin solution is the oblique analogue of Quartimax; it is designed to simplify the description of each variable. The Covarimin solution simplifies the description of each factor and is the oblique analogue of Varimax. Because both these oblique solutions sometimes allow factor axes to become too highly correlated, the Biquartimin solution has been developed which permits the researcher to control the maximum degree of obliqueness, yet optimize a joint function of the Covarimin and Quartimin solutions.

FACTOR SCORES. Beyond simply identifying underlying dimensions of covariation, the researcher using factor analysis sometimes wishes to measure a group of individuals on the factors uncovered in a factor analysis. To do this, he must compute factor scores, which reflect individual differences on the factors.

Factor scores are weighted linear composites or variates which are derived by multiplying an individual's scores on the original variables entered into the factor analysis by a set of weights derived from the factor analysis. This process is repeated separately for weights derived from each of the factors extracted so that each individual receives a new variate score using the weights from each factor.

There are a number of ways to derive variate scores from the results of a factor analysis. Unit weighting is one of the most popular approaches, primarily because of its simplicity. In this approach the researcher defines a "salient" factor loading as one which is at or above a certain level, say .40. All variables which have loadings which can be considered salient are included in the variate score for that factor and those which fall below that level are not included. The variate, or factor, score is obtained simply by adding together the standardized scores for each individual on all variables found to be salient on a given factor. The process is then repeated on each successive factor, usually including a different subset of variables as the salient ones. This process is essentially equivalent to including all variables in the weighted linear composite for each factor, by giving zero weights to those variables which do not load highly on a factor.

A second commonly used method of deriving factor scores is to develop a weighted linear composite for each factor by using the factor loadings as weights. In this approach, each individual's standardized score on each variable is multiplied by the factor loading associated with that variable, on a given factor. The results are cumulated for each factor, across all variables, to arrive at the individual's factor score for that factor. The process is repeated for each succeeding factor, using in each case the loadings on that factor of the full set of variables.

Factor scores can also be derived in another way, using a complete regression solution. In this method, a set of multiple regression weights are developed for each factor, based on the factor loadings and the intercorrelations of the variables which entered into the factor analysis. These regression weights are developed to minimize the errors of prediction in predicting the "true" factor scores from the weighted linear combination based on the regression weights. Actual factor scores are derived in the same way as in the two preceding methods, but the partial regression weights for each factor are used rather than the factor loadings or the 0, 1 weights.

These three methods of developing factor scores do not give equivalent results. Factor scores derived by the regression solution (using an orthogonal matrix) are most nearly orthogonal, or uncorrelated with each other. Factor scores obtained from the unit weighting method tend to be reasonably highly correlated with each other, with the magnitude of the correlation varying as a function of the correlations among the original variables; the factor loading method gives results between the other two methods in terms of the intercorrelations of the obtained factor scores. In terms of the internal consistency reliability of the factor scores derived from the three methods, it appears that regression weighted factor scores are least reliable of the three methods and that the unit weighted scores are the most internally consistent. Thus, the researcher using factor scores must choose the appropriate method in terms of the desired characteristics of the resulting variate scores.

Cluster Analysis

While factor analysis is appropriate for studying the structure of a set of variables in terms of the distribution of each variable's variance across a set of underlying factors, cluster analytic methods are appropriate for categorical placement of variables or objects into subsets. Most cluster analysis approaches consider each variable or object as a unit and group it together with other objects with which it is similar. Clusters resulting from most cluster analysis procedures identify subgroups of objects or variables which are more similar to each other than they are to other variables or objects in the same matrix of interassociations. Thus, while cluster analysis may start with the same matrix of correlations or interassociations as does factor analysis, it frequently yields different results due to its treatment of a variable's variance as an intact unit.

Cluster analysis groups variables or objects by similarity, with the definition of similarity differing for different methods of cluster analysis. Clusters are, therefore, defined as a subset of variables that are more homogeneous with respect to each other than they are to other variables. Homogeneity or similarity is usually statistically defined and, in most cases, based on the idea of minimizing the variance of some similarity index within each cluster. Just as cluster analysis techniques can be used to group objects, variables, or people, extensions of these techniques can be used to group clusters. The grouping of already obtained clusters into "super-clusters" opens the way for the development of a "treelike" structuring of clusters, which may be useful in understanding the similarities among the clusters themselves. An example of the results of an hierarchical cluster analysis is shown in Figure 3.

Clustering methods, therefore, can be differentiated into those which can yield such a clustering of clusters, called the hierarchical methods of cluster analysis, and those which are non-hierarchical, or yield only clustering of objects (Borgen & Weiss, 1971). The choice between the hierarchical or non-hierarchical approaches depends, of course, on the purposes for which the cluster analysis is being done.

Non-Hierarchical Methods

McQuitty (1957a) has developed perhaps the simplest method for a quick cluster analysis of a set of variables, without using calculating or computing equipment. This method, called elementary linkage analysis, has been illustrated on a matrix of interpeople or Q-correlations, where each person has been measured on some multivariate set of observations, and each correlation represents the similarity between two people. In elementary linkage analysis, McQuitty defines a type as a category of persons wherein each person in the type is more like someone else in the type than he is like anyone outside the type. This definition, of course, can also be used in clustering variables, with the result being a subset of variables defined by a group of variables in which each variable is most similar to another variable in that subset. In his later work with non-hierarchical methods of cluster analysis, McQuitty (1961, 1966) changes his definition of a type somewhat, although without destroying the basic logic of the approach. These later methods are superior in some ways to his earlier methods, but lose the attractive characteristic of not requiring computing or calculating equipment to arrive at a classification scheme.

A popular method of cluster analysis which is easily done with a calculating machine was developed many years ago by

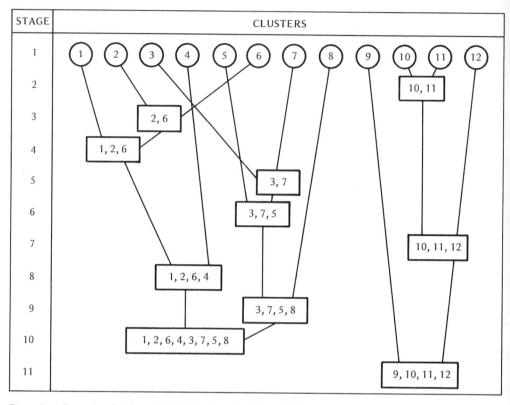

Figure 3.   Example of a hierarchical clustering of twelve variables.

Holzinger and Harman, and later modified by Tryon (Fruchter, 1954). This method defines a cluster in a slightly different way than does McQuitty and, therefore, sometimes arrives at different results. In the Holzinger-Harman-Tryon method of cluster analysis, a cluster is a subset of variables which are grouped together in such a way that the average intercorrelation among the variables in the subset is greater (by a pre-specified amount) than the average correlation of those variables with all other variables not in the cluster. In this way a cluster is defined as a set of variables with high average interrelationships, or a set of variables that are similar to each other, on the average. This method of cluster analysis was popular for many years, because of its logical appeal and computational simplicity,

and only recently is being replaced by more sophisticated computer-based methods.

With the advent of computers, clustering methods are developing rapidly. Tryon (Tryon & Bailey, 1970) has developed a complex set of computer-based clustering systems which interrelate in a system called the BCTRY system of cluster analysis. These methods are derived from a long series of mathematical and statistical work by Tryon and his associates, but are relatively unavailable to the average researcher who desires to group a set of objects for applied purposes. However, applications of Tryon's methods show some practical utility for his techniques.

Cattell and his associates (Cattell, Coulter, & Tsujioka, 1966) have developed a TAXONOME computer program which is designed as a clustering or taxonomic method. Other methods for clustering or classification have been reported by Lingoes (1963), Sawrey, Keller, and Conger (1960), Lorr, Klett, and McNair (1963), Lorr and Radhakrishnan (1967), and Jones (1968), among others. Most of these methods have not been widely used in the applied literature and, hence, their characteristics have not been carefully evaluated. However, they may have specific applications to certain problems; for example, a method by Ball and Hall (1967) which is designed for binary-valued (yes-no) data. Thus, the researcher with a cluster-analytic problem looking for the "best" solution for his data, should carefully evaluate the applicability of these other approaches.

Hierarchical Clustering Methods

McQuitty's (1960) hierarchical syndrome analysis is perhaps the simplest of the hierarchical clustering methods. This method builds on the logic of McQuitty's elementary linkage analysis, clustering together clusters of variables that are logically related to each other. The method begins with all single variables defining a cluster and groups together variables at the initial step to form a first cluster. After that step each cluster is then considered as a new variable at subsequent steps in the procedure, using the same kinds of decision rules originally applied to the single variables. The result is a "tree-structure" consisting of a pyramidal arrangement with several levels. At the lowest level are the single variables. At the next highest level, some variables are grouped into clusters. Going up to the next level the researcher would find some clusters grouped together into "super-clusters." The pyramid continues upward, with the number of super-clusters reduced at each higher level, until finally all clusters derive from a single highest-order super-cluster.

In this way the researcher can graphically examine the structure of his data at a num-ber of levels of generality. The tree-structure shows how the original observations group themselves, and how the groups are in turn grouped. The result is not dissimilar to a family tree, except that it represents an empirical grouping of objects or people based on measured similarity on a number of variables. The groups thus defined can be used for applied purposes in a variety of ways, since they represent homogeneous groups of people (objects, or variables) with a known degree of similarity.

McQuitty's hierarchical syndrome analysis is valuable because the clustering can be done quickly and without either a calculating machine or a computer, once the matrix of interassociations or intercorrelations is available. McQuitty has refined the method (McQuitty & Clark, 1968) so that the resulting clusters are more reliable or replicable, but the new method requires the use of computing facilities.

Ward (1963; Ward & Hook, 1963) has developed a widely used method for hierarchical cluster analysis. The method is available only in computer-based form because of some of the complexities involved in the clustering process. The logic of the method is similar to that of McQuitty's early hierarchical methods, although the decision rules as to when a cluster has been formed are more complex. Ward's approach gives a complete tree-structure in that each step in the pyramidal tree gives a number of clusters smaller by one than the previous step. For example, if twenty persons are to be clustered by Ward's hierarchical method, the number of "clusters" at the first step would be twenty—the number of individuals. At the second step, the two most similar people would be combined to yield nineteen clusters. To complete the third step, which would consist of eighteen clusters, the two most similar "clusters" from step two are combined. This process is repeated at each step until all observations are combined into one super-cluster (see Figure 3).

The method gives an index of cluster

homogeneity at each step. This index reflects the "tightness" of the clusters at that stage in the pyramidal structure. Thus, the researcher can examine this "error function" to determine at what point the grouping of clusters into higher-order clusters begins to result in a set of clusters that are too internally heterogeneous; that is, at what point the clusters begin to look similar to each other. At that point the researcher can conclude that the grouping of clusters into super-clusters is losing more information than is being gained, and he can terminate the clustering procedure. The tree-structure below that point will represent the structure of the original variables into a meaningful hierarchy to the extent that (a) the variables within a cluster bear a resemblance to each other, and (b) each cluster bears some dissimilarity to the other clusters.

Research on and using Ward's hierarchical clustering method supports its utility in problems where a hierarchical structuring of a set of variables is appropriate, although the method is not without its technical problems (Borgen & Weiss, 1970). But Ward's hierarchical clustering method is usable for many practical applications. Veldman (1967) and Jones (1964) give FORTRAN programs for the method.

Cautions in the Use of Clustering Methods

All clustering methods of a given type (i.e., hierarchical or non-hierarchical) do not give the same results. Thus, if the researcher is interested in "the" set of clusters, or "the" hierarchy of clusters deriving from a given set of data, he should analyze the same set of data by more than one method. More reliable conclusions are likely to be drawn concerning the taxonomy of a set of variables if similar results are obtained from two or more methods applied to the same data. It should be noted, in this context, that hierarchical methods can be used to obtain non-hierarchical results simply by examining cluster assignments at a given level of the hierarchical solution. In the same way, through repeated analysis of "cluster scores" the non-hierarchical methods can yield a hierarchical solution. Thus, one approach can be used to verify the results obtained by the other. In the case of contradictory results, reanalysis by a method of the same type (hierarchical or non-hierarchical) would be appropriate.

In addition to analyzing the same set of data by different clustering methods, it is also appropriate to analyze different sets of data by the same method. For example, if the researcher is interested in developing a hierarchical taxonomy of the structure of components of job satisfaction, he might cluster analyze the intercorrelations of job satisfaction component scores for one group of employees. Since some of the intercorrelations are likely determined by chance factors characteristic only of that group of employees, the conclusions drawn from that analysis are likely to be unstable. It is, therefore, appropriate to replicate or repeat the analysis on a different group of subjects using the same measuring instrument. If a similar structure is obtained in the second group, it can be concluded with more certainty that the obtained taxonomy is a stable one.

In the absence of "methodological redundancy," as suggested above, or "replication," the researcher can reduce the possibility of chance effects in his data by using original measurements which are as reliable as possible. In some cases it may be appropriate to use factor analysis of a set of variables prior to cluster analysis, to arrive at a new subset of variates for use in the cluster analysis. Because the factor-analyzed variates represent only the common variance of the original set of variables, they are likely to be more reliable than the original set of variables. Such an approach would be most appropriate where cluster analysis is done on a group of people, measured on a common set of variables, where the objective is to develop homogeneous "people types."

In any event, the results of a cluster

analysis will be dependent on the reliability of the original observations. It is, therefore, incumbent on the researcher to use reliable data in his cluster analysis, and to wherever possible repeat the analysis on another group of subjects and/or by a different method of analysis, to ensure the stability of his results and the generality of his conclusions.

REFERENCES

Armstrong, J. S., & Soelberg, P. On the interpretation of factor analysis. *Psychological Bulletin,* 1968, 70, 361–364.

Ball, G. H., & Hall, D. J. A clustering technique for summarizing multivariate data. *Behavioral Science,* 1967, 12, 153–155.

Borgen, F. H., & Weiss, D. J. Cluster analysis and counseling research. *Journal of Counseling Psychology,* 1971, 18, 583–591.

Cattell, R. B., Coulter, M. A., & Tsujioka, B. The taxonometric recognition of types and functional emergents. In R. B. Cattell (Ed.), *Handbook of multivariate experimental psychology.* Chicago: Rand McNally, 1966.

Cooley, W. W., & Lohnes, P. R. *Multivariate data analysis.* New York: Wiley, 1971.

Dvorak, B. J. Advantages of the multiple cutoff method. *Personnel Psychology,* 1956, 9, 45–47.

Efroymson, M. A. Multiple regression analysis. In R. A. Ralstan & H. S. Wilf (Eds.), *Mathematical methods for digital computers.* New York: Wiley, 1960.

England, G. W. *Development and use of weighted application blanks.* (Rev. ed.) Minneapolis: University of Minnesota, Industrial Relations Center, Bulletin 55, 1971.

Eysenck, H. J. Criterion analysis: An application of the hypothetico-deductive method to factor analysis. *Psychological Review,* 1950, 57, 38–53.

Ezekiel, M., & Fox, K. A. *Methods of correlation and regression analysis: Linear and curvilinear.* New York: Wiley, 1965.

Fruchter, B. *Introduction to factor analysis.* Princeton: Van Nostrand, 1954.

Guilford, J. P. *Fundamental statistics in psychology and education.* (4th ed.) New York: McGraw-Hill, 1965.

Guion, R. M. *Personnel testing.* New York: McGraw-Hill, 1965.

Harman, H. H. *Modern factor analysis.* (2nd ed., rev.) Chicago: University of Chicago Press, 1967.

Hicks, L. E. Some properties of ipsative, normative, and forced-choice normative measures. *Psychological Bulletin,* 1970, 74, 167–184.

Hotelling, H. Relations between two sets of variates. *Biometrika,* 1936, 28, 321–377.

Humphreys, L. G., & Ilgen, D. R. Note on a criterion for the number of common factors. *Educational and Psychological Measurement,* 1969, 29, 571–578.

Jones, K. J. *The multivariate statistical analyzer.* Cambridge: Harvard Cooperative Society, 1964.

Jones, K. J. Problems of grouping individuals and the method of modality. *Behavioral Science,* 1968, 13, 496–511.

Lingoes, J. C. A taxonometric optimization procedure: An IBM 7090 classification program. *Behavioral Science,* 1963, 8, 370.

Lorr, M., Klett, C. J., & McNair, D. M. *Syndromes of psychosis.* New York: Macmillan, 1963.

Lorr, M., & Radhakrishnan, B. K. A comparison of two methods of cluster analysis. *Educational and Psychological Measurement,* 1967, 27, 47–53.

Lykken, D. T. A method of actuarial pattern analysis. *Psychological Bulletin,* 1956, 53, 102–107.

McNemar, Q. *Psychological statistics.* (4th ed.) New York: Wiley, 1969.

McQuitty, L. L. Elementary linkage analysis for isolating orthogonal and oblique types and typal relevancies. *Educational and Psychological Measurement,* 1957, 17, 207–229. (a)

McQuitty, L. L. Isolating predictor patterns associated with major criterion patterns. *Educational and Psychological Measurement,* 1957, 17, 3–42. (b)

McQuitty, L. L. Hierarchical syndrome analysis. *Educational and Psychological Measurement,* 1960, 20, 293–304.

McQuitty, L. L. Typal analysis. *Educational and Psychological Measurement,* 1961, 21, 677–698.

McQuitty, L. L. Multiple rank order typal analysis for the isolation of independent types. *Educational and Psychological Measurement,* 1966, 26, 3–11.

McQuitty, L. L., & Clark, J. A. Clusters from iterative inter-columnar correlational analysis. *Educational and Psychological Measurement,* 1968, 28, 211–238.

Meehl, P. E. Configural scoring. *Journal of Consulting Psychology,* 1950, 14, 165–171.

Meehl, P. E., & Rosen, A. Antecedent probability and the efficiency of psychometric signs, patterns, or cutting scores. *Psychological Bulletin,* 1955, 52, 194–216.

Rulon, P. J., Tiedeman, D. V., Tatsuoka, M. M., & Langmuir, C. R. *Multivariate statistics for personnel classification.* New York: Wiley, 1967.

Rummel, R. J. *Applied factor analysis.* Evanston, Ill.: Northwestern University Press, 1970.

Sawrey, W. L., Keller, L., & Conger, J. J. An objective method of grouping profiles by distance functions and its relation to factor analysis. *Educational and Psychological Measurement,* 1960, 20, 651–673.

Sorenson, W. W. Configural scoring of items for predicting sales success. Unpublished doctoral dissertation, University of Minnesota, Minneapolis, 1964.

Stewart, D., & Love, W. A general canonical correlation index. *Psychological Bulletin,* 1968, 70, 160–163.

Tatsuoka, M. M. *Validation studies: The use of linear multiple regression.* Champaign, Ill.: Institute for Personality and Ability Testing, 1969.

Tatsuoka, M. M. *Discriminant analysis: The study of group differences.* Champaign, Ill.: Institute for Personality and Ability Testing, 1970.

Tatsuoka, M. M. *Multivariate analysis: Techniques for educational and psychological research.* New York: Wiley, 1971.

Taylor, K. E., & Weiss, D. J. Prediction of individual job termination from measured job satisfaction and biographical data. *Journal of Vocational Behavior,* 1972, 2, 123–132.

Thorndike, R. M., Weiss, D. J., & Dawis, R. V. Multivariate relationships between a measure of vocational interests and a measure of vocational needs. *Journal of Applied Psychology,* 1968, 52, 491–496.

Thurstone, L. L. *Multiple factor analysis.* Chicago: University of Chicago Press, 1947.

Tryon, R. C., & Bailey, D. E. *Cluster analysis.* New York: McGraw-Hill, 1970.

U.S. Department of Labor, Manpower Administration. *Manual for the USTES General Aptitude Test Battery: Section II Norms, Occupational Aptitude Pattern Structure.* Washington, D.C.: U.S. Government Printing Office, 1970.

Veldman, D. J. *FORTRAN programming for the behavioral sciences.* New York: Holt, Rinehart and Winston, 1967.

Ward, J. H. Hierarchical grouping to optimize an objective function. *Journal of the American Statistical Association,* 1963, 58, 236–244.

Ward, J. H., & Hook, M. E. Application of an hierarchical grouping procedure to a problem of grouping profiles. *Educational and Psychological Measurement,* 1963, 23, 69–81.

Weiss, D. J. A technique for curvilinear multivariate prediction. Unpublished doctoral dissertation, University of Minnesota, Minneapolis, 1963.

Weiss, D. J. Factor analysis and counseling research. *Journal of Counseling Psychology,* 1970, 17, 477–485.

Weiss, D. J. Further considerations in applications of factor analysis. *Journal of Counseling Psychology,* 1971, 18, 85–92.

Weiss, D. J. Canonical correction analysis in counseling psychology research. *Journal of Counseling Psychology,* 1972, 19, 241–252.

Weiss, D. J., & Dawis, R. V. A multivariate prediction technique for multifunctional predictor-criterion relationships. *Proceedings, 76th Annual Convention of the American Psychological Association,* 1968, 229–230.

CHAPTER 9

Field Research Methods: Interviewing, Questionnaires, Participant Observation, Systematic Observation, Unobtrusive Measures[1,2]

THOMAS J. BOUCHARD, JR.
The University of Minnesota

IN THIS CHAPTER we argue that from the point of view of both science and society field research is as important as laboratory research. This is because the field is where the generality, applicability, and utility of psychological knowledge are put to the test. The field researcher is the mediator of a relevant sociopsychological science. With this perspective in mind we discuss at a very practical level the methods listed in our title. The special characteristics of each method are discussed in detail and each method's peculiar methodological traps are explicated. New uses for old methods are suggested and their wider application recommended. Throughout the chapter we urge that researchers: (1) choose the method that is most likely to serve their purpose rather than the easiest method; (2) use more than one method whenever possible; and (3) focus more on the actual behavior of theoretical or practical concern and less on verbal behavior and test responses than they have in the past.

[1] Preparation of this chapter was supported in part by United States Public Health Service Grant 1 R01 HD 05600-01 to the author. Major revisions and completion of the manuscript occurred while the author was at the Oregon Research Institute, supported by General Research Support Grant RR-05612 from the National Institutes of Health and Grant MH-12972 from the National Institute of Mental Health, United States Public Health Service.

[2] The author is indebted to the following persons for their thoughtful comments on a preliminary version of this chapter: John Campbell, Marvin Dunnette, and Vernon Devine.

INTRODUCTION

Given the context in which this chapter appears it would seem to be unnecessary to spend time justifying the use of field methods as a means of studying human behavior. Yet, it is necessary because field researchers have not developed adequate intellectual justification for their role among either their experimental or applied colleagues. The experimentalist disparages field research and calls for rigor while the applied practitioner ridicules the sterility of the laboratory and calls for relevance. The field researcher finds himself hard put to meet one demand without sacrificing the other. Thus his dilemma. In our opinion creative field research should constitute a synthesis of these apparently conflicting demands. How is this to be done? By testing as rigorously as possible in the field setting the relevance and generality of laboratory-derived concepts. Consider the following example.

In 1941, Barker and his colleagues (Barker, Dembo, & Lewin, 1941) conducted a laboratory experiment which was to become known to almost every student who would subsequently take a course in the behavioral sciences. They found that the frustration of children leads to regressive behavior. More than twenty years later, as part of a field study, a student of Barker's analyzed the records of children's everyday behavior. He reported (Fawl, 1963):

The results ... were surprising in two respects. First, even with a liberal interpretation of frustration fewer incidents were detected than we expected. ... Second ... meaningful relationships could not be found between frustration ... and consequent behavior such as ... regression ... and other theoretically meaningful behavior manifestations. (p. 99)

This example illustrates the different kinds of knowledge that can be obtained by the two types of studies, the different conclusions they may lead to, and the inherent limitations of each. The laboratory study clearly demonstrated a causal link

between frustration and aggression. The field study demonstrated that the phenomenon had very little generality and helped specify the conditions under which the law held (e.g., when the child was forced to remain in the noxious setting and his potential repertoire of responses was so limited that he could not turn to a new class of activities). It also told us something about the frequency of frustrating events in the environment; they were far more infrequent than expected. More than anything else, this example shows us that a workable theory of human behavior will consist not only of a series of if-then laws, but will also contain numerous boundary specifications.

Laboratory experiments seldom deal adequately with boundary conditions or context factors and, therefore, lend themselves to unjustified and often erroneous extrapolations (cf., Berlyne, 1964; Chomsky, 1968). Field settings, on the other hand, allow us to explore boundary conditions in ways which may serve to enhance or delimit laboratory findings and thereby increase our understanding of the various lawful processes under investigation by both types of researchers (McGrath, 1964).

SPECIAL CHARACTERISTICS OF FIELD SETTINGS

Each of the factors to be discussed below is a special characteristic of field settings which is either unavailable or extremely difficult to manipulate in laboratory settings. They are the primary factors a field researcher should be sensitive to and capitalize on in the course of conceptualizing, designing, and carrying out a field study.

The first three—intensity, range, and frequency and duration—are boundary factors. Their greater magnitude in field settings often allows a researcher to explore and perhaps specify the form and limits of a relationship just as a physical scientist specifies a melting point, a boiling point, etc. The analogy to the physical sciences can be pushed further. Just as the point at which a material changes state is of great theoretical interest in the physical sciences, the point at which a behavioral function changes dramatically is of great interest to behavioral scientists. For example, the point of disobedience in the Milgram (1965) studies was characterized by a variety of symptoms of great theoretical, as well as practical, interest. The next three factors, natural time constants, natural units, and complexity, are context or structural factors. They are important features of the natural environment that the experimentalist typically destroys in order to study a phenomenon under controlled conditions. The last two factors, setting effects and representativeness, while not strictly advantages of only field settings, allow the field researcher to ask and test broader kinds of questions than are often asked in the laboratory.

Intensity. An important independent variable may display a range of intensity in the field that could not be generated in the laboratory because of ethical and other restrictions. Firings, layoffs, demotions, and transfers can produce levels of stress that would be unethical for an experimenter to simulate in a laboratory setting. Yet, they occur with great frequency in the world of work.

Range. Phenomena in the field often show a far wider range of variation than could be simulated in the laboratory. Cross-cultural studies can often extend the range even further (Roberts, 1970; Udy, 1964, 1965; Whiting, 1968). Examples that come to mind are: group size, span of control, degree of centralization, complexity, and time span of discretion. Laboratory studies cannot study even in principle the effects of some physical spaces (cf., Sommer, 1969).

Frequency and duration. Laboratory studies encompass a relatively short time span. Human beings have the capacity to buffer wide ranges of stimulation when exposed to them for only short periods (Block, 1968; Sommer, 1968), and experiments may simply fail to provide conditions which cross the response system threshold. Thus, an effect may be shown in the field, but not in the laboratory. Trigger effects are also related to the threshold problem. A small stimulus (trigger) may elicit an effect if predisposing stimuli have occurred repeatedly or for long periods of time.

Natural time constants. System theorists (Berrien, 1968; Buckley, 1967) have sensitized researchers to the fact that some phenomena have natural life spans and that the temporal structure of events is often critical to the outcome of particular manipulations (cf., Savas, 1970). Only field studies allow us to study long temporal structures and to search for natural time units.

Natural units. The field setting is not passive. "Intrinsic orders exist 'out there' and ... these regularities will organize and drive events even though our theories take no notice of them" (Gutman, 1969, p. 162). The field researcher is in a position to seek natural units of behavior, units which occur in conjunction with particular environments. Barker (1968, 1969) calls these eco-behavioral entities (cf., Kelly, 1969; Menzel, 1969).

Setting effects. Studies conducted in certain settings are highly likely to have different outcomes in other settings. Hovland (1959) has suggested that setting effects probably have a strong influence on studies of attitude change. For example, subjects might be open to influence in an educational context, but be much harder to influence in other contexts. This is a simple interaction effect. It is not absurd to assume that there are many higher-order interactions. Field settings are extremely complex. A large number of forces are at work in any given situation. Some of them may be powerful, but subtle and hidden from an observer who does not have an understanding of the antecedent events. Self-selection may have populated the setting only with individuals who have demonstrated a capacity to adapt to the influence of the variable under study. Field settings are open and dynamic in the sense that individuals are continually moving in and out of them.

Thus, a relationship found at time T_1 may not be found at time T_2. All of these factors threaten the validity of any interpretation of an event. Thus, if an effect can be shown to hold in both the lab and the field it can be considered robust and generalizable. Failure to demonstrate an effect in the field should lead a researcher to suspect (among other things) a treatment $\times$ organismic variable interaction due to self-selection, the existence of avoidance or neutralizing mechanisms, or a more powerful main effect due to uncontrolled variables that masks the expected relationship.

Representativeness. While laboratory studies are reasonably strong on representativeness of subjects (e.g., $N = 10$ or more) they are notoriously weak on representativeness of treatments (Feldman & Hass, 1970; Hammond, 1954). A conceptual variable and its empirical realization are not the same thing. Many psychological processes have been demonstrated using only one experimental manipulation. Given the complexity of social-psychological manipulations, a failure to observe an expected effect in the field can be considered a threat to the interpretation of an analogous laboratory study. An example of this problem is the risky-shift phenomenon.

The conceptual variable—tendency of an individual to make riskier decisions in a group than as an individual—had been operationalized in most early studies with only one instrument, the choice dilemma questionnaire. What had appeared to be a striking but simple phenomena became complex when additional measures of the conceptual variable were introduced (Dion, Barron, & Miller, 1971; Clark, 1971; Vinokur, 1971).

Each of the points discussed above illustrates why we must be careful in extrapolating from the small amount of rigorous and carefully worked-out experimental knowledge generated in the laboratory. Indeed there are strong grounds for arguing that with respect to practical issues of wide social concern it is perhaps better to extrapolate or generalize from data gathered in field settings, even if direction of causation remains unknown, than to make use of principles based on rigorously conducted laboratory studies (Meehl, 1971; Willems & Raush, 1969). This is not to imply that scientific knowledge and rigorous procedures should not be used when they are applicable (Becker, 1970; Bouchard, 1971; Campbell, 1969), but rather to emphasize that the context of discovery has hardly been mined while the context of justification has been overburdened with trivial investigations (cf., Argyris, 1968; McGuire, 1967; Ring, 1967).

SPECIAL DIFFICULTIES WITH FIELD STUDIES

The points discussed below are meant to alert the field researcher to the kinds of problems which make it difficult to conduct field studies or draw valid inferences from them. The list is not exhaustive, but is rather selective. Additional problems are discussed later in relation to particular methods.

Causal ambiguity. The study of groups subsequent to their arrival in a situation usually makes it impossible to determine the direction of causation when relationships between variables are found. Kornhauser (1965), for example, compared the mental health of workers at different job levels and found that workers in the lower-skilled jobs were in poorer mental health. He concluded that their occupational situation caused this condition. A plausible alternative explanation is that there is a social class difference (Dohrenwend & Dohrenwend, 1969), perhaps mediated by genetic factors (Goldberg & Morrison, 1963; Turner & Wagenfeld, 1967). The same error underlies the argument of many of those who favor job enlargement because "simplified jobs lead to poorer mental health." The argument may be correct, but correlational studies will never confirm or deny it. Similar interpretive problems plague all studies which contrast groups at different levels of the occupational hierarchy. Hulin and Blood (1968) present an excellent analysis of this particular problem.

A number of researchers have suggested that some of the problems caused by self-selection can be handled by specialized sampling procedures, matching, or covariance analysis (cf., Scott, 1965; Price, 1968). These procedures are very likely to result in systematic unmatching (Meehl, 1970). For example, a researcher may be interested in the relationship between the size of an organization and the personality characteristics of managers. He knows that managers in large organizations have higher IQs than do managers in small organizations so he matches high-IQ managers in small organizations against managers in large organizations. Unfortunately, the managers of small organizations are no longer representative of the population in which the researcher is interested. They lack what Brunswick (1956) called ecological validity (see also Feldman & Hass, 1970). The contrast is between managers of small organizations with high IQs versus unselected managers of large corporations. Such a contrast does not yield data with any generality. Note also that a covariance design is mathematically identical to the matching design and does not overcome the problem, nor does the use of a large number of covariates (Meehl, 1970). Meehl (1970) has concluded "that the ex post facto design is in most instances so radically defective in its logical structure that it is in principle incapable of answering the kinds of theoretical questions which typically give rise to its use" (p. 402).

$N = 1$. Many field studies involve only one organization or subject. While the one-case study is generally sterile scientifically (Campbell & Stanley, 1966) it need not be (Dukes, 1965; Davidson & Costello, 1969; Edgington, 1972; Forehand & Gilmer, 1964). Carefully documented cases which make use of standard instruments may be useful as part of a cumulative record. Data collected in a single case may be compared with previously reported data on the same or different cases. Variation in the perform-ance of one case as a function of environmental variation may be so systematic and regular as to make all alternative interpretations implausible. A well-chosen single case may seriously threaten a traditionally accepted hypothesis. The single case may also represent the sampling of a response to a rare, extreme, and unique event and thereby improve ecological sampling. Brunswick (1956) has argued that "In fact, proper sampling of situations and problems may in the end be more important than proper sampling of subjects, considering the fact that individuals are probably on the whole much more alike than are situations among one another" (p. 39).

We do not advocate the use of $N = 1$ except in exceptional circumstances. The judicious choice of contrasts is still our most powerful methodological strategy (Campbell & Stanley, 1966; Platt, 1964), but research in organizational psychology is in its infancy and the role of tacit knowledge (Polanyi, 1958) is large.

Cost—time—money. Field work of any sort is expensive. With the development of sophisticated instrumentation and more extensive and powerful research designs, it will get even more expensive (Barker, 1968, 1969; Sells, 1969; Schwitzgebel, 1970). One major complaint about field studies is the high-dross rate. That is, a great many "irrelevant" events occur and are recorded before something significant happens and, therefore, much time and money is supposedly spent for very little useful information. We consider this an unwise argument. The fact that important events are rare has been shown to have profound theoretical and empirical implications (Dyck, 1963; Fawl, 1963; Gump & Kounin, 1960). In Barker's (1969) terms "data that are dross for one investigator are gold for another" (p. 39). There is every reason to believe that social science research of any significance is going to get more expensive, not less (Deutsch, Platt, & Senghass, 1971), and it is time to destroy the myth of social science research as cheap.

In summary, field research, like any other enterprise, is beset by both pitfalls and advantages. However, its advantages put it in the position of being the place where the generality, applicability, and utility of psychological knowledge are put to the test. The role of the field researcher is thus an important one from the standpoint of both social utility and scientific advance. His work can enhance the usefulness of scientific theory for applied work and counter erroneous extrapolation and generalization at the theoretical level. The field researcher is the mediator of a relevant social-psychological science.

The remainder of this chapter deals with the many different methods that may be applied in a field investigation. None of them avoids the pitfalls discussed above. Even if they were all used together the resulting data would probably not approximate all that we would need to know. Appropriate combinations, however, may so vastly reduce the number of plausible rival hypotheses that useful practical and theoretical knowledge may be gained. The skilled field researcher will carefully choose as many supplementary methods as necessary in order to conduct meaningful tests of his hypotheses and thereby draw robust conclusions.

The chapter discusses five major methods: interviewing, questionnaire use, participant observation, systematic observation, and unobtrusive measures. Each method is outlined in considerable detail with the intent of facilitating its use by field researchers. Basically, the coverage includes a thorough description of how to use the method or examples of its use, a description and discussion of the major variants of the method, and a discussion of the special problems the user of each method will have to deal with.

Often our discussion takes the form of a series of rules. Generally, they summarize important considerations that are discussed in enough detail to justify them. Unfortunately, many of the rules are not based on empirical evidence, but rather reflect the cumulative experience of previous researchers. Like any set of rules, a researcher should not be constrained from violating them when and if they seem to impede progress toward the fundamental goals of the investigation. However, like most other rules, they did not come about through accident and the need to violate them should always be accompanied by a careful evaluation of the possible consequences.

THE RESEARCH INTERVIEW

Interviewing is widely used as a systematic data-collecting technique in organizational research settings. Few researchers fail to use, at one time or another, some sort of focused conversation with participants. The interview may take place during the exploratory phase, during the course of the research itself, or during the analytic phase where it is used to help interpret data collected by other means. The popularity of the interview and its stepbrother the questionnaire is not an accident. The interview and the questionnaire capitalize on language, the human being's most powerful form of communication. Asking someone for information generally saves an enormous amount of time and effort if that someone is willing and able to supply an answer. However, the great power of the interview and the apparent ease with which it is applied has led to a large number of abuses and misuses. One of the goals of this discussion is to reduce the relative frequency of the abuses and misuses and to enhance the precision and care with which the interview is used.

Setting the Context
for a Successful Interview

Minimizing Status Differentials

Interviews are special forms of social interaction which depend heavily on mutual trust and the goodwill of respondents. If they are to yield useful information, that goodwill and trust must be maintained, cultivated, and validated by the interviewer (Stebbins, 1972). Methodological reports from field studies consistently emphasize the importance of minimizing status differentials in order to maximize trust and thereby increase the productivity of the interview. Recommendations vary from advice to spend some time working on jobs similar to those of the respondent prior to the interview (Blum, 1952), to choosing interviewers with the appropriate demographic and personality characteristics (Benney & Hughes, 1956; Sewell, 1949). Many studies have shown that, in various contexts, such factors as race, sex, age, religion, social class, and education influence the amount of communication occurring in an interview (Benney, Riesman, & Star, 1956; Cannell & Kahn, 1957; Lenski & Leggett, 1960). The practical problem for the researcher is that of obtaining the best fit with the resources available. The problem of fit is most acute at the extremes of the status hierarchy. At the low end of the hierarchy it is sometimes possible to recruit interviewers locally (Goering & Cummins, 1970).

The Inquiring Stance

A second important dimension on which the interviewer and respondent can be contrasted is expertise. This question is seldom discussed in the literature. The overriding assumption appears to be that the researcher is an expert and should be so perceived. According to Argyris (1958), however, "Implying that management knows more than the researcher only seems to increase the insecurity of both the researchers and the administrator" (p. 121).

Nevertheless, it seems to us that it is important to make a clear distinction between expertise (competence as a researcher) and knowledge of the situation at hand. Simplistic as this distinction may seem, it is not always maintained. There is no doubt that in order to establish legitimacy and credibility the researcher must be viewed as an expert; however, in order to maintain reciprocity, the respondent must feel that there is something he can give (Gouldner, 1960). This requires that the researcher cast himself in the role of an "honest inquirer" (Hund, 1959). Apart from its effect on the motivation of the respondents, this stance forces a breadth of perspective on researchers who have a strong tendency to want what they know, rather than want to know. Almost regardless of the kind of data being collected, if the interviewer cannot comfortably put himself in the role of inquirer, he should ask himself if he is posing meaningful questions and if the interview is an appropriate data-gathering instrument for his purposes.

An inquiring stance is important at all levels in the status hierarchy, but probably increases in importance with the expertise and status of the respondent (Gross & Mason, 1953). The higher his status, the more valuable his time and, therefore, the more critical it is that he perceive the inquiry as a valid one, rather than perfunctory. This perspective is transmitted more by the nature of the questions and the way they are asked than by the interviewer's professed purpose (Scott, 1963).

Maintaining Respondent Motivation

Respondent motivation in the interview situation has been conceptualized in a number of ways. The more common "explanations" are altruism, emotional satisfaction, and intellectual satisfaction (Hyman, Cobb, Feldman, Hart, & Slember, 1954; Kinsey, Pomeroy, Martin, & Gebhard, 1965; Richardson, Dohrenwend, & Klein, 1965). Rogers's (1959) self-concept theory is more useful than any other model for organizing thinking about respondent motivation. According to the theory, under conditions of "trust," people find it rewarding to discuss what they know well. By providing conditions that maximize trust and satisfy the needs described above, the interviewer maintains the respondent's interest and motivation (Stebbins, 1972). Minimizing status differentials and taking an inquiring stance are the major strategies one should use for accomplishing these ends. Listed below are a number of tactics useful in achieving them:

1. Maximize privacy. Never interview in a place where you can be overheard.

2. Know whom you are talking to. Know his name and be sure you can pronounce it correctly. It is often possible to obtain background data on an interviewee ahead of time. This is sometimes useful in that it facilitates taking his point of view into account and may minimize misunderstandings. It may, however, bias the interviewer by inducing stereotypes or unwarranted prejudices. A considered judgment is necessary here; one can know too much or too little.

3. Maintain neutrality. Do not take sides on issues that may divide the group you are working with (Argyris, 1958; Caplow, 1956; Scott, 1963).

4. Maintain confidentiality. Under no circumstances should you reveal *anything* you know about one respondent to another respondent. A simple and direct way of demonstrating your intent to maintain confidentiality is to use a coded questionnaire and show how it works. The code can vary from elaborate systems (Kinsey, Pomeroy, Martin, & Gebhard, 1965, p. 60; Astin & Boruch, 1970) to the use of a simple number system instead of names on the answer sheets. Argyris (1958) reports an incident where the foreman tested him to see whether he would leak information. When they found he wouldn't, the work went much more smoothly. Gullahorn and Strauss (1960) recommend adhering to strict confidentiality even when the information requested is common knowledge. Violations of confidentiality constitute a breach of ethical standards (American Psychological Association, 1967) as well as a display of incompetence.

5. Listen. The failure to listen carefully to what a respondent says is a violation of the inquirer stance and a signal that the desired information is not very important. Since much of the information desired by interviewers is already not very important to the respondent, adding insult to injury is inexcusable.

6. Cooling out. Whyte (1960) and Dalton (1967) have pointed out a special problem that sometimes arises and requires special treatment. On occasion, a respondent will reveal too much sensitive material on a first interview. This may cause him to become anxious, particularly if the interviewer is speaking to many people over a long period of time. It may also cause him to "clam up" on subsequent interviews. In such cases, it is recommended that no probing be undertaken and that he be cooled off slowly, the interview ending with some casual small talk. The respondent should also be contacted soon again for further casual discussion in order to allay suspicion and avoid his turning against the researcher. A useful source for dealing with this problem is Goffman's classic paper, "On cooling the mark out" (1952).

7. Inform all respondents about who will be interviewed and how they were chosen. This will eliminate such implicit or explicit questions as "Why me?" and "Who else will this guy talk to?" and put the respondent more at ease.

8. Identify yourself. All respondents should know who you are and, in a general way, what you are doing. They should also be told the amount of time that will be required of them.

Who Should Be Interviewed?

Most research designs call for random or representative samples. Once the sample has been chosen, the researcher should examine carefully the social structure of the group. If the formal leaders and most competent individuals in a unit are not included in the sample because of chance or systematic factors, it is always wise to interview these individuals first. They may be excluded from the analysis later if they were not specified in the original sample (Scott, 1963). Once the formal leaders and most competent members of a unit acquiesce to an interview, it is much easier to interview everyone else (Madge, 1965; Merton, 1947). The researcher should also decide, on the basis of the types of questions he is asking, as well as the social situation, whether he should interview over an extended period of time or mass the interviews. Too much informal communication among interviewees can lead to consensus on issues and questions which may not have existed before the communication, and thereby artificially reduce variance in the data. On the other hand, positive reports about the results of the interview from the initial respondents can reduce anxiety and facilitate data collection. Second, in some cases the investigator may want to interview twice, the first time to get his respondents thinking about the questions, the second time to get their considered opinions.

Last, the interviewer should, in almost all cases, have formal authorization from the chain of command, including union officials when it is relevant. Failure to obtain proper authorization and/or jumping a chain of command can be detrimental to a research project.

Types of Interviews

Interview procedures are usually classified on the basis of question and response format. Table 1 summarizes the various types of interviews when they are classified this way.

Type I interviews are totally structured; the respondent replies to standard questions and is asked to use a specified set of responses. This type of interview is generally given the name structured, directed, closed, or standardized. In spite of their apparent

TABLE 1
FOUR TYPES OF INTERVIEWS CLASSIFIED ACCORDING TO TYPE OF QUESTION AND TYPE OF ANSWER REQUIRED

RESPONSES	QUESTIONS	
	Specified	Unspecified
Specified	I	III
Unspecified	II	IV

narrowness, structured questions can take a variety of forms, for example, multiple-choice, true-false, yes-no, agree-disagree, preference, like-dislike, and identification formats.

Type II interviews have specified questions, but leave the character of the response open. They are often called open-ended or free-response interviews. Again, a variety of formats is possible. A question may require only a single word as a response, such as in a recall task, or it may require considerable elaboration.

There has been much controversy over the relative merits of each of these types of interview. One of the best discussions of this issue is still by Lazarsfeld (1944). In our opinion, the supposed benefits of both types of questions have been overplayed. Dohrenwend (1965) has produced suggestive evidence that open-ended questions do not yield greater efficiency, depth, or validity than structured response formats. The supposed objectivity of structured response is also open to debate (Cahalan, Tamulonis, & Verner, 1947).

Type III interviews do not specify the questions, but do specify the type of response desired. No one to our knowledge has ever made use of this type of interview. The reason appears to be that the data would not be comparable across respondents. Nevertheless, under certain circumstances this procedure could be useful. For example, respondents who spontaneously mention certain concepts might be asked to rate them on a set of semantic differential scales. These responses might then be compared to the responses of another sample or respondents who are asked to rate the same concepts.

Type IV interviews specify neither the question nor the desired response. This interview goes by a variety of names—the clinical interview, the nondirective interview, the unstructured interview, the nonstructured interview, the exploratory interview, the informal interview, etc. It is primarily used as an exploratory tool. See Whyte (1960) for a thorough discussion.

An additional point should be made regarding Types I and II interviews. In some circumstances, the nature of the question is specified, but the specific wording may be formulated by the interviewer in a way that is most appropriate to each respondent. Richardson et al. (1965) call this procedure the nonscheduled standardized interview.

The skilled researcher makes use of a combination of these types and there is no value in touting the merits of a single procedure. In the next section, we will discuss how they might best be combined.

A Recommended Procedure for Conducting Research Interviews

In line with our previous discussion of the need to use complementary methods in field studies, we advocate the use of a mixed strategy when interviewing (Collins, 1970; Lazarsfeld, 1944; Sewell, 1949). Specifically, we recommend a series of "funnel sequences" with feedback loops. Generally, data to be gathered can be subdivided into a limited number of domains. Each domain should be approached first with the broadest and most open questions and unspecified response formats. This approach validates the inquiry perspective recommended in the previous section and familiarizes the interviewer with the conceptual language and level of understanding of the respondent. It allows the interviewer to steer the respondent into the appropriate frame of reference if it is clear that he is "off base." It gives the

interviewer an opportunity to change the language of the more specific questions which follow if this seems necessary. This last point requires some elaboration. We agree with Kinsey et al. (1965) that "it is a mistake to believe that standard questions fed through diverse human machines can bring standard answers" (p. 61). There is no consensus on this issue (cf., Cicourel, 1964, p. 93; Kornhauser & Sheatsley, 1959; Richardson et al., 1965). Some researchers advocate gearing questions to the lowest common denominator while others recommend shifting the phrasing to fit the subject. In spite of varying recommendations, the research data make it clear that if the sample is at all heterogeneous, and if rapport with the respondent is to be maintained, phrasing must shift somewhat from subject to subject (Richardson, 1960). These initial questions also give the respondent a chance to mull the general problem over in his mind and hopefully consider many of the pertinent facts prior to his answering the more specific questions to follow.

More specific questions with fixed response formats should come next. These kinds of questions generally demand very little of the respondent and often he gives very little in terms of motivation and thought. Since it is always possible to pick an alternative haphazardly, if not at random, this is where the funnel sequence pays off. The respondent has had his say, he is now obligated to the investigator, a fairly high motivation is maintained, and the investigator gets an opportunity to make a validity check on responses. If responses to the structured questions contradict the earlier free responses, he can "loop back" and ask why. This poses a difficult problem because it makes possible the introduction of bias and may force an artificial consistency into the data. Some methodologists would argue that no interference should be allowed because both types of responses are a priori equally valid. We take the position that a free response is the more natural manner in which people communicate and it constitutes the "normal" manner of structuring reality. Fixed formats are, on the other hand, artificial and represent the researcher's conception of reality. Nevertheless, the problem of equal validity is not really relevant. The test of the legitimacy of this technique will come when we assess how well it works. There is some evidence that probes of this type can increase the validity of data and do not necessarily introduce bias (Dohrenwend, 1970), and Richardson (1960) has shown that they are extensively used by experienced interviewers without being aware of it. More data is necessary before the issue can be resolved.

Once an area has been covered by both Types I and II questions, the investigator moves to another area and begins a new funnel sequence. If Type III or IV questions are to be used, they should be placed last in whatever funnel sequence they occur.

We very strongly advise against the use of indirect questions. The entire thrust of this discussion of interviewing is predicated on the assumption that directness and clarity maximize the productivity of an interview. Cannell and Kahn (1957) cite four circumstances when indirect questions may be appropriate. They are: (1) when the respondent and interviewer do not share a common language for speaking about a concept and, therefore, do not share a common understanding of it (e.g., dissonance, identification, regression, role conflict); (2) when the respondent cannot report answers directly due to repression or strong emotional fears; (3) when the desired information is very high on social undesirability; and (4) when the stimulus material is too complex to be represented in verbal form. With respect to circumstance (1) above, we would argue that the behavioral indicators underlying the concepts are commonly understood and can almost always be explicated. Gross and Mason (1953) elaborate how they conveyed the concept of role conflict to their respondents using behavior samples to convey their meaning. Circumstances (2) and (3) are variants of the projective hypothesis.

Just as in the case of projective tests, there is no evidence that indirect questions will, in fact, overcome the resistances cited. If indirect questions are used in circumstances (2) and (3), multiple indicators of the direct sort should be included also. We have no quarrel with circumstance (4); a picture should be used if it can ask the question better than a sentence can. To our knowledge, however, no one has ever shown this to be the case. Complex stimuli, such as pictures, are notoriously ambiguous. Apart from the lack of demonstrated validity, a second difficulty with indirect questions is that they generate anxiety and distrust (Whyte, 1957). Last, they violate the inquirer role relationship recommended earlier, and it is likely that they are often "seen through" with the result that the respondents' answers are purposefully distorted (Wax, 1960).

Special Purpose Interviews

The Tandem Interview

The tandem interview is simply an interview conducted by two interviewers. There is only one major report dealing with this procedure (Kincaid & Bright, 1957). That study involved a series of interviews averaging one-and-a-half hours conducted among the "business elite" in their own headquarters by a male and female interview team. The interviewers were research colleagues and both asked questions.

The major advantages of the approach appeared to be the following:

Efficiency. A great deal more ground was covered than is normally possible and recording was simplified.

Increase in rapport. The respondent had the interviewers' complete attention; he was free to talk at a normal pace, and did not need to slow down for note taking. The authors report this had a very favorable effect in that the respondents felt their time was more justifiably spent with two interviewers.

Increase in accuracy of questioning. The two interviewers were able to check each other in case one made an error. The tendency to ask leading questions was reduced and rephrasing of questions was easier. There also seemed to be a greater ability to pull for valid responses when the subject attempted to cover with cliches and facile explanations. It is apparently more difficult to "snow" two people at the same time.

Increase in range and depth of data. The authors felt they had picked up new ideas and probed for details they would not have obtained otherwise.

Increase in accuracy of analysis. Reconstruction of the interview was easier and more complete, and there was less opportunity for personal bias to enter into the interview.

It seems likely that the tandem interview would work best with competent, articulate people who know what they are being interviewed about, and who would not feel that they were being put under duress. It should be particularly productive with people whose time is at a premium. It could also be useful during the exploratory phase of a study.

The Focused Interview

The focused interview (Merton & Kendall, 1946; Merton, Fiske, & Kendall, 1956) is a specialized procedure developed for use on persons who are known to have been involved in a particular situation. Generally, the situation is one which the investigator has controlled and analyzed provisionally prior to the interview. Examples would be a radio or TV program, a filmstrip, a booklet. An interview guide is constructed on the basis of the analysis of the stimulus in order to focus the interview even further.

In spite of the narrowness of the topics treated in such an interview, a highly nondirective procedure is used by the interviewer, who encourages the respondent to structure the stimulus situation. The interviewer generally begins with unstructured questions, moves to semi-structured questions, and ends with structured questions. One unique procedure often used on the focused interview is that of stimulated recall. It entails the graphic representation of the original situation (e.g., playing back of a film or audio or videotape) in order to facilitate recollection and to increase the richness of recall. A device that may be used in conjunction with stimulated recall is the program analyzer. It is simply a mechanical device which allows the respondents to record one dimension of their reaction (by pushing buttons and marking a synchronized moving tape) while the stimulus is being presented. During the interview, the program analyzer is played back with the original stimulus material, and the respondent can be asked why he liked or disliked parts *X, Y,* and *Z.* This procedure partially reinstates the original situation by referring to an ongoing reaction at the time.

The stimulated recall procedure is currently in wide use for studying a variety of interpersonal processes (Bailey & Sowder, 1970). No one seems to have credited Merton and Kendall (1946) with the development of the original technique. Their treatment of how to use the procedure is excellent and well worth reading.

According to Merton and Kendall (1946), effective focused interviews satisfy four interrelated criteria: range, specificity, depth, and personal context.

1. *Range.* The criterion of range can be said to have been approximated when all anticipated and unanticipated responses have been elicited. In order to maximize range, Merton and Kendall recommend that interviewers be extremely careful not to stop too soon, but also not to force topics. This balance is best achieved by using nondirective procedures and not adhering rigidly to fixed questions. Too close an adherence to the interview guide may block unanticipated developments. Transition from one area of discussion to another should be smooth, natural, and, hopefully, introduced by the interviewee. Any topic that comes up should be fully explored before another is introduced.

2. Specificity. The authors admit that most experiences have configural and holistic properties, but they argue cogently that specific slices of experience elicit specific meanings and that these details are of considerable significance. A variety of procedures for achieving specificity are presented. They include reinstatement (stimulated recall), specification of response cause (e.g., What made you feel ... during that section?), explicit reference to stimulus situations, and a variety of others.

3. Depth. Not everything a respondent says is at the same psychological level (cf., Roethlisberger & Dickson, 1939, pp. 272–278). There are times when latent content is more important than manifest content and it is up to the interviewer to monitor depth accurately. A good interview is conducted at the depth appropriate to the problem. Depth is best maintained by taking the attitude that everything is not necessarily true or false and that the respondent may not be capable of saying everything he feels. It is also very important to pay close attention to anxieties, fears, sentiments, and other expressions of affect.

4. Personal context. Fruitful information may be generated by relating the stimulus being studied to the personal context of the interviewee. This is a point at which it may be of considerable importance to know something about the background of the respondent. Two types of context are of importance here, idiosyncratic context and role context. The interviewer should draw on both. This can be done by asking the respondent if he identified in any way with the situation by asking about parallel experience, etc.

The focused interview is often carried out in a group context. We will discuss this procedure in detail below.

The Group Interview

There is no standard group interview procedure. Rather, a number of researchers have interviewed groups and reported on the process. Bogardus (1926) in the earliest paper on the topic claimed that the group interview usefully supplemented the individual interview in that it brought out new data. As a basis for discussion, he used forms with prepared questions on them. Because blunders could be very disruptive to a research project, he suggested that the discussion procedure be carefully worked out ahead of time. He also recommended the use of a leader that everyone knew. Chandler (1954) felt the procedure worked best when all respondents knew the interviewer well, otherwise some participants were afraid to speak up. Edmiston (1944) made the same point and recommended that the group be representative of the unit being studied. Lundberg (1942, p. 371) suggested that the group interview could increase the reliability of some types of data. Wagner (1948), who used a critical incident procedure to collect responses, found that the group procedure took much less time than individual interviews. Thompson and Demerath (1952) commented that the data they obtained from the group procedure was impressive compared to that gathered from individuals. It purportedly had greater depth and scope. They point out that the procedure has a prodding or stimulating quality absent from the individual interview. They also cite the following advantages:

Comments by one member of the group remind others of their experiences or of additional details. Furthermore, since no individual need focus his entire attention on the details of the interviewer's next question, group members have more time for reflection. (p. 150)

They also report that the procedure was very economical and recommended the use of one interviewer to take notes and the other to ask questions. As in the tandem procedure, they note that interaction between the interviewers after the session improves the quality of their notes. Argyris and Taylor (1960), using a similar procedure called the member-centered conference, have also commented on the efficiency of the procedure and the depth and breadth of the data generated. They also recommend two interviewers. Blum (1952) used a version of the group interview in conjunction with a participant observation study. The discussions took place in his apartment following individual interviews held in the respondents' homes. They were booked as feedback sessions on the research. He claims "the information obtained in these sessions was of the greatest research significance. It touched deeper levels and gave insights not obtainable in interview conversations" (p. 41).

Kinsey and his colleagues (Kinsey, Pomeroy, Martin, & Gebhard, 1965) made a different use of groups to gather their data. They point out that by winning the confidence of a group, as a group, they ultimately obtained the confidence of its individual members. "Individuals in any cohesive group are more willing to contribute when they learn from friends that such cooperation does not involve undue embarrassment, and when they observe in the course of time that none of their friends have gotten into difficulty because they have contributed" (p. 28).

The spectacular results of Kinsey et al.—nearly 100 percent of the accessible members of some church congregations—attest to the power of this approach.

The group interview does have some serious limitations, however, and the researcher should consider them before making use of the procedure. Most of the points listed below are from Thompson and Demerath (1952).

1. Scheduling is often very difficult and a missing member can be a serious difficulty.

2. The right mix of people (which is impossible to specify) is necessary or the procedure is useless. Considerations of importance here include status differences, seniority, age, rank, etc.

3. A failure may endanger the entire research project.

4. The procedure does not tap private attitudes well.

Heller (1969) has recently described a procedure called Group Feedback Analysis which achieves many of the aims of both the focused and group interview. Its advantages and disadvantages are essentially identical to those methods.

The procedure has three stages: (1) structured individual instruments are administered to the sample; (2) relevant parts of the data from stage one are fed back to the group (which may range from five to twenty-five) in the form of means and deviations; (3) the ensuing discussion is recorded and content analyzed.

Within this framework, a large number of variations are possible. A number of different kinds of instruments may be used. Individuals may have their own scores fed back. Other group scores may be used for comparison purposes. The discussion can focus on all the data or only selected portions relevant to a particular hypothesis.

The Lengthy Interview

Surprisingly, the question of optimal interview length has received very little systematic attention. One-hour and hour-and-a-half time frames predominate. When more time is needed, a second or third appointment is generally made. Yet, there are times when much longer interviews are necessary.

Gross, Mason, and McEachern (1958) in their study of the role of the school superintendent were able to interview each superintendent only once for eight hours. An excellent report on their method can be found in Gross and Mason (1953). For a variety of reasons, they reversed the funnel sequence described previously and found that this facilitated the long interview considerably. They began the interview with a variety of specific questions dealing with the concepts they were interested in. These were followed by more open-ended questions, the answers to which served as the basis for a focused interview. The interviews took place in the researcher's office, where interruptions were avoided and the interviewer possessed psychological control of the situation. It was also possible under these circumstances to include breathing spells, coffee breaks, and lunch in the procedure. The respondents were unaware that the discussions which took place during coffee breaks and lunch were an integral part of the interview. A variety of question formats was used in order to maintain interest. The authors felt that even though the interviews took eight hours, fatigue was no problem and the procedure had been extremely successful.

Blum (1952) reports that he was able to conduct three-hour-plus interviews in the homes of workers; however, his procedure was exceedingly informal.

The Stress Interview

All interviews create some stress. The inquiry interview which we recommended probably creates the least. Nevertheless, the looping procedure, if used, can be threatening and is akin to the classic stress interview used by police interrogators (cf., Murray, 1948, p. 133). In the research situation, this procedure takes the form of forcefully pointing up weak points and contradictions in the respondents' answers (Murray, 1963; Smith, Bruner, & White, 1956).

Becker (1954) has described a mild stress or pressure technique which consists of starting out the interview at a high level of generality, leading the respondent to commit himself in a particular direction and then expressing skepticism and implying he is a liar. This procedure elicits examples of concrete behavior in areas that are generally avoided, intimated, or treated via innuendo (e.g., racial prejudice, sexual behavior, criminal behavior, even bad breath and body odor). Kinsey and his colleagues (Kinsey et al., 1965) felt they avoided this problem to some extent by assuming that the behavior they were interested in had occurred (e.g., How many times have you had extramarital relations? versus Have you ever had extramarital relations? How often?). Some research (Dohrenwend, 1970) suggests that

leading questions of this sort can be used without eliciting undue bias, and that when properly framed they do not elicit undue stress, but rather set the respondent at ease due to their similarity to normal conversation which is highly directive (Dohrenwend & Richardson, 1964; Richardson, 1960).

Chapple's (1953) technique of varying the interviewer's behavior during the course of the interview is also an effective means of generating stress. He claims it is an effective means of eliciting the respondent's characteristic traits of personality and temperament.

The Automated Interview

We know of no research projects which have used this procedure in organizational settings, but the ready availability of computer software and other electronic equipment in these settings makes it a real possibility. Material can be presented by teletype, cathode ray tube, teaching machine, even audio- and/or videotape.

Most of the research on automated interviewing has been done in the domain of medical history taking and diagnosis. There is not enough data available yet to allow firm conclusions, but it does appear that automated medical interviews are as valid as live interviews (Anderson, 1968; Coombs, Murray, & Krahn, 1970; Eaton, Altman, Schuff, & Sletten, 1970; Fishbein, 1968). A procedure commonly used in the medical domain is that of branching and logic trees. It is striking that social science researchers use this procedure only in the most trivial ways. The main reason, of course, is that they engage in classificatory and diagnostic activity only *after* data collection. As sophistication in the field grows, it will become increasingly useful to sort respondents into subgroups and study different phenomena within those groups (Owens, 1968, 1971). This could be done very efficiently at the time of the interview (or questionnaire administration) with automated equipment. It is virtually impossible to use extensive branching with printed material. A survey of the various automated medical history taking methods and equipment can be found in Budd and Boyd (1970). A potentially very useful device (because of costs and flexibility) soon to be available is the automatic branching and speaking device which administers a branching questionnaire with a taped human voice (Rosov, personal communication, 1972).

The complexity of contingencies which can be achieved with automated equipment is illustrated by a program described by Slack (1971), which conducts a medical interview while monitoring heart rate and keyboard response latency. Questions are contingent upon both these parameters as well as the subject's responses, making the course of the interview dependent on nonverbal as well as verbal information.

A less sophisticated automated procedure is the videotape interview. Virtually no research has been conducted using this method (Dinoff, Clark, Reitman, & Smith, 1969; Dinoff, Stenmark, & Smith, 1970; Dinoff, Newmark, Barnhart, Holm, Stern, & Saunders, 1970) and its potential usefulness is unknown.

A potential user of automated interview systems should examine the literature on computer-assisted instruction (Atkinson & Wilson, 1969; Balan, Browning, Jelin, & Litzler; 1969; Evan & Miller, 1969) and automated psychological testing (Brierley, 1971; Elwood, 1972; Kleinmuntz & McLean, 1968).

The Interviewer— Selection, Training, Monitoring

There is no good evidence that interviewers can be selected on the basis of personality traits or special attitudes (Cannell & Kahn, 1957; Hyman et al., 1954; Richardson, Dohrenwend, & Klein, 1965). Intelligence has been shown to have a moderate negative correlation with errors on the interview form (Guest, 1947, 1954); therefore, selection should be based on intellectual competence if nothing else. Most selection emphasis should, however, go toward minimizing the status differentials discussed previously.

There is also very little data on the training of interviewers (Hauck & Steinkamp, 1964). Most recommendations are based on opinion. Cannell and Kahn (1957) have summarized the major factors which should be covered in a training program as follows:

1. Provide the new interviewers with the principles of measurement; give them an intellectual grasp of the data-collecting function and a basis for evaluating interviewer behavior.
2. Teach techniques of interviewing.
3. Provide opportunity for practice and evaluation by actually conducting interviews under controlled conditions.
4. Offer careful evaluation of interviews, especially at the beginning of actual data collection. Such evaluation should include review of interview protocols. (p. 586)

We would add the following recommendations:

5. Provide training of coding interview responses.
6. Involve the interviewer in the construction of the interview schedule, if possible.

Suggestions one and two are self-evident and need no elaboration. Guest (1954) has demonstrated in a weak, but suggestive, study that extended practice at both interviewing and coding reduces subsequent errors. He does warn that coding practice could result in biasing the interviewer toward what the researcher wants. We strongly recommend training procedures that involve the replaying of taped interviews (preferably videotaped, but audiotaped at minimum) in order to pinpoint errors.

It is often useful to prepare an interviewer's manual. The Michigan Institute for Social Research *Interviewer's Manual* (1969) is a good example to work from.

The problem of potential bias is endemic to the interview method. It is also the case that some "so called" expectation or bias studies cannot be replicated (Friedman, 1942; Lindzey, 1951). In our opinion, the whole problem of experimenter bias has been overplayed in recent years (Barber & Silver, 1968; Snow, 1969). Nevertheless, the careful researcher will take all the precautions possible.

Smith and Hyman (1950) have presented evidence that at the coding level interviewer expectations are even stronger than ideology as a source of bias. Collins (1970) has shown that an interviewer's verbal idiosyncrasies, preferences for certain words, and verbosity bias the recording of open-ended questions and suppress variability in the data. Many studies have demonstrated the effects of verbal reinforcement, some even over the phone (Hildum & Brown, 1956). Matarazzo, Weitman, Saslow, and Wiens (1963) demonstrated that the length of a respondent's answers are directly related to the length of the interviewer's utterances in the interview situation. Shapiro (1970), in a factor analysis of interview data, demonstrated how open-ended questions generated an apparent method factor, which, when carefully examined, turned out to be an interviewer bias factor. When the factor scores for all respondents were ordered by the interviewer, it was clear that groups of respondents interviewed by one interviewer had markedly similar factor scores on the open-ended questions, while all other factor scores displayed considerable variation. This is a useful technique for detecting interviewer bias in open-ended questions. In view of the fact that a few interviewers generally contribute the bulk of the data to most studies, it cannot be assumed that these biases will balance out.

There are no panaceas for this problem. The training procedures discussed previously, plus training relevant to the project, should be used. Incoming transcripts should be monitored carefully. Quick word counts are possible and an examination of protocols will reveal if the replies to some inter-

viewers are much more similar than they should be. Sudman (1966–1967) also discusses a simple scheme which consists of counting selected types of errors for assessing interviewer quality.

Another source of error in interviewer protocols is cheating. There is evidence that cheating is more of a problem than had been thought in the past. Evans (1961) demonstrated that four out of thirteen experienced female interviewers cheated selectively. Case (1971) reports that at least 4 percent of market interviews cannot be verified and at least 25 percent contain serious errors. Roth (1966) indicated that this is a serious problem in sociological field research. Some of the techniques for assessing cheating are postcard follow-ups, spot checks, and telephone follow-ups (Case, 1971). Many investigators now send letters of introduction prior to the interview. If interviewers are aware that such communications are occurring they are less likely to falsify an entire interview. The problem of selective cheating remains, however.

It is tempting to believe that the recording of interviews in toto would eliminate bias and cheating, but then recording itself becomes a variable. Although tape recordings can be made successfully in group settings, they have a strong differentiating effect in the diadic situation. Some respondents will simply not talk with a tape recorder running, while others will speak at length for the record (Whyte, 1960). Second, the existence of a tape which must be transcribed is a threat to the confidentiality which respondents expect. A carefully coded interview would not present such a threat. Hauck and Steinkamp (1964) present a useful discussion of the problems of interviewer supervision.

QUESTIONNAIRE AND INTERVIEW CONSTRUCTION

Like the development of any other measuring instrument in the social sciences, a questionnaire requires a great deal of work before it is ready for field use. The formulation of questions for an interview or questionnaire is still pretty much an art (Noelle-Neumann, 1970; Payne, 1951) and researchers must depend on rules of thumb and past experience more than on empirical data.

Much to the surprise of many novice researchers, a fact is not a fact is not a fact is not a fact. Even what we often consider to be basic experiential data are often coded by human beings according to linguistic conventions and social rules that vary from group to group and individual to individual. Some excellent examples are given by Kinsey et al. (1965, p. 52): lower class individuals are never "ill or injured" although they may be "sick or hurt"; they may "want" but seldom "wish" to do a thing; and they can "see" but they don't "perceive." Even considerable experience in the research context will not always be sufficient for the researcher to avoid these difficulties.

In line with the inquiry perspective outlined earlier it is our opinion that the most efficient and most productive way to formulate effective questions, as well as set a positive framework for the research, is to involve at least some of the respondents in the construction of the questionnaire. If a team of interviewers will be used, it is also wise to involve them in the construction process (Sewell, 1949). The most competent and/or the most influential respondents are generally the best choice. Seldom, if ever, is a hypothesis or theoretical model so complex that it cannot be broken down into components that are understandable to the participants in a study. If the researcher feels he cannot accomplish this we suggest he reexamine his study, because it is unlikely that the answers he will get to his questions will be relevant to his hypotheses. Formulating the objectives of the study in terms that are communicable to the participants constitutes a large part of the problem of operationalizing the hypotheses into a questionnaire. But, this is often the part that is done implicitly and in an unchecked manner. Most researchers move directly from their theory or model to their questions. They generally have a model of the respondents in their heads (cf., Cicourel, 1964, esp. pp. 221–224); however, they don't consult him until the pretest stage, if that soon, and by that time the questionnaire has crystallized to such an extent that it is difficult to change.

The researcher should present his objectives and perhaps some tentative suggestions about how the questions might be asked of his participant. Together they can work out relevant parts of the questionnaire. One discovery that is likely to occur at this point is the range of frames of reference that can be brought to bear on almost any question (cf., Kahn & Cannell, 1957, pp. 556–557). The major objection that has been made to this procedure is that it is unworkable except with relatively intelligent respondents. This is not necessarily true. If the respondents are not able to conceptualize the problem at this level, then the researcher should consider the feasibility of giving ignorance the status of a variable and acknowledging its importance (Cicourel, 1964; Schneider, 1962). This is the only point at which an investigator can evaluate whether or not his procedures are or are not forcing an artificial structure on the respondent's perception of reality.

A second difficulty, which is generally not distinguished from the problem discussed above, is the possibility of questions crystallizing opinions and beliefs. This problem is conceptually, and perhaps empirically, distinguishable from the problem of ignorance. However, even if a question is instrumental in changing vague and loosely structured thoughts into a cohesive and meaningful pattern of responses, that question should not necessarily be seen as invalid.

Formulation and Sequencing of Questions

The participative construction technique does not eliminate the need to scrutinize questions and their sequence. It is wise to subject the questionnaire to criticism from professional colleagues and pretest it on a new sample of respondents. A pretest should also follow any change of questions.

The following rules for evaluating interviews and questionnaires have been culled from many sources, but we have depended heavily on Erdos (1970), Kornhauser and Sheatsley (1959), and Payne (1951). Like any set of rules, they can and should be violated when necessary; however, if they are, the possible consequences should be evaluated. Researchers should not depend on this list exclusively, but rather should use it as a starting point, elaborating, deleting, and modifying for their own situation.

1. *Is the question necessary?* If not, eliminate it. It is the researcher's responsibility to know what he needs and not burden the respondent unnecessarily. Do not collect data because it "might" be used. A review of the literature on almost any topic will reveal that rarely do data collected for other reasons suffice to answer new questions. Questionnaires can become extremely long for no good reason.

2. *Is the questionnaire repetitious?* Does another question serve the same purpose? If so, eliminate it, unless it has been deliberately included to assess reliability or provide convergent validation.

3. *Could the answer be obtained more easily elsewhere—by simple observation or from records?* If so, get it elsewhere. However, do not assume that all files on individuals are complete. They are not. Check them first.

4. *Does the question contain more than one idea? Is it double-barrelled?* If so, break it down. This type of question is almost always ambiguous to both the respondent and the researcher who interprets it. It is possible to use vague and/or double-barrelled questions as projective stimuli (Litwak, 1956), but their use in this manner would seem to demand more extensive validation than most researchers are willing to carry out (Campbell, 1950).

5. *Is the question adequate as it stands, or*

should complementary questions be asked? For example, feelings, knowledge, and behavior often need to be separated.

6. *Can the respondent answer the question?* Does he have the information? If not, don't ask it.

7. *Will the question embarrass the respondent?* If it will, and it is necessary, consider putting it at the end of the questionnaire. Rewording is also possible. For example, instead of "Did you graduate from high school?" one might ask "What grade were you in when you left school?" Even better might be a lead question "Did you get as much education as you wanted?" followed by "What grade were you in when you left school?"

8. *Could it be made more specific or more concrete?* A question that is too general elicits varying frames of reference. The level of generality should depend on the investigator's purpose. Is the level appropriate?

9. *Is the question clear?* Respondents hesitate to reveal that they do not understand a question. Be sure it is clear. Clarity generally correlates with length. Short questions are to be preferred.

10. *Would a memory jogger help?* Can the respondent consult records to gain that information? If so, request that he do so.

11. *Is the question too indirect?* Direct questions are generally preferable. Indirect questions raise suspicion and are annoying but they may be useful; for example, it might be worthwhile to know how many people display spontaneous annoyance or pleasure with something.

12. *Is the response format adequate from a theoretical point of view? Or from the respondent's point of view?* Yes-no formats are useful, but other formats may be more useful. Has ignorance (don't know) been given status? Is the intensity range adequate? Are the alternatives clear?

13. *If precoded answers are given, they will yield far more accurate answers than open-ended questions.* This distinction is similar to that between recognition and

recall scores in learning experiments. Each score has its uses. Be sure the type of score matches your need, and is not simply a function of ease of coding. The word "frequently" as a multiple-choice alternative may mean different things to different people. A specific frequency, such as five times a month, is preferable. Are there sufficient alternatives? This problem is one of the most frequently violated rules in questionnaire construction and generally vitiates the utility of the question as well as antagonizes respondents. Leaving an open alternative, such as "other," is not sufficient. Every alternative must be stated (Noelle-Neumann, 1970).

14. *Is the questionnaire susceptible to an order effect?* First and last questions stand out and randomization is desirable if the questionnaire is homogeneous. The same applies to checklists. Randomization does not do away with context effects. Adding or subtracting items in the middle of a study changes the context of judgment and is generally undesirable (Noelle-Neumann, 1970).

15. *Can the items be arranged so that particular answers preclude the need to answer others?* If so, arrange them this way. You will save time.

16. *Is an item likely to bias those following it?* If such interactions are possible, and undesirable, the items should be separated.

17. *Is the ordering of the questions natural or reasonable?* The order should not be haphazard. It should be easy and comfortable. Consider the following possible orderings: objective-subjective, familiar-unfamiliar, specific-general, past-present, present-past, past-future.

18. *Does the sequence maintain motivation?* A long series of closed-ended questions tends to bore a respondent. Often a change of technique revives interest, for example, card sorting has been shown to be a fast and interesting way to gather a great deal of data (Cataldo, Johnson, Kellstedt, & Milbrath, 1970). Graphic technique can also be used. As we pointed out earlier, it is possible to carry out long interviews with considerable

success if the preparations are adequate and the subject matter is sufficiently interesting. The same is true of long questionnaires (Sletto, 1940). When a great deal of questioning is necessary, an interview followed by a questionnaire should be considered (Magid, Fotion, & Gold, 1962).

19. *Is the opening appropriate?* The first few questions are often critical. Test them thoroughly. They should not arouse resistance, anxiety, or defensiveness. Many questionnaires begin with questions designed to capture the respondent's interest, even if they will not be used in later tabulations (Erdos, 1970, p. 60).

20. *Will the respondent be able to read and understand the questions?* Reading comprehension is consistently overestimated by researchers. A recent Harris poll (*Minneapolis Tribune,* 1970) found the following: (a) 13 percent of the population in the United States over 16 years of age (estimated at 24 percent if refusals are prorated) have serious literacy problems that impair daily life; (b) 34 percent of the sample could not fill out a *simplified* Medicaid application; (c) 8 percent of these with some college training had serious literacy problems. The Project Talent Reading Comprehension Test yielded the same dismal picture.

21. *End the questionnaire (or interview) with a courteous Thank You or similar note of appreciation.*

Design, Distribution, and Documentation of Questionnaires

The best single source of information on the design and distribution of questionnaires is Erdos (1970). There is a large literature on this topic in the marketing and advertising journals as well as the *Public Opinion Quarterly*. Kawash and Aleamoni (1971) also contain many excellent references. All of the points listed below are designed to increase the percentage of returns and they are generally additive:

1. Use quality white (not colored or

tinted) paper and print (do not mimeograph) the questionnaire.

2. Be sure the layout is clean, neat, and uncluttered. Use boxes, lines, and leaders. The questionnaire should look easy.

3. Identify the person or organization conducting the survey. A logo is very useful.

4. Identify the questionnaire with a title. The title should link the respondent to the questionnaire in a meaningful way. Be sure it is truthful or it may backfire.

5. Advance notice through a postcard, letter, or announcement generally increases returns.

6. Incentives of all sorts generally increase return rates. This includes enclosing a ten-cent or twenty-five-cent piece to business executives and doctors, as long as an adequate explanation is enclosed; for example, "The enclosed new coin is just a token of our appreciation, it may brighten the day of a child you know" (from Erdos, 1970, p. 103). Other incentives include an offer to supply a copy of the survey results and an indication of how important the data is to the respondent's organization.

7. A letter should always accompany a questionnaire regardless of whether it was mailed or delivered personally. It should be addressed to the person being surveyed and be signed by the researcher with his status and title indicated (e.g., Research Director). Care should be taken not to bias the data with the content of the letter. A personal signature may or may not increase returns (Kawash & Aleamoni, 1971), but it is unlikely to lower them. Very little is known about how the content of an introductory letter influences response rate. Hendrick, Borden, Giesen, Murray, and Seyfried (1972) varied ingratiation toward both respondent and sender. Their results were very complex.

8. If the questionnaire is to be mailed, send it first class and enclose a stamped reply envelope. Mention this in the letter. The return envelope should be addressed to the same person who signed the letter. If a previous mailing has been used to inform the respondent of the survey, the outside of the envelope should say, "This is the questionnaire we wrote you about." Every effort should be made to differentiate the questionnaire from junk mail.

9. If a questionnaire is to be used in a mail survey, pilot studies can be very useful. They can pinpoint flaws early and if there is a high rate of return the sample size may be reduced. On the other hand, they may suggest that the research is not feasible.

The problem of confidentiality is much greater with questionnaires than with interviews. Even if the questionnaire is coded and the system is explained in the accompanying letter it is doubtful that the same degree of rapport can be achieved. A small proportion of respondents, for example, always tear off the coded numbers. The empirical literature on this problem is mixed. Some studies show no difference between questionnaire and interview data, while others show striking differences (cf., McDonagh & Rosenblum, 1965, and references therein). We recommend transmitting questionnaires in person, if at all possible. There are, however, situations where personalization interacts with confidentiality. Simon (1967) in a study of employees of an industrial firm showed that personalized and individually typed letters had lower returns than form letters. The personalized letters apparently caused the employees to suspect that the assured confidentiality would not be kept.

Often a researcher has a choice of mailing to the respondent's home or place of work. There is no good rule to follow in this situation. Generally if the questions are relevant to the respondent's work and it is convenient for him to fill it out at work then it should be sent there. Alutto (1970) in a survey of the membership of a Chamber of Commerce found that questionnaires that were sent to place of employment yielded a greater completion rate for open-ended questions than those sent to homes. There was no difference for closed-ended questions. The survey dealt with the respondents' attitudes toward university administrators' decision-making procedures.

Ronan (1970) mailed questionnaires to the homes of three groups of workers, managerial-supervisory, salaried, and hourly. The returns were 63.9 percent, 65.3 percent, and 33.8 percent respectively. He does not report whether or not the questionnaires were personalized, but it is likely they were. These results complement Simon's findings.

Low completion rates plague both interview and questionnaire studies. The key question here is "Do the non-responders differ in a meaningful way from the responders?" Two techniques are often used to answer this question. The first is to compare the two groups on available characteristics such as age, sex, place of residence, etc. Ronan, in the study mentioned above, had a return rate of only 33.8 percent for hourly workers. The respondents were compared on demographic characteristics to the entire company and found not to differ. He concluded that there was probably no bias. The logic underlying this reasoning is fallacious. Just because the samples do not differ on demographic variables says nothing about whether they do or do not differ on other more important variables (cf., Gannon, Nothern, & Carroll, 1971). See Meehl (1970) for another version of the matching fallacy. The second procedure often used is to compare the original responders with the waves of respondents generated by follow-up letters. Trends such as decreasing education, age, and income often show up as potential sources of bias. It is better to know something about your sources of error than to deny they exist. It has also been shown that late responders often differ significantly from non-respondents (Williams & Wechsler, 1970). Schwirian and Blaine (1966–1967) showed that the association between variables as well as the population parameters differ across different waves of respondents (blue-collar workers). Since Ronan factor analyzed his data it is possible that he would have obtained different results had he obtained a larger sample. The best solution

to this problem is to plan the questionnaire as carefully as possible in the first place and use follow-up letters to maximize returns. Good procedures can and should get returns from 75 percent to 95 percent (Robin, 1965; Williams & Wechsler, 1970). Smaller returns than this can be useful depending on the goals of the investigator. The procedure that generates one of the highest rates of return is an interview followed by a questionnaire left to be completed at the respondent's leisure (Magid, Fotion, & Gold, 1962).

Numerous studies make extensive use of questionnaire data but do not report the questions asked. In view of the many confounding effects surrounding questionnaires it seems to us that it is imperative that the questionnaire and accompanying letter be made available in full either in appendices or as deposited documents. No editor ought to accept an article based on questionnaire data unless this requirement is met. No empirical discipline should allow it (cf., Sutcliffe, 1972).

We would like to close this section with a note on "questmongering." The questionnaire is being overused and abused as a research technique and as a result its utility is probably decreasing. We strongly urge colleagues not to ask unnecessary questions and to refrain from allowing their students to conduct useless and trite surveys for "educational" purposes.

PARTICIPANT OBSERVATION

The term "participant observation" was apparently coined by Lindeman (1924). In a later book, Hader and Lindeman (1933) give a definition and rationale for the method.

Participant observation is based on the theory that an interpretation of an event can only be approximately correct when it is a composite of the two points of view, the outside and the inside. Thus the view of the person who was a participant in the event, whose wishes and interests were in some way involved, and the view of the person who was not a participant but only an observer, or analyst, coalesce in one full synthesis. (p. 148)

This proposition remains true today. Nevertheless, the vast bulk of industrial and organizational research focuses on the inside view as gathered by questionnaires and interviews. The outside view, careful observation of ongoing behavior, is often ignored. The main reason for this seems to be that the methodology of participant observation is epistomologically suspect (Bruyn, 1963, 1966). We will not deal with this issue in this chapter, but we will note that the problem of how social scientists (as well as everyone else) make their activities "accountable" is coming under sustained scrutiny by a new group of sociologists who go by the label "ethnomethodologist" (Garfinkel, 1967; Weick, 1969).

In spite of the low esteem in which participant observation is held by the "scientific community," it is worth noting that a number of the classic studies in industrial and organizational psychology are based on this methodology (Blau, 1963; Dalton, 1959; Gouldner, 1954; Selznick, 1949). We urge the researcher to carefully examine the potential of this much maligned method. It has strengths which compensate for the weaknesses of other methods. One advantage is that it focuses the researcher's attention on the behavior of individuals rather than simply on their verbal interview or test-taking behavior. This is no small gain in light of the consistent finding that test-taking behavior in the form of attitude and satisfaction measures is consistently unrelated to the behavior of real interest to most investigators (Brayfield & Crockett, 1955; Wicker, 1969). It is difficult to understand why researchers have held so tenaciously to paper and pencil methods rather than turning to a systematic examination of the structure of the behavior of interest (cf., Brandt, 1972; Wernimont & Campbell, 1968).

A second advantage of the method is that it tends to force the researcher to look at the whole man, the whole organization, and the whole environment (social and physical) in an integrated way. Behavior in the field doesn't make sense otherwise. This focus is both compatible with and complementary to the developing emphasis in industrial and organizational psychology on understanding as opposed to a more immediate emphasis on prediction and control as well as the trend toward the use of systems models (Buckley, 1967; Berrien, 1968). If these trends continue, we can expect a welcome upsurge in the use of participant observation as a supplement to other methods.

A third advantage of this method, and perhaps a good reason why every investigator should try it in at least one study, is that it puts him in the context of discovery and facilitates what Merton (1949) calls the serendipity pattern of social research.

The serendipity pattern refers to the fairly common experience of observing an unanticipated, anomalous strategic datum which becomes the occasion for developing a new theory or extending an existing theory. (p. 98)

The Process of Participant Observation

Participant observation is not one, but at least three methods. They are participant observation, enumeration, and informant interviewing (Zelditch, 1962). A researcher may make use of the first method only, or he may combine it with either or both of the other two. He may also combine it with other more systematic techniques.

Participant observation is often described as occurring at four levels (Gold, 1958; Junker, 1960, pp. 35–38). They are:

1. *Complete participant.* This is a wholly concealed role where the researcher surreptitiously becomes a member of the group under study.

2. *Participant as observer.* In this role the researcher is somewhat open about his purpose, but his activities as a participant are kept primary in order to minimize distortion of the situation.

3. *Observer as participant.* In this role the researcher is "publicly known" and perhaps publicly sponsored. At this level informants are heavily used if the researcher is competent enough to develop the appropriate relationships. This is the standard "anthropologist role."

4. *Complete observation.* In this role the researcher is completely open and may use film, videotape, microphones, etc. In our opinion this latter role does not belong under participant observation at all.

This fourfold scheme confounds level of participation and deception. It is possible to separate the two and by dropping level four above generate a 3×2 matrix with six categories.

Below we discuss the implications of each of three levels of participation.

High Level of Participation

A high level of participation entails a heavy commitment of time and energy. A researcher should consider and weigh the value of the data obtained by this method against the effort involved. Often, but not always, this method involves deception or, more accurately, spying. Aside from the ethical difficulties involved with deceptive methods this procedure can lead to disaster if the deception is discovered. Whyte (1951) argues that the risk is seldom worth taking. The psychological burden of such a procedure is extreme and a great deal of training is necessary if the deception is to be successful over any extensive period of time. Since intense participation is of little value unless it is of considerable duration, training is always an important consideration. There is, however, almost no literature on the topic. Sullivan and Queen (1958), in a study of military training, report that in addition to extensive training their observer underwent minor surgery and lost thirty-five pounds. They found that a team approach where the observer met with the rest of the team on weekends reduced the strain of the deceptive role and helped maintain objec-

tivity. A chaplain on the base also served as a contact and functioned in the same capacity. Schwartz and Schwartz (1955) report that the strain of a deceptive role produces symptoms such as anger, resentment, disgust with the subjects of study and that these were signals that the observer was not functioning objectively. They suggest that active participation is more conducive to self-observation and, therefore, sensitizes the observer to possible sources of self-bias.

Complete participation is less obtrusive than partial participation in situations where many individuals are involved—or where most activities are prescribed. When N is small, however, an observer is always in danger of creating and/or severely modifying the phenomenon he is studying. When a number of investigators are incommunicado the danger is severe (cf., Festinger, Riecken, & Schachter, 1956, esp. the methodological appendix). The complete participant (covert or overt) finds it very difficult to record his observations and depends heavily on memory and reconstructive techniques (Dalton, 1967). Many of the new miniaturized recording devices discussed in the hardware section minimize the problem today. Heavy dependency on recollection poses serious problems of proof and should be minimized as much as possible. It has been argued that the complete participant is likely to penetrate more deeply into the social structure he is investigating than a simple observer or interviewer, and thereby generate richer data. Kluckholn (1940), for example, argues that active participation increases the range, relevance, and reliability of data. Range is increased because discussions are freer and relationships relatively open. Relevance is increased because questioning is often in the current situation rather than retrospective. And reliability (precision would be a better term) is increased because levels of depth and intimacy can be achieved that are inaccessible to interviewing. Sampling is also better in that aberrant, atypical, and maladjusted individuals are not the main source of data.

It should be noted that these advantages are not as general as they seem and they apply only to some types of information. The interaction between types of information and methods of data collection will be discussed below. The method by data type interaction does not account for all the variance in opinion on the productivity of active participation. Merton (1947) while discussing a study of the same type, but in a different cultural context than Kluckholn, argues that an unattached observer will get private confidences because the two will never meet again and so the respondent does not experience a sense of self-exposure. Merton does agree with Kluckholn on the problem of informants representing a biased sample and he urges researchers to allot sufficient time to balance out the sampling. It is also important to recognize that complete participation creates restrictions which an overt intermediate participant does not face. The complete participant often cannot change his position to take advantage of special circumstances without threatening his role. His location (status) in the social matrix may also narrow his range of experience and limit his access to certain groups and patterns of activity. Fringe, marginal, and alienated individuals who are often excellent sources of information may be inaccessible. Formal records may not be accessible and systematic interviewing or observation may be impossible (Babchuk, 1962; Blau, 1963, p. 32).

Intermediate Level of Participation

Regardless of whether or not the researcher is incommunicado, the role relationships required to maintain this status are extremely trying. The researcher will consistently find himself being asked for advice or opinions on a variety of subjects. When the research is covert, serious difficulties arise and the researcher is often forced to move into a more active role than he considers desirable in order to maintain his cover. The researcher who has taken the overt approach finds it somewhat easier to emphasize his neutrality on issues and this is generally the course advised by most experienced researchers (Whyte, 1960). There are situations, however, where neutrality is a handicap to the accumulation of valid and useful information. Blum (1952) in a union study at a Hormel plant found that telling things about himself facilitated obtaining information. He called his procedure the interview-conversation and told his respondents he would not ask anything he would not be willing to answer himself. Under these circumstances, he was able to conduct interviews that ran over three hours at one sitting. He was also able to get many of the workers to come to his apartment and participate in very productive quasi-group interviews.

The intermediate participant attempts to gain sufficient rapport to gather the information he needs, but also avoid the "over-rapport" characteristics of some situations. Over-rapport can be a serious problem in that it isolates a researcher from groups that do not relate well to the one he is identified with. Miller (1952) found that over-rapport with union leaders made it difficult to relate to the rank and file and, furthermore, it was impossible to change the situation once it was recognized as a problem. Worse still was the previously mentioned loss of ability to question union leaders about delicate problems without threatening the friendship. Miller suspects that the process of over-rapport may be used by respondents in order to limit what an observer will investigate. He, therefore, recommends a balance between rapport and psychological distance so that the observer can control the situation at all times. Parallel examples of this kind of defensiveness have been reported by Argyris (1952) and Schwartzbaum and Gruenfeld (1969).

Low Level of Participation

The observer who participates marginally always remains an outsider with a special role. He initially creates some resistance and hostility and his effect on respondents is difficult to evaluate. Schwartz and Schwartz (1955) argue that "When the observer attempts to keep himself outside the stream of events he then tends not to recognize his affective reactions or their effects on his observations." In our opinion this is not likely to be a serious problem in most organizational settings. The sensitivity of the observed to the observer is more likely than not to reduce over time and the capacity of the observer is likely to increase. Most researchers report that there is no problem if the observer succeeds in being accepted as a "person." According to Dean (1954), "A person becomes accepted as a participant observer more because of the kind of person he turns out to be in the eyes of field contacts than because of what the research represents to them" (p. 347). Whyte (1955) reports a very similar experience. The observer's perspective will change over time, however, and early observations are likely to be of considerable value later on if only to help calibrate current observations. Therefore, careful recording should begin on day one of a study (Dalton, 1967).

Preparing for a Participant Observation Study

There is very little agreement about how to prepare for and conduct a study using participant observation. Dalton (1967), for example, in a discussion of the methodology underlying his book, *Men Who Manage* (Dalton, 1959), claims: "No explicit hypotheses were formulated in MWM, chiefly for three reasons: (1) I never feel sure that it is relevant for hypothesizing until I have some intimacy with the situation—I think of a hypothesis as a well-founded conjecture; (2) once uttered, a hypothesis becomes obligatory to a degree; and (3) there is danger that the hypothesis will become esteemed for itself and work as an abused symbol for science" (p. 62).

Becker (1958; Becker & Geer, 1960) recommends a more refined strategy that he calls sequential analysis. It consists of three stages: (1) the selection and definition of problems, concepts, and indices; (2) the check on the frequency and distribution of phenomena; and (3) the incorporation of individual findings into a model of the organization under study (p. 271).

Participant observation yields voluminous quantities of raw protocol data. Becker and Geer (1960) report 5,000 single-spaced pages from a medical school study. Blau (1967) reports he has three file cabinets of notes and memos on his *The Dynamics of Bureaucracy* (1963). It seems imperative that an investigator construct some sort of structure prior to entering the field or he will be overwhelmed. Blau (1967), for example, prepared a detailed schedule of research procedures and problems. Each research problem was outlined on a 5 × 8 slip and cross-classified by procedures to be used to study the problem. The file was used in a flexible way and modified as the research proceeded. The flexibility of the method of participant observation also provides nicely for changes of plan. Completing a rigid research design in the field is difficult (Miller, 1954).

There are no fixed rules regarding what should be recorded, but some basic pieces of information are almost always necessary (cf., Selltiz et al., 1960):

1. *Time*. Year, month, day, hour, and second, if necessary.

2. *Location*. Be precise. There are many corridors, men's rooms, etc. A spatial analysis may require precise determinations.

3. *Participants*. Who and in which roles?

4. *Purpose*. Why are they there? Consider both formal and informal reasons.

5. *Function*. What are they doing? Who is doing what to whom?

6. *Frequency and duration*. How often and for how long?

Much of this information can be coded quickly and accurately, but it is essential that it be complete. The sooner the data are recorded the better. On-the-spot recording, even when the research is covert, can be accomplished with a pen and a small piece of paper. A note pad can often be blocked out ahead of time with various spaces representing categories. Pens can be carried on one's clothing. The invention of this method is attributed to Galton. Data recorded in such cryptic forms should be translated as soon as possible, the raw protocols serving as memory crutches.

When no recording at all can be accomplished mnemonics are useful. Lindgren (1939) coded important sequential events by associating them with letters of the alphabet. Essentially this is a plan for remembering (Miller, Galanter, & Pribram, 1960, Chap. 10), that maintains structure and minimizes distortion. Generally, any kind of plan for recall is superior to "going in cold." If key words can be written down during the interaction they can form a useful skeleton for reconstructing the event later on.

When recording is done in the open, the record itself can be very useful if subsequent interviewing is to take place. Melbin (1953) reports that a maplike chart on which he used to plot interactions proved to be a very effective stimulus during subsequent interviewing. It facilitated recall for both the researcher and the respondent.

Even when the researcher is in the open it is sometimes wise not to take notes. Dalton (1967) gives the following reasons for not taking them: (1) informants become guarded when they see the material written down; (2) they would not give the exact report twice, anyhow; (3) the note-taking detracts from careful observation of the informants' visual behavior, intonation, etc.; and (4) it slows the informants down.

Informant Interviewing

One well-recognized, but often ignored, distinction in field research is that between respondent and informant. Respondents are or should be randomly or systematically selected and considered replicable. Informants, on the other hand, are either self-selected or chosen on the basis of knowledgeableness and ability to communicate.

Dean (1954) distinguishes between two types of useful informants and gives a number of characterizations of each type. The first type includes those individuals who are for one reason or another sensitive to what goes on around them. They are:

• The *outsider,* who sees things from the light of another culture, social class, community, etc.

• The *"rookie,"* who is surprised by what goes on and notes the taken-for-granted things that the acclimated miss. And as yet, he may have no *stake* in the system to protect it.

• The *nouveau* status, that is, the person in transition from one role or status to another where the tensions of new experience are raw and sensitive.

• The *"natural,"* that is, the rare and reflective objective person in the field. He can sometimes be pointed out by other intelligent and reflective persons.

The second group is made up of those individuals who, for whatever reason, are more willing to talk than others. They are:

• The *naive informant,* who knows not whereof he speaks: either (1) naive to what the field worker represents, or (2) naive about his own group.

• The *frustrated person* (rebel or malcontent), especially the one who is consciously aware of the blocking of his drives and impulses.

• The *"outs,"* those out of power, but "in-the-know," and critical of the *"ins"*— eager to reveal negative facts about the "ins."

• The *habitué,* "old hand," or *"fixture around here,"* who no longer has a stake or is so accepted that he is not threatened by exposing what others say or do.

• The *"needy" person,* who fastens onto the interviewer because he needs the attention and support. As long as the respondent feels this need, he will talk.

• The *subordinate,* who must adapt to superiors. He generally develops insights to suction the impact of authority, and he may be hostile and willing to "blow his top."

In spite of their self-selected and/or atypical status, informants can and do provide useful information. This information can sometimes be obtained in other ways, but the informant can often supply it faster, more economically, and with a greater degree of accuracy. Campbell (1955) found that carefully selected informants who were not members of crews could judge the morale of ship crews very accurately. Dean (1958) found that some respondents systematically over-reported attendance at union meetings. This spuriously inflated some (not all) of the correlations between attendance and attitudes towards unions in general. Since attendance in this situation was extremely regular, the union officers acting as informants could have supplied the data at a greater level of accuracy than the respondents.

Certain informants may be in a position to know. It would be foolish not to use their information because they are not representative. Secretaries are an excellent example of this group. Informants may also be used as stand-ins for the researcher. It is impossible to be everywhere at once. A qualified informant can often make the appropriate observations. In some cases he can even go further. Dalton (1967) had informants introduce certain agreed-upon topics into discussions, both in his presence and out of it, in order to assess the subjects' reactions.

Since informants are for the most part self-selected, it is important that the researcher strive to include as many representatives of groups he is not in contact with as possible. He should also try to reach as many "normal" members as possible. No matter how hard one tries, it is impossible to counter the distortions introduced when most of one's data comes from the marginal, the disaffected, the hostile, and the pathological.

Informant Motivation

As we suggested above, an informant's motivation may be negative. It may also be positive. In any event, it is important that it be evaluated accurately in order to maintain objectivity and reinforce it, thereby keeping the information coming. A good participant observer continuously asks himself, "Why is this person telling me anything?" Any cues that may be used to index an informant's motivation should be carefully recorded. Wax (1960) suggests that a very common reason why informants supply information is that it gives them a chance to release aggression. This is often revealed in cracks about bureaucratic bungling and administrative stupidity. Sometimes the aggression is highly focused (e.g., against one individual). Sometimes it is diffuse (e.g., against the organization). In each case the distortion likely to be introduced into the data is different. According to Vidich and Bensman (1960), lying to the researcher is a common occurrence "particularly in communities or other relatively self-contained orders which come under the pervasive scrutiny of social research" (p. 191). This problem is likely to be serious when a researcher has misled his informants and has been detected. Under these circumstances he may be repaid in kind.

A problem that comes up at times is "should the investigator pay his informants?" We have a vague and unverified feeling that this has been done. Ethics aside, we believe that this is a bad procedure and is likely to elicit as much misinformation as valid information. An investigator who puts himself in such a situation may be violating the law and even if he isn't, he is putting himself in a position where he is "fair game" for any sort of deception on the part of his informant.

On the positive side, sometimes informants are simply bored, gregarious or curious. These are powerful sources of motivation that minimally distort the information being collected. They should be carefully nurtured. This can be done in a variety of ways. Sometimes it is only necessary to be helpful and friendly as specific occasions demand. Often the researcher can provide transportation, run errands, etc. Wolcott (1970), who was observing a school principal for a good part of three days a week for a year, drove the principal and other administrators to meetings. The conversations he overheard in the car proved to be very useful.

A number of investigators have suggested that the observer provides the informant "with opportunities to express opinions and attitudes without fear of contradiction" (Scott, 1963). An informant may be testing the observer's gullibility and a totally uncritical attitude can lead to the investigator's being thought a fool. An open and honest attitude on the part of the researcher is sometimes more productive than an attempt to maintain strict neutrality (Scott, 1963; Blum, 1952; Gullahorn & Strauss, 1960).

Schwartzbaum and Gruenfeld (1969) have shown that "the amount of time subjects spend in interaction with an observer who has discouraged this behavior may be an important means of distinguishing those supervisors who are well integrated into the organization from those who are tense and anxious about their work" (p. 448). The high interactor was the best integrated. He was seen as less interested in protecting his image than cultivating the researcher as a source of information.

An investigator should always be prepared to elicit and capitalize on the bias-correcting tendencies of subjects. Scott (1963) reports how the comments of some workers would be challenged and corrected on the spot if they were biased and overheard. This, of course, is a tricky business and can be done only under certain circumstances. The group interview discussed earlier is an excellent procedure for capitalizing on this tendency.

The sensitive investigator will maintain the balance of social obligations incurred between himself and his informants, if for no other reason than that he may need their help in the future. Terminating the contacts developed during a study is sometimes quite difficult. Often some quite stringent implicit obligations have been incurred and they may limit what an observer can ethically report. Failure to observe social sanctions of this sort may not hurt the particular investigator but they may seriously affect the ability of future researchers to carry out their work (cf., Cicourel, 1964, p. 66; Editorial, 1958).

Objectivity

Objectivity is a goal for which all researchers should strive, but one which is only approximated, never achieved. Data collected by participant observation is open to more validity threats than that obtained by any other method. Nevertheless, data gathered by such means is more useful than no data at all. Here we discuss ways by which the objectivity of participant observer data can be increased. Many of these items are modified from Bruyn (1963, 1966). The list is purposefully redundant and summarizes much of the material presented in this part of the chapter.

1. Bolster interpretations with data from other sources, such as other observers, structured and unstructured interviews, recordings, pictures, archival data, etc.

2. Separate facts from interpretations. Indeed, this distinction should be maintained at all times. The data base for an interpretation should be recorded at the time the interpretation is made.

3. Distinguish carefully between informant and respondent data.

4. Be aware of your own prejudices, defenses, biases, stereotypes, etc. (Dalton, 1967; Schwartz & Schwartz, 1955).

5. Be sensitive to your own position in the social structure (Bain, 1960).

6. Be aware of the motivations, biases, and prejudices of your respondents and informants (Argyris, 1952).

7. Examine all counter positions carefully and openly. The plight of the worker may indeed be miserable, but it must be understood in the context of management's situation.

8. Observe your subjects in as many different contexts as possible (Becker, 1954).

9. When quantitative terms are used (e.g., many) indicate the percentage of the total group to which you are referring and how you arrived at the figure.

10. Be sensitive to changes in your own attitudes, beliefs, and emotions. Such changes are often cues to a lack of objectivity (Sullivan & Queen, 1958; Schwartz & Schwartz, 1955).

11. Recognize that your subjects are not a random aggregate, but rather a social network. People live, work, and function in groups (Bain, 1960).

12. Avoid over-rapport and do not identify symbolically or emotionally with any subgroup unless it is tactically necessary. Maintain sufficient distance so that your implicit commitments to individuals will not proscribe your movements (Miller, 1954; Jaques, 1951).

13. Be sure that your informants know you will be gathering data from others. If they know you will be checking on them they are less likely to lie.

Reporting

The problem of reporting data from participant observation studies has bothered investigators for a long time. Most of the information is transmitted in narrative form and the reader finds it difficult to assess the objectivity of the report. A number of authors have attached methodological appendices to their work (Dalton, 1959; Blau, 1963; Festinger, Riecken, & Schachter, 1956). These appendices and the methodological reports from other studies have been very valuable in the preparation of this chapter, but they do not objectify the data presented in the original reports. There appears to be no solution to this problem.

The best partial solution we have seen is Becker's (1958) suggestion that participant observers should maintain a natural history of their research and report it pretty much as it occurs.

SYSTEMATIC OBSERVATION TECHNIQUES

Much like the domain of personality measurement, the domain of systematic observation techniques is plagued with the problem of units. There are as many coding or observation schemes as there are personality tests (Herbert, 1970; Weick, 1968). It is doubtful that any recommendations will be widely applicable across all organizational settings. Nevertheless, systematic observation has advantages which deserve to be emphasized in spite of the numerous methodological difficulties encountered in implementing it.

Accurate and comprehensive descriptions of behavior will enable researchers to deal with the criterion problem in a meaningful way. For example, they should prove useful for the development of behaviorally anchored rating scales (Fogli, Hulin, & Blood, 1971) as well as making the job enlargement literature more meaningful.

Observational data can help researchers avoid the fallacy of concluding that behavioral variation exists when behavior has not been studied. As an illustration, there is an enormous body of literature on the Motivation-Hygiene theory that has never linked itself to observed behavior (cf., Dunnette, Campbell, & Hakel, 1967; Grigaliunas & Herzberg, 1971; House & Wigdor, 1967; King, 1970). It is also the case that most of the researchers who use attitude measures implicitly assume that attitudes can be linked to behavior. Yet we know that the majority of the time this assumption is probably invalid (Wicker, 1969). We agree with Williams (1959) that in the long run "no amount of ingenious question construction can serve as an adequate substitute for a detailed empirical description of the social behavior of the subjects of a survey."

Observers often see things that respondents take for granted or are unaware of. Gross (1961) in a study of control of competition in a wholesale manufacturing plant found, when competition was defined as doing similar kinds of work and/or having the same supervisor, that in every informal group not one member was in competition with any other member. Interviews revealed that none of the members was aware of this.

The observer's motivation is much less a source of distortion than the respondent's and, therefore, should generate a more accurate record. In his examination of lunch contacts by workers in a federal enforcement agency, Blau (1963, p. 151) found large discrepancies (39 percent) between reported contacts and actual contacts. These contacts were important both in terms of the status they conferred and the information exchanges which took place. A model which depended on reported contacts would underestimate their ubiquity and miss important parameters in the system.

Conceptual Problems in Observation Studies

Units—imposed or natural? Natural units of behavior generally refer to behavior segments or episodes imposed on a behavior stream when an observer imputes goals and motives to the behavior (Barker, 1963; Dickman, 1963; Scheflen, 1968). Classification of natural behavior units depends on knowledge of context. When behavior is being categorized with an imposed system, it is generally recommended that the use of context be discouraged (Weick, 1968). The major reason for worrying about context effects is that the classification of later responses is dependent upon the classification of earlier responses and artificial consistency may be imposed on the data. This can be a serious problem in hypothesis-testing con-

texts. It is less important when the inquiry is hypothesis-free or exploratory. Nevertheless, the problem deserves more research. Context may either decrease or increase reliability and validity depending upon the level of analysis required.

The problem of deciding whether or not to use "natural units" is a variation on the problem of deciding which sort of data-gathering instrument to use. For example, Willems and Willems (1965) demonstrated that an index of forces toward participation based on coded interviews (natural units) was more predictive of actual participation in five behavior settings (.87) than methods that imposed units (card sort .54, check list .32).

The simplest solution to the problem of which units to use is to choose a standardized scheme which has already been developed and validated. Often, however, standardized schemes are used as second-best alternatives and this "solution" may fail because the operationalization achieved by the scheme is not sufficiently close to the investigator's conceptualization. The coding scheme may be too coarse. A net with a two-inch mesh doesn't catch fish that are only one-inch wide, and the failure to catch fish under two inches doesn't tell us anything about whether or not such fish exist. The coding scheme may be conceptually irrelevant. A phenomenon manifesting itself at the level of grammatical or temporal structure will not be revealed by an analysis of manifest content. A system which is relevant may be insensitive because it has too many or too few categories. More often than not, investigators choose category systems which are too fine and don't reflect the way the behavior of interest is structured (cf., Barker, 1965; Schoggen, 1963).

If available systems do not fit the researcher's needs he will have to construct his own. There are few guidelines for constructing category systems. Good discussions can be found in Katz (1966), Medley and Mitzel (1963), and Weick (1968).

It is sometimes argued that imposed

categories should never be used, but rather that the behavior of interest should be examined for natural units. We feel that this argument is sterile. The theory or problem under consideration should be the prime determinant of the kinds of units to be used. The fruitfulness of the theory should then determine if their use should be continued. Other sciences have found both imposed and natural units useful in answering different kinds of questions.

Passivity versus tempered naturalness. Except for deliberate field experiments, field settings have seldom been purposefully manipulated in order to test hypotheses or facilitate the collection of data. The "hands off" approach is valid for many purposes. Manipulation affects natural time constants which may be fundamental to the phenomena of interest. For example, if certain events occur rarely they may simply be ignored and/or forgotten and seem to have little psychological impact. Increasing their frequency by tempering the environment while decreasing the dross rate, in effect changes the nature of the question the investigator is asking (Gump & Kounin, 1960). Nevertheless, for many purposes, settings are robust and carefully chosen interventions can be used to generate desirable data or test hypotheses. Weick (1968) has labeled this process "tempered naturalness." Dalton (1967) made use of it when he had his informants ask pre-programmed questions in normal conversations in order to find out what people thought about particular events or people.

Tempered naturalness is another name for the "naturalist's alternative." "Manipulate only as much as is necessary to answer your questions clearly and otherwise leave things alone, for there is order even in what seems to you to be the worst confusion..." (Menzel, 1969, p. 91).

Sampling versus comprehensive coverage. Whether the behavior under scrutiny should be sampled or coded comprehensively depends on the purposes of the investigation. Samples of behavior do not convey the same picture as a comprehensive record (Arrington, 1943; Guest, 1955; Soskin & John, 1963) and have less utility as archival data. Samples also destroy intrinsic structure (Barker, 1963) and force the investigator to use imposed units. Hayes, Meltzer, and Wolf (1970) have recently shown that in a discussion task, both the kind of unit of observation chosen (level of complexity) and the sampling rate have an important impact on which conclusions will be drawn about the sequential organization of the behavior observed. This is a relatively unexplored problem and similar difficulties are likely to exist in other domains.

Validity Problems in Observational Studies

Observer validity. Weick (1968, based on Campbell, 1958) presents an extensive list of the ways in which an observer departs from a systematic recording of events. The discussion below is drawn in part from that source. Most observer errors are similar to rating errors and additional material has been drawn from that domain (Guilford, 1954). The sources of error can be classified as content errors, context errors, and errors of bias.

Content errors are due mostly to the operating characteristics of the observer. They are abbreviation, elaboration, middle message loss, and closure and symmetry. Abbreviation refers to simplification and loss of detail in an observation. Almost all observation systems require selection and reduction of observations. There is always the problem of losing important details. Elaboration refers to the addition of unobserved material to a record. Typically, the addition is a logical (expected?) extension to what was observed. Middle-message loss refers to the interviewer's forgetting the center portions of an observation due to primacy and recency effects. Note that if the observer's focus is set at the initiation of interaction, the loss may be at the end of the event. Closure and symmetry refer to the tendency, particularly in ambiguous situations, to complete and/or smooth out an observation on the basis of perceptual as opposed to logical principles. The result of closure and symmetry errors may be abbreviation or elaboration.

Context errors are due primarily to the material or events which surround or are associated with an observation or observer. These are enhancement of contrast, contamination of associated cues, assimilation to prior inputs, and coding relativism. Enhancement of contrast refers to distortion introduced when recordings of observations exaggerate the differences between categories. Typically, this involves enhancing some factors (elaboration) and ignoring or deleting others (abbreviation). Contamination of associated cues refers to the fact that if two cues go together (are somewhat correlated), even if only one is supposed to be focused on, both will come to contribute to coding decisions. Further, if the correlation later breaks down (the cues are no longer associated) the error will be perpetuated. Assimilation to prior inputs refers to the "tendency to distort messages in the direction of identity with previous inputs" (Campbell, 1958, p. 346). Weick (1968) has pointed out that this source of error will bias the data toward typical events and has a tendency to impose more regularity and order than there actually is. Coding relativism refers to the fact that the observer's internal standard for placing a behavior into a category varies as a function of previous behaviors. For example, after recording a series of violent events, behavior that would otherwise be considered vigorous might be coded as relatively subdued.

Errors of bias fall into two groups, judgmental bias and method bias. The judgmental biases are errors of central tendency, logical errors, affective bias, errors of assimilation-contrast, and errors due to prior experience. The method biases are response bias and proximity bias. Errors of central tendency are due to the tendency of observers and raters to hesitate to give extreme ratings or classify events as extreme. Logical errors are due to the fact that judges rate or classify things together on the basis of what they think rather than on the basis of what they observe. A recently discovered version of this error is that of illusory correlations where an erroneous inference about the relationship between two categories of events occurs because of the differential distribution and characteristics of the events (Chapman, 1967). Affective biases occur because of the strong tendency for observers to evaluate everything as either positive or negative and then allow this impression to influence subsequent evaluations. In the rating domain this generates two kinds of error, leniency error and halo effect. Error of assimilation-contrast refers to the fact that on some dimensions observers tend to see others more like themselves than they are and on other dimensions they see others as more different from themselves than they are. See Guilford (1954, p. 280) for examples. Errors due to prior experience refer to the fact that people with a great deal of experience using one system of coding or classification may assimilate it to the new system and distort data compared to coders who did not use the previous system. Response bias refers to observer preferences for particular categories (e.g., yes versus no; true versus false) that are unrelated to the events being recorded. They are often called response styles. Proximity bias refers to the fact that scales or categories adjacent to each other tend to correlate higher than nonadjacent scales. Thus, the proximity of the scales themselves on the coding sheet influences the score.

Two major approaches are available for avoiding or attenuating the variability these errors introduce into the data. They are training and methodological controls. The best way to improve an observer's performance is to teach him to observe systematically. This entails extensive training, the amount varying with the observational system. As with interviewers, observers who understand what the categories mean and what the sources of error are, will perform better than observers who do not understand the scheme and/or have no awareness of various sources of error. Practice with a method followed by group discussion is an effective training procedure. Other procedures include practice with audio- and video-tapes prior to coding live action. For large projects, it is often worthwhile to prepare training manuals and training films (or videotapes). Additional discussion of this topic can be found in Heyns and Zander (1953), Medley and Mitzel (1963), and Weick (1968).

Many errors can also be avoided by using appropriate methodological controls. Categories can be randomized across raters and time periods. Periods of observation can be shortened to reduce fatigue. Recording can be done more promptly in order to reduce forgetting. Continuous feedback can be given on the quality of the data being gathered.

Instrument validity. Films, videotape, audio-tape, etc. *do* distort and lie. Transcripts from these media compound the distortion. Machines are "event recorders" with different operating characteristics than the human sensorium. The camera zooms, foreshortens, doesn't scan as much, works from a relatively fixed locus, sometimes focuses from an unusual angle, and often requires lights which influence the respondent's behavior in subtle ways (Michaelis, 1955). Films differ from videotapes which differ from still photographs and all three differ from audio-tapes and transcripts in obvious and not so obvious ways (McLuhan, 1964). Variance due to instrumentation effects is unexplored territory and casual generalizations from media-specific studies should be avoided.

Respondent validity. Although researchers are aware that respondents may lie on questionnaires and interviews, they are not very sensitive to the possibility that people lie with their behavior. This possibility should always be seriously examined. If respondents can talk for the tape recorder they

can certainly act for the camera (observer). Respondents may also modify their behavior in much more subtle ways in response to observation. Most investigators, however, seem to agree that observations in familiar settings are relatively uncontaminated once the persons being observed have had a chance to adapt (Purcell & Brady, 1966; Soskin & John, 1963). In organizational settings most people are constantly under the informal observation of their peers. The problem of reactivity increases in proportion to the extent that a person's behavior is not typically under some sort of scrutiny.

Situational Classification

The problem of classifying situations or behavior settings is an important one for field researchers because the development of an adequate taxonomy would greatly enhance our ability to compare data gathered by different investigators. At the very least a taxonomy would facilitate the development of empirical generalizations. It would also allow us to speak meaningfully about individual-environment fit (Cronbach, 1957; Endler & Hunt, 1966; Owens, 1968; Pervin, 1968; Sells, 1963). Situational classification shades quickly into ecological psychology and environmental assessment, topics not treated in this chapter. Here we only intend to call the researcher's attention to the issue.

Field work is arduous and often unproductive. One way to increase the probability of generating useful data is to choose settings carefully. Settings are not interchangeable and some settings are far more significant than others (Frederiksen, 1972; Kelly, 1969; Krause, 1970). Serious thought should be given to both the practical and theoretical relevance of a setting (e.g., its representativeness, psychological significance, frequency of usage).

Miller (1958) suggests that interaction situations may be classified in terms of their degree of dependency on other members versus dependency on cues from the problem environment. The higher the degree of "situationality" the less the variation in a participant's behavior is a function of variation in other participants' behavior. Situations may also be defined by the structure of the environment. Socio-fugal space drives people to the periphery of a room, while socio-petal space focuses people toward the center and encourages social interaction (Hall, 1959, p. 215; Sommer, 1969, p. 121).

Observation and/or Coding Schemes Useful in Field Settings

Almost all of the systematic observational and/or coding schemes in existence could be used in field settings if they were appropriately modified and/or applied to records (written, film, etc.) of observations made in the field. Here our treatment is restricted to a few examples from the various areas which have been researched or appear promising. More exhaustive treatments of available schemes in particular areas can be found in Birdwhistell (1970), Boyd and DeVault (1966), Chapple and Sayles (1961), Duncan (1969), Ekman, Friesen, and Taussig (1969), Guest (1960), Herbert (1970), *Journal of Research and Development in Education* (1970), Medley and Mitzel (1963), and Weick (1968).

Analysis of Verbal Material

Content analysis. Content analysis has undergone extensive growth and sophistication with the advent of high-speed computers. Some of the more recent treatments of this technique can be found in Holsti (1968), and Gerbner, Holsti, Krippendorff, Paisley, and Stone (1969). Most computer coding systems are variations of *The General Inquirer* (Stone, Dunphy, Smith, Ogilvie, & Associates, 1966). *The General Inquirer* is a set of computer programs designed to manipulate textual material. It will:

(a) identify systematically, within text, instances of words and phrases that belong to categories specified by the investigator; (b) count occurrences and specified co-occurrences of these categories; (c) print and graph tabulations; (d) perform statistical tests; and (e) sort and regroup sentences according to whether they contain instances of a particular category or combination of categories. (Stone et al., 1966, p. 68)

The categories specified by the user constitute a dictionary. Examples of available dictionaries that might be of use to organizational psychologists are: (1) the Harvard III Psychosociological dictionary which assesses roles, objects, settings, and psychological processes; (2) the Simulmatics dictionary developed to analyze product and corporate images; (3) the Lasswell Value dictionary; (4) the Kranz (1970) activities dictionary.

Content analysis is equally applicable to recordings of interactions and documents and historical records. Protocols may be taken as is or systematically generated by having respondents react to fixed stimuli.

Contentless analysis. Verbal material is structured and directed. Some analytic schemes focus only on these characteristics. The Chapple (1940, 1949, 1962) interaction chronograph was developed to assess the timing and duration of interactions. Lauver (1970) has recently described a simple and inexpensive device for accomplishing this kind of recording. More sophisticated systems have been described by Wiens, Matarazzo, and Saslow (1965), and Hayes (1967, 1969). Examples of the kinds of measures these devices yield are latency, duration, filled time, demand for talking, total verbal output, interruptions, verbal dominance, and various combinations of the above.

Verbal interactions. No interaction scheme has gained wide acceptance for analyzing verbal behavior in any group setting. Bales's (1950a, 1950b) Interaction Process Analysis (IPA) is the most widely used system in social psychology, but it has had little impact on organizational research (cf., Caudill, 1958; Landsberger, 1955). The IPA system is a content-free system with twelve categories focusing on two broad classes of behavior—task and social-emotional orientation. The system has undergone recent modifications which may make it more useful (Bales, 1968; Borgatta, 1962).

Argyris (1965, 1969, 1970) has developed a scheme for categorizing behaviors (verbal) which are hypothesized to inhibit or facilitate interpersonal relationships. Mann (1967) has developed a sixteen-category member-to-leader scoring system for assessing member-feelings toward the leader. Schoonmaker (1966) modified a scheme previously developed by Haire (1955) for studying bargaining behavior. Katz (1966) has briefly described a method of analyzing interpersonal behavior which focuses on role behavior and intentionality. Essentially, the procedure answers the question "who, what, to whom?"

Additional systems for analyzing small-group interaction can be found in Bion (1959), Longabaugh (1963), Hare (1962), Mills (1964), Schultz (1958), and Thelen (1959).

Categorizing Overt Behavior

According to Guest (1960):

No one has yet succeeded in developing a universally applicable typology of behavior categories of observed events. Probably no one will, inasmuch as the purpose for classifying such behavior differs with each separate hypothesis under inquiry. (p. 225)

Scott (1965) issued the same complaint five years later and we can only echo it here.

Guest (1960) has reviewed a large number of individual category systems and is the best single source on the subject. Melbin (1954) has described a recording device (3 × 5 card) that can be used covertly in participant observation studies. The categories answer the question: "Who does what, with whom, when, where, for how long, and under what conditions?" The system is best adapted to situations where the observer will use the data to compile more complete notes at the end of the day. In an

earlier paper, Melbin (1953) described a system of interaction recording that made use of a layout of the floor plan of the setting being studied. Both of Melbin's methods should be adaptable to a variety of coding schemes. Atteslander (1954) has described a similar device.

Guest (1955, 1960) has drawn up a system of classifying incidents involving six dimensions. Each dimension represents a varying number of categories. A fictitious example of an incident is given below. The number in parentheses indicates the number of categories available for that dimension.

Incident No. 1 (10:56 A.M.)
1. Topic: Grievances (16)
2. Place: Department Office (7)
3. Activity: Telephone (12)
4. Contact: General Superintendent (17)
5. Interaction: Foreman initiates, other responds (6)
6. Time: (recorded in quarter minutes)

Guest's system can be modified for use in a wide variety of settings. The data can easily be computer coded and could be used as a basis for individual interviews or Heller's (1969) group feedback analysis.

Many additional but specialized behavior classification systems can be found in the work-sampling literature (cf., Barnes, 1956, 1963; Hansen, 1960; Nadler, 1953).

Self-Observation

All observation data need not be collected by an independent observer. Self-reports of activities in the form of diaries, check lists, etc. have been used intermittently for a long time. Self-reports dealing with all of an individual's activities over a fixed period of time (e.g., a day) are called "time budgets" (Lundberg, Kamarovski, & McInerney, 1934; McCormick, 1939; Sorokin & Berger, 1939). Two major difficulties have prohibited the widespread use of this method. The first is sheer volume of data produced. The second is the unpredictable manner in which human perception and memory select and distort information. The first problem is being overcome as our ability to process large volumes of textual material by computer increases. Kranz (1970) has described a version of the *General Inquirer* (Stone et al., 1966) which should be useful to researchers who wish to make use of the time-budget technique.

The second problem can be solved by using systematic sampling techniques. Carroll and Taylor (1970) have described a procedure which can be used in many organizational settings. It is called the Self-Observation Central-Signaling method (SOCS) and it consists of flickering the lights at a randomly chosen time during each half hour of the day as a signal to the respondents to write down what they are doing. Managers who were not on the plant floor were given two short rings on their phones. A comparison of data collected by the SOCS method and independent observers yielded essentially identical results. Modifications of the SOCS technique using alarm wristwatches and/or personalized transceivers are easily envisioned.

UNOBTRUSIVE MEASURES

The domain of unobtrusive measures is extremely heterogeneous and ill-defined. The major criterion for classifying a method as unobtrusive is that the data generated by the method are not contaminated by reactivity. Thus, the interview is a reactive method because the respondent is aware that he is being tested. Participant observation is a reactive method because the observer (even if he is covert) is a significant source of stimulation that may affect the behavior being emitted by his respondent. Lack of reactivity in a method does not mean that the data generated are valid. There are numerous other sources of invalidity in addition to reactivity. Unobtrusive methods can often, but not always, provide valid data and eliminate the rival hypothesis "reactive measurement effects" (Webb et al., 1966, p. 173). Indeed, many of the methods previously discussed occasionally yield such measures. Webb et al. (1966) have suggested

four large classes of measures—physical traces, archives, simple observation, and measures gathered with hardware. Our discussion is organized around this classification system.

Physical Traces

Physical traces are generally very indirect indicators of psychological and social processes. They are, therefore, most prone to misinterpretation and should be used with caution. An example of this error is the use of indexes of floor wear to assess frequency of use, and indirectly, popularity. Alternative interpretations might be: a bathroom or water fountain was located in the area, the arrangement of furniture allowed no degrees of freedom, the floor material in that area had different characteristics and simply wore faster (poorly calibrated instrument).

Nevertheless, frequency is a useful indicator and it can often be accurately indexed by wear. Data of this sort, for physical surfaces, can be obtained by visual inspection reports from janitors and maintenance records. Files, records, and various data books can be examined to see which sections are used most frequently. Missing pages may serve the same function. Wastebaskets and garbage cans have even been used as sources of information (Hughes, 1958; Shadegg, 1964).

The simple presence of a file cabinet which meets particular government specifications (Department of Defense, 1970) indicates the storage of classified information and may indicate secret research which the field researcher is officially unaware of. Status rankings can still be made by noting the presence of a rug, location (corner, central, peripheral) of an office, access to secretaries and equipment, etc.

Archives

Documents and records can be very useful to a field researcher but their use has been very circumspect because they can never be taken at face value. Even elementary statistics, such as operating costs, are juggled for political reasons (Dalton, 1959).

Angell and Freedman (1953), Madge (1965), Mann (1968), and Webb et al. (1966), all have excellent discussions of the serious limitations of various kinds of documents. In spite of these limitations it should be emphasized that some classic studies of organizational behavior have depended heavily on records (Gouldner, 1954; Selznick, 1949).

The speeches of executives and the organization's own internal statements may be subjected to content and motivational analysis (Donley & Winter, 1970), but they are likely to reveal little. A clinical analysis of actual speeches and news conferences which focuses on slips of the tongue, hesitations, evasive clauses, short replies, etc. is likely to be more diagnostic and informative.

Some documents can be analyzed to yield a literacy index (Plog, 1966; Routh & Rettig, 1969).

In some cases researchers are given access to, and make extensive use of, confidential records (Selznick, 1949). The researcher who does this should have a clear understanding, preferably in writing, of what he can and cannot publish (cf., Whyte, 1959).

Desk calendars, schedule books, and memos can be useful in reconstructing a sequence of events. They may also be useful in the construction of time budgets. Phone bills and records of calls can be used to document a network of contacts. Libraries often record frequency of use of books by whom and when.

A unique source of archival data in the communications industry is "out-takes," field interviews and other material gathered by TV and radio networks, but never shown or published. An analysis of what is shown versus what is gathered would make an interesting study. The fact that there are attempts to subpoena this material testifies to its potential importance. According to Emile de Antonio (Westerbeck, 1970), contacts in the network bureaucracies are always ready to help dig up interesting material. Some organizations may have film material available, gathered for different purposes, but useful to a researcher for establishing base lines or determining past practices.

Rosner (1968) recently made unusual use of archival material by generating an index of innovation from drug company and hospital use records. He assessed how long a hospital took to try new drugs that were periodically announced through listing from the drug companies. Rapid and frequent use was considered indicative of willingness to innovate. Along the same lines, studies of industrial creativity have used number of patents, invention disclosures, number of useful suggestions, etc. as indexes of productiveness (Taylor, Smith, & Ghiselin, 1963). Sick call rates can also be used particularly in isolated situations where the subjects cannot get medical attention elsewhere.

Udy (1964) has made use of the Human Relations Area Files for cross-cultural comparative studies of organizations. A list of the institutions at which these files are located is given in Whiting (1968). Schoenfeldt (1970) gives a list of the major data archives in the Western world readily available to researchers.

Simple Observation

One of the simplest observations a researcher can make is to determine who spoke to whom. A related, but more-often-than-not ignored datum, is where does X place himself with respect to Y? Position and/or spatial arrangements can be used to index behavior (Meharabian, 1969; Wiener, Devoe, Rubinow, & Geller, 1972). The Bogardus social distance scale is a well-known way of transforming spatial concepts into a psychometric mold. Raw spatial measures can be used in much the same way. Cook (1970), Sommer (1969, Chap. 5), Sechrest (1969), and Weick (1968) review a number of studies which show how spatial and approach gradients can be used to index such things as dominance, order of participation, amount of interaction, territoriality, etc. Spatial behavior can be inexpensively recorded using time-lapse photography (Gump, 1969).

Facial and postural clues also convey information about attitudes and intent. Most of this work has not reached the level where it can be of systematic use to organization researchers, but an examination of the literature on the topic is instructive and clinically useful. Reviews have been prepared by Ekman, Friesen, and Ellsworth (1971), Duncan (1969), Rasch and Burke (1963), and Scheflen (1968). Ekman, Friesen, and Taussig (1969), Ekman and Friesen (1969), and Condon (1970) have described sophisticated equipment and methods for analyzing this kind of data.

The use of nonverbal measures is most likely to bear fruit in cross-cultural studies or studies of organizations with significant ethnic mixes (Baxter, 1970; Ekman & Friesen, 1971; Hall, 1959).

Hardware

Very little data are collected in field settings with hardware, yet there is an enormous potential here. Still photography has seldom been used as a means of collecting data. As we pointed out earlier, stills could be used to gather data on spatial behavior. Sayles (1954) and Collier (1957) used photographs as projective tests in a field study, but did not present adequate psychometric data to evaluate the technique. Menzel (1969) has shown how useful photographs can be for the study of primate behavior in field settings. Byers (1964) has provided an excellent introduction to the use of still photography as a systematic recording procedure based on his work with anthropologists.

A far more unobtrusive use of photography is exemplified by the use of infrared sensitive films. Greenhill (1955) recorded audience reactions in the dark with this technique. This was a follow-through on an early suggestion by Galton (1884) that the gross body movement of an audience could be a useful indicator.

General body or locomotor activity can also be assessed unobtrusively using ultrasonic devices (Crawford & Nicora, 1964; Peacock & Williams, 1962). A number of more cumbersome methods have been described by Webb et al. (1966, pp. 152–153).

The movement and/or activity of people can be measured using pedometers and specially adapted self-winding wristwatches called actometers (Schulman & Reisman, 1959). The movement of people and some types of objects past key points can be recorded by photoelectric cells. More specificity can be achieved by planting bugging systems similar to those developed to prevent library thefts (Mueller, 1970).

Continuous monitoring can be achieved with the use of telemetry (Caceres, 1965; Mackay, 1970). The applications in this area are limited only by the researcher's imagination and money. Transmitters are now so small that it is possible to observe "alterations in the pattern of activity in the gut of human subjects to the stress of public speaking" (Mackay, 1969, p. 244).

Transponders which transmit only on receipt of a signal can be used to sample responses and thereby decrease the dross rate. The 3M Company has a tape cassette which can record up to thirty-five days and play back to a computer in two minutes. A great deal of versatile equipment is now available for recording multiple events (Krausman, 1970; Mostofsky, 1970; Sidowski & Spears, 1970).

An extensive study of spontaneous talk by Soskin and John (1963) made use of a voice transmitter carried daily by a husband and wife team. The conversations were recorded by a central receiving station. Purcell and Brady (1966) conducted a similar study with children.

It is also possible to send information to subjects as well as receive it. This information need not be verbal. The feasibility of transmitting Morse code through an electrocutaneous reception apparatus has already been demonstrated (Applied Psychological Services, 1966a, 1966b, 1966c). Intelligible signals may also be mediated through other modalities (Schwitzgebel & Bird, 1970).

Researchers who contemplate the use of behavioral instrumentation should examine the following sources: Baker (1968); Schwitzgebel (1970); Schwitzgebel and Bird (1970); the March 1969 instrumentation issue of the *American Psychologist*; and the Annual Guide to Scientific Instruments published each September by *Science*.

SUMMARY AND CONCLUSIONS

In this chapter, the special characteristics of field settings and the difficulties that research in such settings entails were reviewed. When compared to research in laboratory settings it was concluded that for many purposes field studies could generate extremely useful, practical, and theoretical knowledge.

Five major field methods were described in considerable detail. None of the methods were evaluated relative to each other, however, because it is our firm belief that there is no single best method, in any absolute sense. This is true for all research methods (cf., Runkel & McGrath, 1972, p. 89). Methods are means to ends, no more, no less. The key to good research lies not in choosing the right method, but rather in asking the right question and picking the most powerful method for answering that particular question. Methods are neither good nor bad, but rather more or less useful for answering particular questions at a particular time and place. They serve the purposes of the investigator. At the beginning of this chapter we asserted that a primary purpose of field research was to test the generality, applicability, and utility of psychological knowledge. Here we assert that methods should be chosen in light of these goals. A few examples should illustrate what we mean. Research on Motivation-Hygiene theory has restricted itself almost entirely to self-report techniques (interview-

ing and questionnaires). Most of the criticisms of the theory focus on the inadequacy of this methodology. Additional research which attempts to remedy this problem in a patchwork fashion would be a waste of time. Much more useful for confirming or disconfirming the theory would be data based on systematic observation. On the other hand, the generality of findings based on systematic observation can be tested and generalized to other types of organizations by attempting to answer the same question with interview or questionnaire techniques. A researcher who is ill at ease with a taxonomic system developed by interview and questionnaire technique should not develop a new one using the same technique. A more substantive contribution will be made if he uses observation techniques. In this way, known dimensions are likely to be cross-validated and new dimensions discovered.

These examples share the common characteristic of being instances of multiple operationalism. They specify methods which yield measures that share theoretically relevant components with previously collected measures, but have different sources of error relative to the construct being studied (Webb et al., 1966, pp. 3–5). To the extent that the results converge, our confidence in the generality, applicability, and utility of the proposition studied is increased. To the extent that the results do not converge, our confidence is comparably decreased. We urge all researchers to consider the advantages of methodological heterogeneity and to break the hold that a few favored techniques have on them.

A FINAL NOTE

In this chapter there is no discussion of the ethical questions that arise when many of the methods depicted are put to use. This is not because the issue is unimportant or that a scientific treatise need not concern itself with ethical questions. The issue is extremely important and, therefore, has been treated in an entire chapter in this *Handbook*. We strongly urge potential users of any of these methods to read that chapter and scrutinize the ethical implications of both their goals and methods before embarking on any research project.

REFERENCES

Alutto, J. A. Some dynamics of questionnaire completion and return among professional and managerial personnel: The relative impacts of reception at work site or place of residence. *Journal of Applied Psychology,* 1970, 54, 430–432.

American Psychological Association. *Casebook on ethical standards of psychologists.* Washington, D.C.: American Psychological Association, 1967.

Anderson, J. New self-administered medical questioning. *British Medical Journal,* 1968, 4, 636–638.

Angell, R. C., & Freedman, R. The use of documents, records, census materials, and indices. In L. Festinger & D. Katz (Eds.), *Research methods in the behavioral sciences.* New York: Holt, Rinehart and Winston, 1953.

Applied Psychological Services. Studies into information presentation through novel methods: Information transfer through electrocutaneous stimulation. Report prepared for U.S. Army Electronics Command, Fort Monmouth, New Jersey, April, 1966. Contract No. DA28-043 AMC-00186(e), Wayne, Pennsylvania. (a)

Applied Psychological Services. Studies into information presentation through novel methods: II. Design for a soldier-carried electrocutaneous reception apparatus. Report prepared for U.S. Army Electronics Command, Fort Monmouth, New Jersey, May, 1966. Contract No. DA28-043 AMC-00186(e), Wayne, Pennsylvania. (b)

Applied Psychological Services. Studies into information presentation through novel methods: III. Two-way transfer through electrocutaneous transduction. Report prepared for U.S. Army Electronics Command, Fort Monmouth, New Jersey, July, 1966. Contract No. DA28-043 AMC-00186(e), Wayne, Pennsylvania. (c)

Argyris, C. Diagnosing defenses against the outsider. *Journal of Social Issues,* 1952, 8, 24–34.

Argyris, C. Creating effective relationships in organizations. *Human Organization,* 1958, 17 (1), 34–40.

Argyris, C. *Organization and innovation.* Homewood, Ill.: Dorsey, 1965.

Argyris, C. Some unintended consequences of rigorous research. *Psychological Bulletin,* 1968, 3, 185–197.

Argyris, C. The incompleteness of social-psychological theory: Examples from small group, cognitive consistency, and attribution research. *American Psychologist,* 1969, 24, 893–908.

Argyris, C. *Intervention theory and method: A behavioral science view.* Reading, Mass.: Addison-Wesley, 1970.

Argyris, C., & Taylor, G. The member-centered conference as a research method. In R. N. Adams & J. J. Preiss (Eds.), *Human organization research.* Homewood, Ill.: Dorsey, 1960.

Arrington, R. E. Time sampling in studies of social behavior. A critical review of techniques and results with research suggestions. *Psychological Bulletin,* 1943, 40, 81–124.

Astin, W., & Boruch, F. A "link" system for assuring confidentiality of research data in longitudinal studies. *American Educational Research Journal,* 1970, 7, 615–623.

Atkinson, R. C., & Wilson, H. A., Eds. *Computer-assisted instruction: A book of readings.* New York: Academic Press, 1969.

Atteslander, P. M. The interaction-gram: A method for measuring interaction and activities of supervisory personnel. *Human Organization,* 1954, 13 (1), 28–33.

Babchuk, N. The role of the researcher as participant-observer and participant-as-observer in the field situation. *Human Organization,* 1962, 21 (3), 225–228.

Bailey, K. G., & Sowder, W. T. Jr. Audiotape and videotape self-confrontation in psychotherapy. *Psychological Bulletin,* 1970, 74, 127–137.

Bain, R. K. The researcher's role: A case study. In R. N. Adams & J. J. Preiss (Eds.), *Human organization research.* Homewood, Ill.: Dorsey, 1960.

Baker, R. A. The future of psychological instrumentation. *Behavioral Science,* 1968, 13, 1–17.

Balan, J., Browning, H. L., Jelin, E., & Litzler, L. A computerized approach to the processing and analysis of life histories obtained in sample surveys. *Behavioral Science*, 1969, 14, 105–120.

Bales, R. F. *Interaction process analysis*. Reading, Mass.: Addison-Wesley, 1950. (a)

Bales, R. F. A set of categories for the analysis of small group interaction. *American Sociological Review*, 1950, 15, 258–263. (b)

Bales, R. F. Interaction process analysis. In D. L. Sills (Ed.), *International encyclopedia of the social sciences*. New York: Crowell-Collier and Macmillan, 1968.

Barber, T. X., & Silver, M. J. Fact, fiction, and the experimenter bias effect. *Psychological Bulletin Monograph*, 1968, 70 (6), 1–29.

Barker, R. G. The stream of behavior as an empirical problem. In R. G. Barker (Ed.), *The stream of behavior*. New York: Appleton-Century-Crofts, 1963.

Barker, R. G. Explorations in ecological psychology. *American Psychologist*, 1965, 20, 1–14.

Barker, R. G. *Ecological psychology*. Stanford, Calif.: Stanford University Press, 1968.

Barker, R. G. Wanted: An eco-behavioral science. In E. P. Willems & H. L. Raush (Eds.), *Naturalistic viewpoints in psychological research*. New York: Holt, Rinehart and Winston, 1969.

Barker, R. G., Dembo, T., & Lewin, K. Frustration and regression: An experiment with young children. *University of Iowa Studies in Child Welfare*, 1941, 18, No. 386.

Barnes, R. M. *Work sampling*. New York: Wiley, 1956.

Barnes, R. M. *Motion and time study: Design and measurement of work*. New York: Wiley, 1963.

Baxter, C. Interpersonal spacing in natural settings. *Sociometry*, 1970, 33, 444–456.

Becker, H. S. A note on interviewing tactics. *Human Organization*, 1954, 12 (41), 31–32.

Becker, H. S. Problems of inference and proof in participant observation. *American Sociological Review*, 1958, 23, 652–660.

Becker, H. S., & Geer, B. Participant observation: The analysis of qualitative field data. In R. N. Adams & J. J. Preiss (Eds.), *Human organization research*. Homewood, Ill.: Dorsey, 1960.

Becker, S. W. The parable of the pill. *Administrative Science Quarterly*, 1970, 15, 94–96.

Benney, M., & Hughes, E. C. Of sociology and the interview: Editorial preface. *American Journal of Sociology*, 1956, 62, 137–142.

Benney, M., Riesman, D., & Star, S. A. Age and sex in the interview. *American Journal of Sociology*, 1956, 62, 143–152.

Berlyne, D. E. Emotional aspects of learning. In P. R. Farnsworth, O. McNemar, & Q. McNemar (Eds.), *Annual Review of Psychology*, 1964, 15, 115–142.

Berrien, F. K. *General and social systems*. New Brunswick, N.J.: Rutgers University Press, 1968.

Bion, W. R. *Experiences in groups, and other papers*. New York: Basic Books, 1959.

Birdwhistell, R. L. *Kinesics and context*. Philadelphia: University of Pennsylvania Press, 1970.

Blau, P. M. *The dynamics of bureaucracy*. Chicago: University of Chicago Press, 1963.

Blau, P. M. The research process in the study of the dynamics of bureaucracy. In P. E. Hammond (Ed.), *Sociologists at work*. New York: Anchor Books, 1967.

Block, J. Some reasons for the apparent inconsistency of personality. *Psychological Bulletin*, 1968, 70, 210–212.

Blum, F. H. Getting individuals to give information to the outsider. *Journal of Social Issues*, 1952, 8, 35–42.

Bogardus, E. S. The group interview. *Journal of Applied Sociology*, 1926, 10, 372–382.

Borgatta, E. F. A systematic study of interaction process scores, peer and self-assessments, personality and other variables. *Genetic Psychology Monographs*, 1962, 65, 219–291.

Bouchard, T. J. Jr. Abandon all hope ye who enter here. *Contemporary Psychology*, 1971, 16, 324–325.

Boyd, R. D., & DeVault, M. V. The observation and recording of behavior. *Review of Educational Research*, 1966, 36, 529–551.

Brandt, R. M. *Studying behavior in natural settings*. New York: Holt, Rinehart and Winston, 1972.

Brayfield, A. H., & Crockett, W. H. Employee attitudes and employee performance. *Psychological Bulletin*, 1955, 52, 396–424.

Brierley, H. A fully automated intelligence test. *British Journal of Social and Clinical Psychology*, 1971, 10, 286–288.

Brunswick, E. *Perception and the representative design of psychological experiments*.

(2nd ed.) Berkeley: University of California Press, 1956.

Bruyn, S. The methodology of participant observation. *Human Organization,* 1963, 22 (3), 222–235.

Bruyn, S. *The human perspective in sociology: The method of participant observation.* Englewood Cliffs, N.J.: Prentice-Hall, 1966.

Buckley, W. C. *Sociology and modern systems theory.* Englewood Cliffs, N.J.: Prentice-Hall, 1967.

Budd, H. A., & Boyd, B. R. The acquisition of medical histories by questionnaires. National Center for Health Services Research and Development, Contract No. HSM 110-69-264, 1970.

Byers, P. Still photography in the systematic recording and analysis of behavioral data. *Human Organization,* 1964, 23 (1), 78–84.

Caceres, C. A., Ed. *Biomedical telemetry.* New York: Academic Press, 1965.

Cahalan, D., Tamulonis, V., & Verner, W. Interviewer bias involved in certain types of opinion survey questions. *International Journal of Opinion and Attitude Research,* 1947, 1 (1), 63–77.

Campbell, D. T. The indirect assessment of social attitudes. *Psychological Bulletin,* 1950, 47, 15–38.

Campbell, D. T. The informant in quantitative research. *American Journal of Sociology,* 1955, 60, 339–342.

Campbell, D. T. Systematic error on the part of human links in communication systems. *Information and Control,* 1958, 1, 334–369.

Campbell, D. T. Reforms as experiments. *American Psychologist,* 1969, 24, 409–429.

Campbell, D. T., & Stanley, J. C. *Experimental and quasi-experimental designs for research.* Chicago: Rand McNally, 1966.

Cannell, C. F. Interviewing. In G. Lindzey & E. Aronson (Eds.), *The handbook of social psychology,* Vol. II. Reading, Mass.: Addison-Wesley, 1968.

Cannell, C. F., & Kahn, R. L. *The dynamics of interviewing: Theory technique and cases.* New York: Wiley, 1957.

Caplow, T. The dynamics of information interviewing. *American Journal of Sociology,* 1956, 62, 165–171.

Carroll, S. J. Jr., & Taylor, W. H. Jr. A study of the validity of a self-observational central-signaling method of work sampling. *Personnel Psychology,* 1970, 21, 359–364.

Case, P. B. How to catch interviewer errors. *Journal of Advertising Research,* 1971, 11, 39–43.

Cataldo, E. F., Johnson, R. M., Kellstedt, L. A., & Milbrath, L. W. Card sorting as a technique for survey interviewing. *Public Opinion Quarterly,* 1970, 34, 202–215.

Caudill, W. *The psychiatric hospital as a small society.* Cambridge: Harvard University Press, 1958.

Chandler, M. An evaluation of the group interview. *Human Organization,* 1954, 13 (2), 26–28.

Chapman, L. J. Illusory correlations in observational report. *Journal of Verbal Learning and Verbal Behavior,* 1967, 6, 151–155.

Chapple, E. D. Measuring human relations: An introduction to the study of the interaction of individuals. *Genetic Psychology Monographs,* 1940, 22, 3–147.

Chapple, E. D. The interaction chronograph: Its evolution and present application. *Personnel,* 1949, 25, 295–307.

Chapple, E. D. The standard experimental (stress) interview as used in interaction chronograph investigations. *Human Organization,* 1953, 12 (2), 23–33.

Chapple, E. D. Quantitative analysis of complex organizational systems. *Human Organization,* 1962, 21 (2), 67–87.

Chapple, E. D., & Sayles, L. R. *The measure of management.* New York: Macmillan, 1961.

Chomsky, W. *Language and mind.* New York: Harcourt, Brace and World, 1968.

Cicourel, A. V. *Method and measurement in sociology.* New York: The Free Press, 1964.

Clark, R. D. III. Group-induced shift toward risk: A critical appraisal. *Psychological Bulletin,* 1971, 76, 251–270.

Collier, J. Photography in anthropology: A report on two experiments. *American Anthropologist,* 1957, 59, 843–859.

Collins, W. Interviewers' verbal idiosyncrasies as a source of bias. *Public Opinion Quarterly,* 1970, 34, 416–422.

Condon, W. S. Method of micro-analysis of sound film behavior. *Behavior Research Methods and Instrumentation,* 1970, 2, 51–54.

Cook, M. Experiments on orientation and proxemics. *Human Relations,* 1970, 23, 61–76.

Coombs, G. J., Murray, W. R., & Krahn, D. W. Automated medical histories: Factors determining patient performance. *Computers and Biomedical Research,* 1970, 3, 178–181.

Crawford, M. L. J., & Nicora, B. D. Measurement of human group activity. *Psychological Reports,* 1964, 15, 227–231.

Cronbach, L. J. The two disciplines of scientific psychology. *American Psychologist,* 1957, 12, 671–684.

Dalton, M. *Men who manage.* New York: Wiley, 1959.

Dalton, M. Preconceptions and methods in men who manage. In P. E. Hammond (Ed.), *Sociologists at work.* New York: Anchor Books, 1967.

Davidson, P. O., & Costello, C. G. $N=1$: *Experimental studies of single cases.* New York: Van Nostrand, 1969.

Dean, L. R. Interaction, reported and observed: The case of one local union. *Human Organization,* 1958, 17 (3), 36–44.

Dean, J. P. Participant observation and interviewing. In J. T. Doby (Ed.), *Introduction to social research.* Harrisburg, Pa.: The Stackpole Company, 1954.

Department of Defense. *Industrial security manual for safeguarding classified information.* DoD 5220-22-M, April 15, 1970.

Deutsch, K. W., Platt, J., & Senghaas, D. Conditions favoring major advances in social science. *Science,* 1971, 171, 450–459.

Dickman, H. R. The perception of behavioral units. In R. G. Barker (Ed.), *The stream of behavior.* New York: Appleton-Century-Crofts, 1963.

Dinoff, M., Clark, C. G., Reitman, L. M., & Smith, R. E. The feasibility of video-tape interviewing. *Psychological Reports,* 1969, 25, 239–242.

Dinoff, M., Newmark, C., Barnhart, S., Holm, A., Stern, S., & Saunders, T. R. Reliability of video-tape interviewing. *Psychological Reports,* 1970, 27, 275–278.

Dinoff, M., Stenmark, D. E., & Smith, R. E. Comparison of video-tape and face-to-face interviewing. *Psychological Reports,* 1970, 27, 53–54.

Dion, K. L., Barron, R. S., & Miller, N. Why do groups make riskier decisions than individuals? In L. Berkowitz (Ed.), *Advances in experimental social psychology,* Vol. 5. New York: Academic Press, 1971.

Dohrenwend, B. S. Some effects of open and closed questions on respondent's answers. *Human Organization,* 1965, 24 (2), 175–184.

Dohrenwend, B. S. An experimental study of directive interviewing. *Public Opinion Quarterly,* 1970, 34, 117–125.

Dohrenwend, B. P., & Dohrenwend, B. S. *Social status and psychological disorder.* New York: Wiley, 1969.

Dohrenwend, B. S., & Richardson, S. A. A use for leading questions in research interviewing. *Human Organization,* 1964, 23 (1), 76–77.

Donley, E., & Winter, G. Measuring the motives of public officials at a distance: An exploratory study of American presidents. *Behavioral Science,* 1970, 15, 222–236.

Dukes, W. F. $N=1$. *Psychological Bulletin,* 1965, 64, 74–79.

Duncan, S. Nonverbal communication. *Psychological Bulletin,* 1969, 72, 118–137.

Dunnette, M. D., Campbell, J. P., & Hakel, M. D. Factors contributing to job satisfaction and job dissatisfaction in six occupational groups. *Organizational Behavior and Human Performance,* 1967, 2, 143–174.

Dyck, A. J. The social contacts of some Midwest children with their parents and teachers. In R. G. Barker (Ed.), *The stream of behavior.* New York: Appleton-Century-Crofts, 1963.

Eaton, M. E. E., Altman, H., Schuff, S., & Sletten, I. Missouri automated psychiatry history for relatives and other informants. *Diseases of the Nervous System,* 1970, 31, 198–202.

Edgington, E. S. $N=1$ experiments: Hypothesis testing. *Canadian Psychologist,* 1972, 13, 121–134.

Editorial. Freedom and responsibility in research: The "Springdale" case. *Human Organization,* 1958, 17 (2), 1–2.

Edmiston, V. The group interview. *Journal of Educational Research,* 1944, 37, 593–601.

Ekman, P., & Friesen, W. V. A tool for the analysis of motion picture films or video tape. *American Psychologist,* 1969, 24, 240–243.

Ekman, P., & Friesen, W. V. Constants across cultures in the face and emotion. *Journal of Personality and Social Psychology,* 1971, 17, 124–129.

Ekman, P., Friesen, W. V., & Ellsworth, P. *Emotion in the human face: Guidelines for research and a review of findings.* Oxford: Pergamon Press, 1971.

Ekman, P., Friesen, W. V., & Taussig, T. VID-R and SCAN: Tools and methods in the analysis of facial expression and body movement. In G. Gerbner, O. Holsti, K. Krippendorff, W. Paisley, & P. Stone (Eds.), *Content analysis*. New York: Wiley, 1969.

Elwood, D. L. Test retest reliability and cost analyses of automated and face-to-face intelligence testing. *International Journal of Man-Machine Studies*, 1972, 4, 1–22.

Endler, N. S., & Hunt, J. McV. Sources of behavioral variance as measured by the S-R inventory of anxiousness. *Psychological Bulletin*, 1966, 65, 336–346.

Erdos, P. L. Professional mail surveys. New York: McGraw-Hill, 1970.

Evan, W. M., & Miller, J. R. III. Differential effects on response bias of computer versus conventional administration of a social science questionnaire: An exploratory methodological experiment. *Behavioral Science*, 1969, 14, 216–227.

Evans, F. B. On interviewer cheating. *Public Opinion Quarterly*, 1961, 25, 126–127.

Fawl, C. L. Disturbances experienced by children in their natural habitats. In R. G. Barker (Ed.), *The stream of behavior*. New York: Appleton-Century-Crofts, 1963.

Feldman, C. F., & Hass, W. A. Controls, conceptualization, and the interrelation between experimental and correlational research. *American Psychologist*, 1970, 25, 633–635.

Festinger, L., Riecken, H. W., & Schachter, S. *When prophecy fails*. Minneapolis: University of Minnesota Press, 1956.

Fishbein, M. Automated and computer-based interviewing. *Postgraduate Medicine*, 1968, 43, 224–225.

Fogli, L., Hulin, C. L., & Blood, M. R. Development of first-level behavior job criteria. *Journal of Applied Psychology*, 1971, 55, 3–8.

Forehand, G. A., & Gilmer, B. V. Environmental variation in studies of organizational behavior. *Psychological Bulletin*, 1964, 62, 361–382.

Frederiksen, N. Toward a taxonomy of situations. *American Psychologist*, 1972, 27, 114–123.

Friedman, P. A second experiment on interviewer bias. *Sociometry*, 1942, 5, 378–381.

Galton, F. Measurement of character. *Fortnightly Review*, 1884, 36, 179–185.

Gannon, M. J., Nothern, J. C., & Carroll, S. J. Jr. Characteristics of non-respondents among workers. *Journal of Applied Psychology*, 1971, 55, 586–588.

Garfinkel, H. *Studies in ethnomethodology*. Englewood Cliffs, N.J.: Prentice-Hall, 1967.

Gerbner, G., Holsti, O. R., Krippendorff, K., Paisley, W. J., & Stone, P. J., Eds. *The analysis of communication content: Development in scientific theories and computer techniques*. New York: Wiley, 1969.

Goering, J. M., & Cummins, M. Intervention research and the survey process. *Journal of Social Issues*, 1970, 26, 49–55.

Goffman, E. On cooling the mark out: Some aspects of adaptation to failure. *Psychiatry*, 1952, 15, 451–463.

Gold, R. L. Roles in sociological field observations. *Social Forces*, 1958, 36, 217–223.

Goldberg, E. M., & Morrison, S. L. Schizophrenia and social class. *British Journal of Psychiatry*, 1963, 109, 785–802.

Gouldner, A. W. Patterns of industrial bureaucracy. New York: The Free Press, 1954.

Gouldner, A. W. The norm of reciprocity: A preliminary statement. *American Sociological Review*, 1960, 25, 161–178.

Greenhill, L. P. The recording of audience reactions by infrared photography. Technical report SOECDEVCEN, 269-7-56. Instructional Film Research Program. Pennsylvania State University, University Park, 1955.

Grigaliunas, B. S., & Herzberg, F. Relevancy in the test of motivator hygiene theory. *Journal of Applied Psychology*, 1971, 55, 73–79.

Gross, E. Social integration and the control of competition. *American Journal of Sociology*, 1961, 67, 270–277.

Gross, N., & Mason, W. S. Some methodological problems of eight-hour interviews. *American Journal of Sociology*, 1953, 59, 197–204.

Gross, N., Mason, W. S., & McEachern, A. W. *Explorations in role analysis*. New York: Wiley, 1958.

Guest, L. A study of interviewer competence. *International Journal of Opinion and Attitude Research*, 1947, 1 (4), 17–30.

Guest, L. A new training method for opinion interviewers. *Public Opinion Quarterly*, 1954, 18, 287–299.

Guest, R. M. Foreman at work: An interim report on method. *Human Organization*, 1955, 14 (2), 21–24.

Guest, R. M. Categories of events in field observations. In R. N. Adams & J. J. Preiss (Eds.), *Human organization research*. Homewood, Ill.: Dorsey, 1960.

Guilford, J. P. *Psychometric methods.* New York: McGraw-Hill, 1954.

Gullahorn, J., & Strauss, G. The field worker in union research. In R. N. Adams & J. J. Priess (Eds.), *Human organization research.* Homewood, Ill.: Dorsey, 1960.

Gump, P. V. Intra-setting analysis: The third grade classroom as a special but instructive case. In E. P. Willems & H. L. Raush (Eds.), *Naturalistic viewpoints in psychological research.* New York: Holt, Rinehart and Winston, 1969.

Gump, P. V., & Kounin, J. S. Issues raised by ecological and "classical" research efforts. *Merrill-Palmer Quarterly,* 1960, 6, 145–152.

Gutman, D. Psychological naturalism in cross-cultural studies. In E. P. Willems & H. L. Raush (Eds.), *Naturalistic viewpoints in psychological research.* New York: Holt, Rinehart and Winston, 1969.

Hader, J. J., & Lindeman, E. C. *Dynamic Social Research.* New York: Harcourt, 1933.

Haire, M. Role perceptions in labor-management relations: An experimental approach. *Industrial Labor Relations Review,* 1955, 8, 204–216.

Hall, E. T. *The silent language.* New York: Doubleday, 1959.

Hall, E. T. *The hidden dimension.* New York: Doubleday, 1966.

Hammond, K. R. Representative versus systematic design in clinical psychology. *Psychological Bulletin,* 1954, 51, 150–159.

Hansen, B. L. *Work sampling for modern management.* Englewood Cliffs, N.J.: Prentice-Hall, 1960.

Hare, A. P. *Handbook of small group research.* Glencoe, Ill.: The Free Press, 1962.

Hauck, M., & Steinkamp, S. *Survey reliability and interviewer competence.* Urbana: Bureau of Economic and Business Research, University of Illinois, 1964.

Hayes, D. P. The Cornell datalogger. *Administrative Science Quarterly,* 1969, 14, 222–223.

Hayes, D. P., & Meltzer, L. Bone-conducting microphones. *American Journal of Psychology,* 1967, 80, 619–624.

Hayes, D. P., Meltzer, L., & Wolf, G. Substantive conclusions are dependent upon techniques of measurement. *Behavior Science,* 1970, 15, 265–268.

Heller, F. A. Group feedback analysis. *Psychological Bulletin,* 1969, 72, 108–117.

Hendrick, C., Borden, R., Giesen, M., Murray, E. J., & Seyfried, B. A. Effectiveness of ingratiation tactics in a cover letter on mail questionnaire response. *Psychonomic Science,* 1972, 26, 349–351.

Herbert, J. Direct observation as a research technique. *Psychology in the Schools,* 1970, 7, 127–138.

Heyns, R. W., & Zander, A. F. Observation of group behavior. In L. Festinger & D. Katz (Eds.), *Research methods in the behavioral sciences.* New York: Dryden, 1953.

Hildum, D., & Brown, R. Verbal reinforcement and interview bias. *Journal of Abnormal and Social Psychology,* 1956, 53, 108–111.

Holsti, O. R. Content analysis. In G. Lindzey & E. Aronson (Eds.), *The handbook of social psychology,* Vol. II. Reading, Mass.: Addison-Wesley, 1968.

House, R. J., & Wigdor, L. A. Herzberg's dual factor theory of job satisfaction and motivation: A review of the evidence and a criticism. *Personnel Psychology,* 1967, 20, 369–389.

Hovland, C. I. Reconciling conflicting results derived from experimental and survey studies of attitude change. *American Psychologist,* 1959, 14, 8–17.

Hughes, E. C. *Men and their work.* Glencoe, Ill.: The Free Press, 1958.

Hulin, C. L., & Blood, M. R. Job enlargement, individual differences, and worker responses. *Psychological Bulletin,* 1968, 69, 41–55.

Hund, J. M. Changing role in the interview situation. *Public Opinion Quarterly,* 1959, 23, 236–246.

Hyman, H. H., Cobb, W. J., Feldman, J. J., Hart, G. W., & Slember, C. H. *Interviewing in social research.* Chicago: University of Chicago Press, 1954.

Institute for Social Research. *Interviewer's manual.* Ann Arbor, Mich.: Institute for Social Research, 1969.

Jaques, E. *The changing culture of a factory.* London: Tavistock, 1951.

Journal of Research and Development in Education, 1970, 4 (1).

Junker, B. H. *Field work: An introduction to the social sciences.* Chicago: University of Chicago Press, 1960.

Katz, E. W. A content-analytic method for studying themes of interpersonal behavior. *Psychological Bulletin,* 1966, 66, 419–422.

Kawash, M. B., & Aleamoni, L. M. Effect of

personal signature on initial rate of return of a mailed questionnaire. *Journal of Applied Psychology*, 1971, 55, 589–592.

Kelly, J. G. Naturalistic observations in contrasting social environments. In E. P. Willems & H. L. Raush (Eds.), *Naturalistic viewpoints in psychological research*. New York: Holt, Rinehart and Winston, 1969.

Kincaid, H. V., & Bright, M. The tandem interview: A trial of the two-interviewer team. *Public Opinion Quarterly*, 1957, 21, 304–312.

King, N. Clarification and evaluation of the two-factor theory of job satisfaction. *Psychological Bulletin*, 1970, 74, 18–31.

Kinsey, A. C., Pomeroy, W. B., Martin, C. E., & Gebhard, P. H. *Sexual behavior in the human female*. New York: Pocket Books, 1965.

Kleinmuntz, B., & McLean, R. S. Diagnostic interviewing by digital computer. *Behavior Science*, 1968, 13, 75–80.

Kluckhohn, F. R. The participant observer technique in small communities. *American Journal of Sociology*, 1940, 46, 331–343.

Kornhauser, A. *Mental health of the industrial worker: A Detroit study*. New York: Wiley, 1965.

Kornhauser, A., & Sheatsley, P. Questionnaire construction and interview procedure. In C. Selltiz, M. Jahoda, M. Deutsch, & S. Cook (Eds.), *Research methods in social relations*. New York: Holt, Rinehart and Winston, 1959.

Kranz, P. What do people do all day? *Behavior Science*, 1970, 15, 286–291.

Krause, M. S. Use of social situations for research purposes. *American Psychologist*, 1970, 25, 748–753.

Krausman, D. T. A solid-state cumulative recorder for an analog registry of accumulative events. *Behavior Research Methods and Instrumentation*, 1970, 2 (5), 228.

Landsberger, H. A. Interaction process analysis of professional behavior. *American Sociological Review*, 1955, 20, 566–575.

Lauver, P. J. Inexpensive apparatus for qualifying speech and silence behaviors. *Journal of Counseling Psychology*, 1970, 17, 378–379.

Lazarsfeld, P. F. The controversy over detailed interviews: An offer for negotiation. *Public Opinion Quarterly*, 1944, 8, 38–60.

Lenski, G. E., & Leggett, J. C. Caste, class, and deference in the research interview. *American Journal of Sociology*, 1960, 65, 463–467.

Lindeman, E. C. *Social discovery*. New York: Republic, 1924.

Lindgren, E. J. The collection and analysis of folklore. In Sir F. C. Bartlett, M. Ginsberg, E. J. Lindgren, R. H. Touless (Eds.), *The study of society methods and problems*. London: Routledge, 1939.

Lindzey, G. A. Note on interviewer bias. *Journal of Applied Psychology*, 1951, 35, 182–184.

Litwak, E. A classification of biased questions. *American Journal of Sociology*, 1956, 62, 182–186.

Longabaugh, R. A category system for coding interpersonal behavior as social exchange. *Sociometry*, 1963, 26, 319–344.

Lundberg, G. A. *Social research*. (2nd ed.) New York: Longmans, Green, 1942.

Lundberg, G. A., Kamarovski, M., & McInerney, M. A. *Leisure: A suburban study*. New York: Columbia University Press, 1934.

McCormick, T. C. Quantitative analysis and comparison of living cultures. *American Sociological Review*, 1939, 4, 463–474.

McDonagh, E. C., & Rosenblum, A. L. A comparison of mailed questionnaires and subsequent structured interviews. *Public Opinion Quarterly*, 1965, 29, 131–136.

McGrath, J. E. Towards a "theory of method" for research on organizations. In W. W. Cooper, H. J. Leavitt, & M. W. Shelly III (Eds.), *New perspectives in organization research*. New York: Wiley, 1964.

McGuire, W. J. Some impending reorientations in social psychology: Some thoughts provoked by Kenneth Ring. *Journal of Experimental Social Psychology*, 1967, 3, 124–139.

Mackay, R. S. Biomedical telemetry: Applications to psychology. *American Psychologist*, 1969, 24, 244–248.

Mackay, R. S. *Biomedical telemetry*. (2nd ed.) New York: Wiley, 1970.

McLuhan, M. *Understanding media: The extensions of man*. New York: McGraw-Hill, 1964.

Madge, J. *The tools of social science*. New York: Anchor Books, 1965.

Magid, F. N., Fotion, W. G., & Gold, D. A mail questionnaire adjunct to the interview. *Public Opinion Quarterly*, 1962, 26, 111–114.

Mann, P. H. *Methods of sociological enquiry*. Oxford: Basil Blackwell, 1968.

Mann, R. D. *Interpersonal styles and group development*. New York: Wiley, 1967.

Matarazzo, J. D., Weitman, M., Saslow, G., &

Wiens, A. Interviewer influence on duration of interviewee speech. *Journal of Verbal Learning and Verbal Behavior,* 1963, 1, 451–458.

Medley, D. M., & Mitzel, H. E. Measuring classroom behavior by systematic observation. In N. L. Gage (Ed.), *Handbook of research on teaching.* Chicago: Rand McNally, 1963.

Meehl, P. E. Nuisance variables and the ex post facto design. In M. Radner & S. Winokur (Eds.), *Minnesota studies in philosophy of science, IV.* Minneapolis: University of Minnesota Press, 1970.

Meehl, P. E. Law and the fireside inductions: Some reflections of a clinical psychologist. *Journal of Social Issues,* 1971, 27, 65–100.

Meharabian, A. Significance of posture and position in the communication of attitude and status relationships. *Psychological Bulletin,* 1969, 71, 359–372.

Melbin, M. The action-interaction chart as a research tool. *Human Organization,* 1953, 12 (1), 35.

Melbin, M. An interaction recording device for participant observer. *Human Organization,* 1954, 13 (2), 29–33.

Menzel, E. W. Jr. Naturalistic and experimental approaches to primate behavior. In E. P. Willems & H. L. Raush (Eds.), *Naturalistic viewpoints in psychological research.* New York: Holt, Rinehart and Winston, 1969.

Merton, R. K. Selected problems of field work in the planned community. *American Sociological Review,* 1947, 12, 304–312.

Merton, R. K. *Social theory and social structure.* Glencoe, Ill.: The Free Press, 1949.

Merton, R. K., & Kendall, P. L. The focused interview. *American Journal of Sociology,* 1946, 51, 541–547.

Merton, R. K., Fiske, M., & Kendall, P. L. *The focused interview.* Glencoe, Ill.: The Free Press, 1956.

Michaelis, A. R. *Research films in biology, anthropology, psychology, and medicine.* New York: Academic Press, 1955.

Milgram, S. Some conditions of obedience and disobedience to authority. *Human Relations,* 1965, 18, 57–76.

Miller, F. B. Reistentialism in applied social research. *Human Organization,* 1954, 12 (4), 5–8.

Miller, F. B. "Situational" interactions: A worthwhile concept. *Human Organization,* 1958, 17 (4), 37–47.

Miller, G. A., Galanter, E., & Pribram, K. H. *Plans and the structure of behavior.* New York: Holt, Rinehart and Winston, 1960.

Miller, S. M. The participant observer and "over-rapport." *American Sociological Review,* 1952, 17, 97–99.

Mills, T. M. *Group transformation: An analysis of a learning group.* Englewood Cliffs, N.J.: Prentice-Hall, 1964.

Minneapolis Tribune. Sunday, September 13, 1970.

Mostofsky, D. I. Multiplexed recording of multiple events. *Perceptual and Motor Skills,* 1970, 31, 349–350.

Mueller, M. "Book bugging": A possible answer to library thefts. *Science,* 1970, 167, 361–362.

Murray, H. A., Ed. *Assessment of men.* New York: Rinehart, 1948.

Murray, H. A. Studies of stressful interpersonal disputations. *American Psychologist,* 1963, 18, 28–36.

Nadler, G. Do you know what your supervisors do? *Personnel Psychology,* 1953, 6, 343–354.

Noelle-Neumann, E. Wanted: Rules for structured questionnaires. *Public Opinion Quarterly,* 1970, 34, 191–201.

Owens, W. A. Toward one discipline of scientific psychology. *American Psychologist,* 1968, 23, 782–785.

Owens, W. A. A quasi-actuarial basis for individual assessment. *American Psychologist,* 1971, 26, 992–999.

Payne, S. L. *The art of asking questions.* Princeton: Princeton University Press, 1951.

Peacock, L. J., & Williams, M. An ultrasonic device of recording activity. *American Journal of Psychology,* 1962, 75, 648–652.

Pervin, L. A. Performance and satisfaction as a function of individual-environment fit. *Psychological Bulletin,* 1968, 69, 56–68.

Platt, J. R. Strong inference. *Science,* 1964, 146, 347–353.

Plog, S. C. Literary index for the mailbag. *Journal of Applied Psychology,* 1966, 50, 86–91.

Polanyi, M. *Personal knowledge.* Chicago: University of Chicago Press, 1958.

Price, J. L. Design and proof in organizational

research. *Administrative Science Quarterly,* 1968, 13, 121–134.

Purcell, K., & Brady, K. Adaptation to the invasion of privacy: Monitoring behavior with a miniature radio transmitter. *Merrill-Palmer Quarterly,* 1966, 12, 242–254.

Rasch, P. J., & Burke, R. K. *Kinesiology and applied anatomy.* (2nd ed.) Philadelphia: Lea & Febiger, 1963.

Richardson, S. A. The use of leading questions in nonschedule interviews. *Human Organization,* 1960, 19 (2), 86–89.

Richardson, S. A., Dohrenwend, B. S., & Klein, D. *Interviewing.* New York: Basic Books, 1965.

Ring, K. Experimental social psychology: Some sober questions about some frivolous values. *Journal of Experimental Social Psychology,* 1967, 3, 113–123.

Roberts, K. H. On looking at an elephant: An evaluation of cross-cultural research related to organizations. *Psychological Bulletin,* 1970, 74, 327–350.

Robin, S. S. Procedure for securing returns to mail questionnaires. *Sociology and Social Research,* 1965, 50, 24–35.

Roethlisberger, F. J., & Dickson, W. J. *Management and the worker.* Cambridge: Harvard University Press, 1939.

Rogers, C. R. A theory of therapy, personality, and interpersonal relationships, as developed in the client centered framework. In S. Kock (Ed.), *Psychology: A study of a science,* Vol. III. New York: McGraw-Hill, 1959.

Ronan, W. W. Individual and situational variables relating to job satisfaction. *Journal of Applied Psychology Monograph,* 1970, 54 (1, Part 2).

Rosner, M. M. Administrative controls and innovation. *Behavior Science,* 1968, 13, 36–43.

Rosov, R. J. Personal communication, 1972.

Roth, J. Hired-hand research. *American Sociologist,* 1966, 1, 190–196.

Routh, D. K., & Rettig, K. The mailbag literacy index in a clinical population: Relation to education, income, occupation, and social class. *Educational and Psychological Measurement,* 1969, 29, 485–488.

Runkel, P. J., & McGrath, J. E. *Research on human behavior: A systematic guide to method.* New York: Holt, Rinehart and Winston, 1972.

Savas, E. S. Cybernetics in city hall. *Science,* 1970, 168, 1066–1071.

Sayles, L. R. Field use of projective methods: A case example. *Sociology and Social Research,* 1954, 38, 168–173.

Scheflen, A. E. Human communication: Behavior programs and their integration in interaction. *Behavior Science,* 1968, 13, 44–45.

Schneider, L. The role of the category of ignorance in sociological theory. *American Sociological Review,* 1962, 27, 492–508.

Schoenfeldt, L. F. Data archives as resources for research instruction, and policy planning. *American Psychologist,* 1970, 25, 609–616.

Schoggen, P. Environmental force units in the everyday lives of children. In R. G. Barker (Ed.), *The stream of behavior.* New York: Appleton-Century-Crofts, 1963.

Schoonmaker, A. N. Behavior during collective bargaining negotiations: A multidimensional analysis. Unpublished doctoral dissertation, University of California, Berkeley, 1966.

Schulman, J. L., & Reisman, J. M. An objective measure of hyperactivity. *American Journal of Mental Deficiency,* 1959, 64, 455–456.

Schultz, W. C. *FIRO: A three-dimensional theory of interpersonal behavior.* New York: Holt, Rinehart and Winston, 1958.

Schwartz, M. S., & Schwartz, C. G. Problems in participant observation. *American Journal of Sociology,* 1955, 60, 343–353.

Schwartzbaum, A., & Gruenfeld, L. Factors influencing subject-observer interaction in an organization study. *Administrative Science Quarterly,* 1969, 14, 443–449.

Schwirian, K. P., & Blaine, H. R. Questionnaire return bias in the study of blue collar workers. *Public Opinion Quarterly,* 1966–1967, 30, 656–663.

Schwitzgebel, R. L. Behavior instrumentation and social technology. *American Psychologist,* 1970, 25, 491–499.

Schwitzgebel, R. L., & Bird, R. M. Socio-technical design factors in remote instrumentation with humans in natural environments. *Behavior Research Methods and Instrumentation,* 1970, 2, 99–105.

Scott, W. R. Field work in a formal organization: Some dilemmas in the role of observer. *Human Organization,* 1963, 22 (2), 162–168.

Scott, W. R. Field methods in the study of

organizations. In J. G. March (Ed.), *Handbook of organizations.* Chicago: Rand McNally, 1965.

Sechrest, L. Nonreactive assessment of attitudes. In E. P. Willems & H. L. Raush (Eds.), *Naturalistic viewpoints in psychological research.* New York: Holt, Rinehart and Winston, 1969.

Sells, S. B. Dimensions of stimulus situations which account for behavior variances. In S. B. Sells (Ed.), *Stimulus determinants of behavior.* New York: Ronald Press, 1963.

Sells, S. B. Ecology and the science of psychology. In E. P. Willems & H. L. Raush (Eds.), *Naturalistic viewpoints in psychological research.* New York: Holt, Rinehart and Winston, 1969.

Selltiz, C., Jahoda, M., Deutsch, M., & Cook, S. W. *Research methods in social relations.* New York: Holt, Rinehart and Winston, 1960.

Selznick, P. *TVA and the grass roots.* Berkeley: University of California Press, 1949.

Sewell, W. H. Field techniques in social psychological study in a rural community. *American Sociological Review,* 1949, 14, 718–726.

Shadegg, S. C. *How to win an election.* New York: Toplinger, 1964.

Shapiro, M. J. Discovering interviewer bias in open-ended survey responses. *Public Opinion Quarterly,* 1970, 34, 412–415.

Sidowski, J. B., & Spears, C. A versatile apparatus for measuring the frequencies and durations of animal and human responses. *Behavior Research Methods and Instrumentation,* 1970, 2, 235–238.

Simon, R. Response to personal and form letters in mail surveys. *Journal of Advertising Research,* 1967, 7, 28–30.

Slack, W. Computer-based interviewing system dealing with nonverbal behavior as well as keyboard responses. *Science,* 1971, 171, 84–87.

Sletto, R. F. Pretesting of questionnaires. *American Sociological Review,* 1940, 5, 193–200.

Smith, H. L., & Hyman, H. The biasing effect of interviewer expectations on survey results. *Public Opinion Quarterly,* 1950, 14, 491–506.

Smith, M. B., Bruner, J. S., & White, R. W. *Opinions and personality.* New York: Wiley, 1956.

Snow, R. E. Review of Pygmalion in the class-

room. *Contemporary Psychology,* 1969, 14, 197–199.

Sommer, R. Hawthorne dogma. *Psychological Bulletin,* 1968, 70, 592–595.

Sommer, R. *Personal space: The behavioral basis for design.* Englewood Cliffs, N.J.: Prentice-Hall, 1969.

Sorokin, P. A., & Berger, C. Q. *Time-budgets of human behavior.* Cambridge: Harvard University Press, 1939.

Soskin, W. F., & John, V. P. The study of spontaneous talk. In R. G. Barker (Ed.), *The stream of behavior.* New York: Appleton-Century-Crofts, 1963.

Stebbins, R. A. The unstructured research interview as incipient interpersonal relationship. *Sociology and Social Research,* 1972, 56, 164–179.

Stone, P. J., Dunphy, D. C., Smith, M. S., Ogilvie, D. M., & Associates, Eds. *The general inquirer: A computer approach to content analysis.* Cambridge: M.I.T. Press, 1966.

Sudman, S. Quantifying interviewer quality. *Public Opinion Quarterly,* 1966–1967, 30, 664–667.

Sullivan, M. A. Jr., & Queen, S. A. Participant observation as employed in the study of a military training program. *American Sociological Review,* 1958, 23, 660–667.

Sutcliffe, J. P. On the role of "instructions to the subject" in psychological experiments. *American Psychologist,* 1972, 27, 755–760.

Taylor, C. W., Smith, W. R., & Ghiselin, B. The creative and other contributions of one sample of research scientists. In C. W. Taylor & F. Barron (Eds.), *Scientific creativity: Its recognition and development.* New York· Wiley, 1963.

Thelen, H. A. Work-emotionality theory of the group as organism. In S. Koch (Ed.), *Psychology in the study of a science,* Vol. III. New York: McGraw-Hill, 1959.

Thompson, J. D., & Demerath, N. J. Some experiences with the group interview. *Social Forces,* 1952, 31, 148–154.

Turner, R. J., & Wagenfeld, M. O. Occupational mobility and schizophrenia: An assessment of the social causation and social selection hypothesis. *American Sociological Review,* 1967, 32, 104–113.

Udy, S. H. Jr. Administrative rationality, social setting, and organizational development. In W. W. Cooper, H. J. Leavitt, & M. W.

Shelly II (Eds.), *New Perspectives in organizational research.* New York: Wiley, 1964.

Udy, S. H. Jr. The comparative analysis of organizations. In J. G. March (Ed.), *Handbook of organizations.* Chicago: Rand McNally, 1965.

Vidich, A., & Bensman, J. The validity of field data. In R. N. Adams & J. J. Preiss (Eds.), *Human organization research.* Homewood, Ill.: Dorsey, 1960.

Vinokur, A. Review and theoretical analysis of the effects of group process upon individual and group decisions involving risk. *Psychological Bulletin,* 1971, 76, 231–250.

Wagner, R. A group situation compared with individual interviews for securing personnel information. *Personnel Psychology,* 1948, 1, 93–101.

Wax, R. H. Reciprocity in field work. In R. N. Adams & J. J. Preiss (Eds.), *Human organization research.* Homewood, Ill.: Dorsey, 1960.

Webb, E. J., Campbell, D. T., Schwartz, R. D., & Sechrest, L. *Unobtrusive measures: Nonreactive research in the social sciences.* Chicago: Rand McNally, 1966.

Weick, K. E. Systematic observational methods. In G. Lindzey & E. Aronson (Eds.), *Handbook of social psychology,* Vol. IV. (2nd ed.) Reading, Mass.: Addison-Wesley, 1968.

Weick, K. E. Meaning and misunderstanding. Review of H. Garfinkel: Studies in ethnomethodology. *Contemporary Psychology,* 1969, 14, 357–360.

Wernimont, P. F., & Campbell, J. P. Signs, samples, and criteria. *Journal of Applied Psychology,* 1968, 52, 372–376.

Westerbeck, C. J. Jr. Some out-takes from radical film making: Emile de Antonio. *Sight and Sound,* Summer, 1970.

Whiting, J. W. M. Methods and problems in cross-cultural research. In G. Lindzey & E. Aronson (Eds.), *Handbook of social psychology,* Vol. II. (2nd ed.) Reading, Mass.: Addison-Wesley, 1968.

Whyte, W. F. Observational field work methods. In M. Jahoda, M. Deutsch, & S. Cook (Eds.), *Research methods in the social sciences.* New York: Dryden, 1951.

Whyte, W. F. *Street corner society.* (Rev. ed.) Chicago: University of Chicago Press, 1955.

Whyte, W. F. On asking indirect questions. *Human Organization,* 1957, 15 (4), 21–23.

Whyte, W. F. *Man and organization.* Homewood, Ill.: Irwin, 1959.

Whyte, W. F. Interviewing in field research. In R. N. Adams & J. J. Preiss (Eds.), *Human organization research.* Homewood, Ill.: Dorsey, 1960.

Wicker, A. W. Attitude versus action: The relationship of verbal and overt behavioral responses to attitude objects. *Journal of Social Issues,* 1969, 25, 41–78.

Wiener, M., Devoe, S., Rubinow, S., & Geller, J. Nonverbal behavior and nonverbal communication. *Psychological Review,* 1972, 79, 185–214.

Wiens, A. N., Matarazzo, J. D., & Saslow, G. The interaction recorder: An electronic punched paper tape unit for recording speech behavior during interviews. *Journal of Clinical Psychology,* 1965, 21, 142–145.

Willems, E. P., & Raush, H. L. Interpretation and impressions. In E. P. Willems & H. L. Raush (Eds.), *Naturalistic viewpoints in psychological research.* New York: Holt, Rinehart and Winston, 1969.

Willems, E. P., & Willems, G. J. Comparative validity of data yielded by three methods. *Merrill-Palmer Quarterly,* 1965, 11, 67–71.

Williams, A. F., & Wechsler, H. The mail survey: Methods to minimize bias owing to incomplete response. *Sociology and Social Research,* 1970, 54, 533–535.

Williams, T. R. A critique of some assumptions of social survey research. *Public Opinion Quarterly,* 1959, 23, 55–62.

Wolcott, H. F. An ethnographic approach to the study of school administrators. *Human Organization,* 1970, 29 (2), 115–122.

Zelditch, M. Jr. Some methodological problems of field studies. *American Journal of Sociology,* 1962, 67, 566–576.

CHAPTER 10

Laboratory Experimentation[1]

HOWARD L. FROMKIN
SIEGFRIED STREUFERT
Purdue University

THE FAILURE TO HEED Weick's (1965a) earlier admonishments concerning the disadvantages which arise from the underrepresentation of laboratory experiments has produced a significant vacuum in the data about organizational phenomena. In spite of the unique advantages and valuable contributions of experimental strategies, recent rejection of the laboratory as a legitimate research site constitutes a dilemma to the scientist and administrator who are thereby unable to take advantage of a substantial portion of social psychology. This chapter provides a perspective to bridge the gap between data generated in laboratory experiments and their application to theoretical and practical problems of organizations. The approach resides in judgmental processes which render laboratory findings more serviceable in a two-fold manner. First, in lieu of customary warnings, arguments are presented which mitigate the shibboleths about laboratory experiments (e.g., artificiality and realism, etc.). Second, some suggestions are offered about how prohibitory cautions can be more profitably translated into specific "boundary variables" which vary according to inferences that can be drawn when moving from laboratory to any given domain of application.

---

[1] This paper was prepared in 1970 and was in part supported by a research contract between the Department of Criminal Justice Planning Agency and Purdue University to Howard L. Fromkin and a research contract between the Office of Naval Research, Organizational Psychology Programs, and Purdue University to Siegfried Streufert. The authors gratefully acknowledge the comments of Michael Flanagan and Susan C. Streufert on an earlier draft of this manuscript and several helpful suggestions on a later draft from Ms. Leaetta Hough, editorial assistant to Marvin D. Dunnette.

INTRODUCTION

Laboratory Research and Organizational Behavior

Inspection of the current organizational literature reveals that Weick's (1965a) exhortation in the earlier *Handbook of Organizations* against the neglect of laboratory experimentation is still valid.[2] Some writers reject laboratory data as a legitimate empirical base for knowledge in the social sciences. When attempted, application of the experimental method and/or findings to organizational problems is frequently accompanied by apprehensive statements about such "extrapolations." Recently, a number of critical articles (e.g., McGuire, 1969a; Mosier, 1965; Price, 1968) raise questions about the applicability of laboratory findings for the solution of practical problems. The criticisms receive support from some instances where the results of laboratory studies do not predict how people will behave in real-life situations, such as monitoring radar displays (e.g., Kibler, 1965), space travel (e.g., Chapanis, 1967; Simons, 1964), and education (e.g., Elliott, 1960; Mackie & Christensen, 1967). In addition, the recent identification of a number of "artifacts" associated with laboratory experiments has provided ammunition for attacks aimed at the "artificiality" of the laboratory method. Unfortunately, these artifacts are frequently mistaken as armor for alternative research methods (e.g., Argyris, 1969).[3]

Direct experimentation within organizations is of paramount importance and is required immediately. It is equally clear that data provided by direct experimentation within organizations are currently unavailable, and a multitude of practical considerations hinders future accumulation of such data. The absence of field experimental data in combination with recent invidious rejections of the laboratory constitutes a dilemma to the scientist and to the administrator who want to profit from the rich resources of social science. In spite of general consensus that *all* research methods are useful and required (cf., Lachenmeyer, 1970), organizational laboratory experiments are rarely found and recent skepticism is denying them a place in the total perspective of organizational theory and research.

The present chapter demonstrates the unique and valuable contributions of experimental strategies and discusses undesirable outcomes stemming from their current underrepresentation. In addition, the present chapter proposes a bridge to span the gap between the data of laboratory experiments and their application to theoretical and practical problems of organizations. The chapter is based on the assertion that laboratory data have considerable value for understanding and predicting organizational behavior even though certain "cautions" are in order when one attempts to apply the results of laboratory research. In lieu of the customary inhibitory warnings which do not afford the scientist and/or administrator an avenue to use experimental strategies or data, the present approach focuses on some bases for judgmental processes which render laboratory strategies and findings serviceable to the construction of organizational theory and for application to organizational settings. In short, this chapter provides a structure to bridge the gap between laboratory and organization by (1) presenting some arguments mitigating the speciously convenient criticisms of laboratory research (e.g., generality, artificiality, and realism, etc.) and (2) suggesting how "cautions" may be defined as specific "boundaries" which vary in accordance with

---

[2] Allocation of approximately 50 percent of a recent textbook (Evan, 1971) and an entire issue of *Administrative Science Quarterly* (1969, 41, 155–304) to laboratory experiments on organizations represent the only encouraging exception to the above admonition.

[3] Identification of laboratory "artifacts" provides only false security for research conducted in "natural settings" because the same "artifacts" are found to operate in a wide variety of non-laboratory settings (cf., Argyris, 1952, 1968; Dunnette & Heneman, 1956; Kroger, 1967; Page & Lumia, 1968; Rosen, 1970; Rosen & Sales, 1966; Roethlisberger & Dickson, 1946; Scott, 1962).

the inferences to be drawn when moving from laboratory data to any given domain of application. As such, we undertake the rather ambitious task of providing some useful evaluative tools for *both* the administrator and the researcher.

Definition of Laboratory Experimentation

Many popular conceptions of the phrase "laboratory experimentation" confuse the "laboratory" (or research setting) component with the "experimentation" (or research strategy) component. Unfortunately, criticisms of the former are often erroneously associated with the latter. Common definitions of "laboratory experimentation" usually include three principal characteristics, *all of which are related to the experimentation component.* The first characteristic (e.g., Festinger, 1953; Kaplan, 1964, p. 144; Zelditch & Hopkins, 1961, p. 465) is succinctly summarized by Weick (1965a, p. 198): "Experimental events occur at the discretion of the experimenter." That is, instead of waiting for the conditions of interest to occur, the experimenter creates a situation and manipulates events within the situation. Thus, the experimental strategy of manipulating events (or variables) can be utilized in both natural settings and in laboratory settings.

A second and perhaps "the most important feature of laboratory experiments is that they use controls to identify sources of variation" (Weick, 1965a, p. 198). The control of variables, whether manipulative or statistical, increases confidence in the conclusion that the observed behavior can be attributed to conditions varied by the experimenter because elimination of uncontrolled variables reduces the number of potential alternative explanations (Marx, 1963, p. 11; Marx & Hillix, 1963, p. 6). The idea of control is explored in greater detail below but, suffice to say at this time, "It is in this sense that laboratory observation is superior to naturalistic observation" (Weick, 1965a, p. 198). Although the above control char-

acteristics define the *experimentation component* of the phrase laboratory experimentation, similar control strategies can be used in non-laboratory environments. Third, most descriptions do not define experimentation according to any particular setting, and instead refer to all "situations" where precise measurement of variables are possible. Thus, none of the above defining characteristics of "experimentation" is restricted to any particular environment. Experimentation has been demonstrated in locations as diverse as industrial organizations (e.g., Coch & French, 1948; Morse & Reimer, 1956), paint stores (e.g., Brock, 1965), and university dormitories (e.g., Siegel & Siegel, 1957).

While the above control *strategies* of experimentation can be applied in a wide variety of settings, they are most effectively used in "laboratory" environments. In general, a laboratory is a specifically delineated complex of rooms, which at the very least, is known to subjects as the *Behavioral Science Laboratory in Herman Webster Hall.* Research laboratories may vary from a small room with a table or chairs to a number of rooms with equipment configurations, such as microphones, video cameras, tape recorders, and one-way mirrors (cf., Fromkin, 1969). An important characteristic of many laboratories as a research environment is the greater ease with which the above control strategies can be accomplished.

The above discussion of "laboratory" and "experimentation" raises a distinction which is worthy of note. The variation and control conditions, that is, the "experimentation" component, refer to a *research strategy* which espouses the intentional variation of conditions believed to determine the occurrence of an event (as contrasted with the mere observation of events in situ). The "laboratory" component refers to the *research setting,* which is not necessarily determined by the research strategy, and which may be considered independently of the "experimentation" component. Consequently, criticisms of laboratory experimentation which are traceable to characteristics of research settings do not vitiate the valuable contributions of experimentation to theory and administrative practice.

Cause-Effect Relationships

The aim of laboratory experimentation is to identify cause-effect relationships. In general, the experimenter casts his expectations in the form of a hypothesis, for example, "high worker productivity produces low initiating structure styles of leadership" (e.g., Lowin & Craig, 1968). The stimulus side of the postulated relationship, for example, degree of worker productivity (high versus low) becomes the variable to be manipulated, that is, the "treatment" or *"independent" variable*. For instance, the researcher may decide to vary different levels of productivity so that some subjects supervise highly productive groups and other subjects supervise low productive groups. The level of worker productivity would be *one* of the stimuli to which supervisor subjects are expected to respond. At the same time, the researcher decides which variables to hold constant or to represent identically in both the high and low productivity groups, for example, the age and sex of the workers, or the potential opportunity for and nature of contact between the supervisor subjects and the workers in high and low productivity groups. The response side of the postulated relationship is the variable to be measured or the *dependent variable* of the experiment. The degree of initiating structure shown by the supervisor subjects is only *one* of the response domains which may be measured.

Advantages of Laboratory Experimentation

First, the major advantage of laboratory experimentation is the wide variety of manipulative and statistical *controls* associated with experimental strategies. For example, one unique *defining* procedure of experimentation is the opportunity for *systematic*

variation of the variable (e.g., level of subordinate productivity) which is believed to cause a particular effect (e.g., style of management). The experimenter may manipulate the productivity variable by creating a situation where several subjects supervise the same high levels of subordinate performance and other subjects supervise the same low levels of subordinate productivity. *Systematic* variation of level of subordinate productivity ensures that the stimuli presented to groups within treatments are very similar; that is, all subject supervisors will experience the same high or low levels of productivity. This procedure affords "control" of random variations in productivity.

Another defining procedure of the experimental method is the random assignment of subjects to the different treatment groups. This process of randomization disrupts any potential lawful relationship which may occur when both the treatment variable (X) and a third variable (Z) become associated and together affect the dependent variable (Y). For instance, in the absence of randomization procedures, it is possible that a disproportionately large number of subjects with the same personal characteristics may appear in one or the other of the treatment groups. A relationship between level of productivity and managerial style could then erroneously be attributed to the high or low levels of productivity rather than the unrecognized personal characteristics of the managers. There are a number of other general techniques of control which permit the experimenter to "... prohibit, inhibit, or balance out events" (cf., Weick, 1965a, p. 199) or extraneous variables and thereby increase the clarity of the observed relationship.

The above experimental strategies afford "control" over variables which results in one of the major advantages of laboratory experimentation. These control strategies provide the potential to specify cause-effect relationships; that is, to state with a high degree of confidence that changes in variable X cause changes in variable Y. For example, does managerial style (X) determine productivity (Y)? A number of earlier correlational studies uncovered a relationship between managerial styles and subordinate performance and concluded that specific managerial styles do increase or decrease subordinate performance (cf., Fleishman & Harris, 1962; Fleishman, Harris, & Burtt, 1955; Likert, 1961). More recently, several writers (cf., Carey, 1967, p. 145; Korman, 1966; Vroom, 1964, p. 215) have questioned the direction of this proposed causal sequence and have provided alternative interpretations stressing the likelihood of the reverse process, for example, subordinate productivity (Y) determines leadership style (X). Indeed, a laboratory experiment by Lowin and Craig (1968) has demonstrated that subordinate productivity can produce changes in leadership style. Of course, it is possible that either variable might affect the other.

In other words, the discovery of a correlational relationship between two variables, X and Y, does not guarantee that either X causes Y or that Y causes X. An even more distressing possibility is that neither variations in managerial style produce variations in subordinate performance nor do variations in subordinate performance produce variations in managerial style. Instead, some unrecognized third variable (Z) may interact with both managerial style and subordinate performance. For example, some individual difference factor, such as height or intelligence, may mediate the relationship (cf., reviews by Gibb, 1947, 1954; Mann, 1959; Stogdill, 1948). Of course, correlations are of value as a complementary data base to help understand behavioral phenomena. When sophisticated techniques are used, correlational data can guide the investigator toward more precise isolation of relationships among variables of interest.

Another advantage of experimentation is identified in a recent issue of *Administrative Science Quarterly* which is devoted to laboratory experiments on organizations (Weick, 1969b). These experiments identify

several issues and problems which were previously unrecognized in the world of organization theory, research, and practice. The findings suggest the need for some changes in current conceptualizations which were generated by correlational analysis of organizational behavior. "They [laboratory experiments] illustrate the detection of unnoticed causes, causes that are worth noticing and that bear continued noticing. It seems clear that experimental organizations are as useful for locating problems as for verifying hypotheses" (Weick, 1969b, p. 303). Similarly, Weick's (1969b, pp. 300–303) insightful review of these laboratory experiments clearly reveals the wisdom of increasing the priority of experimental organizations within the diversity of approaches to the study of organizational behavior.

The above advantages of experimental *strategy* should not be weakened by criticisms that would be more accurately focused on the characteristics of the setting in which these strategies are *commonly* utilized. While the value of experimental strategies cannot be doubted, there are indeed problems associated with their application in some laboratory settings. These problems, however, *can* be overcome. This chapter will discuss methods for circumventing many problems that are introduced by laboratory settings. This chapter also describes how the remaining problems can be conceptualized as "boundary variables" and thereby reduced to the realm of judgment.

It is true that some phenomena cannot be studied *directly* in laboratory settings. For example, disasters, erupting volcanoes, tornadoes, and typhoons cannot be manipulated directly by any human agency. There are also a variety of organismic variables at the individual level, for example, sex, race, and physical features, which are impossible to manipulate experimentally. Last, the use of the experiment is sometimes limited by ethical and moral concerns. People cannot be subjected to manipulations which would lead to physical or psychological harm. For example, it would be totally unacceptable to study human grief by deceiving subjects into believing that a loved one had just passed away.[4]

SOME FORMS OF LABORATORY EXPERIMENTATION

The Standard Laboratory Experiment

The literature of industrial and organizational psychology contains laboratory experiments which vary according to a large number of dimensions. The diversity of this research inhibits the identification of the "standard" laboratory experiment. However, for purposes of comparison with experimental simulations (discussed below), some relatively common characteristics can be segregated. For example, subjects are most frequently obtained from a college student population. Subjects typically volunteer for one or two hours of research participation. The use of two or three *independent* variables is the most common practice. Two or three *dependent* variables are generally measured once at one point in time or, at the most, twice during the experiment. Other variables are usually considered only as they relate to the accurate test of a particular theory rather than for their relationship to some particular criterion setting.[5] Since experiments with minor variants of these characteristics are relatively common, greater attention will be devoted to description of simulation.

---

[4] Alternatively, the "genotype" of these phenomena can be studied profitably by transposing the natural event into a laboratory event which "retains the structural properties" and "obeys the same laws" as the original event (Lewin, 1951, p. 164; Zelditch & Evan, 1962, p. 53).

[5] The criterion setting is defined as the specific situation to which a particular experiment is to have relevance or to which the results are to be generalized. For example, if an experiment is studying job satisfaction in the laboratory, then the criterion setting is the actual level and dimensionality of job satisfaction in a particular company or companies.

Simulations

Before examining different forms of simulations that are useful to the organizational researcher, some general comments on simulation techniques are in order. In contrast to the majority of standard laboratory experiments that tend to focus on the specific stimulus characteristics that are contained in the independent variable(s), simulation techniques expose participants to a number of "real-world-like" events. The use of simulation as a pure research technique has varied from relatively simple forms of role-playing experiments (cf., Bem, 1968; Jones, Linder, Kiesler, Zanna, & Brehm, 1968; Penner & Patten, 1970) and experimental simulations (cf., Streufert, Clardy, Driver, Karlins, Schroder, & Suedfeld, 1965) to more or less free simulations (e.g., Kennedy, 1962) and partially or all computerized (man-machine) simulations.[6] Many simulations are intentionally designed to be *partial* replications of real-world events (cf., Zelditch, 1969). On the other hand, some simulations are designed to be perfect miniature replicas of organizations.

Some writers do not distinguish between games, simulations, and role playing. For example, the discussion of simulation techniques by Crano and Brewer (1972) combine these categories of experimentation. The distinction should, however, be made. First, simulations should be distinguished from "parlor games" of the kind discussed by Weick (1965a). Although simulations share some characteristics with games (e.g., the involvement of participants) and are at times referred to as games (cf., Ackoff, Gupta, & Minas, 1962; Shubik, 1960), they differ from games in that the experimenter can manipulate the variables in a simulation to the degree *he wishes*. This does not

---

[6] This chapter does not deal with computer simulations and other computer models of human behavior or organizational behavior. These subject matters have been discussed in detail by Abelson (1968) and Cohen and Cyert (1965).

occur in the "parlor game" which merely defines the rules and the starting position of the players. Such freedom occurs both in the standard laboratory experiment and in experimental simulations.

Simulations are also at times confused with role playing. However, simulations have no more in common with role playing than does the standard laboratory experiment. In a role-playing task a subject is asked to imagine that he is someone else. This procedure is subject to problems (cf., Freedman, 1969). The results obtained by the researcher are questionable since the subject may not be able to imagine the situation sufficiently well to be able to produce the behavior he (or the other) would actually manifest in the real situation (cf., Willis & Willis, 1970). The participant in a simulation does not act as though he were someone else or in an imaginary situation. He completes the task that the experimenters assigned to him in the same way in which he completes a task in the standard laboratory experiment. Simulation techniques make the tasks appear more real to the subject, quite in contrast to role-playing techniques which leave the task imaginary. Indeed, Guetzkow, Alger, Brody, Noel, and Snyder (1963) have demonstrated that their free simulation technique, the Inter-Nation System (INS), is very similar to events in the real world. In fifty-five comparisons of analyses ranging from personal characteristics of decision makers to behaviors of the Inter-Nation System as a whole, two-thirds of the observed events indicated some or much similarity to real-world events. And some simulations have produced rather strikingly accurate prediction, for instance, the simulation of the outbreak of World War I by Charles and Margaret Hermann (1963; Charles Hermann, 1969) or the research by Smoker (1969).[7]

Similarly, high-ranking military officers who visited Streufert's Tactical and Negotiations Simulation acknowledged that the way college sophomores "managed" the movements, deployment of troops and so forth without regard for safety and life was not at all "unlike" the strategic decision making that occurs in the real setting. They hastened to add, however, that the field officers who have to sign letters to the wives of soldiers killed in action feel quite differently.

Simulation techniques have been criticized. Weick (1965a), for example, criticizes simulations on a number of grounds. First, he believes that the complexities of simulated environments might create apathy and confusion. However, neither those working with free simulations, for example, Guetzkow (1962, 1968) and his associates, nor those working with experimental simulations, for example, Streufert (1968) and his associates, have found any evidence for such a contention. Rather, the opposite is true. Participants in simulations tend to experience high levels of involvement.

A typical example of participant involvement is found in Streufert's experimental simulation technique, the University Simulation. At the height of a campus uprising programmed into this simulation, three students are killed and one national guardsman injured. In response to the announcement of a 10:00 P.M. curfew by the (simulated) national guard units on the (simulated) campus of the university, a sub-

---

[7] One should not forget, however, that external validity demonstrated in the outcome of a simulation is not indicative of the functional equivalence of the process underlying the outcome (cf., also Penner & Patten,

1970). The same end result could have occurred because of a variety of interactions among variable dimensions and the associated events. Potential discrepancies between actual and apparent validity may occur in simulations where the experimenter is not in full control of the sequence of events, for example, free simulations. As a result, experimenters using the same or similar methods may, at times, be able to demonstrate external validity while others may not. For instance, while the Hermanns (1963, 1969) successfully replicated World War I conditions in the laboratory, Zinnes (1966) found that data in the INS free simulation did not replicate documented World War I conditions.

ject looked at the converted (very fast moving) clock and said, "We cannot leave this room or we will be killed too." No one objected to that statement or reminded the speaker that this is "just a game." Rather, some other group members nodded or made some other statement of agreement. This happened twice.

Part of the reason for the success of experimental simulation techniques in producing high levels of involvement is, of course, the instruction manual and the program which do *not* permit any unreal event to occur. Part of the success, however, is also due to the selection of environments that are meaningful to the participants. Students, for instance, are concerned about student unrest. The university experimental simulation was conducted during the weeks of the first anniversary of the Kent State killings and students in this game behaved as students. Student interest in Guetzkow's Inter-Nation System (INS) and Streufert's Tactical and Negotiations Simulation is also high. Indeed, simulated environments have been so involving to subjects that they produce "subject demand characteristics"[8] rather than experimenter demand.

Second, Weick (1965a) criticizes simulations because even a minor experimental or design error in a complex environment

_____

[8] Subjects participating in simulations get very involved, and an experimenter watching the subjects through a one-way vision screen or on a video monitor is likely to get involved with the subjects. It is not unusual for a relatively untrained experimenter to empathize or sympathize with the subjects and to try to change slightly some pre-programmed event to give the subjects what they want (e.g., "subject demand characteristics"). Inversely, an experimenter who learns to dislike the participants may want to deny them information that would in his opinion make the subjects happy. These "subject demand characteristics" may occur for at least two reasons: (1) because of the length of time that the experimenter is exposed to the subjects, and (2) because the experimenter himself tends to become involved in the behavior of the subjects that he observed. Subject demand characteristics can be avoided by either pre-programming information that reaches the subjects, or by carefully training the experimenters to avoid these errors. In any case, the contact opportunities between subjects and experimenters should be minimized.

(e.g., a simulation) will make the subject return to the realization that he is in an experiment and will thereby modify his behavior. He quotes Kennedy (1962), who states that "nothing destroys the reality illusion as quickly as an error in the response of the synthetic environment." This is certainly true. However, errors need not occur in well-designed and pretested simulations. Rejecting simulations as a technique because errors *can* occur is akin to rejecting any form of research because the experimenter *could* make a mistake.

Third, Weick (1965a) suggests that an environment may appear realistic to the experimenter but not realistic to the subjects. This problem is easily rectified by pilot research and manipulation checks (cf., Streufert & Streufert, 1969).

Fourth, Weick (1965a) suggests that errors which destroy subjects' feelings of the situation's reality are most likely to occur in moderately complex situations. He states that in extremely complex situations errors are absorbed, while in simpler forms of experimentation they do not occur. Indeed, errors of this kind *can* occur but they *need not* occur. The problem is relatively easily remedied by careful programming of the simulation, by pretesting the method, and by manipulation checks. *Some* of the early forms of simulations might have suffered from the difficulties enumerated by Weick. It is not unusual that innovative techniques need to overcome initial problems. Simulation techniques are now advanced far enough to eliminate their childhood ailments.

There are, however, some settings which are difficult to simulate with students. For example, we cannot simulate actual military combat. The realism of a shell exploding twenty feet away cannot be recaptured in a simulation. Further, it is difficult to simulate accurately a setting if the subjects know nothing about the setting and could care less about it.

Drabeck and Haas (1967) point out that a "realistic simulation" requires real groups. The short-lived, ad hoc group has no history, no future, no linking role expectations or culture. Consequently, different response characteristics can be expected. Drabeck and Haas suggest five properties of group research methods that would produce a realistic simulation: (1) utilization of a real group or an artificial group that is assembled long enough to become real; (2) realistic task characteristics that are familiar to the groups; (3) a realistic ecological environment; (4) interactions with the environment (e.g., input information, feedback, etc.); and (5) avoidance of subjects' awareness that they are participating in an experiment. *Pusko Deception*

Even though a number of these characteristics are also amenable for use in the standard laboratory experiment, they are more easily instituted in simulation techniques. According to Drabeck and Haas (1967), attention to these five characteristics will greatly increase the "realism" of the experiment. More important, however, is that the simulation method may more closely parallel the criterion setting to which the research is to apply. At least for *some* purposes greater similarity can be of considerable value (see the section on Boundary Variables below).

There are various kinds of simulation techniques. To clarify some of these differences, the specific characteristics and implications of the two most prominent simulation methods are discussed below.

Free Simulations

Free simulations, such as the Inter-Nation System (INS) technique developed by Guetzkow and associates (cf., Guetzkow, 1962), broke radically with standard laboratory experimentation techniques. These simulation techniques expose participants to a large number of real-world-like events simultaneously. And sometimes the participants remain in the free simulation setting for considerable periods of time. One might say that experimenters who use this research method are creating field research in the laboratory.

The defining characteristic of free simu-

lation techniques is that events which occur during the simulation are shaped, in part, by the behavior of the participants themselves during the experiment. Subjects are free to modify the inputs to themselves (the independent *within* variables) by their own behavior. A free simulation, then, is a research method: (1) where participants are placed in a complex environment which represents the criterion environment as much as possible; (2) where participants are generally free to behave within the boundaries of established rules and the *interaction* of simulation parameters, participants' own past behavior, and the past behavior of others with whom participants are interacting; (3) where participants attempt through their actions to cope with (change) environmental characteristics or the behavior of other participants; and (4) where ongoing events are determined by the interactions between experimenter-determined parameters and the relatively free behavior of all participating groups.

The advantages of the free simulation technique are its potential relationship to criterion settings, the lack of necessity for concern about controlling confounds (they are part of the setting that is being simulated), and the involvement of the participants and the consequent reduction in experimental artifacts.

It should be noted that many scientists involved in free simulations are not viewing the technique as a research method but rather as a theory.[9] Setting up a simulation as a model requires a considerable knowledge of components and interactions of parameters in the criterion organization. The simulation may then be developed as a model where men interact with parameters and other men (e.g., Guetzkow, 1963),

---

[9] It has been argued that a simulation technique which produces the same outcome as a parallel event in the real world is an approximation of the world. If sequentially a number of real-world events can be reproduced, or for that matter predicted, then the parameters of the simulation and their pre-programmed or specified interactions can be viewed as the simulator's "theory" of the real world.

where men interact with computers, or where all functions of the simulation are operated through computer programs (Abelson, 1968; Guetzkow, 1968). The use of simulation for modeling is interesting and valuable, but it does not qualify as laboratory experimentation in the way it was defined in this chapter. The interested reader who wants to build such simulations is referred to the reviews of this method by Abelson (1968), Hermann (1969), Guetzkow (1971), and Robinson, Hermann, and Hermann (1969).

For those researchers who view free simulations as a technique for *testing* theories, the complex and uncontrolled processes which occur in a free simulation are useful. Since, for instance, intervention in the operations of an ongoing industrial organization or a nation is usually impossible, one recreates as many of their characteristics as possible in a simulated industry or simulated nation and places persons into the simulation as decision makers. Most of the researchers using this technique introduce independent variables into the research design in one of two (or both) ways: (1) they carefully select differential starting positions for individuals or groups in the simulation, or (2) they systematically vary the simulation rules and parameters;[10] for example, they determine in advance which different levels of payoffs should occur if subjects were to engage in certain potential behaviors (e.g., decisions).

Experimental Simulations

The advantages of the standard laboratory experiment and free simulation techniques are clear yet both methods have disadvantages. While the standard laboratory experiment is accused of artificiality, free simulation techniques are dismissed as "laboratory sociology" (e.g., Abelson, 1968). In some, but not all, cases the accusations are accurate. If one's analysis is concerned with variables which occur and/or change during the simulation or "within" the simulation, the free simulation may indeed lack experimental control over variables. Comparisons among groups after group participants have modified or determined events within the different group simulations cannot be legitimately made.

Streufert and associates (e.g., Streufert, Clardy, Driver, Karlins, Schroder, & Suedfeld, 1965) developed a compromise method which maintains the same degree of control over the independent variable as the standard laboratory experiment and also maintains some of the complexities of the free simulation methodologies. Their experimental simulations, for example, the Tactical and Negotiations Simulation and the Hamilton State University Simulation, are complex environments in which subjects participate as decision makers. The manipulation of between-group variables for this experimental technique is identical to that used in the standard laboratory experiment. However, subjects participate in the simulation over longer periods of time (usually six to twelve hours). The experimenters use the elapsed time to manipulate carefully *all* within-group variables by experimental variation, randomization, counterbalancing of stimuli as controls, or employing control groups that are exposed to constant stimulation. All information reaching subjects in experimental simulations is pre-programmed, even though subjects believe that they are determining, at least in part, their own fate. Manipulation checks examine whether participants in experimental simulations continue to believe that they themselves and their alleged opponents (in actuality, simulated programs) are causing current events (Streufert & Streufert, 1969). Another char-

Deception [margin annotation]

---

[10] The term "parameters" will be used to indicate predetermined relationships between a specific subject behavior (e.g., the amount of money spent on employee benefits) and the outcome communicated to the subjects (e.g., satisfaction). The curvilinear relationship between the two variables is a parameter that is chosen by the experimenter either to represent reality or to test certain hypotheses. Parameters are used in free simulations but not in experimental simulations.

acteristic of this method is the rather large number of variables that can be included in the design. Moreover, subjects are more free to behave as they like in this form of research relative to standard laboratory experiments. However, *all* information that reaches participants is entirely pre-programmed. Nevertheless, participants in the experimental simulation believe that they can affect their own fate to some degree; in reality they do not. This defining characteristic renders the experimental simulation more like the standard laboratory experiment than like the free simulation, that is, all independent variables remain under complete control of the experimenter.[11]

Data are collected in the same way as in the standard laboratory experiment (e.g., by responses on paper and pencil measures given during intermissions or through recording subjects' behaviors). In addition, data on behavior *sequences* and group characteristics of participants can be collected and subjected to more elaborate statistical analyses (cf., Streufert, Clardy, Driver, Karlins, Schroder, & Suedfeld, 1965; Streufert, Kliger, Castore, & Driver, 1967). The measured behaviors are not experimenter prescribed or regimented. For instance, groups of subjects are free to make any kind of decision they see fit to make to interact with each other in any way they like, whenever they want, as long as it does not violate the rules of the simulated environment. Another characteristic is the involvement experienced by the participants which is similar to the involvement in free simulation.

There are also some disadvantages which are inherent in experimental simulations. The necessity to make the program believable results in constraints on the number of complexities that can be included. For instance, subjects cannot be given the opportunity to make decisions that would drasti-

cally change the situation in which they find themselves throughout the simulation. On the other hand, the experimental simulation does not share the simplicity of the standard laboratory experiment, and consequently does not eliminate all confounds based on extraneous variables equally well. An experimental simulation is defined as a research method: (1) where participants (subjects) are placed into a complex environment in which they are, at least partly, free to behave as they like; (2) where participants attempt through their actions to cope with (i.e., change) environmental characteristics; (3) where all events (over time) are predetermined; and (4) where the number of independent variables are strictly limited.

Comparison of Methods

Variables and Data Yield

The two most strictly experimental methods that we have discussed are the standard laboratory experiment and the experimental simulation. Both afford greater control over events and both permit inferences about causality. How do they differ?

Both methods can be used to study any phenomenon that is adaptable to the laboratory. However, while the standard laboratory experiment tends to focus on a phenomenon by itself (in isolation) or in interaction with few other phenomena, the experimental simulation tends to focus upon many phenomena in interaction at the same time. The greater complexity of the experimental simulation technique, however, does not affect the number of *independent* variables introduced into the design. The number of variables to which subjects are systematically exposed is limited by the ability of the experimenter to understand potential interactions among them. At most, the number is usually three or four, certainly not more than five. Three to five independent variables can easily be manipulated in the standard laboratory experiment as well as in an experimental simulation. However, while

[11] Experimental simulations must be carefully designed and pretested so that the illusion of participant influence on events is maintained in spite of the characteristics which the predetermined program of events (independent within variable) might have.

the standard laboratory experiment, in general, limits the number of variables that are *present* when the subject is participating in the experiment, the experimental simulation seeks to include as many of these variables at the same time as possible. An attempt may be made to include all the known conditions that are present in the criterion environment at the specific (but invariate) levels at which they exist in the criterion environment. The obtained data then are influenced by more conditions, greater time, and potentially more variables. To the degree to which the presence of these additional variables may affect the behavior of the subjects, the experimental simulation might produce different outcomes than a standard laboratory experiment. Further, the participants in the experimental simulation tend to be more free to behave in their own way since, for instance, their behaviors are not limited to making decision X or decision Y (as is often, but not necessarily, the case in standard laboratory experiments).[12] Finally, more data tend to be collected in experimental simulations which permit more complex analysis of covariance, multivariate analysis of variance, and multidimensional scaling techniques. To produce the same set of multiple results obtained in a single run of an experimental simulation would require many standard laboratory experiments. That, however, does not make the experimental simulation more desirable. Both methods have value. Setting up a good simulation that is not hampered by the problems that Weick mentions tends to take at least a year or two. A good standard laboratory experiment can be designed and completed in a few weeks.

Artifacts

Although artifacts may occur in standard laboratory experimentation, they *can* be

---

[12] Note, however, that much of the behavioral data from the experimental simulation require transformation to numerical values in some rigorous fashion before the experimenter may proceed with statistical analysis.

avoided. Part of the reason for the abundance of artifactual findings in past standard laboratory techniques is that psychologists have only recently become concerned with such matters; the psychology of the psychological experiment is a relatively novel interest of researchers.

Simulations, whether experimental or free, are less subject to some of these artifactual problems. The greater involvement of subjects tends to focus their minds on matters other than the experiment in which they are participating. Further, the experimenter is able to program the experiment so that he has minimal contact with subjects, especially after warm-up periods have ended. The remoteness of time from the initial and only contact with the experimenter is of considerable aid in avoiding both subject-based and experimenter-based response biases.

Control Over Independent Variables

Both the standard and the simulation laboratory experiment maintain control over variables throughout the experiment. This is only partially true for the free simulation. The researcher employing a free simulation is less able to control the events that occur once the simulation has begun. Participants (in interaction with parameters established by the experimenter) can and do modify future information flow to themselves. Thus, even though groups were comparable when the simulation began, after the simulation has started groups may not continue to be comparable.

Confounds

Two kinds of confounds occur in experimental research: confounds planned by the experimenter to achieve some specific effect, for example, intended confounds, and confounds that slip by, in other words, conditions that are due to *unintended* extraneous variables. The intended confound may reflect the use of a constant condition (e.g., guise, instructions and tasks, etc.) which makes an experiment more like the criterion setting, *even though that condition is otherwise unrelated to the independent and dependent variables.* In other cases, the intended confound might merely be an unavoidable by-product of the experimental setting. For instance, when one measures the effects of inconsistent information on attitudes, there must be a source of the inconsistency.

Complex experimental settings often contain more intended confounds than simple laboratory settings. To some degree, these intended confounds increase involvement and can make the experimental situation more like the criterion setting. On the other hand, they might decrease the potential immediate effect that a manipulation of the independent variable has by itself on measured dependent variables. In addition, an incorrectly chosen confound, that is, one that does not occur in the same way in the criterion setting, may make the obtained data of lesser value when application is a desired goal. Intended confounds, then, both help and hinder simulations in comparison to standard laboratory experiments.

Unintended confounds, those of which the experimenter was not aware when he designed his experiments, are also more frequent in simulation settings than they are in the standard laboratory experiment. As a rule, the experimenter who simulates is not able to foresee the effects of all environmental and information variables on the perceptions and behavior of his subjects. This problem can be remedied, in part, by extensive manipulation checks and careful pretesting of any new simulation technique (cf., discussion of "Experimental Procedures: Manipulation Checks" below).

Uninterpretable Interactions

The number of statistical interactions are, in most cases, determined by the experimenter. If he does not want to interpret more than a three-way interaction in an ANOVA design, he merely limits his independent variables to three. This is easily accomplished in the standard laboratory experiment and in the experimental simulation. Free simulations, however, do not permit such an analysis unless one wants to consider all changes over time in the simulation as error. One might be able to introduce some of the differences over time in free simulations into the analysis as covariates; however, the number of covariates that can be used simultaneously is limited. This limitation on covariate analysis is particularly serious when other factors in the analysis consist of *within* levels. If all differences that occur among various runs of a free simulation were introduced into the analysis, then the number of variables would be much too large to analyze and interpret. Even though it might be possible to write computer programs that would calculate F values for, say, fifty-way interactions, the human mind would not be able to interpret their meaning. Free simulations, then, are limited from this point of view. This limitation, however, in no way decreases their value in the "theory building" approach that has been taken by Guetzkow (1968) and others (cf., Guetzkow, Kotler, & Schultz, 1972; Inbar & Stoll, 1972).

Effects of Divergent Pre-experimental Exposure

Experimental psychologists working with rats ensure that all animals used in an experiment are bred from the same strain. This procedure decreases error variance due to interpersonal differences. Except for drawing subjects from the same culture or subculture, the same degree of control cannot be obtained with human subjects. Rats spend their time in identical environments before they are placed into a Skinner box or into a maze. In contrast, people come to an experiment from all sorts of different settings and all sorts of different immediate pre-experimental expectations or experiences. For example, subjects' pre-experimental expectations about wages had a greater effect on the quality of performance than the independent variable, that is, manipulated wages (Evan & Simmons, 1969). Quite different behaviors can be expected from them if they are immediately exposed to the experimental stimuli.

In this case, the standard laboratory experiment is at a disadvantage. Usually the experimenter does not have time to let the subject "adapt out" his previous experience. He cannot afford to keep the subject in a constantly controlled environment for more than an hour or two. Since simulations continue for long periods of time and require pre-training (e.g., via manuals) of the participants, this problem is much more easily solved. A subject who is asked to spend approximately two hours in the simulation room reading the manual will readapt to the new environment, and the pre-experimental experiences will become somewhat less salient. Further, after some time in the simulation has elapsed and the subject is involved in his activities, something that happened hours ago will have less effect. (Note that the latter argument is meaningful only if the conditions to which subjects or groups of subjects are sequentially exposed are randomized.)

Efficiency

Both standard laboratory experimentation and experimental simulation are relatively efficient. The standard lab experiment is simple to run and generally produces a single set of data. Unlike standard laboratory experiments, simulations tend to be very expensive and require elaborate and unusually permanent research space. The experimental simulation is much more difficult and time-consuming to set up and to run, but it can produce more data. The free simulation, on the other hand, does not permit more than a single set of independent (between) variables and does not lend itself to interpretation of effects at several points in time since the "within" determinants of these effects are generally unknown. As an experimental method (not a theoretical representation of reality) the free simulation, then, is considerably less efficient.

Causality

Causality can be inferred in standard laboratory experiments and in experimental simulations. Viewing a phenomenon in greater isolation from other variables, as is possible in the standard laboratory experiment, can contribute greatly to the understanding of the phenomenon itself. Similarly, viewing a phenomenon in simultaneous occurrence with other phenomena, as in the experimental simulation, can contribute to understanding its interactions and its importance in relation to other variables. Inferences from free simulations can be only partial. Again, the uncontrolled effects that participants in free simulations exert on their own environment permit the simulation to take on directions that were not necessarily intended by the experimenter. Further, these uncontrolled effects may not be identified or understood by the experimenter.

Appropriateness of Samples

All experimental techniques are subject to sample problems. The most available subject (and the least expensive one) tends to be the college sophomore who works for credit in one of his classes. For most simulations and most standard laboratory experiments this sample may be inadequate if one intends to generalize to a quite different criterion population (e.g., industrial executives). This problem, however, is not inherent in any technique. An experimenter can gain the cooperation of the criterion population, that is, can have industrial executives perform the functions of industrial executives, and so forth. Those using free simulation techniques have often shown more ingenuity in obtaining criterion members to participate in their research. Nonetheless, all experiments could use samples from criterion populations. Greater understanding of the value of the experiment should make it easier to persuade members of criterion populations to participate.

Cost

The standard laboratory experiment tends to be inexpensive. Most single experiments of this kind cost $5,000 to $15,000. Simulations are much more expensive. They require more extensive and permanent laboratory space as well as more assistants and greater subject costs (since subjects participate for longer time periods). As a rule, a large-scale simulation cannot be run for less than $50,000 per year—even when laboratory space is already available. However, the greater data yield of simulation experiments may make the per unit cost of data as inexpensive or even less expensive as the cost of the standard laboratory experiment.

Measurement of Dependent Variables

There is little difference between the measurement of dependent variables in the standard laboratory experiment and experimental simulations. In either case, dependent measures can be obtained by recording subjects' behavior (e.g., the number of their decisions) or by having subjects complete questionnaires (e.g., attitude scales) during the experiment. In general, the measurement of dependent variables in industrial and organizational psychology does not markedly differ from dependent variable measurement in other related areas of psychology (cf., Webb, Campbell, Schwartz, & Sechrest, 1966). Where special issues of measurement are unique to laboratory experimentation on organizational problems, they are discussed in the various sections of this chapter.

CHARACTERISTICS OF EXPERIMENTAL STRATEGIES

Information Yield

The kind and quantity of data yielded by experimental strategies depends upon the specific purpose and strategy selected by the experimenter. The initial stages of the research process involve many complicated and difficult decisions. To state one rather complex dilemma somewhat simply: does the researcher intend to test theory or hunt phenomena? Of course, some combination of the two is quite possible. According to scientific tradition, theory should precede experimentation, and theory should at best be preceded by observation. Nonetheless, many vital discoveries have been produced through playful, accidental, or unintentional manipulation of phenomena. Some proponents of laboratory research in organizational psychology argue that theory testing is the sine qua non. They suggest that similarity between laboratory research and the organizational setting is unnecessary as long as the bridge can be built via theory (e.g., Zelditch, 1969). Other researchers are more concerned with focusing upon a particular applied problem. While one researcher may study an organizational event in the standard laboratory experiment, another might use experimental simulation, and still another might observe it in the criterion environment, and so forth.

The value of using different research techniques is strikingly clear when the basic research strategies are compared on several continua, such as degree of control of variables, degree of rigor, degree of realism, costs, and so forth. The various strategies yield *different kinds* of information concerning the same question and are, therefore, complementary rather than interchangeable. Every strategy can make a valuable contribution—especially when used interchangeably to compensate for deficiencies of the other strategies. A comprehensive exposition of the above notions is presented by McGrath (1964), Runkel and McGrath (1972), and in the McGrath chapter in this *Handbook*. Therefore, the following brief discussion abstracts only features of McGrath's perspective which are relevant to laboratory strategies.

The information yielded by different strategies is directly related to each strategy's unique model for disposition of the variables circumscribing the problem under scrutiny.

For example, experimental strategies control variables in at least three ways. First, the independent variable(s) is manipulated such that a small number of specific values occur within a single study. In general, the more limited the range of values as compared with range of universe values the greater the potential loss of information for that relevant variable. Experimental manipulation of a variable does, however, facilitate more precise identification of functional relationships. Second, within each treatment condition, the value of the independent variable remains constant throughout the study. Third, the specific values of the independent variable which are used in the study can be randomly selected from the universe of values that the variable assumes.

In sum, with experimental strategies phenomena can be studied in greater depth and detail and with greater precision of measurement in exchange for a reduction with breadth of information. Thus, precision is, at times, obtained at the expense of generality. Before casting any research strategies into an inferior role in the research process, it is important to note that maximum precision and generality (and internal and external validity) are not simultaneously obtainable with any single research strategy or by any single data collection. Thus, when selecting a research method, one typically trades off the desirable aspects of one method for the desirable aspects of another method.

The limitations of experimental strategies with respect to breadth of information are offset by two factors. First, the relatively lower cost (e.g., time, effort, and monetary resources) of laboratory experimentation is conducive to the procedures of partial or complete replication (Sidman, 1960). Such iterative processes extend the information yield and, at the same time, provide valuable evidence regarding the reliability of the findings. Second, the restrictive limitation upon the number of experimental variables results in the greatest information loss when there is no prior knowledge about the problem being studied. However, the potential in-

formation loss due to the experimental control of variables is somewhat nullified by the existence of prior knowledge about most phenomena being studied in organizational psychology.

The contents of the former (March, 1965) and present *Handbook of Organizations* and the burgeoning literature of organizational theory and research from as many as eight disciplines (cf., Dill, 1964) attest to the extensive current state of knowledge about many organizational phenomena. For example, Sells's (1964) taxonomy of organizational behavior includes a battery of 100 relevant variables. An even greater number of theoretically based propositions describing organization behavior may be found in Argyris (1962, 1964), Haire (1959, 1962), Rubenstein and Haberstroh (1960), March and Simon (1958), and Weick (1969a).

Certainly there is an abundance of prior information about many organizational phenomena to which experimental strategies may be appropriately applied. For example, Bass's (1963) experimental test of Likert's (1961) theoretical notions about overlapping committees resulted in some proposed modifications in the theory. In such instances, the use of field strategies is extremely costly due to the high dross rate or the proportion of irrelevant information (Webb, Campbell, Schwartz, & Sechrest, 1966, p. 32), which is encumbered in order to obtain a sampling of a small number of relevant values of the variable(s) of interest to the researcher. Substitution of experimental strategies under these circumstances represents a substantial increase in efficiency without the reduction in scope of information or generality.

Given the extensive literature regarding organizational behavior, testing and sorting out the many concepts, variables, and propositions is required. Platt (1964) pointed out the rapid advances of other fields taking advantage of certain procedures of inductive inference. When applied to the present state of the art in organizational theory, strongest inferences will result from the following recipe suggested by Platt (1964): (1) generate alternative hypotheses; (2) design crucial experiments with alternative possible outcomes where each possible outcome will eliminate one or more of the hypotheses; (3) strive for results with high internal validity; and (4) repeat the procedure with sequential hypotheses to refine the remaining possibilities. It is clear that the experimental method is the most essential ingredient of Platt's recipe (cf., Fromkin, 1968a). Furthermore, most organizational researchers call attention to the interdependence of individual, organizational, and environmental determinants of organizational behavior (cf., Katz & Kahn, 1966; Leavitt, 1964; Sells, 1964; Vroom, 1969; Weick, 1969a). Such *interdependence* requires empirical examination of expected (and unexpected) interactions between the variables associated with each level of analysis. Experimental strategies are also uniquely suited to examine such interactions. We do not need new methods nor theories; we need more representative sampling of known methodologies, with emphasis on the underrepresented standard and simulation laboratory experimentation.

GENERALITY, ARTIFICIALITY, AND REALISM

Generality and Experimentation

Generality is an issue of central concern to researchers in either theoretical or applied areas of research. Generality refers to the extent that effects which occurred in the experimental situation with a particular population of subjects and specific values of the independent variable(s) will occur in the larger untested universes. By definition then, generalization *always* requires extrapolation to realms *not* represented in one's sample, for example, to other populations, to other representations of the independent variable (X), to other representations of the dependent variable (Y), and so forth. It is clear that generality may have several meanings (cf., Campbell & Stanley, 1963, pp. 17–34; Sidman, 1960, pp. 46–67). For example, are

the findings obtained with a particular sample of college students useful for accurately predicting the behavior of all college students or company managers? Are the findings obtained under a particular treatment variable X useful for accurately predicting behavior under other nonidentical representations of X? Are the findings obtained under a particular measurement variable Y useful for accurately predicting behavior under other nonidentical representations of Y?

Although it is important to determine if a relationship is relevant outside the confines of a particular laboratory experiment, generalizations are never logically justified and, to further complicate the issue, there are no objective criteria which yield unequivocal answers to the question of generality. "But we do attempt generalizations by guessing at laws and checking out some of these generalizations in other equally specific but different conditions. In the course of the history of science we learn about the 'justification' of generalizing by the cumulation of our experience in generalizing, but this is not a logical generalization deducible from the details of the original experiment. Faced by this, we do, in generalizing, make guesses as to yet unproven laws, including some not even explored. The sources of external validity are thus guesses as to general laws in the science of a science: guesses as to what factors interact with our treatment variables, and, by implication, guesses as to what can be disregarded" (Campbell & Stanley, 1963, p. 17). Evaluation of generality, then, for example, the decision to act or not act administratively upon the organizational implications of any particular relationship demonstrated in laboratory experiments, is a matter of judgment. The basis for such judgments resides in the identification of critical differences between a specific research setting and a specific organizational setting.

Campbell and Stanley (1963, p. 5) introduce the concepts of *internal* validity and *external* validity to describe how the inappropriate use of any research strategy limits the generality of the research data. Internal validity varies according to whether or not the experimental treatments made a difference; that is, had an effect on the dependent variable. The laboratory setting is most facilitative of procedures which help eliminate or, at least, control extraneous influences which can reduce or result in unintended changes in the dependent variable. Such extraneous variables can render the results uninterpretable and thereby reduce the "internal validity" of the experimental findings. In contrast, "external validity" refers to the degree to which the experimental effects can be generalized to other populations, settings, treatment variables, and measurement dependent variables. Even the most austere laboratory contains cues, such as the setting, the instructions, the response measure, and so forth which can contribute to the subjects' responses. Many of these cues are planned variables. The researcher can select specific variables and specific levels of variables to be *held constant* across groups of subjects to help match the experimental situation to a criterion situation. Events which are not part of a criterion situation can be either eliminated, held constant (at one or several levels), randomized (occur in random order and frequency at all or many of their potential levels), or counterbalanced (occur with equal frequency at all of their potential levels in each cell of the experimental design). These strategies help to produce the necessary conditions for testing a particular theory or help to increase external validity by controlling variables in order to represent a criterion setting.

Much theory-oriented research is relatively unconcerned with external validity, and theoretical concepts tend to be tested in ways which are irrelevant to application. This point of view is described by Aronson and Carlsmith (1968, pp. 22–26). They argue that "experimental realism" (the degree to which the experiment is involving to the subject) is more important than "mundane realism" (the extent to which a laboratory

event is real-world-like). If, they say, an experimental procedure has a good deal of impact, then it need not be presentative of a real-world setting. They also argue that internal validity is more important than external validity because if an intended effect does not occur, one need not worry about its generality. All these arguments are well taken, if all one wants to do is prove one's theory, or disprove someone else's. If, however, one wants to study theory in the laboratory, in relation to a criterion phenomenon, the nonoccurrence of the event in a "mundane" laboratory setting (with external validity) may be as, or even more, important than one's ability to carefully create the event in the laboratory via the powerful manipulation of some perhaps irrelevant variables in the criterion setting.

Without internal validity, an experiment is necessarily doomed to failure. Without external validity, it is of little use to those who would apply the research. Both are equally important. One cannot argue that theory should not be tested. However, if the theory is applicable to a real-world setting (e.g., an organization), the associated laboratory experiment should *reproduce one or more of the conditions that are found in the criterion setting, and it should, if possible, omit all conditions that are never found in the criterion setting.*

The relative importance of internal and external validity might best be demonstrated by an example. Let us assume we could measure the impact of a variable with an "impactometer" with scale values which range from 0 to 50. If the typical impact of an organizational event is 25, and if one were to achieve an impact level of 49 or 50 in the laboratory, then the effect of the impact on behavior in the laboratory might be quite different from the impact on behavior in the organization. This is particularly true when the operations which achieve the high impact level in the laboratory are quite atypical to the organizational setting. Such operations likely produce completely different effects than observed in organizations. In addition, the conditions under which this event occurs in an organization are also quite important if one's experimental findings are to be applied. For example, another variable might interact with our original event when the impact meter reads 25, but not when it reads 50, or vice versa. As a consequence, the obtained phenomenological product of this interaction might be quite different in the two settings, the laboratory and the organization.

Generality and Laboratory Settings

The philosophical question of generality has provoked many individuals to advocate abandonment of experimentation[13] because it is artificial. However, it seems obvious that a lack of realism and artificiality are more an indictment of characteristics of laboratory settings and less a condemnation of experimental methods. Since characteristics of laboratory settings are susceptible to modification, laboratory experiments can vary in their degree of relevance according to the discretion and creativity of the experimenter. A major treatise of this chapter is that the artificiality of laboratories is being unjustly elevated to the status of a fatal flaw. Censorious descriptions of laboratories as artificial are usually based upon perceived differences which are claimed to impose limitations on the generality of laboratory experiments. Careful examination, however, reveals that most of the contended differences either do not exist or are not essential to the occurrence of the criterion stimulus event. Examples of the former are presented below under "Artifacts" and examples of the latter are presented below under "Realism."

---

[13] It is often overlooked that similar problems of generality occur in alternative research settings, such as field interviews (cf., Back, 1962; Becker & Geer, 1957; Cannell & Kahn, 1968; Hakel, Ohnesorge, & Dunnette, 1970), field surveys (cf., Adams & Preiss, 1960; Hyman, 1950; Kornhauser, 1946; Remmers, 1954; Riley, 1962; Sherwood & Nataupsky, 1968; Sills, 1961; Viteles, 1953), field observation (cf., Argyris, 1952; Becker, 1958; Kahn & Mann, 1952; McCall & Simmons, 1969; Scott, 1962; Weick, 1968), and so forth.

The terms "artificiality" and "realism" refer semantically to two points on the same continuum of meaning. Presumably, then, a variable which affects artificiality also affects realism, but in an opposite manner. However, as *commonly used* to describe characteristics of research settings, they refer to quite different phenomena. Artificiality is used to refer to a number of specific variables, allegedly unique to laboratory settings, which are related to the characteristics of the subject population and to the subjects' awareness of their participation in research (cf., Rosenthal & Rosnow, 1969). Realism refers to structural similarities between the research setting and the criterion setting (cf., Evan, 1971; Weick, 1965a). While it may be instructive to explore the validity of this seemingly arbitrary distinction, the following discussion will adopt the customary usage and distinction between the terms.

Artifacts

Experimental research strategies do not prescribe particular kinds of settings. Yet, in practice the vast majority of experiments are performed in settings which, because of their particular characteristics, can be classified as "laboratories." Characteristics associated with "laboratories" may vary from requesting subjects to appear at the "Behavioral Science Laboratory in Herman Webster Hall" to equipment configurations, such as microphones, cameras, and one-way mirrors (cf., Fromkin, 1969) which are present in many experimental settings. The important implication of the laboratory as a customary environment for experimental research is that any or all of the above characteristics potentially promote in subjects an *awareness that they are participants in research;* that is, may impel subjects to believe that, for a short time, their welfare may be protected, and their behavior is being observed, measured, and/or evaluated. This awareness and related phenomena raise a central issue surrounding laboratory experimentation. Can relationships established in laboratories (as described above) be expected to occur unchanged in non-laboratory criterion settings (e.g., organizations)?

Artificiality, as it is commonly used, is viewed as nonrepresentativeness of the laboratory setting which occurs when "...the procedures and experimental treatments are reacted to not only for their stimulus values but also for their role as cues in divining the experimenter's intent" (Campbell & Stanley, 1963, p. 20), the experimenter's expectancies (cf., Rosenthal, 1966, 1969), or arousing evaluation apprehension (Rosenberg, 1965, 1969), etc. It is subjects' responses to such "...extraneous conditions—for the most part social in nature—that affect the experimental variables" (Boring, 1969, p. 5) and thereby contribute to artificiality. Riecken (1962, pp. 33–34) proposes a similar view of the laboratory as a social situation where "...the subject has more than one problem. One is the 'task' that the E sets. Another is what we may, for convenience, call his 'deutero-problem,' meaning his personal problem as defined by three aims.... First, he wants to accomplish his private purposes or get his rewards, for example, pay, course credit, satisfaction of curiosity, self-insight, help with a problem, and so on; second, he wants to penetrate the E's inscrutability and discover the rationale of the experiment—its purposes and the types of judgment that will issue from it; and, third, he wants to accomplish this second aim in order to achieve a third, namely, in order to represent himself in a favorable light or 'put his best foot forward.'"

Thus, it is reasonable to expect that subjects' responses in some laboratory settings will not be determined solely by the treatment variable. In some situations, their responses may be attributed, at least in part, to motives aroused by subjects' awareness of their participation in research. Under some conditions, awareness of participation in research arouses motives which are specific to the perceived role of "subject," and the behavior related to these motives is confounded with responses to the independent variable (cf., reviews by Back, Hood, & Brehm, 1964;

Kintz, Delprato, Mettee, Persons, & Schappe, 1965; Masling, 1966; Reicken, 1962).

The two most widely cited conceptualizations of these motives are demand characteristics (Orne, 1959, 1962, 1969) and evaluation apprehension (Rosenberg, 1965, 1969). In the former role, that is, the "good subject," subjects are motivated to exhibit responses which comply with their percepts of the experimenter's hypothesis. In the latter role, that is, the "apprehensive subject," subjects are motivated to conceal any personal "weaknesses" which the experimenter may be looking for and to present themselves in as favorable a manner as possible.

Recent theory and research on the social psychology of the experiment suggest that the above influences are frequently confounded in the same experiment and may interact with still another extraneous influence, that is, the experimenter's expectancy about experimental outcomes (Rosenthal, 1966, 1969). A third, less frequent, role is the "negativistic subject" who is motivated to deliberately behave in a fashion to disconfirm the experimental hypothesis or to give responses he believes are useless to the experimenter (cf., Masling, 1966; Orne, 1962; Silverman & Kleinman, 1967). Last, there is the "faithful subject" who loyally follows only the experimental instructions and does not respond to cues about the experimenter's hypothesis despite deception and debriefing in prior experiments (Fillenbaum, 1966), or despite suspicions about the true purposes of the experiment (Fillenbaum & Frey, 1970). A number of investigations examined the effects of prior experiences of deception and debriefing upon arousal and manifestation of the above motives in subsequent experiments (cf., Brock & Becker, 1966; Fillenbaum & Frey, 1970; Holmes, 1967; Holmes & Applebaum, 1970; McGuire, 1969b; Silverman, Shulman, & Wiesenthal, 1970; Stricker, 1967). At the present time, there is no unequivocal demonstration of the nature of deception effects.

While the above artifacts are frequently observed in laboratory research, the following discussion reveals that the disparaging criticisms of the laboratory as artificial and ensuing proselytizations for greater attention to alternative research methods are unwarranted.[14] The three major sources of criticism are examined to demonstrate the transitory nature of their "artifactual" status.

Demand Characteristics

Under some conditions, subjects' awareness of their role as subjects and their high regard for the aims of science promote efforts toward being a "good" subject. The "good subject" role is played to contribute to the development of human knowledge by providing data which are useful to science and the experimenter. This is especially likely when subjects perceive the project as very important and meaningful. The concept of the "good subject" role arose from Orne's (1959, 1962) observations of subjects' willingness to place themselves under the complete control of the experimenter without refusing to perform any behavior requested of them in an experimental setting. For example, subjects were observed to persist for hours at a meaningless task (Orne, 1962), to pick up a venomous snake or throw acid at a research assistant (Orne & Evans, 1965).

Subjects' desire to confirm the experimental hypothesis induces subjects to search for information about the experiment—including the pre-experimental "scuttlebutt" (Zemack & Rokeach, 1966), subject recruitment information, experimenter appearance, experimental instructions and procedures, and task requirements—to discover the nature of the experimental hypothesis. Orne (1959) referred to the totality of such cues which reveal the experimental hypothesis as "demand characteristics."

In addition to an examination of adding (Orne, 1962) and copying (Sigall, Aronson,

& Van Hoose, 1970) tasks, verbal conditioning tasks (cf., Levy, 1967) and Asch-type conformity tasks (Horowitz & Rothchild, 1970), the study of demand characteristics has been extended to persuasion and attitude change phenomena. The findings show greater acquiescence to a persuasive message when it is presented in the context of a psychological experiment than in the context of a group discussion, and especially when subjects' responses were *not* anonymous (Silverman, 1968). It is possible that subjects were responding in a manner congruent with their perception that the experiment was designed to show that the messages were persuasive. Alternatively, subjects may have perceived the likelihood of their being persuaded as very great when confronted with sophisticated psychological techniques of persuasion and thereby changed their attitude before receiving the message to protect their self-esteem (cf., McGuire & Millman, 1965). Other research shows that subjects will appear *not* to be persuaded when they perceive that the experimenter equates acquiescence with psychological weakness (Rosenberg, 1965; Silverman & Regula, 1968) and that female subjects are more responsive to demand characteristics of attitude change measures than are male subjects (Silverman, 1968; Silverman & Shulman, 1970).

In contrast to demonstrations of hypothesis confirmation by "good subject" responses to demand characteristics, other studies identify two conditions which produce the opposite tendencies, that is, the "negativistic subject." First, subjects who experienced prior deception, relative to subjects who were merely aware of the practice of deception, were less prone to be "good" subjects by responding to confirm the experimenter's hypothesis (Cook, Bean, Calder, Frey, Krovetz, & Reisman, 1970). Second, Orne (1962, p. 780) suggests that "...when demand characteristics are so obvious that the subject becomes fully conscious of the expectations of the experiment, then there is a tendency to lean over backwards to be honest." Similarly, deliberate confirmation

---

[14] As noted earlier, the same "artifacts" have been found to operate in a variety of non-laboratory settings (cf., Argyris, 1952, 1968; Kroger, 1967; Page & Lumia, 1968; Rosen, 1970; Rosen & Sales, 1966; Dunnette & Heneman, 1956; Scott, 1962; Roethlisberger & Dickson, 1946).

of experimental hypotheses in attitude change studies is predicted when demand characteristics are made too explicit or when subjects are intentionally or incidentally frustrated during the experiment (Silverman & Shulman, 1970, p. 101). Support for the explicit postulate is found in Cook, Bean, Calder, Frey, Krovetz, and Reisman (1970) and for the frustration prediction in Silverman and Kleinman (1967) and Silverman and Shulman (1970).

Before relegating the laboratory experiment to artificial status because of the *potential* operation of demand characteristics, it seems more profitable to understand their dynamics and design a set of controls which allows the researcher to estimate or circumvent their effects. Orne (1962, 1969) recently described three techniques of quasi-controls to delineate the effects of demand characteristics. First, the experimenter may conduct judicious inquiry of the subjects' perceptions during a *post-experimental session*. The aim is to determine what the subjects perceive the experiment is about, what the subjects think the experimenter hopes and expects to find, and how subjects expect others might react in the same situation, etc. This information may reveal what the subjects perceive as "good" responses. There are a number of reasons why information of this nature is difficult to obtain from subjects. For example, subjects will be reluctant to disclose their true perceptions for fear that their experimental responses will be discarded because they caught on to the hypothesis. Similarly, if instructions contain false information to conceal the true hypothesis, subjects may be reluctant to reveal publicly their disbelief and thereby question the experimenter's honesty. It is, therefore, a wise strategy to use someone other than the experimenter to conduct the post-experimental inquiry.

A second technique involves inquiry prior to the experiment—pilot research (cf., Orne, 1959; Riecken, 1962). The non-experiment (Orne, 1969, p. 155) procedure involves selecting a representative sample of subjects to be informed of the instructions and procedures in a manner identical to those which are to be experienced by the experimental subjects. Although they are not actually subjected to the treatment variable, they are asked to imagine themselves as subjects and to respond to the treatment variable by performing the behavior which comprises the dependent variable (e.g., rating scales or actual overt behavior, etc.). But it does not, however, demonstrate whether the obtained results are due to subjects' accurate guessing of what is expected of them (the demand characteristics) or subjects' accurate prediction of their own behavior.

A third technique described by Orne (1959, 1969, pp. 158–159) is the use of *simulators*. In this technique, subjects are asked to pretend that they have been affected by the experimental treatment which they did not actually receive or to which they have been made immune. "For subjects to be able to do this, it is crucial that they be run by another experimenter who they are told is unaware of their actual status, and who is, in fact, unaware of their status" (Orne, 1969, p. 158). Although predominantly to develop hypotheses (cf., Orne, 1959; Orne & Evans, 1965), it can provide valuable information about the nature of experimental subjects' responses.

Orne (1969) refers to post-experimental inquiry, non-experiment, and simulator groups as "quasi-control" groups because, in contrast to standard control techniques which omit the independent variable, subjects are asked to perceive various kinds of information about the independent variables and respond to them as if they were experimental subjects. These procedures do not yield data which permit inferences about the effects of the independent variables. "Rather, they serve to suggest alternative explanations not excluded by the experimental design" (Orne, 1969, p. 160) and apply most specifically to the identification of demand characteristics and how such factors may be affecting the experimental findings. They cannot, however, prove that a particular finding is a function of demand characteristics. More important, quasi-controls can provide information regarding possible ways to manipulate demand characteristics in concert with other experimental variables either as placebo controls (cf., Orne, 1969, pp. 167–173) or as an independent variable (cf., Orne & Scheibe, 1964). The latter procedure involves an additional treatment group which receives the same instructions as other treatment groups but also receives cues identifying the experimental hypothesis. This procedure (cf., Greenwald, 1965; Gustafson & Orne, 1965) affords the firmest foundation for inferences regarding the effects of demand characteristics upon the dependent variable.

Evaluation Apprehension

The underlying assumption of Rosenberg's (1965, 1969) conceptualization of evaluation apprehension is that "...the typical human subject approaches the typical psychological experiment with a preliminary expectation that the psychologist may undertake to evaluate his [the subject's] emotional adequacy, his mental health, or lack of it" (1969, p. 281). This expectation arouses evaluation apprehension or "...an active anxiety-toned concern that he win a positive evaluation from the experimenter, or at least that he provide no grounds for a negative one" (p. 281). The dynamics of the anxiety-toned self-concern are akin to those underlying the approval motive (Crowne & Marlowe, 1964). The resultant response bias occurs when subjects respond to correct (or incorrect) cues of how to do well on the experimental task instead of responding normally to the experimental variables.

The dynamics of evaluation apprehension are seen as having two major components. First, there may be cues in the experimental situation related to the arousal or heightening of evaluation apprehension, for example, cues revealing to subjects that their responses might have significance concerning their personalities. Second, there may be

cues related to hints about the appropriate responses for obtaining favorable evaluation from the experimenter, for example, cues revealing the kinds of responses expected from normal and abnormal persons or mature and immature persons. It appears that either component is sufficient to produce biased responding (cf., Rosenberg, 1969), but the nature of the bias may differ for each component. *When only arousal or heightening cues are present,* subjects must generate their own notions of the appropriate response, and each subject is likely to focus on an idiosyncratic interpretation of unrelated cues. The resulting response bias will appear as *random* error variance. *When only the appropriate response cues are present* (cf., Sigall, Aronson, & Van Hoose, 1970), most subjects are likely to respond relatively uniformly to the same cues. On many occasions, the occurrence of appropriate response cue is correlated with treatment variables and thereby produces *systematic* response bias between treatment groups. In such instances, evaluation apprehension may provide a plausible rival alternative explanation for the effects of the independent variable upon the dependent variable.

In general, evaluation apprehension is aroused or heightened: (1) by cues in the introductory guise (including information on the subject recruitment notices) and/or experimental instructions or procedures which provide hints regarding impending experimental examination of the subject's personal adequacy; or (2) whenever experimental procedures contain surprises or whenever the experimental procedures seem mysterious or deceptive (cf., Rosenberg, 1969, p. 290). More specifically, Rosenberg (1969, p. 306) suggests five broad categories of variables which boost or suppress the evaluation apprehension process: (1) the personality attributes of the subjects (e.g., the need for approval); (2) aspects of the subjects' recent pre-experimental experiences; (3) attributes of the experimental setting; (4) attributes of the experimenter; and (5) attributes of the experimental task. In a series of experiments, Rosenberg (1969) provided support for the effects of some variables in each of the above categories. For example, in contrast to a high evaluation apprehension communication describing the experiment as a "Personality Assessment Project," a low evaluation apprehension communication introduced the experiment as a "Mathematical Psychology Project" and stressed that the investigators were "...interested in integrating the various dimensions or factors involved in social perceptual processes into a more simplified model by a method which statisticians term 'stochastic-inferential' mathematical modeling" (Rosenberg, 1969, p. 311). Alternatively, a communication informing subjects that they were participants in "control groups" of a preliminary investigation for a subsequent research project reduced evaluation apprehension. An example of such a communication is:

Before we can investigate these different factors, however, we have to know how people perceive the feelings and experiences of others when these experimental factors are not present. That is, we need a control, or standardization, group to use as a base line against which we can judge the effects that our experimental factors have on social perception. This is the reason for your participation today. We intend to average the performance of all students participating today, so that we will have a measure of how subjects perform on the task when experimental variables such as fatigue and prior practice are not present. This information will allow us to judge the effects which our experimental variables have when they are used with a subsequent group of students. (Rosenberg, 1969, p. 327)

Various attributes of the experimenter, such as describing him as Dr. So-and-So, a clinical psychologist, or as a person with a "clinical psychological orientation," have been used by Rosenberg (1969) to produce or enhance evaluation apprehension effects. Similarly, Rosenberg (1969) found that endowing the experimenters with a gatekeeper function or with a capacity to withhold the opportunity for some subjects to participate in some future rewarding activity increased the tendency to strive for a favorable evaluation from the experimenters. Therefore, the experimenter's perceived power to control desirable rewards may influence subjects' responses toward securing positive evaluation from him. Attributes of the experimental task which assist the subject in guiding his performance in the direction of favorable evaluation are the degree of ambiguity of the stimuli to which subjects are responding and the degree to which continuous information regarding feedback is available regarding the subjects' task performance. Last, subjects will choose the least effortful response pattern to obtain favorable evaluation by the experimenter (Rosenberg, 1969, p. 300).

To summarize, evaluation apprehension and its effects can be reduced or minimized by assuring that subjects hold two major perceptions regarding the experiment and the experimenter: (1) the purpose of the experiment is more of mathematical or technical nature than an investigation of the subjects' personalities; and (2) the experimenter is *not* interested in individual responses but in normative or nomothetic aspects of responses from groups of individuals.

There appears to be some conceptual confusion between the demand characteristic and evaluation apprehension views. For example, in many situations, it is difficult to determine if subjects' hypothesis-confirming responses are directed toward contributing to scientific knowledge (demand characteristic view) or toward winning the experimenter's approval (evaluation apprehension view). Recently, a strategy unique to laboratory experimentation has been used to examine the relative potency of these two motive states and to determine when subjects' responses are made in the interest of confirming an experimental hypothesis or acquiring a positive evaluation from the experimenter. Sigall, Aronson, and Van Hoose (1970) found that when the two motives require conflicting responses for a numerical task, subjects exhibit tendencies to protect their own image and to "look good" rather than responding to the experimental hypothesis. Similar support for the prepotency of "looking good" has been found in the context of attitude change research. According to Silverman and his associates (Silverman & Shulman, 1970; Silverman, Shulman, & Wiesenthal, 1970), subjects' primary goal is to win the experimenter's approval. When evaluation apprehension is aroused, subjects will respond in the direction of favorable self-presentation—whether or not their responses are congruent or incongruent with the demand characteristics of the experiment.

The experimenter is himself a very prominent source of a variety of cues. A large body of research (discussed below) by Rosenthal and his associates (cf., Rosenthal, 1966; Friedman, 1967) illustrates that the experimenter's expectancies about the experimental outcomes are frequently communicated to subjects by a variety of subtle cues. Subjects who are apprehensive about evaluation by the experimenter are more likely to notice these cues and, correspondingly, respond in a manner to confirm the experimenter's expectancy. To the extent that subjects' responses are made to win the experimenter's approval by confirming his expectations, the dynamics of evaluation apprehension may be viewed as mediating the experimenter expectancy effect. Empirical support for the above notion appears in Rosenberg (1969, pp. 322–336) and Minor (1970).

The above processes of evaluation apprehension are discussed in relation to the supposed artificiality of laboratory findings because they are attributed only to laboratory settings. However, presenting one's self in a favorable manner is a common interpersonal strategy which is frequently observed in a number of *natural* (non-laboratory) settings (cf., Goffman, 1959; Jones, 1964). Similarly, the dynamics of evaluation apprehension are akin to the more general processes of approval motivation (Crowne & Marlowe, 1964) which are frequently manifested as socially desirable responses on psychological tests (cf., Edwards, 1957) in many different environments. For example, many personnel administrators have obtained responses to selection and placement tests which reflect job applicants' attempts to "fake it good" (cf., Guion, 1965).

Experimenter Expectancy

A third major source of potential artifacts derives from the experimenter *himself* and from his *relationships* with subjects. The former involves a variety of variables, such as errors in recording and interpreting data and the age, sex, race, and other personal attributes of the experimenter. The effect of these variables is well documented (cf., Masling, 1966; McGuigan, 1963; Rosenthal, 1966; Sattler, 1970). The latter are related to the experimenter's transactions with subjects and are commonly referred to as "experimenter expectancy" effects. Several literature surveys of more than 100 studies (cf., Barber & Silver, 1968; Friedman, 1967; Kintz, Delprato, Mettee, Persons, & Schappe, 1965; Rosenthal, 1964, 1966, 1967, 1969) review the basic proposition that the experimenter's expectations regarding the experimental outcomes (i.e., his "hypothesis") in some way direct subjects' responses toward confirmation of the experimenter's expectation. Although the findings are not unequivocal (cf., Barber & Silver, 1968), experimenter expectancies in these studies were found to affect a variety of phenomena, such as learning, psychophysical judgments, reaction time, psychological testing, interviewing, and person perception.

Of the variety of available techniques (cf., Rosenthal, 1966), expectancy control groups (e.g., Burnham, 1966) and double-blind procedures are relatively effective methods for assessing the effects of experimenter expectancy. Furthermore, one can minimize the amount of contact between the experimenter and subjects.

A major obstacle to the development of more effective control and elimination procedures is lack of understanding of the processes mediating the experimenter expectancy effect. Of central concern is the question of *how* experimenters transmit their expectancies (or desires) to affect subjects' responses. At first glance, it appears that the expectancy phenomenon can be accounted for by the experimenter's verbal or non-verbal reinforcement of only hypothesis-confirming responses.

While this reinforcement view remains a possibility, there are some data which indicate that the usefulness of operant conditioning with respect to hypothesis-confirming responses is limited (e.g., Adair & Epstein, 1957; Rosenthal, 1966, pp. 289–293), especially since the experimenter expectancy effects seem to occur via experimenter-subject communication during the very early stages of data collection. It appears more likely that para-linguistic and kinetic cues play an equal or more important role (cf., Barber & Silver, 1968; Rosenthal, 1969, pp. 250–254). In order to design procedures which control and/or eliminate the experimenter expectancy effects, the conditions under which the phenomena occur need to be identified. As mentioned earlier, recent research (Minor, 1970; Rosenberg, 1969, pp. 332–336) demonstrates that under some conditions the mere provision of expectancy cues may be a necessary but insufficient condition to produce the expectancy effect. For example, Minor (1970) found that only subjects in the high evaluation apprehension conditions responded to the expectancy effect. A more detailed analysis is required to identify the motives which impel subjects to be attentive and responsive to the subtle cues revealing the experimenter's expectations or desires.

Before condemning *all* laboratory data as artificial, it is wise to note Barber and Silver's (1968) comment that experimenter bias effect is more difficult to demonstrate and appears to be less pervasive than was implied in previous reviews (cf., Kintz, Delprato,

Mettee, Persons, & Schappe, 1965). And, at the very least, the phenomenon is not limited to laboratory research (cf., Dunnette & Heneman, 1956; Viteles, 1953). Amir (1969, p. 338) proposes that the field research supporting the contact hypothesis of race relations may be attributed, at least in part, to the operation of expectancy phenomena: "... respondents in some of the studies have been directly influenced by, and may have tended to comply with the expectations of, research teams or interviewers who generally intended to demonstrate positive attitude change. Similarly, studies in which prestigious persons such as teachers have led subjects through a series of experiences with Negroes suffer from the danger that the research subjects simply cooperated by providing their leader with the changes they knew he was looking for."

Moreover, some persons criticize laboratory findings as nonrepresentative of findings in other settings because subjects are aware of their participation in research and this supposedly arouses motives and behavior unlike the motives and behavior in nonlaboratory settings, for example, organizations. However, in order for these "awareness" phenomena to jeopardize the generalizing of laboratory findings to organizational behavior, it is necessary to assume that the motives and behavior related to awareness are unique only to laboratory settings. The validity of this assumption seems at the very least questionable. For example, the organization is also a social setting whose members are motivated to discover the expectancies of other members and where evaluation apprehension is aroused at least in relation to promotion and/or pay. Indeed, at least one prominent organizational theorist has noted that "... many of the dysfunctions reported between experimenter and subject are similar to the dysfunctions between management and employee" (Argyris, 1968, p. 185). Furthermore, Argyris (1968, p. 188) suggests that the adaptive strategies described above "... are predictable by organizational theory because the relationship between the researcher and the subject is similar to the one between the manager and the employee in formal organizations." Therefore, whether differences exist between the laboratory and the criterion setting and do jeopardize generalizations to the criterion setting are matters of judgment. A basis for making such judgments is found in contemporary theories of organizations and the developing theory of the social psychology of the experiment. A perspective for these judgments, that is, Boundary Variables, is presented toward the end of this chapter.

Perhaps applying the label "artificial" to the laboratory effects of experimenters' expectations upon subjects' behavior is inappropriate because, as Rosenthal (1969, p. 198) notes, the phenomena are of more general theoretical and practical importance. They occur naturally in many social relationships without subjects' awareness of participation in research or without the presence of other stimuli unique to laboratory settings. For example, Merton's (1948) related self-fulfilling prophecy has been found to operate in a variety of natural (nonlaboratory) settings, such as educational systems (Rosenthal & Jacobson, 1968), a summer camp for disadvantaged children (Burnham, 1968), and therapist-patient relationships in clinical settings (Persinger, Knutson, & Rosenthal, 1968), and so forth.

In summary, a substantial body of systematic research reveals that the above artifacts are not as prevalent in laboratory experiments as once claimed, and the same artifacts operate in field settings in association with the strategies proposed as alternatives to laboratory experimentation. Therefore, relegation of laboratory experimentation to a position of lower status relative to other research strategies because of the laboratory's association with these artifacts seems unjustified. Furthermore, the recent accumulation of data and emerging general theory of the social psychology of the experiment provide information about the conditions under which the artifacts operate and information about how the arti-

facts affect various dependent variables. Procedures to assess these effects and circumvent these events when desirable do exist. Thus, the term "artificial" seems an ill-chosen description of laboratory research.

Realism

Although the relationship between resemblance and relevance is the subject of considerable debate, it is often claimed that the experimental settings are more "realistic" when they resemble organizations. However, it is unlikely that any single experiment will resemble a large number of organizations because there is as much variation from one real-life situation to another real-life situation as occurs between the laboratory and real life. For example, male laughter to an off-color joke is more likely to occur in a locker room than at a tea party. Yet one cannot claim that the locker room behavior is more or less "real" than the tea party behavior simply because there are few similarities between the two situations. Similarly, it seems equally irrational to claim that laboratory behavior is less real than organizational behavior simply because there are different variables controlling behavior in the two situations.

The argument that realism requires multiple similarities between laboratory and organizational settings seems greatly exaggerated. While it is true that experiments vary in the degree of resemblance to organizations, a laboratory event is not endowed with greater realism and generality because it occurs in a setting containing several attributes which are similar to characteristics of organizations. It is more likely that only a small number of variables are required to depict organizational phenomena in general. Weick (1965a, pp. 210–226) suggests five attributes: (1) size of work group; (2) duration of interpersonal contacts; (3) ambiguity of performance feedback; (4) significance of performance outcomes; and (5) task interdependence. He suggests that these can be varied, without sacrificing experimental control, to increase the degree of correspondence between laboratory and organizational settings. Other persons, Porter and Lawler (1964), have concluded that organizations also vary in the nature of established formal hierarchical structures (e.g., allocation of decision-making responsibilities), including organizations with no clear "flat" or "tall" structure.

Yet, there is little reason to stipulate any normative list of attributes as important to *every* organizational setting. In many cases it is unnecessary to require arbitrarily the presence of more than one or two of the attributes simultaneously in any single experiment. Rather, the researcher or the administrator, upon examination and analysis of specific criterion organizations or relevant subunits within specific organizations, must determine which attributes are theoretically or practically important to the focal behavior. "Realism" then, like "generality" and "artificiality," may be reduced to a matter of judgment.

In sum, laboratory strategies may vary in the number and kind of organizational properties which can be represented in any single experiment. Furthermore, organizational properties and corresponding laboratory strategies can be selected on the basis of their relevance to a particular theoretical or practical problem of interest to the researcher. *Instead of reinforcing the myth that laboratory settings seldom yield data which are relevant to real-world problems, it is proposed that laboratory settings merely impose identifiable limitations upon the range of criterion situations to which a particular set of laboratory findings may be practically applied.* The potential consumer of laboratory-produced information can decide if the laboratory characteristics of any particular experiment are *critical* for his particular organization and the criterion behavior under consideration.

LABORATORY PROCEDURES

The ensuing examination of experimental strategies may help to eliminate the ill-founded mystique surrounding common laboratory procedures such as setting, subject recruitment, manipulation of independent variables, measurement of dependent variables, and so forth. The discussion also facilitates identification of critical properties of common procedures and thereby enhances the ability to evaluate critical similarities and differences between the (focal) research setting and the (criterion) organizational setting. While the basic procedures of laboratory methodology are presented in a number of sources (cf., Aronson & Carlsmith, 1968; Festinger, 1953; Wiggins, 1968), the literature contains little discussion of procedures for experimental simulations. In general, experimental simulations involve quite similar procedures for manipulation and measurement of independent and dependent variables. However, some differences do exist. Therefore, in addition to a discussion of experimental strategies which apply to laboratory methodology in general, this chapter will consider some strategies which seem particularly relevant for experimental simulations.

Preparing the Cover Story

Once the experimenter selects independent and dependent variables, he is faced with the problems of context. In general, the experimenter devises a credible setting by means of a "cover story." The procedures for the manipulation and measurement of variables are integrated into the cover story in such a way as to have impact on and make sense to the subjects. As discussed earlier, many of the artifacts cited as frequent criticisms of laboratory experimentation can be eliminated or reduced by means of a rationale or instructional set presented to subjects at the beginning of the experiment. In order to inhibit subjects from attempting to decipher the hypotheses, such guises must contain plausible and understandable descriptions of the purposes of the experiment. It is also important that the cover story remain credible throughout the entire experiment. Compulsive attention to details, such as subject recruitment procedures and linking the independent and dependent variable to the content of the cover story, will aid in preventing uncontrolled conjecture and will help allay suspicions. An interesting cover story, developed by Lowin and his associates, contains newspaper advertisements and job interviews to recruit subjects for part-time jobs, such as "office supervisor" for a group of Job Corpsmen who were engaged in secretarial work for a conference of high school English teachers (Lowin & Craig, 1968) or "technician" preparing sparkplugs for a (fictitious) Automotive Research Institute (Lowin, Hrapchak & Kavanagh, 1969). Since the jobs actually take place in a disguised laboratory setting, the experimenters can exercise control over variables and can obtain precise measurement of behavior as it relates to the independent variables. Furthermore, the cover story must stimulate subjects' attention and responsiveness to the manipulations and measures.

Recruiting the Participants

The populations from which subjects are drawn is often unrepresentative of intended criterion populations. Research conducted in university laboratories tends to use college sophomores. They are easy to contact, generally inexpensive, and—because they are participating to get experimental credit for their psychology course—are relatively reliable about showing up. Certainly there are other sources of subjects which could be drawn upon to examine organizational behavior. For example, political decision making in the United States may be examined by using mid-career people from the state department. Military decision making may be studied with career officers, or executives may be asked to participate when high level decision making of a corporation is the focus of research. Using criterion populations decreases the probability of errors due to experience and personality variables which are absent in the college sophomore but are inherent in criterion populations.

Unfortunately, however, it is not always

possible to persuade the department of state to release a number of their employees for research purposes. Similarly, it may not be possible to persuade local industrial organizations to part with large numbers of their executive staff for research. Consequently, some other measures may have to be used. Two methods have been used with some success. The first method attempts to match the criterion population to the persons participating in the simulation via personality tests. The successful work of the Hermanns (1963, 1969), in which the outbreak of the first World War was recreated in the laboratory, used such personality matching. Of course, this procedure does not compensate for differences in experience. However, much research seems to indicate that the degree of experience seems to have little import, at least for decision-making characteristics.

Palola (1967), for example, recruits participants giving them the impression that they were actually hired to perform an important function in the real world and that the laboratory conditions are merely secondary to the task itself. If it is necessary to recruit college sophomores, then the distinction between the task in which they are to participate and other research should be made clear to them, for example, a statement like "You are free to make any decision you want to make, because we are doing this research to provide the agency or company with new ideas about how problems of the kind you will encounter can be solved." This procedure will make the participants feel sufficiently important to forget, at least in part, that they are in an experiment.

Training the Participants

The training of subjects for standard laboratory experiments usually involves little more than a cover story. In addition, the instructions for the subjects are much less complicated than encountered in most simulations. Unless the participants are drawn from the criterion population or are acquainted with the characteristics of the simulated environment, they must be trained (or indoctrinated) in the setting. To some degree this training substitutes for some of the experience of criterion personnel. The experimenter selects the information and belief systems which are typical of the criterion personnel and communicates these to the simulation participants via a manual (described below). Streufert and associates have found in a series of experimental simulations (e.g., Streufert & Streufert, 1969) that college sophomores can be sufficiently indoctrinated to accept a particular point of view and to believe in the "truth" of events that occurred in the simulated setting prior to their participation. They may learn about these events in a manual which they read for some period of time (e.g., two hours) and/or via televised information programs. However, even if participants are drawn from criterion populations, it may be wise to involve them in non-simulation activities for a period of two hours or longer. Such a procedure ensures at least some similarity of pre-experimental exposure, so that differences in mood, or immediate past experience will have little or no serious effect on experimentally measured behavior.

The Simulation Manual

An experimental simulation is programmed so that experimenters merely follow a fixed set of instructions to transmit and receive information (e.g., send typed programmed messages about current events to the groups of subjects and receive written decisions on decision forms from the subjects). While an experimenter's manual is not used in experimental simulations, participants' manuals are used in most simulation techniques. The manuals should be detailed, carefully planned, and should contain a complete statement of the history of the organization with documentation in the form of letters on original stationery, pictures where applicable, and so forth. All the organization's funds, equipment and staff that are available to the subjects (see the

section on Independent Variables) should be clearly delineated. The procedures by which they can be used should be explained in sufficient detail. Subjects should be informed in the manual about any special characteristics of the setting. For instance, if simulated time is to be condensed or expanded in relation to real time, subjects should be so informed in the manual.[15] However, the most important characteristic of the manual should be its *realism*. Just as a simulation does not work well in make-shift rooms, it does not begin well if the manual contains faded ditto pages that supposedly represent letters written by the president of one organization to the president of another organization. A ream of paper printed with the mast head of the organization and personally signed letters are more believable, and consequently more involving. When the manual is realistic, the simulation is more likely to "take." It is, in part, the realism of the setting that distinguishes simulations from simple role-playing techniques.

Preparing the Setting

The environment within which the experiment occurs may resemble the criterion environment in varying degrees. If the criterion environment is very simple, one would find it easy to duplicate it precisely. If, however, the criterion environment is highly complex or varied over time, then some of its important characteristics may be abstracted. To maintain control over the subjects, one may limit their activities. They may be restricted to the laboratory (where they are easily observed and where their behavior can be measured); and they may be required to interact with other groups of subjects in only a pre-planned fashion. Further, one may limit the information flow to

---

[15] If changes in time are made, for example, if time moves faster in the simulation than in the real world, subjects should not be allowed to keep their watches. For that matter, if anything is different in the simulation than it is in the real world, cues that relate to that difference should be carefully removed.

the subjects. They may be prohibited from seeking information from outside sources. Although these procedures are possible for both standard laboratory experiments and simulations, additional precautions must be taken in experimental simulations.

Generally, subjects who participate in an experimental simulation are engaged in their assigned activity for long periods of time, for example, several hours, or even days. Consequently, any procedure that would produce excessive fatigue or boredom (unless that is part of the independent variable) should be avoided. The research rooms should be relatively comfortable. The air conditioning system should be adequate for persons in each room. Sufficient food should be provided to avoid unwanted interference from subjects' physiological needs. Even the aesthetics of the room in which subjects work tends to make a difference. Pleasantly colored rooms without bare walls tend to produce more involved behavior than sterile rooms.

Involvement is a key issue. To produce high levels of involvement the room should be well equipped, and preferably some use should be found for the equipment which is placed in the room. Telephones, charts, relief displays, television receivers and other similar items may be used with considerable success. Subjects should be provided with anything which they might use in the criterion activity. For instance, if high level decision making in an organization is simulated, there should be enough paper, and ideally there should be a supporting staff to keep records and to communicate with supposed other groups, and so forth.

Independent Variables

As observed earlier, one of the major distinguishing features of laboratory experimentation is the controlled manipulation of variables. The researcher's conceptualization of one or more theoretically or practically important variables generally determines the choice of the independent variable(s).

This is the process of translating the conceptual variable(s) into the experimental procedure(s) or, as it is often called, operationalizing the variables. Once operationalized, variables are defined by the experimental procedures. There are no standardized operational procedures for manipulating variables related to organizational behavior. It is an imaginative process which requires ingenuity to match each operationalization with the specific meaning of its conceptualization. A great variety of techniques have been adopted to manipulate independent variables in laboratory experiments. These techniques include simple variations in descriptions of stimulus persons or stimulus situations (e.g., Weick & Nesset, 1968), false reports of interpersonal characteristics (e.g., Fromkin, Klimoski, & Flanagan, 1972) or performance outcomes (e.g., Evan & Simmons, 1969; Goodstadt & Kipnis, 1970), behavioral restrictions such as those encountered in various communication channels (e.g., Carzo & Yanouzas, 1970; Evan & Zelditch, 1961), tape recordings of alleged group interactions (e.g., Aronson & Mills, 1959; Blake & Brehm, 1954), and elaborate scenarios of events such as mock elections which may (Raven & French, 1958) or may not (Julian, Hollander, & Regula, 1969) include confederates.

While independent between-group variables are treated identically for the standard and the simulation laboratory experiment, there are some special procedures for *within-group* treatments which apply more often to experimental simulation techniques and to techniques involving subjects who are apparently hired for a job lasting several hours or several weeks. Such extended time experiments are like simulations in many ways. However, they typically do not use manuals, frequently produce lower levels of participant involvement, and often match the criterion setting more closely than simulations do.

One of the advantages of simulation techniques is their capacity to credibly measure behavior over extended periods of time, providing simultaneously *more* data and data which may be analyzed with statistical within-group analyses. These data are less subject to the increased error produced by differences *between* individuals or between groups. Theoretically, there is no reason why any variable cannot be used as a within-group treatment. For instance, one can measure how different quantities of incoming information (Streufert & Schroder, 1965), different degrees of failure (Streufert & Castore, 1971), different levels of success (Streufert, 1971), or even different forms of leadership style (Streufert, Streufert, & Castore, 1968) and interpersonal climate will affect group decision making, attitudes, efficiency, and so forth. Practically, however, the problems that Weick (1965a) described in simulations must be avoided. In other words, the experiment must remain believable to the participants. Subjects who are informed that they are to some degree influencing their own fate by their behavior should not be presented with information which does not match their behavior. For instance, they should not receive large amounts of information that is irrelevant to their previous actions (cf., Streufert, 1970) and they should not receive information suggesting that they have engaged in behavior (e.g., made decisions) in which they have not engaged. In other words, the experimental sequences or simulation program *must* be designed to appear meaningfully related to the subjects' behavior (cf., Streufert & Streufert, 1969).

Two means can be used to make within-treatment variables highly believable to participants: (1) precise content programming of information and (2) programming of information characteristics. The first requires a highly restricted environment where participants are permitted to engage only in very few and very predictable activities. Precise content programming may not be applicable to all forms of organizational decision making. As long as the criterion setting is well circumscribed with many limitations upon the actions of those working in that setting, content programming might be very useful. If, however, the behavior in the criterion setting is more free of constraints, then the second form of programming may be more applicable.

The second way to keep information flow "real" is to program the characteristic of the information that will be fed to the participants, but not to program the precise content.[16] For instance, when the researcher is interested in the effect of failure on decision makers in a particular organization (cf., Streufert & Castore, 1971), he can determine in advance what percentage of their decisions will result in failure. For all but the failure messages, decision makers might be informed that a particular action of theirs (determined by their past decisions either at random or by design) did achieve the desired end. For the proportion of messages that are to communicate failure, participants might be told that the action did not result in the desired endstate. For instance, when simulating the sales department of a corporation, one could determine in advance what proportion of their product lines, or what proportion of bids, produce or do not produce increased sales. These within treatments over time permit measurement of active behavior and also of perceptions of cost, profit, and of certainty related to future costs and profit, etc. (cf., Streufert & Streufert, 1970).

Simulations and extended time experiments permit division into time periods and each period may be used as a different (within treatment) condition. For instance, when the researcher wishes to analyze the effects of success and failure on the behavior of a sales department, he may expose participants to 20, 40, 60, or 80 percent success in random order. Enough groups should be used (within the treatment condition) to assure that randomization is meaningful. Alternatively,

---

[16] Both types of programming, but particularly this one, should be examined for realism. Pilot research on the perceptions of the programmed variable should be done and manipulation checks and realism checks should be maintained throughout the research program.

if only few groups can be obtained for the research, counterbalancing the order of conditions over time might be a more appropriate procedure.

For extended time experiments or simulations that are sufficiently complex, that is, where the subjects need to learn the skill that is required of the criterion persons, it may be wise to run one or more warm-up periods before beginning to collect data. Using intermediate levels of the variation that is employed as the within independent variable is usually best for warm-up conditions. This has two advantages: it permits the subjects to adapt in advance to the characteristics that can be expected and it permits the experimenter to analyze differences between the warm-up condition(s).

Manipulation Checks

How one translates a conceptual problem into the independent variable of a good research design has been discussed frequently (cf., reviews by Aronson & Carlsmith, 1968; Wiggins, 1968; Festinger, 1953). This discussion need not be repeated here. Some warnings about potential difficulties that can grow out of translation of an organization's problems into research variables may, however, be in order. For example, despite encouraging findings in pilot or pretest research, or for that matter previous operationalizations, it is unwise to assume a priori that operationalizations of conceptual variables will produce the intended differences among treatment groups or that the operationalizations will be free of multiple meanings. Therefore, precautionary measures, such as manipulation checks, are required to assess the effectiveness of the experimental manipulations.

A variety of manipulation checks may be used to assess a number of different aspects of the conceptual variables. For example, Fromkin, Olson, Dipboye, and Barnaby (1971) examined the question of when increments in valuation of a commodity are determined by the perceived scarcity of that commodity. The commodity, nylon hosiery manufactured in France, was presented to subjects under the guise of a marketing research project. Scarcity (the conceptual variable) was operationalized by informing some subjects that only 1,000 pairs (scarce) or over 100,000 pairs (plentiful) were to be distributed in the United States. Two manipulation check items requested subjects to indicate the number of pairs of nylons available and their perceptions regarding the scarcity of the nylons under all conditions. The results show that subjects correctly remembered the *number of pairs* of nylons alleged to be available under both scarce and plentiful conditions; and although the manipulation produced statistically significant differences in the intended direction, subjects unexpectedly perceived the nylons to be very scarce under *both* scarce and plentiful conditions. Tests of the hypothesis revealed that experimental subjects were willing to pay considerably more for both types of nylons in the experiment than they normally pay for nylons on the market, but the hypothesis that subjects were willing to pay *more* money for scarce than for plentiful nylons received only weak support ($p <$ .059). The data from the manipulation check on perceived scarcity provides an explanation for the high valuation of nylons under both scarce and plentiful conditions and potentially explains the corresponding weak spread in valuation of the nylons between scarce and plentiful conditions. Namely, all subjects perceived the nylons as scarce and consequently valued them highly. The above interpretation was facilitated by the inclusion of two distinct kinds of manipulation checks. The first manipulation check (e.g., number of nylons) examined the degree to which subjects remembered the actual instructions. The second manipulation check (e.g., perceived scarcity) examined the degree to which subjects perceived the instructions as intended.

The above discussion shows the utility of extending the manipulation check beyond the specific experimental operations. A secondary advantage of these precautionary procedures is that if significant or large differences between experimental conditions and the manipulation did not take, for the present at least, the experimenter need not look further for explanations of the findings. Moreover, an internal analysis may be performed by dividing subjects into several conditions (e.g., high or low) depending upon their responses to the manipulation checks (cf., Schachter, 1959). For example, only data from those subjects for whom the manipulation took could be analyzed. However, since these supplementary analyses are independent of the random assignment of subjects to experimental conditions, the findings are more suited to the generation of hypotheses for future research rather than for causal statements.

As mentioned earlier, unintended confounds or extraneous stimuli of which the experimenter is unaware, can occur more frequently in simulation settings than in standard laboratory settings. Consequently, it is equally important for the simulation experimenter to establish: (1) whether the experimental manipulation is perceived as intended; (2) what factors subjects perceive as influencing their behavior; and (3) whether subject behavior is modified over time regardless of the manipulation of the independent variable. The design is inadequate if: (1) the experimental manipulation does not work; (2) if subjects indicate that more than 20 percent of their behavior was influenced by the combined effect of randomness, characteristics of the environment, and experimenter factors (see discussion of attribution of causality by Streufert & Streufert, 1969); or (3) if the behavior of control groups varies over time.

A particularly knotty problem is the temporal placement of manipulation checks within the experiment. For example, Lawler (1968a) hired subjects to conduct field interviews for three two-hour sessions with one or two days intervening between each session. The experimental manipulations, that is, "unqualified overpaid" versus "overpaid

due to circumstance" versus "equitably paid," were done at the end of the recruiting interview and prior to the subject's first field interview session. The dependent variable was the quality (number of words recorded by the interviewer—the subject) and quantity of interviews conducted by each subject during the three sessions. The manipulation checks, obtained at the end of the last interviewing session, show that the "unqualified overpaid" subjects did not perceive themselves as more overpaid than "equitably paid" subjects. Since the manipulation checks were not taken immediately after induction of the independent variables, it is difficult to determine whether (1) the manipulations were initially ineffective; or whether (2) the impact of the manipulations was not strong enough to be durable throughout the course of experiment; or whether (3) as Lawler (1968a, pp. 311–312) suggests, unqualified, overpaid subjects reduced their feelings of inequity by increased performance during the first session. Despite the problems which may arise when measures of manipulation effectiveness occur after the measurement of the dependent variables, the strongest causal inferences can be drawn when the manipulation checks are obtained after the measurement of the dependent variables. If the manipulation checks are taken immediately prior to the dependent measures, they may accelerate the process and impact of the manipulations or may provoke awareness or suspicions about the hypotheses and purposes of the experiment. However, the effectiveness of the manipulations may be assessed with pretest control groups or with other independent measures of behavior which are theoretically expected to co-vary with the independent variable.

Construct Validity

The advantage of laboratory data is related to the degree that the experimental manipulation of variables reflect the intended conceptual variables in the absence of alternative explanations. The transition from conceptualizing the variable to operationalizing the variable is difficult because the process involves imperfect translations. Any given set of procedures may contain a number of impurities or extraneous stimuli. The uncontrolled presentation of multiple stimuli within a single translation of the conceptual variable into the operational variable permits a number of interpretations which may compete with the intended interpretation. Either identification and control of extraneous stimuli or elimination of all but the critical stimulus is essential to experimentation because such *unintended* multiple meanings (Aronson & Carlsmith, 1968, p. 13) increase the ambiguity with which one can attribute differences in subjects' behavior to the intended conceptual variable(s). One of the simplest methods for examining the potential potency of alternative explanation is to include some measures which reflect subjects' perceptions of variables, phenomena or intervening processes related to the alternative explanations. The significance of such procedures may be demonstrated by a brief examination of some current controversies which arise in research on equity theory. In order to induce feelings of inequity (Adams, 1965) due to overpayment, several investigators (e.g., Arrowood, 1961; Adams, 1963; Friedman & Goodman, 1967; Lawler, Koplin, Young, & Fadem, 1968; Goodman & Friedman, 1968) informed subjects that they were unqualified to perform the task at the rate they were to be paid, that is, they were overpaid. However, the increments in performance observed under these conditions may also be attributed to subjects' attempts to enhance their self-esteem which may have been abused by the "unqualified" manipulation (cf., Pritchard, 1969). In an attempt to reconcile these alternative explanations, Lawler (1968a) again used "unqualified overpayment" as a condition but also included a condition of "overpayment due to policy" which supposedly did not challenge the subjects' self-esteem. Lawler (1968a, p. 313) did collect supplementary data which

shows that the "unqualified overpaid" groups felt it was "more important to prove that they could do the job" than either the "equitably" or "overpaid by circumstance" groups. There was no difference between the latter two groups. Since the index used to measure subjects' desire to prove their competence was an indirect measure obtained at the end of the experiment, it is difficult to determine if the index reflects the important components of self-esteem or if the subjects' feelings were a product of both the experimental inductions and their task performance. Unfortunately, none of the above studies included a direct measure of self-esteem (e.g., Janis & Field, 1956; Helmreich, Aronson, & LeSan, 1970) and consequently, the self-esteem explanation still remains a plausible alternative explanation of the data.

Furthermore, although Lawler (1968a) found that the "overpaid by circumstance" group felt more overpaid than control subjects, equity theory (Adams, 1968, pp. 315–316) requires that subjects perceive themselves to be unjustly or inequitably paid. Since there were no measures of subjects' perceptions of these dimensions, Lawler's conclusion that expectancy theory (e.g., Vroom, 1964) more adequately explains the findings seems premature.

There are a number of procedures which reduce the tenability of alternative interpretations of operational variables. The process of purification (Aronson & Carlsmith, 1968, p. 15) involves the use of a number of *different* operations of a single conceptual variable which share only the basic properties of that variable. For example, Aronson and Mills (1959) varied the severity of initiation required to gain entrance to a group by requesting subjects to read aloud an embarrassment test which consisted of either twelve obscene words and two descriptive passages of sexual activity (severe initiation condition) or non-obscene words related to sex (mild initiation condition). As predicted, the greater expenditure of unpleasant effort under severe initiation conditions produced greater valuation of a dull tape-recorded group discussion of sex. Several alternative interpretations are offered for these findings (cf., Chapanis & Chapanis, 1964). For example, instead of unpleasant effort, the greater valuation under severe initiation conditions may be attributed to greater sexual arousal evoked by reading obscene words. Greater confidence in the Aronson and Mills (1959) conceptualization and interpretation may be gained if their findings were replicated with a different method of arousing different degrees of unpleasant effort, that is, a different operationalization of their conceptual variable. One step toward eliminating other interpretations or purification was taken when an experiment by Gerard and Mathewson (1966) replicated the Aronson and Mills findings with an emotionality test which consisted of electric shock as the initiation contingency for entrance into a dull group discussion of cheating. The most complete "purification" occurs with a large number of different manipulations of unpleasant effort which differ on a multitude of dimensions. Successful replications eliminate overlap between procedures, thus alternative explanations can be eliminated. Purification may be accomplished with a number of independent and systematic replications (e.g., Aronson & Mills, 1959; Gerard & Mathewson, 1966) or, more efficiently, by involving different operationalizations of the same independent variable within a single experiment (cf., Fromkin, 1968b). Brunswick (1956), Campbell (1957), Campbell and Stanley (1963), and Miller (1957, 1959) extend the idea of using several different dependent variables which are theoretically linked to the independent variable parallels the strategies of construct validation recommended.

Dependent Variables

Since there are several discussions of how to develop dependent variables in the literature, the following discussion is limited to some general statements. More detailed treatment of specific issues is found above under

Artifacts and below under Boundary Variables.

As mentioned earlier, a potential catalyst of behavior in laboratories is the subject's awareness of being in research. Awareness phenomena are not unique to laboratory settings or experimental methods, and can be eliminated from laboratory settings (e.g., Latané & Darley, 1968; Lowin & Craig, 1968). In general, being aware that one is being studied can change behavior in the research setting such that the laboratory behavior is not comparable to behavior as it occurs in natural settings. The intrusion of the measuring instrument may heighten this effect. Consider, for example, a measurement obtained by a movie camera. Managers' responses to union member demands might differ when the camera bore the sign, "Property of United Auto Workers" than when the camera bore the sign, "Property of American Management Association." The measurement procedures and measuring instruments can, under some conditions, introduce unintended additional stimuli into the research setting (laboratory or natural) that elicit confounding responses. The nature of these responses can interact with particular characteristics of the setting and subjects and thereby reduce the generality of the conclusions. This latter problem is discussed below under "Boundary Variables."

The subjects' knowledge of their research participation carries with it, among other cognitions, the idea that their behavior is being *observed*. This can lead to response biases such as the "guinea pig effect" (e.g., Selltiz, Jahoda, Deutsch, & Cook, 1965) or the "reactive effect" (e.g., Campbell, 1957; Campbell & Stanley, 1963; Webb, Campbell, Schwartz, & Sechrest, 1966) that tends to decrease candor. Similarly, subjects may experience a fear of being evaluated or evaluation apprehension (Rosenberg, 1965, 1969) and try to put their best foot forward (Reicken, 1962) by making the most socially desirable response (Crowne & Marlowe, 1964; Edwards, 1957). Most of these problems can be eliminated through the use of unobtrusive measures (Webb, Campbell,

Schwartz, & Sechrest, 1966). (See Evan & Simmons, 1969, for an excellent example of an organization experiment which had multiple measures of the dependent variable.)

Data are collected in both standard and simulation laboratory experiments by counting behaviors (e.g., decisions), by asking subjects to respond on scales, and so forth. Additional information can be obtained by plotting a behavior-flow matrix. Such a matrix is useful in studying the flow of information within an organization, that is, how information is received, processed, and transmitted. For example, Streufert and associates (Streufert, Clardy, Driver, Karlins, Schroder, & Suedfeld, 1965; Streufert, 1970) have repeatedly used a behavior-flow matrix to study complex decision making. A decision plot is made when time is plotted horizontally and decision types are plotted vertically. Every behavior, that is, every decision, becomes a point. Lines can be drawn between points—vertical lines indicating simultaneous occurrence, horizontal lines indicating how long a particular decision type was used, and diagonal lines indicating interrelationships among different kinds of decisions. Moreover, scores such as the number of points (behaviors) within or across categories and the number of diagonals, their points of origin, their length, and their interconnections with other diagonals can be calculated from such a behavior-flow matrix.

If rating scales or similar paper and pencil response measures are desired, the scales can be included on the forms that the participants use to communicate with supposed other groups (e.g., message forms) or forms that they use to record their own behavior as it occurs. The number of scales should be very small since such intrusions might destroy the realism of the situation.

Extended time experiments and simulation afford unique opportunities for collecting data during intermissions. Scales can be included in "interim report" forms. Again, however, there is a limit to the amount of information that should be collected. As a rule, subjects are more conscientious when the length of the time required to complete the form does not exceed five to ten minutes (during each intermission) and does not exceed 25 percent of the length of each work period. This is particularly important when the same scales are administered repeatedly, for example, after each work period. Once the subjects get "turned off" (even if they recover their enthusiasm during the next work period), the data collected during an intermission tend to show more random error. Moreover, subjects should not know in advance when the experimental task is to end because such awareness may influence subjects' responses.

BOUNDARY VARIABLES

Definitions

The presence (or absence) of a factor may be *essential* to the unaltered occurrence of a stimulus response relationship. If that factor occurs in (or is absent from) *only* the research setting or *only* the criterion setting, the difference is referred to as a "critical difference." Critical differences are called "boundary variables," and boundary variables limit the generality of research findings. In order to estimate the extent that results obtained in focal settings[17] will generalize to criterion settings, essential differences between the two settings must be identified. Unfortunately, assuming that the greater the similarity between the two environments, the greater the likelihood that a stimulus-response relationship will be the same in both environments is unwarranted.

---

[17] In the most general sense, the *focal* setting refers to *any* data collection (e.g., laboratory or field) environment and the *criterion* setting refers to *any* environment which is the target of generalization. Criterion settings include laboratory or field research sites as well as non-research settings, such as organizations and so forth. The most general perspective, then, facilitates judgments of generality between different laboratory settings, between laboratory and field research settings, between laboratory and non-research settings (e.g., organizations), between field research and non-research settings (e.g., organizations), between non-research settings (e.g., an organization), and non-research settings (e.g., another organization), and so forth.

Rather, attention should be restricted to just those *differences* that make a difference. Judgments regarding critical differences can be made on the basis of other relevant research findings or, more usually, on the basis of the experience and acumen of the person engaged in the task of comparing or applying research findings. Clearly, trivial differences are dismissed from the analysis.

Research settings are seen as neither artificial nor unreal. Instead, differences between any two environments (e.g., laboratory versus organization) are regarded as identifiable variables. Judgments concerning the applicability of focal setting data for a criterion setting involve a two-step process. The first step is to identify all the boundary variables which are a source of critical differences between the focal and criterion environments.

The second step is prediction of the potency and/or direction of the effects of boundary variables upon stimulus events in focal settings. In many situations, the latter step requires guesses about some (untested or unproven) general laws of behavior. Fortunately, the number of occasions for guesses is continuously being reduced by a useable body of expanding literature describing the operation of artifacts in research settings (cf., Rosenthal & Rosnow, 1969) and the operation of organizational variables (cf., reviews by March, 1965; Weick, 1965a, 1967). It should be remembered that generalization is not, and can never be, a mechanical activity in which conclusions can be drawn with absolute certainty. Rather the consumer of the research data uses his judgment, tempered by experience, to estimate the comparability between existing research and the features of the criterion setting of interest to him.

SOME POTENTIAL BOUNDARY VARIABLES IN EXPERIMENTAL ORGANIZATIONS

In this section we present illustrative examples of common differences between focal research and criterion settings which may become critical for some relationships and thereby attain potential status of boundary variables.[18] The variables discussed here are not necessarily the most influential for any particular criterion setting. In keeping with the present chapter's focus on applying laboratory data to organizational problems, the following discussion of boundary variables uses the laboratory experiment as the focal setting and the organizational environment as the criterion setting. The discussion is organized around two questions: (1) In what ways do variables differ when they occur in the laboratory as compared with their occurrence in an organizational setting? (2) How do subjects' responses to variables in the laboratory differ from the kinds of responses in an organizational setting?

Independent Variables

The following section focuses on elements of the laboratory that disrupt, compete with, or enhance the effect of the independent variables. It is frequently argued that organizational stimuli are not the same when they are in the laboratory. "The very act of bringing a variable into the laboratory usually changes its nature ... you lose some of the original elements and add some others that were not in the original" (Chapanis, 1967, p. 566). For example, the researcher frequently purifies the situation by eliminating the presence of some variables in order to maximize opportunities for the independent variable(s) to be effective. These procedures may produce significant effects in a purified setting, but the effects may become seriously attenuated when the variable occurs in competition with other variables (or impurities) that may exist in the criterion environments. What may be an impurity in the laboratory may be a crucial variable in the criterion setting, hence a boundary variable.

---

[18] A similar application of the boundary variable perspective to problems of race relations in organizations may be found in Fromkin and Ostrom (1974).

Interpersonal Contact

The characteristics or behavior of stimulus persons is often an independent variable in experiments, especially in leadership studies. Interpersonal stimuli may be boundary variables in a number of ways. For example, leaders may attain their status in organizations by appointment from higher authorities, by formal vote of their followers, by the nature of their group participation, or other less formal processes. Theory and research on leadership (e.g., Fiedler, 1967; French, 1956; French & Raven, 1959; Hollander & Julian, 1970) demonstrate dramatically how the manner in which the attainment of the leadership position is crucial to the nature and magnitude of the leader's power to influence his subordinates' behavior. For instance, elected leaders are perceived as more justified in prescribing subordinate behavior, more attractive, and engender more private acceptance of influence (Raven & French, 1958; Julian, Hollander, & Regula, 1969). Since the modes of attaining leadership positions can vary among laboratory settings and among organizational settings, the evidence showing that different modes of leadership attainment can have different effects on subordinate behavior qualifies leadership attainment as a potential boundary variable in some studies. Before applying a particular laboratory finding, the user must first compare the mode of leadership attainment in both settings. If the mode of leadership attainment differs, a boundary variable may exist and generalization may be unwarranted.

The mode and nature of communication between stimulus persons and subjects varies widely among different laboratory studies; they may also differ from the nature of interpersonal communication in organizations, the criterion setting. At one extreme, stimulus persons (e.g., leaders) communicate with subjects via notes (e.g., Cohen, Robinson, & Edwards, 1969; Goodstadt & Kipnis, 1970) or telephone (e.g., Evan & Zelditch, 1961). At the other extreme, stimulus persons communicate with subjects during face-to-face interactions (e.g., Day & Hamblin, 1964; Graen, Orris, & Alvares, 1971; Lowin, Hrapchak, & Kavanagh, 1969; Simmons, 1968). Written communications differ from personal contact on a large number of dimensions. For instance, face-to-face interactions yield a greater amount of information about the physical and psychological attributes of the stimulus persons, as well as conveying a greater number of interpersonal verbal and nonverbal cues (e.g., facial expression or body movements, phonetic variation, etc.). Other research (e.g., Byrne & McGraw, 1964; Triandis, Loh, & Levin, 1966) reveals that the style of the stimulus person's interaction may profoundly alter the intensity and/or direction of subjects' responses. At the same time, it is true that the form of communication within and among organizations varies from personal and telephone contact to written memos (cf., Guetzkow, 1961; Jacoby, 1968; Melcher & Beller, 1967). Since there is no single mode of interaction which characterizes interpersonal interactions in all organizational life, the consumer of laboratory data must examine the criterion setting and judge if the style and form of interpersonal contact are similar to or different from the specific criterion setting (e.g., organizational context) of interest to him.

Characteristics of Stimulus Persons

Age, sex, personality, and/or physical characteristics of stimulus persons may be boundary variables. Some of the personal characteristics which are prominent in laboratory stimulus persons but not in persons in the criterion setting may interact with the independent variable and produce differential responding in subjects. This is a problem in laboratory research too if stimulus persons differ. Experimenters frequently introduce the same person (often a confederate to the experimenter) to each of the treatment groups in order to make the results comparable across treatments (e.g., Day & Hamblin, 1964; Lowin, Hrapchak,

& Kavanagh, 1969). However, when this procedure is adopted, laboratory responses to that stimulus person (the confederate) may still be affected by one or more of *his* idiosyncratic characteristics. For example, the inadvertent choice of a stimulus person who is unexpectedly perceived as highly intelligent or competent can introduce a constant which may be absent from or vary in the criterion setting. In this situation, the difference becomes critical because competence and intelligence are powerful determinants of the magnitude of the leader's influence (cf., Anderson & Fiedler, 1964; Croner & Willis, 1961; Dittes & Kelley, 1956; Hollander & Julian, 1970). Each unique characteristic of the stimulus person which alters the subjects' responses to the independent variable(s) qualifies as a potential boundary variable.

An alternative strategy is to randomly assign different stimulus persons to different treatment groups (e.g., Evan & Zelditch, 1961; Fromkin, Klimoski, & Flanagan, 1972; Goodstadt & Kipnis, 1970; Graen, Orris, & Alvares, 1971; Simmons, 1968). Results obtained with a number of different stimulus persons are more likely to generalize to the criterion setting. Use of the random strategy increases the likelihood of random error in the data, but, at the same time, leads to greater confidence that any unique characteristics of stimulus persons are unimportant as stimulus variables.

Dependent Variables

The measurement of the dependent variable or the manner in which subjects' responses are observed are potential boundary variables. For example, knowledge of being in an experiment can influence behavior in at least two ways: (1) distortion of private responses in favor of public socially approved responses to obtain positive evaluation; and (2) alteration of responses due to a lack of commitment to and/or accountability for any future consequences of behavior. Although awareness phenomena

need not always be salient in laboratory experiments (cf., Evan & Simmons, 1969; Lawler, 1968a; Lowin & Craig, 1968), the measurement procedures may, under some conditions, introduce unwanted stimuli and influence responses in the laboratory.

Awareness of Research

The dependent variable in many laboratory examinations of organizational phenomena has been a self-report measure which requests subjects to rate the competency or desirability of co-workers and so forth. Self-report measures are especially likely to increase the subject's awareness that he is being studied (cf., Cook & Selltiz, 1964, p. 39). First, the underlying purposes of the measures are quite clear, that is, to measure subjects' beliefs, feelings, or orientation toward a stimulus object. Second, the positive and negative implications of each of the response alternatives are in some cases readily apparent to subjects; that is, the respondent can present either a favorable or unfavorable impression of himself by responding at the appropriate end of the scale. Third, the respondent is able to consciously control his responses. However, always identifying self-report measures as a source of critical differences and hence a boundary variable is unwarranted. Awareness-related stimuli can only be considered a boundary variable when they are *not* common to both laboratory and organization. Since the tendency to publicly endorse statements discrepant from one's private beliefs in the service of positive self-presentation is a frequently observed interpersonal strategy in organizations, it is not always desirable to eliminate such determinants of attitudinal responses. Accordingly, awareness-related stimuli cannot always be defined as a boundary variable. Moreover, a number of experimenters have devised creative techniques to disguise the purpose and implications of self-rating scales (e.g., Cook & Selltiz, 1964, pp. 41–43; Webb, Campbell, Schwartz, & Sechrest, 1966).

Dimensionality of Dependent Measures

Since performance is also a frequent dependent variable in laboratory studies of organizational behavior, the nature of the performance measure is an important consideration. For example, laboratory studies of equity theory (cf., reviews by Lawler, 1968b; Pritchard, 1969; Weick, 1965b) show that task performance emphasizes different facets of behavior depending upon the nature of the independent variables being studied. For example, when pay is based on piece rates, performance differences are apt to be reflected more in quality of output; when pay is on a straight hourly basis, performance differences are apt to be reflected more in quantity of output. Thus, the type of measure used for evaluating the dependent variable and its dimensionality must be given careful attention in the context of what may already be known about the parameters to be studied.

Consequences of Behavior

Another way that awareness phenomena may produce a boundary variable is by eliciting laboratory responses characterized by (1) a shortened time perspective, (2) fewer expectations of present accountability for the consequences of behavior, and (3) fewer expectations of future accountability for the consequences of behavior. For example, subjects in laboratory experiments rarely expect their responses to have implications beyond the time they are experimental participants. That is, any positive or negative consequences of behavior are not likely to be very long lasting or extend beyond the time that subjects are in the laboratory. On the other hand, there is some evidence which suggests that laboratory behavior does manifest at least some of the crucial properties of a future orientation.

In several equity theory studies, subjects were hired for part-time jobs which were expected to last only for a short time. In spite of the short-time perspective associated with these temporary employment situations, the performance of unqualified overpaid subjects (e.g., Adams & Rosenbaum, 1962; Adams, 1963; Arrowood, 1961) may be attributed to subjects' fear of losing their jobs (cf., reviews by Weick, 1965b; Lawler, 1968b; Pritchard, 1969). Behavior directed toward job security certainly reflects a future orientation. This interpretation suggests that behavior in situations of short-time perspective may be determined by some of the same factors which determine behavior in ongoing organizations. Similarly, a laboratory experiment by Lowin, Hrapchak, and Kavanagh (1969) employed subjects for temporary jobs and obtained data which approximates the findings obtained by field studies of leadership in many organizations. Last, Schachter, Willerman, Festinger, and Hyman (1961) collected data in field experiments to examine the effects of emotion disruption upon productivity which occurs during industrial changeovers. The Schachter, Willerman, Festinger, and Hyman (1961) findings were replicated in a laboratory experiment by Latané and Arrowood (1963). The laboratory task lasted for only a few minutes. The similarity of field data and laboratory data is a striking demonstration of the phenomenon's generality. As Latané and Arrowood (1963, p. 213) have stated: "This generality becomes the more remarkable when the time span of the two studies is compared. While Schachter, Willerman, Festinger, and Hyman (1961) prolonged their emotional manipulation over two-to-four weeks, we used two minutes; while their subjects had become stereotyped on the same job for untold months, ours had to learn a task in twelve minutes."

Although the response properties and dynamics of future orientation are not clearly understood at the present time, the above data demonstrate that there apparently are phenomena and/or conditions under which the laboratory's short-time perspective will *not* be a source of critical difference between laboratory and organization. A fascinating demonstration of the effects of expanded time references may be found in a recent experiment by Zimbardo, Marshall, and Maslach (1971). Therefore, rather than dismissing all laboratory responses as irrelevant, it seems more realistic to view the laboratory's short-time perspective and any related behavioral implications as a *potential* source of boundary variables. In each situation, the decision must rest upon careful scrutiny of the experimental procedures as compared with a detailed analysis of the phenomenon and criterion environment. The consumer's task is to determine if the difference in time perspective is trivial or critical in each situation.

The problem may become more salient when the dependent variable is obtained with paper and pencil measures. However, behavioroid measures (e.g., Aronson & Carlsmith, 1968, pp. 54–55) are a plausible alternative. Behavioroid measures are based on the assumption that behavioral acts vary on a continuum of consequentiality ranging from anonymous paper and pencil responses to actions which require the performance of effortful and costly tasks over long periods of time. For example, instead of asking subjects to circle a point on a scale which indicates how much they like blacks, one might request subjects to indicate how much time they will devote to taking blacks around campus (e.g., Marlowe, Frager, & Nuttall, 1965) or to sign a legal statement indicating their willingness to be photographed with blacks and giving their permission for circulation of the photograph in a nationwide publicity campaign advocating racial integration (e.g., DeFleur & Westie, 1958).

Behavioroid measures may reduce the short-time perspective because they induce an expanded time reference within which subjects commit themselves to *consequential* behavior. However, subjects must expect to honor their commitment by actually carrying out the behavior. Furthermore, when behavioroid measures imply restrictions on subjects' future behavior, fewer socially desirable responses may be expected than are often obtained on standard paper-and-pencil measures. Similarly, the tendency to modify behavior in order to create a favorable impression on the experimenter may be reduced. That is, when responses are expected to have consequences beyond the laboratory, the anticipation of these consequences may oppose subjects' desire to present a favorable picture of themselves to the experimenter. Although some behavioroid measures are more similar to organizational behaviors than simple ratings, situations do exist in which organizational behavior may have more in common with ratings than with interpersonal behavioral decisions. In such cases, it would be preferable to generalize from data based on simple rating scales than data based on behavioroid or behavioral measures.

Nature of the Task

Experimental tasks vary in their representation of organizational properties on a number of dimensions. When these properties are responsible for critical differences between the laboratory and organization, they qualify as boundary variables. The reader can generate a list of potential *task* boundary variables from the comprehensive classification systems of Shaw (1963) and discussions of task variables (cf., Weick, 1965a, 1967) found elsewhere.

Advantages of the Boundary Variable Concept

The boundary variable approach offers a distinct advantage to the researcher who is interested in matching aspects of the focal setting with critical attributes of the criterion setting. Once identified, the potential boundary variable can be treated experimentally in the laboratory. The experimenter can hold the boundary variable constant at some level which represents its occurrence in the criterion setting. However, this procedure does not yield information about the effects of this variable under different levels of the variable. It remains a potential boundary variable when generalizations are made to other settings. Alternatively, the experimenter can treat the potential boundary variable as an additional independent variable and manipulate it across several levels which are believed to encompass its operation in several criterion settings. The latter strategy yields valuable information about the effects of the variable upon the dependent variable. Under these conditions, the experimenter can determine the effects of the boundary variable and can generalize to a criterion setting with greater confidence by subtracting the effect of the boundary variable.

FIAT MISTURA

It is frequently recognized that the generality of findings in any particular behavioral domain is greatly enhanced by methodological integration. Confirming and/or disconfirming a hypothesis with different methodologies provides the firmest structure for generalization. The advantages of a multimethod approach to the study of organizational behavior (cf., Evan, 1971, p. 4; McGrath, 1964, pp. 533–556; Weick, 1969b, p. 294; Zelditch & Evan, 1962, p. 60) are clear. Yet laboratory experiments are clearly underrepresented. Recent skepticism is depriving them of their rightful place as a legitimate data base in the total perspective of organizational theory and research. Experimental organizations provide unique advantages and critical contributions to the overall research on and theory of organizations. " 'Go back to the lab' seems just as good a recommendation for organizational researchers as does the now fashionable 'Go out into the field.' Previous idle speculation about the worth of laboratory methodology for organizational theory is just that—idle" (Weick, 1969b, p. 303).

The present chapter proposes a concept for bridging the gap between laboratory data and organizational applications. The term "boundary variable" is that concept. Identi-

fication of boundary variables is proposed as an alternative to the iconic notion of absolute restrictions on the use of data beyond their genetic setting. In lieu of dismissing valuable information obtained in the laboratory, consumers can learn the skills of judicious application—an activity which requires both familiarity with existing research and sensitivity to potential boundary variables that may stand between specific studies and specific realms of application.

REFERENCES

Abelson, R. P. Simulation of social behavior. In G. Lindzey & E. Aronson (Eds.), *Handbook of social psychology,* Vol. 2. (2nd ed.) Reading, Mass.: Addison-Wesley, 1968, 274–356.

Ackoff, R., Gupta, S. K., & Minas, J. S. *Scientific method: Optimizing applied research decisions.* New York: Wiley, 1962.

Adair, J. G., & Epstein, J. Verbal cues in the mediation of experimenter bias. Paper presented at the Midwestern Psychological Association Convention, Chicago, May, 1967.

Adams, J. S. Towards an understanding of inequity. *Journal of Abnormal and Social Psychology,* 1963, 67, 422–436.

Adams, J. S. Injustice in social exchange. In L. Berkowitz (Ed.), *Advances in experimental social psychology,* Vol. 2. New York: Academic Press, 1965, 267–299.

Adams, J. S. Effects of overpayment: Two comments on Lawler's paper. *Journal of Personality and Social Psychology,* 1968, 10, 315–316.

Adams, J. S., & Rosenbaum, W. B. Relationship of worker productivity to cognitive dissonance about wage inequities. *Journal of Applied Psychology,* 1962, 46, 161–164.

Adams, R. N., & Preiss, J. J., Eds. *Human organization research.* Homewood, Ill.: Dorsey Press, 1960.

Amir, Y. Contact hypothesis in ethnic relations. *Psychological Bulletin,* 1969, 71, 319–342.

Anderson, L. R., & Fiedler, F. E. The effect of participatory and supervisory leadership on group creativity. *Journal of Applied Psychology,* 1964, 48, 227–236.

Argyris, C. Diagnosing defenses against the outsider. *Journal of Social Issues,* 1952, 8, 24–34.

Argyris, C. *Interpersonal competence and organizational effectiveness.* Homewood, Ill.: Dorsey Press, 1962.

Argyris, C. *Integrating the individual and the organization.* New York: Wiley, 1964, 336.

Argyris, C. Some unintended consequences of rigorous research. *Psychological Bulletin,* 1968, 70, 185–197.

Argyris, C. The incompleteness of social psychological theory: Examples from small group, cognitive consistency, and attribution research. *American Psychologist,* 1969, 24, 893–908.

Aronson, E., & Carlsmith, J. M. Experimentation in social psychology. In G. Lindzey & E. Aronson (Eds.), *Handbook of social psychology,* Vol. 2. Reading, Mass.: Addison-Wesley, 1968.

Aronson, E., & Mills, J. The effect of severity of initiation on liking for a group. *Journal of Abnormal and Social Psychology,* 1959, 58, 379–382.

Arrowood, A. J. Some effects on productivity of justified and unjustified levels of reward under public and private conditions. Unpublished doctoral dissertation, University of Minnesota, Minneapolis, 1961.

Back, K. W. Social research as a communication system. *Social Forces,* 1962, 41, 61–68.

Back, K. W., Hood, T. C., & Brehm, M. L. The subject role in small group experiments. *Social Forces,* 1964, 43, 181–197.

Barber, T. X., & Silver, M. J. Fact, fiction, and the experimenter bias effect. *Psychological Bulletin Monograph Supplement,* 1968, 70, 1–29.

Bass, B. M. Experimenting with simulated manufacturing organizations. In S. G. Sells (Ed.), *Stimulus determinants of behavior.* New York: Ronald Press, 1963, 117–196.

Becker, H. S. Problems of inference and proof in participant observation. *American Sociological Review,* 1958, 23, 652–660.

Becker, H. S., & Geer, B. Participant observation and interviewing: A comparison. *Human Organization,* 1957, 16, 28–32.

Bem, D. J. The epistemological status of interpersonal simulations: A reply to Jones, Linder, Kiesler, Zanna, & Brehm. *Journal of Experimental Social Psychology,* 1968, 4, 270–274.

Blake, R. R., & Brehm, J. W. The use of tape-recording to simulate a group atmosphere. *Journal of Abnormal and Social Psychology,* 1954, 49, 311–313.

Boring, E. G. Perspective: Artifact and control. In R. Rosenthal & R. L. Rosnow (Eds.), *Artifact in behavioral research.* New York: Academic Press, 1969, 1–11.

Brock, T. C. Communicator-recipient similarity and decision change. *Journal of Personality and Social Psychology,* 1965, 1, 650–654.

Brock, T. C., & Becker, L. A. "Debriefing" and susceptibility to subsequent experimental manipulations. *Journal of Experimental Social Psychology,* 1966, 2, 314–323.

Brunswick, E. *Perception and the representative design of psychological experiments.* (2nd ed.) Berkeley: University of California Press, 1956.

Burnham, J. R. Experimenter bias and lesion labeling. Unpublished manuscript, Purdue University, Lafayette, Ind., 1966.

Burnham, J. R. Effects of experimenter's expectancies on children's ability to learn to swim. Unpublished master's thesis, Purdue University, Lafayette, Ind., 1968.

Byrne, D., & McGraw, C. Interpersonal attraction toward Negroes. *Human Relations,* 1964, 17, 201–213.

Campbell, D. T. Factors relevant to the validity of experiments in social settings. *Psychological Bulletin,* 1957, 54, 297–312.

Campbell, D. T., & Stanley, J. C. Experimental and quasi-experimental designs for research on teaching. In N. L. Gage (Ed.), *Handbook of research on teaching.* Chicago: Rand McNally, 1963.

Cannell, C. F., & Kahn, R. L. Interviewing. In G. Lindzey & E. Aronson (Eds.), *Handbook of social psychology,* Vol. 2. Reading, Mass.: Addison-Wesley, 1968, 526–595.

Carey, A. The Hawthorne studies: A radical criticism. *American Sociological Review,* 1967, 32, 403–416.

Carzo, R. Jr., & Yanouzas, J. N. Effects of flat and tall organization structure. *Administrative Science Quarterly,* 1969, 14, 178–191.

Chapanis, A. The relevance of laboratory studies to practical situations. *Ergonomics,* 1967, 10, 557–577.

Chapanis, N., & Chapanis, A. C. Cognitive dissonance: Five years later. *Psychological Bulletin,* 1964, 61, 1–22.

Coch, L., & French, J. P. Jr. Overcoming resistance to change. *Human Relations,* 1948, 1, 512–532.

Cohen, A. M., Robinson, E. L., & Edwards, J. L. Experiments in organizational embeddedness. *Administrative Science Quarterly,* 1969, 14, 208–221.

Cohen, K. J., & Cyert, R. M. Simulation of organizational behavior. In J. G. March (Ed.), *Handbook of organizations.* Chicago: Rand McNally, 1965, 305–334.

Cook, S. W., & Selltiz, C. A multiple-indicator approach to attitude measurement. *Psychological Bulletin,* 1964, 62, 36–55.

Cook, T. D., Bean, J. R., Calder, B. J., Frey, R., Krovetz, M. L., & Reisman, S. R. Demand characteristics and three conceptions of the frequently deceived subject. *Journal of Personality and Social Psychology,* 1970, 14, 185–194.

Crano, W. D., & Brewer, M. P. *Principles of research in social psychology.* New York: McGraw-Hill, 1972.

Croner, M. D., & Willis, R. H. Perceived differences in task competence and asymmetry of dyadic influence. *Journal of Abnormal and Social Psychology,* 1961, 62, 705–708.

Crowne, D. P., & Marlowe, D. *The approval motive: Studies in evaluative dependence.* New York: Wiley, 1964.

Day, R. C., & Hamblin, R. L. Some effects of close and punitive styles of supervision. *American Journal of Sociology,* 1964, 69, 499–510.

DeFleur, M., & Westie, F. Verbal attitudes and overt acts: An experiment on the salience of attitudes. *American Sociological Review,* 1958, 23, 667–673.

Dill, W. R. Desegregation or integration? Comment about contemporary research on organizations. In W. W. Cooper, H. J. Leavitt, & M. W. Shelly II (Eds.), *New perspectives in organizational research.* New York: Wiley, 1964, 39–52.

Dittes, J., & Kelley, H. H. Effects of different conditions of acceptance upon conformity to group norms. *Journal of Abnormal and Social Psychology,* 1956, 53, 100–107.

Drabeck, T. E., & Haas, J. E. Realism in laboratory simulation: Myth or method? *Social Forces,* 1967, 45, 337–346.

Dunnette, M. D., & Heneman, H. Influence of scale administrator on employee attitude response. *Journal of Applied Psychology,* 1956, 40, 73–77.

Edwards, A. L. *The social desirability variable in personality assessment and research.* New York: Dryden, 1957.

Elliott, E. Perception and alertness. *Ergonomics,* 1960, 3, 357–364.

Evan, W. M., Ed. *Organizational experiments: Laboratory and field research.* New York: Harper and Row, 1971, 261–264.

Evan, W. M., & Simmons, R. G. Organizational effects of inequitable rewards: Two experiments in status inconsistency. *Administrative Science Quarterly,* 1969, 14, 224–237.

Evan, W. M., & Zelditch, M. A. A laboratory experiment on bureaucratic authority. *American Sociological Revue,* 1961, 26, 883–893.

Festinger, L. Laboratory experiments. In L. Festinger & D. Katz (Eds.), *Research methods in the behavioral sciences.* New York: Holt, Rinehart and Winston, 1953, 136–172.

Fiedler, F. E. *A theory of leadership effectiveness.* New York: McGraw-Hill, 1967.

Fillenbaum, S. Prior deception and subsequent experimental performance: The "faithful" subject. *Journal of Personality and Social Psychology,* 1966, 4, 532–537.

Fillenbaum, S., & Frey, R. More on the "faithful" behavior of suspicious subjects. *Journal of Personality,* 1970, 38, 43–51.

Fleishman, E. A., & Harris, E. F. Patterns of leadership behavior related to employee grievances and turnover. *Personnel Psychology,* 1962, 15, 43–55.

Fleishman, E. A., Harris, E. F., & Burtt, H. E. *Leadership and supervision in industry.* Columbus: Bureau of Educational Research, Ohio State University, 1955.

Freedman, J. L. Role playing: Psychology by consensus. *Journal of Personality and Social Psychology,* 1969, 13, 107–114.

French, J. R. P. Jr. A formal theory of social power. *Psychological Review,* 1956, 63, 181–194.

French, J. R. P. Jr., & Raven, B. The bases of social power. In D. Cartwright (Ed.), *Studies in social power.* Ann Arbor: Research Center for Group Dynamics, Institute for Social Research, University of Michigan, 1959.

Friedman, A., & Goodman, P. Wage inequity, self-qualifications, and productivity. *Organizational Behavior and Human Performance,* 1967, 2, 406–417.

Friedman, N. *The social nature of psychological research.* New York: Basic Books, 1967.

Fromkin, H. L. Effort and attractiveness: Predictions of reinforcement theory versus predictions of dissonance theory. *Journal of Personality and Social Psychology,* 1968, 9, 347–352. (a)

Fromkin, H. L. Affective and valuational consequences of self-perceived uniqueness deprivation. Unpublished doctoral dissertation, Ohio State University, Columbus, 1968.(b)

Fromkin, H. L. The behavioral science laboratories at Purdue's Krannert School. *Administrative Science Quarterly,* 1969, 14, 171–177.

Fromkin, H. L., & Ostrom, T. M. Laboratory research and the organization: Generalizing from lab to life. In H. L. Fromkin & J. J. Sherwood (Eds.), *Integrating the organization.* New York: The Free Press, 1974.

Fromkin, H. L., Klimoski, R. J., & Flanagan, M. F. Race and task competency as determinants of newcomer acceptance in work groups. *Organizational Behavior and Human Performance,* 1972, 7, No. 1, 25–42.

Fromkin, H. L., Olson, J. C., Dipboye, R. L., & Barnaby, D. A commodity theory analysis of consumer preferences for scarce products. Paper presented at the American Psychological Association Convention, Washington, D.C., September, 1971.

Gerard, H. B., & Mathewson, G. C. The effects of severity of initiation on liking for a group. *Journal of Experimental and Social Psychology,* 1966, 2, 278–287.

Gibb, C. A. The principles and traits of leadership. *Journal of Abnormal and Social Psychology,* 1947, 42, 267–284.

Gibb, C. A. Leadership. In G. Lindzey (Ed.), *Handbook of social psychology,* Vol. II. Reading, Mass.: Addison-Wesley, 1954, 877–920.

Goffman, E. *The presentation of self in everyday life.* New York: Doubleday, 1959.

Goodman, P., & Friedman, A. An examination of the effect of wage inequity in the hourly condition. *Organizational Behavior and Human Performance,* 1968, 3, 350–352.

Goodstadt, B., & Kipnis, D. Situational influences on the use of power. *Journal of Applied Psychology,* 1970, 54, 201–207.

Graen, G., Orris, J. B., & Alvares, K. M. Contingency model of leadership effectiveness:

Some experimental results. *Journal of Applied Psychology,* 1971, 55, 196–201.

Greenwald, A. G. Behavior change following a persuasive communication. *Journal of Personality,* 1965, 33, 370–391.

Guetzkow, H. Organizational leadership in task-oriented groups. In L. Petrullo & B. M Bass (Eds.), *Leadership and interpersonal behavior.* New York: Holt, Rinehart and Winston, 1961, 187–200.

Guetzkow, H., Ed. *Simulation in social science: Readings.* Englewood Cliffs, N.J.: Prentice-Hall, 1962.

Guetzkow, H. Structured programs and their relation to free activity within the international simulation. In H. Guetzkow, C. F. Alger, R. A. Brody, C. Noel, & R. C. Snyder, *Simulation in international relations.* Englewood Cliffs, N.J.: Prentice-Hall, 1963.

Guetzkow, H. Some correspondences between simulations and "realities" in international relations. In M. Kaplan (Ed.), *New approaches to international relations.* New York: St. Martin's Press, 1968.

Guetzkow, H. A decade of life with the internation simulation. In R. G. Stogdill (Ed.), *The process of model building in the behavioral sciences.* Columbus: Ohio State University Press, 1971.

Guetzkow, H., Kotler, P., & Schultz, R. L. *Simulation in social and administrative science.* Englewood Cliffs, N.J.: Prentice-Hall, 1972.

Guetzkow, H., Alger, C. F., Brody, R. A., Noel, R. C., & Snyder, R. C. *Simulation in international relations: Developments for research and teaching.* Englewood Cliffs, N.J.: Prentice-Hall, 1963.

Guion, R. M. *Personnel testing.* New York: McGraw-Hill, 1965.

Gustafson, L. A., & Orne, M. T. Effects of perceived role and role success on the detection of deception. *Journal of Applied Psychology,* 1965, 49, 412–417.

Haire, M., Ed. *Modern organizational theory: A symposium.* New York: Wiley, 1959.

Haire, M. *Organizational theory in industrial practice.* New York: Wiley, 1962.

Hakel, M. D., Ohnesorge, J. P., & Dunnette, M. D. Interviewer evaluations of job applicants' resumes as a function of the qualifications of the immediate preceding applicants: An examination of contrast effects. *Journal of Applied Psychology,* 1970, 54, 27–30.

Helmreich, R., Aronson, E., & LeSan, J. To err is humanizing—sometimes: Effects of self-esteem, competence, and pratfall on interpersonal attraction. *Journal of Personality and Social Psychology,* 1970, 16, 259–264.

Hermann, C. F. *Crises in foreign policy: A simulational analysis.* Indianapolis: Bobbs-Merrill, 1969.

Hermann, C. F., & Hermann, M. G. Validation studies of the inter-nation simulation. China Lake, Calif.: U.S. Naval Ordnance Test Station, December, 1963.

Hollander, E. P., & Julian, J. W. Studies in leader legitimacy, influence, and innovation. In L. Berkowitz (Ed.), *Advances in experimental social psychology,* Vol. 5. New York: Academic Press, 1970, 33–69.

Holmes, D. S. Verbal conditioning or problem-solving and cooperation? *Journal of Experimental Research in Personality,* 1967, 2, 289–294.

Holmes, D. S., & Applebaum, A. S. Nature of prior experimental experience as a determinant of performance in a subsequent experiment. *Journal of Personality and Social Psychology,* 1970, 14, 195–202.

Horowitz, I. A., & Rothchild, B. H. Conformity as a function of deception and role playing. *Journal of Personality and Social Psychology,* 1970, 14, 224–226.

Hyman, H. Problems in the collection of opinion research data. *American Journal of Sociology,* 1950, 55, 362–370.

Inbar, M., & Stoll, C. S. *Simulation and gaming in social science.* New York: The Free Press, 1972.

Jacoby, J. Examining the other organization. *Personnel Administration,* 1968, 31, 36–42.

Janis, I. L., & Field, P. B. A behavioral assessment of persuasibility: Consistency of individual differences. *Sociometry,* 1956, 19, 241–259.

Jones, E. E. *Ingratiation.* New York: Appleton-Century-Crofts, 1964.

Jones, R. A., Linder, D. E., Kiesler, C. A., Zanna, M., & Brehm, J. Internal states or external stimuli: Observers' attitude judgments and the dissonance theory self-persuasion controversy. *Journal of Experimental Social Psychology,* 1968, 4, 247–269.

Julian, J. W., Hollander, E. P., & Regula, C. R. Endorsement of the group spokesman as a function of his source of authority, competence, and success. *Journal of Personality and Social Psychology,* 1969, 11, 42–49.

Kahn, R. L., & Mann, F. C. Developing research partnerships. *Journal of Social Issues,* 1952, 8, 4–10.

Kaplan, A. *The conduct of inquiry: Methodology for behavioral science.* San Francisco: Chandler, 1964.

Katz, D., & Kahn, R. L. *The social psychology of organizations.* New York: Wiley, 1966.

Kennedy, J. L. The system approach: Organizational development. *Human Factors,* February, 1962, 25–52.

Kibler, A. W. The relevance of vigilance research to aerospace monitoring tasks. *Human Factors,* 1965, 7, 93–99.

Kintz, B. L., Delprato, D. J., Mettee, D. R., Persons, C. E., & Schappe, L. H. The experimenter effect. *Psychological Bulletin,* 1965, 63, 223–232.

Korman, A. K. Consideration, initiating structure, and organizational criteria: A review. *Personnel Psychology,* 1966, 19, 349–361.

Kornhauser, A. Are public opinion polls fair to organized labor? *Public Opinion Quarterly,* 1946, 10, 484–500.

Kroger, R. O. The effects of role demands and test-cue properties upon personality performance. *Journal of Consulting Psychology,* 1967, 31, 304–312.

Lachenmeyer, C. W. Experimentation: A misunderstood methodology in psychological and social-psychological research. *American Psychologist,* 1970, 25, 617–624.

Latané, B., & Arrowood, A. J. Emotional arousal and task performance. *Journal of Applied Psychology,* 1963, 47, 324–327.

Latané, B., & Darley, J. M. Group intervention of bystander intervention in emergencies. *Journal of Personality and Social Psychology,* 1968, 10, 215–221.

Lawler, E. E. Effects of hourly overpayment on productivity and work quality. *Journal of Personality and Social Psychology,* 1968, 10, 306–313. (a)

Lawler, E. E. Equity theory as a predictor of productivity and work quality. *Psychological Bulletin,* 1968, 70, 596–610. (b)

Lawler, E. E., Koplin, C. A., Young, T. F., & Fadem, J. A. Inequity reduction over time in an induced over-payment situation. *Organizational Behavior and Human Performance,* 1968, 3, 253–268.

Leavitt, H. J. *Managerial psychology.* (Rev.

ed.) Chicago: University of Chicago Press, 1964.

Levy, L. H. Awareness, learning, and the beneficient subjects as expert witness. *Journal of Personality and Social Psychology,* 1967, 6, 365–370.

Lewin, K. *Field theory in social science.* New York: Harper and Row, 1951.

Likert, R. *New patterns of management.* New York: McGraw-Hill, 1961.

Lowin, A., & Craig, J. R. The influence of level of performance on managerial style: An experimental object-lesson in the ambiguity of correlational data. *Organizational Behavior and Human Performance,* 1968, 3, 440–458.

Lowin, A., Hrapchak, W. J., & Kavanagh, M. J. Consideration and initiating structure: An experimental investigation of leadership traits. *Administrative Science Quarterly,* 1969, 14, 238–253.

McCall, G. J., & Simmons, J. L., Eds. *Issues in participant observation.* Reading, Mass.: Addison-Wesley, 1969.

McGrath, J. E. Toward a theory of method for research on organizations. In W. W. Cooper, H. J. Leavitt, & M. W. Shelly II (Eds.), *New perspectives in organization research.* New York: Wiley, 1964, 533–556.

McGuigan, F. J. The experimenter: A neglected stimulus object. *Psychological Bulletin,* 1963, 60, 421–428.

McGuire, W. J. Theory-oriented research in natural settings: The best of both worlds for social psychology. In M. Sherif & C. W. Sherif (Eds.), *Interdisciplinary relationships in the social sciences.* Chicago: Aldine, 1969, 21–51. (a)

McGuire, W. J. Suspiciousness of experimenter's intent. In R. Rosenthal & R. L. Rosnow (Eds.), *Artifact in behavioral research.* New York: Academic Press, 1969, 13–57. (b)

McGuire, W. J., & Millman, S. Anticipatory belief lowering following forewarning of a persuasive attack. *Journal of Personality and Social Psychology,* 1965, 2, 471–479.

Mackie, R. R., & Christensen, R. P. Translation and application of psychological research. Human Factors Research Incorporated, Santa Barbara Research Park, Goleta, Calif., 1967, Technical Report, 716–717.

Mann, R. D. A review of the relationships between personality and performance in small groups. *Psychological Bulletin,* 1959, 56, 244–270.

March, J. G., Ed. *Handbook of organizations.* Chicago: Rand McNally, 1965.

March, J. G., & Simon, H. A. *Organizations.* New York: Wiley, 1958.

Marlowe, D., Frager, R., & Nuttall, R. L. Commitment to action taken as a consequence of cognitive dissonance. *Journal of Personality and Social Psychology,* 1965, 2, 864–868.

Marx, M. H. The general nature of theory construction. In M. H. Marx (Ed.), *Theories in contemporary psychology.* New York: Macmillan, 1963, 4–46.

Marx, M. H., & Hillix, W. A. *Systems and theories in psychology.* New York: McGraw-Hill, 1963.

Masling, J. M. Role-related behavior of the subject and psychologist and its effects upon psychological data. In D. A. Levine (Ed.), *Nebraska symposium on motivation.* Lincoln: University of Nebraska Press, 1966, XIV, 67–103.

Melcher, A. J., & Beller, R. Toward a theory of organizational communication: Consideration in channel selection. *Academy of Management Journal,* 1967, 10, 39–52.

Merton, R. K. The self-fulfilling prophecy. *Antioch Review,* 1948, 8, 193–210.

Miller, N. E. Experiments on motivation. *Science,* 1957, 126, 1271–1278.

Miller, N. E. Liberalization of basic S-R concepts: Extensions to conflict behavior, motivation, and social learning. In S. Koch (Ed.) *Psychology: A study of science,* Vol. 2. New York: McGraw-Hill, 1959, 196–292.

Minor, M. W. Experimenter-expectancy effect as a function of evaluation apprehension. *Journal of Personality and Social Psychology,* 1970, 15, 326–332.

Morse, N. C., & Reimer, E. The experimental change of a major organizational variable. *Journal of Abnormal and Social Psychology,* 1956, 52, 120–129.

Mosier, C. A. *Survey methods in social investigation.* London: Heinemann, 1965.

Orne, M. T. The nature of hypnosis: Artifact and essence. *Journal of Abnormal and Social Psychology,* 1959, 58, 277–299.

Orne, M. T. On the social psychology of the psychology experiment: With particular reference to demand characteristics and their implications. *American Psychologist,* 1962, 17, 776–783.

Orne, M. T. Demand characteristics and quasi-controls. In R. Rosenthal & R. L. Rosnow

(Eds.), *Artifact in behavioral research*. New York: Academic Press, 1969, 143–179.

Orne, M. T., & Evans, F. Social control in the psychological experiment: Antisocial behavior and hypnosis. *Journal of Personality and Social Psychology*, 1965, 1, 189–200.

Orne, M. T., & Scheibe, K. E. The contribution of non-deprivation factors in the production of sensory deprivation effects: The psychology of the "panic button." *Journal of Abnormal and Social Psychology*, 1964, 68, 3–12.

Page, M. M., & Lumia, A. R. Cooperation with demand characteristics and the bimodal distribution of verbal conditioning data. *Psychonomic Science*, 1968, 12, 243–244.

Palola, E. G. Organizational types and role strains: An experimental study of complex organizations. *Sociology and Social Research*, 1967, 51, 171–184.

Penner, D. D., & Patten, R. L. Comments on the epistemological status of interpersonal simulations. *Representative Research in Social Psychology*, 1970, 1, 62–66.

Persinger, G. W., Knutson, C., & Rosenthal, R. Communication of interpersonal expectations of ward personnel to neuropsychiatric patients. Unpublished data, Harvard University, Cambridge, 1968.

Platt, J. R. Strong inference. *Science*, 1964, 146, 347–353.

Porter, L. W., & Lawler, E. E. The effect of "tall" versus "flat" organization structures on managerial job satisfaction. *Personnel Psychology*, 1964, 17, 135–148.

Price, J. L. Design of proof in organizational research. *Administrative Science Quarterly*, 1968, 13, No. 1, 121–134.

Pritchard, R. D. Equity theory: A review and critique. *Organizational Behavior and Human Performance*, 1969, 4, 176–211.

Raven, B., & French, J. R. P. Jr. Legitimate power, coercive power, and observability in social influence. *Sociometry*, 1958, 21, 83–97.

Remmers, H. H. *Introduction to opinion and attitude measurement*. New York: Harper and Brothers, 1954.

Riecken, H. W. A program for research on experiments in social psychology. In N. F. Washburne (Ed.), *Decisions, values, and groups*. New York: Macmillan, 1962.

Riley, J. W. Jr. Reflections on data sources in opinion research. *Public Opinion Quarterly*, 1962, 26, 313–322.

Robinson, J. A., Hermann, C. F., & Hermann,

M. G. Search under crisis in political gaming, and simulation. In D. G. Pruitt & R. C. Snyder (Eds.), *Theory and research on the causes of war*. Englewood Cliffs, N.J.: Prentice-Hall, 1969.

Roethlisberger, F. J., & Dickson, W. T. *Management and the worker*. Cambridge: Harvard University Press, 1946.

Rosen, N. A. Demand characteristics in a field experiment. *Journal of Applied Psychology*, 1970, 54, 163–168.

Rosen, N. A., & Sales, S. M. Behavior in a non-experiment: The effects of behavioral field research on the work performance of factory employees. *Journal of Applied Psychology*, 1966, 50, 165–171.

Rosenberg, M. J. When dissonance fails: On eliminating evaluation apprehension from attitude measurement. *Journal of Personality and Social Psychology*, 1965, 1, 28–43.

Rosenberg, M. J. The conditions and consequences of evaluation apprehension. In R. Rosenthal & R. L. Rosnow (Eds.), *Artifact in behavioral research*. New York: Academic Press, 1969, 279–349.

Rosenthal, R. Experimenter outcome orientation and the results of the psychological experiment. *Psychological Bulletin*, 1964, 61, 405–412.

Rosenthal, R. *Experimenter effects in behavioral research*. New York: Appleton-Century-Crofts, 1966.

Rosenthal, R. Covert communication in the psychological experiment. *Psychological Bulletin*, 1967, 67, 356–367.

Rosenthal, R. Interpersonal expectations: Effects of the experimenter's hypothesis. In R. Rosenthal & R. L. Rosnow (Eds.), *Artifact in behavioral research*. New York: Academic Press, 1969, 181–277.

Rosenthal, R., & Jacobson, L. *Pygmalion in the classroom: Teacher expectation and pupils' intellectual development*. New York: Holt, Rinehart and Winston, 1968.

Rosenthal, R., & Rosnow, R. L. *Artifact in behavioral research*. New York: Academic Press, 1969.

Rubenstein, A. H., & Haberstroh, C. J. *Some theories of organization*. Homewood, Ill.: Dorsey Press, 1960.

Runkel, P. J., & McGrath, J. E. *Research on human behavior: A systematic guide to method*. New York: Holt, Rinehart and Winston, 1972.

Sattler, J. M. Racial "experimenter effects" in experimentation, testing, interviewing, and psychotherapy. *Psychological Bulletin,* 1970, 73, 137–160.

Schachter, S. *The psychology of affiliation.* Stanford:.Stanford University Press, 1959.

Schachter, S., Willerman, B., Festinger, L., & Hyman, R. Emotional disruption and industrial productivity. *Journal of Applied Psychology,* 1961, 45, 201–213.

Scott, W. R. Fieldwork in a formal organization: Some dilemmas in the role of observer. *Human Organization,* 1962, 22, 162–168.

Sells, H. B. Toward a taxonomy of organizations. In W. W. Cooper, H. J. Leavitt, & M. W. Shelly II (Eds.), *New perspectives in organization research.* New York: Wiley, 1964, 515–532.

Selltiz, C., Jahoda, M., Deutsch, M., & Cook, S. *Research methods in social relations.* (Rev. ed.) New York: Holt, Rinehart and Winston, 1965, 480–499.

Shaw, M. E. Scaling group tasks: A method for dimensional analysis. Technical Report No. 1, 1963, University of Florida, Department of Psychology, Contract NR 170-266, Nonr-580 (11), Office of Naval Research.

Sherwood, J. J., & Nataupsky, M. Predicting the conclusion of Negro-white intelligence research from biographical characteristics of the investigator. *Journal of Personality and Social Psychology,* 1968, 8, 53–58.

Shubik, M. Bibliography on simulation, gaming, artificial intelligence, and allied topics. *Journal of the American Statistical Association,* December, 1960, 736–751.

Sidman, M. *Tactics of scientific research: Evaluation of experimental data in psychology.* New York: Basic Books, 1960.

Siegel, A. E., & Siegel, S. Reference groups, membership groups, and attitude change. *Journal of Abnormal and Social Psychology,* 1957, 55, 360–364.

Sigall, H., Aronson, E., & Van Hoose, T. The cooperative subject: Myth or reality? *Journal of Experimental Social Psychology,* 1970, 6, 1–10.

Sills, D. L. Three "climate of opinion" studies. *Public Opinion Quarterly,* 1961, 25, 571–573.

Silverman, I. Role-related behavior of subjects in laboratory studies of attitude change. *Journal of Personality and Social Psychology,* 1968, 8, 343–348.

Silverman, I., & Kleinman, D. A response deviance interpretation of the effects of experimentally induced frustration on prejudice. *Journal of Experimental Research in Personality,* 1967, 2, 150–153.

Silverman, I., & Regula, C. R. Evaluation apprehension, demand characteristics, and the effects of distraction on persuasibility. *Journal of Social Psychology,* 1968, 75, 273–281.

Silverman, I., & Shulman, A. D. A conceptual model of artifact in attitude change studies. *Sociometry,* 1970, 33, 97–107.

Silverman, I., Shulman, A. D., & Wiesenthal, D. L. Effects of deceiving and debriefing psychological subjects on performance in later experiments. *Journal of Personality and Social Psychology,* 1970, 14, 203–212.

Simmons, R. G. The role conflict of the first-line supervisor: An experimental study. *American Journal of Sociology,* 1968, 73, 482–495.

Simons, J. C. An introduction to surface-free behavior. *Ergonomics,* 1964, 7, 23–36.

Smoker, P. Social research for social anticipation. *American Behavioral Scientist,* 1969, 12, 7–13.

Stogdill, R. M. Personal factors associated with leadership. *Journal of Psychology,* 1948, 25, 35–71.

Streufert, S. The components of a simulation of local conflict: An analysis of the tactical and negotiations game. ARPA Technical Report, Project SD 260, Northwestern University, Evanston, Ill., 1968.

Streufert, S. Complexity and complex decision making: Convergences between differentiation and integration approaches to the prediction of task performance. *Journal of Experimental Social Psychology,* 1970, 6, 494–509.

Streufert, S. Success and response rate in complex decision making. Purdue University, Lafayette, Ind., Office of Naval Research Technical Report #35, 1971.

Streufert, S., & Castore, C. H. Information search and the effects of failure: A test of complexity theory. *Journal of Experimental Social Psychology,* 1971, 7, 125–143.

Streufert, S., & Schroder, H. M. Conceptual structure, environmental complexity, and task performance. *Journal of Experimental Research in Personality,* 1965, 1, 132–137.

Streufert, S., & Streufert, S. C. Effects of conceptual structure, failure, and success on attribution of causality and interpersonal attitudes. *Journal of Personality and Social Psychology,* 1969, 11, 138–147.

Streufert, S., & Streufert, S. C. Effects of failure in a complex decision-making task on perceptions of cost, profit, and certainty. *Organizational Behavior and Human Performance,* 1970, 5, 15–32.

Streufert, S., Streufert, S. C., & Castore, C. H. Leadership in negotiations and the complexity of conceptual structure. *Journal of Applied Psychology,* 1968, 52, 218–223.

Streufert, S., Kliger, S. C., Castore, C. H., & Driver, M. J. A tactical and negotiations game for analysis of decision integration across decision areas. *Psychological Reports,* 1967, 20, 155–157.

Streufert, S., Clardy, M. A., Driver, M. J., Karlins, M., Schroder, H. M., & Suedfeld, P. A tactical game for the analysis of complex decision making in individuals and groups. *Psychological Reports,* 1965, 17, 723–729.

Stricker, L. J. The true deceiver. *Psychological Bulletin,* 1967, 68, 13–20.

Triandis, H. C., Loh, W. D., & Levin, L. A. Race, status, quality of spoken English, and opinions about civil rights as determinants of interpersonal attitudes. *Journal of Personality and Social Psychology,* 1966, 4, 468–472.

Viteles, M. S. *Motivation and morale in industry.* New York: W. W. Norton, 1953.

Vroom, V. H. *Work and motivation.* New York: Wiley, 1964, 215.

Vroom, V. H. Industrial social psychology. In G. Lindzey & E. Aronson (Eds.), *The handbook of social psychology.* Reading, Mass.: Addison-Wesley, 1969, 196–268.

Webb, E. J., Campbell, D. T., Schwartz, R. D., & Sechrest, L. *Unobtrusive measures: Nonreactive research in social sciences.* Chicago: Rand McNally, 1966.

Weick, K. E. Laboratory experiments with organizations. In J. G. March (Ed.), *Handbook of organizations.* Chicago: Rand McNally, 1965, 194–260. (a)

Weick, K. E. The concept of equity in the perception of pay. Paper read at the Midwestern Psychological Association, Chicago, April, 1965. (b)

Weick, K. E. Organizations in the laboratory. In V. Vroom (Ed.), *Methods of organizational research.* Pittsburgh: University of Pittsburgh Press, 1967, 1–56.

Weick, K. E. Systematic observational methods. In G. Lindzey & E. Aronson (Eds.), *Handbook of social psychology,* Vol. 2. Reading, Mass.: Addison-Wesley, 1968, 357–451.

Weick, K. E. *The social psychology of organizing.* Reading, Mass.: Addison-Wesley, 1969. (a)

Weick, K. E. Laboratory organizations and unnoticed causes. *Administrative Sciences Quarterly,* 1969, 14, 294–303. (b)

Weick, K. E., & Nesset, B. Preferences among forms of equity. *Organizational Behavior and Human Performance,* 1968, 3, 400–416.

Wiggins, J. A. Hypothesis validity and experimental laboratory methods. In H. M. Blalock Jr., & A. B. Blalock (Eds.), *Methodology in social research.* New York: McGraw-Hill, 1968, 390–427.

Willis, R. H., & Willis, Y. A. Role playing versus deception: An experimental comparison. *Journal of Personality and Social Psychology,* 1970, 16, 472–477.

Zelditch, M. Jr. Can you really study an army in the laboratory? In A. Etzioni (Ed.), *A sociological reader on complex organizations.* New York: Holt, Rinehart and Winston, 1969.

Zelditch, M. Jr., & Evan, W. M. Simulated bureaucracies: A methodological analysis. In H. Guetzkow (Ed.), *Simulation in social science.* Englewood Cliffs, N.J.: Prentice-Hall, 1962, 48–60.

Zelditch, M. Jr., & Hopkins, T. K. Laboratory experiments with organizations. In A. Etzioni (Ed.), *Complex organizations.* New York: Holt, Rinehart and Winston, 1961, 464–478.

Zemack, R., & Rokeach, M. The pledge to secrecy: A method to assess violations. *American Psychologist,* 1966, 21, 612.

Zimbardo, P. G., Marshall, G., & Maslach, C. Liberating behavior from time-bound control: Expanding the present through hypnosis. *Journal of Applied Social Psychology,* 1971, 1, 305–323.

Zinnes, D. A. A comparison of hostile state behavior in simulated and historical data. *World Politics,* 1966, 18, 474–502.

PART TWO

Individual and Job Measurement and the Management of Individual Behavior in Organizations

Basic Attributes of Individuals in Relation to Behavior in Organizations

MARVIN D. DUNNETTE
The University of Minnesota

INDUSTRIAL AND ORGANIZATIONAL psychology grew out of psychology's early success in describing and measuring differences between people. Psychology as a science and psychologists as practitioners were literally thrust into the world of work by great needs during World War I for the rapid mobilization and utilization of manpower resources. During the twenties and thirties, measurement of individual differences expanded even more, and the implications of such measurement for occupational choice, vocational guidance, counseling, and for programs of personnel selection and job placement in organizations became widely apparent.

Measurement of human attributes remains today as the critically important first step in industrial programs related to all forms of personnel administration and utilization. The four chapters in this Section give systematic attention to what is currently known about the important measurable attributes of humans and how these attributes are related to what people can and will do in work settings.

In choosing to include these four chapters about the methodology and instrumentation available for measuring human attributes, the editor obviously accepts the major thrust of traditional trait concepts and rejects the basic arguments put forward over the last several years by those who claim that human behavior is a function almost exclusively of the situation in which it occurs. The strongest version of the situationist position is that the behavioral generalities and dispositions assumed by trait concepts simply do not exist and that behavior in any particular situation is solely a function of cues and rewards peculiar to that situation. Stagner and Bowers[1] have each sounded strong and persuasive criticisms of such situational extremism. Both authors agree that behavior is indeed more situation specific than trait theorists have traditionally acknowledged, but they also point out that traits, both logically and empirically, have served psychology extremely well as descriptive units, as statements of behavioral probabilities, and as systematizing concepts for helping to understand what would otherwise be seen as disparate and unrelated behavioral episodes. Finally, and most tellingly, both authors note that situationism has failed to recognize sufficiently the person specificity of situations. That is, personal dispositions—traits—may properly be viewed as generalized expectancies which increase the relative probabilities of particular situations being chosen or avoided by particular persons who,

---

[1] See Stagner, R., Traits are relevant—logical and empirical analysis. Paper delivered at the Annual Convention of the American Psychological Association, Montreal, Quebec, Canada, 1973; and Bowers, K. S., Situationism in psychology: An analysis and a critique. *Psychological Review*, 1973, 80, 307–336.

in turn, determine the nature of the reinforcing or aversive qualities of those situations. This is, of course, an interactionist position, and it is this position that is adopted by each of the authors of the following four chapters as he discusses the particular subset of human attributes assigned to him.

In Chapter 11, Dunnette summarizes something of the history of our developing knowledge of the measurement of human aptitudes, abilities, and skills—those measures designated as *Maximum Performance* tests by Cronbach. After reviewing current knowledge relative to aptitude, motor skill, and physical proficiency taxonomies, Dunnette calls attention indirectly to the need for an interactionist position between trait concepts and situationism by noting the existence of two quite distinct taxonomic worlds—one based mostly on standardized test responses, the other based mostly on classifications of work activities and behaviors. The remainder of Chapter 11 is then devoted to a discussion of the nature and relative merits of various strategies for bringing together or linking systematically the two taxonomic worlds. The strategies discussed include Classic Validation, Occupational Aptitude Patterns, Rational Specification, Behavior Validation, Synthetic Validation, and Job and Task Sampling. Dunnette concludes with a call for developing a common taxonomy intermediate between the test world and the work world, arguing that such a system is needed in order to classify jobs, tasks, job dimensions, human attributes, aptitudes, skills, and tests within a common framework taking account of both traditional trait concepts and situational (work) requirements.

In Chapter 12, Holland discusses the major instruments for measuring vocational interests and their practical application to vocational guidance and career counseling. He summarizes the main findings relevant to occupational choice and reviews research evidence about the characteristics and developmental histories of persons with different occupational orientations and at various developmental or life stages. An interactionist orientation between trait concepts and situational characteristics is inherent in the nature of Holland's subject matter. As such, he capitalizes fully in Chapter 12 on the opportunity to convey to the reader much of the excitement and challenge of unraveling more completely the nature of the developmental interplay between the person and his environment in relation to eventual job choice, occupational persistence, and long-term career success.

In Chapter 13, Gough defines personality as a construct or abstraction which helps to account for personal individuality, adaptability, and behavioral dispositions. In elaborating upon personality structure, he, too, adopts an interactionist orientation between trait and situation; throughout, he cites research showing how traits and contexts interact to determine behavioral outcomes. Measures of various personality dimensions and specific personality inventories are presented in the framework of brief reviews of research in such areas as authoritarianism, conformity, need:Achievement, socialization and moral judgment, social maturity, social acuity, origence, field independence, and analytic thinking. Gough also treats personality parameters in relation to research results in such diverse areas as biochemical factors in behavior, effects of stress, managerial styles, and executive effectiveness. Chapter 13 also contains a short appendix with a listing of representative personality inventories and publishers.

In Chapter 14, Owens states explicitly that background data are of enormous importance for both the prediction and comprehension of human behavior. He proceeds to justify his statement with an impressive listing of fifteen logically and empirically based advantages which biodata may offer over other forms of test or inventory information. In the context of my previous comments, background data can also be justified as perhaps the best possible means of merging the worlds of trait and situationally oriented concepts. Previous behavior, as recorded by a standardized background inventory, of necessity, includes behavior predisposed by individual traits as it has been modified by situational parameters. As such, biodata records should indeed aid greatly in the understanding and prediction of future dispositional orientations within particular situational contexts. Background data, as reflected in behavior episodes, may also be regarded as an indirect behavioral expression of the combined effects of the three subareas of personal attributes (aptitudes, interests, personality dimensions) discussed in Chapters 11, 12, and 13. As such, biodata can be argued conceptually to be a step or two closer to the expression of future behavioral observations than other types of test or inventory data. Owens recognizes these possibilities and shows how background measures are indeed related to a spectrum of other measures. In addition, Owens provides practical guidelines for writing, evaluating, weighting, and validating items of biographical information. He concludes the chapter by presenting and discussing his own conceptual model for the future conduct and interpretation of biodata research.

Authors of Chapters 11, 12, 13, and 14 have not given extensive attention to the fact of mean differences between various subgroups (based on sex, age, race, socioeconomic class, etc.) on various tested aptitudes, skills, interests, personality traits, and background experiences. Such differences have, of course, been amply documented and reviewed extensively in books on individual differences by authors such as Anastasi, Tyler, and Vernon. Occasionally, these mean differences have been shown consistently to be substantial. Organizational users of tests and inventories have not infrequently been guilty of attributing more behavioral meaning to such differences than may be warranted; that is, they have neglected to establish the nature of linkages between test and inventory responses and their behavioral implications in the world of work. By setting so-called "test standards" and basing decisions exclusively upon them, some practitioners have committed the error of neglecting a proper assessment of the *total* individual and his overall circumstances. As a result, the process of evaluating human attributes with tests and inventories has received a "bad press" in many circles and has been rejected absolutely in a few.

Proper use of the "instruments"—the tests, inventories, and records of personal background data—discussed in Chapters 11, 12, 13, and 14 *must* take account of their behavioral relevance in the world of work. Obviously, this is far different from saying that they should be discarded or left unused. Research about group differences, how they come about, what their behavioral relevance is, and what, if anything, can or should be done to reduce them must receive more attention. Only with increased knowledge in these areas will the measurement of human attributes, as described in the following four chapters, continue to be the first and most important step in counseling, vocational guidance, career coaching, and other organizational programs intended to promote the wise utilization of our human resources.

CHAPTER 11

Aptitudes, Abilities, and Skills

MARVIN D. DUNNETTE
The University of Minnesota

HUMAN APTITUDES AND SKILLS (physical and motor aptitudes) and their measurement are reviewed in the context of work performance in organizations. The first systematic measures of human attributes were shown to be unrelated to such aspects of human performance as learning ability. By studying very carefully the actual job of learning, Binet, however, did create standard tests predictive of learning success in school, and these became our first measures of intelligence. Throughout the present century, investigators seeking to understand the nature of intelligence have developed, administered, and studied the properties of hundreds of tests. Though persons differ in conclusions drawn from such research, most would agree that no more than fifty distinct aptitudes and skills have been shown to be of practical usefulness for evaluating the potential of individuals for successfully doing different types of work. Parallel with the development of various taxonomies of tested human attributes, other investigators have sought to develop taxonomies within the domain of human work performance. In fact, studies of aptitudes and skills on the one hand and work performance on the other have apparently yielded two quite distinct taxonomic worlds—one based mostly on standardized test responses, the other based mostly on the study and description of actual work performance. Efforts to link the two taxonomies (that is, studies designed to learn exactly what certain tested attributes may mean according to different facets of work performance) have taken many forms. Available strategies are classified and discussed in this chapter according to whether the test performance-job performance linkage is justified by empirical or inferential means and whether it is established at molar or molecular job levels. All strategies have shown reasonably good success in linking and defining the interface between the two taxonomic worlds. Nonetheless, a single taxonomic system is greatly needed in order to provide a common basis for classifying jobs, tasks, job dimensions, human attributes, aptitudes, skills, and tests. Such a system, when developed, will be of great utility in efforts directed at the development and content validation of testing programs designed to aid personnel decision making relevant to work performance in organizations.

SOME DEFINITIONS

This chapter is about certain human attributes, their measurement, and what they have to do with work performance in organizations. One of the most obvious and most readily accessible human characteristics is physical appearance. In their comprehensive review of the literature on physical attractiveness, Berscheid and Walster (1974) show that physical attractiveness is related to almost everything that happens to us, ranging from dating, love, and marriage to perceptions of our own worth, the jobs we're likely to be offered, and even our lifetime happiness. In fact, according to Feldman (1971), a *Wall Street Journal* survey of Pittsburgh University graduates revealed that taller students (6′ 2″ and over) received starting salary offers averaging over 12 percent higher than those who were under six feet tall. However, physical attractiveness, as a directly discernible and measurable attribute, is *not* what this chapter is about. Why not? Primarily because we are concerned here with those human attributes which may affect work performance *directly* without the mediating influence of perceptions based on social interaction. Similarly, this chapter does not discuss attributes, such as sex, race, age, physiognomy, body type, obesity, or any of a number of other such variables that may or may not in some way be correlated with work performance in organizations. Nor are we concerned here with human differences in vocational interests (dealt with in Chapter 12), personality (dealt with in Chapter 13), or life experiences (dealt with in Chapter 14). All these additional attributes bear importantly upon what and how people perform work assignments, but they are *not* aptitudes, skills, or abilities—which need, at this point, to be defined if we are to get on with a discussion of them.

Dictionary definitions for the three words are overlapping and confusing. They include phrases such as "natural tendency or acquired inclination," "propensity," "the quality of being apt," "competence in any field of action," "talents, mental gifts, or endowments," "competent excellence," "the ability that comes from knowledge."

Not very helpful!

In contrast, Cronbach's (1970) distinction between *maximum performance* and *typical behavior* tests is helpful.

We use these [maximum performance tests] when we wish to know how well the person can perform at his best; they may be referred to as tests of ability. The second category [typical behavior] includes those tests that seek to determine his typical performance, that is, what he is likely to do in a given situation or in a broad class of situations. Tests of personality, habits, interests, and character fall in this category.... (Cronbach, 1970, p. 35)

Aptitude, skill, and ability are, therefore, subsumed by Cronbach under the broader term *maximum performance*. Anastasi (1968) carries the distinction further. In contrasting *aptitude* and *achievement,* she states that aptitude denotes performance that "reflects the cumulative influence of a multiplicity of experiences in daily living" (p. 391), whereas achievement denotes performance involving the effects of relatively standardized sets of experiences, such as courses in French, trigonometry, or Gregg shorthand. In the present chapter, the term *aptitude* is used in much the same manner as Anastasi has defined it, and the term *ability* is used in much the same way as Anastasi has defined the term *achievement.* The two terms, clearly, are not separable into mutually exclusive categories; an individual's aptitudes and abilities *both* involve descriptions of current performance, with aptitudes encompassing more general patterns of performance and abilities being more specific. A person may have high verbal *aptitude;* with specialized training, his public speaking *ability* may become very great. Similarly, a person may possess a number of different aptitudes which, when nurtured through an engineering education, will lead to a broad range of competencies or engineering abilities.

Skill is used here to designate physical and motor aptitudes *and* abilities. The critical distinction between aptitude-ability and skill is, for our purposes, the same as that between cognitive and motor-physical. I purposely choose not to attempt a definition of *skill* according to different levels of proficiency or skill acquisition. This is in contrast with the approach used by Super and Crites (1962). They denote skill "as synonymous with *proficiency,* to denote the degree of mastery already acquired in an activity" (p. 73). In contrast, my use of the term *skill* is such that I feel no qualms about saying, for example, that a person possesses "skills" as diverse as finger dexterity, static strength, typing, shooting baskets (with a basketball), or flying an airplane. Here, too, the term obviously is not mutually exclusive of the terms *aptitude* and *ability*. In fact, the "skill" of flying an airplane, though involving a number of motor and physical activities, also involves a number of cognitive proficiencies (abilities) as well.

Perhaps the reader by now suspects that this is all part of a tedious joke. If so, the point is made. No truly satisfying closure can be derived from efforts to define these terms. They all lie within the domain of maximum performance mentioned by Cronbach, and they *are* discriminably different, but subtle nuances are not important. As we proceed, their relative distinctiveness will become more clearly apparent in relation to their behavioral referents and according to their relationships with work performance differences.

AN HISTORICAL PERSPECTIVE

Early Efforts

The reason for having a chapter devoted to aptitudes, abilities, and skills grows out of mankind's centuries old search for an-

swers about the fundamental nature of man. Philosophers' speculations have yielded all sorts of opinions and conclusions. Kant went so far as to argue against a science of psychology because he believed that human feelings, sensations, images, and thoughts could never be accessible to observation and measurement. Even so, the early Greeks were strongly aware of human differences in the ability to learn. Socrates developed and refined tests of how much his students learned, and he used the tests to assess and to enrich their learning. The Greeks also graded boys on an elaborate series of physical tests to keep tab on them as they matured and acquired the skills of manhood. Plato clearly recognized the differing abilities of men and saw the need for accurate assignment of individuals to the particular occupations (soldier, statesman, teacher, etc.) for which they were best suited so that they would make maximum contributions to society.

The modern emphasis on the importance of human differences is usually said (Anastasi, 1958; Tuddenham, 1962) to have begun with an incident occurring in 1796 at the Greenwich Observatory. Maskelyne, the astronomer royal, dismissed his assistant, Kinnebrook, because the latter recorded the times of stellar transits nearly a second later than he (Maskelyne) did. Such "tardiness" in reporting the time at which a star crossed the hairline in the telescope eyepiece was presumed at the time to be merely a matter of careless inattention. In 1816, the curiosity of the astronomer, Bessel, was whetted by reference to the incident in a history of the Greenwich Observatory, and he began to measure differences in times of estimates recorded by various pairs of astronomers. Instead of attributing such discrepancies to carelessness, he suggested that they were stable and interesting qualities of individuals, and they became known as "personal equations." Bessel collected and published data on several trained observers and noted that systematic differences between pairs of observers were also often accompanied by variations in the sizes of the differences from time to time. These observations and the records of them constitute the first instance of what might be called the true measurement of individual differences (that is, the assignment of quantitative values to observable differences in human behavior). Moreover, the measurement is directly in the context of what this chapter is about, for it did involve a concern for measuring a human attribute in relation to its effect on work performance.

But the great thrust forward in observing, describing, and measuring human attributes grew out of concerns about much broader forms of "work performance" than that represented by Bessel's concept of the Personal Equation. In fact, a major impetus toward breaking the Kantian dictum against the study of human nature was provided by the genius of Sir Francis Galton. In his book *Hereditary Genius,* published in 1869, he presented the elements of a system for classifying men according to their eminence (abilities). He stated that true eminence was extremely rare, characterizing only one person out of every 4,000, that *all* human abilities were distributed according to the normal probability curve, and that persons could, therefore, be classified according to the known frequencies of the normal distribution. Galton's first efforts simply ordered people in a number of broad categories. However, he also recognized the desirability of expressing each person's relative standing in the form of a single score or index, and, to do this, he invented the standard score. Galton's concern with eminence and the relative contributions made by persons to society led him and others to seek ways of measuring human differences in learning ability. At first, it was expected that learning ability might be evaluated by such attributes as sensory sensitivity, quickness of response, and various physical proficiencies. As a consequence, the first "mental tests" (used in laboratory investigations, most notably in Wundt's Leipzig laboratory during the late 1800s) consisted of reaction

times (in the tradition of the personal equation) and measures of tactual sensitivity, keenness of vision and hearing, strength of grip, tapping speed, and the like.

Toward Complex Processes

Fortunately, human knowledge and scientific research have frequently been blessed by the presence of certain rebellious or maverick souls who are willing to seek answers to what some may regard as rather simple minded questions. Frequently, their questions grow out of a need, either implicit or explicit, for developing knowledge on which to base quite practical decisions. Thus, it was, in the history of mental testing, that early investigators (Ebbinghaus, 1897; Sharp, 1898; Wissler, 1901) argued and showed empirically that the psychomotor and sensory tests of the day showed absolutely no relationship to differences among children or college students in their acquisition of knowledge or their ability to profit from exposure to learning environments. The demonstration was timely, indeed, for it came at exactly the time when the brilliant French psychologist, Alfred Binet, was beginning his study of learning problems encountered by French school children. In fact, in 1895, he had published an article severely criticizing the practices of sensory and motor testing. With his colleague V. Henri, Binet argued that more complex mental processes should be studied; he emphasized the importance of studying and *measuring* the more complex faculties of memory, imagery, imagination, attention, and comprehension.

During the next decade, Binet tried a number of short tasks designed to tap the complex mental processes of school children. He reasoned that as children grow they are exposed to similar things, and they have opportunities to learn and to develop skills in dealing with the world they live in. To a very real degree he set out to analyze the "job" of learning in school so that he could develop measures that might diagnose, in a standard way, the aptitude for such performance. He came to believe, therefore, that mental ability might be estimated by simply observing how a child copes with tasks similar to the ones he will be asked to face in his day-to-day learning tasks. Binet asked youngsters to identify familiar objects, name the months in order, name coins, arrange scrambled words into meaningful sentences, and define abstract words. These tasks obviously were far more complex and closer to the kind of functioning demanded in the real world than the reaction-time, sensory, and motor tests being espoused by most of the laboratory psychologists of the time.

In 1905, the first Binet Test, consisting of thirty tasks, was published and began to be used in Paris schools. He called his series of tasks a *metrical scale of intelligence,* and with this contribution Binet set off an immediate worldwide response.

It was soon apparent to other investigators that the Binet Test yielded accurate estimates of children's mental status and good predictions of school accomplishment. In this country, Lewis Terman of Stanford University translated, revised, and greatly extended the Binet Test. In 1916, his Stanford-Binet Test was published; it consisted of ninety tasks arranged in order of increasing difficulty. With this test, the measurement of individual differences came of age; an important aspect of human variation had been studied and a measure successfully developed. This development was met with widespread research activity directed toward learning more about this new test and the nature of the underlying construct it was measuring. Major revisions of the Stanford-Binet Test were published in 1937 and 1960.

THE TWO WORLDS OF BEHAVIORAL TAXONOMIES

As a brief aside, please note that a primary reason for Binet's successful unraveling of the "mystery" involving the diagnosis and measurement of learning aptitude was that he studied very carefully the job performance (i.e., learning) he wanted to predict

and inferred from those studies the most likely avenues for measuring human attributes underlying such performance. We shall see, as we continue our excursion through the broad and rocky terrain of aptitude and ability testing, that job and work performance have frequently been ignored—especially by theorists intent on understanding more fully the internal structure of the human mind. In fact, many of the aptitude and skill tests currently available were created and investigated with only a passing nod, at best, given to what they might mean in terms of human work performance in organizations. The existence of two worlds of human behavioral taxonomies (the work world and the test world) will become more evident as we proceed with our discussion of steps taken toward understanding more fully the structure of human attributes and what they may relate to in the world of work.

FROM INTELLIGENCE TO APTITUDES

The existence of multiple aptitudes was yet to be demonstrated during the time that testing, mostly through the impetus of the First World War, experienced its most rapid growth. Nowhere did Binet define intelligence as such, although Tuddenham (1962) states that throughout his career Binet continued to use the vocabulary of faculty psychology, emphasizing different facets of human endeavor as being more or less important. As described by Tuddenham, Binet's later revisions (in 1908 and 1911):

... grew like a mosaic by the gradual accretion of specific test ideas and procedures culled from a lifetime of research . . . earlier, he gave most weight to the power of memory and imagery. Later he stressed attention, conceived broadly as adaptation to new situations. Still later, he described judgment—the power to comprehend and reason—as an essential component in intelligence .... Intelligence was the sum total, or rather the resultant, of all the higher processes in complex interaction, and could be measured only by an extensive sampling of many kinds of behavior.

Regarding intelligence as a product of many abilities, Binet sought in his tests to measure not an entity or single dimension—"general intelligence"—but rather an average level—"intelligence in general." (Tuddenham, 1962, p. 489)

One to Few

Binet's conceptions of intelligence did, therefore, imply the existence and importance of a number of underlying aptitudes which have, of course, been "discovered" and studied extensively over the last fifty years by theoreticians using factor analytic methodology.[1] According to Anastasi (1968), the publication in 1928 of Kelley's *Crossroads in the Mind of Man* paved the way for studies in quest of groupings of aptitudes or *group factors*. He proposed five basic human aptitudes: manipulation of spatial relationships, facility with numbers, facility with verbal material, memory, and speed. Over many years of test development and factor analyses of them, Thurstone, his students, and other investigators (Thurstone, 1938; French, 1951) have proposed about a dozen relatively independent group-

[1] Contemporary thinking emphasizes the existence of multiple aptitudes, but the first theory of trait organization was, of course, due to Charles Spearman, an English statistician and contemporary of Binet. Using correlation to study relationships among a variety of performance areas (based on such measures as school grades, ratings, etc.), he maintained that all intellectual activities share a single common factor, called the *general factor, g,* accompanied by a number of *specific* aptitudes called *s* factors. Essentially, his theory grew out of his observation that most measures of human endeavor were positively correlated. He argued (Spearman, 1904), for example, that a high correlation between grades in French and grades in the study of the classics was evidence of the common action of the *g* factor, but that the correlation was less than perfect because of the singular actions of *s* factors specific respectively to the study of French and of the classics. Later (Spearman, 1927), as he came to work with more and more refined measures of human performance (in contrast to school grades and ratings), he recognized the existence of correlations among similar activities that could not be attributed simply to the so-called *g* factor. In a sense, these intermediate correlations were derived from clusters or groupings of tests similar in the makeup of their *s* factor content, and Spearman designated them as *group factors*.

ings of aptitudes. The seven which have been most frequently corroborated include the following:

V. *Verbal Comprehension:* to understand the meanings of words and their relationships to each other; to comprehend readily what is read; measured most completely by vocabulary knowledge tests.

W. *Word Fluency:* to be fluent in naming or making words; measured best by tests such as anagrams, naming words in a given category (such as all words beginning with the letter C), or forming many words from one larger one.

N. *Number:* to be speedy and accurate in making simple arithmetic computations such as adding, subtracting, multiplying, dividing.

S. *Space:* to perceive fixed geometric or spatial relations among figures accurately and to be able to visualize how they might look if transformed or changed in position.

M. *Memory:* to have good rote memory for paired words, symbols, lists of numbers, or other associates.

P. *Perceptual Speed:* to perceive visual details—similarities and differences—quickly and accurately; probably the same as the speed factor mentioned by Kelley.

I. *Inductive Reasoning:* to be able to discover a rule or principle and apply it in solving a problem, such as determining what is to come next in a series of numbers or words; similar to the inductive processes required in analogy tests.

Few to Many

As most readers undoubtedly are well aware, the classification of human tested abilities has gone on unabated to produce a bewildering array of factored aptitudes. Guilford's research over a period of nearly three decades has perhaps been the most systematic (Guilford, 1956b, 1959, 1967). He views mental organization as lying along three dimensions. Along one dimension are the *operations* (the things a person can do); along a second are the *contents* (the kinds of material or content on which the operations may be performed); and along the third dimension are the *products* (the outcomes or results of the operations being performed on one or more of the contents). The classifications within each of the three areas are as follows:

Operations

1. Cognition—becoming aware of the existence of something.
2. Memory—remembering what was once known.
3. Convergent Thinking—organizing content in such a way as to produce a single correct solution to a problem.
4. Divergent Thinking—utilizing content to produce a wide range or variety of possible solutions to a problem.
5. Evaluation—making judgments or decisions.

Contents

1. Semantic—contents involving language.
2. Symbolic—contents involving numerical ideas and concepts.
3. Figural—contents involving various configurations, patterns, or shapes.

4. Behavioral—contents involving the way persons behave toward one another.

Products

1. Units—bits of information.
2. Classes—groupings of units.
3. Relations—similarities, differences, and contingencies among classes.
4. Systems—groupings of relations.
5. Transformations—concepts of how things change.
6. Implications—projections of concepts to deduce events not yet observed.

A person performing successfully the operations containing semantic content might be said to have high verbal aptitude; a person performing all operations containing symbolic content might have high mathematical aptitude; one performing effectively the operations with figural content might have high spatial aptitude; and a person who could recognize, remember, solve, and evaluate contents involving interpersonal behavior would be said to possess high social aptitude.

A pictorial representation of Guilford's Structure of Intellect model is shown below:

GUILFORD'S STRUCTURE OF INTELLECT MODEL

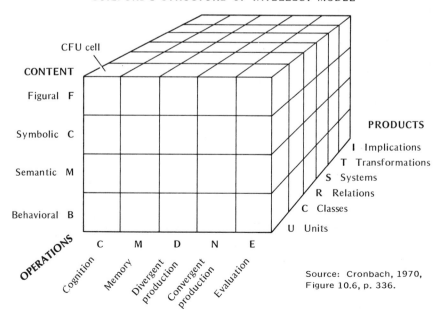

Source: Cronbach, 1970, Figure 10.6, p. 336.

The model posits the possibility of 120 distinct aptitudes based on the 120 cells derivable from five Operations, four Contents, and six Products. This is a far cry indeed from the presumed intentions of Binet when he first set out to develop indicators of school learning ability among Paris school children. The final report summarizing the forty-one technical reports of Guilford's twenty-year Aptitudes Research Project claims the identification of aptitude factors occupying ninety-eight of the 120 hypothesized cells (Guilford & Hoepfner, 1971). Many factor analysts, as noted by Carroll (1972), have argued that Guilford's factor analytic methodology contains a large element of subjectivity which does not lead to undisputable factor identification. Essentially, his method has used orthogonal principal factor rotations "forced" toward best fit solutions against target factor matrices with factor loadings postulated on the basis of the Structure of Intellect model. Perhaps the most damaging evidence against Guilford's approach has been supplied by Horn (Horn, 1967; Horn & Knapp, 1973) who has demonstrated that it is quite possible using the Procrustean methods favored by Guilford to support just about any kind of a priori theory, even those generated randomly. Horn and Knapp (1973) conclude as follows:

Results from factor-analytic studies based on subjective rotational methods thus do not provide a convincing case for a claim that SI theory is valid. This is not to say that results from such analyses *disconfirm* a series of hypotheses or a theory. Such is not the point. The point is that such results provide only about the same support as can also be provided for arbitrary theories of a kind generated by grouping variables at random to represent factors. (p. 42)

Carroll (1972) also summarizes briefly a number of other investigators' (Harris & Harris, 1971; Haynes, 1970) reanalyses by more objective methods of subsets of Guilford's matrices. The study by Haynes yielded a general factor with loadings of .30 or greater on twenty-eight of thirty-four tests he had chosen to represent seventeen of the presumably most clearly established Structure of Intellect factors. Interpretation of the factors derived by Harris and Harris seemed easily compatible with more traditional content interpretations, such as verbal comprehension, arithmetic facility, deductive reasoning, inductive reasoning, and spatial manipulation.

Quite aside from the reality status or inter-investigator agreement about the Structure of Intellect model or the nature and number of aptitudes "discovered" by Guilford and his colleagues, we feel discomfort that the model and the tests designed to confirm it have made almost no contact with dimensions of human endeavor in work settings. Guilford's Structure is a first example, therefore, of what we referred to earlier as the two worlds of behavioral taxonomies. The Structure of Intellect model has been internally oriented, making little or no contact with the real world of human work performance; as such, the theory and the tests designed to test the theory are of little direct use to us for further elaborating and understanding of the patterns of human attributes important for an understanding of work performance in organizational settings.

Divergence, Fluency, and Complexity

A singular contribution by Guilford which no one can deny, however, is his emphasis on the Operations area of Divergent Thinking. School performance, teachers' ratings, learning ability, have typically emphasized convergent thinking—that is, finding a single correct answer to problems. It is no surprise that Binet missed an additional important aspect of human ability, Divergent Thinking. He based his selection of items on ratings of non-test behaviors that failed to emphasize divergent thinking abilities. Attention to divergent thinking operations has yielded a vast amount of research activity which often has been accompanied by the fallacious assumption that tests of such operations might be directly equated with the ability to develop innovative or creative products in productive endeavor. When put to a direct test, however, such measures have nearly always proved to be indicative of little else but scores on other similarly labeled tests. Nonetheless, two aptitudes independent of the usual intelligence measures (at least, among persons with intelligence levels typical of college students), but still predictive of behaviors involving creative production have been identified. They are Ideational Fluency and Preference for Complexity-Asymmetry over Simplicity-Symmetry. Evidence in support of these generalizations has been reviewed by Wallach (1971). Ideational Fluency, as the title implies, involves simply a person's fluency or capacity for generating a large amount of ideational output whether it be in response to Rorschach cards, requests for listing uses for various objects (e.g., a yellow brick), or verbal output in suggesting answers in games of charades. Preference for Complexity-Asymmetry has been measured best by Barron and Welsh (1952) with a test of heterogeneous line drawings selected empirically to differentiate between artists and non-artists.

Careful investigations (Wallach & Wing, 1969; Csikszentmihalyi & Getzels, 1970; Singer & Whiton, 1971) of the role of Ideational Fluency in relation to creative products show it to be related to such diverse outcomes as excellence in art, original writing, winning prizes in state and regional science competitions, building scientific apparatus, and even election to positions of class leadership in school and college. Similarly, the preference for Complexity-Asymmetry has been shown to be related to ratings of the extent to which different practitioners have made significant contributions to fields as diverse as art, architecture, mathematics, and science (Dellas & Gaier, 1970).

As a means of helping to reduce somewhat the confusion induced by the bewilder-ing array of factors suggested by many investigators, a "kit" of reference tests was assembled and distributed by the Educational Testing Service (French, Ekstrom, & Price, 1963). The kit covered twenty-four aptitude factors with two to five tests for measuring each factor.

Many to Few

Very recently, the factors included in the 1963 kit have been reexamined in light of all the research reported over the last decade. Ekstrom (1973) reviews the current status of each of those twenty-four factors and lists also additional factors which recent research suggests may be worthy for investigation in the years ahead. In addition, her report is an excellent source for examining the relationships between these aptitude factors and the various models of intelligence suggested by Thurstone (1938), Cattell (1971), Guilford, Guttman (1970), Royce (1973), and Harris and Harris (1971). The factors retained from the 1963 kit are listed and briefly defined as follows:

1. *Flexibility of Closure:* ability to "hold in mind" a particular visual percept (configuration) and find it embedded in distracting material.

2. *Speed of Closure:* ability to "take in" a perceptual field as a whole, to "fill in" unseen portions with likely material and thus to coalesce somewhat disparate parts into a visual percept.

3. *Associative Fluency:* ability to produce words from a restricted area of meaning.

4. *Expressional Fluency:* ability to supply proper verbal expressions for ideas already stated or to find a suitable expression which would fit a given semantic frame of reference. Expressional fluency differs from ideational fluency in requiring rephrasing of ideas already given instead of the production of new ideas.

5. *Ideational Fluency:* ability to quickly produce ideas and exemplars of an idea about a stated condition or object; the abil-

ity which provides for rapid production of ideas fitting a given specification.

6. *Word Fluency:* facility in producing isolated words that contain one or more structural, essentially phonetic, restrictions, without reference to the meaning of the words; this factor accounts for the ability to rapidly produce words fulfilling specific symbolic or structural requirements.

7. *Induction:* ability in forming and testing hypotheses directed at finding a principle of relationship among elements and applying the principle to identifying an element fitting the relationship; induction, deduction, syllogistic reasoning, and spontaneous flexibility probably combine into a second-order reasoning factor.

8. *Length Estimation:* recommended to be dropped from the next edition of the kit.

9. *Mechanical Knowledge:* recommended to be dropped from the kit revision.

10. *Associative Memory:* ability to remember bits of unrelated material; upon presentation of one part of previously associated but otherwise unrelated material, ability to recall another part.

11. *Span Memory:* ability to recall perfectly for immediate reproduction a series of items after only one presentation of the series.

12. *Number Facility:* ability to manipulate numbers in arithmetical operations rapidly; facility in performing elementary arithmetical operations (typically under speeded conditions); the factor does *not* determine higher mathematical skills or complex mathematical reasoning.

13. *Originality:* ability to produce remotely associated, clever, or uncommon responses.

14. *Perceptual Speed:* speed in finding figures, making comparisons, and carrying out other very simple tasks involving visual perception.

15. *General Reasoning:* ability to solve a broad range of reasoning problems including those of a mathematical nature.

16. *Semantic Redefinition:* ability to imagine different functions for objects or parts of objects and thus use them in novel

ways to accomplish stated purposes; the status of this factor is considered to be tentative; it may be a sub-factor of various flexibility measures.

17. *Syllogistic Reasoning:* ability to reason from stated premises to their necessary conclusion; ability in formal reasoning from stated premises to rule out non-permissible combinations and thus to arrive at necessary conclusions; closely related to Thurstone's original Deductive Reasoning factor.

18. *Spatial Orientation:* ability to perceive spatial patterns or to maintain orientation with respect to objects in space; perception of the position and configuration of objects in space; ability to put together by visual imagination parts that are out of place in a visual pattern and to identify such "out of place" percepts.

19. *Sensitivity to Problems:* research over the last decade suggests that the existence of this factor is ambiguous at best and that it probably should not be included in the revised kit of reference tests.

20. *Spatial Scanning:* speed in visually exploring a wide or complicated spatial field; marker tests for this factor may have to be revised.

21. *Verbal Comprehension:* knowledge of words and their meaning as well as to application of this knowledge in understanding connected discourse; marker tests for the Verbal Comprehension factor are all vocabulary tests.

22. *Visualization:* ability to manipulate or transform the image of spatial patterns into other visual arrangements; ability to manipulate visual percepts (to imagine change in forms) and thus to "see" how things would look under altered conditions.

23. *Figural Adaptive Flexibility:* ability to try out in imagination various possible arrangements of the elements of a visual pattern and thus to converge on one arrangement which satisfies several stated criteria; however, the nature of this factor has not been clearly demonstrated; in order to be included in the revised kit, new types of marker tests will have to be developed.

24. *Spontaneous Semantic Flexibility:*

facility in imagining diverse functions and classifications for objects; this factor probably has not been well demonstrated outside of Guilford's laboratory.

Ekstrom's discussion of the many research studies done to aid in providing further clarification and definition of the above factors suggests that the ones above numbered 8, 9, 16, 19, 20, 23, and 24 have either been shown to be too narrow or that they remain poorly defined by existing "marker" tests. Moreover, of the remaining seventeen factors, Flexibility and Speed of Closure aptitudes (1 and 2) seem indistinct from each other, the four fluency factors are closely related and quite indistinct from Originality (13), General Reasoning (15) is difficult to separate from other reasoning factors, and the Spatial Orientation and Visualization factors (18 and 22) are not easily distinguishable.

The upshot of all this, therefore, is that the following much more brief listing of relatively independent factors seems to do no severe damage to the findings summarized by Ekstrom:

1. Flexibility and Speed of Closure
2. Fluency
3. Inductive Reasoning
4. Associative (Rote) Memory
5. Span Memory
6. Number Facility
7. Perceptual Speed
8. Syllogistic (Deductive) Reasoning
9. Spatial Orientation and Visualization
10. Verbal Comprehension

Remarkably, the years of factorial research since Thurstone's seminal contributions have added only minor modifications to his list of seven Primary Mental Abilities which we already have commented upon earlier in this chapter.[2]

MOTOR AND PHYSICAL SKILLS

So far, we have traced and discussed the development of measures of human cognitive aptitudes—those aptitudes presumed to be important in developing an awareness and understanding of the elements of our environment. We have said nothing about the physical manipulation of objects in the environment. This involves the specification and measurement of *motor skills,* many of which would seem to be relevant to the world of work. For example, the job of secretary involves not only a wide range of cognitive abilities, such as verbal comprehension, perceptual speed, memory, and reasoning, but also, possibly, whatever motor skills may be necessary to handle a typewriter adequately. Scores of other jobs could be named (for example, bricklayer, auto mechanic, and watch repairman) that require relatively greater or lesser amounts of motor proficiency.

---

[2] Ekstrom's list of possible "new" factors and their definitions are listed below (this listing includes only those which Ekstrom regarded as well defined):

(1) *Automatic Processes:* individual differences in processes that are susceptible to a high degree of automatization. (2) *Behavioral Relations and Systems:* ability to judge the interaction between two individuals so as to indicate how one of the individuals feels about the situation. (3) *Chunking Memory:* capacity of the memory to use a limited number of symbols to represent larger amounts of information; appears to offer promise for investigators interested in memory because of its correspondence to processes that have appeared in laboratory studies of memory. (4) *Concept Formation:* a subfactor of induction; despite this, it is suggested that it be included as a separate factor to allow researchers to differentiate between the two steps in the inductive reasoning process: (a) the attainment of the concept from the stimuli, and (b) the selection of other stimuli which do or do not exhibit the concept; the ability to cognize an abstract class or relation, usually by naming. (5) *Integration:* ability simultaneously to bear in mind and to combine or integrate several conditions, premises, or rules, in order to produce the correct response. (6) *Visual Memory:* tests which seem to be the best markers for visual memory include Map Memory, which requires the subject to select the one of five small maps that is an accurate reproduction of a section of a large map previously studied; Plane Formation, which requires the subject to indicate the sections of a grid where planes were seen in a study picture; Position Memory, which requires the subject to recall the items as they appeared on a study page; and Space Memory, which requires the subject to identify the symbols that were located in each section of a study page. (7) *Verbal Closure:* ability to solve problems, requiring the identification of words when some of the letters are missing, disarranged, or mixed with other letters.

Another grouping of skills, similar to motor proficiencies but distinct from them, involves gross physical performances best illustrated probably by differing degrees of competence, proficiency, or physical fitness in various athletic endeavors. Fleishman has studied both motor skills (Fleishman, 1962, 1972) and physical fitness (Fleishman, 1964, 1972) more extensively than any other investigator.

A major conclusion from a wealth of research on motor skills is that these skills are highly specific. Tests designed to measure skills such as finger dexterity, steadiness, speed of response, and eye-hand coordination show low intercorrelations. Summarizing over a decade of factor-analytic results with motor skills tests, Fleishman (1962) concluded that there are eleven fairly independent groupings of motor skills. These are:

1. *Control precision:* involving tasks requiring finely controlled muscular adjustments, such as moving a lever to a precise setting.

2. *Multi-limb coordination:* involving the ability to coordinate the movements of a number of limbs simultaneously, such as packing a box with both hands.

3. *Response orientation:* involving the ability to make correct and accurate movements in relation to a stimulus under highly speeded conditions, such as reaching out and flicking a switch when a warning horn sounds.

4. *Reaction time:* involving the speed of a person's response when a stimulus appears, such as pressing a key in response to a bell.

5. *Speed of arm movement:* involving the speed of gross arm movements where accuracy is not required, such as gathering trash or debris and throwing it into a large pile.

6. *Rate control:* involving the ability to make continuous motor adjustments relative to a moving target changing in speed and direction, such as holding a rod on a moving rotor.

7. *Manual dexterity:* involving skillful arm and hand movements in handling rather large objects under speeded conditions, such as placing blocks rapidly into a form board.

8. *Finger dexterity:* involving skillful manipulations of small objects (such as nuts and bolts) with the fingers.

9. *Arm-hand steadiness:* involving the ability to make precise arm-hand positioning movements that do not require strength or speed, such as threading a needle.

10. *Wrist-finger speed:* involving rapid tapping movements with the wrist and fingers, such as transmitting a continuous signal with a telegraphic key.

11. *Aiming:* involving an extremely narrow ability defined by a test in which the examinee places dots in circles as rapidly as possible.

Fleishman (1964) found that nine factors account for much of the common variance in performance over 100 different physical fitness measures, and he has also developed a manual describing the specific physical tests and their mode of administration for maximizing the accuracy of determining each of the nine factors. As described by Fleishman (1972):

Briefly, the factors and tests identified are as follows: (a) static strength: maximum force that can be exerted against external objects (lifting weights, dynamometer tests); (b) dynamic strength: muscular endurance in exerting force continuously or repeatedly; power of the muscles to propel, support, or move one's body over time (e.g., pull-ups); (c) explosive strength: ability to mobilize energy effectively for bursts of muscular effort (e.g., sprints, jumps); (d) trunk strength: limited dynamic strength specific to trunk muscles (e.g., leg lifts or sit-ups); (e) extent flexibility: ability to flex or stretch trunk and back muscles (twist and touch test); (f) dynamic flexibility: ability to make repeated, rapid, flexing trunk movements; resistance of muscles in recovery from strain (rapid repeated bending over and floor touching test); (g) gross body coordination: ability to coordinate action of several parts of body while body is in motion (cable jump test); (h) gross body equilibrium: ability to maintain balance with nonvisual cues (rail walk test); (i) stamina: capacity to sustain maximum effort requiring cardiovascular exertion (600-yard run-walk). (p. 1020)

As mentioned, the many tests of motor skills and of physical proficiencies are not highly correlated. As a result, in contrast with the factors defined in cognitive areas, motor and physical skills factors are defined by tests with relatively small loadings (i.e., in the 30s and 40s) and low communalities. Motor functions show a high degree of specificity. In fact, one could argue with a fair degree of confidence that Spearman's early conception of a general factor, *g*, accompanied by many specific factors in the cognitive domain *does* apply to the motor skills domain—with the modification, of course, that the emphasis must be placed on the specificity of skills rather than upon any so-called general skill factor.

The area of motor skill and physical testing is complicated even further by Fleishman's and others' findings (Hempel & Fleishman, 1955; Ghiselli & Haire, 1960; Fleishman, 1967; Frederickson, 1969; Hinrichs, 1970; Alvares & Hulin, 1972; Buss, 1973) that the acquisition of motor abilities necessary in the actual performance of work assignments involves different skills at different stages of practice. The typical finding in such investigations is that proficiency in the early phases of learning a new task is related most closely to non-motor factors, such as spatial orientation, mechanical experience, and perceptual speed. With increasing practice, the importance of motor factors increases, tends to level off, and finally to subside to a relatively low level of importance as full task proficiency is accomplished.

Three important implications of these findings are apparent for the industrial psychologist practitioner. First, the prediction of ultimate task performance in motor and physical abilities areas is rendered extremely difficult and must, at the very least, be cognizant of the need to specify what common or standard level of practice or training candidates should have had at the time performance criterion measures are to be gathered. Second, as Fleishman (1972) notes, it may be possible to increase the efficiency of skill training by concentrating throughout the training period on those aptitudes or skills required for final proficiency rather than those required only in the early stages of acquisition. Parker and Fleishman (1961) did indeed show successfully that a specialized training approach designed to take account of different requisite skills at different stages of practice produced faster learning than a more traditional learning approach. The third, and most important, implication of these findings involves the vexing problem that increased specificity in task performance implies that the performance becomes increasingly a function of habits and skills acquired in the specific task being learned. It is crucial to define more fully what the makeup may be of that portion of performance variance now termed as specific to the individual tasks being learned. So far, research efforts in this direction have proven to be unusually intractable and have failed to yield any new evidence for increasing the predictive utility for motor and physical skill measures in relation to the development of task proficiency. However, Anastasi (1968) has pointed out that consideration of the validity of motor tests needs to differentiate between *complex* motor tests that closely resemble or "sample" the criterion performance and tests of the more basic groupings of motor functions or factors discovered by Fleishman. Complex, custom made tests which come close to approximating work samples have typically shown good validities, whereas the commercially available tests of motor skills and physical fitness have shown disappointingly low validities.

Here again, we must face up to the "two worlds of human taxonomy"; in this instance, the problems are perhaps even more complicated than in the case of cognitive taxonomies. The factored taxonomies of standardized motor skill and physical fitness measures, though of theoretical interest, seem *not* to reflect to any satisfying degree the highly specific patterns of human performance in the real work world of organizational settings. Yet, the development and use of work sample type tests is not often practicable because new and different tests would probably need to be developed to match each new and different criterion performance. A middle ground is necessary. Taxonomies of task activities encompassing real work performance may provide a necessary first step. From these, we should be able to infer the nature of human attributes necessary for carrying out various groupings of task and work activities and use either existing or new tests to predict real world work performances.

TAXONOMIES FROM THE WORLD OF WORK

We turn now to descriptions of recent approaches which have focused in some greater detail on behaviors and behavioral taxonomies derived directly from work performance as opposed to test performance.[3]

---

[3] In passing, however, we do not wish to imply that factorial methods for the development of tests—particularly multiple test batteries—have proven entirely useless for predicting work performance in organizational settings. In fact, just the opposite is the case, and several multiple aptitude batteries are in widespread use for such purposes (a brief accounting of their validity "records" for different job and work activities is given toward the end of this chapter). Some of the better known and more widely used factored aptitude test batteries are described below:

1. *General Aptitude Test Battery (GATB).* This battery was developed by the United States Employment and Training Service for use in State Employment Service Offices (Dvorak, 1956). The factors currently covered by the GATB include the following:

N. *Numerical Aptitude:* measured by arithmetic computation and reasoning tests.

V. *Verbal Aptitude:* measured by a vocabulary test.

S. *Spatial Aptitude:* measured by a test involving both the ability to visualize three-dimensional objects in three dimensions and to visualize the effects of moving them in three dimensions.

G. *Intelligence:* a score derived from summing the scores on V, N, and S.

P. *Form Perception:* measured by tests requiring the matching of tools and of geometric forms.

Q. *Clerical Perception:* measured by a test requiring the matching of names.

K. *Motor Coordination:* measured by a test involving placing pencil marks in a series of squares.

F. *Finger Dexterity:* measured by performance tests involving assembly and disassembly of rivets and washers.

M. *Manual Dexterity:* measured by performance tests involving the movement of pegs in a board.

2. *Differential Aptitude Tests (DAT)* (Bennett, Seashore, & Wesman, 1951). These tests are used mostly for educational and vocational counseling of students in grades eight through twelve, but they also have come to be widely used in industry. The DAT battery yields eight scores as follows:

Verbal Reasoning
Numerical Ability
Abstract Reasoning
Clerical Speed and Accuracy
Mechanical Reasoning
Space Relations
Spelling
Grammar

3. *Primary Mental Abilities (PMA).* Several batteries of tests have been published over the years growing out of Thurstone's original factor analytic investigations. The most recent revision was in 1962 and yields scores for five factors: *Verbal Meaning, Number Facility, Reasoning, Perceptual Speed,* and *Spatial Relations.*

4. *Flanagan Industrial Tests (FIT)* (SRA Catalogue for Business, 1974). This battery consists of independent measures of eighteen aptitudes that are reputed to be important, either singly or in combination, in supervisory, technical, office, skilled, and entry jobs. The eighteen tests (requiring five-to-fifteen minutes each) in the FIT battery are adaptations of the Flanagan Aptitude Classification Tests which were developed to measure the critical elements discovered and identified through systematic job analyses of hundreds of occupations, most of which were common to Air Force jobs. The names and brief descriptions of the eighteen tests in the battery are given below:

(1) *Inspection:* measures ability to spot flaws or imperfections in a series of articles quickly and accurately; measures the type of ability required in inspecting finished or semifinished manufactured items. (2) *Memory:* measures ability to remember the codes learned in test 2. (3) *Precision:* measures speed and accuracy in making very small circular finger movements with one hand and with both hands working together; samples ability to do precision work with small objects. (4) *Assembly:* measures ability to "see" how an object would look when put together according to instructions, without having an actual model to work with; samples ability to visualize the appearance of an object from a number of separate parts. (5) *Scales:* measures speed and accuracy in read-

Up to this point, we have only implied possible differences in various taxonomic systems depending upon the data sources used for deriving them. We have given heavy emphasis to factorial investigations, such as those by Thurstone, Guilford, Fleishman, and others because they have been mostly responsible for the nature of the major aptitude and skill tests and batteries currently available for use in predicting work performance in organizations.

However, we turn now to a consideration of other data sources, the taxonomic systems derived from them and their relative usefulness for industrial and organizational behavior and performance prediction.[4]

Behavior Classification in Organizations

Obviously, systematic research efforts directed toward better understanding of work roles in organizations must face problems of behavior classification. We can talk about the impact of organizational variables upon organization members' behavior or the reverse; we can define successful performance in behavioral terms; we can view an individual's past behavior as an indicator of likely future behavior; we can reinforce certain behavior patterns through the use of reward systems. All of these, however, imply that we know how to classify behavior in ways that are meaningful to the problem at hand. It is this root problem of behavior classifica-

---

ing scales, graphs, and charts; samples scale-reading of the type required in engineering and similar technical occupations. (6) *Coordination:* measures ability to coordinate hand and arm movements; involves the ability to control movements in a smooth and accurate manner when these movements must be continually guided and readjusted in accordance with observations of their results. (7) *Judgment and Comprehension:* measures ability to read with understanding, to reason logically, and to use good judgment in practical situations. (8) *Arithmetic:* measures skill in working with numbers—adding, subtracting, multiplying, and dividing. (9) *Patterns:* measures ability to reproduce simple pattern outlines in a precise and accurate way; requires the ability to sketch a pattern as it would look if it were turned over. (10) *Components:* measures ability to identify important component parts. (11) *Tables:* measures performance in reading two types of tables—the first consists entirely of numbers; the second contains only words and letters of the alphabet. (12) *Mechanics:* measures understanding of mechanical principles and ability to analyze mechanical movements. (13) *Expression:* measures feeling for and knowledge of correct English; samples certain communication tasks involved in getting ideas across in writing and talking. (14) *Mathematics/Reasoning.* (15) *Vocabulary.* (16) *Planning.* (17) *Ingenuity.* (18) *Electronics.* (Note: The test manual does not provide description of the exact nature of the content for the last five tests mentioned above.)

5. *Employee Aptitude Survey (EAS)* (Ruch & Ruch, 1963). The EAS battery consists of ten short (five-minute) tests developed primarily for use in industrial and organizational settings. Considering their length, the equivalent form reliabilities are acceptably high, ranging from .75 to .91. Moreover, the authors recom-

mend using the tests in combination with one another as a means of enhancing both the reliabilities and validities of personnel decisions based upon them. The ten tests of the battery include the following: (1) Verbal Comprehension; (2) Numerical Ability; (3) Visual Pursuit; (4) Visual Speed and Accuracy; (5) Space Visualization; (6) Numerical Reasoning; (7) Verbal Reasoning; (8) Word Fluency; (9) Manual Speed and Accuracy; and (10) Symbolic Reasoning. Factorial studies show that the following factors are included in the ten-test battery:

Verbal Comprehension: ability to use words in thinking and communicating.

Number: ability to handle numbers and work with numerical material.

Pursuit: ability to make rapid, accurate scanning movements with the eyes.

Perceptual Speed: ability to perceive small detail rapidly and accurately within a mass of material.

Visualization: ability to visualize objects in three-dimensional space.

Inductive Reasoning: ability to discover relationships and derive principles.

Word Fluency: ability to produce words rapidly, without regard to meaning or quality.

Syntactic Evaluation: ability to apply principles to arrive at a unique solution.

[4] I extend my thanks to Professor George W. England of the University of Minnesota for allowing me to use portions of his unpublished paper, *Behavior Classification in Organizations,* for this section of the chapter. A far more comprehensive survey of concepts and methods used in job taxonomies is given by Prien and Ronan (1971) and by McCormick in Chapter 15 of this *Handbook.*

tion that persists whenever we want to include the concept of behavior in our predictive equations, our explanations or inferences.

The major issues of behavior classification may be stated in terms of:

Objectives: Why we classify behavior
Content: What we want to classify
Methods: How we classify behavior

OBJECTIVE. We focus in this chapter upon a single, primary objective for behavior classification, that of establishing a link between categories of human work performance and categories of human attributes.[5] This broad objective presupposes certain sub-objectives, such as task classification, job classification or the development of job families, worker and employee classification, and the determination and classification of job and worker requirements.

CONTENT AND METHOD. The content question (i.e., what is to be classified) may seem secondary, but actually the answer about what can be classified places bounds on how and for what purposes any given taxonomy may be used. Wheaton (1968) reviewed four bases for behavior classification pre-

viously suggested by Altman (1966) and McGrath and Altman (1966). The four are: behavior description approach, behavior requirements approach, ability requirements approach, and task characteristics approach.

The *behavior description* approach focuses upon observations and descriptions of the behavior that is actually engaged in while performing a task. Emphasis is placed on what *is* done as opposed to what *should be* done, or what *could be* done, or what *must be* done. The *behavior requirements* approach places primary emphasis on behavior that *should be* emitted or which is thought to be required in order to achieve a certain level of performance. Here, one classifies behavior in terms of what *must be* done for successful performance as opposed to what *is* done.

While the behavior description and behavior requirements approaches provide different starting points for determining what is to be classified, they do converge at certain points. For example, a description of behavior common to a group of successful performers is one obvious approach for determining the so-called behavior requirements of the task or set of tasks being studied.

The *ability requirements* approach suggests a classification system in terms of the aptitudes, skills, or other attributes required by a task or set of tasks. The approach is similar to the behavior requirement approach but focuses on human attributes required by the task rather than the actual behavior required by the task. Obviously, the link between task behavior and human attributes must be accomplished by some means involving some degree of human expertise or inferential judgment. Finally, the *task characteristics* approach views the task as a set of conditions which elicit performance. These conditions are imposed upon the operator and have an existence quite apart from the activities they may trigger, the processes they call into play, or the abilities they may require of an operator. The view is that tasks can be described and dif-

---

[5] Though of obvious relevance, we do not intend here to offer an extended argument in support of our obvious assumption that human traits (attributes) do indeed exist to a sufficiently consistent degree across situations so that the prediction of human work performance can realistically be undertaken on the basis of tested aptitudes and skills *apart* from situational modifiers. This is not to say that a taxonomy of situations (Frederiksen, 1972) cannot or should not be taken into account as an aid in enhancing the accuracy of such predictions. Indeed, I have argued strongly (Dunnette, 1963, 1966) that exactly such individualized prediction efforts should be sought. My point simply is to state that I disagree with the thrust of much current emphasis which seems to be seeking to account for human behavior largely in terms of the situation in which it occurs. Quite the contrary is, in my opinion, far closer to reality. The interested and/or skeptical reader may wish to examine Anastasi's examination of evidence bearing on the formation of psychological traits (Anastasi, 1970) and the excellent recent critiques of situationism in psychology by Bowers (1973) and Stagner (1973).

ferentiated according to the intrinsic objective properties which they possess.

Taxonomic Approaches and Results Obtained

BEHAVIOR DESCRIPTION. Taxonomies based on behavior descriptions of jobs and occupations have been carried out most comprehensively and most successfully by McCormick and his colleagues (McCormick & Ammerman, 1960; McCormick, Jeanneret, & Mecham, 1972), and different approaches have been developed by Berliner, Angell, and Shearer (1964), Reed (1967), and Fine (1963). These methods and others are described fully by McCormick in Chapter 15 of this *Handbook*. Thus, only the major results obtained by McCormick et al. are detailed here.

The Position Analysis Questionnaire (PAQ) developed by McCormick and his colleagues contains 189 job elements (defined as a general class of behaviorally related job activities, including those involving behavioral adjustments required by features of the job context or environment) sampling six behavioral areas[6] focused on what employees do to get their jobs done. Each element may be present or not present to different degrees or differ in importance in different degrees for any given job. Cooperation was obtained from seventy industrial organizations, and the PAQ was used by job analysts and supervisors to describe 536 different jobs.[7] Pairs of analysts independently described a subsample of jobs with levels of agreement shown by average cor-

relations ranging between .74 and .89. Factor analysis was utilized on two subsamples of jobs of 268 each divided randomly; component structures were obtained for each and compared by means of Tucker's (1951) coefficient of congruence. Principal Component solutions were derived and rotated via a varimax criterion. Extraction of components was set to terminate when eigenvalues fell below 1.0. The taxonomy of worker behavior dimensions and the percent of common variance attributed to each are shown below according to the analysis across all jobs:

Dimension	Percent Common Variance
Decision/communication/ social	14.1
Skilled activities	9.3
Physical activities/related context conditions	7.3
Equipment/vehicle operation	5.3
Information processing activities	4.8

Because the above dimensions are extremely broad and contain individually so many job elements, separate factor analyses also were conducted within each of the six behavioral areas of the PAQ. These more detailed results are shown in Table 3 of Chapter 15. In each instance, considerably more common variance was accounted for by job dimensions than was the case for the overall analysis. The amounts ranged from 47 percent for Job Context elements to 65 percent for Mediation Process elements. In total, twenty-seven job dimensions were identified and defined according to the elements making them up.

As just one further example of the application of the PAQ, Taylor (1970) used it in a pilot investigation of seventy-six jobs located in four regions of the State Farm Insurance Companies. He "scored" the resulting descriptions according to the dimensions

---

[6] The six behavioral areas and the number of elements in each are as follows: *Information Input* (35), *Mediation Processes* (14), *Work Output* (50), *Interpersonal Activities* (36), *Work Situation and Job Context* (18), and *Miscellaneous Aspects* (36).

[7] The range of jobs represented was very great but did show a distribution which somewhat overrepresented professional, managerial, and clerical jobs at the expense of underrepresenting skilled, semi-skilled, and service occupations. In one phase of the analysis, however, a subsample of 100 jobs representative of the distribution in the labor force was chosen for study.

developed by McCormick et al. (1972) and formed job families on the basis of statistically stable and similar profiles. Six[8] job groupings were derived in this way. Study of the six job family profiles by Taylor shows that the job clusters differ substantially on the following eleven PAQ dimensions:

Perceptual interpretation
Information from people
Decision making
Information processing

Manual control and coordination
Control/equipment operation
Use of finger controlled devices versus physical work
Skilled/technical activities

Communication of decisions/judgments
Staff and related activities
Personally demanding situations

In essence then, Taylor's study shows how a large number of jobs in an organization can be cast against a common taxonomy as a means of discovering important behavioral differences and similarities among them. His approach, as noted, depends entirely upon the use of a standard check list of employee job behaviors (in this instance, the PAQ) as a basis for discovering more fundamental behavior dimensions relevant to work performance. The additional step taken by Taylor of clustering jobs according to similar dimensional profiles, though not an essential ingredient for determining taxonomic categories via the behavior description approach, does yield information of great potential usefulness for a variety of personnel administrative purposes.

BEHAVIOR REQUIREMENTS. The behavior requirements approach for deriving work performance taxonomies differs methodologically from the behavior description approach in one very important way. The approach typically does *not* utilize any standard

check list of job behaviors or elements but seeks instead to generate groupings of critical requirements or behaviors from job incumbents or from persons who have had a wealth of experience with the job or jobs being studied. Approaches to task analysis involving primarily motor response and skilled performance in jobs have been described by Gagné (1962), Gagné and Bolles (1963), Miller (1966), and much more recently by a series of reports from the Taxonomy Project of the American Institutes for Research and summarized most completely by Farina and Wheaton (1971) and Theologus and Fleishman (1971).

For our purposes, however, I believe a far more fruitful taxonomic strategy is the Behavior Observation Scaling methodology growing out of the critical incidents technique pioneered by Flanagan (1954). Though the method was used by several early investigators in studying a variety of executive and supervisory jobs (Flanagan, 1951; Kay, 1959; Williams, 1956), the full usefulness of the method as a classificatory technique for job behavior requirements was not apparent until it was used to determine the behavioral requirements of a nurse's job by Smith and Kendall (1963). Since then, the method has been applied to many different jobs including department managers in retail stores (Campbell, Dunnette, Arvey, & Hellervik, 1973), fire fighters (Heckman, 1973a, 1973b), clerical personnel (Borman, 1974; Palef & Stewart, 1971), grocery clerks (Folgi, Hulin, & Blood, 1971), production foremen in auto assembly plants (Hellervik, Dunnette, & Arvey, 1971), Naval officers (Borman, Dunnette, & Johnson, 1974), several different police functions (Heckman, Groner, Dunnette, & Johnson, 1972; Landy & Farr, 1973), first line supervisors in a large insurance firm (Borman, 1973), and salesmen, research and development scientists, and accountants working for an oil company (Dunnette, Groner, Holtzman, & Johnson, 1972).

Essentially, the methodology involves a series of four to six workshop sessions of about two or three hours each with persons

---

[8] The six job families contained respectively 11, 30, 8, 8, 10, and 9 jobs.

who are very familiar with the job being studied. The primary purpose of these sessions is to elicit stories or anecdotes describing critical incidents that the participants have observed over their years of experience in knowing and working with persons who have been in the jobs being studied. Participants actually write down their stories on forms similar to the ones shown in Figures 1 and 2. Much time is spent during the early portions of such workshops in showing participants the importance of describing job behavior—that is, *what employees actually did* that proved to be successful or unsuccessful and *not what employees who did such things were like.* Thus, a diligent effort is made to avoid obtaining employee attributes or traits in favor of obtaining detailed descriptions of job behaviors—descriptions which, because of the focus on eliciting "suc-

cessful" and "unsuccessful" behaviors, form the basis for categories reflecting the behavioral requirements—desirable and undesirable behaviors—of the jobs being studied. In addition to avoiding traits in these descriptions, workshop participants must also be cautioned against simply focusing their descriptions around the behaviors of just one or a few outstandingly successful or unsuccessful performers. Such a "set" very probably would narrow unduly the range of job behaviors being sampled. Though at first the concept of *behavior* sampling instead of

---

Date _____
Job Described _____
Your Job _____
Your Department _____

PERFORMANCE INCIDENT RECORD FORM

Think back over roughly the last six months to two years, long enough for you to have observed the activities required in the job under consideration. Focus your attention on any specific thing that you saw a person do that made you think of him as a highly effective worker, an average worker, a very ineffective worker, or any shade of effectiveness in between. In other words, think of a specific performance incident that gave you some feeling for how well the individual was doing his job. (Please do *not* record the names of the people involved.)

1. What were the circumstances leading up to the incident?

2. Tell specifically what the individual did that made you think of him as a good, average, or poor performer at that time.

3. How effective is this incident? (circle a number)

   Low 1 2 3 4 5 6 7 8 9 High

4. What performance area does this represent?

Job Described _____

PERFORMANCE INCIDENT FORM

Think back over your career and many things will probably come to mind about what people did in situations. Some of them may be funny, some of them may make you angry to think about them again, while some of them may bring many warm memories. Some or all of these may be job performance incidents. They are noteworthy for our purposes if they are indicative of how well or poorly a person performed his job. In other words, think of a performance incident that gave you some feeling of how a person was performing his job.

1. What were the circumstances leading up to the incident?

2. What did the individual do that made you feel he was a good, average, or poor performer?

3. In which job performance category does this incident fall?

Figure 1. Critical incident record form used to study the job of Naval officer.

Figure 2. Critical incident record form used to study behavior requirements of jobs in general.

people sampling is foreign and rather difficult for most participants to grasp, they nearly always finally experience a kind of "ah ha!" insight, and begin then to pour forth written incidents in large volume; a typical group of twelve to fifteen knowledgeable and conscientious participants will often produce 200 to 300 such incidents over the span of the first two or three meetings.

Next steps involve editing slightly the incidents (being careful to retain the essence of each), forming preliminary performance dimensions, and utilizing later workshop sessions to work out final specifications and definitions for the categories which cover sufficiently the total range of behavioral requirements for the job or jobs being studied. These later steps have been detailed more fully elsewhere (Campbell, Dunnette, Lawler, & Weick, 1970; Campbell, Dunnette, Arvey, & Hellervik, 1973).

In order to give the reader a feeling for the nature of incidents actually gathered and how they ultimately form the basis for a job taxonomy of behavioral requirements, we offer below the following twenty-five inci-

---

1
When "black boxes" in a fire control system began failing, an officer opened one and found that a transistor had failed. By replacing transistors with some purchased locally, the usual repair cost of $165 per box was avoided and four weeks' time saved in making the system operational.

2
An officer used the same training program over and over again without realizing that much of his material was out of date.

3
An officer prepared a series of slide lectures for his training program far in advance of the date he wanted to give them; consequently, when he was ill, someone else was able to continue the program.

4
An officer ignored some parts of his CO's plans on improving morale because he did not agree with them and didn't believe they would work.

5
An officer did nothing about reducing noise levels even though he had to shout to be heard and often could not get the word across to his men.

6
While carrying out his assignment according to his CO's orders, an officer developed a number of new ideas with some potentially better alternatives. The officer submitted a report to his CO in which he discussed the strengths and weaknesses of these new alternatives.

7
An officer anticipated his superior's request for a full report of an accident and had the report ready when his superior called.

8
An officer sent a report to his CO which covered only the first two days of an important four-day mission.

9
An officer in uniform who was drinking and swapping sea stories with several friends at a bar quickly paid the bill and convinced his group to leave when it appeared that several civilians at a nearby table were distressed about their raucous behavior.

10
An officer set a proficiency goal for his training program, developed his training exercises with that goal in mind, and then measured his program's effectiveness against that proficiency goal.

11
An officer who was serving as best man at his brother's wedding showed up fifteen minutes late wearing a dirty and badly wrinkled uniform.

12
An officer was able to repair a malfunctioning sonar unit by using several parts from other pieces of equipment not in use, and thereby restoring the sonar unit to full operation during important surveillance operations.

dents which were elicited from a group of twenty-two Naval Commanders and Captains during workshop sessions undertaken to determine the behavioral requirements of the job of Naval Officer.

The reader may wish to try his hand at classifying these incidents into five categories of behavioral requirements for the job of Naval Officer. Naval officers who participated in the workshop sessions agreed upon categories which they titled: Solving Immediate Problems; Carrying Out Orders: Following Chain of Command; Informing Others Accurately of Relevant Information; Representing the Navy to the Public; and Training Unit and Subordinate Personnel. The behavioral definitions for each of these categories and the incidents which a large majority of officers agreed upon as belonging in each one are given on page 494.

13
When a piece of essential electrical navigation equipment began functioning only intermittently, an officer did nothing. Finally, the unit failed, severely reducing the ship's effectiveness.

14
During difficult maneuvers, an officer refused to carry out his orders until he had questioned his superior at length about them.

15
An officer presented technical information to a civilian audience and used jargon, technical terms, and highly specific examples which most of his audience did not understand.

16
While visiting a friend on the campus of a nearby university, an officer was confronted by a group of loud and unruly students. He talked with them for nearly an hour, and they parted with the feeling that the "Navy isn't so bad after all."

17
During and after training, an officer talked with each trainee to determine how the men were reacting to the training program, what changes, if any, should be made, and whether or not the men felt that the training program was effective.

18
In response to his CO's request for a report on his assignment, an officer wrote down each event in chronological order so that the CO would see how the mission unfolded.

19
An officer at a cocktail party became the center of attention as he complained bitterly about the way "those stupid politicians in Washington are running things."

20
An officer, responsible for overhauling a ship, developed a flow chart which provided a useful framework for checking progress and identifying problems.

21
A personnel problem arose, which an officer noted was covered by a policy statement his CO had recently made, and he proceeded to handle the problem according to that policy.

22
An officer sent a three-week old report to headquarters; the report was seriously out of date and inaccurate.

23
When the command was asked to give an overview of Navy personnel matters to a civilian group, an officer eagerly accepted the assignment and did such a good job that relations between the command and the community were significantly advanced.

24
An officer discouraged his subordinates from taking training courses, because he felt that they were a waste of time.

25
While visiting another unit, an officer spoke disparagingly of his superior and advised others to avoid transferring into his unit.

Source: Borman et al., 1974.

Solving Immediate Problems

To recognize and act upon special problems; to employ imagination, creativity, and initiative in developing solutions; to develop new programs or unique solutions to relieve problems as necessary and appropriate. Includes Incidents 1, 5, 12, 13, 20.

Carrying Out Orders: Following Chain of Command

To carry out assignments as specified; to follow the chain of command; to support policies of higher authorities; to show deference, but not blind adherence to orders from superiors; to constructively criticize policy decisions; and to conscientiously apply standard guidelines whenever possible. Includes Incidents 4, 6, 14, 21, 25.

Informing Others Accurately of Relevant Information

To keep superiors, subordinates, and others fully informed; to transmit information accurately; to be concise and to the point; to present ideas effectively both orally and in writing. Includes Incidents 7, 8, 15, 18, 22.

Representing the Navy to the Public

To project a favorable Navy image; to maintain officer bearing and appearance; to exercise discretion in public behavior; to exhibit professionalism in personal and public contacts; and to accept and carry out reasonable requests from citizen groups. Includes Incidents 9, 11, 16, 19, 23.

Training Unit and Subordinate Personnel

To determine personnel and team training requirements of subordinates; to establish training priorities; to develop effective training programs; to monitor training progress; to keep training programs current and relevant; and to evaluate the results of training programs. Includes Incidents 2, 3, 10, 17, 24.

Along with the above categories of Naval Officer Behavioral requirements, an additional eight categories were identified and defined by the workshop participants and are described by Borman et al. (1974) as follows:

Anticipating, Planning, and Executing

To be alert to task and mission requirements; to anticipate problems and plan for contingencies; to collect and verify information and to organize and employ resources for task accomplishment with economy of effort, and to follow through to completion.

Handling Stressful and Emergency Situations

To recognize and correct potentially dangerous situations; to respond quickly and effectively to take charge during emergencies; to retain composure and remain calm in the face of risks to personal safety; and, if necessary, to jeopardize one's own safety to insure the safety of others.

Integrity

To take required actions as appropriate regardless of personal consequences; to observe and enforce regulations regarding authorized use of equipment and personnel; to behave according to social and ethical standards and to be truthful in all matters; to observe and enforce regulations concerning use of restricted items aboard ship or station.

Responsibility

To carry out assignments as completely as possible; to hold one's self accountable for results; to be reliable and punctual in executing and completing assignments; to make every attempt at meeting expectations and goals; to be prepared physically and mentally for assignments; to set an example of maturity and effectiveness.

Dedication

To seek out and accept increased responsibility; to volunteer for special or dangerous assignments; to sacrifice personal goals for the good of the Navy; to serve without complaint under arduous conditions; and to accept and show commitment to Navy goals.

Motivating Unit and Subordinate Personnel

To contribute to the morale of both assigned personnel and of the entire command; to recognize and utilize appropriately applied commendation and censure techniques; to supervise subordinates without nit picking; to stimulate superior performance by personal example; to set attainable goals for subordinates; to reward jobs well done.

Personal Concern for Subordinates
To show consideration for subordinates' attitudes and frame of mind; to help subordinates and/or their dependents with problems; to express genuine concern for the safety and well-being of personnel; to refrain from exploiting personnel for personal gain.

Consistency and Fairness with Subordinates
To give timely, objective, and accurate performance appraisals; to criticize or reprimand subordinates only in private; to give constructive feedback without appearing to belittle or berate subordinates; to establish and enforce policies uniformly and consistently; to avoid playing favorites; and to keep promises.

Figure 3 below summarizes behavioral categories discovered in a sampling of other investigations that have used the critical incidents methodology to form behavioral requirements for various jobs.

BRIEF RECAPITULATION

It may seem that we have strayed far afield from our intention to discuss aptitudes, skills, and their relation to work performance in organizations. Actually, we have been wandering about some; but, hopefully, not aimlessly, and certainly not astray from our central objective. First, our wandering took us into the person, and we considered briefly the various trait and skill taxonomies that have been developed to help us describe cognitive, motor, and physical proficiency attributes of people. Second, we wandered into the job, and we have considered briefly the various work behavior taxonomies that have been drawn from factorial studies of behavior descriptions and rational or conceptual categorizations of behavioral incidents elicited to show examples of critically good or poor job performance.

LINKING THE TWO WORLDS OF BEHAVIORAL TAXONOMIES

Now, the link must be accomplished between the two sets of taxonomic systems. In one sense, the linkage process is accomplished conceptually by turning to the third approach in behavior classification, the so-called *ability requirements* approach. This orientation asks what human aptitudes, skills, or other attributes are required to carry out a job. Many methods have been used with varying degrees of success. The methods differ from each other in two major ways. First, they differ according to whether the link between human and job taxonomic categories is justified by empirical or strictly inferential means. Second, they differ according to whether the link is established at a molar job level (i.e., by examining overall or global performance in a job) or at a mo-

First Line Supervisors—Insurance Officers (Borman, 1973)
Initiative-Responsibility
Consideration toward Subordinates
Support of Company Policies and Directives
Handling Administrative Detail
Knowing, Understanding, Interpreting Work Procedures
Organizing and Utilizing Manpower Resources

Production Foremen—Transmission and Chassis (Hellervik et al., 1971)	Production Foremen—Auto Assembly (Hellervik et al., 1971)
Making Production	Maintaining Safe and Healthy Working Conditions
Housekeeping	Making Production
Planning, Scheduling Machines, Tools, Supplies	Maintaining Quality **(continued)**

Controlling Direct Labor Costs
Controlling for Quality
Motivating the Work Force
Communicating with the Boss, Other Departments, and Shifts
Cooperating and Dealing with Others in the Plant
Managing the Safety Program
Giving Job Instructions
Attending to Administrative Detail and Following Instructions
Knowing the Technical Aspects of the Job

Communicating Relevant Information to Appropriate Persons
Housekeeping
Gaining Cooperation from the Work Force
Cooperating with Others in the Plant
Using and Allocating Manpower Wisely
Reducing Material Costs
Training Employees
Disciplining the Work Force
Attending to Administrative Detail and Procedures
Displaying a "Management Attitude"

Fire fighters—Grand Rapids
(Heckman, 1973a)

Fire fighting
Attitude
Building Inspection
Desire to Learn
Personal Appearance and Hygiene
Ability to Learn
Courage
Mechanical Work
Public Relations
Driving and Operating Heavy Equipment
Getting Along with Other Fire fighters
Report Writing
Strength and Endurance
Physical Coordination

Fire fighters—St. Paul
(Heckman, 1973b)

First Aid
Getting Along with Other Fire fighters
Driving and Operating Heavy Equipment
Public Relations
Mechanical Work
Taking Effective Action at Fires
Attitude
Desire to Learn
Personal Appearance and Hygiene
Ability to Learn
Courage
Pre-fire Planning
Being Physically Fit

Police Patrolmen
(Heckman et al., 1972)

Crime Prevention
Investigating, Detecting, Following Up on Criminal Activity
Impartial Law Enforcement
Using Force Appropriately
Arresting, Searching, and Transporting Suspects
Crowd Control
Dealing Constructively with the Public
Handling Domestic Disputes
Traffic Maintenance and Control
Maintaining Public Safety
Integrity and Professional Ethics
Commitment, Dedication, Conscientiousness
Team Work
Report Writing

Police Detectives
(Heckman et al., 1972)

Preventing Crime
Developing and Utilizing Informants
Investigating the Scene of a Crime
Arrest, Search, and Seizure
Interrogating at the Scene of a Crime
Interrogating Suspects
Investigating a Case
Report Writing and Paper Work
Appearing in Court
Dealing with Juveniles
Representing Police to the Public
Cooperating with Other Officers and Divisions
Integrity
Conscientiousness and Dedication

Police Sergeants
(Heckman et al., 1972)

Concern for Subordinates
Scheduling, Coordination, Deployment of Manpower
Supervision
Performing Administrative and Inspection Functions
Decision Making and Initiative
Training and Planning
Integrity, Dedication, Conscientiousness
Dealing Effectively with the Public

Police Commanders—Lieutenants and Captains
(Heckman et al., 1972)

Administrative Duties
Communications
Scheduling
Training
Supervision
Commending, Disciplining, Evaluating
Field Command Coordination
Public and Community Relations
Dedication, Integrity, Setting an Example

Grocery Clerks
(Folgi et al., 1971)

Getting Along with Others
Operating a Cash Register
Bagging Groceries
Organizing Work at Checkstand
Handling Money Accurately
Knowledge and Judgment
Conscientiousness

Figure 3. Categories representing behavioral requirements for a variety of jobs discovered and defined via critical incidents methodology.

lecular job level (i.e., by examining performance within subclassifications of a job, such as the dimensions or elements discussed previously. Figure 4 depicts various *ability requirements* approaches for studying and/or estimating future work performance classified according to the two-way classification of Empirical-Inferential and Molar-Molecular. As with most such efforts to organize information, differences among the methods shown in the four cells of Figure 4 are perhaps somewhat indistinct, and, to a degree, arbitrary. Nonetheless, I find the classification useful for organizing much of what remains to be said, and I ask the reader to accept the general plan depicted in Figure 4 if for none other than pedagogic purposes.

1a. Classic Validation

Perhaps the word "Classic" is a poor choice, for I do not intend to convey the notion that this method is to be regarded as a "standard, model, or guide" for validation. Instead, I intend merely to connote something of antiquity or perhaps "historic renown" as concerns the particular method. At any rate, the literature of applied psychology, from the time of Muensterberg (*circa* 1910) to the present, is filled with studies where the possibility of dimensionality of work performance within jobs has been ignored in favor of obtaining global ratings of workers' levels of job performance and correlating their scores on tests against them.

Establishing the link between the two taxonomies in this manner has been one then of essentially ignoring the existence of behavioral taxonomies within jobs and attending instead to how human aptitude taxonomies might be related to global estimates of job performance. Ghiselli has kept track of just about every validation study (both published and unpublished) between the

	EMPIRICAL JUSTIFICATION OF JOB-PERSON LINKAGE	INFERENTIAL JUSTIFICATION OF JOB-PERSON LINKAGE
MOLAR JOB MEASUREMENT	1a. Classic Validation 1b. Occupational Ability Patterns	2a. Rational Specification 2b. Job Samples
MOLECULAR JOB MEASUREMENT	3. Behavior Validation a. Test Scores b. Item Responses	4a. Synthetic Validation 4b. Task Samples

Figure 4. Methods of determining aptitude/ability requirements of jobs classified according to empirical versus inferential justification of person-job relationships and molar versus molecular examination of work performance.

TABLE 1

MEAN VALIDITY COEFFICIENTS FOR VARIOUS APTITUDE AREAS FOR PERFORMANCE IN VARIOUS OCCUPATIONAL AREAS FOR STUDIES BETWEEN 1920–1973

OCCUPATIONAL AREA

APTITUDE AREA	Managers	Clerical Jobs	Sales Clerks	Salesmen	Protective Occupations	Service Occupations	Vehicle Operators	Trades and Crafts
Intelligence	.27(f)	.28(f)	−.03(d)	.33(d)	.22(d)	.27(d)	.16(d)	.25(f)
Spatial Relations	.21(d)	.16(e)	.14(b)	.20(b)	.17(d)	.13(d)	.16(c)	.23(f)
Perceptual Speed	.25(e)	.29(f)	−.02(d)	.23(b)	.21(c)	.10(d)	.17(b)	.24(e)
Motor Abilities	.14(d)	.16(f)	.16(f)	.16(b)	.14(d)	.15(d)	.25(d)	.19(f)

(a) Less than 100 cases
(b) 100 to   499 cases
(c) 500 to   999 cases
(d) 1,000 to 4,999 cases
(e) 5,000 to 9,999 cases
(f) 10,000 or more cases

Source: Ghiselli, 1973.

years 1920 and 1973 that he could lay his hands on, and he has organized the information (Ghiselli, 1966, 1973) to give us a comprehensive overview of how various aptitude measures have fared in relation to these global[9] measures of work performance in organizations. Information[10] contained in Table 1 summarizes his results for a number of broad occupational groupings. The coefficients shown there are averages obtained by converting the validities to zs according to the z transformation, weighting the values by sample size, computing the mean and converting the value to the corresponding r. Though a first impression of the results in Table 1 might suggest that the results are quite poor, the opposite is the case. The data represent an extensive lumping of many different tests, job functions and modes of analysis and, as mentioned, little if any attention given to the specific

facets of work performance to be predicted *within* jobs. Ghiselli (1973) also mentions that the average *maximal* validity coefficients for the twenty-one[11] occupations he summarized ranged between .24 and .46 with an overall average of .35.

In a similar summary of validity studies, Dunnette (1972) and his colleagues[12] reviewed all published and unpublished studies done on non-supervisory jobs relevant to the petroleum refining industry. Again, nearly all job performance measures were global ratings and the groupings of jobs and tests required for summarizing the data probably attenuated the magnitudes of coefficients quite severely. The median validity coefficients for several aptitude areas and four major job areas are shown in Table 2. The magnitudes of median validities are generally somewhat greater than those reported by Ghiselli. Of additional interest are the differences between occupational areas according to the aptitude areas showing the highest median validities; thus, General Intelligence is highest for Operating and Processing, Mechanical Aptitude for Maintenance jobs, Verbal Aptitude in Clerical jobs, and General Intelligence in Quality Control jobs.

[9] Obviously, not *all* the studies summarized by Ghiselli used only global ratings of job success, but he does mention that the large majority of them did do so. Since his analyses do not distinguish between global and more analytic ratings of job behavior, we present his results here to reflect primarily the nature of validity results obtained when global ratings are utilized.

[10] The classification of aptitude areas was done by Ghiselli. The areas are represented by tests similar to the types we have described previously with the exception of the Motor Abilities areas. The tests classified as "Motor Ability" included those measuring finger dexterity, hand dexterity, and tapping speed.

[11] Ghiselli (1973) actually computed averages for twenty-one different job areas which I lumped still further to develop the summary information given here in Table 1.

[12] Richard Arvey and Geula Grinberg Lowenberg.

TABLE 2

MEDIAN VALIDITY COEFFICIENTS FOR VARIOUS APTITUDE AREAS FOR PERFORMANCE IN FOUR OCCUPATIONAL AREAS RELEVANT TO PETROLEUM REFINING

APTITUDE AREA	OCCUPATIONAL AREA			
	Operating and Processing	Maintenance	Clerical	Quality Control
General Intelligence	.32(81)	.20(111)	.17(14)	.24(8)
Numerical	.19(36)	.35(86)	.12(31)	.14(10)
Verbal	—	.29(16)	.22(8)	.16(4)
Mechanical Ability	.20(42)	.38(76)	—	.18(8)
Perceptual Speed	—	.16(43)	.15(5)	—
Spatial Relations	—	.24(34)	.04(10)	—
Motor Skills	.17(9)	.22(65)	.22(19)	.06(2)

Note: Numbers in parentheses represent the total number of coefficients on which the median is based.

1b. Occupational Ability Patterns (OAP)

Given the existence of a useful taxonomy and "instrumentation" for describing human aptitudes, one might assume that differences in abilities required for successfully carrying out different jobs could be discovered by administering test batteries to successful employees in those jobs. This is the essential argument behind the concept of Occupational Ability (or Aptitude) Patterns. Again the job is treated in a molar manner; and implicit in the above assumption is the belief that all persons successfully retained or staying on any given job are there by virtue of relatively homogeneous work performance which, in turn, is made possible by a specific necessary[13] pattern of aptitudes. The concept was first tested empirically by Dvorak (1935), amplified by Paterson and Darley (1936) and carried forth to a kind of ultimate level in the development, norming, and use of the General Aptitude Test Battery. Thus, the GATB norms typically are established and expressed via their empirical linkage with jobs via Occupational Aptitude Patterns. As an example of the approach, we quote below from Super and Crites (1962):

Cutting scores are established for each of the three most important aptitudes found to characterize a group of related occupations, related in that they have the same aptitude requirements. Pattern 3, which is denoted only by a code number, might be called the applied science (professional) field; it is characterized by cutting scores of 125 for General Aptitude and 115 for Numerical and Spatial Aptitudes, and includes two subgroups. One of these is called the Laboratory Science Work group but, consisting of practitioner occupations such as physician and public health officer, might better be called the medical practitioner group; the other is made up of Engineering and Related

Occupations, such as the various kinds of engineers and designers.

Some of the occupations included in these groups are placed there because of the similarity of their known test profiles, each having its own cutting scores which resemble those of the others. Other occupations are included because job analysis data seem to justify this placement. (Super & Crites, 1962, p. 333)

However, Crites (1969) also criticizes the method severely, as in the following quotation:

... establishing Occupational Aptitude Patterns (OAPs) for the General Aptitude Test Battery (GATB), has met with only moderate success. Certainly, there are some OAPs which significantly discriminate not only between occupations but also between more and less successful workers within occupations ... the data in support of many of the GATB OAPs leave much to be desired. Less than half (44 percent) of them are based upon empirical results, but, more importantly, the Ns for most of the occupational groups are quite small. Since the primary statistic used in constituting OAPs has been tetrachoric correlation, and since its sampling error is large for small Ns, little confidence can be had in OAPs derived from such samples. (Crites, 1969, p. 69)

A similar approach is recommended in the manual for interpreting the various aptitude profiles of the Flanagan Aptitude Classification Tests, but no evidence is provided to show that the FACT OAPs were derived empirically by actually testing employees in the various jobs specified.

Direct empirical validation against job performance ratings has not been a requirement in the development of GATB OAPs. Instead, cutting scores have been established according to the belief that workers in the bottom third in score distributions for a given job are not likely to be very successful. As stated in the GATB manual, this generalization serves as only a rough guide because the definition of so-called "poor workers" may well differ according to different jobs, different companies, different locations, and different local labor market conditions.

---

[13] Sufficiency of the aptitude pattern is not typically at issue in the OAP approach. At the time of its development (during the years of the Great Depression), the orientation was more that of vocational guidance and the possibility of suggesting viable options to a counselee rather than trying to assure certain success in whatever endeavor was undertaken.

The GATB OAP cutting scores should not, therefore, be regarded as immutable; they should be modified on the basis of information based on local conditions.

2a. Rational Specification

Persons who are familiar with what a job entails may be able to form good judgments about ability requirements for that job without going to the special effort required by actually administering aptitude tests to persons doing the job. Here again, no formal taxonomy would be available at the job level, though one might be implied in the head of the rater, based on the aptitude taxonomy provided to him for carrying out the ratings. An illustration of this rational or judgmental method is the research done by Desmond and Weiss (1970, 1973). They developed an instrument called the Minnesota Job Requirements Questionnaire (MJRQ) which consisted simply of forty-five statements with five written to be relevant for each of the nine aptitude areas measured by the GATB. The statements were easy to read and understand because they were designed for use by supervisors in estimating the GATB-based aptitude requirements of the jobs they were supervising. Questionnaires were mailed to 344 supervisors of eleven different jobs,[14] and 261 usable returns were received. The returns showed clearly that the ratings were reliable and that they compared quite well with either the GATB-determined OAPs[15] or the ones based on job analyses related to the preparation of the Dictionary of Occupational Titles (U.S. Department of Labor, 1965). The rationally derived OAPs were highly similar to those of the GATB or DOT for seven of the eleven occupations studied. The ones showing most dissimilarity were the occupations of Welder, Baker, Sheet Metal Worker, and Sales Person, and these differences were due mostly to discrepancies with the DOT system which itself is another rationally specified but less systematic approach for determining the aptitude requirements of jobs. In addition, the magnitudes of correlations among pairs of mean supervisor aptitude ratings for the nine aptitude areas of the GATB correlated .38 with the actual magnitudes of correlations among the GATB tests.

In a later study (Desmond & Weiss, 1974), the MJRQ was mailed to 1,019 workers working on the same eleven jobs rated by the supervisors. Analysis of ratings received from 714 respondents showed high congruence with ratings provided by the supervisors ($r = .87$). Their mean ratings also showed equally good agreement with the other OAP methods (GATB and DOT) and, most important, differences among workers on variables, such as satisfaction, age, and tenure showed no important relation to their MJRQ ratings. Also, the magnitudes of correlations among pairs of mean employee aptitude ratings for the various aptitude areas of the GATB correlated .47 with the actual magnitudes of correlations among the GATB tests. Though still based on no specific job or task performance taxonomy and, therefore, suffering from the possibilities of imprecision in looking at the job, the method of Rational Specification as illustrated by Desmond and Weiss seems to have much merit as a quicker and more efficient means of determining OAPs than the strictly empirical approach pioneered by Dvorak.

2b. Job Samples

Because job sampling is similar in method to task sampling, the two are discussed jointly in a later section.

---

[14] The eleven jobs were Mechanical Engineer, Computer Programmer, Dietician, Librarian, Secretary-Stenographer, Welder, Adding Machine Serviceman, Sewing Machine Operator, Baker, Sheet Metal Worker, and Sales Person.

[15] The most rigorous method for designating the required aptitude areas for a given job was based on two requirements: (a) the ability rating for a given job had to differ significantly from the mean rating for that ability on the other jobs considered together; and, (b) the ratings of an ability had to be more consistent among supervisors describing a job than it was for all other supervisors.

3. Behavior Validation

Behavior Validation is contrasted with Classic Validation primarily because tests or item responses are correlated against ratings of behavioral dimensions of job performance instead of against global or Molar ratings of performance. Examples of this approach for linking test taxonomies with job taxonomies may be drawn most readily from validation studies done against specific job dimensions derived via Behavior Observation Scaling methodology.

One recent example of test score validation is given by Borman (1973). After a series of workshop meetings with groups of front line supervisors in an insurance company and with groups of managers a level above these supervisors, Borman derived the following supervisory job performance dimensions from the critical incidents elicited during the workshops.

I. *Initiative; Responsibility:* Expending high degrees of effort and energy toward performing well; taking responsibility to get the job done; actively providing solutions to problems; making suggestions; anticipating problems and moving quickly to solve them *versus* avoiding work and responsibility; expending little or no effort to get the job done; showing a lack of interest in solving unit problems.

II. *Consideration Toward Subordinates:* Awareness of and response to subordinates' needs; understanding subordinates' problems; resolving conflicts among subordinates; displaying interpersonal competence toward subordinates; treating subordinates fairly; supporting subordinates and becoming involved in their self-development *versus* failing to respond positively to subordinates' needs; displaying little or no empathy toward subordinates and their problems; treating subordinates unfairly.

III. *Supporting Company Policies and Directives:* Supporting company policies and upper level management directives or decisions; presenting in a favorable light in-formation passed down from levels higher in the organization; dealing constructively with persons in other units for the good of the Association; cooperating with other units and their personnel; ability to place the role of one's own unit in the context of the whole organization and to react to situations, keeping in mind the "big picture" *versus* failing to support policies, directives, or decisions; dealing ineffectively with other units and their personnel; possessing little or no perspective concerning the relationship between one's own unit and the Association as a whole.

IV. *Handling Administrative Detail:* Maintaining proper records; attending efficiently and effectively to administrative detail; documenting accurately problem behaviors and other actions; meeting deadlines for reports and for other required paper work *versus* maintaining sloppy or inaccurate records; failing to document problem behaviors and other actions; preparing reports improperly or turning them in late.

V. *Knowing, Understanding, and Interpreting Work Procedures:* Knowledge of unit function; ability to understand and interpret procedures and directives; ability to answer work related questions *versus* knowing little about the work being accomplished in one's unit; failing to learn or to understand procedures important for the functioning of one's unit; inability to answer questions related to procedures, directives, or the unit's function.

VI. *Organizing and Utilizing Manpower Resources:* Directing competently the work-related activities of subordinates, including job related training; delegating effectively; maintaining proper degrees of control and authority over subordinates *versus* delegating ineffectively; over- or under-controlling subordinates to the detriment of unit effectiveness; organizing subordinate's activities inefficiently.

As a brief aside, we must note the performance dimensions specified above illustrate a fact common to the Behavior Observation Scaling (BOS) methodology—namely, the job performance areas are by no means restricted to human attributes involving only aptitudes, abilities, and skills. In fact, such a dimension as Displaying Consideration Toward Subordinates would very likely require attributes involving particular patterns of personality and interests as well as (or instead of) any specific aptitude or skill attributes. This stems, of course, from the deliberate effort during BOS workshop sessions to deter participants from focusing upon employee attributes—in the interest of accomplishing the greater objective of sampling employee observations and descriptions of actual job performance instead of sampling the imprecise and potentially erroneous beliefs about what it may take for an employee to be successful. In fact, a major advantage to be gained from the Behavior Validation approach over the so-called Classic approach is that the far more careful specification of performance requirements carries with it the potential for a more informed and less "shotgun" selection of possible predictor measures to be tested empirically against job performance criteria.

Another obvious consequence of all this is that the examples we give here of Behavior Validation necessarily include measures in addition to aptitude tests as possible predictors of the various job performance dimensions.

For example, after examining the performance requirements for the job of first line supervisor, Borman (1973) hypothesized that the following personal attributes would be important correlates of each of the performance dimensions:

I. *Initiative-Responsibility:* decisiveness; self-assurance; initiative; dominance; work ethic; responsibility; supervisory quality.

II. *Consideration Toward Subordinates:* emotional stability; sociability; self-assurance; sociometric popularity.

III. *Supporting Company Policies and Directives:* supervisory quality; self-assurance; status orientation; decisiveness; domi-

nance; emotional stability; responsibility; work ethic.

IV. *Handling Administrative Detail:* interests in occupations of accounting, office work, banking, computer programmer; numerical aptitude; dominance; responsibility, self-assurance; decisiveness; work ethic; clerical aptitude.

V. *Knowing, Understanding, and Interpreting Work Procedures:* numerical aptitude; dominance; responsibility; inferential ability; data interpretation ability; initiative; intelligence; self-assurance.

VI. *Organizing and Utilizing Manpower Resources:* dominance; supervisory quality; self-assurance; status orientation; initiative; decisiveness; work ethic.

Based on the above hypotheses, Borman chose a number of published tests and inventories, administered them to 118 first line supervisors and obtained job performance ratings from both managers and co-workers of each of the supervisors on the dimensions listed above. Correlations between two or more ratings obtained for the same supervisors ranged from .48 to .66 with a median of .59. Using a sophisticated procedure (see Borman, 1973) involving Monte Carlo computer techniques to develop and cross-validate optimal test combinations for many subsamples, Borman developed predictor equations specific to each of the performance dimensions. For each dimension, he started initially with only those scores hypothesized to be important and used a stepwise multiple regression solution with unit weights (instead of least squares solution beta weights). The validities (both for the total Sample and the Cross-Validated Values) obtained are shown in Table 3.

As may be seen, useful validities were obtained for all the supervisory performance dimensions except dimension II, Consideration Toward Subordinates. A special advantage of Behavior Validation as shown here is that the prediction systems may be used to characterize expected job effectiveness in the several different performance areas in-

TABLE 3

VALIDITY COEFFICIENTS FOR REGRESSION EQUATIONS SPECIFIC TO EACH OF SIX PERFORMANCE DIMENSIONS AND FOR AN OVERALL RATING OF EFFECTIVENESS

	Total Sample Value	Cross-Validated Value
I Initiative and Responsibility	.32	.24
II Consideration	.15	.09
III Support of Policies and Practices	.32	.25
IV Handling Administrative Detail	.47	.38
V Knowing, Understanding, and Interpreting	.27	.16
VI Organizing and Utilization	.33	.21
Overall Performance	.37	.30

stead of only an overall or global prediction as is usually the case with methods which fail to consider the dimensional aspects of job behavior.

An additional example of the Behavior Validation approach is provided in a study by Dunnette, Groner, Holtzman, and Johnson (1972). However, they used analyses of item responses to develop "tailor made" prediction scales instead of relying on existing scoring keys from standard tests and inventories. Though the study encompassed three job areas [selling, research and development, and central administrative support functions (accounting, computer processing, etc.)] only one is described here in the interest of economy of time and space. As already mentioned (Dunnette et al., 1972), BOS methodology was employed to discover and define critical performance requirements for the three job functions. Ten areas were found to be common across all three areas. They are listed and defined below:

1. *Knowledge:* possesses information about technical principles, company products, and/or procedures; applies information appropriately to problems arising on the job; uses his experience and training to solve problems, and is not bound to particular methods or techniques or limited in breadth of information.

2. *Objectivity:* interprets information without bias; takes account of all relevant information and does not distort or "color" information to fit preconceived ideas or points of view; and keeps an open mind to viewpoints different from his own.

3. *Alertness:* recognizes unusual opportunities or nonstandard situations; capitalizes on opportunities for increasing sales or improving policies, procedures, or products.

4. *Commitment:* knows, accepts, and supports organizational goals and objectives; sacrifices personal interests when necessary to get the job done; does not shirk responsibility; and works diligently to fulfill commitments.

5. *Initiative:* undertakes needed actions without having to be told; functions effectively without close supervision; is a self-starter; can monitor his own work pace and schedule his own time.

6. *Persistence:* keeps working on a problem, task, or customer even though faced with difficulty and failure; sees things through to a successful outcome; maintains pressure in a patient and relaxed way.

7. *Detail Mindedness:* attends to important details but avoids getting bogged down in unimportant or irrelevant details; keeps tabs on operations and inventories; develops and keeps up-to-date, accurate records; and checks his work to insure that it is free from errors.

8. *Planning and Organizing:* outlines a specific problem for investigation; gathers all relevant information; develops contingency plans; selects priorities and effectively organizes his work and time to meet them; and meets deadlines for assigned reports and projects.

9. *Communicating:* presents ideas, concepts, and arguments accurately and clearly, both orally and in writing; effectively conveys his ideas to others in both group and in one-to-one situations; covers important

points completely, yet concisely; adjusts his presentation to his audience's level of understanding; and is poised and at ease when making presentations.

10. *Working with Others:* keeps relations with co-workers harmonious; cooperates with and helps co-workers; works as part of a team; and keeps superiors, subordinates, and co-workers informed of things relevant to them.

Ratings on these several performance dimensions and on Overall Effectiveness were obtained for each of about 120 accounting-administrative employees from one or more persons above them in the organizational hierarchy. Examination of the intercorrelation matrix among the ten performance areas showed relatively high correlations among several of them. Factor analyses showed that the ten performance areas could be meaningfully summarized according to the four areas in the table at the bottom of the page.

[Ratings on the same scales had also been obtained for 115 salesmen and 100 technical (research and development) personnel. Factor analyses of correlation matrices of their performance ratings yielded essentially the same four factor solutions as the one shown above for Administrative personnel.]

At the same time ratings were obtained, a battery of tests and inventories was administered. Responses to each item of the inventories were examined against each of the Composite rating scores and against the Overall rating in a double cross-validation design. Items showing levels of statistical significance of .10 or lower were examined, and those with no fewer than 10 percent of the respondents in any single response category were unit weighted to form scoring keys separately for each of the two subgroups. The cross-validities of each of the scoring keys were examined in the "other" group (i.e., the group on which it was *not* developed). Keys showing the least shrinkage in the cross-validity samples were then scored for the entire sample and correlated with the Composite Rating Scores.

Tables 4, 5, and 6 show correlations respectively among the Composite Rating (Criterion) scores, the Predictor scoring keys, and between the Predictor keys and the Composite Ratings. The diagonal entries in Table 5 also show the internal consistency (odd-even, Spearman-Brown corrected) reliabilities for each of the scoring keys. The

Composite	Dimensions	Horst (1949) Reliability (Inter-Rater Correlation) of Composite Score
I. Initiative and Persistence	5. Initiative ⎱ 6. Persistence ⎰	.57
II. Personal Commitment	4. Commitment ⎱ 10. Working with ⎰ Others	.48
III. Knowledge Utilization	1. Knowledge ⎱ 2. Objectivity ⎰ 3. Alertness 9. Communicating	.71
IV. Planning, Organizing, Handling Detail	7. Detail Mindedness ⎱ 8. Planning and ⎰ Organizing	.49
O. Overall Rating		.80

TABLE 4

CORRELATION MATRIX* AMONG COMPOSITE RATING SCORES FOR 119 ADMINISTRATIVE PERSONNEL

	I	II	III	IV	0
I	—	15	28	17	60
II	15	—	10	21	51
III	28	10	—	18	65
IV	17	21	18	—	46
0	60	51	65	46	—

   I   Initiative and Persistence
  II Personal Commitment
 III Knowledge Utilization
 IV Planning, Organizing, Handling Detail
  0 Overall Rating
 * Decimal points omitted

TABLE 6

CORRELATION MATRIX* BETWEEN PREDICTOR KEY SCORES AND COMPOSITE RATING SCORES FOR 116 ADMINISTRATIVE PERSONNEL

<table>
<tr><td rowspan="2"></td><td colspan="5">COMPOSITE (CRITERION) SCORES</td></tr>
<tr><td>I</td><td>II</td><td>III</td><td>IV</td><td>0</td></tr>
<tr><td>PI</td><td>66</td><td>08</td><td>32</td><td>10</td><td>45</td></tr>
<tr><td>PII</td><td>03</td><td>63</td><td>-08</td><td>24</td><td>26</td></tr>
<tr><td>PIII</td><td>33</td><td>10</td><td>74</td><td>06</td><td>51</td></tr>
<tr><td>PIV</td><td>17</td><td>26</td><td>04</td><td>67</td><td>34</td></tr>
<tr><td>PO</td><td>48</td><td>18</td><td>54</td><td>23</td><td>61</td></tr>
</table>

*Decimals omitted

  PI   Initiative and Persistence
  PII Personal Commitment
  PIII Knowledge Utilization
  PIV Planning, Organizing, Handling Detail
  PO Overall Rating

Diagonal entries are estimated validities of scoring keys against corresponding Composite Rating Scores.

validity estimates shown in the diagonals of Table 6 are likely to be overestimates of the true validities because scoring keys which failed to cross-validate were dropped from further analyses. However, the correlations between each predictor key and the independently obtained Overall Rating Score represent no artifactual dependency. Moreover, the rank order correlation coefficient of .82 between the magnitudes of corresponding correlations in Tables 4 and 5 suggest that the Predictor Scales map rather closely the pattern of relationships shown among the rated performance dimensions in this particular job area.

To sum up, then, we have described here two empirical studies that illustrate how a carefully conducted dimensional analysis of job performance can contribute to the development of prediction systems designed empirically to link tested personal attributes with those same dimensions of job performance.

4a. Synthetic Validation

As suggested by the empirical studies based on global job (see Tables 1 and 2) ratings and by the results of those utilizing the Behavior Validation procedures described above, the differences in tasks required by different jobs will often result in different patterns of relationships between measures of job proficiency and aptitudes from job to job. It is likely, of course, that much greater consistency would be observed in relationships between test scores and ratings of proficiency for carrying out the actual tasks or elemental behaviors that cut across many different jobs. This is the essential assumption of *synthetic validity*. The approach involves assembling a set of tests to predict proficiency in a job on the basis of the tests' predetermined relationships

TABLE 5

CORRELATION MATRIX* AMONG PREDICTOR KEY SCORES FOR 118 ADMINISTRATIVE PERSONNEL

	PI	PII	PIII	PIV	PO
PI	57	-11	66	21	81
PII	-11	83	-17	22	02
PIII	66	-17	81	-03	80
PIV	21	22	-03	74	25
PO	81	02	80	25	72

*Decimal points omitted

  PI   Initiative and Persistence
  PII Personal Commitment
  PII Knowledge Utilization
  PIV Planning, Organizing, Handling Detail
  PO Overall Rating

Diagonal cells show Spearman-Brown corrected odd-even reliability estimates.

with the specific behavioral elements or components of the job. Presumably, any job can be analyzed into its major elements and a battery of tests tailor-made to sort out applicants who may be expected to show high proficiency in each of the behaviors comprising the major elements of the job. In effect, synthetic validity is the inferring of validity in a specific situation from a logical analysis of jobs into their elements, a determination of test validities for these elements, and a combination of elemental validities into a whole.

By far the most comprehensive investigation of the possibility of linking job taxonomies with person or attribute taxonomies via the process of synthetic validation has been carried out by McCormick et al. (1972). The special and unique advantage of his approach is that he has, in effect, used a common instrument, the PAQ, to establish the linkage between the two taxonomic worlds.

His first step was to secure the cooperation of several of his colleagues from Division 14 of the American Psychological Association in estimating the relevance, importance, or applicability of each of sixty-eight human qualities or attributes to each one of 178 of the 189[16] job elements of the PAQ. Of the sixty-eight attributes, forty-one were specified as aptitudinal and twenty-seven as situational or "adaptability" attrib-

---

[16] Eleven of the job elements of the PAQ require write-in responses and could not, therefore, be used for the attribute ratings. Many of the so-called aptitudinal attributes were such things as depth perception, color discrimination, tactual acuity, and the like. In terms of the human taxonomic qualities we presented earlier in the chapter, the listed attributes can be grouped into relatively fewer aptitude areas as follows:

Cognitive (N = 11)
Verbal Comprehension
Word Fluency
Numerical Computation
Arithmetic Reasoning
Intelligence
Short-term Memory
Visual Form Perception
Perceptual Speed
Closure
Spatial Visualization
Mechanical Aptitude

utes (e.g., "dealing with people," "pressure of time," "working alone," "stage presence," "influencing people," etc.). Ratings were obtained from no fewer than nine and no more than eighteen persons for each of the aptitude attributes. Reliabilities of the mean ratings across the 178 job elements ranged from .85 to .97 with a median of .93. Pairs of job elements were then correlated according to the attribute profiles judged to be relevant or important to them, separately for each of the six major content or substance groupings of the PAQ. Factor analyses of the six correlation matrices yielded factor structures highly similar in most respects to those found when the factorial analyses were made on the basis of descriptions of the 536 jobs across seventy different firms.

The underlying similarity of the two sets of factor structures is, in a way, a kind of first requirement for concluding that fundamental similarities exist between taxonomies based on estimated importance of task elements for getting jobs done and the aptitudinal and adaptive attributes judged to be important in each of those task elements. This is an important finding, for it lays the groundwork for the further argument (basic to the concept of synthetic validity) that if a given kind of work activity, task element, or job dimension is found to be common to different jobs, then the human attributes necessary for doing those jobs ought also to be the same or similar.

McCormick et al. (1972) explain the basic notion of synthetic validity very well:

Motor Skills (N = 10)
Finger Dexterity
Manual Dexterity
Arm/Hand Positioning
Arm/Hand Steadiness
Continuous Muscular Control
Rate of Arm Movement
Eye-Hand Coordination
Eye-Hand-Foot Coordination
Reaction Time
Rate Control
Physical (N = 3)
Dynamic Strength
Static Strength
Explosive Strength

Let us consider, for example, the aptitude requirements of jobs. If by hook or by crook one can identify—in the case of a sample of jobs that do have a particular communality of work activities—the corresponding aptitude(s) that are so required, it would then seem reasonable to assume that the corresponding aptitude(s) would likewise be required in other jobs that have the same communality of work activities. This analogy, repeated for other types of activities and their corresponding aptitudes, would then presumably make it possible to "build up" the total aptitude requirements for any given job synthetically. (pp. 357, 359)

In order to test the synthetic validity model, McCormick obtained GATB scores and GATB validity information from the United States Training and Employment Service for a total of ninety jobs.[17] He chose ninety jobs which corresponded to jobs for which he already had assembled descriptions with the PAQ. The ninety jobs were then ordered in two ways for each of the nine aptitude areas measured by the GATB: first, according to mean scores; and, second, according to the magnitudes of validity coefficients. An ideal next step would have been to demonstrate that the inferences or judgments of required human aptitudes for the nine areas relevant to the GATB aptitudes were correlated positively with the two sets of orderings mentioned above. For example, judgments about the relative importance of Verbal Comprehension across the jobs corresponding to the ninety for which GATB data were available should, according to the synthetic validity model, be highly correlated with mean scores for V across the ninety jobs and with the magnitudes of the validity values for V across the ninety jobs. Similar results would be expected for the other aptitude areas—N, S, P, etc.

Unfortunately, McCormick chose to try a more complicated and, in my opinion, less straightforward test of the synthetic validity

model. He used multiple regression analyses with his factored job dimension scores[18] as independent variables to "predict," in turn, each of the criteria (i.e., mean scores and validity coefficients) for each of the nine GATB aptitude areas. He carried out a double cross-validation of the regression equations he developed and obtained median cross-validated coefficients across all nine aptitudes of .63 and .22 for predicting mean scores and for predicting validity coefficients, respectively.

As mentioned, it is unfortunate that McCormick chose to use the factored job dimension scores because they included much attribute information that is not conceptually relevant to scores on the GATB (e.g., attributes such as Gustatory Acuity, Olfactory Acuity, Empathy, Stage Presence, etc.). Because of this, his results are difficult to interpret—particularly in the context of possible linkages between job behavior taxonomies and taxonomies based strictly on aptitudes and skills as we have been discussing in this chapter.

A similar effort to demonstrate the usefulness of the synthetic validity model was carried out in the area of motor skills by Fleishman and his associates (Theologus & Fleishman, 1971; Levine, Romashko, & Fleishman, 1973). Their first step was the development of a set of thirty-seven rating scales called the Task Assessment Scales (TAS). Here is a partial listing of the several scales making up the Task Assessment Scales:

Perceptual Speed
Flexibility of Closure
Selective Attention
Time Sharing
Choice Reaction Time

---

[17] Note that the ninety jobs were *not* in the same organizations as the jobs for which he had collected PAQ information; the PAQ descriptions had previously been obtained from a number of cooperating industrial firms.

[18] It will be remembered that McCormick previously had shown that twenty-seven dimensions could be used to portray the descriptions of 536 jobs with the PAQ and that twenty-one dimensions resulted from the factor analytic studies of the expert judgments of the human attributes required for each job element of the PAQ.

Reaction Time
Number of Output Units
Number of Elements Per Output Unit
Duration for Which an Output
   Unit is Maintained
Work Load Imposed by Task Goal
Difficulty of Goal Attainment
Number of Responses
Precision of Responses
Response Rate
Simultaneity of Response(s)
Degree of Muscular Effort
Number of Procedural Steps
Dependency of Procedural Steps
Adherence to Procedures
Speed of Limb Movement
Wrist-Finger Speed
Finger Dexterity
Manual Dexterity
Arm-Hand Steadiness
Control Precision
Procedural Complexity
Tutorial Dependency
Natural Dependency
Stimulus Duration
Regularity of Stimulus Occurrence
Variability of Stimulus Location
Operator Control of the Stimulus
Degree of Operator Control
Operator Control of the Response
Feedback
Reaction Time/Feedback Lag
Rapidity of Feedback
Decision Making

Figure 5 shows an example of one of the rating scales, Speed of Limb Movement. They then asked a panel of nine judges to rate each of thirty-eight tasks which had been used in an extensive series of research investigations years earlier by Fleishman (1954).[19] First each judge decided whether

each ability represented by a scale was required for performance of the task; if he decided it was, he was then asked to use the seven-point scale to estimate the lowest level of the ability which a person would need to possess in order to produce errorless performance on the task. Of the thirty-seven ability scales of the TAS, eight were judged to correspond closely with eight of the twelve factors found by Fleishman when he factored the matrix of correlations based on performance scores across the thirty-eight tasks. Table 7 lists the ability scale titles and the corresponding factor titles from the earlier study. Also shown in Table 7 are the correlation coefficients between the mean ability scale ratings on each of the thirty-eight tasks and the factor loadings on each of the factors hypothesized to correspond most closely with each of the abilities rated. With the exception of the Speed of Limb Movement scale, correlations are impressively high. These results show quite conclusively that expert judgments of required abilities for task performance do accurately map the abilities shown factor analytically to be most important for performing those tasks. The next step in establishing the viability of the synthetic validity model requires a demonstration that experts' ratings of required abilities actually correlate with performance on the tasks in addition to reflecting the factor structure underlying the tasks.

Of the thirty-eight tasks, performance on only twenty-seven could be expressed in

---

[19] The names of the tasks used in the earlier studies are listed below:

(1) Precision Steadiness; (2) Steadiness Aiming; (3) Track Tracing; (4) Two-Plate Tapping; (5) Five-Key Tapping; (6) Ten-Target Aiming; (7) Rotary Aiming; (8) Hand-Precision Aiming; (9) Visual-Reaction Time; (10) Auditory-Reaction Time; (11) Minnesota Rate of Manipulation (placing); (12) Minnesota Rate of Manipulation (turning); (13) Purdue Pegboard, Right Hand; (14) Purdue Pegboard, Left Hand; (15) Purdue Pegboard, Both Hands; (16) Purdue Pegboard, Assembly; (17) O'Connor Finger Dexterity; (18) Santa Ana Finger Dexterity; (19) Punch Board; (20) Pin Stick; (21) Dynamic Balance; (22) Postural Discrimination Vertical; (23) Postural Discrimination Angular; (24) Rotary Pursuit; (25) Discrimination Reaction Time; (26) Complex Coordination; (27) Rudder Control; (28) Medium Tapping; (29) Large Tapping; (30) Aiming; (31) Pursuit Aiming I; (32) Pursuit Aiming II; (33) Square Marking; (34) Tracing; (35) Steadiness; (36) Discrimination Reaction Time, Printed; (37) Marking Accuracy; and (38) Log Book Accuracy.

SPEED OF LIMB MOVEMENT

This ability involves the speed with which discrete movements of the arms or legs can be made. The ability deals with the speed with which the movement can be carried out after it has been initiated; it is not concerned with the speed of initiation of the movement. In addition, the precision, accuracy, and coordination of the movement is not considered under this ability.

SPEED OF LIMB MOVEMENT DISTINGUISHED FROM OTHER ABILITIES:

Speed to carry out a movement or response, once initiated.	vs.	Reaction Time (28) and Choice Reaction Time (27); Involve speed of response initiation.
Speed of movement of arms or legs.	vs.	Wrist-Finger Speed (30); Speed of movement of fingers, hands, and wrists.
Speed of movement of arms.	vs.	Manual Dexterity (34): Skilled, controlled arm-hand movements.

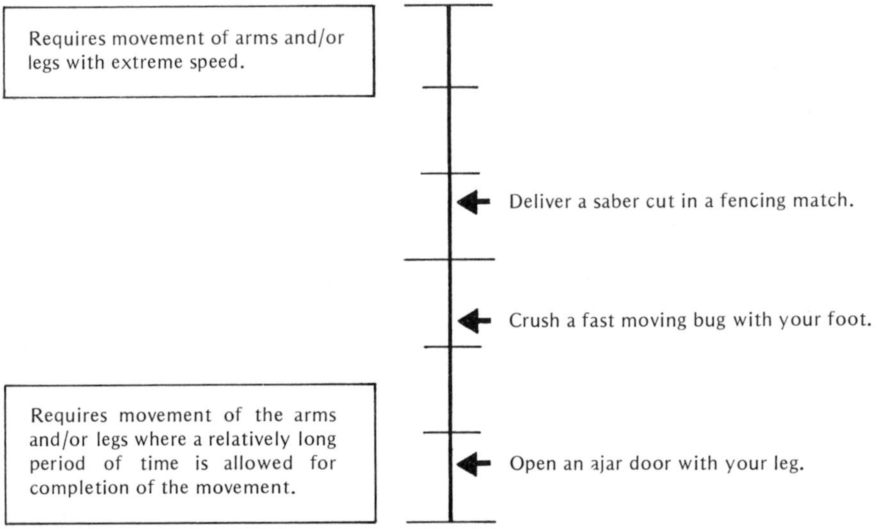

Requires movement of arms and/or legs with extreme speed.

Deliver a saber cut in a fencing match.

Crush a fast moving bug with your foot.

Requires movement of the arms and/or legs where a relatively long period of time is allowed for completion of the movement.

Open an ajar door with your leg.

Figure 5. Definition of speed of limb movement and scale for rating its importance in a task. (Source: Theologus & Fleishman, 1971.)

the form of a common measure (number of units produced per unit time). Of the thirty-seven ability scales for which ratings were available, the number was reduced to six on the basis of inter-rater reliability, degree of variability of ratings across the twenty-seven tasks, and a priori judgments of the logical relevance of the ability to performance on the tasks. Multiple regression was used with ability scale ratings as predictors and performance on the twenty-seven tasks (expressed in number of units per second) as the criterion variable. A corrected (Guilford, 1956a, p. 398) multiple correlation coefficient of .64 was obtained for the three ability scales of Gross Body Coordination, Manual Dexterity, and Arm-Hand Steadiness. Unfortunately, a cross-validation

TABLE 7

CORRELATION COEFFICIENTS BETWEEN MEAN RATINGS ON EIGHT RELEVANT ABILITY SCALES AND FACTOR LOADINGS ON TASKS DEFINING THE FACTOR

Ability Scale	Factor Title	Correlation Coefficient
Choice Reaction Time	Response Orientation	.40
Reaction Time	Reaction Time	.74
Speed of Limb Movement	Rate of Arm Movement	.22
Wrist-Finger Speed	Wrist-Finger Speed	.77
Finger Dexterity	Finger Dexterity	.55
Manual Dexterity	Manual Dexterity	.56
Arm-Hand Steadiness	Arm-Hand Steadiness	.61
Control Precision	Psychomotor Coordination	.62

design was not employed to allow for testing empirically the stability of the multiple correlation coefficient; the number of variables available for the criterion measure precluded the use of a cross-validation design. Nonetheless, this analysis was much more focused than McCormick's in that it examined strictly aptitude and motor skill areas instead of encompassing judgments involving situational, personality (adaptive), and volitional dimensions as well.[20]

Thus, the study provides solid confirming evidence for the utility of the synthetic validation model as a means of linking task or work taxonomies with tested aptitude or standardized motor skills taxonomies. This analysis along with McCormick's provides good evidence that expert inferences about

the ability requirements of job or task elements or dimensions (i.e., when the job is analyzed in the Molecular mode) can be shown to be correlated with both demonstrated levels of ability differences among those elements and differential levels of performance effectiveness and/or validities against performance among those elements.

4b. Job Samples and Task Samples

We have already noted Anastasi's comment (Anastasi, 1968) that complex motor tests built to resemble closely the job performance to be predicted have a good record of validities in contrast with the validities shown by more simple motor tests. Wernimont and Campbell (1968) suggest that samples of desired job behavior should be investigated for their predictive usefulness in other areas and with other kinds of jobs in addition to those involving motor performance. They argue quite convincingly in favor of making more explicit and direct use of the conventional wisdom that "the best indicator of future performance is past performance," and they call for strategies directed toward identifying patterns of behavioral consistency linking meaningful samples of behavior across different contexts (e.g., high school, college, other background experiences, job, etc.) for particular persons or subgroups of persons. According to their consistency model, selection research would begin with a comprehensive study of jobs to discover:

---

[20] The later study by Levine, Romashko, and Fleishman (1973), though utilizing a design somewhat different from the synthetic validity paradigm, also showed the utility of expert judgments concerning ability requirements. They gathered information from fifty-three studies in the vigilance literature and classified them according to which one of four primary perceptual and cognitive abilities (Perceptual Speed, Flexibility of Closure, Selective Attention, Time Sharing) was most important for performance. Differential relationships between performance and time were obtained depending upon the estimated primary ability requirements. This investigation is especially noteworthy because of the relatively great homogeneity which could lead one to anticipate little differentiation of task performance by categories of judged ability requirements. But markedly different performance functions over time were obtained for tasks requiring different primary abilities, attesting to the utility of such expert judgments in evaluating task or dimensional requirements of jobs.

... dimensions of job performance well defined ... by specific behavior incidents ... scaled with respect to their "criticalness" for effective or ineffective performance. (Wernimont & Campbell, 1968, p. 373)

The development empirically of patterns of behavioral consistency is also espoused by Owens (1968), and his approaches and preliminary results in this vein (e.g., the development of behavioral and demographic taxonomies based on background information) are described by him in Chapter 14 of this *Handbook*.

For the purposes of this chapter, it is sufficient to comment briefly about a few noteworthy examples of the development and use of job and task samples. Perhaps the crudest form of a "job sample" is the probationary period or job tryout period used by most companies and government agencies. Most periods are hardly seen as actually sampling how a person is handling the performance requirements of the job, and systematic or standardized procedures are rarely used for evaluating such persons. More usually, the trial period is more a means of estimating an individual's adaptive abilities—such things as getting to work, being on time, getting along with others, listening to directions, etc. Actually, Job Samples are probably of little use unless they are built up on the basis of careful dimensional analyses of the performance requirements of the jobs; such an analysis would then come to involve *task* sampling instead of *job* sampling.

Hinrichs (1970), as mentioned, showed that patterns of proficiency in a job show changes over time, reflecting both a shifting emphasis on task specific aspects of the job and different methods of approaching the learning of various tasks. He was particularly impressed that the most valid prediction of job proficiency at any stage of training was made by tests closely resembling the particular task instead of by tests of more general abilities. As already implied, therefore, careful job analyses can form the basis for taxonomies to be used in developing task samples administered like tests to job incumbents or applicants and their performance measured under conditions standardized according to observers, physical resources available (such as tools), tasks to be accomplished, and various other conditions. Such task samples, linked as they are to the actual dimensions shown to be important to doing the job, can be used in a variety of ways—as measures of criterion performance, as estimates of training proficiency, or as selection tests. The possible utility of developing task samples for criterion purposes was suggested by a review of all studies appearing over the twelve-year span of *Personnel Psychology's* Validity Information Exchange. Lent and his colleagues (Lent, Aurbach, & Levin, 1971a, 1971b) found that 82 percent (205/250) of all studies using "direct" job measures, such as work samples or actual performance records yielded statistically significant validity coefficients. In contrast, only 40 percent (377/948) of the studies using ratings and only 25 percent (47/177) of the studies using "indirect" job measures (such as promotion, tenure, and wage level) yielded statistically significant validities.

Job relevant measures have also frequently been shown to possess relatively high validities for predicting job performance. For example, Dunnette's (1972) summary of validity studies relevant to non-supervisory jobs in the petroleum refining industry showed good levels of median validity for tests of job knowledge and for systematic measures based on job and/or task samples. A summary of these results is shown in Table 8.

Campion (1972) also showed very clearly the special advantages of developing task samples as indicators of job performance. Working with a number of persons with good knowledge of the job of maintenance mechanic, he generated lists of task duties, tasks done in previous jobs by typical applicants, and critical performance tasks. From these lists, tasks were selected which were

TABLE 8

MEDIAN VALIDITY COEFFICIENTS FOR JOB KNOWLEDGE AND JOB OR TASK SAMPLE TESTS FOR FOUR OCCUPATIONAL AREAS IN REFINING

Type of Measure	OCCUPATIONAL AREA Operating and Processing Jobs	Maintenance Jobs	Clerical Jobs	Quality Control Jobs
Job Knowledge Tests	—	.43(190)	.40(105)	—*
Job or Task Samples	.32(18)	.36(18)	.39(2)	—*

Numbers in parentheses indicate the number of coefficients on which the median is based.
* No validity studies of job knowledge or task sample measures were found for quality control jobs.

sufficiently general for use with applicants (i.e., they did not require specialized knowledge of any particular plant or maintenance job). Four "work samples" were designed and standardized and administered along with a set of aptitude tests to thirty-four maintenance mechanics. Correlations between the work sample results, the aptitude test scores, and foremen's ratings of the mechanics' proficiency in three areas are shown in Table 9.

Finch and Impellitteri (1971) discuss several requirements for developing effective task samples as work performance measures. After emphasizing the importance of content validity (see Guion's Chapter 18 in this *Handbook;* also Guion, 1973), they also emphasize that measures should be evaluated for reliability and that they should provide both an end product for evaluation and scoring and samples of work behavior to be observed and evaluated. A good example of evaluating a series of task samples (which taken together constitute a job sample) for psychometric properties is shown in Table 10 where correlations are shown between scores on each of thirty-three tasks of a four-day work sample for Vehicle Mechanic and total score across all elements of the tasks (Engel, 1970). Obviously, the various parts of the work sample show substantial differences in their degree of contribution to the overall score.

Undoubtedly, one of the major advantages of the behavioral scaling methodology described previously is that it offers such a rich source of material for developing task simulations for eliciting behavior of obvious relevance to actual dimensions of job performance. Such steps have been instrumental in developing exercises and simulations making up assessment centers (which are described in greater detail by Finkle in Chapter 20). Their use in this regard is beyond the scope of this chapter because the behavioral dimensions derived via the be-

TABLE 9

CORRELATIONS OF WORK SAMPLE SCORES AND TEST SCORES WITH FOREMEN'S RATINGS OF MECHANICS' PERFORMANCE ON THREE JOB DIMENSIONS (N = 34 MECHANICS)

Predictor Variable (Concurrent)	PERFORMANCE RATING Use of Tools	Accuracy	Overall Mechanical Ability
Work Sample	.66	.42	.46
Mechanical Comprehension	.08	−.04	−.21
General Intelligence	−.23	−.19	−.32
Verbal Comprehension	−.24	−.02	−.04
Numerical Aptitude	.07	−.13	−.10
Perceptual Speed	−.03	−.19	−.09

Source: Campion, 1972, p. 43.

TABLE 10

BISERIAL CORRELATION COEFFICIENTS BETWEEN PERFORMANCE ON EACH EXERCISE OF A VEHICLE MECHANIC WORK SAMPLE AND TOTAL SCORE

Trouble-shooting Exercises		Corrective Action Exercises		Preventive Maintenance Exercises	
1.	.19	1.	.90	1.	.38
2.	.19	2.	.66	2.	.40
3.	.49	3.	.99	3.	.36
4.	.40	4.	.47	4.	.53
5.	.83	5.	.43		
6.	.36	6.	.12		
7.	.30	7.	.57		
8.	.34	8.	0		
9.	.21	9.	.16		
10.	.10	10.	.71		
11.	.50	11.	.30		
12.	.42	12.	.57		
13.	.64				
14.	.15				
15.	.24				
16.	.33				
17.	.20				

Source: Engel, 1970.

havior scaling methodology include many facets outside the aptitude and ability domain (Bray & Campbell, 1968; Dunnette, 1971). It is sufficient to comment that such task simulations have been developed and used successfully for such diverse occupations as management (front line, middle, and senior executive), Army leadership, selling, and protective occupations (patrolmen, sergeants, detectives, and command personnel).

An important potential disadvantage of the behavior scaling methodology as a basis for learning about the dimensionality of jobs and the subsequent development of task samples is that the process must be applied anew to each new job or job situation. At first this seems to rule out widespread use of the method because of the great amount of time and energy to be put into each new study. Two lines of evidence suggest that the disadvantage may be less serious than it appears at first glance.

First, as more and more job areas are submitted to the methodology, areas common to different jobs will begin to be apparent; eventually, a dimensional taxonomy should be developed based on these conceptual analyses of critical requirements which may exhaust a large part of the job domain—similar to the fairly extensive sampling at the level of task elements now provided by McCormick's PAQ. Figure 6 is an illustration of the degree of overlap (or dimensional commonality) that was found among four police job functions, each of which was studied independently with the behavior scaling methodology.

Second, the critical requirements or behavior scaling methodology can be undertaken at varying levels of abstraction; and, it is clearly possible to develop an extremely useful taxonomy of dimensions across jobs which may show quite distinct differences according to specific functional analyses. This type of abstraction is illustrated nicely by the dimensions and critical incidents which were derived for the job of "Naval Officer" and which have been illustrated previously in this chapter. Similar to this line of evidence, but differing slightly in point of emphasis is the possibility that critical incidents may be gathered which are specific to particular occupational areas but which are definitive of the same general overlying dimension. Thus, as we already have seen, ten general dimensions were found to be descriptive across such varying job areas as selling, research and development, and central office-administrative personnel. They were, however, defined according to critical behaviors unique to each function, and these behaviors, in turn, could provide the basic data base for developing task samples for simulations as we have been discussing them in this section.

THE NEED FOR A COMMON TAXONOMY TO LINK THE TWO TAXONOMIC WORLDS

So far, no one has derived a behavioral taxonomy midway between the world of work and the world of human attributes

	Patrolmen	Investigators	Sergeants	Intermediate Commanders
Crime Prevention	X			
Investigating, Detecting, and Following up on Criminal Activity	X			
Using Force Appropriately	X			
Handling Domestic Disputes	X			
Traffic Maintenance and Control	X			
Maintaining Public Safety and Giving First Aid	X			
Teamwork	X			
Investigating the Scene of a Crime		X		
Arrest, Search, and Seizure		X		
Interrogating Suspects		X		
Investigating a Case		X		
Developing and Utilizing Informants		X		
Appearing in Court		X		
Dealing with Juveniles		X		
Cooperating with Other Officers and Divisions		X		
Concern for Subordinates			X	
Communications				X
Commending, Disciplining, and Assigning Efficiency Ratings				X
Training			X	X
Supervision			X	X
Scheduling and Coordinating Manpower			X	X
Decision Making and Field Situations			X	X
Administrative Duties, Report Writing, Paper Work	X	X	X	X
Public Relations and Dealing with the Public	X	X	X	X
Integrity, Dedication, Conscientiousness	XX	XX	X	X

Figure 6. Job performance dimensions derived from analysis of critical requirements separately for patrolmen, investigators, sergeants, and middle command personnel.

measured via standardized tests and inventories. Such a taxonomy could serve a useful purpose as a common reference frame for evaluating and assigning both the important behavioral elements necessary for adequately performing different jobs and the measurable human attributes shown to be necessary for carrying them out. A single taxonomic system which is reasonably exhaustive of both the domains of work behavior and test behavior will ultimately be of great use in programs involving the development and content validation of testing programs designed to aid in making personnel decisions about human work performance.

We have shown in the preceding pages that several methods exist for justifying both rationally and empirically the usefulness of measures of human attributes in describing or predicting how effectively different persons may be expected to carry out various jobs and work functions. Moreover, the evidence shows that job and task performance and corresponding human attributes can be evaluated and sufficiently agreed upon by different judges so that we can take hope that the two taxonomic worlds can be linked successfully. Particularly noteworthy is McCormick's clearcut demonstration that similar factor structures are derived from the intercorrelation matrices of PAQ elements developed from two quite different sets of expert judgments—those involving descriptions (by job analysts) of actual jobs and those involving "guesstimates" (by psychologists) of the aptitudinal and adaptive requirements of the PAQ behavioral elements. In fact, the PAQ probably constitutes an excellent first approximation for developing the common taxonomy that is needed. Further research with it and other behavior description methodologies (such as the BOS methodology) should focus on developing a short, easily administered, and easily understood behavior description inventory which may be used as a common basis for classifying jobs, tasks, job dimensions, human attributes, aptitudes,

skills, and tests and inventories into the same taxonomic system.

REFERENCES

Altman, I. Aspects of the criterion problem in small group research: The analysis of group tasks. *Acta Psychologica,* 1966, 25, 199–221.

Alvares, K. M., & Hulin, C. L. Two explanations of temporal changes in ability-skill relationships: A literature review and theoretical analysis. *Human Factors,* 1972, 14, 295–308.

Anastasi, A. *Differential psychology.* (3rd ed.) New York: Macmillan, 1958.

Anastasi, A. *Psychological testing.* (3rd ed.) New York: Macmillan, 1968.

Anastasi, A. On the formation of psychological traits. *American Psychologist,* 1970, 25, 899–910.

Barron, F., & Welsh, G. S. Artistic perception as a possible factor in personality style: Its measurement by a figure preference test. *Journal of Psychology,* 1952, 33, 199–203.

Bennett, G. K., Seashore, H. G., & Wesman, A. G. *Counseling from profiles: A casebook for the Differential Aptitude Tests.* New York: Psychological Corporation, 1951.

Berliner, D. C., Angell, D., & Shearer, J. Behaviors, measures, and instruments for performance evaluation in simulated environments. Paper delivered at a symposium and workshop on the quantification of human performance, Albuquerque, New Mexico, 1964.

Berscheid, E., & Walster, E. Physical attractiveness. In L. Berkowitz (Ed.), *Advances in experimental social psychology,* Vol. VII. New York: Academic Press, 1974.

Borman, W. C. *First line supervisor validation study.* Minneapolis: Personnel Decisions, Inc., 1973.

Borman, W. C. The rating of individuals in organizations: An alternate approach. *Organizational Behavior and Human Performance,* 1974, 12, 105–124.

Borman, W. C., Dunnette, M. D., & Johnson, P. D. *Development and evaluation of a behavior based Naval officer performance assessment package.* Minneapolis: Personnel Decisions, Inc., 1974.

Bowers, K. S. Situationism in psychology: An analysis and a critique. *Psychological Review,* 1973, 80, 307–336.

Bray, D. W., & Campbell, R. J. Selection of salesmen by means of an assessment center. *Journal of Applied Psychology,* 1968, 52, 36–41.

Buss, A. R. Learning, transfer, and changes in ability factors: A multivariate model. *Psychological Bulletin,* 1973, 80, 106–112.

Campbell, J. P., Dunnette, M. D., Arvey, R. D., & Hellervik, L. W. The development and evaluation of behaviorally based rating scales. *Journal of Applied Psychology,* 1973, 57, 15–22.

Campbell, J. P., Dunnette, M. D., Lawler, E. E., & Weick, K. E. *Managerial behavior, performance, and effectiveness.* New York: McGraw-Hill, 1970.

Campion, J. E. Work sampling for personnel selection. *Journal of Applied Psychology,* 1972, 56, 40–44.

Carroll, J. B. Stalking the wayward factors. *Contemporary Psychology,* 1972, 17, 321–324.

Cattell, R. B. *Abilities: Their structure, growth, and action.* Boston: Houghton Mifflin, 1971.

Crites, J. O. *Vocational psychology.* New York: McGraw-Hill, 1969.

Cronbach, L. J. *Essentials of psychological testing.* (3rd ed.) New York: Harper and Row, 1970.

Csikszentmihalyi, M., & Getzels, J. W. Concern for discovery: An attitudinal component of creative production. *Journal of Personality,* 1970, 38, 91–105.

Dellas, M., & Gaier, E. L. Identification of creativity: The individual. *Psychological Bulletin,* 1970, 73, 55–73.

Desmond, R. E., & Weiss, D. J. *Measurement of ability requirements of occupations.* Research Report No. 34, Work Adjustment Project. Minneapolis: University of Minnesota, 1970.

Desmond, R. E., & Weiss, D. J. Supervisor estimation of abilities required in jobs. *Journal of Vocational Behavior,* 1973, 3, 181–194.

Desmond, R. E., & Weiss, D. J. Worker estimation of ability requirements of their jobs. Unpublished manuscript, 1974.

Dunnette, M. D. A modified model for test validation and selection research. *Journal of Applied Psychology,* 1963, 47, 317–323.

Dunnette, M. D. *Personnel selection and placement.* Belmont, Calif.: Wadsworth, 1966.

Dunnette, M. D. The assessment of managerial talent. In P. McReynolds (Ed.), *Advances in psychological assessment,* Vol. II. Palo Alto: Science and Behavior Books, 1971.

Dunnette, M. D. *Validity study results for jobs relevant to the petroleum refining industry.* Washington, D. C.: American Petroleum Institute, 1972.

Dunnette, M. D., Groner, D. M., Holtzman, J. S., & Johnson, P. D. *Job performance categories and rating scales for sales, technical, and administrative jobs.* Minneapolis: Personnel Decisions, Inc., 1972.

Dvorak, B. J. *Differential occupational ability patterns.* Bulletin 8, Employment Stabilization Research Institute. Minneapolis: University of Minnesota, 1935.

Dvorak, B. J. The general aptitude test battery. *Personnel and Guidance Journal,* 1956, 35, 145–154.

Ebbinghaus, H. Über eine neve Methode zur Prüfung geistiger Fähigkeiten und ihre Andwendung bei Schulkindern. *Zeitschrift Psychologie,* 1897, 13, 401–459.

Ekstrom, R. B. *Cognitive factors: Some recent literature.* Technical Report No. 2, ONR Contract NOOO14-71-C-0117, NR 150-329. Princeton: Educational Testing Service, 1973.

Engel, J. D. *Development of a work sample criterion for general vehicle mechanic.* Technical Report No. 70-11. Fort Knox: Human Resources Research Organization, 1970.

FACT Technical Report. Chicago: Science Research Associates, 1959.

Farina, A. J., & Wheaton, G. R. *Development of a taxonomy of human performance: The task characteristics approach to performance prediction.* Technical Report No. 7. Washington, D. C.: American Institutes for Research, 1971.

Feldman, S. D. The presentation of shortness in everyday life—height and heightism in American society: Toward a sociology of stature. Paper presented before the meeting of the American Sociological Association, 1971.

Finch, C. R., & Impellitteri, J. T. The development of valid work performance measures. *Journal of Industrial Teacher Education,* 1971, 9, 36–50.

Fine, S. A. *A functional approach to a broad*

scale map of work behaviors. HSR-RM-63/2. McLean, Va.: Human Sciences Research, September, 1963.

Flanagan, J. C. Defining the requirements of the executive's job. Personnel, 1951, 28, 28–35.

Flanagan, J. C. The critical incident technique. Psychological Bulletin, 1954, 51, 327–358.

Fleishman, E. A. Dimensional analysis of psychomotor abilities. Journal of Experimental Psychology, 1954, 48, 437–454.

Fleishman, E. A. The description and prediction of perceptual-motor skill learning. In R. Glaser (Ed.), Training research and education. Pittsburgh: University of Pittsburgh Press, 1962.

Fleishman, E. A. The structure and measurement of physical fitness. Englewood Cliffs, N. J.: Prentice-Hall, 1964.

Fleishman, E. A. Performance assessment based on an empirically derived task taxonomy. Human Factors, 1967, 9, 349–366.

Fleishman, E. A. On the relation between abilities, learning, and human performance. American Psychologist, 1972, 27, 1017–1032.

Folgi, L., Hulin, C., & Blood, M. Development of first level behavioral criteria. Journal of Applied Psychology, 1971, 55, 3–8.

Frederickson, C. H. Abilities, transfer, and information retrieval in verbal learning. Multivariate Behavioral Research Monographs, 1969, No. 69-2.

Frederiksen, N. Toward a taxonomy of situations. American Psychologist, 1972, 27, 114–123.

French, J. W. The description of aptitude and achievement tests in terms of rotated factors. Psychometric Monographs, 1951, No. 5.

French, J. W., Ekstrom, R. B., & Price, L. A. Kit of reference tests for cognitive factors. Princeton: Educational Testing Service, 1963.

Gagné, R. M. Human functions in systems. In R. M. Gagné (Ed.), Psychological principles in system development. New York: Holt, Rinehart and Winston, 1962.

Gagné, R. M., & Bolles, R. C. A review of factors in learning efficiency. In E. Galanter (Ed.), Automatic teaching: The state of the art. New York: Wiley, 1963.

Ghiselli, E. E. The validity of occupational aptitude tests. New York: Wiley, 1966.

Ghiselli, E. E. The validity of aptitude tests in personnel selection. Personnel Psychology, 1973, 26, 461–477.

Ghiselli, E. E., & Haire, M. The validation of selection tests in the light of the dynamic character of criteria. Personnel Psychology, 1960, 13, 225–231.

Guilford, J. P. Fundamental statistics in psychology and education. (3rd. ed.) New York: McGraw-Hill, 1956. (a)

Guilford, J. P. The structure of intellect. Psychological Bulletin, 1956, 53, 267–293. (b)

Guilford, J. P. Three faces of intellect. American Psychologist, 1959, 14, 469–479.

Guilford, J. P. The nature of human intelligence. New York: McGraw-Hill, 1967.

Guilford, J. P., & Hoepfner, R. The analysis of intelligence. New York: McGraw-Hill, 1971.

Guion, R. M. Open a new window. Presidential address to the Annual Convention of the American Psychological Association, Montreal, 1973.

Guttman, L. Integration of test design and analysis. Proceedings of the 1969 Invitational Conference on Testing Problems. Princeton: Educational Testing Service, 1970.

Harris, M. L., & Harris, C. W. A factor analytic interpretation strategy. Educational and Psychological Measurement, 1971, 31, 589–606.

Haynes, J. R. Hierarchical analysis of factors in cognition. American Educational Research Journal, 1970, 7, 55–68.

Heckman, R. W. Grand Rapids firefighter test validation study. Minneapolis: Personnel Decisions, Inc., 1973. (a)

Heckman, R. W. St. Paul firefighter test validation study. Minneapolis: Personnel Decisions, Inc., 1973. (b)

Heckman, R. W., Groner, D. M., Dunnette, M. D., & Johnson, P. D. Development of psychiatric standards for police selection: A first year's report. Minneapolis: Personnel Decisions, Inc., 1972.

Hellervik, L. W., Dunnette, M. D., & Arvey, R. D. Development and pretesting of behaviorally defined job performance measures for foremen in Ford Motor Company's transmission and chassis and automotive assembly divisions. Minneapolis: Personnel Decisions, Inc., 1971.

Hempel, W. E., & Fleishman, E. A. A factor analysis of physical proficiency and manipulative skill. Journal of Applied Psychology, 1955, 39, 12–16.

Hinrichs, J. R. Ability correlates in learning a

psychomotor task. *Journal of Applied Psychology*, 1970, 54, 56–64.

Horn, J. L. On subjectivity in factor analysis. *Educational and Psychological Measurement*, 1967, 27, 811–820.

Horn, J. L., & Knapp, J. R. On the subjective character of the empirical base of Guilford's structure-of-intellect model. *Psychological Bulletin*, 1973, 80, 33–43.

Horst, A. P. A generalized expression for the reliability of measures. *Psychometrika*, 1949, 14, 21–31.

Kay, B. R. Key factors in effective foreman behavior. *Personnel*, 1959, 36, 25–31.

Kelley, T. L. *Crossroads in the mind of man: A study of differentiable mental abilities*. Stanford, Calif.: Stanford University Press, 1928.

Landy, F. J., & Farr, J. L. *Police performance appraisal*. University Park: Pennsylvania State University, 1973.

Lent, R. H., Aurbach, H. A., & Levin, L. S. Research design and validity assessment. *Personnel Psychology*, 1971, 24, 247–274. (a)

Lent, R. H., Aurbach, H. A., & Levin, L. S. Predictors, criteria, and significant results. *Personnel Psychology*, 1971, 24, 519–533. (b)

Levine, J. R., Romashko, T., & Fleishman, E. A. Evaluation of an abilities classification system for integrating and generalizing human performance research findings: An application to vigilance tasks. *Journal of Applied Psychology*, 1973, 58, 149–157.

McCormick, E. J., & Ammerman, H. L. *Development of work activity check lists for use in occupational analysis*. WADD-TR-60-77. Lackland Air Force Base, Tex.: Personnel Laboratory, Wright Air Development Division, July, 1960.

McCormick, E. J., Jeanneret, P. R., & Mecham, R. C. A study of job characteristics and job dimensions as based on the Position Analysis Questionnaire (PAQ). *Journal of Applied Psychology*, 1972, 56, 347–368.

McGrath, J. R., & Altman, I. *Small group research: A synthesis and critique of the field*. New York: Holt, Rinehart and Winston, 1966.

Miller, E. E. *A taxonomy of response processes*. Study BR-8. Fort Knox: HumRRo, Division 2, December, 1966.

Owens, W. A. Toward one discipline of scientific psychology. *American Psychologist*, 1968, 23, 782–785.

Palef, S., & Stewart, C. P. Development of a rating scale. *Studies in Personnel Psychology*, 1971, 3, 7–20.

Parker, J. F., & Fleishman, E. A. Use of analytical information concerning task requirements to increase the effectiveness of skill training. *Journal of Applied Psychology*, 1961, 45, 295–302.

Paterson, D. G., & Darley, J. G. *Men, women, and jobs*. Minneapolis: University of Minnesota Press, 1936.

Prien, E. P., & Ronan, W. W. Job analysis: A review of research findings. *Personnel Psychology*, 1971, 24, 371–396.

Reed, L. E. *Advances in the use of computers for handling human factors task data*. AMRL-TR-67-16. Dayton, Ohio: Wright Patterson Air Force Base, April, 1967.

Royce, J. R. The conceptual framework for a multi-factor theory of individuality. In J. R. Royce (Ed.), *Multivariate analysis and psychological theory*. London and New York: Academic Press, 1973.

Ruch, F. L., & Ruch, W. W. *Employee aptitude survey: Technical report*. Los Angeles: Psychological Services, Inc., 1963.

SRA Catalogue for Business. Chicago: Science Research Associates, 1974.

Sharp, S. E. Individual psychology: A study of psychological method. *American Journal of Psychology*, 1898, 10, 329–391.

Singer, D. L., & Whiton, M. B. Ideational creativity and expressive aspects of human figure drawing in kindergarten-age children. *Developmental Psychology*, 1971, 4, 366–369.

Smith, P. C., & Kendall, L. M. Retranslation of expectations: An approach to the construction of unambiguous anchors for rating scales. *Journal of Applied Psychology*, 1963, 47, 149–155.

Spearman, C. "General intelligence" objectively determined and measured. *American Journal of Psychology*, 1904, 15, 201–293.

Spearman, C. *The abilities of man*. New York: Macmillan, 1927.

Stagner, R. Traits are relevant—logical and empirical analysis. Paper presented at symposium on *Traits, persons, and situations: Some theoretical issues*. Annual Convention of the American Psychological Association, Montreal, 1973.

Super, D. E., & Crites, J. O. *Appraising vocational fitness*. (Rev. ed.) New York: Harper and Row, 1962.

Taylor, L. R. Empirically derived job dimensions as a foundation for prediction of organizational behaviors. Unpublished paper, State Farm Insurance Companies, Bloomington, Illinois, 1970.

Theologus, G. C., & Fleishman, E. A. *Development of a taxonomy of human performance: Validation study of ability scales for classifying human tasks.* Technical Report No. 10. Washington, D. C.: American Institutes for Research, 1971.

Thurstone, L. L. Primary mental abilities. *Psychometric Monographs,* 1938, No. 4.

Tucker, L. R. *A method of synthesis of factor analysis studies.* Personnel Research Section Report No. 984. Washington, D. C.: Department of the Army, 1951.

Tuddenham, R. D. The nature and measurement of intelligence. In L. Postman (Ed.), *Psychology in the making: Histories of selected research problems.* New York: Knopf, 1962.

U. S. Department of Labor, U. S. Employment Service. *Dictionary of Occupational Titles,* Vol. II. Washington, D. C.: U. S. Government Printing Office, 1965.

Wallach, M. A. *The intelligence/creativity distinction.* New York: General Learning Press, 1971.

Wallach, M. A., & Wing, C. S. *The talented student: A validation of the creativity intelligence distinction.* New York: Holt, Rinehart and Winston, 1969.

Wernimont, P. F., & Campbell, J. P. Signs, samples, and criteria. *Journal of Applied Psychology,* 1968, 52, 372–376.

Wheaton, G. R. *Development of a taxonomy of human performance: A review of classificatory systems relating to tasks and performance.* AIR-726-12/68/TR-1. Washington, D. C.: American Institutes for Research, 1968.

Williams, R. E. A description of some executive abilities by means of the critical incident technique. Unpublished doctoral dissertation, Columbia University, New York, 1956.

Wissler, C. The correlation of mental and physical traits. *Psychological Monographs,* 1901, 3, No. 16.

CHAPTER 12

Vocational Preferences[1]

JOHN L. HOLLAND
The Johns Hopkins University

Assessment and Classification	Special Populations
Structure and Theory	Practical Applications
Vocational Development	Implications and Strategies
Stability and Change	References

THIS CHAPTER attempts to summarize some of the main findings about vocational interests, vocational choices or preferences, and characteristics of people with different preferences or employed in different occupations. These closely related findings are integrated by assuming that they are the products of a small number of common personal dispositions or constructs. Some research strategies are outlined to make more advantageous use of this knowledge; and some practical applications are indicated.

The need to integrate knowledge of vocational interests, vocational choices, and the characteristics of people in different occupations continues. Although these concepts are closely related, we maintain somewhat separate literatures for vocational interest inventories, vocational choices or preferences, and occupations. The purpose of this chapter is to propose an integration of current knowledge of these concepts, to review the main findings and theories for coping with this knowledge, and to outline some implications for industrial and organizational psychology. Accordingly, preferences for, choices of, and

characteristics of people in or seeking the same or similar occupations are regarded as similar phenomena.

The evidence for seeing vocational interests, vocational choice, and occupational membership in similar dimensions is extensive and growing. For example, people who have scientific interests, those who prefer scientific occupations, and those who engage in scientific occupations are all similar. Recent articles (Campbell & Holland, 1972; Holland, Viernstein, Kuo, Karweit, & Blum, 1970) illustrate that the aspirants for occupations usually resemble the people employed in those occupations. And, although using precise definitions of these concepts or behaviors leads to slightly different results, the similarities are more striking than the differences. Even Crites (1969b), who argues for the distinctions among these

[1] I am indebted to the following people for their counsel in an earlier draft of this chapter. They include: Alexander W. Astin, David L. DeVries, John H. Hollifield, James M. McPartland, Roger A. Myers, Peter H. Rossi, Keith F. Taylor, and Thelma Baldwin Zener.

concepts, concludes that the use of these related concepts produces similar research results.

The usefulness of seeing vocational interests, vocational choice, and occupational membership in similar terms is demonstrated in Crites's encyclopedic account of *Vocational Psychology* and in theoretical work by Crites (1969b), Holland (1966b), Roe (1956), Super, Kowalski, and Gotkin (1967), and others. These varied works suggest that the history of a person's vocational interests, choices, and work experience have continuity and lawfulness rather than disjunctiveness and randomness. This seems eminently rational, and new evidence from diverse sources—work histories, occupational classifications, aptitude batteries, high school and college studies—supports this assumption.

Another way to state the main assumption is to say that vocational interests, vocational choices, and characteristics of people in related occupations are manifestations of a common personal disposition or construct. For instance, it makes sense that a person with scientific interests will seek scientific training and engage in a scientific career, because he has a relatively stable disposition which expresses itself in similar behavior at different ages.

This assumption is used as the main thread for defining the content of the chapter —current knowledge of vocational interests, vocational choices, occupational membership. This content is, in turn, organized as follows:

1. Assessment and Classification. Summarizes current knowledge about the assessment and classification of vocational preferences.

2. Structure and Theory. Outlines some formulations for organizing and interpreting the data.

3. Vocational Development. Discusses the life history of a person's vocational preferences.

4. Stability and Change. Suggests how personal and environmental forces make for predictability of, or lead to change in, vocational preference.

5. Special Populations. Summarizes information about the vocational preferences of blacks and women.

6. Practical Applications. Summarizes information about some common methods for rendering vocational assistance.

7. Implications and Strategies. Suggests some research strategies and practical implications for industrial psychology.

Because it is in a handbook, not an encyclopedia, this review treats only selected topics and uses only selected evidence. For more comprehensive accounts of the same and related materials, the reader should see books by Crites (1969b), Borow (1964), Glaser (1968), Roe (1956), Super and Crites (1962), Super, Starishevsky, Matlin, and Jordaan (1963), Whiteley and Resnikoff (1972), and reviews by Perrone (1966), Tennyson (1968), and Holland and Whitney (1969). In the selection of evidence, the biases are usually in favor of large scale studies with important social outcomes. (The reader will detect a few others.)

ASSESSMENT AND CLASSIFICATION

This section summarizes current knowledge for assessing vocational interests, vocational preferences, vocational choices, and occupational membership, and reviews some promising schemes for classifying this information. For extensive accounts of the assessment process the reader should see the basic books by Strong (1943), Darley and Hagenah (1955), Clark (1961), Super and Crites (1962), and Campbell (1971).

Assessment

A person's vocational interests, preferences, choices, or occupational membership is typically assessed by one or more of three methods: (1) administer an interest inventory; (2) administer a standard questionnaire item; or (3) classify a person's interest inventory scores, questionnaire responses, or current job into an occupational classification. These procedures usually yield similar but not identical results (Campbell & Holland, 1972; Holland, 1963; Holland, Viernstein, Kuo, Karweit, & Blum, 1970; Crites, 1969b).

Explicit definitions are necessary to obtain clear experimental results and comparable findings between studies. To integrate knowledge in larger units, however, breadth of definition or felicitous sloppiness seems necessary. If one demands only moderately positive relationships for results obtained by these different methods, the substantive findings in this field become more intelligible and even exciting.

Interest Inventories

The Strong Vocational Interest Blank, the Kuder Preference Record, and their revisions continue to dominate the attention of practitioners and researchers. Other inventories, such as the Minnesota Vocational Interest Inventory (Clark, 1961), The Vocational Preference Inventory (Holland, 1965), and The Picture Preference Inventory (Geist, 1968) have also generated considerable research about vocational interest but have been used less.

Information about these inventories is now voluminous and scattered throughout the literature. Campbell's (1971) *Handbook for the Strong Vocational Interest Blank* (SVIB) is the largest and most comprehensive summary of the evidence about any single inventory. This companion volume to Strong's (1943) *Vocational Interests of Men and Women* provides an extensive account of the history of the development of the SVIB, including the most recent developments—the development of the basic scales for men and women, administrative indices for detecting errors and response bias, new occupational scales for specific occupations, and new and old data about the retest reliability and validity of both the old and new scales. In addition, the appendices provide 108 pages of empirical detail. Even a casual reader would conclude that the SVIB must be the most well validated inventory in existence.

Current information about the Kuder inventories (Kuder, 1965, 1970) is contained in the manuals of the Kuder inventories: the Occupational Interest Survey, the Kuder Preference Record, etc. Other positive and impressive results appear in journal articles (Madaus & O'Hara, 1967).

Numerous positive findings for the Strong, Kuder, and other inventories attest to their usefulness. At the same time, several problems still need attention:

1. The *evidence* from the use of interest inventories needs a more productive organization or rationale. The old group scales developed by Strong (1943) and the new basic scales developed by Campbell, Borgen, Eastes, Johansson, and Peterson (1968) are useful beginnings. Likewise Kuder's original scales and their derivatives (1965) have served to organize the data for his inventory in useful ways, although Kuder has shown little interest in any theory or classification to revise or interpret his original nine occupational groups.

2. The interest literature still remains largely outside the mainstream of psychology and sociology. The sheer empirical success of these inventories may have relieved interest enthusiasts of the need to cultivate other parts of psychology. Subsequently, neither group—interest types and the other types in psychology—have developed useful dependencies upon one another. Consequently, the interest inventory literature remains a rambling, formless literature integrated only by a few popular inventories and unable to draw on the strengths of personality and learning theory and vice versa.

3. The relative validity and usefulness of different inventories as well as the usefulness of self-expressed vocational interest goes undetermined. Whether the Kuder, Strong, or self-expressed interests are superior to each of the others is not clear (Dolliver, 1969).

Standard Questionnaire Items

Both Kuvlesky and Bealer (1966) and Crites (1969b) have suggested some useful ways to clarify the distinction between vocational preference and choice. Crites's pleas for some standard open-ended question to define vocational choice is a useful idea but will probably go unheeded by researchers. Likewise, the simple questionnaire form devised by Kuvlesky and Bealer (1966) to differentiate preference from choice may go unnoticed. Perhaps their work will, at least, provoke researchers into being clear about whatever definition they do use.

In addition, many people lack the personal resources or opportunity to make vocational choices so that they must accept non-choice jobs. Still others choose jobs for the interpersonal relationships or the context of a job. As a result there are two literatures of vocational preference—one for people with personal resources and opportunity (largely college and technical students) and another for uneducated and poor people. At this time, there is no integration of these diverse orientations. Until psychologists and sociologists tackle the problem more directly we will not know whether an integration is possible, or whether separate theories and literatures are the only solution.

Classifications for Assessment

An employee's current position or interest scores can be used to define his vocational interests and preferences by categorizing his job or high point code in an occupational classification. This procedure has many variants—most of which have gone unexplored —such as classifying all jobs in a work history and developing a single index or category for a person, classifying the jobs a person believes best fit his interests, etc.

Some Assumptions

Most interest inventories rest heavily on the assumption that people perceive occupations and their associated activities accurately and that these perceptions remain the same over long periods of time. Likewise, a person's vocational preferences and vocational choices rest on the same assumptions. If, for example, perceptions of occupations

had no validity, interest inventories would have little or no validity. The national rate of job switching would be much higher, and vocational guidance might depend largely on a cafeteria of work experience.

Fortunately, a few investigators have made rapid progress since 1960, and their work coheres and supports these assumptions. In two major studies O'Dowd and Beardslee (1960, 1967) show that a sample of fifteen occupations are perceived in much the same way by a variety of large samples: faculty, college students, high school students, men versus women. They also demonstrate that occupational stereotypes are complex but can be organized in terms of a few factors which resemble some of the common dimensions found for occupations—especially status. They also show that demographic differences make only small differences in the perception of occupations, and they find little change in stereotypes over four years of college.

Other studies support and fill in more information about occupational stereotypes. Schutz and Blocher (1960), using a sample of 135 high school seniors, found that a student's vocational preference was significantly related to the "vocational sketch" (occupational stereotype) he selected as self-descriptive one week earlier. They, then, suggest how the process of vocational choice might operate and why such stereotypes should have validity. In another study of 679 high school senior boys, Banducci (1968) finds that a student's social status, academic potential, and vocational interests have a small, rather than a large, influence on the accuracy of his occupational stereotypes. At the same time, Banducci extends the work of O'Dowd and Beardslee (1967) and Grunes (1957) by suggesting how several personal characteristics operate in expected ways. For example, bright students have more accurate stereotypes of higher level jobs and poor students have more accurate stereotypes of lower level jobs. In addition, students tend to have more accurate perceptions of occupations which correspond to their dominant scale in their vocational interest profile. In short, Banducci's work illustrates how selective perception functions in a person's occupational search.

Most recently, Marks and Webb (1969) demonstrated that students entering the fields of industrial management or electrical engineering possess "a fairly accurate image —assuming the professionals know what they are talking about—of the typical incumbent of the intended occupation." Their elaborate study of two occupational titles by three levels of experience—freshmen, seniors, and professionals before, during, and after training—closes the door on the argument that inexperienced and experienced people do not see an occupation in the same way. Or, at least, the study renders this argument less plausible. The earlier study by Banducci (1968) contained a Range of Experience Scale (seventy-six items). That scale was unrelated to the accuracy of a student's occupational stereotypes when the effects of social status and academic potential were held constant.

Taken together, these studies of occupational images strongly suggest that stereotypes or generalizations about occupations are stable over time, have validity, and to a lesser degree are selectively perceived according to social status, intelligence, and degree of involvement in the occupation in question.

Classification

The proliferation of interest inventories, special interest scales, and occupational data accelerates the need for classification systems to organize and interpret this information. Although the development of special literatures about the SVIB, the Kuder, and specific occupations has been helpful, the need for classification schemes to put this information together also appears necessary: (1) the sheer amount of occupational information has become practically and intellectually unwieldy; and (2) the financial resources needed to build scales or information pools for all occupations are unlikely to become available. The following paragraphs delineate some of the faults in current occupational classifications and some potential values of improved classifications.

Although current classifications are useful for many purposes, their usefulness is restricted. The use of a particular classification scheme usually yields only a small amount of reliable information. The small informational yield occurs because classifications usually suffer from one or more of the following practical, logical, or scientific deficiencies.

1. They are not comprehensive; they can be used for the classification of only a relatively small number of occupations.

2. They lack an explicit rationale or theory. For instance, the labels assigned to categories frequently lack a clear definition or any elaboration elsewhere. Consequently, the interpretation of data, organized by such classifications is ambiguous, since the meaning of the categories has not been studied and clearly delineated.

3. They lack a clear method for their extension to new fields. Classifications are usually extended or revised by personal opinions rather than by following explicit, logical, or empirical procedures.

4. They classify fields by more than a single, logical, or empirical principle.

5. They are often impractical because they are difficult to use or to teach to others.

6. They lack versatility; that is, they are usually helpful for only one or two purposes. This limitation requires that for many practical and theoretical purposes we must translate the data obtained by one classification into another, a precarious and undesirable activity. For example, educators and researchers usually find that assessment of fitness for an occupation is in one classification, fields of training are in another classification, and occupational information is in still other classifications.

For these reasons, versatile scientific classification systems for occupations become indispensable to the solution of many practical and theoretical problems. For convenience, the classification schemes most relevant to the present chapter are reviewed under the following headings: socioeconomic levels, job content, and worker characteristics.

Prestige and Socioeconomic Levels

Classifications which organize occupations according to prestige, income, educational level, or combinations of these criteria are numerous and relatively easy to form. The Prestige Scale of the National Opinion Research Center (NORC) illustrates perhaps the most useful scale of this type (Hodge, Siegel, & Rossi, 1966). Generally, the NORC Prestige Scale works well in census and research projects because it satisfies the main principles of classification. Levels of prestige are available for each of the main census occupational titles so that it is easy to give a numerical score to occupations or their incumbents, which represents the prestige ranking of that occupation in the eyes of the American public. Consequently, the data obtained from the application of the scale can be interpreted with clarity and confidence.

Job Content

Classifications which organize occupations according to job content are also numerous, but they usually confound job content and job level. Both the U.S. Census and *Dictionary of Occupational Titles* (DOT) illustrate classifications with unfortunate deficits, because their major categories were formed by many principles rather than a single one.

Worker Characteristics

Several attempts have been made to make occupational classifications useful for guidance or placement purposes by organizing occupations according to: (1) needed abilities or aptitudes to do the job; (2) activities performed, interests, personalities, or orientations toward different kinds of activities and problems; or (3) combinations of 1 and 2.

The Minnesota Occupational Rating Scales (Paterson, Gerken, & Hahn, 1953) represent one of the early attempts to organize and categorize occupations according to the kinds of abilities, or talents, needed to perform satisfactorily in an occupation. The Worker Traits Arrangement of the DOT (1965–1966) is a recent, more sophisticated attempt to organize occupations for counseling and placement purposes. This arrangement helps students, workers, and counselors see occupational possibilities in terms of personal traits and needs. In the Worker Traits Arrangement, jobs are "grouped according to kind of work, as well as some combination of worker traits, such as educational development, vocational preparation, aptitudes, interests, temperaments, and physical demands." These classifications make the DOT a more flexible and informative system for standardizing terminology, performing censuses, showing relationships among occupations, exploring occupations, placing job applicants, and coding occupational materials. At the same time, the DOT classification remains an unwieldy tool for some other purposes. The sheer number of classes and subclasses along with the variable criteria for determining classes make the DOT difficult to use and teach to others. Likewise, the rationale for its construction is ambiguous, and the testing of the system has been largely pragmatic (using the system in daily practice) rather than scientific. At the same time, the DOT arrangements have no equal for comprehensiveness, but some revised and abridged classification schemes might serve practitioners and researchers more effectively.

The most sustained, scientific attempt to organize our knowledge of work activities is that of McCormick and his colleagues. Their contribution is not easily summarized because of its long time span, scope, and complexity. Their work has been summarized by McCormick, Jeanneret, and Mecham (1969, 1972).

In their most recent work, McCormick, Jeanneret, and Mecham (1972) developed the Position Analysis Questionnaire (PAQ) as a method for assessing jobs directly. This comprehensive questionnaire contains 189 job elements which are intended to characterize the human behavior required in different jobs.

Data based on the Position Analysis Questionnaire have been used (1) for the purpose of deriving estimates of the human attributes (aptitudes, interests, physical capacities, etc.) that a job requires, and (2) as the basis for identifying job dimensions. Mecham and McCormick (1969a) developed the attribute requirements (sixty-eight) for the job elements (178) in the PAQ. In short, they used PAQ descriptions of individual jobs as data for deriving estimates of the human characteristics needed to perform those jobs. To accomplish this task, sixty-eight attributes were selected as relevant to different kinds of work performance. Raters (primarily industrial psychologists) estimated the relevance of each attribute to the elements of the PAQ. Median attribute ratings were derived, and their inter-rater reliabilities were estimated, most of these being in the .80s and .90s. This estimation of the attribute requirements from the PAQ means that it may be possible to establish useful job requirements using only job analysis data; that is, the usual situational validation of predictors might be ignored. In a related study, Mecham and McCormick (1969b) used the PAQ to estimate the attribute requirements of jobs, and validated these synthetic estimates against data based on the General Aptitude Test Battery (GATB) of the U.S. Employment Service. The results clearly indicate that the PAQ (a comprehensive job analysis) can be used to estimate the aptitudes that jobs require.

Finally, McCormick, Jeanneret, and Mecham (1972) investigated the hypothesis that there is some structure underlying the domain of human work. Using 536 job analyses obtained by the PAQ, they performed principal component analyses of PAQ items which resulted in five overall factors and twenty-seven divisional job dimensions. The divisional dimensions resulted from independent factor analyses of each of the major divisions of the PAQ. They also performed factor analyses of the PAQ item attribute profiles developed by Mecham and McCormick (1969a). The six independent analyses produced twenty-one divisional dimensions. Generally, the job dimensions obtained from job analyses and from attribute profiles appear sensible and consistent with one another as well as with the related literature. Jeanneret and McCormick (1969) concluded that their findings supported their main hypothesis, and the Purdue factors appear to have some valuable implications for job evaluation, selection batteries, and synthetic test validations.

There have been many attempts to organize vocational interest data, but they have rarely resulted in any striking theoretical or practical outcomes. Strong (1943) and others have factor analyzed the scales of the SVIB and found four-to-eight major factors. Norman (1960) analyzed lower level vocational interests using the Minnesota Vocational Interest Inventory and found that six functions account for about 92 percent of the intergroup information. Perhaps Guilford et al. (1954) performed the most comprehensive analyses of vocational interests. The factor analysis of a variety of interest and personality inventories produced six main factors: mechanical, scientific, social welfare, clerical, business, and esthetic. In brief, the results of cluster and factor analyses of interest inventories reveal that a small number of factors account for most of the variance, and these major factors appear to be variations on a few major themes, such as science, people, skilled trades, business, and persuasive interests and activities.

Roe's occupational classification system with eight groups and six levels is related to the sets of interest factors just reviewed. Her occupational groups resemble interest factors and her levels approximate many occupational status measures. A recent study by Roe et al. (1966) shows that her scheme organizes occupational histories in an orderly and impressive way, but the assumption she makes for the relatedness or arrangement of her main groups has received only weak or ambiguous support (Roe et al., 1966; Hutchinson & Roe, 1968). The form of the Roe classification (kinds of occupations by levels of responsibility) appears especially valuable, for it reduces the confounding of interest and levels of talent. Despite these advantages, the Roe classification lacks explicit definitions for groups and levels and a precise rationale or empirical method for its revision or the addition of new occupations.

In several reports, Holland and his colleagues (Holland, 1959, 1966a; Holland, Whitney, Cole, & Richards, 1969; Holland, Viernstein, Kuo, Karweit, & Blum, 1970) have proposed, revised, and tested a classification scheme for occupations which grew out of his development of the Vocational Preference Inventory (Holland, 1965) and a theory of vocational choice (Holland, 1959, 1966b, 1973). Holland's classification is related to earlier vocational interest classifications—particularly to Guilford's six factors of human interest (Guilford et al., 1954).

The present classification (Holland, 1973) of six main categories—Realistic, Investigative, Artistic, Social, Enterprising, and Conventional—and sub-categories, such as Realistic-Investigative or Realistic-Social, etc. —has several desirable characteristics: (1) it implements a theory for interpreting class membership; (2) occupations are classified according to a single, empirical principle; and (3) the classification has been extended to all occupations in the DOT (Viernstein, 1972).

This incomplete review of some occupational classification schemes indicates that few are without flaws. On the other hand, classifications show great promise for structuring both personal assessment data (vocational preferences, work histories, and interest inventory profiles) and occupational data. And, the predictive power of these preliminary schemes is often efficient.

STRUCTURE AND THEORY

The experience with occupational classification systems, the numerous factor analyses of occupational materials, and the literature generally imply an organization or structure for the data obtained from interest inventories and from the concepts of vocational choice, vocational preference, and occupation. The purpose of this section is to suggest a structure, to summarize some advantages of this structural model for occupational knowledge, and to review some popular theories for interpreting this structure, or for interpreting the process and development of vocational preferences.

Structure

The argument for the suggested occupational structure goes as follows: (1) the data about vocational interests, vocational choice, and occupational membership are positively associated, because they represent three methods for assessing the same set of personal dispositions. This, of course, is the main assumption for organizing the present chapter. (2) A common set of dimensions or categories can be obtained not only from these highly correlated methods—vocational interests, choices, and occupational membership—but also many of their correlates—aptitudes, competencies, self-ratings— which are domains normally assumed to be divergent. Briefly, when the information about vocational preference is organized according to a large multimethod and multitrait matrix, a common occupational structure becomes clear.

The data to support these ideas are organized in the next sections. The first section suggests that the data *within* each of several domains have a similar structure. The second section suggests that the data *among* each of several domains are positively associated. And a third section interprets this information. Finally, what follows is a sketch, not a finished painting with every piece of data accounted for. At the same time, it is assumed that a review of all data would not alter the model in any substantial way.

Structure Within Domains

If we review the kinds of factors or dimensions found within each of several domains (aptitudes, interests, personality, occupational membership, and occupational images), some comparable factors appear to be present in most domains. Put another way, no matter what kind of evidence we use, we tend to get similar factors.

For the vocational interest domain, Roe (1956) simply presented Table 1 (on the next page) to show that the occupational categories in her classification resembled the major factors discovered in separate factor analyses by Guilford et al. (1954) and other investigators. And, although Roe engages in no numerical analyses, her table strongly suggests that diverse factor analyses, using different populations and methods, produce similar factors.

More recently, Holland et al. (1969) showed that his six category classifications could be arranged in a hexagon so that the distances among the categories are inversely proportional to the correlations among the categories. Holland's categories are comparable in most respects to Roe's, and the hexagonal ordering of his categories, which were empirically derived, is identical with Roe's circular arrangement of eight categories which has also received empirical support (Roe et al., 1966). Figure 1 illustrates the circular ordering first observed by Cole and Hanson (1971) in both classifications.

These preliminary explorations of or-

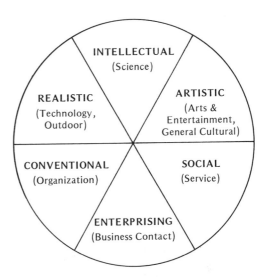

Figure 1. Circular ordering of Holland's categories (in capital letters) and the corresponding ordering of the categories of Roe (in parentheses). (Taken from Cole & Hanson, 1971.)

ganizational plans have received strong support from Cole and her colleagues. In a methodological paper, Cole and Cole (1970) first devised a modified factor-analytic method to visualize the relationships among categories or scales in a single plane. Next, Cole, Whitney, and Holland (1971) applied the Cole analysis to some vocational interest data and found positive evidence for the usefulness of this new configural method. Most recently, Cole and Hanson (1971) compared the scales of the SVIB, the Kuder OIS, Holland's VPI, Clark's MVII, and the ACT Vocational Interest Profile (1970) by applying the Cole configural analysis to each inventory. "The configurations of the scales for all the inventories were found to be similar and to conform to the circular configurations of interest proposed by Roe and Holland."

In short, the results suggest that these diverse inventories assess not only comparable personal dimensions, but also that these dimensions occur in the same order for each inventory, when the Cole configural method is applied. In addition, Cole and Hanson

TABLE 1

THE RELATION OF ROE'S OCCUPATIONAL CATEGORIES TO THE FACTORS FROM SELECTED FACTOR ANALYSES

Classification	Vernon	Thurstone	Darley	Strong	Kuder	Guilford et al.
I. Service	Social welfare vs. administrative Gregarious vs. isolated	People	Welfare uplift	People	Social service	Social welfare
II. Business Contact	Gregarious vs. isolated	People	Business contact	Business	Persuasive	Business
III. Organization	Administrative vs. social welfare	Business	Business detail CPA	Business system	Clerical Computational	Business Clerical
IV. Technology	Scientific vs. display Isolated vs. gregarious	Science	Technical	Things vs. people	Scientific Mechanical Computational	Scientific Mechanical
V. Outdoor	Active vs. verbal				Outdoor	Physical drive Preference for outdoor work
VI. Science	Scientific vs. display Isolated vs. gregarious	Science	Technical	Things vs. people	Scientific	Scientific
VII. General Cultural	Verbal vs. active	Language	Verbal	Language	Literary	Cultural
VIII. Arts and Entertainment	Display vs. scientific	Language	Verbal	Language	Artistic Musical Literary	Aesthetic expression Aesthetic appreciation Cultural Physical drive in some active vs. verbal

Note: Table 1 is Table 11.2 from Roe (1956, p. 148) and retitled for clarity.

have also provided an elegant, statistical reconciliation of earlier contradictory differences among scales with comparable names (i.e., the Mechanical Scale of the Kuder versus the Aviator Scale of the SVIB), and a configural method for plotting and interpreting vocational interest inventory scores and occupational membership.

Most recently, Edwards and Whitney (1972) demonstrated that separate sets of scales, composed entirely of activities, competencies, occupational preferences, or self-ratings, yield similar maps when the Cole configural method is applied. Their factor analyses also revealed that the four different domains of assessment contain the same main factors.

In addition to these precise tests of whether or not similar factors exist from one kind of scale content to the next, much literature, in retrospect, contains maps of main factors that resemble the Cole, Holland, and Roe analyses. Strong's factor maps (see Strong, 1943, Figures 4–12, pp. 146–154) resemble the arrangements that we are rediscovering with newer methods in recent analyses. Robinson, Athanasiou, and Head (1969), using "smallest space analysis," obtain maps for the SVIB, Kuder DD, and the MVII (Figures 3–4, pp. 425–429) that resemble those obtained by Cole and Hanson (1971). In addition, Robinson et al. summarize some of the evidence for the sociological similarity of occupations—largely according to status—but at the same time, their maps of similarity also reflect some of the main interest groups reviewed earlier (Figure 2, p. 421).

Thorndike and Hagen's (1959, p. 37) plot of occupational group means in terms of "high and low quantitative" versus "verbal to mechanical" aptitudes implies that their results for aptitude tests resemble the configurations obtained for interest measures. And O'Dowd and Beardslee (1967) present maps (Figure 4, p. 77) based on their factor analyses of people's perceptions of occupations that also resemble the main

interest factors and the configurations obtained by Cole and Hanson (1971).

To summarize, there is a wide range of evidence that suggests: (1) four-to-eight categories or dimensions of interest account for most interest inventory scales; (2) the relationships among these categories tend to have a characteristic order; (3) similar factors and similar orders are often found from one domain to the next by investigators using a variety of methods; and (4) studies of actual job descriptions also reveal that there are only four-to-eight different kinds of occupations (McCormick et al., 1969).

Relations Among Domains

Vocational interest scales are also positively correlated *across* many domains or classes of psychological variables: personality measures, aptitude tests, self-estimated competencies, perceptual tests, and other psychological and sociological variables. It is in fact difficult to think of variables that are not associated to some degree with vocational interests.

For example, the SVIB scales have been found to be positively correlated with the Edwards PPS (Dunnette, Kirchner, & DeGidio, 1958), Q-sort ratings of personality (Block & Peterson, 1955), objective perceptual performance tests (Crutchfield, Woodworth, & Albrecht, 1958), travel preferences, such as a trip to Yellowstone versus a trip to Las Vegas (Peterson & Pennington, 1969), and the California Psychological Inventory (Gough, 1957; Dunnette et al., 1958). Other investigators have found substantial canonical correlations between the Strong and vocational needs (Thorndike, Weiss, & Dawis, 1968), and the VPI and life goals, self-ratings of ability and personality traits, and potential for achievement (Baird, 1970).

These and other studies rarely result in substantial correlations between interest and personality variables, but the low-to-moderate significant correlations are largely expected ones: people with social interests have high scores on sociability scales, people with scientific interests appear less social, accounting interests go with being orderly, etc. (Cottle, 1950; Gough, 1957; Siess & Jackson, 1970).

An Interpretation

The occurrence of a limited number of factors, their overlap in content from one domain to the next, and the intercorrelation of vocational interests and myriad personal variables fill in another major piece of the puzzle. The evidence implies that the same four-to-eight personal dispositions are expressed in many ways. Or, a small number of personal dispositions may account for what we know about the concepts of vocational interest, preference, choice, and occupational membership.

The usefulness of this assumption can be determined only by vigorous applications of the idea in research and practice. Like a new theory or a new car, careful examination will reveal only limited information. Only vigorous and varied uses of a theory or a car will reveal its strengths and weaknesses. More canonical correlations promise little. At most, they suggest different domains have much in common—something we knew earlier from simple correlations. A more productive step is to explore the various theoretical and practical values of believing by using this working assumption. The experience gained will make clear whether such an assumption is worth further allegiance.

Theory

The extensive work concerned with the *structure* of vocational preferences suggests a useful way to organize most related research and speculation. This tradition has emphasized methods and plans to organize occupational knowledge and to predict occupational choice (occupational classifications, factor analyses, occupational differences).

Another more recent orientation is more concerned with the *processes* of personal development which lead to different vocational preferences. Consequently, the process orientation is more concerned with concepts such as personality development and vocational maturity.

Although these orientations have different goals, they supplement one another. In a sentence, one organizes information about occupations, and the other outlines how people get there. Despite its pragmatic value, this characterization does considerable violence to some of the work that follows. For more sensitive and diverse ways of characterizing vocational theory, see Crites (1969b) and Osipow (1968).

Organization and Prediction

The work of Roe (1956) and Holland (1966b) exemplifies this approach to theory. Although both say something about the development of vocational preference (especially Roe), most of their theoretical and empirical work is closely oriented to their classification schemes and predictions from their application. Both classifications can be traced to earlier factor analytic studies by Strong (1943), Guilford et al. (1954), and others, and both are buttressed, indirectly at least, by more recent work reviewed under "Classification."

In the report "Early Determinants of Vocational Choice," Roe (1957) outlines a theory in which the child's early experiences with his parents are assumed to create or foster "basic attitudes, interests, and capacities which will be given expression in the general pattern of the adult's life, in his personal relations, in his emotional reactions, in his activities, and in his vocational choice." From three characteristic family atmospheres (emotional concentration on the child, avoidance of the child, and acceptance of the child) Roe predicts the resulting adult orientations and the classes of occupations to which such early childhood experience will lead. For example, emotional concentration on the child, which takes the form of overprotectiveness, is assumed to produce children who enter the arts and the entertainment field. In contrast, parental avoidance of the child is assumed to be conducive to the development of scientific interests. Similar predictions about adult vocational choices are made for other parent-child interactions.

Roe's theory of parental influence has generated much empirical investigation and is summarized in Borow (1964), Osipow (1968), and Crites (1969b). Unfortunately, most of the evidence is tenuous, negative, or ambiguous. However, Medvene (1969) recently found that perceived parental attitudes were significantly related to later occupational choice for the occupation of psychology. Medvene may have shown the way to conduct better studies of this subtle problem by carefully specifying the occupational specialities to be studied.

In contrast to the parental influence hypotheses, the occupational classification scheme which Roe (1956) proposed as an integral part of her theory has enjoyed considerable success including much practical usage and positive results. Because of her dissatisfaction with the traditional occupational classifications, Roe developed an occupational classification which explicitly takes into account interests as well as levels of responsibility and training. The first scheme was an 8 × 8 classification with eight groups of occupations identified in terms of "focus of activity." They include (I) Service; (II) Business Contact; (III) Organization; (IV) Technology; (V) Outdoor; (VI) Science; (VII) General Cultural; (VIII) Arts and Entertainment. Each of these classes was also ordered by "level of function" so that for each class there are eight levels ranging from Level 8, "Support, Unskilled," to Level 1, "Innovation and Independent Responsibility." Subsequently, the number of levels was reduced to six and a few occupations were reclassified within this 8 × 6 matrix.

The evidence for the usefulness of Roe's classification and its assumed theoretical properties are contained in reports by Crites (1962), Jones (1965), Osipow (1966), Roe, Hubbard, Hutchinson, and Bateman (1966), Hutchinson and Roe (1968), and others. Of these, the studies by Roe et al. (1966) and Osipow (1966) are especially impressive. Roe and her colleagues (1966) created an 8 × 8 table by applying her classification to all the occupational changes of 804 men for periods up to twenty-two years. Although her sample was not representative, the results clearly suggest that job transitions are orderly rather than random. The majority of changes (68 percent) consist of moving from position to position *within* one of Roe's eight main categories. In short, Roe's classification orders job changes in an efficient way. In addition, her assumption that the eight categories form a circle in which adjacent categories are most closely related also receives support.

Like Roe, Holland's theory of vocational preference attempts to organize occupational knowledge, using a classification, and to predict occupational behavior from a theory of personality types and model environments. In 1959, Holland outlined a theory of vocational choice, and in 1966 and 1973, he provided a more comprehensive, systematic, and testable theory (Holland, 1959, 1966b, 1973).

Holland assumes a six-category typology: Realistic, Investigative, Social, Conventional, Enterprising, Artistic. For each type, a theoretical formulation is offered to explain vocational preference and other behavior. Definitions and techniques for assessing a person's resemblance to a type are provided including scales of the VPI, Strong, and Kuder, choice of occupation, or choice of training. The typology is both a classification of occupations and of persons; that is, the typology can be used to classify and understand occupations or persons.

Vocational choice is assumed to be the result of a person's type, or patterning of types *and* the environment. Holland and his colleagues (Astin & Holland, 1961; Richards

& Seligman, 1968) have found it useful to characterize environments by calculating the distribution of types in a given environment and assuming that the character of an environment emanates from the types which dominate that environment.

The key concepts and assumptions are supplemented by several secondary concepts which can be applied to both a person and his environment. They include:

1. *Consistency.* Some types are more compatible than others; for example, Realistic-Investigative as opposed to Conventional-Artistic. And degrees of consistency are assumed to affect vocational preference—Realistic-Investigatives should be more predictable than Realistic-Socials.

2. *Homogeneity.* Some persons or environments are more clearly defined than others; for instance, a person who closely resembles a single type and shows little resemblance to other types, or an environment dominated largely by a single type.

3. *Calculus.* The relationships among types or occupations can be ordered according to a hexagon in which distances between types or occupational classes are inversely proportional to the size of the correlations between them. This spatial arrangement provides explicit definitions of consistency (three levels) and congruency of person and environment (three or more).

Taken together, the secondary concepts improve predictions and provide degrees of consistency, homogeneity, and congruence. Before the discovery of the hexagonal model it was necessary to resort to all-or-none definitions of consistency and congruity.

The evidence for the usefulness of this theory appears generally positive: Holland and others have established that the formulations for the personality types have some validity (Holland, 1968, 1973; Walsh & Lacey, 1969; Elton & Rose, 1970; Williams, 1972). The usefulness of the occupational classification and its special arrangement—the formation of main categories and subcategories and the discovery of a hexagonal model—receive substantial support in several investigations (Holland, 1966a; Holland, Whitney, Cole, & Richards, 1969; Holland, Viernstein, Kuo, Karweit, & Blum, 1970; Cole & Hanson, 1971). Attempts to document the hypotheses about person-environment interactions have usually received only weak to modest support (Holland, 1968, 1973; Morrow, 1970; Posthuma & Navran, 1970).

Development and Process

The work of Super et al. (1967), Tiedeman, O'Hara, and Baruch (1963), Crites (1969a), Bordin et al. (1963), Vroom (1964), and Blau et al. (1956) illustrate this orientation to a theory of vocational preference. These researchers are concerned with explaining the *process* of vocational preference. They outline the process more explicitly than theories classified as "organization and prediction," and they usually do so in the context of personal development or decision making. Characteristically, they lack a classification or typology, or they only imply a classification.

Of these developmental or decision-oriented formulations, those of Super and Bordin have generated the most research. More recent formulations by Katz (1966) and Kroll, Dinklage, Lee, Morley, and Wilson (1970) have similar orientations and may or may not be more useful. Only more work will make their values clear.

Super and his collaborators hope to predict and understand "career," which they define as the sequence of occupations, jobs, and positions through a person's working life. This definition may be extended to include prevocational and post-vocational positions such as those of students preparing for vocations or those of retired persons.

Although his goals are clear, Super's theorizing is difficult to summarize, because he does not provide a single, explicit formulation. Instead, Super (1971) organizes most of his thinking and research in terms of the following topics: "The differential psychology of occupations (including aptitude and motivation of interest, value, and need theory), the psychology and sociology of life stages and of developmental processes, patterns of career development, vocational maturity, and the phenomonology of decision making."

Super believes only a diffuse statement is possible, because we lack data and knowledge to provide a comprehensive theory. A brief summary of the "segments" in Super's formulation follow.

First, Super believes that the career model is a more useful way to look at vocational preferences and work histories. Although he recognizes the virtues of the older occupational model, the career model draws attention to the developmental, sequential, cumulative character of a person's history of vocational preferences. Consequently, this point of view should lead to career counseling rather than position counseling, to predicting career rather than occupational success.

Second, Super borrowed the concept of life stages from developmental psychology and applied it to a person's vocational behavior. Other thinking by Super and Ginzberg led to the analysis of vocational preference in terms of three periods: fantasy, tentative stages (including interests, capacity, and value), and realistic stages (including exploration, crystallization, and specification).

These stages of exploration, crystallization, choice, and clarification were also refined by Tiedeman, O'Hara, and Baruch (1963) in their development of a model of the decision-making process. Likewise, Havighurst's (1953) theory of developmental tasks is similar to that of life stages. In short, people at any age must perform age-appropriate tasks and success at one stage leads to success at the next stage.

Third, Super's concern with vocational maturity expresses his strategy of focusing on the early stages of vocational development—the exploratory and establishment stages. Consequently, Super and his colleagues (Super, Kowalski, & Gotkin, 1967; Crites, 1965; Gribbons & Lohnes, 1968) have

tried to define, assess, and trace the vocational maturity or development of young people in a wide range of studies.

Fourth, Super views a person's vocational preferences and career patterns as attempts to implement a self-concept. For example, the person selects vocations whose requirements will provide a role which is consistent with his picture of himself. The self-concept model is a useful way to articulate the proceeding orientations or formulations. In short, the self-concept plays a central role in making vocational decisions because it is the product of a person's vocational maturity level, his developmental history with its specific successes and failures in dealing with societal hurdles and experiences; and the self-concept is in process of change from birth to death.

The evidence for the usefulness of Super's formulations is extensive and varied. On the one hand, his formulations have probably affected the work of practitioners more than those of anyone else. On the other hand, the evidence for the validity of his formulations is extensive, but often ambiguous (Hunt, 1967; Super et al., 1967; Gribbons & Lohnes, 1968). Super's reluctance to present a single, clear, and comprehensive statement of his theorizing makes tests of his hypotheses hard to interpret. Perhaps the greatest value of his thinking lies in the programmatic rather than the theoretical orientation his work has provided researchers and practitioners: (1) the usefulness of a developmental view of vocational life and the closely related concepts which Super has initiated or stimulated others to refine and use; and (2) the usefulness of the self-concept model as a way to integrate and understand a person's vocational behavior.

Bordin and his colleagues (Bordin, Nachmann, & Segal, 1963) have also provided a theory of vocational development to account for the process of vocational preference. They propose a matrix of need-gratifying activities, traceable to infantile psychological functions, which will account for all of the gratifications which work can offer. They make an explicit attempt to apply psycho-analytic theory to vocational preference. In their first statement, they illustrate the application of the theory to the occupations of social work, plumbing, and accounting. Using a complex matrix of need-gratifying activities, such as nurturant, oral, and manipulative for one dimension, and categorizations and ratings of degree of involvement, instrumental mode, objects, sexual mode, and affect for another dimension, the authors map and assess each occupation's need-gratifying potential. The resulting characterizations appear instructive.

The investigations performed to test some of the hypotheses in this analytic theory have usually been positive and plausible (Galinsky, 1962; Nachmann, 1960; Segal, 1961; Barry & Bordin, 1967). It is ironic, however, that the chief weakness in the Bordin theory may not be its psychoanalytic base but rather the impracticality of extending the theory to a large number of occupations. The time and labor involved in applying the theory to new occupations restricts its application. If its application could be facilitated, a rapid exploration of its usefulness would become possible.

Assessment

Despite their many virtues, all theories of vocational preference suffer from some theoretical and substantive maladies. These include poor or missing definitions of terms, formulations that "boggle the mind" rather than stimulate investigation, inefficient predictions or no predictive power at all, narrow or excessive scope, and similar problems.

At the same time, current speculation and theorizing appears to have some positive common denominators. The usefulness of occupational classification schemes as well as their potential appears brighter than ever before for organizing occupational information of all kinds. The predictive value of such schemes appears to outrun that usually obtained from more complex procedures. The synthetic validities obtained from job factors only by McCormick, Cunningham, and Thornton (1967) lends additional credence to the values inherent in occupational classification studies.

The perception of vocational behavior as a developmental or lifelong process by all investigators has started a search for linkages over longer spans of time, and for linkages between specialities within psychology itself which have been usually overlooked— especially the relationship of counseling psychology to industrial psychology.

VOCATIONAL DEVELOPMENT

The information about vocational preference is voluminous and accelerating. Investigators, armed with interest inventories and assessment devices of all kinds, have probed children, students, teachers, parents, therapists, employees, retirees, and hospital patients. The strategy here has been to organize this diverse information in the framework of "vocational development" and in the "structure" of occupations. In other words, it appears useful to organize the main threads of evidence according to the life history of a person's vocational preferences, and according to some common occupational categories at each age level. This general orientation carves current knowledge into the following pieces:

1. Elementary and Secondary Students
2. College Students
3. School to Work
4. Employed Adults

This organization is intended to suggest some of the continuities between one stage of life and the next. The assignment of studies to categories is often arbitrary, because many investigations belong to multiple categories. Again, the reader is reminded that this account is a selective review and reformulation.

For a general orientation to the developmental point of view applied to vocational behavior, several authors are especially helpful. White's (1952) *Lives in Progress* provides some vivid, long-term vocational case histories. Crites's (1969c) essay, "Interests," provides a useful history of the definition and the development of interests. *Career Development* by Kroll, Dinklage, Lee, Morley, and Wilson (1970) provides a more comprehensive summary and is usually more readable than the original sources which the authors draw upon. An extensive paper by Jordaan (1971) provides a comprehensive account of the concept of vocational maturity as studied by Super, Crites, and others. Bartlett (1971) also provides a review of the various approaches to the measurement of vocational maturity as well as a more critical analysis. And, Campbell's (1968) report on the development of a cultural change scale from SVIB data provides a provocative technique for assessing cultural change, the context in which vocational development takes place. His interpretation that Americans have become more extroverted—the 1960s as opposed to the 1930s—is persuasive. The recent trends toward socially oriented occupations, and away from engineering and science, support his hypothesis (H. S. Astin, 1967a). In addition, The Cultural Change Scale implies a method for comparing cultures and their relative influence upon vocational development.

Elementary-Secondary Students

New and old studies of vocational preference, using samples of elementary and secondary students, suggest the influence of social status, intelligence, race, sex, and many other variables (Witty & Lehman, 1931; Sewell, Haller, & Straus, 1957; Kohn & Schooler, 1969; Kohn, 1969; Bachman, 1970). Because most studies use only a few selected variables, it is difficult to assess the relative influence of personal and background variables, although social class, education, and intelligence usually outdistance most other variables.

Using a national sample of tenth grade boys, Bachman (1970) has found that boys of high social status are more likely to possess the intellectual abilities demanded in our society for success in school and on the job; and, equally important, they display higher aspirations and more positive self-concepts. Regression analyses reveal that family socioeconomic status influences occupational aspiration more than any other variable, although intelligence contributes some unique variance. Another report by Kohn (1969)—actually a report of three empirical studies of social class—enlarges our understanding of the pervasive outcomes of social class membership on values, self-conception, and work. Kohn documents how characteristic attitudes of parents at different social strata affect their children's vocational aspirations. For example, fathers of high status value self-direction more than conformity to externally imposed standards, whereas fathers of low status value conformity more than self-direction. The implications of these findings for careers appears to be reflected in the studies of careers reported later.

In a large scale study of 127,125 students entering 248 four-year colleges, Werts and Watley (1970) compared fathers' occupations with the probability of children's non-academic achievements in high school—scientific, artistic, oral, leadership, musical, and literary. The results suggest, with unusual clarity, that children excel at their fathers' occupational skills. For instance, sons of scientists tend to win science contests; whereas sons of entrepreneurs have essentially zero probabilities of such success. These and other findings are impressive, because they suggest the strong force of family environment and heredity upon the content and competencies of a student's activities.

The revival of interest in heredity has resulted in more studies of identical and fraternal twins. Using the Minnesota Vocational Interest Inventory, Vandenberg and Stafford (1967) conclude that heredity influences probably affect "the entire occupational spectrum." "The hereditary components influence one's aptitudes and personality traits which in turn influence vocational preferences." And, Nichols (1966) using samples of 498 identical and 319 fraternal twins (assessed with the California Psychological Inventory, the Vocational Preference Inventory, and the Objective Behavior Inventory) found that identicals were more similar than were fraternals in almost all measures.

In their longitudinal studies, Crites (1965), Gribbons and Lohnes (1969), and Super et al. (1967) have made major attempts to analyze the personal and environmental forces affecting a student's vocational preferences. These investigators share a common concern—to specify the developmental processes and experiences that lead to satisfying, mature, and stable vocational preferences in adulthood.

Toward this end, Crites (1965) has developed an attitude scale, The Vocational Development Inventory (VDI), to assess a student's level of vocational development or maturity. This complex scale, measuring several constructs implied by vocational development, such as orientation toward work and involvement in the choice process, can be used as a criterion to assess the effects of treatment designed to promote vocational development in young people, or as a predictor of adaptive vocational behavior at a later age. Of all the tools developed to cope with the assessment of vocational development, Crites's VDI seems most useful for both practitioners and researchers, because it has a clear rationale, an extensive validation, and a simple form (fifty true-false items).

Gribbons and Lohnes (1968, 1969) have studied the vocational preferences and occupational choices of fifty-seven boys and fifty-four girls from about age thirteen to age twenty-five. Using a set of Readiness for Vocational Planning Scales obtained from interviews, and a set of traditional measures, such as socioeconomic status, intelligence, and sex, they related these predictors to successive estimates of vocational maturity, vocational choice, and career patterning. Although their predictions via stochastic processes and other techniques are sometimes weak, their data strongly suggest that the development of a student's vocational preferences is lawful or somewhat predictable. And they demonstrate once again that SES, IQ, and sex are powerful determinants of vocational preference, although the influence of these variables fluctuates from one time to the next. Finally, Gribbons and Lohnes (1969) provide some scales with promising explanatory value for further work. Both the Readiness for Career Planning Scale and the Readiness for Vocational Planning Scales appear to be promising ways to explore the processes of vocational development and to predict career patterns.

Super's most recent findings (Super et al., 1967) are congruent with much of the findings of Gribbons and Lohnes. Super et al. (1967) report that standard measures, such as grades, IQ, and SES (socioeconomic status) are among the best predictors of vocational development (in this case, coping well with the school-to-work transition). Super's longitudinal study of eighth- and ninth-grade boys from about age fourteen to twenty-five also reveals that knowledge of education and training, planning, and interest maturity (SVIB) forecast desirable vocational behavior. The study by Gribbons and Lohnes (1969) reports similar results using somewhat different concepts and definitions.

The developmental studies of Crites, Gribbons and Lohnes, and others—which flow largely from Super's work—have negotiated a large void in our knowledge of the development of vocational preference. They provide a variety of ways to assess a student's progress toward vocational maturity and to link adolescent to adult vocational behavior. What is needed now are more substantial replications of the most promising definitions and predictions along with a clear synthesis of the findings which now rest on diverse instruments and definitions.

Other large scale longitudinal studies by H. S. Astin (1967b), Cooley (1963, 1967),

Flanagan and Cooley (1966), have been more concerned with the prediction of occupational preference or membership than with the analysis of developmental processes. For example, Cooley (1963) traced the occupational preferences of potential scientists versus nonscientists by using an overlapping longitudinal design. In this way, Cooley could examine some of the determinants of vocational preference from the fifth grade to the second year of graduate school. In general, Cooley obtained useful formulae for differentiating science and nonscience students by using ability, interest, temperament, and environmental measures. Among these, interest, temperament, and values inventories (Strong Vocational Interest Blank, Guilford-Zimmerman, Allport-Vernon-Lindsay) were most useful.

The studies by Cooley (1967) and Flanagan and Cooley (1966) reveal that self-predictions of vocational preference (42 percent hits) equal the predictions obtained from ability (38 percent) or motive (42 percent) measures. Using a sample from the same project, H. S. Astin (1967b) showed the predictions of occupational preference could be improved by adding selected environmental characteristics to the usual predictive formula of interests plus ability. In a related study, Barclay (1967) developed a measure of the teacher "press" in different high school curricula by categorizing curricula according to Holland's classification and assessing the most and least preferred students in each curriculum with a battery of inventories and scales. Generally, Barclay found that the students liked by teachers possessed characteristics implied by the classification's theory.

College Students

Perhaps more effort has been devoted to the study of the vocational preferences of college students than any other age group. *The Impact of College on Students* (Feldman & Newcomb, 1969) is a recent and comprehensive summary of this literature,

but the reviews and texts cited earlier are needed to provide a complete knowledge of these diverse studies. Although Feldman and Newcomb concern themselves with students in major fields only, it seems useful to regard major fields as a reliable estimate of vocational choice.

Their review reiterates what others have found at both younger and older age levels. Students enrolled in different curricula show some special characteristics, and students in different fields or with different interests appear to come from different social and economic backgrounds. Differences of opinion center on the degree or clarity of the personal characteristics which we can attribute to a field or group of vocational preferences, such as "science" or "education."

The accentuation hypothesis, which Feldman and Newcomb propose, also appears to apply to people at other age levels. They suggest that a student's major field tends to accentuate the personal characteristics a student brings to his field of study. In more general terms, young people, college students, and employed adults may seek out congenial situations which in turn reinforce the very traits that led to the selection of the particular vocational preference, training, or occupation.

Other work by Flanagan et al. (1964), Davis (1965), Folger, Astin, and Bayer (1970), Astin and Panos (1968), Krulee, O'Keefe, and Goldberg (1966), Werts (1968), Katz, Korn, Leland, and Levin (1968), Dunteman, Anderson, and Barry (1966) provides massive amounts of information about the correlates and determinants of vocational preference among college students. These large scale studies clearly document substantial differences among college students seeking different occupations. At the same time, this mountain of new data increases the need for comprehensive plans to organize and interpret student vocational preferences and their correlates. As Feldman and Newcomb discovered earlier, the use of tests and scales common to several student samples is only a limited, and often impossible, way to interpret group differences. Nevertheless, the magnitude of these recent studies provides a rich ore for ambitious prospectors that has never been available before.

These massive studies of concurrent relationships have been accompanied by a smaller number of diverse, longitudinal studies of the vocational preferences of college students. The substantive outcomes are usually clear, but the theoretical contributions are sometimes obscure; that is, the relationships between the empirical analyses and theoretical statements are often ambiguous. Despite these shortcomings, the analyses usually strongly support the idea that students in different fields have different personalities and that the college experience often "accentuates" or reinforces what the student brings to his college or field of study. Some outstanding examples of this longitudinal work follow.

In several large scale national samples, Astin and Panos (1968) studied the influence of college characteristics upon a student's choice of occupation and major field. Generally, their results are helpful in analyzing the influence of college environments as they relate to vocational decision making because their study included both personal and environmental data as well as some estimates of the relative contribution of each to vocational decisions. Astin and Panos conclude that:

1. About three-fourths of the students changed their long-term career plans after entering college, but the percentage of those who changed varied greatly from field to field (50-to-95 percent).

2. The patterns of change in career choice and in field of study were not random. Students who changed their plans tended to switch to fields that were related to their initial vocational choice.

3. In general, the student's career choice tended to move into closer conformity with the most popular career choices among his fellow students.

This "progressive conformity hypothesis"

of Astin and Panos resembles the "accentuation hypothesis" of Feldman and Newcomb as well as the "congruity" and "birds of a feather" hypotheses assumed by the man on the street and most researchers. The Astin and Panos findings are impressive, because they flow from a large national study of 127,212 students that used extensive controls (input-output design) and a comprehensive assessment of the college environment. For a complete account of the virtues of Astin's input-output designs, the reader should see A. W. Astin (1970a, 1970b). The origin and development of Astin's environmental inventory for assessing colleges (The Inventory of College Activities) is summarized in another extensive report (A. W. Astin, 1968).

Using Project Talent data, Cooley (1967) examined the interactions which took place among interests, abilities, and career plans. This complex longitudinal study suggests that as students move from the ninth to twelfth grades, their vocational interests, abilities, and career plans converge or become more congruent. In a related study, Cooley and Lohnes (1968) devised the career development tree, a method for showing the patterns of successive occupational preferences or occupations, and applied this model to the five-year data in Project Talent. For example, 55 percent of the twelfth grade boys who planned college physical science programs were pursuing science careers five years after high school. These and other findings suggest that felicitous categorizations at different age levels are a useful way to organize career data.

Holland (1968) tested the usefulness of his revised theory (Holland, 1966b) in a large, diverse sample of college students. Generally, the formulations for the personality types received more support in the 1968 study than in the earlier ones (e.g., Holland, 1963), although the hypotheses about person-environment interactions still received only weak support. Once again, the evidence suggested that students in different fields have different personal characteristics. There was also some evidence to support the congruity hypothesis that students are more likely to remain in fields which are populated by the majority of the student body. In another longitudinal study, using the Holland Occupational Classification, Holland and Whitney (1968) found support for the Astin and Panos finding that successive student occupational preferences are not random. For example, "79 percent of the men indicate successive vocational choices that are related or lawful rather than random" (Holland & Whitney, 1968, p. 16). A special classification scheme for women yielded similar and equally efficient predictions.

In a four-year study of college students at Northwestern, Krulee, O'Keefe, and Goldberg (1966) provided much needed information about the influences that lead to occupational choice and change: aspirations, values, career expectations, curriculum evaluations, personal preferences, and family background. This investigation is an unusually comprehensive source of data about the choice of training and vocation, and the personal attitudes and orientation that lead to a change in choice. Although these researchers emphasize the influence of identity processes on occupational choice, the relationship between theories of identity and their experimental activities are tenuous; that is, ideas from identity theory guided the design and data collection, but only a few explicit hypotheses about student identity were tested.

In other large scale studies, both Davis (1965) and Werts (1967) found that "deviant" students tend to switch their preferences to career choices that are more compatible with their personal characteristics.

School-to-Work

The transition from school to work has received relatively little interest until recently. Taken together, the recent work of psychologists and sociologists outlines more clearly how young people maintain or change their vocational aspirations as they move from school to their first several jobs.

In a large-scale study of "school leavers" in England, Veness (1962) assessed students for their aspirations and expectations of work—what they want to be, to do. This comprehensive and sensitive study of how children view their future jobs forms a rich source of data and ideas about the first stage of the school-to-work transition. In general, Veness's work reinforces the importance of some common determinants of vocational aspiration such as talents, interests, and social status.

Super et al. (1967) studied the school-to-work transition in the context of Super's thinking about vocational development. Using special theoretical measures to assess vocational coping behaviors, scaled career outcomes, and occupational outcomes, they tried to predict a student's vocational behavior from earlier assessments of vocational maturity and common measures or records, such as IQ, SES, and school grades.

Among the vocational maturity measures, a boy's knowledge of education and training requirements, planning activity, and interest maturity (SVIB) score appear "conceptually and empirically useful" in forecasting adult vocational behavior. At the same time, standard measures such as IQ, SES, and grades obtained in high school predict the same career behaviors just as efficiently. To summarize, "those who are well endowed personally and environmentally, who aim high, who take the more demanding school program, who earn good grades in junior and in senior high school, and who use the extra resources ... in school and in out-of-school activities, tend to handle their post-high-school careers better, and to be more successful and satisfied in their jobs, than do boys who lack these characteristics, do not act thus, and do not use these resources." In short, high school graduates with more resources (internal and external) cope more successfully with their vocational problems.

Recent sociological studies extend and reinforce these findings. The prestige level of a person's first job is positively correlated with being white and well educated. The point of entry into the labor force is, in turn, positively related to the eventual occupational level a man attains ten years later (Ornstein & Rossi, 1970). In a similar study, Zeller, Shea, Kohen, and Meyer (1970) show that people with lower levels of skill and training have more difficulty in finding jobs and that they usually obtain jobs of lower prestige and income. The vocational difficulties of young men of low SES are further compounded, because they receive less vocational counseling and the counseling they do receive is poor (Simpson & Harper, 1962).

Employed Adults

This section attempts to organize what we know about vocational preferences from the assessment of adult workers. For convenience, this knowledge is categorized as follows:

1. Occupational Differences (characteristics of workers with different vocational preferences).

2. Developmental Histories (prevocational experience of workers with different vocational preferences).

3. Work Histories (career patterns and determinants).

Occupational Differences

As always, new information about differences among individual occupations or groups of occupations continues to grow. For instance, Strong Vocational Interest Blank scales have been developed from large samples for computer programmers (Perry & Cannon, 1967), fashion models (Campbell, 1967), stewardesses and dental assistants (Harmon & Campbell, 1968), Catholic priests (Lepak, 1968), and community recreation administrators (Roys, 1967). These interest scales are a valuable source of information about the occupational incumbents which a student can obtain directly from the recent Strong Handbook (Campbell,

1971), since it contains the keys for all the Strong scales.

The manuals of the SVIB, the Kuder Preference Record, and the Differential Aptitude tests are some of the best single sources of data about occupational differences. Likewise, *Appraising Vocational Fitness* (Super & Crites, 1962), reports and summarizes similar evidence. More recently, Ghiselli (1966) has organized the predictive validity of aptitude tests according to occupations. In short, the evidence about occupational differences is extensive, but the organization and interpretation of this evidence remains unfinished. Although occupations differ in many ways, the major and minor characteristics—interests, aptitudes, personality, values, intelligence—attributed to workers in different occupations are often unclear and debatable (see Super & Crites, 1962; Crites, 1969b; Holland, 1971b).

Although it does not appear obvious, or even desirable, to many researchers, the need to organize this voluminous material into more manageable and interpretable categories seems imperative. The recent substantial results from the diverse classifications by Roe et al. (1966) and McCormick et al. (1967) strongly imply that the development of occupational classifications has great promise for organizing, predicting, and interpreting occupational behavior.

Developmental Histories

Since Fryer's (1931) pioneering work, there has been a small but increasingly useful and scientifically sound group of studies concerned with the history or development of a person's vocational preferences from a young age to his current employment. (Some of these studies concerned primarily with adolescents were reviewed earlier.)

Fryer's first studies of occupational preferences were case histories. More recently, Bordin and his students (Bordin et al., 1963) performed a variety of clinical and experimental studies to learn how various developmental experiences are related to the vocational choices of engineers, physicists, clinical psychologists, dentists, social workers, lawyers, accountants, and writers. These small scale, pioneering studies provide some positive evidence and many plausible hypotheses and ideas for thinking about the relation of personal development to vocational preference. Other studies by Roe (1951) and Norton (1953) are also a valuable source of hypotheses about the origin and history of vocational preferences.

Another group of studies has relied on large scale surveys of the life histories of engineers, lawyers, physicians, and other professionals (Laurent, 1951; Kulberg & Owens, 1960; Chaney & Owens, 1964). These studies have always yielded results that are statistically significant and easily interpreted. For example, Kulberg and Owens (1960) correlated a 100-item life history form with the scores of mechanical engineering freshmen on the engineering scale of the SVIB and with two of Dunnette's (Dunnette, 1957; Dunnette, Wernimont, & Abrahams, 1964) engineering function scales (pure research and sales engineering). The results suggest that the typical engineer has a history of painful or somewhat unsuccessful personal-social relationships and that he has a history of superior performance in science along with more enjoyment of quantitative and practical courses rather than in linguistic and social studies. And, the prospective engineer "has a history of long career planning, of liking to work with things and ideas as opposed to people, and of enjoying creative work and disliking routine." These results, and those obtained from other structured history forms, appear to reinforce many of the findings obtained from earlier small-sample clinical studies. Laurent's study (1951) of engineers paints a similar picture and provides some model histories of other occupations which are also convincing and consistent with some of the traits attributed to those professions. Laurent finds that lawyers have come from families characterized by much social activity. His findings dovetail with the Roe and Siegelman study

(1964) in which they found that the amount of family social activity was related to a college student's preference for the law.

At this point, there seems to be sufficient evidence for someone to organize these histories of individual occupations into occupational categories to obtain a more explicit account of their apparent coherence and to separate the more crucial from the less crucial life experiences. To summarize, the results from the developmental studies suggest that people in different occupational groups have characteristic histories. There is no longer a question of whether there are typical patterns of personal development. The question now is what are the typical patterns of personal development, and how might they be put to scientific and practical use.

Work Histories

The studies of work histories or career patterns are largely atheoretical and few in number, because psychologists and sociologists have, until recently, concerned themselves more with the problems of adolescence, such as choosing and preparing for a career. At the same time, recent career studies have begun to suggest that careers are more orderly than many have assumed, and that some useful methods and ideas exist for analyzing and interpreting the history of a person's successive vocational preferences.

Most career studies can be categorized as longitudinal studies of the relationship between training and current occupation or the study of a single transition. A smaller number are concerned with either a theoretical analysis of multiple job transitions or the application of some theoretical ideas to the data, or both.

The amount of information about the relation of training to present occupation is substantial, but poorly organized (or highly specific) and atheoretical. Despite these difficulties, these studies clearly demonstrate that there is a strong positive relationship between vocational preference (as assessed by choice of training or field of study) and current vocational preferences (as assessed by employment in current occupation) for periods of up to thirty-five years. In addition, if a person's vocational preferences are organized with almost any classification scheme, the relationship between early and late occupational preferences is markedly increased.

For example, a National Science Foundation survey (1963) of 40,000 college graduates—at bachelor's, master's, and professional degree levels—finds that, two years after getting their degrees, most students had secured jobs which were related to their major fields of study. Needless to say, the degree of relatedness varied greatly among fields. Using the same data over a five-year interval, Sharp (1970) reports similar and more readily interpretable relationships. For example, 87.1 percent of the health graduates are employed in health professions five years later; 77.3 percent of engineering graduates are employed as engineers. In contrast, only 58.7 percent of the business and commerce graduates are employed in business and managerial occupations. This study, like most surveys and occupational analyses, suffers because it was necessary to use a conventional classification system with all its scientific weaknesses.

Other surveys provide similar information. Miller (1968) used census data to examine the relationship between formal training and current occupation. Her national sample of experienced labor, aged twenty-two to sixty-four, had either completed three or four years of college or some type of formal occupational training.

For those who had completed three or more years of college the relationship between field of college major and current occupation appears in general to be quite close. However, there is some indication, among males at least, that as workers become older they tend to move into managerial activities and out of the direct pursuit of the occupation for which their college or professional training prepared them.

The relationship between training and current occupation is somewhat more difficult to interpret for those whose formal education stopped before the completion of three years of college. Except for three occupations—professional nurses, barbers, and hairdressers where licensing requirements are quite rigid—none of the thirty-one occupations for which the study provides both specific occupation and specific training data had as much as three-fifths of their workers with training directly in the occupation pursued, and most had considerably less than half with such training. Nevertheless, a relatively high proportion of workers in many of these occupations had had some type of formal training for their current occupation.

Other smaller scale studies, using more homogeneous populations, usually produce clearer results. Doyle (1965), using a sample of college graduates from a single college who had been out of college either five or ten years, found that 70 percent of the alumni remain in their initial occupational fields. McKenzie and Magoon (1966), using a sample of University of Maryland graduates, found that only 43 percent believed their training was "essential" to their job, although 69 percent would major in the same field if they had a chance to reenter college. A study of Harvard alumni by Bateman and Roe (1966) revealed that student occupational plans as college seniors and as employees or students five years later are the same for 68 percent of a sample of 127. Over an eight-year period—from precollege to four years past the senior year—Watley (1968), using National Merit Scholars ($N = 3,673$), reported that only a few fields keep at least 50 percent of their initial recruits. However, a casual inspection of Watley's data suggests that if it were reorganized in terms of broad classes of vocational preferences, the level of stability of vocational choice would show a marked increase. In another recent study of college graduates (University of Maine), Lucy (1971) found statistically significant and strong positive relationships between the category of a student's major field and the category of his current occupation using Holland's classification. Contingency coefficients for 6 × 6 tables range from .64 for a twenty-five-year interval to .74 for a fifteen-year interval. These are impressive findings since Lucy's study spanned time intervals of ten to thirty-five years (803 alumni from the classes of 1935, 1940, 1945, 1950, 1955, 1960).

In general, these relatively simple studies of vocational preferences are rarely very analytical, but they do imply that shifts in vocational preferences are lawful rather than random. And, there is a tendency for such shifts to become less frequent with age. Another report (Parnes, Egge, Kohen, & Schmidt, 1970) reveals that in a representative sample of middle-aged men only one in ten changed employers in a one-year period, whereas an earlier report reveals that four in ten young men make job changes over a one-year period (Zeller, Shea, Kohen, & Meyer, 1970).

These studies of career preference and work history are complemented in useful ways by the studies of sociologists who have been more concerned with the level or prestige of a man's occupation than the kind of work he performs. In addition, sociologists have been more concerned with understanding and manipulating the social system or structure that surrounds the individual worker. Although these characterizations are overdrawn, they capture the main emphases of these different orientations to the study of occupational life.

Recent work history studies by Rossi, Coleman, and Blum illustrate the values and possibilities that are inherent in more sophisticated analyses of a man's career and the forces assumed to affect his career. This research group collected comprehensive, retrospective life history data for a national sample of men aged thirty to thirty-nine. For each man, they obtained his work and educational history in addition to a great range of background data and tried to secure a month-to-month record of a man's life from age fourteen to thirty-nine. Blum, Kar-

weit, and Sorensen (1969) then devised a computer storage and retrieval program so that only a single tape was needed to store the massive data. This efficient storage and retrieval system was made possible by recording only *changes* at a particular time rather than using a standard set of positions for each person. An important consequence of this computer program is that it makes standard data analyses more practical and greatly facilitates a wide range of analyses which otherwise might be impractical and expensive for small computers. But perhaps the chief advantage of this computer program is that it stimulates the researchers to consider the data from several points of view; for example, "time" can mean a man's age or an actual calendar date, or time can be contingent upon a related event, such as a man's occupation during the month in which he was married. In short, the data form a chemistry set rather than a single set of knitting directions.

A study by Coleman, Blum, and Sorensen (1970) illustrates some of these possibilities. These investigators used the retrospective life history data described earlier to study the effect of various personal and background data upon a person's occupational success from his first job to his job ten years later. Using simple correlational and multiple regression techniques, they found that the occupational status of a person's first job depends more upon his educational attainment than upon any other factor. Likewise, education has a stronger effect on the last job than does any other characteristic, including the status of first job. The status of first and last jobs are moderately intercorrelated (.51 for whites and .40 for blacks). These findings suggest that the *level* or status of a job may be as predictable as the *kind* of work a person prefers. What seems to be called for now is an integration of the occupational dimensions preferred by psychologists and sociologists in the same studies.

In another study, using the same data, Sorensen (1970) developed a mathematical model of the decision to leave a job. He then substituted real data in his theoretical regression equation and obtained the predicted linear relationship between the logarithm of the probability of moving and age. These and other studies illustrate the wide range of quasi-experimental studies that a well-designed instant longitudinal study program can facilitate (Ornstein & Rossi, 1970).

STABILITY AND CHANGE

So far we have found some helpful methods—tests, inventories, and classifications—for predicting the vocational area in which a person will find success and satisfaction—especially satisfaction. And, we have some productive classifications for organizing occupational knowledge. A precise statement of these conclusions would provoke some debate. At the same time, a useful understanding of perhaps the major scientific question—What personal and impersonal forces serve to maintain or change a person's vocational preference?—goes unanswered and only occasionally investigated.

A persuasive explanation of the processes of stability and change would have pervasive, practical application. The creation of vocational guidance devices, services, and systems could become more rational and effective. And the development of educational, business, and national policies about many occupational problems could, likewise, become more beneficial and less costly. Instead, parents, educators, and practitioners must now rely on rule-of-thumb techniques fired at students and employees in shotgun fashion. The following sections outline current knowledge about the stability or prediction of vocational preference and some possible explanations for change.

Stability

The prediction of a person's future vocational preference has been a common preoccupation of both psychologists and lay-

men. And, although the study of career patterns or job transitions is superseding the study of a single transition, such as the relation of the kind of training to the nature of a man's job over different intervals of time, the analysis of a single transition—a single unit of a career—has been helpful in explaining the forces that affect a career. In short, the prediction of occupational membership and career pattern are complementary investigations—each with its special virtues. Whether we are interested in persons or social systems, careers or occupations, both points of view contribute useful information about occupational life.

Studies of the prediction of vocational preferences greatly exceed studies planned to understand the processes inherent in stability and change. This disparity may exist because psychologists have been so busy trying to show that psychological tests work. Even the few studies of process usually lean heavily on tests for their explanation of change. In addition, the study of change in preference or personality has been one of the most refractory problems in psychology; that it has been neglected is easily understood.

Self-Predictions

Until recently, self-predictions of vocational preference have been regarded as unreliable and unworthy of research. However, Holland and Whitney (1968) demonstrated that the predictive validity of a college student's vocational preference over eight to twelve months was about twice as efficient as his highest scale score on the Vocational Preference Inventory.

This finding led to several more substantial studies. From a review of only large scale longitudinal studies ($N > 3,000$), Whitney (1969) concludes that "a person's expressed vocational choice predicts his future employment about as well as interest inventories or combinations of personality and background characteristics." The studies reviewed earlier under "vocational development" reveal similar trends; initial vocational preferences usually have a statistically significant stability. Equally important, if vocational preferences are organized by a classification, the efficiency of self-prediction is markedly increased. For example, without any classification, self-predictions have an efficiency (percentage hits) of about 50 percent for college males, but with an eight-category classification scheme, hits increase to 68 percent (Roe et al., 1966).

More recent studies also suggest that self-predictions usually equal or exceed predictions from tests or inventories. For women, Stahmann (1969) found that self-predictions of field of graduation exceeded those obtained from interests (Occupational Interest Inventory) and achievement (Cooperative Achievement test scores). For men, self-predictions and OII scores were approximately equal. Using Project Talent data, Richards (1970) concludes that it is more accurate and efficient to use a high school student's self-prediction to forecast his choice of major field than multiple predictive equations based on a wide range of aptitude and interest variables. In a subsequent analysis, devoted to the prediction of occupational choice over a five-year interval, Richards (1971) concludes that self-predictions (one item) and test scores (optimally weighted composites of 45 to 109 test scores) are about equally efficient. And Foreman and James (1969) show that self-predictions of interest and inventoried interests tend to converge for those areas of interest which the client considers relevant. This valuable study of concurrent relationships needs to be extended to a longitudinal one. As it stands, the Foreman and James study implies that people learn what concerns them, but we need to know if this selective perception of interests makes a predictive difference.

Tests, Inventories, and Grades

The prediction of vocational preference over varying periods of time from a few months to thirty years makes up a substantial literature that is difficult to summarize. Dolliver (1969), Whitney (1969), and Rose and Elton (1970) have enumerated some of the difficulties in comparing different predictive techniques or inventories and have suggested some solutions. In general, predictive comparisons of different tests, techniques, and variables are not comparable with respect to time interval, task, and classification, so that most studies stand as unique, sometimes unintegratable, studies.

Despite these weaknesses, two areas of work show that both the kind and level of a person's vocational preference is predictable and, therefore, somewhat stable over long periods of time. Campbell's recent book (1971) provides the most substantial predictive summary in existence for the SVIB. Recent studies by Stone and Athelstan (1969) and Harmon (1969) illustrate this approach to the study of occupational preference and clearly demonstrate that the kind, content, or focus of a person's vocational preference has stability. A clear estimation of how much stability there is remains unanswered. Likewise, the relative efficiency of tests, inventories, and self-prediction is unclear.

Another set of studies and summaries show that the *level* of a person's vocational preference is also somewhat predictable. Perhaps the most outstanding studies are by Ghiselli (1969), who provides a summary of his theory of managerial talent, and who (Ghiselli, 1966) summarizes what we know about the validity of aptitude tests. Earlier studies and summaries by Stewart (1947) and Thorndike and Hagen (1959) suggest that the level of a person's occupational preference is positively correlated with various intellectual aptitudes. More recent studies (Little, 1967; Heath & Strowig, 1967; Droege, 1968; Lipe, 1970) also show low-to-moderate positive correlations between a variety of tests, demographic variables (GATB, Project Talent test battery, high school grades) and *level* of vocational preference. Like the predictions of *kind* of vocational preference, the present studies possess many ambiguities or lack information for comparisons of the relative efficiency of different techniques and variables.

Possible Explanations

Little effort has been devoted to understanding the processes that lead to changes in vocational preference. What is known comes from a few studies that were direct attempts to explain change and from a larger number of studies in which change in vocational preference was a peripheral concern. Despite this lack of research interest, the results of these direct and indirect attempts imply several plausible hypotheses which are worthy of continued interest and exploration.

They include: (1) people change their vocational preferences in response to positive reinforcement from others, especially when the "others" are numerous and significant to the person concerned; (2) indecision about change in, or instability of, a person's preference may reflect competency and health rather than confusion and maladjustment; and (3) changes in vocational preference often appear lawful rather than random, as if the person were searching for a preference that represents a better fit. These and other potential explanations are implied in reports by Fryer (1931), Bordin and Wilson (1953), Dressel (1954), Dunkleberger and Tyler (1961), and others. To clarify this evidence, studies have been characterized as concerned largely with personal or environmental explanations of change.

Personal Characteristics

In their four-year longitudinal study of college students, Astin and Panos (1968) show that a student's stability of vocational choice is a function of numerous personal characteristics: initial choice, degree sought, sex, race, and other factors. Their regression analyses indicate that "the sex of the student entered into the prediction of more careers ... and with generally larger weights, than did any other personal characteristic except initial choice of a career and of a major field." Males choose masculine, and women choose feminine, occupations. In the present context, changers move to fields populated primarily by their own sex.

Other studies show that people who maintain their vocational preference also have high retest correlations on an interest inventory. The most substantial study of this kind is by Cooley (1967) who found that high school students (Project Talent) with high retest interest inventory scores are most likely to maintain their initial plans. Conversely, students with low retest correlations are more likely to change their vocational preference in the four-year interval between the ninth and twelfth grades. Bordin and Wilson (1953) and Petrik (1969) report similar findings. The explanatory value of such results is limited, although they suggest that non-changers see themselves in reliable ways and in ways that are probably consistent with their vocational preference. In contrast, the low retest reliabilities for changers probably reflects their changing conception of themselves, but the data say little about the influences or processes leading to such changes.

Another study (Dunkleberger & Tyler, 1961) suggests more clearly what personal forces may affect a change in vocational preference. These investigators categorize high school students as "changers" and "non-changers" according to the rank order of their SVIB scores obtained in the eleventh and twelfth grades. Changers and non-changers were then compared on the California Psychological Inventory and the Edwards Personal Preference Schedule. They conclude that "changers" on the SVIB "may be ... capable, well-adjusted individuals who have a wide variety of interests ... and who change their attitudes as they obtain more experience and information."

These hypotheses receive some support from other studies which suggest that students change their vocational choices to achieve a closer congruency between the demands of a field and their estimation of their own fitness, and in response to a variety of environmental influences or supports. For example, Werts (1967) finds that changers leave fields where they have less ability than the non-changers, that sons who chose their fathers' occupations were less likely to change plans, and that students are more likely to change to fields where they are more like the other students with respect to social class. In another longitudinal study, Holland and Nichols (1964) presented both changers and non-changers with a standard item of explanation (alternatives possessed identical content) and learned that changers and non-changers ranked their "reasons" for staying in or leaving a field in almost identical order. Both rank highest "a field where I can make the best use of my interests and abilities."

To summarize, some evidence of uneven quality suggests that a person's individual characteristics, especially his conception of these characteristics, leads to change in vocational preference as a way to achieve greater congruity, success, and satisfaction.

Environmental Influences

The evidence for the influence of the environment on a person's vocational preference is more substantial. The studies reviewed in the "Vocational Development" section strongly imply that a college student's vocational preference is manipulated by the patterning of reinforcement he receives from fellow students. "The student's career choice tended to move into closer conformity with the more popular career choices among fellow students" (Astin & Panos, 1969, p. 132). The Brown experiment (1966) provides a vivid and convincing demonstration that the proportions of peers with science or nonscience goals in a stu-

dent's dorm floor clearly influence a student's tendency to maintain or change goals. In Brown's experimental study, students in the minority fields (only 25 percent were in science) tended to move to majority fields (75 percent were in nonscience) when both groups lived on the same floor of a dormitory. The reverse situation also held. When nonscience students (25 percent) live with science students (75 percent), nonscience students tend to switch to science fields.

The hypothesis supported in the college studies also appears to hold for some studies of older men. For instance, Benjamin's (1968) thirty-one-year longitudinal study of 229 engineers leads him to conclude: "(1) The interests of engineering students were fairly stable.... (2) Interest changes that did occur reflected a tendency to become more like men-in-general. (An occurrence that can be interpreted as a giving-in to the popular reinforcements).... (5) Men select occupations which will provide outlets for their early acquired personal characteristics; but they also, as a result of continuing life experiences (...occupational role and function),...become very much like others in the same occupation." (Again, this occurrence can be regarded as giving in to the reinforcements of one's peers and significant others.)

Several other studies strongly suggest that the significant others in a student's life belong to the same or similar field of training. For example, Holland (1964) in a predictive study found that a student's friends tend to fall in the same or related field. In a more convincing study, Williams (1967) discovered that pairs of roommates who request reassignment tend to come from different fields and that the most common incompatible roommate pairs are science-business combinations or investigative-enterprising types. Finally, Hogan et al. (1972) extended the similarity-attraction hypothesis to activities and vocational interests. Using a standard experimental design for testing the similarity-attraction hypothesis, Hogan clearly demonstrates that students expect to like people who have interests like their own rather than people with divergent interests.

SPECIAL POPULATIONS

The vocational development and achievement of blacks and women are of special interest. On the one hand, the welfare of these special populations has, until recently, attracted little scientific study. And, on the other hand, what little we do know about their vocational development and achievement highlights most of the major influences that affect the vocational preferences of all populations. In short, the cultural treatment of blacks and women provides some unusually vivid illustrations of the processes of stability and change in vocational development.

The most current and comprehensive information about the labor market experience of women and blacks is contained in two major reports by Parnes and his colleagues (Shea, Roderick, Zeller, & Kohen, 1971; Shea, Spitz, & Zeller, 1970). These studies of the employment status of women are in the process of becoming five-year longitudinal studies. The vast range of detailed information in these reports make them impossible to summarize, but, among other things, these reports do document the many ways in which the culture molds the aspirations, employment opportunities, and rewards for women and blacks, both young and old.

For instance, it seems clear that the culture (parents, schools, and others) teaches women and blacks, in contrast to white men, to aspire to a narrower range of occupational possibilities and to expect less vocational achievement, and the culture reinforces this early education by discriminatory training, hiring, and promotional practices so that the expectations of women and blacks are confirmed.

That these outcomes are probably cultural or learned, rather than innate, appears factual in the case of women, because some measures of talent (for example, intelligence) related to occupational achievement shows no essential mean differences between men and women. In the case of blacks, the evidence is not so clear. On the other hand, until blacks receive a full share of socioeconomic resources there is no precise way to resolve these ambiguities.

These interpretations for black men are reinforced by another important series of studies described earlier under "Vocational Development." These and other studies (Coleman, Blum, & Sorensen, 1970; Ornstein & Rossi, 1970) reveal that black and white males with equal amounts of education attain different levels of initial and subsequent job success. H. S. Astin's study (1969) of women doctorates in 1957 and 1958 ($N = 1,979$) provides another comprehensive account of the various ways in which the vocational preferences of talented women are influenced in special ways—domestic problems, employer discrimination, educational experience.

The main themes in these large scale, national surveys of blacks and women are extended and often reinforced by many smaller scale studies. Gysbers, Johnston, and Gust (1968) and Rezler (1967a, 1967b) have found that homemakers and career-oriented women have different interests, attitudes, and life histories. Elton and Rose (1967) found that the vocational preferences of women are attributable to differences in personality as well as sex role. Other studies by Watley and Kaplan (1971), Faunce (1968), and H. S. Astin (1968) provide additional information about women with different vocational preferences, their career difficulties, the effects of their high school training, etc. And Rossi (1965), Useem (1960), and Gardner (1971) have attempted to explain the shortage of female scientists or to interpret the changes taking place in the lives of women. Small scale studies of black high school and college students appear to reflect similar cultural barriers and expectations for blacks. Witty, Garfield, and Brink (1941) found that postal work, music, medicine, law, and teaching were more popular among black than white male high school students. Hager and Elton (1971) report that black male college freshmen are more apt to have social service rather than scientific interests. In this case, the authors relied upon a factor analysis of the SVIB. Other studies about the *level* of vocational aspiration are unclear and often conflicting (Shappell, Hall, & Tarrier, 1970; Nelson, 1968; Kuvlesky & Thomas, 1971).

Taken together, the vocational preferences of women and blacks reveal how cultural influences play a powerful role in the shaping of a person's vocational development. It seems reasonable to conclude then that the stability and special qualities of vocational preferences of white males are maintained, in part, by similar cultural forces rather than by some innate unfolding alone.

PRACTICAL APPLICATIONS

The 1960s have been characterized by a resurgence of interest in vocational behavior and by the development of plans, systems, and methods for the facilitation of vocational exploration, preparation, and decision making. The range of alternatives in previous years (principally, one-to-one and group counseling) has been increased to include computer-assisted vocational exploration, vocational experience kits, non-computerized vocational counseling simulations, and vocational guidance systems. In addition, considerable substantive work, with and without theoretical stimulation, now provides a better understanding of the life history of a person's vocational preferences so that educators, researchers, and developers can create more effective interventions.

Whether or not these new approaches will lead to a major shift in the methods used to promote better vocational decisions remains in doubt. Fortunately, the sheer increase in population appears to have played a large role in the development of this new generation of interventions (the absurdity of one-to-one counseling became vivid), and

such pressure should continue to militate for interventions of low cost and high benefit. The following sections outline some representative plans for facilitating a person's vocational development, new methods and techniques, and some preliminary evaluations of these interventions.

Plans and Systems

Different agencies and individuals have proposed a wide range of plans or systems for accelerating vocational development. These plans range from abstract, theoretical, and sometimes ambiguous formulations to specific, systematic, and operational schemes.

Most recently, the Office of Education has outlined three "career education models," which might be more appropriately labeled "three general plans for promoting more adaptive vocational behavior among children and adults." The three plans would be "school-based," "employer-based," and "home-community-based" and would be devised "to serve all Americans" (*Education Daily*, May 27, 1971). These plans for more comprehensive vocational education for youth and adults represent a major attempt to promote vocational awareness, vocational exploration, and vocational preparation in junior and senior high schools, colleges, and technical institutes. This ambitious undertaking will attempt to provide help for everyone and to link together the scattered efforts of schools, colleges, technical institutes, and employers. That such a major effort is needed seems clear, but what will come of this development-oriented, atheoretical effort is unclear.

In a theoretically oriented plan, Hershenson (1969) suggests some techniques to promote a student's vocational development. He assumes that two levels of assistance are needed: "facilitation (promoting normal development) and remediation (actively removing serious blocks to development)." Using his earlier formulation of five vocational life stages (social-amniotic, self-differentiation, competence, independence, commitment), Hershenson outlines some techniques to help students through each of the five transitions. For instance, a student in the self-differentiation stage, who has attained a satisfactory differentiation but has difficulty in defining his competencies, may profit from traditional guidance procedures such as taking aptitude and ability tests, experiencing work samples, and learning about his performance (alias feedback). Briefly, a person with a relatively accurate self-concept can use information about his potentials and competencies. Hershenson's perceptive article is one of only a few that attempts to integrate theoretical thinking and daily practice. Although it is only a first attempt, Hershenson's report is a useful beginning, for he outlines how better theories could be of great value and how practical problems can be redefined in potentially useful, theoretical terms.

Ehrle (1970) offers a more restricted plan; that is, providing occupational information to students. Ehrle categorizes the methods of providing information according to verbal vocational experience (books, charts, tapes, films, etc.), directed experiential learning (employer visits, career days), and actual experience. And he advocates gaming and simulation: "for illustrating important facts, for focusing on long range planning required in making educational-vocational decisions, for familiarizing students with decision-makng tools necessary for vocational maturity, for creating high involvement on the part of participants, and for allowing many decisions to be made in a few hours." Although Ehrle helps to organize our thinking about the use of information, he neglects the issues, evidence, and rules for integrating personal needs and informational techniques. We need to know more accurately what works best with what kind of person for what cost. A recent book (Blocher, Dustin, & Dugan, 1971) epitomizes these needs. Their book, *Guidance Systems,* is an excellent review of what a wide range of specialists think about vocational guidance, social organizations, infor-

mation systems, human development, and other related topics. The authors present a vast array of problems, ideas, techniques, and possibilities, but they do not propose a single, comprehensive plan to cope with the vocational problems of students.

Perhaps the most comprehensive and largely operational plan for providing occupational information to elementary and secondary students is contained in the Project Plan sponsored by American Institutes of Research (Flanagan, 1968). Project Plan is a system of individualized education which provides learning units according to a student's needs and talents.

Vocational education and vocational guidance units have been developed and integrated into this major instructional plan (Hamilton & Webster, 1971). For the primary grades, instructional units were created to give students an appreciation of occupational life and then integrated into social studies learning units. In the intermediate grades (five to eight), students are introduced to job families based on Project Talent data. Consequently, students learn what job families or clusters they resemble and what preparation is needed. Future work will probably provide practice in decision making by having students make plans for hypothetical students. At the high school level, students are provided with more specific and concentrated experience in setting their educational-vocational planning. Students are provided a wide range of common vocational exploration techniques and experiences, such as occupational films, reading materials, work simulation kits, audiotapes, and occupational representatives. Finally, students are encouraged to make specific, post-high school plans and are given some role-playing training to facilitate job or college interviews.

The distinctive characteristics of the guidance system within Project Plan are its long time span, comprehensiveness, and integration within the curriculum. The plan rests largely on pragmatic techniques that appear to, or are known to, help. The underlying formula for the plan is mainly informational: students need accurate and reliable information about themselves and occupations, and they need to acquire more rational strategies for processing self and occupational knowledge.

Methods, Systems, Tests

The growth of a few comprehensive plans for vocational education has been accompanied by a burgeoning of test batteries, computerized vocational information systems, and other less comprehensive devices and methods for accomplishing similar objectives.

Tests

Test publishers and testing agencies continue to devise more comprehensive assessment batteries. Both the American College Testing Program (1970) and the Educational Testing Service for the College Entrance Examination Board (1969) have developed vocational guidance batteries for Junior College students. Both programs provide students and counselors large amounts of information about a student's aptitudes and interests, but both programs leave the integration of the information largely up to the counselor and student. However, neither program has examined the effects of the information upon students.

In one sense, these large scale testing programs attempt to facilitate the work of counselors and faculty who work in the one-to-one tradition of vocational counseling. They have succeeded in improving the collection and transmission of more student information, but whether or not these programs improve the quality of a student's vocational development needs investigation.

Computer-based Vocational Guidance Systems

The planning and development of computer-based vocational guidance systems has been one of the major developments of the last five years. These developments have been summarized in a recent conference report (Computer-based Vocational Guidance Systems, 1969), which is organized according to theoretical considerations (really very few), problems of implementation, and specific vocational guidance systems under development. In general, investigators have tried to develop guidance systems to provide educational and vocational information, to simulate model counselor-client interactions, and to give students practice in decision making.

The Willowbrook Computerized Vocational Information System (Harris, 1969) is one of the few operational systems. Using Roe's and Holland's theorizing, Harris and her colleagues have developed vocational exploration programs in which students are shown some of the relationships between their personal characteristics and occupational requirements. Harris reports a survey of a random sample of 290 first-time users that is very positive: (1) 83 percent felt they learned something about themselves; (2) 69 percent believed they learned something new about occupations; and (3) 74 percent felt better able to choose an occupation. These and other findings are a bright beginning. Other studies of users and nonusers should provide more definitive estimates of the effects of the Computerized Vocational Information System (CVIS).

Simulation and Training

Many investigators have developed relatively small scale, short term simulations, reinforcement techniques, or training programs to promote desirable vocational behaviors, such as seeking more occupational information, making more rational vocational decisions, behaving appropriately in job interviews, or becoming more aware of one's interests and competencies. Some of these new methods are more concerned with providing students with vocational counseling at low cost while others are more concerned with providing special stimulation or experience. Both methods are concerned with practical goals, and both kinds of intervention are beginning to provide a clearer understanding of how vocational preferences are affected by experience.

Krumboltz and his colleagues (Krumboltz & Schroeder, 1965; Sheppard, 1967; Baker, 1968; Ryan, 1969) have shown that reinforcement techniques are helpful in getting students to seek relevant occupational information or overcome decision-making problems. These results are especially valuable, because the authors have found some techniques that make students seek information—a task rarely achieved by conventional exhortations. These techniques include reinforcing any student information-seeking behavior in several interviews, listening to a tape in which the counselor again reinforces information-seeking or using an occupational experience kit. In a related study, Bergland and Krumboltz (1969) began the study of *when* students are ready for career exploration. Students were administered simulated occupational experience kits at grades 9, 10, 11, and 12 and then tested for information-seeking behavior. This experiment suggests that the eleventh graders were a little more susceptible to the influence of the experience kits. Useful as this experimental study is, the question of the timing of vocational interventions remains a vast problem considering the numerous studies needed to examine all the possibilities—different interventions at different times and in different combinations.

The development of occupational simulation kits (Krumboltz, 1971) provides new practical tools which can be used to help both students and researchers. These kits resemble the chemistry kits which used to be popular as Christmas gifts. The present kits provide materials so that students can experience some of the common and simple tasks involved in particular occupations. For instance, in the appliance serviceman kit a student must test electrical circuits to find the defective component in a foil-lined schematic of a malfunctioning iron. The salesman kit requires a student to prepare a sales presentation geared to the interests or needs of a prospective customer. So far, these work simulations have served largely to provide complex stimuli for many useful experiments. More comprehensive tests of their usefulness are now possible because the kits are now available for general use.

The Life Career Game (LCG) is another development designed to simulate some aspects of a person's career, especially to give students an appreciation of the decisions that must be made about jobs, education, family life, and leisure (Boocock, 1966, 1968). The LCG provides a less explicit experience than that provided by the Krumboltz Occupational Experience Kits. Generally, experimental studies of the effects of the LCG have been disappointing. Johnson (1971) found that playing the LCG with or without discussion had no effect on ninth-grade students' awareness of life decisions, exploratory activity, or time competency. But Boocock (1966) found some positive effects such as students agreeing "that it is hard to plan your life ahead" after playing The Life Career Game. More important outcomes, like more adaptive career behaviors, remain unanswered.

Special treatments devised to affect a student's vocational preference, interest pattern, and self-knowledge continue to give mixed results. Plotkin (1967) found that occupational information classes increased the vocational interest patterns of slow learning eleventh- and twelfth-grade boys. But Pilato (1969) found that three vocational guidance treatments (taking an interest inventory, studying an occupational classification, and relating their interests to the occupational classification) produced only a few positive results.

The Work-Sample Program (Jewish Employment and Vocational Service, 1968) is an elaborate set of twenty-eight work samples classified according to level and kind of work. Clients can use the work-sample program to explore their abilities and to learn and adapt to various occupational tasks and roles. Although the work-sample program was developed to help people not amenable to conventional techniques (disadvantaged, alienated, disturbed), the work-sample program appears to be one logical extension of the occupational experience kits that should be, with modification, helpful for large portions of the general population. The first experimental study of the effectiveness of the work-sample program is positive and encouraging, although the first evaluation is not without flaws. The Life Skills Programs devised by Adkins (1970) would be a valuable adjunct to such a program. Adkins has emphasized the need to teach poor people in explicit ways and has devised some of the materials for such teaching. For example, the curriculum track, Managing a Career, includes concrete training units about interviews, tests, and application blanks. Educational Resources (1970) has produced an audio course in which tape cassettes can be run from ten to thirty hours to achieve similar goals.

Several investigators have devised methods to make vocational counseling a cheaper process and to reach larger numbers of people. Both of the following approaches simulate what counselors and clients normally do in vocational counseling.

Magoon (1969) developed the Effective Problem Solving (EPS) counseling model, a self-directed learning program for people who are uncertain about their vocational preference. Small groups of students (four or five) meet with a counselor who orients students to a set of structured materials that require a student to read and provide information about himself and occupations. Students go through the materials at their own pace and use the counselor as a consultant. The forms filled out by the student simulate the assessment of self and possible occupational alternatives that counselors and clients cope with in traditional counseling.

The EPS is assumed to have some special advantages in addition to lowered costs. Some of the most important advantages include more thorough and systematic assessment and planning, more client responsibility, and better grasp of the process of assessment and decision making. For a fuller account of this promising method, the reader should see Magoon's extensive report (1969) as well as a modification of Magoon's program by Danish, Graff, and Gensler (n.d.).

Holland's (1971a) Self-Directed Search (SDS) resembles Magoon's Effective Problem Solving model. Both were planned to reach large numbers of people at low cost and both simulate the traditional vocational counseling process. The SDS differs from the EPS in that the SDS is briefer but less thorough, oriented to a single rather than several theories, and requires little or no supervision during the process of administration.

The Self-Directed Search (SDS) is a self-administered, self-scored, and self-interpreted vocational counseling tool. The SDS includes two booklets. To use the SDS, a person fills out the assessment booklet and obtains a three-letter occupational code. He then uses the three-letter code to search for suitable occupations in the occupational classification booklet. In short, the SDS provides a vocational counseling experience by simulating what a person and his counselor do in several interviews.

Evaluation

There is a marked need for a more complete knowledge of the effects of these new devices. The resources to use everything in any quantity are not available. And the traditional studies of validity are not sufficient, for we also need to know the effects of playing a career game or of undergoing a simulated counseling experience, and how to organize groups of these techniques and devices into systems of intervention for a high rate of desirable assistance at low cost. To do this, a more concerted attempt to think through systems of intervention in terms of a theory, or a theory of interventions, may be especially advantageous. Such a theory would specify what behaviors are desirable at what stages and would suggest how, when, and for whom interventions would be most effective.

IMPLICATIONS AND STRATEGIES

This review of what is known about a person's life history of vocational preferences implies some research strategies for making more efficient predictions and for obtaining clearer understanding of the process of vocational development. This selective review also implies some strategies for improving the future practice of industrial and organizational psychology. The following sections attempt to outline these ideas. To balance this subjective appraisal and to obtain a more comprehensive view, the reader will find it useful to compare Crites (1969b), and Super, Roe, and Tiedeman in *Perspective in Vocational Development* (Whiteley, 1972).

Research Strategies

Several ideas appear useful for organizing the diverse information about vocational preferences, for obtaining more insight into the personal and environmental forces involved in forming a person's vocational preferences, and for making more efficient predictions of vocational behavior. These strategies for research and speculation include: (1) occupational classifications are needed to structure and explain the vast array of substantive knowledge concerned with vocational preference, vocational choice, and occupational membership; (2) the application of reinforcement theory promises to clarify the processes involved in stability and change of vocational preference; and (3) the investigation of interpersonal competency may lead both to a greater understanding of "vocational maturity" along with other vocational behavior and to more efficient predictions of vocational achievement. These interpretations of needed research are only a few of many, but they appear especially promising for the problems at hand.

Occupational Classification

This selective account of the vocational literature, and the more extensive reports by others, reveal a great need for better ways to organize and explain the vast array of occupational data. Some common problems make this need clear. It is not practical to maintain files for even 1,000 of the 30,000 occupations; it is difficult to comprehend occupational differences across more than ten categories; it is usually necessary to combine data from several occupations into single categories even in studies of great size, and investigators often perform such classifications in ignorant ways or by following implicit unexamined rules. In addition, occupational classifications are needed to house and organize new occupational information so that practitioners are not required to remember a horde of specific details (which they cannot do anyway) and teachers can teach personnel workers self-sustaining occupational plans rather than large amounts of specific data which take longer to learn and are easily forgotten. These and other common problems show the pervasive need for better occupational classification.

These obvious needs are reinforced by the thinking of others and by the substantive success of recent classificatory work. For example, Owens (1968) has suggested a developmental-integrative model for a single scientific discipline of psychology. An important part of his model lies in grouping people according to their patterns of prior experience so that we could develop laws for different types and sub-types rather than going to either extreme—studies of individuals or whole populations. For this purpose, Owens suggests the use of scored autobiographical forms. In the present context, the structure, reviewed earlier, which appears common to most occupational classification schemes appears especially helpful for identifying groups and subgroups that have similar personal histories and characteristics. Such a technique is unusually practical, for investigators could use either existing interest inventory scales or only vocational preferences categorized according to one or more occupational classifications.

The substantial predictive validity of classification schemes has been reviewed earlier in the sections on "Assessment and Classification" and "Structure and Theory." Although a definitive assessment is not yet possible, the evidence so far suggests that classification schemes yield predictive hits at least at the level of multiple regression formulas and frequently at a higher level at less cost. The substantive success of classification schemes may occur because "categories sort people not traits." That is, qualitative methods may be most appropriate for selected human problems. Trait-oriented methods (for example, multiple regression) ignore the natural organization of traits in making predictions. With more resources devoted to the development of classifications, more efficient and rational schemes appear possible. Several other ideas and developments lend credence to the promise of occupational classification.

Aspirational, educational, and work histories can be integrated and examined by categorizing a person's preferences from early childhood until he dies murmuring "I wish I had been a racing car driver." In this way the history of one's vocational preferences provide powerful data for understanding human growth and development as well as vocational behavior.

Since classifications imply at least a primitive theory, they can become a convenient vehicle for organizing not only the data for a single individual but also the whole range of occupational knowledge. Using only a limited number of categories, a classification can be used to organize occupational knowledge of all kinds: work histories of successful and unsuccessful workers, interactions of productive and unproductive worker-super-visor combinations, characteristics of people in different occupations, environmental characteristics of different occupations, and occupational findings of any kind.

The development of prestige scales by sociologists to assess occupational levels provides another relatively independent occupational dimension. Taken together, the interest and prestige classifications provide powerful ways to organize occupational information according to kind and level. The use of these schemes in tandem should clarify many of the ambiguities that flow from more primitive or traditional classificatory schemes, since their use will sort occupations into more homogeneous groups.

Reinforcement Theory

Another strategy for understanding a person's vocational preferences is to apply reinforcement terms. Seen in this way, a person's vocational preferences are contingent upon multiple, partial reinforcements received from birth to death from the personal and impersonal aspects of his environment. The increase in stability of vocational preference with age may reflect the increasing amount of positive reinforcement that most people receive as they increase their ability to locate situations where they will receive an increasing number of positive reinforcements. Consequently, people change less and less with age as they are reinforced more and more for a decreasing range of behavior.

Certain common sense explanations seem consistent. For example, if you want to change the way you do your job or play new roles, it is often necessary to change jobs or employers. In reinforcement terms, a person must find a new employer who will reinforce him in different ways. In short, even the most simple application of reinforcement theory in conjunction with the main substantive theme—the great stability of vocational preferences—provides an appealing interpretation.

Other folklore may have similar explanations. The belief that it is destructive to remain on a single job for many years may have validity because a single long-term job provides a massive reinforcement of only a few coping behaviors. Consequently, many potential skills and behaviors remain dormant. Likewise, the increasing rigidity of behavior often observed with increasing age may result from the effect of narrow job demands rather than some inherent qualities of the person. Or, jobs make people over as well as vice versa.

This global and incomplete formula orders many other findings in plausible ways. For example, a child's parents, social class, and school provide a vast range of positive and negative reinforcements depending upon the parents' income, education, and physical setting. The changes in aspiration in adolescence and adulthood may reflect the differential reinforcement a college student or adult worker receives from his school, college, or work environment. The differences in vocational preference for men and women strengthen the same hypothesis. The college-effects studies which show that students tend to switch to the most popular or largest fields offer strong support for the power of reinforcement. For instance, students in popular fields receive more mutual reinforcement from students in the same field, more family support, financial, and physical resources.

The tools and concepts used to study vocational preference are easily translated into reinforcement terms. An interest inventory is a technique for securing a record of a person's partial reinforcements. Therefore, his scores tell us what motivates him, what positive and negative experiences he has had and what people have taught him to think about himself. Occupational classification systems are methods for organizing similar sets of reinforcements.

This cursory account suggests only a few of the ways that reinforcement thinking can be used. The work of the Minnesota team is a more vivid and comprehensive application of reinforcement theory to vocational

behavior (Lofquist & Dawis, 1969). Vroom's hypotheses (1964) about vocational motivation can also be interpreted in terms of reinforcement theory. The empirical success of these approaches and the ease with which the evidence can be translated into reinforcement terms strongly imply that other investigators should profit from similar effort.

Finally, the application of reinforcement theory or other learning principles appear especially helpful for explaining the processes of vocational development. At the same time, learning theories are not very helpful for organizing the content of vocational preference. For example, the Minnesota theory of vocational adjustment might profit from the incorporation of a practical typology so that the theory could deal more effectively with both the *process* and the *content* of vocational adjustment. Their current attempt to develop a typology via reinforcer patterns of supervisors is theoretically valuable but grossly impractical as a scientific strategy (Borgen, Weiss, Tinsley, Dawis, & Lofquist, 1968).

Interpersonal Competency

Several problems (the need for efficient predictions of vocational achievement, the limited usefulness of vocational maturity research, and the increasing demand for interpersonal competency as our society becomes "transient") suggest that a more active investigation of interpersonal competency may provide assistance in alleviating all three of these difficulties. For example, vocational maturity appears to be a special case of personal and interpersonal competence. Likewise, there is some evidence that suggests interpersonal competence plays a large role in vocational achievement. And predictions of the future work environment stress an increasing need for interpersonal competency. The following discussion outlines how interpersonal competency contributes to many adaptive vocational behaviors and reviews some supportive evidence.

There is considerable evidence that personal competence (especially interpersonal competence) may be a major determinant of diverse vocational behavior, including the choice of occupation, the level of that choice, the ability to cope well with transitions from job to job, and the eventual level of vocational attainment. Personal competence is composed of those adaptive dispositions and skills which facilitate a person's ability to cope with other people and to face the vicissitudes of life by relying selectively on one's inner resources and the resources of the environment, including people, institutions, tools, or information. An interpersonal competency scale (Holland & Baird, 1968) forms the base for the above definition and much of the accompanying discussion.

A person with high interpersonal competency, as opposed to a person with low interpersonal competency, is more likely to aspire to a high level occupation, because high interpersonal competency is associated with high aspiration, self-confidence, dominance, etc. (Hereafter, individuals with high interpersonal competency or low interpersonal competency are referred to as HIC or LIC.) HICs actively seek and obtain jobs because they are more independent and aggressive. They get and use occupational information because they engage in pre-decision search, and because their interpersonal relationships are likely to be supportive and of a wide range.

HICs are more likely to keep a job or advance on a job, because they have the interpersonal resources to appraise or diagnose other workers and supervisors, to be well liked, to make socially adaptive responses in stressful situations, to take initiative, and to learn from others, since they are more open to information and advice from others.

HICs reach high levels of vocational success, because occupational level—as assessed by the NORC Scale (National Opinion Research Center) or the Occupational Level Scale (OL) of the Strong—is positively related to social competence, dominance, sociability, vocational maturity (Bartlett, 1968; Bohn, 1966; Crites, 1969a), specialization level, and other correlates implying high levels of competency, self-direction, self-confidence, and aspiration.

Last, HICs are more apt to make orderly and constructive, if not self-enhancing, job transitions, because they are more likely to anticipate blind alleys and desirable alternatives. They also cope well with the stresses and diagnostic problems inherent in transitions, such as the assessment of potential supervisors, the assessment of self, especially in relation to self versus possible alternatives, and the need to find and evaluate needed information.

The origin and development of HIC may occur in the following ways: HICs are more apt to originate in families of high social status where good nutrition and health are more likely. As a child, the HIC gets more attention, practice, and reinforcement for acquiring interpersonal competence. In a sense, he grows up in the major league of interpersonal competency. He gets a wide range of experience and has more intellectual and physical resources in the home to help him acquire both a sense of competency and identity. His well-educated parents usually pass on habits of self-direction, self-confidence, and high aspiration.

As the HIC moves from occupational choice to training, and from job to job, he is in a position to have his competence increased by more training, experience, and reward. Presumably, HICs may go downhill like anyone else, but because stability seems more characteristic of work behaviors, it appears that HICs become LICs only after a marked series of failures. Likewise, LICs become HICs (if at all) only by a slow accretion of successful reinforcements. For example, recall the general inability of a great variety of training experiences to rectify underachievement in schools.

Several studies suggest that social status promotes social competence. A person's social status is positively correlated with his scores on occupational status scales such as the Occupational Level Scale of the Strong. The OL Scale is, in turn, positively correlated with a great range of variables often associated with achievement and occupational status. Using the data of the Oakland Growth Study, Elder (1968) found that the use of the OL Scale in 1938 for a sample of sixty-three boys was positively correlated with their educational level and occupational status in 1958, and with their scores on the California Psychological Inventory in 1953–1954 on capacity for Status, Achievement via Conformity, Achievement via Independence, and Intellectual Efficiency. This trail of evidence suggests that social status may promote several aspects of social competence.

Kohn's studies (1969) of parental values strongly implies that high SES parents foster self-direction. And at the adult level, Ghiselli's Initiative and Occupational Level Scale clearly distinguishes three gross occupational levels (Ghiselli, 1969). Other work by Gordon (1967) implies that the rewards of interpersonal relations are positively related to social level; that is, there are more possibilities for satisfying activities and interpersonal relations at high levels of SES.

Schneider and Stevens (1971) recently found that placement readiness (an individual's degree of specification, crystallization, exploration) was clearly related to dominance and independence. Super et al. (1967) in their longitudinal study of young men found that those "who are well-endowed personally and environmentally ...handle their post-high school careers better." At an older age level, Bray and Grant (1966) found that salary progress in business management is associated with high ratings or scores on administrative and interpersonal skills, intellectual ability, lack of passivity, and control of feelings. In a related longitudinal study, Meyer and Cuomo (1964) report that engineers who become managers, as opposed to those who do not, are rated higher in poise, self-confidence, aggressiveness, sophistication, business conscientiousness, status drive, education, and experience. Using a representative sample of

male work histories, Sorensen (1970) found that men with high levels of education who held jobs of high prestige were more likely to change jobs. Taken together, these studies imply that job-seeking may depend heavily on some interpersonal competencies and attitudes, such as self-confidence and dominance. This is not to say that chance and other factors, such as intelligence, special aptitudes, and dispositions, do not play an important role in the vocational behaviors considered here.

Practical Implications

Current knowledge of vocational preference is a useful source of ideas for the future conduct of industrial and organizational psychology. A few implications which appear to have special promise for application to everyday problems are outlined here. But before doing so, it seems helpful to stress the need to make a greater effort to lean on the record of a person's whole life rather than upon that particular segment preferred by one's scientific specialty: developmental, vocational counseling, industrial, or organizational psychology. Although we are undergoing a race for clarity and micro-theory, it still seems helpful to step back and look at the main characteristics of a life. In the case of a person's vocational preferences, there appear to be some long-term continuities that industrial psychologists could capitalize upon, if they made more energetic attempts to do so.

The implications for practice have been categorized as (1) Vocational Agriculture, or the creation of better jobs and working environments; (2) Vocational Transience, and the need to cultivate interpersonal competency; and (3) Personnel Work, or some applications to traditional personnel functions.

Vocational Agriculture

The shift from working with individuals to working with groups and organizations is not only more economical but also demands a shift from treating a person's job environment as a relatively unimportant force to treating his environment as a major influence. The redesign of jobs, environments, and work organizations requires better models for predicting and understanding the processes of person-person, person-environment interactions. Current knowledge of a person's vocational interests, and the vocational interests of his co-workers, provides a simple set of techniques and formulations for these tasks. Because a person's vocational preferences are an index of personality and competency, his preferences can be used to restructure jobs, to interpret possible new worker-supervisory interactions, etc. The history of a person's vocational preferences, in conjunction with an occupational classification, can be used to explore transfers, second careers, and retirement activities. But perhaps most important, a knowledge of vocational preferences is one main source for the redesign of vocational environments. A skillful use of this knowledge should foster the creation of environments that stimulate, reward, and develop the activities, competencies, and goals of people with different vocational preferences. The manipulation and design of whole working environments, difficult as it is to conceive of, promises to be more economical and beneficial than earlier remedial activities with individuals. Last, the use of classification schemes to assess college and work environments by Astin and Panos (1968) and McCormick et al. (1972) strongly suggest that industrial organizations could profit from the auspicious beginnings made in these investigations. Astin and McCormick provide a variety of techniques for assessing organizational environments that range from the simple to the complex; and equally important, they have an impressive record of empirical success.

Vocational Transience

The acceleration of change in contemporary life increases the need for more people with higher levels of interpersonal competency. The earlier section on "Interpersonal Competency" also details the need to foster interpersonal competency and outlines a formulation for its development. We also need to teach more explicitly what little is known about transience as a way to reduce its disorganizing impact on many people. Again, there is good reason to believe that a person's vocational interests or his history of preferences provide a first index for understanding what kinds of people tolerate change best, and what techniques or supports might be most helpful for what kinds of people.

Personnel Work

The traditional personnel functions might be facilitated by a cultivation of our knowledge of vocational preference. For example, work histories could be analyzed in theoretical terms using one or more classification systems. It is now possible to study work histories as scientific rather than as artistic problems. The selection, placement, and reassignment functions could also take advantage of classification schemes as methods for organizing and understanding occupational data. In addition, the use of vocational preference inventories and classification schemes provides powerful tools for reducing the great variety of individual differences to a workable few. For example, interest inventories and occupational classifications provide practical techniques for the study of job satisfaction, worker motivation, and job enrichment. A worker's interest inventory or occupational classification can be used to form homogeneous groups so that treatment effects, motivations, and satisfactions can be related to common kinds of personalities.

REFERENCES

Adkins, W. R. Life skills: Structured counseling for the disadvantaged. *Personnel and Guidance Journal,* 1970, 49, 108–116.

American College Testing Program. *The ACT career planning profile.* Iowa City: Author, 1970.

Astin, A. W. *The college environment.* Washington, D.C.: American Council on Education, 1968.

Astin, A. W. The methodology of research on college impact, I. *Sociology of Education,* 1970, 43, 223–254. (a)

Astin, A. W. The methodology of research on college impact, II. *Sociology of Education,* 1970, 43, 437–450. (b)

Astin, A. W., & Holland, J. L. The environmental assessment technique: A way to measure college environments. *Journal of Educational Psychology,* 1961, 52, 308–316.

Astin, A. W., & Panos, R. J. *The educational and vocational development of American college students.* Washington, D.C.: American Council on Education, 1968.

Astin, H. S. Patterns of career choices over time. *Personnel and Guidance Journal,* 1967, 45, 541–546. (a)

Astin, H. S. Career development during the high school years. *Journal of Counseling Psychology,* 1967, 14, 94–98. (b)

Astin, H. S. Career development of girls during the high school years. *Journal of Counseling Psychology,* 1968, 15, 536–540.

Astin, H. S. *The woman doctorate in America.* New York: Russell Sage Foundation, 1969.

Bachman, J. G. *Youth in transition: The impact of family background and intelligence on tenth-grade boys,* Vol. II. Ann Arbor, Mich.: Institute for Social Research, 1970.

Baird, L. L. The relation of vocational interests to life goals, self-ratings of ability and personality traits, and potential for achievement. *Journal of Counseling Psychology,* 1970, 17, 233–239.

Baker, R. D. Orienting stimuli in vocational problem-solving as factors in promoting career information-seeking. *Dissertation Abstracts,* 1968, 29, 1417.

Banducci, R. Accuracy of stereotypic perceptions of types and levels of occupations in relation to background and personal characteristics of high school senior boys. Unpublished doctoral dissertation, University of Iowa, Iowa City, 1968.

Barclay, J. R. Approach to the measurement of teacher "press" in the secondary curriculum. *Journal of Counseling Psychology,* 1967, 14, 552–567.

Barry, W. A., & Bordin, E. S. Personality development and the vocational choice of the ministry. *Journal of Counseling Psychology,* 1967, 14, 395–403.

Bartlett, W. E. Vocational maturity and personality variables of manpower trainees. *Vocational Guidance Quarterly,* 1968, 17, 104–108.

Bartlett, W. E. Vocational maturity: Its past, present, and future development. *Journal of Vocational Behavior,* 1971, 1, 217–229.

Bateman, T., & Roe, A. College seniors' plans and their implementation. Center for Research in Careers, Harvard Studies in Career Development, Harvard University, Cambridge, 1966, No. 47.

Benjamin, D. R. A thirty-one year longitudinal study of engineering students' interest profiles and career patterns. *Dissertation Abstracts,* 1968, 28, 4441.

Bergland, B. W., & Krumboltz, J. D. An optimal grade level for career exploration. *Vocational Guidance Quarterly,* September, 1969, 29–33.

Blau, P. M., Gustad, J. W., Jessor, R., Parnes, H. S., & Wilcock, R. C. Occupational choice: A conceptual framework. *Industrial Labor Relations Review,* 1956, 9, 531–543.

Blocher, D. H., Dustin, E. R., & Dugan, W. E. *Guidance systems.* New York: Ronald Press, 1971.

Block, J., & Peterson, P. Q-sort item analyses of a number of Strong vocational interest inventory scales. Officer Education Research Laboratory, Maxwell, Alabama, May, 1955.

Blum, Z. D., Karweit, N. L., & Sorensen, A. B. *A method for the collection and analysis of retrospective life histories.* Center for Social Organization of Schools, Report No. 48. Baltimore: Johns Hopkins University, 1969.

Bohn, M. J. Vocational maturity and personality. *Vocational Guidance Quarterly,* 1966, 15, 123–126.

Boocock, S. S. An experimental study of the learning effects of two games with simulated environments. *American Behavioral Scientist,* 1966, 10, 8–17.

Boocock, S. S. *Life career.* New York: Western Publishing, 1968.

Bordin, E. S., & Wilson, E. H. Changes of interest as a function of shift in curriculum orientation. *Educational and Psychological Measurement,* 1953, 13, 297–307.

Bordin, E. S., Nachmann, B., & Segal, S. J. An

articulated framework for vocational development. *Journal of Counseling Psychology,* 1963, 10, 107–117.

Borgen, F. H., Weiss, D. J., Tinsley, H. E., Dawis, R. V., & Lofquist, L. H. *Occupational reinforcer patterns.* Bulletin 48, Industrial Relations Center. Minneapolis: University of Minnesota, 1968.

Borow, H., Ed. *Man in a world of work.* Boston: Houghton Mifflin, 1964.

Bray, D. W., & Grant, D. L. The assessment center in the measurement of potential for business management. *Psychological Monographs,* 1966, 80 (17, Whole No. 625).

Brown, R. D. Peer group influence in a college residence hall. Unpublished doctoral dissertation, University of Iowa, Iowa City, 1966.

Campbell, D. P. The vocational interests of beautiful women. *Personnel and Guidance Journal,* 1967, 45, 968–972.

Campbell, D. P. Changing patterns of interests within the American society. *Measurement and Evaluation in Guidance,* 1968, 1, 36–49.

Campbell, D. P. *Handbook for the Strong vocational interest blank.* Stanford: Stanford University Press, 1971.

Campbell, D. P., & Holland, J. L. Applying Holland's theory to Strong's data. *Journal of Vocational Behavior,* 1972, 2, 353–376.

Campbell, D. P., Borgen, F. H., Eastes, S. H., Johansson, C. B., & Peterson, R. A. A set of basic interest scales for the Strong vocational interest blank for men. *Journal of Applied Psychology Monographs,* 1968, 52 (6, Part 2), 1–54.

Chaney, F. B., & Owens, W. A. Life history antecedents of sales, research, and general engineering interests. *Journal of Applied Psychology,* 1964, 48, 101–105.

Clark, K. E. *The vocational interests of nonprofessional men.* Minneapolis: University of Minnesota Press, 1961.

Cole, N. S., & Cole, J. W. L. *An analysis of spatial configuration and its application to research in higher education.* ACT Research Report No. 35. Iowa City: American College Testing Program, 1970.

Cole, N. S., & Hanson, G. *An analysis of the structure of vocational interests.* ACT Research Report No. 40. Iowa City: American College Testing Program, January, 1971.

Cole, N. S., Whitney, D. R., & Holland, J. L. A spatial configuration of occupations. *Journal of Vocational Behavior,* 1971, 1, 1–9.

Coleman, J. S., Blum, Z. D., & Sorensen, A. B. *Occupational status changes for blacks and non-blacks during the first ten years of occupational experience.* Center for Social Organization of Schools, Report No. 76. Baltimore: Johns Hopkins University, 1970.

College Entrance Examination Board. *Comparative Guidance and Placement Program.* New York: College Entrance Examination Board, 1969.

Computer-based vocational guidance systems. Washington, D.C.: Superintendent of Documents, Catalog No. FS 5.225:25053, 1969.

Cooley, W. W. Career development of scientists. Cooperative Research Project No. 436, Office of Education, Graduate School of Education, Harvard University, Cambridge, 1963.

Cooley, W. W. Interactions among interests, abilities, and career plans. *Journal of Applied Psychology Monographs,* 1967, 51 (5, Whole No. 640).

Cooley, W. W., & Lohnes, P. R. *Predicting development of young adults.* Contract No. OE-610-065. Palo Alto, Calif.: Project TALENT Office, American Institutes for Research and University of Pittsburgh, 1968.

Cottle, W. C. A factorial study of the multiphasic Strong, Kuder, and Bell inventories using a population of adult males. *Psychometrika,* 1950, 15, 25–47.

Crites, J. O. An interpersonal relations scale for occupational groups. *Journal of Applied Psychology,* 1962, 46, 87–90.

Crites, J. O. Measurement of vocational maturity in adolescence: I. Attitude test of the Vocational Development Inventory. *Psychological Monographs,* 1965, 79 (2, Whole No. 595).

Crites, J. O. *The maturity of vocational attitudes in adolescence.* Iowa City: University of Iowa, 1969. (a)

Crites, J. O. *Vocational psychology.* New York: McGraw-Hill, 1969. (b)

Crites, J. O. Interests. In R. L. Ebel (Ed.), *Encyclopedia of educational research.* New York: Macmillan, 1969, 678–686. (c)

Crutchfield, R. S., Woodworth, D. G., & Albrecht, R. E. *Perceptual performance and the effective person.* Personnel Laboratory, U.S. Air Force, ASTIA Document No. AD-151-039. Lackland Air Force Base, Tex.: 1958.

Danish, S. J., Graff, R. W., & Gensler, S. A. *The self-help vocational decision-making* booklet: *An adaptation of Magoon's effective problem-solving manual.* Carbondale: Student Counseling and Testing Center, Southern Illinois University, n.d.

Darley, J. G., & Hagenah, T. *Vocational interest measurement.* Minneapolis: University of Minnesota Press, 1955.

Davis, J. A. *Undergraduate career decisions.* Chicago: Aldine, 1965.

Dolliver, R. H. Strong vocational interest blank versus expressed vocational interests: A review. *Psychological Bulletin,* 1969, 72, 95–107.

Doyle, R. E. Career patterns of male college graduates. *Personnel and Guidance Journal,* 1965, 43, 410–414.

Dressel, P. L. Interests: Stable or unstable. *Journal of Educational Research,* 1954, 48, 95–102.

Droege, R. C. GATB longitudinal validation study. *Journal of Counseling Psychology,* 1968, 15, 41–47.

Dunkleberger, C. J., & Tyler, L. E. Interest stability and personality traits. *Journal of Counseling Psychology,* 1961, 8, 70–74.

Dunnette, M. D. Vocational interest differences among engineers employed in different functions. *Journal of Applied Psychology,* 1957, 41, 273–278.

Dunnette, M. D., Kirchner, W. K., & DeGidio, J. Relations among scores in Edwards Personal Preference Schedule, California Psychological Inventory, and Strong Vocational Interest Blank for an industrial sample. *Journal of Applied Psychology,* 1958, 42, 178–181.

Dunnette, M. D., Wernimont, P. & Abrahams, N. Further research on vocational interest differences among several types of engineers. *Personnel and Guidance Journal,* 1964, 44, 484–493.

Dunteman, G. H., Anderson, H. E. Jr., & Barry, J. R. *Characteristics of students in the health related professions.* Rehabilitation Research Monograph Series, No. 2. Gainesville: University of Florida, 1966.

Educational Resources, Inc. *The world of work.* New York: P. O. Box 353, 1970.

Edwards, K. J., & Whitney, D. R. A structural analysis of Holland's personality types using factor and configural analysis. *Journal of Counseling Psychology,* 1972, 19, 136–145.

Ehrle, R. A. Vocational maturity, vocational evaluation, and occupational information. *Vocational Guidance Quarterly,* September, 1970, 41–45.

Elder, G. H. Jr. Occupational level, achievement motivation, and social mobility: A longitudinal analysis. *Journal of Counseling Psychology,* 1968, 15, 1–7.

Elton, C. F., & Rose, H. A. Significance of personality in the vocational choice of college women. *Journal of Counseling Psychology,* 1967, 14, 293–298.

Elton, C. F., & Rose, H. A. Male occupational constancy and change: Its prediction according to Holland's theory. *Journal of Counseling Psychology,* 1970, 17, Part 2, No. 6.

Faunce, P. S. Personality characteristics and vocational interests related to the college persistence of academically gifted women. *Journal of Counseling Psychology,* 1968, 15, 31–40.

Feldman, K. A., & Newcomb, T. M. *The impact of college on students.* San Francisco: Jossey-Bass, 1969.

Flanagan, J. C. Individualizing education. Paper presented at American Psychological Association convention, San Francisco, 1968.

Flanagan, J. C., & Cooley, W. W. *Project Talent: One-year follow-up studies.* Cooperative Research Project No. 2333. Pittsburgh: University of Pittsburgh, 1966.

Flanagan, J. C., Davis, F. B., Dailey, J. T., Shaycoft, M. F., Orr, D. B., Goldberg, I., & Neyman, C. A. *The American high school student.* Cooperative Research Project No. 635. Pittsburgh: University of Pittsburgh, 1964.

Folger, J. K., Astin, H. S., & Bayer, A. E. *Human resources and higher education.* New York: Russell Sage Foundation, 1970.

Foreman, M. E., & James, L. E. Vocational relevance and estimated and measured test scores. *Journal of Counseling Psychology,* 1969, 16, 547–550.

Fryer, D. *The measurement of interests.* New York: Holt, 1931.

Galinsky, M. D. Personality development and vocational choice of clinical psychologists and physicists. *Journal of Counseling Psychology,* 1962, 9, 299–305.

Gardner, J. Sexist counseling must stop. *Personnel and Guidance Journal,* 1971, 49, 705–714.

Geist, H. A ten-year follow-up of the Geist picture interest inventory. *California Journal of Educational Research,* 1968, 19, 198–206.

Ghiselli, E. E. *The validity of occupational aptitude tests*. New York: Wiley, 1966.

Ghiselli, E. E. Managerial talent. In D. Wolfle (Ed.), *The discovery of talent*. Cambridge: Harvard University Press, 1969.

Glaser, B. G., Ed., *Organizational careers*. Chicago: Aldine, 1968.

Gordon, R. A. Social level, social disability, and gang interaction. *American Journal of Sociology*, 1967, 73, 42–62.

Gough, H. G. *Manual for the California psychological inventory*. Palo Alto, Calif.: Consulting Psychologists Press, 1957.

Gribbons, W. D., & Lohnes, P. R. *Emerging careers*. New York: Teachers College Press, Columbia University, 1968.

Gribbons, W. D., & Lohnes, P. R. *Career development from age 13 to age 25*. Final report, 1969. Project No. 6-2151, Grant No. OEG-1-7-062151-0471. Washington, D.C.: Office of Education.

Grunes, W. F. Looking at occupations. *Journal of Abnormal and Social Psychology*, 1957, 54, 86–92.

Guilford, J. P., Christensen, P. R., Bond, N. A. Jr., & Sutton, M. A. A factor analysis study of human interests. *Psychological Monographs*, 1954, 68 (4, Whole No. 375).

Gysbers, N. C., Johnston, J. A., & Gust, T. Characteristics of homemaker and career-oriented women. *Journal of Counseling Psychology*, 1968, 15, 541–546.

Hager, P. C., & Elton, C. F. The vocational interests of black males. *Journal of Vocational Behavior*, 1971, 1, 153–158.

Hamilton, J. A., & Webster, W. J. Occupational information and the school curriculum. *Vocational Guidance Quarterly*, March, 1971, 215–219.

Harmon, L. W. Predictive power over ten years of measured social service and scientific interests among college women. *Journal of Applied Psychology*, 1969, 53, 193–198.

Harmon, L. W., & Campbell, D. P. Use of interest inventories with nonprofessional women: Stewardesses versus dental assistants. *Journal of Counseling Psychology*, 1968, 15, 17–22.

Harris, J. A. The Willowbrook computerized vocational information system. In *Computer-based vocational guidance systems*. Washington, D.C.: U. S. Government Printing Office, Superintendent of Documents, Catalog No. FS 5.225:25053, USGPO, 1969.

Havighurst, R. J. *Human development and education*. New York: Longmans, Green, 1953.

Heath, B. R. G., & Strowig, R. W. Predicting occupational status for non-college-bound males. *Personnel and Guidance Journal*, 1967, 46, 144–149.

Hershenson, D. B. Techniques for assisting life-stage vocational development. *Personnel and Guidance Journal*, 1969, 47, 776–780.

Hodge, R., Siegel, P. M., & Rossi, P. H. Occupational prestige in the United States, 1925–1963. *American Journal of Sociology*, 1966, 72, 286–295.

Hogan, R., Hall, R., & Blank, E. An extension of the similarity-attraction hypothesis to the study of vocational behavior. *Journal of Counseling Psychology*, 1972, 19, 238–240.

Holland, J. L. A theory of vocational choice. *Journal of Counseling Psychology*, 1959, 6, 35–44.

Holland, J. L. Explorations of a theory of vocational choice and achievement: II. A four-year prediction study. *Psychological Reports*, 1963, 12, 537–594.

Holland, J. L. *Explorations of a theory of vocational choice: V. A one-year prediction study*. Moravia, N.Y.: Chronicle Guidance Professional Service, 1964.

Holland, J. L. *Manual for the vocational preference inventory*. Palo Alto, Calif.: Consulting Psychologists Press, 1965.

Holland, J. L. A psychological classification scheme for vocations and major fields. *Journal of Counseling Psychology*, 1966, 13, 278–288. (a)

Holland, J. L. *The psychology of vocational choice*. Waltham, Mass.: Blaisdell, 1966. (b)

Holland, J. L. Explorations of a theory of vocational choice: VI. A longitudinal study using a sample of typical college students. *Journal of Applied Psychology*, 1968, 52, 1–37.

Holland, J. L. *Counselor's guide for the self-directed search*. Palo Alto, Calif.: Consulting Psychologists Press, 1971. (a)

Holland, J. L. Review of J. O. Crites: Vocational psychology. *Contemporary Psychology*, 1971, 16, 148–150. (b)

Holland, J. L. *Making vocational choices: A theory of careers*. Englewood Cliffs, N.J.: Prentice-Hall, 1973.

Holland, J. L., & Baird, L. L. An interpersonal competency scale. *Educational and Psychological Measurement*, 1968, 28, 503–510.

Holland, J. L., & Nichols, R. C. The development and validation of an indecision scale: The natural history of a problem in basic research. *Journal of Counseling Psychology,* 1964, 11, 27–34.

Holland, J. L., & Whitney, D. R. Career development. *Review of Educational Research,* 1969, 39, 227–237.

Holland, J. L., & Whitney, D. R. *Changes in the vocational plans of college students: Orderly or random?* ACT Research Reports No. 25. Iowa City: American College Testing Program, Research and Development Division, April, 1968.

Holland, J. L., Whitney, D. R., Cole, N. S., & Richards, J. M. Jr. *An empirical occupational classification derived from a theory of personality and intended for practice and research.* ACT Research Report No. 29. Iowa City: American College Testing Program, 1969.

Holland, J. L., Viernstein, M. C., Kuo, H., Karweit, N. L., & Blum, Z. D. *A psychological classification of occupations.* Baltimore: Center for Social Organization of Schools, Report No. 90, Johns Hopkins University, 1970.

Hunt, R. Z. Self and other semantic concepts in relation to choice of a vocation. *Journal of Applied Psychology,* 1967, 51, 242–246.

Hutchinson, T., & Roe, A. Studies of occupational history: II. Attractiveness of occupational groups of the Roe system. *Journal of Counseling Psychology,* 1968, 15, 107–110.

Jeanneret, P. R., & McCormick, E. J. *The job dimensions of "worker-oriented" job variables and their attribute profiles as based on data from the position analysis questionnaire.* Report No. 2, 1969. Lafayette, Ind.: Occupational Research Center, Purdue University, Contract Nonr-1100(28), Office of Naval Research.

Jewish Employment and Vocational Service. *Work samples.* Philadelphia: 1913 Walnut Street, 19103, 1968.

Johnson, R. H. *Effect of the life career game on decision-making variables at the ninth grade level.* Doctoral dissertation, University of Missouri. Ann Arbor, Mich.: University Microfilms, 1971, No. 71-3343.

Jones, K. J. Occupational preference and social orientation. *Personnel and Guidance Journal,* 1965, 43, 574–579.

Jordaan, J. P. Vocational maturity: The construct, its measurement, and its validity. Paper presented at International Association for Applied Psychology; XVIIth International Congress, Liege, Belgium, July 25–30, 1971.

Katz, J., Korn, H. A., Leland, C. A., & Levin, M. M. *Class, character, and career: Determinants of occupational choice in college students.* Stanford: Institute for the Study of Human Problems, Stanford University, 1968.

Katz, M. A model of guidance for career decision making. *Vocational Guidance Quarterly,* 1966, 15, 2–10.

Kohn, M. L. *Class and conformity.* Homewood, Ill.: Dorsey Press, 1969.

Kohn, M. L., & Schooler, C. Class, occupation, and orientation. *American Sociological Review,* 1969, 34, 659–678.

Kroll, A. M., Dinklage, L. B., Lee, J., Morley, E. D., & Wilson, E. H. *Career development: Growth and crisis.* New York: Wiley, 1970.

Krulee, G. K., O'Keefe, R., & Goldberg, M. *Influence of identity processes on student behavior and occupational choice.* Cooperative Research Project No. 5-0809. Evanston, Ill.: Northwestern University, 1966.

Krumboltz, J. D. *Job experience kits.* Chicago: Science Research Associates, 1971.

Krumboltz, J. D., & Schroeder, W. W. Promoting career planning through reinforcement. *Personnel and Guidance Journal,* 1965, 43, 19–26.

Kuder, G. F. *Manual for general interest survey, form E.* Chicago: Science Research Associates, 1965.

Kuder, G. F. *Manual for occupational interest survey, form DD.* Chicago: Science Research Associates, 1970.

Kulberg, G. E., & Owens, W. A. Some life history antecedents of engineering interests. *Journal of Educational Psychology,* 1960, 51, 26–31.

Kuvlesky, W. P., & Bealer, R. C. A clarification of the concept "occupational choice." *Rural Sociology,* 1966, 31, 265–276.

Kuvlesky, W. P., & Thomas, K. A. Social ambitions of Negro boys and girls from a metropolitan ghetto. *Journal of Vocational Behavior,* 1971, 1, 177–187.

Laurent, H. Jr. A study of the developmental backgrounds of men to determine by means of the biographical information blank the relationship between factors in their early backgrounds and their choice of professions.

Unpublished doctoral dissertation, Western Reserve University, Cleveland, Ohio, 1951.

Lepak, R. C. Development of a "Catholic Priest" scale on the Strong vocational interest blank. *National Catholic Guidance Conference Journal,* 1968, 12, 261–268.

Lipe, D. Trait validity of airline stewardess performance ratings. *Journal of Applied Psychology,* 1970, 54, 347–352.

Little, J. K. The occupations of non-college youth. *American Educational Research,* 1967, 4, 147–153.

Lofquist, L. H., & Dawis, R. V. *Adjustment to work.* New York: Appleton-Century-Crofts, 1969.

Lucy, W. T. A study designed to test the validity of selected formulations from John Holland's theory of vocational choice. Unpublished doctoral dissertation, University of Maine, Orono, 1971.

McCormick, E. J., Cunningham, J. W., & Thornton, G. C. The prediction of job requirements by a structured job analysis procedure. *Personnel Psychology,* 1967, 20, 431–440.

McCormick, E. J., Jeanneret, P. R., & Mecham, R. C. *The development and background of the position analysis questionnaire.* Office of Naval Research, Contract Nonr-1100 (28), Report No. 5. Lafayette, Ind.: Occupational Research Center, Purdue University, 1969.

McCormick, E. J., Jeanneret, P. R., & Mecham, R. C. A study of job characteristics and job dimensions as based on the Position Analysis Questionnaire. *Journal of Applied Psychology,* 1972, 56, 347–368.

McKenzie, J. D., & Magoon, T. M. *Subsequent vocational and educational status of Arts and Sciences graduates of 1963.* Counseling Center, Research Report No. 1-66. College Park: University of Maryland, 1966.

Madaus, G. F., & O'Hara, R. P. Vocational interest patterns of high school boys: A multivariate approach. *Journal of Counseling Psychology,* 1967, 14, 106–112.

Magoon, T. M. Developing skills for educational and vocational problems. In J. D. Krumboltz & C. E. Thoresen (Eds.), *Behavioral counseling.* New York: Holt, Rinehart and Winston, 1969, 343–396.

Marks, E., & Webb, S. C. Vocational choice and professional experience as factors in occupational image. *Journal of Applied Psychology,* 1969, 53, 292–300.

Mecham, R. C., & McCormick, E. J. *The rated attribute requirements of job elements in the position analysis questionnaire.* Office of Naval Research Contract Nonr-1100 (28), Report No. 1. Lafayette, Ind.: Occupational Research Center, Purdue University, 1969. (a)

Mecham, R. C., & McCormick, E. J. *The use of data based on the position analysis questionnaire in developing synthetically derived attribute requirements of jobs.* Office of Naval Research Contract Nonr-1100 (28), Report No. 4. Lafayette, Ind.: Occupational Research Center, Purdue University, 1969. (b)

Medvene, A. M. Occupational choice of graduate students in psychology as a function of early parent-child interactions. *Journal of Counseling Psychology,* 1969, 16, 385–389.

Meyer, H. H., & Cuomo, S. Q. *Characteristics of young engineer managers.* Report No. 4. Management Development and Employee Relations Services. Schenectady, N.Y.: General Electric, 1964.

Miller, A. R. *Current occupation and past training of adult workers.* (mimeo.) Office of Statistical Standards, Statistical Evaluation Report No. 7, Bureau of the Budget. Washington, D.C.: Superintendent of Documents, U.S. Government Printing Office, 1968.

Morrow, J. M. Jr. Satisfaction with choice of college major: A test of Holland's theory of vocational choice. Unpublished doctoral dissertation, University of North Carolina, 1970.

Nachmann, B. Childhood experience and vocational choice in law, dentistry, and social work. *Journal of Counseling Psychology,* 1960, 7, 243–250.

National Science Foundation. *Two years after the college degree.* NSF Report 63–26. Washington, D.C.: U.S. Government Printing Office, 1963.

Nelson, J. C. Interests of disadvantaged and advantaged Negro and white first graders. *Journal of Negro Education,* 1968, 37, 168–173.

Nichols, R. C. *The resemblance of twins in personality and interests.* Research Report No. 8. Evanston, Ill.: National Merit Scholarship Corporation, 1966.

Norman, W. T. A spatial analysis of an interest domain. *Educational and Psychological Measurement,* 1960, 20, 347–361.

Norton, J. L. Patterns of vocational interest development and actual job choice. *Journal of Genetic Psychology,* 1953, 82, 235–262.

O'Dowd, D. D., & Beardslee, D. C. *College student images of a selected group of professions and occupations.* USOE, Cooperative Research No. 562 (8142). Middletown, Conn.: Wesleyan University, 1960.

O'Dowd, D. D., & Beardslee, D. C. *Development and consistency of student images of occupations.* Cooperative Research Project No. 5-0858. Rochester, Mich.: Oakland University, 1967.

Ornstein, M. D., & Rossi, P. H. *Going to work: An analysis of the determinants and consequences of entry into the labor force.* Center for Social Organization of Schools, Report No. 75. Baltimore: Johns Hopkins University, 1970.

Osipow, S. H. Consistency of occupational choices and Roe's classification of occupations. *Vocational Guidance Quarterly,* Summer, 1966, 285–286.

Osipow, S. H. *Theories of career development.* New York: Appleton-Century-Crofts, 1968.

Owens, W. A. Toward one discipline of scientific psychology. *American Psychologist,* 1968, 23, 782–785.

Parnes, H. S., Egge, K., Kohen, A. I., & Schmidt, R. M. *The pre-retirement years.* Columbus: Center for Human Resource Research, Ohio State University, 1970.

Paterson, D. G., Gerken, C. D'A., & Hahn, M. E. *Revised Minnesota rating scales.* Minneapolis: University of Minnesota Press, 1953.

Perrone, P. A. Vocational development. *Review of Educational Research,* 1966, 36, 298–307.

Perry, D. K., & Cannon, W. M. Vocational interests of computer programmers. *Journal of Applied Psychology,* 1967, 51, 28–34.

Peterson, R. A., & Pennington, A. L. SVIB interests and product preferences. *Journal of Applied Psychology,* 1969, 53, 304–308.

Petrik, N. D. Test-retest reliability of the SVIB and differing curricular experience. *Proceedings of the 77th Annual Convention of the American Psychological Association,* 1969, 4, 687–688.

Pilato, G. T. The effects of three vocational guidance treatments on some aspects of vocational preference and self-knowledge. *Dissertation Abstracts,* 1969, 29, 3919.

Plotkin, A. L. The effect of occupational information classes upon the vocational interest patterns of below average, adolescent males. *Dissertation Abstracts,* 1967, 27, 2895.

Posthuma, A. B., & Navran, L. Relation of congruence in student-faculty interests to achievement in college. *Journal of Counseling Psychology,* 1970, 17, 352–356.

Rezler, A. G. Characteristics of high school girls choosing traditional or pioneer vocations. *Personnel and Guidance Journal,* 1967, 45, 659–665. (a)

Rezler, A. G. The joint use of the Kuder preference record and the Holland vocational preference inventory in the vocational assessment of high school girls. *Psychology in the Schools,* 1967, 4, 82–84. (b)

Richards, J. M. Jr. Who studies what major in college? Paper presented at the American Psychological Association convention, Miami, Florida, 1970.

Richards, J. M. Jr. The prediction of career plans. In J. C. Flanagan et al., *Five years after high school.* Palo Alto, Calif.: American Institutes for Research, 1971.

Richards, J. M. Jr., & Seligman, R. Faculty and curriculum as measures of college environment. Paper presented at the American Psychological Association convention, San Francisco, 1968.

Robinson, J. P., Athanasiou, R., & Head, K. B. *Measures of occupational attitudes and occupational characteristics.* Ann Arbor, Mich.: Institute for Social Research, 1969.

Roe, A. A psychological study of physical scientists. *Psychological Monographs,* 1951, 43, 121–235.

Roe, A. *The psychology of occupations.* New York: Wiley, 1956.

Roe, A. Early determinants of vocational choice. *Journal of Counseling Psychology,* 1957, 4, 212–217.

Roe, A., & Siegelman, M. *The origin of interests.* Washington, D.C.: American Personnel and Guidance Association, 1964.

Roe, A., Hubbard, W. D., Hutchison, T., & Bateman, T. Studies of occupational histories: I. Job changes and the classification of occupations. *Journal of Counseling Psychology,* 1966, 13, 387–393.

Rose, H. A., & Elton, C. F. Ask him or test him? *Vocational Guidance Quarterly,* Summer, 1970, 28–32.

Rossi, A. S. Women in science: Why so few? *Science*, 1965, 148, 1196–1202.

Roys, K. B. Vocational interests of community recreation administrators using the SVIB. *Journal of Applied Psychology*, 1967, 51, 539–543.

Ryan, T. A. Reinforcement techniques and simulation materials for counseling clients with decision-making problems. *Proceedings of the 77th Annual Convention of the American Psychological Association*, 1969, 4, 693–694.

Schneider, L. R., & Stevens, N. D. Personality characteristics associated with job-seeking behavior patterns. *Vocational Guidance Quarterly*, 1971, 19, 194–200.

Schutz, R. A., & Blocher, D. H. Self-concepts and stereotypes of vocational preferences. *Vocational Guidance Quarterly*, 1960, 8, 241–244.

Segal, S. J. A psychoanalytic analysis of personality factors in vocational choice. *Journal of Counseling Psychology*, 1961, 8, 202–208.

Sewell, W. H., Haller, A. O., & Straus, M. A. Social status and educational and occupational aspiration. *American Sociological Review*, 1957, 22, 67–73.

Shappell, D. L., Hall, L. G., & Tarrier, R. B. School motivation and occupational orientation. *Vocational Guidance Quarterly*, December, 1970, 97–103.

Sharp, L. M. *Education and employment*. Baltimore: Johns Hopkins Press, 1970.

Shea, J. R., Roderick, R. D., Zeller, F. A., & Kohen, A. I. *Years for decision: A longitudinal study of the educational and labor market experience of young women*, Vol. I. Columbus: Center for Human Resource Research, Ohio State University, 1971.

Shea, J. R., Spitz, R. S., & Zeller, F. A. *Dual careers: A longitudinal study of labor market experience of women*, Vol. 1. Columbus: Center for Human Resource Research, Ohio State University, 1970.

Sheppard, L. E. Effects of a problem-solving procedure for stimulating vocational exploration. *Dissertation Abstracts*, 1967, 28, 943–944.

Siess, T. F., & Jackson, D. N. Vocational interests and personality: An empirical integration. *Journal of Counseling Psychology*, 1970, 17, 27–35.

Simpson, R. L., & Harper, I. Social origins, occupational advice, occupational values, and work careers. *Social Forces*, 1962, 40, 264–271.

Sorensen, A. B. The occupational mobility process: An analysis of the decision to leave a job. Paper presented at Seventh World Congress of the International Sociological Association, Varna, Bulgaria, 1970.

Stahmann, R. F. Predicting graduation major field from freshman entrance data. *Journal of Counseling Psychology*, 1969, 16, 109–113.

Stewart, N. AGCT scores of Army personnel grouped by occupation. *Occupations*, 1947, 26, 5–41.

Stone, T. H., & Athelstan, G. T. The SVIB for women and demographic variables in the prediction of occupational tenure. *Journal of Applied Psychology*, 1969, 53, 408–412.

Strong, E. K. Jr. *Vocational interests of men and women*. Stanford: Stanford University Press, 1943.

Super, D. E. The future of vocational development theory. In J. M. Whiteley (Ed.), *Perspectives in vocational development*. Washington, D.C.: American Personnel and Guidance Association, 1972.

Super, D. E., & Crites, J. O. *Appraising vocational fitness*. (Rev. ed.) New York: Harper and Row, 1962.

Super, D. E., Kowalski, R. S., & Gotkin, E. H. *Floundering and trial after high school*. Career Pattern Study, Monograph IV. Cooperative Research Project No. 1393. New York: Teachers College, Columbia University, 1967.

Super, D. E., Starishevsky, R., Matlin, N., & Jordaan, J. P. *Career development: Self-concept theory*. New York: College Entrance Examination Board, 1963.

Tennyson, W. W. Career Development. *Review of Educational Research*, 1968, 38, 346–366.

Thorndike, R. L., & Hagen, E. *Ten thousand careers*. New York: Wiley, 1959.

Thorndike, R. M., Weiss, D. J., & Dawis, R. J. Canonical correlation of vocational interests and vocational needs. *Journal of Counseling Psychology*, 1968, 15, 101–106.

Tiedeman, D. V., O'Hara, R. P., & Baruch, R. W. *Career development: Choice and adjustment*. New York: College Entrance Examination Board, 1963.

U. S. Department of Labor, Manpower Administration. *Dictionary of occupational titles: Occupational classification*, Vol. II.

Washington, D.C.: Superintendent of Documents, USGPO, 1965.

Useem, R. H. Changing cultural concepts in women's lives. *Journal of the National Association of Women Deans and Counselors,* 1960, 24, 29–34.

Vandenberg, S. G., & Stafford, R. E. Hereditary influences on vocational preferences as shown by scores of twins on the Minnesota Vocational Interest Inventory. *Journal of Applied Psychology,* 1967, 51, 17–19.

Veness, T. *School leavers: Their aspirations and expectations.* New York: Humanities Press, 1962.

Viernstein, M. C. *The extension of Holland's occupational classification to all occupations in the Dictionary of Occupational Titles. Journal of Vocational Behavior,* 1972, 2, 107–121.

Vroom, V. H. *Work and motivation.* New York: Wiley, 1964.

Walsh, W. B., & Lacey, D. W. Perceived change and Holland's theory. *Journal of Counseling Psychology,* 1969, 16, 348–352.

Watley, D. J. Stability of career choices of talented youth. Evanston, Ill.: National Merit Scholarship Corporation, Research Report No. 2, 1968.

Watley, D. J., & Kaplan, R. Career or marriage? Aspirations and achievements of able young women. *Journal of Vocational Behavior,* 1971, 1, 29–43.

Werts, C. E. Career changes in college. *Sociology of Education,* 1967, 40, 90–95.

Werts, C. E. Paternal influence on career choice. *Journal of Counseling Psychology,* 1968, 15, 48–52.

Werts, C. E., & Watley, D. J. Paternal influence on talent development. Evanston, Ill.: National Merit Scholarship Corporation, Research Report No. 4, 1970.

White, R. W. *Lives in progress.* New York: Holt, Rinehart and Winston, 1952.

Whiteley, J. M., & Resnikoff, A., Eds. *Perspectives in vocational development.* Washington, D.C.: American Personnel and Guidance Association, 1972.

Whitney, D. R. Predicting from expressed vocational choice: A review. *Personnel and Guidance Journal,* 1969, 48, 279–286.

Williams, C. M. Occupational choice of male graduate students as related to values and personality: A test of Holland's theory. *Journal of Vocational Behavior,* 1972, 2, 39–46.

Williams, J. E. *Conflict between freshman male roommates.* Research Report No. 10-67. College Park: Counseling Center, University of Maryland, 1967.

Witty, P., Garfield, S., & Brink, W. A comparison of the vocational interests of Negro and white high school students. *Journal of Educational Psychology,* 1941, 32, 124–132.

Witty, P. A., & Lehman, H. C. A study of vocational attitude and intelligence. *Elementary School Journal,* 1931, 31, 735–746.

Zeller, F. A., Shea, J. R., Kohen, A. I., & Meyer, J. A. *Career thresholds: A longitudinal study of the educational and labor market experiences of male youth,* Vol. 2. Columbus: Center for Human Resource Research, Ohio State University, Columbus, October, 1970.

CHAPTER 13

Personality and
Personality Assessment

HARRISON GOUGH
University of California, Berkeley

THE PSYCHOLOGY OF PERSONALITY attends to the ways in which individuals resemble each other and to the ways in which they differ. Measurement seeks to specify and calibrate these dimensions of variation. Personality theory, once merely the elaboration of personal world views, has now moved closer to the scientific ideal of a consensually confirmed set of facts, propositions, and instrumentalities directed to the comprehension of defined problems. Any theory of personality must answer three questions: (1) How is personality defined? (2) What motivates behavior? and (3) How is personality structured, that is, what are the key dimensions and how are they interrelated? A possible fourth question concerns directionality: What are the aims, goals, and even ultimate purposes of human life? Significant current research includes studies of authoritarianism, conformity, need:achievement, moral development, social judgment, creativity, analytic thinking, sleep and dreaming, biochemical factors in behavior, genetics, population, heart disease and the effects of stress on physical well-being, and managerial styles and executive effectiveness.

The variations in thought and behavior that differentiate one person from another constitute a key facet of what is meant by the concept of personality. When we meet someone for the first time we scrutinize him carefully—his speech, dress, manner, and modes of reaction—so as to detect his individuality and the way in which he stands apart from others. At the same time we note his resemblance to others and the degree to which his behavior may conform to patterns that we have previously come to understand. Thus, even in our first perceptions of personality, we intuitively recognize, as Kluckhohn and Murray (1953) once noted, that everyone is in some respects like all other persons, like some others, and (finally) like no other individual.

This particularity, if we may call it that, is a very interesting phenomenon, however, as it cannot just go in any direction. There is a sort of target, or lawfulness, in the development of individuality. A literary creation, for example, can be different from

571

anything seen in life and, yet, sensed as "right" or "wrong" in its expression of human individuality. For each kind of variation there seems to be a sort of inherent logic and structure toward which the observed example seeks to move. One function of literature is to delineate these types or syndromes of reaction, and as we come to know a Meursault, an Ahab, a Don Fabrizio, or a Raskolnikov, we sense the veridicality of the portrait each author has drawn. What is more, we gain deeper insight into the meanings of alienation, obsession, grace, and evil. The student of personality must concern himself with life, including the literature that derives from life.

Biography and autobiography stand one step removed from the analyses of the novelist, and together constitute another great reservoir of insight and information for the student of personality. Documents such as Wells's *Experiment in Autobiography* (1938), the *Parallel Lives* of Plutarch (46–120 A.D.), and even Goodspeed's *A Life of Jesus* (1950) can be cited as examples. Each attempts to depict essences and to discover the causes as well as the apparent aims of behavior. Lest the reader worry, at this point, that he has stumbled into an apologia for unscientific and unchecked intuitionism, let it be noted that the leading psychologists of the past fifty years have been pleased to contribute their own autobiographical sketches to the five-volume *History of Psychology in Autobiography* (Murchison, 1930, 1932, 1936; Boring et al., 1952; Boring & Lindzey, 1967), and that anyone who seeks knowledge of the emergence of psychology as a scientific discipline must pay at least some attention to these sources.

Personality, it may be concluded, encompasses more than the laboratory scientist and quantitatively minded researcher can at present bring under scrutiny, and the student of personality must, therefore, attend to other sources of information, including the insights vouchsafed by art and literature

and the lessons to be intuited from his own experience.

Present-day study of personality also rests on concepts and theories derived from the medical and psychiatric clinic. Hippocrates (460–357 B.C.) proposed that the body was composed of four humors—black bile, blood, yellow bile, and phlegm—and that excesses or deficiencies of each of these substances produced characteristic forms of malfunctioning. Galen (130–200 A.D.) later suggested perhaps the first typology of personality, based on these humors, in which melancholic (depressed), sanguine (buoyant), choleric (irritable), and phlegmatic (apathetic) modes of reaction were specified.

In more modern times, Kraepelin (1856–1926) and Bleuler (1857–1939) developed diagnostic concepts (e.g., the manic-depressive and schizophrenic psychoses) and Freud (1856–1939) advanced his basic theoretical notions concerning mental structure (id, ego, and superego) and dynamics (e.g., repression and projection). Recent work on the role of amino acids in brain functioning (see Schildkraut, 1965), the psychology of sleep and dreaming (see Dement, 1965; Kleitman, 1939), the location of drive and reward centers in the brain (Olds & Olds, 1965), and the nature of the electrophysiological rhythms that accompany thought and fantasy (see Kamiya, 1969) has produced new information that is only now being assimilated into personality theory and the general conceptualization of human behavior.

What Toffler (1970) has called "future shock," the feeling that events and experiences are moving too rapidly to permit integrated comprehension, is a problem for the personologist of today just as it is for the citizen who watches the kaleidoscopic transformations of his life in too many sectors. The neat patterns of even ten years ago, when personality theory could be approached as an orderly tour through the elegant edifices erected by great scholars between 1900 and 1960, are being erased by the constant flow of new facts and new knowledge. Already, except for purely historical purposes, it is probably wiser to approach the field of personality by way of topics of relevance and available evidence than by way of the commendable but rapidly eroding theoretical systems of yesterday. In keeping with this admonition, the discussion to follow will center principally on problem areas and will only incidentally deal with the formal systems and grand designs of the past.

COMMON SENSE QUESTIONS

Before going into the specific problem areas to which research has been directed, we should look at some of the broad questions about personality that come easily to mind. One of these must certainly be that of definition: Just what is meant by the term "personality"? Perhaps the most heroic struggle with this query was that of Allport (1937) who devoted thirty-one pages of his classic textbook to a response. After considering historical, theatrical, theological, philosophical, juristic, sociological, biosocial, omnibus, psychiatric, and other definitions, Allport put forward the following formulation: "Personality is the dynamic organization within the individual of those psychophysical systems that determine his unique adjustments to his environment" (Allport, 1937, p. 48). This definition stresses key notions that anyone would recognize as important, such as the individuality of each person, the interplay of inner and outer forces, and the capacity of the system to change in response to demands from within or without.

Later writers on personality have either tended to accept Allport's formulation (cf., Lazarus, 1971; Maddi, 1968; Sanford, 1968), or have stressed the multiplicity of working viewpoints and the fact that significant progress in the understanding of human behavior may be achieved even while definitional issues remain unresolved. Hall and Lindzey (1957, p. 9), for example, state that no substantive definition of personality can be used in any very general way, and add that personality in any specific inquiry is defined by the empirical methods of inquiry espoused by the investigator. McClelland (1951) concluded that personality is a complex inference from the totality of a subject's behavior, and that the goal of this inference is to provide an acceptable conceptualization of the person's behavior in all of its detail. Wiggins, Renner, Clore, and Rose (1971) stress the incompleteness of any single perspective, and suggest that biological, experimental, social, and psychometric perspectives are all required if the diversity of personality is to be adequately apprehended.

A second concern dictated by common sense has to do with motivation: What prompts people to think, act, move about, and seek goals in their behavior? The biological nature of the human organism provides an important part of the answer to this question, for man is as subject to hunger, thirst, and the need for new experience as any other animal. Maslow (1968) has posited a motivational hierarchy, in which "deficiency motives"—physiological and self-protective needs—must first be satisfied, but once satisfied give way to "being motives," such as belonging, love, esteem, and self-actualization. Man as a social organism and at work is largely under the push of these "B-motives," and hence rewards, such as approval and recognition, are of great importance, and the drive to do something in one's own individual and unique manner may be the most compelling of all. The implications of Maslow's ideas for managerial and personnel issues have been discussed by many writers (cf., Centers & Bugental, 1966; Haire, 1964).

At one time the notion of instincts was predominant (an instinct may be defined as a species-specific, unlearned, organized, and goal-directed pattern of behavior), and human action was seen as the expression of these innate drives. McDougall (1923) was a leading spokesman for this viewpoint, and Veblen (1914) posited an "instinct of workmanship." Instinct doctrine subsequently tumbled because of its cumbersomeness (the list of instincts eventually became almost as long as the varieties of behavior that were to be explained) and its tautological weaknesses. Psychodynamic psychology also furnished an important series of motivational concepts, from the Eros (love) and Thanatos (death and aggression) of Freud to organ inferiority and the resulting compensatory drives postulated by Adler.

Motivational concepts played a major role in the writings of the Gestalt psychologist Lewin (1935, 1936). In his topological psychology (a psychology of field-relationships), Lewin stressed notions such as the valences of goal objects, barriers, impeding locomotion (movement) toward these objects, and the interplay of psychological forces in the life space of the individual. Many of Lewin's concepts are directly relevant to issues in personnel and industrial psychology. Consider, for example, worker output. Any observed level of productivity, according to Lewin, is best viewed as a homeostatic equilibrium, a compromise between forces tending to augment or increase and those tending to constrain or diminish. To raise the level of this equilibrium it is necessary to pay attention to both inhibiting and energizing forces. A bonus for higher productivity (positive vector) might not lead to a significant change in level unless fears of being accused of rate-busting (negative vector) are simultaneously allayed. Group discussion and decision making were the methods Lewin found to be most effective in reducing negative vectors tending to suppress new or intensified effort.

The "need-press" theory of Murray (1938) should also be mentioned. A need, according to Murray, is a motive force in the individual having directional and energic (quantitative) properties; press refers to the directional tendency that an object or situation exerts as it impinges upon an individual. Behavior, it follows, is a resultant of the dynamic interplay between needs and press. Murray identified a series of twenty-seven manifest and eight latent needs, and proposed scales and other devices for assessing their presence and strength; need: achievement, need:nurturance, need:order, and need:understanding are among the variables proposed by Murray. The TAT or Thematic Apperception Test developed by Morgan and Murray (1935), in which stories are told in response to pictures and then rated for needs and thematic content, is still widely used in personality assessment. Later tests, such as Edwards's Personal Preference Schedule (1953), the Adjective Check List (Gough & Heilbrun, 1965), and the Personality Research Form (Jackson, 1967) contain scales addressed to needs as defined by Murray.

The cognitive emphasis in Murray's work has also been echoed in subsequent endeavor. McClelland, Atkinson, Clark, and Lowell (1953), for example, published an extensive analysis of the need:achievement variable. Festinger (1957), in his studies of cognitive dissonance, documented the motivating power generated by the doubts and uncertainties of decision making. Perhaps the ultimate example of a cognitive motivation is found in man's striving for competence (White, 1959).

With regard to work, probably the major motivational theory at the present time is that of Herzberg (1966; Herzberg, Mausner, & Snyderman, 1959). Two classes of work inducements are postulated—extrinsic and intrinsic. The former includes items such as pay, working conditions, and job security; the latter comprises recognition for superior performance, having responsibility for one's own duties, and advancement to higher positions. The role of extrinsic factors is to prevent job dissatisfaction, whereas intrinsic factors promote job satisfaction. The theory has stimulated a considerable volume of research (cf., House & Wigdor, 1967), but with somewhat equivocal results (see

Dunnette, 1967; Hulin, 1966; Wernimont, 1966). A worthwhile by-product of work on the "motivator-hygiene" or MH hypothesis has been the development of assessment tools, including the 144-item Job Motivation Inventory (Kahoe, 1966), the Choice Motivation Scale (Hamlin & Nemo, 1962), and even the Picture Motivation Test (Kunca & Haywood, 1969) for use with children.

A recent study by Clark (1970) of 271 public school administrators illustrates the kind of findings yielded by the Herzberg MH theory. These Ss took the Kahoe Job Motivation Inventory and the California Psychological Inventory (Gough, 1957). The JMI was scored for two major clusters— motivator (intrinsic) job orientation versus hygiene (extrinsic) orientation. These two clusters were then correlated with the eighteen scales of the personality inventory, to see if scales more indicative of self-actualization and creativity would co-vary with the motivator factor, and if scales associated with conventionality and inflexibility would co-vary with the hygiene factor. The results were moderately in support of these expectations: the motivator factor correlated positively with psychological-mindedness and tolerance for both sexes (197 males, 67 females), and the hygiene factor correlated negatively with flexibility and social presence. The magnitudes of the coefficients, however, were modest, the largest single value being a $+.39$ between the motivator factor and psychological-mindedness for females.

Although not strictly a theory of motivation, Holland's (1973) schema of vocational choice possesses drive-generating implications. Holland posited six modes of response to cultural demands and opportunities; realistic, investigative, artistic, social, enterprising, and conventional. Personality and vocational types are defined on the basis of these factors taken alone or in combination. Job choice, job performance, and even life circumstances can then be forecast from the typological classification.

A third question concerns the structuring of personality, the identification of major facets or "dimensions," and the organization of dispositions with respect to centrality, visibility, and importance. Cattell (1946, 1950) and Eysenck (1947) have been among the leading writers on this topic. Eysenck has argued that many significant aspects of personality can be conceptualized as interactions between two basic dimensions or factors—the stable versus unstable, and the introverted versus extraverted. The notions of Hippocrates and Galen, previously mentioned, can be reinterpreted in Eysenck's formulation (cf., Eysenck & Eysenck, 1963); for example, in the quadrant defined by instability and introversion one finds the melancholic temperament, and descriptions such as pessimistic, sober, anxious, and reserved; in the quadrant defined by instability and extraversion one finds the choleric temperament, and descriptions such as excitable, impulsive, aggressive, and touchy. Personality or internal problems are associated with the first quadrant indicated, whereas behavioral or conduct problems are more often found in the second. Eysenck has developed two self-descriptive assessment devices to aid in the measurement of these two dimensions, the Eysenck Personality Inventory (Eysenck & Eysenck, 1963) and the Maudsley Personality Inventory (Eysenck, 1959). Either can be given in from ten to fifteen minutes, and although they are susceptible to faking, both furnish statistically reliable indices of the introversion-extraversion and normal-neurotic factors.

Cattell (1946) began with a list of 171 personality variables, drawn from previous rosters of trait names and descriptors, and used this list of 171 terms to represent the "personality sphere." Surface traits were then defined by examining the intercorrelations of these 171 variables and by noting the clusters formed by variables correlating positively ($r \geq .60$) with each other. They are referred to as surface because their similarity can be identified through study of trait ratings gathered from observers, without recourse to more analytic psychometric methods.

Examples of surface traits would be sociability versus shyness (sociable, gregarious, and intrusive versus shy, seclusive, and reserved) and integrity-altruism versus dishonesty, undependability.

By means of factor analysis a less obvious but mathematically more basic covariation can be detected, and factors or clusters identified in this manner are designated source traits. From standing on these source traits, the manifest ratings on the surface traits and the 171 initial trait variables can at least theoretically be reconstructed. Source traits, therefore, constitute statistically powerful dimensions of personality, and should be equally useful in forecasting behavior and response in significant non-test situations. Cattell has developed a self-descriptive personality inventory to measure sixteen of these source traits (Cattell, 1949; Cattell & Eber, 1964), including the following: schizothymia (aloof, cold) versus cyclothymia (warm, sociable), threctia (timid, shy) versus parmia (adventurous, thick-skinned), and praxernia (conventional, practical) versus autia (Bohemian, unconcerned). A somewhat related device, also based on factorial technique, is the Guilford-Zimmerman Temperament Indicator (Guilford & Zimmerman, 1949) which contains ten scales including those for general activity, ascendance, and emotional stability.

Trait psychology leads easily to type psychology, in which salient and recurring dispositions are grouped together and mnemonically labeled. Thus an "introvert"—viewed as a kind of person—may be characterized by traits of persistence, rigidity, autonomic nervous system imbalance, and innumerable typifying habitual responses (cf., Eysenck, 1951). Jung (1923) was a major advocate of type theory, proposing classifications such as introverted, extraverted, intuitive, thinking, and feeling. His concepts are also embodied in several personality inventories including the Myers-Briggs Type Indicator (Myers, 1962) and Gray-Wheelwright (Gray & Wheelwright, 1946).

A fourth question to consider is directionality, that is, the aim of behavior. Immediate actions are often easily related to proximate goals, but what about long-term trends and distant and even unattainable targets? Teleology—the contention that natural processes are influenced by purpose and that events seek a defined resolution—has never been a popular philosophical concept among scientifically minded psychologists. Nonetheless, many students of personality have been unwilling to divest themselves of the belief that goals and ends do act on the personality.

Allport (1961) appealed to Charlotte Bühler's concept of *Bestimmung,* a term more or less signifying "directedness." In her study of some two hundred life histories most seemed to be ordered or steered toward a designated goal or goals. The more mature the personality, Allport added, the more marked and clearly focused the *Bestimmung.* Individuals appear to be able to tell when they are developing or moving toward a distant goal or value, and when they are marking time or experiencing a diversion. *Radix,* Wertheimer's term for the ruling passion or goal-object of a life, is another expression pertaining to this presumed phenomenon of directionality. Still another is Erikson's concept of identity (Erikson, 1950), in which the individual seeks and feels compelled to move toward some sense of completeness and integration that he cannot as yet define or specify, but that he wants desperately to achieve and knows he can recognize. The existentialist creed that man must transcend himself in order to know himself should also be noted.

But what of the logic of positivism, the physical realities of life and man's biological nature? Can concepts such as identity, self-actualization, and "becoming" (Allport, 1955) be squared with the constraints set by these givens? On this point, let us permit Allport to speak for himself (1961, p. 563):

Precisely what do we mean when we say that the normal personality is relatively free to program his own identity? Not that he is liberated from all his drives (he still must sleep, eat, obtain oxygen, and he is strongly goaded by sex needs, by angry impulses, by ego defenses). Not that he is entirely free from his early learning—many dispositions and attitudes acquired in childhood will be with him to the end. Not that he is independent of the continuous stream of "nutriment" that the environment gives him to reward and sustain his cultural attitudes and to insure his conformity to the roles he must play in family, in occupation, and in society.

All these pressures exist. But *becoming* is the process by which all these forces are employed by the creative urge to program a style of life for oneself. The basic existential urge to grow, pursue meaning, seek unity, is also a "given." It is a major fact—even more prominent in man's nature than his propensity to yield to surrounding pressures. It is this desire for autonomy, for individuation, for self-hood, for existential uniqueness that enters into the shaping of the product.

A final common sense distinction to be considered is that between healthy and unhealthy manifestations of behavior, the sane versus the insane. This distinction, which seems so easy to make, is more difficult than meets the eye. An important theme in personality and psychiatric theory of the past fifteen to twenty years has been the notion that mental health and illness represent to some extent mere point of view, not fixed and reliable criteria. Szasz (1961) has advanced the notion that labeling an individual as mentally ill sets up behavioral constraints that soon lead to the outcomes the diagnosis envisaged. Sarbin (1964, 1967) has argued that at least some of the descriptive terms of abnormal psychology, for example, "anxiety," are reifications of mythical entities rather than valid referents of observable behavior, and that "mental illness"—used as anything other than a convenient metaphor —is illogical and should be dropped from psychological discourse. Other writers such as Scheibe (1970), Goffman (1963), and Laing (1967) have stressed the effects of stigma on the identity and value systems of those who are in one way or another labeled as deviant by the culture in which they live.

The laymen's belief that there is indeed such a thing as mental illness is not, of course, without its scientific supporters. Ausubel (1961) concluded that personality disorder is disease, as disease is defined and conceptualized medically and psychiatrically, and Ellis (1967), although stressing the need to avoid pejorative use of the concept of mental illness, concluded that the term has value as a shorthand descriptor of a person who behaves in a consistently ineffectual and bizarre manner.

On the positive pole of the continuum problems also arise. Barron (1965) has shown that highly creative persons in architecture, literature, and other pursuits typically manifest more pathology on personality tests, such as the Minnesota Multiphasic Personality Inventory (Hathaway & McKinley, 1943), than unselected members of these same professions; but there is more to this story, as these creative individuals were also characterized by unusual levels of ego strength and personal resourcefulness (Barron, 1965, pp. 62–63):

... it has always been a matter of pride in self-consciously artistic and intellectual circles to be, at the least, eccentric. "Mad as a hatter" is a term of high praise when applied to a person of marked intellectual endowments. But the "divine madness" that the Greeks considered a gift of the gods and an essential ingredient of the poet was not, like psychosis, something subtracted from normality; rather, it was something added. Genuine psychosis is stifling and imprisoning; the divine madness is a liberation from "the consensus." If this is so, then we would expect to find evidence of an enhancement of ego strength in our creative individuals, so that greater psychopathology and greater personal effectiveness would exist side by side. Psychometrically, such a pattern would be quite unusual.... Nevertheless, just such an unusual pattern is found....

MacKinnon (1965) has shown the close fit between his empirical data on creative versus less creative architects and Otto

Rank's three-stage theory of normal, neurotic, and creative man, in which the third and highest level of individual fulfillment can only be reached by way of the acceptance and then resolution of neurotic conflict. Personal adjustment seen as the integrated acceptance of the totality of one's feelings and dispositions, without denial or repression, is a formulation congruent with the therapeutic goals of Rogers (1961), Sullivan (1953), and psychoanalysis in general.

A brief summary of the above comments on common sense issues in conceptualizing personality may now be offered. Personality is not a thing or tangible object to be defined and identified, but rather an inference or abstraction that calls to mind the individuality, adaptability, and characteristic dispositions of the human organism. Our view of personality must attend to motivational factors, ranging from the biological and metabolic needs of man as a living being through interpersonal and social responsiveness on up to the evocation of goals and ideals and even undefinable end-points of the evolutionary process. Although personality is largely a differentiating concept, there are dimensions and facets that are present in varying degrees in everyone, and that can be identified and measured. Personality assessment is that branch of study concerned with the specification of these dimensions of variation and the construction of tests and measuring devices for their calibration. Finally, from a scientific standpoint, some of the obvious everyday distinctions among people—such as mentally healthy versus mentally ill—are not easy to make and may even to some extent be illusory. No one can be freed forever from inner stress and external conflict; adjustment, therefore, is not the absence of these problems, but a way of reacting to them.

DOMAINS OF RESEARCH

In this section of our survey of personality we shall take up a series of key variables and domains of functioning that research has revealed to be important. In most of the instances to be reported a scale or assessment method has been developed to permit reliable identification of the variable. This is not a trivial matter, as the cumulative growth of knowledge about facets or aspects of personality depends on linkage between one study and another; measuring devices can help to provide such linkage. Another consideration in choosing examples for this section has to do with relevance to the fields of personnel and industrial psychology. The issues selected for discussion either have an already demonstrated significance for practical affairs, or can be easily extrapolated to the world of work.

The initial example comes from the classic study of Adorno, Frenkel-Brunswik, Levinson, and Sanford (1950) on the authoritarian personality. This project developed scales for ethnocentrism, political and economic conservatism, and anti-Semitism, in addition to its best-known index, the F scale for authoritarianism. In its final form, the F scale included thirty items, such as "Obedience and respect for authority are the most important virtues children should learn" and "If people would talk less and work more, everybody would be better off." Ss selected because of higher or lower scores on this scale were subsequently contrasted on interview behavior, test scores, life situation, and other kinds of observation. Out of the thousands of bits and pieces of information so generated, a cohesive portrait of the high-scorer gradually emerged, one that revealed him to be categorical and judgmental in his reactions to others, intellectually rigid, repressive of his own inner life, hostile in response to restraint, deferential to those above and exploitative of those below, fearful of social change, distrustful, self-pitying, and self-serving. This is, of course, an exaggerated interpretation phrased so as to vivify the ultimate implications of high scores on the scale; fortunately, few individuals will score high enough to warrant literal application of these inferences.

As might be expected, industrial psyhologists have made good use of the F cale. Vroom (1959) found that employees n a delivery company who were low on the F scale tended to work more productively under democratic leaders, while workers who were higher on the F scale tended to produce more under directive supervision. Kernan (1964) found, as might be expected, that laboratory training in human relations methods for supervisory engineers did not lead to changes on the F scale.

One would hypothesize that the F scale would relate negatively to quality of performance in any setting demanding sensitivity to the feelings of others, tact, ability to adapt to complex and changing situations, and the like. However, its utility is impaired by two difficulties. The first is the almost total transparence of the scale, and as a consequence its easy fakability. The second is the growing societal worry about invasion of privacy and the use of very personal and dogmatic statements such as those included in this measure. A current trend, therefore, toward more subtle and indirect variants of the F scale, measures that are addressed to the authoritarianism dimension (or to parts of it), but that are less contaminated by flamboyant and objectionable assertions. Christie's scale for Machiavellianism (Christie & Geis, 1971) is one example of these devices; Rokeach's measures of dogmatism and "opinionation" (Rokeach, 1960), are widely used although they are only a shade less assertive than the original F scale; the California Psychological Inventory scale for Tolerance (Gough, 1951, 1957) is a third offshoot of this domain.

Conformity versus independence of judgment is a second variable warranting discussion. The research paradigm here was introduced by Asch (1951, 1956), who pitted an experimental subject against a panel of confederates reporting false conclusions in regard to perceptual judgments. Faced with these opinions, the experimental S could either remain independent (hold to his initial judgment), or yield. The index of independence derived from the Asch procedure

was reliable, but expensive. An innovation introduced by Crutchfield (1955) utilized five electronic displays in which information conveyed by the experimenter led each S to view himself as a minority of one. By interspersing problems offering a false consensus among those calling for authentic decision making, a reliable score was accumulated of the number of times an individual had yielded. This score was subcategorized by kind of decision, including judgments about size, illumination, length, and other aspects of physical reality on the one hand, and subjective preferences on the other. By gathering private information a day or two ahead of the experimental sessions, Crutchfield was able to register personal preferences of his Ss and then to see if these preferences would be abandoned in the face of group pressure to the contrary.

The Crutchfield apparatus furnishes more data per unit of time and money than the original Asch paradigm, but is still too expensive for routine use in selection and personnel evaluation. Probably the briefest index of the independence-conformity continuum currently available is the twenty-two-item personality inventory scale developed by Barron (1953c) in item analyses of test protocols gathered from participants in Asch's experiments. High-scorers on Barron's scale, in addition to behaving independently in the experimental situation, tend to be creative at work and to value the originality of ideas, prefer change and variety to routine and certainty, and do not particularly admire stringent self-discipline and tireless devotion to duty (Barron, 1963).

Conformity to a socially or interpersonally defined standard need not always be an index of inadequate ego functioning. In the perceptual domain, in fact, alignment with modal views appears to be an indicator of functional integrity. One example of a measure based on this notion is the Group Conformity Ratio (GCR) of the Picture-Frustration Test (Rosenzweig, Fleming, & Clark, 1947). Certain frequently recurring responses to the cartoon situations contained in this test are defined as "conformity" indicators, and a total score is tallied by counting the number of such responses an individual gives. Persons scoring higher on this GCR variable tend to reveal greater ego strength and superior social adjustment.

Another example is the conformance score on the Sarbin-Hardyck (1955) stick figures. Consensual choices of descriptors for a series of stick figure drawings were first established. On subsequent samples, a conformance score was defined by the number of times the respondent chose the modal label. In a sample of ninety-one college males, the conformance score correlated +.51 with personal adjustment as rated from the MMPI profiles of these Ss by three skilled interpreters. Finally, we may note Berg's "deviation hypothesis" (Berg, 1955); this hypothesis states that persons who differ from an established pattern of "bias" (response) on insignificant matters will also differ from established patterns of response on significant issues. Deviance in inference, perception, or even preference, on the basis of this hypothesis, can be considered to some extent at least as a diagnostic cue for psychopathological reactions of many kinds. What this last group of studies seems to suggest is that the effectively functioning organism must be alert to a sort of reality principle, and must be capable of matching its perceptions to the givens of its physical and social surround. Moreover, once these impressions are formed, they should not lightly be dismissed in response to environmental pressures or contrary social views, and the individual should always be prepared for those occasions in which social consensus will be incorrect and misleading.

Murray's concept of need:achievement (Murray, 1938) is the third variable to be touched on in this section. An impressive amount of work has been carried out on need:achievement by McClelland, Atkinson, and others (see Atkinson, 1964; McClelland, 1955, 1961; McClelland, Atkinson, Clark, & Lowell, 1953; McClelland & Winter, 1969). Murray classified n:ach under the heading of actions that express ambition, will-to-power, and the desire for accomplishment and prestige, and offered the following definition (Murray, 1938, pp. 80–81): "To overcome obstacles, to exercise power, to strive to do something difficult as well and as quickly as possible." The strength of the need is typically inferred from stories told in response to the Thematic Apperception Test (Morgan & Murray, 1935), although Murray had also proposed questionnaire items to be used in its assessment (e.g., "I feel I am driven to ever greater efforts by an unslaked ambition"; "I feel the spirit of competition in most of my activities"; and "Ambition is a gallant madness").

Laboratory experimentation revealed that Ss whose TAT stories contained a large number of achievement themes did persist more diligently on anagrams and other tasks than Ss scoring low on n:ach. Later work on the need suggested that fear of failure—as distinguished from need for achievement—had to be considered and the functioning of the variable was redefined by Atkinson (1964) to take account of these two facets. For example, a success-oriented S would be hypothesized to work hardest at a task of intermediate difficulty having 50/50 chance of success; this is because a task with high odds for success would have little incentive value, whereas a task of low probability for success would discourage effort even if the incentive was great. An S fearing failure (high anxiety concerning failure) would experience greatest dismay in the 50/50 situation, and would avoid such tasks; he would prefer a very easy task with success assured—or a very difficult one on which failure could carry no stigma.

A more parsimonious statement of the theory has been given by Campbell, Dunnette, Lawler, and Weick (1970, p. 352) who write:

... the tendency to approach a task with the intention of performing successfully (T_s) is multiplicative function of the strength of the achievement motive (M_s), the subjective prob ability of success (P_s), and the valence or incentive value of success (I_s). That is, $T_s = M_s \times P_s \times I_s$. Conversely, the behavioral tendency to avoid failure by avoiding the task (T_f) is a multiplicative function of the strength of the need to avoid failure (M_{AF}), the subjective probability of failure (P_f), and the incentive value of failure (I_f). That is, $T_f = M_{AF} \times P_f \times I_f$. For any given task the observed behavioral tendency is the resultant of T_s and T_f.

Need:achievement studies in business and industry have indicated that managers score higher than persons in other kinds of jobs, Americans score higher than those tested in other countries, more effective exceed less effective managers, and there is some tendency for persons in higher-level jobs to attain higher *n:ach* scores than those in lower positions. The relationships underlying these generalizations, however, are not strong enough to permit forecasting for the individual case.

Although the TAT is not particularly time-consuming or expensive to administer, it is difficult to score if more than two or three variables are to be estimated. Objective measures of *n:ach* have been developed, including the achievement scales of the Edwards Personal Preference Schedule (Edwards, 1953) and the Adjective Check List (Gough & Heilbrun, 1965). The record of personality inventories in personnel selection studies to date, unfortunately, has not been encouraging (cf., Guion & Gottier, 1965).

A somewhat different approach to assessing achievement drive is taken on the California Psychological Inventory (Gough, 1957), where two variants are identified: achievement in settings demanding conformance to rule and structure, and achievement in settings demanding creation of form and method. The form-enhancing facet is assessed by a scale called "achievement via conformance" (*Ac*), and the form-creating facet by a scale called "achievement via independence" (*Ai*). Domino (1968, 1971) has carried out several studies to test the implications of this distinction and the validity of the two scales in settings where

one of the motives should be more relevant than the other. In one analysis (Domino, 1968), courses were classified according to whether the instructor's demands were more conformist or independent. The *Ac* scale correlated higher than *Ai* in courses of the former classification and in the latter the magnitudes were reversed. In a second analysis (Domino, 1971), *S*s were chosen according to high-low standing on *Ac* and *Ai* and then assigned to one of four introductory psychology sections taught by the same instructor. Two sections were taught in a manner stressing independence, and the other two in a manner stressing conformance. There was a very significant interaction effect, in which students high on *Ai* and low on *Ac* did better in a section stressing independence and less well in one stressing conformance; students high on *Ac* and low on *Ai* manifested a contrasting trend.

The conformance-independence distinction in the functioning of the achievement drive has obvious implications for performance in many settings. Where the work situation is highly structured, methods of procedure known and stipulated, and criteria of effectiveness clear and unambiguous, the *Ac* variant will be relevant and should be predictive of the quality of work; where the situation is inchoate, methods unknown or optional, and criteria of effectiveness emergent, the *Ai* variant will be more relevant than *Ac* and should be more predictive of the quality of performance.

Socialization and moral judgment constitute a fourth classification for which interesting measures are available. Kohlberg (1963, 1964) distinguished six stages of moral reasoning, grouped into three levels: pre-moral, conventional or role-conforming morality, and morality based on personally authenticated ethical principles. A developmental as well as philosophical gradient is implied, and Kohlberg has specified typical behaviors between the ages of seven and sixteen that are associated with each step ahead. In the pre-moral period, for example, the child obeys rules in order to win favor or avoid punishment; in the period of conventional morality he conforms to avoid disapproval by others; in the stage of moral maturity he acts so as to avoid self-condemnation. Kohlberg's method of assessment consists of a set of hypothetical "moral dilemmas" embodying twenty-five moral concepts that appear to be cultural universals. The response given to a dilemma can be rated according to the level of morality it implies, and by accumulating the ratings on each item a total score is obtained.

In keeping with the Piagetian background of his work, Kohlberg views the developmental pattern as having a significant maturational component, that is, as not something that is brought about by social learning and cultural inculcation of rules. Not all students of behavioral development would agree with this conclusion; Bandura and Walters (1963), for example, place greater emphasis on the effects of social learning in leading to self-disciplined behavior in the adult.

Kohlberg's implicit notion that an intuitional ethic represents a higher form of moral development than an ethic derived from consensus has also been questioned. Hogan (1970, p. 206), for example, makes this statement:

Philosophers have typically maintained that neither the ethics of personal conscience nor the ethics of social responsibility represents a necessarily higher form of morality, and that the two viewpoints are equally defensible on moral grounds. Within psychology, however, there seems to be a tendency to assign greater virtue to moral judgments based on the dictates of personal conscience. Thus, it has been argued that persons who subordinate the rule of law to a higher moral principle while making moral judgments are, by definition, the most mature.

Hogan's analysis of this issue led him to suggest that preference for the ethics of personal conscience as against the ethics of social responsibility was a dispositional matter, having roots in childhood, adult experience, and personality structure. To test this idea, Hogan developed a "Survey of Ethical Attitudes" containing moral dilemmas of the Kohlbergian variety and also multiple-choice completion items contrasting the two forms of moral outlook. Two thirty-five-item parallel scales were completed, including items such as the following: "An unjust law (a) should be obeyed, (b) should be disobeyed"; "A man's conscience is a better guide to conduct than whatever the law might say"; and "All civil laws should be judged against a higher moral law." Correlations between the two forms ranged from .88 to .94 in different samples. High scores on the Survey indicate preference for positive law (social basis), low scores a preference for natural law (personal basis).

To examine the personality correlates of the measure, it was given to students at two colleges along with several well-known personality and aptitude tests. The two forms of the Survey correlated $+.40$ and $+.39$ with the "thinking" scale of the Myers-Briggs Type Indicator (Myers, 1962); $-.50$ and $-.58$ with the "intuition" scale of that same test; .01 and .00 with the $D48$ test of intellectual ability (Black, 1963); .17 and .22 with the Edwards (1957) social desirability scale; .38 and .34 with the socialization scale of the California Psychological Inventory; and $-.34$ and $-.32$ with the psychological-mindedness scale of that same instrument. The Survey was also given to members of a college fraternity, and adjectival descriptions of each person were gathered from five peers, using the Gough Adjective Check List (Gough & Heilbrun, 1965): adjectives with largest positive correlations (hence used more often to describe males preferring the ethics of social responsibility) included thoughtful, good-natured, conventional, conscientious, helpful, and honest; and adjectives with largest negative correlations (hence used more often to describe males preferring the ethics of personal conscience) included rebellious, uninhibited, charming, cynical, sarcastic, and vindictive. Hogan's results appear to confirm his contention that preference for individual as against social morality derives from a broad and identifiable pattern of personality factors.

Another questionnaire method for getting at social maturity is based on the CPI (Gough, 1966, 1971). Study of 2,146 nondelinquent and 881 delinquent males permitted the specification of a six-scale index of social maturity, including dominance, responsibility, socialization, and flexibility weighted positively, and conventionality and desire to create a good impression weighted negatively. Cross-validation of the index on 2,482 non-delinquent versus 409 delinquent males gave rise to a biserial correlation of .63. The index was later applied to men from fourteen different occupational groups, and then the index's ranking of these groups was compared with ratio scaling ranks assigned by college students. For example, dentists were ranked in second place on social maturity by the raters and in third place by mean score on the index, bankers were put in fourth place by the raters and in second by the index, and machinists were placed in the fourteenth rank by both methods. The rank-order correlation between test and raters was .83. The index appears to possess reasonable validity for identifying general trends and relationships, and has also shown utility in the identification of individual instances of dereliction and wrongdoing (cf., Lefcourt, 1968).

Social judgment is the next variable to be considered. Variously referred to as social acuity, social perceptiveness, sensitivity, empathy, person perception, social intelligence, and social insight, this factor has an obvious relevance to the behavior of men in groups, and as one would expect has been the object of considerable study. E. L. Thorndike (1920) listed social intelligence as one of the three major forms of intelligence (the others being abstract and mechanical), and recently Guilford (1967) has added social intelligence to the set of measurable facets in his theory of intellect. Over the years, tests such as the George Washington University Social

Intelligence Test (Moss, Hunt, & Omwake, 1930), the Kerr Empathy Test (Kerr & Speroff, 1947), the Chapin Social Insight Test (Chapin, 1939, 1967), and the Sargent Insight Test (Sargent, 1953) have been published.

Although early evaluations of the validity of devices such as these were largely negative (cf., Thorndike & Stein, 1937), more recent work (Gough, 1965) has suggested that the Chapin test may be of value. In several different samples, the Chapin scale was found to relate to creativity in science and engineering, persistence in graduate work in psychology, and ratings of social insight among staff members of social service agencies. The test contains twenty-five items, each offering a social or interpersonal vignette, followed by statements that either diagnose the nature of the conflict presented or that indicate better and poorer steps to be taken in its resolution. It can be administered in from twenty to thirty minutes, and scored in seconds.

The concept of empathy (Einfuhlung), first introduced by Theodor Lipps (1851–1914), dealt with the disposition of an observer to assume the posture and facial expression of another. By means of this motoric mimicry the onlooker comes to experience vicariously the feelings and attitudes of the person observed. The notion of empathy was also applied by Lipps to the perception of geometric forms and illusions (cf., Boring, 1942); for example, in perceiving the Müller-Lyer illusion the acute-angled wings curtail mental activity whereas the extended wings free it, leading the second line to be seen as longer than the first even though both are of identical length.

Over the years, the term "empathy" has gradually come to signify the cognitive apprehension of another person's feelings and state of mind, and "empathy" has been used in the title of several tests. One of the best known is the Kerr Empathy Test (Kerr & Speroff, 1947). However, this instrument, in spite of its name, is not a direct measure of the function as it asks the respondent to estimate the reactions of people-in-general, not those of a particular individual. The reviews of this test (cf., Hall, 1965; R. L. Thorndike, 1959) have also been rather pessimistic. A more promising measure is that of Hogan (1969), who developed a personality scale to identify persons judged to be high or low on empathic talent. Representative items include "As a rule I have little difficulty in 'putting myself into other people's shoes' "; "I enjoy the company of strong-willed people"; and "I frequently undertake more than I can accomplish." In cross-validating samples of both sexes and different age levels, the Hogan scale correlated approximately .40 with criteria of empathy or social acuity.

Sound movies have been used in studies of social acuity, particularly by Cline (1953, 1964). Cline's method is to present viewers with a series of filmed interviews, after each of which the observer is asked to complete a post-diction test (guessing what the interviewee in the film did at various key decision-making points in his past life), and to guess how the S described himself and was described by others on an adjective check list. Accuracy on these tasks turns out to correlate significantly with ratings of general effectiveness, independence of judgment, and even personal soundness. For practical application, the full set of nine "Cline movies" is too long and time-consuming, but the method has great potential. An extremely valuable assessment tool would be provided if the series could be reduced to a half-hour device including four or five brief interviews and reliable subscales for post-diction and personal inference.

Creativity is the sixth topic to be considered in this section. Again, because of the vast amount of research on this subject, attention will be focused principally on measures possessing promise for operational usage. For broader discussion of the psychology of creativity, the reader may consult books such as those by Anderson (1959), Barron (1968), Getzels and Jackson (1962),

Parnes and Harding (1964), Taylor (1964), Torrance (1962), and Vernon (1970).

The major impetus for current research on creativity came from Guilford's (1950) presidential address to the American Psychological Association, in which he documented the incredible inattention of psychologists to this topic (only 186 of 121,000 titles in a twenty-three-year period of the *Psychological Abstracts* had anything to do with creativity, originality, imagination, or related topics), and also issued a stirring call for new work on the problem. Guilford and his colleagues (cf., Guilford, 1966; Wilson, Guilford, & Christensen, 1953) have heeded this admonition and have introduced a series of tests for original and "divergent" thinking that many investigators have employed. An example is the "unusual uses test" in which the respondent is asked to think of new uses for everyday objects, for example a button. The responses are then rated for rarity (infrequency), remoteness, and appropriateness. Mednick (1962) has stressed the importance of the remoteness factor in association, and has developed a convenient test (Mednick & Mednick, 1967) to assess the capacity to produce associations of this kind.

The centrality of the cognitive element in creative thinking may suggest to some that creative achievement may be classified as merely a facet or aspect of intellectual achievement in general. However, at least with respect to conventional measures of intelligence, creative potential does not appear to be adequately appraised by tests of intellectual ability (cf., Cropley, 1966; Getzels & Jackson, 1962; Welsh, 1971). Getzels and Jackson scaled their Ss along continua of intelligence and rated creativity, and paid special attention to those high on the latter but not the former. Welsh has proposed even more specific classifications of these two dimensions, calling the former "intellectence" and the latter "origence." An individual scoring high on intellectence, but low on origence, will tend to manifest a kind of pragmatic, unimaginative problem-solving ability, whereas the individual high on both will seek new and unusual solutions to these same problems. Welsh has also constructed scales on the Strong Vocational Interest Blank (Welsh, 1971) and Adjective Check List (Welsh, 1969) for four quadrants of interaction that are generated by the two dimensions. The *S*-4 variant—low on origence and high on intellectence—is described by Welsh as efficient, logical, and methodical, cathecting difficult tasks that can be solved by systematic application of rational procedures derived from abstractions, and as being introversive in temperament.

The measure used by Welsh as a marker in the development of the origence factor was the art scale of the Figure Preference Test (Welsh, 1959). This art scale is available in two forms: the original sixty-five-item Barron-Welsh (BW) version (Barron & Welsh, 1952), and a revised sixty-item version (Welsh, 1969) with a 30/30 split on like versus dislike items. The original Barron-Welsh scale was also slightly modified by dropping three items, leaving a sixty-two-item measure with twenty-four like responses and thirty-eight dislike. The validity of the art scales in ranking samples according to creative achievement has been remarkable. Barron (1965, p. 22) presents a table giving almost perfect correspondence between common sense ranking for creativity of some seventeen samples (e.g., creative architects, writers, scientists) and the mean scores of these groups on the sixty-two-item BW scale.

Another promising line of measurement has involved the rating of projective test protocols for originality or creativity. The "O" or original response to Rorschach Inkblot cards has been noted since the method was first introduced in 1921, and later work (cf., Barron, 1955) has found the Rorschach variable to be of value in the study of creativity. Perhaps even more successful, however, has been the special scoring of free response tasks such as the Franck Drawing Completion Test (Franck & Rosen, 1949).

Schimek (1954) reported excellent results for this device, and other investigators (e.g., Anastasi & Schaefer, 1971; Barron, 1958) have confirmed these findings.

Indirect self-report scales for creativity are also available. These measures, of course, identify personal attitudes and self-conceptions that are reliably associated with creative expression; they do not assess the function itself. Two such scales on the Adjective Check List have given encouraging results, a fifty-nine-item index developed by Domino (1970) and a twenty-seven-item cluster by Smith and Schaefer (1969). Both scales identify individuals who tend to be imaginative, impulsive, nonconforming, and spontaneous in thought and behavior. Welsh's origence measure on the Adjective Check List (Welsh, 1969) should be mentioned again in this context. Several attempts have also been made to develop personality inventory scales for the creative temperament (cf., Barron, 1953b, 1953c; Gough, 1957). Several of these devices were used by Domino (1969) in a study of the mothers of more and less creative sons; he found the mothers of more creative offspring to score higher on measures associated with creative attainment.

Tests and methods such as those described above have been applied with good results to various occupational and professional samples. Architects have been extensively studied by MacKinnon and Hall (cf., Hall & MacKinnon, 1969; MacKinnon, 1960, 1962) who found more creative practitioners to be characterized by higher scores on the Barron-Welsh Art Scale, higher scores on the perception and intuition scales of the Myers-Briggs Type Indicator, lower scores on the economic scale of the Allport, Vernon, and Lindzey (1951) Study of Values, lower scores on the banker and office man scales of the Strong Vocational Interest Blank (Strong, 1943), and higher scores on Barron's independence scale (Barron, 1953c). Other occupational groups include artists and writers (Drevdahl & Cattell, 1958; Helson, 1970), mathematicians (Helson,

1971; Helson & Crutchfield, 1970), engineers (Harris, 1960; McDermid, 1965), scientists (Roe, 1952; Taylor, 1959), students of science (Garwood, 1964; Parloff & Datta, 1965), and business managers (Barron & Egan, 1968).

The last topic to be discussed in this section is "field independence" or "field articulation" (Witkin, Lewis, Hertzman, Machover, Meissner, & Wapner, 1954; Witkin, Dyk, Faterson, Goodenough, & Karp, 1962). Articulated or independent perception, in contrast to global or dependent perception, occurs when the individual is able to perceive items or components as discrete from an organized ground when the field is structured, or if unstructured, to impose organization and to utilize this structure in coping with the perceptual phenomenon.

Among the tests evaluated as measures of an analytic-independent mode of perceptual functioning, two have consistently stood out as providing valid differentiations. One of these is the "rod-and-frame" test in which a movable rod is presented visually in a frame that may be tilted to left or right; the task of the S is to adjust the rod to true verticality, having no background cues and nothing for guidance save the misleading frame and his own sense of gravitational orientation. The other is the "embedded figures test" in which the task is to find a simple figure embedded in a complex figure; the test consists of a series of such problems, and both group and individual forms are published. The rod-and-frame apparatus, originally quite cumbersome, has recently been made available as a portable device for use in individual testing (Oltman, 1968).

Extensive study of the field articulation hypothesis in age-differentiated (Witkin, Goodenough, & Karp, 1967), cross-cultural (Witkin, 1967), mentally retarded (Witkin, Faterson, Goodenough, & Birnbaum, 1966), and clinical (Witkin, 1965; Witkin, Lewis, & Weil, 1968) samples has shown that field independence has an almost astonishing range of implications for effective function-

ing and ego strength. Psychopathology, of course, can occur at either end of the continuum, but forms will differ. At the global or field-dependent pole, problems of identity diffusion, passivity, alcoholism, ulcer, obesity, character disorder, and hallucinatory states are more common, whereas at the analytic or field-independent pole problems of extrapunitiveness, paranoia, obsessive-compulsive reactions, and delusional thinking are more frequent. The critical factor seems to be the coherence and cohesiveness of the ego defensive system: the greater this coherence the more likely is the individual to be on the articulated or field-independent side of the continuum.

If the rod-and-frame and embedded figure methods were merely tools for use in psychiatric settings they would be of little importance to this review. The evidence, however, is that both have much broader consequences and that high-scorers on both devices will tend to cope more effectively with ambiguous and misleading stimuli encountered in everyday life, including work. The embedded figure method, based on Gottschaldt's stimuli, has also been developed as a testing technique by Crutchfield (Crutchfield, Woodworth, & Albrecht, 1958). The Crutchfield test has been shown to relate to effective performance in a variety of settings, and to identify persons (high-scorers) who are judged by others to be insightful, reliable, and able to cope with complexity.

Although all three of the assessment devices discussed above are "cognitive," in that they call on problem-solving dispositions rather than on preferences and points of view, they also appear to pertain to stylistic qualities that are pervasive in their expression. Furthermore, the practical problems encountered in using the three procedures are minimal. The portable rod-and-frame apparatus can be set up almost anywhere and administered to a subject in less than half an hour. The individual form of the embedded figures can take up to an hour, but the group form can be given in from ten to forty-five minutes. Crutchfield's adaptation of the Gottschaldt Figures can be administered either individually or to groups in from five to ten minutes.

In the perceptual field, a phenomenon that more or less maximizes the role of misleading cues is the visual illusion. One would expect field-independent Ss on Witkin's procedures to be less susceptible to these illusions, and indeed there is evidence to suggest that this is true (cf., Gardner, 1961; McGurk, 1965). There is also evidence to indicate that susceptibility to illusions, such as the Müller-Lyer, decreases with increasing age. However, there are complicating factors in that susceptibility to other illusions increases with age, for example, the Ponzo illusion (Leibowitz & Judisch, 1967); the cultural environment also seems to have an effect, with persons living in a more "carpentered" environment (Segall, Campbell, & Herskovits, 1966) being more susceptible to the Müller-Lyer illusion and persons from more primitive regions being more susceptible to the vertical-horizontal.

In spite of these problems, it should be possible to develop an assessment tool based on visual illusions; Gough and McGurk (1967) have proposed such an instrument, a thirty-item multiple choice test that can be given in twenty minutes. Scores on this test show an age-developmental gradient, confirmed in cross-cultural study (Chandra, 1972; Gough & Delcourt, 1969; Gough & Hug, 1968; Gough & Meschieri, 1971), and also correlate significantly with the rod-and-frame and Crutchfield's hidden figures test.

ADDITIONAL DOMAINS OF ASSESSMENT

In this section attention is directed to a series of research topics in which assessment methods are being used. Coverage will be briefer than in the preceding section, and emphasis will be placed upon new procedures or on promising new applications of older methods. The purpose of this section is to give a glimpse of the wide variety of current work in which personality appraisal is playing a part.

One of these domains is that of sleep and dreaming. After the pioneering work on sleep and wakefulness by Kleitman (1939), the discovery of the relationship between rapid eye movements (REM) and dreaming (Aserinsky & Kleitman, 1953), and studies of dream deprivation (Dement, 1960), a large number of researchers became interested in the scientific study of sleep and dreams and since 1960 there has been a great expansion of well-documented information. Sleep is now known to involve four stages, recognizable by various cues including typical electroencephalographic tracings. The distribution of stages is not even throughout the night, and stage one (REM) sleep in which most dreaming takes place, tends to recur frequently during the last third of the night.

The possibilities for personality analysis in regard to sleep and dreaming are almost infinite—for example, are different personality patterns associated with the predominance of one or more of the four stages of sleep, are "good sleepers" differentiated from "poor sleepers," are there diagnosable changes in personality factors attendant on deprivation of each stage of sleep, and are there differences in the amount of sleep needed by persons of contrasting temperament?

The question of good versus poor sleepers has been studied by Monroe (1967), using the MMPI. Monroe found good sleepers (i.e., persons who fall asleep quickly, seldom wake up before morning, and have little subjective difficulty in regard to falling asleep or staying asleep) to score higher on the Barron ego strength scale (Barron, 1953a) and lower on the scales for depression, psychasthenia, schizophrenia, social introversion, and anxiety (Welsh, 1956). Another study considered the question of the amount of sleep needed (Hartmann, Baekeland, Zwilling, & Hoy, 1971), using the MMPI and CPI to assess personality. Clear differences were noted between long and short sleepers, with the former being less confident and assertive and more suppressive in ego control, and the latter more self-assured and forceful, but less adept in the management of aggressive impulse.

Biochemical factors in personality have long been matters of interest, beginning with the body fluids or humors postulated by Hippocrates. In the early twentieth century, discoveries concerning the functioning of the endocrine glands led to enthusiastic pronouncements about hormonal influences on behavior (cf., Berman, 1921). Even after setting aside these early and excessive claims for hormonal stimulation, important relationships remain and current scientific writing (cf., Whalen, 1967) continues to attend to these factors. An obvious example of the impact of biochemical balance on mood and behavior is found in the personality changes attendant on menstruation in the human female.

In the last fifteen years a great deal of work has been done on the adrenal catecholamines, epinephrine and norepinephrine, and other biogenic amines (compounds formed from amino acids and having neuroregulatory functions in human biology). These compounds have been related to the experiencing of fear and anger (Ax, 1953), depression (Prange, 1964), and the clinical syndrome known as Parkinson's disease (cf., Barchas, Stolk, Ciaranello, & Hamburg, 1971): in fear, there is an increase of epinephrine in the blood, whereas in anger norepinephrine levels rise; in depression, the catecholamine hypothesis specifies an insufficiency of norepinephrine at synapses in the central nervous system; and in Parkinson's disease there is a deficiency of dopamine (another catecholamine) in the basal ganglia of the brain. For excellent reviews of current work on neuroregulatory agents in behavior, the reader is referred to a chapter by Barchas, Stolk, Ciaranello, and Hamburg (1971), and to papers by Schildkraut (1965) and Schildkraut and Kety (1967).

Among the psychological assessment tools that have been used in studies addressed to biochemical and hormonal factors may be mentioned the Multiple Affect Adjective Check List (Zuckerman & Lubin, 1965), the Clyde Mood Scale (Clyde, 1963), and Spielberger's State-Trait Anxiety Inventory (Spielberger, 1966). The Menstrual Distress Questionnaire (MDQ) developed by Moos (1968b, 1969) for assessing kind and degree of menstrual distress should also be noted here. This questionnaire contains eight components—pain, concentration, behavioral change, autonomic reactions, water retention, negative affect, arousal, and control. Different kinds of profiles are easily recognized on the MDQ, and the instrument is a convenient tool for correlational study against other criteria. For example, Moos (1968a) has used the MDQ to demonstrate that women using oral contraceptives scored lower than nonusers on subscales in five of the eight components.

The family environment in which children's personalities are shaped is the third area of research to which brief attention will be directed. Some nineteen years ago (Bateson, Jackson, Haley, & Weakland, 1956), the "double-bind" hypothesis was advanced; this hypothesis specifies a faulty pattern of communication in which closely related but sharply incongruent messages are relayed. For example, a mother might tell a daughter "Have some cookies, I made them especially for you" and then about the time the first bite is taken adding "You'll have to start dieting soon because you're overweight." The recipient of such a pair of messages is in something of a "bind," the authors contended, and the result is to create confusion concerning interpersonal communication and in extreme cases to provoke schizophrenic withdrawal. Lidz, Fleck, and Cornelison (1965) also studied families of schizophrenic patients and pointed out conditions of "marital schism" (chronic and extreme discord) in which the child is used as a pawn, and "marital skew" in which one parent capitulates to a dominant but seriously disturbed partner. Singer and Wynne (1963) and Mishler and Waxler (1965) have also contributed to current conceptions of the "schizophrenogenic family."

One of the most important measurement outcomes of this line of work was the application of Q-sort technique (cf., Block, Patterson, Block, & Jackson, 1958) to the description of parents. Block's 100-item California Q-set (Block, 1961) is an excellent tool for this kind of characterization, as it includes both descriptive and inferential items of the kind that clinicians use in formulating a diagnostic portrait. The advantage of the Q-deck is that each observer is recorded in a way that permits comparison with any other observer; also, his attention is addressed to the complete set of items so that oversights, momentary lapses of memory, etc., are forestalled by the technique of eliciting his reactions.

In a later study (Block, 1971), Q-methodology was adapted in a very successful manner to the study of longitudinal trends in the development of normal personality. For this study Block and his collaborators introduced three new Q-sorts: a 104-item deck for use in describing adolescents; a sixty-three-item deck for describing the interpersonal behavior of adolescents; and a ninety-two-item deck for describing the familial environment. Judges could then read the accumulated files on the Ss of the study, their family history archives in the project, etc., and then sort the different decks so as to give an organized and analytic picture of the S's functioning and his familial milieu. Changes over time could be noted by contrasting Q-sortings based on data from T-1 with those based on data from T-2, T-3, and so on.

Factor analysis of the basic 100-item Q-deck data on the Ss of the study permitted the identification of five typologies for males and six for females. All other sources of contemporary and longitudinal data were then analyzed against these typologies, including the interpersonal Q-sorts derived from junior high school recordings, from senior high school observations, and from subsequent observations during adulthood, and similar examination was carried out for the other Q-decks, test scores, and demographic information. This incredibly rich source of material allowed the formulation of interpretive resumés for each type that are exceedingly informative. It is unfortunate that space does not allow the quotation of these summaries; the reader who is interested in the use of objective techniques and statistical analysis in the study of elusive but important dynamic issues is encouraged to consult Block's (1971) book, *Lives Through Time*.

The Q-sort method can be adapted to the study of many problems (cf., Block, 1961), and new decks of statements prepared for use in specific settings. For example, Gough and Woodworth (1960) prepared a fifty-six-item Q-deck for use with research scientists, containing statements such as "indifferent to the practical implications of his own research" and "is good at developing short cuts and approximation techniques." Cluster analysis (Tryon & Bailey, 1966) identified eight stylistic dispositions, including the "diagnostician," "methodologist," and "esthetician." A subsequent French application of the deck (Bonnardel & Lavoëgie, 1965) to a sample of 113 chemists supported the generality of the type patterns.

A forty-five-item deck for use with public administrators was developed on an Italian sample (Gough & Parisi, 1967; Gough, Misiti, & Parisi, 1968), and then translated and used in a comparison of American and Italian federal administrative officials (Gough, Misiti, & Parisi, 1971). This deck included statements such as "A leader should not enter into relationships of personal friendship with his subordinates"; "When interviewing an applicant for a job it is wise not to let him know what one thinks of his prospects"; and "In public administration personal initiative is a necessary quality at every level." Six administrative styles were identified—the innovator, the mediator, the actionist, the moderate, the achiever, and the realist—and it was noted that American administrators put more emphasis on personal warmth and positive reinforcement of subordinates than did their Italian counterparts. In this regard it should be recalled that Haire, Ghiselli, and Porter (1966), in their international study of managerial thinking, found Italian industrialists to stress the distinction between higher- and lower-level positions.

Q-sort and adjective check list methods are also beginning to be used in the study of physical and geographic environments (cf., Craik, 1971), permitting the identification of landscape typologies, and of people who prefer environments of different kinds. These same methods can be used to assess the social and psychological climates of industrial and other organizations (cf., Moos & Houts, 1968; Stern, 1970).

The next example of a significant area of research in which personality assessment is playing a part is that of behavioral genetics (cf., Hirsch, 1967; Lindzey, Loehlin, Manosevitz, & Thiessen, 1971; McClearn, 1970), and in particular current studies of twins (Gottesman & Shields, 1966). Most of the work of thirty or more years ago on this topic was concerned with intellectual functioning and its possible heritability. In the past five to ten years, researchers have begun to employ personality measures and some interesting findings on personality inventory scales are beginning to emerge (cf., Gottesman, 1966; Nichols, 1965; Schoenfeldt, 1968). For example, Gottesman (1962) found that on the MMPI those scales reflecting hysterical and hypochondriacal neuroses tended to have low heritability quotients (i.e., to be environmentally determined), whereas scales assessing anxiety, depression, and schizoid withdrawal had substantial genetic (heritable) components. After re-

viewing the Gottesman and other studies, however, Lindzey, Loehlin, Manosevitz, and Thiessen (1971) conclude that although genotypic factors may have a significant influence on personality, their specific impact is too complex to permit any conclusions at this time concerning greater or lesser heritability of individual scales or measures.

Research on family planning and population control is next in this series. Although major studies of population trends in the United States in the 1940s and 1950s did not yield very encouraging findings with respect to personality assessment (cf., Fawcett, 1970), current work is beginning to identify some promising leads. For example, MacDonald (1970) found that women with an "internal" orientation toward control on Rotter's locus of control questionnaire (Rotter, 1966) were more likely to use birth control methods than those with an "external" orientation. Rodgers and Ziegler (1968) found that reliable use of the contraceptive pill (ovulation suppressor) could be forecast by pairing the scores of husband and wife on certain personality variables; for example, if husband scored higher than wife on the CPI dominance scale pill usage was more reliable. Bakker and Dightman (1964) noted that women who were inconsistent in using the pill scored lower on the 16PF (Cattell, 1949) scale for emotional maturity and higher on surgency than control *S*s who were more consistent.

The occurrence of undesirable side effects from use of the pill has also been noted, with up to 25 percent of women discontinuing usage and stating that they will not use the pill again (Ratner, 1967). Bakker and Dightman (1964) also reported personality test data comparing women on the pill who did or did not complain of side effects; the complainers, as might be expected, scored higher on most of the scales of the MMPI, and on the exhibition, autonomy, intraception, succorance, endurance, and heterosexuality scales of the Edwards Personal Preference Schedule (Edwards, 1953).

A final example of research findings

under this subtopic concerns the responses of men to surgical sterilization (vasectomy). A four-year follow-up by Ziegler, Rodgers, and Prentiss (1969) showed that whereas the Ss gave favorable subjective reports on the aftermath of the operation, MMPI retest scores indicated an increase in anxiety and internal distress. Five of the Ss who showed markedly adverse changes in adjustment following vasectomy were found to have had significantly higher Mf (femininity) scores on the preoperative testing with the MMPI.

The assessment of psychopathology by means of structured devices has long been a field of active work among personality psychologists. The best known of the wide-band tools for this purpose is the Minnesota Multiphasic Personality Inventory (Hathaway & McKinley, 1943). In recent years, some quite useful measures of individual syndromes have been introduced. Among these should be mentioned the Hamilton (1960, 1967) twenty-one-item rating scale for depression, Beck's (Beck, Ward, Mendelson, Mock, & Erbaugh, 1961) twenty-one-item depression inventory, Zung's (1965) twenty-item self-rating scale for depression, the twenty-eight-item depression rating scale of Wechsler, Grosser, and Busfield (1963), and the ten-item rating scale for paranoid schizophrenia (Venables & O'Connor, 1959). Brief indices of overall adjustment or psychiatric status have also been developed in recent years, including, for example, the sixteen-item brief psychiatric rating scale of Overall and Gorham (1962) and Langner's (1962) twenty-two-item screening index. These measures resemble earlier screening tools, such as the 195-item Cornell Medical Index (Brodman, Erdmann, Lorge, & Wolff, 1949), except in length.

Another trend in psychiatric and medical research has been the development of measures related to personality syndromes implicated in particular kinds of illness. A number of years ago Klopfer (1954, 1957) examined Rorschach protocols of patients with slow-growing and fast-growing cancers, correctly post-dicting the actual status

of nineteen out of twenty-four records reviewed. Patients with fast-growing cancers tended to be ego-defensive, with strong motivations to adjust to reality and to maintain independent functioning; patients in the slow-growing category tended to be looser in their conceptual organization, less self-disciplined, and lower on ego strength. An MMPI scale to differentiate between patients of the two kinds was developed by Blumberg (1954). Later work (cf., Bahnson & Bahnson, 1969) has suggested that personality variables play a part in the incidence of cancer as well as in response to the disease. Loss, separation, depression, and despair have been noted as antecedents to the onset of the illness, and repressive ego defenses are characteristic of the vulnerable population. Bahnson (Bahnson & Bahnson, 1969) has developed a fifty-item adjective check list to assess five of the factors postulated as having critical relevance.

Psychological susceptibility to coronary heart disease is another problem that has received extensive study (cf., Jenkins, 1971), and a coronary-prone kind of temperament (called "Pattern A") has been defined by Friedman, Rosenman, and their collaborators (cf., Rosenman, Friedman, Strauss, Wurm, Kositchok, Haan, & Werthessen, 1964). Pattern A behavior is characterized by intense desire to attain self-selected goals, competitiveness, need for recognition and advancement, responsiveness to due-dates and time deadlines, propensity to accelerate the rate of physical and mental activity, and heightened mental and physical alertness. Pattern B behavior, the antithesis of Pattern A, is found among coronary-resistant Ss.

Pattern A tendencies have been reliably assessed by a battery of measures (Bortner & Rosenman, 1967), and by a simple fourteen-item rating scale in which each item consists of two adjectives—one associated with Pattern A behavior and the other with Pattern B (Bortner, 1969). Examples would be "never late—casual about appointments" and "fast (eating, walking, etc.)—slow doing things." The S checks his position on each one-and-a-half-inch continuum (marked at opposite poles by the terms indicated), and then distance from the B-pole is measured to the nearest one-sixteenth inch. The fourteen-item scale was able to reproduce interviewers' classifications of thirty-eight A and twenty-three B Ss with 64 percent accuracy, and an abbreviated seven-item version attained a 65 percent hit rate. Heightened cholesterol levels in the blood, hypothesized by many clinicians as a precursor of cardiac illness, may also be predictable from personality measures. Jenkins, Hames, Zyzanski, Rosenman, and Friedman (1969) found significantly higher blood lipid readings for male Ss scoring high on the CPI socialization scale and low on the inventory scale for self-acceptance.

Pioneers in psychosomatic medicine (Alexander, 1939; Dunbar, 1938; Saul, 1935) stressed the fact that physical illness was often antedated by a period of psychological discomfort and turbulence. The methodology of study and evidence produced were largely clinical, that is, based on the observations and inferences of the examining physician. An implicit idea was that the organism was able to tolerate a fixed amount of stress, but once this threshold was surpassed pathogenic consequences could be anticipated. If stress is conceived as any experience requiring a coping reaction, the possibility comes to mind of tallying the number of stressful experiences (positive or negative) over a period of time. This approach was in fact taken by Rahe and his collaborators (Holmes & Rahe, 1967; Rahe, 1968; Rahe, McKean, & Arthur, 1967), leading to the development of a forty-two-item Schedule of Recent Experiences (SRE). Various experiences, for instance, buying a new car, getting married, death of a member of one's family, are assigned standard weights according to their judged impact. Ss with above average scores on the SRE during a two-year interval were later found to suffer a higher incidence of illness.

Shorter time-spans also are significant. Rahe, Mahan, Arthur, and Gunderson (1970) studied 2,684 men at sea, relating the occurrence of illness to SRE scores during the six months preceding embarkation. In from six to eight months at sea, two-thirds of the men reported to the sick bay at least once. A high-risk group composed of the 30 percent of men with highest scores on the SRE had 50 percent more illnesses than the 30 percent of the men with lowest scores on the schedule; in one outbreak of acute bacillary dysentery, the frequency of illness was twice as great among high-risk as among low-risk men. Life change indices have also been found to differentiate between college students suffering from colds, sore throats, and upper respiratory infections (Jacobs, Spilken, Norman, & Anderson, 1970).

To terminate this section, several studies relating personality assessment data to success in business and management will be mentioned. An excellent brief review of the assessment of managerial talent has been contributed by Dunnette (1971), and a more extended discussion may be found in a recent book by Campbell, Dunnette, Lawler, and Weick (1970). Among the best known of the assessment programs for selecting managers is that developed by Bray and his colleagues for the American Telephone and Telegraph Company (Bray & Grant, 1966). The "multiple assessment programs," of which Bray's is an example, typically use a wide array of procedures including the interview, ability tests, situational tasks, and personality inventories, such as the Personality Research Form (Jackson, 1967), Omnibus Personality Inventory (Heist & Yonge, 1968), Ghiselli's (1968) decision-making scale, and others mentioned previously in this chapter. Variables are generated from these assessments, such as observers' ratings of general effectiveness and administrative skills, performance on specific group tasks, and scores on scales from the various tests.

In the Bray study, forecasts and ratings made of college and noncollege assessees were checked against progress in the company six to eight years later. Of fifty-eight Ss who had been advanced on up to the middle management level or above, the assessors had predicted this rate of promotion for forty-six and had failed to predict it for twelve; of seventy-two who had not progressed beyond the first level, the predictors had given low ratings to sixty-eight. Using an increase in salary criterion over the same period, significant correlations were obtained with staff ratings of general effectiveness and administrative skills, among others. Personality tests generally gave lower and, to some extent, inconsistent coefficients. After surveying the AT&T program and others, Dunnette (1971) concluded that the multiple assessment method does possess validity for identifying managerial talent, beyond what could be achieved by use of individual differences measures (i.e., test scores) alone or in combination.

Harrell (1969, 1970) administered a battery of eleven tests, such as the Strong Vocational Interest Blank (Strong, 1943), MMPI, and Guilford-Zimmerman Temperament Survey (Guilford & Zimmerman, 1949) to members of seven classes of the Stanford Graduate School of Business, and then followed up the graduates after intervals of five years. For graduates who took employment in large business, those with higher salaries scored higher on the management orientation scale of the Strong, the *Ma* (hypomania) scale of the MMPI, the general activity and social interest scales of the Guilford-Zimmerman, and the initiative, self-assurance, and decision-making scales of the Ghiselli Self-Description Inventory (Ghiselli, 1956a, 1968). For those going into small business, higher earnings were associated with higher scores on personnel manager scale of the Strong, *Pd* (psychopathic deviate) and *Pa* (paranoia) scales of the MMPI, ascendance and thoughtfulness scales of the Guilford-Zimmerman, and factor *C* (consideration for others) of the Leadership Opinion Questionnaire (Fleishman, 1960), and lower scores on a version of the California *F* scale for authoritarianism (Adorno, Frenkel-Brunswik, Levinson, & Sanford, 1950).

Rawls and Rawls (1968) administered the Edwards Personal Preference Schedule (EPPS) and CPI to sixty of 150 executives in a utilities company, contrasting thirty highly successful and thirty less successful Ss, matched on age and length of service in the organization. The more successful executives scored significantly higher on the EPPS scales for dominance, heterosexuality, and aggression, and lower on its scales for deference and order. On the CPI, more successful executives scored lower on self-control and femininity, and higher on dominance, capacity for status, sociability, social presence, self-acceptance, intellectual efficiency, psychological-mindedness, and flexibility. Biographical data were also reviewed, and showed the more successful were younger when they learned to swim and began to drink alcoholic beverages, and were more often elected as leaders of their groups. Baker's dissertation (1971) might also be noted, as it revealed successful stock market speculators to be characterized by a similar pattern of scores on the CPI.

CONCLUDING REMARKS

An "activist" approach to the study of personality and personality assessment has been adopted in this chapter. That is, interest has been centered on perceiving, appraising, diagnosing, and knowing, and on the prediction of what individuals will do in defined settings. Personality tests and related tools have been mentioned in regard to these specific substantive areas of interest, rather than as ends in themselves, and theories about personality have similarly been subordinated to the problems of forecasting and conceptualizing behavior in different contexts. Not every example employed will have an immediate or easy applicability to man at work, but even the most peripheral will be relevant to the broad view of human behavior that modern science and humanitarian concerns bid us to take.

Given the vast array of assessment methods at the disposal of the practitioner, an obvious need is for some sort of actuarial procedure to select variables and treat them in concert. Years ago, Meehl (1954) pointed out that actuarial prediction is at least as accurate as the ordinary man's intuition, adding (1956) that configural and nonlinear combinations of scores should do even better than the simple linear forecasting equations largely in use up to the time of his survey. A recent evaluation (Goldberg, 1969) of prediction from multivariate tools suggests that linear methods may be hard to surpass; in differentiating between neurotic and psychotic MMPI profiles, an unweighted combination of five scales ($L + Pa + Sc - Hy - Pt$) identified in an earlier study (Goldberg, 1965), equaled or exceeded the classificatory accuracy of any of the other methods examined, including those using moderator variables (cf., Ghiselli, 1956b, 1960; Saunders, 1956), profile typologies (Lykken & Rose, 1963; Marks & Seeman, 1963), and more complex mathematical techniques such as those derived from the Bayes theorem (cf., Pankoff & Roberts, 1968). In the foreseeable future, it would seem, anyone using tests to make predictions of recurrent and reasonably well specified criteria would be well-advised to try regression methods and other linear techniques.

Diagnostic thinking often involves a sequence of ordering Ss to classes or typologies, the end point being a cell in which the certainty of classification is maximized. The decision-tree model invoked here has been put to good use in simulating the diagnostic thinking of psychiatrists (Spitzer & Endicott, 1969). Diagno-II, as one of the Spitzer-Endicott decision trees is called, uses a ninety-six-variable input (age, sex, and ninety-four scaled judgments from an interview), and incorporates fifty-seven decision points leading to forty-six different diagnostic verdicts. Diagnoses given by Diagno-II agree with psychiatrists as well as the psychiatrists agree with each other. Kleinmuntz (1963) has used basically the same procedure with the MMPI, and the method can easily be applied to test scores as well as to subjective inferences or ratings. The decision-tree method is ordinarily linear at each choice point, but the system of decisions will be nonlinear. It, too, can be recommended to practitioners who must make forecasts from assessment data.

Other interesting and even ingenious methods for enhancing predictive accuracy and improving the intelligibility of personality measures are being studied. Goldberg (1970) has found that an equation based on the forecasting behavior of an individual—where his informational source is known and specifiable, as it is in the case of a test profile—tends to be more accurate on cross-validation than the person himself. Should we employ man or a model of man, Goldberg asks, and the perhaps tantalizing answer is that if accuracy is the desideratum we should use the model. A subsequent study by Wiggins and Kohen (1971) suggests that the admonition may also hold for committee decisions, such as the forecasting of performance in graduate education. Another development in this same domain is the series of computerized interpretations of test profiles, particularly of the MMPI (cf., Finney, 1966; Fowler, 1967; Klett & Pumroy, 1971; Rome et al., 1962).

Cautionary notes on the need to attend to context and the specifics of a given situation in predicting behavior have been sounded by Mischel (1968) and Peterson (1968), among others. The strongest version of this "situationist" position is that the kind of generality of drive and disposition assumed by personality measurement does not exist, and that behavior in any particular situation is solely a function of cues and rewards imbedded in that situation. A more moderate formulation is that general or pervasive dispositions will always be modified and influenced by the cue-reward system in any given context.

Much work on prediction from personality measures has observed this latter formulation, either implicitly or explicitly, and one of the standard texts on personality assessment (Stern, Stein, & Bloom, 1956) places great weight on the inclusion of environmental variables in the forecasting conceptualization. Megargee's studies on dominance (cf., Fenelon & Megargee, 1971; Megargee, 1969; Megargee, Bogart, & Anderson, 1966) provide excellent examples of how context may moderate behavior. He found that when a two-person task was defined so as to stress task solution, a personality measure of dominance had no relationship to the assumption of leadership; however, when instructions were phrased so as to define the task as an indicator of leadership, Ss scoring higher on dominance assumed leadership in 90 percent of the dyads. These findings held for males. When males and females were paired, a single exception was observed: low-dominant males assumed leadership when paired with high-dominant females; post-task interviews suggested that Ss in these pairings were aware that role expectations had triumphed over personal dispositions. Domino's studies (Domino, 1968, 1971) of the interaction between achievement drive and classroom demands also illustrate how context and personal dispositions interact in the generation of situation-specific behavior. Personality assessment, it is clear, must attend in its forecasts to the specifics of the situation in which the criterion behavior is to occur.

A final comment concerns the need for the practitioner of personality assessment to develop professional skill in the use and interpretation of his tools. This need has long been appreciated by users of projective devices, such as the Thematic Apperception Test and Rorschach, and excellent manuals for clinical interpretation are available (cf., Beck, 1944, 1945; Klopfer & Davidson, 1962; Murstein, 1963). Advocates of structured testing devices are also beginning to provide material relevant to the analysis of individual cases (cf., Callis, West, & Ricksecker, 1964; Carson, 1969). There are indeed many occasions when, as Meehl (1957) once said, the tester must be ready to use his head instead of the equation. When this occurs he must have the kind of familiarity with his methods and readiness to think inductively that will permit him to render valid professional judgments. With this assertion

we return to the ideas expressed at the start of this chapter: The personality assessment psychologist must be responsive to himself and to others in a human and intraceptive manner; that is, he cannot be merely a technician or the master of a set of methods used in a purely algorithmic fashion.

APPENDIX

DESCRIPTIONS AND PUBLISHERS' ADDRESSES FOR A REPRESENTATIVE LISTING OF PSYCHOLOGICAL ASSESSMENT DEVICES

Brief Self-Report Devices

Adjective Check List. 300 adjectives scored for twenty-four variables, such as self-control, personal adjustment, and need:achievement. *Time:* 10 minutes. *Publisher:* Consulting Psychologists Press.

Eysenck Personality Inventory and *Maudsley Personality Inventory.* Fifty-seven-item (EPI) and forty-eight-item (MPI) tests, scored for extraversion and neuroticism (EPI and MPI), and faking (EPI only). *Time:* 10 minutes. *Publisher:* Educational and Industrial Testing Service.

Gordon Personal Profile. Eighteen items scored for ascendancy, responsibility, emotional stability, and sociability. *Time:* 10 minutes. *Publisher:* Harcourt Brace Jovanovich.

The IPAT Anxiety Scale Questionnaire. Forty items scored for five components of anxiety and two overall indices of "overt" and "covert" anxiety. *Time:* 10 minutes. *Publisher:* Institute for Personality and Ability Testing.

Personnel Reaction Blank. Seventy items scored for an "honesty-dependability" factor. *Time:* 15 minutes. *Publisher:* Consulting Psychologists Press.

State-Trait Anxiety Inventory. Forty items scored for anxiety-proneness ("trait") and current level of anxiety ("state"). *Time*: 10 minutes. *Publisher*: Consulting Psychologists Press.

Longer Self-Report Devices

California Psychological Inventory. 480 items scored for eighteen interpersonal variables, such as dominance, responsibility, tolerance, achievement by independence, and flexibility. *Time*: 50 minutes. *Publisher*: Consulting Psychologists Press.

Comrey Personality Scales. 180 items scored for eight factor dimensions, such as trust, orderliness, emotional stability, extraversion, and empathy. *Time*: 40 minutes. *Publisher*: Educational and Industrial Testing Service.

Dimensions of Temperament. Twenty forced-choice sets (each with ten items) scored for ten factor dimensions, such as sociable, ascendant, tough-minded, active, and responsible. *Time*: 45 minutes. *Publisher*: The Psychological Corporation.

Edwards Personal Preference Schedule. 210 items scored for fifteen "needs," such as achievement, order, affiliation, dominance, and aggression. *Time*: 40 minutes. *Publisher*: The Psychological Corporation.

Guilford-Zimmerman Temperament Indicator. 300 items scored for ten factor analytic traits, such as general activity, sociability, emotional stability, objectivity, and thoughtfulness. *Time*: 40 minutes. *Publisher*: Sheridan Psychological Services.

Minnesota Multiphasic Personality Inventory. 566 items scored for thirteen standard scales including lie, hypochondriasis, depression, paranoia, and schizophrenia; also special scales, such as anxiety, ego strength, and control. *Time*: 60 minutes. *Publisher*: The Psychological Corporation.

Myers-Briggs Type Indicator. 166 items scored for four Jungian polarities, extraversion-introversion, sensation-intuition, thinking-feeling, and judgment-perception.

Time: 45 minutes. *Publisher*: Educational Testing Service.

Omnibus Personality Inventory. 385 items scored for fourteen scales, such as thinking introversion, estheticism, autonomy, anxiety level, and altruism. *Time*: 45 minutes. *Publisher*: The Psychological Corporation.

Personal Orientation Inventory. 150 items scored for twelve scales, such as innerdirected, self-actualizing value, existentiality, synergy, and acceptance or aggression. *Time*: 30 minutes. *Publisher*: Educational and Industrial Testing Service.

Personality Research Form. 440 items scored for fifteen standard and seven additional scales, including achievement, autonomy, endurance, play, abasement, and succorance. *Time:* 45 minutes. *Publisher:* Research Psychologists Press.

Sixteen Personality Factor Questionnaire. 187 (Forms A and B) items, or 105 (Form C) items scored for sixteen factors, such as schizothymia-cyclothymia, desurgency-surgency, simple-sophisticated, and dependent-self-sufficient. *Time:* 45 minutes. *Publisher:* Institute for Personality and Ability Testing.

Measures of Personal Values

Study of Values. Forty-five items scaled for six values—theoretical, economic, aesthetic, social, political, and religious. *Time:* 30 minutes. *Publisher:* Houghton Mifflin Company.

Survey of Interpersonal Values. Thirty items scored for support, conformity, recognition, independence, benevolence, and leadership. *Time:* 15 minutes. *Publisher:* Science Research Associates.

Measures of Vocational Interests

Holland Vocational Preference Inventory. 160 occupational titles scored for eleven scales, including realistic, intellectual, artistic, enterprising, and status. *Time:* 20 minutes. *Publisher:* Consulting Psychologists Press.

Kuder Preference Record—Vocational. 168 items (Form C) scored for eleven variables, including mechanical, computational, musical, social service, and outdoor. *Time:* 45 minutes. *Publisher:* Science Research Associates.

Minnesota Vocational Interest Test. 158 items scaled for twenty-one nonprofessional jobs (e.g., baker, plumber, and sheet metalsmith), and nine work areas (e.g., electronics and mechanical). *Time:* 45 minutes. *Publisher:* The Psychological Corporation.

Self-Directed Search. Sixteen-page *Assessment Booklet* and eight-page *Occupations Finder.* Booklet is self-scored for Holland's six occupational categories, and for types derived from these categories. The *Finder* furnishes 456 suggested occupations for the various types. *Time:* Two hours for testing and review of occupations in the *Finder.* *Publisher:* Consulting Psychologists Press.

Strong Vocational Interests Blanks. Male form (revised edition) includes 399 items scored for fifty-four occupational interests plus other variables. Women's form scored for thirty-two occupations. *Time:* 50 minutes. *Publisher:* Stanford University Press.

Strong-Campbell Interest Inventory. 325 items scored for six general occupational themes, twenty-three basic interest scales, and 124 occupational scales, plus several administrative indices. Same form used for both sexes, with male and female scales indicated on the profile sheet. *Time:* 30 minutes. *Publisher:* Stanford University Press.

Other Tests

Chapin Social Insight Test. Twenty-five items scored for social insight. *Time:* 30 minutes. *Publisher:* Consulting Psychologists Press.

Embedded Figures Test. Group form contains eighteen items. *Time:* 20 minutes. *Publisher:* Consulting Psychologists Press.

Holtzman Ink Blot Technique. Two forms, each containing forty-five inkblots suitable for group-testing; yields twenty-two scores, such as rejections, location, space, form appropriateness, and color. *Time:* 75 minutes. *Publisher:* The Psychological Corporation.

Leadership Opinion Questionnaire. Forty items scored for structure (the degree to which the individual is task-oriented), and consideration (concern for others and for warmth in human relations). *Time:* 20 minutes. *Publisher:* Science Research Associates.

Rod-and-Frame Test. Portable apparatus for individual testing. *Time:* variable. *Manufacturer:* The Polymetric Company.

Rorschach Inkblot Test. Ten inkblots for use in individual testing. *Time:* variable. *Publisher:* Grune and Stratton.

Thematic Apperception Test. Twenty cards in each series (male or female) for use in individual testing. *Time:* variable. *Publisher:* Harvard University Press.

Welsh Figure Preference Test and *Barron-Welsh Art Scale.* 400 figures (WFPT) in group-testing booklet format scored for eighteen variables, such as symmetry, complexity, and artistic perception. Briefer eighty-six-item version (BWAS) scored for original and revised art scales. *Times:* 50 and 20 minutes. *Publisher:* Consulting Psychologists Press.

Publishers' Addresses

Consulting Psychologists Press
577 College Avenue
Palo Alto, Calif. 94306

Educational and Industrial Testing Service
P.O. Box 7234
San Diego, Calif. 92107

Educational Testing Service
Princeton, N.J. 08540

Grune and Stratton
381 Park Avenue South
New York, N.Y. 10017

Harcourt Brace Jovanovich
757 Third Avenue
New York, N.Y. 10017

Harvard University Press
Cambridge, Mass. 02138

Houghton Mifflin Company
110 Tremont Street
Boston, Mass. 02107

Institute for Personality and Ability Testing
1602 Coronado Drive
Champaign, Ill. 61822

Polymetric Company
1415 Park Avenue
Hoboken, N.J. 07030

The Psychological Corporation
304 East 45th Street
New York, N.Y. 10017

Research Psychologists Press
Goshen, N.Y. 10924

Science Research Associates
259 East Erie Street
Chicago, Ill. 60624

Sheridan Psychological Services
P.O. Box 837
Beverly Hills, Calif. 90213

Stanford University Press
Stanford, Calif. 94305

REFERENCES

Adorno, T. W., Frenkel-Brunswik, E., Levinson, D. J., & Sanford, R. N. *The authoritarian personality*. New York: Harper and Row, 1950.

Alexander, F. Psychological aspects of medicine. *Psychosomatic Medicine,* 1939, 1, 1–18.

Allport, G. W. *Personality: A psychological interpretation*. New York: Henry Holt, 1937.

Allport, G. W. *Becoming: Basic considerations for a psychology of personality*. New Haven: Yale University Press, 1955.

Allport, G. W. *Pattern and growth in personality*. New York: Holt, Rinehart and Winston, 1961.

Allport, G. W., Vernon, P. E., & Lindzey, G. *Study of values: Manual of directions*. (Rev. ed.) Boston: Houghton Mifflin, 1951.

Anastasi, A., & Schaefer, C. E. The Franck drawing completion test as a measure of creativity. *Journal of Genetic Psychology,* 1971, 119, 3–12.

Anderson, H. H., Ed. *Creativity and its cultivation*. New York: Harper and Row, 1959.

Asch, S. Effects of group pressure upon the modification and distortion of judgments. In H. Guetzkow (Ed.), *Groups, leadership, and men*. Pittsburgh: Carnegie Press, 1951, 177–190.

Asch, S. E. Studies of independence and submission to group pressure: I. A minority of one against a unanimous majority. *Psychological Monographs,* 1956, 70 (9, Whole No. 416).

Aserinsky, E., & Kleitman, N. Regularly occurring periods of eye motility, and concomitant phenomena during sleep. *Science,* 1953, 118, 273–274.

Atkinson, J. W. *An introduction to motivation*. Princeton: Van Nostrand, 1964.

Ausubel, D. P. Personality disorder *is* disease. *American Psychologist,* 1961, 16, 69–74.

Ax, A. F. The physiological differentiation between fear and anger in humans. *Psychosomatic Medicine,* 1953, 15, 433–442.

Bahnson, M. B., & Bahnson, C. B. Ego defenses in cancer patients. *Annals of the New York Academy of Sciences,* 1969, 164, 546–559.

Baker, W. G. Personality correlates of stock market speculation. *Dissertation Abstracts International,* 1971, 31 (7-B), 4376.

Bakker, C. B., & Dightman, C. R. Psychological factors in fertility control. *Fertility and Sterility,* 1964, 15, 559–567.

Bandura, A., & Walters, R. H. *Social learning*

and personality development. New York: Holt, Rinehart and Winston, 1963.

Barchas, J. D., Stolk, J. M., Ciaranello, R. D., & Hamburg, D. A. Neuroregulatory agents and psychological assessment. In P. McReynolds (Ed.), *Advances in psychological assessment,* Vol II. Palo Alto, Calif.: Science and Behavior Books, 1971, 260–292.

Barron, F. An ego-strength scale which predicts response to psychotherapy. *Journal of Consulting Psychology,* 1953, 17, 327–333. (a)

Barron, F. Complexity-simplicity as a personality dimension. *Journal of Abnormal and Social Psychology,* 1953, 68, 163–172. (b)

Barron, F. Some personality correlates of independence of judgment. *Journal of Personality,* 1953, 21, 287–297. (c)

Barron, F. The disposition toward originality. *Journal of Abnormal and Social Psychology,* 1955, 51, 478–485.

Barron, F. The psychology of imagination. *Scientific American,* 1958, 199, 151–166.

Barron, F. *Creativity and psychological health.* Princeton: Van Nostrand, 1963.

Barron, F. The psychology of creativity. In *New directions in psychology II.* New York: Holt, Rinehart and Winston, 1965.

Barron, F. *Creativity and personal freedom.* New York: Van Nostrand, 1968.

Barron, F., & Egan, D. Leaders and innovators in Irish management. *Journal of Management Studies,* 1968, 5, 41–60.

Barron, F., & Welsh, G. S. Artistic perception as a factor in personality style: Its measurement by a figure-preference test. *Journal of Psychology,* 1952, 33, 199–203.

Bateson, G., Jackson, D. D., Haley, J., & Weakland, J. Toward a theory of schizophrenia. *Behavioral Science,* 1956, 1, 251–264.

Beck, A. T., Ward, C. H., Mendelson, M., Mock, J., & Erbaugh, J. An inventory for measuring depression. *Archives of General Psychiatry,* 1961, 4, 561–571.

Beck, S. J. *Rorschach's test: I. Basic processes.* New York: Grune and Stratton, 1944.

Beck, S. J. *Rorschach's test: II. A variety of personality pictures.* New York: Grune and Stratton, 1945.

Berg, I. A. Response bias and personality: The deviation hypothesis. *Journal of Psychology,* 1955, 36, 3–9.

Berman, L. *The glands regulating personality.* New York: Macmillan, 1921.

Black, J. D. *Preliminary manual, the D48 test.*

Palo Alto, Calif.: Consulting Psychologists Press, 1963.

Block, J. *The Q-sort method in personality assessment and psychiatric research.* Springfield, Ill.: Charles C Thomas, 1961.

Block, J. *Lives through time.* Berkeley: Bancroft Books, 1971.

Block, J., Patterson, V. L., Block, J., & Jackson, D. D. A study of the parents of schizophrenic and neurotic children. *Psychiatry,* 1958, 21, 387–397.

Blumberg, E. M. The results of psychological testing of cancer patients. In J. A. Gengerelli & F. J. Kirkner (Eds.), *The psychological variables in human cancer.* Berkeley: University of California Press, 1954, 30–61.

Bonnardel, R., & Lavoëgie, M. S. Recherche sur la caractérisation des chercheurs scientifiques. *Journal de Psychologie Normal et Pathologique,* 1965, 62, 333–349.

Boring, E. G. *Sensation and perception in the history of experimental psychology.* New York: Appleton-Century-Crofts, 1942.

Boring, E. G., & Lindzey, G., Eds. *A history of psychology in autobiography,* Vol. V. New York: Appleton-Century-Crofts, 1967.

Boring, E. G. et al., Eds. *A history of psychology in autobiography,* Vol. IV. Worcester, Mass.: Clark University Press, 1952.

Bortner, R. W. A short rating scale as a potential measure of pattern A behavior. *Journal of Chronic Disease,* 1969, 22, 87–91.

Bortner, R. W., & Rosenman, R. H. The measurement of pattern A behavior. *Journal of Chronic Disease,* 1967, 20, 525–533.

Bray, D. W., & Grant, D. L. The assessment center in the measurement of potential for business management. *Psychological Monographs,* 1966, 80 (17, Whole No. 625).

Brodman, K., Erdmann, A. J. Jr., Lorge, I., & Wolff, H. G. The Cornell medical index: An adjunct to medical interview. *Journal of the American Medical Association,* 1949, 140, 530–534.

Callis, R., West, D. N., & Ricksecker, E. L. *The counselor's handbook: Profile interpretation of the Strong vocational interest blanks.* Urbana, Ill.: R. W. Parkinson, 1964.

Campbell, J. P., Dunnette, M. D., Lawler, E. E. III, & Weick, K. E. Jr. *Managerial behavior, performance, and effectiveness.* New York: McGraw-Hill, 1970.

Carson, R. C. Issues in the teaching of clinical MMPI interpretation. In J. N. Butcher

(Ed.), *MMPI: Research developments and clinical applications.* New York: McGraw-Hill, 1969, 41–53.

Cattell, R. B. *Description and measurement of personality.* New York: World Book, 1946.

Cattell, R. B. *Manual for forms A and B: Sixteen personality factor questionnaire.* Champaign, Ill.: Institute for Personality and Ability Testing, 1949.

Cattell, R. B. *Personality: A systematic, theoretical, and factual study.* New York: McGraw-Hill, 1950.

Cattell, R. B., & Eber, H. W. *Handbook for the sixteen personality factor questionnaire.* Champaign, Ill.: Institute for Personality and Ability Testing, 1964.

Centers, R., & Bugental, D. E. Intrinsic and extrinsic job motivations among different segments of the working population. *Journal of Applied Psychology,* 1966, 50, 193–197.

Chandra, S. An assessment of perceptual acuity in Fiji: A cross-cultural study with Indians and Fijians. *Journal of Cross-Cultural Psychology,* 1972, 3, 401–406.

Chapin, F. S. Preliminary standardization of a social insight scale. *American Sociological Review,* 1939, 5, 157–166.

Chapin, F. S. *The Chapin social insight test.* Palo Alto, Calif.: Consulting Psychologists Press, 1967.

Christie, R. C., & Geis, F., Eds. *Studies in Machiavellianism.* New York: Academic Press, 1971.

Clark, W. H. Relationships of motivational orientations to personality characteristics. *APA Experimental Publication System,* 1970, 6, #201A.

Cline, V. B. The assessment of good and poor judges of personality using a stress interview and sound-film technique. Unpublished doctoral dissertation, University of California, Berkeley, 1953.

Cline, V. B. Interpersonal perception. In B. A. Maher (Ed.), *Progress in experimental personality research.* New York: Academic Press, 1964, 221–284.

Clyde, D. J. *Manual for the Clyde mood scale.* Coral Gables, Fla.: University of Miami, Biometric Laboratory, 1963.

Craik, K. H. The assessment of places. In P. McReynolds (Ed.), *Advances in psychological assessment,* Vol. 2. Palo Alto, Calif.: Science and Behavior Books, 1971, 40–62.

Cropley, A. J. Creativity and intelligence. *British Journal of Educational Psychology,* 1966, 36, 259–266.

Crutchfield, R. S. Conformity and character. *American Psychologist,* 1955, 10, 191–198.

Crutchfield, R. S., Woodworth, D. G., & Albrecht, R. E. Perceptual performance and the effective person. *Personnel Laboratories Report,* WADC-TN-58-60, ASTIA Document No. 131039, Lackland Air Force Base, Texas, 1958.

Dement, W. The effect of dream deprivation. *Science,* 1960, 131, 1705–1707.

Dement, W. C. Dreams and dreaming. *International Journal of Neurology,* 1965, 5, 168–186.

Domino, G. Differential prediction of academic achievement in conforming and independent settings. *Journal of Educational Psychology,* 1968, 59, 256–260.

Domino, G. Maternal personality correlates of son's creativity. *Journal of Consulting and Clinical Psychology,* 1969, 33, 180–183.

Domino, G. Identification of potentially creative persons from the adjective check list. *Journal of Consulting and Clinical Psychology,* 1970, 35, 48–51.

Domino, G. Interactive effects of achievement orientation and teaching style on academic achievement. *Journal of Educational Psychology,* 1971, 62, 427–431.

Drevdahl, J. E., & Cattell, R. B. Personality and creativity in artists and writers. *Journal of Clinical Psychology,* 1958, 14, 107–111.

Dunbar, H. F. *Emotions and bodily changes.* (2nd ed.) New York: Columbia University Press, 1938.

Dunnette, M. D. Review: Work and the nature of man, by Frederick Herzberg. *Administrative Science Quarterly,* 1967, 12, 170–173.

Dunnette, M. D. The assessment of managerial talent. In P. McReynolds (Ed.), *Advances in psychological assessment,* Vol. 2. Palo Alto, Calif.: Science and Behavior Books, 1971, 79–108.

Edwards, A. L. *Manual for the Edwards personal preference schedule.* New York: Psychological Corporation, 1953.

Edwards, A. L. *The social desirability variable in personality assessment and research.* New York: Dryden, 1957.

Ellis, A. Should some people be labeled mentally ill? *Journal of Consulting Psychology,* 1967, 31, 435–446.

Erikson, E. H. *Childhood and society.* New York: W. W. Norton, 1950.

Eysenck, H. J. *Dimensions of personality.* London: Routledge, Kegan Paul, 1947.

Eysenck, H. J. The organization of personality. *Journal of Personality,* 1951, 20, 101–117.

Eysenck, H. J. *Maudsley personality inventory.* London: University of London Press, 1959.

Eysenck, H. J., & Eysenck, S. B. G. *Eysenck personality inventory.* London: University of London Press, 1963.

Fawcett, J. T. *Psychology and population.* New York: The Population Council, 1970.

Fenelon, J. R., & Magargee, E. I. Influence of race on the manifestation of leadership. *Journal of Applied Psychology,* 1971, 55, 353–358.

Festinger, L. *A theory of cognitive dissonance.* Evanston, Ill.: Row Peterson, 1957.

Finney, J. C. Programmed interpretation of MMPI and CPI. *Archives of General Psychiatry,* 1966, 15, 75–81.

Fleishman, E. A. *Manual for the leadership opinion questionnaire.* Chicago: Science Research Associates, 1960.

Fowler, R. D. Jr. Computer interpretation of personality tests: The automated psychologist. *Comprehensive Psychiatry,* 1967, 8, 455–467.

Franck, K., & Rosen, E. A projective test of masculinity-femininity. *Journal of Consulting Psychology,* 1949, 13, 247–256.

Gardner, R. W. Cognitive controls of attention deployment as determinants of visual illusions. *Journal of Abnormal and Social Psychology,* 1961, 62, 120–127.

Garwood, D. S. Personality factors related to creativity in young scientists. *Journal of Abnormal and Social Psychology,* 1964, 68, 413–419.

Getzels, J. W., & Jackson, P. W. *Creativity and intelligence: Explorations with gifted students.* New York: Wiley, 1962.

Ghiselli, E. E. Correlates of initiative. *Personnel Psychology,* 1956, 9, 311–320. (a)

Ghiselli, E. E. Differentiation of individuals in terms of their predictability. *Journal of Applied Psychology,* 1956, 40, 374–377. (b)

Ghiselli, E. E. The prediction of predictability. *Educational and Psychological Measurement,* 1960, 20, 3–8.

Ghiselli, E. E. Some motivational factors in the success of managers. *Personnel Psychology,* 1968, 21, 431–440.

Goffman, E. *Stigma: Notes on the management of spoiled identity.* Englewood Cliffs, N.J.: Prentice-Hall, 1963.

Goldberg, L. R. Diagnosticians versus diagnostic signs: The diagnosis of psychosis versus neurosis from the MMPI. *Psychological Monographs,* 1965, 79 (9, Whole No. 602).

Goldberg, L. R. The search for configural relationships in personality assessment: The diagnosis of psychosis versus neurosis from the MMPI. *Multivariate Behavioral Research,* 1969, 4, 523–536.

Goldberg, L. R. Man versus model of man: A rationale, plus some evidence, for a method of improving on clinical inferences. *Psychological Bulletin,* 1970, 73, 422–432.

Goodspeed, E. J. *A life of Jesus.* New York: Harper and Row, 1950.

Gottesman, I. I. Differential inheritance of the psychoneuroses. *Eugenics Quarterly,* 1962, 9, 223–227.

Gottesman, I. I. Genetic variance in adaptive personality traits. *Journal of Child Psychology and Psychiatry,* 1966, 7, 199–208.

Gottesman, I. I., & Shields, J. Contributions of twin studies to perspectives on schizophrenia. In B. A. Maher (Ed.), *Progress in experimental personality research,* Vol. 3. New York: Academic Press, 1966, 1–84.

Gough, H. G. Studies of social intolerance: II. A personality scale for anti-Semitism. *Journal of Social Psychology,* 1951, 33, 247–255.

Gough, H. G. *Manual for the California psychological inventory.* Palo Alto, Calif.: Consulting Psychologists Press, 1957.

Gough, H. G. Imagination: Undeveloped resource. In *Proceedings, first annual conference on research developments in personnel management.* Los Angeles: University of California Institute of Industrial Relations, 1957, 4–10. (Reprinted in S. J. Parnes & H. F. Harding, Eds., *A source book for creative thinking.* New York: Scribner's, 1962, 217–226.)

Gough, H. G. A validational study of the Chapin social insight test. *Psychological Reports,* 1965, 17, 355–368.

Gough, H. G. Appraisal of social maturity by means of CPI. *Journal of Abnormal Psychology,* 1966, 71, 189–195.

Gough, H. G. Scoring high on an index of social maturity. *Journal of Abnormal Psychology,* 1971, 77, 236–241.

Gough, H. G., & Delcourt, M. J. Developmental increments in perceptual acuity among Swiss and American school children. *Developmental Psychology,* 1969, 1, 260–264.

Gough, H. G., & Heilbrun, A. B. Jr. *The adjective check list manual.* Palo Alto, Calif.: Consulting Psychologists Press, 1965.

Gough, H. G., & Hug, C. Perception de formes géométriques et d'illusions chez des enfants Français et Américains. *Journal International de Psychologie,* 1968, 3, 183–190.

Gough, H. G., & McGurk, E. A group test of perceptual acuity. *Perceptual and Motor Skills,* 1967, 24, 1107–1115.

Gough, H. G., & Meschieri, L. Cross-cultural study of age-related differences in perceptual acuity. *Journal of Consulting and Clinical Psychology,* 1971, 37, 135–140.

Gough, H. G., & Parisi, D. La tecnica del *Q*-sort nello studio dei funzionari direttivi dell'amministrazione pubblica (the *Q*-sort technique in the study of managerial personnel in public administration). *Rivista di Psicologia Sociale,* 1967, 14, 107–127.

Gough, H. G., & Woodworth, D. G. Stylistic variations among professional research scientists. *Journal of Psychology,* 1960, 49, 87–98.

Gough, H. G., Misiti, R., & Parisi, D. Contrasting managerial perspectives of American and Italian public administrators. *Journal of Vocational Behavior,* 1971, 1, 255–262.

Gough, H. G., Misiti, R., Parisi, D. Il *Q*-sort del pubblico funzionario: Dati normativi e implicazioni diagnostiche (the Public Administrator's *Q*-sort Deck: Normative data and diagnostic implications). *Rivista di Psicologia Sociale,* 1968, 15, 323–343.

Gray, H., & Wheelwright, J. B. Jung's psychological types, their frequency of occurrence. *Journal of General Psychology,* 1946, 34, 3–17.

Guilford, J. P. Creativity. *American Psychologist,* 1950, 5, 444–454.

Guilford, J. P. Basic problems in teaching for creativity. In C. W. Taylor and F. E. Williams (Eds.), *Instructional media and creativity.* New York: Wiley, 1966, 71–103.

Guilford, J. P. *The nature of human intelligence.* New York: McGraw-Hill, 1967.

Guilford, J. P., & Zimmerman, W. S. *The Guilford-Zimmerman temperament survey.* Beverly Hills, Calif.: Sheridan Supply Co., 1949.

Guion, R. M., & Gottier, R. F. Validity of personality measures in personnel selection. *Personnel Psychology,* 1965, 18, 135–164.

Haire, M. *Psychology of management.* (2nd ed.) New York: McGraw-Hill, 1964.

Haire, M., Ghiselli, E. E., & Porter, L. W. *Managerial thinking: An international study.* New York: Wiley, 1966.

Hall, C. S., & Lindzey, G. *Theories of personality.* New York: Wiley, 1957.

Hall, W. B. Review of the empathy test. In O. K. Buros (Ed), *Sixth mental measurements yearbook.* Highland Park, N.J.: Gryphon Press, 1965, 214–215.

Hall, W. B., & MacKinnon, D. W. Personality inventory correlates of creativity among architects. *Journal of Applied Psychology,* 1969, 53, 322–326.

Hamilton, M. A rating scale for depression. *Journal of Neurology, Neurosurgery, and Psychiatry,* 1960, 23, 56–62.

Hamilton, M. Development of a rating scale for primary depressive illness. *British Journal of Social and Clinical Psychology,* 1967, 6, 278–296.

Hamlin, R. M., & Nemo, R. S. Self-actualization in choice scores of improved schizophrenics. *Journal of Clinical Psychology,* 1962, 18, 51–54.

Harrell, T. W. The personality of high earning MBAs in big business. *Personnel Psychology,* 1969, 23, 457–463.

Harrell, T. W. The personality of high earning MBAs in small business. *Personnel Psychology,* 1970, 23, 369–375.

Harris, D. Development and validity of a test of creativity in engineering. *Journal of Applied Psychology,* 1960, 44, 254–257.

Hartmann, E., Baekeland, F., Zwilling, G., & Hoy, P. Sleep need: How much sleep and what kind? *American Journal of Psychiatry,* 1971, 127, 1001–1008.

Hathaway, S. R., & McKinley, J. C. *Manual for the Minnesota multiphasic personality inventory.* Minneapolis: University of Minnesota Press, 1943.

Heist, P., & Yonge, G. *Manual for the omnibus personality inventory.* New York: Psychological Corporation, 1968.

Helson, R. Sex-specific patterns in creative literary fantasy. *Journal of Personality,* 1970, 38, 344–363.

Helson, R. Women mathematicians and the creative personality. *Journal of Consulting Psychology,* 1971, 36, 210–220.

Helson, R., & Crutchfield, R. S. Mathematicians: The creative researcher and the average Ph.D. *Journal of Consulting and Clinical Psychology,* 1970, 34, 250–257.

Herzberg, F. *Work and the nature of man.* Cleveland: World Book, 1966.

Herzberg, F., Mausner, B., & Snyderman, B. B. *The motivation to work.* (2nd ed.) New York: Wiley, 1959.

Hirsch, J., Ed. *Behavior-genetic analysis.* New York: McGraw-Hill, 1967.

Hogan, R. Development of an empathy scale. *Journal of Consulting and Clinical Psychology,* 1969, 33, 307–316.

Hogan, R. A dimension of moral judgment. *Journal of Consulting and Clinical Psychology,* 1970, 35, 205–212.

Holland, J. L. *Making vocational choices: A theory of careers.* Englewood Cliffs, N.J.: Prentice-Hall, 1973.

Holmes, T. H., & Rahe, R. H. The social readjustment rating scale. *Journal of Psychosomatic Research,* 1967, 11, 213–218.

House, R. J., & Wigdor, L. A. Herzberg's dual factor theory of job satisfaction and motivation. *Personnel Psychology,* 1967, 20, 369–390.

Hulin, C. L. Review of Herzberg's work and the nature of man. *Personnel Psychology,* 1966, 19, 434–437.

Jackson, D. N. *Personality research form manual.* Goshen, N.Y.: Research Psychologists Press, 1967.

Jacobs, M. A., Spilken, A. Z., Norman, M. M., & Anderson, L. S. Life stress and respiratory illness. *Psychosomatic Medicine,* 1970, 32, 233–242.

Jenkins, C. D. Psychologic and social precursors of coronary disease. *New England Journal of Medicine,* 1971, 284, 244–255, 307–317.

Jenkins, C. D., Hames, C. G., Zyzanski, S. J., Rosenman, R. H., & Friedman, M. Psychological traits and serum lipids: I. Findings from the California psychological inventory. *Psychosomatic Medicine,* 1969, 31, 115–128.

Jung, C. G. *Psychologische typen.* Zurich: Rascher, 1921. English edition, *Psychological types.* London: Kegan Paul, 1923.

Kahoe, R. D. Development of an objective factorial motivation-hygiene inventory. Unpublished doctoral dissertation, George Peabody College, Nashville, Tenn., 1966.

Kamiya, J. Operant control of the EEG alpha rhythm and some of its reported effects on consciousness. In C. Tart (Ed.), *Altered states of consciousness.* New York: Wiley, 1969, 507–517.

Kernan, J. P. Laboratory human relations training: Its effect on the "personality" of supervisory engineers. *Dissertation Abstracts,* 1964, 25, 665–666.

Kerr, W. A., & Speroff, B. J. *The empathy test.* Chicago: Psychometric Affiliates, 1947.

Kleinmuntz, B. MMPI decision rules for the identification of college maladjustment: A digital computer approach. *Psychological Monographs,* 1963, 74 (14, Whole No. 577).

Kleitman, N. *Sleep and wakefulness.* Chicago: University of Chicago Press, 1939.

Klett, C. J., & Pumroy, D. K. Automated procedures in psychological assessment. In P. McReynolds (Ed.), *Advances in psychological assessment,* Vol. 2. Palo Alto, Calif.: Science and Behavior Books, 1971, 14–39.

Klopfer, B. Discussion of paper by E. M. Blumberg on results of the psychological testing of cancer patients. In J. A. Gengerelli & F. J. Kirkner (Eds.), *The psychological variables in human cancer.* Berkeley: University of California Press, 1954, 62–65.

Klopfer, B. Psychological variables in human cancer. *Journal of Projective Techniques,* 1957, 21, 331–340.

Klopfer, B., & Davidson, H. H. *The Rorschach technique: An introductory manual.* New York: Harcourt, Brace, and World, 1962.

Kluckhohn, C., & Murray, H. A. Personality formation: The determinants. In C. Kluckhohn, H. A. Murray, & D. M. Schneider (Eds.), *Personality in nature, society, and culture.* (2nd ed.) New York: Knopf, 1953, 53–67.

Kohlberg, L. The development of children's orientations toward a moral order: I. Sequence in the development of moral thought. *Vita Humana,* 1963, 6, 11–33.

Kohlberg, L. The development of moral character and moral ideology. In M. L. Hoffman & L. W. Hoffman (Eds.), *Review of child development research,* Vol. 1. New York: Russell Sage Foundation, 1964, 383–432.

Kunca, D. F., & Haywood, N. P. The measurement of motivational orientation in low mental age subjects. *Peabody Papers in Human Development,* 1969, 7, No. 2.

Laing, R. D. *The politics of experience.* New York: Ballantine, 1967.

Langner, T. S. A twenty-two item screening

score of psychiatric symptoms indicating impairment. *Journal of Health and Human Behavior,* 1962, 3, 269–276.

Lazarus, R. S. *Personality.* (2nd ed.) Englewood Cliffs, N.J.: Prentice-Hall, 1971.

Lefcourt, H. M. Serendipitous validity study of Gough's social maturity index. *Journal of Consulting and Clinical Psychology,* 1968, 32, 85–86.

Leibowitz, H. W., & Judisch, J. M. The relation between age and the magnitude of the Ponzo illusion. *American Journal of Psychology,* 1967, 80, 105–109.

Lewin, K. *A dynamic theory of personality.* New York: McGraw-Hill, 1935.

Lewin, K. *Principles of topological psychology.* New York: McGraw-Hill, 1936.

Lidz, T., Fleck, S., & Cornelison, A. R. *Schizophrenia and the family.* New York: International Universities Press, 1965.

Lindzey, G., Loehlin, J., Manosevitz, M., & Thiessen, D. Behavioral genetics. *Annual Review of Psychology,* 1971, 22, 39–94.

Lykken, D. T., & Rose, R. Psychological prediction from actuarial tables. *Journal of Clinical Psychology,* 1963, 19, 139–151.

McClearn, G. E. Behavioral genetics. *Annual Review of Genetics,* 1970, 4, 437–468.

McClelland, D. C. *Personality.* New York: William Sloane, 1951.

McClelland, D. C., Ed. *Studies in motivation.* New York: Appleton-Century-Crofts, 1955.

McClelland, D. C. *The achieving society.* Princeton: Van Nostrand, 1961.

McClelland, D. C., & Winter, D. G. *Motivating economic achievement.* New York: The Free Press, 1969.

McClelland, D. C., Atkinson, J. W., Clark, R. A., & Lowell, E. L. *The achievement motive.* New York: Appleton-Century-Crofts, 1953.

McDermid, C. D. Some correlates of creativity in engineering personnel. *Journal of Applied Psychology,* 1965, 49, 14–19.

MacDonald, A. P. Jr. Internal-external locus of control and the practice of birth control. *Psychological Reports,* 1970, 27, 206.

McDougall, W. *Outline of psychology.* New York: Scribner's, 1923.

McGurk, E. Susceptibility to visual illusions. *Journal of Psychology,* 1965, 61, 127–143.

MacKinnon, D. W. Genus architectus creator varietas Americanus. *Journal of the American Institute of Architects,* 1960, 34 (3), 31–35.

MacKinnon, D. W. The nature and nurture of creative talent. *American Psychologist,* 1962, 17, 484–495.

MacKinnon, D. W. Personality and the realization of creative potential. *American Psychologist,* 1965, 20, 273–281.

Maddi, S. R. *Personality theories: A comparative analysis.* Homewood, Ill.: Dorsey Press, 1968.

Marks, P. A., & Seman, W. *Actuarial descriptions of abnormal personality: An atlas for use with the MMPI.* Baltimore: Williams and Wilkins, 1963.

Maslow, A. H. *Toward a psychology of being.* (2nd ed.) New York: Harper and Row, 1968.

Mednick, S. A. The associative basis of the creative process. *Psychological Review,* 1962, 69, 220–232.

Mednick, S. A., & Mednick, M. T. *Examiner's manual: Remote associates test—college and adult forms 1 and 2.* Boston: Houghton Mifflin, 1967.

Meehl, P. E. *Clinical versus statistical prediction.* Minneapolis: University of Minnesota Press, 1954.

Meehl, P. E. Clinical versus actuarial prediction. In *Proceedings of the 1955 invitational conference on testing problems.* Princeton: Educational Testing Service, 1956, 136–141.

Meehl, P. E. When shall we use our heads instead of the formula? *Journal of Counseling Psychology,* 1957, 4, 268–273.

Megargee, E. I. Influence of sex roles on the manifestation of leadership. *Journal of Applied Psychology,* 1969, 53, 377–382.

Megargee, E. I., Bogart, P., & Anderson, B. J. Prediction of leadership in a simulated industrial task. *Journal of Applied Psychology,* 1966, 50, 292–295.

Mischel, W. *Personality and assessment.* New York: Wiley, 1968.

Mishler, E. G., & Waxler, N. E. Family interaction processes and schizophrenia: A review of current theories. *Merrill-Palmer Quarterly,* 1965, 11, 269–315.

Monroe, L. J. Psychological and physiological differences between good and poor sleepers. *Journal of Abnormal Psychology,* 1967, 72, 255–264.

Moos, R. H. Psychological aspects of oral contraceptives. *Archives of General Psychiatry,* 1968, 19, 87–94. (a)

Moos, R. H. The development of a menstrual distress questionnaire. *Psychosomatic Medicine,* 1968, 30, 853–867. (b)

Moos, R. H. Typology of menstrual cycle symptoms. *American Journal of Obstetrics and Gynecology,* 1969, 103, 390–402.

Moos, R. H., & Houts, P. S. Assessment of the social atmosphere of psychiatric wards. *Journal of Abnormal Psychology,* 1968, 73, 595–604.

Morgan, C. D., & Murray, H. A. A method for investigating fantasies: The thematic apperception test. *Archives of Neurology and Psychiatry,* 1935, 34, 289–306.

Moss, F. A., Hunt, T., & Omwake, K. T. *The social intelligence test.* Washington, D.C.: George Washington University, 1930.

Murchison, C., Ed. *A history of psychology in autobiography,* Vols. I, II, III. Worcester, Mass.: Clark University Press, 1930, 1932, 1936.

Murray, H. A. *Explorations in personality.* New York: Oxford University Press, 1938.

Murstein, B. I. *Theory and research in projective techniques (emphasizing the TAT).* New York: Wiley, 1963.

Myers, I. B. *Manual (1962): The Myers-Briggs type indicator.* Princeton: Educational Testing Service, 1962.

Nichols, R. C. The national merit twin study. In S. G. Vandenberg (Ed.), *Methods and goals of human behavior genetics.* New York: Academic Press, 1965, 231–243.

Olds, J., & Olds, M. Drives, rewards, and the brain. *New directions in psychology,* Vol. II. New York: Holt, Rinehart and Winston, 1965, 327–410.

Oltman, P. K. A portable rod-and-frame apparatus. *Perceptual and Motor Skills,* 1968, 25, 503–516.

Overall, J. E., & Gorham, D. R. The brief psychiatric rating scale. *Psychological Reports,* 1962, 10, 799–812.

Pankoff, L. D., & Roberts, H. V. Bayesian synthesis of clinical and statistical prediction. *Psychological Bulletin,* 1968, 70, 762–773.

Parloff, M. B., & Datta, L. Personality characteristics of the potentially creative scientist. In *Science and psychoanalysis,* Vol. VIII. New York: Grune and Stratton, 1965, 91–106.

Parnes, S. J., & Harding, H. F., Eds. *A source book for creative thinking.* New York: Scribner's, 1964.

Peterson, D. R. *The clinical study of social behavior.* New York: Appleton-Century-Crofts, 1968.

Prange, A. J. Jr. The pharmacology and biochemistry of depression. *Diseases of the Nervous System,* 1964, 25, 217–221.

Rahe, R. H. Life change measurement as a predictor of illnesses. *Proceedings of the Royal Society of Medicine,* 1968, 61, 1124–1126.

Rahe, R. H., McKean, J. D., & Arthur, R. J. A longitudinal study of life change and illness patterns. *Journal of Psychosomatic Research,* 1967, 10, 355–366.

Rahe, R. H., Mahan, J. L., Arthur, R. J., & Gunderson, E. K. E. The epidemiology of illness in naval environments: I. Illness types, distribution, severities, and relation to life change. *Military Medicine,* 1970, 135, 443–452.

Ratner, H. Oral contraception drop-out rate. *Science,* 1967, 155, 951.

Rawls, D. J., & Rawls, J. R. Personality characteristics and personal history data of successful and less successful executives. *Psychological Reports,* 1968, 23, 1032–1034.

Rodgers, D. A., & Ziegler, F. J. Social role theory, the marital relationship, and use of ovulation suppressors. *Journal of Marriage and the Family,* 1968, 30, 584–591.

Roe, A. *The making of a scientist.* New York: Dodd, Mead, 1952.

Rogers, C. R. *On becoming a person: A therapist's view of psychotherapy.* Boston: Houghton Mifflin, 1961.

Rokeach, M. *The open and closed mind.* New York: Basic Books, 1960.

Rome, H. P., Swenson, W. M., Mataya, P., McCarthy, C. E., Pearson, J. S., Keating, F. R. Jr., & Hathaway, S. R. Symposium on automation techniques in personality assessment. *Proceedings of the Staff Meetings of the Mayo Clinic,* 1962, 37 (3), 61–82.

Rosenman, R. H., Friedman, M., Strauss, R., Wurm, M., Kositchok, R., Haan, W., & Werthessen, N. T. A predictive study of coronary heart disease: The Western collaborative group study. *Journal of the American Medical Association,* 1964, 189, 15–22.

Rosenzweig, S., Fleming, E. E., & Clark, W. Revised scoring manual for the Rosenzweig picture-frustration study. *Journal of Psychology,* 1947, 24, 165–208.

Rotter, J. B. Generalized expectancies for internal versus external control of reinforcement. *Psychological Monographs*, 1966, 80 (1, Whole No. 609).

Sanford, N. Personality: The field. *International Encyclopedia of the Social Sciences*, 1968, 12, 587–606.

Sarbin, T. R. Anxiety: Reification of a metaphor. *Archives of General Psychiatry*, 1964, 10, 630–638.

Sarbin, T. R. On the futility of the proposition that some people be labeled "mentally ill." *Journal of Consulting Psychology*, 1967, 31, 447–453.

Sarbin, T. R., & Hardyck, C. D. Conformance in role perception as a personality variable. *Journal of Consulting Psychology*, 1955, 19, 109–111.

Sargent, H. D. *The insight test: A verbal projective test for personality.* New York: Grune and Stratton, 1953.

Saul, L. J. A note on the psychogenesis of organic symptoms. *Psychoanalytic Quarterly*, 1935, 4, 476–483.

Saunders, D. R. Moderator variables in prediction. *Educational and Psychological Measurement*, 1956, 16, 209–222.

Scheibe, K. E. *Beliefs and values.* New York: Holt, Rinehart and Winston, 1970.

Schildkraut, J. J. The catecholamine hypothesis of affective disorders: A review of supporting evidence. *American Journal of Psychiatry*, 1965, 122, 509–522.

Schildkraut, J. J., & Kety, S. S. Biogenic amines and emotion. *Science*, 1967, 156, 21–30.

Schimek, J. Creative originality: Its evaluation by use of free-expression tests. Unpublished doctoral dissertation, University of California, Berkeley, 1954.

Schoenfeldt, L. F. The hereditary components of the project TALENT two-day test battery. *Measurement and Evaluation in Guidance*, 1968, 1, 130–140.

Segall, M. H., Campbell, D. T., & Herskovits, M. J. *The influence of culture on visual perception.* Indianapolis: Bobbs-Merrill, 1966.

Singer, M. T., & Wynne, L. C. Differentiating characteristics of the parents of childhood schizophrenics, childhood neurotics, and young adult schizophrenics. *American Journal of Psychiatry*, 1963, 120, 234–243.

Smith, J. M., & Schaefer, C. E. Development of a creativity scale for the adjective check list. *Psychological Reports*, 1969, 25, 87–92.

Spielberger, C. D., Ed. *Anxiety and behavior.* New York: Academic Press, 1966.

Spitzer, R. L., & Endicott, J. Diagno II: Further development in a computer program for psychiatric diagnosis. *American Journal of Psychiatry*, January Supplement, 1969, 125, 12–21.

Stern, G. G. *People in context: The measurement of environmental interaction in school and society.* New York: Wiley, 1970.

Stern, G. G., Stein, M. I., & Bloom, B. S. *Methods in personality assessment.* New York: The Free Press, 1956.

Strong, E. K. Jr. *Vocational interests of men and women.* Stanford, Calif.: Stanford University Press, 1943.

Sullivan, H. S. *The interpersonal theory of psychiatry.* New York: W. W. Norton, 1953.

Szasz, T. *The myth of mental illness: Foundations of a theory of personal conduct.* New York: Hoeber-Harper, 1961.

Taylor, C. W. The identification of creative scientific talent. *American Psychologist*, 1959, 14, 100–102.

Taylor, C. W., Ed. *Creativity: Progress and potential.* New York: McGraw-Hill, 1964.

Thorndike, E. L. Intelligence and its uses. *Harper's Magazine*, 1920, 140, 227–235.

Thorndike, R. L. Review of the empathy test. In O. K. Buros (Ed.), *Fifth mental measurements yearbook.* Highland Park, N.J.: Gryphon Press, 1959, 120–121.

Thorndike, R. L., & Stein, S. An evaluation of the attempts to measure social intelligence. *Psychological Bulletin*, 1937, 34, 275–285.

Toffler, A. *Future Shock.* New York: Random, 1970.

Torrance, E. P. *Guiding creative talent.* Englewood Cliffs, N.J.: Prentice-Hall, 1962.

Tryon, R. C., & Bailey, D. The BCTRY system of cluster and factor analysis. *Multivariate Behavioral Research*, 1966, 1, 95–111.

Veblen, T. *The instinct of workmanship.* New York: Macmillan, 1914.

Venables, P. H., & O'Connor, N. A short scale for rating paranoid schizophrenia. *Journal of Mental Science*, 1959, 105, 815–818.

Vernon, P. E., Ed. *Creativity: Selected readings.* Baltimore: Penguin Books, 1970.

Vroom, V. H. Some personality determinants of the effects of participation. *Journal of Abnormal and Social Psychology*, 1959, 59, 322–327.

Wechsler, H., Grosser, G. H., & Busfield, B. L.

The depression rating scale. *Archives of General Psychiatry*, 1963, 9, 334–343.

Wells, H. G. *Experiment in autobiography.* New York: Ryerson Press (McGraw-Hill), 1938.

Welsh, G. S. Factor dimensions A and R. In G. S. Welsh & W. G. Dahlstrom (Eds.), *Basic readings on the MMPI in psychology and medicine.* Minneapolis: University of Minnesota Press, 1956, 264–281.

Welsh, G. S. *Preliminary manual, the Welsh figure preference test.* (Res. ed.) Palo Alto, Calif.: Consulting Psychologists Press, 1959.

Welsh, G. S. *Gifted adolescents: A handbook of test results.* Greensboro, N.C.: Prediction Press, 1969.

Welsh, G. S. Vocational interests and intelligence in gifted adolescents. *Educational and Psychological Measurement*, 1971, 31, 155–164.

Wernimont, P. F. Intrinsic and extrinsic factors in job satisfaction. *Journal of Applied Psychology*, 1966, 40, 41–50.

Whalen, R. E. *Hormones and behavior.* Princeton: Van Nostrand, 1967.

White, R. W. Motivation reconsidered: The concept of competence. *Psychological Review*, 1959, 66, 297–333.

Wiggins, J. S., Renner, K. E., Clore, G. L., & Rose, R. J. *The psychology of personality.* Reading, Mass.: Addison-Wesley, 1971.

Wiggins, N., & Kohen, E. S. Man versus model of man revisited: The forecasting of graduate school success. *Journal of Personality and Social Psychology*, 1971, 19, 100–106.

Wilson, R. C., Guilford, J. P., & Christensen, P. R. The measurement of individual differences in originality. *Psychological Bulletin*, 1953, 50, 362–370.

Witkin, H. A. Psychological differentiation and forms of pathology. *Journal of Abnormal Psychology*, 1965, 70, 317–336.

Witkin, H. A. A cognitive-style approach to cross-cultural research. *International Journal of Psychology*, 1967, 2, 233–250.

Witkin, H. A., Goodenough, D. R., & Karp, S. A. Stability of cognitive style from childhood to young adulthood. *Journal of Personality and Social Psychology*, 1967, 7, 291–300.

Witkin, H. A., Lewis, H. B., & Weil, E. Affective reactions and patient-therapist interactions among more differentiated and less differentiated patients early in therapy. *Journal of Nervous and Mental Disease*, 1968, 146, 193–208.

Witkin, H. A., Faterson, H. F., Goodenough, D. R., & Birnbaum, J. Cognitive patterning in mildly retarded boys. *Child Development*, 1966, 37, 301–316.

Witkin, H. A., Dyk, R. B., Faterson, H. F., Goodenough, D. R., & Karp, S. A. *Psychological differentiation: Studies of development.* New York: Wiley, 1962.

Witkin, H. A., Lewis, H. B., Hertzman, M., Machover, K., Meissner, P. B., & Wapner, S. *Personality through perception.* New York: Harper and Row, 1954.

Ziegler, F. J., Rodgers, D. A., & Prentiss, R. J. Psychosocial response to vasectomy. *Archives of General Psychiatry*, 1969, 21, 46–54.

Zuckerman, M., & Lubin, B. *Manual for multiple affect adjective check list.* San Diego: Educational and Industrial Testing Service, 1965.

Zung, W. W. K. A self-rating depression scale. *Archives of General Psychiatry*, 1965, 12, 63–70.

CHAPTER 14

Background Data[1]

WILLIAM A. OWENS
The University of Georgia

FOLLOWING A BROAD INTRODUCTION to background data, this discussion narrows to a treatment of the scored autobiographical data form as the vehicle of choice. A definition of this vehicle lays stress on the objective measurement of prior experience. Types of items are indicated and evaluated; and the construction of an instrument is discussed. The topics of keying items, weighting, combining, and interpreting them follow. The major issue of validity is dealt with under the subordinates of predictive utility; common criteria and functions served; use in classification; artifacts and limitations; and stability across cultures, age, race, and sex groups, and companies. A brief treatment of reliability is followed by a discussion of the relationships of biodata dimensions to a spectrum of other measures. Finally, a conceptual model for biodata research is reviewed and evaluated, and suggestions are made regarding the industrial utility of both isoteric and more catholic approaches.

INTRODUCTION

To the student of human behavior, the importance of background data as an aid to both prediction and comprehension is enormous. Just after the turn of the century Galton (1902) stated, "The future of each man is mainly a direct consequence of the past—of his own biological history, and of those of his ancestors. It is, therefore, of high importance when planning for the future to keep the past under frequent review, all in its just proportion." If we accept the sagacity of Galton's statement, we are left with the question of how to implement his suggestion.

Forty years later, as though in response to Galton, Allport (1942) reviewed the use of personal documents in psychological science. He listed them as including autobiographies, questionnaires, verbatim recordings, diaries, letters, and expressive and projective

---

[1] The writer has striven for an organized and coherent treatment of the topic; references are used for documentation and illustration as appropriate. The reader should *not* assume an exhaustive citation of the literature since many excellent studies are not quoted. A bibliography may be obtained from The Smith-Richardson Foundation, Greensboro, North Carolina, if this is desired.

productions. He also noted that biographical data had been employed in studies of attitudes and that there was apparent concern with criteria for the life history. All in all, Allport characterized the use of personal documents prior to 1920 as "uncritical," but noted that properly handled they *do* conform to the requirements of science. Somewhat more pointedly Guthrie (1944) stated, "An individual's ... past affiliations, political and religious, offer better and more specific predictions of his future than any of the traits that we usually think of as personality traits. When we know how men adjust themselves through learning to their situation, and also know the situations to which they have been exposed, ... we know the men themselves and there is no need to speculate concerning the deeper reaches of the soul until we can explore these with similar knowledge."

More or less parallel with the foregoing sorts of research and speculation, work was proceeding on the objective scoring of the application blank, the device representing the most immediate forebearer of the scored biodata form. Thus, at the 1894 Chicago Underwriters' meeting (see Ferguson, 1961), Colonel Thomas L. Peters of the Washington Life Insurance Company of Atlanta, Georgia, proposed that one way to improve the selection of life insurance agents "would be for managers to require all applicants to answer a list of standardized questions, such as the following: Present residence? Residences during the previous ten years? Birth date and place? Marital status? Dependent or not dependent for support on own daily exertions? Amount of unencumbered real estate? Occupation during previous ten years? Previous experience in life insurance selling? For what companies? For what general agents? When and where? Claims, if any, for unsettled accounts? References?" Such a list had been developed and used, said Peters, by his associates in the Georgia Association of Life Insurers. So it was not a group of psychologists, as many have believed, but a group of businessmen who created what is truly the granddaddy of standardized personal history and application blanks.

In 1915 Woods (see Ferguson, 1961, 1962) attempted an empirical analysis of the responses of good and poor salesmen to the individual items of an application blank, and in 1917 Scott, following Woods's lead, included an application blank or personal history record among his "Aids in the Selection of Salesmen." By 1922 Goldsmith had published an article on "The Use of the Personal History Blank as a Salesmanship Test" in which the procedures of empirical item analysis and weighting were made quite explicit. Only three years later Manson (1925) reported on combining items for sales selection via multiple R, Kenagy and Yoakum (1925) examined background factors and personal data in relation to general sales success, and Cope[2] (see Anon., 1925) suggested their potential value in selecting public employees. Although it seems to have been reported only in his book, Viteles (1932) completed a study during 1926 in which he established that an objective scoring scheme for an application blank could be useful in the selection of taxicab drivers. Indeed, cross-validated on 188 new hires a given critical score would have rejected 60 percent of poorest earners, 18 percent of average, and 22 percent of best. The course seemed charted and the ship under weigh.

Just when the notion of casting the item options of an application blank into multiple choice form first emerged is not clear. What is clear is that the military establishment of World War II enjoyed considerable success in their use of a scored biodata form. Thus, Guilford and Lacey (1947) reported average validities of 0.35 to 0.40 in predicting success of Air Force student pilots in training and comparable rs for navigators of 0.25 to 0.30. Similarly, Parish and Drucker (1957) reported on a sixteen-year research program by the Adjutant General's Office (AGO), U.S. Army, and noted that the biodata blank had been the most consistently

---

[2] Methodology and data credited to Gertrude V. Cope.

successful device for predicting peer and tactical officer ratings of leadership in OCS ($r = 0.45$). They also noted that a specially constructed inventory key predicted a pass versus resign criterion to the extent of an r of 0.50. Among closely related lines Roy, Brueckel, and Drucker (1954) found the biodata blank more valid ($r = 0.26$) than any combination of ten tests of aptitude, attitude, and physical proficiency in predicting ROTC leadership ratings of officers and cadet peers at six schools ($N = 2003$). Findings in the massive Officer Integration Program were essentially similar.

In any event, the Personnel Research Branch, AGO, U.S. Army held a central place in activities involving wartime and early postwar uses of scored autobiographical data. Within this group, none has been a more outspoken champion and exponent of the biodata approach than Henry (1966), around whom much of the productive activity has taken place. He has repeatedly commented that Richardson, Bellows, and Henry have found it their single best predictor of a broad spectrum of industrial criteria, and has documented this finding through some twenty-five studies done at The Standard Oil Company (New Jersey) and its affiliates (Vol. II, 1962). In addition, he has stimulated both conferences (1966) and research (for example, see Owens & Henry, 1966) in a fashion which clearly makes him a focal point in recent developments.

Before we proceed further in a manner which implies that the scored autobiographical data blank represents *the* method of choice in gathering background data, let us briefly take stock: (1) The S himself would not have to supply the data—parents, friends, and acquaintances could provide it, but vital subjective reactions would be lost. (2) The questionnaire format is not essential—letters, recordings, and autobiography could be given after-the-fact interpretation, but the method is laborious, often unreliable, and usually lacking in relevance to a given criterion. (3) The interpretation would not have to be objective and the blank "scored"—yet the projective interpretation of "open-ended" statements is slow, expensive and of apparently poor relative validity; and the post hoc establishment of more objective scoring categories or protocols is tedious, may involve substantial sampling error, and is beset with some subjectivity in the interpretation of a particular response. All in all, research does and should continue with such other techniques as the weighted application blank (see England, 1961; or Fleishman & Berniger, 1967). Indeed, several application blank studies are referred to in what follows because most response data cast in that form could also be obtained on a biodata inventory. However, devices of the former sort tend to be shorter, less systematic, and more purely empirical than the latter—characteristics which make it more difficult and less profitable to review studies which utilize them. In short, the relatively recent upsurge of interest in biodata must be based upon some rather general perception of advantages afforded—real and fancied—which we should examine before proceeding. Some of them are as follows:

1. Biodata is obviously another format for the traditional selection or employment interview with the advantages that (a) every interviewee is asked the same questions in exactly the same way, and (b) the value judgments made by the "interviewer" are standardized, relevant, and of known validity.

2. It essentially represents an extension and revision of the existing and accepted application blank.

3. Studies by Mosel and Cozan (1952) and by Keating, Paterson, and Stone (1950) both suggest that correlations between information provided by the applicant and that obtained from previous employers are very high; virtually all rs reported range from 0.90 to 0.99. This is impressive accuracy of reporting *for these selected sorts of verifiable items*.

4. Biodata is useful in appraising significant, noncognitive characteristics among employees at levels such that substantial and

relatively homogeneous abilities can be inferred from prior performance and/or academic record (for examples, see Smith et al., 1961; Laurent, 1962; or Taylor et al., 1965).

5. Biodata represents an appealing exploratory device. For example, if good and poor foremen are discriminated by an item dealing with amount of education, the presence of a mental ability test in a subsequent selection battery may well be indicated.

6. Biodata items can encompass both predictors and criteria. To illustrate, one item response may indicate a research versus administrative preference and k-1 items may then be examined for the correlates and possible predictors of this preference (Albright & Glennon, 1961).

7. The biodata item has both intuitive and intrinsic validity probably based on the fact that it speaks directly to a central measurement axiom; namely, that what a man *will do* in the future is best predicted from what he *has done* in the past.

8. Biodata items make it possible to achieve real understanding quite beyond the unvarnished fact of empirical prediction. An examination of discriminating item responses can tell a great deal about what kinds of employees remain on a job and what kinds do not, what kinds sell much insurance and what kinds sell little, or what kinds are promoted rapidly. Insights obtained in this fashion may serve anyone from the initial interviewer to the manager who formulates personnel policy.

9. The usual empirical derivation of both items and scoring keys tends to assure that only job-relevant questions will be asked, and that answers will be evaluated only in terms of their relationship to subsequent job success. There can, thus, be no justified complaints of willful discrimination against minority groups. Nor is there any "hidden exploration of the psyche" in the sense belabored by Gross (1962) or Packard (1964).

10. In contexts both academic and industrial, biodata has proven itself at least as good a criterion predictor as cognitive measures and less highly correlated with race. (See later discussion on Validity.)

11. With tests in general and personality questionnaires in particular the subjects of some rather scathing current criticism, biodata may well enjoy better acceptance than the former, and will almost certainly be more valid than the latter.

12. Because both items and factors have great independence, biodata makes an excellent device for the contexts of differential prediction or classification.

13. Because biodata may be regarded as measuring both earlier input variables and prior experience, it lends itself nicely to conceptual modeling, the evaluation of developmental theory and heuristic functions.

14. Since the measurement practitioner is often unsure of the antecedents of what he measures, it may be noted that causal-type inferences can be approached by relating biodata based patterns of prior experience to scores on tests or questionnaires of concern (Kulberg & Owens, 1960; Chaney & Owens, 1964).

15. As will be indicated in what follows, biodata is an efficient, robust, and highly valid predictor of a broad spectrum of very practical criteria.

DEFINITION

Having narrowed our concerns to the foregoing extent, let us now attempt a definition of scored autobiographical data. Objective or scorable autobiographical data as inputs for predictive, diagnostic, or counseling purposes are typically secured by use of some more or less standardized form, a Biographical Information Blank (BIB), a Biographical Data Form, an Application Blank, an Interview Guide, an Individual Background Survey, or something similar. The data form has commonly been composed of multiple choice items which permit the respondent to describe himself in terms of demographic, experiential, or attitudinal variables presumed or demonstrated to be related to personality structure, personal adjustment, or success in social, educational, or occupational pursuits. Usually the items have called for "factual" data but those which have tapped attitudes, feelings, and value judgments resulting from experience have not been excluded. Excepting the demographic area, the time referred to by the items should be in the past. Two important features of the data are that they are: (1) self-reports (autobiographical), and (2) in a format which lends itself to conventional psychometric evaluations and interpretations.

ITEMS

Although a definition is useful, examples of several types of items may still add clarity. These follow.

Some Types of Biodata Items

1. *Yes–No*
   Have you found your life to date to be pleasant and satisfying?
2. *Continuum, single choice*
   What is your weight?
   (a) under 135 pounds
   (b) 136 to 155 pounds
   (c) 156 to 175 pounds
   (d) 176 to 195 pounds
   (e) over 195 pounds
3. *Non-continuum, single choice*
   What was your marital status at college graduation?
   (a) single
   (b) married, no children
   (c) married, one or more children
   (d) widowed
   (e) separated or divorced
4. *Non-continuum, multiple choice*
   Check each of the following from which you have ever suffered.
   (a) allergies
   (b) asthma
   (c) high blood pressure
   (d) ulcers

(e) headaches
(f) gastrointestinal upsets
(g) arthritis

5. *Continuum, plus "escape option"*
   What was your length of service in your most recent full-time job?
   (a) less than 6 months
   (b) between 6 months and 1 year
   (c) 1 to 2 years
   (d) 2 to 5 years
   (e) more than 5 years
   (f) no previous full-time job
6. *Non-continuum, plus "escape option"*
   When are you most likely to have a headache?
   (a) when I strain my eyes
   (b) when I don't eat on schedule
   (c) when I am under tension
   (d) January first
   (e) never have headaches
7. *Common stem, multiple continua*
   Over the past 5 years, *how much* have you enjoyed each of the following? (Use continuum 1 to 4 at right below.)
   (a) loafing or watching TV
   (b) reading
   (c) constructive hobbies
   (d) home improvement
   (e) outdoor recreation
   (f) music, art, or dramatics, etc.

   (1) very much
   (2) some
   (3) very little
   (4) not at all

In the experience of the writer, continuum items—that is, items in which the response options lie along either an apparent or a demonstrated continuum—are preferable to non-continuum items, in terms of both validation probability and adaptability to subsequent statistical analysis. Similarly, single choice (choose one option) items are superior to multiple choice; since, in the latter, positive endorsers are often spread rather thinly over a number of categories, thereby giving rise to the familiar "thin-splits" problem in analysis. Escape options are sometimes a necessary evil, although they often attract so few endorsers that they could as well be discarded. If they are "slotted into" a continuum, it is often unclear where they belong; if they are not, and are retained, one must contemplate the analysis of a dichotomous item involving the escape option versus all others. Dichotomous items, of course, often involve so coarse a grouping as to result in a loss of information. The fact that point estimates of correlations based upon them are affected by the level of the dichotomy is also of concern.

CONSTRUCTION

If we assume that a potential investigator has reached a decision regarding item format, what guidelines may be provided with respect to item content favoring validity? A finding by Williams (1961) is germane. He constructed and assembled a questionnaire of ninety-eight items to predict a criterion of enlistment or non-enlistment in advanced Air Force Reserve Officer's Training Corps (AFROTC). Before administering his questionnaire, Williams discovered that he was able to enunciate a specific hypothesis for thirty-five of his items, of which sixteen, or 45 percent, ultimately validated; in the remaining list of sixty-three items where a specific hypothesis was either vague or nonexistent, he found that only eight items, or 12 percent, ultimately validated. The moral seems clear; although one may include some items because they have priorly demonstrated validity in reasonably similar circumstances, biodata items are much more likely to validate if they are knowledgeably beamed at a specific target.

Pursuing the question of appropriate item content further, Larsen et al. (1967) conducted a study directed specifically at the development of guidelines. They twice administered a sixty-five-item questionnaire to ninety-one seniors in business and forty-nine in engineering with instructions to (1) answer honestly and (2) answer like a job

applicant; order effects were controlled. Chief criteria were "behavioral faking," that is, actual changes in item response; and "objectionability," that is, a rating on a five-point scale with a checking of up to three reasons. The authors' conclusions are of interest. With respect to faking, they state: (1) self-evaluation items with options differing only in degree should be avoided; (2) self-description items with options differing in nature but *not* degree should be avoided; (3) items dealing with past behavior should be favored. On the topic of item objectionability they indicate: (1) that self-description items with qualitatively differing options are also poor in this context; (2) that items which force the S to choose among uniformly favorable or unfavorable options are resisted; but (3) that items dealing with past and present behavior and with opinions, attitudes, and values are among the most acceptable. Items dealing with family relationships did not encourage faking but could clearly become so personal as to be offensive.

Smart (1968) was also concerned with the objectionability of items. He had forty college students rate their willingness to answer each of the items of a BIB. He then had five graduate students examine the best and poorest items and develop rules for producing the one or avoiding the other. A new group of five graduate students applied the ten overlapping rules developed and predicted item objectionability (low willingness), as originally rated with considerable success. A study by Majesty (1967) is of interest in this same context because it implies that rational screening of items may be effective in avoiding bias. He had 1,036 students on six college campuses either complete or rate 295 information blank items and found that sex, race, and religion could be discriminated—virtually as well with rational as with empirical keys. Of his items, 47 percent did so discriminate, demographic items most and self-description items least. Happily, it is the latter which also appear to be superior predictors of other criteria. For example, Buel (1971) attempted to build a seventy-eight-item biodata form composed of strictly historical items and found that sixteen validated; he then paraphrased the items in such fashion that opinion, attitude, and value dimensions were implied and found that thirty-three validated. The implications seem clear; of course, biodata items should be in historical format. However, if opinions, attitudes, and values shine through them it is because this is the stuff of which some major dimensions of prior experience are composed.

If we shift our attention from concerns with probable item validity to concerns with probable reliability, it becomes appropriate to review a study by Owens et al. (1962). The investigators employed retest consistency as a criterion for the development and evaluation of biodata items and suggested rules for item writing, such that this criterion might be better satisfied. Their method utilized, first, an inspection of consistent and inconsistent items with a view to deriving rules; second, the "blind" sorting of items by five independent judges to evaluate rule conformity versus nonconformity; and, third, a determination of the relationship of conformity to retest consistency. Four rules satisfied a statistical criterion of significant association. These were as follows:

1. Brevity is desirable; an actual word count indicated substantial differences between consistent and inconsistent items in this regard. (Complexity of ideas is, of course, a corollary.)

2. Whenever possible, numbers should be used to graduate or scale, and to define options or alternatives.

3. Either all response options or alternatives should be covered or an "escape" option should be provided.

4. Items, particularly item stems, should carry a neutral or a pleasant connotation for the respondent.

Rule 4, of course, seems suggestively congruent with the findings of Highland and Berkshire (1951) to the effect that forced-choice "blocks" are best composed entirely of positive statements, a finding confirmed in volume three of the *Social Science Research Reports* of The Standard Oil Company (N.J.) (1962b).

SCORING AND INTERPRETATION

The items of a biodata inventory are typically keyed in one of two ways: First, each option may be scored as a binary variable with either unit weights or weights which reflect both the direction and the magnitude of criterion group differences; or second, the options may be regarded as lying along a continuum and may be assigned either progressive unit weights or an irregular series. Studies bearing on the relative merits of the two approaches are not numerous, although one by Lecznar & Dailey (1950) is relevant. They report keying biodata inventories in two ways: (1) by the "pattern of response" method where gradients of phi coefficients are considered for the responses *to an item as a whole;* and (2) by the conventional method in which item options are evaluated independently. They found that the two methods yielded comparable initial validities, but that the pattern of response key showed less shrinkage in cross-validation. The writer's experience also recommends scoring items as units, though based upon the continuum procedure previously mentioned.

In any event, once items have been keyed, a question arises as to how best to combine them to serve a given purpose. Several possibilities exist. (1) A total score may be a simple sum of weighted or unweighted item scores which have in common only their relationship to a criterion. (2) Whether by rational sorts and iteration, by highly correlated triads expanded to maximum saturation, or by some other method, relatively homogeneous clusters of items may be identified and scores from them optimally weighted, via multiple R, for the prediction of a given criterion. Various writers have published to this point, among them DuBois, Loevinger, and Gleser (1952); Berkeley (1953); Pickrel (1954); and Matteson,

Osborn, and Sparks (1969). Berkeley compared the usual empirical method with the combination of scores from homogeneous clusters and summarized his findings as follows: (1) the empirical keys showed higher criterion correlations in the initial validation sample; (2) the empirical keys showed greater shrinkage; (3) neither method yielded superior cross-validities; and (4) the homogeneous keys were psychologically meaningful, but the empirical keys were not. The report by Matteson et al. (1969) is clear, well-documented and provides computer program flow charts. For classification purposes one might wish to anchor clusters to orthogonal factors in the interest of minimizing factor intercorrelations and maximizing *differential* validities. The point, however, is more hypothetical than real since the average intercluster correlation reported by both DuBois et al. (1952) and Berkeley (1953) was only 0.15.

Differential weighting of either binary or continuum options or items is, of course, most profitable, as Guilford (1954) has noted, when tests are short and item intercorrelations low. Thus, the items of weighted application blanks, quite appropriately, are usually assigned differential weights (see England, 1961). Empirically scored biodata blanks, on the other hand, are not usually short, and homogeneous clusters are, by definition, highly intercorrelated. It, therefore, follows that differential weighting of biodata options or items will not usually be profitable. On the other hand, *if* items are arranged in some approximate order of quality from best to poorest, Clark and Gee (1954) have clearly indicated that both reliability and discrimination of a total score are damaged when one descends down the list far enough to include items which add less unique than error variance. Thus, a longer inventory or sub-scale is not always superior to a shorter one.

In the context of adding a biodata inventory to an existing test battery, both Malloy (1955) and Webb (1960) have suggested the superiority of a criterion composed of deviate scores over the usual criterion. Deviate scores are equal to the difference between predicted and actual criterion values, using predictors other than the one in question. The correlation between the new predictor and this residual variance is a part correlation and the method is directed at assuring that the new predictor will make a unique contribution. The conception seems solid, but difference scores of this sort are often so unreliable that the investigator with these purposes in mind may be wise to validate his items against both normal and deviate criterion values.

Two final conceptions which relate to both construction and interpretation of biodata items represent unique contributions. First, Ferguson (1967) has suggested an IQ-like approach. In the sales area, for example, he states that the most useful type of biodata item is one correlating with net worth or age; that is, one measuring economic developmental maturity. Clearly, for example, it does not have the same significance for a man of forty-five to have $50,000 worth of life insurance as for a man of thirty to have this same amount. Thus, responses to such items must be age normed. More broadly, Ferguson's (1967) position is that an operationally defined scale based upon items which have developmental significance in the given context will be a solid predictor, and that this rationale will obviate the need for much "cut-and-try," empirical research. The idea is an ingenious one and the indication that some items need age norming is noteworthy. If a problem exists it may lie in the sagacity required to identify the dimension having developmental significance in the particular context of immediate concern. Second, Helmreich et al. (1971) employed a thirty-nine-item life history questionnaire to predict success among 115 male aquanauts. All were Navy enlistees and composed five classes in training to be Divers Second Class. Success was defined in terms of ability to work effectively under water, to get along with teammates, and to adjust to stress, and all were expressed in terms of pass versus fail and success in training criteria. What is remarkable in this study is not so much the careful wording of items and the fine criterion prediction but the fact that twelve items are answered nineteen times—once for each year of S's life. The authors feel that this items-times-years response matrix reveals developmental trends of great significance. The conception is innovative and further research should soon illuminate its more obvious pros and cons.

VALIDITY

One of the unmixed and conspicuous virtues of scored autobiographical data has been its clear and recognized tendency to be an outstanding predictor of a broad spectrum of external criteria. For example, Ghiselli (1966) in his summary on *The Validity of Occupational Aptitude Tests* reported that when validities were averaged across a number of occupations, personal data predictors led all the rest. Their average correlations with criteria of trainability and proficiency were 0.44 and 0.41, respectively. The writer selected seventy-two biodata studies on which he felt otherwise unable to comment and sorted them twice—once with respect to the criteria the inventories were designed to predict, and again with respect to the stated or implied selection function to be served. (Results at right.)

Since differences between companies, instruments, and criteria tend to attenuate results, it is instructive to examine criterion validities within a company where such differences are usually smaller. Thus, in The Standard Oil Company (N.J.) studies (Vol. II, 1962b), the following data were obtained: (1) in ten studies with skilled craftsmen and applicants a biodata form showed a median correlation of 0.45 with a criterion usually consisting of multiple alternation rankings on overall job performance; (2) in two studies of Engineering and Technical Personnel a biodata form showed correlations of 0.30 and 0.27 with the preceding cri-

n	Criterion to be predicted	$av.r_v$
17	sales success (ten life and casualty)	0.35
12	performance in clerical or office jobs	0.48
12	mixed criteria of military performance	*
	six pilot selection and training	
	two courts martial or incipient criminality	
10	high-level talent and/or creativity	0.48
6	managerial performance or potential	*
4	factory jobs	*
3	MBAs, leadership, and earnings	*
3	credit risk	0.62
2	vehicle drivers	*
3	misc.	*
72		

n	Selection function to be served
35	positive; interest in high job performance
18	positive; interest in survivors versus non-survivors
11	positive; interest in advancements, salary increases, etc.
8	negative; interest in segregation of poor performers or nonperformers
72	

* Data either inappropriate, not in correlational form, too limited, or too heterogeneous.

terion; (3) in studies of commercial-type office personnel a biodata form showed a median correlation of 0.40 with alternation rankings on overall job performance; (4) a biodata form for supervisors correlated 0.43 and 0.38 with the same ranking criterion; (5) in fifteen studies, a biodata form from the Early Identification of Management Potential (EIMP) project showed a median correlation of 0.35 with various criteria of managerial success.

Five individual studies seem worthy of a brief comment either because the criteria are of current interest or because the format and findings are unusual. (1) Baehr et al. (1968) found a Personal History Index one of the best of a large battery of measures directed at the prediction of police patrolman performance ratings and tenure. She also found prediction better within majority and minority groups than across all Ss, and better than average within selected job performance defined subsets of Ss. (2) Plag and Goffman (1967) found that, beyond the Armed Forces Qualification Test (AFQT), biodata variables enhanced the prediction of five criteria of the military effectiveness of naval trainees; indeed, although the AFQT score was significantly related to all five criteria, it was the prime predictor of only one. (3) Gantz et al. (1969) have reported finding the Biographical Inventory for Research and Scientific Talent (BIRST) of Smith et al. (1961) the best of a battery of heavily noncognitive predictors of promotion rate for a sample of 118 scientists and engineers. (4) In a study conducted by Richardson, Bellows, Henry, and Company (1971), a brief biodata form was administered to black, disadvantaged males ($n = 477$) and females ($n = 225$) from three cities who subsequently received job placement through their State Employment Service Offices. Prime criteria were tenure through three months and six months, and total correlations across cities ranged from 0.37 to 0.53. The results have clear social significance, and they extend the spectrum of valid biodata prediction down to very low educational and socioeconomic levels. Finally, (5) in a rare study of the construct validity of a biodata device Erickson et al. (1970) have reported comparing sixty high scoring scientists or engineers with fifty-seven low scorers across a broad spectrum of other measures of creativity, interest, motivation, and personality. Results indicate a close agreement between obtained results and expectations from theory; they also suggest that ratings may be less valid measures of creativity than BIRST scores.

Studies which relate scores on biodata instruments to various criteria of academic performance are numerous but have somewhat restricted relevance to present purposes. Only four which seem to argue to some potentially significant dimensions of trainability will, therefore, be noted here for their implications in that context. As long ago as 1940, Asher and Gray administered a thirty-item personal history blank to freshmen at the University of Kentucky and empirically keyed fifteen items to predict grade-point average. They found: (1) that biodata scores correlated only 0.07 with a measure of general mental ability; (2) that biodata score was a better predictor of "survival-corrected" grade average ($r = 0.40$); but (3) that mental ability score was a better predictor of uncorrected grade average ($r = 0.52$). Some twenty years later, Anastasi, Meade, and Schneiders (1960) broadened the criterion to include general academic desirability and adjustment expressed in a trichotomy. Cross-validation one year subsequent to key development produced the following validities: high versus low groups, 0.55; high versus average groups, 0.35; and average versus low groups, 0.26. The authors also noted that the biodata inventory appeared superior for this purpose to measures of aptitude, achievement, personality, and interest. More recently the Institute for Behavioral Research in Creativity (IBRIC, 1968) has published a manual for their biodata inventory, Alpha, in which they report correlations of 0.58 and 0.60 between their 300-item form J and the first semester grades of male and female freshmen, respectively, at Ohio University. Comparably, Prediger (1969) using a Project Talent sample of over 20,000 Ss obtained a cross-validated point-biserial correlation of 0.60 between score on a 246-item biodata inventory and a criterion of college attendance versus nonattendance. It may even be germane to note that DuBois's (1967) Test of Adult College Aptitude (TACA) designed for evening division students includes a first section of twenty-two biodata items along with a second section of fifty-four of the usual cognitive items, verbal and numerical. The point need not be labored further; that is, trainability in the fairly restricted senses implied can be predicted rather well from score on an empirically keyed biodata inventory.

If we shift our concern from selection to classification, and from simple to differential validity, it will be recognized that biodata offers many almost unique advantages. Biodata items tend to show very low intercorrelations, rationally sorted clusters tend to be relatively independent (Siegel, 1956), and oblique rotations of biodata factors tend to coincide almost perfectly with orthogonal rotations. When these characteristics are combined with high validity and the relative independence of scores on biodata scales from those of other measuring devices, particularly cognitive, the case for their potential utility in classification is impressive. Indeed, a study by Lunneborg (1968) suggests that biographical data have greater relative utility in the making of differential than in the making of absolute predictions. A number of investigators have contributed to our knowledge along the lines implied. Laurent (1951) found measurable differences in the early backgrounds of lawyers, engineers, and physicians. Levine and Zachert (1951) reported eight keys on a 125-item biodata inventory to be good and unique predictors of grades in twenty-four Air Force technical schools. Albright and Glennon (1961) identified forty-three biodata items which discriminated petroleum research scientists oriented toward supervision from those desiring to remain in research—rewards equal. Morrison et al. (1962) factored three criteria and seventy-five discriminating biodata items which had been administered to 418 petroleum research scientists; they found substantial profile differences across the five resulting factors for Ss rated highly on either productivity or creativity versus those with a high "hard data" ranking on creativity.

A recent and compelling study is one by Baehr and Williams (1967), who administered a 150-item biodata form to an occupationally heterogeneous sample of 680 males. One hundred twenty-five items were factored by the principal axis procedure with subsequent rotations of the accepted factors to both an equamax criterion of orthogonal simple structure and a promax criterion of oblique simple structure. Ability of the fifteen oblique factors to discriminate the ten occupations was tested through application of an analysis of variance to the fifteen factor scores across the ten groups. Each factor showed some differences between pairs of occupations significant at or above the 5 percent level. The authors applied four reasonable criteria and concluded that eight factors showed substantial promise in the context of occupational classification. Clearly, coherent scores from biodata inventories do show great promise in the context of personnel classification.

Above and beyond the empirical fact that they are good predictors, many critical questions still surround the use of biodata inventories. First, we lack longitudinal evidence over substantial periods of time to indicate, as of 1971, that what S says he did in 1955 is really what he did. We do have a small bit of relevant evidence, but all too little. Keating, Paterson, and Stone (1950) reported on the validity of work history data obtained by interview in 1940–1942 and independently checked. Although, in correlational terms, the validities were very high—0.90 to 0.98—the vehicle was not biodata, the reports were obtained in a counseling context and the variables concerned were those subject to direct check. Similarly, Mosel and Cozan (1952) checked records of applications for employment and found high agreement between applicant claims and verifications by past employers on weekly wages, duration of employment and job duties. All correlations save one were 0.90 or over. Validity was not a function of either time span or sex, but wages were less accurately stated than was duration of employment, where both refer to recent jobs. It is apparent on examining this area of vital concern that we must plan and conduct longitudinal studies on the validity and accuracy of our basic data, and that we must do so at the earliest possible opportunity.

Second, pleased with good validity co-efficients, we have tended to ignore some of the potential artificialities of our data. Only a few writers have been really critical. Brumback (1969) has revisited the con-tamination issue and noted that, if a biodata form is being used to predict a rating cri-terion, the latter may be contaminated by either real information or stereotypes de-rived from the former. The study of item faking and objectionability by Larsen et al. (1967) has been priorly reported. Klein and Owens (1965) conducted a study on the same topic in which they demonstrated that items validated against a subjective, "trans-parent criterion," like ratings, are more likely to be fakable than those validated against an objective, "hard data" criterion. Thus, college interviewers instructed to re-spond to a biodata inventory like creative engineers tend to select responses relating to rated rather than to "patent index" cre-ativity. Some halo of good general impres-sion onto specific traits seems to be implied. Although the issue is clearly broader than biodata, Hughes, Dunn, and Baxter (1956) have shown how "leaking" tips to applicants can progressively erode the validity of a weighted application blank used in the selec-tion of life insurance agents. Or, on yet another theme, the IBRIC manual for bio-data form Alpha (1968) states a relatively consistent finding in concurrent studies; that is, the best key, predictively, is one based upon items which reflect self-confidence. Such items tend to generalize across both criteria and studies and to emerge in the form of first factors from factor analyses (see Thomson & Owens, 1964). Is this good or bad? If it indicates some generalization of validity, it is clearly good. If, on the other hand, it means only that one who is successful on a job comes to know it and to be more confident as a result, then it is bad; and correlations based on it are spu-rious, since the job applicant could not have such confidence prior to his job experience.

In any event, it is clear that we must devote the same attention to possible artifacts of biodata response that we have already in-voked in the evaluation of other varieties of questionnaires.

Third, an interesting issue concerns the robustness of biodata prediction and structure across cultures; age, race, and sex groups; and companies. With respect to the first, Cassens (1966) factor analyzed sixty-two scaled biodata items directed at the early identification of management potential (EIMP). Ss were 105 North Americans working in the United States, seventy-four North Americans working in Latin Amer-ica, and 382 Latin Americans from five countries. A Spanish translation of the items was used with the Latin American Ss. Ten factors were identified, nine of which were common to all three groups. This factor stability was achieved in spite of shifts in item loadings. A further exploration of Cas-sens's third group was conducted by Frye (1967), who computed factor scores for each S on each of five factors. He entered these into successive analyses of variance with two criteria of classification—job function and country. After obtaining four significant interactions out of five, Frye concluded that the structure of an organization determines who will rise to the executive level, but that the characteristics of persons who reach this level are affected by organizational assign-ment as well as country. He agreed with Cassens on the desirability of characterizing Ss and groups with factor scores as opposed to item responses.

With a somewhat different purpose in mind, Laurent (1970) administered four questionnaires, including two biodata forms already empirically validated on 443 United States managers, to 800 employees in three European countries. All sigmas were sig-nificantly larger and all means save one higher in the European samples. Of special interest is the fact that one biodata form, which had correlated 0.44 with a criterion of success in the United States, correlated 0.55, 0.59, and 0.61 with a comparable criterion in the European sample. Two of the differences represented are statistically significant. Explanations are not easily come by; Laurent feels that biodata must be assessing basic, rather culture-free characteristics. The larger European sigmas may also reflect less test sophistication or a more highly stratified society.

Schmuckler's (1966) purpose was to evaluate the stability of biodata dimensions across age groups. His Ss were 439 middle management executives from a large international petrochemical company. At testing, 166 were under age twenty-five, 206 were between twenty-five and thirty, and 117 were thirty or older. His biodata blank consisted of sixty-two scaled items, and he employed a principal components analysis with an orthogonal rotation to factor the data. Eleven factors were identified; ten were common to the two youngest groups and the eleventh was unique to the oldest. In general, similar factor structures were identified for the three age groups, but the specific items loading on a factor varied from sample to sample as did the factor loadings. In a somewhat more empirical vein, Rawls and Rawls (1968) identified 110 of 179 biodata items which discriminated thirty more versus thirty less successful executives of a southern utility company. Among sixty male college students chosen for comparable personality profile and curriculum, ninety-nine items discriminated apparent student leaders from the balance. Of these 110 and ninety-nine items, eighty-seven discriminated both groups. Such a finding clearly implies both the age stability of items and the possibility of selecting college seniors with management potential. In this same context, Kirkpatrick (1968), after an interval of five years, readministered an eleven-page weighted application blank to 324 of an original 1,129 chamber of commerce applicants for executive positions. The original criterion had been a forced-choice rating of job performance. In spite of a shift to a dollar criterion, the author found (1) that the old key was still valid; and (2)

that the construction of a new thirty-five-item key would involve only the dropping of four "old items" and the adding of four "new ones."

A number of investigators are currently concerned with the question of bias in testing. A study by Sparks (1965a) is of particular interest because he used a biodata inventory to predict scores on a series of five cognitive tests normally employed in personnel selection. The criterion is, thus, unbiased in the sense that it is objective. Ss were applicants for a given job with a large, southern oil refinery; 517 were classified as white and ninety-one as Negro. Although all pairs of mean test scores obtained by the two groups were significantly different, correlations between biodata scores and test scores did not differ significantly for the two ethnic groups. To the same point, Cherry (1969) observed no moderator effects of race or socioeconomic status in predicting cognitive test score from a fifty-five-item biodata form. Although they are not drawn from industry, results reported by The Richardson Foundation (1968) are noteworthy because of the sample size involved. The Alpha inventory (IBRIC, 1968) was administered to 8,321 white and 2,000 black North Carolina male high school students and a biserial correlation of -0.02 between race and inventory score obtained. In a subsample, this score correlated 0.65 and 0.40 with Grade Point Average (GPA) for whites and blacks, respectively. Thus, the small correlation with race is by no means attributable to generally poor prediction, although the fact of better prediction for the whites may argue for the desirability of differential keying, as noted by Baehr et al. (1968).

Owens (1971) and Schoenfeldt (1970b) administered an identical biodata form of 118 items to approximately 1,000 male college freshmen and 900 female college freshmen at a large southeastern university. Independent factor analyses of the items, by sex, resulted in the identification of fifteen interpretable factors in the female data and thirteen in the male data. (See Table 1.) An examination of common item loadings suggests that four factors are completely or nearly identical, that six others are quite similar, and that only five "female factors" and three "male factors" are reasonably characteristic of a single sex. If scores on the two sets of factors are used as multiple predictors of such objective "criteria" as other test scores, the one does about as well as the other. However, if subgroups are formed on the basis of the distances between factor score profiles, it appears most reasonable to identify twenty-three common pat-

TABLE 1
BIODATA FACTORS—MALE AND FEMALE COLLEGE STUDENTS

Factor Name—Males (n = 1,037)		Rank	% Variance
I.	Warmth of Parental Relationship	1	3.5
*II.	Emotional Maturity or Adjustment	17	1.2
III.	Intellectualism	4.5	2.3
IV.	Academic Achievement (Self-Perceived)	2.5	3.1
V.	Social Introversion	2.5	3.1
VI.	Scientific Interest	10	1.8
VII.	Socioeconomic Status	7	2.1
VIII.	Independence/Dominance	6	2.2
IX.	Parental Control versus Freedom (bipolar)	8	2.0
*X.	Literary-Historical Interest	11	1.6
XI.	Positive Academic Attitude	12.5	1.5
XII.	Sibling Friction	18	1.1
XIII.	Religious Activity	15.5	1.3
XIV.	Athletic Interest	4.5	2.3
XV.	Social Desirability	9	1.9
*XVI.	Family Size	19	0.9
*XVII.	Math Achievement (or Math-English Discrepancy)	12.5	1.5
*XVIII.	Interest in Vocational Courses	15.5	1.3
*XIX.	English Achievement	14	1.4
			36%

* Not used for subsequent subgrouping

Factor Name–Females (n = 897)		Rank	% Variance
I.	Warmth of Maternal Relationship	1	4.3
II.	Leadership (Social)	2	3.2
III.	Academic Achievement (Self-Perceived)	3	3.1
IV.	Parental Control versus Freedom (bipolar)	5	2.4
V.	Cultural-Literary Interests (Reading)	6	2.0
VI.	Scientific-Artistic Interest	9	1.8
VII.	Socioeconomic Status	4	2.6
VIII.	Expression of Negative Emotions (Anger)	11	1.7
*IX.	T.V. (Daytime)	16	1.4
X.	Athletic Participation	7	1.9
XI.	Conformity to Female Role	9	1.8
XII.	Maladjustment	9	1.8
XIII.	Popularity with Opposite Sex	12.5	1.6
*XIV.	Math versus English	14.5	1.5
XV.	Positive Academic Attitude	14.5	1.5
*XVI.	Only Child	18	1.1
*XVII.	Language Achievement	19	1.0
XVIII.	Daddy's Girl	17	1.3
XIX.	Social Maturity	12.5	1.6
			38%

* Not used for subsequent subgrouping

terns in the male data versus fifteen in the female. Somewhat circularly, the female subgroups are not discriminated as well by the factors as the male.

Moving on from an evaluation of the influences of age, race, and sex to the possible influence of company, a study by Buel (1966) is germane. In brief, he took fifty-nine empirically keyed items from a study of physical scientists in a research laboratory by Smith et al. (1961), and introduced them into a 118-item biodata form administered under his cognizance to research personnel in a major pharmaceutical research and manufacturing organization (Buel, 1965). Original criteria had been creativity and productivity, and validity coefficients had ranged from 0.52 to 0.61. Of the original fifty-nine items, fifty were significantly related to criteria of the second study. Buel classified these into those requiring previous experience (nine) and those requiring none (forty-one). He then related each to patents, publications, and forced-choice supervisory ratings as criteria. Validities ranged from 0.34 to 0.51, with the exception of one r of 0.57 for total key versus a forced distribution criterion of creativity, and one insignificant r of 0.14 for the "no previous experience" items versus the supervisory rating criterion.

All in all, the available evidence would seem to suggest that the major dimensions of biodata response are quite stable across cultures, age, race, and sex groups, and companies.

RELIABILITY

Any question regarding the reliability of biodata inventories or scales is a subject for equivocation. The intrinsic correlations between biodata items are very low. Therefore, a device involving selections of items which result from empirical keying, and have in common only their agreement with a given criterion, will have to be of considerable length to be reliable. On the other hand, items which correlate highly with a common factor or a common core of items may be expected to compose brief scales of quite satisfactory reliability. For example, the IBRIC manual (1968) for biodata form Alpha reports retest reliabilities of 0.82 to 0.88 for ninth grade students in a North Carolina junior high school. The keys were empirical and directed at the prediction of academic performance and creativity. Number of items scoring is not specified, but means approximating 100 imply that it is substantial. Similarly, Chaney (1964) readministered an eighty-two-option form to forty-nine male college students who had received the first administration nineteen months earlier. He obtained a retest estimate of 0.85. By contrast, Baehr and Williams (1967) report K-R twenty estimates for factorial scales of four to thirteen items which range from 0.43 to 0.76. Ss were a vocationally heterogeneous sample of 680 males. Comparably Bryson (1969), who employed factorial scales of five high-loading items each, obtained average retest estimates over a one-week interval approximating 0.90. Subjects were forty college males.

NOMOLOGICAL NET

It is entirely appropriate to wish to allocate biodata to some position within the network of variables which constitutes the measurement domain. The task, however, is not singular but plural, since biodata is not *one* measure of *one* dimension but multiple measures of multiple dimensions. Thus, one must first decide the essential dimensionalities and then decide how each relates to some of the key variables in the domain. Hopefully, all will recognize the difficulties inherent in this undertaking; the biodata dimensions are not ultimates, marker or reference variables of choice do not obtrude themselves, and relationships observed are conditioned by the characteristics of the Ss to whom both instruments are administered, to name a few.

In any event, the first task, that of identifying biodata dimensions, may be substantially simplified by discarding results obtained through the factoring of only criterion valid items. If computer capability restricts one to a small matrix, it is clearly more profitable to factor valid than presumably invalid items. However, just as clearly, this procedure results in a non-representative selection of items from the total biodata domain. Happily, there are at least two recent investigations in which the selection of items to be factored was either quasi-random or systematic. Owens[3] (1968) selected and developed items for a biodata inventory in order to fill a matrix defined by developmental input variables and types of prior experiences on one axis and by such modifying dimensions as noxity, eucity, and complexity of experience on the other. A pool of some 2,000 continuum-type items resulted, and this was reduced by successive stages involving both rational and statistical analysis to 659, 389, and 275 items (see Bryson, 1969). This last represented the largest single matrix the investigators could factor with the computer capability available to them. These items were administered to a sample of 1,037 freshman males and 897 freshman females at a southeastern state university. The resulting matrices of item intercorrelations were factored separately for the two sexes by the method of principal axes (see Schoenfeldt, 1970a). Unities were entered on the diagonals in order that a profile of component scores, rather than estimated factor scores, might ultimately be obtained for each S. In each case, all factors with roots larger than 1.00 were extracted and three rotations to an orthogonal varimax criterion of simple structure were examined (Kaiser, 1958). In both instances, application of the usual criteria recommended a solution involving no more than nineteen factors accounting for 36 percent of the variance in the male data and for a corresponding 38 percent in the female data. Six factors in the former and four in the latter were discarded as ambiguous, overly abbreviated, or inappropriate to subsequent

purposes, leaving the thirteen male and fifteen female factors already referred to in Table 1.

The second recent factor analysis of "criterion-free" items is the one by Baehr and Williams (1967) already commented upon in the context of classification uses of biodata. Of the fifteen primary factors identified by them, the authors felt that the first eight "offer the most potential for operational use." It is of considerable interest to compare these factors derived from different items, administered to Ss both older and with occupational experience, to those of Table 1. The Baehr and Williams factors follow:

1. *School Achievement:* this factor contains items implying both academic success and positive academic attitudes. It seems closely related to both male Factors 4 and 11 of Table 1.

2. *Higher Educational Achievement:* this factor could have no counterpart in the prior analysis because it relates to the holding of a bachelor's degree, a job, etc.

3. *Drive:* the authors defined this factor as inner drive to be outstanding, attain high goals, supervise others, and achieve advancement. Male Factor 8 from the prior analysis seems to contain the earlier hallmarks of these characteristics.

4. *Leadership and Group Participation:* this dimension is defined as a desire to contact others as shown in memberships and organized activities. Male Factor 15 from the prior analysis involves many of the same connotations and Factor 5 many opposite ones.

5. *Financial Responsibility:* this factor deals with financial status and the handling of finances. Male Factor 7 from Table 1 is directly comparable.

6. *Early Family Responsibility:* this factor represents an "own family" orientation which could have no direct counterpart among college freshmen.

7. *Parental Family Adjustment:* as implied, this factor is related to a happy parental home experience. Male Factors 1, 9,

---

[3] With the assistance of Dr. M. J. Driver.

and 12 from the prior analysis contain more specific dimensions of this sort.

8. *Situational Stability:* this factor has specific reference to mid-life occupational stability which college freshmen clearly could not have experienced.

It is, of course, true that a rational comparison of factors is not definitive. On the other hand, a rather striking disagreement between these two analyses would not be entirely surprising, and such disagreement does not seem to emerge. If they are accepted as reasonably representative of the kinds of dimensions which are identified in the factorial study of biodata, a question remains as to their correlates in other cognitive and noncognitive measurement domains. Data of this sort are implied by, but not made explicit in, the report on assessment of patrolmen by Baehr et al. (1968). Owens (1971), on the other hand, administered a number of reference or marker variables to his Ss and correlated each of them with each biodata factor in the context of predicting the former from the latter. These correlations appear in Tables 2 and 3, with the exception of the biodata factor correlations with selected and representative scales of the Strong Vocational Interest Blank which appear in Table 4. Two characteristics of the data in these tables seem noteworthy. First, most of the substantial relationships seem plausible and appear to "make sense"; and, second, the typical multiple R is of substantial magnitude and does not compare badly with similar estimates of the correlation between predicted and obtained academic average. Clearly, biodata is a complex vehicle, related to, and capable of predicting quite well, a broad spectrum of scores on a wide variety of other measures.

PLACE IN PSYCHOLOGY

Research involving biodata has been subject to more or less constant criticism on the basis that quite good prediction is achieved, but that it is accompanied by modest, if existent, gains in understanding. There has also appeared to be a not unreasonable feeling that research in this area has been somewhat insular, neither seeking nor defining its relationship to the larger body of psychology. Thus Guilford (1959) has quite properly observed that biodata research has been characterized by an empirical shotgun approach to prediction, largely devoid of both theory and generality. Similarly, Dunnette (1962) reviewed selected biodata applications to the problem of predicting managerial and executive success and stressed the need for moving beyond simple prediction to a greater emphasis on the finding of causal relationships. Closer to the position of Guthrie (1944), and somewhat antecedent to that of the writer, Dailey (1960) has expressed the view that biodata captures a relatively direct representation of that everyday behavior of the individual which constitutes the essential criterion for both assessment and measurement. He goes on to recognize the need for a systematic approach to the interpretation and use of biodata. Against this backdrop of some uneasiness, criticism, and dissatisfaction, the writer would propose that biodata be regarded as providing a postmortem view of the development of the individual—an inverted pyramid of many recent and a few remote events the validity of which is limited chiefly by the insight of its author and by the memory and intention of the respondent.

If we adopt this view of biodata as a measure of prior experience, we can immediately establish one functional relationship with the broader domain of measurement. One of our most basic measurement axioms holds that the best predictor of what a man *will do* in the future is what he *has done* in the past. The criterion validity of biodata, which directly implements this axiom, is thus quite in accord with expectation. A corollary of interest and significance would hold that Ss who have behaved similarly in the past should continue to behave similarly in the future. If this corollary of the axiom is correct, and we now have statistical methods

TABLE 2

RELATIONSHIP OF BIODATA FACTORS TO SCORES ON REFERENCE VARIABLES ("Betas" and Rs)

Reference Battery Variables	Biographical Factors — Males									
	Warmth of Parental Relationship	Academic Achievement	Social Introversion	Athletic Interest	Pseudo-Intellectualism	Aggressive/Independence (Verbal)	SES	Parental Control vs Freedom	Positive Adjustment Response Bias	Scientific Interest
Academic Achievement										
High School GPA		653								
SAT. V		170	184			257				
SAT. M		158					165			
SAT. Total		182	180			193	168			
Social Attitude										
Radical vs Conservative	-202					295				
Tender vs Tough Minded										
F Scale										
Direct F	213		190			-170			-154	
Reverse F	115									
Total F	244		193			-175			-150	
Crown Marlowe										
Social Desirability									297	190
Rotter's										
Internal vs External									-187	
Purdue Values Inventory										
Cognitive Values						352				203
Social Religious Conform.	317		194			-195		-157	-177	
Economic Values			243			-200				
Personal Goals										
Physical Goals	195		-192	522						
Short-Term Goals			-154						-144	
Long-Term Goals						193				
Emotional Reactions										
Positive Emotionality					129				-124	
Negative Emotionality					258				-345	
Inhibition	-148		129							
Exposure			-160			236			-187	
General Outlook Inventory										
Integrative Complexity			-165		207	453				
Conceptual Simplicity					177				-342	
Hierarchical Complexity			-180			273			-153	
Maudsley Personality Invent.										
Extraversion			-605	183		162				
Neuroticism									-474	

Note: p, p^2 and p_c refer to the unbiased estimates of rho, rho-squared, and rho cross-validated respectively. The formulas for these estimates were provided by Claudy (1969).

ALL NUMBERS ARE EXPRESSED IN THOUSANDTHS.

Positive Academic Attitude	Religious Activity	Sibling Friction	Emotional Maturity or Adjustment	Literary-Historical Interest	Family Size	Math Achievement	Interest in Vocational Courses	English Achievement	R	R^2	ρ	ρ^2	ρ_c
				256	-161	-156	160	146	725	525	718	515	712
									604	365	594	352	585
				362					536	287	523	272	510
							177		510	260	496	245	482
	-191								514	264	500	248	486
	297		139						429	184	410	166	391
	127								472	223	456	206	440
									248	061	208	041	167
			-150						501	251	486	235	472
199		246							566	320	554	306	543
-154									355	125	331	107	306
210	264		166						543	295	531	280	519
211									647	418	638	406	630
						-192	-177		538	289	525	274	512
									624	390	615	377	606
									316	100	287	081	258
									258	066	220	046	182
									293	086	261	066	229
									512	262	498	246	484
									296	088	265	068	233
									385	148	363	130	341
			-155						597	357	587	343	577
									549	301	536	286	524
158									483	234	468	217	453
-161									692	479	685	468	678
									593	352	583	338	573

Multiple Correlation

TABLE 3

RELATIONSHIP OF BIODATA FACTORS TO SCORES ON REFERENCE VARIABLES ("Betas" and Rs)

Reference Battery Variables	Biographical Factors — Females									
	Warmth of Maternal Relationship	Social Leadership	Academic Achievement	SES	Parental Control vs Freedom	Cultural vs Literary Interest	Athletic Participation	Scientific/Artistic Interest	Conformity to Female Role	Maladjustment
Academic Achievement										
High School GPA			602	-177						
SAT. V			282			253	-289			
SAT. M			248							
SAT. Total			308			161	-259			
Social Attitude										
Radical vs Conservative	-162					215			-192	
Tender vs Tough Minded		158							173	
F Scale										
Direct F						-158			148	
Reverse F										
Total F						-185			185	
Crown Marlowe										
Social Desirability										-268
Rotter's										
Internal vs External										176
Purdue Values Inventory										
Cognitive Values		181				323		217		
Social Religious Conf.	265					-225			291	
Economic Values						-191	184			
Personal Goals										
Physical Goal		204					530	179		
Short-Term Goals						-119				
Long-Term Goals		175								151
Emotional Reactions										
Positive Emotionality		115						117		
Negative Emotionality					175				181	263
Inhibition								180		
Exposure		197			157					213
General Outlook Inventory										
Integrative Complexity		285				291		268		
Conceptual Simplicity									224	164
Hierarchical Complexity	166	163								
Maudsley Personality Invent.										
Extraversion		396	-170	180						-364
Neuroticism										532

Note: p, p^2 and p_c refer to the unbiased estimates of rho, rho-squared, and rho cross-validated respectively. The formulas for these estimates were provided by Claudy (1969).

ALL NUMBERS ARE EXPRESSED IN THOUSANDTHS.

Expression of Negative Emotions	Social Maturity	Popularity with Opposite Sex	Positive Academic Attitude	Daddy's Girl	T.V. (Daytime)	Math vs English	Only Child	Language Achievement	Multiple Correlation				
									R	R^2	ρ	ρ^2	ρ_c
						194			722	521	715	510	708
		-258							616	379	605	365	594
		-211				309			517	268	502	250	487
		-278							590	348	578	333	566
					-160		-150		491	241	474	223	457
		-161		185					444	197	425	178	405
									402	162	379	142	356
				108					216	047	162	024	107
									444	197	424	178	404
-270	180		183						562	316	549	300	536
					148				356	126	328	106	301
	228								529	280	514	263	500
-161			215		177				620	385	610	370	599
		196				161			449	201	429	183	410
									633	400	623	386	613
		160							319	102	288	081	256
									346	120	318	099	289
									262	069	221	047	179
170									470	221	452	203	434
					-191				405	164	383	145	360
									460	212	442	193	423
	265						-188		621	385	610	371	600
202									474	224	456	206	438
	265		225						497	247	480	229	464
164	192	193			150				720	518	713	507	706
176					193				657	431	648	418	639

TABLE 4
RELATIONSHIP OF BIODATA FACTORS TO SELECTED SCALES OF THE STRONG VIB ("Betas" and Rs)

Biodata Factors   Males

SVIB Occupational Group	Parental Warmth	Intellectualism	Academic Achievement	Social Introversion	Scientific Interest	Socioeconomic Status	Independ./Domin.	Parental Control	Positive Academic Attitude	Sibling Friction	Religious Activity	Athletic Interest	Social Desirability	Multiple R	Cross-Validated R
Physician I				.133	.477								.131	.50	.50
Physicist II		-.136		.249	.435		-.088		-.152			-.195	.105	.56	.58
Air Force Officer III		.095			.263	-.076					.105	.240		.38	.37
Carpenter IV		-.239	-.159	.160	.185	-.169	-.305		-.271			.106		.55	.50
Social Wkr. V		.212	.105	-.158	-.264	.107	.317		.187	.077		-.115		.53	.48
Musician Performer VI		-.088	-.136				.108	.091	-.190			-.297		.40	.35
CPA Owner VII		.102	.190		-.215	.077	.141		.168		-.140			.39	.23
Purchasing Agent VIII	.101		-.093		.134	-.113	-.306			-.125	-.089	.233	-.122	.46	.41
Real Estate Sales IX			-.086	-.248	-.483						-.166	.220	-.077	.59	.49
Author-Journalist X	-.083				-.108	.121	.114		-.105		-.132	-.218		.34	.35
Pres. Mfg. Firm XI				-.110	-.217				-.084	-.115	-.138			.31	.20
Com. Rec. Ad'n. XII		.228	.089	.299	-.301		.240		.209	.099	.093	.233	-.091	.59	.56

and a computer capability to evaluate it, then we shall in many senses be reinterpreting the time-honored experimentalists' identification of individual differences with error variance. Instead, it will be our view that such variance is composed of three components: (1) mean biodata-defined subgroup differences based upon distinctive patterns of prior experience; (2) within subgroup individual differences, per se; and (3) error, in the classical sense of random or "chance" variance.

Over the past several years the writer[4] has been employing biodata in accordance with the foregoing rationale. This research has been guided and integrated by the evalu-

ation of a conceptual model (see Figure 1) which has its roots in the priorly enunciated axiom and corollary. The figure is in some senses a flow chart, and it can be most easily explained in terms of the operations which it implies. Accordingly, in overview, the circle at the left represents a large sample of Ss—say all freshmen at a given university. These Ss are first administered a comprehensive biodata form designed to cover the salient dimensions of their prior experience. The dimensions are identified via a principal axis factor analysis with unities on the diagonals, and each S is identified by a profile of his component scores across the several factorial dimensions. Distances between these profiles compose a D^2 matrix (Cronbach & Gleser, 1953; Mahalanobis, 1936) from which Ss are hierarchically grouped (Ward & Hook, 1963) into "families" of

_____
[4] Major assistance has been provided by Drs. Rebecca Bryson, J. B. Bryson, M. J. Driver, P. R. Pinto, and L. F. Schoenfeldt.

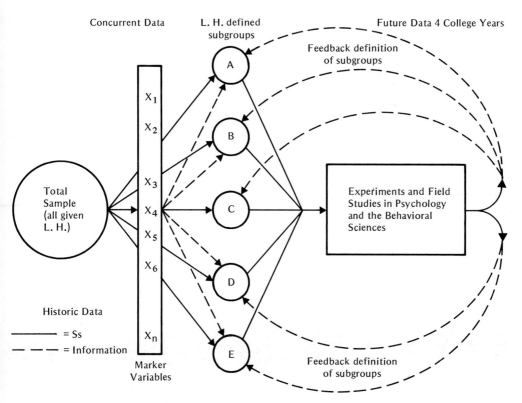

Figure 1.   A conceptual model for biodata research.

closely similar profiles representing similar patterns of prior experience. These subsets or families are represented by the smaller circles lettered A through E. The tendency of Ss within these subsets, who have exhibited internally similar and externally differential prior behaviors, to continue to so behave in the future is evaluated in three ways. First, the letters X_l to X_n represent marker or reference variable tests selected as useful in characterizing the subgroups. The distinctiveness of subgroup behaviors is initially evaluated in terms of their tendency to score differentially across this spectrum of reference measures. Second, the entire college careers of these Ss may be regarded as being composed of a series of potential field studies in which the differential behaviors of the subsets are revealed and evaluated. Thus, differences may be expected in academic achievement, in major chosen, in activities selected, in real and perceived health, in disciplinary infractions recorded, etc. Third, selected subgroups may be hypothesized to differ in their performances in a variety of controlled, experimental situations. These situations are so chosen as to cover the major behavioral domains, that is, sensation, perception, learning, memory, etc., and to represent experimental contexts in which prior experience may reasonably be expected to play a role. Finally, feedback from the three contexts is collated and summarized, by subgroup, to provide an ever-expandable taxonomy of subset behaviors.

Given the foregoing outline, an attempt may now be made to provide a few of the specifics subsumed by it. Systematic development and administration of the biodata inventory have been priorly described under the heading of Nomological Net. Factors derived appear in Table 1. However, certain methodological matters not previously dealt with seem to warrant discussion. Subgrouping of Ss for pattern of prior experience was accomplished as follows: Each S was represented by a profile of his (or her) virtually uncorrelated factor scores across the thirteen

(or fifteen) factors. Distances between each profile and each other were summarized in terms of the D^2 statistic of Cronbach and Gleser (1953). The hierarchical grouping technique of Ward and Hook (1963) was then applied to the resulting matrix of D^2 values. Because of computer limitations it was necessary to break the total sample down into subsamples, or blocks, and then to match subgroups across blocks. This was accomplished by combining from the separate blocks those subgroups which were essentially collinear in the discriminant space of the biodata. A recognized deficiency in the grouping procedure has been that it is sequential, and that an individual remains in the subgroup to which he was originally assigned even though the group average may migrate away from him. Special procedures were, therefore, developed to optimize the fit of each individual to a subgroup, or to remove him from the structure entirely if he either failed to fit any group well (an isolate $-<5\%$) or fitted more than one group equally well (an overlap $->20\%$). Because of these ambiguities, approximately 25 percent of Ss in the present sample were not ultimately assigned to a subgroup. Clearly, the seriousness of an assignment error in the overlap case depends upon the similarity of the groups overlapped. This similarity is now being evaluated in terms of (1) the D^2 distance between the two or more subgroups in question, and (2) the criterion similarities in the given subgroup behaviors. If the differences are relatively minor, overlap Ss may be assigned to the most proximal group with an attendant and drastic reduction in ungrouped cases.

Before proceeding to the central question of the behavioral meaning of subgroup membership, it seems vital to comment briefly on subgrouping as an inferential procedure. Here Schoenfeldt (1966) has demonstrated that hierarchically grouping Ss in accordance with the paradigm described does produce substantially parallel subgroups in two independent samples. More recently, he has pursued three designs for cross-validating subgroup assignment (see Schoenfeldt, 1970b). First, the freshmen of 1970 were allocated to the subgroups of 1968, with the result that there was a small loss of fit; 67 percent were assignable to subgroups in 1970 instead of the 75 percent of 1968. Second, the subgroups of 1968 and the parallel subgroups of 1970 were each ranked for the common criterion variable of mean predicted grade-point average. The between-ranks correlation was 0.89 ($p < .001$) for the males and 0.73 ($p < .01$) for the females. Third, two canonical discriminant analyses were run, one for each sex, employing SAT-V, SAT-M, and high school GPA to maximally differentiate the biodata subgroups of 1968. In each case two significant canonical dimensions emerged and were identified as high school grade point average and SAT-V; the two variables accounted for 78 percent of the variance in the male

analysis and for 73 percent in the female analysis. In Figures 2 and 3 (female and male) the dots indicate the locations of the 1968 group centroids in the two-dimensional discriminant space, and the squares the locations of the parallel centroids of 1970. (Two male groups and one female group were deleted because they failed to replicate.) As an estimate of the magnitude of displacement of the groups of 1970 from those of 1968, it should be noted that one change of quadrant exists in the female data and four in the male. The rule, however, is a relatively small change in location indicating substantial stability of the subgroup structure. Finally, Anderson (1972) conducted an analysis of data derived from 5,370 Ss on three different university campuses. Essentially, subgroups were identified in the data composite and their differential affinities for institution were examined. In accordance with expectation, Ss from the Universities

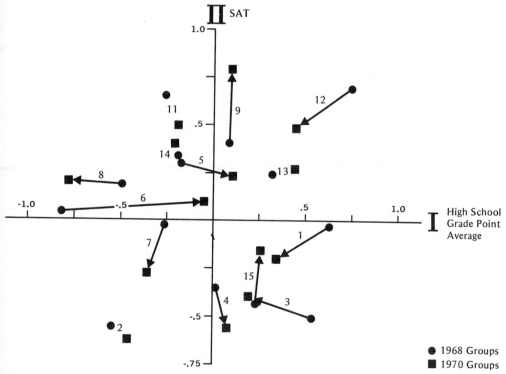

Figure 2.   Female group centroids in discriminant space.

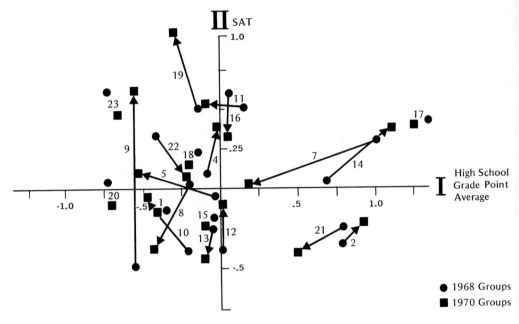

Figure 3.   Male group centroids in discriminant space.

of Georgia and Kentucky overlapped extensively in their subgroup memberships, but students from Purdue overlapped the other two much less.

If we accept the foregoing evidence of the inferential meaning of subgrouping, we may then turn our attention to the question of the behavioral significance of subgroup membership. First then, Tables 5 and 6 will show that the subgroups do respond very differently to a broad spectrum of other tests, questionnaires and indexes *not* employed in their definition. Not shown are differences of the same sort across the various scales of the Strong VIB. The Reference Measures, which follow, are numbered to correspond with the numbers in the tables.

1. High school grade point
2. SAT-Q
3. SAT-V
4. SAT-total
5. Radicalism
6. Tender-mindedness
7. Direct F
8. Reverse F
9. Total F
10. Social desirability
11. Externalization
12. Cognitive values
13. Social, religious conformity
14. Economic values
15. Physical goals
16. Short-term goals
17. Long-term goals
18. Positive emotionality
19. Negative emotionality
20. Inhibition
21. Exposure
22. Integrative complexity
23. Conceptual simplicity
24. Hierarchical simplicity
25. Extraversion
26. Neuroticism

Second, in the academic field study context subgroup differences have been demonstrated with great consistency. Sometimes selected subgroups and a prior hypothesis were involved, and sometimes all the subgroups and no such hypothesis. In any event, some examples of observed differences follow: differences in the proportion of "good" Rorschach responses (Frazer, 1971); differences in academic performance (Schoenfeldt, 1970b); differences in tested creativity (Halpin, 1972); differences in the tendency to under- or over-achieve (Klein, 1972); differences in pattern of vocational interests

TABLE 5

MAGNITUDES OF DIFFERENCES BETWEEN SUBGROUP MEANS ON REFERENCE MEASURES (MALES)[a]

Group	N	1	2	3	4	5	6	7	8	9	10	11[b]	12	13	14	15	16	17	18	19	20[b]	21	22	23	24	25	26
1	40	H							H																			
2	39	L	L		L																				H			
3	62			H		H	H	L		L				L		L				H	L		H	H	H	H	H	H
4	31			H	L																		L	L		L	H	H
5	25		H	H	L									H		H							H	L		L	H	
6	16	H	H	H	H	H	H	H		H	H																	
7	12			L	L	L		L	H	H													L	L	H	H	L	H
8	39	H	L																									
9	29					H		H		H					H				H	H		H		H		H	H	H
10	24		H	L	H	H	H	H		L													L	L	L			
11	20																	L				H		H				
12	39											H	H			L				L			L		L			
13	54										L														L			
14	26	H			H		H	H								L					H							
15	22															L								L				
16	22	H	H	H	H	H					H		H			H		H				L	L	H		L		
17	20		H	H	H							H	H													L		
18	19	L			H		H			L					L				H	H				L		H		
19	10	H				H	H			L						L						L		L		H	H	
20	36	L								L								L								H	L	L
21	22	H				L				L						L						L		L		L	L	H
22	30									L				L										L		H	H	L
23	21	L				H		L		L				L		L								L	L		H	

Total 658

[a] H = Group mean is more than .5 S.D. above grand mean.
L = Group mean is more than .5 S.D. below grand mean.
[b] Differences among subgroup means were significant, excepting variables 11 and 20.

TABLE 6
MAGNITUDES OF DIFFERENCES BETWEEN SUBGROUP MEANS ON REFERENCE MEASURES (FEMALES)[a]

Group	N	1	2	3	4	5	6	7[b]	8[b]	9	10	11	12	13	14	15	16	17	18	19	20	21	22	23	24	25	26
1	73	H																									
2	65	L	L		L																						
3	59	H																									
4	38															H											
5	47	L					H				L					L							L			L	H
6	41				L		L													H		H	L			L	H
7	56		L								H									L		L					
8	41				H	H							H	L							H		H	L			
9	22																			H	H		H	H			
10	35		H																				H			L	H
11	42	H	H										H	L	L												
12	20	H													L												
13	70													L		H		H				H					H
14	15																	H									
15	43																										H

Total 667

[a] H = Group mean is more than .5 S.D. above grand mean.
L = Group mean is more than .5 S.D. below grand mean.
[b] Differences among subgroup means were significant, excepting variables 7 and 8.

(Jones, 1970); differences in proportion of male homosexuals (Lewis & Schoenfeldt, 1972); differences in proportion of drug users (Strimbu & Schoenfeldt, 1972); differences in proportion of campus leaders (Boardman, 1972); differences in social desirability (which moderates the similarity-attraction), relationship (Jones, 1971), etc. As this is written, freshmen Ss of 1968, now seniors, have completed a so-called College Experience Inventory of eighty-five items, and preliminary analyses indicate that members of the differing subgroups tend to walk different pathways through the university (Feild, 1973).

Third, in the experimental domain, subgroups selected to address an hypothesis have been observed to differ in persistence with the motor method when learning the stylus maze (O'Neill, 1972); to differ in recall as a function of interest area (Helms, 1972); to differ in persuasibility (Hatcher, 1970); and to differ in social desirability, which serves as a moderator of the similarity-attraction relationship observed to be greater within subgroups (Bowditch, 1969). In addition, Hughes (1970) has reported a significant interaction between subgroup membership and frequency of usage in a verbal learning paradigm.

To date, the writer is aware of only three industrial studies utilizing the procedures outlined here; namely, those of Taylor, Ruda, and Pinto. Taylor (1968), through the courtesy of Paul Sparks at Humble Oil and Refining, obtained the responses of 444 male, managerial employees to the Richardson, Bellows, and Henry biodata form B. Using essentially the present methodology, he found that 84 percent of his salesmen in a primary sample of 222 came from three of nine subgroups. He then employed a minimum distance classifier to assign the remaining 222 to the subgroups of the primary sample. Within this cross-validation sample he found 83 percent of his salesmen in three parallel subgroups.

Ruda (1970) had 458 executives of a large midwestern oil company complete a 247-item personal history form. Top-level executives also ranked their subordinates' performances. All Ss were subgrouped employing the methods previously described and thirteen subgroups were identified. Distance from superior's to subordinate's subgroup was found to be negatively related to rated performance of subordinate. In addition, this distance measure of rater versus ratee similarity was found to moderate relationships between biodata dimensions themselves and rated subordinate performance.

In the study by Pinto (1970) a comprehensive biodata form, plus certain standardized tests, were administered to 2,060 salesmen. For purposes of analysis the sample was split into subsamples A and B. The Ss of subsample A were then subgrouped, and the Ss of subsample B were assigned to these subgroups with only a 10 percent loss in fit. Termination reports constituted the criterion, which was predicted via three models. In the first, other measures were employed to predict within biodata subgroup, but no moderator effects were observed. In the second, a multiple R generated in subsample A from the non-biodata predictors vanished on cross-validation in subsample B. However, in the third, the biodata subgroups showed clear differential affinities for the criterion, and the magnitudes of these affinities correlated 0.66 ($p < .01$) in subsamples A and B.

What important facts emerge from this brief review? First, persons who have behaved similarly in the past *do* tend to exhibit both similar concurrent and future behaviors. Second, confidence in the post hoc validity of biodata based subgrouping *does* seem justified; indeed, some 80 percent of our results to date are positive. It thus seems reasonable to assume, following Taylor, Ruda, and Pinto that subgroup membership *will* argue for a wide variety of differential behaviors of industrial moment and significance. How shall we then proceed?

The conceptual model discussed contains

provision for feedback from the behaviors of the subgroups to an ever-expanding compendium of these behaviors. Ultimately included should be such information as early background; pattern of test scores; academic achievements; choice of career; pattern of extracurricular activities; behavior in any controlled or experimental contexts; type of job held; ratings on a broad spectrum of job behaviors; community activities; promotion rate and channel, etc. Such a taxonomy of subgroup behaviors would be of interest and utility to persons in many branches of psychology. The experimentalist could be provided with background homogeneous subsets of Ss expected to exhibit somewhat more homogeneous behaviors than a random sample; an analog of the genetically pure strains of rats, or other laboratory animals, currently employed for a similar purpose. The social psychologist might be intrigued with whether intra-subgroup similarity is recognized and followed by attraction, a relationship potentially moderated by such variables as general social desirability. The student of measurement will see the differing patterns of antecedents of his Ss, how these argue for particular test and questionnaire scores, and may even add the variable of subgroup membership to his prediction equations. The developmental psychologist may wish to avail himself of an opportunity to test, with retrospective data, such major hypotheses as those of optimal input and behavioral consistency. Both the educational and the clinical psychologist will perceive a context in which to examine for the presence of a possible interaction between "kind of person," as defined by subgroup, and a treatment variable—instructional method in the one case and therapeutic method in the other. Indeed, quite outside of the field of psychology, the economist might wish to examine subgroup differences in spending patterns; the political scientist to study differential subgroup affinities for political philosophy; and the geographer to wonder whether or not there exists such an affinity of subgroup for the populations of isolated regions. The list could be extended but the point would remain the same—that is, the endeavor is an integrative one in which many fields of psychology, indeed of behavioral science, have a common stake.

INDUSTRIAL UTILITY

In order to maintain continuity, it seems appropriate to first discuss the utility of the approach involving the biodata-based subgrouping of Ss and then to expand to include a more catholic and less systematic view. Accordingly, the grouping approach potentially offers at least four types of industrial applications. First, it may be used in the selection context; clearly, the overlap of a subgroup and a criterion group represents an empirical probability. Second, the approach has relevance to personnel classification in general and to the maximum manpower context in particular. Here Schoenfeldt (1972) has carefully delineated a model which relates biodata subsets, viewed as kinds of persons, to kinds of jobs as derived from the Position Analysis Questionnaire of McCormick, Jeanneret, and Mecham (1969). Third, the grouping approach lends itself to an employee counseling application. Thus, an employee just beginning his career with a company could have his biodata profile matched with the mean profile of that subgroup of existing employees which his profile most closely resembles. In effect, this would predict for the subsequent behavior of the individual, all of the behavior already known to characterize the subgroup. The joint task of counsellor and counsellee would then be to plan intervention strategies where the projection proved unpalatable to either. Fourth, the grouping approach offers industry an opportunity to determine, through the administration of a biodata form requiring perhaps an hour, that subset to which an S most probably belongs. If the industrial correlates of subset membership have been comprehensively determined, the modal characteristics of the subset may reasonably be attributed to the individual, with the result that one hour of testing time could be made to provide a more comprehensive characterization of an S than a week spent in a well-organized assessment center. Clearly, the success of such a procedure faces at least two contingencies. First, the industry in question must administer the given biodata form to all, or a large sample, of their present employees, and must be prepared to follow this by finding the affinity of subgroup for each of a broad spectrum of criteria of performance. Second, the matching of individual biodata profile to subgroup mean profile must be reasonably accurate. This matter has been previously discussed.

At any rate, some of the more apparent advantages of the subgrouping approach are as follows:

1. It is enormously efficient measurement which confers upon the individual, on the basis of the administration of a single biodata form, all of the behavioral tendencies which are known to characterize that biodata subset in which he holds membership.

2. Preliminary evidence suggests that a number of criteria which are not very well predicted, directly, may be expected to have quite strong affinity for biodata subgroup. Thus, let us assume that some inverse of number of unexcused absences constitutes a criterion of "responsibility"; this variable itself has not been easy to predict, yet it does appear to have quite strong differential subset affinity. Evidence of this sort implies that subset membership, as a binary variable, should enter a number of multiple regressions of a criterion variable upon biodata scale predictors. Tesser (1971) has shown that this is indeed the case.

3. If several biodata subsets have affinity for the same criterion, there is presumptive evidence to suggest that the differences between them may represent stylistic differences in performance. Thus, Taylor (1968) found that three of his nine subsets of managerial personnel contained over 83 percent of the salesmen in his entire sample (base rate 31 percent). Interestingly enough, inspection of their characteristic responses implies that one is heavily saturated with once visible college athletes; one with Ss who show a college history of success in verbal activities and of elevation to elective offices, and one with highly motivated Ss who work longer and harder than their fellows. Implications for the study of managerial styles are readily apparent.

4. Since neither biodata items nor scales are empirically validated against a given criterion, the post hoc observation of subgroup affinity for criterion group (percent overlap) is, in this sense, an unbiased estimate which is subject to sampling fluctuation but not to the shrinkage customary in empirical studies.

5. It seems entirely possible that biodata will attract increasing attention in the larger context of organizational effectiveness. The "kinds of persons" on whom climate variables may be expected to impact differentially are well defined by biodata subsets.

6. A business or industry which commits itself to characterizing the subsets in terms of their common and differential criterion behaviors initiates a system which will grow more valuable as more data are accumulated and evaluated. Ultimately, the meaningfulness of a statement to the effect that John Jones belongs to subset X is as great as our knowledge of the behaviors which adhere to such subset membership.

To turn to a more eclectic view, biodata seems likely to be employed to serve many of the following purposes in the years immediately ahead.

1. With Equal Employment Opportunity Commission (EEOC) and Office of Federal Contract Compliance (OFCC) applying substantial deterrent pressures to industrial testing, biodata may be used either to predict test scores, and indirectly their criterion correlates, or to directly predict the criterion variables themselves. (See, for example, Sparks, 1965b; Harding et al., 1961.)

2. Under the pressures recognized in number 1 above, biodata may come into increasing prominence as a relatively race-and-culture-fair predictor.

3. In view of the fact that there are numerous biodata correlates of differential age changes in mental abilities (see Gilmer, 1963), it seems reasonable to anticipate a longitudinal study of cause and effect relationships. If the biodata-appraised characteristics are antecedent to the intellective changes, biodata could be used to predict which management candidates could be expected to display most intellectual growth, or least decline, subsequent to selection.

4. Because biodata has proven to be an excellent predictor of measured interests, job tenure, and choice behavior, it seems likely to find increasing use in the prediction of an expanded range of motivation-saturated criteria.

5. Biodata devices will undoubtedly continue to be particularly useful in discriminating among persons whose status argues that they must be relatively homogeneous with respect to mental ability, for example, scientists, executives, the creative, etc.

6. If subjects with similar biodata-defined backgrounds are of greater than average compatibility, then the efficiency of the work force may depend to a very important extent on discovering who should work with whom.

7. Because biodata scales tend to be of high validity, and because biodata items and both cluster and factor scales are characterized by very low intercorrelations, it is apparent that the substance of biodata lends itself uncommonly well to the construction of devices to fit the personnel classification function.

In summary, the predictions of Galton (1902) and Guthrie (1944) have been amply fulfilled. Past behavior, as recorded in background data, is indeed an excellent predictor of future behavior. What is new, strangely enough, is our recognition that it *is* precisely this past behavior or prior experience which scored autobiographical data primarily measures. Given this recognition, many new perspectives are possible. We can build conceptual models, and we can envision the role and place of biodata devices in the area of measurement and in the broader domains of psychology and the behavioral sciences. It is too early to definitively predict the shape of research to come, but it is not too early to note that the vistas are intriguing and the effort of great promise.

REFERENCES

Albright, L. E., & Glennon, J. R. Personal history correlates of physical scientists' career aspirations. *Journal of Applied Psychology,* 1961, 45, 281–284.

Allport, G. W. The use of personal documents in psychological science. *Social Science Research Council Bulletin,* 1942, No. 49.

Anastasi, A., Meade, M. J., & Schneiders, A. A. The validation of a biographical inventory as a predictor of college success. *Educational Testing Service,* 1960, V, 81 pp.

Anderson, B. B. An inter-institutional comparison on dimensions of student development: A step toward the goal of a comprehensive developmental-integrative model of human behavior. Unpublished doctoral dissertation, University of Georgia, Athens, 1972.

Anonymous. A method of rating the history and achievements of applicants for positions. *Public Personnel Studies,* 1925, 3 (7), 202–209. (Methods and data credited to Gertrude V. Cope.)

Asher, E. J., & Gray, F. E. University of Kentucky: Relation of personal history data to college success. *Journal of Educational Psychology,* 1940, 31, 517–526.

Baehr, M., & Williams, G. B. Underlying dimensions of personal background data and their relationship to occupational classification. *Journal of Applied Psychology,* 1967, 51, 481–490.

Baehr, M., Furcon, J. E., & Froemel, E. C. Psychological assessment of patrolman qualifications in relation to field performance. Washington, D.C.: Superintendent of Documents, US GPO, 1968.

Berkeley, M. H. A comparison between the empirical and rational approaches for keying a heterogeneous test. *USAF Human Resources Research Center Bulletin,* 1953, 53–54.

Boardman, W. K., Calhoun, L. G., & Schiel,

J. H. Life experience patterns and development of college leadership roles. *Psychological Reports,* 1972, 31, 333–334.

Bowditch, J. L. Biographical similarity and interpersonal choice. Doctoral dissertation, Purdue University, Lafayette, Ind., 1969.

Brumback, G. B. A note on criterion contamination in the validation of biographical data. *Educational Psychological Measurement,* 1969, 29 (2), 439–443.

Bryson, J. B. The dimensions of early human experience. In W. A. Owens (Chrmn.), *Developmental implications of biographical data.* Symposium presented at the meeting of the Southern Society for Philosophy and Psychology, Miami, April, 1969.

Buel, W. D. Biographical data and the identification of creative research personnel. *Journal of Applied Psychology,* 1965, 49, 318–321.

Buel, W. D. A note on the generality and cross-validity of personal history for identifying creative research scientists. *Journal of Applied Psychology,* 1966, 50, 217–219.

Buel, W. D. Personal communication, 1971.

Cassens, F. P. *Cross-cultural dimensions of executive life history antecedents.* Greensboro, N.C.: The Creativity Research Institute, The Richardson Foundation, 1966.

Chaney, F. B., & Owens, W. A. Life history antecedents of sales, research, and general engineering interest. *Journal of Applied Psychology,* 1964, 48, 101–105.

Cherry, R. L. Socioeconomic level and race as biographical moderators. *Dissertation Abstracts International,* 1969, 30 (4-B), 1937.

Clark, K. E., & Gee, H. Selecting items for interest inventory keys. *Journal of Applied Psychology,* 1954, 38, 12–17.

Claudy, J. G. An empirical investigation of small sample multiple regression and cross-validation. Unpublished doctoral dissertation, University of Tennessee, Knoxville, 1969.

Cronbach, L. J., & Gleser, G. Assessing similarity between profiles. *Psychological Bulletin,* 1953, 50, 456–473.

Dailey, C. A. The life history as a criterion of assessment. *Journal of Counseling Psychology,* 1960, 7, 20–23.

DuBois, P. H. Test of adult college aptitude (TACA). Manual for administration scoring and interpretation. *Research in Education (ERIC),* 1967, 2 (12), ED011985.

DuBois, P. H., Loevinger, J., & Gleser, G. C. The construction of homogeneous keys for a biographical inventory. *USAF Human Resources Research Bulletin,* 1952, 52–58.

Dunnette, M. D. Personnel management. *Annual Review of Psychology,* 1962, 13, 285–314.

England, G. W. *Development and use of weighted application blanks.* Dubuque, Iowa: William C. Brown, 1961.

Erickson, C., Gantz, B. S., & Stephenson, R. W. Logical and construct validation of a short form biographical inventory predictor of scientific creativity. Paper read before American Psychological Association, Miami, 1970.

Feild, H. S. Subgroup and individual differences in the quasi-actuarial assessment of behavior: A longitudinal study. Unpublished doctoral dissertation, University of Georgia, Athens, 1973.

Ferguson, L. W. The development of industrial psychology. In B. H. Gilmer (Ed.), *Industrial psychology.* New York: McGraw-Hill, 1961, 18–37.

Ferguson, L. W. *The heritage of industrial psychology.* Hartford: Author, 1962.

Ferguson, L. W. Economic maturity. *Personnel Journal,* 1967, 46 (1), 22–26.

Fleishman, E. A., & Berniger, J. Using the application blank to reduce office turnover. In E. A. Fleishman (Ed.), *Studies in personnel and industrial psychology.* Homewood, Ill.: Dorsey Press, 1967, 39–46.

Frazer, R. W. Differential perception of individuals subgrouped on the basis of biodata responses. Unpublished doctoral dissertation, University of Georgia, Athens, 1971.

Frye, R. *Analysis of patterns of life history antecedents of executives from different countries.* Greensboro, N.C.: The Creativity Research Institute, The Richardson Foundation, 1967.

Galton, F. *Life history album.* (2nd ed.) New York: Macmillan, 1902.

Gantz, B. S., Erickson, C., & Stephenson, R. W. Test prediction of promotion rate and job satisfaction for scientists and engineers. Paper read at California State Psychological Association, San Diego, 1969.

Ghiselli, E. E. *The validity of occupational aptitude tests.* New York: Wiley, 1966.

Gilmer, R. S. A factorial approach to the life history correlates of intellectual change. Unpublished doctoral dissertation, Purdue University, Lafayette, Ind., 1963.

Goldsmith, D. B. The use of the personal

history blank as a salesmanship test. *Journal of Applied Psychology,* 1922, 6, 149–155.

Gross, M. L. *The brain watchers.* New York: Random, 1962.

Guilford, J. P. *Psychometric methods.* (2nd ed.) New York: McGraw-Hill, 1954.

Guilford, J. P. *Personality.* New York: McGraw-Hill, 1959.

Guilford, J. P., & Lacey, J. I., Eds. Printed classification tests. *AAF Aviation Psychology Research Program Reports.* Washington, D.C.: GPO, 1947, No. 5

Guthrie, E. R. Personality in terms of associative learning. In J. McV. Hunt (Ed.), *Personality and the behavior disorders,* Vol. 1. New York: Ronald Press, 1944, 49–68.

Halpin, W. G. A study of the life histories and creative abilities of potential teachers. Unpublished doctoral dissertation, University of Georgia, Athens, 1972.

Harding, F. D., & Bottenberg, R. A. Effect of personal characteristics on relationships between attitudes and job performance. *Journal of Applied Psychology,* 1961, 45, 428–430.

Hatcher, J. C. Differential persuasibility: Subgrouping on the basis of experiential data. Unpublished master's thesis, University of Georgia, Athens, 1970.

Helmreich, R., Bakeman, R., & Radloff, R. The life history questionnaire: Prediction of performance in Navy diver training. University of Texas, Austin, Social Psychology Laboratory, Report 18, 1971.

Helms, W. Biodata subgroup differences in recall and clustering of interest area stimulus words. Unpublished master's thesis, University of Georgia, Athens, 1972.

Henry, E. R. (Chrmn.) *Research conference on the use of autobiographical data as psychological predictors.* Greensboro, N.C.: The Creativity Research Institute, The Richardson Foundation, 1966.

Highland, R. W., & Berkshire, J. R. A methodological study of forced choice performance rating. *Research Bulletin,* Human Resources Research Center, San Antonio, 1951, 51–59.

Hughes, J. F., Dunn, J. F., & Baxter, B. The validity of selection instruments under operating conditions. *Personnel Psychology,* 1956, 9, 321–324.

Hughes, M. J. Biodata subgroup differences in serial verbal learning. Unpublished doctoral dissertation, University of Georgia, Athens, 1970.

Institute for Behavioral Research in Creativity (IBRIC). *Manual for Alpha biographical inventory.* Greensboro, N.C.: Predictions Press, 1968.

Jones, E. L. The affinity of biodata subgroups for vocational interest. Paper read at Georgia Psychological Association, Atlanta, May, 1970.

Jones, E. L. The relationship among biographical similarity, perceived similarity, and attraction in the roommate situation. Unpublished master's thesis, University of Georgia, Athens, 1971.

Kaiser, H. F. The varimax criterion for analytic rotation in factor analysis. *Psychometrika,* 1958, 23, 187–200.

Keating, E., Paterson, D. G., & Stone, C. H. Validity of work histories obtained by interview. *Journal of Applied Psychology,* 1950, 34, 1–5.

Kenagy, H. G., & Yoakum, C. S. *The selection and training of salesmen.* New York: McGraw-Hill, 1925.

Kirkpatrick, J. J. A second cross-validation of an executive weighted application blank. Proceedings of 76th Annual Convention, American Psychological Association, 1968, 3, 581–582.

Klein, H. A. Personality characteristics of discrepant academic achievers. Unpublished doctoral dissertation, University of Georgia, Athens, 1972.

Klein, S. P., & Owens, W. A. Faking of a scored life history as a function of criterion objectivity. *Journal of Applied Psychology,* 1965, 451–454.

Kulberg, G. E., & Owens, W. A. Some life history antecedents of engineering interests. *Journal of Educational Psychology,* 1960, 51, 26–31.

Larsen, R. H., Swarthout, D. M., & Wickert, F. R. Objectionability and fakability of biographical inventory items. Paper read at Midwestern Psychological Association, Chicago, 1967.

Laurent, H. A study of the developmental backgrounds of men to determine by means of the biographical information blank the relationship between factors in their early background and their choice of professions. Digest of doctoral dissertation, Western Reserve University, Cleveland, 1951. Greensboro, N.C.: The Creativity Research Institute Press, The Richardson Foundation.

Laurent, H. Early identification of management talent. *Management Record,* 1962, 24 (5), 33–38.

Laurent, H. Cross-cultural cross-validation of empirically validated tests. *Journal of Applied Psychology,* 1970, 54, 417–423.

Lecznar, W. B., & Dailey, J. T. Keying biographical inventories in classification test batteries. *American Psychologist,* 1950, 5, 279.

Levine, A. S., & Zachert, V. Use of biographical inventory in the Air Force classification program. *Journal of Applied Psychology,* 1951, 35, 241–244.

Lewis, M. A., & Schoenfeldt, L. F. Developmental interest factors associated with homosexuality. Unpublished manuscript, University of Georgia Library, Athens, 1972.

Lunneborg, C. E. Biographic variables in differential versus absolute prediction. Proceedings, 76th Annual Convention of the American Psychological Association, 1968, 3, 233–234.

McCormick, E. J., Jeanneret, P. R., & Mecham, R. C. The development and background of the position analysis questionnaire (PAQ). Occupational Research Center, Purdue University, Lafayette, Ind., June, 1969.

Mahalanobis, P. C. On the generalized distance in statistics. Proceedings of the National Institute of Science (India), 1936, 12, 49–55.

Majesty, M. S. *Identification of race, sex, and religion through life history.* Springfield, Va.: The Clearinghouse for Federal Scientific and Technical Information, AD 695–827, 1967.

Malloy, J. The prediction of college achievement with the life experience inventory. *Educational and Psychological Measurement,* 1955, 15, 170–180.

Manson, G. E. What can the application blank tell? *Journal of Personnel Research,* 1925, 4, 73–99.

Matteson, M. T., Osburn, H. G., & Sparks, C. P. *A computer-based methodology for constructing homogeneous keys with applications to biographical data.* Houston: Personnel Psychology Services Center, University of Houston, 1969, Report 1.

Morrison, R. F., Owens, W. A., Glennon, J. R., & Albright, L. E. Factored life history antecedents of industrial research performance. *Journal of Applied Psychology,* 1962, 46, 281–284.

Mosel, J. L., & Cozan, L. W. The accuracy of application blank work histories. *Journal of Applied Psychology,* 1952, 36, 365–369.

O'Neill, P. J. Stylistic differences in maze learning. Unpublished doctoral dissertation, University of Georgia, Athens, 1972.

Owens, W. A. Toward one discipline of scientific psychology. *American Psychologist,* 1968, 23, 782–785.

Owens, W. A. A quasi-actuarial basis for individual assessment. *American Psychologist,* 1971, 26, 992–999.

Owens, W. A., & Henry, E. R. *Biographical data in industrial psychology: A review and evaluation.* Greensboro, N.C.: The Creativity Research Institute, The Richardson Foundation, 1966.

Owens, W. A., Glennon, J. R., & Albright, L. E. Retest consistency and the writing of life history items: A first step. *Journal of Applied Psychology,* 1962, 46, 329–332.

Packard, V. *The naked society.* New York: McKay, 1964.

Parish, J. A., & Drucker, A. J. Personnel research for Officer Candidate School, USA TAGO Personnel Research Branch Technical Research Report, 1957, No. 117, 22 pp.

Pickrel, E. W. The relative predictive efficiency of three methods of utilizing scores from biographical inventories. *USAF, Human Resources Research Center Bulletin,* 1954, 54–73.

Pinto, P. R. Subgrouping in prediction: A comparison of moderator and actuarial approaches. Unpublished doctoral dissertation, University of Georgia, Athens, 1970.

Plag, J. A., & Goffman, J. M. The armed forces qualification test: Its validity in predicting military effectiveness for Naval enlistees. *Personnel Psychology,* 1967, 20, 323–339.

Prediger, D. J. New procedures for scoring psychological measurements: Development of moderated scoring keys for psychological inventories. *Research in Education (ERIC),* 1969, 4 (05), ED024887.

Rawls, D., & Rawls, J. R. Personality characteristics and personal history data of successful and less successful executives. *Psychological Reports,* 1968, 23, 1032–1034.

Richardson, Bellows, Henry, & Co. Predicting job tenure among ES applicants and program tenure among WIN clients through the use of biographical information, Washington, D.C., 1971.

Roy, H., Brueckel, J., & Drucker, A. J.

Selection of Army and Air Force reserve training corps students. *USA Personnel Research Branch Notes,* 1954, 28, 9 pp.

Ruda, E. S. The effect of interpersonal similarity on management performance. Unpublished doctoral dissertation, Purdue University, Lafayette, Ind., 1970.

Schmuckler, E. *Age differences in biographical inventories: A factor analytic study.* Greensboro, N.C.: The Creativity Research Institute, The Richardson Foundation, 1966.

Schoenfeldt, L. F. The grouping of subjects into homogeneous subsets: A comparison and evaluation of two divergent approaches. Unpublished doctoral dissertation, Purdue University, Lafayette, Ind., 1966.

Schoenfeldt, L. F. Life experience subgroups as moderators in the prediction of educational criteria. Paper read before the American Educational Research Association, Minneapolis, 1970. (a)

Schoenfeldt, L. F. Non-test variables in the prediction of educational progress. In E. E. Dudek (Chrmn.), *Use of non-test variables in admission, selection, and classification operations.* Symposium presented at the meeting of the American Psychological Association, Miami, September, 1970. (b)

Schoenfeldt, L. F. Maximum manpower utilization: Development, implementation, and evaluation of an assessment-classification model. Invited address before American Psychological Association, Honolulu, September, 1972.

Siegel, L. A biographical inventory for students: I. Construction and standardization of the instrument. *Journal of Applied Psychology,* 1956, 40, 5–10.

Smart, B. D. Reducing offensiveness of biographical items in personnel selection: A first step. *Studies in Higher Education,* 1968, 95, 14–21.

Smith, W. J., Albright, L. E., Glennon, J. R., & Owens, W. A. The prediction of research competence and creativity from personal history. *Journal of Applied Psychology,* 1961, 45, 59–62.

Sparks, C. P. Prediction of cognitive test scores by life history items: Comparison across two different ethnic groups. Houston: Author, 1965. (a)

Sparks, C. P. Using life history items to predict cognitive test scores. Houston: Author, 1965. (b)

Standard Oil Co. (N.J.) *Social science research reports: Selection and placement,* Vol. II. New York: Author, 1962. (a)

Standard Oil Co. (N.J.) *Social science research reports: Performance review and evaluation,* Vol. III. New York: Author, 1962. (b)

Strimbu, J. L., & Schoenfeldt, L. F. Life history subgroups in the prediction of drug usage patterns and attitudes. Unpublished manuscript, University of Georgia Library, Athens, 1972.

Taylor, C. W., Ellison, R. L., & Tucker, M. F. *Biographical information and the prediction of multiple criteria of success in science.* Salt Lake City: University of Utah, 1965.

Taylor, L. R. A quasi-actuarial approach to assessment. Unpublished doctoral dissertation, Purdue University, Lafayette, Ind., 1968.

Tesser, A. On evaluating multi-dimensional constructed groups. Athens, Ga.: Author, 1971.

The Richardson Foundation, The Creativity Research Institute. *A report on the preliminary findings of the North Carolina Talent Study.* Greensboro, N.C.: Author, 1968.

Thomson, R. W., & Owens, W. A. A factorial study of the life history correlates of engineering interests. *American Psychologist,* 1964, 19, 478 (abstract).

Viteles, M. *Industrial psychology.* New York: W. W. Norton, 1932.

Ward, J. H., & Hook, M. E. Application of a hierarchical grouping procedure to a problem of grouping profiles. *Educational and Psychological Measurement,* 1963, 23, 69–81.

Webb, S. C. The comparative validity of two biographical inventory keys. *Journal of Applied Psychology,* 1960, 44, 177–183.

Williams, W. E. Life history antecedents of volunteers versus nonvolunteers for an AFROTC program. Paper read at Midwestern Psychological Association, Chicago, 1961.

The Practice of Industrial and Organizational Psychology

ROBERT M. GUION
Bowling Green State University

THE IDEA OF "PROFESSIONAL PRACTICE" means different things to different people. To some it implies an art, highly developed, distinctive in method, finely honed by expert tutelage and extensive experience. To others it represents the application of some fundamental and generalizable body of knowledge; for example, there are fields of professional practice such as applied music (distinguishable from musical theory) or applied science (distinguishable from a parent body of scientific knowledge). From the latter view, if we believe that psychology is the science of behavior, it follows that professional practice in applied psychology is the application of scientific generalizations where they are available or of the methods of scientific research when the parent science has not provided the necessary general theory.

Whether art or science, professional practice implies the use of established techniques, or technology, for the solution or alleviation of genuine and important human problems. Whatever the emphasis, the technology is some sort of composite of art, science, and methodology. We may speak of the methodology of science or of the methodology of art, but it is not very useful to speak of methodology alone. By itself, methodology implies something too rigorous and systematized to be a true art form, but it does not offer implications rich enough in substance to be the stuff of science. Nevertheless, the practice of industrial and organizational psychology has most often been understood simply as the application of method. This is unfortunate; it needs also to be understood as the application of the judgments and intuitions of artistry and in terms of the system and generality of science.

Observation is the cornerstone of both art and science. To be effective for either, observation requires established method. McCormick, in Chapter 15 on job analysis, writes of the problems of systematizing observations of jobs and of the tasks that comprise them. (The word "observation" is used here in a very broad sense; what it is intended to imply here is classified by McCormick in a very detailed list of methods of analysis including but not restricted to the direct observations of the job analyst himself.) More important perhaps than the descriptions of method is McCormick's persistent emphasis on the variety of purposes of job analysis and his insistence that purposes be specified. Observations without clearly defined objectives tend to be aimless indeed, neither scientifically sound nor professionally useful.

Observations of jobs, of machines and tools used in the performance of jobs, of work places, and of the work environment more generally are described in Chapter 16 by Chapanis in terms of a rather specific class of purposes: to design jobs, their components, and their settings to match the capacities and limitations of the workers. Although engineering psychology was once concerned almost exclusively with man-machine systems, the chapter by Chapanis shows that it has developed into a much broader field of applied science relevant to nearly all of the social problems of the relationship of man to his environment. In a very real sense, engineering psychology offers an alternative model for traditional industrial psychologists to consider in approaching their traditional problems. Mason Haire once suggested that it is peculiar that a field called *engineering* psychology should show more concern than traditional psychologies with molding the environment to fit the person. Chapanis may have helped resolve the apparent paradox by having pointed out that humane professional practice requires sound knowledge from many sources and an objective concern, in planning or in designing programs or equipment, for the implications of anticipated actions.

The "criterion problem" is often viewed more with reverence and awe than with planning or action; it is nevertheless the most traditional problem in the various facets of industrial and organizational psychology. Quite properly, Smith recognizes in Chapter 17 that the observation of dependent variables is essentially a measurement problem; for example, that observations by qualified observers must be systematized and quantified if the practices of the profession or the hypotheses of the science are to be evaluated adequately. Smith also gives further emphasis to the necessity for clear statements of purposes in professional practice: "The first requirement of a criterion is that it be relevant—to some important goal of the individual, the organization, or society." Various professional activities can be directed toward different and perhaps equally important goals; clearly, no single criterion concept is going to be equally appropriate to all goals. Even within

the concerns of a single purpose, the question of single as opposed to multiple criteria is very real; it is to be answered, as Smith ably points out, by the logic and the data in the problem at hand.

Of the kinds of professional practice generally considered "traditional," the most traditional of all is probably employment testing and the use of related employment aids. It would be pleasant to write that the most traditional activity has been the validation of selection procedures, but that would be false; for most of the last twenty years, at least, validity has been more often assumed than determined. The technology of employee selection is, however, a matter of testing assumptions (or hypotheses) by deliberate design. Guion, giving rather short shrift to the important questions of employee recruitment and placement in recognition of the actual state of the technology, describes in Chapter 18 the designs and systems by which relatively low-risk hypotheses are formulated and tested in the processes called validation. The formulation of hypotheses is or should be applied science, the validation of hypotheses is applied methodology, but the act of making an employment decision is, as a unique event, still an art. Guion recommends that the technological focus be directed increasingly to further investigations of the decision process itself and, in so doing, move beyond notions of test validation to more fundamental notions of selection research. That recommendation is but one of several suggestions for moving industrial and organizational psychology toward a firmer scientific basis by seeking greater generalizability of the validities of professional hypotheses.

Another traditional problem area is personnel training, an area described by Hinrichs in Chapter 19 with some ambivalence. As matters currently stand, little that passes as personnel training can be called applied science. There is, of course, the "same tired list of 'principles' derived out of learning research" appearing in various textbooks, but these principles, according to Hinrichs, are generally ignored in the professional practices of training specialists. Nevertheless, the trends are toward greater, not less, reliance on formal training activity, despite the weakness of the scientific base. According to Hinrichs, although "the practitioners are doing little to build a psychology of training, they must be doing something right; it can't all be a big fraud." Even though there are those who are not sure they can agree with his optimism, most practitioners can agree as Hinrichs argues forcefully for a "better way"; his argument ties together many of the concerns of the preceding chapters. He calls for clear identification of task variables, competent measurement of dependent variables, and reasonable efforts to select qualified trainees; his call comes in a systems model context. The systems analogy is used for the formal training system, for the personal system of skill acquisition, and for an interacting organizational system. Hinrichs also supplies a useful rubric for examining various training methods. When he comes to the inevitable plea for further research, he does so with the justification that he has offered a framework within which such research may be conceptualized and developed.

The chapters from McCormick's through Hinrichs's tend to emphasize the methodology and research design of applied science. Beginning with Finkle's Chapter 20 on assessment centers, the emphasis appears to shift to one on the arts and theories of professional practice. Assessment centers for both selection and training have proliferated in recent years. Each is somehow different from others, bearing the imprimatur of its own developer, yet each is seen as a variation on a common theme emphasizing group processes and internally varied approaches to measurement. The growth of these professional centers is not entirely a blessing; Finkle expresses concern over the concomitant growth of "faddish commercialism" in the initiation of new centers, a faddishness probably made possible by the absence of clearly enunciated purposes for

many of the variations and by the further absence in many cases of serious attempts to evaluate either an assessment center as a whole or any of its constituent parts. It is paradoxical that the original AT&T assessment center approach, which has been systematically and exhaustively evaluated in the Bell system, is widely copied in everything except the processes of systematic evaluation. It is certainly not that the AT&T studies have answered all possible questions; each variation creates its own new questions. The developers of each assessment center seem to identify for themselves the constructs they wish to assess even though, as Finkle points out, little attention is given to estimating either the reliability or the construct validity of the assessment of any given construct.

Quite different in both content and form is Chapter 21 by Thomas on the management of conflict. This is no "how-to-do-it" prescription for professional techniques. Rather, it is a body of theory, drawn from a variety of sources, intended to be helpful to those who are responsible for management in conflict situations. Conflict is probably always a fact of organizational life, although it seems periodically to be intensified. Unfortunately, it is not a fact of life widely studied by the scientifically oriented organizational psychologist, nor have systematic programs for its management been developed by those more oriented toward the artistry of professional practice. Much of the literature cited by Thomas comes from sociology and social psychology; relatively little has been contributed by people whose primary concern is for the effective functioning of organizations. It is devoutly to be hoped that industrial and organizational psychologists concerned with management processes will turn in increasing numbers to the systematic testing of hypotheses derived from Thomas's chapter.

The same might be said to some degree of Beer's Chapter 22 on organizational development, although this is certainly a topic that has produced a considerable literature on professional practices. The faddishness Finkle abhors in assessment centers is also found in much that is done in the name of organizational development (affectionately known as "O.D."). This is not surprising; Beer points out that the field is relatively young and that there has been little time for evaluative research. Professional practice in organizational development stems from the research of social psychology, from theories of attitude change, and from the practices of laboratory training. Beer, following Lewin, has provided a chain-like structure of "unfreezing," "change," and "refreezing" in which the various kinds of diagnostic and process interventions now a part of the repertory of organizational development can be understood and theoretically evaluated. It is Beer's contention that O.D. technology "goes far beyond applied research"—that it actually creates the changes for which traditional research merely sets a stage.

Both Thomas and Beer are concerned with the social psychology of groups. In contrast, Chapter 23 by Miner and Brewer presents a clinical concern with individuals. In any organization, some individuals are ineffective; Miner and Brewer apply principles derived from the professional practice of clinical psychology to the managerial practice of coping with ineffective performance. Their approach is the control model; to control, one identifies individuals who consistently perform below a definable minimum standard and subsequently takes managerial action intended to bring performance to an acceptable (not necessarily high or optimum) level. Unlike Beer, who sees traditional selection and training as outmoded tools for organizational change, Miner and Brewer consider effective selection a means of partially preventing instances of ineffective performance. They point out, however, that even the best selection and training effort is imperfect and that ineffective performance may always be expected to occur. Their major emphasis, then, is on the methods of control that need to be introduced. After describing various classes of perform-

ance problems (e.g., absenteeism, alcoholism, and physical or cultural handicaps), they describe some recommended corrective procedures. Examples include changing work roles, disciplinary actions, counseling, and special training. Despite the fact that many of the problems are clinical, Miner and Brewer remark on the degree to which management practice apparently fails to utilize the research and concepts of clinical practice. There is much room for improvement in the attempts to manage poor performance, and much of the needed improvement must come from the development of industrial clinical psychology as a coordinated field of study.

The chapters on conflict management, on organizational development, and on the management of ineffective performance share a common emphasis on the management process within an organizational setting. Together, they exemplify a more recent emphasis sometimes termed "organizational" psychology in distinction from the more traditional emphases embodied in what is more likely to be termed "industrial" or "personnel" psychology. This is not wholly uniform use of words; there are, for example, programs in graduate schools known as organizational programs that are not distinguishable from some programs in personnel psychology.

This is more than merely a word game; the playing with words arises because of a distinction in approaches to professional practice more fundamental than that one group focuses more on management than does the other. It may well be that the essential distinction between the old and the new in professional practice in this hyphenated field of industrial-organizational psychology is a difference in the relative weighting of data and research method on the one hand against models and theories on the other. Traditional topics in industrial psychology have stressed data and the means by which dependable data may be acquired. This is not to say that theory is ignored in the chapters that are more traditional; McCormick has written of theoretical taxonomies of tasks, Chapanis writes from the theoretical orientation of a systems approach (or of applied experimental psychology), Smith provides a three-dimensional approach for the organization of thinking about criteria, Guion's "rational foundation for predictive validity" is based on psychometric theory and on the argument that each use of employment tests should have a theoretical foundation, Hinrichs provides a theoretical framework in which to integrate learning theory, training systems, and organizational goals, and Finkle's treatment of assessment centers is generously laced with theoretical constructs to be assessed. Nevertheless, in all of these chapters, the emphasis is on "how to do it" and on the methodological problems of evaluating how well "it" has been done. In contrast, the chapters stressing managerial and organizational processes are more concerned with presenting a rationale for what is to be done and for getting on with the doing—with or without evaluative validating research. Again, this is not to say that the theoretical structures have no support in data; all three of these chapters have cited research results liberally. Their emphasis, however, is on the theoretical inferences to be drawn from data and logic in tandem and on logical deductions that can fill in the gaps in empirical knowledge. The advance of technology in this hyphenated field requires both approaches: an empirical matching of prediction with outcome, and a logical internal consistency of ideas. Both are historically respected approaches to Truth, and it is certain that Truth is always a scarce commodity. The evaluation of what is done under either the newer or the more traditional approach will not be properly based on ideas of which is the better route to Truth but on hard evaluations of how well each has carried out its own task.

These two sets of chapters (or the approaches they represent) cannot be distinguished in intentions of practicality. Traditional industrial psychology may have often been impractical, but not by intent. To the contrary, a common criticism of the field has been its atheoretical pragmatism, a preoccupation with daily operating problems to the exclusion of more general theories of behavior at work. The newer concerns grouped under organizational psychology are also pragmatic. Theory-building is not the end in itself. Building a theory in organizational psychology, as it is being practiced, is done to provide a guide to management practice. In fact, it might result in *better* theory if there were more rather than less attention given to theory construction itself. One student complained rather stridently (but also rather accurately) that organizational psychology seems to encourage each practitioner to become his own theoretician, the result being a field overrun with minor modifications of the modifications others have made of someone else's theory.

All of this has been introduction to a comment on Jacoby's Chapter 24 on consumer psychology. Jacoby argues that consumer psychology is a field apart from either organizational or industrial psychology and that its inclusion in this *Handbook* is, therefore, peculiar. He writes from the perspective of an outsider looking at industrial and organizational psychology to see if there is any ground common to his own field. The result is a well-balanced welding of data and theory that makes the envious industrial-organizational psychologist plead for the outsider to come in. Jacoby provides insightful as well as entertaining evidence that, in consumer psychology, at least, there is and ought to be a two-way street joining the professional practice of the consumer psychologists to the basic research of the scientists. He then suggests that a similar sort of interaction between consumer psychology and industrial-organizational psychology could enrich both and provide a sort of validation of ideas. His example is a $2 \times 2 \times 2$ extension of the two-factor theory of work motivation-job satisfaction.

The Jacoby chapter does superbly what all of the other chapters on professional practice do in abundance also: it suggests areas for useful research. Although this section of the *Handbook* is principally devoted to the technology of professional practice, each chapter in it provides clear and rich direction for future research. One can only wonder how many dissertation topics will be drawn from these pages.

At the outset, these introductory comments referred to the art, the methodology, and the science of that technology comprising the professional practice of industrial and organizational psychology. Comments on the chapters themselves, however, considered a slightly different trinity: art, method, and theory. This does not suggest a confusion of theory with science; rather, it suggests that much of the scientific foundation for practice may come internally from the ranks of industrial-organizational psychologists themselves. These chapters, taken as a group, make surprisingly little use of the basic theories and findings of experimental psychology. Sometimes the relevance of laboratory findings to the organizational setting is merely ignored; sometimes, it is explicitly rejected. There are, to be sure, practices built plainly on laboratory and field investigations in social psychology and in theoretical psychometrics. For the most part, however, these chapters suggest strongly that industrial and organizational psychology must take the initiative to broaden its own scientific base.

CHAPTER 15

Job and Task Analysis

ERNEST J. McCORMICK
Purdue University

THIS CHAPTER BEGINS with a brief overview of various aspects of job analysis and job analysis methods. The primary focus of the chapter, however, is in terms of systematic approaches to the analysis of human work, including a discussion of various major efforts that have been made in this direction, such as functional job analysis, the use of task inventories, and other forms of structured job analysis questionnaires, such as the Position Analysis Questionnaire (PAQ). In addition, there is a discussion of the use of structured job analysis questionnaires as the direct basis for establishing aptitude requirements of jobs and of compensation rates for jobs, thus possibly eliminating conventional test validation procedures and job evaluation procedures.

In large part, the entire domain of industrial and organizational psychology and the related aspects of personnel administration and management have their roots in the interface of people with their jobs. The human "problems" in business and industry are reflected to a substantial degree in terms of such criteria as job performance, absenteeism, labor turnover, grievances, job satisfaction, etc. Some of the statistical "variance" of these and other criteria can, of course, be related to any of a number of variables within the work context, such as individual differences, the social and organizational context of work, incentives, and the nature of supervision; but any such listing of possible sources of variance would be incomplete without consideration of the nature of the jobs in question. In more operational terms, the conventional facets of personnel administration and management cover personnel selection and placement, training, personnel appraisal, the establishment of incentive systems (including job evaluation), the establishment of organizational relationships, manning programs, safety programs, etc. To varying degrees these and other management functions are intertwined with the jobs in question. Further, the functions associated with job design, system development, industrial engineering, and human factors engineering also have very direct implications in terms of the nature of human work, and thus should not be carried out in a vacuum, but should be pursued in full recognition of their implications in terms of the nature of the human work activities that would ultimately be influenced by them.

The job-related aspects of these numerous nooks and crannies of the various domains naturally place an emphasis upon the availability of relevant job information that—for the particular purpose in hand—can contribute positively to the problems at hand. The importance of job-related information to these various objectives has, of course, long been recognized, as reflected, for example, by the job-analysis programs of many organizations, the operations of the United States Training and Employment Service (UST&ES), and the research carried out by various organizations, both private and public. If one looks outside the confines of the organization, the implications of job-related information are extended into other areas, such as vocational counseling, educational and training programs, and a wide range of psychological and economic studies that have job-related orientations.

Although various apparent needs for job-related information have stimulated efforts over the years to develop such data, it must be granted that the efforts along these lines have tended to be rather unsystematic and to be more subjective than objective, and have been shrouded in verbiage that does not lend itself to systematic analyses. Certainly for some purposes the conventional approach to job analysis and job description has served (and will continue to serve) very useful purposes. But the widespread implications of job-related data argue for more systematic research approaches to this domain. In this connection, it is encouraging to know that in recent years there have been certain significant efforts in the direction of the more systematic study of human work, and more systematic approaches to the processes of collection and analysis of job data.

THE COLLECTION OF JOB AND OCCUPATION INFORMATION

Fundamental to any given purpose that requires job-related information is the need to make some determination as to the type of information to be obtained and the method of so doing. Thus, as one takes some-

thing of an overview of the field of job and task analysis, it is appropriate first to consider the processes of collection of job and occupation information, including some of the pros and cons of various such approaches.

Aspects of the Job Analysis Process

With some notion as to the purposes of a job analysis program in mind, someone needs to make a determination regarding each of various aspects of the approach to be used in the actual collection of job-related data. There are at least four such aspects, these being set forth in the form of questions as follows:

1. What *type(s)* of information is to be obtained?

2. In what *form* is the information to be obtained (and usually presented)?

3. What *method* of analysis will be used?

4. What *agent* will be used? (Usually the "agent" will be an individual, such as a job analyst, but in isolated circumstances it may be a device, such as a camera.)

Let us touch on these separately, indicating in each instance some of the alternatives.

Type of Job Analysis Information

Following are some of the types of information that might be elicited by job-analysis procedures.

Work Activities

Job-oriented activities (description of the work activities performed, expressed in "job" terms, usually indicating what is accomplished, such as galvanizing, weaving, cleaning, etc.; sometimes such activity descriptions also indicate how, why, and when a worker performs an activity; usually the activities are those involving active human participation, but in certain approaches they may characterize machine or system functions)

    Work activities/processes
    Procedures used

Activity records (films, etc.)
Personal accountability/responsibility
Worker-oriented activities
Human behaviors (behaviors performed in work, such as sensing, decision making, performing physical actions, communicating, etc.)
Elemental motions (such as used in methods analysis)
Personal job demands (human expenditures involved in work, such as energy expenditure, etc.)
Machines, tools, equipment, and work aids used
Job-related tangibles and intangibles
Materials processed
Products made
Knowledge dealt with or applied (such as law or chemistry)
Services rendered (such as laundering or repairing)
Work performance
Work measurement (i.e., time taken)
Work standards
Error analysis
Other aspects
Job context
Physical working conditions
Work schedule
Organizational context
Social context
Incentives (financial and nonfinancial)
Personnel requirements
Job-related knowledge/skills (education, training, work experience, etc. required)
Personal attributes (aptitudes, physical characteristics, personality, interests, etc. required)

Form of Job Analysis Information

The form of job analysis information refers essentially to the distinction in terms of its qualitative versus quantitative features, or in some instances in terms of its "degree" along a qualitative-to-quantitative scale.

Qualitative (this end of the scale is characterized by typically verbal, generally narrative, descriptions in the case of certain types of information, such as job content, or qualitative statements about such items of information as working conditions, social context, personnel requirements, etc.)

Quantitative (this end of the scale is characterized by the use of "units" of job information, such as: job tasks; specific worker behaviors, such as making color discriminations, handling materials, etc.; oxygen consumption during work; production per unit of time; error rates per unit of time; noise level; size of work group; aptitude test standards; ratings of job characteristics; etc.)

Methods of Collection of Job Information

Among the methods of collection of job information are the following:

1. Observation
2. Individual interview (interview with job incumbent)
3. Group interview (interview with several job incumbents as a group)
4. Technical conference (conference with experienced personnel)
5. Questionnaire: structured
6. Questionnaire: open-ended
7. Diary
8. Critical incidents (records of worker behaviors that are "critical" in terms of characterizing very good or very poor job performance)
9. Equipment design information (blueprints and other design data of equipment being developed)
10. Recordings of job activities (films, mechanical recordings of certain job activities, etc.)
11. Records (available records, such as maintenance records, etc.)

Agent Used in Collecting Job Information

In most instances the "agent" is an individual, but in some circumstances a device of some sort is used. Following is a listing of possible agents.

Individuals
   Job analyst
   Supervisor
   Incumbent
Devices
   Cameras
   Physiological recording devices
   "Force" platforms (for recording physical movements in three dimensions)
   Other devices

Discussion

One could contemplate other aspects of job information that might also be added to the above list, such as, for example, the level of specificity of the information. (Work activity data, for example, can be characterized in terms of very minute detail, such as elemental motions, or at a very gross level.)

Considering the above four facets, we can envision many combinations thereof, such as (in the most common case) *job-oriented work activities* (type of information) being recorded as *essay descriptions* (qualitative form), on the basis of *observation* (method), by an *analyst* (agent). Needless to say, certain combinations are manifestly impossible; for example, an incumbent, as the agent, obviously cannot use the observation method on himself.

Job Analysis: Past and Present

Looking back, we would generally have to concede that the study of human work has presented a fairly dismal impression, highlighted with only a few bright spots here and there. The lamentations about the generally unsatisfying historical state of the art have been variously expressed, such as by Kershner (1955): "As is patently evident, job analysis has been a sort of handmaiden serving in various ways a variety of needs and all the while floundering in a morass of semantic confusion." And Ramras (1969),

in retrospect, makes the following observations: "We all know the classic procedures of occupational analysis. One man watched and noted the actions of another man at work on his job. The actions of both men were biased, and the resulting information varied with the wind, especially the political wind. But the information got to the personnel manager, who used it to jog his memory when he was hiring other people."

Of the various deficiencies of conventional job analysis procedures, probably the sharpest criticism is that the typical essay descriptions of job activities are not adequately descriptive of the jobs in question, especially in the case of jobs that deal primarily with decision and communication activities (such as managerial, supervisory, professional, technical, etc.). In discussing this rather central problem, Cowan (1969) points out that one problem in job analysis has been that of simulating in verbal form jobs which are composed of a large number of important, independent, and nonverbal job elements.

Despite the problem of "verbal simulation" and the other difficulties that haunt the job analyst, however, we should agree with Cowan (1969) that traditional job descriptions serve a number of useful purposes in manpower management.

Granting the positive contributions of conventional job analysis approaches, there still seems to be something that is missing in the brew. Somehow one's pervading sense of queasiness leads to the conclusion that, with some notable exceptions, the study of human work has generally been more in the domain of the arts than of the sciences. Perhaps to express it differently, the study of the human work (which occupies a major part of man's lifetime) probably has not generally benefited from the systematic, scientific approaches that have been characteristic of other domains of inquiry, such as the study of physical phenomena, biological phenomena, or of the behavior of man himself (as through psychological and sociological research).

Recent Developments

As pointed out above, however, the study of human work during the bygone years has not been entirely unsystematic and lacking in the scientific approach. We could cite a number of examples to illustrate this, such as: some of the techniques of the industrial engineers, such as the measurement of the time of elemental motions; the measurement of physical effort by the work physiologists; numerous quantitative studies dealing with job evaluation methods (although these concern more use of the job analysis information than its collection); and some of the work of the United States Training and Employment Service (Lewis, 1969). But more particularly, in recent years there have been certain developments that offer very encouraging prospects of pulling some phases of job analysis out of the doldrums. These developments are not panaceas for all phases of job analysis or all circumstances; but for certain uses in some situations they might be considered a breakthrough. Probably the common denominator of these developments is in the identification and use of "units" of job-related information of some given type, that thus lends the resulting data to more systematic analysis and application. Such developments usually involve the use of structured questionnaires or taxonomies. Typical of these developments are the following: the use of job inventories as developed by the Personnel Division of the Air Force Human Resources Laboratory (Christal, 1969; Morsh, 1969); and the Position Analysis Questionnaire (PAQ) that provides for the analysis of jobs in terms of worker-oriented job elements (McCormick, Jeanneret, & Mecham, 1969). Some of these will be elaborated later.

Discussion

In our discussion here, we will want to take an overview of some of the various approaches to the study of human work. In doing so, however, we will tend to dwell in particular on some of the more systematic, quantitatively oriented procedures. We should point out, however, that, although the past several years perhaps have been witness to at least a small quantum step on the road toward the development of a science of human work, the millenium in this effort is by no means here or around the corner.

Conventional Job Analysis

The conventional job-analysis programs obviously vary in some of their features, but their communalities probably are more pronounced than their differences. As the basis for a brief discussion of conventional job analysis procedures, the practices of the United States Training and Employment Service (UST&ES) will be used. In drawing upon illustrative material from the UST&ES, however, it should be recognized that certain features of their job analysis program represent extensions and elaborations that are not typical of the programs of many individual organizations.

The coverage provided for in their job analysis schedule, as illustrated in the *Handbook for Analyzing Jobs* (1972)[1] provides for identification information, a job summary, work performed ratings, worker trait ratings, and a description of tasks, along with other information. As indicated earlier, the description of work activities creates the most serious headaches because of the dependence upon the analyst's skill in verbal description to "reproduce" on paper the job as it exists in its actual setting. Part of a job analysis schedule is shown in Figure 1, in particular the job summary and the description of tasks.[2] One point might be added here, however, namely, that the description

---

[1] *Handbook for Analyzing Jobs.* Manpower Administration, U.S. Department of Labor. Washington, D.C.: Superintendent of Documents, Stock Number 2900-0131, 1972.

[2] For guidelines and specific procedures used by the UST&ES in its job analysis procedures, the reader is referred to the *Handbook for Analyzing Jobs,* ibid.

PARTS OF JOB ANALYSIS SCHEDULE
U.S. DEPARTMENT OF LABOR, MANPOWER ADMINISTRATION

Job: Dough Mixer (Bakery Products Industry)

4. Job Summary:

   Operates mixing machine to mix ingredients for straight and sponge (yeast) doughs according to established formulas, directs other workers in fermentation of dough, and cuts dough into pieces with hand cutter.

15. Description of Tasks:

    1. Dumps ingredients into mixing machine: Examines production schedule to determine type of bread to be produced, such as rye, whole wheat, or white. Refers to formula card for quantities and types of ingredients required, such as flour, water, milk, vitamin solutions, and shortening. Weighs out, measures, and dumps ingredients into mixing machine.

    2. Operates mixing machine: Turns valves and other hand controls to set mixing time according to type of dough being mixed. Presses button to start agitator blades in machine. Observes gages and dials on equipment continuously to verify temperature of dough and mixing time. Feels dough for desired consistency. Adds water

or flour to mix measuring vessels and adjusts mixing time and controls to obtain desired elasticity in mix.

3. Directs other workers in fermentation of dough: Prepares fermentation schedule according to type of dough being raised. Sprays portable dough *Trough* with lubricant to prevent adherence of mixed dough to trough. Directs DOUGH-MIXER HELPER in positioning trough beneath door of mixer to catch dough when mixing cycle is complete. Pushes, or directs other workers to push, troughs of dough into fermentation room.

4. Cuts dough: Dumps fermented dough onto worktable. Manually kneads dough to eliminate gases formed by yeast. Cuts dough into pieces with hand cutter. Places cut dough on proofing rack and covers with cloth.

5. Performs miscellaneous duties: Records on work sheet number of batches mixed during work shift. Informs BAKE SHOP FOREMAN when repairs or major adjustments are required for machines and equipment.

Figure 1. Portions of a job analysis schedule used by the U.S. Training and Employment Service. This illustration deals with the job of dough mixer, and shows a part of the Job Summary and Description of Tasks sections.

---

of the work performed section should make it clear *what* the worker does, *how* he does it, and *why* he does it. These aspects in some instances may be fairly manifest, but if they are not, the analyst should go out of his way to insure that they are indeed brought out.

Functional Occupational Classification Approach

In the last number of years, the United States Training and Employment Service has developed, and used experimentally, a new approach to job analysis; this effort is what is referred to as a functional occupational classification project (Lewis, 1969). The specific features of this approach are reflected in the *Handbook for Analyzing Jobs* (1972), and the results of the approach are reflected in part in the current edition of

the *Dictionary of Occupational Title* (DOT) (1965).

The functional occupational classification data consist in part of extensions and organization of the kinds of data obtained during regular job analysis activities, and in part comprise certain new types of information (or analyses of other information). The approach provides for five categories of information, as follows: (a) worker functions; (b) work fields; (c) machines, tools, equipment, and work aids; (d) materials, products, subject matter, and services; and (e) worker traits.

Worker Functions

The analysis procedure is predicated on the assumptions that each job involves some relationship to data, people, and things, and hat the involvement of people in each of hese areas can be viewed as a hierarchy. The structure of these hierarchies is shown n Table 1.

In the practice of the UST&ES, each job s classified in terms of its involvement, by assigning (in each case) the code for the category (actually the level) that is considered to characterize the job.

Work Fields

The work fields consist of organizations of specific methods that are characteristic either of (a) machines, tools, equipment, or work aids, and directed at common technological objectives; or (b) techniques designed to fulfill socioeconomic purposes. There are ninety-nine such categories; for example, drafting, riveting, and sawing.

Machines, Tools, Equipment, and Work Aids

There is provision for identifying the particular items of these types that are used by workers.

Materials, Products, Subject Matter, and Services

Jobs are characterized in terms of the particular items of these types that are involved, using a list of 580 categories derived from the commodities index of the *Standard Industrial Classification Manual* and from educational classifications or subject matter fields. Some examples are: lumber and wood products; field crops; business services; administration; and meteorology.

Worker Traits

The worker traits aspect provides for an analyst to rate each job in terms of worker traits. This consists of traits in the following categories:

Training time (general educational development, and specific vocational preparation, rated on numerical scales)

Aptitudes (seventy-one aptitudes, rated on five-point scale)

Interests (five pairs of bipolar interests)

Temperaments (twelve categories of occupational situations to which workers must adjust)

Physical demands (six categories, each with specific sub-categories)

Working conditions (seven categories with specific sub-categories)

Discussion

Any given job can be characterized in terms of the various types of categories described above; in some instances, there is provision for rating the job on some characteristics. The end-result of this is that jobs

TABLE 1
WORKER FUNCTION HIERARCHY OF FUNCTIONAL OCCUPATIONAL CLASSIFICATION OF UNITED STATES TRAINING AND EMPLOYMENT SERVICE

Data	People	Things
0 Synthesizing	0 Mentoring	0 Setting-Up
1 Coordinating	1 Negotiating	1 Precision Working
2 Analyzing	2 Instructing	2 Operating-Controlling
3 Compiling	3 Supervising	3 Driving-Operating
4 Computing	4 Diverting	4 Manipulating
5 Copying	5 Persuading	5 Tending
6 Comparing	6 Speaking-Signaling	6 Feeding-Offbearing
	7 Serving	7 Handling
	8 Taking Instructions-Helping	

Note: The hyphenated factors Speaking-Signaling, Taking Instructions-Helping, Setting-Up, Operating-Controlling, Driving-Operating, and Feeding-Offbearing are single functions.

can be categorized or quantified on each of many different characteristics, thus lending the data so gathered to more quantitative description, summarization, and analysis.

Task Description and Analysis

There are many variants of the processes of task description and analysis, but there is also something of an underlying theme. The theme relates to the dissection of human work into "tasks," and the further analysis thereof. Such dissection is carried out for various purposes, but the dominant objectives are those of training and system development.

Before proceeding, however, let us clarify the distinction that has been made between *task description* and *task analysis*. Miller (1962) makes the point that a task description may be best understood as a statement of requirements, in particular a description of what has to be accomplished. Such description is essentially in "operational" terms, typically describing a physical process, the description specifying such aspects as the cues (or stimuli) which the person should perceive in the task environment and the related responses which he makes. On the other hand, Miller characterizes task analysis in terms of the "behavioral understanding" of the task requirements. As related to possible training objectives, task analysis tends to be focused on the human performance requirements and the skills and knowledges that need to be developed in order for people to be able to perform the task as described.

Task Description and Analysis in System Development

Task description and analysis processes for system development purposes have been used in particular by, or on behalf of, the military services (especially the United States Air Force). In the case of systems being developed, the intent of such programs has been that of "predicting" the job activities of personnel who ultimately would be involved in the operation or maintenance of the system. At various stages during the process, analyses are made on the basis of the features and operational requirements of the system (as it is then envisioned) of the tasks that would be involved. If such analyses indicate that some tasks or combinations thereof could not be performed adequately by personnel, the design of the system may then be modified accordingly. As the system is developed the task description and analysis tends to become more and more definitive until, toward the end of the development process, it becomes essentially a specification of the training for personnel who would be involved in the system.

One point should be added about task description and analysis in this context. Since the "system" does not exist as an entity during this process, and since there are, therefore, no personnel who actually are engaged in the jobs in question (since the jobs actually do not then exist), the task description and analysis must be inferred from an analysis of the physical equipment of the system as it "exists" in the form of drawings, blueprints, and other descriptions, and of any intermediate prototypes or models that may be created. In this frame of reference, the task description and analysis process undergoes a series of "approximations" over time, becoming progressively "closer" to the activities of the "final" system.[3]

---

[3] The use of task analysis in this context is discussed in more detail in a technical report of the Wright Air Development Division (WADD Technical Report 60-593, December, 1960). As one phase of the development of systems, the Air Force has developed the concept of the *personnel subsystem* that embraces the various aspects of personnel planning for each system. One part of this program consists of developing the Qualitative and Quantitative Personnel Requirements Information (QQPRI), which is substantially based on task analysis information. This program is described further in a report by Demaree, Marks, Smith, and Snyder (1962).

Task Description and Analysis for Training

In discussing task description and task analysis in the training context, let us first clarify further the distinction that is commonly made between these two. Cunningham and Duncan (1967) make the point that task description specifies the *terminal* (end-of-course) *performance* of trainees, and thus the *content* of training. On the other hand, task analysis relates to "behavioral categories" that are relevant to learning—behavioral categories, such as identification, short-term and long-term recall, decision making, making multiple discriminations, applying concepts, applying principles and rules, etc. The "learning" conditions that would be optimum for these different behavioral categories presumably would be different for each such category. Because of this tie-in between learning conditions and behavioral categories, task analysis (which is in part directed toward the analysis of tasks in terms of such categories) is then the handmaiden of training *methods*. Training *content* (the focus of task description) typically does not itself provide inklings about appropriate training methods to be used. Rather, the training methods should be predicated upon the "behavioral categories" involved in the activities—and the learning conditions that presumably are optimum for learning the behaviors in question.

TASK DESCRIPTION. Miller (1962) states the opinion that each *task activity* consists of the following:

1. An indicator on which the activity-relevant indication appears
2. The indication or cue which calls for a response
3. The control object to be activated
4. The activation or manipulation to be made
5. The indication of response adequacy, or feedback

Thus, the *indicator* is in a sense an external source that gives rise to some *indication or cue* to make a response by *activation or manipulation* of some control object, with there being some subsequent indication of *response adequacy or feedback*. The indication to trigger the response may appear all at once, or it may have to be assembled by the human by recall through periods of time. The feedback may be proximal (as by feel of a control) or distal (as by hearing an engine start). The critical features of task description can then be characterized as follows:

Indication (stimulus) → Activation (response) → Feedback

This formulation can be envisioned as the framework for many common activities, such as:

Alarm clock rings → Turn off alarm → Peace and quiet returns Car approaching from side street → Honk horn → Car stops

This formulation also is fairly straightforward in its application to many types of essentially physical tasks. However, Cunningham and Duncan (1967) call our attention to the fact that, although the formulation is appropriate to most repetitive tasks, there are problems in applying it to some non-repetitive (physical) tasks. (And it might be added, parenthetically, that the problems are magnified in attempting to describe tasks that are more cognitive in nature and in which observable physical activities are nominal.) The difficulties referred to by Cunningham and Duncan relate to both the cues and responses. In some (if not many) industrial jobs, for example, there is no readily identifiable cue to trigger a given response. Rather, the cues may consist of combinations of indications (in some cases distributed through time), but these may be vague and, therefore, defy delineation. Further, Cunningham and Duncan report that, in their efforts to specify the cues used by some workers, they could not identify any objective observable cues and had to resort to teasing out subjective responses from the workers; and in certain instances, they found that such subjectively reported cues were not really the ones used by the workers.

They also report problems in trying to spell out, definitively, in some task descriptions the nature of the response to be made. One facet of the problem relates to the fact that dissimilar but *functionally* equivalent responses may be made on different occasions to the same cue. And in some circumstances, workers were observed to make responses without any preceding cue to trigger it. There also are problems of ambiguity with respect to specifying the nature of the feedback in some tasks.

Although Miller (1962) has taken cognizance of some of these problems, Cunningham and Duncan (1967) argue for a somewhat more flexible approach to task description than that proposed by Miller and others. They propose, in effect, that although it seems sensible to consider each such ingredient, one should not be a slave to the procedures and forms by obediently putting down an "entry" for each such ingredient (if in fact it makes no sense to do so, or if any such entry would be redundant or trivial). They go on to make the point that the fact that the method of observation cannot be applied rigorously to task description does not necessarily mean that such description cannot be rigorous; rather, this argues for recognition of the dependence on the subjective aspects of the process.

TASK ANALYSIS. As indicated above, task analysis is concerned in part with analyzing the behavior components that are involved in tasks, with the view toward developing training methods that are reasonably appropriate to such components. This objective has led to various attempts to develop some

taxonomy of tasks or activities. One such scheme proposed by Gagné (1965) is called a cumulative learning sequence, and consists of six categories as follows: (a) stimulus-response connections; (b) chain of relationships (motor or verbal); (c) multiple discriminations; (d) concepts; (e) simple principles or rules; and (f) complex principles or rules. He postulates the notion that this is essentially a hierarchy in the sense that the learning at any given level subsumes learning at the lower levels (with the possible exception of the "chain of relationships"). The potential relevance of such a formulation to training methods can be reflected by the following series of assumptions:

1. Any given task can be characterized in terms of one of these categories.

2. For any given category there is some optimum approach to learning (such as how to learn multiple discriminations, concepts, etc.).

3. Therefore, the specific training method for the task should be predicated on the learning approach that is most relevant for the category that represents the nature of the task.

There are, however, some hitches in this possible approach. Annett and Duncan (1967), for example, express the opinion (somewhat supported by evidence) that Gagné's formulation is not invariably a hierarchy; in other words, learning of, say, simple principles and rules, does not necessarily depend upon learning at each and every lower level in the sequence. And further (and perhaps more basic) it probably can be said that, at this stage of affairs, there is no manifestly optimum learning procedure or approach for each such category of the hierarchy; thus, the bridge between any given category of learning task and a corresponding (optimum) training method is a fairly shaky one.

These and other reflections lead Annett and Duncan to the unsatisfying conclusion that a method of analyzing tasks which reliably prescribes the training procedures required probably does not exist. They go on to suggest that one way of building up such a method would be to begin with a provisional set of categories for which there is some evidence of relatively specific training methods and conditions (such as might now be done in the case of multiple discriminations and chains of relationships). Beyond this, it would be necessary to test the value of providing specific methods and conditions in training people on the various components of real tasks.

The business of the world (including the training business) cannot stop until research provides complete, unambiguous answers. Thus, even though task analysis procedures do not yet lead in all cases to definitive answers to training problems, training must be continued (even if in some instances not as efficiently as might be wished). Hopefully, research might ultimately resolve some of the presently vexing aspects of this problem.

Task Description and Analysis Approaches

Recognizing some of the limitations of task description and analysis, and the qualms expressed by various people relating thereto, let us illustrate without much elaboration certain specific schemes or approaches that have been used.

TASK DESCRIPTION FORM. An example of a task description form presented by Miller (1962) is given as Figure 2. This shows only the headings used and a couple of job elements. Note in particular the elements of control, activity, and indication (as discussed above).

TASK EQUIPMENT ANALYSIS FORMS FOR AIR FORCE (TEA). In the United States Air Force some type of task equipment analysis form (TEA) is used in connection with their task analysis activities. Figure 3 illustrates the format developed and used by the

JOB ELEMENT FORM						
Duty 1. Adjust system				POSITION Line mechanic—Radar system		
TASK	TIME minutes		ELEMENTS			REMARKS Alternatives and/or precautions
	In seq.	Out seq.	CONTROL	ACTIVITY	INDICATION (Include when to do task and frequency of task)	
1.1 Adjust radar receiver	40	40	⟶		Adjust every 25 hours of a/c time. See a/c log.	
			1.1.1 POWER ON Button	Press	Inverter starts and makes audible hum, pilot light comes on, range indicator lights come on, tiltmeter pointer comes on scale.	Avoid starting system with covers removed from high voltage units: personal hazard
			1.1.2 AC voltage adjustment (screwdriver)	Turn	AC voltmeter aligns to 117 ±4 volts.	

Figure 2. Portion of one task description form showing a couple of illustrative activities. This form provides for the identification of the control to be used, the activity (i.e., the response to be made), and the indication. (From Miller, 1962.)

TASKS (GROSS TASK) (SUB-TASKS)	Take-Off (Example of Gross Task)	Radio Position Report (Example of Sub-Task	Identification of task a. Include alternate tasks b. List tasks in operational sequence
VEHICLE EQUIPMENT	Throttle, Stick, Rudder Pedals	ARC _____	Equipment task is performed on.
SUPPORT EQUIPMENT AND PERSONNEL	Control Tower	Communication Station	Personnel performing task—number and type. Other personnel or equipment supplying information or services.
DISPLAYS	RPM Instrs. Gyro Instrs. T.P.T.	Pilot Light or Switch Position, Clock	What operator sees, hears, feels, smells, etc. This must include all the critical elements needed for decision, including controls which may also serve as displays.
DIAGNOSIS AND DECISION	Recognizes that steps preliminary to take-off are satisfactory	Recognizes Time for Report	(1) Mental and/or physical process before initiating action. (2) Consideration of alternates (other possible decisions).
ACTION	Pushes Throttle Forward	Depresses Mike Button	What does operator do? Consider possible erroneous actions. Define the control(s) involved, their location, and tolerance.
FEEDBACK	Increased RPM: Appearance of Runway; Sound of Engine	Clicks in Earphones; Verbal Responses from Ground	What indications does pilot get of effect of his action?
INCIDENCE	Once Per Sortie	Every _____ Minutes	How often is pilot called on to perform this activity?
TIME	30 Sec.	10 Sec.	How long does this action take? Consider overlap or interference with other actions and total time requirement.
REMARKS			Degree of confidence on task existence during operational procedures.

Figure 3. Illustration of task equipment analysis form (TEA) used in task analysis by U. S. Air Force. (From Snyder, 1960.)

then Wright Air Development Division; it includes illustrative tasks and notes and comments relative to the analysis procedure. Modifications of this as developed by HRB-Singer, Inc. are shown in Figure 4, as presented by Snyder (1960). This figure shows the column headings of two forms, namely those for operator personnel and for maintenance personnel, since some variations are appropriate for these two types of jobs.

A TASK DESCRIPTION PROCEDURE. As another illustration of task description approaches, a few features of that proposed by Dean and Jud (1965) will be given. The viewpoint reflected by their procedure is limited to that of the trainer or educator who analyzes the basic steps of any job so he can successfully teach it to somebody else. (In doing so, the intent should be that of presenting material at the level of detail necessary to describe a familiar procedure to some one who does not know it.)

The approach is summarized below, and is illustrated in part by the common use of the telephone, but on the assumption that the trainee has never seen one before.

1. Write each step on a card, each step consisting of a stimulus and response as:
   Stimulus: When the phone rings,
   Response: pick up the phone.
   Stimulus: If you hear a busy signal (rapid buzzing sound),
   Response: hang up immediately.
2. Use the imperative form of verb:
   Right: Next, turn the dial clockwise until your finger is stopped by a small silver bar.
   Wrong: Next, the dial should be recessed.
3. Explain technical terms:
   Example: If you do not hear a DIAL-TONE (steady buzzing sound), HANG UP (replace the receiver on the phone as you found it).
4. Rationale for steps: If it seems desirable to record the rationale of a step (i.e., the reason the step is performed)

for future reference, do so on the back of the card.
5. Place cards in sequence: In doing so it usually occurs that at some stage in a sequence there is a *branching,* such that a *discrimination* or decision needs to be made by reason of differing stimuli (or conditions) that occur. Such *branching* (as opposed to a strictly *linear* sequence) is reflected by placing those cards that represent alternative responses side-by-side instead of one below the other. This arrangement is illustrated in Figure 5, the particular example being an abbreviated version of the series of discriminations a bank teller makes in checking endorsements on a deposited check. In branching situations, the task statements need to be expressed clearly in terms of the specific circumstances under which each response is made.

DISCUSSION. The use of forms and procedures such as those illustrated above is reasonably straightforward in well-structured jobs in which the cues and their corresponding responses can be fairly well spelled out. As suggested by Annett and Duncan (1967), however, adaptations need to be made in less-routinized and less-structured jobs.

Job Inventories

A job inventory (also referred to as a task inventory) is a form of structured job-analysis questionnaire that consists of a listing of tasks, usually the tasks being those which are relevant to the jobs within some occupational area.[4] The "tasks" as incorporated in job inventories usually consist only of a statement of the activity as such, omitting the cues and feedback features as dis-

---

[4] The term *check list* has also been used for what is referred to here as a job inventory. Although the term *check list* may be appropriate in some instances, it implies simply a "checking" of items, whereas most job inventories require more elaborate responses, such as ratings.

FORM FOR OPERATOR PERSONNEL

Duties, Tasks, and Sub-Tasks	Display		Decisions
	Description	Critical Values	

(Continuation)

Control		Feedback	Incidence	Time	Remarks
Description	Action				

FORM FOR MAINTENANCE PERSONNEL

Duties, Tasks, and Sub-Tasks	Systems Equipment	Service Equipment	Displays		Decisions
			Description	Critical Values	

(Continuation)

Control		Feedback	Incidence	Time	Cycle	I & D Code	Task B & C Explanation	Remarks
Description	Action							

Figure 4. Column headings of task analysis forms developed by HRB-Singer, Inc. for use in connection with the U. S. Air Force task analysis activities. Headings for two forms are shown, one for operator personnel and the other for maintenance personnel. (From Snyder, 1960.)

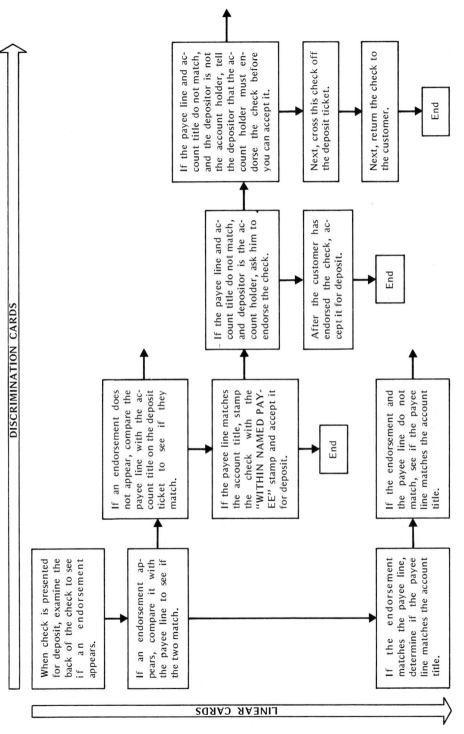

DISCRIMINATION CARDS

When check is presented for deposit, examine the back of the check to see if an endorsement appears.

If an endorsement appears, compare it with the payee line to see if the two match.

If an endorsement does not appear, compare the payee line with the account title on the deposit ticket to see if they match.

If the payee line matches the account title, stamp the check with the "WITHIN NAMED PAYEE" stamp and accept it for deposit.

End

If the payee line and account title do not match, and depositor is the account holder, ask him to endorse the check.

After the customer has endorsed the check, accept it for deposit.

End

If the payee line and account title do not match, and the depositor is not the account holder, tell the depositor that the account holder must endorse the check before you can accept it.

Next, cross this check off the deposit ticket.

Next, return the check to the customer.

End

If the endorsement matches the payee line, determine if the payee line matches the account title.

If the endorsement and the payee line do not match, see if the payee line matches the account title.

LINEAR CARDS

Figure 5. Illustration of the arrangement of task description cards of part of the operation of handling deposited bank checks. In particular, this shows the arrangement of tasks in a *linear* sequence (those below one another) versus a *branching* (those placed beside each other). (From Dean & Jud, 1965.)

cussed above in task description and analysis. Examples shown later will illustrate their nature. Job inventories usually are completed by incumbents as the basis for reporting some job-related information about the incumbents' positions; however, in some instances they may be completed by someone other than an incumbent, such as by a supervisor (who might thus describe an incumbent's position).

The job inventory technology has been developed over the last several years primarily by the Personnel Division of the Air Force Human Resources Laboratory (Christal, 1969; Morsh, 1969; Morsh & Archer, 1967). However, the methodology has also been adopted by certain other military services both in the United States and elsewhere; and there have been at least a few other organizations—private and governmental—that have used some form of job inventory for research or operational purposes.

The Nature of Job Inventories

In its final form, a job inventory usually is characterized by two dominant features, namely, the list of tasks and provision for some response(s).

Task listing. The list of tasks included in an inventory typically includes virtually all the tasks that might be performed by incumbents in the occupational field in question. In the military services an occupational field usually embraces a variety of jobs within some relatively broad, but related, domain of work, such as medical services or aircraft maintenance. The tasks usually are grouped within broader categories of duties. An example of part of a job inventory is shown as Figure 6. In final form, an inventory might include anywhere from 100 to 200, up to 400, or 500 or more, tasks.

Responses to job inventories. Usually the job incumbent completes an inventory as related to his own position. In a very simple case, he may simply indicate whether he does, or does not, perform a particular task.

If this is all that is required, the inventory is, in effect, a simple check list. However, it is usually the practice to ask for further responses to the individual tasks. There are many options in this regard, but they generally are referred to as primary and secondary task rating factors (Morsh & Archer, 1967). The primary task rating factors provide for an indication for each task of the relevance of that task to the position, such as in terms of time, importance to the position, how much "part of the job" the task represents, or how frequently the task is performed.

In connection with reporting time spent, it has been the experience of the Air Force that a relative time-spent scale usually is better than one based on absolute time or percentage of time. The relative time-spent scale used by the Air Force is given below (Morsh & Archer, 1967):

Relative Time-Spent Task Rating Scale. Compared with other tasks you do in your job, the time you spend on the task you are rating is:
1. Very much below average
2. Below average
3. Slightly below average
4. About average
5. Slightly above average
6. Above average
7. Very much above average

Another scale, the Hemphill part-of-job scale, was developed by Hemphill (1959) for use by executives, but has been found to be quite acceptable for use by Air Force officers (Cragun & McCormick, 1967). This scale is shown below in slightly modified form:

Part-of-job Task Rating Scale.
0. Definitely not part of the position
1. Under unusual circumstances is a minor part of position
2.
3.
4. A substantial part of the position
5.
6.
7. A most significant part of the position

Listed below is a duty and the tasks which it includes. Check all tasks which you perform. Add any tasks you do which are not listed. Then rate the tasks you have checked.	CHECK	TIME SPENT	IMPORTANCE
H. INSTALLING AND REMOVING AERIAL CABLE SYSTEMS	✓ IF DONE	1. Very much below average 2. Below average 3. Slightly below average 4. About average 5. Slightly above average 6. Above average 7. Very much above average	1. Extremely unimportant 2. Very unimportant 3. Unimportant 4. About medium importance 5. Important 6. Very important 7. Extremely important
1. Attach suspension strand to pole			
2. Change and splice lasher wire			
3. Deliver materials to lineman with snatch block and handline			
4. Drill through-bolt holes and secure suspension clamps on poles			
5. Install cable pressurization systems			
6. Install distribution terminals			
7. Install pulling-in line through cable rings			
8. Load and unload cable reels			
9. Load lashing machine with lashing wire			

Figure 6. Portion of a job inventory for the outside wire and antenna systems career field of the Air Force. (From Morsh & Archer, 1967.)

In the use of this scale the incumbent is asked to consider and weigh the importance, frequency of occurrence, relevance, or other factors which he thinks will determine the extent to which the task is a "part" of his position.

There are quite a number of secondary rating factors that have been used, most of these eliciting more subjective responses of the incumbent about the task. Some of these are of a continuous nature, and others of a categorical nature. Some examples are listed below (Morsh & Archer, 1967):

1. Continuous variable task rating factors
   (a) Complexity of the task
   (b) Criticality of task to unit mission
   (c) Difficulty of learning the task
   (d) Difficulty of learning the task by OJT
   (e) Difficulty of task performance
   (f) Experience needed for task performance
   (g) Extent of training in school or work experience
   (h) Satisfaction in performing task
   (i) Special training necessary to perform task
   (j) Supervision required in task performance

(k) Technical assistance required to perform task

(l) Time spent in task during entire career

(m) Training emphasis task should have

(n) Training required for task performance

2. Categorical variable task rating factors. Method of learning (usually with categories representing different ways of learning the task)

3. Special training required (usually expressed in terms of amount)

4. Task performance (expressed as "can do now" or in terms of time that would be required to learn)

When inventories are completed by someone other than the incumbent (as by a supervisor), the primary rating factors might be used as the basis for eliciting his perception of the position. In addition, he might be asked to use certain of the secondary rating factors. Or he might be asked to use specially adapted scales, including scales for use in evaluation of subordinates, such as relative proficiency or time to learn (to become proficient) as reported by Swanson (1969).

Development of Job Inventories

As indicated above, a job inventory typically is developed for an occupational area. Given the area to be covered, the development of a job inventory is admittedly a time-consuming chore and, therefore, should be undertaken only when the scope and importance of its use would justify the effort. Archer and Fruchter (1963) report that "typical" preliminary inventories should be completed in three to four weeks, but that those for more complex technical jobs might take about twice that long.

A final inventory is typically the product of the work of a job analyst and of technical advisors. The procedures used by the Air Force are spelled out by Morsh and Archer

(1967) and Archer and Fruchter (1963), and represent a very substantial amount of experience. Although the details will not be repeated here, the major steps will at least be mentioned.

SELECTION OF SOURCE MATERIALS. As a starter, the job analyst responsible for the development of an inventory usually begins by locating source materials that may be descriptive of the occupational area. Such materials might include training materials of various types, instruction manuals relating to equipment used, relevant organizational directives, relevant technical reports, texts, etc. Such an accumulation of material can serve to provide the analyst with some background in the area, and may also be used by him as the basis for the development of a preliminary inventory.

DEVELOPMENT OF PRELIMINARY INVENTORY. In the development of preliminary inventories by the Air Force, it is typically the practice to have the job analyst do so on the basis of the source materials mentioned above. In this general method, Archer and Fruchter (1963) describe two alternative approaches. One of these consists of developing a large pool of task statements from the source materials and then organizing them into "duty" groupings. The other consists of starting off with a "duty outline," and then developing task statements within the framework of each duty or sub-duty. For various reasons they propose the second approach.

On the other hand, preliminary inventories can be developed by first asking a sample of job incumbents to list activities that they perform, or to ask technical experts to list the activities they know to be performed in the occupational area in question. In either case, the analyst then consolidates the statements, eliminating duplications, thus ending up with a single list of tasks. In addition, he edits the statements, working them into a reasonably consistent form.

The form of task statements conforms

to certain ground rules, such as those prescribed by Morsh and Archer (1967), some of which are summarized as follows: (1) they should describe actual job activities (and not qualifications, skills, training, etc., or "responsibilities"); (2) they should be brief, clear, and unambiguous so that they are easily understood by the incumbent; (3) they should be so worded that the task rating scales (such as "time spent") make good sense when applied to them; (4) they should be worded in the first person, present tense, with the "I" understood, such as "Operate...," "Write...," "Clean...," and *not* "Operates...," "Writes...," "Cleans...." Generally, one would tend to characterize job activities that are reasonably identifiable as discrete units of work, that have discernible beginnings and endings, and that in the normal course of events are executed completely by an individual. In doing so, however, one should avoid the Scylla of excessive minutia (such as "Remove bolts that hold generator") and the Charybdis of excessive generality (such as "Repair motor vehicles"), and rather seek an intermediate level on the specificity-to-generality scale (such as "Repair generators").

REVIEW OF INVENTORIES. A preliminary inventory is then typically reviewed by several or many technical advisors (experts in the occupational area) for various purposes, such as adding (writing in) any tasks that have been omitted; indicating if any listed tasks should be consolidated, broken down further, or eliminated; and judging whether the task statements as given are clear in their meaning, or whether they should be reworded to make them more understandable to an ultimate incumbent. Such a review might be arranged by mail or might be carried out during an interview with the technical advisors, either individually or as a group.

PREPARATION OF FINAL INVENTORY. The analyst then reviews the suggestions of the several technical advisors, and works up a final inventory that generally takes advantage of their suggestions. In case of questions, or significant differences between and among advisors, the review process might be repeated with an intermediate form of the inventory, before preparation of a final form.

In the final form there usually is provision for incumbents to write in tasks that are not in the inventory. This makes it possible to spot tasks that may have been missed somewhere along the line. But more particularly this provides for identifying new tasks, thus furnishing data for up-dating inventories with dynamic changes in an occupational area.

In the preparation of the final form of an inventory there is usually provision for the incumbent to record certain types of biographical data, in particular those which might be relevant in later statistical summaries and analyses to be carried.

Administration of Job Inventories

One of the plus marks for job inventories is that they can be completed by typical job incumbents without special training. However, in most situations it is desirable to arrange for the incumbents to be gathered together for the purpose of completing the inventories, to provide a reasonably quiet, undisturbed environment, and to provide the opportunity for respondents to ask questions if in fact they have any.

Reliability of Job Inventory Information

The reliability of the responses of individuals to job inventories most logically should be determined on the basis of two administrations to the same sample of subjects, preferably a week or two apart, but not too long apart (because of the possibility of changes in job content over a period of time). Several such analyses have been made. Some of these analyses are given below, in particular those of (a) McCormick and Ammerman (1960); (b) Birt (1968); and (c) Cragun and McCormick (1967).

Response or scale	(a)	(b)	(c)
Task occurrence	.70 & .73	.87	.63, .64 & .65
Time spent on task	.61	.83	.62
Part-of-position (of task)		.83	.63
Importance (of task)			.56
Difficulty (of task)		.47	.35

The time span between the two administrations in the case of the coefficients from Cragun and McCormick (c) was several weeks, which may account for the somewhat lower coefficients.

Such coefficients can be viewed as reflecting the reliability of individuals when responding to individual task statements on two different occasions. However, one can also view the reliability of job information in a much broader context. Considering consolidated data from a job inventory completed by a sample of job incumbents, one could ask this question, as phrased by Christal (1969): "If we were to go out and get a second sample (of subjects), would we get the same results?" An answer to Christal's question is provided in the form of correlations between the "percent performing" the various tasks in an inventory resulting from two subsamples, and corresponding correlations of the "time spent" responses of those in the two subsamples. The correlations reported by Christal are quite persuasive. For thirty-five samples, representing ten career fields and a total of 9,822 cases, the medians (of the thirty-five correlations) were as follows:

Task rating factor	Median correlation
Percent performing	.978
Time spent	.957

As another indication of reliability of job inventory information, Birt (1968) examined the possible effect of differences in inventory responses of twenty airmen as given to two inventories a week apart on their hypothetical "assignments" to actual vacancies which had been "described" in terms of the same basic inventory. He used an "affinity" index which reflected the degree of relationship of a "person" profile to each "job" profile. Actually, affinity indexes were derived in thirteen different ways (that need not be described here). For a given method, it was possible to correlate an individual's affinity indexes for the forty-nine vacancies as these indexes resulted from the two administrations of the inventory. These correlations, averaged across the twenty airmen, ranged from .92 to .99 for the thirteen methods, with a median of .96. These results indicate that the possible "assignments" of airmen, as they might be made by a computer matching of men and positions, would not be markedly affected by whatever differences there are in inventory responses on two different occasions.

Although the reliability of responses of individuals to individual tasks tends to be rather moderate, when the many bits and pieces of inventory data are pooled, either for an individual, and especially across individuals, the stability of job information data is generally very respectable. Such stability can be considered fully adequate for use of the resulting data for many practical purposes.

Reliability of responses—however measured—does not, of course, provide evidence of the validity thereof, although it does strongly imply that there must be underlying truth. With regard to the question of validity, however, Christal (1969) reports briefly the efforts of a group of trainers in the Air Force who refused to accept the validity of occupation survey results in their area, and set about to gather evidence that the data were in error; yet, at the end of their investigation, they had to accept the inventory results as being basically valid.

Summarization of the Job Inventory Responses

The data collected with job inventories lends itself to numerous forms of summarization and analysis. One such example is given in Table 2. This particular illustration shows some of the data summarized from an Air Force job inventory administered to 425 medical laboratory specialists. The data presented shows: percent of those who perform each task; the mean time spent by those who perform the task; the mean percent of time spent (on the task) by all specialists; and the cumulative percent of time spent by all specialists across the tasks already listed.

JOB AND OCCUPATION STRUCTURES

In searching for some order and system in this world of ours, people have developed classifications or taxonomies of biological organisms, of material substances, and (in the domain of human life) of human be-

havior—even of the jobs and occupations people pursue. A taxonomy of things or phenomena is predicated on manifestations of certain similarities and differences between and among the individual cases being classified. There are various approaches to the development of taxonomies, as discussed by Theologus (1969), these having been developed and applied especially in the biological sciences. Certain of these, specifically the Linnaean and Darwinian approaches, depend heavily upon subjective opinions regarding the bases of classification in the actual classification of specific organisms or objects. On the other hand, numerical taxonomy places emphasis on repeatability and objectivity, thus aiming toward the establishment of classifications based on stable, objectively derived, data bases. Existing taxonomies in the job and occupational area probably have some parallels to these alternative approaches, although the bias proposed here is that of the numerical approach, with its focus on the use of reasonably objective data.

TABLE 2
PARTIAL JOB DESCRIPTION OF MEDICAL LABORATORY SPECIALIST
BASED ON JOB INVENTORY RESPONSES (N = 425)

Task	% who perform task	Mean % time spent by those who perform	Mean % time spent by all specialists	Cumulative % time spent by all specialists
Collect blood specimens directly from patients	91.02	1.75	1.59	1.59
Perform blood count	85.84	1.58	1.36	2.95
Perform differential cell counts	85.84	1.51	1.29	4.24
Prepare and process specimens	86.82	1.45	1.26	5.51
Perform hematocrit tests	85.64	1.46	1.25	6.76
Prepare blood smears	86.82	1.41	1.23	7.99
Examine urine specimens microscopically	84.38	1.43	1.21	9.20
Clean area and equipment aseptically	77.83	1.48	1.16	10.35
Perform glucose tests	83.50	1.38	1.15	11.51
Perform albumin tests	83.20	1.38	1.15	12.66
Perform specific gravity tests	83.01	1.38	1.15	13.80
Test blood for ABO grouping and ABO subgrouping	77.15	1.14	0.88	30.42
Crossmatch blood	70.12	1.24	0.87	31.29
Identify immature blood cells	82.81	1.05	0.87	32.16
Examine specimens microscopically	77.83	1.08	0.84	33.00
Perform antibiotic sensitivity test	71.68	1.16	0.83	33.83
Type blood of donors and recipients	72.46	1.12	0.81	34.65

Job Descriptors

In any event, the development of job or occupation taxonomies is predicated upon the characteristics of jobs and occupations—whether subjectively judged or quantified. In this connection there are, of course, many different facets or kinds of attributes that conceivably could serve in some way as the basis of a taxonomy for some purpose (Farina, 1969). For our purposes these various characteristics will be referred to as *job descriptors*.

In general, individual job descriptors are of two types—qualitative and quantitative. *Qualitative* descriptors are those which are categorical, or nominal, in nature. Such descriptors either "apply" or "do not apply" to individual jobs. At a very specific level one could thus characterize jobs as to whether they do, or do not, involve out-of-town travel, or reading blueprints, or driving a vehicle; at a grosser level jobs can be characterized in terms of professional, clerical, etc., or on the basis of other broadly conceived classes (although such allocation typically is predicated on the basis of syndromes of more specific descriptors). On the other hand, *quantitative* descriptors are those in which jobs are characterized in terms of degree, such as amount of physical effort required or the amount of time involved in, say, personal contacts. It should be noted that some descriptors can be characterized in either qualitative (i.e., categorical) or quantitative terms.

For purposes of the present discussion some types of job variables will be mentioned, but these will not comprise an exhaustive listing. Before so proceeding, however, two points should be made that are relevant to the discussion of taxonomic approaches mentioned above. In the first place, the possible use of any job descriptor in a taxonomy in some circumstances is based on rational considerations, and in other circumstances is based on quantitative job data. In the second place, the classification or quantification of individual jobs in terms of specific variables can be based on subjective judgments and evaluations, or on essentially objective data or observations relating to the jobs.

Job Content

One of the most commonly recognized types of job descriptors is that of job content; that is, the nature of the work activities that incumbents perform. Usually job content is viewed in the framework of job-oriented activities, but it can also be viewed in the framework of worker-oriented activities. Job content, of course, can be characterized at various levels of specificity or generality.

CLERICAL JOB FUNCTIONS. One example of a systematic analysis of job content variables of a job-oriented nature is reported by Chalupsky (1962). In this study, a check list of thirty-three clerical operations was used in analyzing a sample of 192 jobs. The operations included such items as analyzes, compiles, plans, and translates. The 192 jobs were represented by complete job descriptions provided by the United States Training and Employment Service. A factor analysis of the data resulted in the identification of five factors, as follows: inventory and stockkeeping; supervision; computation and bookkeeping; communication and public relations; and stenography-typing and general clerical. Each of these can be viewed as representing a reasonably stable cluster of the more specific clerical functions which, in the world of work, typically tend to occur in combination with each other. (It might be added that a parallel analysis of the same jobs using a check list of fifty-eight clerical knowledge items resulted in the identification of factors that corresponded very closely with these, except that the last factor was broken down into two, namely, stenography-typing and filing and general clerical.) In this study, the descriptors of job content can be viewed at two levels, namely, at the level of the thirty-three clerical operations and at the level of the several factors.

WORK PERFORMANCE FACTORS OF HEALTH OFFICERS. As another illustration of the use of factor analysis of job content, Brumback and Vincent (1970) describe a fairly large-scale survey of commissioned officers of the Public Health Service in which 3,719 officers used a job inventory to report their own work activities. The resulting responses were subjected to factor analysis in order to identify the different functional areas of work represented by the sample. A total of twenty-six such functional work areas (i.e., factors) were identified, a few of which were: performing public health inspection and control activities; conducting surveys (such as epidemiological investigations); and preparing and testing samples for contaminants or disease agents.

In large part, this analysis was made with the possible objective in mind of providing a more appropriate basis for personnel appraisal, in particular, one that might be more job-oriented than person-oriented.

JOB FACTORS OF HIGH-LEVEL POSITIONS. As another illustration of a systematic approach to the study of descriptors of job content, Baehr (1967) carried out a factor analysis of a job analysis questionnaire called the Work Elements Inventory that consisted of 122 "generic" job elements that might be relevant to supervisory, management, sales, and other higher-level positions. The factor analysis was based on data provided by 600 job incumbents who used the inventory to describe their own positions, and generated the factors, here grouped into four areas:

Organization
  1. Setting organizational objectives
  2. Improving work procedures and practices
  3. Promoting safety attitudes and practices

  4. Developing and implementing technical ideas
Leadership
  5. Judgment and decision making
  6. Developing group cooperation and teamwork
  7. Coping with difficulties and emergencies
Personnel
  8. Developing employee potential
  9. Supervisory practices
  10. Self-development and improvement
Community
  11. Promoting community-organization relations
  12. Handling outside contacts

JOB DIMENSIONS BASED ON PAQ JOB DATA. Mention was made earlier of the Position Analysis Questionnaire (PAQ). This questionnaire consists of job elements of a worker-oriented nature, that characterize human "behaviors" in jobs. Each such element, of course, can be thought of as a job descriptor by itself. But further, such job elements can be subjected to statistical analyses (such as factor and principal components analyses) to identify broader descriptors. Two such studies have been carried out with PAQ-based data, one reported by Jeanneret and McCormick (1969) using the first form of the PAQ (Form A), and the other by Marquardt and McCormick (1973; June 1974). Both of these consisted of principal components analyses of two "sets" of data based on the PAQ, one set dealing with "job data" (data from PAQ analyses of jobs) and the other from "attribute profiles" of the PAQ job elements. (The analyses based on the attribute profiles will be discussed later.) Since the job data study by Marquardt and McCormick (June 1974) was based on the more recent PAQ (Form B) and involved a large sample of jobs, the results of this will be presented here. This consisted of principal components analyses of PAQ data for 3,700 jobs. One such analysis, an "overall" or general analysis, was carried out with the ratings for the 3,700 jobs on virtually all of the PAQ job elements (182 job elements). Other analyses were carried out separately for the job elements within each of the six divisions of the PAQ.

The results of these principal components analyses are given in Table 3 in the first column. (Reference will be made to the second column later.) Since it is not feasible here to present the voluminous data on the loadings of the job elements on the components, only the titles of the components are given. These are referred to as job dimensions.

These dimensions can be interpreted as reflecting the "organization" of human job behaviors; that is, the extent to which job behaviors tend to group themselves together in the world of work.

Attribute Requirements of Jobs

Aside from characterizing jobs in terms of job content descriptors, they can also be characterized in terms of their human "requirements"; that is, the nature (and possibly degree) of the human attributes (qualities, abilities, etc.) that presumably contribute to satisfactory job performance. Such requirements most typically are established for individual jobs on the basis of judgments (such as those of job analysts), but in some instances (and more defensibly) on the basis of statistical validation procedures. However, one would wish for a more analytical approach to this process than has been practiced in the past. In this connection, there is the initial question regarding the identification of the relatively independent attributes that are relevant to job performance. Further, it would be useful to have some well-founded, systematic procedure for specifying the attributes required for various types of human work activity. A couple of probing efforts along these lines will be discussed briefly.

HUMAN ABILITIES IN TASK PERFORMANCE. As one such effort, the American Institutes for Research has embarked on a program for the development of a taxonomy of human performance, in particular for providing a unifying set of variables for describing human task performance. (Such a common task-descriptive language would lend itself to various purposes, such as relating human performance in one task to that observed in other tasks, or for applying the results of task-related research to operational tasks.) In this regard, Fleishman (1967) differentiates between what he refers to as an *ability* (a general trait of the individual which has been inferred from certain response tendencies) and a *skill* (the level of proficiency on a specific task or group of tasks). He postulates the notion that the development of proficiency (i.e., skill) on any given task is predicated in part on the possession of relevant basic abilities.

As one phase of the research program of the American Institutes of Research, Theologus, Romashko, and Fleishman (1970)

TABLE 3
SUMMARY OF JOB DIMENSION TITLES[a]

Job Dimensions Based on Job Data	Job Dimensions Based on Attribute Profile Data
Division 1: Information Input	
J1-1 Perceptual Interpretation	A1-1 Visual Input from Devices/Materials
J1-2 Evaluation of Sensory Input	A1-2 Evaluation of Visual Input
J1-3 Visual Input from Devices/Materials	A1-3 Perceptual Input from Processes/Events
J1-4 Input from Representational Sources	A1-4 Verbal/Auditory Input/Interpretation
J1-5 Environmental Awareness	A1-5 Non-Visual Input
Division 2: Mental Processes	
J2-6 Decision Making	A2-6 Use of Job-Related Knowledge
J2-7 Information Processing	A2-7 Information Processing

Continued

TABLE 3 (cont.)

Job Dimensions Based on Job Data	Job Dimensions Based on Attribute Profile Data

Division 3: Work Output

J3–8 Manual/Control Activities	A3–8 Manual Control/Coordination Activities
J3–9 Physical Coordination in Control/Related Activities	A3–9 Control/Equipment Operation
J3–10 General Body Activity versus Sedentary Activities	A3–10 General Body/Handling Activities
J3–11 Manipulating/Handling Activities	A3–11 Use of Foot Controls
J3–12 Adjusting/Operating Machines/Equipment	
J3–13 Skilled/Technical Activities	
J3–14 Use of Miscellaneous Equipment/Devices	

Division 4: Relationships with Other Persons

J4–15 Interchange of Ideas/Judgments/ Related Information	A4–12 Interpersonal Communications
J4–16 Supervisory/Staff Activities	A4–13 Signal/Code Communications
J4–17 Public/Related Personal Contact	A4–14 Serving/Entertaining
J4–18 Communicating Instructions/Directions/ Related Job Information	
J4–19 General Personal Contact	
J4–20 Job-Related Communications	

Division 5: Job Context

J5–21 Potentially Stressful/Unpleasant Environment	A5–15 Unpleasant Physical Environment
J5–22 Potentially Hazardous Job Situations	A5–16 Personally Demanding Situations
J5–23 Personally Demanding Situations	A5–17 Hazardous Physical Environment

Division 6: Other Job Characteristics

J6–24 Attentive Job Demands	A6–18 Work Schedule I
J6–25 Vigilant/Discriminating Work Activities	A6–19 Job Responsibility
J6–26 Structured versus Unstructured Work Activities	A6–20 Routine/Repetitive Work Activities
J6–27 Regular versus Irregular Work Schedule	A6–21 Attentive/Discriminating Work Demands
J6–28 Work/Protective versus Business Clothing	A6–22 Work Attire
J6–29 Specific versus Non-Specific Clothing	A6–23 Work Schedule II
J6–30 Continuity of Work Load	

General (G) Dimensions

G–1 Decision/Communication/Social Responsibilities	(No overall analyses made)
G–2 Environmental Demands/General Body Control	
G–3 Equipment/Machine Operation	
G–4 Unnamed	
G–5 Manual Control Activities	
G–6 Office/Related Activities	
G–7 Evaluation of Sensory Input	
G–8 General/Public-Related Personal Contact	
G–9 Use of Technical/Related Materials	
G–10 General Physical Activities versus Sedentary Activities	
G–11 Hazardous/Personally Demanding Situations	
G–12 Attentive/Vigilant Work Activities	
G–13 Unnamed	
G–14 Supervision/Coordination	

ᵃ The dimensions based on job data and on attribute profile data are arranged by PAQ division in parallel columns for comparative purposes. Within any given division there may be dimensions based on the two sources which may be identical, or nearly so. However, the ordering and numbering of dimensions within each division is not intended to reflect corresponding dimensions.

crystallized at least a tentative listing of human abilities that have relevance to human task performance, and developed scales for use in classifying tasks in terms of such abilities. An initial listing of fifty such abilities was used, these being based primarily on previous factor analyses of human performance in the sensory, perceptual, cognitive, psychomotor, and physical areas. These were used experimentally in a couple of pilot studies, and were then reduced to thirty-seven, each with its own definition and rating scale.[5] The rating scales consist of seven points, each one having three benchmark tasks to represent specified scale positions as aids in rating other tasks.

As one phase of the study, two groups of raters rated the degree to which each of the thirty-seven abilities was required for performance on each of six hypothetical tasks. The pooled reliability correlations (i.e., intraclass correlations) for groups of ten or twenty raters were about .90 and .91 for the two groups. Although the reliability of ratings of individual raters was fairly modest, the pooled ratings take on very respectable reliability.

JOB DIMENSIONS BASED ON PAQ ATTRIBUTE DATA. The listing of human abilities developed by Theologus, Romashko, and Fleishman (1970) mentioned above probably reflects about the most adequate inventory of such abilities available, and thus provides a

---

[5] These thirty-seven abilities are: (1) Verbal comprehension; (2) Verbal expression; (3) Ideational fluency; (4) Originality; (5) Memorization; (6) Problem sensitivity; (7) Mathematical reasoning; (8) Number facility; (9) Deductive reasoning; (10) Inductive reasoning; (11) Information ordering; (12) Category flexibility; (13) Spatial orientation; (14) Visualization; (15) Speed of closure; (16) Flexibility of closure; (17) Selective attention; (18) Time sharing; (19) Perceptual speed; (20) Static strength; (21) Explosive strength; (22) Dynamic strength; (23) Stamina; (24) Extent flexibility; (25) Dynamic flexibility; (26) Gross body equilibrium; (27) Choice reaction time; (28) Reaction time; (29) Speed of limb movement; (30) Wrist-finger speed; (31) Gross body coordination; (32) Multilimb coordination; (33) Finger dexterity; (34) Manual dexterity; (35) Arm-hand steadiness; (36) Rate control; (37) Control precision.

reasonably sound set of descriptors of human abilities for use in characterizing individual tasks or jobs. Aside from the use of these (or other) attributes as descriptors of job requirements, one can also analyze such requirements on an across-job basis. One such approach consisted of a factor analysis based on the "attribute-profiles" of job elements of the PAQ. The attribute profiles were developed on the basis of two studies, one by Mecham and McCormick (1969a) with Form A of the PAQ, and the other by Marquardt and McCormick (1972) with Form B. In both instances industrial psychologists rated the relevance of seventy-six human attributes to the job elements of the PAQ, using a six-point scale. Most of the thirty-seven abilities reported above by Theologus, Romashko, and Fleishman (1970) were included. There were from eight to eighteen raters per attribute, and the pooled reliability of the ratings were generally in the upper 80s and lower 90s. The attribute profile for a job element consisted of the median ratings for the seventy-six attributes. In the principal components analyses of these profiles, the profiles for the job elements were correlated. Principal components analyses were carried out separately for the job elements in each of the six divisions of the PAQ.

The results of the principal components analyses are given in the second column of Table 3. These job dimensions can be interpreted as reflecting the extent to which job elements tend to be grouped in terms of their common profiles of attribute requirements. It will be noted in Table 3 that a number of the job dimensions based on the attribute profile data correspond substantially with some of those based on job data (as given in the first column). Such similarities in job dimensions appeared despite the differences in the nature of the input data.

Job Evaluation Factors

In the typical point system of job evaluation the descriptors used in characterizing jobs consist of factors of various types, such as education, experience, mental demands, physical requirements, responsibility, hazards, working conditions, etc. Individual jobs are evaluated in terms of each factor included in the system, and values are assigned to the jobs based on such evaluations. These values, summed across the different factors, provide a total value for each job which, in turn, is converted into a base wage or salary rate, such as illustrated in Figure 7.

Job Interrelationships

Virtually any kind of job descriptor can be used as possible common denominators to reflect similarities and differences between and among jobs (and positions). Although similarities and differences in terms of descriptors can be judged subjectively, a systematic approach to the study of human work argues for a more quantitative basis for the analysis of job interrelationships, using descriptors (of whatever sort) that

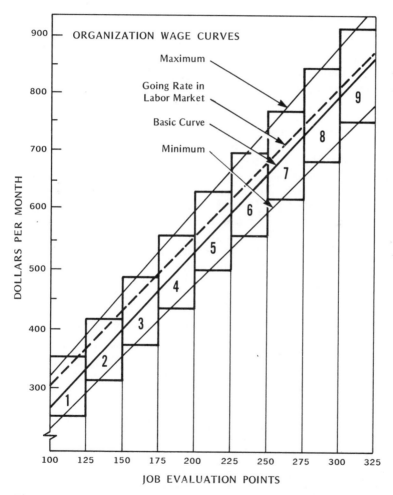

Figure 7. Illustration of an "organization" wage curve, and of one pattern of conversion of job evaluation points into rates of pay. In this particular example, the point values are converted into nine pay grades, each of which has a range of rates. (From McCormick & Tiffin, *Industrial Psychology*, 6th ed., 1974, Figure 15.5.)

characterize jobs in categorical or quantitative terms, such provided for with structured job analysis questionnaires.

Identification of Job Types

At one level of analysis, one might wish to identify, statistically, those positions which, for practical purposes, have reasonably common *combinations* of characteristics, such that they might be considered as comprising a separate job.

JOB TYPES BASED ON HIERARCHICAL GROUPING TECHNIQUE. One statistical technique that can be used for this purpose is a hierarchical grouping technique, as reported by Ward (1963). By an iterative procedure it is possible to build up groups of positions, each group consisting of those positions which have substantial communality in the tasks (or job elements) that characterize them. As used in the United States Air Force these groups are referred to as job types. An example of such an analysis is reported by Harding and Downey (1964), on the basis of data from 1,664 engineering officers who completed a job inventory. The hierarchical grouping technique resulted in the statistical identification of seventeen job types. Examples of the types of data resulting from this analysis are given in Table 4. This shows, for each of three resulting job types, certain data that illustrate the basis for the identification of the job types, specifically the percent of individuals who performed each of the few tasks, and the cumulative percent of time spent by those within the job type devoted to those tasks. In these listings, the last entry in the cumulative percent column represents the percent of time devoted by individuals in the job type to those activities that define the job type in question.

Although the hierarchical grouping technique as illustrated in Table 4 was used with "time" devoted to tasks as the basis for relating positions to each other, other bases can also be used, such as simply the number of tasks (or job elements) in common between two jobs (or positions).

JOB CLUSTERS BASED ON SAMOA METHODOLOGY. Another statistical procedure, the Systematic Approach to Multidimensional Occupational Analysis (SAMOA), has been used by the United States Navy in a series of studies relating to the identification of job "clusters." One such analysis was carried out by Carr (1967) with the positions in the engineering departments of naval destroyers. A job inventory consisting of 135 tasks was completed by 350 personnel, the resulting data being used to identify "clusters" of men whose patterns of tasks were reasonably similar. For this purpose, a "coefficient of compositional similarity" (CCS) was computed for each pair of men, as follows:

$$\text{CCS} = \frac{Id}{Id + Un_1 + Un_2}$$

where: Id = No. of tasks identical between man 1 and man 2
Un_1 = No. of tasks unique to man 1
Un_2 = No. of tasks unique to man 2

This coefficient was used in the SAMOA procedure as the basis for statistical analyses to identify clusters of men whose combinations of tasks were reasonably similar, five such clusters being thus identified. Further, each such cluster was characterized in terms of a statistically derived index on each of three "TOC" dimensions (T = Technical; O = Organizational; and C = Communicational). The clusters and their indexes on these dimensions are:

Cluster	T	O	C
1. Propulsion and auxiliary	4	3	3
2. Apprentice	1	2	2
3. Assistant	2	1	2
4. General	4	3	3
5. Refrigeration and air conditioning	2	4	3

Although the development of the dimension values will not be given, they were derived in a reasonably objective manner. With such dimensions then quantified, it was possible to represent the five clusters in a three-dimensional manner as shown in Figure 8.

TABLE 4
ILLUSTRATIVE TASKS FROM JOB INVENTORY
THAT CHARACTERIZE EACH OF THREE JOB TYPES
OF ELECTRONIC ENGINEERS IN AIR FORCE
WITH DATA ON PERFORMANCE OF THOSE WITHIN JOB TYPE

Job types and tasks	Percent of group performing	Cumulative percent of time spent
Research Engineer		
Conduct theoretical studies and in-house experimentation on proposed techniques	87	20
Design experimental circuitry	74	34
Carry out original analytical work	58	46
—		
Evaluate test results and prepare reports	32	60
Perform engineering evaluations of proposed systems	32	71
—		
Provide guidance to contractors	13	86
Test Project Engineer		
Participate in test activities as a member of the launch or flight crew	72	21
Supervise technicians or other engineers	75	40
—		
Design and develop instrumentation systems	25	65
—		
Assist in developing plans for tests	15	84
Monitor safety systems and procedures	9	85
Program Administrator		
Provide administration and technical direction	79	15
Perform liaison with higher headquarters, contractors, and using commands	69	27
—		
Forecast technical requirements	43	52
—		
Formulate advanced plans to improve technical capability	18	73
Assist in conducting and reviewing actions of boards and development teams	15	75

Note: Dashes represent tasks, or groups of tasks, that are not represented here.

Job Families

The discussion above illustrated the use of systematic approaches to the identification of positions or jobs which form relatively homogeneous clusters or job types. Systematic approaches can also be used for relating jobs or positions to each other at a broader level that might be referred to as job families. A "job family" can, of course, be predicated upon any of several characteristics—or perhaps various syndromes of characteristics. In one such study McCormick, Finn, and Scheips (1957) developed a series of "patterns" of job requirements, such that the jobs that fall in each pattern might be thought of as a job "family." The data for this study were based on a sample of 4,000 jobs which the United States Training and Employment Service was using in a broader study. Each job had been analyzed in terms of forty-four different variables (aptitudes, interests, temperaments, physical demands, etc.). These data were subjected to factor analysis, with seven factors being identified, as follows:

1. Mental and educational development versus adaptability to routine

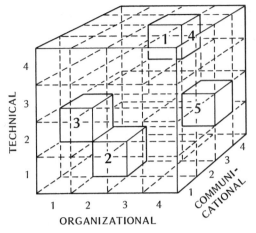

4

TECHNICAL 3

2

1

1   2   3   4

ORGANIZATIONAL

COMMUNI-CATIONAL

Figure 8. Illustration of five clusters of naval engineering department positions in terms of their values on three dimensions (Technical, Organizational, and Communicational). See text for identification of clusters. (From Carr, 1967.)

2. Adaptability to precision operations
3. Body agility
4. Artistic ability and esthetic appreciation
5. Manual art ability
6. Personal contact versus adaptability to routine
7. Heavy manual work versus clerical ability

In turn, a factor score was derived for each factor, producing a "profile" of factor scores for each job. Varying combinations of "high" and "low" factor scores were then used as the basis for characterizing each possible "pattern" of job requirements (or job families). As an aside, it might be added that most of the 4,000 jobs fell into a limited number of the possible patterns.

Other Job Interrelationships

The availability of quantifiable job data and statistical methods offers the opportunities for quite an assortment of analyses. As an example of one such analysis, Mc-Cormick and Asquith (1960), in one phase of a study dealing with manning guidelines for naval vessels, analyzed the relationship for each of six groups of officers and enlisted

personnel as well as the relationship of job activities for each of the several individuals from day to day *across time* (over a period of about two weeks) as contrasted with the activities *between individuals* of each work group for the same day. The data used consisted of times for various activities as reported by incumbents using daily diaries. An average intercorrelation of these times was computed for each individual *across time* for the several days, and also for each day *between individuals* within each group. Although our interest here is more in terms of methodology than of results as such, the results are summarized briefly below. The data given are *means* of the average intercorrelations of individuals across time and of those between individuals of each such group for the separate days.

	Coefficients	
	Range	*Mean*
Across time (for individuals)	.03 to .92	.42
Between individuals (within each group for same day)	−.12 to .73	.21

These correlations can be interpreted as follows: on the average, the similarity of the work activities of individuals from day to day (i.e., across time) is represented by a mean coefficient of about .42, whereas on the average, the similarity of the work activities of the several individuals within each of the work groups (i.e., between individuals) is represented by a coefficient of .21.

Existing Job Classification Systems

Job descriptors serve as the common denominators for bundling jobs together into specific job categories, and in some instances for relating these categories to each other into a total classification system or taxonomy. Some such taxonomies are of a very simple nature, such as the pay-grade structure of individual organizations, as based on job evaluations (in such an instance, the variable in common to those in a particular category is, of course, the pay-grade evaluation). There are, however, certain job classification systems that provide for a systematic organization of all, or many, jobs into a complete structure to serve some purpose or objective. Certain such systems are in operational use, whereas others exist more as formulations for possible specific uses (although the extent of their actual use by an individual organization may not be known). The basis for at least some existing systems is in terms of rational considerations, and the classification of individual jobs in specific categories is essentially subjective. In certain schemes, the structure has been established on the basis of more objective, quantitative data, and the allocation of jobs is accordingly more objective. A few of the better known classification systems will be described briefly.

Bureau of the Census

The United States Bureau of the Census uses an occupational classification system for classifying people in the labor force in terms of present or past occupation. This system consists of ten major occupational categories as follows (United States Bureau of the Census, Population Division, Technical Paper 18, 1968):

Professional, technical, and kindred workers
Farmers and farm managers
Clerical and kindred workers
Sales workers
Craftsmen, foremen, and kindred workers
Operatives and kindred workers
Private household workers
Service workers, except private household
Farm laborers and foremen
Laborers, except farm or mine

The Dictionary of Occupational Titles (DOT)

In its operations, the United States Training and Employment Service provides for the classification and coding of applicants and of available positions by the use of an occupational classification system that is incorporated as a part of the *Dictionary of Occupational Titles* (DOT). The major occupational categories are as follows:

1. Professional, technical, and managerial occupations
2. Clerical and sales occupations
3. Service occupations
4. Farming, fishery, forestry, and related occupations
5. Processing occupations
6. Machine trades occupations
7. Bench work occupations
8. Structural work occupations
9. Miscellaneous occupations

Within these occupational categories are less than a hundred occupational divisions (such as occupations in life sciences, computing and account-recording occupations, printing occupations, and packaging and materials-handling occupations); these are identified by a two-digit code. At the next level (a three-digit code) are about 560 more specific occupational groups (such as physicians and surgeons, mail carriers, hoisting and conveying occupations, and tailors and dressmakers). The basis for the occupational groups is essentially that of job content as judged by analysts.

It should be added that the jobs in the *Dictionary of Occupational Titles* are also characterized in terms of other variables, in particular the worker traits mentioned earlier (including training time, aptitudes, interests, temperaments, physical demands, and working conditions), and the relationship with the data, people, and things hierarchies.

A Psychological Classification of Occupations

Another type of occupational classification is that developed over the years by Holland et al. (1970). The classification is based on a theory of personality types. The underlying rationale is that vocational choice, and presumably vocational success, are a function of personality factors, and that personality types are in fact reflected by vocational choice. The initial classification scheme developed in 1959 was essentially of an a priori nature. It has been further developed and tested, and is now reasonably well supported by empirical data. The basic classification is given below:

R: Realistic occupations. (Includes skilled trades, many technical, and some service occupations.)

I: Investigative occupations. (Includes scientific and some technical occupations; this group was originally designated as Intellectual occupations.)

A: Artistic occupations. (Includes artistic, musical, and literary occupations.)

S: Social occupations. (Includes educational and social welfare occupations.)

E: Enterprising occupations. (Includes managerial and sales occupations.)

C: Conventional occupations. (Includes office and clerical occupations.)

The classification system provides for an occupation to be coded in terms of three of these classifications, such as E S C for salesmen; this code means that salesmen resemble people in Enterprising (E) occupations most of all, but they resemble people in Social (S) and Conventional (C) occupations to a lesser degree. Holland et al. (1970) represent the relationships among these classes with a hexagon, as shown in Figure 9. The values shown on the lines between the individual classes are correlations (for a sample of 1,234 college students) of their scores on the Vocational Preference Inventory (VPI), which provides scores reflecting vocational interests as related to the six classes. In general, the hexagon is so presented that close relationships (i.e., higher correlations) are represented by shorter distances, and more distant relationships by longer distances.

A special tabulation of data was carried out at Purdue University for 832 jobs for which Position Analysis Questionnaires (PAQ) were available, to provide the basis for relating such data (actually job dimension scores), to Holland's classification. The

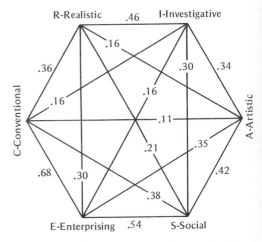

Figure 9. Hexagonal model for interpreting inter- and intra-class relationships between the classifications of Holland et al. (1970) occupational classification system. The values are correlations (for a sample of college students) of Vocational Preference Inventory (VPI) scores, the six scores reflecting interests as related to the six occupational classes.

resulting analyses, reported by Holland et al. (1970), reflected a reasonable relationship between the PAQ data and Holland's classifications, and also provided the basis for expanding the occupations included in Holland's classification.

Career Fields

Certain organizations, especially the military services, organize various jobs into career fields or career ladders, in which specific jobs are depicted in something of a pyramid, reflecting the typical, or (more generally) the planned, progression of personnel from lower level up to higher level positions. Each such ladder represents a separate career area, such as electric computer repair, accounting and finance, preventive medicine, and jet engine mechanic.

Since the usual context in which such career fields are used is that in which some "planning" of careers is involved, the development and implementation of such a program requires various analyses and decisions, such as: the identification of the "job types" as they actually exist; the possible restructuring of such job types; the determination of the "level" of each job type; and the possible establishment of subareas within which promotional sequences would be expected to take place. In large part, the structuring of a career field must be predicated on rational, judgmental considerations. However, the development of reasonably objective, relevant data can, of course, provide more "substance" on which to base such decisions. For example, the use of job inventories can reflect the (existing) patterns of tasks that occur in positions, and thus contribute to the identification of job types and of relating job types to each other on the career ladder; and systematic job evaluation procedures can aid in the establishment of appropriate levels (and pay grades) for jobs within the ladder.

The concept of career fields and the development of formalized structures that represent typical (or desired) progression ladders has been promulgated primarily by the military services, presumably because of the large number of personnel involved. There are, of course, many occupational areas in civilian life that can be viewed as career fields within which there are common, or rational, progression sequences that have not been formally crystallized; the "formal" recognition of a career field as such is very much a matter of administrative desirability (as in the military services). But whether formally so crystallized or not, the occupational structure in question can serve as a blueprint of typical progression within the occupational domain, and, by implication, aid in career planning, including the implications for desirable training and for planning job experiences to facilitate the occupational development of the individuals in question.

APPLICATION OF JOB-RELATED INFORMATION

The collection and manipulation of job-related information obviously should serve some purposes other than those of keeping job analysts, typists, and computer operators busy. Some of the potential uses and applications of such information have been mentioned in passing or have been discussed above. Although the potential uses of job information are many, the following overview may give an impression of some of the primary frames of reference in this regard.

Frame of reference in use of job-related information:

Individual
  Vocational guidance
  Vocational preparation
Organization
  Manpower planning
  Job design
  Job evaluation
  Recruiting
  Selection and placement
  Training
  Personnel appraisal
Labor relations
  Management-union relations
Public policy and administration
  Legal aspects: standards, licensing, certification, etc.
  Public employment services
  Public training and education programs
  Social security administration
  Safety programs
Research objectives
  Population analysis (economic, social, etc.)
  Behavioral research related to job or occupational characteristics

Let us now single out a few such purposes or objectives for specific focus. But in so doing, let us speculate a bit about possible uses in addition to touching on actual uses.

Job Design

The design of jobs can be approached from various angles. Davis (1961), for example, indicates that the approaches to job design can be characterized as: (1) process-centered or equipment-centered (in which jobs are designed by specializing activities or functions or by applying rational methods to determine minimum production time); (2) worker-centered (in which particular emphasis is placed on designing jobs so as to enhance worker motivation and job satisfaction); and (3) a combination of these two. The worker-centered approach is the one that is associated with the relatively recent interest in job enlargement, or what Herzberg (1968) refers to as job enrichment. Its central precept is that people tend to gain greater job satisfaction from jobs that are enlarged (or enriched) as contrasted with those that are not so enlarged (or enriched). The basis for change is one that is at issue, with Herzberg arguing quite vehemently against simply "enlarging" jobs by adding more activities (and thus increasing the variety). Rather, in line with his own theories, he would argue for "enriching" jobs by "vertical" loading (that is, in terms of increased authority, accountability, decision making, reduction of controls, etc.) rather than by "horizontal" loading (which, as he puts it, consists of simply adding more "meaningless" tasks). This position is in line with his hypothesis that positive job satisfaction can occur only when the job content makes it possible for the "motivator" factors to come into play (these being responsibility, achievement, recognition, growth, etc.).

At this reading, it is probably not possible to set forth any *validated* set of guidelines regarding the enlargement of jobs that would have reasonably general utility in enhancing job satisfaction. (For example, despite Herzberg's arguments, the relative advantages of vertical versus horizontal loading have not been thoroughly explored.) What seems to be missing is some systematic analysis of the relationship between specific job characteristics on the one hand, and job satisfaction on the other hand—taking into account also the pervading aspects of individual differences and of individual interests. Now that it is possible to characterize jobs in terms of job dimensions (such as those based on the Position Analysis Questionnaire), it may be possible to systematically examine some such relationships.

In the absence of such analytical data, one needs to be a bit cautious in making pronouncements about job enlargement efforts. Recognizing such qualifications, however, tentative generalizations seem to suggest themselves. To begin with, most personnel tend to react favorably to job enlargement, thus tending to support the hypothesis that job enlargement may serve to enhance motivation and job satisfaction. And it should be added that the experiments with job enlargement generally have indicated that productivity has not suffered from such programs, and in some instances has been improved. On the other hand, there are also indications that some individuals do not prefer "enlarged" jobs.

Job Evaluation

The typical approaches to job evaluation involve the use of conventional job descriptions by members of a job evaluation committee as the basis for making some sort of evaluative judgments regarding individual jobs. The bases of these evaluations depend upon the particular job evaluation system in use. Conventional systems differ in two major respects, namely the *basis* of evaluation and the *method* of evaluation. These are depicted below, along with the four basic types of systems that characterize each possible combination.

	Basis of evaluation	
Method of evaluation	Individual job factors	Job as an entity
Comparison with defined standard (absolute judgment)	Point system	Classification system
Comparison with other jobs (relative judgment)	Factor comparison system	Ranking system

Objectives of Job Evaluation Systems

The features of these four basic types of systems will not be described here.[6] The

---

[6] These systems are discussed elsewhere, such as in H. B. Maynard (Ed.), *Industrial Engineering Hand-*

basic objectives of job evaluation systems (of whatever nature) are those of: (1) providing a common base for evaluation of jobs in such a manner that individual jobs *within* an organization will have wage or salary scales *relative to each other* that are reasonably acceptable to the personnel in question; and (2) providing a basis for establishing a basic wage or salary structure that has some reasonable relationship to the going rates for corresponding jobs in the labor market. Thus, a job evaluation system should result in job values that have a rather respectable correlation with going rates in the labor market. The widespread use of job evaluation systems (especially the point system) implies the general acceptance of such systems as the basis for establishing wage or salary rates.

Job Evaluation Based on Structured Job Information

The conventional approaches to job evaluation provide for evaluation of jobs as entities, or of major job factors. Although job evaluations based on such approaches have been reasonably well accepted, it would seem that a more analytical approach might also be used in this process, perhaps with some modest improvement in arriving at job values. Such an approach would be predicated on the identification and use of behaviorally related common denominators of jobs which, in turn, might have their own labor market "values" resulting from supply and demand factors. Thus, the total "value" of a given job might be "built-up" on the basis of the particular combination, or mix, of such common denominators and their individual implicit values.

The Position Analysis Questionnaire (PAQ) described earlier was used in testing such an approach, since it provides for characterizing jobs in terms of worker-oriented job elements. And in turn, the job dimensions derived from the PAQ might serve as the basis for characterizing jobs in terms of

book (New York: McGraw-Hill, 1963), Section 6, Chapter 5.

broader groupings of such elements (Jeanneret & McCormick, 1969).

JOB SAMPLE. The study in question, reported by Mecham (1970) and Mecham and McCormick (1969b), was based on data for a sample of 340 jobs. Job analyses, using the PAQ (Form *A*), were obtained on a strictly voluntary and confidential basis from forty-five different organizations which supplied completed PAQs in connection with the larger job dimension research program. The sample used in this study included 340 jobs, specifically those for which wage or salary data were reported. The sample contained jobs in each occupational category given in the *Dictionary of Occupational Titles* except for Category 4 (farming, fishing, forestry, and related occupations).

CONVERSION OF WAGE AND SALARY DATA TO A METRIC. Wage and salary rates were supplied with reference to various time periods (i.e., hourly wage, weekly salary, monthly salary, etc.) by different organizations and, therefore, it was necessary (for statistical purposes) to convert all such rates to a common time base. The average monthly compensation rate was selected as this common time base.[7]

ANALYSIS PROCEDURE. As a first step in analyzing the data, the job sample was randomly divided into two subsamples (Sample *A* with 165 jobs and Sample *B* with 175 jobs). Secondly, the data in Samples *A, B,* and the

---

[7] This rate was computed as follows: Average monthly compensation = 173 multiplied by hourly wage rate; *or* 4.333 multiplied by weekly salary; *or* 1.00 multiplied by monthly salary; *or* 1/12 multiplied by yearly salary. The computations were based on the rationale that employees typically work forty hours per week and receive pay during vacations. While this may not be strictly true in all cases, it was thought that this was generally a reasonable assumption. When organizations supplied wage or salary information for a job in terms of a wage range (e.g., $100–$150 per week), the average wage or salary was computed (in this case, $125 per week). This average wage or salary per time period was then converted to the average monthly compensation rate using the computational procedures described above.

combined sample were independently evaluated to determine the presence of meaningful variables predictive of wage and salary rates; this was done using a correlational and regression analysis approach. Three different types of predictor variables were evaluated with respect to each of the three samples (*A*, *B*, and combined). The three types of predictors used were: (1) responses to individual job elements of the PAQ; (2) job dimensions scores based on "overall" dimensions; and (3) job dimension scores for the twenty-seven dimensions based on the "divisions" of the PAQ as the dimensions were derived from job data obtained with the PAQ.

As a third step, the predictors and their respective weights (derived using a stepwise regression analysis procedure) for Sample *A* were used to predict compensation rates in Sample *B* and vice versa. This step constituted a double cross-validation procedure in which cross-validation coefficients were derived by correlating predicted rates with observed rates (Sample *B* observed rates were correlated with rates predicted from Sample *A* predictors and weights, and vice versa). The basic procedure is shown graphically in Figure 10.

After the cross-validation coefficients had been derived using the procedure above, Samples *A* and *B* were combined, and predictors identified and their respective weights were computed. It would be expected that the combined sample would yield the optimum combination of predictors and weights for any of the three types of predictors (i.e.,

job elements, "overall" job dimensions, and "division" job dimensions).

As a fourth and final step, the residuals (observed rate—predicted rate = residual) obtained with the optimum prediction equations (for each of the three types of predictors) were compared by "50-dollar" predicted compensation classes. This procedure was designed to determine if prediction was better in some sections of the compensation range than in others. Additionally, the standard deviation of residuals in each "50-dollar" class was computed as a way of determining the range of mis-prediction for each class. Finally, the generalized expected standard deviation of observed compensation rates around predicted compensation rates was computed and plotted.

SELECTION OF JOB EVALUATION PREDICTORS. To select a set of tentative predictors from the 189 possible PAQ job elements, responses to each PAQ job element in each sample were correlated with wage and salary rates for that sample. The fifteen job elements having responses with the highest positive correlations and the ten having the most negative correlation in each sample were selected as tentative predictors. These twenty-five job elements for each sample comprised the job element set used later in the stepwise regression procedure. The "overall" job dimensions and "division" job dimensions were used without any such selection procedure since it was not necessary to reduce the number of predictors in these analyses.

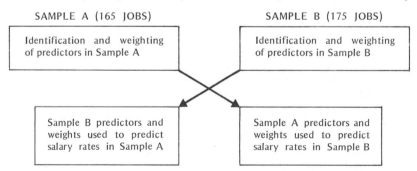

SAMPLE A (165 JOBS)   SAMPLE B (175 JOBS)

Identification and weighting of predictors in Sample A

Identification and weighting of predictors in Sample B

Sample B predictors and weights used to predict salary rates in Sample A

Sample A predictors and weights used to predict salary rates in Sample B

Figure 10.   Illustration of double cross-validation procedures used in job evaluation study with the Position Analysis Questionnaire (PAQ).

The next step involved subjecting all tentative predictors in each set for each sample to a "build-up" stepwise regression analysis. This procedure produced sets of final predictors and corresponding regression weights for each sample on each type of predictor. Because the job elements (twenty-five) used as tentative predictors and the "division" job dimensions (twenty-seven) did not produce important increases in predictive power beyond the ninth step, only these nine are reported as final predictors. With the remaining predictor set, "overall job dimension scores," all five dimension scores were used.

DOUBLE CROSS-VALIDATION. Following the identification of final predictors and the derivation of regression weights, the double cross-validation procedure was undertaken. (As will be noted later, some shrinkage in the multiple correlation coefficients did occur but was of a minor nature, ranging from less than .01 in the case of predictions made with the "overall" dimensions scores to about .05 with predictions based on the "division" dimension scores.)

RESULTS. The multiple correlation coefficients computed as part of the regression analysis for each set of predictors within each sample are given in Table 5. These coefficients ranged from .83 to .90 for the various job samples (A, B, and combined). As noted above, the shrinkage in cross-validation was fairly nominal.

An examination of the pattern of relationships between job evaluation points and monthly compensation rates was made by dividing the entire range (from about $375 to $1,525 per month) into twenty-five classes. Although there were variations by class intervals, the basic relationship appeared to be linear, except for the lower end of the scale, which tended to veer up a bit. However, there were very few jobs in the lower class intervals, so the pattern for these categories must be viewed cautiously.

The standard deviation of the compensation rates of jobs within each class interval can be viewed as an indication of "misprediction." In general, it was found that the range of mis-prediction was narrower for lower level jobs than for higher level jobs; further, the range increased progressively as the predicted compensation rate increased, the increase in range being virtually a constant ratio of the compensation rates.

DISCUSSION. The basic hypothesis explored in this phase of the study was that behaviorally related job elements (such as those incorporated in the Position Analysis Questionnaire) or data based on them, would have an important and predictable relationship to rates of monetary compensation on an across-the-board basis. In general, the results of the study supported this contention. The multiple correlations with compensation rates, of three sets of data based on the PAQ, ranged from .83 to .90 for two initial samples of

TABLE 5
MULTIPLE CORRELATION AND CROSS-VALIDATION COEFFICIENTS
OF REGRESSION EQUATIONS BASED ON JOB DATA OF
THE PAQ USED TO PREDICT COMPENSATION RATES

Nature of Data	Initial Sample		Cross-validated Sample*		Combined Sample
	A	B	B	A	
Overall Dimensions (5)	.83	.87	.87	.83	.85
Dimensions from PAQ Divisions (9)	.87	.90	.85	.83	.87
Individual Job Elements (9)	.87	.89	.86	.86	.87

* The regression equation developed from the initial Sample A (or B) was then cross-validated by applying it to Sample B (or A).

jobs, and from .83 to .87 when regression equations based on each of those two samples were used to predict the other. The results generally suggest the possibility that, with additional research, it might be possible to develop an operational job evaluation system based on the PAQ that might have reasonable validity as a predictor of monetary compensation.

In this connection a postscript might be added about a separate analysis that was carried out independently by an insurance company. This consisted of an analysis of the relationship between predicted job values (based on regression equations derived from the present study) as related to actual salary rates (median monthly base salary) for seventy-four jobs (Taylor, 1970). The resulting correlation (double-checked for accuracy) was 0.93.

Personnel Specifications

The personnel specifications for any given job presumably should set forth the personal attributes that are related to satisfactory performance on the job. Such specifications generally have been established on the basis of judgment, or on the basis of statistically validated relationships between predictors (test scores, biographical data, etc.) and relevant criteria of job success. There is growing evidence, however, to suggest that such specifications can be established on the basis of job component validity (what has sometimes been referred to as synthetic or generalized validity).

Specifications Based on Judgments

It is probable that most personnel specifications are established on the basis of the judgments of employment managers and other personnel officials, and in some instances by psychologists. Not very much is known, however, about the validity of such judgments. Some indications on this score came from an investigation by Trattner, Fine, and Kubis (1955). They had available the mean test scores on each of ten aptitude tests for workers in each of ten jobs. Separately, eight job analysts estimated the mean aptitudes (for the ten aptitudes) required for each of the ten jobs, these estimates being based on written job descriptions. Another group of eight analysts made similar ratings based on actual observation of the jobs. Correlations of the estimated aptitudes with the mean test scores were computed for each group of analysts, these correlations being given below for two groups of aptitudes:

	Analysts using job descriptions	Analysts using observation
Mental and perceptual aptitudes	.60	.71
Physical aptitudes	.01	.27

Although these data need to be interpreted with some reservations, they do suggest that analysts can estimate the *level* of mental and perceptual requirements of jobs more adequately than they can physical aptitudes.

As another approach to the judging of personnel specifications, Parry (1968) compared the *estimates* of validity coefficients (for three groups of employees and for fourteen tests and sub-tests) with the *actual* validity coefficients, and found only a moderate degree of relationship. However, the study did not comprise a really rigorous analysis, so the results of this study also need to be accepted with reservations.

Based on very modest bits and pieces of data, with a fairly heavy dose of subjective judgment thrown in, we probably can set forth the following surmises about personnel specifications set forth on the basis of judgments: that such judgments probably have at least moderate validity, but perhaps more for some kinds of requirements than for others; that "level" of such requirements can be estimated more adequately than the degree of their "validity"; and that such estimates will be enhanced by increased familiarity with the jobs in question.

Specifications Based on
Statistical Validation

To date the method of establishing personnel specifications that has the general blessings of psychologists is that of empirical, statistical validation of predictors (tests, personal data, etc.) against appropriate criteria (preferably of job performance); such an approach preferably should be through a follow-up procedure in which the tests are administered to job applicants (but not used in selection or placement) with test data being analyzed later against a subsequently derived criterion. With an adequate sample of personnel on a given job, such statistical analyses generally provide a sound basis for deriving personnel specifications.

Job-Component Validity

One would wish to avoid undue dependence on subjective evaluations in establishing personnel specifications; and frequently, it is not possible to identify predictors by statistical validation, if for no reason other than limited sample sizes. Thus, one would hope that there might be some reasonably objective procedure that would make it possible to establish valid specifications, especially in those circumstances in which empirical statistical validation is not possible or practical.

CONCEPT OF JOB-COMPONENT VALIDITY. This leads into the concept of job-component validity, or what has been referred to by Lawshe (1952) as synthetic validity. Job-component validity is predicated on the assumption that any given job component or activity (or basic job characteristic) that occurs in substantially the same form in different jobs would have the same "requirements" as far as the personnel are concerned (McCormick, 1959). If, in some way, one could identify what the human requirements are for any given job component, it would then presumably be possible to "build up" the total requirement for any given job, knowing what job components (or characteristics) exist in the job. This basic notion is reflected in Table 6, in which certain hypothetical job components are listed (A, B, C, D,..., N), along with the human "attribute" required to perform each (a, b, c, d,..., n). Each of three jobs (X, Y, and Z) is "described" in terms of the importance of each component. The level of the requirement for each *attribute* for a given job is a function of the *importance* of the component for which the attribute is required. The total job requirement, in turn, is the summation of the thus-derived requirements for the individual attributes. This is an overly simplified model; in practice, the "building-up" of total job requirements is not this straightforward.

The J-Coefficient

Actually there have been only a few efforts to develop job-component approaches

TABLE 6
SIMPLIFIED HYPOTHETICAL EXAMPLE OF APPLICATION OF
CONCEPT OF JOB-COMPONENT VALIDITY

Job component	Attribute required for component	Importance of component in given jobs			Total attribute requirements for jobs		
		Job X	Job Y	Job Z	Job X	Job Y	Job Z
A	a	5	1	0	5a	1a	—
B	b	1	0	5	1b	—	5b
C	c	0	4	1	—	4c	1c
D	d	3	0	2	3d	—	2d
—	—	—	—	—	—	—	—
N	n	0	3	1	—	3n	1n

for use in establishing personnel specifications. One such approach is that of the J-Coefficient developed by Primoff (1955, 1959) for use by the United States Civil Service Commission for selecting tests for trades and industrial jobs in the federal service. The basic instrument used is a job analysis blank that consists of fifty-five job elements, each of which is defined. Examples include the following: works rapidly; dexterity of hands and arms; keenness of vision; initiative; public contacts; and reasoning. (It should be added that a number of the job elements tend to characterize human traits or qualities that might be required in jobs rather than job behaviors as such.) Any given job is rated by several persons who are familiar with the job, such as incumbents or supervisors. The job is rated in terms of the importance of each job element to the job, using the following scale:

Code	Value	
0	0	Element is not present in the job
V	1	Element is present in the job but not of extreme importance
+	2	Element is present and of extreme importance to the job

The ratings of the several raters are then added together. By a process that need not be described here, a "matrix of test values for J-Coefficient" has been developed that consists of what might be thought of as weights for each of various Civil Service tests as related to each of the job elements. A partial matrix is given in Figure 11, for a few of the job elements included in the matrix.

In the case of any given job, the J-Coefficient for any specific test is based on the *test values* of the individual job elements (as given in this matrix) and the *importance* of the individual elements as rated for the job. The derivation of these J-Coefficients involves a procedure that will not be reported here. These procedures lead to the selection of specific tests to be used, and to the weighting of these tests for personnel selection purposes. In certain studies in which the J-Coefficient has been used for developing test batteries actual validation of tests against job-related criteria have also been carried out. The results of such comparisons indicate that the J-Coefficient approach is a reasonably satisfactory method for developing test batteries.

The Position Analysis Questionnaire (PAQ)

The most extensive studies relating to job component validity have involved the use of the PAQ. Two series of such studies have been carried out, one by Mecham (1970) and Mecham and McCor-

JOB ELEMENT	TEST (arbitrary labels)				
	Test A	Test B	Test C	– – –	Test N
1. Work rapidly	44	47	20		21
2. Strength	2				
—					
8. Estimate size of object		07	05		

Figure 11. Partial matrix of test values of J-Coefficient. The complete matrix covers fourteen tests and fifty-five job elements. (From Primoff, 1955.)

mick (1969c) with Form *A* of the PAQ, and the other by Marquardt and McCormick (July 1974) wtih Form *B*. The results of both were in reasonable agreement, but since the second one was based on Form *B* of the PAQ and included a larger sample of jobs, it will be summarized here.

SAMPLE OF JOBS USED. In this phase of the study, 659 positions were used. These were positions within the total group of about 8,000 for which PAQs were available, and for which test validity data had been published or were otherwise available from the United States Training and Employment Service. The positions used corresponded to a total of 141 "jobs" in terms of the Employment Service data.

CRITERIA. The ultimate test of the validity of a "method" of developing job requirements based on the concept of job-component validity would be to try out the system over a period of time to see if it generally results in the selection of satisfactory personnel for various jobs. For purposes of the present study a more modest approach was undertaken in which test validity data available primarily from the United States Training and Employment Service were used as the basis for the "criteria" against which (tentative) job-component job requirements could be tested. For illustrating the approach used, first let us consider a single attribute, specifically an attribute for which there is a corresponding test in the General Aptitude Test Battery (GATB) of the United States Training and Employment Service. Next let us select a sample of jobs for which test scores based on that test are available, and for which we have derived a set of job requirements based on job components. Given such data, it seems that one approach to the testing of requirements so derived would be that of correlating these job requirements for the jobs with the mean test scores of people on corresponding jobs. This approach would be predicated on the assumption that jobs tend to differ in the "level" of a given attribute required for successful performance, and that people somehow tend to gravitate into jobs which are commensurate with their own abilities. If these assumptions are reasonably valid, it follows that, for a given attribute, the differences in the mean test scores of people on various jobs would reflect in a very gross way the varying job requirements, on that attribute, of the jobs in question. There are potential loopholes in this chain of reasoning (but there is also some fairly substantial support for it). Recognizing some of the possible loopholes, for purposes of this pilot "test" of a system of deriving job requirements based on job components, the mean test scores of personnel on each of the several jobs in the sample were used as one set of criterion values.

Another related criterion that was used was the test score for incumbents on each job that was one standard deviation below the mean. This was called a "potential cutoff score" since it would more likely approximate the test cutoff score used in actual practice than the mean test score (although in practice a cutoff score usually is influenced by labor market conditions).

Considering the same set of data (that is, a set of job requirements for a sample of jobs derived from their individual components, and test-score data for incumbents on such jobs), there is another possible way of teasing out some indication of the "validity" of the job requirements so derived. This involves the coefficients of validity of test scores against appropriate performance criteria for samples of people on those jobs. A validity coefficient, in a sense, is a reflection of the relative "importance" of a test (or of the attribute that the test measures) in relationship to the criterion. For a given attribute, if one can somehow derive—on the basis of the components present in individual jobs—indexes of the "requirements" of various jobs for that attribute, these attribute indexes could then be correlated with the coefficients of validity, for corresponding jobs, of a test that presumably measures that attribute. Thus, a third criterion used consisted of the validity coefficients of tests for jobs that corresponded to the positions used in this phase of the project.

SUMMARY OF DATA USED. The basic data used in the job component validity study then consisted of the following:

1. Data provided by the United States Training and Employment Service for each of 141 "jobs" consisted of (a) mean test score of a sample of incumbents on each job, the tests being the nine tests of the General Aptitude Test Battery (GATB); (b) the score for the incumbents that was one standard deviation below the mean; and (c) a validity coefficient for each job on each of the nine tests, with certain exceptions (for certain tests coefficients were not available for a few jobs).

2. PAQ analyses of 659 positions that corresponded with the 141 jobs mentioned above. (PAQ data were available in many instances for two or more positions that corresponded with a single job.)

REGRESSION ANALYSIS WITH JOB DIMENSION SCORES. In testing the "validity" of job requirements based on job components, job dimension scores (component scores) were first derived for the 659 sample positions, these being derived separately for the two sets of job dimensions mentioned above, specifically: (1) the thirty dimensions derived from the principal components analysis of the six divisions of the PAQ as based on job data for 3,700 jobs; and (2) the twenty-three dimensions resulting from the principal components analysis of the six divisions of the PAQ as based on the attribute profiles of the job elements. Similar analyses were carried out with these two sets of job dimension scores.

Once both sets of job dimension scores were derived for the 659 positions, each set was divided into two subsamples (A and B). The dimension scores for each subsample of jobs were then separately correlated with each of the three criteria described above, the resulting correlations then being subjected to a build-up stepwise regression analysis.

Once regression equations were computed for each of the two subsamples of jobs (A and B) on each of the nine GATB tests for all three criteria (mean test scores, potential cutoff scores, and validity coefficients), a double cross-validation procedure was carried out. This procedure involved the use of the regression equations developed with subsample A to predict the criterion values in subsample B and vice versa. This provided some indication of the shrinkage which one could expect from use of the subsample regression equations. As a final step, the subsamples were combined and regression analyses were performed for both criteria on each of the nine tests. In the resulting regression equations eight or nine job dimensions were retained. The analyses give some indication of the relative importance of individual attributes for a given job, expressed as a predicted mean test score, potential cutoff score, or validity coefficient, independently for each of the nine tests.

RESULTS. The primary results of this multiple regression analysis of job dimension scores against the three criteria are given in Table 7. This shows the results from the use of both types of job dimensions; that is, those based on job analysis data and those based on attribute profiles of the job elements. That table shows the results of the combination of the two subsamples, A and B. With respect to the double cross-validation scheme, it might be added that the shrinkage tended to be most pronounced in the case of predictors which did not yield high multiple correlation coefficients in the two subsamples.

It can be seen that the dimensions based on job data tend to be slightly better predictors of the criteria than are the dimensions based on attribute data, but the difference is negligible. It can also be seen that mean test scores and potential cutoff scores are considerably more predictable than validity co-

TABLE 7

**MULTIPLE CORRELATIONS OF COMBINATIONS OF JOB DIMENSION SCORES
BASED ON JOB DATA AND ON ATTRIBUTE PROFILE DATA
AS RELATED TO THREE CRITERIA BASED ON GATB TEST SCORES OF JOB INCUMBENTS
FOR COMBINED SAMPLE OF ONE HUNDRED AND FORTY-ONE JOBS**

GATB test	Criterion and PAQ data base					
	Mean test scores		Potential cutoff scores		Validity coefficients	
	Job data	Attribute data	Job data	Attribute data	Job data	Attribute data
G—Intelligence	.73	.74	.74	.75	.38	.36
V—Verbal	.76	.75	.77	.77	.39	.33
N—Numerical	.74	.73	.74	.74	.39	.31
S—Spatial	.67	.66	.68	.65	.44	.38
P—Form perception	.65	.63	.65	.62	.32	.28
Q—Clerical perception	.74	.71	.73	.69	.34	.27
K—Motor coordination	.75	.73	.73	.70	.26	.23
F—Finger dexterity	.59	.56	.54	.53	.39	.36
M—Manual dexterity	.46	.47	.42	.44	.40	.32
Median coefficient	.73	.71	.73	.69	.39	.32

efficients. The lower predictability associated with validity coefficients is probably, in part, a reflection of their relatively unstable nature; such instability is associated with such factors as small sample sizes and restricted range, unreliable criteria, etc. On the predictor side of the coin, certain steps might be suggested for future work to improve the already respectable relationships which were found in this study. One such step might consist of the use of more than one analyst, supervisor, or incumbent to complete the PAQ for each job to be analyzed; these PAQ ratings by several persons well acquainted with the job could then be pooled into a composite PAQ rating which would probably tend to be more stable and hence provide greater potential predictability. In addition, and where possible, validation data should be gathered on the specific jobs actually analyzed with the PAQ. This would obviate the matching process required in this study and hence minimize or eliminate the possibility of a mismatch between job analysis, validation, and normative data.

In brief, it seems to be possible to establish reasonably valid job requirements (expressed in terms of mean test scores or potential cutoff scores) for a wide variety of jobs *strictly* on the basis of data on job components of the jobs, as resulting from analysis of jobs with a structured job analysis questionnaire, such as the Position Analysis Questionnaire (PAQ). To the extent that this can be done, it would eliminate the need for the conventional validation of tests in at least certain specific situations in industry.

DISCUSSION

Job information can be used either in the context of individual positions or jobs, or in some "collective" context. A young person going through vocational counseling or an employment interviewer, for example, is largely concerned with individual positions or jobs, and should have job-related information available that lends itself to such purposes. On the other hand, job information can be used more for some "collective" purpose, such as the development of the basis for a job evaluation program, the establishment of the basis for job-component validity, etc. For such "collective" purposes, it is especially useful to have job-related data of a quantitative nature, and it is largely in connection with such purposes that a plea has been made for developing such data. In the context of the use of job information relative to individual positions or jobs, such quantitative data sometimes can also be useful (such as test-score profiles, measures of physiological costs, time typically spent on various tasks, etc.). But some such purposes can well be served by more conventional, descriptive forms of job-related information, such as typical essay-type job descriptions (which, despite some shortcomings, can characterize the functions and activities of jobs within an organization). Thus, although the recent years have seen the development of certain techniques that contribute to the quantification of job-related information, the use of such approaches on an across-the-board basis should not be viewed as a universal panacea. Rather, given some purpose or objective that involves some job-related information, one should plan for the collection of the type and form of information that seems reasonably optimum for the purpose at hand.

REFERENCES

Annett, J., & Duncan, K. D. Task analysis and training design. *Occupational Psychology,* 1967, 41, 211–221.

Archer, W. B., & Fruchter, D. A. *The construction, review, and administration of Air Force job inventories.* Lackland Air Force Base, Tex.: Personnel Research Laboratory, Aerospace Medical Division, PRL-TDR-63-21, AD-426 755, August, 1963.

Baehr, M. E. *A factorial framework for job descriptions for higher-level personnel.* Chicago: Industrial Relations Center, University of Chicago, 1967.

Birt, J. A. The effect of the consistency of job inventory information upon simulated airmen reassignment. Unpublished doctoral dissertation, Purdue University, Lafayette, Ind., June, 1968.

Brumback, G. B., & Vincent, J. W. Factor analysis of work-performed data for a sample of administrative, professional, and scientific positions. *Personnel Psychology,* 1970, 23, 101–107.

Carr, M. J. The SAMOA method of determining technical, organizational, and communicational dimensions of task clusters. San Diego: U.S. Naval Personnel Research Activity, Technical Bulletin STB 68–5, November, 1967.

Chalupsky, A. B. Comparative factor analyses of clerical jobs. *Journal of Applied Psychology,* 1962, 46, 62–66.

Christal, R. E. Comments by the chairman. In *Proceedings of 19. Division of Military Psychology Symposium: Collecting, analyzing, and reporting information describing jobs and occupations.* (77th Annual Convention of the American Psychological Association.) Lackland Air Force Base, Tex.: Personnel Research Division, Air Force Human Resources Laboratory, September, 1969, 77–85.

Cowan, J. Discussion. In *Proceedings of 19. Division of Military Psychology Symposium: Collecting, analyzing, and reporting information describing jobs and occupations.* (77th Annual Convention of the American Psychological Association.) Lackland Air Force Base, Tex.: Personnel Research Division, Air Force Human Resources Laboratory, September, 1969, 71–72.

Cragun, J. R., & McCormick, E. J. *Job inventory information: Task and scale reliabilities and scale interrelationships.* Lackland Air Force Base, Tex.: Personnel Research Laboratory, Aerospace Medical Division, PRL-TR-67-15, November, 1967.

Cunningham, D. J., & Duncan, K. D. Describing non-repetitive tasks for training purposes. *Occupational Psychology,* 1967, 41, 203–210.

Davis, L. E. The concept of job design and its status in industrial engineering. In *Symposium on human factors in job design.* (American Psychological Association.) Santa Monica, Calif.: Systems Development Corporation, Report SP-611, November, 1961.

Dean, E. C., & Jud, R. A. How to write a task analysis. *Training Directors' Journal,* November, 1965, 19 (11), 9–22.

Demaree, R. G., Marks, M. R., Smith, W. L., & Snyder, M. T. *Development of qualitative and quantitative personnel requirements information*. Wright-Patterson Air Force Base, Ohio: Behavioral Sciences Laboratory, Aerospace Medical Division, MRL-TDR-62-4, December, 1962.

Dictionary of occupational titles: Vol. I. Definitions of titles; Vol II. Occupational classification. (3rd ed.) U.S. Training and Employment Service. Washington, D.C.: U.S. Government Printing Office, 1965.

Farina, A. J. Jr. *Development of a taxonomy of human performance: A review of descriptive schemes for human task behavior*. Washington, D.C.: American Institutes for Research, AIR-726-1/69-TR-2, January, 1969.

Fleishman, E. A. Development of a behavior taxonomy for describing human tasks: A correlational-experimental approach. *Journal of Applied Psychology*, 1967, 51, 1–10.

Gagné, R. M. *The conditions of learning*. New York: Holt, Rinehart and Winston, 1965.

Handbook for analyzing jobs. Manpower Administration, U.S. Department of Labor. Washington, D.C.: U.S. Superintendent of Documents, Stock Number 2900-0131, 1972.

Harding, F. D., & Downey, R. L. Jr. *Electronic engineer job types in the Air Force Systems Command*. Lackland Air Force Base, Tex.: Personnel Research Laboratory, Aerospace Medical Division, PRL-TDR-64-8, March, 1964.

Hemphill, J. K. Job descriptions for executives. *Harvard Business Review*, 1959, 37, 55–67.

Herzberg, F. One more time: How do you motivate employees? *Harvard Business Review*, 1968, 46, 53–63.

Holland, J. L. et al. *A psychological classification of occupations*. Baltimore: Center for Social Organization of Schools, Johns Hopkins University, Research Report No. 90, November, 1970.

Jeanneret, P. R., & McCormick, E. J. *The job dimensions of "worker-oriented" job variables and of their attribute profiles as based on data from the Position Analysis Questionnaire*. Lafayette, Ind.: Occupational Research Center, Purdue University, Report No. 2, June, 1969.

Kershner, A. M. *A report on job analysis*. Washington, D.C.: Office of Naval Research, ONR Report ACR-5, 1955.

Lawshe, C. H. Employee selection. *Personnel Psychology*, 1952, 5, 31–34.

Lewis, L. Job analysis in the United States

Training and Employment Service. In *Proceedings of 19. Division of Military Psychology Symposium: Collecting, analyzing, and reporting information describing jobs and occupations*. (77th Annual Convention of the American Psychological Association.) Lackland Air Force Base, Tex.: Personnel Research Division, Air Force Human Resources Laboratory, September, 1969, 33–41.

McCormick, E. J. The development of processes for indirect or synthetic validity: III. Application of job analysis to indirect validity. A symposium. *Personnel Psychology*, 1959, 12, 402–413.

McCormick, E. J., & Ammerman, H. L. *Development of worker activity check lists for use in occupational analysis*. Lackland Air Force Base, Tex.: Personnel Laboratory, Wright Air Development Division, WADD-TR-60-77, July, 1960.

McCormick, E. J., & Asquith, R. H. *An analysis of work patterns of CIC personnel for CVA-59 class ships*. Washington, D.C.: The Clifton Corporation, 1960.

McCormick, E. J., Finn, R. H., & Scheips, C. D. Patterns of job requirements. *Journal of Applied Psychology*, 1957, 41, 358–364.

McCormick, E. J., Jeanneret, P. R., & Mecham, R. C. *A study of job characteristics and job dimensions as based on the Position Analysis Questionnaire*. Lafayette, Ind.: Occupational Research Center, Purdue University, Report No. 6, 1969.

Marquardt, L. D., & McCormick, E. J. *Attribute ratings and profiles of job elements of the Position Analysis Questionnaire (PAQ)*. Lafayette, Ind.: Occupational Research Center, Department of Psychological Sciences, Purdue University, Report No. 1, 1972.

Marquardt, L. D., & McCormick, E. J. *Component analyses of the attribute data based on the Position Analysis Questionnaire (PAQ)*. Lafayette, Ind.: Occupational Research Center, Department of Psychological Sciences, Purdue University, Report No. 2, 1973.

Marquardt, L. D., & McCormick, E. J. *The job dimensions underlying the job elements of the Position Analysis Questionnaire (PAQ), Form B*. Lafayette, Ind.: Occupational Research Center, Department of Psychological Sciences, Purdue University, Report No. 4, June, 1974.

Marquardt, L. D., & McCormick, E. J. *The*

utility of job dimensions based on Form B of the Position Analysis Questionnaire (PAQ) in a job component validation model. Lafayette, Ind.: Occupational Research Center, Department of Psychological Sciences, Purdue University, Report No. 5, July, 1974.

Mecham, R. C. The synthetic prediction of personnel test requirements and job evaluation points using the Position Analysis Questionnaire. Unpublished doctoral dissertation, Purdue University, Lafayette, Ind., January, 1970.

Mecham, R. C., & McCormick, E. J. *The rated attribute requirements of job elements in the Position Analysis Questionnaire*. Lafayette, Ind.: Occupational Research Center, Purdue University, Report No. 1, January, 1969. (a)

Mecham, R. C., & McCormick, E. J. *The use in job evaluation of job elements and job dimensions based on the Position Analysis Questionnaire*. Lafayette, Ind.: Occupational Research Center, Purdue University, Report No. 3, June, 1969. (b)

Mecham, R. C., & McCormick, E. J. *The use of data based on the Position Analysis Questionnaire in developing synthetically derived attribute requirements of jobs*. Lafayette, Ind.: Occupational Research Center, Purdue University, Report No. 4, June, 1969. (c)

Miller, R. B. Task description and analysis. In R. M. Gagné (Ed.), *Psychological principles in system development*. New York: Holt, Rinehart and Winston, 1962.

Morsh, J. E. Job analysis in the United States Air Force. *Personnel Psychology*, 1964, 17, 7–17.

Morsh, J. E. Collecting, analyzing, and reporting information describing jobs in the United States Air Force. In *Proceedings of 19. Division of Military Psychology Symposium: Collecting, analyzing, and reporting information describing jobs and occupations*. (77th Annual Convention of the American Psychological Association.) Lackland Air Force Base, Tex.: Personnel Research Division, Air Force Human Resources Laboratory, September, 1969.

Morsh, J. E., & Archer, W. B. *Procedural guide for conducting occupational surveys in the United States Air Force*. Lackland Air Force Base, Tex.: Personnel Research Laboratory, Aerospace Medical Division, PRL-TR-67-11, September, 1967.

Parry, M. E. Ability of psychologists to estimate validities of personnel tests. *Personnel Psychology*, 1968, 21, 139–147.

Primoff, E. S. *Test selection by job analysis: The J-Coefficient*. Washington, D.C.: U.S. Civil Service Commission, Assembled Test Technical Edition, May, 1955.

Primoff, E. S. The development of processes for indirect or synthetic validity: IV. Empirical validations of the J–Coefficient. A symposium. *Personnel Psychology*, 1959, 12, 413–418.

Ramras, E. M. Discussion. In *Proceedings of 19. Division of Military Psychology Symposium: Collecting, analyzing, and reporting information describing jobs and occupations*. (77th Annual Convention of the American Psychological Association.) Lackland Air Force Base, Tex.: Personnel Research Division, Air Force Human Resources Laboratory, September, 1969, 75–76.

Snyder, M. B. Methods for recording and reporting task analysis information. In *Uses of task analysis in deriving training and training equipment requirements*. Wright-Patterson Air Force Base, Ohio: Wright Air Development Division, WADD Technical Report 60-593, December, 1960.

Swanson, J. B. Job inventory information: Inventory and scale reliability. Unpublished master's thesis, Purdue University, Lafayette, Ind., January, 1969.

Taylor, L. R. Personal communication, October, 1970.

Theologus, G. C. *Development of a taxonomy of human performance: A review of biologic taxonomy and classification*. Washington, D.C.: American Institutes for Research, AIR-726–12/69-TR-3, December, 1969.

Theologus, G. C., Romashko, T., & Fleishman, E. A. *Development of a taxonomy of human performance: A feasibility study of ability dimensions for classifying human tasks*. Washington, D.C.: American Institutes for Research, AIR-7-26-1/70-TR-5, January, 1970.

Trattner, N. H., Fine, S. A., & Kubis, J. F. A comparison of worker requirement ratings made by reading job descriptions and by direct observation. *Personnel Psychology*, 1955, 8, 183–194.

Ward, J. H. Jr. Hierarchical grouping to optimize an objective function. *Journal of the American Statistical Association*, 1963, 58, 236–244.

CHAPTER 16

Engineering Psychology

ALPHONSE CHAPANIS
The Johns Hopkins University

ENGINEERING PSYCHOLOGY is primarily concerned with the discovery and application of information about human behavior in relation to machines, tools, jobs, and work environments. The ultimate goal of the field is to help in the design of equipment, tasks, work places, and work environments so that they best match worker abilities and limitations. This chapter provides an overview of engineering psychology, its philosophy, its subject matter, and its methods.

The chapter begins with a consideration of man as a component of man-machine systems and illustrates some principles in the selection and design of information displays, the design of controls, and the dynamics of powered control systems.

However important it may be to worry about dials, gauges, knobs, and levers, some of the most challenging and intricate problems of engineering psychology arise in the design of large man-machine systems and the integration of man into those systems. It is at this point that engineering psychology comes closest to traditional industrial psychology, for the design of systems requires the psychologist to consider the selection of workers, their training, the design of the system hardware and its environments, and the design of operating rules, instructions, and procedures. Because the evaluation of man-machine systems involves the behavior of both men and machines, the engineering psychologist is often intimately involved in this evaluation process.

The real-world orientation of engineering psychology has resulted in the recognition of some methodological issues that confront applied psychologists everywhere. This has led to a healthy reappraisal of the relevance of laboratory findings to the real world. In particular, attention has focused on the dependent variables that are used in experimentation and on their relationship to the criteria that are used in the evaluation of systems.

Engineering psychology faces some problems and difficulties that will determine its ultimate vigor and growth. Most important, perhaps, is that the field is still not able to show convincingly that its principles and findings are effective in the design of systems. Perhaps for that reason, engineering psychology is still not as well accepted by design engineers as its potential would seem to warrant.

INTRODUCTION

Engineering psychology is primarily concerned with the discovery and application of information about human behavior in relation to machines, tools, jobs, and work environments. The ultimate goal of the field is to help in the design of equipment, tasks, work places, and work environments so that they best match worker abilities and limitations. As we shall see later in this chapter, however, the words *jobs, tasks,* and *worker* should be interpreted in their broadest possible senses, for engineering psychology is just as much concerned with the mental work of computer operators, air traffic controllers, and office workers, as with the physical labor of foundry workers, stevedores, and miners.

Within the past few years engineering psychologists have started to expand their horizons by applying their principles and methodologies to a variety of contemporary social problems: education, medicine, law enforcement, architecture, city planning, highway and transport design, and pollution.[1] This newly developed concern with man's relationship to the total environment around him implies a much broader definition of the field than has heretofore been the case. At this time it is not entirely clear how much emphasis will eventually be given to these broader social issues in contrast to the more traditional concerns with machine systems that have dominated the field up to this time.

ENGINEERING PSYCHOLOGY, HUMAN FACTORS ENGINEERING, AND ERGONOMICS. Other terms that are closely allied to engineering psychology are *human factors engineering, human engineering,* and *ergonomics.* Human factors engineering, or its less-preferred equivalent, human engineering, is a term used almost exclusively on the North Amer-

ican continent. Elsewhere in the world, *ergonomics* is the word that most closely approximates its American counterpart. Although the terms human factors engineering and ergonomics look and sound quite different, this dissimilarity is more the result of historical accident than of any genuine distinction between the fields they represent. For all practical purposes, human factors engineering and ergonomics may be considered synonymous.

The rapid growth of human factors engineering has not been without its problems. Disagreements have occurred between professional subgroups, several professional societies currently vie with each other to be the spokesman for the profession, and some specialists have rejected the label *human factors* for others such as bioastronautics, biodynamics, bioengineering, bioinstrumentation, biosciences, biotechnology, crew systems technology, life sciences engineering, man-machine systems engineering, and manned systems technology. Despite these signs of malcontent, Kraft's useful (1970) survey of the field concludes that no single collective term has emerged as a substitute for human factors engineering.

The distinction between engineering psychology and human factors engineering (or ergonomics) has also been the topic of considerable debate in professional circles. The point of view most consistent with current practice and thought has human factors engineering as the general term for the field that is concerned with human performance, behavior, and training in man-machine systems; the design and development of man-machine systems; and systems-related biological or medical research.[2] Viewed in this way (see Figure 1), human factors engineering draws upon parts of such human sciences as anatomy, anthropometry, applied physiology, environmental medicine,

---

[1] See, for example, the March, 1969, issue of the journal *Consulting Engineer* which contains seventeen articles all bearing on the topic, "Human Factors in Urban Design."

[2] The terms *human factor* or *human factors* and *human engineering* have also been used to refer to what might be more correctly called problems of human relations in industry (see, for example, Gow, 1930; Magoun, 1932; O'Connor, 1928; Tannenbaum, 1966).

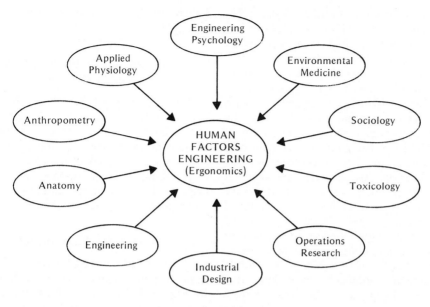

Figure 1. Some areas of specialization contributing to human factors engineering.

sociology, and toxicology, as well as parts of engineering, industrial design, and operations research. In this schema engineering psychology may be properly viewed as one of the disciplines contributing to the broader field of human factors engineering.

Despite the intensity of the debates that have occasionally developed over these definitions of fields and sub-fields, such problems of nomenclature are more academic than real. In his practical work, the engineering psychologist needs to know enough about related disciplines so that he can use them in arriving at sensible and informed design decisions. Rather than calling engineering psychology a distinct entity, it would be more correct to say that this name is an administrative convenience and a common label useful for identifying certain courses and curricula offered in many universities. Since somewhat more than a third of all people currently engaged in human factors work have come into it by way of psychology (Kraft, 1970), engineering psychology is one of the educational routes through which a large number of profes-

sional people enter into the field of human factors engineering. That in itself is perhaps reason enough for engineering psychology to retain its distinctive name.

ENGINEERING PSYCHOLOGY VERSUS INDUSTRIAL PSYCHOLOGY. Industrial psychology traditionally regarded the job as a constant, a given. The primary task of the industrial psychologist was to select workers who were best suited to do the job and then to mold or shape them further through training and other strategies. Engineering psychology took the opposite point of view. The worker was regarded as a biological and psychological constant with many innately determined abilities and limitations. The engineering psychologist viewed his task as that of changing the machines and the tools with which man worked, or the environment in which he worked, to make the job better suited to the man.

This distinction between these two fields of psychology can no longer be maintained as sharply as has been drawn here. On the one hand, textbooks of industrial psychology (see, for example, Blum & Naylor, 1968; Fleishman, 1967; Tiffin & McCormick, 1965) now include chapters or sections on engineering psychology. Indeed, the fact that a chapter such as this one has been included in a handbook of industrial and organizational psychology is evidence enough that industrial psychologists recognize the contributions engineering psychology has to offer. On the other hand, newer emphases and interests in systems engineering, discussed later in this chapter, have made it clear that machines cannot be designed for an abstract man; they have to be designed for particular people. Aircraft are designed to be piloted by highly select, highly trained operators. Automobiles, on the other hand, are designed for use by almost any adult. The systems approach recognizes that equipment design cannot be divorced from considerations of personnel selection and training, topics that have been traditionally the province of the industrial psychologist.

These two converging streams tend to blur the lines of demarcation between engineering and industrial psychology. Indeed, an intriguing possibility is that industrial psychology will eventually absorb engineering psychology, as some writers seem to feel, or that engineering psychology, with its emphasis on systems, will one day claim industrial psychology for itself.

THE SCOPE OF THIS CHAPTER. This chapter tries to provide an overview of engineering psychology, its philosophy, its subject matter, and its methods. We begin with man as a component of man-machine systems, turn to a consideration of systems and the systems approach, and conclude with some problems and difficulties with the field. In keeping with the distinction I drew earlier between engineering psychology and human factors engineering, my emphasis in this chapter will be on the former, that is, on psychological studies of machine design and of man at work. That still encompasses such a very considerable subject matter that

I shall only be able to touch on some of the highlights.

MAN AS A COMPONENT OF A MAN-MACHINE SYSTEM

Engineering psychology began by studying the individual operator and the machine with which he worked. Since a substantial amount of the typical engineering psychologist's time is still taken up with problems of this kind, it is appropriate that we also begin with psychological studies of man as a component of a man-machine system.

A Man-Machine Model

A simplified but useful way of looking at man in man-machine systems is illustrated in Figure 2. In any machine system, the human operator first has to sense and perceive something. The thing he senses is usually some sort of a machine display. A display may be any of a thousand or more things—the position of a pointer on a dial, a red light flashing on a control panel, the readout of a digital computer, the sound of a warning buzzer, a spoken command issuing from a loudspeaker, or the feel of a certain kind of control. He may also get important information from the machine itself, for example, from a noisy bearing, the rhythmic vibration of a smooth running engine, or the unbroken contrast of fabric coming out of a loom.

Having sensed the display, the man has to interpret it, understand it, perhaps do some mental computation, and reach a decision. In so doing, the operator often uses other important human abilities—his ability to remember, to compare what he perceives with past experiences, to coordinate what he perceives with strategies he may have formed in the past for handling similar events, and to extrapolate from his perceptions and past experiences to the solution of novel problems. He is not necessarily aware that he is doing all these things. His

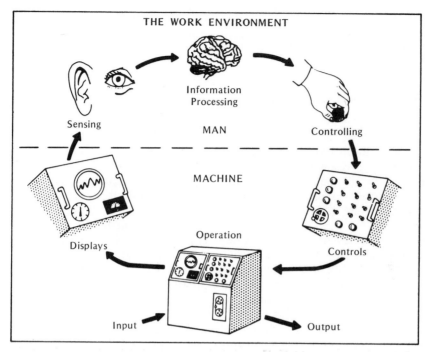

Figure 2. The man-machine model.

behavior may be so well practiced or routine that his decisions may be made almost reflexly, just as an experienced driver may decide almost unconsciously whether to stop when he sees a green traffic light change to yellow. In textbooks of psychology, these functions are often discussed under the heading of the higher mental processes. Engineering psychologists, however, tend to use machine terminology instead of more ordinary psychological terms. In keeping with this bias, Figure 2 refers to these higher mental processes collectively as information processing.

Having reached a decision, the human operator normally takes some action. This action is usually exercised on some type of control—a push button, lever, crank, pedal, switch, or handle. Man's action upon one or more of these controls exerts in turn an influence on the machine, which in turn alters its output and its displays. Many times, of course, a machine operator monitoring a process may decide to do nothing. That is still regarded as an important human output.

A man-machine system does not exist in isolation; it exists in an environment of some sort. Since the nature of this environment usually influences man's efficiency and performance, the engineering psychologist is often concerned with environmental factors as well.

Information Displays

The man-machine model described above provides a convenient framework for summarizing some of the main content areas of engineering psychology. Machine displays are one conventional point of entry into the man-machine cycle, because it is through such displays that the machine communicates to its human operator. For this reason, a considerable amount of work has been devoted to studies of displays and the ways in which they should be selected and designed.

The Selection of a Sense Channel

Although man has available a dozen or so sense channels that could conceivably be used to receive information from machine systems, only three—vision, hearing, and the sense of touch or vibration—have been exploited to any great extent. Of the three, vision and hearing are the two that are most often used.

Many factors influence an engineer's decision to use one form of communication rather than another. Cost, engineering feasibility, and existing communication links are some of the things he must consider. In addition, engineering psychologists have directed attention to the human factors relevant to the selection and design of a communication system. The first question that needs to be answered in this connection is: Which sensory-input channel should be used for receiving information from the communication link? Most often this question may be interpreted to mean: Should we design for human eyes or ears?

The choice of the communication channel between machine and man depends on the type of information that is to be transmitted, the way it is to be used, the location of the man, the environment in which the man operates, and the nature of the sense organ itself. For example, our ears, unlike our eyes, can receive information from all directions. Moreover, we can't close our ears the way we close our eyes. These properties make the ears well suited to the reception of emergency and warning signals. Such considerations have been organized by engineering psychologists into the recommendations that follow:

VISUAL MEANS OF COMMUNICATION. In general, visual means of communication (television, teletype, radar, written or printed materials, dials, gauges, and so on) are more appropriate when:

1. The message to be transmitted is complex or abstract, or contains technical or scientific terms.

2. The message to be transmitted is long.

3. The message needs to be referred to later. (Visual means of communication lend themselves well to producing durable copies, so that the message can be filed, stored, and referred to at will.)

4. The message deals with spatial orientation or with the locations of points in space. (Showing someone how to get from point A to point B with the help of a map is much easier than trying to do the same thing using only spoken words.)

5. The state of a system (temperature, pressure, rate of flow) has to be compared with some base line or normal operating condition.

6. There is no urgency in the transmission of the message.

7. The available auditory channels are overloaded or are likely to be saturated with messages.

8. The auditory environment is not suitable for the transmission of aural communications. (For example, visual messages are often more suitable for transmitting information in such noisy places as in the immediate vicinity of a high-speed printing press or jet aircraft.)

9. The operator's job allows him to stay in one spot. (In order to receive visual messages the recipient must have his eyes focused on the receiving unit or must be sufficiently close to it so that he can see the message when it arrives.)

10. The machine or system output consists of many different kinds of information (e.g., engine temperature, cylinder pressure, RPM, speed, fuel consumption) which must be displayed simultaneously, monitored, and acted upon from time to time.

AURAL MEANS OF COMMUNICATION. Aural forms of communication (telephones, annunciator systems, buzzers, warning signals, sirens, gongs, and so on) are generally more suitable when:

1. The message is simple and uncomplicated. (For example, the words "Okay" and "No" are very easily transmitted aurally.)

2. The message is short.

3. Speed of transmission is important. (If you want to signal someone to "Look out!" an auditory message is probably the best way to do it. Auditory signals, in general, have greater attention-getting value than visual ones.)

4. The message does not need to be referred to later.

5. The message deals with events in time and with a particular point in time. (For example, if you want to signal someone exactly when to launch a missile or start a race, an auditory communication system will enable you to pinpoint this time easily and with precision.)

6. Visual channels of communication are likely to be overloaded.

7. The environment is not suited to the reception of visual messages. (For example, in the presence of excessive vibration, or in the absence of all illumination, an auditory transmission system may be the only one feasible.)

8. The operator has to move around a lot. (I have already remarked that our ears are always alert for messages and that messages can be received from any direction. If the operator must continually move about in the work environment, an aural form of communication, for example, a paging system, is more likely to get through to him.)

9. There is a chance that the operator may be subjected to anoxia, certain noxious fumes and gases, or to the effects of high positive acceleration. (The auditory system is much more resistant than the eye to anoxia of the brain. An operator can hear messages when he may be temporarily blind because of lack of oxygen. Oxygen lack may occur from ascent to high altitudes, from the inhalation of certain kinds of noxious fumes and gases, and from positive acceleration which drains blood from the head.)

10. The problem is one of detecting a signal in the presence of noise. (The ear is a very sensitive frequency analyzer. That is why you can hear, or single out for perception, the sound of an individual instrument from the sound of an entire orchestra. The eye, by contrast, is a frequency synthesizer. It responds to a collection of wavelengths of light with a single unitary sensation from which it is impossible to isolate individual components. The ability of the ear to detect a particular signal in the presence of many other sounds makes the ear a very sensitive detector in systems such as sonar.)

This brief evaluation[3] of the relative advantages and disadvantages of the visual and auditory channels of communication makes it clear that there are many situations in which it is appropriate to use one, and many other situations in which it is appropriate to use the other. In any case, one should not try to make the eyes or ears do jobs for which they are not suited.

The Visual Display of Information

The sense of sight renders remarkable psychological service as an information channel. Man's eyes are his major source of contact with his environment. They furnish him with his primary means of knowing things and of finding his way about in life. Think, for example, of the wealth of information you have gained from the books, magazines, and newspapers that you have read so far in your life. Small wonder, then, that the sense of sight is so heavily exploited in man-machine systems.

Engineering psychologists have given a great deal of attention to visual displays and even a partial listing of the kinds of research they have done makes an impressive catalogue of applied visual problems. The list includes studies on the design of magnification aids such as binoculars, optical range finders, and telescopes; cathode-ray

---

[3] For a more thorough comparison of man's sense channels, see Mowbray and Gebhard (1961).

tubes, radar scopes, and television screens; warning and signal devices; highway signs; letters, numerals, and type faces; graphic displays such as tables, graphs, and nomographs for presenting quantitative information in publications and reports; and dials, gauges, and instruments of all kinds (see, for example, McCormick, 1970; Morgan et al., 1963; Woodson & Conover, 1966). Since it is impossible to do justice to this range of topics in a few pages, I have selected a few representative problems to talk about below.

MECHANICAL INDICATORS AND THEIR USES. The outcome of a considerable amount of research and experience has led to the principle that visual displays in general, and dials and indicators in particular, should be designed and selected to give a human operator the kind of information he needs in the way that he can best use it. The application of this principle to indicators requires first that we know something about the functions such devices serve.

One purpose of indicators is to provide exact numerical readings. You use a clock to find out the time, and, if you are rushing to make a plane connection, you want to know the time exactly. You use a thermometer to find out the exact temperature of the room you are in, the roast you have in your oven, or the photographic developer you use in the basement darkroom. Compasses, thermometers, speedometers, kilowatt-hour meters, tachometers, and thousands of other indicators are used to provide operators with exact quantitative readings.

Sometimes dials and indicators are used only for check-reading purposes—to get a GO, NO-GO, or OK, NOT-OK type of indication. An example is the temperature indicator on the dashboard in many modern cars. Most people don't care about the exact engine temperature of their automobiles and there is no reason for them to know. All they really need to know is whether everything is within its normal operating range and whether everything is holding steady. For check reading it is often

not necessary to use a dial or indicator at all. Oftentimes a warning light is all that is required. Warning lights, however, do not conveniently provide information about more complex types of check reading—those that show rates of change or the amount and direction of deviation from some normal operating condition.

The two functions discussed so far are concerned with the transmission of information from machine to man. Sometimes, however, a visual indicator is linked to a control so that an operator can verify information he puts into a machine. When you set the thermostat for your furnace, you need some sort of an indicator to tell you exactly what instructions you have given the system. This is a homely example of a type you can find repeated hundreds of ways in machine shops, factories, airplanes, and ships.

When the helmsman of a ship tries to keep his vehicle on a compass heading of 210°, he performs a tracking task. Gusts of wind, waves, and ocean currents tend to force the vehicle off its course from time to time. The task of the helmsman is to make the proper corrective movements with his wheel so that the number 210° is brought back under the index marker whenever it drifts off. In a large ship, deviations occur relatively slowly and infrequently. In a small ship, or in an aircraft, they may happen rapidly and often. However fast the action, the task is primarily a tracking task.

There is always some danger in trying to summarize complex recommendations in a simple way. One difficulty is that indicators may occasionally be used for several purposes. Then, too, there are sometimes special considerations that override any general rule one could make. If we keep these precautions in mind, Figure 3 can be taken as a useful summary of the relative advantages and disadvantages of three kinds of indicators for the uses described above. A + means that the indicator is suited to that function, an empty cell means that the indicator is only fair or questionable for that

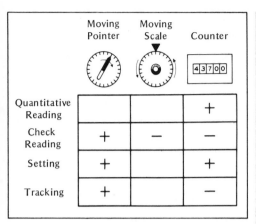

	Moving Pointer	Moving Scale	Counter
Quantitative Reading			+
Check Reading	+	−	−
Setting	+		+
Tracking	+		−

Figure 3. Recommended uses for three basic types of mechanical indicators.

Figure 4. A moving-scale indicator of a type in common use.

application, and a — means that you should generally avoid using that indicator for the purpose shown.

THE MOVING-SCALE INDICATOR. According to Figure 3, the moving-scale indicator does not show up very well at all. The trouble with this indicator is that there is no way to design it without violating one of three important principles. They are:

1. The scale and the knob (or crank or wheel) that controls it should move in the same direction. So, for example, when you turn the knob clockwise, the scale should move clockwise. When you turn the control counterclockwise, the scale should move counterclockwise.

2. A clockwise rotation of the knob should increase the settings on the scale; a counterclockwise rotation should decrease settings.

3. The numbers of the scale should increase in a clockwise direction around the scale because scales are read more easily when numbers progress in this way.

There is no way to design an indicator of this type so that all three rules are satisfied at the same time. A common compromise is illustrated in Figure 4, where the numbers increase in a counterclockwise direction around the scale. Incidentally, can you read the setting on that dial?

The indicator in Figure 5 makes use of the recommendations in Figure 3 by substituting a direct reading counter for the scale. In this case the operator rotates the knurled

Figure 5. The moving-scale indicator in Figure 4 has been redesigned for easier readability.

flange around the outside of the control. Clockwise rotation of the flange increases the numbers in the windows; counterclockwise rotation decreases them. Both of these devices are available commercially from the same company. Studies of these two types of indicators (Weldon & Peterson, 1957) show that the one in Figure 5 leads to far fewer setting and checking errors than the one in Figure 4.

THE DESIGN OF LETTERS AND NUMERALS. Letters and numerals in signs, labels, dials, and visual displays of all sorts are so ubiquitous and so important that engineering psychologists have devoted a considerable amount of attention to their design and to the factors that influence their legibility. As is so often the case with applied problems, the solutions are by no means as simple as we would like.

The first and most important conclusion one can draw from a considerable amount of research on the problem is that no single style of letters and numerals is best for all conditions. A good starting point, however, is the NAMEL set, so-called because it is the outcome based on research done primarily at the Navy Medical Equipment Laboratory. This set, illustrated in Figure 6, has stood up so well in repeated tests that it has been incorporated into military standards (MIL-C-18012). Note that the characters have no serifs or other embellishments. Except for the I, J, L, and W, the letters are

Figure 6. The NAMEL letters and numerals.

as wide as they are high. The numerals, except for the 1, have a height:width ratio of 5:3.

Now for a few of the special conditions that complicate the story. One important distinction is between front-lighted and transilluminated displays. Figure 6 is an example of a front-lighted display. The letters and numerals are printed on a surface that is illuminated from in front and the viewer sees the display by reflected light. Examples of transilluminated displays are the pedestrian WAIT and WALK signs that one sees at busy street corners. Many instrument panels and control consoles also use transilluminated labels. For such displays the letters themselves are cut out of an opaque mask. Since the light source is behind the mask, the letters are luminous on a black or dark background. Transilluminated, or luminous letters, are subject to irradiation, that is, the white tends to spread out over the black surround so that white lines appear wider than they really are. The phenomenon of irradiation means that the stroke widths of characters should be narrower if they are transilluminated than if they are front-lighted. For most ordinary illuminated letters on a dark background the stroke widths in Figure 6 should be reduced about a third, that is, to about one-eighth to one-tenth the heights of the characters. As the brightness of letters and numerals increases, the stroke width needs to be reduced correspondingly. For extremely bright letters this may mean using stroke widths that are only $\frac{1}{40}$th that of the height of the character.

Letters and numerals used under daylight conditions outdoors come in two common variations: black letters and white backgrounds, and white letters and black backgrounds. For the former, the stroke widths in Figure 6 are nearly ideal, but the widths of the letters should be reduced to about three-quarters of their heights. For white letters on black backgrounds, the best width to height ratio is about the same as for black letters on a white background, that is, about 3:4, but the stroke widths should be reduced to about half of those shown in Figure 6.

This brief excursion into the legibility of numerals and letters by no means exhausts the variety of conditions under which they can be used or the complexities that are associated with alternative uses. For example, I have not even touched on type styles for printing. This would get into problems of a somewhat different sort from mere legibility. Still, this discussion illustrates some of the kinds of work that has been done on this important class of display problems and some of the conclusions that have derived from that work. For more complete treatments of these topics see McCormick (1970) and Woodson and Conover (1966).

The Auditory Display of Information

Even though it normally ranks only second best, the auditory sense channel is an important vehicle of communication between man and machine and between man and man. Think of the many important ways in which aural signals help us to get along in our world of machines. The ringing of an alarm clock wakes us in the morning. The telephone rings. We answer it and talk to someone miles away to set up an appointment later in the day. The burbling of the coffee maker assures us that the preparation of breakfast is proceeding on schedule. These examples are only a few of the thousands of sounds, noises, and signals that assail our ears continually throughout the course of a day and communicate information to us.

Aural communication systems can be grouped into two main classes: (a) tonal signaling systems such as gongs, buzzers, bells, diaphones, horns, whistles, sirens, and other similar sounds, and (b) speech communication systems. In general, tonal signaling systems are to be preferred when:

1. The message is extremely simple.
2. The listener has had special training in the meaning of coded signals. "Take

cover" and "All clear" siren signals are of no use unless people know what kind of a signal means what.

3. The message calls for immediate action.
4. Speech signals are overburdening the listener.
5. Conditions are unfavorable for receiving speech signals. Tonal signals can be heard in noise that would make speech unintelligible.
6. Secrecy is important. Speech can be readily understood by unintentional listeners, whereas it is possible to devise coded tonal or noise signals that cannot be interpreted unintentionally.
7. Speech communication channels are overloaded.
8. Speech will mask other speech or annoy listeners for whom the message is not intended.

By contrast, speech communication systems are generally preferred when:

1. Flexibility of communication is necessary.
2. It is necessary to be able to identify the source of the message.
3. The listener has had no special training in the meaning of coded signals.
4. Rapid two-way exchanges of information are necessary.
5. The message deals with a future time requiring some preparation. In the countdown preparatory to the launch of a space vehicle, the rhythmic sequence of words "... nine, eight, seven, six ..." enables a number of listeners to prepare for and to arrive simultaneously at the final word in the sequence, "ignition." A series of identical tonal signals under the same circumstances is often miscounted. A word countdown also enables listeners to take actions at specific times in the sequence, as, for example, at the count of "fifteen."
6. Stress might cause the listener to forget the meaning of a code for tonal signals.

HUMAN FACTORS IN THE DESIGN OF TONAL SIGNALING SYSTEMS. Tonal signaling systems are used in auditory Morse code, in sonar, in aircraft navigation and guidance systems, and in a variety of alarm and warning devices. The main human factors problems associated with such systems are the special characteristics of various signals that accommodate them for certain uses, and a variety of technical factors that can be included under the heading of signal processing and control. The latter include such things as signal-to-noise relationships, the masking of sound by noise, various ways of filtering to enhance the audibility of signals in the presence of unwanted noise, and the selection of optimum signal levels, durations, and sequences. Since these topics get into some fairly complex technical material, I shall forego any more discussion of them here and refer the interested reader to Morgan et al. (1963).

SPEECH COMMUNICATION SYSTEMS. Human factors in speech communication systems can be roughly grouped into three main areas:
1. Human engineering the language.
2. Human engineering the components of speech systems.
3. Human engineering the speech communication systems as a whole.

In studying these problems and in arriving at solutions to them engineering psychologists rely heavily on the results of intelligibility tests—elaborate tests of speech communication carried out with carefully selected talkers, listeners, communication equipment, and speech test materials. For a fuller treatment of these methods see Chapanis (1959) and Morgan et al. (1963).

HUMAN ENGINEERING THE LANGUAGE. Research and practical studies have shown that it is often possible to communicate more effectively by altering a language, by using it in certain prescribed ways, or by constructing a specialized language for specific purposes. Recent research on time-compressed speech illustrates one of these approaches and suggests some potentialities that have not yet been fully exploited. Underlying

this research are new developments in electronics that make it possible to play back recorded messages at accelerated rates without changing speech quality. In short, these techniques provide time compression without concomitant bandwidth compression. In a test of time-compressed speech, Sticht (1968) had subjects of three mental aptitude levels listen to a recorded sample of speech on a scientific subject and then answer questions on what they had heard. The results in Figure 7 reveal some losses in compre-

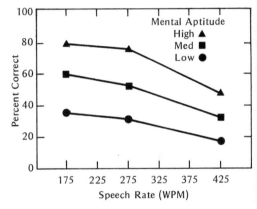

Figure 7. Comprehension scores for each of three groups of subjects as a function of message presentation rate. (After Sticht, 1968.)

hension as the speech rate is increased above normal. Since professional oral readers speak at a rate of about 175 words per minute, rates of 275 and 425 words per minute represent speech compressions of 36 percent and 59 percent respectively. These gains in speed are greater than the losses in accuracy shown in Figure 7. The net gain is revealed clearly when the same data are plotted as listening efficiency curves (Figure 8). Some possible applications of this technique are in education, in computer systems, and in systems for the recording and later readout of stored voice messages.

A different example of human engineering the language is the construction of the international word-spelling alphabet that has been adopted by the International Civil Aviation Organization (ICAO). When

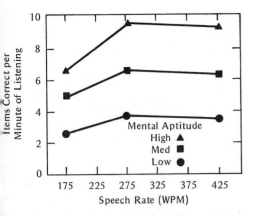

Figure 8. The data in Figure 7 have been replotted as listening efficiency curves. (After Sticht, 1968.)

TABLE 1
INTERNATIONAL WORD-SPELLING ALPHABET ADOPTED BY THE INTERNATIONAL CIVIL AVIATION ORGANIZATION (ICAO)

Alpha	November
Bravo	Oscar
Charlie	Papa
Delta	Quebec
Echo	Romeo
Foxtrot	Sierra
Golf	Tango
Hotel	Uniform
India	Victor
Juliet	Whiskey
Kilo	X Ray
Lima	Yankee
Mike	Zulu

communication links are poor, or when noise is excessive, it is sometimes necessary to spell each word you are trying to communicate. Although this procedure is tedious and time consuming, it is very effective. Its effectiveness can be increased by picking words that begin with each of the letters of the alphabet and saying the words instead of the letters. This technique is known as *word spelling*. A considerable amount of research has gone into getting suitable lists of words for this purpose. Among other things, such words should be easy to pronounce, readable by persons with all sorts of educational backgrounds, and easily distinguishable from one another. In addition, if the words are to be used internationally they need to be recognizable when spoken by and to persons of different nationalities and accents. Finding a list of words to satisfy these requirements was no easy task. Years of research finally resulted in the set shown in Table 1. To communicate the word *stop,* for example, the talker says, "sierra, tango, oscar, papa."

Other ways of human engineering the language are discussed in Chapanis (1965b) and Morgan et al. (1963).

HUMAN ENGINEERING THE COMPONENTS OF SPEECH SYSTEMS. There are many things an engineer can do in the design or selection of components to make speech communica-

tion more effective for special purposes. Microphone noise shields, noise-cancelling microphones, automatic gain control (AGC), peak clipping with re-amplification, and heterodyne clipping are some of the devices and techniques that can improve the performance of components. To illustrate a few of the many principles that can be put to use, following are some of the specific ways in which headsets can be modified to increase their effectiveness in noisy environments:

1. Slightly better intelligibility of speech can be obtained with earphones that are connected out of phase. *Out of phase* means that when the diaphragm of one earphone moves towards the center of the listener's head the diaphragm of the other moves away from it. This is just the opposite of the customary way of connecting earphones. Although the gain is small, it is measurable and the change needed to bring it about electrically is quite simple.

2. Delaying the arrival of a speech signal to one ear by about 500 micro-seconds relative to that delivered to the other ear also results in a measurable improvement in intelligibility.

3. Binaural headsets are more effective than monaural ones when the listener is in noise.

4. The signal from the talker's microphone, that is, the talker's voice, is usually returned to him via his earphones. This

feedback signal is called the side tone. Since talkers usually adjust their vocal effort to compensate, within limits, for changes in the level of the side tone, keeping the side tone weak will help maintain a high signal-to-noise ratio. Talkers also tend to speak more slowly when the side tone is weak and this in turn improves the intelligibility of speech.

5. Passing the side tone signal through either a high-pass or a low-pass filter before it enters the headset also causes talkers to increase their vocal effort and to enunciate their speech more precisely—both of which tend to improve the intelligibility of speech.

6. A delay of about 0.05 seconds in the arrival of the side tone also tends to make talkers increase their level of effort and speak more slowly.

HUMAN ENGINEERING THE SPEECH COMMUNICATION SYSTEM AS A WHOLE. Speech communication systems are usually designed as a whole, that is, the individual components and the language are selected to match each other and to work together in effective combinations. Such systems can, of course, be designed to meet any of a large number of special communication needs. The eight variations of a system in Figure 9 illustrate a few of the complicated technical considerations that are involved in this kind of work.

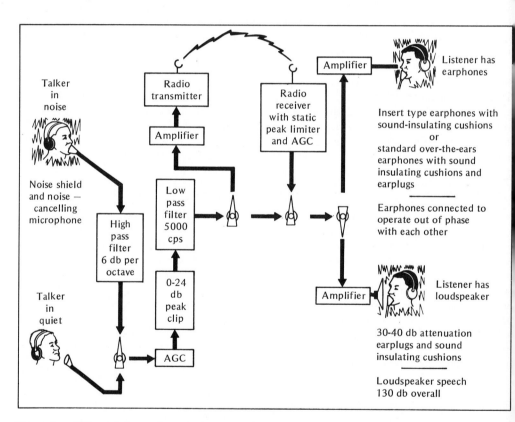

Figure 9. Eight variations of a speech communication system for use in extremely intense noise. The variations include all combinations of: talker in quiet versus talker in noise; a direct communication channel versus a radio link between the talker and listener; and listener with earphones versus listener with loudspeaker. (After Morgan et al., 1963.)

The Design of Controls

The preceding few sections have been concerned with sensory inputs to the human operator—with ways in which machines can effectively convey information to their human counterparts. As the man-machine model in Figure 2 shows, however, there is an output side to the human operator's job as well. In most man-machine systems the operator receives information through his several senses, processes this information in a variety of ways, and then takes some sort of action. That action is normally exerted through a control of some kind, for example, a push button, knob, crank, or lever. Research and experience have shown that the ways in which controls are designed may have important effects on the speed and accuracy with which human actions are exercised on machines. We turn now to a few of the concepts and principles that apply to the design of controls.

Picking the Right Control for the Job

As was the case with the design of information displays, the first step in designing controls for effective human use is to pick the best control for the job. In itself, a control is neither good nor bad. It is merely appropriate or inappropriate. A push button is fine for starting a motor, but it is not a good way of steering a car; a knob is a good way of controlling the flow of water through a faucet, but hardly an efficient way of entering data into a computer.

Controls in common use fall into twelve basic classes: hand push buttons, foot push buttons, toggle switches, rocker switches, rotary switches, slide switches, knobs, cranks, thumbwheels, levers, handwheels, and pedals. Table 2 shows some recommended uses for these various kinds of controls. This table does not tell the whole story, however; additional considerations that enter into the choice of a control are given below.

TABLE 2
RECOMMENDED CONTROLS FOR VARIOUS TYPES OF TASKS*

For SMALL forces and	use
2 discrete settings	Hand push button, foot push button, toggle switch, slide switch, or rocker switch
3 discrete settings	Finger push button, toggle switch, or rotary selector switch
4 to 24 discrete settings	Bank or array of finger push buttons, rotary selector switch, or detented thumbwheel
25 or more discrete settings	Bank or array of finger push buttons
Small range of continuous settings	Knob, lever, or thumbwheel
Large range of continuous settings	Crank

For LARGE forces and	use
2 discrete settings	Detent lever, large hand push button, or foot push button
3 to 24 discrete settings	Detent lever
Small range of continuous settings	Handwheel, rotary pedal, or lever
Large range of continuous settings	Large crank

* After Morgan et al., 1963.

MATCHING CONTROLS TO LIMBS. Although it is theoretically possible to use many different parts of the human body to activate controls, only the hands and feet are customarily used for this purpose. Perhaps the most important rule to observe in this connection is that none of the limbs should be overburdened. If the operator has a number of controls to use, they should be distributed among the four limbs.

Since the four limbs differ in their capabilities, controls should be selected to match those capabilities. Generally speaking, many controls of many different kinds can be assigned to the hands, but not more than two simple controls should be assigned to each foot. Since most people are right-handed, the major load should be assigned to the right hand. Finally, controls that must be adjusted rapidly and with great precision should be assigned to the hands; those requiring the application of large forces to the feet.

MATCHING CONTROLS TO MOVEMENTS. Controls should mimic the movements they produce in the system. For example, a lever that moves up and down conforms naturally to the up and down movements of a hoist and the clockwise rotation of a crank conforms naturally to the movement of a crane to the right. When the movements of a control are naturally and easily associated with the movements of a display, vehicle, or machine component, the two are said to be compatible.

COMBINING FUNCTIONALLY RELATED CONTROLS. When an operator uses a large number of controls, it is often advantageous to have related controls combined. Many switches for lighting systems combine an on-off switch with a continuously variable dimmer. Since these are functionally related operations, they are sensibly combined.

The principal advantages of combined controls are that they reduce the number of movements required to operate a number of controls, they help the operator use several controls at the same time or in sequence, and they save space. In combining controls, however, it is important not to violate other human-engineering principles, such as optimum *control-display ratios* and *natural movement relationships*.

MATCHING CONTROLS TO THE WORKING ENVIRONMENT. Man-machine systems work in many different kinds of environments and the characteristics of these environments may have some important implications for control selection and design. Some of these are:

1. Cold temperatures produce stiffness in an operator's hands and feet and reduce his dexterity. If the operator wears gloves or mittens he will have greater difficulty in manipulating small devices and may have to have more than normal amounts of separation between controls.

2. Heat generally causes operators to perspire. Perspiration often limits the amount of force an operator can apply with his hands and may hamper his finger dexterity as well.

3. Vibration and oscillation reduce manual dexterity and make it more difficult for operators to make smooth, continuous movements.

4. Acceleration and g-forces may prevent an operator from applying his full force on a control and may make it difficult for him to reach controls.

5. Restrictive garments, heavy work clothes, shoulder harnesses, and seat belts often make it difficult for an operator to reach and operate controls effectively.

6. The normal working position of the operator, that is, whether he is sitting or standing, affects his mobility and the choice and location of controls.

Factors in the Design of Controls

A number of design factors keep cropping up in connection with many types of controls. Perhaps the most important of these are control-display ratios, direction-of-movement relationships, methods of coding controls, and methods of preventing accidental activation. One of these topics is discussed in some detail below.

DIRECTION-OF-MOVEMENT RELATIONSHIPS AND OPERATOR EXPECTATIONS. Studies of errors made in operating controls reveal that reversal errors, errors made by moving a control in the wrong direction, are relatively common. For example, I invariably turn the windshield wiper knob the wrong way when I want to turn off the windshield wipers on my family automobile. Other examples of this kind may perhaps occur to you. At first glance, one might suppose that errors of this kind are caused by inattention, carelessness, or lack of training. Further analysis, however, reveals that such errors often occur because controls move in directions that are contrary to the way in which people expect them to move. In some cases, human expectations about control movements are so universal that they have been termed *population stereotypes*.

When controls, control arrangements, and control-display movements conform to population stereotypes, we find in general that:

1. Reaction time, or decision time, is shorter.

2. The first control movement the operator makes is more likely to be correct.

3. The operator can use the control faster and make adjustments with greater precision.

4. The operator can learn to use the control (or the control-display combination) much faster.

People are remarkably adaptive and can often learn to compensate for deficiencies in equipment design. It is not surprising, therefore, to find that operators can learn to use controls that do not move in expected directions, and that they can adapt to layouts that do not conform to population stereotypes. The danger, however, is that when operators are under stress or anxiety, these learned habits often break down, with the

result that the operator reverts to more natural (though incorrect) movements. The experimental evidence on this point is so strong that we may adopt it as a general principle: Do not require operators to make unnatural movements, especially since it is so easy to design equipment properly in the first place.

An illustration of the way in which this kind of research is done, and of its practical consequences, comes from two studies done on the design of keysets for the entry of numerical information. At the time when AT&T was considering the possibility of replacing the dial on telephones with a series of push buttons, Lutz and Chapanis (1955) made a study of six different configurations of ten keys. The keysets were made up with blank keys, that is, with no marks or designations on them. Each of a carefully selected, stratified sample of people was asked to show where they would expect to find each of the ten digits on these keysets. Of the six keysets tested, the one on the left in Figure 10 yielded the greatest amount of

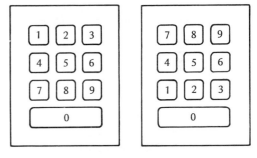

Figure 10. The telephone (left) and adding machine (right) layouts of a numeric entry device.

consistency. For that keyset, most people expected the digits to increase from left to right and from top to bottom. They expected the 0 to be the odd key at the bottom.

The Lutz and Chapanis study, of course, merely confirmed the existence of a population stereotype. It did not provide any evidence about performance. That came from a study by Conrad and Hull (1968). These investigators compared the telephone arrangement (the one on the left in Figure 10) with the adding-machine arrangement (the one on the right in Figure 10). The telephone layout was found to be better in both speed and accuracy, thus confirming the results of the expectancy study by Lutz and Chapanis.

Compatible control-display movement relationships have been studied with many kinds of controls, displays, and arrangements of both. A few highly dependable movement stereotypes are shown in Figure 11.

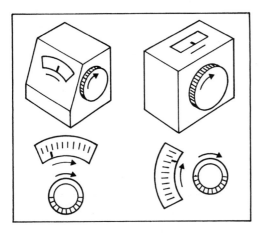

Figure 11. A few highly dependable control-display movement stereotypes. (After Loveless, 1962.)

The Dynamics of Powered Control Systems

Although principles regarding the selection and design of individual controls find ready application in a variety of situations, much more interesting and challenging problems of control design are encountered in machine systems in which the design of the control interacts in complex ways with the dynamics of the system itself. These complex interactions usually occur in powered control systems.

A simple way of illustrating the problem is to compare what happens when a man digs a hole with a hand shovel and with a power shovel. In the former instance, man applies muscular power to the tool, the shovel, and the tool in turn affects the environment—the soil in which he is digging. He can manipulate the tool in a variety of ways, angle it more or less steeply, apply more or less force on it, and use it as a lever, cutting device, scraper, or scoop. In all cases, the outcome is directly related to the force the man applies to the tool and the way in which he uses it.

Contrast this situation with what happens when an operator uses a giant power shovel. The human operator no longer applies muscle power to the environment, that is, the soil in which he is digging. The "muscle power" comes from the engine of the shovel itself. The function of the operator's control is to regulate the power source in such a way that his "tool" will do the job he wants to get done. The operator is, in this case, much further removed from the actual job being done, and his control actions may be related to the performance of his machine only in very complex and indirect ways. Sensory processes, thought processes, and skill, rather than muscle-power, are the operator characteristics required by powered control systems. Powered control systems are so ubiquitous in our modern technological society that engineering psychologists have devoted a great deal of attention to them—not only to understand their characteristics, but also to find out how best to integrate man into them.

Closed-loop Control Systems

Many powered man-machine systems can be diagrammed as in Figure 12. The system has (on the left in the figure) a display which usually portrays continuously changing information. The operator senses this information, ordinarily through his eyes or ears, and moves his control, or controls, accordingly. The output, or output signal, from the operator's control (X_c) initiates some action in the machine. The output of the machine (X_m) constitutes the system output. As used here, machine refers

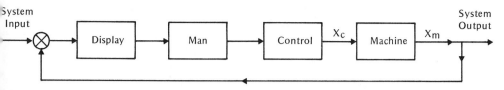

System Input · System Output

Figure 12. Block diagram of a closed-loop, powered control system.

to all the components of the system other than the display, the man, and the controls which the man operates. The thing that makes this a closed-loop system is that information about the performance of the system is fed back to the display. The display, therefore, combines information about the input and the system output.

Driving an automobile is a familiar illustration of a closed-loop system. The system input is the panorama of the winding road, the stream of vehicular traffic, and the outline of the front end of the driver's own automobile framed in his windshield. What the driver sees (the display) is partly a function of objects not under his control (the road) and partly under his control (the position of his car on the road). The controls are, of course, the steering wheel, accelerator, and brake. The outputs of these controls act upon the machine (the automobile) to yield the system output (the movements of the automobile).

It's easy to find other examples of closed-loop systems that fit this model. Here are a few:

• Flying an airplane
• Diving a submarine
• Steering a ship
• Operating a power shovel
• Controlling the water level above and below a dam
• Controlling the flow of liquids in a continuous-process chemical plant

Good human engineering practice is required in the design of every part of closed-loop systems—on the displays and controls, for example—but our primary concern at the moment is with the dynamics of the machine itself, that is, the way in which the control output is transformed into a system output.

ZERO-ORDER CONTROL. The simplest kind of system (Figure 13) is a zero-order one in which the operator's control movements (X_c) directly determine the system output (X_m). K is a constant representing the *gain, amplification,* or *gearing ratio.*

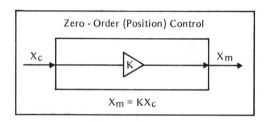

Zero - Order (Position) Control

$$X_m = KX_c$$

Figure 13. Zero-order control.

In the top line of Figure 14 are two sets of hypothetical control movements. Both show a sequence of movements starting with the control at a neutral (or zero) position. The control is displaced in one direction (for example, to a or c), held there for a short period of time, and returned to the neutral position. After another short period of time the control is displaced in the opposite direction (for example, to b or d), held there for a short period of time, and returned once more to the neutral position. The sequence of control movements at the left on the top line of the diagram shows mathematically exact *step inputs.* Although no control operates with such instantaneous precision, this artificial example will help to illustrate the nature of the control dynamics in each of the systems discussed. The sequence of control movements on the right is somewhat more realistic because it shows the control moving gradually from one position to another. Notice that the total displacement for the control movements on the

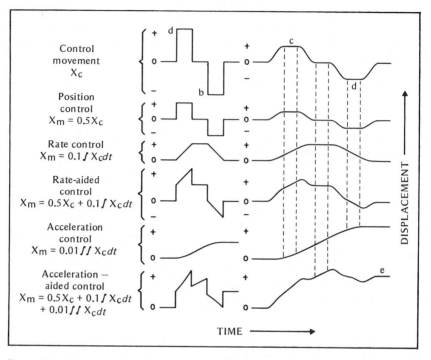

Figure 14. The top line shows two sets of hypothetical control movements. Underneath are the corresponding movements of the system (system output) for each of several kinds of control systems. (From Chapanis, 1960.)

right, that is, from 0 to c or from 0 to d, is only half those on the left, that is, from 0 to a or from 0 to b.

The curves in the second line of Figure 14 show the system output for each of these control sequences when a zero-order control system links the two. The curves representing the system output have exactly the same shapes as those representing the control output, being merely reduced by the factor K (0.5 in this example). K could, of course, be greater than 1, in which case the system output would be greater than the control output.

FIRST-ORDER CONTROL. The next level of complexity, a first-order control (upper half of Figure 15) is one in which the operator's control directly determines the rate of change of the machine output. This is commonly

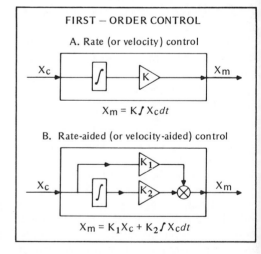

Figure 15. Two types of first-order control system.

called a *rate control,* or *velocity control* system. The third line of Figure 14 shows the machine output of a rate control system for each of the two control sequences in the top line. Note that a displacement of the control produces a rate of change of position in the machine—that rate of change in the machine being proportional to the displacement of the control. An automobile approximates a first-order control system. A fixed displacement of one of the controls (the accelerator) produces a constant velocity in the system output (the forward movement of the automobile).

First-order control systems very often include the lower-order position term as well, in which case they are called *rate-aided,* or *velocity-aided* control systems (see the lower half of Figure 15). The output of such a control system, illustrated by the curves in the fourth line of Figure 14, is the algebraic sum of both the position and the velocity components of the system, that is, the two curves on line four are the sums of the curves on the two lines immediately above it. In the design of rate-aided systems, an extremely important consideration is the proper selection of values for the constants K_1 and K_2, or, to be more exact, the ratio K_1/K_2, called the *rate-aiding constant.* A considerable amount of research suggests that the best all around value for this ratio is 0.5, with values between 0.2 and 0.8 constituting an acceptable range. The values in Figure 14 were selected because they are useful to illustrate the point graphically; they are clearly inappropriate for any real control system.

SECOND-ORDER CONTROL. Still more complexity is shown in the second-order control system in the upper half of Figure 16. Here the output of the operator's control determines the acceleration of the machine output. The schematic representation of such a system output is shown in the fifth line of Figure 14. Note that when the operator's control is displaced and held at a fixed position the

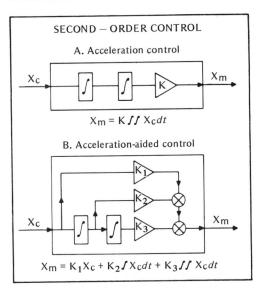

Figure 16.   Two types of second-order control system.

machine movement keeps increasing at a faster and faster rate. When the operator's control is returned to its neutral position after an initial displacement, the machine continues to change its position at a constant rate. To stop the machine movement the operator must make another displacement in the opposite direction, that is, from 0 to *b,* or from 0 to *d,* and then back to neutral.

Second-order control systems frequently include both lower-order terms, one for position and one for rate. Such systems (illustrated in the lower half of Figure 16) are commonly called *acceleration-aided* systems. The performance of such a system is shown in the bottom line of Figure 14. As in the case of rate-aided systems, the selection of the appropriate constants is a critical matter if a man is to use the system effectively. Research suggests that these constants should be in the ratio 1:2:8 or 1:4:8. The constants in Figure 14 have been selected for their graphical convenience, and are clearly unsuited for any real control system.

HIGHER-ORDER CONTROL. One can find control systems of still higher order, the steering system of a large ship being a good example. In this case, the position of a hydraulic valve in the rudder control system results in a rate of movement of the rudder. The position of the rudder, in turn, results in an angular acceleration of the moving ship and the angular position (heading) of the moving ship results in a rate of change of lateral position with respect to the desired course. This is a fourth-order control system.

COMPLEXITY OF CONTROL MOVEMENTS AND CONTROL ORDER. Implicit in the curves contained in Figure 14 is a principle of great importance: As control order increases, the operator's control has to go through increasingly complex movements to produce a simple change in the system output. This is shown more dramatically in Figure 17, which reverses the relationships shown in Figure 14. In Figure 17, the desired system output is shown in the top line. Below it are

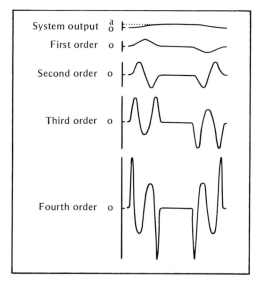

Figure 17. The top line represents the movement, or output of a system. The curves below show the control movements in systems of various orders that would produce the response in the top line. (From Kelley, 1968.)

the control movements that an operator would have to make to produce that system output. In the case of a fourth-order system such as the ship steering system mentioned above, the operator has to make an absolute minimum of five changes in the direction of motion of his control to make the ship execute a simple change in heading.

Even more troublesome than the complexity of the control movement itself is the fact that in higher-order systems a control movement bears no obvious relation to the movement of the system. This lack of correspondence between control movements and system responses in higher-order systems is clearly illustrated in Figures 14 and 17. For this reason control movements in such systems have to be learned by rote or by what has sometimes been called muscle sense. Learning to make correct control movements is even more difficult when the time scale illustrated in Figures 14 and 17 is so drawn out that it is difficult for a human operator to know until much later whether his movement produced any response, much less the correct one. The acme of systems of this kind has perhaps been reached in the gigantic supertankers that are now plying our seas. These are ships of such enormous mass, and of such colossal dimensions, that a control movement may not result in a perceptible change in the direction of the ship until as much as five minutes later! The wonder is that there have been so few collisions and other accidents involving ships of this kind.

PREDICTOR DISPLAYS FOR POWERED CONTROL SYSTEMS. This brief excursion into powered control systems is perhaps sufficient to suggest some of the complexities human operators face when they are involved with them. A variety of solutions, and partial solutions, has been studied and tested to cope with these problems. "Quickening," control and display augmentation, historical displays, command displays, and predictor displays are some of the devices that have turned out to be useful. In this section, I scuss the last one of these in a little more etail.

A predictor display shows an operator what the behavior of the system will be in he future. It does this by means of a special omputing device that extrapolates from resent conditions. Figure 18 is a schematic iagram showing how such a display would e integrated into a control system. The ontrolled element can be a plane, ship, or ther vehicle, an elevator, a nuclear reactor, r, in fact, any manually controlled dynamic ystem that responds in a way that can be neasured by appropriate instruments and imulated by electronic or other means.

The heart of the predictor system is a ast-time model of the output or behavior of he system that is being controlled. The nodel can be mechanical, electromechanical, r electronic, and, if the last, the model may se analog, digital, or hybrid simulation nethods. Sensing instruments in the real ystem provide part of the basic inputs to the nodel. The other main part of the basic input comes from the programmer, which generates signals based on control actions the

operator could, or most likely would, make during the prediction period. One useful program assumes that the operator will move his control to either extreme. Under these circumstances the display presents the operator with the boundaries of the entire range of system performance, or the "maneuvering envelope" within which a vehicle will operate. Such displays may also take account of limits that are imposed on the behavior of the system for other reasons, for example, maximum tolerable stresses a vehicle can withstand or maximum g-forces that can be tolerated by an operator.

Studies by engineering psychologists (see, for example, Kelley, 1968) have shown that in some systems predictor displays have reduced the amount of training required almost to the point of eliminating it. In other systems, predictor displays have made it possible for human operators to control systems that would otherwise be almost literally impossible to master. Although these displays are by no means the answer to all the control problems of powered control systems, they are a dramatic illustration of the gains that

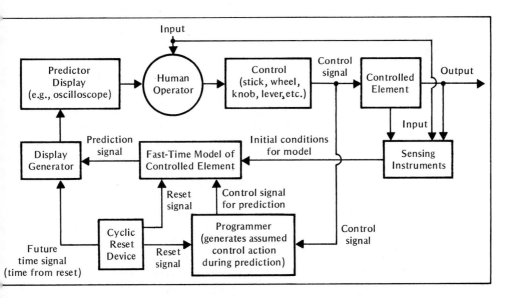

Figure 18. Block diagram of a manual control system incorporating a predictor display. (From Kelley, 1968.)

can be achieved when machine systems are properly designed for human use.

THE SYSTEMS APPROACH

However important it may be to worry about dials, gauges, knobs, and levers, some of the most challenging and intricate problems of engineering psychology arise in the design of large man-machine systems and the integration of man into these systems. At this point, we come face to face with what may appear to be an inconsistency in terminology. I have just discussed powered control systems and it is indeed proper to speak of those problems as *systems* problems. But our modern technological society contains systems within systems. Powered control systems are generally small, although not necessarily simple, systems. They typically involve a man and a machine. What follows will be concerned with much larger systems—systems typically made up of many men and many machines or machine components. Examples of such large systems are a factory, a nationwide telephone network, a nuclear submarine, an air traffic control system, or a computerized banking system.

Costs and Tradeoffs

One way in which engineering psychology differs from its more traditional academic relatives is in its concern with the overall performance of a system. To maximize overall performance the engineering psychologist recognizes that he may occasionally have to compromise about individual parts of it. This philosophy comes directly from systems engineering and the engineer's approach to design.

To make effective compromises or tradeoffs, the consequences of decisions have to be expressed in the same units. For most systems, cost is the common unit used for measuring the consequences of design decisions. It is a commonly understood measure and it is a measure that makes sense to engineers, businessmen, and workers alike.

A full cost equation for a man-machine system includes a large number of terms:

Value of a system = value of all the goods and services produced by the system
+ incidental or "spinoff" values
− cost of the prime equipment
− cost of replacement parts and maintenance
− material costs of operating the system (e.g., raw materials)
− cost of accidents, errors, breakage, or wastage
− cost of job aids, auxiliary equipment and tools, and manuals
− cost of selecting personnel to operate the system
− cost of training personnel to operate the system
− personnel costs of operating the system (e.g., salaries and wages)
− social costs of operating the system (e.g., long-term effects of pollution)

Some terms in this equation are extremely difficult to compute for some systems. For example, what is the *value* of the system that takes men to the moon? Moreover, some of these costs have been identified only recently. For years the indirect social or human costs of creating and operating some of our systems have been largely ignored. Only recently have we become sensitive to the impact of some of our machine systems on natural resources, land values, public health, and the development of cities and suburbs. Nonetheless, the fact that we cannot compute some of these values and costs should not keep us from thinking about them. Even though we cannot always supply numbers, this equation, or one like it, is the basis on which systems designers, industrialists, city planners, and government officials reach their decisions.

Almost every term in the equation above involves human considerations, directly or indirectly, and it is this that makes it of direct concern to the engineering psychologist. In general, most people agree that we should try to maximize the value of a system, the term on the left-hand side of the equation. To increase the value of the system, we should decrease costs and this brings us up squarely to the issue of tradeoffs. Let's see what this means in practical terms.

One of the main costs of a system is that of the prime equipment, the hardware of the system. In trying to reduce costs, a designer may eliminate certain safety features and, in so doing, may inadvertently increase the costs arising from accidents, errors, and wastage. Here, then, is a tradeoff that could be disadvantageous. Wittingly or unwittingly, the designer traded off reliability, or safety, against the cost of the equipment. As another example, the engineering or industrial psychologist may increase the number of job aids for a system, thereby adding to the cost of the system, a generally undesirable thing to do. He may, however, knowingly trade off these costs against other possible savings. By spending $50,000 more on the development of better job aids, he may reduce personnel training costs by $100,000, and decrease the costs of accidents, errors, and wastage by another $150,000. Such a tradeoff is well worth it.

Engineering psychology involves many tradeoffs of this kind. The fact that we cannot put precise monetary values on them does not mean that we can ignore them. The costs and tradeoffs are there, whether or not we can measure them precisely.

The Personnel Subsystem

In dealing with large systems problems, Air Force engineering psychologists coined the term *personnel subsystem* to refer to all those parts of a system in which human considerations are directly involved. The personnel subsystem contrasts with the *hardware subsystem,* those parts of a system that involve strictly material, physical, or engineering considerations. Although there is something about the sound of personnel subsystem that reveals its military origins, it is nonetheless a term that is generally accepted

in engineering psychology today. The personnel subsystem combines some conventional aspects of industrial psychology with certain elements of man-machine design of the kind that has been discussed. Figure 19 is a convenient way of identifying the major elements of the personnel subsystem and their various interrelationships.

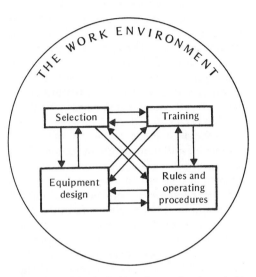

Figure 19. The basic ingredients of systems design and their interrelationships.

Selection

A man-machine system is not complete unless there are people to operate and maintain it. In staffing a system, the engineering psychologist tries to answer many important questions. What kinds of people will be needed to operate the system? What sorts of things will each person do? How many people will be needed? How will these people be selected and trained? How will they be supervised and evaluated? These are people-oriented questions dealing with the "design" of the people elements of a system.

Problems of personnel selection are familiar grounds for most psychologists. The techniques, test devices, and statistical methods of personnel selection for systems operation are very much the same as those used by industrial psychologists everywhere. However, even conventional practices change when incorporated into the modern systems idea. For one thing, personnel psychologists used to accept the job as given—a fixed quantity with definite requirements. In these terms, the job of the personnel psychologist was to find people who could do that particular job. Indeed, this point of view still dominates most textbooks of personnel psychology today. The systems approach has changed that simple view. To the engineering psychologist the job is not a fixed quantity, but a variable, something to be changed and manipulated until a final design has been realized. As a variable, systems can usually be made to fit any of a large number of different kinds of people. This new approach calls for genuine interaction between the design of the selection system and the equipment elements of a system. For example, if the engineer designs a computer, or a radar, for on-the-spot repairs, selection devices will have to pick operators who have some sophisticated electronic skills. On the other hand, if the engineer designs the system with modular replaceable, or throwaway units, operators who are selected for the job need have only rudimentary, or even no electronic skills.

Cost often helps systems designers and engineering psychologists arrive at decisions about alternatives such as these. Assume that a highly complicated system can be built for $1 million, but that it requires operators with high skill levels. Assume further that the system can be designed with much simpler logic and circuitry but at a cost of $1.25 million. By estimating the costs of selecting and training operators at the two different skill levels, the engineering psychologist can help the systems designer make a decision about the complexity, and cost, of the system that he should build. These considerations mean that *base rates* as used by personnel psychologists (see, for example, Dunnette, 1966) can be manipu-

lated much more directly than personnel psychologists have heretofore assumed. Complicated equipment designs generally mean low base rates; redesign of equipment to make it simpler generally means that base rates can be increased.

The second important way in which the systems approach has altered some traditional concepts of personnel selection has come about because the engineering psychologist, more than the conventional industrial psychologist, is typically concerned with novel systems. This means that he cannot necessarily depend on an available pool of experienced or trained labor. Since the system has not yet been constructed, he may not even have criteria against which to test the adequacy of his selection devices. He must instead make his criteria on a priori grounds.

To illustrate, the industrial psychologist who works for a large motor car company has a comparatively easy job of setting up selection tests for workers to man a production line. The automobile industry is well established, its products and techniques change little from year to year, and the assembly lines at Ford, Chrysler, and General Motors are very much the same. There is, moreover, a large and often mobile labor force upon which the personnel director can draw. Contrast this situation with that faced by the team selecting the first astronauts. A booster, launching system, capsule, and tracking and recovery system would have been of no use at all without someone ready and trained to ride that first capsule. Since the system was the first of its kind, the selection team could not draw on previous experience and was not even entirely sure what criteria should be used. Now that we have some experience with space flight, the selection problem has become easier. We know that some of the original criteria were of no help in selecting successful space candidates; conversely, we know now that criteria not originally included in the selection battery are important.

Essentially this same situation is duplicated with almost every first version of a system that is designed, built, and completed. The first nuclear power plant would have been of no use without a work force selected and trained to operate it. The first supersonic aircraft to be put into commercial operation required crews picked and ready to fly it. And so on. Different systems have varying amounts of novelty. In some cases, there are systems similar to the one being designed and the selection teams can depend on a reasonable amount of transfer from the old to the new systems. In other cases, however, the novel elements in a system may be so many and so important that the psychologist must use all his intuitive and analytical skills to derive a reasonable selection battery. Fortunately or unfortunately, depending on how you look at it, this century has been characterized by the number of radically new, innovative systems that have been created in response to the needs of our society. This means that some of the specialized techniques developed by engineering psychologists (see, for example, Chapanis, 1970b) to cope with these problems may eventually be incorporated into more conventional personnel selection practices.

Training

As Figure 19 suggests, personnel training cannot be considered independently of personnel selection and neither can it be divorced from considerations of equipment design. In general, the more highly selected the people, the less training they will need. Conversely, less highly selected people need more training. Both selection and training interact with the complexity of the system: the more complex the system, the more stringent the selection and training requirements. A good illustration of how equipment design interacts with training requirements appears in the material on powered control systems that was discussed earlier in this chapter. Months of training that had been required for operators to master certain kinds of control systems were almost entirely eliminated when these systems were provided with predictor displays.

The nature of most systems problems precludes reliance on personnel selection alone to supply the manpower needs of the system. For this reason, the engineering psychologist usually has to plan a training program to give the selected personnel the level of skills they need to operate the system effectively. Special complications of training for the operation of systems of the kind with which we are most concerned are: (1) long lead times are often required; (2) operators must be trained to operate systems that are not yet in existence; (3) operators of many modern systems must be trained as a team, not as individual operators; and (4) training has to be directed to handling rare emergency situations that are critical for the system when they occur.

It takes about forty-two months to train an air traffic controller to do an effective job. Similarly, the astronauts who have landed on the surface of the moon spent years learning the skills needed for this venture. Operators of complex modern systems may need to spend a very long time in training, perhaps as much time as may be required to build the system. If the operators of such systems are to be ready when the system is finished, their training must be started while the system is still being designed. They must learn to operate a system that doesn't exist and that may be changed further during the final stages of design. Learning to fly a high speed jet aircraft is difficult enough; learning to fly a supersonic aircraft that hasn't yet been built introduces still further difficulties for the learner, the teacher, and the designer of the training program.

Many modern systems use teams of operators who must coordinate their activities and work together if the system is to function effectively. As an example, a civilian air traffic control center guides and directs air traffic for hundreds of miles around a large metropolitan airport. Since the skies are so large, and the number of planes in them so many, the air space around an airport is divided into sectors, with a controller in charge of each sector. If the traffic control center is to do its job well, there must be a smooth transfer of responsibility from one controller to another as planes change sectors. This involves highly developed team performance. Such team performance does not just happen; it is the result of training.

A characteristic of many modern industrial systems is that they have become automated to various degrees and they have relegated the human operator more and more to the status of a monitor, trouble-shooter, and maintenance man. Although these jobs are at some times not very active, they are nonetheless highly important. An automated oil refinery or electric generating plant represents an extremely large capital investment. Breakdowns and emergencies that cause the system to be inoperative are not only costly, but may have other larger consequences as well, for example, explosions and power blackouts. Emergencies are, of course, rare events and they often come in unexpected guises. Training operators to anticipate and to take appropriate corrective action for any of the large number of emergencies that could happen in a complicated modern system requires special attention.

TRAINING DEVICES. Many modern systems are such complex assemblages of men and machines that training would, theoretically, be best carried out on the job. The cost of doing that is so prohibitive and, in many cases, so potentially dangerous that substitute procedures have to be used. Among these substitutes are simulators, or training devices, of one sort or another. Training simulators are models of a system that try to duplicate the essential ingredients of the system. Through the use of such simulators operators can develop in safety the skills they will need when they work on the system itself. Although a simulator is generally smaller, simpler, and cheaper than the system it mimics, it is nonetheless a system itself. For this reason, the design of a training device includes most of the problems that are encountered in the design and construction of any system. In addition, the design of training devices involves some additional problems not ordinarily encountered in working systems. Since the simulators are to be used for training purposes, they must have built into them devices for measuring the performance of trainees, for providing feedback, or knowledge of results, to the trainee, and for simulating a wide variety of emergency conditions.

Training simulators are used so widely in industry and in the military services that they have become big business in themselves and have become the major preoccupation of a great many engineering psychologists.

One of the most difficult questions that has to be resolved in the design of simulators is the fidelity with which the training device should mimic the actual system. If the fidelity of a training device is high, it begins to approximate the system itself and becomes as expensive as the system. If the fidelity of the training device is low, it is cheaper to construct but may result in little or no positive transfer from the training equipment to the system. Ideally, a training device should have as much fidelity as is required to provide the greatest amount of positive transfer of training per dollar. Where that point lies, however, is a question for which we have no ready answer.

Although research on learning has probably had more time, effort, and talent devoted to it than any other area in experimental psychology, a disappointingly small amount of laboratory research on learning has any direct applicability to the design and construction of practical training devices and curricula (Mackie & Christensen, 1967). Indeed, some of the best work on training devices and simulators is done by engineers, not by psychologists. This situation may be a reflection of the sterility of a great deal of modern psychological research which, in its attempt to remain pure, builds elaborate theories about unimportant kinds of behavior.

Operating Procedures

Another element of systems design consists of the instructions, operating procedures, and rules that set forth the duties of each operator in a system. Some rules may specify how the system is supposed to behave with regard to other systems, or in the space through which it operates. Navigation rules, for example, establish which of two vessels has the right of way when their paths intersect. Although many operating procedures and rules are arbitrary, a good set of them contributes greatly to safe and orderly operations.

The most important subset of rules and operating procedures is the technical manuals—the instruction booklets, operating instructions, and maintenance guides—that accompany equipment. This has been a sadly neglected area of both industrial psychology and engineering psychology. Only recently has evidence been assembled to show that the design and wording of the written materials accompanying equipment may be at least as important as the design of the equipment itself (Chapanis, 1965a). In some situations even experienced maintenance men are able to understand and follow no more than about 75 percent of the instructions they are given in the manuals they have to use (Sinaiko & Brislin, 1970). A partial explanation for the severity of these problems can be found in some data reported by Sticht (July, 1969). Figure 20 compares the readability of technical manuals used in five military occupational specialties with the average reading levels of

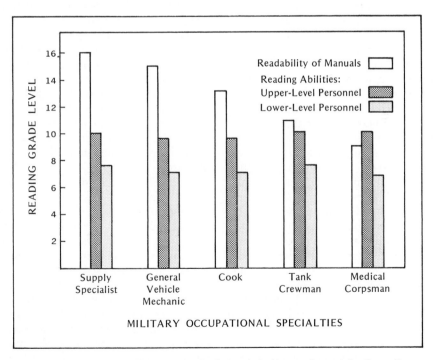

Figure 20. Average reading grade levels for technical manuals used in five military occupations compared with the average reading abilities of personnel in those occupations. (After Sticht, 1969.)

men in those occupational specialties. In four of the five military jobs, the average reading level of the manuals exceeds the average reading ability of the men in those specialties and, in some cases, by very substantial amounts. Such discrepancies become even more apparent when we look at instructions prepared for people who do not speak English as their native tongue (see, for example, Sinaiko, Guthrie, & Abbott, 1969). In the light of such evidence, it is not surprising that errors, accidents, and wastages of enormous proportions can be traced directly to the difficulties people have in reading and interpreting the printed materials that come with the equipment they are supposed to use.

Several conspicuous characteristics of the recent work in this area deserve special comment. The first is that it has been done almost entirely by and for the military services. In a sense, the interest of the military services in these problems parallels the development of engineering psychology, which itself received its first major impetus from that direction. Only much later, after they had proven their worth in the design of weapons of war, were the data and findings of engineering psychology adapted to more general industrial situations. In like manner, it is the military services that have had to come to grips with these problems of instructions and manuals primarily because the problems have been so overwhelming they could not be ignored. To make complex equipment available to a broad cross section of men, the words that accompany the equipment have to be adapted to those men. This realization has culminated in some large projects, such as PIMO (the Presentation of Information for Maintenance and Operation), a systematic attempt to reorganize technical manuals and instruction booklets throughout the United States Air Force.

These military origins do not mean that problems of presenting information are any less serious in industrial and other situations. The gobbledegook of "governmentese" has been for years the favorite subject of ridicule by newspaper columnists and other writers. Indeed, there is probably no better example of the mismatch between people and words than the instructions that are sent out with Federal income tax forms. Literally millions of mistakes, costing the Internal Revenue Service millions of dollars to track down and rectify, are made each year by taxpayers who cannot figure out how to prepare their returns properly. To turn to examples more closely related to the subject of this chapter, manuals prepared by IBM to teach programming have earned a well-deserved reputation for being esoteric and turbid. Similarly, the difficulty of following "easy-to-assemble-it-yourself" instructions is a theme common to innumerable jokes and cartoons. One can even find an occasional study on communications within selected industries. For example, de Montmolin and his colleagues (1970) empirically devised sets of natural language codes, artificial language codes, and symbols to decrease errors in the goods forwarding process of the central stores of a tobacco firm, Régie Francaise. These errors had previously been traced to ambiguous labeling on the cigarette cartons. To sum up, then, it is likely that problems of communication are no less serious in commerce and industry than they are in the military services. It's rather that the business world hasn't yet come to realize how serious they are.

A second feature of this new work is that it is empirical. People have been talking and writing for years about the simplification of paper work in business and industry and about the simplification of writing in general (see, for example, Flesch, 1946). Rarely, however, have those efforts been accompanied by studies of the behavioral consequences of bad writing. Now, however, we are beginning to see for the first time experiments that try to validate principles of effective communication by observing how people respond to it.

Although the preparation of good equipment manuals requires an effective writing style, it demands a lot more as well. Technical manuals are, after all, technical. They are full of charts, drawings, tables of data, and technical terms. An effective manual requires that all of these elements be considered together and assessed in terms of their total impact on the user. The new work on communication takes all these factors into account.

The last interesting characteristic of this kind of work is that it is being done by engineering psychologists and other applied scientists, not by psycholinguists and similar language experts. It is significant, for example, that some of the first, and best, experiments on the design of tables, graphs, and nomographs were done by engineering psychologists (Carter, 1946a,b; Connell, 1947). In like manner some of the most effective rules for the writing of technical manuals have been prepared by engineering psychologists (Sinaiko & Brislin, 1970). Pure linguistic science has been singularly unhelpful in dealing with these problems of the real world. In fact, there is even some evidence that linguistic science may actually hinder the discovery of practical solutions to our problems of communication. In their study of words and labels for the French tobacco industry, de Montmolin and his collaborators (see above) conclude that some of their empirical results are the reverse of what would have been expected on the basis of both common sense and the theoretical work of some linguists.

Equipment Design

The fourth element of systems design is the design of the basic equipment used in the systems. This is the oldest part of engineering psychology, the part that is most fully developed, and the one that still occupies the greatest number of engineering psychologists. It encompasses all the material that has already been discussed earlier in this chapter under the heading of man as a component of a man-machine system.

The Work Environment

The final ingredient of systems design is the environment in which men and machines work. The important variables of the work environment range from those that are commonly found in industrial environments, such as lighting, noise, temperature, humidity, ventilation, pollutants, and contaminants, to more exotic ones, such as anoxia, acceleration (g-forces), radioactivity, and weightlessness, that are less commonly found in industrial situations.

Acceptable tolerance levels for most environmental variables have been tabulated and are available in many handbooks (see, for example, Morgan et al., 1963). Table 3 is an example of only one out of many such sets of data. Those in Table 3 are useful for specifying tolerable noise levels in situations where noise is relatively continuous throughout the entire frequency spectrum (for ex-

TABLE 3
**SPEECH-INTERFERENCE LEVELS (IN DB) THAT BARELY PERMIT
RELIABLE CONVERSATION AT VARIOUS DISTANCES AND VOICE LEVELS**

Distance between talker and listener (ft.)	Normal voice level	Raised voice	Very loud	Shouting
0.5	71	77	83	89
1	65	71	77	83
2	59	65	71	77
3	55	61	67	73
4	53	59	65	71
5	51	57	63	69
6	49	55	61	67
12	43	49	55	61

ample, ventilation noise in offices, the noise in most engine rooms, and the noise around milling machines). The SIL (speech interference level) is the arithmetic average of the decibel levels of the noise in the three octave bands of 600–1,200, 1,200–2,400, and 2,400–4,800 hertz.

The principal difficulties with many of the data available on the work environment are that (1) very little is known about the effects of multiple environmental stresses (for example, the combined effects of high temperatures, reduced ventilation, high noise levels, and vibration), and (2) most of the available data are for young healthy males. Very little is known about tolerance levels for women, for middle-aged and older workers, and for workers with various minor bodily disabilities. Despite the volumes of data already available, the unanswered questions in this area are more numerous than those we can answer with certainty.

Both the engineering psychologist and the industrial psychologist are in an anomalous position regarding these environmental problems. First, there are several well-established groups of engineers, for example, illuminating engineers, acoustic engineers, and heating, ventilating, and air conditioning engineers, among others, who consider themselves expert on environmental problems. Although psychologists have, to be sure, contributed a great deal of experimental data on the effects of these variables on human performance, it is perhaps correct to say that the bulk of the data has come from the work of specialists who do not identify themselves as psychologists. Indeed, some environmental problems, in particular those dealing with tolerable levels of radioactivity, pollutants, and contaminants, are usually considered to be more medical or physiological than psychological problems.

Even more serious, perhaps, is that these environmental problems are a part of systems *engineering*. The typical engineering psychologist is, in spite of his specialized training, a psychologist and not an engineer.

For instance, he can easily find in handbooks what are acceptable light levels for various kinds of jobs, but he is not likely to know very much about the fixtures, luminaires, and light sources needed to provide the appropriate lighting. This same observation can be made about ventilation systems, air filters, acoustic shields, and the many other devices that make environments livable and comfortable.

Perhaps the best way of summing up the position of the engineering psychologist with respect to this class of problems is to say that at present he serves best as a consultant on environmental problems when there is no one on the systems design team better qualified than he to deal with them. He can identify the important environmental problems to be considered in the design of the system, set up acceptable tolerance limits for each environmental variable, and monitor the design of equipment for the control of the relevant environmental variables. In executing his decisions and recommendations, however, the engineering psychologist needs to work with and through someone who is qualified to do engineering design work.

Interrelationships Among the Variables

The last thing that needs to be said about Figure 19 and the design of systems is that everything interacts with everything else. I have already commented on and illustrated the tradeoffs possible among personnel selection, personnel training, and equipment design. These are so important that they are worth calling to your attention again at this point.

Tradeoffs apply equally to operating rules and instructions. For example, complex instructions require highly selected and highly trained personnel. In addition, when equipment is complicated, instructions and operating rules tend to be complicated as well. Simple instructions, on the other hand, can be used by less highly selected and less highly trained operators. Similarly, when the design of equipment is simplified, operating rules and procedures can also be simplified.

Finally, Figure 19 does not show, but should show, interrelationships between the work environment on the one hand, and personnel selection, training, equipment design, and operating procedures, on the other. A simple example will suffice. In designing a system for use in torrid regions, one can select people better able to withstand these temperatures, or one can design the system with air conditioning so that ordinary people can operate the system. The physical environment also interacts with operating procedures because the latter usually specify such things as the duration of work and rest periods, and the pace or rate at which work is done. In these ways, operating procedures may be used to compensate for otherwise intolerable temperatures or other extreme environmental conditions.

In Summary

The systems designer and the engineering psychologist view a system as a complicated set of interrelationships between people, training, equipment design, operating procedures, and the environment. All these variables are elements in their equations, and all can be manipulated to optimize the final product. Moreover, when a system fails it does not fail for any one reason. It usually fails because the people who are trying to operate the system are either unable to cope with the way the system is designed or to follow the procedures they are supposed to follow in the environment in which the system has to operate. Anticipating and preventing such failures are done typically by varying one or more of the five basic elements above.

Systems Evaluation

After a system has been designed, and the components and subsystems have been built and put together, the whole system—men and machines—is exercised to find out what it will do. Systems evaluations serve one or more of the following purposes:

1. To find out what the system will do; in particular, to find out whether it will do the things it was designed to do.

2. To compare the system with other systems.

3. To discover ways of improving the system.

4. To prepare a series of operating procedures for using the system best.

A full systems evaluation runs into all the problems of human experimentation familiar to psychologists: human variability; motivation; contamination of performance with the effects of learning, fatigue, and boredom; and so on. Although we do not have answers for all the difficulties of human experimentation, we have developed methods for overcoming many of them. Since techniques such as counterbalancing, randomizing, and statistical manipulation are generally unfamiliar to engineers, the engineering psychologist, with his knowledge of the tactics and strategies of human experimentation, can help design systems evaluations to provide more reliable and realistic indications of what the man-machine combination can and cannot do. Indeed, this is one of the areas in which engineering psychologists have made some of their most significant impacts.

Because systems evaluations differ in some important ways from the carefully controlled laboratory experimentation with which experimental psychologists are usually familiar, the engineering psychologist cannot let his adherence to the strict methods of laboratory experimentation blind him to methods that may be somewhat less precise, but more productive. In their work, engineering psychologists use a variety of methods, some borrowed from other areas of psychology, some borrowed from industrial engineering, and some devised to meet their own needs. A few of the methods that have proven especially valuable are the analysis of accidents and near-accidents, activity analysis and other direct observational techniques, simulation methods, and the study of critical incidents (see Chapanis, 1959; Meister & Rabideau, 1965).

A FEW METHODOLOGICAL ISSUES

Doing laboratory research in psychology is easy. Problems can be, and typically are, selected according to an experimenter's own interests. Dependent and independent variables can be picked for their ease of control and manipulation in the laboratory, not for any practical goals. The principal criterion used in judging a piece of pure laboratory research is whether it contributes some new piece of information that we have not had previously. The whole business is rather like a game in which the primary emphasis is on following the rules.

Applied research is much more demanding than that. Questions for research cannot be selected according to the momentary interests of the experimenter; they are dictated by the requirements of the problem. Variables cannot be selected for their ease of manipulation in the laboratory; they have to be relevant to some real life purpose. They have to be useful. Finally, the value of a piece of applied research is determined not by its adherence to the formal rules of the game of science, but by the stern criteria of: "Does it really work?" and "Does it make any practical difference?"

A piece of laboratory research, once published, is in the literature for a very long time. If subsequent research should prove it wrong, no great harm is done. Studies that are wrong keep getting cited in the literature, if for no other reason than to provide a proper historical background for new publications. In this sense, laboratory studies, even if they have been disproved, continue to earn credits for their authors. One can always shrug off such findings with the off-hand statement that "After all, that's the nature of scientific progress."

The harsh requirements of applied research, on the other hand, do not permit so cavalier an attitude about outcomes. An engineering psychologist who reaches a conclusion that this or that is the best way of designing the controls for a space vehicle does so with the awful realization that what he says may cost lives and waste millions of dollars. Moreover, his failures are there in plain view for all to see. Such considerations have forced engineering psychologists to come face-to-face with some methodological issues that have not been faced by their more academic colleagues.

The Relevance of Laboratory Findings to the Real World

Most academically trained psychologists do not appreciate the limitations of laboratory studies for solving the practical problems of the world. On the contrary, in our graduate schools we teach our students that laboratory experiments are an infallible way of discovering the truth about the world around us. We rebut popular beliefs about human behavior by citing the results of laboratory experiments. And in professional and scientific arguments we appeal to the data of laboratory experiments in much the same way that learned men, centuries ago, appealed to the authority of Aristotle or Thomas Aquinas.

Yet the fact of the matter is that most laboratory experiments in psychology have only very limited relevance for the solution of practical problems (Chapanis, 1967). At best, laboratory experiments are rough and approximate models of real-life situations. A laboratory experiment can select only a few independent variables for test. Unsuspected interactions in real life may nullify or even reverse conclusions reached in the laboratory. Variables change when they are brought into the laboratory. While the control of extraneous or irrelevant variables in the laboratory may increase the precision of an experiment, the effects discovered may be so small that they are of no practical consequence. The dependent variables used in laboratory experiments are usually variables of convenience, rarely selected for their relevance to any practical situation. Further, the methods used to present variables in the laboratory are often artificial and unrealistic. Taken together, these considerations mean that engineering psychologists can generalize only with extreme caution from the results of laboratory experiments to the solution of practical problems.

On Criteria

Some of the most difficult questions for the engineering psychologist have to do with criteria that are relevant to his work. The questions are relatively easy to frame; the solutions, unfortunately, difficult to find. Nonetheless, it is useful to state questions properly even if answers are not immediately forthcoming.

The Essential Nature of an Experiment

An experiment may be described simply as a deliberately arranged situation in which the experimenter: (1) varies some factors (the independent variables), while (2) minimizing the influence of some other factors that are not of interest to him at the moment (the controlled variables), (3) in order that he may measure changes in behavior (the dependent variables) that are the result of, or are produced by, the independent variables.

An essential problem in this chain has to do with the selection and choice of dependent variables in our research. The question may be phrased in this way: "How do we decide what kind of output, index, or criterion to measure when we do an experiment?"

On the Number of Dependent Variables

Any competent researcher can think of a great many different dependent variables to use for any experiment. Let's take a relatively simple and circumscribed problem—the problem of evaluating the legibility of type. In their comprehensive review on this topic, Cornog and Rose (1967) found that over the years investigators have used an astonishing variety of dependent variables in studying this problem. Some of them are: (1) the amount of meaningful information retained after reading connected prose or text; (2) the time taken to read a sample of connected text; (3) errors made in recognizing individual symbols; (4) the number of symbols recognized per unit time; (5) the number of words or symbols that can be read on either side of a fixation point; (6) recognition thresholds measured in terms of the distance at which symbols first become identifiable; (7) recognition thresholds in terms of the amount of light at which symbols first become identifiable; (8) speed in transcribing symbols into a machine; (9) errors in transcribing symbols into a machine; (10) eye-blink rate during reading; (11) heart rate during reading; and (12) nervous muscular tension during reading.

This list by no means exhausts the dependent variables that have been used in this kind of research, but it will perhaps convey some idea of the diversity of measures that can be used with even a fairly limited kind of problem. Remember that the independent variable was in every case some variation in typography.

If we turn to a more general kind of problem, for example, the effects of noise on human behavior, we find that the number of dependent variables increases greatly. Table 4 gives a partial list of some that have been used in studies of this kind. This list can, of course, be multiplied several times by subdividing each of the variables in it. For example, one can take at least two separate measures, speed and accuracy (or errors), in tasks such as cancelling c's, name checking, and number checking. Time estimation can easily be divided into four different measures: the estimation of short

TABLE 4
A PARTIAL LIST OF DEPENDENT VARIABLES THAT HAVE BEEN USED IN STUDYING THE EFFECTS OF NOISE ON HUMAN BEHAVIOR*

Annoyance value of the noise	Minnesota Clerical Test
Auditory fatigue	Minnesota Form Board Test
Blood oxygen saturation	Monitoring lights
Blood pressure	Monitoring steam pressure gauges
Cancelling c's	Muscle tension
Clock-watching	Name checking
Critical flicker fusion	Number checking
EEG	Palmar sweating
EMG	Peristaltic contractions
Extrapolating the movement of a	Pulse rate
visual target	Respiration amplitude
Finger volume	Serial reaction time
Flow of gastric juices	Somatic complaints
Hearing loss	Subjective feelings such as irritation
Inserting a stylus into a moving	and distraction
tape containing irregularly-	Time estimation
sized and irregularly-spaced	Trembling
holes	Word fluency

* From Plutchik, 1959.

time intervals, the estimation of long time intervals, the estimation of filled time, and the estimation of unfilled time. Each of these tests tends to give results that differ from each other (Woodrow, 1951). EEG records yield several different measures. And so on.

Let's take one more example. Imagine that you are designing an experiment and that you want to use a measure of psychomotor performance as a dependent variable. How many different measures do you have to pick from? No one really knows. When Fleishman and Hempel (1954) made their factor analytic study of dexterity, however, they used fifteen different tests. In a later study of physical proficiency and manipulative skill (Hempel & Fleishman, 1955) they used forty-six different tests, and in a still later article on complex psychomotor performance (Fleishman & Hempel, 1956), they used twenty-three different tests. Collectively these add up to eighty-four separate tests, each of which claims to be a measure of some sort of psychomotor performance. You could use any one of them as a dependent variable.

Dependent Variables May Be Unrelated

A disconcerting thing about dependent variables is that they are often unrelated. Examples are so numerous you merely need to scan through abstracts and summaries of research studies in almost any issue of any journal to find them. The literature abounds with experiments in which results obtained with one dependent variable seem to be unrelated to those obtained with some other dependent variable. For example, in the three factor analytic studies referred to above, Fleishman and Hempel discovered five orthogonal (that is, independent) factors among their fifteen tests of dexterity, fifteen orthogonal factors among their forty-five tests of physical proficiency and manipulative skill, and nine orthogonal factors among their twenty-three complex psychomotor tests. This is a total of twenty-nine unrelated and independent factors all falling under the general heading of psychomotor performance.

The non-relatedness of many dependent variables in human research has two important implications that are worth dwelling on for a moment. First, although investigators may use the same words in describing their respective experiments, this does not mean that they are really talking about the same things. So when you see a number of experiments that purport to have measured the effects of something on psychomotor performance, or on complex decision making, or on vigilance, it is important to look closely at the exact dependent measures that have been used in those experiments. The data may or may not refer to the same human functions. The second implication is that we have to choose carefully and wisely when we plan applied research. If our experiments are to be meaningful, our dependent measures must have some relation to the tasks in the real-life problem that we are investigating.

On Systems Criteria

At this point, we need to turn the problem around and ask about the criteria that are important in industrial and engineering work. Let's approach the problem this way. When you are trying to decide what kind of a new automobile to buy, what factors do you consider? Do you judge an automobile by what it will do to your blood pressure, respiration rate, or brain wave pattern? I doubt it. I am equally sure that you are not at all concerned about what the automobile might do to your critical flicker threshold, your reaction time, or to that hypothetical quantity that has been called your "spare mental capacity" (Brown & Poulton, 1961). On the contrary, I strongly suspect that you will make your decision on the basis of one or more of the following:

Appearance
Availability of service and parts
Cost
Ease of handling
Economy of operation
Frequency of repair record
Luggage storage capacity
Riding qualities
Safety features
Size
Speed

To generalize, the value or worth of a system is normally judged by several criteria. These criteria are not necessarily all compatible. In the case of automobiles, for example, speed and economy of operation are, in general, incompatible. Faster, high performance cars are usually more costly to operate than those that have less power. Criteria also vary greatly from system to system and many criteria are specific to particular systems. Among the criteria that might be used to evaluate an automated assembly line in a factory are the number of units produced per unit time, and the amount of raw materials wasted during the manufacturing process. Criteria that are specific to telephonic communication systems are the naturalness of the transmitted voice signals, and freedom from cross talk. Military systems are frequently evaluated by a criterion of kill probability. And so on.

Table 5 lists a "baker's dozen" of important criteria (in the right-hand column) that apply to many, if not most, man-machine systems. I think these criteria are self-explanatory. Other things equal, the better of two systems is the one that (a) has a longer anticipated life, (b) has the more pleasing appearance, (c) is more comfortable for the people who use it, (d) is more convenient, (e) is easier to operate or use, (f) is more familiar, (g) is cheaper to buy, (h) is quicker to repair, (i) requires fewer operators, (j) is cheaper to operate, (k) breaks down less often, (l) is safer, and (m) can be used with less highly trained personnel. Criteria like these are the real indicators of system performance and they are the criteria with which the engineering psychologist has to come to grips if he is to do his job properly.

Human considerations enter into every one of the systems criteria in Table 5. What may not be so obvious, however, is that the human considerations almost always get in-

TABLE 5
SOME COMMON DEPENDENT MEASURES (OR CRITERIA) USED IN ERGONOMIC AND HUMAN FACTORS RESEARCH (IN THE COLUMN ON THE LEFT) AND SOME GENERAL SYSTEMS CRITERIA (IN THE COLUMN ON THE RIGHT)*

Experimental criteria	Systems criteria
Accuracy (or, conversely, errors)	Anticipated life of the system
Cardiovascular responses	Appearance
Critical flicker fusion	Comfort
EEG	Convenience
Energy expenditure	Ease of operation or use
Muscle tension	Familiarity
Psychophysical thresholds	Initial cost
Ratings (e.g., of annoyance, comfort, etc.)	Maintainability (e.g., mean time to repair)
Reaction time	Manpower requirements
Respiratory responses	Operating cost
Spare mental capacity	Reliability (e.g., mean time to failure)
Speed	Safety
Trials to learn	Training requirements

* From Chapanis, 1970a.

volved in compromises of one sort or another—in the kinds of tradeoffs which have already been referred to several times in this chapter. Psychologists working in their laboratories are often unaware of these conflicting requirements, but they are there nonetheless. The necessity for making such compromises often explains why abstract laboratory findings cannot be accepted at face value in the practical world of systems design. Systems criteria are not neat and simple linear transformations of the outcomes of basic research.

The Relation Between Dependent Variables and Systems Criteria

In the left-hand column of Table 5, I have listed some dependent variables, or experimental criteria, as they appear in psychological and human factors journals. Although this is, of course, a highly abbreviated list, it is a set of dependent variables used over and over again.

As you look at the two columns of this table, there seems to be little or no correspondence between them. It is difficult to see what some of the experimental criteria in the left-hand column have to do with any of the systems criteria in the right-hand col-

umn. Moreover, a number of systems criteria do not seem to be measured by any of the experimental criteria. One of the most important methodological questions with which engineering psychology has to come to grips is the following: "How can variables like those in the left-hand column be matched to those in the right-hand column?" An alternative way of posing the problem is to ask: "Of all the possible dependent variables that an engineering psychologist could use in any experiment, how can he pick those that will have the greatest amount of transfer to the criteria that will be used in the design and evaluation of a man-machine system?" The answers to these questions are neither obvious nor simple.

Let me illustrate with just one of the predicaments we run into when we try to translate experimental findings into terms that are relevant for the real world. Consider, for example, the system criterion of comfort. Surely, we can all agree that we should try to increase the comfort of operators in any system. But how exactly do you measure comfort? What are the ingredients that contribute to it? Is the anthropometric design of seats and workplaces relevant to comfort? Of course. How about environmental factors, such as lighting, noise, and vibration? Are they important factors in comfort? Yes. Do subjective feelings, such as feelings of security, contribute to an operator's comfort? Most decidedly. What this means is that comfort is not a unitary thing that can be assessed by any single experimental variable. On the contrary, comfort is a combination of many things—physical dimensions, physiological responses, and psychological feelings. To assess comfort properly, we need to measure many different aspects of man, his performance and behavior.

What is true about comfort applies equally to all the other systems criteria listed in Table 5. The implications of this are far-reaching. It is unlikely that we shall ever be able to assess systems criteria with just a single experimental measure. We need instead to concentrate on finding combinations of experimental variables, and the proper weights to assign to those variables, to arrive at some kind of an overall index of what is relevant and important. This is indeed a formidable task, but one that must be tackled if we are to progress beyond the trivial. An intriguing aspect of this point of view is that it brings engineering psychology close to personnel psychology once again. The assessment and prediction of systems criteria from the dependent variables of psychological experiments are similar to what personnel psychologists have been trying to do for years when they use test results to predict such complex systems criteria as absenteeism, salesmanship, or managerial ability. The contexts are different but, on close inspection, the problems are basically very much the same.

SOME PROBLEMS AND DIFFICULTIES

Although engineering psychology has had a turbulent, shaky, and erratic childhood, it appears to have grown into a vigorous, lusty, and healthy young adult. It has shown that it can survive in the harsh world of applied science and it does seem to say

something that can contribute to the general welfare of society. Still, the field is beset with some serious difficulties, the resolution of which is not entirely clear at the moment. Three major ones are discussed below.

How Effective is Engineering Psychology?

To those of us in the field it is obvious that engineering psychology is important in industry and systems design. Others, however, are not necessarily convinced. Questions that pragmatic businessmen or engineers sometimes ask are: "What good are human factors?" "What evidence can you give me that they work?" These are reasonable questions to expect from anyone who must show that his expenditures are sensible and likely to yield profits or tangible benefits. As Kraft's (1970) survey clearly shows, engineering psychologists and human factors specialists agree that one of the major problems confronting the field is that of demonstrating the "cost-effectiveness" of their contributions. However they are worded, the questions are easy to pose. Their answers, on the other hand, involve some methodological issues that are annoyingly complex.

On the Importance of Human Factors in Systems

One way of approaching the questions posed above is to show the importance of human factors to system performance. On this score there is no lack of evidence. Here, for example, is a portion of the text with which Meister et al. (1968) begin their report:

The contribution of human error to the unreliability of overall system performance has been ... illustrated ... empirically by Meister (1967). In [that] study, approximately 24% of overall system unreliability could be attributed to the effect of human error. In 1960, Shapiro et al. reported on a survey of several major missile systems and reported that the percentage of equipment failures caused by human error ranged from 20% to 53% of the total failures reported. Willis (1962) estimates "that 40% of the problems uncovered in missile testing derive from the human element; 63.6% of the (shipboard) collisions, flooding and grounding could be blamed upon human error. Reports produced by the United States Air Force indicate that human error was responsible for 234 of 313 aircraft accidents during 1961."[4]

It is even more impressive that every year some 55,000 persons are killed, and an additional 1,500,000 are injured, in street and highway accidents throughout the United States. Over 20,000 workers are killed, and some 25,000,000 are injured, in on-the-job accidents every year. The estimated annual cost to our nation of these deaths and injuries has been estimated to run into the tens of billions of dollars. Moreover, everyone agrees that human error accounts for a substantial fraction of this awesome carnage.

However impressive it may be to cite such statistics, we have, in all honesty, to admit that they do not really answer our basic question. Sensible, rational, and unequivocal prescriptions for decreasing these frightful tolls have eluded scientists, engineers, lawmakers, and police officials alike. Nor can engineering psychologists yet claim any greater successes than have been achieved by some of the more or less intuitive solutions tried by lawmakers and law enforcement officials. In short, to say that systems are plagued with human errors does not mean that human factors specialists know how to reduce those errors.

On the Nature of Acceptable Evidence

The problems are further complicated by the difficulty of providing acceptable evidence to prove that human factors really work. For a laboratory scientist, or a personnel psychologist, the most direct way to

prove the effect of a variable A is to test two otherwise identical groups—one with and the other without A. If the researcher can demonstrate a significant difference between the two groups on some sort of a criterion measure, most people would agree that he has good evidence for the genuine effectiveness of variable A. Such a simple, straightforward technique is virtually impossible to use in systems design. No one would seriously consider designing two manufacturing plants, two subway systems, or two airports, one with and the other without a systematic human factors program, just to test the value of human factors. The cost alone is prohibitive.

Failing that kind of direct, unequivocal evidence, engineering psychologists are forced to fall back on less satisfactory, although technically feasible, methods. One of these is to compare a system before and after the application of systematic human factors engineering. Engineering psychologists are sometimes called in to advise about systems in operation; when even though a plant, office, or system is working, it is obvious to someone in charge that it is not working well. It may even be apparent that the reason the system is not working well has to do in some way with the people in the system. Assume that the consultant comes in, studies the system, and suggests a number of important changes, which are made. Assume further that there is a significant increase in the output, or efficiency, of the system after the changes are made. How good is this evidence? Not very. There are at least two things wrong with it. First, the dangers of arguing from this kind of before and after comparison were illustrated dramatically in the Hawthorne experiments years ago (see Chapanis, 1959, pp. 73–75, 230–233). In addition to the presumed human factors improvements, many other changes may also have occurred, and in this kind of study it is impossible to determine with certainty which of the changes is responsible for the effect. The second major difficulty with such before and after evi-

---

[4] The references cited in this quotation are all part of the irregular technical report literature not readily available to me. I have not, therefore, cited them in the references.

dence is that when a system has already been put into operation, the best an engineering psychologist can do is to make some rather superficial modifications in it. The major decisions (for example, decisions about the allocation of functions to men and machines or the number of operators needed to man a console) have already been made. Once a system has been designed and put into operation, it is almost impossible to go back and undo those major decisions, even if they should later turn out to have been incorrect.

Evidence From Component and Subsystem Design

The other kind of support available to show the value of engineering psychology is from experiments on the bits and pieces of systems. Here we are on firmer ground. A good example of this kind of work is a paper by Teel (1971) which reviews three studies conducted at Autonetics: one in inspection, one in manufacturing, and one in missile silo safety. In all three cases the data show that human factors engineering yielded returns far in excess of the cost of the studies conducted. One of those studies is reviewed here to show the kind of evidence on which Teel's conclusions are based.

The study dealt with the performance of electronic assemblers who had to put eighty-seven discrete components in their proper locations on a $3'' \times 3''$ ceramic printed-circuit module. The assemblers normally worked from narrative instructions and drawings in an operator instruction document. Approximately 20 percent of the completed boards contained at least one misplaced component.

To try to reduce both assembly time and errors, a human factors staff member and an industrial designer developed an experimental work station which projected assembly instructions onto the module board. The station consists of a filmstrip projector, a filmstrip of instructions, numerically sequenced kits of parts, and a structure to tie these elements together. The circuit board

is held on the work surface in a jig, and assembly instructions are projected onto it. The projected instructions show a number identifying the kit of components that is to be used and a series of light arrows showing where and in which direction each component is to be inserted. When all the components in one kit have been assembled, the operator advances the filmstrip to the next frame for instructions on the placement of the parts contained in the next kit.

A comparison of the standard and experimental work stations was made with six assemblers who had no previous experience with the type of module that served as the test item. All assembled the module four times. They used the standard method on the first and fourth trials and the experimental method on the second and third trials. The results show that the new station reduced assembly time by 64 percent and errors by 75 percent.

The reduction in assembly time (Table 6) was estimated to save the company seven times the cost of the human engineering study that preceded the change. However

TABLE 6
THE VALUE OF AN IMPROVED WORK STATION FOR ELECTRONIC ASSEMBLERS*

Number of systems produced/year	190
Number of modules/system	44
Number of modules assembled/year	8,360
Assembly time/module with standard method	76 min.
Assembly time/module with projection station	28 min.
Time savings/module with projection station	48 min.
Cost saving/module ($\frac{8}{10}$ hour $\times$ \$4.20)	\$ 3.36
Cost saving/year (\$3.36 $\times$ 8,360)	\$28,090
Cost of study	
Human factors engineering time	\$ 2,000
Subject time	\$ 450
Design of work station	\$ 750
Implementation (three stations)	\$ 1,000
Total	\$ 4,200

* From Teel, 1971.

impressive they may be, these figures are underestimates because of two additional considerations: (1) The value of the error reduction should also have been included in the figures. However, it was not evaluated primarily because of the impossibility of getting reliable estimates of the cost of identifying and correcting misplaced components. (2) Savings will accrue to the company as long as the projection work station is used. Continuing costs of the station will be limited largely to the preparation of new filmstrips.

In Summary

To sum up, then, engineering psychology is in the curious position of having a great many principles which most people believe to be valid and useful. Proving that usefulness in any scientifically rigorous way, however, is much easier said than done. Collecting evidence of this kind is something to which engineering psychologists need to devote more attention.

The Search for an Identity

Like so many young adults in our contemporary society, engineering psychology seems to be searching for an identity. Despite their name, engineering psychologists are not engineers and, in the eyes of some of their colleagues, neither are they psychologists. This ambiguous status has several consequences, one of which is reflected in endless debates about whether human factors specialists are better trained in departments of engineering or in departments of psychology. The issue is by no means clear and it is not likely to be settled definitively in the next decade.

To an engineer an engineering psychologist is, first and foremost, a psychologist, and most of the time the engineer is right. This simple truth immediately makes the engineering psychologist a second-class citizen in the world of industry and systems, for it is engineers, not psychologists, who design, build, and install equipment. In a

sense, the engineering psychologist can never play a direct role in any equipment problem. He can only advise, argue, cajole, and sometimes say, "I told you so." Except in the simplest and usually the most trivial applications, the engineering psychologist is forced to work through someone who can translate his recommendations and suggestions into workable pieces of hardware. It's often a touchy and delicate position in which to find oneself.

Since most engineering psychologists seem to get into the field through experimental psychology, one might suppose that engineering psychologists would find a more comfortable home among their psychologist colleagues. Such, unfortunately, has not generally been the case. Throughout the history of psychology, most academic experimentalists have had a distaste for any kind of psychology that is in any way applied. Indeed, the rewards in academic life and in the professional world of psychology more often accrue to the theoretical, the pure, and the basic psychologists than to those who use their science for the solution of the problems of the world. The grudging tolerance of engineering psychology by the academic world means, among other things, that there are no genuine programs of education for this specialty. Although courses in engineering psychology are widely taught, not a single department in the country can claim a well-integrated curriculum which turns out engineering psychologists with the skills they really need to have.

In his useful survey of the field, Kraft (1970) asked human factors specialists what they actually do. The most commonly mentioned activities, among the seventy-three on his list, include:

1. man-machine analysis
2. control-display requirements
3. design of work stations
4. development of operator procedures
5. control-display development
6. task-equipment analysis
7. surveillance of engineering design
8. time-line functional analysis
9. mock-up development

10. human error analysis

11. mission simulation

12. system safety analysis

This list of activities is impressive not only because of the highly technical content of the topics in it, but also because it seems so completely unrelated to the content of academic psychology. Small wonder, then, that the typical psychology department finds it so difficult to accept and integrate such arcane and esoteric subject matters into its comfortable and familiar world of mazes, nonsense syllables, and Mueller-Lyer illusions.

Although engineering psychology would seem by its very name to be the offspring of, and to belong to, two different professions, in actual fact it is more nearly correct to say that it is ignored by both parents. Neither fish nor fowl, the engineering psychologist is most often a self-developed person, one who has through his own perseverance trained himself in spite of, rather than with the help of, academic programs. The net result is that training in engineering psychology is spotty, the field lacks cohesiveness, and the people in it are not always sure to whom they should pledge their intellectual allegiance.

Acceptance of Engineering Psychology in Systems Engineering

Although engineering psychology has established some significant beachheads in industry, a survey of engineering textbooks shows that the field is not generally recognized by engineers. Chestnut (1965) devotes only one page of the more than 600 pages in his book to man as an operator and as an element in a man-machine system. Hall (1962) allocates about a page and a half to human factors. Machol (1965) is a bit more generous with a brief chapter in which, however, man is considered only as an abstract information processor. Although Shearer et al. (1967) mention a driver and a steersman in their introductory chapter, the rest of the book never again refers to man, his characteristics, or his behavior. A mere three pages in Wilson's book (1965)

are concerned with human factors. More important, for every book on systems engineering that mentions the human operator, one can find another in which the words *human, man, human factors,* and *psychology* do not appear. Even such a brief excursion into the literature provides enough evidence to justify the conclusion that engineering psychology, or human factors engineering, has not made a strong impression on the systems engineers who write textbooks on the subject.

Engineers' Use of Human Factors

Even though engineers who write textbooks pay little attention to engineering psychology, one might expect that practicing engineers would. Unfortunately, engineering psychologists often discover that their views are given little attention, even when they are members of a systems design team. This impression is confirmed by Meister and Farr (1966), who conducted an experiment in which each of thirty design engineers was asked to design two products according to elaborate specifications: (1) a weapons assignment and control station, and (2) a self-contained portable test set for circuit modules that are used with a radio navigation device. After observing their designers at work, and after analyzing the products of their efforts, Meister and Farr concluded that their designers had little or no interest in human factors, human factors information, or in the application of human factors criteria to design. Moreover, they neither possessed nor read human factors handbooks and, although they stated verbally that they were concerned with the human aspects of their products, their behavior in practice was consistently negative toward user or operator requirements.

In another elaborate study, Meister et al. (1968) tried to assess to what extent designers are influenced by manpower and personnel resources data in their work. In that study, each of six engineers was given three months to design the propellant transfer and pressurization subsystem (PTPS) for the Titan III space launch system. The Titan III PTPS is a large bi-propellant transfer subsystem used in the ground fueling of a fixed base, two-stage booster for scientific payloads. This subsystem is responsible for receiving propellants from railroad cars, for storing propellants in ready storage vehicles for a period of up to twenty days, and for transferring the stored propellants to the booster tanks. The propellant consists of a mixture of nitrogen tetroxide and unsymmetrical dimethylhydrazine and hydrazine. Since all these substances are highly volatile and extremely toxic either individually or in combination, their handling and storage automatically require the most stringent safety provisions.

The designers worked from an elaborate set of specifications and engineering standards. Three of the designers were told that they should design for personnel with low-skill levels; the other three, that they should design for personnel with high-skill levels. Skill levels were in every case defined. The results of the study showed that manpower requirements and information about personnel resources do exert some influence on the design of equipment, but that the influence is only moderate. By and large, engineers were disappointingly unaware of, or indifferent to, personnel considerations.

Some Reasons for the Inadequate Use of Human Factors Information

If we are willing to grant that engineering psychology can make some desirable contributions to industry and the design of machine systems, why don't engineers pay more attention to it? The two Meister studies cited above identify three possible reasons for the inadequate use of human data in the design process.

FAULTY TIMING. All too often human factors recommendations come after, rather than before, significant engineering design decisions have been made. The typical engineering psychologist, lacking all but a minimal background in engineering, finds himself dependent on the flow of engineering information to him as the basis for his contributions. As a result, he fails to participate in the preparatory work that is so important for the decisions that are subsequently made. Unfortunately, it is precisely during that preparatory phase that fundamental decisions are made. These decisions, once made, are extremely difficult to reverse later. In this connection, it is important to emphasize the relatively informal nature of the process that leads to basic design decisions. Formal paper work most often merely summarizes decisions that have already been made informally. To be effective, therefore, the engineering psychologist cannot wait for written documents if he is to have any effect on design decisions. This lesson, unfortunately, has not yet been learned by the profession.

INADEQUATELY EXPRESSED RECOMMENDATIONS. A second and perhaps even more important reason why human factors recommendations are not applied is that they are not expressed in terms that engineers understand and can make use of. To illustrate, the following is a description of the capabilities of a person with somewhat less than average skills—a so-called "three-level" person—as prepared by Air Force psychologists:

Three-level—Performs simple manual operations readily (without assistance), but may require assistance (supervision or use of manuals) with more complex operations, particularly those involving a combination of tasks or requiring significant decisions involving extrapolation of data or judgment. Performs simple responses quickly; shows hesitation or significant delay with more complex ones. Has a low error probability (1–5%) for simple or moderately complex operations, which rises to extremely high level for complex operations (50%).

Let's assume for the moment that the description is a valid one. What does it mean to a design engineer? Not very much.

First, how is a design engineer to know which decisions are "significant" and which are not? What decisions involve "extrapolations" and what do not? What are "simple responses," what are "complex" ones? And so on. Even more important is that the design engineer has no conception of what such a description means in terms of specific equipment design. Can such a so-called "three-level" person correctly interpret a conventional micrometer? Can he understand how to insert data into a computer through a conventional teletype keyboard? Is there some special way that a keyboard should be redesigned for such a person? How many dials can such a person monitor simultaneously? Three? Five? Ten? A hundred? Without such concrete information, the designer is literally lost. He doesn't use the human information because he doesn't know what it means. And, if the truth were to be stated bluntly, the engineering psychologist often doesn't know either. If we are to make an impact on the world of design, a great deal more needs to be done to translate our recommendations about human behavior into terms that are specific, concrete, and understandable.

THE NATURE OF THE DESIGN BUSINESS. A third, although perhaps somewhat less cogent, reason for the failure of human factors recommendations to be accepted can be traced to the engineers themselves and to the nature of their work. In general, designers give human considerations a low priority, and for understandable reasons. The typical designer is constantly plagued by a host of requirements—specifications, costs, schedules, and deadlines, just to name a few—that clamor and compete for his attention. System development is usually chaotic and almost always behind schedule. Given the pressures under which he works, it is not surprising that he should give low priority to those considerations he is least able to understand and that come to his desk last. The moral of this is that if he wants to be heard, the engineering psychologist needs

to get into the design process early and to present his message more lucidly than do those with whom he must compete.

A Final Note of Optimism

Although the problems and difficulties discussed in the foregoing sections are realistic, they may leave the impression that things are really much worse than is indeed the case. In actual fact, there is reason for optimism about the prospects for engineering psychology and the human factors business.

Consider first that the field is scarcely two decades old. Prior to 1950 there was only one company with an established human factors engineering program. By 1956 the number of industrial programs had grown to twenty-four, and by 1968 to 178. The growth of educational programs is no less impressive. In 1947 the first known course in engineering psychology was offered at The Johns Hopkins University. Today, approximately fifty-seven educational institutions have some kind of human factors or engineering psychology program. Of these, twenty-five are offered in schools or departments of engineering, twenty-one in departments of psychology, and the remainder under other auspices.

Although these and other indices of past growth are reassuring, it is in looking into the future that we find our greatest reason for optimism. The growth of new and different tools, machines, and systems continues at a rate that shows no signs of diminishing. In addition, one sees everywhere trends pointing to the growth, development, and reorganization of most of our social systems: transportation, criminal enforcement and the administration of justice, housing, education, energy resources and power, health and medicine, housing, social welfare, and recreation. At the same time there is at all levels of society a demand that these reorganized social systems do more than meet man's needs in terms of physical numbers. We now demand that they improve the "quality" of man's life as well (see, for example, Clausen, 1971). In the last analysis, technology, machines, systems, and institutions are devised for only one purpose, and that is to serve man. The need now is to build systems that not only serve man, but that serve him well. These are human factors considerations of staggering dimensions.

In the decades to come one unexpected and powerful source of support for engineering psychology will be an ally that is already doing much to shape the future of the field. Our judicial system, laws, and tradition equate human error with human fault and responsibility. The legal profession, however, has been quick to realize that engineering psychology puts human error in a larger and more accurate perspective, that is, as a basically predictable phenomenon in a complex industrial society (see, for example, Goodman, 1968; Peters, 1968). A number of important trials have succeeded in establishing a new legal philosophy: When an engineer can predict, or could have predicted, human miscalculations in the operation of a machine, it is his duty to protect workers against the hazards that he could, or should, have foreseen. Not only is this an ethical and legal maxim, but it makes sound engineering sense as well. As pointed out repeatedly in this chapter, safety, convenience, and comfort are more readily and fully guaranteed and implemented at the design stage. They are also achieved at the lowest cost when such factors are planned for at the drawing board.

Since the monetary settlements and punitive damages awarded by our courts are often substantial in amount, they constitute a powerful incentive to engineers, designers, manufacturers, and industrialists to insure that human considerations have been adequately taken into account. At the same time, these same developments impose equally demanding requirements on the engineering psychologist, for it is up to him to defend, against strong and hostile opponents, the validity of his claims and assertions. In this way, these new social forces are creating a future that is at once challenging, hopeful, and frightening. The future is truly exciting. In meeting its new responsibilities it is even possible that engineering psychology will eventually do more for academic experimental psychology than experimental psychology has done for it.

REFERENCES

Blum, M. L., & Naylor, J. C. *Industrial psychology: Its theoretical and social foundations.* New York: Harper and Row, 1968.

Brown, I. D., & Poulton, E. C. Measuring the spare 'mental capacity' of car drivers by a subsidiary task. *Ergonomics,* 1961, 4, 35–40.

Carter, L. F. Relative effectiveness of presenting numerical data by the use of tables and graphs. Report #TSEAA-694-1, Aero Medical Laboratory, Air Materiel Command, Dayton, Ohio, April, 1946. (a)

Carter, L. F. A study of the best design of tables and graphs used for presenting numerical data. Report #TSEAA-694-1C, Aero Medical Laboratory, Air Materiel Command, Dayton, Ohio, September, 1946. (b)

Chapanis, A. *Research techniques in human engineering.* Baltimore: Johns Hopkins Press, 1959.

Chapanis, A. Human engineering. In C. D. Flagle, W. H. Huggins, & R. H. Roy (Eds.), *Operations research and systems engineering.* Baltimore: Johns Hopkins Press, 1960, 534–582.

Chapanis, A. Words, words, words. *Human Factors,* 1965, 7, 1–17. (a)

Chapanis, A. *Man-machine engineering.* Monterey, Calif.: Brooks/Cole, 1965. (b)

Chapanis, A. The relevance of laboratory studies to practical situations. *Ergonomics,* 1967, 10, 557–577.

Chapanis, A. Relevance of physiological and psychological criteria to man-machine systems: The present state of the art. *Ergonomics,* 1970, 13, 337–346. (a)

Chapanis, A. Systems staffing. In K. B. De Greene (Ed.), *Systems psychology.* New York: McGraw-Hill, 1970, 357–382. (b)

Chestnut, H. *Systems engineering tools.* New York: Wiley, 1965.

Clausen, A. W. Towards an arithmetic of quality. *Human Factors Society Bulletin,* 1971, 14 (1), 1–2, 5–8.

Connell, S. C. The relative effectiveness of presenting numerical data by the use of scales and graphs. Report #TSEAA-694-1M, Aero Medical Laboratory, Air Materiel Command, Dayton, Ohio, December, 1947.

Conrad, R., & Hull, A. J. The preferred layout for numerical data-entry keysets. *Ergonomics,* 1968, 11, 165–173.

Cornog, D. Y., & Rose, F. C. *Legibility of alphanumeric characters and other symbols: II. A reference handbook.* National Bureau of Standards Miscellaneous Publication 262-2. Washington, D.C.: U.S. Government Printing Office, 1967.

de Montmolin, M., Morin, P., & Régnier, J. Recherches expérimentales de sémiologie graphique. *Metra,* 1970, Special Series Number 15.

Dunnette, M. D. *Personnel selection and placement.* Belmont, Calif.: Wadsworth Publishing, 1966.

Fleishman, E. A., Ed. *Studies in personnel and industrial psychology.* (Rev. ed.) Homewood, Ill.: Dorsey Press, 1967.

Fleishman, E. A., & Hempel, W. E. Jr. A factor analysis of dexterity tests. *Personnel Psychology,* 1954, 7, 15–32.

Fleishman, E. A., & Hempel, W. E. Jr. Factorial analysis of complex psychomotor performance and related skills. *Journal of Applied Psychology,* 1956, 40, 96–104.

Flesch, R. *The art of plain talk.* New York: Harper and Brothers, 1946.

Goodman, R. M. A trial lawyer looks at human factors. *Human Factors Society Bulletin,* 1968, 11 (6), 1–2.

Gow, C. R. *Foundation for human engineering.* New York: Macmillan, 1930.

Hall, A. D. *A methodology for systems engineering.* New York: Van Nostrand, 1962.

Hempel, W. E. Jr., & Fleishman, E. A. A factor analysis of physical proficiency and manipulative skill. *Journal of Applied Psychology,* 1955, 39, 12–16.

Kelley, C. R. *Manual and automatic control.* New York: Wiley, 1968.

Kraft, J. A. Status of human factors and biotechnology in 1968–1969. *Human Factors,* 1970, 12, 113–151.

Loveless, N. E. Direction-of-motion stereotypes: A review. *Ergonomics,* 1962, 5, 357–383.

Lutz, M. C., & Chapanis, A. Expected locations of digits and letters on ten-button keysets. *Journal of Applied Psychology,* 1955, 39, 314–317.

McCormick, E. J. *Human factors engineering.* (3rd ed.) New York: McGraw-Hill, 1970.

Machol, R. E., Ed. *System engineering handbook.* New York: McGraw-Hill, 1965.

Mackie, R. R., & Christensen, P. R. *Translation and application of psychological research.* Technical Report 716-1, Human Factors Research, Inc., Santa Barbara Research Park, Goleta, Calif., 1967.

Magoun, F. A. *Problems in human engineering.* New York: Macmillan, 1932.

Meister, D., & Farr, D. E. The utilization of human factors information by designers (U). Unnumbered technical report, Systems Effectiveness Laboratory, The Bunker-Ramo Corporation, Canoga Park, Calif., September, 1966.

Meister, D., & Rabideau, G. F. *Human factors evaluation in system development.* New York: Wiley, 1965.

Meister, D., Sullivan, D. J., & Askren, W. B. The impact of manpower requirements and personnel resources data on system design. Report #AMRL-TR-68-44, Aerospace Medical Research Laboratories, Wright-Patterson Air Force Base, Ohio, September, 1968.

Morgan, C. T., Cook, J. S. III, Chapanis, A., & Lund, M. W., Eds. *Human engineering guide to equipment design.* New York: McGraw-Hill, 1963.

Mowbray, G. H., & Gebhard, J. W. Man's senses as informational channels. In H. W. Sinaiko (Ed.), *Selected papers on human factors in the design and use of control systems.* New York: Dover Publications, 1961, 115–149.

O'Connor, J. *Born that way.* Baltimore: Williams and Wilkins, 1928.

Peters, G. A. Product liability and 'forensic engineering.' *Bar Bulletin* (Los Angeles County Bar Association), 1968, 43, 367–369, 385.

Plutchik, R. The effects of high intensity intermittent sound on performance, feeling, and physiology. *Psychological Bulletin,* 1959, 56, 133–151.

Shearer, J. L., Murphy, A. T., & Richardson, H. H. *Introduction to system dynamics.* Reading, Mass.: Addison-Wesley, 1967.

Sinaiko, H. W., & Brislin, R. W. Experiments

in language translation: Technical English-to-Vietnamese. Research Paper P-634, Institute for Defense Analyses, Science and Technology Division, Arlington, Va., July, 1970.

Sinaiko, H. W., Guthrie, G. M., & Abbott, P. S. Operating and maintaining complex military equipment: A study of training problems in the Republic of Vietnam. Research Paper P-501, Institute for Defense Analyses, Science and Technology Division, Arlington, Va., July, 1969.

Sticht, T. G. Some relationships of mental aptitude, reading ability, and listening ability using normal and time-compressed speech. *The Journal of Communication,* 1968, 18, 243–258.

Sticht, T. G. Literacy demands of publications in selected military occupational specialities. Draft Professional Paper, Human Resources Research Office, Division Number 3 (Recruit Training), George Washington University, Washington, D.C., July, 1969.

Tannenbaum, A. S. *Social psychology of the work organization.* Belmont, Calif.: Wadsworth Publishing, 1966.

Teel, K. S. Is human factors engineering worth the investment? *Human Factors,* 1971, 13, 17–21.

Tiffin, J., & McCormick, E. J. *Industrial psychology.* (5th ed.) Englewood Cliffs, N.J.: Prentice-Hall, 1965.

Weldon, R. J., & Peterson, G. M. Effect of design on accuracy and speed of operating dials. *Journal of Applied Psychology,* 1957, 41, 153–157.

Wilson, W. E. *Concepts of engineering system design.* New York: McGraw-Hill, 1965.

Woodrow, H. Time perception. In S. S. Stevens (Ed.), *Handbook of experimental psychology.* New York: Wiley, 1951, 1224–1236.

Woodson, W. E., & Conover, D. W. *Human engineering guide for equipment designers.* (2nd ed.) Berkeley: University of California Press, 1966.

CHAPTER 17

Behaviors, Results, and Organizational Effectiveness: The Problem of Criteria[1]

PATRICIA C. SMITH
Bowling Green State University

DECIDING WHAT CRITERIA one wants to predict, manipulate, or conceptualize is the first problem of the scientist. Three dimensions seem to cover most criteria: the time-span to be covered, the specificity desired, and the closeness to organizational goals to be approached. These determine the logic of the criteria chosen, their relevance, reliability, and salability. Suggestions are given for improving criteria.

"The criterion" is certainly one of the key problems in industrial and organizational psychology, as evidenced by the massive efforts designed to clarify its theory and to improve its measurements. (For example, see such reviews as those of Kendall, 1956; Wallace & Weitz, 1955; Katzell, 1957; Taylor & Nevis, 1961; Weitz, 1961; Biesheuvel, 1965; Wallace, 1965; Guion, 1967; Owens & Jewell, 1969; Bray & Moses, 1972.) Determination of policies concerning organiza-

tional structure, managerial and employee development, conditions of work, design of jobs, incentive plans, leadership styles, selection, placement, transfer and promotion, and organizational objectives requires comparisons of criterion measures.

The dictionary (Funk & Wagnalls, 1963) defines a criterion as a "standard or rule by which a judgment can be made." In psychology it has come to mean a dependent or predicted measure for judging the effectiveness of persons, organizations, treatments, or predictors of behavior, results, and organizational effectiveness.

[1] I thank R. A. H. Goodfellow, O. W. Smith, J. Scheffers, and J. P. Wijting for their critical readings of the manuscript.

REQUIREMENTS OF A CRITERION

The first requirement of a criterion is that it be relevant to some important goal of the individual, the organization, or society. Determination of relevance is, however, a matter of judgment. Some group or person must decide which activities are most relevant to success. Once these activities have been identified, efforts must then be directed toward developing psychometrically sound measures of these activities. The measure of a criterion should be neither contaminated with irrelevant variance nor deficient in terms of measuring the important objectives of the organization and of the people in it.

Neither the criterion nor the measure of it should be biased or trivial (Ghiselli & Brown, 1955, Chap. 4). In order to insure the importance of a criterion, careful analysis is required for the understanding of the goal or goals of the individual, organization, or society. Some goals are obvious. Some may be equally important, yet obscure and inadequately formulated. For the latter, criteria must be developed. These criteria are achieved only via analysis and understanding so that valid measures can be applied or devised. Consequently, relevancy, the first requirement for a criterion, consists of two parts. One is the validity of the goal which is judged to be important. The second is the validity of the measure(s) of the goal achievement. This requirement is parallel to the requirement that a test be valid.

Reliability is the second requirement of a criterion. It involves agreement between different evaluations, at different periods of time and with different although apparently similar measures. Reliability is usually said to set the upper limit of validity (Ryan & Smith, 1954, pp. 46–56; Wallace & Weitz, 1955; Blum & Naylor, 1968, p. 182) and of the predictability of effects of treatments. Reliability may, of course, be estimated or operationalized in several different ways, and these estimates may occasionally yield quite different values for the same criterion measure. For example, test-retest stability could be low even though internal con-

sistency estimates derived at particular points in time may be high. Occasionally, therefore, and depending upon the type of "reliability" that is computed, the upper limit of validity may not be rigidly set by the value found for reliability. Dunnette (1966, pp. 35–36) discusses some anomalies wherein validity may not necessarily be limited by the size of reliability.

A criterion measure must in addition be practical—available, plausible, and acceptable to those who will want to use it for decisions. Psychologists are seldom the decision makers, and they must consider the market for their ideas. It is a temptation to predict that which is predictable (e.g., Kurtz, 1937), rather than that which ought to be predicted as a basis for decisions.

MULTIDIMENSIONALITY OF CRITERIA

The Search for the Criterion

The use of the single noun "criterion" has been misleading. It has stemmed from the false search for measures which would be related to what Thorndike (1949) called the "ultimate criterion."

The ultimate criterion is the complete final goal of a particular type of selection or training. For example, it might have been agreed that the final goal in the selection and training of Air Force bombardiers was that they should under conditions of combat flying drop their bombs in every case with maximum precision upon the designated target. The ultimate goal in the selection and training of insurance salesmen might be that each man sell the maximum amount of insurance which would not be allowed to lapse and that he continue actively as an insurance salesman for an extended period of years. The ultimate criterion for a production line worker might be that he perform his task, maintaining the tempo of the line, with the minimum of defective products requiring rejection upon inspection, that he be personally satisfied with the task to such an extent that he is not a source of unrest and conflict with other workers, and that he continue in the job for an extended period of time. It can be seen that the ultimate goal is stated in very broad terms and in terms that are often not susceptible to practical quantitative evaluation. Furthermore, it is usually not entirely accurate to specify a single and unified ultimate goal. The bombardier had to fire a gun as well as drop bombs. The life insurance salesman must keep records and in many instances manage an office, as well as sell to customers. Even with the production line worker we have indicated considerations of contentment and permanence on the job as well as simple performance. A really complete ultimate criterion is multiple and complex in almost every case. Such a criterion is ultimate in the sense that we cannot look beyond it for any higher or further standard in terms of which to judge the outcomes of a particular personnel program.

In practice, the complete ultimate criterion is rarely, if ever, available for use in psychological research. (Thorndike, 1949, p. 121)

As the quotation indicates, no single measure can fully express success or failure. Yet a single decision must somehow be made about each individual, organization, or treatment—hence the search for composites which properly represent the full complexity of the underlying measures.

There are several bases for combining measures into a single summary criterion measure. The first is statistical, based on intercorrelations of measures. If different measures are not highly correlated, then a composite is illogical, cancelling out important bits of information, pro and con. But if several measures can be shown to be highly intercorrelated or to represent a single factor, then construction of a combined measure is reasonable. An example of a statistical composite is given by Edgerton and Kolbe (1936), who obtain a composite by *maximizing* differences between individuals in terms of composite criterion scores and minimizing differences in scores on different criterion variables within the individual. Convergence of several criteria is illustrated by French (1954), who combined ratings from classmates, upperclassmen, and officers to obtain a single, reliable criterion of leadership. There are many other examples

of successful combinations of criteria, but always to a rather limited goal.

The second basis is economic. If organizational goals can be reduced to common measurement scales such as dollars, then we can combine apparently diverse criteria. Brogden and Taylor (1950) have suggested the combination of varied criteria into a single measure of profits versus costs to the organization. Reminding management of the monetary importance of personnel decisions has great practical appeal. But, as Wallace and Weitz (1955) point out in their excellent discussion of criteria, converting all objectives to monetary terms is impractical. For one thing, neither indirect labor costs nor satisfaction of employees can be so converted; public relations goals such as "good will" can similarly not be translated readily into dollars and cents.

A third basis for combining is judgmental, either by direct estimations by policy makers of the relative importance of various criteria or by "capturing" operational policies by analysis of actual decisions made. (A good reference on policy capturing is Slovic & Lichtenstein, 1971.) Either of these has the advantage of taking the decision concerning weighting out of the hands of psychologists and putting it in the hands of the people who are paid to make policy. (This is not to say that psychologists should not help to serve as agents for change in policy, but only that they should recognize their consultative and, perhaps, persuasive roles.) Fiske (1951) argues that explicit policy and empirical research can substitute for judgment in development of criteria. We can only wish him good luck.

ARGUMENTS AGAINST THE SINGLE CRITERION

Establishment of a single criterion appears to many as a hopeless quest. There are two reasons, one logical and one empirical. Logically, all components of a single criterion measure should be expected to represent different aspects of a unitary concept or different ways of measuring the same characteristic. Combining such variables as production and absences seems like adding olives and toothpicks to obtain the alcoholic content of drinks. Especially clear pleas for multiple criteria have been made by Otis (1940), Toops (1944), Guion (1961), Weitz (1961), Dunnette (1963), Biesheuvel (1965), Guion (1965), Wallace (1965), Ronan and Prien (1966), and Roach and Wherry (1970). They argue that success is not unitary, for different jobs for the same person, for different persons on the same job, or for different aspects of the same job for the same person. Ghiselli (1960) points out that two persons may achieve equivalent total performance with quite different patterns of behavior, and hence, logically, evaluation of either treatments or individual differences should be made on the basis of different measures.

The second reason for rejecting the single criterion concerns the obtained interrelationships among criterion measures and predictive measures in empirical studies. An overwhelming majority of studies involving statistical analyses of sets of criterion measures finds that these analyses rarely yield a single general factor. In other words, several criterion measures are necessary to account for the variance in a criterion correlation matrix. To mention only a few studies, Ewart, Seashore, and Tiffin (1941), Rush (1953), Grant (1955), Stark (1959), Seashore, Indik, and Georgopoulos (1960), Forehand (1963), Ronan (1963), Schultz and Siegel (1964), Wiley (1964), Siegel and Pfeiffer (1965), and Kirchner (1966) all reported multidimensionality of criteria. This convergence of evidence should partly answer the arguments of Marks (1967), who argued that unreliability contributes to the "apparent" complexity of criteria. We shall see further evidence of multidimensionality as we survey the empirical results.

The argument has progressed to a consideration of how many criteria should be utilized. This question will prove to be an empirical one in each case. When a single composite will cover most of the variance in a set of criteria, then that composite should be used to represent them, and other criteria sought. When several dimensions are involved, several sets of criteria or composites will be required.

CLASSIFICATION OF CRITERIA

We can classify criteria in a three-dimensional framework, as illustrated in Figure 1, which represents a cutaway diagram of kinds of criteria. The first dimension is the time span covered. The second is the degree of specificity of the criterion (as related to our discussion of multidimensionality above). The third is the closeness of the relationship to criteria based on the goals of individuals, organizations, or society.

Time Span Covered

Criterion measures can be obtained either very soon after actual on-the-job behavior has occurred or many years afterwards. We may have, for example, a count of the number of times a worker stops his work for a rest break (Smith & Lem, 1955), which is very short-term, or a rating of success based on life history data including salary (Bingham & Davis, 1924), which is long-term. What is apparently the same criterion measure can involve different behaviors and abilities at different periods of time. It has been long known (Kornhauser, 1923; Blankenship & Taylor, 1938; McGehee, 1948; Smith & Gold, 1956) that performance early in the learning period does not necessarily correlate highly with later performance. More recent studies substantiate those findings (Ghiselli & Haire, 1960; Bass, 1962; Prien, 1966; MacKinney, 1967). These changes may represent changes in organizational demands with increased time on the job (Prien, 1966; Seashore & Yuchtman, 1967). They also may reflect a shift in the abilities being used. Factor structure shifts (Fleishman & Fruchter, 1960) and the correlation with predictive tests changes (Ghiselli & Haire, 1960) with time. All this leads to a plea for longitudinal studies (e.g., Ghi-

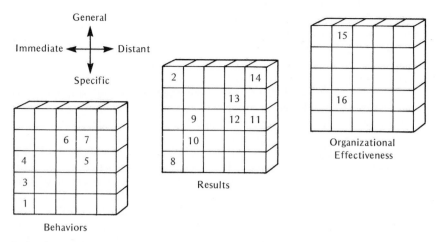

Figure 1. Dimensions of criteria.

selli, 1956; Guion, 1967) and consideration of the dynamic nature of criteria. Too often, mere convenience, rather than the relevance to long-term performance, has dictated the use of measures.

The time span dimension has implications for the prediction of criterion measures. The time span of a manipulation or a predictor should be matched to the time span of the criterion measure. Thus, changes in the short-run situation, such as a bonus for attendance, could be expected to be reflected only in such short-term behaviors as absences and tardiness, and not necessarily in long-term job satisfaction. The latter might be more affected by policy toward promotions, which is long-term. There should be a match in time span. And predictors should be measuring those characteristics of individuals which will be relevant at the particular point in time in which criterion measures will be gathered.

Specificity

Criteria vary also in their specificity-generality. Some may refer to very specific aspects of behavior (or effectiveness) on the job, while others give a summary estimate. Here the literature on multidimensionality of criteria is relevant (see above), although

multidimensionality occurs across all of our classifications of criteria.

Regardless of the time span, criteria can differ in the specificity with which they refer to descriptions of performance versus global estimates. At one extreme we have a rater check whether a certain behavior has been observed (Flanagan, 1954) and on the other we have results combined into the composite dollar criterion (Brogden & Taylor, 1950). Another pair of examples is the tabulation of absence in a department (Stark, 1959) versus a composite of indices (Kurtz, 1937). Again there are implications for prediction and manipulation. Change in a single variable cannot be expected to have much effect on a general criterion. Since there are multiple factors causing change in general performance, the effect of any one will probably be small. Conversely, a test of general interest in the job cannot be expected to predict very precisely the specific criterion of absences. If possible, the relative degree of specificity in a manipulation or predictor should be matched to the specificity of the criterion measure.

Closeness to Organizational Goals

Most important in classifying criteria is the dimension that concerns the closeness of the required decisions in relation to organizational and societal goals. Criteria range from the description of actual behavior, through evaluation of results, to estimates of the effects upon the organization and society. Ideally, of course, it would be these last estimates which we would hold in mind in doing any research on policy making. Organizational goals such as economic stability, growth, and flexibility, and societal goals such as contribution toward individual well-being and growth, economic and social vitality of the community, and general productivity are the kinds of goals toward which our efforts are directed. But unfortunately, these are not always the dependent variables in which investigators are interested.

One reason is that such goals may appear to be inaccessible to the investigator. Actually, criteria and their measures can be developed for these goals. The practical difficulty is that investigators in general do not have the financial support for these types of investigations. Lacking this support, organizations and society are deprived of long-term projects and their evaluation in favor of short-term projects which may "pay off" sooner.

Another reason is that a particular manipulation or prediction is frequently much removed from organizational goals, can be expected to have only a minute effect on the total picture, and correlation with a measure of organizational effectiveness would probably be small, even though it might prove statistically significant. Moreover, a global or molar organizational evaluation would not permit diagnosis of the extents of achievement of more specific goals.

This dimension involves, first, the combination of specific human behaviors into generalizations about results (such as ratings or summary personnel statistics; cf., Guion, 1961), and second, the combination of a number of these generalizations to evaluate their impact on organizations, individuals, or society. Both steps involve prob-

lems, many of which will be discussed more fully below.

Here let us note briefly that the making of a generalization concerning results from specific behaviors involves a consideration of how they are to be combined. Whitlock (1963) indicates that there is a psychophysical law relating single behavioral elements to overall judgments. The log of the ratio of observations of effective performance to observations of ineffective performance is linearly related to the log of summary evaluative ratings, indicating that observations actually enter equally (without differential weighting) into a summary evaluation. Whether this is the manner in which observations *should* be combined is another matter. Perhaps a regression equation can do a better job than human judgment.

Ghiselli (1956) points out that there is individuality in the way components should be put together to obtain an overall estimate of results. Each individual can achieve results in his own manner, using different job behaviors and different abilities. Guion (1967) also points out that the dimensionality of criteria may be peculiar to each individual.

The step from results to organizational effectiveness is also large. If results which are not really important to organizational goals are weighted in making a judgment, then the final criterion is contaminated. If important aspects are omitted or not weighted enough, the criterion is deficient (Ghiselli & Brown, 1955). The evaluation of contamination or deficiency is judgmental. In my opinion, this judgment has to be made by management; this sort of decision is what management is paid for. But the psychologist can help in several ways.

He can ask directly for a judgment of importance. This judgment can be obtained either before or after the results of any comparison are in. After results have been obtained one can at least take into account whether certain aspects of the criterion are predictable or not (Kurtz, 1937). Weighting by importance has to be approached with caution, however (Ewen, 1967), since it, like other methods of weighting, may add nothing to validity. Rating of importance, however, is dependent upon the presence of the factor being rated (Smith & Landy, 1969). The psychologist can apply cost accounting principles to achieve a composite, as suggested by Brogden and Taylor (1950) and Likert and Seashore (1963). The difficulty here is that some aspects of organizational effectiveness are much easier to put into monetary terms than others, perhaps biasing the result in favor of the obvious and the short term. Or, he can apply statistical techniques to determine more clearly what are the bases of policy decisions. He can determine the weights actually given to various factors in making policy decisions on an intuitive basis, and systematize the weighting of those factors.

The large literature concerning policy capturing cannot be reviewed here. Only a small portion of the research has been concerned with industrial problems, largely for practical reasons. All the methods require a large number of stimuli to be judged by each judge or by a number of comparable judges, and hence the methods are typically applicable only in large homogeneous organizations. It is no wonder that such research has been conducted either in military settings or with manufactured stimuli (such as persons simulated in the form of personnel folders) rather than actual subjects to be judged.

Various procedures have been used to group judges according to similarity of their policies. JAN (Judgment Analysis, Christal, 1968; Naylor & Wherry, 1965) groups raters according to the degree of similarity or homogeneity of their multiple regression equations for predicting standing on a single criterion measure from the various cues they used in making their judgments (Williams, Harlow, Lindem, & Gab, 1970). Alternative ways of grouping by the the use of profiles of factors are PROF (Profile of Fac-

tors Method, Wherry & Naylor, 1966) and COPAN (Component Profile Analysis, Maguire & Glass, 1968), which use factors rather than item scores for greater reliability.

These methods show great promise for those situations in which sufficiently large groups of persons can be judged. An excellent review of such methodology is given by Slovic and Lichtenstein (1971).

In any case, we are trying to move from results to what Astin (1964) calls conceptual criteria, that is, "a verbal statement of important or socially relevant outcomes based on the more general purposes or aims of the sponsor" (Astin, 1964, p. 809).

DIRECT OBSERVATIONS OF BEHAVIORS

Criteria are seldom actual records of behavior, unfortunately, and the behaviors "slab" is not heavily represented. We could, for example, go out on the production line armed with a stopwatch, time the elements of movement involved in the job, and summarize their variability by computing standard deviations. These could be used as indices of fatigue. The indices are on the behaviors slab, and quite specific and short term. The relationship to organizational objectives is remote. These measures belong in Cell 1 in Figure 1. McGehee and Owen (1940) timed actual rest pauses taken, as did Smith and Lem (1955), showing them to be responsive to short-term manipulations (scheduling of rest periods and size of work lot). These, too, are specific, belonging in Cell 1.

Flanagan (1949) established the critical incidents technique, in which specific job behaviors which are critical to satisfactory or unsatisfactory performance are elicited by interview of superiors, subordinates, and co-workers, and then translated into a check list of behaviors actually observed, so that these incidents can be summed to obtain an overall evaluation. (The end results belong on the results "slab," short-term, and general; see Cell 2.) The technique has proved especially useful with personnel on whom a large number of incidents can be observed, as in the military. It would be difficult to adapt to the observation of managerial personnel, for example, for whom no two incidents may be alike. It has led to further attempts emphasizing direct observation of behavior.

Critical incidents have been used with favorable results by Kirchner and Dunnette (1957), among others. Kay (1959, p. 270) on the other hand found that "judges throughout actually were incapable of assessing the degree of likelihood of effective, average, and ineffective foremen doing that which was described in the critical incident." The problem seems to be that of opportunity to observe, rather than the format itself. We shall have more to say on that point later.

Another example of criterion measurement on the behavior slab is the interesting technique of Whitlock, Clouse, and Spencer (1963) in which observers tallied accident behaviors, or unsafe performances (see Cell 3, Figure 1). They report fairly high reliability for accident data but a relatively low correlation with actual injuries.

One that is much older, however, is the anecdotal report form, which stems from clinical and medical observation—the free verbal report of incidents (a technique for which we can give no primary reference). It involves someone's recording every incident of interest in a person's behavior. It can be commended for its thoroughness and condemned for its impracticality as it relies upon the conscientiousness of reporting by busy individuals, and, what is probably worse, their literary style. We cannot expect dramatic reporting from the ordinary observer. These reports belong in Cell 4, as immediate and somewhat more general.

But it is these observations that have to take place if our criterion measures are to be soundly based on fact. The trick is to obtain records of actual job behaviors before the process of selective recall distorts the impressions. Whitlock's (1963) psychophysical law indicates that favorable and unfavorable impressions acquire unitary weights in combination, which indicates the need for a more detailed basis of recording.

One approach is to ask observers to record at least sketchy notes on their observations on the job, not expecting them to write biographical portraits of the people they observe but merely to note a date and some reminder of the incident with some generalizations (see Cell 4, Smith & Kendall, 1963). (The job anecdote file suggested by Guion, 1965, is similar.) This approach by no means solves the problem of incomplete observations, since observation is usually squeezed in between many more urgent duties. It is at this point that many rating systems fail; they cannot enforce observation.

Another approach is to place a special observer into the situation with no duty except to observe and record. The observer can be either a participant behaving as if he were no different from any other worker [a good example was Owen's (McGehee & Owen, 1940) participation as a clerk in an office in which changes in rest pauses were introduced] or an obvious outsider, as in the work curve studies (Roethlisberger & Dickson, 1938; Rothe, 1946a,b, 1947, 1951; Rothe & Nye, 1958, 1959, 1961; Smith, 1953; see Cell 1). The use of an observer greatly improves the quality of the obtained data, but is costly and may disrupt the customary activities of the people being observed.

Another approach is to take the person being rated or observed off the job into a special situation. One type is the simulation of the job, used most conspicuously for the evaluation of the readiness of astronauts for space flights. It has been used successfully for evaluating proficiency in maintenance checking (Besnard & Briggs, 1967) in which there was no difference in errors between the simulator and the operational equipment groups. It has been used broadly in dangerous or highly critical work (see Cell 5).

Standard flights in pilot evaluation and a check list of items descriptive of a pilot's performance were evaluated in a summary by Viteles (1945), and have been used systematically more recently.

For executives, whose jobs are even more variable, the simulation has been largely on the basis of the In-Basket Test (Frederiksen, Saunders, & Ward, 1957) and assessment centers (see Chapter 20 of this *Handbook*). The In-Basket Test presents to the executive or manager a sample of incoming mail and memos, and records how he sorts, prepares for action, gets work accomplished, and seeks guidance from others. A complicated system, or rather several systems, of scoring are produced. Reliabilities vary from zero to high depending on scoring category. But the technique shows significant (if low) relationships to ratings from higher management (Meyer, 1970). It is a promising type of criterion at the managerial level. (See Cell 6.)

The assessment centers of large companies serve the same function and also take the manager or executive away from the job for observation. For example, the Sohio Assessment Program (Finkle & Jones, 1970) uses a job sample of managerial activities as well as peer ratings in the evaluation of progress and performance of managers, without any reliance on ratings by other managers. The program is aimed at assessing discrete aspects of performance, assessed from tests and situational exercises. Thomson (1970) reports much greater reliabilities at the assessment center than in the working situation; the actual supervisors were more lenient and demonstrated more halo (see below) than did the observers at the center. (Perhaps the observers were concentrating more upon observation.)

Grant and Bray (1966) report the extensive assessment center activities at American Telephone and Telegraph in which interviews, projective techniques, and situational tests were used with significant success to predict managerial effectiveness. Again, observation of behavior is intensive, intentional, and predicts later performance. Assessment centers are somewhat distant and general. (See Cell 7.)

We cannot emphasize too strongly that observation of actual behavior on the job or, if necessary, off the job is the core of establishment of a successful criterion. Without careful observation, we cannot make valid ratings or evaluate the meaning of so-called objective or "hard" criteria discussed below.

EXAMINATION OF RESULTS

The results "slab" contains two sets of criteria—the "hard" criteria obtained from organizational records such as absences and turnover, and the "soft" criteria obtained from ratings. The first maintains the appearance of objectivity; the second is frankly judgmental.

Hard Criteria

Company records furnish data for evaluation of performance, both specific and general and long- and short-term. They represent material available from payroll, insurance, and personnel records, without explicit use of ratings or other evaluation, although, as we shall see, evaluation has entered into every figure in the books.

Tardiness

A short-term specific criterion is tardiness. Its short-term characteristics are emphasized by one of the very few studies using tardiness as a criterion (Mueser, 1953). It was not rain, but bright sunny days that were related to tardiness. It belongs in the lower left corner of the second "slab" in Figure 1 (see Cell 8).

Absences

Absences can be measured in a number of different ways. The base may differ as in percentages of scheduled working hours absent versus number of occasions absent (regardless of the number of days involved in an occasion). They may be broken down into absences attributable to different causes, as illness, personal, excused or unexcused, despite the difficulty in ascertaining the actual cause. In any case, indices of absences behave differently as criterion measures both among themselves and as compared with other criterion measures, and with predictive measures. Kerr, Koppelmeir, and Sullivan (1951) found, for example, a correlation of $-.44$ between unexcused absences and job satisfaction, while total absences correlated .51 with job satisfaction. (There was no control for job level.) Metzner and Mann (1953) also found frequency of absence superior as a criterion to the actual days lost. Huse and Taylor (1962) report that the total absence frequency is the most reliable absence measure.

Situational factors may greatly affect this index, as is indeed true for all the so-called "hard" criteria. Behrend (1953) points out that absence rate is affected by the labor market conditions at the time. Stark (1959) points out that absences may be a function of factors beyond the control of the manager, and absences are used not only as a criterion of individual performance but also as a criterion of effectiveness of foremen. The relationship of absences to personal history and organizational characteristics is different in larger than in smaller units, and for blue- and white-collar workers (Baumgartel & Sobol, 1959). Argyle, Gardner, and Cioffi (1958) note that absenteeism was not related to either turnover or productivity (using departments as the units of analysis), which agrees with Ronan's (1963) finding that the factor structure and weightings of various criteria shift from plant to plant, and with the situational variability reported by both Lyons (1972) and Porter and Steers (1973). Clearly, absences should not be blindly adopted as criteria. They should be located as fairly short-term, medium specific results (see Cell 9), and should not be expected to relate closely with more general, long-term organizational goals.

Accidents

This notoriously unreliable set of measures (Ghiselli & Brown, 1955, p. 344, for example) is nevertheless important to some organizational goals, including humanitarian and economic ones, to which fingers can be easily pointed. The problem is that most accidents are, by definition, beyond any person's immediate control. The best solution, in all probability, is to return to the behaviors "slab" and observe accident behaviors (Whitlock, Clouse, & Spencer, 1963). Barring this more careful inspection of behavior, statistics need to be compiled on the actual record, which is not a very satisfactory process if one is interested in individual accident performance. Accident statistics based on group data are more reliable. Daniels and Edgerton (1954) validated ratings by superiors against the percent of damaged vehicles in motor units, and found a significant relationship. But Ronan (1963) again finds no consistent factor structure for his injury index (visits per year) and lost time accidents in his analysis of multiple criteria.

The problem of the base for accident figures is worse than that for absence figures. One can compute accidents per hours worked, pieces produced, miles driven or flown, or trips taken, giving entirely different results. Like any other errors, including mistakes in executive decisions, more errors will be made with more opportunity for error, and hence the rate should be taken into account. On the other hand, it seems reasonable to penalize a person for moving too rapidly and taking unwarranted risks of error.

The decision to use one base or another should be a logical one having to do with what treatments, conditions, or measures are to be related to the criterion. Accidents are relatively immediate, specific results. (See Cell 10.)

Tenure or Turnover

Length of service has been used as a criterion in many test validation studies, and has proved to be predictable. A complete review of the literature up to 1964, including the studies of predictive validity, is given by Schuh (1967). Turnover, sometimes defined as the number of terminations divided by the average number in the working force and sometimes as the average number of terminations and accessions divided by the average number in the working force, is used to assess the effectiveness of groups, or of supervisors of groups. In any case the decision of an employee to terminate is a long-term decision, but moderately specific, and belongs at the right middle of the results "slab" (see Cell 11). It should not be expected to respond to minor changes, such as shifting the schedule of rest pauses.

Turnover is related to the alternative job openings that are available (Behrend, 1953; Tiffin & Phelan, 1953; Stark, 1959) and hence may reflect factors beyond the control of management. It is apparently not related to absences but is related to productivity (Argyle, Gardner, & Cioffi, 1958). It will continue to be popular and important as a criterion because of its obvious relationship to costs and returns, and hence, to organizational goals.

Sales

For evaluating performance of sales personnel, actual dollar sales are an obvious choice as a criterion. But it, too, has pitfalls. For example, Rush (1953) found four factors in fifteen scales measuring sales knowledge and performance in different ways, three of these involving different measures of sales. It makes a difference, for example, whether we measure percentage of quota achieved or average monthly volume. Taylor, Schneider, and Symons (1953) found similarly that basic salary for salesmen was a more predictable criterion than bonus earnings (in a system supposedly adjusting for differences in ability). When we go to studies of differences in groups, we find fairly good reliability of measures of group turnover and sales productivity per man (Weitz & Nuckols, 1953). State by state, clusters of nineteen measures showed five factors, including the absolute size of the state. This factor illustrates an important problem in the use of sales as a criterion: It should be adjusted in some way for the potential of the sales territory. Ideally, we would have actual norms for each territory, so that performance could be compared with the norms, but accumulation of such data is difficult, and ratings of difficulty of territory have to be substituted. This criterion would appear to be a fairly long-term, fairly general result. (See Cell 11.)

Production

Direct measures of output would seem to be closest to organizational goals and most desirable to use as criteria. They are short term and moderately general. (See Cell 9.) They are very effective in the ideal (for psychologists) situation in which there is only one job in the entire population to be examined, as in the handkerchief factory studied by Smith and Gold (1956) in which half the employees ran the handkerchiefs through the machines the long way and the other half ran them crossways with the same average production for each group. But that is not at all typical in the working world. Often, in order to enhance sample size, similar but different jobs are combined and must, therefore, be put on a comparable basis. This equating requires that for each job we estimate what is "normal" production, and express productivity as a ratio to normal or standard. Herein lies the rub.

Time study of the jobs must precede the setting of standard rates of production, and this study must include some rating of the effort and skill of the person who is observed and timed. (For a clear description see Krick, 1962.) This rating is rife with errors of rating (see, for example, Argyle,

Gardner, & Ciotti, 1958; Lifson, 1953; Ryan, 1947). These errors are perhaps one reason that records of production have not proven to be as useful or as popular for criterion purposes as was once hoped (Schultz & Siegel, 1961).

A related criterion is the length and shape of learning curves. Lefkowitz (1970) showed the effect of training on productivity of sewing machine operators, as did Smith and Taylor (1956). In both studies the progress of learning was not linear. Thus, a criterion measure should be taken in relation to the actual learning curve rather than a linear rate of progression. It is also probable that learning curves should be evaluated for each element of a complex skill, since certain elements respond more to practice than others do (Barnes, 1963). Rates of improvement in test performance also may occur at different rates for various elements making up the performance (e.g., Salvendy, Seymour, & Corlett, 1970). Again, the shapes of acquisition curves are discerned only with difficulty, and the criterion should be developed only with the help and judgment of a number of careful judges. They are relatively long-term and moderately general results (see Cell 12).

Job Level and Promotions

The extent to which an individual reaches a high or higher job level has been used as a criterion, a fairly long-term and global or general one, on the results "slab" (see Cell 13). The extent to which promotions are a valid criterion is limited by the fact that many factors other than performance may affect promotions, such as political expediency, organizational structure, and labor market conditions. Nevertheless, promotions represent a chips-on-the-board decision concerning the value of a person to the organization. Job level should be evaluated in terms of some standard job evaluation scheme. However, actual promotions are frequently not based on performance evaluation, but rather word-of-mouth and other informal evaluations, and hence, may reflect many situational factors (Campbell, Dunnette, Lawler, & Weick, 1970). Nevertheless, job level has been used by several investigators including Henry (1948) and Bentz (1968) with success. It should be corrected for years in service as we shall see below.

Salary

The same rationale—that actual operational decisions have been based on performance—makes salary level an appealing criterion, particularly at the managerial and professional levels. Bingham and Davis (1924) and Gifford (1928) used dollars as a criterion. The recognition of the importance of years on the job appeared explicitly somewhat later. A significant, if inadequately statistically documented book, is that of Jaques (1961), concerning the normal progression curves for equitable payment. A follow-up in the United States, accompanied by means and variances, is certainly warranted. Jaques examined, for a number of employees, their salary gains and computed lines of best fit for persons starting at a given initial level. Relationships between obtained curves and extrapolated curves are certainly impressive. Years seem to be related curvilinearly to gains in salary, but, more importantly, the relationship seems to be predictable. It takes a major change in job level to break the steady normal progression of salary with age. (Don't take a job below your proper asking price; you won't make it up later.)

This steady increase with age has led to corrections of job or promotional level according to years of tenure. Hulin (1962) used a number of corrections, the most sophisticated of which was probably obtaining the difference between salary increase and the salary increase predicted on the basis of tenure.

Even corrected, this criterion runs the risk of contamination, since many factors besides individual merit may influence salary. For example, internal politics, or scarcity of personnel in a special field may affect the situation. Nonetheless, it represents a long-term, global result (see Cell 14).

Soft Criteria

As we have seen, the so-called hard criteria all involve some subjective components. Human judgment enters into every criterion from productivity to salary increases. Merit rating as well as evaluation of causes of accidents or absences involves a subjective evaluation. In this process, some common errors exist. Many rating procedures have been developed which attempt to reduce or eliminate these errors.

Common Errors

LENIENCY AND SEVERITY. The first common error is that of leniency. Ratings tend to be bunched toward the favorable end of the rating scales. The average person is rated as above average, making for a displacement of the mean, and skewness. The reasons are multiple. In the first place, there is real selection of persons to be rated. The worst have actually been fired or transferred. Moreover, the rater is usually in the position of judging his own competence along with that of the person being rated; if a superior rates his subordinates as incompetent, it reflects upon his own competence as a supervisor. These factors, together with normal human kindness, make for a bunching at the favorable end of the rating scales (Thorndike, 1949; Bass, 1956; Sharon & Bartlett, 1969).

The opposite can also occur: One way to appear good is to devalue the people around you, and this mechanism can affect ratings—the error of severity. This error can be detected only by a low mean rating and positive skewness. Again, this error is very hard to detect because what is really needed is a number of ratings of different groups.

SEQUENTIAL EFFECTS. The judgment of an item on a rating scale may be affected by the items which precede it, either more or less favorably. This error can be controlled only by randomizing orders of presentation.

DISTRIBUTION ERRORS. These represent deviations from the expected more or less normal distribution curve. The errors usually indicate failure to discriminate. When persons or products are being rated, the ratings tend to pile up in the middle of the distribution. (This error may be compounded with the errors of severity or leniency to give a leptokurtic and skewed distribution.) When items describing people are being rated, raters tend to pile up *items* at the *ends* of the scales, avoiding the middle (Cliff, 1959; Rotter & Tinkleman, 1970). It is difficult to write neutral items, as has been reported by attitude scalers, although Obradović (1970) seems to have managed to locate items of approximately neutral attractiveness. The trick seems to be to write double-barreled statements or very general ones. Anchoring statements on the scale on which items are to be rated will shift the distribution—a positive anchor making for a shift from neutral to negative, and vice versa. In any case, the distributions of ratings should be checked before they are used.

INTERCORRELATIONAL ERRORS. The first such error is the all-pervasive halo effect, which means that rating on one characteristic spills over to affect ratings on other characteristics, resulting in high intercorrelations among ratings for supposedly different characteristics or behaviors. Halo can be either favorable or unfavorable—it merely represents the failure of the rater to differentiate. The prevalence of the error has been frequently reported. Two examples will suffice. Turner (1960) factor analyzed twenty different measures of criterion performance of foremen, and found two factors, one involving all the ratings (halo), and the other involving employee relationships, including nonrating measures. Vielhaber and Gottheil (1965) found, amusingly, a correlation of .31 between ratings based only on name and home address and ratings by peers and superiors after fourteen weeks at West Point.

Contributing to halo are the effects of contrast and similarity. Some raters rate in relationship to their own self-ratings—either contrasting others to themselves or assuming similarity to themselves. Training seems to be the solution.

The logical error is more difficult to handle. It is difficult to tell when it is an error and when it is a legitimate inference. The individual rater has a pattern of correlations which he assumes among traits in others, and which remains when the effect of halo is removed through partial correlation (Koltuv, 1962). Without such a set of assumptions, hardly any rating would be possible; the problem is to eliminate false generalizations or at least to systematize the assumptions held. There is considerable agreement concerning the structure of personality, both for complete strangers and for persons well known to each other (Passini & Norman, 1966, 1969). This fact gives some hope for retaining the valid intercorrelations and eliminating the idiosyncratic ones. Psychologists have been misled, in my opinion, by the hope that traits and factors on jobs would prove to be orthogonal, when in reality they are intercorrelated to greater or lesser degrees. This intercorrelation does not mean that they cannot be assessed separately; it means only that the final results will be interrelated.

Types of Rating Scales

Rating scales can be classified along each of the dimensions we have proposed for criteria, and scales can be constructed to fit any of the cells we have discussed. They can be directed toward very short or very long time spans. They can be very specific, or quite global covering only an overall estimate of performance. And they can be directed toward behavior or toward organizational goals. But they need to be classified further.

Most of these classifications have to do

with format which may have relatively little effect on the resulting evaluation. Blumberg, DeSoto, and Kuethe (1966) found remarkably small effect of rating scale format, although raters, ratees, traits, and some of their interactions were significant. Stockford and Bissell (1967), on the other hand, found "a marked influence on the value of ratings" when descriptive scales were compared with the less effective evaluative scales. This finding agrees with that of Yuzuk (1961). Madden and Bourdon (1964) also found differences in results from different formats, with no general principle emerging. Hence, we must consider format seriously.

DIRECT ESTIMATION. Direct estimation of evaluative level is made using formats that ask directly the question, how good is the ratee? The answer may be recorded on a graphic scale typically running from left to right with a few verbal anchors such as excellent, good, average, poor, and unsatisfactory placed beneath the scale, although in its pure form it has anchors only at the extremes. Some more specific scales have been constructed vertically, with the good end at the top (Champney, 1941; Smith & Kendall, 1963), which has the advantage of permitting more detailed verbal anchors to be inserted along the scale. In any case, the method is characterized by estimating psychological distance directly by measuring distance along the linear scale. Numeric scales evaluate by asking for a number to represent the level of performance, and are usually combined with some verbal anchoring system (Blumberg et al., 1966). Similarly, alphabetic scales use letters of the alphabet (which are characteristically later transformed into numbers). Some of the direct estimation scales use verbal anchors directly, and later transform these into numbers. A novel symbolic rating scale is the General Motors "Faces" scale (Kunin, 1955), which represents a series of faces from a scowling frown to a pleased grin. Checks made on this symbolic scale, too, are transformed into numbers.

RANKING. Ordering of persons can be achieved, without asking for direct estimations of distance along a scale, by some version of ranking. For example, persons to be evaluated may be simply ranked from best to poorest along any relevant dimension(s). These ranks may be treated under a number of assumptions (see Guilford, 1954, pp. 178–195) to give more direct estimations of distances between persons, and to permit the combination of rankings of different persons by more than one rater. Or every individual (ratee) may be paired with every other individual (ratee) to permit pair comparisons, and respondents' preferences may be treated (see Lawshe, Kephart, & McCormick, 1949; Guilford, 1954, pp. 154–176; Edwards, 1957; Torgerson, 1958) to yield psychological distance between the ratees. Though one of the best of the scaling methods psychometrically, this method has the disadvantage of requiring a large number of judgments per judge (all possible pairs of ratees) and considerable computation. Another method to achieve ordering is the use of forced distribution ratings—requiring the rater to put a fixed percentage of persons into each of several categories, on the assumption of a normal distribution. This assumption is so seldom warranted in the actual industrial situation where people have been discharged, promoted, and cajoled to increase productivity in relation to their previous performance that this method is not recommended. The method has also been shown to be affected by rater bias (Klores, 1966).

TEST CONSTRUCTION METHODS. These can be used to achieve a scale of cumulative points. This approach implies that norms will be used to achieve an estimate of distance between persons. The most common procedure is to use an unweighted check list in which adjectives or descriptive statements are merely checked as applying or not applying to the individual being rated. Each favorable response is given a positive weight and each unfavorable one typically a zero weight to

give a total score. The old scale by Hartshorne and May (1929) is an example of an unweighted scale. So also is the very much more sophisticated critical incidents approach (Flanagan, 1954; Buel, 1960), which involves collecting examples of good and bad behaviors which are to be used as a check list for evaluation. The advantage of this approach is the emphasis on observation of behavior. The disadvantages are the difficulty in obtaining actual concrete behaviors that can be observed and noted. Except in the military situation, it has become necessary to use broad generalizations, losing the huge advantage of emphasis on observation.

The use of expected behaviors (Smith & Kendall, 1963) rather than actual observations at least permits observers to generalize from specific observations to other specific predictions of behavior so that actual behavior is incorporated in the rating procedure. That judges indicate the dimension to which each expected behavior pertains facilitates clarity of scale definition. The scaling of expectations permits one method of weighting behaviors.

There are several approaches to weighting of a scale. Some examples of weighted scales are those of Ferguson (1947), Knauft (1948), and Uhrbrock (1950, 1961). Ferguson (1947) scaled a number of statements about managers by a modified method of equal appearing intervals (Richardson & Kuder, 1933) to establish a weighted scale of success. This method gave a scale that proved useful in evaluating managers in a variety of situations with different raters reporting. Knauft (1948) simplified the procedure by eliminating the comparison with an external criterion measure and established alternate forms of scales for two jobs. The last big step in weighting of items was made by Uhrbrock (1961), who scaled 2,000 (presumably) all-purpose items. (His first scaling was concerned only with foremen, but this restriction is not made clear in his last report.) His efforts were aimed at forced-choice matching of items (see below), but his items, scaled by equal-appearing intervals, could just as well be used for a weighted check list. On the assumption of an underlying overall dimension of goodness, he has furnished us with a pool of items for use in constructing a weighted check list of descriptions of behavior for almost any job—so long as we wish a global rating.

Any of these can be transformed into an unweighted scale, simply by using unitary weights. There is no strong evidence that weighting actually improves the psychometric properties of a scale. A common approach is to "score" a ratee according to the median scale value of the items chosen by the rater as being descriptive of his job performance. A potential problem in the use of the median has been pointed out by Jurgensen (1949). If an individual ratee has been given credit for a large number of positive items, his median score will actually be lower than that of a ratee who was endorsed for only a few very highly rated items. Jurgensen recommends instead a strictly algebraic weighted score.

Semantic differential scales are a type of weighted check list in which weightings are obtained at the same time as ratings. The individuals are described along seven-point bipolar scales covering a dimension of meaning (Osgood, Suci, & Tannenbaum, 1957). Performance is described according to locations on scales defined by pairs of bipolar adjectives (such as *good* ... *bad*). The scales are not really equal-interval scales (Heise, 1969), and they are not *always* bipolar (Mordkoff, 1965). There seems to be no great advantage over simple unweighted check lists or direct numerical rating scales.

ITEMS AS SCALED STANDARDS. The psychologist may set up a series of items as scaled standards against which an individual may be judged. These items may be used as anchors, usually along a graphic rating scale. For a global rating scale, Uhrbrock's (1961) items seem ideally suited. I once attempted to scale adjectives by the method of paired comparisons so that they might be used as scaled anchors for an evaluative rating scale. A deficiency of the method became apparent: the adjectives were pre-screened by normal item analysis techniques for low dispersions of ratings; the items became unscalable by paired comparisons because there was insufficient overlap of judgments.

Forced choice is a special technique designed to reduce the effects of rating errors and faking (Sisson, 1948). The procedure involves the presentation of groups of items matched for general desirability but differentiated in terms of their predictive performance against some overall criterion (for formats, see Guilford, 1954, pp. 154–176). Forced choice ratings are perhaps more valid and less susceptible to faking (Taylor & Wherry, 1951; Izard & Rosenberg, 1958; Zavala, 1965; Scott, 1968) than more direct rating scales, but still subject to bias (Travers, 1951; Kay, 1959; Howe & Silverstein, 1960; Howe, 1960). Four positively worded statements proved a valid, reliable, bias-resistant and acceptable format (Berkshire & Highland, 1953). There is some convergent validity (Taylor, Schneider, & Clay, 1954; Prien & Kult, 1968). The use of items of neutral attractiveness proved valid (Obradović, 1970) against a forced distribution rating. The forced choice format requires pretesting items for desirability, and is based on the belief that raters must be deceived concerning what they are rating and the interpretation of the rating. It also gives a global summary rating of performance. It is opposed to the multiple-measured approach recommended in the present presentation.

The forced-choice format attempts to overcome the errors of leniency or severity by concealing from the rater the meaning of his ratings. This is done by constructing rating scales such that it is not immediately obvious how different responses are scored. This effort to conceal the scoring system has, in practice, often led to a contest between the administrator and the rater. A rater, intent on giving favorable ratings, can beat the system, however, merely by rating each person in the same way as a formerly rated and high-scoring person. Any attempt to interpret scores or to give feedback to the ratee is also made very difficult by the concealed scoring system inherent in the approach.

The matching of alternatives according to social desirability also poses a problem since judged desirability depends upon the situation and the judges. The whole field of attitude measurement depends upon these differences, which undercut forced-choice matchings.

Forced choice also introduces another systematic source of error. In a typical combination of four alternatives in forced choice, two are dead items, used only as decoys. These items also attract positive endorsements. For example, "honest" may be a nonscored (nondifferentiating between high and low ratees) item, although it may be legitimately endorsed about a very good candidate. This effect introduces error variance. I prefer a more direct and more specific method of evaluation.

Results from forced-choice ratings belong at various places on the cube, depending entirely on the items included.

Another technique is that of scaled expectations (Smith & Kendall, 1963; Maas, 1965; Kendall & Hilton, 1965; Dunnette, Campbell, & Hellervik, 1968; Fogli, Hulin, & Blood, 1971), which sets up a scale for each dimension to be rated on desirability of behaviors which the rater might expect a ratee to demonstrate. These scaled behaviors serve as anchors for raters who have agreed upon the desirability and the dimension which each item represents. The scales are used with raters similar to or preferably the same as those who construct the scales. The advantages of the procedure are use of the raters' own terms, the specificity of the behavior rated, the emphasis upon observation, the lack of ambiguity of meaning of the anchors, and high scale reliabilities (in the upper .90s). The disadvantage is the necessity for collaboration of a number of raters in constructing the scales

—a disadvantage that may well be a psychological advantage due to the training achieved.

INDIVIDUALS AS SCALED STANDARDS. An early example was the man-to-man scale (Guilford, 1954, pp. 269–270). This scaling method used actual people as anchors against which employees were to be compared. Ideally, the same anchor men should be used in all departments doing the rating, permitting comparison from department to department. The difficulties encountered were primarily lack of knowledge of the same key men by different raters and inequality of units from man to man. Ross (1966) has solved these problems and proposed a modern man-to-man scale suitable for overall, global ratings of performance based on a two-pronged approach. Each rater in an organization ranks not only his own subordinates, but also non-subordinates (reference persons) in other departments with whom he has had recent contact who are comparable to benchmark persons in his own department. Moreover, all evaluations of benchmarks are transformed to V values, a type of standard score based on the rank of the individual within the reference group, and his overall standard score (transformed from ranks within his own department) for general performance, job level, and educational level. The procedure permits cross-referencing of ratings by different raters with different groups of subordinates, and takes into account the anchoring of individual rating scales. It seems to be a practical solution to the criterion problem when a single global criterion is wanted, although it would seem to be unwieldy for the construction of separate scales for different characteristics.

CONSTRUCTING SCALES. For most criterion problems, scales have to be constructed especially for the particular research or administrative purpose involved. Overall evaluation is suitable for discharge, promotion, and similar decisions. Most research, counseling, training, or transfer decisions require separate scales for separate dimensions of performance. Several investigators have recommended that the scales should be descriptive rather than evaluative (e.g., Flanagan, 1954; Smith & Kendall, 1963). Stockford and Bissell (1967) report that descriptive scales are "more reliable, less influenced by bias, and show less deviation in leniency and severity than is characteristic of ratings on 'subjective' or *evaluative* scales." Scales should be defined briefly and so also should levels within each scale (Madden, 1964). There is disagreement about whether it is worthwhile to scale the anchors more finely than favorable-unfavorable (e.g., Bass, 1956), although the idea of scaling has proved to be beguiling (Uhrbrock, 1950, 1961; Smith & Kendall, 1963). Actually the entire attitude-scaling literature is relevant to measurement of attitudes toward employees (cf., Edwards, 1957; Torgerson, 1958; Fishbein, 1967).

There are two psychometric problems that arise in anchoring scales: locating defining statements on the correct scale and at the right place on that scale. An attempt to solve these problems is retranslation of expectations. Briefly, the persons who are to rate indicate and define the dimensions along which descriptions are to be made. They then write examples of behavior to be expected of persons along each scale. Other raters independently allocate these examples to the dimensions to see if there is agreement as to their meaning. Independently, they are assigned numbers to indicate position along the relevant scale. Examples (and scales) about which there is low agreement are eliminated (Smith & Kendall, 1963; Fogli, Hulin, & Blood, 1971). The procedure leads to examples with high scale reliabilities.

Training of Raters

The success of these anchoring procedures depends in my opinion on the training of the raters. Attempts to use the scales by persons who had not been trained in rating resulted in relatively low success (Hakel, 1966).

Training should include instruction on the principles of rating, participation in selection of items and follow-up. Such training "raises the reliability of, and reduces the effects of bias on, the merit ratings that are given their subordinates" (Stockford & Bissell, 1967). In the Smith and Kendall (1963) study, extensive conferences were held covering rating errors, observation, and implications of observed behavior for future behavior. Raters participated—and that is important—in defining the areas to be evaluated, in defining the levels of each area, in writing examples of behavior, in allocating examples to areas, and in indicating the scale value of each example. A crucial aspect is the observation and recording of relevant behaviors. Another important aspect is the fact that conferences on evaluation seem a natural forum for participative discussion of supervisory practices.

Who Should Observe and Evaluate?

No amount of training can improve a rater if that rater has had no opportunity to observe the ratee's behavior. This fact makes the choice of the rater crucial. The choice is usually made on the basis of expediency rather than potential accuracy of rating. Yet the rater is more important than the technique (Bayroff, Haggerty, & Rundquist, 1954).

QUALIFICATION OF RATERS. There are some data on qualifications of good raters. The obvious takes place: superior intelligence and effectiveness are associated with less biased and more reliable ratings (e.g., Schneider & Bayroff, 1953; Stockford & Bissell, 1967). Some people are consistently better in terms of validity of ratings than others (Wiley & Jenkins, 1964). Familiarity of rater with ratee is also a key factor in quality of rating (Besco & Lawshe, 1959). The relation of initiating structure to consideration is related to variability of ratings, emphasis on production, overall level of rating, and absence of leniency (Klores, 1966).

More effective managers valued initiative, persistence, broad knowledge, innovation, and planning as contrasted with less effective supervisors, who emphasized cooperation, company loyalty, teamwork, accepting suggestions, and tact and consideration (Kirchner & Reisberg, 1962). Stockford and Bissell (1967) found that in their study the ratings reflected "primarily the personal-social relationships between supervisor and subordinate rather than the output of the subordinate in question."

SUPERIORS. The answer to the question of who should rate has usually been the immediate supervisor, and possibly a more remote one. All of the previously cited literature concerns such ratings. They have the advantages of face validity, acceptability, and availability, although it is frequently difficult to find more than one rater familiar enough with the ratee to achieve an independent estimate of reliability. There is frequent reason to question the actual opportunity by the supervisor to observe behavior on the job. There are alternatives.

PEERS. The most popular alternative is peer rating. Peer (or "buddy") ratings take two principal forms—the nomination of peers as best or poorest on some dimension or ranking from best to poorest (Hollander, 1954). The earliest applications were to military leadership and were concerned with the *prediction* of success in Officers' Candidate School and combat performance (with notable success). The early evidence is well summarized by Hollander (1954). The ratings do not reflect merely popularity (Wherry & Fryer, 1949; Hollander, 1956, 1965). Nevertheless, Doll and Longo (1962) corrected peer ratings for perceived "antisocial" characteristics of ratees to increase predictive validity. Peer ratings are valid even when administered with an administrative set (Hollander, 1957). Peer ratings are more stable over time than supervisors' (sergeants') ratings (Gordon & Medlund, 1965). French (1954) developed a single reliable criterion based on a combination of ratings by officers, upperclassmen, and classmates.

Civilian applications are fewer. Again, predictive validity was established against promotion (Roadman, 1964). Tucker, Cline, and Schmitt (1967) found no convergent validity between peer ratings and superior ratings. Peer ratings seem to be tapping a different source and/or type of information even though French (1954) did see fit to develop a combined criterion from peer and superior ratings. Peer ratings should probably be examined as separate criteria particularly for leadership (Wherry & Fryer, 1949). Additional industrial applications are needed, especially in identification of leadership potential. The threat to management of allowing nominations from the rank and file is undoubtedly responsible for hesitancy in the use of peer ratings. They should, nevertheless, be considered seriously. Peers, after all, have the opportunity to observe. Borman (1974) showed, in fact, that peers and superiors not only provide different perceptions of job performance but that they actually evaluate different aspects of performance in very different ways. Moreover, superiors' ratings of subordinates suffered reduced reliability when the superiors used scales which had been developed by subordinates. Similarly, the peer ratings provided by subordinates of each other suffered from low reliability when they were based on the scales developed by superiors.

SUBORDINATES. Ratings by subordinates do not agree with superiors' ratings (Fleishman, Harris, & Burtt, 1955; Rambo, 1958; Besco & Lawshe, 1959; Tucker et al., 1967) although they identify some aspects of promotability (Mann & Dent, 1954). Besco and Lawshe (1959) compared ratings of leadership (Rambo, 1958) by employees and general foremen with ratings by higher managers concerning departmental effectiveness. Superiors' ratings were related only to consideration. Superiors' and subordinates' ratings are tapping different dimensions of performance. Perhaps more information can be obtained from the classroom situation, where the resistance to subordinates' ratings is probably less.

SELF. Self-ratings have been even less used —except in the enormous job satisfaction literature. In performance evaluation, they have been avoided because of the obvious possibility of bias. Kirchner (1966) found a significant (if low) relationship between superior and self-ratings. Thornton (1968) found a bias in favor of self, and a relationship of that bias to lack of promotability, despite a positive correlation on some characteristics between superior and self-ratings. Lawler (1967) on the other hand found disagreement between self-ratings and both peer and supervisors' ratings. The use of self-ratings in performance appraisal interviews is emphasized by Bassett and Meyer (1968). They used self-ratings as a basis of an interview with the ratee, and report less defensiveness and fewer complaints with the procedure. It is in their sort of counseling setting that self-appraisals seem most promising.

JOB SATISFACTION. Job satisfaction is a goal in itself. It has been evaluated in numerous ways (see Chapter 30 in this *Handbook*) with differing results. We can refer again to Figure 1. Job satisfaction measures can vary, particularly on the time span dimension. Measures taken in the framework of a short time span can be expected to relate to short-term behaviors such as tardiness or rest pauses, while measures with a long-term reference can be expected to relate to long-term behaviors such as terminations and job choice. Job satisfaction should serve as a criterion for evaluation of such treatments as leadership training, organizational structure, communications networks, and job enrichment. The self-evaluation seems to be the logical choice for such criteria.

ASSESSMENT OBSERVERS. Evaluation can be made by psychologists or management personnel in assessment centers, in which situational exercises may be engaged in, testing

may take place, and group discussions may be held. It is difficult to determine whether the measures are criterion or predictive measures; they are sometimes one and sometimes the other. That they can have predictive validity against more remote criteria (about Cell 7 against Cell 13) has been demonstrated by Grant and Bray (1966). Predictive validity has been demonstrated also for salesmen (Bray & Campbell, 1968).

EXAMINATION OF OUTCOME: IMPROVING INFERENCE

We now proceed to the outcomes or organizational effectiveness slab. Here we are concerned with decisions based on inferences from results. These inferences involve moving from either hard or soft criteria to decisions concerning organizational effectiveness. They usually involve combining several criteria.

The Problem of Weighting

Direct Weighting by Management

Management makes the decisions concerning courses of action to be taken on the basis of evidence. But the choice of how to weight different aspects of evidence to form the decision is usually quite unsystematic. The psychologist can help by asking for formal judgments of the amount of weight to be placed on various aspects of results or evidence contributing to the decision. These judgments may be either objective or highly subjective. The mere formalization of policy helps, but is difficult to obtain.

Policy Capturing

Sometimes the psychologist can help by using statistical techniques to "capture" the weighting given by management to various items of information. We have discussed policy capturing previously, but here we are concerned with its application to organizational effectiveness. Here, artificial stimuli or simulated aspects of evidence believed to be part of the decision matrix can be presented to executives who will be asked to make hypothetical decisions based on their own views of which combinations may lead to greatest organizational effectiveness. This essentially is the strategy used by Borman and Dunnette (1974) when they sought judgments from Naval officers about the relative effectiveness of the personnel subsystems of 100 simulated ships. Then, the decision process can be made more systematic in at least two ways, based on the predictive equations summarizing the judges' evaluations: First, future decisions might be turned over to computers; and second, feedback could be given to the executives in training sessions focused on helping them to improve the consistency of their own judgments (Slovic & Lichtenstein, 1971). In these days when complex decisions related to such matters as air pollution and public opinion have to be balanced against immediate corporate profits, research in this broad area is sorely needed.

The Dollar Criterion

The use of immediate corporate profits as a criterion becomes less and less plausible. We need criteria that reflect the societal and long-term organizational goals as well as the economic ones. It is important, nonetheless, that the psychologist working in industry apply some cost accounting to his work—that is, if he prefers to retain his job during recessions. He is referred to Likert and Seashore (1963) and a good accounting text for his do-it-yourself kit. The dollar criterion, as Brogden and Taylor (1950) formulated it, seems to belong to a fairly immediate, general criterion of organizational effectiveness (about Cell 15).

The Problem of Contamination-Deficiency

The problem of contamination and deficiency is most urgent at the level of organizational effectiveness. We can include unwanted sources of variance in our organizational measures, as, for example, ethnic, racial, political, and familial preferences, and we can exclude other, particularly long-term sources, such as planning for the future R&D efforts. (One firm actually forbids the purchase of capital equipment unless it can be paid for out of annual profits in that operating unit!) To the extent to which contamination occurs, the criterion measure tends to drift off the chart shown in Figure 1. Deficiency leads it toward the immediate and specific (try Cell 16). This problem is what Astin (1964) called the problem of conceptual criteria.

In one sense, this problem is the central problem of criteria. If operational decisions are based on contaminated or deficient grounds, no degree of care in the results or behaviors segments will preserve organizational effectiveness. The operational problem here is that we have nothing to lean on but administrative judgment, which can build an Edsel out of pieces of reasonably sound criterion research.

Validation by the Multitrait-Multimethod Matrix

The validity of a particular method of measuring a criterion variable may be determined relatively efficiently by evaluation of convergent and discriminant validity (Campbell & Fiske, 1959). Briefly, a measure should agree with other measures of the same trait more closely than with measures using the same method of measurement designed to measure different traits. In factor analytic terms, the measure should load more highly on a trait factor than on a method factor. The factor approach in my opinion is less susceptible to the effects of small fluctuations in the size of correlation coefficients than the Campbell-Fiske model. Either the inspection of the correlation matrix or factor analysis will evaluate the extent to which a measure is central to the concept being evaluated. Either requires the time to take multiple measures using a variety of methods, which will not be popular with management.

Most criteria have not been validated at all; they have been established by fiat. Convergence and discrimination seem to be minimal requirements before an entire decision-making process is to be constructed on the basis of a measure. A little salesmanship by the psychologist to management is in order here.

The Dynamic Nature of Criteria

The time dimension in Figure 1 is an important one. The "same" measure has different factorial structure at different points in time (Fleishman & Hempel, 1954; Fleishman & Fruchter, 1960). Ghiselli (1956) has emphasized that relations between tests and criteria are not necessarily stable, and that changes in performance occur over very long periods of time.

Longitudinal studies of criteria in actual practice are in order. This is one task for psychologists in industry who can undertake longitudinal projects, and who have the courage to sell them to management. Only when we have real-life studies of the relative stability of relationships between treatments or predictors and criteria over time can we know when to generalize from a single study to a general problem. We live in a time in which it is necessary to use law to enforce even one-shot test validations, and in which experimenters use college sophomores in one-hour laboratory experiments to generalize to the world of the long working life of people. Studies such as those of Fleishman and Fruchter (1960) on telegraphers in which the structure of abilities changed with both treatments and abilities need to be extended. There, the actual observed behaviors shifted with time and, consequently, so did the relationship of a (various) predictor(s) with a criterion (criteria).

Managers, with the help of psychologists, need to decide at what stage(s) in progress measures should be taken as criteria. This decision should invoke all of the considerations involved in the time dimension.

Individual Styles

The results slab involves the combination of behaviors into results. This combination is complicated by the fact that different people achieve an end of the same value by a different combination of behaviors. Ghiselli (1956) emphasized this problem of personal styles in limiting prediction of performance by a single regression equation of tests (or behaviors) against a single criterion measure. One manager achieves production by a strong emphasis on human relations, for example, while another emphasizes production control. Ghiselli implies that subjects be separated according to styles and that prediction be attempted only within a given style. This procedure, unfortunately, greatly diminishes the N. It holds the promise, however, of raising our obtained relationships.

Use of Criteria in Counseling

Development of employees (or managers) by feeding back the strong and weak points in their performance as indicated by criterion measures and devising plans for improvement has been one of the explicit aims of top management. Yet, the procedure is seldom used. One of the reasons is that criteria developed for administrative purposes are personally very threatening and discussion of them leads to defensiveness and deflation (Meyer, Kay, & French, 1965). Defensiveness can be reduced by making sure the person evaluated can participate in planning for his own improvement (Meyer et al., 1965; French, Kay, & Meyer, 1966; Bassett & Meyer, 1968). But, it seems desirable to separate the salary evaluation aspects of rating from the counseling aspects.

Successful combination of administrative (promotional) and counseling interviews has been reported in an assessment center (Acker & Perlson, 1971) perhaps because these applicants were volunteers for the program. At any rate, counseling, to an even greater degree than research, requires that multiple criteria be gathered which are psychologically discriminable and capable of being communicated effectively.

How to Determine an Organizational Criterion

The procedure for developing a criterion has been clearly summarized by Guion:

1. Analyze the job and/or the organizational needs by new, yet-to-be-developed techniques.
2. Develop measures of actual behavior relative to the behavior expected, as identified in job and need analysis. These measures are to supplement measures of the consequences of work—the so-called objective criteria commonly tried at present.
3. Identify the criterion dimensions underlying such measures by factor analysis or cluster analysis or pattern analysis.
4. Develop reliable measures, each with high construct validity, of the elements so identified.
5. For each independent variable (predictor), determine its predictive validity for *each one* of the foregoing criterion measures, taking them one at a time. (Guion, 1961, p. 148)

This procedure allows judgment concerning weighting of different criteria *after* the empirical data are in—finally allowing some weighting according to predictability. Movement to the organizational "slab" occurs only when behaviors and results have been analyzed.

RECURRENT PROBLEMS

Relevance and Reliability of Observation and Rating

Observation and interpretation hold the key to establishment of effective criteria. These are related to the convergence and discriminability of both the observational measures and the combined rating that results from those observations.

Establishing the reliability of judgments is essential, as is the correlation of behaviors with results and results with organizational effectiveness. These steps have seldom been performed; investigators would improve their effectiveness if they would do so.

Who Should Evaluate?

As our discussion has indicated, most criteria boil down to ratings. The crucial recurrent problem is who should rate. The first level requires that those people rate who have observed actual behavior, which strongly suggests peer ratings. The second level requires inferences from the first, which suggests supervisors' ratings. The third level is managerial, and is poorly represented in our diagram. Here the psychologist can help pull the results together, but the final decision about how to use such judgments belongs to top management.

Multidimensionality and the Use of Multiple Measures

The search for *the* elusive criterion continues despite strong evidence that it does not exist. The fact of multidimensionality poses a practical problem at the level of organizational effectiveness. Various objectives have to be weighted in making decisions. Organizational goals have to be spelled out, including community responsibilities. Nowhere is this problem more evident than in the area of minority employment (see Chapter 18), where community goals are often in conflict with economic goals. Executive decisions have to be made.

Criteria for different purposes need to be separated. They should parallel the predictors or treatments in generality and immediacy. More than one measure should be taken if possible at the required level so that convergence can be evaluated.

Equivalence of Measures

Finally, one measure cannot be freely substituted for another without establishing equivalence, which means much more than high intercorrelation. It involves similar correlations with other variables and similar responses to treatments (see Gulliksen, 1950; Smith, Kendall, & Hulin, 1969, pp. 152–158; Smith, Smith, Baumgartel, Gliner, & Goodale, 1971). Thoughtless substitution of one rating for another or one measure of absences for another can greatly disrupt relationships with other variables and hence resulting decisions.

TOWARD AN INTEGRATION OF CRITERION MODELS

Three criterion models and the possibility of their integration through construct validation have been discussed by James (1973). Since the models discussed by James are the same as the ones presented in this chapter, a brief review of his comments and suggestions serves a useful summarizing role for what has been said here.

His discussion focuses on three criterion models: (1) the ultimate criterion model [as developed by Thorndike (1949) and as presented in this chapter]; (2) the multiple criterion model [as articulated by Ghiselli (1956), Guion (1961), Dunnette (1963), Wallace (1965), and Schmidt and Kaplan (1971) and discussed in this chapter]; and (3) the general criterion model represented by the view of managerial effectiveness presented by Campbell, Dunnette, Lawler, and Weick (1970). The last model differs from the multiple model only to the extent of specifying the major components and probable internal dynamics of the multiple measures required in efforts to understand performance effectiveness. In this sense, I have implied use of the general model throughout this chapter by specifying the various types and levels of measurement that may be desirable in any concerted effort to measure the facets of job performance.

The major thrust of James's argument is that the three models can best be melded into an integrated approach to analysis of criteria through the theory and technology of construct validation (Cronbach & Meehl,

1955). This follows directly the counsel of Kavanagh, MacKinney, and Wolins (1971) when they state that since the ultimate criterion "can best be described as a psychological construct ... the process of determining the relevance of the immediate to the ultimate criterion becomes one of construct validation" (p. 35). The case for construct validation as a central point of methodological and theoretical emphasis in criterion research and development is easy to make. Construct validation is the method of choice because it is the only way of understanding *what* is being measured by criteria which cannot be validated by the traditional methods of empirical validation. In particular, as pointed out by James (1973), "the need to identify criterion constructs becomes crucial whenever contaminated measures, such as ratings, are employed, especially multiple ratings from different sources, or whenever operationally defined objective criteria (typically global) are not available" (p. 79). In other words, an orientation toward construct validation in criterion research is the best way of guarding against a hopelessly incomplete job of criterion development. In essence, *all* the possible sources and measures of performance variation discussed in this chapter need to be given an opportunity to be studied within the nomological net of each ultimate criterion construct. These should include measures sampling all degrees of complexity, all relevant time periods, and all levels of measurement—behavioral, results, and organizational consequences. Coverage should include but not be restricted to such measures as behaviorally based performance ratings developed by and completed by several raters; objective measures of job performance, ability, motivation-satisfaction morale; measures of situational parameters; and global measures of organizational outcomes. A full and complete understanding of the ultimate constructs of performance effectiveness in any specific job-person-organization setting can best be gained by an ongoing and continuing program of construct validation.

REFERENCES

Acker, S. R., & Perlson, M. R. Can we sharpen our management of human resources? *Behavioral Sciences Applications,* Corporate Personnel Department, Olin Corporation, 1971.

Argyle, M., Gardner, G., & Cioffi, F. Supervisory methods related to productivity, absenteeism, and labour turnover. *Human Relations,* 1958, 11, 23–40.

Astin, A. W. Criterion-centered research. *Educational and Psychological Measurement,* 1964, 24, 807–822.

Barnes, R. M. *Motion and time study.* (5th ed.) New York: Wiley, 1963.

Bass, B. M. Reducing leniency in merit ratings. *Personnel Psychology,* 1956, 9, 359–369.

Bass, B. M. Further evidence on the dynamic character of criteria. *Personnel Psychology,* 1962, 15, 93–97.

Bassett, G. A., & Meyer, H. H. Performance appraisal based on self-review. *Personnel Psychology,* 1968, 21, 421–430.

Baumgartel, H., & Sobol, R. Background and organizational factors in absenteeism. *Personnel Psychology,* 1959, 12, 431–443.

Bayroff, A. G., Haggerty, H. R., & Rundquist, E. A. Validity of ratings as related to rating techniques and conditions. *Personnel Psychology,* 1954, 7, 93–114.

Behrend, H. Absence and turnover in a changing economic climate. *Occupational Psychology,* 1953, 27, 69–79.

Bentz, V. J. The Sears experience in the investigation, description, and prediction of executive behavior. In *Predicting managerial success.* Ann Arbor, Mich.: Foundation for Research in Human Behavior, 1968, 59–152.

Berkshire, J. R., & Highland, R. W. Forced-choice performance rating. *Personnel Psychology,* 1953, 6, 355–378.

Besco, R. O., & Lawshe, C. H. Foreman leadership as perceived by superiors and subordinates. *Personnel Psychology,* 1959, 12, 573–582.

Besnard, G. G., & Briggs, L. J. Measuring job proficiency by means of a performance test. In E. A. Fleishman (Ed.), *Studies in personnel and industrial psychology.* (Rev. ed.) Homewood, Ill.: Dorsey Press, 1967.

Biesheuvel, S. Personnel selection. *Annual Review of Psychology,* 1965, 16, 295–324.

Bingham, W. V., & Davis, W. T. Intelligence test scores and business success. *Journal of Applied Psychology,* 1924, 8, 1–22.

Blankenship, A. B., & Taylor, H. R. Prediction of vocational proficiency in three machine operations. *Journal of Applied Psychology,* 1938, 22, 518–526.

Blum, M. L., & Naylor, J. C. *Industrial psychology: Its theoretical and social foundations.* New York: Harper and Row, 1968, Chapter 7.

Blumberg, H. H., DeSoto, C. B., & Kuethe, J. L. Evaluation of rating scale formats. *Personnel Psychology,* 1966, 19, 243–259.

Borman, W. C. The rating of individuals in organizations: An alternate approach. *Organizational Behavior and Human Performance,* 1974, 12, 105–124.

Borman, W. C., & Dunnette, M. D. *Selection of components to comprise a Naval Personnel Status Index (NPSI) and a strategy for investigating their relative importance.* Minneapolis: Personnel Decisions, 1974.

Bray, D. W., & Campbell, R. J. Selection of salesmen by means of an assessment center. *Journal of Applied Psychology,* 1968, 52, 36–41.

Bray, D. W., & Moses, J. L. Personnel selection. *Annual Review of Psychology,* 1972, 23, 545–576.

Brogden, H. E., & Taylor, E. K. The dollar criterion: Applying the cost accounting concept to criterion construction. *Personnel Psychology,* 1950, 3, 133–154.

Buel, W. D. The validity of behavioral scale items for the assessment of individual creativity. *Journal of Applied Psychology,* 1960, 44, 407–412.

Campbell, D. T., & Fiske, D. W. Convergent and discriminant validation by the multi-trait-multimethod matrix. *Psychological Bulletin,* 1959, 56, 81–105.

Campbell, J. P., Dunnette, M. D., Lawler, E. E. III, & Weick, K. E. Jr. *Managerial behavior, performance, and effectiveness.* New York: McGraw-Hill, 1970.

Champney, H. The measurement of parent behavior. *Child Development,* 1941, 12, 131–166.

Christal, R. E. JAN: A technique for analyzing group judgment. *The Journal of Experimental Education,* 1968, 36, 24–27.

Cliff, N. Adverbs as multipliers. *Psychological Review*, 1959, 66, 27–44.

Cronbach, L. J., & Meehl, P. E. Construct validity in psychological tests. *Psychological Bulletin*, 1955, 62, 281–302.

Daniels, H. W., & Edgerton, H. A. The development of criteria of safe operation for groups. *Journal of Applied Psychology*, 1954, 38, 47–53.

Doll, R. E., & Longo, A. A. Improving the predictive effectiveness of peer ratings. *Personnel Psychology*, 1962, 15, 215–220.

Dunnette, M. D. A note on *the* criterion. *Journal of Applied Psychology*, 1963, 47, 251–254.

Dunnette, M. D. *Personnel selection and placement*. Belmont, Calif.: Wadsworth Publishing, 1966.

Dunnette, M. D., Campbell, J. P., & Hellervik, L. W. *Job behavior scales for Penney Co. department managers*. Minneapolis: Personnel Decisions, 1968. (Cited in J. P. Campbell, M. D. Dunnette, E. E. Lawler III, & K. E. Weick Jr., *Managerial behavior, performance, and effectiveness*. New York: McGraw-Hill, 1970, 119–123.)

Edgerton, H. A., & Kolbe, L. E. The method of minimum variation for the coordination of criteria. *Psychometrika*, 1936, 1, 185–187.

Edwards, A. E. *Techniques of attitude scale construction*. New York: Appleton-Century-Crofts, 1957.

Ewart, E. S., Seashore, S. E., & Tiffin, J. A factor analysis of an industrial merit rating scale. *Journal of Applied Psychology*, 1941, 25, 481–486.

Ewen, R. B. Weighting components of job satisfaction. *Journal of Applied Psychology*, 1967, 51, 63–73.

Ferguson, L. W. The development of a method of appraisal for assistant managers. *Journal of Applied Psychology*, 1947, 31, 306–311.

Finkle, R. B., & Jones, W. S. *Assessing corporate talent*. New York: Wiley, 1970.

Fishbein, M., Ed. *Readings in attitude theory and measurement*. New York: Wiley, 1967.

Fiske, D. W. Values, theory, and the criterion problem. *Personnel Psychology*, 1951, 4, 93–98.

Flanagan, J. C. Critical requirements: A new approach to employee evaluation. *Personnel Psychology*, 1949, 2, 419–425.

Flanagan, J. C. The critical incident technique. *Psychological Bulletin*, 1954, 51, 327–355.

Fleishman, E. A., & Fruchter, B. Factor structure and predictability of successive stages of learning Morse code. *Journal of Applied Psychology*, 1960, 44, 97–101.

Fleishman, E. A., & Hempel, W. E. Jr. Changes in factor structure of a complex psychomotor test as a function of practice. *Psychometrika*, 1954, 18, 239–252.

Fleishman, E. A., Harris, E. F., & Burtt, H. E. Leadership and supervision in industry. *Bureau of Education Monographs # 33*. Columbus: Ohio State University, 1955.

Fogli, L., Hulin, C. L., & Blood, M. R. Development of first-level behavioral criteria. *Journal of Applied Psychology*, 1971, 55, 3–8.

Forehand, G. A. Assessments of innovative behavior: Partial criteria for the assessment of executive performance. *Journal of Applied Psychology*, 1963, 47, 206–213.

Frederiksen, N., Saunders, D. R., & Ward, B. The in-basket test. *Psychological Monographs*, 1957, 71, No. 9 (Whole No. 438).

French, J. R. P. Jr., Kay, E., & Meyer, H. H. Participation and the appraisal system. *Human Relations*, 1965, 18, 3–20.

French, J. W. The validity of some objective personality tests for a leadership criterion. *Educational and Psychological Measurement*, 1954, 14, 34–49.

Funk & Wagnalls. *Standard college dictionary*. (Text ed.) New York: Harcourt, Brace, & World, 1963.

Ghiselli, E. E. Dimensional problems of criteria. *Journal of Applied Psychology*, 1956, 40, 1–4.

Ghiselli, E. E. Differentiation of tests in terms of the accuracy with which they predict for a given individual. *Educational and Psychological Measurement*, 1960, 20, 675–684.

Ghiselli, E. E., & Brown, C. W. *Personnel and industrial psychology*. New York: McGraw-Hill, 1955.

Ghiselli, E. E., & Haire, M. The validation of selection tests in the light of the dynamic character of criteria. *Personnel Psychology*, 1960, 13, 225–231.

Gifford, W. W. Does business want scholars? *Harper's Magazine*, 1928, 156, 669–674.

Gordon, L. V., & Medlund, F. F. The cross-group stability of peer ratings of leadership potential. *Personnel Psychology*, 1965, 18, 173–177.

Grant, D. L. A factor analysis of managers'

ratings. *Journal of Applied Psychology,* 1955, 39, 283–286.

Grant, D. L., & Bray, D. W. The assessment center in the measurement of potential for business management. *Psychological Monographs,* 1966, 80 (Whole No. 625).

Guilford, J. P. *Psychometric methods.* New York: McGraw-Hill, 1954, 274–278.

Guion, R. M. Criterion measurement and personnel judgments. *Personnel Psychology,* 1961, 14, 141–149.

Guion, R. M. *Personnel testing.* New York: McGraw-Hill, 1965.

Guion, R. M. Personnel selection. *Annual Review of Psychology,* 1967, 18, 191–216.

Gulliksen, H. *Theory of mental tests.* New York: Wiley, 1950.

Hakel, M. D. Jr. Perceiver differences in interpersonal perceptions: An analysis of interrater agreement on scaled-expectation rating scales in an employment interview setting. Unpublished doctoral dissertation, University of Minnesota, Minneapolis, 1966.

Hartshorne, H., & May, M. A. *Studies in service and self-control.* New York: Macmillan, 1929.

Heise, D. R. Some methodological issues in semantic differential research. *Psychological Bulletin,* 1969, 72, 406–422.

Henry, W. E. Executive personality and job success. *AMA Personnel Series,* 1948, #120.

Hollander, E. P. Buddy ratings: Military research and industrial implications. *Personnel Psychology,* 1954, 7, 385–395.

Hollander, E. P. The friendship factor in peer nominations. *Personnel Psychology,* 1956, 9, 425–447.

Hollander, E. P. The reliability of peer nominations under various conditions of administration. *Journal of Applied Psychology,* 1957, 41, 85–90.

Hollander, E. P. Validity of peer nominations in predicting a distant performance criterion. *Journal of Applied Psychology,* 1965, 49, 434–438.

Howe, E. S. Further comparisons of two short-form derivations of the Taylor manifest anxiety scale. *Psychological Reports,* 1960, 6, 21–22.

Howe, E. S., & Silverstein, A. B. Comparison of two short-form derivatives of the Taylor manifest anxiety scale. *Psychological Reports,* 1960, 6, 9–10.

Hulin, C. L. The measurement of executive success. *Journal of Applied Psychology,* 1962, 46, 303–306.

Huse, E. F., & Taylor, E. K. Reliability of absence measures. *Journal of Applied Psychology,* 1962, 46, 159–160.

Izard, B. R., & Rosenberg, S. Effectiveness of a forced-choice leadership test under varied experimental conditions. *Educational and Psychological Measurement,* 1958, 18, 57–62.

James, L. R. Criterion models and construct validity for criteria. *Psychological Bulletin,* 1973, 80, 75–83.

Jaques, E. *Equitable payment.* New York: Wiley, 1961.

Jurgensen, C. E. A fallacy in the use of median scale values in employee check lists. *Journal of Applied Psychology,* 1949, 33, 56–58.

Katzell, R. A. Industrial psychology. *Annual Review of Psychology,* 1957, 8, 237–268.

Kavanagh, M. J., MacKinney, A. C., & Wolins, L. Issues in managerial performance: Multitrait-multimethod analyses of ratings. *Psychological Bulletin,* 1971, 75, 34–49.

Kay, B. R. The use of critical incidents in a forced-choice scale. *Journal of Applied Psychology,* 1959, 43, 269–270.

Kendall, L. M., & Hilton, T. L. Rationale and results of an attempt to develop behaviorally anchored rating criteria for students in graduate schools of business administration. Paper presented at 73rd American Psychological Association Convention, September 5, 1965.

Kendall, W. E. Industrial psychology. *Annual Review of Psychology,* 1955, 6, 217–250.

Kerr, W. A., Koppelmeir, G., & Sullivan, J. J. Absenteeism, turnover, and morale in a metals fabrication factory. *Occupational Psychology,* 1951, 25, 50–55.

Kirchner, W. K. Relationships between supervisory and subordinate ratings of technical personnel. *Journal of Industrial Psychology,* 1966, 3, 57–60.

Kirchner, W. K., & Dunnette, M. D. Using critical incidents to measure job proficiency factors. *Personnel,* 1957, 34, 54–59.

Kirchner, W. K., & Reisberg, D. J. Differences between better and less effective supervisors in appraisal of subordinates. *Personnel Psychology,* 1962, 15, 295–302.

Klores, M. S. Rater bias in forced-distribution performance ratings. *Personnel Psychology,* 1966, 19, 411–421.

Knauft, E. B. Construction and use of weighted check list rating scales for two industrial situations. *Journal of Applied Psychology*, 1948, 32, 63–70.

Koltuv, B. B. Some characteristics of intra-judge trait intercorrelations. *Psychological Monographs*, 1962, 76, 33 (Whole No. 552).

Kornhauser, A. W. A statistical study of a group of specialized office workers. *Journal of Personnel Research*, 1923, 2, 103–123.

Krick, E. V. *Methods engineering*. New York: Wiley, 1962.

Kunin, T. The construction of a new type of attitude measure. *Personnel Psychology*, 1955, 8, 65–78.

Kurtz, A. B. The simultaneous prediction of any number of criteria by the use of a unique set of weights. *Psychometrika*, 1937, 2, 95–101.

Lawler, E. E. III. The multi-trait-multi-rater approach to measuring managerial job performance. *Journal of Applied Psychology*, 1967, 51, 369–381.

Lawshe, C. H., Kephart, N. C., & McCormick, E. J. The paired comparison technique for rating performance of industrial employees. *Journal of Applied Psychology*, 1949, 33, 69–77.

Lefkowitz, J. Effect of training on the productivity and tenure of sewing machine operators. *Journal of Applied Psychology*, 1970, 54, 81–86.

Lifson, K. A. Errors in time-study judgments of industrial work pace. *Psychological Monographs*, 1953, 67, No. 5 (Whole No. 358).

Likert, R., & Seashore, S. E. Making cost control work. *Harvard Business Review*, 1963, 41, 96–108.

Lyons, T. F. Turnover and absenteeism: A review of relationships and correlates. *Personnel Psychology*, 1972, 25, 271–281.

Maas, J. B. Patterned scale expectation interview: Reliability studies on a new technique. *Journal of Applied Psychology*, 1965, 49, 431–433.

McGehee, W. Cutting training waste. *Personnel Psychology*, 1948, 1, 331–340.

McGehee, W., & Owen, E. B. Authorized and unauthorized rest pauses in clerical work. *Journal of Applied Psychology*, 1940, 24, 605–614.

MacKinney, A. C. An assessment of performance change: An inductive example. *Organizational Behavior and Human Performance*, 1967, 2, 56–72.

Madden, J. M. Comparison of three methods of rating-scale construction. *Journal of Industrial Psychology*, 1964, 2, 43–50.

Madden, J. M., & Bourdon, R. D. Effects of variations in rating scale format on judgment. *Journal of Applied Psychology*, 1964, 48, 147–151.

Maguire, T. O., & Glass, G. V. Component profile analysis (COPAN)—An alternative to PROF. *Educational and Psychological Measurement*, 1968, 28, 1021–1033.

Mann, F. C., & Dent, J. K. The supervisor: Member of two organizational families. *Harvard Business Review*, 1954, 32, 103–112.

Marks, M. R. Review of Ronan, W. W., & Prien, E. P., Toward a criterion theory: A review and analysis of research and opinion. *Personnel Psychology*, 1967, 20, 216–218.

Metzner, H., & Mann, F. Employee attitudes and absences. *Personnel Psychology*, 1953, 6, 467–485.

Meyer, H. H. The validity of the in-basket test as a measure of managerial performance. *Personnel Psychology*, 1970, 23, 297–307.

Meyer, H. H., Kay, E., & French, J. R. P. Jr. Split roles in performance appraisal. *Harvard Business Review*, 1964, 43, 124–129.

Mordkoff, A. M. Functional versus nominal autonomy in semantic differential scales. *Psychological Reports*, 1965, 16, 691–692.

Mueser, R. E. The weather and other factors influencing employee punctuality. *Journal of Applied Psychology*, 1953, 37, 329–337.

Naylor, J. C., & Wherry, R. J. Sr. The use of simulated stimuli and the "JAN" technique to capture and cluster the policies of raters. *Educational and Psychological Measurement*, 1965, 25, 969–986.

Obradović, J. Modification of the forced-choice method as a criterion of job proficiency. *Journal of Applied Psychology*, 1970, 54, 228–233.

Osgood, C. E., Suci, G. J., & Tannenbaum, P. H. *The measurement of meaning*. Urbana: University of Illinois Press, 1957.

Otis, J. L. The criterion. In W. H. Stead, C. Shartle, & Associates, *Occupational counseling techniques*. New York: American Book Co., 1940.

Owens, W. A., & Jewell, D. O. Personnel selection. *Annual Review of Psychology*, 1969, 20, 419–446.

Passini, F. T., & Norman, W. T. A universal conception of personality structure? *Journal* of *Personality and Social Psychology*, 1966, 4, 44–49.

Passini, F. T., & Norman, W. T. Ratee relevance in peer nominations. *Journal of Applied Psychology*, 1969, 53, 185–187.

Porter, L. W., & Steers, R. M. Organizational, work, and personal factors in employee turnover and absenteeism. *Journal of Applied Psychology*, 1973, 80, 151–176.

Prien, E. P. Dynamic character of criteria: Organizational change. *Journal of Applied Psychology*, 1966, 50, 501–504.

Prien, E. P., & Kult, M. Analysis of performance criteria and comparison of a priori and empirically derived keys for a forced-choice scoring. *Personnel Psychology*, 1968, 21, 505–513.

Rambo, W. W. The construction and analysis of a leadership behavior check list for industrial managers. *Journal of Applied Psychology*, 1958, 42, 409–415.

Richardson, M. W., & Kuder, G. V. Making a rating scale that measures. *Personnel Journal*, 1933, 12, 36–40.

Roach, D. E., & Wherry, R. J. Performance dimensions of multi-line insurance agents. *Personnel Psychology*, 1970, 23, 239–250.

Roadman, H. E. An industrial use of peer ratings. *Journal of Applied Psychology*, 1964, 48, 211–214.

Roethlisberger, F. J., & Dickson, W. J. *Management and the worker*. Cambridge: Harvard University Press, 1938.

Ronan, W. W. A factor analysis of eight job performance measures. *Journal of Industrial Psychology*, 1963, 1, 107–112.

Ronan, W. W., & Prien, E. P. *Towards a criterion theory: A review and analysis of research and opinion*. Greensboro, N.C.: The Richardson Foundation, 1966.

Ross, P. F. Reference groups in man-to-man job performance rating. *Personnel Psychology*, 1966, 19, 115–142.

Rothe, H. F. Output rates among butter wrappers: I. Work curves and their stability. *Journal of Applied Psychology*, 1946, 30, 199–211. (a)

Rothe, H. F. Output rates among butter wrappers: II. Frequency distributions and a hypothesis regarding the "restriction of output." *Journal of Applied Psychology*, 1946, 30, 320–327. (b)

Rothe, H. F. Output rates among machine operators: I. Distributions and their reliability. *Journal of Applied Psychology*, 1947, 31, 384–389.

Rothe, H. F. Output rates among chocolate dippers. *Journal of Applied Psychology*, 1951, 35, 94–97.

Rothe, H. F., & Nye, C. T. Output rates among coil winders. *Journal of Applied Psychology*, 1958, 42, 182–186.

Rothe, H. F., & Nye, C. T. Output rates among machine operators: II. Consistency related to methods of pay. *Journal of Applied Psychology*, 1959, 43, 417–420.

Rothe, H. F., & Nye, C. T. Output rates among machine operators: III. A nonincentive situation in two levels of business activity. *Journal of Applied Psychology*, 1961, 45, 50–54.

Rotter, G. S., & Tinkleman, V. Anchor effects in the development of behavior rating scales. *Educational and Psychological Measurement*, 1970, 30, 311–318.

Rush, C. H. Jr. A factorial study of sales criteria. *Personnel Psychology*, 1953, 6, 9–24.

Ryan, T. A. *Work and effort*. New York: Ronald Press, 1947.

Ryan, T. A., & Smith, P. C. *Principles of industrial psychology*. New York: Ronald Press, 1954, 46–58.

Salvendy, G., Seymour, W. D., & Corlett, E. N. Comparative study of static versus dynamic scoring of performance tests for industrial operators. *Journal of Applied Psychology*, 1970, 54, 135–139.

Schmidt, F. R., & Kaplan, L. B. Composite versus multiple criteria: A review and resolution of the controversy. *Personnel Psychology*, 1971, 24, 419–434.

Schneider, D. E., & Bayroff, A. G. The relationship between rater characteristics and validity of ratings. *Journal of Applied Psychology*, 1953, 37, 278–280.

Schuh, A. J. The predictability of employee tenure: A review of the literature. *Personnel Psychology*, 1967, 20, 133–152.

Schultz, D. G., & Siegel, A. I. Generalized Thurstone and Guttman scales for measuring technical skills in job performance. *Journal of Applied Psychology*, 1961, 45, 137–142.

Schultz, D. G., & Siegel, A. I. The analysis of job performance by multidimensional scaling techniques. *Journal of Applied Psychology*, 1964, 48, 329–335.

Scott, W. A. Comparative validities of forced-choice and single-stimulus tests. *Psychological Bulletin,* 1968, 70, 231–244.

Seashore, S. E., Indik, B. P., & Georgopoulos, B. S. Relationships among criteria of job performance. *Journal of Applied Psychology,* 1960, 44, 195–202.

Seashore, S. E., & Yuchtman, E. Factorial analysis of organizational performance. *Administrative Science Quarterly,* 1967, 12, 377–395.

Sharon, A. T., & Bartlett, C. J. Effect of instructional conditions in producing leniency on two types of rating scales. *Personnel Psychology,* 1969, 22, 251–263.

Siegel, A. I., & Pfeiffer, M. G. Factorial congruence in criterion development. *Personnel Psychology,* 1965, 18, 267–280.

Sisson, E. D. Forced-choice: The new Army rating. *Personnel Psychology,* 1948, 1, 365–381.

Slovic, P., & Lichtenstein, S. Comparison of Bayesian and regression approaches to the study of information processing in judgment. *Organizational Behavior and Human Performance,* 1971, 6, 649–744.

Smith, O. W., & Landy, F. Grid versus graphic scaling of importance and presence of some college experiences. *Perceptual and Motor Skills,* 1969, 29, 146.

Smith, O. W., Smith, P. C., Baumgartel, R., Gliner, J., & Goodale, J. Psychology of the scientist: XXX. Replication: What is it? *Perceptual and Motor Skills,* 1971, 33, 691–697.

Smith, P. C. The curve of output as a criterion of boredom. *Journal of Applied Psychology,* 1953, 37, 69–74.

Smith, P. C., & Gold, R. A. Prediction of success from examination of performance during the training period. *Journal of Applied Psychology,* 1956, 40, 83–86.

Smith, P. C., & Kendall, L. M. Retranslation of expectations: An approach to the construction of unambiguous anchors for rating scales. *Journal of Applied Psychology,* 1963, 47, 149–155.

Smith, P. C., & Lem, C. Positive aspects of motivation in repetitive work: Effects of lot size upon spacing of voluntary work stoppages. *Journal of Applied Psychology,* 1955, 39, 330–333.

Smith, P. C., Kendall, L. M., & Hulin, C. L. *The measurement of satisfaction in work*

and retirement. Chicago: Rand McNally, 1969.

Smith, P. C., & Taylor, J. G. An investigation of the shape of learning curves for industrial motor tasks. *Journal of Applied Psychology,* 1956, 40, 142–149.

Stark, S. Research criteria of executive success. *Journal of Business,* 1959, 32, 1–14.

Stockford, L., & Bissell, H. W. Establishing a graphic-rating scale. In W. E. Fleishman (Ed.), *Studies in personnel and industrial psychology.* (Rev. ed.) Homewood, Ill.: Dorsey Press, 1967.

Taylor, E. K., & Nevis, E. C. Personnel selection. *Annual Review of Psychology,* 1961, 12, 403–405.

Taylor, E. K., & Wherry, R. J. A study of leniency in two rating systems. *Personnel Psychology,* 1951, 4, 39–47.

Taylor, E. K., Schneider, D. E., & Clay, H. Short forced-choice ratings work. *Personnel Psychology,* 1954, 7, 245–252.

Taylor, E. K., Schneider, D. E., & Symons, N. A. A short forced-choice evaluation form for salesmen. *Personnel Psychology,* 1953, 6, 393–401.

Thomson, H. A. Comparison of predictor and criterion judgments of managerial performance using the multitrait-multimethod approach. *Journal of Applied Psychology,* 1970, 54, 496–502.

Thorndike, R. L. *Personnel selection.* New York: Wiley, 1949.

Thornton, G. C. The relationship between supervisory- and self-appraisals of executive performance. *Personnel Psychology,* 1968, 21, 441–455.

Tiffin, J., & Phelan, R. F. Use of the Kuder preference record to predict turnover in an industrial plant. *Personnel Psychology,* 1953, 6, 195–204.

Toops, H. A. The criterion. *Educational and Psychological Measurement,* 1944, 4, 271–297.

Torgerson, W. S. *Theory and methods of scaling.* New York: Wiley, 1958.

Travers, R. M. W. A critical review of the validity and rationale of the forced-choice technique. *Psychological Bulletin,* 1951, 48, 62–70.

Tucker, M. F., Cline, V. B., & Schmitt, J. R. Prediction of creativity and other performance measures from biographical information among pharmaceutical scientists. *Journal of Applied Psychology,* 1967, 51, 131–138.

Turner, W. W. Dimensions of foreman performance: A factor analysis of criterion measures. *Journal of Applied Psychology,* 1960, 44, 216–223.

Uhrbrock, R. S. Standardization of 724 rating scale statements. *Personnel Psychology,* 1950, 3, 285–316.

Uhrbrock, R. S. 2,000 scaled items. *Personnel Psychology,* 1961, 14, 375–420.

Vielhaber, D. P., & Gottheil, E. First impressions and subsequent ratings of performance. *Psychological Reports,* 1965, 17, 916.

Viteles, M. S. General review and summary: Five years of research, a summary of outcomes. *Psychological Bulletin,* 1945, 42, 489–526.

Wallace, S. R. Criteria for what? *American Psychologist,* 1965, 20, 411–417.

Wallace, S. R., & Weitz, J. Industrial psychology. *Annual Review of Psychology,* 1955, 6, 217–250.

Weitz, J. Criteria for criteria. *American Psychologist,* 1961, 16, 228–231.

Weitz, J., & Nuckols, R. C. A validation study of "How supervise?" *Journal of Applied Psychology,* 1953, 37, 7–8.

Wherry, R. J., & Fryer, D. H. Buddy ratings: Popularity contest or leadership criteria? *Personnel Psychology,* 1949, 2, 147–159.

Wherry, R. J. Sr., & Naylor, J. C. Comparison of two approaches—JAN and PROF—for capturing rater strategies. *Educational and Psychological Measurement,* 1966, 26, 267–286.

Whitlock, G. H. Application of the psychophysical law to performance evaluation. *Journal of Applied Psychology,* 1963, 47, 15–23.

Whitlock, G. H., Clouse, R. J., & Spencer, W. F. Predicting accident proneness. *Personnel Psychology,* 1963, 16, 35–44.

Wiley, L. Relation of characteristics ratings to performance ratings. *Journal of Industrial Psychology,* 1964, 2, 7–15.

Wiley, L., & Jenkins, W. S. Selecting competent raters. *Journal of Applied Psychology,* 1964, 48, 215–217.

Williams, J. D., Harlow, S. D., Lindem, A., & Gab, D. A judgment analysis program for clustering similar judgmental systems. *Educational and Psychological Measurement,* 1970, 30, 171–173.

Yuzuk, R. P. The assessment of employee morale. Columbus: The Ohio State University Bureau of Business Research, 1961, Monograph No. 99.

Zavala, A. Development of the forced-choice rating scale technique. *Psychological Bulletin,* 1965, 63, 117–124.

CHAPTER 18

Recruiting, Selection, and Job Placement[1]

ROBERT M. GUION
Bowling Green State University

TECHNOLOGY IN EMPLOYEE SELECTION is more highly developed than in recruiting or placement; therefore, the major emphasis is on selection. Selection technology stems historically from concepts of test validation, and discussions of both criterion-related and descriptive validities are offered. Validation for most tests and other employee selection methods is seen as the empirical testing, where possible and appropriate, of rationally developed hypotheses about individual, situational, or subgroup characteristics which may influence job behavior or its effects. It is recognized that some employee selection procedures are appropriately validated by demonstrations that they are descriptive of skills or knowledge judged necessary to effective job performance. Attention is given to social and statistical problems of bias in measurement and in prediction. A brief survey of relevant civil rights regulations and legal decisions is included. An epilogue offers suggestions for programs of employee selection research.

Organizations need people. People need jobs. By some process, the needs of organizations and the needs of people must be matched. The process of personnel selection views the matching problem from an organizational perspective, but without ignoring the "people" perspective. It first identifies the employer's needs, and it selects from among available people those whose interests and abilities best fit the employer's needs.

In the early days of industrialization, a foreman went where the applicants were assembled, pointed at those who looked strongest, and sent the rest away. With later sophistication, decisions were based on recommendations from existing employees, or physical examinations, or references from friends or previous employers, or conversations or interrogations called interviews, or written interviews called application blanks, or something called tests. Whether simple or sophisticated, employers try to get some

[1] Most of this chapter was written while the author was on sabbatical leave with the Educational Testing Service, Princeton, New Jersey. The stimulating and permissive atmosphere that greatly facilitated the writing is acknowledged with gratitude.

descriptive understanding of each applicant before deciding whether to hire, reject, or hold out a little longer in hopes of finding someone better than the best at hand.

This is a glib account because the decision itself is often glib. One does not know whether one applicant is "better" than another unless a reasonably precise distinction is made between those characteristics genuinely useful in job performance and those merely desired. One man once expressed his employment policy in these words, "We hire only the kind of people I wouldn't mind having my own daughter work beside." Translated, he meant clean, well-groomed men and women whose manners, language, and moral attitudes were "nice." These qualifications were relevant to his attitudes and habits of doing business (e.g., offering summer employment to offspring of executives and preferred customers), but they had little to do with performance on specific jobs.

Purely descriptive considerations of age, sex, race, ethnic background, personal appearance, inferred attitudes, manner of dress or manner of speaking, educational or work histories, special skills, credit ratings, and many other characteristics have often been of paramount importance in deciding who shall and who shall not be hired. That some of these considerations have become illegal is beside the point; the point is that personnel selection is often based on matching descriptions of applicants with an employer's stereotype of the kind of people he would like to have around. Where this is true, regardless of the level of sophistication in description, the sophistication in selection is little higher than that of the finger-pointing foreman.[2]

When a notion of who will be nice to have around is firmly grounded in business reasoning, descriptions begin to make sense.

Few would argue with a policy statement to the effect that it is nice to have employees who are productive, are likely to stay, will show up regularly for work, and will not steal. It is an appropriate policy to hire those who will work well and dependably at the tasks they are paid to perform. Unfortunately, however, one cannot describe or measure job performance before it occurs.[3] Therefore, one must assume, and if possible demonstrate, that the characteristics described prior to employment are in fact related to subsequent characteristics of performance on the job.

Such assumptions are working hypotheses, and they have guided selection decisions since Gideon watched men drinking from a brook. Without them, the selection decision based solely on description is no more than the exercise of prejudice. Employment "standards" (a frequent euphemism for prejudice) that specify whites, or short-haired males, or shapely women, without specifying how these descriptive characteristics may be related to performance on the job, are based on purely personal preference rather than on considered business interests.

There are three options for making selection decisions among applicants whose job performance is not known in advance. Option 1 is randomization. If one finds, in a specific instance, that he simply has no defensible hypothesis, his best option may be to select at random and not bother with description at all. This option is usually mentioned facetiously; it deserves more serious consideration, because sometimes the only alternative to random selection is biased selection.

Where a defensible hypothesis is formulated, and where the variables of the hy-

---

[2] Which may not be all bad. Those early foremen apparently knew well the demands of the jobs to be filled. Some of them, at least, did something right; productivity in the early days of industrialization, as seen in retrospect, is the envy of many modern industrialists.

[3] This point seems to have been overlooked in the wording of the Supreme Court in its decision in *Griggs* v. *Duke Power* (1971): "What Congress has forbidden is giving these devices and mechanisms controlling force unless they are demonstrably a reasonable *measure* of job performance" (p. 11; italics added). Substituting "predictor" for "measure" would be more realistic and presumably express the intent of the Court.

pothesis can be acceptably operationalized, there are two other options. The preferred, Option 2, is to test the hypothesis and, if it proves tenable, to select employees on the basis of a *demonstrated* relationship between the applicant characteristic and measures of performance on the job. Frequently, such empirical investigation is not possible. In these situations, the remaining option, Option 3, is to base selection decisions on the *assumed* or *hypothesized* relationships.

The legitimacy of Option 1 lies in the absence of reasonable alternatives. The legitimacy of Option 2 lies in the acceptability of the measures, particularly those of job performance, and of the methods used in testing the hypothesis. The legitimacy of Option 3 lies in the degree to which the hypothesis itself is well-grounded in careful observations and prior research results. Although little will be said about Option 1 (the option of last resort), the bulk of this chapter will be concerned with these questions of legitimacy.

Prologue

The application of psychology to personnel selection is well established; it is the hallmark of "traditional" industrial psychology. We seem, however, to be at a point in history when the practice and the thought of leaders of the field are ready to change. It is too soon to describe the "new" thought or even to predict what it will be. There is, however, ample justification for taking a hard look at what is generally considered the best practice. In this chapter we shall try to see where we are, how we came to this point, and where we have fallen short of the best practice as tradition has defined it.

Despite the inclusiveness of the title, this chapter will emphasize the selection process and the research which gives it foundation. Recruiting or placement are not less important processes; to the contrary, respectively, they probably are more vital and more profitable to the organization. An organization's success in recruiting defines the applicant population with which it will work; selection is more pleasant, if not easier, when any restriction of range or skewness of distribution is attributable to an overabundance of well-qualified applicants. And a well-conceived and fully operational plan of differential placement can maximize the returns from investments in employment programs. Unfortunately, the contributions and confusions of the literature, the central social pressures, and the facts of contemporary practice conspire to place the emphasis on selection. Nevertheless, a brief commentary on each of these other facets of employment psychology may help provide a setting within which the selection process may profitably be viewed.

RECRUITING. The seriousness with which an organization views the recruiting function is probably a function of the tightness of the labor market. When area unemployment is high, personnel managers may be able to fill jobs adequately by sitting and waiting. When organizations must compete vigorously for available talent, recruiting becomes an active, expensive priority.

What little research on recruiting has been reported has been concerned with such questions as the expected yield from different recruiting sources. If research identifies one source of recruiting as providing a better yield—in absolute numbers, quality, or special characteristics—it indicates where recruiting dollars should be spent. It leaves unanswered the question of why one source is more useful than another. It would be useful to look for any unique characteristics of people attracted through different sources. Not only would such research provide some understanding of the superiority of various sources, but it might provide clues about variables to consider in predicting performance.

The search for understanding has not typified recruiting research, but there have been a few efforts to move in this direction in college recruiting. Behling, Labovitz, and Gainer (1968) identified three "theories" of recruiting: (1) that applicants choose jobs logically by comparing offers for such objective factors as salary, benefits, and specific indicators of opportunity; (2) that people make choices on highly subjective grounds, depending upon organizational characteristics they perceive as satisfying their own personal needs; and (3) that applicants cannot really differentiate among offers and, therefore, base choices on physical facilities and other "critical" but fleeting contacts with the firms making offers. A solid theoretical basis for recruiting practice, these authors suggest, would involve some combination of these points of view. The second of the "theories," the one dealing with more subjective factors, was the basis of research reported by Tom (1971). In a study that should stimulate much more work in this area, Tom was able to show a similarity of self-report profiles and profiles of perceptions of organizations students wanted to join.

PLACEMENT. If an applicant is considered for a single job, a simple decision is possible; that is, the applicant may either be selected for the position or rejected. This is selection. Placement, or classification, is more complex, deciding where to assign the applicant if he is hired. Usually there is more than one job opening, and it is useful to consider an applicant for positions other than the one advertised or sought. Effective placement has advantages both for the organization and the applicant; potential effects include greater work proficiency and stability and greater job satisfaction as well.

Selection and placement are often treated independently, but the major difference is in methodological history. Research on selection has ordinarily used correlation theory to compare variations in applicant traits to variations in subsequent performance of those who are hired. Research on placement has used interpersonal comparisons such as comparing a set of applicant characteristics with the characteristics of successful groups in various job classifications. In this sense,

selection is a special case of placement; the applicant is selected if he is more like successful rather than nonsuccessful members of the group for which he is considered, and he is rejected if the reverse is true. Moreover, even the methodological differences are more apparent than real; for example, a discriminant function analysis for a placement decision is not different from a multiple regression equation if the criterion is dichotomized.

A number of mathematically sophisticated procedures have been suggested for placement decisions. Cronbach and Gleser (1965) are among those who have presented methods based on statistical decision theory; Rulon, Tiedeman, Tatsuoka, and Langmuir (1967) offered a somewhat simpler approach based on the concepts of profile analysis. Neither has sparked any great outpouring of research in employment settings. Except in military applications, the principal interest in the mathematics of placement has been from theoreticians rather than practitioners. Therefore, few examples are available to describe an existing technology.

The usual approach to placement consists of a succession of selection predictions (Ghiselli, 1956b). That is, the applicant is first considered for the job most needing to be filled. If he qualifies, he is placed on that job. If not, he is considered for the next most important job in the organization's priorities, and so on until a place is found in the hierarchy of organizational requirements that he will fit—or until he is totally rejected. Such a procedure may be casual or systematic, depending upon (a) the degree of formality in establishing and communicating to decision makers the relative priorities among job openings and (b) the validity of the assessment procedures used in evaluating candidates for each job.

The latter *may* be equated with the problem of validity to be discussed in the context of the more limited selection problem. There are, however, some relatively straightforward methods specifically related to placement. Many of these have long been known, discussed both by Ghiselli and Brown (1955) and Ryan and Smith (1954). One of the easiest to apply consists of a simple matching of an applicant's profile of scores on several variables with a corresponding profile of a successful group on each of the alternative jobs. This concept is easy to apply but less easy to develop. It requires, in effect, a series of variables that distinguish successful from less successful members in each of several different job classifications—and, moreover, do so in different patterns or at different levels.

A similar situation exists with regard to the use of successively different cutting scores, either on a single variable or a composite of several. This implies vertical placement, that is, placement in one of a series of jobs in a hierarchy requiring varying degrees of the same characteristics. This is a useful form of placement where (a) minimum levels of acceptable proficiency can be clearly defined, (b) test scores associated with minimum proficiency can be validly determined, and (c) jobs can be ordered along a continuum of minimum test scores. Where jobs differ in the kinds rather than amounts of traits required, one may simply use the multiple regression approach to make several different predictions for an applicant and place him where his predicted performance will have the greatest utility for the organization.

All of the approaches to placement discussed so far have generally taken an organizational point of view, the view that there are diverse jobs to be done and that individuals must be optimally assigned somewhere within that diversity. There is another point of view, that of counseling employees regarding choice points within career ladders. The use of personal history items has been successful with engineers, where a choice must be made between research and administrative fields (Albright & Glennon, 1961). Similar decisions must be made at an earlier career point by medically trained health personnel. For instance, Howell and Newman (1967) used bio-

graphical items to predict success differentially in four possible health science career ladders. They met with little success in predicting peer ratings of successful performance, but they did develop a set of scoring keys deemed useful for career counseling. Perhaps the counseling point of view, in which the responsibility for decision is shared between the personnel officer and the candidate himself, may prove more useful than the statistical models of placement. It should at the very least promote higher levels of job satisfaction.

SELECTION. Efforts in recruitment and in placement are evaluated largely from a frame of reference dominated by the selection problem. To select for any given job, job family, or total organization, we must identify the characteristics or variables that influence performance. We must recruit where we have good chances of finding whatever personal characteristics are so identified, and we must place—either with or without the aid of computers—people with the desired characteristics in jobs or departments where they and the hiring organization can profit. Where the characteristics that influence performance are not personal (e.g., situational variables), then the organization must modify circumstances to enhance performance. It would seem, therefore, useful at this stage in the development of employment psychology to stay with the central problem of selection.

TEST VALIDATION: THE TRADITIONAL MODEL

A Brief History of Employment Psychology

The central focus in the history of employment psychology was on tests—formal, standardized samples of behavior yielding some sort of measure of one or more applicant characteristics. Psychologists did not invent tests; both Gideon and Plato had advocated military aptitude tests centuries before Galton and Cattell. If they did not invent tests, however, psychologists certainly did stress them—in many forms and in many situations. Cattell (1890) described ten tests he was using before the turn of the century; implicit in his discussion of his work is the assumption that he could in time discover tests of mental ability that would relate to performance in college. By 1894 the tests were systematically given to students at Columbia University and, in 1901, Wissler published accounts of the Pearsonian correlations between mental ability tests and academic performance at Columbia (Hull, 1928). Shortly thereafter, Munsterberg (1913) did his classic study for selection of streetcar motormen. When World War I broke out, Otis, "with commendable generosity and patriotism" (Hull, 1928, p. 17), turned over to the Army his work on paper and pencil tests, giving birth to the famous "Alpha" and "Beta" tests for screening and classification.

When that war was over, applied psychologists turned their attention in earnest to the problem of employee selection. An extensive, three-installment journal article outlined in detail the principles and practices of "Measurement in Vocational Selection" (Freyd, 1923). It is discouraging that little of substance has been added or changed in the half century since then. In fact, much that was accepted as good practice in the textbooks of the 1920s (Hull, 1928; Kornhauser & Kingsbury, 1924; Link, 1924) has dropped from contemporary typical practice more from atrophy than from obsolescence.

Freyd's prescription began with selecting a department where the greatest savings for the employer can be made. From that point, Freyd's outline is a sequence of ten steps.

Job analysis was Step 1. The purpose was to discover the characteristics leading to success or failure. It was not treated casually: "What is here meant is a more or less protracted, objective, and systematic study of the behavior of individuals actually engaged in the particular activity" (Hull, 1928, p. 282).

Step 2 was designating the criterion, a single measure. The criterion concept was fuzzy even from the early days. Where Freyd referred to a "criterion of success" or "criterion of vocational accomplishment," Hull wrote of the criterion as the measure of "actual aptitude" which the test approximated. Freyd clearly distinguished vocational selection from vocational guidance. Hull and others seemed to combine the two enterprises; as a result, the focus was usually more on the test than on the criterion.

Step 3 was to select "subjects for the experiment," and several rules were given. Although Freyd was not worried about using present employees, he recognized that objections "vanished" when applicants alone were the subjects. He indicated that the sample should exclude those whose standing on the criterion derived from chance or "special advantages," or who had previous knowledge of the tests, or sensory or motor defects, or literacy problems. Sex or age differences were to be studied.

Step 4 was to develop a list of the abilities required for success. The list was supposed to be exhaustive, and procedures were recommended for evaluating individual entries in the list. Step 5 was to find or devise the appropriate measuring instruments, and they were not restricted to tests. Step 6 was to administer them "under carefully controlled conditions" to the selected subjects. Results of the testing were to be statistically compared with criterion scores as Step 7. Step 8 was the combination of measures for optimal correlation. The last three comprise what is now known as validation; in that era the evaluation process was more often called "testing the tests" (Hull, 1928; Kornhauser & Kingsbury, 1924). Hull in particular, but others as well, strongly advocated using two or three times as many tests as were expected for actual use because of the belief that even educated guesses would be frequently wrong and because of expected but unpredictable differences in the correlations of tests with criteria.

Step 9 was "to justify them [the measuring instruments] by comparing their predictive accuracy with that of the methods of selection already in use." Step 10 came only if that comparison were favorable: to install the new measures, be sure they were being properly used, and "continuously check up on their predictive accuracy and adjust them to changes in the type of applicant and industrial demands" (Freyd, 1923, p. 218).

This is marvelously up to date. This chapter may be a contemporary outline, but it will differ little; it is built on the foundation of orthodoxy laid in Freyd's era. Stripped of its pejorative connotations, the notion of orthodoxy implies authenticity, an accepted or established rightness. Historical developments to roughly 1950 can be summarized as the "tenets of orthodoxy" in personnel selection:

1. *The purpose is to predict future job performance.* "It is...essential to know whether the scores are in any useful sense predictive of subsequent success in the occupation" (Bingham, 1937, p. 216). Earlier, Kornhauser and Kingsbury italicized the question, "Does the test enable us to make better predictions as to people's fitness for the job...?" (1924, p. 45).

2. *Predictors and criteria should be selected on the basis of job analysis.* The study of the job should provide clues about potential predictors of job performance; "...the tests which are to be experimented with can be chosen only on the basis of some more or less plausible relationship between particular tests and the sort of duties performed in the job to be filled" (Kornhauser & Kingsbury, 1924, p. 47).

3. *Measuring instruments must be standardized.* "In order for measurements of persons taken at varying times to be comparable, the procedure of the test must be uniform. It would lead to chaos if physical measurements were made by uncorrected scales or rulers which varied considerably

with temperature or season" (Freyd, 1923, p. 232).

4. *Tests should be empirically evaluated.* Link (1924) had said that no test had any significance before it was tried out; more bluntly, "A personnel selection program which does not involve empirical checks of the selection procedures against criteria of job success is at best a static and untested one. At worst it may be outright charlatanism" (Thorndike, 1949, p. 119).

5. *Validation is situation-specific.* "...if maximum value is to be attached to test scores the conditions under which the applicants are employed with the use of tests should reproduce in general the conditions under which they were employed when the tests were evaluated" (Freyd, 1923, p. 381). Strong arguments were presented by Kornhauser and Kingsbury (1924) for not assuming constancy of validities, despite their belief that "some few tests" (such as typing tests) had generalizable validity.

6. *More than one test should be used.* Hull (1928) insisted that a battery of four or five tests or more must be developed if the criterion in all its complexity was to be predicted with maximum efficiency.

7. *But only one criterion should be used.* Freyd presented a list of possible criterion measures, from which "a criterion" could be selected. "If the experimenter believes that any one of these criteria is inadequate to express the employee's vocational accomplishment, there is no reason why several of them may not be combined or averaged" (Freyd, 1923, p. 223).

8. *Tests are preferred over "non-test" predictors.* "The experimenter will not limit himself to any particular type of measuring instrument, but those in which he will be most interested are tests and questionnaires" (Freyd, 1923, p. 231).

9. *Individual differences should be recognized in evaluating tests.* "If men and women are both employed in the occupation, it will be necessary to examine the results for sex differences, and if need be, to

evaluate the test separately for the two sexes...if proper sampling does not permit a limited range of ages then some correction should be made for age differences" (Freyd, 1923, p. 225).

10. *Tests are supplements to existing employment procedures.* It was loudly disclaimed that tests would supplant interviews, reference checks, and other procedures; final decisions were to be made by interviewers. But Freyd was honest: "But the test score should be the deciding point. The function of the interviewer then becomes that of conserving the time of the tester by eliminating those applicants with gross defects..." (p. 380).

Such was the standard view of personnel selection among industrial psychologists of the middle of this century. The technology had been sharpened by the successes of both military and industrial applications during World War II; for example, methods of job analysis and test construction were improved, tests sometimes approached factorial purity, and classification received as much statistical thought as did selection. Psychologists could do better what they had been doing all along.

With the tenets of orthodoxy supported by success, personnel selection began to slip out of the central focus of industrial psychology by the late 1950s. If not all problems were solved, they were at least deemed under control. Personnel selection was often left to personnel managers or technicians or secretaries while psychologists attended more to attitudes, morale, leadership, and in general the psychological problems of managing an already selected work force.

The applications of orthodoxy became pro forma. The commandment to use two or three times as many tests in a trial test battery as might be needed in the final version was typically forgotten; in fact, even "testing the tests" was often done casually if at all. It was a period in which "everybody knew" tests were wonderful, and an employer could be in style without spending any development money by simply adopting the tests and test standards used by someone else. Non-psychologists were unaware of the many things that could go wrong in a testing program, and psychologists were often too busy with the newly increased scope of their discipline to worry very much about it.

Myart v. *Motorola* (French, 1965) and the 1964 Civil Rights Act sparked a reluctant rebirth of interest in employee selection. It was at first defensive, a reiteration of one major theme of orthodoxy that tests are better than non-tests and should, therefore, not be challenged.

This point of view had its friends in Congress, and a protective clause was written into the 1964 Civil Rights Act:

Notwithstanding any other provision of this title, it shall not be an unlawful practice for an employer...to give and to act upon the results of any professionally developed ability test provided that such test, its administration or action upon the results is not designed intended, *or used* to discriminate because of race, color, religion, sex, or national origin. (Bureau of National Affairs, 1964; italics added)

The key phrase was "or used." This phrase emphasizes outcome as well as intent; a test that inadvertently discriminates against any of the protected classes could be considered just as illegal as one that did so on purpose. The notion of test bias was not new or unknown, and the possibility of inadvertent discrimination was faced in a number of symposia, articles, and monographs.

Both the Equal Employment Opportunity Commission (EEOC) and the Office of Federal Contract Compliance (OFCC) in the United States Department of Labor have published documents regulating the use of tests (EEOC, 1966, 1970; OFCC 1968, 1971).[4] These documents were essen

---

[4] The Equal Employment Opportunity Coordinating Council, created by the EEO Act of 1972, is at this writing preparing a more comprehensive document to serve as common regulations of OFCC, EEOC, the

tially a reiteration of orthodoxy in employment testing. They emphasized the need for hypotheses based on careful job analysis, cautioned against biased criteria, and in general required that tests be empirically validated. Two important considerations seemed to be new, but neither is especially heretical. First, the definition of a test was greatly extended to include many of the things not formerly called tests. The term was extended to include "all other formal, scored, quantified, or standardized techniques of assessing job suitability including, for example, personal history and background requirements which are specifically used as a basis for qualifying or disqualifying applicants or employees, specific educational or work history requirements, scored interviews, biographical information blanks, interviewers' rating scales and scored application forms" (OFCC, 1971).[5] Second, these documents insist that tests be validated not only for the total applicant population as a whole, but ("where technically feasible") independently for minority and non-minority subgroups, pretty much as Freyd (1923) had long ago suggested for sex groups.

These documents have not always been warmly received. Along with some administrative procedures of enforcement, they have stimulated controversy. The most valuable aspect of such controversy is that it forces employment psychologists to reexamine its most orthodox assumptions and practices. From this new look at established ideas, some aspects of orthodoxy may be reaffirmed while others may be dropped or changed. This is, of course, a continuing process and

___

United States Civil Service Commission, and the United States Department of Justice.

[5] The present discussion, like the history it encapsulates, began with the personnel selection problem and gradually shifted to problems of employment testing. There is no implication that testing is equated with the total employment process; the shift simply reflects the reality that tests have been the preeminent items of concern. Perhaps the modern definitions of "test" in these regulations may move toward equating these terms.

was underway long before federal regulation was a consideration; federal regulation, however, is hastening the process.

The Four Faces of Validity

The historical account must take special notice of the *Technical Recommendations for Psychological Tests and Diagnostic Techniques* (American Psychological Association et al., 1954), superseded later by the *Standards for Educational and Psychological Tests and Manuals* (American Psychological Association, 1966). The issues stimulating these documents were more clinical and educational than industrial, and the content was more concerned with the information that should be presented in a manual than with the professional practices of users. The earlier *Standards* were nevertheless important to employment psychology because of their presentation of four aspects of validity; a later revision, more oriented toward problems of test use, discusses the implications of each for employment testing (American Psychological Association et al., 1974). Each of these four terms refers to the process of investigation through which the accuracy of inferences to be derived from test scores may be evaluated (Cronbach, 1971). That process is called validation, and it takes many forms; in the final analysis, the judgment that a test is sufficiently "valid" for employment office use should be based on a comprehensive and integrated set of investigations, perhaps of all four aspects.[6] Some of these validations evaluate inferences about the relationship of test scores to a criterion; these are the criterion-related validities, *predictive* and *concurrent*. Some of the validations assess the more nearly intrinsic mean-

___

[6] Classical test theory, in its mathematical formulation, refers to "the validity of the test." This is a shorthand phrase appropriate for a formula or conversation; however, it is misleading for two reasons: (1) validity is not singular, and it is erroneous to speak of "the" validity, and (2) validity is not really a property of the test itself but of the use to be made of it, that is, the inferences to be drawn from the scores.

ing of test scores; here they are called the descriptive validities, *content* and *construct*.

Other adjectives have been used in the literature: face validity, factorial validity, discriminant validity, and on ad nauseam. Although the multiplicity of adjectives may suggest confusion, each of these specialized terms is in some way related to one of the four basic kinds of validity.

CRITERION-RELATED VALIDITIES. Testing, particularly employment testing, is often an indirect means by which inferences are made about something other than the test and the trait it may be presumed to measure. One may use a test as a means of drawing inferences about performance not yet attempted or about measures more difficult to obtain. In such uses, the "something other" is the criterion. Criterion-related validities can (under appropriate circumstances) be computed; a test may have as many computed criterion-related validities as there are criteria against which to validate. One validity coefficient may describe the accuracy of inferences about quality of performance, another about speed, and still another about the probability of early termination; the test may be highly valid for one, moderately valid for another, and of no validity at all for the third.

Investigations of predictive validity may be distinguished from those of concurrent validity on the basis of a time interval. In predictive validation, a period of time elapses between measurement of the predictor and measurement of the criterion; during this period of time, something happens—some treatment (such as training) is presented, experience is gained, or some intervening event can be identified. In contrast, concurrent validation collects both types of measurement at the same time, or at least the measurements are so contiguous in time that no discernable change in conditions or in subjects may be assumed. Of these, predictive validation is the proper model for employment testing. The tester's problem is to predict some future behavior

or event after the applicant is put to work; only predictive validity is directly related to that purpose. Concurrent validity is often used as an estimate of or substitute for predictive validity, but it is really not a very dependable estimate at all (Guion, 1965a).

Not every correlation is evidence of validity. Acceptance of correlation as validity implies acceptance of the correlated criterion as an important concept in vocational success and as a good measure of that concept. Such faith is often unwarranted.

DESCRIPTIVE VALIDITIES. The primal function of a test is descriptive. One tests in order to describe the characteristics of those tested, usually in quantitative terms. One seeks evidence of content validity when using test scores to infer descriptions of achievement or mastery in a clearly defined area of knowledge or skill. One seeks evidence of construct validity when using test scores to infer the degree to which theoretical attributes describe the person tested. The difference between these kinds of inferences is small: the difference between an attribute that can be relatively easily defined (specific classes of achievement) and one which is derived (i.e., constructed) from a network of scientific laws and observations. However, the difference between the kinds of investigations necessary to support contentions of validity of the two kinds is great.

Descriptive validities differ, then, from criterion-related validities in that their focus is on the test itself while the focus in criterion-related validity is on an external variable of greater interest. There are other important differences. A statement of criterion-related validity is established narrowly, on a specific set of data, whereas judgments of content or construct validity are established by a much broader basis of data and of inference. Moreover, a statement of criterion-related validity can be expressed by an apparent precision of two or three decimal places; descriptive validities are more broadly judged as adequate, marginal, or inadequate.

The idea of content validity is primarily drawn from educational testing, and it may need some special modification to be fully appropriate for evaluating employment tests. Typing tests are frequently accepted for employment use on the grounds of content validity without careful examination of an argument that typically sounds something like this: the job requires typing, the test measures typing ability, ergo, the test has content validity. It does, but the evaluation is superficial and betrays lack of familiarity with the subject.

In developing a test to measure a specific universe of tasks or observations, the test developer must define that universe with some care. In doing so, he specifies a "universe of admissible operations" (Cronbach, 1971) and develops the test as a representative sample of that universe. It is evaluated by noting correspondence of test development procedures to the basic definition of the content area. An empirical method of evaluating content validity under this procedure could be developed. It would call for the development, independently, of two test samples and then comparing the results. The procedure is closely allied to equivalent-form reliability: it differs in that the emphasis is on procedural equivalence in content sampling more than on statistical equivalence.

The development of a typing test with content validity appropriate for employment use might begin with job analysis to determine the specific kinds of typing tasks to be performed on the job, for example, typing invoices, compiling and typing lists, and typing short letters from recorded dictation. Specific job tasks could be listed, perhaps with a percentage frequency rating, and a typing test could be constructed so that it includes all kinds of tasks in an appropriate ratio. Content validity is usually not quantified, but it could then be established empirically (although the writer knows of no instances to cite) either by comparing independently developed forms or by correlating the percentage weights of tasks in the test with the similar weights in the job

analysis. Although such quantification is not being done, and might be suspect if it were, it illustrates the essential nature of the judgment process involved in reaching the conclusion that a test has content validity.

The assumption of a clean distinction between content validity and predictive validity is the same false distinction often made between achievement and aptitude tests. When one gives a typing test to a job applicant, he is not really very much interested in past attainments. His concern is with future performance. A typing test of high content validity may not have much predictive validity (Guion, 1965a). What is more to the point, however, is that judgments of content validity leave unanswered an important job-related question: How much of the validly measured achievement does the job require? If a speed test for typing is deemed to have sufficient content validity, how fast must one type for satisfactory initial performance? The answer would probably vary from one situation to another; different answers might be found for situations where typing consists of preparing invoices in contrast to typing from recorded dictation. To find the answer, something very much like a short-term predictive validation could be done. Supervisors could be asked for an immediate evaluation of new employees; scores on the test could be compared to those evaluations and optimal cutting scores defined empirically.

In short, content validity may not be a fully satisfactory evaluation of an employment test for use with relatively inexperienced applicants, although it should often be considered in the total evaluation. There are, however, two specific sorts of measurement where investigations into content validity are fully appropriate. One of these is for selection of experienced personnel, as in upgrading or promotion, where the new job is an extension of skills or information learned on an old one or in specialized training. The other, obviously enough, is for the evaluation of criterion measures. Whether a work sample or ordinary production data, it is appropriate to ask whether the measure obtained is representative of the universe of tasks the worker is expected to perform.

The word "content" refers to a fairly well-defined category of experience, such as shorthand or typing skill, knowledge of basic electronics, or a cab-driver's knowledge of his city's geography. The word "construct," on the other hand, refers to "categories that are deliberate creations chosen to organize experience into general law-like statements" (Cronbach, 1971, p. 462). Construct validation is, therefore, more theoretical and requires a bigger data base. It involves inquiry into the nature of the traits being measured by a test (or by a criterion, for that matter); that is, "...determining the degree to which certain explanatory concepts or constructs account for performance on the test" (American Psychological Association, 1966). In the simplest case, the assessment of construct validity involves three steps: (1) hypotheses about the trait being measured and its relation to something else, that is, a measure of the trait; (2) data carefully gathered to test such hypotheses; and (3) inferences about the adequacy of the hypotheses in explaining the data collected.

It is tempting to engage in a full discussion of the fascinating and extremely important concept of construct validity; the philosophical foundations are by no means clearly established (Bechtoldt, 1959; Campbell, 1960; Cronbach & Meehl, 1955; Ebel, 1961; Loevinger, 1957), a fact which has given rise to a frequent if fatuous assertion that "no one really knows what construct validity is." Nevertheless, this discussion will be restricted to the role of judgments of construct validity in employment psychology— a role which, while important, is highly specialized. Moreover, the emphasis will be on criterion constructs; job success, or any component of it, is probably the most important construct of all in employment testing.

Construct validity is important when one is primarily concerned with understanding the nature of the attribute being measured. It represents a greater concern with the intrinsic character of a measurement than with its utility. It involves relationships between the measure of concern and other measures as a guide to understanding. An example in criterion development may serve to clarify.

Consider an attribute of job performance for inspectors at an assembly conveyor, detection of defects, measured by a simple count of the number of defects found each day. There are several obvious problems. One does not know, for example, the "correct" number of defects. Moreover, the simple count does not take into account the degree to which a defect is glaring or subtle, nor is it clear that each counted defect was in truth defective.

If one would do the research necessary to evaluate the construct validity of counted defects, several studies would be appropriate. He could, for example, develop a work sample and correlate the simple count with performance on a known sample. He could devise a special training program, and determine whether those who were trained had higher counts than those who were not. If there were some way to identify customer complaints and trace them to the individual inspector, the simple count could be correlated with customer complaints. It might be hypothesized that the ability to detect defects is a composite of special forms of visual acuity and attention span; the simple count, along with work sample scores, acuity measures, and measures of visual attention, could be factor analyzed. The measure could be correlated with measures of possible contaminants, such as the age of the equipment producing the objects to be inspected, in the anticipation (or hope) of low correlations. From this large network of research data, inferences would then be drawn about the nature of the construct itself and about the value of the simple measure. It is important, although quite incidental to understanding the construct validity of a measure, that some correlated measures could be predictors and evaluated as such by assessing their predictive validities.

Large-scale study of criterion constructs through such networks of research data is rare, but research on the construct validity of criteria is by no means unknown. One explores the construct validity of ratings when he investigates length of service as a possible contaminant. Lawler (1967) was investigating the construct validity of his set of ratings when he used the multi-trait-multi-method matrix using peer, self, and supervisory ratings. Gunderson and Nelson (1966) did similar studies following factor analytic research. One suspects that greater attention to the construct validity of criterion measures would pay real dividends. If one has a clear understanding of the nature of the constructs measured and of the contaminating influences, hypotheses about predictors can be more clearly formulated and defended, and contaminants can be incorporated into the prediction scheme.

Efforts to assess construct validity are much more frequently made with tests. A published test with a well-filled manual has much of the work already done, with a substantial amount of known information about what the test does or does not correlate with. The literature may include experimental and factor analytic studies. One may be able, even without further research, to evaluate with reasonable confidence the construct validity of each of several alternative tests under consideration.

There is, however, no justification for assuming that a test judged on adequate grounds to be a highly valid measure of a desired construct is in fact useful as an employment tool. It is of no value to justify a claim that a test has high construct validity as a measure of, let us say, spatial visualization abilities, unless one also has solid grounds for claiming that performance on the job requires spatial visualization.

VALIDITY AND THE EMPLOYMENT PROCESS. Predictive validation is the most appropriate

research paradigm for employment testing. The writer, at the present time, takes a moderately orthodox position; it is a tenet of orthodoxy that one shall attempt, if at all possible, to compute predictive validity and to base one's decisions about the use of the test on such validity. If a well-designed validation study can be done, it should be; the "meaningfulness" of tests should be largely derived from such study.

Nevertheless, a caveat is appropriate. *A predictive validity coefficient is not necessarily a good appraisal of the appropriateness of a test as a selection instrument.* This is more than a recognition that some traits may be prerequisite without being predictive in a correlative sense (Hedberg & Baxter, 1957). Rather, the statement is more a recognition that even the most fundamental tenets deserve to be questioned. Ebel (1961) has, for example, criticized the entire concept of validity in all four guises. He suggests that one should ask of a test only that it be meaningful in operational definition, in its relationships to other variables, and in its reliability. Dunnette (1963b) has followed suit, suggesting "that coefficients of *practical* validity (concurrent and predictive) be accorded a lower position in the status hierarchy and that they be used simply as one of a number of kinds of evidence to lend meaning to test behavior" (p. 252; italics in original). Whether one wants to eliminate the concept or merely reduce its role, an evaluation of the relative importance of predictive validity requires three considerations.

First, the uncritical acceptance of the predictive paradigm is too often accompanied by an equally uncritical acceptance of the criterion measure, and many criteria are charitably described as casual. Too often the criterion measure is restricted to what is easily measured without regard for the inclusion of more important aspects of performance. Moreover, even a carefully developed criterion measure may frequently be subject to severe and often inexplicable contaminations. Ideally, an empirical validity coefficient measures the communality of constructs on either side of the prediction equation. In practice, it may represent correlation with contaminants as much as correlation with essential constructs of performance.

Such a situation is illustrated in Figure 1. Suppose a test of arithmetic reasoning is used to predict performance on a salvage and repair operation as rated by the super-

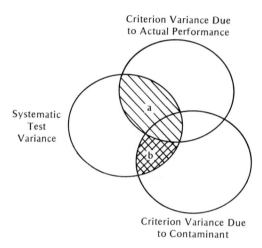

Figure 1. Representation of spurious validity statement due to correlation between test scores and criterion contaminants.

visor. The total systematic test variance is principally due to some form of logical thinking, but some of it may be due to verbal ability. Suppose further that there are two main sources of systematic variance in supervisory ratings: (1) the intended variance, demonstrated salvage skill, and (2) contaminant variance stemming from the supervisor's erroneous tendency to equate salvage skill with verbal indications of superior intelligence—being able "to talk a good job." In these circumstances, the validity of the basic hypothesis (that test scores predict actual performance) is represented by the shaded area *a*, but the obtained validity coefficient is represented by the total of the shaded areas *a* and *b*. The obtained statement of validity is misleading because it

represents to an appreciable degree the correlation between test scores and an irrelevant contaminant. One might, of course, argue that the test also contains the contaminant; however, the contaminating test variance has no influence on the predictions unless there is a correlated contaminant in the criterion. Much effort has been expended in trying to purge tests of unwanted variance; such effort is more urgently needed for the purging of criteria and for clarifying what a criterion measure is supposed to represent (Wallace, 1965).

Second, solid predictive validation is often not possible. Occasionally, concurrent validation *can* be used as a substitute even though it is likely to be unsatisfactory. Frequently, however, no useful criterion-related study can be done; for instance, there may not be enough people, there may be an excessive restriction of range (Peterson & Wallace, 1966), and it may be impossible to obtain a satisfactory performance measure. (Examples occur where the nature of job performance is too diverse, as in many professional occupations, or where the individual's contribution to group performance cannot be teased out.) For these situations, it is not so much the paradigm that is at fault as the circumstances in which the paradigm is to be applied. It might be possible to generalize predictive validity from other studies, if there are enough of them for the same sort of job to yield some kind of consensus. Indeed, if that were the case, the consensus would probably be a better indicator of predictive validity than a single study. Unfortunately, there are too few occasions when a consensus about a specific test can be satisfactorily identified.

Finally, there are different ideas about the place of a valid test (by whatever definition) in the total employment process. Some see the test as the basis for decision; in this role, predictive validity has obvious importance. Others see the test as simply another, albeit perhaps superior, input into a human decision process. In this view, the test must be "meaningful" if it is to result in good decisions; that is, the test must be a genuine help to the decider. The real job of prediction is done by a person, not by a test. The important evaluation of a test, in this view, is its construct validity or its meaningfulness, and if predictive validation is possible, fine. If this view is carried to its logical conclusion, the decision maker *is* the test, and his *decisions* should be validated according to the predictive paradigm.

DEVELOPING RATIONAL HYPOTHESES

Concentration on test validation encourages a fundamental error; the problem is not one of evaluating tests, it is one of developing and validating hypotheses. Too much attention has been given to "testing" and not enough to "predicting."

Rundquist (1969) suggests less attention to statistical technique and more to psychological thinking. He argues that man is an open system working as part of a larger open system. In an open system, any given outcome can have a variety of antecedents. Satisfactory performance by one man may be due to characteristics different from those producing satisfactory performance by another. The point was made schematically by Dunnette (1963a, 1974) as shown in Figure 2. Independent selection batteries are introduced for three different groups of people, and still there are those for whom none of the batteries is appropriate. Each battery represents a different valid hypothesis about the relationships between applicant characteristics and job performance. The diagram implies that prediction can be improved by this "individualizing" approach; it also implies a background of extensive and carefully reasoned research.

Too often, employment tools are adopted not only "without meaningful study" (*Griggs* v. *Duke Power,* 1971), but without much serious thought. The adoption of any selection standard implies a hypothesis, but in routine testing the hypothesis is not even acknowledged, let alone clearly enunciated.

The task of formulating clear hypotheses should be accorded a central position in employment psychology. The form of the hypothesis should most often be functional, such that $Y = f(X)$, where Y is the important criterion construct to be predicted and X is the variable or set of variables which the investigator has reason to believe is relevant to Y. The nature of the relationship (linear, parabolic, exponential) may also be hypothesized, or it may be left to empirical investigation. What must be specified is the reasoning that selects the variables on the two sides of the equation.

Criterion Constructs: What to Predict

Criteria are not interchangeable or equivalent; one cannot proceed as if it made no difference what criterion is used in personnel research. The very first task is to determine what is to be predicted. Sometimes criterion constructs emerge almost volcanically from specific organizational problems: excessive turnover or absenteeism, low quality, or low productivity. More frequently they must be inferred from an analysis of jobs or of organizational needs; even obvious criteria should not be accepted without critical examination.

One must decide on the degree of generality sought. If the pressures for improved selection are organization-wide, such as a turnover problem plaguing all departments of a broad organization, then the criterion needs to have broad applicability reflecting general rather than job-specific concerns. If the pressure stems from excessive labor costs of specific operations, then criteria will need to be more specifically tied to individual jobs or groups of jobs. The pioneers of employment psychology were advised to "consult the cost accountant to find the department in which increased efficiency in selecting employees would bring about the greatest economic saving to the firm" (Freyd, 1923, p. 218); this is not bad advice even now.

Most often, the concerns are for perform-

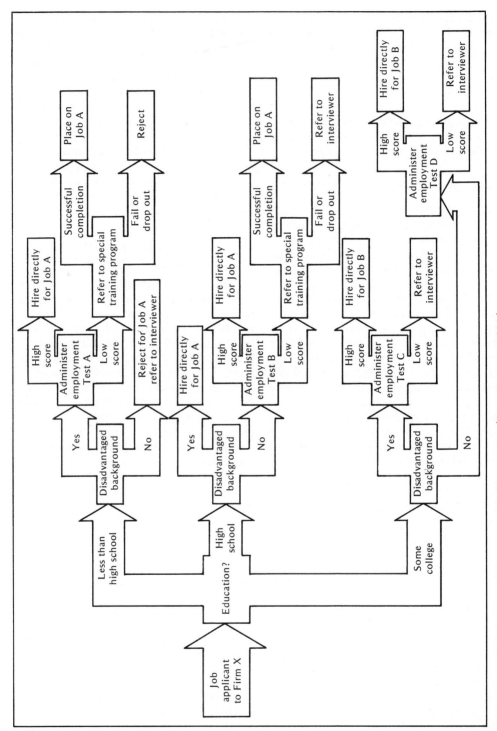

Figure 2.   Dunnette's model of the personnel decision process. (From Dunnette, 1974.)

ance on a job, and criteria should be related to specific jobs or job families. For the most part, criterion constructs are found through careful studies of individual jobs, even where jobs with like performance requirements will later be grouped for validation purposes. Knowledge of what a person does, how he goes at it, why he does it, or how important it is (in terms of time, urgency, uniqueness, or whatever)—all such information can be examined to infer the crucial or defining task activities, personal behaviors, or areas of responsibility. One should not rush too quickly to seek measures; the first task is to develop a *conceptual definition* of the critical aspect of performance to be predicted.

The emphasis must be on defining *critical* concepts. Little improvement can be expected in performance simply by predicting a trivial aspect of performance. Identifying the critical may require some preliminary hypothesizing. In one organization, for example, it was suggested from job analysis that the crucial aspect of a riveter's job performance is neither quantity nor reject rate but the rhythm of work which contributes to both. It was said (although not verified by data) that a new worker with low productivity can still be expected to become a fast, accurate riveter if he first develops a sense of rhythm on the job. If the crucial measure is one of rhythm, then the appropriate concept is not rate of work but variability in performance. As a worker develops his own rhythm, according to this point of view, his output becomes more consistent; as workers develop more consistent output rates, it is suggested, they also become faster and more accurate.

Such assumptions should be verified before a major personnel research is based on them. They are reasonable in view of the series of studies on output rates reported by Rothe (e.g., Rothe, 1946, 1947, 1951; Rothe & Nye, 1959, 1961) suggesting that consistency may be a function of motivation. The point here is not whether they are

sound, but that they were based on an analysis of the work performed.

ORGANIZATIONAL VALUES. Many aspects of job performance and related behavior involve questions of relative value. Examples include traditional aspects of proficiency: work volume, quality, safety, and perhaps production consistency or predictability. Other values include various aspects of trainability, motivation to work, rate of personal career development, stability of the work force, and perhaps basic honesty or responsibility. Each of these identifies in rough form, needing refinement and precision of definition in practical use, the "ball park" in which criterion constructs are to be found.

Consideration of organizational values provides a guide to priorities. Is rate of production more or less important in the performance of a job than quality? Insofar as both are valued, in some designated combination, is the combination of greater or less value to the organization than the trainability or stability of the work force? There is a fallacy in these questions—the notion that choices must be made between competing values; but such questions can help in developing a list of priorities: which hypotheses are to be developed? It is not likely, for every job, that every kind of criterion concept will become the focal point of personnel research. Decisions must be made and the hard task of setting priorities should not be nudged aside by the simple expedient of using ratings of overall performance.

There is often a strong pragmatic desire to seek a single, all-inclusive criterion concept. For relatively simple jobs, this may be feasible. For most jobs, the reality is that different aspects of performance are in fact independent, and multiple criteria can and should be identified (Dunnette, 1963b; Ghiselli, 1956a; Guion, 1961, 1965a).

Schmidt and Kaplan (1971) offered a resolution of what they see as conflict between those who have advocated multiple criteria and those who have advocated the inclusive single criterion (Toops, 1944; Brogden & Taylor, 1950; Nagle, 1953). It is not certain, however, that a controversy has raged; it seems more an evolution of concepts. With a technological concept of "the validity" of a test, the single criterion was indeed indispensible. The literature of the 1940s and early 1950s not only demanded single criteria but showed how to achieve them with at least some functional unity, such as the "dollar criterion" (Brogden & Taylor, 1950). It became apparent, however, that single-factor criteria could not be counted on (Seashore, Indik, & Georgopoulos, 1960), and in the late 1950s and throughout the 1960s, the emphasis has been on functional unity in criterion constructs, even if more than one variable must, therefore, be predicted.

If controversy does exist, the arguments seem to be (a) that in the final analysis, a single hire-or-reject decision must be made, and (b) that a single criterion such as a dollar criterion represents a single coherent economic construct. Elsewhere (Guion, 1961), this writer has argued it is more rational to give different weights to different predictions at that final point of decision than to combine functionally independent elements at the outset of one's research. The arguments would have followed the same line if economic rather than psychological constructs had been used as illustrations; the savings attributable to increased production are functionally independent of the savings attributable to increased stability of the work force and should, therefore, be predicted independently. The implication in either case is that more than one hypothesis may be necessary to maximize prediction.

CONFERENCES. Knowledge of the job, in the light of organizational values, can lead directly to criterion concepts if informed people are assembled in conference. An excellent description of this approach is the Smith and Kendall (1963) report on the development of rating scales for nurses. Be-

fore any attempt was made to develop measures (in this case ratings), supervising nurses were brought together and asked to identify the dimensions along which nursing performance should be evaluated. As practicing nurses, they had a substantial body of detailed knowledge of the job itself; specific job descriptions were not necessary. Moreover, as agents of hospital management, they had rather clear pictures of organizational value systems, and they could combine value judgments with detailed knowledge to tease out the crucial dimensions of nursing behavior.

Criterion Measurement

Criterion measures are operational definitions of inferred constructs. Development of the construct is a matter of knowledge and wisdom; development of the corresponding measure is a matter of technology. The requirements of effective criterion measurement have been detailed by Smith in Chapter 17 of this *Handbook* and require no elaboration here. Only one point will be stressed.

That point is the need to assess the construct validity of measures chosen as criteria. There are many approaches, such as systematic investigations of various sources of bias through correlational, experimental, or factor analytic methods. This is, admittedly, a prescription for hard investigative work, but a casual approach to the development and evaluation of criteria can only be expected to provide casual results. It is reasonable to suppose that prediction can be improved if criterion constructs are carefully thought through and the operational measures carefully studied for construct validity.

Of the various methods of criterion measurement, simulation and work sampling deserve special consideration for personnel selection programs. Ghiselli (1966) has shown that trainability is a more predictable class of criteria than proficiency. It is useful, however, to show that training has indeed produced proficiency. Actual performance is subject to many influences that may not be known at the time of prediction; daily performance measures may be influenced by variations in training programs or motivation, quality or style of supervision, wage systems, work group characteristics, and many other variables that are unknowns at the time a hiring decision must be made. It is feasible, however, to measure and to predict maximum performance capability, which can often be defined by simulation or work sample exercises. If as much attention were given to the development of good work sample criteria as has been given to the development of predictors, the potential savings would seem much greater than those to be realized through research based on the criterion at hand.

Predictor Constructs

The identification and operational definition of criterion constructs is only one side of the equation. The essence of hypothesis formation is the identification and operational definition of variables that will predict criterion performance or will in some sense influence such prediction.

The choice of such variables is too often based on stereotypes. Regardless of the type of job, there are certain characteristics (reminiscent of the Boy Scout Law, according to Hakel & Schuh, 1971) that seem always to be in demand by interviewers.

It is better if background thinking is more specifically related to the criterion constructs chosen as targets for prediction. Such thought should be guided by three principles: (1) Complex behavior cannot be fully predicted by simple means; one should not ordinarily be satisfied to postulate a single predictor. (2) Complex behavior is in part a function of the characteristics of the individual, but only in part; it is also a function of the stimulus variables in the situation. We have been too long hung up on tests (i.e., measures of individual traits); if we turn our attention to the question of how best to predict a criterion, we would typically recognize potential predictors other than individual traits. It is not necessary at this point to ask whether situational or demographic variables would combine with individual traits in a linear fashion or would interact with them; at this point it is important only that they be considered in the formulation of the hypothesis. (3) Complex behavior is not likely to be optimally predicted in the same way for all sorts of people. There is nothing inherently sensible in the idea that all applicants should be herded through an absolutely identical process in reaching employment decisions; the Dunnette model in Figure 2 is once again an appropriate reference. Obviously, it is not feasible to develop a separate prediction equation for every individual; it is feasible, however, to develop separate prediction equations for logically different subgroups.

The completion of a prediction hypothesis, therefore, calls for the consideration of three kinds of variables: individual traits, situational stimuli, and variables for subgroup classification. The latter are sometimes termed moderators, that is, variables that may influence the relationship between a predictor and a criterion. (At a later stage, when the predictor constructs have been identified, additional variables such as response styles might enter into consideration as artifacts of the measurement.) Consideration of the possible kinds of variables requires a thorough knowledge of the literature, aided by reference to some specific sources.

INDIVIDUAL TRAITS. This *Handbook* will provide the first step in searching the literature; what one needs first is a fairly comprehensive understanding of the range and variety of human characteristics upon which to draw, and the third section of this volume, Chapters 11 through 14, should certainly place such information in a convenient package. No further attempt will be made in this chapter to catalog traits.

Various reviews will also prove helpful.

TABLE 1
MEAN VALIDITY COEFFICIENTS FOR CLERICAL OCCUPATIONS

	General Clerks		Recording Clerks		Computing Clerks		All Clerks	
	Train.	Prof.	Train.	Prof.	Train.	Prof.	Train.	Prof.
Intellectual Abilities	.46f	.31f	.48f	.26e	.52f	.24e	.47f	.27f
Intelligence	.46f	.36e	.43f	.26e	.54d	.21d	.48f	.30f
Immediate Memory		.29f	.32d	.36d	.46a	.26c	.32d	.30d
Substitution	.21d	.24d	.24c	.23c	.34b	.24c	.24d	.24e
Arithmetic	.49f	.26e	.50f	.26d	.51d	.28d	.50f	.26f
Spatial and Mechanical Abilities	.35f	.14d	.30f	.18d	.52d	.28d	.33f	.20e
Spatial Relations	.40e	.14c	.32e	.16d	.55c	.25d	.36f	.19d
Location		.05b	.24c	.12c	.49a	.30b	.27c	.17d
Mechanical Principles	.32e	.20a	.28f	.23d	.54c	.27c	.30f	.25d
Perceptual Accuracy	.40b	.26e	.41e	.26d	.31b	.31d	.40e	.27f
Number Comparison	.40b	.25d	.29b	.29d	.35b	.32d	.34c	.27e
Name Comparison	.40b	.29d	.35b	.33c	.19a	.34d	.35c	.31d
Cancellation		.22c	.58b	.19d	.11a	.24d	.49b	.21d
Pursuit		−.17a	.21b	.12b		.35a	.21b	.12b
Perceptual Speed		.40b	.42e			.46b	.42e	.42c
Motor Abilities	.34a	.16d	.15d	.17d	.14b	.09d	.15d	.15e
Tracing		−.09a	.17b	.11b	.08a	.42b	.15b	.19b
Tapping		.13b	.23b	.15b	.16b	.16b	.21c	.15d
Dotting			.13b	.17c	.16a	.03c	.18b	.12d
Finger Dexterity	.34a	.14c	.09c	.25b		−.11b	.09c	.24d
Hand Dexterity		.29c	.30a	.16a		−.05a	.30a	.11b
Arm Dexterity		.16b	.09a	−.09a		.34a	.09a	.11b
Personality Traits		.36b		.14c		.19b		.23d
Personality	.17d	.30c		.18c		.17b	.17d	.24d
Interest	.17d	.30c		−.01b		.23b	.17d	.12b

a. Less than 100 cases
b. 100 to 499 cases
c. 500 to 999 cases
d. 1,000 to 4,999 cases
e. 5,000 to 9,999 cases
f. 10,000 or more cases
From Ghiselli, 1966b.

Typically, such reviews focus on the measures themselves. One who has some understanding of the traits measured can look beyond the specific references to the concepts they imply.

Perhaps the first reference to consult is Ghiselli's monograph (1966b), a compilation of the average validities found in studies where tests, jobs, and criteria are classified in various ways. Table 1 illustrates the kind of information provided; two kinds of criteria, three kinds of clerical jobs, and twenty-five categories of tests (including five major classes) are used; suggestions of the reliability of mean validities are given by the footnotes describing total Ns of the studies upon which the averages are based. An average validity of .58 where cancellation tests are used to predict trainability of recording clerks is suspect since it involved a small total N; a mean validity of .49, on the other hand, seems quite dependable for using arithmetic tests to predict trainability of general clerks since it is based on a total N of more than 10,000 cases.

The detailed table is summarized for quick visual reference in Figure 3. If one has a criterion construct that fits well the trainability category and wants to predict it among general office clerks, Figure 3 tells him quickly that the chances are quite good that a measure of intellectual ability will work, while the odds are not very favorable for personality traits.

In addition, there are reviews of specialized areas. Dorcus and Jones (1950) published a general review; Guion and Gottier (1965) reviewed validities of personality measures; Korman (1968) reviewed research on the selection of managers; Lent, Aurbach, and Levin (1971a, 1971b) surveyed Validity Information Exchange reports; Schuh (1967a, 1967b) reviewed research on the prediction of tenure; Zedeck (1971b) has reviewed research on moderators. Various textbooks could also be consulted for evaluative reviews (e.g., Albright, Glennon, & Smith, 1963; Dunnette, 1966b; Guion, 1965a; Lawshe & Balma, 1966). A search

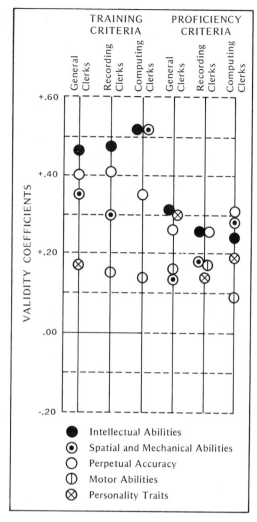

Figure 3. Mean validity coefficients of tests for clerical occupations. (From Ghiselli, 1966b.)

of abstracts and various bibliographies may turn up specific studies quite similar to the one contemplated.

Conferences with the people who know the situation best—job incumbents, supervisors, industrial engineers, inspectors—can help the psychologist take a new and fresh look at everything in the process: criteria, predictors, moderators, measurement techniques, and general help in organizing the research project. Systematic efforts to solicit the thinking of such people should be a part of the planning of all personnel research. The investigator's principal task is to imagine what individual traits might be assessed in the prediction of his chosen criterion. His imagination is guided by his knowledge of what has worked in similar kinds of situations in the past, and it can be guided as well by the intuitions and experience of people more familiar with the nuances of performance on the job in question.

None of this can quite replace firsthand observation of work in progress. Something very much like old-fashioned introspection occurs when, through systematic observation, one sees clearly what is done, what methods and materials are used, what muscle groups or sensory processes are called upon, and so on. Better yet, where feasible, would be an actual trial of the task, although one should remember that the procedures of the learner are not necessarily those used after experience.

The development of hypotheses should not be restricted to the identification of predictor variables; individual traits may also serve as potential moderators. Examples abound. Ghiselli (1968) and Kipnis (1962) have shown that motivational variables moderate aptitude validities. Similarly, Betz (1971) reported that job satisfaction moderated predictions of success; subgrouping applicants on the basis of predicted job satisfaction might, therefore, be considered. Applicant expectations, perhaps as assessed in some measure of organizational image (Tom, 1971) would be worth further consideration as possible moderators. Even variables that, for policy reasons, would not be used in prediction, such as age, could be included in research so that the relative importance of usable variables could be assessed more clearly (cf., Plante & Stewart, 1971).

SITUATIONAL PREDICTORS. There are fewer broad guides in the literature to examine for situational variables relevant to the predic-tion equation.[7] The problem is that environmental factors influencing performance have not been considered very often in attempting predictions during the hiring process. Perhaps the only systematic exception to this general statement occurs where selection is done within the framework of systems analysis, and these variables are considered more from a training point of view in such applications (Rundquist, 1969).

There are many potentially important situational variables, but only a few have been reported in studies relevant to selection. In the selection of managers, variables of organizational climate (Stanton, 1960) or work-group autonomy (Ghiselli & Lodahl, 1958) might be considered. Selection of managers or salesmen who must work in a far-flung enterprise might consider such variables as the nature of the territory or specific management practices (Ferguson, 1958; Knauft, 1949; Wallace & Twitchell, 1949). Leadership preferences of subordinates might influence performance of leaders (Stanton, 1960); it could be argued that leadership styles of supervisors could influence the performance of subordinates—either as a direct predictor of performance or as a moderator interacting with subordinate traits. In short, any management practice which is suggested in the literature or the folklore of management suggests in turn a variable originally put forth on the assumption that it influences job performance and is, therefore, appropriately considered as a possible predictor or moderator.

The point is perhaps best made with reference to an experimental study reported by Frederiksen, Jensen, and Beaton (1972). Two situational variables were manipulated in the simulation: "organizational climate" (either the organization encouraged imaginative solutions to problems or required close adherence to rules and regulations) and "supervisory climate" (either global or

---

[7] Two sections of this *Handbook* may be helpful, the section on "Attributes of Organizations" and the following section entitled, "Behavioral Processes in Organizations."

detailed). It was the interaction of these that produced the most marked effect on performance; a consistent climate (e.g., innovative-global or rules-detailed) yielded productivity on an in-basket exercise significantly higher than did the inconsistent climate. If these results can be generalized, the prediction of performance within a single organization (whether innovative or rigid) should take into account not only the traits of the applicants but also the supervisory styles of their proposed bosses; to do otherwise would be to tolerate explainable error in prediction.

POPULATION SUBGROUP CHARACTERISTICS. Standard textbooks on individual differences (cf., Anastasi, 1958) describe differences of subpopulation averages on various traits. For example, differences can be cited associated with sex, age, race, socioeconomic status, and degree of urbanization. People are not all alike; for people who differ in specific ways, test score predictions and interpretations may also differ. Variables that define identifiable subpopulations may serve as direct predictors or as moderators.

Traditional personnel selection recognizes the importance of subgroup differences in its recommendation that validity studies be done with a representative sample of the applicant population; major changes in the applicant mix of characteristics have long been suspected of influencing validity. Subgroup characteristics, therefore, have important implications for recruiting.

There is a further sense in which subgrouping can improve prediction. The moderator concept applies to the influence of the moderator variable on a specific predictor-criterion relationship. It might also serve to identify subgroups for which quite different predictors are appropriate (Ghiselli, 1960a; Shott, Albright, & Glennon, 1963). Aside from possible legal implications (to be discussed independently below), there is no a priori reason to assume that the performance of men is necessarily predicted optimally from the same variables used for predicting performance of women; the same could be said of differential prediction based on race, or age, or socioeconomic status, or expected patterns of job satisfaction.

Selection of Measures

With predictor and moderator constructs specified, the hypothesis is fully formulated, but cannot be tested or used until operational definitions have been accepted. Traditionally, preferred predictors have been called tests. One should not feel bound by narrow concepts of testing. When the emphasis is correctly placed on the task of predicting criterion performance rather than on simply validating tests, the traditional conception of a test expands. Personal history items such as those on application blanks, specific items of information drawn from interviews, global judgments made by interviewers or others, and specific educational or work history requirements must be considered as tests. Each of them is, in effect, an operational definition of something deemed importantly related to performance on the criterion to be predicted. Each of them is a hurdle to be "passed" if one is to get the job.

The narrower conception will be here discussed as "psychological tests" rather than as employment tests; psychological tests are those that are intended to measure skills, abilities, aptitudes, or personality characteristics through psychometrically standardized samples of behavior. That this definition could also include such things as personal history forms or interviewer guides, but does not, simply emphasizes the artificiality of designating some predictors as psychological tests and others as something different.

PSYCHOLOGICAL TESTS. The writer has contrived a set of demonstration data with three different "tests" to predict a dichotomous criterion. Score distributions on one test are markedly different for those who are "superior" or "other." (The biserial r is .60.)

The "superior" and "other" groups have identical distributions of scores on the other two tests (i.e., validities are zero). However, one of these "invalid tests" correlates .72 with the "valid test."

This is not far out of line for correlations between tests presumably measuring the same things, such as two respectable measures of general mental ability. Suppose one must decide which of two mental ability tests, correlating .72 according to the best evidence, should be used. Suppose further that no appreciable differences can be detected in item content, reliability, or time requirements. Could it be reasonably assumed that the two tests would have equal validities? Probably not. Probably only a specific research study could clearly show that one test is or is not superior to the other. We could belabor the point, but it seems fruitless; few investigators are likely to accept the burden of trying out tests they do not expect to use.

Information can be found to give one measure an edge over competing measures. It can be drawn from manuals, from textbook reviews, or from test reviews (such as the *Mental Measurements Yearbooks* edited by Buros, 1938, 1941, 1949, 1953, 1959, 1965, 1972). In reading a test manual, one looks first for evidence of competence in test construction: clarity of purpose, adequacy of research samples, presentation of evidence rather than of marketing claims, specificity of standardization of administration and scoring, correlations with other measures of the same and of discriminably different constructs, and other statistical data. Normative tables can be examined to determine difficulty level, discriminability, and normality of distribution in samples like the population expected. Reliability data can be evaluated, along with validities in similar situations for other users. Alternative tests can be examined and choices made on such technical matters as evidences of reliability, predictive validity, and most importantly construct validity along with such practical considerations as face validity (palatability in

the employment office) and cost. The general literature may give clues to extraneous variables that might influence scores. It is also worthwhile to consider test security; a test that is available everywhere may not be a standard stimulus for all applicants.

PERSONAL HISTORY. Biographical data rank high in popularity among researchers. Some use of application blanks ranks in sophistication with finger-pointing, but personal history questionnaires can be relevant theoretically (cf., Ramfalk, 1957; Super, 1960). Groups of personal history items can be put together in an internally consistent scale to measure specific traits; single items may also be used as predictors. Rarely, however, does one encounter networks of data for inferring construct validity of personal history predictors. This may be troublesome in the present context of formulating a hypothesis, but the fact remains that personal history data often provide the best predictions (e.g., Loudermilk, 1966; Plag & Goffman, 1967).

Personal history is not assessed solely by self-report. Reference ratings continue to be used, although Browning (1968) found them no better in predicting teacher ratings than Mosel and Goheen (1959) had reported in the Civil Service study. Brenner (1968) reported on a specific kind of personal history, high school teachers' ratings of work habits in school, as a valid predictor of supervisory production ratings. Since self-reports in the application blank format are subject to distortion (Goldstein, 1971), novel approaches to gathering personal history data in ethical ways deserve serious attention.

INTERVIEWS. The interview is the most widely used employment technique, but it also seems the most in disrepute. Early research demonstrated the unreliability of the judgments of experienced interviewers (Hollingworth, 1922). When Wagner (1949) did his comprehensive review, he noted that interviews tended to be unreliable and, therefore, of questionable validity. He concluded, among other things, that the validity of an interview is probably highly specific both to the unique situation and to the interviewer as an individual; the implication, which could not be supported from the available evidence, was that some interviewers make judgments that are more valid than those of others. Another theme in his review was that interviewing could be a means of assessing specific traits related to the kind of success to be predicted, preferably those traits where other, and perhaps better, techniques cannot be used.

Following Wagner's review by a decade and a half were a series of reviews: Mayfield (1964), Ulrich and Trumbo (1965), and Webster (1964), the latter reviewing a series of experimental studies done within the framework of the Canadian Army. These reviews were no more favorable, painting a dismal picture of interviewer agreement and, from Webster, of the manner in which decisions were reached. Much experimental research on the interviewing process surfaced in the wake of these reviews. Little of it has watched actual interviews, as had been done earlier (Daniels & Otis, 1950; Anderson, 1960). Instead, "simulated" interviews became the mode for investigations. Major centers of research have been the Life Insurance Agency Management Association (Carlson, 1967, 1968, 1971; Carlson & Mayfield, 1967; Mayfield & Carlson, 1966) and the Minnesota-Ohio State axis (Dunnette & Hakel, 1966; Hakel, 1971; Hakel, Dobmeyer, & Dunnette, 1970; Hakel & Schuh, 1971); many others, however, have studied interviewing from one perspective or another (e.g., Antia, 1971; Blakeney & MacNaughton, 1971; Bolton & Hickey, 1969).

Some generalizations seem to be emerging. First of all, matters may not be quite so hopeless for the interview as has been believed; the problems of unreliability and poor validity are still prevalent, but here and there are cases where some interviewers, in some situations, made judgments that yielded substantial coefficients of validity.

Ghiselli (1966a), as one illustration, reported a biserial r (corrected for restricted range) of .51, where even the uncorrected coefficient of .35 was not inconsequential. Another apparent success story is in assessment center interviews (Grant & Bray, 1969).

Second, a major determiner of final judgment is for most interviewers the first impression; Hakel (1971) has suggested that the classical unreliability of interviewer judgments may be due largely to the wide differences that exist in first data and first impressions. Negative information seems to carry more weight than does favorable information (although the amount of favorable information may be important as well). Incidentally, it has also been shown that different interviewers disagree about whether certain items of information should be considered favorable or unfavorable—another factor contributing to the unreliability of interviews. Other determiners of final judgment seem to be how information is presented to the interviewer, whether applicants appear singly or in batches, and reasonably enough, how many people the interviewer needs to hire. Experience is apparently not a factor.

Such research has undeniable value. The validity of interviews will be low until interviewers make their judgments more reliably. A major function of the interviewer will always be to integrate the totality of information available and to make the final employment decision to hire, reject, or hold in abeyance. Research demonstrating that interviewers do not integrate full sets of information is a prelude to research on how they may be induced to do so, and to do so validly.

Most interviewing research reported to date does not, however, speak to the interview as a means of operationally defining specific constructs within a rational hypothesis. In this regard, the advice that can be given is still in the stage of unsupported "how to do it" statements. It may be firmly recommended that interviewing be done under congenial but standardized circumstances and that special interviewer guides be developed. It may be recommended that specific rating scales for specific traits, preferably behaviorally anchored scales (Maas, 1965), be placed at the disposal of the interviewer and that he receive training in their use. When such advice is followed, then studies may be undertaken to determine whether the resulting ratings have the desired construct and predictive validity.

The Rational Foundation for Predictive Validity

A procedure has been outlined in unusual detail and emphasis for hypothesis formation in personnel selection: (1) Identify clearly and with logical precision the important criterion constructs, basing judgments on data from job or situation analysis. (2) Obtain operational definitions of these constructs, and be sure they exhibit satisfactory construct validity. (3) Postulate predictor and moderator variable constructs on the basis of informed opinion. (4) Select measures and find evidence upon which to infer their descriptive validities—content validity if the constructs measured on either side of the equation are defined as samples of the same universe of work behavior, construct validity if the postulated relationship is quasi-theoretical.[8]

By the time an investigator has done all of this, he has something more than a hypothesis. He has a firm, rational foundation for predictive validity, and, more often than not, the hypothesis is likely to be confirmed in predictive validation.

This is true only when the logical steps are carefully and intelligently followed. The

[8] Where content validity is appropriate, the functional equation, $Y = f(X)$, may be considered an identity; Y and X are simply different definitions of the same content domain. Where Y is a job performance construct and X is a different construct (an aptitude), then (1) the equation represents at least a piece of a theory, even where it is no further elaborated, and (2) the measures of both Y and X must have adequate construct validity for their respective sides if the theory is to be tested adequately.

tradition in personnel research is not firmly on the side of rational or theoretical foundations. To the contrary, the tradition has been best illustrated by the saying, "if it works, use it." The tradition has served well, and it should not be unduly criticized. Trying out prospective variables on the basis of hunch, informed intuition, or simple availability has at times yielded valuable results. It is not too pragmatic to say that a result that works is useful whether its history be rational or serendipitous. However, the rationally developed hypothesis has a better chance to work, and it is defended more meaningfully.

The total task of personnel research is, of course, unfinished when one has *only* the rational foundation for predictive validity. As with any other hypothesis in any field of research, its validity is subject to empirical test. Nothing in these comments is intended to indicate that a rationally developed hypothesis is an adequate substitute for empirical validation. It is intended, however, to suggest that a well-developed rational hypothesis may be of more value to an organization than a half-baked empirical study.

Whenever an idealized predictive validation is not feasible, some compromises are needed. The first level of compromise is still empirical: one might be able to do concurrent validation even when the door is closed to predictive studies. (Reservations about the value of such substitution have already been expressed.) Several factors, however, may prevent any empirical validation study at all. Validation with small Ns or variances, or against a criterion that measures nothing of importance with respect to the job (or measures poorly something important), may be of less value than no study at all; in such circumstances a carefully developed and well-supported hypothesis, as a rational prototype of the empirical study that could not be done properly, may prove superior. The development of the hypothesis, more than raw empiricism, may constitute meaningful study of the selection problem.

THE VALIDATION PROCESS: HYPOTHESIS TESTING

To assert that a good hypothesis is better than a poor study is no excuse to avoid empirical validation. Even the most carefully formulated hypothesis must be tested if at all possible; hypothesis-testing is what validation is all about.

Two rather fundamental kinds of arguments can be made for empirical validity studies. First, it is arrogant to assume that because one is a professional psychologist he really knows what will work and what won't. Parry (1968) demonstrated this to the embarrassment of nine of her ten psychologists, whose predictions of validity did not correlate significantly with actual validities in a series of studies.

Second, it is the most defensible definition of the quasi-judicial term, "job-related." What had been described here as the rational foundation for predictive validity (meaning the full set of data and arguments supporting the hypothesis) is evidence that tests suggested by that hypothesis are job-related. If those in an adversary position disagree, however, the issue might be resolved on the basis of which side argues better. A preferred resolution would be based on empirical data demonstrating the degree of relationship between test performance and job performance.

Simple Designs: Bivariate Relationships

The simplest hypothesis puts one variable on each side of the equation. This simple case is practical, it is involved in more complex hypotheses, and it illustrates important points about data gathering and analysis.

DATA COLLECTION. Two general approaches to data collection correspond to the two approaches to empirical validity. The most directly applicable design is predictive: predictor data are gathered and, ideally, held in abeyance without consideration in the hiring process. For those who are hired, after a waiting period, criterion data are collected. With both sets of data available, relationships can be determined. Alternatively, presently employed people provide the data, being taken from their places of work for "testing"; in this approach criterion data are available at about the same time predictor data are gathered. Regrettably, this seems the more common approach. Where memory for how one would have answered earlier, or job experience, or absence of anxiety may influence scores, the common approach is not very good. (Concurrent research is usually done to estimate results of predictive validation, but there is no particular reason to restrict it so. It could also be used to assess the construct validities of either predictors or criteria, an application too often overlooked in personnel research.)

Within either design, certain rules of research technique should be followed. These are discussed in most standard texts, but they may be briefly summarized here:

1. Contaminants should not be allowed to influence correlations; for example, where supervisory ratings are criteria, the supervisors should rate without knowledge of predictor data.

2. Data should be obtained under standardized conditions. Interviewing, testing, and completion of personal history forms should be done with some standard privacy, at least in part so that distractions will not be highly variable from one applicant to another. Time limits or specific oral instructions should be uniform for all. If interviews are to seek information, that information should be sought within a reasonably standardized context.

3. Motivation should be maximized. Specific attempts to increase motivation probably have a positive effect only up to some point; beyond that, they are self-defeating. The recommendation is, therefore, difficult to carry out. Nevertheless, applicant motivation is an extremely important variable in interviewing as well as in testing; unless the job is made to seem desirable, the applicant

who is "just shopping" will not do his best and may be lost to the organization.

4. Data must be recorded accurately. Scoring or editing predictor data during a research study is usually done carefully, with a strong enough desire for accuracy so that some of it may even be double-checked. Criterion data, however, are likely to contain serious errors. They are often drawn from files that have been more or less carefully maintained, and not necessarily in the same form or by the same rules, from one time period to another. It has been said so often that it becomes tiresome, but no substantial personnel research program can be carried on unless there is a well-working system of personnel accounting; records must be kept and kept accurately.

DATA ANALYSIS. The latter principle applies equally well to data analysis. It is a source of amazement that people who can be very careful in scoring data seem to see no reason to verify key-punching: Wolins (1962) even gave cause to wonder if the arithmetic is correct in reports in psychological journals; if such error occurs in the journals, the frequency of error must be still greater in unmonitored in-house reports.

Data analysis seeks to answer four kinds of questions in evaluating any form of assessment: (1) Is there any dependable relationship at all between the characteristic as measured and performance on the job; that is, can the possibility of a purely chance relationship be ruled out? (2) If so, what is the nature of that relationship? (3) Again if so, how strong or how useful is that relationship? (4) What use should be made of the relationship; that is, how should it be applied in making decisions about individual applicants? These are the questions to be answered in the process called validation.

First, is there a relationship? In correlational language, this can be answered by computing a correlation ratio (eta).[9] If eta

is not significantly different from zero, the answer is negative and the validation process stops. The same is true in contingency analysis if one obtains a nonsignificant chi square.

Dunnette (1966a) criticized the notion of significance testing rather intemperately but cogently. If N is very large, tests of statistical significance allow one to reject the null hypothesis with a very small relationship, an act of building "theoretical castles on the quicksand of merely rejecting the null hypothesis" (Dunnette, 1966a, p. 155). Certainly, the statistical test of the null hypothesis is not sacred; moreover, it is not fully appropriate for employment usage.

It is useful to remind ourselves what, precisely, a test of the null hypothesis is about. The null hypothesis says that, *if* in the total population from which we have drawn a sample there is no relationship, and *if* the sample at hand were drawn randomly from that population, and *if* we were then to draw an infinite number of further samples of the same size also at random, *then* a departure from null as large or larger than that in our observed sample would occur a given proportion of the time. If that proportion is no greater than 5 percent, according to tradition, we may suspect that the null hypothesis is not so good. In practice we go further; we behave as if we accept the alternative hypothesis that a relationship does in fact exist in the total population. Every time a predictor is adopted for operational use (with or without the statistical background), it is implicit that the hypothesis of a true relationship is accepted, that representativeness of the sample is assumed, and that new samples are expected to give the same or similar results.

The samples, of course, are not drawn at random, and the population (i.e., the applicant mix) changes from time to time, but we behave as if we consider these points trivial—as in fact we do. As a result, many tests validated for employment use in the decade following World War II by rejection of the null hypothesis have continued in use as instruments of employment de-

---

[9] Typically, of course, r is computed and tested for significance. This is making the linear assumption prematurely; a nonsignificant r does not rule out useful nonlinear relationships.

cision on the basis of assumptions neither examined nor tenable (cf., Morrison & Henkel, 1970; Tversky & Kahneman, 1971).

It is not suggested that tests of the null hypothesis be dropped from the validation strategy; rather, it is suggested that they be used primarily to avoid misleading impressions from otherwise impressive results from small samples. If a set of data "passes" the test of the null hypothesis (allowing its rejection with due regard to specified confidence intervals), that fact is merely justification for going ahead to the remaining questions. If the data do not "pass," then the hypothesized predictor should be abandoned, modified, or shelved for further data; it should not be considered for operational use.

The second question inquires into the nature of the relationship; is it linear or something else? By what regression equation or pattern of expectancies may the criterion be predicted? As a rule, it can be expected to be linear (Tupes, 1964), although one cannot invariably count on such convenient simplicity (Guion, 1965a; Kahneman & Ghiselli, 1962). Computers have simplified things for personnel research; although most statistical packages turn out product moment correlation coefficients with incredible speed, they can almost as easily be programmed to yield etas, scattergrams, and even higher order moments. (The latter may identify, for example, constraints against various corrections or other assumptions.) It is convenient to make the linear assumption, but careful examination of scatterplots will sometimes reveal other potentially useful relationships if Ns are large enough.

The third question, if there is a specific, reliable relationship, how strong is it? The answer is given by correlation coefficients or by measures of group overlap or errors in classification. That is, the answer is typically given through descriptive statistics —statistics describing the sample already hired and on the job.

Descriptive statistics are subject to several kinds of known error and may be corrected in making inferences about future samples.

Correlation coefficients can be corrected for restriction of range or for unreliability in the criterion (or in the predictor, if one can provide a reason for doing so). Theoretical expectancy charts (Lawshe, Bolda, Brune, & Auclair, 1958) can be constructed from original or corrected correlations; going this far, however, involves the assumption of a normal bivariate surface, an assumption too often unchecked. To make such corrections simply because one knows how to do so can be quite misleading; errors can be avoided by looking at the nature of the data with care.

Too often statistical elegance is simply a substitute for proper procedure. Statistical tools are useful and can, within limits, compensate for inadequacies in data (as in simple range restriction corrections). Overreliance on such tools, however, may mask basic weaknesses in data. Lawshe (1969) issued a beautiful summons to return to reality:

... very often, the statistical nicety of present methods suggests or implies an order of precision which is not basically inherent in the data. Psychological measurements at this point in time, are quite unreliable; to suggest otherwise by using unwarranted degrees of statistical precision is for the psychologist to delude others, and perhaps to delude himself. (p. 122–123)

The logic of statistical correction is nevertheless useful in evaluating practical utility; decisions to use or not to use a predictor should not be based on the absolute size of a correlation. Base rates and selection ratios are equally important. It would seem useful to consider the context and to translate any statistical inference into more practical terms; Curtis and Alf (1969) suggested as such practical indices (a) the possible increase in criterion mean, (b) the expected increase in the percentage of those who are satisfactory, and, where more than two criterion categories are appropriate, (c) the percentage increase in the desirable criterion categories.

The fourth question requires a policy

decision—a decision that must take empirical information into account. There are four options: (1) not to use it at all, (2) use it to "cream" the applicants—that is, to pick the cream of the crop, (3) use it to identify applicants with minimal qualifications, or (4) use it only in conjunction with other predictors or moderators. If there is no evidence of a relationship, the predictor should not be used at all. If the policy is to "cream" the applicants, the triangular scatterplots are not very helpful. If minimum qualifications are sought, then the clarity of criterion definition, patterns of curvilinearity, and the standard error of estimate must be considered. In short, policy decisions are better grounded if data are considered in making them.

Multivariate Models

Most criteria are complex and can be predicted better by a battery than by a single predictor. Most fully developed hypotheses are multivariate. The basic approaches to multivariate research are the same as with bivariate models. The choice is between predictive and concurrent validation, and there is the same need for control in data collection and analysis. Differences are primarily in analysis, the need for cross-validation, and subsequent use. Nothing close to justice can be given these methods, so they will simply be briefly mentioned.

ADDITIVE MODELS. One way to combine predictors is to add them together. The composite is not a measure, that is, it is not interpreted as an attribute, but it can be treated as a single variable and validated by bivariate methods.

Weights for combining variables could be set by policy. It may, for example, be felt that each predictor is just as important as any other and that, therefore, all should be equally weighted. The data will often outsmart the policy makers; nominal weights may be equal, but effective weights probably

are not. Dispersions of the various distributions, reliabilities of individual measures, their intercorrelations—all of these determine in specific ways the effective contribution of each measure to the composite (Richardson, 1941).

Weighting is often done through multiple regression; several computer programs are available to develop optimal weights for maximizing correlation. There are, however, other purposes that might dictate other approaches to weighting. Horst (1966) has identified several: (a) to maximize dispersion of the composite, (b) to achieve specific conditions of skewness or kurtosis to increase discrimination in certain parts of the distribution, (c) to maximize reliability, or (d) to get differential estimates of different criteria. One might also weight to maximize common factor variance; in one study (Stone & Athelstan, 1969) such weights gave better prediction in cross-validation than did those from multiple regression. In employment practice, the purpose is ordinarily to weight for maximum validity.

For any of these purposes, weights are mathematically determined from the sample at hand. Just as with other descriptive statistics, optimal weights may be somewhat different for subsequent groups of applicants; it may be strongly recommended that, rather than carrying beta weights (or b coefficients) to illusory levels of accuracy, rough rounding, perhaps to integers, is probably enough.

Where differential weights are derived, cross-validation is necessary. That is, the weights should be applied to a new sample from the same population to determine whether the intended effect is repeated. For example, multiple regression weights are tested in a new sample to determine how much shrinkage may be found in the multiple correlation coefficient. In a sense, it may be argued that the use of approximate, rounded weights reduces the need for cross-validation since they are much like the arbitrary weighting of parts of a single test.

To the extent that such weights are approximations of mathematically derived weights, however, the logic of cross-validation still applies, and a new sample is probably needed—even if less urgently. Even if the weights are so far removed from those derived mathematically as to seem purely arbitrary, the logic of replication, always important, still applies.[10]

Any composite should make sense. Every addition of a variable to the predictor battery increases disproportionately the opportunities for error; the composite is subject to errors not only in the correlation of a variable with the criterion but also in all intercorrelations. A combination badly needing examination recently came to the writer's attention: a battery of four variables including two apparent suppressors (i.e., variables with negative weights to eliminate or suppress irrelevant variance in the other variables). There was no cross-validation and no explanation of the suppressor effect. When it is recognized that replicable suppressor effects are rare, one has a right to be suspicious of an unverified equation with two of them.

SUBGROUPING. One or more variables may be used as a basis for assigning applicants to a subgroup; predictor variables may then be validated within each subgroup independently. The subgrouping variable has become known as a moderator variable. Variables which correlate with cross-products of predictor and criterion, which correlate with systematic errors of prediction, or which pro-

vide significant interactions with predictors may serve as bases for subgrouping with the expectation that improvement in prediction will occur in some subgroups.

Under some circumstances a moderator might enter a composite in a single equation for the total group. Rock (1969) has shown how to estimate the gain in predictive efficiency from the more general polynomial equation using the formula

$$1 - \hat{R}_p{}^2 = [(n_1\sigma_y{}^2(1 - R_1{}^2) \\ + n_2\sigma_y{}^2(1 - R_2{}^2), \\ \ldots, n_g\sigma_y{}^2(1 - R_g{}^2)) \\ /\sum_{g=1}^{G} n_g]/\sigma_y{}^2$$

where

$\hat{R}_p{}^2 = $ estimate of the multiple correlation squared that would be obtained if a polynomial equation incorporating moderator (grouping variable) terms in both linear as well as cross-product forms were used.

$R_g{}^2 = $ multiple correlation squared within the g-th group as defined by the grouping or moderator variable.

If the decision is that the variable can best be used in subgrouping (which will usually be the case), the prediction system is sequential. Applicants are first classified on the subgrouping variable; the appropriate prediction formula for each group is then applied. If the basis for subgrouping itself involved prediction (as in predicting probable behavioral style or level of job satisfaction), it is conceivable that something markedly different from the moderator concept would be involved. Instead of applying a different regression equation to the same predictors, one might wish to apply totally different sets of predictors. This is an extension of individual dimensionality of criteria (Ghiselli, 1956a). One retail clerk, for example, may develop a good sales record on the basis of product knowledge com-

---

[10] That is, repeating a research study and finding substantially similar results enhances one's faith in the hypothesis tested. Many things might change in a subsequent study: There may be changes in population, in the criterion predicted, or in weights assigned to specific predictors. Cross-validation is the process of checking a given set of weights on a new sample from the same population. The term is often applied, erroneously, to examples of replication, validity extension, or validity generalization when the stability of weights is not at issue. Perhaps the most embarrassing example of this confusion is Guion & Gottier (1965).

bined with personal dominance, whereas another may build such a sales record by first building customer goodwill. If clerks were to be subgrouped on the basis of such differences in style, different predictors of sales might be necessary for the different subgroups. This concept has not yet been adequately explored.

What has been explored is the basic principle of subgrouping, and the results have not been exciting. Raubenheimer and Tiffin (1971) seemed to have success with a modification of the Ghiselli prediction-of-predictability concept (1960b). Zedeck (1971a) attempted unsuccessfully to identify moderators by discriminant function analysis and was also unsuccessful in a search for a "joint moderator" (Zedeck, Cranny, Vale, & Smith, 1971). In his general review of the problem (Zedeck, 1971b), he suggested that unreliability of moderators, along with other statistical problems, might explain why moderator effects have often not held up under cross-validation.

He has probably not, however, had the final word. A series of six articles was grouped together in the June, 1972, issue of the *Journal of Applied Psychology* as a feature section on moderator variables (Abrahams & Alf, 1972a, 1972b; Dunnette, 1972; Ghiselli, 1972; Velicer, 1972a, 1972b). The section features debates (e.g., Abrahams & Alf *versus* Dunnette) on the propriety and inherent error in various methods of identifying potential moderators as well as more theoretical contributions. The general reaction to the series expressed by Ghiselli is appropriately cautious; he suggested that moderators may be "as fragile and elusive as that other will-o-the-wisp, the suppressor variable" (Ghiselli, 1972, p. 270).

Elusive or not, moderator variables *are* occasionally found and even replicated. As Ghiselli pointed out, the implications of this fact may be profound for psychometric theory, and the theoretical implications may ultimately hold greater practical importance than the immediate application of any single finding.

SYNTHETIC VALIDITY. Lawshe (1952) introduced the term, "synthetic validity," meaning "the inferring of validity in a specific situation from a logical analysis of jobs into their elements, a determination of test validity for these elements, and a combination of elemental validities into a whole" (Balma, 1959, p. 395). Three approaches to the concept can be identified, but none is established. One is a direct approach using traditional validation of predictors against criterion elements (Guion, 1965b). Another approach identifies predictors with high means for those who are on jobs demanding certain task elements (Lawshe & Steinberg, 1955; McCormick, Chapter 15 in the *Handbook*). The third is the J-Coefficient approach of the United States Civil Service Commission (Primoff, 1955). None of these approaches has produced a substantial literature.

The common thread is that jobs are analyzed into elements, test correlates of the elements (or performance in the element) are identified, and the correlates of the elements of a given job are combined to form a test battery for that job. Any evaluation of the scheme is ultimately based on the degree of correspondence between predicted and actual performance on a composite criterion.

It should be noted that the three approaches to synthetic validity are conceptually different. Direct validation against criterion elements is a form of criterion-related validity. In a sense, so also is the approach of associating high mean scores with specific elements, although this is more closely related to placement decisions than to traditional correlational analysis. The J-Coefficient may, however, be more closely related in concept to content validity. It is not concerned with the content validities of specific tests, in any conventional sense, but it may be considered a measure of the content validity of a battery of tests. It is computed by correlating weights assigned through job analysis to specific job elements (expressed in psychological terms) against "beta" weights of tests designed to measure each element. The latter weight is determined by expert judgment influenced by a growing body of empirical data where test scores are treated as the dependent variable and job elements as the independent variable in a multiple regression equation. In this sense, it is a measure of the correspondence of the content of the job, as judged by competent analysts, and the job-relevant content of the tests. Wherry (1955) argued on theoretical grounds that it is, nevertheless, a useful estimate of what is now called criterion-related validity.

PATTERN ANALYSIS. There has been a slight but persistent interest in looking at the configuration of traits rather than their cumulative magnitude. Those in a specific configuration—a type (Tryon & Bailey, 1970) or an ulstrith (Toops, 1959)—could be treated as having a probability of success distinctly different from those of other configurations of the same variables. A variation on the theme is profile comparison, where a specially desired profile is identified and individual applicants can be ranked quantitatively on how well their own profiles fit the standard.

Such approaches are intuitively appealing; they move toward individualizing the prediction process. There are, however, some disadvantages, mainly that enormous Ns are required. A recent application makes the point well; the use of pattern anaylsis in prediction was apparently successful, but it could not be cross-validated since all of the 1,525 cases were needed to do the pattern analysis (Tanofsky, Shepps, & O'Neill, 1969).

A general comment seems appropriate to all non-additive approaches: results are unlikely to hold up well from one sample to another. In multiple regression, the rules of combination are well established, yet cross-validation is necessary to assess the degree of shrinkage when the formula developed on one sample is applied to another. No such rules exist for configural or moderated relationships or for synthetic validities; the newer techniques are simply not as "safe" as established notions of linear regression. The need for cross-validation is correspondingly more important.

Decision Models

The original publication of the Cronbach and Gleser monograph (1957) sparked interest in the application of decision theory to employment psychology. The fundamental point of view is that tests, interview judgments, or other predictors are useful in the employment process only insofar as they facilitate an employment decision. Research has followed two different lines. One problem investigated is that of using valid data; that is, how can decision rules be developed so that the "best" decisions are made? Such investigations represent an extension of the validation process. The other problem is to understand what happens in decision making; that is, how does the decision maker process various kinds of information in arriving at a decision? This is an important line of investigation for the improvement of the administrative processes of using valid data (perhaps in combination with unvalidated data), but it is not a part of the validation process unless the resulting decisions are themselves treated as predictors and validated. This line of investigation has been surveyed by Slovic and Lichtenstein (1971).

A major contribution of decision theory is its emphasis on base rates (Meehl & Rosen, 1955; Rorer, Hoffman, LaForge, & Hsieh, 1966). Use of a test where base rates are extreme may result in *more* errors of prediction than the a priori probabilities. Many employers, as one example, are concerned with internal theft; presumably, a device to identify thieves in advance would be welcomed by these employers. To validate such a device, two criterion groups would be needed: (1) those who are identified as thieves, and (2) those who are not. If one-fifth of the employees do in fact steal, and of those one-fifth are caught (Ash, 1971), then the first group includes only 4 percent of the total—an extreme base rate. A "valid" predictor, given an optimal cutting score, would probably correctly identify many of the thieves, but (unless it were nearly perfectly valid) it would also identify many of the non-thieves incorrectly as thieves. The frequency of "false positives" would increase the errors above 4 percent. The seriousness of this problem depends on the utilities involved; if the savings from correct identification of potential thieves is considerably greater than the costs of incorrectly labeling an applicant a thief, the predictor might have net utility as a decision tool.

A common application of decision theory is to establish "optimum" cutting scores. The optimal cutting score can be defined by a minimum loss function; unless special assumptions are made regarding relative costs of false positives, false negatives, and perhaps additional recruiting, the optimal cutting score is that point at which a phi coefficient would be maximum (Guttman & Raju, 1965).

"Optimum" in this context is a mathematical, not an operating term. Unless the criterion groups are so precisely designated that a satisfactory group is clearly satisfactory and the unsatisfactory group clearly is not, "optimum" cannot be interpreted as the point above which (or below which, or within which, if two of them) applicants are predicted to meet performance qualifications or standards. Nor does the "optimum" speak to the question of an expected selection ratio; perhaps the designated optimum cutting score would permit the selection of 70 percent of the applicant population, whereas only 40 percent (or perhaps 80 percent) will be hired. The "optimum" cutting score should probably be taken as a basis for computing utility or percentage of misclassifications to evaluate validity, with no implication for administrative action.

The designation of a specific cutting score, no matter how derived, fails to take into account the standard error of measurement or the standard error of estimate. This

writer advocates, if cutting scores are to be used, the designation of three categories of applicant: those above the cutoff and eligible for selection, those to be rejected for being below the cutoff, and those in a band of about two standard errors around the cutoff for whom the decision is to be made wholly on other grounds.

This is not psychometrically sound from an organizational point of view. If there is an additional variable to consider for those in the middle range and it is valid, then that variable should be added to the prediction equation for all subjects; to do otherwise is to settle for less validity than is possible. To use a less valid means of decision making in this middle range is to reduce the validity of the test at hand. All in all, validities will be maximized, and total errors in classification minimized, if this suggestion is not followed.

It is made, however, from an individualized point of view. It *is* psychometrically sound to recognize that the true score of an individual applicant is not necessarily equal to the observed score. Where a decision is a close one on the basis of validated data, and where an applicant has something else in his favor, then it seems just that he receive the benefit of any doubt. And where he has *nothing* else in his favor, it seems a reasonable parallel to withhold such benefit. Admittedly, the argument is intuitive and sentimental rather than rigorous.

BIAS: SOCIAL AND STATISTICAL

This has been an essentially traditional treatment of personnel selection. From the outset, the intent has been to see where we are, how we got there, and where we have fallen short. The latter is most easily discovered in equal employment policies in relation to tests. The Motorola case (French, 1965) and the Tower amendment to the then pending Civil Rights Bill led to some general questioning of assumptions and practices in personnel recruiting, selection, and placement. The questions were not as embarrassing as the fact that no one really knew very much about the possibly illegal discriminatory aspects of personnel procedures, including tests; the issue simply hadn't been faced.

The cry was that tests were racially biased. The evidence proposed was that blacks usually obtained lower mean scores than whites; such evidence does not support a view of racial bias because it ignores relationships of test scores to criteria. However, few organizations could provide any validity data at all and fewer still had data on racial or sex differences in predictor or criterion performance. Nearly ten years after Motorola, we have scholarly debate, governmental regulation, and decisions at law to think about, but firm answers are elusive. The scholarly debate may move our thinking forward to genuinely new ideas; in the meantime, governmental regulation and decisions at law will be based on the existing traditions of "how to do it" and the national policy to do it fairly.

Patterns of Discrimination

An effective personnel tool discriminates —in a statistical sense. It is, therefore, appropriate to differentiate *fair* discrimination —the statistical power to distinguish those who can do the job well from those who cannot—from unfair discrimination.[11] "Unfair discrimination exists when persons with equal probabilities of success on the job have unequal probabilities of being hired for the job" (Guion, 1966, p. 26).

---

[11] In a personal communication, Dr. William Enneis has pointed out that the terms "fair" and "unfair" have no legal significance; that is, there is no such thing in law as "fair discrimination," and "unfair discrimination" is legally redundant. The problem, of course, is in the two quite distinct meanings of the word "discriminate." In the legal sense, to discriminate is to act with prejudice; thus unfairness is implied. In the statistical sense more familiar to specialists in measurement, to discriminate is to differentiate or to make clear distinctions, and the making of such distinctions in a non-prejudicial manner is the technical problem at hand.

In regression language, a related definition was offered by Cleary (1968, p. 115):

A test is biased for members of a subgroup of the population if, in the prediction of a criterion for which the test is designed, consistent non-zero errors of prediction are made for members of the subgroup. In other words, the test is biased if the criterion score predicted from the common regression line is consistently too high or too low for members of the subgroup.

A slightly different variant is Dunnette's (1974):

... unfair discrimination against a minority group occurs when, over the long run, a firm's personnel decisions yield higher proportions of reject-errors for members of the minority group than for members of the non-minority group.

Statistically, these are all different. The first is concerned with individual prediction and reflects differences in correlations, slopes, and intercepts. The second is similar but is concerned with continuous predictions. The third is concerned less with individual predictions than with group effects.

Despite the differences, however, there are some similarities. Each allows the rejection of those who cannot do the job. Each seeks more accurate prediction of performance. Each asserts that decision makers should look for and act upon possible differences in validity.

This has become known as the problem of differential validity, a term which should imply much more than merely a difference in correlation coefficients for different groups. Consideration of differences in validity should also take into account possible differences in slopes and intercepts of regression equations. Differences in means and standard deviations in the two variables are also important considerations in possible differential validity.

Bartlett and O'Leary (1969), working from and extending the Cleary definition, identified eleven patterns of validity differences to consider in questions of racial bias

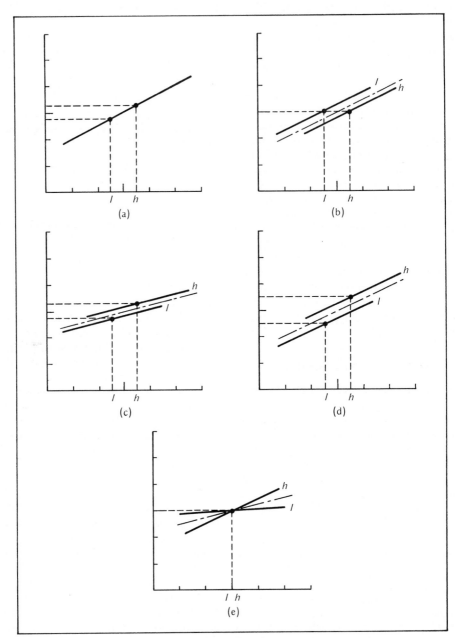

Figure 4. Five cases of differences in validity for two subgroups.

in prediction. For simplicity, we shall consider only five cases, as shown in Figure 4. The axes are drawn in sigma units so that the slope of the regression of y on x indicates degree of correlation; equal Ns and standard deviations are assumed. Means of two subgroups are shown for both predictor and criterion variables. Broken lines show a composite regression.

In (a) and (c), the lower group is a full standard deviation below the higher group on the predictor and half a standard deviation below the higher group on the criterion. In (b), the lower group is a standard deviation below the higher on the predictor, but there is no difference on the criterion. In (d), the lower group is a full standard deviation below the higher group on both measures. In all four situations, correlations for the two groups are equal, although in (b), (c), and (d) the intercepts differ. In (e), means are equal but correlations differ; as drawn, the correlation for the "lower" group is near zero.

In such cases, the recommendation of Kirkpatrick, Ewen, Barrett, and Katzell (1968) has become rather standard: predict separately for the two groups. In this way, in all five illustrations, candidates for employment will be selected on the basis of the predicted criterion performance, with equal standards applied for all; fairness by the first two definitions, at least, will be assured. If instead a single regression based on the total sample is used, (a) is still "fair," but each of the other cases shows a pattern of over-and-under-prediction. The early notion of test bias is shown as (b), where something has depressed predictor scores markedly but has no influence on criterion performance. In (d), criterion performance is as much influenced by the biasing factor as is the test, and test bias is not assumed; however, there would be unfair discrimination in employment *unless* the different regressions were used for prediction. An intermediate case is shown as (c), where the biasing factor has only half as much influence on criterion measurement as on pre-

dictor measurement. Again, however, errors in prediction can be minimized by using the separate regression equations. A somewhat different situation is posed in (e), where the composite regression produces reversed patterns of prediction error at the different ends of the predictor scale, and where the group with the lower correlation is one in which the predictor provides no appreciable improvement over chance. Here differential prediction means that the predictor is used for the group with the higher correlation and not with the other group: one must find another predictor that will work for the lower group or perhaps be reduced to random selection. (The assumption of equal Ns in these examples should be remembered.)

It all seems very straightforward. Before accepting the recommendation to use independent prediction in every case, however, let us start over with a different basic argument about the nature of fairness. Fair discrimination could be defined as that which would be based on a flawless criterion, without a predictor. The degree of unfairness in the use of the predictor is the amount of departure from this hypothetical ideal. The use of the predictor is fair to, let us say, the lower group to the extent it selects proportionately as many as would have been selected on a flawless criterion (Thorndike, 1971).

Assume a cutoff at the composite mean, with a desirable level of job performance at the composite criterion mean. Further, assuming normal distributions, some simple calculations produce the data shown in Table 2. If a fair predictor is one that selects as many in each group as would be directly selected by the criterion itself, then (d) and, under these unique conditions, even (e) are "fair" while the others, including (a), are not. In the others, the percentage of the low scoring group achieving the specified criterion level is greater than the percentage above the cutting score. In short, the situation that is "fair" when fairness is defined in terms of individual expectancy of pre-

TABLE 2
EFFECTS OF DIFFERENCES IN MEANS
AND VARIANCES ON SELECTION IN FIVE CASES*

| Case | r | Lower Group | | | Higher Group | |
		% Selected on Criterion	% Selected on Predictor	Diff.	% Selected on Criterion	% Selected on Predictor
a	.50	40	31	9	60	69
b	.50	50	31	19	50	69
c	.25	40	31	9	60	69
d	.50	31	31	0	69	69
e	.50; .05	50	50	0	50	50

* Based on five hypothetical cases shown graphically in Figure 4.

diction is *not* "fair" when fairness is defined in terms of group proportions (Thorndike, 1971)[12] and vice versa.

At this point there is a temptation to say the issue is one of policy (which kind of fairness do you want?), and move on to technical matters. There are several technical factors to consider which, taken as a group, make the question of differential validity far more complex than it at first appeared. Without much discussion, here are some further problems:

1. Where there is validity in one group and not in the other, the difference may be due to very small *N*s in one of the groups (Boehm, 1972). Farr, O'Leary, and Bartlett (1971) report that some variant of this case accounts for almost all of their cases of differential validity; their black sample *N*s seem to hover around thirty. One should question whether such apparent differences are real; in one case an *r* of .20 was significant for 268 whites, but .20 was *not* significant for twenty-eight blacks. In this case, *r*'s, slopes, and intercepts may all be equal. Clearly, comparing each *r* to zero is not the appropriate comparison; the appropriate comparison to determine if race is a moderator is to compare the correlations to each other. Certainly a correlation of .20 is not significantly different from another correla-

[12] The problem was further complicated by Darlington (1971), who gave four mathematical definitions of fairness and showed that, for practical purposes, all are incompatible.

tion of .20 (Humphreys, 1973; Zedeck, 1971b).

2. Apparently different equations with parallel slopes may appear to over-predict rather than under-predict for the lower scoring group because of test unreliability. Linn and Werts (1971) have shown that, where one group mean is below the mean of the other group on both test and criterion, unreliability of the measures may produce different intercepts with parallel slopes. Thus, unreliability increases the likelihood that the higher scoring group's regression equation will over-predict for the lower group.

3. Apparently different regression equations may be due to the inclusion or exclusion of a second predictor in the regression equation. Where two correlated predictors form an unbiased composite, use of one variable alone may appear to be biased (Linn & Werts, 1971).

4. If the variance of one group is appreciably lower than the variance of another, the standard errors of estimate would differ even where there is no difference in the validity coefficient (Einhorn & Bass, 1971). Figure 5, on the left, shows this situation; on the right the same problem is shown but with a difference in correlation. The horizontal line indicates an acceptable level of job performance. In the example on the left, all members of Group 2 could be accepted while some members of the group with the larger variance would have to be rejected

in order to have all accepted candidates perform satisfactorily. In the example on the right, the same pattern would be found despite the fact that the predicted performance of Group 1 is higher than that of Group 2. Thus "fair" selection according to the Guion definition (based on probabilities of achieving satisfactory performance) might select those with the lower predicted criterion score, which would perhaps be "unfair" in terms of an alternative definition.

It is apparent that we have become pretty confused by the whole topic of moderators and subgrouping, topics that have been restricted to correlation coefficients. Race could, perhaps, be a genuine moderator, forming a point biserial correlation with the cross-products of test and criterion or with errors in prediction around a single regression line. If so, one ethnic group alone would, under certain conditions, provide a validity coefficient higher than could be obtained combining the two.

This is, in itself, not a very helpful statement, since differences in the absolute magnitude of validity coefficients or overlap statistics seem less important in the context of questions of relative predictor means, criterion means, variances, reliabilities, slopes, intercepts, standard errors, and other problems not yet discussed. It is ironic that most of the research on differential validity to date has concentrated on the magnitude of correlation coefficients. Linn and Werts expressed it well: "When complications such as possible bias in the criterion, different within group slopes, different within group reliabilities, and small samples of minority students (and employees) are added to the above problems, the investigation of test bias would seem to be an exceedingly difficult task requiring considerable skill and caution" (p. 4). To which this writer utters a fervent "amen"!

Criterion Bias

If the problem of investigating possible predictor bias is difficult, the problem of criterion bias is appalling. One should, of course, examine one's criteria, especially ratings, to attempt to evaluate the possibility; however, mean differences between men and women or between black and white are, in themselves, no more evidence of unfair bias in criteria than in predictors.

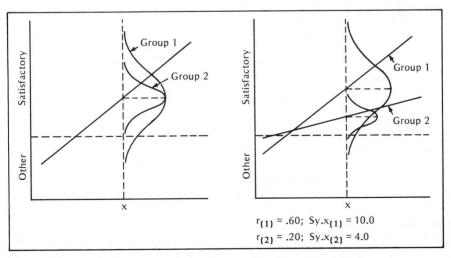

Figure 5. Groups with different standard errors of estimate. (Adapted from Einhorn & Bass, 1971.)

$r_{(1)} = .60; \ S_{y \cdot x_{(1)}} = 10.0$

$r_{(2)} = .20; \ S_{y \cdot x_{(2)}} = 4.0$

Farr et al. (1971) cited data that can be used for discussion. One of their samples was comprised of prison correctional officers. Attendance records of 322 whites and forty-nine blacks indicated that blacks were absent roughly twice the mean number of days as whites; because of the variability in each sample, however, the difference was not statistically significant and it seems appropriate to rule out criterion bias. Mean supervisory ratings were closer, but variances were small and the difference was statistically significant ($t = 2.09$). On still another criterion, whether the supervisor felt it necessary to extend the six-months-on-the-job probationary period for a second six months, the difference was highly significant ($t = 4.93$).

On the objective, countable criterion there is no reliable evidence of a systematic bias by race. Supervisory ratings do appear to be slightly biased against blacks, and there is a pronounced bias in the use of extended probation. Or is there? Is the use of extended probation, as one possible example, due to an affirmative action program that has brought in groups of black employees below the usual standards with the view that additional training would bridge the gap? Is there a greater tendency to fire a white than to extend his probationary period? Do the lower supervisory ratings suggest that after extending probation they still didn't have the heart to fire some people who really never were qualified? Or does the apparently smaller bias effect of supervisory ratings mean that in time supervisors begin to get over their prejudicial feelings? About all that really can be said is that such data serve as projective tests; one can read into them what he will. The fact remains, however, that no outside data exist to tell whether an observed difference is evidence of bias or simply descriptive.

What to do? Not much of a prescription can be offered. The options fall along a continuum. At the easiest end one can shrug it all off and simply assume that a criterion is a criterion is a criterion and, good or bad, is to be predicted. Indeed, very often this may be all that can be done. At the other end of the continuum is a detailed study of the construct validity of the criterion measure—a set of correlates, a set of predictions come true, a pattern of events and relationships. But even the most elaborate of studies will never completely determine whether observed ethnic differences in performance are due to bias or to "real" differences.

Language Handicaps

Much has been said about the use of tests fairly when choosing men and women, or blacks and whites. Too little attention is given to those groups who are more comfortable in a language other than English.

Some people who are bilingual may be fluent and comfortable in either language; others who are bilingual may have severely limited vocabulary and linguistic skill in both languages.

The effects of bilingualism are varied and complex. They cannot be adequately summarized in any single generalization . . . . Under certain conditions, intellectual development may be aided by bilingualism; under other conditions, it may be seriously retarded. Emotional as well as intellectual factors probably contribute to the specific effects of bilingualism in particular cases. In testing any bilingual groups, such as immigrants or children of immigrants, however, the possible influences of language handicap on test performance must be given serious consideration. *It cannot be generally assumed that such individuals can be adequately measured with a verbal test, despite their apparent mastery of English* (Anastasi, 1968, p. 243; italics added).

For an appreciable segment of American society, English is not the first language learned. Spanish-speaking people whose heritage may be Mexican, Cuban, or Puerto Rican make up a part of the applicant pool or labor market in most sections of the country; some efforts are being made to provide employment opportunities more widely to American Indians. Many Orientals are also included in a labor market that assumes, with or without justification, that English is their first language of choice. It is entirely possible that a moderator effect may be found with useful frequency by subgrouping according to language heritage (as opposed simply to language skill); suggestions of genuine moderator effects were found in the ETS-Civil Service studies of cartographers (Campbell, 1972), and Casavantes (1972) has suggested that possibly more moderating effects could have been identified in a more representative sampling of Spanish-speaking applicants.

Canada has a related problem in providing equality of employment opportunity for its French-speaking minority. Clearly, one cannot solve the problem simply by providing French translations of English tests; individual words in a vocabulary test simply will not translate with the same nuances and interrelationships. However, French and English tests can be built to the same specifications to provide essentially equivalent tests (Lavallée & Thivierge, 1970).

Such a solution may be inadequate, however, for testing such groups as the Spanish-speaking migrants if they lack full communicative skill in both languages. On this problem the writer is long on questions but short on proposals for solutions.

The Law and Personnel Testing

"Perhaps public regulation will return personnel testing, at least, to psychologists" (Guion, 1967). That statement seems naive, now that testing is within the province of lawyers, and psychologists speak knowingly of legal requirements. Once a sloppy or incompetent piece of work could be castigated within the family; now it may be against the law.

The Civil Rights Act of 1964 has several provisions related to selection, recruiting, termination, and promotion of employees, but this discussion is restricted to the role played by employment tests in making decisions. Briefly, it is an unlawful employ-

ment practice to make decisions so as to discriminate against individuals on the basis of race, color, religion, sex, or national origin; it is also illegal to follow a "pattern or practice" of discrimination. A parallel bar to discrimination in employment is Executive Order 11246 applying to Federal contractors. Both the Equal Employment Opportunity Commission (EEOC), established by the Civil Rights Act, and the Office of Federal Contract Compliance (OFCC) of the United States Department of Labor, established to administer the Executive Order, seek to abolish unfair practices of recruiting, selection, promotion, wage policy, and general working conditions. These two agencies are not always in perfect accord; moreover, the federal regulations are sometimes in conflict with state laws, particularly in regard to the employment of women, and different courts seem to have made decisions in specific cases that may not be consistent. In short, "neither the legal doctrines nor their effects can be described definitely" (Harvard Law Review, 1971, p. 1112).

The EEOC has issued Guidelines (1970) and the OFCC has issued an Order (1971) regulating the use of tests. These documents are essentially the same and will be discussed together as "the federal documents."[13] They begin with a statement of faith in testing when it is done properly, promptly followed by doubts that testing is typically done properly. An examination of some EEOC and court cases suggests that the scepticism may be warranted. There are many cases where there were no validation attempts at all. Examples include *Arrington* v. *Massa-*

---

[13] Some may know that I have been involved in the development of these documents. It should be recognized that disagreements can be expected among those who share authorship, and between psychologists' intentions and court readings, on the interpretation of specific points. The comments here, therefore, should be understood as my personal opinions carrying no special weight. They are certainly not to be construed in any way as representing the policy of the Office of Federal Contract Compliance, or of its Testing and Selection Advisory Committee, with which I was explicitly identified.

chusetts Bay Transportation Authority (2 FEP Cases 371)[14], where the judge wrote, "At best the defendant has used the test on the unsupported assumption that better test takers are also better drivers or collectors." Other horror stories include allegations of shorter time limits for black applicants (EEOC Decision 71-1155, 3 FEP Cases 388), cutoff scores based on prior knowledge that blacks will be largely excluded (*Baker* v. *Columbus School District*, 3 FEP Cases 719), or requiring subordinates to falsify scores of black applicants (*Tidwell* v. *American Oil*, 3 FEP Cases 1007).

The courts and EEOC decisions have, on several occasions, supported the use of tests. Statistical evidence was presented and accepted at the district court level for educational requirements and flight time standards in *Spurlock* v. *United Airlines* (3 FEP Cases 839). The EEOC decisions have supported test use with no evidence of validity because there was also no evidence of disproportionate impact (Decisions 71-1471 and 71-1525, 3 FEP Cases 667 and 669).

What the documents require is evidence of validation wherever there is a disparate rate of rejection for minorities compared to non-minorities, or men compared to women. There must be some reason to suggest violation of the law before the documents take force. Otherwise, there is no legal requirement for any kind of validation. One might say that organizations have the right even to be fairly stupid in their employment practices so long as they are stupid fairly.

The emphasis is on empirical validity; the documents presume that predictive validity will most often be the appropriate model, while recognizing that in many

situations content validity is more appropriate (cf., Decision 70630, 2 FEP Cases 588). The phrase, "where technically feasible," is repeated frequently in recognition that all too often small Ns or the unavailability of useful criteria preclude meaningful empirical study. In such cases, construct validity may be defended (although the expert witness who first enters the thicket of explaining construct validity in court is to be pitied), or validity may be inferred by generalization from other situations if those situations are similar in job content, organizational context, and applicant populations. In short, despite some poorly informed criticism of excessive stringency (cf., Harvard Law Review, 1971; opinion in *King* v. *Georgia Power*, 3 FEP Cases 767), the federal documents identify predictive validity as a general model and recognize that it is not always possible to follow. Followed or not, evidence of some kind of validity is required consistent with APA *Standards*, and this implies some concern with procedures of data gathering and analysis, appropriateness of sampling, and job and situational characteristics.

Where the psychologists who drafted the documents wrote of validation, the courts speak of job relatedness; these terms are not necessarily the same. Consider the decision of the Supreme Court in *Griggs* v. *Duke Power* (3 FEP Cases 175): "On the record before us, neither ... requirement ... is shown to bear a demonstrable relationship to successful performance of the jobs for which it was used. Both were adopted ... *without meaningful study* of their relationship to job-performance ability" (*Griggs* v. *Duke Power*, 1971; italics added). What constitutes meaningful study? Surely an empirical validation study based on a hypothesis derived from careful job analysis would be a meaningful study, but must it be so complete to satisfy the courts? Would not the study necessary to arrive at what has here been termed "the rational foundation for predictive validity" be a "meaning-

---

[14] The Bureau of National Affairs (1969, 1971, 1972a, 1972b) publishes a subscription service of Fair Employment Practice (FEP) cases dating to the effective data of the 1964 Civil Rights Act. Citation to specific cases in this chapter will be to this service, giving volume number and page. For example, the famous decision in *Griggs* v. *Duke Power* is referenced as "3 FEP Cases 175," indicating page 175 of Volume 3.

ful study"? In fact, would not such a study be more meaningful than a casual, concurrent effort to correlate scores on tests adopted for no clearly articulated reason against ratings hastily gathered under threat of legal action?

There is another interesting phrase in that decision to be considered in interpreting the federal documents. It was said, "What Congress has forbidden is giving these devices and mechanisms *controlling force* unless they are demonstrably a reasonable measure of job performance" (*Griggs* v. *Duke Power,* 1971; italics added). Where a decision is based almost entirely on test scores, as is implicit in the documents, the test has "controlling force." Does it have "controlling force" where it is simply information and where the decision is made clinically (as, for example, in an assessment center)? If not, must it be validated? It is entirely possible that judicial opinion may weigh the argument as more important than the correlation (cf., Jacksonville Terminal, 3 FEP Cases 862).

The documents define "test" very broadly. Almost anything that is scalable, including nominal scales, is included if used as a basis for personnel decisions. If an employer has disparate rates of rejection, but argues that he does not "use tests" (a difficult argument under such a broad definition), he may be called upon to validate his "unscored procedures." To do so, of course, he must systematize them, and they become tests under the definition! The effect of this seeming circularity is to suggest that one cannot avoid the necessity to comply with these documents simply by abandoning the use of "tests" which can be validated in standard ways.

Both documents require that ethnic or sex subgroup data be independently generated and analyzed, "where technically feasible," to look for possible differential validity, although no specific prescription is provided. To date, cases have been too much concerned with the basic problem of vali-

dation in general to say much on differential validity.[15] The documents say only that where there are differential rates of rejection, evidence is needed that the test is relevant to job performance for the group placed at a disadvantage by the test.

Suggestions

Perhaps a Handbook should contain some advice on what to do; certainly in no area are psychologists asked with greater urgency how to handle the problems created by their technology. There are unresolved technological issues, such as those of differential validity, but employers must take defensible action without waiting for the resolutions. Therefore, with much trepidation, some advice is offered.

First of all is the subject of differential validity. Always check for it in all aspects: means, slopes, intercepts, standard errors, and correlations (or expectancy equivalents of these). Then look at the resulting information with a sceptical eye. True differences between validity coefficients are not commonplace (Boehm, 1972). A false assumption of differential validity may result in fewer jobs for minorities and less accurate prediction. In the ETS-Civil Service Commission studies of three occupations and two minorities (Campbell, 1972), 144 pairs of correlations of aptitude tests against ratings yielded only two significant differences. Moreover, there were as many instances where validities for blacks were higher than those for whites, as the reverse. The situation was essentially similar when job knowledge tests and work samples were used as criteria.

Where there is a clear and significant difference in regression, the minority group may have a lower regression line than the whites. Some employers may nevertheless use the common regression equation because it will result in hiring a larger proportion

---

[15] However, see *U.S.* v. *Detroit Edison,* 6 FEP Cases 612.

of the minorities. This is a decision that should be made very carefully. There is support for it in the knowledge that it is at least partly due to unreliable measurement. There is further support for it in the motivation to do something positive to enhance employment opportunities for the minorities, whether that motivation stems from concern or from fear of the law.

The latter argument should not be carried too far. It connotes too often a paternalistic arrogance of "being nice" to undeserving people. Moreover, one may question how nice it really is. If the disparity in regressions is really great, then the use of common regression overpredicts performance for many minority members. Stated more directly, such a policy may result in hiring a greater proportion of minorities who fail. This seems of dubious social value. It reinforces stereotypes (both within and outside the minority group), lowers organizational productivity and raises costs, and invites charges of reverse discrimination. The latter point is more serious than it may at first seem; preoccupation with such charges may continue to delay the time when employment decisions are in fact color-blind decisions based on competent judgment of job qualifications. One should not expect to wipe out suddenly the effects of economic injustice through the simple expedient of differential regression.[16]

The above comments have argued both sides of the issue without clear resolution; we can apologize for the confusion without settling it. In general, it seems there are so many factors producing spurious and un-

reliable subgroup differences that greater reliability will ordinarily lie with the use of a composite unless the differences are truly convincing (Guion, 1972). This advice is counter to that of an earlier, more naive time (Guion, 1966). But one must beware of arrogant advocacy of simple solutions to complex problems.

Nowhere is this truth dramatized better than by Dunnette (1974). He has prepared hypothetical data where a predictor yields validity coefficients of .66 and .45 for blacks and whites, respectively. Going beyond the validity coefficients, he determined the utility associated with various cutting scores, estimating such things as costs of recruiting and screening, ordinary training, remedial training, societal costs for welfare of a portion of those not employed, and even riot costs. In his example, the direct costs to the employer are least when his use of the predictor results in rejection rates of 60½ percent for blacks and 22½ percent for whites. However, the *total* cost, including costs to the community in which the employer does business, is least when this uncommonly valid predictor is overlooked entirely. This, as Dunnette points out, is the moral dilemma faced by many employers. Employers are in fact instruments of social policy. As such they cannot continue employment practices which systematically reject minority applicants. Neither can they be the instruments of an outmoded and unwanted paternalism.

EPILOGUE

The selection of a new employee is an administrative act. It is also an art, applied freshly each time an administratively responsible person faces each new applicant. It is the administrator, in each situation, who makes the decision.

The traditional role of the industrial-organizational psychologist is to provide information to be considered in making that decision. To this end he develops and tests hypotheses about applicant characteristics that can be used to predict employee per-

---

[16] Since the manuscript for this chapter was prepared, there have been additional studies in the literature and further analyses. A summary of nineteen reports by Schmidt, Berner, and Hunter (1973) casts doubt on the merits of the hypotheses of differential prediction or of single-group validity. It should be understood, however, that their finding (that reported incidence of either phenomenon occurs with about chance frequency) applies only to the use of race as a moderator of the validities of aptitude tests. There are as yet no substantial data on other moderators or on race as a moderator of other types of predictors.

formance and shows how to assess them. Presumably, where valid tests are available, the employment decision is itself made more valid—a presumption rarely checked since the decision process itself is rarely studied.

The industrial-organizational psychologist can move a further step in his usefulness by studying and validating the decision process itself. Perhaps one of his more crucial tasks for the years immediately ahead is to determine how valid predictor data, obtained in a standardized fashion, are or should be combined with sporadically available materials of unknown validity about people (and similarly uncertain data about organizational needs) in making the ultimate decision to hire, reject, or file. He can help the decision maker gain insights into his own decision policies, by determining the actual effective weights various kinds of information may have, and by determining which decision makers (or which policies) result in the most valid decisions. He might, for example, apply a Bayesian formula containing both empirical and subjective probabilities, in which the decision maker can plug in his impressions along with the empirical expectancies from validated predictors. But even having done all of this, the contribution of the industrial-organizational psychologist remains technological because it is situational.

His self-image, however, calls for him to be a scientist, not a technician. This requires that he develop a firm scientific footing for technological application—a set of generalizable laws. We cannot presume at this time to be very definitive about the nature of such generalizations, or even how we are to move beyond situationalism to achieve them. We must, however, get them on the agenda for personnel research. We must formulate hypotheses that are relevant to a job (or to a specified set of sub-tasks), identify possible constraints, and define limits of generalizability.

Industrial-organizational psychology faces, in this era and in this arena, two not-easily-compatible problems. One of these is to follow the governmental regulations governing testing which currently reflect the technological reality of situational demands. The other is to develop a science. It is not unreasonable to assume that, if proper precautions are taken, it is possible for scientific generalizations to lead also to fair decisions.

It is time to distinguish between selection research and test validation. Selection research is the broader, more inclusive term, and its scope is the entire decision process. Properly conducted, it will treat simultaneously many kinds of variables other than applicant characteristics—but it will *include* information about applicant characteristics. Full-scale selection research can be more fruitful if, among other things, such information is valid. It would be useful to provide a foundation for comprehensive selection research by providing test validation research of a sufficiently comprehensive and controlled scope to provide generalizable rather than situational statements of test validities.

Why is it that, after a half century, we have so little to say about generalized validity? Is it simply a matter of inertia—that once in the set of situational validity we have never pulled out? Probably not. Is it because of excessive reliance on ratings—ratings which are subject to a wide variety of purely situational and even individual influences? This seems more plausible. Is it because we have been too preoccupied with "validating tests" to give full attention to the more precise problem of predicting performance through whatever variables may influence it? This, too, seems plausible when one reflects on the absence of selection research including situational variables.

One approach to generalizable validity is a modification of one form of synthetic validity that has never been adequately publicized and which could move toward a scientific basis for the art of decision: the J-Coefficient. Basic data could be obtained systematically from a wide variety of settings, following a predictive model. Only employees who prove "satisfactory" would be retained in analysis. For these, coefficients similar to Primoff's beta coefficients (Primoff, 1955) could be computed and the standard J-Coefficient could be determined.

Another step forward calls for the creation of what might be termed "instant criteria." An example is suggested by Grant and Bray (1970) in their use of the Learning Assessment Program (LAP) for telephone company craftsmen. In the LAP, a series of learning tasks is abstracted from a total training program. It is designed to represent the total learning required; with programming, it can be learned in as little as four days instead of several weeks. If such abstractions should prove feasible for general application, they would not only reduce a major obstacle to predictive validation studies—the amount of time required for completion—but, by removing much of the idiosyncratic influence on real-life criterion performance, would move away from the purely situational.

Another path is termed "synthetic criteria" by Mullins and Usdin (1970). They provided profile cards for each of 100 subjects showing graphically their performance on each of a set of predictors; expert judges (either training instructors or psychologists) were asked to rank the subjects in terms of deciles of predicted performance in rating. Regression weights were determined by multiple correlation and the resulting predictions were compared with actual criteria after training. Mullins and Usdin were quite optimistic about the implications of their finding, suggesting even that it might become feasible to dispense with empirical validation as it is known now. Such enthusiasm is a bit premature; the correspondence with actual validities varied according to (a) the school studied, (b) the number of experts used, (c) the method of synthesis, and (d) the predictor set chosen, and there was no consideration of minority subgrouping or other forms of bias. Nevertheless, the study is an approach worth pursuing; with refinement, it might well provide a synthetic

or instant criterion and thereby move the technology one step closer to science.

Experimental studies could be conducted. Standard work samples could be developed either for jobs or for task elements. Subjects could be sought in a wide variety of systematically varied settings. The design might systematically look for autocratic versus democratic supervision; large versus small organizations; narrow occupational functions versus wide; small versus large span of control, etc. To the extent that such factors do not influence covariance of tests and work samples, generalizable validity could be assumed. The special advantage of the work sample lies in its freedom from day-to-day or situational influences on the criterion; the work sample would, of course, be relatively free from motivational fluctuations, peer pressures, supervisory quality, etc.

Such studies require massive industry-wide or public support. Perhaps, however, there is enough recognition that employers need to know what they are doing when they make employment decisions to promote such broad-based research. The difficulty is not the massiveness of the direct research problem, but the number of unsolved indirect problems. Foremost among these is the fact there is as yet no adequate taxonomy of either situations (Frederiksen, 1972) or of tasks (Fleishman & Stephenson, 1970), although progress is being made on both. As the dimensions of tasks become more clearly understood, performance on those dimensions can be more clearly predicted and the limitations on the generalization of such prediction more precisely understood.

REFERENCES

Abrahams, N. M., & Alf, E. Jr. Pratfalls in moderator research. *Journal of Applied Psychology*, 1972, 56, 245–251. (a)

Abrahams, N. M., & Alf, E. Jr. Reply to Dunnette's "Comments on Abrahams's and Alf's 'Pratfalls in moderator research.'"

Journal of Applied Psychology, 1972, 56, 257–261. (b)

Albright, L. E., & Glennon, J. R. Personal history correlates of physical scientists' career aspirations. *Journal of Applied Psychology*, 1961, 45, 281–284.

Albright, L. E., Glennon, J. R., & Smith, W. J. *The use of psychological tests in industry.* Cleveland: Howard Allen, 1963.

American Psychological Association, American Educational Research Association, & National Council on Measurement Used in Education (Joint committee). Technical recommendations for psychological tests and diagnostic techniques. *Psychological Bulletin*, 1954, 51, 201–238.

American Psychological Association. *Standards for educational and psychological tests and manuals.* Washington: American Psychological Association, 1966, 40 pages.

American Psychological Association, American Educational Research Association, & National Council on Measurement in Education. *Standards for educational and psychological tests.* Washington: American Psychological Association, 1974, 76 pages.

Anastasi, A. *Differential psychology.* (3rd ed.) New York: Macmillan, 1958.

Anastasi, A. *Psychological testing.* (3rd ed.) New York: Macmillan, 1968.

Anderson, C. W. The relation between speaking times and decision in the employment interview. *Journal of Applied Psychology*, 1960, 44, 267–268.

Antia, K. A. Contribution of the interview to the selection of higher-level personnel. *Studies in Personnel Psychology*, 1971, 3, 7–20.

Ash, P. Screening employment applicants for attitudes toward theft. *Journal of Applied Psychology*, 1971, 55, 161–164.

Balma, M. J. The development of processes for indirect or synthetic validity (a symposium: 1): The concept of synthetic validity. *Personnel Psychology*, 1959, 12, 395–396.

Bartlett, C. J., & O'Leary, B. S. A differential prediction model to moderate the effects of heterogeneous groups in personnel selection and classification. *Personnel Psychology*, 1969, 22, 1–17.

Bechtoldt, H. P. Construct validity: A critique. *American Psychologist*, 1959, 14, 619–629.

Behling, O., Labovitz, G., & Gainer, M. College recruiting: A theoretical base. *Personnel Journal*, 1968, 47, 13–19.

Betz, E. L. An investigation of job satisfaction as a moderator variable in predicting job success. *Journal of Vocational Behavior*, 1971, 1, 123–128.

Bingham, W. V. *Aptitudes and aptitude testing.* New York: Harper, 1937.

Blakeney, R. N., & MacNaughton, J. F. Effects of temporal placement of unfavorable information on decision making during the selection interview. *Journal of Applied Psychology*, 1971, 55, 138–142.

Boehm, V. R. Negro-white differences in validity of employment and training selection procedures: Summary of research evidence. *Journal of Applied Psychology*, 1972, 56, 33–39.

Bolton, D. L., & Hickey, M. E. Effect of interviews on teacher selection decisions. *Journal of Applied Psychology*, 1969, 53, 501–505.

Brenner, M. H. Use of high school data to predict work performance. *Journal of Applied Psychology*, 1968, 52, 29–30.

Brogden, H. E., & Taylor, E. K. The dollar criterion: Applying the cost accounting concept to criterion construction. *Personnel Psychology*, 1950, 3, 133–154.

Browning, R. C. Validity of reference ratings from previous employers. *Personnel Psychology*, 1968, 21, 389–393.

Bureau of National Affairs. *The Civil Rights Act of 1964.* Washington: Bureau of National Affairs, 1964.

Bureau of National Affairs. *Fair employment practice cases,* Vol. 1. Washington, D.C.: Bureau of National Affairs, 1969.

Bureau of National Affairs. *Fair employment practice cases,* Vol. 2. Washington, D.C.: Bureau of National Affairs, 1971.

Bureau of National Affairs. *Fair employment practice cases,* Vol. 3. Washington, D.C.: Bureau of National Affairs, 1972. (a)

Bureau of National Affairs. *Fair employment practice cases,* Vol. 4. *Labor Relations Reporter* series, 1972. (b)

Buros, O. K., Ed. *The 1938 mental measurements yearbook.* Highland Park, N.J.: Gryphon, 1938.

Buros, O. K., Ed. *The 1940 mental measurements yearbook.* Highland Park, N.J.: Gryphon, 1941.

Buros, O. K., Ed. *The third mental measure-

ments yearbook. Highland Park, N.J.: Gryphon, 1949.

Buros, O. K., Ed. *The fourth mental measurements yearbook.* Highland Park, N.J.: Gryphon, 1953.

Buros, O. K., Ed. *The fifth mental measurements yearbook.* Highland Park, N.J.: Gryphon, 1959.

Buros, O. K., Ed. *The sixth mental measurements yearbook.* Highland Park, N.J.: Gryphon, 1965.

Buros, O. K., Ed. *The seventh mental measurements yearbook.* Highland Park, N.J.: Gryphon, 1972.

Campbell, D. T. Recommendations for APA test standards regarding construct, trait, or discriminant validity. *American Psychologist,* 1960, 15, 546–553.

Campbell, J. T. Principal results of the study and conclusions. In L. A. Crooks (Ed.), *An investigation of sources of bias in the prediction of job performance.* Princeton: Educational Testing Service, 1972.

Carlson, R. E. Selection interview decisions: The effect of interviewer experience, relative quota situation, and applicant sample on interviewer decisions. *Personnel Psychology,* 1967, 20, 259–280.

Carlson, R. E. Employment decisions: Effect of mode of applicant presentation on some outcome measures. *Personnel Psychology,* 1968, 21, 193–207.

Carlson, R. E. Effect of interview information in altering valid impressions. *Journal of Applied Psychology,* 1971, 55, 66–72.

Carlson, R. E., & Mayfield, E. C. Evaluating interview and employment application data. *Personnel Psychology,* 1967, 20, 441–460.

Casavantes, E. J. Implications for Spanish-Americans. In L. A. Crooks (Ed.), *An investigation of sources of bias in the prediction of job performance.* Princeton: Educational Testing Service, 1972.

Cattell, J. McK. Mental tests and measurements. *Mind,* 1890, 15, 373–380.

Cleary, T. A. Test bias: Prediction of grades of Negro and white students in integrated colleges. *Journal of Educational Measurement,* 1968, 5, 115–124.

Cronbach, L. J. Test validation. In R. L. Thorndike, *Educational measurement.* (2nd ed.) Washington: American Council on Education, 1971, 443–507.

Cronbach, L. J., & Gleser, G. C. *Psychological tests and personnel decisions.* Urbana: University of Illinios Press, 1957.

Cronbach, L. J., & Gleser, G. C. *Psychological tests and personnel decisions.* (2nd ed.) Urbana: University of Illinois Press, 1965.

Cronbach, L. J., & Meehl, P. E. Construct validity in psychological tests. *Psychological Bulletin,* 1955, 52, 281–302.

Curtis, E. W., & Alf, E. F. Validity, predictive efficiency, and practical significance of selection tests. *Journal of Applied Psychology,* 1969, 53, 327–337.

Daniels, H. W., & Otis, J. L. A method for analyzing employment interviews. *Personnel Psychology,* 1950, 3, 425–444.

Darlington, R. B. Another look at "cultural fairness." *Journal of Educational Measurement,* 1971, 8, 71–82.

Dorcus, R. M., & Jones, M. H. *Handbook of employee selection.* New York: McGraw-Hill, 1950.

Dunnette, M. D. A modified model for test validation and selection research. *Journal of Applied Psychology,* 1963, 47, 317–323. (a)

Dunnette, M. D. A note on *the* criterion. *Journal of Applied Psychology,* 1963, 47, 251–254. (b)

Dunnette, M. D. Fads, fashions, and folderol in psychology. *American Psychologist,* 1966, 21, 343–352. (a)

Dunnette, M. D. *Personnel selection and placement.* Belmont, Calif.: Wadsworth Publishing, 1966. (b)

Dunnette, M. D. Comments on Abrahams's and Alf's "Pratfalls in moderator research." *Journal of Applied Psychology,* 1972, 56, 252–256.

Dunnette, M. D. Personnel selection and job placement of the disadvantaged: Problems, issues, and suggestions. In H. L. Fromkin & J. J. Sherwood (Eds.), *Integrating the organization.* New York: The Free Press, 1974.

Dunnette, M. D., & Hakel, M. D. Interpersonal perception and behavior prediction in the employment interview. Paper presented at convention of American Psychological Association, New York, 1966.

Ebel, R. L. Must all tests be valid? *American Psychologist,* 1961, 16, 640–647.

Einhorn, H. J., & Bass, A. R. Methodological considerations relevant to discrimination in employment testing. *Psychological Bulletin,* 1971, 75, 261–269.

Equal Employment Opportunity Commission. *Guidelines on employment testing procedures.* Washington: Equal Employment Opportunity Commission, 1966.

Equal Employment Opportunity Commission. Guidelines on employee selection procedures. *Federal Register,* August 1, 1970, 35 (No. 149), 12333–12336.

Farr, J. L., O'Leary, B. S., & Bartlett, C. J. Ethnic group membership as a moderator of the prediction of job performance. *Personnel Psychology,* 1971, 24, 609–636.

Ferguson, L. W. Life insurance interest, ability, and termination of employment. *Personnel Psychology,* 1958, 11, 189–193.

Fleishman, E. A., & Stephenson, R. W. *Development of a taxonomy of human performance: A review of the third year's progress.* Technical Progress Report 3, R70-11. Washington, D.C.: American Institutes for Research, September, 1970.

Frederiksen, N. Toward a taxonomy of situations. *American Psychologist,* 1972, 27, 114–123.

Frederiksen, N., Jensen, O., & Beaton, A. E. *Prediction of organizational behavior.* Elmsford, N.Y.: Pergamon, 1972, 333 pages.

French, R. L. The Motorola case. *The Industrial Psychologist,* 1965, 2, 20–50.

Freyd, M. Measurement in vocational selection: An outline of research procedure. *Journal of Personnel Research,* 1923, 2, 215–249, 268–284, 377–385.

Ghiselli, E. E. Dimensional problems of criteria. *Journal of Applied Psychology,* 1956, 40, 1–4. (a)

Ghiselli, E. E. The placement of workers: Concepts and problems. *Personnel Psychology,* 1956, 9, 1–16. (b)

Ghiselli, E. E. Differentiation of tests in terms of the accuracy with which they predict for a given individual. *Educational and Psychological Measurement,* 1960, 20, 675–784. (a)

Ghiselli, E. E. The prediction of predictability. *Educational and Psychological Measurement,* 1960, 20, 3–8. (b)

Ghiselli, E. E. The validity of a personnel interview. *Personnel Psychology,* 1966, 19, 389–394. (a)

Ghiselli, E. E. *The validity of occupational aptitude tests.* New York: Wiley, 1966. (b)

Ghiselli, E. E. Interaction of traits and motivational factors in the determination of the success of managers. *Journal of Applied Psychology,* 1968, 52, 480–483.

Ghiselli, E. E. Comment on the use of moderator variables. *Journal of Applied Psychology,* 1972, 56, 270.

Ghiselli, E. E., & Brown, C. W. *Personnel and industrial psychology.* (2nd ed.) New York: McGraw-Hill, 1955.

Ghiselli, E. E., & Lodahl, T. M. Evaluation of foremen's performance in relation to the internal characteristics of their work groups. *Personnel Psychology,* 1958, 11, 179–187.

Goldstein, I. L. The application blank: How honest are the responses? *Journal of Applied Psychology,* 1971, 55, 491–492.

Grant, D. L., & Bray, D. W. Contributions of the interview to assessment of management potential. *Journal of Applied Psychology,* 1969, 53, 24–34.

Grant, D. L., & Bray, D. W. Validation of employment tests for telephone company installation and repair occupations. *Journal of Applied Psychology,* 1970, 54, 7–14.

Griggs vs. *Duke Power Company,* 401 U.S. 424 (1971).

Guion, R. M. Criterion measurement and personnel judgments. *Personnel Psychology,* 1961, 14, 141–149.

Guion, R. M. *Personnel testing.* New York: McGraw-Hill, 1965. (a)

Guion, R. M. Synthetic validity in a small company: A demonstration. *Personnel Psychology,* 1965, 18, 49–63. (b)

Guion, R. M. Employment tests and discriminatory hiring. *Industrial Relations,* 1966, 5, 20–37.

Guion, R. M. Personnel selection. *Annual Review of Psychology,* 1967, 18, 191–216.

Guion, R. M. Implications for governmental regulatory agencies. In L. A. Crooks (Ed.), *An investigation of sources of bias in the prediction of job performance.* Princeton: Educational Testing Service, 1972.

Guion, R. M., & Gottier, R. F. Validity of personality measures in personnel selection. *Personnel Psychology,* 1965, 18, 135–164.

Gunderson, E. K., & Nelson, P. D. Criterion measures for extremely isolated groups. *Personnel Psychology,* 1966, 19, 67–80.

Guttman, I., & Raju, N. S. A minimum loss function as determiner of optimal cutting scores. *Personnel Psychology,* 1965, 18, 179–185.

Hakel, M. D. Similarity of post-interview trait rating intercorrelations as a contributor to interrater agreement in a structured employment interview. *Journal of Applied Psychology*, 1971, 55, 443–448.

Hakel, M. D., Dobmeyer, T. W., & Dunnette, M. D. The relative importance of three content dimensions in overall suitability ratings of job applicants' resumes. *Journal of Applied Psychology*, 1970, 54, 65–71.

Hakel, M. D., & Schuh, A. J. Job applicant attributes judged important across seven diverse occupations. *Personnel Psychology*, 1971, 24, 45–52.

Harvard Law Review. Employment discrimination and Title VII of the Civil Rights Act of 1964. *HLR*, 1971, 84, 1109–1316.

Hedberg, R., & Baxter, B. A second look at personality test validation. *Personnel Psychology*, 1957, 10, 157–160.

Hollingworth, H. L. *Judging human character*. New York: Appleton, 1922.

Horst, P. *Psychological measurement and prediction*. Belmont, Calif.: Wadsworth Publishing, 1966.

Howell, M. A., & Newman, S. H. Prediction of work area specialization among professional health personnel. *Personnel Psychology*, 1967, 20, 89–110.

Hull, C. L. *Aptitude testing*. Yonkers, N.Y.: World Book, 1928.

Humphreys, L. G. Statistical definitions of test validity for minority groups. *Journal of Applied Psychology*, 1973, 58, 1–4.

Kahneman, D., & Ghiselli, E. E. Validity and nonlinear heteroscedastic models. *Personnel Psychology*, 1962, 15, 1–11.

Kipnis, D. A noncognitive correlate of performance among lower aptitude men. *Journal of Applied Psychology*, 1962, 46, 76–80.

Kirkpatrick, J. J., Ewen, R. B., Barrett, R. S., & Katzell, R. A. *Testing and fair employment*. New York: New York University Press, 1968.

Knauft, E. B. A selection battery for bake shop managers. *Journal of Applied Psychology*, 1949, 33, 304–315.

Korman, A. K. The prediction of managerial performance: A review. *Personnel Psychology*, 1968, 21, 295–322.

Kornhauser, A. W., & Kingsbury, F. A. *Psychological tests in business*. Chicago: University of Chicago Press, 1924.

Lavallée, L., & Thivierge, J. P. Étude d'équivalence entre les examens de la connaissance des langues français et anglaise utilisés dans la fonction publique. *Studies in Personnel Psychology*, 1970, 2, 62–73.

Lawler, E. E. III. Management performance as seen from above, below, and within. *Journal of Applied Psychology*, 1967, 51, 247–253.

Lawshe, C. H. What can industrial psychology do for small business (a symposium 2): Employee selection. *Personnel Psychology*, 1952, 5, 31–34.

Lawshe, C. H. Statistical theory and practice in applied psychology. *Personnel Psychology*, 1969, 22, 117–124.

Lawshe, C. H., & Balma, M. J. *Principles of personnel testing*. New York: McGraw-Hill, 1966.

Lawshe, C. H., & Steinberg, M. D. Studies in synthetic validity: I. An exploratory investigation of clerical jobs. *Personnel Psychology*, 1955, 8, 291–301.

Lawshe, C. H., Bolda, R. A., Brune, R. L., & Auclair, G. Expectancy charts: II. Their theoretical development. *Personnel Psychology*, 1958, 11, 545–560.

Lent, R. H., Aurbach, H. E., & Levin, L. S. Predictors, criteria, and significant results. *Personnel Psychology*, 1971, 24, 519–533. (a)

Lent, R. H., Aurbach, H. A., & Levin, L. S. Research design and validity assessment. *Personnel Psychology*, 1971, 24, 247–274. (b)

Link, H. C. *Employment psychology*. New York: Macmillan, 1924.

Linn, R. L., & Werts, C. E. Considerations for studies of test bias. *Journal of Educational Measurement*, 1971, 8, 1–4.

Loevinger, J. Objective tests as instruments of psychology theory. *Psychological Reports* (monograph Supp. 9), 1957, 635–694.

Loudermilk, K. M. Prediction of efficiency of lumber and paper mill employees. *Personnel Psychology*, 1966, 19, 301–310.

Maas, J. B. Patterned scale expectation interview. *Journal of Applied Psychology*, 1965, 49, 431–433.

Mayfield, E. C. The selection interview: A reevaluation of published research. *Personnel Psychology*, 1964, 17, 239, 260.

Mayfield, E. C., & Carlson, R. E. Selection interview decisions: First results from long-term research project. *Personnel Psychology*, 1966, 19, 41–53.

Meehl, P. E., & Rosen, A. Antecedent probability and the efficiency of psychometric signs, patterns, or cutting scores. *Psychological Bulletin*, 1955, 52, 194–216.

Morrison, D. E., & Henkel, R. E., Eds. *The significance test controversy*. Chicago: Aldine, 1970.

Mosel, J. N., & Goheen, H. W. The Employment Recommendation Questionnaire: III. Validity of different types of references. *Personnel Psychology, 1959, 12*, 469–477.

Mullins, C. J., & Usdin, E. Estimation of validity in the absence of a criterion. *AFHRL-TR-70-36*, 1970.

Munsterberg, H. *Psychology and industrial efficiency*. Boston: Houghton Mifflin, 1913.

Nagle, B. F. Criterion development. *Personnel Psychology, 1953, 6*, 271–289.

Office of Federal Contract Compliance. Validation of tests by contractors and subcontractors subject to the provisions of Executive Order 11246. *Federal Register*, September 24, 1968, 33 (No. 186), 14392–14394.

Office of Federal Contract Compliance. Employee testing and other selection procedures. *Federal Register*, October 2, 1971, 36 (No. 192), 19307–19310.

Parry, M. E. Ability of psychologists to estimate validity of personnel tests. *Personnel Psychology, 1968, 21*, 139–147.

Peterson, D. A., & Wallace, S. R. Validation and revision of a test in use. *Journal of Applied Psychology, 1966, 50*, 13–17.

Plag, J. A., & Goffman, J. M. The Armed Forces Qualification Test: Its validity in predicting military effectiveness for naval enlistees. *Personnel Psychology, 1967, 20*, 323–340.

Plante, L., & Stewart, C. P. The prediction of key-punch training success. *Studies in Personnel Psychology, 1971, 3*, 77–86.

Primoff, E. S. *Test selection by job analysis*. Washington, D.C.: U.S. Civil Service Commission, Test Technical Series No. 20, 1955.

Ramfalk, C. W. *Top management selection*. Stockholm: Swedish Council for Personnel Administration, 1957.

Raubenheimer, I., van W., & Tiffin, J. Personnel selection and the prediction of error. *Journal of Applied Psychology, 1971, 55*, 229–233.

Richardson, M. W. The combination of measures. In P. Horst (Ed.), The prediction of personal adjustment. *Bulletin*, No. 48. New York: Social Science Research Council, 1941.

Rock, D. A. The identification and utilization of moderator effects in prediction systems.

Research Bulletin RB-69-32. Princeton: Educational Testing Service, April, 1969.

Rorer, L. G., Hoffman, P. J., LaForge, G. E., & Hsieh, K. Optimum cutting scores to discriminate groups of unequal size and variance. *Journal of Applied Psychology, 1966, 50*, 153–164.

Rothe, H. F. Output rates among butter wrappers: II. Frequency distributions and an hypothesis regarding the "restriction of output." *Journal of Applied Psychology, 1946, 30*, 320–327.

Rothe, H. F. Output rates among machine operators: I. Distributions and their reliability. *Journal of Applied Psychology, 1947, 31*, 484–489.

Rothe, H. F. Output rates among chocolate dippers. *Journal of Applied Psychology, 1951, 35*, 94–97.

Rothe, H. F., & Nye, C. T. Output rates among machine operators: II. Consistency related to methods of pay. *Journal of Applied Psychology, 1959, 43*, 417–420.

Rothe, H. F., & Nye, C. T. Output rates among machine operators: III. A non-incentive situation in two levels of business activity. *Journal of Applied Psychology, 1961, 45*, 50–54.

Rulon, P. J., Tiedeman, D. V., Tatsuoka, M. M., & Langmuir, C. R. *Multivariate statistics for personnel classification*. New York: Wiley, 1967.

Rundquist, E. A. The prediction ceiling. *Personnel Psychology, 1969, 22*, 109–116.

Ryan, T. A., & Smith, P. C. *Principles of industrial psychology*. New York: Ronald Press, 1954.

Schmidt, F. L., & Kaplan, L. B. Composite versus multiple criteria: A review and resolution of the controversy. *Personnel Psychology, 1971, 24*, 419–434.

Schmidt, F. L., Berner, J. G., & Hunter, J. E. Racial differences in validity of employment tests: Reality or illusion? *Journal of Applied Psychology, 1973, 58*, 5–9.

Schuh, A. J. Application blank items and intelligence as predictors of turnover. *Personnel Psychology, 1967, 20*, 59–63. (a)

Schuh, A. J. The predictability of employee tenure: A review of the literature. *Personnel Psychology, 1967, 20*, 133–152. (b)

Seashore, S. E., Indik, B. P., & Georgopoulos, B. S. Relationships among criteria of job performance. *Journal of Applied Psychology, 1960, 44*, 195–202.

Shott, G. L., Albright, L. E., & Glennon, J. R. Predicting turnover in an automated office situation. *Personnel Psychology,* 1963, 16, 213–219.

Slovic, P., & Lichtenstein, S. Comparison of Bayesian and regression approaches to the study of information processing in judgment. *Organizational Behavior and Human Performance,* 1971, 6, 649–744.

Smith, P. C., & Kendall, L. M. Retranslation of expectations: An approach to the construction of unambiguous anchors for rating scales. *Journal of Applied Psychology,* 1963, 47, 149–155.

Stanton, E. S. Company policies and supervisors' attitudes toward supervision. *Journal of Applied Psychology,* 1960, 44, 22–26.

Stone, T. H., & Athelstan, G. T. The SVIB for women and demographic variables in the prediction of occupational tenure. *Journal of Applied Psychology,* 1969, 53, 408–412.

Super, D. E. The biographical inventory as a method for describing adjustment and predicting success. *Bulletin of the International Association of Applied Psychology,* 1960, 9, 18–39.

Tanofsky, R., Shepps, R. R., & O'Neill, P. J. Pattern analysis of biographical predictors of success as an insurance salesman. *Journal of Applied Psychology,* 1969, 53, 136–139.

Thorndike, R. L. *Personnel selection.* New York: Wiley, 1949.

Thorndike, R. L. Concepts of culture-fairness. *Journal of Educational Measurement,* 1971, 8, 63–70.

Tom, V. R. The role of personality and organizational images in the recruiting process. *Organizational Behavior and Human Performance,* 1971, 6, 573–592.

Toops, H. A. The criterion. *Educational and Psychological Measurement,* 1944, 4, 271–297.

Toops, H. A. A research utopia in industrial psychology. *Personnel Psychology,* 1959, 12, 189–297.

Tryon, R. C., & Bailey, D. E. *Cluster analysis.* New York: McGraw-Hill, 1970.

Tupes, E. C. A note on "validity and nonlinear heteroscedastic models." *Personnel Psychology,* 1964, 17, 59–63.

Tversky, A., & Kahneman, D. Belief in the law of small numbers. *Psychological Bulletin,* 1971, 76, 105–110.

Ulrich, L., & Trumbo, D. The selection interview since 1949. *Psychological Bulletin,* 1965, 63, 100–116.

Velicer, W. F. Comment on the general inapplicability of Ghiselli's moderator system for two predictors. *Journal of Applied Psychology,* 1972, 56, 262–265. (a)

Velicer, W. F. The moderator variable viewed as heterogeneous regression. *Journal of Applied Psychology,* 1972, 56, 266–269. (b)

Wagner, R. The employment interview: A critical summary. *Personnel Psychology,* 1949, 2, 17–46.

Wallace, S. R. Criteria for what? *American Psychologist,* 1965, 20, 411–417.

Wallace, S. R., & Twichell, C. M. Managerial procedures and test validities. *Personnel Psychology,* 1949, 2, 17–46.

Webster, E. D., Ed. *Decision making in the employment interview.* Montreal: Eagle, 1964.

Wherry, R. J. *A review of the J-Coefficient.* Washington, D.C.: U.S. Civil Service Commission, Assembled Test Technical Series No. 26, July, 1955.

Wolins, L. Responsibility for raw data. *American Psychologist,* 1962, 17, 657–658.

Zedeck, S. Identification of moderator variables by discriminant analysis in a multi-predictable group validation model. *Journal of Applied Psychology,* 1971, 55, 364–371. (a)

Zedeck, S. Problems with the use of "moderator" variables. *Psychological Bulletin,* 1971, 76, 295–310. (b)

Zedeck, S., Cranny, C. J., Vale, C. A., & Smith, P. C. Comparison of "joint moderators" in three prediction techniques. *Journal of Applied Psychology,* 1971, 55, 234–240.

CHAPTER 19

Personnel Training

JOHN R. HINRICHS
International Business Machines Corp.

The Personnel Training Scene in the 1970s	Training Techniques
A Systems Viewpoint	References

THE AREA OF PERSONNEL TRAINING in organizations is reviewed, with the conclusion that little systematic psychological knowledge about the field has been developed. An open-systems viewpoint is employed to help clarify the nature of the training process. This analysis moves from a review of the skill acquisition system at the level of the individual trainee, to the supra-system of the training department, and finally to the total organizational system in which the training department operates. The signal and maintenance inputs, systems operator, outputs, and feedback loops for each of these systems are discussed. A final section reviews various popular training methodologies, classifying them into content, process, and mixed techniques. Research needs in the area of personnel training are reviewed in the concluding section.

To a considerable extent the field of personnel training is where it all comes together when we describe the practice of industrial and organizational psychology. Or at least it is where it all *should* come together. To be effective, training in organizations must rest soundly on the bedrock of all of the other topics discussed in the chapters in this section. An effective job and task analysis is essential to determining training needs: (1) evaluations of behavior, performance, and effectiveness—criteria—are as essential to the evaluation of training success as they are to the development of selection strategies; (2) training is often a critical component in obtaining the optimal match between people and hardware; (3) the determination of the best solution to an organizational staffing problem may resolve itself into a choice between emphasis on recruiting and selection versus training and development; and so forth for the other issues discussed in this section of the *Handbook*. So, in our discussion of the psychology of personnel training, we assume some familiarity with the total spectrum of applied organizational and industrial psychology.

The field of personnel training is a many faceted though imprecisely delimited area of theory, knowledge, and practice. We shall attempt to cover all aspects. In the first section of this chapter we shall review the nature of the personnel training scene in the mid-1970s. The review will attempt to answer the question of whether there is, in fact, currently such a thing as a psychology of personnel training. The answer comes out as a qualified "maybe."

Next, we shall turn to an attempt to develop a conceptual scheme for describing what's involved in most training efforts. This scheme, using the framework of open-systems theory, is intended to be sufficiently broad to cover all aspects of skill acquisition, including motor skills, cognitive skills, and interpersonal skills. Then a generalized model is developed which attempts to describe the training process in idealized terms as one among a repertoire of many possible responses to organizational problems. The model flows from the determination of training needs through implementation and evaluation. Next, we turn our attention to a description of the major training techniques currently in use in organizations. The description includes a brief review of research evaluating the major methodologies. Finally, we conclude with some speculation about future training needs of organizations and current and future research directions which these needs suggest.

THE PERSONNEL TRAINING SCENE IN THE 1970s

A recent chapter in the *Annual Review of Psychology* (Campbell, 1971) provides a comprehensive assessment of the personnel training scene in organizations as it has evolved to the end of the decade of the sixties. It is not a particularly bright assessment.

Following our independent excursion into the literature, we would tend to agree with this assessment and conclude that:

1. The field of training in organizations is dominated by practitioners, most of whom are non-psychologists. As a result, right from the start it is probably not too realistic to expect much progress in the development of a psychology of training.

2. The major emphasis, in most organizations, tends to be on the "training program." The premium and organizational reward in real life most often is on doing something—anything seen as being responsive to organizational needs. In the rush to

"do something," the practitioners all too often lose sight of the problem. A voluminous catalog of training programs undoubtedly provides a euphoric comfort that problems are being solved as well as providing a measure of job security for the program implementor and administrator.

3. With the premium on generating programs and relatively less concern with definition of the problems, program design becomes eclectic. Fads move in and out of use with the greatest of ease.

4. There is little or no concern today with using theory in the design of programs, much less with building new theory. The good program is one that is attention-getting, dramatic, contemporary, or fun. Whether or not it changes behavior becomes secondary. And whether or not insights evolve for modifying the program to maximize results or for building new programs is of small concern.

5. Within this framework, of course, there is precious little research on the effectiveness of training. Most programs are sold and accepted on faith. What evaluation there is is global and program-specific, with few generalizable insights useful for theory building. This is especially true in business and industry; psychologists seem to have played much more of a role in the design and evaluation of training efforts in the military than they have in the private sector of our economy, and most of our few generalizations about training are indebted to military-sponsored research.

6. This situation is very similar to what it was back in the 1950s or even the forties. While the content and emphasis of personnel training may have changed, the way in which training in organizations is designed and implemented has evolved very little (McGehee & Thayer, 1961).

Against this rather disorganized backdrop, one might question why it is that training has survived as a viable organizational activity in business. And survive it has! Estimates of man-hours expended and dollars devoted to training each year in

American industry will boggle the mind. And the trend is not toward less reliance on training, but toward more (Mesics, 1969). While the practitioners are doing little to build a psychology of training, they must be doing something right; it can't all be a big fraud.

Undoubtedly many things are being done right, or at least well. In all probability training often does contribute both to individual and to organizational effectiveness. A body of expertise and lore regarding what seems to work has evolved. But we would contend that training could be done better.

We would point out that it is as important to understand *why* certain things work as it is to identify *which* ones work so that insights may be generalized to new areas. We would suggest, therefore, that to achieve this, the technology of training should be built less on ad hoc considerations and more on general principles derived from systematic research. The alternative is for a review of the field in the 1980s to read much the same as a review in the seventies.

Is There A Psychology of Personnel Training?

Almost without exception textbooks in industrial and organizational psychology repeat the same tired list of "principles" derived out of learning research when they deal with the topic of training—distribute practice, motivate the learner, make the learning task similar to the final task, etc. (Blum & Naylor, 1968; Korman, 1971). Such principles, however, have been ignored by training practitioners with amazing regularity, except to the extent that they find their way into program design as a result of the administrator's "common sense" about what works best. This suggests that either: (1) practitioners (management) are stupid to ignore such "principles" which will demonstrably increase training effectiveness and reduce costs, or (2) the "principles" are of little or no value in the real (non-laboratory) world.

As in most things, there is probably an element of truth in both possibilities. As Gagné (1962) points out, there are very clearly many instances in which these ubiquitous "principles" are of no help, or may even be counter-productive to the enhancement of training effectiveness. Thus, we would conclude that today there is no such thing as a complete, universally accepted, identifiable, and verifiable psychology of training. Any description of training practices invariably is a mishmash of different frames of reference reflecting how the field has evolved without direction or unifying theory. For example, today different training activities are classified in terms of: (1) technique (e.g., T.V. training, computer-assisted instruction, programmed instruction, simulations, encounter training, etc.); (2) population (e.g., training of the hardcore and handicapped, management development, etc.); or, (3) objective (e.g., training in problem solving, creativity training, career updating, organization development, sensitivity, etc.). It is practically impossible to develop any meaningful description of the psychology of personnel training around such a conceptual monstrosity.

As a result, we must scrap both descriptions of current practices and attempts to organize around learning "principles" derived from laboratory research and evolve a more all-inclusive conceptual framework for the classification of training efforts in organizations. Such a dilemma in the training area is reminiscent of similar concern with developing a classification scheme for learning in general. For example, Jensen's (1967) three-dimensional space for representing classes of variables in learning tasks has considerable parallel to the different descriptive frames of reference which have evolved by natural process in the training field. Jensen's scheme entails dimensions of (a) learning content and modality (verbal, spatial, visual, etc.); (b) learning procedures (pacing, distribution of practice, etc.); and (c) types of learning (conditioning, motor, etc.) (Jensen, 1967, p. 123).

Jensen concludes that there has been an extremely meagre sampling of research within the cubes described by the intersection of these dimensions. His further concern with the lack of research clarifying interactions of learning variables with subjects in this (or any other) conceptual framework —not to mention his concern over the lack of research to delineate the genotypes of between-subject variation associated with the phenotypes of learning he describes— is equally applicable to the field of training in organizations. If most research in the basic area of learning has tended to occur without reference to any unifying taxonomy, this is certainly true of the applied field of training in organizations.

Perhaps it is too much to ask that a cohesive taxonomy of training variables be developed to provide a framework for building a psychology of training. After all, if learning research has not progressed very far beyond the more or less arbitrary selection of tasks from various points in Jensen's "types/procedures/contents" taxonomy—or any other taxonomy—it may be completely unrealistic to call for coordinated research on the interactions operating in the field of training. But without a unifying conceptual framework and coordinated research designs, training will continue to be an ad hoc field and our response to the question of whether or not there is such a thing as a psychology of personnel training will continue as a qualified "maybe." The comments of McGehee and Thayer (1961) over a decade ago are still pertinent today; let's hope they are not still pertinent a decade from now. "Sporadic research, however brilliant, will not give us answers to the many problems concerning learning which are required if we are to make training a useful management tool. What is required to answer these problems is systematic research" (McGehee & Thayer, 1961, p. 179).

What is needed is a description in behavioral and organizational terms of what is involved in the training process. This description should be sufficiently general that it encompasses all of the current training techniques being used in organizations, appropriate for all of the special populations which are used to describe training, and for all of the specific objectives for which training programs are implemented. It must also be possible to fit all of the various learning "principles" into this training description in a meaningful and cohesive way. Then out of this, hopefully, it should become clear which are the key considerations and points of leverage at both the individual and the organizational level which must be attended to in maximizing the effectiveness of personnel training.

Training Defined

Training may be defined as any organizationally initiated procedures which are intended to foster learning among organizational members. Needless to say, the desired learning is in a direction which is intended to contribute to overall organizational objectives. *Learning* may be thought of as a process by which an individual's pattern of behavior is changed by experience—for our purposes, the catalytic experience of exposure to the training activity. So, training is a systematic intentional process of altering behavior of organizational members in a direction which contributes to organizational effectiveness (King, 1964, p. 125; McGehee & Thayer, 1961, p. 3; Warren, 1969, p. 3).

Such a definition in its barest form sounds manipulative; the organization supports a program designed to alter behavior of its members toward increasing their contribution to organizational objectives. To be sure, some training can and does approach manipulation (such as some programs of attitudinal indoctrination or forced attendance of managers in sensitivity training groups).

However, the vast majority of training in business and industry is anything but manipulative. As a matter of fact, training is the area of personnel activity where the goals of the organization and the goals of the individual today can be in closest harmony. Training is where organizational and individual development can merge; where personal and corporate growth can occur simultaneously. So, while the motivation for instituting and supporting training almost always springs from the organization's desire to enhance its effectiveness, the outcomes of training do not have to be dedicated exclusively to that end.

We shall return to this point later as we build our conceptual model of the training process and make the point that where the balance of outcomes leans too heavily toward the exclusive benefit of organizational objectives, training efforts will lose their effectiveness, and vice versa. In other words, effective training programs must demonstrably contribute to the satisfaction of both the trainee's personal goals as well as the organizational goals.

In setting up a model of training in organizations, we shall look upon learning as the alteration of behavior in its broadest sense. For our purpose, the term *behavior* will include any aspect of human activity, cognition, or feeling. A behavior becomes learned when one experiences a new way of acting, thinking, or feeling, finds the new pattern gratifying or useful, and incorporates it into the repertoire of behaviors.

Any behavior that has become learned can be thought of as a *skill*. Thus, as Fleishman (1967) points out in his discussion of motor skills, "the term skill refers to the level of proficiency on a specific task or limited groups of tasks." In terms of *training*, learning is task oriented; it is the process of skill enhancement. This distinction is relatively easy to develop in the area of motor skills—operating a turret lathe, playing baseball, flying an airplane—but the same concepts and definitional process can be extended to the areas of cognitive and interpersonal skills—communication skills in making a speech, leadership skills in managing a department, interpersonal skills in holding an interview. Training, then, is directed toward a specific skill designed to enhance the level of proficiency of that skill on a specific task or group of tasks.

In contrast to skills, *abilities* may be thought of as more basic and enduring attributes of an individual. Abilities themselves may to some extent be learned, but they are usually of a more general and permanent nature and less task specific than is true of skills. We may think of abilities as individual difference variables which people bring to the training situation. As such, the concept of ability is an important one in the design and administration of training activities; it is a key component on the input side of the training process, as we shall elaborate when we develop our model.

The concept of skill provides an important dimension which can be used as a basis for developing a taxonomy of current day training activity. It is also useful for identifying some of the key variables which must be taken into consideration in the development and selection of training techniques and in the process of evaluating training effectiveness. We may think in terms of three broad classes of skills which apply in organizational settings:

1. *Motor skills,* which are entailed in the manipulation of the physical environment based upon appropriate response patterns of the body musculature.

2. *Cognitive skills,* in which we include the acquisition of patterns of attitudes and beliefs.

3. *Interpersonal skills,* most often thought of in terms of self-awareness and in effective functioning within social processes and interactions.

While it is true that many training programs end up imparting skills in more than a single one of these areas, the primary thrust of a specific training activity is usually beamed at skill acquisition within a single area. For simplicity, we shall view training programs as being relatively "pure" in terms of their objectives for imparting skills in a single one of these three areas; in practice, we recognize that training is never completely "pure" in its objectives or effects.

A SYSTEMS VIEWPOINT

The nature of the training process, when reviewed as a series of procedures to foster skill acquisition, immediately suggests an open systems model of what's involved. Components of the model should be readily apparent to those with even a brushing acquaintance with systems theory: inputs (trainees, organizational resources); some type of systems operator (individual learning processes, the "training program"); and outputs (skilled personnel, organizational success). Systems feedback occurs through the training evaluation procedures, either research based or informal.

While such a concept of training is very "in" in the personnel and training literature, most descriptions of industrial training practices in systems terms are shallow and do little to clarify what's going on. For example, Warren (1969) devotes an entire book to training as a system, but does not move appreciably beyond developing and describing the flow chart of the training process. Such descriptions may be useful as a check list of what not to overlook in designing and conducting training programs, but they do not provide insight into the dynamics of the training process which can lead to generalizations for maximizing its effectiveness.

Glaser (1962, p. 6) outlines the principal components of an instructional system as: (a) instructional goals, (b) entering behavior, (c) instructional procedures, and (d) performance assessment. Overlying each of these are research and development logistics. Such system concepts have made their most important impact on training in the military. This is a natural outgrowth of the influence of human factors psychologists in the design of training for military personnel. The emphasis has been on designing training procedures for imparting skills which are very often specific to a particular military need—such as manning a specific weapons system—and the instructional systems tends to be viewed as an extension, if not a subsystem, of the design of the weapons system itself. Crawford (1965) provides several examples from the military of how training can be an integral sub-part of a broader "parent system." In business and industry, however, talk about systems concepts seems largely borrowed from the military but is actually used very little in the design of training programs.

We would like to explore some of the main points of consideration in viewing personnel training as an open system in order to see if we can find a framework for better understanding the key factors in the training process. We should point out, however, that this is certainly not a definitive treatment; it will be a mixture of theory (drawn heavily upon concepts from Berrien, 1968, in his discussion of general and social systems), as well as concepts from general writings on training, learning "principles," and experience.

First of all, it is clear that there are three levels of analysis that we can assume. One of the beauties of systems theory is that we can move from one to another of these levels with relative ease in developing a total picture of training in organizations. Our systems oriented discussion will flow from the micro to the macro.

The first level of analysis will assess the process of skill acquisition in systems terms. This is training at the level of the *individual;* it is concerned with the inputs, the outputs, and the intervening operators which are at the base of the training process. The feedback process at this level concentrates on the evaluation of performance or skill of individual trainees. This feedback component deals with individual difference variables of skill and performance and the assessment of change in these variables as a result of the training intervention.

For the next level of analysis we move to a discussion of the systems involved at the level of the *training program.* Here the key variables are the ones most often of concern to personnel and training people—trainee selection and program design. The evaluation procedures are group based: does the management development program enhance the overall effectiveness of the organization's management team; is the retraining program for technicians successful in providing an acceptable fraction of an obsolescent technician group with updated or changed skills; and so forth.

The final level of analysis is from the point of view of the *total organization*. Here the training function is viewed as one among many which can contribute to desired organizational objectives. The system operator at this level is one designed to compare the potential effectiveness of various organizational subsystems and to conduct the cost/benefit analysis of trade-offs from alternate courses of action available to the organization. The evaluation procedure assesses such questions as the relative efficiency of training versus such alternatives as recruitment, merger or acquisition, changes in technologies, altered markets, or revised net to gross financial objectives.

Skill Acquisition System

The system operator at the level of the skill acquisition system is the individual trainee. The operator consists of all of the processes by which learning occurs in an individual. As Fitts (1962) illustrates in his discussion of factors in complex skill training, there can be a broad array of dynamic feedback loops or subsystems involved in learning at the individual level. These deal with variables of sensory interactions, central nervous system dynamics, response interactions, environmental dynamics, and machine display and control dynamics. As it is beyond the scope of our discussion of personnel training to dwell on these dynamic feedback loops, we shall adopt the expedient recommended by Berrien (1968, p. 17) by treating this system operator as a "black box" and focusing our attention on the role of inputs, outputs, and feedback at the level of the individual trainee. Figure 1 provides a diagram of the major components of a skill acquisition system developed within this framework.

Berrien differentiates two classes of system inputs: (1) maintenance, and (2) signal. Maintenance inputs are those which energize the system; they are the source of energy to keep it going. Signal inputs, on the other hand, are the ones which are most crucial to formal achievement or, in our instance, skill acquisition. The signal is

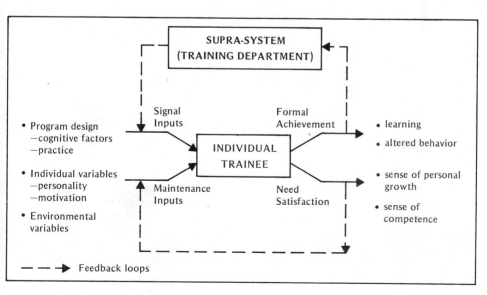

Figure 1.   Skill acquisition system.

what is processed by the system and transferred as output to the supra-system; without signal input there would be no formal achievement of the system.

Sorting out the different functions of maintenance and signal inputs can help to clarify some of the key features in skill acquisition. Both maintenance and signal inputs are essential to the proper functioning and continued operation of the system. However, they must exist in some appropriate ratio to one another so that there is enough maintenance input to insure that the system operates, while at the same time not so much that it drowns out the signal inputs.

MAINTENANCE INPUTS. Maintenance inputs tend to be thought of as "givens" in terms of factors which sustain the system, but it is important to recognize, as we shall elaborate later, that they can be influenced during the course of skill acquisition through the feedback process. For our skill acquisition model, we may think of two general classes of maintenance inputs. The first are *individual variables,* which are the "givens" an individual brings to the skill acquisition situation. An extensive list of such variables could be prepared, and would probably fall within this framework:

Ability: or the extent to which the individual possesses the basic "horsepower" to perform the task at hand. Does the individual have the mental ability to learn what is expected of him? Does he have the muscle ability to perform the motor task? Does he have the visual acuity to learn the discrimination task?

Personality: the whole spectrum of personality variables can come into play here. Especially key is the self-confidence or self-esteem that the individual has in his ability to carry on the behavior required in order to acquire the desired skill.

Motivation: here we would include all the kinds of motivational variables which operate on the individual and tend to shape his behavior—need for achievement, competence, power, security, etc., or instrumentality and valence factors—with no necessity for getting into a specific argument about the most "correct" description of need or motivation variables operating in the skill acquisition system.

The second general category of maintenance input are *organizational and social system variables.* We conceive of these very broadly as factors in the immediate training environment and the broader organizational and social environment which serve as maintenance inputs to skill acquisition. They include such things as: (1) overall organizational norms, role expectations, policies, support, recognition, etc.; (2) formal and informal rewards of pay, job security, awards, enhanced job competence, advancement potential, etc.; (3) supportive supervision, managerial pressure, and expectations; and (4) peer recognition, pressure, acceptance, and the informal social system. By and large, these are the maintenance inputs which are most under the control of the organization and which can be varied to ensure that training takes place.

We certainly do not claim to have been exhaustive in these lists of individual and social system variables; our purpose has been to suggest that there are a variety of factors which support and sustain the skill acquisition system and are crucial to its maintenance, but which, in and of themselves, do not determine the formal achievement of training objectives.

SIGNAL INPUTS. On the other hand, signal inputs to the system are the main determiners of formal achievement. They may be thought of as the training manipulations. Again we can describe two broad classes of signal inputs—cognitive and practice:

Cognitive inputs consist of information on the nature of the skills which are to be acquired. They are essentially the educational component of training and include such things as:

1. definition and statement of specific training objectives

2. setting of performance goals and standards

3. instructions, orders, and directives

4. demonstrations and role models with regard to desired terminal behaviors

5. information and data presented via lecture, textbook, audiovisual techniques, etc.

The manipulation of cognitive signal inputs is the process of getting the individual to understand the nature of the terminal behaviors desired as a result of training—even in skill areas where the desired response is emotional rather than cognitive. Examples of such inputs designed to increase awareness of skills which are to be internalized are such things as: (a) a lecture, film, or discussion session on techniques in a training program on "How to interview"; (b) a demonstration of the steps involved in operating a drill press; (c) a programmed instruction course in how to write and debug a computer program. We shall go so far as to say that all *training* (though not necessarily all learning) has some cognitive component to it. If there is such a thing as training activity which is purely experiential (perhaps some encounter groups border on this, though even here there is usually a cognitive component), we shall not include such activities under the rubric of training. All training must go beyond the mere learning process to include some systematic effort to impart cognitive awareness of the terminal behaviors desired as a result of the training.

Practice in the behaviors which represent the objectives of the training process is the second class of signal input to all training. Our basic definition of learning suggests that a skill will not be acquired until it is practiced ("behavior becomes learned when one experiences a new way of acting, thinking, or feeling, finds the new pattern gratifying or useful, and incorporates it into the repertoire of behavior"). The amount of practice entailed in training may vary, but for skills to be acquired, training inputs must be more than just cognitive.

It is in this area of practice that most of the "do's" and "don'ts" of learning theory find their way into texts on industrial and organizational psychology—considerations of massed versus distributed practice, whole versus part learning, over-learning, degree of similarity of practice and task elements as a determiner of transfer, and so forth. We tend to agree with McGehee and Thayer (1961, pp. 78–79) that such principles have not been adequately validated in the industrial setting to warrant their wholesale application. The types of variables covered by the so-called "principles" should be viewed more as heuristics to be considered in designing the conditions of practice than as any kind of absolute guidelines. Fully as important, if not more so, will be considerations of the nature of the behaviors which it is desired to impart through the training, the population being trained, time and resources available to be spent on practice, relative importance of practice versus cognitive inputs for the attainment of terminal behaviors, and so forth.

There are several points with regard to practice, however, which do seem generalizable and which fit in well with our systems view of skill acquisition. First of all, the level of difficulty of the practice task should be such that the trainee experiences early and visible success. For an easy task, this may be achieved through practice on a total task; more difficult tasks may have to be broken down into components which are capable of being mastered with relative ease. The success experience is important because of its reward value for beginning to fix the signal input of practice into memory as learning. Success is also important because of its role in enhancing the important maintenance inputs of trainee self-confidence and supportive organizational and social system variables. As we shall explore in more detail later, such impact occurs through feedback loops which must be built into the skill acquisition system. Success is a prerequisite for learning and must be built into the practice situation at an early stage.

Secondly, practice, if it is at all complex and broken down into components, should follow a logical sequence. Each subsequent practice of the behavior should represent an extension of the skills required over the previous practice. This should be a gradual building in level of difficulty and complexity leading up to practice on the complete task, which has been defined as the desired terminal behavior. Practice which is invariant in terms of level of difficulty tends to become boring and non-rewarding; practice which is stopped after it is mastered or which is cumulative in terms of required level of ability will facilitate learning.

Finally, a point closely related to the previous one is that it is important that the skills required for each level of performance be mastered before moving on to the next level. However, in most tasks individuals vary considerably in their rate of skill acquisition, and this requirement plus the requirement of not over-practicing to the point of boredom emphasizes the need for individualizing training in most situations. To the extent feasible, it is important to let trainees progress through the sequence of practice stages which is optimal for their own individualized skill acquisition. Lock-step training efforts beamed at the "average" trainee will miss the mark for most individuals. In the applied setting, the potential for individualized training is best realized through some of the auto-instructional techniques and on-the-job approaches to personnel training.

OUTPUTS. Berrien (1968) refers to two behavioral outputs from a social system: formal achievement (FA) and group need satisfaction (GNS). For our discussion at the level of the individual, we may think of Formal Achievement as the skills acquired and of individual rather than Group Need Satisfaction (GNS). These variables fit within the same type of model as that discussed by Berrien.

Berrien points out that it is the signal inputs which are transferred into learning; cognitive and practice inputs result in the acquisition of skills which are the formal achievement of the system. The maintenance inputs of individual and organizational and social system variables merely maintain the system and make it grow. For the system to continue to exist, the formal achievement outputs must be of use to the supra-system; in the skill acquisition model, skills which are acquired must be of use to the organization's training system. To the extent they are not, they represent waste and lead to entropy (even though they may serve as useful inputs to other systems pertinent to either the individual or to the organization). Where the formal achievement—skills acquired—are not adequate to satisfy the needs of the supra-system, the training system will either fail or be altered through the feedback mechanism. Thus the concept of feedback is important in understanding the role of outputs in the relationship between the system and the supra-system.

FEEDBACK. Feedback is a key element of systems theory and is the one most often discussed in models based upon the theory. The major functions of feedback are (a) to control output by sending messages generated by the output back to the input regulator; (b) to maintain a relatively steady state of system operation even in the face of external variables which would cause it to fluctuate; and (c) because of this, to increase the probability that the system will survive in the face of external pressures. Feedback operates on signal inputs primarily from formal achievement outputs, as well as on maintenance inputs primarily through need satisfaction outputs.

In the case of a physical system, a typical example would be a process control system in an oil refinery. When some output from the process gets out of its prescribed tolerances (Formal Achievement), feedback is used to adjust the input stream (signal) either by changing the mixture of materials flowing through the process or by changing the physical characteristics of the reaction taking place so that the output returns to the prescribed tolerance levels.

In our training analogy, if a process of skill acquisition for an individual is not meeting quality and quantity standards which are expected (Achievement), appropriate feedback should serve to alter the signal inputs. At the cognitive level, this could mean resetting the individual's goals which have been established for skill acquisition, demonstrating the correct method which is to be employed, re-explaining the objectives, etc. In terms of practice, alteration in signal inputs in terms of sequencing, difficulty level, amount of time spent, etc., may be employed.

Berrien's analysis of the feedback mechanism in social systems seems useful in our training analogy. He contends that feedback of formal achievement outputs has an impact on signal inputs by traveling a loop through the supra-system. In our training model, feedback flows through the formal training system, personified by the instructional staff which has the responsibility for setting objectives, designing and carrying out the program, and evaluating progress. In short, the extent to which individual behavior is being altered is evaluated by the training system and impacts the design of the instructional process or training manipulation for each individual trainee, as well as the design of future programs.

The action of the feedback loop of formal achievement through the training system is essentially the process of individualizing instruction. It is the classic model of a "good" educational system; the teacher beams the instruction at the level of competence of the individual trainee and adjusts accordingly: "low achievers" or "slow learners" are decelerated; "high achievers" are accelerated; individual levels of achievement are periodically assessed or tested throughout the educational period, etc.

Similar concerns should exist in industrial training, though undoubtedly often do not. Probably a major determiner of the success of skill acquisition, especially in the

area of complex skills, is the extent to which there is interaction between the training system and the individual trainee and the extent to which training input adjusts itself to the degree of formal achievement. The participative instructor-based techniques, such as conference methods, case study, or role playing can do this to some extent. Probably part of the success of programmed instruction is the built-in feedback mechanism. Conversely, we would expect techniques with low feedback potential (lectures, films, etc.) to be relatively ineffective.

All of the measurement technologies for assessing individual differences are appropriate for evaluating individual skill acquisition for building this feedback loop. Most have been discussed in detail in other chapters. Most frequently, however, such evaluation occurs quite informally. It is usually a judgmental process which is part of the ongoing instructional procedure. However, the very persuasive research on experimenter effects (Rosenthal, 1963) and implications for skill acquisition of teacher expectations suggests a real need for more objective and nonreactive approaches to the assessment of formal achievement in skill acquisition and for the systematic feedback of such data through the training process to alter signal inputs. There is a tremendous amount we need to learn about this whole procedure.

Feedback from Need Satisfaction outputs, in contrast to formal achievement, operates primarily on maintenance inputs. They do not necessarily work through the supra-system but operate directly on the inputs which affect the individual and on his interaction with the broader social system variables, such as his intrinsic rewards, his self-confidence, and his organizational and peer group role. When there is positive feedback—needs that are satisfied through the skill acquisition process—maintenance inputs to the system will be continued and the system will be sustained. When there is negative feedback, the system tends to run down. Training must provide individual need satisfaction for the skill acquisition system to be maintained.

Berrien provides an understanding of the relationship between Formal Achievement and Need Satisfaction by positing differential roles for the sub- and supra-systems in determining the function of feedback. He suggests that the *subsystem* controls the lower limit of Group Need Satisfaction and the upper limit of Formal Achievement; on the other hand, the *supra-system* controls the upper limit of GNS and the lower limit of Formal Achievement.

For a training system (the supra-system, in terms of skill acquisition) this suggests that there has to be at least some minimum acceptable level of Formal Achievement—skill acquisition—for the subsystem to be maintained; without some tangible results, the training activity is not likely to be continued. At the same time, most training departments do not see themselves functioning purely to enhance the need satisfaction of trainees; an upper limit on individual need satisfaction will tend to be imposed in the interest of maintaining some minimal level of Formal Achievement.

The subsystem, however, tends not to exert all of its energies toward the attainment of Formal Achievement objectives; there is an upper limit to just how much an individual or group will direct its energies to Formal Achievement. On the other hand, there is also some lower limit to the amount of personal or group satisfaction which the individual must experience to continue to participate in the activity; an activity without some intrinsically satisfying aspect will not be maintained for long.

All of which says that there must be some mutuality of goal satisfaction inherent in the skill acquisition process. Where the balance tips too heavily either to the organization or to the individual, the activity will not be sustained. Balance is maintained through the system feedback loops, and survival is tied to the extent the feedback mechanism works to maintain a relatively steady state of system operation.

Fortunately, as we pointed out in the introduction to this chapter, of all of the areas of applied psychology the field of training is where this type of balance is able to be maintained most closely and where the goals of the organization and the individual can be most in agreement. For this reason, skill acquisition systems should be capable of considerable stability; perhaps this is why the training function has flourished even in the face of rather haphazard design, imprecisely understood objectives, and sporadic evaluation. In large measure, skill acquisition systems must be inherently stable and healthy systems. At least their history would suggest this, and the concept of balance between Formal Achievement and Need Satisfaction from open systems theory may help to explain why.

The Training System

We have already touched upon the extent to which the skill acquisition system is a subsystem of a larger system devoted to the training function. We may think of this training system as encompassing most of the activities usually included in a discussion of training in organizations; in an organizational sense, it consists of all of the things falling within the responsibility of the training department. A discussion of these components within the framework of open systems theory may put this traditional picture into a somewhat different perspective.

Usually discussions of training departments outline four major roles or objectives:

1. To determine training needs.

2. To identify or select those individuals who should participate in training.

3. To design and conduct training programs. (We have already seen that this activity includes the processing of feedback information from the skill acquisition system which is developed within specific training programs. This feedback works through the training system to then modify signal inputs to the skill acquisition system.)

4. The evaluation of training and the assessment of the effectiveness of specific techniques in programs.

We may think of the attainment of these objectives as the formal achievement of the training system and shall discuss them more fully later. But first, let us complete our picture of the training department in a system's framework. The main features of this system are presented in Figure 2.

SIGNAL INPUTS. Signal inputs to the training system come from the total organizational system, and specifically from executive management of the organization. Essentially, these inputs may be thought of as the charter which determines the training department's training activity in the organization. They consist of broad objectives which have been set for ensuring the availability of skilled manpower as well as company policy and directives with regard to the formal role of the training department.

MAINTENANCE INPUTS. These inputs are closely tied to the formal charter of the training department and are those attributes which ensure the formal existence of the department. They include such things as adequate funds and budget, staff allocation,

facilities, and the flow of trainees from the organization.

NEED SATISFACTION OUTPUTS. These may be thought of as recognition in the organization of the extent to which the training department fulfills its charter. When successful training programs have been designed and implemented and overall training objectives achieved, recognition of this will be satisfying to the training department. Feedback of need satisfaction from the training system affects maintenance inputs to training in several ways. For one, as trainees go through the program and find it satisfying—"a good course"—and useful to them, the satisfied feedback spreads through the organization and tends to build up demand for the program. Such feedback also tends to increase support for the program from management and ensure maintenance through adequate funding and staffing.

FORMAL ACHIEVEMENT OUTPUTS. One of the major activities of a training department is to engage in a systematic evaluation of training needs in order to set detailed training

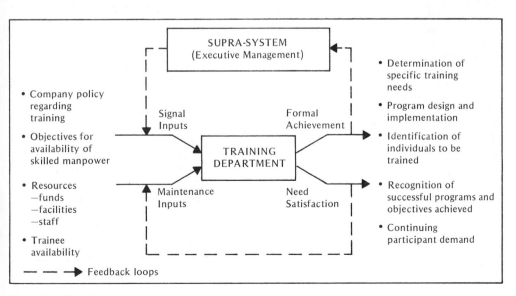

Figure 2. Training system.

objectives and also to develop programs and implement training techniques designed to attain these objectives. It may be useful to think of these activities as the formal achievement of the training system.

McGehee and Thayer (1961) point to two major activities in the setting of training objectives. These are "operations-analysis" and "man-analysis." Bass and Vaughan (1966) have in mind similar functions when they discuss "job analysis" and "manpower analysis" for the determination of training needs. Operations analysis consists of studies designed to determine what behaviors employees must exhibit if they are to perform effectively in their assigned job functions.

Operations analysis is the orderly and systematic collection of data about an existing or potential industrial task or a cluster of tasks usually called a "job." Its purpose is to determine just what an employee must be taught in order to perform the task or job so that he contributes maximally to the attainment of organizational goals. An operations analysis will result in the following data concerning a task or a task cluster: (1) standards of performance for the task or job; (2) if a task cluster or "job," the identification of the tasks which make up the job; (3) how each task is to be performed if standards of performance are to be met; (4) the skills, knowledge, and attitudes which are basic to the performance of each task in the required manner. (McGehee & Thayer, 1961, pp. 63–64)

There is nothing magical or unique about operations-analysis for the determination of training needs. The philosophy and techniques presented in the chapters on job and task analysis, as well as on criterion development, are fully appropriate to studies within the training system designed to specify the terminal behaviors desired from the training process. A specific terminal behavior—effective performance within a clearly understood task—is set up as the desired end product of the training situation and the basis against which training programs are developed and techniques are selected.

Man-analysis, in contrast to operations analysis, focuses on employees performing within specific roles. The intention is to identify whether or not employees are performing their assigned tasks effectively, and if not, whether training can increase their effectiveness and specifically what type of training is required. The general procedures of performance evaluation and personnel assessment discussed in other chapters of this section are appropriate and fully applicable. Where the evaluation procedure utilized in the skill acquisition system should be thought of as assessing the skills or proficiencies of an individual trainee in a kind of $N = 1$ design, man-analysis evaluates the proficiency of employees versus group norms coming out of the operations analysis to identify individuals who should be trained.

With a clear statement of training objectives, both in terms of task requirements and individuals identified to be trained, the formal achievement output of the training department then becomes one of the signal inputs to the skill acquisition system. This occurs through the selection of specific techniques and development of programs designed to achieve the stated objectives. Ideally, this is a rational process of selecting techniques which have been demonstrated to have maximum utility for imparting the desired terminal behaviors and putting these techniques together into a cohesive training program.

It is in this area of selecting training techniques and developing programs that training administration today is more art than science. It is here that very little is known, as research evaluation has not revealed which techniques or combinations of techniques are most effective for achieving specific objectives. There is room for a considerable amount of research to build a systematic catalog of training approaches or techniques in terms of their utility for achieving specific results. At least that is the position taken by some psychologists when they comment on the training scene (Campbell, 1971).

When we view the problems involved in developing such a systematic catalog, however, it is not too surprising that most frequently training design is based more on common sense and experience than on research. When we complicate the picture with additional considerations—which Campbell, Dunnette, Lawler, and Weick (1970) have termed modifiers (such as cost of training, time available both on the part of the trainee and instructor, the availability of facilities and equipment, questions of who trains and the competence of the staff, ability considerations of trainees, motivational considerations involved in adult training or training disadvantaged populations)—then the permutations which would be involved in a systematic program of research become unmanageable. Not that we do not need comprehensive research to help us to do a more intelligent job of training program design. But, at the current state of knowledge, we would suspect that there would be a significantly greater return by concentrating primarily on a sound evaluation of training needs. This should be through carefully conducted operations-analysis and man-analysis as a base for informed judgment and rationality in deciding upon techniques, either singly or in combination, designed to accomplish training objectives.

Gagné (1962) makes a strong case for this approach when he suggests "principles" which reflect the critical components of training design:

1. Any human task may be analyzed into a set of component tasks which are quite distinct from each other in terms of the experimental operations needed to produce them.
2. These task components are mediators of the final task performance; that is, their presence insures positive transfer to a final performance, and their absence reduces such transfer to near zero.
3. The basic principles of training design consist of: (a) identifying the component tasks of a final performance; (b) insuring that each of these component tasks is fully achieved; and (c) arranging the total learning situation in a sequence which will insure optimal mediational effects from one component to another.

The examples which Gagné gives are from military training research—for example, a motor task of flexible gunnery, a fixed procedure of operating a radar, or a trouble-shooting procedure in repairing complex equipment. Gagné makes a convincing point that simple practice is often not the best approach to learn such tasks. For example, detailed analysis of a motor skill task will often identify a cognitive component which is critical to performance; task practice without mastery of the cognitive component may be at best inefficient and at worst useless. He makes the point that careful adherence to the classical learning "principles" will be of considerably less utility in training than careful task analysis and attention to sequencing in training design.

In a practical sense, it is much easier to see how this applies with regard to the tangible tasks from military operations which Gagné describes than how the task analysis approach should apply in a more diffused area as in management training. However, at the very least, training departments would be well advised to make an effort to be more precise than the typical programs of many management development departments.

For example, having pinned down the fact that an organization will expend money and time to develop the leadership of its management population, a typical reaction of the training department is to jump in with a "program." Characteristic responses are:

1. "Let's brush off that same program we gave last year."
2. "The ABC company is doing XYZ; we should, too."

3. "Obviously our employees need to know some of X, some of Y, and a little of Z. We shall put together a training smorgasbord which covers the waterfront."

Only rarely is time spent in determining in detail just what the training should accomplish. Usually there is a very imprecise idea of the specific tasks toward which managers should be trained. Even less is there any understanding of the basic components which make up that task. Finally, there is seldom a determination of how to achieve proficiency in each component task, or how to link tasks together to form proficiency in the total task. In effect, there is seldom a real rational analysis of how the training program should be constructed, much less any carefully controlled research. As a result, very often such programs in the management development area tend to be:

1. beamed toward some preconceived objective or value system often associated with some particular school of thought in the behavioral sciences, such as "Theory Y," "Grid Training," "Need Achievement training," or "Transactional Analysis" (Campbell, 1971). Such training usually says little about the specific behaviors expected of the manager.

2. focused on a single technique as a panacea: T-groups, O.D., role playing, Kepner Tregoe. The emphasis is on applying techniques with which the trainer is familiar, with the result that very often the procedure ends up being seen by the trainee as of questionable relevance to his job performance.

3. short term, with no follow-through to the job situation and reinforcement or updating. Training is not viewed as an ongoing aspect of the manager's development but more as a course or program which, once completed, indicates that development has been accomplished.

The problems in taking an analytical approach to the design of management development training, however, have been well outlined by Campbell, Dunnette, Lawler, and Weick (1970). If in fact, as they conclude after their extensive review of the literature, we have only an imprecise picture of what managers actually do on their jobs, especially in such nebulous areas as human relations, how can we specify the task components which should be addressed by training? If we don't even know what the total task is with any degree of precision, we certainly cannot identify component tasks.

This then says that there is a need for much more comprehensive and behavior-oriented research in the components of task *performance* as a base for the design of training programs. Just because it has not been done does not mean that it is impossible. Without research, there is little prospect of significant advances in developing a psychology of training or improving on the relatively meagre return which evaluation research suggests for many management development programs.

Another of the crucial considerations in the design of training which Gagné discusses is the optimal sequencing of training applications to arrive at a final objective. The problem results from the fact that most often a training needs analysis determines that multiple training techniques or approaches should be employed. How should these several approaches be tied together into a total program?

A logical approach might say, for example, that for a complex skill acquisition need, such as in the development of managerial skills or in learning to conduct an interview, an optimum sequence of training would involve (a) first, some education at the cognitive level in basic concepts; (b) next, skill practice; and (c) finally, some training in attitudinal and interpersonal awareness. So, a manager training program with broad objectives might move from content-oriented techniques (lectures, or presentations on finance, management practices, etc.) to skill training (business games, in-baskets, etc.) to interpersonal training (group dynamics exercises, T-groups, etc.). We shall describe a number of these specific techniques later in this chapter.

Another approach for determining optimal sequencing can use an empirical orientation. Bass and Vaughan (1966, p.

134) describe how the optimum sequence for aviator training was determined by looking at the patterns of correlations among performance on various key sub-components of training, such as instruments, gunnery, navigation, etc. As an example of this approach, assume a task made up of five sub-component tasks. Consider that performances on these tasks are intercorrelated like this:

	a	b	c	d	e
Task a	—	.35	.32	.40	.43
Task b		—	.70	.17	.52
Task c			—	.10	.45
Task d				—	.38
Task e					—

Such patterning of correlations suggests that some sub-component tasks are more highly related to certain tasks than others. For example, sub-tasks *b* and *c* are highly correlated, and we might expect that skills learned on one task might transfer to a high degree of performance on the other. Therefore, they should probably be placed close together in the training sequence.

By rearranging the order of the different tasks, it may be possible to produce a correlation matrix in which the magnitude of the coefficients increases as one goes down the columns and decreases when one goes across the rows. In effect, the matrix is one in which each element is maximally related to its adjacent elements. For our example, we would expect maximum transfer to occur when training is sequenced in this order:

	c	b	e	a	d
Task c	—	.70	.45	.32	.10
Task b		—	.52	.35	.17
Task e			—	.43	.38
Task a				—	.40
Task d					—

FEEDBACK. The classical feedback loop in a training system is the process of training evaluation—either through formal or informal research. Evaluation research is most likely to concentrate on formal achievement outcomes from training, and as such, the feedback will serve as a corrector of signal inputs. Such feedback occurs through the organizational system to sustain or modify training policy and objectives or the allocation of resources and effort to training. Based upon the results of research evaluations, the training department may then redefine the objectives of training, tune up or change the techniques which have been put together into the program, or change or redefine the criteria for attendance in the program as originally developed through the man-analysis procedures.

In general, there has not been a great deal of attention to rigorous research-based training evaluation on the part of industrial training departments. Perhaps because of this, training evaluation has become almost a favorite whipping boy of some texts. For example, Warren (1969, p. 8) goes so far as to state that: "If any general rule for a training function were to be stated, it would be: 'If you can't measure it, don't train for it'." Although such a statement is sheer nonsense, it does illustrate the extent to which lack of evaluation in training is seen as a problem area.

We shall not attempt to present a detailed review of training evaluation procedures. The texts devoted to experimental design, measurement, and quantitative techniques provide the background necessary for understanding some of the technical problems involved in training evaluation research. For two specific texts dealing with most aspects of conducting evaluative research in training, see American Institutes for Research (1970) and Hesseling (1966).

We take the strong position that attempts at training evaluation which are not experimental, do not have pre-post measures, and do not have adequate control groups, are not really evaluations. Surveys of participants' reactions (happiness sheets), post-training measures only, and studies which do not utilize control groups are not very useful in providing the information we need for assessing training effectiveness. On the other hand, we do need broad designs which assess the utility of various approaches for achieving specific objectives under various moderating circumstances of ability levels, time available, costs, etc.

However, there have been a number of forceful arguments (e.g., Argyris, 1968) that it is not possible to evaluate training, particularly in such areas as attitude change, motivation, or sensitivity. The contention is that measurement in and of itself is an intervention. Although there are some compelling aspects to these arguments, we would contend that evaluation should at least be attempted, although only attempted under appropriate experimental designs. But, as we pointed out above, we also feel that there may in fact be more benefit from a careful predetermination of training needs and task analysis prior to the design of training programs than there will be from elaborate broad designs attempting to evaluate results.

The Organizational System

The third system which must be considered in any discussion of training within organizations is that which is embedded in the executive management of the total organization. The key aspects of this system as it is pertinent to training are outlined in Figure 3. The total organizational system, of course, is concerned with more than training, but for the training system to survive, it has to interact with this supra-system to obtain maintenance inputs of funding and resources as well as direction and support.

INPUTS TO THE ORGANIZATIONAL SYSTEM. The maintenance inputs which sustain the total organizational system are, of course, the overall profitability or vitality of the enterprise as well as the availability of resources for continued success. Very importantly, such resources include manpower, but they also include other factors like markets, raw materials, money, and technology.

The signal inputs to the organizational system that are crucial to its interaction with the training system are such things as:

1. Basic business plans and objectives.
2. Information on quality and quantity of manpower available currently and for tasks for the future.

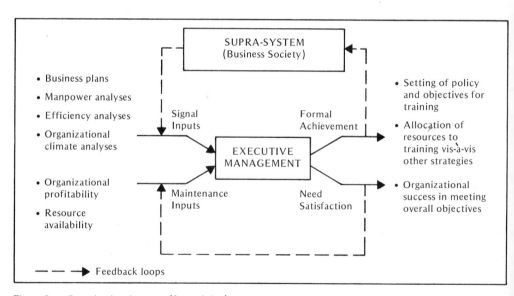

Figure 3.   Organizational system (for training).

3. Efficiency data, including such things as cost information with regard to labor, equipment, overhead; utilization information with regard to equipment, manpower; and planned performance data, quality data, etc.

4. Information on organizational climate, including objective indicators of attitudinal or motivational health of the enterprise (strikes, turnover, absence data, etc.) as well as specially conducted measurements of organizational climate through survey procedures.

A concept such as human resources accounting (Likert, 1967) comes very close to being the type of systematic input to the organizational system which is necessary for it to function effectively in determining the allocation of effort and resources to the training system. Analysis of the human resource in financial terms permits the organizational system to undertake the cost/benefit analysis which is necessary for a rational decision to support training versus the allocation of resources toward other strategies for attaining organizational objectives.

OUTPUTS FROM THE ORGANIZATIONAL SYSTEM. The need satisfaction output is obviously tied to organizational success in meeting overall objectives. When the organization is successful, the needs of the organization members are satisfied and such satisfaction feeds back to maintain the system.

The *formal achievement* of the organizational system, at least with regard to training, can be thought of as a policy decision to maintain a training department and support training, specific objectives set for this activity, and the allocation of resources (money, facility, staff) to training vis-à-vis other potential organizational activities.

The process by which this is done has been termed "organization analysis" by McGehee and Thayer. They define this as "determining where within the organization training emphasis can and should be placed" (McGehee & Thayer, 1961, p. 25). Thus organization-analysis looks at all of the

kinds of factors which we have listed as signal inputs (plans, manpower, efficiency data, organizational climate), evaluates the costs involved and the benefits to be derived from training as opposed to other strategies for obtaining organizational objectives, and then determines the overall policy with regard to training.

One of the problems with this type of analysis in industrial organizations is that the utility and value of training too often are taken for granted. Perhaps because of the positive values surrounding education in our society, proposals for training rarely have a negative reception by business executives who in other matters will take a hard and analytical approach. Also, it is surprising how frequently training will be accepted almost as an end in itself, without a careful analysis of how it contributes to the broader business objectives.

There is a real need, at the level of the organizational system, to recognize that training is not a panacea. There needs to be a careful weighing of alternative strategies, including, for example, altered recruiting strategies, changed personnel policies regarding such things as pay or job security, automation, or the introduction of new equipment, alterations in general business objectives, or changes in the design of jobs. In the job design area, for example, Fiedler (1965) suggests that there should be more emphasis on placing managers in job situations which resonate more appropriately with their basic managerial style and personality rather than trying to train managers in different management styles. Perhaps a more efficient alternate strategy to management development might be a better selection and *placement* process for managers. At the very least, we are suggesting that there is a need for more rational analysis of alternate strategies in the decision to fund training and to support it with formal organizational policy.

The *feedback* loop from the training subsystem operates through the organizational system as an assessment of the degree to which training does or does not contribute to the objectives of providing skilled manpower. The evaluation is one of whether or not training has had an impact on operating data of skilled manpower availability, efficiency indexes, or organizational climate. If it does, support continues; if it does not, support is reduced or strategies changed.

Thus our overall model of the training process in organizations suggests a dynamic interaction between the organizational system and the training system, which in turn is built on top of a dynamic interaction between the training system and the skill acquisition system. All three of these systems must be considered in developing an overview of the training process. In the following section, we shall shift our vantage point back to the specific training system and evaluate some of the major training techniques in use today.

TRAINING TECHNIQUES

Having determined the nature of tasks (terminal behaviors) desired as a result of training and of the component tasks which make up these terminal behaviors, the next concern of a training department is to determine which techniques to use in the training program in order to optimize learning (achieve the greatest amount of learning with minimum expenditure of time and money). We have already touched on the major problems in making such a determination, and it would now be appropriate to review some of the main techniques available to training departments in making this decision.

There are few books on training which fail to describe in some detail the major techniques currently being used. Therefore, we do not intend to give these techniques more than outline coverage in the discussion which follows.

The prevalent training techniques tend to group themselves into three categories, based upon their most common usage. We have given them labels of:

1. *Content* techniques of training, which are designed to impart substantive knowledge or information on a cognitive level.

2. *Process* techniques, mainly intended to change attitudes, develop awareness of self and others, and impact the trainee's interpersonal skills.

3. *Mixed* training techniques, which may have both an information transmitting function as well as an attitude change function.

The literature on training reports little comparative research on the various techniques which is useful in deciding which techniques to use to achieve which specific objectives. Most of the evaluation is based on logical analysis or common sense. It is in this area, in addition to the area of task analysis, in which there is the greatest need for systematic research in an effort to build a true psychology of industrial training.

McGehee and Thayer (1961) outline a number of criteria which have to be weighed in deciding upon techniques for achieving various objectives. These include:

1. The kinds of behavior to be acquired (motor skills, concepts, verbal skills, attitudes, etc.).
2. The number of employees to be trained.
3. The ability level of trainees.
4. Individual differences among trainees.
5. Cost in relation to various factors.
6. The incorporation of alleged learning principles such as motivation, opportunity for practice, reinforcement, knowledge of results, meaningfulness, and overlearning. (McGehee & Thayer, 1961, pp. 195–196)

We would certainly add to this list previous experience based upon systematic evaluation of the results achieved by different techniques within the milieu of the specific organization.

Content Oriented Techniques

We have included under the general framework of content techniques designed to impart knowledge the techniques of lecture, audiovisual aids, programmed instruction (PI), and computer-assisted instruction (CAI).

LECTURE TECHNIQUE. The lecture technique is familiar to everyone, at least everyone who has attended some kind of formal schooling. Almost universally it has been criticized in discussions of training techniques. For example, Korman (1971) outlines the major problems with the lecture method as:

1. It perpetuates the authority structure of traditional organizations with implications of negative behavior. Korman suggests that the degree to which learning is not self-controlled is a negative contributor to performance (Pressey, 1965).

2. Except in the area of cognitive knowledge and conceptual principles, there is probably limited potential transfer from the lecture to the actual skills required to do the job.

3. The high verbal and symbolic requirements of the lecture method may be threatening or incapable of being handled by people with low verbal or symbolic experience or aptitude. Individuals from relatively deprived educational, social, and economic backgrounds may have more difficulty than those from higher levels in learning through the lecture procedure. Where there are language barriers, as in an international group of trainees, the lecture method may be relatively ineffective.

4. The lecture method does not permit individualized training based upon individual differences in ability, interests, and personality. Similarly, the lecture method is not flexible to provide feedback and reinforcement systematically to trainees.

Despite all these problems, however, the lecture method is still widely used in industry, in large measure probably because of widespread familiarity with it from its use in the general educational system. Patten (1971) points out that it is frequently used effectively when skilled lecturers are employed and where it is appropriate. It also can be economical. He emphasizes the necessity for a question and answer period following the lecture. The lecture should rarely be relied upon as the sole method of instruction; it can have some utility as a preliminary training method to provide cognitive awareness prior to skills training, particularly where the instructor possesses significant knowledge about the topic not otherwise accessible to the trainees.

AUDIOVISUAL TECHNIQUES. The use of various audiovisual devices is usually included in the list of training techniques. Actually, these should probably not be thought of as stand-alone techniques, as in practice they are usually used as supplements or aids in conjunction with other approaches to the training process. Audiovisual devices include the old standbys of films, slides, filmstrips, records, flannel boards, etc. Use of such training equipment received a big spurt during World War II when there was a need to train large numbers of military and civilian personnel, a shortage of qualified instructors, and a need for a certain amount of uniformity in the training. Now such equipment is part and parcel of any training effort.

Some of these training aids, films, or records, have many of the disadvantages of the lecture. They treat trainees as a passive audience. At the same time, however, they "capture" experts in a topical area to ensure the quality and correctness of the material presented. In the area of films particularly, extensive research has isolated many technical considerations which are important for effectiveness. Professional guidance and assistance should certainly be sought in the preparation of films (McGehee & Thayer, 1961, p. 194).

Recent new technologies such as tape cassettes and television can be thought of as an extension of traditional technologies, though they present some very important new possibilities when used in a feedback mode. Although tapes and TV are used to present content, the ability to individualize immediate feedback can be a powerful tool in process-oriented training, for example in demonstrating the implications of particular trainee behaviors.

The big benefits of audiovisual aids are the ability to cover large numbers of trainees, relatively low costs per trainee, uniformity of training content, and the variety which can be built into the training context through their use. They are being employed as supplements to training efforts ranging all the way from traditional lectures to highly unstructured encounter groups.

AUTO-INSTRUCTIONAL TECHNOLOGIES. Among the newest content-oriented training techniques which have received a great deal of attention are two which are beamed specifically at self-instruction: programmed instruction (PI) and computer-assisted instruction (CAI). In focusing on these new approaches, however, we should not lose sight of the fact that auto-instructional techniques are probably the oldest form of instructional procedures; probably more learning takes place simply by reading an appropriate book than by any other technology.

However, the new technologies of programmed instruction and CAI provide an exciting extension to this procedure. Programmed instruction burst on the training scene in the late 1950s and was immediately followed by exuberant predictions of fantastic results and a rash of applications and "teaching machine" hardware. Two major approaches to PI have been employed:

1. Linear programs which progress in a regular stepwise fashion through the instructional material ensuring positive reinforcement and gradual building of competence and achievement.

2. Branching techniques which selectively lead the trainee into subroutines when he demonstrates problems in mastering the materials. The key features in PI have been

fully described in several texts and will not be repeated in detail here (see, for example, Foundation for Research on Human Behavior, 1961).

Advocates of the approach point out that programmed instruction, when carefully done, has a number of very strong arguments in its favor:

1. It involves the trainee by requiring active response.

2. It is individualized and self-paced rather than under the authoritarian control of a trainer.

3. Knowledge of results can provide immediate reinforcement for correct responses in a non-threatening (private) manner.

4. Challenge and interest can be built into the learning sequence by branching techniques and humorous or unexpected responses within the programmed format.

5. Updating and revision of the program can be done at will, based upon data and experience acquired through use.

6. Perhaps most important, writing the program requires careful organization and pre-study of the content of what is to be included, optimum sequencing of the content, and testing—a process which should precede all training program designs but which seldom does.

In view of all of these positive factors, it is not surprising that PI has found significant utility in many instances, both in the academic community and in industry. The major positive effects seem to be in savings in training time although some industrial studies have demonstrated enhanced performance as a result of training under PI versus traditional lecture procedures (Goldberg, Dawson, & Barrett, 1964; Hedberg, Steffen, & Baxter, 1965; Hughes & McNamara, 1961).

However, PI is not a panacea. It is costly, appropriate to a somewhat limited range of training objectives where content is clear and objectives readily identifiable, and because of its low social involvement probably of limited use where one of the training objectives is the facilitation of social interaction. A recent extensive review of research evaluating PI versus other training methodologies (Nash, Muczyk, & Vettori, 1971) suggests that in view of the high costs of preparing program texts a more rigorous criterion of "practical superiority" rather than statistical should be applied in evaluating PI. Under this criterion there is little indicated superiority in learning and retention for PI; and the time savings may be an artifact of self-pacing versus a controlled learning environment, rather than a result of the PI methodology. This review suggests considerable caution in the decision to develop PI materials. However, PI has found considerable use among the array of training techniques.

Computer-assisted instruction (CAI) is a logical extension of the PI methodology. CAI puts the learning program in storage in a computer system and fosters training through interaction between the trainee and the system. Seltzer (1971) describes uses of CAI for drill and practice, tutorial instruction, and dialogue. He debates the utility of CAI in specific areas on considerations of whether or not the computer can do better than more traditional methods, and whether or not there are less expensive ways to achieve the same goals.

On balance, Seltzer concludes:

1. The high costs of CAI will probably limit its utility.

2. It is not clear that it presents any significant improvement over the more traditional modes of drill and practice.

3. The technology for using the computer in a true dialogue mode of instruction is not sufficiently advanced.

4. There are probably some instances in which the potential power of the technique in the tutorial mode would justify its use.

Two other approaches to the use of the computer in an interactive setting show it to be clearly superior to other procedures. These are for information storage and retrieval of large scale data banks and libraries and for simulations and gaming in various models of real world situations.

Research studies done in industry comparing CAI with PI suggest that there may be savings in time with CAI, but it is unclear whether there are significant differences in performance or achievement (Schwartz & Haskell, 1966; Schwartz & Long, 1967). There is need for additional research in this area.

A study of auto-instructional techniques in vigilance training not involving either PI or CAI (Attwood & Wiener, 1969) suggests several possible reasons for the effectiveness of the approach. Primarily, Attwood and Wiener suggest that self-control over the training sequence makes the task more interesting and involving. Also, in the interaction with hardware they suggest there is a "pin-ball machine effect" increasing the trainee's motivation to perform, with the sole reward being knowledge of results and self-satisfaction in performance. Particularly for learning a dull task like vigilance, anything which can inject "fun" into the situation should have a positive effect.

Mixed Techniques

There are a number of commonly used training techniques which may be used to impart both substantive knowledge or content as well as to achieve some of the objectives set for the more process-oriented techniques: attitude change, awareness, interpersonal effectiveness. These include techniques such as conference methods, case studies, simulators and games, and various on-the-job techniques.

CONFERENCE DISCUSSION TECHNIQUES. According to a recent survey of training practices, the conference or discussion technique ranks high in terms of frequency of use (Utgaard & Dawis, 1970). The conference or discussion technique contains a number of elements which should make it superior to the pure lecture or auto-instructional techniques:

1. It can engender considerable involvement of the trainees with an increase in mo-

tivation to understand the concepts under discussion and the desire to participate.

2. It provides an opportunity for clarification of any misunderstandings.

3. Feedback is possible either from the conference leader or from the other participants which can serve as a powerful reward or punishment.

Conference techniques may be used both for enhancing the understanding of conceptual and cognitive information and for the development of attitudes among the trainees. Because of this potential multiple use, we have included it among the "mixed" techniques.

Most of the people who advocate the conference technique do so primarily based upon an intuitive feeling of its superiority over the lecture technique, its degree of widespread use, and its relative ease of implementation, rather than on rigorously controlled research studies evaluating its effectiveness. Bass and Vaughan (1966, p. 98) cite one study which demonstrated greater behavioral change—less error in a performance rating task among a management population—as a result of training by the conference method in comparison with a control group and a group trained by the lecture method.

Several problems are prevalent in the use of the conference or discussion technique. First of all, it is limited to use by relatively small groups. Secondly, in practice, conference sessions are often poorly organized, and as Planty, McCord, and Efferson (1948, p. 182) point out, the conference can become "a conversational boat ride on uncharted seas to an unknown port." Finally, effective conference leadership requires considerable skill and finesse, particularly when the conference is used in a "process" mode. Skill is required to ensure that all trainees have an opportunity to participate, that diverging points of view are fully aired, that feedback from the group is not unduly punitive for diverging points of view, and that the discussion does in fact proceed toward some predetermined objective rather than wandering aimlessly.

CASE STUDY/INCIDENT PROCESS. The case study method is one which has a long history of use in certain academic settings, but has also found extensive use in industrial training. As Patten (1971, p. 144) points out "using cases on an intermittent basis is perhaps the easiest way to make the transition from traditional cognitive styles of learning in orthodox training classrooms to more dynamic learner-involved participatory and existential styles of learning." The case is essentially a description of some area of activity with which it is hoped the trainees will become familiar. Through study and analysis of the case and discussion, it is hoped that the trainees' behavior will be impacted in several ways. First of all, case study requires understanding, logical thinking, and analysis on the part of trainees. It often forces the trainee to extrapolate from incomplete information and to develop the implications of a situation presented in the case. Frequently, judgment and decision making are entailed, as there is usually not one single best solution to the case. Finally, through discussion of implications and consequences, the trainees receive feedback about the appropriateness of their analysis and decision making. Thus, case study analysis can be a dynamic and involving learning experience, useful both for imparting substantive knowledge about an area of concern as well as for teaching approaches to decision making and problem solving.

The incident process is similar to the case study, except that only a limited scenario is presented initially, and the trainees must develop the pertinent information about the case through a series of questions and answers with the trainer. The trainer provides only information specifically requested by the trainees.

There are several pitfalls inherent in the case process. First of all, it is difficult to know just how much information to include in the case; if too much detail is provided it becomes unwieldy; if it is too limited, the situation seems overly artificial and the necessary information for a fully balanced judgment is not available. Also, the role of the discussion leader is extremely important. Without active leadership there is a tendency for case analysis to become solution-oriented rather than understanding-oriented, for participants to concentrate on finding fault with the positions of others and for the analysis to be relatively superficial. Very little conclusive research on the utility of the case method is reported in the literature.

SIMULATIONS. One of the long-standing "principles" of training, which has both research justification and considerable common sense appeal, is the concept that practice on a task requiring behaviors as near as possible to those that will be used in the final task will enhance transfer of skills from the training to the job situation and will be an efficient means for carrying out the training. This is the rationale behind the use of simulators.

Simulators are in wide use in many kinds of training requiring the acquisition of motor skills. They have also been widely used in instances which have to couple motor and cognitive skills into total performance. For example, a significant part of the training for aviators, submarine officers, or other military personnel involves simulators. A major component of training for astronauts involves complex and ingenious simulators of the space environment in which they will operate. Simulators of various kinds are also used in a variety of industrial training situations. Most of the research on such "hardware" simulators has been carried out for the military (Valverde & Youngs, 1969).

The simulation approach is particularly useful where there are complex interdependencies among groups of people and hardware and considerable teamwork required for effective operation. Boguslaw and Porter (1965) describe the major considerations in the design of team training for effective performance in complex systems. Their frame of reference is primarily from the military.

In recent years, simulators have found increasing use in non-motor skill areas. Specifically, business games may be thought of as simulations of the operation of an enterprise. Here trainees manipulate a model of an organization or some component part of an organization to try to maximize certain outcomes. Various degrees of competition between teams of trainees may be built into these exercises. Business games, if they entail any degree of complexity, almost always utilize a computer to carry out the simulation.

Such games have a number of appealing aspects which suggest they may be very useful for training. Depending upon the degree to which they mirror real life organizations, they should provide for considerable transfer from the training to the job situation. They are dynamic and permit one to see the consequences of his decisions. At the same time they are non-punitive, in that mistakes or bad decisions will not result in actual loss, as a mistake made by an astronaut in a simulator will not result in his actually crashing on the moon. Games are intrinsically motivating and often build up a high level of involvement. They may also deal with a variety of factors important to the total management situation and thus impart understanding of finance, personnel, manufacturing, distribution, etc.

Some of the problems with business games are that:

1. They often do not encourage or allow normal approaches, but limit behavior to those programmed in the situation.

2. Trainees may become too involved in the game per se and neglect to critique the effectiveness of their behavior.

3. There is a tendency to "lock in" to whatever strategy proves effective in order

to "win the game," rather than experimenting.

4. There may be some question of the degree of realism of the gaming situation as well as of the degree to which the game situation is related to the trainees' at-home situation.

5. Participation in the game may be costly, particularly where extensive computer time is entailed.

The in-basket is a specialized form of simulator which can be thought of as a cross between a case study and a game. The trainee works through a pile of typical correspondence and responds to the problems which are raised in a fashion supposedly modeling the kind of behavior needed in a real life situation.

Perhaps because of the "face validity" of many simulators and the extent to which they are employed for specific training objectives, there is a surprising absence of conclusively controlled research to test their effectiveness or to identify general principles for their design. The exception is some of the hardware oriented research conducted for the military.

ON-THE-JOB TRAINING TECHNIQUES. There are a host of techniques which are essentially designed to enhance learning while the trainee is actually performing in the job setting. It should not be too surprising that these techniques are among those cited as being most frequently used in a recent survey of training practices (Utgaard & Dawis, 1970). Examples of on-the-job approaches are:

1. *Job instruction training* essentially is the process of having a trainer explain the job to the trainee, observe his performance, and provide feedback about his performance. It is a straightforward process of breaking a new employee in on a new job, and is the most frequently used technique.

2. *Orientation training* is merely a systematic effort to ensure that a new employee has all of the basic information he needs to function effectively.

3. *Apprentice training* is like a period of internship in which the trainee works under the guidance of an experienced supervisor for a specified period of time before achieving journeyman status.

4. *Performance appraisals* in many organizations fulfill a training and development function by providing feedback about the appropriateness of on-the-job behavior and performance.

5. *Coaching* is the process of ensuring that training and learning occur in the day-to-day man-manager relationship.

6. *Job rotation* is widely used in management development as a technique to systematically ensure that trainees are exposed to a variety of organizational functions.

7. *Assistantships* or various committee assignments similarly are used to provide personnel development.

All of these on-the-job techniques are based upon the philosophy that people learn a job best by doing it. However, this conclusion may or may not be justified, and there are a number of obvious problems with many of the on-the-job programs:

1. They may be inefficient, resulting in low productivity and waste.

2. There may be low involvement of the trainee in the training process, particularly in a program like job rotation in which he is not an incumbent in the job for a long enough period to really learn very much and is not motivated to dig in because he knows he will move on in the near future.

3. The quality of instruction diffused through an on-the-job situation may be less competent than instruction concentrated in the training department.

4. Too often in the on-the-job situation training takes second place to getting the job out.

However, in spite of these drawbacks on-the-job techniques are probably the most widely used approaches to training in industry today. Probably because they seem so "common-sensical" and easy to use, there has been little research on the effectiveness of these procedures. One study (Goodacre,

1963), which attempted to sort out the effects of a revision in the performance appraisal system, on-the-job coaching, and special instruction in enhancing man-management practices, was confounded with essentially very ambiguous results.

Process Oriented Techniques

We have included under the category of process oriented techniques a number of approaches which are distinguished by heavy reliance upon the interaction among trainees. The major emphasis without exception is on behavioral or attitudinal change, rather than on imparting cognitive knowledge. Such processes are used for developing interpersonal insights—awareness of self and of others—for changing attitudes and for practice in human relations skills, such as leadership or the interview.

ROLE PLAYING. Role playing techniques have their origin in psychotherapy, but have found wide use in industrial settings for imparting sales, leadership, and interviewing skills, as well as other skills. The essence of role playing is to create a realistic situation, as in the case study approach, and then have the trainees assume the parts of specific personalities in the situation. The success of the technique depends heavily upon the extent to which the individual throws himself into the role, rather than merely acting. Then, the participants in the role playing interact to solve the problem presented in the case. In the process, they receive considerable feedback about the impact of their behaviors from other members of the role playing session. Advocates of role playing say that it is highly involving, that the cases can be meaningful if carefully developed, and that it provides practice in personal interaction and problem solving which can closely simulate real life conditions.

On the negative side (1) there is danger that trainees will feel that the role playing exercise is childish, (2) they may revert to overacting and neglect focusing on the problem solving, (3) the trainer has no control over the immediate reinforcement or rewards which are in the hands of other trainees in the interaction process, and (4) the technique is somewhat limited in the number of people that can be involved, is time consuming, and relatively expensive.

Research on the effectiveness of role playing shows that it can be useful in increasing the supervisor's sensitivity to an employee's feelings when used in conjunction with case study and adequate discussion (Lawshe, Bolda, & Brune, 1959). It has also been determined that the strength of prior attitudes about role playing is an important determiner of the degree of attitude change. There is a greater degree of attitude change when people play roles at variance with their own points of view, and greater acceptance of the technique when they are placed in roles which are congruent with their original view (Elbing, 1967).

SENSITIVITY TRAINING. The training area which has probably received more attention than any other in recent years is sensitivity or T-group training. The approach has increased in attention and its use has evolved and developed since the mid-1940s. Along with the increasing use of the technique, there has been a growing volume of research attempting to evaluate the effectiveness of T-group training.

A detailed description of all of the purposes which have been attempted to be served by T-group training is beyond the scope of this chapter. A list of the most common T-group objectives has been synthesized from much of the literature by Campbell, Dunnette, Lawler, and Weick (1970, p. 239) and includes the following:

1. To give the trainee an understanding of how and why he acts toward other people as he does and of the way in which he affects them.
2. To provide some insights into why other people act the way they do.
3. To teach the participants how to "listen,"

that is, actually hear what other people are saying rather than concentrating on a reply.

4. To provide insights concerning how groups operate and what sorts of processes groups go through under certain conditions.
5. To foster an increased tolerance and understanding of the behavior of others.
6. To provide a setting in which an individual can try out new ways of interacting with people and receive feedback as to how these new ways affect them.

The classical model of the T-group is one of a meeting without an agenda in which participants discuss questions dealing with the "here and now" of the group process. The discussion explores why participants behave the way they do, how they perceive one another, and the feelings and emotions which are generated in the interaction process. The discussion is steered away from cognitive or intellectual aspects of problems and from prior or future events and concentrates instead on the behavioral processes operating at the moment.

Over the years, a variety of modifications and extensions of this basic model have developed to the point where at the present time there is certainly no single monolithic model for the T-group. These include such things as grid training, instrumented laboratories, mini-labs, marathon labs, etc.

The T-group experience is designed to be highly involving for the trainee. He becomes personally involved in what is going on as it deals with many aspects of his basic personality. He is highly motivated to participate. The only problem is that it is not always clear what the motivation is for that participation—whether it is to improve his interpersonal skills for the job situation or to defend his self-concept. Another problem with T-groups is that only small numbers of trainees can be included and the process is relatively expensive. Also, reinforcement of behavior comes from the group and is not controlled in any systematic fashion by the trainer. Finally, but not least, there may be a considerable amount of psychological stress associated with the T-group experience, and

instances of breakdown and severe trauma have been recorded.

House (1967) lists a number of issues which must be considered in the choice to use T-group training.

1. Are the changes that T-group training induces the kind required for more effective leadership behavior?
2. Can the organization tolerate the changes in the individual if the T-group is successful?
3. Can the candidate tolerate the anxiety involved in the T-group process?
4. What are the credentials of the T-group leaders?

House lists a number of ethical considerations including questions of organizational concern for personal well-being, privacy, forced attendance, and extent of organizational responsibility if an employee experiences emotional collapse as a result of participation in a T-group.

There have been several extensive reviews of research evaluating sensitivity training (Campbell & Dunnette, 1968; House, 1967). The reviews outline that there are considerable problems in undertaking effective research in such nebulous areas as sensitivity training and that most of the studies vary widely in quality and degree of control employed. Campbell and Dunnette (1968) conclude that in terms of external criteria of behavioral change on the job, T-group training probably does have an impact. Several studies do seem to demonstrate that participants exhibit changed behavior when back on the job. Such behavioral changes, however, have not been tied to changes in organizational effectiveness by the research studies reviewed. Also, most changes in behavior are individual and unique, making it difficult to assess any common trends of effectiveness out of the T-group experience. As a generalization, the research suggests that people who are motivated to change become most involved in the program and in fact do change; on the other hand, it is clear that many people do not become involved and do not change their behaviors.

On the internal level, the extent to which self-perceptions and personality are changed as a result of T-group exposure is not clear.

MODELING. Recently there has been put together a management skills training procedure which links several approaches into a coordinated learning system (Goldstein & Sorcher, 1974). The key component is modeling of the behaviors to be learned using film or video. The focus is on supervisory behaviors in interpersonal situations, and the sequence of learning activities includes:

1. a clear statement of the behaviors to be applied

2. a filmed model or demonstration situation of the skills being applied

3. practice through role playing for each trainee

4. social reinforcement of correct behaviors, in the practice situation, and

5. planning by each trainee in how to transfer the skills back to his or her specific job situation.

The technique appears to have great promise, based upon initial evaluation of results.

Research Needs

Throughout this chapter the reader has probably sensed a certain amount of frustration over the wasteland of training research. For an activity that consumes as much time, effort, and money in contemporary organizations as training does, it is truly amazing that there is not a really solid research base to ensure that training may be designed and carried out in the most efficient possible manner. We can only echo the rather strong statement by Campbell, Dunnette, Lawler, and Weick (1970) regarding management training, and point out that it applies equally to all training: "First, we must state quite bluntly that there is simply a great need for more research and for a wider variety of research. This may sound trite, but we are frankly surprised by the extremely limited nature of managerial

training studies done thus far.... Taken together, questions related to what techniques are best for what kinds of content and how such combinations are related to managerial behavior show that the need for more and broader research has reached alarming proportions" (pp. 480–481).

There is a clear need for research on the key parameters of training in organizations at all three levels of analysis which we used in developing our system's model: the individual, the training department, and the total organization. The first priority should probably reside at the level of the training department. Here there is a need for comprehensive attention to more effective procedures for determining just what training should be undertaken. The orientation should be one of understanding the behavioral bases of effective performance in industrial tasks. The basic questions are those raised by programs of man-analysis and operations-analysis: "What are the skills required for effective performance and to what extent is training needed to impart these skills?"

In addition to task analysis to develop a behavioral taxonomy of jobs, such research should be aimed toward building basic metrics for evaluating training needs with regard to specific jobs. Check lists or rating instruments need to be developed which are behaviorally based and standardized with normative information. Such instruments, then, can be used for assessing the appropriateness of job behavior of specific employees in specific positions and for identifying areas of ineffective behavior where training may be called for. The instruments also can be used as the base for evaluating whether or not training has any impact on task behaviors.

The second level of research should be a comprehensive program to assess the role of various variables for impacting the skill acquisition process. There is a need for systematic research looking at variables of different training techniques, instructional procedures, and trainee variables, and their interactions for imparting the skills identified as necessary from a task analysis. The key variables in such a program of research will look at these things: (1) different training techniques, either singly or in combination; (2) moderating effect of different training conditions, such as conditions of practice, feedback, reinforcement; and (3) trainee variables, including individual differences of ability and motivation, but also differences in trainee population parameters, such as race, age, sex, etc.

Clearly a taxonomy of training variables which looks at all permutations and combinations of such variables is not possible; a *systematic* program of research to look at the most likely combinations, however, does need to be carried out.

A final level where research is needed is in the role of training in the total organizational system. There is a real lack of research here, but the few studies and insights that have been generated suggest that there is a great deal more we need to know. For example, research on the effectiveness of leadership training (House, 1968) suggests that very often behavioral changes imparted by the training program are short lived when the manager gets back into the organizational setting. Unless he returns to a supportive climate, there is very little long-term continuing effect of training. Similar results have been found with regard to T-group training.

Likewise, there are some fairly strong indications of similar effects with regard to training for the hard-core disadvantaged. Much more important than training manipulations, personal background, or attitudes is the climate in the organization in which the hard-core employee finds himself (Friedlander & Greenberg, 1971).

These trends suggest that one possible fruitful research manipulation in the evaluation of manager training, for example, would be not to train at all. A comparative evaluation of the job effectiveness and success of managers who participated in training programs in comparison with a group that did not receive training might reveal that much of the blind faith which organizations have in management development is of questionable justification.

Such considerations talk very clearly to the need for more longitudinal research in the total career development process. Such research could look at the role of training versus other variables which impact careers, such as placement, leadership, organizational climate, and task design. The focus should be on assessing the role of such variables as determiners of effective task behavior as well as of career growth.

The research needs outlined here are extensive. It is certainly not realistic to expect that any individual organization is going to undertake the comprehensive program of research needed to develop a full taxonomy of tasks, to assess all of the factors in the interactions which impact skill acquisition, or to undertake comprehensive longitudinal studies to compare the usefulness of training versus other procedures for impacting job behaviors. However, an individual organization at least should think in terms of a more systematic program of research to cover the key variables of importance to its situation.

At the same time, there needs to be some broader framework so that research conducted within individual organizations is cumulative and can be compared. Perhaps the framework for the necessary broad taxonomy should be laid out by some coordinating agency or body, and individual organizations encouraged to structure their research so that it contributes to the overall framework. Campbell, Dunnette, Lawler, and Weick (1970) outline such a relationship when they suggest comprehensive programs of research to be undertaken in "halfway houses" located between universities and business organizations. They suggest that such research be undertaken in extension programs of business schools and university research institutes. They also believe that managerial training organizations will have to be set up almost exclusively for research purposes. Such institutes would attempt to build cooperation for follow-up purposes with participating business organizations.

It is clear that without some systematic attention to broad scale research on the training process, the field is not going to advance much beyond the rather disorganized state which currently exists. With all of the money, time, and effort going into conducting training, it should be possible to gain support to do the basic research needed for building a better understanding of the critical determiners of effective training in organizations.

REFERENCES

American Institutes for Research. *Evaluative research: Strategies and methods.* Pittsburgh: AIR, 1970, 160 pages.

Argyris, C. Some unintended consequences of rigorous research. *Psychological Bulletin,* 1968, 20, 185–193.

Attwood, D. A., & Wiener, E. L. Automated instruction for vigilance training. *Journal of Applied Psychology,* 1969, 53, 218–223.

Bass, B. M., & Vaughan, J. A. *Training in industry: The management of learning.* Belmont, Calif.: Wadsworth Publishing, 1966, 164 pages.

Berrien, F. K. *General and social systems.* New Brunswick, N.J.: Rutgers University Press, 1968, 231 pages.

Blum, M. L., & Naylor, J. C. *Industrial psychology: Its theoretical and social foundations.* New York: Harper and Row, 1968, 633 pages.

Boguslaw, R., & Porter, E. H. Team functions and training. Chapter II in R. M. Gagné (Ed.), *Psychological principles in system development.* New York: Holt, Rinehart and Winston, 1965, 387–416.

Campbell, J. P. Personnel training and development. *Annual Review of Psychology,* 1971, 22, 565–602.

Campbell, J. P., & Dunnette, M. D. Effectiveness of T-group experiences in managerial training and development. *Psychological Bulletin,* 1968, 70, 73–104.

Campbell, J. P., Dunnette, M. D., Lawler, E. E. III, & Weick, K. E. Jr. *Managerial behavior,*

performance, and effectiveness. New York: McGraw-Hill, 1970, 546 pages.

Crawford, M. P. Concepts of training. Chapter 9 in R. M. Gagné (Ed.), *Psychological principles in system development.* New York: Holt, Rinehart and Winston, 1965, 301–341.

Elbing, A. O. Jr. The influence of prior attitudes on role-playing results. *Personnel Psychology,* 1967, 20, 309–321.

Fiedler, F. E. Engineering the job to fit the manager. *Harvard Business Review,* 1965, 43, 115–122.

Fitts, P. M. Factors in complex skill training. In R. Glaser (Ed.), *Training research and education.* Pittsburgh: University of Pittsburgh Press, 1962, 177–199.

Fleishman, E. A. Individual differences and motor learning. Chapter 8 in R. M. Gagné (Ed.), *Learning and individual differences.* Columbus, Ohio: Merrill, 1967, 165–191.

Foundation for Research on Human Behavior. *Programmed learning: Evolving principles and industrial applications.* Ann Arbor: University of Michigan, 1961, 179 pages.

Friedlander, F., & Greenberg, S. Effect of job attitudes, training, and organization climate on performance of the hard-core unemployed. *Journal of Applied Psychology,* 1971, 55, 287–295.

Gagné, R. M. Military training and principles of learning. *American Psychologist,* 1962, 17, 83–91.

Gagné, R. M., Ed. *Learning and individual differences.* Columbus, Ohio: Merrill, 1967, 265 pages.

Glaser, R., Ed. *Training research and education.* Pittsburgh: University of Pittsburgh Press, 1962, 596 pages.

Goldberg, M. H., Dawson, R. I., & Barrett, R. S. Comparison of programmed and conventional instruction methods. *Journal of Applied Psychology,* 1964, 48, 110–114.

Goldstein, A. P., & Sorcher, M. *Changing supervisor behavior.* New York: Pergamon Press, 1974, 90 pages.

Goodacre, D. M. Stimulating improved man management. *Personnel Psychology,* 1963, 16, 133–143.

Hedberg, R., Steffen, H., & Baxter, B. Insurance fundamentals: A programmed text versus a conventional text. *Personnel Psychology,* 1965, 18, 165–172.

Hesseling, P. *Strategy of evaluation research.*

Assen, Holland: Van Gorcum, 1966, 359 pages.

House, R. J. T-group education and leadership effectiveness: A review of the empiric literature and a critical evaluation. *Personnel Psychology*, 1967, 20, 1–32.

House, R. J. Leadership training: Some dysfunctional consequences. *Administrative Science Quarterly*, 1968, 12, 556–571.

Hughes, J. L., & McNamara, W. J. A comparative study of programmed and conventional instruction in industry. *Journal of Applied Psychology*, 1961, 45, 225–231.

Jensen, A. R. Variety of individual differences in learning. Chapter 6 in R. M. Gagné (Ed.), *Learning and individual differences*. Columbus, Ohio: Merrill, 1967, 117–135.

King, D. *Training within the organization*. London: Tavistock, 1964, 274 pages.

Korman, A. K. *Industrial and organizational psychology*. Englewood Cliffs, N.J.: Prentice-Hall, 1971, 398 pages.

Lawshe, C. H. Jr., Bolda, R. A., & Brune, R. L. Studies in management training evaluation: Chapter II. The effects of exposures to role playing. *Journal of Applied Psychology*, 1959, 43, 287–292.

Likert, R. *The human organization: Its management and value*. New York: McGraw-Hill, 1967, 258 pages.

McGehee, W., & Thayer, P. W. *Training in business and industry*. New York: Wiley, 1961, 305 pages.

Mesics, E. A. *Education and training for effective manpower utilization: An annotated bibliography on education and training in work organizations*. Ithaca, N.Y.: Cornell University, 1969, 157 pages.

Nash, A. N., Muczyk, J. P., & Vettori, F. L. The relative practical effectiveness of programmed instruction. *Personnel Psychology*, 1971, 24, 397–418.

Patten, T. H. Jr. *Manpower planning and the development of human resources*. New York: Wiley, 1971, 737 pages.

Planty, E. G., McCord, W. S., & Efferson, C. A. *Training employees and managers*. New York: Ronald Press, 1948, 278 pages.

Pressey, S. C. Two basic neglected psychoeducational problems. *American Psychologist*, 1965, 20, 391–395.

Rosenthal, R. On the social psychology of the psychological experiment: The experimenter's hypothesis as unintended determinant of experimental results. *American Scientist*, 1963, 51, 268–283.

Schwartz, H. A., & Haskell, R. J. Jr. A study of computer-assisted instruction in industrial training. *Journal of Applied Psychology*, 1966, 50, 360–363.

Schwartz, H. A., & Long, H. S. A study of remote industrial training via computer-assisted instruction. *Journal of Applied Psychology*, 1967, 51, 11–16.

Seltzer, R. A. Computer-assisted instruction: What it can and cannot do. *American Psychologist*, 1971, 26, 373–377.

Utgaard, S. B., & Dawis, R. V. The most frequently used training techniques. *Training and Development Journal*, 1970, 24, 40–43.

Valverde, H. H., & Youngs, E. J. *Annotated bibliography of the training research division reports, 1950–1969*. Wright-Patterson Air Force Base, Ohio: Air Force Human Resources Laboratory, Air Force Systems Command, 1969, 199 pages.

Warren, M. W. *Training for results: A system approach to the development of human resources in industry*. Reading, Mass.: Addison-Wesley, 1969, 239 pages.

CHAPTER 20

Managerial Assessment Centers

ROBERT B. FINKLE
The Standard Oil Company (Ohio)

ASSESSMENT CENTER ACTIVITIES are reviewed highlighting the similarities and dissimilarities among a number of installations which have been described, to date, in available periodicals. Similarities, reflecting early work done by AT&T, are noted to feature: assessment in groups, assessment by groups, and the use of multiple techniques with emphasis on situational exercises. Differences among the reviewed programs are seen as significant in both scope and impact and become the focus of elaboration throughout the chapter. Among the differences reviewed are varying practices with respect to: purpose, choice and training of assessors, choice of techniques, methods of collecting, weighing and recording data, approaches to reporting and feedback, research conducted, and professional guidance provided. Short summaries are provided covering most of the original published research on assessment centers. Concern is expressed for a faddish commercialism growing out of the assessment center label and a plea made for professional guidance and research.

In 1969, at a meeting of The Executive Study Conference, Dr. Erwin K. Taylor referred to assessment centers reported on by a number of business organization representatives as "Variations on a Theme...." Similar reference, of course, might be made to human beings, automobiles or snowflakes without obvious implications of limitations or narrowness. Nevertheless, Dr. Taylor's remark is quite apt as a description of assessment center activity in the sixties and sets a constructive foundation for reviewing recent developments and for speculating about future ramifications in the field of applied group assessment. The term "assessment center" as described in this chapter refers to a group-oriented, standardized series of activities which provide a basis for judgments or predictions of human behaviors believed or known to be relevant to work performed in an organizational setting. The scope of this writing will be further narrowed by covering only work that would be defined as managerial—hence the title "Managerial Assessment Centers." Clearly, most of the technology and procedures described would apply equally well to many non-managerial assessment activities.

THE THEME

Dr. Taylor further attributed the theme to Dr. Douglas W. Bray and in doing so was alluding to assessment activities begun by the American Telephone & Telegraph Company in 1956. The original model was a longitudinal research study of college hires, known as "The Management Progress Study" (Bray, 1964a). Subsequent programs at the managerial level included assessment centers in Bell Telephone affiliated companies designed to select first level foremen, and centers operated by AT&T to assess higher levels of management in some of the Bell companies (Bray, 1964b). In response to the AT&T theme, assessment centers were initiated in Standard Oil of Ohio in 1962, then subsequently in IBM, Sears, General Electric, J. C. Penney, and, by this writing, in over 1,000 organizations.[1] Several consulting firms, such as Personnel Decisions, Inc. of Minneapolis, Minnesota, were known to offer assessment center services with others prepared to advise and assist companies in setting up centers. At least one organization specialized in offering psychological assessment center materials, and workshops on how to conduct assessment centers were being offered by several groups including the American Management Association.

Four characteristics seem to contribute most significantly to the theme of these assessment activities, as inspired by the initial AT&T effort: assessment in groups, assessment by groups, use of multiple measurement techniques with heavy emphasis on situational exercises, and a special appeal to management.

Assessment In Groups

The assessment center approach is distinguished from most previous managerial

assessment approaches by the nearly universal practice of operating with fixed-sized groups of assessees. Typical is the choice of groups of twelve. The selection of twelve assessees facilitates division of the main group into six-party groups for the carrying out of situational exercises—often leaderless group discussions. Group assessment also permits the use of peer evaluations.

Testing for managerial prediction, as with other testing, has often been done via group test administration, particularly under in-company direction. For example, programs such as those conducted at Sears by Bentz (1967) and at Standard Oil of New Jersey by Laurent (1962) in the fifties and sixties were designed to predict managerial success and could be administered on an individual or group basis in response to practical determinations of efficiency and convenience. However, testing done by consulting organizations to assess managerial talents was most commonly done on an individual-at-a-time basis, partly due to practical demands of scheduling, but fundamentally due to an emphasis on clinical instruments and techniques which required man-for-man exposures of each assessee to a psychologist. In essence, then, the assessment center approach to the prediction of managerial talent contrasts with typical consultant assessment being done in groups and typical in-company assessment being done in fixed-sized groups to permit standardized inter-group activities.

Assessment By Groups

The use of several assessors and the roles these assessors play also set assessment centers apart from approaches to managerial assessment done previously. Though the qualifications and backgrounds of the assessors vary from program to program, the use of a team of evaluators is universal. Again, this practice is most strongly inspired, perhaps, by the commitment to use group situational exercises. But in addition to one or more roles in generating assessment information,

---

[1] Byham reported in 1969 that the following firms and government agencies had implemented multiple assessment procedures: AT&T, Standard Oil Company (Ohio), IBM, Caterpillar Tractor Co., General Electric Co., Sears, Roebuck & Company, Minnesota Mining & Manufacturing Co., Olin-Mathieson Chemical Corp., Wolverine Tube Co., Wickes Corp., J. C. Penney Co., The Peace Corps, the Internal Revenue Service, and the Oak Ridge Atomic Energy Facility. His estimate of over 1,000 was made in 1973.

the assessment staff usually acts as a team in evaluating the information generated and in establishing at least a skeleton for a report of the results for each assessee. This team approach, as with the practice of assessing in groups, should be recognized as a difference in degree and role, as contrasted with earlier managerial assessment approaches, rather than as a fundamental difference in method. Many in-company programs and consulting assessment services have used staff members both to generate and evaluate information. The team approach in modern assessment centers is simply cited here as a universal characteristic which contrasts, to some extent at least, with many previous efforts.

Multiple Methods

The use of several testing and assessment techniques is characteristic of most assessment centers though the use of multiple methods of assessment is not, of course, unique, a point elaborated by Taft (1959). Most managerial assessment programs have employed several techniques—typically interviewing, objective testing and, with some, projective testing. Use of the latter has been more characteristic of assessment by consulting firms than by permanent "internal" staffs of companies or other organizations.

The featured "new" technique in assessment centers has been the situational exercise. In the modern day assessment centers the situational exercises may have consisted of individually administered "In-Basket" problems followed by questionnaires or interviewing or both. Or they may be group problems or discussions followed by peer ratings or questionnaires. With this addition, the multiple methods drawn upon for currently operating management assessment centers will include all or nearly all of the following:

OBJECTIVE TESTS. Instruments in which scores or weights have been preassigned to discrete answers, usually presented in multiple-choice format. These tests may measure mental abilities, knowledge, skills, attitudes, interests, values or personality characteristics. They may be timed or untimed, are usually administered in paper-and-pencil format, and can be given individually or in groups with a minimum of training for those administering and scoring them. They lend themselves readily to quantitative analysis and verification. For elaboration on objective testing and evaluation techniques, the reader is referred to basic texts (Anastasi, 1968; Cronbach, 1966), to reviews by Buros (1959, 1961), and to test publication catalogues (Psychological Corporation, 1971; Science Research Associates, 1971).

PROJECTIVE TESTS. Instruments to which responses are provided to ambiguous or loosely structured or defined stimuli. Interpretation of the responses is made by specially trained and experienced professionals who produce descriptive analyses of the persons being tested. Testing must be done individually if the responses are oral, but can be done on a group or individual basis if the responses are written. In assessment centers, when used at all, the most common techniques have been the Thematic Apperception Test and a form of sentence completion test. The *Handbook of Projective Techniques* (Murstein, 1965) reviews these and other projective instruments.

INTERVIEWING. Interviewing can be attempted by anyone from well-trained professionals to untrained laymen. It can vary in structure, standardization of interpretation and in the mood or climate in which it is conducted. Output of the interviewer can be a simple repetition or summation of information and opinion offered by the interviewee, an interpretation of response and conduct, or an evaluation of the interviewee as the result of the exposure. Interviews can, of course, be conducted individually, by a panel of interviewers or as a sequence of two or more interviewers. Reviews of the contribution of interviewing to personnel activities occur periodically and comprehensive ones have been by Wagner (1949), Mayfield (1964), and Ulrich and Trumbo (1965).

SITUATIONAL EXERCISES. Such activities are more or less standardized exposures of one or more assessees to one or more assessors under conditions and performing tasks believed to simulate work exposures or at least to elicit performance that generalizes to the work environment. The simplest examples of situational exercises are job sample tests such as typing tests, driving tests (the actual driving part), and field tests in apprenticeship safety training. Examples typical of those used in assessment centers are the In-Basket exercise, leaderless group discussions, and group gaming activities.

Tracing to military selection procedures in Germany and Great Britain, the situational exercise was first featured in the United States in activities of the OSS Assessment Staff (1948) during World War II. An early review of the technique was covered in a symposium at the 1953 meeting of the American Psychological Association, where presentations were made by Flanagan, Fiske, Bass, Carter, Kelly, and Weislogel (1954). In current applications, most of these exercises simulate problems encountered by individuals or groups in business or other forms of organizational life. Observations of performance are made and judgments or descriptions of the behavior of individuals are developed. Bass (1954) reviewed the leaderless group discussion technique. The In-Basket exercise was introduced in the early 1950s by Frederiksen (1957) and its industrial application was later reviewed by Lopez (1966). References to other simulation techniques have occurred in writings by Thornton (1964), Wollowick and McNamara (1969), and Byham (1970).

PEER RATINGS. Having assessment carried out in groups makes it possible to obtain peer evaluations in a number of ways. These may consist of rankings or ratings by the assessees themselves judging each other in overall ways, such as who contributed most effectively in a just-completed situational exercise. Or they may call for assessees to rate one another on specific characteristics or traits similar to or identical with traits to be judged by the assessors from the other information generated. Research on and applications of this technique have been reported by Hollander (1954, 1957), Weitz (1958), and Roadman (1964).

The Appeal

Perhaps the most striking characteristic of assessment centers, at least to date, is the relatively favorable reaction of laymen in the organizations in which they have been established. Businessmen appear to be more ready to accept this open, standardized, relevant assessment process.

Persons with any business or other managerial experience have had to form judgments about work performance and potential from several similar types of exposure: interviewing—as with hiring or other job filling; record examination—as in resumes or written materials; observation of work or reports on work observations by other supervisors; occasional observation of individual contribution at meetings or conferences; casual contact. By contrast, many managers have been quite skeptical of the value of tests and have been encouraged in their skepticism by such eloquent, if not entirely constructive, appeals for common sense as presented in *The Organization Man* (Whyte, 1956). The assessment center theme gives the manager a close approximation to all of his usual exposures (interviewing, work observation, background data, formal and informal observation of individual contribution), but under more standardized conditions and with the opportunity to share reflections and judgments with other managers given similar exposure. At the same time, most assessment programs play down the use of formal tests—the object of most managerial skepticism about formal assessment. The result is a strong appeal and a sharp growth in assessment center activity. Further reflections on this reaction have been presented elsewhere (Finkle & Jones, 1970).

VARIATIONS

But what of the variations on this theme? What are they and what significance do they have for persons considering, developing, using, or evaluating assessment centers?

Since variations in the most specific sense are nearly infinite in number, this review will cover the principal differences noted among the more established and publicized programs and will approach these differences in the following topic areas: purposes and uses, instruments, assessor composition and training, integration procedures, reports, and professional participation and guidance.

Purposes and Uses

Of all the variations on the assessment center theme that will be discussed, certainly the most basic are the variations of purpose. Desirably and appropriately, evidences have been and will continue to be required to demonstrate the validity of the assessment process. The fundamental definition of validity is that an instrument should measure what it is supposed to measure. Varieties of purpose, therefore, will set the stage for varieties of criterion choice and methodology in verification; this will be discussed later.

A strong contextual factor in the established purpose of the assessment activity is the organizational makeup of the company, or other organizational entity, in which the activity is to be conducted. Some organizations, by their size and structure, present a large number of like or similar management jobs, or at least present a series of well-defined levels of management responsibility. Examples of such structures, among companies with assessment centers, are the Bell Telephone Companies, Sears, and J. C.

Penney. But other organizations may have single or relatively few incumbents for each of a large number of unique management positions, many of which are molded, to some extent at least, to feature the strengths, experiences, and styles of specific individuals.

In the first type of organization where a large number of relatively homogeneous jobs exist, the purpose of the assessment activity is quite likely to help with a specific decision such as the suitability of individuals for a particular type or level of management job. This purpose implicitly or explicitly presumes a recognized set of critical requirements for success in the higher level work. Also assumed in most assessment efforts directed to this purpose is a common knowledge and agreement among higher level managers, who will be assessors, as to the managerial and administrative skills and styles that will indicate the capacity to meet the critical requirements of the job. Fortunately, research can provide some means of verification of these assumptions and of the judgments made in their application.

With the second organizational circumstances described earlier, namely when jobs and job requirements are more heterogeneous throughout the management ranks, the purpose of the assessment activity must be defined differently or, as is sometimes unfortunately the case, left ambiguous. In the Sohio program, the purpose is to establish reliable and valid judgments about the extent to which each assessee possesses each of several personal characteristics believed to be relevant, in varying degrees, to success in a multiplicity of management assignments, defined or yet to be defined. Other programs, such as the General Electric one, stress development as the primary purpose. All too often, however, clear focus is not given to the purpose and an uneasy suspicion can arise that the activity itself, or the general exposure it produces, may be the goal.

The key differences referred to above were with respect to the avowed primary purposes of certain programs. But even programs proclaiming relatively similar primary purposes may lay quite different emphases on secondary or additional objectives. The assessment center activities most publicized to date seem to include among their various purposes one or more of these five: (1) the decision that an assessee does or does not qualify for a particular job or level of job; (2) a set of decisions as to how the assessees rate on a series of defined variables; (3) a prediction of the long-range potential of each assessee; (4) judgments associated with the development of each assessee; and (5) the development of the assessor in the assessment role. Which one or ones of these purposes a particular program features will have considerable bearing on the content and process of the program and, most importantly, on the methodology employed in verification (validation). Some examples of the influence of purpose on design follow.

With the objective being to determine qualifications for a particular job or level of job, the verification task features the development of a criterion of success on the targeted job or level. The key decision in the assessment program would have been a simple recommendation that an assessee was or was not qualified for promotion. This decision may, of course, have been expressed in more than a dichotomous fashion. For example, predictor scores expressing degrees of confidence of success or degrees of predicted success might be available. In any event, the fundamental design would seem to be one of predicted validity between the predictor scores and the measure of job success of those actually promoted.

If the objective is the documentation of trait judgments, validation becomes a task of establishing the validity of the predictions regarding each of the characteristics rather than verification of a global success or failure prediction. Presumably this validation of the trait judgments could take the form of agreement between the assessment judgments of these traits and subsequent or concurrent measures of the same traits derived either

in similar fashion, that is, through reassessment, or in different fashion, that is, from ratings derived from on-the-job performance evaluations. In the second approach, the adequacy of the "criterion" measures, presumably derived from performance ratings, might be highly debatable, particularly if these criterion measures are collected under conditions of poorer standardization than are the assessment judgments. Since the traits or characteristics are constructs that should bear consistent and predictable interrelationships among themselves and with the various assessment techniques contributing to their formulation, the multi-trait-multimethod design of Campbell and Fiske (1959) seems quite appropriate as an analysis tool. This has application with or without the inclusion of concurrent or subsequent information independently derived from assessment or appraisal inputs. Fundamentally, however, it must be recognized that the "judgment of traits" purpose in assessment begs the question of how the characteristics measured should be selected, weighted, or supplemented to accomplish promotion decisions. Although the psychologist may wish to offer assistance in the standardization and verification of this decision-making process, it should be recalled that this purpose for assessment was chosen to cover circumstances where there is little or no similarity in job content across the managerial positions in the organization—hence producing significant variations in critical requirements for success.

The purpose in assessment of predicting long-range potential is perhaps the most tenuous of those attempted in such programs; still, considerable interest will quite likely be evidenced in this purpose by the upper management of an organization. The very willingness to attempt the prediction, let alone verify it, requires acceptance of the premise that a relatively fixed set of characteristics will relate to level of success in the organization. Some are unwilling to subscribe to this premise. For those who do however, an appropriate design for verifica tion would seem to be that pursued by the former Personnel Research group of the Exxon Corporation, then identified as Standard Oil of New Jersey (see Laurent, 1962). The design featured a multiple correlation between predictor variables and a criterion of level of business success by age.

When the purpose of the assessment information is to diagnose developmental needs, the task of validation becomes, if anything, even more complex—even to the extent where it is the practice in some circles to waive the verification entirely. But if verification is to be attempted, it now becomes a matter of supporting the accuracy of the diagnosis which advocates change in the assessee's knowledge, skill, style, values, interests, or whatever. Beyond that, full verification of the developmental objectives of the program would seem to call for confirmation that "prescriptions" for development are effective in that they are found to produce new or sharpened behaviors. Finally, it would be desirable to verify that these changes correlate significantly with increased success at some specified job, with level of success, or with rate of promotion. If specific behavioral changes were not pursued for verification, at least the entire process of developmental diagnosis and prescription might be compared with the absence of the process or with a control process to determine the aggregate improvement in numbers of persons reaching some success criterion as the result of the assessment developmental efforts. To the writer's knowledge, no such verification efforts have been attempted in connection with developmentally oriented assessment programs.

If the prime purpose of the program is the development of assessors in the assessment role, the verification task is somewhat similar to the one just covered. If taken beyond simple testimonial evidence, such verification would seem to call for before-and-after measurements matched with a control group. Some attention would need to be given to identifying what behaviors of the manager are the target for change, and

in what way. One likely focus would be on the appraisal skills of the manager. Appraisals completed by the manager following his development as an assessor might be expected to evidence fewer rating problems such as halo, central tendency, and leniency. Though such objectives could be defined and efforts made to measure their attainment, the author again has no knowledge of efforts to conduct such verification analysis in connection with current assessment center programs.

As complicated as these verification approaches can be when related to a specifically defined purpose, the difficulty of the task will be compounded when several purposes are attributed to the program. For example, a program may feature the near-term decision to promote or not to promote. But it may also produce a report describing abilities and characteristics, estimating potential, advocating development actions and espousing the benefits of serving as an assessor. All categories of verification reviewed above would seem appropriate—a cornucopia for the disinterested researcher, a Herculean challenge for the applied practitioner.

Instruments

The types of assessment instruments which may be used in assessment centers are broadly classed as objective, situational, sociometric, and projective. Marked variety can occur with respect to each of these classes including the omission of the entire class.

OBJECTIVE TESTS. Among objective tests, broadly referred to as paper-and-pencil tests, assessment centers may make use of such mental ability instruments as the School and College Ability Tests, the Miller Analogies Test, the Watson Glaser Critical Thinking Appraisal, and the Wesman Personnel Classification Series; and such personality, value, and interest inventories as the Gordon Personal Inventory, the Guilford-Martin Personality Inventory, the Edwards Personal

Preference Schedule, the Allport-Vernon-Lindzey Study of Values, and the Strong Vocational Interest Blank (Buros, 1959, 1961). These and comparable tests are purchased from test publishers (Cronbach, 1966, p. 609). They may be interpreted in accordance with the publisher's descriptions and interpretations of their content, or they may be analyzed by the assessment center director and weighted or interpreted in accordance with such studies in the context of their use. In any event, these objective tests are generally standardized instruments developed by professionals; but to the author's knowledge, no two centers have made use of the same combination of such tests. A survey reflecting variation in test use, as well as in other factors, was made by Bender (1973).

SITUATIONAL EXERCISES. Even greater variety may be found in the choice, development, and application of situational exercises used in assessment centers. Here not only do differences occur in the apparent content, as judged by the label or general format of the exercise, but also considerable variation is contributed simply because many, if not most, situational exercises are either privately developed by each company or organization establishing an assessment center or are "borrowed" from another center and typically applied in the new context with significant modification. Only recently have standardized situational exercises become available for purchase as are paper-and-pencil tests (Development Dimensions, 1973). Even among standardized forms, the variety of task is quite broad including group or individually administered games, such as manufacturing exercises or stock market tasks; leaderless group (usually six-man) discussion topics, such as promotion decisions, business expansion problems, disciplinary situations, or even nonbusiness questions like school board or draft board problems; individual tasks such as prepared or impromptu talks, written reports, mock interviewing, or "irate" customer phone calls.

Perhaps the most commonly used situational exercise, though it too is omitted from a few programs, is the In-Basket (Lopez, 1966). Typically, in the In-Basket exercise, the assessee has the task of sorting an accumulation of mail, reports, notes, etc. received at a manager's desk. He is to dispose of these materials by giving instructions in writing as to their appropriate handling. Variations in the application of this basic approach center around two factors: the development of the exercise and its interpretation. Development can consist simply of a relatively hasty accumulation of materials surrounding a real or mythical job with little thought to rationales for analysis. Or it may produce a well-studied series of documents chosen to elicit specific categories of response established through careful prior statistical analyses. As with other situational exercises, standardized In-Basket tests can now be purchased for use in assessment centers, thus enabling an organization unwilling or unable to undertake the elaborate development of an instrument to improve on what might otherwise be a very haphazard and superficial approach.

Interpretation of In-Basket material can vary from judgments or scores derived from an inspection or analysis of the materials to a review of reasons offered by the assessee on a questionnaire or in an interview as to why he took certain actions in handling the materials. Such follow-up interviews are usually conducted by management representatives on the assessment staff and call for the interviewers to judge certain administrative and supervisory skills and abilities in accordance with prescribed standards and/or their own views as successful managers. Interestingly, therefore, this one instrument, the In-Basket, can be used for assessment in a highly quantified, actuarially supported fashion, or in a far more subjective, interview-based, almost clinically treated fashion. Obviously, the output will vary, across these differences, in reliability, validity, and relevance.

Other exercises bearing a common label

may also be applied in widely diverse ways. For instance, a stock market exercise, designed originally at Sohio in 1962 to support a risk-taking construct, was modified by IBM to serve as a warm-up exercise and, by title at least, has appeared in a variety of other programs including an application at Penney's which features both intra-team and inter-team competition under conditions of stress.

SOCIOMETRIC RATINGS. Sociometric ratings or peer ratings (Weitz, 1958) have been used in some programs. When used, they may be in the form of follow-up questionnaires to group situational exercises. In this application, each assessee may be asked to rank, rate, and/or comment on the performance of his associates in the exercise. Ranking, ratings, or comments on peers may also be elicited from the assessees at other times in the program, often near the end. As with situational exercises, peer ratings are probably developed and applied individually by each organization establishing an assessment center and will, therefore, appear in as many formats as there are centers making use of them.

PROJECTIVE INSTRUMENTS. Projective tests were used in the AT&T Management Progress Study, in AT&T executive-level assessment centers, and are now used in the Sohio program. The projective instruments employed in these programs were the Thematic Apperception Test and one or another form of a sentence completion test (Murstein, 1965). Few other centers seem to have included projective techniques in their efforts. The inclusion or exclusion of this technique constitutes a rather significant difference in instrument choice, which calls for some speculation as to cause.

The primary circumstances and rationales supporting the inclusion of projective instruments in the assessment effort seem to be the following: The technique provides a unique approach to assessment in that it allows for a broad analysis of personality characteristics by a clinically trained professional. Somewhat the same contribution can be made by having clinical psychologists conduct interviews of all assessees. But with limited time, this might preclude having management representatives conduct interviews—a debatable trade-off—since the manager cannot handle the projective techniques whereas the clinical psychologist can handle both the interview and the projectives. An alternative is having managers conduct follow-up interviews to a situational exercise such as an In-Basket problem. Still, if the program rationale calls for a full check-and-balance approach to techniques, as well as to assessors, the projective instruments in the hands of well-qualified psychologists comprise an established but unique technique. Also, when the purpose of the program is to describe (predict) behavioral constructs, rather than simply produce a potential rating or a "go, no-go" promotion decision, the projective instruments may be better suited to contribute to judgments about some of the variables than any other technique available. This is particularly true when the choice of behavior variables or constructs to be rated is based on relevance rather than ease of eliciting, reliability, or even validity, of measurement. Clearly, all constructs included must be measured with sufficient reliability to support validity and with sufficient validity to be useful. Nevertheless, such characteristics as originality and achievement motive may be seen as of critical relevance to enough placement decisions to justify their inclusion even when they cannot be predicted with as high a validity as some other characteristics of less critical import. If the projective techniques can contribute uniquely to judgments of such characteristics, their inclusion can become important and perhaps even necessary. Finally, inclusion of projectives in a program where managers (laymen) contribute as assessors provides an overt demonstration that the skilled professional can offer a somewhat unique perspective to personality analysis. This is most creditable when the projective reports cover characteristics, such as impact or personal acceptability, that can also be judged from other available techniques, as well as cover characteristics, such as relationship with authority or need for structure, that may be less well supported by other techniques. Giving managers this opportunity to judge both the clinical psychologist and his projective techniques builds confidence in the depth of the group assessment program and lays a firmer foundation for acceptance of other professional services, such as counseling, consulting, and individually administered assessments.

By contrast with the above rationales for including projectives in a group assessment program, there are several reasons why they may not be included. Typically, testing programs for selection and promotion in medium and large organizations have heretofore been directed by psychologists with strong psychometric training and persuasion and who are most familiar with standardized procedures such as paper-and-pencil tests and inventories, weighted biographic forms and patterned interviewing. These professionals often choose to rely exclusively on the instruments and techniques in which they are personally trained and experienced and may have a dim view of projective techniques, which lend themselves less well to straightforward actuarial verification.

There may be a bit of self-fulfilling prophecy in the view of psychometricians toward the validity of projectives when they apply classical psychometric techniques in the analysis. This is particularly likely when the prime program objective is to predict or judge the qualifications of persons for movement to a specific job or level of job. Given this objective, a global, success-fail criterion for validation is typically defined for judging the contribution of various predictors. Reports from projective instruments are awkward to handle in such analyses since they must first be coded or quantified. Then too, their contribution, as with all predictors actuarially weighted, will be limited to the maximization of reliably measured inputs

related to the particular criterion choice. To the extent that the criterion choice is faulty, excessively parsimonious or vulnerable to change in time, more stable constructs from the projectives which might have overridden these changes will be lost. Accordingly, projectives vitiated in this way by actuarial weighting may not add enough unique value to justify their cost in time and a specially qualified staff. It can also be argued that the inclusion of projectives, and psychologists to interpret them, may be seen as inconsistent with the flavor given assessment by the situational exercises in which emphasis is placed on standardizing and sharpening the normal and overt means by which managers make judgments about work-associated performance.

Assessor Composition and Training

In the Management Progress Study of AT&T, the assessment staff was comprised of behavorial scientists—principally psychologists. Subsequent programs established in the Bell System for assisting in promotion decisions to first line management made exclusive use of management representatives as assessors. The Sohio program employs a staff of two psychologists, three managers, and a program director (who is not a psychologist). An AT&T executive level assessment program used psychologists with some use of managers, as does the program offered by Personnel Decisions for application across companies. Most programs, however, have followed the lead of the Bell System's lower management programs and have featured management representatives as assessors.

Variation in assessor use also occurs among the programs as to how frequently these representatives should change. Some programs use a fixed group of managers as staff for several months; other programs use managers for only one program. Arguments for frequent change in the managerial assessment staff stress the value of managers becoming more sophisticated in making human judgments and gaining firsthand conviction about the efficiency and effectiveness of the program and the supporting staff. Arguments for less frequent change of managers as assessors concern the importance of greater stability in the program and greater efficiency of using well-trained assessors, rather than undergoing the cost of continuous training.

High in the order of procedures that differ significantly across programs is the amount of time devoted to the training of assessors. Some programs may devote two or three weeks to assessor training in which they employ lectures, films, discussions, and practice sessions on interviewing, objective and comprehensive observation, note taking and report preparation. One program loads a tightly packed seven-day schedule with such training activities while still another program includes only about six hours of assessor orientation in a compact five-day program.

These differences in composition and training of management assessors are, as with other differences across various assessment programs, a function of the objectives, the environment, the program format, and the convictions of those establishing the program. When the improvement of managers in their skill to make human judgments is given high priority in the objectives of a program, then a high ratio of assessors to assessees, possibly one to one, is likely. In addition, manager training and process discussion time is likely to be high; as a result managers are given shorter times as members of the assessment staff so that more can have exposure to the program. If the environment is one of close economic concern, there may be less training time within the total program time, and a higher assessee-to-assessor ratio—possibly four to one. When the format of the program is made up almost exclusively of inputs and judgments by management assessors, without counterbalancing inputs and judgments by professionals, there is likely to be more time devoted to management training time and the practice of holding managers longer on

the assessor assignment. Finally, a professional setting up the program will establish more management assessor training time if he feels that in the program being designed the inputs and judgments of managers and psychologists would, in the matter of training, differ significantly, and that the difference would favor the psychologist in terms of producing more valid results. It is then clear that a variety of situational factors bear on assessor composition and training and that these differences should be added to the others whose effects will have to be resolved, hopefully with research support, in the total context of a particular assessment program.

Integration Procedures

On the surface, there would seem to be less difference across assessment programs in the combining and judging of inputs than in some other program phases. The most common pattern seems to be that of a case-by-case, that is, assessee-by-assessee, review of assessment data by the assessment staff and the reduction of this input to a series of ratings. (Intellectual measures derived from tests may be taken directly and not used as input to rating judgments.) Typically, rating scales with descriptive statements at points along the scale are rated independently by staff members. Only differences beyond a specified tolerance zone are discussed. Rather fundamental differences can result, however, from the choices made in the variables or personal characteristics to be rated. Programs show some agreement if variables are judged by their labels as shown in Table 1.[2]

Still, the variation from program to program in number of variables from ten to over twenty suggests either fundamental differences in the choice of characteristics, in the semantic levels of specificity, or in both. More significant, perhaps, is the rec-

---

[2] Variables listed here are from reports by members of the respective organizations at some point in time as cited. Obviously, any program may be changed in content as the result of experience so that these lists may no longer represent variables currently in use.

TABLE 1

COMPARISON OF VARIABLES FROM SELECTED PROGRAMS

AT&T (Bray & Grant, 1966)	IBM (Hinrichs, 1969)	Sohio (Thompson, 1970)	IRS (DiCostanzo & Andretta, 1970)	Wolverine Tube Division of Universal Oil Products (McConnell, 1969)
Organization and planning	Self-confidence	Amount of participation	Decision making	Intellectual ability
Decision making	Written communications	Oral communication	Decisiveness	Oral communication skills
Creativity	Administrative ability	Personal acceptability	Flexibility	Written communication skills
Human relations skills	Interpersonal contact	Impact	Leadership	Leadership
Behavior flexibility	Energy level	Quality of participation	Oral communications	Creativeness
Personal impact	Decision making	Personal breadth	Organization and planning	Self-objectivity
Tolerance of uncertainty	Resistance to stress	Orientation to detail	Perception and analytic ability	Behavior flexibility
Resistance to stress	Planning and organizing	Self-direction	Persuasiveness	Primacy of work
Scholastic aptitude	Persuasiveness	Relationship with authority	Sensitivity to people	Realism of expectations
Range of interests	Aggressiveness	Originality	Stress tolerance	Range of interests
Inner work standards	Risk taking	Understanding of people		Energy and drive
Primacy of work	Oral communications	Drive		Acceptance
Oral communications skills		Potential		Organization and planning
Perception of social cues				Initiative
Self-objectivity				Decision making
Energy				Motivation
Realism of expectations				
Bell System value orientation				
Social objectivity				
Need advancement				
Ability to delay gratification				
Need for superior approval				
Need for peer approval				
Goal flexibility				
Need for security				
Staff prediction				

ognition that both the choice and the meaning of chosen variables are clearly a function of the methods and techniques of generating data input. For example, the In-Basket produces input particularly appropriate for judgments of administrative skill; group exercises produce inputs well suited for judgments of interpersonal competence; projective analyses produce inputs more associated with judgments of motivation and personality dimensions; mental ability tests will, of course, contribute to judgments about intellectual functioning. Whatever the labels and definitions are for the selected variables, therefore, the meaning of variables within a program is strongly a function of the choice of instruments available to provide input for the judgments made.

Other possible sources of differences in the integration phase of assessment programs are: the extent of standardization, induced by format or training, associated with the development of input data from situational exercises and interviews; the thoroughness with which rating scales used to collect judgments in the integration session have been developed, including definitions, bench mark descriptions, and empirical scaling; the process for sharing input and recording judgments with consideration for sequence of input, independence of ratings, rules for resolving, and/or recording differences of opinion, opportunity for modification of scales, or addition of comments; provision for formation and documentation of supplementary judgments on such factors as best utilization, constraints on type of supervision to be received, needs for development; if a judgment of potential is to be made, as it is in most, but not all, programs, the definition of potential with reflections on time, level, area of activity, and overriding conditions. And overriding all these areas for possible differences is the likelihood that most programs will make changes from time to time in their choice, definition, or scaling of variables, in their choice or use of input instruments, or in their techniques and procedures for performing the integration task.

Reports

At some stage, the rating judgments must be consolidated and developed into a final report package. Most assessment programs have adopted the practice begun in the Bell System of preparing a relatively comprehensive narrative report for each assessee. Examples of such reports have been offered by Byham (1970), and Bray and Grant (1964). The content of the report will be guided, of course, by the variables and factors judged in the program which, in turn, were influenced, as was suggested earlier, by the choice of instruments and techniques. Beyond this, considerable variance will occur from program to program in accordance with ground rules established for report preparation. Some programs, for example, Sohio, limit written reports to documentation of judgments, data, and opinion developed by and/or agreed to by the entire assessment staff. Not included in these reports are statements contributed by one staff representative on performance or background information derived from a single source, such as the interview, the background questionnaire, or a particular situational exercise. The emphasis here is on requiring the assessment staff to offer only statements about how the assessee may be expected to behave in the future. Interpretation and generalization from firsthand exposure to reports of exercise behavior, interview information, and recorded background are not left to the as-yet-unidentified "to whom it may concern" reader of the report. More typically, however, assessment reports, as with the J. C. Penney and Bell System programs, offer rather full elaboration on the observed situational exercise behavior as well as on the background of the assessee. Possibly the intent in such reports is to contribute more meaning to the variable judgments, possibly to justify them to the assessee. A similar sharing of background data is characteristic of assessment reports prepared by private consulting organizations reporting individual assessment results.

An area of practical, as well as strategic,

concern in assessment report writing that seems to have attracted little or no research, but which plagues anyone performing the task, is that of presenting information in a manner which can be understood on a general good-bad continuum. Several things can be seen to contribute to this problem. Relevant is the old saw where one fellow cheerfully greets another with "How's your wife?" only to be asked "Compared with what?" The assessment committee making judgments about an assessee has presumably been guided toward a certain normative or relativity position. Such judgments may be made relative to the assessee's peers, relative to his potential peer level if he is moved to a specific higher level, relative to the incumbents of a specific, higher level job, or relative to management in general. Less likely are comparisons with the general population (too broad) or simply with the other eleven or so assessees in the program at one time (too narrow). Still, no matter how well targeted the basis for comparison may be, the judgment of any particular reader may vary from the aggregate perspective of the assessment committee.

Some of the problems of writing properly understood assessment statements may derive from characteristics of management level appraisal statements in organizations. Many performance evaluation appraisals are written in somewhat bland style with more highlighting of the positive than of the negative. Several conditions and attitudes seem to reinforce this practice. One is a general conservative feeling that "the written word will haunt you." Another is a concern that negative appraisal statements may trigger corrective action with ensuing unpleasantness. Still another is a loyalty to subordinates that is further intensified when departmental barriers are strongly defined. Finally, the tie between appraisals and motivation contributes to a strong positive flavor, particularly when appraisals are closely reviewed with subordinates. Whether influenced by these or other factors, many

professionals, inside and outside the business organization, have adopted a similar style in writing assessment reports. Rather typically, some reports on assessments of current management done on an individual basis by outside agencies are almost entirely expressed in positive terms with negatives "suggested" so lightly as to be undetected by many casual readers.

The task of the assessment report writer of conveying to the reader the normative relativity determined by the assessment committee with respect to each reported judgment is, accordingly, a difficult one which merits more attention and research than seems to have so far been forthcoming. Although this source of variation from center to center has been reflected upon only briefly and in general terms in writings about assessment, we suspect that it contributes significantly to variations in actual use, and, therefore, value, of assessment information.

Research Including Validation

As was mentioned earlier, a body of research publication has begun to evolve on the subject of assessment centers. We shall not attempt here to cover this material in detail since most of it is available to interested readers, but rather will simply identify and summarize the principal contributions. It should be noted that material reported to date falls into three broad categories. The first comprises research on specific techniques or approaches to prediction of managerial potential that predates the AT&T Management Progress Study or deals with assessment approaches different in type from the AT&T model. Typical of such contributions are Laurent (1962) on Early Identification of Management Potential work at Standard Oil of New Jersey (Exxon); Bentz (1967) on prediction of executive success at Sears; Campbell et al. (1962) on work by Psychological Research Services of Western Reserve University; Hilton et al. (1955); Albrecht et al. (1964). The second category includes research on current assessment centers, with principal attention being focused on the AT&T, Sears, Sohio, and IBM programs. The third category consists of reports summarizing and evaluating research of either of the types mentioned above. Included here are articles by Dunnette (1971) and Taft (1959), and symposiums at the annual APA professional meetings, such as those chaired by Finkle in 1963, Kirchner in 1964, and Byham in 1971.

The following are brief summations of the professional reports in the second category above—those on assessment centers:

Bentz, V. J. Validity of Sears assessment center procedures. In W. C. Byham (Chm.), *Validity of assessment centers.* Symposium presented at the American Psychological Association, Washington, D.C., September, 1971. (a)

This paper summarized the development of the Sears Assessment Center Procedures and follow-up efforts to date on three "classes" of management trainees. The program was based on an executive model featuring four generalized areas: use of mental ability, openness to change, administrative skill and decision making, and emotional strength. The procedures were developed through intensive research on a small executive sample that revealed encouraging validity (over 100 significant correlations) for In-Basket, two-group problem-solving simulations and the Sears Executive Battery including the Sears Factored Personality Scale, all in prediction of a wide range of criteria including subjective ratings from personnel directors and immediate superiors, a job (upward) mobility index, and a salary progress index. Follow-up study of the resulting multiple assessment battery provided support (several hundred significant correlations) for many of the predictors when compared with performance judgments based on performance elements and on factor-derived perform-

ance variables—the criterion judgments being formed six months after, twelve months after and, in some instances, between one and two years after, the assessments. These studies are seen as steps in a continuing research program in which the "real validity from the data lies considerably in the future."

Bentz, V. J. The Sears longitudinal study of management behavior. In A. C. MacKinney (Chm.), *Longitudinal approaches in management research: Working examples.* Symposium presented at the American Psychological Association, Washington, D.C., September, 1971. (b)

This paper placed the Sears Assessment Center in perspective with the broader Sears Longitudinal Study of Executive Behavior. The overall study was presented as encompassing the management trainee initial selection process (thirty-nine variables), the data collection during a nine-month formal training program (twenty-one variables), the Assessment Center data (seventy variables) and the career-future stage which includes periodic assessments of job performance (fifty-four variables to date). The sequential sampling of yearly groups of college graduates is expected to permit ready replication, technique refinement, new purposes and even altered project design. Representative findings were reviewed including the factor structure of the In-Basket and of the three Leaderless Group Situations employed in the Assessment Center and significant relationships indicated in several samples between predictors and criteria and across predictors.

Bray, D. W., & Grant, D. L. The assessment center in the measurement of potential for business management. *Psychological Monographs,* 1966, 80 (17).

The assessment process in the Bell System's Management Progress Study and the results of several analyses of the process were discussed. Included were studies of assessment staff evaluations, contributions to the process of selected techniques, and relationships of assessment data to subsequent progress in management. The results, based on 355 young managers, indicated that the assessors' evaluations were influenced considerably by their overall judgments, and also included many intra-individual discriminations; all of the techniques studied made some contribution to the judgments. Situational methods (group exercises and In-Basket) had considerable influence; paper-and-pencil ability tests had somewhat less; personality questionnaires the least. The relationships between assessor judgments and subsequent progress in management, though covering only a relatively short time period, indicated that the assessors' predictions were quite accurate. A complex of personal characteristics was more predictive of progress than any single characteristic; some of the characteristics, however, appeared to have higher relationships to progress than others. The situational methods and paper-and-pencil ability tests were more predictive of progress than the personality questionnaires.

Campbell, R. J., & Bray, D. W. Assessment centers: An aid in management selection. *Personnel Administration,* 1967, 30, 6–13.

This article describes the Bell System Assessment Center Program. It outlines process and rating procedure and reports research evidence in layman's terms. A follow-up on 506 men in this longitudinal study shows high-rated men more likely to be above average after attaining first-line management jobs (68 percent versus 46 percent) and to be viewed as having higher future potential (50 percent versus 31 percent).

Carleton, F. O. Relationships between follow-up evaluations and information de-

veloped in a management assessment center. Paper presented at the American Psychological Association Convention, Miami Beach, 1970.

Based on follow-ups of 122 men going through the Standard Oil (Ohio) assessment program, managers' ratings on thirteen scales were used as a criterion two-and-one-half to five years after the program. Various reports show moderate (high .20s) relationships with managers' behavioral ratings. Higher correlations (.30s and .40s) were found when the predictor was a composite committee report, especially with a later judgment of management potential (.65).

Dodd, W. E., & Kraut, A. I. Will management assessment centers ensure selection of the same old types? *Proceedings of the Annual Convention of the American Psychological Association,* 1970, 5 (Pt. 2), 569–570.

Data collected from 573 sales trainees in 1965–1966 (training ratings and three Gordon personality tests) were correlated with subsequent evidence of management potential (selection to a management assessment program and performance in the program). Those selected for assessment were found to be higher on training ratings and leadership and lower on independence. Only the training ratings and ascendancy were related to assessment performance. Salesmen predicted to do well in assessment but who were not selected were low on conformity. Results are discussed in terms of coordinating early identification of management potential to assessment performance, thereby breaking the hold of conformity on present selection procedures.

Donaldson, R. J. Validation of the internal characteristics of an industrial assessment center program using the multi-trait-multi-method matrix approach. Doctoral dissertation, Case Western Reserve University. Ann

Arbor, Mich.: University Microfilms, 1969, No. 70-5088.

This study of the Sohio assessment program focused on the judgments of the assessment staff, which represent the end products of this assessment process and on the relationship of selected source data to these end products. The assessment staff was separated into two rater groups, managers and psychologists, while the source data were represented by peer raters, self-raters, and test information. The two assessment rater groups and the three types of source data were each thought to measure three proposed assessment dimensions within the FACT program. The results demonstrated that the manager raters and psychologist raters who compose the assessment staff were able to agree upon and discriminate among the three proposed assessment dimensions. The two assessment rater groups were found to use comparable methods, and the assessment dimensions proved to be dependent constructs. The peer rating data, the self-rating data, and the projective test data did contribute to the judgments of the assessment staff. The data suggested that the assessment ratings were more independent of self-rating than they were of peer rating data. Auxiliary analyses revealed that assessment raters' measures of the proposed Basic Intellectual Capacity dimension were reflecting something other than what was being measured by the objective tests.

Finley, R. M. Jr. An evaluation of behavior predictions from projective tests given in the Sohio assessment center. Paper presented at the American Psychological Association Convention, Miami Beach, 1970.

Behavior predictions based on projective tests in Sohio's program were examined for two samples—109 and 119 assessees, respectively. Correlations were high with assessment committee's ratings, but low with later supervisor's judgments. Only three of thirteen traits showed convergent validity in an early sample. Committee ratings also correlated highly with supervisor's rating. Better results for more recent samples were attributed to refined procedures as well as shorter time interval to criterion.

Ginsburg, L. R., & Silverman, A. The leaders of tomorrow: Their identification and development. *Personnel Journal,* 1972, 51, 662–666.

Utilizing a one-day assessment center, the authors compared assessment ratings of thirty-seven administrative personnel in a hospital to their present job performance. Validity coefficients were reported for ratings of dimensions assessed with a median coefficient of .34.

Grant, D. L., & Bray, D. W. Contributions of the interview to assessment of management potential. *Journal of Applied Psychology,* 1969, 53 (1, Pt. 1), 24–34.

Interviews of 348 men from the Management Progress Study were coded and compared with assessment center evaluations. The interview data were found to contribute to assessment center evaluations. Judgments of career motivation and to a lesser extent work motivation and control of feelings appear to have been influenced by the interview information. Judgments of interpersonal skills were reinforced, if not influenced by the interview reports. Several of the interview variables, especially those reflecting career motivation, dependency needs, work motivation, and interpersonal skills were found to be directly related to progress in management.

Grant, D. L., Katkovsky, W., & Bray, D. W. Contributions of projective techniques to assessment of management potential. *Journal of Applied Psychology,* 1967, 51 (3), 226–232.

The contributions of projective techniques to assessment-center staff evaluations and the relationships of projective variables to progress in management were presented. The projective data were obtained by coding reports written by a clinical psychologist from three projective instruments. Analyses of the data showed that the projective reports particularly influenced the assessment staff in rating such characteristics as work motivation, passivity, and dependency. In addition, several of the projective variables were reliably related to progress in management, especially those pertaining to leadership and achievement motivation. The findings clearly indicated that relevant information on managerial motivation was obtained from the projective reports.

Greenwood, J. M., & McNamara, W. J. Inter-rater reliability in situational tests. *Journal of Applied Psychology,* 1967, 51 (2), 101–106.

A study was conducted to determine the degree of inter-rater reliability in situational tests and the relative effectiveness of professional and nonprofessional evaluators in this type of situation. The results indicated that the reliability of observer ratings and rankings was reasonably high in several different situational tests. Of particular significance was the finding that adequate reliability could be obtained from the use of nonprofessional evaluators in business-oriented situational tests.

Hardesty, D. L., & Jones, W. S. Characteristics of judged high potential management personnel: The operations of an industrial assessment center. *Personnel Psychology,* 1968, 21, 85–98.

Two psychologists and three business managers judged the management potential of approximately 180 candidates in the Sohio assessment program. Those

judged high scored significantly higher on various tests (SCAT total, Doppelt Math Reasoning, etc.), sociometric ratings (leadership, general effectiveness), and on various other measures, than those judged low in business potential. Various biographical differences between the high and low groups were presented.

Hinrichs, J. R. Comparison of "real life" assessments of management potential with situational exercises, paper-and-pencil ability tests, and personality inventories. *Journal of Applied Psychology,* 1969, 53, 425–433.

This concurrent validity study questioned whether there might be other less time-consuming and less expensive methods of obtaining as good data as assessment procedures provide. Forty-seven candidates were rated on their assessment center performance. These same men were rated using information (personnel records) already available. Except for ratings on a factor dealing with interpersonal behavior, overall ratings of management potential based on careful review of company records were as highly correlated with assessment center rating scale factors as were overall ratings of management potential based upon the two-day program. Also reported was a moderate concurrent validity ($r = .37$) between assessment program evaluation and relative salary standing as criterion, which contrasted with an insignificant relationship ($r = .10$) between executive ratings and the criterion.

Jaffee, C. L., Bender, J., & Calvert, O. L. The assessment center technique: A validation study. *Management of Personnel Quarterly,* Fall, 1970, 9–14.

Although not conclusive because of small sample size and brief time exposure, this analysis of an assessment program in the Nuclear Division of Union Carbide Corporation showed an encouraging trend supporting the assessment center technique as a dependable tool for inclusion in the total process of selecting new supervisors. In the control group, the supervisors promoted before the assessment center program were, by and large, effective; however, in a few cases, these superiors were considered by some of the individuals interviewed to have some serious weakness. In no case did this type of comment appear in regard to the experimental group.

Keepers, T. D. An investigation of some of the relationships between test protocols and clinical report using a computerized analysis of text. *Dissertation Abstracts,* 1968, 29 (2-B), 771–772.

TAT stories and Sentence Completion tests of sixty assessments done in and for industry were submitted to computerized content analysis along with the psychological reports derived from the above tests over eighty-three conceptual dimensions defined in the "Harvard III Psychological Dictionary." Scores for each conceptual category were derived by dividing the frequency count of use in each document by the length of the document, categories were rank ordered by percentage of use, and correlational comparisons were made between kinds of documents (i.e., S-C versus TAT, S-C versus Report, TAT versus Report, and S-C and TAT versus Report), as well as between the various report writers. Results showed that: (1) Frequent conceptual content in any set of protocols was mirrored by relatively frequent use of the same conceptual content in the report; (2) Different report writers did not show systematic bias; (3) TAT and S-C conceptual content overlap (average $r_s = .49$) in contributing to reports, and analysis suggested that intellectual defenses had a greater chance of being expressed on the S-C; (4) The vocational rather than clinical intent of the reports was evident; and (5) Reports made use of a significant amount of information in the protocols as judged by the correlation between the combined protocols and reports (average $r_s = .62$). This correlation is higher than the one between TAT and Report (average $r_s = .47$) and slightly lower than the correlation between S-C and Report (average $r_s = .66$).

Kraut, A. I., & Scott, G. J. Validity of an operational management assessment program. *Journal of Applied Psychology,* April, 1972, 56 (2), 124–129.

The validity of an assessment program is examined by reviewing the career progress of 1,086 employees in sales, service, and administrative functions after they were assessed. Although participants were nominated on the basis of being promotable, raters found that more than one-quarter were unqualified, and the others were widely differentiated. Ratings were used to move men into first-line management, but the relationship of ratings to first promotions is moderate enough to reduce fears of "crown prince" or "kiss of death" effects. Nor does participation seem to de-motivate these employees. Assessment ratings are substantially correlated with two major criteria, second-level promotions and demotions from first-line management.

McConnell, J. J., & Parker, T. An assessment center program for multi-organizational use. *Training and Development Journal,* March, 1972, 26, 6–14.

This study compared assessment ratings of seventy first-line supervisors to ratings of their present job performance. Subject samples ($N = 70$) included groups from three manufacturing organizations and a bank. Assessment ratings correlated $r = .57$ with job performance ratings for the combined sample. In analyses using fewer subjects, support was also established for test-retest assessment reliability ($N = 21$; $r = .74$) and for the effectiveness of training of line managers to make reliable judgments of traits ($N = 129$; $r_{avg.} = .90$).

Thompson, H. A. Comparison of predictor and criterion judgment of managerial performance using the multi-trait-multimethod approach. *Journal of Applied Psychology,* December, 1970, 54 (6), 496–502.

The multi-trait-multimethod matrix technique was used to examine the predictive validity of ratings of management potential derived from an industrial assessment center program. The subjects were seventy-one professional, technical, and lower level managerial personnel. Psychologists' and managers' ratings on thirteen assessment dimensions were correlated with supervisors' ratings of current job performance on the same dimensions. Ratings obtained of on-the-job performance were lower in quality than the predictor ratings. The median reliability of the criterion ratings was .52 compared to median reliabilities of .85 and .89 for the psychologists' and managers' ratings, respectively. Supervisors failed to differentiate the various dimensions. Results are compared with findings of other studies that used this technique to determine the sources of unreliability in the criterion.

Wollowick, H. B., & McNamara, W. J. Relationship of the components of an assessment center to management success. *Journal of Applied Psychology,* 1969, 53, 348–352.

Reported was a predictive study to determine the validity of assessment programs, and the extent of data they provide beyond that of other sources (paper-and-pencil tests). A subjective over-all rating correlated .37 with criterion of change in position level. However, statistical combination of test scores, exercise scores, and personal characteristic scores yielded slightly higher validities for each than for the subjective rating. Further, combining all three evaluative areas yielded

a multiple R of .62, nearly doubling the criterion variance accounted for. It was concluded that situational exercises significantly improved the prediction over tests alone, and that some statistical method of generating a final evaluation might be superior to the subjective method.

Although the work summarized is commendable as an indication of professional examination, guidance, and contribution, it should be recognized that work of this sort must be pursued on a continuous basis in connection with all assessment programs. Such study may produce new techniques, new knowledge or even new methodologies. Most of it, however, will simply provide the necessary verification that the techniques employed in a particular program do, in fact, function as intended in that circumstance and over time. As uninspiring as this may sound, it is quite critical to the successful future of assessment centers.

As was stated earlier, one of the common characteristics of assessment centers is the appeal this process has for managers. Though quite an asset to those promoting a program, this appeal may be short lived if the substantive value of the program cannot also be demonstrated. Though nonprofessionals may react favorably to the logic and openness of an assessment effort, they will be quick to reject a superficial, invalid approach once its true nature has been revealed.

A final comment on research should be added. The variations in objectives, climate, situational factors, staffing, etc. that characterize assessment center programs should alert professionals themselves to the dangers of universal or overly parsimonious approaches to development, analysis and verification. Reviews of research to date (see Dunnette, 1971) show, fortunately, some adaptation of technique to varying circumstances. But too much may still be done in conventional ways and on conventional problems. A recent paper by Guion (1971) advocates a more constructive verification model along synthetic validity lines and calls also for more study of the actual use of assessment information in organization decisions. Some elaboration on both of these points, variation in research and detailed description of use, is offered by Finkle and Jones (1970).

Feedback to Assessees

Most programs provide for direct feedback to the assessee about the evaluation of his performance at the assessment center. Differences occur, however, in the timing, in who performs the feedback and the manner and detail with which it is conducted. Some programs include feedback to assessees as part of the program itself while others arrange for feedback after formal reports are developed. The former arrangement is almost always handled by management members of the assessment staff; the latter plan may be handled by professional personnel who were associated directly or indirectly with the assessment process. Little has been written about the detail presented in feedback or about training provided those who are to give the feedback. Kraut (1972, 1973) has reported favorable reactions by assessees to assessment as an aid to their self-development. Opinions differ among center administrators on whether assessees should be allowed to read or even be given copies of written results as contrasted with their being given only oral feedback. Arguments favoring the reading or possession of a written report stress fairness and improved communications. Those favoring an oral report feel that an open two-way discussion of each reported judgment constitutes better communication than straight reading and is, therefore, fairer; they argue, too, that a written report can be misused.

As with other phases of assessment, the problem or questions associated with the feedback vary depending upon the purposes of the program. Feedback is, perhaps, more straightforward and less threatening when associated with programs that feature a near-term, go-no-go decision of promotion to a specific job or job level or with programs that stress development. Even then it would seem important to establish structure and training for those providing feedback so that suggestions for development are realistic and assessees do not become subject to well-meaning but uncontrolled and unsophisticated guidance. But when more complex personal characteristics are being reflected with a view to career determination and potential, the need for skilled counselors is even greater. Particularly difficult is the handling of advice and reflection about long-range potential since the person providing feedback may, himself, be unsure of factors critical to long-term success in a particular organization.

Whatever the method, it is seemingly both desirable and important in the eyes of those designing programs to provide open and thorough feedback to the assessees themselves.

Professional Participation and Guidance

Some reflections have already been offered as to the differences across assessment centers in the use of psychologists, or other trained professionals, as participants in the program. A few centers have used professionals only, some have used a mixture of professionals and managers, while many have made no use of professionals at all. These comparisons refer to participation in the assessment process either to generate information or to weigh information to form judgments or, most often, both. Such differences in staffing may be attributed to some of the many variations already discussed, such as purpose of the program, choice of instruments, belief in presence or absence of quality, differences between psychologists and managers, or belief that in a mixture of professional and lay assessors, the latter would be overwhelmed by the former. Then, too, the decision to use or not use professionals in the assessment process may be based on far more pragmatic considerations, such as the number of professionals in or readily available to the organization, the cost of using well-qualified professionals, or the anticipated acceptance of professionals in the organization.

This brings us to the more critical variation among assessment centers with respect to professionals, namely, the extent to which qualified professionals play a significant role in the development and analysis of the program. This chapter has addressed itself to variations on a theme. Upon close inspection, the theme is essentially a popular packaging of previously tried techniques with heavy emphasis on situational activities that permit lay judgments of group and individual behavior. The variations encompass differences in purpose, climate, technique, staffing, training of staff, process of decision making, choice of decisions to be made, method of report, feedback, and use. The technical complexity of this morass of behavioral considerations is extensive. It is fully as broad as the topic of testing. Beyond that, it reflects much of the complexity and uncertainty of performance rating literature and practice and draws rather liberally from even broader areas, such as decision making, change of behavior, management style, and organizational climate. All of these areas have been the objects of study and research by industrial and organizational psychologists (*Annual Review of Psychology*). Though many contributions to understanding and technique have come from these efforts, no claim has been made for a fully supported, comprehensive body of knowledge in any of these subject areas, let alone across them, which might serve as a sound basis for the confident pursuit of assessment goals and practices along clear and proven paths. By contrast, the more one is familiar with applied research and theory in these areas, the more one is aware of the gaps, the inconsistencies, the pitfalls and, in the terms of one writer, the "counter-intuitive" (Forrester, 1971) effects of real life interactions.

The implications of these circumstances for assessment centers are clear. The truths that human behavior is complex, that there are no pat answers, and that even "experts" do not always agree are arguments *for* professional guidance, not against. As tempting as it may appear, the ready availability of group exercises is, in and of itself, hardly a case for a "do-it-yourself" approach to assessment centers any more than the availability of scalpel and suture recommends a "do-it-yourself" approach to brain surgery.

How, then, will professional guidance help? Generally, despite differences in specific training and experience, the professional should bring these things to the assessment center effort: a fuller, more realistic, and more broadly accepted perspective of human behavior; experience with, understanding of, and/or skill in the use and application of testing instruments; an awareness of the need for verification of assumptions and the personal skill, or knowledge of where to obtain assistance in such verification; objectivity and quality of advice born out of professional obligation and reputation. These are solid attributes and should contribute to a sound assessment program well beyond the early favorable reactions attributable primarily to surface appeal. They could easily make the difference between a successful or an unsuccessful effort.

EFFECTS AND CONSEQUENCES

Having reviewed the core concept of assessment centers, the variations associated with their design and operation and the demands placed upon research and verification by these variations, it is important to reflect, at least briefly, on the effects of and reactions to such programs in the organizations in which they are installed. The appeal of the usual assessment program was noted earlier to be one of the universal characteristics of such programs. The openness and surface relevance of the situational exercises and the participation in the judgmental process by managers produce enthusiastic reactions by most who associate with the activity. It seems that few managers who have served as staff contributors fail to describe their experience in positive terms. But, like testimonial reaction to training programs, this form of expression may or may not be an index of lasting benefit received. The attraction to managers of the assessment process may also be explained, at least in part, by the entertainment and change of pace the exposure provides and by the heady experience of manipulating and judging other human beings. The extent to which one company's assessment center gives signs of approaching a standardized cocktail party supports a concern that the process, in the wrong hands, might become little more than a fraternity initiation. A possible effect, seemingly negative, is an enchantment with the process to the exclusion of an acceptance and use of the product of that process in actual manning decisions.

Quite opposite to this is the problem of overuse by some managers in their personnel decisions. By overuse is meant a blind following of assessment data without effort to seek corroboration based on performance records or other available judgments. Whether this tendency stems from a reluctance to make decisions or is due to a strong conviction about the accuracy of assessment information is immaterial; it still represents extreme practice. And as with most extremes, it may have limitations. The most obvious negative is that even if the validity of the assessment judgments is greater than any one other set of judgments, the combination of all available judgments might well be still greater. The difficulty of supporting or refuting this hypothesis does not make it any less pertinent; those making day-to-day decisions must reckon with the likelihood of its validity. A less obvious limitation of an overreliance on assessment information is the possibility that a few errors in judgment attributed without corroboration to the assessment information may greatly overshadow a much larger number of sound judgments made with appropriate reliance on the assessment information. A few glaring errors attributed to the assessment judg-

ments could upset the entire program without a fair reflection on the aggregate improvement in decisions achieved by adding assessment information to that which would otherwise be the sole basis for the decisions.

One effect of establishing an assessment center is the need to assure appropriate controls for the circulation and retention of assessment reports. This need is not, of course, unique to assessment centers since it applies to any form of assessment or appraisal data. Nevertheless, it is also a critical problem for assessment centers.

The party chiefly concerned with the confidential treatment of assessment results is the assessee himself. If the assessees as a group are keenly disturbed by any portion of the assessment program, the life of the program will most certainly be limited as these assessees themselves move into positions of greater impact. The distribution of assessment information to persons not needing it or able to use it as a significant factor in corporate decisions is a clear basis for complaints about invasion of privacy. Few employees claim that taking physical examinations is an invasion of privacy because they are justified in assuming that the information is handled on a need-to-know basis and with professional control. But when personal information is requested and disseminated with little or no evidence of need or of professional control, concerns for invasion of privacy may well arise.

The key to developing appropriate controls for the handling of such information is the identification of the principal type of decision to be made from the information. Programs such as those of the Bell System and Sohio that clearly feature promotion or placement decisions and relegate development to a strictly secondary role make the identification of principal decisions relatively simple. Other programs that reflect multiple use of the information without commitment to priority of use make this identification more difficult. However, with the principal decisions identified as well as possible, the tightest treatment of confidentiality, short of not using the data at all, would seem to be to limit the viewing of assessment reports to those individuals who have significant authority to make the primary decisions. Following this thesis, the best example of who should *not* see the assessment information when it is primarily or exclusively designed for promotion decisions is the assessee's current supervisor since, in most organizations, he produces appraisal input to the decision, but does not make it. Exposing the data to the individual's immediate supervisor may reinforce a paternalistic locking of the assessee to his boss, whereas the assessee, singled out as having stronger than average potential for his peer group, might well move past his boss in the foreseeable future. Even when the primary purpose of the assessment program is development, the present supervisor has a rather limited perspective for advising the assessee in his career development and can contribute to on-the-job development without, or at best with only a selected portion of, the assessment data. Someone at a higher level of management and someone in a staff role representing the corporate development of manpower may well be in a more appropriate position to guide and counsel the assessee in his longer-range corporate development. Controls, then, constitute still another phase of an assessment program that must be tailored to the purpose of, and surrounding conditions associated with, the program.

A final question for consideration of effects that grow out of the adoption of an assessment activity is that of how long the judgments produced in the process should be considered to be valid or appropriate for use. The Management Progress Study of AT&T included a reassessment of the originally assessed participants in the study after eight years and found good evidence for stability in some, but not all, of the characteristics measured in the program (Campbell, 1968; Bray, Campbell, & Grant, 1973). Longitudinal validity studies at Sohio showed, with most variables, similar validities for groups with longer exposures (two to five years) between assessment and field criterion measures, and with shorter exposure (less than two years) between assessment and field criterion measures. These studies provide encouragement for those who seek stability in the variables judged in the assessment process, but do suggest the need for analysis to support or refute a priori assumptions about stability. By contrast, some programs feature developmental objectives. Presumably, these programs assume that styles, characteristics, and skills judged in the program are susceptible to significant change in a desired direction in response to planned efforts. Verification of these assumptions would seem at least as complex and as necessary as when stability is desired, yet studies along these lines have not, to the writer's knowledge, been reported. Finally, what of those programs that claim an essentially balanced dual purpose of helping with placement or promotion decisions and with developmental efforts? Though seemingly paradoxical, certain assumptions can be enunciated to support this dual objective. Promotion decisions might be based on some variables; development decisions on others. Or promotion decisions might be based on near-term use of variables believed, over time, to be receptive to planned, positive change. Whatever the assumptions, however, the verification task becomes more complex but none the less important. These reflections on stability add further support to the argument for sophisticated analysis and consultation.

CONCLUSIONS

The 1960s have seen the evolvement of the assessment center as a model for managerial evaluation and development. The early seventies find rapid, fad-like growth of the application of this model in business and other organizations. The key components of this model, derived from early and continued activities at AT&T, are assessment in groups, assessment by groups, and use of multiple techniques with emphasis on situational exercises. In most organizations, the model has been welcomed by management. Despite the common characteristics, many basic differences characterize the content and application of assessment center programs. Among these are: form and climate of the organization or organization component in which the center is established; purpose or purposes of the program; choice of assessees; choice and training of assessors; choice of techniques; choice of characteristics to be measured or judged; methods of collecting, weighting, and recording data; preparation, style, and use of reports; research conducted and reported; and professional guidance provided. The volume of reported research on assessment centers has been encouraging although most of it has been addressed, thus far, to four programs—AT&T, Sohio, IBM, and Sears, with the principal contributor being the Bell System. This research and subsequent reviews of it have featured analyses of the data-generation process and of the data itself, possibly to the exclusion of examining the use and value of the data in organizational decision making. Furthermore, the reporting of and summarization of this research, as even in this chapter, under the generic caption of "assessment centers," permits and fosters the inference that there is a professionally endorsed entity worthy of purchase, rental, or trial by organizations believing themselves to have any or all of the multifarious needs to which various assessment center programs have been addressed. Despite the popular common label, there is no such entity but only a variety of programs, each of which must be evaluated in the context of its own objectives and circumstances.

With variations outweighing the theme, with research endorsing several programs but perhaps suggesting an entity that is more superficial than real, with activities subsumed under the label "assessment centers" clearly covering a whole gamut of complex behavioral sub-disciplines—with these conditions amid the growing signs of faddish commercialism, the most critical factor in further applications would clearly seem to be the need for continued close, qualified, professional guidance and ad hoc verification and control. And yet, given such professional attention, the "theme" concepts of the assessment center package can, and hopefully will, emerge as helpful and much needed input to critical organizational manpower decisions.

REFERENCES

Albrecht, P. A., Glaser, E. M., & Marks, J. Validation of a multiple assessment procedure for managerial personnel. *Journal of Applied Psychology,* 1964, 48, 351–360.

Anastasi, A. *Psychological testing.* (3rd ed.) New York: Macmillan, 1968.

Annual Review of Psychology. Palo Alto, Calif.: Annual Reviews, Inc.

Bass, B. M. The leaderless group discussion. *Personnel Psychology,* 1954, 7, 470–477.

Bender, J. M. What is "typical" of assessment centers? *Personnel,* July-August, 1973, 50, No. 4.

Bentz, V. J. The Sears experience in the investigation, description, and prediction of executive behavior. In F. R. Wickert & D. E. McFarland (Eds.), *Measuring executive effectiveness.* New York: Appleton-Century-Crofts, 1967, Chapter 7, 147–205.

Bentz, V. J. Validity of Sears assessment center procedures. In W. C. Byham (Chm.), *Validity of assessment centers.* Symposium presented at the American Psychological Association, Washington, D.C., September, 1971. (a)

Bentz, V. J. The Sears longitudinal study of management behavior. In A. C. MacKinney (Chm.), *Longitudinal approaches in management research: Working examples.* Symposium presented at the American Psychological Association, Washington, D.C., September, 1971. (b)

Bray, D. W. The assessment center method of appraising management potential. In J. W. Blood (Ed.), *The personnel job in a chang-*

ing world. New York: American Management Association, 1964. (a)

Bray, D. W. The management progress study. *American Psychologist,* 1964, 19, 419–420. (b)

Bray, D. W., & Grant, D. L. Situational tests in assessment of managers. *Management games in selection and development.* Proceedings of The Executive Study Conference, May 5–6, 1964. Princeton: Educational Testing Service, 1964, 121–138.

Bray, D. W., & Grant, D. L. The assessment center in the measurement of potential for business management. *Psychological Monographs,* 1966, 80 (17).

Bray, D. W., Campbell, R. J., & Grant, D. L. *The management recruit: Formative years in business.* New York: Wiley-Interscience, 1973.

Buros, O. K., Ed. *The fifth mental measurements yearbook.* Highland Park, N.J.: Gryphon, 1959.

Buros, O. K., Ed. *Tests in print.* Highland Park, N.J.: Gryphon, 1961.

Byham, W. C. The uses of assessment centers. Unpublished paper presented at Spring, 1969 meeting of The Executive Study Conference, 1969.

Byham, W. C. Assessment center for spotting future managers. *Harvard Business Review,* July-August, 1970, 150–160, plus appendix.

Byham, W. C. (Chm.) Validity of assessment centers. Symposium presented at the meeting of the American Psychological Association, Washington, D.C., September, 1971.

Byham, W. C., & Thornton, G. C. III. Assessment centers: A new aid in management selection. *Studies in Personnel Psychology,* 1970, 2 (2), 21–35.

Campbell, D. T., & Fiske, D. W. Convergent and discriminant validation by the multitrait-multimethod matrix. *Psychological Bulletin,* 1959, 56, 81–105.

Campbell, J. T. et al. Assessments of higher-level personnel: I through VII. *Personnel Psychology,* 1962, 15 (1, 2, 3, 4).

Campbell, R. J. Career development: The young business manager. Paper presented at the annual meeting of the American Psychological Association, San Francisco, 1968.

Campbell, R. J., & Bray, D. W. Assessment centers: An aid in management selection. *Personnel Administration,* 1967, 30, 6–13.

Carleton, F. O. Relationships between follow-up evaluations and information developed in a management assessment center. Paper presented at the American Psychological Association Convention, Miami Beach, 1970.

Cronbach, L. J. *Essentials of psychological testing.* (2nd ed.) New York: Harper and Row, 1966.

Development Dimensions, Inc. *Catalogue of assessment and development exercises.* Pittsburgh: Development Dimensions, Inc., 1973.

DiCostanzo, F., & Andretta, T. The supervisory assessment center in the Internal Revenue Service. *Training and Development Journal,* 1970, 24(9), 12–15.

Dodd, W. E., & Kraut, A. I. Will management assessment centers ensure selection of the same old types? *Proceedings of the Annual Convention of the American Psychological Association,* 1970, 5 (Pt. 2), 569–570.

Donaldson, R. J. Validation of the internal characteristics of an industrial assessment center program using the multi-trait-multimethod matrix approach. Doctoral dissertation, Case Western Reserve University. Ann Arbor, Mich.: University Microfilms, 1969, No. 70-5088.

Dunnette, M. D. Multiple assessment procedures in identifying and developing managerial talent. In P. McReynolds (Ed.), *Advances in psychological assessment,* Vol. II. Palo Alto, Calif.: Science and Behavior Books, 1971.

Finkle, R. B. (Chm.) Multiple approach assessment programs. Symposium presented at the annual meeting of the American Psychological Association, Philadelphia, August, 1963.

Finkle, R. B., & Jones, W. S. *Assessing corporate talent: A key to managerial manpower planning.* New York: Wiley-Interscience, 1970.

Finley, R. M. Jr. An evaluation of behavior predictions from projective tests given in the Sohio assessment center. Paper presented at the American Psychological Association Convention, Miami Beach, 1970.

Flanagan, J. C., Fiske, D. W., Bass, B. M., Carter, L. F., Kelly, E. L., & Weislogel, R. L. Situational performance tests: A symposium. *Personnel Psychology,* 1954, 7, 461–498.

Forrester, J. W. Counter-intuitive behavior of social systems. *Technology Review,* Alumni Association of the Massachusetts Institute of Technology, 1971, 73 (3).

Frederiksen, N., Saunders, D. R., & Wand, B. The in-basket test. *Psychological Monographs,* 1957, 71 (9), (Whole No. 438), 28 pages.

Ginsburg, L. R., & Silverman, A. The leaders of tomorrow: Their identification and development. *Personnel Journal,* 1972, 51, 662–666.

Grant, D. L., & Bray, D. W. Contributions of the interview to assessment of management potential. *Journal of Applied Psychology,* 1969, 53 (1, Pt. 1), 24–34.

Grant, D. L., Katkovsky, W., & Bray, D. W. Contributions of projective techniques to assessment of management potential. *Journal of Applied Psychology,* 1967, 51 (3), 226–232.

Greenwood, J. M., & McNamara, W. J. Interrater reliability in situational tests. *Journal of Applied Psychology,* 1967, 51 (2), 101–106.

Guion, R. M. A research model for managerial selection. Paper presented at the meeting of the International Congress of Applied Psychology, Liège, Belgium, July, 1971.

Hardesty, D. L., & Jones, W. S. Characteristics of judged high potential management personnel: The operations of an industrial assessment center. *Personnel Psychology,* 1968, 21, 85–98.

Hilton, A. C. et al. The validity of personnel assessments by professional psychologists. *Journal of Applied Psychology,* 1955, 39, 287–293.

Hinrichs, J. R. Comparison of "real life" assessments of management potential with situational exercises, paper-and-pencil ability tests, and personality inventories. *Journal of Applied Psychology,* 1969, 53, 425–433.

Hollander, E. P. Buddy ratings: Military research and industrial implications. *Personnel Psychology,* 1954, 7, 385–393.

Hollander, E. P. The reliability of peer nominations under various conditions of administration. *Journal of Applied Psychology,* 1957, 41, 85–90.

Jaffee, C. L., Bender, J., & Calvert, O. L. The assessment center technique: A validation study. *Management of Personnel Quarterly,* Fall, 1970, 9–14.

Keepers, T. D. An investigation of some of the relationships between test protocols and clinical report using a computerized analysis of text. *Dissertation Abstracts,* 1968, 29(2-B), 771–772.

Kirchner, W. K. (Chm.) In-company experiences with multiple-approach executive assessment programs: Theory versus reality. Symposium presented at the meeting of the American Psychological Association, Los Angeles, September, 1964.

Kraut, A. I. A hard look at management assessment centers and their future. *Personnel Journal,* May, 1972, 317–326.

Kraut, A. I. Management assessment centers in international organizations. *Industrial Relations,* 1973, 12, No. 2.

Kraut, A. I., & Scott, G. J. Validity of an operational management assessment program. *Journal of Applied Psychology,* April, 1972, 56 (2), 124–129.

Laurent, H. Early identification of managers. *Management Records,* May, 1962, 33–38.

Lopez, F. M. Jr. Evaluating executive decision making: The in-basket technique. *AMA Research Study 75.* New York: American Management Association, 1966.

McConnell, J. H. The assessment center in the smaller company. *Personnel,* 1969, 46 (2), 40–46.

McConnell, J. J., & Parker, T. An assessment center program for multi-organizational use. *Training and Development Journal,* March, 1972, 26, 6–14.

Mayfield, E. C. The selection interview: A reevaluation of published research. *Personnel Psychology,* 1964, 17, 239–260.

Murstein, B. I., Ed. *Handbook of projective techniques.* New York: Basic Books, 1965.

Office of Strategic Services (OSS) Assessment Staff. *Assessment of men.* New York: Rinehart, 1948.

Psychological Corporation. *The Psychological Corporation test catalog.* New York: 1971.

Roadman, H. E. An industrial use of peer ratings. *Journal of Applied Psychology,* 1964, 48, 211–214.

Science Research Associates, Inc. *Test and management tools.* Chicago: 1971.

Slevin, D. P. The assessment center: Breakthrough in management appraisal and development. *Personnel Journal,* April, 1972, 51, 255–261.

Taft, R. Multiple methods of personality assessment. *Psychological Bulletin,* 1959, 56, 333–352.

Thompson, H. A. Comparison of predictor and criterion judgment of managerial performance using the multi-trait-multimethod approach. *Journal of Applied Psychology,* December, 1970, 54 (6), 496–502.

Thornton, R. F. Situational tests for management selection. *Management games in selection and development.* Proceedings of The Executive Study Conference, May 5–6, 1964. Princeton: Educational Testing Service, 1964, 89–105.

Ulrich, L., & Trumbo, D. The selection interview since 1949. *Psychological Bulletin,* 1965, 63, 100–116.

Wagner, R. The employment interview: A critical summary. *Personnel Psychology,* 1949, 2, 17–46.

Weitz, J. Selecting supervisors with peer ratings. *Personnel Psychology,* 1958, 11, 25–35.

Whyte, W. H. Jr. *The organization man.* New York: Simon and Schuster, 1956.

Wollowick, H. B., & McNamara, W. J. Relationship of the components of an assessment center to management success. *Journal of Applied Psychology,* 1969, 53, 348–352.

CHAPTER 21

Conflict and Conflict Management[1]

KENNETH THOMAS
University of California, Los Angeles

A BALANCED VIEW of conflict is emerging in the literature which recognizes that conflict can have constructive or destructive effects, depending upon its management. To aid in conflict management, two general models of conflict are synthesized from the literature—a process model and a structural model. The process model focuses upon the sequence of events within a conflict episode, and is intended to be of use when intervening directly into the stream of events of an ongoing episode. The structural model focuses upon the conditions which shape conflict behavior in a relationship, and is intended to help in restructuring a situation to facilitate various behavior patterns. The chapter concludes with some general observations on the state of the conflict literature.

INTRODUCTION

Conflict, like power, is one of those fascinating but frequently abused and misunderstood subjects. Like any potent force, conflict generates ambivalence by virtue of its ability to do great injury or, if harnessed, great good. Until recently, social scientists have been most aware of conflict's destructive capability—epitomized by strikes, wars, interracial hostility, and so on. This awareness seems to have given conflict an overwhelming connotation of danger and to have created a bias toward harmony and peacemaking in the social sciences. However, a more balanced view of conflict seems to be emerging. More and more, social scientists are coming to realize—and to demonstrate—that conflict itself is no evil, but rather a phenomenon which can have constructive or destructive effects depending upon its management.

In this chapter, I have tried to assemble a body of theory which will be helpful in managing industrial and organizational conflict, and I have attempted to put that theory into a coherent and understandable form.

[1] I wish to thank Dave Jamieson for his able help in reviewing the conflict literature, and Ralph Kilmann and the members of the Human Systems Development Study Center, UCLA, for their comments on an earlier draft of this paper. Portions of this work were supported by UCLA and the Division of Research of the Graduate School of Management, UCLA.

Specifically, I have surveyed the conflict literature for relevant concepts, hypotheses, and findings, interpreted that material in the context of my own theoretical framework, and integrated that material into two complementary models of conflict. Where there were appreciable gaps in those assembled models, I have also filled in with hypotheses of my own.

The literature relevant to industrial and organizational conflict is in need of integration. Much of this literature is specialized according to organizational arena—for example, the interface between union and management, between superior and subordinate, between different departments, and so on. This situation makes it difficult for students, theorists, and practitioners specializing in one area to benefit from the concepts and models of other areas. Moreover, there is a great deal of research outside the boundaries of organizations which has yielded concepts and insights of great potential relevance to the study of conflict in organizational settings. This research, from experimental gaming, small group research, social conflict, international relations, etc., is also largely specialized and unintegrated.

It is presumed here that the dynamics underlying conflict behavior in one area will be relevant to conflict in other areas. This assumption was spelled out in an editorial of the first issue of the *Journal of Conflict Resolution* (1957, p. 2):

Many of the patterns and processes which characterize conflict in one area also characterize it in others. Negotiation and mediation go on in labor disputes as well as in international relations. Price wars and domestic quarrels have much the pattern of an arms race. Frustration breeds aggression both in the individual and in the state. The jurisdictional problems of labor unions and the territorial disputes of states are not dissimilar. It is not too much to claim that out of the contributions of many fields a general theory of conflict is emerging.

This chapter, then, will focus upon material which appears relevant to conflict phenomena in all arenas of organizations.

Definition of Conflict

Before proceeding any farther, it is important that conflict be defined. In the behavioral sciences, the word "conflict" has no single, clear referent. When used by psychologists, the word often denotes incompatible response tendencies within an individual. For example, ambivalence may be called "approach-avoidance conflict" (Levinger, 1957). Likewise, the term may be used to mean role conflict—competing response tendencies within an individual stemming from the requirements of different roles which he occupies (Kahn et al., 1964).

In this chapter attention will be restricted to the type of conflict which occurs *between* social units. These social units may be individuals, groups, or organizations. Moreover, the discussion will be restricted to conflict between *two* social units, which will be referred to as "dyadic conflict." Conflict phenomena between more than two units involves the formation of coalitions, and the discussion of such "political" behavior is outside the scope of this chapter.[2]

Even with such restrictions, however, there is no consensus among researchers on a specific definition of "conflict." A painstaking review of conflict literature conducted by Fink (1968) revealed a large number of divergent usages, including fourteen different criteria for simply distinguishing conflict from competition! Within the organizational conflict literature, Pondy (1967) likewise found a number of divergent specific definitions ranging over objective conditions, emotions, perceptions, and behavior. Rather than attempt to argue that one of these specific definitions was really conflict, Pondy recommended that "conflict" be used in a generic sense to include all these phenomena.

Taking a cue from Pondy, then, I shall

---

[2] The reader interested in coalitions should refer to Gamson (1964) and Caplow (1968). Perhaps the most well-known study of coalitions in organizational politics was reported by Dalton (1959).

adopt a more general working definition of dyadic conflict. Dyadic conflict will be considered to be a *process* which includes the perceptions, emotions, behaviors, and outcomes of the two parties. Specifically, in order to differentiate conflict processes from other processes, I shall say that conflict is the process which begins when one party perceives that the other has frustrated, or is about to frustrate, some concern of his.[3] Later in the chapter, this definition will be further developed into a process model of dyadic conflict. Meanwhile, however, it should be pointed out that this working definition includes a wide variety of phenomena, since a party may be frustrated by actions ranging from intellectual disagreement to physical violence.

Effects of Conflict

As was mentioned earlier, attitudes toward conflict appear to have shifted over the past twenty or thirty years. The human relations movement, with its emphasis upon the personal and organization costs of conflict, implied that conflict was to be avoided or eliminated (Kelly, 1970; Litterer, 1966; Baritz, 1960). There is now a more general recognition that interpersonal and intergroup conflict often serves useful functions.[4]

Some recurrent themes in discussions of positive effects of conflict are as follows:

First, a moderate degree of conflict may not necessarily be viewed as a cost by the parties involved. Theories of motivation are shifting from notions of tension reduction to the view that organisms tend to maintain optimal levels of stimulation (Allport, 1953; Hunt, 1963; Driver & Streufert, 1964). It is increasingly recognized that too little stimu-

[3] The noun "party" and the pronoun "him" will often be used in this chapter to denote a social unit involved in a conflict. These terms are used for convenience, and are not intended to limit the discussion to individuals.

[4] For example, this view has recently been expressed by sociologists (Coser, 1956; Van Doorn, 1966), psychologists (Schmidt & Tannenbaum, 1960; Blake & Mouton, 1964; Deutsch, 1971; Hoffman et al., 1962), economists (Boulding, 1964), and organization theorists (Pondy, 1967; Thompson, 1960; Litterer, 1966).

lation or tension (boredom) may be as unpleasant to a person as an excess of it. Under conditions of low tension, people may welcome or seek out the novelty of divergent opinions, the challenge of competition, and at times, the excitement of overt hostilities. Deutsch (1971, p. 48) mentions that conflict stimulates interest and curiosity, and that "conflict is often part of the process of testing and assessing oneself and, as such, may be highly enjoyable as one experiences the pleasure of full and active use of one's capacities."

Second, the confrontation of divergent views often produces ideas of superior quality. Divergent views are apt to be based upon different evidence, different considerations, different insights, different frames of reference. Disagreements may thus confront an individual with factors which he had previously ignored, and help him to arrive at a more comprehensive view which synthesizes elements of his own and others' positions. The ideology of the university has long stressed the importance of the free exchange of ideas in the pursuit of knowledge. In a study of medical researchers, Pelz (1956) found that researchers who discussed their work with colleagues of different orientations were more likely to be high performers. Hoffman (1959; Hoffman & Maier, 1961) found that groups composed of members with different interests tended to produce higher quality solutions to a variety of problems than did homogenous groups. On the basis of a number of his own group decision-making studies, Hall (1971, p. 88) concluded that "conflict, effectively managed, is a necessary precondition for creativity."

Third, aggressive behavior in conflict situations is not necessarily irrational or destructive. Rapoport (1966) identified two basic models of international conflict which also appear to describe alternative views of conflict in organizations. According to the first model, the participants in a conflict fall under the influence of strong nonrational forces which push the parties toward increasingly destructive behavior. Viewed in this way, conflict resembles a dangerous disease which should be suppressed. Janis and Katz (1959) point out that the majority of past research on intergroup and interpersonal conflict has focused upon its destructive aspects, helping to promote this view. According to the second model, however, conflict behavior is the instrumental, goal-oriented behavior of two largely rational parties. As such, the parties remain in greater control of the situation, and the outcome need not be destructive.

Indeed, the aggressive pursuit of apparently conflicting goals by two parties may well lead to constructive outcomes. March and Simon (1958, p. 129) and Litterer (1966) state that such conflict tends to initiate a search for ways of reducing the conflict. Since one party's gains are not necessarily another party's losses, two parties actively seeking to improve their own conditions may thus succeed in finding new arrangements which benefit them both (Follett, 1941). In a very real sense, such new arrangements constitute progress for the parties and for the organization. Viewed from this perspective, the suppression of conflict may have the effect of impeding progress and maintaining the status quo (Van Doorn, 1966).

A few useful side effects of conflict have also been noted. Litterer (1966) noted that conflict within an organization may call attention to systemic problems which require change. Hostility between groups also tends to foster internal cohesiveness and unity of purpose within groups (Coser, 1956; Blake & Mouton, 1961). Finally, power struggles often provide the mechanism for determining the balance of power, and thus for adjusting the terms of a relationship according to those realities (Coser, 1956).

Recognition of useful consequences of conflict, of course, does not mean that conflict is regarded as intrinsically good instead of intrinsically bad. The destructive consequences of conflict in organizations are well known. What does seem to be emerging is a more balanced view of conflict which recognizes cost and benefit, danger and promise.

With the recognition that conflict can be both useful and destructive, the emphasis has shifted from the elimination of conflict to the *management* of conflict. The goal of conflict management has been variously stated as keeping conflicts productive or at least not destructive (Deutsch, 1971, p. 53), or as keeping conflicts creative and useful (Kahn & Boulding, 1964, p. 76).

Conflict Models

The shift in emphasis from the elimination of conflict to conflict management requires a more discriminating understanding of conflict phenomena. In order to manage conflict, we must understand what sort of conflict behavior is most likely to lead to constructive outcomes and which behaviors tend to be either unproductive or destructive. Then we must begin to identify the variables which influence the occurrence of those behaviors, so that we can develop productive intervention strategies and tactics.

The remainder of the chapter will be spent developing two models of dyadic conflict—a process model and a structural model. Together, the two models are my attempt to integrate and build upon some of the insights in the conflict literature. Both models focus upon the conflict-handling behavior of the conflict parties, and both models attempt to understand that behavior. However, in reviewing the literature, it became apparent that researchers attempt to "understand" conflict phenomena in different ways—hence the two models.

PROCESS MODEL. One form of research attempts to understand conflict phenomena by studying the internal dynamics of conflict episodes. Here the objective is commonly to identify the events within an episode and to trace the effect of each event upon succeeding events. From this perspective, conflict is very much an ongoing process. I have, therefore, referred to the model which incorporates this sort of research as a "process model" of conflict.

To illustrate the focus of the process model, let us examine a hypothetical conflict episode between Sales and Production department supervisors:

Sales has promised a customer an early delivery date on a given item. When informed of this during a meeting, the Production supervisor feels frustrated because that delivery date would throw off his whole production schedule. He has carefully planned his schedule in order to maximize the productive capacity of his equipment. Perceiving that covering Sales' promise is incompatible with the efficiency of his own department, the Production supervisor attempts to make the Sales supervisor change the promised delivery date. Annoyed at this response, and disturbed by the idea of disappointing the customer, the Sales manager resists this influence attempt and tries to convince the Production manager to meet the delivery date. In the resulting discussion, both parties become more hostile and argumentative. The meeting adjourns, leaving the two parties deadlocked.

In examining this episode, the process model is concerned with identifying events —for example, the frustration of one party, his conceptualization of the situation, his behavior, the reaction of the other party, and the final agreement or lack of agreement. Having identified those events, the model is then concerned with the influence of each event upon the following events—for example, how did each manager's conceptualization of the issue influence his behavior, how does one manager's behavior influence the other's, and how is the form of the final agreement influenced by their behavior?

This sort of knowledge would tend to be helpful in influencing an ongoing episode. Knowing what effects one's own behavior would have upon others would help a party manage the behavior which occurs during an episode. Knowing the likely effects of behavior upon outcomes would help the party steer interaction toward a desirable outcome. Such knowledge would presumably be of use to the two principal parties as well as to third parties—mediators, arbitrators, supervisors, committee chairmen, etc.

STRUCTURAL MODEL. Other research attempts to understand conflict phenomena by studying how underlying conditions shape events. Here the objective is to identify parameters which influence conflict behavior, and to specify the form of that influence. Because these conditions or parameters are relatively fixed or slow changing, I have referred to the model which incorporates this research as a "structural model" of conflict.

As a means of illustrating the focus of the structural model, let us examine the relationship between the Sales and Production managers with a view toward identifying the underlying variables which shape the parties' behavior:

Negotiations between the department heads are largely confined to biweekly meetings convened by the vice president of operations. This procedure shapes the behavior of both parties —complaints accumulate and smolder until meeting time; and the formality of the meeting and the presence of their boss minimizes risk taking. At the same time, the boss's presence provides a resolution mechanism which is sometimes utilized when they deadlock: his arbitration provides an alternative to continuing power struggles. Formal rules and past agreements by the two parties eliminate conflicts on issues which are unambiguously covered by those rules and agreements. However, because of the abundance of rules, disagreements which do occur tend to be win-lose issues over the interpretations of those rules. Social pressures from other parties help to keep the competition from escalating uncontrollably, although the prevailing organizational norms do not encourage problem solving. The Production manager tends to be somewhat more competitive and hostile than the Sales manager. This difference is partly due to the Production manager's personality: he is an older, up-from-the-ranks manager who fought his way through the Depression. However, competitive behavior by both department heads is encouraged by the members of their departments, each of which has come to view the other department as an enemy. Underlying many of the issues which arise between the two department heads is some very real conflict of interest stemming from tight performance indices and tightening organizational resources. Both parties have high stakes in these issues.

In examining this relationship, the structural model is concerned with identifying the pressures and constraints which bear upon the parties' behavior—for example, social pressures, personal predispositions, established negotiation procedures and rules, incentives, and so on. Furthermore, the structural model attempts to specify the effects of these conditions upon behavior—for example, in what way do peer pressures influence behavior, how does frequency of interaction influence conflict behavior, and how do various personal motives shape one's conflict behavior?

This understanding of structural influences would tend to be helpful in altering variables to produce long-run changes in conflict-handling behavior in a situation: Personnel may alter hiring or promotion policies to favor more collaborative individuals, incentive schemes may be changed, new rules made, new meeting procedures instituted, etc.

NEED FOR BOTH MODELS. Having identified and differentiated these models, something needs to be said about their interrelationship. First, the two models complement each other. The structural model tends to be useful for suggesting systemic changes, while the process model tends to be helpful in managing an ongoing system. The structural model suggests long-run improvements in relationships, while the process model helps one cope with crises. And so on. Both models, and the tactics which they suggest, are necessary for effective conflict management.

Secondly, the two models are presented separately for convenience and because they seem to reflect somewhat different research literatures. In reality, of course, they fit together into one larger view of conflict structure and process. The structural variables constrain and shape the process dynamics, while knowledge of the process dynamics helps one predict the effects of structural variables.

PROCESS MODEL OF DYADIC CONFLICT

The first model to be developed is the process model, which identifies and examines the events within a conflict episode. Pondy (1967) and Walton (1969) note that conflict in a dyadic relationship tends to occur in cycles. Pondy refers to a given conflict cycle as an episode. Within a relationship, each episode is partially shaped by the results of previous episodes and in turn lays the groundwork for future episodes.

The process model of dyadic conflict to be developed in this chapter is shown in Figure 1. This model depicts five main events within an episode from the viewpoint of one of the parties: frustration, conceptualization, behavior, other's reaction, and outcome.

Briefly, the episode is produced by the party's experiencing of frustration, present or anticipated, to the realization of one of his goals. If the experienced frustration is dealt with consciously, the party will then conceptualize the situation. This is the point at which the conflict becomes salient to the party. In Walton's terms, the conflict becomes defined as an "issue."

Based largely upon his conceptualization of the situation, the party then engages in behavior vis-à-vis the other party to cope with the situation. "Behavior" is used here in a general sense so as to include avoidance or withdrawal as well as more assertive behaviors.

The other party then reacts to this behavior. The loop in Figure 1, between behavior and conceptualization, represents

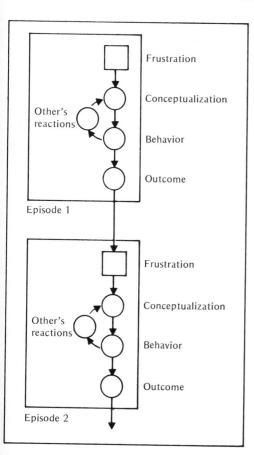

Figure 1. Process model of dyadic conflict episodes.

the effects upon the party of the other's reaction to his behavior. The party's initial behavior may initiate a more or less prolonged interaction between himself and the other. Each party's behavior serves as a stimulus for the other's response. During the course of this interaction, each party's conceptualization of the conflict issue may change, affecting his behavior accordingly.

When the interaction on a given issue stops, some sort of outcome has occurred. Depending upon the preceding behaviors, this outcome might take various forms— joint agreement, domination by one party, joint avoidance of the issue, unresolved disagreement, etc. In Walton's terms, the outcome has "consequences" for both parties.

Pondy (1967) speaks of these consequences as the "conflict aftermath."

The outcome of a given episode sets the stage for subsequent episodes on the same issue. Specifically, the outcome is likely to determine the degree to which the goals of the two parties continue to be frustrated, and thus the likelihood that the experienced frustration will provoke another interchange in the future.

Let us now consider the events in the model in more detail.

Frustration

Conflicts appear to stem from one party's perception that another party frustrates the satisfaction of one of its concerns. The word "concern" is used here as a blanket term to include more specific concepts like needs, desires, formal objectives, and standards of behavior. In the literature, conflicts have been traced to a variety of such concerns. For example, status concerns have been linked to conflict in interpersonal relations (Whyte, 1948), interdepartmental relations (Seiler, 1963), and union-management relations (Walton & McKersie, 1965). Autonomy concerns have been shown to produce conflicts in relations between supervisors and subordinates (Argyris, 1957), as well as between departments (White, 1961). Other cited concerns involve formal objectives, promotion, scarce economic resources, behavioral norms and expectations, compliance with rules and agreements, values, and various interpersonal needs.

Just as concerns vary widely, frustrating behaviors take a number of forms. Conflict episodes might stem from: disagreement, denial of a request, violation of an agreement, insult, active interference with performance, vying for scarce resources, breaking a norm, diminishing one's status, ignoring one's feelings, etc.

Conceptualization

The next event in the process model of conflict involves the party's conceptualization of the situation. As will be discussed, this appears to involve a definition of the conflict issue in terms of the concerns of both parties plus some notion of possible action alternatives and their outcomes.[5] The process model considers how particular conceptualizations influence conflict-handling behavior, and how escalation and other changes in behavior stem from changes in a party's conceptualization.

The element of subjective reality appears to be crucial in understanding and influencing a party's conflict-handling behavior. As Allport said, "The way a man defines his situation constitutes for him its reality" (1955, p. 84). Deutsch (1969) argues that there is no necessary relationship between the "objective" characteristics of the situation and a party's conflict behavior, elaborating a number of ways in which subjective reality intervenes. However, surprisingly little psychological theorizing and research appear to have been done on the conceptualization of conflicts by the parties involved.

DEFINING THE ISSUE. The first element in a party's conceptualization of a conflict situation is his definition of the issue involved. Operationally, this appears to involve some assessment of the primary concerns of the two parties—the party's own frustrated concern and his perception of the concern which led the other party to perform the frustrating action. For example: "I want a raise, but my boss wants to reduce departmental expenditures"; "The union wants an additional sixteen cents, but management prefers to give twelve cents"; "I want to receive

more air time during meetings, but so does the Marketing vice president."

A party in a given conflict situation may define the issue in a number of ways. There is no one "objective" issue, but rather a series of possible definitions. Three dimensions of a party's definition of a given issue seem relevant here: egocentricity, insight into underlying concerns, and the "size" of the issue. These three dimensions appear important in terms of their influence upon the party's subsequent conflict-handling behavior.

"Egocentricity" refers to defining the issue solely in terms of one's own concerns. For example, "We need another maintenance man, but the maintenance supervisor won't lend us one," or "The union wants another sixteen cents an hour, but management doesn't want us to have it." The contrasting mode is the appreciation of the other party's own concern. For example, "We need another maintenance man, but the maintenance supervisor needs him for another project"; or "The union wants another sixteen cents an hour, but management would prefer to invest that money in new equipment." This distinction has not been developed in the literature, but would appear to be important. Specifically, an egocentric definition of a conflict issue fails to recognize the other party's concern and makes subsequent cooperation less likely.

Related to egocentricity, but more general, is a party's insight into underlying concerns. At one extreme, a party may think only in terms of the specific issue contested: "My boss wants me to adopt a new form for my weekly reports, but I prefer the old one." By contrast, the party may instead identify more basic concerns which are responsible for both parties' stands. For example: "I can't afford the time required to complete the new, longer form, but my boss needs information which wasn't on the old form." Several theorists have pointed out that the appreciation of underlying concerns increases the likelihood that a solution can be reached which satisfies those concerns for both parties (Follett, 1941; Deutsch, 1969; Walton, 1969).

---

[5] This "conceptualization" need not be a thoughtful analysis. Party may respond habitually, or "without thinking," in many situations. In these instances, however, we can still think of Party as behaving in accordance with "performance programs" which have been evoked by the situation (March & Simon, 1958, pp. 139–142). These programs are in effect conceptualizations based upon past experiences with similar situations. However primitive, these programs contain a definition of the situation and salient alternatives.

Follett (1941) referred to such solutions as "integrative" solutions. Using the current example, for instance, defining the issue in the second manner may suggest the possibility of a shorter form which focuses upon the information most useful to the boss.

Identifying underlying concerns may be difficult, however. Eisinger and Levine (1968) maintain that such concerns are often unconscious in labor-management relations. Walton (1969) points out that personal or "emotional" concerns are often viewed as less acceptable than more "substantive" concerns in organizations. As a result, these concerns may be unrecognized by the parties involved, but may be expressed by bringing up more substantive and acceptable issues. Walton (1969) refers to these substantive issues as "umbrella issues," while Schutz (1958) calls them "goblet" issues. The underlying concerns have sometimes been referred to as "hidden agendas" (e.g., Stagner & Rosen, 1965). Without identifying emotional concerns, these goblet issues may appear particularly mystifying and difficult to resolve. Muench (1960, 1963) used a clinical psychological approach to help identify underlying issues in union-management negotiations.

The notion of "size" of an issue was developed by Fisher (1964). Fisher noted that wars tend to be fought over large issues, and conversely that large issues are difficult to resolve short of war. His recommendation for conflict management was, therefore, a form of "issue management"; namely, the "fractionation" of large issues into smaller ones:

The danger inherent in big disputes and the difficulty of settling them suggest that, rather than spend our time looking for peaceful ways of resolving big issues, we might better explore the possibility of turning big issues ... into little ones. (Fisher, 1964, p. 92)

Fisher identified five aspects of the size of an issue: the parties on each side, the immediate physical issue, the immediate issue of principle, the substantive precedent which settlement will establish, and the procedural precedent which settlement will establish. Regarding the parties, for example, a grievance might be regarded as between a worker and his supervisor, between the local union and the company, or between organized labor and big business. Concerning the immediate physical issue, a supervisor and his subordinate might discuss the subordinate's substandard performance on a given task, poor performance on a number of tasks, or the general quality of the subordinate's work. Regarding principle, Sales and Manufacturing might simply discuss whether to sacrifice a production schedule for the sake of a last minute customer order, or they might invoke the principles of customer service versus efficiency. Substantive precedent is increased when the parties decide they are "going to settle this thing once and for all." Procedural precedent becomes involved when the parties become concerned that they not establish a pattern of yielding to demands. The upshot of Fisher's discussion, then, is that conflicts are most easily resolved when they are defined as occurring between the people directly involved, are limited to a single concrete issue, are not treated as matters of principle, and are considered as isolated instances to be weighed on their own merits.

SALIENT ALTERNATIVES. The second aspect of a party's conceptualization of the conflict situation is his awareness of action alternatives and their outcomes. By "action alternatives" is meant the possible final actions of conflict episodes which represent dispositions of the conflict issue—a maintenance supervisor dispatches an additional maintenance man, a union is granted an additional five cents an hour, etc. A given party, being less than omniscient, is assumed to be aware of a relatively small set of alternatives in the conflict situation at any given time (Simon, 1957), which we shall call the set of his "salient" alternatives. The party is also assumed to have some notion of the probable outcomes of these salient alternatives for both parties—specifically, the degree to which the concerns of both parties would be satisfied. These salient alternatives, together with their probable outcomes for both parties, determine the party's view of the conflict of interest between himself and the other party.

It appears useful here to introduce the joint outcome space as a format for representing the party's conceptualization of alternatives and their outcomes.[6] Figure 2

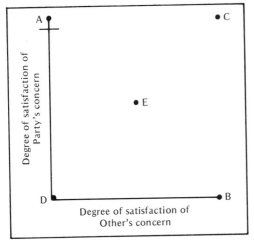

Figure 2.   The joint outcome space.

represents Party's conceptualization of the joint outcome space for himself and Other. The horizontal and vertical axes represent the degree to which the Party perceives that Other's concern and Party's concern, respectively, would be satisfied by a given alternative. Point *C* represents an alternative which is seen as satisfying the concerns of both parties. Point *D* represents relatively complete frustration of both parties' concerns. At Point *A,* Party satisfies his concern while

Other is frustrated; while the opposite is true at Point *B.* Point *E* represents an alternative which yields some, but incomplete, satisfaction to both parties.

When Party's set of salient alternatives deviates from Point *C,* he is assumed to be aware of conflict of interest between himself and Other.[7] Because no alternative is perceived which allows both parties to simultaneously satisfy their concerns, Party perceives that each represents an obstacle to the other's satisfaction.

Again, researchers have noted that a party's perception of conflict of interest is to some extent independent of the objective situation. For example, Blake et al. (1964, p. 31) refer to the win-lose "assumption," and Walton and McKersie (1965, p. 19) suggest that "The fact that certain items often become the subject of distributive bargaining is explained as much by a party's perception as by the inherent nature of the agenda item." In the present case, a party's definition of a conflict issue is asserted to influence the type and degree of conflict of interest which he perceives by suggesting different patterns of alternatives. The four modal patterns shown in Figure 3 will be considered.

Figure 3a depicts an "either/or" conceptualization of a conflict issue. Here, conflict of interest is total: the only outcomes seen are total satisfaction and total frustration and each party's satisfaction is seen as occurring at the expense of the other. This conceptualization is referred to by Blake et al (1964) as "win-lose," and is an example of what Hayakawa (1963) termed "the two valued orientation." Such a conceptualization might be suggested by defining an issue egocentrically, "Either I get *X* or I don't,"

[6] The joint outcome space was used by Galtung (1965) and is common in the bargaining literature (Luce & Raiffa, 1957). Payoff matrices provide an alternative representation of conflict situations (Walton & McKersie, 1966; Thibaut & Kelley, 1959) and are used extensively in the two-person experimental game literature. The joint outcome space is used in the current instance because patterns of outcomes are easier to visualize.

[7] There exists no agreed upon unambiguous definition of conflict of interest. Bergström (1970) has discussed some of the ambiguities in the concept. Axelrod (1967) developed axiomatically a measure of conflict of interest using the joint outcome space. However, he assumed continuous alternatives and a convex range of outcomes—assumptions which appear unjustified in terms of the perceptions of many conflict parties.

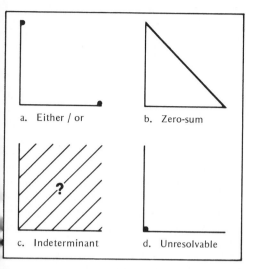

Figure 3.   Patterns of conflict of interest.

or in terms of a specific point of contention, "Whether or not we do Y." Such phrasings admit of only two possibilities. Either/or conceptualizations are also likely under conditions of high stress and strong ego involvement. Under high stress, new alternatives are unlikely to be perceived (Osgood, 1961) and parties' conceptualizations of the situation tend to become simpler (Schroder et al., 1967; Walton, 1969). With increasing ego involvement in a position, parties tend to reject intermediate positions and to associate them with the opposing position (Sherif & Hovland, 1961), leading to a polarized either/or view of alternatives.

The zero-sum conceptualization in Figure 3b is similar, but less extreme. This conceptualization is somewhat more sophisticated than the previous one—the party has identified a dimension rather than two points. For example, the issue may now involve the amount of time or money spent on a new product line, rather than the decision of whether or not to develop it. Or the issue may now involve allocation of responsibility for a past event, rather than deciding who was to blame and who was innocent (Gragg, 1964). Here, a range of intermediate settle-ments are recognized as possibilities—compromises between the preferred alternatives of the two parties. Some degree of satisfaction is seen as simultaneously possible for both parties, although increases in one party's satisfaction are still at the expense of the other.

In the "indeterminant" conceptualization in Figure 3c, the party's definition of the issue does not imply a specific set of alternatives. Such a conceptualization is apt to be the result of defining the issue in terms of the underlying concerns of the two parties. For example, in a dispute between sales and production, the issue may be defined as quickness of delivery versus efficient utilization of production facilities. Because there is no a priori relationship between these two concerns, finding alternatives becomes an empirical matter. If the party is optimistic (Blake et al., 1964) he may seek to identify integrative alternatives. If so, what was formerly a distributive issue may be rephrased as an integrative problem (Walton & McKersie, 1965), namely, "How can we furnish quick delivery without sacrificing production efficiency?"

Figure 3d represents a party's conceptualization of an unresolvable issue. Such a conceptualization might stem from not understanding an issue well enough to cope with it, from defining conflicts in terms of big, unresolvable issues (Fisher, 1964), or from the perception that both parties are unalterably attached to their positions. Unresolvable issues are depicted as frustrating to both parties. Although neither party is seen as gaining at the other's expense, strong conflict of interest remains in the sense that each party is seen as an obstacle to the other's satisfaction.

To sum up the material on conceptualization, then, it has been asserted that Party's conceptualization of a conflict situation is a critical, and often ignored, influence upon his behavior. In a given situation, it is possible for Party to define a conflict issue in a number of different ways. Different definitions suggest issues of different "size" or importance to Party, giving him different stakes in a conflict. In addition, each definition suggests a different pattern of salient alternatives and outcomes, which may in turn produce a markedly different perception of the conflict of interest present in the situation. As we shall see later, Party's perception of stakes and conflict of interest have an important influence upon his behavior.

Behavior

Following frustration and conceptualization, the third event in the process model involves the party's conflict behavior. In this section, we shall consider three components of behavior—orientation, strategic objectives, and tactics—and the determinants of each. Since the distinction among these three entities is frequently overlooked in the literature, let's consider a familiar example. Clyde and Lucille have a reasonably successful marriage. Both have basically collaborative orientations toward important issues which come up between them; they like each other and try to resolve issues so that both parties are satisfied. However, on one particular afternoon, a crucial professional football game is on TV at the same time as a rerun of Lucille's favorite Sinatra movie. Although they would like to collaborate, each regretfully perceives a conflict of interest. And because the preferred program is important to each, both Clyde and Lucille attempt to see their own program. (Their strategic objective on this issue is to win.) Accordingly, each adopts various mild tactics which they think may bring the other around—reading favorable reviews in the newspaper, citing the importance of their program, appealing to a sense of fairness, and so on. To be sure, orientation, strategic objectives, and tactics are interrelated. However, they are to some extent independent since they respond in part to different variables. The collaborative orientation is partly a response to their mutual identification, while the competitive strategic objectives are partly a response to the perceived conflict of interest, and the

tactics are partly shaped by each party's knowledge of the other. All three sets of influences are important in understanding the resulting behavior.

ORIENTATION. The model categorizes a party's orientation on the basis of the degree to which he would like to satisfy his own concern and the degree to which he would like to satisfy the concern of the other. Figure 4 uses the joint outcome space to plot five such orientations—competitive, collaborative, avoidant, accommodative, and sharing —together with their preferred outcomes. Although the names and conceptualizations are somewhat different, this categorization scheme stems most directly from the work of Blake and his colleagues (Blake & Mouton, 1964; Blake et al., 1964; Hall, 1969).

Before discussing the orientations in Figure 4 individually, some comments on the complexity of this scheme are in order. A five-category scheme is obviously more complicated and difficult to master than a dichotomous differentiation like cooperative-uncooperative. The latter is appealing in its simplicity and is still used extensively in the

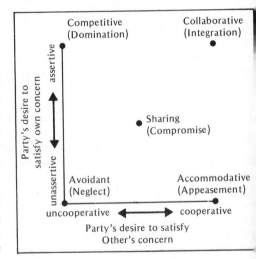

Figure 4. Five conflict-handling orientations, plotted according to Party's desire to satisfy own and Other's concerns.

experimental game approach to conflict research. However, the cooperative-uncooperative dichotomy appears to greatly oversimplify the more complex range of options available to the conflict party.

A stronger case can be made for the present two-dimensional scheme. The cooperative-uncooperative distinction represents one dimension which might accurately reflect the thinking of Party's opponent: "Does he want to cooperate and help me satisfy my concerns, or doesn't he?" However, a different distinction is more likely to be reflected in the thinking of Party and his constituents, namely, "Does Party actively strive to achieve his own concerns, or doesn't he?" Both distinctions in fact reflect important dimensions which are analytically independent: the degree to which one attempts to satisfy the other's concern and the degree to which one assertively pursues one's own concerns.

A great deal of unnecessary sacrifice or competition seems to stem from confusing these two dimensions or reducing them to a single dimension. When cooperation is assumed to be in opposition to pursuing one's own concerns, cooperation comes to mean sacrifice, and asserting one's needs; ("standing up for one's rights") comes to mean putting up a fight.

Returning to the five orientations in Figure 4, the competitive orientation represents a desire to win one's own concerns at the other's expense, namely, to dominate. In the context of labor relations, Donnelly (1971, p. 373) refers to relationships which are based upon this orientation as "conflict" relationships: "...both parties desire to exercise whatever legal bargaining power they have in a given situation. No quarter is yielded...." Blake et al. (1964) refer to such relationships as "win-lose power struggles."

By contrast, an accommodative orientation focuses upon appeasement—satisfying the other's concerns without attending to one's own. Under such an orientation, a party may be generous or self-sacrificing for the sake of their relationship. Donnelly refers to relationships in which this orientation is common as "accommodation" relationships: "...long-run motives center around the desire for agreement." Blake et al. refer to this pattern as "peaceful coexistence." Interestingly, Follett (1941) did not explicitly consider this orientation, but revealed her attitude toward it when she referred to being "mushy" during negotiations.

The sharing orientation is intermediate between domination and appeasement. It is a preference for moderate but incomplete satisfaction for both parties—for compromise. Party gives up something and keeps something. Horse-trading in union-management negotiations reflects this orientation (Patten, 1970). Blake et al. refer to this orientation as "splitting the difference," since Party seeks an outcome which is intermediate between the preferred outcomes of both parties.

In contrast to sharing, the collaborative orientation represents a desire to *fully* satisfy the concerns of both parties—to integrate their concerns. Donnelly describes collaborative union-management relationships as "cooperative": "Neither party is interested in the exercise of advantage; rather, both parties are seriously intent upon reaching a mutually beneficial agreement." Blake et al. (1964) and Walton and McKersie (1965) refer to collaborative orientations as "problem solving" orientations.

The remaining orientation, avoidance, reflects indifference to the concerns of either party. Blake et al. describe this orientation as an instance of withdrawal, isolation, indifference, ignorance, or reliance upon fate. The words "evasion," "flight," and "apathy" have also been used to describe this orientation. Stagner and Rosen (1965) have discussed the prevalence and consequences of this orientation in the work setting.

Let us now consider the cooperative dimension in Figure 4 in more detail. Karen Horney's (1945) categorization of interpersonal behavior into movement toward, against, and away from the other appears relevant here. Cooperation involves movement toward the other—attempts to satisfy other's concerns. Collaboration and accommodation are certainly cooperative in this regard. By contrast, competition and avoidance are uncooperative, involving movement against and away from the other, respectively. Sharing is moderately cooperative, since it contains a limited amount of movement toward the other as well as a limited amount of competitive movement against. Thomas's (1971) findings seem to support this classification. In a study of interdepartmental relations, managers rated their peers on a number of items, including conflict-handling behaviors and measures of cooperativeness. Ratings of cooperativeness varied negatively with ratings of behavior associated with competition and avoidance, and positively with behavior associated with collaboration and accommodation.

The cooperativeness of Party toward Other is to a large extent a function of his identification with Other. Party's identification may range from positive identification through indifference to hostility. Attention to Other's satisfaction through collaboration or accommodation appears to be a manifestation of identification. If two parties have agreed upon important issues in the past or agree on common ends, then they may feel sufficient goodwill toward each other to approach disagreement cooperatively. An uncooperative orientation, on the other hand, may stem from indifference to the other's outcomes or from a desire to injure the other. In the former case, frustration of the other's concern is an incidental by-product of Party's motives: the conflict remains impersonal (Coser, 1956) or "object-centered" (Fink, 1968). In the latter case, however, intended frustration is part of Party's motivation. The conflict is personalized or "opponent-centered," and competition and avoidance may constitute aggression for its own sake (Dollard et al., 1939; Berkowitz, 1962).

The second dimension in Figure 4, assertiveness, was referred to by Blake et al. (1964) as the active-passive dimension. It represents the extent to which Party is interested in satisfying his own concerns.[8] The assertiveness of Party's orientation is in part a result of the strength of Party's concern, or what Blake et al. (1964) call Party's "stakes" in the conflict. The most assertive orientations, competition and collaboration, require the greatest immediate outlay of energy—to compete and problem-solve, respectively. Hence, they require some degree of commitment to one's concern. By contrast, avoidance and accommodation require less energy —Party has only to do nothing or go along with Other. In matters of little import to Party, he is, therefore, apt to drift into avoidance or accommodation. Sharing is intermediate in assertiveness and energy expenditure.

STRATEGIC OBJECTIVES. As the discussion shifts to strategies and tactics, it will be useful to think about the joint outcome space in still another way—as composed of an integrative and a distributive dimension.[9] (See Figure 5.) Any point (outcome) in the space can be thought of as having an integrative and a distributive component. The integrative component is, roughly speaking, the total amount of satisfaction for both parties. The distributive component is the proportion of that satisfaction going to each party. In other words, the integrative dimension represents the size of the pie available to both parties; the distributive dimension represents the way they divide it up.

Party can be thought of as having some notion of what is feasible along both of these dimensions. His notion of the degree of integration possible is implied by his conceptualization of the issue, namely, the

_____

[8] This dimension corresponds to the instrumental meaning of "aggressiveness" used by Storr (1968)—attempting to overcome obstacles to one's satisfaction. I have not used this term here because the word "aggression" has unfortunately been restricted by most psychologists to denote intentionally injurious behavior.

[9] Although they did not explicitly use the joint outcome space, the terms "integrative" and "distributive" were used by Walton and McKersie (1965).

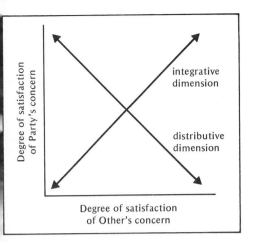

Figure 5. Integrative and distributive dimensions in the joint outcome space.

type and degree of conflict of interest which is present. His assessment of the power and commitment of Other influences what he can hope for along the distributive dimension (Donnelly, 1971).

In the process model, these notions of feasibility interact with Party's preferred outcomes (orientation) to result in some sort of strategic objective. For example, if Party would prefer domination but finds his opponent strong, he may decide to aim for a compromise of some sort. No matter what his preferences, if Party conceptualizes the issue as unresolvable, he is likely to settle for no decision. If Party prefers integration and has an indeterminant conceptualization of the issue, he may search for an integrative solution. And so on.

TACTICAL BEHAVIOR. An exhaustive treatment of specific tactics is beyond the scope of this chapter. Space does not permit consideration of tactics for avoiding issues, appeasing Other, or striking equitable compromises.[10] Rather, attention will be restricted to competitive and collaborative

[10] See Blake and Mouton (1964) for a discussion of these tactics in the interpersonal context and Blake et al. (1964) for their equivalents in the intergroup context.

tactics—distributive tactics intended to increase one's own satisfaction at Other's expense, and integrative tactics intended to increase joint satisfaction. These are the tactics which have received most attention in the literature. They are also the tactics most likely to occur on issues which are important to a party.

First, let us consider competitive tactics. These tactics come in a number of forms because Party may have a variety of power bases which can be used to influence Other. French and Raven (1959) identified six such bases of power: information power, referent power, legitimate power, expert power, coercive power, and reward power. The use of these power bases in conflict situations is discussed by Raven and Kruglanski (1970). Briefly, Party uses information power competitively when he furnishes information to convince Other that Party's preferred alternative should be chosen. This may involve selective or misrepresentative information (Walton & McKersie, 1965) and may degenerate into win-lose arguing (Blake & Mouton, 1964). Party uses referent power by appealing to Other's attraction to Party. Legitimate power, which depends upon accepted rules or principles of proper behavior, is especially relevant in formal organizations: supervisors may "pull rank" on subordinates, the union may appeal to contract clauses, etc. Expert power is used when Party uses any superior knowledge which Other may attribute to Party: "Take my word for it—I know about these things." Coercive power is based upon threats of punishment—strikes, lockouts, sabotage, withdrawal of cooperation on other issues, etc. Finally, Party uses reward power by promising rewards if Other complies—cooperation on later issues, promotions, etc.

Walton and McKersie (1965) lump together the competitive use of these tactics under the heading of "bargaining." Assume that each party has a preferred outcome or "target" along the distributive dimension. Then, paraphrasing Walton and McKersie, Party's competitive use of the above tactics is intended to serve one or more of the following tactical purposes: (1) to make Party's target appear acceptable to Other: "It wouldn't really be so bad for you"; (2) to convince Other that his target is not worth insisting upon: "You wouldn't really be happy with that anyway, and besides it would cost you to hold out for it"; (3) to present Other's target as unacceptable to Party: "Under no circumstances could I settle for X"; and (4) to persuade Other that it is worthwhile to Party to hold out for his target: "I'm willing to stay here all night."

Bargaining stances vary in intensity from "hard bargaining" through "soft bargaining" (Walton & McKersie, 1966), depending upon how much one demands and the risks one is willing to take. In moderately strong form, however, bargaining tactics include some characteristic behaviors which have important consequences. First, Party withholds or misrepresents information—the strength of his concern, his preferences for various alternatives, the consequences of alternatives for himself and Other, and so on. This misrepresentation and rationing of information reduces the trust level between parties. Secondly, Party commits himself to his preferred alternative, reducing flexibility and effectively redefining an issue as winlose. And thirdly, Party may employ threats. Such coercive tactics tend to produce hostility or negative identification toward Party (Raven & Kruglanski, 1970).

Collaborative tactics, called "problem-solving" tactics by Walton and McKersie, involve quite different behaviors. Essentially, problem-solving tactics are designed to increase joint gain by finding alternatives which satisfy the concerns of both parties. Walton and McKersie identify three steps in the problem-solving process: (1) identifying the essential or underlying concerns of both parties, (2) searching for alternatives and identifying their consequences for both parties, and (3) identifying the alternative which is most jointly satisfying.[11]

The specifics of these problem-solving steps will not be considered here. The interested reader should consult Walton and McKersie (1965) or Blake et al. (1964). However, some general characteristics of problem-solving tactics are important here. First, effective problem solving requires the candid exchange of *accurate* information—Party's underlying concerns, his assessment of the probable outcomes of various alternatives, and his satisfaction with those probable outcomes. Second, problem solving requires a flexible, exploratory stance—to redefine issues in the light of new insights, to search for and be open to new alternatives, and to explore their consequences. And last, such behaviors require trust in Other—trust that Other is giving accurate information, trust that Other will not exploit Party's flexibility, and trust that Other will not use his knowledge of Party's preferences to his own bargaining advantage.

It is apparent that bargaining and problem-solving tactics tend to interfere with each other (Walton & McKersie, 1966). Bargaining tends to reduce the trust, candor, and flexibility required for problem solving. Likewise, the disclosures made during problem solving and the positive affect generated by it tend to discourage subsequent misrepresentation and bargaining.

Interaction

The fourth phase of the process model involves interaction. Party's behavior is viewed as initiating a sequence of behaviors from the two parties. Again considering events from Party's viewpoint, Other's behavior is seen as influencing Party's behavior in a number of ways.

The discussion of interaction which follows will examine that process from two different perspectives. First, Party's behavior will be portrayed as strongly influenced by

---

[11] Follett (1941, p. 36) stressed a preliminary step: "The first step ... is to bring the differences into the open." This is the confrontation step which precedes problem solving proper. Problem solving is referred to as confrontation by Lawrence and Lorsch (1967), although it seems that interpersonal confrontation might also be a first step in a bargaining stance.

a number of psychological dynamics which are triggered by Other's behavior. This perspective, which is widespread in the psychological literature, focuses upon the "reactive" aspects of Party's behavior. To balance the picture somewhat, attention will then shift to the more self-conscious efforts of the parties to manage the conflict between them.

DYNAMICS OF ESCALATION/DE-ESCALATION. During the course of negotiations with Other, Party's orientation, strategic objectives, and tactics may change as a reaction to Other's behavior. For example, Party's orientation may change when the stakes change or when Other's behavior alters Party's identification with him; Party's strategic objectives may change with his perceptions of Other's power and the degree of conflict of interest between them; and Party's tactics may change to reflect his trust and respect for Other.

Such changes are frequently described in terms of the escalation/de-escalation dimension. Escalation usually denotes an increase in the level of conflict, however that term is defined. Escalation might involve: increasing the number or the size of issues disputed, increasing hostility between parties, increasing competitiveness, pursuing increasingly extreme demands or objectives, using increasingly coercive tactics, and decreasing trust.

This section will cover eleven dynamics which occur during negotiations. Most of these refer to the dynamics of escalation and de-escalation. As such, they have special relevance for mediators and for other third parties who are concerned with conflict management.

1. The first dynamic involves the concept of revaluation. Follett (1941) maintained that parties rarely actually give in to their opponents. Instead, agreements usually accompany changes in a party's conceptualization of an issue. Coming into conflict with Other and hearing Other's arguments may lead Party to "revaluate" his definition of the issue and his preferred alternative. For example, revaluation may occur when Party realizes that his preferred alternative has undesirable consequences for other important concerns. Marketing may stop pressing for short lead times on an order when they learn that such lead times would force Production to neglect other important orders; Management changes its position when it realizes that its preferences would be counter to existing regulations; and so on. While it may occur under any circumstances, revaluation is facilitated by open communication, trust, and the use of persuasive rather than coercive tactics—in short, by collaboration and problem solving.

2. Self-fulfilling prophesies (Merton, 1957) are common in conflict phenomena. The behavior Party receives from Other is to some extent a response to Party's *own* behavior. Walton and McKersie (1965) hypothesized that problem solving tends to encourage problem solving responses and that bargaining tends to elicit bargaining responses. Deutsch (1949) hypothesized the same for cooperation and competition. In the context of interdepartmental relations, Thomas and Walton (1971) found that managers reported using tactics which were similar to those they saw the other party using: forcing was related positively to Other's forcing, and negatively to Other's candor and accommodation; candor was related positively to Other's candor, and negatively to Other's forcing and avoiding. The upshot of this is that Party's orientation toward the other and his trust or distrust toward Other have some tendency to be reinforced by generating the predicted behavior in Other—regardless of the other's original orientation.[12] For example, if a foreman sees a union steward as competitive and, therefore, fights him on every issue, he may actually prod the steward into fighting.

---

[12] In the experimental gaming literature, players' tactics have been found to correlate highly with the tactics of their opponents (Rapoport & Chammah, 1965). Kelley and Stahelski (1970) found that competitive game behavior elicited responses from *cooperatively* oriented subjects which made the latter appear to have a competitive orientation—even to neutral observers.

Likewise, if a subordinate avoids confronting his boss because he believes the boss would not respond to his needs, the boss, in his ignorance of his subordinate's needs, will not respond to them.

3. A number of biases occur in Party's perceptions of Other. To begin with, Party is largely unaware of Other's motives. Party is familiar with the reasons behind his own actions, since he has planned them himself. But since he is not usually privy to Other's thinking, the reasons behind Other's behavior are often unknown. His own actions, therefore, appear quite reasonable to him, while the behavior of Other often appears arbitrary. What he sees as a necessary move on his part might be seen as an arbitrary and unjustified attack if made by the other party. For example, Defense Department statements frequently contrast the enemy's "arbitrary acts of aggression" with our own "protective reactions." In addition, Party is selective in his perception of Other's behavior. Depending upon his level of trust or suspicion toward Other, he looks for different things (Deutsch, 1969). If suspicious, he is vigilant for signs of threat, competition, hostility, and conflict of interest —which he is then more likely to find. With this bias, he underestimates the commonalities between parties (Blake & Mouton, 1961) and may miss the other's cooperative overtures and signs of goodwill.

4. Another source of bias stems from cognitive simplification. We have already noted that cognitive simplification may result in a win-lose conceptualization of issues. Here, we are more concerned with Party's perception of himself and Other. Party's perceptions tend to become more black-white under stress, threat, and ego involvement; but some of these simplifications also fulfill Party's need for cognitive consistency or dissonance reduction (Osgood, 1961; Festinger, 1964). As these simplifications occur, Party is less able to simultaneously see good and bad qualities in himself or Other—Party becomes good in all respects while Other becomes bad. Blake and Mouton

(1961) have demonstrated these distortions in intergroup conflict. To some extent these distortions increase the stakes for Party because he is defending good against evil, and he accordingly becomes more righteous. In addition, Party's identification with Other diminishes as Other becomes less likable. The extreme case of such distortions occurs in holy wars, where defenders of the faith righteously butcher infidels. But a significant amount of these distortions also occurs across bargaining tables, between departments, and elsewhere in organizations.

5. Communication is the medium through which Party's misperceptions can be corrected: Other's communications may lead Party to revaluate his own position, to recognize Other's actual orientation and to revise his stereotype of Other. However, communications tend to become distorted with perceived conflict of interest or with competitive behavior (Raven & Kruglanski, 1970). Trust is diminished as either party uses communications to manipulate or coerce the other or as either party becomes suspicious that the other is doing so. With diminished trust, Other's communications cease to be believed or even listened to, and Party concentrates on getting his own message across. In the context of labor relations, Stagner and Rosen (1965) referred to such communication patterns as the "dialogue of the deaf." After a while, as communication attempts prove fruitless, communications channels cease to be used at all (Deutsch & Krauss, 1962), and both parties may communicate only through their actions.

6. Breakdowns in communications enable both parties to develop and maintain their distorted views of each other and to feed their mutual hostility. Newcomb (1947) used the term "autistic hostility" to describe hostility which develops in the absence of communication, and went on to develop the thesis that persistent hostility varies with the degree to which a party's perception of a relationship "remains autistic, its privacy maintained by some sort of barriers to communication" (p. 69). At the extreme,

political assassinations may be performed by parties whose autistic and withdrawn personalities enable them to fantasize their targets as devils and themselves as heroes; and army morale (largely dependent upon hostility) is maintained by preventing fraternization with the enemy.

7. As hostility and distrust increase, Party's tactics tend to become coercive (Raven & Kruglanski, 1970). Each of the remaining bases of Party's power tends to disappear with increasing hostility. Information power becomes ineffective as Other becomes suspicious of Party and ceases to listen to him. Expert power becomes ineffective with Other's mistrust and lack of respect. Party has no referent power, or has *negative* referent power when Other ceases to identify with him. Party's legitimate power becomes ineffective when Other sees him acting arbitrarily. Even reward power may become ineffective when Other views gifts from Party as tainted or as bribes. As Party perceives that these types of influence are ineffective, he tends to fall back upon coercive power—threatening various unfavorable consequences for Other if Other does not comply with Party's preferences: "I've tried to be reasonable with you, but that's over now. If you don't do X by Wednesday . . . you'll have to pay the consequences."

8. After competing with Other to satisfy his initial concern, Party may lose sight of his initial concern and simply compete with Other for its own sake. This phenomenon has been called goal substitution or goal displacement. Party's objective becomes beating Other, even if it means sacrificing some of his own concerns. Party may see himself as saving face, getting even, teaching Other a lesson, showing Other he can't get away with it, etc. Like the battered fighter, his satisfaction comes from being able to say, "You ought to see the other guy."

9. Competition between the parties may spread to other issues. This "proliferation" of issues is discussed by Walton (1969) and Deutsch (1969). New issues (or revived old issues) become opportunities for Party to "seize the high ground" (Walton, 1969) in his ongoing struggle with Other: "While we're on that subject, how about the time *you* did such and such." We may find that the parties bicker over issues that they would otherwise have no trouble resolving, and take apparently unreasonable positions merely to oppose the other.

10. As this competitiveness spreads and is accompanied by cognitive simplification, Party may perceive that the basic concerns of the two parties are generally incompatible. At this point, it may appear to Party that the relationship cannot continue: "This organization isn't big enough for the both of us." And Party may try to drive Other away: Production tries to eliminate Maintenance as a separate department, one politician demands another's resignation, management tries to destroy a union, etc.

11. Where substantial hostility and cognitive simplification exist, Walton (1969) notes that the parties must ventilate their feelings to each other and state the issues which divide them before they can begin to seek an integrative solution. In his terms, a "differentiation" phase precedes the integration phase. Ventilating feelings, or "getting it off your chest," produces a catharsis (Dollard et al., 1939) for Party—a reduction in hostility toward Other. In order for catharsis to occur, however, Other must listen to Party's negative feelings. If Other ignores them or counters with abuse toward Party, Party's hostility toward Other will increase. If both parties succeed in ventilating their feelings to each other, the reduced hostility will remove some of the tendencies toward cognitive simplification, allowing the parties to develop a more balanced perception of themselves and the issues. As the parties appreciate similar interests and positive characteristics in each other, the succeeding integration phase may even involve considerable positive feelings: "You know, he's not really such a bad guy."

CONFLICT MANAGEMENT IN THE DYAD. So far, the conflict behavior of two interacting parties has been considered as a reaction to events and conditions, and as influenced by emotional and cognitive forces largely beyond their control. Although the parties to a conflict *are* responsive to a number of such forces, this view of conflict phenomena is incomplete and misleading. In the remaining part of this section, attention will be given to the manner in which parties, during interaction, manage their own conflict behavior.

As mentioned earlier, the view that conflict parties are the pawns of external forces is widespread in the literature (Rapoport, 1966). Probably the most notorious example involves Richardson's (1960) mathematical model of an arms race, in which the rate of armament of each side responds to the other's armaments.[13] The model implies that nations, under many circumstances, will engage in continually escalating arms races. Richardson (p. 12), however, qualified his model by saying: "The equations are merely descriptive of what people would do *if they did not stop to think*" (italics mine).

During interaction, parties *do* stop to think about the consequences of their actions. However, there has been very little research to tell us when, how, and to what extent. As Janis and Katz (1959) noted, social science researchers have tended to focus upon the destructive tendencies in human conduct—perhaps because, like the news media, we find destruction more eye-catching.

Walton et al. (1966) had expected interdepartmental relationships between Sales and Production to polarize toward either collaboration or competition. They reasoned that relationships which combined both would be unstable, since bargaining behavior tends to encourage more bargaining behavior and to discourage problem solving, while problem solving would likewise encourage more problem solving and interfere with bargaining. In a study of six interdepart-

_____
[13] Richardson's model is reviewed by Rapoport (1966) and Patchen (1970).

mental relationships, however, they found that those relationships were spread over the collaborative-competitive dimension, with two in the mid-range. Clearly, one possible explanation is that at least some of those managers had stopped to think about the consequences of competitive behavior and had managed the degree of competition in their relationships.

Within the literature, there is some recognition that conflict parties may anticipate both the long-run and short-run consequences of their behavior. Donnelly (1971) points out that union and management bargaining teams can be viewed as having long-term goals as well as short-run objectives, and that they may restrict their exercise of bargaining power in accordance with those long-term goals. For example, in what Donnelly refers to as the "aggressive" type of relationship, both parties seek the upper hand over the long haul, but also accept the organizational security of the other. Hence they compete, but do not allow competition to escalate to the point of endangering the other's existence. In the "accommodation" relationship, the parties recognize that bargaining power may shift from issue to issue, and adopt the long-term objective of maintaining agreement or harmony. Accordingly, they drastically limit the use of any bargaining power which might create hostility and endanger that long-term harmony.

A party's anticipation of the short-run consequences of his behavior upon the other is a major part of the Walton and McKersie (1965) model of labor negotiations. In that model, Party engages in three types of tactics toward Other—distributive tactics, integrative tactics, and "attitudinal structuring" tactics. In attitudinal structuring, Party uses his knowledge of the effects of his behavior to shape Other's trust, hostility, and orientation during negotiations. The tactics may involve behavior which is unrelated to the issue at hand, such as compliments, expressing common interests, discussing common friends, and so on. However, attitudinal structuring tactics may also involve Party's integrative and distributive tactics. Specifically, since distributive tactics (bargaining) interfere with positive attitudinal structuring, Party may moderate his bargaining tactics in order to maintain Other's trust, identification, and cooperation.

Bales (1950) appeared to recognize that moderating one's competitiveness is often a tactic intended to promote positive interpersonal sentiments in groups. In his process rating system, the Interaction Process Analysis, Bales included passive acceptance and compliance (accommodation) as a positive social-emotional response rather than a task response. Compromise could likewise be included in that category.

Outcome

The final event in the process model is the outcome of the conflict episode. When interaction between the parties ceases, some outcome has occurred, whether it is an explicit agreement of some sort or a tacit agreement to let the issue drop. In this section, some of the short-run consequences of these outcomes will be briefly considered. Then the discussion will shift to some of the longer-run outcomes of Party's behavior for Party, for Other, and for the organization which includes them both.

CONFLICT AFTERMATH. The outcome of a specific conflict episode involves more than a substantive agreement. There are residual emotions—frustration from the new agreement, and hostility or mistrust stemming from the other party's behavior during negotiations. There may also be stereotypes, perceptions of incompatibility, long-term goals concerning the other, and so on. All of these constitute what Pondy (1967) termed the "conflict aftermath." The elements of this aftermath set the stage for subsequent episodes between the parties.

All of these short-term consequences will not be discussed in detail here. Many are simply instances of dynamics we have already covered. One set of consequences does

seem important, however—the effects of the form of the substantive agreement upon subsequent episodes. Follett (1941) noted that an *integrative* agreement constituted a true resolution of the issue: since both parties are satisfied, no issue or problem remains. However, other forms of agreements are apt to be only temporary settlements. In the case of neglect, compromise, accommodation, and domination by one party, some residual frustration remains in one or both parties. Issues settled by such agreements are apt to recur: "The conflict will come up again and again in some other form, for...we give up part of our desire, and because we shall not be content to rest here, sometime we shall try to get the whole of our desire."[14]

LONG-TERM EFFECTS. Adopting a more general or long-term view, let us now consider the outcomes of Party's behavior with respect to Other's goal attainment, Party's goal attainment, and the goal attainment of the organization which includes Party and Other.

By definition, Other's goal attainment is expected to be furthered by Party's cooperative behavior—collaborative or accommodative. Two studies provide evidence that Other perceives this to be the case. In a study of superior-subordinate relations, Burke (1970) found that subordinates perceived conflict to be handled most constructively when they perceived supervisors as adopting accommodative or collaborative tactics, and least constructively when supervisors adopted competitive or avoidant tactics.[15] Thomas (1971) found similar results in interdepartmental relations, where managers' satisfaction with interdepartmental

---

[14] Follett (1941, p. 35).

[15] Burke interpreted these responses at face value, as measures of the effectiveness of dyadic decision making. Placing less faith in the respondents' capacity to be objective, and recognizing that their observations are limited to their own frames of reference, these responses are interpreted here as merely the subordinate's satisfaction with his supervisor's behavior and its effects.

negotiations varied positively with collaborative and accommodative behavior by their counterparts in other departments, and negatively with competition and avoidance.

Reinforcement theory would suggest that Other's attraction to Party would increase with Party's collaboration and accommodation, and would decrease with Party's competition and avoidance. This seems to be true with one important exception: accommodation does not necessarily generate attraction. In the context of interdepartmental relations, Thomas (1971) found that managers reported more trust and less annoyance as they perceived other managers to be more accommodating; but no increase in respect for the other's abilities. Laboratory findings by Thibaut and Riecken (1955) suggest that accommodation is viewed more favorably when it is perceived as voluntary and less favorably when it is viewed as compliance to pressure. Accommodation by supervisors (who have power to say "no") may, therefore, generate more attraction than accommodation by peers or subordinates.

In terms of Party's attainment of his own substantive objectives, it might initially be expected that assertive behavior—collaboration and competition—would tend to produce successes, whereas unassertive behaviors would not. Again, however, the relationship is more complex. A number of studies have demonstrated a relationship between collaboration and promotability in organizations—Blake and Mouton (1964), Thomas (1971), and Dutton and Walton (1966). On the other hand, although competition may produce short-run advantages for Party, the long-run consequences of competition may involve hostility and competition from Other, with accompanying delays, deadlocks, and inefficiencies in their joint decision making. Dutton and Walton (1966) report that supervisors were unhappy with managers whose interdepartmental relations evolved into mutual competition. Thomas (1971) found no relationship between competitive behavior and promotability. Blake

and Mouton (1964), however, concluded that competitive tactics may be a useful backup approach when collaboration fails to be effective.[16]

The literature also provides some indication that collaboration, in addition to promoting substantive achievements, promotes the satisfaction of personal needs. In a study within research and development teams, Aram et al. (1971) found that team collaboration was positively related to several measures of member self-actualization and well being. By contrast, Dutton and Walton (1966) observed that managers involved in competitive interdepartmental relations experienced considerable frustration and anxiety. No comparative data are available for the effects of accommodation, compromise and avoidance.

In terms of organizational goal achievement, Lawrence and Lorsch (1967) found that organizational performance was related to inter-unit collaboration in three different industries. Since an organization is the composite of its sub-parts, it makes intuitive sense that behavior which meets the needs of both parties to an inter-unit conflict would produce more aggregate goal attainment for the organization. For example, consider the case where Sales and Production are in conflict over delivery dates: Sales desires to please customers by promising quick delivery while Production is concerned with preserving an efficient production schedule (which is often disrupted by emergency runs). If the two departments

---

[16] Clearly, more research needs to be done on the relationship of conflict-handling behaviors to individual performance. Blau (1955) found that the relationship of competition to performance within a department was mediated by work-group norms, with competitive behavior being negatively related to performance where cooperative norms existed. Similarly, although Thomas (1971) found accommodation to be negatively related to promotability in his study, frequent accommodation might be more functional in organizational climates with strong cooperative norms. Other mediating variables might include: one's supervisor's values, the ability of Other to retaliate, and any intrinsic conflict of interest in the central issues.

succeed to some degree in finding an integrative solution which allows quicker delivery at no added production costs, then the organization has become that much more effective and has developed a comparative advantage over its competitors. The same reasoning could be applied to the confederation consisting of management and union.

Third Party Process Interventions

Before proceeding to the structural model, some attention will be given to the implications of the process model for third party process intervention. This section is not intended to be a survey of the literature on process intervention, but rather a brief discussion of the salient implications of the model.

COLLABORATION. The material in the "outcome" section implies that, on the whole, mutual collaboration is a desirable state of affairs—for the organization and for the parties themselves. To be sure, there are exceptions. Schmidt and Tannenbaum (1960) argue that there is no single "right" way to handle conflict—that the third party may occasionally avoid or repress conflicts which appear unresolvable in the time available, for example, or that he may choose to sharpen some issues into more intense "conflict" (competition). Clearly, more research needs to be done in this area. On the whole, however, the model and the data suggest that joint collaboration toward integrative outcomes is frequently a worthy objective for the third party's efforts.

DE-ESCALATION. The dynamics of escalation suggest a number of tactics aimed at reducing competition and encouraging problem solving. They involve: motivating the parties, establishing communication, reducing hostility and distrust, and aiding problem solving.

The third party may attempt to provide incentives for resolving or de-escalating the conflict by pointing out the costs of continued competition. To the extent that the parties are interdependent, the impracticality of severing connections can also be stressed.

The third party may also reopen communications, serving as a communications link himself until he can bring the parties together. Many of his efforts will need to be directed toward getting the parties to listen to each other and to perceive the other's points accurately. A variety of techniques have been used to increase the accuracy of Party's perception of Other's position. The third party may restate or translate Other's points to Party. He may also ask Party to paraphrase or repeat Other's points (Rogers & Roethlisberger, 1952). Going somewhat farther, he may ask both parties to exchange roles and play the other's part during dialogue (e.g., Johnson, 1967).

Reducing hostility and building trust are often referred to as "conciliation" within labor-management negotiations (Rehmus, 1965). The third party may question the black-white stereotypes of Party. He may interpret Other's behavior and rationale, and point out Other's cooperative gestures toward Party. He may also show Party how Party's own behavior is influencing Other. Finally, the third party may encourage both parties to work through their hostile feelings. This encouragement may involve: being authentic himself, providing supportiveness toward the speaker, and ensuring that the other party listens.

Acting as mediator during the more substantive aspects of negotiations, the third party may encourage problem solving. He may help the parties voice and define their underlying concerns. This may involve separating issues and searching through the underbrush of proliferated issues until the central issues can be identified. He can question win-lose assumptions and pose the issue as an integrative problem. Finally, he can help the parties find integrative solutions.

CONFRONTATION. In addition, however, the material on conflict management within the dyad suggests that the parties may avoid, accommodate, or compromise on some issues as a way of maintaining harmony. Where the third party perceives that some important issue is being dealt with in this manner, he may attempt to move the parties towards a more collaborative or problem-solving approach to the issue. As in the case of de-escalation, the third party may attempt to build trust, provide a model of collaborative behavior, and aid in substantive problem solving.

Another tactic, however, is to increase the parties' perceived stakes in the issue as a way of eliciting more assertive behavior from them—pointing out the frustration of each party, defining an issue in larger terms, etc. The third party may even appeal to the self-respect of Party: "Are you going to let him do that to you?" This may amount to "sharpening an issue into conflict," in Schmidt and Tannenbaum's (1960) terms, or inducing a "differentiation phase" in Walton's (1969) terms. However, the third party's eventual objective here is to achieve collaborative or problem-solving behavior after the issue has been confronted.

STRUCTURAL MODEL

In contrast to the process model, the structural model of dyadic conflict is relatively unconcerned with discrete conflict episodes. The structural model gives up some clinical understanding of specific episodes in order to highlight the central behavioral tendencies within a given dyadic relationship. Thus, the model is concerned with the aggregate mix of behaviors used by the two parties during negotiations—the prevalence of collaboration, competition, avoidance, etc.

Furthermore, rather than identifying the events within conflict episodes, the structural model is concerned with the underlying parameters which shape those episodes. Specifically, the model is concerned with a number of pressures and constraints upon the parties. Each party's behavior is viewed as the resultant of those pressures and constraints, and behavioral change is seen as the consequence of changes in the configuration of these variables.

The structural model is represented in Figure 6. Briefly, the two circles represent the two interacting parties in the dyad. The conflict behavior of the two parties is seen as shaped by four types of structural variables. First, both parties are seen as having behavioral predispositions which stem partially from their motives and abilities. Second, both parties are subject to pressure from their surrounding social environments. Third, the parties respond to the conflict incentives in the situation—the conflict of interest between them, and their stakes in the

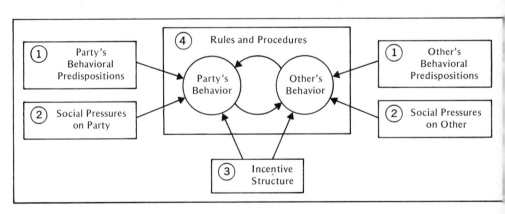

Figure 6.   Structural model of dyadic conflict.

relationship. Last, the interaction of the two parties is seen as occurring within a framework of rules and procedures which constrain their behavior—decision rules, negotiating procedures, and procedures for third-party involvement.[17]

Let us now consider in greater detail these four components of the structural model and their effects upon conflict-handling behavior. In discussing each of these categories of structural variables, I have not attempted to cover all the relevant research findings and theoretical speculations in the literature. The literature on personality alone would be overwhelming. Rather, I have tried to give the reader a feel for the variety of structural variables which shape conflict episodes, and to cite some of their more salient influences upon behavior. Where findings and theory are sketchy, I have also tried to provide some theory.

Behavioral Predispositions

The first variable which shapes Party's behavior is his own set of behavioral predispositions. For example, Stagner (1962) demonstrated that labor relations at the plant level were to some extent responsive to the personalities of stewards and managers. This is not to say that Party has inflexible traits and that his behavior does not vary from situation to situation. Rather, Party is assumed to have some *tendencies* in his behavior.

Berkowitz (1962) noted that individuals can be thought of as having a hierarchy of responses for dealing with conflict situations. At the top of that hierarchy is what Blake and Mouton (1964) call a "dominant style" of response. This is the behavior which Party

tends to use habitually and feels most comfortable with. If that behavior seems inappropriate in a given situation or fails to work, Party may fall back upon the next response in his hierarchy—his "back-up style." And so on down the hierarchy. For example, a given supervisor may tend to be collaborative, approaching issues with his subordinates in a problem-solving manner. However, when he feels that one subordinate is taking advantage of him, or when no integrative solution can be found on a given issue, he may fall back to a more competitive stance and attempt to use his power to suppress the subordinate's objections. If that does not work, he may withdraw. And so on. In the same situation, different supervisors would be expected to vary in their selection of behaviors.

Party's response heirarchy can be thought of as partially shaped by his motives and abilities. For example, problem solving is easier for creative people (Follett, 1941) and people who can deal cognitively with complex issues (Schroder et al., 1967). Competition is an outlet for individuals with high needs to exercise power or dominance (Stagner, 1962; Raven & Kruglanski, 1970). Managers with high affiliative or interaction needs may be more sensitive to other's feelings and may, therefore, lean towards accommodation (Stagner, 1962; Bass & Dunteman, 1963). And managers who are "task-oriented" may be more interested in confronting and solving problems (Bass & Dunteman, 1963).

Some evidence from the experimental gaming literature suggests that personality differences are most likely to show up in behavior under relatively non-threatening circumstances. In a comprehensive review of personality studies involving experimental games, Terhune (1970) found that high conflict of interest, anticipated threat from opponents, and actual competition from opponents tend to minimize the effects of personality. It is as if threat tends to reduce us all to a common denominator. Under such

---

[17] This model does not concern itself with feedback effects. In actuality, the interaction of the parties and the outcomes of their conflicts alter the predispositions of the parties, social pressures, incentive structures, and decision mechanisms. See, for example, Newcomb et al. (1965, pp. 12–15), Dubin (1957), and Thibaut (1968).

circumstances, the noncoercive responses in an individual's response hierarchy may seem ineffective (Raven & Kruglanski, 1970), leaving coercive tactics and a competitive orientation.

Social Pressure

The second set of influences in the structural model are social pressures from outside the dyad. During conflict episodes, Party's behavior may be influenced by social pressure from a number of directions. In this section, we shall consider two sources: from groups which Party represents, and from neutral parties or bystanders. These two sets of pressures will be called "constituent pressure" and "ambient social pressure," respectively.

CONSTITUENT PRESSURE. Blake et al. (1964) distinguish between conflicts over "personal matters," in which Party is acting for himself, and "group matters," in which Party is acting as a representative for a group. They point out that, as a representative, Party is often not free to negotiate according to his own preferences and judgments. Rather, as a group representative, Party is subject to the group's evaluation of him as a hero or as a traitor. Group norms sanction representative behavior which the group perceives as contributing to group goals, and punish other behavior.

Such sanctions may vary from group to group. The effectiveness of many informal sanctions, such as social isolation, is apt to vary with the attractiveness of the group to Party (Festinger et al., 1950). In formal groups, representatives may also have to contend with formal sanctions. For example, Megginson and Gullett (1970) note that unions are "quasi-political" organizations: union representatives must maintain popularity in order to retain office, and contract agreements reached by representatives must be ratified by the electorate.[18]

Representatives are not bound to the preexisting expectations of their constituents, of course. They may play an active role in modifying those expectations. This process is referred to as "intra-organizational bargaining" by Walton and McKersie (1965, Chaps. 8, 9). The interested reader may refer to Walton and McKersie for a more detailed account of the dynamics and tactics involved in this process. In the present section, we shall restrict attention to the broad implication of constituent pressure for Party's behavior.

One would expect that the added responsibility of representing others would increase Party's assertiveness in negotiating with Other. The literature more specifically suggests that social pressure from constituents is usually toward *competitive* behavior. In part, this competitive tendency may reflect the effect of group interaction upon attitudes toward risk. The competitive bravado sometimes observed in group strategy-setting meetings is reminiscent of "risky shift" phenomena. In a number of experiments, Wallach and Kogan (1965) and their colleagues[19] have frequently found that group discussion of an issue produces shifts in individual preferences toward riskier behavioral strategies.

There is another important set of group influences upon competition, however. Competition with other groups tends to serve a number of functions for the internal dynamics of a given group. Perhaps most important, competition and hostility toward other groups tend to strengthen the leadership hierarchy within a group, and to increase cohesion and unity of purpose (Coser, 1956; Blake & Mouton, 1961). The common goal of defeating an enemy tends to produce ingroup collaboration, and the group tends to

---

in frequency, underscoring the importance of constituent pressures upon union representatives.

[19] A description of the early risky shift research is contained in Jones and Gerard (1967, pp. 628–639). Recent reviews of research on this topic (Pruitt, 1971a, 1971b; Cartwright, 1971), while not questioning that risky shifts are frequent, have stressed that their occurrence is contingent upon various factors.

---

[18] Recently, Stern and Pearse (1968) noted that rank-and-file rejections of settlements had been increasing

close ranks behind its leadership. Coser (1956) notes, therefore, that a group may have some motive to search for and maintain enemies. In unions, Megginson and Gullett (1970) note that union officials have a vested interest in maintaining hostile relations with management in order to reduce inter-member bickering and to ensure their own continued support.

Once the hostility and competitive orientation exist, constituents may demand strongly competitive stances from their representatives. Walton and McKersie (1965, p. 350) state that constituents may be unsatisfied with agreements which have been reached by problem solving, quoting one union negotiator as saying, "The boys will only accept a contract when they are convinced I have taken a 'pound of flesh' from the company." Likewise, Stern and Pearse (1968) cite a case in which the attempts of union representatives to de-escalate competition with management led union members to question the integrity of those representatives.

Walton and McKersie (1965, p. 351) suggest that problem solving may be reconciled with constituent pressures by "bringing the constituents face to face with the realities of the situation," thus increasing communication between representatives and membership, and involving the membership in informed problem solving activities on issues. Stern and Pearse (1968) report a case in which these tactics were successfully utilized within a union, enabling the collaborative negotiation of a contract while increasing membership confidence in their representatives.

AMBIENT SOCIAL PRESSURE. Party may also be exposed to social pressures from various more-or-less neutral observers or bystanders —pressures regarding proper conflict behavior. These pressures may reflect the norms, values, and interests of some larger system of which the dyad is a part—for example, cultural values, organizational and work group norms, and public interest. To a large extent, it is the existence of bystanders, to-gether with their ability to employ sanctions against the two parties, which gives strength to these standards of behavior.

Some pressures come from formal authorities. In the case of labor-management negotiations, for example, the government may employ moral suasion (Megginson & Gullett, 1970, p. 502) to end strikes or to encourage the parties to adopt softer bargaining positions. The government may also threaten the use of sanctions, such as fines, or threaten to intervene through legislation or compulsory arbitration. The possibility of such actions lends weight to the government's pressures. The case is similar for formal authority within an organization. A supervisor may employ suasion to influence conflict-handling behavior between subordinates. For example, Thomas and Walton (1971) found that supervisory emphasis on cooperation tended to be accompanied by more collaborative and accommodative interdepartmental behavior by subordinates. Underlying this suasion is the supervisor's ability to impose formal sanctions upon the subordinate or to impose new policies to settle the conflict issue.

Other pressures have less formal sources. Public opinion may be a factor in labor disputes—solely because both parties wish to avoid public disapproval or because such disapproval may have adverse economic effects upon the company and union. Within an organization, conflicting managers and workers are subject to peer pressures. Peers may employ social sanctions such as isolation, but may also withhold substantive aid. For example, Blau (1955) found evidence which suggests that cooperative norms within one work group were enforced by diverting work from workers who competed with others, thus lowering their performance.[20]

The most common objective of ambient social pressure appears to be the prevention of disruption for the larger system. Thus, there are commonly norms within the system forbidding violence and constraining the

---

[20] Blau's findings are summarized and interpreted in Zaleznik and Moment (1967, pp. 362–365).

use of coercive power. For example, March and Simon (1958, p. 131) predict that organizations encourage persuasive and problem-solving approaches to internal conflicts to the exclusion of bargaining behavior. They also predict that there will be less pressure toward these "analytic" approaches to conflict *between* organizational systems: open bargaining and the use of coercion are more likely between company and union, for example, than within either. Even here, however, there remains some public and governmental pressure within the larger system that the parties seek agreement rather than resorting to force, that is, that they bargain "in good faith" (Blake et al., 1964).

Beyond restricting coercion and violence, however, norms sometimes generalize to the point of discouraging *any* assertive conflict-handling behavior. Storr (1968, Chap. 8) observes that our Western civilization encourages the repression of aggressive feelings—that we are used to thinking of aggression as "bad" rather than regarding it as a drive which is necessary for gaining mastery over the environment.[21] Litwin and Stringer (1968) note that organizations vary in the degree to which they encourage conflict to be accepted and dealt with, including this variable as one dimension of "organizational climate." Blake and Mouton (1964) note that some supervisors create work group atmospheres in which interpersonal conflicts are avoided or smoothed over. Finally, Bennis and Shepard (1956) argue that small groups, in their development, tend to pass through stages in which interpersonal conflicts are seen as threatening to group harmony and are suppressed.

Using Walton's (1969) terminology, such norms constitute "barriers" to the expression of assertive conflict behavior. These barriers will sometimes provide cooling off periods

and prevent competition and escalation on what appear to be unresolvable issues (Walton, 1969; Schmidt & Tannenbaum, 1960). However, they also discourage the confrontation of issues which could be resolved by problem solving. In controlling conflict behavior, then, such norms tend to discourage resolution of underlying conflict issues. Moreover, Walton (1969, p. 90) notes that these norms may drive conflicts underground to take less overt but more destructive competitive forms, and that suppressed issues and feelings may accumulate to make an eventual confrontation more intensely violent and destructive.

Dysfunctional norms are susceptible to change. Several authors have stated that norms function as though they are based upon shared, but often unvoiced and unexamined assumptions. Bion (1961) noted this in therapy groups, and Freire (1970) observed the same for culturally shared norms. In the case of organizational or group norms which suppress assertive conflict behavior, it is as though members have reached an implicit consensus that such behavior is threatening or dangerous to them. A third party may succeed in altering dysfunctional norms by making these assumptions explicit to an organization or group and having that body examine their validity and consequences (Schein, 1969, Chap. 6).

Incentive Structure

The third source of influence upon the behavior of the conflict parties is what we shall call their "incentive structure." "Incentive structure" is used in a very broad sense here to mean the interrelationship between the concerns of the two parties—the manner in which the satisfaction of Party's concerns is linked to the satisfaction of Other's concerns. For example, two executives may find themselves in competition for promotion to a single vacant position. Union and management may both desire to keep a company in operation, but the union's overriding concern for higher salaries may be

---

[21] Storr uses the term "aggression" to refer to behavior directed against obstacles to one's satisfaction. Thus, aggressive behavior, in his sense, would include problem solving as well as competition. He does not restrict the use of this term to behavior which is directed against others.

incompatible with management's great concern for increased dividends to stockholders. And so on.

In the process model, we were concerned with a party's conceptualization of issues as a determinant of his behavior. That conceptualization was one event in the sequence of events involved in a conflict episode. In the structural model, however, we are concerned with the effect of various *conditions* upon emergent behavior. Therefore, we are concerned with the "realities" of the issues which affect the concerns of both parties. Subjective reality seems more relevant to the process model, while objective reality seems more relevant to the structural model.[22]

In the structural model, we shall view the mix of conflict behavior used by a party as influenced by two aspects of the incentive structure—the stakes involved in the relationship, and the extent to which there is conflict of interest between the concerns of the parties. The stakes for Party are defined loosely as the importance to Party of those concerns of his which depend upon the behavior of Other. This importance is considered in relationship to the importance of other concerns which Party holds. For example, an executive's stakes in his relation-

ship with his janitor may be relatively low, involving the tidiness of his office; while his stakes in his relationship with the company president are considerably higher, involving job security, pay, etc. Likewise, the Sales department may have high stakes in their relationship with Production, involving their ability to honor sales orders, while they have lower stakes in their direct relationships with Maintenance, involving only occasional repairs of office equipment.

In this context, conflict of interest refers to the general degree of incompatibility versus compatibility between the concerns of Party and Other. For example, our executive may have no conflict of interest with his janitor over the tidiness of his office, since the janitor is paid on the basis of office tidiness. By contrast, there may be a great deal of conflict of interest between Sales and Production over the acceptance of unusual orders, the acceptance of small production orders, and scheduling of production runs. In most real-world situations, the conflict of interest in a relationship may be subject to only gross estimation.

Axelrod (1970) develops a fairly detailed definition of conflict of interest and hypothesizes that conflict of interest, so defined, tends to produce "conflictful" (competitive) behavior. In a review of Axelrod's work, however, Tanter (1971) takes Axelrod to task for not considering the impact of stakes upon the relationship between conflict of interest and behavior. In the present model, stakes and conflict of interest are viewed as interacting in their effects upon behavior. High stakes could lead to either competition or collaboration, depending upon the conflict of interest present; and conflict of interest would not be expected to produce competition if the stakes were trivial. We shall discuss this interaction in more detail after considering stakes and conflict of interest individually.

STAKES. In the literature, the notion of Party's stakes in a relationship has often been phrased in terms of Party's *dependence*

---

[22] This helps to explain Bernard's (1951) observation that "conflict," by which she seems to mean conflict of interest, has tended to be defined subjectively by psychologists and objectively by sociologists. Bernard argued for the adoption of an objective definition. For our purposes, however, objective and subjective reality are both necessary to understand the course of events in a dyad. Subjective reality has the more direct influence upon behavior, and one would often be naive to assume that subjective reality is an accurate representation of objective reality. However, one cannot understand the origins of subjective reality without taking objective reality into account. Objective reality, unfortunately, is not directly observable. In this sort of research, objective reality must often be operationalized as the subjective reality of the researcher. If the researcher perceives underlying concerns which the parties are unaware of, then those are treated as the objective, underlying concerns of the two parties. Likewise, if the researcher perceives an integrative alternative which the parties overlook, then he concludes that there is no necessary objective conflict of interest between the parties.

upon Other.[23] Essentially, the more Party depends upon Other in some way for the satisfaction of important concerns, the greater are Party's stakes in his relationship with Other. This dependence may take a variety of forms. In relations among individuals, the satisfaction of many of Party's interpersonal needs may be dependent upon Other's behavior. For example, if Party has high affiliative needs, he may be dependent upon Other for friendly behavior. Workflow patterns and responsibilities within an organization determine functional dependence—the extent to which Party's adequate performance of his job depends upon the adequate performance of Other (Kahn et al., 1964). For example, it may be vital to Accounting to receive accurate information from Sales, and a supervisor may be almost totally dependent upon his subordinates' performance of a number of tasks. The necessity of distributing resources among parties creates another type of interdependence. For example, the allocation of company funds is vital to union and management; two executives may each have some stake in getting their share of work from a secretary whom they share; and Sales and Production may each have to adjust their budget requests to the requests of the other. Finally, the necessity of coordinating work between two parties may create interdependence around the timing or scheduling of activities (March & Simon, 1958).[24] For example, it may be necessary for Sales to coordinate sales orders and promised delivery dates with Production's scheduling.

Other things being equal, Party is expected to be more assertive in those relationships where stakes are highest. In such relationships, Party is more likely to invest the time and energy required for the bar-

gaining or problem solving necessary to obtain satisfactory outcomes. Based upon data on functional dependence between managers, Kahn et al. (1964, p. 212) concluded:

Role senders who are dependent on the focal person's performance are usually unrelenting in their pressures on him because diminishing the pressures would jeopardize their own job efficiency ... their personal investment in the performance of the focal person is too great for them to relax their pressures.

In addition to being more assertive, Party is expected to be more sensitive to Other's behavior where high stakes are involved. In the context of interdepartmental relations, Thomas (1971) found highest correlations between managers' perceptions of Other's behavior and annoyance with Other under very high functional dependence.

These dynamics suggest some interesting implications for relationships involving asymmetric dependence between parties. March and Simon (1958) note that the decision of whether or not to negotiate a given issue can itself be a conflict issue in organizations. Such issues would be likely to occur in relationships with asymmetric dependence, where the parties have different stakes and, therefore, different motivation to negotiate. For example, a local union might be presumed to be relatively more dependent upon the company than vice versa: the company mediates nearly all of the union's concerns, while the company is also concerned with customers, suppliers, competitors, stockholders, etc. Under these circumstances, we would expect the union to get more emotionally involved in labor-management issues, to be more assertive in addressing issues, and to prefer more frequent negotiations. By contrast, the company management might be more likely to feel that the union was "getting upset over nothing" and to frequently react by avoiding contact or attempting to smooth over an issue—less assertive behaviors. One could hypothesize similar tendencies in superior-subordinate

[23] See March and Simon (1958), Emerson (1962), Kahn et al. (1964), Pondy (1966), Thompson (1967), Thomas and Walton (1971).

[24] Using Thompson's (1967) categorization, work-flow dependence is a form of "sequential" dependence, resource distribution is "pooled" interdependence, and coordination is "reciprocal" interdependence.

relationships where the superior has several subordinates, or in interdepartmental relationships with asymmetric dependence.[25]

CONFLICT OF INTEREST. The notion of compatibility versus incompatibility of concerns occurs in the literature under a variety of labels. For example, Walton (1970) speaks of integrative versus distributive situations, Deutsch (1949) discusses promotively interdependent versus "contriently" interdependent goals, Blake and Mouton (1961) and Thibaut and Kelley (1959) speak of a state of "competition" between the desires of the parties, Bernard (1951, 1957) uses the term "conflict" to denote incompatibility of values, and so on.

Walton and McKersie (1965, p. 5) differentiate between issues and problems: issues are areas of common concern in which the objectives of the parties are assumed to be incompatible, and problems are areas of concern which do not involve fundamental incompatibilities between objectives. I would like to modify their scheme slightly to define "common problems" as areas of

interdependence which largely involve commonality of interest, and to define "competitive issues" as areas which largely involve conflict of interest. Areas which involve a potential for either will be called "mixed issues." Figure 7 shows archetypal representations of a competitive issue, mixed issue, and common problem. The shaded areas indicate possible joint outcomes. In Figure 7a, a competitive issue, it is impossible for both parties to jointly satisfy their concerns.[26] In Figure 7c, a common problem, the two parties have a common stake in attaining favorable outcomes—each party's increases in satisfaction are accompanied by increases for the other. In Figure 7b, however, a mixed issue, there is no necessary relationship between the outcomes of the two parties: integrative solutions are possible but so are wins and losses, depending upon the conceptualizations and behaviors of the parties.

First, let us consider competitive issues. The conflict of interest in competitive issues appears to have two sorts of origins, both involving scarce resources. The most straightforward form occurs when two parties have to allocate resources between them—money, promotion, status, work force, committee speaking time, etc. Here, conflict

---

[25] In many situations of *highly* asymmetric dependence, however, the more dependent party may exercise some caution in his assertiveness. Here, the greater dependence of Party upon Other gives Other a source of coercive power which he may use upon Party. Kahn et al. (1964, p. 212) concluded that highly dependent managers may mitigate their assertiveness "for fear of the consequences." In many settings, however, we would expect organizational norms and third-party pressures to restrict the exploitation of dependent parties by parties with such power advantages.

[26] Competitive issues are represented in their most general or inclusive form here—to include possibilities of deadlocks and other sub-optimal outcomes. In order to simplify presentation here, strictly zero sum issues and either/or issues are regarded as more specific forms of this general pattern.

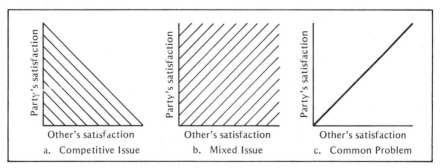

Figure 7.   Three types of decision areas.

of interest exists to the extent that the summed aspirations of the two parties exceed the quantity of resource available (Thibaut & Kelley, 1959). For example, Walton and McKersie (1965, p. 18) note that in union-management negotiations, the most basic conflicts of interest often center around incompatible desires for economic resources, and White (1961) found chronic interdepartmental conflict of interest where different departments desired jurisdiction over programs. However, conflict of interest may also occur when parties have different, or "differentiated" concerns—different individual motives, different departmental objectives, interest in different topics, etc. Differentiation itself does not imply conflict of interest: people with different knowledge and interests may learn from each other, relationships can meet several needs and objectives, and so on. Rather, it appears that differentiation involves conflict of interest only when there are insufficient means or resources to meet both parties' concerns at a given time—when time is too scarce to enable one party to attend to the other's concerns, when there is insufficient money or manpower to achieve two departmental goals simultaneously, etc. For example, Collins and Guetzkow (1964, Chap. 5), in reviewing the effects of personality differences upon group decision making, conclude that such differences tend to create most conflict under time pressure—when there is insufficient time to satisfy the differentiated concerns of the parties. Resources like time and funds, however, tend to be generally scarce in organizations, so that Lawrence and Lorsch (1967) found that, on the whole, differentiation between organizational units posed an obstacle to integration. Because of the crucial role played by resource availability in creating conflict of interest, Cyert and March (1963) identified organizational "slack"—an overabundance of organizational resources—as an important factor in reducing inter-unit conflict.

Research has tended to link conflict of interest to uncooperative behavior. In his classic field experiment, Sherif (1958; Sherif & Sherif, 1956, Chaps. 6, 9) created intergroup conflict of interest in a boys' camp by establishing competitive sports events for desirable prizes. As a result, each group developed hostile attitudes toward the other and, even outside of the sports events, adopted uncooperative behavior—ranging from assertive and hostile (competitive) behavior to avoidance. In a laboratory setting, Blake and Mouton (1961) created conflict of interest between pairs of groups by asking the two groups to evaluate the relative quality of papers written by each group. The resulting behavior was markedly competitive: group members sought to undermine the other group's position without understanding that position, and group representatives took unyielding negotiating postures. In a study of interdepartmental relations in industry (Thomas & Walton, 1971), managers indicated that competitive and, to a lesser extent, avoidant behavior was more common in relationships where conflict of interest was prevalent.

By contrast, the commonality of interest in common problems is expected to produce cooperative behavior. On such problems, Party's own outcomes become more satisfactory when Other's outcomes become more satisfactory. It is thus to Party's advantage to help, or at least not interfere with, Other's efforts (Deutsch, 1949). This formulation suggests that Party will tend to either collaborate with Other or go along with Other's wishes (i.e., accommodate).

In his previously mentioned field experiment, Sherif (1958) created commonality of interest between groups after they had become competitive and hostile. His "superordinate goals" encouraged *active* collaboration by both groups, since the goals, which were highly desired by both groups, could not be attained by either group's individual efforts. With this change in incentives, the two groups collaborated to achieve the superordinate goals; and a series of such tasks succeeded in reducing intergroup hostility. In the area of labor relations, the

Scanlon Plan (Lesieur, 1958; Lesieur & Puckett, 1969) appears to have produced some increase in union-management cooperation by creating commonality of interest in the form of profit-sharing plans.[27] The Tavistock Institute has pioneered a form of collaborative incentive within work groups (Emery, 1959; Trist et al., 1963): reversing the trend toward differentiation of job responsibilities between workers, this approach has encouraged shared responsibility between work-group members for various group tasks.

In contrast to common problems and competitive issues, mixed issues may permit either cooperative or competitive behaviors. One can think of competitive issues as encouraging uncooperative behavior and of common problems as encouraging cooperative behavior (Deutsch, 1949). However, mixed issues do not appear to encourage either; rather they *allow* either. For example, consider a disagreement over which course of action to follow. Each party is assumed to have some concern that the insights which have led him to his position be reflected in the dyad's decision. The parties may adopt either cooperative or uncooperative behaviors: they may, for example, attempt to integrate their insights into a decision which is at least as good as either party's position, or each party may attempt to impose his position upon the other.

The parties' selection of behavior on mixed issues is asserted to be influenced by the relative importance and frequency of competitive issues versus common problems in the relationship as a whole. Through the dynamics described in the process model, behavior on any mixed issues which arise is assumed to respond to the identification, trust, and other results of cooperative or uncooperative behavior in other decision areas. Thus, the same substantive disagreement would be more likely to be approached cooperatively by parties with mainly common interests than by parties with mainly conflicting interests. One tends to discuss issues with allies and to debate them with enemies.[28]

JOINT EFFECTS OF STAKES AND CONFLICT OF INTEREST. The predicted joint effects of these two variables upon Party's aggregate conflict-handling behavior in a relationship are shown in Figure 8. Here we are concerned with Party's predominant behavioral mode or behavioral tendency, recognizing that his behavior will vary to some extent from issue to issue. Basically, since higher stakes are expected to result in more assertive behavior while common interests result in cooperative behavior, Figure 8 is quite similar to Figure 4 in the process model.

Briefly, considerable conflict of interest is expected to produce competition when Party has a great deal at stake.[29] However, when he has relatively little at stake in a relation-

---

[27] The use of profit-sharing plans, along with some of their shortcomings, is discussed in Stagner and Rosen (1965, pp. 126–128).

[28] At this point, I feel a need to clarify the relationship of common problems to the present conflict models. I have assumed that conflict phenomena are a *subset* of decision-making phenomena. Specifically, as long as decision making is seen by both parties as progressing toward resolving common problems, I have chosen to exclude such phenomena from the scope of conflict. Conflict occurs when some sort of interference takes place between the parties—when one party frustrates some concern held by another. These disruptions and the concerns which underlie them constitute the issues which are conceptualized and dealt with by the parties in the process model of conflict. Therefore, the *process* model excludes the conceptualization of common problems. In seeking an integrative outcome to a conflict, the parties may redefine an issue as an integrative problem, but it is not common problems themselves which spawn conflict episodes. Likewise, a conflict issue may arise while two parties are discussing a common problem, but it is not the common problem itself which constitutes the conflict issue. However, the presence within a relationship of decision areas which are characterized by common interests is assumed to influence behavior in the conflict episodes which *do* occur. Thus, the presence of common problems in a relationship is included in the structural model as an influence upon conflict-handling behavior.

[29] Conflict of interest and high stakes may also create competitive deadlocks between the parties. Under these conditions, the parties may engage in avoidance (withdrawal), if this is feasible. See, for example, Pondy (1966, p. 249) and Blake et al. (1964, Chap. 6).

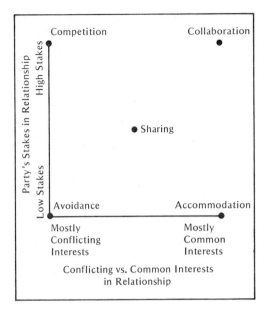

Figure 8. Predominant conflict-handling behavior of Party as a function of stakes and aggregate conflict of interest in a relationship.

ship in which there is considerable conflict of interest, he is expected to be more likely to avoid issues. Essentially, such issues may constitute minor annoyances in his routine which he may neglect in favor of matters which are more important to him. Viewing Other as an unpleasant source of minor irritations, he may physically avoid Other or at least avoid confronting those issues. For example, a busy Maintenance supervisor may avoid one Production foreman who often wants his men's services; a supervisor may discourage subordinate complaints by keeping his door shut; and so on.

Likewise, considerable commonality of interest is assumed to produce collaboration in relationships where Party has a great deal at stake. However, when Party has relatively little at stake in a relationship in which there is commonality of interest, he is expected to engage in more accommodation. Again, he is expected to devote his energy to relationships in which he has greater stakes. With common interests, he can generally trust Other's intentions and may lose little

by deferring to Other's wishes. For example, if a researcher is engaged in several joint research projects, he is likely to devote the least energy to the least important of them, relying upon his colleague's judgment and generally accommodating his wishes.

Little systematic data on sharing (compromise) are available in the literature. A predisposition toward sharing would appear to be most frequent in relationships with intermediate stakes and intermediate conflict or commonality of interest. With intermediate stakes, Party may be willing to give up some satisfaction, but not all; and Party may, therefore, invest the moderate time and energy required for compromise, but not the greater time and energy required for more assertive behaviors. Proposing compromises has elements of both cooperation and noncooperation, yielding something to Other but also holding out something for oneself, so that it would appear to be less likely in the cooperative climate created by extreme commonality of interest or the uncooperative climates created by extreme conflict of interest. To be sure, compromise may be an eventual *outcome* of competitive processes where neither party can win, but a preference for compromise as a behavioral *orientation* would appear more likely in these intermediate situations.

Rules and Procedures

The final set of influences upon the behavior of the parties stems from the rules and procedures which are relevant to their joint decision making. These rules and procedures make up the established decision-making machinery which governs the negotiations of the two parties. At any given moment, this machinery serves to constrain and shape the behavior of the parties who interact within it. I have tried to sort out three components of this machinery: decision rules which dictate substantive decisions on issues, negotiation procedures which constrain the interaction of the two parties, and procedures for the involvement of third parties to resolve conflict issues through mediation or arbitration.

DECISION RULES. By "decision rules" is meant those mutually accepted rules that specify which alternatives are to be selected or avoided when issues arise. These decision rules contrast with procedural rules, which specify how one negotiates rather than what one decides. Decision rules might include the formal rule that Sales must allow a five-day lead time on Production orders; the informal agreement that two departments share responsibility for certain types of errors; the norm that a supervisor should give his subordinates a chance to develop professionally; and so on. In his treatment of industrial relations systems, Dunlop (1958) visualized the actors as surrounded by a "web of rules" which stem from management, workers, and government.

Rules tend to arise or to be created to cover sensitive issues between parties (Thibaut & Kelley, 1959, Chap. 8). If Sales and Production frequently come into conflict over the length of lead times on production orders, then a number of rules will tend to emerge to govern this issue. Such rules might take the form of formal agreements between the two departments, informal expectations on the basis of past precedent, or organizational rules imposed upon the two departments to manage their conflict. Dubin (1957) spoke of informal rules as the "common law of the plant."

In their most effective form, rules serve to prevent conflict behavior. Both parties yield some of their personal power and freedom as an accepted rule acquires influence over them both (Thibaut & Kelley, 1959). When issues arise which are clearly covered by an accepted rule, both parties follow the rule rather than using tactics to try to satisfy their own concerns. In time, the behavior dictated by the rule may become automatic, so that a situation is no longer even conceptualized as a conflict issue. For example, Sales personnel may automatically tell customers that orders can-

not be filled in less than five days, no longer recognizing any conflict with Production over lead times. Such rules are often efficient in the sense that they avoid the time, energy, and potential hostility of conflict episodes.

When they do not eliminate awareness of conflicts, rules still tend to transform the base of power used in a conflict episode. During negotiations over an issue covered by a rule, either party may appeal to the rule as an impersonal source of legitimate power (Thibaut & Kelley, 1959; Raven & Kruglanski, 1970).[30] Raven and Kruglanski (1970) note that exercising such power is less likely to generate hostility than is coercive power.

However, rules also have a number of drawbacks in their effects upon conflict behavior. First, rules discourage problem solving in individual cases. Over time, accepted rules take on a quality of moral obligation (Thibaut & Kelley, 1959). Deviations from the rule are often regarded as wrong, even though a particular case might be more satisfactorily handled for both parties by coming to some other agreement. Essentially, as the rule becomes stronger, the merits of a particular case and the degree to which both parties' concerns are satisfied become less relevant.

Second, it is my observation that rules promote black-white thinking which may encourage win-lose competition on issues. For some reason, applying rules to behavior seems to generate two-valued thinking: right-wrong, correct-incorrect, should-shouldn't, guilty-innocent. Inevitably, rules are ambiguous—the implications of one rule are unclear, or it is unclear which rule to apply. In such cases, disagreements over rules are

---

[30] This behavior—invoking established decision rules—is difficult to classify in our five-category scheme of conflict behavior. Blake and Mouton (1964, Chap. 6) associated such behavior with the sharing (compromise) orientation, possibly because reliance upon established rules and traditions prevents integrative solutions and tends, over the long haul, to result in only moderate goal satisfaction for both parties.

apt to be conceptualized as "either/or" issues and are likely to result in competitive arguments: "That's the right way" versus "That's the wrong way"; "Yes I should" versus "No you shouldn't"; and so on. Because the functionality of alternatives for both parties becomes irrelevant, few criteria exist to resolve the dispute.

Third, formal rules may proliferate. While general guidelines and informal agreements tend to occur in low threat situations, formal rules are most likely in situations of higher threat (Thibaut, 1968). In the context of interdepartmental relations, for example, Walton et al. (1966) found more formalized decision rules in competitive relationships. In such situations, decision rules may proliferate as each party seeks to control the other and protect himself. As disagreements occur over ambiguities in the rules, more detailed rules may be established to attempt to cover those ambiguities. Patten (1970) notes that continued collective bargaining has resulted in longer and more detailed labor contracts. The bureaucracy literature (e.g., Merton, 1957), likewise, notes the tendency for rules to proliferate as supervisors seek to control subordinates and subordinates seek clarification of existing rules. One cost of such proliferated rules is that an inordinate amount of time and energy may be required to deal with these rules: the parties must spend time scanning and mastering the rules before acting. Also, special legalistic machinery may have to be created to deal with interpreting rules and handling disputes.[31] Finally, if there are too many rules for a party to master, he may be unwilling to take positions on issues for fear of violating some rule (Thibaut & Kelley, 1959) and may thus adopt a conservative, avoidant orientation toward issues.

NEGOTIATION PROCEDURES. The two parties are not likely to interact randomly. More frequently, there are procedures which govern their frequency of interaction, the sequencing of issues, length of sessions, formality of presentation, number and composition of people present, and so on. These procedures may vary in formality from convenience and habit to elaborately formalized regulations. For example, all issues between R&D and Accounting may be filtered through the two department heads, who meet only monthly when they present formal proposals to a company-wide budget committee. Union-management negotiations may occur every few years between a fixed set of representatives who begin negotiations by reading formal proposals covering a large number of issues. Each morning, a Maintenance supervisor may meet informally with a Production supervisor to consider maintenance issues. Sales personnel in a given plant may interact informally with Production supervisors whenever important issues arise. And so on.

As a vehicle for considering the effects of negotiation procedures upon behavior, let us look at common procedures in labor-management contract negotiations.[32] First, the long period between negotiations discourages collaboration by allowing hostile stereotypes to develop (Newcomb, 1947), by preventing consideration of issues when facts are fresh, and by allowing issues to accumulate. Second, formal presentations encourage competition by increasing each side's commitment to their stated position. Third, consideration of several issues during a given negotiation tends to prevent settling each on its own merits: each tends to be seen as linked to the others (Fisher, 1964), so that they may be used in horse trading rather than problem solving (Patten, 1970). Fourth, filtering issues through a fixed set of representatives tends to discourage problem solving if those representatives are less knowledgeable concerning the facts of specific issues (Lawrence & Lorsch, 1967).

Considering such influences leads Patten (1970) to observe that the structure of

---

[31] Patten (1970) observed that the labor relations literature is becoming increasingly legalistic.

[32] For a discussion of the relationship between procedures and behavior in interdepartmental relations, see Walton et al. (1966).

collective bargaining is itself the source of a great deal of competition. However, he also noted that the structure of collective bargaining is seldom questioned, so that the adversary viewpoint it produces is often taken for granted—even in the literature. Kerr (1954) also noted that labor-management negotiation procedures tend to become complex and rigid over time, until conflict negotiations become stylized and even ceremonial.

However, a number of procedural innovations *have* been tried which have succeeded in increasing the level of union-management collaboration in different organizations. For example, the Rogers Company[33] pioneered a form of open-ended bargaining in which either side could initiate negotiations whenever problems arose, thus preventing issues and hostilities from accumulating until the contract expiration date. An important feature of the Scanlon Plan (Lesieur, 1958; Lesieur & Puckett, 1969) was the creation of union-management contact throughout the organization. McKersie (1964; McKersie & Shropshire, 1962) reported a reduction in the competitive use of grievances in relations between International Harvester and the United Auto Workers when grievance-handling procedures were changed. Under the new procedures, grievances were handled when they arose, by the people directly involved, and with no written records. The quickness of action appeared to prevent hostilities from building and allowed settlement when the facts were still available; restricting negotiations to people directly involved meant that an issue could be considered on its own merits rather than in the context of other issues between union and management; and the informality and lack of written materials served to increase flexibility and reduce concern with precedent.

Blake et al. (1964, Chap. 12) reported that more integrative settlements were reached during contract negotiations when negotiation procedures were altered to encourage problem solving. Small union-management teams were formed for fact-

finding on individual issues under consideration. Then larger groups met to generate alternatives, examine their implications for the concerns of union and management, and rank the alternatives in order of preference. Only then did the entire group of negotiators meet to determine the final settlements on the several issues. This procedure prevented premature commitment to alternatives, encouraged the consideration of each issue on its own merits, and fostered an exploratory, problem-solving orientation. The early collaboration on fact-finding may also have generated mutual trust and identification between the parties.

MEDIATION AND ARBITRATION MECHANISMS. When a dyad is unable to reach agreement on an issue, there are apt to be mechanisms by which third parties may become actively involved in the decision-making process in an attempt to reach a settlement. Such mechanisms may be voluntary or compulsory. Prolonged competitive conflict episodes have costs for a system, so that the system has a vested interest in developing mechanisms to terminate such episodes (Galtung, 1965). Moreover, the parties themselves have some interest in avoiding the costs of a prolonged conflict episode (Coser, 1961; Blake et al., 1964, Chap. 4; Stagner & Rosen, 1965, Chap. 8).

Mediation and arbitration mechanisms are perhaps most formally developed and most noticeable in union-management relations. For example, many union-management contracts provide for binding arbitration of disputes over the interpretation of the contract's terms (Stagner & Rosen, 1965, pp. 112, 113), while state and federal governments provide mediation services for the negotiation of labor contracts. However, mediation and arbitration mechanisms are also prevalent within organizations, although they may be less formal. For example, Blake et al. (1964, Chap. 4) note that supervisors in an organization are frequently called upon to mediate or arbitrate conflicts between subordinates. In addition, members of the Personnel department may be avail-

---

[33] Cited in Walton and McKersie (1965, p. 45).

able as mediators in interdepartmental conflicts; and unresolved issues may sometimes be arbitrated by ad hoc or standing organizational committees. Finally, Scott (1965) notes the prevalence of formal and informal appeals systems in organizations for settling superior-subordinate conflicts.

Let us consider mediation first. In mediation, the third party's role is that of helper or consultant to the dyad. The mediator does not impose a settlement upon the dyad. Rather, his role is to help the two parties locate and agree upon some mutually acceptable alternative. As such, he may utilize tactics similar to the third-party tactics covered in the process model or those suggested by Walton (1969). As Rehmus (1965) pointed out, little systematic data have been collected on the behavior of mediators, or the effects of mediators upon negotiations. Still, the behavior of the mediator is apparently directed towards eliciting problem solving or compromise from the conflict parties. Through his behavior, the mediator may also help the parties arrive at a more productive and less competitive pattern of negotiation for their relationship as a whole (Walton, 1969, Chap. 13).

In contrast, arbitration is expected to be rather mixed in terms of its effects upon conflict behavior within the dyad. In arbitration, the parties yield responsibility for arriving at an agreement, and a settlement is dictated by the arbitrator instead. First, let us consider the positive side of arbitration. Most importantly, arbitration terminates competitive deadlocks on specific episodes and may thus prevent escalation beyond acceptable levels. Secondly, however, an insightful arbitrator, by virtue of his experience and relative objectivity, may also be able to identify more integrative settlements than the parties themselves are able to perceive (although this is also true of mediators). For example, Mason (1969) recommended a corporate planning method in which the advocates of two competing plans debate in front of a planning group: essentially acting as an arbitrator, the planning group uses the debate to identify the key insights of each plan and attempts to integrate them into a final plan.

On the negative side, however, I would expect arbitration to do little to reduce existing hostility between the parties and would expect frequent arbitration to actually promote some degree of competition. Relieved of the responsibility for arriving at ultimate decisions with the other party, each party may be less concerned with the effects of his behavior before the arbitrator. This behavior would be analogous to disputing children accusing each other in front of their parents; or to a separated couple fighting via their attorneys during divorce litigation.

In addition, the intergroup research of Blake and Mouton (1961) demonstrates the likelihood of negative reactions to arbitrated decisions: to the extent that the decision favors one group over another, the "losing" group tends to view the decision as invalid and the arbitrator as unfair. In the case of labor relations, Stagner and Rosen (1965, Chap. 8) note that unions may ignore arbitration decisions when the arbitrators appear unfair. Blake and Mouton (1964, p. 54) quote one experienced arbitrator as saying that "the best arbitration judgments are ones that make neither group feel like winners." In any case, gaining the commitment of the parties to arbitrated settlements is apt to be a difficulty, so that arbitrated settlements may frequently be only temporary respites.

RECAP OF THE CONFLICT MODELS

Conflict can be represented by two different models which focus on separate aspects of conflict phenomena and have complementary uses for the practitioner:

1. *The Process Model.* Focuses upon the *sequence of events* which transpire within a conflict episode, and is particularly useful when one is faced with the need to understand and intervene directly into the stream of events of an ongoing episode.

2. *The Structural Model.* Focuses upon

the *conditions* which shape conflict behavior in a relationship, and is useful in restructuring a situation to facilitate desired kinds of behavior patterns.

The two models suggest different sets of diagnostic questions for practitioners interested in understanding and managing specific conflicts. Those diagnostic questions are presented in Tables 1 and 2.

STATE OF THE LITERATURE

Thus far conflict has been defined, its functionality and dysfunctionality discussed, a model of the conflict process in dyads developed, and a model developed of the structural variables which shape conflict behavior in relationships. At this point, it seems fitting to conclude by making some general observations on the state of the conflict literature. Briefly, I shall note that research is noticeably lacking in some specific areas, that there is a need for more integrative theory and systematic research, and that validated instruments for measuring conflict behavior are needed.

Specific Areas for Research

Reviewing the literature for the process model turned up three general areas which seem particularly in need of further research:

TABLE 1
DIAGNOSTIC QUESTIONS FROM THE PROCESS MODEL

Key Questions	Relevant Conflict Events
1. What perceived loss or threat of loss has led each party to perceive a conflict?	1. Frustration
2. How does each party define the conflict issue? • Does each party have an accurate perception of the other's concerns? • Is the issue posed superficially rather than in terms of underlying concerns? • Would alternative definitions of the issue be more helpful in suggesting integrative solutions to the conflict?	2. Conceptualization
3. How does each party pursue his objectives in dealing with the other party? • What is his underlying orientation in approaching the conflict issue—competitive, collaborative, sharing, avoidant, accommodative? • What assumptions underlie his choice of strategies and tactics?	3. Behavior
4. How is each party's behavior influenced by the behavior of the other? • What ongoing dynamics seem to be producing the escalation or de-escalation? • Is each party aware that the other's behavior is partly a response to his own? • What efforts are the parties making to manage their own conflict?	4. Interaction
5. If things proceed as they are going, what are apt to be the short-term and long-term results of this episode—both substantive and emotional? • What foreseeable effects will this episode have upon subsequent episodes?	5. Outcome

TABLE 2
DIAGNOSTIC QUESTIONS FROM THE STRUCTURAL MODEL

Key Questions	Relevant Conditions
1. Does the general makeup of either party predispose him toward the use of specific conflict-handling modes? • Are those predispositions compatible with the requirements of his position? • To what extent could his behavior be changed through training experiences?	1. Behavioral predispositions
2. (a) Is either party acting as representative for a larger set of individuals? • What expectations do they have of his behavior? • How much power do they have over him? • To what extent can they monitor his negotiating behavior?	2. (a) Social pressures: constituent
2. (b) Who are the other, relatively neutral, onlookers? • What sort of behavior will they encourage or discourage? • How much power do they have over the parties?	2. (b) Social pressures: ambient
3. (a) How much is at stake for the parties in this relationship? • In what ways is each party dependent upon the other? • Is either party more vitally concerned with the outcome of negotiations than the other?	3. (a) Incentives: stakes
3. (b) What is the relative importance and frequency of competitive issues versus common problems in the relationship as a whole? • To what extent have resource scarcities created conflict of interest between the parties? • In what ways have differentiated responsibilities created conflict of interest?	3. (b) Incentives: conflict of interest
4. (a) Are there many rules which dictate or constrain settlements on specific issues? • To what extent are the parties free to problem-solve on important issues?	4. (a) Rules and procedures: decision rules
4. (b) How are the behaviors of the parties shaped by the format of their negotiations? • How frequently do the parties interact? • When and where are meetings held? • What are the number and composition of people present? • How formally are the negotiations conducted?	4. (b) Rules and procedures: negotiation procedures
4. (c) What provisions are there for involving third parties? • Are skilled third parties available to help the parties resolve their own disputes? • Does the larger system have provisions for terminating conflict episodes by imposing settlements when the parties deadlock?	4. (c) Rules and procedures: mediation and arbitration mechanisms

the functionality of various conflict-handling behaviors, conflict management within the dyad, and the parties' conceptualization of issues.

FUNCTIONALITY OF CONFLICT BEHAVIORS. It is only relatively recently that researchers have come to realize that conflict could have functional outcomes. Our notions concerning the functionality of conflict-handling behaviors are still relatively primitive and undifferentiated. For example, a disturbing amount of research in experimental gaming concerns itself with the simplistic dichotomy of cooperative behavior versus uncooperative behavior, and is directed at identifying factors which increase cooperation. Underlying this research, there appears to be a basic assumption that cooperation is good and noncooperation is bad.

The five-category classification for conflict behavior used in this article appears more useful for investigating the functionality of conflict behaviors in organizations. But here still, it is relatively easy to latch on to one behavior, collaboration, as the functional or "white hat" behavioral mode. To be sure, the research cited in the process model shows that collaboration tends to be related to managerial promotability and to organizational effectiveness in some settings. However, the general issue of functionality appears much more complex.

First, Pondy (1967) noted that functionality must be judged according to a set of criteria, and that the functionality of a given behavior may well depend upon the criteria adopted. Many international relations researchers, for example, appear to regard international goodwill as a value in its own right, leading them to consider joint cooperation as functional.[34] By contrast, organizational researchers and consultants are more apt to adopt organizational criteria related

to performance—to getting things done. Thus, it is important for organizational research to take assertiveness into account as well as cooperation, so that joint collaboration or problem solving tends to be regarded as functional. From this perspective it is tempting to view non-collaborative behaviors as irrational behavioral mistakes or miscalculations made by parties who lack our own behavioral science insights. However, it is apparent that the conflict parties themselves have their *own* set of objectives or criteria, and that their selection of conflict behaviors is more likely to be understood in terms of their functionality for meeting those objectives. We have noted, for example, that competition with outgroups may be functional for ingroup harmony, and that different behaviors may be instrumental in satisfying different interpersonal needs.

Second, it is apparent that the functionality of a specific conflict-handling behavior may vary over issues and situations. For example, consider the functionality of a manager's behavior for his own promotability in the organization. The manager should not expend much time or energy on issues where little is at stake. He would be wise to avoid confronting issues which would escalate into costly or unresolvable conflicts. In dealing with competitive others, or in situations with high conflict of interest, competition may result in more favorable outcomes. The manager may be especially cooperative in his handling of conflicts with those who rate his performance. And his conflict behavior with peers and subordinates may vary with his supervisor's notions of proper behavior.

CONFLICT MANAGEMENT WITHIN THE DYAD. It was noted during the discussion of the process model that conflict research has tended to focus upon destructive tendencies in conflict episodes—tendencies toward escalation, for example. By contrast, we know relatively little about the conflict management practiced within the dyad—the avoidance of some issues, conciliation activities,

---

[34] This observation, together with the fact that experimental gaming is often used in peace research, may help to explain why the cooperative-uncooperative distinction has been retained in the experimental game literature.

attempts to de-escalate competition and convert competition to collaboration, etc. Everyday experience suggests that such activities are common, even though they are sometimes ineffectual.

CONCEPTUALIZATION. It is surprising that so little research has been done concerning a party's conceptualization of conflict issues. Party's behavior is based in large measure upon his conceptualization: his definition of the issue appears to determine his view of the stakes involved, and his awareness of alternatives appears to determine his view of the conflict of interest present. Moreover, there is no necessary relationship between objective reality and Party's conceptualization (Deutsch, 1969). Hence, Party's conceptualization of a conflict issue appears to be a key leverage point in conflict management.

In the two conflict models, a number of influences upon Party's conceptualization have been hypothesized and Party's conceptualization has been hypothesized to influence Party's behavior in a number of ways. The investigation of these influences and of third party influences upon Party's conceptualization appears to be a critical area for empirical research.

Conflict Theory as a Whole

The organizational conflict literature is largely specialized according to organizational arena, and research studies are often focused upon narrow sets of variables. This pattern seems understandable for an applied field where researchers are often concerned with specific problems. However, I would like to stress the desirability of developing more integrative theory and more comprehensive research strategies.

INTEGRATIVE THEORY. The theory and research relating to organizational conflict seems largely segmented and unintegrated. Although there are several pieces of quality research and many important theoretical

insights, the theoretical ties between them are often unclear. Researchers look at different manifestations of conflict, different independent variables, and so on. It is easy to get the impression that conflict is a general label for a number of largely unrelated phenomena—strikes, absenteeism, arguing, budget disputes, religious schisms, tensions, and so forth.

This chapter met a need of mine to begin integrating insights in that scattered literature—to look for those basic events and structural variables which appear helpful in understanding the various manifestations of conflict in dyads. It is my opinion that the literature would benefit from more of this theoretical integration. An established body of integrated conflict theory would be useful in relating the different conflict literatures and in suggesting applications of findings from one organizational arena to another. A general integrated theory would also be helpful in generating research hypotheses, diagnosing conflicts, and in teaching.

COMPLEX MODELS. It is also my opinion that our conceptualization of conflict phenomena would benefit by becoming more complex. In assembling the structural model, it became apparent that conflict-handling behavior is shaped by a variety of structural variables—by personal predispositions, rules, procedures, incentives, organizational norms, constituent pressures, and so on. This complexity is seldom reflected in the theory and research in our field. In approaching a conflict relationship, the practitioner and the researcher apparently tend to take many of these variables for granted. The result is likely to be that the researcher develops an oversimplified view of the determinants of behavior in a setting, and that the practitioner overlooks some possible change strategies—or some variables which will interfere with his change attempts.

I view the structural model in this chapter as a first step toward a more complete and useful model. The present model designates several categories of variables which influence conflict behavior and specifies the expected form of some of those influences. It needs to be tested and expanded. What variables have been omitted, what influences oversimplified? How do the structural variables interact to influence behavior? How does behavior feed back to influence the structural variables? And how do the structural variables tend to vary together? If expanded by answering these questions, the structural model would eventually become a systems model of conflict with strong predictive power, and with implications for system change strategies.

As it is now, I hope that this model may serve to generate comprehensive research which can begin to answer the questions above by addressing structural influences in their complexity.

Validated Instruments

Finally, despite its popularity as a topic, empirical research on conflict behavior in organizations is still somewhat sparse. Progress in research and theory would be aided greatly by the availability of validated instruments for measuring conflict behavior.

Self-assessment measures for behavioral classification schemes similar to the one in this chapter have been used by Blake and Mouton (1964), Lawrence and Lorsch (1967), Hall (1969), and Thomas and Walton (1971). However, at present, there is little in the way of validity data on any of them. Thomas (1971) discusses the validity problem in some detail. Essentially, there is some evidence that subjects have difficulty comprehending and distinguishing some of the behavioral categories, and some evidence of a strong social desirability response bias. Clearly, more care needs to be devoted to developing and validating these instruments.

But in addition, there is a need to develop scoring systems for coding ongoing conflict behavior. Freed from the biases inherent in self-assessment measures, such scoring systems would ultimately provide

the most objective data on conflict-handling behavior.

REFERENCES

Allport, G. W. The trend in motivational theory. *American Journal of Orthopsychiatry*, 1953, 23, 107–119.

Allport, G. W. *Becoming*. New Haven: Yale University Press, 1955.

Aram, J. D., Morgan, C. P., & Esbeck, E. B. Relation of collaborative interpersonal relationships to individual satisfaction and organizational performance. *Administrative Science Quarterly*, September, 1971, 16, 289–296.

Argyris, C. *Personality and organization: The conflict betwen system and the individual*. New York: Harper and Brothers, 1957.

Axelrod, R. Conflict of interest: An axiomatic approach. *Journal of Conflict Resolution*, March, 1967, 11, 87–99.

Axelrod, R. *Conflict of interest*. Chicago: Markham, 1970.

Bales, R. F. *Interaction process analysis: A method for the study of small groups*. Reading, Mass.: Addison-Wesley, 1950.

Baritz, L. *The servants of power*. Middletown, Conn.: Wesleyan University Press, 1960.

Bass, B. M., & Dunteman, G. Behavior in groups as a function of self, interaction, and task orientation. *Journal of Abnormal and Social Psychology*, May, 1963, 66, 419–428.

Bennis, W. G., & Shepard, H. A. A theory of group development. *Human Relations*, 1956, 9, 415–457.

Bergström, L. What is a conflict of interest? *Journal of Peace Research*, Summer, 1970, 197–219.

Berkowitz, L. *Aggression: A social psychological analysis*. New York: McGraw-Hill, 1962.

Bernard, J. The conceptualization of intergroup relations. *Social Forces*, March, 1951, 29, 243–251.

Bernard, J. Parties and issues in conflict. *Journal of Conflict Resolution*, June, 1957, 1, 111–121.

Bion, W. R. *Experiences in groups, and other papers*. London: Tavistock, 1961.

Blake, R. R., & Mouton, J. S. Reactions to intergroup competition under win-lose conditions. *Management Science,* July, 1961, 7, 420–435.

Blake, R. R., & Mouton, J. S. *The managerial grid.* Houston: Gulf Publishing, 1964.

Blake, R. R., Shepard, H. A., & Mouton, J. S. *Managing intergroup conflict in industry.* Houston: Gulf Publishing, 1964.

Blau, P. M. *The dynamics of bureaucracy.* Chicago: University of Chicago Press, 1955.

Boulding, K. E. *Conflict and defense: A general theory.* New York: Harper and Row, 1963.

Boulding, K. E. Two principles of conflict. In R. L. Kahn & E. Boulding (Eds.), *Power and conflict in organizations.* New York: Basic Books, 1964.

Burke, R. J. Methods of managing superior-subordinate conflict: Their effectiveness and consequences. *Canadian Journal of Behavioral Science,* April, 1970, 2, 124–135.

Caplow, T. *Two against one: Coalitions in triads.* Englewood Cliffs, N.J.: Prentice-Hall, 1968.

Cartwright, D. Risk taking by individuals and groups: An assessment of research employing choice dilemmas. *Journal of Personality and Social Psychology,* December, 1971, 20, 361–378.

Collins, B. E., & Guetzkow, H. *A social psychology of group processes for decision making.* New York: Wiley, 1964.

Coser, L. *The functions of social conflict.* New York: The Free Press, 1956.

Coser, L. The termination of conflict. *Journal of Conflict Resolution,* December, 1961, 5, 347–354.

Cyert, R. M., & March, J. G. *A behavioral theory of the firm.* Englewood Cliffs, N.J.: Prentice-Hall, 1963.

Dalton, M. *Men who manage.* New York: Wiley, 1959.

Deutsch, M. A theory of cooperation and competition. *Human Relations,* 1949, 2, 129–152.

Deutsch, M. Conflicts: Productive and destructive. *Journal of Social Issues,* January, 1969, 25, 7–41.

Deutsch, M. Toward an understanding of conflict. *International Journal of Group Tensions,* January-March, 1971, 1, 42–54.

Deutsch, M., & Krauss, R. M. Studies in interpersonal bargaining. *Journal of Conflict Resolution,* 1962, 6, 52–76.

Dollard, J., Doob, L., Miller, N., Mowrer, O. H., & Sears, R. R. *Frustration and aggression.* New Haven: Yale University Press, 1939.

Donnelly, L. I. Toward an alliance between research and practice in collective bargaining. *Personnel Journal,* May, 1971, 50, 372–379, 399.

Driver, M. J., & Streufert, S. The 'general incongruity adaptation level' (GIAL) hypothesis: An analysis and integration of cognitive approaches to motivation. Institute Paper No. 114, Institute for Research in the Behavioral, Economic, and Management Sciences, Krannert Graduate School of Industrial Administration, Purdue University, Lafayette, Ind., 1964.

Dubin, R. Industrial conflict and social welfare. *Journal of Conflict Resolution,* June, 1957, 1, 179–199.

Dunlop, J. T. *Industrial relations systems.* New York: Holt, Rinehart and Winston, 1958.

Dutton, J. M., & Walton, R. E. Interdepartmental conflict and cooperation: Two contrasting studies. *Human Organization,* Fall, 1966, 25, 207–220.

Eisinger, R. A., & Levine, M. J. The role of psychology in labor relations. *Personnel Journal,* September, 1968, 47, 643–649.

Emerson, R. M. Power-dependence relationships. *American Sociological Review,* 1962, 27, 31–41.

Emery, F. E. *Characteristics of socio-technical systems.* Document No. 527. London: Tavistock Institute of Human Relations, 1959.

Festinger, L., Schachter, S., & Back, K. *Social pressures in informal groups: A study of human factors in housing.* New York: Harper and Row, 1950.

Festinger, L. *Conflict, decision, and dissonance.* Stanford: Stanford University Press, 1964.

Fink, C. F. Some conceptual difficulties in the theory of social conflict. *Journal of Conflict Resolution,* December, 1968, 12, 412–460.

Fisher, R. Fractionating conflict. In R. Fisher (Ed.), *International conflict and behavioral science: The Craigville papers.* New York: Basic Books, 1964.

Follett, M. P. In H. C. Metcalf & L. Urwick (Eds.), *Dynamic administration: The collected papers of Mary Parker Follett.* New York: Harper and Brothers, 1941.

Freire, P. Conscientization: Cultural action for freedom, Part III. *Harvard Education Review,* August, 1970, 40, 452–477.

French, J. R. P. Jr., & Raven, B. H. The base of social power. In D. Cartwright (Ed.),

Studies in social power. Ann Arbor: University of Michigan, 1959, 150–167.

Galtung, J. Institutionalized conflict resolution. *Journal of Peace Research,* 1965, 4, 348–397.

Gamson, W. A. Experimental studies of coalition formation. *Advances in Experimental Social Psychology,* 1964, 1, 81–110.

Gragg, C. I. Whose fault was it? *Harvard Business Review,* January-February, 1964, 42, 107–111.

Hall, J. *Conflict management survey: A survey of one's characteristic reaction to and handling of conflicts between himself and others.* Houston: Teleometrics, Inc., 1969.

Hall, J. Decisions, decisions, decisions. *Psychology Today,* November, 1971, 5, 51–54, 86–87.

Hayakawa, S. I. *Language in thought and action.* (2nd ed.) New York: Harcourt, Brace and World, 1963.

Hoffman, L. R. Homogeneity of member personality and its effect on group problem solving. *Journal of Abnormal and Social Psychology,* January, 1959, 58, 27–32.

Hoffman, L. R., & Maier, N. R. F. Quality and acceptance of problem solutions by members of homogeneous and heterogeneous groups. *Journal of Abnormal and Social Psychology,* March, 1961, 62, 401–407.

Hoffman, L. R., Harburg, E., & Maier, N. R. F. Differences and disagreement as factors in creative group problem solving. *Journal of Abnormal and Social Psychology,* March, 1962, 64, 206–214.

Horney, K. *Our inner conflicts: A constructive theory of neurosis.* New York: W. W. Norton, 1945.

Hunt, J. McV. Motivation inherent in information processing and action. In O. J. Harvey (Ed.), *Motivation and social interaction, cognitive determinants.* New York: Ronald Press, 1963, 35–94.

Janis, I. L., & Katz, D. The reduction of intergroup hostility, research problems and hypotheses. *Journal of Conflict Resolution,* March, 1959, 3, 85–100.

Johnson, D. W. Use of role reversal in intergroup competition. *Journal of Personality and Social Psychology,* October, 1967, 7, 135–141.

Jones, E. E., & Gerard, H. B. *Foundations of social psychology.* New York: Wiley, 1967.

Journal of Conflict Resolution. Editorial, March, 1957, 1, 1–3.

Kahn, R. L., & Boulding, E., Eds. *Power and conflict in organizations.* New York: Basic Books, 1964.

Kahn, R. L., Wolfe, D. M., Quinn, R. P., Snoek, J. D., & Rosenthal, R. A. *Organizational stress: Studies in role conflict and ambiguity.* New York: Wiley, 1964.

Kelley, H. H., & Stahelski, A. J. Social interaction basis of cooperators' and competitors' beliefs about others. *Journal of Personality and Social Psychology,* 1970, 16, 66–91.

Kelly, J. Make conflict work for you. *Harvard Business Review,* July-August, 1970, 48, 103–113.

Kerr, C. Industrial conflict and its mediation. *American Journal of Sociology,* November, 1954, 60, 230–245.

Lawrence, P. R., & Lorsch, J. W. Differentiation and integration in complex organizations. *Administrative Science Quarterly,* June, 1967, 12, 1–47.

Lesieur, F. G., Ed. *The Scanlon plan: A frontier in labor-management cooperation.* Cambridge: M.I.T. Press, 1958.

Lesieur, F. G., & Puckett, E. S. The Scanlon plan has proved itself. *Harvard Business Review,* September-October, 1969, 47, 109–118.

Levinger, G. Kurt Lewin's approach to conflict and its resolution: A review with some extensions. *Journal of Conflict Resolution,* December, 1957, 1, 329–339.

Litterer, J. A. Conflict in organizations: A re-examination. *Academy of Management Journal,* September, 1966, 9, 178–186.

Litwin, G. H., & Stringer, R. A. Jr. *Motivation and organizational climate.* Cambridge: Harvard University Press, 1968.

Luce, R. D., & Raiffa, H. *Games and decisions: Introduction and critical survey.* New York: Wiley, 1957.

McKersie, R. B. Avoiding written grievances by problem solving: An outside view. *Personnel Psychology,* Winter, 1964, 17, 367–379.

McKersie, R. B., & Shropshire, W. W. Jr. Avoiding written grievances: A successful program. *The Journal of Business,* April, 1962, 35, 135–152.

March, J. G., & Simon, H. A. *Organizations.* New York: Wiley, 1958.

Mason, R. O. A dialectical approach to strategic planning. *Management Science,* April, 1969, 15, 403–414.

Megginson, L. C., & Gullett, C. R. A predictive model of union-management conflict. *Personnel Journal,* June, 1970, 49, 495–503.

Merton, R. K. *Social theory and social structure.* (Rev. ed.) Glencoe, Ill.: The Free Press, 1957.

Muench, G. A. A clinical psychologist's treatment of labor-management conflicts. *Personnel Psychology,* 1960, 13, 165–172.

Muench, G. A. A clinical psychologist's treatment of labor-management conflicts: A four-year study. *Journal of Humanistic Psychology,* 1963, 1, 92–97.

Newcomb, T. M. Autistic hostility and social reality. *Human Relations,* 1947, 1, 69–86.

Newcomb, T. M., Turner, R. H., & Converse, P. E. *Social psychology: The study of human interaction.* New York: Holt, Rinehart and Winston, 1965.

Osgood, C. E. An analysis of the cold war mentality. *Journal of Social Issues,* 1961, 17, 12–19.

Patchen, M. Models of cooperation and conflict: A critical review. *Journal of Conflict Resolution,* September, 1970, 3, 389–407.

Patten, T. H. Jr. Collective bargaining and consensus: The potential of a laboratory training input. *Management of Personnel Quarterly,* Spring, 1970, 9, 29–37.

Pelz, D. C. Some social factors related to performance in a research organization. *Administrative Science Quarterly,* 1956, 1, 310–325.

Pondy, L. R. A systems theory of organizational conflict. *Academy of Management Journal,* September, 1966, 9, 246–256.

Pondy, L. R. Organizational conflict: Concepts and models. *Administrative Science Quarterly,* September, 1967, 12, 296–320.

Pruitt, D. G. Choice shifts in group discussion: An introductory review. *Journal of Personality and Social Psychology,* December, 1971, 20, 339–360. (a)

Pruitt, D. G. Conclusions: Toward an understanding of choice shifts in group discussion. *Journal of Personality and Social Psychology,* December, 1971, 20, 495–510. (b)

Rapoport, A. Models of conflict: Cataclysmic and strategic. In A. de Reuck & J. Knight (Eds.), *Conflict in society.* Boston: Little, Brown, 1966, 259–288.

Rapoport, A., & Chammah, A. M. *Prisoner's dilemma: A study in conflict and cooperation.*

Ann Arbor: University of Michigan Press, 1965.

Raven, B. H., & Kruglanski, A. W. Conflict and power. In P. Swingle (Ed.), *The structure of conflict.* New York: Academic Press, 1970, 69–109.

Rehmus, C. The mediation of industrial conflict: A note on the literature. *Journal of Conflict Resolution,* March, 1965, 9, 118–126.

Richardson, L. F. In N. Rashevsky & E. Trucco (Eds.), *Arms and insecurity: A mathematical study of the causes and origins of war.* Pittsburgh: Boxwood Press, 1960.

Rogers, C. R., & Roethlisberger, F. J. Barriers and gateways to communication. *Harvard Business Review,* July-August, 1952, 30, 46–52.

Schein, E. H. *Process consultation: Its role in organization development.* Reading, Mass.: Addison-Wesley, 1969.

Schmidt, W. H., & Tannenbaum, R. The management of differences. *Harvard Business Review,* November-December, 1960, 38, 107–115.

Schroder, H. M., Driver, M. J., & Streufert, S. *Human information processing.* New York: Holt, Rinehart and Winston, 1967.

Schutz, W. C. The interpersonal underworld. *Harvard Business Review,* July-August, 1958, 36, 123–135.

Scott, W. G. *The management of conflict: Appeal systems in organizations.* Homewood, Ill.: Irwin-Dorsey, 1965.

Seiler, J. A. Diagnosing interdepartmental conflict. *Harvard Business Review,* September-October, 1963, 41, 121–132.

Sherif, M. Superordinate goals in the reduction of intergroup conflict. *The American Journal of Sociology,* January, 1958, 63, 349–356.

Sherif, M., & Hovland, C. I. *Social judgment: Assimilation and contrast effects in communication and attitude change.* New Haven: Yale University Press, 1961.

Sherif, M., & Sherif, C. W. *An outline of social psychology.* (Rev. ed.) New York: Harper and Brothers, 1956.

Simon, H. A. *Administrative behavior: A study of decision-making processes in administrative organization.* (2nd ed.) New York: Macmillan, 1957.

Stagner, R. Personality variables in union-management relations. *Journal of Applied Psychology,* 1962, 46, 350–357.

Stagner, R., & Rosen, H. *Psychology of union-*

management relations. Belmont, Calif.: Brooks/Cole Publishing, 1965.

Stern, I., & Pearse, R. F. Collective bargaining: A union's program for reducing conflict. *Personnel,* May-June, 1968, 45, 61–72.

Storr, A. *Human aggression.* New York: Atheneum, 1968.

Tanter, R. Review of *Conflict of interest* by Robert Axelrod. *Administrative Science Quarterly,* September, 1971, 16, 365–366.

Terhune, K. W. The effects of personality in cooperation and conflict. In P. Swingle (Ed.), *The structure of conflict.* New York: Academic Press, 1970.

Thibaut, J. The development of contractual norms in bargaining: Replication and variation. *Journal of Conflict Resolution,* March, 1968, 12, 102–112.

Thibaut, J. W., & Kelley, H. H. *The social psychology of groups.* New York: Wiley, 1959.

Thibaut, J. W., & Riecken, H. W. Some determinants and consequences of the perception of social causality. *Journal of Personality,* 1955, 24, 113–133.

Thomas, K. W. Conflict-handling modes in interdepartmental relations. Unpublished doctoral thesis, Purdue University, Lafayette, Ind., 1971.

Thomas, K. W., & Walton, R. E. Conflict-handling behavior in interdepartmental relations. Research Paper No. 38. Division of Research, Graduate School of Business Administration, UCLA, 1971.

Thompson, J. D. Organizational management of conflict. *Administrative Science Quarterly,* March, 1960, 4, 389–409.

Thompson, J. D. *Organizations in action.* New York: McGraw-Hill, 1967.

Trist, E. L., Higgin, G. W., Murray, H., &

Pollack, A. B. *Organizational choice.* London: Tavistock, 1963.

Van Doorn, J. A. A. Conflict in formal organizations. In A. de Reuck & J. Knight (Eds.), *Conflict in society.* Boston: Little, Brown, 1966, 111–133.

Wallach, M. A., & Kogan, N. The roles of information, discussion, and consensus in group risk taking. *Journal of Experimental Social Psychology,* January, 1965, 1, 1–19.

Walton, R. E. *Interpersonal peacemaking: Confrontations and third party consultation.* Reading, Mass.: Addison-Wesley, 1969.

Walton, R. E. How to choose between strategies of conflict and collaboration. In R. T. Golembiewski & A. Blumberg (Eds.), *Sensitivity training and the laboratory approach.* Itasca, Ill.: Peacock, 1970.

Walton, R. E., Dutton, J. M., & Fitch, H. G. A study of conflict in the process, structure, and attitudes of lateral relationships. In A. H. Rubenstein & C. J. Haberstroh (Eds.), *Some theories of organization.* Homewood, Ill.: Irwin, 1966.

Walton, R. E., & McKersie, R. B. *A behavioral theory of labor negotiations: An analysis of a social interaction system.* New York: McGraw-Hill, 1965.

Walton, R. E., & McKersie, R. B. Behavioral dilemmas in mixed-motive decision making. *Behavioral Science,* September, 1966, 11, 370–384.

White, H. Management conflict and sociometric structure. *American Journal of Sociology,* September, 1961, 67, 185–199.

Whyte, W. F. *Human relations in the restaurant industry.* New York: McGraw-Hill, 1948.

Zaleznik, A., & Moment, D. *The dynamics of interpersonal behavior.* New York: Wiley, 1967.

CHAPTER 22

The Technology of Organization Development

MICHAEL BEER
Harvard University

THIS CHAPTER PRESENTS a framework for conceptualizing and evaluating the growing social technology of organization change and development (OD). The historical foundations for OD are discussed briefly. The many techniques and methods of OD, from laboratory training to job enrichment, are described within an organizing framework and evaluated in terms of current research and theory. Structured and unstructured laboratory training methods are discussed and reasons for their success and failure offered. Their role in OD is placed in perspective. Next, diagnostic methods, ranging from survey feedback to less quantitative methods, such as confrontation meetings, are discussed. Process interventions, including team building, meeting processing, intergroup meetings, counseling, task forces, and interpersonal peacemaking are described, and relevant research and theory provided. Structural interventions and inventions, such as job enrichment, matrix structures, the Scanlon Plan, and Human Asset Accounting are described and evaluated. Their role in OD is also placed in perspective. Finally, the question of how these techniques can be integrated into a strategy of OD is discussed. Pre-programmed strategies, such as Grid OD, are contrasted with more organic consultant-centered strategies. The role of the consultant and his qualifications are explored briefly.

INTRODUCTION

The primary contribution of industrial psychologists to organizational effectiveness has been the development of technologies for selecting and training organizational members. While making a significant contribution, these technologies have not met many important problems faced by organizations. For example, the increasing rate of change in science, technology, information, markets, and individual needs and expectations (Toffler, 1970) has placed a premium on an organization's ability to change. Indeed, individual and organizational adaptability has become critical to the organization's ability to survive in its environment. Yet, selection programs are based on criteria of effectiveness which represent the organization's capacity to cope in the past, not its requirements for coping with the future. Such selection programs maintain the status quo (Wallace, 1970). In addition, training programs are often ineffective in their attempt to change behavior. For example, human relations training, based primarily on cognitive inputs, often fails to create significant changes in supervisory behavior. And, when these programs do change behavior, they are often in conflict with leadership or organizational climate (Fleishman, Harris, & Burtt, 1955; Sykes, 1962), which prevents permanent transfer of training into the organizational setting.

Moreover, substantial evidence has accumulated that organizations are much more than a collectivity of individuals. It is becoming clear that an organization is a complex social system (Katz & Kahn, 1966; Stogdill, 1959) whose outputs are dependent upon human inputs of abilities, needs, values, and expectations, on social processes at the interpersonal, group, and intergroup level (Argyris, 1962; Blake & Mouton, 1964; Dickson & Roethlisberger, 1966; Likert, 1961, 1967; McGregor, 1960), and on the organization's internal environment of technology (Trist & Bamforth, 1951) and structure (Burns & Stalker, 1961; Lawrence & Lorsch, 1967b; Woodward, 1967). Figure 1 shows the complex interactive relationship between inputs, processes, internal environment, and outputs.

Selection and training methods address the problem of organizational effectiveness through attempts to improve the quality of organizational inputs. Their focus on the individual ignores the important influence of social processes and the organization's internal environment on individual behavior and organizational outputs. Industrial and organizational psychologists need a technology for developing organizations as total systems.

The field of organization development (OD) has spawned a wide variety of techniques for dealing with organizations as total systems. These techniques, while sometimes based on previous research and theory, are often the result of creative practitioners responding to a variety of organizational problems and needs. They now constitute a growing social technology for intervening in, changing, and developing organizations.

What today is called OD can be traced to the unsuccessful, yet innovative, attempt by Mayo and his colleagues (Mayo, 1933; Roethlisberger & Dickson, 1939) to bridge the gap between individual needs and organizational reality. The counseling program at the Hawthorne plant of Western Electric was the first attempt to intervene directly in the organization's social process. Its failure to do so effectively stemmed from the fact that the counselors did not view themselves as change agents. They operated more as therapists, listening and reflecting,

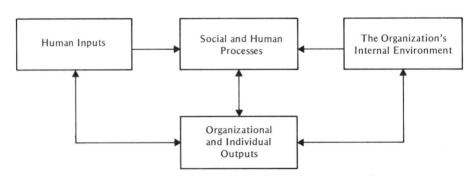

Figure 1.   Organization's internal environment of technology.

but never utilizing their data to intervene and create change (Dickson & Roethlisberger, 1966). The Hawthorne plant counseling program was followed by the development of perhaps the most important educational invention of the twentieth century—laboratory training. Though it is primarily a powerful training technique, laboratory training has been applied systematically to organizations as a means of changing organizational culture, and has influenced the development of OD. Laboratory training is discussed in the first section of this chapter.

Many of the innovative techniques for intervening in the social processes of the organization owe their origin to the principles and models on which laboratory training is founded. They are: (1) Data feedback and action-research (Lewin, 1946); (2) The use of groups for individual and group change; (3) The use of groups as agents of change (Cartwright, 1951); and (4) Participation as a means for achieving ownership of change (Coch & French, 1948). These technologies will be discussed in section two in this chapter:

1. Diagnostic technologies which depend on data and feedback as a means for changing organizations, and

2. Process technologies such as team building, which extend the method of laboratory training to the development of work groups.

Though diagnostic and process technologies have provided a means of changing organizational processes, they have not proven to be sufficient by themselves. Job and organization structure (Lawrence & Lorsch, 1969; Rice, 1953), personnel systems (Alfred, 1967; Lesieur, 1958), and financial control systems (Likert, 1967) are also important aspects of organizations. The third section in this chapter will review new organizational inventions and techniques for changing the structural constraints of the organization. The last section of this chapter will review approaches to organization change which integrate several OD technologies. The question of how to integrate technologies to achieve change has received relatively little attention to date and remains one of the key problems requiring solution before OD can achieve its full potential.

Organization development is still in its infancy and to date little research on its effectiveness exists. Therefore, this chapter will be more descriptive than evaluative. Where evaluative research is not available, an attempt has been made to place the various techniques in perspective through the use of conceptual models and theory. Kurt Lewin's model (Schein, 1961), which is most frequently used, conceptualizes change as a three-stage process of:

1. *Unfreezing:* a decrease in the strength of old attitudes, values, or behaviors resulting from information or experiences which disconfirm one's perception of self, others, or events.

2. *Changing:* the development of new attitudes, values, or behaviors through identification or internalization.

3. *Refreezing:* the stabilization of change at a new equilibrium state through supporting changes in reference group norms, culture, or organizational policy and structure. The power of each technology may be estimated by the extent to which provision for all three stages of change is made in its design. The power of a technology will also be discussed in terms of whether it is likely to change organizational inputs, processes, or outputs. A technology which changes all of these is more pervasive and powerful than one which changes only one or two.

LABORATORY TRAINING

The National Training Laboratories (NTL) sponsored its first sensitivity training program in Bethel, Maine, in 1947. Under the early guidance of Leland Bradford, Kenneth Benne, and Ronald Lippitt, NTL spearheaded the development of laboratory training as a tool for individual growth and group development. Later, through the efforts of Blake and Shepard at

Esso, laboratory training was used as a tool for organizational change and development. Blake's experience at Esso led him to some basic modifications in the laboratory training design which resulted in the instrumented laboratory (Blake & Mouton, 1962), an important and increasingly used variation of the original unstructured laboratory. For nearly twenty years laboratory training has been a major tool for organization development and a cornerstone for the new social technology of OD. Its role and potential effectiveness as an OD tool must, therefore, be understood.

The Unstructured Laboratory

In its original form a T-group is a small, unstructured, face-to-face group ranging in size from approximately ten to fifteen individuals who do not know each other (stranger group). No activities or agenda are planned. A trainer is present as a resource, guide and model, but not as a formal leader or chairman. With no structure planned and with no prior common experiences to discuss, group members' own behavior exhibited in their struggle to deal with the lack of structure becomes the agenda. "Here-and-now" behavior, in the language of T-groups, is the subject matter for learning. The main mechanism for learning is non-evaluative feedback received by each individual from other group members. This feedback creates a certain amount of anxiety and tension which causes the individual to unfreeze and begin to consider alternative values, attitudes, and behaviors. When feedback is accompanied by anxiety and embedded in group norms which value personal risk taking, owning up to feelings, collaboration, and supportiveness, an atmosphere of "psychological safety" (Schein & Bennis, 1965) is created which reduces defensiveness and resistance to self- and group examination. Self-examination leads to experimentation with new attitudes, values, assumptions, and actual behavior, thus allowing the development of new internal

states and external behavior provided they are reinforced by the group.

This description of a T-group reflects a number of theories (Hampden-Turner, 1966; Harrison, 1965; Schein & Bennis, 1965) about what happens in laboratory training. These theories share the common assumption that a laboratory training experience may confront the participant with new experiences and data which disconfirm his perceptions of himself and of the world around him. In accordance with balance theory (Festinger, 1957; Heider, 1958), T-group theorists maintain that the disequilibrium which results from such disconfirming experiences is followed by attitude changes, then new behavior, and finally a new awareness which constitutes a reintegration and new balance. A participant may experience this "developmental cycle" several times during the course of a T-group.

Learning Goals and Outcomes

Learning outcomes of laboratory training are seen as possible at the individual, group, and organizational level (Campbell & Dunnette, 1968; Seashore, 1968). At the individual level participants may increase awareness of their own behavior, their sensitivity to the behavior of others, and they may change their own attitudes and behavior. More importantly, a laboratory training experience may increase a person's confidence and ability to analyze continually his own interpersonal behavior for the purpose of changing and improving its effectiveness. Learning how to learn is potentially the most important outcome of laboratory training at the individual level.

Learning outcomes at the group level may include a better understanding of group formation and process as they affect risk taking, creativity, participation, conflict management, decision making (Argyris, 1966), and commitment. These may be translated into more effective group action in the back-home organization if a large enough proportion of any one work group has attended a laboratory. Traditional values and assumptions underlying the management of organizational phenomena such as intergroup conflict, power, influence, status, leadership, and culture may also come into question in a T-group. A more realistic understanding of these organizational problems and the assumptions underlying them may increase organizational effectiveness (Argyris, 1964b). Increased effectiveness may come about through changes in individual attitudes and behavior, but may also result from increased individual skill in diagnosing these organizational problems and intervening successfully to eliminate them in the back-home organization.

Do T-groups achieve these learning goals? Campbell and Dunnette (1968), in an extensive review of research, conclude that T-group training does induce change in individual behavior in the back-home setting. Increased sensitivity, more open communication, and increased flexibility in role behavior are among the most frequently found changes. They conclude that changes in self-perception and attitudes also occur, but that other training experiences probably also achieve these same results. Buchanan (1969), surveying much of the same literature, concludes that T-groups result in more openness, receptivity and awareness, greater tolerance of difference, and a reduction of extreme behavior. There also appears to be substantial evidence that behavioral skills, such as listening and soliciting feedback, increase and that cognitive style also changes. Finally, House (1967) concludes that T-groups change leadership style, create less dependence on others, result in less demand for subservience from others, and stimulate better communication through better listening. These research findings offer substantial support for the claim that T-groups have learning outcomes at the individual and perhaps at the group level. However, these reviews also indicate that it is often difficult to specify ahead of time the kind and extent of training outcomes for each individual (Campbell & Dunnette, 1968) and that these

outcomes are quite varied. What are the reasons for this variance and what is the implication for the translation of individual change into improved individual, group, and organizational performance?

Reasons For Varied and Unpredictable Outcomes

1. The term, T-group, or sensitivity training, is an umbrella for a large number of variations in experience-based learning technology (Dunnette, 1970). Some T-groups are aimed at heightening feelings and experience; others are intended for personal growth and development; still others are aimed at improving management and organizational effectiveness. Thus, different T-groups seek different outcomes. In addition, T-groups vary in content. Some T-group experiences involve only learning in an unstructured group; other T-group experiences include blocks of time for cognitive learning; still other T-group experiences, particularly those designed for improving managerial and organizational effectiveness, include simulations of the task and organizational environment. Finally, trainer "styles" will affect the nature of the experience in the primary T-group and the overall design of the T-group program; that is, the degree to which other non-T-group technologies are included in the training design. Research findings (Buchanan, 1969) indicate that duration of the laboratory, trainer behavior and the extent of feedback and goal setting all affect learning outcomes.

2. There is undoubtedly an interaction between the individual's personality, attitudes, values, and expectations prior to T-group and the T-group experience itself. This interaction probably results in different behavior during the laboratory and different outcomes for different individuals (Buchanan, 1969; Campbell & Dunnette, 1968). For example, Harrison and Lubin (1965) found that "work-oriented" people changed more than "person-oriented" individuals. They hypothesized that the culture shock

of the T-group for the more task-oriented person was the major reason for this.

3. The membership of T-groups varies. As originally designed, T-groups were attended by strangers for the purpose of personal learning and growth. However, as T-group technology was used more and more for the purpose of organizational change and development, the composition tended to move from "stranger groups" to "cousin groups" (individuals from the same organization who do not work together) and "family groups" (a boss and his subordinates) (Kuriloff & Atkins, 1966). Thus the particular composition of the T-group may result in different outcomes. In support of this, Morton and Wight (1964) reported that family T-groups resulted in more transfer of change to the organization than cousin groups. While unfreezing and learning effects are likely to be greater in stranger groups because of the relative safety of this environment, refreezing of behavior and transfer of learning to the back-home environment are likely to be greater in cousin and family groups. Degree of group homogeneity in personality also seems to affect learning outcomes (Buchanan, 1969).

4. A variety of training outcomes is likely to occur due to differences in participants' back-home situations. The learning of any two individuals may be identical, but the behaviors exhibited on the job will vary depending on which new behaviors and attitudes happen to be supported by their respective organizational cultures. For example, Underwood (1965) found that the extent to which new behaviors are seen as contributing to effectiveness (and are presumably supported by others) will depend on organizational norms. In other words, even if T-groups were always to result in the same learning, final attitude and behavioral outcomes will vary depending on the back-home environment.

From the discussion above it should be clear that the crucial question surrounding T-groups is not whether they are effective, but rather under what circumstances they are effective and, therefore, when and how they should be used in an OD program. This question will be discussed following the next section on the instrumented laboratory.

Instrumented Versus Unstructured Laboratory Training

Reviews on the effectiveness of laboratory training have typically lumped all forms of such training together. Yet, research indicates that the design of the laboratory training program is an important variable in determining results. The instrumented training laboratory, for example, Blake and Mouton's (1962) Managerial Grid Laboratory, is significantly different from the traditional T-group.

The key difference between the instrumented laboratory and the T-group lies in the former's planned and structured nature. Participants work in groups much like the T-group, although the size of the group is typically smaller (between five and eight participants). Groups are in competition with each other and are given specific tasks on which to work. The content of the exercises provides cognitive learning. In the case of the Managerial Grid Laboratory (Blake & Mouton, 1964), the content centers around a two-dimensional grid (one dimension of the grid represents people-oriented behavior and the other, production-centered behavior), which provides a framework for understanding leadership and managerial behavior. Participants typically prepare solutions to problems or fill out questionnaires as part of pre-work to test their understanding of the Managerial Grid. During the session, participants must develop a consensual team solution for each of the tasks they worked on individually. These group activities generate individual and group behavior and provide experiential data for individual and group self-examination. Since questionnaires based on the Grid framework are used to collect perceptions of individual and group functioning, experiential learning occurs within a common conceptual framework and reinforces the cognitive learning goals of the laboratory. Thus, the instrumented laboratory provides cognitive and experiential learning, learning about content and process. Moreover, the instrumentation reduces dependence on the trainer as facilitator, interpreter of behavior, and/or teacher, and allows line managers to be instructors for in-company programs, an important part of Blake and Mouton's strategy for change. Blake and Mouton's leadership in developing the instrumented laboratory has been followed by others. For example, Morton's Organization Development Laboratory (Morton & Bass, 1964) is similar to the Managerial Grid in its use of structure, planned exercises, and feedback through questionnaires.

Little sound research on the effectiveness of the Managerial Grid Laboratory in changing individual and group behavior is available. Many of the studies amount to subjective reports of participants after completion of the training. Smith and Hanour (1969) found a trend toward more participative managerial values and a small increase in openness of communication in meetings and in one-to-one relationships. The biggest changes occurred in meetings and work group behavior, but in general the changes were small. Similarly, Beer and Kleisath (1967) report significant shifts in opinions about ideal leadership behavior (in the expected direction) following the Grid Laboratory and also improvements on a number of organizational dimensions one year following laboratory attendance by all salaried employees in one organization.

Unstructured Versus Instrumented Laboratory Training

T-groups would seem to have as their greatest advantage the capacity to intensively involve participants and create an awareness of process at the interpersonal level. The instrumented laboratory seems to have an advantage in its ability to direct and focus learning in specific, preselected areas, and in creating awareness of group process through formal critique. The lack of structure and reliance on the trainer as a reference for learning provides little content control in the "pure" T-group and the focus on interpersonal factors is often at the expense of attention to group process. Hall (1970) arrives at the conclusion that instrumented laboratories, such as Grid, best optimize three criteria: (1) participant involvement, (2) control over content, and (3) focus on process. Wilson, Mullen, and Morton (1968) report that a very high percentage of participants who six months before attended Morton's Organization Development Laboratory and a similarly high percentage of participants who eighteen months before attended a sensitivity training session claimed that the experience was of value to them. However, those who went through the instrumented laboratory showed significantly greater improvement as managers, as members of a team, in building team effort in their organizations, and in communication with others at work. Unfortunately, the study had many flaws and as yet a final conclusion cannot be reached.

Laboratory Training and Organization Development[1]

Undoubtedly, laboratory training can have powerful unfreezing effects on individuals during and immediately following the training experience. The off-site session, the stranger group, the "cultural island" reinforced by laboratory norms, and the feedback can undermine the individual's clarity of self and his integration of past behavior and attitudes. Indeed, the individual often sees himself and his past managerial behavior as less than optimal when compared with newly learned expectations. Blake, for example, finds a considerable drop after

[1] In this discussion T-groups and instrumented laboratories will be lumped together, although clearly most of the research on which the discussion is based has been on T-groups.

training in percentage of laboratory participants who report themselves as 9,9 managers (managers equally high in concern for people and productivity). Similarly, laboratory training probably changes individual expectations of what is ideal organizational behavior, and this is displayed through less favorable perceptions of the organization immediately after training (Zand, Steele, & Zalkind, 1967) and in changed perceptions of what constitutes an ideal organizational climate (Golembiewski & Carrigan, 1970). The implication of these findings is that only when individuals have learned to be more aware of their own and others' behavior can they become aware of and develop new expectations for organizational behavior. Thus, to unfreeze an organization and pave the way for change, individuals need to be intra- and interpersonally aware (Tannenbaum, 1971), and they need to perceive themselves and their organizations as less than ideal.

That such unfreezing occurs and allows the learning of new skills and attitudes seems to be indicated by research findings of increased sensitivity, greater openness in communication, and greater flexibility in role behavior (Campbell & Dunnette, 1968). However, it is in the transfer of the new attitudes and skills to daily organizational life that laboratory training as a single and only technology of change falls short. Argyris (1971) believes that T-groups motivate new behaviors but provide little skill in how to use them on the job; that is, they do not build sufficient competence for effective utilization of these behaviors in the task environment and this in turn creates barriers to organization development and change.

Buchanan (1969) cites three development efforts that successfully overcame the transfer problems through systematic application of laboratory training throughout the company. In a sales organization the systematic application of T-group technology to a sales organization resulted in significant movement toward a "System 4" climate (see Likert, 1967) eighteen months after training

(Golembiewski & Carrigan, 1970). The effects of laboratory training were probably enhanced by a confrontation of organizational issues immediately after the T-group and a facilitating experience one year later.

Beer and Kleisath (1967) report similar findings after systematic application of the Managerial Grid Laboratory to all salaried exempt employees in one division of a company. Changes in leadership style, group process, responsibility, and delegation were found over a one-and-a-half year time period. Satisfaction with supervisory behavior increased for salaried nonexempt employees who did not attend the Grid Laboratory, indicating that the new supervisory behavior transferred back into the organization. However, research in the same division three years later indicated the continuation of poor intergroup relationships (Beer, 1970). These problems were to be dealt with by a subsequent phase of the Grid OD program which was to translate laboratory learning into improved intergroup relations. This phase never took place and the changes never occurred, thus demonstrating the limitations of laboratory training when it is the only OD intervention.

Attempts to increase transfer also frequently take the form of "including in the training experience people and/or activities associated with the job, while still retaining a focus on behavior in the laboratory" (Buchanan, 1967). Likewise, Shepard (1965) suggested that laboratory training be applied to family groups so that a new structure of work relationships is built at the same time that a new viewpoint is developed by group members. This application of T-group technology will be discussed in the section on team development later in this chapter. The consultant is also important in assuring transfer of learning (Friedlander, 1968). His role prior to and following laboratory training can be critical in assuring that the new attitudes and skills are transferred into the organizational setting.

However, even if the transfer of learning occurs, the new skills and attitudes may not always contribute to organizational effectiveness or may take some time to be felt. One finding (Bass, 1967; Deep, Bass, & Vaughan, 1967) suggests that T-group experience actually reduces effectiveness in a simulated business situation; another (Wagner, 1965) suggests that there is a time period of uncertainty and trial-and-error as participants regress from their learned behavior, then overcompensate, and finally apply their new learning efficiently.

There are other reasons for considering alternatives to laboratory training. One reason is a conflict between laboratory training values and the organization's values (Bennis, 1969). Another reason is that persons opposed to T-group values may not attend such a program (Argyris, 1971). At such times other less threatening interventions should be used.

The strength of laboratory training probably lies in its ability to modify organizational inputs (individual needs, expectancies, values, abilities, and cognitive frameworks). However, additional technologies and multiphase programs are needed to ensure transfer and refreezing of new attitudes and behaviors (Blake & Mouton, 1968b; Buchanan, 1968; Marrow, Bowers, & Seashore, 1967).

The remainder of this chapter will be devoted to OD technologies which are used to supplement laboratory training and often to replace it.

DIAGNOSTIC INTERVENTIONS

Part of the transfer problem associated with laboratory training comes from the fact that there are no built-in mechanisms for focusing unfrozen states of participants and their new learning about self and organization on relevant and important organizational problems. Systematic and planned improvement of an organization requires diagnosis (Beckhard, 1969) of its various subsystems (i.e., production department, research and development group) and processes (i.e., decision making, communica-

tion). To facilitate this, the social sciences have developed an elaborate research technology which can be used to measure the social-psychological state of an organization. These range from numerous questionnaire techniques to measure attitudes (Edwards, 1957; Shaw & Wright, 1967), leadership behavior (Stogdill & Coons, 1957), group process (Hemphill, 1956), and organizational climate (Likert, 1967; Litwin & Stringer, 1968) to interviews and observation. Because the very process of conducting research may contaminate and change the subject (individual or organization), unobtrusive measures of organizational behavior (Webb, Campbell, Schwartz, & Sechrest, 1966) have received considerable attention.

The relative merits of each of these measurement techniques have been widely discussed and argued. It seems rather clear that each method has certain advantages and disadvantages and that an integrated research approach (Whyte, 1963) which draws on the strengths of each of these methods is the most valid means of diagnosing organizational problems, understanding organizational behavior (Alderfer, 1967; Beer, 1971b), and evaluating the effects of organization development efforts (Beer, 1970). Probably the most efficient and effective sequence of diagnostic methods starts with observation, is followed by a semistructured interview, and is completed with a questionnaire intended to measure precisely problems identified by the earlier diagnostic steps. This sequence provides a funnel effect, moving from emphasis on "band-width" to emphasis on "fidelity" of measurement.

Of the three traditional methods, the questionnaire survey holds the greatest promise for *efficiently* obtaining data about the functioning of large-scale social systems. It has the further advantage of standardization and, therefore, offers the possibility of comparing data across organizational units. However, the questionnaire's greatest disadvantage lies in its inflexibility and, therefore, in its inability to identify problems not previously anticipated by the researcher. Too often psychometrically sound questionnaires are designed to measure theoretical constructs or variables, not to identify organizational problems. Too often they do not provide sufficient qualitative information to fully understand what is happening in the organization. Supplementing questionnaires with interviews and observations is one answer. Innovation in questionnaire development and use is another answer.

The "Corporate Excellence Rubric" developed by Blake and Mouton (1968a, 1969) is an operationally oriented (as compared to theoretically oriented) way of viewing organizational behavior, performance, and results. In *Corporate Excellence Diagnosis* (Blake & Mouton, 1968a), they have translated this framework into a book of scales that can be used to diagnose organizational problems and review progress of change efforts. The six major activities of Human Resources, Financial Management, Operations, Marketing, R&D, and Corporate are assessed by means of ratings and open-ended comments. The scales are designed to be used by managers as a preliminary to discussion.

In order to overcome the problem of inflexibility, Rosen and Komorita (1969) developed an "Ipsative Consequence Model." There is no predetermined structure of items. Subjects list both positive and negative consequences of a potential change and then rate them in terms of subjective utility and probability. This eliminates the negative effects of a structured questionnaire and the disadvantage of interviews which require trained personnel; yet, the advantages of both of these methods are still retained. The Ipsative Consequences Model allows diagnosis of potential problems prior to organizational change, thus aiding the planning of change, or it can be modified to assess the consequences of change.

Heller (1969) suggests "Group Feedback Analysis" as a means of extending questionnaire methodology. After a questionnaire survey is completed, subjects are convened for feedback of the data and an unstructured discussion. Heller reports that more understanding is obtained from this diagnostic method than is provided by the questionnaire alone.

Data Gathering For Whom?

Who needs to understand data gathered about organizational functioning during the diagnostic phase? Traditional research methods are geared to provide understanding for the social scientist. Organizational members are told as little as possible about the purpose of the research. As Argyris (1968) has pointed out, this approach places organizational members in a dependent relationship with the researcher and can have many of the negative effects of Theory X management (McGregor, 1960), such as resistance, falsification of data, lack of cooperation with the researcher, and lack of commitment to organizational change implied by the findings.

When the purpose of gathering data is change, organizational members, even more so than the OD consultant, must understand the data and develop an awareness of problems facing the organization. They, not the social scientist, must develop a commitment to organizational change. What is needed are diagnostic methods which involve organizational members in the process of identifying and diagnosing organization problems. Psychometric soundness and issues of statistical reliability and validity become relatively unimportant in comparison with the issue of commitment to the needed change.

Post-Laboratory Diagnosis

A technique often used by OD consultants to accomplish these objectives is the post-laboratory diagnosis. If members from a single organizational unit are attending a training laboratory, the unfreezing effects of the laboratory and the cognitive learning about organizations which occur there can be used effectively by having participants diagnose organizational problems immediately following the laboratory experience. Blake and Mouton (1968a) suggest this approach for organizations utilizing the Managerial Grid Laboratory. Following the week-long laboratory seminar, organization members diagnose the culture of their organization by completing individually an organization culture questionnaire and then developing a consensual answer for each question. They then present their views to key managers who are present for this last part of the training program. The culture questionnaire employed for this purpose is based on the same cognitive framework used throughout the week's training.

In effect, the laboratory training experience teaches participants the concepts necessary for an accurate diagnosis, unfreezes them sufficiently to view their organization differently than they otherwise would, and provides a climate for risk taking and confrontation. A similar approach has been used following T-groups (Golembiewski & Carrigan, 1970).

The post-laboratory diagnosis would seem to be a more effective intervention than the laboratory experience alone, or a diagnosis alone. The structure of a questionnaire and/or the stimulus of a guided group discussion about organizational problems is a natural way to channel the unfreezing and learning effects of the laboratory experience into changes in organizational functioning and behavior. It is a step toward achieving transfer from laboratory training to organizational change.

Survey Feedback

Mann and his associates were among the first to depart from traditional training techniques (Mann, 1957; Mann & Likert, 1952; Neff, 1965). They developed the survey feedback approach as a means of creating change. Survey feedback interventions combine diagnosis as a means of focusing change efforts on organizationally relevant problems and group methods as a medium for unfreezing and change.

The survey feedback process is a collaborative effort between consultant and organizational members in gathering data about organizational processes, analyzing this data, interpreting it, and action planning for change and improvement. This process normally starts with a questionnaire, although interview data can also be used (Beckhard, 1966). It is important that the client system own the data and, therefore, their involvement in developing the questionnaire items becomes an important step in the process (Chase, 1968). The consultant can be helpful in this process by suggesting questions based on preliminary interviews with a small sample of organization members and by providing help in the formulation of items and development of scales. Intuitively, the degree of involvement in questionnaire development seems important in determining ownership of the findings; however, not enough research has been done on this to conclude one way or the other.

Data are fed back to the client system through a series of interlocking conferences with family units starting at the top and moving down through the organization systematically. The meeting is best scheduled, planned, and led by the line manager (Klein, Kraut, & Wolfson, 1971) after the data are fed back to him by the consultant. The consultant may help in the planning and is present during the feedback session as a resource for interpreting the data. He helps the group to problem solve and plan for needed change and to critique its own process during the meeting (Miles, Hornstein, Callahan, Calder, & Schiavo, 1966).

The three components of survey feedback interventions are data, group meeting, and process analysis. Each uniquely contributes to the change process (Miles et al., 1966).

1. *Data:* Survey feedback data usually deal with organizational issues such as roles, intergroup relations, supervision, communication, organizational policy and employee

satisfaction, and attitudes. Neff (1965) has suggested that data about organizational performance also be included in the feedback process. In contrast, data generated in laboratory training is primarily concerned with individual's self, interpersonal relations, and group process. Furthermore, in survey feedback the questionnaire mediates the feedback process, while in laboratory training the trainer and group are the mediators. In survey feedback, most of the data are objective and about "there-and-then" problems (things that have happened on the job prior to the meeting), while in laboratory training the data are mostly subjective and "here-and-now" (individuals' feelings and perceptions about other T-group members and the T-group itself). As in laboratory training, the role of survey data is to corroborate the client's beliefs about the state of the organization, or *disconfirm* beliefs, thereby unfreezing the client and encouraging *inquiry* concerning the reasons for the data. The key to making survey feedback data as powerful a tool for unfreezing as the here-and-now data of laboratory training lies in its relevancy. The data should be broken down to reflect the specific condition of the department or group receiving the feedback rather than the organization as a whole. The greater the relevancy of the data the greater the likelihood that organizational members will be involved with the data and committed to subsequent change. Wakeley (1964) has found that relevancy and involvement can be increased by getting managers to forecast attitude survey results. This method probably helps bring into sharper focus confirming and disconfirming data, thereby creating greater unfreezing and encouraging inquiry.

2. *Group Meetings:* An important part of the survey feedback process is that it takes place in family group meetings. Meetings have been found to result in more satisfaction with the feedback process and perception of greater information utilization than feedback through written reports (Klein

et al., 1971). Similarly, multiple meetings were found by Klein, Kraut, and Wolfson to be more effective than a single meeting. Meetings are effective because they probably have an unfreezing effect by creating pressure on individuals to own up and clarify their views for the group. The group meeting also creates pressure on individuals to evaluate their views about problems in light of the prevailing viewpoint in the group. Thus, if effective problem solving is done by the group, members are likely to arrive at greater agreement about the real problem and develop more change momentum. The group meeting can unfreeze existing beliefs about problems, change individual and group perceptions of these problems, and refreeze a new group awareness and belief through group pressure. The group becomes the medium of change (Cartwright, 1951). Support for this comes from a recent finding (Chase, 1968) that the most effective changes are ones which take place during a feedback meeting in which the group identifies its problems, decides to change, and determines the direction for change.

Myers (1967) reports a feedback process in which the manager appoints a committee of employees to analyze data and make recommendations for change. This method does not seem to take advantage of the unfreezing and change potential inherent in the family group meetings. As in the Coch and French (1948) study of participation, direct involvement in the change is likely to bring about more commitment to the change and more favorable consequences than indirect involvement through a temporary group of representatives. A family unit's direct involvement in the feedback process also enhances the group's potential to change and adapt after the survey feedback process is over. Indeed, the open discussion and sharing of feelings about the group's problems in front of the boss can create an immediate change in the capacity of the group to deal with these problems later. Once problems have been openly discussed with the authority figure, it is easier to do so in the future. However, such an open discussion may be difficult to achieve (Chase, 1968) immediately and may only develop with the help of a third party and after "word has gotten around" that the first few conferences went well and did not result in anyone being hurt or fired.

3. *Process Analysis:* The consultant can provide the stimulus for the group to analyze its own process during the feedback session. Thus, the meeting can generate here-and-now behavior at the individual and group level which in itself may provide significant learning. Openness, collaboration, problem solving, and decision making can be examined with the help of the third party. A consultant who facilitates process analysis can provide useful learning for group members and can significantly improve the group's output. Evidence for the latter comes from the study by Klein et al. (1971) in which it was found that communication and involvement were positively related to group member satisfaction with the survey feedback process and perceptions that feedback data would be utilized. Chase (1968) reported significantly better problem solving and meeting outputs when a consultant was present. Most survey feedback interventions reported in the literature have not recognized the contribution that experiential learning, coming from process examination during survey feedback meetings, makes in achieving behavioral and organizational change.

It is clear that survey feedback is much more than questionnaires and reporting of results. A sophisticated diagnosis without the follow-up steps of interlocking conferences throughout the organization will not result in acceptance and utilization of the data (Mann, 1957). Though evaluation research on the survey feedback technology is limited, there is some evidence to suggest that the feedback process itself can effect change. The original Detroit Edison work (Baumgartel, 1959; French, Lawshe, & Mann, 1956) showed that groups which had

more intensive feedback sessions and a consultant present showed more favorable change in attitudes when compared with groups who had less intensive feedback sessions and controls who had no feedback. One of the key changes was in perception of supervisory behavior (Baumgartel, 1959), which may indicate that the feedback process helped open up channels of communication normally blocked by hierarchy and power differentials. Thus, survey feedback may equalize power (Leavitt, 1965) and thereby increase communication, information flow, confrontation of problems—all important dimensions of organizational health. Chase (1968) reports that the survey feedback model was effective in equalizing power, so that even in an extremely threatening environment confrontation occurred.

In order to create lasting change, survey feedback must be followed up. Frohman (1970) found that consultant involvement after survey feedback resulted in more change than when such follow-up did not occur. Miles et al. (1969) report a failure of the survey feedback intervention in a school system probably due to lack of action planning following the feedback and failure to provide continued support for and planning of further organization development. Not surprisingly, transfer into organizational life will not be achieved unless goals for change are developed. Survey feedback, like laboratory training, cannot be an isolated event and must be related in some way to a broader OD program. Neff (1965) suggests that action planning on specific problems is important to the success of the survey feedback method. Frohman and Shashkin (n.d.) review a number of successful OD programs in which the survey feedback method was an integral part of a larger effort.

Interview Feedback

The survey feedback method is an attempt to combine scientific rigor in measurement with feedback techniques and thereby increase the probability that the data will be utilized. As Chase (1968) suggests, however, scientific rigor is much less crucial than ownership of the data and commitment to action. Without commitment to the action program even the best data are useless in effecting change. Mean scores on a rating scale are "cold" (McLuhan, 1964) and impersonal and may fail to stimulate conflict about important issues. On the other hand, the semi-structured interview has the advantage of flexibility, which increases the probability that specific problems will surface and be stated in a language familiar to everyone. Beckhard (1966) reported a case study where the survey feedback was used successfully.

The Confrontation Meeting

The confrontation meeting (Beckhard, 1967) is designed to bring together a large segment of an organization so that members are directly involved in problem identification and action planning for organizational improvement.

The confrontation meeting can mobilize an organization toward an action plan in a shorter period of time than the survey feedback, usually an afternoon and morning. Therefore, it is probably best used when an organization faces some sort of crisis or stress, such as the loss of a key customer, a new top manager, a new product, or a new area of business. In these situations there is often a wide gap between the perceptions of top management and those closer to the problem at a lower level.

A consultant is present during the meeting; however, the general manager of the organization opens the meeting. He describes the purpose of the meeting and attempts to create a supportive climate so that individuals will take the personal risks needed to surface problems. Assurances are made about the anonymity of the data.

A large group which consists of as many as fifty or sixty people (several levels of an organization) is divided into smaller groups of five or six individuals, each small group consisting of people from different organization units and levels. Bosses and subordinates are not placed in the same group. The top group meets as a group, but without the general manager. The assignment is "Think of yourself as a person with needs and goals in this organization, and think of the total organization. What are the behaviors, procedures, ways of work, attitudes, etc., that should be different so that life would be better around here?" (Beckhard, 1967).

Lists of items are made in an hour. Each group reports the problem list to the larger group. The lists are then combined into categories by the leaders with help from the consultant. This usually takes a half-day. The following morning new groups are formed along functional and expert lines which fit the problem categories identified. The senior person in the organization for that functional or problem area heads the group. They go through the list and select three or four items which affect them most, discuss these, problem solve, and determine action and timetables for beginning work on the problem. They also select additional items to which top management should give the highest priority. A partial plan to communicate to the rest of the organization about the meeting is developed. Each group reports to the total group the results of their work, and the meeting ends. Beckhard recommends a follow-up meeting to review progress toward the goals developed during the confrontation meeting. Both follow-up and positive action on the results of the meeting are critical; otherwise, a loss in trust and credibility results.

Beckhard feels that the qualities which make the confrontation meeting a useful technology are that it provides rapid diagnosis, catharsis, involvement in problem identification and problem solving; increases influence of lower levels, thereby increasing commitment; shortcuts normal bureaucratic barriers to decision making; and enhances quality of decisions by placing the problems where the information is. Undoubtedly, organizational members come out of a confrontation meeting with a similar view of what needs to be done.

The chief difference between the confrontation meeting and the other data feedback methods described above is the direct involvement of organizational members in the diagnosis. In the other diagnostic methods the questionnaire and/or the consultant's interview are the means of generating data. The consultant's feedback of the data is the catalyst for confrontation and problem solving. In the confrontation meeting there is no intermediate step. This is its greatest advantage and at the same time its greatest pitfall. There is no question that data generated by organizational members themselves is "hot" (McLuhan, 1964), and, therefore, real to them and easy to own. However, this very quality of the meeting may be threatening to organizational members. And without openness problems will not surface. Not surprisingly then, crisis situations, which seem to generate willingness to take personal risks and to tackle problems, are regarded as the best environment for a confrontation meeting. A climate of openness is crucial for a successful confrontation meeting. In short, the meeting is an attempt to stimulate the type of communicating that should have been occurring in the organization all along by creating a special situation where openness can occur.

The process and product of the confrontation meeting are the strongest evidence for its contribution to organizational effectiveness. Thus, the nature of the problems identified and their importance to organizational performance is one measure of this technique's usefulness. Bennis (1969) described a confrontation meeting in a small R&D firm where problems of competitiveness between project teams, lack of decisions about future direction, and questions about the manager's leadership were identified. Several changes occurred as a result of the meeting, including the appointment of an administrative manager to take over some

of the leadership in managing the firm. More recently, a confrontation design was effectively utilized to prevent the shutdown of a plant due to unprofitable operations. The plant was able to reduce its loss rate from $1,000,000 a year to $200,000 a year within a year after the confrontation meeting (Huse & Barebo, 1970).

Confrontation meetings have not been used often enough and data are scarce. Research is needed on the organizational conditions for which it is best suited, the accuracy of the diagnosis, and the effectiveness of problem solutions under these various conditions.

Other Diagnostic Technologies

The trend in the field of OD seems to be going in the direction of less rigorous, more organic, and more involving techniques for diagnosing organizational states. The emphasis is on getting organizational members directly involved in diagnosis, and in the problem solving and goal setting which must follow if improvements are to occur. The assumption underlying this trend, and a correct one in this writer's view, is that organizational members engaged in this type of diagnostic process will feel ownership of the findings and thus develop a commitment to correcting the problem. They will also learn how to diagnose organizational problems. They will become more process aware and readier to recognize process problems on their own in the future. A number of these more organic and involving diagnostic technologies have been developed in the systems group of TRW (Fordyce & Weil, 1971), discussed briefly below.

Sensing

This is essentially an unstructured group interview through which a manager can inform himself directly about the feelings, attitudes, and problems at lower levels of the organization not normally accessible to him. The group session can be tape recorded for wider use later. Several types of groups (functional groups, horizontal groups, diagonal slices, professional groups, etc.) may be chosen depending on the problems or needs of the manager. Huse and Beer (1971) report on the use of this tool, which helped a plant manager keep in constant touch with the feelings of hourly employees.

The Manager's Diagnostic Meeting

The top manager or his principal assistant, a staff assistant or assistants who have broad contacts within the organization, representatives from various levels of the organization, and a consultant meet as a team to assess the effectiveness of the organization and to determine where and if change is needed. The team may gather information by the sensing method, questionnaires, or interviews. The emphasis of this tool is on diagnosis and pooling of information periodically, although recommendations for change in goals and strategies can result.

The Family Group Diagnostic Meeting

This meeting is a vehicle through which a work group gathers data about its own performance, critiques it, and decides on further steps for change, if necessary. The manager suggests categories in which information is to be gathered, such as planning, achieving goals, what is done best, what is done worst, and how the group works together and with other groups. These categories can be given at the meeting, but, preferably, the categories are given before the meeting. Data generated are discussed and re-categorized by major themes and actions planned (for example, a team building meeting or intergroup meeting discussed later in this chapter). The meeting is a simple way for a group to generate its own data, rather than relying on a third party to do it. All the advantages of direct involvement are inherent in this method,

although there may be limited openness if the group has had no previous development and a supportive climate does not exist.

The Organization Mirror

The organization mirror allows an organizational unit to obtain feedback from a number of key interfaces (user of a staff service, customers, suppliers, etc.). A third party gathers data ahead of time and presents the information at the beginning of the meeting. The outsiders (individuals from other organizational units) fishbowl to discuss and interpret data. Then the insiders fishbowl to discuss what they heard the outsiders say and identify issues needing clarification. The meeting then goes on to an identification of major problems, problem solving, and action planning for improvement.

Diagnostic Interventions In Perspective

All of the diagnostic interventions discussed above are designed to generate data either about the organization as a whole or about one organizational unit. The methods differ in their research rigor and in the degree of involvement by organization members. Observation, questionnaires, and the interview in the hands of a skilled professional can probably provide the most sophisticated and detailed picture of what is going on in the organization, but they do not involve organization members in the process and, therefore, generate less ownership of the data and commitment to change. The manager-developed questionnaire and, to an even greater extent, the various data generating meetings provide a less elegant data base, but result in more ownership of the diagnosis.

The inverse relationship between scientifically rigorous research methods and commitment to change creates a continuing dilemma for the change agent (Lawrence & Lorsch, 1969). He must weigh the trade-off between quality of diagnosis and commitment through involvement. The more sophisticated consultant or questionnaire-centered diagnosis should be the choice in situations where the problems are not urgent; the client feels a clear hurt; the problems are not obvious; there is little previous experience in the organization with OD and less process awareness; there is low trust within the organization and low probability of open self-diagnosis; and/or the change agent is trusted and perceived as competent. Participative and organic approaches to diagnosis should be the choice where problems are critical; the client does not feel a clear hurt; problems are not difficult to see; the individuals in the organization are aware of organizational process; there is a fair amount of trust between organizational members; and/or the change agent has not had a chance to build expert influence or trust. Few situations will point to a clear-cut and obvious choice between the organic, client-centered diagnosis, and the more rigorous, consultant-centered diagnosis. The considerations just listed will have to be weighed and traded off. If sufficient time exists, it may even be possible to use both approaches to diagnosis, thereby gaining the benefits of both. Many questions about the situational conditions which must be considered in choosing a diagnostic method remain unanswered and await further experience and research.

The diagnostic interventions discussed in this section utilize groups as the means of generating data and as the medium for problem solving and goal setting. This is as it should be. Research in group dynamics suggests (Cartwright, 1951) that the group should be used as the source of data, the target of change, and the agent of change. Furthermore, the group process itself has beneficial effects beyond the specific problems being dealt with. Communication is improved, relationships are built, a climate of supportiveness and openness which can carry over into the task environment is developed.

Action planning and goal setting are integral parts of most of the interventions described above. Kolb, Winter, and Berlew (1968) found that persons who set training goals during a T-group were perceived by the trainers and by themselves to change more. Action goals probably provide a clear view of the path which has to be taken to create change (Campbell, Dunnette, Lawler, & Weick, 1970), a path or a means not previously understood. Indeed, not setting goals following data feedback has probably been the cause for failure in some situations (Miles et al., 1969).

Are the diagnostic interventions discussed in this section effective in creating change? The data are limited but suggest that they can be. From the theoretical point of view discussed in the previous paragraphs, there is reason to believe that they will create unfreezing and, to some extent, change and refreezing. The whole process of data feedback, problem solving and goal setting is so clearly linked to the organizational health dimensions of confrontation, undistorted communication, and clear goals (Beckhard, 1969) that relevance of these interventions to organizational health and effectiveness seems apparent. Diagnostic interventions can change organizational behavior and refreeze it, but in this they are less powerful than laboratory training and other interventions (which will be discussed in the remainder of this chapter). That is, diagnostic interventions are probably better in identifying problems and unleashing the willingness to change than they are at actually creating conditions for behavior change and refreezing. For this reason, diagnostic interventions are usually followed by process interventions which can capitalize on the readiness for change evoked by diagnostic interventions.

PROCESS INTERVENTIONS

The primary emphasis of diagnostic interventions is developing an awareness of organizational problems. Yet, diagnostic interventions are more than a technique for generating data; they are also a means for beginning the process of change. Nevertheless, to accomplish these changes and to refreeze appropriate behavior, a number of techniques for direct intervention in various interpersonal, group, and organizational processes have been developed. The purposes of these "process interventions" is to eliminate problems and to create conditions for permanent change.

Process interventions are specially created situations which allow the examination and change of ongoing relationships and interactions in the context of the actual task environment. While immediate problems are being worked on, organizational members are learning by doing. New behaviors which emerge and are encouraged during the course of the intervention can be the beginning of a learning cycle when these new behaviors *successfully* resolve work problems immediately and later. In a sense, the change agent indirectly takes over the management process by creating a situation in which managers and employees will look at problems in new ways and solve them through means not normally used. The probability of permanent change in the organization is enhanced because the new behaviors are practiced in performing ongoing tasks within the context of the family group and/or organizational setting. Thus, transfer of individual learning to relevant organizational situations, a problem for laboratory training, is not a problem for process interventions. In addition, refreezing of new behaviors and attitudes is enhanced by the shared experience of the work group and the pressure of new norms adopted by the group during the time of the intervention. The conditions usually created to make this happen are: (1) feedback of data about how organizational members view other organizational members, organizational processes, and/or organizational problems; (2) the presence of the change agent as a catalyst; (3) an offsite location; and (4) the creation and enforcement by the change agent of norms which ensure psychological safety and a problem-solving approach to conflict.

In simple terms, process interventions are based on the assumption that new behavior, when successful, will lead to attitude and value changes, and these changes in turn will reinforce the new behaviors. The assumption that behavior change can and must come first in the change process is supported by Skinner's (1953) work in operant conditioning and by Bandura's (1969) application of behavior therapy.

Process interventions can differ in depth. Some, such as those which deal with meeting behavior, are not particularly value laden or central to the individual's self-identity or the organization's culture. Other interventions, such as team development, can be emotionally laden and quite central to the individual's or group's sense of self. Which intervention is appropriate depends on the problem and, importantly, the readiness of the client (Harrison, 1970).

Process interventions typically repeat the cycle of data gathering, feedback, discussion, problem solving and action planning we have seen in the diagnostic interventions. What distinguishes a process intervention from a diagnostic intervention is its focus on one or more specific human or organizational processes identified as problems in an earlier diagnosis, and relatively greater emphasis on changing and refreezing organizational behavior and functioning.

Processing Meetings

Meetings are a way of life in every organization. They are used as means of communication, coordination, problem solving and decision making. Due to the multiple purposes of meetings and to their crucial importance in resolving key task problems, meetings can play an important part in the organization's effectiveness. Furthermore, problems in interpersonal, intragroup, and intergroup relationships can affect the quality of a meeting and its outcomes.

Meetings are a time when people and process come together and offer a unique opportunity for data gathering, process improvement, and improvement in organizational effectiveness. Not surprisingly then, meetings have been found useful for both organizational diagnosis and OD interventions (Argyris, 1971; Beer, 1971b; Pieters, 1971; Schein, 1969).

The OD consultant can ask questions or gather impressions about the process he is observing while the meeting is in progress or at its conclusion. His presence can stimulate a critique of the meeting itself, as well as discussion about organizational problems which surfaced during the meeting. Feedback by the consultant can cover the content of the meeting, quantity of communication, interaction patterns, quality of communication (extent of openness, evaluative communication, exploration, etc.), nature of conflict resolution, boss-subordinate relationships, and intergroup relations. The consultant may also provide feedback to individuals after the meeting, depending on the problem and situation.

Schein (1969) reports extensive use of meeting interventions as a process consultation tool. In one instance his critique of a meeting resulted in substantial change in the meeting structure and agenda. More specifically, operational problems had been discussed together with policy questions in the same meeting; yet, the nature of these problems and the process they require are quite different. The first calls primarily for communication and a tightly run meeting; the second calls for exploration of ideas and a loosely run meeting; that is, two different climates and processes are required. Process critique led to two meetings with different agenda.

Tape recordings of meetings can be used as the feedback mechanism. This allows a detailed analysis of the interaction and if desired, the participants can critique the meetings later. Argyris (1971) found that his procedure resulted initially in unfreezing and then commitment to organizational development. Weber (1971) also demonstrated the effectiveness of this type of feedback mechanism. He used video feedback techniques with groups of college students

engaged in a task, and obtained significant favorable changes in several of Bales's interaction categories.

Extensive research evidence concerning the effectiveness of meeting process interventions does not exist. Specifically, information is needed about the long-term impact of various interventions and feedback technique, on later meetings, individual behavior outside of meetings, and other organizational variables. This writer agrees with Schein (1969), who suggests that while the analysis of the process of a meeting may not look like a powerful OD intervention, it is, in fact, quite powerful. Indeed, an elaborate technology for analyzing the process of problem solving and decision making in meetings will probably be developed. For example, organizations may provide centers, equipped with videotape and manned by professionals, for work groups interested in analysis and development of their meeting behavior.

Team Development

The primary work group is probably the most important subsystem within an organization. Its importance in shaping organizational behavior prompted Likert's (1961) view of an organization as a series of small groups linked by individuals who are members in one group and leaders in another. It is, therefore, not surprising that group development has received so much emphasis. Team building, often called team development, is perhaps the most advanced and most frequently used of all the OD technologies.

What Is Team Development?

Team development interventions start with data gathering about group processes and problems. These data are obtained through interviews conducted by the consultant and/or by means of questionnaires. Data discussed in team development meetings may include leadership behavior, interpersonal problems and process, roles, trust, communication, planning and decision making, goals, delegation, technical and task problems, and barriers to effective group and organizational functioning.

Shortly after the data have been collected, the work group meets off-site in order to avoid day-to-day pressures. Usually the meeting lasts three days although it can be as short as a day and a half or as long as a week. During the meeting the consultant feeds back the data to the group. Usually problems are categorized and placed on charts for presentation, discussion, and prioritization. The group then sets the agenda for the remainder of the meeting. The group decides whether to tackle interpersonal problems before planning problems, or leadership problems before communication problems. Often the consultant suggests those problems which, when tackled first, make subsequent discussion and problem solving easier. The discussion of each area is followed by action planning.

Throughout the team development meeting, the consultant plays at least four roles. First, he functions as a process consultant helping the group critique the process of its interactions. He promotes group norms conducive to confronting and solving conflict. He also functions as a resource person on questions or problems related to the behavioral sciences. When appropriate, he functions as a teacher on subjects such as leadership, group process, conflict resolutions, etc. The consultant may also act as a counselor to individuals during or following the team meeting.

The objective of team development is the removal of immediate barriers to group effectiveness and the development of self-sufficiency in managing group process and problems in the future. The removal of some of the barriers is underway by the end of the first meeting, if problems have been confronted and discussed. During this first meeting, the group is dependent upon the consultant to develop a climate conducive to risk taking. The group, however, must learn to maintain that climate without the con-

sultant. Follow-up interventions are frequently required. Probably several team development experiences and sometimes laboratory training are needed to assure an open climate without the consultant's presence. We do not yet fully understand what it takes to create a self-sufficient group.

Four Models For Team Development

There are many variations of team development, although most include the action-research model of data, feedback, and action planning. They all involve to varying degrees group participation, self-examination, problem confrontation, and goal setting. The assumption underlying all types of team development efforts is that persons who are closest to the task situation can solve their own problems if a catalyst—a third party—facilitates the confronting of conflict and problem solving. Within this broad framework, however, there are four separate models of team development. These models may be used in pure form or, as is most often the case, they can be mixed and integrated to varying degrees in each team development intervention. The situation, the team itself, and the consultant all determine which model or mix is to be utilized.

THE GOAL-SETTING MODEL. Goals influence individual and group behavior. They influence the direction, coordination, and extent of group effort. Moreover, participation in the setting of goals influences the degree of commitment to those goals and the motivation to work toward those goals (Likert, 1961). Group goal setting generates more commitment because decision making is more explicit (Pelz, 1958), and an individual's agreement to pursue certain goals is reinforced by group norms (Lewin, 1947; Bennett, 1955).

One form of team building involves group members in the process of developing individual and group goals with the help of a consultant (Beckhard, 1966). Goals are set for end results such as productivity, sales, and profits. They may also be set to change the organization's internal environment and its processes where such changes are needed to accomplish end result goals or improve attitudes (Likert, 1959). The process is iterative and is followed periodically by the group. The purpose of this team-building approach may simply be to energize a group to become more goal- and action-oriented with respect to issues that they all know exist. In this form the goal-setting model of team building is similar to the survey or interview feedback intervention described earlier. Beckhard (1969) has used the goal-setting model to work out solutions to problems identified in interviews prior to the team development session. Another purpose of the goal-setting team meeting may be to help the group learn how to participate in the goal-setting process as a group. The consultant accomplishes this purpose by helping the group plan meetings and by functioning as a process consultant during the meetings.

THE INTERPERSONAL MODEL. The assumption underlying this team development model is that an interpersonally competent group can function more effectively as a team (Argyris, 1962). A group in which there is sharing of feelings, mutual supportiveness, and non-evaluative communication is one which develops mutual trust and confidence. As trust develops, individuals in the group are more willing to cooperate (Deutsch, 1964), take personal risks in the group, and communicate more frequently, accurately, and openly. A climate is created where conflict can be confronted, problems effectively solved, and effective decisions made (Argyris, 1966). Increased cooperation and group cohesiveness will also lead to higher commitment to group goals and enhance team effectiveness and productivity (Seashore, 1954).

One approach to developing effective interpersonal relations in a primary work unit is to apply the T-group technology directly to a family unit. The group may go away for a week and in an unstructured setting begin to explore their perceptions of each other, their relationships, and how they function as a group. The group deals with behaviors observed in the context of the work environment, not just "here-and-now" behavior typically addressed in stranger groups. For example, job related issues of power, status, and authority are dealt with (Shepard, 1965). Shepard points out that the risks in a family group laboratory are far greater than in the stranger laboratory and, therefore, must be preceded by much greater preparation of group members through personal consultation, development of trust, seminars, and attendance at a stranger laboratory. Kuriloff and Atkins (1966) describe the use of T-group technology with a family unit which was composed of three organizational levels. They report improvements in performance as evidenced by the accomplishment of an extremely difficult goal by the group.

Blake and Mouton (1962) conducted some of their earliest work with the interpersonal team-building model. The sessions lasted from several days to a week and were held away from the work site in order to increase "leveling." The purpose was to explore defensiveness, to understand how others felt, and to clear up barriers to cooperation. One problem usually dealt with was the boss's inability to recognize his subtle influence over others. Problems of deference, dominance, competition, control, listening, and resistance were also typically dealt with.

One typical approach involves the collection of interpersonal data by the consultant prior to a team-building meeting. Each group member considers every other member's behavior and then for each person, including the boss, lists three or more behaviors which help or hinder team and organizational effectiveness. An important opening step in the meeting is a presentation by the consultant of the rules which will govern the meeting and the feedback process. The group then discusses one group

member at a time, using wall charts of helping and hindering factors as a take-off point.
It is customary to discuss the boss first in
order to reduce anxiety and create a climate
where further risks can be taken. The charts
provide a means for getting into interpersonal feedback quickly; they eliminate the
unproductive "warm-up period" so common
in group development. Moreover, the behavior on the charts and the feedback are
generally task related. Major barriers to interpersonal and group effectiveness are dealt
with and hopefully the new openness transfers to the work environment.

ROLE MODEL. A "role" represents that set of
behaviors which a person in one organizational position feels obligated to perform
and which persons in other organizational positions expect that person to perform (Kahn, Wolfe, Quinn, Snoek, &
Rosenthal, 1964). A group, therefore, is a
series of overlapping roles and much of the
behavior in a group can be understood in
terms of individuals' perceptions of their
roles. In fact, role differentiation (Guetzkow, 1968; Lawrence & Lorsch, 1967b) appears to be important to organizational effectiveness and is an underlying cause for
problems in intergroup conflict and coordination.

Using the notion of a group as a set of
interdependent roles, Bennis (1966) has
speculated that if group members better
understood their role space and that of
others, conflict and ambiguity might be
reduced and more energy might be available
for task relevant behavior. Many variations
of role perception and clarification meetings
are being used as a means of developing
more effective groups. Recently Dayal and
Thomas (1968) reported the use of a Role
Analysis Technique (RAT) for examining
role interdependence in a newly formed
organization. In general, the team discusses
the purpose of each role, expectations
that each role occupant has of others in his
group, and the obligation of each role occupant to others. More specifically, each group

member comes prepared with a description
of his role and how it fits into the objectives
of the group and the organization. The
individual whose role is being discussed lists
the activities which constitute his role and
these are discussed. Agreement is sought on
the makeup of the role. The individual then
lists his expectations of each role occupant
in the group who, in his opinion, affects his
own role performance. He also obtains the
other group members' expectations of him—
his role obligation. Each individual is held
responsible for writing up the major points
covered during the meeting.

No evaluation of this or similar techniques is available. Dayal and Thomas
(1968) report that many interpersonal and
organizational issues surface in the discussions and that communication improves
and becomes more fluid and meaningful.
They feel it is a less threatening way of
dealing with interpersonal problems than is
possible with the interpersonal team-building model. The exchange of role perceptions has been found by this writer to be a
useful technique for confronting and dealing with many problems facing groups, including interpersonal relations, power, intergroup relations, and leadership.

Harrison (1973) has developed a "Role
Negotiations" approach to team building
which also attempts to deal with group issues through a focus on role behavior rather
than interpersonal behavior. He claims that
this approach is more suited to the reality
of many organizational settings in which
power, coercion, and competitiveness are a
reality. The Role Negotiations technique
makes the basic assumption that people in
organizations prefer a fair negotiated settlement to a state of unresolved conflict. The
change process is essentially one of bargaining and negotiation in which two or more
members agree to change behavior in exchange for some desired change on the part
of the other. Each person is asked to list on
a piece of paper, one for each person in the
group, those things which the other person
should *do more* or *do better,* those things

which the other should *do less,* and those things which should *not be changed.* Agreements are negotiated and contracted for in writing. Harrison feels that this approach can resolve major conflicts and group problems without having to get into feelings and emotions.

THE MANAGERIAL GRID MODEL. As a follow-up to the Managerial Grid Laboratory, Blake and Mouton (1968b) have designed a team development meeting which draws heavily on previous learning in the Grid Laboratory. Each group spends a week applying the Grid framework to an examination of its own functioning. Prior to the meeting each individual fills out instruments about the quality and nature of teamwork and individual performance. This includes what he sees as his own barriers to effectiveness and what he sees others doing to enhance or reduce group effectiveness. Each individual also indicates what he feels would be an ideal culture for the group. The information in the questionnaires determines the content of the team development. During the meeting the group tries to arrive at a consensus about the culture of the group and the problems facing it. Initially, differences typically exist. In trying to resolve those differences, information is exchanged and conflict is confronted. When the group reaches a consensus about the team's actual functioning and their ideal functioning, they compare the two. In this way needs are identified and plans for individual and team development can be made.

Grid team development is likely to cover many of the issues dealt with by the other models. However, there are two key differences. First, the heavy use of instrumentation makes it possible for a group to proceed without an OD consultant. According to Blake and Mouton, only the top group requires consultant help. Groups below that level proceed with the help of an organizational member who has been trained to monitor team development meetings. Secondly, "unfreezing" is intended to occur

when the group recognizes differences between their ideal and actual group functioning. The recognition of disparity also leads the group to systematically plan and develop a 9,9 culture (a pattern of management which integrates concern for people and production through participation). A disadvantage of Grid team development lies in its standardization, which might prevent a group from dealing with its most pressing and important problems first. Problems are dealt with when the design provides for the discussion of the relevant data. Some managers have found the standardization and instrumentation cumbersome and frustrating.

Application Of Team-Building Technology

Team development interventions rarely rely on only one model. For example, roles cannot be discussed without getting into interpersonal issues, and goals cannot be discussed without dealing with roles or some notion of an ideal state. This writer has found that the role, interpersonal and goal models, can be integrated into a three-day team development meeting. The first day is used for role clarification; the second for interpersonal feedback using the helping and hindering format described in the section on "The Interpersonal Model." The third day is used for discussion and action planning from a list of organizational problems. Recent experience has shown that a team-building meeting can be opened successfully with interpersonal feedback, thus creating more openness at the outset. A rapid start is facilitated by posting all data on charts.

The team development interventions can be used with project teams or task forces, new family and functional teams (composed of individuals in the same discipline within an organization). In the development of a new team the objective is to clarify goals and roles so that lack of mutual understanding does not create a barrier to the accomplishment of the task. A climate of supportiveness and openness can be created through the use of the interpersonal team-building model. Furthermore, since a history of previous behavior does not exist, an unstructured T-group approach in which feedback is based on here-and-now behavior may be appropriate. Wakeley and Shaw (1965) developed a new plant management team using an integrated approach and a week of training in a simulated task environment. The simulated task environment included typical plant-opening problems which were presented to the team through in-baskets and telephone calls. The results were (1) team members were in greater agreement about the frequency with which they would have to work together on the actual job and (2) team members were in greater agreement about the perceived effectiveness of each person and the team. In addition, the plant had the most effective start-up in company history. These results suggest that team development technology may be effectively applied to new groups, particularly when the design incorporates preparation for the anticipated task environment.

The systems group at TRW extensively applied team development to new project teams (*Business Week*, 1971; Fordyce, 1968). The problems which face such a team are similar to those facing a family team and, therefore, the same techniques are applicable. There are some differences, however. If team members retain a primary job and functional affiliation, the functional differentiation is likely to result in conflict between members (Lawrence & Lorsch, 1967b). A project team integrator (Lawrence & Lorsch, 1967a) with special training in resolving conflict and coordinating activity is needed to assist the development of a project team. With the increasingly temporary nature of organizations a sophisticated technology of new team development is needed. A combination of existing team development techniques and simulations of the task environment will provide

the basis for this technology. Hundert (1971) reports on a three-day workshop for project teams which incorporated "lecturettes," group exercises, an experience in project team functioning within a simulated environment, and start-up of actual project team work with a consultant present. Much more development work and research are needed, however.

Empirical and Theoretical Support for Team Development

Consultants and participants alike typically judge team development efforts as successful (Davis, 1970). However, evidence other than the testimony of clients or consultants is necessary. But such research is sparse. Friedlander (1967) did, however, systematically evaluate team development technology. He found that a team development intervention with four family groups created significant increases (when compared with eight control groups) in member ratings of group problem-solving effectiveness, approachability of the leader, mutual influence, and personal involvement. Intragroup trust and effectiveness of meetings did not increase. The team development sessions were off-site for four to five days. The objectives were to identify problems facing the work group system, to develop solutions, and to plan the implementation of the solutions (the goal-setting, problem-solving model). In addition, interpersonal and group processes were also explored (interpersonal model). A later examination of the same data (Friedlander, 1968) showed that consultant involvement prior to team development and the amount of follow-up after team development were related to amount of change. Once again, the consultant's role, which will be more fully discussed later, proved to be very important.

Three other studies support assumptions on which team development interventions are based. In a community relations training program (Lippitt, 1949) trainees who attended as a team changed more than trainees who attended as individuals. Riecken (1952) found those attending a volunteer work corps who continued to have contact with other participants in their developmental experience were most likely to retain attitude change. Both of these studies support a basic assumption of team development. That is, changes in attitudes and behavior are more likely and more permanent when an established group goes through training together and operates as a group later, thereby providing support for and reinforcement of change.

Moreover, team development makes sense intuitively. For instance, the development program is tailored to fit the needs and problems of the particular group. Each group, with a consultant's help, establishes a process relevant for its situation, group membership, leader, task, and organizational environment. The emergence of contingency theories of leadership and organization (Fiedler, 1964; Hersey & Blanchard, 1969; Lawrence & Lorsch, 1967b; Tannenbaum & Schmidt, 1958) are further support for a process such as team development which attempts, through open communication and confrontation of conflict, to develop better fit between people, task, and group process.

Team development or group development is perhaps the most powerful and pervasive OD technology available to the change agent. Its design provides data for diagnosis and unfreezing, incorporates experiential learning, and provides the means for refreezing new behavior. Furthermore, the process of team development is likely to change organizational inputs (needs, values, skills) and a wide variety of group and organizational characteristics and functions (leadership, group cohesiveness, communication, planning). Through problem identification it can also effect immediate change in organizational outputs.

We are likely to see innovation in the technology of group development in the future. Videotape feedback or brief question-naires filled out regularly and frequently are likely to be used to provide more real time data for group analysis and critique with the help of a consultant. Simulations and gaming will increasingly be used in the future as a means of systematic group assessment and development.

Intergroup Interventions

Integration and collaboration are key ingredients in the organization's ability to adapt to its environment. Organizations which have to respond to considerable change must maintain a system of relationships which connect interdependent groups (Bennis, 1966; Lawrence & Lorsch, 1967b). And as the environment demands more rapid response, organizational hierarchy becomes less and less viable as a means for resolving conflict. Groups must learn to resolve conflict at their level, and for this reason, managing intergroup relations takes on greater and greater importance.

Intergroup relations are probably a function of: (1) contextual factors surrounding the relationship, (2) attributes of the relationship, and (3) management of the interface between groups (Walton & Dutton, 1969). Some antecedents of interdepartmental conflict such as incentives and rewards, physical barriers to communication, task interdependence, and jurisdictional ambiguities (Walton, Dutton, & Cafferty, 1969) require structural changes in the organization. In order to effect such changes, managers with sufficient authority to redesign the organization must be involved. Eliminating such contextual factors will be discussed in a later section, "Environmental Interventions and Inventions."

However, in many instances it is not in the interest of organizational effectiveness to remove contextual determinants of conflict. For example, the intergroup conflict created by organizational differentiation is essential to the organization's ability to cope with its environment (Lawrence & Lorsch, 1967b). The interventions to be discussed in this section are not aimed at preventing conflict, but rather at helping groups manage their conflict productively.

Consequences Of Win/Lose Conflict

Win/lose conflict between two groups has a predictable effect on what happens within each group and on what happens between them (Blake, Shepard, & Mouton, 1964; Sherif, Harvey, White, Hood, & Sherif, 1961). One of the most important and potentially damaging consequences is the perception that the other group is malicious. Once this occurs, they see their disagreement as inevitable because the personalities of individuals in the other group are now seen as the main causes of the conflict and these are not perceived as changeable. Other perceptual distortions develop also. For example, each group sees only the best parts of itself and the worst parts of the other group. Objectivity, which is necessary for effective problem solving, is lost. Negative stereotypes are developed and reinforced by group norms, which in turn reinforce the negative perceptions and attitudes. Thus, win/lose conflict tends to be a self-fulfilling prophecy. Once it is assumed that the other group is bad, each group acts accordingly to cope with this perceived situation, thus evoking more negative behavior. Intervention is clearly necessary at this stage because the groups are unable to manage the conflict themselves.

Blake et al. (1964) review a number of different strategies groups use to resolve win/lose conflict. These strategies are based on implicit and explicit assumptions about the inevitability of the conflict and the possibility and probability of agreement. When conflict is viewed as inevitable and no possibility for agreement is seen, it is unlikely that an intervention will lead to a relationship of trust and a problem-solving approach to the conflict. Third-party decisions and arbitration can solve the immediate problem but will not change the relationship. When groups are not interdependent, isolation and withdrawal can be an effective

strategy in dealing with win/lose conflict. However, in most intergroup relationships within organizations, interdependence and common goals exist. When this is so, consultant interventions are recommended.

The Intergroup Laboratory

Based on substantial research on intergroup conflict, Blake and his associates (Blake et al., 1964) have developed an intergroup laboratory. The laboratory generally has the following format:

1. The groups meet at a location away from their work setting. Norms which will enhance the development of honesty, open feedback, and problem solving are present and discussed at the start of the meeting. The goals of the meeting are described as the exploration of mutual perceptions, the discussion of problems in the relationship, and the development of solutions or action plans for improving the relationship.

2. Each group is then asked to meet separately and with the help of a consultant develop an image of itself and an image of the other group. These might include a statement of roles as well as statements reflecting the group's feelings about itself and the other group.

3. The groups are brought together for an exchange of images. During this exchange, the groups are asked to listen and refrain from making explanations or statements.

4. A period of time is then allotted for clarification of images. In this phase of the laboratory, each group is allowed to ask questions but statements, explanations, justifications, or accusations are not permissible.

5. The groups are again separated and asked to diagnose the present relationship based on the exchange of images. They are asked to answer the question, "Why does the other group see us as they do?"

6. The groups are brought together to exchange their diagnoses.

7. The groups working together develop a consolidated list of key issues and sources of friction.

8. Working together, the groups develop action plans for changing their relationship and may, in fact, solve some specific problems. A follow-up meeting is planned.

The laboratory format has been applied with some modifications to the relationship between labor and management (Blake, Mouton, & Sloma, 1965; Hundert, 1974), functional groups in an industrial setting (Beer et al., 1971; Blake et al., 1964; Golembiewski & Blumberg, 1967), headquarters and a field organization (Blake & Mouton, 1962), contractor and sub-contractor (Fordyce & Weil, 1971), foreign service officers and the administrative staff of the State Department (Bennis, 1969), and mergers (Blake & Mouton, 1964; Blansfield, Blake, & Mouton, 1964; Blumberg & Wiener, 1971).

Modifications To The Basic Design

Modifications to the design are many, depending on the situation. Beckhard (1969) does not ask groups to generate a self-image. He simply asks them to develop a list of what exasperates them about the other group and what they think the other group is saying about them. Fordyce and Weil (1971) present as an optional step preliminary interviewing of the parties or the use of sensing (see earlier section on diagnostic interventions), in order to prepare the consultant or the key managers for the laboratory. Whether two groups or more attend also depends on the situation. Pieters (1971) reports the inclusion of a Sales Service group in a Sales/Production intergroup meeting where Sales Service was the integrating and intermediate unit in the relationship. Much of the data the groups generated about each other provided important information for this third group about their required role in the interface. The specific procedures vary, too. Golembiewski and Blumberg (1967) applied a "3D" procedure in a meeting of several functional groups all brought together at the same time. Each group was asked to pick three other groups with which it needed to meet, "thereby creating a free market for confrontation." Groups were then asked to develop images of all three groups and through a successive set of meetings between pairs, intergroup confrontation meetings were held, and many diverse interfaces were dealt with at once. The extensiveness of the training also varies. Blake and Mouton (1962) spent two days in intra-team development prior to getting a headquarters and field group together. During the intergroup laboratory they combined members of the two groups into smaller subgroups based on functional similarity and had them work on interpersonal issues as well as problem identification and solution. Others have stressed the importance of getting the two groups to work through to solution some specific problems prior to the end of the meeting, thereby providing the groups with a success experience based on the trust-confrontation problem-solving model.

The Merger Laboratory, as Blansfield et al. (1964) describe it, departs even further from the traditional design. The acquirer and acquired group meet with behavioral scientists to air their feelings and concerns about the merger so that the human dimensions of the situation become evident. Next, the two groups are asked to compare employee benefit programs, to ask for clarification, and to plan modifications. This stage is aimed at removing security issues as potential barriers to further work. Following this, key managers from the acquiring group are asked to "fishbowl" and discuss their plans for integrating the two companies, and these plans are revised on the basis of questions asked by the acquired group. Next, the acquired group meets in a fishbowl before the buyers to discuss aspects of internal operations, pointing out possible shortcomings of the merger. Based on the fishbowls, the discussion turns to the expectations that functional groups from the two organizations have of each other and to potential barriers to collaboration. Then each group meets with a behavioral scientist to discuss in depth their own internal relationships and operational problems with special attention on how these can affect the integration. Finally, the acquired group identifies those operational policies and procedures which are unique to itself and of value to the acquiring group. The acquired group examines its own practices and procedures to identify those which could be deterrents to integration.

This laboratory, with its use of the fishbowl and workshop approach, is similar to the Organization Mirror (discussed in the section on diagnostic interventions). The emphasis on working through problems takes the group beyond the cathartic and diagnostic stage of image exchange into actual problem solving. This is an intervention which not only allows examination of the process, but helps shape it in a training setting. Blumberg and Wiener (1971) tried a similar approach in a merger but utilized Likert's Organizational Climate Questionnaire to get each group to look at itself and to jointly plan the culture of the newly integrated organization.

The key elements in the intergroup laboratory are: (1) open communication of feelings and perceptions in an environment of listening and supportiveness, (2) the identification by each unit of things it could do better or differently, (3) an opportunity for each organizational unit to help the other group and be helped by the other group on specific problems, and (4) planning follow-up action. An element which is not common to all designs is the degree of emphasis on person-to-person relationships across groups. The data on intergroup conflict suggest that it is primarily a group phenomenon rather than an interpersonal phenomenon. Nevertheless, there may be times when work on interpersonal relations across groups is required.

Other Intergroup Interventions

There are a number of interventions in intergroup conflict which depart significantly from the techniques just described and should be mentioned. Blake et al. (1964)

describe a case in labor/management conflict in which the consultant had access to only one party. In this instance management went through a laboratory to learn about intergroup conflict through experiencing it. The consultant then spent a period of time with the client as an observer and interviewer to obtain firsthand data about the actual conflict. This was followed by a Norm-Setting Conference in which management came to an agreement that they wanted a relationship of cooperation between themselves and labor. The conference created conditions which allowed management to initiate action toward collaboration in the actual labor/management conflict. In subsequent interchanges with the union, the consultant intervened several times to prevent management from behaving in a way that would escalate a win/lose relationship. Muench (1960) also reports the use of the diagnostic-consulting approach with management in a labor/management conflict.

Sykes (1964) also had access to only one group in an intergroup conflict. He conducted interviews within the one group and found that asking individuals to give specific examples of behavior in order to support their stereotype of the other group caused reexamination and eventual change of the unfounded stereotype. Once the group leaders openly expressed these new attitudes, the group members also openly expressed the new attitudes. The group, however, never admitted to having changed its perception of the other group. Due to practical constraints which may make it impossible to bring both parties together, approaches such as these, which do not rely on the participation of both parties, are a useful addition to the repertoire of intergroup interventions.

Evidence Of Effectiveness

The bulk of the evidence on the effectiveness of the intergroup laboratory or other intergroup interventions comes from subjective reports by behavioral scientists who were involved in the intervention itself (Beckhard, 1969; Bennis, 1969; Blake et al., 1964; Blumberg & Wiener, 1971; Muench, 1960; Sykes, 1964). Golembiewski and Blumberg (1967) have provided the only evaluation that goes beyond the consultant's estimate of results. They measured the extent to which members from three groups wanted to get along with the other groups before and after a three-way confrontation. Generally positive changes were found. Changes in attitudes appeared to be related to the extent of involvement in the exercise. While such attitudinal data are useful, they do not shed any light on the behavioral consequences of the intergroup confrontation meeting. Beer, Pieters, Marcus, and Hundert (1971) report a case study in which intergroup confrontation meetings were used as part of a larger change effort aimed at improving integration. Changes in integration were noted in the organization, but the contribution of the intergroup meetings was not known at the time the case was reported. Recent analysis of that data suggests that the intergroup laboratory may have been an important contributor to the change. When compared with control groups which did not go through an intergroup laboratory, the perceptions and attitudes of those groups which did attend an intergroup laboratory changed substantially.

Much more research is needed, not only on the effectiveness of the intergroup laboratory and other interventions, but on the conditions under which they can be effective. It is likely that effectiveness of these interventions is highly dependent on the organization in which they are embedded, the nature of the conflict between the groups and its causes, the leaders of the two groups and their willingness to solve problems, behavior in the laboratory, and probably the design of the meeting itself. The greatest impact of the intergroup meeting is not on past issues and feelings, but on new issues and problems (Blake et al., 1964). This suggests that measuring attitudes about past issues and comparing them with post-

meeting attitudes about those issues may not be relevant. What is needed are data on how new problems are handled. Because follow-up is critical and as much as five years may be required to change some relationships, research on the effects of the intergroup laboratory must be longitudinal and must account for the effects of consultant follow-up (Blake et al., 1964).

Theoretical Foundations Of Intergroup Interventions

Since research on the effectiveness of intergroup interventions is limited, an evaluation of intergroup interventions cannot be based on empirical data. Nevertheless, intergroup interventions can be evaluated on logical grounds. The intergroup laboratory is based on the assumption that by bringing both parties together in a face-to-face meeting, relationships will improve and a problem-solving approach to conflict resolution will develop (Blake et al., 1964). Sherif (1958) points out, however, that attempts to get conflicting groups together can backfire because communication opportunities are used for further accusation and recriminations. Even favorable information is likely to be interpreted or misinterpreted to fit existing negative stereotypes. Theoretically, the design of the intergroup laboratory prevents the strengthening of stereotypes by establishing norms regarding conduct during the laboratory. Specifically, norms for giving and receiving feedback prohibit groups from making accusations and from defending their position. Constructive behavior is thereby encouraged and selective listening reduced.

Sherif (1958) also concludes that a group is likely to see a leader's attempt to reduce conflict with another group as a betrayal of its position unless the groups have a superordinate goal. In most intergroup interventions a superordinate goal does exist. Indeed, the existence of a superordinate goal is a key assumption underlying the applications of the intergroup laboratory. Most of the case studies described have dealt with sub-groups of one organization (i.e., Sales and Production) where there is never a real question about the commonness of goals. In conflicts between labor and management, prime contractor and sub-contractor, seller and customer, the superordinate goal may be more difficult to see for the participants in the conflict. A superordinate goal may not exist between seller and customer because of the competitive system in which the participant groups are embedded. Cohen and Petrella (1971) have pointed out that much of OD technology, and intergroup technology in particular, is based on the interdependence-love-trust model rather than the power-competition model. They suggest that in some cases a power-competition model is more appropriate. That is, helping the client to be independent and to establish power may be a more useful intervention than helping two groups develop mutual trust and interdependence. In this writer's view, their criticism of the love-trust model is appropriate where, in fact, interdependence is not required and a superordinate goal does not exist. More and more, however, interdependence is a reality in our complex society. Nevertheless, they have opened another area of intergroup interventions which needs investigating. Likewise, Walton and Dutton (1969) and Seiler (1963) point out the importance of "task-related asymmetries" (unequal power, status, or competence) as antecedents to conflict. One strategy may be to help the lower power group increase its power through increasing its competence, thereby removing a cause of the conflict and creating conditions for better relationships. Beer (1971b) reports on the impact of perceived incompetence as a factor in the relationship between a marketing group and other departments. Increasing the competence and effectiveness of the marketing group was one of the strategies for improving integration and probably played as important a role in improving integration as did the intergroup laboratories (Pieters, 1971; Marcus, 1971).

Where perceptual distortions and stereotypes exist in the context of superordinate goals, the intergroup laboratory seems well founded. The meeting is likely to break down such stereotypes by confronting each group with actual behavior that is inconsistent with the stereotype. In a setting where norms of supportiveness and listening are enforced, real communication is likely to begin, thereby allowing problem solving. Allport (1954) felt that eliminating stereotypes as a mechanism for attitude change is futile since they are merely rationalizations to support long held attitudes. In intergroup relations, however, stereotypes reinforced by group norms are often the only support for attitudes and behavior which prevent intergroup collaboration. Deeply engrained attitudes developed in early childhood experiences are not at issue.

Theoretically, the intergroup laboratory is a moderately powerful technology. Its design takes groups through the full cycle of change and development. More specifically, the exchange of perceptions can unfreeze attitudes; and the meeting norms, consultant interventions, and actual problem solving during the meeting itself can create new attitudes and behavior. Refreezing of new attitudes and behavior is likely to occur through action planning, that is, planning to alleviate the conditions which led to the conflict. The main deficiency of the intergroup laboratory probably lies in its relative lack of power to change individual values and attitudes toward collaboration. However, laboratory training and team building are powerful interventions for modifying these organizational inputs and may be an effective intervention prior to an intergroup laboratory. The principal advantages of the intergroup laboratory are its effects on the intergroup process itself and organizational outputs. Efficiency, for example, is likely to increase if some immediate problems were solved during the meeting.

The technology for improving intergroup relations is still in its infancy, although it appears to have gotten a promising start. We need a greater variety of interventions which recognize the practical difficulties of bringing two groups together. The attempts of Cohen and Petrella (1971) and Blake et al. (1964) to solve an intergroup conflict by working with only one group is a good start. A distinction between intergroup relations (affect) and integration (behavior) is also needed in planning effective intergroup interventions (Beer, 1971b). Changing intergroup relations may require an intergroup laboratory which will break the self-fulfilling prophecy inherent in win/lose conflict. However, a change in attitudes may not lead to improvements in coordination and integration unless structural changes are also made. More attention will have to be given to incorporating an examination of structural issues in the intergroup laboratory.

Temporary Task Forces

Often an organizational diagnosis reveals specific and immediate task problems (such as excessive cost or unclear business strategy) which are barriers to organizational effectiveness. Temporary task forces can be created to deal with these problems. Such task forces are different from temporary or permanent task forces which are created to accomplish non-routine but recurring work, such as product development and business management (Lawrence & Lorsch, 1967b).

The temporary task force is based on the assumptions that: (1) assigning experts to a problem is likely to result in a high quality solution (Maier, 1963); (2) if various levels of the organization are involved, conditions for mutual influence are created (Lewin, 1951); and (3) if a large number of organizational members participate, commitment to the recommendations will increase (Beckhard, 1969; Coch & French, 1948; Fleishman, 1965).

Analyses of a successful and an unsuccessful task force (Drought, 1967) have shown that in order for the task force approach to work, the following conditions must be met:

1. The task must be clearly defined.
2. The task must be relevant to the skills and interests of the participants chosen.
3. The task force must be composed of several organizational levels including superiors and subordinates; however, the group must not be so large as to be unmanageable.
4. Time must be taken for the group to evolve adequate working relationships.
5. Bosses of committee members must be supportive so that open communication can be achieved.

Task forces have been used to review and recommend new personnel policies and practices (Drought, 1967), to solve system-wide process problems in a school (Schmuck, Runkel, & Langmeyer, 1969), to solve quality problems (Rubenstein, 1971), and to achieve significant cost reductions and operations improvements (Beckhard, 1966; Mitchell, Koppes, Neukom, & Reavis, 1971).

One objective of a task force is to generate diverse and relevant data about a problem that would not be available if it were tackled by the functional organization. Thus, as mentioned earlier, success is dependent on the quality of communication and the relationships established in the group. The OD consultant's typical approach to this problem has been to help groups establish the necessary openness through team development (Beckhard, 1969; TRW Systems Group, 1969). Chambers, Mullick, and Goodman (1971) suggest a somewhat different approach. They modified the Delphi method developed at Rand (Dalkey, 1969). To avoid typical communication problems, a "coordinator" (in this case an operations researcher) collects each task force member's data prior to the first meeting and, if needed, prior to subsequent meetings. The coordinator remains on the task force to help members arrive at decisions using decision models he supplies. The coordinator functions as the central processor of information, and thereby reduces group process problems, distortion of information, and withholding of information. The difficulty with the approach, of course, is that task force members do not learn how to work on their own. They remain dependent on the consultant. Nevertheless, the approach may be effective in a situation where conditions for group development do not exist and/or there is insufficient time to go through the process.

Temporary task forces are among the least powerful OD interventions. Their problem or task orientation assures some immediate change in organizational outputs (productivity, efficiency, employee satisfaction); however, relatively little permanent modification of organizational inputs (needs, values, abilities, or expectations) and organizational processes (leadership, group effectiveness, intergroup relations, planning) is likely to occur. Task forces are not particularly effective in unfreezing an organization or creating permanent change in individuals' behavior or organizational processes. They must be accompanied by other interventions, such as the confrontation meeting, to provide the stimulus for unfreezing and other process interventions or training to create lasting change in organizational inputs and processes.

More and more uses for temporary task forces are being found. In the future, task forces which deal with non-routine or non-linear tasks will operate collaterally with the hierarchical organization (Zand, 1971). We shall see the use of task forces extended outside the organization to include customers, suppliers, sub-contractors, or members of the community (Walton, 1971). Task forces will also be utilized to diagnose organizational problems and provide the impetus for organization change and renewal. Furthermore, training and development packages will be devised to help such task forces achieve effective functioning quickly (Hundert, 1971).

Counseling and Third-Party Consultation

The counseling program at the Hawthorne plant of Western Electric constituted the first major attempt at grappling with the human problems existing at the individual-organization interface. The Hawthorne researchers had intervened in the organization's process as experimenters and had found that it added to their understanding of organizations and made a difference (Dickson & Roethlisberger, 1966). Their research interviewing allowed them to experiment with new ways of behaving with workers. A new role of counselor emerged which had no precedent in industrial organizations. The counselor's role at the Hawthorne plant was the precursor to the third-party consulting, coaching, and counseling role which is an important process intervention in today's broader storehouse of OD technologies.

As originally conceived, the counseling program at the Hawthorne plant failed and was discontinued in 1956. The counselor was to have been the link between the data obtained in the counseling sessions and management. This important component was lost as the counseling program grew. As Dickson and Roethlisberger point out so well, the data somehow remained in the files. The counselors, operating on the Rogerian client-centered therapy model (Rogers, 1951) listened, reflected, and sometimes interpreted what the client said about himself and his relationship with others. However, they did not intervene or develop active strategies for dealing with the problems they were hearing. In the Rogerian model, the counselor focuses on the individual, not the problem (Leavitt, 1965). The counselor does not assist in problem solving.

Counseling

Counseling and coaching of individuals can, however, be viewed in action-oriented terms and can play an important part in a broader effort to create organizational change (Dayal & Thomas, 1968). The OD consultant as a third party can use his direct knowledge of what is happening in the organization to help a person improve his ability to observe and process data about himself (Schein, 1969). In the role of counselor, the change agent can help a manager identify and work on individual problems which are blocking progress in the larger change effort. A counselor may learn something about a person and feed that information back to the individual (Schein, 1969), or he may feed back his own reactions to the person (Argyris, 1961). In both cases, the counselor would be operating on the reality therapy model (Glasser, 1965). The counselor can then take an active role in helping the client to identify alternative behavioral solutions. He can actively help the individual in becoming skilled in these behaviors, thereby taking on the role of coach (Meyer, Kay, & French, 1965). The consultant-counselor may help the individual manager change through modeling (Sofer, 1962) the desired behavior in their two-person interaction or through role-playing of an anticipated interaction.

Recently, the techniques of Gestalt therapy (Herman & Phillips, 1971) have been introduced to the practice of organization development. These techniques differ from many conventional OD practices in their emphasis on developing self-supports for individuals, rather than environmental (team or group) supports. Authenticity is stressed as a key value, even when this involves behaviors that are seemingly undesirable. Herman and Phillips believe that many OD practitioners attempt to solve problems prematurely and thus do not facilitate a real solution.

In Gestalt therapy, the third party helps the individual become aware of core issues by: (1) helping him experience extremes (polarization); (2) helping him to become more aware of how he blocks his own goal attainment (truncating his power); and (3) encouraging him to stay with difficult intra- and interpersonal transactions until he has truly finished with them (closure). Development is seen as a natural extension of the individual's authentic style, not as change to someone else's model. Though this therapeutic model seems more individual than problem oriented, clearly it is more action oriented than the Rogerian nondirective therapy model.

Interpersonal Peacemaking

The consultant may be a third party to conflict between two persons. The costs of such conflict to the individuals and organization are lost energy, dysfunctional behavior, and lack of adaptability. There are many ways in which such conflict can be controlled or its consequences minimized, but it can only be resolved if the underlying issues are confronted and dealt with. This may happen in a team-building or intergroup confrontation meeting, but often a separate intervention is needed to cope directly with a severe two-person conflict. Walton (1969) describes three cases involving such conflicts, provides a diagnostic model for them, and outlines the conditions for effective confrontation and third-party tactics in a planned two-person confrontation.

Conflict over substantive issues requires bargaining and problem solving with a third party present. Conflict involving emotional issues requires a restructuring of perception and working through of feelings with a third party present. Most interpersonal conflicts have both components. The third party must create conditions for productive interpersonal confrontation. Both parties must be motivated to improve the relationship and must perceive power equality in the confrontation situation. The third party must promote norms for constructive confrontation, reassure parties, and employ his process skills to promote an effective meeting. He can assist the processing of reliable and accurate communication by paraphrasing, summarizing, and/or translating. Moreover, the third party must ensure an optimal level of tension during the meeting. Walton further points out that confrontation efforts by the two parties must be synchronized in terms of their readiness and so it is best to let the parties determine the timing. Once the parties are engaged, Walton has found it useful to phase the interaction so that differences are aired first. This phase is then followed by efforts at "integration" of the differences (finding a common ground for agreement).

The success of an interpersonal confrontation is dependent on the context of the confrontation (neutrality of site, time available, etc.) and the interventions of the third party; for example, refereeing, restating issues, offering observations, etc. (Fordyce & Weil, 1971; Walton, 1969). Walton outlines the role attributes of a third party which are important in resolving two-person confrontations. These are probably important for any consultant role. The attributes are:

1. High professional expertise regarding social processes.

2. Low power over fate of principals.

3. High control over processes in confrontation setting.

4. Moderate knowledge about the principles, issues, and background factors.

5. Neutrality or balance with respect to substantive outcomes, personal relationships, and conflict resolution methodology.

The confrontation between two persons is a special case of the other process technologies already discussed. According to Sherwood (1971), the objective of a confrontation is to negotiate a contract between two persons, thereby explicitly setting new ground rules for the relationship. Third-party consultation and counseling differs from the other process technologies in that it relies more heavily on neutrality of the consultant and his professional skills. In a sense, the consultant or counselor is the technology.

Counseling is primarily aimed at the individual's attitudes and behavior (organizational inputs) and, therefore, cannot be expected to have major impact on organizational processes and outputs. Third-party consultation will have its major impact on interpersonal process, with some possibility of learning at the individual level and some possibility of increasing organizational out-

puts. Of the two technologies, third party consultation is more powerful. Both technologies are dependent on other events to refreeze changes which do occur. For these reasons, both counseling and third-party consultation are usually used in conjunction with other diagnostic and process technologies.

ENVIRONMENTAL INTERVENTIONS AND INVENTIONS

Organizations have been changing for a long time without any of the diagnostic or process technologies discussed above and without benefit of laboratory training or education of any kind. Management, operating on the basis of classical organizational theory or technological models, such as Scientific Management and, more recently, Operations Research, changed significant structural, technological, and task variables in the organization with the intent of improving organizational performance (Leavitt, 1965). While changes in these variables rarely had specific behavioral change objectives, they had many unintended behavioral consequences. What Leavitt calls the "people-approaches" to change grew out of the realization that the other approaches did not adequately account for the dynamics of human behavior and the importance of participation in change (Coch & French, 1948; Leavitt, 1965). Since the classic work of Trist & Bamforth (1951) and the ensuing view of an organization as a socio-technical system, a number of new approaches to organization development have emerged which, like the technological approaches, change the organization's internal environment. However, unlike the technological approaches, these newer approaches have specific behavioral outcomes and objectives clearly in mind. These more recent approaches rely on what Shepard (1965) calls "situational induction." That is, the constraints of the situation shape behavior. Education and process interventions are not relied on to create the change, although they can obviously be utilized to help consolidate change.

It has been recognized for some time that organizational structure, technology, and administrative controls inhibit participation, frustrate maturity and psychological success, and can cause severe psychological problems (Argyris, 1957, 1971; Herzberg, 1966; McGregor, 1960; Trist & Bamforth, 1951). If this is so, then surely these factors could be changed to create the opposite effect. For example, changes in technology and task can create a culture which allows greater self-actualization (Margulies, 1969). Walton (1967) has concluded that, particularly at lower levels in the organization (first-line supervisors and below), changes in formal structure, procedures, and economic incentives should be the primary means for creating a participative process of management. Interventions in the social process of the organization, while helpful, should be supplementary. Argyris (1971) also emphasizes the importance of structural changes at lower levels in the organization.

Clearly, interventions in the organization's internal environment[2] have a place in an OD program. Social scientists have intervened with some success in the organization's structure and roles (Chapple & Sayles, 1961; Lawrence & Lorsch, 1969), control and accounting system (Likert, 1967), job structure (Chapple & Sayles, 1961; Davis, 1957; Ford, 1969), and pay and personnel systems (Alfred, 1967; Beckhard, 1970; Lesieur, 1958).

Job Design

Jobs in organizations have typically been designed on the basis of scientific management principles. The scientific management school (Taylor, 1911) assumes that dividing

work into simple and specialized jobs results in more efficiency and control over people and production, requires less skilled workers, and leads to greater profitability. In the past twenty years a number of studies have demonstrated that when jobs are designed in accordance with these assumptions, there are unintended and undesirable outcomes (Argyris, 1964a; Blauner, 1964; Davis, 1957; Guest, 1955; Richardson & Walker, 1948; Walker & Guest, 1952; Worthy, 1950). These studies have shown that work which requires little skill, is machine paced and repetitive and provides little feedback of results, often leads to dysfunctional outcomes. For example, such work often leads to dissatisfaction, surface attention to work, depersonalization, and feelings of alienation and frustration due to lack of feelings of success. Studies show these psychological effects lead to social and economic costs, such as poor mental health, reduced longevity, higher incidence of coronary problems, high turnover and absenteeism, resistance to change, low product quality, and labor/management problems (see *Work in America,* 1973).

Experiments In Response To Awareness

The growing awareness that routine and unchallenging jobs may have motivational costs greater than the apparent economic benefits led to a number of experiments in job design (Conant & Kilbridge, 1965; Davis, 1957; Davis & Valfer, 1965; Davis & Werling, 1960; Elliott, 1954; Maher, Overbagh, Palmer, & Piersol, 1969; Pelissier, 1965; Sorcher & Meyer, 1968). These efforts were not guided by any systematic conceptual or theoretical framework. Rather, the attempt has been to reverse the trend toward unchallenging work by enlarging jobs so that the worker performs a longer sequence and variety of operations, schedules his own work, inspects and tests the quality of his work, sets up and maintains his own equipment, and controls his own

---

[2] The concept of internal environment refers to the many structural characteristics of an organization and is to be distinguished from Lawrence and Lorsch's (1967b) concept of organizational environment.

operation (Davis, 1957). These goals have been achieved by rotating persons through jobs (Wood & Okum, 1946), by combining several jobs which together constitute a total or whole task (Biganne & Stewart, 1963; Huse & Beer, 1971; Marks, 1954; Tangerman, 1953), and by forming autonomous work groups which are responsible for assigning, rotating, and scheduling work, and for completion of the total task (Huse & Beer, 1971; Kuriloff, 1963; Rice, 1953; Woodhead, 1943).

Theoretical Impetus

Herzberg's motivation-hygiene theory (Herzberg, Mausner, & Snyderman, 1959) has been a major impetus for the use of job design as a technique for increasing employee satisfaction and motivation (Ford, 1969; Paul, Robertson, & Herzberg, 1969). Given that conditions which lead to dissatisfaction with hygiene factors are minimized, the theory suggests that employee motivation will be enhanced if employees experience achievement, responsibility, advancement, recognition, and growth in competence (i.e., motivators). Herzberg strongly states that only changes in the work itself can affect satisfaction (of motivator needs), and that human relations training, better pay, and better working conditions only prevent dissatisfaction. Myers (1968), who has applied and researched Herzberg's theory at Texas Instruments, distinguishes between adding more operations to a job, which he calls "horizontal job loading," and adding more responsibility to the job, "vertical job loading." The latter is felt to be much more desirable and potentially effective because it provides more of an opportunity for the satisfaction of motivator needs. The term, "job enrichment," is now used to denote the more desirable practice of vertical job loading, while the term, "job enlargement," has come to be associated with the supposedly less desirable practice of horizontal loading.

Current Status

Job enrichment has been used extensively as a technology of organizational development (Anderson, 1970; Foulkes, 1969; Gooding, 1970; Rush, 1971). By and large, these job enrichment applications have been considered successful. Lawler (1969), in reviewing ten studies where jobs had been enriched, concludes that job enrichment did have positive effects on behavior in every one of the studies reviewed. In all ten cases quality was affected positively, whereas quantity of production was positively affected in only four. Anderson (1970) similarly concluded that job enrichment reduces costs mainly through its effects on quality of production. He also concluded that job enrichment reduces indirect labor costs (quality inspectors, schedulers, supervisors, etc.). Anderson's conclusions suggest that productivity increases because employees take on more responsibilities while producing the same quantity with higher quality.

Job enrichment also seems to have been generally successful in increasing satisfaction and motivation (Biganne & Stewart, 1963; Ford, 1969; Marks, 1954). These findings are supported by a number of correlational studies which show the expected relationship between job characteristics and satisfaction.

With few exceptions, job enrichment applications have lacked appropriate controls and methodological rigor (Hulin & Blood, 1968). While in this writer's view there seems to be little doubt about the general effectiveness of a job design strategy for increasing satisfaction, motivation, and job performance, many questions remain about the specific effects. Are the effects, as Lawler and Anderson suggest, primarily on quality and not quantity of production? Does job enrichment result in more work per unit time? Does the worker maintain quantity of production while taking on new responsibilities? What are the effects with respect to satisfaction, motivation, resistance to change, innovation, labor relations, training and learning time, and expense? Furthermore, job enrichment applications have typically involved a number of simultaneous changes in variety of work, autonomy, amount of feedback the employee gets, amount of responsibility required, degree of task identity or wholeness, and the degree to which working with others is required. Are all the changes equally important? Unfortunately, few jobs have been redesigned by means of horizontal or vertical loading only. Lawler (1969) concludes both are probably necessary and for theoretical reasons vertical loading is more important (Porter & Lawler, 1968). Little solid evidence exists regarding which job dimensions are critical and what specific effects a change in any one of the dimensions will have. In short, many empirical questions remain unanswered and prevent the development of a sophisticated technology of job design.

The motivation-hygiene theory of Herzberg (Herzberg, Mausner, & Snyderman, 1959) does provide a theoretical basis for the technology of job enrichment and has proven useful in applications. Ford (1969) and his associates at AT&T designed a two-day "Work-Itself" workshop for supervisors and managers of the client department. The workshop includes: (1) a review of Herzberg's theory; (2) a free association "green light" session in which supervisors give their ideas about how the job in question is to be redesigned; and (3) a "red light" session during which participants evaluate whether the changes suggested will, in fact, provide the worker a greater opportunity for motivator need satisfaction, or whether the changes reflect improvements in hygiene. The use of Herzberg's theory has provided a systematic framework for a technology of job enrichment at AT&T. However, there is considerable controversy over the validity of Herzberg's theory (House & Wigdor, 1967; Whitsett & Winslow, 1967), and its status

is in question. Since its status is in question, the technology which is based on it is also in question. Equally important, the theory has not specified which job dimensions (e.g., autonomy, variety, etc.) satisfy which motivator needs, nor does it deal with the question of how worker characteristics or background interact with the motivating conditions.

New Theoretical and Research Underpinning For Job Design

If the technology of job design is to reach maturity, a better means for measuring job characteristics and understanding their relationship with satisfaction, motivation, and performance must be developed. Turner and Lawrence (1965) developed a measure of six "requisite task attributes" based on a review of the literature and on an a priori conceptual framework. The six attributes are: (1) variety; (2) autonomy; (3) required interaction; (4) optional interaction; (5) knowledge and skill required; and (6) responsibility. These six measures were sufficiently correlated that they were combined into a Requisite Task Attribute Index (RTA). The questionnaires and rating scales developed by Turner and Lawrence constitute a systematic attempt to measure attributes of a job and will probably be the forerunner of more sophisticated, but similar, measures needed in the future. The importance of this should not be underestimated. Without such measures it is impossible to know if a proposed job change did, in fact, make a difference (Beer, 1968). Perhaps more importantly, the Turner and Lawrence research provides an insight into the interaction between individual differences and job characteristics. They found that urban and small-town workers reacted differently (satisfaction and absenteeism) to jobs with a high RTA index (enriched jobs). There was a significant positive correlation between RTA and satisfaction and a significant negative correlation between RTA and absenteeism for the small-town sample, but not for the urban sample. Cultural background seems to moderate the relationship between the characteristics of the job and psychological and behavioral outcomes.

Blood and Hulin (1967) and Hulin and Blood (1968) provide additional data to substantiate the importance of individual differences in determining reaction to enriched jobs. They found that workers who hold traditional values about work and achievement respond positively to complex jobs, while workers who are alienated from work (as urban workers might be expected to be) respond negatively to complex jobs. They propose a three-dimensional model which specifies the relationship between worker alienation, job characteristics, and satisfaction with work (Hulin & Blood, 1968).

Hackman and Lawler (1971) carried the investigation of individual differences and their interaction with job characteristics further. Based on expectancy theory (Porter & Lawler, 1968; Vroom, 1964), they propose that employee motivation and satisfaction will be enhanced when: (1) the process of work allows satisfaction of higher order needs; (2) the individual has strong higher order needs; (3) the individual experiences satisfaction of these needs as a result of his own effort; and (4) the individual learns to expect such valued outcomes. It is suggested by Hackman and Lawler that the satisfaction of higher order needs through work may, in fact, arouse these and other needs (Alderfer, 1969; Maslow, 1954), rather than satiate them, thereby assuring continued motivation. They propose that jobs will provide higher order need satisfaction when: (1) workers feel personally responsible for a meaningful portion of the work; (2) work outcomes are intrinsically meaningful; and (3) feedback about performance is provided. The Turner and Lawrence measures of variety, autonomy, task identity, and feedback were used to measure these job conditions. Hackman and Lawler (1971) found that when jobs are high on these job conditions, employees with strong higher order needs have higher job satisfaction, are absent from work less frequently, and are rated by supervisors as doing higher quality work than employees with weak or few higher order needs.

Job Design In Perspective

Research and experiments in job design have clearly demonstrated that certain job characteristics are related to desirable psychological and performance outcomes, although these need considerably more specification and quantification. The research has also shown (Blood & Hulin, 1967; Hackman & Lawler, 1971; Turner & Lawrence, 1965) that individual differences are an important moderator variable. The reported success of job enrichment may be due in part to the populations with which it has been tried. Therefore, awareness of where and how job enrichment is to be applied is needed. There has been considerable discussion about employee participation in planning job enrichment. The importance of individual differences would suggest that participation, or at least an opportunity for self-selection or self-paced job enrichment is an important element in the job enrichment process but further investigation is needed. We need to better understand the effects of participation and/or opportunity for self-selection on ownership of the job change, expectations that may or may not be met, and the state of the person-job equilibrium which results. The biggest advantage of the autonomous work group (Kuriloff, 1963; Rice, 1953) as an approach to job enrichment may be in the freedom individuals have in the group to accept responsibility when they are ready.

A question that has not been answered and is begged by all the research to date is the effect of an enriched job on individual needs themselves. Hackman and Lawler (1971) and Alderfer (1969) suggest that satisfying higher order needs creates stronger higher order needs. If man is viewed as a dynamic growing being, as opposed to a static being, concern about individual differences may be unwarranted. Research (Goodman & Baloff, 1968; Hall & Nougaim, 1968; Hinrichs, 1970; Korman, 1968; Locke, 1968; Zander, Forward, & Albert, 1969) and theory (Festinger, 1957) suggest that task-related experiences can be viewed as independent variables with effects on needs, attitudes, and expectations. Thus, the best strategy may be to provide an enriched job for people who are not ready for it in the hope that they will grow into it. Experience with job enrichment suggests that such a process does take place (Huse & Price, 1970; Margulies, 1969). Much more research is needed on the extent to which the situation can induce new needs and expectations. We must know the precise discrepancy between individual readiness and job challenge which will induce need changes with the least human and economic costs. It is likely that some sort of graded and self-paced job sequence is the optimal job enrichment strategy.

From a practical point of view, however, the issue of individual differences and job design may be moot. Technology must and is often applied uniformly because jobs are interdependent and individualized jobs can present the organization with complex personnel problems in placing employees and satisfying their needs for equity in pay and status. An equally viable strategy of job enrichment may be to redesign jobs in accordance with motivational, behavioral, and psychological outcomes the organization needs in order to meet its mission. Those individuals who cannot adjust may leave, providing the organization an opportunity to select new people who fit the new job design philosophy.

Job Design And Organizational Context

No discussion of job design as an OD technology is complete without mention of the organizational context in which job redesign occurs and the possible effects on the program. The organization's culture, social processes, technology, union/management relationships and pay systems, to mention just a few context variables, affect the job enrichment program and are, in turn, affected by it.

The extent of trust that exists between workers and management certainly will determine the extent to which employees accept job enrichment. Van de Groff and Gispen (1970), for example, report a failure in job redesign due to lack of trust. Beer and Huse (1970) report that employees were at first suspicious about job enrichment and that a climate of trust was needed.

Alderfer (1969) reports that job enrichment resulted in greater satisfaction with opportunities to use skills and abilities, but less satisfaction with the amount of respect from one's boss. This was especially true for employees with seniority. Apparently redesign put a strain on the interpersonal relationship between boss and subordinate. He concludes that job enrichment can create difficulties with the boss. This finding is similar to Ford's (1969) experience with job enrichment. He found that job redesign changes the role of the supervisor as tasks previously performed by the supervisor are delegated to the subordinate. This can result in a change in the superior/subordinate relationship and can be threatening to the supervisor. Steps have to be taken to deal with this problem whenever job enrichment is planned.

Beer and Huse (1972) report on the interaction of pay systems and pay satisfaction with job enrichment. They point out that increases in responsibility and involvement are seen by workers as requiring increases in pay in order for their perceptions of equity to be maintained. However, traditional job evaluation plans do not always provide for more pay as responsibility increases because responsibility is given little weight in the plan. The extent to which pay problems arise out of job enrichment is not fully understood. Ford (1969) reports nothing about pay in his description of the AT&T efforts. But if the findings of Beer and Huse are correct, job enrichment efforts may require redesign of pay systems and reevaluation of jobs to maintain employee perceptions of equity in pay.

Moreover, job enrichment programs may run into serious problems in unionized plants. Much of what job enrichment seeks to do will eliminate the frustrations on which unionism is founded and, therefore, can cause union resistance. The union contract (Beer, 1971a) tends to freeze the relationship between management and labor and makes it difficult to change roles and relationships. Myers (1971) reports that unions are often threatened by job enrichment. They see it as unilateral infringement of their prerogatives in prescribing roles and reward systems. He suggests that both unions and management must be involved in the process, with management taking the first step. He describes several successful efforts in which both management and labor were involved.

The nature of the manufacturing technology has an important influence in determining the extent to which job enrichment is possible, the cost benefits of job enrichment, and the means by which the program can be carried out. Clearly the job characteristics of autonomy, variety, task identity, and feedback are not equally possible in all technologies. For example, task identity is difficult in a process technology, where many thousands of pounds of a material are processed by a manufacturing line in one hour (i.e., chemicals, soap, fertilizer). On the other hand, conditions of autonomy and feedback may be easier to create in an automated process technology (Blauner, 1964; Shepard, 1967) than in heavy assembly technology.

Job enrichment may entail quite different techniques and procedures, and different obstacles, depending on the technology (Anderson, 1970). For example, employee participation, a question discussed earlier, may make sense in the service industry, but may be impossible in the heavy assembly or process industries. In the heavy assembly industry, capital investment in equipment may make it virtually impossible to introduce job enrichment. When it is introduced, the aim seems to be first to set up a job module that encompasses a subassembly or sub-unit of the total product, such as the washer pump at Maytag (Biganne & Stewart, 1963). Another approach in heavy industry or in process technologies that may accomplish the objectives of job enrichment without the cost of redesigning whole assembly lines or plants is the use of work teams around assembly lines, processing units, or modular parts of lines. In the electronics industry, where change is rapid and technology obsolesces quickly, enrichment is accomplished by asking workers to solve problems at their own work stations or in teams (Roche & MacKinnon, 1970).

The interaction of technology and job redesign is critical. To date little is known about the trade-off between motivational or psychological benefits of job enrichment and its costs (capital investment, training, loss of efficiency, etc.). These trade-offs will have to be known if job enrichment is to become a sophisticated OD technology.

Personnel Systems

Organization development practitioners have tended to separate their sphere of activity from the traditional concerns of personnel administration. OD is the new approach and personnel administration is the old. The conceptual distinction between developmental and maintenance activities (Herzberg, 1966) has further separated these two areas. Yet, personnel practices can be an important lever for changing and/or supporting change in organization inputs, processes, and outputs.

Pay Systems

Pay is very important to people and it receives a considerable amount of their attention and time. It is, therefore, a means by which the organization can and does transmit important messages to employees about the kind of organization they are working in, how it operates, and what is expected of them. Because pay is so important, pay systems can provide the stimulus for behavior change and the pay itself can provide the reinforcement. In effect, pay can be a change agent (Lawler, 1971).

However, pay systems have not been thought of as change agents, and little research exists. The Scanlon Plan (Lesieur, 1958) has been the most widely applied incentive plan and is consistent with research and theory on motivation and organizations. Simply stated, the plan is a profit-improvement-sharing plan by which employees and management share in cost savings on the basis of a pre-agreed base line ratio of costs to sales. Its unique feature is the elaborate system of employee-management committees through which employees participate in the evaluation of suggestions and in decisions leading to their implementation. McGregor (1960) calls the Scanlon Plan an important social invention and gives it considerable attention as a mechanism for implementing a philosophy of participative management. Walton (1967) provides extensive rationale as to why a formal system of participation, such as the Scanlon Plan, has advantages over informal leader-centered participation for employees at lower levels in the organization. Among the reasons given are that: (1) prescribed rules and roles make it easier for lower level employees with less verbal and human relations skills to adopt new behavioral patterns; (2) hourly workers do not identify with the organization and have somewhat lower ego needs and needs for involvement; (3) extrinsic incentives are necessary to stimulate the behaviors required in a participative climate.

Puckett (1958) provides impressive evidence that the Scanlon Plan has produced increases in productivity. Its effect on the organization is less clearly understood because most organizations that introduce the plan also make other interventions to change the organizational climate. Lawler (1971) concludes, however, that pay systems like the Scanlon Plan and the Lincoln Electric Plan (1951) have produced more democratic cultures, as well as higher productivity.

Pay may indeed be an important and as yet an unexplored lever for change. Beckhard (1970) reports the offer of a pay increase as a way to get the union to allow employees to participate in cost reduction task forces. Pay was apparently successful in unfreezing the union and management from their polarized positions. The pay increase stimulated new behavior, and the intrinsic rewards and positive feelings coming from participating in the task forces will hopefully sustain the new behavior. Finally, Lawler (n.d.) suggests that employees participate in the design of pay systems to achieve more understanding and trust of the system. He reports data (1969) which demonstrate that participation in pay design results in more intended behavior change than do nonparticipative changes. These results point to participation in pay system design as a potentially powerful intervention.

Staffing Systems

A free labor market inside the corporation created by a job posting system could be extremely important in changing the culture of an organization. Alfred (1967), a student of McGregor, suggests that job posting does this in the following ways: (1) it gives the employee authority over his career now held by the boss and thereby equalizes power; (2) it provides more open feedback to employees about their performance as they are accepted or rejected for jobs for which they apply; and (3) a supervisor of a department with a poor work climate will have trouble attracting applicants from within the company and will, therefore, be forced to change. Texas Instruments and Polaroid are known to be using such a system, but no evaluation is available. The extent to which the system can create a climate change or is dependent on a climate of openness and trust is not known. It is possible that subordinates who would like to transfer out of a department may not be able to do so if they fear retaliatory measures from their boss.

Organization Structure and Roles

We are going through an era where new structural and role models for organizations are developing. Just as bureaucracy and its associated roles might be viewed as an invention of the industrial revolution (Bennis & Slater, 1968), so "ad hocacy" (Toffler, 1970) and its associated roles might be viewed as an invention of the post-industrial era. It is imperative that the OD consultant understands this revolution in organizational form. Inventions in organization structure and roles can provide useful solutions to problems that the OD consultant may encounter.

Many of these problems are likely to be caused by the inadequacy of the bureaucratic model for the changing environment in which more and more organizations find themselves. Burns and Stalker (1961) found more organic organizational forms in successful electronic companies and concluded that project teams and other temporary groups are required in such dynamic environments. Lawrence and Lorsch (1967b), studying organizations operating in three different environments ranging from certain to uncertain, found consistent relationships between environment and organization structure. They describe these structural characteristics in terms of the extent of differentiation between functional groups and the mechanisms which integrate the various functions. Organizations in more uncertain environments tended to develop both temporary and permanent teams which cut across the traditional functional organization (matrix organization). Furthermore, a new role, which Lawrence and Lorsch called the integrator role (Lawrence & Lorsch, 1967a), emerged and was critical to achieving integration within these new structures.

Lawrence and Lorsch (1969) propose that systematic diagnosis of the organization's environment and the structure and functioning required by that environment is an important and viable approach to organization development. Beer et al. (1971) describe the effects that structural and role changes (introduction of project teams and the integrator role made in accordance with the Lawrence and Lorsch model) have on integration and organization culture. They conclude that the effects of the changes are in line with what the Lawrence and Lorsch theory predicts when project teams are embedded as overlays in a bureaucratic structure. In order to be successful, a project team needs an appropriate task, effective integration, appropriate team composition, and a supportive management environment (Beer et al., 1971).

More recently Zand (1971) proposed that the dilemma of choosing between the bureaucratic or authoritarian organization and the organic or participative organization is best solved when a person or organization uses both or multiple styles. For routine and linear tasks the bureaucratic-authoritarian model should be used, but when the task changes and is non-routine and nonlinear, the organic-participative model should be used. It is clear that new structural and role models are emerging and will provide OD consultants with new solutions to some of the problems they encounter.

Financial Control Systems

Financial controls influence organizational behavior. Their design is, therefore, critical to the organization's effectiveness and efficiency (Barnard, 1938). They can prevent dysfunctional change and induce functional change (Haberstroh, 1965). Typically, however, financial controls are designed from the point of view of the accountant, rather than the behavioral scientist, and generally fail to have the functional influence on behavior that they might. However, systems can be designed which will create and maintain the desired behavior. If integration is the desired behavior Baumler (1971), based on his research, suggests important parameters that need to be considered when designing a financial control system intended to promote integration.

Human Asset Accounting is a recent invention which promises to provide an important new tool for changing organizations. It is based on the research and theory of Likert (1961, 1967) and his associates (Likert & Bowers, 1969) at the Institute for Social Research. This research shows the relationship between organizational processes and organizational results. Longitudinal studies indicate that measures of attitudes and managerial behavior are more highly correlated with organizational outputs of productivity and profitability over the long term than the short term. That is, managerial attitudes and behavior seem to have a long-range effect. Unfortunately, most organizations use conventional accounting data and methods, and information about a manager's attitudes and behavior is not entered into the accountant's books. Consequently, the relationships between such variables and organizational outputs have not been apparent. Clearly, an accounting system that accounts for such variables is needed. Such a system was developed at the R. G. Barry Corporation (1970). The first step was incorporation of outlay costs at the individual level, such as recruiting, training, and replacement costs. A second step will be the inclusion of each person's dollar value based on competence and potential. The next step will be development of a system for amortizing these assets on the basis of an anticipated rate of competence obsolescence. Additional steps planned include the valuation of relations that individuals have with outside contacts, such as customers, and the valuation of organizational health states (Brummet, Pyle, & Flamholtz, 1969).

The idea of valuing in dollar terms the human dimension of the organization at the individual, group, and organizational level is indeed an exciting idea and deserves significant developmental research in the future. Many of the problems organizations face often result because managers do not understand how their decisions impact the human component of the system. Consequently, short-range decisions with unaccounted and unanticipated costs are made. By the time the human problems resulting from these decisions surface, they are often difficult, if not impossible, to deal with. In the domain of social and human activities, the best solution to a problem is its prevention. Interpersonal and intergroup conflict often results in polarized attitudes; and once polarization occurs, conflict resolution and change are difficult. If knowledge about effects of decisions were available before the decisions were implemented, some human problems would probably have been avoided. For example, it might have been possible to prevent the alienation of workers and the resulting cost if the impact of management's decisions in technology and labor relations could have been measured in dollar terms at the time they were made. With the formation of unions the labor/management relationship has stabilized in a polarized state, making organization change extremely difficult.

Placing quantitative values on the condition of organizational processes promises to dramatically influence the decision-making processes and culture of organizations. Perhaps Human Asset Accounting will influence organizational culture and decision-making processes even more dramatically than laboratory education and process interventions. However, more research is needed on these effects if the potential impact of human asset accounting as a technology of organization development is to be fully understood.

Environmental Interventions In Perspective

Changes in the organization's internal environment probably have more powerful unfreezing effects than any other category of OD technologies reviewed in this chapter. This is mainly because they come down from the top and create a new situation which "forces" people to behave differently. For example, the creation of a project organization forces individuals from different functional groups to meet and interact on an assigned problem. If the *group* is held clearly accountable for project results, strong motivational forces are unleashed to confront problems and collaborate. However, changes of this type may be less powerful in changing attitudes, values, or skills and in refreezing new behaviors so that they become independent of the initial conditions which induced them. This is so because environmental interventions do not deal in a developmental way with organizational inputs (needs, values, skills) or organizational processes, such as leadership, teamwork, communication, and so on. In the case of the project organization, conditions for changing organizational inputs and processes are created, but unless followed by educational and/or process interventions which directly affect individual skills and attitudes as well as group process, the chances of successful and permanent organizational change are slim.

Changes in the internal environment of the organization are often based on the legal and formal power of management to change things. Therefore, the likelihood that those affected by the change will feel ownership for the change and be committed to the change is low; the likelihood that resistance and/or dysfunctional behavior will follow the change is high. The dilemma facing organization development consultants is how to gain the unfreezing benefits of situationally induced change and the resultant increase in the pace of change without losing the crucial elements of free choice, understanding, and commitment to

change. We must learn how to do this (Argyris, 1971). Bass (1970) has suggested some ways of gaining commitment from others when their involvement in the planning stage is not possible. With reasonable success, Beer et al. (1971) have applied some of these suggestions in communicating structural changes to a large organization. Considerably more work needs to be done before environmental interventions can be integrated with OD technologies which assume that ownership of change is necessary for effective change to take place.

INTEGRATED TECHNOLOGIES

As stated in the introduction to this chapter, organizational outcomes are a function of the interaction among the following: (1) individual needs, values, expectations, and abilities which constitute the organization's inputs; (2) interpersonal, group, and intergroup processes; and (3) organizational structure, job structure, controls, and administrative systems which constitute the organization's internal environment. We have reviewed in this chapter means for changing the organization's inputs, processes, and internal environment. However, each approach alone is limited in its scope and capacity for effecting change. For example, laboratory education is a technology for changing organizational inputs. But, as experience and research have shown, unfreezing or changing organizational inputs does not necessarily create permanent change in organization behavior, regardless of the power of the technique and the amount of change created in the individual. From the realization that individual change is insufficient came a technology for changing organizational processes, particularly at the interpersonal, group, and intergroup level. Completely independent of these developments came new approaches that are primarily aimed at changing structure, jobs, and systems.

If OD is to effect change in the total organizational system, the various approaches to change must be integrated in a meaningful way. There are two ways to accomplish this: (1) a consultant can integrate the technologies; or (2) integration can be achieved by preprogramming some sequence of interventions, based on a systematic theory or set of assumptions about how organizations change. The former approach would yield a different program of interventions for every organization and problem, and the latter would be a standardized approach by which every organization would follow a prescribed sequence on the road to self-renewal. Regardless of the means of integration, OD will achieve maturity as a scientifically based technology for changing organizations when we have sufficient understanding of the change process to prescribe an effective and efficient integration of interventions.

Grid Organization Development

Blake and Mouton (1969) pioneered the development of an integrated preprogrammed OD technology. Their program rests on three assumptions about organizations (Dutton, 1969): (1) individuals and organizations reduce dissonance between their self-image and reality; (2) organizations "satisfice" at levels of functioning and performance below their potential; and (3) a tremendous amount of energy is devoted to dysfunctional behaviors resulting from self-deception. The net result of all this is what Blake has called "cultural drag." The organization is unable to adapt and change in response to internal and external problems.

Based on these assumptions Blake and Mouton have developed a six-phase OD program. It starts with instrumented laboratory training and ends with problem solving and an action program aimed at changing organization functioning at the process and content level.

The program includes the following steps:

Phase I   A Grid laboratory-seminar for all organizational members, starting at the top.

Phase II   Team development for all groups in the organization, starting at the top.

Phase III   Intergroup confrontation meetings at the major group/group interfaces.

Phase IV   The development of an ideal organizational model (process, structure, and culture) by the top team of the organization. The top team prepares by reading books and is assisted by a number of instruments and models, including the Corporate Excellence Rubric described earlier in this chapter.

Phase V   Temporary task forces implement parts of the ideal strategic model.

Phase VI   The organization measures the change and is hopefully at a more effective level of functioning.

Phases I, II, and III have been described in detail earlier in the chapter. Phases IV, V, and VI utilize the temporary task force approach also described earlier to mobilize the organization's energy toward change. Thus, Blake and Mouton have integrated these approaches and in many cases themselves developed the various approaches. They assume that organizational change must start with individual change as the unfreezing mechanism, and that process problems at the interpersonal, group, and intergroup levels must be dealt with before changes in strategy and the organization's internal environment can take place. In effect, self-deception resulting from dissonance reduction must be overcome by increasing individual and organizational self-awareness. This process begins the change and must precede the planning of the new internal organizational environment (policy, structure, systems). Furthermore, the Grid OD program is based on the assumption, supported by research discussed in the section on laboratory training, that individual change can be maintained only if it is supported with group change and culture change. Finally, managers self-administer the program. Participation of managers as instructors is a key mechanism for increasing understanding and commitment to change by those in powerful positions. A basic assumption in the Grid OD program is that those who must change will do so if they plan the change. Thus, the organization and its culture is the target of change in Grid OD. Grid is not, as so often assumed, an individual or management development program.

Does Grid OD create effective and efficient change? There is little research to answer this question. Blake, Mouton, Barnes, and Greiner (1964) report that a multiphase OD program increased profits through cost reduction (an increase of several million dollars) and that there was a 31 percent increase in the number of meetings, an increase in transfers within the organization, and a higher frequency of promotions from the ranks of younger managers. More success in solving organizational problems and a shift in attitudes toward the 9,9 goal of Grid were also reported. It is probable that Grid OD did affect the organization significantly, but the extent of the impact is not clear. First, the attitude data were post-hoc. Secondly, there were interventions by Blake as a consultant which changed the plant/headquarters relationship prior to the start of the OD program (Greiner, 1967). These interventions probably prepared the way for Grid OD at the plant but make it difficult to assess the exact impact of the program itself. However, the intervention at the plant/headquarters interface prior to Grid is in line with Blake's assertions that change must start at the top and, therefore, does not take away from the success of Grid at the plant level. Furthermore, in broad-aimed change programs of the Grid type, the exact impact of any one aspect of the technology is less important than the total impact (Beer, 1970).

The importance of starting at the top with Grid, a basic tenet of the technology,

is supported by an evaluation of Grid in a large Federal agency over a period of three years (Greiner, Leitch, & Barnes, 1968). They found no change in organizational climate, but attribute it to total lack of change by top management due to factors in their organizational environment. The failure of Grid OD in this instance does not reflect on the technology so much as it reflects on the need to use it appropriately or ensure that appropriate conditions exist. In fact, the failure supports the assumption that Grid OD must start at the top.

More research on Grid OD is needed. One of the key questions which remains unanswered is whether organization development would progress more quickly if changes in structure, roles, and systems were to precede interventions at the individual and process levels. Could Phases IV and V precede Phases I, II, and III, and how might this be done? Furthermore, we must find out if, due to the amount of instrumentation involved, Grid is too tedious and cumbersome for managers and, therefore, reduces their enthusiasm for the OD process.

The Grid can also be criticized for not integrating more systematically and pragmatically the technologies which are aimed at changing the organization's internal environment. Changes in structure, roles, jobs, and systems are expected as a result of Phases IV and V, but mechanisms are not built in for systematic examination of these areas. Nevertheless, Grid OD is a major contribution to the technology of OD and, considering the state of the art, is probably a very effective and efficient tool for organization change.

Consultant-Based Integration

Probably the most efficient OD program, from the point of view of time and energy, is one where a consultant has been involved in planning the integration of a series of technologies. He can pinpoint the organizational dimensions and components where major barriers to effectiveness exist and plan interventions accordingly.

Many integrated programs have been developed in this way. For example, Seashore and Bowers (1963) integrated changes in policies, structure, individuals' cognitive framework, and interpersonal and group process. The result was significant change in a number of organizational dimensions. Marrow, Bowers, and Seashore (1967) report an extremely successful effort at changing the climate and performance of an acquired company through the integration of the following interventions: (1) a new production system was introduced; (2) a vestibule training program was established; (3) coaching for substandard employees was introduced; (4) problem-solving meetings were held at various levels; (5) T-groups were held for top management and supervisors; (6) a change in the compensation system was introduced; (7) low performers were fired; and (8) selection tests were introduced. The effects of each intervention are not known, but the inclusion of laboratory training, diagnostic interventions, process interventions, and environmental interventions makes it one of the best examples of an integrated OD program. The trend toward eclectic and integrated approaches in OD is further exemplified by a five-year plant level OD program (Beer & Huse, 1972; Huse & Beer, 1971), which included data feedback, job enrichment, changes in structure, changes in policy, third-party peacemaking, consultant coaching and feedback, and intergroup problem-solving meetings. Schmuck, Runkel, and Langmeyer (1969) provide some evidence that integrating technologies is the most effective approach. An integration of laboratory training, skill training, and consultant follow-up was more effective than skill training and follow-up alone, consultant intervention alone, or laboratory training alone. Beckhard (1966); Dayal and Thomas (1968); Dyer, Maddocks, Moffitt, and Un-

derwood (1970); Schmuck et al. (1969), and Waters (1968) report other integrated programs.

To date little evidence exists about the relative impact of each technology in an integrated program and the organizational level or situation in which each technology is most appropriate. However, enough evidence is accumulating to make the following statements:

1. Appropriate structural and role changes (environmental interventions) can precede supporting educational and process interventions in creating permanent behavioral and cultural change (Beer et al., 1971). That is, environmental interventions, such as structural and role changes, provide the stimulus for unfreezing. Educational and process interventions help develop behavioral skills, attitudes, and a culture necessary for achieving the objectives of the structural change. This approach is contrary to Blake's Grid OD model and the model used by many consultants. Their model stresses the importance of laboratory education as the first step in OD.

2. Changes in organization structure, job structure, formal procedures, and systems are likely to be more effective interventions at lower levels in the organization than are process or educational interventions. The reverse holds for higher levels in the organization (Argyris, 1971; Beer & Huse, 1972; Ford, 1969; Walton, 1967).

3. Consultant involvement is critical to the success of many OD technologies described in this chapter. Friedlander (1968) reports that consultant involvement with some groups before and after a family group laboratory resulted in significantly improved group effectiveness when compared with groups who did not have such consultant involvement. He concludes that consultant involvement may be more important than variations in trainer role and behavior or differences in laboratory climate and content. Frohman (1970) reports that survey feedback supplemented with con-

sultant help and guidance in the application of new approaches resulted in more change than survey feedback alone. The role of the consultant in preparing for change and following up on an intervention needs more research. Such research will probably reveal the critical part the consultant plays in OD efforts.

The Consultant

No research is available about the qualities of an effective consultant. In this writer's experience, the consultant's professional and interpersonal competence is as important, and perhaps more important, than the OD technologies themselves. Argyris (1971) suggests that an effective consultant should not be evaluative, attributive, or inconsistent even though the client is. Thus, he must be relatively independent of his immediate climate and culture. Argyris (1971) also suggests that the consultant must possess self-awareness and a high degree of self-confidence if he is to take the risks involved in confronting clients with their own behavior and if he is to stay independent of the client's culture. The work by Sofer (1962) suggests that the OD consultant needs skills as a clinician and therapist, and must be a model for the client. Walton (1969) believes that the consultant must maintain a neutral, non-threatening role, yet develop expert power with his clients. Certainly, the consultant must play a number of different roles (Bennis, 1965) as teacher, counselor, consultant, and manager of an OD program. Moreover, for balanced and integrated programs in large organizational systems he must be an integrator (Lawrence & Lorsch, 1967a) of a number of technologies, approaches, and departments which interface with the change effort (personnel department, engineer group, financial control group, operations research).

As Dickson and Roethlisberger (1966) suggested about counseling, OD consulting is as much a person specialization as a task specialization. The change agent must possess behavioral science knowledge, research skills, and clinical skills. These make up his "technical bag" and constitute expert power as a source of influence with the client. Additionally, he must possess the personality and interpersonal competence to use himself as the instrument of change. These are the sources of his referent power. Finally, the consultant must possess the intermediate orientation of an integrator, coordinating between various departments and mixing disciplines, technology, theories, and research findings organically, not mechanically. Thus, the consultant himself is potentially the most important OD technology available; yet, to date, little systematic knowledge exists about the individual attributes of an effective change agent.

SUMMARY

This chapter has been an attempt to present a framework for conceptualizing and evaluating a growing social technology for changing and developing organizations. This technology allows behavioral scientists to intervene and change the organization's inputs, processes, and internal environment. Much of it holds great promise, but considerable research is needed to better understand under what circumstances the various techniques can be used effectively and how they can be integrated into large-scale organization development efforts. The field of organization development tends to be dominated by change efforts which use one technology or one approach to organization change. It still has no established theory for changing organizations as total systems. Such a theory will probably emerge from the technology already developed and from experiences gained in applying that technology. This theory should provide a better understanding of how and when various technologies are applicable and how they can be integrated. In the meantime, OD technology provides applied behavioral scientists with powerful tools for changing organizations. These tools go far beyond applied research, the primary means for changing organizations in the past.

REFERENCES

Alderfer, C. P. Convergent and discriminant validation of satisfaction and desire measures by interviews and questionnaires. *Journal of Applied Psychology,* 1967, 51, 509–520.

Alderfer, C. P. An empirical test of a new theory of human needs. *Organizational Behavior and Human Performance,* 1969, 4, 142–175.

Alfred, T. M. Checkers or choice in manpower management. *Harvard Business Review,* 1967, 45 (1), 157–167.

Allport, G. W. *The nature of prejudice.* New York: Doubleday, 1954.

Anderson, J. W. The impact of technology on job enrichment. *Personnel,* 1970, 47 (5), 29–37.

Argyris, C. *Personality and organization: The conflict between system and the individual.* New York: Harper and Row, 1957.

Argyris, C. Explorations in consultant-client relationships. *Human Organization,* 1961, 20, 121–133.

Argyris, C. *Interpersonal competence and organizational behavior.* Homewood, Ill.: Irwin, 1962.

Argyris, C. *Integrating the individual and the organization.* New York: Wiley, 1964. (a)

Argyris, C. T-groups for organizational effectiveness. *Harvard Business Review,* 1964, 42 (2), 60–74. (b)

Argyris, C. Interpersonal barriers to decision making. *Harvard Business Review,* 1966, 44 (2), 84–97.

Argyris, C. Some unintended consequences of rigorous research. *Psychological Bulletin,* 1968, 70 (3), 185–197.

Argyris, C. *Management and organizational development: The path from Xa to Xb.* New York: McGraw-Hill, 1971.

Bandura, A. *Principles of behavior modification.* New York: Holt, Rinehart and Winston, 1969.

Barnard, C. I. *The functions of the executive.* Cambridge: Harvard University Press, 1938.

Bass, B. M. The anarchist movement and the T-group. *Journal of Applied Behavioral Science,* 1967, 3, 211–226.

Bass, B. M. When planning for others. *Journal of Applied Behavioral Science,* 1970, 6, 151–171.

Baumgartel, H. Using employee questionnaire results for improving organizations. *Kansas Business Review,* December, 1959, 2–6.

Baumler, J. V. Defined criteria of performance in organizational control. *Administrative Science Quarterly,* 1971, 16, 340–349.

Beckhard, R. An organization improvement program in a decentralized organization. *Journal of Applied Behavioral Science,* 1966, 2, 3–25.

Beckhard, R. The confrontation meeting. *Harvard Business Review,* 1967, 45 (2), 149–155.

Beckhard, R. *Organization development: Strategies and models.* Reading, Mass.: Addison-Wesley, 1969.

Beckhard, R. Planned change in organizational systems. Invited address presented at the meeting of the American Psychological Association, Miami Beach, September, 1970.

Beer, M. Needs and need satisfaction among clerical workers in complex and routine jobs. *Personnel Psychology,* 1968, 21, 209–222.

Beer, M. Evaluating organizational and management development programs: Trials, tribulations, and prospects. In *Evaluation of psychological programs in organizations.* Symposium presented at Bowling Green State University, Bowling Green, Ohio, December, 1970.

Beer, M. Organizational climate: A viewpoint from the change agent. In *Organizational climate.* Symposium presented at the American Psychological Association, Washington, D.C., September, 1971. (a)

Beer, M. Organizational diagnosis: An anatomy of poor integration. In *Improving integration between functional groups: A case in organization change and implications for theory and practice.* Symposium presented at the American Psychological Association, Washington, D.C., September, 1971. (b)

Beer, M., & Huse, E. F. Improving organizational effectiveness through planned change and development. Unpublished manuscript, Corning Glass Works, Corning, N.Y., August, 1970.

Beer, M., & Huse, E. F. A systems approach to

organizational development. *Journal of Applied Behavioral Science,* 1972, 8 (1), 79–101.

Beer, M., & Kleisath, S. The effects of the managerial grid lab on organizational and leadership dimensions. In S. S. Zalkind (Chm.), *Research on the impact of using different laboratory methods for interpersonal and organizational change.* Symposium presented at American Psychological Association, Washington, D.C., September, 1967.

Beer, M., Pieters, G. F., Marcus, S. H., & Hundert, A. T. Improving integration between functional groups: A case in organization change and implications for theory and practice. Symposium presented at American Psychological Association, Washington, D.C., September, 1971.

Bennett, E. B. Discussion, decision, commitment, and consensus in "group decision." *Human Relations,* 1955, VIII, 251–274.

Bennis, W. G. Theory and method in applying behavioral science to planned organizational change. *Journal of Applied Behavioral Science,* 1965, 1, 337–360.

Bennis, W. G. *Changing organizations.* New York: McGraw-Hill, 1966.

Bennis, W. G. *Organization development: Its nature, origins, and prospects.* Reading, Mass.: Addison-Wesley, 1969.

Bennis, W. G., & Slater, P. *The temporary society.* New York: Harper and Row, 1968.

Biganne, J. F., & Stewart, P. A. Job enlargement: A case study. Research series No. 25, State University of Iowa, Iowa City, Bureau of Labor and Management, 1963.

Blake, R. R., & Mouton, J. S. The instrumental training lab. In I. R. Weschler & E. H. Schein (Eds.), *Issues in sensitivity training.* Washington, D.C.: National Training Laboratories, 1962.

Blake, R. R., & Mouton, J. S. *The managerial grid.* Houston: Gulf, 1964.

Blake, R. R., & Mouton, J. S. *Corporate excellence diagnosis: The phase 6 instrument.* Austin: Scientific Methods, 1968. (a)

Blake, R. R., & Mouton, J. S. *Corporate excellence through grid organization development: A systems approach.* Houston: Gulf, 1968. (b)

Blake, R. R., & Mouton, J. S. *Building a dynamic corporation through grid organization development.* Reading, Mass.: Addison-Wesley, 1969.

Blake, R. R., Mouton, J. S., & Sloma, R. L. The union management intergroup laboratory. Strategy for resolving intergroup conflict. *Journal of Applied Behavioral Science,* 1965, 1, 25–57.

Blake, R. R., Shepard, H. A., & Mouton, J. S. *Managing intergroup conflict in industry.* Houston: Gulf, 1964.

Blake, R. R., Mouton, J. S., Barnes, L. B., & Greiner, L. E. Breakthrough in organization development. *Harvard Business Review,* 1964, 42 (6), 133–155.

Blansfield, M. G., Blake, R. R., & Mouton, J. S. The merger laboratory. *Training Directors Journal,* 1964, 18 (5), 2–10.

Blauner, R. *Alienation and freedom.* Chicago: University of Chicago Press, 1964.

Blood, M. R., & Hulin, C. L. Alienation, environmental characteristics, and worker responses. *Journal of Applied Psychology,* 1967, 51, 284–290.

Blumberg, A., & Wiener, W. One from two: Facilitating an organizational merger. *Journal of Applied Behavioral Science,* 1971, 7, 87–102.

Brummet, R. L., Pyle, W. C., & Flamholtz, E. G. Human resource accounting in industry. *Personnel Administration,* 1969, 32 (4), 34–46.

Buchanan, P. C. Crucial issues in organizational development. In G. Watson (Ed.), *Change in school systems.* Washington, D.C.: National Training Laboratories, 1967.

Buchanan, P. C. *Reflections on a project in self-renewal in two school systems.* Washington, D.C.: National Training Laboratories, 1968.

Buchanan, P. C. Laboratory training and organization development. *Administrative Science Quarterly,* 1969, 14, 466–480.

Burns, T., & Stalker, G. M. *The management of innovation.* London: Tavistock, 1961.

Business Week. Teamwork through conflict. March 20, 1971, 44–50.

Campbell, J. P., & Dunnette, M. D. Effectiveness of T-group experiences in managerial training and development. *Psychological Bulletin,* 1968, 70 (2), 73–103.

Campbell, J. P., Dunnette, M. D., Lawler, E. E., & Weick, R. E. *Managerial behavior, performance, and effectiveness.* New York: McGraw-Hill, 1970.

Cartwright, D. Achieving change in people: Some applications of group dynamics theory. *Human Relations,* 1951, 4, 381–392.

Chambers, J. C., Mullick, S. K., & Goodman, D. A. Catalytic agent for effective planning. *Harvard Business Review,* 1971, 49 (1), 110–119.

Chapple, E. D., & Sayles, L. R. *The measure of management.* New York: Macmillan, 1961.

Chase, P. A survey feedback approach to organization development. In *Proceedings of the executive study conference.* Princeton: Educational Testing Service, November, 1968.

Coch, L., & French, J. R. P. Jr. Overcoming resistance to change. *Human Relations,* 1948, 1, 512–533.

Cohen, A. M., & Petrella, T. Power: What is the OD consultant's response to separateness, risk, and fight? Paper presented at the Fall National OD Network Conference, New York, October, 1971.

Conant, E. H., & Kilbridge, M. D. An interdisciplinary analysis of job enlargement: Technology, costs, and behavioral implications. *Industrial and Labor Relations Review,* 1965, 18, 377–395.

Dalkey, N. C. The Delphi method: An experimental study of group opinion. RM-5888-PR. Rand Corporation research memo., June, 1969.

Davis, L. E. Job design and productivity: A new approach. *Personnel,* 1957, 33, 418–430.

Davis, L. E., & Valfer, E. S. Intervening responses to changes in supervisor job designs. *Occupational Psychology,* 1965, 39, 171–189.

Davis, L. E., & Werling, R. Job design factors. *Occupational Psychology,* 1960, 34, 109–132.

Davis, S. Building more effective teams. *Innovation,* 1970 (15), 32–41.

Dayal, I., & Thomas, J. M. Operation KPE: Developing a new organization. *Journal of Applied Behavioral Science,* 1968, 4, 473–506.

Deep, S., Bass, B. M., & Vaughan, J. Some effects on business gaming of previous quasi-T-group applications. *Journal of Applied Psychology,* 1967, 51, 426–431.

Deutsch, M. Cooperation and trust: Some theoretical notes. In W. Bennis, E. Schein, D. Berlew, & F. Steele (Eds.), *Interpersonal dynamics.* Homewood, Ill.: Dorsey Press, 1964.

Dickson, W. J., & Roethlisberger, F. J. *Counseling in an organization: A sequel to the Hawthorne researches.* Cambridge: Harvard University, School of Business Administration, Division of Research, 1966.

Drought, N. E. The operations committee: An experience in group dynamics. *Personnel Psychology,* 1967, 20, 153–163.

Dunnette, M. Should your people take sensitivity training? *Innovation,* 1970, 14, 42–55.

Dutton, J. M. Review of R. R. Blake & J. S. Mouton, Corporate excellence through grid organization development: A systems approach. *Administrative Science Quarterly,* 1969, 14, 608–610.

Dyer, W. G., Maddocks, R. F., Moffitt, J. W., & Underwood, W. J. A laboratory-consultation model for organization change. *Journal of Applied Behavioral Science,* 1970, 6, 211–227.

Edwards, A. L. *Techniques of attitude scale construction.* New York: Appleton-Century-Crofts, 1957.

Elliott, J. D. *Increasing office productivity through job enlargement.* New York: American Management Association Office Management Series, No. 114, 1954.

Festinger, L. *A theory of cognitive dissonance.* Evanston, Ill.: Row, Peterson, 1957.

Fiedler, F. E. A contingency model of leadership effectiveness. In L. Berkowitz (Ed.), *Advances in experimental social psychology.* New York: Academic Press, 1964, 49–80.

Fleishman, E. A. Attitude versus skill factors in work group productivity. *Personnel Psychology,* 1965, 18, 253–266.

Fleishman, E. A., Harris, E. F., & Burtt, H. E. *Leadership and supervision in industry.* Columbus: Ohio State University, Bureau of Educational Research, 1955.

Ford, R. N. *Motivation through work itself.* New York: American Management Association, 1969.

Fordyce, J. K. A task-process approach to organization development. In *Proceedings of the executive study conference.* Princeton: Educational Testing Service, November, 1968.

Fordyce, J. K., & Weil, R. *Managing with people: A manager's handbook of organization development methods.* Reading, Mass.: Addison-Wesley, 1971.

Foulkes, F. K. *Creating more meaningful work.* New York: American Management Association, 1969.

French, J. R. P. Jr., Lawshe, C. H., & Mann, F. C. Training for effective leadership. In *Planning and training for effective leader-*

ship. Ann Arbor, Mich.: Foundation for Research on Human Behavior, 1956.

Friedlander, F. The impact of organizational training laboratories upon the effectiveness and interaction of ongoing work groups. *Personnel Psychology,* 1967, 20, 289–307.

Friedlander, F. A comparative study of consulting processes and group development. *Journal of Applied Behavioral Science,* 1968, 4, 377–399.

Frohman, M. A. An empirical study of a model and strategies for planned organizational change. Unpublished doctoral dissertation, University of Michigan, Ann Arbor, 1970.

Frohman, M. A., & Shaskin, M. The practice of organization development: A selective review. Unpublished manuscript, n.d.

Glasser, W. *Reality therapy.* New York: Harper and Row, 1965.

Golembiewski, R. Personal communication, 1971.

Golembiewski, R. T., & Blumberg, A. Confrontation as a training design in complex organizations: Attitudinal changes in a diversified population of managers. *Journal of Applied Behavioral Science,* 1967, 3, 525–547.

Golembiewski, R. T., & Carrigan, S. B. Planned change in organization style based on the laboratory approach. *Administrative Science Quarterly,* 1970, 15, 79–93.

Gooding, J. It pays to wake up the blue-collar worker. *Fortune,* 1970, LXXXII (3), 133–139.

Goodman, P., & Baloff, N. Task experience and attitudes toward decision making. *Organizational Behavior and Human Performance,* 1968, 3, 202–216.

Greiner, L. E. Antecedents of planned organization change. *Journal of Applied Behavioral Science,* 1967, 3, 51–86.

Greiner, L. E., Leitch, D. P., & Barnes, L. B. The simple complexity of organizational climate in a governmental agency. In R. Tagiuri & G. H. Litwin (Eds.), *Organizational climate.* Cambridge: Harvard University, Graduate School of Business Administration, Division of Research, 1968.

Guest, R. H. Men and machines: An assembly-line worker looks at his job. *Personnel,* 1955, 31, 496–503.

Guetzkow, H. E. Differentiation of roles in task-oriented tasks. In D. Cartwright & A. Zander (Eds.), *Group dynamics: Research*

and theory. (3rd ed.) New York: Harper and Row, 1968.

Haberstroh, C. J. Organization design and systems analysis. In J. G. March (Ed.), *Handbook of organizations.* Chicago: Rand McNally, 1965.

Hackman, J. R., & Lawler, E. E. III. Employee reactions to job characteristics. *Journal of Applied Psychology,* 1971, 55, 259–286.

Hall, D. T., & Nougaim, K. E. An examination of Maslow's need hierarchy in an organizational setting. *Organizational Behavior and Human Performance,* 1968, 3, 12–35.

Hall, J. The use of instruments in laboratory training. *Training and Development Journal,* 1970, 24 (5), 48–55.

Hampden-Turner, C. M. An existential learning theory and the integration of T-group research. *Journal of Applied Behavioral Science,* 1966, 2, 367–386.

Harrison, R. Group composition models for laboratory design. *Journal of Applied Behavioral Science,* 1965, 1, 409–432.

Harrison, R. Choosing the depth of organizational intervention. *Journal of Applied Behavioral Science,* 1970, 6, 181–202.

Harrison, R. Role negotiation: A tough-minded approach to team development. In W. G. Bennis, D. E. Berlew, E. H. Schein, & F. I. Steek (Eds.), *Interpersonal dynamics.* (3rd ed.) Homewood, Ill.: Dorsey Press, 1973.

Harrison, R., & Lubin, B. Personal style, group composition, and learning. *Journal of Applied Behavioral Science,* 1965, 1, 286–301.

Heider, F. *The psychology of interpersonal relations.* New York: Wiley, 1958.

Heller, F. A. Group feedback analysis: A method of field research. *Psychological Bulletin,* 1969, 72 (2), 108–117.

Hemphill, J. K. *Group dimensions: A manual for their measurement.* Columbus: Ohio State University, Bureau of Business Research, Research Monograph No. 87, 1956.

Herman, S., & Phillips, R. Applications of gestalt in OD Workshop presented at Fall National OD Network Conference, New York, October, 1971.

Hersey, P., & Blanchard, K. H. *Management of organizational behavior: Utilizing human resources.* Englewood Cliffs, N.J.: Prentice-Hall, 1969.

Herzberg, F. L. *Work and the nature of man.* Cleveland: World Publishing, 1966.

Herzberg, F. L., Mausner, B., & Snyderman, B. *The motivation to work.* New York: Wiley, 1959.

Hinrichs, J. R. Psychology of men at work. In P. Mussen & M. Rosenzweig (Eds.), *Annual Review of Psychology,* Vol. 21. Palo Alto, Calif.: Annual Reviews, Inc., 1970.

House, R. J. T-group education and leadership effectiveness: A review of the empiric literature and a critical evaluation. *Personnel Psychology,* 1967, 20, 1–32.

House, R. J., & Wigdor, L. A. Herzberg's dual-factor theory of job satisfaction and motivation: A review of the evidence and a criticism. *Personnel Psychology,* 1967, 20, 369–389.

Hulin, C. L., & Blood, M. R. Job enlargement, individual differences, and worker responses. *Psychological Bulletin,* 1968, 69 (1), 41–55.

Hundert, A. T. Problems and prospects for project teams in a large bureaucracy. In *Improving integration between functional groups: A case in organization change and implications for theory and practice.* Symposium presented at the American Psychological Association, Washington, D.C., September, 1971.

Hundert, A. T. Application of the organization development process to intergroup conflict: A case with union and management. In *Organization development: Fad or innovation in applied behavioral science.* Symposium presented at the American Psychological Association, New Orleans, August, 1974.

Huse, E. F., & Barebo, C. A. Personal communication, 1970.

Huse, E. F., & Beer, M. Eclectic approach to organizational development. *Harvard Business Review,* 1971, 49 (5), 103–112.

Huse, E. F., & Price, P. S. The relationship between maturity and motivation in varied work groups. Presented at the meeting of the American Psychological Association, Miami, September, 1970.

Jaques, E., & Brown, W. *The glacier project papers.* Carbondale: Southern Illinois University Press, 1965.

Kahn, R. L., Wolfe, D. M., Quinn, R. P., Snoek, J. D., & Rosenthal, R. A. *Organizational stress: Studies in role conflict and ambiguity.* New York: Wiley, 1964.

Katz, D., & Kahn, R. L. *The social psychology of organizations.* New York: Wiley, 1966.

Klein, S. M., Kraut, A. I., & Wolfson, A. Employee reactions to attitude survey feedback: Study of the impact of structure and process. *Administrative Science Quarterly,* 1971, 16, 497–514.

Kolb, D. A., Winter, S. K., & Berlew, D. E. Self-directed change: Two studies. *Journal of Applied Behavioral Science,* 1968, 4, 453–471.

Korman, A. K. Self-esteem, social influence, and task performance: Some tests of a theory. Proceedings of seventy-sixth annual convention, *American Psychological Association,* 1968, 3, 567–568.

Kuriloff, A. H. An experiment in management: Putting theory Y to the test. *Personnel,* 1963, 40 (6), 8–17.

Kuriloff, A. H., & Atkins, S. T-group for a work team. *Journal of Applied Behavioral Science,* 1966, 2, 63–94.

Lawler, E. E. III. Job design and employee motivation. *Personnel Psychology,* 1969, 22, 426–435.

Lawler, E. E. III. *Pay and organizational effectiveness: A psychological view.* New York: McGraw-Hill, 1971.

Lawler, E. E. Participation in pay. Unpublished manuscript, Institute for Social Research, University of Michigan, Ann Arbor, n.d.

Lawler, E. E., & Hackman, R. J. Impact of employee participation in the development of pay incentive plans: A field experiment. *Journal of Applied Psychology,* 1969, 55 (6), 467–471.

Lawrence, P. R., & Lorsch, J. W. New management job: The integrator. *Harvard Business Review,* 1967, 45 (6), 142–151. (a)

Lawrence, P. R., & Lorsch, J. W. *Organization and environment: Differentiation and integration.* Cambridge: Harvard University, Graduate School of Business Administration, Division of Research, 1967. (b)

Lawrence, P. R., & Lorsch, J. W. *Developing organizations: Diagnosis action.* Reading, Mass.: Addison-Wesley, 1969.

Leavitt, H. J. Applied organizational change in industry: Structural, technological, and humanistic approaches. In J. G. March (Ed.), *Handbook of organizations.* Chicago: Rand McNally, 1965.

Lesieur, F. G., Ed. *The Scanlan plan: A frontier in labor-management cooperation.* Cambridge: M.I.T., Industrial Relations Section, 1958.

Lewin, K. Action research and minority problems. *Journal of Social Issues,* 1946, 2, 34–64.

Lewin, K. Group decision and social change. In E. E. Maccoby, T. Newcomb, & E. Hartley (Eds.), *Readings in social psychology.* New York: Holt, Rinehart and Winston, 1947, 330–344.

Lewin, K. *Field theory in social science.* New York: Harper and Brothers, 1951.

Likert, R. Motivational approach to management development. *Harvard Business Review,* 1959, 37 (4), 75–82.

Likert, R. *New patterns of management.* New York: McGraw-Hill, 1961.

Likert, R. *The human organization: Its management and value.* New York: McGraw-Hill, 1967.

Likert, R., & Bowers, D. G. Organizational theory and human resource accounting. *American Psychologist,* 1969, 24, 585–592.

Lincoln, J. F. *Incentive management.* Cleveland: Lincoln Electric, 1951.

Lippitt, R. *Training in community relations.* New York: Harper and Brothers, 1949.

Litwin, G. H., & Stringer, R. A. Jr. *Motivation and organizational climate.* Cambridge: Harvard University, Graduate School of Business Administration, Division of Research, 1968.

Locke, E. A. Motivational effect of knowledge of results: Knowledge or goal setting? *Journal of Applied Psychology,* 1967, 51, 324–329.

Locke, E. A. Toward a theory of task motivation and incentives. *Organizational Behavior and Human Performance,* 1968, 3, 157–189.

Locke, E. A., Bryan, J. F., & Kendall, L. M. Goals and intentions as mediators of the effects of monetary incentives on behavior. *Journal of Applied Psychology,* 1968, 52, 104–121.

McGregor, D. *The human side of enterprise.* New York: McGraw-Hill, 1960.

McLuhan, H. M. *Understanding media.* New York: McGraw-Hill, 1964.

Maher, J. R., Overbagh, W., Palmer, G. T., & Piersol, D. T. Enriched jobs mean better inspection performance. *Industrial Engineering,* November, 1969, 23–26.

Maier, N. R. F. *Problem-solving discussions and conferences.* New York: McGraw-Hill, 1963.

Maier, N. R. F. *Psychology in industry.* (3rd ed.) Boston: Houghton Mifflin, 1965.

Mann, F. C. Studying and creating change: A means to understanding social organization. In *Research in industrial human relations.* Industrial Relations Research Association, Publication No. 17, 1957, 146–167.

Mann, F. C., & Likert, R. The need for research on communicating research results. *Human Organization,* Winter, 1952, XI, 15–19.

Marcus, S. H. Findings: The effects of structural, cultural and role changes on integration. In *Improving integration between functional groups: A case in organization change and implications for theory and practice.* Symposium presented at the American Psychological Association, Washington, D.C., September, 1971.

Margulies, N. Organizational culture and psychological growth. *Journal of Applied Behavioral Science,* 1969, 5, 491–508.

Marks, A. R. N. An investigation of modifications of job design in an industrial situation and their effects on some measures of economic productivity. Unpublished doctoral dissertation, University of California, 1954.

Marrow, A. J., Bowers, D. G., & Seashore, S. E., Eds. *Management by participation.* New York: Harper and Row, 1967.

Maslow, A. H. *Motivation and personality.* New York: Harper and Row, 1954.

Mayo, E. *The human problems of an industrial civilization.* New York: Macmillan, 1933.

Meyer, H. H., Kay, E., & French, J. R. P. Jr. Split roles in performance appraisal. *Harvard Business Review,* 1965, 43 (1), 123–129.

Miles, M. B., Hornstein, H. A., Callahan, D. M., Calder, P. H., & Schiavo, R. S. Data feedback and organization change in a school system. Presented at the meeting of the American Sociological Association, August, 1966.

Miles, M. B., Hornstein, H. A., Callahan, D. M., Calder, P. H., & Schiavo, R. S. The consequences of survey feedback: Theory and evaluation. In W. G. Bennis, K. D. Benne, & R. Chin (Eds.), *The planning of change.* (2nd ed.) New York: Holt, Rinehart and Winston, 1969.

Mitchell, M. D., Koppes, D. L., Neukom, D. R., & Reavis, T. E. Organization development at Newark. Unpublished report. Oakland, Calif.: Kaiser Aluminum & Chemical, 1971.

Morton, R. B., & Bass, B. M. The organizational training laboratory. *Training Directors Journal,* 1964, 18 (10), 2–18.

Morton, R. B., & Wight, A. A critical incident evaluation of an organizational training laboratory. (working paper) Akron, Ohio: Aerojet General Corporation, 1964.

Muench, G. A. A clinical psychologist's treatment of labor-management conflicts. *Personnel Psychology,* 1960, 12, 165–172.

Myers, M. S. How attitude surveys can help you manage. *Training Directors Journal,* 1967, 21 (10), 34–41.

Myers, M. S. Every employee a manager. *California Management Review,* 1968, X (3).

Myers, M. S. Overcoming union opposition to job enrichment. *Harvard Business Review,* 1971, 49 (3), 37–49.

Neff, F. W. Survey research: A tool for problem diagnosis and improvement in organizations. In S. M. Miller, & A. W. Gouldner (Eds.), *Applied sociology.* New York: The Free Press, 1965.

Paul, W. J., Robertson, K. B., & Herzberg, F. L. Job enrichment pays off. *Harvard Business Review,* 1969, 47 (2), 61–78.

Pelissier, R. F. Successful experience with job design. *Personnel Administration,* 1965, 28, 12–16.

Pelz, E. R. Some factors in "group decision." In E. E. Maccoby, T. M. Newcomb, & E. L. Hartley (Eds.), *Readings in social psychology.* (3rd ed.) New York: Holt, Rinehart and Winston, 1958.

Pieters, G. R. Changing organizational structures, roles, and processes to enhance integration: The implementation of a change program. In *Improving integration between functional groups: A case in organization change and implications for theory and practice.* Symposium presented at the American Psychological Association, Washington, D.C., September, 1971.

Porter, L. W., & Lawler, E. E. III. *Managerial attitudes and performance.* Homewood, Ill.: Irwin, 1968.

Puckett, E. S. Measuring performance under the Scanlon plan. In F. G. Lesieur (Ed.), *The Scanlon plan: A frontier in labor-management cooperation.* Cambridge: M.I.T., Industrial Relations Section, 1958.

R. G. Barry Corporation. *Annual Report,* 1970.

Rice, A. K. Productivity and social organization in an Indian weaving shed: An examination of some aspects of the socio-technical system of an experimental automatic loom shed. *Human Relations,* 1953, 6, 297–329.

Richardson, F. L. W. Jr., & Walker, C. R. *Human relations in an expanding company.* New Haven: Yale University, Labor and Management Center, 1948.

Riecken, H. *The volunteer work camp: A psychological evaluation.* Reading, Mass.: Addison-Wesley, 1952.

Roche, W. J., & MacKinnon, N. R. Motivating people with meaningful work. *Harvard Business Review,* 1970, 48 (3), 97–110.

Roethlisberger, F. J., & Dickson, W. J. *Management and the worker: An account of a research program conducted by the Western Electric Company, Hawthorne Works, Chicago.* Cambridge: Harvard University, 1939.

Rogers, C. R. *Client-centered therapy.* Boston: Houghton Mifflin, 1951.

Rosen, H., & Komorita, S. S. A decision paradigm for action research: Problems of employing the physically handicapped. *Journal of Applied Behavioral Science,* 1969, 5, 509–518.

Rubenstein, S. P. Participative quality control. *Quality Progress,* January, 1971.

Rush, H. M. F. *Job design for motivation.* Conference Board Report No. 515. New York: The Conference Board, Inc., 1971.

Schein, E. H. Management development as a process of influence. *Industrial Management Review,* 1961, II (2), 59–77.

Schein, E. H. *Organizational psychology.* Englewood Cliffs, N.J.: Prentice-Hall, 1965.

Schein, E. H. *Process consultation: Its role in organization development.* Reading, Mass.: Addison-Wesley, 1969.

Schein, E. H., & Bennis, W. G. *Personal and organizational change through group methods: The laboratory approach.* New York: Wiley, 1965.

Schmuck, R. A., Runkel, P J., & Langmeyer, D. Improving organizational problem solving in a school faculty. *Journal of Applied Behavioral Science,* 1969, 5, 455–490.

Seashore, C. What is sensitivity training? *News and Reports,* 1968, 2 (2).

Seashore, S. E. *Group cohesiveness in the industrial work group.* Ann Arbor: University of Michigan, Survey Research Center, 1954.

Seashore, S. E., & Bowers, D. G. Changing the structure and functioning of an organization: Report of a field experiment. *University* of Michigan, Institute for Social Research, Survey Research Center, 1963, Monograph No. 23.

Seiler, J. A. Diagnosing interdepartmental conflict. Harvard Business Review, 1963, 41 (5), 121–132.

Shaw, M. E., & Wright, J. M. Scales for the measurement of attitudes. New York: McGraw-Hill, 1967.

Shepard, H. A. Changing relationships in organizations. In J. G. March (Ed.), Handbook of organizations. Chicago: Rand McNally, 1965, 1115–1143.

Shepard, J. M. Functional specialization and work attitudes. In P. Mussen & M. Rosenzweig (Eds.), Annual review of psychology, Vol. 21. Palo Alto, Calif.: Annual Reviews, Inc., 1967.

Sherif, M. Superordinate goals in the reduction of intergroup conflict. American Journal of Sociology, 1958, 43, 349–356.

Sherif, M., Harvey, O. J., White, B. J., Hood, W. R., & Sherif, C. W. Intergroup conflict and cooperation: The robbers cave experiment. Norman: University of Oklahoma Book Exchange, 1961.

Sherwood, J. J. Planned renegotiation: A norm-setting OD intervention. Paper presented at New Technologies in Organization Development Conference, New York, October, 1971.

Skinner, B. F. Science and human behavior. New York: Crowell-Collier and Macmillan, 1953.

Smith, P. B., & Hanour, T. The impact of phase I managerial grid training. Journal of Management Studies, 1969, 6, 318–330.

Sofer, C. The organization from within. Chicago: Quadrangle Books, 1962.

Sorcher, M., & Meyer, H. H. Motivating factory employes. Personnel, 1968, 45 (1), 22–28.

Stock, D. A. A survey of research on T-groups. In L. P. Bradford, J. R. Gibb, & K. D. Benne (Eds.), T-group theory and laboratory method. New York: Wiley, 1964.

Stogdill, R. M. Individual behavior and group achievement. New York: Oxford University Press, 1959.

Stogdill, R. M., & Coons, A. E. Leader behavior: Its description and measurement. Ohio State University, Bureau of Business Research, 1957, Research Monograph No. 88.

Sykes, A. J. M. The effect of a supervisory training course in changing supervisors' perceptions and expectations of the role of management. Human Relations, 1962, 15, 227–243.

Sykes, A. J. M. A study in changing the attitudes and stereotypes of industrial workers. Human Relations, 1964, 17, 143–154.

TRW Systems Group. Manager's guideline: Organization development. April, 1969.

Tangerman, E. J. Every man his own inspector, every foreman his own boss at Graflex. American Machinist, 1953, 7 (3), 7.

Tannenbaum, R. Organizational change has to come through individual change. Innovation, 1971 (23), 36–43.

Tannenbaum, R., & Schmidt, W. H. How to choose a leadership pattern. Harvard Business Review, 1958, 36, 95–101.

Taylor, F. W. Scientific management. New York: Harper, 1911.

Toffler, A. Future shock. New York: Random, 1970.

Trist, E. L., & Bamforth, K. W. Some social and psychological consequences of the long-wall method of coal-getting. Human Relations, 1951, 4, 3–38.

Turner, A. N., & Lawrence, P. R. Industrial jobs and the worker. Cambridge: Harvard University, Graduate School of Business Administration, 1965.

Underwood, W. J. Evolution of laboratory method training. Training Directors Journal, 1965, 19 (5), 34–40.

Van de Groff, M. H. K., & Gispen, J. H. Work stratum. Progress, The Unilever Quarterly, 1970 (4).

Vroom, V. H. Work and motivation. New York: Wiley, 1964.

Wagner, A. B. The use of process analysis in business decision games. Journal of Applied Behavioral Science, 1965, 1, 387–408.

Wakeley, J. H. One way to get meaningful results from attitude surveys. Personnel, 1964, 41 (6), 43–47.

Wakeley, J. H., & Shaw, M. E. Management training: An integrated approach. Training Directors Journal, 1965, 19 (7), 2–13.

Walker, C. R., & Guest, R. H. The man on the assembly line. Cambridge: Harvard University Press, 1952.

Wallace, S. R. Issues in criterion development. In Evaluation of psychological programs in organizations. Symposium presented at

Bowling Green State University, Bowling Green, Ohio, December, 1970.

Walton, R. E. Contrasting designs for participative systems. *Personnel Administration,* 1967, 30, 35–47.

Walton, R. E. *Interpersonal peacemaking: Confrontations and third-party consultation.* Reading, Mass.: Addison-Wesley, 1969.

Walton, R. E. Frontiers beckoning the organizational psychologist. Invited address presented at the meeting of the American Psychological Association, Washington, D.C., September, 1971.

Walton, R. E., & Dutton, J. M. The management of interdepartmental conflict: A model and review. *Administrative Science Quarterly,* 1969, 14, 73–84.

Walton, R. E., Dutton, J. M., & Cafferty, T. P. Organizational context and interdepartmental conflict. *Administrative Science Quarterly,* 1969, 14, 522–542.

Waters, C. A. Building internal resources for organizational development. In *Proceedings of the executive study conference.* Princeton: Educational Testing Service, November, 1968.

Webb, E. J., Campbell, D. T., Schwartz, R. D., & Sechrest, L. *Unobtrusive measures: Nonreactive research in the social sciences.* Chicago: Rand McNally, 1966.

Weber, R. J. Effects of videotape feedback on task group behavior. In *Job attitudes and behavior.* Paper session presented at the meeting of the American Psychological Association, Washington, D.C., September, 1971.

Whitsett, D. A., & Winslow, E. K. An analysis of studies critical of the motivator-hygiene theory. *Personnel Psychology,* 1967, 20, 391–415.

Whyte, W. F. *Toward an integrated approach for research in organizational behavior.* Ithaca, N.Y.: Cornell University, New York State School of Industrial and Labor Relations, 1963. Reprint Series No. 155.

Wilson, J. E., Mullen, D. P., & Morton, R. B. Sensitivity training for individual growth: Team training for organization development. *Training and Development Journal,* 1968, 22 (1), 47–53.

Wood, A., & Okum, M. L. Job rotation plus that works. *American Machinist,* 1946, 96 (9).

Woodhead, E. A. Jobs break-down under group study plan. *Electrical World,* 1943, 120 (4).

Woodward, J. *Industrial organization: Theory and practice.* London: Oxford University Press, 1967.

Work in America. Report of a special task force to the Secretary of Health, Education, and Welfare. Cambridge: M.I.T. Press, 1973.

Worthy, J. C. Organizational structure and employee morale. *American Sociological Review,* 1950, 15, 169–179.

Zand, D. Collateral organizations. Workshop presented at Fall National OD Network Conference, New York, October, 1971.

Zand, D. E., Steele, F. I., & Zalkind, S. S. The impact of an organizational development program on perceptions of interpersonal, group, and organizational functioning. In S. S. Zalkind (Chm.), *Research on the impact of using different laboratory methods for interpersonal and organizational change.* Symposium presented at the meeting of the American Psychological Association, Washington, D.C., September, 1967.

Zander, A., Forward, J., & Albert, R. Adaptation of board members to repeated failure or success in their organization. *Organizational Behavior and Human Performance,* 1969, 4, 56–76.

CHAPTER 23

The Management of Ineffective Performance[1]

JOHN B. MINER
Georgia State University

J. FRANK BREWER
University of Maryland

THE CONCEPT OF PERFORMANCE failure is considered within the context of organization theory and the control model. The discussion focuses on organizational performance standards, causes of negative deviations, and corrective procedures that may be introduced to restore effective performance levels. A final section deals with the nature of current company practice in this area. Although the chapter deals with a number of topics, such as training, job enlargement, and the culturally disadvantaged, which are considered elsewhere in this *Handbook,* it treats these topics from a different viewpoint—as they relate to ineffective performance. As contrasted with other chapters, this one is concerned with industrial clinical psychology.

Just as organizational psychology has its origins in, and owes much to, social psychology, the study of ineffective work performance has a continuing debt to clinical psychology. The clinician, however, is concerned with causes and treatments of a different nature from those which are of interest to the student of ineffective performance. While clinical psychology focuses on those individuals who fail to meet *society's* criteria and standards for adequate emotional, motivational, and intellectual adjustment, ineffective performance is defined in relation to criteria and standards established by a considerably smaller social unit—the employing *organization.*

THE CONTROL MODEL APPLIED TO INEFFECTIVE PERFORMANCE

Ineffective performance and the use of procedures designed to correct it may be best understood when viewed in the context of the control model. This model serves to call attention to cases where some deviation from established standards occurs. With

[1] The literature reviewed extends through 1970.

regard to performance, this refers to the employee whose work behavior departs from existing role prescriptions so markedly that it is below a minimum acceptable level. Where ineffective performance exists, some type of corrective procedure is needed if an improvement up to an acceptable level is to be achieved. Thus, the control, and accordingly the management, of ineffective performance involves identifying those individuals whose work is consistently below a minimum standard, and then taking action to raise their performance to an acceptable level. Dealing with ineffective performance differs from attempting to improve performance to the highest level possible and from preventative efforts to avoid performance declines in that failure has actually occurred prior to the time action is taken. The topics considered in this chapter, therefore, may be viewed in relation to the same conceptual framework that is used in production control, quality control, inventory control, cost control, and the like. However, in this instance the factor to which the control model is applied is human performance.

Performance Criteria and Standards

Minimum acceptable levels which define ineffective performance are frequently established by the immediate superior on a judgmental basis, although in the context of management by objectives there may be some degree of participation by the employee himself in setting standards (Steinmetz, 1969). Subjective standards of this kind vary somewhat from manager to manager and even at different points in time with the same manager. For most purposes it seems best to define ineffective performance in terms of what is *considered* unsatisfactory. This means that two employees whose performance is identical could be labeled effective and ineffective because differing standards are applied to each. Under such circumstances, the ineffective performance might be viewed as caused in part, or even entirely, by the manager's standard

setting process. Thus ineffective performance which occurs only because it is defined as such by superiors can be subsumed under the ineffective performance concept and can be handled in terms of the control model. Corrective action in such cases requires a revision of managerial standards or the introduction of more objective indexes of performance. It is one of the advantages of objective performance measures that their use reduces the frequency of ineffective performance by managerial definition only.

Minimal acceptable levels of performance are established either implicitly or explicitly on a number of criteria. Performance is a multidimensional concept and the variables that constitute it vary from job to job depending on the existing role prescriptions. Typical performance dimensions are: quantity of output, quality of output, absenteeism, impact on the performance of others, contribution to internal stress and conflict, and dishonest behavior. It is apparent that an individual can fail relative to one of these criteria and perform quite acceptably on others. The usual practice is to consider a person ineffective if he performs below the minimum acceptable level on any dimension that is relevant to his job.

Ultimately what is relevant to a person's job must be determined in relation to the task and maintenance goals of the organization. Excessive absenteeism, very poor quality work, behavior which constantly foments conflict with no positive consequences, and the like do have a meaningful relationship to goals. However, just as ineffective performance may be caused by establishing unusually high standards, it also may be caused by introducing performance criteria that are not goal-related. In such cases, performance failure is still usually considered to exist since there is in fact a problem situation, but as with inappropriate standards, the failure may be viewed in part or entirely as a matter of definition. A solution can be achieved only if the performance criterion which is not goal-relevant can be eliminated. Criteria of this kind which appear with some frequency in the business world include kinship, religion, race, and ethnic group (Powell, 1969).

Strategic Factors Contributing to Ineffective Performance

In many of its applications the control model has been used without detailed attention being given to the causes of the deviation from standard. The major concerns have been with establishing the standard, measuring the deviation, and setting up a feedback mechanism or some similar procedure to correct the deviation.

When the control model is applied to human performance, however, it is apparent that corrective procedures cannot be effective unless information is available regarding the causal factors which were strategic in producing the performance failure. Once one has established the various causes which have combined to produce a given instance of ineffective performance, it is possible to consider whether the impacts of one or more

of these various strategic forces can be removed or blunted, and whether doing this will serve to establish a satisfactory level of performance. With performance control automatic correction of extreme deviations is not possible. The appropriate corrective procedure must be selected based on a comprehensive understanding of causation. As in medicine, a treatment must be chosen which is appropriate to the nature of the disorder, if a cure is to be achieved.

As a variety of cases of performance failure have been collected and studied, various writers have developed lists of potential strategic factors. These lists are of considerable value in dealing with specific cases, since the factors noted may be treated as hypotheses, which are then checked against available knowledge of the individual and his environment. Those factors which are confirmed to operate in a particular case constitute the strategic causes and provide a basis for the choice of a corrective procedure. Three such lists of possible strategic factors are given in Table 1. It is apparent that the lists have much in common, al-

TABLE 1

LISTS OF STRATEGIC FACTORS CONTRIBUTING TO INEFFECTIVE PERFORMANCE

Ginzberg, Miner, Anderson, Ginsburg, and Herma (1959): Military Organizations
1. The personality of the soldier
   a. Physical condition
   b. Intelligence
   c. Emotional stability
   d. Motivation
2. The soldier and his family
   a. Separation
   b. Breakup
3. The immediate group
   a. Cohesion
   b. Leadership
4. The military organization
   a. Investment
   b. Planning and improvisation
   c. Discipline and over-permissiveness
   d. Assignment
5. Conflict of cultural values
   a. Equity
   b. Religious and moral values
6. Situational stress
   a. Location
   b. Combat

Continued

TABLE 1 (Continued)

Miner (1963; 1966; 1975): Business Organizations
1. Intelligence and job knowledge
   a. Insufficient verbal ability
   b. Insufficient special ability other than verbal
   c. Insufficient job knowledge
   d. Defect of judgment or memory
2. Emotions and emotional illness
   a. Continuing disruptive emotion (anxiety, depression, anger, excitement, shame, guilt, jealousy)
   b. Psychosis (with anxiety, depression, anger, etc., predominating)
   c. Neurosis (with anxiety, depression, anger, etc., predominating)
   d. Alcoholism and drug problems
3. Individual motivation to work
   a. Strong motives frustrated at work
   b. Unintegrated means to satisfy motives
   c. Excessively low personal work standards
   d. Generalized low work motivation
4. Physical characteristics and disorders
   a. Physical illness or handicap, including brain damage
   b. Physical disorders of emotional origin
   c. Inappropriate physical characteristics
   d. Insufficient muscular or sensory ability
5. Family ties
   a. Family crises
   b. Separation from an emotionally significant family
   c. Social isolation
   d. Predominance of family considerations over work demands
6. The groups at work
   a. Negative consequences associated with group cohesion
   b. Ineffective management
   c. Inappropriate managerial standards or criteria
7. The company
   a. Insufficient organizational action
   b. Placement error
   c. Organizational over-permissiveness
   d. Excessive span of control
   e. Inappropriate organizational standards or criteria
8. Society and its values
   a. Application of legal sanctions
   b. Enforcement of cultural values by means not connected with the administration of the law
   c. Conflict between job demands and cultural values as individually held (equity, freedom, morality, etc.)
9. Situational forces
   a. Negative consequences of economic forces
   b. Negative consequences of geographic location
   c. Detrimental conditions of work
   d. Excessive danger
   e. Problems in the work itself

Steinmetz (1969): Business Organizations
1. Managerial and organizational shortcomings
   a. Lack of proper motivational environment
   b. Personality problems
   c. Inappropriate job assignment
   d. Improper supervision
   e. Lack of training
   f. Failure to establish duties

TABLE 1 (Continued)

2. Individual, personal shortcomings of the employee
   a. Lack of motivation
   b. Laziness
   c. Personality clashes
   d. Dissatisfaction with job assignment
   e. Failure to understand one's duties
   f. Chronic absenteeism
   g. Alcoholism
   h. Mental illness
   i. Chronic illness
   j. Senility
   k. Sex
3. Outside influences
   a. Family problems
   b. Social mores
   c. Conditions of the labor market
   d. Governmental actions
   e. Union policies
   f. Climate

though they differ in the fineness with which categories are established. In most instances failure occurs as a consequence of an interaction between characteristics of the individual and aspects of his organizational context; to these may be added outside factors related to the family, the culture, and the environmental situation. It is rare to find only a single strategic factor; complex determination is the rule.

Reducing the Incidence of Ineffective Performance

There are several approaches that may be used to reduce the incidence of ineffective performance in an organization:

1. Select individuals for employment who have a low probability of failure.

2. Establish performance standards at such a low level that failure rarely occurs.

3. Identify strategic factors and introduce corrective procedures as quickly as possible.

4. Terminate the employment of all ineffective performers as soon as they are identified.

Of these four, the initial two are essentially preventive in nature, rather than controlling, and are considered in other chapters of this volume. Good selection procedures

without doubt can serve to reduce performance failure, but it is doubtful that they can ever provide a complete solution because of changing individuals and work contexts. Low standards also can reduce the incidence of failure; however, the achievement of task and/or maintenance goals can be expected to suffer as a result and organizational survival may be threatened, particularly in the profit-making sector.

Research bearing on certain strategic factors and on corrective procedures is considered at some length in later sections of this chapter. In order for strategic factors to be identified and appropriate corrective action initiated quickly, however, managers must develop a fund of knowledge in this area. The effects of management development and educational programs designed to provide this knowledge are considered in this section. Data relevant to a strategy of immediate firing when ineffective performance occurs are also considered.

TRAINING IN DEALING WITH INEFFECTIVE PERFORMANCE. Several courses have been developed to familiarize managers with the causes of ineffective performance and with the various corrective approaches that may be taken (Belasco & Trice, 1969; Miner,

1965; Steinmetz, 1969). These courses utilize group discussion techniques, case analysis, and the lecture method. The most extensive research has been directed to the identification of changes produced by the lecture method, although studies have been conducted to evaluate the effectiveness of training based entirely on the analysis of cases and of a course utilizing the conference leadership discussion pattern, based on case materials and content-oriented questions.

One study conducted in the business setting utilized fifty-six research and development managers in the experimental group and thirty controls (Miner, 1965). The experimental subjects took a course consisting primarily of lectures fashioned around the Miner list of strategic factors noted in Table 1. Comparison of measures taken before and after the course indicated that a major impact was in the area of managerial motivation. The managers in the experimental group developed more positive attitudes to authority figures, a higher level of power motivation, more positive attitudes toward the masculine role, and a greater interest in routine administrative tasks; they were resistant to a decline in competitive motivation which the control group experienced, presumably as a result of certain organizational changes. A follow-up analysis carried out five years after the training had been completed, comparing promotion rates and performance ratings of managers in the R&D department who had had the course with those of managers who had not, indicated a definite superiority for the former. The managers in the experimental group had been much more successful in spite of the fact that both groups were at the same average managerial level and had the same rated potential for advancement at the time training occurred.

A similar course has also been evaluated in the context of an undergraduate program in business administration, again using experimental and control groups. The same changes in managerial motivation that were found in the R&D study appeared in this research, as well as a clear increase in competitive motivation and a greater desire to assume a differentiated role. These changes were still in evidence a year and a half after completion of training. In contrast, a course which focused entirely on the analysis of cases of ineffective performance failed to yield any evidence of change in a college student group.

However, Belasco and Trice (1969) did identify certain changes resulting from their course which utilized the conference leadership discussion pattern, based on case materials. These researchers employed a Solomon four-group design with a total of 133 industrial supervisors. Changes in attitudes toward deviant behavior, in self-reported action in dealing with problem employees, and in knowledge related to ineffective performance were investigated. The changes identified were not large, but there was evidence of a shift to significantly greater knowledge about problem employees, to attitudes indicative of less favorable evaluations of problem employees, and to more favorable action patterns in dealing with ineffective performance. Although this research did not deal with changes in managerial motivation directly, indirect evidence based on post-training interviews suggests that the training did tend to serve as a means of increasing the supervisors' identification with the managerial role.

Taking the Miner (1965) and Belasco and Trice (1969) research together, it seems evident that the various courses having a strong content emphasis related to the sources and correction of ineffective performance yield not only an increase in knowledge, but a change in motivation such that there is a greater tendency to view oneself as a real manager. Research to date suggests that this shift in managerial motivation and identification is the major consequence of the training. It probably accounts for the development of somewhat less favorable attitudes toward problem employees noted in the Belasco and Trice study.

FIRING AS A SOLUTION TO INEFFECTIVE PERFORMANCE. There is no question that in many companies firing has been and often still is the preferred solution to problems of performance failure. Yet this approach has become hedged with so many constraints, both internal and external to the organization, that often it is not feasible. Furthermore, it can be as costly as taking corrective action. Thus, in many cases it is easier and more efficient to manage ineffective performance and reduce its incidence than to rely on involuntary terminations. This does not deny that there are situations where the termination route is feasible and in fact desirable, as with organizations which are able to utilize an up or out policy. Even in these instances, however, an analysis of the strategic factors producing failure will permit some type of cost-benefit evaluation of the various decision alternatives. It is always possible that, even when firing is a readily available solution, a full exploration of alternatives will reveal that retention with some type of control procedure applied to performance is preferable. Firing with full knowledge that available corrective procedures have a low probability of success or are excessively costly is one thing; firing as a blanket policy applied to all instances of performance failure is a much more questionable managerial practice.

Among the constraints on firing is the fact that company payments toward unemployment compensation are based on an experience-rating procedure that penalizes a firm for high involuntary turnover rates. Furthermore, a number of companies have policies requiring severance payments to individuals who are separated against their will subsequent to an initial probationary period. Although these may not be paid in discipline cases, a unionized firm that utilizes firing extensively as a solution to performance failure can expect to make severance payments in a rather large number of instances.

This is only one of the pressures related to unionization. If there is a possibility that dismissal represents an unfair labor practice, a firm may have to reinstate with back pay. This can be ordered by a Labor Relations Board or by the courts. Even if a company wins such a case, the costs in time and money can be sizable. Formal grievances are frequently filed in discharge cases and these may well require arbitration. In one series of over 300 discharges appealed to an arbitrator, only 46 percent were sustained. In 19 percent the men were reinstated with full back pay; the remainder were reinstated but with some pay loss (American Arbitration Association, 1957).

Strikes in response to a firing that is considered unfair are common in firms that do not have a no strike clause incorporated in the union contract. Even where a no strike agreement does apply over the period of the agreement, slowdowns and other types of retaliatory action may occur. The only realistic solution to these varied union pressures may be eventual reinstatement.

Internal pressures against firing need not be mediated through the union. Employees may consider a discharge inequitable and take action to make things difficult for the responsible manager or retaliate against the company in some way. Even where a manager does not view this as likely, he may hesitate to fire because of the enmity his action might create or because he feels guilty about discharging a man. Especially in the case of long-service employees and at the management level, strong social pressures against firing are characteristic in most organizations.

Externally, there is always the possibility that a company that frequently resorts to discharge may create a negative image for itself in the local labor market. The number and quality of applicants may be curtailed and recruiting costs may rise. In some instances the antagonism generated toward the company may influence the sale of products and other business dealings.

Finally, there are the costs associated with personnel turnover of any kind. These relate to recruiting, selecting, and training a replacement; to bringing a new man to full capacity; to the compensatory efforts of others while the new man is being developed. Taken as a whole, these factors exert a strong pressure on many firms for performance control rather than discharge. The remainder of this chapter is concerned with the identification of causes and the development of solutions where ineffective performance is in evidence.

SPECIFIC PROBLEM AREAS

Research on specific types of ineffective performance and on the relationships between strategic factors and performance is extremely uneven. Certain problem areas have attracted a great deal of attention for a number of years. Alcoholism and the handling of alcoholic employees, for instance, has been the subject of numerous studies. Other problem areas, such as drug addiction, have only recently become a significant source of performance failure, and thus, the total accumulated research is still meager. But there are also long-standing problem areas such as chronic disciplinary cases that have attracted practically no research and give little evidence of doing so in the future. These imbalances between problem areas are clearly reflected in the following discussions, which deal with insufficient time on the job (absenteeism, turnover), accident repetition, alcoholism, drug addiction, emotional disorders, physical handicaps, and the culturally handicapped.

Insufficient Time on the Job

Studies of time on the job fall into two major categories—absenteeism and turnover. Absenteeism is the more relevant of the two for the present purposes since excessive absence from work is usually viewed as constituting ineffective performance; absenteeism is one of the dimensions on which performance is evaluated. Turnover is much less directly related to ineffective performance. The control model is rarely applicable to it, since once a person has separated corrective action is impossible. Yet there is a sense in which voluntary separations after relatively

short periods of employment can be considered as instances of performance failure; the individual fails to make himself available to do the work for which he was hired.

ABSENTEEISM. Research dealing with the causes of absenteeism is of three types. These are studies dealing with illness, either psychological or physical or both; studies dealing with structural variables; and studies dealing with attitudinal variables.

Illness consistently emerges as the most important cause of absenteeism. It is generally estimated to account for from one-half to two-thirds of all absences. Within the broad category of illness, reports from both practicing professionals (Sternhagen, 1969) and researchers (Willings, 1968) indicate that the primary causation is psychological. Some of the most frequently noted psychological problems are personal maladjustment, emotional disorders, alcoholism, and drug addiction. These will be considered later in this chapter.

Much of the research dealing with structural variables has yielded negative results. Absenteeism fails to correlate with compensation (Metzner & Mann, 1953; Willings, 1968), growth potential of the job (Metzner & Mann, 1953), ability to utilize skills (Metzner & Mann, 1953), work load (Gerstenfeld, 1969; Willings, 1968), and amount of required overtime (Lindquist, 1958). On the other hand, both Sternhagen (1969) and Willings (1968) have found that employees who receive sick pay are absent nearly twice as much as those who do not. Gerstenfeld (1969), Lindquist (1958), and Odiorne (1955) all report significant relationships between physical working conditions (heat, light, machine maintenance) and absenteeism.

A considerable amount of research has been done relating absence rates to job attitudes, in part at least because the subject has been a matter of some controversy. Much of the controversy appears to have arisen out of conflicting operational definitions of job satisfaction and from over-generalization of findings. A review of the literature, with particular attention to the precise questions asked, indicates that certain types of employee dissatisfaction relate to absenteeism, but not all types.

Significant relationships are present with worker attitudes toward immediate superiors (Mayo, 1945; Willings, 1968) and toward co-workers and the work group (Metzner & Mann, 1953). Absenteeism does not consistently correlate with attitudes toward management practices (Hauser, 1961), perceived equity of the company compensation structure (Ross & Zander, 1957), or overall satisfaction with the company, except where the overall satisfaction measure focuses primarily on attitudes toward the supervisor, co-workers, and the work group. Metzner and Mann (1953) found satisfaction with work group relations inversely related to absence rates for white collar men working in low skill jobs and for blue collar men, but not for white collar women or white collar men working in higher level jobs. They hypothesize that at the higher skill levels satisfaction with monetary factors and quality of supervision are more important determinants of absenteeism and also that being absent is a less acceptable alternative at this level. The very high absenteeism rates of the female white collar workers (twice those of the men) appear to be determined largely by off-the-job factors.

TURNOVER. Unlike absenteeism, turnover appears to correlate frequently with overall satisfaction measures dealing with organizational and industry variables (Morse, 1953; Schuh, 1967; Hauser, 1961). Among the factors found related to turnover are worker attitudes toward management practices, quality and nature of working conditions, actual size of wages, degree to which the company is perceived as treating its employees fairly (Metzner & Mann, 1953), and amount of required overtime (Lindquist,

1958). Ross and Zander (1957) found that the extent to which the job precluded satisfaction being derived from family or community sources was related to high turnover.

Turnover is also closely associated with the type of work-group dissatisfactions noted in the discussion of absenteeism, and with certain intrinsic aspects of the job. Telly (1970) compared relatively high and low turnover shops of the Boeing Company and found much greater felt inequity in the shops experiencing the greatest number of separations. Inequity was most pronounced with regard to the outcomes of supervision, leadman, working conditions, intrinsic aspects of the job, and social aspects of the job. Similarly, a study conducted in a plant of the General Electric Company, and focusing on cases where employment was often of very short duration, established that more authoritarian foremen had much higher turnover rates (Ley, 1966).

Accident Repetition

Accidents are most frequent in the age range from seventeen to twenty-eight and decline steadily after that to reach a low point in the late fifties and the sixties (Schulzinger, 1956). The tendency for individuals to experience more frequent injuries during their early years in the labor force is one of the most stable findings in the accident field (Haddon, Suchman, & Klein, 1964). Another such finding is that women represent a much lower risk insofar as accident repetition is concerned than men (MacIver, 1961).

Other evidence indicates that those individuals who have high injury rates in one year are the ones who are most likely to have high rates the following year. In one study, those who had no accidents the first year were found to have an average of .69 the second year, while those with nine the first year had 5.14 the second (Tiffin & McCormick, 1965). Additional analyses carried out to determine whether the hazards associated with specific jobs could account for these findings produced negative results. When differences in job danger were controlled, the same pattern was still present in the data.

Findings of this kind are consistent with the widely held opinion that injuries are not merely a direct function of the degree to which the working environment contains hazardous features; that instead there are reasonably stable and enduring personality characteristics that predispose people to accident repetition (Farmer & Chambers, 1939). It is true that training deficiencies and the fact that younger workers are more likely to be new on the job could account for part of the injury-age relationship (Van Zelst, 1954). But these cannot explain all the findings. For one thing the increase during the early years is far too marked. For another, the injury rates do not reach their highest level until age twenty-two, even though skill deficiencies are more pronounced at younger ages.

Contrary to the earlier view that differences in accident frequencies can be accounted for entirely in terms of chance fluctuations (Mintz & Blum, 1949), it does appear that there are certain individuals who are consistently more susceptible to injuries than others. This tendency appears to be more pronounced during a specific period of life, however. Research into the personality characteristics of accident repeaters tends to support the accident proneness view. There appear to be some consistent differences between those with high and low rates of injury.

In one study, sentence completion test responses were related to accident rates (Davids & Mahoney, 1957). High rates were associated with low trust, low sociocentricity, low optimism, resentment, and very negative employment attitudes. Another investigation involved the testing of a group of individuals with extremely high injury-frequency rates (LeShan, 1952). There was evidence of a lack of warm emotional relationships with others. Most had a number of acquaintances, but were not close to them. In addition, these accident prone individuals exhibited a marked, and often unreasonable, hatred of their superiors at work as well as of other authority figures. Other findings were a high level of concern about health matters, even though actual illness tended to be rare, and a strong desire for increased social status, coupled with very little accomplishment in this regard. Emotionally disturbing situations were often handled by misperceiving and distorting the world around them so as to make it less threatening. As a result these people often made bad mistakes in judgment. They did little planning for the future and were very impulsive.

This latter finding is consistent with data from another study indicating that those with high injury-frequency and injury-severity rates are likely to act with a high degree of muscular speed even though they lack the visual capacity to comprehend a situation with equal rapidity (Drake, 1940). The same tendency to impulsive risk taking appears to be reflected in the repeated finding that a score obtained when the Banker scale (cautiousness) of the Strong Vocational Interest Blank is subtracted from the Aviator scale (adventuresomeness) is closely associated with a high accident rate (Kunce, 1967).

Taken as a whole the research provides a rather consistent picture of the accident prone person. Because their high injury rates are not normally maintained throughout life, it seems most appropriate to view accident proneness as a transient personality maladjustment that is most likely to appear in the years before age thirty. The major motivation behind the repeated accidents themselves appears to be a desire to impress others by resorting to sudden and very risky decisions and behavior. This impulsiveness is often combined with a strong hatred of superiors and a consequent defiance of rules and policies established by these people. Thus, safety regulations are deliberately flouted, not only as a means of impressing others with one's skill or bravery, but as a way of attacking and resisting management. Under such circumstances exposure to danger becomes particularly frequent for these employees. With an exposure level this high it is not surprising that they are in fact injured on a number of occasions. There is something of the quality of an addiction in the repeated exposure to hazard, even though under normal circumstances the work might not be considered very dangerous at all.

In some instances, this pattern may be supplemented as a result of certain additional personality processes. Hatred toward superiors and other authority figures can generate considerable guilt, and a wish, whether conscious or unconscious, to escape this guilt by being punished. To the extent punishment is viewed as a means of atoning for one's sins, it may be desired. For people such as this an accident may be equated with punishment, and a strong desire to suffer injury may develop at periodic intervals when guilt becomes too pronounced. Under such circumstances the accident may even be a serious or half-hearted suicide attempt.

This interpretation does not deny the existence of other factors contributing to accident repetition, such as differences in exposure to hazards; in sensory, neural, and motor functioning; in the intellectual capacity for correctly recognizing and making judgments concerning hazards; in experience and training; in the extent of exposure to pertinent social and other environmental stresses; and in susceptibility to physical trauma (Haddon, Suchman, & Klein, 1964). Some apparently very useful models for understanding the accident process, not just accident repetition, have in fact been developed using variables of this kind. Gordon (1949) considers the interactions among the host (worker), the agent (germ, loose board), and the environment in which the host and agent interact. A similar framework, which views accidents as progressing through a series of stages of which the actual injury is only the final outcome, has been developed by Suchman (1961).

Alcoholism

Because of drinking on the job, hangovers, and anxiety, alcoholics often turn out insufficient work or work of poor quality, but absenteeism is the primary consequence for performance. In one company (Observer & Maxwell, 1959), a group of known alcoholics lost 2.5 times as many days from work as a group of nonalcoholics of similar sex, age, length of service, job type, and ethnic background. These absences were not entirely a direct result of drinking; the alcoholics had 3.6 times as many accidents. The off-the-job accident rate was particularly high. Other studies have confirmed the very high accident rates among alcoholics (Brenner, 1967). As might be anticipated from the preceding discussion of accident repeaters, personality factors appear to play a significant role in the generation of severe and frequent injuries among alcoholics (Selzer, 1969; Smart et al., 1969).

One of the most difficult problems in the management of alcoholism is identification, since it is characteristic for employees to cover up for their alcoholic friends. Based on a study of approximately 200 members of Alcoholics Anonymous, it appears that among the best indicators are considerable absenteeism, leaving work during the morning or at the noon hour, and improbable excuses for absences (Trice, 1957). Inconsistencies tend to appear in these stories, and there is frequent mention of colds, flu, stomach upsets, and virus conditions. On the job such symptoms of hangovers as red eyes and a flushed face are often in evidence, as well as hand tremors and the smell of either alcohol or breath cleansers. Work tends to be accomplished in spurts and slumps. There may be temperamental outbursts and an unusual amount of suspiciousness. Also problems outside work are likely to arise, in particular financial difficulties, marital discord, and difficulties with neighbors.

Psychological research related to alcoholism has focused on such factors as the way in which alcohol influences performance and the personality characteristics of alcoholics. The former has been a topic of research interest for a number of years (Jellinek & McFarland, 1940). Where the amount of alcohol taken is not excessive and the task relatively simple, the effects on performance appear to be minimal (Lewis, 1969; Vogel-Spratt, 1967). As the amount of alcohol increases, perceptual and psychomotor performance begins to deteriorate with reaction time and coordination being influenced first (Indeström & Cadenius, 1968). The young are affected more than those who are older (Wilson, Barbariak, & Koss, 1970), and it is clear that chronic alcoholics build up a resistance to performance decrement such that an intake of up to thirty ounces per day has no impact on performance of simple motor tasks (Talland et al., 1965). There is other evidence indicating that alcohol may cause distortion of time estimates (Rutschmann & Rubinstein, 1966), that it may serve to reduce the suppressing effects of punishment on behavior (Vogel-Spratt, 1967), and that it may have a facilitating influence on performance in situations where emotional arousal might otherwise prove disruptive (Greenberg & Carpenter, 1957).

Although early research relating personality and attitude measures to alcoholism was successful in developing procedures that may be used to identify alcoholics both in the employment situation and after hiring, it did not succeed in identifying typical personality patterns either prior to, during, or subsequent to the disorder (Sutherland, Schroeder, & Tordella, 1950; Syme, 1957). More recent research, however, has tended to amplify certain themes that were embedded in some of the earlier studies, with promising results.

A study of a group of employed alcoholics revealed that beneath a "hypernormal" facade were major dependency problems (Hurwitz & Lelos, 1968). Although 30 percent had largely surrendered to their dependency wishes, in the manner of hospitalized alcoholics, the remainder were experiencing intense conflicts on this score, often with hostility a prominent result. A similar stress on the role of dependency conflict emerged from the research of others, such as McCord and McCord (1963) and Bacon, Barry, and Child (1965). In another instance, alcoholics were found to give up very easily in performing mental arithmetic problems under the stress of experimental harassment; they did not care about making a show of competence (Rosenberg, 1969).

An additional promising body of research has been developed by McClelland and his co-workers (McClelland & Winter, 1969). They find that alcoholism is closely associated with strong power motivation, which is frustrated either at work or in other contexts. Although it is too early to say whether this finding is interrelated with that of dependency conflict, it does seem that heavy drinking can be a means of satisfying underlying dependency needs while at the same time experiencing strong fantasies of power. Thus it might be anticipated that drinking would disrupt work performance most when the job frustrates dependency and power needs; that when the power to control others is lacking, the possibility of forcing others to serve one's dependency needs is lacking as well.

Several typologies have been developed to aid in the diagnosis and treatment of alcoholism. Of these, the Jellinek (1960) classification system appears most useful (Block, 1970). The first type demonstrate continued reliance upon the effects of alcohol for relief of physical or emotional pain. They display no loss of self-control and are capable of abstaining, even though their drinking does have a disruptive impact on the family and work performance. There are no withdrawal signs and the disorder need not progress further. The second type are similar to the first except that gastritis, cirrhosis, and other complications associated with excessive alcohol intake are in evidence. The major incentive for drinking is social, but because of the various physical effects the impact on job performance may be sizable.

With the third type there is definite physical dependence on alcohol, accompanied by craving and loss of control, and when drinking ceases, by withdrawal symptoms. Behavioral changes are clearly in evidence. The fourth type are similar except that loss of control is less pronounced. There is a clear inability to abstain, but the individual may not be aware of this fact. Many of these individuals are regular wine drinkers and because wine is widely used in their culture have no thought of not drinking regularly. Yet, job performance does suffer. Finally, there are the periodic alcoholics who drink heavily for a period of time and then either cease because of loss of consciousness or because their drinking is forcibly stopped. Weekend alcoholics who lose part of the work day or all of it on Friday and require Monday to recover are in this category; so, too, are individuals who disappear into an alcoholic society for weeks or even months. Extended periods without heavy drinking do not make these people any less alcoholic.

Drug Addiction

Much of the available research related to drug addiction is of the laboratory variety, dealing with performance effects, although some studies of the impact of long-term use on employment have been made as well. The level of knowledge in this area, however, is currently well below that of alcoholism.

Studies with marijuana indicate that chronic users are influenced less than those who use it rarely. The same amount that will produce considerable impairment in the intellectual and psychomotor performance of those who have had little prior experience with the drug normally has little effect on regular users; there may even be a facilitation effect (Weil, Zinberg, & Nelson, 1969). As the amount of marijuana increases, there is a shift from tranquility, apathy, and mild euphoria to distortions of perceptions, especially regarding time, and finally, with large amounts to disorientation and hallucinations (Leonard, 1969). Although in the extreme states delirium is clearly manifest, identification of the regular marijuana user is often very difficult. On the other hand, the United States has had little experience with long-term use. Studies in other countries indicate that despite differences in cultural backgrounds, the consistent result is the development of lethargy and sloth to the point where job performance is greatly impaired if it is possible to keep a job at all (Asuni, 1964; Benabud, 1957; Sagoe, 1966).

The amphetamines yield much the same symptom picture as marijuana, although in general the changes are less intense (Partridge, 1967). Relatively small amounts have been shown to have no effect on the performance of complex mathematical tasks. However, they do lead to an exaggerated self-appraisal of one's performance and a greater propensity to take risks (Hurst, Weidner, & Radlow, 1967). Neither amphetamines nor barbiturates appear to have much impact on initial learning. Yet recall is affected unless it occurs in the same state as the original learning took place (Bustomane et al., 1968). The consequence for performance would appear to be a strong incentive to continue use on the job once use has been initiated, in order to maintain competence.

In contrast to drugs such as marijuana and the amphetamines, the opiates such as heroin tend to create a physical addiction similar to that alcohol may produce, rather than a purely emotional addiction. Heroin appears to provide the user with relief from frustration, panic, and reactive hostility by creating a temporary feeling of well-being (Torda, 1968). The impact on work and employment is likely to be massive. In a longitudinal study based on a follow-up of penal records of fifty-three heroin addicts by

Defluer, Ball, and Snarr (1969), 43 percent were considered to be following permanent criminal careers selling drugs and stealing; they had little or no legitimate employment as adults. Another 34 percent were following sporadic criminal careers interspersed with short periods of legitimate employment, usually in relatively low level service positions. An additional 6 percent were supported by families. The remaining 17 percent were able to maintain steady employment in adult life. Often the work was of a high status nature and paid reasonably well. Such employment not only provides the money that heroin addiction requires, but also the freedom to adjust one's work and hide the addiction.

Stress, Emotion, and Emotional Disorder

Environmental stress, strong emotions (especially negative ones such as anxiety, depression, and anger), and the presence of emotional disorder are closely associated. The severity of emotional disturbance is directly related to the number of situations that are stressful for an individual, the frequency or duration of exposure to such situations, the intensity of the emotion aroused, and the degree of ego strength available to handle emotion (Miner, 1963, 1966, 1975).

STRESS AND EMOTION. A variety of studies have been conducted dealing with the interacting relationships among stress, negative emotion, and various aspects of performance. A frequent source of difficulty is the manner in which work roles are defined and transmitted. Both role conflict and role ambiguity have been found to have negative consequences (Kahn et al., 1964; Rizzo, House, & Lirtzman, 1970). Impressionistic evidence points to the stress-producing impact of sizable discrepancies between individual capabilities and job demands, and the consequent impact on performance (Jaques, 1966). Further support for this position comes from studies relating role

overload to serum cholesterol levels and to the incidence of coronary disease (Sales, 1969; Sales & House, 1970). It appears that when role overload is present, in that the individual is faced with an obligation to do more than he is able in the time available, the effects upon health can be sizable. Similar negative consequences for health appear to be associated with low levels of job satisfaction.

Studies conducted at the Institute for Social Research of the University of Michigan appear to add to this list of job-related stresses. Because much of the data are correlational, however, the nature of the causal processes cannot be specified with certainty. Low status, management responsibility, technological change, temporal requirements of shift work and threats to self-esteem in appraisal systems have all been found associated with tension, anxiety, or indexes of pathology (Kahn & French, 1962; Zander & Quinn, 1962). On the matter of the introduction of technological change through automation, Mann and Williams (1962) found that anxiety was increased, but other evidence suggests that this reaction is a relatively short-lived function of fear of the unknown (Browne, 1966).

Although research dealing with physical stresses such as noise, loss of sleep, and extreme temperatures has indicated a negative impact on performance with some consistency (Gagné, 1962; McCormick, 1964), some of the most interesting findings relate to the extent to which these effects are moderated by work factors (Wilkinson, 1969). The effects of physical stresses appear to be influenced by a variety of factors such as duration of the work period, familiarity with both the stress and the work, motivational level, the nature of the task, the aspect of performance measured, and the presence of other stresses in the work environment.

Research on relationships between negative emotions, such as anxiety, and performance does not always indicate detrimental effects (Carron & Morford, 1968). However, the characteristic finding is that these emotions *can* yield major decrements in a variety of aspects of performance (Basowitz et al., 1955). Whether they will in fact do so depends on a number of factors including in particular the intensity of the anxiety experienced and the particular nature of the task (Dunn, 1968; Spielberger, 1966).

EMOTIONAL DISORDER, EMPLOYMENT, AND PERFORMANCE. The evidence cited indicates that environmental stresses and negative emotions may influence performance in a variety of ways. The overall tendency is to contribute toward failure, but there are many exceptions. Extrapolating to the more extreme conditions of emotional pathology, one might expect a similar trend—a correlation with ineffective performance which is significant, but far from +1.00. The data appear to support this conclusion, while raising a number of questions regarding relationships between job level and emotional symptoms.

Symptoms of emotional illness are particularly likely to interfere with work when the individual is employed in a higher-level position. Jobs requiring only limited skill are much less vulnerable to emotional disruption. In a series of studies of British factory workers at the unskilled level, the existence of emotional symptoms had no relationship with performance level (Markowe, 1953). Yet within groups of skilled workers ineffective performance was associated with the presence of severe anxiety, depression, feelings of inadequacy, and frequent outbursts of anger and jealousy (Peck & Parsons, 1956). Research conducted among factory supervisors also indicates that the less effective are often emotionally disturbed (Steiner, 1953). Consistent with these findings, experimental research has established that intense emotional arousal has little effect on stereotyped work performance, but a very negative effect when the work becomes less stereotyped and requires considerable thought (Schachter et al., 1961). When the work is automatic and routine, as are most semiskilled jobs, extreme emotional upset has little impact on performance. When the work has a stronger cognitive element, as with higher level positions, the same emotional pattern is disruptive.

One might anticipate that under these circumstances individuals who are emotionally disturbed would be found more frequently in positions at the lower occupational levels, if they are to remain in the labor force at all. Considerable evidence supports this conclusion (Kornhauser, 1965; Miner & Anderson, 1958b). Consistent with this finding, emotional disorder has been found to be related to lower educational attainment and intelligence (Miner & Anderson, 1958a), lower socioeconomic status (Petras & Curtis, 1968; Phillips, 1967), and to problems in occupational adjustment (Bean, Myers, & Pepper, 1964; Bamdas, 1969).

There is controversy, however, as to the cause of the strong association between emotional symptomatology and occupational level. Longitudinal evidence indicates that disproportionate numbers of men who are known to be emotionally disturbed subsequently gravitate to low-skill occupations; either they fail at higher levels and move back or they never achieve a higher level (Miner & Anderson, 1958b). On the other hand, evidence has been presented to support the view that routine, boring work itself may operate as a *cause* of emotional disturbance (Argyris, 1964; Kornhauser, 1965; Lambruschini, 1967). There seems little doubt from the findings noted in connection with the preceding discussion of stress and emotion, and from other data on the precipitating causes of breakdown that certain stresses in the occupational sphere can be a source of emotional disorder (Beisser & Glasser, 1968; Klumbies, 1967).

However, there is serious doubt whether routine, highly specialized work based on considerable division of labor is the major determinant of the high frequency of emotional disturbance in low level jobs. On the one hand, there is the finding that those who are already disturbed tend to gravitate to such positions. On the other hand, there is considerable evidence that in the urban context (where the research suggesting a negative *causal* effect of routine work has been done) the elimination of routine can be expected to have few positive consequences (Blood & Hulin, 1967; Hulin & Blood, 1968). This evidence indicates that urban blue collar workers are primarily alienated from middle-class, work-related values and norms and that accordingly considerations related to routine work and job enlargement have little meaning for them one way or the other.

Physical Handicaps and Deficiencies

The available research consistently indicates that those physically handicapped people who are able to maintain regular employment and who are placed in the right type of job typically perform in an entirely satisfactory manner (Barker, 1953; Ehrle, 1961). In fact there is evidence that absenteeism (Feldman, 1953) and accident rates for certain handicapped groups (Block & Campbell, 1963) may well be less than among the physically normal.

Many handicapped people develop competencies which allow them to compensate for their impairments. Thus, blind people often develop more accurate hearing and neuromuscular activity than those with normal sight (Angel, 1969). Compensating capabilities of this kind can be a major source of performance effectiveness, if the individual is placed in a position where they are relevant to the task. Thus, job placement becomes a crucial factor determining the level of performance of handicapped people.

There are also some clear variations in relation to employment among different types of handicaps. Orthopedic disabilities tend to be less disruptive of performance than other types of disabilities, with the result that a greater proportion of this particular group is able to maintain employment (Anglin, 1963). Employment rates among epileptics are considerably lower, partly because of seizures, but also because of the high frequency of personality problems in this group (Wright & Trotter, 1968). On the other hand, among epileptics whose seizures are medically controlled and who do maintain employment, job performance levels are in no way depressed.

A study comparing individuals suffering from cardiovascular disorders or diabetes with matched controls indicated that the handicapped group did have a higher absenteeism rate (Wyshak, Snegireff, & Law, 1961). However, this was largely due to differences among those employed in production jobs. Outside of production, the absenteeism rates for the handicapped and control groups were much the same. Consistent with this result, it has been found that among cardiovascular patients who are subsequently reemployed, the duration of employment is considerably longer for those who are in managerial and professional positions than for those reemployed at lower levels (Sigler, 1967). It appears, however, that of all cardiovascular patients who are reemployable, 25 to 40 percent do not return to regular work (Wright & Trotter, 1968). They tend to react to the disorder with passivity and considerable anxiety.

Among the deaf who are employed, there is no evidence of deficiencies in any aspect of performance (Wright & Trotter, 1968). Those in management tend to rate their work high and they exhibit greater employment stability than those who are not handicapped. Yet there is a disproportionate concentration of the deaf in manual occupations, with very few in professional, technical, clerical, sales, or service positions. Generally, these employees are viewed by their superiors as having little chance for advancement in spite of their satisfactory work.

Taken as a whole the research evidence on the physically handicapped seems to indicate that performance failure is somewhat less likely in this group than among the emotionally disturbed and mentally retarded (Wright & Trotter, 1968). However, this situation results in large part from the fact that many of the more severely handicapped do not enter the labor force. In addition, companies and welfare agencies alike have given much attention to appropriate job placements for the handicapped, with apparently favorable results.

Consequences of aging. The early research in gerontology dealing with sensory and motor abilities consistently indicated that a decline does occur with age (Birren, 1959; Pressey & Kuhlen, 1957; Welford, 1958, 1959). This was found to be true of speed of movement, dexterity and coordination, physical strength, visual and auditory sensitivity, and perceptual speed. More recent research has generally substantiated the early conclusions, while adding certain qualifications. For instance, it now appears that continued practice, of the kind that might occur in an occupation or through athletic participation, can moderate the decline in speed of movement to a substantial degree (Pacaud, 1963). Furthermore, it has been shown that differences between young and older workers in speed of response are related more to differences in the cognitive associative aspects of the task than to the motor aspects (Birren, Riegel, & Morrison, 1963).

For most sensory and motor abilities the decline starts in the late twenties and is gradual in nature. There are major differences among individuals, however. As a result the variation in any given ability within a group of men in their sixties will be much greater than within a group of twenty-year-olds. Thus, although deficiencies of this kind are increasingly likely to cause performance failure as life progresses, there is no reason to assume that physical deficiencies will necessarily contribute to ineffectiveness in an older employee.

In fact, there are studies which suggest the impact of this decline on actual job performance may be minimal in many instances. An analysis of production records for 6,000 clerical workers in five government agencies and twenty-one different companies indicated that there were essentially no differences associated with age (United States Department of Labor, 1960). The occupations were primarily of a routine nature—typists, keypunch operators, and various clerks engaged in filing, posting, and sorting activities. In contrast, studies carried out among factory workers in the men's footwear, men's clothing, and household furniture industries did indicate a decline in the performance of the older workers, with the number of ineffectives increasing steadily above the age of forty-five.

Whether or not older workers are prone to become ineffective appears to depend upon the extent to which a reduction in physical capacities makes a difference in the particular type of work and upon the extent to which it is possible to compensate for the physical changes. Performance in many occupations, including those of a clerical nature, is dependent more on intellectual than physical abilities. Certain intellectual components, such as general knowledge and verbal ability, tend to show a rise with age (Birren, Riegel, & Morrison, 1963). Others, such as memory, learning, and arithmetic skills, generally show a decline, but this effect is modified both by initial level and continued practice. People who are initially above average in these abilities and who use them frequently in their work show little if any decline (Craik, 1965; Inglis, Sykes, & Unkus, 1968). In an overall sense, then, the intellectual sphere is less affected by age and consequently people in primarily intellectual jobs are less likely to become ineffective as they grow older.

On the other hand, those in manual jobs, such as factory workers, are vulnerable to the effects of aging. Although they typically can perform various job duties as well as those who are much younger, they cannot repeat the operations over and over again at the same rate (Welford, 1958). Even the strength which is required in connection with most unskilled positions is entirely within the capabilities of most employees of more advanced age; but many cannot maintain the pace. If they are pressed to increase their output, quality will fall off badly. When left to their own devices, most older workers who have experienced some decline in a job-related ability will concentrate on accuracy, since an almost complete elimination of errors is the only way they can approach an adequate overall performance level. Where this type of compensatory effort is not possible, as in jobs where there is machine pacing, ineffective performance is likely to be a concomitant of advancing age.

The Culturally Handicapped

Society has only recently become concerned about the culturally handicapped or disadvantaged. The result of this concern has been a sizable increase in programs designed to provide regular employment to this group (Doeringer, 1969). Although definitions of the culturally handicapped differ considerably, they range upward from that of the hard core unemployed. A profile of this latter group includes the following (Adelberg, 1969):

1. Unemployed and has been for eighteen months.
2. Never received any skill training.
3. Parents were unskilled.
4. Lives with one-and-one-half families.
5. Needs eyeglasses and dental work.
6. Has seen a doctor only once in his life.
7. Has no transportation.
8. Has a sixth grade education and only a fourth grade mathematics background.
9. Is usually a minority group member.

Whatever the definition of the culturally handicapped, they are certainly people who have had difficulty in obtaining jobs that are stable, pay good wages, and provide pleasant working conditions. They are ac-

customed to low wages, dead-end employment, undesirable working conditions, and what they view as inequitable supervision. They have work habits and expectations about jobs that are incompatible with the performance norms of higher wage enterprises (Doeringer, 1969). It is in this sense, as well as in terms of education and skill training, that they are culturally disadvantaged.

Performance of the culturally handicapped. A number of companies have reported on their experiences in hiring groups of culturally handicapped workers who, under normal circumstances, would not have been able to join their work forces. The National Industrial Conference Board (Janger & Schaeffer, 1970) has collected information from several of these companies with programs for the disadvantaged. The results are surprisingly consistent. The Equitable Life Insurance Company program had a turnover rate of 45 percent for the first six months of employment and 67 percent for the first year, which was three times the normal rate. The major problems were lateness and absenteeism. General Motors reported a turnover rate of 47 percent for the first six months, with unsatisfactory work and excessive absenteeism the primary difficulties. At International Harvester 80 percent were gone within two months. The conclusion drawn from the Conference Board studies is that the problems are related to, or stem from, a lack of basic education or skills training, inability to manage one's personal affairs, a lack of knowledge of the general and specific requirements of the work situation, inability to defer satisfactions, suppressed hostility toward whites on the part of minority group members, and low motivation.

Employer complaints about the culturally handicapped often center around behavioral considerations—lateness, absenteeism, voluntary turnover, theft, and insubordination (Piore, 1969). There is reason to believe that the most reliable workers, in terms of lateness and absenteeism, remain employed for the shortest periods of time (Friedlander & Greenberg, 1969). Thus, there is a reciprocal relationship between turnover and effectiveness. Furthermore, workers who have previously held jobs which paid a high rate and who were born in the urban north tend to leave quickly (Purcell & Cavanagh, 1970). It appears that those culturally handicapped individuals who do remain in their jobs tend to come from the rural south and have a history of very low wages whenever they have been employed. Their performance, especially in terms of behavioral considerations, is usually poor. Without special consideration and the utilization of corrective procedures aimed at producing adaptation to the cultural norms associated with steady employment, these people are very likely to appear in lists of ineffective performers. Many will leave without giving any notice at all.

SPECIFIC CORRECTIVE PROCEDURES

A great variety of corrective procedures may be used in an attempt to move performance to an effective level. Among these are job redesign, promotion, transfer, demotion, management development, training, changes in supervision, changes in compensation, personnel policy modification, threats, disciplinary actions, counseling, medical treatment, and psychotherapy. The nature of the corrective procedure that will prove effective depends on the strategic factors causing performance failure. In addition, the success of a corrective effort depends on the extent to which it is possible to bring the procedure chosen fully and completely to bear on the problem. There are considerations, such as the availability of resources and the degree to which treatment approaches have been perfected, which operate as constraints both within an employing organization and outside it.

The discussion which follows does not attempt to consider all possible corrective procedures in detail. Many of these are treated in other chapters of this volume as they apply to the whole range of human performance, not just the ineffective. This chapter is concerned primarily with changed role prescriptions, threat and discipline, counseling and related approaches, and training. These are the areas in which a literature has developed focused specifically on problems of ineffective performance.

Changed Role Prescriptions

The requirements of a man's work may be changed either by shifting him to another position or by redesigning his current job. The objective in either case is to get the individual into a job which he can perform effectively. In larger companies with widely varied types of work, transfer may provide a meaningful solution; in smaller companies of a specialized nature it is less likely to do so, and some kind of reassignment of tasks to create a job that can be performed effectively becomes the preferred alternative. In the same way firms with a very flat managerial hierarchy may offer little opportunity to use promotion as a solution; but vertical job enlargement may provide an alternative. It may not be possible to demote people who are already in low level positions, but job simplification can achieve a similar result.

A NEW JOB. Moving an individual into a new position may be an appropriate response to a variety of sources of difficulty. In the intellectual area either demotion or transfer may be required, depending on the nature of the abilities that are lacking. Jobs with emotional, motivational, and physical requirements that are more appropriate may be located. Problems related to the family are often solved by changing the location of work or the amount of travel. A more suitable work group or style of supervision can be achieved through reassignment. So, too, can a value climate better fitted to the individual, or a more appropriate physical working situation.

In general, transfer is most easily accomplished and appears to work best in a remedial sense when the person is in an entry-level, early career position, and when there is a clear alternative in which his capabilities can be used (Weatherbee, 1969). Although from an organizational maintenance viewpoint promotion of an ineffective employee may create many difficulties, it can be a valuable corrective procedure especially in clear-cut cases of underplacement, where an employee is strongly motivated to do the things a higher position requires and perhaps to achieve the status that goes with such a job. Demotion, on the other hand, is most appropriate when, because of manpower shortages or for other reasons, an individual has been moved to too high a level. Usually such overplacement has its origins in relative intellectual deficiency or in emotional problems.

A CHANGED JOB. Changes in assigned tasks or in the physical work context are particularly appropriate for the physically handicapped, for older workers, and for those with high accident rates. A great deal of attention has been given to specific modifications that may be made in various jobs so that people with particular handicaps may perform effectively in them (International Labor Office, 1969). Similarly, much has been done in the field of safety engineering to change jobs to eliminate hazards, so that the possibility of injury, irrespective of the personality dynamics of the individual, is reduced (Heinrich, 1959).

Much the same kind of job redesign to fit specific needs of individuals has been recommended in cases of emotional disorder (McMurry, 1959). The research of Kornhauser (1965) and others suggests that job enlargement with the elimination of routine and specialization may have a positive impact in this regard. However, the subsequent analysis by Hulin and Blood (1968) seems to indicate that substantial effects from job enlargement can be expected only among white collar workers and among

blue collar workers outside the large cities. In addition, there would seem to be a real risk in some cases that enlarging a job either vertically or horizontally may only serve to eliminate the employment haven that makes it possible for an emotionally disturbed person to function at all.

There appears to be considerable research evidence indicating that job enlargement can have a positive impact on motivation under certain circumstances, and thus contribute to improved performance. There is reason to believe this approach will be more effective where the quality of work is low than where quantity is the problem (Lawler, 1969). Job enlargement may also prove useful where insufficient time on the job is a matter of concern, either in the form of excessive absenteeism (Dekar, 1969) or rapid turnover (Ford, 1969). Results with blue collar workers suggest that this group is less responsive to extending the scope of the job either vertically or horizontally (Ford, 1969; Sexton, 1967) than others, and that accordingly job enlargement should be applied as a corrective procedure at the lower levels in manufacturing plants only where there is very good reason to anticipate success. On the other hand, more consistently positive results can be anticipated at the foreman level (Davis, 1966).

PERSONNEL POLICY MODIFICATION. A final corrective procedure which yields changed role prescriptions is personnel policy modification, either in the sense of actually altering existing policies (or introducing new ones) or in the sense of permitting exceptions. Policies can operate to produce widespread alienation in a work force with a resulting increase in cases involving insufficient time on the job (Brown, 1970). Although little attention has been given in the literature to the modification of policies and little research has been conducted in the area of policy planning generally, practical experience clearly indicates that this is an area of considerable significance for the handling of performance failure. In a number of respects, it overlaps with the discussion of threat and discipline which follows.

Threat and Discipline

A type of corrective action that may be applied in instances where motivational factors are strategic is the use of managerial power to either threaten or actually invoke negative sanctions. This approach appears particularly useful when the standards of conduct or productivity held by the individual are low. Unfortunately, however, threat and discipline are often applied in cases where the failure is attributable to intellectual or physical factors, or to emotional problems. In such instances, where motivation is not a major factor, punishment can do more harm than good.

The typical approach is for a superior to demand improved performance and couple this demand with a threat that negative sanctions will be invoked if change does not occur. The alternative to this, and often the end result of the former approach as well, is a formal disciplinary action carried out in the manner specified by organizational rules or the union contract. The usual sequence of formal actions is warning, suspension without pay, and discharge, depending on the number of violations in a given time period (Stessin, 1960; Wollenberger, 1963). In actual practice, however, supervisors do not resort to formal disciplinary actions nearly as often as they could in terms of the infractions that occur (Maier & Danielson, 1956). In general, it appears that more positive results are obtained if the formal, judicial approach can be avoided. Discipline clearly has very limited reform possibilities, but it does serve to point up the existence of a problem in performance, which may then be solved in other ways, and it does have a corrective effect with some people (Booker, 1969).

One of the areas in which threat has been used with positive results is in the control of excessive absenteeism. Spot checks at home by visiting nurses and other members of an organization's health unit often uncover sick leave abuses and help to reduce them (Johnson, 1969; McFarland, 1952). Some firms have introduced point systems whereby different types of absences warrant charging different amounts of points against the individual with discharge the ultimate consequence, if the point total reaches a specified level in a given time period (Kearns, 1970). On the other hand, some companies have introduced positive sanctions such as providing rewards for unused sick leave in the form of extra compensation, credit toward retirement, and the like (Campbell, 1970; Korner, 1967). These "buyback" procedures can yield positive results in reducing absenteeism, but such a policy can prove costly and have a negative impact on employee health.

There is also information bearing on the use of threat and discipline with other types of problems. Accident repetition and compliance with safety rules are best considered in terms of their motivational bases (Magee, 1967). Negative attitudes toward authority among the accident prone may be circumvented by having safety rules developed on a participative basis. Enforcement of these rules and disciplinary procedures then become matters related to compliance with group norms, rather than of authoritarian repression, which only stimulates rebellion and a flouting of regulations. It seems clear in terms of the personality dynamics involved that threat and discipline administered from above are unlikely to yield positive results in cases of accident repetition; if the authority factor can be removed, there is a better chance.

Experience with threat and discipline in the handling of addictions is extensive, especially in the case of alcoholics. The evidence is clear in indicating that punitive procedures based on a moralistic conception of the problem are not very effective (Siegler & Osmond, 1968). On the other hand, threat and discipline, including the prospect of loss of employment, appear to be by far the most effective means of motivating alcoholics, and probably drug addicts as well, to seek assistance and treatment (Presnall, 1966, 1967). Thus it appears that an approach which emphasizes discipline in relation to performance deficiencies, coupled with appropriate treatment programs aimed at correcting the disorder and restoring effective performance, provides the best solution.

In one study of 102 cases of discharged employees—thirteen emotionally disturbed and eighty-nine alcoholics—that went to arbitration, 55 percent of the cases were reversed by the arbitrator, with the result that employment was restored (Trice & Belasco, 1966). Follow-up of these cases indicates that for three-quarters of the employees, the experience of discharge and subsequent reinstatement did not result in correction of the ineffective performance. Many were fired again or left voluntarily, or if working at the time of follow-up were considered unsatisfactory. The evidence from this study indicates rather clearly that corrective discipline alone is relatively futile.

Counseling and Related Approaches

The history of counseling in industry began with a department established in the Ford Motor Company in 1914. The Ford program was not focused on ineffective performance, but rather served to advise employees generally on personal affairs and to assist them with health, legal, and family problems. Highly paternalistic in nature, it met considerable employee resistance and eventual abandonment (Bellows, 1961). Almost all such general programs since have failed to survive over an extended period. The much discussed Western Electric program, which was originally established to achieve a widespread "Hawthorne effect," lasted for twenty years, but was discontinued in 1956 (Dickson & Roethlisberger, 1966).

In recent years, industrial counseling has tended to focus more on specific types of employee problems, has involved the industrial clinical psychologist to a much greater extent, and has been more widely viewed as a corrective procedure for ineffective performance. Limited-goal programs of this kind have been successful. At the higher executive levels, they are frequently staffed with outside psychological consultants (Flory, 1965), while at lower levels, the more typical approach is to employ a staff clinical psychologist. The emphasis is on working out relatively mild adjustment problems that may be hampering performance effectiveness. More severe emotional disorders are normally referred for outside treatment. If the problem appears to require more than perhaps ten or fifteen one-hour sessions, the employee is invariably advised to seek help on a private basis. Some firms, in fact, reject all internal adjustment counseling of this type on the grounds that such matters are the sole responsibility of the individual (Dunnette & Kirchner, 1965).

In contrast to counseling by specialists with considerable psychological training, a number of companies have attempted to foster increased participation by immediate superiors in a counseling role. Here counseling merges into coaching. Many management development programs have been directed toward explicating this role. However, much of what is done in the name of superior-subordinate counseling actually has very little to do with the correction of ineffective performance.

Counseling by those without extensive psychological training can win acceptance from employees and can contribute to the handling of ineffective performance (Berg, 1970; Hunt & Lichtman, 1969). On the other hand, there are clearly many cases where a superior cannot deal with the problem and does best to refer the individual to an appropriate source equipped to do so. In such instances, it is usually considered advisable for a manager to restrict his own comments to matters closely related to the individual's job performance (Committee on

Occupational Psychiatry, 1965). The same holds true when an emotionally disturbed person returns to work after treatment. A superior contributes most to restoring effectiveness when he stresses the worker role and performance rather than the patient role and illness (Simmons, 1965).

A particularly difficult problem in counseling arises in connection with the culturally handicapped. In order to obtain meaningful results with this group, it appears necessary to achieve some degree of empathy in the relationship. Counseling works best when both participants are on or near the same level of functioning (Carkhuff, 1969). Yet, by definition the supervisors and counselors who deal with the culturally disadvantaged in the employment context typically have a very different relationship to the culture. At the very least there are major socioeconomic and class differences which drastically impede communication and acceptance (Vontress, 1970). As a consequence, counseling with the culturally handicapped to improve performance effectiveness, although potentially very rewarding, has not consistently produced a large proportion of successes (Janger & Shaeffer, 1970).

ALCOHOLISM CONTROL PROGRAMS. A sizable number of companies have established formalized alcoholism control programs. Almost without exception these programs involve some relationship with Alcoholics Anonymous, which is generally considered to be the most valuable single resource available to a company for help with drinking problems, although a variety of other referral sources are used as well (Habbe, 1969).

The early programs placed considerable stress on educating supervisors regarding such things as the disease progression, symptoms, counseling, and treatment sources (Presnall, 1966). More recently, programs have shifted away from this emphasis on making the supervisor a diagnostician and

counselor to a concern with getting the alcoholic to a treatment source, such as Alcoholics Anonymous, as quickly as possible. Under this approach supervisors are informed of company policies and procedures for referral, trained to observe work behavior that indicates performance problems, instructed regarding the use of discipline to motivate seeking help, and advised to avoid discussing drinking with the employee except to indicate that the company handles problems in this area like any other health problem. The emphasis is consistently upon keeping the supervisor's role focused on work performance.

A number of factors are frequently noted as necessary to a successful alcoholism control program (Presnall, 1967; Trice, 1968). Among these are a policy emphasis on drinking as a health problem, early identification through impaired performance, union participation, consistent efforts to ensure that supervisors take action when performance declines, use of company records such as those for absenteeism to aid identification, and the effective use of discipline.

Programs that have followed these lines have had surprisingly high levels of success. One source reports company programs achieving recovery rates in the range of 50 to 70 percent of all cases (Presnall, 1967); another reports a range of 65 to 85 percent for industrial programs, as contrasted with 30 percent for the general public (Cohen, 1969). These figures may be somewhat inflated due to the selection of cases (the most easily treated being the most easily identified) and short follow-up periods. Yet the Consolidated Edison Company program, which appears to have had considerable success in identifying employed alcoholics and which has used a five-year follow-up period to establish recovery, reports a 55 percent rate (Franco, 1968). When contrasted with the findings from treatment evaluation studies conducted among such groups as hospitalized alcoholics (Belasco & Trice, 1969), these results are very impressive.

Training and Development

Much of what is done in using training and development procedures for purposes of correcting performance failure differs little from the use of these procedures as input-improving mediators (Miner, 1969). Typically, where some type of training is viewed as the appropriate solution to an instance of ineffective performance, instruction is given on the job, or the individual is included in a group development effort along with others who might benefit from the training, but who are not considered ineffective. It is rare to find a company training or management development program constructed specifically for the purpose of correcting major performance deficiencies and applied only to individuals deemed to be failing. In large part this is the case because ineffective performance comes in many individual varieties, and it is thus unlikely that a company will be faced with a number of ineffective employees who, at approximately the same point in time, give evidence of having similar problems and need the same type of training to correct them.

The major exceptions occur where a company has deliberately hired a number of individuals with similar potentialities for failure, as a result of community pressure. These people might be physically handicapped in some way or they may have been hospitalized previously for emotional disorders. Recently, however, the major pressure has been in the area of the culturally disadvantaged. Here training has been widely applied to cope with the performance deficiencies of groups of individuals who have been hired in response to pressures both from the community and from the value and normative systems of executives themselves.

The content of the more successful among these training programs for the culturally handicapped has been surprisingly similar (Adelberg, 1969; Doeringer, 1969; Janger & Schaeffer, 1970). Four aspects appear frequently.

1. Basic education and skills training.

2. Counseling and supportive services, including help in managing personal affairs.

3. Pre-assignment training in work orientation and specific job requirements.

4. On the job training.

Which among these requires the greatest emphasis depends on the specific composition of the group. Topics such as money management, health, where to find help, career development, arithmetic, remedial reading, dress, manners, grammar, spelling, and composition may not need much attention, but experience suggests that even among those who have been to high school they are often important (Stoessel, 1970).

A number of problems that may undermine the effectiveness of training programs for the culturally disadvantaged have been noted by Gray and Borecki (1970). Among the most important of these are the following: Trainees have often been found to want to personalize their learning experiences to a point where there is a breakdown in teaching effectiveness. Instructors, being from a considerably different background, have a tendency to permit the trainees to use their disadvantaged background as a crutch. Not infrequently details are sacrificed in order to get the larger picture across. When trainees cannot see the relevance of what they are asked to learn for the expected job and when rewards for undergoing training are small, learning suffers. Abstract principles are meaningless unless illustrated repeatedly with practical examples.

Difficulties have frequently arisen because training programs were not supported by higher level management and because they produced double standards for performance in the same work setting (Janger & Shaeffer, 1970). The culturally handicapped may be permitted to continue employment without discipline in spite of absenteeism rates and other performance features which are not handled with the same degree of permissiveness in the regular work force. The result can be considerable resentment. Supervisors often need training in dealing with this type of problem (Margulies, 1970). Sensitivity training for regular members of the organization has been considered as one solution (Sullivan, 1970). Clearly, the success of training for the culturally handicapped is not merely a function of interactions between trainees, instructors, and/or supervisors (Goodman, 1969). Aspects of the organizational environment may prove crucial; so, too, may the actions of the government agency involved, if there is governmental sponsorship. The potential for interpersonal conflict surrounding these programs seems to be very high indeed. This apparently is one reason why insufficient time on the job has often continued to be a major problem. Yet it remains true that on the job training has proved a much more successful method of aiding the culturally handicapped than other, institutional approaches (Levitan & Mangum, 1969).

COMPANY EXPERIENCE AND PRACTICE

Further insight into some of the problems and approaches considered in this chapter may be obtained from the results of a survey conducted late in 1970.[2] Data were obtained from 100 companies located

[2] The survey was conducted jointly by the American Society for Personnel Administration and The Bureau of National Affairs, Inc. The results presented here are based on an analysis of the questionnaire data made by the authors. The assistance of John V. Schappi, Associate Editor of The Bureau of National Affairs, Inc., and Mary Green Miner, Director of BNA Surveys, in making this information available to us is greatly appreciated.

throughout the United States. The companies varied considerably in size. Although some large corporations were included, approximately half had less than 1,000 employees. The industry composition of the sample was diverse. The respondents listed themselves as managers of personnel, industrial relations and/or employee relations in seventy-six cases, with six more indicating that they were vice presidents without specifying the functional area; in all probability they had personnel and industrial relations under their jurisdiction. Other titles mentioned with some frequency were employment manager, manager of administrative or management services, medical director, nurse, and manager of wage and salary administration. The survey questions focused on alcoholism, drug addiction, and emotional illness.

Tables 2 and 3 provide evidence on the prevalence of these problems. The extent to which these figures are based on actual company statistics presumably varies considerably from company to company. A rather large number of respondents did not provide estimates for one or more employee groups. Several firms did not have any production employees at all. The data indicate that alcoholism is most prevalent among production employees. Other statistically significant differences are the low use of marijuana among managers and the higher incidence of hard drug addiction among production workers. The estimates for emotional illness do not differ significantly across employee groups. If anything, the absolute values

TABLE 2
MEAN ESTIMATED PERCENTAGES OF VARIOUS EMPLOYEE GROUPS WITH LISTED PROBLEMS

	Office		Production		Management	
	N	X̄	N	X̄	N	X̄
Alcoholism	56	1.9	54	3.2	57	1.9
Marijuana use	45	.7	41	1.2	47	.1
Hard drug addiction	43	.1	36	.4	46	.1
Emotional illness						
requiring treatment	55	1.4	49	1.4	55	1.3
Totals		4.1		6.2		3.4

TABLE 3
ESTIMATED PREVALENCE OF PROBLEMS COMPARED
WITH TWO YEARS PREVIOUSLY (N = 100)

Problem	Lower	Same	Higher	Not Indicated
Alcoholism	4	56	11	29
Drug use	1	29	26	44
Emotional illness	1	47	17	35

given in Table 2 would appear to be on the conservative side, presumably as a result of undetected cases. Estimates based on studies within companies having highly effective case identification procedures, for instance, place the overall alcoholism figure for employees in business, industry, and civilian government at 5.3 percent (National Council on Alcoholism, 1968).

From Table 3 it appears that all three types of problems are increasing, although it may be that the data reflect only differential sensitivity to these problems among the respondents. However, drug use is viewed as increasing more rapidly than either alcoholism or emotional illness, a finding which is consistent with the facts on drug use nationally. There is also a statistically significant difference in the "Not Indicated" column between alcoholism and drug use. Apparently the respondents feel more confident that they know what is happening in the alcoholism area than with drugs.

Observation and reports by superiors are noted most frequently as the methods used to detect problems, as compared with such procedures as checks of absenteeism records, annual physical examinations, home visits by a nurse or supervisor, tests of urine for drugs, checks of the frequency and nature of requests for medical and counseling assistance, and checks of arrest records. Table 4 provides data on the use of various techniques to aid supervisors in detecting problems and also in dealing with them. Policy statements, supervisory training, and lists of outside referral sources are used significantly more often for alcoholism. Consultation with the company physician is used *less* often for drug cases. The "None indicated" frequencies indicate clearly that companies tend to do a good deal to help supervisors insofar as alcoholism is a problem among subordinates, while providing assistance in the area of emotional illness somewhat less often, but that they are much less likely to do anything with regard to drug problems. Once again the data suggest that companies know what is happening and are coping much more effectively in the alcoholism area than is the case with the relatively new problem of drugs.

TABLE 4
TECHNIQUES USED TO AID SUPERVISORS IN DEALING
WITH EMPLOYEES HAVING PROBLEMS (N = 100)

Techniques	Alcoholism	Problem Drug Use	Emotional Illness
Policy statement or written suggestions	20	8	5
Supervisory training meetings	25	8	13
Consultation with company physician	46	27	41
Consultation with staff psychologist	13	7	12
List of outside referral sources	27	11	18
None indicated	30	60	44

TABLE 5
TECHNIQUES USED IN DEALING WITH EMPLOYEES HAVING PROBLEMS (N = 100)

Problem	Discipline Short of Discharge	Discharge	In-house Counseling	Referral to Outside Agency	None Indicated
Alcoholism	46	28	69	65	5
Use of marijuana	14	25	19	17	55
Use of hard drugs	9	33	16	17	49
Serious emotional illness	10	3	41	73	18

Table 5 indicates the extent to which discipline, counseling, and outside referrals are used. Discipline short of discharge is used significantly more often with alcoholics, presumably in large part to motivate treatment since the in-house counseling and referral to outside agency frequencies are also high in this group. Discharge is rarely applied in the case of serious emotional illness, but is reported with about equal frequency for alcoholism and drug use. Internal counseling is used by relatively few companies for drug users, more frequently for emotional illness, and very often for alcoholism. Outside referral is also rare in drug cases. In fact, about half of the companies did not indicate any of these techniques being applied with drug cases. To some extent this is a reflection of the low drug use frequencies noted in Table 2, especially among firms with no production employees; but it is apparent that companies do not know quite what to do in this area.

Further data on the techniques noted in Table 5 are given in Tables 6 through 9. On an overall basis, among employees with the types of problems considered in the survey, it appears that although the threat of discipline is extensively used, there is a wide divergence of opinion on its effectiveness as a corrective procedure (see Table 6). Among the sources of counseling noted in Table 7, the personnel department is noted most frequently, the immediate supervisor and staff medical personnel are indicated as intermediate, and a staff psychologist is least frequently used. Most of the firms do use some

TABLE 6
USE OF THREAT OF DISCIPLINE TO ENCOURAGE EMPLOYEES HAVING PROBLEMS TO SEEK TREATMENT (N = 100)

	Frequency
Threat of discipline used and considered effective	44
Threat of discipline used but not noted as effective	39
Threat of discipline not used	14
No indication	3

kind of counseling for one or more types of problems.

Table 8 provides information on specific outside resources utilized and in particular on those resources with which liaison has been established. A comparison of Tables 5 and 8 suggests that in the case of emotional illness at least, outside referral may well occur without any regular liaison having been established. Outside psychiatrists, outside psychologists, and hospitals and clinics are used significantly less often for drug addiction than for alcoholism or emotional illness. Alcoholics Anonymous is noted much more frequently for alcoholism, but

TABLE 7
EXTENT TO WHICH COUNSELING IS OFFERED TO EMPLOYEES HAVING PROBLEMS (N = 100)

Source of Counseling	Frequency
Immediate supervisor	31
Personnel department	66
Staff medical personnel	41
Staff psychologist	10
No counseling offered	14

TABLE 8
EXTENT TO WHICH LIAISON HAS BEEN ESTABLISHED WITH OUTSIDE RESOURCE FACILITIES FOR HELP IN DEALING WITH INDICATED PROBLEMS (N = 100)

	Alcoholism	Drug Addiction	Emotional Illness
Outside psychiatrists	27	8	38
Outside psychologists	18	7	21
Hospitals and/or clinics	43	13	37
Alcoholics Anonymous	48	4	5
Clergy	23	9	14
Police	10	13	2
Local committees and agencies	7	6	2
No indication of liaison with outside resource facilities	35	72	50

some companies apparently use it for other problems as well. Alcoholics are referred to the clergy by significantly more companies than are drug addicts, and the police are noted infrequently as a source of help with emotional illness. The previous pattern where little information is provided on drug cases, somewhat more on emotional illness, and considerably more on alcoholism is again in evidence.

A question dealing with the effectiveness of these outside resources yielded the results given in Table 9. There is a clear dichotomy, with hospitals and clinics, Alcoholics Anonymous, and outside psychiatrists noted more frequently than outside psychologists, the police, local committees and agencies, and the clergy. These results are, of course, not independent of the frequency of use.

TABLE 9
EXTENT TO WHICH OUTSIDE RESOURCES ARE NOTED AS MOST EFFECTIVE (N = 100)

	Frequency
Outside psychiatrists	14
Outside psychologists	4
Hospitals and/or clinics	20
Alcoholics Anonymous	19
Clergy	0
Police	1
Local committees and agencies	1

Although not in the same sense an outside resource, data obtained on union cooperation are also interesting. Of the sample firms thirty-seven did not have unions. Among those that did, the majority, thirty-nine, had sought union cooperation in dealing with employees having problems; twenty-four had not. When cooperation had been sought, it was reported to be helpful by thirty-two of the thirty-nine firms. It is not known why certain firms did not seek union cooperation, but no doubt in some cases there was little reason to anticipate that it would be helpful. Nevertheless, the overall trend of the data are such as to suggest that this is an area in which union-management cooperation can be obtained, with mutual advantage to all concerned.

A final section of the questionnaire dealt with such personnel matters as leave policies and medical insurance coverage. As indicated in Table 10 the data on leave policies tend to be similar for alcoholism and emotional illness, but deviate considerably in the case of drug addiction. There are no significant differences between the former two. The drug addicts are lower than the other two on regular paid sick leave only and higher on immediate termination without leave. They are lower than the alcoholics on regular paid sick leave followed by unpaid leave and higher than the alcoholics in the "No indication" category. Clearly, if a company has any leave policy related to drug addiction, it tends to be a stiffer one than with the other problems studied. This same pattern is present in the medical insurance coverage data of Table 11. Drug addicts are

TABLE 10
LEAVE POLICIES APPLIED TO EMPLOYEES NEEDING TIME OFF
FOR RECOVERY OR REHABILITATION (N = 100)

Leave policy	Alcoholism	Problem Drug Addiction	Emotional Illness
Regular paid sick leave only	31	18	41
Unpaid leave only	21	16	17
Regular paid sick leave followed by unpaid leave	24	12	20
No leave; termination only	7	22	0
No indication	17	32	22

significantly less likely to be covered. It also appears that the respondents are less certain as to whether they are covered or not. Emotional illness is more frequently covered than alcoholism.

TABLE 11
EXTENT TO WHICH MEDICAL INSURANCE
COVERS ANY PART OF THE COST
OF TREATMENT (N = 100)

Problem	Coverage Yes	No	No Indication
Alcoholism	69	21	10
Drug addiction	52	29	19
Emotional illness	83	11	6

CONCLUSION

In reviewing the literature related to the management of ineffective performance, one cannot help but be struck by the fact that so little of the research and so few of the concepts derive from the nuclear field of industrial clinical psychology. The citations which follow are from a great variety of fields, each of which overlaps with the subject matter of this chapter to some small degree. Included are industrial relations, personnel management, psychiatry, vocational guidance, clinical psychology, industrial psychology, management, human engineering, sociology, public health, pharmacology, social psychology, personality theory, organization theory, occupational rehabilitation, experimental psychology, medicine and labor economics, as well as a number of more specific areas which have become a focus for sizable research efforts such as the study of alcoholism and geriatrics. In fact, at the present time it appears that industrial clinical psychology is more appropriately described as an area of practice and in terms of certain focal problems than as a coordinated field of study or discipline.

The great need for research which deals directly with the key variables of the control model such as performance criteria and standards, strategic factors, and corrective procedures, and with the relationships among them is probably the most striking conclusion that emerges from this chapter. We know a great deal about certain specific problem areas and a few corrective procedures; other problem areas and most corrective procedures have been studied very little. But the greatest gap in our knowledge is at the core of the management of ineffective performance. How does the control model function to contribute most effectively to the attainment of organizational goals?

REFERENCES

Adelberg, M. Industrial training of the hardcore unemployed. *Personnel,* 1969, 46, No. 6, 22–28.

American Arbitration Association. *Procedural and substantive aspects of labor-management arbitration: An AAA research report.* New York: The Association, 1957.

Angel, J. L. *Employment opportunities for the*

handicapped. Chicago: World Trade Academy Press, 1969.

Anglin, R. A. *The governor's study of the utilization—present and potential—of disabled persons in state government* (W. Va.). Charleston, W. Va.: 1963.

Argyris, C. *Integrating the individual and the organization.* New York: Wiley, 1964.

Asuni, T. Sociopsychiatric problems of cannabis in Nigeria. *Bulletin of Narcotics,* 1964, 16, 2, 17–28.

Bacon, M. K., Barry, H., & Child, L. I. A cross-cultural study of drinking: II. Relations to other features of culture. *Quarterly Journal of Studies on Alcohol,* 1965, Supp. No. 3, 29–48.

Bamdas, B. S. The working ability of schizophrenic patients having neurosis-like symptoms. *Social Psychiatry,* 1969, 4, 115–120.

Barker, R. G. *Adjustment to physical handicap and illness: A survey of the social psychology of physique and disability.* New York: Social Science Research Council, 1953.

Basowitz, H. et al. *Anxiety and stress.* New York: McGraw-Hill, 1955.

Bean, L. L., Myers, J. K., & Pepper, M. P. Social class and schizophrenia: A ten-year follow-up. In A. B. Shostak & W. Gomberg (Eds.), *Blue collar world: Studies of the American worker.* Englewood Cliffs, N.J.: Prentice-Hall, 1964, 381–391.

Beisser, A. R., & Glasser, N. The precipitating stress leading to hospitalization. *Comprehensive Psychiatry,* 1968, 9, 50–61.

Belasco, J. A., & Trice, H. M. *The assessment of change in training and therapy.* New York: McGraw-Hill, 1969.

Bellows, R. *Psychology of personnel in business and industry.* Englewood Cliffs, N.J.: Prentice-Hall, 1961.

Benabud, A. Psychopathological aspects of the cannabis situation in Morocco. *Bulletin of Narcotics,* 1957, 9, 4, 1–16.

Berg, I. A. Employee counseling in a well-rounded personnel program. *Public Personnel Review,* 1970, 31, No. 3, 185–189.

Birren, J. E. Sensation, perception, and modification of behavior in relation to the process of aging. In J. E. Birren, H. A. Imus, & W. F. Windle (Eds.), *The process of aging in the nervous system.* Springfield, Ill.: Charles C Thomas, 1959, 143–166.

Birren, J. E., Riegel, K. I., & Morrison, D. F. Intellectual capacities, aging, and man's environment. In R. H. Williams, C. Tibbitts, & W. Donahue (Eds.), *The process af aging,* Vol. 1. New York: Atherton Press, 1963, 9–45.

Block, J. R., & Campbell, W. J. Physical disability and industrial safety. *Personnel Journal,* 1963, 42, No. 3, 117–120.

Block, M. A. *Alcohol and alcoholism: Drinking and dependence.* Belmont, Calif.: Wadsworth Publishing, 1970.

Blood, M. R., & Hulin, C. L. Alienation, environmental characteristics, and worker responses. *Journal of Applied Psychology,* 1967, 51, 284–290.

Booker, G. S. Behavioral aspects of disciplinary action. *Personnel Journal,* 1969, 48, 525–529.

Brenner, B. Alcoholism and fatal accidents. *Quarterly Journal of Studies on Alcohol,* 1967, 28, 517–528.

Brown, D. R. Do personnel policies alienate employees? *Personnel Administration,* 1970, 33, No. 1, 29–37.

Browne, R. C. Automation and stress. *Journal of Psychosomatic Research,* 1966, 10, 73–75.

Bustomane, J. A. et al. Learning and drugs. *Physiology and Behavior,* 1968, 3, 553–555.

Campbell, E. I. Sick leave abuses and what to do about it: A look at government employees. *Personnel,* 1970, 47, No. 6, 42–48.

Carkhuff, R. R. Critical variables in effective counselor training. *Journal of Counseling Psychology,* 1969, 16, 238–245.

Carron, A. V., & Morford, W. R. Anxiety, stress, and motor learning. *Perceptual and Motor Skills,* 1968, 27, 507–511.

Cohen, W. J. Revolution in mental health. *Personnel Administration,* 1969, 32, No. 2, 4–8.

Committee on Occupational Psychiatry of the American Psychiatric Association. *The mentally ill employee: His treatment and rehabilitation.* New York: Hoeber Medical Division, Harper and Row, 1965.

Craik, F. I. M. The nature of the age decrement in performance on dichotic listening tasks. *Quarterly Journal of Experimental Psychology,* 1965, 17, 227–240.

Davids, A., & Mahoney, J. T. Personality dynamics and accident proneness in an industrial setting. *Journal of Applied Psychology,* 1957, 41, 303–306.

Davis, L. E. The design of jobs. *Industrial Relations,* 1966, 6, 21–45.

Defleur, L. B., Ball, J. C., & Snarr, R. W. The

long-term social correlates of opiate addiction. *Social Problems,* 1969, 17, 225–234.

Dekar, A. D. Absenteeism: A fact of life. *Personnel Journal,* 1969, 48, 881–888.

Dickson, W. J., & Roethlisberger, F. J. *Counseling in an organization.* Cambridge: Graduate School of Business Administration, Harvard University, 1966.

Doeringer, P. B. *Programs to employ the disadvantaged.* Englewood Cliffs, N.J.: Prentice-Hall, 1969.

Drake, C. A. Accident proneness: A hypothesis. *Character and Personality,* 1940, 8, 335–341.

Dunn, J. A. Anxiety, stress, and the performance of complex intellectual tasks: A new look at an old question. *Journal of Consulting and Clinical Psychology,* 1968, 32, 669–673.

Dunnette, M. D., & Kirchner, W. K. *Psychology applied to industry.* New York: Appleton-Century-Crofts, 1965.

Ehrle, R. A. The marginally employable in a changing economy. *Journal of Rehabilitation,* 1961, 27, No. 4, 16–17.

Farmer, E., & Chambers, E. G. *A study of accident proneness among motor drivers.* Report No. 84. London: Industrial Health Research Board, Medical Research Council, 1939.

Feldman, S. The labor market for the handicapped. *Employment Security Review,* 1953, 20, No. 9, 8–11, 39.

Flory, C. D., Ed. *Managers for tomorrow.* New York: New American Library, 1965.

Ford, R. N. *Motivation through the work itself.* New York: American Management Association, 1969.

Franco, S. C. Consolidated Edison's experience with a program on drinking problems. In United States Civil Service Commission, *The first step.* Washington, D.C.: Government Printing Office, 1968, 17–19.

Friedlander, F., & Greenberg, S. Work climate as related to the performance and retention of hard-core unemployed workers. *Proceedings, 77th Annual Convention, American Psychological Association,* 1969, 607–608.

Gagné, R. M. *Psychological principles in system development.* New York: Holt, Rinehart and Winston, 1962.

Gerstenfeld, A. Employee absenteeism: New insights. *Business Horizons,* 1969, 12, No. 5, 51–57.

Ginzberg, E., Miner, J. B., Anderson, J. K., Ginsburg, S. W., & Herma, J. L. *Breakdown*

and recovery. New York: Columbia University Press, 1959.

Goodman, P. S. Hiring and training the hardcore unemployed: A problem in system definition. *Human Organization,* 1969, 28, No. 4, 259–269.

Gordon, J. E. The epidemiology of accidents. *American Journal of Public Health,* 1949, 39, 504–515.

Gray, I., & Borecki, T. B. Training program for the hard-core: What the trainer has to learn. *Personnel,* 1970, 47, No. 2, 23–30.

Greenberg, L. A., & Carpenter, J. A. The effect of alcoholic beverages on skin conductance and emotional tension: I. Wine, whiskey, and alcohol. *Quarterly Journal of Studies on Alcohol,* 1957, 18, 190–204.

Habbe, S. *Company controls for drinking problems.* Personnel Policy Study No. 218. New York: National Industrial Conference Board, 1969.

Haddon, H., Suchman, E. A., & Kline, D. *Accident research.* New York: Harper and Row, 1964.

Hauser, A. Absenteeism and labor turnover in the manufacturing industries of the Dakar area. In The Commission for Technical Cooperation in Africa South of the Sahara, *Absenteeism and labor turnover.* Abidjan: Commission for Technical Cooperation in Africa South of the Sahara, 1961, 113–129.

Heinrich, H. W. *Industrial accident prevention.* New York: McGraw-Hill, 1959.

Hulin, C. L., & Blood, M. R. Job enlargement, individual differences, and worker responses. *Psychological Bulletin,* 1968, 69, 41–55.

Hunt, R. G., & Lichtman, C. M. Counseling of employees by work supervisors: Concepts, attitudes, and practices in a white collar organization. *Journal of Counseling Psychology,* 1969, 16, 81–86.

Hurst, P. M., Weidner, M. F., & Radlow, R. The effects of amphetamine upon judgments and decisions. *Psychopharmacologia,* 1967, 11, 397–404.

Hurwitz, J. I., & Lelos, D. A multi-level interpersonal profile of employed alcoholics. *Quarterly Journal of Studies on Alcohol,* 1968, 29, 64–96.

Indeström, C. M., & Cadenius, B. Time relations of the effects of alcohol compared to placebo: Dose response curves for psychomotor and perceptual test performances and blood and urine levels of alcohol. *Psychopharmacologia*, 1968, 13, 189–200.

Inglis, J., Sykes, D. H., & Unkus, M. N. Age differences in short term memory. In S. S. Chown & K. F. Riegel (Eds.), *Psychological functioning in the normal aging and senile aged*. New York: Karger, 1968, 18–43.

International Labor Office. *Adaptation for the disabled*. Geneva, Switzerland: ILO, 1969.

Janger, A. R., & Schaeffer, R. G. *Managing programs to employ the disadvantaged*. Personnel Policy Study No. 219. New York: National Industrial Conference Board, 1970.

Jaques, E. Executive organization and individual adjustment. *Journal of Psychosomatic Research*, 1966, 10, 77–82.

Jellinek, E. M. *The disease concept of alcoholism*. New Haven, Conn.: Hillside Press, 1960.

Jellinek, E. M., & McFarland, R. A. Analysis of psychological experiments on the effects of alcohol. *Quarterly Journal of Studies on Alcohol*, 1940, 1, 272–371.

Johnson, E. H. Control of sick leave. *Personnel Journal*, 1969, 48, 35–39.

Kahn, R. L. et al. *Organizational stress: Studies in role conflict and ambiguity*. New York: Wiley, 1964.

Kahn, R. L., & French, J. R. P. A summary and some tentative conclusions. *Journal of Social Issues*, 1962, 18, 3, 122–127.

Kearns, J. C. Controlling absenteeism for profit. *Personnel Journal*, 1970, 49, 50–52.

Klumbies, G. Pathogenic job conflicts. *Psychotherapy and Psychosomatics*, 1967, 15, 33–34.

Korner, R. A. Buyback of unused sick leave: A cost evaluation technique. *Personnel Journal*, 1967, 46, 646–648.

Kornhauser, A. *Mental health of the industrial worker: A Detroit study*. New York: Wiley, 1965.

Kunce, J. T. Vocational interests and accident proneness. *Journal of Applied Psychology*, 1967, 51, 223–225.

Lambruschini, C. Role of short term psychotherapy for the prevention of neurosis in laborers. *Psychotherapy and Psychosomatics*, 1967, 15, 38.

Lawler, E. E. Job design and employee motivation. *Personnel Psychology*, 1969, 22, 426–435.

Leonard, B. E. Cannabis: A short review of its effects and the possible dangers of its use. *British Journal of Addiction*, 1969, 64, 121–130.

LeShan, L. L. Dynamics of accident-prone behavior. *Psychiatry*, 1952, 15, 73–80.

Levitan, S. A., & Mangum, G. L. *Federal training and work programs in the sixties*. Ann Arbor: Institute of Labor and Industrial Relations, University of Michigan, 1969.

Lewis, E. G. Sensory phenomena following ingestion of varying doses of alcohol. *Quarterly Journal of Studies on Alcohol*, 1969, 30, 618–633.

Ley, R. Labor turnover as a function of worker differences, work environment, and authoritarianism of foreman. *Journal of Applied Psychology*, 1966, 50, 497–500.

Lindquist, A. Absenteeism and turnover as a consequence of unfavorable job adjustment. *Acta Sociologica*, 1958, 3, 2–3.

McClelland, D. C., & Winter, D. G. *Motivating economic achievement*. New York: The Free Press, 1969.

McCord, W., & McCord, J. *Origins of alcoholism*. Stanford: Stanford University Press, 1963.

McCormick, E. J. *Human factors engineering*. New York: McGraw-Hill, 1964.

McFarland, R. A. *Human factors in air transportation*. New York: McGraw-Hill, 1952.

MacIver, J. *Behavioral approaches to accident research*. New York: Association for the Aid of Crippled Children, 1961.

McMurry, R. N. Mental illness in industry. *Harvard Business Review*, 1959, 37, No. 2, 79–86.

Magee, R. H. How to build motivation into safety rules. *Personnel Journal*, 1967, 46, 88–91.

Maier, N. R. F., & Danielson, L. E. An evaluation of two approaches to discipline in industry. *Journal of Applied Psychology*, 1956, 40, 319–323.

Mann, F. C., & Williams, L. K. Some effects of the changing work environment in the office. *Journal of Social Issues*, 1962, 18, 3, 90–101.

Margulies, N. An integrated approach to supervisory training for hiring the hard-core. *Training and Development Journal*, 1970, 24, No. 8, 42–44.

Markowe, M. Occupational psychiatry: An historical survey and some recent researches. *Journal of Mental Science*, 1953, 99, 92–101.

Mayo, E. *The social problems of an industrial civilization*. Cambridge: Harvard University Press, 1945.

Metzner, H., & Mann, F. Employee attitudes and absences. *Personnel Psychology,* 1953, 6, 467–485.

Miner, J. B. *The management of ineffective performance.* New York: McGraw-Hill, 1963.

Miner, J. B. *Studies in management education.* New York: Springer, 1965.

Miner, J. B. *Introduction to industrial clinical psychology.* New York: McGraw-Hill, 1966.

Miner, J. B. An input-output model for personnel strategies. *Business Horizons,* 1969, 12, No. 3, 71–78.

Miner, J. B. *The challenge of managing.* Philadelphia: Saunders, 1975.

Miner, J. B., & Anderson, J. K. Intelligence and emotional disturbance: Evidence from army and veterans administration records. *Journal of Abnormal and Social Psychology,* 1958, 56, 75–81. (a)

Miner, J. B., & Anderson, J. K. The postwar occupational adjustment of emotionally disturbed soldiers. *Journal of Applied Psychology,* 1958, 42, 317–322. (b)

Mintz, A., & Blum, M. L. A re-examination of the accident proneness concept. *Journal of Applied Psychology,* 1949, 33, 195–211.

Morse, N. C. *Satisfactions in the white collar job.* Ann Arbor: University of Michigan Press, 1953.

National Council on Alcoholism. *Prevalence of alcoholism among employees.* New York: NCA, 1968.

Observer (pseudonym), & Maxwell, M. A. A study of absenteeism, accidents, and sickness payments in problem drinkers in one industry. *Quarterly Journal of Studies on Alcohol,* 1959, 20, 302–312.

Odiorne, G. S. Some effects of poor equipment maintenance on morale. *Personnel Psychology,* 1955, 8, 195–200.

Pacaud, S. Psychological and psychomotor functions in aging. In R. H. Williams, C. Tibbitts, & W. Donahue (Eds.), *Process of aging,* Vol. 1. New York: Atherton Press, 1963, 45–63.

Partridge, M. Drug addiction: A brief review. *International Journal of Addictions,* 1967, 2, No. 2, 207–220.

Peck, R. F., & Parsons, J. W. Personality factors in work output: Four studies of factory workers. *Personnel Psychology,* 1956, 9, 49–79.

Petras, J. W., & Curtis, J. E. The current literature on social class and mental disease in America: Critique and bibliography. *Behavioral Science,* 1968, 13, 382–398.

Phillips, L. Socioeconomic factors and mental health. *American Journal of Orthopsychiatry,* 1967, 37, 410–411.

Piore, M. J. On-the-job training in the dual labor market: Public and private responsibilities in on-the-job training of disadvantaged workers. In A. R. Weber, F. H. Cassell, & W. L. Ginsburg (Eds.), *Public-private manpower policies.* Madison, Wis.: Industrial Relations Research Association, 1969, 101–132.

Powell, R. M. *Race, religion, and the promotion of the American executive.* Columbus: College of Administrative Science, Ohio State University, 1969.

Presnall, L. P. *Alcoholism and employees.* New York: National Council on Alcoholism, 1966.

Presnall, L. P. *Recent findings regarding alcoholism in industry.* New York: National Council on Alcoholism, 1967.

Pressey, S. L., & Kuhlen, R. G. *Psychological development through the life span.* New York: Harper and Row, 1957.

Purcell, T. V., & Cavanagh, G. F. Alternative routes to employing the disadvantaged within the enterprise. In G. S. Somers (Ed.), *Proceedings of the Twenty-Second Annual Winter Meeting, Industrial Relations Research Association,* 1970, 66–77.

Rizzo, J. R., House, R. J., & Lirtzman, S. I. Role conflict and ambiguity in complex organizations. *Administrative Science Quarterly,* 1970, 15, 150–163.

Rosenberg, C. M. Anxiety in alcoholics. *Quarterly Journal of Studies on Alcohol,* 1969, 30, 729–732.

Ross, I. C., & Zander, A. Need satisfactions and employee turnover. *Personnel Psychology,* 1957, 10, 327–338.

Rutschmann, J., & Rubenstein, L. Time estimation, knowledge of results, and drug effects. *Journal of Psychiatric Research,* 1966, 4, 107–114.

Sagoe, T. E. C. Narcotics control in Ghana: A case study. *Bulletin of Narcotics,* 1966, 18, 2, 5–13.

Sales, S. M. Organizational role as a risk factor in coronary disease. *Administrative Science Quarterly,* 1969, 14, 325–336.

Sales, S. M., & House, J. Job satisfaction as a

possible contributor to risk of death from coronary disease. *Proceedings, 78th Annual Convention, American Psychological Association,* 1970, 593–594.

Schachter, S. et al. Emotional disruption and industrial productivity. *Journal of Applied Psychology,* 1961, 45, 201–213.

Schuh, A. J. The predictability of employee tenure: A review of the literature. *Personnel Psychology,* 1967, 20, 133–152.

Schulzinger, M. S. *The accident syndrome.* Springfield, Ill.: Charles C Thomas, 1956.

Selzer, M. A. Alcoholics at fault in fatal accidents and hospitalized alcoholics: A comparison. *Quarterly Journal of Studies on Alcohol,* 1969, 30, 883–887.

Sexton, W. P. Organizational and individual needs: A conflict? *Personnel Journal,* 1967, 46, 337–343.

Siegler, M., & Osmond, H. Models of drug addiction. *International Journal of Addiction,* 1968, 3, No. 1, 3–24.

Sigler, L. H. Reemployment of the elderly cardiac. *Geriatrics,* 1967, 22, No. 9, 97–105.

Simmons, O. G. *Work and mental illness.* New York: Wiley, 1965.

Smart, R. C. et al. Physiological impairment and personality factors in traffic accidents of alcoholics. *Quarterly Journal of Studies on Alcohol,* 1969, 30, 440–445.

Spielberger, C. D. *Anxiety and behavior.* New York: Academic Press, 1966.

Steiner, M. E. The search for occupational personalities. *Personnel,* 1953, 29, 335–343.

Steinmetz, L. L. *Managing the marginal and unsatisfactory performer.* Reading, Mass.: Addison-Wesley, 1969.

Sternhagen, C. J. Medicine's role in reducing absenteeism. *Personnel,* 1969, 46, No. 6, 28–38.

Stessin, L. *Employee discipline.* Washington, D.C.: Bureau of National Affairs, 1960.

Stoessel, L. Opportunity for the disadvantaged. *Training and Development Journal,* 1970, 24, 4, 28–30.

Suchman, E. A. A conceptual analysis of the accident phenomenon. *Social Problems,* 1961, 8, 241–253.

Sullivan, J. F. Assimilating the newly employed hard-core. *Training and Development Journal,* 1970, 24, No. 9, 44–48.

Sutherland, E. H., Schroeder, A. M., & Tordella, A. B. Personality traits and the alcoholic: A critique of existing studies. *Quarterly Journal of Studies on Alcohol,* 1950, 11, 548–561.

Syme, L. Personality characteristics and the alcoholic: A critique of current studies. *Quarterly Journal of Studies on Alcohol,* 1957, 18, 288–302.

Talland, G. A. et al. Practice and alcohol's effects on motor skills and attention: A supplementary report on an experiment in chronic intoxication and withdrawal. *Quarterly Journal of Studies on Alcohol,* 1965, 26, 393–401.

Telly, C. S. Inequity and its relationship to turnover among hourly workers in the major production shops of the Boeing Company. In W. G. Scott & P. P. Le Breton (Eds.), *Managing complex organizations.* Academy of Management Proceedings, held in Chicago, 1970, 119–124.

Tiffin, J., & McCormick, E. J. *Industrial psychology.* Englewood Cliffs, N.J.: Prentice-Hall, 1965.

Torda, C. Comments on the character structure and psychodynamic processes of heroin addicts. *Perceptual and Motor Skills,* 1968, 27, 143–146.

Trice, H. M. Identifying the problem drinker on the job. *Personnel,* 1957, 33, 527–533.

Trice, H. M. Key elements in successful alcoholism programs. In United States Civil Service Commission, *The first step.* Washington, D.C.: Government Printing Office, 1968, 27–30.

Trice, H. M., & Belasco, J. A. *Emotional health and employer responsibility.* Ithaca, N.Y.: New York State School of Industrial and Labor Relations, Cornell University, 1966.

United States Department of Labor. *Comparative job performance by age: Office workers.* Bulletin No. 1273. Washington, D.C.: Government Printing Office, 1960.

Van Zelst, R. H. The effect of age and experience upon accident rate. *Journal of Applied Psychology,* 1954, 38, 313–317.

Vogel-Spratt, M. Alcohol effects on human behavior under reward and punishment. *Psychopharmacologia,* 1967, 11, 337–344.

Vontress, C. E. Counseling blacks. *Personnel and Guidance Journal,* 1970, 48, 713–719.

Weatherbee, H. Y. Steering marginal performers to solid ground. *Personnel,* 1969, 46, No. 4, 34–44.

Weil, A. T., Zinberg, N. E., & Nelson, J. M

Clinical and psychological effects of marijuana in man. *International Journal of Addictions,* 1969, 4, 427–451.

Welford, A. T. *Aging and human skill.* London: Oxford University Press, 1958.

Welford, A. T. Psychomotor performance. In J. E. Birren (Ed.), *Handbook of aging and the individual.* Chicago: University of Chicago Press, 1959, 562–613.

Wilkinson, R. T. Some factors influencing the effect of environmental stressors upon performance. *Psychological Bulletin,* 1969, 72, 260–272.

Willings, D. The absentee worker. *Personnel and Training Management,* 1968, 31, No. 12, 10–12.

Wilson, A. S., Barbariak, J. J., & Koss, W. A.

Effects of alcoholic beverages and congeners on psychomotor skills in old and young. *Quarterly Journal of Studies on Alcohol,* 1970, 31, Supp. No. 5, 115–129.

Wollenberger, J. B. Acceptable work rules and penalties: A company guide. *Personnel,* 1963, 40, No. 4, 23–29.

Wright, G. N., & Trotter, A. B. *Rehabilitation research.* Madison: University of Wisconsin, 1968.

Wyshak, G., Snegireff, L. S., & Law, A. F. *Cardiacs and diabetics in industry.* Springfield, Ill.: Charles C Thomas, 1961.

Zander, A., & Quinn, R. The social environment and mental health: A review of past research at the Institute for Social Research. *Journal of Social Issues,* 1962, 18, 48–66.

CHAPTER 24

Consumer and Industrial Psychology: Prospects for Theory Corroboration and Mutual Contribution[1]

JACOB JACOBY

Purdue University

AFTER EXAMINING THE RELATIONSHIP of consumer psychology to industrial psychology and concluding that the two were fundamentally different and independent sub-domains of psychology, it was noted that both consumer and organizational psychology trace much of their conceptual and methodological underpinnings back to social psychology. The basic contention of the chapter is that it would probably be of mutual benefit to organizational and consumer psychology for each to examine the manner in which equivalent social psychological constructs have been considered and developed by the other. Attention is then directed to exploring two representative points of contact: motivation and the interwoven subject of communication, leadership, and change. Primary emphasis was devoted to considering how the concepts and findings of consumer psychology might prove useful to organizational psychology, and several applications to such topics as equity theory and expectancy theory were proposed. The chapter concludes by noting that, to the extent that similar findings can be obtained in both domains when similar concepts and methods are involved, the generality and validity of these findings and of the underlying psychological constructs are substantially enhanced.

---

[1] The reader is encouraged to familiarize himself with the related consumer psychological literature appearing since this chapter was written in 1971 for additional findings and insights. However, the approach to concept stretching employed throughout this chapter still remains valid.

A note of deep appreciation is expressed to Howard L. Fromkin, Leon B. Kaplan, Charles W. King, Robert Perloff, and Robert Pritchard for having read and commented on an earlier draft of this manuscript.

INTRODUCTION

The traditional view of consumer and industrial psychology is that the former—along with personnel, organizational, and human engineering psychologies—is subsumed under the latter (e.g., *American Psychologist*, 1965; Guion, 1965; Katzell, 1958). Industrial psychology is considered to be a subdiscipline of psychology, and consumer psychology to be a specialty within that subdiscipline (although some definitions of industrial psychology have to be stretched to make this point, cf., Guion, 1965, p. 817). Perhaps this view was justified at one point when two conditions obtained: the consumer and industrial psychologist were probably one and the same person and the only psychologist in the organization, and these early consumer psychologists were primarily management oriented and interested in the consumer qua purchaser, that is, in adding to the profits of the firm. However, there are some fundamental distinctions between the other specialties of industrial psychology, taken as a whole, and consumer psychology which give one cause to doubt the lineage as outlined.

As early as 1958, Katzell, in his review of the field of industrial psychology, noted that consumer psychology "has a different set of dependent and independent variables" (p. 237). At a most basic level, industrial psychology is concerned with the behavior of people inside (industrial) organizations as workers and producers of goods, while consumer psychology is concerned with the behavior of people outside of organizations as purchasers and users of these goods. Industrial psychologists are primarily interested in how to make organizational members (i.e., employees) happier, more productive, or both, with the ultimate purpose being to develop more efficient and effective organizations. It is thus a management-oriented discipline. Consumer psychology, while historically management-oriented, is in the main no longer so. Consumer behavior includes both purchase and consumption components,[2] and many consumer psychologists are now more interested in the consumer qua consumer than in the consumer qua purchaser (Krugman, 1968; Perloff,

1963, 1964). The advent of consumerism as an emerging cultural force has provided additional impetus, and one now finds consumer psychologists and the results of their labors just as likely to be employed by the consumer (through the government or consumer action groups) as by the manufacturer (cf., Jacoby, 1971a).

Thus, while consumer psychology is obviously an applied form of psychology, it is not so obviously a specialty of industrial psychology. From the perspective of many consumer psychologists, industrial and consumer psychology are siblings in the household of applied psychology, sharing a common parentage in the more fundamental areas of psychology. As such, the relationship more closely resembles one of lateral peership than anything hierarchical.

Evidence that the two are indeed separate fields is reflected in a variety of ways. First, it is the exception (e.g., Tiffin & McCormick, 1965) rather than the rule for introductory texts on industrial psychology to contain a chapter on consumer psychology. In contrast, basic texts dealing with the more general notion of "applied" psychology (e.g., Anastasi, 1964; Hepner, 1966) invariably do devote some portion to consumer behavior and treat this separately from industrial/organizational psychology. Second, surveys regarding the content of the nonacademic industrial psychologist's job reveal that "marketing and consumer research" plays an inconsequential role—only about 5 percent of industrial psychologists report such activities to constitute a significant proportion of their total function (MacKinney & Dunnette, 1964). Finally, while each and every human being is a consumer, not each and every adult human being works within an organization. To be sure, organizations are omnipresent and affect everyone's way of life, but not necessarily in any direct fashion vis à vis the manner in which individuals may earn a living.

And so consumer psychology—that branch of psychology which studies the dynamics underlying decisions and behavior

---

[2] In some instances the "consumer" may also become a seller, as when he sells the home he is living in or the stocks he owns. Unfortunately, the psychological dynamics underlying consumer behavior qua salesmanship have received scant empirical attention.

regarding the acquisition, use, and disposition of products, services, time, and ideas (Jacoby, 1969)—is potentially a much broader field than industrial psychology. Indeed, it could be argued, tongue-in-cheek, of course, that industrial psychology should be subsumed under consumer psychology (e.g., selection of a job represents a form of consumption and this becomes especially obvious when there are many job openings for every qualified individual, i.e., during a "buyer's market").

Probably the greatest point of similarity between consumer and industrial psychology occurs with that specialty of industrial psychology variously known as industrial-social (Haire, 1954; Vroom & Maier, 1961) or organizational (Bass, 1965; Leavitt, 1962; Leavitt & Bass, 1964; Schein, 1965) psychology. While the traditional areas of industrial psychology (e.g., selection and placement) are more concerned with R-R types of relationships, both consumer and organizational psychology tend to focus on S-R relationships. In the process of trying to understand human behavior in their respective contexts, both consumer and organizational psychology can trace a major portion of their conceptual and methodological heritage back to social psychology. Indeed, it is easy to conceptualize social psychology as the apex of a triangle which has organizational and consumer psychology at the two base points. Consumer psychology has drawn most heavily from the social psychological literature on attitudes, communication, and persuasion, while organizational psychology has traditionally focused on the social psychological studies of leadership and group behavior.

The direction of information flow along the social-organizational-consumer triangle need not, indeed has not, been all one way. Both organizational and consumer psychology provide excellent testing grounds for general social psychological propositions. While social psychology is essentially a broad-gauged and basic discipline, the validity of its propositions must eventually be examined in specific contexts. Together, the working-producing and buying-using contexts account for the vast majority of contemporary man's waking hours, and it is only natural that social psychological concepts be incorporated into and tested in these domains (cf., Jacoby, 1974a). While the social psychologist's laboratory provides a superb setting for rigorously testing explicit hypotheses, the field provides an excellent setting in which to establish construct validity or generality of these findings (Campbell & Stanley, 1963).

If consumer and industrial/organizational psychology are siblings spawned from the same social psychological parent, what can be said of their relationship to each other? Our objective in this chapter is to suggest some preliminary answers to this question. This will be done primarily by examining how several social psychological concepts have been borrowed, sometimes re-labeled, and utilized in consumer and industrial psychology. Throughout, there has been a deliberate attempt to stretch concepts and ideas, to be explorative, heuristic, and purposefully speculative, in the hope that examining the manner in which a concept has been utilized in one domain will provide insights leading to thoughts about how it may be applied in the other.

Several factors ought to be noted before we proceed. First, many of the "findings" of consumer psychology are frequently based on the results of only one or two studies appearing in the published literature. Indeed, it is only in the last few years that one can discern the emergence of a systematic, programmatic orientation to consumer behavior research. As a function of this lack of replication and questionable generality, many of the findings cited more closely approximate hypotheses than verified statements of fact.

Second, while both consumer and industrial psychology, as disciplines of empirical inquiry, have existed for a comparable length of time (and both may trace their birth to Scott, 1903, 1908a, 1908b, 1911a, 1911b, as documented by Ferguson, 1962), the pace and amount of published literature generated in industrial psychology seems to have far outstripped that of consumer psychology. Perhaps one reason for this is that business firms seem quite willing to share knowledge regarding the management of people but considerably less willing (almost to the point of being phobic) to share information on consumer reaction to product development and promotional efforts. Indeed, it wasn't until the early 1960s, with the advent of the *Journal of Advertising Research* and the *Journal of Marketing Research,* that consumer behavior articles began appearing in any significant numbers. As a consequence, organizational psychology has a greater number of well-developed, comprehensively examined constructs and well-documented findings. Logically, it would seem to have more to offer the developing field of consumer psychology than vice versa, and indeed it has. For example, the three major integrated conceptual statements regarding consumer behavior (Engel, Kollat, & Blackwell, 1968; Howard & Sheth, 1969; Nicosia, 1966) all reflect the substantial influence of March and Simon's (1958) now classic work on organizations. Given the orientation of this *Handbook,* however, the focus will be on how consumer psychology can add to the development of industrial psychology rather than vice versa.

Finally, some of the findings of consumer psychology may appear as "old hat" to industrial psychologists. This probably should be viewed as a desirable and encouraging state of affairs in that it reflects a certain degree of construct validity for both domains. As Vroom (1969, p. 197) has pointed out, ultimately "statements about the determinants of behavior in organizations should be derivable from general theories capable of explaining behavior in other situations." Howard and Sheth (1969, p. 295) argue in similar fashion that "buying behavior in most cases is merely a part of the interrelated total ongoing pattern, and not a unique kind of behavior independent of other daily activities."

Vroom and Maier (1961, p. 413) note that "research in industrial social psychology has been based on two general types of models. The first treats the individual as the unit of analysis...[while the] second kind of conceptual model treats the social system as the unit of analysis." Inasmuch as a consideration of all actual and potential points of contact between consumer and social industrial psychology is beyond the scope of this chapter, attention has been limited to representative issues from each of these research traditions. The social system approach is represented by the interrelated processes of communication, leadership, and effecting change, while the individual level of analysis is represented by various approaches to the subject of human motivation.

COMMUNICATION, LEADERSHIP, AND CHANGE

Both organizational and consumer psychology are vitally interested in influencing behavior and in the factors that affect and determine such influence. Cyert and MacCrimmon (1969, p. 589) assert that:

The study of behavior within organizations must include an analysis of the organizational processes used to influence participants to behave in particular ways. Behavior is primarily influenced by *authority,* that is, by control over reward and punishment and by *persuasion* (and the reinforcement of these methods through status and prestige), or by any combination of these. (Italics ours)

Organizations will sometimes rely primarily or entirely on persuasive communications to generate compliance with organizationally determined desiderata. Situations such as these usually occur when the direct application of authority either would be illegitimate, would violate the "psychological contract" (Schein, 1965), or when it is believed that more rapid acceptance would ensue, morale would not suffer, etc., if persuasive techniques were employed in preference to the direct execution of formal, legitimate authority.

Marketer-advertisers rarely possess the power of direct authority over consumers that is available to management when dealing on an internal matter with members of the firm. Consequently, consumer psychologists direct a great deal of attention to the study of persuasive communications. *Communication* has been defined as a process whereby a source transmits a message over or through a particular medium to a receiver. *Persuasion* is that variety of communication in which a source exerts an influence upon the response tendencies and/or actual behavior of the receiver.

As one considers the manner in which persuasive communication has been examined in the industrial and consumer contexts, certain basic similarities in conceptualization, if not in terminology, become apparent. More specifically, the topic of "formal communication" in the organizational context (see Porter & Roberts, 1976, Chap. 35) reflects essentially the same characteristics as does the subject of "advertising" in the consumer context. In similar fashion, informal communication is roughly comparable to and may be equated with word-of-mouth advertising, informal leaders in organizations with opinion leaders in the marketplace, organizational change agents with consumer innovators, and the acceptance of organizational change with the acceptance of innovations (i.e., new products, brands, etc.). Our purpose in this section is to examine the results of investigations in the consumer behavior domain regarding word-of-mouth advertising, opinion leaders, consumer innovators and innovations, while attempting to note some of the implications that these findings have for organizational behavior. We are aware, however, that there are probably many implications for organizational behavior which we will

no doubt fail to recognize. The reader is, therefore, not only invited but urged to allow his creative, synthesizing faculties free rein and to participate in this exercise.

Word-of-Mouth Processes and Informal Communication

In his comprehensive reviews of the topic (1967a, 1967b), Arndt defines word-of-mouth (WOM) advertising as: "oral, person-to-person communication between a perceived noncommercial communicator and a receiver concerning a brand, a product, or a service offered for sale" (1967a, p. 190). While Arndt delimits this definition to instances in which the communicator is in direct, face-to-face contact with the receiver, consideration of the "housewives exchanging information over the phone" stereotype suggests that WOM probably encompasses any oral transmission of product-, brand-, or service-related information. This is consistent with Cox's (1963) description of WOM as simply entailing "conversations about products." Note also that Arndt's definition says nothing regarding interpersonal influence nor persuasive communications, but simply focuses upon the exchange of information between individuals (cf., King & Summers, 1970, p. 44). The fact that the source may or may not have any intent to persuade or that the receiver may be persuaded even if the source had no such intentions (cf., Miller, 1966; Nilsen, 1957) is irrelevant. The distinguishing characteristic of WOM advertising, and that which differentiates it from personal selling, is that the source is perceived by the receiver to be *independent* of the manufacturer, advertiser, and/or seller.

Thus, in the implications for organizational behavior to be drawn below, we are not considering informal job-related conversations such as those that take place between a supervisor and subordinate or conversations generated in lieu of official, written memoranda (cf., Melcher & Beller, 1967).

Rather, we are concerned with the relatively ignored subject of oral communication regarding aspects of organizational life which typically occur outside the formal organizational channels (as defined by the organizational chart), and in which the communicator is perceived to be operating independently of the organization or its representatives. Stated somewhat differently, we are referring to the communication network in organizations which defines the structure of that amorphous entity known as the "informal organization" (cf., Jacoby, 1968), and sometimes referred to as the "grapevine" (Davis, 1959).

Reports of effective use of WOM advertising during the 1930s and early 1940s do exist. However, it was the work by investigators at Columbia University's Bureau of Applied Social Research on interpersonal communication and influence with respect to voting behavior (Berelson, Lazarsfeld, & McPhee, 1954; Lazarsfeld, Berelson, & Gaudet, 1948), the diffusion of a new drug in communities of physicians (Coleman, Katz, & Menzel, 1957; Coleman, Menzel, & Katz, 1959; Menzel & Katz, 1955–1956), and on purchasing behavior (Katz & Lazarsfeld, 1955), coupled with Rogers's (1962) excellent compilation of the research on the adoption and diffusion of agricultural innovations, which provided the impetus for studying word-of-mouth processes in the consumer context. In general, these studies demonstrated that personal sources produced greater exposure to information about the product and, in particular, had greater impact on behavior related to that product than any other type of information source. Moreover, they suggested an intriguing modification of the earlier conceptualization of mass media communication, namely, the "two-step flow of communication" model (cf., Katz, 1957a,b). According to this model, information and influence flow "*from* [the formal, mass media sources] *to* opinion leaders and *from them* to the less active sections of the population" (Lazarsfeld, Berelson, & Gaudet, 1948, p. 151). Let

us, for the moment, defer consideration of the opinion leaders and focus primarily on word-of-mouth processes of communication.

The vast majority of studies conducted in the consumer behavior context indicate that word-of-mouth information plays a significant role in making the consumer aware of the product and in affecting his decision to buy or not to buy that product, brand, or service. Arndt has commented that in "general, word of mouth emerges as one of the most important, possibly *the* most important source of information for the consumer" (1967a, p. 238).

Word-of-mouth communication can serve either as a facilitating or retarding force on product acceptance. However, word-of-mouth transmitters appear more likely to transmit favorable than unfavorable information. Engel, Blackwell, and Kegerreis (1969) found word of mouth for a new automotive service to be "decidedly favorable," while Engel, Kegerreis, and Blackwell (1969) reported that forty dissatisfied customers of this service showed no greater use of word of mouth than did forty satisfied customers. Arndt (1967c, p. 293) found that 57 percent of the word-of-mouth conversations for a new brand of coffee were favorable, 39 percent neutral, and only 4 percent negative. In other words, to the extent that one can translate these findings to the organizational context, there is more reason to believe that informal organizational communication operates to the firm's advantage than otherwise. It is, therefore, not something to be feared and discouraged by management but to be understood and, if possible, used to further organizational goals.

However, from the receiver's perspective, negative word of mouth has greater impact than favorable word of mouth. In Arndt's (1967c) study, 42 percent of those not exposed to word-of-mouth communication (i.e., the "controls") did purchase the new brand of coffee. In comparison, 54 percent of those exposed to favorable word of mouth, but only 18 percent of those exposed to negative word of mouth, made such a purchase.

Verbalized dissatisfactions are, therefore, probably more detrimental to the firm than verbalized satisfactions are beneficial.

Another important aspect of word-of-mouth information concerns the point in the decision process at which it exerts its significant influence. In deciding to incorporate a brand or product into his regular usage pattern, the consumer, according to the most generally accepted and copied model of the adoption process (cf., Rogers, 1962; Rogers & Shoemaker, 1971), moves through stages of awareness, interest, evaluation, trial, and adoption. There is almost unanimous agreement in the literature that formal (mass media) and informal (word of mouth) sources of information play different roles and may act in complementary rather than competing fashion (cf., Cox, 1967). The mass media seem to be best equipped to create awareness, while word of mouth is the most important source of information in the later stages, particularly in the evaluation stage. This suggests that in those instances where the organization relies on persuasion rather than authority to influence member behavior, formal communications are the best means of indicating what actions are deemed desirable. However, informal communication sources will determine how this information is evaluated and whether or not there will be compliance. Moreover, Sheth's (1968) finding, that word of mouth leads to more rapid adoption than when mass media are the source of the information, suggests that informal communication sources will be more likely to produce rapid compliance than will formal communication sources.

Cunningham (1967) presented data which indicate that word-of-mouth is engaged in more often and has greater impact on purchases for new products than for established products, thereby suggesting the increased importance of informal communication when attempting to introduce organizational change. There are also data to indicate the information exchange usually takes place horizontally rather than vertically, that is, between individuals of similar age and status (Feldman & Spencer, 1965; Katz, 1957a; King & Summers, 1967) and that, within these strata, individuals will tend to search for others perceived to be more competent than themselves (Feldman, 1966; King & Summers, 1967).

In a significant extension of the two-step model, in which the information flow is viewed as being unidirectional (i.e., from the media to the opinion leaders and from them to the masses), Bauer (1963) and Cox (1963) contended that consumers have "information needs" which prompt them to take a more active, information-seeking role in the communication process. Cox (1963) cited evidence to indicate that such information seeking, where non-opinion leaders initiate conversations with opinion leaders and where opinion leaders seek out information from the mass media, may take place at least as often as does information receiving. Similarly, Cunningham (1967) found that about half the word-of-mouth activity engaged in by his subjects was of the traditional information-receiving variety, while about half was of the information-seeking variety. Moreover, consumers pay more attention to information they have sought than to information volunteered to them (Arndt, 1967c).

The significance of such information seeking should not be undervalued. Organizational members are in all likelihood not passive recipients of formal communications. They, too, must have information needs regarding their various relationships with and within the organization. Hence, they are likely to initiate conversations and seek out information pursuant to the satisfaction of these needs, and it would be in an organization's best interest if it could learn to use all channels of information to which it had access, including word-of-mouth, in order to satisfy these needs.

Finally, while the social psychological laboratory studies of rumor transmission suggest that word of mouth is an unreliable and frequently distorted form of communication, "most of the research on message transmission conducted in naturalistic settings has found word of mouth relatively reliable and undistorted" (Arndt, 1967a, p. 233). As an example, Davis (1959, p. 350) estimated that between 90 and 95 percent of grapevine information in the typical business organization is true. These differences between laboratory and field findings have been attributed to the motives of the communicator. "In a product situation, the knowledge that the receiver of word of mouth can buy the product and thus check the veracity of the message would appear to discourage extreme exaggerations" (Arndt, 1967a, p. 234). In other contexts (e.g., battlefield units, financial circles, and probably within most organizations), non-veridical information transmission can lead to serious consequences for both the transmitter and receiver alike.

Several possible explanations have been offered to account for the apparently greater persuasive impact of word-of-mouth processses relative to that of the formal mass media. Some of these are based on two particularly important characteristics of WOM communication, namely, (a) that negative as well as positive information may be exchanged, and (b) that WOM is a two-way rather than a one-way form of communication. The first factor implies that the information from a WOM source is more likely to represent a balanced rather than a one-sided view, as is the case with the mass media. In turn, this suggests that WOM sources are perceived to be less biased and more trustworthy (Arndt, 1967a, p. 205; Cox, 1963), and there is considerable evidence in the social psychological literature to indicate that more trustworthy sources have greater persuasive impact. Some of the effectiveness of such trustworthy sources is probably because they are less likely to engage the defense mechanisms of the receiver, particularly those of selective attention, perception, and retention, nor are receivers likely to adopt a critical evaluative posture with respect to information stemming from such a source (Bauer, 1967).

The flexibility provided by two-way communication permits the occurrence of several other factors which also serve to enhance the effectiveness of word-of-mouth influence. First, "interpersonally communicated information can often be tailored to meet an individual's particular information needs" (Cox, 1963, p. 64). Moreover, "a consumer may be able to develop a great deal more information about a product through consumer channels—particularly information concerning product performance and the social or psychological consequences of a purchase decision" than it may be possible to obtain from the more formal sources of product information (Cox, 1963, p. 64). Finally, the feedback aspect of two-way communication would tend, even by itself, to increase the accuracy with which the information is transmitted.

Another set of factors posited to explain the greater persuasive impact of WOM relates to the social aspects of the process. "In contrast to the mass media, personal contacts [can] offer social support" (Arndt, 1967a, p. 205). Moreover, WOM communication is often backed up by subtle social pressures and surveillance. It may also serve a "legitimizing" function by giving the stamp of approval for intended or actual purchase behavior (Engel, Kegerreis, & Blackwell, 1969).

In sum, the evidence indicates word-of-mouth to be a potent force affecting consumer decision processes and purchasing behavior. The findings in the consumer behavior sphere suggest that informal organizational communication processes are probably similarly important and deserve considerably more attention and study than they have heretofore received (Davis, 1959; Jacoby, 1968).

Opinion Leaders and Informal Leaders

According to the two-step flow model, some people—the opinion leaders—play a more significant role in the word-of-mouth communication-influence process than do others. A study by Myers (1966) provides one of the more clear-cut examples of the importance of opinion leaders. A new product (Armour's Chicken and Rice dinner) was introduced to women in fifteen established ladies' social groups. The opinion leader served as the source of introduction in nine of these groups and a non-leader in the remaining six groups. Each of the fifteen introducer-sources was given free samples of the product and asked to serve it to her family and, within two days, to give some of the samples to her friends and ask them to serve it to their families. For the nine groups in which the opinion leader was the introducer, most of the other women's attitudes changed in the same (i.e., favorable) direction as that of the introducer. The attitudes of women in the other six groups, however, appeared to change more in a direction opposite to that of their non-opinion leader introducer's. This and considerable other evidence suggests that opinion leaders exert a significant effect on both opinions and actual purchasing behavior.

Consideration of the function served by opinion leaders suggests a basic equivalence with the notion of communication "relay points" or "message centers" (Cyert & March, 1955; Shannon & Weaver, 1949) and with the more recently advanced notion of organizational "linking pins" (Likert, 1961). In other words, while the head of a formal organizational unit serves as a linking pin or relay point for information exchange between his supervisor and peers at one level and his subordinates at another, the evidence regarding the opinion leader cited below suggests that the organization's "informal leaders" probably serve the identical linking pin function in the firm's informal organization. Consequently, the informal opinion leader provides the logical starting point for those wishing to exert an impact on the organizational system via word-of-mouth processes. The more we know about the characteristics and motives of the opinion leader, the easier it should be to identify him and utilize his unique and valuable talents.

Research thus far has identified several characteristics of the opinion leader. Perhaps most important is that "no matter what their sphere of influence, opinion leaders do actually exceed non-opinion leaders in mass media exposure in general" (Katz & Lazarsfeld, 1955, p. 311) and in exposure to mass media relevant to their particular spheres of influence in particular (Summers, 1970). This suggests that informal leaders within the organization are probably more attuned to the communications emanating from the formal sources than are their non-leader colleagues. It should also be pointed out that there is evidence to indicate that opinion leaders also receive more information from personal information sources and are more influenced by what others have to say than by information supplied by the formal sources (Katz & Lazarsfeld, 1955; Sheth, 1968). These findings suggest a multi-step rather than the traditional two-step flow described above.

Other characteristics of opinion leaders are that they: (a) seem to conform more closely to the norms of the social system than does the average group member (Rogers & Cartano, 1962); (b) tend to participate in more social activities than do followers (Rogers, 1962); (c) are generally of the same social class as those they influence; (d) tend to have slightly higher status and be more cosmopolitan in the sense of being oriented beyond the local community (Rogers, 1962); and (e) are considered to be more competent than their followers (Katz & Lazarsfeld, 1955). Sheer physical mobility and proximity are also factors. Opinion leaders must be accessible and in contact with people in order to be able to exert any influence (Howard & Sheth, 1969, p. 313; King & Summers, 1967).

Dichter (1966) suggested that there are four primary bases for opinion leadership motivation. First, product involvement may serve to stimulate word-of-mouth communication, particularly to the extent that the opinion leader's experience with the product produces either moderately pleasurable or moderately unpleasurable experiences. It is probably true that organizational opinion leaders will exhibit greater involvement with organizational issues than will most other organizational members. This suggests that periodically collecting attitudinal, satisfaction, and morale data from these individuals should enable management to accurately forecast the attitudes, satisfaction, and morale of the entire organization at some later point in time. This also suggests that, providing one can locate the opinion leaders, word-of-mouth processes are likely to be activated to the extent that opinion leaders can be involved in the activity or issue in question. Second, self-involvement will sometimes play a major role in motivating opinion leaders to talk about the product. Such conversations may serve such purposes as gaining attention, showing connoisseurship, suggesting status, giving the impression that the opinion leader has inside information, seeking confirmation of his judgment, and/or asserting superiority. Third, the opinion leader may be motivated simply by an altruistic concern for others. Thus, appealing to such altruism may be sufficient to activate word-of-mouth communication. Finally, advertising for the product may be entertaining in and of itself and, therefore, provide the stimulus for product-related conversations. This suggests that the content of formal communications will be talked about to the extent that they are made interesting.

Arndt (1967a) suggested several other partially overlapping motivating factors including interest and ego involvement in the product category, the drives to reduce cognitive dissonance or to establish cognitive clarity, as an ego defense mechanism (e.g., the embarrassed hostess may save face by blaming the cake mix), and because such conversations may serve as a means to other ends. These findings are perhaps best summarized by noting that opinion leaders become opinion leaders to satisfy their own needs (Cox, 1967, p. 615).

Two additional findings regarding opinion leadership are of particular relevance for organizational psychologists. First, opinion leaders tend to be more active receivers of information about new products, tend to have more favorable attitudes toward such new products (Summers & King, 1969), and tend to be positive, facilitating change agents (King & Summers, 1970). To the extent that there is a common denominator across opinion leadership in the consumer context and being an informal leader in the organizational context, this suggests that informal leaders may be more receptive to organizational change than other organizational members and may, in many instances, serve to facilitate the introduction and acceptance of planned organizational change.

Moreover, opinion leadership seems to be a general phenomenon (Katz & Lazarsfeld, 1955, p. 321), with a moderate degree of overlap existing across spheres of influence (Gross, 1969; Jacoby, 1974b; King & Summers, 1970; Summers & King, 1971). This suggests that informal leaders may possess similar broad leadership capacity and influence, and that the effort and funds expended by the organization to locate and identify them may turn out to be a fairly good investment. Management might make use of opinion leaders in at least two different ways: (a) simply to assess their motives, attitudes, morale, etc., in order to formulate some idea of what the organization as a whole is likely to be thinking and the direction it may be going in; and (b) through the judicious "planting" of information, management might be able to make the opinion leader serve as a positive communication link in the pursuit of organizational goals.

There are at least two different strategies which could be adopted in trying to identify the organizational counterparts of opinion leaders. First, consistent with the older "trait" approach applied to formal leaders, investigators might attempt to locate individuals within the organization who manifest the characteristics cited above as being possessed by opinion leaders. A second, more dynamic approach would be to start with the basic communication network notion from which concepts of opinion leadership volved. Given that opinion leaders are much more active participants in the communication process than their followers, both as receivers and transmitters of formal and informal communications, one could attempt to identify those individuals in the organization who process (i.e., receive and transmit) more organizationally relevant information than do others. A methodology for mapping the informal organizational structure of large, complex organizations, which, as a by-product, is capable of being used for such purposes, has already been developed (Jacoby, 1968).

An alternative to identifying existing informal leaders is to actually create them. Success in this regard has been reported by Mancuso (1969), who has provided guidelines for the types of individuals most likely to become opinion leaders. According to Mancuso, potential opinion leaders must possess mobility, status, and confidence. Of these three, he considers mobility—the frequency of contact the individual has with others—to be the most critical. Moderately high status is desired but difficult to manipulate. Consequently, Mancuso advocates selecting individuals who already exhibit the desired degree of status. Finally, confidence is viewed as being primarily a function of having the relevant information and being knowledgeable. According to Mancuso, this factor is probably the easiest to manipulate. One simply provides the potential opinion leader with the necessary information or makes him aware of where such information can be found. Mancuso reports that the application of his full technique has yielded impressive results, and it would seem that an experimental attempt to apply these in an organizational context might prove equally worthwhile.

Innovators as Change Agents

Related to the entire issue of word-of-mouth communication and opinion leadership is the acceptance of innovations (i.e., change) in the marketplace. *Innovations* are most frequently defined as any form of a product that has recently become available in a market (Rogers, 1962; Engel, Kollat, & Blackwell, 1968), while *innovators* are those individuals who are among the first to incorporate (i.e., "adopt") the innovation into their regular purchasing and usage behavior. Over time, the way any given product is adopted by all those who eventually do adopt it follows normal distribution. Innovators are typically designated as those who are among the first $2\frac{1}{2}$ to 10 percent to adopt; later groups are designated in turn as: early adopters, early majority, late majority, and laggards (cf., Rogers, 1962; Rogers & Shoemaker, 1971). There is considerable evidence to indicate that innovators and early adopters play a significant role, basically through word-of-mouth communication, in the subsequent diffusion of an innovation through the population at large (Arndt, 1967c; Bell, 1963; Bohlen et al., 1968; Coleman, 1960; Coleman, Katz, & Menzel, 1966; Frank, Massy, & Morrison, 1964; King, 1963; Lazer & Bell, 1966; Robertson, 1968; Rogers, 1962). Thus, even though they are not responsible for the introduction of change, they may be considered change agents in the sense that they provide the initial toehold and act as instigators to facilitate the acceptance of change by others. Given that the vast majority, perhaps as high as 90 percent (Rogers & Stanfield, 1968), of the new products introduced annually are rejected by consumers, identification of the innovation-prone individual has assumed tremendous practical importance. Generalizations from the investigations just cited indicate that, with respect to socio-demographic characteristics, innovators tend to be younger, more mobile, educated, literate, privileged (i.e., have more discretionary income relative to their peers), and to have somewhat higher income and status. Personality characteristics most often cited in connection with innovators are venturesomeness (i.e., possessing favorable attitudes toward trying new ideas and products) and the tendency to take greater risks than non-innovators. Open-mindedness has also recently been demonstrated to be significantly associated with innovation proneness (Jacoby, 1971b; Coney, 1973).

With respect to information processing behavior, innovators appear to be more exposed to all forms of communication. This includes marketer-dominated (e.g., advertising), consumer-dominated (e.g., word of mouth), and neutral (e.g., *Consumer Reports*) sources (Arndt, 1967a, p. 215; Bohlen, 1968). They are more frequently asked for their opinion by others and are more prone to relate unsolicited experiences to others (Engel, Kegerreis, & Blackwell, 1969). They also tend to hear about innovations much earlier than do the non-innovators, and they engage in extensive and systematic search for relevant information regarding the innovation (Berning & Jacoby, 1974; Engel, Blackwell, & Kegerreis, 1969).

Finally, several studies indicate that there is some overlap between being an opinion leader and being an innovator (Baumgarten, 1971; Robertson, 1971). Conceivably, innovators may simply be that class of opinion leaders most likely to respond favorably to new products.

The implications for organizational management beyond those already adumbrated may be as follows: Basically, and for one reason or another, it is usually quite difficult to get most organizational members to accept organizational change. One known method of increasing the likelihood of planned change being accepted is to have the organizational members who will be affected participate in the planning and introduction of such change (e.g., Coch & French, 1948). Based on the findings presented above, another possibility would be to utilize the innovators already existing within the organization to assist in the critical information dissemination function. Possibly, as a function of such participation, they might accept the change themselves and then persuade others to do likewise.

The innovator-change agent could be identified either by assessing those already in the organization's work force for the identifying characteristics and/or a specific innovation-proneness inventory could be administered to all incoming employees, and records maintained of the scores of all such individuals. Then, as change was contemplated, the organization could make certain that each of these change agents received as much relevant and supporting information as possible, making sure, of course, not to activate psychological reactance (Brehm, 1966).

In this regard, several features of Mancuso's (1969) procedure to "create" opinion leaders are also worth noting. It involved inviting individuals believed to possess the requisite characteristics of mobility and status to join a select "panel of leaders" for the purpose of evaluating new products on a regular basis, providing these people with substantial information regarding this commodity, encouraging them to discuss their choices and opinions with their friends, encouraging their contributions and incorporating these when appropriate, and providing them with periodic feedback. Could not such a procedure be adopted by an organization in an attempt to create an ongoing panel of opinion leader-change agents? Moreover, based on the known effects that participation in the planning of change has on the subsequent acceptance of change, it may be possible to achieve just as good (and perhaps even better) acceptance of planned organizational change by having only the organization's informal-opinion leaders participate in the formulation of such change rather than everyone being affected.

Stimulus Object Characteristics Affecting the Acceptance of Innovations

Certain characteristics of products and conditions under which they are introduced (Hart & Jacoby, 1973) have been found to affect the acceptance of innovations. Considerable recent research (cf., Cox, 1967) indicates that the greater the perceived risk associated with a given product, the less likely it is to achieve acceptance. Marketers introducing new products will frequently use money-back guarantees, "cents-off" coupons, and other similar devices to lessen the perceived risk. Analogously, managers wishing to introduce and gather acceptance for organizational change should seek to develop means of reducing the amount of risk likely to be perceived by organizational members. There are various types of perceived risk—psychological, social, physical, financial, and functional (Kaplan, Szybillo, & Jacoby, 1974)—each of which should probably be borne in mind by managers planning an organizational change.

Other evidence indicates that "buyers under time pressures are less apt to adopt a new brand" (Howard & Sheth, 1969, p. 325). Perhaps, then, it would be better to introduce major organizational change gradually rather than all at once. Such a piecemeal approach is consistent with techniques used to reduce perceived risk.

Based on his review of the literature, Rogers (1962) has proposed the following factors as affecting the rate of adoption: relative advantage, compatibility, communicability, complexity, and divisibility. Relative advantage refers to the consumer's perception that the new product offering is superior, at least in some important respects, to the products it supersedes. Compatibility refers to the goodness of fit between the new product and the values and past experiences of the individual. The poorer the fit, the less likely it is to be accepted. The implications of relative advantage and compatibility for promoting a planned organizational change are obvious.

Communicability refers to how easy it is for individuals to discuss the new product. The more difficult it is to communicate about a product, the slower its rate of acceptance. Products which are highly visible are usually those which are easiest to communicate about. Relatedly, complexity refers to the degree to which a new product is difficult to understand or use. Complex

products are unlikely to be diffused rapidly. Finally, divisibility refers to whether a product can be broken down into smaller "pieces" (e.g., can one buy a single bottle, or must one buy a six-pack?). Consumers forced to buy either large units or quantities of a new product are less likely to do so, probably because of the perceived risk involved. Combined, these factors also suggest that managers would do well to introduce organizational change piecemeal, with each piece being simple enough and perhaps made graphic enough so as to be easily communicable.

Perhaps the most appropriate means of concluding this section on informal communication, leadership, and acceptance of change is to note that the findings from the consumer behavior context can only begin to suggest the importance of these same phenomena for organizational behavior.[3] Whether or not they do assume such significance in the organizational sphere, where authority and direct control are also available for use in influencing the membership, is an empirical question. However, to the extent that we can accurately extrapolate from these findings, it would appear that a substantial research effort devoted to exploring these relatively neglected issues may well pay large dividends for those interested in understanding and affecting organizational behavior.

MOTIVATION

Content Versus Process Approaches

The subject of motivation is of central concern to almost all branches of psychology, and this is no less true of both consumer and organizational psychology. Campbell, Dunnette, Lawler, and Weick (1970) have classified the various theoretic orientations to motivation into "content" and "process"

---

[3] The reader interested in pursuing these topics is directed to additional relevant work by Barnett (1953), Carter and Williams (1957, 1959), Gillfillian (1935), and Mansfield (1960, 1961a, 1961b).

approaches. The former are primarily concerned with identifying specifically *"what it is within an individual or his environment that energizes and sustains behavior"* (p. 341), while the latter are concerned with identifying the major classes of variables and mechanics which underlie *how* motives operate to determine behavior.

Another way one might conceptualize this distinction is in terms of arousal versus direction. While the content approaches attempt to answer the question of what activates the individual to begin with, the process approaches are concerned with answering the question of why an individual engages in one particular activity at a specified point in time out of the wide variety of activities of which he is capable; that is, why did behavior take the specific direction that it did? This implies, probably correctly, that the process theories are inextricably related to choice behavior and decision making in that the individual, either consciously or unconsciously, is always selecting one direction (or behavioral alternative) and rejecting others.

To a certain extent, the content-process distinction postulated by these industrial psychologists parallels the distinction made between *primary* and *selective* buying motives (Nicosia, 1966, p. 33). Primary motives are defined as those that lead to the purchase or use of a broad class of products or services (e.g., a car), while selective motives are those that influence the selection of a particular type or brand of the product (e.g., Plymouth). In a sense, primary motives activate behavior while selective motives direct it. Again, the development of such parallel structures and concepts in separate disciplines, if occurring independently, does provide an encouraging amount of consensual and construct validity.

A Two-Factor Content Approach

The number of general content theories is legion and the more common systems (Maslow, 1954; Murray, 1938), or deriva-

tives thereof, have found their way into both organizational and consumer psychology. Probably the premiere example of a content formulation unique to the organizational context is to be found in the work of Herzberg and his colleagues (Herzberg, 1966; Herzberg, Mausner, & Snyderman, 1959). Briefly, they distinguish between intrinsic and extrinsic motivational factors. Intrinsic factors roughly translate into those associated with job content, in particular, those things that make one's work personally rewarding and satisfying. Extrinsic factors, on the other hand, are primarily associated with job context, referring to such things as the quality of one's supervision, working conditions, and company policies and practices. According to this theory, intrinsic factors mediate job satisfaction while extrinsic factors mediate job dissatisfaction. The basic tenet of the theory is that the two types of factors are independent—extrinsic factors have no effect upon feelings of satisfaction and intrinsic factors have no impact upon feelings of dissatisfaction. Parenthetically, these formulations are consistent with Katz's (1964) hypothesis that the factors which motivate an individual to join an organization are frequently different from those motivational factors which keep him there and/or those motivational factors which predispose him to perform above and beyond the level expected of him.

Due to a substantial body of disconfirming studies, Herzberg's formulations are currently considered by many to be discredited (cf., Campbell, Dunnette, Lawler, & Weick, 1970; Porter, 1966). Even so, observations from the consumer context suggest that there may be some merit in categorizing motivational factors according to such a framework. For example, it has often been noted that "the right price is only one of the criteria on which the success of a new brand turns, but if the price is not right, it alone can be responsible for its failure" (Gabor & Granger, 1965, p. 150). Similarly, the fact that most brands in a given product category possess warranties may not make the individual more likely to buy any one of them or to be happy with them once purchased, but failure to have a warranty may definitely rule a brand out. Foote (1961), then Manager of the Consumer and Public Relations Research Program for General Electric, has commented:

In the electrical appliance business, we have been impressed over and over by the way in which certain characteristics of products come to be taken for granted by consumers, especially those concerned with basic functional performance or with values like safety. If these values are missing in a product, the user is extremely offended. But if they are present, the maker or seller gets no special credit. . . .

A similar state of affairs exists in the automotive field, where consumers invariably rank safety first in importance when it comes to buying a car, yet cite power, comfort, and appearance as the factors which satisfy them most. Finally, while interacting with a pleasant salesperson in clean and pleasant surroundings may not bring about a sale, dealing with a rude salesman in an unpleasant environment will usually kill that sale.

In other words, it appears that many factors important in buying a product will, by their presence or absence, either positively or negatively affect behavior and/or subsequent satisfaction, but not both. These examples suggest a dual system, comparable to Herzberg's in many essential respects, in which one set of factors operates as "facilitators" and others as "inhibitors" of behavior —or is it satisfaction? The distinction is probably important. Herzberg's formulations have been involved with the determinants of satisfaction and dissatisfaction, not with the determinants of performance. Yet, as many an investigation has shown (cf., Brayfield & Crockett, 1955; Vroom, 1964), these two factors are not directly related. Moreover, some of the examples just provided refer entirely to purchase behavior, some entirely to satisfaction with the purchase, and some to a combination of behavior and satisfaction. This suggests that perhaps another dimension ought to be crossed with the facilitator-inhibitor dimension, namely, a behavior-satisfaction dichotomy.

Finally, some facilitators and inhibitors might be of short- or long-term duration (e.g., a rude salesperson may be considered a short-term inhibitor, while lack of a warranty is of considerably greater duration), thereby suggesting a third relevant dimension.

The result of these speculations about Herzberg's formulations in the consumer behavior context is a conceptually richer, eight-celled structure (facilitators versus inhibitors X behavior versus satisfaction X long term versus short term), and it is perhaps in more complex frameworks such as this that evidence in support of Herzberg's formulations might be found. However, regardless of whether Herzberg's formulations are or are not substantiated in this organizational context, they do offer an interesting and potentially worthwhile point of departure for research into the motivational determinants of consumer purchasing behavior and post-purchase satisfaction.

Finally, it has been noted (Campbell, Dunnette, Lawler, & Weick, 1970, p. 381) that Herzberg's fundamental postulate of independence between intrinsic and extrinsic factors remains untested. To the extent that equivalent factors can be identified in consumer behavior, testing the independence hypothesis in a consumer behavior context, where it might be somewhat easier to manipulate independent variables and to measure dependent variables, might be possible.

Process Approaches: Expectancy Theory

While the content approaches are interesting to speculate about, it is probably the process approaches which offer the greatest possibilities for mutual contribution. Campbell, Dunnette, Lawler, and Weick (1970) described three basic process approaches: stimulus-response (drive X habit) theory;

expectancy theory; and equity theory. Some S-R formulations have been applied to consumer behavior—witness Howard's (1968) applications to buyer behavior in general, and Farley and Kuehn's (1965) application to brand loyalty. These attempts, however, have not yielded any significant departures from the more general and better known formulations, nor do they seem to provide fresh insights for organizational behavior. Consequently, our emphasis will be on the expectancy and equity approaches.

The wellsprings of expectancy theory are to be found in the works of Tolman (1932) and Lewin (1938), with subsequent development coming primarily from the personality and social psychologists (Atkinson, 1958; Edwards, 1954; Peak, 1955; Rotter, 1955; Rosenberg, 1956, 1960; Fishbein, 1967). In essence, expectancy theory maintains that the motivational force to engage in any given behavior out of a set of alternative behaviors is a composite of the perceived likelihood that that given behavior will result in attaining certain outcomes, weighted by the desirability (value or importance) that the individual attaches to each of these outcomes. (Note: Use of the phrase *outcome desirability* in contrast to the more generally accepted term *value importance* is intentional. The word *outcome* plays a significant role in the conceptual elaboration of the expectancy model as described below, while the word *desirability* reflects the fact that an outcome need only be considered desirable or undesirable, not necessarily important, in order to have motivating properties.)

Thus, we have four primary variables to be considered for each individual: a set of possible behavioral alternatives; a set of outcomes; the desirability to the individual of each of these outcomes; and the individual's perception of the likelihood that engaging in each of the alternative behaviors will lead to each of the outcomes. For any individual at a given point in time, a motivational force is calculated by applying the following basic formula:

$$MF\ A_a = \Sigma(DO_k \cdot EA_a O_k)$$

where:

$MF\ A_a =$ the motivational force of alternative a,

$DO_k\quad =$ the desirability of outcome k,

$EA_a O_k =$ the expectancy that selecting alternative a will result in obtaining outcome k.

Expectancy theory thus reflects its Lewinian heritage in that it is a phenomenological field theory. It is the alternatives, outcomes, desirabilities, and expectancies as perceived by the individual and exist for him at that point in time (i.e., his immediate psychological field) which determine the direction of his behavior (i.e., which behavioral alternative he selects), not necessarily objective reality. Consequently, the dynamic nature of motivated behavior is placed into a static, cross-sectional mold.

Expectancy theory was formally introduced into the industrial psychological literature via Vroom's (1964) "instrumentality" theory of worker motivation. It has subsequently been extended and made more explicit by Graen (1969), Porter and Lawler (1968), and Campbell, Dunnette, Lawler, and Weick (1970). A simplified composite version suggested by these formulations is presented in Figure 1. Under the Behavioral Alternatives column is included the set of those behavioral acts considered possible by the individual under the circumstances (i.e., his "evoked set"; cf., March & Simon, 1958). Assume that we have a manager confronted with a subordinate who has recently started to arrive late for work every day. The manager's task is to decide upon the best course of action at that particular point in time (e.g., personally chew the subordinate out; continue to ignore it; ask him to see a personnel counselor; fire him; ask the boss what to do; etc.). The Level I Outcome column lists all of the possible direct consequences which might result (e.g., he will start to arrive on time; his work output will

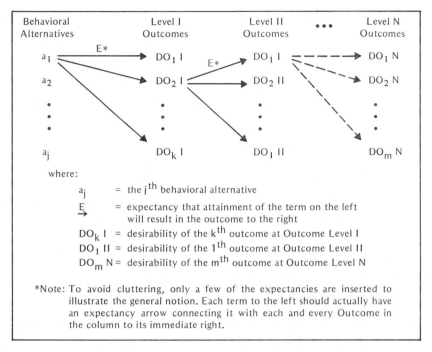

where:

a_j = the jth behavioral alternative

$\underset{\rightarrow}{E}$ = expectancy that attainment of the term on the left will result in the outcome to the right

$DO_k\,I$ = desirability of the kth outcome at Outcome Level I

$DO_1\,II$ = desirability of the 1th outcome at Outcome Level II

$DO_m\,N$ = desirability of the mth outcome at Outcome Level N

*Note: To avoid cluttering, only a few of the expectancies are inserted to illustrate the general notion. Each term to the left should actually have an expectancy arrow connecting it with each and every Outcome in the column to its immediate right.

Figure 1.   A composite industrial psychology expectancy model of motivation.

decrease; others in the office will start to come in late; the boss will be disturbed; etc.). Level II Outcomes are those consequences one step removed (e.g., if, as a result of counseling, he starts to come in on time and his productivity does not suffer, then it will lead to: praise from the boss; a raise; greater respect from the manager's other subordinates; etc.). Eventually we come to Level N Outcomes which describe the basic needs of individuals much as contained in the traditional content formulations (e.g., need for love, respect, power, etc.). Finally, the Ds and Es in Figure 1 represent the *desirability* of each of the specific outcomes to the individual and the *expectancy* —essentially a subjective probability estimate —that engaging in the specific behavior (or attainment of a previous level outcome) will lead to the specific outcome under consideration.

While the second through nth level outcomes are heuristic and interesting to consider, difficulty arises in specifying which outcomes are at which particular level. It is very likely that there are many outcomes which will be at different levels for different people and which will vary within one person over time. Probably because of such operational difficulties, no empirical work bearing on this aspect of the expectancy model exists.

The expectancy formulation raises many questions and, as noted by Campbell, Dunnette, Lawler, and Weick (1970, pp. 381–383), the literature of industrial psychology provides no data as yet to answer many of these. Two questions in particular attract our attention: (1) What is the relative contribution of expectancies and desirabilities to the motivation of individuals? (2) How do expectancies come about and how are they influenced? While investigators have only recently started to apply the expectancy formulation to consumer behavior, these applications do provide some tentative answers to these two questions.

It is very easy to apply the basic expectancy model to consumer behavior by considering the alternative courses of action that the individual can take to be represented by a set of specific brands or products that he can buy. Consider the individual who intends to purchase a single brand from among an array of fifteen different brands of toothpaste displayed in front of him. Assume further that all brands in his "evoked set" (i.e., those brands which he considers to be viable alternatives in his decision process, cf., March & Simon, 1958; Howard & Sheth, 1969) are contained in this display. The set of alternatives is thus clearly defined. Moreover, the first level outcomes are generally well-known in regard to most commonly purchased consumer products. For example, most consumers want a toothpaste to freshen breath, clean teeth, be good tasting, and prevent decay. Consequently, it is possible, using common purchasing situations, to set up realistic, less ambiguous tests of the model than may be possible in an organizational framework.

Results from such investigations are illuminating. Hansen (1969), in a series of six experiments, found that outcome desirability and perceived expectancy are predictive of both preference statements and choice behavior in simulated purchasing situations but neither, taken separately, was as good a predictor as total score. Moreover, the number of outcomes that are salient (i.e., used by the individual to a significant degree in making his choice judgment) are few. Subjects given anywhere from three to ten appropriate outcomes across the six experiments tended to reduce the number of outcomes considered by assigning desirability ratings of zero to several outcomes. When the three most desirable outcomes were taken for each subject, predictions were as good as those based on the total number of outcomes. Finally, Hansen found that the expectancies and outcome desirabilities were "highly independent."

Somewhat at variance with these findings is the work of Sheth and Talarzyk (1970). These investigators used a sample of 1,272 respondents from a national sample of female heads of households and six different product categories (frozen orange juice, mouthwash, toothpaste, toilet tissue, lipstick, and brassieres). Each product category contained five brands and five appropriate outcomes. These authors found that, without a single exception in the thirty tests they conducted, the expectancies demonstrated greater predictive power of overall purchase attitudes than did the outcome desirabilities. Moreover, combining the perceived expectancies and outcome desirabilities, as specified by the general formula, resulted in a considerable *lowering* of the predictive power, as opposed to using the expectancies alone. This finding is analogous to the effect that adding a cue with weak predictive power will have on decision making performance (Dudycha & Naylor, 1966; see also Cox, 1962). Two possible explanations were offered for these results. First, in the process of expressing expectancies on a scale anchored to specific outcomes, outcome desirabilities are probably already incorporated by the subject. Second, outcome desirabilities "are not specific to a brand but rather general for a product class. Why should they, therefore, be predictive of variances in the attitudes toward specific brands?" (Sheth & Talarzyk, 1970, p. 13).

As one considers the manner in which the expectancy model has been applied to the consumer behavior context, it is possible to see the nature of the outcomes in a different perspective, one which has implications for understanding the genesis of the expectancies. What follows represents a speculative attempt by the author to extend the basic expectancy model so as to encompass more of the elements and mechanisms involved in consumer behavior motivation. It is believed that the resultant formulation more accurately describes the relationships which actually exist and is more capable of capturing the dynamic flow of motivation. In the spirit of this chapter, perhaps this modification developed to suit a consumer context will provide insights for new ways in which the model might be applied to phenomena in both social and industrial/ organizational psychology.

The expectancy models adopt what is essentially a "pull" perspective of motivation. In other words, it is a combination of desired outcomes weighted by their respective expectancies which *attracts* the individual to one (or perhaps a select few) of the behavioral alternatives. And yet there are other motivational factors which can and do determine the behavioral response. Consider the outcomes notion as applied to the purchase of toothpaste. The salient outcomes, as noted earlier, are usually given to be: decay prevention, fresh breath, good taste, and cleaner teeth. Yet, what one's dentist recommends, what one sees and hears from advertising, whether one likes the advertisements for one brand and dislikes the advertisements for another, whether one is price conscious and motivated to get the best deal for the money, one's past experience with the various brands, etc. also exert a motivational influence and affect the direction of behavior, that is, the selection of one specific brand over another. These are not desired *outcomes* in the sense that this concept has been utilized but, rather, are motivational *inputs*. Stated somewhat differently, outcomes refer to the consequences (e.g., obtaining fewer cavities or whiter teeth) perceived as ensuing or likely to ensue from having taken a specific action, while inputs are the antecedent factors which "push" the individual to take specific courses of action. Inputs "lead to" a given action, while outcomes are perceived as likely to "result from" having taken that action.

The more commonly used term "values" (Rosenberg, 1956) can thus be partitioned into antecedent (input) and consequent (outcome) values. Antecedent and consequent are not meant to imply that these occur at temporally distinct periods in the mind of the individual. They simply take cognizance of the fact that some motivational forces lead to or push an individual to take a certain course of action, while other motivational forces arise from considering the consequences likely to arise from each of the alternatives being considered and serve to attract or pull the individual toward some alternative(s) and away from others.

The notion of functional consequences is critical here. Outcomes refer to the primary *functional* aspects of the alternatives in the product set; they are the basic purpose for buying and/or using the product to begin with. Inputs, on the other hand, are those motivational factors other than perceived functional consequences which influence the selection of one specific behavioral alternative over the other available alternatives. For example, one might like the advertising or packaging for Brand *A* over Brand *B* and may, if these were the only two motivational factors operating, be motivated to buy Brand *A*. Yet such motivational factors can in no way be considered outcomes in the same sense as preventing cavities or cleaning teeth would be.

At this point the model would appear as in Figure 2, and the formula for obtaining the motivational force of each alternative is as follows:

$$MF\,A_a = f \Sigma\,(SI_i \cdot LI_iA_a) + \Sigma\,(DO_k \cdot EA_aO_k)$$

where:

$MF\,A_a$ = the motivational force of alternative *a*,

SI_i = the significance of input *i*,

LI_iA_a = the likelihood that input *i* will lead to selecting alternative *a*,

DO_k = the desirability of outcome *k*,

EA_aO_k = the expectancy that selecting alternative *a* will result in obtaining outcome *k*.

The term significance is used to represent the importance of the input to the individual and would be assessed through questions such as: "How important are your dentist's

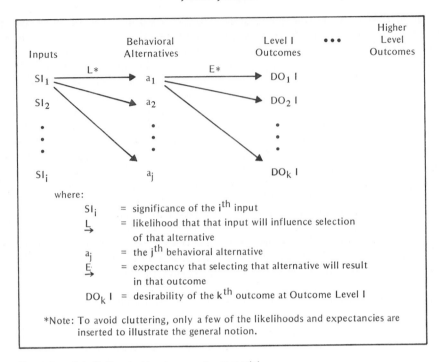

Figure 2.   A basic input-outcome expectancy model.

recommendations to you when it comes to buying toothpaste?" The likelihoods tie the inputs to specific alternatives and are assessed through questions such as: "How likely is it that what your dentist recommends will lead you to buy Brand X?"

As with Herzberg's formulations, money is the factor which might appear most likely to provide the greatest difficulty in classifying. To illustrate: While we would consider price of the brand to be an input factor, it may appear to be an outcome when phrased in more general terms like "saving money." However, reference to the primary functional criterion provides the solution. One does not buy toothpaste in order to save money, but to whiten teeth, prevent cavities, etc. Consequently, price would be treated as an input factor.

However, this does suggest an interesting question. If first order outcomes are related to higher order outcomes, is it not possible for immediately relevant inputs to be related

to higher order inputs? For example, could not the importance of price (an immediately relevant, first order input) to the individual be a function of his need to save money and be thrifty (a second order input), and could not this in turn be a function of his need for self-esteem (or some other higher level need)? In other words, perhaps there is a parallel structure on the input side which mirror-images the structure on the outcome side, with both structures eventually terminating in a common pool of basic human needs à la the context taxonomies.

Moreover, separating inputs from outcomes and placing the variables in this format suggest an answer to the question regarding the genesis of outcome expectancies. More specifically, it is conceivable that the expectancies about the purchase of Brand X leading to outcome k are simply a function of selected inputs. In other words, the expectancy that buying Crest will prevent tooth decay is probably a function of what one's dentist recommends, knowledge that this is one of the few brands to have received the American Dental Association's Council on Dental Therapeutics' seal of approval, one's past experience with the brand up to that point in time ("I switched to Crest ten years ago and haven't had a cavity since"). Furthermore, not only do inputs determine the expectancies, they are also capable of determining the number and importance of the first level outcomes. For example, advertising has been instrumental in establishing whiter teeth and "need to smell good" (an outcome appropriate for products such as deodorants, colognes, etc.) as first level outcomes possessing high desirability in contemporary American society by tying them to higher level outcomes (e.g.,

"If my teeth are white and I smell good, I will probably get promoted, be liked by everyone, and get the girl in the ad"). And so inputs can affect outcomes without having to go through the brand alternatives.

Thus, with the emergence of feedback loops, what was initially a static cross-sectional model of motivation begins to take on certain dynamic properties. Inasmuch as motivation operates as a dynamic process to begin with, this is perceived to be an advantage over the completely static models.

The resultant model may now be depicted as in Figure 3. Note that the various components are situated along an abstract-to-concrete continuum, with the most basic human needs representing the most abstract level and the alternatives (in this case, ob-

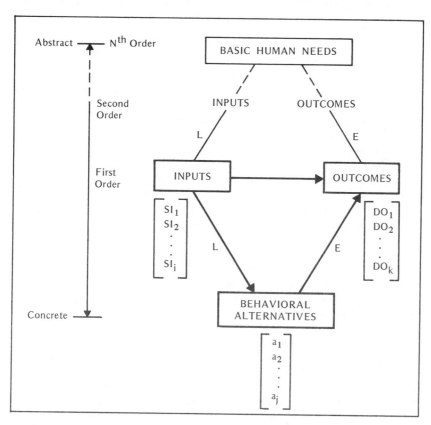

Figure 3. The structure of a motivational state for person P at time T: The complete expectancy-frame model.

jectively observable and denotable brands) available to the individual at that point in time and defining his psychological field constituting the most concrete level.

The dashed lines from the second to the nth order level are meant to suggest two things. First, the number of intermediate levels and position of specific values in the structure probably vary across individuals and possibly within each individual from time 1 to time 2. Second, not all basic human needs funnel down to affect behavior. Some are *relevant* and others *irrelevant* to the choice situation. The latter may be disregarded from further consideration while the former are further partitioned into those that are *functionally* relevant (i.e., perceived outcomes) and those that are *nonfunctionally* relevant (i.e., perceived inputs).

While the inclusion of basic human needs and higher order inputs and outcomes serves to place the model into broader conceptual perspective, it is probably true that empirical tests of the model's ability to predict specific behaviors need only be confined to the first order inputs, outcomes, and alternatives. Fortunately, it is at these levels that operationalization is easiest (Jacoby & Olson, 1974). However, to adequately understand the motivational process one must trace the first order inputs and outcomes to their root source.

The model is not truly dynamic in the sense of representing a continuous motivational flow. Rather, it suggests a sequence of discrete points which, given adequate measurement, collectively serve to adumbrate the motivational flow. It is analogous to the frames of a motion picture film and may be termed a "frame model" of the motivational process.

Each frame, as illustrated in Figure 3, represents the individual's motivational state at a given point in time. Note that Figure 3 reflects the fact that inputs, which can determine the selection of a particular alternative, can affect outcomes directly. Note, also, that the influence of the outcomes on the inputs is not explicitly outlined. This is because each frame, which represents the

individual's phenomenological field at a specific point in time, always reflects *anticipated* rather than actual consequences. The effects of actual consequences which have occurred as the result of selecting an alternative at a prior point in time (Time 1) have already been incorporated into the psychological field (under past experiences and in the reevaluation of the inputs) and are now ready to influence the next behavioral decision. Each frame represents the here and now; the situation existing at the time that the measurement is taken. It is theoretically possible to "shoot" as many frames both before and after a behavioral act and over as many behavioral acts (i.e., trials) as one wants, but each frame represents the motivational state of the individual at the point in time at which it was taken. Shifts in perceived significance and desirability values for given inputs and outcomes, respectively, are noted by comparing the appropriate values across frames, not through intra-frame analysis.

Finally, the model is capable of, and indeed ideal for, coping with intra-individual conflict situations. Obviously, as it now stands, there is built-in conflict between the competing brands in the alternative set, and there can be conflict within the set of first order inputs (e.g., "I like the ad for Brand X, but my dentist says it's bad for my teeth") and within the set of first order outcomes (e.g., the toothpaste formulas yielding greatest whitening ability generally contain a high number of abrasives harmful to tooth enamel). However, the frame concept also suggests that we apply the model to different strata of conflict as they occur over time. For example, the alternatives in the individual's phenomenological field at Frame 1 may be: buy a Christmas present for the wife; wash and wax the car; watch a football game. Given that the individual opts to buy the present, Frame 2 might include an electric toaster, electric knife, and small portable TV. Subsequent to deciding on one of these, Frame 3 would include the various brands perceived as being viable purchase alternatives. Assuming that one can "shoot" frames as easily as they can be conceptualized, the frame concept enables us to follow the psychodynamic flow and processes underlying motivated behavior.

Process Approaches: Equity Theory

Equity theory is essentially a social comparison theory in which an individual evaluates his "inputs into" versus "outputs derived from" a given situation relative to those of another, where this other may be another person, a class of people, an organization, or the individual himself relative to his experiences from an earlier point in time. To the extent that the individual perceives an imbalance in this relationship (i.e., inequity), it is postulated that he will experience dissatisfaction and be motivated to engage in some kind of activity which will restore equity. This relatively simple notion has its roots in the social exchange theories of Homans (1961) and Thibaut and Kelley (1959). Thus far it has been applied to the organizational sphere by Blau (1964), Jaques (1961), Patchen (1961), Schein (1965), Weick (1966), among others, and most formally by Adams (1963, 1965), with this latter variant later being extended by Pritchard (1969).

At its most basic level, equity theory refers to the psychologically perceived economics of human exchange in which an individual exchanges something of value to him in order to obtain something else he values. The governing principle of equity theory would seem to be "to give equal value for value received" (Adams, 1965, p. 278). In an industrial context, what one gives (i.e., the inputs) includes such factors as age, seniority, experience, education, demonstrated past performance, etc., while common outputs include pay, praise, promotion, increased responsibility, and the like. As Pritchard (1969) has noted, almost any factor (e.g., salary) may be considered as an input or outcome, depending upon the circumstances.

Let us now consider a set of counterpart notions in the consumer behavior sphere,

bearing in mind, first, that our approach is more in the spirit of hypothesis generation than hypothesis testing and, second, that our frame of reference is primarily one in which the individual operates on an "internal standard" (Pritchard, 1969, p. 205), that is, uses himself and his past experiences as the "comparison other."

Cost, effort, and time expended may be conceived of as the common consumer inputs for products received. These three classes of input variables are generally positively correlated—usually, the more expensive an item (e.g., a car, home), the greater the amount of time and effort invested in carefully selecting the output. There are, however, instances of input trade-off, for example, busy, well-to-do people are more likely to use money rather than time and/or effort as an input (cf., Jacoby, Szybillo, & Berning, 1974).

In general, however, price is the most important input in the consumer context, and the "equal value for value received" principle is reduced to "you get what you pay for." In a substantial number of product categories, in fact, time and effort inputs are held relatively constant (e.g., as when several brands of the same product are available at the same location), and price is the only input free to vary. Consideration of this simplified situation offers several insights for equity theory development.

While common sense suggests that in most instances consumers will try to buy an item at the lowest price possible, data indicate that this is generally not true. Consumers tend to have a notion of what the "fair price" of a commodity might be, both for established products (Gabor & Granger, 1964; Gabor, Granger, & Sowter, 1971; Kamen & Toman, 1970, 1971; Monroe, 1971; Scitovsky, 1944–1945) and, with surprisingly low variance, even for new and about-to-be introduced products (Peterson, 1970). Moreover, the fair price for an item is usually defined not by a specific point, but by an acceptable *range* of prices bound by upper and lower limits (Gabor & Granger, 1964, 1965, 1966; Kamen & Toman, 1970; Monroe

& Venkatesan, 1969; Monroe, 1970). With respect to this range, Engel, Kollat, and Blackwell (1968, p. 429) comment as follows:

So long as the price of a product falls within the acceptable zone, price may not be a criterion. However, if price exceeds the upper *or lower* range of acceptable prices, price becomes important and the product in question is rejected. (Italics ours)

This implies that under certain conditions, reduction in price may lead to a reduction in demand, while increase in price may lead to an increase in demand, and there is substantial evidence in support of these hypotheses (Gabor & Granger, 1965; Gabor, Granger, & Sowter, 1971; Oxenfeldt, 1958; Wasson, 1965). An experiment by Leavitt (1954) indicated that consumers more often selected the higher priced of two alternative brands for products such as cooking sherry, moth flakes, razor blades, and floor wax when the only information differentiating the two was price. More significantly, they were more prone to selecting the higher priced alternative when this price differential was large than when it was small.

Other evidence indicates "that the 'right' price has a wide latitude for some commodities and practically none for others" (Gabor & Granger, 1964, p. 42). For example, an individual "may feel that $20.00 is a fair price for a given type of electric shaver *and* also for a bracelet. However, his range might be from $17.50 to $22.50 in the case of the shaver, but from $10.00 to $35.00 in the case of the bracelet" (Kamen & Toman, 1970, p. 35). When compared to the "price paid last," consumers not only exhibit considerable readiness to buy at a lower price, "but also a substantial degree of willingness to accept prices which exceed it" (Gabor & Granger, 1965, p. 148).

Finally, though many people do avail themselves of special "sales"—a condition of temporarily lowered inputs for identical outputs—the restoration of pre-sale prices rarely

seems to generate experiences of inequity. In a similar vein, these "rules of the game" even seem to apply to situations like buying a car, then finding out and accepting the fact that the guy down the street bought the identical car for less money.

What does this body of literature imply for equity theory generally and as it is applied to organizational behavior? First and foremost, it substantiates the intrinsic validity of the equity formulations and suggests that equity in exchange may be a rather general phenomenon engaged across a wide spectrum of human behavior. Second, it suggests that equity operates within a *range,* that is, that there are upper and lower thresholds between which any and all input/output ratios are acceptable. It is only when input/output ratios move out of this range, in *either* direction, that motivational forces are activated to restore equity. Third, just as the range varies in size as a function of the type of product being considered, it may vary in size for different types of organizational activities. For example, existing federal legislation requires that males and females be paid the same (an output) for the same work (an input), indicating that, in this case, the acceptable range may be a focused point. However, it says nothing regarding differential output when such output is in terms of praise or recognition. This suggests a series of studies to determine just what the acceptance range is for selected organizational activities as perceived by specific, relatively homogeneous groups of employees (where homogeneity is defined in terms of the likelihood that these people will use each other as comparison others).

Fourth, the work of Gabor and Granger (1964, 1965, 1966) and Leavitt's (1954) experiment, in which subjects selected the higher priced of two alternatives because they believed it to be of higher quality, provide support for Pritchard's (1969, p. 209) hypothesis that individuals operating on an internal standard will prefer a high input-high output situation to one of low input-low output. Whether this would still be true under conditions in which high input would strain the resources of the individual remains an empirical question. Indeed, the question of "how high is high, and how low is low?" has not yet been answered by any of the equity theorists, except in a relative sense (i.e., an input or output is high only to the extent that it is perceived by the individual to exceed the value of the input or output for the comparison other).

Fifth, the fact that the same output can be had for less input at one point in time (e.g., during a sale) than another without generating feelings of inequity suggests that timing and other "rules of the game" are probably strong mediators of whether such feelings will be experienced or not. To the extent that the rules (norms) themselves are considered equitable, feelings of inequity will not result from the perception that, according to these rules, selected others were able to secure a more favorable input/output ratio than oneself. Accordingly, the statement "Charlie bought his car during their special sale and I bought mine two weeks later" may represent the acknowledgement of equity rather than inequity.

Sixth, these as well as other data in the consumer behavior sphere fail to corroborate Pritchard's contention that "Person will tend to maximize outcomes" (1969, p. 206). Generally speaking, consumer behavior data reflect "satisficing" (March & Simon, 1958, p. 141), rather than maximizing behavior.

Finally, while predictions made by equity theory regarding underpayment are generally supported, the predicted effects of overpayment have not been satisfactorily demonstrated (Pritchard, 1969, p. 204). In part, this is due to the nature of the manipulations typically employed, as these tend to activate feelings of self-esteem and thereby contaminate the data. Again, it may be that the consumer context, with its clearly specified inputs and outputs, offers an excellent opportunity for conducting such theory validation research.

CONCLUDING REMARKS

Given that both consumer and organizational psychology have borrowed extensively from social psychology, the basic objective of this chapter has been to suggest that each might have something to gain by examining the manner in which equivalent social psychological concepts have been considered by the other. The approach has been intentionally speculative, devoted primarily to conjecturing how the variables and findings of consumer psychology might prove useful for those primarily interested in organizational behavior.

The obvious time and space constraints limited consideration to only two broad topics. However, many more could have been examined in similar fashion. For example, one could start by selecting specific social psychological concepts and note how these might be reflected in both the organizational and consumer contexts. Decision making, both of the individual and group variety, and attitudes would be high up on the list of concepts to be so examined. Other specific possibilities include the need for esteem (which corresponds to "conspicuous consumption" and "snob appeal products" in the consumer sphere and the notion of status or "status symbols" in the organizational sphere), and the risky shift phenomenon (as it might be reflected in both family purchase decisions and in organizational conference and meeting behavior).

Another possible approach would be to start with a concept indigenous to one domain and consider how it could possibly be applied to the other. As examples, brand switching could be equated with job switching (cf., March & Simon, 1958, pp. 106–108; Nicosia, 1966, pp. 108–112), selling with recruiting (selling a job), product design with man-machine (human factors) applications, and market segmentation with work group segmentation (e.g., managers versus foremen, line versus staff, etc.). Finally, additional possibilities for mutual contribution exist with respect to considering the common methodologies and techniques employed in organizational and consumer psychology (e.g., surveys, interviews, questionnaires, attitude scales and other attitude measuring devices, etc.). It should be kept in mind that the possibilities cited are meant to be suggestive, not exhaustive, and numerous others certainly exist.

However, the utility that one domain has for the other goes beyond serving as a rich source of hypotheses. As suggested in the section on motivation, the consumer context, because it contains a large number of variables which are more amenable to control and easier to bring into the laboratory, provides some unique opportunities for testing certain organizational hypotheses. The reverse may also be true; the organizational context, under some conditions, may be able to provide opportunities for cleaner tests of hypotheses regarding consumer behavior.

Finally, investigators cannot help but be encouraged when propositions regarding behavior derived and applied in one domain can also be demonstrated to explain behavior in other domains. Perhaps the greatest utility of exercises such as this one, both for the respective domains and for psychology in general, is the possibility of more firmly establishing the more general applicability of many of the theories and models of social psychology. It can only be hoped that this chapter will stimulate some of the research necessary for establishing this greater generality.

REFERENCES

Adams, J. S. Toward an understanding of inequity. *Journal of Abnormal and Social Psychology,* 1963, 67, 422–436.

Adams, J. S. Inequity in social exchange. In L. Berkowitz (Ed.), *Advances in experimental social psychology,* Vol. 2. New York: Academic Press, 1965, 267–299.

American Psychological Association. Guidelines for doctoral education in industrial psychology. *American Psychologist,* 1965, 20, 822–831.

Anastasi, A. *Fields of applied psychology.* New York: McGraw-Hill, 1964.

Arndt, J. Word of mouth advertising and informal communication. In D. F. Cox (Ed.), *Risk taking and information handling in consumer behavior.* Cambridge: Harvard University Press, 1967, 188–239. (a)

Arndt, J. *Word of mouth advertising.* New York: Advertising Research Foundation, 1967. (b)

Arndt, J. Perceived risk, sociometric integration, and word of mouth in the adoption of a new product. In D. F. Cox (Ed.), *Risk taking and information handling in consumer behavior.* Cambridge: Harvard University Press, 1967, 289–316. (c)

Atkinson, J. W., Ed. *Motives in fantasy, action, and society.* Princeton: Van Nostrand, 1958.

Barnett, H. G. *Innovation: The basis of cultural change.* New York: McGraw-Hill, 1953.

Bass, B. M. *Organizational psychology.* Boston: Allyn and Bacon, 1965.

Bauer, R. A. The initiative of the audience. *Journal of Advertising Research,* 1963, 3, 2–7.

Bauer, R. A. Source effect and persuasibility: A new look. In D. F. Cox (Ed.), *Risk taking and information handling in consumer behavior.* Cambridge: Harvard University Press, 1967, 559–578.

Baumgarten, S. A. The male fashion change agent on the college campus. Unpublished doctoral dissertation, Purdue University, Lafayette, Ind., 1971.

Bell, W. E. Consumer innovators: A unique market for newness. In S. A. Greyser (Ed.), *Toward scientific marketing. Proceedings of the winter conference of the American Marketing Association, 1963.* Chicago: American Marketing Association, 1963, 85–95.

Berelson, B., Lazarfeld, P., & McPhee, W. *Voting: A study of opinion formulation in a presidential campaign.* Chicago: University of Chicago Press, 1954.

Berning, C. A. K., & Jacoby, J. Patterns of information acquisition in new product purchases. *Journal of Consumer Research,* 1974, 1 (2), 18–22.

Blau, P. *Exchange and power in social life.* New York: Wiley, 1964.

Bohlen, J. M., Coughenour, C. M., Lionberger, H. F., Moe, E. O., & Rogers, E. M. Adopters of new farm ideas. In H. H. Kassarjian & T. S. Robertson (Eds.), *Perspectives in consumer behavior.* Glenview, Ill.: Scott, Foresman, 1968, 351–361.

Brayfield, A. H., & Crockett, W. H. Employee attitudes and performance. *Psychological Bulletin,* 1955, 52, 396–428.

Brehm, J. W. *A theory of psychological reactance.* New York: Academic Press, 1966.

Campbell, D. T., & Stanley, J. C. *Experimental and quasi-experimental designs for research.* Chicago: Rand McNally, 1963.

Campbell, J. P., Dunnette, M. D., Lawler, E. E. III, & Weick, K. E. Jr. *Managerial behavior and human performance.* New York: McGraw-Hill, 1970.

Carter, C. F., & Williams, B. R. *Industry and technological progress: Factors governing the speed of application of science.* London: Oxford University Press, 1957.

Carter, C. F., & Williams, B. R. The characteristics of technologically progressive firms. *Journal of Industrial Economics,* 1959, 7, 87–104.

Coch, L., & French, J. R. P. Jr. Overcoming resistance to change. *Human Relations,* 1948, 1, 512–532.

Coleman, J. S., Katz, E., & Menzel, H. The diffusion of an innovation among physicians. *Sociometry,* 1957, 20, 253–270.

Coleman, J. S., Katz, E., & Menzel, H. *Medical innovation: A diffusion study.* Indianapolis: Bobbs-Merrill, 1966.

Coleman, J. S., Menzel, H., & Katz, E. Social processes in physicians' adoption of a new drug. *Journal of Chronic Diseases,* 1959, 9, 1–9.

Coleman, R. P. The significance of social stratification in selling. *Proceedings of the American Marketing Association,* December, 1960, 171–184.

Coney, K. A. Dogmatism and innovation: A replication. *Journal of Marketing Research,* 1973, 9, 453–455.

Cox, D. F. The measurement of information value: A study in consumer decision making. In W. S. Decker (Ed.), *Emerging concepts in marketing. Proceedings of the Winter Conference of the American Marketing Association.* Chicago: American Marketing Association, 1962, 413–421.

Cox, D. F. The audience as communicators. In S. A. Greyser (Ed.), *Toward scientific marketing.* Chicago: American Marketing Association, 1963, 58–72.

Cox, D. F. Risk taking and information handling in consumer behavior. In D. F. Cox (Ed.), *Risk taking and information handling in consumer behavior.* Cambridge: Harvard University Press, 1967, 604–639.

Cunningham, S. M. Perceived risk as a factor in informal communications. In D. F. Cox (Ed.), *Risk taking and information handling in consumer behavior.* Cambridge: Harvard University Press, 1967, 265–288.

Cyert, R. M., & MacCrimmon, K. R. Organizations. In G. Lindzey & E. Aronson (Eds.), *The handbook of social psychology,* Vol. 1. Reading, Mass.: Addison-Wesley, 1969, 568–611.

Cyert, R. M., & March, J. G. Organizational structure and pricing behavior in an oligopolistic market. *American Economic Review,* March, 1955, 129–139.

Davis, K. Making constructive use of the office grapevine. In K. Davis & W. G. Scott (Eds.), *Readings in human relations.* New York: McGraw-Hill, 1959.

Dichter, E. How word of mouth advertising works. *Harvard Business Review,* 1966, 44, 147–166.

Dudycha, L. W., & Naylor, J. C. Characteristics of the human inference process in complex choice behavior situations. *Organizational Behavior and Human Performance,* 1966, 1, 110–128.

Edwards, W. The theory of decision making. *Psychological Bulletin,* 1954, 51, 380–417.

Engel, J. F., Blackwell, R. D., & Kegerreis, R. J. How information is used to adopt an innovation. *Journal of Advertising Research,* 1969, 9, 3–8.

Engel, J. F., Kegerreis, R. J., & Blackwell, R. D. Word of mouth communication by the innovator. *Journal of Marketing,* 1969, 33, 15–19.

Engel, J. F., Kollat, D. T., & Blackwell, R. D. *Consumer behavior.* New York: Holt, Rinehart and Winston, 1968.

Farley, J. V., & Kuehn, A. A. Stochastic models of brand switching. In G. Schwartz (Ed.), *Science in marketing.* New York: Wiley, 1965, 444–464.

Feldman, S. P. Some dyadic relationships associated with consumer choice. In R. M. Haas

(Ed.), *Science technology and marketing.* Chicago: American Marketing Association, 1966, 758–776.

Feldman, S., & Spencer, M. The effect of personal influence in the selection of consumer services. In P. D. Bennett (Ed.), *Proceedings of the Fall conference of the American Marketing Association.* Chicago: American Marketing Association, 1965, 440–452.

Ferguson, L. W. *The heritage of industrial psychology.* Hartford, Conn.: Finlay Press, 1962.

Fishbein, M. A. Attitude and the prediction of behavior. In M. A. Fishbein (Ed.), *Readings in attitude theory and measurement.* New York: Wiley, 1967, 477–492.

Foote, N. N. *Consumer behavior: Household decision making,* Vol. 4. New York: New York University Press, 1961.

Frank, R. E., Massy, W. F., & Morrison, D.˙G. The determinants of innovative behavior with respect to a branded, frequently purchased food product. In *Proceedings of the American Marketing Association.* Chicago: American Marketing Association, 1964, 312–323.

Gabor, A., & Granger, C. W. J. Price sensitivity of the consumer. *Journal of Advertising Research,* 1964, 4, 40–44.

Gabor, A., & Granger, C. W. J. The pricing of new products. *Scientific Business,* 1965, 3, 141–150.

Gabor, A., & Granger, C. W. J. Price as an indicator of quality: Report on an inquiry. *Economica,* 1966, 33, 43–70.

Gabor, A., Granger, C. W. J., & Sowter, A. P. Comments on "Psychophysics of prices." *Journal of Marketing Research,* 1971, 8, 251–252.

Gillfillian, C. S. *The sociology of invention.* Chicago: Follett, 1935.

Graen, G. Instrumentality theory of work motivation: Some experimental results and suggested modifications. *Journal of Applied Psychology,* Monograph, 1969, 53, No. 2, Part 2.

Gross, E. J. Support for a generalized marketing leadership theory. *Journal of Advertising Research,* 1969, 9, 49–52.

Guion, R. M. Industrial psychology as an academic discipline. *American Psychologist,* 1965, 20, 815–821.

Haire, M. Industrial social psychology. In G. Lindzey (Ed.), *The handbook of social psychology,* Vol. 2. Reading, Mass.: Addison-Wesley, 1954, 1104–1123.

Hansen, F. Consumer choice behavior: An experimental approach. *Journal of Marketing Research,* 1969, 6, 436–443.

Hart, E. W. Jr., & Jacoby, J. Novelty, recency, and scarcity as predictors of perceived newness. *Proceedings, 81st annual convention of the American Psychological Association,* 1973, 8, 839–840.

Hepner, H. W. *Psychology applied to life and work.* (4th ed.) Englewood Cliffs, N.J.: Prentice-Hall, 1966.

Herzberg, F. *Work and the nature of man.* Cleveland: World Publishing, 1966.

Herzberg, F., Mausner, B., & Synderman, B. *The motivation to work.* (2nd ed.) New York: Wiley, 1959.

Homans, G. C. *Social behavior: Its elementary forms.* New York: Harcourt, Brace and World, 1961.

Howard, J. A. Learning and consumer behavior. In H. H. Kassarjian & T. S. Robertson (Eds.), *Perspective in consumer behavior.* Glenview, Ill.: Scott, Foresman, 1968, 93–103.

Howard, J. A., & Sheth, J. N. *The theory of buyer behavior.* New York: Wiley, 1969.

Jacoby, J. Examining the "other" organization: A methodology for studying the informal organizational structure of complex organizations. *Personnel Administration,* 1968, 31, 36–42.

Jacoby, J. Toward a definition of consumer psychology: One psychologist's views. Paper delivered as part of a symposium entitled "Toward a definition of consumer psychology," 77th Annual Convention of the American Psychological Association, Washington, D.C., September, 1969.

Jacoby, J. Training consumer psychologists: The Purdue University program. *Professional Psychology,* 1971, 2, 300–302. (a)

Jacoby, J. A multi-indicant approach for studying new product adopters. *Journal of Applied Psychology,* 1971, 55, 384–388. (b)

Jacoby, J. Is consumer psychology the legitimate child of social psychology? Presidential address to the Division of Consumer Psychology, 82nd annual convention of the American Psychological Association, New Orleans, 1974. (Revised version, in press, *American Psychologist.*) (a)

Jacoby, J. The construct validity of opinion

leadership. *Public Opinion Quarterly,* 1974, 38 (1), 81–89. (b)

Jacoby, J., & Olson, J. C. An extended expectancy model of consumer comparison processes. In S. Ward & P. Wright (Eds.), *Advances in consumer research,* Vol. I. Urbana, Illinois: Association for Consumer Research, 1974, 319–333.

Jacoby, J., Szybillo, G. J., & Berning, C. A. K. Time and consumer behavior: Interdisciplinary neglect of a fundamental relationship. In R. Ferber (Ed.), *Synthesis of consumer behavior: A project report to the National Science Foundation,* in preparation. Available as *Purdue Papers in consumer psychology,* 1974, No. 139.

Jaques, E. *Equitable payment.* New York: Wiley, 1961.

Kamen, J. M., & Toman, R. J. Psychophysics of prices. *Journal of Marketing Research,* 1970, 7, 27–35.

Kamen, J. M., & Toman, R. J. Psychophysics of prices: A reaffirmation. *Journal of Marketing Research,* 1971, 8, 252–257.

Kaplan, L .B., Szybillo, G. J., & Jacoby, J. The varieties of perceived product risk: A cross-validation. *Journal of Applied Psychology,* 1974, 59 (3), 287–291.

Katz, D. The motivational basis of organizational behavior. *Behavioral Science,* 1964, 9, 131–146.

Katz, E. The two-step flow of communication: An up-to-date report on an operating hypothesis. *Public Opinion Quarterly,* 1957, 20, 61–78. (a)

Katz, E. The two-step flow of communication. *Public Opinion Quarterly,* 1957, 21, 67–68, 73–76. (b)

Katz, E., & Lazarsfeld, P. F. *Personal influence: The part played by people in the flow of mass communications.* Glencoe, Ill.: The Free Press, 1955.

Katzell, R. A. Industrial psychology. *Annual Review of Psychology,* 1958, 9, 237–268.

King, C. W. Fashion adoption: A rebuttal to the "trickle down" theory. In S. Greyser (Ed.), *Proceedings of the winter conference of the American Marketing Association.* Chicago: American Marketing Association, 1963, 108–128.

King, C. W., & Summers, J. O. Dynamics of interpersonal communication: The interaction dyad. In D. F. Cox (Ed.), *Risk taking and information handling in consumer behavior.* Cambridge: Harvard University Press, 1967, 240–264.

King, C. W., & Summers, J. O. Overlap of opinion leadership across consumer product categories. *Journal of Marketing Research,* 1970, 7, 43–50.

Krugman, H. E. Consumer behavior. *International encyclopedia of the social sciences.* New York: Macmillan and The Free Press, 1968, 349–354.

Lazarsfeld, P. F., Berelson, B., & Gaudet, H. *The people's choice.* (2nd ed.) New York: Columbia University Press, 1948.

Lazer, W., & Bell, W. E. The communication process and innovation. *Journal of Advertising Research,* 1966, 6, 2–8.

Leavitt, H. J. A note on some experimental findings about the meaning of price. *Journal of Business,* 1954, 27, 205–210.

Leavitt, H. J. Toward organizational psychology. In G. B. von Haller (Ed.), *Walter Van Dyke Bingham.* Pittsburgh: Carnegie Institute of Technology Press, 1962, 23–30.

Leavitt, H. J., & Bass, B. M. Organizational psychology. In P. R. Farnsworth (Ed.), *Annual review of psychology,* Vol. 15. Palo Alto, Calif.: Annual Reviews, 1964, 371–398.

Lewin, K. *The conceptual representation and the measurement of psychological forces.* Durham, N.C.: Duke University Press, 1938.

Likert, R. *New patterns of management.* New York: McGraw-Hill, 1961.

MacKinney, A., & Dunnette, M. D. The industrial psychologist's job. *Personnel Psychology,* 1964, 17, 271–280.

Mancuso, J. R. Why not create opinion leaders for new product introductions? *Journal of Marketing,* 1969, 33, 20–25.

Mansfield, E. Acceptance of technological change: The speed of response of individual firms. (Mimeo.) Pittsburgh: Graduate School of Industrial Administration, Carnegie Institute of Technology, 1960.

Mansfield, E. Technological change and the rate of imitation. *Econometrica,* 1961, 29, 741–766. (a)

Mansfield, E. Innovation, size of firm, and market structure. (Mimeo.) Pittsburgh: Graduate School of Industrial Administration, Carnegie Institute of Technology, 1961. (b)

March, J. G., & Simon, H. A. *Organizations.* New York: Wiley, 1958.

Maslow, A. H. *Motivation and personality.* New York: Harper and Row, 1954.

Melcher, A. J., & Beller, R. Toward a theory of organization communication: Consideration in channel selection. *Academy of Management Journal,* 1967, 10, 39–52.

Menzel, H., & Katz, E. Social relations and innovations in the medical profession: The epidemiology of a new drug. *Public Opinion Quarterly,* Winter, 1955–1956, 19, 337–352.

Miller, G. R. On defining communication: Another stab. *Journal of Communication,* 1966, 26, 88–99.

Monroe, K. B. The measurement of price thresholds: Psychophysics and attitudes of acceptance. In D. L. Sparks (Ed.), *Broadening the concept of marketing.* Chicago: American Marketing Association Fall conference proceedings, 1970, 120.

Monroe, K. B. Psychophysics of prices: A reappraisal. *Journal of Marketing Research,* 1971, 8, 248–250.

Monroe, K. B., & Venkatesan, M. The concepts of price limits and psychophysical measurement: A laboratory experiment. In P. R. McDonald (Ed.), *Marketing involvement in society and the economy.* Chicago: American Marketing Association Fall conference proceedings, 1969, 345–351.

Murray, H. A. *Explorations in personality.* New York: Oxford University Press, 1938.

Myers, J. G. Patterns of interpersonal influence in the adoption of new products. In R. M. Hass (Ed.), *Science technology and marketing.* Chicago: American Marketing Association, 1966, 750–757.

Nicosia, F. M. *Consumer decision processes.* Englewood Cliffs, N.J.: Prentice-Hall, 1966.

Nilsen, T. R. On defining communication. *The Speech Teacher,* 1957, 6, 10–18.

Oxenfeldt, A. R. *Establishing a new product program: Guides for effective planning and organization, Report No. 8.* New York: American Management Association, Marketing Division, 1958.

Patchen, M. *The choice of wage comparisons.* Englewood Cliffs, N.J.: Prentice-Hall, 1961.

Peak, H. Attitude and motivation. In M. R. Jones (Ed.), *Nebraska symposium on motivation.* Lincoln: University of Nebraska Press, 1955, 149–188.

Perloff, R. Roles of consumer and psychology in consumer psychology. *Psychological Reports,* 1963, 13, 931–933.

Perloff, R. The work of the industrial psychologist in relation to consumers and the public. *Business and Society,* 1964, 4, 23–24.

Peterson, R. A. The price-perceived quality relationship: Experimental evidence. *Journal of Marketing Research,* 1970, 7, 525–528.

Porter, L. W. Personnel management. *Annual Review of Psychology,* 1966, 17, 395–422.

Porter, L. W., & Lawler, E. E. *Managerial attitudes and performance.* Homewood, Ill.: Dorsey-Irwin, 1968.

Porter, L. W., & Roberts, K. H. Communication in organizations. In M. D. Dunnette (Ed.), *Handbook of industrial and organizational psychology.* Chicago: Rand McNally, 1976.

Pritchard, R. D. Equity theory: A review and critique. *Organizational Behavior and Human Performance,* 1969, 4, 176–211.

Robertson, T. S. Social factors in innovative behavior. In H. H. Kassarjian & T. S. Robertson (Eds.), *Perspectives in consumer behavior.* Glenview, Ill.: Scott, Foresman, 1968, 361–370.

Robertson, T. S. *New product diffusion.* New York: Holt, Rinehart and Winston, 1971.

Rogers, E. M. *Diffusion of innovations.* New York: The Free Press, 1962.

Rogers, E. M., & Cartano, D. G. Methods of measuring opinion leadership. *Public Opinion Quarterly,* 1962, 26, 435–441.

Rogers, E. M., & Shoemaker, F. F. *Communication of innovations: A cross-cultural approach.* New York: The Free Press, 1971.

Rogers, E. M., & Stanfield, J. D. Adoption and diffusion of new products: Emerging generalizations and hypotheses. In F. M. Bass, C. W. King, & E. Pessemeier (Eds.), *Applications of the sciences in marketing management.* New York: Wiley, 1968.

Rosenberg, M. J. Cognitive structure and attitudinal affect. *Journal of Abnormal and Social Psychology,* 1956, 53, 367–372.

Rosenberg, M. J. An analysis of affective-cognitive consistency. In C. I. Hovland & M. J. Rosenberg (Eds.), *Attitude organization and change.* New Haven: Yale University Press, 1960, 15–64.

Rotter, J. B. The role of the psychological situation in determining the direction of human behavior. In M. R. Jones (Ed.), *Nebraska symposium on motivation.* Lincoln: University of Nebraska Press, 1955.

Schein, E. H. *Organizational psychology.* New York: Prentice-Hall, 1965.

Scitovsky, T. Some consequences of the habit of judging quality by price. *The Review of Economic Studies,* 1944–1945, 12 (2), No. 32.

Scott, W. D. *The theory of advertising.* Boston: Small, Maynard, 1903.

Scott, W. D. *The psychology of advertising.* Boston: Small, Maynard, 1908. (a)

Scott, W. D. *The psychology of advertising in theory and practice.* Boston: Small, Maynard, 1908. (b)

Scott, W. D. *Increasing human efficiency in business.* New York: Macmillan, 1911. (a)

Scott, W. D. *Influencing men in business.* New York: Ronald, 1911. (b)

Shannon, C. E., & Weaver, W. *The mathematical theory of communication.* Urbana: University of Illinois Press, 1949.

Sheth, J. N. Perceived risk and the diffusion of innovations. In J. Arndt (Ed.), *Insights into consumer behavior.* Boston: Allyn and Bacon, 1968, 173–188.

Sheth, J. N., & Talarzyk, W. W. Relative contribution of perceived instrumentality and value importance components in determining attitudes. Paper presented at the 1970 Fall conference of the American Marketing Association. An abstract appears in D. L. Sparks (Ed.), *Broadening the concept of marketing.* Chicago: American Marketing Association, 1970, 35.

Summers, J. O. The identity of women's clothing fashion opinion leaders. *Journal of Marketing Research,* 1970, 7, 178–185.

Summers, J. O., & King, C. W. Interpersonal communication and new product attitudes. In P. R. McDonald (Ed.), *Marketing involvement in society and the economy. Fall conference proceedings.* Chicago: American Marketing Association, 1969, 292–299.

Summers, J. O., & King, C. W. Overlap of opinion leadership: A reply. *Journal of Marketing Research,* 1971, 8, 259–261.

Thibaut, J. W., & Kelley, H. H. *The social psychology of groups.* New York: Wiley, 1959.

Tiffin, J., & McCormick, E. J. *Industrial psychology.* (5th ed.) Englewood Cliffs, N.J.: Prentice-Hall, 1965.

Tolman, E. C. *Purposive behavior in animals and men.* New York: Appleton-Century-Crofts, 1932.

Vroom, V. H. *Work and motivation.* New York: Wiley, 1964.

Vroom, V. H. Industrial social psychology. In G. Lindzey & E. Aronson (Eds.), *The handbook of social psychology,* Vol. 5. Reading, Mass.: Addison-Wesley, 1969, 196–268.

Vroom, V. H., & Maier, N. R. F. Industrial social psychology. *Annual Review of Psychology,* 1961, 12, 413–446.

Wasson, C. R. The psychological aspects of price. In C. R. Wasson (Ed.), *The economics of managerial decision: Profit opportunity analysis.* New York: Appleton-Century-Crofts, 1965, 130–133.

Weick, K. E. The concept of equity in the perception of pay. *Administrative Science Quarterly,* 1966, 11, 414–439.

PART THREE

Description and Measurement of Organizations and of Behavioral Processes in Organizations

SECTION V.

Attributes of Organizations and Their Effects on Organization Members

J. RICHARD HACKMAN
Yale University

INDUSTRIAL AND ORGANIZATIONAL PSYCHOLO-GISTS have traditionally—and validly—viewed behavior in organizations as jointly determined by characteristics of the individual organization members, and the characteristics of the organization itself. Research in industrial psychology, however, has been heavily skewed toward the individual. Substantial knowledge now is available about the attributes of individuals which are important for understanding behavior in organizations; less is known about the organizational side of the equation.

While the translation from broad, organizational-level concepts to immediate, proximal influences on individual organization members is always difficult, the chapters in this section may provide some help. The chapters provide a number of new ways of conceptualizing and researching organizational attributes, and both summarize and extend what currently is known about the effects of such attributes on behavior within organizational systems.

The chapters in the section are roughly ordered in terms of how "molar" the perspective of each chapter is. Thus, the section begins with an examination of the environment of organizations themselves, and ends with a detailed assessment of one set of structural devices (control systems) which can have rather direct effects on the day-to-day behavior of individuals in organizations.

In Chapter 25, Starbuck attacks the large and diffuse issue of the relationship between organizations and their environments. In the opening pages of the chapter, Starbuck focuses on the question of demarcation; that is, where does the organization end and the environment begin? The way in which this question is answered, it turns out, has some provocative implications for how one goes about researching organizations—and, indeed, what organizations actually are and are not.

One of the major contributions of the Starbuck chapter is the presentation of a systematic framework for analyzing the logical associations which are possible between organizational characteristics and environmental characteristics. Within each cell of the framework, extensive bibliographic references are provided—which should be of considerable help to the reader in organizing and making sense of the massive literature having to do with organization-environment relations.

The chapter concludes with a discussion of the dynamics of organization-environment relations over time. Special attention is given to some thorny methodological problems which must be overcome by researchers who choose to construe organizations as long-lived, dynamic, adaptive systems operating in a fluid environment. Throughout the chapter Starbuck keeps a sharp eye out for both methodological and conceptual-philosophical issues which must be confronted if the complex, two-way relationships between organizations and their environments are to be better understood.

Chapter 26 also deals with organizations as total units, but takes as organizing focus the widely popular (but often amorphous) concepts of organizational "structure" and "climate." This chapter, by Payne and Pugh, provides a systematic and detailed look at organizational structure and climate from three different perspectives:

1. How structure and climate are affected by the context or environment of the organization—providing some interesting points of linkage with Chapter 25.

2. How structure and climate affect the attitudes and behavior of organization members.

3. How organizational structure and organizational climate themselves interrelate.

Throughout the chapter, special attention is given to comparisons between objective and subjective strategies for measuring structure and climate. The authors document the great diversity of ways the concepts have been operationalized and measured—and show how research findings can be significantly altered by the measurement strategy used. The chapter concludes with a summary of what is and is not known about the correlates of organizational structure and climate—and with both a pessimistic and optimistic view of the future of these concepts in research on organizations.

In Chapters 25 and 26 the external boundaries of organizations are viewed as significant for understanding both the structural makeup of organizations and the relationships between organizations and their environments. Adams in Chapter 27 also focuses attention on organization boundaries —and examines in considerable detail the special roles organizations develop for carrying out the "acquisition" and "disposal" functions which must take place at system boundaries.

Central to the chapter is a new structural model of organizational boundary systems, which specifies both the unique properties of boundary roles and the major sources of influence on the behavior of people who occupy such roles. Particular emphasis is given to the "bargaining" activities required of boundary role occupants. Research evidence relevant to each of the major sources of influence on boundary role behavior is reviewed, including several findings which have emerged from recent research prompted by the Adams model.

Throughout the chapter, the interdependencies among the components of the model are emphasized, and compelling arguments are advanced for the importance of considering behavior at organizational boundaries in "systems" terms.

Graen in Chapter 28 also takes a systems approach to understanding roles and role behavior in organizations. The particular focus of the chapter, however, is the process by which organization members learn, adjust to, and influence the definition of their organizational roles and jobs.

The chapter is based on the premise that the traditional, "fixed slot" model of organizations is becoming an increasingly inappropriate organizational form for contemporary society. Instead, Graen argues, organizations must become more capable of dealing quickly and effectively with fluid, fast-changing environments—and this will require a more open, dynamic process of role and job definition.

The model of the "role-making process" proposed in Chapter 28 is one contribution toward this end. Based on contemporary role theory and motivational theory, the model views the role-making process as continuous and always incomplete, as the individual and the organization adapt and readapt to each other. One organizational attribute which receives special attention in the chapter is the nature of the organizational reward system. The reward system is seen as one of the crucial "assimilating mechanisms" in the role-making process.

The last half of the chapter focuses on issues of research strategy relevant to study of role-making processes in organizations. Graen argues that traditional research procedures are likely to miss the mark in the study of role making and other dynamic processes in organizations, and an alternative "open systems" research strategy is proposed. The chapter concludes with the presentation of some recent data which illustrate and test parts of the role making model.

In Chapter 29, Lawler provides a simultaneously detailed and broad-ranging review of control systems—a particular structural feature which is increasingly present in contemporary work organizations. After reviewing several types of control systems (and the reasons why certain managers prefer some types of systems over others), Lawler launches into an extended discussion of the effects of control systems on behavior in organizations. He first shows how control systems can have dysfunctional consequences for organizations (for example, by increasing the level of "bureaucratic" behavior among members, and by eliciting invalid data about system performance). Then attention turns to the reasons for such dysfunctional outcomes, and some suggestions are made for how member resistance to control systems can be decreased and how control systems can be used to prompt increased *self*-control on the part of organization members.

A distinguishing feature of the chapter is the use throughout of a "thermostat" model of organizational controls. As each substantive question is dealt with, the response is framed in terms of the operation of a thermostat—for example, by asking "Who sets the standards," "What is sensed or measured," "Who acts as the discriminator," "What kind of action is taken to turn on or off the activity," and so on.

CHAPTER 25

Organizations and Their Environments

WILLIAM H. STARBUCK

University of Wisconsin-Milwaukee

ASSUMING ORGANIZATIONS can be sharply distinguished from their environments distorts reality by compressing into one dichotomy a melange of continuously varying phenomena. Studies allowing for mutual interpenetrations between organizations and environments could reveal conditions which determine organizations' independence from their environments, could generate job and organizational taxonomies and measures of effectiveness, and most importantly, could revolutionize the concept of what an organization is.

Organizations' environments are largely invented by organizations themselves. Organizations select their environments from ranges of alternatives, then they subjectively perceive the environments they inhabit. The processes of both selection and perception are unreflective, disorderly, incremental, and strongly influenced by social norms and customs. One consequence is great variety in how organization-environment relations have been conceptualized. Another consequence is unexploited opportunities for studying organizational perception systems.

There are two distinct strategies for studying organizational adaption over time. The first strategy treats an organization as a flexible system which persists by changing its structure and form. Studies taking this approach will have to use more interventionist techniques and emphasize predictive validity more than they have in the past. The second strategy views organizations as successions of static structures which are endlessly replaced: the histories of individual organizations become comparatively unimportant artifacts of the tasks and rules societies impose on organizations, and research studies emphasize evolutionary models of large aggregates of organizations.

INTRODUCTION

This chapter is symbolized by Jonah trying to swallow the whale.

Several weeks of preparatory reading demonstrated how extensive and heterogeneous is the literature on organization-environment relations. Not only has there been no comprehensive summary of what is known, but some of the most interesting and relevant studies have been published in journals which organization theorists ordinarily ignore. So a thorough review and synthesis would bring genuine benefits. Moreover, the literature is riddled with intriguing and potentially fruitful, but partially developed, notions that cry out for elaboration and theoretical cultivation. And there are more than a few conceptual vestibules that open onto whole vistas of unexplored research terrain. It was not difficult to outline a chapter which promised to be socially useful without boring anyone.

The finished document deviates somewhat from its initial outline, however. Close examination disclosed that only a book could effectively summarize what has already been written, and quite a long book would be needed at that. Bringing immature ideas to ripeness could not be adopted as a primary objective because of time constraints: at least for this author, ideas will not mature according to a schedule. So the central thrust had to become the pointing out of portals which evidently lead to vast unexplored regions, together with enough editorial comments about theory and method to facilitate the work of exploration. But even this restricted objective exploded into an unmanageably large task during the writing process, as each opened door revealed a long gallery of doors to be opened. In consequence, the material to follow covers less than one-third of the originally planned content.

The chapter is composed of three main sections, each divided into several sub-sections. The first, titled *Boundaries,* is concerned with the demarcation between an organization and its environment. The second, titled *Domains, Roles, and Territories,* discusses the logical associations between organizational and environmental characteristics. And the third, titled *Adaptation, Evolution, and Research Strategy,* is devoted to the dynamics over time of organization-environment relations. However, all three sections possess similar general orientations —indicating some fundamental philosophical issues and the methodological dilemmas they create, surveying alternative conceptual formulations and their implications for research strategy, and identifying subject areas in which research effort ought to be especially productive. None seriously attempts to synthesize a body of knowledge, although two tables in the middle section do sketch conceptual frameworks and fill them with bibliographic references which it is hoped other researchers will find useful.

The net result cannot fail to persuade researchers that the study of organization-environment relations offers adequate scope for them to expend their time and to release their energies. One can easily avoid being bored by familiar, carefully worked out ideas and integrated sets of concepts. Unless he consciously seeks to do so, one researcher is unlikely to find himself even brushing against another's territory. Not only do the puzzles not unravel themselves, but a large percentage resemble Gordian knots. And very modest searches will uncover questions about which no relevant data have ever been collected.

Merely the vision of such opportunities must be irresistibly attractive...to people with a craving for whale.

BOUNDARIES

One difficulty inherent in studying organizations' relations with their environments is that organization must be distinguished from environment. Even talking about an organization's environment implies that the organization differs from its environment. Yet the two are not separate, and a boundary between them is partially an arbitrary invention of the perceiver (Child, 1969, 1972; Thompson, 1962).

An organization displays some of the properties of a cloud or magnetic field. When one is far enough inside it, he can see its characteristics and effects all about him; and when one is far enough outside it, he can see that it comprises a distinctive section of social space. But as he approaches the boundary, the boundary fades into ambiguity and becomes only a region of gradual transition that extends from the organization's central core far out into the surrounding space. One can sometimes say "Now I am inside" or "Now I am outside," but he can never confidently say "This is the boundary."

In fact, organizational boundaries are even more ambiguous than those of clouds and magnetic fields. A cloud or magnetic field can be identified by the presence of a single phenomenon—water droplets or magnetic force. An organization cannot be identified by the presence of a single phenomenon, because organization implies the conjunction of several related but imperfectly correlated phenomena. Consider the variety of definitions of organization. One consequence is that an organization has different shapes and different boundaries depending on which organizational phenomena are observed and on who does the perceiving. Another consequence is that a specific organizational component may appear to be central as measured by some phenomena and appear to be peripheral as measured by other phenomena, and a specific environmental component may be proximate according to some phenomena and remote according to others.

At least the foregoing are conjectures based on experiential evidence. Organizational boundaries have not been studied in an empirically systematic fashion. There have been, of course, studies of intra-orga-nizational authority, influence, and clique structures, but these have assumed that the organizational boundary is known, and have focused on individuals falling within the boundary. There have been studies of job involvement, role conflict, and competition between organizational and professional norms, but these have aggregated individuals from many different organizations. An apparently smooth and continuous boundary according to multi-organizational data might only signify that discrete, discontinuous boundaries occurred in different places in different organizations. The multi-organizational studies have also assumed that only persons falling within some defined boundary are relevant. Finally, existing studies have concentrated on a single organizational phenomenon or on a cluster of closely associated phenomena, searching for correlations and consistencies rather than for orthogonalities and inconsistencies. A given individual is only likely to be central on one dimension and peripheral on another if the two dimensions are distinctly different.

A Not-Entirely-Hypothetical Example

To see whether his conjectures about centrality and peripherality make sense, and to see what might be disclosed by systematic studies, the author fabricated measurements from case evidence about a manufacturing firm with which he has had extensive contact. He listed specific people with whose work he was familiar, wrote down what he knew about their behaviors, and estimated the measurements that might be obtained by a real study. Unfortunately, the list of people was not very long and it contained several people having similar jobs, so a supplementary list was drawn up of other people whose activities were familiar and who worked in or dealt with firms like the one being approximated. To provide weak insurance against the author's prejudices, all of the fabricated measurements were components of scales—such as frequencies, per-

Distance From Company's Center	DIMENSION 1 Psychological Job Investment (Hours Spent on Activities Directly Affecting the Company, Times Job Involvement)	DIMENSION 2 Social Visibility (Hours Spent in Social Interaction Relevant to Company, Times Numbers of People[1] Talked to at One Time)	DIMENSION 3 Influence on Resource Allocation (Expected[2] Increments in the Values of the Company's Resource Flows)	DIMENSION 4 System Response Speed (Reciprocal of the Median Time For Decisions to Take Effect)
1	Vice-president heading division President	Telephone switchboard operator	President	Telephone switchboard operator
	Plant manager Sales manager at plant level Production scheduler at plant level Analyst on operations research staff Accountant on corporate staff Salesman Production planner at plant level	President	Vice-president heading division	
		Vice-president heading division	Plant manager	
3		Plant manager Sales manager at plant level Department foreman in plant	Sales manager at plant level	
	Unskilled worker in plant Corporate lawyer, part-time	Analyst on operations research staff Salesman Typist in secretarial pool	Production scheduler at plant level	Unskilled worker in plant
	Telephone switchboard operator	Production scheduler at plant level Production planner at plant level Corporate lawyer, part-time — Midpoint of boundary two Accountant on corporate staff	Union's bargaining representative Competing firm's president	
10		Unskilled worker in plant	— Gap within boundary one	Typist in secretarial pool
	Typist in secretarial pool Competing firm's president Competing firm's salesman — Midpoint of boundary two	Competing firm's salesman Competing firm's president Union shop steward, part-time — Midpoint of boundary one — Gap within boundary one	Corporate lawyer, part-time — Midpoint of boundary two Department foreman in plant Production planner at plant level Accountant on corporate staff	Department foreman in plant
32	Union shop steward, part-time Competing firm's production scheduler	Competing firm's production scheduler Outside member, board of directors Union's bargaining representative	— Midpoint of boundary one Salesman Large, regular customer Telephone switchboard operator Agent for internal revenue service Outside member, board of directors Analyst on operations research staff	Midpoint of boundary two
	— Midpoint of boundary one — Gap within boundary one		Union shop steward, part-time	Union shop steward, part-time
100			Unskilled worker in plant Competing firm's production scheduler Competing firm's salesman	
316	Union's bargaining representative Outside member, board of directors Agent for internal revenue service Large, regular customer		Typist in secretarial pool	

Boundary labels appearing in the columns: Boundary two, Boundary one.

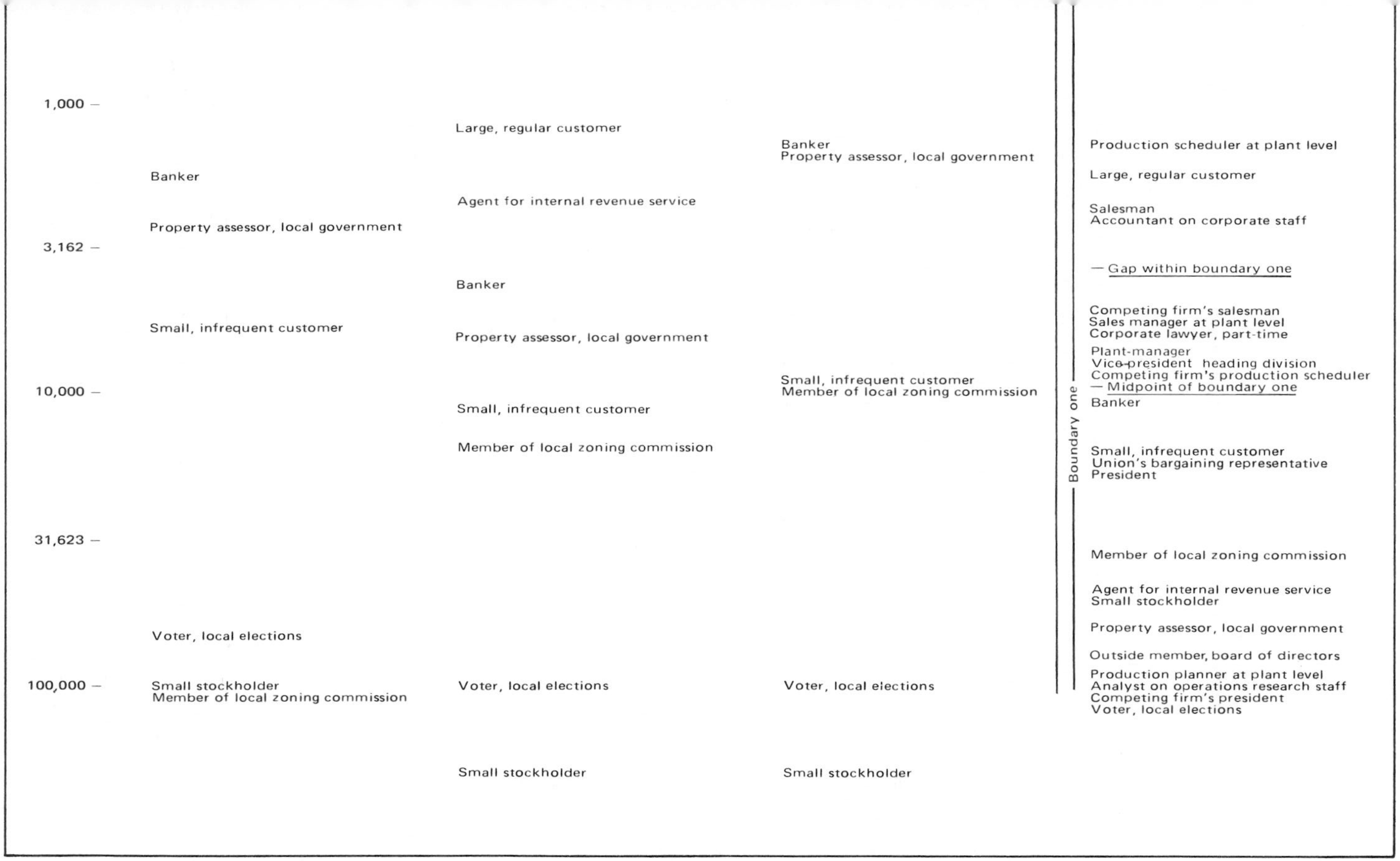

Figure scale values: 1,000 — 3,162 — 10,000 — 31,623 — 100,000 —

Boundary one

Column (rightmost, at boundary one):
- Production scheduler at plant level
- Large, regular customer
- Salesman
- Accountant on corporate staff
- — Gap within boundary one
- Competing firm's salesman
- Sales manager at plant level
- Corporate lawyer, part-time
- Plant-manager
- Vice-president heading division
- Competing firm's production scheduler
- — Midpoint of boundary one
- Banker
- Small, infrequent customer
- Union's bargaining representative
- President
- Member of local zoning commission
- Agent for internal revenue service
- Small stockholder
- Property assessor, local government
- Outside member, board of directors
- Production planner at plant level
- Analyst on operations research staff
- Competing firm's president
- Voter, local elections

Other dimension entries:

- Banker
- Property assessor, local government
- Small, infrequent customer
- Member of local zoning commission
- Voter, local elections
- Small stockholder

- Large, regular customer
- Banker
- Property assessor, local government
- Agent for internal revenue service
- Banker
- Property assessor, local government
- Small, infrequent customer
- Member of local zoning commission
- Voter, local elections
- Small stockholder

- Banker
- Property assessor, local government
- Small, infrequent customer
- Voter, local elections
- Small stockholder
- Member of local zoning commission

1. All people are counted equally, independent of their affiliations with the subject firm.
2. The expectation allows for the probability that taken decisions will actually be implemented.

Figure 1. Distances, on four dimensions, from a manufacturing firm's center.

centages, upper and lower bounds, and rates per unit of time—and not the scales themselves.

Figure 1, based on these fabricated measurements, shows the positions of various people on four scales that can be interpreted as measuring distances from the organization's center. The measurements have been exponentially transformed so that all four scales have approximately the same range. Obviously many other scales could be presented, and some of the alternative scales probably represent more important dimensions than those in Figure 1. For example, one could examine the hours spent in prescribed role activities or the amounts of pay received from the firm. If the sets of insiders and outsiders can be meaningfully defined, one could look at social visibility within the set of insiders, or at the ratio of inside to outside visibility (Haire, 1959). The four dimensions in Figure 1 were chosen because they show rather different patterns and because they do not assume the set of insiders is known.[1]

The subsets labeled Boundary 1 are those including both people who are conventionally regarded as members of the firm (a member of the board of directors, a typist, an operations research analyst) and people who are conventionally regarded as members of other organizations (the union's bargaining representative and shop steward, a competing firm's president and salesman). One rule that might be adopted to distinguish insiders from outsiders is that an insider is inside on all dimensions and an outsider outside on all dimensions. As shown in Table 1, this rule implies that none of the twenty-eight people is an insider and that only the voter in local elections is an outsider. A second rule would be that an insider is inside the midpoints of the boundaries on all dimensions and that an outsider is

outside all the boundary midpoints. If Boundary 1 is taken as a premise, this rule identifies seven insiders and eight outsiders, and leaves thirteen people in the boundary category. However, identifying new sets of insiders and outsiders implies that the boundary should be redefined. A new boundary implies further changes in the sets of insiders and outsiders, and further changes in the boundary itself. The final results of following these iterative cycles to their logical conclusions are shown as Boundary 2. According to the midpoints of the Boundary 2 subsets, there are no insiders and eleven outsiders.

Boundary 2 implies that, although one can identify some people who fall outside a given organization, no one is an insider with respect to all of the organization's activities. This is partly a consequence of the inverse relationship between a decision's magnitude and its time-span of implementation. Small decisions are implemented promptly; large decisions concern the future and may never be put into effect, because the farther into the future one plans, the less chance there is that one's plans will be realized. The lack of insiders may also partly result from the curvatures of the four scales. The midpoint of a scale segment is quite sensitive to the scale's metric properties, and if any of the example scales were monotonically transformed in a nonlinear fashion, the boundary midpoints would be shifted.

Boundary 2 has the advantage that it is defined on the basis of observed behaviors rather than on the basis of social conventions. But the midpoints criterion has the disadvantage that it ignores the potential existence of a discrete organizational boundary: a discrete boundary would not necessarily fall near the center of a boundary region. If there were discrete boundaries between the firm and its environment, they would appear as gaps in the scales of Figure 1. A gap implies that everyone is either unambiguously inside and above the gap, or unambiguously outside and below the gap. Unfortunately, however, one cannot claim

[1] The range of possible dimensions is suggested by Barker's (1968) inventory of the behaviors in a Midwestern city and by Aguilar's (1967) descriptions of the allocations of information gathering tasks among managers.

TABLE 1
INSIDERS AND OUTSIDERS AMONG THE PEOPLE LISTED IN FIGURE 1

Criterion	Insiders	Outsiders
Above the Boundary 1 subsets on all four dimensions, or below the Boundary 1 subsets on all four dimensions	None	Local voter
Above the midpoints of the Boundary 1 subsets on all four dimensions, or below the midpoints of the Boundary 1 subsets on all four dimensions	Department foreman Divisional vice-president Plant manager Sales manager Production scheduler Staff accountant Corporate lawyer	Local voter Small stockholder Zoning commissioner Small customer Property assessor Banker IRS agent Outside director
Above the midpoints of the Boundary 2 subsets on all four dimensions, or below the midpoints of the Boundary 2 subsets on all four dimensions	None	Local voter Small stockholder Zoning commissioner Small customer Property assessor Banker IRS agent Outside director Large customer Competitor's scheduler Union's steward
Above the largest gaps in the Boundary 1 subsets on all four dimensions, or below the largest gaps in the Boundary 1 subsets on all four dimensions	Production scheduler	Local voter Small stockholder Zoning commissioner Small customer Property assessor Banker IRS agent Outside director

that a gap exists until he has enumerated everyone, because one cannot say no one falls within a given region until he can say where everyone does fall. This is a practically insurmountable hurdle, given that everyone must encompass people in the organization's environment, and given that the relevant gaps are likely to be surrounded by people who would not traditionally be considered organizational members. Nevertheless, Figure 1 illustrates this idea by identifying the largest gaps within each instance of Boundary 1. And Table 1 shows that the gaps criterion identifies the same group of outsiders as did the midpoints criterion, but the gaps criterion identifies the production scheduler as the sole insider.

Some Research Problems Suggested by Centrality Measurements

If the empirical hurdles to discovering gaps in the organization-environment transition can be overcome, one payoff would be the sorting out of various conceptualizations of organization-environment relations. For example, Dill (1958), Emery and Trist (1965), Evan (1965, 1966), Haire (1959), Levine and White (1961), Normann (1971), and Terreberry (1968) have assumed that organization can be distinguished from environment and that environmental components can be dichotomized as relevant or irrelevant. This implies that there should be at least two gaps in each organization-environment dimension: one gap identifying everyone unambiguously as an insider or outsider, and another gap separating relevant outsiders from irrelevant ones. The example of Figure 1 suggests that neither gap exists in an absolute sense, and that organization-environment dimensions are either continua or so different from each other that composite dimensions are continua (Hoiberg & Cloyd, 1971). Child (1972), Guetzkow (1966), Litwak and Hylton (1962), Miller (1972), Thompson (1962), and Weick (1969) have taken the latter view.

Gaps or no, measures of the organization-environment transition are a necessary first step toward discovering conditions making organizations more or less independent of their environments. For instance, Beesley (1955) and Stinchcombe (1965) have argued that organizations breed more organizations, by training organization founders and by creating demands for the outputs of organized activities; and Stinchcombe also proposed that the prevalence of organizations increases with the society's literacy and schooling rates, with its degree of urbanization, and with its utilization of monetary transactions.[2] If new organizations are not

always created by decomposing old organizations, more organizations per capita imply more organizational memberships per capita. And if nearly everyone belongs to some organization, or if organization memberships are restricted to an elite sub-population, more memberships per capita imply more organizational interdependence. Therefore, organizations might become more interdependent as their societies become more literate, monetary, and the like.

On the other hand, the logic linking the preceding propositions becomes binding only in extreme cases, and all real societies may fall into the non-extreme ranges where logical necessity fades into ambiguity. Two important contingencies are the society's norms about role compartmentalization and about organizations' purposes. It could be that organizationally sparse societies create broad-purpose organizations and insist that role behaviors in different organizations be logically compatible; and it could be that organizationally dense societies create narrow-purpose organizations and encourage membership schizophrenia (Stinchcombe, 1965, p. 146). Societies also differ in the constraints they impose on organizational memberships. Centrally planned economies ordinarily require that the political party be represented on all economically relevant policy-making bodies, whereas the United States (at least officially) proscribes overt participation in business firms by members of the federal government and members of competing firms (Berle & Means, 1967; Chatov, 1971; Gordon, 1961; Pfeffer, 1972a). Bennis (1970) forecasted, "This idea of the mono-organizational commitment will likely erode in the future where more and more people will create pluralistic commitments to a number of organizations," but he did not explain why.

The argument that organizational density induces organizational interdependence

[2] Stinchcombe's propositions are far from self-evident, and they are difficult to document. Relevant statistics do not exist for most societies; the available statistics are often non-comparable; and there is a high probability one will only discover that literacy, schooling, and so forth increase the accuracy and exhaustiveness of a society's recordkeeping. Moreover, an unpublished pilot study by Carlos Bertero suggested that nations fall into at least three distinct subsets (highly developed economies, highly undeveloped economies, and two-class societies composed of a small, affluent class and a large, impoverished class): the correlations representing Stinchcombe's propositions were very small within each subset; the functional forms differed from subset to subset; and correlations across all three subsets were suppressed by confounding of the highly developed and the two-class societies. It is also doubtful that Stinchcombe's propositions are valid when the variables reach their upper ranges. In the United States, for example, monetary transactions have become abnormal and are becoming rare: one pays with a promise, which is an individualistic rather than a universalistic good, but affluence has become so high that the individualistic character of promises is no longer a dominating liability. And the social norms about management practice have become so stringent that literacy

has become nearly irrelevant. Organization founders are no longer expected to be able to read the legal or even the financial documents an organization must have; one hires lawyers and accountants to read for (not to) one.

emphasizes the importance of people and roles, and it is essentially opposite to the argument usually put forth about the differences between oligopolies and purely competitive markets. The latter emphasizes the importance of information and perception, saying that interdependence only affects behavior when the total number of interdependent organizations is small enough for one organization to perceive the others as unique individuals and small enough to enable stable coalitions (Caves, 1967; Stigler, 1968). When the total number of interdependent organizations becomes very large, inter-organizational perceptions diffuse and generalize, and the potential impacts of one organization on another dwindle in relative importance. An organization in a densely populated sector should behave in terms of the sector's general properties, and should assume that its own behaviors will not change the sector's properties. When the number of interdependent organizations becomes very small (but greater than one), inter-organizational perceptions differentiate among the other organizations, and the potential impacts of any one organization on another rise in significance. An organization in a sparsely populated sector should forecast other organizations' behaviors, including the other organizations' responses to its own acts. Since such forecasts are neither easy nor reliable, and since the small number of relevant parties makes direct negotiation feasible, sparsely populated sectors are inclined to form coalitions (Aiken & Hage, 1968; Caves, 1967; Friesema, 1970; Levine & White, 1961; Litwak & Hylton, 1962; Pfeffer, 1971).

In the late nineteenth century and early twentieth, a great many large business firms were created either as voluntary coalitions of small firms or as attempts by some wealthy owners to impose control. Ever since, it has been popular to predict that industry is becoming more concentrated and interdependent (Emery & Trist, 1965; Terreberry, 1968). Economic statistics suggest that some industries (automobiles, flour, glass, malt liquors) have clearly increased in concentration, that some industries (cement, chemicals, fertilizers, paper and pulp) have clearly decreased in concentration, and that the overall trend across all industries has been negligible (Caves, 1967, pp. 32–35; Steindl, 1965, pp. 187–221; Stigler, 1968, pp. 74–88; Weiss, 1965). However, the economic time series are founded on artificially defined industries that may or may not exist in the real world of organizational behavior. The time trends might look quite different if data such as those in Figure 1 were used to establish the relative influences of competitors, customers, suppliers, government agencies, and so forth, and then sets of interdependent organizations were identified on the basis of actual behaviors. Indeed, Levine (1972) has mapped some networks of banks and industrial firms created by interlocking directorates. This is precisely the kind of analysis that is needed, but interlocking directorates are only one form of inter-organizational relationship and far from being the most important form.

Centrality data analogous to Figure 1 offer the opportunity for at least two more lines of research. First, one could establish an empirical weighting function for measures of organizational effectiveness (Seashore & Yuchtman, 1967; Yuchtman & Seashore, 1967). Or more realistically, one could discover how weighting functions and measures of effectiveness vary. If an organization has different shapes and different boundaries from the viewpoints of different observers, effectiveness depends on the observer's frame of reference (Friedlander & Pickle, 1968). Second, the scales of Figure 1 clearly describe people in an unsatisfactory way, because one foreman may do quite different things from another. However, from centrality data, one could establish job taxonomies based on similar role profiles, establish organizational taxonomies based on similarities in the ways influences are distributed, and probably eliminate (explain) a lot of the variance in present observations of job involvement, morale, pay, status, and the like.

But the most important consequence of

such data would be a revised concept of what organizations are. If the fabricated measures in Figure 1 approximate reality, this would be more a revolution than a revision, for the fabricated measures imply that one should stop thinking of organizations as distinguishable subsets of society, and start thinking of them as hills in a geography of human activities (Pock, 1972). Social groups and networks would appear as mounds and ridges on the organizational hills, and societies and economies would appear as islands and continents (Crozier, 1972; Hoiberg & Cloyd, 1971; Levine, 1972).

Since there are many activity dimensions, one must choose the dimensions he wishes to map—just as geographers must choose whether to map altitudes, climates, population densities, or transport networks—and the shapes of organizational hills will shift as functions of the dimensions mapped. On the basis of Figure 1, a map of psychological job investment would show a set of interdependent organizations as a cluster of plateaus separated from each other by shallow valleys, and separated from the general population of organizations by deep valleys; a map of response speed would show each organization as a steep spire rising from an undulating plain. In either case, some people conventionally classified as organization members would be undifferentiated from the population at large, and other people would be difficult to assign to a specific organization.

This view of organization is hardly new. It is latent in many texts on organizations, social psychology, social anthropology, and industrial structure (e.g., Katz & Kahn, 1966, pp. 30–70), and the maps one could draw are kindred to the organization chart and the sociogram. However, no one has yet collected the data needed to convert a general orientation into a perceptual frame of reference, and when someone does, the topography of organization theory itself should be transformed.

At present, virtually all organizational research implicitly or explicitly assumes or-

ganizations can be sharply distinguished from their environments. A given person or phenomenon is inside or outside, or relevant or irrelevant. This practice is analogous to trying to develop a physics of gases on the basis of a dichotomy like breathable-unbreathable, which scrambles together and ignores fine gradations in temperature, pressure, and chemical composition. The dichotomy makes such strong monotonicity assumptions and discards so much information that it is nearly valueless, and yet its acceptability as a measurement standard blocks systematic observations of temperature, pressure, and composition. Such simple and useful relations as Boyle's and Avogadro's Laws may indefinitely remain undiscovered.

DOMAINS, ROLES, AND TERRITORIES

Studies of organization-environment relations are also complicated by the ambiguous, relativistic character of organizational environments (Barker, 1968; Weick, 1969). To no small degree, an organization's environment is an arbitrary invention of the organization itself. The organization selects the environments it will inhabit, and then it subjectively defines the environments it has selected.

Environmental selection. Taking into account the multitudinous dimensions along which environments can vary and the many values each dimension can assume, an organization has potential access to a vast number of environments. And since the organization occupies just a few of these locations, it effectively selects some alternatives from the complete set. At least, that is an abstract conceptualization: the actual selection processes are neither explicit, thoughtful, nor orderly.

Many environments are excluded from consideration by constraints which the organization imposes unreflectively or unconsciously, through assumptions and values that are inherent in the organization's decision-making procedures (Buck, 1966; Starbuck & Dutton, 1973). One reason why criteria are implicit, rather than explicit, is that the organization acquired them by imitating other organizations in its social reference group. Since the tendency is to imitate choices rather than rules for choosing, the organization is not forced to consider what the rules are; and even if the rules themselves have been imitated, there is no contrast with what neighboring organizations do to make the organization consider why it does what it does. Another reason for criteria being implicit is that selection processes are activated incrementally (Mintzberg, 1972; Normann, 1971). An organization only examines its environmental choices because external pressures, such as the actions of competing organizations, raise doubts about the viability of its present environment (Hedberg, 1973, 1974; Terreberry, 1968); and the organization only reevaluates those environmental segments which are under attack. Selection criteria supporting the unthreatened environments remain implicit, even though they may be logically inconsistent with criteria being explicitly applied in the threatened domains.

On the whole, the nature of implicit selection criteria is less strongly determined by an organization itself than by its neighbors—the surrounding system of organizations which Evan (1966) called the organization-set. Members of the organization-set provide the examples for imitation (Chandler, 1962; Richman & Copen, 1972; Starbuck & Dutton, 1973; Stinchcombe, 1965). They make the attacks which instigate environmental reassessments, and then they constrain the directions incremental revisions can take (Clark, 1965; Levine & White, 1961; Maniha & Perrow, 1965; Thompson & McEwen, 1958; Weick, 1969). They set prices, costs, and available resources. And they preserve and transmit managerial traditions. Since implicit criteria filter out nearly all environmental alternatives and leave only a small number for explicit consideration (Cyert et al., 1956), an organization's

ultimate environmental selections are strongly affected by the properties of its organization-set; and so the degrees to which specific organizations occupy appropriate environments are partially controlled by organizational social systems as wholes (Levine & White, 1961; Hirsch, 1972).

Once a set of environmental alternatives has been explicitly identified, the organization must select some to inhabit. But organizations' choices among explicit alternatives are none too systematic (Cohen et al., 1972; Cyert et al., 1956; Normann, 1971). Some environmental alternatives possess special prominence because they predate the choice question and even the organization, or because they are accompanied by unusually large amounts of information. Other alternatives are judged promising or unpromising on the basis of a priori theories that owe as much to folklore and myth as to analysis and evidence. Alternatives which are actually explored tend to be evaluated with whatever data can be easily and quickly acquired. Some alternatives are rejected because of initial impressions that would not be substantiated by investigation, and others become final contenders on equally superficial grounds.[3] Not infrequently, the evaluation data are provided by other organizations which are advocating the selection of particular alternatives—potential customers or suppliers, communities seeking industrial employers, and so on.

Of course, noise and disorder in the selection process degrade the association between organizational and environmental properties. Even if an organization would attempt to assess its idiosyncratic strengths and weaknesses and to choose environments which matched and complemented them, it would likely end up inhabiting environments whose properties were only loosely correlated with its idiosyncracies. But in addition, nearly all organizations find it im-

---

[3] There is some evidence that people lack effective heuristics for deciding how much data to acquire before making a decision (Beach, 1966; Phillips et al., 1966; Starbuck & Bass, 1967).

possible to assess themselves and choose matching environments (Starbuck & Dutton, 1973; Wildavsky, 1972). They find it difficult to acknowledge and to discuss their own inadequacies and incompetences. They avoid strategic specialization, both because diversification is seen as a hedge against risk and because specialization concentrates intra-organizational power in the hands of persons having appropriate expertise. They seek reassurance in goals and solutions that have the endorsement of universal acceptance and use. And insofar as possible, they avoid talking about ultimate goals and values at all, preferring to escape interpersonal conflict and to maintain an atmosphere of co-operative problem solving. The result is that organizations rarely achieve even the degree of environmental compatibility attainable with badly conducted selection processes, and the overwhelming majority of organizations inhabit environments characterized by extremely weak appropriateness (Bell, 1974; Starbuck & Dutton, 1973).

ENVIRONMENTAL PERCEPTION. The second aspect of the environmental invention process is perceptual relativity. The same environment one organization perceives as unpredictable, complex, and evanescent, another organization might see as static and easily understood.

Inter-organizational perception differences are partially analogous to the differences between two individual humans. Every perception system encounters difficulties in discovering reality inductively; and to learn an environment's causal structure solely through observation of naturally occurring phenomena is virtually impossible, because autocorrelations among successive observations can be produced either by a variable's dependence on its own past values or by interdependence among groups of variables. The abstract feasibility of sorting out correct from incorrect explanations only becomes practically relevant after the perceiver has accumulated literally tens of thousands of successive observations, and by that time, the causal structure may well have shifted to a new form. Consequently, a perceiver's ability to organize and interpret his observations depends very strongly on the theories and beliefs he holds a priori, and he tends to learn what he already believed (Clark, 1970, 1972; Dill, 1962).

The degree to which an environment is simple and predictable is especially contingent on prior beliefs. Suppose, for example, a problem solver starts out with the premise that his environment is fundamentally simple—being decomposable into just a few broad classes of phenomena which follow smooth, easily expressed trends—but that actual events are to some extent randomly determined in the sense that they include erratic components unique to a specific time and circumstance. The problem solver sets about discovering continuous, readily understandable patterns, and because that is what he seeks, any observational components implying complexity and discontinuity are perceived as random deviations about average patterns. He also aggregates his observations across different times and circumstances in order to distill out generally valid truths. Competing problem solvers, for instance, are perceived as specific realizations of a large, general class, and they are individually uninteresting because competitive behavior should be characterized on the basis of its uniformities across different individuals.

The chance this problem solver will ever be forced to question his initial preconceptions is so small as to be negligible. His every experience, having both general, explicable components and unique, random components, fits neatly into his perceptual framework and confirms the wisdom underlying his prior beliefs. If the accuracy of his predictions is low, it is nevertheless as high as the environment allows, and he need only look to his neighbors to see that their predictions have comparable accuracy. Of course, his neighbors obtained their prior beliefs through the same socialization process as the problem solver himself, and they use similar analytic methods.

But organizational perceptions are even more relativistic than those of individuals.

One reason is that organizations are exceptionally conscious of and inclined to accept social reality. They hire personnel from neighboring organizations and imitate their methods; they form coalitions (e.g., trade associations) with other organizations for the purpose of acquiring environmental data and influencing environmental variables; they send personnel to inter-organizational training programs and conventions; they encourage personnel to belong to professional associations and to adopt professionally approved methods. They also devote substantial resources to consensus development and distill out the common elements from members' heterogeneous experiences. Such collective socialization processes homogenize perceptions across different organizations and reduce each organization's sensitivity to the unique and unusual characteristics of its own environments.

Consensus production has the additional effect of eliciting affective commitments to existing, socially approved perceptions, and so heightening the dependence of organizational perception systems on prior beliefs. Yet, consensus production is only one of several processes that reduce the amount of ambiguity an organization can assign to its current knowledge in anticipation of future learning, that create inertia against the incorporation of new perceptions, and that institutionalize data collection formats which reinforce prior beliefs. For example, organizations tend to crystallize and preserve their existing states of knowledge whenever they set up systems to routinely collect, aggregate, and analyze information, whenever they identify and allocate areas of responsibility, whenever they hire people who possess particular skills and experiences, and whenever they plan long-range strategies and invest in capital goods (Aguilar, 1967; Child, 1972; Dill, 1962; Mintzberg, 1972; Normann, 1971). It is literally as well as poetically true that organizations cast their prior beliefs in steel and concrete.

Finally, organizations normally play influential, active roles in their own environments (Weick, 1969). Partly because they seek environments which are sparsely inhabited by competitors (locating one's fish-and-chips shop at least 200 yards from the existing ones), partly because they subjectively define their products and outputs in ways that emphasize distinctions between themselves and their competitors (the only one of the Chinese restaurants in Lafayette, Indiana, which specializes in *Northern* Cantonese cuisine), partly because they infer what environmental possibilities exist on the basis of past and present experiences (young people are more likely than middle-aged ones to use marijuana), and partly because they must impose simplicity on extremely complex interrelationships (eight competitors might be treated as distinct individuals, but 800 cannot be), organizations perceive their environments as systems in which they themselves constitute important components. And to no small extent, these perceptions validate both themselves and organizations' beliefs about environmental structure. It is primarily in domains where an organization believes it exerts influence that the organization attributes changes to its own influence, and in domains where an organization believes itself impotent, it tends to ignore influence opportunities and never to discover whether its impotence is real. Of course, someone who launches a marriage agency on the premise that people have difficulty finding suitable mates is likely to observe that his clients have found it difficult to find suitable mates. Moreover, it is the beliefs and perceptions founded on social reality which are especially liable to self-confirmation. A lone baker who increases his flour inventory because he thinks the flour price will rise for a few weeks and then fall might well be wrong, but if many bakers respond to a shared, collective forecast by increasing their inventories, their expectations will quite probably be confirmed.

ANALYTICAL STRATEGIES AND ENVIRONMENTAL DIMENSIONS. The foregoing discussion implies that organization-environment relations constitute highly complex and ambiguous stimuli to persons who are trying to observe them. Naturally enough, these ambiguous stimuli have evoked a heterogeneous range of responses from different observers.

Organization theorists have taken at least five different approaches—as outlined in Table 2—toward describing the environmen-

TABLE 2
DIFFERENT APPROACHES TO DESCRIBING ORGANIZATIONAL ENVIRONMENTS

	Type Code
Description of those environmental elements with which organizations have immediate, direct interactions	
Primary emphasis on the environmental elements involved in or created by inter-organizational relationships	
As perceived by the subject organization, including subjective characterizations of how the environment might or should appear	1
As perceived by an outside observer who is interested in how the environment actually does appear	2
Inclusive characterization of all immediately active, environmental elements	
As perceived by the subject organization, including subjective characterizations of how the environment might or should appear	3
As perceived by an outside observer who is interested in how the environment actually does appear	4
As perceived by an outside observer who is interested in both how the environment does appear and how it might or should appear	5
Description of those environmental elements with which organizations have remote, indirect interactions	
Inclusive characterization of all environmental elements	
As perceived by an outside observer who is interested in how the environment actually does appear	6

tal elements which have direct, immediate effects on organizational behaviors. One group of theorists has emphasized primarily the effects of inter-organizational relations, whereas another group has adopted inclusive viewpoints in which inter-organizational relations are merely components. Within each of these general groups, there have been subgroups differing in the stresses they placed on data obtained from organizational members versus data obtained from outside observers, and differing in the emphases they placed on prescriptive versus descriptive information. These perceptual orientations have further been elaborated into at least twenty terminological variations, as set forth in Table 3. One theorist's "domain" may be virtually identical with another's "role," and quite different from a third's "domain"—but this kind of confusion is typical of social science nomenclature, particularly in comparatively undeveloped subject areas.

The complexity of organization-environment relations and the ambiguity of organizational boundaries imply also that different perceivers will disagree about what constitute dimensions of the organization and what constitute dimensions of the environment. For example, this author would argue that an organization's technology, its perceptual characteristics, or its ability to predict future events are more properly dimensions of the organization itself than dimensions of its environment. However, Dill (1958), Evan (1966), Khandwalla (1970), Normann (1969), and Thompson (1967) have classified as environmental dimensions such technological characteristics as the disruptiveness of environmental inputs or the range of technology. Duncan (1972, 1973), Emery and Trist (1965), Khandwalla (1970, 1972), Lawrence and Lorsch (1967), McWhinney (1968), and Thompson (1967) have treated an organization's inability to predict future events as environmental uncertainty. And Dill (1958), Duncan (1972), Lawrence and Lorsch (1967), and Thompson (1967) have put into the environmental category such perceptual characteristics as clarity of information or time span of feedback.

This kind of conceptual disagreement is, to some extent, irresolvable. Phenomena in-

TABLE 3

TERMS USED TO DESCRIBE ORGANIZATIONAL ENVIRONMENTS

Type code*	Term and user	Definition	Process by which specification is achieved	Behavioral implications
1	Domain (Levine & White,1961; Thompson, 1967)	The specific goals (activities) an organization wishes to pursue and the functions undertaken in order to pursue these goals; e.g., the domains of health agencies include the diseases covered, the population served, and the kinds of services rendered.	Domains are defined through competition and negotiation with neighboring organizations. Domain consensus is sought in order to minimize competition.	An organization must fulfill the commitments implicit in its domain or lose control of the domain to other organizations.
1	Organizational saga (Clark, 1970, 1972)	The collective understanding within an organization that it possesses a unique history of accomplishment.	Sagas are conceived and initiated by a single man or a small cadre.	The existence of a saga induces unity among organizational members and helps nonmembers to differentiate the subject organization from others.
2	Industry (Chamberlin, 1962; in general use, particularly by economists)	One or more organizations competing in the production of substitutable products. Product characteristics (i.e., substitutability) are as perceived by customers or clients.	Conceptually, industries are defined through the combined effects of such processes as product research, advertising, geographic migrations, or legal protection of patents and trademarks. Pragmatically, industries are defined by the Bureau of the Census.	Industry characteristics determine the forms and extent of competition, prices and profit levels, and the content of intra-organizational decision rules (e.g., the need to forecast competitors' behaviors).
2	Organization-set (Evan, 1965, 1966)	The set of other organizations whose roles interlock with the roles of a subject organization.		Characteristics of an organization-set affect the forms of competition and cooperation with other organizations, flows of information and personnel between organizations, and a subject organization's internal structure, decision making, effectiveness, public image, and self-image.
2	Organizational role (Maniha & Perrow, 1965)	The goals and tasks undertaken by an organization.	Because they seek support for their own activities, neighboring organizations assign goals and tasks to a subject organization.	

* Type codes are taken from Table 2.

TABLE 3 (Continued)

Type code*	Term and user	Definition	Process by which specification is achieved	Behavioral implications
3	Domain (McWhinney, 1968)	What aspects of the environment are of concern, what phenomena should be noticed, and what variables are used as decision criteria.	Leaders select the domains of concern.	Different environments determine organizations' decision methods. The importance of domain problems depends on the environment's causal texture, being greatest when the environment is a turbulent field.
3	Strategy set (Chamberlain, 1968)	An organization's plan for the configuration of environmental relations it wishes to achieve over a future time horizon.		
3	Subenvironment (Lawrence & Lorsch, 1967)	The environment of one organizational department as perceived by the organization's members.		Environments differ in their degrees of uncertainty (clarity of information, uncertainty of causal relationships, time span of feedback). Different degrees of uncertainty require different degrees of intra-organizational differentiation and integration.
3	Territory (Child, 1972; Normann, 1969)	The subset of an organization's domain which the organization seeks to dominate.	Territories result from strategic choice by a dominant coalition within the organization.	Environments do not directly determine organizational attributes; organizational attributes are determined by the dominant coalition's interpretation of the environment.
4	Behavior setting (Barker, 1968; Wicker, 1972)	An environment having temporal and physical boundaries, and associated with recurring behavior patterns which are compatible with and related to the environmental setting.	Behavior settings are established through trial and error learning, through observational and instructional learning, through people choosing settings, and through settings choosing people.	People try to maintain the existence of behavior settings which provide satisfactions.
4	Domain (Normann, 1969, 1971; Child, 1972)	Those parts of the environment with which an organization constantly interacts. Defined primarily in terms of the characteristics of products and of competing organizations.	Product variations are attempts to defend or exploit an established domain; product reorientations are attempts to change a domain.	Organizations have established cognitive frameworks for perceiving and interpreting events which occur within their domains. Strategic changes within an existing domain are accommodated within the existing organizational structure.

TABLE 3 (Continued)

Type code*	Term and user	Definition	Process by which specification is achieved	Behavioral implications
4	Market (in general use, particularly by economists and students of business administration)	The set of customers and clients who make use of a subject organization's products or of competing (highly substitutable) products.	Markets are directly defined by customers' perceptions of products, but these are in turn affected by product characteristics, advertising, geographic migrations, and so forth.	Market characteristics determine sets of competing organizations (industries), forms of competition (e.g., the extent of non-price competition), and the content of intra-organizational decision rules (e.g., price policies).
4	Role (Rhenman, 1972)	An organization's exchange relations with its environment.		
4	Territory (Rhenman, 1972)	Those parts of its environment which an organization actually dominates.	An organization establishes its territory through market penetration which, in turn, is achieved by imitating successful organizations, identifying badly served sub-markets, redefining its product space, and introducing new technology.	
5	Niche (Starbuck & Dutton, 1973)	An environmental configuration that facilitates the survival of one organizational species.	Niches are defined partly by environmental properties and partly by organizational properties (requirements and capabilities).	Organizations generally avoid adaptation to niches.
5	Subenvironment (Bell, 1974)	The environment of one organizational department as perceived, at least in part, by an outside observer.		Departments tend to adapt to their environments. However, since different departments face environments of different types, organizations face highly differentiated environments.
5	Task environment (Dill, 1958, 1962)	Those parts of the environment (customers, suppliers, competitors, regulatory agencies) which are potentially relevant to goal setting and goal attainment. Any one organization faces multiple task environments.	Task environments are defined through internally and externally generated goal changes.	Environmental characteristics affect such intra-organizational properties as decentralization and work group relations.
6	Distant environment (Child, 1972)	Everything beyond an organization's domain.		

TABLE 3 (Continued)

Type code*	Term and user	Definition	Process by which specification is achieved	Behavioral implications
6	Secondary environment (Normann, 1969, 1971)	Everything beyond an organization's domain.		Organizations lack rules for attending to and decoding information from secondary environments. Moreover, changes of an organization's domain change its structure.
6	Value environment (Normann, 1969)	That subset of the secondary environment which sets norms and makes evaluations.		

volving interactions between organization and environment necessarily reflect the characteristics of both. Consider, for instance, an organization which (or whose environment) has a long time span of feedback for price changes; that is, after a price change, a rather long time elapses before the organization notices such responses as changed product demand or changed prices sought by competitors. If the long time lapse occurs because customers and competitors are price insensitive and do not even notice that the price was changed, one could argue that slow feedback is an environmental property. On the other hand, one could argue that slow feedback is an organizational property if the long time lapse occurs because the organization has inadequate and insensitive perceptual mechanisms, as in the classic case of a manufacturing firm which attends only to the orders it receives from wholesalers and ignores what happens at the retail level. But of course, such pure cases do not occur in reality. Every organization has some perceptual mechanisms which are less effective and sensitive than they might be, and every environment ignores some organizational activities.

Nevertheless, organization theorists could reduce the frequency of conceptual confusion and disagreement by the simple expedient of avoiding concepts which include interactions between organization and environment. Time span of feedback, for example, could be replaced by two concepts: the environment's reaction speed and the organization's reaction speed; and there would probably be stronger consensus that an environment's reaction speed is an environmental characteristic and that an organization's reaction speed is an organizational characteristic. But even in this case, the debate is not fully resolved. An environment's reaction speed to price changes could be substantially different from its reaction speed to advertising changes, and hence an aggregated reaction speed to marketing changes would depend on the organization's propensities for price or advertising changes.

Again, confusion can be reduced through more detailed specification ("the environment's reaction speed to . . ."), but the residual ambiguity can never be entirely erased, because interactive phenomena are intrinsically dependent on both participants in the interaction.

It would also help if concept formulators adhered to the principle that measures based solely on subjective data provide information about the subject, not about his environment. If one were presented with a study of Harry Brown's relation to his "environment" in which the only data about Harry's environment were Harry's self-reports, one would expect to find concepts like cognitive balance (or congruence or consonance) appearing prominently in the analysis, and one would not, in the absence of corroborating evidence, accept Harry's description of his environment as being objectively realistic. Even if Harry were multiplied into all the inhabitants of a town, one would expect the analyst to make statements of the form "The inhabitants of Brownville perceive their environment as offering equal opportunity to all," rather than "The Brownville environment offers equal opportunity to all."

By contrast, the studies which have tried to measure organizations' environmental uncertainty (Duncan, 1972, 1973; Khandwalla, 1972; Lawrence & Lorsch, 1967) have depended entirely upon subjective data obtained from the organizations' members, and yet they have spoken as if environmental uncertainty were a characteristic of some objectively real environment. There is a fairly strong case for saying that uncertainty is inevitably a characteristic of a perceiver rather than of a perceived situation, and hence that studies of environmental uncertainty are inevitably studies of ideology and attitude structure. Somewhat the same point can be made about any study which measures both organizational and environmental properties with organization members' self-reports: the logic of reality becomes comparatively irrelevant and the logic of ideology dominates. And even if organizational properties are measured in some objective fashion, it can be argued that the realism of environmental perceptions is irrelevant: organization members should adapt their organizations to the environments which they believe exist, whether their perceptions would be objectively confirmed or not. So the usefulness of subjective perceptions, including environmental uncertainty, is not in question. What is in question is whether data about perceived environments should be treated as if they were data about real environments, and whether uncertainty should ever be considered an environmental characteristic.

Table 4 lists some studies reporting or discussing the effects of environments on organizations. No attempt has been made to be exhaustive. The emphasis, rather, has been on recent studies and on studies representing a variety of viewpoints.

TABLE 4
EFFECTS OF ENVIRONMENTS ON ORGANIZATIONS

Affected elements within an organization's strategic problem	Environmental category exerting the effect		
	Physical	Primarily macro-social	Primarily micro-social
Valuations placed on organizational inputs and outputs	Block 1 No direct effects	Block 5 Concepts of value Social norms about self-interest and social responsibility Motives for, and satisfactions from, working Organizational role concepts	Block 9 Characteristics of potential and actual exchange partners Characteristics of competing organizations
Constraints imposed on organizational inputs, outputs, and control variables	Block 2 Characteristics of locations Localizations Properties of materials Scarcities Ubiquities	Block 6 Organizational role concepts Social stratifications Geographic migrations and regional development Macro-social integration technology Organizational existence criteria Physiological characteristics of animals and people	Block 10 Constraints imposed by exchange agreements Characteristics of exchange media The degree of strategic interdependence between competing organizations
Relations between inputs, outputs, and control variables within organizations	Block 3 Conversion relations Physical regularities	Block 7 Social distributions, norms, and role concepts Abstract characteristics of the macro-social environment Examples afforded by existing organizations Intra-organizational coalitions Range of feasible technology	Block 11 Forms of cooperation with exchange partners Characteristics of actual exchange partners and competing organizations The degree of strategic interdependence between competing organizations

TABLE 4 (Continued)

Ubiquitous effects across all of the above elements	*Block 4* No direct effects	*Block 8* Central government regulation General economic conditions Social norms about administrative and strategic behaviors, exchange relations, and knowledge ownership Taxes and subsidies	*Block 12* Characteristics of exchange agreements The ambiguity of roles played by neighboring organizations The degree of competition among competing organizations

Block 1: No direct effects because valuation is a subjective act. Indirect effects include the high value of salt on the desert, the restrictions and taxes on smoke emission, variations in the salability of air-conditioning equipment, the low cost of plankton, the high cost of tin, and variations in the usefulness of fertilizers.

Block 2:
(a) Characteristics of locations such as altitude, accessibility, and climate.
(b) Localizations, such as the geographic distributions of oil, of sunlight, and of rubber trees.
(c) Properties of materials, such as hardness, radioactivity, and toxicity.
(d) Scarcities, such as rare minerals, truffles, and sandy beaches.
(e) Ubiquities, such as water vapor, bacteria, and oxygen.

Block 3:
(a) Conversion relations such as photosynthesis, $E = mc^2$, and $HCl + NaOH = H_2O + NaCl$.
(b) Physical regularities such as Newton's laws, the periodic table of elements, and Mendel's laws.

Block 4: No direct effects—see Block 1.

Block 5:
(a) Concepts of value as reflected in life-styles and traditions, consumption patterns and living standards, invested capital per capita, and the foci of socialization (Adelman & Morris, 1967; Caudill, 1961; Coleman, 1961; Crecine, 1969; Diamond, 1958; Florence, 1964; Friedlander & Pickle, 1968; Gibson, 1969; Hagen, 1962; Harshbarger, 1972; Kirlin & Erie, 1972; Landsberger, 1970; Lee, 1948; McClelland, 1961; Mack, 1956; Parsons, 1960; Perrow, 1970; Roos & Roos, 1970; Singh & Drost, 1971; Starbuck, 1966; Stone & Rowe, 1966; Thompson, 1967; P. E. White, 1974; Yamey, 1966; Zigler & Child, 1969).
(b) Social norms concerning the comparative importance of self-interest and social responsibility, as reflected in the acceptance of profit

as a criterion of organizational performance, the emphasis on long-or short-run performance criteria, the importance of stable or full employment, and the structures of organizational perception systems (Baldwin, 1964; Bass & Franke, 1972; Bennis, 1970; Cheti, 1964; Cyert & March, 1963; Eisenstadt, 1965a, 1965b; Friedlander & Pickle, 1968; Galbraith, 1967; Gordon, 1961; Levitt, 1958; Miner, 1971; Narver, 1971; Nichols, 1969; Nove, 1969; Perrow, 1970; Pondy, 1969; Reiss & Bordua, 1967; Richman, 1965; Rose, 1967; Stinchcombe, 1965; Tawney, 1921; Tumin, 1964; Veblen, 1904; Walton, 1967; Weber, 1965; Williamson, 1964).

(c) Motives for, and satisfactions from, working (Argyris, 1957; Blau, 1963; Blauner, 1964; Burns, 1966; Centers & Bugental, 1966; Child, 1969; Form & Geschwender, 1962; Friedlander, 1965; Goldthorpe et al., 1968; Handyside & Speak, 1964; Hulin, 1966; Katzell et al., 1961; Kerr & Siegel, 1954; Lang, 1965; Lenski, 1961; McClelland, 1961; March & Simon, 1958; Perrow, 1961a; Richman & Copen, 1972; Seeman, 1959; Slocum & Topichak, 1972; Starbuck, 1965; Stinchcombe, 1965; Turner & Lawrence, 1965; Udy, 1961; Vroom, 1964; Wanous & Lawler, 1972; Weber, 1930; Wernimont & Fitzpatrick, 1972; Wild & Kempner, 1972; Zurcher et al., 1965).

(d) Organizational role concepts
1. Administrators versus policy makers (Allison, 1972; Armstrong, 1965; Astiz, 1969; Bayley, 1969; Bidwell, 1965; Burns & Stalker, 1961; Eisenstadt, 1965a, 1965b; Graham, 1968; Harris, 1969; Janowitz, 1964; Kaufman, 1960; Krauss, 1971; Lang, 1965; Lindblom, 1968; Lowi, 1972; March & Simon, 1958; Medvedev, 1971; Novick, 1967; Ono, 1971; Peabody & Rourke, 1965; Perrow, 1961b; Schollhammer, 1971; Seidman, 1970; Takamiya, 1972; Weber, 1947; Wolman, 1972).

Table Continued

TABLE 4 (Continued)

2. Employers ~~versus employees~~ (Abegglen, 1958; Behrend, 1957; Child, 1964; Elliott, 1960; Foskett, 1969; Kerr et al., 1960; March & Simon, 1958; Rice, 1963; Schein & Ott, 1962; Starbuck, 1965; Stinchcombe, 1965; Udy, 1959; Wedderburn, 1971; Zahn, 1969).

3. Intimates versus strangers (Crozier, 1964; Davis, 1968; Goffman, 1959; Hall, 1959; Levy, 1966; Lupton & Wilson, 1959; O'Brien et al., 1971; Richman & Copen, 1972; Tajfel, 1969; Triandis & Vassiliou, 1972).

4. Owners versus non-owners (Beed, 1966; Berle & Means, 1967; Child, 1969; Florence, 1964; Galbraith, 1967; Gordon, 1961; Grabowski & Mueller, 1972; Heath et al., 1968; Landsberger, 1969; Larner, 1966; Lempert & Ikeda, 1970; Levine, 1972; Marris, 1964; Marx, 1967; Monsen et al., 1968; Nichols, 1969; Nonet, 1969; Pondy, 1969; Strange, 1972; Villarejo, 1961, 1962).

5. Superiors versus subordinates (Armstrong, 1965; Bendix, 1963; Bidwell, 1965; Blumberg, 1969; Clark & McCabe, 1970; Cole, 1972; Crozier, 1964; Cummings et al., 1971; Cummings & Schmidt, 1972; Denhardt, 1969; England & Lee, 1971; Goodman & Moore, 1972; Graves, 1972; Haire et al., 1966; Hickson et al., 1974; Hofstede, 1972; Kavčič et al., 1971; Kelly, 1968; Luckham, 1971; Milne, 1970; Miner, 1971; Mulder, 1971; Nath, 1968; Peterson, 1972; Richman & Copen, 1972; Schollhammer, 1971; Stinchcombe, 1965; Turner & Lawrence, 1965; Udy, 1959; Weber, 1965).

6. Workers versus nonworkers (Abegglen, 1958; Argyris, 1957; Blauner, 1964; Davis, 1968; Dibble, 1965; Dubin, 1956; Eisenstadt, 1965b; Goldthorpe et al., 1968; Lefton & Rosengren, 1966; Levy, 1966; Neuloh, 1966; Richman & Copen, 1972; Seeman, 1959; Shimmin, 1962; Smith, 1968; Wachter, 1972; Wilensky, 1966; Udy, 1961, 1970; Zurcher et al., 1965).

Block 6:
(a) Organizational role concepts—see Block 5d.
(b) Social stratification distributions
  1. Ethnic and ethical distributions (Becker, 1957; Bellah, 1964; Blau & Scott, 1962; Boehm, 1972; Cressey, 1969; Danet, 1971; Ellis, 1969; Featherman, 1971; Form & Miller, 1960; Gael & Grant, 1972; Gustafsson, 1963; Hagen, 1962; Helper, 1969; Lenski, 1961; Levy, 1972; Light, 1972; Peacock, 1968; Sheth, 1968; Slocum & Strawser, 1972; Stinchcombe, 1965; Thurow, 1969; Weber, 1930; Weiker, 1969; Whitt et al., 1972; Zborowski, 1969).

2. Distributions of skills and knowledge (Abrahamson, 1967; Adams, 1968; Adelman & Morris, 1967; Ajiferuke & Boddewyn, 1971; Axelrod et al., 1969; Becker, 1964; Blau & Scott, 1962; Burrage, 1972; Coleman et al., 1966; Collins, 1971; Coombs, 1968; Florence, 1964; Galbraith, 1968; Hall, 1968; Hirsch, 1968; Layton, 1969; Litt, 1969; Milne, 1970; J. I. Nelson, 1972; Nonet, 1969; Perrucci & Gerstl, 1969; Simpson, 1970; Stinchcombe, 1959, 1965; Weiker, 1969).

3. Distributions of wealth, power, and influence across people (Adelman & Morris, 1967; Baran & Sweezy, 1966; Belknap & Steinle, 1963; Blankenship & Elling, 1962; Coleman, 1961; Demerath & Thiessen, 1966; Dibble, 1965; Durkheim, 1933; Eisenstadt, 1965a; Florence, 1964; Form & Miller, 1960; Hagen, 1962; Kolko, 1962; Kovak, 1972; Landsberger, 1970; Larner, 1966; Lupton & Wilson, 1959; Marx, 1967; Miliband, 1969; Miller, 1958, 1970; Mills, 1956; Montgomery, 1972; Myrdal, 1963; Nove, 1969; Perrucci & Pilisuk, 1970; Prest & Stark, 1967; Schumpeter, 1934; Stinchcombe, 1965; Thurow, 1969).

4. Distributions of wealth, power, and influence across organizations (Allen, 1965; Baran & Sweezy, 1966; Burrage, 1972; Cook, 1962; Edwards, 1955; Elling & Halebsky, 1961; Form & Miller, 1960; Freeman et al., 1963; Levy, 1966; Lieberson, 1971; Litt, 1969; Medvedev, 1971; Miller, 1970; Perrow, 1961a; Rotwein, 1964; Schiller, 1969; Starbuck, 1965; Stinchcombe, 1965; Warren, 1967).

5. Distributions of activities, functions, and responsibilities across organizations (Axelrod, 1970; Baty et al., 1971; Burrage, 1972; Eisenstadt, 1965a, 1965b; Florence, 1964; Form & Miller, 1960; Galbraith, 1956, 1967; Goldman, 1960; Harris, 1969; Hollander, 1961; Kriesberg, 1955; Landsberger, 1969; Levy, 1966; Lieberson, 1971; Litt, 1969; Mansfield, 1968; Montgomery, 1972; Nelkin, 1972; Scherer, 1965; Selznick, 1949; Sunkel, 1971; Zahn, 1969).

(c) Geographic migrations of people—such as invasions, emigrations, urbanization, and tourism—and the development of geographic regions (Adams, 1968; A. M. Voorhees & Associates, 1964; Chandler, 1962; Cressey,

Table Continued

TABLE 4 (Continued)

1969; Demerath & Thiessen, 1966; Florence, 1964; Greenwald, 1972; Hamilton et al., 1969; Hyrenius et al., 1967; Katz & Eisenstadt, 1965; Layton, 1969; Lowry, 1964; McKinney & Bourque, 1971; Morrill, 1965; Petersen & Thomas, 1968; Stephan, 1971; Thomas, 1958; Weber, 1930; Weintraub et al., 1969).

(d) Technology for macro-social integration
1. Systems for generating and transmitting electric power.
2. Systems for transmitting goods and people, such as airlines, buses, canals, highways, railroads, and rivers (Ben et al., 1965; Chandler, 1962; Esposito & Esposito, 1971; Fogel, 1964; Hoover & Moses, 1968; Kerr & Siegel, 1954; Litterer, 1961; Locklin, 1966; McKinney & Bourque, 1971; Nelson, 1959; Shaw & Abrams, 1966; Smith et al., 1968; Stephan, 1971; Thompson, 1967; Turner & Lawrence, 1965).
3. Systems for transmitting information, techniques, and values, such as families, radio-telephone-television systems, newspapers and magazines, school systems, and voluntary associations (Abelson & Bernstein, 1963; Abrahamson, 1967; Aguilar, 1967; Ajiferuke & Boddewyn, 1971; Allen & Cohen, 1969; Baty et al., 1971; Bidwell, 1965; Carroll, 1969; Coombs, 1968; Form & Miller, 1960; Gensch, 1969; Hall, 1959; Hansen & Weisbrod, 1969; Harris, 1962; Harrison, 1972; Hirsch, 1972; Illich, 1971; McKinney & Bourque, 1971; Mansfield, 1968; Miller, 1972; Miller & Wager, 1971; J. I. Nelson, 1972; Rogers & Shoemaker, 1971; Schiller, 1969; Sunkel, 1971; Weinberg, 1967; Zigler & Child, 1969).
4. Systems for transmitting wealth, such as banks, dowry, governmental taxes and loans, inheritance, and savings and loan associations (Adelman & Morris, 1967; De-Leeuw & Gramlich, 1968; Goody et al., 1971; Lorie, 1968; Marcus, 1967; Reeves, 1970; Saulnier & Halcrow, 1968; Selden, 1968; Shaw, 1968; Wilson, 1968; Wildavsky, 1964).

(e) Criteria for organizational existence, such as bankruptcy criteria, legally admissible forms, and rules of incorporation (Altman, 1971; Crum, 1953; Marcus, 1967; Reeves, 1970; Stinchcombe, 1965; Wilcox, 1960; P. E. White, 1974).

(f) Physiological characteristics of animals
1. Characteristics of nonhuman animals—for example, whales reproduce slowly, kangaroos are difficult to fence, cattle are docile but delicate, and viruses cause disease.

2. Characteristics of human beings, such as addiction, aging, attentiveness, biological periodicities, endurance, height, intelligence, learning rates, metabolism, reach, sex, strength, and weight.

Block 7:
(a) Social distributions, norms, and role concepts affecting intra-organizational decision processes and problem solving—see Blocks 5b, 5d, and 6b.
(b) Abstract characteristics of the macro-social environment
1. Structural intricacy or causal complexity (Emery & Trist, 1965; McWhinney, 1968; Terreberry, 1968).
2. Reaction or response speed (Emery & Trist, 1965; Lawrence & Lorsch, 1967; Miller, 1972; McWhinney, 1968; Terreberry, 1968).
(c) Examples for imitation afforded by the methods and structures of existing organizations, and diffusions of managerial style and organizational forms in geographic or social space (Acheson, 1972; Alchian, 1950; Bowden, 1965; Carroll, 1969; Chandler, 1962; Crozier, 1972; Downie, 1958; Flores, 1972; Litterer, 1961, 1963; Ono, 1971; Richman & Copen, 1972; Schollhammer, 1971; Starbuck & Dutton, 1973; Stinchcombe, 1965; Winter, 1964; Wright, 1971).
(d) Intra-organizational coalitions and interest groups, as functions of extra-organizational values and social distributions and as determinants of intra-organizational conflict and control (Abrahamson, 1967; Axelrod, 1970; Bass & Franke, 1972; Berle & Means, 1967; Burns, 1966; Child, 1972; Crozier, 1964; Cyert & March, 1963; Dahrendorf, 1959; Dalton, 1959; Eisenstadt, 1965a; Flanders, 1966; Friedlander & Pickle, 1968; Galbraith, 1967; Gordon, 1961; Hill, 1969; Kaufman, 1960; Kerr & Siegel, 1954; Kirlin & Erie, 1972; Marris, 1964; Marx, 1967; Miller & Thomas, 1971; Perrow, 1961b; Pondy, 1969; Rogers, 1968; Schollhammer, 1971; Stocking & Mueller, 1957; Tumin, 1964; Weinshall, 1971; Williamson, 1964).
(e) The range of feasible technology available for adoption, the diffusion of technological information among organizations, achievable returns to scale, or available automation techniques (also see Block 6d; Adelman & Morris, 1967; Bain, 1954; Beesley, 1955; Bowden, 1965; Burns & Stalker, 1961; Carroll, 1969; Caves, 1967; Fetter & Thompson, 1971; Florence, 1964; Hoover & Moses, 1968; Kernan & Schkade, 1972; Kilbridge & Wester, 1966;

Table Continued

TABLE 4 (Continued)

Landsberger, 1970; Layton, 1969; Leibenstein, 1960; Litterer, 1961, 1963; Normann, 1969; Perrow, 1970; Pondy, 1969; Scherer, 1970; Starbuck, 1965, 1966; Stigler, 1968; Thompson, 1967; Tilton, 1971; Utterback, 1971).

Block 8:

(a) Governmental planning, legislation, and regulation about prices, quantities, and qualities of goods and services and about allocations of goods and services among individuals and organizations (Averch & Johnson, 1962; Bernstein, 1955; Caves, 1967; Chatov, 1971; Child, 1969; Clemens, 1950; Edwards, 1967; Galbraith, 1967; Kohlmeier, 1970; Lang, 1965; Locklin, 1966; McArthur & Scott, 1969; Meade, 1968; Means, 1962; R. R. Nelson, 1972; Nove, 1969; Posner, 1971; Reiss & Bordua, 1967; Richman, 1965; Scherer, 1970; Schultze, 1968; Shonfield, 1965; Stigler, 1971; Tivey, 1966; Vickers, 1959; Voigt, 1962; Wilcox, 1960).

(b) General economic conditions as reflected in prices, incomes, employment rates, and tax rates, and indirectly in life-styles, migration rates, rates of innovation, and the importance of governmental policies (Adams, 1968; Altman, 1971; Becker & Stafford, 1967; Chandler, 1962; DeLeeuw & Gramlich, 1968; Fromm, 1970; Greenwald, 1972; Hall & Hitch, 1939; Hall & Mansfield, 1971; Hammel, 1969; Loescher, 1959; Marcus, 1967; Nelson, 1959; Palen, 1969; Scherer, 1970; Schmookler, 1966; Schultze, 1968; Stanback, 1969; Starbuck, 1968a; Stone & Rowe, 1966; Tannenbaum, 1965; Weymar, 1968; White, 1970; Zymelman, 1965).

(c) Social norms concerning the legitimacy of administrative and strategic behaviors, such as acceptable inter-organizational relations, legal and illegal competitive behaviors and employment practices, and legitimate modes of organizational control (Allen, 1968; Berliner, 1957; Caves, 1967; Child, 1969; Christie & Geis, 1970; Clark, 1961; Cressey, 1969; Crozier, 1964; Downie, 1958; Granick, 1960; Grove, 1962; Hall & Hitch, 1939; Kaysen & Turner, 1959; Kelly, 1968; Kessel, 1958; Loescher, 1959; Means, 1962; Nonet, 1969; Nove, 1969; Parry, 1966; Phillips, 1962; Reiss & Bordua, 1967; Richardson, 1966; Richman, 1965; Scherer, 1970; Shonfield, 1965; Stigler, 1968; Stinchcombe, 1965; Voigt, 1962; Wedderburn, 1971; Wilcox, 1960; Winter, 1964).

(d) Social norms concerning exchange relations, including expectations about the impersonality of bargaining and negotiation, the liabilities of buyers and sellers, and the structure of the credit and monetary system (Bloch, 1969; Hawkins, 1963; Heath et al., 1968; Lefton & Rosengren, 1966; Levy, 1966; Rados, 1969; Rose, 1967; Udy, 1959; Weber, 1947; Yamey, 1966).

(e) Social norms concerning the ownership of knowledge as reflected in patent rights, access to education, and research secrecy (Abrahamson, 1967; Becker, 1964; Caves, 1967; Coleman et al., 1966; Coombs, 1968; Crane, 1972; Hansen & Weisbrod, 1969; Harris, 1962; Hirsch, 1968; Hoenack, 1971; Illich, 1971; Kahn, 1962; Levitt & Feldbaum, 1971; Machlup, 1962, 1968; Mansfield, 1968; Neumeyer, 1971; Scherer, 1965, 1970; Stigler, 1971; Weinberg, 1967).

(f) Taxes and subsidies, on small versus large businesses, on tangible versus intangible property, on old versus new property, on earned versus inherited wealth, on stable versus erratic incomes, on different social units (e.g., families, old people, nonprofit corporations), on different spending patterns (e.g., gifts, education, luxuries, rent), and on different economic activities (e.g., importing, short-term investment, farming, polluting) (Adelman & Morris, 1967; Chamberlain, 1968; Council for Economic Education, 1960; Esposito & Esposito, 1971; Finger, 1971; Fromm, 1970; Krzyzaniak & Musgrave, 1963; Mansfield, 1968; Miliband, 1969; Posner, 1971; Recktenwald, 1971; Reeves, 1970; Robertson, 1968; Rolph et al., 1968; Shonfield, 1965; Stanback, 1969; Stigler, 1971).

Block 9: Also see Block 5.

(a) Characteristics of potential exchange partners (clients, coalition members, community residents, constituents, customers, governmental bodies, suppliers)

  1. The number of potential exchange partners (Blau & Scott, 1962; Caves, 1967; Demerath & Thiessen, 1966; Fidler, 1967; Hasenfeld, 1972; Kelly, 1968; Lakshmanan & Hansen, 1965; Litterer, 1961; Mohr, 1969; Normann, 1969; Scherer, 1970; Stigler, 1968).

  2. The size distribution (market concentration) of organizations which are potential exchange partners (Normann, 1969; Scherer, 1970; Thompson, 1967).

(b) Characteristics of actual exchange partners

  1. The number of exchange partners (Barker, 1968; Evan, 1966; Fetter & Thompson, 1971; Morgan, 1949; Normann, 1969).

  2. The heterogeneity or diversity of exchange

Table Continued

TABLE 4 (Continued)

partners at one time (Bell, 1973; Dill, 1958; Khandwalla, 1970; Lawrence & Lorsch, 1967; Thompson, 1967).

3. Various characteristics of exchange partners such as aggressiveness, organizational forms, power, prestige, rates of technological change, size, technical abilities, or values and motives (also see Blocks 5, 6, and 8; Ben-David, 1968; Blankenship & Elling, 1962; Britt & Galle, 1972; Cartter et al., 1968; Corwin, 1972; Crecine, 1969; Danet, 1971; Dibble, 1965; Dill, 1965; Duncan, 1972; Eisenstadt, 1965a; Elling & Halebsky, 1961; Engwall, 1973; Evan, 1966; Form & Miller, 1960; Galbraith, 1956; Hamilton et al., 1969; Harshbarger, 1972; Hasenfeld, 1972; Kelly, 1968; Kerr & Siegel, 1954; Lawrence & Lorsch, 1967; Levine & White, 1961; Levy, 1972; Loescher, 1959; McKie, 1959; Maniha & Perrow, 1965; Newman & Logan, 1955; Nonet, 1969; Normann, 1969; Rogers, 1968; Scherer, 1970; Schmookler, 1966; Schneider, 1972; Selznick, 1949; Simpson & Gulley, 1962; Starbuck, 1971; Starbuck & Dutton, 1973; Tannenbaum, 1965; Thompson, 1967; Turner & Lawrence, 1965; Warner & Low, 1947; Weiss, 1966b).

(c) Characteristics of organizations competing in input acquisition (purchasing) or in output acceptance (marketing)

1. The number of competing organizations; that is, is the market monopolistic, duopolistic, oligopolistic, or perfectly competitive? (Averch & Johnson, 1962; Barker, 1968; Caves, 1967; Chamberlin, 1962; Eisenstadt, 1965a; Emery & Trist, 1965; Evan, 1966; Kaysen & Turner, 1959; Lang, 1965; Leibenstein, 1960; Litwak & Hylton, 1962; Loescher, 1959; McKie, 1959; McWhinney, 1968; Normann, 1969; Phillips, 1962; Scherer, 1970; Smith, 1964; Stigler, 1968; Williamson, 1965).

2. The size distribution (market concentration) across competing organizations (Allen, 1965; Bell & Murphy, 1969; Collins & Preston, 1969; Comanor, 1967b; Comanor & Wilson, 1967; Edwards, 1955; Emery & Trist, 1965; Khandwalla, 1971; McKie, 1959; Mann, 1966; Normann, 1969; Qualls, 1972; Rotwein, 1964; Scherer, 1970; Stern & Morgenroth, 1968; Stigler, 1968; Weiss, 1965, 1966b).

3. The degree of output heterogeneity (product differentiation) across competing organizations (Allen, 1965; Caves, 1967; Chamberlin, 1962; Comanor, 1967b; Edwards, 1955; Galbraith, 1956; Goldman, 1960;

Khandwalla, 1970, 1971; Litwak & Hylton, 196. Loescher, 1959; McKie, 1959; Normann, 1969; Passer, 1953; Perrow, 1970; Pfeffer, 1971; Rotwein, 1964; Scherer, 1970; Smith, 1964; Starbuck & Dutton, 1973; Stigler, 1968; U.S. National Commission on Food Marketing, 1966; Weiss, 1965).

4. The rate of technological change among competing organizations (Ben-David, 1968; Burns & Stalker, 1961; Comanor, 1967a; Duncan, 1972; Galbraith, 1956; Harshbarger, 1972; Kahn, 1961; Lawrence & Lorsch, 1967; Mansfield, 1968; Normann, 1971; Passer, 1953; Phillips, 1962; Scherer, 1965, 1970; Schmookler, 1966).

5. Various characteristics of competing organizations such as distribution channels, fixed costs, organizational structures, product diversification, reaction speed, technical abilities, vertical integration, or values and motives (also see Block 7c; Carter, 1967; Clark, 1961; Comanor, 1967a; Esposito & Esposito, 1971; Gort, 1962; Hall & Hitch, 1939; Hawkins & Radcliffe, 1972; Leibenstein, 1960; Loescher, 1959; McCarthy, 1964; Phillips, 1962; Scherer, 1970; L. J. White, 1972).

Block 10: Also see Block 6.

(a) Constraints and conditions imposed by agreements with various exchange partners, such as admissible ranges of customers, geographic territory, or products and services (also see Blocks 6, 8, 9b, 11a; Allen, 1968; Buck, 1966; Hawkins & Radcliffe, 1972; Maniha & Perrow, 1965; Pashigian, 1961; Starbuck, 1965; Stocking & Mueller, 1957; Yamey, 1966).

(b) Characteristics of exchange media (credit, goods, inaction, information, labor, money, policies, products, raw materials, services)

1. Variability (consistency, heterogeneity, reliability) over time in resources made available or outputs sought (also see Block 8b; Bonini, 1963; Dill, 1958; Emery & Trist, 1965; Fetter & Thompson, 1971; Greenwald, 1972; Khandwalla, 1970; Pugh et al., 1969; Starbuck, 1965, 1966, 1968a; Thompson, 1967).

2. Various characteristics of exchange media such as availability, bulkiness, complexity, perishability, reliability, substitutability, and uniqueness (also see Blocks 2, 5, 6, 7, 8; Aguilar, 1967; Carter, 1967; Cartter et al., 1968; Dill, 1958; Jacoby et al., 1971; Levine & White, 1961; Misra & Jain, 1971; Thompson, 1967; Wernimont & Fitzpatrick, 1972). Table Continued

TABLE 4 (Continued)

(c) The degree of strategic interdependence between competing organizations

1. The potential importance of forecasting, influencing, and reacting to the actions of individual competitors, as present in duopolistic and oligopolistic markets in contrast to monopolistic and perfectly competitive markets (Chamberlin, 1962; Emery & Trist, 1965; Fellner, 1949; Schérer, 1970).

2. The degree to which organizations actually attempt to forecast, influence, and react to the actions of individual competitors; that is, organizations' awareness of their interdependence with their competitors (Chamberlin, 1962; Fellner, 1949; Friedman, 1968; Kaysen & Turner, 1959; Litwak & Hylton, 1962; Scherer, 1970; Stern & Morgenroth, 1968).

3. The degree of consensus among differentiated competitors concerning each organization's exclusive domain, territory, or sphere of influence (also see Blocks 6b5, 10a, 11a; Edwards, 1955; Kahn, 1961; Levine & White, 1961; Normann, 1969; Pfeffer, 1971; Rhenman, 1972; Thompson, 1967).

4. Competitive, financial, social, and technological barriers to market entry (also see Blocks 6, 8; Bain, 1954, 1956; Caves, 1967; Comanor, 1967a, 1967b; Eisenstadt, 1965a; Esposito & Esposito, 1971; Leibenstein, 1960; McKie, 1959; Mann, 1966; Passer, 1953; Qualls, 1972; Scherer, 1970; Stigler, 1971; Tilton, 1971; Weiss, 1965).

Block 11: Also see Block 7.

(a) Forms of cooperation with exchange partners and potential competitors, such as cartels, coalitions, collusions, contracts, cooptations, coordinations, joint ventures, licensing agreements, mergers, parallel actions, and reciprocal purchases (Aiken & Hage, 1968; Assael, 1969; Baker & Schulberg, 1970; Baty et al., 1971; Blois, 1972; Chandler, 1962; Clark, 1961; Clark, 1965; Desai, 1966; Downie, 1958; Fellner, 1949; Fog, 1960; Friesema, 1970; Gordon, 1961; Gort, 1962; Guetzkow, 1966; Kahn, 1961; Kaysen & Turner,

1959; Levine, 1972; Levine & White, 1961; Litwak & Hylton, 1962; Loescher, 1959; Macaulay, 1963; McKie, 1959; Mascarenhas, 1972; Miller, 1963; Mott, 1968; Nelson, 1959; Newton, 1971; Pashigian, 1961; Perrow, 1970; Pfeffer, 1971, 1972a, 1972b; Phillips, 1962; Pugh et al., 1969; Scherer, 1970; Stocking & Mueller, 1957; Tannenbaum, 1965; Thompson & McEwen, 1958; van de Vall, 1970; Voigt, 1962; Warren, 1967; Weiss, 1965; Weymar, 1968; P. E. White, 1974; White et al., 1971).

(b) Characteristics of actual exchange partners—see Block 9b.

(c) Characteristics of competing organizations—see Block 9c.

(d) The degree of strategic interdependence between competing organizations—see Block 10c.

Block 12: Also see Block 8.

(a) Characteristics of exchange agreements such as completeness, covertness, enforceability, explicitness, formality, illegality, and stability (also see Blocks 8c, 8d, 11a; Guetzkow, 1966; Levine & White, 1961; Macaulay, 1963; Scherer, 1970).

(b) The ambiguity (versus clarity) of roles played by neighboring organizations—also see Block 10c

1. Membership overlap with competing organizations and exchange partners (also see Block 6b3; Aldrich, 1971; Berle & Means, 1967; Curtis, 1971; Evan, 1966; Form & Miller, 1960; Guetzkow, 1966; Lieberson, 1971; Lupton & Wilson, 1959).

2. Overlap between competing and cooperating organizations (also see Blocks 10c3, 11a; Form & Miller, 1960; Guetzkow, 1966; Levine, 1972; Normann, 1969; Perrow, 1970).

(c) The degree of competition (conflict, hostility, rivalry, stress) among competing organizations (also see Block 12b2; Britt & Galle, 1972; Clark, 1961; Demerath & Thiessen, 1966; Desai, 1966; Hawkins & Radcliffe, 1972; Khandwalla, 1970, 1971; Lang, 1965; Maniha & Perrow, 1965; Perrow, 1970; Phillips, 1962; Scherer, 1970).

The organizing principle for Table 4 is a partitioning of effects according to where they arise in the environment and according to how they affect the organization. The environment was originally divided into the categories of physical, macro-social, and micro-social, where macro-social denotes that variations tend to occur at a national, cul-

tural, or international level of aggregation, and where micro-social denotes that variations tend to occur across local communities, industries, or markets. However, there was substantial redundancy between the macro-social and micro-social categories—phenomena tended to appear in both lists—so the redundancy was reduced by changing the categories to physical, primarily macro-social, and primarily micro-social.

Where effects occur within, organizations could be described in many ways. One could, for example, separate phenomena according to whether they primarily affect individuals, work groups, departments or divisions, or whole organizations; or one could separate the effects having primary impacts on task structure, social structure, or ideological structure. The author opted for still another schema: to partition effects according to how they might change an organization's long-run strategic planning. Do the primary impacts fall on

1. the valuations assigned to organizational inputs or outputs, whether by insiders or outsiders?

2. the constraints which organizational inputs, outputs, and control variables must satisfy? or

3. the intra-organizational conversion relations between inputs, outputs, and control variables?

Since it would hardly be argued that organizations do, in fact, analyze their long-run strategies so formally as this schema implies, and since many phenomena had to be listed under two or three categories, it is not obvious the schema is a good one.

The labels and categories actually filling the blocks of Table 4 are not designed according to a general schema, but were developed inductively from the content of an initial subset of the references. It might be that the headings now associated with many references ought to be further subdivided, and that the headings now associated with few references ought to be deleted, but the number of references under each heading may also say more about this author's knowledge than about knowledge in general.

Table 5 inverts the theme of Table 4, and lists some studies reporting or discussing the effects of organizations on their environments. As before, the categories and labels were constructed inductively on the basis of an initial group of references.

There should also be, in principle, a sixth table devoted to the ways organizational perceptions vary as functions of organizational characteristics. Organizations obviously differ in the attentions they pay to various environmental phenomena, in the mechanisms they establish for environmental perception (Aguilar, 1967), and consequently in the amounts and kinds of perceptual distortions they experience. Some of these differences—perhaps most—are dictated by environmental properties and are imbedded in Table 4. But to the extent organizations exercise discretion over their own behaviors, perceptual distortions should also vary with such organizational characteristics as structuring of activities or operating variability (Pugh et al., 1969), as well as with the characteristics of perceptual mechanisms themselves. One ought to be able to say, for example, customer-oriented organizations usually perceive customers' desires more realistically than do organizations which are not customer-oriented.

No such table can be presented. For one thing, there is the obvious dilemma of trying to sort out which organizational characteristics (including perceptual distortions) are environmentally determined and which are discretionary. Organization theorists do not agree about which phenomena belong in which category; and even if they did, there have been no empirical studies directed toward measuring the comparative sizes of environmental and discretionary effects. What would be needed would be studies methodologically similar to Pondy's (1969) effort to measure the impact of managerial discretion on administrative employment, but expanded to include an enormous number of environmental variables and an even more enormous number of organizations from different societies. Such studies are far into organization theory's future, and in the meantime, it seems organization theorists should devote themselves to research projects about which there can be conceptual agreement.

In addition, however, there have been no systematic studies of organizations' perceptual distortions. There are anecdotes like the stories of the Edsel automobile or Amer-

TABLE 5
EFFECTS OF ORGANIZATIONS ON ENVIRONMENTS

Organizational activity exerting the effect

Column key (Organizational activity exerting the effect):

- A — Technological policies
- B — Educational and research activities
- C — Geographic moves and expansions
- D1 — Activities by governmental agencies
- D2 — Influence on governmental policies
- D3 — Participation in community power structure
- E1 — Inter-organizational coalitions
- E2 — Advertising and public relations
- E3 — Control of evaluation criteria
- F1 — Policies toward exchange partners
- F2 — Exchange strategies
- F3 — Range of inputs and outputs
- F4 — Intra-organizational structure and methods
- F5 — Organizational membership criteria
- F6 — Conditions of employment and work

Affected elements within an organization's environment	A	B	C	D1	D2	D3	E1	E2	E3	F1	F2	F3	F4	F5	F6
Characteristics of locations	x	x		x	x	x									
Localizations	x	x	x	x	x										
Properties of materials	x	x		x											
Scarcities	x	x	x	x	x			x							x
Ubiquities	x		x	x	x			x	x		x				
Conversion relations	x	x													
Physical regularities		x													
Concepts of value	x	x	x	x	x	x	x	x	x	x	x			x	x
Norms about self-interest and social responsibility	x	x	x	x	x	x	x	x	x			x	x	x	x
Motives for and satisfactions from working	x	x	x	x	x			x	x	x	x		x	x	x
Organizational role concepts	x	x	x	x	x	x	x	x	x	x		x	x	x	x
Social stratification distributions	x	x	x	x	x	x	x	x	x	x	x	x	x	x	x
Geographic migrations and regional development	x	x	x	x	x	x	x	x		x		x	x		x
Technology for macro-social integration	x	x	x	x	x	x	x	x	x	x					
Criteria for organizational existence	x	x		x	x	x	x		x	x	x		x		
Physiological characteristics of animals and people	x	x	x	x	x	x		x		x	x	x	x	x	x
Abstract characteristics of the macro-social environment	x	x	x	x	x	x	x			x	x	x	x	x	x
Examples afforded by existing organizations	x	x	x	x	x	x	x	x	x	x	x	x	x	x	x
Intra-organizational coalitions	x	x	x	x	x	x	x		x	x	x		x	x	
Range of feasible technology	x	x	x	x	x	x	x	x		x	x	x		x	x
Governmental planning and regulation	x	x	x	x	x	x	x	x		x	x	x	x	x	x
General economic conditions	x	x	x	x	x				x		x		x	x	x
Norms about administrative and strategic behaviors	x	x	x	x	x	x	x	x	x	x	x	x	x	x	x
Norms about exchange relations	x	x	x	x	x			x	x	x	x	x			x
Norms about knowledge ownership	x	x	x	x	x	x	x		x	x	x	x	x	x	
Taxes and subsidies	x	x	x	x	x	x		x	x	x				x	x
Characteristics of potential exchange partners	x	x	x	x			x		x	x	x	x		x	
Characteristics of actual exchange partners	x	x	x	x	x	x	x		x	x	x	x		x	x
Characteristics of competing organizations	x	x	x	x	x	x	x	x		x	x	x	x	x	
Constraints imposed by exchange agreements	x	x	x	x		x				x	x	x		x	
Characteristics of exchange media	x	x	x	x	x	x	x	x	x	x	x	x	x	x	x
Degree of interdependence between competitors	x	x	x	x	x			x	x		x	x	x	x	
Forms of cooperation with exchange partners	x	x	x	x	x	x	x			x	x	x	x	x	
Characteristics of exchange agreements	x	x	x	x	x				x	x	x	x		x	
Ambiguity of neighboring organizations' roles	x	x	x	x	x	x	x					x		x	x
Degree of competition among competitors	x	x	x	x	x	x	x	x	x	x	x	x	x	x	x

TABLE 5 (Continued)

A. Technological policies, such as natural resource exploration, extraction, and replacement, the mechanization of production and investments in physical capital, or pollution and waste disposal (Ben-David, 1968; Blauner, 1964; Bowden, 1965; Cameron et al., 1972; Carter, 1967; Caves, 1967; Collins, 1971; Commoner, 1971; Cooper, 1972; Dill, 1965; Fisher et al., 1962; Fogel, 1964; Heroux & Wallace, 1972; Hicks, 1972; Kilbridge & Wester, 1966; Layton, 1969; Mansfield, 1968; Marx, 1967; Moore, 1963; Narver, 1971; Neering et al., 1972; Neuloh, 1966; Scherer, 1970; Schiller, 1969; Schmookler, 1966; Smith, 1968; Stephan, 1971; Stettner, 1966; Taylor, 1971; Whitt et al., 1972).

B. Educational and research activities, such as indoctrination and training programs, or direct influence on organizations which perform educational and research activities (Altman & Nathans, 1972; Ben-David, 1968; Bidwell, 1965; Clark, 1972; Clark et al., 1968; Collins, 1971; Denhardt, 1969; Dill, 1965; Fiedler, 1972; Form & Miller, 1960; Friedlander & Greenberg, 1971; Hansen & Weisbrod, 1969; Illich, 1971; Kaufman, 1960; Layton, 1969; Levy, 1972; Lowry, 1972; Machlup, 1962, 1968; McKinney & Bourque, 1971; Mansfield, 1968; Mansfield, 1972; Nelkin, 1972; J. I. Nelson, 1972; Neumeyer, 1971; O'Brien et al., 1971; Perlstadt, 1972; Roos & Roos, 1970; Scherer, 1970; Schmookler, 1966; Schultz, 1971; Schwartz, 1968; Starbuck, 1965; Sunkel, 1971; Weinberg, 1967; Wynia, 1972).

C. Geographic moves and expansions, such as the development of the multinational firm or military invasions (A. M. Voorhees & Associates, 1964; Esposito & Esposito, 1971; Fidler, 1967; Fogel, 1964; Form & Miller, 1960; Greenwald, 1972; Heroux & Wallace, 1972; Lakshmanan & Hansen, 1965; Lawer, 1972; Levinson, 1971; McKinney & Bourque, 1971; Paquet, 1972; Servan-Schreiber, 1968; R. Vernon, 1971; Weintraub et al., 1969; Wilson, 1954).

D. Attempts to alter community or macro-social environments
   1. Regulating and controlling activities by governmental agencies—see Table 4, especially Block 8.
   2. Influence exerted on governmental policies through coups and revolutions, information control, lobbying, political contributions, and support of interest groups (Andrews, 1972; Astiz, 1969; Axelrod, 1970; Bernstein, 1955; Caves, 1967; Chatov, 1971; Cook, 1962; Dahl, 1961; Edwards, 1959;

Epstein, 1969; Finer, 1955, 1956; Hacker, 1965; Krauss, 1971; Lieberson, 1971; Lowi, 1972; Lowry, 1972; McConnell, 1966; Milbrath, 1963; Miller, 1958; Peabody & Rourke, 1965; Perrow, 1970; Pfeffer, 1972a; Rourke, 1969; Scherer, 1970; Schultze, 1968; Stigler, 1971; Strange, 1972; Tannenbaum, 1965; Wilson, 1961).
   3. Influence on the behaviors of nongovernmental organizations through participation in community power structures (Belknap & Steinle, 1963; Blankenship & Elling, 1962; Demerath & Thiessen, 1966; Elliott, 1960; Form & Miller, 1960; Freeman et al., 1963; Kovak, 1972; McConnell, 1966; Maniha & Perrow, 1965; Miller, 1958, 1970; Mills, 1956; Newton, 1971; Perrow, 1961b; Perrucci & Pilisuk, 1970; Pfeffer, 1972a; Schaffer & Schaffer, 1970; Simpson & Gulley, 1962; Strange, 1972; Turk, 1969, 1970; P. E. White, 1974; Wolman, 1972).

E. Attempts to alter micro-social environments
   1. Inter-organizational coalition, cooperation, and coordination (see Block 11 of Table 4; Allen, 1965; Beesley, 1955; Bell & Murphy, 1969; Bidwell, 1965; Corwin, 1972; Elling & Halebsky, 1961; Rotwein, 1964; Turk, 1970).
   2. Advertising and public relations programs, including efforts to publicize organizational structure, strategy, and performance (Borden, 1942; Brown, 1972; Carlson, 1968; Cheit, 1964; Comanor & Wilson, 1967; Esposito & Esposito, 1971; Form & Miller, 1960; Galbraith, 1956; Gibson, 1969; Goldman, 1960; Hawkins, 1963; Hollander, 1961; Kovak, 1972; Lief, 1958; Long, 1962; Peabody & Rourke, 1965; Rourke, 1961, 1969; Scherer, 1970; Schmalensee, 1972; Sloan, 1964; Stanton, 1970).
   3. Control of the criteria by which an organization is externally evaluated, including discretionary decisions about the amounts and timing of profits and dividends (Brittain, 1966; Elton & Gruber, 1968; Friedlander & Pickle, 1968; Galbraith, 1967; Hasenfeld, 1972; Hawkins, 1963; Kaplan & Roll, 1972; Kravis, 1968; Krzyzaniak & Musgrave, 1963; Kuehn, 1969; Larner, 1966; Marris, 1964; Monsen et al., 1968; Pondy, 1969; Reeves, 1970; Scherer, 1970; Walter, 1967; Williamson, 1964).

F. Organizational strategy and structure
   1. Responsiveness to and discrimination among clients, customers, sponsors, and suppliers (Belknap & Steinle, 1963; Blois,
Table Continued

TABLE 5 (Continued)

1972; Brown & Lambe, 1972; Caudill, 1961; Edwards, 1959; Fetter & Thompson, 1971; Galbraith, 1956, 1967; Hanson, 1969; Hasenfeld, 1972; Helper, 1969; Kovak, 1972; Lefton & Rosengren, 1966; Lempert & Ikeda, 1970; Litt, 1969; Long, 1962; Machlup, 1949; Marcuse, 1964; Medvedev, 1971; Nonet, 1969; Reiss & Bordua, 1967; Rosengren & Lefton, 1970; Scherer, 1970; Stanton, 1970; Starbuck & Dutton, 1973; Strange, 1972; D. T. A. Vernon, 1971; Wolman, 1972; Wolters, 1970; Zimmerman, 1972).

2. Exchange strategies—the kinds of media exchanged and exchange agreements made, including, for example, the prices, quantities and qualities of outputs, brand identification and product differentiation, and efforts to prevent competitive entry (Allen, 1968; Andrews, 1972; Bain, 1956; Brown & Lambe, 1972; Caves, 1967; Demerath & Thiessen, 1966; Edwards, 1959; Fisher et al., 1962; Fog, 1960; Hall & Hitch, 1939; Jacoby et al., 1971; Kahn, 1962; Kaysen & Turner, 1959; Leibenstein, 1960; McKie, 1959; Markham, 1951; Narver, 1971; North, 1966; Pashigian, 1961; Passer, 1953; Scherer, 1970; U.S. National Commission on Food Marketing, 1966; D. T. A. Vernon, 1971; Weiss, 1966a; L. J. White, 1972; Wilcox, 1960; Wolman, 1972; Yamey, 1966).

3. Range of inputs and outputs, diversification, and vertical integration (Belknap & Steinle, 1963; Blois, 1972; Caves, 1967; Chandler, 1962; Channon, 1972; Edwards, 1955; Gort, 1962; Hawkins & Radcliffe, 1972; Hicks, 1972; Kirlin & Erie, 1972; Larson & Porter, 1959; Lieberson, 1971; Litterer, 1961; Mancke, 1972; Maniha & Perrow, 1965; Mohr, 1969; Newman & Logan, 1955; Perlstadt, 1972; Reeves, 1970;

Scherer, 1970; Selznick, 1949; Starbuck, 1965; Starbuck & Dutton, 1973; Stephan, 1971; Wilson, 1954; Zimmerman, 1972).

4. Intra-organizational structure and decision methods, job design and allocations of responsibility, degrees of formality and routineness (Aiken & Hage, 1966; Allison, 1972; Argyris, 1957; Bidwell, 1965; Blau, 1963; Chandler, 1962; Crecine, 1969; Cyert & March, 1963; Hall & Hitch, 1939; Kelly, 1968; Kirlin & Erie, 1972; Kohn, 1971; McArthur & Scott, 1969; Montgomery, 1972; Moore, 1963; Perrow, 1961b; Porter & Lawler, 1965; Rourke, 1969; Scherer, 1970; Starbuck, 1966; Williamson, 1964).

5. Criteria for organizational membership and for participation in organizational policy making (Aldrich, 1971; Bennis, 1970; Berle & Means, 1967; Blankenship & Elling, 1962; Bloch, 1969; Boehm, 1972; Brown, 1972; Collins, 1971; Crawford, 1971; Dill, 1965; Elling & Halebsky, 1961; Gael & Grant, 1972; Gordon, 1961; Kaufman, 1960; Lieberson, 1971; J. I. Nelson, 1972; Perlstadt, 1972; Pinnelli, 1971; Selznick, 1949; Slote, 1969; Strange, 1972; Weinberg, 1967; Zimmerman, 1972).

6. Terms of employment, wages, and the safety and comfort of working environments (Abegglen, 1958; Adams, 1968; Argyris, 1957; Becker, 1957; Bloch, 1969; Blumberg, 1969; Cartter et al., 1968; Child, 1969; Dill, 1965; Dubin, 1956; Flanders, 1966; Friedlander & Greenberg, 1971; Goldthorpe et al., 1968; Hamilton, 1967; Hicks, 1972; Kohn, 1971; Kravis, 1968; Lang, 1965; Levitt, 1958; Marx, 1967; Miller & Thomas, 1971; Moore, 1963; Palen, 1969; Scherer, 1970; Schultz, 1971; van de Vall, 1970; Weiss, 1966b).

ican policy in Vietnam. These suggest perceptual distortions vary substantially with the perceiver's organizational role, and an organization's perceptions are quite heterogeneous. Nevertheless, they also suggest various organizational properties—such as reward and punishment systems, centralization and decentralization of decision authority, or redundancy in intra-organizational communications—which may influence the homogeneity and realism of perceptions throughout an organization. There have also

been systematic studies which collected both objective and subjective data about environmental properties. But these studies have either ignored one or the other of the two kinds of data, or they have combined the two through a statistical technique such as factor analysis. None seem to have analyzed how subjective perceptions systematically deviate from objective evidence, let alone how perceptual distortions vary with organizational characteristics. In short, this is research terrain awaiting cultivation.

ADAPTATION, EVOLUTION, AND RESEARCH STRATEGY

The ease with which one can discover questions on which little or no systematic research has been done suggests that the subject of organization-environment relations offers opportunities for quick, dramatic research progress. Although this promise appears real, its fulfillment will depend strongly on judicious choices of research questions and methods. The complexity and richness of organization-environment relations imply high frequencies of logical ambiguities, simultaneous relations, and spurious correlations. Statistically significant correlations will probably be easily come by; substantively significant correlations will probably be rare; and truly profound discoveries will probably require research techniques radically different from those organization theorists presently use.

FEW ORGANIZATIONS OR MANY? One strategic choice the researcher faces is whether to study just a few organizations or many. Assuming the total resources available for data collection are predetermined and independent of the number of organizations studied, observing more organizations means observing fewer characteristics of each organization or obtaining fewer consecutive observations of each variable. So someone seeking to build and document a complex, dynamic theory should investigate comparatively few organizations at one time, and someone working toward a simple, static theory should observe many organizations simultaneously (Starbuck, 1968b).

One can debate whether organization theorists ought to be giving first priority to complex, dynamic theories or to simple, static theories, of course; but so many research topics remain unexplored that assigning priorities among them is substantially an act of faith. It is as if, on the basis of their first impressions, the blind men tried to decide which part of the elephant should have first priority for further investigation.

For the time being, there is latitude to indulge the personal preferences of leg-men, tail-men, and trunk-men.

Still, it is important to recognize that fairly superficial choice criteria—like the number of organizations studied—may embody rather profound substantive issues. A researcher who opts for trunks is likely to find himself studying elephants; one who opts for tails is likely to find himself studying peacocks; and the two may find themselves with much greater comparability problems than the legendary blind men faced.

At least as they are normally conducted, studies of many organizations reveal rather effectively the general behavioral propensities which permeate cultures, industries, and similar aggregates; but the disclosures are so macroscopic and diffuse that an analyst glimpses only the grossest causal relationships, and one suspects that the composite pattern is as much an artificial product of aggregation techniques as a valid insight into real behavior. For example, if guided by average statistics, one might get the impression that small corporations grow into middle-sized ones, and eventually into large corporations (Crum, 1953; Steindl, 1965). However, nearly all small corporations simply go out of business before they are ten years old; the highest percentage of middle-sized corporations are less than two years old; and a very respectable proportion of the largest corporations are essentially new births. The implication (neither supported nor denied by published statistics) is that most large corporations were at least middle-sized at birth, and only a very small portion grew from modest beginnings.

This aura of artificiality can be greatly reduced—and to some extent replaced by a sense of immediate, live, causally connected activity—through intensive studies of one or two organizations. However, case studies normally impress observers with the high proportion of organizational resources devoted to apparently unique, idiosyncratic, or nonrecurring activities, thereby casting suspicion that the studied organization is unrepresentative. Even a case example which has been chosen on overt criteria to typify some large class of organizations would almost certainly persuade a sufficiently intimate observer that it possesses enough atypical properties to render it a poor basis for generalization. So people who study just one or two organizations tend to observe the deviant and peculiar details characterizing single organizations, whereas people who study many organizations simultaneously tend to discover aggregate, general propensities to which few, if any, organizations conform exactly.

Large-sample studies are also comparatively effective sources of information about environmental constraints, such as legal restraints on organizational forms and behaviors, natural resource limitations, or technological feasibilities. Truly operational constraints must manifest themselves in the behaviors of large numbers of organizations, since a law which virtually no one observes can hardly be considered an effective constraint. On the other hand, it is very difficult to think of environmental constraints which are not (or cannot be) violated by specific, individual organizations. Sometimes the violations are surreptitious and clandestine, as in the case of most criminal activities, and sometimes the violations are overt and socially sanctioned, as in the case of most patented production techniques. But in any event, one cannot depend on case studies alone to reveal the existence and forms of environmental constraints, because the case being studied may violate some, or even many, of the constraints which bind other organizations.

A constraint creates both a limitation and an opportunity at the same time. Laws forbidding the sale of heroin present quasi-monopolistic opportunities for organizations which are prepared to and able to behave illegally; a patent advantages the patent holder precisely because it restricts the behaviors of other organizations. And analogous dualities are implicit in many of the aggregate behavioral propensities exposed by large-sample studies. Substantial returns to scale in automobile manufacture contribute to the market being dominated by high-volume, semi-standard products; but this mass market also, by leaving some customers unsatisfied, makes possible the existence of such small-volume manufacturers as Morgan, Bristol, and Stutz. One cannot expect large-sample studies to disclose how such idiosyncratic opportunities come to be identified and exploited, because large-sample methodology has difficulty coping with non-random deviations from aggregate patterns. Studies of carefully selected individual organizations are far more effective for that.

The foregoing might be summarized by saying large-sample studies show the anatomy of conformity, whereas small-sample studies show the anatomy of deviance. To the extent one must understand deviance in order to comprehend conformity—and conversely—the two types of studies complement one another. But they are not simply two sides of the same coin.

DYNAMIC ADAPTATION VERSUS STATIC EVOLUTION? Interlocked with the issue of how many organizations to study is the question of whether the researcher perceives organizations as relatively long-lived, dynamic systems which adapt themselves to environmental changes, or he perceives them as relatively short-lived, static structures which are selected for environmental fitness through survival-of-the-fittest competition.

Researchers who undertake small-sample studies tend, on the whole, to develop models in which an organization shifts continuously from one form to another. Some of these shifts are responses to intra-organizational stresses and learning; some are reactions to such environmental pressures as competitors' behaviors, technological changes, and governmental policies; and some represent initiatives in which the organization seeks to redefine its strategy and its environment. Yet, they all take place concurrently, interacting with one another, so that the observer never perceives a system developing in a controlled environment and displaying properties which clearly generalize to many environments, and more importantly, so that any description of how the organization looks at one time is about as representative and meaningful as a single frame from a reel of motion picture film. The researcher finds himself trying to assemble a complete motion picture of a highly flexible, nearly fluid system that displays more persistence and cohesion than structure and form.

Clearly, it is no trivial task simply to describe this sort of adaptive system. Verbal characterizations tend to vibrate between painfully detailed anecdotes and poetic ambiguities. Although there exist mathematical methods capable of describing quite complex dynamic systems, these methods require expertise in topics which have been ignored or deemphasized by most mathematical social scientists: even if someone invests the massive effort to create a realistic mathematical model, practically no one will understand what his model says. Computer simulation offers a compromise between the verbal and the mathematical, but the promise remains potential. The handful of published computer simulations either have concentrated on one microscopic subsystem of a real, observed organization, or have vaguely generalized about the qualitative properties of hypothetical, abstract organizations. Moreover, computer simulations have a propensity for luring researchers into Bonini's paradox—the more realistic and detailed one's model, the more the model resembles the modeled organization, including resemblance in the directions of incomprehensibility and indescribability.

But if describing the adaptation of a flexible, dynamic system is difficult, gathering the data to document an insightful description is even more challenging. In order to maximize his theory's potential for generalization, the researcher must distinguish among the various kinds of changes mentioned above: those instigated by intra-organizational stresses and learning, those instigated by environmental forces, and those representing the organization's strategic initiatives. Yet the data he traditionally has available combine all of these phenomena in a single, intermingled, unreproducible, and uncontrollable stream; and in a very real sense, the only appropriate statistical tools are those designed for samples of size one.

Data gathering strategies vary along many dimensions, of course, but two strategic dimensions appear to be particularly critical during the present stage of organization theory's development. An analyst must decide whether to emphasize the postdictive explanation of events which have already taken place, or to attempt the predictive extrapolation of events which are going to occur. He must also choose between passively observing events which transpire naturally, or actively intervening to force certain events to happen (Starbuck, 1974).

Sciences (and organization theory has been no exception) seem inevitably to begin in the passive-postdictive mode. The doctor collects his patient's medical history; the geologist records earth movements and the patterns generated by past movements; the economist compiles the periodic statistics which add up to an economic history. Then one or more theories are advanced to explain what has been observed—a tentative diagnosis, a conjecture about the earth's development, a macro-economic model.

And these passive-postdictive biases are healthy for a science's early development. They highlight the most prominent, nonpathological phenomena. They reduce distortions arising from scientists' observational activities. They minimize the costs of proposing erroneous theories and thereby stimulate the invention and unbiased evaluation of alternative hypotheses. They discourage the premature rejection of partially deficient theories and promote processes of revision, modification, correction, combination, and elaboration. They decrease personal associations between specific scientists and specific observations, concepts, or philosophies. They permit standards of scientific achievement to develop in relative autonomy from extra-scientific payoffs.

However, it is important that a science start diverging from its initial passive-postdictive mode as soon as it grows strong enough to do so. For one thing, until the doctor acts upon one of his diagnostic conjectures and prescribes a treatment, the patient can receive no benefit. But there are several intrinsically scientific reasons of equal or greater importance.

First, as long as the costs associated with promulgating erroneous theories remain low, there is little incentive to eliminate erroneous theories and hence to discriminate carefully between better hypotheses and worse ones. Defective hypotheses tend to be retained long after their deficiencies have become obvious; comparisons among alternative theories tend to be vague and inconclusive; data measurement techniques need not be honed to maximum sharpness; and scientists generally behave as if they do not take their science seriously.

Second, because people proposing postdictive theories know in advance what phenomena their conjectures must explain, all serious proposals are consistent with the most prominent empirical facts, and all appear to perform almost equally well. Differences between postdictive theories always lie in their abilities to explain comparatively unimportant phenomena, or what the theories' proponents believe to be comparatively unimportant phenomena; and postdiction must give way to prediction before the differences between theories are exposed clearly and unambiguously.

Third, autonomous scientific development gradually shifts from fertility to sterility. Scientific disciplines develop social structures and codes of behavior which, for all of their fundamental virtues, can become intellectual prisons that stifle innovation, creativity, and progress. So to prevent this progression toward sterility from actually coming about, the autonomy of disciplinary development should be moderated and disrupted by extra-disciplinary influences (Gordon & Marquis, 1966; Starbuck, 1974). One of the most obvious ways to inject extra-disciplinary values is to transform the science into an actively interventionist activity that seeks to bring about desired states of affairs, because criteria of desirability are extra-scientific and evoke influence attempts by any affected, nonscientific, social systems.

Fourth, an exclusive emphasis on naturally occurring phenomena produces data distributions dominated by uninteresting events—nearly everyone has brown eyes, nearly all rock formations are stable, nearly all prices are the same as they were last week. In order to acquire the kinds of data that facilitate comparisons among theories, in quantities that make these comparisons conclusive, the scientist must achieve some degree of experimental control over that which he observes. At the very least, he must be able to select settings likely to yield interesting, revealing observations—meaning that he has predicted what he will observe—and to demonstrate convincingly his theory's effectiveness and completeness, he must extrapolate a trajectory from past events and then intervene and engineer events which deviate from the predicted trajectory. The latter endeavors put science all the way into an active-predictive mode.

Finally, a point that is especially relevant for organization theorists who perform small-sample studies: the passive-postdictive mode contravenes analyses of organizations as flexible, adaptive systems. An adaptive system is both reactive and selectively active. It reacts to changes in and signals from its environment, and possesses a characteristic repertoire of response patterns. It also selects environmental settings to which it is capable of responding, and either learns new reaction patterns that match its environment's requirements, or undertakes to modify its environment's properties to bring them into line with its own capabilities (Normann, 1971). So to analyze such a system effectively, a researcher must strive to distinguish among and to comprehend individually the system's short-run immediately programmed reactions, its flexibilities for learning new reaction patterns or rigidities for preserving old ones, and its long-run strategies for selecting or creating appropriate environmental settings.

A researcher can use several analytic approaches to gathering separate data about each of these adaptive subsystems. He can observe the system's reactions to regular oscillatory inputs of different frequencies; observe its reactions to sudden, step-like shocks; observe its reactions to introductions of informational noise; observe its reactions to disruptions of internal and external information channels; and so on. However, naturally occurring phenomena do not often match one of these analytic approaches, partly because almost all events are merely sequences of routine and expected behaviors by both the organization and its environment, and partly because the various observational conditions are all scrambled together in an uncontrolled, but nonrandom, melange. Either researchers must depend on having the good luck to observe natural events of unusual sorts—implying acceptance of a slow and decelerating rate of scientific progress—or they must intervene and exert some degree of experimental control. The net result is that organization theorists will be impelled to undertake experimental manipulations simply to ensure that their science maintains a reasonable rate of progress. And since organizations are purposeful systems which do not tend to accept interventions purely for the sake of scientific progress, which tend to demand plausible forecasts of the consequences of proposed interventions, and which tend to place evaluations on alternative interventions, experimental manipulations are virtually certain to be amplified into full-scale, active-predictive investigations.

In sum, the organization theorists who perceive organizations as relatively long-lived, dynamic, and adaptive systems are confronted by major methodological challenges which are calling for innovations in research strategy. A gradual transition from the traditional passive-postdictive mode of data gathering to an active-predictive mode appears inevitable, although one might debate the speed with which active-predictive activities will be embraced. Another potential transition lurks in the deficiencies of current descriptive methods. That no truly adequate descriptive medium exists seems clear, but no one knows what alternative media are going to be invented and made available for adoption.

STATIC, EVOLUTIONARY MODELS. On the other hand, one does not have to emphasize organizations' adaptive properties. Most of the researchers who undertake large-sample studies, at least implicitly, take the position that organizations are relatively stable, static structures. They stress the properties each organization displays right now, and the similarities and differences among comparable organizations, without regard for trajectories of change within the histories of single organizations.

This is not to suggest that it is plausible for organization theorists to ignore social change. After all, change is constant (to coin a phrase). It is plausible, however, to perceive any given organization as having a static structure at any given time, and then to perceive social change as a birth and death process which alters the set of existing organizations.

Birth and death processes can even be introduced within the life history of a single organization. That is, one can think of a social system which is continuously the same organization by legal, geographic, or other criteria as also being an envelope containing a sequence of discretely different organizations at different times, according to other criteria for organizational existence. Consider, for example, a small manufacturing plant which is sold to a large, conglomerate corporation, the former owner being retained as plant manager and no sudden, drastic changes being made in who is employed or what is manufactured. Based on distributions of customers, products, and inventories, on assignments of activities among employees, or on geographic location, one might argue that the original organization still survives. But based on who receives the profits, on the legal form of organization, or on methods of accounting, one might argue that the previous firm no longer exists and a new organization has been born.

Death and rebirth has traditionally been an accepted description for bankruptcies, mergers, ownership changes, and similar legally demarcated transitions. Very modest extrapolation will extend this description to cover large-scale turnovers in managerial personnel, major reorganizations of operating divisions, or drastic strategic reorientations. And from there, it begins to appear reasonable to characterize as death and rebirth virtually any kind of reorganization, reassignment of roles, or revision of decision rules. One soon finds himself perceiving organizations as evanescent structures indeed, static at any given time, but often on the brink of being discarded and replaced by newer forms.

The birth and death viewpoint brings forth once again the centrality of two dilemmas that have perennially plagued organization theory. Since the organization that died long ago according to one definition probably still exists according to another, how one operationally defines an organization strongly affects what one learns about organizations. It also makes a great deal of difference what criteria one uses to measure the magnitudes of social changes, because a process that appears as a smooth, continuous flow by one set of criteria appears as a sequence of discrete and distinct stages by other criteria. However, long histories of debate have produced little, if any, movement toward consensus about how these issues should be resolved, and the solutions individual researchers endorse remain very much matters of personal preference. It

would be unrealistic to forecast any imminent revolutions.

The birth and death viewpoint also implies that organization theorists can assign low priority to understanding adaptation within the life history of a single organization, and can concentrate instead on macroscopic views of adaptation. The high priorities should be assigned to understanding what tasks and rules a society imposes on its organizations, how these task and rule assignments translate into organizational birth and death rates and into measures of survival fitness, and what frequency distributions across different types of organizations result. All societally important adaptive processes manifest themselves by shifting whole populations of organizations, and the central task is to comprehend these population motions rather than the motions of individual organizations within their sub-populations. It is not even essential to understand how individual organizations are able to violate aggregate rules or to deviate from aggregate trends for brief time periods: these are merely noise in the overall development of a large-scale social system, and researchers should first seek to perceive the total system with such noise filtered out.

Stepping back and getting a macroscopic perspective makes any single organization appear ephemeral. One is immediately struck by the very high death rates among newly created organizations: among industrial firms, approximately half survive less than two years and four-fifths less than ten years (Crum, 1953; Marcus, 1967; Steindl, 1965). Then one also realizes that even lifetimes of fifty to one hundred years may appear short in comparison to the speeds with which organizational populations shift (Stinchcombe, 1965). Statistically, it probably makes little difference whether a group of existing organizations are remodeled to extend their life spans, or they are destroyed now and some new organizations are created (although the organizations' members undoubtedly have opinions about the more desirable course).

A macroscopic perspective also suggests the possibility that population movements fit into an evolutionary model. Evolution is essentially a matching process by which an environment comes to be inhabited by an appropriate set of residents. The environment's properties translate into fitness criteria that influence the birth and survival probabilities of various potential residents, gradually reducing the proportions of less fit residents and raising the proportions of more fit residents. Some environmental properties, such as the presence or total absence of certain resources, determine fitness criteria directly—for example, people having large lung capacities are better suited to living at high altitudes. Other environmental properties, such as limitations on the total supplies of certain resources, determine the basis on which residents compete with each other for survival—for example, limited water supplies imply competition for water. This second type of population shift has been labeled survival-of-the-fittest.

Evolutionary concepts have the potential to contribute significantly to our understanding of organizations. Organizational environments clearly differ in their propensities to give birth to various types of organizations, in the rules they require organizations to obey, in the tasks they reward organizations for performing, and in their criteria for organizational existence. Organizations often compete with each other for environmental resources; imitation evidently produces an inheritance-like transmission of characteristics from one generation to the next; and births and deaths are statistically important organizational phenomena. As a matter of fact, it is astonishing that organization theorists have not built up a substantial body of research on organizational evolution. But such is the case. Aside from Stinchcombe's (1965) work, the main writings on organizational evolution have come in domains which most organization the-

orists ignore: empirical studies by economists of long-run changes in industrial composition (e.g., Beesley, 1955; Downie, 1958; Esposito & Esposito, 1971; Mann, 1966; Marcus, 1967; Qualls, 1972; Scherer, 1970; Stigler, 1968; Weiss, 1965), and theoretical discussions, also by economists, of the effects of competition and financial constraints on firms' internal decision rules (Alchian, 1950; Downie, 1958; R. R. Nelson, 1972; Winter, 1964, 1971). One of the most stimulating analyses from an organization theorist's vantage point is Levins's (1968) *Evolution in Changing Environments,* a purely biological treatment that has not yet sifted into the social sciences. So in principle, organizational evolution is another vein of high-grade intellectual ore waiting to be mined.

But before anyone plunges enthusiastically ahead, he should recognize that evolutionary models have limitations which are capable of fully disillusioning the overly optimistic. Not only do previous attempts to apply evolutionary concepts in the social sciences (e.g., Alland, 1970; Sahlins & Service, 1960) imply that evolutionary propositions have strong propensities for degenerating into vacuous tautologies, but there is at least one methodologically fundamental limitation to the inferences one can draw. The constraints imposed by environmental properties are not, in general, sufficiently restrictive to determine uniquely the characteristics of their organizational residents.

For example, one attempted application of evolutionary theory was the argument that survival-of-the-fittest implied all firms maximize profits: any firm which did not use profit-maximizing decision rules would be at a competitive disadvantage in comparison to firms which did, would lose financial support, and would be driven out of business. Fairly extensive debates—in which articles by Alchian (1950) and Winter (1964) presented the key counterarguments —demonstrated that such strong conclusions should not be drawn. Firms only compete with other firms, and it is far from obvious that any existing firms have discovered profit-maximizing decision rules. Some firms might accidentally hit on non-optimal decision rules which produce the same behaviors as profit-maximizing decisions, and thus maximize profits for fallacious reasons. Because there is continuous change in the environment and in the behaviors of the competing firms, a profit-maximizing firm must adapt both ceaselessly and erratically, and the kinds of incremental adaptation used by firms are unlikely to maintain accurate tracking. Since such financial supporters as stockholders, suppliers, and bankers do not shift their resources quickly, a non-profit-maximizing firm can survive for quite a long time; and in addition, a study by Simon (1956) suggests that a firm holding a modest resource inventory might survive indefinitely. Financial sources, not being omniscient, might mistakenly withdraw their support from firms which are maximizing long-run profits, and support instead firms which are maximizing short-run profits, with the result that all true profit maximizers would be driven out of business. And so on. The list of contingencies is quite long.

Evolutionary propositions should contain information about intra-organizational behaviors in the sense that evolution should make some behaviors more prevalent and other behaviors less so. But evolutionary selection will not ordinarily be strong enough that only one mode of intra-organizational behavior will enable an organization to survive, and it may be that survival can be achieved through many, many different modes of behavior.

Such ambiguity should be especially characteristic of organizational evolution. For one thing, organizations actively manipulate and restructure their environments. They try to change environmental properties which are acting as constraints and impeding their survival. And for another thing, organizations' environments are themselves largely composed of other organizations that are all changing at the same time, so that both organizations and their environments are evolving simultaneously toward better fitness for each other. Since neither knows the other's ultimate state, there is certain to be a great deal of exploratory behavior, and this variation becomes itself a constraint on the pattern of evolution —a constraint which increases the range of possible outcomes. Consequently, models of organizational evolution are likely to be composed of weak statements about change propensities, such as inequalities involving partial derivatives, rather than statements about what changes will definitely occur.

Nevertheless, evolutionary models remain one of the more promising topics which organization theorists have not thoroughly explored, and evolutionary models should be especially attractive to those organization theorists who perform large-sample studies. It seems plausible that, because organizational populations evolve more slowly than individual organizations adapt, it will be possible to make stronger predictions about large systems of organizations than about single cases. And one could reasonably argue that good theories about organizational populations should be a high priority objective because of their applicability to social policies and their potential for benefiting whole societies.

REFERENCES

Abegglen, J. C. *The Japanese factory*. Glencoe, Ill.: The Free Press, 1958.

Abelson, R. P., & Bernstein, A. A computer simulation model of community referendum controversies. *Public Opinion Quarterly,* 1963, 27, 93–122.

Abrahamson, M., Ed. *The professional in the organization*. Chicago: Rand McNally, 1967.

Acheson, J. M. Accounting concepts and economic opportunities in a Tarascan village: Emic and etic views. *Human Organization,* 1972, 31, 83–91.

Adams, W. *The brain drain*. New York: Macmillan, 1968.

Adelman, I., & Morris, C. T. *Society, politics & economic development.* Baltimore: Johns Hopkins Press, 1967.

Aguilar, F. J. *Scanning the business environment.* New York: Macmillan, 1967.

Aiken, M., & Hage, J. Organizational alienation: A comparative analysis. *American Sociological Review,* 1966, 31, 497–507.

Aiken, M., & Hage, J. Organizational interdependence and intra-organizational structure. *American Sociological Review,* 1968, 33, 912–930.

Ajiferuke, M., & Boddewyn, J. Socioeconomic indicators in comparative management. *Administrative Science Quarterly,* 1971, 15, 453–458.

Alchian, A. A. Uncertainty, evolution, and economic theory. *Journal of Political Economy,* 1950, 58, 211–221.

Aldrich, H. Organizational boundaries and inter-organizational conflict. *Human Relations,* 1971, 24, 279–293.

Alland, A. Jr. *Adaptation in cultural evolution.* New York: Columbia University Press, 1970.

Allen, G. C. *Japan's economic expansion.* London: Oxford University Press, 1965.

Allen, G. C. *Monopoly and restrictive practices.* London: Allen and Unwin, 1968.

Allen, T. J., & Cohen, S. I. Information flow in research and development laboratories. *Administrative Science Quarterly,* 1969, 14, 12–19.

Allison, G. T. *Essence of decision.* Boston: Little, Brown, 1972.

Altman, E. I. *Corporate bankruptcy in the United States.* Lexington, Mass.: Heath Lexington Books, 1971.

Altman, S. M., & Nathans, R. The university and approaches to problems of state and local governments. *Policy Sciences,* 1972, 3, 339–347.

A. M. Voorhees & Associates. Multi-purpose centers for the Baltimore region: Market potential. Washington: A. M. Voorhees & Associates, 1964.

Andrews, K. R. Public responsibility in the private corporation. *Journal of Industrial Economics,* 1972, 20, 135–145.

Argyris, C. *Personality and organization.* New York: Harper and Brothers, 1957.

Armstrong, J. A. Sources of administrative behavior: Some Soviet and Western European comparisons. *American Political Science Review,* 1965, 59, 643–655.

Assael, H. Constructive role of interorganizational conflict. *Administrative Science Quarterly,* 1969, 14, 573–582.

Astiz, C. A. *Pressure groups and power elites in Peruvian politics.* Ithaca, N. Y.: Cornell University Press, 1969.

Averch, H., & Johnson, L. L. Behavior of the firm under regulatory constraint. *American Economic Review,* 1962, 52, 1052–1069.

Axelrod, J., Freedman, M. B., Hatch, W. R., Katz, J., & Sanford, N. *Search for relevance.* San Francisco: Jossey-Bass, 1969.

Axelrod, R. *Conflict of interest.* Chicago: Markham, 1970.

Bain, J. S. Economies of scale, concentration, and the condition of entry in twenty manufacturing industries. *American Economic Review,* 1954, 44, 15–39.

Bain, J. S. *Barriers to new competition.* Cambridge: Harvard University Press, 1956.

Baker, F., & Schulberg, H. C. Community health care-giving systems: Integration of inter-organizational networks. In A. Sheldon, F. Baker, & C. P. McLaughlin (Eds.), *Systems and medical care.* Cambridge: M.I.T. Press, 1970, 182–206.

Baldwin, W. L. The motives of managers, environmental restraints, and the theory of managerial enterprise. *Quarterly Journal of Economics,* 1964, 78, 238–256.

Baran, P. A., & Sweezy, P. M. *Monopoly capital.* New York: Monthly Review Press, 1966.

Barker, R. G. *Ecological psychology.* Stanford: Stanford University Press, 1968.

Bass, B. M., & Franke, R. H. Societal influences on student perception of how to succeed in organizations. *Journal of Applied Psychology,* 1972, 56, 312–318.

Baty, G. B., Evan, W. M., & Rothermel, T. W. Personnel flows as interorganizational relations. *Administrative Science Quarterly,* 1971, 16, 430–443.

Bayley, D. H. *The police and political development in India.* Princeton: Princeton University Press, 1969.

Beach, L. R. Accuracy and consistency in the revision of subjective probabilities. *IEEE Transactions on Human Factors in Electronics,* 1966, HFE-7, 29–37.

Becker, G. S. *The economics of discrimination.*

Chicago: University of Chicago Press, 1957.

Becker, G. S. *Human capital.* New York: National Bureau of Economic Research, 1964.

Becker, S. W., & Stafford, F. Some determinants of organizational success. *Journal of Business,* 1967, 40, 511–518.

Beed, C. S. The separation of ownership from control. *Journal of Economic Studies,* 1966, 1 (2), 29–46.

Beesley, M. The birth and death of industrial establishments: Experience in the west midlands conurbation. *Journal of Industrial Economics,* 1955, 4, 45–61.

Behrend, H. The effort-bargain. *Industrial and Labor Relations Review,* 1957, 10, 503–515.

Belknap, I., & Steinle, J. G. *The community and its hospitals.* Syracuse: Syracuse University Press, 1963.

Bell, F. W., & Murphy, N. B. Impact of market structure on the price of a commercial banking service. *Review of Economics and Statistics,* 1969, 51, 210–213.

Bell, G. D. Organizations and the external environment. In J. W. McGuire (Ed.), *Contemporary management: Issues and viewpoints.* Englewood Cliffs, N.J.: Prentice-Hall, 1974, 259–282.

Bellah, R. N. Religious evolution. *American Sociological Review,* 1964, 29, 358–374.

Ben, C., Bouchard, R. J., & Sweet, C. E. Jr. An evaluation of simplified procedures for determining travel patterns in a small urban area. *Highway Research Record,* 1965, 88, 137–170.

Ben-David, J. *Fundamental research and the universities.* Paris: Organization for Economic Co-operation and Development, 1968.

Bendix, R. *Work and authority in industry.* New York: Harper and Row, 1963.

Bennis, W. A funny thing happened on the way to the future. *American Psychologist,* 1970, 25, 595–608.

Berle, A. A., & Means, G. C. *The modern corporation and private property.* (Rev. ed.) New York: Harcourt, Brace and World, 1967.

Berliner, J. S. *Factory and manager in the USSR.* Cambridge: Harvard University Press, 1957.

Bernstein, M. H. *Regulating business by independent commission.* Princeton: Princeton University Press, 1955.

Bidwell, C. E. The school as a formal organization. In J. G. March (Ed.), *Handbook of organizations.* Chicago: Rand McNally, 1965, 972–1022.

Blankenship, L. V., & Elling, R. H. Organizational support and community power structure: The hospital. *Journal of Health and Human Behavior,* 1962, 3, 257–269.

Blau, P. M. *The dynamics of bureaucracy.* (Rev. ed.) Chicago: University of Chicago Press, 1963.

Blau, P. M., & Scott, W. R. *Formal organizations.* San Francisco: Chandler, 1962.

Blauner, R. *Alienation and freedom.* Chicago: University of Chicago Press, 1964.

Bloch, H. D. *The circle of discrimination.* New York: New York University Press, 1969.

Blois, K. J. Vertical quasi-integration. *Journal of Industrial Economics,* 1972, 20, 253–272.

Blumberg, P. *Industrial democracy.* New York: Schocken, 1969.

Boehm, V. R. Negro-white differences in validity of employment and training selection procedures: Summary of research evidence. *Journal of Applied Psychology,* 1972, 56, 33–39.

Bonini, C. P. *Simulation of information and decision systems in the firm.* Englewood Cliffs, N.J.: Prentice-Hall, 1963.

Borden, N. H. *The economic effects of advertising.* Chicago: Irwin, 1942.

Bowden, L. W. *Diffusion of the decision to irrigate.* Chicago: Department of Geography, University of Chicago, 1965.

Britt, D., & Galle, O. R. Industrial conflict and unionization. *American Sociological Review,* 1972, 37, 46–57.

Brittain, J. A. *Corporate dividend policy.* Washington: Brookings Institution, 1966.

Brown, D. S. The management of advisory committees: An assignment for the 70s. *Public Administration Review,* 1972, 32, 334–342.

Brown, S. A., & Lambe, T. A. Parking prices in the central business district. *Socio-Economic Planning Sciences,* 1972, 6, 133–144.

Buck, V. E. A model for viewing an organization as a system of constraints. In J. D. Thompson (Ed.), *Approaches to organizational design.* Pittsburgh: University of Pittsburgh Press, 1966, 103–172.

Burns, T. On the plurality of social systems. In J. R. Lawrence (Ed.), *Operational research and the social sciences.* London: Tavistock, 1966, 165–177.

Burns, T., & Stalker, G. M. *The management of innovation*. London: Tavistock, 1961.

Burrage, M. The group ties of occupations in Britain and the United States. *Administrative Science Quarterly*, 1972, 17, 240–253.

Cameron, P., Robertson, D., & Zaks, J. Sound pollution, noise pollution, and health: Community parameters. *Journal of Applied Psychology*, 1972, 56, 67–74.

Carlson, R. O. Public relations. In D. L. Sills (Ed.), *International encyclopedia of the social sciences*, Vol. 13. New York: Macmillan and The Free Press, 1968, 208–217.

Carroll, T. W. *SINDI 2*. East Lansing: Computer Institute for Social Science Research, Michigan State University, 1969.

Carter, A. P. Changes in the structure of the American economy, 1947 to 1958 and 1962. *Review of Economics and Statistics*, 1967, 49, 209–224.

Cartter, A. M., Reder, M. W., McKersie, R. B., Tolles, N. A., & Henle, P. Wages. In D. L. Sills (Ed.), *International encyclopedia of the social sciences*, Vol. 16. New York: Macmillan and The Free Press, 1968, 397–429.

Caudill, W. Around the clock patient care in Japanese psychiatric hospitals. *American Sociological Review*, 1961, 26, 204–214.

Caves, R. *American industry*. (2nd ed.) Englewood Cliffs, N.J.: Prentice-Hall, 1967.

Centers, R., & Bugental, D. E. Intrinsic and extrinsic job motivations among different segments of the working population. *Journal of Applied Psychology*, 1966, 50, 193–197.

Chamberlain, N. W. *Enterprise and environment*. New York: McGraw-Hill, 1968.

Chamberlin, E. H. *The theory of monopolistic competition*. (8th ed.) Cambridge: Harvard University Press, 1962.

Chandler, A. D. Jr. *Strategy and structure*. Cambridge: M.I.T. Press, 1962.

Channon, D. F. *The strategy and structure of British enterprise*. Cambridge: Graduate School of Business Administration, Harvard University, 1972.

Chatov, R. The problem of independent regulatory agency behavior—a sociological systemic and equilibrium approach. (working paper) Berkeley: School of Business Administration, University of California, 1971.

Cheit, E. F. The new place of business: Why managers cultivate social responsibility. In E. F. Cheit (Ed.), *The business establishment*. New York: Wiley, 1964, 152–192.

Child, J. Quaker employers and industrial relations. *Sociological Review*, 1964, 12, 293–315.

Child, J. *The business enterprise in modern industrial society*. London: Collier-Macmillan, 1969.

Child, J. Organizational structure, environment, and performance: The role of strategic choice. *Sociology*, 1972, 6, 1–22.

Christie, R., & Geis, F. L. *Studies in Machiavellianism*. New York: Academic Press, 1970.

Clark, A. W., & McCabe, S. Leadership beliefs of Australian managers. *Journal of Applied Psychology*, 1970, 54, 1–6.

Clark, B. R. Interorganizational patterns in education. *Administrative Science Quarterly*, 1965, 10, 224–237.

Clark, B. R. *The distinctive college*. Chicago: Aldine, 1970.

Clark, B. R. The organizational saga in higher education. *Administrative Science Quarterly*, 1972, 17, 178–184.

Clark, B. R., Anderson, C. A., & Halsey, A. H. Education. In D. L. Sills (Ed.), *International encyclopedia of the social sciences*, Vol. 4. New York: Macmillan and The Free Press, 1968, 509–533.

Clark, J. M. *Competition as a dynamic process*. Washington: Brookings Institution, 1961.

Clemens, E. W. *Economics and public utilities*. New York: Appleton-Century-Crofts, 1950.

Cohen, M. D., March, J. G., & Olsen, J. P. A garbage can model of organizational choice. *Administrative Science Quarterly*, 1972, 17, 1–25.

Cole, R. E. *Japanese blue collar*. Berkeley: University of California Press, 1972.

Coleman, J. S., Campbell, E. Q., Hobson, C. J., McPartland, J., Mood, A. M., Weinfeld, F. D., & York, R. L. *Equality of educational opportunity*. Washington: U.S. Government Printing Office, 1966.

Coleman, R. P. The significance of social stratification in selling. In M. L. Bell (Ed.), *Marketing: A maturing discipline*. Chicago: American Marketing Association, 1961, 171–184.

Collins, N. R., & Preston, L. E. Price-cost margins and industry structure. *Review of Economics and Statistics*, 1969, 51, 271–286.

Collins, R. Functional and conflict theories of

educational stratification. *American Sociological Review,* 1971, 36, 1002–1019.

Comanor, W. S. Market structure, product differentiation, and industrial research. *Quarterly Journal of Economics,* 1967, 81, 639–657. (a)

Comanor, W. S. Vertical mergers, market powers, and the antitrust laws. *American Economic Review, Papers and Proceedings,* 1967, 57, 254–265. (b)

Comanor, W. S., & Wilson, T. A. Advertising market structure and performance. *Review of Economics and Statistics,* 1967, 49, 423–440.

Commoner, B. *The closing circle.* New York: Knopf, 1971.

Cook, F. J. *The warfare state.* New York: Macmillan, 1962.

Coombs, P. H. *The world educational crisis.* London: Oxford University Press, 1968.

Cooper, R. Man, task, and technology. *Human Relations,* 1972, 25, 131–157.

Corwin, R. G. Strategies for organizational innovation: An empirical comparison. *American Sociological Review,* 1972, 37, 441–454.

Council for Economic Education. *Taxation and foreign trade.* New York: Asia Publishing House, 1960.

Crane, D. *Invisible colleges.* Chicago: University of Chicago Press, 1972.

Crawford, M. P. Retirement and disengagement. *Human Relations,* 1971, 24, 255–278.

Crecine, J. P. *Governmental problem solving.* Chicago: Rand McNally, 1969.

Cressey, D. R. *Theft of the nation.* New York: Harper and Row, 1969.

Crozier, M. Bureaucracy as a cultural phenomenon: The French case. In M. Crozier, *The bureaucratic phenomenon.* London: Tavistock, 1964, 209–314.

Crozier, M. The relationship between micro- and macrosociology. *Human Relations,* 1972, 25, 239–251.

Crum, W. L. *The age structure of the corporate system.* Berkeley: University of California Press, 1953.

Cummings, L. L., & Schmidt, S. M. Managerial attitudes of Greeks: The roles of culture and industrialization. *Administrative Science Quarterly,* 1972, 17, 265–272.

Cummings, L. L., Harnett, D. L., & Stevens, O. J. Risk, fate, conciliation, and trust: An international study of attitudinal differences among executives. *Academy of Management Journal,* 1971, 14, 285–304.

Curtis, J. Voluntary association joining: A cross-national comparative note. *American Sociological Review,* 1971, 36, 872–880.

Cyert, R. M., & March, J. G. *A behavioral theory of the firm.* Englewood Cliffs, N.J.: Prentice-Hall, 1963.

Cyert, R. M., Simon, H. A., & Trow, D. B. Observation of a business decision. *Journal of Business,* 1956, 29, 237–248.

Dahl, R. A. *Who governs?* New Haven: Yale University Press, 1961.

Dahrendorf, R. *Class and class conflict in industrial society.* Stanford: Stanford University Press, 1959.

Dalton, M. *Men who manage.* New York: Wiley, 1959.

Danet, B. The language of persuasion in bureaucracy: "Modern" and "traditional" appeals to the Israel customs authorities. *American Sociological Review,* 1971, 36, 847–859.

Davis, S. M. Entrepreneurial succession. *Administrative Science Quarterly,* 1968, 13, 402–416.

DeLeeuw, F., & Gramlich, E. Staff economic study: The federal reserve-MIT econometric model. *Federal Reserve Bulletin,* 1968, 54, 11–40.

Demerath, N. J. III, & Thiessen, V. On spitting against the wind: Organizational precariousness and American irreligion. *American Journal of Sociology,* 1966, 71, 674–687.

Denhardt, R. B. Bureaucratic socialization and organizational accommodation. *Administrative Science Quarterly,* 1969, 13, 441–450.

Desai, M. An econometric model of the world tin economy, 1948–1961. *Econometrica,* 1966, 34, 105–134.

Diamond, S. From organization to society: Virginia in the seventeenth century. *American Journal of Sociology,* 1958, 63, 457–475.

Dibble, V. K. The organization of traditional authority: English county government, 1558 to 1640. In J. G. March (Ed.), *Handbook of organizations.* Chicago: Rand McNally, 1965, 879–909.

Dill, W. R. Environment as an influence on managerial autonomy. *Administrative Science Quarterly,* 1958, 2, 409–443.

Dill, W. R. The impact of environment on organizational development. In S. Mailick & E. H. Van Ness (Eds.), *Concepts and issues in administrative behavior.* Englewood Cliffs, N.J.: Prentice-Hall, 1962, 94–109.

Dill, W. R. Business organizations. In J. G. March (Ed.), *Handbook of organizations.* Chicago: Rand McNally, 1965, 1071–1114.

Downie, J. *The competitive process.* London: Gerald Duckworth, 1958.

Dubin, R. Industrial workers' worlds: A study of the "central life interests" of industrial workers. *Social Problems,* 1956, 3, 131–142.

Duncan, R. B. Characteristics of organizational environments and perceived environmental uncertainty. *Administrative Science Quarterly,* 1972, 17, 313–327.

Duncan, R. B. Multiple decision-making structures in adapting to environmental uncertainty: The impact on organizational effectiveness. *Human Relations,* 1973, 26, 273–291.

Durkheim, E. *The division of labor in society.* New York: Macmillan, 1933.

Edwards, C. D. Conglomerate bigness as a source of power. In the National Bureau of Economic Research report, *Business concentration and price policy.* Princeton: Princeton University Press, 1955, 331–359.

Edwards, C. D. *The price discrimination law.* Washington: Brookings Institution, 1959.

Edwards, C. D. *Control of cartels and monopolies.* Dobbs Ferry, N.Y.: Oceana, 1967.

Eisenstadt, S. N. Bureaucracy, bureaucratization, markets, and power structure. In S. N. Eisenstadt, *Essays on comparative institutions.* New York: Wiley, 1965, 177–215. (a)

Eisenstadt, S. N. Political orientations of bureaucracies in centralized empires. In S. N. Eisenstadt, *Essays on comparative institutions.* New York: Wiley, 1965, 216–250. (b)

Elling, R. H., & Halebsky, S. Organizational differentiation and support: A conceptual framework. *Administrative Science Quarterly,* 1961, 6, 185–209.

Elliott, O. *Men at the top.* London: Weidenfeld and Nicolson, 1960.

Ellis, W. W. *White ethics and black power.* Chicago: Aldine, 1969.

Elton, E., & Gruber, M. The effect of share repurchase on the value of the firm. *Journal of Finance,* 1968, 23, 135–149.

Emery, F. E., & Trist, E. L. The causal texture of organizational environments. *Human Relations,* 1965, 18, 21–32.

England, G. W., & Lee, R. Organizational goals and expected behavior among American, Japanese, and Korean managers—a comparative study. *Academy of Management Journal,* 1971, 14, 425–438.

Engwall, L. Business behavior: The cigarette case. *Marquette Business Review,* 1973, 17, 59–72.

Epstein, E. M. *The corporation in American politics.* Englewood Cliffs, N.J.: Prentice-Hall, 1969.

Esposito, L., & Esposito, F. F. Foreign competition and domestic industry profitability. *Review of Economics and Statistics,* 1971, 53, 343–353.

Evan, W. M. Toward a theory of interorganizational relations. *Management Science,* 1965, 11, B-217-B-230.

Evan, W. M. The organization-set: Toward a theory of interorganizational relations. In J. D. Thompson (Ed.), *Approaches to organizational design.* Pittsburgh: University of Pittsburgh Press, 1966, 174–191.

Featherman, D. L. The socioeconomic achievement of white religio-ethnic subgroups: Social and psychological explanations. *American Sociological Review,* 1971, 36, 207–222.

Fellner, W. J. *Competition among the few.* Clifton, N.J.: Augustus M. Kelley, 1949.

Fetter, R. B., & Thompson, J. D. Simulation of a hospital subsystem: The maternity service. In J. M. Dutton & W. H. Starbuck (Eds.), *Computer simulation of human behavior.* New York: Wiley, 1971, 387–399.

Fidler, J. E. Commercial activity location model. *Highway Research Record,* 1967, 207, 68–84.

Fiedler, F. E. Predicting the effects of leadership training and experience from the contingency model. *Journal of Applied Psychology,* 1972, 56, 114–119.

Finer, S. E. The political power of private capital. (Part I) *Sociological Review,* 1955, 3, 279–294.

Finer, S. E. The political power of private capital. (Part II) *Sociological Review,* 1956, 4, 5–30.

Finger, N. *The impact of government subsidies on industrial management.* New York: Praeger, 1971.

Fisher, F. M., Griliches, Z., & Kaysen, C. F. The costs of automobile model changes since 1949. *Journal of Political Economy,* 1962, 70, 433–451.

Flanders, A. The internal social responsibilities

of industry. *British Journal of Industrial Relations,* 1966, 4, 1–21.

Florence, P. S. *Economics and sociology of industry.* London: C. A. Watts, 1964.

Flores, F. The applicability of American management practices to developing countries: A case study of the Philippines. *Management International,* 1972, 12 (1), 83–95.

Fog, B. *Industrial pricing policies.* Amsterdam: North-Holland, 1960.

Fogel, R. W. *Railroads and American economic growth.* Baltimore: Johns Hopkins Press, 1964.

Form, W. H., & Geschwender, J. A. Social reference basis of job satisfaction: The case of manual workers. *American Sociological Review,* 1962, 27, 228–237.

Form, W. H., & Miller, D. C. *Industry, labor, and community.* New York: Harper Brothers, 1960.

Foskett, J. M. *Role consensus.* Eugene: Center for the Advanced Study of Educational Administration, University of Oregon, 1969.

Freeman, L. C., Fararo, T. J., Bloomberg, W. Jr., & Sunshine, M. H. Locating leaders in local communities: A comparison of some alternative approaches. *American Sociological Review,* 1963, 28, 791–798.

Friedlander, F. Comparative work value systems. *Personnel Psychology,* 1965, 18, 1–20.

Friedlander, F., & Greenberg, S. Effect of job attitudes, training, and organization climate on performance of the hard-core unemployed. *Journal of Applied Psychology,* 1971, 55, 287–295.

Friedlander, F., & Pickle, H. Components of effectiveness in small organizations. *Administrative Science Quarterly,* 1968, 13, 289–304.

Friedman, J. W. Reaction functions and the theory of duopoly. *Review of Economic Studies,* 1968, 35, 257–272.

Friesema, H. P. Interjurisdictional agreements in metropolitan areas. *Administrative Science Quarterly,* 1970, 15, 242–252.

Fromm, G., Ed. *Tax incentives and capital spending.* Washington: Brookings Institution, 1970.

Gael, S., & Grant, D. L. Employment test validation for minority and nonminority telephone company service representatives. *Journal of Applied Psychology,* 1972, 56, 135–139.

Galbraith, J. K. *American capitalism.* Boston: Houghton Mifflin, 1956.

Galbraith, J. K. *The new industrial state.* London: Hamish Hamilton, 1967.

Galbraith, J. R. Achieving integration through information systems. *Academy of Management, Proceedings of the 28th Annual Meeting,* December, 1968, 111–120.

Gensch, D. H. A computer simulation model for selecting advertising schedules. *Journal of Marketing Research,* 1969, 6, 203–214.

Gibson, D. P. *The thirty billion dollar negro.* London: Macmillan, 1969.

Goffman, E. *The presentation of self in everyday life.* Garden City, N.Y.: Doubleday Anchor, 1959.

Goldman, M. I. Product differentiation and advertising: Some lessons from Soviet experience. *Journal of Political Economy,* 1960, 68, 346–357.

Goldthorpe, J. H., Lockwood, D., Bechhofer, F., & Platt, J. *The affluent worker.* London: Cambridge University Press, 1968.

Goodman, P. S., & Moore, B. E. Critical issues of cross-cultural management research. *Human Organization,* 1972, 31, 39–45.

Goody, J., Irving, B., & Tahany, N. Causal inferences concerning inheritance and property. *Human Relations,* 1971, 24, 295–314.

Gordon, G., & Marquis, S. Freedom, visibility of consequences, and scientific innovation. *American Journal of Sociology,* 1966, 72, 195–202.

Gordon, R. A. *Business leadership in the large corporation.* (2nd ed.) Berkeley: University of California Press, 1961.

Gort, M. *Diversification and integration in American industry.* Princeton: Princeton University Press, 1962.

Grabowski, H. G., & Mueller, D. C. Managerial and stockholder welfare models of firm expenditures. *Review of Economics and Statistics,* 1972, 54, 9–24.

Graham, L. S. *Civil service reform in Brazil.* Austin: University of Texas Press, 1968.

Granick, D. *The red executive.* London: Macmillan, 1960.

Graves, D. A cross-cultural comparison of managerial behavior in England and France. *International Studies of Management & Organization,* 1972, 2, 105–116.

Greenwald, H. P. Patterns of authority in two herding societies: An ecological approach.

Administrative Science Quarterly, 1972, 17, 207–217.

Grove, J. W. *Government and industry in Britain.* London: Longmans, 1962.

Guetzkow, H. Relations among organizations. In R. V. Bowers (Ed.), *Studies on behavior in organizations.* Athens: University of Georgia Press, 1966, 13–44.

Gustafsson, B. Types of religious institutionalization. In N. Ehrenstrom & W. G. Muelder (Eds.), *Institutionalism and church unity.* London: SCM Press, 1963, 123–143.

Hacker, A., Ed. *The corporation take-over.* New York: Anchor Books, 1965.

Hagen, E. E. *On the theory of social change.* Homewood, Ill.: Dorsey Press, 1962.

Haire, M. Biological models and empirical histories of the growth of organizations. In M. Haire (Ed.), *Modern organization theory.* New York: Wiley, 1959, 272–306.

Haire, M., Ghiselli, E. E., & Porter, L. W. *Managerial thinking.* New York: Wiley, 1966.

Hall, D. T., & Mansfield, R. Organizational and individual response to external stress. *Administrative Science Quarterly,* 1971, 16, 533–547.

Hall, E. T. *The silent language.* New York: Doubleday, 1959.

Hall, R. H. Professionalization and bureaucratization. *American Sociological Review,* 1968, 33, 92–104.

Hall, R. L., & Hitch, C. J. Price theory and business behaviour. *Oxford Economic Papers,* 1939, No. 2, 12–45.

Hamilton, H. R., Goldstone, S. E., Milliman, J. W., Pugh, A. L. III, Roberts, E. B., & Zellner, A. *Systems simulation for regional analysis.* Cambridge: M.I.T. Press, 1969.

Hamilton, R. F. *Affluence and the French worker in the fourth republic.* Princeton: Princeton University Press, 1967.

Hammel, E. A. *The pink yo-yo.* Berkeley: Institute of International Studies, University of California, 1969.

Handyside, J. D., & Speak, M. Job satisfaction: Myths and realities. *British Journal of Industrial Relations,* 1964, 2, 57–65.

Hansen, W. L., & Weisbrod, B. A. *Benefits, costs, and finance of public higher education.* Chicago: Markham, 1969.

Hanson, P. *The consumer in the Soviet economy.* Evanston: Northwestern University Press, 1969.

Harris, R. L. The effects of political change on the role set of the senior bureaucrats in Ghana and Nigeria. *Administrative Science Quarterly,* 1969, 13, 386–401.

Harris, S. E. *Higher education.* New York: McGraw-Hill, 1962.

Harrison, G. S. Flow of communication between government agencies and Eskimo villages. *Human Organization,* 1972, 31, 1–9.

Harshbarger, D. The strain towards irrelevance. *Human Relations,* 1972, 25, 253–263.

Hasenfeld, Y. People processing organizations: An exchange approach. *American Sociological Review,* 1972, 37, 256–263.

Hawkins, D. F. The development of modern financial reporting practices among American manufacturing corporations. *Business History Review,* 1963, 37, 135–168.

Hawkins, K., & Radcliffe, R. Competition in the brewing industry. *Journal of Industrial Economics,* 1972, 20, 20–41.

Heath, D. B., Erasmus, C. J., & Buechler, H. C. *Land reform and social revolution in Bolivia.* New York: Praeger, 1968.

Hedberg, B. Uncertainty reduction and action programs in organizational transition from growth to non-growth. (working paper) Berlin: International Institute of Management, 1973.

Hedberg, B. Reframing as a way to cope with organizational stagnation. (working paper) Berlin: International Institute of Management, 1974.

Helper, R. *Racial policies and practices of real estate brokers.* Minneapolis: University of Minnesota Press, 1969.

Heroux, R. L., & Wallace, W. A. On the development of new communities. *Socio-Economic Planning Sciences,* 1972, 6, 387–407.

Hicks, F. Making a living during the dead season in sugar-producing regions of the Caribbean. *Human Organization,* 1972, 31, 73–81.

Hickson, D. J., Hinings, C. R., McMillan, C. J., & Schwitter, J. P. The culture-free context of organization structure: A trinational comparison. *Sociology,* 1974, 8, 59–80.

Hill, W. The goal formation process in complex organizations. *Journal of Management Studies,* 1969, 6, 198–208.

Hirsch, P. M. Processing fads and fashions: An

organization-set analysis of cultural industry systems. *American Journal of Sociology,* 1972, 77, 639–659.

Hirsch, W. *Scientists in American society.* New York: Random House, 1968.

Hoenack, S. A. The efficient allocation of subsidies to college students. *American Economic Review,* 1971, 61, 302–311.

Hofstede, G. H. Experiences with Gordon's surveys of personal and interpersonal values in an international business school. (working paper) Lausanne: Institut pour l'Etude des Méthodes de Direction de l'Entreprise, 1972.

Hoiberg, E. O., & Cloyd, J. S. Definition and measurement of continuous variation in ecological analysis. *American Sociological Review,* 1971, 36, 65–74.

Hollander, S. C. Measuring the cost and value of marketing. *Business Topics,* 1961, 9 (3), 17–27.

Hoover, E. M., & Moses, L. N. Spatial economics. In D. L. Sills (Ed.), *International encyclopedia of the social sciences,* Vol. 15. New York: Macmillan and The Free Press, 1968, 95–108.

Hulin, C. L. Effects of community characteristics on measures of job satisfaction. *Journal of Applied Psychology,* 1966, 50, 185–192.

Hyrenius, H., Holmberg, I., & Carlson, M. *Demographic models: DM3.* Göteborg: University of Göteborg, 1967.

Illich, I. *De-schooling society.* New York: Harper and Row, 1971.

Jacoby, J., Olson, J. C., & Haddock, R. A. Price, brand name, and product composition characteristics as determinants of perceived quality. *Journal of Applied Psychology,* 1971, 55, 570–579.

Janowitz, M. *The military in the political development of new nations.* Chicago: University of Chicago Press, 1964.

Kahn, A. E. The chemical industry. In W. Adams (Ed.), *The structure of American industry.* New York: Macmillan, 1961, 246–252.

Kahn, A. E. The role of patents. In J. P. Miller (Ed.), *Competition, cartels, and their regulation.* Amsterdam: North-Holland, 1962, 308–346.

Kaplan, R. S., & Roll, R. Investor evaluation of accounting information: Some empirical evidence. *Journal of Business,* 1972, 45, 225–257.

Katz, D., & Kahn, R. L. *The social psychology of organizations.* New York: Wiley, 1966.

Katz, E., & Eisenstadt, S. N. Some sociological observations on the response of Israeli organizations to new immigrants. In S. N. Eisenstadt, *Essays on comparative institutions.* New York: Wiley, 1965, 251–271.

Katzell, R. A., Barrett, R. S., & Parker, T. C. Job satisfaction, job performance, and situational characteristics. *Journal of Applied Psychology,* 1961, 45, 65–72.

Kaufman, H. *The forest ranger.* Baltimore: Johns Hopkins Press, 1960.

Kavčič, B., Rus, V., & Tannenbaum, A. S. Control, participation, and effectiveness in four Yugoslav industrial organizations. *Administrative Science Quarterly,* 1971, 16, 74–86.

Kaysen, C., & Turner, D. F. *Antitrust policy.* Cambridge: Harvard University Press, 1959.

Kelly, J. *Is scientific management possible?* London: Faber and Faber, 1968.

Kernan, J. B., & Schkade, L. L. A cross-cultural analysis of stimulus sampling. *Administrative Science Quarterly,* 1972, 17, 351–358.

Kerr, C., & Siegel, A. The interindustry propensity to strike—an international comparison. In A. Kornhauser, R. Dubin, & A. M. Ross (Eds.), *Industrial conflict.* New York: McGraw-Hill, 1954, 189–212.

Kerr, C., Dunlop, J. T., Harbison, F. H., & Myers, C. A. *Industrialism and industrial man.* Cambridge: Harvard University Press, 1960.

Kessel, R. A. Price discrimination in medicine. *Journal of Law and Economics,* 1958, 1, 20–53.

Khandwalla, P. N. Environment and the organization structure of firms. (working paper) Montreal: Faculty of Management, McGill University, 1970.

Khandwalla, P. N. The effect of competition and firm size on the decentralization of top management decisions: An empirical study. (working paper) Montreal: Faculty of Management, McGill University, 1971.

Khandwalla, P. N. Uncertainty and the "optimal" design of organizations. (working paper) Montreal: Faculty of Management, McGill University, 1972.

Kilbridge, M., & Wester, L. An economic

model for the division of labor. *Management Science*, 1966, 12, B-255–B-269.

Kirlin, J. J., & Erie, S. P. The study of city governance and public policy making: A critical appraisal. *Public Administration Review*, 1972, 32, 173–184.

Kohlmeier, L. M. Jr. *The regulators*. New York: Harper and Row, 1970.

Kohn, M. L. Bureaucratic man: A portrait and an interpretation. *American Sociological Review*, 1971, 36, 461–474.

Kolko, G. *Wealth and power in America*. New York: Praeger, 1962.

Kovak, R. M. Urban renewal controversies. *Public Administration Review*, 1972, 32, 359–372.

Krauss, W. R. Toward a theory of political participation of public bureaucrats. *Administrative Science Quarterly*, 1971, 16, 180–191.

Kravis, I. B. Income distribution: Functional share. In D. L. Sills (Ed.), *International encyclopedia of the social sciences*, Vol. 7. New York: Macmillan and The Free Press, 1968, 132–145.

Kriesberg, L. Occupational controls among steel distributors. *American Journal of Sociology*, 1955, 61, 203–212.

Krzyzaniak, M., & Musgrave, R. A. *The shifting of the corporation income tax*. Baltimore: Johns Hopkins Press, 1963.

Kuehn, D. A. Stock market valuation and acquisitions: An empirical test of one component of managerial utility. *Journal of Industrial Economics*, 1969, 17, 132–144.

Lakshmanan, T. R., & Hansen, W. G. A retail market potential model. *Journal of the American Institute of Planners*, 1965, 31, 134–143.

Landsberger, H. A., Ed. *Latin American peasant movements*. Ithaca, N.Y.: Cornell University Press, 1969.

Landsberger, H. A. A framework for the cross-cultural analysis of formal organizations. In H. A. Landsberger (Ed.), *Comparative perspectives on formal organizations*. Boston: Little, Brown, 1970, 1–16.

Lang, K. Military organizations. In J. G. March (Ed.), *Handbook of organizations*. Chicago: Rand McNally, 1965, 838–878.

Larner, R. J. Ownership and control in the 200 largest nonfinancial corporations, 1929 and 1963. *American Economic Review*, 1966, 54, 777–787.

Larson, H. M., & Porter, K. W. *History of Humble Oil & Refining Company*. New York: Harper Brothers, 1959.

Lawer, N. D. The relocation of the United States Public Health Service. *Public Administration Review*, 1972, 32, 43–48.

Lawrence, P. R., & Lorsch, J. W. *Organization and environment*. Cambridge: Graduate School of Business Administration, Harvard University, 1967.

Layton, C. *European advanced technology*. London: Allen and Unwin, 1969.

Lee, D. Are basic needs ultimate? *Journal of Abnormal and Social Psychology*, 1948, 43, 391–395.

Lefton, M., & Rosengren, W. R. Organizations and clients: Lateral and longitudinal dimensions. *American Sociological Review*, 1966, 31, 802–810.

Leibenstein, H. *Economic theory and organizational analysis*. New York: Harper Brothers, 1960.

Lempert, R., & Ikeda, K. Evictions from public housing: Effects of independent review. *American Sociological Review*, 1970, 35, 852–860.

Lenski, G. *The religious factor*. Garden City, N.Y.: Doubleday, 1961.

Levine, J. H. The sphere of influence. *American Sociological Review*, 1972, 37, 14–27.

Levine, S., & White, P. E. Exchange as a conceptual framework for the study of interorganizational relationships. *Administrative Science Quarterly*, 1961, 5, 583–601.

Levins, R. *Evolution in changing environments*. Princeton: Princeton University Press, 1968.

Levinson, C. *Capital, inflation, and the multinationals*. London: Allen and Unwin, 1971.

Levitt, M., & Feldbaum, E. Policy making and the patent system: A test of the democratic theory. (working paper) Washington: Department of Political Science, Howard University, 1971.

Levitt, T. The dangers of social responsibility. *Harvard Business Review*, 1958, 36(5), 41–50.

Levy, B. Effects of "racism" on the racial bureaucracy. *Public Administration Review*, 1972, 32, 479–486.

Levy, M. J. Jr. *Modernization and the structure of societies*, 2 vols. Princeton: Princeton University Press, 1966.

Lieberson, S. An empirical study of military-industrial linkages. *American Journal of Sociology,* 1971, 76, 562–584.

Lief, A. *It floats.* New York: Rinehart, 1958.

Light, I. H. *Ethnic enterprise in America.* Berkeley: University of California Press, 1972.

Lindblom, C. E. *The policy-making process.* Englewood Cliffs, N.J.: Prentice-Hall, 1968.

Litt, E. *The public vocational university.* New York: Holt, Rinehart and Winston, 1969.

Litterer, J. A. Systematic management: The search for order and integration. *Business History Review,* 1961, 35, 461–476.

Litterer, J. A. Systematic management: Design for organizational recoupling in American manufacturing firms. *Business History Review,* 1963, 37, 369–391.

Litwak, E., & Hylton, L. F. Interorganizational analysis: A hypothesis on co-ordinating agencies. *Administrative Science Quarterly,* 1962, 6, 395–420.

Locklin, D. P. *Economics of transportation.* (6th ed.) Homewood, Ill.: Irwin, 1966.

Loescher, S. M. *Imperfect collusion in the cement industry.* Cambridge: Harvard University Press, 1959.

Long, N. E. *The polity.* Chicago: Rand McNally, 1962.

Lorie, J. H. Securities markets. In D. L. Sills (Ed.), *International encyclopedia of the social sciences,* Vol. 14. New York: Macmillan and The Free Press, 1968, 136–143.

Lowi, T. J. Four systems of policy, politics, and choice. *Public Administration Review,* 1972, 32, 298–310.

Lowry, I. S. A model of metropolis. Santa Monica: RAND Corporation, RM-4035-RC, 1964.

Lowry, I. S. Reforming rent control in New York City: The role of research in policymaking. *Policy Sciences,* 1972, 3, 47–58.

Luckham, A. R. Institutional transfer and breakdown in a new nation: The Nigerian military. *Administrative Science Quarterly,* 1971, 16, 387–405.

Lupton, T., & Wilson, C. S. The social background and connections of "top decision makers." *Manchester School of Economic and Social Studies,* 1959, 27, 30–51.

McArthur, J. H., & Scott, B. R. *Industrial planning in France.* Cambridge: Division of Research, Harvard Business School, 1969.

Macaulay, S. Non-contractual relations in business: A preliminary study. *American Sociological Review,* 1963, 28, 55–67.

McCarthy, J. L. The American copper industry: 1947–1955. *Yale Economic Essays,* 1964, 4, 64–130.

McClelland, D. C. *The achieving society.* Princeton: Van Nostrand, 1961.

McConnell, G. *Private power and American democracy.* New York: Knopf, 1966.

Machlup, F. *The basing-point system.* Philadelphia: Blakiston, 1949.

Machlup, F. The supply of inventors and inventions. In National Bureau of Economic Research (Eds.), *The rate and direction of inventive activity.* Princeton: Princeton University Press, 1962, 143–167.

Machlup, F. Patents. In D. L. Sills (Ed.), *International encyclopedia of the social sciences,* Vol. 11. New York: Macmillan and The Free Press, 1968, 461–472.

Mack, R. P. Trends in American consumption and the aspiration to consume. *American Economic Review, Papers and Proceedings,* 1956, 46, 55–68.

McKie, J. W. *Tin cans and tin plate.* Cambridge: Harvard University Press, 1959.

McKinney, J. C., & Bourque, L. B. The changing South: National incorporation of a region. *American Sociological Review,* 1971, 36, 399–412.

McWhinney, W. H. Organizational form, decision modalities and the environment. *Human Relations,* 1968, 21, 269–281.

Mancke, R. B. Iron ore and steel: A case study of the economic causes and consequences of vertical integration. *Journal of Industrial Economics,* 1972, 20, 220–229.

Maniha, J., & Perrow, C. The reluctant organization and the aggressive environment. *Administrative Science Quarterly,* 1965, 10, 238–257.

Mann, H. M. Seller concentration, barriers to entry, and rates of return in thirty industries, 1950–1960. *Review of Economics and Statistics,* 1966, 48, 296–307.

Mansfield, E. *The economics of technological change.* New York: W. W. Norton, 1968.

Mansfield, R. The initiation of graduates in industry. *Human Relations,* 1972, 25, 77–86.

March, J. G., & Simon, H. A. *Organizations.* New York: Wiley, 1958.

Marcus, M. Firms' exit rates and their determinants. *Journal of Industrial Economics,* 1967, 16, 10–22.

Marcuse, H. *One dimensional man*. Boston: Beacon Press, 1964.

Markham, J. W. The nature and significance of price leadership. *American Economic Review*, 1951, 41, 891–905.

Marris, R. *The economic theory of "managerial" capitalism*. New York: The Free Press, 1964.

Marx, K. *Capital*. New York: International Publishers, 1967.

Mascarenhas, R. C. A conceptual framework for understanding autonomy for public enterprises in India. *Academy of Management Journal*, 1972, 15, 65–75.

Meade, J. E. Is "the new industrial state" inevitable? *Economic Journal*, 1968, 78, 372–392.

Means, G. C. *Pricing power and the public interest*. New York: Harper Brothers, 1962.

Medvedev, Z. A. *The Medvedev papers*. New York: St. Martin's Press, 1971.

Milbrath, L. W. *The Washington lobbyists*. Chicago: Rand McNally, 1963.

Miliband, R. *The state in capitalist society*. New York: Basic Books, 1969.

Miller, D. C. Industry and community power structure: A comparative study of an American and an English city. *American Sociological Review*, 1958, 23, 9–15.

Miller, D. C. *International community power structures*. Bloomington: Indiana University Press, 1970.

Miller, G. A., & Wager, L. W. Adult socialization, organizational structure, and role orientations. *Administrative Science Quarterly*, 1971, 16, 151–163.

Miller, J. G. Living systems: The organization. *Behavioral Science*, 1972, 17, 1–182.

Miller, M. J., & Thomas, C. W. Structurally-generated alienation and organizational effectiveness in total institutions. (working paper) Richmond: Department of Sociology, Virginia Commonwealth University, 1971.

Miller, R. A. Exclusive dealing in the petroleum industry: The refiner-lessee dealer relationship. *Yale Economic Essays*, 1963, 3, 223–247.

Mills, C. W. *The power elite*. London: Oxford University Press, 1956.

Milne, R. S. Mechanistic and organic models of public administration in developing countries. *Administrative Science Quarterly*, 1970, 15, 57–67.

Miner, J. B. Changes in student attitudes toward bureaucratic role prescriptions during the 1960s. *Administrative Science Quarterly*, 1971, 16, 351–364.

Mintzberg, H. Research on strategy-making. *Academy of Management Proceedings*, 1972, 90–94.

Misra, S., & Jain, S. Effect of fittingness, type of goods, and type of slogan on brand awareness. *Journal of Applied Psychology*, 1971, 55, 580–585.

Mohr, L. B. Determinants of innovation in organizations. *American Political Science Review*, 1969, 63, 111–126.

Monsen, R. J., Chiu, J. S., & Cooley, D. E. The effect of separation of ownership and control on the performance of the large firm. *Quarterly Journal of Economics*, 1968, 82, 435–451.

Montgomery, J. D. Allocation of authority in land reform programs: A comparative study of administrative processes and outputs. *Administrative Science Quarterly*, 1972, 17, 62–75.

Moore, W. E. Industrialization and social change. In B. F. Hoselitz & W. E. Moore (Eds.), *Industrialization and society*. Paris: UNESCO-Mouton, 1963, 299–359.

Morgan, J. N. Bilateral monopoly and the competitive output. *Quarterly Journal of Economics*, 1949, 63, 371–391.

Morrill, R. L. Migration and the spread and growth of urban settlement. *Lund Studies in Geography, Series B*, 1965, 26, 1–208.

Mott, B. J. F. *Anatomy of a coordinating council*. Pittsburgh: University of Pittsburgh Press, 1968.

Mulder, M. Power equalization through participation? *Administrative Science Quarterly*, 1971, 16, 31–38.

Myrdal, G. *Challenge to affluence*. New York: Pantheon, 1963.

Narver, J. C. Rational management responses to external effects. *Academy of Management Journal*, 1971, 14, 99–115.

Nath, R. A methodological review of cross-cultural management research. *International Social Science Journal*, 1968, 20, 35–62.

Neering, M., Williams, C., Faught, W., Avioli, P., Maylie, J., Sterling, D., & Pantell, R. H. Stanford land use study. *Socio-Economic Planning Sciences*, 1972, 6, 409–419.

Nelkin, D. *The university and military research*. Ithaca, N.Y.: Cornell University Press, 1972.

Nelson, J. I. High school context and college plans: The impact of social structure on aspirations. *American Sociological Review,* 1972, 37, 143–148.

Nelson, R. L. *Merger movements in American industry, 1895–1956.* Princeton: Princeton University Press, 1959.

Nelson, R. R. Issues and suggestions for the study of industrial organization in a regime of rapid technical change. In V. R. Fuchs (Ed.), *Policy issues and research opportunities in industrial organization.* New York: National Bureau of Economic Research, 1972, 34–58.

Neuloh, O. A new definition of work and leisure under advanced technology. In J. Stieber (Ed.), *Employment problems of automation and advanced technology.* London: Macmillan, 1966, 200–212.

Neumeyer, F. *The employed inventor in the United States.* Cambridge: M.I.T. Press, 1971.

Newman, W. H., & Logan, J. P. *Management of expanding enterprises.* New York: Columbia University Press, 1955.

Newton, J. W. Cooptation among community decision organizations. (working paper) Waltham, Mass.: Florence Heller School for Advanced Studies in Social Welfare, Brandeis University, 1971.

Nichols, T. *Ownership, control and ideology.* London: Allen and Unwin, 1969.

Nonet, P. *Administrative justice.* New York: Russell Sage Foundation, 1969.

Normann, R. Organization, mediation and environment. Stockholm: Swedish Institute for Administrative Research, Report Nr. UPM-RN-91, 1969.

Normann, R. Organizational innovativeness: Product variation and reorientation. *Administrative Science Quarterly,* 1971, 16, 203–215.

North, D. C. *Growth and welfare in the American past.* Englewood Cliffs, N.J.: Prentice-Hall, 1966.

Nove, A. *The Soviet economy.* (2nd rev. ed.) London: Allen and Unwin, 1969.

Novick, D., Ed. *Program budgeting.* Cambridge: Harvard University Press, 1967.

O'Brien, G. E., Fiedler, F. E., & Hewett, T. The effects of programmed culture training upon the performance of volunteer medical teams in Central America. *Human Relations,* 1971, 24, 209–231.

Ono, T. Modernization of business administration in Japan. *International Studies of Management & Organization,* 1971, 1, 274–291.

Palen, J. J. Belief in government control and the displaced worker. *Administrative Science Quarterly,* 1969, 14, 584–593.

Paquet, G., Ed. *The multinational firm and the nation state.* Don Mills, Ontario: Collier-Macmillan Canada, 1972.

Parry, A. *The new class divided.* New York: Macmillan, 1966.

Parsons, T. *Structure and process in modern societies.* New York: The Free Press, 1960.

Pashigian, B. P. *The distribution of automobiles.* Englewood Cliffs, N.J.: Prentice-Hall, 1961.

Passer, H. C. *The electrical manufacturers: 1875–1900.* Cambridge: Harvard University Press, 1953.

Peabody, R. L., & Rourke, F. E. Public bureaucracies. In J. G. March (Ed.), *Handbook of organizations.* Chicago: Rand McNally, 1965, 802–837.

Peacock, J. L. *Rites of modernization.* Chicago: University of Chicago Press, 1968.

Perlstadt, H. Goal implementation and outcome in medical schools. *American Sociological Review,* 1972, 37, 73–82.

Perrow, C. Organizational prestige: Some functions and dysfunctions. *American Journal of Sociology,* 1961, 66, 335–341. (a)

Perrow, C. The analysis of goals in complex organizations. *American Sociological Review,* 1961, 26, 854–866. (b)

Perrow, C. *Organizational analysis.* Belmont, Calif.: Wadsworth Publishing, 1970.

Perrucci, R., & Gerstl, J. E., Eds. *Engineers and the social system.* New York: Wiley, 1969.

Perrucci, R., & Pilisuk, M. Leaders and ruling elites: The interorganizational bases of community power. *American Sociological Review,* 1970, 35, 1040–1057.

Petersen, W., & Thomas, B. Migration. In D. L. Sills (Ed.), *International encyclopedia of the social sciences,* Vol. 10. New York: Macmillan and The Free Press, 1968, 286–300.

Peterson, R. B. A cross-cultural perspective of supervisory values. *Academy of Management Journal,* 1972, 15, 105–117.

Pfeffer, J. Organizational ecology: A system resource approach. (working paper) Stanford: Graduate School of Business, Stanford University, 1971.

Pfeffer, J. Size and composition of corporate boards of directors: The organization and its environment. *Administrative Science Quarterly,* 1972, 17, 218–228. (a)

Pfeffer, J. Merger as a response to organizational interdependence. *Administrative Science Quarterly,* 1972, 17, 382–394. (b)

Phillips, A. *Market structure, organization and performance.* Cambridge: Harvard University Press, 1962.

Phillips, L. D., Hays, W. L., & Edwards, W. Conservatism in complex probabilistic inference. *IEEE Transactions on Human Factors in Electronics,* 1966, HFE-7, 7–18.

Pinnelli, A. Female labour and fertility in relationship to contrasting social and economic conditions. *Human Relations,* 1971, 24, 603–610.

Pock, J. C. Definition and maintenance of organizational boundaries. (working paper) Portland, Ore.: Reed College, 1972.

Pondy, L. R. Effects of size, complexity and ownership on administrative intensity. *Administrative Science Quarterly,* 1969, 14, 47–61.

Porter, L. W., & Lawler, E. E. III. Properties of organization structure in relation to job attitudes and job behavior. *Psychological Bulletin,* 1965, 64, 23–51.

Posner, R. A. Taxation by regulation. *Bell Journal of Economics and Management Science,* 1971, 2, 22–50.

Prest, A. R., & Stark, T. Some aspects of income distribution in the U.K. since World War II. *Manchester School of Economics and Social Studies,* 1967, 35, 217–243.

Pugh, D. S., Hickson, D. J., Hinings, C. R., & Turner, C. The context of organization structures. *Administrative Science Quarterly,* 1969, 14, 91–114.

Qualls, D. Concentration, barriers to entry, and long run economic profit margins. *Journal of Industrial Economics,* 1972, 20, 146–158.

Rados, D. L. Product liability: Tougher ground rules. *Harvard Business Review,* 1969, 47 (4), 144–152.

Recktenwald, H. C. *Tax incidence and income redistribution.* Detroit: Wayne State University Press, 1971.

Reeves, T. C. *Foundations under fire.* Ithaca, N.Y.: Cornell University Press, 1970.

Reiss, A. J. Jr., & Bordua, D. J. Environment and organization: A perspective on the police. In D. J. Bordua (Ed.), *The police.* New York: Wiley, 1967, 25–55.

Rhenman, E. *Organization theory for long-range planning.* New York: Wiley, 1972.

Rice, A. K. *The enterprise and its environment.* London: Tavistock, 1963.

Richardson, G. B. The pricing of heavy electrical equipment: Competition or agreement? *Bulletin of the Oxford University Institute of Economics and Statistics,* 1966, 28, 73–92.

Richman, B. M. *Soviet management.* Englewood Cliffs, N.J.: Prentice-Hall, 1965.

Richman, B. M., & Copen, M. *International management and economic development.* New York: McGraw-Hill, 1972.

Robertson, D. B. *Should churches be taxed?* Philadelphia: Westminster Press, 1968.

Rogers, D. *110 Livingston Street.* New York: Random House, 1968.

Rogers, E. M., & Shoemaker, F. F. *Communication of innovations.* New York: The Free Press, 1971.

Rolph, E. R., Pechman, J. A., Harberger, A. C., Netzer, D., Due, J. F., & Shoup, C. S. Taxation. In D. L. Sills (Ed.), *International encyclopedia of the social sciences,* Vol. 15. New York: Macmillan and The Free Press, 1968, 521–560.

Roos, L. L. Jr., & Roos, N. P. Administrative change in a modernizing society. *Administrative Science Quarterly,* 1970, 15, 69–78.

Rose, A. M. Confidence and the corporation. *American Journal of Economics and Sociology,* 1967, 26, 231–236.

Rosengren, W. R., & Lefton, M., Eds. *Organizations and clients.* Columbus, Ohio: Merrill, 1970.

Rotwein, E. Economic concentration and monopoly in Japan. *Journal of Political Economy,* 1964, 72, 262–277.

Rourke, F. E. *Secrecy and publicity.* Baltimore: Johns Hopkins Press, 1961.

Rourke, F. E. *Bureaucracy, politics, and public policy.* Boston: Little, Brown, 1969.

Sahlins, M. D., & Service, E. R., Eds. *Evolution and culture.* Ann Arbor: University of Michigan Press, 1960.

Saulnier, R. J., & Halcrow, H. G. Credit. In D. L. Sills (Ed.), *International encyclopedia of the social sciences,* Vol. 3. New York: Macmillan and The Free Press, 1968, 461–471.

Schaffer, A., & Schaffer, R. C. *Woodruff.* Chapel

Hill: University of North Carolina Press, 1970.

Schein, E. H., & Ott, J. S. The legitimacy of organizational influence. *American Journal of Sociology,* 1962, 67, 682–689.

Scherer, F. M. Firm size, market structure, opportunity, and the output of patented inventions. *American Economic Review,* 1965, 55, 1097–1125.

Scherer, F. M. *Industrial market structure and economic performance.* Chicago: Rand McNally, 1970.

Schiller, H. I. *Mass communications and American empire.* New York: Augustus M. Kelley, 1969.

Schmalensee, R. *On the economics of advertising.* Amsterdam: North-Holland, 1972.

Schmookler, J. *Invention and economic growth.* Cambridge: Harvard University Press, 1966.

Schneider, B. Organizational climate: Individual preferences and organizational realities. *Journal of Applied Psychology,* 1972, 56, 211–217.

Schollhammer, H. Organization structures of multinational corporations. *Academy of Management Journal,* 1971, 14, 345–365.

Schultz, T. P. Rural-urban migration in Colombia. *Review of Economics and Statistics,* 1971, 53, 157–163.

Schultze, C. L. *The politics and economics of public spending.* Washington: Brookings Institution, 1968.

Schumpeter, J. A. *The theory of economic development.* Cambridge: Harvard University Press, 1934.

Schwartz, R. A. Corporate philanthropic contributions. *Journal of Finance,* 1968, 23, 479–497.

Seashore, S. E., & Yuchtman, E. Factorial analysis of organizational performance. *Administrative Science Quarterly,* 1967, 12, 377–395.

Seeman, M. On the meaning of alienation. *American Sociological Review,* 1959, 24, 783–791.

Seidman, H. *Politics, position, and power.* New York: Oxford University Press, 1970.

Selden, R. T. Money: Velocity of circulation. In D. L. Sills (Ed.), *International encyclopedia of the social sciences,* Vol. 10. New York: Macmillan and The Free Press, 1968, 447–453.

Selznick, P. *TVA and the grass roots.* Berkeley: University of California Press, 1949.

Servan-Schreiber, J.-J. *The American challenge.* New York: Atheneum, 1968.

Shaw, E. S. Financial intermediaries. In D. L. Sills (Ed.), *International encyclopedia of the social sciences,* Vol. 5. New York: Macmillan and The Free Press, 1968, 432–439.

Shaw, G. S., & Abrams, J. W. Demand forecasting for airline scheduling. In D. B. Hertz & J. Melese (Eds.), *Proceedings of the fourth international conference on operational research.* New York: Wiley, 1966, 444–457.

Sheth, N. R. *The social framework of an Indian factory.* New York: Humanities Press, 1968.

Shimmin, S. Extra-mural factors influencing behaviour at work. *Occupational Psychology,* 1962, 36, 124–131.

Shonfield, A. *Modern capitalism.* London: Oxford University Press, 1965.

Simon, H. A. Rational choice and the structure of the environment. *Psychological Review,* 1956, 63, 129–138.

Simpson, M. E. Social mobility, normlessness, and powerlessness in two cultural contexts. *American Sociological Review,* 1970, 35, 1002–1013.

Simpson, R. L., & Gulley, W. H. Goals, environmental pressures, and organizational characteristics. *American Sociological Review,* 1962, 27, 344–351.

Singh, B., & Drost, H. An alternative econometric approach to the permanent income hypothesis: An international comparison. *Review of Economics and Statistics,* 1971, 53, 326–334.

Sloan, A. P. *My years with General Motors.* Garden City, N.Y.: Doubleday, 1964.

Slocum, J. W. Jr., & Strawser, R. H. Racial differences in job attitudes. *Journal of Applied Psychology,* 1972, 56, 28–32.

Slocum, J. W. Jr., & Topichak, P. M. Do cultural differences affect job satisfaction? *Journal of Applied Psychology,* 1972, 56, 177–178.

Slote, A. *Termination.* Indianapolis: Bobbs-Merrill, 1969.

Smith, J., Meyer, J. R., & Schnore, L. F. Transportation. In D. L. Sills (Ed.), *International encyclopedia of the social sciences,* Vol. 16. New York: Macmillan and The Free Press, 1968, 129–144.

Smith, M. A. Process technology and powerlessness. *British Journal of Sociology,* 1968, 19, 76–88.

Smith, R. A. *Corporations in crisis.* Garden City, N.Y.: Doubleday, 1964.

Stanback, T. M. Jr. *Tax changes and modern-*

ization in the textile industry. New York: National Bureau of Economic Research, 1969.

Stanton, E. *Clients come last.* Beverly Hills, Calif.: Sage Publications, 1970.

Starbuck, W. H. Organizational growth and development. In J. G. March (Ed.), *Handbook of organizations.* Chicago: Rand McNally, 1965, 451–533.

Starbuck, W. H. The efficiency of British and American retail employees. *Administrative Science Quarterly,* 1966, 11, 345–385.

Starbuck, W. H. Organizational metamorphosis. In R. W. Millman & M. P. Hottenstein (Eds.), *Promising research directions.* State College, Pa.: Academy of Management, 1968, 113–122. (a)

Starbuck, W. H. Some comments, observations, and objections stimulated by "Design of proof in organizational research." *Administrative Science Quarterly,* 1968, 13, 135–161. (b)

Starbuck, W. H. Concerning a misspecified specification. *Sociometry,* 1971, 34, 214–226.

Starbuck, W. H. The current state of organization theory. In J. W. McGuire (Ed.), *Contemporary management: Issues and viewpoints.* Englewood Cliffs, N.J.: Prentice-Hall, 1974, 123–139.

Starbuck, W. H., & Bass, F. M. An experimental study of risk-taking and the value of information in a new product context. *Journal of Business,* 1967, 40, 155–165.

Starbuck, W. H., & Dutton, J. M. Designing adaptive organizations. *Journal of Business Policy,* 1973, 3 (4), 21–28.

Steindl, J. *Random processes and the growth of firms.* London: Charles Griffin, 1965.

Stephan, G. E. Variation in county size: A theory of segmental growth. *American Sociological Review,* 1971, 36, 451–461.

Stern, L. W., & Morgenroth, W. M. Concentration, mutually recognized interdependence and the allocation of marketing resources. *Journal of Business,* 1968, 41, 56–67.

Stettner, L. Survey of literature on social and economic effects of technological change. In J. Stieber (Ed.), *Employment problems of automation and advanced technology.* London: Macmillan, 1966, 451–479.

Stigler, G. J. *The organization of industry.* Homewood, Ill.: Irwin, 1968.

Stigler, G. J. The theory of economic regulation. *Bell Journal of Economics and Management Science,* 1971, 2, 3–21.

Stinchcombe, A. L. Bureaucratic and craft ad-

ministration of production. *Administrative Science Quarterly,* 1959, 4, 168–187.

Stinchcombe, A. L. Social structure and organizations. In J. G. March (Ed.), *Handbook of organizations.* Chicago: Rand McNally, 1965, 142–193.

Stocking, G. W., & Mueller, W. F. Business reciprocity and the size of firms. *Journal of Business,* 1957, 30, 73–95.

Stone, R., & Rowe, D. A. *The measurement of consumers' expenditure and behaviour in the United Kingdom, 1920–1938.* Cambridge: Cambridge University Press, 1966.

Strange, J. H., Ed. Citizens' action in Model Cities and CAP programs: Case studies and evaluation. *Public Administration Review,* 1972, 32, 377–470.

Sunkel, O. Underdevelopment, the transfer of science and technology, and the Latin American university. *Human Relations,* 1971, 24, 1–18.

Tajfel, H. Social and cultural factors in perception. In G. Lindzey & E. Aronson (Eds.), *The handbook of social psychology,* Vol. 3. Reading, Mass.: Addison-Wesley, 1969, 315–394.

Takamiya, S. Group decision-making in Japanese management. *International Studies of Management & Organization,* 1972, 2, 183–196.

Tannenbaum, A. S. Unions. In J. G. March (Ed.), *Handbook of organizations.* Chicago: Rand McNally, 1965, 710–763.

Tawney, R. H. *The acquisitive society.* London: G. Bell, 1921.

Taylor, J. C. Some effects of technology in organizational change. *Human Relations,* 1971, 24, 105–123.

Terreberry, S. The evolution of organizational environments. *Administrative Science Quarterly,* 1968, 12, 590–613.

Thomas, B., Ed. *Economics of international migration.* London: Macmillan, 1958.

Thompson, J. D. Organizations and output transactions. *American Journal of Sociology,* 1962, 68, 309–324.

Thompson, J. D. *Organizations in action.* New York: McGraw-Hill, 1967.

Thompson, J. D., & McEwen, W. J. Organizational goals and environment: Goal-setting as an interaction process. *American Sociological Review,* 1958, 23, 23–31.

Thurow, L. C. *Poverty and discrimination.* Washington: Brookings Institution, 1969.

Tilton, J. E. *International diffusion of technol-*

ogy. Washington: Brookings Institution, 1971.

Tivey, L. J. *Nationalisation in British industry.* London: Cape, 1966.

Triandis, H. C., & Vassiliou, V. Interpersonal influence and employee selection in two cultures. *Journal of Applied Psychology,* 1972, 56, 140–145.

Tumin, M. Business as a social system. *Behavioral Science,* 1964, 9, 120–130.

Turk, H. Comparative urban studies in interorganizational relations. *Sociological Inquiry,* 1969, 39 (1), 108–110.

Turk, H. Interorganizational networks in urban society: Initial perspectives and comparative research. *American Sociological Review,* 1970, 35, 1–19.

Turner, A. N., & Lawrence, P. R. *Industrial jobs and the worker.* Cambridge: Graduate School of Business Administration, Harvard University, 1965.

Udy, S. H. Jr. "Bureaucracy" and "rationality" in Weber's organization theory: An empirical study. *American Sociological Review,* 1959, 24, 791–795.

Udy, S. H. Jr. Technical and institutional factors in production organization: A preliminary model. *American Journal of Sociology,* 1961, 67, 247–254.

Udy, S. H. Jr. *Work in traditional and modern society.* Englewood Cliffs, N.J.: Prentice-Hall, 1970.

U.S. National Commission on Food Marketing. *Special studies in food marketing, technical study number 10.* Washington: U.S. National Commission on Food Marketing, 1966.

Utterback, J. M. The process of technological innovation within the firm. *Academy of Management Journal,* 1971, 14, 75–88.

van de Vall, M. *Labor organizations.* New York: Cambridge University Press, 1970.

Veblen, T. *The theory of business enterprise.* New York: Charles Scribner's, 1904.

Vernon, D. T. A. Information seeking in a natural stress situation. *Journal of Applied Psychology,* 1971, 55, 359–363.

Vernon, R. *Sovereignty at bay.* New York: Basic Books, 1971.

Vickers, G. Is adaptability enough? *Behavioral Science,* 1959, 4, 219–234.

Villarejo, D. Stock ownership and the control of corporations. *New University Thought,* 1961, 2 (1), 33–77.

Villarejo, D. Stock ownership and the control of corporations. *New University Thought,* 1962, 2 (2), 47–65.

Voigt, F. German experience with cartels and their control during the pre-war and post-war periods. In J. P. Miller (Ed.), *Competition, cartels, and their regulation.* Amsterdam: North-Holland, 1962, 169–213.

Vroom, V. H. *Work and motivation.* New York: Wiley, 1964.

Wachter, M. L. A labor supply model for secondary workers. *Review of Economics and Statistics,* 1972, 54, 141–151.

Walter, J. E. *Dividend policy and enterprise valuation.* Belmont, Calif.: Wadsworth Publishing, 1967.

Walton, C. C. *Corporate social responsibilities.* Belmont, Calif.: Wadsworth Publishing, 1967.

Wanous, J. P., & Lawler, E. E. III. Measurement and meaning of job satisfaction. *Journal of Applied Psychology,* 1972, 56, 95–105.

Warner, W. L., & Low, J. O. *The social system of the modern factory.* New Haven: Yale University Press, 1947.

Warren, R. L. The interorganizational field as a focus for investigation. *Administrative Science Quarterly,* 1967, 12, 396–419.

Weber, C. E. Intraorganizational decision processes influencing the EDP staff budget. *Management Science,* 1965, 12, B-69–B-93.

Weber, M. *The Protestant ethic and the spirit of capitalism.* London: Allen and Unwin, 1930.

Weber, M. *The theory of social and economic organization.* London: Collier-Macmillan, 1947.

Wedderburn, K. W. *The worker and the law.* (2nd ed.) Harmondsworth: Penguin, 1971.

Weick, K. E. *The social psychology of organizing.* Reading, Mass.: Addison-Wesley, 1969.

Weiker, W. F. The Ottoman bureaucracy: Modernization and reform. *Administrative Science Quarterly,* 1969, 13, 451–470.

Weinberg, I. *The English public schools.* New York: Atherton, 1967.

Weinshall, T. D. Two conceptual schemes of organizational behaviour. *Management International,* 1971, 11 (6), 43–54.

Weintraub, D., Lissak, M., & Azmon, Y. *Moshava, kibbutz, and moshav.* Ithaca, N. Y.: Cornell University Press, 1969.

Weiss, L. W. An evaluation of mergers in six industries. *Review of Economics and Statistics,* 1965, 47, 172–181.

Weiss, L. W. Business pricing policies and inflation reconsidered. *Journal of Political Economy,* 1966, 74, 177–187. (a)

Weiss, L. W. Concentration and labor earnings. *American Economic Review,* 1966, 56, 96–117. (b)

Wernimont, P. F., & Fitzpatrick, S. The meaning of money. *Journal of Applied Psychology,* 1972, 56, 218–226.

Weymar, F. H. *The dynamics of the world cocoa market.* Cambridge: M.I.T. Press, 1968.

White, H. C. *Chains of opportunity.* Cambridge: Harvard University Press, 1970.

White, L. J. The American automobile industry and the small car, 1945–70. *Journal of Industrial Economics,* 1972, 20, 179–192.

White, P. E. Resources as determinants of organizational behavior. *Administrative Science Quarterly,* 1974, 19, 366–379.

White, P. E., Levine, S., & Vlasak, G. J. Exchange as a conceptual framework for understanding interorganizational relationships: Applications to nonprofit organizations. In A. R. Nègandhi (Ed.), *Organization theory in an interorganizational perspective.* Kent, Ohio: Center for Business and Economic Research, Kent State University, 1971, 35–52.

Whitt, H. P., Gordon, C. C., & Hofley, J. R. Religion, economic development, and lethal aggression. *American Sociological Review,* 1972, 37, 193–201.

Wicker, A. W. Processes which mediate behavior-environment congruence. *Behavioral Science,* 1972, 17, 265–277.

Wilcox, C. *Public policies toward business.* (Rev. ed.) Homewood, Ill.: Irwin, 1960.

Wild, R., & Kempner, T. Influence of community and plant characteristics on job attitudes of manual workers. *Journal of Applied Psychology,* 1972, 56, 106–113.

Wildavsky, A. B. *The politics of the budgetary process.* Boston: Little, Brown, 1964.

Wildavsky, A. B. The self-evaluating organization. *Public Administration Review,* 1972, 32, 509–520.

Wilensky, H. L. Work as a social problem. In H. S. Becker (Ed.), *Social problems.* New York: Wiley, 1966, 117–166.

Williamson, O. E. A dynamic theory of interfirm behavior. *Quarterly Journal of Economics,* 1965, 79, 579–607.

Williamson, O. E. *The economics of discretionary behavior.* Englewood Cliffs, N. J.: Prentice-Hall, 1964.

Wilson, C. *The history of Unilever.* London: Cassell, 1954.

Wilson, H. H. *Pressure group.* New Brunswick, N.J.: Rutgers University Press, 1961.

Wilson, J. S. G. Banking. In D. L. Sills (Ed.), *International encyclopedia of the social sciences,* Vol. 1. New York: Macmillan and The Free Press, 1968, 512–522.

Winter, S. G. Jr. Economic "natural selection" and the theory of the firm. *Yale Economic Essays,* 1964, 4, 225–272.

Winter, S. G. Jr. Satisficing, selection, and the innovating remnant. *Quarterly Journal of Economics,* 1971, 85, 237–261.

Wolman, H. Organization theory and community action agencies. *Public Administration Review,* 1972, 32, 33–42.

Wolters, R. *Negroes and the great depression.* Westport, Conn.: Greenwood, 1970.

Wright, R. W. Organizational ambiente: Management and environment in Chile. *Academy of Management Journal,* 1971, 14, 65–74.

Wynia, B. L. Executive development in the federal government. *Public Administration Review,* 1972, 32, 311–317.

Yamey, B. S., Ed. *Resale price maintenance.* London: Weidenfeld and Nicolson, 1966.

Yuchtman, E., & Seashore, S. E. A system resource approach to organizational effectiveness. *American Sociological Review,* 1967, 32, 891–903.

Zahn, G. C. *The military chaplaincy.* Toronto: University of Toronto Press, 1969.

Zborowski, M. *People in pain.* San Francisco: Jossey-Bass, 1969.

Zigler, E., & Child, I. L. Socialization. In G. Lindzey & E. Aronson (Eds.), *The handbook of social psychology,* Vol. 3. Reading, Mass.: Addison-Wesley, 1969, 450–589.

Zimmerman, J. F. Neighborhoods and citizen involvement. *Public Administration Review,* 1972, 32, 201–210.

Zurcher, L. A. Jr., Meadow, A., & Zurcher, S. L. Value orientation, role conflict, and alienation from work: A crosscultural study. *American Sociological Review,* 1965, 30, 539–548.

Zymelman, M. A stabilization policy for the cotton textile cycle. *Management Science,* 1965, 11, 572–580.

CHAPTER 26

Organizational Structure and Climate[1]

ROY PAYNE
University of Sheffield

DEREK S. PUGH
London Graduate School of Business Studies

THE PURPOSE OF THIS CHAPTER is to review work focusing on the concepts of organizational structure and organizational climate. This involves examining studies which relate the two constructs themselves as well as studies which explore the determinants of each (e.g., organizational contextual features such as technology and size). The review is organized around a distinction between objective and subjective methods of measurement. These two methods of measurement are not synonymous with structure and climate, and it is argued that both structure and climate can, and have been, measured by both methods. The validity of structure and climate is investigated by systematically reviewing studies according to the various combinations possible for the structure and climate/objective and subjective distinctions (e.g., objective structure and subjective structure, subjective structure and subjective climate). A final section looks at the relationship between measures of organizational climate and individual factors such as job satisfaction. Attention is drawn to the need to distinguish whether such studies use the individual or the organization as the unit of analysis. Consistent patterns are difficult to find, particularly when subjective measures are used. The reader is invited to draw his own conclusions about the value of future work on these two concepts and is helped towards this evaluation by being offered a pessimistic and an optimistic interpretation of the chapter.

---

[1] We are grateful to Richard Hackman and Diana Pheysey for detailed comments on an earlier draft of this chapter and Marvin Dunnette for his patience.

INTRODUCTION

The organizational setting limits and influences people's behavior, and thus interests the psychologist. Since it is often difficult to relate variables such as organization size, structure, and technology to changes in human behavior, only the past decade of psychological research has started to use such factors to explain changes in the more traditionally chosen variables of morale, job satisfaction, and leadership style. Such acceptance of "the reality of the structured social relationship" (Pugh, 1969) has generated study of concepts such as control, authority, and power as well as leadership, authoritarianism, and influence, and represents the beginning of "organizational psychology."

This chapter surveys some important structural aspects of organizations and their interrelationships and examines their effects on the attitudes and behavior of individuals in organizations. At this level too, the concepts studied have developed considerably in the last decade. The enormous philosophical impact of the open systems concept (Katz & Kahn, 1966) with its distinguishing features of interaction with the environment and feedback loops, has transformed industrial and social psychologists' traditionally specific and static concerns with morale, job satisfaction, and job performance into more general and dynamic interests in the organization as an environmental setting for individual and group behaviors. Discovering how the organization is a psychologically meaningful environment for individual organization members has led to the concept of "organization climate."

Influences on Organizational Structure and Climate

Organizational climate research, like systems analysis, has examined "context" or environmental features such as structure. Figure 1 summarizes a simple systems model of the relationships considered in this survey. The headed arrows suggest the direction of the more important relationships. Although each conceptual box relates to every other and is affected by the wider environment and culture, the arrows indicate the stronger of these relationships.

Moving from left to right across Figure 1, organizational context represents those variables (Pugh, Hickson, Hinings, McDonald, Turner, & Lupton, 1963) which influence organizational structure. We feel that an organization, or a person starting one, has a goal or purpose; and if the organization is independent of other organizations, it has the decision-making power to organize its resources such as people, money, and equipment to achieve this goal. Although strategic choices (Child, 1972) have often determined the development of organizational structure, the technology, the number and variety of employees, and other entities such as trade unions or owners upon which the organization depends may also constrain the structure. These variables then provide a context for the structure.

To define the context of organizational structure, we can think about available structure alternatives such as (1) specialization and professionalization of roles with consequent sectional interests versus generalist roles with emphasis on common organizational goals; (2) procedural standardization and simplified, routine jobs versus enlarged job descriptions with emphasis on individual skills and personal contributions; and (3) hierarchical authority relationships and communication channels restricted to vertical interactions versus general participation and multi-directional communication.

Different structures might, then, produce different climates. Highly specialized, highly prescribed roles in a centralized authority system are unlikely to encourage entrepreneurial risk taking, for example. Because organizational climate is influenced by organization members' individual perceptions and is, thus, relatively subjective, it occurs in a box with broken lines in Figure 1. Climate describes the characteristic behavioral processes in a social system at one

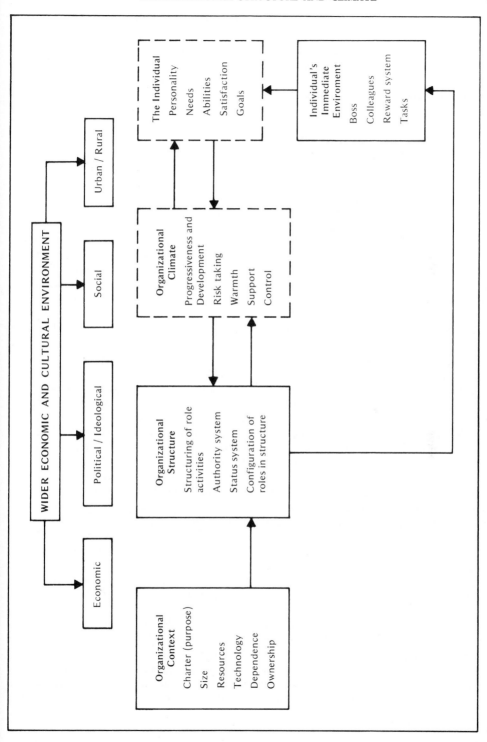

Figure 1. Major influences on organizational structure and climate.

particular point in time. These processes reflect the members' values, attitudes, and beliefs which thus have become part of the construct. Given "climate's" geographical analogy, the organizational context and structure variables are the hills and rivers or physical features of the geographical area. Climate dimensions such as progressiveness and development, risk taking, warmth, support, and control correspond to temperature, rainfall, and wind velocity which have been generated by the interactions of physical features with the sun's energy. Social systems' equivalent energy sources are people who also create and are part of the climate. Although both physical and social climates may affect their respective structures, the context and structure of a social system are more stable than its people, whose energies may not always be spent in predictable cycles.

The individual is in a box with broken lines, too. A person's personality, needs, abilities, satisfactions, and goals affect his perceptions and thus indirectly influence the measure of the climate. As Figure 1 shows, the "true" climate also influences individuals' characteristics and experiences.

An individual's characteristics are also partly determined by his immediate environment, which, in turn, is affected by the structure of the organization. In this chapter, we do not explore the effects of structure on immediate job environment and on the individual. Section V deals with this subject.

Finally, such organizational and individual constructs exist in the wider economic and cultural environment of the real world. Although this environment may directly affect each of these variables, a sequential effect is also possible. An economic or cultural change may produce changes in an organization's purpose, resources, and technology (context). The structure may be adaptable and respond to such changes or may have to change itself, thus creating changes in climate, a person's immediate job environment, and ultimately the individual himself.

Objective and Subjective Measurement

There are two types of organizational measurement. "Objective" measurement implies a direct assessment of organizational properties without any conceptual transformations; here, a member is only an informant about available measurement instruments such as an organization chart or performance records. "Subjective" measurement implies indirect assessment of organizational properties by instruments which measure group perceptions; here, a member is a respondent to instruments with statements such as, "The jobs in this organization are clearly defined and logically structured," or "The employees here are constantly being checked for rule violation." The distinction between objective and subjective measurement does not directly relate to that between structure and climate, each of which can be measured by both methods. Many studies of structure have used subjective methods, and "climate" encompasses many objective phenomena such as labor turnover, absenteeism, and lateness statistics. This chapter, then, will use these two basic distinctions between structure and climate, and between subjective and objective forms of measurement, to outline the literature as follows:

(a) The Concept and Measurement of Organizational Structure

(b) The Concept and Measurement of Organizational Climate

(c) The Relationship Between Perceptual Measures of Structure and Perceptual Measures of Climate

(d) The Relationship Between Objective Measures of Structure and Perceptual Measures of Climate

(e) The Relationship Between Objective Measures of Structure and Objective Measures of Climate

(f) The Relationship Between Organizational Climate and Characteristics of Individual Members

(g) Summary of Findings and Discussion

The authors know of no relevant studies

which have compared perceptual measures of structure and objective measures of climate.

THE CONCEPT AND MEASUREMENT OF ORGANIZATIONAL STRUCTURE

This section will explore the concept of organizational structure and review Max Weber's writing on bureaucracy. An outline of the subjective and objective measures of structure reveals its multidimensionality. Certain contextual features such as organizational size, technology, and degree of dependence on other organizations have consistent relationships with structural dimensions, particularly when they have been measured with objective instruments. Also, there are newer forms of organizational structure such as organic and matrix structures for which measurement instruments have not yet been developed.

Most research workers have used a connotative rather than a denotative definition of organization structure. Definitions have included suggestions or implications beyond the actual meaning of the construct. However, such systematic descriptions and analyses of organizational processes and behaviors have made us aware of their distinctive regularities. For example, let us look at Pugh's description:

All organizations have to make provision for continuing activities directed towards the achievement of given aims. Regularities in such activities as task allocation, the exercise of authority, and co-ordination of functions are developed. Such regularities constitute the organization's structure, and sociologists have studied systematic differences in structure related to variations in such factors as the objectives of the organization, its size, ownership, geographical location, and technology of manufacture, which produce the characteristic differences in structure of a bank, a hospital, a mass production factory or a local government department. (Pugh, 1966, p. 239)

Weber's analysis of a modern bureaucracy (Weber, 1947) has also influenced our present conceptualization of structure. His elements of bureaucratic organizations, as distinguished from traditional and charismatic organizations, included: (1) a continuous organization of official functions bound by rules; (2) a specified sphere of competence for each office; (3) offices organized in a clearly defined hierarchy; (4) specified rules or norms which regulated the conduct of an office; (5) separation of an official from ownership of the means of production or administration; (6) the office as the official's primary job; (7) written and recorded administrative acts, decisions, and rules; (8) a free contractual relationship for each office; and (9) candidate selection and appointment on the basis of technical qualifications, with a system of promotion according to achievement and seniority. Weber's description was idealized, and did not empirically correspond to the structure of most organizations. However, we may regard his concepts as potential dimensions for locating organizations; they have offered a convincing analysis of bureaucratic structure and have provided a heuristic model for the operationalization of the concept of structure (Udy, 1959; Hall, 1963; Hage & Aiken, 1967; Pugh, Hickson, Hinings, & Turner, 1968).

Configurational Measures of Structure

The earliest studies of organizational structure concentrated on configurational aspects of structure such as span of control, number of levels, and organizational size rather than on Weber's analysis. Management writers such as Urwick (1947) prescribed a span of control over a maximum of six people, but Worthy (1950) argued that larger spans of control provided greater opportunity for individual development, and cited a study with a positive relationship between size of span and morale. Since other factors such as organizational size and function also related to span (Entwistle & Walton, 1961), and size affected morale (Porter & Lawler, 1965), researchers have become interested in a whole framework of related structure variables. Woodward (1965) and Hickson, Pugh, and Pheysey (1969) related the span of control practiced by first-line supervisors to the technical advancement of a particular production system. Although this argued against one absolute, ideal span-of-control number, the more successful organizations did have spans of control close to the median of their particular production group type.

An example of the configurational tradition linked to a Weberian approach has been the work of Blau and Schoenherr (1971), who studied the relationships among structural variables in fifty-three financial agencies of the United States government. They suggested that increasing size generated structural differentiation along various dimensions at decelerating rates, and that both vertical and horizontal structural differentiations enlarged the administrative component. However, Argyris (1972) pointed out that these findings might have related to specific civil service organizations which had finite budgets, high-level positions which were difficult to enter, and limited marketing or service functions. Organizations with traditional, administrative management should show positive relationships between the number of employees and structural differentiation along various dimensions.

Many studies have related structural elements such as the number of organizational levels to dependent variables such as productivity, effectiveness, and morale. In Porter and Lawler's review (1965) of such studies, flat structures seemed more effective and satisfying in small companies with less than 5,000 members, but there was no particular trend relating structure to these variables in larger companies.

Other configurational studies have tried to identify the proportion of nonproductive (administrative, supportive) roles to productive (work flow) ones (Terrien & Mills, 1955; Anderson & Warkov, 1961; Haas, Hall, & Johnson, 1963). Given "Parkinson's Law," it is heartening that these studies have suggested that the administrative component decreases as organizational size increases, probably due to economies of scale.

Hall (1972) suggested that the relationship was curvilinear; this may relate to problems of coordination in large organizations.

Such configurational studies have had understandable, clear data with definite numbers. In a comprehensive review on centralization versus decentralization, Porter and Lawler (1965) found that only one out of four studies operationalized its principal variable, and argued that research could not advance until we have differentiated between different degrees of centralization. In the mid-1960s such attempts began to appear.

Perceptual Measures of Structure

Hall (1963) selected six concepts about organization structure which were based on Weber's assumptions, treated them as continuous dimensions, and tried to measure them. The six aspects of structure were: (1) a well-defined hierarchy of authority; (2) a division of labor which was based on functional specialization; (3) a system of rules which covered the rights and duties of positional incumbents; (4) a system of procedures for dealing with work situations; (5) impersonality of personal relationships; and (6) selection for employment and promotion based on technical competence. Hall measured each dimension with a series of statements rated for degree of applicability to a person's job. In his first study using the measures, Hall gave the questionnaires to a random sample of personnel from all levels and functions in ten organizations. There were perceived structural differences between departments with nonuniform, uncertain tasks and those with predictable, uniform tasks; the nonuniform task departments were significantly less bureaucratic on half of the dimensions.

Hall and Tittle (1966) characterized whole organizations on the same bureaucratic dimensions and related these dimensions to organization size, number of organizational segments or divisions, and organizational concern with manipulating ideas versus objects. To deal with the problems of members' different perceptions about structure and of treating the bureaucracy as a configurative unity, Hall and Tittle arranged the mean scores for each dimension into a distribution for five data categories and formed a Guttman scale of bureaucracy along five sub-dimensions: (1) impersonality of operation; (2) hierarchy of authority; (3) division of labor; (4) specificity of procedures; and (5) complexity of rules. An organization that scored positively on the first sub-dimension was, thus, highly likely to score positively on all the others. In twenty-five different organizations, organizational size had a significant but low association with bureaucracy. Also, bureaucracies seemed to deal with objects rather than ideas, and to concern themselves less directly with people and more with things.

Hage and Aiken (1967) expanded and refined Hall's perceptual measures in a study of sixteen welfare agencies. Their analysis of variance of the data showed significant differences between organizations, but not between organizational levels or occupational groups. Such results may be related to their sample, which had rather homogeneous occupations but very different organizational sizes. Hage and Aiken also used a fairly good mean organizational score which was calculated from a random sample of organizational positions; they showed that this mean score correlated highly with means computed from all individual scores (median correlation +0.87). These writers (Hage & Aiken, 1966, 1967, 1969; Aiken & Hage, 1967) found that organizations with more professionally trained men had less rule observation and more participative decision making. Organizations with more people involved in decision making were less bureaucratic; and the more participative, less bureaucratic structures produced lower alienation from work and expressive alienation (Aiken & Hage, 1967). Multiple correlations which used structural dimensions as independent variables and program change and alienation as dependent variables were .75 or higher.

However, how generalizable have these findings been? Although Hage and Aiken argued that their sixteen organizations represented a universe, they also said that studies should relate to a particular time and a particular place. Their unusually homogeneous population may have contributed to their high multiple correlations; another relevant factor may have been that they added together individual scores to create organizational scores. Guilford (1965) showed some interesting examples of how correlation coefficients can be distorted in this way. Thus, Hage and Aiken quoted, but ignored, Bachman, Smith, and Slesinger (1966), who advised examining structural effects only when individual effects had been held constant by partial correlation.

Certainly, the use of perceptual measures of organizational properties has generated methodological and interpretive difficulties. It is fortunate that the next development of organizational measures attempted to describe organizations in a more objective way (Pugh et al., 1968; Pugh, Hickson, & Hinings, 1969).

Objective Measures of Structure

One of our projects (Pugh et al., 1963) initially sought to develop valid and reliable measures of organization structure and context. We utilized a sample of fifty-two extremely varied manufacturing and service organizations in the English Midlands, each of which employed at least 250 persons. We included manufacturing firms which made strip steel, toys, double decker buses, chocolate bars, injection systems, and beer, and service organizations such as chain stores, municipal departments, transport companies, insurance companies, and a savings bank. Forty-six of these organizations comprised a stratified random sample by size (number of employees) and Standard Industrial Classification (type of product or service). Our tests for the internal scalability of measures utilized the entire sample; tests of relationships between structure variables used only the stratified sample. Although it was difficult to set up universally applicable methods, we wanted to assess organizations of as wide a range as possible. There were structured interview schedules for several main executives; these contained objective questions such as, "Are there written operating instructions for direct workers?" We directed specific questions to executives who were responsible for particular areas, and then got formal confirmations of their responses. For example, we may have asked the production manager about written operating instructions and then requested an actual set of instructions as evidence. Finally, we gathered information from public records and other sources to obtain measures such as an index of individuality of ownership.

We arranged individual item responses into a previously developed (Pugh et al., 1963) scheme and then into cumulative measures which characterized the organization. The following organizational variables were measured:

Contextual Variables

Origin and History—private versus public founding, and the history of changes in ownership and location

Ownership and Control—public versus private ownership and the number and type of owners

Size—number of employees, net assets, and market position

Charter—the nature and range of goods and services

Technology—the degree of integration in work processes

Interdependence—the extent of dependence on customers, suppliers, and trade unions

Structural Variables

Specialization—the degree of division into specialized roles

Standardization—the degree of standard rules and procedures

Formalization—the degree of written instructions and procedures

Centralization—the degree of decision-taking authority at the top

Configuration—long versus short chains of command and role structures, and percentage of "supportive" personnel

These measures varied widely in number, type, complexity, and sophistication. For example, location was assessed by one relatively crude measure, number of operating sites; however, the main standardization scale had 128 dichotomous items which formed two sub-scales based on factor analysis. When possible, we used factor analysis within the main variables to confirm their existence as factors and to identify and operationalize subsidiary factors. We also applied general dichotomous or Guttman procedures to relevant scales to confirm internal validity. Thus, there were 132 fully operational measures for characterizing organizations, which ranged from simple dichotomies to large multi-item scales (Levy & Pugh, 1969).

We then examined interrelationships separately within the sets of contextual (Pugh, Hickson, & Hinings, 1969) and structural (Pugh et al., 1968) variables and also studied the relationships between contextual variables (treated as independent variables) and structural variables (treated as dependent variables).

A principal component factor analysis of structural interrelationships produced the factors shown on the following page.

We used the first three of these factors to create an understandable empirical taxonomy of organization structures (Pugh, Hickson, Hinings, & Turner, 1969). Organizations were divided into those scoring High, Medium, and Low on Factor 1 (Structuring of Activities) and into High and Low on each of Factors 2 (Decision-taking Authority) and 3 (Means of Control), thereby yielding a twelve-cell organizational taxonomy. Figure 2 shows that seven of the twelve possible cells contained one or more organizations, and these seven organizational types were designated, respectively, as: Full Bureaucracy, Nascent Full Bureaucracy, Workflow Bureaucracy, Nas-

Factor	*Component Scales*
Structuring of Activities—the degree of employee behavior which was defined by specialist jobs, routines, procedures, and formal written records	Specialization Standardization Formalization
Concentration of Authority—the degree of decision-taking authority which was concentrated at the top or outside the organization, if it was part of a larger company	Centralization Degree of autonomy of chief executive
Line Control of Work Flow—the degree of control which was exercised by line personnel versus impersonal procedures	Number of subordinates per supervisor (few versus many) Degree to which written records of role performance were collected (low versus high)
Relative Size of Supportive Component—the relative number of nonproductive personnel or auxiliary support to main work-flow	% of clerks % of non-workflow personnel

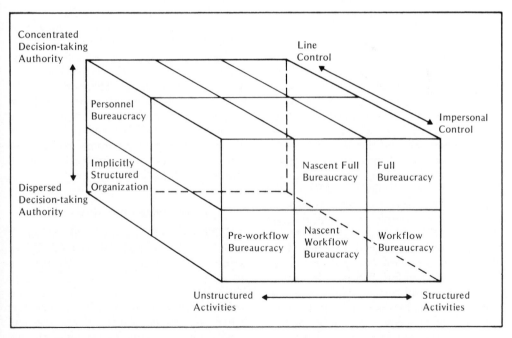

Figure 2. An empirical taxonomy of structures of work organizations. (From Pugh, Hickson, Hinings & Turner, 1969.)

cent Workflow Bureaucracy, Pre-workflow Bureaucracy, Personnel Bureaucracy, and Implicitly Structured Organization.

We then examined the relationships between contextual and structural variables. The two major dimensions of context, organization size and technology, helped predict the structuring of activities dimension; large organizations which had complex but highly integrated production technologies tended to structure and prescribe in detail the nature of people's work activities. Dependence predicted concentration of authority; organizations often concentrated decision-taking authority at the top when they were dependent on or owned by some other organization. Thus, decision taking in organizational branches was more centralized than in autonomous organizations. Inkson, Pugh, and Hickson (1970), Hinings and Lee (1971), and Hickson, Hinings, McMillan, and Schwitter (1974) replicated these results.

In his replication study which used a diverse "national" sample of eighty-two United Kingdom organizations, Child (1972) questioned our positive relationship between dependence and centralization. Here, structuring of activities and centralization were negatively correlated, which caused the concentration of authority factor to disappear. Child suggested that those structural dimensions which were related to the prescribed and autonomous content of job activities also helped describe a framework of administrative control. He cited Hinings and Lee's replication (1971), which concluded that degree of regulation of behaviors varies inversely with centralization. Blau and Schoenherr's study of United States employment security agencies (1971) also found that formal procedures encouraged decentralization and flexible decision making. We can partly explain these controversial results by remembering the different kinds of samples used. The Pugh et al. (1963) sample contained more "dependent" organizations than did the Child study. This altered the distribution of centralization

scores and changed the relationship between the centralization dimension and the other structural variable.

Table 1 presents the correlation matrices for three structural and three contextual variables from six different studies.

We have put lines around those correlations which differed by at least .50 across the six studies and have arbitrarily called them "unstable" relationships. For example, centralization of authority had unstable relationships with all but one of the other variables. We did not put lines around the correlations between dependence and centralization because of the extent of the sampling differences already mentioned. Thus, centralization's instability may have been due to sampling problems, or perhaps to statistical inadequacy of its scale (Mansfield, 1973). Sampling differences may also help explain the relative instability of dependence and technology, as measured by the Aston scale of workflow integration. The large correlation between size and technology (.75) on a United States sample of manufacturing organizations may have reflected a cultural characteristic.

However, some of the relationships were strikingly stable. Correlations such as those between functional specialization and size, functional specialization and workflow integration, dependence and workflow integration, and specialization and role definition should generate some fruitful hypotheses about organizational control processes (Child, 1972).

Nonbureaucratic Structures

How can we measure nonbureaucratic structures? Burns and Stalker's (1961) descriptive study suggested a mechanistic-organic (later called "organismic"; Burns, 1963) dimension. Their mechanistic end was very similar to Weber's ideal bureaucracy; it had precisely defined functional roles and a hierarchical structure of control, authority, and communications. Their organic end went beyond a mere antithesis and made

TABLE 1
CORRELATIONS BETWEEN OBJECTIVE MEASURES OF STRUCTURE AND
CONTEXT VARIABLES FROM SIX STUDIES

		Structure			Context	
		Functional Specialization	Role Definition	Centralization of Authority	Size	Technology (Work-flow Integration)
Structure	Role Definition	.47 .43 .71 .67 .67 .40				
	Centralization of Authority	-.50 -.25 -.40 -.56 -.04 .03	.22 .33 -.13 -.21 -.40 .42			
Context	Size	.67 .80 .82 .63 .34 .49	.08 .41 .39 .56 .40 .49	-.09 -.01 -.37 -.56 -.63 .38		
	Technology (Work-flow Integration)	.44 .27 .64 .41 .68 .13	.11 .26 .45 .09 .36 .06	-.22 .25 -.30 .14 .17 .17	.15 .21 .75 .24 .29 .12	
	Dependence	-.36 .00 .05 .32 .30 .11	-.04 .52 .14 .40 .40 .31	.72 .60 .59 -.03 .23 .55	-.06 .11 -.10 .21 .11 .02	-.05 .23 .04 .19 .11 -.04

Order of studies and correlations is:

Pugh et al. (1969)—46 manufacturing and service organizations (UK)

Inkson et al. (1970)—21 manufacturing organizations (USA)

Payne & Mansfield (1973)—14 manufacturing organizations (UK)

Inkson et al. (1968)—25 manufacturing organizations (UK)

Child (1972)—82 manufacturing and service organizations (UK)

Hickson et al. (1971)—24 manufacturing organizations (Canada)

 = unstable relationships

prescriptions such as being responsible for one's own problems; it had a network form and based position authority upon expertise settled by consensus.

Burns and Stalker's formulation, then, emphasized our present lack of research information on nonbureaucratic structures, a name which itself has suggested a lack of positive identification. "Implicitly struc-tured" organizations (Pugh, Hickson, Hinings, & Turner, 1969) which seem to show much traditionalism may also have been one form of nonbureaucracy. However, many other different forms of nonbureaucratic structure may develop, particularly in organizations which are facing complex environmental changes (Burns & Stalker, 1961; Lawrence & Lorsch, 1967; Bennis, 1966;

Leavitt, 1962). Hopefully, future research will generate measuring instruments suitable for such structures.

The Relationship Between Perceptual and Objective Measures of Structure

Studies which compare perceptual and objective measures of organizational structure have been rare. Turner (1965) compared Hall's perceptual measures with the objective ones of Pugh et al. (1968). He used Pugh's original sample of fifty-two organizations to select three organizations which had sharply contrasting structures, and asked personnel in each of them to complete the Hall bureaucracy scales. Turner ranked the organizations on both the Hall and the Pugh et al. measures, and found very low agreement between the sets of dimension-organization rankings. Rankings on centralization or standardization measures in two organizations differed by more than two units; eight sets of rankings differed by one unit; rankings on formalization or specialization measures in only two organizations agreed perfectly. This comparison, then, offered little validation of Hall's first four dimensions, particularly since Turner selected divergent organizations which should have shown the differences relatively easily.

Pennings collected data on the Pugh and Hall scales from ten manufacturing organizations. His low "inter-approach" (objective versus subjective measures) correlations "call into question the assumption that the different instruments tap identical structural attributes and suggest that some of the scales lack satisfactory stable discriminatory measuring ability" (Pennings, 1971, p. 1).

Studies which have not explicitly compared perceptual and objective measures can also help us. Inkson, Hickson, and Pugh (1968) used abbreviated Pugh et al. objective scales (Inkson, Pugh, & Hickson, 1970) on forty Birmingham manufacturing and service organizations. They also gathered perceptual data about the role perceptions of the chief executive and his eight or so immediate subordinates and found three relevant dimensions: (1) role routine, or the immediate and long-term changes in a role; (2) role definition, or the fixed limits and authority constraints of a job; and (3) role formalization, or the formal prescriptions and documents for a job. They calculated the executives' mean score on each dimension for every company; each of these mean scores has been treated as a perceptual measure of standardization and formalization. Table 2 shows the correlations between the perceptual and objective structural measures.

Although Inkson et al. hypothesized that all three dimensions of role perception would relate positively to structuring of activities and centralization of authority, only role formalization varied directly with these objective measures of bureaucratic structure; role routine and role definition varied inversely. When only the twenty-five manufacturing organizations were considered, the relationships were even stronger. However, the authors suggested that the executives in the bureaucratic, larger organizations might have had positions "above" those positions which involved formal activity structuring and probably had relatively innovative, creative jobs. Perhaps data from a sample which included employees at lower levels in the organization would support the original hypothesis; certainly, adequate sampling of all the various organizational subgroups is important in accurately measuring group perceptions.

Inkson, Schwitter, Pheysey, and Hickson (1971) replicated and extended this study with a sample of seventeen Ohio (USA) manufacturing organizations. They gave the role perception measures to managerial levels throughout the organizational hierarchy. Table 3 gives correlations between objective structural measures and subjective role measures for groups of both senior executives and managers from all levels.

Comparison of Tables 2 and 3 shows differences between British and American ob-

TABLE 2
CORRELATIONS BETWEEN OBJECTIVE AND SUBJECTIVE MEASURES OF STRUCTURE
FOR 40 BRITISH MANUFACTURING AND SERVICE ORGANIZATIONS

		Objective Measures		Subjective Measures		
		Structuring of Activities	Centralization	Role Routine	Role Definition	Role Formalization
Objective Measures	Log Size	.61	-.11	-.31	-.26	.29
	Structuring of Activities		.24	-.56	-.28	.19
	Centralization of Authority			-.22	-.16	.42
Subjective Measures	Role Routine				.39	-.06
	Role Definition					.44

(From Inkson, Hickson, & Pugh, 1968.)

TABLE 3
CORRELATIONS BETWEEN OBJECTIVE AND SUBJECTIVE MEASURES
OF STRUCTURE FOR 17 U.S. MANUFACTURING ORGANIZATIONS

		Objective Measures				Subjective Measures					
		Structuring of Activities		Centralization		Role Routine		Role Definition		Role Formalization	
		Top	All	Top	All	Top	All	Top	All	Top	All
Objective Measures	Log Size	.79	.79	-.41	-.41	-.39	-.28	-.21	.51	.57	.71
	Structuring of Activities			-.36	-.36	-.33	-.01	.20	.62	.52	.66
	Centralization of Authority					.50	.43	.21	-.16	-.37	-.30
Subjective Measures	Role Routine							.18	.22	-.22	-.36
	Role Definition									.76	.71

Top = Chief executive and immediate subordinates only

All = Managers from all levels

(From Inkson, Schwitter, Pheysey & Hickson, 1971.)

jective structural variables relationships. In the United States sample, size related more strongly to activity structuring and correlated more negatively with centralization of authority; also, activity structuring varied inversely with centralization of authority. In the entire British sample, activity structuring and centralization varied directly; these relationships also held true for the subsample of twenty-five manufacturing organizations.

The relationships between the objective and perceptual structural measures were also slightly different for the two samples. In the United States study, both size and activity structuring generally correlated positively with role definition and role formalization; in the British study, they correlated negatively with role definition and positively with role formalization. Accordingly, in the latter sample, there was a weaker relationship between the two perceptual measures.

On a matched sample of fourteen of these organizations, Inkson, Schwitter, Pheysey, and Hickson (1970) showed that United States organizations had a higher mean score on objective measures of activity structuring and role formalization. There was also a significant difference between the two countries' subjective measures of role formalization. Certainly, this has pointed to cultural differences in the structural features themselves as well as in their interrelationships.

Our concern, however, is defining relationships between objective and perceptual measures of structural variables. Greater size and activity structuring seem to have led to more perceived formalization of roles; in the United States, an increase in role definition also occurred, particularly when lower level managers were included in the sample. No data from any group of managers has supported the expectation that greater size and activity structuring would lead to perception of more routine jobs; indeed, all the data except from the United States managers of all levels have shown fairly strong negative relationships. Merton's belief (1940) that bureaucracy would lead to routine, predictable jobs that helped create the bureaucratic personality seems false for the sample of senior managers. As expected, more centralization of authority led to higher perceived role routine in United States manufacturing organizations ($r = .43$) and also in the British subsample of manufacturing organizations ($r = .13$). The relationships between perceived and objective structural measures in the United States sample, even with the lower level managers, had directions closer to those hypothesized, than did those relationships in the British sample. However, the unusual negative relationship between size and routine in both sets of data may have been dependent on their use of professionally oriented managers in larger companies who perceived innovation as part of their jobs. Managers in bigger companies may be successfully legislating for change in role prescriptions; Texas Instruments now has an effective, if somewhat mechanistic, system for encouraging and supporting innovative ideas.

Thus, the managers in the smaller, less bureaucratic organizations perceived their jobs as more routine. Researchers should try to replicate this result with a larger sample of organizations and different measures of role routine; Inkson et al.'s finding may have been a function of their particular measuring instrument. Inkson's study also lacked a perceptual measure of decentralization.

Following the path of Inkson et al. (1968), Child and Ellis (1973) used a sample of seventy-eight organizations and 787 senior managers. They also found that activity structuring related positively to role formalization and role definition, and related negatively to role routine, although correlations were smaller. Centralization was associated with jobs that were more routine ($r = .45$) but less formalized ($r = -.31$). A $-.57$ correlation between managers' perceived authority ratings and objective centralization scores showed that the former may have been providing subjective measures of centralization; thus, more centralized organizations probably gave their managers a narrower range of authority. Child felt that this relationship, surprisingly strong for a group of the most senior managers, might have related to the centralization measures themselves—high centralization scores meant that many decisions remained at the chief executive level or even went outside the organization to another board.

Have perceived and objective measures of structure, then, validated each other? The two ways of operationalizing structuring have shown only moderate relationships with each other. However, the two ways of operationalizing centralization of authority have been more strongly correlated with each other. Certainly, our past research has produced many interesting ideas, and points to a need for more accurate measures of structure which will show convergent validity with each other.

Cross-sectional Studies of Structure

Investigators of organizational structure originally concentrated on measuring configuration variables (ratios of particular job roles and levels); only later did they use perceived and then objective measures to dimensionalize other aspects of structure. Current studies of all three types have established several reasonably stable relationships across varying samples. The dimensions of specialization, standardization, and formalization have seemed highly interrelated, and have also been primarily related to the contextual feature of size. Technology appears to have been related to specialization in smaller degree, and had its primary impact on certain configurational features such as the first line supervisor's span of control and the proportions of personnel in specialized departments such as maintenance and production control. In all except one study, dependence was strongly related to diffusion of authority.

Thus, a reasonably stable conceptual framework which related context variables such as size, technology, dependence, and ownership patterns to structural dimensions such as specialization, formalization, and centralization has emerged from the comparative cross-sectional studies. However, comparative studies of "nonbureaucracies" are lacking.

Longitudinal and Dynamic Studies of Structure

Since a formal authority structure is a construct derived from the activities of organizational members, it is sometimes considered a subject in its own right. However, a formal authority structure has also provided a framework for the study of members' attitudes and behavior, and of the processes behind organizational stability and change. Longitudinal and dynamic studies can help to develop convincing causal explanations; cross-sectional correlational studies can only infer causal hypotheses.

Thus, Aldrich (1972) emphasized the use of causal models and path analysis to relate structural variables. He suggested that Pugh et al. unduly stressed size as a determinant of structure, and argued that technology was more relevant. In a stimulating series of responses to Aldrich, Hilton (1972), Heise (1972), and Pugh and Hickson (1972) debated the value of path analysis as a tool for helping with causal analysis. All agreed that causal models required longitudinal data to reveal the processes by which organizations (a) remained in a relatively steady state, and (b) changed.

Unfortunately, there have been few such longitudinal studies. Using the Pugh et al. measures (1968), Inkson, Pugh, and Hickson (1970) compared two samples at two points in time and found similar relationships between context (size, technology, dependence) and structure (structuring of activities, concentration of authority). Then, they compared the structural and contextual features of fourteen "workflow bureaucracies" (Pugh, Hickson, Hinings, & Turner, 1969) at two points with an intervening period of four to five years. Although technology and dependence measures remained the same over time, organizational size decreased 5 to 10 percent, on the average. However, the structuring scores themselves usually showed a significant increase of about 10 percent, and concentration of authority scores significantly decreased about 33⅓ percent.

These results concurred with the developmental sequence implied by Pugh's taxonomy of structures (Pugh, Hickson, Hinings, & Turner, 1969). Inkson, Pugh, and Hickson hypothesized the operation of an organizational "rachet mechanism"; here size increases would bring structuring increases, but size decreases would not result in structuring decreases, at least on a short-term basis. However, in Pugh et al.'s study, decreased concentration of authority accompanied increased structuring.

Although the Inkson, Pugh, and Hickson study (1970) was longitudinal, it only implied the actual change processes of organizational structure. Comparative studies of change processes are lacking, although some descriptive studies are available (Pettigrew, 1973; Dalton, 1959; Crozier, 1964; Gouldner, 1954; Guest, 1962). To look at processes on a large comparative scale, we must rely on the organizational climate studies which reflect people's perceptions of what occurs in organizations.

THE CONCEPT AND MEASUREMENT OF ORGANIZATIONAL CLIMATE

This section will describe major organizational climate factors which have been operationalized with several measures. We define climate by distinguishing between objective and subjective measures. Some climate dimensions also seem to be structural measures. Thus, we organize the rest of the chapter around the subjective-objective and structure-climate distinctions.

Tagiuri and Litwin (1968) have summarized several writers' definitions of climate. Campbell, Dunnette, Lawler, and Weick (1970) also offered a definition, and usefully described four major dimensions of organizational climate: (1) individual autonomy; (2) degree of structure imposed on the position; (3) reward orientation; and (4) consideration, warmth, and support. Of these, individual autonomy was perhaps the clearest composite and included individual responsibility (Litwin & Stringer, 1968), agent independence (Schneider & Bartlett, 1970), rules orientation (Kahn, Wolfe, Quinn, Snoek, & Rosenthal, 1964), and Tagiuri's factor which dealt with opportunities for exercising individual initiative. Keystones of this dimension were the freedom of the individual to be his own boss and reserve considerable decision-making power for himself and his lack of constant accountability to higher management.

The degree of structure imposed upon the position included Litwin and Stringer's structure, Schneider and Bartlett's managerial structure, Tagiuri's first factor dealing with direction and objectives, and Kahn et al.'s closeness of supervision. The principal element was the degree to which superiors established and communicated a job's objectives and the methods for accomplishing them.

The grouping of reward orientation included Litwin and Stringer's reward factor, Schneider and Bartlett's general satisfaction factor, Kahn et al.'s promotion-achievement orientation, and Tagiuri's being with a profit-minded and sales-oriented company. Although these factors did not hang together as well as those in the previous two groups and varied a great deal in breadth, the reward element appeared to have been present in each.

The dimension of consideration, warmth, and support was less clear than the previous three. Managerial support (Schneider & Bartlett, 1970) and nurturance of subordinates (Kahn et al., 1964) seemed quite similar. Since supervisory practices helped determine this characteristic, Litwin and

Stringer's warmth and support also seemed to belong here. Although Tagiuri's factor of working with a highly competitive and competent superior did not clearly mesh with a human relations composite, it appeared to refer to the support and stimulation received from one's superior.

Orientation to development and progressiveness may have been another important climate dimension. Stern (1970), Pace (1968), and Gorman and Malloy (1972) all identified major climate factors, each of which concerned fostering people's development and encouraging the growth and application of new ideas and methods.

Campbell et al. pointed out that their first two dimensions were similar to the first two structural dimensions Pugh et al. (1968) obtained from objective data. Individual autonomy and concentration of authority may have both resulted from a decentralized authority system. Degree of structure was similar to structuring of work activities. Although it was encouraging that two methods of data collection were so similar, these two climate factors may really have been only alternative ways of measuring structural variables.

Other writers, already cited, used subjective methods to measure structural factors. Hall (1963), Hage and Aiken (1967), and Bonjean and Grimes (1970) have all used the Hall scales to measure bureaucracy variables. They gave scales which measured these concepts to members of an organization, and represented the organization's structure by the mean of the individual responses. Aiken and Hage (1967) grouped responses for positions at different organizational levels, and then grouped across positions to obtain a structural score for the organization. Although these measures were conceptually different from climate dimensions, the two were operationally similar. Schneider (1972, p. 2) made the same point: "Previous literature in organizational climate has confused the perception of structural characteristics, events of behavior, and the summary climate perceptions." Thus, we

feel that some climate dimensions should have been treated as structural variables; it has been easy for social science to produce a "new" concept and treat it as a modern field of study. Morale, job satisfaction, and work alienation have had almost three separate literatures, although operational measures of each have had much in common. Some currently developing areas of sociology, action theory (Silverman, 1970) and ethnomethodology (Garfinkel, 1967) are not only similar themselves, but also resemble the more phenomenological viewpoints in psychology such as those of Stout (1896), Lewin (1951), and Kelly (1955).

However, if we treat some of the major components of climate as structural variables, then what is climate? Payne (1971) has described climate as "a molar concept reflecting the content and strength of the prevalent values, norms, attitudes, behaviors, and feelings of the members of a social system which can be operationally measured through the perceptions of system members or observational and other objective means" (p. 156). Two peculiarities of this definition were its generalization to any arbitrarily defined social system and its inclusion of both objective and subjective measures. Payne's definition of climate was similar to Likert's concept of an intervening variable (1967); Likert's management systems themselves may be seen as climate measures.

Likert's (1967) description of causal, intervening, and end-result variables emphasized the conceptual differences between organization structure and organization climate. Here, organization structure became a causal variable, and climate, an intervening variable. Let us look at his descriptions:

The "causal variables" are independent variables which determine the course of development within an organization and the results achieved by the organization. These causal variables include only those independent variables which can be altered or changed by the organization and its management. General business conditions, for example, although an independent variable, is not included amongst the causal list. Causal variables include the structure of the organization and management's policies, decisions, business and leadership strategies, skills and behavior.

The "intervening" variables reflect the internal state and health of the organization, e.g., the loyalties, attitudes, motivations, performance goals, and perceptions of all members and their collective capacity for effective interaction, communication and decision making.

The "end-result" variables are the dependent variables which reflect the achievements of the organization, such as its productivity, costs, scrap-loss, and earnings. (p. 26)

Payne's definition also stressed the rather crude distinction between objective and subjective measures. Although Payne's dichotomy needed some clarification of terms, it was certainly a start in categorizing means of data collection. Barker (1965) pointed out, "The characteristics of data-generating systems, including the details of the coupling between psychologists and phenomena, are almost limitless" (p. 1).

Barker (1965) himself distinguished between T and O data. In T data the psychologist acted as a mere transducer or "docile receiver, coder, and transmitter of information about the input, interior conditions, and output of psychological units" (p. 1); examples included Barker's field observations of the "stream of behavior." In O data, the psychologist was both a transducer and an operator, because "the psychologist, here, is coupled into the psychological unit as an operative part of it, regulating input, and/or influencing interior conditions, and/or constraining output" (p. 3). Experiments, structured interviews, and questionnaires (self-reports and reports by others about a person) produced O data. Barker's distinction corresponded to, but was not synonymous with our distinction between objective (T data) and subjective (O data). For example, the Pugh et al. (1968) measures of structure contained questions such as, "Is there a memo form?" and "Can I see it?" which

had reasonable face validity as objective (T) data; however, the psychologist controlled the input (O data). We classified these as objective data because the questions referred to environmental rather than psychological phenomena, and the psychologist acted largely as a transducer.

The rest of this section explores the utility of the distinctions between structure and climate and between their objective and subjective operationalizations. Figure 3 summarizes the differences between these concepts and gives examples of different types of data for each category.

Most measures of organizational climate contain subjective measures of both structure and climate dimensions. Hall's (1963) operationalizations of Weber's dimensions of bureaucracy were subjective measures. Barker (1963) suggested using observational techniques to classify behavior settings and behavior episodes and thus, to objectively measure organizational climate. These would reveal existing norms, reinforced behavior patterns, and the frequency of various groups' activities. If such information was collected over extended time periods, it could also provide structural data which would reveal role relationships, reward patterns, and communication patterns. Here, these data could illustrate the *possibility* of objective measures of climate dimensions such as warmth, support, risk taking, and developmental press. Various statistics such as absence, lateness, and turnover could also provide objective indices about behavioral and attitudinal norms of the organization such as "voting with the feet." Each of the previously discussed Aston measures and those of Blau and of Worthy, have represented an objective measure of organizational structure.

The Relationship Between Perceptual and Objective Measures of Climate

There have been very few studies which have examined the convergent validity of

	Climate	Structure
Subjective	Stern's Organizational Climate Index Litwin and Stringer's Organizational Climate Questionnaire	Hall's dimensions of bureaucracy Litwin and Stringer's scale of Structure in their Organizational Climate Questionnaire
Objective	Barker's Behavioral Episodes Critical Incidents labour turnover absenteeism and lateness statistics	Dimensions of Structure as measured by Pugh et al. and by Ronan and Prien

Figure 3. Subjective and objective operationalizations of climate and structural variables.

climate measures by comparing objective and subjective measures. This has been due to the concept's infancy as well as the high cost of collecting observational data from several organizations. Barker (1963) and Barker and Gump (1964) have given many examples of behavioral descriptions which have led to excellent, objective climate data.

Barker (1963) compared the effects of being a student in large versus small public high schools. The students from the small high schools "entered the same number of behavior settings (although there were fewer available); held important, responsible, and central positions in a greater number of the settings; experienced more attractions and more pressures toward participation in the settings; entered a wider variety of behavior settings; and held important, responsible, and central positions in a wider variety of the settings" (p. 33).

Throughout the seventeen weeks of the study, students from small high schools held "central, responsible positions" as members and officers of widely varying types of organizations on an average of 3.7 behavior set-

tings per student. Students from the large high school showed an average of only .6 behavior settings per student. Also, students from small schools held important positions in twice as many different settings as those from the large school. These data supported Barker's theory that "the students of the small high schools (with fewer than optimal inhabitants per setting) were more strongly motivated, engaged in more varied activities, and were more responsibly involved than the students of the large school (with more than optimal inhabitants per setting)" (p. 33). Also, they provided an excellent description of climate in different schools as shown by their students' activities and involvements.

Astin and Holland (1961) compared perceptual and objective climate measures. They used the College Characteristics Index (Pace & Stern, 1958) for a perceptual measure and the Environmental Assessment Technique (EAT) for an objective measure. The EAT was a rather crude measure, possibly much better suited to academic organizations than to business, welfare, or trade union organizations. It was an eight-variable index based on institutional size, student intelligence, and the proportion of students studying various subjects. They classified subjects into categories according to Holland's (1959) theory of vocational choice: (1) realistic (agriculture, forestry, engineering); (2) intellectual (natural sciences, math, philosophy); (3) social (education, nursing, sociology); (4) conventional (accounting, business studies, economics); (5) enterprising (public administration, political science); and (6) artistic (arts, music, foreign language) orientations.

Using a sample of thirty-six schools, Astin and Holland obtained sizable correlations between different EAT and CCI dimensions such as size and aggression (.64), intelligent factor and understanding (.70), realistic orientation and humanities and social sciences (−.81), intellectual orientation and deference (−.55), social orientation and narcissism (.59), conventional orientation and passivity (.42), enterprising orientation and humanities and social sciences (.79), artistic orientation and sensuality (.69).

Astin (1963) further validated the EAT by relating it to thirty-nine climate-like items such as, "students are more inclined to pursue their own individual projects than to engage in group activities." Seventy-five percent of the correlations were significantly different from zero; student intelligence accounted for the largest percentage of the variance in the climate items.

Stern (1970) related organizational culture dimensions to objective indicators of school climate such as teacher absenteeism, teacher turnover, and pupil absenteeism. He derived his culture dimensions from a joint factor analysis of the Activities Index (AI) and the College Characteristics Index (CCI). The AI was a personality measure based on thirty Needs derived from the work of Murray (1938); both the AI and CCI were constructed around the same thirty needs. Stern studied these two measures separately and together, and was primarily concerned with their interaction. When factoring the two measures jointly, he argued that internal environment (CCI) and personalities (AI) together represented the culture of the organization. His Joint Factor, Second Order Factor Analysis produced six factors: (1) protective culture; (2) achievement needs; (3) development press; (4) emotional culture; (5) friendliness needs; and (6) submissiveness needs.

Only the first and fourth factors were genuine "culture" factors which contained first order factors from the AI and CCI. In a study of forty schools, Stern found that protective culture related −.62 to pupil absenteeism and that achievement needs related +.45 to pupil absenteeism. When the socioeconomic level of the school was held constant, these relationships stayed at −.58 and +.58, respectively. Thus, a protective culture kept people in the school, but when teachers communicated a high need for achievement, pupil absenteeism increased. Protective culture and achievement needs were inversely related $(r = -.70)$. No other factors related to these indices of objective climate.

Hutchins and Nonneman's (1966) Environment Inventory for Medical Schools related scores on six factors to Astin's previously described objective climate measures. Medical Schools with a climate of high intrinsic motivation had a student body with great scientific orientation, intellectualism, and aestheticism and low social orientation and conventionality. A climate of extrinsic motivation showed generally reverse relationships. The inventory's one major factor of general esteem showed the same relationships, but with slightly lower correlations. Quite clearly, the climate in these schools strongly reflected the abilities and academic values of the students.

In the study, medical school resources (finance, staff, size of faculty, percent of research students, faculty-student ratios) were also related to the perceived climates. Schools which had better financial resources and more favorable staff-student ratios had climates higher on general esteem and intrinsic motivation. Fewer resources were associated with feelings of being under extrinsic motivation and of receiving "encapsulated training."

Thus, these few studies have suggested that perceptual climate measures have some validity and do correlate with objective, nonperceptual climate indicators. Theoretically, some of these relationships have been pretty tame. It was almost tautological to show a positive relationship between staff and students of high intelligence and high resources and a climate seen as intellectual and of high esteem; the entry requirements determined these factors. However, it also would have been discouraging if such indicators had not validated each other. Results of these studies may be limited to educational institutions; here, selected members might determine climate and performance more than in other organizations such as hospitals, government, and industry. Nevertheless, the Astin studies have shown that fairly simple statistical descriptions of an organization can say something important.

THE RELATIONSHIP BETWEEN PERCEPTUAL MEASURES OF STRUCTURE AND PERCEPTUAL MEASURES OF CLIMATE

The length of this section reveals the psychologist's love for questionnaires. In surveying the better known organizational description inventories (e.g., Hemphill, 1956; Likert, 1967; Litwin & Stringer, 1968), we try to carefully maintain the distinction between structure and climate. We find that: (1) relationships between perceived measures of structure are relatively stable across different studies; (2) an organization perceived as bureaucratic does not have a climate perceived as cold, threatening, or low in cohesiveness; (3) organizations perceived as having decentralized decision taking do tend to have climates perceived as warm, supportive, and encouraging risk taking; and (4) relationships between climate

dimensions are not stable across different studies.

Hemphill's "Group Dimensions Description Questionnaire"

This title might imply that a "group" dimensions questionnaire does not measure organizational climate. However, Hemphill (1956) has suggested that his questionnaire tried "to arrange all social collectivities in a meaningful set of orthogonal (independent) dimensions" (p. 7). Indeed, his instrument has been used to describe both small groups and large organizations.

Subjects rated 150 statements on a five-point scale which extended from "Definitely True" to "Definitely False." The questionnaire contained thirteen dimensions which measured the degree to which the group had (1) autonomy; (2) control over its members; (3) formal procedures; (4) a pleasant atmosphere; (5) a homogeneous membership; (6) members' knowledge of each other; (7) stability; (8) stratification of status; (9) cohesion; (10) clear goals; (11) easy or difficult entry requirements; (12) member involvement; and (13) amount of participation of members in group affairs.

Two of Hemphill and Westie's (1950) criteria for constructing the group dimensions were applicability to all social collectivities and unidimensional scaling. Pheysey and Payne (1970) gave Hemphill's instrument to groups of managers and found that the permeability dimension was inappropriate for groups in which membership allocation was determined by some larger organization. Also, both these authors and Findikyan and Sells (1964), in a large study with 976 respondents, found that each of several dimensions reflected more than one organizational characteristic.

Thus, Pheysey and Payne classified the remaining eight dimensions into "Climate and Process" and "Structure" categories. The Climate dimensions were Intimacy, Participation, Polarization, Potency, and viscidity; the structure dimensions included autonomy, flexibility, and stratification. They felt that autonomy was similar to the organizational concept of decentralization, and that flexibility was the inverse of structuring of work activities (Pugh et al., 1968). Stratification resembled the organizational indicator, height of hierarchy or vertical span.

We reproduce Table 4 from Pheysey and Payne to show the correlation matrix for three structural variables and two climate variables in each of two studies, those of Hemphill (1956) with 100 persons who represented 100 groups and Findikyan and Sells (1964) with 967 persons who represented sixty groups. The three structural dimensions were related. Autonomous groups were more flexible and less stratified; thus, one of Hemphill's major factors which came

out of the dimensions was "Behavior regulation appearing as social structure." Autonomy and flexibility (informality) were negatively related to potency; thus, members of these organizations had important reference points outside their particular groups. Autonomous social systems, however, were more viscid (cohesive), as predicted by the human relations school. Bureaucracy or lack of it (flexibility) seemed to have been unrelated to viscidity (cohesiveness) (r's = .05, .08); however, stratified groups were less cohesive.

Likert's "Management Systems"

Unfortunately, Likert's own measures did not utilize his beautiful differentiation among causal, intervening, and end-result variables. This was surprising since he had

TABLE 4
INTERCORRELATIONS OF SOME PERCEIVED STRUCTURAL AND PERCEIVED CLIMATE VARIABLES FROM THE HEMPHILL GROUP DIMENSIONS DESCRIPTION QUESTIONNAIRE

			Structure		Climate	
			Flexibility (Informality)	Stratification	Potency	Viscidity (Cohesiveness)
Structure	Autonomy	a	0.36	-0.58	-0.45	0.24
		b	0.46	-0.42	-0.24	0.23
	Flexibility (Informality)	a		-0.35	-0.35	0.05
		b		-0.35	-0.45	0.08
	Stratification	a			0.04	-0.34
		b			0.12	-0.46
Climate	Potency	a				0.16
		b				0.07

a = correlations reported by Hemphill, 1956
    N = 100 persons representing 100 groups

b = correlations reported by Findikyan & Sells, 1964
    N = 967 persons representing 60 groups

(From Pheysey & Payne, 1970.)

stated that: "It is valuable to recognize in any diagnosis, or analysis of an enterprise which variables are causal, which intervening, and which end-result" (Likert, 1967, p. 138). Although his book *The Human Organization* contained four questions about organization performance which clearly tapped end-result variables, these were excluded from his revised instrument in Appendix II. Also, Appendix III of his book described causal, intervening, and end-result variables in organizations in some detail, but did not link these to particular measures. For example, causal variable $A,1$ was "the extent to which the principle of supportive relationships permeates the company," and intervening variable $A,5$ was "the extent to which members of the organization feel that the atmosphere of the organization is supportive." However, it was unclear whether item number 3 in Likert's questionnaire, "the extent to which superiors display supportive behavior towards others" (p. 197), operationalized a causal or an intervening variable. However, since a causal variable "must be subject to deliberate alterations or changes by the organization" (p. 141), we have classified nineteen out of fifty-one of Likert's measurements as causal variables; this has not fitted neatly with Likert's grouping of the variables. We feel item $3,c,(1)$, the "point at which downward communication is initiated" was a causal variable; and item $3,c,(2)$, the "extent to which superiors willingly share information with subordinates," and item $3,c,(3)$, the "extent to which communications are accepted by subordinates" were intervening variables.

We can then classify these causal variables as measures of organization structure. Many of Likert's items related to the level of participative decision making; thus, we have classified as centralization measures about half of the items previously identified as causal variables. Item $5,f$, "the extent to which subordinates are involved in decisions related to their work," then, measured centralization; item $5,d$, "the extent to which technical and professional knowledge is used

in decision making," measured specialization. We tentatively decided the other half of the items indicated the extent of an organization's standardization and formalization; however, many of these items related to participative management as well as to bureaucracy. An example was item $7,e$, "the extent to which control data (accounting, productivity, cost, etc.) are used for self-guidance or group problem solving by managers and non-supervisory employees, or used by supervisors in a punitive, policing manner."

We might want to test the theoretical question, "How does the extent of centralization-decentralization affect intervening organizational climate variables?" However, many of the items in Likert's measures reflected value judgments, so that any causal or intervening variables in System 4 management were "good," and those in System 1, "bad"; thus, his measures represented only general "good" or "bad" evaluations of a company. All of Likert's causal, intervening, and end-result variables were highly intercorrelated. Likert reported that the correlation matrix of his measures could be summarized by one factor; the total score for all variables then correlated 1.00 with this factor.

Taylor and Bowers (1970) used Likert's measure to develop an instrument specifically for organizational climate. Although it was an improvement and had a five-factor solution via Guttman's (1968) Smallest Space Analysis, intercorrelations between all scales except one were at least .70. Thus, this instrument, too, had a large general factor.

However, Pugh (Pugh et al., 1968; Pugh, Hickson, Hinings, & Turner, 1969) had already identified several structural dimensions. Other factor analyses of climate measures ascertained the independence of dimensions such as structuring of work environment, and warmth or considerateness (Campbell et al., 1970). If Likert's measures were valid, decentralized, unstructured, and less bureaucratic, organizations would have loyal members, high morale, and high productivity. However, we feel Likert's measures were inadequate to test hypotheses which related structural and climate variables.

Tagiuri's "Executive Climate Questionnaire"

This questionnaire was developed (1968) to assess executive climate. Tagiuri distinguished between this type of climate and managerial climate, which pervaded the whole organization, and was a specialized term that reflected management's philosophy about the nature of man. Items from the "Executive Climate Questionnaire" were rated on a seven-point scale and covered areas of the company, top management, company policy, the job, the department, my superiors, my associates, my subordinates, and advancement.

Tagiuri factors analyzed data from 232 members of the Advanced Management Program at Harvard University, and produced the following five factors: (1) policies lead to clear direction and guidance; (2) professional atmosphere (and status bases); (3) qualities of superiors; (4) qualities of department (or group with whom the manager works); and (5) emphasis on results combined with executive autonomy and satisfaction.

Only Factor 1 was a causal variable, in Likert's terms, or a structural variable in ours; as a structural component, it seemed to represent the executive level equivalent of structuring of work activities. If we treat the other four factors as genuine climate variables, we find that the structural factor had little or no relationship with the climate factors. The strongest correlation was between Factors 1 and 3 ($r = .31$); Factors 1 and 4 correlated .25. These relationships suggested that good top management produced (or was attracted to) companies that had clear goals and policies; these goals, then, produced an effective working group atmosphere among the company executives.

Since these relationships were small, however, many other factors must have affected each of these dimensions.

Litwin and Stringer's Organizational Climate Questionnaire

This questionnaire was developed (1968) to test the hypothesis that different environments demand or arouse different types of motivation. Litwin and Stringer based their motivational theory on the work of Atkinson (1964) and McClelland, Atkinson, Clark, and Lowell (1953). Using groups playing a business game, they experimentally manipulated leadership style and produced different climates which aroused different needs; success in these different climates, then, depended on arousal of the appropriate kinds of motivation. They theorized that bureaucratic and somewhat authoritarian leadership would arouse the need for power; informal and friendly leadership would arouse the need for affiliation; and leadership which stressed high productivity, personal goal-setting and individual responsibility would arouse the need for achievement. Both experimental and field studies moderately supported these hypotheses.

Their climate index had fifty items, each of which was rated on a four-point scale from "Definitely Agree" to "Definitely Disagree." Its nine scales included (1) structure of work; (2) responsibility-willingness to take; (3) reward-degree of positive; (4) risk-willingness to take; (5) warmth; (6) support-trust; (7) standards of performance; (8) conflict-openness to; and (9) identity-loyalty.

Structure of work was very similar to the Pugh et al. factor of structuring of activities and was a structural variable. Responsibility concerned motivating people to make decisions, but also included a strong element of decentralization. This scale, thus, had items such as, "Supervision in this organization is mainly a matter of setting guidelines for your subordinates; you let them take responsibility for the job," and

"Around here management resents your checking everything with them; if you think you've got the right approach you just go ahead." We have regarded responsibility as a measure of centralization-decentralization.

Table 5 presents the correlation matrix of the nine climate scales, and utilizes the responses of 518 managers, supervisors, technicians, specialists, and salesmen in a wide variety of business organizations. The two structural scales were almost independent of each other. Responsibility was positively related to most of the genuine climate scales. If we accept responsibility (decentralization) as a causal variable, it seemed to have led to a climate where people took risks ($r = .52$), were rewarded for taking them ($r = .50$), and felt the warmth ($r = .46$) and support ($r = .47$) to aim for the high standards set ($r = .42$). This pattern led to a feeling of identity with or loyalty to ($r = .51$) the organization.

Structure of work had its highest corre-

TABLE 5
INTERCORRELATIONS OF THE CLIMATE SCALES IN THE LITWIN AND STRINGER IMPROVED CLIMATE QUESTIONNAIRE (FORM B)

		Structure	Climate						
		Responsibility (Decentralization)	Reward	Risk	Warmth	Support	Standards	Conflict	Identity-Loyalty
		2	3	4	5	6	7	8	9
Structure	1. Structure of Work (Structuring of Activities)	.18	.24	.18	.28	.34	.38	.28	.31
	2. Responsibility (Decentralization)		.50	.52	.46	.47	.42	.30	.51
Climate	3. Reward			.48	.54	.49	.29	.39	.56
	4. Risk				.41	.43	.49	.44	.42
	5. Warmth					.57	.22	.31	.69
	6. Support						.33	.48	.59
	7. Standards							.34	.41
	8. Conflict								.35

The five highest correlations are underlined.

N = 518 managers, supervisors, technicians, specialists, and salesmen in different business organizations

(From Litwin & Stringer, 1968.)

lation with setting standards. Perhaps developing standard policies, procedures, and control information allowed a company to define its standards and set higher ones when necessary; feedback affected the level of aspiration. However, the correlation was not very strong ($r = .38$), and structure of work had only weak relationships with the other climate variables. If the measures were valid, however, a reasonable degree of structure was compatible with a climate of support ($r = .34$), identity ($r = .31$), and willingness to take a risk ($r = .18$). These small, yet positive correlations argued against the idea that a bureaucratic organization would stifle one's willingness to take a risk, or decrease perceived warmth and support. Indeed, the hypothesis based on bureaucratic dysfunction (March & Simon, 1958) suggested that structure and these climate variables would be negatively correlated. Although the 518 managers in Litwin and Stringer's study probably did not fully represent all organizational situations, their responses have suggested that "organization" or structuring in organizations is not necessarily bad.

Meyer (1968) used Litwin and Stringer's measure to compare two General Electric plants with similar production operations but different management orientations. One plant utilized participative, Theory Y principles, and the other, Theory X principles. Although structure was not measured, the Theory Y plant seemed low on structuring of activities and decentralized, and the Theory X plant, just the opposite. The Theory X plant was less successful than the Theory Y plant, but it was still "a profitable and generally successful business" (p. 160).

On the climate measure, the two plants were similar on structure and standards; the Theory Y plant was higher on responsibility, risk, rewards, warmth, and identity. However, the management decided to get rid of the Theory X manager, even though the evidence herein reviewed does not support the belief that "organization" or structuring in organizations is necessarily a bad thing.

Halpin and Croft's Climate Scale and Hall's Bureaucracy Scales

George and Bishop (1971) used perceptual measures to study organizational climate and structure. They gave the *Organizational Climate Description Questionnaire* or *OCDQ* (Halpin & Croft, 1963) and the *Structural Properties Questionnaire* (Bishop, George, & Murphy, 1967), which was a slightly modified version of the Hage and Aiken scales (1967), to 296 teachers in fifteen elementary schools. Since they used Component Analysis, we cannot quote correlations between various structural and climate measures. However, the four structural variables must have been positively correlated because they formed part of two major components. Also, these two components had sizable vector weights in a canonical correlation between structural and climate variables; thus, there was some relationship between structure and climate. However, George and Bishop's results were slightly confusing because the sixteen personality dimensions of the 16 P.F. (Cattell, 1957) were also entered in the same component analysis, and were, therefore, part of the components. These personality factors contributed at least 43.6 percent of the variance in each of the twenty components. George and Bishop's results suggested that (1) school structures which were perceived as formalized, centralized, complex, and having professional latitude produced climates which were perceived as low in consideration and intimacy and high in production emphasis; and that (2) schools with climates which were high on disengagement, hindrance, and intimacy had structures which allowed some professional latitude and were centralized, slightly formalized, and low on complexity.

Inkson and Hickson's Measures of Perceived Structure and Role

In 1968 Inkson, Hickson, and Pugh developed an instrument to measure senior managers' perceptions of organizational roles. They wanted to describe the following relationships: (a) between Pugh et al.'s objective measures of organizational structure (1968) and perceived degree of role formalization, role definition, and role routine; and (b) between organizational structure and the degree to which managers expected other managers to behave in an innovative manner, the degree to which managers were perceived to behave in an innovative way, and the degree of perceived interpersonal conflict among senior managers. We have already considered the relationships between the objective and subjective measures of organization structure. However, using the measures of innovative expectation, innovative behavior and interpersonal conflict as climate variables, we can examine the relationships between perceived structural and perceived climate variables in this study and in those of Inkson et al. (1971) and Child and Ellis (1973).

Table 6 compares the correlations between the perceived structural and perceived climate variables across the three studies. Although Child's scales were sometimes slightly short because his factor analysis separated some of the items, they were substantially the same as those in the other studies. We have drawn lines around those correlations which were very different across at least two of the studies; this happened in about half of the relationships. These differences were often quite large, and were not always related to United States-United Kingdom sample variations. For example, the correlations between role formalization and innovative expectations were positive, negative, and almost zero across the three studies. We have not tried to decide which of the three studies best fits our hypotheses. Generally, Table 6 shows decreasing stability for relationships between perceived structural variables, relationships between perceived climate variables, and relationships between perceived structure and perceived climate. This finding may have been a function of the inherent instability of perceptual measures in general, or of Inkson et al.'s particular measures. Since the data

from Hemphill's questionnaire reflected these same three types of relationships, and these correlations were very uniform across two studies (Table 4), perhaps Inkson's particular measures were at fault.

This section has, thus, suggested a fairly clear relationship between perceived decentralization and climate characteristics such as cohesiveness, warmth, consideration and support, and openness to conflict. When people have perceived a decentralized structure, they have also perceived a climate supportive of some risk taking and conflict. This has agreed with our last section's clear relationships between objective and subjective measures of centralization. However, perceived structuring of work through bureaucratic procedures has not necessarily led to a climate which was low in warmth and cohesiveness. Although these relationships varied across different studies, they were not particularly strong and have seemed to best approximate zero. Finally, relationships between perceived structure measures have been more reliable across studies than have been relationships between perceived climate measures.

THE RELATIONSHIP BETWEEN OBJECTIVE MEASURES OF STRUCTURE AND PERCEPTUAL MEASURES OF CLIMATE

This section examines the effect of structure on climate. Since organizational size is so pervasively related to structural variables, it is also necessary to consider the effect of size on climate. One hypothesis behind work of this kind is that larger, more bureaucratic organizations produce a climate which encourages conformity, alienation, rule following, suspicion, deference, and little commitment to work (March & Simon, 1958). Empirically, however, organizational size relates to climate variables in a different manner. Relationships may be in the hypothesized direction, but quite small or even in the opposite direction. Structural variables are not so widely related to climate, and different structural variables can affect

TABLE 6
CORRELATIONS BETWEEN PERCEIVED STRUCTURE AND PERCEIVED CLIMATE VARIABLES FOR THREE STUDIES

			Structure			Climate	
			Role Formalization 1	Routine 2	Definition 3	Innovative Expectations 4	Innovative Behavior 5
Structure	Routine 2	a.	-.24				
		b.	-.22				
		c.	.00				
	Definition 3	a.	.43	.26			
		b.	.76	.18			
		c.	.49	.34			
Climate	Innovative Expectations 4	a.	.35	-.66	.07		
		b.	-.34	.17	.04		
		c.	.10	-.48	-.27		
	Innovative Behavior 5	a.	.09	-.44	-.06	.50	
		b.	.01	.44	-.01	-.02	
		c.	.33	-.37	.06	.34	
	Interpersonal Conflict 6	a.	-.01	.47	.10	-.39	-.44
		b.	.11	.01	.09	-.24	-.12
		c.	.36	.03	.08	-.02	.37

(a) 25 Birmingham, U.K. manufacturing organizations, top managers only.
(From Inkson, Hickson, & Pugh, 1968.)

(b) 17 Ohio manufacturing organizations, top managers only.
(From Inkson, Schwitter, Pheysey, & Hickson, 1971.)

(c) 78 British manufacturing and service organizations, top managers only.
(From Child & Ellis, 1973.)

the same climate variable in different ways. Thus, both structure and climate are multidimensional, and consequent interactions are too complex to substantiate simple hypotheses about the effects of bureaucracy on attitudes and behavior. This section tries to account for such complexity and confusing relationships.

There have been very few studies which have utilized objective structural measures and perceptual climate measures, even if we accept organizational size as the minimal indicator of structure. The work of Pugh et al. has been embarrassingly conspicuous.

Indik (1965) did a good job of conceptually and empirically defining the relationships between size, bureaucratic structure, and climatic outcomes. Figure 4 represents his Prototype Paradigm which related independent variable such as size, mediating variables such as organizational and psychological processes, and dependent variables such as member behavior. Indik tested

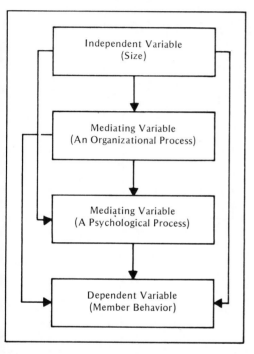

Figure 4. Prototype paradigm.
(From Indik, 1965.)

directional hypotheses which related the variables in this paradigm across three different groupings of organizations—32 package delivery organizations, each of which had 15–16 members; 36 automobile sales dealerships, each of which had 25–132 members; and 28 voluntary-membership, educational-political organizations, each of which had 101–2,989 members.

We reproduce Figure 5 from Indik (1965) to show these correlations for each of the groupings. Indik operationalized four different organizational process variables: (1) amount of job and task specialization

represented the number of different job titles in the organization, and conceptually, was an objective measure of structure; (2) amount of higher-level interpersonal control was a perceptual measure of centralization, or the amount of influence reputedly held by each of several different organizational levels; (3) amount of communication; and (4) lack of coordination were also perceptual organizational process variables, and indicated climate. Amount of communication expressed how free people felt to discuss personal problems with their superior; lack of coordination measured how well people saw eye-to-eye on matters. The psychologically based variables were all perceptual climate measures. Lack of absence and turnover were two operationalizations of the dependent variable, tendency to participate, and were objective climate indicators which reflected commitment and loyalty.

Although Indik's mixture of structural and climate operationalizations of organizational process may not have greatly affected this study's results, it did change the process concept itself. Generally, his results confirmed his directional hypotheses for independent, mediating, and dependent variables; however, these results were decreasingly clear for delivery organizations, auto sales dealerships, and voluntary organizations. Large size led to a higher task specialization, less communication, less coordination, but not to increased higher-level control. These results supported Pugh et al.'s (1968) findings, that increased size was related to increased structuring of activities, but not to increased centralization. Since Indik's organizations were smaller than those in the Pugh study, this was useful information. Particularly in the delivery organizations, both size and the organizational process variables had the anticipated relations with the psychological process variables. Size, organizational process, and psychological process variables all had direct effects on the dependent variable, tendency to participate; also, Indik used

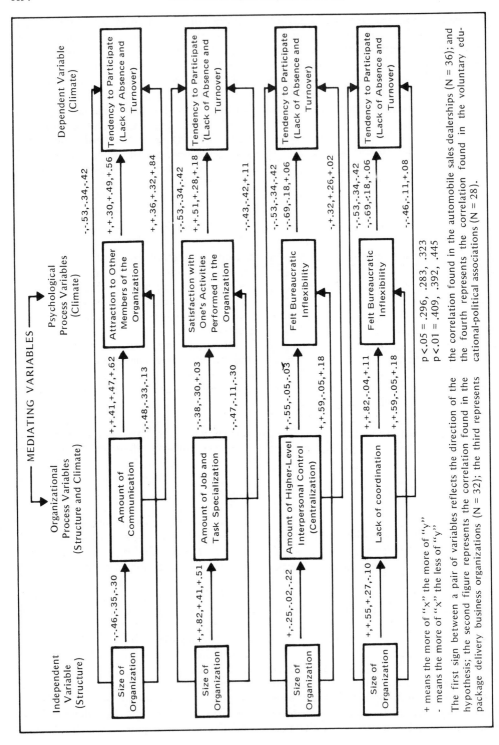

Figure 5. Schematic diagram. (From Indik, 1965.)

partial correlations to show that each of these independent and mediating variables accounted for independent portions of this variance. These results supported the suggestion that structural variables such as size and task specialization affect climate. It was less certain how centralization influenced climate; however, the data from the delivery organizations suggested that more centralization (higher-level control) led to lower felt bureaucratic inflexibility, lower absence, and lower turnover. This unexpected finding awaits confirmation.

Inkson et al. (1968, 1971) used Pugh et al.'s structural variables in conjunction with perceptual measures of both structural and climate variables such as expectations of innovative role behavior, degree of actual innovative behavior, and perceived interpersonal conflict. We have already given details of these studies. Table 7 presents correlations between the structural and climate variables for each study.

We have shown the data for each of three groups—top managers from twenty-five Birmingham manufacturing organizations,

top managers from seventeen Ohio manufacturing organizations, and managers from all levels of seventeen Ohio manufacturing organizations. The first two groups were, thus, directly comparable.

The samples from the two countries showed strikingly different relationships. In the Birmingham sample, larger size and higher structuring of activities correlated with higher expectations of innovative roles, a greater amount of innovative behavior, and less interpersonal conflict about decisions among the top management. In the Ohio sample of top managers, only the last relationships between the structural variables and interpersonal conflict held true (r's $= -.12, -.18$). Top managers in the larger and more structured Ohio organizations expected and perceived less innovative behavior in their organizations.

In the Birmingham sample, centralization of authority was completely unrelated to all the climate variables. However, top managers in more decentralized Ohio companies tended to report less innovative behavior among their colleagues. Further-

TABLE 7
CORRELATIONS BETWEEN OBJECTIVE STRUCTURAL AND PERCEIVED CLIMATE VARIABLES
IN 25 BIRMINGHAM, UK AND 17 OHIO, USA MANUFACTURING ORGANIZATIONS

Structural Variables	Climate Variables								
	Innovative Role Expectations			Innovative Behavior			Interpersonal Conflict		
	B'ham Top Mgrs.	Ohio Top Mgrs.	Ohio Mgrs. all levels	B'ham Top Mgrs.	Ohio Top Mgrs.	Ohio Mgrs. all levels	B'ham Top Mgrs.	Ohio Top Mgrs.	Ohio Mgrs. all levels
Structural Variables Log Size	.46	-.28	-.56	.16	-.36	-.08	-.43	-.12	.11
Structuring of Activities	.55	-.19	-.32	.26	-.41	-.03	-.34	-.18	.04
Centralization of Authority	.02	-.16	-.05	.01	.46	.19	.02	.43	.36

1. Birmingham study: Inkson, Hickson, & Pugh, 1968.
2. Ohio study: Inkson, Schwitter, Pheysey, & Hickson, 1971.

more, managers from all levels of the more decentralized Ohio organizations reported less interpersonal conflict.

In a replication of these studies, Child and Ellis (1973) examined a sample of 787 of the very top executives in seventy-eight organizations. They found that the organizational structure variables were generally unrelated to managers' expectations of innovative behavior (r's $\propto$ 0); a similar pattern emerged between structure and perceived innovative behavior. However, standardization and formalization were each slightly correlated with perceived questioning of authority (r's $= .22, .19$); when organizational size was controlled by partial correlation, these relationships were even stronger. Again, when size was partialled out, specialization, formalization, and standardization each correlated about .30 with perceived interpersonal conflict; these correlations represented the strongest relationships. Centralization was unrelated to interpersonal conflict ($r = 0$), but showed a strong negative correlation with expected ($r - .40$) and perceived ($r = -.20$) innovative behavior. The last relationship increased to $-.30$ when organizational size was held constant.

The relationships between structuring of activities and each of the perceived organizational climate variables except interpersonal conflict varied widely across the three studies, although their measures and subjects were reasonably comparable. For example, these correlations were positive (Inkson et al., 1968), zero (Child & Ellis, 1973), and negative (Inkson et al., 1971).

Centralization was also a confusing variable. Inkson et al. (1968) showed almost zero correlations between centralization and each of several climate variables. The 1971 Inkson study demonstrated negative correlations between decentralization and both perceived interpersonal conflict and perceived innovative behavior. It was surprising that greater decentralization was associated with less innovative behavior. Child and Ellis's study (1973) suggested that

greater decentralization would lead to more expected and perceived innovative behavior; however, decentralization was unrelated to perceived interpersonal conflict. Child and Ellis used path analysis to show that the correlation between centralization and expected innovative behavior was much smaller when one considered the two role variables, role routine, and level of perceived authority.

Although these studies have illustrated the complexity of the relationships, we still do not completely understand the large differences across the three studies. Cultural and developmental differences probably contributed to some of the variance between the US and UK studies, but the cause of the rest of the variance has been unclear.

Payne and Pheysey (1971) used the Pugh et al. structural measure to contrast three organizations of different structural types. They compared these organizations' climates, as perceived by supervisors and managers. Two organizations had similar sizes (350–400 members) and production technologies. One of these (ASTON) was relatively bureaucratic and centralized, and the other (BRUM) was unbureaucratic and decentralized. The third organization (CARRS) had about 3,000 members, and was bureaucratic and centralized. ASTON had a climate very different from that of BRUM. As hypothesized, the bureaucratic ASTON had a conventional climate, which was concerned with rules and administratively efficient; although more centralized, members of ASTON questioned authority more and felt psychologically closer to their leader than did the members of BRUM. However, the strength of ASTON's last two relationships may have been due to another structural variable, the length of the vertical hierarchy. Since ASTON had only five vertical levels and BRUM had eight, ASTON's leaders probably had more similar status. ASTON was also perceived as being more dynamic and progressive; this organization scored significantly higher on scales such as scientific and technical orientation, industriousness, future orientation, and readiness to innovate.

Payne and Pheysey also compared ASTON's and CARRS's climates since they had different sizes but relatively the same type of bureaucratic, centralized structure. The smaller ASTON was perceived as more rules-oriented and more administratively efficient, but had a higher concern for its employees' involvement and leaders who were not psychologically distant. This smaller company was also much more industrious, more oriented to the future and to intellectual and scientific matters, and more prepared to innovate. These findings agreed with those of Indik (1965); size seems to have affected climate even with structural processes held constant.

Thus, different aspects of structure such as size, degree of bureaucracy, centralization, and hierarchical span have had separate and independent effects on the social processes and psychological climate of an organization. This independence of effects has helped explain the inconsistent relationships between structural and climate variables across studies which utilized similar conceptions and operationalizations of these variables.

In other sections, different operationalizations of centralization/decentralization have shown consistent relationships with an open, warm, and supportive climate. In confusing contrast, several bureaucratic variables in this section did not have consistent relationships with these and other climate variables. Furthermore, authors did not identify and probably lacked the methodology to define the intervening variables which might have explained those differences. Exceptions to this chaos were the moderately strong relationship between organizational size and structuring of activities and between size, and some (Inkson et al., 1971; Child & Ellis, 1973), although not all (Pugh, Hickson, Hinings, & Turner, 1969; Inkson et al., 1968), operationalizations of centralization.

Size has related more pervasively to different climate variables than has any other single structural variable. It correlated (mean $r = .25$) with all the climate variables in the Inkson et al. (1968) study, with expectations of innovative behavior in the Ohio study (Inkson et al., 1971), and with all the climate variables except perceived innovative behavior in the Child and Ellis (1973) study. Payne and Mansfield (1973) studied fourteen manufacturing organizations, and found that organizational size showed a correlation of at least .34 with each of sixteen (out of twenty) scales of organizational climate. Stern (1970) also showed that larger colleges had climates which were lower on his dimension of intellectualism.

Certainly, future organizational research must consider the pervasive effect of size. Either it must utilize statistical controls, or make comparisons within particular ranges. Child and Mansfield (1972) have shown that contextual and structural variables may differ significantly across industries; thus, size and technology may need to be controlled simultaneously. However, statistical controls can be applied validly only with organizational samples *much* larger than in previous analyses.

THE RELATIONSHIP BETWEEN OBJECTIVE MEASURES OF STRUCTURE AND OBJECTIVE MEASURES OF CLIMATE

This section summarizes the data which relate the organizational structure variable of size to objective and statistical climate measures such as lateness, sickness, and turnover records. Data which have used other, perhaps more adequate, structural measures are lacking, and existing relationships are small. Incidence of lateness, absence, and turnover is slightly higher in larger organizations; thus, large organizational size does seem to have negative consequences. A decentralized structure helps combat the negative effects of size and bureaucracy. Seemingly, it will be worthwhile to pursue studies which utilize objective structure and climate measures.

In this section, we shall again treat organizational size as the primary indicator of structure, to increase the number of relevant studies. Objective climate measures will include the behavioral descriptions of Barker and Gump (1964) as well as statistics on absenteeism, labor turnover, and labor disputes; statistics on accidents and productivity are also possible indicators of commitment and involvement in an organizational climate.

Porter and Lawler (1965) summarized the relationships between size of an organizational subunit and each of several objective climate measures (Table 2, p. 35). Size varied directly with absenteeism in ten studies and in a curvilinear manner in another; in a twelfth investigation, the two variables were unrelated. Three out of four studies showed correlations between size and labor turnover. In two studies, larger organizations had more labor disputes. The relationships between size and accidents were positive in three investigations, curvilinear in two more, and negative in a sixth. Finally, the correlations between size and productivity varied the most; there were three curvilinear and two negative relationships, and one positive and one zero relationship.

Dunteman (1966) used data from 234 industrial manufacturing organizations to examine the relationships between organizational conditions and organizational members' behavior. This volunteer sample of companies comprised 8 percent of the 2,938 organizations which were representative of all United States manufacturing organizations. Dunteman found that aversive job behaviors such as lateness, turnover, and grievances were independent of each other and unrelated to size. He cited Palmer's (1961) study of 188 manufacturing companies in which aversive job behaviors were also related to each other, but unrelated to organizational size. However, larger firms

did experience more strikes, perhaps because they were more unionized. Dunteman concluded that, "Neither size nor age was appreciably related to measures of personnel performance (i.e., what we have treated as objective climate) and organizational functioning. Personnel performance and organizational functioning varied with factors that could be controlled (e.g., recreation and savings-investment programs) rather than with the enduring and unalterable conditions of an organization such as size and age" (p. 304). Dunteman also noted that, "The most significant aspect of this investigation is its demonstration of the complex relationships that can be expected to exist between various organizational attributes and behaviors" (p. 304). Such studies have, then, considered the structural variable of size; they have also followed Indik's (1965) conceptualization, and have examined the degree of implied specialization and standardization in bureaucratic systems. However, none of them has measured the degree of centralization of decision taking.

Weiss (1957) studied centralization, but didn't measure size; nevertheless, his findings were useful. He administered a twenty-two-item check list of decisions to members of sixty firms and asked them to list the location of the role that was responsible for each decision. Thirty-four firms supplied additional data on labor turnover, absenteeism, accidents, and grievances. There were no significant differences in labor statistics between centralized and decentralized companies, as inferred from one-tailed t-tests; however, the more decentralized companies generally had the more favorable figures.

More recently, Prien and Ronan (1971) surveyed 107 firms, and found a small negative relationship between three indicators of company size and production workers' length of service (r's $\sim -.21$). The next largest correlations were between length of service and the fact that the company conducted time studies. Length of service was unrelated to variables which had loadings on specialization and standardization factors.

These data which have related objective structural and climate measures have not been totally adequate; however, they have suggested that organizational size was related to aversive job behaviors such as absenteeism (Porter & Lawler, 1965). Porter and Lawler felt that subunit size might be more important than organizational size. Indeed, the small-group research which has shown negative correlations between group size and variables such as job satisfaction and performance probably has supported this interpretation. Such relationships to climate may have been due to increased bureaucratic procedures and controls, a greater number of hierarchical levels (Pugh et al., 1968), or even more communication problems, all of which are usually associated with larger organizational size. Probably, all three of these factors have been important. Structural features such as greater participation through decentralization seem to have decreased status differentials, and thus had a positive effect on objective climate indicators; again, this effect was small. Although Barker's (1963) study described some processes by which size affects behavior, it dealt with educational organizations whose members had freer choice of activities than did those of work organizations; thus, Barker's study had limited implications in our framework.

We do need more structural (factorial) and process studies to examine structure and climate variables and accordingly, to understand the workings of work systems. Since relationships have been unstable across investigations which have utilized perceptual measures, objective indicators may prove to be more useful.

THE RELATIONSHIP BETWEEN ORGANIZATIONAL CLIMATE AND CHARACTERISTICS OF INDIVIDUAL MEMBERS

Figure 1 shows the two-way interaction between organizational climate and the individual. Thus, the individual's own needs, satisfactions, and goals influence his perception of the organizational climate; and that climate in turn affects these same satisfactions, goals, and behaviors. Indeed, Pace and Stern (1958) originally theorized that the concept of climate might improve understanding of individual attitudes and behavior; it would operationalize the E (Environment) in Lewin's formula $B = f(P \times E)$.

How, then, have measures of climate helped us further understand human behavior? To adequately evaluate this question, we must differentiate among different operationalizations of climate, individual, and group variables. First, we might collect data from an individual about his perceptions of climate and relate these to other individual variables such as job satisfaction. Second, we might give an individual a mean organizational climate score derived from his and others' perceptions of climate and relate this to other variables which characterize the individual. This latter method, however, results in the same climate scores for all the individuals in an organization. More commonly, we want to measure climate variance between individuals and may calculate an individual's "climate discrepancy score," which reflects the difference between his score and the group's mean climate score; we then relate this discrepancy score to some independent variables. Finally, we might measure individuals within a given organization on variables such as job satisfaction, personality, or performance and calculate a group or organizational score for each of these variables; we might then relate these to the group or organizational climate score. In this last case, we have grouped individual attributes to produce an organizational score; the organization has, thus, become the unit of analysis. The rest of this section concerns these three strategies.

The Relationship Between Individuals' Climate Scores and Other Individual Variables

This sub-section summarizes some studies which relate individuals' perceptions of organizational climate to individuals' personalities and job attitudes. Correlations are moderately strong, but researchers must be careful in assigning causality.

Stern (1970) explored the association between a person's needs and his perception of climate. He and others used Murray's (1938) needs-press theory as a framework for both a personality measure and a climate measure. Surprisingly, however, joint factor analyses of these two measures showed little overlap between them. We would have expected that personality would have affected perceived environment, particularly since these two variables had a common conceptual basis.

George and Bishop (1971) used Cattell's (1957) sixteen PF to measure personality, Halpin and Croft's (1963) OCDQ to measure organizational climate, and Hall's bureaucracy scales to measure perceived organization structure. They hypothesized that, "The type of organizational climate perceived is directly related to the degree of compatibility found between the organizational structural characteristics and the individual personality traits of its members" (p. 468). The authors demonstrated the expected relationships between the three sets of variables; schools with particular kinds of structures and climates attracted teachers with particular personality traits.

However, since all three measures were perceptual, we might have also hypothesized that an individual's personality would affect his perception of both climate and structure, and thus, the relationship between them. Although most of George and Bishop's more significant components (factors) contained both personality and structural variables, the personality variables comprised the bulk of the variance. Thus, it would have been interesting to have held personality constant and examined the relationship between perceived climate and perceived structure.

Friedlander and Margulies (1969) used an adapted version of the *Organizational Climate Description Questionnaire* (Halpin & Croft, 1963) to measure climate. One could argue that two OCDQ scales, hindrance and production emphasis, derived their meanings from structural variables and may have, thus, reflected perceived structure. For example, hindrance described "those feelings by members that they are burdened with routine duties and other requirements deemed as busy work; their work is not being facilitated." Production emphasis represented "management behavior characterized by close supervision; management is highly directive and insensitive to communication feedback" (p. 174). However, we feel that these scales denoted an organization's values and practices, and thus, measured climate.

Friedlander and Margulies related eight dimensions of the adapted climate instrument to three satisfaction dimensions, interpersonal relationships, task-involved self-realization, and opportunities for recognizable advancement. These were developed from a factor analysis by Friedlander (1963). They administered questionnaires to 114 employees, 110 of whom were rank and file workers in an electronics firm. Six of the climate dimensions showed significant correlations with all three satisfaction dimensions; the climate dimensions of aloofness and production emphasis did not have any correlations which were significantly different from zero. A multiple regression analysis produced the following results:

Satisfaction Dimension	Climate Predictors (Beta Weights)	R
Interpersonal Relationships	Esprit (.38) Hindrance (−.30) Thrust (.21)	.73
Task-Involvement	Thrust (.31) Hindrance (−.35)	.54
Advancement	Thrust (.36) Intimacy (.30) Hindrance (−.18)	.63

Thus, each of the three satisfaction dimensions was associated with a climate high in thrust and low in hindrance.

To further explore the relationship between climate and satisfaction, Friedlander and Margulies separated their subjects into those who placed high and low values on the satisfaction dimensions. The high value group maximized satisfaction in a climate of high thrust, high intimacy, and low hindrance. The low value group maximized satisfaction in a climate high in esprit, low in dissension, and low in disruption (disengagement). This study demonstrated well, then, the interaction between personality and environmental variables.

Schneider and Hall (1973) conducted a similar study with parish priests. They studied a self-perceived work climate which focused on the job itself and its immediate environment, and was, thus, different from organizational climate. Work climate was probably a more appropriate concept since parish priests work in very small groups. Schneider and Hall related self-perceived work climate to five satisfaction dimensions of the *Job Description Index* (Smith, Kendall, & Hulin, 1969) and to a semantic differential scale of self-image. The semantic differential scale produced three factors: supportive (helpful, sincere), intellectual, and involved (active, committed).

Table 8 shows the correlations between four factors from the work climate scale and each of five JDI and three self-image dimensions. There were moderately strong relationships between each of the work climate scales and each of the satisfaction dimensions except pay. The correlations between work climate and self-image were weaker but made sense. Priests who perceived themselves as supportive, intellectual, and involved had meaningful work and felt accepted by others. Priests' self-image scores were negatively correlated with perceived superior effectiveness; this may have reflected projection, and was not too surprising.

The authors also had some unpublished data which related climate and satisfaction. Eight organizational climate scales (Payne & Pheysey, 1971) were correlated with three JDI scales—work, superiors, and colleagues. The subjects for these data were 348 managers, supervisors, and staff personnel from a manufacturing company employing about

TABLE 8
CORRELATIONS BETWEEN PERCEIVED ASSIGNMENT VARIABLES
AND PERCEIVED CAREER EXPERIENCE FOR 199 CURATES

| Perceived Assignment Variables (Work Climate) | Perceived Career Experience | | | | | | | |
| | Satisfaction (JDI) | | | | | Self-Image | | |
	Work	Pay	Promotion	Supervision	People	Supportive	Intellectual	Involved
Superior Effectiveness	.20	.03	.12	.68	.29	.04	-.14	-.14
Work Challenge and Meaning	.52	.01	.18	.28	.26	.14	.20	.21
Personal Acceptance	.25	-.01	.17	.06	.39	.17	.15	.15
Supportive Autonomy	.35	.06	.13	.72	.31	.11	-.07	-.09

(From Hall & Schneider, 1973.)

8,000 people. Sixteen of the twenty-four possible correlations between climate and satisfaction ranged between .20 and .44.

Litwin and Stringer (1968) performed one of the few experimental studies of the effect of organizational climate on individuals. While students played a business game over an eight-day period, Litwin and Stringer manipulated the leader's style to produce different climates. They demonstrated that a given leadership style produced a characteristic climate which, in turn, aroused a particular motive as measured by the TAT (McClelland, Atkinson, Clark, & Lowell, 1953). The leadership style which was controlling and based on authority produced a climate with high structure, low reward, high punishment, and low risk taking; this climate, in turn, aroused the power motive. Although an aroused motive was temporary and lasted only during the experiment, this work demonstrated how we can create or alter climate in a small group, and how climate can then arouse a motive appropriate for its demands.

Thus, these studies which used the individual as the unit of analysis showed moderate relationships between climate and satisfaction. The Schneider and Hall results have suggested that climate measures which focused on an individual's immediate job showed stronger correlations with satisfaction than did organizational climate measures. We use Figure 1 to emphasize our lack of knowledge about the causal direction of these relationships; over time, the causality probably occurs in both directions. Given the association between satisfaction and climate, however, it would be wise to partial out satisfaction when relating climate and other variables such as performance, labor turnover, and absence.

Less clear was the relationship between climate and personality variables. However, it seems worthwhile to explore how discrepancies between personality and climate relate to satisfaction and performance. We review these studies in the next sub-section.

The Relationship Between Individuals' Climate Discrepancy Scores and Other Individual Variables

The relationships between individual climate discrepancy scores and other variables such as job satisfaction have been small. The common variance may have reflected variance from the interaction between persons and environments, the persons themselves, or their perceptions about their environments.

Pervin (1967) studied the interaction of personality and environment with a semantic differential instrument called the *Transactional Analysis of Personality and Environment* (TAPE). He asked subjects to rate each of six concepts on fifty-two semantic-differential adjectives, and used a three-mode factor analysis to simultaneously explore factors in the scales, concepts, and organizations (colleges). Pervin discovered thirteen factors which reflected climate features of the colleges. These factors and samples of their related scales included:

Factors

1. Warm-Cold
2. Goal-directed Activity
3. Scholarship
4. Optimism-Alienation

Sample Scales

Warm-Cold; Sociable-Unsociable
Motivated-Undirected;
    Industrious-Tranquil
Research-Application; Scholarly-
    Non-scholarly
Relaxed-Tense; Optimistic-
    Pessimistic.

The six concepts rated were college, self, students, faculty, administration, and ideal college. He calculated discrepancy scores across concepts such as college versus ideal college and self versus students, and related these scores to satisfaction with life at college. High discrepancies between self and college and between college and ideal college were positively related to dissatisfaction scores. A —.36 to +.77 range in correlations between self-college discrepancy scores and sixteen satisfaction items for form *A* illustrated the variability between the relationships, but generally supported the notion that congruent personality and environment were associated with satisfaction.

Pervin also studied the correlations between discrepancy scores and satisfaction across subjects for each of eleven public and ten private colleges. He reported the mean, median, range and the number of significant ($p \leq .05$) correlations between the discrepancy scores and each of the sixteen satisfaction items in both public and private college samples. The mean of the mean correlations across the sixteen satisfaction items for the eleven public colleges was .20, and for the ten private colleges was .26. Thus, with the organization as the unit of analysis, discrepancy scores accounted for 4 to 7 percent of the variance in satisfaction with college life. Pervin (1968) has suggested that "Discrepancy scores appear to relate better to the criterion variables than simple perceptions of self, students, faculty, administration, or college" (p. 61). The data from the previous section have not substantiated these results, which may have been idiosyncratic to the TAPE.

Stern (1970) reported the work of Bergquist (1961), who found that high school graduates whose personalities were more congruent with their college climates were more satisfied with college. Fishburne (1967) used Stern's instruments to show that West Point military cadets who voluntarily left the academy had personalities discrepant from the climate. However, Froe (1962) found that students whose need patterns were most congruent with college press were least likely to utilize their abilities; he explained these results by citing the low academic press in the particular college.

Stern (1970) also presented a detailed clinical study of a girl, Gail Kristus, who had difficulties adjusting to her environment. He used data from his personality and climate measures to diagnose inconsistency between her personal needs and values and her environment. He also related this discrepancy (deviancy) of a person on both personality and perceived climate to perceived institutional problem areas of decision making, faculty quality, leisure resources, and political freedom. There were no relationships between either personality or environment discrepancy and problem areas. If we interpret the latter variable as satisfaction with the institution, we may say that discrepancy scores were unrelated to this dependent variable in this study.

Andrews (1967) reported a field study conceptually similar to these discrepancy studies. Two Mexican firms had very different climates or value orientations. One was highly achievement-oriented, economically effective, ready to change, and progressive; and the other was power-oriented and generally less successful economically. Andrews gave the *Thematic Apperception Test* (TAT) to top level managers in the two firms to measure their need for achievement (*N* Ach) and need for power (*N* Pow). He also used the number of promotions and salary increases during the preceding four-year period to measure performance. There were no differences in motivational measures between the two organizations; however, the managers that had progressed most in each firm were those whose personal needs were most congruent with the values of the organization.

Although we suggested earlier that psychologists developed the concept of climate to measure the interaction of environment and personality, and thus better predict behavior, there have been surprisingly few studies which have related these two variables. Generally, these have supported the hypothesis that individual environment compatibility enhances behavior and attitudes. The percentage of variance explained in the dependent variables has not been large, and disappointingly, has not been significantly greater than that explained by zero-order correlations between personality or ability measures and performance. For example, Ghiselli (1966) summarized several studies showing .20–.30 validity correlations for occupational selection tests. Relating discrepancy scores to other variables has created the problem of allocating variance to the personality variable, the environmental variable, or some interaction of the two. Accordingly, Wall and Payne (1973) emphasized that discrepancy scores can be misleading and suggested the use of raw scores and part or partial correlations to explore relationships and interactions. Stern (1970) has been the only person who has addressed this problem. In his work with culture factors, he separated discrepancy components between (1) the person's total culture score and the organizational mean culture score $(C\text{-}c)$, (2) the need (personality) component $(N\text{-}n)$, and (3) the press (climate) component $(P\text{-}p)$. As previously reported, none of these was related to any of the six perceived institutional problems.

Thus, on the whole, discrepancy scores have not explained how personality, environment, or the interaction between the two relates to other variables.

The Relationship Between Group Climate Scores and Group Personality Attributes

Several studies have shown moderately strong relationships between group or organizational climate scores and group personality scores. However, these studies' lack of agreement in defining organizational climates and the varied personalities of their members have raised questions about their empirical and theoretical value.

Although the concept of climate was originally developed for use as an environmental variable in Lewin's equation $B = f(P \times E)$, it quickly became a tool for understanding the organization itself. In-

deed, Stern (1970) eventually criticized on technical grounds the two individual approaches discussed in the previous subsections. He said that "the two sets of measures (climate and personality) cannot be reconciled with one another in a simple scale-for-scale correspondence of variables of the same name" (p. 192).

Stern felt that it was more meaningful to analyze personality-press relationships across organizations or colleges rather than individuals. Indeed, his suggested method did produce high correlations between personality and climate scales. "The generally large positive entries along the main diagonal reflect the fact that students characterized by any specific need are to be found at institutions with appropriate press" (p. 202). Stern factor-analyzed a joint personality-climate matrix which used organizational means as raw data. This factor analysis produced five "culture" dimensions: expressive, intellectual, protective, vocational, and collegiate. To estimate the relative contributions of the personality and climate components of the culture factors, Stern separated the variables' loadings on each of the new composite factors into the personality-climate subsets, calculated the means and variances for each subset separately, and normalized these. These standard scores were directly comparable. Stern showed that, "There are differences between the types of men attending each kind of liberal arts college. The independent males have needs that contribute to the maintenance of a college culture that is intellectual and noncollegiate. They differ, then, from denominational men who are oriented towards protectiveness and non-expressive needs, and from the university men, who reveal no single strong need" (p. 216).

Stern also calculated indices of dispersion and of dissonance between an individual and his culture, which had arisen either from differences in personality or from perceptions of the environment. Cultural heterogeneity or dispersion was roughly similar across schools. Seemingly, the only similarity across particularly heterogeneous schools was the ongoing experience of organizational change. Public institutions were more dissonant than private ones; the amount of dissonance between need and press in a given school was related to the heterogeneity of the students, rather than of the environments. Dissonance between an individual and his culture was unrelated to an individual's deviance from his cultural norm. Cultural variability within male academic programs was related to the number of reported problems such as organizational decision making, faculty quality, academic quality, and social and political freedom. Cultural diversity was unrelated to the nature of the physical plant.

Stern (1970) also calculated correlations between his main factors in the *College Characteristics Index* (CCI), a climate measure, and several performance variables. Table 9 shows the correlations between his

TABLE 9
CORRELATIONS BETWEEN MEASURES OF ACADEMIC QUALITY AND INTELLECTUAL PRESS CLIMATE SCORE (CCI)

Measure of Academic Quality	N	r with Climate Score
Knapp-Greenbaum Index: scholars per 1,000	50	.80
Percentage of graduates receiving Ph.D., 1936-1956	37	.76
Percentage of Merit Scholar entrants, 1956	41	.49
Merit Scholars per 1,000, 1960	25	.59
National Merit Scholarship Qualifying Test means	38	.71
CEEB-SAT Verbal means	16	.83
CEEB-SAT Mathematical means	16	.34

(From Stern, 1970.)

Intellectual Press factor and various measures of academic quality.

It is hard to detect a causal relation between these indices. Stern said only that "The intellectual climate of an institution is closely related to the quality of its students" (p. 141). He cited similar findings from Astin's work with nonintellectual factors, and suggested that "The very fact that our own data show that the characteristics of students are appropriate to the colleges they attend might be offered as evidence against the effort to promote intellectual values wholesale. But data like those of Astin (1964) simply indicate that such institutions are organized in ways relevant to the *resources* possessed by their constituency, and not whether the colleges are also relevant to adolescent purposes" (p. 172). Although his criticisms pertained specifically to institutions whose major concerns were developing people, they also, more generally, referred to many other formal organizations. Certainly, Stern has illustrated our lack of understanding about manipulating environmental climates to increase people's motivation, achievement, and satisfactions.

Using a sample of twenty-eight different medical schools as the units of analysis, Hutchins and Nonneman (1966) related personality factors and perceived climate. They correlated both mean *Allport-Vernon-Lindzey Values* (1951) scores and mean *Edwards Personal Preference* scores with climate. Schools which had students with high economic values and low aesthetic values had climates with high extrinsic motivation and encapsulated training. Schools which had students with theoretical, noneconomic, nonreligious, and aesthetic values had climates with high intrinsic motivation. Correlations ranged between −.40 and +.79. None of the values scores were significantly related to general esteem. Relationships between the *Edwards Personal Preference* scores and climate also seemed intuitively logical. Schools which had students with low achievement, low autonomy, low aggression, high abasement, high order, and high nurturance scores had encapsulated training climates. Schools which had students with high achievement, high autonomy, high dominance, low deference, and low order scores had intrinsically motivating climates. The least convincing associations were between general esteem and students with low autonomy, high affiliation and low change; these correlations were generally .45.

Hutchins and Nonneman also related school climate and exam performance. Schools which had climates high on intrinsic motivation, low on extrinsic motivation, and encapsulated training did the best on exams. This seemed to support Stern's (1970) and Astin's (1964) findings that the climate in a given college or school reflected student-body characteristics such as intelligence, achievement orientation, and independence.

In summary, our two sub-sections which have related organizational climate and individual variables have generally suggested that personality and job satisfaction are related to perceived climate. The exception to this was Stern's finding. It seems likely, then, that relationships which have utilized group or organizational scores as summaries of individual scores may have been at least partly explained by the individual scores themselves. Certainly, we must investigate these relationships by partialling out such individual effects. Pheysey, Payne, and Pugh (1971) did this for small groups of managers. Several relationships with significant zero-order correlations disappeared when Pheysey et al. controlled for individual effects with second-order partial correlations. Seemingly, then, Hutchins and Nonneman (1966), Pervin (1967), and George and Bishop (1971) may have overestimated their results. However, these authors' interpretations that the characteristics of organizational members strongly influence climate or culture have been compelling. We might expect that future use of partial correlations will reduce, rather than remove, such relationships.

Conclusions

Finally, let us review the relationships between organizational climate and characteristics of individual members, and between climate and group characteristics of members. An individual's perceptions about climate were related to his personality and job attitudes. However, studies which investigated the differential effects of person-environment fit were relatively scarce and not well designed. It was difficult to determine if the results were related to the interaction of person and environment, to the person alone, or to his perceptions about the environment. Theoretically, however, such research has been intriguing, and should be pursued with Stern's (1970) useful techniques.

At the organizational level of analysis, relationships between personality and perceived environments seemed much stronger; clearly, the people in a system have affected the development of its climate. Methodologically, however, this type of research has presented some problems. For example, Schneider (1972), Payne and Mansfield (1973), and Gorman and Malloy (1972) all showed that perception of organizational climate varied with organizational level. People higher in an organization had more positive views about that organization. Stern (1970) also presented evidence for subcultural (departmental) heterogeneity within colleges. Seemingly, climate perceptions were varied, and a group score may not have adequately reflected a given organizational climate. Thus, Payne and Mansfield (1973) have examined the relationships between the variance in climate scores and certain contextual and structural variables. They found that larger organizations generally had more variance in climate.

However, climate means and variances alone may not have adequately represented that variable's diversity within a given organization. Future researchers need to develop measures which reflect a pattern of scores within an organization. Perhaps they could utilize a matrix of horizontal and vertical organizational divisions and thus employ related techniques for repertory grid analysis or hierarchical clustering. Such suggestions also apply to variables such as job satisfaction and personality. Here, too, the use of group or organizational means appears questionable. Although relationships with mean scores may be empirically robust (Astin, 1964; Stern, 1970), we feel that studies which utilize complex scores will have more empirical and theoretical utility.

Finally, in interpreting and evaluating this section's studies, we should remember McNemar's (1955) warning: "The researcher who is cognizant of the assumptions requisite for a given interpretation of a correlation coefficient and who is also fully aware of the many factors which may affect its magnitude will not regard the correlational technique as an easy road to scientific discovery" (p. 768). Surely, this section has emphasized some of the difficulties inherent in defining and explaining such correlations.

SUMMARY OF FINDINGS AND DISCUSSION

How, then, can we summarize the literature on organizational structure and climate? Several conclusions seem justified.

Relationships between perceptual and objective measures of structural variables were not strong. However, in general, relationships between different objective measures of structure were fairly stable. Exceptions to this were the widely varying correlations between decentralization and role definition and between decentralization and organizational size; also, the positive correlations between technology and size differed in strength, although this difference may have arisen from sampling characteristics. Organizational size was a staunch determinant of structuring of work variables. Technological differences in production methods affected those structural features related to the production process. The smaller the organization, the more pervasively technology influenced structure. Also, more dependent organizations had more centralized decision-taking structures.

Relationships between different perceived climate measures were less stable than were relationships between different perceived structure measures. Present climate measures tapped about five main factors; two of these, individual autonomy and degree of structure imposed on position, seem to have paralleled the two major structural variables of concentration of authority and structuring of work activities. However, measures of perceived climate were different across hierarchical levels; thus, mean climate scores may have masked important variations.

Perceptual measures of climate variables such as openness, warmth, consideration, and support showed associations with perceptual measures of centralization. In general, climate measures did not show any generalizable relationships with perceptual measures of structuring of work activities. However, organizational size did influence perceived climate. Objective measures of centralization and structuring of activities were also related to perceived climate measures; these relationships differed in size and direction in an unpredictable way across different samples. Organizational size showed moderate correlations with objective climate measures such as absenteeism, labor turnover, and number of grievances. We found no studies which compared perceptual measures of structure and objective measures of climate.

Individual characteristics such as personality, intellectual ability, and job satisfaction probably moderated perceptions of climate. However, climate researchers have rarely considered either these effects or the previously mentioned structural ones, so that findings were not always clearly interpretable. A large discrepancy between an individual's needs and personality and his environment's potential to fulfill such needs led to lowered satisfaction and satisfactoriness. However, past research on such discrepancies had several methodological difficulties, and definitive statements are not yet possible.

A Pessimistic Conclusion

Certainly, such problems of methodology and interpretation could lead to a pessimistic view about the literature on organizational structure and climate. Different operationalizations of each of the structural and climate measures have shown low correlations with each other. This lack of convergent validity has suggested that the past measures have been inadequate. Perceptual measures of each of the structural and climate variables have varied so much among themselves that mean scores were uninterpretable. Even worse, different positions in the structural hierarchy have shown systematic differences in measures of perceived organizational climate and structure. Thus, past studies which ignored these issues were probably misleading. It is understandable, then, why they have not found stable relationships between different organizational variables. Furthermore, we have no useful theory to predict likely differences due to sampling. Organizations are so complex we have fallen into a trap (Forrester, 1969, as quoted by Miller, 1972):

Complex systems differ from simple ones in being "counter-intuitive," i.e., not behaving as one might expect them to. They are remarkably insensitive to changes in many system parameters, i.e., ultrastable. They stubbornly resist policy changes. They contain influential pressure points, often in unexpected places, which can alter system steady states dramatically. They are able to compensate for externally applied efforts to correct them by reducing internal activity that corresponds to those efforts. They often react to a policy change in the long run in a way opposite to their reaction in the short run. (p. 150)

The next part of Forrester's argument is particularly relevant:

Intuition and judgment generated by a lifetime of experience with the simple systems that surround one's every action create a network of expectations and perceptions that could hardly be better designed to mislead the unwary when he moves into the realm of complex systems. (p. 150)

This chapter's research, then, has largely been performed by the unwary. Future research can ignore most of these studies and utilize a completely different approach. We need deep involvement from the members of a complex system to gather meaningful data which accurately reflect these people's experiences. The researcher must create a relationship of trust and openness with his research clients to avoid the unintended consequences of rigorous research (Argyris, 1968). The researcher needs to swap data explanations with his subjects so that interpretations are more realistic. Idiosyncratic and time-consuming work of this kind makes comparative research on a large scale presently impossible. When thousands of such detailed cases exist, then we may again attempt comparative research.

An Optimistic Conclusion

More optimistically, we have developed several new methods for measuring dimensions of organization structure and climate. Although subjective and objective operationalizations seemed to have produced different relationships within each of these dimensions, each of the dimensional measures has discriminated across organizations. Both objective configurational and objective procedural and role measures of organizational structure have differentiated between different organizational systems so that distinctive structural profiles have emerged. Also, context and structure have shown many stable interrelationships.

Different climates have had predictable effects on satisfaction; both climate (Likert, 1967; Hutchins & Nonneman, 1966) and organizational structure (Woodward, 1965) may have been related to organizational performance. The conceptual similarity between results based on objective structure measures and perceptual climate measures (Campbell et al., 1970) has been very encouraging and has provided the basis for the convergent validity of both types of measures. We need more work on all types of measures, however, to establish their validities.

The use of subjective measures and group scores to represent social systems has presented many methodological problems and thus is an exciting challenge. Clearly our model of an individual within a system has necessitated data about both his position in the system and his individual characteristics. Facet design and analysis (Foa, 1968) may be a possible way to utilize this information. Also, the use of carefully chosen samples may explain many of the unexpected relationships in the past.

This review has suggested the potential benefits of exploring multimethod variance for a particular organizational concept. We do not have to assume that understanding comes only from low multimethod variance. Instead, we may use our knowledge of all results to more adequately define the nature of the measures. This approach should help us more fruitfully explore the relationships in a complex reality.

Finally, we must link the comparative and process approaches (Pugh, 1969). Comparative cross-sectional studies are theoretically dry since anything beyond a statistical analysis is only inferential. However, different process case studies often cannot be compared, are on a small scale, and overgeneralize. An effective combination of these approaches implies a need for an adequate sample of respondents appropriately placed in each of an adequate sample of organizations. Cross-sectional surveys and process studies must interrelate and complement each other if compelling theories of organizational behavior are to emerge.

The way forward is clear. We can benefit from the ability to design organization structures and to create climates which are appropriate to particular goals and needs.

Furthermore, the planning and implementation of social changes will be more feasible with such knowledge. Thus, research which improves our understanding of organizational structure and climate will make an important contribution to our future.

REFERENCES

Aiken, M., & Hage, J. Organizational alienation: A comparative analysis. *American Sociological Review,* 1967, 31, 497–507.

Aldrich, H. Technology and organizational structure: A reexamination of the findings of the Aston group. *Administrative Science Quarterly,* 1972, 17, 26–43.

Allport, G. W., Vernon, P. E., & Lindzey, G. *Study of values.* Boston: Houghton Mifflin, 1951.

Anderson, T. H., & Warkov, S. Organizational size and functional complexity: A study of administration in hospitals. *American Sociological Review,* 1961, 26, 23–28.

Andrews, J. D. W. The achievement motive and advancement in two types of organizations. *Journal of Personality and Social Psychology,* 1967, 6, 163–169.

Argyris, C. Some unintended consequences of rigorous research. *Psychological Bulletin,* 1968, 70, 185–197.

Argyris, C. *The applicability of organizational sociology.* London: Cambridge University Press, 1972.

Astin, A. W. Further validation of the environment assessment technique. *Journal of Educational Psychology,* 1963, 54, 217–226.

Astin, A. W. Distribution of students among higher educational institutions. *Journal of Educational Psychology,* 1964, 55, 276–287.

Astin, A. W., & Holland, J. L. The environmental assessment technique: A way to measure college environments. *Journal of Educational Psychology,* 1961, 52, 308–316.

Atkinson, J. *An introduction to motivation.* Princeton: Van Nostrand, 1964.

Bachman, J. G., Smith, C. G., & Slesinger, J. A. Control, performance, and satisfaction: An analysis of structural and individual effects. *Journal of Personality and Social Psychology,* 1966, 4, 127–136.

Barker, R. G. On the nature of the environment. *Journal of Social Issues,* 1963, 19, 17–38.

Barker, R. G. Explorations in ecological psychology. *American Psychologist,* 1965, 20, 1–14.

Barker, R. G., & Gump, P. V. *Big school, small school.* Stanford: Stanford University Press, 1964.

Bennis, W. G. Organizational developments and the fate of bureaucracy. *Industrial Management Review,* 1966, 7, 41–55.

Bergquist, H. E. *A correlate of college satisfaction.* Unpublished thesis, School of Education, University of Chicago, 1961.

Bishop, L. K., George, J. R., & Murphy, M. *Structural properties questionnaire. Form I.* (working paper) Claremont Graduate School, Claremont, Calif., 1967.

Blau, P. M., & Schoenherr, R. A. *The structure of organizations.* New York: Basic Books, 1971.

Bonjean, C. M., & Grimes, M. D. Bureaucracy and alienation: A dimensional approach. *Social Forces,* 1970, 48, 365–373.

Burns, T. Industry in a new age. *New Society,* January, 1963, 17–20.

Burns, T., & Stalker, G. *The management of innovation.* London: Tavistock, 1961.

Campbell, J., Dunnette, M. D., Lawler, E. E., & Weick, K. E. *Managerial behavior, performance, and effectiveness.* New York: McGraw-Hill, 1970.

Cattell, R. G. *Handbook for the 16 P. F. questionnaire.* Champaign, Ill.: Institute of Personality and Ability Testing, 1957.

Child, J. Organization structure and strategies of control: A replication of the Aston study. *Administrative Science Quarterly,* 1972, 17, 163–177.

Child, J., & Ellis, T. Predictors of variation in managerial roles. *Human Relations,* 1973, 26, 227–250.

Child, J., & Mansfield, R. M. Technology, size, and organization structure. *Sociology,* 1972, 6, 369–393.

Crozier, M. *The bureaucratic phenomenon.* London: Tavistock, 1964.

Dalton, M. *Men who manage.* New York: Wiley, 1959.

Dunteman, G. H. Organizational conditions and behavior in 234 industrial manufacturing organizations. *Journal of Applied Psychology,* 1966, 50, 300–305.

Entwistle, D., & Walton, J. Observations on the

span of control. *Administrative Science Quarterly,* 1961, 5, 522–533.

Findikyan, N., & Sells, S. B. *The dimensional structure of student campus organizations.* Fort Worth: Institute of Behavioral Research, Texas Christian University, 1964.

Fishburne, F. J. *An investigation of the use of the activities index and the college characteristics index as predictors of voluntary attrition at the U.S. Military Academy.* Unpublished master's thesis, Ohio State University, Columbus, 1967.

Foa, U. A. Three kinds of behavioral changes. *Psychological Bulletin,* 1968, 70, 460–473.

Forrester, J. W. *Urban dynamics.* Cambridge: M.I.T. Press, 1969.

Friedlander, F. Underlying sources of job satisfaction. *Journal of Applied Psychology,* 1963, 47, 246–250.

Friedlander, F., & Margulies, N. Multiple inputs of organizational climate and individual value systems upon job satisfaction. *Personnel Psychology,* 1969, 22, 171–183.

Froe, O. D. Some research activities concerned with non-intellective factors in student achievement at Morgan State College. In K. M. Wilson (Ed.), *Institutional research on college students.* Atlanta: Southern Region Education Board, 1962.

Garfinkel, H. *Studies in ethnomethodology.* Englewood Cliffs, N.J.: Prentice-Hall, 1967.

George, J. R., & Bishop, L. K. Relationship of organizational structure and teacher personality characteristics to organizational climate. *Administrative Science Quarterly,* 1971, 16, 467–475.

Ghiselli, E. The validity of occupational selection tests. New York: Wiley, 1966.

Gorman, L., & Malloy, E. *People, jobs, and organizations.* Dublin: Irish Management Institute, 1972.

Gouldner, A. *Patterns of industrial bureaucracy.* New York: The Free Press, 1954.

Guest, R. *Organizational change.* Homewood, Ill.: Dorsey Press, 1962.

Guilford, J. P. *Fundamental statistics in psychology and education.* New York: McGraw-Hill, 1965.

Guttman, L. A general non-metric technique for finding the smallest co-ordinate spaces for a configuration of points. *Psychometrika,* 1968, 33, 469–506.

Haas, E., Hall, R. H., & Johnson, N. J. The

size of the supportive component in organizations. *Social Forces*, 1963, 42, 9–17.

Hage, J., & Aiken, M. Program change and organizational properties. *American Journal of Sociology*, 1966, 72, 503–519.

Hage, J., & Aiken, M. Relationship of centralization to other structural properties. *Administrative Science Quarterly*, 1967, 12, 72–92.

Hage, J., & Aiken, M. Routine technology, social structure, and organizational goals. *Administrative Science Quarterly*, 1969, 14, 366–376.

Hall, D. T., & Schneider, B. Organizational climates and careers: The work lives of priests. New York: Seminar Press, 1973.

Hall, R. The concept of bureaucracy: An empirical assessment. *American Journal of Sociology*, 1963, 69, 32–40.

Hall, R. H. *Organizations: Structure and processes*. Englewood Cliffs, N.J.: Prentice-Hall, 1972.

Hall, R. H., & Tittle, C. A note on bureaucracy and its correlates. *American Journal of Sociology*, 1966, 72, 267–272.

Halpin, A. W., & Crofts, D. B. The organizational climate of schools. *Administrators Notebook*, 1963, 11, 4 pages.

Heise, D. R. How do I know my data? Let me count the ways. *Administrative Science Quarterly*, 1972, 17, 58–61.

Hemphill, J. K. *Group dimensions: A manual for their measurement*. Columbus: Ohio State University, 1956.

Hemphill, J. K., & Westie, C. M. The measurement of group dimensions. *Journal of Psychology*, 1950, 29, 325–342.

Hickson, D. J., Hinings, C. R., McMillan, C. J., & Schwitter, J. P. The culture-free context of organization structure. *Sociology*, 1974, 8, 59–80.

Hickson, D. J., Pugh, D. S., & Pheysey, D. C. Operations, technology, and organization structure: An empirical reappraisal. *Administrative Science Quarterly*, 1969, 17, 44–54.

Hilton, G. Causal inference analysis: A seductive process. *Administrative Science Quarterly*, 1972, 1, 44–54.

Hinings, C. R., & Lee, G. Dimensions of organization structure and their context: A replication. *Sociology*, 1971, 5, 83–93.

Holland, J. L. A theory of vocational choice. *Journal of Counseling Psychology*, 1959, 6, 35–45.

Hutchins, E. B., & Nonneman, A. J. *Construct validity of an environmental assessment technique for medical schools*. Technical Report No. L661. Evanston, Ill.: Association of American Medical Colleges, 1966.

Indik, B. P. Organizational size and member participation: Some empirical tests of alternative explanations. *Human Relations*, 1965, 18, 339–350.

Inkson, J. H., Hickson, D. J., & Pugh, D. S. *Administrative reduction of variances in organization and behavior*. London: British Psychological Society, Annual Conference, 1968.

Inkson, J. H., Pugh, D. S., & Hickson, D. J. Organization context and structure: An abbreviated replication. *Administrative Science Quarterly*, 1970, 15, 318–329.

Inkson, J. H., Schwitter, J. P., Pheysey, D. C., & Hickson, D. J. A comparison of organization structure and managerial roles, Ohio, U.S.A., and the Midlands, England. *Journal of Management Studies*, 1970, 7, 347–363.

Inkson, J. H., Schwitter, J. P., Pheysey, D. C., & Hickson, D. J. *Comparison of Birmingham, England and Ohio, U.S.A. organizations*. Unpublished paper, University of Aston, Birmingham, England, 1971.

Kahn, R. L., Wolfe, D. M., Quinn, R. P., Snoek, J. D., & Rosenthal, R. A. *Organizational stress: Studies in role conflict and ambiguity*. New York: Wiley, 1964.

Katz, D., & Kahn, R. L. *The social psychology of organizations*. New York: Wiley, 1966.

Kelly, G. A. *The psychology of personal constructs*. New York: W. W. Norton, 1955.

Lawrence, P. R., & Lorsch, J. W. *Organization and environment*. Cambridge: Harvard Business School, 1967.

Leavitt, H. *Toward organizational psychology*. Reprint No. 117. Pittsburgh: Graduate School of Industrial Administration, Carnegie Institute of Technology, 1962.

Levy, P. M., & Pugh, D. S. Scaling and multivariate analyses in the study of organizational variables. *Sociology*, 1969, 3, 193–213.

Lewin, K. *Field theory in social science*. New York: Harper Brothers, 1951.

Likert, R. *The human organization*. New York: McGraw-Hill, 1967.

Litwin, G. H., & Stringer, R. A. *Motivation and organizational climate*. Cambridge: Harvard University, 1968.

McClelland, D. C., Atkinson, J. W., Clark,

R. A., & Lowell, E. L. *The achievement motive.* New York: Appleton-Century-Crofts, 1953.

McNemar, Q. *Psychological statistics.* New York: Wiley, 1955.

Mansfield, R. M. Bureaucracy and centralization: An examination of organizational structure. *Administrative Science Quarterly,* 1973, 18, 477–488.

March, J. G., & Simon, H. A. *Organizations.* New York: Wiley, 1958.

Merton, R. K. Bureaucratic structure and personality. *Social Forces,* 1940, 18, 560–568.

Meyer, H. H. Achievement motivation and industrial climates. In R. Tagiuri & G. H. Litwin (Eds.), *Organizational climate: Exploration of a concept.* Cambridge: Harvard University, 1968.

Miller, J. G. Living systems: The organization. *Behavioral Science,* 1972, 17, 1–182.

Murray, H. *Explorations in personality.* New York: Oxford University Press, 1938.

Pace, C. R. The measurement of college environments. In R. Tagiuri & G. H. Litwin (Eds.), *Organizational climate: Exploration of a concept.* Cambridge: Harvard University, 1968.

Pace, C. R., & Stern, G. G. An approach to the measurement of psychological characteristics of college environments. *Journal of Educational Psychology,* 1958, 49, 269–277.

Palmer, G. J. *Incentive conditions and behavior in 188 industrial manufacturing organizations.* Project NR 170-478. New Orleans: Tulane University, 1961.

Payne, R. L. Organizational climate: The concept and some research findings. *Prakseologia,* NR 39/40/ROK, 1971.

Payne, R. L., & Mansfield, R. M. Relationships of perceptions of organizational climate to organizational structure, context, and hierarchical position. *Administrative Science Quarterly,* 1973, 18, 515–526.

Payne, R. L., & Pheysey, D. C. G. G. Stern's Organizational climate index: A reconceptualization and application to business organizations. *Organizational Behavior and Human Performance,* 1971, 6, 77–98.

Pennings, J. M. *A comparison of measures of organizational structure: A validation attempt.* Sixty-sixth Annual Meeting of the American Sociological Association, Denver, Colorado, 1971.

Pervin, L. A. A twenty college study of student × college interaction using TAPE. *Journal of Educational Psychology,* 1967, 58, 290–302.

Pervin, L. A. Performance and satisfaction as a function of individual-environment fit. *Psychological Bulletin,* 1968, 69, 56–68.

Pettigrew, A. *The politics of organizational decision making.* London: Tavistock, 1973.

Pheysey, D. C., & Payne, R. L. The Hemphill group dimensions description questionnaire: A British industrial application. *Human Relations,* 1970, 23, 473–497.

Pheysey, D. C., Payne, R. L., & Pugh, D. S. The influence of structure at organization and group levels. *Administrative Science Quarterly,* 1971, 16, 61–73.

Porter, L. W., & Lawler, E. E. Properties of organization structure in relation to job attitudes and behavior. *Psychological Bulletin,* 1965, 64, 23–51.

Prien, E. P., & Ronan, W. W. An analysis of organization characteristics. *Organizational Behavior and Human Performance,* 1971, 6, 111–131, 215–234.

Pugh, D. S. Modern organization theory: A psychological and sociological study. *Psychological Bulletin,* 1966, 66, 235–251.

Pugh, D. S. Organizational behavior: An approach from psychology. *Human Relations,* 1969, 22, 345–354.

Pugh, D. S., & Hickson, D. J. Causal inference and the Aston studies. *Administrative Science Quarterly,* 1972, 17, 273–276.

Pugh, D. S., Hickson, D. J., & Hinings, C. R. An empirical taxonomy of work organization structures. *Administrative Science Quarterly,* 1969, 14, 115–126.

Pugh, D. S., Hickson, D. J., Hinings, C. R., McDonald, K., Turner, C., & Lupton, T. A conceptual scheme for organizational analysis. *Administrative Science Quarterly,* 1963, 8, 289–315.

Pugh, D. S., Hickson, D. J., Hinings, C. R., & Turner, C. Dimensions of organization structure. *Administrative Science Quarterly,* 1968, 13, 65–105.

Pugh, D. S., Hickson, D. J., Hinings, C. R., & Turner, C. The context of organization structures. *Administrative Science Quarterly,* 1969, 14, 94–114.

Schneider, B. *The perception of organizational climate: The customer's view.* Unpublished paper, University of Maryland, College Park, 1972.

Schneider, B., & Bartlett, C. J. Individual differences and organizational climate II: Measurement of organizational climate by the multi-trait, multi-rater matrix. *Personnel Psychology,* 1970, 23, 493–512.

Schneider, B., & Hall, D. T. Towards specifying the concept of work climate: A study of Roman Catholic diocesan priests. *Journal of Applied Psychology,* 1973, 56, 447–455.

Silverman, D. *Theory of organizations.* London: Heinemann, 1970.

Smith, P. C., Kendall, L., & Hulin, C. *The measurement of satisfaction in work and retirement: A strategy for the study of attitudes.* Chicago: Rand McNally, 1969.

Stern, G. G. *People in context: Measuring person-environment congruence in education and industry.* New York: Wiley, 1970.

Stout, G. F. *Analytical psychology,* Vol. I. London: Sonnenschein, 1896.

Tagiuri, R. Executive climate. In R. Tagiuri & G. H. Litwin (Eds.), *Organizational climate: Exploration of a concept.* Cambridge: Harvard University, 1968.

Tagiuri, R., & Litwin, G. H. *Organizational climate: Explorations of a concept.* Cambridge: Harvard University, 1968.

Taylor, J. C., & Bowers, D. G. *The survey of organizations.* Ann Arbor: Institute for Social Research, University of Michigan, 1970.

Terrien, F. W., & Mills, D. L. The effect of changing size upon the internal structure of organizations. *American Sociological Review,* 1955, 20, 11–13.

Turner, B. *A pilot study for the replication and possible validation of R. Hall's study of perception of bureaucracy.* Unpublished undergraduate thesis, University of Birmingham, 1965.

Udy, S. Bureaucracy and rationality in Weber's organization theory: An empirical study. *American Sociological Review,* 1959, 24, 791–795.

Urwick, L. F. *The elements of administration.* London: Pitman, 1947.

Wall, T. D., & Payne, R. L. Are deficiency scores deficient? *Journal of Applied Psychology,* 1973, 58, 322–326.

Weber, M. The theory of social and economic organization. Glencoe, Ill.: The Free Press, 1947.

Weiss, E. C. Relations of personnel statistics to organization structure. *Personnel Psychology,* 1957, 10, 27–42.

Woodward, J. Industrial organization: Theory and practice. New York: Oxford University Press, 1965.

Worthy, J. C. Organizational structure and employee morale. *American Sociological Review,* 1950, 15, 169–179.

CHAPTER 27

The Structure and Dynamics of Behavior in Organizational Boundary Roles[1]

J. STACY ADAMS
University of North Carolina

THE NEED FOR EFFECTIVE organizational boundary functions increases as the turbulence of an organization's environment increases. At present, turbulence is high and will increase, probably exponentially, in the future. Attention to boundary functions and to behavior in boundary roles is, therefore, indicated.

Presented in this chapter are: (1) a discussion of organizational boundary functions and of boundary role behavior; (2) a structural model of organizational boundary systems; (3) a discussion of important variables of which boundary role behavior is a function; (4) a limited discussion of experiments and untested hypotheses relating to these variables; and (5) an analysis of the dynamic interactions among the variables. The chapter concludes with a brief statement on the conceptual status of behavioral disciplines in the larger scheme of things.

INTRODUCTION

A condition of organization survival is effective interaction with the external environment of the organization. This condition becomes most evidently essential as societies grow, develop, and differentiate, as the level of interdependence and interaction among social units increases, as competition for decreasing resources grows, and as intergroup conflict increases. Transactions with other systems are required in order that organizations may obtain necessary inputs and dispose of their outputs. These acquisition and disposal requirements are general and, therefore, apply to all organizational systems, be they industrial, educational, political, religious, social, military, etc. Organizations require raw materials and fabricated parts, capital, personnel, technology, information, "goodwill," legitimacy, and other inputs in order to fulfill their produc-

[1] Much of the conceptual and empirical work reported in this chapter is the result of stimulating discussions with my former students Robert L. Frey Jr., John G. Holmes, Dennis W. Organ, and James A. Wall in an informal seminar between 1969 and the present. I am very grateful to them. I also wish to thank the Graduate School of Business Administration, University of North Carolina, the General Electric Company, the Smith Richardson Foundation, and the National Science Foundation (Grant GS 35124) for providing generous support.

tive activities (their "mission" or "purpose") and they require the means and environment to dispose of their goods, services, information, and other productive outputs. The disposal of outputs, in turn, permits acquisition of new inputs either through direct exchange procedures or indirectly by influence on sources of inputs. For example, a manufacturing firm will sell its productive output and acquire new inputs with its proceeds. In other organizations, such as a state highway department, the process is less direct. The highway department obtains new inputs by influence of legislative and other bodies and bases its influence, in part, on the quality of service rendered and on the promise of the quality of services to be given in the future, the latter, of course, being at least partially validated by the former.

The acquisition and disposal functions of organizations require specialized organizational roles (Katz & Kahn, 1966; Kahn et al., 1964). They will be called boundary roles. These are commonly the roles of marketing and sales personnel, purchasing agents, dispatchers and traffic men, personnel recruiters, admission and placement staffs, advertising and public relations workers, information and intelligence gatherers and purveyors, legislative representatives, negotiators and bargaining agents, and others whose activities place them at organization boundaries for the purpose of effecting transactions with the environment. Although the particular, discrete activities engaged in are various, they nevertheless share certain important properties and they are differentiated from the role activities of persons operating more or less entirely within an organization, such as persons engaging principally in production, managerial, and maintenance activities.

UNIQUE PROPERTIES OF BOUNDARY POSITIONS

Boundary positions have a number of unique properties deriving from their struc-

tural relationship to other roles and from the fact that occupants of these positions must effect transactions with external agents. First, the occupant of such a position—named here the boundary role person or BRP—is more distant, psychologically, organizationally, and often physically, from other members of his organization than they are from each other, and he is closer to the external environment and to the agents of outside organizations; second, he represents[2] his organization to the external environment; and, third, he is his organization's agent of influence over the external environment.

BRP Distance

The BRP's distance from his fellow members potentially weakens his organizational bonds, as does his relative closeness to the outside environment. Influence by the parent organization over him may be weaker than over other members, or may require greater energy to achieve a given level of influence. Distance from the organization and proximity to the external world may also generate suspicion of the BRP and a strong desire to monitor his behavior, as will be discussed in several contexts later.

Conversely, knowledge by the BRP that he is removed from his parent organization may both give him greater behavioral freedom in performing tasks than is possessed by other members and, simultaneously. arouse anxiety about how he is perceived "back home." It is well known, for example, that overseas personnel frequently express concern about their distance from their organization, even though they may be enjoying unusual perquisites. The feelings

---

[2] Representation, as used herein, is intended to denote information-presenting behavior particularly, not, as Vidmar (1971) suggests, to denote bargaining on behalf of someone. We wish to distinguish conceptually between representation and influence attempts directly designed to secure certain organization outcomes. Admittedly, the distinction may be fragile under some conditions.

are often reinforced by visits and audits that are clearly in the nature of "checks."

In general, it is hypothesized that constituent suspicion of the BRP and desire to monitor his behavior, and BRP anxiety about how constituents perceive him are monotonically increasing functions of the distance between BRP and parent organization. Furthermore, the slopes of the functions will be moderated by the character of the environment in which a BRP represents his organization or effects transactions on its behalf, the slope of the functions being steeper if the environment is perceived as inimical than if it is benign or friendly. This is diagrammed in Figure 1.

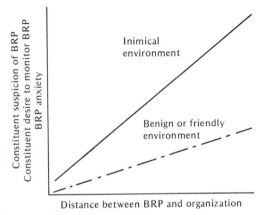

Figure 1. Effects of distance between BRP and organization.

BRP as Representative

In their representational function BRPs are the "face" of the organization. Indeed, a primary activity of some boundary positions, particularly at the highest levels, is "putting on a face" in order to facilitate organization environment transactions and to obtain social support and legitimation. All BRPs, to a greater extent than others, represent to the external environment the organization's preferences, needs, beliefs, attitudes, norms, aspirations, and other characteristics. As Katz and Kahn (1966) have noted, the BRPs face outward in their representational

function. The representations are both calculated and unwitting, veridical and not (Goffman, 1969). Impression management is a part of the boundary role and the BRP is often selected, in part, for his ability to create an impression consistent with organizational objectives. As a result, quite atypical organization members may be selected for boundary positions, which has implications for the BRP's interpersonal relations with fellow members, who are in some sense his constituents.

At the same time as they represent their organization, effective transactions require that BRPs have knowledge of and be sensitive to the preferences, needs, beliefs, attitudes, norms, and aspirations of the external organizations with which they are dealing. Without this, successful impression management, negotiation and bargaining are, at best, made difficult or a matter of chance since successful transactions must, in the long run at least, be successful from the point of view of both a BRP's organization and the external organization. He must, in effect, perform two representational tasks: He must reflect his own system to the outside and he must reflect the outside inwardly. Under some conditions, accurate representation of the external world is of paramount importance, as when the function of the information is to permit the organization to adapt to external events. Under other conditions, the function of representation is secondary and designed to subserve another function, such as influence of organization members. This, in effect, constitutes impression management of the BRP's own constituents.

When representation by the BRP is manipulatively designed to influence selectively either insiders or outsiders, it may be primarily coping or defensive behavior on his part. It is coping behavior if it is functionally related to the achievement of organization outcomes. For example, a BRP may exaggerate his organization's assets to a government commission in order to make it appear that the return on investment is relatively low and, thus, to make it possible to obtain more favorable price or rate rulings. Similarly, a BRP may exaggerate to his constituents an outside organization's plight in order to have them moderate their expectations, which he believes are so high as to prevent a transaction from being concluded. Distorted representation is defensive if the primary object of the behavior is to protect the BRP as a person and if such service potentially conflicts with the achievement of organization outcomes (Katz & Kahn, 1966). A BRP may, for example, grossly understate the bargaining discretion given to him by his organization so that his opponents cannot attribute to him personally such characteristics as intransigence and exploitativeness and, therefore, "blame" him for stress in the course of bargaining. An illustration of defensive representation of the external world to constituents is the salesman who misreports consumer apathy to justify low sales. Another is the politician who exaggerates external threat to the nation in order to garner votes.

BRP as Influence Agent

As influence agent the BRP attempts to influence the behavior of other persons and organizations whose preference orderings typically differ from his own organization's. Simultaneously, the BRP is the target of representations and influence attempts by external agents. Since these representations and influences characteristically conflict with his organization's interests, the BRP must, in turn, transmit them to his constituents and frequently attempt to alter their initial preference orderings. In effect, the BRP is both the influencer and the recipient of influence from insiders and outsiders. This basic characteristic leads potentially to higher levels of role conflict and tension for the BRP than for other organization members; influences his approach to and manner of bargaining, and the outcomes he achieves; has implications for how the internal constituents of his organization perceive, eval-

uate, and trust him; affects his job satisfaction; and influences the strength of his organization bonds (Kahn et al., 1964).

The BRP who bargains with an external agency on behalf of his organization must not only attempt to reach an agreement with outsiders, but must also obtain agreement from his own group as to what constitutes an acceptable agreement with the external organizations. The BRP is at the crunode of a dynamic, dual conflict in which the outcomes of conflict resolution attempts (however tentative) in one conflict become inputs to the second conflict, the outcomes of which then become new inputs to the first conflict, and so on. The dynamic, mutually causative nature of the process is suggested in Figure 2, in which arrows represent influence attempts. Most studies of bargaining have failed to examine this aspect of the process. They have typically placed subjects in decision-making situations requiring them to interact only with an opponent, whereas bargainers in a wide range of situations act on behalf of one or more persons and are influenced by them as well as by an external opponent.

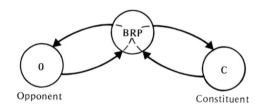

Figure 2. Dynamic, dual conflict of BRP in bargaining.

In part as a result of the fact that BRPs may have to settle for transaction outcomes that are less than maximum, in part because they are sensitive to, and, indeed, because they may "speak for" other organizations, and partly because they are organizationally, physically, and psychologically closer than constituents to the external organizations— often perceived as the "opponent," the "enemy," or the "competition"—their loyalty to the organization may be suspect, and they may be perceived as being more likely than other members to deviate from norms and to defect. From these considerations there are a number of derivative consequences. First, the organization sets up mechanisms to monitor and to ensure the loyalty and norm-adherence of BRPs. Examples are the periodic "inspirational" meetings held for sales forces in businesses and regulations governing the length of foreign duty tours, which are also, of course, direct or indirect forms of norm-sending by the parent organization. Second, BRPs must *display* their loyalty and norm-adherence to a greater extent than do other organization members, although, in fact, their loyalty and norm-adherence may under some conditions be greater and more rigid than that of other members. To the degree organizational membership is attractive to BRPs, their display of fealty may be correlated with the extent to which they perceive their fidelity is suspected. The more they feel their behavior and beliefs are suspect, the more they will display their loyalty, the more they will *be* loyal to the organization and its norms, and the more narrowly, rigidly, and exclusively they will interpret organizational norms and demands. Paradoxically, a corollary consequence of being suspect and of rigid norm interpretation is to *apply* norms and demands inflexibly in bargaining transactions and, therefore, possibly to reduce bargaining effectiveness, at least over the long run. That is, there may result an intransigent demand for maximum outcomes rather than a quest for optimal outcomes. This line of reasoning is consistent with findings by Druckman et al. (1970), Vidmar (1971), and Vidmar and McGrath (1970), and will be discussed again in this chapter.

A third consequence deriving from the suspicion attached to boundary role positions is conflict for the incumbent. The organizational need for optimal outcomes, whether explicit or not, and the need for BRPs to display their loyalty and norm-adherence are often incompatible. For example, allow-ing a vendor a given margin of profit in order to achieve an optimal outcome in obtaining organizational inputs may give the appearance that the negotiator is disloyal; giving economic aid to a socialist nation may be perceived as ideological treachery; advocating birth control as a practical matter in a poor urban area may be labeled as doctrinal heresy or as a form of genocide; and advertising the democratic character of the Army in order to attract recruits may appear to violate norms about authority and discipline. The essence of many such conflicts is that there is role sending both about the outcomes to be achieved (strike an optimal bargain, give succorance to the poor, etc.) and about some of the means to achieve them (don't allow much profit margin to the vendor, don't advocate birth control, etc.). As mentioned earlier, conflict also arises from being sensitive to two sets of needs, norms, and values, those of the BRP's own organization and those of the external organization with which he is interacting. Imbalanced weighting of either set will result in a less than optimal outcome and in a possible charge of disloyalty; but even if the bargainer achieves an *objectively* optimal outcome for his organization, he risks being perceived as ineffective or disloyal or both.

In the remainder of this chapter a structural model of boundary role behavior is presented. This is followed by a discussion of variables of which boundary role behavior is a function and by analyses of the complex, dynamic relationships among these variables. Emphasis is placed on environmental transactions requiring influence by BRPs in bargaining contexts. This emphasis on negotiation, as distinguished from more purely representational activities of BRPs, is chosen because there exists a large literature on negotiation and conflict resolution which is singularly useful in suggesting hypotheses about boundary behavior and which, in turn, may be enlightened by a systemic approach to boundary transactions. The illustrative use of bargaining situations should not suggest, however, that what follows is an analysis and review of bargaining: The focus of interest is behavior in organization boundary roles.

MODEL OF ORGANIZATIONAL BOUNDARY ROLES

The major existing theory relevant to boundary role behavior is found in role theory, especially as developed in the work of Kahn et al. (1964) and Katz and Kahn (1966), in the theory of labor negotiation by Walton and McKersie (1965), in the work of Evan (1966) on interorganizational relations, and in organization system theory (e.g., Berrien, 1968; Easton, 1965; Rice, 1963, 1969; Miller & Rice, 1967; Thompson, 1967; March & Simon, 1958). There is, of course, highly relevant work in diverse areas, for example, by Schelling (1960) and Rapoport (1960) on conflict resolution, by Sherif et al. (1961) and Sherif (1966) on intergroup conflict, by Thibaut and Kelley (1959) on small groups, and by many writers on organizational behavior. There are also numerous studies concerned with bargaining process which are significant (see reviews by Rapoport & Orwant, 1962; Becker & McClintock, 1967; Gallo & McClintock, 1965; Vinacke, 1969; Gergen, 1969). Almost all investigations consider negotiators in "isolation" and fail to examine the complex, interactive effects of negotiators being men "caught in the middle" of internal and external forces. Despite its high quality and relevance, the work cited does not constitute a comprehensive, articulated theory of boundary role behavior. There is need to begin the development of such a theory, to analyze the structural system properties of boundaries and of boundary positions and roles, to specify the major variables of which boundary role behavior is a function, and, especially significantly, to state the complex, dynamic interrelations among these variables. What follows is a beginning, hopefully suggestive enough to encourage further work.

Structural Model

The structural properties of boundary roles are presented in Figure 3. An organization is viewed as a bounded, open system effecting transactions with its external environment, such as with another organization. The transactions are undertaken by the occupant of a boundary role (BRP_A) with a counterpart (BRP_B) on behalf of his organization, which consists of himself and some "constituents" (C_{A1}, etc.). His counterpart, BRP_B, if acting on behalf of an organization, is also assumed to have constituents (C_{B1}, etc.) by whom he is influenced (arrows 5, 6, 7). The constituents in a given system may

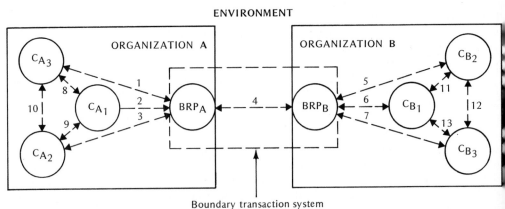

Boundary transaction system

Figure 3.   Structural model of organization boundary systems.

influence each other and may either be in agreement or disagreement about the organization's preferences, the *BRP*, etc. (arrows 8, 9, 10, and 11, 12, 13). One constituent, for example C_{A1} or C_{B1}, may act as spokesman for other constituents or for the organization when dealing with his BRP. Two (or more) BRPs engaged in a transaction are conceived as constituting a distinct open system, the boundary transaction system, the boundaries of which overlap and include portions of organizations A and B.

The BRP of a given organization is subject to the influence of his constituents, as individuals or as a group (arrows 1, 2, and/or 3), and to influence by his counterpart (arrow 4). He may also be influenced by a "third party interventionist" (Douglas, 1962; Walton, 1969), but this is omitted from consideration for present purposes. Reciprocally, the BRP may influence his constituents and his opposite. To the degree that the preference orderings relevant to a transaction are different for the BRP's organization and the opposite organization (or person), the BRP is the recipient of conflicting influence attempts. The influence attempts by constituents on the BRPs constituting a boundary transaction system are major inputs to that system (omitting third party intervention inputs from consideration). In turn, influence by BRPs on their respective constituencies are principal outputs from the boundary transaction system and are inputs to their organizations.

The model identifies the major structural features of organization boundary transactions and makes explicit the essential interactive character of boundary roles. To understand and to predict the behavior of BRPs and the transaction outcomes they achieve for their organizations, it is evident that investigating either only the effects of constituent-related or opponent-related variables at one time is insufficient. This results in misleading conclusions, or, at best, in incomplete knowledge. The simultaneous actions of internal and external system variables perforce suggest interactions among variables. Thus, experimental designs must permit these to occur and data analyses must seek evidence in statistical interactions. This does not preclude the observation of statistical main effects, of course; but interactions constitute the critical tests of hypotheses stating that behavior such as bargaining is a joint function of several intra-system and system-environment variables. For example, in an early investigation of boundary role in which BRPs conducted simulated labor-management negotiations, Frey and Adams (1972) found that opponent behavior (external system variable) and constituent role pressure (internal system variable) interacted strongly and best predicted negotiation outcomes achieved. They concluded that an open system view, incorporating internal and external variables as elements of an interlocking system, was the most fruitful approach to the prediction and understanding of the behaviors and perceptions of BRPs in intergroup conflict. Other studies by Organ (1970), Holmes (1971), and Wall and Adams (1974) also support this conclusion.

Variables of Which Boundary Role Bargaining Is a Function

The structural model of organization boundary systems (Figure 3) does not identify directly the variables of which boundary role bargaining is a function. The structural properties, however, permit deduction of what are the major classes of variables: *They are the attributes of components of the model and attributes of relationships among components.* The major classes of variables so deduced are identified in Table 1. Some relationships among components, while logically possible, appear implausible or relatively unimportant at this time and are, therefore, not listed.

It is not the purpose of this chapter to develop an exhaustive list and to discuss all variables of which boundary role bargaining, much less all boundary role behavior, is a

TABLE 1
CLASSES AND OPERATIONAL EXAMPLES OF VARIABLES
OF WHICH BOUNDARY ROLE BEHAVIOR IS A FUNCTION

Classes of Variables	Operational Examples
A. Attributes of components	
1. Organization, A or B	1. A has competitive bargaining norms; A's earnings are low.
2. Boundary transaction system	2. System has specific interaction norm.
3. BRP_A or BRP_B	3. BRP_B speaks tough; BRP_A is high achiever.
4. Constituents in A or B	4. C_{A_1} is an outcome maximizer.
5. Environment, excluding B or A	5. Unemployment rate is low; money scarce.
B. Attributes of relationships among components*	
1. Organizations A and B	1. Outcomes have zero-sum structure; A more powerful than B.
2. Organization and its BRP	2. Organizational membership attractive to BRP.
3. Constituent or constituent group and BRP	3. C_{A_1} distrusts BRP_A; C_{A_1} has reward power over BRP_A; BRP behavior visible to C's.
4. BRP_A and BRP_B	4. BRP_B has referent power over BRP_A; BRP's distrust each other.
5. Constituents, e.g., C_{A1} and C_{A2}; C_{B1}, C_{B2}, and C_{B_3}	5. C_{A1} and C_{A2} disagree on BRP_A bargaining posture.
6. Boundary transaction system and organization A or B	6. System is distant from A.
7. Environment and organization A or B	7. A is dependent on environment for X.
8. Environment and boundary transaction system	8. Public pressure on transaction system to reach a settlement.

* All possible relationships are not identified; some appear less plausible or consequential than others.

function. Instead, a limited set of variables falling in several of the classes identified in Table 1 and having special interest to the author and his students will be discussed in detail, together with some speculations, hunches, and hypotheses. Importantly, the interrelationships among these variables will be given special attention, not only because they interact but because sets of these variables are related in such ways that they form closed, dynamic loops having deviation amplifying or counteracting consequences. The significance of these complex, dynamic "mutual causal processes" (Maruyama, 1963) for understanding system behavior generally and boundary behavior specifically is profound.

BRP ORGANIZATION BARGAINING NORMS. Organizations typically have implicit or explicit norms on the posture or approach to bargaining that should be taken by their agents. They can be characterized as lying on cooperative-competitive, distributive-integrative, maximizing-optimizing continua. The last, in particular, implies the temporal aspects of such norms. Maximizing transaction outcomes implies a short-term point of view—single transactions considered to the exclusion of possible later ones. Optimizing, on the other hand, suggests a perspective which comprehends transaction outcomes within a set of expected transactions over a period of time. In a laboratory experiment, Holmes (1971) operationally designed a temporal element into his manipulation of distributive and integrative organization norms and found marked effects on agreements achieved by BRPs. Many more agreements resulted from normative pressures to optimize with respect to time than from maximizing pressures. Furthermore, this resulted in the achievement of greater net outcomes over time for the BRPs' own organizations.

In general, as discussed in detail later,

there would tend to be associated, or to develop, with maximizing norms close monitoring of BRP behavior by constituents and little trust, fairly tough, inflexible bargaining patterns by BRPs, low BRP referent power over their counterparts, and poor bargaining outcomes *over the long run,* whereas the reverse would obtain under optimizing norms. Such predicted statistical main effects are of interest in their own right, as are the main effects observed in many investigations of cooperation and competition in interpersonal and inter-organizational bargaining (e.g., Deutsch & Krauss, 1962; Walton, & McKersie, 1965; Organ, 1970; Frey & Adams, 1972). However, main effects of bargaining norms, although accounting for a substantial proportion of bargaining behavior and organization outcome variance, are of less interest than the interaction of these norms with other variables, especially those that are attributes of the external system. Discussion of such interactions will follow in later sections of this chapter, but a brief example is appropriate at this point. Holmes (1971) found that distributive and integrative pressures by constituents on how BRPs should bargain with the representative of another organization interacted both with the opponent's bargaining posture (distributive or integrative) and with whether or not the opponent's constituents agreed or disagreed among themselves about the bargaining tactics their representative should adopt. These interactions had the effect of greatly enhancing or reducing differences *apparently* due entirely to organization bargaining norms when viewed as simple main effects. Furthermore, there is evidence in a study by Wall (1972) that normative influences on BRPs may change over cycles of transactions. His subjects (constituents) altered normative directives about *how* to bargain as a function of the first negotiation. In sum, statistical main effects are partly illusory and one is led to the conjecture that past investigations reporting main effects of cooperation and competition in bargaining may have yielded only partial information

because the theoretical and experimental perspectives taken did not permit certain interactions to be observed. The influence of cooperative and competitive bargaining postures is better understood if considered as occurring within a systemic fabric of dynamically interacting variables, some internal, others external to a given organization.

VISIBILITY OF BRP's BEHAVIOR TO HIS CONSTITUENTS. The extent to which a BRP's behavior and performance are known in his organization varies. Little or much information may be had about the *outcomes* he achieved, such as the terms of a contract settlement, and about the *means* used by the BRP in concluding a transaction, such as the discrete tactics employed, whether his posture was tough and uncompromising or flexible and cooperative, what he communicated to the opponent, and how friendly or hostile interaction was. In varying degrees the organization may monitor outcomes, the means of achieving them, or both. Constituents may choose to monitor closely or loosely either or both the BRP's means of achieving outcomes or the outcomes proper, but the ease of doing this is not invariant. Certain kinds of transactions take place in "closed" sessions or in secrecy, which make observation of ongoing bargaining and related behavior impossible. Only the outcome of such sessions may be directly observable; thus, though an organization may wish to monitor "means behavior," circumstances preclude it or force indirect inferences which are subject to noise and bias. The spatial and organizational distance of the BRP from his organization and the lack of communication between them may also make ongoing bargaining behavior relatively invisible or unreliable. This is frequently true of "field representatives" and agents of several kinds.

As bargaining behavior proper may be difficult to observe, so may it be that the outcomes cannot be fully known and assessed until some time has elapsed—for example, because the outcome is contingent upon events unpredictable or uncontrollable by two negotiating parties (e.g., a contract "pegged" to an economic index) or because there is a necessary delay in the manifestation of the outcome (e.g., the economic results of the merger of two companies). Boundary transaction outcomes may also be difficult to apprehend simply because they are partly or wholly unmeasurable. This is certainly the case with respect to some public welfare transactions. For example, an agreement achieved between a governmental agency and a group of the public may render objectives so vague, so complex, or so compromised that they are not readily measurable. Or the measurement technology that is required may not exist (cf., Gross, 1966).

The visibility of the BRP's behavior should, generally, influence the variability—the "flexibility"—of his behavior: The greater the visibility, the less the variability, provided there are at least some normative expectations about his behavior. The effect should be more pronounced when means behavior, as distinguished from an outcome achieved, is visible and monitored. The visibility variable also should interact with the trust placed in a BRP by his constituents. Close monitoring of the BRP's behavior is inconsistent with trusting him highly. Thus, the effects of trust would be negated by close observation of the BRP's activities. As an experiment by Strickland (1958) on supervision and trust suggests, an organization that monitors closely the behavior of BRPs is likely to distrust them and to suspect their competence. Wall and Adams (1974) found related evidence when they observed that constituents whose organization lost money were likely to distrust their BRPs and to monitor them more closely, especially if the BRPs had failed to conform with directives on how to bargain.

Some data on the effects of visibility of the BRP's behavior have been obtained by Organ (1970). He showed that BRPs who believed that their constituent could not observe their ongoing negotiating behavior were much more likely to deviate from norms sent by their constituent than were BRPs who thought their behavior was highly visible. Low visibility was also associated with lower reported BRP tension. These results are encouraging but leave unanswered questions about the differential effects of means and outcome behavior visibility on BRP perceptions of constituent evaluations, on means behavior, and on outcome performance. Similarly, in an extension of Wall and Adams's (1974) work, the reliability of the information (or its source) obtained by constituents should be investigated to determine how this variable influences their evaluations of a BRP. Generally, information about BRP bargaining behavior proper may be obtained directly by constituent observation, through the BRP, through third parties, or through some combination of these with varying degrees of credibility and "noise." Information credibility when the BRP is the source should, furthermore, be mediated by the constituent's general trust in the BRP and the extent to which he perceives that distorting information has instrumental value to the BRP in obtaining personal gratification.

BRP PERCEPTION OF OPPONENT BARGAINING BEHAVIOR. The relationship between the bargaining behavior of BRP and the perceived exploitativeness or reasonableness of his opposite's bargaining behavior has been partially established. In an experiment by Gruder (1968), the BRP negotiated more demandingly and more competitively if his counterpart was seen as exploitative. Frey and Adams (1972) showed that BRPs in a simulated labor-management negotiation who dealt with an "exploitative" counterpart sent him, on the average, much more demanding messages than did BRPs who faced a cooperative counterpart and that the settlements made were a joint function of a BRP's perception of the opponent as exploitative or cooperative and of whether he felt trusted or distrusted by his constituent. The latter interaction revealed specifically that BRPs who faced a cooperative opponent and were distrusted by their constituents conceded very much less in negotiations than did BRPs in any other condition, BRPs in all conditions having been directed to be tough bargainers. In sum, then, this study showed that while role sending from the BRP to this counterpart is more demanding when the opponent is exploitative, the exploitativeness of the opponent does not lead to small concessions by the BRP; instead, the smallest concessions are made when the BRP faces a cooperative counterpart, feels he is distrusted by his parent organization, and has been enjoined by it to be tough.

A similar result was obtained in the comparable conditions of a later, more complex study by Frey (1971). In that experiment, some results of which are given in Table 2, Frey found that the *verbal* behavior of the opponent (either conciliatory or demanding), as distinguished from his actual bargaining behavior (exploitative or cooperative), which was manipulated independently, had significant effects on the magnitude of concessions made by the BRP.

He conceded less when his opponent sent conciliatory messages. This effect, however, was due almost wholly to the very small concessions made by BRPs whose constituents told them to bargain exploitatively. This tendency to concede much less when the opponent speaks in a conciliatory manner and when the BRP is urged to be tough is greatly enhanced if the BRP believes his constituent distrusts him and if the conciliatory verbal behavior of the opponent is belied by his exploitative bargaining behavior. What might appear at first glance as "taking advantage of a sucker" is much more complex. There is evidence in Frey's data for a process of sanctioned retribution. When a BRP is directed by his constituent to be exploitative and the opponent is verbally conciliatory but bargains exploitatively, which makes him appear manipulative and dishonest, the BRP "zaps" him by conceding vastly less than under any other condition. Similar behavior by the BRP is not apparent, however, if he has been enjoined to bargain cooperatively.

TABLE 2
MEANS OF BRP CONCESSIONS TO UNION SPOKESMAN IN CENTS

| | | Constituent gives BRP: | | | |
| | | "Be cooperative" directives | | "Be exploitative" directives | |
		Trust	Distrust	Trust	Distrust
Opponent bargains cooperatively	Opponent verbally conciliatory	61.56	53.44	40.67	37.44
	Opponent verbally demanding	49.22	52.56	54.67	48.56
Opponent bargains exploitatively	Opponent verbally conciliatory	61.44	40.11	26.89	22.00
	Opponent verbally demanding	62.44	55.67	43.00	45.67

Adapted from Frey, 1971, with permission.

A laboratory investigation by Holmes (1971) casts additional light on the effects of perceptions of the opponent on boundary role behavior. In a factorial design, he manipulated type of role pressure from the BRP's three constituents (competitive versus cooperative), constituent group structure (ingroup in consensus versus ingroup in dissensus), bargaining behavior of the opponent (competitive versus cooperative), and group structure of the opponent's three constituents (outgroup in consensus versus outgroup in dissensus). Although the BRP's perceptions of his opponent's being either competitive or cooperative had highly significant main effects on the BRP's bargaining behavior, many more agreements being made when the opponent's behavior was cooperative, the basic behavior pattern of the BRP is much more complex and is described by Holmes as a "triangle effect" reminiscent of a behavior pattern identified by Kelley and Stahelski (1970). The BRP complied with the role pressures of his constituents when he negotiated with a cooperative opponent, but the effects of the role pressures were smaller with a competitive opponent, because a BRP urged to be cooperative by his constituents tended to assimilate toward the behavioral style of his external counterpart. The occurrence of this pattern was dependent upon the structure of the ingroup and outgroup constituencies. A powerful "triangle effect" in the BRP's behavior was evident only when either the ingroup or the outgroup was in a state of dissensus; it was absent when consensus existed in these groups. Holmes's (1971) data for the ingroup consensus and dissensus conditions are shown in Figure 4. They will be discussed again at a later point, as will the interaction between opponent behavior and constituent distrust found by Frey and Adams (1972).

EXPECTATION OF FUTURE INTERACTION BE-TWEEN BRP AND OPPONENT. Leaving out of consideration the possibility that a certain negotiating posture may prevent the com-

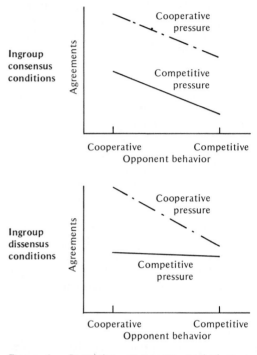

Figure 4. Bargaining agreements reached as a function of constituent role pressure, opponent behavior, and ingroup structure. (Adapted from Holmes, 1971, with permission.)

pletion of a transaction and that a negotiator may have no acceptable alternative to reaching an agreement with a given person or organization, competitiveness of bargaining by a BRP (as measured by bargaining concessions, for example) should be a decreasing, monotonic function of the BRP's expectation of conducting future transactions with a particular opposing BRP or organization. If a BRP expects that a transaction with a given other BRP or organization will occur only once, how demanding, tough, and intransigent he can be is limited only by "what the market will bear" and by his willingness to go that far, since there is no need to consider the future consequences of such negotiating behavior—for example, that the opponent would retaliate or be forced to find other organizations to deal with. If, on the other hand, a BRP anticipates negotiating with another system more than once, he must consider the implications of his bargaining behavior in one transaction for subsequent transactions. In effect, he must consider long-term equilibrium over a number of transactions. Furthermore, this must be with respect to two dimensions of the BRP's relationship with his opponent, the functional and the socio-emotional. The first is related principally to organization outcomes produced through bargaining and entails prediction of the effects of bargaining in one transaction on the expected outcome value of a *set* of transactions, including the present one and uncertain ones in the future. The long-term socio-emotional relationship between a BRP and his opponent must also be contemplated by the BRP. A tough or exploitative stance in a given transaction is likely to stress the boundary transaction subsystem socio-emotionally, which implies not only that future transactions may be unpleasant, but also that they may be more difficult to complete at a given outcome level.

Expectation of future interaction between a BRP and an opponent should result in main effects on such variables as outcomes achieved, concessions made, and verbal behavior toward the opponent. Lower outcomes, more concessions, and more conciliatory behavior should be observed when repeated negotiations are expected than when they are not. However, interaction effects with organization bargaining norms, for example, are also predictable. Taking frequency of concessions to illustrate, a cooperative organization bargaining norm should result in very frequent concessions when the BRP expects repeated transactions since the norm is congruent with making concessions to establish long-term equilibrium. Furthermore, the BRP cannot easily be faulted: He *is* being cooperative and, also, the *future* consequences of his concessions on aggregate long-term outcomes are invisible. If the BRP anticipates only one transaction with an opponent, a cooperative organizational norm should lead to few

concessions. The norm is incongruent with achieving desirable outcomes in a single transaction and it should be discounted in importance by the BRP in favor of achieving high outcomes, on the not unreasonable assumption that constituents are ultimately more concerned with the magnitude of outcomes than with how they were achieved. A quite different situation obtains if the organization bargaining norm is competitive. Under the expectation of only one transaction, the BRP should make a minimal number of concessions since the norm is consistent with the one-transaction context and should lead to high immediate outcomes. Not many more concessions would be predicted, however, if the BRP anticipates future transactions with the opponent. Though it may, in fact, be dysfunctional in obtaining high outcomes over the long run, making few concessions leads to large immediate outcomes, it is obedient to norms, and its possible future consequences on outcomes are invisible. The "triangular" interaction just described is diagrammed in Figure 5. More complex, three-way interactions can be predicted if the effects of such a variable as visibility of the BRP's behavior is also considered. If, for example, the BRP's ongoing bargaining behavior is highly visible to constituents who have directed him to negotiate cooperatively, the very small number of concessions the BRP is predicted to make under one-time transaction conditions would not obtain. Concerned with *how* he bargains because his behavior is visible to constituents, the BRP should make more concessions to the opponent. In general, high visibility of bargaining tactics would eliminate the triangular pattern depicted in Figure 5, leaving only evidence of main effects.

SYSTEM EFFECTIVENESS. Organizations vary with respect to the performance effectiveness of different boundary and internal functions, as well as in regard to their overall effectiveness. Overall effectiveness, whether high or low, permits few, if any, objective evalua-

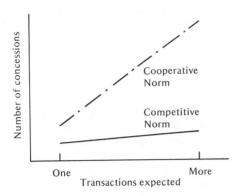

Figure 5. Predicted effects of bargaining norms and expected frequency of transactions on number of concessions made.

tions of the performance of subsystems, although if overall effectiveness were high the comfortable, but perhaps illusory, conclusion might be drawn that all was well. Much less can the performance of individuals, such as BRPs, be inferred from overall system effectiveness. Yet, these very inferences are commonly made. A person is assumed to be performing well because measures of organization effectiveness are satisfactorily high. Conversely, one may observe a person's being blamed for organization reverses for which he had no responsibility.

Such seemingly illogical actions are not simply a function of simplistic thinking, stupidity, or other aberrations. They stem principally (one need not go so far as to assume *no* aberrations) from the nature of the information available to make appropriate inferences about causes and effects in organizations and in smaller and larger systems. Information about the behavior of boundary role occupants is often lacking, unreliable, or only indirectly and complexly related to it. As a result, constituents may evaluate BRP performance on the basis of overall system effectiveness. Some of the consequences were observed by Wall (1972) in an experiment that addressed itself in part to the problem raised here.

In his experiment, constituents playing the role of sales managers were given information that their company had earned or lost $1,500. They were also informed that their BRP, a salesman, had conformed or not conformed with their instructions to bargain competitively or cooperatively with the buyer of another organization, or they were given no information about their BRP's bargaining behavior. In effect, the conformity conditions constituted high visibility conditions with respect to obedience, whereas the condition of no information created a condition of very low visibility, to use reference terms introduced earlier. Both information, or the lack of it, about BRP conformity with instructions and about the system effectiveness significantly influenced constituent evaluations of BRPs and of their performance. Although constituents had no objective data permitting specific *performance* evaluations of their BRPs, those in companies earning money rated BRPs and their performance significantly better than did those in companies losing money. Information about conformity with directive had comparable effects. Conforming BRP were judged more highly than nonconforming BRPs. The absence of information about BRP behavior resulted in intermediate evaluations, which, however, were much nearer to those made of conforming than of nonconforming BRPs. System effectiveness and BRP conformity interacted strongly to affect evaluations of the BRP. The general nature of the interaction was that lack of information about behavior conformity greatly accentuated negative evaluation when the system was losing money and enhanced positive evaluations when the system made money.

Wall (1972) also found that information about system effectiveness and BRP conformity produced effects on constituent evaluations of BRP loyalty. The data are reproduced in Table 3. The implications of these data are examined more fully when the "distrust cycle" is discussed in a later

TABLE 3
CONSTITUENT EVALUATION OF BRP LOYALTY AS A FUNCTION OF SYSTEM EFFECTIVENESS AND BRP CONFORMITY

	Conformity with Constituent Directives		
	BRP con- forming	No infor- mation on con- formity	BRP not con- forming
System effective	1.41	1.92	3.53
System ineffective	2.67	3.80	4.40

Adapted from Wall, 1972, with permission.

section. It may be noted here, however, that by affecting evaluated loyalty there results a series of events which either further increases constituent distrust of the BRP through closed, deviation amplifying loops or counteracts distrust through deviation counteracting loops.

STRUCTURE OF BRP AND OPPONENT CONSTITUENT GROUPS. Bargaining norms sent by constituents to a BRP about how he should behave, competitively or cooperatively, for example, were shown earlier to have important main and interactive effects. The norm transmitted to the BRP may be unambiguous or noisy, however. A socio-psychologically important source of norm ambiguity results from divisiveness among the BRP's constituents, which Holmes (1971) has labeled dissensus. As reported earlier, he found that constituent ingroup consensus and dissensus affected BRP performance; also, that perceptions of the opposing BRP were influenced.

In Holmes's study, norm-sending was transmitted directly to the BRP and he was the subject of influence. The BRP is not the subject of influence in norm-sending by the opponent's constituency, of course, but the supposed influence on the opposing BRP is nevertheless relevant to the BRP's bargaining behavior. If he believes consensus exists among outgroup constituents, he may

infer that his counterpart's behavior is involuntary. If, on the other hand, he knows that the outgroup is in a state of dissensus, he may perceive his opponent's behavior as being much more voluntary, as being a matter of choice, and that the opponent is hostile or peaceful, likable or unlikable, etc., depending on his bargaining stance. These attributions under conditions of outgroup dissensus should, in turn, be associated with the bargaining behavior adopted by the BRP in response to the opponent. This is precisely what Holmes demonstrated when he observed a significant triple interaction between a BRP's own organization norm (cooperative versus competitive), outgroup structure (consensus versus dissensus), and opponent behavior (cooperative versus competitive). The data he obtained formed a pattern very similar to that presented in Figure 4. When the opponent's constituents disagreed on the bargaining posture to be adopted, a BRP directed to be cooperative was highly cooperative if the opponent was cooperative, but was extremely competitive if the opponent was also competitive. If the BRP was enjoined by his constituents to be competitive he was extremely competitive, whether his opposite behaved cooperatively or competitively. When the opponent's constituents were in agreement, however, no interaction of opponent behavior and bargaining norms were evident.

From Holmes's (1971) investigation it appears that disagreement among *either* one's own constituents or the opponent's constituents reduces a BRP's willingness or ability to obey instructions to cooperate when the opponent bargains competitively. Although the net effects are comparable, the underlying psychological processes must be different. In the case of ingroup dissensus, a BRP appears to be released from having to conform with cooperative norms (from two out of three constituents) that might result in exploitation by a competitive opponent. Processes activated by outgroup dissensus seem quite different. Holmes's experimental observations suggest that the BRP's bargaining behavior under instructions to be cooperative are mediated by his perceptions of the *meaning* of cooperative and competitive behavior by the opponent when outgroup constituents appear to disagree about how their representative should bargain. Outgroup dissensus implies to the BRP that his opponent has some choice in the behavior he adopts. If he bargains cooperatively, the BRP perceives that it is genuine cooperation and that the opponent is honest, peaceful, likable, and pleasant, and he responds by being highly cooperative himself. If the opponent behaves competitively, on the other hand, the BRP perceives not only that such bargaining is unnecessary, since the opponent is not under unanimous constituent pressures, but that the opponent is deceptive, hostile, unlikable, and unpleasant, and he responds in kind by being extremely competitive. This is evidence, again, that relatively complex interactions among internal and external system variables explain the bargaining behavior of boundary role occupants.

TIME PRESSURE TO COMPLETE TRANSACTIONS. Both the nature of some transactions and the characteristics of environments in which organizations exist can limit the time available to conclude transactions and can, therefore, create time pressure constraints on BRPs. This, in turn, should influence their bargaining behavior. Some transactions are arbitrarily time bound. For example, a settlement between two parties must be concluded within a certain period or else a third party may inflict penalties. Other transactions are intrinsically time constrained, at least for one party. For example, perishable goods must be sold within a short time, or, in a special case of perishability, a man must propose marriage before a girl's affection wanes. Some organizations exist in relatively turbulent environments. Since adaption to external events requires an increase in activities (including boundary transactions)

it follows that the time available for any given activity is reduced—assuming no *deus ex machina*. Environmental change may, therefore, result in time pressure.

The effect of time pressure on a BRP is difficult to predict—at least as a main effect—since the effects should be significantly mediated by organization norms, bargaining behavior of the opponent, perception of the opponent's time constraints, and visibility of the BRP's behavior to his constituents. In general, however, increased time pressure to conclude a transaction should result in increased concessions and lower outcomes (cf., Komorita & Barnes, 1969), because time can be viewed as a negotiable commodity in the transaction (and is formally so viewed in certain financial instruments involving time-related discounts). If time pressure is unequally distributed among BRPs in a boundary transaction system, concessions made by a given BRP should be proportional to the share of pressure exerted on him by time.

ATTRACTIVENESS OF ORGANIZATION MEMBERSHIP TO THE BRP. Attractiveness of membership is defined as strength of desire to retain membership. Control of this variable is important in some investigations, but it is also of some interest for substantive reasons. Do outcomes achieved by a BRP for his organization vary as a function of his organization's attractiveness to him? A direct relationship between attractiveness and outcomes can be predicted from the fact that lower (or higher) attractiveness should lead to smaller (greater) influence by the organization, which should result in greater (smaller) relative influence on the BRP by the opposing BRP, more (fewer) concessions by him, and lower (higher) outcomes for his organization.

If both attractiveness of the BRP's organization and the toughness of his opponent's bargaining behavior are varied independently in an experiment, and if no strong organization norms exist as to BRP means behavior, the effects on concessions should be

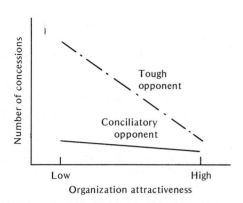

Figure 6. Predicted effects of organization attractiveness and opponent behavior on number of concessions made.

observable both in statistical main effects and interactions as suggested in Figure 6. Low attractiveness should result in frequent concessions when the opponent is tough and competitive, whereas only a small number of concessions would be expected when attractiveness is high and the opponent tough. On the other hand, when the opponent is conciliatory and cooperative, both low and high organization attractiveness should result in fairly few concessions. When the opponent is conciliatory, there is little need to make concessions in either condition of attractiveness. When he is demanding, however, his relative influence is high over a BRP whose organization has little attraction, which should lead to many concessions. But if the BRP is highly attracted to his organization, his desire to maintain his organizational membership should induce him to make few concessions, since many concessions would be perceived as endangering his membership.

Other questions also suggest themselves. Assuming relatively high initial organization attractiveness and a low level of monitoring of BRP behavior, does later introduction of surveillance result in the BRP's perceiving that his constituents trust him less? Does this, in turn, affect his desire to retain his organizational membership? With what effect on outcomes obtained? These questions bear not only on BRP behavior, which is viewed as a joint function of variables internal and external to an organization, but also on the theoretical relationship between organization attractiveness and constituent trust.

CONTROL OVER BRP OUTCOMES. Organizations typically have a measure of control over their members' outcomes—for example, pay, prestige, status, job satisfaction. Control over the BRP's outcomes is no exception, but in relation to him the organization must compete to some extent with outcomes to the BRP that are under the control of external organizations—often the "opponent." Clearly, the success achieved by the BRP in negotiation is partly under the control of the outsider, who also exercises a measure of control over the atmosphere under which transactions take place—pleasant, congenial, or harsh and stressful. There may also be control over illegitimate rewards. Such dual control—internal and external—over BRP outcomes sharpens problems of "conflict of interest" and, of course, bears importantly on the questions of perceived trust and organizational loyalty discussed below.

In general, it would be predicted that the greater the amount of control exercised by constituents over a BRP's outcomes, the more he will comply with organizational norms and demands. The relationship is probably straightforward in the instance of extrinsic outcomes, such as monetary payoffs. In the case of such outcomes as organizational climate, however, the relationship may be more complex. It is assumed that the more favorable the organizational climate, the more rewarding or attractive organizational membership is. Consequently, manipulation of organizational climate should have effects comparable to the control of extrinsic outcomes. But important dimensions of organizational climate include trust among members and degree of autonomy and discretion members have in performing tasks. It is suggested that these aspects of organizational climate will be continually strained in the case of the BRP and that, therefore, control over this outcome to the BRP will be difficult or "noisy." The more the trust and the greater the autonomy the BRP perceives, the more likely he will strive for optimal, rather than maximal, solutions, and thus yield, tend to appear "cooperative" with the opponent, develop friendly relations with him, and so on. However, to be discussed later, this behavior is likely to decrease perceived constituent trust in the BRP and increase organizational monitoring of his behavior. This state of affairs is, in turn, likely to be perceived by the BRP as distrustful and punitive. The BRP is likely to anticipate these consequences of his behavior and may, therefore, refrain from engaging in such behavior, thus avoiding lower or punitive outcomes. The paradox is noteworthy, for it is suggested that a rewarding organizational climate may be self-destructive and may lead eventually to less organizational effectiveness in boundary transactions than might be supposed. The process described is not, however, a *necessary* state of affairs. It should be found to hold particularly when organization norms are competitive and when goals have a maximization structure.

TRUST IN BRP. The occupants of boundary roles, by virtue of their position in the organization structure, are subject to role sending from persons in the external environment, and, in a great range of situations, the behavior required is to some degree opposite to that demanded by role sending emanating from the BRP's constituents because of differences in preference orderings. To conclude a transaction, the BRP may have to yield something or forego an outcome desired by his organization. Thus, there exists an apparent objective basis for distrusting the BRP. The more he concedes or foregoes, the greater the possible distrust by constituents. Furthermore, with any experience, the BRP will perceive the

level of trust in which he is held by his constituents.

Another aspect of boundary role behavior bearing on trust is the extent, proximity, and apparent congeniality of contact between the BRP and his opposite in the external environment. The greater, the closer, and the friendlier the relationship appears to be, the more suspect the BRP's loyalty may be and the more likely he may be seen as a potential defector. Again, it is assumed that the BRP will typically be sensitive to these perceptions on the part of his fellow organization members.

Two questions of some interest arise in relation to trust in the BRP. First, how does the behavior of the BRP influence the degree of trust in which he is held by his own organization members and the extent to which he is perceived as likely to defect? Do variations in the degree he yields to the opponent relate systematically to variations in how much fellow members trust him and in how likely they believe he would defect? The data reported by Wall (1972) bear on this. In his experiment he observed that salesmen (BRPs) in an organization that lost money were perceived by constituents as much less loyal than salesmen whose firm made money. The constituents of organizations losing money, as compared to those in profit-making organizations, were also distinctly less likely to indicate they would choose their BRP for a later "confidential mission." Wall also noted that BRPs who were said to have deviated from organization norms were distrusted by their constituents, whereas those who conformed were trusted, an effect independent of organization outcomes achieved. An additional finding was that constituents expressed greater desire to monitor BRP behavior if their firms had lost money or if they had evidence that their representatives had deviated from organization bargaining norms.

Secondly, how do variations in the BRP's perceptions of how much he is trusted relate to his boundary role behavior? A hypothesis receiving considerable support is that the

BRP in a bargaining situation will yield less, be less flexible, and be more demanding as perceived distrust increases and that, as a result, the opponent will become more intransigent, which leads to lower organization effectiveness and, then, to greater distrust of the BRP by his constituents. Data from Organ (1970) and Frey and Adams (1972) show that constituent distrust of the BRP increases the toughness of his behavior, although this effect is complex. In the Frey and Adams (1972) study, for example, the constituent trust variable interacted with the manipulated bargaining style of the opponent. BRPs who were distrusted by their constituent and perceived their opponent's behavior to be cooperative were much tougher bargainers than BRPs in other conditions.

Gruder (1968) has shown that if one bargainer is perceived as exploitative (i.e., tough), his counterpart reacts in the same manner. This finding received strong support from Holmes's data (1971). The relationship between the opponent's toughness and outcomes to the BRP's organization may be inferred directly from a study by Komorita and Barnes (1969), in which they found that a demanding bargaining posture increased outcomes (i.e., if the opponent gains, the BRP may lose). Finally, Wall and Adams (1974) have unequivocally shown that BRPs are distrusted by their constituents if the organization is ineffective (loses money).

Although the research cited is enlightening, further research is indicated. It would be of interest, for example, to determine the effects of the attractiveness of organizational membership to the BRP upon the influence of constituent trust. Constituent distrust should be much more significant to BRPs for whom continued organizational membership is important. If a BRP values his membership highly and perceives he is distrusted by constituents, he should be found to bargain more demandingly and to make fewer concessions than if membership is not highly valued. Although it is known that

tension and felt conflict are high among BRPs (Kahn et al., 1964; Organ, 1970), no data on organization attractiveness are available. It might be hypothesized, however, that there is a positive relationship between constituent distrust and tension, and an inverse one between tension and organization attractiveness. If this is true, it follows that increasing constituent distrust of the BRP would lead to lower organization attractiveness and a decrease in the effect of distrust upon the BRP's bargaining behavior. In the limiting case, organization attractiveness could become so low as to induce the BRP to sever his association with the organization.

Distrust of BRPs, whatever its basis, is likely to involve deviation amplifying and counteracting mutual causal processes (Maruyama, 1963), as suggested in Figure 7. Arbitrarily beginning with the distrust variable, although a cycle may be "entered" at any point, an increase in constituent distrust (D) promotes increased monitoring of BRP behavior (M) (Strickland, 1958), as well as increased perceived distrust by the BRP (P), which is also increased by monitoring of his behavior, since surveillance implies distrust; an increase in perceived distrust (P) increases the toughness of the BRP's bargaining behavior (B) (Organ, 1970; Frey & Adams, 1972); this will, in turn, induce the opponent to adopt a tougher bargaining posture (O) (Gruder, 1968); intransigent bargaining by the opponent should lead to reduced organizational effectiveness (E) (Wall, 1972); finally, a decrement in organizational effectiveness will enhance constituent distrust of the BRP (D). In addition, an increase in tough BRP bargaining behavior (B), provided it is visible, is assumed to lower constituent distrust (D) and vice versa, at least in organizations that value "toughness" in what they perceive to be adversary relationships.

Because these variables are causally interrelated in closed cycles or loops, changes in any one or more of them induce changes in the others *and* further changes in them-

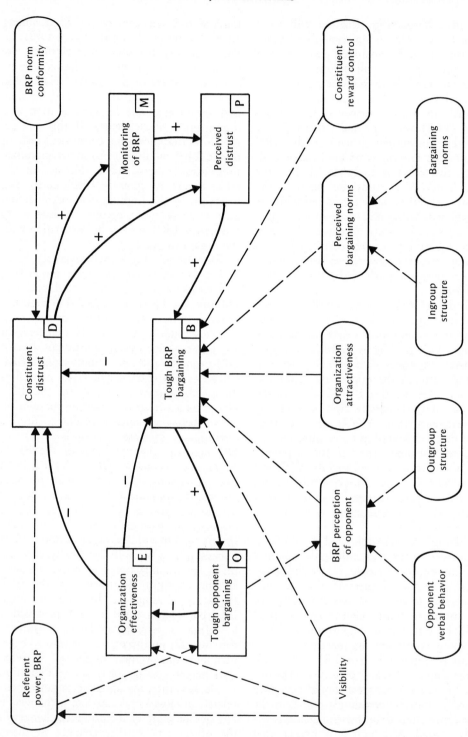

Figure 7. Deviation amplifying and counteracting mutual causal processes involving constituent distrust of BRP and other variables. (Solid arrows indicate causal direction of relationships between variables, and + and - signs indicate whether they are positive or negative.)

selves, the latter being either amplifying or counteracting. The closed loops, D M P B O E D and D P B O E D, are deviation amplifying: Increases in distrust further increase it and decreases lead to further decreases. There are also in the system of variables depicted two deviation counteracting loops, D M P B D, and D P B D: An initial increase in distrust will cause distrust later to decrease, while an initial decrease will lead to an eventual increase. A deviation amplifying loop that is part of the system but does not directly involve constituent distrust is B O E B: An increase, for example, in B causes an increment in O, which reduces E, which, in turn, results in a further increase in B, at least to some limiting values of E, beyond which the BRP might capitulate or cease bargaining.

Through sequential cycles, effects throughout the system of variables become more complex: The counteracting effect of a loop such as D P B D, which leads, for example, to a decrease in D at the end of the first cycle, is itself counteracted in the second cycle through loops D P B D and D M P B D, leading in time to a stable value of distrust. But the same decrease in D in the first cycle would be amplified through loops D M P B O E D and D P B O E D. The net effects of both deviation amplifying and counteracting processes through a single cycle and over a sequence of cycles are obviously difficult to estimate in the absence of specific quantitative data on the magnitude of the relationships between variables and in the absence of other information, such as on the differential lag of various effects. For example, a complete cycle of effects in loop D P B O E D might be supposed to require more time than in loop D P B D. At this stage of research the relative power of the several positive and negative feedback loops, to use more common though less descriptive terms, has not been assessed. A guess is that their combined effective power over a series of cycles limits maximization and minimiza-

tion of the value of any of the interacting variables, but produces instability in the values assumed by the variables.

As stated earlier, the system of interacting variables in Figure 7 may be "entered" at any point. Thus, a change or deviation induced in any variable will "cycle through" the system, every other variable in the system being changed. An initial deviation in constituent distrust (D) may, for example, be set off by BRP conformity with norms. Wall (1972) has shown that if constituents think that their BRP disobeyed normative directives on how to bargain, they were perceived as disloyal, whereas they were evaluated as loyal if they conformed. Data from Gruder (1968), Organ (1970), Frey and Adams (1972), and Holmes (1971) identify a number of variables that affect the toughness (cooperativeness-competitiveness, integrativeness-distributiveness) of the stance taken by a BRP in dealing with an opponent. Most of these have already been discussed, but may be reviewed briefly. Opponent bargaining behavior, opponent verbal behavior, and outgroup constituent structure influence a BRP's perception of his opponent, which in turn determines how tough he will be. The structure of a BRP's own constituency affects his perception of his organization's bargaining norms, and this, then, influences his bargaining posture. The degree to which a BRP believes his behavior is visible to his constituents has been shown by Organ (1970) to influence his bargaining posture such that it is more consonant with organization bargaining norms under conditions of high visibility. Similarly, the visibility of organization outcomes should affect BRP behavior. Although Frey and Adams (1972) found no effect of constituent control over BRP pay on the BRP's bargaining behavior with an opponent, there is reason to hypothesize such a relationship, as explained earlier. Similarly, although no empirical evidence exists to support a relationship between attractiveness of organization membership to a BRP and the toughness of his bargaining stance, there are theoretical grounds for predicting this, as noted earlier.

If, through the effects of the above variables, the bargaining behavior of a BRP is altered at any point in time, constituent distrust will be affected—either directly in the B D relationship or through the B O E D. Such effects on distrust would then cycle through the system. It may be presumptuous at this stage of development to refer to the process depicted in Figure 7 as the "distrust cycle" in constituent-BRP organizational relationships. There is still much to learn. Nevertheless, the dynamic relationships shown have the value of impressing the need and usefulness of viewing sociopsychological phenomena both in spatial and temporal systemic terms. The variables identified in the cycle are neither independent elements nor simple pairs of covarying entities, but a set of dynamically interacting elements.

RELATIVE POWER OF THE BRP AND THE OPPONENT. In general, the greater the relative power possessed by the BRP over his counterpart, the more advantageous should be the outcomes of his bargaining. One form of power, however, generates special problems. The occupant of a boundary role may have to depend to a significant extent on the referent power (French & Raven, 1960) he possesses over the opposing BRP, that is, the degree to which he is liked and is socially attractive to his opponent, since he has no legitimate power and usually little reward, coercive, and expert power over his opponent. If this power is not immediately given, it must be cultivated. If friendship with the opponent, as part of referent power, is apparent to members of the BRP's own organization, there is increased likelihood that his loyalty will be suspect and that his means behavior will be closely monitored, since evidence of friendship implies possible referent power by the opponent over the organization's BRP. Some derivative consequences already have been hypothesized

to be dysfunctional, for example, leading to tougher, less flexible, and, therefore, possibly less adaptive negotiating over the long run. Such bargaining behavior, perhaps perceived as exploitative or unreasonable by the opponent, would appear as inconsistent with liking the BRP, reduce his social attractiveness, and, thus, tend to diminish *his* referent power. These processes are illustrated in Figure 8 and form closed dynamic loops which are connected to the system of variables represented in Figure 7. Loops R D M P B R, R D P B R, D M P B D, and D P B D are all counteracting: An increase in *visible* referent power subsequently decreases referent power and vice versa.

If it is assumed that BRPs are aware of the above relationships between their referent power and constituent distrust, they will attempt to hide existing friendly relations with the opponent and to impress the opposite on their constituents (in part reflected in the B D relationships shown in Figures 7 and 8), the latter being a phenomenon commonly observed during the course of conflictful negotiations in labor-management and international affairs. Such impression management should, furthermore, be substantially more probable when organization bargaining norms are competitive rather than cooperative, and when the BRP is highly attracted to maintain his organization membership than when he is not. Another method of counteracting distrust generated by visibly friendly relations with the opponent might be to try to achieve visibly high outcomes by aggressive, tough bargaining tactics. However, as suggested in Figure 7, this is likely to elicit reactance by the opponent and, thus, to reduce outcomes to the BRP's organization.

CONCLUSION

The growth of societies places increasing demands on the boundary functions of social units. As the units increase in number, the interactions among them, involving the transfer of energy, goods, services, informa-

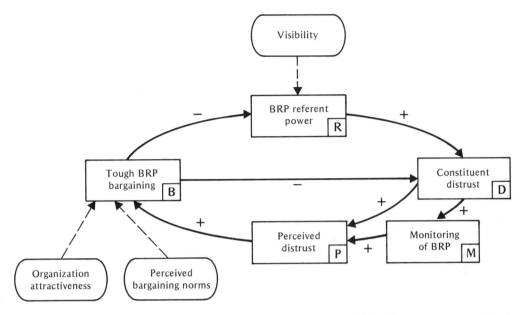

Figure 8. Deviation counteracting mutual causal processes involving BRP referent power, constituent distrust, and other variables. (Refer to Figure 7.)

tion, and other entities, increase exponentially. Better understanding of boundary functions and processes is, therefore, distinctly indicated.

A step toward such understanding was made here by analyzing some of the essential structural properties of boundary transaction systems and the dynamic behavioral processes allied with them. The nature of the structural elements identified and their relationships implied interdependence and interaction. In our research, therefore, we predicted and sought evidence in the form of statistical interactions. This much was deliberate. As evidence for the existence of important, predicted interactions grew, however, it became clear that some variables not only interacted but did so in mutually causative, self-closing cycles that were either deviation amplifying or counteracting over time. Though such processes are not new to psychology or to other sciences, their recognition in the present context is of some importance. First, it suggests a very different approach to organizational psychology than

has typified most work. The essence of organizational psychology is interaction among organization components and between them and the external environment. Thus, not only must interactions among variables be a focus of attention, but a search must be undertaken for those that feed back on themselves. Secondly, the identification of variables interacting in amplifying and counteracting mutual causal processes suggests fertile ground for organizational and social engineering. The best of such activities in the past have been characterized by modification of only one or a few variables. If less than a complete systemic perspective of all major interacting variables is had, the consequences of modification must be uncertain, and in the case of social programs, costly in human terms.

Although the question of organizational intervention has not been discussed, it is not inappropriate to close with a comment on this, albeit in a broader context than the term is traditionally used. In a sense, the only fundamental root for intervention is the systemic perspective of organizational behavior that has been urged. If intervention is successful, however, the very processes that have been examined here will be basically altered. The direction of causal processes may be changed, as may the sign of relationships between variables. In this respect, there is a fundamental distinction between the physical and social sciences as Gergen (1969) has suggested. The results of research in the former disciplines do not affect the phenomena studied by them (although they typically have immense effects on other phenomena). The fruits of research in the social sciences, however, affect the very functions being investigated. Man, as a cognitive organism, alters his behavior as a function of new knowledge about his behavior. His beliefs about economic and psychological processes, for example, may be so altered by the social sciences that the processes are basically altered. A conclusion is inevitable: A systemic perspective of organizational behavior—any behavior—must include that perspective as an element of the system because it shapes some of the behavior in the system.

REFERENCES

Becker, G. M., & McClintock, C. G. Value: Behavioral decision theory. In P. R. Farnsworth et al. (Eds.), *Annual Review of Psychology*. Palo Alto, Calif.: Annual Reviews, 1967, 239–286.

Berrien, F. K. *General and social systems*. New Brunswick, N.J.: Rutgers University Press, 1968.

Deutsch, M., & Krauss, R. M. Studies in interpersonal bargaining. *The Journal of Conflict Resolution*, 1962, 6, 52–76.

Douglas, A. *Industrial peacemakings*. New York: Columbia University Press, 1962.

Druckman, D., Solomon, D., & Zechmeister, K. The influence of negotiator's role and negotiating set on children's distribution of resources. Unpublished manuscript, Institute for Juvenile Research, Chicago, 1970. (Quoted in Gruder & Rosen, 1971.)

Easton, D. *A systems analysis of political life*. New York: Wiley, 1965.

Evan, W. B. The organization set: Toward a theory of interorganizational relations. In J. D. Thompson (Ed.), *Approaches to organizational design*. Pittsburgh: University of Pittsburgh Press, 1966, 177–180.

French, J. R. P. Jr., & Raven, B. H. The bases of social power. In D. Cartwright & A. Zauder (Eds.), *Group dynamics: Research and theory*. (2nd ed.) Evanston, Ill.: Row, Peterson, 1960.

Frey, R. L. Jr. The interlocking effects of intergroup and intragroup conflict on the bargaining behavior of representatives. Unpublished doctoral dissertation, University of North Carolina at Chapel Hill, 1971.

Frey, R. L. Jr., & Adams, J. S. The negotiator's dilemma: Simultaneous in-group and out-group conflict. *Journal of Experimental Social Psychology*, 1972, 4, 331–346.

Gallo, P. S., & McClintock, C. G. Cooperative and competitive behavior in mixed-motive games. *Journal of Conflict Resolution*, 1965, 9, 68–78.

Gergen, K. J. *The psychology of behavior exchange*. Reading, Mass.: Addison-Wesley, 1969.

Goffman, E. *Strategic interaction*. Philadelphia: University of Pennsylvania Press, 1969.

Gross, B. M. *The state of the nation: Social systems accounting*. London: Social Science Paperbacks, 1966.

Gruder, D. L. Effects of perception of opponent's bargaining style and accountability to opponent and partner on interpersonal, mixed motive bargaining. Unpublished doctoral dissertation, University of North Carolina at Chapel Hill, 1968.

Holmes, J. G. The effects of the structure of intragroup and intergroup conflict on the behavior of representatives. Unpublished doctoral dissertation, University of North Carolina at Chapel Hill, 1971.

Kahn, R. L., Wolfe, D. M., Quinn, R. P., Snoek, J. D., & Rosenthal, R. A. *Organizational stress: Studies in role conflict and ambiguity*. New York: Wiley, 1964.

Katz, D., & Kahn, R. L. *The social psychology of organizations*. New York: Wiley, 1966.

Kelley, H. H., & Stahelski, A. J. Social interaction basis of cooperators' and competitors' beliefs about others. *Journal of Personality and Social Psychology*, 1970, 16, 66–91.

Komorita, S. S., & Barnes, M. Effects of pressures to reach agreement in bargaining. *Journal of Personality and Social Psychology,* 1969, 13, 245–252.

March, J. G., & Simon, H. A. *Organizations.* New York: Wiley, 1958.

Maruyama, M. The second cybernetics: Deviation amplifying mutual causal processes. *American Scientist,* 1963, 51, 164–179.

Miller, E. J., & Rice, A. K. *Systems of organization.* London: Tavistock, 1967.

Organ, D. W. Some factors influencing the behavior of boundary role persons. Unpublished doctoral dissertation, University of North Carolina at Chapel Hill, 1970.

Rapoport, A. *Fights, games, and debates.* Ann Arbor: University of Michigan Press, 1960.

Rapoport, A., & Orwant, C. Experimental games: A review. *Behavioral Science,* 1962, 7, 1–37.

Rice, A. K. *The enterprise and its environment.* London: Tavistock, 1963.

Rice, A. K. Individual, group, and intergroup processes. *Human Relations,* 1969, 22, 565–584.

Schelling, T. C. *The strategy of conflict.* New York: Oxford University Press, 1960.

Sherif, M. In common predicament: Social psychology of intergroup conflict and cooperation. Boston: Houghton Mifflin, 1966.

Sherif, M., Harvey, O. J., White, B. J., Hood, W. R., & Sherif, C. W. *Intergroup conflict and cooperation: The robber's cave experiment.* Norman: University of Oklahoma Press, 1961.

Strickland, L. Surveillance and trust. *Journal of Personality,* 1958, 26, 200–215.

Thibaut, J. W., & Kelley, H. H. *The social psychology of groups.* New York: Wiley, 1959.

Thompson, J. D. *Organizations in action.* New York: McGraw-Hill, 1967.

Vidmar, N. Effects of representational roles and mediators on negotiation effectiveness. *Journal of Personality and Social Psychology,* 1971, 17, 48–58.

Vidmar, N., & McGrath, J. E. Forces affecting success in negotiation groups. *Behavioral Science,* 1970, 15, 154–163.

Vinacke, W. E. Variables in experimental games: Toward a field theory. *Psychological Bulletin,* 1969, 71, 293–317.

Wall, J. A. The effects of the constituent's informational environment upon the constituent-boundary role person relationship. Unpublished doctoral dissertation, University of North Carolina at Chapel Hill, 1972.

Wall, J. A. Jr., & Adams, J. S. Some variables affecting a constituent's evaluations of and behavior toward a boundary role occupant. *Organizational Behavior and Human Performance,* 1974, 11, 390–408.

Walton, R. E. *Interpersonal peacemaking: Confrontation and third-party consultation.* Reading, Mass.: Addison-Wesley, 1969.

Walton, R. E., & McKersie, R. B. *A behavioral theory of labor negotiations.* New York: McGraw-Hill, 1965.

CHAPTER 28

Role-Making Processes Within Complex Organizations[1]

GEORGE GRAEN
University of Illinois

THE PARTICULAR WAY a person comes to behave in his or her organizational role may be a function of not only the formal, written job descriptions and other documents of this kind, but also of the events which occur during the period when the person is progressing from the status of "newcomer" in a particular position to that of "established incumbent" in that position. If these role-making processes can be documented as important determiners of role behavior, this would help to explain our rather consistent failures to improve the functioning of complex organizations through changes in the formal, written documents. Moreover, future attempts at organizational renewal would be expected to show higher success rates by incorporating an understanding of role-making processes into change programs.

INTRODUCTION TO ROLE-MAKING SYSTEMS

Organizational members accomplish their work through roles; these roles are sets of behaviors that persons expect of occupants of a position. Organizations frequently divide complex tasks into specialized activities, assigning activities to particular roles, and integrating the outputs of the activities into a final product or service. An organization may operate at an extremely efficient level due to superior technology, advantageous positions in its various input and output markets, and a very appropriate type of role-system for its participants. Consequently, it is of practical as well as theoretical importance to understand the role-making systems within organizations.

Role-making systems are those processes whereby the participant in the organization:

[1] The author would like to thank the following individuals for their contributions to our attempt to understand organizational assimilation: Anice Birge, Jim Cashman, Fred Dansereau, Joan Graen, Bill Haga, Carline Haga, Bill Hoel, Virginia Ingersoll, Chip Johnson, Tom Johnson, Toby Kahr, John Newman, Warren Nielsen, Dean Orris, and Len Slobodin. The author gratefully acknowledges several helpful suggestions on this chapter from Ms. Leaetta Hough, editorial assistant to Marvin D. Dunnette.

(a) acquires knowledge about the content of the constraints and demands placed upon his behavior and the sources of those constraints and demands, (b) receives and sends persuasive communications regarding his behavior in the role, (c) accepts a particular pattern of behavior, and (d) modifies this pattern over time. The role-making system thus determines behavior in terms of the direction and magnitude of energy expended at a given point in time and the changes in expenditures that occur over time.

The determinants of role-making systems can be classified into three major categories: (1) physical-technological systems, (2) social-cultural systems, and (3) person systems (McGrath, Chap. 31, this *Handbook*). For a given role, the physical-technological systems represent the constraints and demands that are imposed by the *accepted* beliefs about those physical and technological systems. Given a specific function to be performed by a person in the focal role, the accepted beliefs about the relevant physical and technological systems may rule out completely a subset of ways to perform that function and may partially order the utility of a number of other ways to perform that function. These beliefs need not be verifiable to serve as mechanisms; they need only be accepted. The canons of engineering, systems design, and operations research are examples of these beliefs.

The social-cultural systems represent the constraints and demands that are imposed by the *accepted* beliefs about the social and cultural systems. As with the physical-technological systems, the social-cultural systems may rule out a subset of ways to perform a given function and may partially order the utility of a number of other ways to perform that function. These beliefs also only need be accepted to be determinants. Legal, ethical, and social norm systems are examples of these beliefs.

Finally, the person systems represent the constraints and demands imposed by the *accepted* beliefs about the person systems that highlight the actor for the role. The person systems may rule out completely one subset of ways and partially order the utility of another subset of ways to perform a given function. As with the other two sets of systems, the person systems need only be accepted. Models of the basic nature of man are examples of these belief systems.

Theoretically, combinations of these three sets of systems should uniquely determine the behavior of a person in a particular role at a given point in time. However, all members of an organization do not necessarily share the beliefs. Several factors complicate the determination process: (a) ambiguity, (b) conflict, and (c) load. For example, a new person in an organizational role may need to acquire knowledge about many relevant beliefs before he can perform in the role. For this new person, the behaviors that are appropriate for his role may be underdetermined and ambiguous for him. The processes that inhibit and enhance the acquisition of this knowledge are part of the role-making system. As we shall see, the mechanisms that channel this knowledge may have a high noise component on both the sending and receiving ends. Even so, clearly communicating this knowledge does not necessarily determine behavior in the role. Instead, the reduction of ambiguity may increase the awareness of conflicting beliefs. The new person may discover that his beliefs are incompatible with those of other participants regarding how he should perform his role. His immediate superior may demand that he perform his role in one way, his colleagues may prefer a second way, and he may prefer a third way. The processes that resolve this potential conflict represent yet another part of the role-making system.

Another complicating factor is loading. The new person has limited capacities to acquire new knowledge to behave in certain ways. When the situation overwhelms these limits, the new person may respond in dysfunctional manners, and avoid these situations in the future. The processes that produce the coping behaviors required to deal with these instances of overload are another part of the role-making system.

A most important complicating factor is that these belief systems change over time. The environments of roles are dynamic and the rate of change is increasing at an astounding rate. As Dunnette (1972) so eloquently stated:

The seventies and beyond will be the *Era of Coping with Transience*. If we succeed, the chances for a better world are good. If we fail, humanity will be rocketed into a crisis of adaptation from which it will not survive, and we will witness (as we may, indeed, be witnessing in microcosm) the total breakdown of adaptation that Toffler refers to as *Future Shock*.

What is the transient society? Primarily, it is change, accelerated beyond the wildest notions, coupled with impermanence throughout society and a loss of any sense of stability. In the words of C. P. Snow, "the rate of change has increased so much that our imagination can't keep up," and according to our colleague, Warren Bennis, "No exaggeration, no hyperbole, no outrage can realistically describe the extent and pace of change. . . . In fact, only the exaggerations appear to be true."

Transience is the temporariness of modern life. It is the impermanence of objects, the nomadic wanderings of people, the fleeting quality of human interactions, the cracking at the seams of organizational bureaucracies, and the kinetic blizzard of information and ideas.

People increasingly are alienated, "turned off," deadened, apathetic in response to change and often unwilling to cope with newness. The atmosphere is laden with words, images, noise, poisons, and dirt. Sensory systems are turning inward, seeking renewal of feeling through drugs or its explosive and unrestrained expression in groups characterized by warmth and support, transient though they may be.

Revered institutions are shattering and breaking down. Religion—as the interaction between man and his personal God—is dwindling. For many, God is indeed dead. The nature of marriage as well as the basic structures of all sorts of personal and organizational commitments are changing wildly. Symptoms include the increasing rates of divorce, liberalized laws governing marital dyads and communes, a breakdown of nationalism, and the rampant turnover and shifting about among companies of college students during the first several years of employment.

People suddenly are becoming aware of the discontinuities of consumption but also of the contaminating effects of our consumption-oriented and still burgeoning population. This, coupled with what amounts to be widespread consumer loss of faith in not only products but also ideas, information, and ultimately, technology, has laid the groundwork for a "people's revolt."

And, finally, our society is witnessing conflict on a massive scale. Our recent history in learning partially to cope with management-labor conflict offers only modest clues for coping with black versus white, old versus young, the power elite versus the power weak, man versus woman, and straight versus hip. (Adapted from Dunnette, 1972)

Why Study Role-Making Systems?

The challenge of transience will demand the invention and utilization of new organizational forms. These new forms will be designed for decisive and immediate adaptation to the contingencies of their environments. As Bennis (1966) has pointed out, survival of organizations in the future will depend upon their ability to cope and adapt to meet the changing demands of their environments. The criteria for evaluating the goodness of organizational designs are undergoing basic revision.

The bureaucratic model of organization that has served rather well until the second half of the twentieth century is becoming increasingly incompatible with our changing environments. This model works best for harnessing routine, predictable human muscle and mechanical energy in situations involving stable environments and a work force that has been socialized to accept the legitimacy of economic coercion.

Although the present dysfunctions of the bureaucratic model are many, the future dysfunctions of this organizational form will probably lead to its demise. The primary characteristic of this organizational form is its *over-determination* of events.

The model assumes that there exists "one best way" of performing any given function. Once this one best way has been accepted, all structures and functions are programmed in detail. Unknowns in the situation are filled by simplifying assumptions: The environments of the organization are assumed to be stable; the complexities of the human participants are simplified through the mechanism of partial inclusion (Katz & Kahn, 1966) in which human participants are required to leave most of their personality outside of the organization.

Machine-like capabilities of the participants are required and only these are allowed expression. Thus, the program is assumed to be complete.

To ensure that only the specified events occur and in the prescribed manner, elaborate control systems are established. Hierarchical and overlapping monitoring and authority systems are devised to produce "fail-safe" and "zero defect" outcomes. Overpowering reward and punishment systems further determine that the details of the program will be performed religiously.

This organizational form by overdetermining behavior in organizations produces machine-like outputs and becomes itself machine-like. Relationships and behaviors crystallize into hardened habit systems that resist modification. Performance tends to narrow and settle on the minimum standards. Only those behaviors specifically prescribed are performed by the participants. Only defensible actions are taken; standard procedure becomes the bible, and change in any aspect of the program meets with resistance. In short, like most single-purpose machines, the organization designed along the lines of the bureaucratic model becomes obsolete with changes in technology and other environmental conditions.

The remainder of this first section of the chapter will be devoted to a discussion of two models of the processes of job or role making in complex organizations: One of these models views the job as a complete and stable entity while the other model views the role as incomplete and dynamic. Throughout this chapter, the terms "job" and "role" will be interchangeable. (Perhaps after more is known about the role-making process an empirically defensible distinction between the two terms can be made.) The next section will present a motivational formulation that seems to be useful in our attempts to conceptualize and investigate the role-making process. Following this section, some empirical work on reward systems as assimilation mechanisms will be presented and discussed. The last part of the chapter will be concerned with generating research questions, devising methods of seeking answers, and attempting to apply these methods to answering these questions about the role-making processes.

Fixed Job Model

Traditional models of organization assume that role-making processes should be designed in the abstract. Only after experts designed these processes were people selected to fill the roles. These established roles were assumed to be fixed and people were required to fit themselves into these roles.

Based upon these assumptions, selection models were devised to select the right man for the job. A modern version of this kind of model is represented by Dawis and Lofquist (1969). According to this model, two matching processes are prescribed at the initial selection stage but no adjustments are prescribed after the person assumes the role. The two matching processes are in terms of the ability to perform the particular job in an adequate fashion and in terms of the adequacy of the job rewards for the person. The optimal situation would be when the person selected possesses both the set of abilities that perfectly *match* those required to perform the job adequately and the set of preferences that perfectly *match* those outcomes inherent in the job.

This model assumes that not only are job situations unchanging over time in terms of required abilities and outcomes, but also that people are stable over time in terms of the abilities and preferences they possess.

After the person has been selected and placed on a particular job, he is expected to fit neatly into the role situation with little or no help from the organization. Difficulties in adjusting to the role, according to this formulation, indicate that the matching procedures were faulty.

The blame for these difficulties in role making rests upon the new person and the selection system.

A usual concomitant of this situation is an acceptance of turnover as a necessary by-product of the selection system. New people who do not fit their roles adequately are rejected from the organization. This completes the cycle of events—selection, fitting, rejection.

The most discouraging aspect of this situation is that the system is prematurely closed. Instead of high turnover leading to attempts to understand and correct the role-making systems, high turnover tends to be accepted as a fact of organizational life. The basic assumptions of this model were not questioned until recently.

A series of studies by Ford (1969) within AT&T has produced some rather dramatic reductions in turnover. A study of telephone service representatives in eight different locations reduced resignations and dismissals by over 13 percent for a six-month period. Moreover, comparing the reduction for special treatment groups to those of the corresponding control groups produced a reduction of over 22 percent in resignations and dismissals.

This special treatment was not an improved selection system. It was an attempt to change the role in significant ways. The jobs of the service representatives were "enriched" by adding new duties and responsibilities—duties and responsibilities that were formerly the sole prerogative of their supervisors. The service representatives were allowed to make decisions regarding credit ratings, amount of deposit, denial of service, and giving of credit without the supervisor's approval. They also were given direct feedback regarding the consequences of their actions without the mediation of their supervisor. In sum, the basic assumption of the fixed job was violated, producing gratifying reduction in the formerly accepted turnover phenomenon.

Another series of studies by Paul and his associates (Paul, Robertson, & Herzberg, 1969) performed in Great Britain also questions the "fixed-job" model. Jobs are being changed in significant ways and apparently producing functional consequences for both organizations and participants. These "enrichment" studies have not focused upon the role-making processes as such. Rather, they have focused upon the impact of radically upgrading jobs by introducing meaningful challenges to people.

These enrichment studies should serve to demonstrate some inadequacies of the fixed-job model with its consequent acceptance of turnover. In addition, the enrichment studies illustrate the need for not only a changing-job model but also for a changing-person model. The over-simplified fixed-job model that assumes that the most fit person will remain in the job by personally surviving can no longer be accepted as useful.

Interpersonal Role-Making Model

Kahn, Wolfe, Quinn, Snoek, and Rosenthal (1964) proposed a role-set model which included some aspects of the role-making systems discussed earlier. According to the interpersonal role-making model, the behavior of a person in his organizational role is a function of role pressures, intrinsic satisfactions, and occupational identity. Other persons who have some vested interest in the way a focal person performs his job exert role pressure. This set of individuals who are interdependent with the focal person are called his "role-set." The role-set attempts to shape the focal person's behavior through the role-episode process. In this role episode, the role-set member sends information about how he prefers the focal person to perform the role and attempts to gain compliance by implying the consequences of acceptance and rejection of this request. The focal person's ensuing behavior indicates compliance or noncompliance, and this is feedback to the role sender regarding the impact of his messages. This completes the role-sending episode. If the behavior is not acceptable to the role sender, he may initiate another episode.

These episodes may continue over the entire role-making period and involve every member of the role-set. In this manner, a complex series of social interactions is assumed to occur that influence the behavior of the person in his organizational role. Important parameters of the role-sending episode are organizational constraints and demands, social and interpersonal factors, and person factors.

This role-set model assumes that the apparent completeness of the initial organizational design is somewhat of a fiction. Indeed, Kahn et al. (1964) in *Organizational Stress* documented the incompleteness of the formal organizational design. In a national sample of employed males, 35 percent lacked

clarity about the scope and responsibility of their jobs and 38 percent lacked enough information to do their jobs adequately.

One of the crucial mechanisms that is assumed to modify the role during the process of assimilating a new member into the organization, in addition to the authority, technological, and workflow demands placed upon the organization by its environment, is the interpersonal exchange relationships between the new role incumbent (member) and his immediate supervisor (leader). Although other members of the new person's role-set can enter the negotiation of the definition of the new person's role, their bargaining tools are limited to informal sanctions. Only the leader is granted the authority to impose formal sanctions to back up his negotiations.

The interpersonal role-making model involves a leader and a member and is shown in Figure 1. According to this model, adapted from Katz and Kahn (1966) discussed above, the leader holds a set of expectations regarding the appropriate role behavior of the member (Role Expectation). The leader communicates his expectations

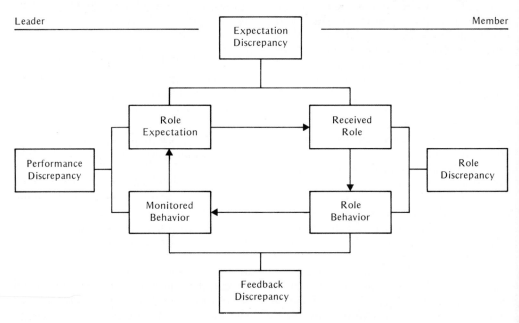

Figure 1. Model of the interpersonal role-making model involving a leader and a member.

to the member through a number of different channels. Although these expectations may be misinterpreted due to noise in the communications process, the member receives and interprets these sent expectations (Received Role). Based partly upon these received roles, the member may modify his role behavior. The feedback to the leader concerning the impact of his sent role is transmitted by the member's role behavior (Monitored Behavior). If the leader interprets the role behavior of the member as sufficiently discrepant from his role expectations, he may decide to communicate this to the member and thus initiate another cycle of events.

Although the Katz and Kahn model specifies a number of complicating factors, the model fails to specify that the member may negotiate with the leader in several manners in addition to resisting the sent roles. An additional means that the member may employ would be to attempt to modify the leader's role expectations directly. In this manner, the member would be conceptualized as an active problem solver in the role-defining process.

The complicating factors that Katz and Kahn refer to include organizational factors, interpersonal factors, and personality factors. Organizational factors refer to the situational characteristics of the role within the organizational matrix. The interpersonal factors refer to the dyadic relationships between the leader and the member. Finally, personality factors refer to the style and preferences of the leader and the member and the compatibility between these two actors.

In the interpersonal role-making model four discrepancy factors make the model amenable to research. None of these four factors would usually be known to both actors. The *expectation discrepancy* is the difference between the role expectation held by the leader and that received by the member. Only an outside observer with access to both sources of information would be in a position to assess this factor. This expectation discrepancy is an index of the noise in the role-sending system. This factor may operate to enhance or inhibit the role-making process depending upon the operation of the interpersonal and personality factors.

Role discrepancy is the difference between what the member perceives to be his leader's role expectations and the member's current role behavior. Only the member and an outside observer usually would have information on this discrepancy. In role terminology, this role discrepancy would be an index of the member's perceived conflict between his and his leader's definition of the role. We would expect this discrepancy to be related to the member's role attitudes.

Feedback discrepancy is the difference between the member's role behavior and the leader's perception of that behavior. Only an outside observer could assess this factor. This feedback discrepancy is an index of noise in the feedback system.

Finally, *performance discrepancy* is the difference between the leader's role expectations and his perception of the member's current role behavior. Usually only the leader and an outside observer would have information on this discrepancy. In role terminology, this discrepancy is an index of perceived conflict between the leader's expectations and his member's role behavior. We would expect this discrepancy to be related to the leader's evaluation of his member's performance.

A SYSTEM FOR INFLUENCING ROLE-MAKING CHOICES

A motivational model that can be integrated with the interpersonal role-making model is the interdependent role-systems model. According to this formulation of the pressures on the organizational member to perform certain role behaviors and not others, role relevant forces are generated by three sets of demands: (1) organizational or situational demands, (2) social or role-set demands, and (3) personal or personality demands. The organizational demands are those demands which are legitimized by the organization through the mechanism of the employment contract. Organizations specify in some detail the obligations of a person who accepts each organizational role. These obligations include the activities that must be performed at some specified level of excellence, various proscriptions and prescriptions relating to organizational rules and procedures, and certain authority relationships to other organizational roles. For employment to begin, an individual must accept these basic role specifications. Once an individual is inducted into an organization, the process of assimilating him into the role-system begins.

Such activities as training, rewarding, and punishing may be part of this process. Finally, after the individual has been integrated into the relevant role-systems, the process of maintaining these systems in a state of balance begins. The maintenance process consists of structuring the reward system of the organization in such a manner that the individual will be rewarded for organizationally defined appropriate role behavior and not for inappropriate behavior. Thus, the organization maintains contingencies between appropriate behavior and its mediated rewards and punishments.

The second set of demands on the role incumbent are the social or role-set demands (Katz & Kahn, 1966). A role set for a particular role incumbent includes all incumbents (excluding his immediate superiors) of roles that are dependent upon his role behavior and have a vested interest in how he performs his role. These other individuals promise or threaten and thereby attempt to influence him to perform his role in a certain manner.

The third and final set of demands on the role incumbent are the personal or personality demands. When the individual joins the organization, he has already experienced an elaborate socialization process. Through this process, the individual has internalized a complex array of beliefs, values, norms, and expectancies about himself and his physical and social environment. These products of socialization are vital to the individual's identity as a person. They serve as psychological buoys in the individual's attempts to cope with unpredictable situations and as landmarks to help locate the often fine lines between: (a) rational and irrational, (b) conformity and independence, (c) ethical and unethical, and (d) healthy and sick.

Thus, placed in an organization, the individual attempts to integrate his organizational role and his personal belief systems. This adjustment process may be quite painful for the individual if the role requires behaviors that are incompatible with the individual's basic beliefs. In extreme cases, this adjustment process fails completely due to the inability to modify adequately either the role demands or the personal demands. In less extreme cases, the individual can integrate the role and personal demands in a satisfactory if not optimum manner. Thus, the individual brings to his organizational role a set of personal demands.

An example of conflict among the three sets of demands is as follows: Suppose that for a particular role we find that nearly all role activities can be represented by six repetitive cycles of behavior: (a) monitoring, (b) learning, (c) communicating, (d) maintaining, (e) planning and decision making, and (f) routine tasks. Further suppose that we observe a role incumbent over an extended period of time and record the amount of time and energy he expends in each of these six behavior cycles. Table 1 shows the results of our observations in terms of the proportions of the total time and energy actually expended on role-related activities. Suppose, also, that we have assessed the role-incumbent's perceptions of the organizational, role-set, and personal demands for each of the six behavior cycles shown in Table 1.

According to Table 1, our role incumbent is faced with conflicting demands from the three sources of pressure. The organization demands 40 percent routine tasks, 20 percent monitoring, 15 percent communicating and planning, and 5 percent learning and maintaining. In contrast, his role-set demands 50

TABLE 1
PROPORTIONS OF TIME AND ENERGY

Behavior Cycle	Organizational Demands U P	Role-Set Demands U P	Personal Demands U P	Actual Expenditure P
Monitoring Events	(0) .20	(0) .05	(5) .05	.05
Learning New Skills	(1) .05	(2) .05	(4) .25	.25
Communicating	(2) .15	(4) .10	(3) .10	.10
Maintaining Structure	(3) .05	(5) .50	(2) .10	.05
Planning and Decision	(4) .15	(3) .10	(1) .30	.15
Routine Tasks	(5) .40	(1) .20	(0) .20	.40
Total	1.00	1.00	1.00	1.00

Note: U is the expected utility of compliance; P is the proportion of total time and energy for organizational activities. Total time and energy for organizational activities is a variable quantity that depends upon the individual's allocation to non-organizational activities. Rating of these proportions may differ among (1) role incumbent, (2) role-set members, (3) other organizational members, and (4) outside observer.

percent maintaining, 20 percent processing, 10 percent communicating and planning, and 5 percent monitoring and learning. Finally, he personally demands 30 percent planning, 25 percent learning, 20 percent routine tasks, 10 percent communicating and maintaining, and 5 percent monitoring. Somehow our role incumbent must cope with these conflicting demands. A motivational formulation that offers some help in our attempts to understand the allocation process is presented in the next section.

Focusing on the Supervisor

To simplify the situation for purposes of discussion, let us consider only the reactions of the immediate supervisor as seen by a particular focal person at one point in time. Let us assume that the focal person sees only two alternative patterns for allocating his time and energy. One of these patterns is preferred by his supervisor over the other pattern. This other pattern might be preferred by the focal's peers. The supervisor legitimately can mediate various organizational outcomes for the focal person. Some of these outcomes may be seen as rewards by the focal person, such as achievement feedback on tasks, recommendations for promotions or increases in salary, praise, and inter-

personal acceptance and support. Others of these outcomes may be viewed as punishments by the focal person, such as interpersonal rejection, admonishment, and recommendations for a salary cut, demotion, or dismissal.

The effective supervisor can be expected to establish a relationship between behavior and outcomes in such a manner that desired behavior leads to the attainment of outcomes viewed as rewarding, whereas undesired behavior leads to outcomes seen as punishments.

One difficulty in establishing such contingencies between behavior and subsequent rewards and punishments is that behavior must somehow be evaluated as desirable or undesirable. The supervisor may decide to use many categories or just a few, but he must use at least two. Whatever categorization system the supervisor selects must be such that he can use it consistently for all of his members at any one point in time and for each of his members over different points in time. Although the supervisor may employ 100 categories in judging the desirability of the role behavior of his members, he may employ as few as two or three gross categories for his distribution of rewards and punishments. He may collapse his 100-category system into three reward and punishment categories such that those members receiving the top third of the rating would be categorized as "winners," those receiving the middle third as "hired-hands," and those receiving the bottom third as "losers." Under this system the supervisor would attempt to give the "winners" the most rewards and the fewest punishments, the "losers" just the reverse, and the "hired-hands" fewer rewards than the winners but more than the losers and fewer punishments than the losers but more than the winners.

If the supervisor employed the above system, one might expect his members to be more attentive to his three-category ratings than to his 100-category ratings. The former system possesses concrete consequences for his members because it serves as the basis for his differential treatment of them. In contrast, the latter system is merely the personal accounting system used to derive the reward and punishment categories. It may make little difference to the members if they are in the 75th or the 85th category of the 100-category system, but it should make a difference if they are "winners" or merely "hired-hands."

If the supervisor sought to maximize the impact of his reward and punishment contingencies on his subordinates' behavior, he would attempt to distribute the available rewards and punishments based upon the personal preferences of his members. For those judged to be "winners," he would attempt to give them the rewards that they personally found most attractive, and for the "losers," he would attempt to give them the punishment that they found least attractive. Equally important, the supervisor would attempt to maintain these contingencies in a consistent and unambiguous manner and to communicate these contingencies to his members.

Instrumentality

The above notions regarding contingency management were derived from Instrumen-tality Theory (Peak, 1955; Rosenberg, 1956; Georgopoulos, Mahoney, & Jones, 1957; Vroom, 1964; Dulany, 1961, 1968; Fishbein, 1967; Graen, 1969). Instrumentality is conceptualized as the relationship a member perceives between an outcome category such as "winner" and the occurrence of other more or less preferred consequences. Like the correlation coefficient, perceived instrumentality ranges from $+1.00$ through 0.00 to -1.00. For example, an instrumentality of $+1.00$ indicates that the member believes that reward must be a consequence of being a "winner"; and instrumentality of -1.00 indicates that he believes that reward cannot be a consequence of being a "winner," and an instrumentality of 0.00 indicates that he sees no relationship between the reward and being a "winner."

In addition to the perceptions of the contingencies between outcome categories and various other outcomes, a second component of the instrumentality formulation is the preference of the member for each of the outcomes. These preferences may be viewed as the relative degree of attraction of various rewards and punishments. Attractions are assumed to vary from high positive values through zero to high negative values. Positive values of attraction indicate preferences for attaining the outcome; negative values indicate the reverse, and a zero value indicates indifference toward attaining the reward or punishment.

According to this instrumentality formulation, the value of an outcome category, such as being classified as a "winner," is a monotonically increasing function of the algebraic sum of the products of (a) the perceived instrumentalities between being a "winner" and the occurrence of various other rewards and punishments and (b) the preferences for these other outcomes. Less formally, the value of being a "winner" depends upon how useful it is seen for achieving rewards and avoiding punishments. Some support for this type of linkage has been provided by Peak and her colleagues (Carlson, 1956; Rosenberg, 1956; Peak,

1960) and by Fishbein and his associates (Anderson & Fishbein, 1965; Fishbein, 1967).

If the supervisor manages effectively, his members should view the performance categories in the following manner: Being rated a "winner" is much more valuable than being rated either a "hired-hand" or a "loser." If the supervisor does not manage properly, the three categories may be viewed by his members as equally valuable (seen as only one category) or viewed as two equally valuable and one different (two categories). Another possibility might be that some of the members can discriminate all three categories while other members can only discriminate two or even one category. Obviously, if only one category is perceived (all three categories have the same value for the member), the contingency between rewards and punishments and behavior is irrelevant, and behavior will not be determined by the reward system.

A final component of the instrumentality model is "expectancy." Expectancy is the subjective probability that performing an act, such as superior effort, will lead to a particular outcome such as attaining the rating of "winner." If the member expects that there is no way he can become a "winner," he probably would not try to achieve this rating. Expectancy is assumed to vary from 0.00 to 1.00. Expectancy of 0.00 indicates a belief that the member has no chance of achieving the rating, and an expectancy of 1.00 indicates that he is certain to achieve the rating. According to this model, expectancy is viewed as moderating the relationship between the value of a category and actual behavior. Desired behavior by the member is not expected unless the outcome category has a high value for the member, and the expectancy (subjective probability) that desired role behavior will lead to this outcome category is high. In addition, the expectancy that less desired behavior also will lead to this reward category should be low.

The Choice

To illustrate the instrumentality model consider the choice facing a particular focal person. As shown in Figure 2, the tendency of a person to perform the supervisor's preferred pattern as opposed to the peers'

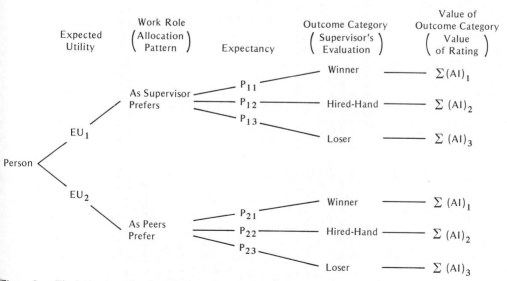

Figure 2. The instrumentality formulation of choice alternatives.

TABLE 2
CALCULATION OF NET VALUES OF EACH OF THREE OUTCOME CATEGORIES

Treatment Actions (Outcomes) by Supervisor (Contingent upon Type of Outcome Category)	Attraction of Treatment Outcomes (A)	"Winner"		Outcome Category "Hired-Hand"		"Loser"	
		(I)*	(AI)₁	(I)*	(AI)₂	(I)*	(AI)₃
Achievement Feedback	5	.5	2.5	−.4	−2.0	−.5	−2.5
Promotion	4	.4	1.6	−.2	−.8	−.4	−1.6
Raise in Pay	3	.3	.9	.0	.0	−.3	−.9
Praise	2	.2	.4	.2	.4	−.2	−.4
Acceptance	1	.1	.1	.4	.4	−.1	−.1
Transfer	0	.0	.0	.5	.0	.0	.0
Rejection	−1	−.1	.1	.3	−.3	.1	−.1
Admonishment	−2	−.2	.4	.1	−.2	.2	−.4
Relative Pay Cut	−3	−.3	.9	−.1	.3	.3	−.9
Demotion	−4	−.4	1.6	−.3	1.2	.4	−1.6
Dismissal	−5	−.5	2.5	−.5	2.5	.5	−2.5
Net Value of Outcome Category			11.0		1.5		−11.0

* I indicates perceived probability (see Editor's Note, footnote 2, p. 1213).

preferred pattern depends upon (1) his perceived value of the role consequences (the sum of the products of attractions and perceived instrumentalities), and (2) the probability that striving for a given rating will lead to being so rated (expectancy). The supervisors' preferred pattern will have a higher probability of being selected by the member to the extent that the expected utility of this pattern is greater than that for the alternative pattern.

An example of how the expected utility estimates could be calculated for a person is as follows: Suppose that the person's preferences (attractions) for various role outcomes are as shown in Table 2. Further assume that the probabilities (instrumentalities)[2] that supervisory ratings (Outcome Categories) would lead to various Treatment Actions are as shown in Table 2. The perceived net value of each Category Outcome for any given person would be the sum of the products between the preference or attraction levels of various Treatment Actions and their corresponding "instrumentality determined" contingent probabilities. In this example, the net values of the Outcome Categories are 11.0, 1.5, and −11.0 for the "winner," "hired-hand," and "loser" categories, respectively. The results of the calculation reflect the assumption that the net value of each Category Outcome depends upon how instrumental it is for attaining other outcomes (Treatments) and the relative attraction of these other outcomes.

The final step in estimating expected utilities of various behaviors or Allocation Patterns requires estimates of the subjective probabilities or Expectancies between each Allocation Pattern and the attainment of each Outcome Category. Suppose that our person estimates the matrix of expectancies (subjective probabilities) shown in Table 3.

Now, we can calculate the expected utilities associated with the two Allocation Patterns as follows:

$$EU_1 = [P_{11} \times \Sigma(AI)_1]$$
$$+ [P_{12} \times \Sigma(AI)_2]$$
$$+ [P_{13} \times \Sigma(AI)_3]$$
$$5.95 = .60 \, (11.0) + .30 \, (1.5)$$
$$+ .10 \, (-11.0)$$
$$EU_2 = [P_{21} \times \Sigma(AI)_1] + [P_{22} \times \Sigma(AI)_2] + [P_{23} \times \Sigma(AI)_3]$$
$$.90 = .20 \, (11.0) + .60 \, (1.5)$$
$$+ .20 \, (-11.0)$$

where:

EU_1 = Expected utility of supervisor's pattern.

P_{11} = Expectancy that supervisor's pattern will lead to the winner category. (See Table 3.)

$\Sigma(AI)_1$ = Net value of the winner category. (See Table 2.)

P_{12} = Expectancy that supervisor's pattern will lead to the hired-hand category. (See Table 3.)

$\Sigma(AI)_2$ = Net value of the hired-hand category. (See Table 2.)

P_{13} = Expectancy that supervisor's pattern will lead to the loser category. (See Table 3.)

---

[2] *Editor's Note:* Instrumentalities are conceptualized as correlation coefficients which may, of course, be converted through regression equations into probabilities. Thus, a person's perceptions of linkages between Category Outcomes and various Treatment Actions are probabilities, ranging from −1.00 to +1.00, derived through regression from the underlying perceived instrumentalities.

TABLE 3
EXPECTANCIES THAT PARTICULAR WORK ROLES
WILL RESULT IN PARTICULAR OUTCOME CATEGORIES

Work Role Allocation Pattern	Outcome Category Expected			Total
	"Winner"	"Hired-Hand"	"Loser"	
As Supervisor Prefers (P_1)	.60 (P_{11})	.30 (P_{12})	.10 (P_{13})	1.00
As Peers Prefer (P_2)	.20 (P_{21})	.60 (P_{22})	.20 (P_{23})	1.00

$\Sigma(AI)_3 =$ Net value of the loser category. (See Table 2.)

$EU_2 =$ Expected utility of peers' pattern.

$P_{21} =$ Expectancy that peers' pattern will lead to the winner category. (See Table 3.)

$P_{22} =$ Expectancy that peers' pattern will lead to the hired-hand category. (See Table 3.)

$P_{23} =$ Expectancy that peers' pattern will lead to the loser category. (See Table 3.)

Within this model, the tendency to perform the Allocation Pattern preferred by the supervisor is predicted to be an increasing monotonic function of the difference between the expected utilities of the two patterns $(EU_1 - EU_2)$. This relative expected utility can vary from high positive through zero to high negative values. Positive values indicate tendencies to perform the supervisor's pattern; negative values indicate the reverse, and zero values indicate tendencies toward neither of the patterns. It should be noted that positive category attraction can be offset by uncertainty and vice versa, and that the expected utilities of both acts must be considered.

Complicating Factors

An additional set of consequences that moderate the relationship between relative expected utility and behavior involves the psychological risks associated with performing each of the alternatives. These psychological risks involve both external and internal forces. The external forces are generated by people other than the supervisor, who, having a "vested" interest in the person's role behavior, attempt to influence him (Katz & Kahn, 1966). These influence attempts place additional contingencies upon the person's behavior in the form of various promised or threatened consequences of compliance or noncompliance, such as gratification, deprivations, and punishments. A further complicating factor is the possibility that these interested others may prescribe competing alternative behavior. In a situation where compliance with one legitimate influence attempt renders compliance with another impossible or impractical, role conflict exists for the person. This conflict, being uncomfortable, will lead the person to reduce it in the least painful manner and to avoid it in the future. In modern organizations that are characterized by a high degree of interdependence, the presence of these external forces is the rule rather than the exception. Therefore, external forces must be recognized as contributors to the psychological risk associated with role behavior.

Another source of psychological risk involves internal forces. These internal forces are embedded in the person's hopes and fears regarding the intrinsic or personal consequences of his role behavior. Some examples of favorable consequences are the personal satisfactions associated with performing the act (e.g., expressing valued abilities and completing challenging tasks) and the satisfaction associated with performing the role behaviors in a preferred manner (e.g., expressing self-determination and independence). In contrast, some examples of unfavorable consequences are fatigue, frustration, threats to both physical and psychological health and well-being, opportunity costs, and possible cognitive inconsistencies. In short, a person has more at stake in his tendency to perform one pattern of behavior rather than another than the expenditure of more or less effort.

Of course, all of these potential risks are not salient for every person and all role behaviors. However, these risks must be recognized as potential determiners of role actualization. Although it would be nice if the determiners of role performance did not include such a complex set of conditions, these conditions must be hypothesized and investigated before we can hope to understand role behavior.

Including all of these considerations, the model can be restated in the following manner:

Role Behavior = (Relative Expected Utility)w_0 + (Resultant External Pressure)w_1 + (Resultant Internal Pressure)w_2

where,

"Resultant External Pressure" is the sum of the perceived amount and direction of external pressure relevant to act_1 relative to that of act_2.

"Resultant Internal Pressure" is the sum of the products of preference and instrumentality for all relevant intrinsic consequences of act_1 relative to that of act_2.

w_0, w_1, w_2 are beta weights of a linear, multiple regression equation that may take any values.

Organizational reward systems can be viewed as critical in the process wherein individuals come to perform the role behavior that the organization prefers. Indeed, a reward system can be viewed as a mechanism through which the individual is assimilated into the organization.

In the following section two studies will be examined which highlight some important characteristics of organizational reward systems as assimilating mechanisms.

STUDIES OF REWARD SYSTEMS AS ASSIMILATION MECHANISMS

Graen (1969) reported a study in which participants, working at similar temporary jobs in the same organization, worked under different reward systems. Three different reward systems were investigated. The first reward system consisted of merely monitoring individual performance and providing feedback to participants (control group). The second reward system included the first and emphasized effective performance by giving a pay increase as an incentive for future continued effectiveness (obligation group). The rationale for this second reward system was that participants might be grateful for the pay increase and feel obligated to continue to earn that pay increase. The third reward system included the first and emphasized effective performance by giving achievement feedback and offering future achievement feedback contingent upon future effective performance (contingency group). The rationale for this third reward system is that it yields a predictable system for participants. If the contingencies between performance and rewards are established and maintained by the organization in an unambiguous manner, participants can predict rather accurately the consequences of their performance and in a sense achieve some control over their payoffs.

The participants, who were 169 women, worked at computer-related, clerical tasks for two days. The tasks involved extracting specified bits of information from a huge matrix of numbers on computer tape. A single best method of performing each task was emphasized during the skill acquisition activities. This was considered the role behavior the organization preferred.

The reactions of the participants under the three reward systems, although working at the same tasks, at the same time, in the same room, and under the same conditions, were rather different. (See Table 4.) The participants who worked under the "Obligation" reward system showed higher satisfaction with their salary than participants working under either the "Contingency" reward system or the "Control" reward system. Those persons working under the "Contingency" system demonstrated higher satisfaction with their achievement feedback and the recognition they received than those working under the other two systems.

The participants working under the three reward systems also differed regarding their estimates of the instrumentality of their organizational role. Those working under the Contingency system felt their organizational role was more instrumentally related to the attainment of achievement

TABLE 4
**REACTIONS OF PARTICIPANTS TO THE DIFFERENT
ORGANIZATIONAL REWARD SYSTEMS**

Organizational Reward System	Satisfaction with Role Outcomes	Instrumentality of Role Performance	Value of Role Performance
Contingency System Monitoring and Feedback of Individual Performance AND Explicit Emphasis on Excellence and its Contingencies	*Achievement Feedback **Recognition Salary	**Achievement Feedback **Recognition **Human Relations Salary	*Achievement Feedback *Recognition *Policies and Practices *Working Conditions Salary
Obligation System Monitoring and Feedback of Individual Performance AND Explicit Emphasis on Salary Increases as Incentives for Future Performance	Achievement Feedback Recognition **Salary	Achievement Feedback Recognition Human Relations *Salary	Achievement Feedback Recognition Policies and Practices Working Conditions Salary
Control System Monitoring and Feedback of Individual Performance ONLY	Achievement Feedback Recognition Salary	Achievement Feedback Recognition Human Relations Salary	Achievement Feedback Recognition Policies and Practices Working Conditions Salary

 * Significantly higher at $p < .05$
** Significantly higher at $p < .01$

feedback, recognition, and personal treatment than persons working under either of the other two systems. Those working under the Obligation system saw their role as having higher instrumentality for the attainment of pay increases than did those under the other two systems.

The value of role performance also showed differences among the three reward systems. Only those under the Contingency system perceived high overall value for role performance. In terms of the initial rationale for the Contingency system, the reactions of the participants under this system appear to be compatible. That is, the relationship between role performance and the rewards became more predictable for the participants. As a consequence of these more predictable relationships, participants viewed role performance as more instrumental in gaining preferred outcomes than those under the other systems. Moreover, they valued the role performance more than persons in either the contingency group or control group.

Effective Performer Model

The effective performer model predicts that role performance is a function of the beliefs of the role incumbent. Role incumbents are expected to perform well to the extent that they believe that role performance will lead to highly desired payoffs, whereas poor performance will not. An important factor in this model is the link between performance and the payoff (expectancy). Unless this link can be established and maintained, the effective performer model simply does not apply.

Results from the Graen (1969) study discussed above support the effective performer model. Estimates derived from the model were similar to the actual overall role satisfaction of the participants under all three systems: Contingency (.61), Control (.43), and Obligation (.22). However, actual overall role satisfaction can be influenced by a large number of variables from outside of the situation, such as those things that a participant may bring to the role. One way to partial out the impact of these outside influences and thereby focus more directly on the impact of the reward system is to consider only those changes that occur within the organization beginning at a time immediately before the reward system is established until a time somewhat after that system has been put into effect (Harris, 1963). In this manner each participant can serve as his own control. If we consider only these changes for the participants, the correlations between the estimates of the effective performer model and the actual changes over time (improvements) are shown in Table 5. Thus, even though the correlations between predicted and actual overall role satisfaction showed significant relationships under all three conditions, the correlation between the predicted and the improvement in overall role satisfaction showed significant relationships for only those under the Contingent (.46) and the Control (.23) systems and not for those under the Obligation (.02) system.

The improvements in role performance were predicted by the effective performer model with differential accuracy for the three reward systems. Only under the Contingency system were the relationships significant between the estimates of the model and the actual improvements in performance. Neither the Control nor the Obligation system produced other than near-zero relationships.

This study demonstrated that the effec-

TABLE 5
CORRELATIONS BETWEEN THE PREDICTIONS OF THE
EFFECTIVE PERFORMER MODEL AND THE ACTUAL OUTCOMES

Organizational Reward System	Overall Role Satisfaction		Improvement in Role Performance	
	Actual	Improvement	Task A	Task B
Contingency System Monitoring and Feedback of Individual Performance AND Explicit Emphasis on Excellence and its Contingencies	.61**	.46**	.35**	.43**
Obligation System Monitoring and Feedback of Individual Performance AND Explicit Emphasis on Salary Increases as Incentives for Future Performance	.22*	.02	−.12	.05
Control System Monitoring and Feedback of Individual Performance ONLY	.43**	.23*	.08	.04

NOTE: Improvement (residual gains) scores are the post-treatment scores with the pretreatment scores partialled out.
* $p < .05$
** $p < .01$

tive performer model can account for some changes (improvements) in role performance. Under the Contingency reward system, changes in role performance were partly a function of the instrumentalities of role performance and the expectancy that the increased expenditure of effort on the task would lead to more effective performance (the Effective Performer model). When feedback linked role performance with the valued payoffs as seen by the participants, improvements in role performance occurred. Moreover, perceived instrumentalities were responsive to the content of feedback. This suggests that the value of the various payoff positions can be modified by the organization by manipulating perceived instrumentalities.

For a review of the research on instrumentality models, see Mitchell and Biglan (1971) and Miner and Dachler (1974).

Piece Rate versus Hourly Rate

Pritchard, Dunnette, and Jorgenson (1972) report on a study designed to assess the behavior of participants on a temporary job working under two different reward systems. One reward system based pay directly upon measured performance (piece-rate system). The other reward system based pay upon role incumbency and minimum acceptable performance (hourly rate system). Special efforts were made to ensure nearly identical conditions for all participants with the single exception of the reward system. The tasks involved processing catalog orders for a retail department store.

Differences in the performance of the participants under the two different reward systems emerged after only three days. Those participants working under the piece-rate system consistently narrowed their output to the cutting points of the pay system. The piece-rate system contained the following cutting points:

(a) Below 16 units per hour, the pay was, say, $.08 per unit;

(b) From 16 to 22 units per hour, the pay was, say, $1.60 per hour;

(c) From 23 to 29 units per hour, the pay was, say, $2.00 per hour;

(d) Over 29 units per hour, the pay was, say, $2.40 per hour.

The cutting points were 16, 23, and 30 units per hour. Output above each of these cutting points, but below the next higher cutting point, merited no additional compensation and apparently the participants working under this system learned these contingencies rather quickly. The average number of units produced per hour above these cutting points but below the next higher cutting point was 1.75 for the first day, .63 for the second day, and .36 for the third day.

Those working under the flat hourly rate tended to increase the number of units that they produced per hour over the first three days. The average number of units per hour that they produced was 16.21 for the first day, 19.29 for the second day, and 20.42 for the third day. In addition, those participants working under the piece-rate system showed less positive evaluations than those under the hourly system regarding the overall situation and particularly the work itself, the pay system, and their fellow participants even during the very first day on the job.

At the beginning of the fourth day, the reward systems were changed for the participants. Those who had worked under the hourly system were placed under the piece-rate system and vice versa. The group that was now on the piece-rate system also tended to learn the contingencies quickly. Their performance tended to converge just slightly above the cutting points. The average number of units per hour above the cutting points, but below the next higher cutting point, was 1.03 the first day, .65 the second day, and .67 the third day under the piece-rate system. The group that was now on the hourly rate system showed no increase in performance over the three days on the hourly system; indeed, their performance decreased. The average number of units per hour for this group was 20.19 for the first day, 18.87 for the second day, and 17.72 for the third day. Moreover, on the very first day of the change in reward systems, compared with those now on the hourly rate, those on the piece rate for the first time showed less positive evaluation of the overall situation and especially the pay system and their organizational supervisors.

However, the average hourly performance of the participants under the two reward systems demonstrated a clear superiority for the piece-rate system over the hourly rate system. The group working under the piece-rate system consistently produced at a much higher level throughout the period than the group working under the hourly rate system. If the performance trend for the piece-rate system were called "outstanding" performance, the trend for the hourly rate would be merely "moderate" performance. This superiority of the piece-rate system was maintained over the entire six days even though the groups were changed after the third day. After the reward systems were exchanged between the two groups, the average performance on the fourth day showed dramatic shifts from the third day. The group newly assigned to the piece-rate system demonstrated a sharp improvement in performance to a level close to that of the former group under the piece-rate system. In contrast, a corresponding decrease was shown in the performance of the group newly assigned to the hourly system.

The effect of the reward system was clearly to increase the expenditure of effort of the participants. This was shown by the over time results and the shifts in performance corresponding to the changes in the reward systems. Even though the participants reacted affectively less favorably to the piece-rate system, they obviously expended more effort in response to its contingencies.

This study illustrates that reward systems can produce rather immediate and signifi-cant differences in the behaviors of participants. By insuring that other factors in the work setting are similar for all participants and varying only the reward system, this design allows us to assess the effects of the reward mechanism. Although this study did not produce the necessary information to allow us to understand the complete dynamics of these reward mechanisms, the results do suggest that different reward systems can influence expectancy and hence performance.

In future studies, organizational assimilation studies might seek to determine the relative contribution of other factors associated with reward systems. Some of these factors might be associated with the reward system itself (e.g., arbitrary cutting points with empty intervals or the machine-model of man that the piece-rate system implies), and some of the factors might be associated with alternative methods of establishing and maintaining the reward systems (e.g., arbitrary, fixed systems or participative, negotiated systems). Equally important, the interactions between these factors and other aspects of the ongoing enterprise should be repeatedly assessed over time (e.g., role conflicts, role ambiguities, and role loads of the participants from various sources and concerning several content areas).

Although these two studies clearly showed the impact of various reward systems on the attitudes and behavior of newcomers into organizations, both studies focused on the expenditure of effort in role performance. While this interest in the expenditure of effort is deeply rooted in previous research and theory in psychology, the directional component of motivation is also relevant to organizational behavior. If the major defining characteristic of organizational behavior is its functional interdependence (March & Simon, 1958), the behavior of participants must be coordinated such that their products can be integrated in efficient and effective manners. On a highly interdependent set of tasks, it may not be functional for a subset of the team to be expending a great deal of effort in order to produce at a high rate while the remaining members are overwhelmed with that output.

RESEARCH QUESTIONS REGARDING ROLE-MAKING PROCESSES

Organizations must recruit and select persons to perform the patterns of behavior that produce the outputs that justify their continuance. For most organizations, the available human talent is sufficiently differentiated through genetic endowment and environmental modification that some minimal activity to seek out and acquire certain people is believed to be worth the effort. Although the criteria for selecting the right people are often open to question, the belief that certain people can make significantly higher contributions to the organization than certain other people is so strong that recruitment and selection activities are deeply embedded in the fabric of almost all organizations.

Most of our systematic knowledge concerning these recruitment and selection processes has been derived from the organization's frame of reference. A vast literature on the *techniques* of recruitment and selection exists; however, little is known about the *processes* of recruitment and selection even from the organization's point of view (Campbell, Dunnette, Lawler, & Weick, 1970).

Technique development primarily is concerned with discovering the "one best" procedure for a specified situation. In contrast, process investigation is concerned primarily with discovering the critical events that modify the outcomes during the ongoing episode. The ongoing phenomena, the understanding and description of the *process of becoming,* seem more important.

One consequence of focusing on processes rather than techniques is the realization that processes involving the organizational assimilation of human participants can be understood fully only by considering the changing situations from the vantage points of each of the actors. Taking only the point of view of the organization's representative and not that of the recruit while attempting to investigate the inducement function must lead to a one-sided and incomplete understanding of this process.

Consider the inducement process. From the organization's perspective this represents the recruitment process. In contrast, from the recruit's frame of reference it is essentially a process of self-presentation. This process should answer different important questions for each party. For the organization's representative the recruit usually attempts to convey the image of his potential contribution in the most glowing terms. Similarly, the organization's representative attempts to portray the organization in the "best" light. The interaction between these two "sales" representatives can be characterized in most cases as a mutual attraction process. The recruit attempts to divine the type of person that the organization is seeking and to present his image in such a manner that he uniquely suits the model. On the other side, the organization's representative attempts to infer the kind of position the recruit is seeking and to present the available position(s) in a way to offer at least the *opportunity* for the realization of this sought position.

Although this process represents the initial exchange between the new recruit and the organization and may provide the bases for an entire set of expectations and attitudes concerning the organization, very little is known about this process. Several questions regarding the functions and dysfunctions of this process can and should be asked: Does the source and/or content of organizational aggrandizement produce unrealistic expectations from the participants? To what extent is the induction process based upon the "probable future" as opposed to the "relatively certain present" in terms of the behaviors and outcomes of the recruit and the organization? Would periodic reality testing be helpful within this process?

Once both the recruit and the organization share a reciprocal interest, the process of opting is activated. From the organization's frame of reference, this is called the selection process. In contrast, from the recruit's frame of reference it is a negotiating process. This opting process answers a set of questions for each party. The organization must decide whether or not the recruit has the potential to more than compensate for the costs incurred by the organization. Similarly, the recruit must decide whether or not the organization has the potential to more than compensate for the costs incurred by the individual.

Although this process is usually characterized from the organization's point of view as the organization selecting from among the willing suitors, an opting process often is the more critical frame of reference. If the selection process is the only frame of reference considered, the resultant procedures might alienate and/or drive away the best recruits. The overemphasis on the organization's point of view at the expense of that of the recruit can cost the organization dearly in terms of losing high potential people who are apt not to join the organization and by alienating recruits who do join the organization.

Another possible consequence of the overemphasis on the organization's frame of reference is that the bargaining process between the organization's representative and the recruit is not given its due attention. This initial interaction probably provides the bases for many expectations and attitudes of each part. Unfortunately, this critical process of establishing the terms and conditions of the relationship between the recruit and the organization tends to be ignored. Indeed, the myth that the organization through some objective procedure unilaterally establishes and faithfully maintains an equitable reward structure for all its par-

ticipants is reinforced in the literature. Thus the nature as well as the outcomes of these negotiations should be understood to enhance its functions and minimize its dysfunctions for both parties.

Role Defining

Once the recruit opts to accept the organization's initial demands and promises and the organization accepts those of the recruit, the recruit is assigned the status of a new incumbent of what is usually a partially defined organizational role within an ongoing unit. The significance of the other members of the unit for the new incumbent will depend partially upon the degree of functional interdependence within the unit. This significance can vary from no significance—the rare situation where the new incumbent has complete autonomy and independence of action and consequence and where no other participant has any vested interest in how he performs his role—to critical significance—the situation where the new incumbent is completely interdependent with the other participants in his unit in terms of both actions and consequences.

Beginning with the introduction of the new incumbent into his role situation, the realities of the situation increasingly modify and elaborate the "promise" and the probabilities of those promises occurring. The new incumbent begins to learn about his role situation in terms of immediate assignments and expected behavior patterns. He begins to receive communications from a variety of fellow participants implying expected behaviors from him. Through these communications, the new incumbent gradually identifies the set of participants who have a vested interest in his role behavior. This set usually includes the organization's formal representatives—his immediate supervisor and perhaps his supervisor's boss. Moreover, this set usually will include at least some other participants who work closely with him—some of his peers both within and outside of his unit and his sub-ordinates if he has any. The impact of these other participants on the new incumbent depends upon both their dependence on him and his dependence on them and the means available to each party to communicate demands and to influence compliance.

If we assume for the moment that the new incumbent is adequately interdependent in the above sense with the organization's representative (his immediate supervisor) and a group of other participants who share a fairly homogeneous set of expectations regarding the new incumbent's role behavior (his interdependent others), the notion that only *one* frame of reference exists for the organization is too simplistic.

In the event that the role expectations of the interdependent others split into two conflicting sets, we would want to add additional frames of reference (Getzels & Guba, 1954; Gross, Mason, & McEachern, 1958).

Considering the role-defining process from the organization's frame of reference, the process should answer the question of how the new personality can be fitted into the established patterns of work behavior. What is he really like? What are his behavior potentials, temperaments, attitudes, and expectations? Which of his characteristics are compatible with established patterns of role behavior? Which are incompatible? A basic part of this process might be one of cognitive incorporation. The organization's representative must construct a model of the new incumbent that will serve as a basis for the organization's relations with and treatment of the person. That this process is subject to the biases of the superior has been described by McGregor (1960, 1967). Moreover, the dysfunctions of these biases can handicap and dehumanize an organization. The significance of Theory X and Theory Y is not that superiors have vastly different models of subordinates' basic natures. On the contrary, they are significant because these models distort the process by which superiors come to understand their subordinates and consequently how they relate to

their subordinates. In this manner, Theory Y may be as dysfunctional as Theory X. If the subordinate is best characterized by the Theory X model, treating him as a Theory Y person could be as depersonalizing as the reverse. In short, the organization must perceive its participants as accurately as possible and the role-defining process should be designed to serve this function faithfully.

From the frame of reference of the role set or the group of interdependent others, this aspect of role defining should answer the question of how this new personality can be integrated into the established patterns of interpersonal relations. What should be his social status? What kind of a person is he? Moreover, from the new incumbent's point of view, the process should answer the question of how he can integrate his personality into both the working (organizational) and interpersonal (social) relations that are currently established. He must learn not only the locations of the johns, but also his prescribed role in both the working and interpersonal patterns. He must begin to understand how events occur in the situation and his role in these events. In short, he must learn who the people are, what they are, and where and when they make a difference with respect to his role.

Most organizations provide some minimal activity to provide some answers to these questions. These activities are called orientation and training programs. The content of the information communicated during these activities usually consists mainly of things the organization thinks the participant should know: information on the organization's benefit programs, public relations material on the goodness of the organization, and a lengthy list of rules, admonitions, and the consequences of rule violation.

Unfortunately, the usual orientation and training programs are one-way communications systems that fail to define much of the role. Thus, much of the role explication is left to the new incumbent and his superiors and peers, without the benefit of formal organizational assistance. Moreover, the nature of the information required to construct valid or even workable replicas is usually inhibited by norms concerning information exchange during day-to-day work activities. However, the superior must construct at least a partial replica of the new incumbent to be used as a basis for working relationships. In addition, the other participants will construct their replicas of the new person to be used as a basis for interpersonal relationships. Possibly of greater import, the new incumbent must construct replicas of his organizational role vis-à-vis his organizational superior, and his organizational role vis-à-vis his significant others. Although these replicas need not be perfectly valid constructs, they must at least provide a basis for inferring workable relationships (Graen, Dansereau, & Minami, 1972). Without benefit of such replicas, one is faced with all of the difficulties of working with a stranger. In interdependent situations, where the quality of one's work is dependent upon the quality of another's work and the integration of these products, working with a stranger simply will not do.

Closely dependent upon the progress of this first aspect is a second aspect of the role-defining process. This second aspect should answer the question of how the new incumbent will modify the established patterns of both role behavior and interpersonal relations. In this process, the new incumbent may modify the established behavior patterns and may have his own behavior patterns modified. This adaptation process can vary from the situation where the new incumbent is forced into the pre-established behavior patterns (a maximum of accommodation and a minimum of manipulation on the part of the new incumbent) to the situation where the new incumbent modifies the situation to suit his personality (a minimum of accommodation and a maximum of manipulation by the new incumbent).

The basic process involved can be characterized as negotiated role definition. Pressures are exerted and counter-pressures generated to somehow shake the interdependent unit into a differentiated yet coordinated system. Pressures to reestablish previous normal patterns of behavior may simply overwhelm the new incumbent. However, the new incumbent may modify the pre-established order to enhance his own potentials. Although this negotiation process may be threatening to all participants, it may also establish a pattern of behavior that could correct inequities in the previous pattern. New working relationships may prove more productive and desirable than the old. New interpersonal relations and coalitions may be superior to the old. Though some may lose in the process, others may gain. Although change at first blush is often threatening, once the process begins, the inherent promise of improvement helps to sustain the activity.

During this negotiation process someone, perhaps everyone, in an interdependent unit must give and take. Somehow, the new incumbent (a complete open system) must become part of a larger system. He may be forced to simply fill a programmed slot in the pattern of activities, or he may force a complete reorganization of the unit.

From the frame of reference of the organization's representative and the immediate superior, the new incumbent is viewed traditionally as merely an interchangeable component in the system. Thus, the new incumbent should be made (selected, oriented, trained, rewarded, and/or punished) to fit the slot. However, to accomplish this fitting, one must ignore most of the individual's personality demands. The unintended consequences of this procedure will provide material for sociological theses for a long time to come (Merton, 1940; Selznick, 1949; Gouldner, 1954).

From the new incumbent's frame of reference, he may conform to the traditional view of himself and simply accept being fit into a pre-established slot, or he may reject the traditional view of himself and struggle to modify his pre-established role (Ziller, 1964, 1965). If the new incumbent is encouraged to modify his role, what will be the consequences for him and the other participants in his unit? What will be the nature of the process by which a new order is worked through? Can this process be understood and facilitated? If so, by whom?

The role-defining function is perhaps the most critical one for all participants. During this process, the new patterns of work and social behavior become established (Lieberman, 1956). Questions of who does what, when, how, and with respect to whom are answered. This process completes the organization's incomplete program for the unit. In this way, the organization's plan or design for the unit becomes operational.

Unfortunately, this role-defining process may be quite painful for the new incumbent; he may fail completely due to an inability to modify adequately either his personal demands or the organization's demands. However, the role-defining process may move toward establishing a new order, even in spite of the protests of the new incumbent. The question of whether or not this negotiation process necessarily must be a win-lose competition or a zero-sum game must be asked. Moreover, what is the role of unequal social power in this process? Does the process of unequal power necessitate the win-lose competition? If we somehow equate the social power of the participants during the adaptation process, can the participants be assisting in establishing a pattern that will be satisfactory or better from each of the frames of reference? If so, how can this be accomplished?

Contribution Function

The contribution process addresses the extent to which an incumbent seeks to realize his potential or unique capabilities within the organizational context (Katz, 1964). From the new incumbent's frame of reference, he seeks to impose some of his identity on his role. In other words, the new incumbent seeks to make his mark on his role.

In contrast, the organization seeks to minimize the unique contribution of its participants by maintaining standardized roles.

To maintain standardized roles, the organization depersonalizes its rules by requiring that new incumbents express *only* specified potentials. Roles are filled by incumbents, not personalities, and incumbents are treated as partial personalities by the organization. This *fiction* tends to perform the function of maintaining the standardized nature of organizational roles which can be filled by interchangeable incumbents. In this manner, the problem of replacing personnel can be minimized. According to this fiction, one does not replace a personality, but only an incumbent. Fitting an incumbent into a programmed role is relatively simple compared with the task of fitting a personality into that same role. The optimum situation, according to this fiction, would be for the new incumbent to bring only his role-specified potentials into the organization, leaving his residual personality at the front gate.

From the role-set point of view, a similar fiction is maintained. Other interdependent participants seek stable and predictable relations with the new incumbent. Thus, the new incumbent is ascribed a given social status and assigned a social role within the pattern of interpersonal relationships. This particular status and role is maintained by social pressures of various sorts. Deviations from this social role have certain consequences for the new incumbent and in extreme cases, the social role of the new incumbent may be as depersonalizing as his organizational role. Hopefully, the new incumbent can modify both the organizational role and the social role.

The contribution process can be characterized as bargaining. The bargaining between the new incumbent and the organization's representative includes the exchange of time and effort for organizational influence. The immediate superior trades legitimate influence (of which the organization has a monopoly) for behavior of the new incumbent over and above that specified by the employment bargain. Examples of such behaviors are the following: (a) expending unusual amounts of time and energy at critical periods, (b) producing exceptionally high quality work on certain vital projects, (c) intervening in interpersonal conflicts to cool emotionally disruptive situations within the unit, (d) doing things designed to make the supervisor look good in the eyes of his superiors, and (e) performing various protective acts to keep the unit from looking bad. These behaviors and many more are not required as a condition of employment, but they could prove to be the difference between success and failure for the unit (Katz, 1964).

During the contribution process, the new incumbent and his immediate superior strike a bargain regarding the nature and frequency of these extra-role behaviors that the new incumbent will perform and the content and extent of latitude the superior will grant the new incumbent in exchange. Tannenbaum's notions (1962) regarding an expanding influence pie rather than a fixed influence pie seem relevant. Under what conditions and during what kind of process does the expanding influence pie situation hold?

Regarding the social role, a similar exchange process takes place. The new incumbent exchanges behaviors designed to enhance the status, cohesiveness, and relationships of his role set relative to those of other groupings (Jones & Jones, 1964). His interdependent others reciprocate with idiosyncrasy credit (Hollander, 1964). In this way, the new incumbent is allowed to deviate and thus modify his social role. In a sense, in exchange for his contributions he is given greater latitude in what is socially acceptable behavior for him.

Involvement

Another set of questions that must be answered concerning the new incumbent in the organization concerns the extent of his ideological involvement in the organization. From the new incumbent's frame of reference, he seeks to answer the extent to which he can identify his vocation within the ide-

ology of the organization. The nature of this involvement process can be characterized as one of conversion. Although both the organization's representatives and the interdependent others play critical roles in this process, the relationships have less of an exchange nature than of a supportive nature. The superior must convince the new incumbent, by his example as well as by his treatment of the new incumbent, that the organization deserves the commitment of its participants. Not only must the superior feel this commitment but he must also treat the new incumbent in a manner that communicates that the organization does indeed take care of its own. In addition, other participants must reinforce this conception of the organization as an instrument of societal value. The organization must have a mission that overwhelms individual and special interest group goals.

Although this involvement process can possibly produce the greatest and most enduring changes in human behavior within organizations, we know very little about it. We can identify organizations that have achieved this "we-feeling" among its participants and even a few that have lost it; however, we do not understand the phenomenon.

In the above sections we have asked many questions. In the next section we will discuss methods which may help in the search for answers.

METHODOLOGICAL ISSUES IN ROLE-MAKING RESEARCH[3]

Concrete Behavior Setting

Most studies purporting to investigate behavior in organizations fail to adequately describe, much less explore, the parameters of the "concrete" setting in which the behavior of interest occurs. Instead, studies

---

[3] Portions of this section were presented at the Academy of Management in Atlanta, August, 1971. The intellectual contributions of Marvin D. Dunnette to this section are manifestly acknowledged.

are typically designed to gather data relevant to some abstract hypothesis or model and often the hypothesis of interest does not include statements concerning the conditions under which the phenomenon should operate. Moreover, the study design usually does not employ procedures for assessing the "concrete" behavior setting in much detail. Indeed, the description of the "concrete" setting is frequently the perceptions and beliefs of the interested participants.

Consequently, these studies cannot produce information relevant to the establishment of boundary conditions for the hypothesis or model. If the results of the study are compatible with the hypothesis or model, the results are simply tallied on the support side of the ledger. If the results are incompatible, the tally is sometimes placed on the negative side of the ledger. The reviewer who attempts to integrate the results of a series of these studies is faced with a frustrating task. Usually no consistent pattern of relationships can be found because information about the concrete setting for each study is not sufficiently detailed or has not been collected in any systematic fashion. Examples of this unfortunate state of affairs are the research on the relationship between employee attitudes and employee performance (Brayfield & Crockett, 1955; Herzberg, Mausner, Peterson, & Capwell, 1957; Vroom, 1964) and the research on the relationship between leadership styles and leadership performance (Anderson, 1966; Campbell, Dunnette, Lawler, & Weick, 1970; Graen, Alvares, Orris, & Martella, 1970; Korman, 1966; Vroom, 1964).

We are not simply proposing that more variables be assessed in empirical studies but that greater attempts be made to understand the concrete setting for the behavior under investigation. The understanding of the concrete setting deserves as much research attention as the particular phenomenon under investigation. The literature on demand characteristics, experiment effects, and unintended consequences of laboratory research has important implications for research on behavior in organizations. These alternative explanations for the results of laboratory studies imply that the concrete behavior setting of the laboratory has not been researched adequately. Before a researcher can clearly interpret the results of his laboratory experiment, he must have a good understanding of his concrete setting. If this is required for the simplified concrete setting of the laboratory experiment, the requirement applies doubly to the complex settings in organizations (see Runkel & McGrath, 1972).

In some respects, the task of the researcher in attempting to understand the concrete setting of his study is very similar to that of the new person who accepts a participant role in that setting. Both must acquire knowledge concerning the source and content of constraints and demands upon behavior from the various sets of systems: physical-technological systems, social-cultural systems, and person systems. Both must seek to assess the operations of ambiguity, conflict, load, and change in the setting. A main difference between the task of the new person and that of the researcher is that the new person must live in the concrete setting while the researcher only visits the setting.

This difference between visiting and residing may have important consequences for researchers in organizations. Unless the researcher can convince the participants in the study that he understands and accepts the obligations of his visitor status, full cooperation may not be given to the researcher. In a real sense, to be granted full cooperation by the participants, the researcher must himself go through a role-making process in interaction with the participants. As sociologists have been saying for years, to understand human behavior in organizations, we must study them from both the inside as well as the outside as concrete settings.

Our current fixation with "steady state" or present state research is not likely to produce understanding of the role-making systems. Although the usual situation within organizations may be a state of relative stability (steady state), knowledge about the role-making systems that can lead to prescriptive recommendations and successful interventions must be derived from longitudinal studies of the role-making systems in operation. These role-making systems would be expected to be activated when a significant disruption of the ongoing pattern of activity occurs, such as a new person joining a unit or a change in role assignments.

Needed are research designs that explore and test these systems over the complete cycle of events, that select the research settings that promise to produce measureable outcroppings of the role-making systems in operation, that attend equally to the concrete setting and role-making systems, that explore, monitor, probe, and test these systems over their entire cycle of activity.

Closed System

Argyris (1970) has attacked what he labels "rigorous research" on organizations. He implies that rigorous research can be characterized as a fairly routinized and predictable set of activities. Moreover, the rigorous research model assumes that the exploration of the unknown can be most efficiently mapped through a set of standard operating procedures. According to Argyris, the standard procedures for rigorous research are the following: First, the researcher explores the relevant literature and consults with knowledgeable colleagues. Second, the researcher organizes his ideas into a conceptual framework, defines them conceptually and operationally, and logically derives his hypotheses. Third, the researcher selects his research site, his research instruments, and his sampling design. The procedures for developing instruments, and sampling designs, we are told, are clearly detailed in books on research methods. Fourth, a pretest is conducted. Fifth, the data are collected and analyzed statistically. Again, the procedures for performing these activities are available in books on research design.

We are told that the emphasis in "rigorous research" is upon "(1) clearly defined objectives, (2) rationality, (3) simplification and specialization, and (4) direction and control." These are some of the defining characteristics of a bureaucratic organization. Thus Argyris predicts that the consequences of rigorous research will be similar to those of the bureaucratic organization. Some of these unintended consequences are (1) physical withdrawal, (2) psychological withdrawal, (3) overt hostility, (4) covert hostility, (5) emphasis on material rewards as a reason for participation, and (6) collective action by subjects against the researcher.

Perhaps a more descriptive label for the research procedures outlined by Argyris would be "closed system" research. Additional characteristics of "closed system" research have been detailed by Dunnette in his paper on "Fads, fashions, and folderol" (1966). In contrast to the procedures given by Argyris, research aimed at producing valid understanding of phenomena occurring within ongoing organizations should be characterized as creative problem solving. As such, research cannot be programmed in detail. The so-called "rigorous" designs are inappropriate for research on organizations, not only because they may have unintended consequences as pointed out by Argyris, but also because they fail to achieve the intended consequences of discovering valid relationships.

Integrating the Study and the Organization

Research designed to understand the role-making systems must integrate the research system and the organizational systems. Ideally, behavior that the research design imposes can be legitimized by the organizational representatives and accepted by the participants as role-relevant activities. The investigator needs to make a special effort to involve the organization and the participants.

An important aspect of this integration process is the role-making activities of the researchers. The researchers must relate to the participants in a way that creates relationships of trust, support, and honesty. The initial "confrontation of strangers," to use Goffman's (1959) phrase, must develop into a sharing relationship over time. Indeed, treating organizational representatives and participants as colleagues would be optimal.

Open Systems Design

Let us illustrate some major elements of what we call the "open systems" design. "Open systems" design hopefully will connote a shift in our thinking about role making from static, independent, machine- or computer-like operations to more dynamic, interdependent, partially undefined, and interacting systems requiring feedback, even negative feedback. In moving from fixed or closed systems models to more open systems models we sacrifice the security of a sense of closure for the risky opportunity to discover more valid understanding.

Some salient characteristics of an open systems design are the following:

1. *The study is designed to seek an understanding of the phenomenon of interest within the context in which it is embedded rather than attempting to substantiate hypotheses across all contextual conditions.*

This characteristic applies to the intent of the researcher. One would expect that a high tolerance for ambiguity should be helpful to avoid prematurely closing the net around the phenomenon of interest. The basic goal of such a study, simply stated, is to produce a testable set of notions about the order underlying the ongoing series of events (see Platt, 1964).

2. *Research questions are stated such that they contain as few as possible prior unproven assumptions about the nature of the actors, their behaviors, or the context under investigation.*

In our investigations of the role-making processes, we posed the research question in this manner: As a newcomer becomes an established incumbent, what set of outcropping from the actors, their behaviors, and the context change? What is the direction of

change? If we followed a more closed model, we might have used the assumptions underlying Max Weber's bureaucratic model of organizations. This model assumes that organizational roles are defined completely by the authoritative, technological, and workflow demands placed upon the organization by its environments. Once the role is defined by these demands, it is fixed and stable. Making this assumption, our attention would be focused on the process by which people are encouraged to conform to the pre-defined role. Our approach was to test empirically the validity of this assumption in concrete situations.

Furthermore, we might have assumed one of a number of ideal-typical models of man (Schein, 1965). Here we have a wider selection: (a) one-factor models of the dominant motivation of man (economic man, social man, or achieving man), (b) two-factor models of man (Adam and Abraham), and even (c) a hierarchy of needs model. Each of these models of man restricts the scope of the study and might blind us in our attempt to understand the phenomenon of interest in the concrete situation.

3. *The investigator carefully assesses organizational settings and selects one as a research context based upon the expected operation of the phenomenon of interest, the emergence of measurable outcropping relevant to the actors, their behavior, and the organizational context, and the assurance that required quality controls on data and flexibility of procedures can be established and maintained.*

The organizational setting that we selected in one of our studies was the entire administrative hierarchy of a service organization in a large public university. This setting promised to meet all of the requirements for an open systems study. The subject organization was composed of sixty people from the director on down. Approximately half of the people were in new positions and a third of the people were new to the organization. This setting appeared likely to reveal the operation of whatever processes affect the transition from new-comer to established incumbent. Fortunately for the study, the newcomers were assuming positions that represented a vertical cross-section of the administrative hierarchy. Control and flexibility were possible through the cooperation of the director and the associate directors. Even though the content of the interview was not known at the outset of the study, the design included personal interviews with each of the sixty focal people for at least one hour and with the immediate supervisor of each focal person concerning that focal person for one-half hour on four different occasions: during the second month, the fourth month, the seventh month, and the ninth month of tenure.

4. *At the beginning of the investigation, the scope of interest must be wide enough to ensure that the major portions of the complete context and the entire time cycle of the phenomenon of interest will be covered. Through iterations of testing and refining measures throughout the study and attempting at each stage to understand more and to document this understanding, the study successively approximates the crucial set of variables.*

During the initial interview as much attention was given to the past history and current circumstances of the organization and its environments as was devoted to the actors and their behaviors. Throughout the study, the reactions and insights of the participants were used to test and refine instruments, to generate alternative hypotheses, and to add, delete, and modify measures. At the end of each set of interviews, our understanding of the processes and the context was evaluated and necessary changes were made for the following set of interviews. At the end of the third wave of interviews no changes were made due to an absence of negative feedback. Either the organizational participants had given up on us or we had narrowed to an acceptable set of variables.

5. *Heavy emphasis is placed upon increasing the validity of the data by including many procedures to decrease sources of bias and error and enhance quality.*

Many attempts were made to involve the participants in the procedures and outcomes of the project. After the usual discussions between the director and research staff and associate directors and the research staff but before the initial set of interviews, a large group meeting that included most of the participants was held to describe the study, introduce the staff, and answer questions. During the initial interview, the study was again described and discussed, credentials and ground rules were exchanged, and information was collected. A "confrontation of strangers" aptly describes this initial interview with each party testing the other. During the second set of interviews, several of the participants asked to have their first interviews discounted. They did not want to "own" information from their first interviews.

Apparently our quality control procedures had served to place some of our participants in an untenable position. We had so much information, from them and from other members of the organization, that asking some of the same questions a second time and perhaps again in the future probably made maintaining a spurious role without detection a near-impossible task.

This *interactive assessment* procedure may be criticized on the grounds that getting so close to participants could be reactive in terms of changing the variables in the act of assessing their value. An alternative procedure might be to attempt to reduce the opportunity for this reactivity by employing *unobtrusive measures* (Webb, Campbell, Schwartz, & Sechrest, 1966). A major disadvantage of this procedure as we view it is that the unobtrusive measures that would be sensitive to role-making outcroppings probably would involve violations of the relationships of honesty, trust, and respect between researcher and participant. We believe that "Super-spy" procedures, while unobtrusive, are likely to do more damage to the research endeavor in the long run than the information they produce would be worth.

The potential effects of reactivity can be estimated within *a series* of research studies. The understanding derived from a series of studies employing potentially reactive procedures can be tested in new settings using less potentially reactive measures and the results assessed. The fear of using potentially reactive procedures should not be used as an excuse to avoid researching the role-making process.

6. *In terms of analysis, an open systems design requires that the results not only show statistical significance, but more importantly, that they demonstrate "consistent patterns of integrated and significant results." Searches are made for the conditions under which the results might show different consistent patterns (interactions or moderating conditions). It requires that we analyze our data far beyond the mere finding of significant results—beyond publishable results—to ensure that the results demonstrate consistency beyond that which we report.*

Implications

This theoretical position assumes that to understand the behavior and performance of individuals and groups within complex organizations, an open systems approach that incorporates the *interactions* among the individual, his group, and his organization should be adopted and programmed into systematic research. This position is similar to that of Katz and Kahn (1966) and their mentor, Lewin (1951). It goes beyond Katz and Kahn, but not Lewin, by attempting to determine the magnitudes and behavior effects of the many sources and kinds of pressures that impinge upon the individual in his organizational role. Moreover, this position accepts the necessity to consider a wide range of phenomena as influencing behavior within organizations, including those which have been viewed traditionally as within separate areas. For example, the traditional approach has been to view the study of the

individual's feelings, cognitions, and behavior as the proper concern of the personality researcher; the study of the feelings, cognitions, and behavior of individuals within groups as the appropriate area of the social researcher; the study of the feelings, cognitions, and behavior of groups within complex organizations as the parlance of the organizational researcher. Although each of these groups of researchers has made important contributions within the constraints of their respective areas, these essentially isolated contributions have a slight probability of producing an integrated understanding of the complex of pressures that interact to influence the behavior of individuals and groups within complex organizations. We hope that this proposed approach will help speed the realization that the boundaries of the three areas are not only contrived but also inhibit our progress toward the understanding of the mysteries of organizational phenomena.

In the next section, two recent attempts to apply these ideas about open systems design will be presented and discussed. The first study investigates the organizational assimilation of newcomers into various office worker roles during their probationary period. The second study builds upon the first and investigates the role-making process of managers during a period of reorganization.

OPEN SYSTEMS DESIGNS ON ORGANIZATIONAL ASSIMILATION

Clerical Study

A recent study by Graen, Orris, and Johnson (1973) was designed to investigate the organizational assimilation of office workers into clerical and secretarial roles within a large public university. This study used an open systems design to investigate the processes whereby a "newcomer" to the organization becomes an "established incumbent."

The design of the study called for repeated monitoring of the organizational assimilation process at six different points during the first six months of the newcomer's tenure. At each monitoring point, information was collected from three different sources: (a) the newcomer, (b) his immediate supervisor, and (c) his designated peer representative. All information was collected from newcomers in small group meetings with a member of the research staff during working hours. Small group meetings lasted about one hour per session with the newcomers and about one-half hour per session with the supervisors and the peer representatives. The monitoring periods for each newcomer were the first week, the second week, the fourth week, the twelfth week, the sixteenth week, and the twentieth week of tenure (time since joining the organization).

At about the eighteenth week of tenure for the newcomer, feedback sessions were held to exchange information with the participants. These sessions lasted one full working day. During the morning a small group of newcomers (ten to twelve) would exchange information with three members of the research staff. During the afternoon the immediate supervisors of the newcomers would join the newcomers and the staff members in the exchange of information.

The newcomers who participated in this study were all new to the university (previous employees of the university were not included in the study) and had accepted clerical or secretarial positions in any of the eight largest employing departments of the university during a six-month period. The eight departments were Physics, Chemistry, Computer Science, Library, Admissions and Records, Administrative Data Processing, Business Office, and Dean of Students.

One of the significant outcomes of this study was the demonstration of meaningful and measurable outcropping during the assimilation period. Although the procedures employed in this study should be refined for use in future studies, these procedures suggest several useful ways of monitoring the processes that occur during the period of or-

ganizational assimilation. Some of these procedures that will be discussed include: (a) the extent of involvement of the new (focal) person in various role activities; (b) role preferences, ambiguities, and conflicts concerning the extent of involvement of the focal person in various role activities from three different perspectives (focal, focal's supervisor, and focal's peer); (c) role satisfaction of the focal person; (d) role performance; and (e) instrumentality variables.

The extent of involvement of the focal person in various role activities was assessed at weeks 1, 2, 4, 12, and 16. The assessment of involvement was based on fourteen activities. Some of these activities were seeking personal fulfillment, planning for peak loads of work, becoming an accepted member of the staff, performing high quality work, dealing with conflicting pressures, doing the basic job, and changing the job. The results on involvement in these activities showed "reasonable" trends over the sixteen-week period. Seeking personal fulfillment and attempting to change the job were maintained at rather constant levels throughout the period. In contrast, becoming an accepted member of the staff, performing the basic job, and performing high quality work showed sharp declines during the first few weeks followed by rather constant trends. The only activity showing a significant increase over time was dealing with conflicting pressures. The reasons for increased involvement in dealing with conflicting pressures (which will be discussed shortly) were abundant. Finally, as expected, those activities that concerned learning and mastery of the role and going to others for help declined significantly over the period. Although these results may be evaluated as documenting the intuitively obvious, intuition may be valid but without documentation; it also may be invalid.

Role Readiness

One dimension that served to order the data of this study was called "role readiness." Role readiness was defined by the newcomer's evaluation of the relevance of the job to his future work plans. If the job was seen as having little or no relevance to the work the newcomer intended to perform in the future, the newcomer was categorized as a "role rejector." On the other hand, if the job was seen as possessing a fair degree of relevance to his future work, the newcomer was categorized as a "role accepter." Somewhat surprisingly, close to 40 percent of the monitored group fell into the role-rejecting category. To determine whether this was an atypical sample from the population in view of the high proportion of people who indicated little or no relevance in their jobs for future work, a control sample of newcomers was drawn from the same population and assessed for role readiness. Supporting the results on the monitored sample, the control sample showed also the identical proportions of accepters and rejectors. Equally surprising, an analysis of the demographic characteristics of accepters and rejectors failed to reveal any differences in age, sex, education, marital status, previous work experience, occupation of spouse, or the like. In short, role readiness was not related to any of the reasonable demographic characteristics, although as we shall see, it was related to most of the outcropping of the assimilation processes.

The role preferences of the focals and the supervisors and peers regarding how the focals should modify their involvement in each activity was assessed at four time periods. Also assessed were the focals' perceptions of the above preferences of their supervisors and peers. An example of the results is shown in Figure 3. This figure shows the preferences of the focals (FF), their supervisors (SS), and the focals' perceptions of their supervisors' preferences (SF) for role rejecting persons and role accepting persons separately. As shown in this figure, the focals' preferences in performing high quality work declined significantly for both groups over the period; the focals' percep-

tions of the supervisors' preferences were low relative to those of the focal during the first two weeks and tended to decline significantly over the entire period for both groups; the actual preferences of the supervisors showed significantly different trends for role readiness groups. The trend for role rejecting was sharply increasing over time; whereas, the trend for role accepting was comparatively flat throughout the period.

The discrepancy between the focals and their supervisors can be seen by comparing the trend for the focals' preferences to that for the supervisors' preferences. The difference between these two trends for the role rejecting is relatively high during the first week, lower during the second week, and increases in the opposite direction for the last two time periods. In contrast, this difference for the role accepting decreases from the first to at least the twelfth week. Although this discrepancy can be assessed by outside observers, this does not necessarily imply that the parties were aware of their differences. Before the parties can be aware of this discrepancy, the situation must be rather unambiguous. An estimate of role preference ambiguity can be made by comparing the trends for the supervisors' actual preferences and that for the focals' perception of their supervisors' preferences. The differences between these two trends for the role rejecting show generally increasing ambiguity over the monitored period. In sharp contrast, and more of what one would expect during assimilation, the differences between the two trends for the role accepting show generally low and slightly decreasing ambiguity over time.

The most dramatic trends between role accepting and role rejecting persons were shown in the ambiguity between what the supervisor wanted the focal to do and the focal's reading of these preferences summed over all fourteen activities. The difference increased monotonically throughout the period for role rejecting persons. In contrast, the role accepting showed slightly higher ambiguity than role rejecting at the first

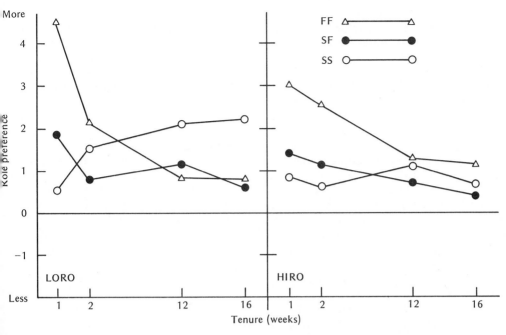

Figure 3. Supervisor's demands (SS), supervisor's demands as seen by focal (SF), and focal's preferences (FF) concerning performing high quality work for role-rejecting (LORO) and role-accepting (HIRO) focal people.

week, but at the second week the ambiguity of the role accepting declined sharply and remained at a low level throughout the period. The role rejecting began at week one with slightly less ambiguity regarding their supervisor's preferences, but instead of maintaining this advantage, their ambiguity increased in magnitude at each succeeding period. On the other hand, their role accepting colleagues reduced their ambiguity to a low level by the second week and maintained this level until at least the end of the period. The increasing divergence between the ambiguity of the two role readiness groups over time suggests that the processes producing this ambiguity between the focal and his supervisor remained quite active at sixteen weeks.

Role attitudes and satisfactions were assessed toward both particular aspects of the role situation and the overall role situation. The results on overall role satisfaction using the Hoppock (1935) measure show a trend

that is monotonically decreasing with time in the role. Although the role accepting focals begin with and maintain throughout a much higher level of satisfaction than the role rejecting focals, the over time trends did not interact for these two groups. This illustrates the erosion of overall role satisfaction as a function of time in the situation. However, the higher overall satisfaction of the role accepting as compared to the role rejecting was maintained until at least the twentieth week of tenure. Also at the twentieth week of tenure, the supervisors of the focals were asked to estimate the overall role satisfactions of their new people. The results were somewhat surprising. The supervisors estimated the role satisfaction of the role accepting focals quite close to their actual level. In sharp contrast, these supervisors estimated the satisfaction of the role rejecting focals as being only slightly lower than their estimates for the role accepting focals and much higher than the actual level of this group. Apparently, even after twenty weeks of working with these people, the supervisors did not appreciate the low level of overall role satisfaction of the role rejecters.

This apparent insensitivity to the new people might have implications for the other estimates made by supervisors concerning new people. For example, although the supervisors rated the performance of the role accepting focals significantly higher than the rejecting focals over the entire period, do these ratings really reflect the role performance of the new people? Is it possible for a supervisor to accurately evaluate the role performance of a person without getting close enough to that person to be aware of his overall satisfaction with the role situation?

Finally, the instrumentalities of following the various role preferences were assessed for twelve role outcomes. These twelve role outcomes included such things as achieving personal fulfillment, becoming an accepted member of the staff, earning praise from the supervisor, feeling a sense of pride in the work, and earning a wage increase. Each focal person indicated: (a) his attraction to each outcome, (b) the instrumentality of following his own role preferences for the attainment of each outcome, (c) the instrumentality of following his supervisor's role demands for the attainment of each outcome, and (d) the instrumentality of following his peers' role demands for the attainment of each of these outcomes. As might be expected from the above, the role accepting focals saw the outcomes as more attractive for them than did the role rejecting focals, and saw, following both their own preferences and those of their supervisors, as having greater instrumentality for the attainment of these outcomes than did their role rejecting colleagues. Only the instrumentality of following the role demands of their peers failed to discriminate between these two role readiness groups.

In addition to showing that assimilation processes can produce a number of measurable outcroppings, these measurable outcroppings suggest that a three-phase process of organizational assimilation applied in this concrete situation. During the first two weeks of tenure, the newcomer modified many of his role relevant beliefs, often in a rather dramatic manner. Possibly as a consequence of confronting the concrete role situation (a set of tasks rather than a vague label for his role; a particular person rather than a name of a supervisor; a concrete setting rather than the name of the department, and the like), the newcomer changed many beliefs about the role and his part in the setting. Also during this "Initial Confrontation" phase, the immediate supervisor of the newcomer formed a first impression of the newcomer's role performance. Although supervisors discriminated rather well in terms of the effectiveness of performance even at this early period, they tended to show optimism regarding the future performance of the newcomers. In other words, the supervisors tended to rate the future performance of the newcomer higher than they rated the newcomers' present performance. During this initial phase, the peers apparently were aware of the newcomer, but did not pay a great deal of attention to him.

During the second phase, from about the second week to the twelfth week of the newcomer's tenure, the newcomer was allowed and indeed expected to cope with the role and the situation and to make an adequate adjustment primarily on his own. From the view of the newcomer, the supervisor had called a "time out" period regarding his (the supervisor's) part in the assimilation process, and the newcomers' overall role satisfaction gradually eroded over this period. The communications mechanism between the newcomer and his supervisor produced increasing levels of ambiguity in several critical areas of role behavior. The readiness of the newcomers to accept the organizational role and its contingent obligations seemed to play an increasingly important part in the effectiveness of the communications process. Those newcomers who readily accepted the role and its obligation somehow reduced the ambiguity between what their supervisor preferred and what they perceived their supervisor as preferring regarding their role behavior. In contrast, those newcomers who had a more negative reaction to the role and its obligation showed increasing ambiguity between the demands of their supervisor and their perception of those demands.

At the onset of the third and final phase, about the twelfth week, the supervisors evaluated the *progress* of the newcomers as required by probationary procedure. If they found them wanting, they began to take immediate corrective action. However, the communications mechanisms were not calibrated for all newcomers and the increased demands from the supervisor were not accurately received by all newcomers. The consequence of this increase in demands, coupled with the faulty mechanism for communicating these demands, was a sharp increase in the ambiguity between the newcomer and his supervisor, especially for those newcomers who needed special help in adjusting to the role situation. The peers also evaluated the progress of the newcomers during this period. If the peers found the newcomers wanting in terms of their criteria, they increased the magnitude of their demands on the newcomers. Again the communication mechanisms were not calibrated for all dyads, and the increased demands resulted in greater ambiguity between what the established peer demanded, and what the newcomer perceived the peer as demanding, especially for those newcomers who needed special help in adjusting to the role situation. Although the overall role satisfaction of the new people declined at a sharp rate during this period, especially for those newcomers who needed the most help in adjusting to the role, the supervisors did not detect this rather dramatic difference between the role rejecting and role accepting newcomers' level of overall satisfaction.

Three Phases

A reasonable reconstruction of this concrete organizational assimilation process thus would include the three more or less distinct phases of *Initial Confrontation, Working Through,* and *Integrating.* During the initial confrontation phase, the newcomer had to cope with the discrepancies between his expectations about the situation and his assessment of the concrete situation. The magnitude and direction of change in the newcomer's beliefs that are relevant to the role situation should generally be a function of the differences between his past role experiences and his present role situation. This "disillusionment phenomenon" of high expectations for an organizational role before it is experienced but followed by much lower satisfaction after that role is experienced may be a rather general phenomenon.

Vroom and Deci (1971) found this to be the case for graduate students attaining master's degrees in industrial administration and subsequently joining business organizations. These investigators found that a significant decline in role attitudes occurred from the period before experiencing the organization and after one year in that organization. Moreover, these less favorable attitudes about the organization were maintained for at least two and one-half years. This past disillusionment may affect the role readiness of a newcomer. If the disillusionment is too severe, the newcomer may overreact by rejecting the role as basically incompatible with his personality and still accept the organizational position, however, as a visitor. Once this occurs, the task of persuading the newcomer to reject the visitor perspective and become a resident must be accomplished before that newcomer can be integrated into the ongoing role system. Once a newcomer is "turned-off" by the role situation to this extent, the task of "turning-on" must be accomplished before the task of integrating the newcomer can be accomplished. We need more work on these phenomena to help us understand the antecedents, mechanisms, and consequence of the disillusionment with the role situation.

Perhaps the most that can be accomplished in the first phase would be to delay the full impact of the disillusionment until the newcomer is prepared to cope with it. During the second phase, the working through processes might involve the newcomer, his supervisor, and some of his peers attempting to negotiate a mutually favorable set of understandings regarding roles and working relationships. Although in this study the second phase was characterized by the newcomer attempting to make an essentially unassisted adjustment, this phase could be the critical working through phase of the assimilation process. At this time, the newcomer has a fair grasp of his role, has begun polishing the required skills, and has developed at least acquaintanceships with his role-set members. He is now ready to learn more and to establish working relationships with his role-set members, especially his supervisor. If the newcomer's role-set members are ready and able to assist in this working through process, perhaps the role ambiguity and conflict demonstrated in this study can be significantly reduced. Perhaps, through a negotiating process, the overlap between the *subjective organization* of the newcomer and his supervisor can be increased substantially. Ideally, such a working through would increase the overlap among the subjective organizations (the role situation as seen by a participant) of all members of the newcomer's role-set.

If the goal of the second phase is to increase the role clarity among members of the newcomer's role-set, one goal of the third phase is the integration of the newcomer into the ongoing role-set. The decrease in role ambiguity that could result from the working through processes would result very likely in the recognition of role conflicts. Only after sufficient clarity is achieved can the lines of conflict be seen. Although the realization of role conflict may be painful to the participants, the integration of the newcomer into the role-set requires that these conflicts be negotiated. Some conflicts will be resolved and others will be accepted as unresolvable by the participants. The result of this process is the involvement of the newcomer in the matrix of the role-set.

One outcome which may be partially due to the process of organizational assimilation is turnover. By the end of the fourth month 23 percent of the role rejecting and 10 percent of the role accepting newcomers had left the organization. At the end of the summer session 59 percent of the role rejecting and 25 percent of the role accepting newcomers had left the organization. Finally, at the beginning of the new academic year only 27 percent of the role rejecting and 55 percent of the role accepting newcomers were still on their jobs.

This phenomenon of withholding information and support from some types of newcomers was suggested in an investigation by Alderfer (1971). In this study of the same bank that Argyris (1954) had examined some fifteen years earlier, Alderfer found that the bank had initiated a program some ten years earlier to augment the management ranks with college graduates ("new types") selected for their aggressiveness. At the time Argyris examined the bank, he found that it was largely attracted to and peopled by the "right type." The "right type" was characterized as the stereotype of the nervous, submissive, timid bank clerk. The importation of the "new types" created the opportunity for confrontations between the "right" and the "new" types. The interactions between people from these two groups were described by Alderfer as a process of avoiding confrontations by not working through the barriers to accurate communications. Although the resultant noise in the communications between these two types of people was not documented in this situation, the ambiguity between these two types would be expected to be massive.

An all too easy reaction to this situation by the proponents of the fixed job model would be that the "wrong type" of people were being hired for these jobs. Therefore, if those rejecting the role could be identified as "misfits" during the selection process, they should not be hired. During the selection process, the "winners" should be sorted out from the "losers" and only the "winners" should be hired.

Although this expedient approach may

appeal to administrators as a short-run solution to an immediate problem, in the longer run this approach may lead to a hardening of the attitudes of the established participants against the acceptance of newcomers. In effect the policy of the organization becomes one of selecting the right types and promoting self-adjustment through trial and error. At the extreme, this policy toward newcomers can turn even the most role ready newcomer into a role rejector in a short period of time. In addition, the costs of alienating those newcomers who could make highly significant contributions to the organization are overlooked by the fixed job approach. Organizational renewal depends upon the organizational assimilation of these wrong types.

Fortunately, the organization probably cannot identify subsequent role rejectors early. Although these newcomers identified themselves to the research staff under certain conditions, these people probably would not identify themselves to the organization's selection officers for fear of being rejected for the position for which they are applying.

Next, we turn to a study that built upon and hopefully profited from the earlier clerical study. In this study, we sought answers to the many questions raised by the clerical study. The highest priority question was: By what mechanism could an organizational assimilation process completely reject approximately 40 percent of its newcomers?

Managerial Study

This investigation (by Dansereau, Graen, & Haga, 1975; Haga, Graen, & Dansereau, 1974) was designed to study the organization assimilation of administrators into a service organization of a large public university. Much of the design and procedure of this study was described earlier as the illustration of the "open systems" design for research. As mentioned in that section, the entire administrative hierarchy of sixty positions was investigated over a nine-month period. Although about one-half of these people were in new positions and about a third of the people were newcomers to the organization, a more significant datum, as we shall see, was that a full 88 percent of the dyadic relationships involving a supervisor and his members were new. In terms of these relationships, almost everyone in this organization was faced with a role-making task of some magnitude. Another important characteristic of this situation was that the organization was attempting to change its image by de-emphasizing its "bricks and mortar" function while emphasizing its "professional service" function. This attempt to move from an orientation toward the physical plant to one toward service to clients reflected a national trend for this type of service organization.

One improvement of this study over the clerical study was the procedure used to assess job behavior. (See also Hinrichs, 1964; Carroll & Taylor, 1969.) In this study, the managers were asked individually to generate an exhaustive list of their present job activities. During the first interview (the second month after reorganization), each manager developed such a list of his present activities with the help of the interviewer. An "aided recall" procedure was used to help the manager list as many of his activities as possible in the manager's own words. The procedure called for the interviewer first to elicit the initial list from the manager. Next, the interviewer asked for definitions and elaborations of the activities on the initial list. After this, the interviewer asked the manager (a) to estimate his present involvement in each activity and (b) to estimate the involvement that his supervisor preferred of him. At each stage, the manager was encouraged to add, delete, or change any activity that he desired.

This same procedure was followed for all managers in the organization. During the same period a second interviewer talked to only the supervisors of managers in the sample. This interviewer employed the "aided recall" procedure to develop lists of activities for each of the supervisor's people. After the list of activities for a particular subordinate had been generated, the supervisor was asked: (a) to estimate the involvement in each activity that he expected of that person, and (b) to estimate that person's present level of involvement.

The data from these lists of activities were collated and analyzed. Contrary to what one might expect, even with our aided recall procedure, the managers tended to give only partial lists of their activities. Often a manager would omit an activity that was considered critical by his supervisor or his colleague. To overcome the many problems of individualized and partial lists, a master list of activities was constructed for the managers. This master list in the managers' language was exhaustive but was not completely mutually exclusive. It contained twenty-two different activities from "individual counseling" to "experimenting with organizational procedures."

During the second wave of interviews (the fourth month after reorganization), the master list was used in both the interviews with the managers about their own jobs and those with the supervisors about each of the manager's jobs. The interviewers encouraged the participants to add or change activities as they desired and to evaluate the master list. No items were added or changed and the evaluations were quite favorable. Some of the managers wanted to use the master list as a basis for a job evaluation study. This idea was not discouraged at the time. This master list was used again at seven and nine months to collect involvement data from both the focal managers and their immediate supervisors. In all four sets of interviews the focal managers were asked to estimate their involvement in each of the twenty-two activities: (a) in terms of what they were presently doing, and (b) in terms of what their supervisor wanted them to do. On the other side of the relationship, the supervisor was asked to estimate the involvement of each of his focal managers in each of the same twenty-two activities: (a) in terms of what he wanted them to do, and (b) in terms of what they were doing.

In addition to the involvement information, both the focal managers and their supervisors were asked about the working relationships between the supervisor and the manager. The managers were asked about their attitudes toward the situation, their professional orientation, and other matters.

Two fairly uncorrelated dimensions called "Professional Orientation" and "Negotiation Latitude" were found to order the data of this study. "Professional Orientation" was defined by membership in professional associations and subscriptions to professional journals. "Negotiation Latitude" was defined by the participant's perception of his supervisor's flexibility in allowing him to make changes in his job and his supervisor's willingness to use formal authority to help solve a problem on the member's job. Professional orientation and negotiating latitude were each treated as dichotomous dimensions. Although each of these two dimensions ordered the data singly, their combined effect failed to order the data in any consistent fashion.

Professional Orientation

Considering the involvement of the participants in their various job activities, professional orientation showed significant differences on many activities: (a) what the focal person said he was doing, (b) what his supervisor said he was doing, (c) what his supervisor expected him to do, and (d) what the focal person perceived that his supervisor expected him to do. Asking what the focal person felt his supervisor wanted him to do indicated an overwhelming ambiguity for the total sample. Approximately 80 percent of all responses on this dimension were "don't know." Even at the ninth month, the ambiguity of the focal person regarding his supervisor's expectations had not decreased. In addition, the correspondence between what the focal said he was doing and what the supervisor said the focal was doing showed gross differences. Although the supervisor said that he knew what his people were doing, the accuracy of his perceptions did not warrant much confidence.

On most activities, the professionals indicated higher levels of involvement than the nonprofessionals. Moreover, the supervisors indicated higher levels of present involvement and higher levels of expected involvement for the professionals than the nonprofessionals. These differences were maintained over time. However, the patterns of involvement suggested that the focal people were not necessarily following the expectations of their supervisors. Indeed, these patterns suggested almost no relationship between what the focal said he was doing and either (a) what the supervisor said the focal was doing, or (b) what the supervisor said he expected the focal to do. Apparently the exchange of information between the focal and his supervisor did not provide sufficiently accurate data to either party regarding involvement in activities.

These findings on involvement suggest that the supervisor forms an idealized model of how a person in a given position should perform his job. Based upon this model, the supervisor judges the activities of the person as he sees them, probably using a few rather gross categories, such as "too much," "too little," and "appropriate involvement." Obviously, the supervisor cannot continuously monitor the activities of his people. Unless he detects some difficulty, he assumes that the focal's activities are appropriate.

Both supervisors and focals distinguished between professional and nonprofessional in terms of involvement in activities; however, the results showed that although the supervisor indicated that he gave different treatment to the professional and the nonprofessional, the focals failed to perceive this differential treatment. In fact, the most unexpected finding concerning professional orientation was the utter lack of significant differences in work attitudes. Even satisfaction with the work itself, the supposed hallmark of the professional, failed to distinguish between professionals and nonprofessionals.

In view of this last finding one may question the validity of the measure of professional orientation. However, the job defining measures strongly supported the validity of this measure of professional orientation. The participants were asked to indicate the usefulness of (a) job descriptions, (b) schooling, (c) professional societies, (d) professional journals, and (e) personal contacts in helping them define their jobs. The only significant differences were that the professionals showed higher values on the usefulness of professional societies and professional journals than did the nonprofessionals.

In summary, the professional orientation appears to be useful in ordering the involvement data from both the focal and the supervisor and the data on how the supervisor perceives his treatment of his people. However, it appears not to be useful to order the focal's attitudes or his perception of how his superior treats him. Perhaps this indicates that the profession helps to define role behavior but is silent regarding the proper attitudinal reactions of the professional.

Negotiating Latitude

On involvement in activities, negotiating latitude showed significant differences on the correspondence between what the supervisor said the focal was doing and what the supervisor expected the focal to be doing. The "negotiating" (high negotiating latitude) focals were seen by their supervisors as doing more what their supervisor expected than were the "constrained" (low negotiating latitude) focals. This difference in correspondence between the negotiating and the constrained increased in magnitude over time. The correspondence remained high and relatively constant for the negotiating focals but began high and decreased over time for the constrained focals. This indicates that those in the negotiating group were seen by their supervisors as continuing to do as they were expected, whereas those in the constrained group were seen by their supervisors as progressively deviating more from that expected. In addition, as was the case for professional orientation, negotiating latitude showed significant differences on many activities. Supervisors indicated higher levels of involvement expected for the negotiating focals than the constrained focals. Moreover, negotiating focals indicated higher levels of involvement in communicating and administering activities than those indicated by constrained focals. Equally important, these differences were maintained over time.

Negotiating latitude ordered the data concerning supervisors' treatment of the participants. The supervisors indicated that they treated negotiating and constrained focals differently. In agreement, the participants indicated that they received this different treatment. The attitudinal consequences of this differential treatment were consistent. The attitudes of the two groups were similar at four months but became increasingly different at seven months. The general trends for overall (Hoppock, 1935) and outcome satisfaction over time were similar to the trends of what the supervisor expected and what the supervisor saw the focals doing. The negotiating group started with favorable attitudes and maintained them throughout, while the constrained started with favorable attitudes but became progressively less favorable over time. One of the largest differences in attitudes between the two groups was toward their interpersonal relations with their supervisors. In short, whatever negotiating latitude was tapping, its contribution to the evaluative reactions of the participants was pervasive and large.

What was "negotiating latitude" measuring? Obviously, we had a handle on an important phenomenon, but what was its nature? Negotiating latitude was assessed at all four points during the nine months of the study. Over this time period it showed high stability. Thus, few people were moving from negotiating to constrained, or vice versa over time. The measure taken at the second month was used to define the dimension.

What can happen before the second month that could be related to these distant (in time) outcomes? Whatever "negotiating latitude" was, it demonstrated the following characteristics:[4]

1. It was formed relatively early in the development of the relationship between the supervisor and his member (before the second month) and remained relatively stable (.60) over at least nine months.

2. It was indicated by a member's perception of his supervisor's willingness to help the member cope with his job during the second month after reorganization.

3. It was not related to professional orientation, job type, level in the organization, employment history, education, age, tenure, sex, race, or life cycle.

4. It was not related to leadership style (in fact, 85 percent of all units of two or more members contained both negotiating and constrained focals).

5. It did not interact with either professional orientation or job type on any of the variables below.

6. It was related to correspondence between what the supervisor expected a focal to do and what that superior saw the focal doing (job performance). Negotiating focals were seen as conforming to expectations; whereas constrained focals were seen as deviating progressively from expectations over time.

7. It was related to the level of involvement the supervisor expected and to that which the member reported (with negotiating showing higher involvement than that shown by constrained).

8. It was related consistently over time to the supervisor's treatment of his members. Negotiating members reported receiving higher job latitude, more information, greater influence in decisions, more support of their actions, and greater consideration of

---

[4] These findings have been replicated and extended in three separate role-making studies using similar open-systems designs. These subsequent investigations support the generalizability of this network of relationships.

their feelings and needs than that reported by constrained members. Supervisors indicated that negotiating members required higher amounts of these outcomes than those required by constrained members to perform their jobs adequately and without undue dissatisfaction.

9. It was related to the severity of job problems involving immediate supervision. Both supervisor and member reports indicated that constrained members experienced more severe problems with supervision than that experienced by negotiating members.

10. It was related to work attitudes consistently over time. Negotiating members indicated more positive attitudes toward the overall job situation, work itself, supervision, and outcomes received than constrained members.

11. The above relationships between negotiating latitude and involvement, supervisory treatment, job problems, and attitudes were in predictive as opposed to concurrent or postdictive time sequences. The dichotomy between negotiating and constrained members was based upon data taken during the second month after reorganization, whereas the dependent variables were assessed at later times, for example, four, seven, and nine months after reorganization.

A Suggested Interpretation

These findings suggest that our predecessors in social psychology may have misled us into believing that informal groups within large organizations cannot include a supervisor and his subordinates in the same unit. We were led to believe that common interests, whether threats or goals, can only be shown by organizational peers and never by people at different levels in the organization. Based on these notions, the supervisor is assumed to possess interests that must be incompatible with those of his people. It is this assumed incompatibility that prevents the supervisor and his members from developing into an informal group (Argyris, 1964; Likert, 1961). These findings suggest

that such an "impossible" informal coalition can and did form within organizational units.

Consider the situation facing a supervisor in a large, functionally interdependent organization. According to the closed systems beliefs about formal organization, the supervisor is assumed to possess adequate authority to control the events for which he is held responsible. Each position in the supervisor's unit is assumed to be completely programmed by the role-system. The supervisor's main function is to enforce the role proscriptions and prescriptions on his subordinates. In actuality, this set of beliefs map the ongoing situation very poorly. The supervisor rarely has adequate control over the events within his area of responsibility. Each position in his unit is peopled by a complex individual who must somehow define his role in spite of the outdated job description. The supervisor's main function is not to enforce the incomplete and often contradictory sets of rules and procedures but to somehow influence the events that must occur for his unit to perform its many functions. To do this, he must depend upon his people for much more than they can legitimately be required to do. Somehow he must enlist at least some of his people as "special" assistants or he probably will fail. An alternative that is sometimes attempted is for the supervisor to do everything required himself and delegate nothing. The usual consequence of this is role overload and eventual exhaustion.

If the supervisor intends to enlist some of his people as informal assistants, he must somehow reward them for their services. He can do this by employing his authority to give special treatment to these assistants. Without formal sanctions to reinforce this special status, the relationship between the supervisor and his assistants takes on greater significance. The assistants must have confidence and trust that their supervisor will reciprocate for their extra efforts. To earn this trust, the supervisor must consistently treat his assistants as favored. He cannot punish them and formally they can do little wrong. Once a member becomes an informal assistant of the supervisor, the supervisor cannot reject an assistant without overwhelming justification in the eyes of his other informal assistants. Without such justification, the supervisor may become suspect and lose all of his informal assistants.

The supervisor probably will not enlist all of his people as informal assistants. This enlistment of informal assistants increases the dependence of the supervisor upon his informal assistants. This is a potential cost to the supervisor. If an informal assistant creates a problem, the supervisor must accept some personal responsibility for the consequences without recourse to completely blaming the member. Moreover, the possibility of such an event occurring is increased due to the wider latitude given the informal assistants. If the supervisor enlists all of his members as informal assistants, he becomes greatly dependent upon them. At the extreme, the supervisor may find himself dominated by his informal assistants.

The question of the selection of informal assistants is an interesting one. On what basis are these members identified? The supervisor would tend to select members who are compatible with him in terms of work competence and interpersonal skills and people he can trust to do the right thing. A member who is too competent may threaten him, while one too incompetent may embarrass him. Probably most importantly, the supervisor must select those members that he can trust without watching closely. In many, perhaps most, cases the members identify themselves through their relations with the supervisor. In some cases the selection probably is made based upon the supervisor's prejudices concerning race, religion, or ethnic background.

Based upon our results, the selection process probably occurs very early in the development of the relationship between supervisor and member. It could be that the enlistment of a member as an informal assistant involves the development of the relationship via a somewhat different process from that which would occur with an ordinary member. Again according to our results, the unselected member becomes aware of his inferior status gradually over time. Possibly the subtleness of these developments enhances some of the dysfunctional consequences.

If this interpretation is essentially correct, units within large, interdependent organizations become differentiated on an informal basis into informal assistants and ordinary members. The formal responsibilities of the supervisor that may be impossible under the formal structure may become practical under the differentiated structure. In this way, the many functions of the unit can be performed in a satisfactory manner without undue strain on either the supervisor or the members. The informal assistants accept additional duties and responsibilities, but are compensated by increased latitude in defining, possibly enriching jobs, and special treatment from the supervisor. If the selection of informal assistants can be justified to the ordinary members, possibly the special treatment by the supervisor could be legitimized and thus not alienate the ordinary members. That nonprofessionals did not react negatively to the special treatment the supervisors gave the professionals suggests that differential treatment can be accepted as proper if the basis for the distinction can be justified to the members.

This model of unit differentiation during organizational assimilation is compatible with the results of the clerical study. If the role-accepting members were accepted as informal assistants to the supervisor and the role rejecting were rejected as ordinary members, the results are compatible. The informal assistants receive the special attention of the supervisor and the ordinary members do not. Over time, the informal assistants are integrated into the unit, while the ordinary members drift slowly out of the organization.

In the situation within the bank that Alderfer (1971) described, it would be interesting to investigate the differences in the developing relationships between supervisors and young managers. One would predict that a supervisor who was the "right type" might select as his informal assistants young managers who were also "right types." Moreover, one might expect that a "new type" supervisor might prefer "new types" as his informal assistants.

Although this model is speculative at the present time, it does serve to summarize in a rather consistent manner a large and complex set of results. Hopefully, such a model will serve as a tool in our attempts to understand in a scientific manner how it is that large and complex organizations can perform their functions as efficiently as they do in spite of the logical impossibility of their performing at these levels based upon the acceptance of closed systems beliefs about organizational functioning.

Concluding Note

The fixed and closed systems model of organizational assimilation with its assumptions of nineteenth century bureaucratic theory fails to order the data from contemporary organizations. Although this outdated model may work tolerably under conditions of relative stability, under conditions of change the model fails utterly. Under conditions of change, inputs into the organization may be too variable in both characteristics and dynamics. People, technology, information and other inputs may be changing so rapidly that fixed models would be clearly inadequate.

In contrast, the role-making model that views organizational participants as "carriers" of organization allows for such dynamics. Participants interpret rules and procedures in ways that may permit and possibly may promote the functioning of the unit. People prefer not to behave as machines within organizations. As soon as they are given some latitude, they begin to work through their own patterns of behavior. They will seek to rationalize their behavior in terms of some goals—real or imagined.

Within interdependent units, people work out their behavior patterns based upon the enforced demands of the organization and the preferences of the participants (Weick, 1969). Over time the participants test the demands of the organization that create difficulties for them. If these demands are not enforced, the demands are modified. In these ways, the formal job descriptions and standard procedures become outdated while they're being revised.

Complex organizations tend to be ambiguous systems even to their participants. Although rules and procedures are sometimes useful to organizations, their functional utility decreases greatly under conditions of change. Under conditions of relative stability, rules and procedures may help to reduce ambiguity and increase predictability, but under conditions of change these same rules and procedures may prevent people from adapting to the demands to perform their functions in efficient manners.

It is time that we started to question the unproven assumptions of the fixed and closed systems model and began to seek more empirically based answers to the many questions involving the role-making processes.

REFERENCES

Alderfer, C. P. Effect of individual, group, and intergroup relations on attitudes toward a management development program. *Journal of Applied Psychology*, 1971, 55, 307–311.

Anderson, L. R. Leader behavior, member attitudes, and task performance of intercultural discussion groups. *Journal of Social Psychology*, 1966, 69, 305–319.

Anderson, L. R., & Fishbein, M. A. Prediction of attitude from the number, strength, and evaluative aspect of beliefs about the attitude object: A comparison of summation and congruity theories. *Journal of Personality and Social Psychology*, 1965, 1, 437–443.

Argyris, C. *Organization of a bank*. New Haven: Labor and Management Center, Yale University, 1954.

Argyris, C. *Integrating the individual and the organization.* New York: Wiley, 1964.

Argyris, C. *Intervention theory and method.* Reading, Mass.: Addison-Wesley, 1970.

Bennis, W. G. The decline of bureaucracy and organization of the future. In W. G. Bennis (Ed.), *Changing organizations.* New York: McGraw-Hill, 1966, 3–15.

Brayfield, A. H., & Crockett, W. H. Employee attitudes and employee performance. *Psychological Bulletin,* 1955, 52, 396–424.

Campbell, J. P., Dunnette, M. D., Lawler, E. E., & Weick, K. E. *Managerial behavior, performance, and effectiveness.* New York: McGraw-Hill, 1970.

Carlson, E. R. Attitude change through modification of attitude structure. *Journal of Abnormal and Social Psychology,* 1956, 52, 256–261.

Carroll, S. J., & Taylor, W. H. Validity of estimates by clerical personnel of job time proportions. *Journal of Applied Psychology,* 1969, 53, 164–166.

Dansereau, F. Jr., Graen, G., & Haga, W. J. A vertical dyad linkage approach to leadership within formal organizations: A longitudinal investigation of the role-making process. *Organizational Behavior and Human Performance,* 1975.

Dawis, R. V., & Lofquist, L. H. *Adjustment to work: A psychological view of man's problems in a work-oriented society.* New York: Appleton-Century-Crofts, 1969.

Dornbusch, S. A. The military academy as an assimilating institution. *Social Forces,* 1955, 33, 316–321.

Dulany, D. E. Hypotheses, habits in verbal "operant conditioning." *Journal of Abnormal and Social Psychology,* 1961, 63, 251–263.

Dulany, D. E. Awareness, rules, and prepositional control: A confrontation with S-R behavior theory. In T. R. Dixon & D. L. Horton (Eds.), *Verbal behavior and general behavior theory.* Englewood Cliffs, N.J.: Prentice-Hall, 1968.

Dunnette, M. D. Fads, fashions, and folderol in psychology. *American Psychologist,* 1966, 21, 343–352.

Dunnette, M. D. Research needs of the future in industrial and organizational psychology. *Personnel Psychology,* 1972, 25, 31–40.

Fishbein, M. A. Attitude and the prediction of behavior. In M. A. Fishbein (Ed.), *Readings in attitude theory and measurement.* New York: Wiley, 1967, 477–492.

Ford, R. N. *Motivation through the work itself.* New York: American Management Association, 1969.

Georgopoulos, B. S., Mahoney, G., & Jones, N. A path-goal approach to productivity. *Journal of Applied Psychology,* 1957, 41, 345–353.

Getzels, J. W., & Guba, E. G. Role conflict and effectiveness: An empirical study. *American Sociological Review,* 1954, 19, 164–175.

Goffman, E. *The presentation of the self in everyday life.* New York: The Free Press, 1959.

Gouldner, A. W. *Patterns of industrial bureaucracy.* Glencoe, Ill.: The Free Press, 1954.

Graen, G. Instrumentality theory of work motivation: Some experimental results and suggested modifications. *Journal of Applied Psychology Monograph,* 1969, 53 (Whole No. 2, Part 2).

Graen, G., Alvares, K., Orris, J. B., & Martella, J. Contingency model of leadership effectiveness: Antecedent and evidential results. *Psychological Bulletin,* 1970, 74, 285–296.

Graen, G., Dansereau, F., & Minami, T. Dysfunctional leadership styles. *Organizational Behavior and Human Performance,* 1972, 7, 216–236.

Graen, G., Orris, J. B., & Johnson, T. Role assimilation processes in a complex organization. *Journal of Vocational Behavior,* 1973, 3, 395–420.

Gross, N., Mason, W., & McEachern, A. W. *Exploration in role analysis: Studies of the school superintendency role.* New York: Wiley, 1958.

Haga, W. J., Graen, G., & Dansereau, F. Jr. Professionalism and role making within a service organization: A longitudinal investigation. *American Sociological Review,* 1974, 39, 122–133.

Harris, C. W., Ed. *Problems in measuring change.* Madison: University of Wisconsin Press, 1963.

Herzberg, F., Mausner, B., Peterson, R. O., & Capwell, D. F. *Job attitudes: Review of research and opinion.* Pittsburgh: Psychological Services of Pittsburgh, 1957.

Hinrichs, J. R. Communications activity of industrial research personnel. *Personnel Psychology,* 1964, 17, 193–204.

Hollander, E. P. *Leaders, groups, and influence.* New York: Oxford University Press, 1964.

Hoppock, R. *Job satisfaction.* New York: Harper and Brothers, 1935.

Jones, R. G., & Jones, E. E. Optimum conformity as an ingratiation tactic. *Journal of Personality,* 1964, 32, 436–458.

Kahn, R. L., Wolfe, D. M., Quinn, R. P., Snoek, J. D., & Rosenthal, R. A. *Organizational stress: Studies in role conflict and ambiguity.* New York: Wiley, 1964.

Katz, D. The motivational basis of organizational behavior. *Behavioral Science,* 1964, 9, 131–146.

Katz, D., & Kahn, R. L. *The social psychology of organizations.* New York: Wiley, 1966.

Korman, A. K. Consideration, initiating structure, and organizational criteria: A review. *Personnel Psychology,* 1966, 19, 349–361.

Lewin, K. Behavior as a function of the total situation. In K. Lewin, *Field theory in social science.* New York: Harper and Brothers, 1951.

Lewin, K. *Field theory in social science.* (D. Cartwright, Ed.) New York: Harper and Brothers, 1951.

Lieberman, S. The effects of changes in roles on the attitudes of role occupants. *Human Relations,* 1956, 9, 385–402.

Likert, R. *New patterns of management.* New York: McGraw-Hill, 1961.

McGrath, J. E. Stress and behavior in organizations. In M. D. Dunnette (Ed.), *Handbook of industrial and organizational psychology.* Chicago: Rand McNally, 1976.

McGregor, D. *The human side of enterprise.* New York: McGraw-Hill, 1960.

McGregor, D. *The professional manager.* New York: McGraw-Hill, 1967.

March, J. G., & Simon, H. A. *Organizations.* New York: Wiley, 1958.

Merton, R. K. Bureaucratic structure and personality. *Social Forces,* 1940, 18, 560–568.

Miner, J. B., & Dachler, P. D. Personnel attitudes and motivation. In P. H. Mussen & M. R. Rosenzweig (Eds.), *Annual review of psychology.* Palo Alto, Calif.: Annual Reviews, 1974.

Mitchell, T. R., & Biglan, A. Instrumentality theories: Current uses in psychology. *Psychological Bulletin,* 1971.

Paul, W. J., Robertson, K. B., & Herzberg, F. Job enrichment pays off. *Harvard Business Review,* March-April, 1969, 61–78.

Peak, H. Attitude and motivation. In M. R. Jones (Ed.), *Nebraska symposium on motivation.* Lincoln: University of Nebraska Press, 1955, 149–188.

Peak, H. The effect of aroused motivation attitudes. *Journal of Abnormal and Social Psychology,* 1960, 61, 463–468.

Platt, J. R. Strong inference. *Science,* 1964, 146, 347–352.

Pritchard, R. D., Dunnette, M. D., & Jorgenson, D. O. Effects of equity and inequity on worker performance and satisfaction. *Journal of Applied Psychology Monograph,* 1972, 56, 75–94.

Rosenberg, M. J. Cognitive structure and attitudinal effect. *Journal of Abnormal and Social Psychology,* 1956, 53, 367–372.

Runkel, P. J., & McGrath, J. E. *Research on human behavior: A systematic guide to method.* New York: Holt, Rinehart and Winston, 1972.

Schein, E. H. *Organizational psychology.* Englewood Cliffs, N.J.: Prentice-Hall, 1965.

Selznick, P. *TVA and the grass roots.* Berkeley: University of California Press, 1949.

Tannenbaum, A. S. Control in organizations: Individual adjustment and organizational performance. *Administrative Science Quarterly,* 1962, 7, 236–257.

Vroom, V. H. *Work and motivation.* New York: Wiley, 1964.

Vroom, V. H., & Deci, E. L. The stability of past decision dissonance: A follow-up study of job attitudes of business graduates. *Organizational Behavior and Human Performance,* 1971, 6, 36–49.

Webb, E. J., Campbell, D. T., Schwartz, R. D., & Sechrest, L. *Unobtrusive measures: Nonreactive research in the social sciences.* Chicago: Rand McNally, 1966.

Weick, K. E. *The social psychology of organizing.* Reading, Mass.: Addison-Wesley, 1969.

Ziller, R. C. Individuation and socialization: A theory of assimilation in large organizations. *Human Relations,* 1964, 17, 341–360.

Ziller, R. C. Toward a theory of open and closed groups. *Psychological Bulletin,* 1965, 64, 164–182.

CHAPTER 29

Control Systems in Organizations

EDWARD E. LAWLER III
University of Michigan

Types of Control Systems	Self-Control and Intrinsic Motivation
Individual Behavior in Organizations	How Many Control Systems?
Dysfunctional Effects of Control Systems	References
Reward Systems	

THE IMPACT OF CONTROL SYSTEMS on the behavior of individuals in organizations is analyzed. A thermostat model of control is developed and related to the absence or presence of five behaviors: (1) resistance to control systems, (2) bureaucratic behavior, (3) falsifying control system data, (4) intrinsic motivation, and (5) extrinsic motivation. A review of the literature shows that how control systems are structured strongly influences whether these behaviors will be present in organizations. Particularly important in determining the impact of a control system seems to be its relationship to the organization's reward system. When extrinsic rewards are related to the control system measures, extrinsic motivation, falsification of data, resistance, and bureaucratic behavior are all present. The research also suggests that control systems which are effective in producing extrinsic motivation are often poor for the purposes of planning and coordination.

All viable, complex organizations contain control systems of some type. Although in most formal organizations they are very visible and important, little behavioral research has been done on their impact. A number of organization theorists (e.g., Haire, 1959; Tannenbaum, 1968) have pointed out that social systems tend to become uncoordinated and disintegrate unless some mechanism is introduced to prevent this from happening. Control systems are one important mechanism used to accomplish this. As Tannenbaum (1968) points out, "organization is impossible without some form of control."

Small, poorly differentiated organizations typically do not have extensive formalized control systems. However, large organizations, where specialization of function exists, typically contain a number of formal well-developed control systems. These are the organizations with the greatest need for control systems because they have the most severe coordination and information processing problems. How organizations handle their coordination problems has been shown by Lawrence and Lorsch (1967) to significantly influence their effectiveness. According to their study, different environments demand that organizations have varying degrees and kinds of differentiation and integration if they are to be successful.

A number of organization theorists have argued that control systems are instituted in organizations because management feels it needs information about what is going on lower down in the organization (Woodward, 1970). This information is used by management for many purposes: to coordinate the activities of different parts of the organization, to plan for the future of the organization, to take corrective action where problems exist, and to specify and monitor the behavior of lower level members of the organization. Merton (1940), for example, argues that control systems develop out of management's attempt to obtain control over the behavior of members of the organization as the organization grows larger and more complex. This attempt usually takes the form of rules, regulations, standard procedures, and an information system that reports on how adequately the prescribed behavior is performed.

Eilon (1962) maintains that four elements are necessary before a control system, whether simple or complex, is established— objective setting, planning, execution, and information gathering. Objectives have to be set in relation to the behavior that is desired; plans have to be made about how these objectives can be reached, the plans have to be executed, and information has to be gathered about the effectiveness of the action. These are not always discrete sets of activities, but they do seem to define the minimum elements that must be present if it is to be said that a control system exists. Planning, setting standards, and action are all prerequisites of control. Without some concept of what should be done, it is impossible to make any assessment of what has in fact been done.

There is some confusion in the behavioral science literature about the meaning of control. Sometimes it is used to mean to direct, to influence, or to determine the behavior of someone else. This rather general way of defining control has its roots in the study of influence and power and has led to some interesting research. However, in discussing the role of control systems in the present chapter, this definition is not used. Rather, in agreement with Eilon's definition, control refers to the task of ensuring that planned activities are producing the desired results (Woodward, 1970). The focus of this chapter is on how control systems impact on the behavior of the members of organizations. How a control system impacts on behavior is heavily influenced by both the nature of the system and the nature of the people. Thus, the first part of the chapter is devoted to defining control systems and looking at the key ways in which they differ. This is followed by a brief discussion of the determinants of human behavior. These two sections serve as an introduction to the major focus of the chapter, which is on how different types of control systems impact on behavior. Based upon the literature and psychological theory, consideration is given to when the dysfunctional effects of budgets, management information systems, and other control systems are likely to appear and to how control systems influence both intrinsic and extrinsic motivation.

TYPES OF CONTROL SYSTEMS

Most organizations contain many control systems. They include such systems as budgets, performance appraisals, management information systems, books of administrative rules, regulations and procedures, and production reports. Although no really adequate classification system for control systems exists, a number have been suggested. For example, control systems can be classified according to the kind of data gathered. Most systems deal with one of three kinds of data: financial, production, or administrative. Control systems also can be classified according to the purpose or purposes they serve in the organization. Some exist mainly for measuring performance in order to increase extrinsic motivation. Others exist to provide top management with information they need for long-range planning. Still others exist primarily to provide ongoing feedback to employees about how they are performing their jobs.

Reeves and Woodward (1970) propose two continua for classifying control systems: personal-mechanical and unitary-fragmented. The personal-mechanical dimension refers to how control is exercised in an organization. An example of a personal control system is the owner-manager who gives instructions to his employees and monitors their work. Examples of mechanical systems are such impersonal controls as cost control systems, quality control systems, and the automatic control systems of continuous flow production plants.

The unitary-fragmented dimension refers to how various control processes are linked with each other. Some firms try to relate different control systems so that an overall integration of managerial control (unitary system) exists. Other firms do not establish such linkages. Thus, a control system can be characterized as either integrated or not, and the control systems of a firm can be similarly classified.

Rackham and Woodward (1970) have classified the control systems of a number of firms according to the two dimensions above. Unit and small batch production firms tend to have unitary and mainly personal control systems while process production firms tend to unitary and impersonal control systems. This work represents an interesting first attempt to relate characteristics of organizations to characteristics of their control systems. Further research of this type can help us understand more fully why organizations develop the kind of controls they do and should also give us a better idea of the frequency with which the different kinds of control systems are present in organizations.

McKelvey (1970) and others have drawn an analogy between a thermostat furnace system and the control systems that operate in many organizations. This is a useful analogy because it helps to elaborate upon Eilon's idea about what functions are present in a control system and suggests an approach to classifying control systems. The thermostat system that controls the heating level in a room consists of (1) a *sensor* that measures the temperature of a room, (2) an adjustable device that sets a *standard* which is the desired temperature (often this is a temperature band), (3) a *discriminator* that compares the sensed information with the standard, (4) an *effector* that responds to the discriminator by turning the activity (furnace) on or off, (5) some wires for *communication,* (6) the *activity* itself, in this case the furnace, and (7) a source of *energy* that powers the activity.

Many of the control systems that operate in organizations contain these same seven functions. Probably the closest analogy to the thermostat model in most organizations is the budget system. Like the thermostat, the budget measures only one particular aspect of performance (financial expenditure), standards are set (budgetary goals), budgetary performance is compared with the standard (often by a controller or superior), action is taken when a deviance occurs from the standard, communication takes place in the form of financial reports, and an activity, spending money, takes place that derives its energy from the motivation of the people in the system. This analysis has not gone far enough, however, if we are interested in the impact of control systems on behavior. Admittedly, the thermostat analogy is a good one, but to predict people's reactions to the budget we need to know more about the system and how it operates than whether it has the same seven functions as the thermostat. Just knowing there is a sensor and a discriminator, for example, is not enough. We also need to know the answers to the following questions that are concerned with how the functions are performed:

1. What does the sensor actually measure? That is, what kind of behavior is it sensitive to? Just as in understanding the impact of temperature, it is important to know something about humidity, it is impor-

tant, in organizational control systems, to know which behavior is and is not measured by the system.

2. Who sets the standards? Are they unilaterally set by a superior, or are they jointly set by the subordinate and his superior? Involved here are questions of participation, power sharing, and leadership style.

3. Who or what acts as the discriminator? Here it is important whether the superior, the actor himself, a staff person, or someone else acts as the discriminator.

4. What kind of action is taken to turn the activity on or off? Are rewards and punishments used to motivate the behavior?

5. Who receives the communication concerning deviations from the standard? Do they go to the person whose behavior is being measured? Do they go to the person and someone else (e.g., his boss)? Involved here are the issues of whether the organization is counting on self-control to operate (information only to person) and what kind of feedback the person gets about his performance.

6. What is the activity? Can it be measured? Is it essential that it be performed? How well is it measured by the sensor?

7. What is the basic source of motivation for the activity? Is it extrinsic or intrinsic?

Not all control systems are as close to the thermostat model as is the budget. In some systems, several of the elements are missing or poorly developed. For example, many organizations have rules and regulations about how activities, like customer relations, are to be performed, but they have no really well-developed sensor or measure of how they are being performed. Production reports, unlike the thermostat, sometimes do not operate on the basis of standards and deviance from that standard. They simply sense and report how much of a given activity has taken place.

It is the thesis of this chapter that the best way to analyze how people will react to a particular control system is to focus on the questions suggested by the thermostat model rather than by relying on one or more of the other ways of classifying control systems. These questions are concerned directly with the determinants of behavior, whereas the classification systems presented earlier operate at levels that are more removed from the determinants of behavior. It is not possible to predict the reactions of people to control systems from knowing whether they are mechanical or personal systems. If we know how the information from each is used and how the standards are set, however, it is possible to predict behavior because these are the things which influence behavior. Undoubtedly, mechanical and personal systems *do* have different effects on behavior, but it is because they differ on more fundamental grounds, such as who receives information and how it gets used. Thus, these issues are emphasized throughout the discussion of the behavioral impact of organizational control systems which follows, because they are helpful guidelines for showing when control systems are likely to produce dysfunctional consequences, such as invalid information, resistance, and rigid bureaucratic behavior, and such functional consequences as extrinsic motivation and self-control.

INDIVIDUAL BEHAVIOR IN ORGANIZATIONS

Closely tied to the control systems in most organizations is the reward system. Reward systems are needed in organizations because the behaviors needed by the organization (i.e., working on an assembly line) frequently are behaviors which people will not perform unless they are given some sort of extrinsic reward. The control system specifies the behavior that the employees must perform, and the reward system is created to reward those people who perform in the desired manner. The performance measurement part of most control systems is crucial here because it provides information about who should be rewarded and/or punished. In a sense, the reward system helps to provide the motivational mechanism that makes the control system viable.

When behavioral scientists have focused on reward and control systems, they have usually pointed out how reward and control systems can end up defeating the purposes for which they were established, that is, making the organization more effective (March & Simon, 1958). They point out that people often rigidly adhere to rules to the detriment of the organization's goals, and that they manage to distort the information that is processed by the communication system. These dysfunctional behavioral reactions certainly do occur, and they will be discussed more fully; however, control systems can and often do play a vital and functional role in organizations.

Even though behavioral scientists have at times been critical of control systems, they have not gone so far as to suggest that they are unnecessary. No one denies that with large size and specialization of function some sort of information and control system is needed. What behavioral scientists like McGregor (1960) have suggested is a new motivational basis for the operation of an organization's control system. They have pointed out that people can be motivated by things other than the formal rewards and punishments offered by the organization. They further argue that because of people's intrinsic motivation to do well, a "properly" administered control system will motivate people to exercise *self-control*. That is, people will perform their jobs as specified regardless of whether formal rewards and punishments are tied to their behavior. This emphasis on the role of self-control is particularly strong in the writings of Argyris (1964), Likert (1961), McGregor (1960), and Tannenbaum (1968). It has led critics of this viewpoint to argue that if the traditional control system approach ignores human motivation and can be referred to as "organizations without people," then the self-control idea smacks of "people without organization."

The control system and its tie-in to the formal reward system is so basic to what many people think an organization is that it is not surprising the idea of self-control is equated with no control. The evidence is mixed, but it does suggest that under certain conditions people can exercise self-control and that when they do, self-control can eliminate many of the problems that occur when control systems operate solely on the basis of formal rewards and punishments. The challenge is to specify when self-control is likely to be effective and when it isn't. This can be done with some degree of certainty by considering what is known about human behavior. Basic to any discussion of control systems is some conception of the nature of human beings. As Argyris (1957) states, implicit in any control system is a set of assumptions about what causes human behavior. He points out, for example, that traditional reward-based control systems seem to assume that:

1. Man is rational and motivated to maximize his economic gain.

2. Man is not a social animal.

3. Man can be treated in a standardized manner.

4. Man needs to be stimulated by management if he is to work.

This set of assumptions about human behavior does not, of course, fit with what is known; in fact, it is precisely because people don't fit these assumptions that control systems often lead to dysfunctional behavior. Before we consider the kinds of dysfunctional reactions that control systems produce, however, it is necessary to give a brief overview of what is known about the determinants of human behavior.

Expectancy Theory

During the last ten years, expectancy theory has been successfully used by a number of psychologists to understand individual behavior in organizations (see Lawler, 1973, for a review). This theory makes a number of assumptions about the nature of individuals that are different from those that

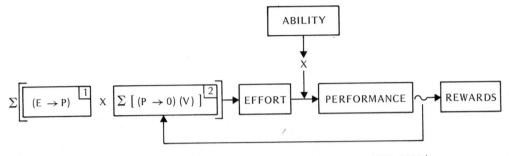

Figure 1.   Extrinsic motivation model. (From Porter & Lawler, 1968; Lawler, 1970, 1971.)

underlie traditional control systems. A considerable amount of evidence supporting its validity exists, and it appears to be capable of explaining the kinds of reactions that control systems produce.

A number of different authors have stated expectancy-type theories. They all emphasize that people set performance goals for themselves and that people are forward-looking in the sense that they are concerned about what kind of outcomes their behavior will produce. Figure 1 presents an expectancy model based upon earlier models developed by Porter and Lawler (1968) and Lawler (1970, 1971). It shows the relationship that exists among expectancy, instrumentality, importance attitudes, and extrinsic motivation. A separate slightly different model is needed to deal with intrinsic motivation; this is shown in Figure 2. The first term in the models, $E \rightarrow P$, refers to a person's subjective probability about the likelihood that he can perform at a given level; or in other words, that effort on his part will lead to successful performance. This term can be

thought of as varying from 0 to 1. As a general rule, the less likely a person feels that performing at a given level is possible, the less likely it is he will try to perform at that level (Vroom, 1964). The models also show that this $E \rightarrow P$ probability is directly influenced by self-esteem. The higher a person's self-esteem, the more realistic will be the $E \rightarrow P$ subjective probabilities. A person's $E \rightarrow P$ probabilities are also, of course, strongly influenced by the situation and by previous experience in that and similar situations.

The second factor that influences motivation is made up of a combination of a number of beliefs about what the outcomes of successful performance will be and about the valence of these outcomes (Box 2). As Figure 1 shows, the person's subjective probability that performance will lead to an outcome $(P \rightarrow O)$ should be multiplied by the valence of that outcome (V). Although the model doesn't show it, outcomes gain their valence from their ability to satisfy the needs individuals have. Maslow's (1954)

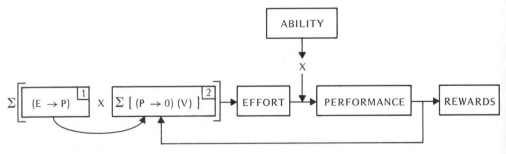

Figure 2.   Intrinsic motivation model.

need hierarchy theory provides a reasonable list of the needs most people have. It includes basic physiological needs and a need for security as well as social, esteem, and self-realization needs. Valence is considered to vary from $+1$ (very desirable) to -1 (very undesirable), and the performance to outcome probabilities to vary from $+1$ (performance sure to lead to outcome) to O (performance not related to outcome). The products of all probability times valence combinations are summed for all outcomes that are seen to be related to performance. Hence, this second factor will be larger, the more positively valent rewards are seen to be obtained as a result of good performance, and the less negatively valent outcomes are seen to result from performance. The final link in the model is a wavy line that connects performance to rewards. It is drawn as a wavy line to indicate that extrinsic rewards do not always follow directly from performance. Figure 1 also shows that a feedback loop from the strength of the connection between performance and outcomes to the $P \rightarrow O$ probability exists. This is included to illustrate the importance of learning in determining what a person's performance outcome probabilities will be in a situation (Graen, 1969). Clearly, the degree to which performance has been closely followed by outcomes in past similar situations will influence the person's beliefs about what outcomes performance will lead to now and in the future.

The two factors that so far have been said to influence the strength of a person's extrinsic motivation to perform in a given manner are (1) the person's belief that effort can be converted into performance, and (2) the net attractiveness of the events that are felt to stem from the performance. These two factors combine multiplicatively so if the first is zero or if the second is zero or negative, there will be no motivation to perform effectively. If a person doesn't believe that performance will follow from effort, he or she will not be motivated to perform even though feeling it will lead to a number

of desirable outcomes. Similarly, unless performance is seen to lead to positive outcomes, the person will not be motivated to perform even if he or she is sure putting forth effort will lead to performance. On the other hand, the greater the product of these two factors, the greater will be the motivation to perform.

The intrinsic motivation model is particularly important when control systems are considered because of the recent emphasis on self-control. It is similar to the one presented for extrinsic motivation with two exceptions: The first is that it shows the $E \rightarrow P$ probability as influencing the $P \rightarrow O$ probabilities. This is included because much of the research on achievement motivation has shown that achievement motivation comes into play only when certain $E \rightarrow P$ probabilities exist. Both Atkinson (1964) and McClelland (1955, 1961) have suggested that the highest intrinsic motivation results when effort is seen to have only a 50-50 chance of leading to performance. Under the 50-50 condition, a number of intrinsic rewards are tied to performance that do not come into play when there is certainty that effort will lead to good performance. Feelings of achievement, accomplishment, and growth are often seen to result from successful performance when there is less than a perfect relationship between effort and performance. Thus, in some instances motivation may be highest when the effort to performance probability is around .5 because of the potential influence of this belief on $P \rightarrow O$ beliefs.

The intrinsic reward model also differs from the extrinsic one in that it shows a more direct connection between performance and rewards (straight line). This comes about because the rewards are given by individuals to themselves and thus are closely related to behavior. Because of this close connection and the strong $P \rightarrow O$ connections it causes, intrinsic rewards can be very significant motivators.

Although both of these models go beyond the data that presently exist, there is evidence to support much of the thinking in them.

The models suggest that $E \rightarrow P$ beliefs and $P \rightarrow O$ beliefs should be related to performance, and a number of studies have shown these connections (Galbraith & Cummings, 1967; Georgopoulos, Mahoney, & Jones, 1957; Hackman & Porter, 1968; Lawler & Porter, 1967; Porter & Lawler, 1968; Spitzer, 1964). The two models also lead to the prediction that $E \rightarrow P$ and $P \rightarrow O$ beliefs should be more highly correlated with future performance than with present or past performance, and one study has suggested that this is true (Lawler, 1968). They suggest that attitudes about the value of rewards should be related to performance only where those rewards are related to performance, and one study has found this (Schneider & Olson, 1970). In summary, a number of studies have provided fairly consistent support for the specific empirical hypotheses that are suggested by the expectancy models of motivation.

Motivation and Performance

The strength of a person's motivation to perform is most directly reflected in effort; that is, in how hard he or she tries to perform. This effort expenditure may or may not result in good performance (Lawler & Porter, 1967) since the person must possess the necessary abilities in order to perform the job well. A number of authors (e.g., Lawler, 1966; Maier, 1955; Vroom, 1964) have argued that motivation and ability combine multiplicatively in order to determine performance. A similar view is presented in Figures 1 and 2. Ability is shown to combine multiplicatively with effort in order to make the point that if ability is zero, performance will also be zero. In other words, unless both ability and effort are high, there cannot be good performance. Great amounts of effort cannot completely take the place of ability. Although it is not shown in the model, situational blocks and incorrect perceptions of what is appropriate behavior can often prevent performance

from being high even when ability and motivation are high.

DYSFUNCTIONAL EFFECTS OF CONTROL SYSTEMS

There is no question that control systems often produce behavior which is dysfunctional. Three types of behavior have received the most attention: (1) rigid bureaucratic behavior, (2) resistance, and (3) the production of invalid information. These will be discussed in turn and an effort will be made to specify when control systems are likely to produce these behaviors.

Bureaucratic Behavior

Blau (1955) has made the point that control systems can lead to employees behaving in rigid ways that are dysfunctional as far as the goals of the organization are concerned. This phenomenon, which is referred to as bureaucratic behavior, has also been described by a number of other authors. It consists of individuals behaving in ways that are called for by the control system, but that are dysfunctional as far as the generally agreed upon goals of the organization are concerned. Bureaucratic behavior comes about because people often act in whatever way helps them look good on the measures used by control systems. In many cases this is a functional outcome, but in others it is not. It is those cases in which bureaucratic behavior is dysfunctional that have "caught the eye" of behavioral scientists. At this point in time, there are a number of examples of this phenomenon in the literature.

Blau (1955) analyzed the operation of a department in a public agency of a state government. The agency's "major responsibility is to serve workers seeking employment and employers seeking workers" (p. 19). The tasks performed by the organization included interviewing clients, helping them to fill out application forms, counseling them, and referring them to jobs. These activities were seen by the organization as instrumental to the accomplishment of the objectives of the organization, and a control system was instituted to be sure that they were done. As a basis for evaluating the individual interviewers, statistical records were kept by managers of such things as how many interviews a particular interviewer conducted. The effect of the control system was to motivate the employees to perform those behaviors that were measured by the system (e.g., interviewing). Unfortunately, this did not always contribute to the organizational goal of placing workers on jobs. As Blau points out:

An instrument intended to further the achievement of organizational objectives, statistical records constrained interviewers to think of maximizing the indices as their major goal, sometimes at the expense of these very objectives. They avoided operations which would take up time without helping them to improve their record, such as interviewing clients for whom application forms had to be made out, and wasted their own and the public's time on activities intended only to raise the figures on their record. Their concentration upon this goal, since it was important for their ratings, made them unresponsive to requests from clients that would interfere with its attainment. (p. 43)

Berliner (1961) has described the situation faced by plant managers in the Soviet Union. They are typically placed on a production-based pay incentive plan and are given unreasonably high production goals on the assumption that this is best for the overall economy.

...the bonus system is an effective device for eliciting a high level of managerial effort, but in the context of excessively high production targets, it induces management to make certain types of decisions that are contrary to the intent of the state. The production of unplanned products, the concealment of production capacity, the falsification of reports, and the deterioration of quality are the unintended consequences of the system of managerial incentives.

...the incentives that motivate managers to strive for the fulfillment of their production targets are the same incentives that motivate them to evade the regulations of the planning system. Because of the tightness of the supply system ... managers are compelled to defend their enterprise's position by over ordering supplies, by hoarding materials and equipment, and by employing expediters whose function it is to keep the enterprise supplied with materials at all costs, legal or otherwise. (p. 369)

Cohen (1966), in discussing the Soviet situation, points out that the dysfunctional consequences which occur because of the managers' rigid obsession with meeting their production goals should not be taken as evidence that the American system is necessarily better. The American system stimulates its own form of societally dysfunctional behavior. According to him, "the American system is admirably contrived to encourage deviance on an enormous scale in the area of merchandising" (p. 83). The reason for this is simply that American "control" and reward systems pay off not on productivity but on profits.

Babchuk and Goode (1951) have provided an interesting case study that highlights how control systems, when combined with rewards, can cause employees to behave dysfunctionally. They studied a selling unit in a department store where a pay incentive plan was introduced to pay employees on the basis of sales volume. Total sales initially increased, but this was done in a way that was not functional as far as the long-term goals of the organization were concerned. There was considerable "sales grabbing" and "tying up the trade," as well as a general neglect of such unrewarded and unmeasured functions as stock work and arranging merchandise for displays.

It is possible to cite a number of other examples of situations where employees respond to control systems with rigid control-system-oriented behavior that is dysfunctional from the point of view of the goals of the organization. In fact, the negative connotation that has become attached to the initially neutral term bureaucracy stems from just this kind of behavior. All too often in large bureaucracies the control system seems to do more to prevent the goals of the organization from being accomplished than to help them be accomplished. What is needed at this point is not more evidence that the phenomenon exists but a better analysis of why it exists.

A number of sociologists have talked about the phenomenon (e.g., Merton, 1940; Selznick, 1949; Gouldner, 1954); their views have been summarized by March and Simon (1958). Merton's explanation is contained in Figure 3. It shows that rigidity stems from the emphasis on reliability; and from the need to defend individual actions. However, Merton does not explain why *all* individuals do not respond this way to the emphasis on reliability, nor does he say anything about the conditions which favor people responding this way. Clearly, everyone does not respond to control systems

with rigid behavior all the time. People are often willing to "break the rules" in order to get things done. Frank (1959), in discussing Soviet management practices, has noted that managers often violate some standards and even laws in order to keep their organization functioning effectively. This in fact occurs so much that it has become socially legitimate. One of the most effective forms of labor bargaining is a work-to-rules action. What this means is that unlike "normal" times, the employees follow the rules closely, observing the letter of the law, and as a result the organization functions much less effectively. It is also obvious that organizations differ widely in the degree to which the members rigidly respond to the rules and measures set up by the control system (Burns & Stalker, 1961). Part of the explanation for this difference rests in the nature of the control systems that are used in different organizations and part of it rests in the nature of the individuals that work in different organizations.

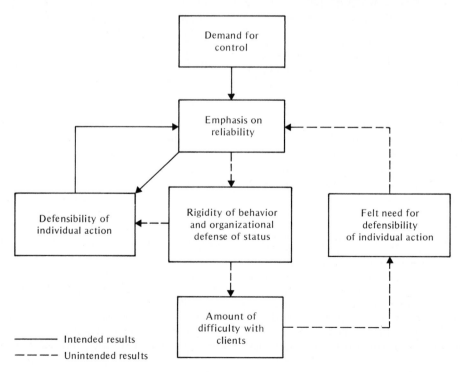

Figure 3.   The simplified Merton model. (From March & Simon, 1958; Merton, 1940.)

It is possible to state some general characteristics of control systems and of people that make rigid bureaucratic behavior particularly likely to occur. This can best be done by looking at some of the questions that were raised in the discussion of the thermostat model and by looking at several others concerning the nature of individuals.

WHAT IS SENSED OR MEASURED? Rigid dysfunctional bureaucratic behavior occurs when the control system does not adequately measure the kinds of behavior that must be performed if the organization is to function effectively. This usually happens because the system is not set up to measure *all* the behaviors a person should perform. It may also happen because for a particular job there is no simple measurable output that contributes to organizational effectiveness, and the control system has to measure the process a person goes through rather than the results obtained. This can cause the person to focus more on the process than on what is being contributed to organizational effectiveness. The study by Babchuk and Goode (1951) provides a good example of a control system that failed to measure all the necessary or relevant behavior, while the one by Blau (1955) shows what can occur when systems measure activities rather than results.

Performing according to the control system only becomes a problem and is regarded as dysfunctional bureaucratic behavior when the sensor measures are in some way inadequate. In most cases control-system-oriented behavior is not dysfunctional. In fact, the effectiveness of many organizations is based upon the fact that most of the time people let the control system guide their behavior. For example, the measures of productivity which are taken for most jobs often encourage employees to be more productive and to emphasize productive behavior rather than those nonproductive behaviors which are not measured.

WHO SETS THE STANDARDS? The Russian example described by Frank (1959) illustrates the point that if the standards are seen as unreasonable by the participants, they are particularly likely to engage in dysfunctional behavior in order to reach these standards. That is, if the standards are set in such a way that they can only be achieved by dysfunctional behavior such as falsifying reports, abusing equipment, and the neglect of other important activities, then such behavior is likely to occur. It is possible that if the employees were allowed to participate in the setting of standards they would be more likely to see them as reasonable and acceptable. This could come about either because the participation process would produce more reasonable goals or because it would lead to a better understanding of and psychological commitment to the goals. There is evidence which shows that participation can increase goal acceptance; however, at this time there is none which shows that it can reduce bureaucratic behavior (Vroom, 1964; Lawler, 1973).

If the goals are not set by the person, a logical case can be made that it is important who the person is that does set them. The more expertise and organizational legitimacy the standard setter has, the less likely dysfunctional behavior is to result. Expertise is important because it should influence the reasonableness of the standards which are set; legitimacy is important because of the hierarchical nature of organizations and people's expectations about who should and should not control their job activities. When standards are set by someone who is not seen as a legitimate setter (e.g., remote staff person), it may be easier to justify engaging in dysfunctional behavior.

WHO ACTS AS THE DISCRIMINATOR? Based upon the extrinsic motivation model it would seem that the more the discrimination function is performed by someone other than the actor, the more the control system will be adhered to and the greater the potential for bureaucratic behavior. Once an outsider becomes involved, the possibility exists that rewards can be given on the basis of how the person performs the behavior that is measured by the control system. The rewards that are given may be formal rewards (e.g., pay, promotion) or they may be simply approval or disapproval as shown by the discriminator. As is stressed by expectancy theory, once valued rewards become involved the person's behavior is going to be influenced by what he or she feels must be done in order to obtain them. The perception may well develop that rewards depend on the control system measures if someone with reward power acts as the discriminator. Based on this reasoning and expectancy theory, if the discriminator function is performed by a person's superior, the chances of rigid adherence to the system will be greater than if it is performed by a staff person or some other outside agent who lacks reward power.

WHO GETS THE INFORMATION AND HOW IS IT USED? Very much related to the issue of who acts as the discriminator is the issue of who gets the information about the adequacy of the performance and how this information is used. The more it is used as a basis for the giving of rewards and punishments, the more people will be motivated to look good in terms of the measures. The expectancy model clearly points out that when people see a given behavior as leading to extrinsic rewards they value, they will be motivated to carry out this behavior. Thus when information from the control system is fed to the superior and used as a basis for rewarding or punishing people, it follows that employees will be very concerned about looking good on the measures. This in turn sets up the possibility of people demonstrating the kind of rigid bureaucratic behavior that is often dysfunctional.

WHAT ARE THE PEOPLE LIKE? Expectancy theory emphasizes that how people respond to reward systems is very much a function of how much they value the rewards that are involved. If they do not value the rewards, they are not likely to perform the behavior required to obtain the rewards. This has obvious implications for understanding which

individuals are likely to respond to control systems with rigid bureaucratic behavior. Those individuals who value the rewards that are given on the basis of the information that is provided by the control system are the ones who are particularly likely to try to look good on the measures. Therefore, they will be the ones who are most likely to engage in dysfunctional behaviors in order to look good. On the other hand, if the information from the control system is not used as a basis for the giving and withholding of rewards and punishments, there should be no relationship between individual differences in reward value and bureaucratic behavior.

HOW OBVIOUS ARE ORGANIZATIONAL GOALS? One of the things that seems to contribute to bureaucratic behavior is the lack of any clear-cut generally accepted set of organizational goals (Selznick, 1949). When organizational goals are not clear and generally accepted, there is a tendency for individuals to focus on organizational subunit goals. This is particularly true in large organizations where specialization of function exists and where employees are rewarded on the basis of measures of subunit performance (Lawrence & Lorsch, 1967). In fact, subunit identification may take place even when the organization's goals are clear if a high degree of structural differentiation exists within the organization. In many cases goal differentiation is functional because good subunit performance leads to effective organizational performance; in other cases, however, organizational performance may suffer (Wildavsky, 1964). There are times when "good" subunit performance as defined by the control system is not what the organization needs, and yet it unavoidably occurs (Frank, 1959). The Russian example of the plant managers illustrates this point quite well.

Often "good" subunit performance occurs even though clear organizational goals exist, because the lack of any general acceptance of them discourages individuals from behaving in ways that despite their contribution to organizational effectiveness make their subunit look "bad." This is particularly likely to be true in work organizations when individuals have not been involved in the setting of the organization's goals.

SUMMARY. Overall our discussion suggests that rigid bureaucratic behavior which may be dysfunctional is most likely to occur when the following conditions exist:

1. The control system measures are not inclusive enough or do not measure goal accomplishment adequately.

2. The standards in the control system are set too high and by someone other than the actor.

3. The discrimination function is performed by an outsider who has reward power.

4. The information from the control system goes to a person who can and does use it as a basis for giving rewards.

5. The people subjected to the control system value the rewards given by the reward system.

6. The organization goals are not clear and/or generally accepted.

7. A high level of subunit identification exists.

Invalid Data

All control systems need valid data about what is occurring in the organization if they are to be effective; yet, behavioral scientists have shown repeatedly that accurate and valid information is often not forthcoming (see, e.g., Wilensky, 1967). As Argyris (1964) points out, control systems tend to be effective and to produce valid information for the unimportant and programmed problems and to produce invalid information for the important and non-programmed problems.

There is evidence to suggest that control systems produce two kinds of invalid data. They produce invalid data about what can be done and they produce invalid data about what has been done. The first kind of in-

valid data makes planning very difficult, while the second makes the control of day-to-day activities very difficult. The research on budgets and on piece rate payment systems provides a number of good examples of situations where organizations are given invalid data about what is possible. In order to understand how and why invalid data occurs, it is worth reviewing a few of the case studies that have illustrated this phenomenon.

Whyte (1955) has provided some graphic case examples of how individuals distort the data that are fed into production measuring systems. Most of Whyte's examples are cases where individuals under pay incentive systems distort data about the kind of production that is possible on a given job. The following quote illustrates one worker's attitude toward the measurement system and the time study men who run it.

"... you got to outwit that son-of-a-bitch! You got to use your noodle while you're working, and think your work out ahead as you go along! You got to add in movements you know you ain't going to make when you're running the job! Remember, if you don't screw them, they're going to screw you! ... Every movement counts! ...

"Remember those bastards are paid to screw you," said Starkey. "And that's all they got to think about. They'll stay up half the night figuring out how to beat you out of a dime. They figure you're going to try to fool them, so they make allowances for that. They set the prices low enough to allow for what you do."

"Well, then, what the hell chance have I got?" asked Tennessee.

"It's up to you to figure out how to fool them more than they allow for," said Starkey.

"... When the time-study man came around, I set the speed at 180. I knew damn well he would ask me to push it up, so I started low enough. He finally pushed me up to 445, and I ran the job later at 610. If I'd started at 445, they'd have timed it at 610. Then I got him on the reaming, too. I ran the reamer for him at 130 speed and .025 feed. He asked me if I couldn't run the reamer any faster than that, and I told him I had to run the reamer slow to keep the hole size. I showed him two pieces with oversize holes that the day man ran. I picked them out for the occasion! But later on I ran the reamer at 610 speed and .018 feed, same as the drill. So I didn't have to change gears—and then there was a burring operation on the job too. For the time-study man I burred each piece after I drilled and reamed, and I ran the burring tool by automatic feed. But afterwards, I let the burring go till I drill 25 pieces or so; and I just touched them up a little by holding them under the burring tool." (Whyte, 1955, pp. 15–18)

Gardner (1945) has also pointed out that employees often give invalid data in industry and provides an example of how it can occur.

In one case, a group, who worked together in assembling a complicated and large sized steel framework, worked out a system to be used only when the rate setter was present. They found that by tightening certain bolts first, the frame would be slightly sprung and all the other bolts would bind and be very difficult to tighten. When the rate setter was not present, they followed a different sequence and the work went much faster.

Argyris (1951, 1964), Hofstede (1967), and others have pointed out that employees also often provide misleading data when they are asked to give budgetary estimates. Not surprisingly they usually tend to ask for much larger amounts than they need because they realize that their budget request will be cut and in order to play the game, they must come in with a high initial budget figure. On the other hand, in instances where a low budget estimate is needed in order to get a budget or project approved (e.g., under some Program Planning and Budgeting Systems, Lyden & Miller, 1968), a low estimate is submitted. The budget bargaining process managers go through with their superiors is not too dissimilar from the one that goes on between the time study man and the worker who is on a piece rate plan or work standard plan. The time study man and the superior both

try to get valid data about what is possible in the future, and the employees who are subject to the control system often give invalid data and try to get as favorable a standard, or budget, as they can.

How frequently do employees consciously provide invalid data when standards and budgets are being set? It is impossible to come up with any hard figures, but the research on standard setting suggests that it happens much of the time (Lawler, 1971). There is less evidence with respect to how often it occurs in the setting of budgets, but the data suggest it happens much of the time there too. In this situation as in the standard setting situation, low trust typically exists, and as a study by Mellinger (1956) shows, when low trust exists people are likely to conceal data or to communicate invalid data.

There are also a number of examples in the behavioral science literature of cases where employees have fed invalid information about what has happened into the control system. Again it is difficult from the literature to determine just how often this overt falsification occurs, but it probably is not as common as the practice of making consciously invalid estimates of what is possible. Undoubtedly one reason for this dissimilarity between the two processes is that it is easier to catch and punish an employee who has misreported what has happened than it is to catch and punish one who has consciously given an erroneous estimate.

Roethlisberger and Dickson (1939) in their classic study of the Bank Wiring Room point out how employees can manage the kind of production reports that go outside their work group. In this case, the employees were on a pay incentive plan and they wanted to show a consistent daily production figure. They did this by not reporting what they produced on some days and reporting things as having been produced that were never produced. Similar examples have been cited by others who have looked at the way employees react to financial incentive systems (e.g., Whyte, 1955; Lawler, 1971).

There are also data available which suggest that employees will consciously feed invalid information into management information systems (e.g., Argyris, 1971; Mumford & Banks, 1967; Pettigrew, 1970, 1972, 1973). Such falsification often occurs in order to cover up any errors or poor performance that has occurred. Employees also feed invalid data to the management information systems in order to make the system look bad and to discourage people from using it. Often there is strong resistance to management information systems and employees try to make them fail. The behavioral basis for this resistance will be discussed later. At this point it is sufficient to note that it is present and that one way it appears is in the form of invalid data being given to the system. Giving the system invalid data can be a very effective way to resist a system since it can lead to the system reporting obviously illogical and incorrect data, and this can discourage management from relying on the system.

Finally, it should be noted that invalid data may be fed into a control system simply because the system demands the data and it is not available. Sometimes control systems demand data that simply is not and cannot be collected. Faced with this situation an employee may choose to estimate the data rather than to admit that it does not exist or to give up on the system. This would seem to be a particular problem where computer-based management information systems are being installed. They often call for historical cost, production, and other data that simply are not available (Argyris, 1971). It seems to have frequently happened in Vietnam when commanders were asked to provide data on the number of enemy that were killed and wounded.

Despite the fact that much of the research on the production of invalid data is from case studies, it is possible to state with some exactitude the conditions under which control systems are likely to be faced with in-

valid data input. This can be done by referring to the questions suggested earlier about the nature of control systems and by looking at the characteristics of individuals that were outlined in the expectancy theory model.

WHAT IS MEASURED? There is relatively little evidence on the degree to which different kinds of measures are likely to produce distorted data. One obvious point does need to be made, however, about the nature of the data that are collected. Employees are more likely to try to distort subjective data than objective data. For one thing falsifying subjective data is easier to do and the possible repercussions are less. It also relates to the general point that biasing is most likely to occur where uncertainty exists (March & Simon, 1958; Pettigrew, 1970). This means that a manager is more likely to report that morale is high when it is low and that a group of subordinates is working well when they are working poorly than he is to report that he did make his budget when he didn't. Or in the case of a commander in Vietnam, he is more likely to report invalid data on enemy casualties than he is on his own. One implication of this, of course, is that organizations need to mistrust measures of subjective dimensions, particularly when the sensor is the person responsible for the measure, and when the measure will be used for evaluative and reward purposes.

It is also worth noting that the more important the organization considers the measure to be, the more likely it is to be distorted. This relates to Argyris's (1964) point that organizations have their greatest difficulty gathering data when important issues are involved. Organizationally important measures are more likely to make a difference in a person's life, and because of this increased importance there is greater pressure to look good on them. This pressure may be either internally generated by the person or externally generated by the reward system in the organization. In short, measures of important dimensions are more likely to be distorted because they can make a difference to a person, and, therefore, according to expectancy theory there should be more motivation present to distort the measures.

WHO SETS THE STANDARDS? There is some evidence which suggests that when standards are set by others, and when they are seen as unreasonable, invalid data are likely to be produced (Hofstede, 1967). The piece rate incentive studies show how employees distort data when standards are set by time study engineers. Interestingly, there are studies which suggest this may not happen when the standards are set by the people. For example, Gillespie (1948) has reported on a study where workers were allowed to participate in setting rates. According to him (p. 95):

When a new job was to be quoted, the job description was sent to the shop and the men got together and worked out methods, times, and prices; the result went back via the foremen to the sales department in order that a quotation could be sent. I was, as said above, surprised and horrified at this unplanned, nonspecialized and dishonesty-provoking procedure and set out to improve organization and method. As I went deeper into the study of department economics I found:

   a. The group's estimates were intelligent.
   b. The estimates were honest and enabled the men, working consistently at a good speed, to earn a figure LESS THAN THAT COMMON TO SIMILAR SHOPS ON ORGANIZED PIECEWORK.
   c. The overhead costs were lower than they would have been if the shop was run on modern lines.

There is also reason to believe that when standards are set by outsiders and particularly when they are seen as unreasonable, individuals are more likely to give invalid data about what is actually being accomplished. The Russian example cited earlier illustrates how people react when unreasonably high rates are set by outsiders. Since this violates their sense of fairness, they feel it is legitimate for them to act unfairly in order to reach the standard. This may mean distorting the data in order to look good. The point is that unreasonable standards set by others can both put pressure on an individual to give invalid data and a means for psychologically justifying the giving of invalid data. Falsification of data needn't occur simply because standards are set unilaterally by someone else, particularly if the person has legitimacy as a standard setter. It is likely to occur, however, if the standards are set by someone else and are seen as high and difficult to reach.

WHO ACTS AS THE DISCRIMINATOR? The more the individual whose behavior is being measured is in the position of acting as the discriminator and sensor of his or her own behavior, the greater the possibility there is for invalid data. If the individual reports the data and compares it to the standard, it is easier for him or her to distort it than if it were done by someone else who must be misled or deceived. Whether he or she actually will distort it under these conditions is probably very much influenced by how the data will be used and who receives them.

WHO RECEIVES INFORMATION AND HOW IS IT USED? Probably the most important determinant of whether individuals will give invalid data to the control system is how the data will be used. If the data are estimates of future activity or simply statements of the current activity level and they are to be used *only* for high level organization planning purposes, then there is a reasonable chance that valid data will be given, or at least that the data will not be consciously falsified. Nevertheless, even here valid data might not be forthcoming if the employees feel that by giving the information they will lose control of a planning process in which they should be involved.

The greatest chance of an individual consciously distorting data exists in situations where the data will be communicated to people in the organization who are in a position to evaluate, reward, and punish, and where the individual believes that the data will be used as a basis for determining rewards in the organization. This follows directly from the expectancy theory model that was presented earlier and has been shown by a number of studies (Argyris, 1951; Dalton, 1959; Stedry, 1960; Tannenbaum, 1962; Becker & Green, 1962). Expectancy theory points out that individuals will behave in ways that will maximize the rewards that they will receive. In certain situations they may well perceive that the only way they will receive the rewards that they want is to distort the data that are used for evaluating them. In most cases this means distorting the data in order to receive extrinsic rewards like pay or promotion.

A dramatic example of individuals withholding data in order to obtain money is present in the research on the giving of blood (Titmus, 1971). In the United States many so-called commercial blood banks in large cities pay donors for the blood they give. In large cities there is a high incidence of patients coming down with hepatitis after they have received transfusions. The research shows that the incidence of hepatitis is much higher among patients receiving commercial blood than among those receiving free blood. Apparently the blood of paid donors is more likely to contain hepatitis than is the blood of voluntary donors. The reason for this is that blood banks have to rely on their donors to give accurate medical histories in order to prevent harmful blood from being collected. However, as Titmus points out (p. 151):

... it has been repeatedly shown that paid donors—and especially poor donors badly in need of money—are, on the average and compared with voluntary donors, relatives and friends, more reluctant and less likely to reveal a full medical history and to provide information about recent contacts with infectious disease, recent inoculations, and about their diets, drinking and drug habits that would disqualify them as donors.

Read (1959) has documented the tendency of subordinates to withhold information from their superiors. According to his study, managers tend to withhold information about such issues as fights with other units, unforeseen costs, rapid changes in production, insufficient equipment, and so on. Read also reports that the tendency to restrict information was most severe among managers who were classified as being high upward mobiles.

Obviously not all individuals whose performance looks poor in terms of some control system deal with this poor appearance by trying to distort the data that are produced by the system. For one thing, there is the possibility of being caught, and the individual may regard the consequences of this as being much more undesirable than any of the consequences of just looking bad on the measures. There also are important individual difference factors involved that will be discussed next.

WHAT ARE THE PEOPLE LIKE? One relevant individual difference variable is the degree to which the employees value the rewards that are perceived by them to be related to the control system. The obvious prediction from expectancy theory is that the more the individual values the rewards that are perceived to depend upon the data gathered by the control system, the more likely he or she is to provide invalid data in order to obtain the rewards. Thus it is not surprising that in the Read study the upwardly mobile managers were the ones who were most likely to withhold any negative data.

There are other individual difference factors that are possibly relevant here, but there is little research to substantiate just how important these traits are. Part of the reason for this lack of research is the difficulty of measuring many of the relevant individual difference factors. For example, it would seem that the more the individual feels alienated from the organization and its goals the more likely he or she would be to provide invalid data. Unfortunately, there are no well-developed measures of this kind of alienation. Similarly, it would seem that an individual's self-image would be very important in determining willingness to feed a control system invalid data. This might be described as an honesty-dishonesty dimension or as a dimension that involves whether the individual has a self-concept that includes bending the rules in order to beat the game and obtain what is desired. Again, however, there are no individual difference measures that tap this kind of trait very well.

WHAT IS THE ACTIVITY? It has already been suggested that the more difficult an activity is to measure the more likely invalid data will be produced. This suggests that measures evaluating group activities as well as measures of processes are likely to produce invalid data. Typically, the process a person goes through in order to achieve an end result is more difficult to measure than is the result itself. For example, how a sale is accomplished is difficult to measure, while whether it is accomplished is rather easily measured in a reliable and valid way. There are also many activities that are performed by a group which have no results that are easily measured on an individual basis. For example, it is often difficult to measure the contribution of individual authors when a book is jointly written.

If the activity is essential to the continued existence of the organization, then it may be particularly difficult for the individual to feed the organization invalid performance data because any errors will be very obvious in the long term. However, it still may be possible to give invalid data about what is possible, as people regularly do when budgets and pay incentive systems are involved.

STRUCTURAL FACTORS. Wilensky (1967) has discussed the relationship between a number of structural factors and the production of invalid data. According to his analysis such things as large numbers of organization levels, emphasis on rank, high degrees of specialization, and interdepartmental rivalry all tend to encourage the generation and transmission of invalid data. Many of these points follow from what is known about communication. The more links that are involved in the sending of a communication, the more distorted it tends to become (Krech, Crutchfield, & Ballachey, 1962). Also, one-way communication tends to produce less accurate communication. Thus it is not surprising that such things as number of levels and emphasis on rank influence the accuracy of information transmission since they tend to encourage one-way communication and the passing of messages through many links.

SUMMARY. Overall our discussion suggests that invalid data about both what is happening and what is possible are most likely to be fed to the control system by individuals when the following conditions exist in the system:

1. The data are subjective in nature.

2. The data are measuring a dimension that the individual sees as reflecting on his or her competence in an important area.

3. Standards are set by a process which does not allow participation by the individuals being measured and the standards are seen as being unreasonable.

4. The individual has control over the information gathering and the discriminator function.

5. The information is given to an individual's superior, who uses it to evaluate the individual for the giving and withholding of significant rewards and punishments.

6. The individual values the rewards that are related to the data and the individual is alienated from the system.

7. The activity is not one that produces clear-cut outcomes and is difficult to measure.

8. The activity is not one that is so important to the functioning of the organiza-

tion that if it is not performed adequately the organization will cease functioning.

Resistance to Control Systems

Every discussion of the behavioral problems associated with control systems points out that they often meet strong resistance from the people who are affected by them. Rarely, however, do these discussions point out that control systems can also fulfill some important needs that people have and that for this reason many people want a control system to be present. Because of the attractive and unattractive features of control systems, employees often express a sense of ambivalence toward them (Hall & Lawler, 1969). Before discussing why people want control systems, however, let us consider some of the reasons why they tend to resist them.

Virtually every author who discusses control systems tends to explain the resistance to them in terms of their being perceived as a threat to the need satisfaction of employees (e.g., Argyris, 1971; Mumford & Banks, 1967; Caplan, 1971; Pettigrew, 1970; Whisler, 1970a, 1970b). They then go on to emphasize how control systems can threaten the satisfaction of a number of different needs. This same theme emerges regardless of whether the control system being discussed is a pay system, or a management information system. Lawler (1971) and Whyte (1955) have shown how the imposition of a performance measurement system can threaten the satisfaction of social, esteem, and security needs. Argyris (1951) and others have shown how budgets can do the same things. Along similar lines, Argyris (1971), Mumford and Banks (1967), and Whisler (1970b) have pointed out how computer-based management information systems can threaten the satisfaction of social, security, esteem, autonomy, and self-actualization needs. Pettigrew (1970, 1972) has also pointed out that control systems often significantly change the power and status relationships in an organization. The question that remains to be answered concerns why control systems tend to be seen as such significant threats to the satisfaction of so many needs and why they can significantly change the power relationships in organizations. There are a number of reasons for this, the most significant of which will be discussed next.

CONTROL SYSTEMS CAN AUTOMATE EXPERTISE. Control systems can automate or computerize jobs that presently are considered to require "expertise" (Pettigrew, 1970, 1973; Carroll, 1967). The effect of this on a person can be to make superfluous a skill that is difficult to develop and is a source of respect. This phenomenon seems to occur most frequently when management information systems are installed. Such systems can have a tremendous impact on the nature of middle and lower level management jobs. They can, for example, make costing, purchasing, and production decisions that previously were the essence of many management jobs. Because of this Leavitt and Whisler (1958) have pointed out that the potential is present for the elimination of many management jobs. This has not yet happened, and it may never happen, but many still say that the potential exists for automating or computerizing many jobs. As Carroll (1967) has pointed out, "all indications point to a 'rationalization' and 'depersonalization' of managerial work."

This phenomenon certainly is not restricted to managerial jobs. Pettigrew has provided an example of how stock order clerks saw computerization as potentially making unnecessary the skills that they had developed to do their jobs. It didn't turn out that way, but the point is they feared it would happen. Mumford and Banks (1967) have studied the impact of computerization on white collar jobs in a bank. They also found that computerization was seen as making useless the expertise that had been built up in some jobs.

Control systems probably are seen by people as threatening their need satisfaction in a number of areas when they reduce the degree of expertise necessary to do a job and when they automate, standardize, and rigidify work. Particularly relevant would appear to be satisfaction in the status, autonomy, and security need areas. Security because the person may feel more expendable, status because what the person is respected for can become valueless, and autonomy because the new system may seriously restrict the person's freedom to perform the job by requiring certain repetitive activities (Argyris, 1971).

CONTROL SYSTEMS CAN CREATE NEW EXPERTS AND GIVE THEM POWER AND AUTONOMY. Pettigrew (1970, 1973) gives an excellent example of how the installation of a highly computerized MIS (Management Information System) created a new power elite in one organization. This resulted in considerable jockeying for position within the organization and resulted in some groups' power and status being reduced. The individuals who ended up in control of the system, however, gained in power; they not only didn't resist the system, they pushed for its expansion. In another paper, Pettigrew (1972) stresses how information can be a source of power in an organization and how the individuals who run the new MIS can find themselves in the sometimes powerful and satisfying role of gatekeeper.

It is probably safe to assume that every time a control system has been implemented, there is some group that has gained as a result of its installation and another that has lost. The group that has lost typically has seen its power, status, autonomy, and job security reduced as a result of the new control system. In the case of budgets, the winners typically are the accountants that run them. In the case of incentive systems, it is the time-study men, and in the case of complex MIS, it is the computer experts and staff people who run them. These people support the system because the

system helps them; at the same time there are usually others who are losing power to these people. These "losers" are the ones who resist the new systems.

CONTROL SYSTEMS HAVE THE POTENTIAL TO MEASURE INDIVIDUAL PERFORMANCE MORE ACCURATELY AND COMPLETELY. Certain kinds of control systems can increase the degree to which performance is validly measured in an organization. They can improve the validity of the performance measurement process by improving both the accuracy of the performance data collected and also its inclusivity. For example, moving from a simple superior's rating of performance to a performance evaluation system based upon both quantitative responsibility accounting data and production data can increase the accuracy of the performance measurement data which are available. It seems logical that employees who feel it will reflect positively on their performance and increase their own position in the organization will welcome it. The opposite may be true for those who see the installation of such an objective evaluation system as threatening to their job security, their status, and their power in the organization. Thus, in most situations while one group probably will favor better measurement another group is likely to resist it.

Argyris (1971) has talked about how MIS can lead to leadership based more on competence than on power. In many ways this point is similar to the one being made here. Both are pointing out that with better performance data the highest level of need satisfaction is more likely to go to the more competent (as measured by the system). This is a positive outcome for some, but it may be resisted by those who doubt their own competence in the areas measured but have satisfactory positions.

New control systems often are resisted because they measure aspects of performance that have not previously been measured. The installation of a MIS or a budgeting system, for example, often means that an aspect of a manager's performance not measured before will be measured. Again some managers will seek this out while others will resist it. Specifically, those managers who see themselves as doing poorly in the area that is about to be measured would be expected to resist the installation of the new control system. It might also be resisted because it would tend to restrict the manager's freedom to perform. The more that is measured, the less freedom there is to disregard certain aspects of performance in order to do well in those areas that are measured.

A human resources accounting system (Likert & Bowers, 1969; Brummet, Flamholtz, & Pyle, 1968) is an interesting example of a new control system that might be expected to be resisted by many managers. When working properly it measures how a manager handles the human assets for which he or she is responsible. It should be able to tell whether a manager has liquidated them in order to obtain short-term profits or increased them in order to help the organization grow. At the moment organizations rarely measure managers' performance in this area and managers often liquidate these human assets in order to look good on those dimensions that are measured (Rhode & Lawler, 1973). If human asset values were measured it would pose a severe threat to those managers who tend to manage without regard to these values (see Argyris, 1953, for an example of this type of manager) since their performance will look worse. This would threaten them in the esteem, security, and autonomy need areas. Thus, it seems safe to predict that human asset accounting or for that matter any measurement system that makes performance measurement more inclusive will be supported by some, but seen as a need satisfaction threat by others.

CONTROL SYSTEMS CAN CHANGE THE SOCIAL STRUCTURE OF AN ORGANIZATION. Mumford and Banks (1967) stress the point that changes in a control system can produce major changes in the social relationships in

an organization. They can break up social groups, pit one friend against another (e.g., pay incentive systems), create new social groups, and as was pointed out earlier, by creating new experts they can change the status and power of organization members. This is no more dramatically illustrated than when pay incentive plans, work measurement systems, and computerized management information systems have been installed or altered. As Mumford and Banks (1967) report, changes in these systems have a strong impact on the social relations in the organization. Some people have less opportunity to form friendships after the changes have been made, others have more. Some people end up pitted in a competitive way against people with whom they formerly had cooperative relationships. Because of the impact of control systems on social need satisfaction it is not surprising that some employees see control systems as threats to their social need satisfaction and resist the installation of such systems.

CONTROL SYSTEMS CAN REDUCE OPPORTUNITIES FOR INTRINSIC NEED SATISFACTION. Hackman and Lawler (1971), following the earlier work of Lewin and others concerned with psychological success and intrinsic satisfaction, have specified some of the conditions that must exist if these feelings are to be experienced. According to them, psychological success and intrinsic satisfaction will be experienced as a result of effective performance when a task has the following characteristics: (1) a high degree of task identity, (2) feedback is available about performance, (3) a high degree of autonomy is possible in how it is performed, and (4) a high degree of variety is present so that the person will be challenged by the job. According to this view all four characteristics have to be present if the person is to experience psychological success and intrinsic satisfaction as a result of good job performance.

Most information systems can help provide feedback about performance; thus they can help create opportunities for psychological success. However, they also can reduce the opportunities that are available for experiencing psychological success, if as often happens they end up reducing the amount of autonomy by specifying in considerable detail how things have to be done on the job. This frequently happens in the case of jobs where incentive pay and budget systems are in effect, and it has happened to other jobs because of the installation of management information systems. If as Carroll (1967) says, more real time decisions are completely automated and made by centralized information systems, it certainly appears that it is likely to happen to many lower-level jobs in organizations. The feedback they provide may not compensate for the decrease in autonomy they can cause, and as a result they can prevent people from experiencing intrinsic satisfaction as a result of effective performance. Naturally, when people see that the control system will reduce their autonomy and thereby their opportunities for experiencing psychological success and intrinsic satisfaction, they will resist the system if they value these kinds of experiences.

Desire for Control Systems

There are at least three different reasons why employees might want to be subject to a control system. It is doubtful that all of them will affect a person at the same time, but it is also likely that at least one of them will affect each person at any time. This means that for most people the idea of being subject to a control system has both positive and negative features. In many cases the negatives outweigh the positives and for this reason resistance to control systems frequently surfaces.

Perhaps the most important positive function a control system can perform for an individual is to give feedback about task performance. Since most control systems measure the performance of individuals and groups, the potential exists for an individual

to find out from the control system how his or her performance compares with that of others. Not all control systems provide this kind of information; often all the person receives is a series of meaningless numbers.

Several social psychological theories have pointed out that individuals are strongly motivated to find out how their performance compares with that of relevant others. Festinger (1954) first made this point in his social comparison theory; more recently it has been stressed by Pettigrew (1967). Both Festinger and Pettigrew stress that people look to the performance of comparison others in the sense that they pick people whom they see as similar to themselves and they then compare their performance in a situation with the performance of this other person. If their performance compares favorably, they tend to feel good about it and if it compares unfavorably they tend to feel poorly about it. This social comparison process would seem to be particularly likely to come into play in situations where no absolute standard of performance exist. For example, a baseball player's batting average is only good or bad in comparison with other players' batting averages.

In addition to the work on social comparison theory there is a substantial body of research which shows that people want information on how well they are performing and that when they get it they tend to perform better (Vroom, 1964; Hackman & Lawler, 1971). Since control systems can provide feedback, they potentially can be seen as desirable by employees who want feedback.

Lawler (1971) has pointed out that many people have a sense of trepidation or fear about getting valid feedback on their job performance and for this reason tend to have ambivalent feelings about performance evaluation sessions. On the one hand they want to know how they are doing, but on the other hand they know the feedback may not be pleasant to receive and that it may not be communicated in a pleasant, easy-to-hear manner. There is a great deal of evidence to suggest that superiors tend not to handle these sessions well (Campbell, Dunnette, Lawler, & Weick, 1970). They tend to give highly evaluative and sometimes punitive feedback that does not help the person grow and develop. Thus, even though the person wants feedback there may be a great deal of hesitancy about receiving it, particularly if the process which is used to communicate it is one the person doesn't trust and is not comfortable with.

In addition to providing feedback, control systems tend to structure tasks, define how they are to be done and indicate how performance on them will be measured. As has already been stressed this can go so far as to eliminate any feeling of autonomy and thereby reduce employees' chances of experiencing psychological success and intrinsic satisfaction. However, most individuals see some degree of structuring and controlling as desirable. On the extreme are the high F-scale people who want a lot of structure and clear-cut rules and procedures. These people seek jobs where extensive control systems are in effect. Probably more typical, however, are people who want a moderate amount of structure in the world. They will resist a control system that is too rigid and constricting, but welcome one that helps define jobs better and gives some performance feedback. A number of psychoanalytic theorists have observed that people do not want complete freedom (Fromm, 1941). They want some sort of limits, rules, regulations, etc. to be in operation. This, of course, suggests that control systems that strike the proper balance between autonomy and control will be seen as desirable by many people.

It has been stressed by some writers that most control systems place an individual in a dependent situation (Argyris, 1957) because he is told what to do and how to do it and then his behavior is monitored. It has been further argued that the dependent situation is worsened when the reward system is tied in with the control system and the individual is only rewarded when he or she performs in a particular way. Admittedly this represents a dependent situation, but does it represent a severe one? It is interesting to compare this case with a situation where rewards are given on an arbitrary or random basis so that the employee cannot influence the rewards that are received. This situation would seem in many ways to place the individual in an even more severe dependent position. This is perhaps best illustrated by the cartoon which shows two rats in a Skinner box and one rat is saying to the other, "Boy, have I got this guy trained. Every time I press this bar he gives me a pellet." This cartoon nicely highlights the point that this is in fact a two-way dependent situation. The rat is dependent on the experimenter, but in some ways the experimenter is dependent upon and obligated to the rat. A similar situation exists where pay incentive systems are in effect. The employee does have some control over what rewards are received and for this reason is not in as severe a dependent situation as he or she would be in if it were not possible to influence the kinds of rewards that could be received. From this perspective the greatest dependent situation is one where rewards are given on an arbitrary and capricious basis because the individual cannot control the reception of the rewards that are desired.

There is evidence that sometimes a majority of the workers in an organization prefer to work where pay is based on performance (Lawler, 1971). When asked why they like this type of pay system, many of them talk in terms of the kind of control it gives *them* (Viteles, 1953; Whyte, 1955). There is also evidence to suggest that the reason many employees do not favor pay incentive plans is that they don't trust management to administer them fairly. It is not that they don't like the control it could give them; quite the contrary, they seem to believe that because of the way the plan would be run it would not give them that control. Thus it appears that control systems which are tied into reward systems may, under certain conditions, be sought by employees rather than resisted by them.

Factors Influencing the Amount of Resistance to Control Systems

Now that we have considered some of the reasons why resistance to control systems exists and some of the reasons why control systems are desired, we are in a position to state some of the conditions under which resistance is likely to be present. As with other dysfunctional reactions to control systems, the amount of resistance which appears is determined by both the characteristics of the control system and the characteristics of the individuals who are involved.

WHAT IS MEASURED? Based on the discussion so far there appear to be two ways in which what is measured can be crucial in determining the amount of resistance to a control system. If the control system measures performance in an area that has not been measured before or that has not been stressed before, the system will be resisted by those people who do not see themselves as performing well in that area. This point is in line with the earlier discussion, which stressed that control systems which measure behavior in new areas will be seen by some people as threatening to their security, esteem, and perhaps autonomy.

Control systems that take over the measurement of things that previously have been measured by other means are also likely to be resisted. As was pointed out above, control systems often take over measurement and decision-making responsibilities that previously were performed by employees (sometimes on an "expert" basis). Where this happens the control systems will be resisted by the people whose skills are being replaced. They will resist them because they threaten their job security, status, and autonomy. Of course this will not always

happen, since under some conditions the institution of the system may lead to the upgrading of the people doing the job and to the elimination of certain tedious parts of their job. The point simply is that any time a control system takes over or changes the duties of a person the potential for strong resistance is present. The resistance may or may not be based on accurate perceptions of what the impact of the system will be; however, in one sense it doesn't matter whether the perceptions are accurate because if they are present, there will be resistance.

WHO SETS THE STANDARDS? Control systems are often resisted because of the standards that they use. There is good reason to believe that participation in standard setting by the person being measured can be an effective way to reduce resistance to the standards and thereby to the control system. A great deal of research suggests that participation under certain conditions can reduce the amount of resistance that is manifested toward the introduction of any change. In the classic study on this topic, Coch and French (1948) found that participation reduced the motivational and morale problems that were associated with a change in work procedures. Mann and Williams (1960) found that resistance to the introduction of a computer was greatly reduced by participation. In this situation, managers met and discussed the changes for several years before they took place. Miller (1960) and Mumford and Banks (1967) have reported on studies where participation was not used in the installation of control systems and the resistance was high. Their conclusion is that with participation there probably would have been less resistance.

Strauss (1963) and others have seriously questioned the value of participation in reducing resistance to change, and some later studies have shown (French, Israel, & As, 1960) that participation does not always reduce resistance to change. This raises the question of why participation reduces resistance under any set of conditions. A number of explanations have been offered, but three seem to be most valid. The first makes the point that with real participation people actually have a chance to shape the nature of the change that is being instituted. Presumably because they are motivated to protect their need satisfaction they influence the change in ways that make it less threatening to them than a change designed by someone else. Thus because of participation the change may actually be less threatening to the satisfaction of their needs and for this reason be resisted less. This line of reasoning seems particularly applicable to the setting of standards and leads to the prediction that control systems with participatively developed standards will be resisted less because they will be seen as less threatening to the individuals, and they actually will be less threatening.

A number of studies have pointed out that some of the resistance to control systems that occurs is irrational (e.g., Mumford & Banks, 1967; Pettigrew, 1970, 1973). It is irrational in the sense that it is based upon large amounts of misinformation. Most major organizational changes tend to produce a tremendous number of rumors. Not infrequently these rumors have only a small basis in fact and make the change look worse than it is. This is not surprising since it follows from some of the early research on rumors. Allport and Postman (1947) have pointed out that rumors are particularly likely to occur on topics which are important and where there is ambiguity about what is occurring. Control systems certainly are important, and when little participation takes place there is often a great deal of ambiguity about what is going on. Allport and Postman also point out that people tend to fill out rumors to make them fit their own organization of the world. They elaborate on facts, make inferences, etc., until the rumor no longer resembles the fact that started the rumor. In situations where people are anxious because a major change is anticipated, the rumors which circulate often paint a much more threatening picture than the one which actually exists. This leads to resistance because people see the control system as threatening their need satisfaction.

One obvious way to reduce resistance that is based upon erroneous information is to communicate valid information. This is often done by organizations on a top-down, one-way basis. Unfortunately, people don't always believe one-way communications and even when they do they often do not get answers to their questions. Thus, good communication in sensitive areas must almost be by necessity two way in nature; therefore, the relevance of participation to the issue of communication and resistance to change. One thing participation requires is good communication; thus, where participation takes place, one would expect people to be better informed about the nature of any change. In some cases this should lead to less resistance to change because the valid picture will be less threatening than the invalid one. If, however, the valid picture is a threatening one, then, obviously, participation will not eliminate resistance and may in fact increase it.

Miles (1965) and others have suggested that participation may reduce resistance to change because when people participate in developing changes they feel a sense of ownership of those changes. This sense of ownership creates a condition whereby it becomes important to the people that these changes be successfully introduced. It becomes important because their self-esteem and feelings of competence are tied to the successful introduction of the changes (Vroom, 1964). Under these conditions not only are people unlikely to resist the changes, they are motivated to carry them out. The prediction, then, is that when people participate in developing changes they will be less likely to resist them because they will feel a sense of commitment to seeing the changes successfully introduced. In other words, they will see the satisfaction of certain of their needs as being tied to their successful implementation.

These three explanations are not mutually exclusive; all can, and probably often do, operate at the same time. They are also probably not equally powerful. There are relatively little data to indicate how important the various explanations are and how often they operate to reduce resistance. Still, it is possible to speculate about their relative potency. Probably the major reason that participation reduces resistance is that it allows people to shape changes that better fit their needs. Probably of less importance is the fact that with participation the change is owned by the people, and of least importance is the informational effect. If the information effect were strong, it would seem that better communications alone should be able to reduce resistance, yet there is little evidence that this actually occurs. Power equalization seems to be necessary for resistance to be significantly lowered. There really are no strong data based reasons for stating that ownership of the change is a less important factor than restructuring the change to better fit the needs of the people. It does seem, however, that the latter is a phenomenon that is more likely to occur and one that can make a concrete, easily noticeable difference in things like standards.

Employee participation need not be limited to standard setting but can be used in the design of the entire control system. What research there is suggests that under many conditions this will reduce resistance.

If the individual is not involved in the standard setting process and the other aspects of designing the control system, then it would seem to be important that it be done by someone with high expert power and considerable reward power. Otherwise, it seems inevitable that it will be resisted as being unfair and not relevant.

WHO ACTS AS THE DISCRIMINATOR? It would seem that if the individual acts as the discriminator there should be less resistance to the control system than if another person acts as the discriminator. This prediction follows from two points: First, if the individual acts as the discriminator it means that he or she will receive performance feedback and this is something the individual wants to receive. Second, when an individual acts as discriminator he feels that he can control the data that are passed on to his superior and the rest of the system. This can be important if the individual feels that the system is likely to produce data which will threaten his need satisfaction. If the individual acts as the discriminator, then the possibility exists of distorting or withholding negative data. This may allow the individual to avoid many of the negative repercussions that might come from a control system. A control system that has an outside agent acting as the discriminator makes such distortion more difficult, and as a result, the individual sees it as potentially threatening to his or her need satisfaction. If performance is poor under these conditions, there is little that the performer can do to prevent this information from being passed on to the rest of the organization.

WHO RECEIVES THE INFORMATION AND HOW IS IT USED? It has already been stressed that individuals are more likely to accept control systems if they receive the feedback from them. If they act as the discriminator, they will get the feedback directly, but even if someone other than themselves acts as the discriminator they can still receive feedback from the discriminator. If they do get the feedback then their "need to know" can be satisfied by the control system, providing, of course, the data are presented in meaningful terms. Naturally if the installation of a control system offers people something they value (e.g., feedback about performance), they are less likely to resist its installation than if it offers nothing of value. If social comparison theory and psychological success theory are correct and people do value feedback about their performance then control systems that provide it should be resisted less than those that do not.

Likert (1961) has pointed out that the

amount of resistance to a control system is very much determined by who gets the information in addition to the person who is being measured. He correctly notes that when the data are passed on to the individual's superior or to others in the organization, resistance to the system is likely to be increased. It is particularly likely to be high if the information is used as a basis for determining the level of reward that an individual will receive. When rewards are involved there is always a threat to a person's need satisfaction level. However, if the control system does not provide performance data to the superior or to higher levels in the organization, then the system may fail to fulfill several of its most important functions, for instance, providing higher levels in the organization with the information they need to coordinate and plan future activities. Likert, recognizing this dilemma, suggests that superiors be given data only on the performance of the group of people who report to them. Thus no data on an individual's performance would be passed on to a superior; instead such data would go only to the individual. Superiors would receive combined data on the performance of all their subordinates; as a result they would be unable to identify the performance of any one of their subordinates. Superiors would, however, know how the performance of their group of subordinates compares with that of other similar groups.

Likert suggests that a similar pattern could be followed up the hierarchy so that no superior would receive individual data on the performance of his or her subordinates. This should reduce the resistance to control systems on the part of many people. However, it also would prevent the use of control system data for the purpose of giving and withholding rewards and punishments on an individual basis. This could be very damaging from the point of view of extrinsic motivation. If the extrinsic motivation system is to operate effectively, some sort of individual performance measures are needed, unless, of course, the organization decides to use a group or company-wide incentive plan. Thus, Likert's approach should reduce resistance to control systems, but at the cost of also reducing extrinsic motivation. The question of when or whether extrinsic rewards should be used to motivate behavior will be discussed in a later section.

WHAT ARE THE PEOPLE LIKE? The assumption that the people who resist control systems will be those who see them as threatening their need satisfaction leads to some interesting predictions about who will resist control systems. For instance, it seems that the greatest resistance should come from those that have the most to lose; that is, those established, satisfied employees whose jobs will be affected by the change. The least resistance should come from those who are in a poor position to begin with and whose potential for gain is the greatest. Mumford and Banks (1967) provide data from their study of banks to support the view that the most established workers do offer the greatest resistance to new control systems. According to them, "In banking, and this may be true of other office situations, resistance to change will not come from the apathetic individual who does not like his job, is not involved enough with it to join a union, and has not got the company's interests at heart. On the contrary, this kind of person may be for change because he will not see it as threatening his interests.... The kind of man who's likely to oppose ... innovation ... is probably one of the bank's most esteemed employees, identified with the interests of the bank and fits in well.... He likes his job ... has plans to get on and believes he can achieve this ambition" (p. 113).

Pettigrew (1970) has provided an example of one type of person who may seek the installation of a control system, that is, the person whose skills are needed to run the system. In his example, a computer was being installed and the programmers and systems analysts who worked on the system very much supported its introduction. For them its installation meant a direct increase in their power, status, and value and thus it is not surprising that they wanted the control system to go into effect.

There don't appear to be any examples in the literature of another point with respect to who might profit from the installation of a control system. It is quite possible that some of the people who are subject to a control system might see its installation as advantageous because it will reflect positively on them. For example, a manager who does a good job of dealing with and developing people might favor a human resources accounting system because it would point up how well he or she is doing in a particular area that is presently not being measured. This same phenomenon could occur whether the control system is a human resource accounting system or a management information system.

Although there is no evidence to suggest that certain kinds of people are particularly likely to perceive changes as having a negative impact on them, it is likely that certain personality factors may be relevant here. In particular it would seem that low self-esteem people may be more likely to see changes as threatening to them. One other personality factor that may be important is the person's degree of authoritarianism. From the research on high authoritarian people it would seem that they should be more favorable to control systems than low authoritarian people. They, for example, seek structure and are most comfortable in clear superior-subordinate situations.

SUMMARY. Overall our discussion suggests that resistance to control systems is most likely to be present when:

1. The control system measures performance in a new area.

2. The control system replaces a system that people have a high investment in maintaining.

3. The standards are set without participation.

4. The results from the control system are not fed back to the people whose performance is measured.

5. The results from the control system are fed to higher levels in the organization and are used by the reward system.

6. The people who are affected by the system are relatively satisfied with things as they are and they see themselves as committed to the organization.

7. The people who are affected by the system are low in self-esteem and authoritarianism.

REWARD SYSTEMS

So far we have discussed three behavioral problems that arise when control systems are present in organizations. In discussing each of them it has been stressed that they are likely to be particularly severe when the information from the control systems is used as a basis for rewards and punishments. One way to reduce the amount of resistance to a control system, to decrease the amount of bureaucratic behavior associated with it, and to increase the amount of valid data fed into it is to say that the data from the control system will not be used by the reward system. In fact, at this point, it may be tempting to conclude that control systems should never be tied into reward systems. In many cases this may be the right conclusion, but in others it clearly is not.

Relating Rewards to Performance

Divorcing the control system from the reward system may eliminate one set of problems while creating another. Specifically, it may create a condition where no one will be motivated to perform well in the area measured by the control system because there is no extrinsic motivation present. The main reason behavioral problems appear when rewards are tied into control systems is that people are motivated to look good on the measures taken by the control system. This can be a dysfunctional motivation, but it can also be a very functional one. It can be the major motivation that causes people to perform their jobs in ways that make the organization effective. In most cases this type of extrinsic motivation is more functional than dysfunctional, because without it most control systems simply would not work.

In short, separating the reward and control systems may reduce invalid data, bureaucratic behavior, and resistance to control systems, but it may also reduce the motivation to perform well unless intrinsic motivation is present. Later the conditions under which intrinsic motivation is likely to be present will be discussed. However, at this point it is important to try to specify the conditions under which it is functional to tie the reward system to measures of performance. The following are some of the factors that influence how functional relating rewards to performance is.

INCLUSIVENESS OF PERFORMANCE MEASURES. It has already been stressed that performance measurement systems can cause problems when they do not measure all the behavior that is needed for effective job performance. They cause problems because the employees tend to overemphasize those aspects of performance that are measured. This tendency is naturally exaggerated when performance in those areas that are measured determines the level of their rewards. In cases where inclusive measures are not available, it may well be best not to relate rewards to performance.

OBJECTIVITY OF PERFORMANCE MEASURES. The point has often been made that objective performance measures have many advantages and should be used where possible. There are, however, many situations where objective measures do not exist for individual or even group performance. One way of dealing with such situations is to measure performance on the basis of larger and larger groups until some objective measures can be found. Another approach is to measure performance on the individual or small group level and to use admittedly subjective measures. This is possible in some situations but not in others. The key factor in determining whether this approach is feasible is

the degree of superior-subordinate trust. The more subjective the measure, the higher the degree of trust needed, because without high trust there is little chance that the subordinate will believe that rewards are fairly based upon performance. Further, the more subjective the measures, the more the individual may be able to distort them in order to look good. Figure 4, which is taken from Lawler (1971), illustrates the relationship between trust and the objectivity of the performance criteria showing that, even with the most objective system, some trust is still required if the individual is to believe in the system. It also shows that unless a high degree of trust exists, reward systems based on subjective criteria have little chance of success.

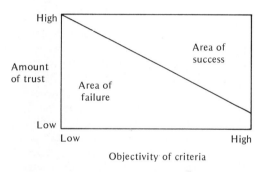

Figure 4. Relationship of trust and the objectivity of performance criteria to success of the program. (From Lawler, 1971.)

INFLUENCES ON MEASURES OF PERFORMANCE. There are many measures that are generated by control systems that are either partially or totally not influenced by the performance of many organization members (e.g., profits). Tying the rewards of employees to a measure that they cannot influence will increase their frustration and desire to distort the data that are fed into the control system. Further, as the motivation model presented earlier indicates, if a reward system is going to motivate employees, the performance measure upon which the rewards are based must be one that the individual feels will reflect accurately the effectiveness of his or her performance. The criteria must, in short, be within the employee's control in the sense that when the employee behaves effectively the measure will reflect it. Rewarding individuals on the basis of measures they cannot influence is likely to produce efforts on the part of the employees to distort the data and resist the system.

In summary, serious thought should be given to *not* tying rewards to control system measures of performance in jobs where:

1. The level of trust is low.

2. Individual performance is difficult to measure.

3. Performance must be measured subjectively.

4. Relatively inclusive measures of performance cannot be developed.

Organizational Factors

Lawler (1971) has pointed out that in the case of one extrinsic reward, pay, there are a number of organizational factors which influence what the impact will be of relating it to performance. The same point is valid for other extrinsic rewards. The relating of extrinsic rewards to control system measures of performance in some types of organizations has one effect, while in others it has a quite different effect. Organizational factors also influence the kind of measures that can be collected. Climate, technology, and structure are organizational factors which are relevant here.

ORGANIZATIONAL CLIMATE. The reward system in an organization must fit the human relations climate of that organization for it to operate effectively. Consider for a moment the suggestion that employees participate in measuring their performance. In the kind of organization that generally adopts a democratic or participative approach to management, participative performance appraisals develop naturally. On the other hand, in an autocratically run organization it is unlikely that meaningful participation can ever develop as it requires a climate of openness and trust. This is particularly

likely to be a problem for autocratic organizations in which subjective measures of performance have to be used.

What kind of reward control system relationship will work in an organization that is characterized by an autocratic management style? The evidence suggests that plans which tie rewards to "hard" criteria, such as quantity of output, profits, or sales, and thus require a minimum level of trust, stand a much better chance of succeeding than approaches which depend on joint goal setting and soft criteria. The problem for traditional organizations occurs in jobs where no objective performance data are produced by the control systems and where trust and participation are needed if extrinsic rewards are to act as an incentive. In this situation if the organization ties extrinsic rewards to control system measures, then invalid data and rigid bureaucratic behavior are likely to result.

TECHNOLOGY. The kind of product an organization produces influences how the production process is structured; this in turn influences the appropriateness of different reward systems. Woodward (1958, 1965) distinguishes among industrial organizations that engage in mass production, unit production, and process production. Giving rewards on the basis of individual measures of performance makes sense in unit and mass production plants, but it rarely makes sense in a process production firm. Giving rewards based on plant-wide control system performance measures is well suited to many process production plants but not to most unit and mass production plants. This difference arises because of the difficulty of gathering adequate control system measures of individual perfomance in process production organizations. In many nonindustrial professionally staffed service organizations, such as hospitals and schools, good control system measures of individual performance often cannot be developed. If an effort is made under these conditions to tie rewards to control measures, the likely result is the type of bureaucratic behavior Blau (1955) found in his study.

In short, the type of product an organization produces influences the technology and production method of the organization. Production methods differ in the degree to which individual performance is identifiable and measurable by the control system. Because of this, organizations that differ in the kinds of products they produce need different reward system-control system relationships if they are to avoid the dysfunctional outcomes that often accompany inappropriate relationships.

ORGANIZATION STRUCTURE. Several aspects of organization structure affect the kind of reward system-control system relationships that are appropriate for an organization. Size is a crucial variable. Another is the degree of centralization. Small organizations can do things that large organizations cannot. They can, for example, use bonus pay plans that are based upon organization-wide performance. In a small organization, most employees feel that their behavior affects the performance of the total organization. In a large organization this is not likely to be true (except at the very top), and as a result a plan that rewards on the basis of organization-wide performance will not motivate most people.

The degree of centralization-decentralization affects the kind of performance criteria data that can be gathered by the control system. In a centralized organization, for example, the performance of a sub-part, or a particular plant, is often difficult to measure unless a decentralized responsibility-based accounting system is used. Even if it is possible to measure an individual plant's performance, this is often not a good criterion upon which to base rewards because the plant employees often are not in control of the plant. As a result they do not feel responsible for the plant's performance. If substantial decision-making power is vested in the central office and local plant management is evaluated and rewarded on the basis

of how the plant performs, the local management will resent this discrepancy and engage in behavior designed to defeat the control system. This seems to be less likely to happen when decision making is decentralized and accounting data are gathered on sub-parts of the organization.

Table 1, which is adapted from Lawler (1971), summarizes the relevance of organizational factors to the kinds of pay plans that can be used successfully. The human relations climate of an organization, its production technology, its size, and its degree of centralization all affect the kind of pay system that is appropriate for an organization. Each of these factors limits the possible types of performance-based pay plans that can be successfully used. In order to determine what kind of plan can be used in a specific organization, one must classify the organization according to each of four variables listed in Table 1. An organization might, for example, practice authoritarian management, engage in mass production, and be large and centralized. Since each of the factors (being of a certain size, having a highly centralized administration, etc.) serves to rule out some kinds of pay plans, it is possible that for some organizations there is simply no pay plan that can be labeled appropriate. In these organizations it is advisable not to try to tie the pay system to control system measurements of performance; instead pay should be determined on other bases. In fact, in many types of organizations there is no really satisfactory way of tying pay to control system measures of performance.

In summary, a number of organizational factors influence whether extrinsic rewards should be distributed on the basis of control system measures of performance in order to generate extrinsic motivation. In many situations rewards should not be tied to the control system measures of performance because the cost in terms of resistance, bureaucratic behavior, and invalid information can be expected to exceed any gains in extrinsic motivation. It is also true that some kind of

TABLE 1
RELEVANCE OF FOUR ORGANIZATIONAL FACTORS TO PAY PLANS

Human relations climate	Authoritarian	Need objective hard criteria; pay clearly tied to performance
	Democratic	Can use participative goal setting and softer criteria
Production type	Mass and unit	Can usually develop hard criteria; rewards on individual or small group basis
	Process	Need to encourage cooperation; individual performance not highly visible or measurable
	Professional organizations (i.e., hospital, school, consulting firms)	Individually based plans; soft criteria; high individual involvement in own evaluation
Size	Large	Organization-wide bonuses poor for all but a few top-level managers
	Small	Organization-wide bonuses possible in some situations
Degree of centralization	Centralized	Hard to base performance on subunit (i.e., plant) performance
	Decentralized	Pay can be based on profit center or subunit performance for members of management

From Lawler, 1971.

motivation for effective performance is usually needed if the organization is to survive. Intrinsic motivation does represent a potential alternative to extrinsic motivation, and it will be discussed next.

SELF-CONTROL AND INTRINSIC MOTIVATION

At the heart of the writings of many behavioral science-oriented organization theorists is the idea that people can exercise self-control. McGregor (1960), for example, lists internal motivation and control as one of the assumptions underlying his statement of Theory Y. The exercise of self-control refers to employee behavior which is functional in terms of the goals of the organization as defined by the control system, and which is motivated by something other than the fear of punishment or the hope of extrinsic reward. In short, it refers to behavior which is functional and which is intrinsically motivated.

Argyris (1964), McGregor (1960), and Tannenbaum (1968) have given numerous examples of the occurrence of intrinsically

motivated and internally controlled behavior. Self-control offers an interesting contrast to control based on extrinsic rewards. As has been stressed, control based on extrinsic rewards can be too "effective" in the sense that it leads to people being too responsive to the control system, which in turn leads to a number of dysfunctional consequences. Self-control represents a possible alternative because it makes external control superfluous. If, for example, a person is motivated to fulfill a budget because it leads to a sense of accomplishment, it is not necessary to offer a pay increase as well. The intrinsic motivation makes the extrinsic motivation unnecessary.

There are also many situations where it is difficult to get extrinsically motivated control systems to operate functionally. In these situations the only real alternative may be to have self-control operate, particularly if, as Tannenbaum (1968) says, it can be "more effective than that of other systems." The questions that need to be answered, however, concern when self-control will operate and just how effective it can be. As the following sections will show, there is some research showing it is more likely to operate when the control systems provide feedback, allow participation, and have standards that are moderately difficult to reach.

Feedback

Feedback or knowledge of results seems to be crucial to the exercise of self-control because it performs two important functions. First, it gives the individual the information that is needed in order to correct his or her behavior when it deviates from the standard or desired behavior. Second, feedback provides the intrinsic motivation that will lead the person to perform at the standard or in an effective way. Thus, the suggestion is that feedback makes it possible for the person to exercise self-control because it gives needed information, as well as providing the motivation for self-control to be exercised.

Vroom (1964) refers to two kinds of information that people get from feedback. The first is information about how they are performing at the time they are performing. He refers to this as the cue function of feedback and says it can contribute to good performance even on tasks that have been performed many times. Annett and Kay (1957) have shown a sudden increase in performance with greater cue feedback and sudden decrease with reduced cue feedback. An example of reduced cue feedback would be a blindfolded driver.

The second kind of information which people get from feedback is information about performance success that comes after the task has been performed. A number of early psychological learning studies have shown that this kind of feedback is necessary if task performance is to improve. For example, Thorndike (1927) found that subjects showed no improvement in drawing lines of specified lengths unless they were told whether they were "right" or "wrong." Elwell and Grindley (1938) found no improvement in subjects' attempts to hit a bull's eye unless they could see where they

hit. Finally, Bilodeau, Bilodeau, and Schumsky (1959) found no improvement in performance on a lever-displacing task unless subjects were told the kind of errors they were making. More studies could be cited, but the point seems obvious: feedback is necessary for self-control to operate because without it the person will not know how to correct his or her behavior.

Despite the existence of considerable data about the importance of feedback, employees often do not receive feedback on their performance either while they are performing or after they have completed their task performance. Bingham (1932), for example, cites a case where firemen stoking furnaces received little feedback about how they were performing. The addition of some feedback devices (instruments in this case) allowed them to receive feedback, and their performance improved as a result. Some control systems do provide feedback but they provide it too late to allow the person to exercise self-control. Learning theorists have for a long time stressed the importance of immediate feedback on performance. If a person is going to exercise self-control, the feedback is needed most while he or she is still performing the task; failing this, if behavior change is to take place, the person at least needs it while the memory of the performance is still clear. Financial information systems where the reports are delayed until several months after the performance, and surveys of customer reactions to interactions with company employees months earlier, are two examples of delayed control system feedback that make self-control difficult.

Maier (1955), Viteles (1953), Vroom (1964), and others have suggested that feedback can motivate workers to perform more effectively. A number of laboratory studies have shown that when provided with knowledge of their results subjects will work longer and harder (Arps, 1920; Locke & Bryan, 1967; Manzer, 1935; Johanson, 1922; Smode, 1958). These studies typically make no attempt to specify the conditions under which feedback will have these effects and they fail to specify why feedback influences motivation.

In the study mentioned earlier, Hackman and Lawler (1971) have attempted to do this. They assume that feedback motivates because it allows the performer to experience intrinsic rewards and that this creates the expectancy that performance will lead to intrinsic rewards. They further argue that the person is likely to experience intrinsic rewards only on certain kinds of tasks. Tasks that are challenging, whole or identifiable, and which allow the person some performance autonomy are hypothesized to be tasks which will be motivating if feedback is present. Their data provide some support for their argument. It is not clear from the data that feedback must exist for intrinsic motivation to be present. The evidence is clear, however, that when present, feedback can contribute to intrinsic motivation and thereby to a person's willingness to exercise self-control. Formal information and control systems are sources of feedback and thus their existence can encourage self-control.

Participation

Central to much of the writing on self-control is the argument that participation encourages self-control. According to Tannenbaum (1968), "the relative success of participative approaches...hinges, not on reducing control, but on achieving a system of control that is more effective" (p. 23). Tannenbaum argues that with participation there is greater control because those influence attempts that are made are more effective and because self-control exists. Like Likert (1961) he argues that the amount of control in an organization is not fixed. With participation, total control is supposed to increase while with authoritarian management it decreases. With participation, control presumably increases from the superior's point of view because with it subordinates do what has been agreed on, while under other leadership styles, there is less certainty that things will be carried out. With participation, subordinates feel they have more control because they have a chance to influence what they are going to do. Thus, with participation, both superiors and subordinates should feel they have more control.

Both Tannenbaum and Likert present data which show that the influence pie is seen as bigger in some organizations than in others. Likert, for example, presents data showing that employees in high-producing departments feel that they and their superiors have more influence than employees in low-producing departments feel they and their superiors have. Likert, as does Tannenbaum, presents other data which suggest that in participative organizations workers see more control to be present. The data, however, do not show the amount of control employees at different levels in the organization feel they have. The studies typically rely on the lower-level members of the organization giving data on how much control they feel they and others have. It is not surprising that with participation they feel they have more control, but it is hard to trust their view of the amount of control others in the organization have. What is needed to make the case that with participation more total control exists is additional data on the amount of control experienced by people at all levels in organizations where participation is being practiced.

Assuming that participation does lead to lower-level employees having greater control, the question becomes how do they use that control. Do they use it to behave in ways that are functional from the point of view of the organization? In other words, do they exercise what has been called in this chapter self-control? If they do, those organizations which have lower-level members participate in decisions should be more effective. Tannenbaum (1968) has summarized his work that is relevant on this point and states "organizations with influential rank-and-file memberships can be as effective as organizations with relatively uninfluential members." He goes on to add that organizations with "influential leaders and members are likely to be more effective than organizations with less influential members and/or leaders." Thus, it seems that when the lower-level members of an organization feel they have control it does not decrease the effectiveness of the organization and it may in fact increase it under certain conditions. Overall the argument seems to be that when lower-level participants in an organization are given an opportunity to participate they feel they have more influence, and because of this, they exercise self-control which sometimes increases organizational effectiveness. However, the evidence cited by Tannenbaum and Likert to support this participation → self-control → organizational effectiveness chain is very sketchy and incomplete. Particularly lacking are data to support the self-control-organizational effectiveness link of the chain.

A number of other studies have looked at the participation → self-control relationship. They seem to suggest that when people are given the opportunity to participate in decision making they are likely to exercise self-control. Some of these studies have already been discussed in the section of this chapter concerned with participation and resistance to change. There it was argued on the basis of several studies that participation may reduce resistance to change because when people participate in changes they feel a sense of ownership of the changes and, therefore, are motivated to see them put into effect. The same argument can be made with respect to the effect of participation on people's willingness to perform according to certain standards. In this case, participation in the setting of standards may lead to people feeling a sense of ownership of the standards and to being motivated to live up to the standards. Studies like the classic Lewin, Lippitt, and White (1939) study on leadership style in boys' groups suggest this can happen. In this study, boys in a democratically led work group showed the greatest self-control. Unlike other groups, they continued to be productive even when their leader was not present.

A study by Bavelas (reported in French, 1950) also shows that participation in goal setting can lead to high commitment to participatively developed goals and that this commitment leads to people being more motivated to perform in whatever way will result in the goals being realized. A number of other studies (e.g., Bachman, 1962; Lewin, 1947; Lawrence & Smith, 1955; Morse & Reimer, 1956; Strauss in Whyte, 1955; Vroom, 1960) make this same point. Thus it seems safe to conclude that participation can influence an individual's intrinsic motivation and self-control. It seems to influence it because, as Vroom (1964) points out, people become "ego involved" in decisions in which they have had an influence. The decisions become their decisions and they develop expectancies to the effect that when the decisions are successfully implemented they will experience such intrinsic rewards as feelings of competence and self-esteem. Because of this, they work to implement the decision even though no extrinsic rewards are involved.

The degree to which participation leads to this kind of intrinsic motivation or self-control is strongly limited by certain individual difference factors. For example, it is obviously not likely to appear among people who are not motivated by intrinsic outcomes. As the Vroom (1959, 1960) and the French, Israel, and As (1960) studies have shown, it does not tend to appear when people prefer directive leadership. It is possible that after experience with participation people's preferences for it may change so that in the long term most people will respond favorably to it. However, there is little evidence to show that this kind of change can and will take place.

Vroom (1964), in commenting on the effects of participation, has pointed out that some of the positive effects of participation on productivity may be due to its effect on decision quality. That is, with participation, not only are people more committed to the goals and standards that are set but they set more reasonable and higher quality goals. There is some evidence to suggest that this does happen. For example, in both the Strauss and the Bavelas studies the employees did set higher goals and this, when combined with their high commitment to these goals, led to higher productivity. However, it is not clear that participation will always lead to better quality decisions. In fact, there are many cases where it probably does not. Vroom in another chapter in this volume attempts to specify some of the conditions under which improved decision quality might be expected.

Perhaps the best way to summarize the present discussion of the effects of participation is to state that self-control is likely to exist when control systems have participatively set standards. Participation seems to lead to a greater commitment to decisions that are made. When a commitment exists, people exercise self-control because they are intrinsically motivated to carry out the decision. Whether this will result in higher productivity or greater organizational effectiveness is a function of the nature of the decision that is made.

Goal Difficulty

Much of the work on achievement motivation stresses that it is highest on tasks that participants see as moderately difficult (Atkinson, 1964). Apparently when people are performing a task on which they see themselves as having about a 50-percent chance of performing successfully (that is, when $E \to P$ is .5), effective performance of the task becomes very valent to them. It is attractive to them because it becomes associated with feelings of achievement and competence. This finding would seem to indicate that control system standards and goals which are seen as moderately difficult to achieve will produce the most intrinsic motivation. Thus budgets, production standards, etc. should be set so that employees have about a 50-percent chance of achieving

them, if achievement motivation is to be maximized.

According to expectancy theory, if goals are set so that there is less than a 50-percent chance of achieving them, they will look too difficult to achieve and people will abandon any hope of achieving them. If they are very easy to achieve, they will be seen as not challenging and intrinsic motivation will not come into play. However, as Lawler (1971) points out, when they are seen as easy to achieve, the motivation to accomplish them still may be high because of the effect of extrinsic motivation. Extrinsic motivation can be at its maximum only when the $E \to P$ probability is 1.

Three studies have considered the relationship between the perceived difficulty of obtaining a given budget and the motivation of people to achieve that budget. The first was a laboratory study involving 108 students (Stedry, 1960). Later Stedry and Kay (1964) did a field experiment designed to test some of the ideas developed in the lab study. Unfortunately, neither study provides strong support for the view that budget difficulty impacts on motivation. In the first study, Stedry used a 3×4 factorial design that varied budget level and aspiration level. He found aspiration level to have a strong influence such that performance was highest for those subjects formulating a high aspiration level. This finding incidentally fits with the work of Locke (Locke & Bryan, 1967) on the motivating power of goal setting. As far as budget difficulty was concerned only difficult-to-achieve budgets seemed to have a positive influence on performance. In the case of this study a difficult-to-achieve budget was one that was achieved 39 percent of the time, while a moderately difficult one was achieved 59 percent of the time. Thus Stedry's results come close to the 50-percent probability of success suggested by Atkinson for maximum achievement motivation.

The field experiment of Stedry and Kay (1964) is inconclusive because of the small number of subjects that participated (seventeen foremen divided into four groups). The data do suggest, however, that where difficult goals are perceived as "impossible," performance tends to be lower than when either normal goals or difficult goals are given that are perceived as "challenging." The data also suggest that the worker's acceptance or rejection of the goal has a strong influence on performance.

Hofstede (1967) has done a questionnaire study that also looks at the effect of goal difficulty on performance. Based on his study he concludes (p. 160) that Budgets and Standards "will have a more positive effect on motivation when they are tighter and less easily attained. This works up to a certain limit: beyond this limit, tightening of standards reduces motivation." Thus, Hofstede's data support the view that goal difficulty is important and that goals can be both too difficult and too easy. Unfortunately, Hofstede's study has substantial methodological difficulties. The study lacks independent measures of motivation and budget tightness and the measures used (particularly those of motivation) are open to question.

Despite the methodological problems with the studies that have been done they are in agreement. They all suggest that self-control is most likely to be present when standards or budgets are set that have approximately a 50-percent chance of being obtained. Very difficult goals seem to have a positive effect on performance only when they are accepted. Easy goals seem to have little positive effect because even if they are accomplished nothing is achieved.

In the discussion of participation, it was stressed that it may be successful because it influences people's tendencies to accept goals and standards that are set. Hofstede states that where participation exists moderately difficult goals are particularly likely to be set. Putting all this together suggests that participation may affect performance positively when it leads to moderately difficult goals being set and accepted. It also follows that if moderately difficult goals can be set

and accepted without participation, then participation may not be needed in order to maximize motivation and self-control, although it still might have positive effects in terms of information exchange.

Summary

The evidence suggests that people are likely to exercise self-control and be intrinsically motivated to perform well when they perform tasks that provide feedback, and which have standards or goals that are moderately difficult to achieve and are accepted by them. Participation in control system design can help lead to moderately difficult goals being set and accepted by employees. Some individual difference factors also seem to be relevant. Self-control seems to be most likely to be present in people who desire intrinsic rewards. Participation seems likely to be helpful in producing self-control only among individuals who desire and are comfortable with power equalization in decision making.

Organizational Factors and Self-Control

In the discussion of the advisability of control based upon extrinsic rewards, it was stressed that in some situations extrinsic rewards should not be tied to the control system because the dysfunctional consequences are likely to outweigh the advantages. One possibility is that in those situations where control by extrinsic rewards is not possible, self-control can be used instead. It was also stressed that it is particularly difficult to use extrinsic rewards where low trust exists, authoritarian management is practiced, and no hard performance criteria exist. Our discussion of self-control would seem to indicate that these are also the conditions under which self-control is not likely to be possible. Without trust, participative management, and fairly objective criteria it is hard to imagine that moderately difficult goals could be set and accepted. Further, without measures of performance that are somewhat objective and trusted it is unlikely that the people who are subject to the control system will feel that they are receiving valid feedback on their performance. Thus, it does not seem that self-control can be expected to operate in those situations where extrinsic control cannot operate effectively. Just the opposite seems to be true; those organizational conditions that favor the establishment of an effective extrinsic reward system also favor the creation of self-control and intrinsic motivation.

One obvious implication of this conclusion is that certain kinds of organizations simply are not in a position to effectively control the behavior of their members. Ironically, it is those organizations that were developed to use external control over the behavior of their members (i.e., autocratically run bureaucracies) that find themselves unable to use control systems well. They were never designed to use self-control, and the external control which they were designed to use cannot operate without significant negative side effects.

HOW MANY CONTROL SYSTEMS?

Stedry (1960) in his discussion of budgets has suggested that more than one budget may be needed in an organization. He correctly points out that budgets like most control systems are expected to perform multiple functions in an organization and that an appropriate budget for one function may not be appropriate for another. He distinguishes between the kind of budgets that are needed for planning purposes and those that are needed for motivational purposes. For planning purposes, the best estimate of what is possible is needed. In order to maximize intrinsic motivation budgetary goals that will be achieved slightly less than 50 percent of the time are needed. Thus Stedry concludes that separate budgets are necessary for planning and intrinsic motivation. Hofstede (1967), based on his own research and that of Stedry, also calls for multiple budgets.

It is hard to disagree with the view that control systems which are good for one purpose tend not to be good for others and that, therefore, multiple systems may be needed. If anything, the present discussion argues that separate budgets for planning and motivation as suggested by Stedry and Hofstede are really not enough. Our discussion emphasizes that it is important to distinguish between intrinsic and extrinsic motivation because a control system that is good for one may not be good for the other. This suggests that different systems are needed for planning, intrinsic motivation, and extrinsic motivation if these functions are to be performed most effectively. In some cases, decisions may be made not to try to accomplish one or more of these functions, and in these cases, of course, multiple control systems may not be necessary.

Stedry's (1960) point that different goal difficulties are needed for planning and for intrinsic motivation correctly identifies one of the reasons why different systems may be needed. Maximum intrinsic motivation seems to be produced when goals or standards are set at a moderate level and maximum extrinsic motivation seems to be present when they are set at a lower level. Motivation from all sources may be highest when they are set somewhere in between these two levels, so that goals are high enough for some intrinsic motivation to be present but not so high that the extrinsic rewards offered for goal accomplishment are seen as unobtainable. Finally, effective planning may require their being set at another level.

There is also a question about whether the same amount and kind of participation is desirable when control system standards are being set for planning, extrinsic and intrinsic motivation. It has already been stressed that participation can be helpful when goals are being set for intrinsic motivation; it also seems logical that if people have some information they should be involved in setting goals for planning. The problems arise when participation is used and the goals or standards that are set are to be used for extrinsic rewards as well as for planning and intrinsic motivation.

Usually where goals are being set for planning purposes or for intrinsic motivation purposes the employees can be counted on to give valid data. However, when goals and standards are being set for the purpose of distributing extrinsic rewards, like pay, there is a strong motivation for employees to give invalid data. It is to their economic advantage to get the standard or goal set as low as possible because with low-level goals they have the greatest chance of profiting financially. The research reviewed earlier on such things as piece rate incentive systems shows that this does happen and that often standards get set which are too low to be intrinsically motivating. They sometimes turn out to be accurate for planning but only because employees restrict and manage their production so that they will be accurate. This doesn't always have to happen and in organizations where superior/subordinate relations are good and trust is high, it may not. However, in most cases goal setting for extrinsic rewards needs to be handled differently from goal setting for planning and intrinsic motivation.

Earlier evidence was presented to show that when control systems are tied into reward systems employees tend to produce invalid data both about what they can do and about what they are actually doing. This doesn't always happen but it happens often enough so that it creates problems when the same data are used for planning, intrinsic motivation, and as a basis for the distribution of extrinsic reward. Both planning and intrinsic motivation depend upon valid data. Crucial to effective planning is valid data and feedback about what has happened. To the extent that this is not available, it is unrealistic to expect that effective planning and intrinsic motivation will be present. In most organizations it probably is not reasonable to assume that data collected for the purpose of distributing extrinsic rewards are valid data.

In summary, then, there seem to be a number of reasons why different control systems may be needed for different purposes. These include the willingness of people to give valid data, the level at which standards must be set for different purposes, and the possibility of using participation in developing control systems that are designed to perform different functions. Still there are immense practical problems in establishing multiple control systems in an organization. Perhaps the most severe of these would be convincing people that they really are separate. People certainly will suspect that information given for planning might be used to set standards for extrinsic reward purposes. Similarly, they may believe that the intrinsic and extrinsic reward systems are related. Meyer, Kay, and French (1965) found a tendency for this to happen when they tried to get individuals to set goals that would be intrinsically motivating. Unfortunately, there is very little research on the whole idea of having multiple independent control systems. It, like many of the important psychological problems associated with control systems, has been too long ignored.

Personality and Different Types of Control Systems

So far the focus has been on how different control systems affect behavior. At this point it seems appropriate to consider what is known about how personality factors affect which type of system is chosen. Traditional organization theory (Koontz & O'Donnell, 1968) stresses that a person's authority should be commensurate with his responsibility. In other words, no one should be held responsible for something that he or she cannot control. Responsibility and authority might be roughly commensurate at lower levels in organizations, but at higher levels responsibility almost always exceeds authority. Managers are held accountable for things they have only partial control over (e.g., corporate profits). A manager may cope with this gap between his responsibility and his authority in many ways. One of the most common is to develop an elaborate control system. Burns and Stalker (1961) talk about the social isolation of executives and their anxieties over whether they are getting valid data about what is happening in the organization. It is not hard to imagine that executives often fantasize that things are not going well in the organization but that people are not providing them with information about the problems. Executives have been heard to proclaim that they only hear about the problems after they have been solved (Argyris, 1957, 1964; Haire, 1956).

A smooth functioning control system obviously can partially relieve an executive's anxieties about what is going on "down there." It can be reassuring to get daily or weekly production reports, etc., showing that things are going well. Thus, these data may often be collected, reworked, and analyzed, even though they are not needed for anything but the reduction of executive anxiety.

If executive anxiety reduction is one of the functions served by control systems, we should expect some relationship between the type of control system in an organization and the personalities of the top people in that organization. Unfortunately, little research exists that is relevant to this point. Jaques has stated, "my own recent experience has impressed upon me how much institutions are used by their individual members to reinforce individual mechanisms of defense against anxiety" (1956, p. 478). However, he presents little data to support the view that people create particular conditions in organizations primarily in order to reduce their anxiety.

Attempts have also been made to relate personality characteristics to the type of accounting system used in organizations. Sorter and Becker (1964) sought to relate the types of depreciation used by companies to the personalities of their chief financial officers. The personality measure used was the California F-scale. After some very questionable manipulations of the data (dropping deviant cases), the authors report results that they interpret as showing a relationship between the accounting system used and the F-scale scores. The relationships found were in the direction of the firms with high F-scale executives using more conservative methods of accounting and tending to be rigid in their practices. Despite the fact that the data are not strong, they are suggestive of the fact that accounting systems may be affected by the personality of the executives of an organization.

At this point, the hypothesis that a relationship may exist between an organization's control systems and the personalities of its executives must be regarded as highly tentative because data in support of it are far from substantial. The hypothesis is, however, a lead that appears worth pursuing. It would be very interesting to know, for example, if in an organization systematic personality and leadership style differences exist between those managers who rely heavily on control systems for their management styles and those who don't. Similarly, it would be interesting to know if firms with elaborate hierarchically administered control systems have executives with different personality types than do other firms. One would expect that the high-control organizations would be populated by executives with higher anxiety, rigidity, F-scale and conservatism scores, to mention a few possibilities. The difficult thing in making between-organization comparisons of this type is to identify the executives who actually influence the kind of control system that exists in the organization.

One of the reasons that Sorter and Becker got such weak results may well have been that they failed to get data from the key people who actually made the accounting decisions. In the case of many organizations it may be difficult to identify just who has responsibility for instituting the particular control systems that are used. However, this may not be such a significant problem if, as has been suggested (Bowen, 1971), there is such a thing as a typical personality type in most organizations. If there is a similar personality among the top people in an organization, it may be sufficient merely to obtain personality measures on a sample of the top-level people and to relate these measures to the type of control systems that exist in the organization.

In considering the relationship between personality and control systems, it is important to note the strong impact of another variable, namely the degree of stress the organization is encountering. A number of writers have pointed out that when organizations enter crisis periods, they tend to tighten up their internal systems (e.g., Argyris, 1953; Hermann, 1963). Usually this means that they tend to emphasize their control systems more (e.g., cut budget, get out more reports). Based on our discussion of the impact of personality on a manager's reactions to control systems, it would seem that stress and crisis would be particularly likely to be dealt with through control system changes in those organizations with rigid and insecure managers. Emphasizing and elaborating the control system is a concrete behavior that a manager can perform to cope with the crisis he or she views the organization to be facing. If the manager personally is insecure during the time of stress, he or she may be particularly likely to look for concrete, controlling types of behavior to perform as a means of reducing anxiety. This, of course, may or may not help the organization to deal effectively with the crisis. It may be that the best way to deal with a particular crisis is *not* to tighten controls but to loosen them (see, e.g., Janowitz, 1959; Burns & Stalker, 1961). The prediction is, however, that in organizations populated by a certain personality type the almost inevitable reaction to stress and crisis will be to tighten the control system.

In summary, it is clear from studies like that done by Lawrence and Lorsch (1967) that control systems are needed for many important functional reasons in organizations. There is also some research suggesting that the kind of systems present in a particular organization and the degree to which they are emphasized may be determined by personality traits and anxieties of the top management of the organization. This suggests in turn that in order to understand the kinds of control systems that exist in an organization, it may be useful to look at both personality factors and such organizational and environmental factors as type of production and rate of environmental change. This has not been done and, indeed, very little research has been done on why organizations end up with the control systems they have. Efforts directed toward improving the types of control systems in organizations could profit from this kind of research since it might help point out what needs to be done to get organizations to adopt more effective control systems.

REFERENCES

Allport, G. W., & Postman, L. *The psychology of rumor.* New York: Holt, 1947.

Annett, J., & Kay, H. Knowledge of results and skilled performance. *Occupational Psychology,* 1957, 31, 69–79.

Argyris, C. *The impact of budgets on people.* New York: Controllership Foundation, 1951.

Argyris, C. *Executive leadership.* New York: Harper and Row, 1953.

Argyris, C. *Personality and organization.* New York: Harper and Row, 1957.

Argyris, C. *Integrating the individual and the organization.* New York: Wiley, 1964.

Argyris, C. Management information systems: The challenge to rationality and emotionality. *Management Science,* 1971, 17, 275–292.

Arps, G. F. Work with knowledge of results versus work without knowledge of results. *Psychological Monographs,* 1920, 28 (3, Whole No. 125).

Atkinson, J. W. *An introduction to motivation.* Princeton: Van Nostrand, 1964.

Babchuk, N., & Goode, W. J. Work incentives in a self-determined group. *American Sociological Review*, 1951, 16, 679–687.

Bachman, J. G. Some motivation effects of control in a task situation as a function of ability. Unpublished doctoral dissertation, University of Pennsylvania, Philadelphia, 1962.

Becker, S., & Green, D. Budgeting and employee behavior. *The Journal of Business*, 1962, 35, 392–402.

Berliner, J. S. The situation of plan managers. In A. Inkeles & K. Geiger (Eds.), *Soviet society: A book of readings*. Boston: Houghton Mifflin, 1961, 361–381.

Bilodeau, E. A., Bilodeau, I. M., & Schumsky, D. A. Some effects of introducing and withdrawing knowledge of results early and late in practice. *Journal of Experimental Psychology*, 1959, 58, 142–144.

Bingham, W. V. Making work worthwhile. In W. V. Bingham (Ed.), *Psychology today*. Chicago: University of Chicago Press, 1932, 262–271.

Blau, P. M. *The dynamics of bureaucracy*. Chicago: University of Chicago Press, 1955.

Bowen, D. D. *An evaluation of motivational similarity in work groups*. Unpublished doctoral dissertation, Yale University, New Haven, 1971.

Brummet, R. L., Flamholtz, E. G., & Pyle, W. C. Human resource measurement: A challenge for accountants. *The Accounting Review*, 1968, 43, 217–224.

Burns, T., & Stalker, G. M. *The management of innovation*. London: Tavistock, 1961.

Campbell, J. P., Dunnette, M. D., Lawler, E. E., & Weick, K. E. *Managerial behavior, performance, and effectiveness*. New York: McGraw-Hill, 1970.

Caplan, E. *Management accounting and behavioral science*. Reading, Mass.: Addison-Wesley, 1971.

Carroll, D. C. Implications of on line, real-time systems for managerial decision making. In C. A. Myers (Ed.), *The impact of computers on management*. Cambridge: M.I.T. Press, 1967, 140–166.

Coch, L., & French, J. R. P. Jr. Overcoming resistance to change. *Human Relations*, 1948, 1, 512–532.

Cohen, A. K. *Deviance and control*. Englewood Cliffs, N.J.: Prentice-Hall, 1966.

Dalton, M. *Men who manage*. New York: Wiley, 1959.

Eilon, S. Problems in studying management control. *International Journal of Production Research*, 1962, 1.

Elwell, J. L., & Grindley, G. C. The effect of knowledge of results on learning and performance I: A coordinated movement of the two hands. *British Journal of Psychology*, 1938, 29, 39–53.

Festinger, L. A theory of social comparison processes. *Human Relations*, 1954, 7, 117–140.

Frank, A. G. Goal ambiguity and conflicting standards: An approach to the study of organization. *Human Organization*, 1959, 17, 8–13.

French, J. R. P. Jr. Field experiments: Changing group productivity. In J. G. Miller (Ed.), *Experiments in social psychology*. New York: Mc-Graw-Hill, 1950.

French, J. R. P. Jr., Israel, J., & As, D. An experiment on participation in a Norwegian factory. *Human Relations*, 1960, 13, 3–19.

Fromm, E. *Escape from freedom*. New York: Farrar and Rinehart, 1941.

Galbraith, J., & Cummings, L. L. An empirical investigation of the motivational determinants of task performance: Interactive effects between instrumentality-valence and motivation-ability. *Organizational Behavior and Human Performance*, 1967, 2, 237–257.

Gardner, B. B. Human relations in industry. Chicago: Irwin, 1945.

Georgopoulos, B. S., Mahoney, G. M., & Jones, N. W. A path-goal approach to productivity. *Journal of Applied Psychology*, 1957, 41, 345–353.

Gillespie, J. J. *Free expression in industry*. London: Pilot Press, 1948.

Gouldner, A. W. *Patterns of industrial bureaucracy*. Glencoe, Ill.: The Free Press, 1954.

Graen, G. Instrumentality theory of work motivation: Some experimental results and suggested modifications. *Journal of Applied Psychology Monograph*, 1969, 53, 1–25.

Hackman, J. R., & Lawler, E. E. Employee reactions to job characteristics. *Journal of Applied Psychology Monograph*, 1971.

Hackman, J. R., & Porter, L. W. Expectancy theory predictions of work effectiveness. *Organizational Behavior and Human Performance*, 1968, 3, 417–426.

Haire, M. *Psychology in management*. New York: McGraw-Hill, 1956.

Haire, M. *Modern organization theory.* New York: Wiley, 1959.

Hall, D. T., & Lawler, E. E. Unused potential in research and development organizations. *Research Management,* 1969, 12, 339–354.

Hermann, C. F. Crisis and organizational viability. *Administrative Science Quarterly,* 1963, 8, 61–82.

Hofstede, G. H. *The game of budget control.* Assen, Netherlands: Van Gorcum, 1967.

Janowitz, M. Changing patterns of organizational authority: The military establishment. *Administrative Science Quarterly,* 1959, 3, 473–493.

Jaques, E. Social systems as defense against persecutory and depressive anxiety. In M. Klein et al. (Eds.), *New directions in psychoanalysis.* London: Tavistock, 1956.

Johanson, A. M. The influence of incentive and punishment upon reaction-time. *Archives of Psychology,* 1922, 8, No. 54.

Koontz, H., & O'Donnell, C. *Principles of management.* (4th ed.) New York: McGraw-Hill, 1968.

Krech, D., Crutchfield, R. S., & Ballachey, E. L. *Individual in society.* New York: McGraw-Hill, 1962.

Lawler, E. E. Ability as a moderator of the relationship between job attitudes and job performance. *Personnel Psychology,* 1966, 19, 153–164.

Lawler, E. E. A correlational-causal analysis of the relationship between expectancy attitudes and job performance. *Journal of Applied Psychology,* 1968, 52, 462–468.

Lawler, E. E. Job attitudes and employee motivation: Theory, research, and practice. *Personnel Psychology,* 1970, 23, 223–237.

Lawler, E. E. *Pay and organizational effectiveness: A psychological view.* New York: McGraw-Hill, 1971.

Lawler, E. E. *Motivation in organizations.* Monterey, Calif.: Brooks/Cole, 1973.

Lawler, E. E., & Porter, L. W. Antecedent attitudes of effective managerial performance. *Organizational Behavior and Human Performance,* 1967, 2, 122, 142.

Lawrence, L. C., & Smith, P. C. Group decision and employee participation. *Journal of Applied Psychology,* 1955, 39, 334–337.

Lawrence, P. R., & Lorsch, J. W. *Organization and environment.* Cambridge: Division of Research, Graduate School of Business Administration, Harvard University, 1967.

Leavitt, H. J., & Whisler, T. L. Management in the 1980s. *Harvard Business Review,* 1958, 36, 41–48.

Lewin, K. Group decision and social change. In T. M. Newcomb & E. L. Hartley (Eds.), *Readings in social psychology.* New York: Holt, 1947, 330–344.

Lewin, K., Lippitt, R., & White, R. K. Patterns of aggressive behavior in experimentally created social climates. *Journal of Social Psychology,* 1939, 10, 271–299.

Likert, R. *New patterns of management.* New York: McGraw-Hill, 1961.

Likert, R., & Bowers, D. G. Organizational theory and human resources accounting. *American Psychologist,* 1969, 24, 585–592.

Locke, E. A., & Bryan, J. F. *Goals and intentions as determinants of performance level, task choice, and attitudes.* Washington, D.C.: American Institute for Research, 1967.

Lyden, F. J., & Miller, E. G., Eds. *Planning, programming, and budgeting: A systems approach to management.* Chicago: Markham, 1968.

McClelland, D. C. Some social consequences of achievement motivation. In M. R. Jones (Ed.), *Nebraska symposium on motivation.* Lincoln: University of Nebraska Press, 1955, 41–64.

McClelland, D. C. *The achieving society.* Princeton, N.J.: Van Nostrand, 1961.

McGregor, D. *The human side of enterprise.* New York: McGraw-Hill, 1960.

McKelvey, W. W. *Toward an holistic morphology of organizations.* Santa Monica: Rand Corporation, 1970.

Maier, N. R. F. *Psychology in industry.* (2nd ed.) Boston: Houghton Mifflin, 1955.

Mann, F. C., & Williams, L. K. Observations on the dynamics of a change to electronic data processing equipment. *Administrative Science Quarterly,* 1960, 5, 217–256.

Manzer, C. W. The effect of knowledge of output on muscular work. *Journal of Experimental Psychology,* 1935, 18, 80–90.

March, J. G., & Simon, H. A. *Organizations.* New York: Wiley, 1958.

Maslow, A. H. *Motivation and personality.* New York: Harper and Row, 1954.

Mellinger, G. D. Interpersonal trust as a factor in communication. *Journal of Abnormal and Social Psychology,* 1956, 52, 304–309.

Merton, R. K. Bureaucratic structure and personality. *Social Forces,* 1940, 18, 560–568.

Meyer, H. H., Kay, E., & French, J. R. P. Jr. Split roles in performance appraisal. *Harvard Business Review,* 1965, 43, 123–219.

Miles, R. E. Human relations or human resources? *Harvard Business Review,* 1965, 43, 148–163.

Miller, B. *Gaining acceptance for major methods changes.* Research study No. 44. New York: American Management Association, 1960.

Morse, N. C., & Reimer, E. The experimental change of a major organizational variable. *Journal of Abnormal and Social Psychology,* 1956, 52, 120–129.

Mumford, E., & Banks, O. *The computer and the clerk.* London: Routledge and Kegan Paul, 1967.

Pettigrew, A. M. *A behavioral analysis of an innovative decision.* Unpublished doctoral dissertation, University of Manchester, 1970.

Pettigrew, A. M. Information as a power resource. *Sociology,* 1972, 6, 187–204.

Pettigrew, A. M. *The politics of organizational decision making.* London: Tavistock, 1973.

Pettigrew, T. F. Social evaluation theory: Convergence and applications. In D. Levine (Ed.), *Nebraska symposium on motivation,* Vol. 15. Lincoln: University of Nebraska Press, 1967, 241–311.

Porter, L. W., & Lawler, E. E. *Managerial attitudes and performance.* Homewood, Ill.: Irwin-Dorsey, 1968.

Rackham, J., & Woodward, J. The measurement of technical variables. In J. Woodward (Ed.), *Industrial organization: Behavior and control.* London: Oxford University Press, 1970, 19–36.

Read, W. Factors affecting upward communication at middle management levels in industrial organizations. Unpublished doctoral dissertation, University of Michigan, Ann Arbor, 1959.

Reeves, T. K., & Woodward, J. The study of managerial control. In J. Woodward (Ed.), *Industrial organization: Behavior and control.* London: Oxford University Press, 1970, 37–56.

Rhode, J. G., & Lawler, E. E. Auditing change: Human resource accounting. In M. D. Dunnette (Ed.), *Work and nonwork in the year 2001.* Monterey: Brooks/Cole, 1973, 153–177.

Roethlisberger, F. J., & Dickson, W. J. *Management and the worker.* Cambridge: Harvard University Press, 1939.

Schneider, B., & Olson, L. K. Effort as a correlate of organizational reward system and individual values. *Personnel Psychology,* 1970, 23, 313–326.

Selznick, P. *TVA and the grass roots.* Berkeley: University of California Press, 1949.

Smode, A. F. Learning and performance in a tracking task under two levels of achievement information feedback. *Journal of Experimental Psychology,* 1958, 56, 297–304.

Sorter, G. H., & Becker, S. W. Corporate personality as reflected in accounting decisions: Some preliminary findings. *Journal of Accounting Research,* 1964, 2, 183–196.

Spitzer, M. C. *Goal-attainment, job satisfaction, and behavior.* (Doctoral dissertation, New York University.) Ann Arbor, Mich.: University Microfilms, 1964, No. 64–10, 048.

Stedry, A. *Budget control and cost behavior.* Englewood Cliffs, N.J.: Prentice-Hall, 1960.

Stedry, A. C., & Kay, E. *The effects of goal difficulty on performance.* Publication BRS-19. Crotonville, N.Y.: Behavioral Research Service, General Electric, 1964.

Strauss, G. Some notes on power-equalization. In H. J. Leavitt (Ed.), *The social science of organization.* Englewood Cliffs, N.J.: Prentice-Hall, 1963, 39–84.

Tannenbaum, A. Control in organizations: Individual adjustment and organizational performance. *Administrative Science Quarterly,* 1962, 1, 236–257.

Tannenbaum, A. S. *Control in organizations.* New York: McGraw-Hill, 1968.

Thorndike, E. L. The law of effect. *American Journal of Psychology,* 1927, 39, 212–222.

Titmus, R. M. *The gift relationship.* New York: Pantheon, 1971.

Viteles, M. S. *Motivation and morale in industry.* New York: W. W. Norton, 1953.

Vroom, V. H. Some personality determinants of the effects of participation. *Journal of Abnormal and Social Psychology,* 1959, 59, 322–327.

Vroom, V. H. *Some personality determinants of the effects of participation.* Englewood Cliffs, N.J.: Prentice-Hall, 1960.

Vroom, V. H. *Work and motivation.* New York: Wiley, 1964.

Whisler, T. L. *The impact of computers on organizations.* New York: Praeger, 1970. (a)

Whisler, T. L. *Information technology and organizational change.* Belmont, Calif.: Wadsworth Publishing, 1970. (b)

Whyte, W. F., Ed. *Money and motivation: An analysis of incentives in industry.* New York: Harper and Row, 1955.

Wildavsky, A. *The politics of the budgetary process.* Boston: Little, Brown, 1964.

Wilensky, H. L. *Organizational intelligence.* New York: Basic Books, 1967.

Woodward, J. *Management and technology.* London: Her Majesty's Stationery Office, 1958.

Woodward, J. *Industrial organization: Theory and practice.* London: Oxford University Press, 1965.

Woodward, J., Ed. *Industrial organization: Behavior and control.* London: Oxford University Press, 1970.

SECTION VI.

Behavioral Processes in Organizations

J. RICHARD HACKMAN
Yale University

THE CHAPTERS IN THIS SECTION focus on the actual behavioral processes which determine what happens in organizations on a day-to-day basis. Included are processes located primarily within the individual (Chapters 30–32) and processes that are mainly interpersonal in nature (Chapters 33–37). All chapters in the section, regardless of the locus of the behavioral process under examination, explicitly address the interaction between organization members and the organizational environment. And all examine the consequences of these focal behavioral processes for the subsequent states of the social system and of the individual.

It is assumed throughout the section that it is not sufficient for industrial and organizational psychologists to focus attention primarily either on the attributes of organizations or on the attributes of individuals *qua* individuals. Instead, the assumption is that new understandings about organizational behavior will derive mainly from examinations of ongoing behavioral processes which involve inputs from *both* individuals and the organizational surround. The reason for this assumption is that the behavioral processes which take place in organizational settings serve as the vehicles through which conflicting inputs from individuals and the environment must be dealt with—and through which latent opportunities for individual-organization integration may be identified and pursued. Moreover, it can be argued that it is precisely such points of interaction that offer the most leverage for

effecting *changes* in individual and interpersonal behavior in organizations. Thus, many of the chapters in the section offer insights into strategies for modifying ongoing behavioral processes in organizations—toward the end of improving both system performance effectiveness and the quality of the organizational experience for individual organization members.

The section begins with a multi-faceted analysis of behavioral processes surrounding one of the most widely used concepts in industrial-organizational psychology: namely, job satisfaction. In Chapter 30, Locke carefully disassembles the concept of job satisfaction, analyzes the nature and function of each component, and puts it all together again complete with some suggestions about how it might be more appropriately and effectively used in the future.

The Locke chapter is *not* yet another comprehensive review of the literally thousands of studies which have used some measure of job satisfaction. Instead, the chapter focuses on general and conceptual issues surrounding job satisfaction, and evaluates current measurement and usage of the concept in terms of the conceptual framework proposed. Thus, the chapter is selective, evaluative, and heavily oriented toward recommendations for ways problems, theories, and research methodologies can be reformulated on the basis of a more clear-cut understanding of the concept of job satisfaction. Throughout the chapter special attention is given to the causal antecedents of satisfaction in organizations, to the behavioral consequences of satisfaction and dissatisfaction, and to methodological problems and opportunities associated with use of the concept.

In Chapter 31, McGrath attacks the question of stress in organizational settings—and how it affects the performance of individuals in their organizational roles. McGrath sets the stage for his analysis by first proposing separate frameworks for understanding (a) the dynamics of stress and (b) behavior in organizations. He then puts the two frameworks together and shows how increases (or decreases) in stress levels can affect organizational behavior.

Particular attention is paid the question of task and role performance under stress. McGrath calls into question the traditional inverted "U" relationship between stress-induced arousal and performance effectiveness. Instead, he argues, the relationship between arousal and performance may be positive and monotonic—if certain extraneous factors, such as task difficulty, are held constant. The chapter concludes with a discussion of several different types of stress which can occur in organizations, the kinds of experiences these stressors induce in organization members, and the ways individuals can effectively cope with each type of stress.

Chapter 32, by MacCrimmon and Taylor, provides a broad and interdisciplinary view of the decision-making process. One of the unusual features of the chapter is its organization in terms of the *strategies* that decision makers can bring to bear on various types of choice situations in various environmental circumstances. Empirical literature regarding each of the strategies is reviewed, and the normative implications of using each strategy are explored. Particular attention is given to the strategic options open to decision makers in three different types of environments—those characterized by uncertainty, by complexity, and by conflict.

After reviewing and exploring the relationships among problem types, environmental conditions, and decision strategies,

the authors turn to the characteristics of the decision maker himself. In this concluding section, a number of attributes of the decision maker which affect both strategic choices about decision making and decision-making effectiveness are reviewed and evaluated.

In Chapter 33, Hackman reviews the multiplicity of effects that groups can have on the beliefs, attitudes, and behavior of individuals in organizations. In attempting to identify those social processes and events which have particularly potent effects on individual organization members, the chapter draws upon two bodies of research findings: (1) the massive social psychological literature on "social influence," and (2) the more modest literature on group processes in organizational settings. After reviewing and organizing current knowledge relevant to group influences on individuals in organizations, Hackman develops the implications of these phenomena for (a) individual work effectiveness on various tasks and jobs, and (b) the health and effectiveness of the group as a whole.

Vroom in Chapter 34 provides both a review of major historical trends in the study of group and organizational leadership, and proposes a new conceptual paradigm for the analysis of leadership practices. Throughout the chapter, various theories and empirical research programs on leadership are evaluated not only on conceptual and technical adequacy, but also on the degree to which they offer practical guidance for improving leadership effectiveness. By and large, existing research and theory are found wanting when assessed against this latter criterion.

The new approach proposed by Vroom explicitly is intended to provide normative guidance on the question of "How much—and what kind of—participation will be effective for this particular type of problem in this particular set of organizational circumstances?" The theory treats leadership as essentially a decision-making activity, and proposes that the nature of the problem and of the organizational situation are critical moderators of the effectiveness of various leadership "styles."

Chapter 35 attacks the enormous—if amorphous—problem of "communication in organizations." This chapter, by Porter and Roberts, attempts to draw from the considerable research literature on communications those conceptual paradigms and empirical generalizations which have particular relevance for understanding communicative behavior in work organizations.

After first reviewing the prescriptive implications of various organizational theories for how communication should take place in organizations, the authors turn to research evidence about what actually does happen when people communicate at work —and why. Research findings are summarized from two major groups of studies: (1) those which focus on the person-to-person activities involved in the communication process, and (2) those which examine organizational factors which affect and redirect that process. The chapter concludes with a discussion of methodological problems involved in doing research on communication in organizations, and with some suggestions about research strategy which—if adopted— should increase the usefulness of future research on the topic.

In Chapter 36, Alderfer explores the nature and consequences of change processes which occur in organizations. The chapter draws material about change from a variety of conceptual and empirical traditions, and integrates it in terms of a new and provocative conceptual paradigm. The first section of the chapter lays the groundwork for the remainder by proposing an "open systems" model for describing and analyzing change processes. Change, in this context, is viewed as movement from one "steady state" to another—and as following the same general pattern regardless of whether the entity which changes is an individual, a group, or a total organization.

The conceptual framework proposed is used to explore the nature of both steady states and change processes at all three levels of analysis. Research findings about individuals, groups, and organizations changing are reviewed and evaluated in terms of the open systems framework. The chapter concludes with a discussion of the implications of both the framework and the empirical findings reviewed for the development of a more adequate technology for social change.

In Chapter 37, Barrett and Bass examine selected organizational processes from a cross-cultural perspective. The chapter probes the degree to which culture and national identity affect what happens in organizations—and what the consequences of various organizational practices are for both individuals and the institutions themselves. Four consequential themes are examined in cross-cultural perspective: (a) the motivation to work; (b) management and supervision; (c) testing and assessment; and (d) training and development activities.

The chapter shows that some variables and processes are, for all practical purposes, reasonably universal—that is, they operate the same way, and with similar consequences, across cultural and national boundaries. It also is found, however, that many processes and relationships often taken as "given" within the United States are significantly altered—and sometimes reversed in direction—once one leaves the North American continent. The chapter and the section conclude with a discussion of the utility of cross-cultural studies of organizational phenomena, and with a plea for further development of the methodological and conceptual apparatus that will be required to most beneficially pursue such studies.

CHAPTER 30

The Nature and Causes
of Job Satisfaction[1]

EDWIN A. LOCKE
University of Maryland

STRESSING A CONCEPTUAL APPROACH to the subject of job satisfaction, this chapter begins with a historical overview of major theories of job attitudes, including those of Scientific Management, the Hawthorne Researchers, and Cognitive Growth advocates. The concept of job satisfaction is then analyzed and distinguished from related concepts. After basic job dimensions affecting job attitudes are discussed, the major process and content theories of job satisfaction are critically analyzed. Major findings concerning both the causes and effects of job satisfaction are then summarized. Sections on measurement problems and research strategies in the study of job attitudes are followed by recommendations for future research. Especially advocated are studies of the methods of mental functioning (e.g., thinking processes) of satisfied and dissatisfied employees.

INTRODUCTION

A thorough review of the literature on job satisfaction by Herzberg, Mausner, Peterson, and Capwell in 1957 included 1,795 references on the subject. A recent APA literature search using the key words "job satisfaction" (and related terms) yielded 556 references on the topic between 1967 and early 1972. Prorating this average of about 111 per year back through 1958 yields a total of 999 in that interval. Summing the above three figures gives a total of 3,350 articles (or dissertations) on the subject to date. This must be considered a minimum figure since neither literature search was totally exhaustive.

Obviously a comprehensive review of the

[1] The author acknowledges the helpful comments and suggestions of Anne H. Locke, and Drs. Marvin D. Dunnette, J. Richard Hackman, Olin W. Smith, and Patricia C. Smith in the preparation of this chapter.

1297

literature of even the last decade would be impossible here. Nor would it necessarily be desirable since much of this literature is trivial, repetitive, and inconclusive.

The purpose of this chapter is threefold: (1) to *summarize and integrate* theory and research pertaining to major issues in the area of job satisfaction; (2) to *evaluate* this research from the point of view of the validity of theories, findings, and approaches prevalent in this area; and (3) to *make recommendations* concerning possible reformulations of problems or theories and for new research methodologies and areas of research.

I. Historical Overview

While systematic attempts to study the nature and causes of job satisfaction as such did not begin until the 1930s, the important role played by a worker's "attitudes" in determining his actions in the job situation was recognized long before. Taylor, for example, said of scientific management in 1912:

... it is not a new scheme of paying men ... it is not time study ... it is not motion study ... in its essence, scientific management involves a complete mental revolution on the part of the workingman engaged in any particular establishment or industry.... And it involves the equally complete mental revolution on the part of those on the management's side .... (1970, pp. 67–68)

The great revolution that takes place in the mental attitude of the two parties under scientific management is that both sides take their eyes off the division of the surplus as the all-important matter, and together turn their attention toward increasing the size of the surplus until this surplus becomes so large that it is unnecessary to quarrel over how it shall be divided. (Ibid., pp. 69–70)

By "attitude" Taylor meant much more than just feelings; he meant the workers' philosophy concerning cooperation with management and their view of their own self-interest. He implicitly assumed that a worker who accepted the scientific management philosophy and who received the highest possible earnings with the least amount of fatigue would be satisfied and productive.

The problem of fatigue reduction which had been a primary concern of both Taylor and Gilbreth (1970) continued to be investigated during World War I and into the 1930s. The Industrial Health and Fatigue Research Boards in Great Britain carried out extensive investigations of the effects of hours of work and rest pauses on fatigue and performance (e.g., see Vernon, 1921; Wyatt, 1927). Other researchers in Great Britain, Germany, and the United States made extensive studies of the effects of such environmental factors as illumination, ventilation, and noise on fatigue. (Summaries of this research may be found in Burtt, 1931; Ryan, 1947; Viteles, 1932.)

The British researchers were also responsible for some of the earliest studies of industrial boredom and monotony. Among the organizational antidotes to boredom suggested by the British investigators were: piece rate incentives; smaller lot or batch sizes; rest pauses; increased work variety (horizontal enlargement); and social interaction (Wyatt, Fraser, & Stock, 1929). Another suggested antidote was music (Wyatt, Langdon, & Stock, 1937). The relationship between individual traits such as intelligence and boredom was also investigated.

It is ironic, in view of later developments, that Mayo's "first inquiry" (1970, pp. 379ff.) into the problem of industrial dissatisfaction involved a textile mill in which excessive fatigue due to lack of adequate rest pauses appeared to be the central problem.[2]

---

[2] It is interesting that Mayo refused to accept the introduction of rest pauses as an adequate explanation of the dramatic reduction of turnover and improvement in attitudes achieved in this study (cf., Mayo, 1970, pp. 387–388). Like Roethlisberger and Dickson's interpretation of the Hawthorne studies, he preferred to emphasize the Human Relations element, that is, the fact that the men had been talked to and listened to by management. It would have been interesting to

The Hawthorne studies which Mayo and his colleagues initiated in the late 1920s also began as a study of the effects of such factors as rest pauses and incentives on productivity. But the emphasis soon shifted to the study of "attitudes" when the employees failed to react in a mechanistic manner to these changes. In short, the Hawthorne researchers "discovered" what Taylor had observed decades before: that workers have minds, and that the appraisals they make of the work situation affect their reactions to it. As with Taylor, the term attitude, as the Hawthorne researchers used it, referred to more than just job satisfaction. It included the employees' view of management, of the economic situation at the time, their hypotheses about the purpose of the studies, their moods, etc.

The interpretations of the Hawthorne studies (Mayo, 1960; Roethlisberger & Dickson, 1939) stressed the role of the informal work group and supervisory practices in shaping employee attitudes and performance. Concomitantly, the role of economic incentives was downgraded on the grounds that workers were more interested in social relationships than money and were too irrational or unintelligent to make meaningful economic calculations (Roethlisberger & Dickson, 1939, pp. 531ff.). It should be noted that there is good reason to doubt the validity of the Hawthorne researchers' conclusions concerning the role of money in employee motivation (e.g., see Carey, 1967; Sykes, 1965).

Two years after Mayo's preliminary report on the Hawthorne studies appeared, Hoppock (1935) published the first intensive study of job satisfaction. He used samples which included most employed adults in one small town and 500 schoolteachers from several dozen communities. Hoppock's orientation was not toward any particular management philosophy; rather, his results

and interpretations emphasized the multiplicity of factors that could affect job satisfaction, including both factors that had been studied previously (fatigue, monotony, working conditions, supervision) and those which were only to be emphasized later (achievement).

The Hawthorne studies rather than Hoppock's were to shape the trend of research for the next two decades, however. The outgrowth of this work, along with the studies of leadership stimulated by the needs of the armed forces in World War II, was the "Human Relations" movement. As noted above, this view stressed the central importance of the supervisor and the work group in determining employee satisfaction and productivity. Leaders of this movement in the postwar years were industrial sociologists such as Homans (1950) and Whyte (1955), and psychologists such as Fleishman (1972), Halpin and Winer (1957), Likert (1961), and Marrow et al. (1967), the latter two being the foremost advocates of participatory management.

The Human Relations movement may have reached the peak of its influence in the late 1950s or perhaps early 1960s. The publication of Herzberg, Mausner, and Snyderman's monograph in 1959 signaled the beginning of a new trend which was to refocus attention on the work itself, a factor which had been ignored or de-emphasized by nearly everyone except the Industrial Health Research Board. (For another exception see Ryan, 1947.) The emphasis this time, however, was on vertical rather than horizontal job enlargement. The new emphasis suggested that real satisfaction with the job could only be provided by allowing individuals enough responsibility and discretion to enable them to grow mentally. The method of improving employee morale and performance through redesign of the work itself has gained rapidly in popularity in the last decade with two major reports appearing in the last few years (Ford, 1969a; Maher, 1971).

In retrospect, three major schools of

---

observe what the outcome of this study would have been if the employees had been listened to, but the rest periods had not been introduced.

thought or historical trends can be identified concerning the factors believed to be most conducive to employee job satisfaction. The *Physical-Economic School* emphasized the role of the physical arrangement of the work, physical working conditions and pay. Its major proponents were Taylor and the British Industrial Health Research Board and most American researchers of the 1920s. The *Social* (or *Human Relations*) *School,* beginning in the 1930s, emphasized the role of good supervision, cohesive work groups, and friendly employee-management relations. Its proponents were the Hawthorne investigators, and more recently industrial sociologists and the Michigan and Ohio State leadership researchers. The contemporary *Work Itself* (or *Growth*) *School* emphasizes the attainment of satisfaction through growth in skill, efficacy, and responsibility made possible by mentally challenging work.

While these "schools" represent somewhat of an oversimplification of the actual trends in research, since the schools themselves overlap in time and all three are prevalent to some degree today, they provide a useful framework for summarizing major historical trends. (See Herzberg, 1967, and Schein, 1965, for further descriptions of these and other trends.)

II. The Concept of Job Satisfaction

The definition of the concept of job satisfaction must begin with an identification of its epistemological roots. Since satisfaction is an emotional response, the meaning of the concept can only be discovered and grasped by a process of introspection, that is, an act of conceptual identification directed to one's mental contents and processes. *Job satisfaction may be defined* (for the present) *as a pleasurable or positive emotional state resulting from the appraisal of one's job or job experiences.* This definition is systematically elaborated as the chapter progresses.

While most industrial psychologists accept this definition, at least by implication, in practice it is common to find them using "operational definitions" of the concept, that is, "job satisfaction is whatever my (arbitrarily chosen) measure of it measures." Unfortunately, this procedure evades the basic question, namely, *what is it* that you are measuring when you measure job satisfaction? Every measurement operation presupposes an explicit or implicit *conceptual definition* of the phenomenon being measured. If this were not the case, the researcher would have no idea what to measure and no basis on which to choose among alternative methods of measuring it. The choice of any measure must be defended on the grounds that it actually measures what the investigator set out to measure. (The issue of validation is dealt with in VIII below.) The problem is not solved by declaring that one is measuring what one is measuring and proceeding on one's way.

The concept of job satisfaction is related to but distinguishable from the concepts of *morale* and *job involvement.* Both morale and satisfaction refer to positive emotional states which may be experienced by employees. Viteles (1953, p. 284) cites the following definition of morale: *"Morale is an attitude of satisfaction with, desire to continue in, and willingness to strive for the goals of a particular group or organization."* Two differences in emphasis from the concept of satisfaction stand out here: first, morale is more future-oriented, while satisfaction is more present and past-oriented; and second, morale often has a group referent (based on a sense of common purpose and the belief that group goals can be attained and are compatible with individual goals), while satisfaction typically refers to the appraisal made by a single individual of his job situation. One could view morale as being caused, in part, by job satisfaction, in that a person who achieves his job goals or is making progress toward them should feel more confident about the future than one who is not so successful.

Job satisfaction must also be distinguished from *job involvement* (Lodahl & Kejner, 1965). To involve means to "preoccupy or absorb fully" (*Random House Dictionary of the English Language*). A person who is involved in his job is one who takes it seriously, for whom important values are at stake in the job, whose moods and feelings are significantly affected by his job experiences and who is mentally preoccupied with his job. Thus, a person who is highly involved in his job should be more likely to feel extremely satisfied or extremely dissatisfied with it (depending upon his degree of success), while an uninvolved person would have less extreme emotional reactions to the same or analogous job experiences.

III. Basic Job Dimensions

A job is not an entity but a complex interrelationship of tasks, roles, responsibilities, interactions, incentives, and rewards. Thus a thorough understanding of job attitudes requires that the job be analyzed in terms of its constituent elements.

The most popular approach to identifying these elements has been factor analysis: a number of job attitude items are responded to by a group of employees, the responses are intercorrelated, and then grouped into "factors," each factor consisting of items that correlate more highly with each other than with other items. The basic elements are then inferred from the content of the items in each factor.

Unfortunately, this procedure leads to almost as many different factor structures as there are studies. The results depend upon the particular items that the researcher happens to include, the nature of the employee sample tested, the particular jobs involved, the environment in which the employees work, and the methods of analysis used on the data.

While such grouping may be useful for certain purely statistical purposes (e.g., obtaining uncorrelated dimensions for use as predictors or criteria), this approach does not substitute for or even verify a *conceptual* analysis of job dimensions. (It should be noted that an implicit conceptual analysis underlies and is presupposed by every attempt to make up items for inclusion in an attitude survey.) For example, a high correlation between two attitude items does not prove that the two attitude objects are the same. The fact that they are correlated *statistically* does not prove that they are the same *in reality*. It only proves that the individuals in that sample are *evaluating* the two elements similarly. Such similar evaluations could mean either that the employees actually discriminate between the elements but appraise them in the same way, or that they do not discriminate between them (perhaps because the items are ambiguous) and are answering *as if* the two were the same. An unfortunate practical consequence of grouping items into factors solely on a statistical basis is that dimensions which are conceptually distinguishable and which might show different relationships to other variables often get lumped together.

Thus far statistical procedures, such as factor analysis, have added little to our understanding of basic job dimensions. And to the degree that the availability of such "sophisticated" statistical procedures has encouraged attempts at measurement in the absence of thorough conceptual analyses, one could say that understanding has even been retarded. Furthermore, such advanced statistical techniques are not even necessary for most research purposes. The particular job dimensions to be studied can just as easily be isolated conceptually according to the particular goals of the researcher. Thus in some cases one might desire only the employee's general attitude toward pay, while in other cases one might wish to break down pay attitudes into various sub-dimensions (attitude toward absolute level of pay; toward pay equity; toward pay raises and their basis; toward bonus and overtime policies; toward pay security; etc.).

The typical job dimensions that have been studied by previous investigators include the following:

Work: including intrinsic interest, variety, opportunity for learning, difficulty, amount, chances for success, control over pace and methods, etc.

Pay: including amount, fairness or equity, method of payment, etc.

Promotions: including opportunities for, fairness of, basis for, etc.

Recognition: including praise for accomplishment, credit for work done, criticism, etc.

Benefits: such as pension, medical, annual leave, paid vacations, etc.

Working Conditions: such as hours, rest pauses, equipment, temperature, ventilation, humidity, location, physical layout, etc.

Supervision: including supervisory style and influence; technical, human relations, and administrative skill, etc.

Co-Workers: including competence, helpfulness, friendliness, etc.

Company and Management: including concern for the employee as well as pay and benefit policies.

The above dimensions may be adequate for some purposes, but it should be noted that this type of classification mixes two different levels of analysis, namely, *Events or Conditions* (the first six elements in the above list), and *Agents* (the last three elements in the above list). Since every Event or Condition is ultimately caused by someone or something, and since every Agent is liked or disliked because he is perceived as having done (or failed to do) something, a more logical type of analysis might involve a consideration of not only Events and Agents separately, but also the interaction between them. (An example of such a scheme designed to test Herzberg's theory is shown in section V below.)

Two advantages of the Event/Agent distinction are that it allows and encourages the study of *causal attribution,* an important new area of research in personality theory

(Weiner, Frieze, Kukla, Reed, Rest, & Rosenbaum, 1971), and it suggests a method of determining the reasons for employees' attitudes towards various job Agents such as supervisors (i.e., determining the Events and Conditions which they are perceived as causing or bringing about).

As to the issue of how to combine the various specific factors into broader classes, one possibility with respect to Events would be a three-category system: the *Work* (task activity, amount, smoothness, achievement, variety, etc.); *Rewards* (promotion, responsibility, money, and verbal recognition); and *Context* (social and physical working conditions, benefits, etc.). One obvious way to classify Agents would be: *Self* (which should be added to the above list) versus *Others;* other possibilities are In-Company versus Outside of Company, and Human versus Nonhuman. Again, the particular combinations used would best be made in terms of the purposes of the researcher than in terms of statistical considerations.

IV: Causal Models of Job Satisfaction

Causal *models* of job satisfaction attempt to specify the types or classes of variables (needs, values, expectancies, perceptions, etc.) considered causally relevant, as well as how these variables combine to determine overall job satisfaction. Such models, which Campbell, Dunnette, Lawler, and Weick (1970) call *process* theories, are to be distinguished from *content* theories, which attempt to identify the specific needs or values most conducive to job satisfaction. The latter type of theory is examined in the next section.

Virtually all theorists on the subject of emotion would agree that in some sense an individual's affective reactions are dependent upon an interaction between the person and his environment. Considerable differences of opinion exist, however, concerning just which mental processes determine these reactions.

Expectancies

Some theorists have argued that an individual's affective reactions depend upon the discrepancy between what his environment offers or what he attains, and what he has adapted to or expects (e.g., Ilgen, 1971; McClelland, Atkinson, Clark, & Lowell, 1953; Spector, 1956). Most studies relating expectancies to satisfaction, however, have failed to control adequately for (or even attempted to measure) the effects of values (goals, desires, aspirations) or to separate them from expectancy effects. This writer has remarked elsewhere that the reaction one experiences in response to an unexpected event or outcome is *surprise* (Locke, 1969). Whether the surprise is pleasant or unpleasant depends upon whether the deviation from expectancy is in a direction one values or a direction one disvalues (Locke, 1967). For example, a promotion or raise will ordinarily give pleasure whether it is expected or not, while a demotion or reduction in salary will be unpleasant whether it is expected or not.

It is possible that expectancy as such could influence one's emotional reactions indirectly, however. When a person expects a pleasant event to occur, he often begins to anticipate the actual event and the pleasure it will bring, for example, by fantasizing or contemplating its consequences or by telling others about it. If the event then fails to come about, it may be more disvalued than if it had not been expected in the first place, perhaps due to the heightened contrast between the anticipated success and the failure which results. On the other hand, a person who expects failure in attaining some value may have time to erect defenses against it or to activate coping mechanisms that will lessen the disappointment.[3]

[3] A commonly used coping mechanism is to convince oneself that the value being sought is really not as important as one thought it was originally. (See Table 6 of this chapter.) A commonly observed defense mechanism is repression (the automatized blocking of

Note that in the above examples, expectancy functions to influence the timing of the evaluation process and/or the intensity of the evaluations. Expectancy does not replace or supplant value judgments; it simply affects their operation.

Needs

A number of theorists have argued that it is the degree to which the job fulfills or allows the fulfillment of the individual's needs that determines his degree of job satisfaction (e.g., Lofquist & Dawis, 1969; Morse, 1953; Porter, 1962; Schaffer, 1953; Wofford, 1971). However, few, if any, of the theorists who subscribe to this view provide an adequate definition of the concept of need; nor do they distinguish this concept from related concepts, such as value.

The concept of need arises from the fact that the existence of living organisms is conditional; life depends upon a specific course of goal-directed action. The concept of need refers to those conditions which are required to sustain the life and well-being of a living organism. With respect to man, two interrelated categories of needs can be distinguished: (1) *Physical needs:* the requirements of a healthy, properly functioning body (e.g., food, water, air, rest); and (2) *Psychological needs:* the requirements of a healthy, properly functioning consciousness (e.g., sensory stimulation, self-esteem, pleasure). The reason that man has psychological as well as physical needs is that his mind (his cognitive capacity, his conceptual faculty) is his means of survival (Rand, 1964).

It must be stressed that needs are *objective requirements of an organism's survival and well-being*. They exist (that is, are required) whether the organism has knowledge of them or not. They exist whether the organism consciously desires these con-

a thought or feeling from entry into conscious awareness).

ditions (and the actions required to attain them) or not. To take a simple example on the level of physical needs, man has a need for Vitamin B-12; but nobody could have valued (desired) this vitamin before it was discovered. Similarly, a child deprived of sensory stimulation still needs such stimulation to develop normally whether he realizes it or not.

Values

The concept of need must be distinguished from the concept of value. A value "is that which one acts to gain and/or keep" (Rand, 1964, p. 15). It is that which one regards as conducive to one's welfare. A value is what a person consciously or subconsciously desires, wants, or seeks to attain. Thus, while needs are "objective" in that they exist regardless of what the person wants, values are "subjective"[4] in the sense that they are "in consciousness" (that is, they are standards in the person's conscious or subconscious mind). While needs are innate (inborn), values are acquired (learned). Thus, while all men have the same basic needs, men can (and do) differ in what they value. While his needs confront man with the requirement of action, his values determine his actual choices and emotional reactions.

A number of theorists have stated explicitly that it is the (perceived) job situation in relation to the individual's values that is the most direct determinant of job satisfaction (Katzell, 1964; Locke, 1969; Likert, 1961; Pelz & Andrews, 1966; Rosen & Rosen, 1955; Smith, Kendall, & Hulin, 1969). It should be noted that most of the so-called need theorists referred to earlier use that term as if it were synonymous with the term value.

Despite extensive theoretical and empirical support for the general view that satisfaction results from value attainment, it is not the whole story. Several further issues remain to be discussed, namely: What is the relation of value importance to satisfaction? How do the various value judgments that an individual makes combine to produce overall job satisfaction? And what happens when an individual's values contradict or conflict with his needs?

To answer these questions, the concept of value must be discussed in more detail. All values have two attributes (Rand, 1966): *content,* or what is wanted or valued; and *intensity,* or how much it is wanted or valued. An individual's values, ranked as to importance, would represent his *value hierarchy.*

This writer has argued elsewhere that every emotional response reflects a dual value judgment: the *discrepancy* (or relation) between what the individual wants (including how much he wants) and what he perceives himself as getting, and the *importance* of what is wanted (or that amount of what is wanted) to the individual (Locke, 1969).[5] Thus, it was argued that accurate estimates of affect intensity (e.g., degree of job satisfaction) reflect both percept (or cognition)-value discrepancy and value importance.[6] If this is the case, then

---

[4] By "subjective" in this context is meant "in the conscious or subconscious mind." The term is *not* intended to be interpreted in the philosophical sense as meaning arbitrary or devoid of any rational, objective basis.

[5] It was not sufficiently stressed in previous articles that: (a) a person is not always conscious of his values, a fact which makes for severe measurement problems; and (b) a person's values are interrelated in that the reason a person values one thing may be that it is a means of gaining some more fundamental value (e.g., achievement in work brings a sense of efficacy). Thus a given value does not operate independently of the person's total value system.

[6] This is true only if satisfaction is measured in such a way that it reflects the actual *amount* of pleasure produced by a job element or gained from a job experience. Furthermore, two different meanings of the term importance must be distinguished: (a) important in an abstract sense in the context of the person's value hierarchy, and (b) "important to change right now" (because it is the worst aspect of the job as it is today). With respect to the theory proposed, it is importance in the first respect that is intended. (See Mobley & Locke, 1970, for a further discussion of this point.)

overall job satisfaction would be the sum of the affect ratings pertaining to the individual job elements. Weighting the individual job satisfaction estimates by value importance (which in practice seems to be of no practical benefit, e.g., Decker, 1955; Ewen, 1967; Mikes & Hulin, 1968; Schaffer, 1953) would, in this view, be redundant since importance is already reflected in these ratings (Mobley & Locke, 1970; see also footnote 6).

The above conceptualization is illustrated in Figures 1 and 2, which show satisfaction (hypothetically) with pay and temperature as a function of value-percept discrepancy and importance. (See Locke, 1969, for illustrative empirical data.) Observe that the shape of the function depends (in part) on the particular value involved. The pay functions are linear, because most people cannot get "too much" pay. In contrast, the temperature functions are bell-shaped, because people prefer moderate temperatures to extreme ones. Functions with other shapes are also possible. Such shapes will differ not only for different values but for different individuals.

It will be noted that importance affects the relative intensity of satisfaction or dissatisfaction produced by a given percept-

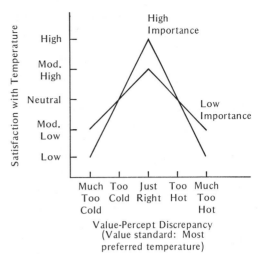

Figure 2. Hypothetical function relating value-percept discrepancy and importance to satisfaction with temperature.

value discrepancy. The slope of the pay function is steeper for those who consider pay to be more important. In the case of temperature, the quadratic trend is stronger for those who consider temperature to be more important. Importance, therefore, affects the *range of affect* which a given value can produce. Given a random distribution of percept-value discrepancies, more important values will lead to greater overall variability in affect than less important values. This relationship is represented graphically in Figure 3. (For illustrative data see Mobley & Locke, 1970.) The influence of importance on affect variability may explain the findings that: the correlation between satisfaction with more important values (or "needs") and overall satisfaction is higher than the corresponding correlation(s) for less important values (Ewen, 1967; Schaffer, 1953), and that the correlation between various job attributes and satisfaction is higher for individuals who want them more than for those who want them less (Hackman & Lawler, 1971).

The foregoing analysis provides a possible solution to the conflict between what Vroom has called the "subtractive" model

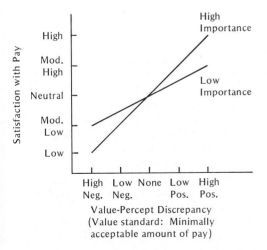

Figure 1. Hypothetical function relating value-percept discrepancy and importance to pay satisfaction.

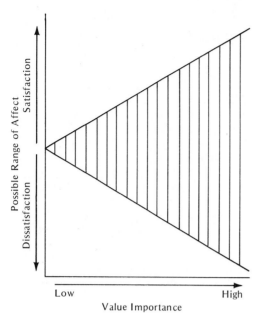

Figure 3. Hypothetical function relating value importance to possible range of affect.

and the "multiplicative" model of satisfaction (Vroom, 1964, pp. 162ff.). The subtractive model views affect as a function of percept (cognition)-value discrepancy (or "need" fulfillment) alone, but ignores the effect of value importance. The multiplicative model views satisfaction as a function of the product of the perceived amount of the value (offered by the job) and value importance but ignores value-percept discrepancy. Both views fail to distinguish between the *amount of the value wanted* by the person and *how much the person wants that amount,* that is, the importance of the value (or the desired amount of it) to him. These two elements may be correlated but they are not identical. (Further confounding of these two concepts may easily occur in the process of measurement, so that subjects asked to rate discrepancy may implicitly "weight" it by importance; similarly, subjects asked to rate importance may implicitly include a rating of discrepancy.)

Thus, if S stands for satisfaction, V_c stands for value content (including the amount wanted), P stands for the perceived amount of the value provided by the job, and V_i stands for value importance, the subtractive model asserts that $S = V_c - P;$ while the multiplicative model claims that $S = V_i \times P$. If this writer's view had to be expressed mathematically, it would be of the general form: $S = (V_c - P) \times V_i$ with the qualification that the point(s) of inflection and the point(s) of neutrality (no satisfaction, no dissatisfaction) would have to be discovered empirically in order to correctly determine the direction of the importance weighting. Depending upon the particular value standard used in the formula, and the shape of the function, either the absolute or the arithmetic $V_c - P$ difference might be appropriate.

While the above model offers something approaching an integration of the subtractive and multiplicative models, *the actual formula presented above is misleading* in that it assumes ratio scale measurement of variables which are hard to measure even on an ordinal scale. Furthermore, the formula pertains only to single values, whereas most emotional reactions are the result of multiple value appraisals (see footnote 5).

Need-Value Conflicts

It was stated above, as a general proposition, that job satisfaction was a function of value attainment. However, since it is the existence of needs which gives rise to the requirement of action, and, therefore, to the requirement of pursuing values, it would be self-contradictory to claim that any value was as good as another or that all values will yield the same degree of pleasure once attained. This becomes obvious as soon as one grasps that *the ultimate biological function of man's values is to direct his actions and choices so as to satisfy his needs.*

It is also clear that all men do not value that which they need; for example, it is obvious that the basic values of alcoholics and drug addicts are blatantly self-destructive. Since need frustration results in pain or discomfort (either psychological or physical), any pleasure gained from attaining a value which contradicts or is incompatible with a need will necessarily be diluted in quality or quantity or duration as compared with a value that is compatible with one's needs.

This diminution in pleasure may not be noticed in the short run, but should, other things being equal, become increasingly manifest in the long run. For example, in the realm of physical needs the effects of insufficient rest or a poor diet may not be noticed for days or weeks or even years, but eventually one will pay the price. The same principle applies to psychological needs. A man who, for instance, evaded every psychological conflict and threat by the use of defense mechanisms might "get away with it" for a while, in that his anxiety would be temporarily reduced, but ultimately he would become incapable of coping with reality and would become neurotic or psychotic.

Summary

Job satisfaction results from the perception that one's job fulfills or allows the fulfillment of one's important job values, providing and to the degree that those values are congruent with one's needs. It still remains to discuss the nature of man's needs. Theories of man's needs and their relationship to job satisfaction are discussed in the next section.

V. Major Content Theories of Job Satisfaction

Content theories attempt to specify the particular needs that must be satisfied or the values that must be attained for an individual to be satisfied with his job. Two major theories have dominated the contemporary scene: Maslow's Need Hierarchy theory and Herzberg's Motivator-Hygiene theory.

MASLOW'S NEED HIERARCHY THEORY

Maslow's theory (Maslow, 1954, 1970)[7] asserts that man has five basic categories of needs: *physiological* needs, including food, water, air, etc.; *safety* needs, including freedom from physical threats and harm as well as economic security; *belongingness* and *love* needs; *esteem* needs of two types: the need for mastery and achievement, and the need for the recognition and approval of others; and the need for *self-actualization,* which is defined as "the tendency ... to become actualized in what he is potentially" or "the desire to become more and more what one is, to become everything that one is capable of becoming" (Maslow, 1954, pp. 91–92).

The theory argues further that these needs are arranged in a hierarchy of "prepotency" or dominance, the order from most to least prepotent being that given above. According to Maslow, the less prepotent needs are neither desired nor sought until the more prepotent needs are satisfied or fulfilled. Thus, for example, the need for safety will not motivate behavior or produce satisfaction when attained until the physiological needs are fulfilled; similarly, the need for self-actualization will not become operative until all four of the more prepotent needs (physiological, safety, belongingness, self-esteem) are fulfilled. Maslow does not claim that the more prepotent needs have to be fully satisfied before the less prepotent ones operate, but rather that the more prepotent ones will always be relatively more fulfilled than the less prepotent ones. He also recognizes that there are individual exceptions to his theory, for example, people who would give up everything for the sake of their ideals.

Maslow did not develop a specific theory of work motivation as such, but the implica-

[7] All quotations cited are from the 1954 edition, but all may be found almost verbatim in the 1970 edition. Furthermore, all aspects of the theory discussed here are basically unchanged in the later edition.

tions of his theory for the design of incentive systems by management are obvious. The optimal job environment for a given employee would be the one which corresponded most closely to his position on the need hierarchy.

Logical Criticisms

1. LACK OF PROOF OF NEEDS. Maslow offers no proof that the list of needs which he proposes are, in fact, needs. While the existence of physiological needs is well established enough not to require further proof, the same is not true of the remainder of the list. On what grounds, for example, does Maslow claim that man has a need for self-esteem?[8] And on what basis does he assert that self-esteem is based on the approval of others? Some psychotherapists would argue that basing one's self-esteem on the opinions of others is a sign of neurosis (Blumenthal, 1969). It is also confusing when Maslow lumps together into a single need category such diverse factors as freedom from physical harm and economic security. Physical harm is directly life-threatening, but economic insecurity is not.

2. UNINTELLIGIBILITY. It is virtually impossible to find an intelligible definition of the concept of self-actualization in Maslow's writings. For example, to "become more and more what one is" is self-contradictory. To become "everything that one is capable of becoming" is impossible if taken literally, since every person is metaphysically capable of becoming an almost unlimited number of things. A person who tried to become self-actualized in this respect would probably become neurotic due to unresolvable conflicts among the thousands of choices open to him (e.g., with respect to character, occupation, activities, friends, etc.). As Maslow defines it, the term self-actualization has no

coherent meaning and cannot be used to explain anything. (The issue of whether this concept could be redefined so as to become intelligible is dealt with later in this section.)

3. CONFUSION BETWEEN NEEDS AND VALUES. The distinction between needs and values was drawn in section IV of this chapter. Maslow appears to recognize the distinction, but implies that it is irrelevant since he believes that "most often, under good conditions, what [man] wants is what he needs (what is good for him) in order to avoid sickness" (1954, p. 125), that is, that there is a near-perfect correspondence between needs and values. This is simply not true. While needs by definition are innate and universal, one can observe that men differ enormously in what they value both within and between cultures; furthermore, psychotherapists' offices, hospitals, jails, and graveyards are full of people whose values not only failed to bring them pleasure, but which were blatantly self-destructive and self-defeating.

Maslow also claims that needs can "*disappear permanently*" (1954, p. 147). While values can disappear (i.e., be changed or replaced), needs cannot, since they are part of an organism's nature. Needs can only be fulfilled or frustrated.

Maslow also claims that, "The organism tells us what it needs (and, therefore, what it values) by sickening when deprived of these values" (1954, pp. 152–153). This is precisely what the organism does not do. The experience of pain, discomfort, or suffering does serve as a *signal* to the organism that *some need* has been frustrated; but the experience of suffering as such does not automatically endow an individual with knowledge as to *what need* has been frustrated. Nor does it tell him, once the need has been identified, *how* specifically to go about satisfying it. To cite an obvious example, thousands of children used to die of or be crippled by polio. The existence of this illness, however, did not tell Jonas Salk how

---

[8] This writer agrees that man has a need for self-esteem (though not with Maslow's alleged basis for it), but Maslow has not shown why man has such a need.

to develop his vaccine, nor did it identify the nature of the organism causing polio. All of this had to be discovered by years of painstaking research, methodical experimentation, and excruciating mental effort (Carter, 1967). The nature of man's needs (both physical and mental) and how to satisfy them must be discovered by his mind.

It has already been stated that all men have a hierarchy of values, but this hierarchy differs with each man, and a given hierarchy may or may not correspond to the individual's actual needs.

4. CONFUSION BETWEEN ACTIONS AND DESIRES. Maslow is somewhat inconsistent about just what his theory is a theory of. At one point he claims that it is a theory of action, that is, that more prepotent needs will always be more fulfilled or satisfied than less prepotent needs (1954, pp. 100–101). Elsewhere, however, he claims that the theory postulates only *felt desires* to act (1954, p. 99), and admits that these felt desires may not be expressed in action. These two views obviously have different implications for predicting and explaining actions and attitudes.

5. SATISFIED NEEDS AND THE NEED HIERARCHY. The basis for Maslow's hierarchy theory is the premise that "a satisfied need is not a motivator" (1954, p. 105). While this, strictly speaking, may be true, it is also true that no human need is ever permanently satisfied as the result of a single act or series of actions. It is in the nature of needs that they must be continually and repeatedly fulfilled if the organism is to survive. Furthermore, Maslow admits that "behavior tends to be determined by several or *all* of the basic needs simultaneously rather than by only one of them" (1954, p. 102). This would seem to contradict the idea of need satisfactions occurring in a fixed hierarchical order.

Research Findings

Blackler and Williams have aptly observed that, "it has proved easy to interpret

situations by his [Maslow's] model, but rather more elusive to actually test it out" (1971, p. 291). In practice, it has been common for researchers to cite findings (e.g., differences in "need satisfaction" between job levels) as being "consistent" with Maslow's theory, but rare for them to make direct tests of it using the longitudinal method. The two studies that have been done using such an approach have not shown strong support for it (Hall & Nougaim, 1968; Lawler & Suttle, 1972; see review of recent research by Miner & Dachler, 1973).

Conclusion

Despite the "intuitive" appeal of Maslow's need hierarchy theory, there is little firm support for its major thesis of a fixed hierarchy of needs which automatically governs action. It is not necessarily what a man needs but what he *values* most strongly that dominates his thoughts and actions. Since values are acquired rather than innate, since men have the capacity to choose their values, and since men are not omniscient, such values may or may not be congruent with their needs. Furthermore, the individual's value hierarchy may put (known) physical needs first or it may not. In the case of a teen-ager who takes drugs which he knows to be dangerous solely in order to "belong" to his peer group, the desire for acceptance (and the illusion of self-esteem) clearly overrides his desire for physical well-being. Any value *can* dominate action, including self-destructive values.

HERZBERG'S MOTIVATOR-HYGIENE THEORY

The original basis for the Motivator-Hygiene (or two-factor) theory was a study of some 200 engineers and accountants who were asked to describe a time when they felt especially satisfied and a time when they felt especially dissatisfied with their job (Herzberg, Mausner, & Snyderman, 1959). These "critical incidents" were then classified by grouping those together that "seemed to go together" and recording the frequency with which each category was mentioned.

Incidents classified as involving the work itself, achievement, promotion, recognition, and responsibility, were frequently mentioned as sources of satisfaction, but much less often as sources of dissatisfaction. This group of factors was labeled "Motivators" and was asserted to involve mainly aspects of the work itself.

Incidents classified as involving supervision, interpersonal relations, working conditions, company policies and salary were frequently mentioned as causes of job dissatisfaction, but less frequently as causes of satisfaction. This group of categories was labeled "Hygienes" and was asserted to involve primarily the context in which the work was performed.

Thus, the theory argues that job satisfaction and dissatisfaction result from different causes; satisfaction depends on Motivators while dissatisfaction is the result of Hygiene factors.

Herzberg later expanded his theory by tying these findings to a specific view of the nature of man (Herzberg, 1966). He argued that there are two separate and unrelated classes of human needs: physical needs which man shares with animals, and psychological needs whose root is man's possession of a reasoning mind. The need to use one's mind, which he calls psychological growth, is satisfied by such actions as increasing one's knowledge, making abstract integrations, creative activity, being effective in ambiguity, developing individuality, and the like. (If the concept of self-actualization were to be made intelligible, the above criteria might be a more promising approach than those suggested by Maslow.)

Herzberg argued further that these two sets of needs operate in different ways. Physical needs, he claimed, motivate action according to a pain-avoidance (tension reduction) principle. When frustrated they produce discomfort; when fulfilled they produce a relief from discomfort but no positive pleasure. In contrast, the need for growth motivates action only in a positive sense. Attaining growth brings pleasure, but failure to grow does not bring displeasure.

The two-factor theory of job satisfaction parallels this dual theory of man's needs. The Hygiene factors operate only to frustrate or fulfill man's physical needs, while the Motivators serve to fulfill or frustrate man's growth needs.

Logical Criticisms

1. MIND-BODY DICHOTOMY. Herzberg's view of man's nature reveals a profound and unwarranted mind-body dichotomy. He argues that man has a "dual nature," each part operating according to opposite principles and unrelated to the other, viz., "to use one's brains is a need system of itself, divorced from any connection with, or dependence on, the basic biological stresses" (1966, p. 51). In fact, man's mind has a great deal to do with his physical needs. *It is by means of his mind that he discovers the nature of his physical as well as his psychological needs and how to satisfy them.* The reason that he needs to use his mind productively is *ultimately* a biological one: his mind is his means of survival (Rand, 1964). Just as a neurotic is less fit to survive than a normal person, so a psychotic is less fit to survive than a neurotic. (The reason that mentally ill people do not drop dead as soon as they develop a problem is that psychological problems do not ordinarily lead to destruction as quickly as physical ones, and because such people are usually cared for by people whose minds are functioning properly.)

2. UNIDIRECTIONAL OPERATION OF NEEDS. There is little justification for the view that either psychological or physical needs cause affect only in one direction. The tension-reduction view of motivation has been thoroughly discredited even for animals (Cofer & Appley, 1964; White, 1959). Furthermore, such acts as eating and drinking

in man involve much more than simply the avoidance of hunger or thirst pangs; for example, the pleasure of taste itself is involved. Similarly, as any psychotherapist can testify (Herzberg's theory of mental health notwithstanding; see 1966, pp. 77ff.) a, if not *the,* primary cause of the unhappiness of neurotics is their lack of self-esteem (failure to grow in Herzberg's model). It is not due to lack of food, water, air, or toilets.

3. LACK OF PARALLEL BETWEEN MAN'S NEEDS AND THE MOTIVATOR AND HYGIENE FACTORS. Herzberg's attempt to draw a parallel between man's animal (physical) needs and Hygiene factors on the one hand, and his growth needs and Motivators on the other, does not hold up under close scrutiny. For example, Hygiene factors such as managerial decisions and supervisory actions may have direct consequences for the individual's interest in his work, his success, advancement, and responsibility. Herzberg himself (Herzberg et al., 1959) found that the two main second level factors causing job dissatisfaction were unfairness and lack of growth, both of which have more to do with psychological than with physical needs. On the other hand, Motivator factors may involve physical as well as psychological needs. For example, a man may dislike his work because it is too physically demanding or dangerous or dirty.

4. INCIDENT CLASSIFICATION SYSTEM. There are numerous logical inconsistencies in Herzberg's incident classification system. For example, if an employee reports that the work is too easy or too hard, it is classified in the "work itself" category, but if there is too much or too little work, it is classified as "working conditions." Similarly, if the worker is praised or criticized for his work, it is classified as "recognition," but if credit is given or withheld, it is classified as "supervision (interpersonal)" (Herzberg et al., 1959, Appendix II). Further, if the employee reports being given new responsibility, it is classified as "responsibility," but if the super-

visor will not delegate responsibility, it is called "supervision (technical)," and if the company does not allow him enough, it is called "company policy" (Herzberg, 1966, Appendix).

Schneider and Locke (1971; based on Hahn, 1959) observed that these inconsistencies are caused or made possible by a fundamental confusion in Herzberg's classification system. This confusion is between the *event or condition* that causes the employee to feel satisfied or dissatisfied, and the *agent* (person, organization, or thing) which caused this event or condition to come about. Herzberg's system includes a random mixture of both, with all of the Motivator factors turning out to be events or conditions (work, achievement, advancement, responsibility, and recognition), while the major Hygiene factors are agents (company, supervisor, co-workers). Frequency comparisons between event and agent categories are meaningless, since they involve different levels of analysis. Every event logically implies at least one agent, and every agent implies at least one event or condition brought about by that agent. A refined and expanded version (from Locke, 1973) of the event/agent category system developed by Schneider and Locke (1971) is shown in Tables 1 and 2.

5. DEFENSIVENESS. Vroom (1964) has observed that Herzberg's results might be an artifact of defensiveness on the part of the employees. Thus, to avoid any threat to their self-image, they take credit for the satisfying events that occur while blaming others for dissatisfying occurrences.

Defensiveness is such a well-known phenomenon that some serious attempt to answer this criticism is clearly needed. Herzberg (1966, pp. 130–131) has made only one attempt to answer it, and insofar as this writer has been able to decipher the answer, it consists solely of logical fallacies (e.g., question-begging, diverting the issue). Bobbitt and Behling's (1972) more recent attempt to answer it is also unconvincing (Locke, 1972a).

TABLE 1
SATISFYING AND DISSATISFYING EVENT CATEGORIES

Satisfying Events	Dissatisfying Events
1. *Task Activity:* enjoyed the work task or task activity itself (regardless of external rewards or outcomes). Given a desired task assignment. Saw the work as important, significant, or meaningful.	*Task Activity:* did not enjoy or disliked the work or task activity itself (regardless of external rewards or outcomes). Given a disliked or undesired task assignment (e.g., a dirty job). Saw the work as unimportant, insignificant, or meaningless.
2. *Amount of Work:* amount of work just right; neither too much nor too little; work was easy to do (no specific success involved).	*Amount of Work:* not reasonable; too much or too little; work was especially hard or difficult (no specific failure involved).
3. *Smoothness:* work went smoothly without (temporary) distraction or interruption; work done efficiently (but no specific success involved).	*Smoothness:* work did not go smoothly. Temporary interruptions or distractions; wasted time; work done inefficiently. (*Note:* if actual failure, use #4 below).
4. *Success* (work achievement in relation to some standard): finished a task; completed an assignment or project; solved a problem; reached a work goal; met a deadline; did a job especially well or fast or skillfully; improved performance; had a project or solution accepted by others; saw ultimate success of work; getting a contract (if success was most salient); reaching a sales figure if it represents a standard of achievement.	*Failure* (work failure in relation to some standard): did not finish a task; did not complete an assignment or project; did not solve a problem; failed to reach a work goal; did not make a deadline; did a job especially poorly or slowly or unskillfully; failed to improve performance or did worse than before; had a project or solution rejected by others; saw ultimate "failure" of work because not used or results of work damaged or destroyed; failed to get contract or reach sales figure (if failure was most salient); caused an accident (see also #11).
5. *Promotion:* to a higher position; promise of promotion.	*Demotion or Lack of Promotion:* did not get a desired promotion or promised promotion; no opportunity for promotion (blocked opportunity).
6. *Responsibility:* was increased; given special assignment (not necessarily promoted).	*Responsibility:* was not increased as desired or as promised; did not get special assignment that wanted to get; too much responsibility; given responsibility without adequate training; reduction of responsibility; unclear responsibility.
7. *Verbal (or implied Verbal) Recognition of Work:* praised, thanked, complimented, given credit, given award, or special recognition for a piece of work or for performance in general (by company, supervisor, co-workers, subordinates, etc.); given high rating for work.	*Negative Verbal (or implied Verbal) Recognition or Lack of Recognition For Work:* criticized, blamed, not thanked, not complimented, not given credit or credit stolen by another, not given award, given reprimand, insulted for a piece of work or for performance in general (by company, supervisor, co-workers, subordinates); false accusation; given low rating for work; gesture or look of disapproval; complaint about product or work.
8. *Money:* received a monetary raise or bonus or tip; made a profit; got money for overtime work; promise of a raise; getting a contract (if money was more salient; see also #4).	*Money:* did not receive a desired raise or promised money bonus; did not make a profit; no overtime pay; no tip or low tip; salary or raise unfair (compared to others); failed to get contract or sale (if money was most salient; see also #4).

TABLE 1 (continued)

Satisfying Events	Dissatisfying Events
9. *Interpersonal Atmosphere:* in general was pleasant; everyone was getting along well together, polite, friendly, interesting conversations; pleasant nonwork interaction with others (e.g., office party); praised for nonwork action. (Note: do not use this if praise was for work; see #7).	*Interpersonal Atmosphere:* in general was unpleasant; everyone was getting along poorly, hostile, unfriendly, touchy, etc.; obscene language used in presence; dull conversation; unpleasant nonwork interaction with others; criticized for nonwork action. (Note: do not use this if criticized for work; see #7).
10. *Physical Working Conditions* pleasant: weather, temperature, humidity, air, machinery, hours of work, location, physical surroundings of work, etc.	*Physical Working Conditions* unpleasant: weather, temperature, humidity, air, machinery, hours of work, location, failure to get desired time off; physical surroundings of work, etc.
11. *Uncodable or Other:* e.g., outcome of union election, etc.	*Uncodable or Other:* e.g., outcome of union election; accident (that does not belong in #3 or #4 above), etc.

From Locke, 1973. Copyright 1973 by the American Psychological Association. Reprinted by permission.

TABLE 2
SATISFYING AND DISSATISFYING AGENT CATEGORIES

1. *Self* (the respondent).

2. *Supervisor* or other specific superior or superiors of respondent.

3. *Co-worker(s)* of respondent (someone at same level in organization or colleague in profession).

4. *Subordinate(s)* of respondent (someone at lower level in organization or profession).

5. *Organization,* management, or organizational policies. (No particular person or persons cited.)

6. *Customer(s)* of respondent (including students, patients, buyers, etc.).

7. *Nonhuman agent* (nature, machinery, weather, neighborhood, equipment, "God," etc.).

8. *No agent* indicated (e.g., luck, the "breaks," "that's the way it is") or "do not know," or unclassifiable.

From Locke, 1973. Copyright 1973 by American Psychological Association. Reprinted by permission.

6. THE USE OF FREQUENCY DATA. Herzberg's results are based entirely on frequency data. He compared the relative frequency with which the various categories were mentioned as sources of affect. If one is to infer a theory of human nature from such data, one assumption that must be made is that the responses are caused solely or mainly by attributes of the persons answering (i.e., their needs and values). However, as Herzberg himself acknowledges (1966, p. 127), the reports of satisfying and dissatisfying incidents gathered with his method are also determined by the actual nature of the jobs held by the employees (see also Vroom, 1964, p. 128). Thus, while one reason that failure is not often mentioned as a source of dissatisfaction may be that it does not cause displeasure when it occurs, another reason may be that *it simply does not occur very often* since most people are fairly well matched to their jobs and thus are able to perform them successfully.

One way to avoid such difficulties in interpretation is to use an *intensity* approach, that is, to ask employees to think of a time when: they succeeded, failed, were recognized and were criticized, and to have them indicate the degree to which each event affected their attitude toward their job.

7. DENIAL OF INDIVIDUAL DIFFERENCES. Herzberg has consistently minimized or denied

the existence of individual differences among employees as to reported sources of satisfaction and dissatisfaction. While it is defensible to argue that all men have the same needs (by the very nature of needs), it is not defensible to argue that they all have the same values. Yet it is the individual's values that are the most direct determinants of his emotional reactions to the job (Locke, 1969). Hulin (1971) and Hulin and Blood (1968) have presented convincing evidence that all employees do not value jobs which allow them the opportunity for psychological growth. Even Ford (1969a), who accepts Herzberg's theory, acknowledges that all workers do not respond positively to job enrichment programs.

Herzberg could answer this criticism, however, by arguing that employees who do not value or attempt to attain psychological growth through their work will not attain the same quality or quantity (or duration) of satisfaction from their work[9] as those who do value and seek it, the reason being that these workers' values conflict with their needs. This writer would tend to agree with Herzberg on this point. The whole issue, however, suggests the need for further research to test the hypothesis systematically.

Research Findings

One problem involved in testing Herzberg's theory is that the theory itself has not been consistently stated by Herzberg. King (1970), for example, has identified five different versions of it from Herzberg's writings. Due to space limitations it will not be possible to discuss each version here; rather, the theory will be discussed mainly from the point of view of a "weak" version of King's theory V: satisfaction is determined predominantly by Motivators and dissatisfaction predominantly by Hygienes.[10] Other versions will be referred to incidentally. (See King, 1970, for details of each version.)

When Herzberg's method, including his classification system, is used, his original aggregate pattern of results is replicated consistently (Herzberg, 1966), though not universally (House & Wigdor, 1967), and not if the data are analyzed on an individual basis (Schwab & Heneman, 1970). Unfortunately, Herzberg's is virtually the only method that does consistently replicate the original aggregate findings (House & Wigdor, 1967; King, 1970). And in view of the aforementioned flaws in Herzberg's method, these failures to replicate must be regarded as casting serious doubt on the validity of his theory.

Schneider and Locke (1971), for example, used the event/agent classification system shown in Tables 1 and 2 to analyze critical incident reports from four white collar samples. They found that the same classes of events were seen as responsible for *both* satisfaction and dissatisfaction. These were mainly task related, Motivator-type events (categories 1–7 in Table 1).

Four replications (two using blue collar subjects) of the event findings can be found in Locke (1973). Table 3 shows the combined results for these four replications plus Sample D from Schneider and Locke (1971), which employed the same methodology.[11] Of the ten chi-squares on the individual Event categories, only four were significant and in the direction predicted by Herzberg's theory. Three were significant in the opposite direction, and three were not significant.

---

[9] This is not to deny that some workers can satisfy the need for growth from other, off-the-job activities. This, however, does not change the argument; such workers would still attain less pleasure from their jobs than workers whose jobs allowed for growth.

[10] The strong version states that satisfaction comes *only* from Motivators and dissatisfaction comes *only* from Hygienes.

[11] The problem of unequal numbers of incidents or events being reported for satisfaction and dissatisfaction was solved by having each respondent in these samples indicate the *most important* event responsible for his satisfying and dissatisfying experience and the agent *most responsible* for this event.

TABLE 3
FREQUENCY OF MOTIVATOR AND HYGIENE EVENTS AS
SATISFIERS AND DISSATISFIERS FOR FIVE SAMPLES[a]

Event Category	Frequency as:		χ^2
	Satisfier[b]	Dissatisfier[b]	
1. Task Activity	40	39	0.00
2. Amount of Work	9	27	9.24**
3. Smoothness of Work	11	32	10.55**
4. Achievement/Failure	114	64	13.37**
5. Promotion	20	13	1.39
6. Responsibility	33	8	14.90**
7. Recognition	81	93	1.00
8. Money	35	20	3.89*
9. Interpersonal Atmosphere	17	40	9.59**
10. Working Conditions	7	26	11.19**
ALL MOTIVATORS (1–7)	308	276 ⎫	6.75*
ALL HYGIENES (8–10)[c]	59	86 ⎬	

* $p < .05$
** $p < .01$
[a] From Schneider and Locke (1971, Sample D) and Locke (1973).
[b] Only the incident rated as most important in causing the attitude was classified for each subject.
[c] Incidents not classifiable using the above categories were not included in the analysis.

The overall chi-square based on a Motivator-Hygiene split (categories 1–7 versus 8–10) was significant at the .05 level, due almost entirely to the Hygiene factors being mentioned more often as dissatisfiers than as satisfiers. (None of the chi-squares for the individual samples was significant, indicating that even the latter result is not a "robust" one.) Motivators were mentioned almost equally often as satisfiers and dissatisfiers and accounted for more than 76 percent of the events in both cases.

With respect to agents, the data of Schneider and Locke (1971) and Locke (1973) show a consistent trend in the direction of the self being given credit for satisfying events relatively more often than it is blamed for dissatisfying events as compared with non-self agents. These results suggest the possibility of defensive bias.

A recent study by Wall (1973) yields direct evidence for the defensiveness thesis. Wall asked seventy-seven employees of a chemical process company to describe sources of job satisfaction and dissatisfaction for three different time periods. In each

period, scores on a measure of "ego-defensiveness" correlated significantly with the proportion of all dissatisfying factors mentioned which were Hygienes in Herzberg's system. Since most of Herzberg's Hygiene factors are agents (other persons), these results support the notion that his results are partly an artifact of the defense mechanism of projection.

Wernimont (1966) attacked the problem of defensiveness by having subjects classify their incidents (using Herzberg's categories) according to a forced-choice format. His results were similar to the event results of Schneider and Locke. However, Wernimont's method has been criticized by Herzberg (1966, pp. 150ff.) on the grounds that the forced-choice procedure compelled subjects to attribute their attitudes to causes which did not apply to the incident at all. This may be true, in part, but it does not explain why the effect of this procedure is to yield the particular pattern of results Wernimont obtained.

Whatever the merits of Wernimont's study, the problem of defensive bias still remains as a probable contaminating factor in Herzberg's results.

The problem of undue reliance on frequency data was avoided by Lindsay, Marks, and Gorlow (1967), who used the intensity method described earlier. They had subjects think of specific incidents of achievement and failure and the like and then asked them to indicate the intensity of the effects of these events on job satisfaction. They found that achievement acted as both a satisfier and a dissatisfier. This study has also been attacked on the grounds that the format used was confusing to the subjects and that separate scales for satisfaction and dissatisfaction were not used (Whitsett & Winslow, 1967).

However, a recent unpublished study by Cortese (1972) which avoided these problems obtained similar results. He asked nineteen nurses and nursing assistants to think of a time when they experienced each of seven Motivator events and each of three Hygiene events at both a "good" and a "bad" level (achievement, failure, high pay,

low pay, etc.) using Schneider and Locke's (1971) event categories. The subjects rated the effect of each event on a satisfaction and a dissatisfaction scale, respectively. The data, shown in Table 4, indicate that both Motivator and Hygiene events led to significant effects on both positive and negative attitudes, though the effects of Motivators on satisfaction tended to be greater than their effects on dissatisfaction. Interestingly, the pattern for Hygiene events was the same; they had significant effects on both satisfaction and dissatisfaction, but somewhat greater effects on satisfaction. Thus, the effects of Motivator and Hygiene factors were similar rather than opposite. However one interprets these results, they do not support Herzberg's theory.

These basic findings were replicated in a class project in which the present writer had students ask employees ($N = 36$) to think of four specific job incidents: a time when they achieved and failed, and a time when interpersonal relations or working conditions were good and poor. The effects

TABLE 4
EFFECTS OF MOTIVATOR AND HYGIENE EVENTS ON INTENSITY OF SATISFACTION AND DISSATISFACTION

| Event Category | Mean Effect on: | | t^b on difference | df. |
	Satisfaction[a]	Dissatisfaction[a]		
1. Task Activity	4.37[c]	3.29[c]	3.06*	31
2. Amount of Work	3.88	3.88	0	32
3. Smoothness of Work	3.88	3.47	1.05	31
4. Achievement/Failure	4.68	3.87	2.74*	32
5. Promotion	4.71	3.17	3.64*	18
6. Responsibility	3.29	2.63	1.34	20
7. Recognition	4.47	3.70	1.92	27
8. Money	4.18	4.20	0.05	20
9. Interpersonal Atmosphere	4.11	2.86	3.20*	24
10. Working Conditions	3.65	3.89	0.54	24
11. Other	4.40	3.80	1.64	28
ALL MOTIVATORS (1–7)	4.18	3.43		
ALL HYGIENES (8–11)	4.08	3.69		

* p < .01
[a] Measured on a 5-point scale: 1 = event gave no pleasure (displeasure), to
                                              5 = event gave enormous pleasure (displeasure)
[b] t for independent samples was used due to incomplete data.
[c] All means are significantly different from 1 (= no affect).
From Cortese, 1972.

of each of these four incidents were indicated on separate job satisfaction or dissatisfaction scales. The results are shown in Table 5. Again, the effects of both achievement (a Motivator) and interpersonal relations or working conditions (Hygiene factors) were significant in both directions. The effects were greater on satisfaction than on dissatisfaction, but the Motivator and Hygienes did not differ from each other in their ability to produce satisfaction or dissatisfaction, respectively.

A possible explanation for the more intense effects of "good" job events on satisfaction than of "bad" events on dissatisfaction lies in the agent data obtained from the frequency studies reported above. Since individuals are more likely to take credit for satisfying events and to blame others for dissatisfying events, they are presumably less "ego involved" in the latter than in the former. Such reduced involvement would tend to lessen the intensity of the affective reaction. Another possible explanation is repression based on the desire not to acknowledge or feel disappointment or failure.

Comparing these results with those obtained with the frequency method (using the Schneider-Locke event/agent classification system), there is agreement in only one main respect: both Motivators and Hygienes lead to both satisfaction and dissatisfaction. Otherwise, the two methods do not show the same pattern. For example, while Hy-

gienes are not mentioned very often as causes of either satisfaction or dissatisfaction, when they do occur, they affect attitudes just as intensely as the Motivators.

The reason for this was suggested by the data gathered for the class project mentioned above. It was found that in 60 percent of the cases where Hygienes were mentioned as sources of satisfaction or dissatisfaction, the reason given was *they facilitated or interfered with the employee's ability to perform his assigned work tasks* or were associated with Motivator factors such as Recognition. In other words, the Motivators were not independent of the Hygiene factors but were causally interrelated with them. To give an example, a twenty-five-year-old male economic consultant reported that the reason why "excellent interpersonal relations on [a] project" caused him to feel satisfied was that "the job went smoothly and the goal was accomplished." Similarly, a "very uncooperative work group" made him feel dissatisfied because "progress towards job accomplishment [was] extremely slow."

A number of early correlational tests of the Motivator-Hygiene theory, involving concurrent estimates of the statistical variance in overall job satisfaction accounted for by satisfaction with specific Motivator and Hygiene factors, were also criticized on the grounds that they did not use separate scales for satisfaction and dissatisfaction (Whitsett & Winslow, 1967). However, recent studies

TABLE 5
EFFECTS OF ACHIEVEMENT/FAILURE AND INTERPERSONAL RELATIONS (OR WORKING CONDITIONS) ON INTENSITY OF SATISFACTION AND DISSATISFACTION

Event Category	Mean Effect on:	
	Satisfaction[a]	Dissatisfaction[a]
Achievement/Failure	4.08[b]	3.33[c]
Interpersonal Relations or Working Conditions	4.22[d]	3.03[e]

[a] Same scales used as shown in Table 4, note a.

[b,c,d,e]: t-tests for correlated data (35 d.f.); b vs. c, t = 3.26 (p < .01); d vs. e, t = 5.01 (p < .01); b vs. d, t = −0.65 (ns); c vs. e, t = 1.16 (ns). All means are significantly different from 1 (= no affect).

(Hulin & Waters, 1971; Waters & Roach, 1971b; Waters & Waters, 1969, 1972) which employed separate satisfaction and dissatisfaction scales also failed to show consistent support for the theory or any of its versions. These latter studies suggested that both Motivator and Hygiene factors correlated with both satisfaction and dissatisfaction, with the Motivator factor correlations most often being higher than those for Hygienes.

Studies employing more abstract ranking procedures (Friedlander, 1964) also suggest that Motivator and Hygiene factors cause both satisfaction and dissatisfaction, with the Motivators being more causally potent.

Herzberg (1966) and his supporters (Whitsett & Winslow, 1967) have been quite critical on methodological grounds of studies which do not support the two-factor theory. Some of these criticisms are not without foundation (e.g., the possible biases involved in the use of abstract ranking procedures); but one is struck by the enormous inconsistency with which these criticisms are applied. They are always applied to disconfirming studies and never to confirming studies. Furthermore, when they are applied to disconfirming studies, the particular parts of these studies which support the theory are excluded from the main criticism and accepted as valid while the disconfirming parts are rejected even though both sets of findings were obtained with the same method (e.g., Herzberg, 1966, pp. 145–146, 151).

Similarly, evidence to the effect that Motivator factors can be sources of employee dissatisfaction (even evidence reported by Herzberg himself, 1966, p. 127) is shrugged off with the explanation that such evidence is based on a "misinterpretation of . . . feelings" (1966, p. 84; see also p. 128). While it is true that people can misinterpret their feelings, nowhere in his writings does Herzberg provide any evidence for his thesis as it applies to reports of dissatisfying work. He simply asserts it.

One is ultimately forced to the conclusion that a double standard is being used by supporters of the theory in evaluating the evidence based on the a priori assumption that the Motivator-Hygiene theory is valid. This procedure is known in logic as the fallacy of question-begging or assuming what one sets out to prove. (For a case of openly acknowledged bias, see Bockman, 1971, p. 186).

Conclusion

In one respect, Herzberg has made a major contribution to our knowledge and understanding of the nature of job satisfaction. This contribution stems from his stress on the importance of psychological growth as a precondition of job satisfaction and his showing that such growth stems from the work itself. This has led to many fruitful suggestions concerning how jobs might be redesigned to allow for greater psychological growth. While Herzberg was not the first theorist to posit the existence of such needs, his work has served to focus attention on the importance of psychological growth and its relation to work and has been a major impetus to applied research (Ford, 1969a; Maher, 1971).

On the other hand, Herzberg's insistence on the idea of two unipolar continua (one pertaining only to dissatisfaction and involving Hygienes and the other pertaining only to satisfaction and involving Motivators) seems indefensible, both logically and empirically. Furthermore, adherence to this view is really unnecessary from the point of view of emphasizing the importance of work in facilitating psychological growth.

For example, the experiments on job enrichment conducted by advocates of Herzberg's theory (Ford, 1969a; Maher, 1971) do *not,* in fact, presuppose the validity of the *unipolar continuum* aspect of Herzberg's theory. They only assume that factors in the work itself are an important source of positive attitudes. These studies all involve restructuring jobs so as to make the work more satisfying. No researcher has yet tried to test the other side of the Motivator coin by redesigning the work so as to produce dissatisfaction. Nor is there any practical reason why any organization should wish to do so.

On this point, it is ironic to note that Ford (1969a), who originally supported the idea that job enrichment would lead to increased job satisfaction, later suggested that this might be an incorrect assumption and that the major effect of enrichment in the realm of attitudes might be to increase job *involvement* (1969b). One of the consequences of greater involvement is that the potential is greater for both satisfaction *and* dissatisfaction.

Finally, Herzberg's treatment of supervisory practices as Hygiene elements is entirely spurious and ultimately contrary to the implicit assumptions of his theory and even to some of his own statements (e.g., see Herzberg et al., 1959, p. 135). While Herzberg's official theory makes the supervisor out to be an environmental appendage who can only cause (or not cause) dissatisfaction, when the theory is applied to industry, the supervisor is given an important new role— one that is not implied in any of the "Human Relations" theories: *the role of a redesigner of the work itself. The supervisor is, in effect, regarded as an agent whose job is to (help) increase opportunities for psychological growth.* The job of the supervisor, in this view, is to help his subordinates to gain values, especially task values (Locke, 1970a).

Summary

Combining the most defensible aspects of each of the theories discussed above, we can expand our definition of job satisfaction as follows: It is hypothesized that *job satisfaction results from the appraisal of one's job as attaining or allowing the attainment of one's important job values, providing these values are congruent with or help to fulfill one's basic needs. These needs are of two separable but interdependent types: bodily or physical needs and psychological needs, especially the need for growth. Growth is made possible mainly by the nature of the work itself.*

VI. Causal Factors in Job Satisfaction: A Survey of Major Findings

The categorization scheme used in this section follows (selectively) the classification of major aspects of the job delineated in section III above. Since a complete summary of the literature is obviously impossible here, the discussion will emphasize important findings and integrating principles.

EVENTS AND CONDITIONS

Work

Work attributes that have been found to be related to work interest and satisfaction include: opportunity to use one's valued skills and abilities; opportunity for new learning; creativity; variety; difficulty; amount of work; responsibility; non-arbitrary pressure for performance; control over work methods and work pace (autonomy); job enrichment (which involves increasing responsibility and control); and complexity (e.g., see Alderfer, 1967; Cooper, 1970; Ford, 1969a; Hackman & Lawler, 1971; Hall & Lawler, 1971; Herzberg et al., 1957, 1959; Lawler & Hall, 1970; Locke, 1973; Maher, 1971; Morse, 1953; Patchen, 1970; Pelz & Andrews, 1966; Vroom, 1964; Walker & Guest, 1952).

While each of the above factors is conceptually distinguishable from the others, there is one element which they share in common, the element of *mental challenge* (see, on this point, Barnowe, Mangione, & Quinn, 1972). New learning, creativity, autonomy, coping with difficulties, and being responsible for decisions regarding the organization of the work, all involve the use of one's conceptual faculty. Further, a person's valued skills and abilities nearly always include his mental skills, directly or by implication.

In the absence of an adequate mental challenge or in the presence of a work task that is accomplished automatically (with no effort, skill, or thought required), one experiences *boredom,* which is the converse of interest. Wyatt, Langdon, and Stock (1937) noted many years ago after extensive investigations of British workers that "boredom arises when the mental processes involved in work fail to occupy and to hold the focus of attention" (p. 65).[12] Boredom is the result of unused mental capacity.

If the challenge of the work is sufficiently great and is accepted by the employee, he should become both interested and *involved* in the job (Ford, 1969b; Patchen, 1970). One reason that challenge stimulates involvement is that it requires the exercise of individual judgment and choice, and thereby makes oneself the main causal agent in performance. Actions and outcomes for which one takes personal responsibility will ordinarily produce greater affect than those for which one is not responsible, because more of oneself (i.e., one's ego) is involved in the job. Another reason is that coping with challenge requires effort and the expenditure of effort requires *commitment* to the goals one is seeking.

Just as too little challenge can result in dissatisfaction, so can too much. If the degree of challenge is so great that the individual cannot successfully cope with it, he will experience a sense of failure and frustration with his work. If the challenge is moderate, in the sense that success is difficult but possible, then the individual will experience pleasure and satisfaction.[13] It has been found in numerous studies that

achievement on the task or *success* in problem solving or in reaching specific standards of competence is an important determinant of task and work satisfaction (Herzberg, 1966; Locke, 1965; Turner & Miclette, 1962; Vroom, 1964). Thus, there must not only be opportunities or challenges on the job, but these challenges must be successfully overcome for the individual to experience pleasure. The individual does not have to experience final success for this to occur so long as he experiences *improvement* (Hilgard, 1942) or *progress* toward a final goal (Locke, Cartledge, & Knerr, 1970).

There is evidence that a person's feelings of achievement or accomplishment are enhanced if he works on or completes a "whole" piece of work or if his personal contribution to the whole is clear and visible. Achievement is also enhanced if there is a definite feedback from some source (another person or the task itself) regarding the degree of achievement attained (Hackman & Lawler, 1971).

The root of the pleasure of achievement is man's need to cope successfully with his environment in order to survive. Successful coping yields a sense of efficacy or competence in dealing with reality (see White's, 1959, concept of competence motivation), and a sense of pride in oneself (Turner & Miclette, 1962). In Herzberg's (1966) terminology, efficacy satisfies the need for psychological growth.

An important precondition of work satisfaction is that the individual find the work itself *personally interesting* and meaningful (Herzberg et al., 1959; Strong, 1943). An employee will not automatically like a task simply because it is challenging or because he has mastered it. He also has to like it for its own sake. This means that a man

---

[12] Many writers have argued that employees on repetitive jobs use fantasy and daydreaming to reduce boredom (though Smith, 1955, did not find support for this). Some have argued that jobs which demand no attention are less boring than jobs which demand partial attention because daydreaming is easier in the former case. Perhaps employees who daydream do not experience total boredom, but it does not follow that what they experience is of interest. Daydreaming may best be viewed as a relief from boredom rather than an arouser of interest, in the same way that Baldamus (1961) views "traction" as a relief from tedium but not a positive pleasure in itself.

[13] Atkinson and Feather (1966) argue that the pleasure experienced with achievement is a negative linear function of difficulty. They define difficulty, however, as probability of success. Defined in this way the hy-

pothesis that pleasure decreases in intensity as probability of success increases has not received strong support in the literature (e.g., Locke, 1967). It might be more defensible to define difficulty more broadly, such as in terms of the total amount of effort required; the total time required; the degree of intelligence and problem-solving skill needed; the amount of information that must be integrated, etc.

must choose the line of work *because he likes it,* not because someone else told him to like it, or because he is trying to prove something (e.g., that he is a big shot).

Another determinant of work satisfaction which is frequently overlooked in this age of technology is the *absence of physical strain.* Chadwick-Jones (1969), for example, found reduced physical effort to be the main source of satisfaction for a group of English workers who were transferred from a pre-automated to an automated steel plant. The fact that 76 percent of the workers were interviewed five years or more after the transfer had taken place indicates that this preference was more than a temporary phenomenon. The basis for the preference for physically light work is presumably the individual's need for bodily well-being.

INDIVIDUAL DIFFERENCES. Research summarized by Hulin (1971) and Hulin and Blood (1968) shows quite clearly that all employees do not consciously value, desire, or seek mentally challenging work. There are intriguing statistical differences between job levels in this respect and possibly urban-rural and Catholic-Protestant differences as well (Turner & Lawrence, 1965). The interesting theoretical question which these findings pose is: Do employees who do *not* value or seek mentally challenging work get the same quality, quantity, and duration of satisfaction from their work as do those who do seek (and successfully cope with) such work? Does work *mean* the same thing to both types of individuals? This writer thinks not; but more research on this question is clearly warranted. Studies by Friedmann and Havighurst (1962) and Morse and Weiss (1962) suggest that there are important differences between job levels in the meaning of work with the lower levels more often viewing work only as a means to keep busy or to earn a living, while the higher level workers more often view it as pleasurable in itself and as a means of fulfilling a variety of psychological needs.

The fact that employees at higher job levels are more likely to want and to get

mentally challenging work than employees at lower job levels may explain, in large part, the almost universal finding of a positive relationship between job level and job satisfaction.

Pay

A recent monograph by Lawler (1971) has summarized most of the research to date on the subject of pay satisfaction. Lawler contrasts "discrepancy" theory—the view that pay satisfaction depends upon the difference between obtained pay and valued[14] pay—and "equity" theory—the view that pay satisfaction is a function of obtained pay in relation to the individual's perceived inputs and outputs in relation to other people holding similar jobs.

While Lawler views these two models as basically different, this writer regards the theories as involving two different levels of explanation. *Discrepancy theory posits a model of pay satisfaction, while equity theory provides content for that model.* The latter theory identifies *some* of the factors that determine what an individual's desired level of pay will be.

Factors that have been hypothesized to determine equity level include: (1) *individual traits,* such as age, seniority, education, and experience; (2) *individual actions,* such as effort expenditure, output quantity, output quality, creative innovation; and (3) *job attributes,* such as challenge, level of responsibility, time span of discretion. (For various views of the determinants of perceived equity, see Adams, 1965; Homans, 1961; Jaques, 1961; Lawler, 1971; Patchen, 1961; Whyte, 1955.)

According to equity theory these factors are judged on a *comparative* basis so that an

---

[14] The value standard to be used in explaining pay satisfaction is complex since in one sense almost everyone "wants" an infinite amount of pay. This writer suggests using, among others, the individual's "minimally acceptable" amount as a standard. This was used to construct (hypothetically) Figure 1. This standard represents the crossover point between satisfaction and dissatisfaction, so that negative discrepancies are increasingly disvalued and positive discrepancies are increasingly valued.

individual who possesses more of certain traits or works harder or has a more demanding job than another individual (in the same department, company, union, profession, etc.) thinks he should be paid more money.

It is clear that individuals who believe they are inequitably paid are dissatisfied with their pay. Equity theory also predicts that overpayment will lead to just as much dissatisfaction with pay as underpayment. Laboratory research indicates, however, that individuals who are overpaid (according to the experimenter's announcement to the subject as to what constitutes equitable payment) are just as satisfied with their pay as, though not more satisfied than, equitably paid subjects (Pritchard, Dunnette, & Jorgenson, 1972).

With respect to the latter finding, it will be recalled that "discrepancy theory" predicts a linear function relating pay to pay satisfaction (see Figure 1), under the assumptions that pay is a generally valued commodity, and that all other factors are held constant. In the typical equity experiment, however, all other factors are not equal, since an explicit attempt is made to induce feelings of guilt and inferiority in overpaid subjects. This presumably results in a *conflict between two values among those subjects:* money and justice. The result of this conflict would be that the greater pleasure derived from the additional money would be offset by the displeasure resulting from the knowledge that one did not deserve it. Thus, the resulting satisfaction would be no greater than that obtained from equitable payment.

In the long run, of course, equity theory would claim that individuals take actions or make judgments aimed at reducing their guilt (e.g., modifying effort, reappraising the desirability of other aspects of the job). It is not clear, however, just how these activities would affect pay satisfaction.

Unlike the typical laboratory study, however, real-life employees are not usually told that they are being overpaid or that they are not competent to perform the duties they have just been hired to perform. In the present writer's opinion this artificiality in the laboratory studies of equity, in addition to the extremely short time spans typically involved, severely limits (if not negates) the generality of the results of these studies insofar as overpayment is concerned (e.g., see Lawler, Koplin, Young, & Fadem, 1968; Vroom, 1970). In real life, it is more typical for employees who are paid more highly than would seem equitable to simply adjust their conception of equitable payment to justify what they are getting. (Has anyone ever met a $20,000-a-year plumber who felt guilty?)

It should be added that the concept of equity is so loose that it allows for enormous variation in individual interpretation, for example, in the nature of the reference group used for comparison, in the particular aspects of equity to be considered, etc.[15]

While equity considerations do influence the value standards which employees use to evaluate their pay, they are certainly not the only factors involved. Pay values are also influenced by the individual's personal financial situation (e.g., expenses) and by his own economic aspirations. Such values are also affected by the amount of pay he has received previously; for example, Hinrichs (1969) and Zedeck and Smith (1968) found that employees' judgments of a "just, meaningful raise" depended on the absolute amount of their present pay. Larger raises were needed with larger starting amounts.

The root of the desire for pay as such is the individual's desire to satisfy his physical needs (food, shelter, clothing, etc.). But it can mean much more than this. Money also serves as a symbol of achievement (McClelland, 1961), as a source of recognition, and as a means of obtaining other values (e.g., leisure, works of art, etc.). To some it

---

[15] Thus, it is very easy for an individual to switch his standards of equity in such a way as to always give himself the highest possible level of "equitable" payment. It is especially easy to justify "overpayment" by finding some other person or group who is equally highly paid and who is comparable in some way to oneself.

is a status symbol; to others it means security; to others it allows greater freedom of action in all areas of life. In some cases salary is interpreted as reflecting management's concern for the individual employee

The basis of the desire for equitable pay is the desire for *justice* or fairness; that is, for returns or rewards commensurate with one's actions.

INDIVIDUAL DIFFERENCES. Nearly all occupational groups consider either amount of pay and/or employment security to be relatively important (Herzberg et al., 1957; Smith, Kendall, & Hulin, 1969). Recent research by Ingham (1970) in England suggests the interesting hypothesis that blue collar employees who choose to work in large organizations (e.g., 3,000 or more) are motivated mainly by economic considerations (and are attracted to these organizations because of their higher pay), while those who choose to work in smaller firms (less than seventy) are more attracted by work variety and the informal social relationships than by monetary considerations. Dalton has described one group of industrial rate-busters who were motivated primarily by money as "country-born (or middle-class born), lone-wolf, Republican, money-saving, and investing worker[s], without outside interests." In contrast, those who made below-average earnings were characterized as "city-born, gregarious, New Deal Democratic, spending worker[s] with hobbies that cost money and bring no economic return" (reported in Whyte, 1955, p. 46).

Promotion

Satisfaction with promotions can be viewed, like pay, as a function of the frequency of promotion in relation to what is desired and the importance of promotion to the individual. Again the equity concept provides some content for this model.

All employees do not agree, however, on what constitutes equity. While American culture has always stressed merit or ability to do the job as being the standard of justice

in promotion, there are large subgroups of the population that do not share this view. Public firms and unionized firms are more likely than private and nonunionized firms to stress passing examinations (civil service requirements) and seniority (years on the job or in the firm) as a basis for promotion.

While equity (however defined) is one factor that influences a person's value standard concerning desired number of promotions, again it is not the only factor. It is easily conceivable that an employee could appraise the promotion system in his company as fair, and yet still be dissatisfied with his chances for promotion simply because there were none. Such an individual's value standard would depend upon his personal ambitions and career aspirations.

Alternatively, an individual might view the promotion system in his firm as unfair and still be personally satisfied with it, because he does not desire to be promoted. Since a promotion ordinarily entails an increase in responsibility and work difficulty, an individual who does not feel up to such a challenge (e.g., who has low self-esteem or who is at the limit of his ability) will not desire to be promoted or will at least be in conflict at the prospect. Promotions which require the individual to give up other important values (such as community ties in the case of a promotion that requires moving) may also be unattractive to some employees (Bray, Campbell, & Grant, 1974).

The roots of the desire for promotion would include: the desire for psychological growth (made possible by the greater responsibility); the desire for justice (if one has earned the promotion); the desire for higher earnings; and the desire for social status (for those who base their self-image on what others think of them).

INDIVIDUAL DIFFERENCES. It is well known that business executives value promotions highly (Bray et al., 1974; Campbell, Dunnette, Lawler, & Weick, 1970), perhaps as highly as any occupational group in our society. This reflects the very high degree of personal ambition in these individuals. One would expect that self-esteem and self-confidence would affect the desire for promotion at all occupational levels, although this issue has not been frequently researched.

Verbal Recognition

Usually the subject of recognition is discussed under the topic of supervision, but in keeping with the present method of classification it is discussed here separately as an event.

Virtually all employees value being praised for their work and being given credit where credit is due, especially by supervisors and colleagues whose judgment they respect. Similarly, most employees disvalue being criticized or not getting credit for their work accomplishments. Locke (1973) found recognition to be one of the single most frequently mentioned events causing job satisfaction and dissatisfaction, especially among blue collar workers. Researchers using Herzberg's methodology found it to be one of the most frequently mentioned satisfactions, and (despite his illogical classification system) also found it to be the fourth most frequently mentioned dissatisfier (using people rather than incidents as the unit of analysis; summarized in House & Wigdor, 1967).

Another important function of recognition for work is that it provides feedback concerning the competence of one's job performance. Thus praise indicates that one has done a job correctly, according to the standards of one's superiors, while criticism indicates that one has not met their standards. Depending upon the form in which such feedback is given, it can be used to correct past errors and to set future goals for performance (Locke, Cartledge, & Koeppel, 1968).

The desire for recognition is typically attributed to the desire or need for self-esteem or a positive self-concept. However, this view takes for granted the validity of the theory (already questioned in section V

above) that genuine self-esteem comes from the approval of others. Nevertheless, it is clear that many people do, in fact, *attempt* to gain self-esteem by gaining the approval of significant others.

A motive for recognition that has not received sufficient emphasis is the desire for justice. Another is the desire for knowledge, which in turn helps one to become more efficacious.

INDIVIDUAL DIFFERENCES. Individuals with low self-esteem should be most dependent on recognition and most emotionally affected by it (positively and negatively). Furthermore, there is evidence that females are more sensitive than males to interpersonal job factors of this type (Herzberg et al., 1957), though the ultimate causes are probably cultural rather than biological.

Working Conditions

There are far too many aspects of working conditions to make any thorough summary possible here. Generally, employees value physical surroundings which are not dangerous or uncomfortable. With respect to features such as temperature, humidity, ventilation, lighting, and noise, moderate rather than extreme degrees are preferred since extremes (e.g., too much heat, too little light) cause physical discomfort and reduce one's ability to work. Most employees also value a location close to home, new (rather than old) buildings, cleanliness (including clean air), and adequate tools and equipment (Barnowe et al., 1972).

It is this writer's impression that physical working conditions such as those mentioned above, unless they are extremely good or bad, are usually taken for granted by most employees. They do not become salient unless some explicit standard of comparison is available (e.g., see Chadwick-Jones, 1969, p. 50). Such standards are most obviously present where the working conditions change over time (e.g., moving into a new building) or when the individual changes jobs.

The basic principles underlying the employee's preference for pleasant working conditions are: (1) the desire for physical comfort, based on his physical needs; and (2) the desire for conditions which facilitate (and/or do not block) the attainment of his work goals.

Mott, Mann, McLoughlin, and Warwick (1965) have shown that attitudes toward shift work are determined in large part by the worker's perception of the degree to which his hours of work facilitate or interfere with his valued off-the-job activities (see also Chadwick-Jones, 1969, pp. 87ff.; Vroom, 1964, pp. 155ff.).

Both Herzberg (1966) and Whyte (1955) have observed that complaints about physical working conditions are sometimes symbols or manifestations of deeper frustrations (e.g., anxiety, personal problems, distrust of management, dislike for the work itself) and soon disappear when these problems are resolved.

INDIVIDUAL DIFFERENCES. Herzberg et al. (1957) argue that women tend to consider working conditions to be more important than men and factory workers consider them more important than office workers. The latter is also true of hours of work. In fact, it is reasonable to assume that those who enjoy their work would view *hours of work* in exactly the opposite way from those who do not like their work. For the man who loves his work and is absorbed in it, the usual complaint is there is not enough time in the working day to get everything done that he wants to do. In contrast, the man who dislikes his work would prefer to get it over with as fast as possible so that he can do things which he enjoys more.

AGENTS

The Self

One of the most unresearched subjects in the area of job attitudes is the individual's view of himself and the way in which this view affects what he seeks for pleasure on the job and how various job experiences and conditions affect him. The concept of *self-esteem* is clearly a crucial factor in this regard. Korman (1968) has argued that whereas high self-esteem employees get more pleasure from task success than from failure, low self-esteem persons do not. Leonard and Weitz (1971), however, failed to replicate this finding.

One could predict that high self-esteem persons as compared to low self-esteem persons would: (1) be more likely to value challenging tasks; (2) find the pleasures resulting from achievement to be more intense and enduring; (3) be more likely to want promotions for reasons of justice and the desire for more responsibility and less likely to want them for status reasons; (4) be less likely to value prestige, approval, and verbal recognition as sources of self-assurance (e.g., see Greenhaus, 1971); (5) be less emotionally affected by criticism; (6) experience fewer conflicts and feelings of anxiety on the job; (7) be less defensive and employ fewer defense mechanisms.

The whole issue of attribution of causality is now being researched on a wide scale by personality theorists (e.g., see Weiner et al., 1971). Many investigators (e.g., Lewin, 1963) have found that people tend to dissociate themselves from failure by projecting it onto external sources. This defense mechanism is motivated by the desire to protect self-esteem against threat. On the positive side, Argyris (1964) has argued that individuals will experience pleasure with success only to the degree that they perceive themselves as causally responsible for it.

Supervisors, Co-workers, and Subordinates

It has been found consistently that subordinates like supervisors who are "Considerate" (Vroom, 1964) and "Employee Centered" (Likert, 1961). The term Consideration emerged from the Ohio State factor analytic studies (Halpin & Winer,

1957). The items in the Consideration scale involve such supervisory traits or actions as friendliness, praising good performance, listening to subordinates' opinions, and taking a personal interest in them (Fleishman, 1972). The term Employee Centered emerged from the Michigan studies and has a similar meaning.

While not denying the above findings, a somewhat different perspective on the issue is taken here. This perspective is based on a distinction between two different types of human relationships; these types may be called *Functional* and *Entity* relations.[16] In a Functional relationship the bond between two (or more) persons consists of specific *services* they can provide for each other, for example, a shopkeeper providing a customer with a product in return for money. An exchange of specific actions or material values is involved. Each person is valued for what he can do for the other rather than as an end in himself.

In an Entity relationship, the bond is between *persons,* not services. The attraction is based on mutual liking of or admiration for the other person qua person rather than on an exchange of specific services. The attraction is to the other person as a whole rather than to any particular extrinsic value he can provide. Romantic love would be the most clear-cut example of an entity relationship; a friendship (though less intense than a love relationship) would be another example.

Long-term Functional relationships which entail extensive and frequent contact among the parties can develop into Entity relationships as, for example, in the case where a scientist falls in love with his research assistant or a doctor with his nurse or patient.

It is typical for *both* types of relationship to play a role in determining the degree of attraction between supervisor and subordinate and among co-workers at the same hierarchical level. Specifically:

1. Since the basis of a *Functional* attraction is the gaining of values, a subordinate will like his superior to the extent that he sees the superior as providing him with or helping him to attain important job values (this view was previously presented in Locke, 1970a, 1970b). These values can be divided into two broad classes:

   (a) *Task-related values:* interesting and challenging work, help in attaining work goals, freedom from interruptions, good equipment, etc.

   (b) *Rewards for task performance:* promotion, pay raises or high earnings, verbal recognition.

In this model, the supervisor is seen as a *value facilitator.* Thus this is basically an "instrumentality" approach but in a more direct way than has been the case in previous studies (e.g., Evans, 1970; House, 1971). As noted earlier, one original (though not explicitly stated) contribution of Herzberg's theory is that it views the supervisor as having a new role (one not recognized by most previous theorists)—that of a task or job enricher.

The concept of value facilitation would also explain the attitude of a supervisor toward his subordinate (an issue seldom researched by industrial psychologists). A supervisor should value his subordinates to the degree that they help to attain the supervisor's work goals. Thus, supervisors should like subordinates who are reliable and competent (unless they are seen as a threat) and cooperative in accepting and completing

---

[16] The writer first learned of this distinction from a lecture by N. Branden. The philosophical base for it was laid by Aristotle in his *Nichomachean Ethics,* who distinguished among three types of friendship: "Friendships of utility" were those in which the attraction was based on what each person could do for the other. "Friendships of goodness" were those based on mutual admiration of the other's virtues and values. These two types correspond closely to the concepts of functional and entity attraction, respectively. Aristotle's third, intermediate type was called "Friendships of pleasure" and involved a shallow, short-term, emotional attraction between individuals based on the pleasure and amusement they could provide for one another (e.g., adolescent love).

work assignments. Similarly, employees should like co-workers who help them with their work tasks or to achieve some common goal and who facilitate their getting rewards.

2. *Entity* relationships are based on attraction between persons qua persons, rather than persons qua value facilitators. A superficial type of entity attraction to another person will generally occur when that other person has a "nice personality," viz., when he is pleasant, friendly, polite, benevolent, and the like, providing he is viewed as sincere.[17] A more profound type of entity attraction, however, requires a perception of *fundamental similarity in basic attitudes, values, or philosophy* (Byrne, 1969). Individuals are generally attracted to and feel most comfortable with people who are "like them" or "see things" the way they do, especially "important" things. Certain actions of one person toward another may facilitate attraction even though they have no direct functional significance. One of these is taking a personal interest in the other person. Examples of such actions on the part of a supervisor would involve interactions with his subordinate which were not directly job related or required by the job, for example, asking about and being aware of his subordinate's health or personal problems; discussing personal matters; discussing off-the-job activities; being aware and considerate of the subordinate's idiosyncracies, personal tastes, preferences, and feelings.

It is logical to assume that the greatest degree of overall liking for another person in the work place will arise when both entity and functional attractions are high. However, it is clearly possible to like, for example, one's supervisor "as a supervisor" but not "as a person," and vice versa.

---

[17] A person who is "nice" but insincere is disliked because he is perpetrating a type of fraud: he is projecting an entity attraction for the victim when actually he wants something from him (i.e., the attraction is purely functional). The same type of deception is involved when a person marries for money.

The above distinction between functional and entity relationships suggests a somewhat different method of designing "attitude toward the supervisor" questionnaires than has been followed heretofore. A functional type of questionnaire would determine the degree to which the supervisor is seen as facilitating, inhibiting, or not affecting subordinate value attainment; while an entity questionnaire would look at the degree to which the supervisor is perceived as sharing the values of his subordinates and taking a personal interest in them.

Many of the supervisory characteristics found by previous investigators to be related to employee satisfaction (e.g., Barnowe et al., 1972; Dubin, Homans, Mann, & Miller, 1965; Hill & French, 1967; Likert, 1961; Mann & Hoffman, 1960; Pelz, 1951, 1967; Rosen, 1969; Tosi, Chesser, & Carroll, 1972) can be interpreted within this framework. Others, such as participation, may fit into both, depending upon the context. For example, participation gives the subordinate more influence, especially with respect to task values, but it may also be interpreted as indicating that the supervisor is concerned with his personal feelings and opinions.

Company and Management

All of the *functional* activities described above as applicable to supervisors would also apply to the organization as a whole. The organization can determine the nature of the individual's work tasks, his work load, his degree of responsibility, his promotional opportunities, his rate of pay, and the physical conditions of work. In fact, the organization has more ultimate control over these factors than does the employee's immediate supervisor.

The concept of entity attraction does not apply as obviously to the relationship between an employee and the organization as it does to that between an employee and his supervisor, since the former is a more impersonal type of relationship than the latter.

Two other concepts that have been used to describe organizational policies are: (1) *role conflict,* the degree to which role expectations are incompatible or self-contradictory; and (2) *role ambiguity,* the degree to which role expectations are vague, unclear, or undefined. Both have been found to be associated with job dissatisfaction (House & Rizzo, 1972; Kahn, Wolfe, Quinn, Snoek, & Rosenthal, 1964).

Benefits have not been found to have a strong influence on job attitudes, although there may be exceptions for certain categories of employees (e.g., pre-retirees vis-à-vis the pension plan, etc.).

Summary

Job satisfaction results from the attainment of values which are compatible with one's needs. Among the most important values or conditions conducive to job satisfaction are: (1) mentally challenging work with which the individual can cope successfully; (2) personal interest in the work itself; (3) work which is not too physically tiring; (4) rewards for performance which are just, informative, and in line with the individual's personal aspirations; (5) working conditions which are compatible with the individual's physical needs and which facilitate the accomplishment of his work goals; (6) high self-esteem on the part of the employee; (7) agents in the work place who help the employee to attain job values such as interesting work, pay, and promotions, whose basic values are similar to his own, and who minimize role conflict and ambiguity.

VII. The Consequences of Job Satisfaction

There are two reasons for being concerned with the phenomenon of job satisfaction. First, it can be viewed as an end in itself, since happiness, after all, is the goal of life. Secondly, it can be studied because it contributes to other attitudes and outcomes. While there is evidence that job satisfaction does have effects, the findings must be interpreted with great caution.

Effects on Other Attitudes

Since one's job is part of one's life, it is logical to expect job satisfaction to influence life satisfaction. Kornhauser (1965), Iris and Barrett (1972), and Weitz (1952) have found significant correlations between attitudes toward the job and those toward life.

Less obvious is the effect of job satisfaction on family attitudes and other off-the-job activities. Kornhauser (1965) found positive correlations among attitudes toward these areas. One mechanism by which such an effect might occur would be emotional generalization or "spillover." The cause-effect relationship could, of course, work in both directions; that is, work attitudes could affect family attitudes and vice versa. In addition, certain personality traits could affect both sets of attitudes.

An individual's job attitudes can also affect his view of himself. Herzberg et al. (1959), for example, found that satisfying job experiences (e.g., achievement, recognition) often increased the individual's self-confidence. One would also expect an equal and opposite effect as a result of dissatisfying experiences, although Herzberg did not find this. (This could be due to his illogical classification system, however; see section V.) As noted earlier, the effect of such job experiences or outcomes on the individual's self-concept should be dependent, in part, on whether he attributes them to himself or to external agents.

Effects on Physical Health and Longevity

Burke (1969/1970) found significant correlations between job and/or non-job satisfactions and such subjectively reported physical symptoms as fatigue, shortness of breath, headache, sweating, and ill health. Herzberg et al. (1959) found that subjects reported physical symptoms, such as headaches, loss of appetite, indigestion, and nausea following dissatisfying job incidents.

Whyte (1955, based on work by Dalton) reports that 18 percent of the workers in one plant who were neither "restricters" nor "rate busters," and who were, therefore, presumably in conflict over whether to maximize earnings or to adhere to the group output norm, were being treated for ulcer problems, whereas no individual who was a consistent rate buster or restricter was troubled by this problem.

Steelworkers on highly automated and subjectively boring jobs were reported by Chadwick-Jones (1969) to complain frequently of being extremely fatigued, presumably due to the low level of arousal induced by their work tasks (cf., Scott, 1966). The fatigue was experienced as being qualitatively different from ordinary physical fatigue, however, since it was not induced by exertion but by boredom.

In a one-hour laboratory experiment, Sales (1969) found a significant negative relationship between the subjects' enjoyment of the task and changes in their level of serum cholesterol during the work period. Since high cholesterol levels are thought to be a precursor of coronary heart disease, this finding implies a relationship between dissatisfaction and the incidence of such disease. In a later study, Sales and House (1971) found correlations as high as $-.83$ between job satisfaction and rate of mortality from arteriosclerotic heart disease (with social status partialed out) using occupational *groups* or professions as the unit of analysis. These results must be interpreted with caution, however, since other possible causal factors were not ruled out.

More convincing is a longitudinal study of individuals by Palmore (1969) in which he correlated a number of physical and attitudinal variables measured at the beginning of the study with a Longevity Quotient (observed years' survival after a physical examination divided by expected years' survival based on actuarial tables). *The single best overall predictor ($r = .26$; $N = 268$) of longevity was work satisfaction* (defined as a feeling of general usefulness and ability to fulfill a meaningful social role). The second best overall predictor ($r = .25$) was the interviewer's rating of the subject's overall happiness. Both factors predicted longevity better than either physical functioning ($r = .21$) or tobacco use ($r = -.19$).

An extensive review of the medical-psychological literature by Jenkins (1971) found numerous studies which reported associations between coronary disease and job complaints such as boredom, feeling ill at ease, and interpersonal conflict. Other studies reviewed by Jenkins point to a "coronary prone" behavior pattern characterized by extreme competitiveness, impatience, perfectionism, and an inability to relax. Some of these studies were longitudinal, but others reported only concurrent relationships.

The above results relate to the very fascinating field of psychosomatic medicine in that they suggest a causal relationship between psychological states and bodily functioning. Even the longitudinal studies reported above are correlational and, therefore, do not prove causality. Future studies should look for causal mechanisms that would explain the correlational results, perhaps along the lines of the Sales (1969) study described above.

Effects on Mental Health

The experience of dissatisfaction itself is an unpleasant psychological state; furthermore, the existence of this state implies conflict since it means the employee is holding a job that he would prefer to avoid (at least in some respects). This suggests the possibility of a relationship between satisfaction and mental health.

The most systematic study of the relationship of job satisfaction to mental health is that of Kornhauser (1965). He developed an index of mental health from six component indices involving: anxiety and tension, self-esteem, hostility, sociability, life satisfaction, and personal morale (versus despair and anomie). Kornhauser found consistent relationships between satisfaction and the total mental health index among three levels of blue collar automobile workers.

The strongest relationship between specific job attributes (as perceived by the workers) and mental health was for the attribute of "chance to use abilities." This aspect of the work itself was discussed earlier (see sections V and VI) as being related to mental challenge which in turn was related to satisfaction of the individual's need for psychological growth.

An alternative interpretation of the above correlation is that the job structure (or rather the poor fit between the job requirements and the employee's mental capacity) is a cause (or more precisely, one of the causes) of both the dissatisfaction and the mental health problems. On the other hand, certain traits of the employees may predispose them to select jobs which prevent them from growing.

It is also worth noting that "human relations" factors had little or no relationship to the mental health of the work population studied by Kornhauser.

Effects on Action

The view that job satisfaction was a causal factor in job behavior, especially level of performance or output, was an outgrowth of the Hawthorne studies. This is ironic in that (1) previous work had indicated that there was no necessary relationship between satisfaction and productivity; and (2) the Hawthorne findings themselves proved no such relationship.

On the first point, longitudinal laboratory studies by Thorndike (1917) and Poffenberger (1928) had both shown that performance could remain constant or even improve while the individual's feelings of fatigue or dissatisfaction were increasing.

On the second point, what the Hawthorne researchers actually found was that when certain changes were made in the work environment (e.g., rest pauses, hours of work, incentive system, type and degree of supervision, etc.), both performance and morale improved (Roethlisberger & Dickson, 1939). In no case did they show that satisfaction as such led to higher output.

An understanding of the nature of the relationship between job satisfaction and job behavior is only possible if one first understands the nature of emotions and their relationship to action.

It has been argued that emotions are the form in which one experiences value judgments (Arnold, 1960; Locke, 1969, based on Rand, 1964), the causal sequence being: object (situation) → perception (cognition) → appraisal (value judgment) → emotion. If the individual appraises the perceived object as furthering his existence or well-being (by the standard of his values), he will experience a positive emotion; if he appraises the object as a threat to his well-being, he will experience a negative emotion. The value appraisal producing the emotion is subconscious and automatic; furthermore, the individual may not be aware of the values which cause his response (or even the emotion itself), especially if the emotion is complex or if he is a poor introspector.

Locke (1970b), based on Arnold (1960), has argued that emotions involve (as part of the experience of emotion itself) action tendencies; that is, felt urges to action. The two basic urges were asserted to be approach and avoidance of the valued or disvalued object or situation. Such action tendencies, however, do not necessarily lead to overt action. There are numerous action alternatives open to a person in the face of an emotion. A broad classification of these alternatives is presented in Table 6.

Thus, in order to know how an individual will act in response to an emotion, one would have to know which action alternative(s) he will select. This will be affected by such factors as his values, beliefs, and methods of thinking; the constraints and opportunities offered or presented by the

TABLE 6
CLASSIFICATION OF ACTION ALTERNATIVES FOLLOWING POSITIVE AND NEGATIVE EMOTIONS[a]

Positive appraisals
1. Approach object; retain object; repeat act
2. If satiated or if anticipate future boredom (or failure): switch activities; set new goal; choose new task; pursue new endeavor

Negative appraisals
1. Avoid object; leave situation
2. Change object
   a. Physical attack; destroy, damage, injure object or person (threaten attack)
   b. Persuasion; complain; argue; convince agent to modify his actions; bargain; criticize; harass
   c. Change own actions or performance (if they are disvalued object)
3. Change reaction to object
   a. Modify content or hierarchy of own values (self-persuasion; therapy)
   b. Modify estimate of relationship between situation or object and one's values
   c. Use ego-defense mechanisms: psychological withdrawal; repression; evasion; rationalization; projection; fantasy; displacement, etc., to distort perception or appraisal of situation
4. Tolerate situation (focus on valued aspects of situation); postpone action until later date
5. Repeat previous action (rigidity, compulsion)

[a] Reprinted with changes from Locke (1970b), by permission of Academic Press.

situation; and the specific object which is perceived as beneficial or harmful to the individual.

Let us now consider some specific findings on the relationship of job satisfaction to action.

ABSENCES AND TERMINATION. Since the basic action tendencies following job satisfaction and dissatisfaction are approach and avoidance, the most obvious behavioral prediction would be a relation between job dissatisfaction and such actions as absences, termination, and lateness.

Lateness as an action category has not often been studied, but virtually all major reviews of the literature have found consistent significant relationships between job

dissatisfaction, and absenteeism and turnover (Brayfield & Crockett, 1955; Herzberg et al., 1957; Schuh, 1967; Vroom, 1964). More recent studies have supported these earlier findings (e.g., Atchison & Lefferts, 1972; Kraut, 1970; Taylor & Weiss, 1972; Waters & Roach, 1971a; Waters & Roach, 1973).[18] Especially interesting is Hulin's (1968) quasi-experimental field study in which an increase in satisfaction and a reduction in turnover were observed following management-instituted changes designed to increase satisfaction in problem areas uncovered in an earlier, correlational study (Hulin, 1966).

A recent study by Ingham (1970) suggested that absenteeism could be affected by the *type* of satisfaction(s) gained from the job. Ingham found that employees in small plants (less than seventy employees) were less likely to be absent than employees in larger (more than 3,000 employees) plants despite being equal in degree of overall job satisfaction. However, employees in the smaller plants felt a greater degree of personal obligation to the company than was the case with employees in larger plants, who worked mainly for the money. While the conclusions of this study are not definitive, they suggest a number of hypotheses regarding causal factors which affect absenteeism aside from the amount of overall satisfaction as such.

While reported correlations between amount of satisfaction and absenteeism or turnover have been consistent and significant, they have not been especially high (usually less than .40), the reason being that most employees do not act solely on the basis of their feelings. Other factors that would typically be considered in reaching a decision to be absent or terminate would include: personal obligations to one's employer, financial need, and the availability of other jobs.

[18] A more recent review of this literature by Porter and Steers (1973) is fully consistent with the earlier findings.

In view of the numerous replications of the relationship between satisfaction and withdrawal from the job, it would seem that little will be gained from additional studies along these same lines. Further progress is unlikely until detailed studies are made of those who *deviate* from the regression line; that is, those who do *not* act in strict accordance with their degree of job satisfaction. To explain the actions of such people will require the identification of causal factors other than feelings.

COMPLAINTS AND GRIEVANCES. Complaints and grievances are by definition a response to (perceived) dissatisfaction with some aspect of the work situation. Fleishman and Harris (1962) found that high grievance rates were found in departments where the supervisors were rated low in Consideration and high in Initiating Structure, a combination which presumably results in dissatisfaction with the supervisor. However, since this study was done across departments, other possible causal factors, such as differences in the nature of the jobs, were not controlled. This is potentially important because grievances may be either about, or a displacement of dissatisfaction with the work itself. The latter is evidenced by the observation that job enlargement or enrichment sometimes leads to a dramatic decrease in the evidence of employee complaints and grievances (e.g., see Ford, 1969a; Maher, 1971). Such displacements may also be motivated by personal problems, that is, dissatisfaction with oneself.

PRODUCTIVITY. Just as reviews of the literature have shown consistently that job satisfaction is related to absences and turnover, they have been equally consistent in showing negligible relationships between satisfaction and level of performance or productivity (Brayfield & Crockett, 1955; Herzberg et al., 1957; Vroom, 1964).

A number of writers (e.g., Locke, 1970b; Porter & Lawler, 1968) have argued that an alternative way to conceptualize the satis-

faction-productivity relationship is to view the second as a cause of the first rather than vice versa. Even Ford, a supporter of Herzberg, writes that "good performance—good productivity in a useful task—leads to good employee job attitudes" (1969a, p. 97; for supporting evidence, see Siegal & Bowen, 1971). The conditions under which high productivity would lead to high satisfaction would be: (1) when high productivity leads to the attainment of the individual's important job values, for example, task values such as success and achievement, and rewards such as promotion, recognition, high earnings, and the like; and (2) when such production was not attained at such a high cost as to undermine the pleasure of attainment (e.g., fatigue) or to negate other values (e.g., family relationships).

The conditions under which high satisfaction would encourage high subsequent productivity are far more complex. There is no reason to expect any simple relationship, because level of productivity has little or no relationship to approach or avoidance of the job as such. To know what level of productivity would follow a given degree of satisfaction, one would have to have answers to at least the following questions:

1. On what was the individual's (past) satisfaction based; that is, what were the main objects or conditions producing it? For example, if past satisfaction was attained from high productivity, one could expect the action to be repeated. But if it was attained from (or despite) low productivity, there would be no reason to expect high production in the future. Or if the main reasons for being satisfied were the pay and style of supervision, neither of which was contingent upon good performance, there would be little reason to expect high production subsequently. If satisfaction was derived from the work itself, one might expect the individual to work persistently in the future, but not necessarily at a fast rate.

2. What types of actions does the individual anticipate will bring him value attainment and, therefore, pleasure in the fu-

ture (Locke, Cartledge, & Knerr, 1970)? An individual who worked hard and was satisfied in the past might not expect to be so in the future if company policies had changed in some significant way. Individuals do not usually act blindly according to what brought them success in the past; they also guide their actions in anticipation of future conditions.

3. Which among the many action alternatives possible to an individual will he choose in response to satisfaction or dissatisfaction? In response to poor performance which he finds unrewarding, an individual might take any of the following actions: give up and perform more poorly than before; muddle along at the same level; try to improve; quit his job; ask for a transfer; file a grievance; or beat his dog. (See Locke, 1970b, Table 2, for examples of action alternatives following positive and negative appraisals of the job as a whole, and of specific aspects of the job situation.)

4. On the basis of the foregoing considerations, what explicit or implicit performance goals does the individual set (Locke, 1970b)?

5. Does the individual have the knowledge and ability to attain a high level of performance, assuming that he tries to do so?

It is obvious from the above that the effect of satisfaction on performance is highly complex and indirect. (For a detailed discussion of various theories concerning this relationship, see Schwab & Cummings, 1970.)

Herzberg et al. (1959) have argued for a direct effect of satisfying experiences on job performance, with the positive effects of satisfaction (and, therefore, of Motivators) being more frequent than the negative effects of dissatisfaction (and, therefore, of Hygienes). Aside from the fact that Herzberg reports only perceived and recalled rather than objectively measured performance effects, his study did not show any overall relationship between level of satisfaction and level of production. He only showed a relationship between specific job experiences and specific types of recalled action responses.

Schwab, DeVitt, and Cummings (1971) attempted to replicate Herzberg's frequency findings by having their subjects rate the degree to which satisfying and dissatisfying experiences affected their productivity on a scale of intensity. They found, contrary to Herzberg, that the effects of Motivator and Hygiene experiences were exactly parallel. When either was favorable (that is, a source of satisfaction), they led to an equal degree of perceived performance improvement; when either was unfavorable (a source of dissatisfaction), they led to no perceived change in performance.

One interesting aspect of the latter finding is its close parallel to the results obtained by Cortese and the present writer described in section V (see Tables 4 and 5) when they tested Herzberg's theory of satisfaction using the intensity method. In both cases Motivators and Hygienes led to equal degrees of satisfaction or performance improvement, and to equal but smaller (or nonexistent) degrees of dissatisfaction or performance decline.

A possible interpretation of the findings reported by Herzberg et al. (1959) and Schwab et al. (1971) is that both satisfaction and performance were jointly affected by the specific job experiences in question. Ford (1969a), for example, found that changing the challenge and responsibility of the work itself led to improvement in both job satisfaction and job performance among several groups of AT&T employees.

Both logic and research suggest that it is best to view productivity and satisfaction as *separate outcomes* of the employee-job interaction, and to expect causal relationships between them only in special circumstances.

Work variability. When investigating the relationship between performance and attitudes, it has been standard practice to use overall output or output rate as the criterion. However, there are other aspects of performance that could be used. One of them is output variability. Wyatt, Fraser, and Stock (1929) found a relationship between degree of boredom experienced with the work and the magnitude of variability in output among production workers. This effect was explained as being the result of lapses of attention. To this writer's knowledge, no replication of this finding has yet been attempted. If such an effect were to occur, it should be most pronounced in cases where the work was self-paced and where workers were not aiming for specific output goals or quotas.

Rate of learning. Another aspect of performance that has not been extensively investigated is rate of learning. Wyatt, Langdon, and Stock (1937) found that the most bored workers showed much slower improvement in learning their work tasks than did the least bored workers, even when controlling for initial ability. Attempted replications of this finding are certainly in order. Again this relationship would only be expected if other incentives (goals, money bonuses) were not operating.

Other actions. There are other actions that could, under certain circumstances, result from job satisfaction or dissatisfaction. Lateness, leaving early, and taking longer-than-authorized lunch, coffee, and/or rest breaks are ways of temporarily avoiding the job situation. These types of actions have not often been studied, however, probably because of the difficulty of obtaining valid measurements of them.

There is only slight evidence for a relationship between dissatisfaction and accidents (Vroom, 1964). Hersey (1952) argues for a causal relationship between the presence of high *or* low emotional states and worker accidents. One possible mechanism by which such states might affect accident rate would be through distraction of the individual's attention from the job and/or distorting his judgment. Alternatively, certain traits in the individual, such as hostility

or alcoholism (see Haddon, Suchman, & Klein, 1964), might predispose him to be both dissatisfied with his job and prone to engage in accident-producing behaviors.

Summary

Job satisfaction, itself or in combination with the conditions (both in the individual and the job environment) which bring it about, has a variety of consequences for the individual. It can affect his attitude toward life, toward his family, and toward himself. It can affect his physical health and possibly how long he lives. It may be related (indirectly) to mental health and adjustment, and plays a causal role in absenteeism and turnover. Under certain conditions, it may affect other types of on-the-job behavior as well. However, job satisfaction has no direct effect on productivity.

VIII. The Measurement of Job Satisfaction

Rating Scales

Most researchers have followed the lead of Hoppock (1935) in using direct verbal self-reports to measure job satisfaction. The formats used have included Likert scales, Thurstone-type scales, "faces" scales, and lists of adjectives requiring a "yes," "no," or "?" response. Of these the Cornell Job Description Index or JDI (Smith, Kendall, & Hulin, 1969), which employs the latter format, has been described as the most carefully developed scale to date (Vroom, 1964). The JDI includes five scales pertaining to work, pay, promotions, people (co-workers), and supervision. Each scale contains nine or eighteen items. A compilation of different job satisfaction measures may be found in Robinson, Athanasiou, and Head (1969).

One problem inherent in many rating scales is the inclusion of items which are *descriptive* in nature (e.g., "job keeps me on my feet") along with items which are strictly evaluative (e.g., "boring," "satisfying"). The problem with the former type of item is scoring; unless the individual's value standard is known (or unless there are no individual differences in values with respect to that attribute), scoring errors are bound to be made for some individuals. Also evaluative and descriptive items may show different relationships with other variables (Maas, 1966; Smith et al., 1969, p. 157; Yuzuk, 1961).

Some researchers do not measure satisfaction directly but rather infer it by measuring its alleged causes. For example, Porter (1962) uses as a measure of satisfaction the discrepancy between how much of some aspect the individual reports getting and how much he thinks he should get. While this general method may be defensible to an extent (see section IV), Porter's approach does not distinguish between what one "should get" and what one wants. Also, value or "need" importance is not included in the satisfaction calculations.

Some problems common to all self-description inventories include: (1) the assumption of perfect (or at least reasonably good) self-insight, which means both the capacity and willingness to introspect; and (2) the assumption of a common core of meaning across individuals in interpreting the scales or items.

Neither assumption is really valid. Not all individuals are aware of or able to identify their feelings (about their jobs or about themselves). Nor do all individuals interpret a given item in the same way.

Overt Behavior

No one but a confirmed behaviorist would be foolish enough to advocate the use of overt behavior as a measure of job satisfaction. This approach is clearly inadequate because there is no known behavior which would satisfy the minimal criteria needed to justify it, namely: (1) the behavior inevitably follows the experience of satisfaction; that is, satisfaction is always expressed in this particular way; (2) the behavior occurs

with a frequency or intensity that is directly proportional to the intensity of the attitude experienced; and (3) no causal factors other than satisfaction influence the behavior, or if so, their influence can be precisely calculated.

Action Tendency Scales

The view of emotions propounded in the previous section asserts that the action *tendencies* of approach and avoidance are inherent in the experience of positive and negative emotional reactions, respectively. This suggests a specific approach to the measurement of job attitudes, namely, asking the individual to report the action tendencies which he experiences in relation to his job and/or its component elements. This approach would neither ask the individual how he feels as such, nor how he acts as such, but rather *how he feels like acting* (or how he would act if no other factors but his feelings were guiding his actions). Some examples of the type of question that would be congruent with this approach are listed in Table 7.[19] While these items apply mainly to attitudes about the job as a whole, not to its elements, relevant items could easily be designed for specific job attributes.

While this approach does assume some self-insight on the part of the respondent, such items may require less self-knowledge than items which ask for estimates of satisfaction as such. Furthermore, such questions may have more of an absolute frame of reference than do evaluative questions. For example, Smith et al. (1969) have noted that an employee may respond to questions concerning his job satisfaction based on a frame of reference which takes account of the alternative jobs available. Thus, different frames of reference could make the responses of different employees non-com-

---

[19] Preliminary interviewing with these items suggests that some of them elicit answers more indicative of job involvement than of job satisfaction. This was discovered by applying the procedure of logical validation described in section VIII to these items.

TABLE 7
SAMPLE ITEMS FOR AN ACTION TENDENCY
INTERVIEW SCHEDULE FOR JOB SATISFACTION

1. When you wake up in the morning, do you feel reluctant to go to work?
2. Do you ever feel reluctant to go home from work at night because of the enjoyment you are getting from your job?
3. Do you often feel like going to lunch at work sooner than you do?
4. Do you feel like taking a coffee or rest break more often than you should?
5. Do you ever wish you could work at your job on evenings or weekends?
6. Are you sometimes reluctant to leave your job to go on a vacation?
7. When you are on vacation, do you ever look forward to getting back to work?
8. Do you ever wake up at night with the urge to go to work right then and there?
9. Do you ever wish holidays or weekends would get over with so that you could go back to work?
10. If you were starting over in your working career, would you lean toward taking the same type of job you have now?
11. Would you be tempted to recommend your present job to a friend with the same interests and education as yours?
12. Do you ever feel like just walking out on this job for good?
13. When you are at work, do you ever wish you could be somewhere else?
14. Do you think you will be reluctant to retire when the time comes, if you still have this same job?
15. Do you ever feel like working right through lunch break?
16. Do you ever feel like going home early from this job?
17. When you are on your way to work, do you ever feel like going somewhere else instead?
18. How would you feel about working overtime at this job without extra pay?
19. If you inherited a million dollars tomorrow, how would you feel about keeping this job?
20. Would you like to find a better job than this one as soon as possible?

parable. On the other hand, action tendency questions may be less subject to such distortions since one does not need much of a frame of reference to know whether he feels like going to work or not.

It is interesting to note that Kornhauser (1965, p. 160) found that action tendency questions (e.g., "If you could ... start all over, would you choose the same type

of work you are in now or a different type of work?") revealed a higher degree of overall job dissatisfaction among blue collar employees than did more direct affect ratings.

Interviews

It is unfortunate that interviews have been used relatively infrequently to assess job satisfaction. Two reasons for not using them have clearly been the problems of objectivity and disagreement among interviewers. A third has been the total man-hours required as compared with rating scales. On the other hand, there are many potential advantages to interviews; for example: the meaning of the responses can be determined; contradictions can be explained or corrected; individuals with poor self-insight can be assessed more accurately; misinterpretations of the items can be corrected, etc. Furthermore, interviews can probe more in depth and can use an approach to question-asking which is best suited for each individual based on his knowledge, degree of education, and perspective.

The problem of subjectivity might be overcome by training, by structuring (although excessive structuring would destroy the purpose of the interview), and by having other assessors listen to tapes of the interviews to prevent idiosyncratic interpretations.

Critical Incidents

The publication of Herzberg et al.'s (1959) monograph pointed, by implication, to a much neglected aspect of the study of job satisfaction, namely, the measurement of its *qualitative* aspect. Most previous work had put major emphasis on quantitative measurement. (Herzberg's study also looked at the *temporal* or duration aspect of satisfaction, although this has not been followed up by later researchers.) Herzberg's focus was not on how much satisfaction or dissatisfaction individuals experienced, but on the particular sources of those feelings derived from a description of specific experiences.

The justification for this is not only that the particular types of events producing satisfaction may affect the amount (and/or duration) of satisfaction or dissatisfaction experienced, but there may be implications for action as well. Ingham (1970), as noted earlier, found that differences in the type, but not the amount, of satisfaction experienced by employees in small and large plants were related to rate of absenteeism.

The major advantage of the critical incidents approach to the study of job attitudes is that it is much less cognitively demanding on the subject than are the approaches which employ abstract rating scales.

Logical Validity

A major problem with job attitude measurement (as with the measurement of any mental state) is that of validation. I would propose a new type of validity which, though related to some conventional types (e.g., content), is different from them in its emphasis. I call this new type *logical validity*. Logic is "the art of noncontradictory identification" (Rand, 1966). What this means is that *for a measurement to have logical validity, it must be integrated in noncontradictory fashion with all pertinent information relevant to the phenomenon being measured*. One element of logical validity would be content validity which, in this case, would involve the logical relationship between the conceptual definition of the concept or phenomenon being measured and the methods used to measure it (e.g., the particular content of the questions asked the subject). For example, one would not logically ask a person his mother's age in order to determine his job satisfaction. Logical validity does not stop here, however, since the use of "logical" methods (questions) does not guarantee that the subject will interpret them in the same way that the questioner does. The subject's interpretation can only be determined by careful questioning.

It must be stressed that this procedure is not a matter of determining convergent and discriminant validity (cf., Locke, Smith, Kendall, Hulin, & Miller, 1964). In the latter procedure, a number of different measures of the same construct are used and the one that shows the least method bias and that is most representative of those used is chosen as the most valid. As Smith et al. (1969) point out, however, this procedure does not prove that *any* of the measures are actually valid.

Logical validity would require, in the above instance, that the contradictions among the individual's responses to different items or scales used to measure the same phenomenon be resolved, for example, by pointing out the contradiction to him and by further discussion with the subject. For example, in the Kornhauser study mentioned above, it would have been interesting to ask specific workers to explain apparent discrepancies between their expressed job satisfaction and their stated reluctance to choose the same line of work again. When such a procedure is followed, it will usually be found that in answering the different questions or scales, the subject misread one of the items, or was using a different frame of reference in the two cases, or interpreted one or more items idiosyncratically, etc.

Note that by this procedure, *it is the measurements, not the measures, that are being validated*. There is *no* assumption that a given method or set of questions is valid for every person, since people differ in their knowledge, their verbal ability, their frames of reference, their introspective capacity, and their willingness to communicate.

Logical validity as defined here should not to be confused with construct validity, which involves integrating specific measurements of psychological contents or processes into a theoretical network. The problem with the latter procedure is that if the predicted theoretical interrelationships do not emerge, the researcher is faced with the problem of deciding whether it is his theory or his measure which is at fault. Furthermore, if, as is typical, *some* of the predictions came out to *some* degree, this leaves the results open to numerous and varied interpretations. Construct validity deals with the issue of what the measurements, once made, relate to. It does not deal firsthand with the problem of whether the original measurements are valid in the first place. Two good examples in the literature of the problems involved in determining construct validity are LPC (least preferred co-worker) and N ach (need for achievement). After more than a decade and scores of studies (or hundreds in the case of N ach) in which these measures were correlated with everything in sight, no one is yet clear on just what these measures actually measure. Significantly, no one apparently has taken the trouble to interview the subjects in depth and to ask them what they think their responses mean and why.

Summary

The rating scale approach and its variants has been by far the most commonly used method of measuring job satisfaction. It is suggested that other methods be used as well, including action tendency reports, critical incidents, and interviews. A logically valid measure of job satisfaction would be one that integrates and is consistent with all the pertinent evidence one has concerning the employee's feelings about his job.

IX. Research Methods and Strategies in the Study of Job Satisfaction

Correlation

By far the most frequently used method in the study of job satisfaction has been that of correlation. To take a specific example, the majority of studies designed to determine the effects of supervisory behavior have used the procedure of correlating measures of such behavior with subordinate attitudes and productivity. The resulting correlations are then arbitrarily interpreted as indicating a causal relationship, and the direction of causation is arbitrarily asserted to be that the

supervisor's behavior is the cause of the employee's actions or reactions. This may be called the method of *correlation with speculation,* because, while an explanation of the results may be offered, alternative explanations of the findings are neither seriously explored nor ruled out. In the case of research on supervision, recent experimental findings provide support for a causal interpretation directly opposite to the one typically made (Lowin & Craig, 1968).

Sometimes, correlations between variables are presented with little attempt being made to explain them at all, for example, relationships between age or tenure and job satisfaction, sex differences in satisfaction, the effects of group size on behavior or attitudes. In interpreting the results of factor analyses or multiple correlations, the term "percent of variance accounted for" is often used with the implication that accounted for means accounted for in a *causal* rather than a *statistical* sense.

The method of presenting correlations between variables without any attempt to identify the nature of phenomena which caused the relationship to occur has been called the method of *correlation without explanation* (Locke, 1969).

While the method of correlation may be useful for the purposes of suggesting causal hypotheses, it is not a method of scientific proof. A correlation, by itself, explains nothing. Even the cross-lagged correlation technique, while it helps clarify temporal relationships, does not show *how* the alleged cause causes its effect, as would be required of any full causal explanation (on this issue, see Locke, 1972b). Nor does this technique rule out other explanations.

To give an example of a study which attempts to go beyond this method, that is, to provide a defensible explanation of a correlational finding, consider the research of Ingham (1970) discussed earlier. He attempted to explain an observed positive correlation between company size and absenteeism by reference to the values of the individual workers and the interaction of these values with the reward structure of the different sized companies. He found that employees in large plants were attracted mainly by the high wages, whereas those in smaller plants valued the work variety and close interpersonal relations to be found in such settings. The result in both cases was a match between values and rewards leading to equal *degrees* of overall job satisfaction in both types of plants. The difference in absenteeism was explained by the differences in the *type* of satisfaction involved. Workers in the small plants obtained more pleasure from the work itself and had a more personal relationship with their superiors than was the case in the larger plants. The latter difference produced a greater feeling of personal obligation and identification with the company in the case of the smaller firms, which in turn produced a lower absence rate.

A related example of going beyond correlations (mentioned in section VII) would be the attempt to explain the reasons for "off-quadrant" cases, for example, individuals whose absence rate is not congruent with their degree of job satisfaction, that is, who fail to quit despite being dissatisfied or who terminate despite being satisfied.

To explain a correlation, especially a correlation between some external situation and individual action, one would have to identify at least *some* of the *causal mechanisms* involved, for example, the individuals' needs, values, emotions, beliefs, expectancies, cognitive processes, and the like (Locke, 1972b). The failure of an individual's feeling or attitude about a particular object to correlate with his behavior indicates that other attitudes (beliefs, etc.) which were not measured are guiding his actions.

Experimentation

The laboratory experiment has the advantage that environmental variables (and to some extent subject variables) are controlled, but the results of such studies are limited in their generalizability for obvious reasons.

Field studies involve a far more natural work context than do laboratory studies but suffer from limitations in the ability to control all relevant causal factors. Despite this problem, field studies have been extremely influential in the history of industrial psychology (e.g., Taylor's studies of the principles of Scientific Management, the Hawthorne studies, studies of the effects of participation and of job enrichment, etc.). Presumably practitioners and theorists alike have more confidence in findings derived from such studies than in findings arrived at by other methods.

Individual Case Studies

Researchers must make a trade-off between scope and depth in research, and the tendency in the job satisfaction area has been overwhelmingly to sacrifice depth in the interests of scope. Thus, most research studies involve the use of many subjects and a great variety of (often superficial) measures at the expense of a thorough understanding of any given individual. This pattern is logically associated with the preference for questionnaires over interviews, since in-depth studies virtually necessitate the latter.

This imbalance is unfortunate for a number of reasons. First, questionnaires do not easily tap the more basic (fundamental) and less verbalized (and/or repressed) values of the individual, whereas case studies using interviews are ideal for this purpose. Second, as noted in the previous section, interviews allow for the identification of individual differences in question interpretation as well as in the specific meaning of the answers. Third, case studies can be very valuable as a source of hypotheses about the psychodynamics of job satisfaction. Such hypotheses might never emerge from a questionnaire study because the relevant questions would not have been asked. Fourth, case studies can be used to test certain hypotheses, since it only takes one case to disprove the generality of a theory. Fifth, case studies give one a much fuller and more integrated picture of the whole individual than is possible in large-scale studies using pencil and paper measures. Finally, and related to the previous point, case studies encourage the use of the *longitudinal method*. With the exception of Strong's (1943) studies of vocational interests, it has been almost unheard of in job satisfaction research to study the same individual across time, yet such studies might provide valuable insights concerning the long-range determinants of job attitudes (e.g., see Bray et al., 1974). Especially interesting would be studies of how individuals cope with job dissatisfaction (Seashore, 1972).

Summary

The methods of "correlation with speculation" and "correlation without explanation" have been vastly overused in job satisfaction research. More extensive use of alternative methods, such as experimentation and longitudinal case studies using interviews, is recommended.

X. Recommendations for Future Research: The Psycho-epistemology of Job Satisfaction

A number of recommendations were made (or implied) in previous sections concerning promising areas for future research. Among them were: (1) the development of value-importance-satisfaction functions for various job elements, individuals, and employee groups; (2) the measurement of the meaning of work for employees who do not value mentally stimulating work tasks and, more generally, the effects of need-value conflicts on satisfaction; (3) the study of "second level" values, that is, values which underlie specific or surface values; (4) the relation of self-esteem to job satisfaction; (5) the development of functional and entity attraction scales for rating supervisors; (6) the effects of job dissatisfaction and conflicts on physical health; (7) systematic studies of how employees choose among alternative courses of action in response to positive and negative appraisals of the job; (8) the use of

action tendency measures of job satisfaction; (9) a more extensive use of experimental and interview methods and studies of single individuals at all stages of job attitude research; (10) more research aimed at identifying causal mechanisms and less use of "correlation without explanation."

There is a line of research related to the last point which this writer believes to be so potentially important as to be worth a separate discussion. This line of research could be called the "psycho-epistemology of job satisfaction" or "the psycho-epistemology of the satisfied worker." Blumenthal (1969) has defined psycho-epistemology as *"the study of man's cognitive processes from the aspect of the interaction between the conscious mind and the automatic functions of the subconscious"* (No. 7, p. 4). Or put more briefly, psycho-epistemology is the study of man's methods of mental functioning.

What types of cognitive processes would be likely to affect an individual's attitude toward his job, over and above the particular content of his values and the job conditions and experiences which he encounters? Here are some examples:

General Emotional Maladjustment

Several investigators have found that workers who are habitually bored or dissatisfied with their jobs are also generally maladjusted; that is, they are also dissatisfied with other aspects of their life (Hoppock, 1935; Smith, 1955). A plausible interpretation of these findings is that certain traits in the worker himself (e.g., thinking disorders, conflicts) are responsible for the poor attitudes in all areas. Detailed explorations of the thinking processes and emotional problems of such individuals would be needed to identify the roots of such problems.

Emotional Generalization

Individuals differ greatly in the degree to which they use emotional generalization. One type could be called "perceptual-emotional generalization" in that it involves appraising objects according to their superficial or easily perceivable characteristics and the emotions they invoke rather than their essential properties (e.g., disliking a supervisor because he looks like one's father and ignoring his actual personality traits). Another type could be called "spatio-temporal emotional generalization," in that it entails evaluating objects or situations which are in temporal or spatial proximity in the same way (e.g., generalizing dislike of one's supervisor to one's pay, work, co-workers, and working conditions).

Self-Other Comparisons

Equity theory assumes, apparently as a fact of human nature, that people use only social standards to evaluate their pay, which standards then govern their pay satisfaction. Even if one were to accept this assumption (which this writer does not), there are obviously enormous individual differences in the frequency with which people compare themselves with others, in whom they choose to compare themselves with, and in the significance which they attach to the differences they discover.

This is also true in areas other than pay. For example, individuals who succeed in reaching a work goal sometimes get very little pleasure from their success, because they compare themselves with someone who could have done the same job faster or better. Similarly, employees who receive promotions may compare themselves with those in higher positions or those who were promoted sooner and feel inferior or even resentful that it took so long.

Defensiveness

Individuals who are defensive will obviously react to criticisms from supervisors and co-workers differently from non-defensive individuals. For example, those who characteristically employ the mechanism of *projection* will tend to blame others for their

own errors and, therefore, dislike these others more than would non-projectors. Herzberg (1966) has noted that workers who dislike their work may *displace* this frustration onto the working conditions. Another common mechanism is *repression,* or the blocking of certain thoughts, ideas, emotions, or conclusions from entry into conscious awareness. Repression not only blocks out painful emotions (though not without consequences); it can reduce the intensity of positive ones as well.

Coping With Stress and Dissatisfaction

Some individuals experience far more anxiety and tension than others under conditions of external pressure or stress. One factor which determines how an individual will react to stress is his ability to maintain a consistent *task focus* (Wine, 1971). Similarly, coping with failure and dissatisfaction requires that one identify their causes and make plans for corrective action.

There are numerous ways of failing to cope rationally with stress, including blind, impulsive action (panic, aggression); worry and ruminating (focusing on how terrible the whole situation is); daydreaming (letting the mind fantasize passively); refusing to become involved (making a joke of the whole thing); and physical withdrawal (escape).

Goal-setting

The process by which individuals go about setting goals in their work and developing aspirations with respect to pay, promotions, and career development has important implications for the way they appraise themselves and their job, yet such processes have rarely been studied except in the narrow confines of laboratory experiments. Of special importance here are the level at which such goals are set in relation to the individual's capabilities and the degree to which the individual sets goals according to his own independent judgment as opposed to the judgments and assertions of others.

Motivation by Positives and Negatives

Various researchers and theorists have distinguished between individuals who are motivated primarily by positives, for example, the desire for achievement; and those motivated by negatives, for example, the desire to avoid failure or criticism, etc. Such differing value orientations have very different implications for the types of tasks an individual will choose, the persistence with which he will work on them, and the degree of risk he will be willing to take (Atkinson & Feather, 1966), not to mention the degree and quality of pleasure he will gain from reaching such goals.

These are only a few of the numerous types of cognitive processes which have implications for an individual's satisfaction with his job. The measurement problem in the realm of mental operations is, of course, enormous. But this should not deter investigators from this line of research. Little progress will be made in understanding job satisfaction if investigators study only what is easy to measure instead of what is important.

XI. Overall Summary

More than 3,300 studies on the subject of job satisfaction have been published to date. The early (pre-1930) studies stressed the effects of physical conditions of work (including fatigue) and pay on worker attitudes. In the 1930s the Hawthorne studies focused attention on social factors such as supervision and the work group. This influence largely dominated thinking until the late 1950s, when researchers and theorists began to examine the effects of the work itself on worker attitudes. The contemporary scene reveals a growing interest in the identification of work attributes that will reduce boredom and increase job involvement.

From the point of view of process theory, job satisfaction may be viewed as the pleasurable emotional state resulting from the perception of one's job as fulfilling or allowing the fulfillment of one's important job values, providing these values are compatible with one's needs. (Values refer to what one considers beneficial, whereas needs are the conditions actually required for one's well-being.)

From the point of view of content theory, neither Maslow's Need Hierarchy theory nor Herzberg's Motivator-Hygiene theory provides an adequate specification of the particular job conditions conducive to job satisfaction. Both suffer from numerous logical inconsistencies and from lack of empirical support. Herzberg's theory, however, does provide a useful distinction between physical (bodily) and psychological (mental) needs, and identifies cognitive growth as a major psychological need that can be fulfilled through work.

Previous research indicates that work satisfaction is engendered by work which is varied, allows autonomy, is not physically fatiguing, which is mentally challenging and yet allows the individual to experience success, and which is personally interesting. Satisfaction with rewards such as pay, promotions, and recognition depends on the fairness or equity with which they are administered and the degree to which they are congruent with the individual's personal aspirations. Satisfaction with working conditions depends on their compatibility with the individual's physical needs and the degree to which they facilitate the attainment of his work goals.

The employee will be satisfied with agents in the work situation (supervisors, subordinates, co-workers, management) to the degree that they are seen as facilitating the attainment of his work goals and work rewards, and to the degree that these agents are perceived as having important values in common with him. The former type of relationship is called *functional*, because it stresses what one individual can do for the other. The latter type is called an *entity* relationship, because it involves a response to the other person as an end in himself.

Role conflict and ambiguity should be minimized to avoid dissatisfaction.

High self-esteem individuals will experience more pleasure in their work, other things being equal, than individuals with low self-esteem.

Job dissatisfaction, alone or in combination with other factors, can have a variety of consequences, including effects on individual's other attitudes, physical health, absences, turnover, and grievances. However, there is no direct effect of satisfaction on productivity. The opposite cause-and-effect relationship will hold in cases where high production leads to the attainment of important job values.

Job satisfaction researchers have relied too much on rating scales to measure job satisfaction and too little on interviews. It is argued that measurements of job satisfaction should have *logical validity,* which means that the measurements should integrate all relevant knowledge about the individual and the phenomenon being measured. Research in this area has also relied too heavily on correlational studies and could benefit from more case studies and in-depth interview studies.

Future research would benefit from examining individual differences in the mental operations which characterize (the psycho-epistemology of) the satisfied and dissatisfied worker.

REFERENCES

Adams, J. S. Inequity in social exchange. In L. Berkowitz (Ed.), *Advances in experimental social psychology,* Vol. 2. New York: Academic Press, 1965, 267–299.

Alderfer, C. P. An organizational syndrome. *Administrative Science Quarterly,* 1967, 12, 440–460.

Argyris, C. *Integrating the individual and the organization.* New York: Wiley, 1964.

Arnold, M. B. *Emotion and personality: Psychological aspects,* Vol. 1. New York: Columbia University Press, 1960.

Atchison, T. J., & Lefferts, E. A. The prediction of turnover using Herzberg's job satisfaction technique. *Personnel Psychology,* 1972, 25, 53–64.

Atkinson, J. W., & Feather, N. T. *A theory of achievement motivation.* New York: Wiley, 1966.

Baldamus, W. Efficiency and effort. London: Tavistock, 1961.

Barnowe, J. T., Mangione, T. W., & Quinn, R. P. The relative importance of job facets as indicated by an empirically derived model of job satisfaction. Unpublished report, Survey Research Center, University of Michigan, Ann Arbor, 1972.

Blackler, F., & Williams, R. People's motives at work. In P. B. Warr (Ed.), *Psychology at work.* Baltimore: Penguin, 1971, 283–303.

Blumenthal, A. The base of objectivist psychotherapy. *The Objectivist,* 1969, 8, Nos. 6 & 7.

Bobbitt, H. R., & Behling, O. Defense mechanisms as an alternate explanation of Herzberg's motivator-hygiene results. *Journal of Applied Psychology,* 1972, 56, 24–27.

Bockman, V. M. The Herzberg controversy. *Personnel Psychology,* 1971, 24, 155–189.

Bray, D. W., Campbell, R. J., & Grant, D. L. *Formative years in business.* New York: Wiley, 1974.

Brayfield, A. H., & Crockett, W. H. Employee attitudes and employee performance. *Psychological Bulletin,* 1955, 52, 396–424.

Burke, R. J. Occupational and life strains, satisfaction, and mental health. *Journal of Business Administration,* Winter, 1969/1970, 1, 35–41.

Burtt, H. E. *Psychology and industrial efficiency.* New York: Appleton, 1931.

Byrne, D. Attitude and attraction. In L. Berkowitz (Ed.), *Advances in experimental social psychology,* Vol. 4. New York: Academic Press, 1969, 36–89.

Campbell, J. P., Dunnette, M. D., Lawler, E. E., & Weick, K. E. Jr. *Managerial behavior, performance, and effectiveness.* New York: McGraw-Hill, 1970.

Carey, A. The Hawthorne studies: A radical criticism. *American Sociological Review,* 1967, 32, 403–416.

Carter, R. *Breakthrough: The saga of Jonas Salk.* New York: Pocket Books, 1967.

Chadwick-Jones, J. K. *Automation and behaviour.* New York: Wiley, 1969.

Cofer, C. N., & Appley, M. H. *Motivation: Theory and research.* New York: Wiley, 1964.

Cooper, R. *Memorandum on motivation.* England: School of Business Studies, University of Liverpool, 1970.

Cortese, J. J. The two-factor theory: A revision of classification systems. Unpublished manuscript, Department of Business Administration, University of Maryland, College Park, 1972.

Decker, R. L. A study of three specific problems in the measurement and interpretation of employee attitudes. *Psychological Monographs,* 1955, 69, No. 16 (Whole No. 401).

Dubin, R., Homans, G. C., Mann, F. C., & Miller, D. C. *Leadership and productivity.* San Francisco: Chandler, 1965.

Evans, M. G. The effects of supervisory behavior on the path-goal relationship. *Organizational Behavior and Human Performance,* 1970, 5, 277–298.

Ewen, R. B. Weighing components of job satisfaction. *Journal of Applied Psychology,* 1967, 51, 68–73.

Fleishman, E. A. *Manual for the supervisory behavior description questionnaire.* Washington, D.C.: American Institutes for Research, 1972.

Fleishman, E. A., & Harris, E. F. Patterns of leadership behavior related to employee grievances and turnover. *Personnel Psychology,* 1962, 15, 43–56.

Ford, R. N. *Motivation through the work itself.* New York: American Management Association, 1969. (a)

Ford, R. N. The obstinate employee. *Public Opinion Quarterly,* 1969, 33, 301–310. (b)

Friedlander, F. Job characteristics as satisfiers and dissatisfiers. *Journal of Applied Psychology,* 1964, 48, 388–392.

Friedmann, E. A., & Havighurst, R. J. Work and retirement. In S. Nosow & W. H. Form (Eds.), *Man, work, and society.* New York: Basic Books, 1962, 41–55.

Gilbreth, F. B. Science in management for the one best way to do work. In H. F. Merrill (Ed.), *Classics in management.* (Rev. ed.) New York: American Management Association, 1970, 217–263.

Greenhaus, J. H. Self-esteem as an influence on occupational choice and occupational satisfaction. *Journal of Vocational Behavior,* 1971, 1, 75–83.

Hackman, J. R., & Lawler, E. E. Employee reactions to job characteristics. (Monograph). *Journal of Applied Psychology,* 1971, 55, 259–286.

Haddon, W., Suchman, E. A., & Klein, D. *Accident research.* New York: Harper and Row, 1964.

Hahn, C. P. Collection of data for utilization in curriculum planning of the U.S. Air Force Academy. Contract #AF 41 (657)-204, March, 1959.

Hall, D. T., & Lawler, E. E. Job pressures and research performance. *American Scientist,* 1971, 59, 64–73.

Hall, D. T., & Nougaim, K. E. An examination of Maslow's need hierarchy in an organizational setting. *Organizational Behavior and Human Performance,* 1968, 3, 12–35.

Halpin, A. W., & Winer, B. J. A factorial study of the leader behavior descriptions. In R. M. Stogdill & A. E. Coons (Eds.), *Leader behavior: Its description and measurement.* Columbus: Ohio State University, Bureau of Business Research, Research Monograph No. 88, 1957, 39–51.

Hersey, R. B. Emotional factors in accidents. In H. W. Karn & B. H. Gilmer (Eds.), *Readings in industrial and business psychology.* New York: McGraw-Hill, 1952, 211–217.

Herzberg, F. *Work and the nature of man.* Cleveland: World Publishing, 1966.

Herzberg, F. The motivation to work. In E. A. Fleishman (Ed.), *Studies in personnel and industrial psychology.* (Rev. ed.) Homewood, Ill.: Dorsey Press, 1967, 282–287.

Herzberg, F., Mausner, B., & Snyderman, B. *The motivation to work.* New York: Wiley, 1959.

Herzberg, F., Mausner, B., Peterson, R. O., & Capwell, D. F. *Job attitudes: Review of research and opinion.* Pittsburgh: Psychological Service of Pittsburgh, 1957.

Hilgard, E. R. Success in relation to level of aspiration. *School and Society,* 1942, 55, 423–428.

Hill, W. W., & French, W. L. Perceptions of the power of department chairmen by professors. *Administrative Science Quarterly,* 1967, 11, 548–574.

Hinrichs, J. R. Correlates of employee evaluations of pay increases. *Journal of Applied Psychology,* 1969, 53, 481–489.

Homans, G. C. *The human group.* New York: Harcourt, Brace & World, 1950.

Homans, G. C. *Social behavior: Its elementary forms.* New York: Harcourt, Brace & World, 1961.

Hoppock, R. *Job satisfaction.* New York: Harper, 1935.

House, R. J. A path goal theory of leader effectiveness. *Administrative Science Quarterly,* 1971, 16, 321–338.

House, R. J., & Rizzo, J. R. Role conflict and ambiguity as critical variables in a model of organizational behavior. *Organizational Behavior and Human Performance,* 1972, 7, 467–505.

House, R. J., & Wigdor, L. A. Herzberg's dual-factor theory of job satisfaction and motivation: A review of the evidence and a criticism. *Personnel Psychology,* 1967, 20, 369–390.

Hulin, C. L. Job satisfaction and turnover in a female clerical population. *Journal of Applied Psychology,* 1966, 50, 280–285.

Hulin, C. L. Effects of changes in job satisfaction levels on employee turnover. *Journal of Applied Psychology,* 1968, 52, 122–126.

Hulin, C. L. Individual differences and job enrichment: The case against general treatments. In J. R. Maher (Ed.), *New perspectives in job enrichment.* New York: Van Nostrand, 1971, 159–191.

Hulin, C. L., & Blood, M. R. Job enlargement, individual differences, and worker responses. *Psychological Bulletin,* 1968, 69, 41–55.

Hulin, C. L., & Waters, L. K. Regression analysis of three variations of the two-factor theory of job satisfaction. *Journal of Applied Psychology,* 1971, 55, 211–217.

Ilgen, D. R. Satisfaction with performance as a function of the initial level of expected performance and the deviation from expectations. *Organizational Behavior and Human Performance,* 1971, 6, 345–361.

Ingham, G. K. *Size of industrial organization and worker behaviour.* England: Cambridge University Press, 1970.

Iris, B., & Barrett, G. V. Some relations between job and life satisfaction and job importance. *Journal of Applied Psychology,* 1972, 56, 301–304.

Jaques, E. *Equitable payment.* New York: Wiley, 1961.

Jenkins, D. C. Psychologic and social precursors of coronary disease (II). *New England Journal of Medicine,* 1971, 284, 307–317.

Kahn, R. L., Wolfe, D. M., Quinn, R. P., Snoek, J. D., & Rosenthal, R. A. *Organizational stress: Studies in role conflict and ambiguity.* New York: Wiley, 1964.

Katzell, R. A. Personal values, job satisfaction, and job behavior. In H. Borow (Ed.), *Man in a world at work.* Boston: Houghton Mifflin, 1964, 341–363.

King, N. Clarification and evaluation of the two-factor theory of job satisfaction. *Psychological Bulletin,* 1970, 74, 18–31.

Korman, A. K. Task success, task popularity, and self-esteem as influences on task liking. *Journal of Applied Psychology,* 1968, 52, 484–490.

Kornhauser, A. W. *Mental health of the industrial worker: A Detroit study.* New York: Wiley, 1965.

Kraut, A. I. The prediction of employee turnover by employee attitudes. American Psychological Association, 1970.

Lawler, E. E. *Pay and organizational effectiveness: A psychological view.* New York: McGraw-Hill, 1971.

Lawler, E. E., & Hall, D. T. Relationship of job characteristics to job involvement, satisfaction, and intrinsic motivation. *Journal of Applied Psychology,* 1970, 54, 305–312.

Lawler, E. E., & Suttle, J. L. A causal correlational test of the need hierarchy concept. *Organizational Behavior and Human Performance,* 1972, 7, 265–287.

Lawler, E. E., Koplin, C. A., Young, T. F., & Fadem, J. A. Inequity reduction over time and in an induced overpayment situation. *Organizational Behavior and Human Performance,* 1968, 3, 253–268.

Leonard, S., & Weitz, J. Task enjoyment and task perseverance in relation to task success and self-esteem. *Journal of Applied Psychology,* 1971, 55, 414–421.

Lewin, K. Psychology of success and failure. In T. W. Costello & S. S. Zalkind (Eds.), *Psychology in administration.* Englewood Cliffs, N.J.: Prentice-Hall, 1963, 67–72.

Likert, R. *New patterns of management.* New York: McGraw-Hill, 1961.

Lindsay, C. A., Marks, E., & Gorlow, L. The Herzberg theory: A critique and reformulation. *Journal of Applied Psychology,* 1967, 51, 330–339.

Locke, E. A. The relationship of task success to task liking and satisfaction. *Journal of Applied Psychology,* 1965, 49, 379–385.

Locke, E. A. Relationship of success and expectation to affect on goal-seeking tasks. *Journal of Personality and Social Psychology,* 1967, 7, 125–134.

Locke, E. A. What is job satisfaction? *Organizational Behavior and Human Performance,* 1969, 4, 309–336.

Locke, E. A. The supervisor as "motivator": His influence on employee performance and satisfaction. In B. M. Bass, R. Cooper, & J. A. Haas (Eds.), *Managing for accomplishment.* Lexington, Mass.: Heath Lexington, 1970, 57–67. (a)

Locke, E. A. Job satisfaction and job performance: A theoretical analysis. *Organizational Behavior and Human Performance,* 1970, 5, 484–500. (b)

Locke, E. A. In "defense" of defense mechanisms: Some comments on Bobbitt and Behling. *Journal of Applied Psychology,* 1972, 56, 297–298. (a)

Locke, E. A. Critical analysis of the concept of causality in behavioristic psychology. *Psychological Reports,* 1972, 31, 175–197. (b)

Locke, E. A. Satisfiers and dissatisfiers among white collar and blue collar employees. *Journal of Applied Psychology,* 1973, 58, 67–76.

Locke, E. A., Cartledge, N., & Knerr, C. S. Studies of the relationship between satisfaction, goal-setting, and performance. *Organizational Behavior and Human Performance,* 1970, 5, 135–158.

Locke, E. A., Cartledge, N., & Koeppel, J. Motivational effects of knowledge of results: A goal-setting phenomenon? *Psychological Bulletin,* 1968, 70, 474–485.

Locke, E. A., Smith, P. C., Kendall, L. M., Hulin, C. L., & Miller, A. M. Convergent and discriminant validity for areas and rating methods of job satisfaction. *Journal of Applied Psychology,* 1964, 48, 313–319.

Lodahl, T. M., & Kejner, M. The definition and measurement of job involvement. *Journal of Applied Psychology,* 1965, 49, 24–33.

Lofquist, L. H., & Dawis, R. V. *Adjustment to work.* New York: Appleton-Century-Crofts, 1969.

Lowin, A., & Craig, J. R. The influence of level of performance on managerial style: An experimental object-lesson in the ambiguity of correlational data. *Organizational Behavior and Human Performance,* 1968, 3, 440–458.

Maas, J. B. Satisfaction with work as indexed by income level. Unpublished doctoral dissertation, Department of Psychology, Cornell University, Ithaca, New York, 1966.

McClelland, D. C. *The achieving society.* Princeton: Van Nostrand, 1961.

McClelland, D. C., Atkinson, J. W., Clark, R. A., & Lowell, E. L. *The achievement motive.* New York: Appleton-Century-Crofts, 1953.

Maher, J. R., Ed. *New perspectives in job enrichment.* New York: Van Nostrand, 1971.

Mann, F. C., & Hoffman, R. L. *Automation and the worker.* New York: Holt, Rinehart and Winston, 1960.

Marrow, A. J., Bowers, D. G., & Seashore, S. E. *Management by participation.* New York: Harper and Row, 1967.

Maslow, A. H. *Motivation and personality.* New York: Harper and Row, 1954 (2nd ed., 1970).

Mayo, E. *The human problems of an industrial civilization.* New York: Viking Press, 1960 (originally published 1933).

Mayo, G. E. The first enquiry. In H. F. Merrill (Ed.), *Classics in management.* (Rev. ed.) New York: American Management Association, 1970, 379–388.

Mikes, P. S., & Hulin, C. L. Use of importance as a weighting component of job satisfaction. *Journal of Applied Psychology,* 1968, 52, 394–398.

Miner, J. B., & Dachler, P. D. Personnel attitudes and motivation. In P. H. Mussen & M. R. Rosenzweig (Eds.), *Annual review of psychology.* Palo Alto, Calif.: Annual Reviews, 1973, 24, 379–402.

Mobley, W. H., & Locke, E. A. The relationship of value importance to satisfaction. *Organizational Behavior and Human Performance,* 1970, 5, 463–483.

Morse, N. C. *Satisfactions in the white-collar job.* Ann Arbor: University of Michigan, Survey Research Center, 1953.

Morse, N. C., & Weiss, R. S. The function and meaning of work and the job. In S. Nosow & W. H. Form (Eds.), *Man, work, and society.* New York: Basic Books, 1962, 29–35.

Mott, P. E., Mann, F. C., McLoughlin, Q., & Warwick, D. P. *Shift work*. Ann Arbor: University of Michigan, 1965.

Palmore, E. Predicting longevity: A follow-up controlling for age. *The Gerontologist,* 1969, 9, 247–250.

Patchen, M. *The choice of wage comparisons.* Englewood Cliffs, N.J.: Prentice-Hall, 1961.

Patchen, M. *Participation, achievement, and involvement on the job.* Englewood Cliffs, N.J.: Prentice-Hall, 1970.

Pelz, D. C. Leadership within a hierarchical organization. *Journal of Social Issues,* 1951, 7, No. 3, 49–55.

Pelz, D. C. Influence: A key to effective leadership in the first-line supervisor. In E. A. Fleishman (Ed.), *Studies in personnel and industrial psychology.* (Rev. ed.) Homewood, Ill.: Dorsey Press, 1967, 407–416.

Pelz, D. C., & Andrews, F. M. *Scientists in organizations.* New York: Wiley, 1966.

Poffenberger, A. T. The effects of continuous work upon output and feelings. *Journal of Applied Psychology,* 1928, 12, 459–467.

Porter, L. W. Job attitudes in management: I. Perceived deficiencies in need fulfillment as a function of job level. *Journal of Applied Psychology,* 1962, 46, 375–384.

Porter, L. W., & Lawler, E. E. *Managerial attitudes and performance.* Homewood, Ill.: Dorsey Press, 1968.

Porter, L. W., & Steers, R. M. Organizational, work, and personal factors in employee turnover and absenteeism. *Psychological Bulletin,* 1973, 80, 151–176.

Pritchard, R. D., Dunnette, M. D., & Jorgenson, D. O. Effects of perceptions of equity and inequity on worker performance and satisfaction. (Monograph). *Journal of Applied Psychology,* 1972, 56, 75–94.

Rand, A. The Objectivist ethics. In A. Rand (Ed.), *The virtue of selfishness.* New York: Signet, 1964, 13–35.

Rand, A. Concepts of consciousness. *The Objectivist,* 1966, 5, No. 9, 1–8.

Robinson, J. P., Athanasiou, R., & Head, K. B. *Measures of occupational attitudes and occupational characteristics.* Ann Arbor: Survey Research Center, University of Michigan, 1969.

Roethlisberger, F. J., & Dickson, W. J. *Management and the worker.* Cambridge: Harvard University Press, 1939.

Rosen, N. A. *Leadership change and work-group dynamics.* Ithaca, N.Y.: Cornell University Press, 1969.

Rosen, R. A. H., & Rosen, R. A. A suggested modification in job satisfaction surveys. *Personnel Psychology,* 1955, 8, 303–314.

Ryan, T. A. *Work and effort.* New York: Ronald Press, 1947.

Sales, S. M. Organizational role as a risk factor in coronary disease. *Administrative Science Quarterly,* 1969, 14, 325–336.

Sales, S. M., & House, J. Job dissatisfaction as a possible risk factor in coronary heart disease. *Journal of Chronic Diseases,* 1971, 23, 861–873.

Schaffer, R. H. Job satisfaction as related to need satisfaction in work. *Psychological Monographs,* 1953, 67, No. 14 (Whole No. 364).

Schein, E. H. *Organizational psychology.* Englewood Cliffs, N.J.: Prentice-Hall, 1965.

Schneider, J., & Locke, E. A. A critique of Herzberg's incident classification system and a suggested revision. *Organizational Behavior and Human Performance,* 1971, 6, 441–457.

Schuh, A. J. The predictability of employee tenure: A review of the literature. *Personnel Psychology,* 1967, 20, 133–152.

Schwab, D. P., & Cummings, L. L. Theories of performance and satisfaction: A review. *Industrial Relations,* 1970, 9, 408–430.

Schwab, D. P., & Heneman, H. G. Aggregate and individual predictability of the two-factor theory of job satisfaction. *Personnel Psychology,* 1970, 23, 55–66.

Schwab, D. P., DeVitt, H. W., & Cummings, L. L. A test of the adequacy of the two-factor theory as a predictor of self-report performance effects. *Personnel Psychology,* 1971, 24, 293–303.

Scott, W. E. Activation theory and task design. *Organizational Behavior and Human Performance,* 1966, 1, 3–30.

Seashore, S. E. Defining and measuring the quality of working life. Unpublished report, Institute for Social Research, University of Michigan, Ann Arbor, 1972.

Siegal, J. P., & Bowen, D. Satisfaction and performance: Causal relationships and moderating effects. *Journal of Vocational Behavior,* 1971, 1, 263–269.

Smith, P. C. The prediction of individual differences in susceptibility to industrial monotony. *Journal of Applied Psychology,* 1955, 39, 322–329.

Smith, P. C., Kendall, L. M., & Hulin, C. L. *The measurement of satisfaction in work and retirement.* Chicago: Rand McNally, 1969.

Spector, A. J. Expectations, fulfillment, and morale. *Journal of Abnormal and Social Psychology,* 1956, 52, 51–56.

Strong, E. K. *Vocational interests of men and women.* Stanford: Stanford University Press, 1943.

Sykes, A. J. M. Economic interest and the Hawthorne researches. *Human Relations,* 1965, 18, 253–263.

Taylor, F. W. What is scientific management? In H. F. Merrill (Ed.), *Classics in management.* (Rev. ed.) New York: American Management Association, 1970, 67–71.

Taylor, K. E., & Weiss, D. J. Prediction of individual job termination from measured job satisfaction and biographical data. *Journal of Vocational Behavior,* 1972, 2, 123–132.

Thorndike, E. L. The curve of work and the curve of satisfyingness. *Journal of Applied Psychology,* 1917, 1, 265–267.

Tosi, H. L., Chesser, R. J., & Carroll, S. J. A dynamic model of certain aspects of the superior-subordinate relationship. *Eastern Academy of Management,* 1972.

Turner, A. N., & Lawrence, P. R. *Industrial jobs and the worker.* Cambridge: Harvard University Press, 1965.

Turner, A. N., & Miclette, A. L. Sources of satisfaction in repetitive work. *Occupational Psychology,* 1962, 36, 215–231.

Vernon, H. N. *Industrial fatigue and efficiency.* New York: Dutton, 1921.

Viteles, M. S. *Industrial psychology.* New York: W. W. Norton, 1932.

Viteles, M. S. *Motivation and morale in industry.* New York: W. W. Norton, 1953.

Vroom, V. H. *Work and motivation.* New York: Wiley, 1964.

Vroom, V. H. Industrial social psychology. In V. H. Vroom & E. L. Deci (Eds.), *Management and motivation.* Baltimore: Penguin, 1970, 91–106.

Walker, C. R., & Guest, R. H. *The man on the assembly line.* Cambridge: Harvard University Press, 1952.

Wall, T. D. Ego-defensiveness as a determinant of reported differences in sources of job satisfaction and job dissatisfaction. *Journal of Applied Psychology,* 1973, 58, 125–128.

Waters, L. K., & Roach, D. Relationship between job attitudes and two forms of withdrawal from the work situation. *Journal of Applied Psychology,* 1971, 55, 92–94. (a)

Waters, L. K., & Roach, D. The two-factor theories of job satisfaction: Empirical tests for four samples of insurance company employees. *Personnel Psychology,* 1971, 24, 697–705. (b)

Waters, L. K., & Roach, D. Job attitudes as predictors of termination and absenteeism: Consistency over time and across organizational units. *Journal of Applied Psychology,* 1973, 57, 341–342.

Waters, L. K., & Waters, C. W. Correlates of job satisfactions and job dissatisfactions among female clerical workers. *Journal of Applied Psychology,* 1969, 53, 388–391.

Waters, L. K., & Waters, C. W. An empirical test of five versions of the two-factor theory of job satisfaction. *Organizational Behavior and Human Performance,* 1972, 7, 18–24.

Weiner, B., Frieze, I., Kukla, A., Reed, L., Rest, S., & Rosenbaum, R. M. *Perceiving the causes of success and failure.* New York: General Learning Press, 1971.

Weitz, J. A neglected concept in the study of job satisfaction. *Personnel Psychology,* 1952, 5, 201–205.

Wernimont, P. F. Intrinsic and extrinsic factors in job satisfaction. *Journal of Applied Psychology,* 1966, 50, 41–50.

White, R. W. Motivation reconsidered: The concept of competence. *Psychological Review,* 1959, 66, 297–333.

Whitsett, D. A., & Winslow, E. K. An analysis of studies critical of the motivator-hygiene theory. *Personnel Psychology,* 1967, 20, 391–415.

Whyte, W. F. *Money and motivation.* New York: Harper and Row, 1955.

Wine, J. Test anxiety and direction of attention. *Psychological Bulletin,* 1971, 76, 92–104.

Wofford, J. C. The motivational basis of job satisfaction and job performance. *Personnel Psychology,* 1971, 24, 501–518.

Wyatt, S. Rest pauses in industry. (A review of the results obtained.) Industrial Fatigue Research Board, Great Britain, 1927, Report No. 42.

Wyatt, S., Fraser, J. A., & Stock, F. G. L. The effects of monotony in work. Industrial Fatigue Research Board, Great Britain, 1929, Report No. 56.

Wyatt, S., Langdon, J. N., & Stock, F. G. L. Fatigue and boredom in repetitive work. Industrial Health Research Board, Great Britain, 1937, Report No. 77.

Yuzuk, R. P. *The assessment of employee morale*. Columbus, Ohio: Bureau of Business Research, Monograph No. 99, 1961.

Zedeck, S., & Smith, P. C. A psychophysical determination of equitable payment: A methodological study. *Journal of Applied Psychology*, 1968, 52, 343–347.

CHAPTER 31

Stress and Behavior in Organizations[1]

JOSEPH E. McGRATH
University of Illinois

Stress   References
Behavior in Organizations

WE ARE HERE CONCERNED with stress and behavior in organizations. It must be admitted at the outset that "stress" is not a very precise concept. Nor is "behavior in organizations," for that matter. So our first task will be to lay out a framework in which we try to tell the reader how we will use these imprecise terms of "stress," "behavior," and "organizations."

The first section deals with stress. In it we discuss some of the key substantive and methodological issues in the stress area, and lay out a general paradigm for conceptualizing stress. The latter part of that section describes, in some detail, a recent study in which we tried to test a stress theory, derived from the key substantive propositions in the stress area, within a realistic setting. That study led us to question some of the central premises of "stress theory," and to the formulation of a new model of stress, arousal, and performance. The new model has some dramatic implications for theory and practice.

The second section deals with behavior in organizations. It starts with a general framework from which we can derive six potential "sources" of stress. Then, each of these six sources is examined, in turn, in relation to our stress model. The chapter ends with a brief commentary on problems and potentialities for future research on stress and behavior in organizations.

I. STRESS

A. The Nature of the Problem

In recent years, the term "stress" has been used widely, and with widely varying meanings, in the behavioral science literature.

Cofer and Appley (1964), Appley and Trumbull (1967), Weitz (1970), Sells (1970), Kahn (1970), McGrath (1970b), and others have commented upon the currency, and the imprecision of use, of the term. We will not enter the definitional argument here. Rather, we will beg the question by trying to lay out a four-stage paradigm which encompasses the "stress prob-

[1] Research leading to this chapter was supported in part under Grant AF1161-67, AFOSR (J. E. McGrath, Principal Investigator).

lem"—its origin, its effects on the "stressee," his reactions, and their consequences. It is this four-stage "stress chain" or "stress cycle" with which we will be concerned.

A distinction which is important to the focus of this chapter has to do with a limitation on the kinds of stress which will be considered here. By and large, we are interested in stresses which arise in the context of person-to-person behavior. We will call this social-psychological stress (see McGrath, 1970b, p. 4). We mean here roughly what Cofer and Appley (1964, p. 441) mean by *psychological* as distinct from *systemic* stress, and what Lazarus (1966) means by psychological and sociological, as distinct from physiological, levels of stress. But, following Lazarus (1966), the limitation refers not so much to classes of variables measured as to the manner in which we will interpret the variables. Thus, for example, we do not mean to exclude physiological data, but will look upon such data as evidence of social-psychological states or processes, rather than attempt to investigate the physiological processes and mechanisms which produce these states. Nor will we exclude purely physical variables (e.g., cold, noise); rather, we will deal with them as they become antecedent conditions contributing to social-psychological events. So, we will be concerned with interpreting events in the "stress cycle" from a social-psychological perspective. We will be primarily concerned, of course, with viewing that stress cycle as it operates within organizational settings.

Within that context, then, let us consider a working definition of "stress" as we will use it—a definition not so much of *what stress is,* but rather of the sets of conditions which we will require before treating a situation as "having" stress "in" it.

Stress involves an interaction of person and environment. Something happens "out there" which presents a person with a demand, or a constraint, or an opportunity for behavior. From a definitional standpoint, the extent to which that demand is "stressful" depends on several things. (From an empirical standpoint, it likely depends on many other things as well.) First, it must be perceived by the "stressee." Second, it must be interpreted by him, in relation to his ability to meet the demand, circumvent, remove, or live with the constraint, or effectively use the opportunity. Third, he must perceive the potential consequences of successfully coping with (i.e., altering) the demand (constraint, opportunity) as more desirable than the expected consequences of leaving the situation unaltered.

So there is a *potential for stress when an environmental situation is perceived as presenting a demand which threatens to exceed the person's capabilities and resources for meeting it, under conditions where he expects a substantial differential in the rewards and costs from meeting the demand versus not meeting it.*

It is tempting to suggest that the *degree* to which the demand exceeds the capability (as perceived), and the *degree* of differential rewards and costs (consequences) expected from meeting versus not meeting the demand, reflect the *amount* of stress experienced. Such a proposition could be expressed as:

$$(1)\ ES = C\ (|D - A|);$$

where ES is experienced stress; C is the differential consequences (rewards and costs) of successfully meeting versus not meeting the demand; D is the perceived demand and A is the perceived ability to cope with it.

This formulation implies: (a) that the demand and the capability (as perceived) must be substantially *out of balance* for it to be worth speaking of "stress"; (b) that an imbalance in *either* direction may be stressful; thus, an "underload" of environmental demand, as in studies of stimulus impoverishment, may lead to stress, as well as overload, although they may lead to different reactions and consequences; (c) that the differential consequences anticipated from meeting the demand versus failing to meet it must be substantial; and (d) that these

P.E fit model

6 thry

differential consequences may arise from high versus low rewards and/or from low versus high costs. A formulation such as this is implied in several recent treatments of stress (e.g., McGrath, 1970c; Sells, 1970; Kahn, 1970).

But it may be unwise to accept such a formulation, especially the mapping of *size* of discrepancy between perceived demand and capability to amount of experienced stress. In a recent study of stress (Lowe & McGrath, 1971), which will be examined at length later in this chapter, the data suggest that arousal (as indexed by pulse rate) seemed to vary with consequences of favorable versus unfavorable outcome, *and with uncertainty of outcome*. If so, then the proper formulation would be:

$$(2) \quad ES = (C)(K - |D - A|)$$ (f bl)

where *ES, C, D,* and *A* are as before and *K* is a constant. Here, the *closer* perceived demand is to perceived ability (regardless of direction), the larger the second term (uncertainty) and the greater the experienced stress (if one can consider arousal as evidenced by pulse rate to be a reasonable operational definition of experienced stress). This formulation is important to the definitional problem because it implies precisely the opposite of formula (1). Formula (2) implies that experienced stress, or at least arousal, increases as perceived demand and ability approach each other, rather than as they get out of balance. This reformulation, the evidence giving rise to it, and its implications, will be of central concern later in this chapter.

B. Some Propositions About Stress

Empirical research on social-psychological factors in stress has been somewhat inconclusive, to date. Nevertheless, it is possible to adduce several general themes, or propositions, from that research literature. We will briefly describe a set of six general themes here. These six themes all have received some empirical support, and thus may represent a useful set of working hypotheses. They are still considerably short of being solid empirical generalizations, however, and they are also less than a fully-articulated theory. (For further discussion of these themes, and references to research evidence about them, see McGrath, 1970a.)

Theme 1: Cognitive Appraisal. Subjectively experienced stress is contingent upon the person's perception of the situation. That is, emotional, physiological, and behavioral responses viewed as indices of subjectively experienced stress are greatly influenced by the person's interpretation of the "objective" or external stress situation.

Theme 2: Experience. Past experience, in the form of familiarity with the situation, past exposure to the stressor condition, and/or practice or training in responses to deal with the situation, can operate to effect the level of subjectively experienced stress from a given situation, or to modify reactions to that stress.

Theme 3: Reinforcement. Positive and negative reinforcements—past successes and failures—can operate to reduce or enhance, respectively, the level of subjectively experienced stress from a given situation. This is an extension of theme 2.

Theme 4: The Inverted U. There is a nonlinear, probably non-monotonic, perhaps inverted U-shaped, relationship between degree of stress (as subjectively experienced) and level or quality of performance. The most pervasive form of this theme hypothesizes that, at low levels of arousal, performance is "poor"; that increases in stress up to some optimal level (optimal, that is, for that particular individual and that particular task performance) enhance performance; but that further increases in stress beyond that optimal level lead to performance decrements. (We will have much more to say about the inverted-U relation later.)

Theme 5: Task Differences. The nature of the tasks or activities in which the person is involved, and the relationship of those activities to the stressor conditions, influence the direction and shape of the relationships between subjectively experienced stress, task performance, and ensuing consequences. (Task factors affecting performance will also be treated later.)

Theme 6: Interpersonal Effects. The presence or absence of, and the activities of, other persons in the situation influence both the subjective experience of stress, and behavior in response to stress, in several partially conflicting ways. Presence or activity of other people can increase arousal level. Other people can act as sources of potential irritation and antagonism when exposure is for long periods of time. Other people are sources of potential affiliative, self-esteem, and other interpersonal rewards. Other people may be sources of potential facilitative or contrient interdependence with respect to performance of tasks. Some of these functions may operate to increase arousal, some to reduce it, some to modify task performance independent of arousal levels. And it is evident that which of these functions will operate, and how strongly, depends on the who, what, when, and where of the situation.

C. Some Complicating Problems

The six themes just listed, while representing reasonable working hypotheses, are less empirically solid than one might wish. Primarily, their "validity" suffers from several very general, but very fundamental, methodological problems. Most of these methodological problems pervade much social and psychological research; but they apply with special force in studies of human stress. Again, we will merely list some of these general problems, which represent both limitations on our present knowledge and issues which need to be dealt with in future research on stress. (For further discussion of these and related problems see McGrath, 1970e.)

1. THE METHODS-VARIANCE ISSUE: The information obtained from any set of observations is, in part, a function of (and, indeed, an artifact of) the methods used to make the observations, and the "experimental conditions" under which these observations are made. Thus, evidence built upon a single measure of stress, or upon a single type of stressor condition, is of limited generalizability. Much of the evidence in the stress research literature is based on studies using a single index of stress, or using variations in a single stressor condition, or both. The value of such evidence is necessarily weakened because there is no way to estimate the "artifact" due to the specific measurement techniques used (method variance). (See Campbell & Fiske, 1959; McGrath, 1970d.)

2. THE RESPONSE-PATTERN ISSUE: When separate measures of stress agree, we can interpret this as convergent evidence of a general "stress" effect. When they disagree, however, we are posed with a dilemma: shall the disagreement be interpreted as a lack of convergent validity, hence evidence against the usefulness of at least some of the measures; or, shall it be interpreted as reflecting *differentiated patterns* of response, with each component of the pattern (i.e., each separate stress measure) reflecting an important aspect of the total response to stress. One prominent example of work which follows the latter view is Lacey's (1967) research on the directional fractionation hypothesis. Lacey holds that, for certain types of tasks or situations (e.g., information acquisition), skin conductance increases while heart rate *decelerates;* while for other situations (e.g., information processing or "mental work"), both skin conductance and heart rate increase. Whether such non-convergent results are to be interpreted as evidence of non-convergence of "alternative" measures, or as evidence of differential response patterns, depends on the viewpoint and the theoretical stance of the investigator.

3. THE INDIVIDUAL-DIFFERENCES ISSUE: Different individuals may react differently to the same (objective) situation; and the same

individual may react differently to two different, presumably stressful, situations. In part, this problem is taken into account, at least conceptually, by the "cognitive appraisal" theme, and by the "experience" and "reinforcement" themes indicated above. But in part it represents a continuing dilemma for investigators seeking general relationships between (presumed) "stressor" conditions and observed reactions to them.

4. THE ISSUE OF COMPARABILITY OF STRESSOR CONDITIONS: One serious limitation of research on stress has been the lack of appropriate metrics for calibrating levels or intensities of stressor conditions, and for "cross-calibrating" levels of different stressor conditions in comparable terms. Many different conditions have been studied as "stressor" conditions. Little has been done to "map" degrees of one kind of stressor condition into levels or degrees of another. Consequently, we really have no basis for anticipating whether any two studies of stress, using different stressor conditions (e.g., shock, noise, cold, isolation), *should* give comparable results. In other words, we are not in a position to tell whether "stress" is a broad concept or is highly situation-specific. To put it facetiously: how many volts of shock are equivalent to three scale-units of interpersonal disagreement on an attitude issue, or to one hour of isolation? Not only does such an issue face all of the normal problems of comparability of measures taken in different terms, but, since the person's "translation" of the situation is so crucial in the experience of stress (theme 1), those mappings (of volts to hours or scale units) are likely to differ from one individual to another.

5. THE ISSUE OF REALISM: There is always some "artificiality" about behavior measured in a study. This artificiality increases the more the investigator exercises control over or carries out manipulations of conditions, and the more he makes use of obtrusive measurement techniques. Stress studies done in laboratory settings are especially subject to effects of "artificiality," because by the very nature of the setting the "subject" knows he is in an experiment and (presumably) that he is "protected" against extreme levels or durations of painful or noxious conditions. Furthermore, the "rewards," as well as the "pains," that can ensue from his behavior are likely to be attenuated in the laboratory setting. Studies in natural settings present their own limitations, of course, but they do offer the chance to study behavior under "stressor" conditions which are, and are perceived to be, "real," and which portend real and substantial consequences if they are not reckoned with.

But the limitations of natural settings for the study of stress should not be overlooked. While it is true that natural settings have more potential for gains and pains to the individual, and are more likely to find him performing under "natural" motivational circumstances, it is also the case that individuals tend to select, develop, or shape the behavior settings in which they participate so that they offer "acceptable" or "manageable" levels of stress. And by and large this shaping (preventive coping) takes place long *before* the investigator arrives on the scene. So, a *potential* for high levels of stress in natural settings does not always get translated into an observation period during which stress is actually high.

These methodological issues, together, pose serious problems, both for the interpretation of existing evidence about stress and for the planning of future research on stress. If we want to untangle the somewhat conflicting strands of the stress problem, we will need to utilize: (a) multiple measures of subjective stress or arousal; (b) "stressor" conditions which vary in more than a "high" versus "low" fashion and which can be "calibrated" in degree independent of subjective reactions to them; and (c) conditions generating relatively substantial "degrees" of stress, because they have important consequences for the responding person. We will describe later, a study which attempted to reckon with these methodological issues while testing several of the themes listed earlier.

D. A Paradigm for the Study of Stress

The preceding comments on definitions, themes, and problems in the study of social psychological stress make it clear that we are dealing with a complex, important, widely studied, but imprecise concept. To give some skeleton to our subsequent sections, let us lay out a frame of reference which makes explicit some rather crucial distinctions in this area, some of which are implied in the prior discussion and some of which are frequently overlooked in stress research.

We can view a "stress situation" as composed of a four-stage, closed-loop cycle. It begins with some condition(s) or set of circumstances in the socio-physical environment. If the situation is perceived by the focal person (with reference to whom it is a potentially stressful situation) as leading to some undesirable state of affairs if left unmodified (or some desirable state of affairs if modified), then it becomes a "stressful situation"—whether that perception is accurate or not. The focal person then "chooses" some response alternative (including escape or inaction). Then, he executes that response with the intention of changing his relation to the situation (in a "favorable" direction). That response does, in fact, have *some* consequences for him and for the situation though not necessarily the intended ones. (See Figure 1.)

These four stages are connected by four *linking processes,* and it is these linking processes which provide the substance for the study of stress. The first of these processes, which links stage *A* with stage *B,* is what Lazarus (1966) has called "cognitive appraisal," what Hackman (1970) has called redefinition, and what is indicated in Figure 1 simply as the *appraisal process.* The *experience* of stress or threat, as a subjective state, is a function of such appraisal—

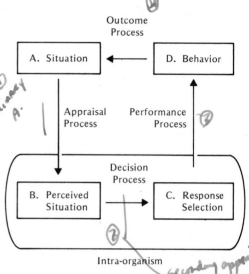

Figure 1. A paradigm for analysis of the stress cycle.

whether the appraisal is accurate or not. (Under some conditions, subjective stress may occur as the result of appraisal of an "objectively" benign environment; conversely, a really dangerous situation may not be perceived as such and thus may not lead to subjective stress.)

The second process link, between stage *B* and stage *C,* is essentially a *decision-making process.* It involves relating the situation (as perceived) to the available alternatives, and "choosing" a response or set of responses intended to deal with the undesirable features of the situation. Lazarus (1966) has used the term "secondary appraisal" to refer to this process. The operation and effectiveness of this process will depend on (a) the outcome of the prior appraisal process; (b) the organism's past experience; (c) his current state (e.g., fatigue); and (d) the contents and organization of his response repertoire and his available resources.

The third link, between stage *C* and stage *D* of the cycle, is the *response process* or performance. It results in a set of behaviors which, in principle, can be evaluated in terms of quantity, quality, and speed. The level of performance depends on ability, on task difficulty, and on the standards (of quality, quantity, speed) used to assess performance.

There is a fourth process link, between stage D (behavior) and stage A (situation). This is the link between the behavior of the focal person and its consequences for the situation. It is the *outcome,* or effect, or change process. This link is often overlooked, perhaps because it occurs "outside" the individual. While the extent to which the chosen response results in desired behavior depends on the performer's ability to execute his decision (i.e., to do what he intends to do), the extent to which the behavior results in desired (or undesired) changes in the situation depends not only on the level of performance, but also on several other factors which are *not* under control of the focal person:

(a) The performance level, and timing, of others who are in facilitative interdependence with the focal person (teammates).

(b) The performance level, and timing, of others who are in contrient interdependence with the focal person (opponents).

(c) The nature, strength, and certainty of the behavior-situation effect.

Performance and Outcome: It is important to put some special emphasis on the outcome link, for both substantive and methodological reasons. When we do laboratory studies, we usually arrange conditions so that the behavior-to-situation (or outcome) link is assured to be perfect ($r = 1.00$), in order to study the performance link or the decision link. The "cycle" of a behaving system becomes, in the laboratory experiment, the stimulus-response sequence of a trial. In field studies, on the other hand, we frequently ignore the distinction between performance and outcome. We tend to *make hypotheses about* performance (response choice-behavior relations), but *test them* by observing the combined (and confounded) double link of *performance and outcome* (relation of response choice to situation effect). But if other factors (teammates, opponents, or chance) can

influence outcomes, as we have argued above, then we are working with quite low-grade information about either performance or outcome relationships with such a strategy.

Suppose, for example, that there is a perfect 1-to-1 link between response selection and behavior (that is, the focal person *can* do exactly what he *decides* to do), but there is a rather low relation between level of performance and outcome. If one wishes to test a hypothesis about level of performance, but one assesses performance by measuring the situational consequences of that performance, he would be led to believe that the performance relationship (doing what one decides to do) is rather weak or insignificant, when in fact it is not.

All of this may seem to be playing with words, so let us put the argument in a concrete form. In a recent study of stress among little league baseball players (Lowe & McGrath, 1971), a deliberate attempt was made to measure, separately, the level of performance of batters and the desirability of outcome of the time at bat. For the former, we used ratings of how hard (hence, how far) the batter hit the ball (with appropriate adjustments for walks, strikeouts, and bunts). Outcome was scored with respect to how the time at bat affected results of the game: number of bases gained by batter and runners, number of runs scored, number of outs. We computed correlations between performance and outcome, for each of sixty players, with the N of each correlation being the set of all of that player's times-at-bat during an entire season (ranging from 15 to nearly 100). Those correlations were all positive and ranged widely for different players. Their median was near .50. A correlation of .50, between performance and outcome, means that only about 25 percent of the variance in *consequences* of times at bat was predictable from level of performance of the batter. If we had tried to test any relationship between some antecedent condition (e.g., experienced stress, as measured by pulse rate) and performance, and if we had mistakenly used "outcome" (runs scored, etc.) instead of "performance" (the batter's behavior with the bat), we would almost certainly have concluded "no relationship" even if the "real" relationship was nearly perfect.

Now the reader surely must be asking, "What has little league baseball got to do with our topic?" Baseball is not "life," and a little league is only one very special instance of an organization, if it is that. What makes the finding worth retelling here is that it represents a case where one can easily distinguish between, and separately measure, performance and outcome. It is often hard to measure performance and outcome separately in "real" organizations; but this fact does not weaken the logical need for doing so. Indeed, the "teammate errors," "opponent play," and "chance" factors which can operate to turn a little league weak ground ball into a four run event, or a well hit line drive into an inning-ending double play, are the *same kinds* of exogenous factors which downgrade the link between "how well I do my job" and "what I get out of doing my job well" in real life organizations. We will return to this very crucial distinction between performance and outcome (and to the little league study) later in the chapter.

The Process Links: One of the reasons for laying out the four-stage stress cycle is because it seems likely that the functional relations differ between different stages— that is, that the four process links have different "shapes." Earlier in this section, we mentioned the widely espoused hypothesis of an inverted U-shaped relationship between "stress" and "performance." See Mc-Grath, 1970a, for references to studies of the inverted-U function. In the present schema, that hypothesis would seem to refer to the third link (from stage C to stage D). But it has been *tested* as if it referred to a double or even triple link (from A to D, or B to D). The present framework would lead one to expect *different* shaped functions for each of the links.

For instance, there may be a direct, linear relation for the first link (between stage A and stage B): the greater the *real* demand of the situation, the greater the *perceived* demand, other things being equal. But this relation must be viewed as quite imperfect, to the extent that individual factors (e.g., experience) affect the appraisal process. Furthermore, it is the *uncertainty* (that is, the "closeness" of perceived demand and perceived ability) which affects arousal, or experiences threat. Moreover, the individual has to "care about" meeting the demand (i.e., consequences) before he experiences "stress."

The second link (stage B to stage C) might well represent either a positive or a negative function, depending on other conditions. Zajonc's (1965) work on social facilitation suggests that increased arousal ("subjective stress") functions so as to "rigidify" the response hierarchy, making well-learned responses even more dominant over less well-learned ones. If the best-learned responses are the "right" ones, such stabilizing of the response hierarchy would enhance the effectiveness of the response choice. But if the best-learned responses are *not* correct (from the point of view of the investigator), results will likely be "scored" as poor performance (of the "right" response). We may speculate that one of the reasons why "experience" seems to modify "stress" or the effects of stress is that prior practice in appropriate responses makes them more likely to occur under arousal conditions.

It is the third link (from stage C to stage D) to which the inverted-U function would seem to apply if it applies at all. The rationale here is that a moderate amount of "arousal" would enhance the quality of performance, through its activating effect (cf., Scott, 1966), but that further increases would degrade performance, presumably through "interference" of fear or anxiety or through "disorganization." But the better learned the chosen response (stage C), the better it will be executed (stage D). Hence, considering what was said about link two, this might lead to better performance when the best-learned responses are "correct," poorer performance when they are not "correct," rather than to a U-shaped function. This very crucial third link will be the focus of a later section of this chapter.

For the fourth link (stage D to stage A), we can posit no specific function. The shape of the outcome relationship depends in large part on factors in the situation (and in the researcher's evaluation of it) over which the focal person may have little control. One set of these derive from the nature of the situational definition of "success"—whether it is dichotomous or by degrees. Another has to do with whether a given outcome level ensues compellingly, or only probabilistically, from a certain performance level. Still others have to do with whether outcome success is entirely dependent on the focal person's performance level, or on the interaction of his, others', and opponents' performance; and whether the *effect* of the focal person's behavior is influenced by chance. All of these represent different functional relationships.

Given that there may be different functional forms for the four process links, then we can utilize the "themes" listed earlier as guiding hypotheses only if we first spell out *where* each theme fits into the four-stage framework—which process links it affects—and how each process operates.

E. Stress, Arousal, and Task Performance

We have already referred several times to a recent study (Lowe, 1971; Lowe & McGrath, 1971) of stress in little league play. In that study, we tried to test several of the six themes listed earlier, and to do so in a way that dealt with the methodological issues raised earlier.

Results of that study indicate that several central premises of current "stress theory" are in error. Notably, they call into question: (a) the inverted-U relation between stress and performance; (b) the nature and antecedents of arousal; and (c) the role of

experience in affecting stress and performance. This evidence has led us to formulate a new model of stress which, if correct, has some rather revolutionary implications both for stress theory and for its applications in organization. We will describe that study, its results, and our new stress model here, so that the implications of the new model can be applied to the issues to be discussed in later sections.

1. *The Study:* As indicated before, there is a widespread belief in the theoretical proposition that stress leads to arousal, in a linear fashion, and that the relation of arousal to performance is curvilinear. Considerable research evidence has been interpreted as lending support, or partial support, to this view. Some of this evidence is reviewed by McGrath (1970e).

One limitation of this proposition has been that much of the supporting evidence has been based on studies in which post hoc reinterpretations have had to be made about the nature of the independent variable (personal or situational stress) in order for resulting data to be construed as supporting the famous inverted-U. Sometimes this has been done by redefining stress levels ("high" versus "low" become "moderate" versus "low"). Often this redefinition has been done by deciding, post hoc, that the intended "high" level of stress was not really very high, but only moderate—hence the expected downward slope of the right-hand side of the curve did not occur.

Another aspect of the inverted-U hypothesis which causes some misgivings is the awkward theoretical premises used to account for the curvilinearity. Most of the explanatory effort has been devoted to accounting for why low levels of stress should produce low levels of performance, while moderate stress yields higher levels of performance—the left-hand side of the inverted-U. Here the explanation has been fairly well argued in terms of activation theory (e.g., Scott, 1966). However, activation theory certainly does not account for the right-hand side of the inverted-U—the decrease in performance from moderate to high levels of stress. Indeed, this side of the function has usually been taken for granted—"of course" performance deteriorates under very high levels of stress—and the left portion has been taken as problematical, to be accounted for by activation theory. In one recent treatment (Scott, 1966), the author spends one sentence stating the *assumption* of the right-hand side of the stress-performance curve, and the remainder of a lengthy article mustering evidence to account for the left-hand side.

Still another troublesome feature of the U-shaped function, one that has made it more difficult to pin down strong supporting evidence, is the premise that the U-shaped function holds only within-individual and within-situation. In other words, it is not expected that two individuals would have their maximum performance level at the same level of "objective stress"; nor that the same person would have his maximum at the same stress level for two different tasks or in two different situations. While both of these are quite reasonable premises, they add greatly to the difficulty of generating compelling evidence, especially evidence *refuting* the U-shaped function.

A proper test of these hypotheses requires some rather demanding conditions. There must be some basis for identifying situations which differ in "stressfulness" or "demand." What is needed is not just a presence-absence or high-low dichotomy, but a *set* of situations which can at least be ordered in the degree of demand which they impose. *Multiple* levels are needed if we are to test the inverted-U hypothesis. Furthermore, the inverted-U hypothesis implies that the stressfulness of situations varies from one individual to another for a given task, and from one task to another for the same individual. Thus, a reasonable test of that hypothesis requires placing the *same* persons in a series of situations, which vary in degree of demand but which call for performance of essentially the same task. Since the effect of a demand situation will depend on the per-

son's cognitive appraisal of that situation—"one man's meat is another man's poison"—some means must be devised to ensure that all persons *appraise* the set of situations as differentially demanding, and at least rank order them in the same order as to their demand.

We also wanted to test the effects of past experience (and reinforcement) on the demand-stress-performance-outcome cycle. This required a test situation in which participants varied appreciably in amount (and reward value) of past experience in the same class of situations. Furthermore, it must be possible to distinguish, and to measure reliably, the focal person's *performance* (i.e., what he does) and the *outcome* of that performance (i.e., how his behavior affects the situation).

Finally, our working definition states that the perceived consequences of successful versus unsuccessful performance in the situation must be substantial for the situation to be demanding or stressful. This can probably best be obtained in situations which are more or less realistic—that is, where people are engaging in activities that they care about rather than taking part in "an experiment."

We were fortunate to find a situation which made it possible to meet all of these requirements, namely, little league baseball. We were even more fortunate, through splendid cooperation of parents, coaches, league officials, and players, to be able to carry out a study encompassing all (sixty) players of all (four) teams of a league for all (thirty-six) games of the 1969 season.

The "time at bat" was chosen as the unit of activity. For each at-bat sequence, the following measures were obtained:

(a) Arousal or experienced stress: Pulse rate, breathing rate, and a measure of behavioral activity during the waiting period in the "on deck" circle.

(b) Batting performance: A rating of how *well* the batter hit the ball (distance and trajectory of the ball).

(c) Favorableness of outcome: Computation of an index based on base runners advanced, runs scored, and outs made.

(d) Situational demand (situation criticalness, *SC*): Calculation of an index of the degree to which a favorable versus an unfavorable outcome of the time at bat would affect team success in the game (in terms of runs ahead or behind, innings, outs, and base runners).

In addition, pulse rate and breathing rate were obtained on each player before the game, and pulse rate after the game. An index of game criticalness (*GC*) (in terms of potential effect of the game on the team's season success) was computed for each game.

Players ranged in age from ten to twelve. This age differential represents marked differences in experience and in practice on the task.[2]

2. *Results*: Results of the little league study led us to the following conclusions. First, differences in situational demand *do* lead to differences in arousal (pulse rate, *PR*). This relationship is positive monotonic. It holds when all individuals are aggregated, and it also holds for the majority of persons individually. It holds when differences in situational demand are indexed by demand of the specific situation (*SC*), and it holds even more strongly for differences in demand of the situation as a whole (*GC*). The same relationships hold for breathing rate (*BR*) as for pulse rate, though less strongly.

Second, age, considered as an index of experience, *does not* yield differences in arousal (*PR* or *BR*). With each age group, there is a positive linear relation between demand and arousal, as noted above. Age yields neither a main effect on arousal, nor does it interact with demand level in affecting arousal. However, age *does* yield an effect on performance. Older (more experienced) boys *perform better* than younger ones, and do so at each level of demand.

[2] The study included more detailed measures of past experience and reinforcement, which will not be discussed here. See Lowe (1971).

The most crucial findings, though, have to do with the relation between demand and performance. Here, the evidence led us to a reformulation. We expected a positive linear relation between demand and arousal, an inverted-U relation between arousal and performance, and, therefore, an inverted-U relation between demand and performance.

The first hypothesis was supported: There was a positive linear relation between demand (*SC* or *GC*) and arousal (*PR* or *BR*). There also was an inverted-U relation between demand (*SC* or *GC*) and *absolute* level of performance as hypothesized.

But the hypothesis that arousal has a curvilinear relation with performance (which should have followed logically as the connecting link between the other two hypotheses) simply did not appear to be supported in the data. Indeed, at *any given level* of demand, including very high demand, the *higher the arousal* the *better the performance*. This, of course, should not have been the case at high levels of demand, since at high demand, arousal is expected to be very high and performance is (therefore?) *expected* to be very low. This anomaly led us to further analyses.

Data were rearranged by series; that is, all six of a team's games against a given opposing team (e.g., team *A* versus team *B*) were considered as a set. These were put into 4 × 4 matrices (with empty diagonals), one for each measure. Thus, there was a matrix for average team performance (of each team against each opponent), a matrix for average team pulse rate (of each team against each opponent), etc.

It was apparent that poor team performances occurred mainly when the team was pitted against one of the better opposing teams. This led us to recognize the perfectly obvious point that differences in opponent task ability represented, for the referent team, differences in *task difficulty*. Furthermore, the situations of very high demand (high *GC*) tended to occur *against better opposing teams*.

With this in mind, we made a "correction" for task difficulty (ability of opposing pitching). With this correction, the curvilinear (inverted-U) relation between demand and performance *disappeared,* and there remained:

(1) *A positive linear relation* between demand and arousal.

(2) A *positive monotonic relation* between demand and performance.

(3) A *positive monotonic relation* between arousal and performance.

We then found that we were able to predict average team performance against any given opponent (team *A* against team *B*), with considerable accuracy, in terms of three linear components: (1) team *A*'s average task ability for the whole season; (2) team *B*'s average task ability (viewed as task difficulty for team *A*); and (3) team *A*'s level of arousal (pulse rate) during its games against team *B*;

$$P_{A-B} = \bar{P}_A + \bar{P} \ (TD_B) + K \ (AR_{A-B})$$
where:

P_{A-B} = Performance of team *A* against team *B*:

$\bar{P}_A$ = Average performance of team *A*:

TD_B = Task difficulty of team *B*, which is average performance of all teams when opposing team *B*;

AR_{A-B} = Arousal of team *A* when playing team *B*, measured as average pulse rate of team *A* against team *B*, minus league average pulse rate;

and K is a constant (for which .1 was a best fit in the Lowe study).

These results seem to say that, rather than there being an inverted-U relation between demand and performance or between arousal and performance, if one takes account of task difficulty, then performance *increases monotonically with increasing demand,* and *with increasing arousal.*[3]

The appearance of the curvilinear relation between demand and performance arises because, in the nature of things, increasing situational demand often carries with it increases in (objective) task difficulty as well as increases in arousal. While arousal is related to performance in a positive fashion, task difficulty is related to performance in a negative fashion. The inverted-U, then, apparently arises when *both* of these two processes (arousal and task difficulty), with their opposite effects, are allowed to operate simultaneously as mediators between demand and performance. (See Figure 2.) At low levels of demand, performance is relatively poor *because* arousal is low. At high levels of demand, absolute level of performance is low, *not because* arousal is high, but *in spite of it* and because task difficulty is high.

Furthermore, results indicate that experience *does not* affect arousal; older boys are neither more nor less aroused than younger ones at a given demand level, and both older and younger boys are sensitive to (i.e., have differential arousal for) different levels of demand. But experience *does* affect performance, probably through changes in ability. Older boys, while no more or less aroused than younger boys, have higher levels of task performance *at each level of demand.*

Examination of the team and individual data also led us to question our previous assumptions about how situational demand operates to increase stress or arousal. We had previously thought that arousal would depend on the potential valence of the outcome (i.e., consequences to the team of winning versus losing the game, *GC,* or of a successful versus unsuccessful batting performance, *SC*), and the probability of obtaining a successful outcome (i.e., the perceived task difficulty relative to perceived ability). In this formulation, arousal or experienced stress would increase as *either*

---

[3] The reader may wonder if we really had "high" arousal, or only moderate. Our data include average pulse rates exceeding 120 beats per minute in the high situational stress conditions. We believe this is "high"!

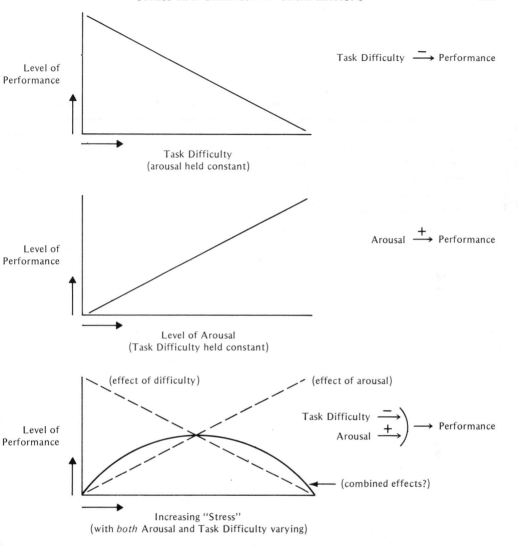

Figure 2.   Diagram of the inverted-U relation as a hypothetical function of task difficulty and arousal.

valence of consequences *or* probability of failure increased. Thus $ES = AR = (C)(D - A)$, where ES is experienced stress; AR is arousal; C = consequences of successful versus unsuccessful outcome; D = perceived difficulty; and A = perceived ability.

Our reexamination of the data led us to conclude that arousal tended to be high when there were high consequences (i.e., high potential gain *or* loss could accrue to the team from a successful versus unsuccess-

ful outcome) *and* when there was *much uncertainty about the outcome* (that is, when the opposing team was neither clearly weaker nor clearly stronger). Arousal was low when outcome did not affect team success very much (i.e., consequences low), or when the team was highly likely to lose (*p* failure high) *or* highly likely to win (*p* success high). So, we might predict level of arousal to be the product of perceived consequences and perceived uncertainty:

$$ES = AR = (C) (K - | D - A|),$$

where K is a constant. Here, arousal is high when $D - A$ is *small,* whereas the earlier formulation postulated that arousal would be high when $D - A$ was *large.* It is not the threat of probable failure (to meet the task demand) for tasks with important consequences, but rather the *uncertainty* of success on such important tasks, which leads to maximum arousal. Arousal (experienced stress) is lower when confidence about a successful outcome is *high or low.*

3. *Reformulation of the model:* These findings led us to reformulate our working model of stress with three key points of difference: A positive rather than an inverted-U relation between arousal and performance; the role of uncertainty in arousal; and the role of experience in arousal and performance. These add up to a dramatic re-

formulation of the nature of human stress and its effects. Moreover, if this new model is replicated and validated, it suggests an array of intervention strategies for improving task performance in realistic settings.

The new model (see Figure 3) postulates that variations in performance demands of an objective situation have three separate and direct effects:

(a) an increase in consequences (i.e., in the difference between the rewards and costs of a successful task outcome on the one hand, and the rewards and costs of task failure on the other) (line #2 in Figure 3);

(b) an increase in perceived task difficulty (line #3 in Figure 3); and

(c) an increase in actual task difficulty (line #1).

The effectiveness of *Task Performance* is some function of three factors:

(a) difficulty of the task (line #10);

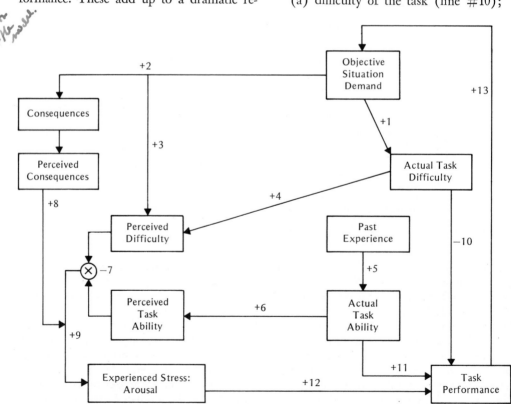

Figure 3. A reformulation of the stress model.

(b) *ability* of the person(s) (line #11); and

(c) *arousal* (line #12).

Ability depends on experience (line #5) (as well as on "talent").

Arousal, in turn, depends on *perceived consequences* (line #8), and on *uncertainty* (line #9).

Uncertainty depends on the closeness (line #7) of *perceived task difficulty* (which is affected both by the situation and by actual task difficulty) (line #3 and line #4) and *perceived ability* (line #6) (which is affected by ability and experience, and probably other factors). *Uncertainty is at a maximum when perceived difficulty is equal to perceived ability.* Arousal is a *product* of consequences and uncertainty.

Task difficulty has a negative monotonic relation to performance (line #10): the more difficult the task, the poorer the performance, virtually by definition. Task ability has a positive monotonic relation to performance (line #11) virtually by definition. Arousal, we postulate, has a positive monotonic relation (line #12)—*not* an inverted-U relation—to performance. The higher the arousal, the better the performance, up to and including *very* high levels of arousal. (Our data included average pulse rates exceeding 120 beats per minute in the high arousal conditions.)

4. Some Implications: This reformulation suggests certain rather powerful implications. For one thing, suppose one wished to improve task performance. Our revised model implies three routes:

(a) Make the task actually easier.

(b) Increase the individual's actual ability.

(c) Increase the individual's arousal.

"Making the task easier," or redesigning the job, the tools, or the job procedures, has been a favored technique to improve performance in work organizations since the early time and motion movement years ago. Of course, it is not always possible to make a task easier, for all worthwhile tasks, but we have in the past operated on the assumption that to do so would be an unmixed

blessing as far as improved task performance is concerned. More recent research would tend to dispute this. Our model suggests that task redesign might have both of two effects on performance: (1) a positive direct effect through reducing actual task difficulty; and (2) a possible negative indirect effect by reducing *perceived* task difficulty, which might thereby decrease uncertainty and reduce arousal. This suggests that, when perceived ability is already at or near perceived difficulty (the condition for maximum uncertainty and one condition for maximum arousal), *reducing* objective task difficulty may backfire. However, when the individual feels "over-matched"—that is, when he perceives task difficulty as greatly exceeding his ability—a reduction in actual task difficulty, or any other means to reduce perceived task difficulty, should improve performance both directly and through increased arousal.

A second way to improve performance would be through increased task ability. Presumably, this can be done through training and practice—again, a favorite solution for work organizations. However, if experience increases actual ability but also increases perceived ability, which in turn reduces uncertainty and decreases arousal, task performance may suffer. On the other hand, if perceived ability is very low relative to perceived difficulty, training that leads to increased ability *and* increased perceived ability should be an unmixed blessing, yielding positive effects on task performance both directly and indirectly via increased arousal.

The third route to improved task performance suggested by the model is through increases in arousal. For this route, any of several factors might be utilized.

(a) If perceived difficulty is close to perceived ability, then uncertainty should be maximum and the level of arousal should depend on perceived consequences. Under these conditions, performance should be increased due to increased arousal only if there is an increase in perceived consequences.

This could perhaps be fostered by convincing the individual of the importance of the outcome for him, for his group, or for some other valued object (as in the classic appeal to "...win one for the Gypper..."). Or, perhaps, arousal could be increased by tapping some other motivational component through incentives external to the situation (e.g., money, fear of reprisal).

(b) If perceived ability is much higher than perceived difficulty, then presumably the individual will be overconfident of success and his arousal will be low. If his perceptions are accurate—if he really is much more competent than the task demands—then this favorable set of circumstances *may* lead to task success even with relatively low arousal. But if either of his perceptions is in error—if he is not as task competent as he thinks, or if the task is more difficult than he thinks—then the less favorable relation between actual ability and task difficulty, along with low arousal, should portend task failure. Under these circumstances, arousal can be increased (according to the model) either by *increasing* perceived difficulty or by decreasing perceived ability.

(c) If perceived ability is way *below* perceived difficulty, we presumably have the situation where there is no hope of task success, hence arousal is low. If these perceptions are accurate, that is, if the focal individual really is grossly overmatched, then increases in arousal probably will not be sufficient to offset the unfavorable relation of ability to task difficulty. But if objective ability and task difficulty are actually close, although the individual mis-perceives his own ability as too low or task difficulty as too high (leading to low arousal), then techniques to improve his self-confidence and techniques to lower his estimate of task difficulty may increase arousal and lead to task success.

(d) Finally, it is possible (but not testable in our data) that a number of other kinds of stressors, or arousing or activating stimulus conditions, could serve to increase arousal in addition to the factors shown in the figure (consequences, perceived ability, perceived difficulty). Zajonc (1965) has shown, for example, that presence of other people, even an unseen audience, functions to increase arousal. Stress researchers have used shock, white noise, and other extraneous stimuli as "stressors"—presumably because they increase arousal. Any of these might serve to increase arousal, hence performance, but our present formulation does not encompass them.

It should be noted that, according to our formulation, techniques designed to increase arousal through increasing perceived consequences, or through arousal conditions exogenous to the model, should always lead to increased arousal and (relatively) improved performance. But techniques designed to increase or decrease perceived task ability, or to increase or decrease perceived task difficulty, will work toward increased arousal and improved performance *only if* they operate to increase *uncertainty* of outcome by bringing perceived difficulty and perceived task ability closer together. If such operations *increase* the perceived difficulty-perceived ability discrepancy, however, and thereby reduce uncertainty, this will in turn *reduce* arousal and lead to poorer performance. It is not the *direction* of change of the perception (that is, increased versus decreased perceived ability or perceived difficulty) that is determinate, but rather the direction of change of the perceived difficulty-perceived ability *relationship*.

The reformulation has some implications for selection, as well as for intervention strategies such as those suggested above. Given the inverted-U hypothesis, and the "individual differences" hypothesis which says that persons differ in how much "stress" they can take before performance drops off, it is an easy inferential step to begin seeking persons who are "stress resistant"—that is, who do not get very highly aroused as stress increases from low to moderate to high, hence who are expected (under the inverted-U hypothesis) to "resist" performance decrement that is supposedly associated with very high arousal. Indeed, considerable effort has been spent in research to select such "stress resistant" persons, but with little success.

If our present formulation is correct, we would expect that persons selected as "stress resistant," other things equal, would perform *less well* than persons operating at higher arousal levels. This would not only account for the lack of success in selection for "stress resistance," but would also suggest the desirability of trying to identify "arousal prone" people, or at least persons who respond to task situations with sufficient arousal to achieve successful task performance.

II. BEHAVIOR IN ORGANIZATIONS

A. A Conceptual Framework

Let us suppose that "behavior in organizations" represents a particular subset of human behaviors. Let us suppose, further, that "behavior in organizations" is distinguished as a special subset of behavior, not by involving different forms of behavior, but rather by occurring within a context whose parameters (e.g., size, formal purpose, division of effort, etc.) denote those social arrangements we normally label "organizations"—as distinct from crews or classrooms or communities or committees or campsites or communes.

Let us suppose, still further, that we can consider behavior as the interaction of three conceptually independent "systems," namely:

(a) The physical and technological environment in which the behavior takes place;

(b) The social medium, or patterns of interpersonal relations, within which the behavior occurs; and

(c) The "person system" or "self-system" of the focal person whose behavior is to be considered.

When we talk about behavior as occurring within a triplet of embedding systems, we intend to imply that those systems interact or intersect. It may be useful to look at the intersections—geometrically represented (see Figure 4)—and to consider what concepts might be used to label portions of the space.

The three systems can be viewed as intersecting two at a time. The intersection of "physical environment" and "social environment" represents what Barker (e.g., Barker & Wright, 1955) calls the Behavior Setting, and it is so labeled. It is the joint operation of a physical milieu in conjunction with what Barker calls "standing patterns of behavior" and what we will call social patterns.

The intersection of the person system and the physical-technological environment is labeled "Tasks," whereas the intersection of the person system and the social environment is labeled "Roles." Much of what we mean by "role" represents the performance of tasks—but some aspects of role represent relationships which transcend specific tasks and even specific behavior settings. Similarly, much of what we mean by task performance is subsumed under the concept of role behavior—but not all of it, since much task behavior takes place without there being a crucial element of interpersonal interdependence.

If behavior occurs as the intersection of the three systems of physical environment, social environment, and person, and if we examine the three two-system intersections and label them as Behavior Setting, Role, and Task, we then derive another order of specification or definition of behavior, namely: Behavior occurs as the interaction of task, role, and behavior setting.

Building on this framework, let us examine the idea of "behavior in organizations." We can delimit that concept in a number of ways. For example, if we focus on identification of the Person System involved in the behavior, we could hold that behavior in organizations ought to include *any* behavior of a "member" of the organization, whether or not that behavior takes place "in" the physical or social setting of the organization (that is, all of circle *C*).

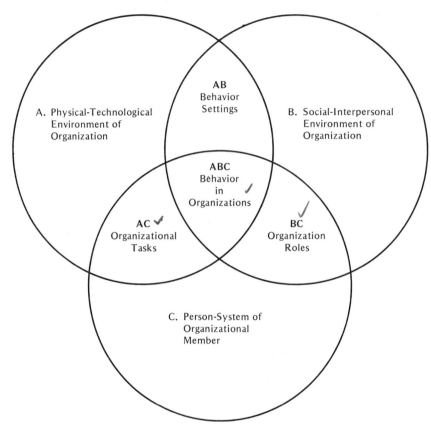

Figure 4. Three embedding systems for behavior in organizations.

With this set, observations such as the small town schoolteacher being seen in the bar on Saturday night, or the principal who beats his wife, are to be considered data about "behavior in organizations," for the school system as an organization.

Alternatively, focusing on the physical environment system, we could hold that "behavior in organizations" refers to any behavior which takes place within the time-place-thing boundary defined as "belonging" to the organization (all of circle *A*). With this set, our data on "behavior in organizations" for a work organization is not only burdened with the rummy game in the back of the warehouse and the surreptitious smoking in the men's room, but also with the thoughts, words, and deeds of any casual visitor to the premises.

A third possibility is to focus on the social environment, and to count as relevant data any behavior which takes place in reference to those social patterns which structure that environment (that is, all of circle *B*). With this set, we would have to consider behaviors of the sort fostered by the organization (e.g., high productivity) whether performed by organizational members or on organizational tasks or otherwise.

Each of these very broad sets seems to include much behavior which we may not wish to treat as central to the study of "behavior in organizations." Perhaps a very narrow specification, also flowing from the framework indicated in Figure 2, will serve us better. We propose, then, that we focus our concern on "behavior in organizations" defined as *the actions of organizational members, on organizational tasks, in organizational roles, in organizational behavior settings.* Instead of requiring any one of the three embedding systems to be relevant, as in the prior broad specifications, this narrow specification calls for the relevance of *all three* embedding systems before we will consider the behavior as included in our study of "behavior in organizations." We will adopt this as a working position for the time being; but it is probably overly narrow and we will likely have to "loosen" it later on in our analysis.

This way of conceptualizing behavior may offer one further advantage, for definitional or delimitation purposes. One can view an "organization" as a "thing" analytically separate from its members by considering it as a set of *behavior settings,* as *a set of tasks,* or as *a set of roles.* The set of behavior settings can exist and can be defined without reference to any persons, but requires the specification of a physical-technological domain and of a structured social system. The set of tasks can be defined without reference to the social relations involved, but requires specification of the physical-technological domain and of the person or membership domain. Role patterns can be specified without reference to the physical-technological environment, but require specification of the social organization and of the membership domain. (A more direct way of saying these things is that you can't have a role or a task, but you can have a behavior setting, without reference to any occupants. Conversely, you can't have a role or a behavior setting, but you can have a task, without reference to a social order; and you can't have a behavior setting or a task, but you can have a role, without reference to a physical-technological environment.)

Hence, one can view an organization as a set of behavior settings, which yet need to be "peopled" before they can become actualized. Or, one can consider an organization as a set of tasks, which yet need to be given a social ordering before they can become an organization. Or, one can consider an organization as a set of roles, which yet need to be placed in a time-place-thing context before they can be enacted. Each of these may be a useful stance for different purposes.

B. The Framework in Relation to the Stress Cycle

When we consider the relations of "stress" to "behavior in organizations," the present frame of reference is useful in still another way. "Stress" can arise from various origins, and these origins map in a rather straightforward way *to the three embedding systems and the three two-system intersects.* In other words, the framework indicates six "classes" of stress, or sources of stressful situations, namely:

1. Task-based stress (difficulty, ambiguity, load, etc.).
2. Role-based stress (conflict, ambiguity, load, etc.).
3. Stress intrinsic to the behavior setting (e.g., effects of crowding, of undermanning, etc.).
4. Stress arising from the physical environment itself (e.g., extreme cold, hostile forces, etc.).
5. Stress arising from the social environment, in the sense of interpersonal relations (e.g., interpersonal disagreement, privacy, and isolation, etc.).
6. Stress within the person system, which the focal person "brings with him" to the situation (e.g., anxiety, perceptual styles, etc.).

It is conceded that these six "sources of stress" are not totally separate. Their arbitrary separation may aid our study, though. It is likely that *effects* of the stress differ depending on the source. It is also likely that effective behaviors for *coping* with stress, and especially organizational "design" procedures for *preventing* its occurrence, may differ for stresses arising from these six different sources. Thus, we will treat stresses arising from each of these sources separately, and try to make the best of the overlap we will find.

If it is true that stress can arise from any of six different sources, then the "outcome" link which was drawn in Figure 1 should reflect a connection between the behavior of the focal person and that particular source of stress. So, depending on the source of the stressful condition (task, role, etc.), coping behaviors need to be "aimed" at changing different aspects of the situation. (This is not to say that the focal person always "reads" the source of stress accurately—indeed, he may not even "read" the presence of stress accurately. But he responds in terms of what he does perceive to be the case, not what "really is" the case.)

In any event, if it is true that "stress" which affects behavior in organizations can arise from any of six sources, then it seems reasonably to follow that the effects of that stress (i.e., the four process links in the cycle) should be traced in terms of these six sources. That is to say, if we have an "event" which we wish to interpret as a potential "stress event"—that is, as an instance of the stress cycle—we should try to trace matters from an originating condition (of one of six classes), through appraisal, decision, performance, and outcome, back to *a change* (or lack of change) *in the originating condition* (i.e., the source).

Let us consider that the four-stage cycle shown in Figure 1 starts from whichever aspect of the situation is the source of the stress condition: task, role, behavior setting, physical environment, social environment, person. For the moment, let us presume that, in the general case, a stress arising from a given source requires an outcome which affects that source. In other words, a task-based demand requires action which affects the "state of the task" or the relation of the

person to the task; a role-based demand requires action which yields role-related effects; and so forth. If the focal person misreads the source or nature of the stressing condition, and "aims" his coping behavior at the "wrong" aspect of the situation, he will surely not achieve effective coping, in the sense of removing or overcoming the stressor condition. This set of circumstances is pictured in Figure 5.

But even if focal person "attacks" the "wrong" source of stress with his coping behavior—for example, if he tries to solve a role-based problem with a task change—his "coping" behavior will have *some* effects, hence, will alter circumstances for the next phase of the cycle. Indeed, sometimes stress from a given source (e.g., social environment) can effectively be "removed" by coping behavior which operates with respect to another source (e.g., by "self-change," which then adapts to or conforms to social norms).

So in the general case, we should think of *six potential sources* of stressful conditions, and *six sets of outcomes* of stress and behavior in reaction to it. This elaborated version of the stress cycle is shown in Figure 6.

Figure 6 suggests that the stress cycle is relatively complicated. There is an array of potential sources of stress (and a number of possible stressor conditions within each). These sources map to the "systems" and "intersects" underlying behavior—task, role, behavior setting, physical and social environment, and person. There is an equivalent array of potential "perceived sources" of stress, in the "eye of the beholder," and there is not necessarily a one-to-one mapping between them (that is, the focal person may mis-perceive the source of stress). For any given situation (as perceived), there is an array of potential responses—potential coping behaviors. These are not specified in Figure 6, because they are particular to the different sources of stress. That is, there is a separate set of potential responses for task-based stress, role-based stress, etc. (The cop-

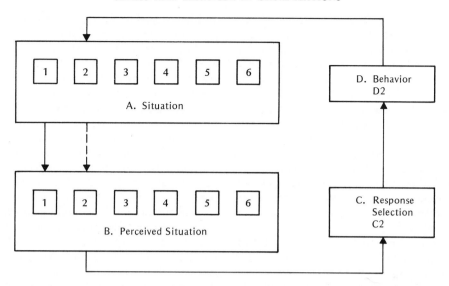

In the illustration, it is assumed that the stress actually arises from source 1, but that focal person misperceives it as arising from source 2, thus selects and executes a response which affects source 2 but not source 1. Therefore, the original condition that operates as a source of stress continues unmodified by the coping behavior.

Figure 5.   Illustration of an incomplete "stress cycle" due to misperception of the source of stress.

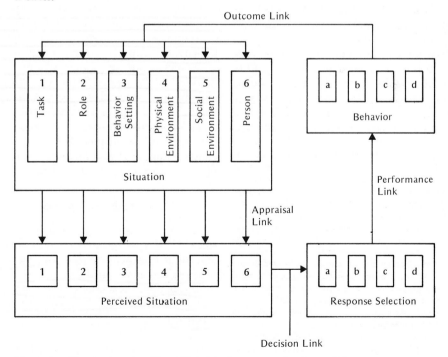

Figure 6.   The stress cycle with multiple input sources and outcome links.

ing responses are "nested" within the perceived sources of stress.) Similarly, there is an array of potential behaviors following from each of the "selected" coping responses, which also are not specified in Figure 6, and which are parallel to (one-to-one with) the responses. Each behavior can be "assessed" in terms of a complex of quality (or accuracy), quantity (or intensity or magnitude), and speed (or timing). Then there is an array of potential effects, or outcomes, which parallels the sources or inputs. The operation of a given cycle must be considered in terms of *its effects on all six sources* or aspects of the situation.[4]

Perhaps a hypothetical example will help to clarify some of the implications of Figure 6. Suppose there is an external "stressor" in the form of an increase in task load or difficulty for a certain organizational member, *A*. Suppose, further, that he perceives this change in task demand as being important to him (i.e., high consequences), and as posing a demand which he may or may not be able to handle (i.e., high uncertainty). In our model, he should presumably undergo high arousal (i.e., stress).

Now, there are a lot of ways he might respond to this (i.e., response selection). One would be to shift part of his work load to someone else, or to fail to perform part of his task. Either of these might violate role expectations which others hold for him,

and hence lead to a change in role demands on him—a new source of stress.

Alternatively, he might try to isolate himself from additional task and role demands by modifying his physical environment—by closing his door, putting a "do not disturb" sign on it, taking his phone off the hook. All of these are behaviors aimed at modification of the behavior setting. They might or might not help him solve the problem; and they might or might not create new stresses (e.g., from other persons who try to reach him by phone).

Still another response might be to change his task performance procedures—to do the task in a new way. He might or might not have the intended outcome (i.e., meeting the task demand); and it might or might not lead to generation of additional "stresses"—including those from the "self," such as anxiety, headaches, and the like.

Thus, we cannot really deal with the problem in terms of "the stressor," or "the response," or "the effect." Rather, we have to think of the stress cycle as a complex set of processes which reflect the individual's continuing—and *two-way*—interchange with his environment. This interchange involves a whole array of "sources," of "alternatives," of "responses," and of "effects"—and the total *set* of these operates as a "system." This notion of a complex of sources and of responses to stress is elaborated further, later in the chapter. We turn, now, to consideration of stress and behavior for each of the six sources of stress, in turn.

C. Tasks and Stress

There has been much emphasis in stress research, and in research on organizations, regarding task performance. But tasks, and task performance, can have any of at least four functional relations to the stress cycle, and these have not always been distinguished.[5]

---

[4] There are still further complexities which are not indicated by Figure 6. One set of these are potential feedback loops within the cycle. For example, behavior, and the focal person's own reaction to it, may affect his appraisal of the situation and/or his response selection, independent of its situational consequences. Another set of complications arises because the "systems" and "intersects" which make up the "situation" are themselves interlocked, and in a kind of equilibrium. Changes in any one of them—for example, to remove a stressor condition—may have adverse and unanticipated consequences for one or more other aspects of the situation. For example, efforts to cope with a task-based stressor may be carried out in such a way that it produces role-based problems that did not exist previously. Thus, a full representation of the stress cycle would show many crisscrossing and back-looping arrows that do not appear in Figure 6.

[5] The first three of these are parallel to the set of categories identified by Hackman (1970).

1. Tasks can themselves be the source of stress; they can impose demands which threaten to exceed the capabilities of the focal person. (Case I, performance of stressful tasks.)

2. Tasks can be performed during periods in which stressors from other sources are operating. (Case II, task performance under stress conditions.)

3. Tasks can be performed in order to remove or reduce some stressful condition. (Case III, task performance as a coping behavior.)

4. Task performance, or decrements in it, can be viewed as an indicant of stress. (Case IV, task performance as a measure of stress.)

These four roles of task performance are laid out in Figure 7.

These distinctions may be useful because the different functional roles of tasks in the stress cycle seem to suggest different kinds of relations between amount of stress and level of task performance. In Case I, when the task itself is the source of stress—that is to say, when the task is "difficult," relative to the focal person's task performance capabilities—then the more difficult ("stressful") it is, the poorer the level of task performance, virtually by definition. This describes an inverse or negative relation between task-based stress and task-performance effectiveness, *other things being equal.*

In contrast, for Case II, when we talk about performing a task while some other kind of stressor condition is operating (e.g., cold in the arctic, shock in the laboratory, interpersonal friction in the office), it may well be that the availability of the task, as an attention and effort absorber, actually reduces the otherwise stressful effects of such other conditions. On the other hand, if the stressor condition operates so as to distract the focal person from the task, its presence should decrease task performance effectiveness. Thus, performing a task while under stress may have two quite different results:

(a) A reduction in "subjective stress" compared to what would have been the case

had a "task" not been available to perform.

(b) A decrease in the effectiveness of task performance, compared to what would have been the case, had no external stressor been present. This represents a very complex relationship, an *interdependence* between task performance and experienced stress rather than the usual assumption of a functional dependence of task performance on the level of stress.

In Case III, where the performance of a task is itself a coping behavior designed to remove or reduce the effect of some stressor, we again have some interesting possibilities. Here let us assume that the focal person is performing a usual task, A, indigenous to his role in the organization, when some stressor condition, X, unrelated to that task, begins to impinge upon him. He then ceases work on task A, and executes task B—some "stress reducing" or "stressor eliminating" activity. With respect to task B, level of performance of the task should relate *inversely* to level of stress by definition: the better he does the coping task, B, the less the stressing condition will continue to affect him. The shape of the presumed relation is the same as in Case I, but the logical direction of the relation is reversed. With respect to task A, however—the ongoing "normal" activity which was interrupted by the stressor and by the coping behavior of task B—task performance effectiveness *is reduced perhaps to zero* during the period of time involving the coping behavior. Thus, onset of a task-extraneous stressor might have several consequences:

(a) A cessation of performance of task A (ongoing activity), hence, at least a temporary reduction in task performance effectiveness on task A.

(b) Initiation of task B (the coping task), for which the higher the level of performance, the more (or sooner) the reduction of stress (and the sooner the resumption of task A).

Among other things, this case calls to our attention (a) the importance of specifying *which* of multiple tasks is to be the referent

Case I   Performance of a stressful ("difficult") task:

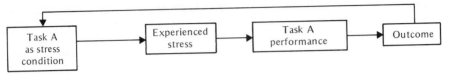

Case II   Performance of a task under stressful conditions:

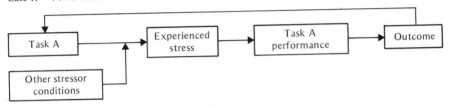

Case III   Performance of a task to cope with stress:

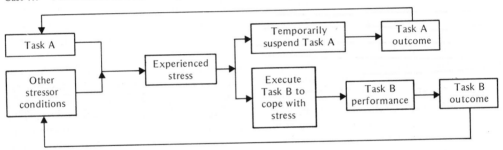

Case IV   Performance of a task inserted to measure stress:

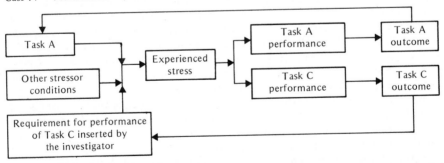

Key: Task A is the "normal" or ongoing task activity in which the focal person is engaged at the time of onset of the stress cycle.

Task B is a task activity undertaken by focal person in order to remove/reduce some stressor condition.

Task C is a task *not* "normal" to the situation which is inserted by the investigator in order to get a measure of stress or of its effects.

Figure 7.   Four functional roles of tasks in the stress cycle.

of any stress-performance relation we may wish to study; and (b) the crucialness of the temporal aspects of the situation.

Case IV is somewhat special, in that it refers to the way in which a research investigator "treats" task performance scores, rather than to a different functional role of the task in situ. Sometimes investigators insert certain kinds of tasks—not indigenous to the organizational setting—in order to obtain measures of performance (on "standardized" tasks) which are to be considered as evidences of stress or of the effects of stress. Such insertion of tasks-to-be-performed not only is a frequent occurrence in laboratory studies, but is relatively often done in field studies. Performance on a pursuit rotor after return from a more or less dangerous aircraft mission, or performance on a backward digit sequence task under simulated combat-stress conditions, are examples of the latter. In such cases, it cannot be taken for granted that the insertion of the task is not reactive vis-à-vis the stressor conditions. It may indeed be the case, as in Case II, that the inserted task absorbs the focal person's attention and effort, and acts to reduce stress below what it would have been had no such task been inserted. At the same time, it is reasonable to suppose that such inserted tasks are not themselves stressful, since failure to do "well" on them may have no consequences for the focal person's normal role performance or for his ability to cope with the stress condition. Thus, scores from such inserted tasks may well represent not so much measures of stress as *manipulations* which reduce stress.

As an aside, it seems perfectly reasonable to consider lots of activities other than psychomotor tasks as being "performance of inserted or extraneous tasks." One can view filling out a questionnaire, or an adjective check list, or answering questions by an interviewer, as having much the same effect on stress as performing on a pursuit rotor task. Subjective reports by study participants may be reactive in any usage (see Webb et al., 1966), but they may have an additional reactive effect in stress research: their presence may operate as a "distractor" to reduce subjective stress.

1. *Some Parameters of Task-Based Stress:* Tasks which are themselves "stressful" (Case I) may be so because of any of at least three properties: difficulty, ambiguity, and load.[6] First, a task can be too *difficult;* that is, it can pose performance requirements which exceed the performance capabilities of the focal person. If the high jump bar is placed at 6'8" and I can jump only 5'10", that task is too difficult for me. Again, of course, the experienced stressfulness of a task demand will depend on the focal person's *perceptions* of the demand, of his own capabilities, and of the pain-and-gain consequences of his failure to meet the demand. In the example above, I will not be "stressed" by the task (at *that* time) if I don't know (how high it is), if I think I can (jump high enough), or if I don't care (about succeeding on the task).

A second way in which a task can be a source of stress is if there is *ambiguity* about what the task requires, and/or about what standards are relevant to judge performance on it. This is perhaps a very prevalent form of task-based stress in organizations, because many organizational tasks are assigned in the form of statements of goal, or "ideal states," rather than in the form of operational procedures to be followed. We would have an "ideal state" task, for example, if a football coach sent in the instruction: "make a touchdown." We would have an operational task if, instead, he sent in the instruction: "run play 32B." In the former case, the focal person is left with knowledge about the intended outcome (which he probably already had), but little to go on by way of response selection. We may often have a similar state of affairs in organizations,

---

[6] These parameters of task-based stress are similar to those by Hackman (1970). They are also similar to the kinds of role-based stress dealt with by Kahn et al. (1964).

when assigned tasks are such things as "increase sales next month," "...assigned responsibility to get out the annual report on time...," "avoid all unnecessary expenses ...," and the like.

Not only is the lack of clear-cut operational requirements in assigned tasks a frequent source of stress, but there is also often an ambiguous relationship between performance (my *behavior* on the task) and outcome (my *success* in reaching the intended goal). Other things equal, *the more uncertain the relation between effectiveness of performance on the task* (quality, quantity, or speed) *and outcome of that performance* (desired change in the situation), the more stressful the situation. To the extent that the performance-outcome relation depends on (a) the cooperative work of associates; (b) the work of "opponents"; (c) the arbitrariness or whim of others (superordinates, "outside judges," etc.); or (d) chance events, to that extent, task "success" is ambiguous even given highly effective task performance, and the situation is likely to be stressful for the focal person.

Notice that the proposition stated in the previous paragraph refers to the degree of uncertainty in the performance-outcome relation, not to the level (degree of difficulty) of performance set as the standard of success. *Both* level of difficulty of task (i.e., level of performance needed for probable success) and level of certainty of success (i.e., probability of success given any specific level of performance) can contribute to the stressfulness of a task demand. This relationship is pictured in Figure 8. Three different standards of difficulty (A, B, and C) are shown on the ordinate. The outcome level to be yielded from performance at each of eight levels (P_1 to P_8) is shown as a set of distributions. The variance of each distribution is an indication of the *degree of uncertainty of outcome success*, given a performance at that level of competence.

A third way in which a task can be a source of stress, in addition to difficulty and ambiguity, is through *task load*. A given

focal person may be responsible for a set of tasks, each of which he can do, but which are paced in time so that he cannot do all of them, or do them quickly enough or long enough, to handle the total task load. In one sense, this problem can be dealt with better under role-based stress, since it is not the specific task(s) which place the unmeetable demand, but the total collection of tasks which fall into focal person's (role) responsibility. In another sense, this is a problem of task difficulty, where difficulty arises from demands for combinations of quantity or speed rather than from a demand for quality of performance.

2. *Tasks and Response Selection:* There are lots of different "tasks" narrowly defined, and lots of different "stress situations." The response alternatives available are, to some degree, specific to each task and situation. There are some *general* classes of response, however, and there are some general "principles," or "themes," or "processes" involved in response selection.

First, there is always the "do nothing" alternative. Closely allied is the response: "keep on doing what I was doing" (before the onset of the stressor). There is also the response: "leave the situation"—physically or psychologically.

If we assume that there is a task (or a set of tasks) indigenous to the situation (task A), in which the focal person is engaged at the time of "onset" of a "stressing condition," then we can reasonably talk about: (a) responses aimed at continuing that task(s) (task A), and (b) responses aimed at removing, reducing, offsetting, or otherwise coping with the stressor condition (task B). When the task itself is the source of stress (Case I), through its difficulty, ambiguity, or load, then "continuing the task" and "coping with the stressor" tend to be one and the same. If the "stress" comes from some source other than the task (as in Case II or Case III), then to "cope with the stressor condition" is, to some degree, to abandon performance on the ongoing task (task A).

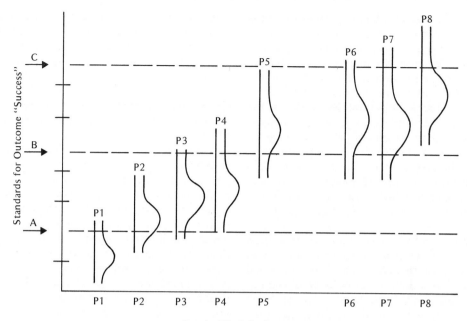

Level of Task Performance
P_1 through P_8 ordered levels of task performance.

A. Easy task
B. Medium task
C. Difficult task

Figure 8 shows a hypothetical set of distributions of "outcome levels" for each of eight performance levels (P_1 through P_8). The portion of each distribution which exceeds a given outcome standard (A, B, or C) represents the *probability* that a performance *at that level* will yield a successful task outcome. Thus, a performance at level P_1 will occasionally be successful against an "easy" standard (A, easy task), but never against a medium or difficult standard. Performance at level P_5 will "succeed" for an easy task standard (A) and usually for a medium task standard (B), but seldom or never against a difficult task standard (C).

Figure 8.   Relation between level of task performance and attainment of task success.

It is probably useful to consider the focal person as potentially engaged in a whole spectrum of "tasks" or responses—including the one or more tasks indigenous to his role, the one or more tasks or response alternatives by which he might cope with various potential stressors, and the one or more "escape" responses. Indeed, we can consider the focal persons as having, at any point in time, a full spectrum (or repertoire) of possible responses, and then proceed to ask a series of questions such as the following:

(a) Under a certain set of conditions, C_0 (for example, when the task is routine and no "other" stressor conditions are operating), what is the probability of response $r_{i1}, r_{i2}, \ldots, r_{in}$?

(b) When conditions change from C_0 to C_1 (for example, when some "outside" stressor begins to operate at above-threshold levels), what is now the probability of response $r_{i1}, r_{i2}, \ldots, r_{in}$?

But since people often engage in more than one response, simultaneously or in rapid succession in a time-sharing fashion, we might consider the distribution of frequency of each of the alternative responses within some finite period of time. We can now talk about different "situations" (sets of conditions, C_0, C_1, ..., C_j) in terms of their effects on the distribution of frequencies of the response alternatives. Such changes might come from onset of a "stressor" in the physical environment (noise, cold, etc.), from a change in possibilities offered by the behavior setting (e.g., a new occupant, hence, a new "target" of behavior), or from a change in any "source" (e.g., person, role, etc.). Indeed, a "change" in conditions could be defined in terms of whether or not, and the degree to which, there is a *shift in distribution of frequency of response alternatives*.

Zajonc (1965) has postulated that presence of other persons leads to an increase in arousal, and that one effect of such increased arousal is a shift in probability of various response alternatives. Specifically, he holds that increased arousal increases the probability of selection of the dominant (i.e., most probable, best-learned) response, with a consequent decrease in the probability of all other responses. Under conditions where the best-learned response is in fact an effective response for dealing with the situation (e.g., if it is a "correct" response on the ongoing task, *and* if the "stressor" can be removed or circumvented by successful completion of the task), arousal leads to improved performance (of the response that gets selected). However, Zajonc's work also implies that, if the dominant response is not an effective one, arousal degrades performance. This could come about in two general ways. First, if successful task completion requires acquisition of new responses (i.e., "learning"), then arousal which increases the probability that an "old," well-learned response will be selected, will in fact decrease the probability of an effective performance (i.e., acquiring or exhibiting a "new" response). This is the case which Zajonc treats. In addition, if the "stressor" condition is not connected to the ongoing task, then if arousal increases the probability of a (dominant) response which is aimed at successful completion of that ongoing task,

it will *decrease* the probability of responses aimed at removal of the stressor condition. This effect, or something akin to it, has been spoken of in terms of the "focusing" effects of stress, in terms of "functional blindness" resulting from arousal (e.g., Crider, 1970, p. 182), in terms of "residual attention" to secondary tasks (e.g., Roscoe, 1970).

Now, this poses a problem for the stress investigator. If stress from some non-task source leads to *enhancement of performance* of the ongoing task (by making the best-learned response more probable than it was) and *a failure to perform some other task* which would have coped with the stress, then the direction of the relationship between arousal (resulting from stress) and performance *depends on whether the investigator chooses to measure performance with respect to task A* (the ongoing primary task) *or task B* (the task which would have coped with the stressor).

Let's consider a trivial example. John is manning a radarscope in the DEW line. He is alone in the room. The door blows open, and bitter cold wind begins to operate as a stressor condition. But he would have to *leave* the scope (thereby reducing at least temporarily the effectiveness of his performance on his assigned task) in order to close the door (thereby "coping with" the stress). On the other hand, if he continues to man the scope in spite of the cold (and perhaps even do it more alertly *because* of the cold), then it is clear that he is not effectively performing the coping task (shutting the door). How is it possible for John to exhibit "effective performance" for both tasks? In the short run, he cannot. (He can, of course, do both tasks ineffectively—he can leave the scope to get a hot cup of coffee but not close the door.) *The decision* (by the investigator) *as to which task is the one John should do and the decision by the investigator as to the criterion by which performance will be assessed, determine whether the investigator will discover that stress improves task performance or degrades it.*

The point, here, is that we need to conceptualize the focal person's performance as a "battery of potential responses"—some having to do with the ongoing tasks, some having to do with coping with the stressor conditions, some having to do with the individual's psychological state. We must be prepared to measure "performance" on all of these responses. Then, we can more reasonably ask: *what* shift in response distribution results from stress (of various degress and kinds), rather than *whether* "performance" gets better or worse.

Suppose that Zajonc is right, and that the proposition is general in that it applies to arousal from any source and to performance on various kinds of tasks. If arousal leads to an increase in the probability of the already-most-probable response, then performance will "improve" with respect to that response but "degrade" (or cease) with respect to all other possible responses. What we mean by a learning task (in Zajonc's sense of acquisition of a new response) is that "correct" performance requires that the previously most-probable response *not* occur and that some particular *other* response—presumably in the repertoire but low in the hierarchy—does occur. It would also follow, then, that *any new* response (as in the "learning" case), or an effective response to any "new" task (or stimulus), would be *less* likely to occur under arousal. Thus, we would expect something like the "functional blindness" which reportedly occurs for extraneous stimuli under arousal (Crider, 1970, p. 182); and we would expect the kind of fixation, perseveration, or focusing of attention and effort which is often said to accompany "stress" (arousal).

Perhaps, in natural settings, there tends to be a shift in "task requirements" (e.g., addition of new and crucial stimulus conditions, or increase in standards for success) as the situation goes from moderate to "high" levels of stress. If arousal operates to enhance performance of the most probable response, which was previously appropriate but is now inadequate because it doesn't reckon with the added task requirements, then that should lead at "high" levels of stress to the downward performance function predicted by the inverted-U hypothesis —*if we measure performance with respect to the now expanded task requirements.* We would postulate that some of the past findings supposedly showing the inverted-U function may have come about because task requirements were allowed (by the investigator) to shift—a special case of increased task difficulty—and performance at high stress levels was assessed with respect to such an expanded (more difficult) task. This could readily occur, for example, if the investigator mistakenly measures outcome (the situation-effect of focal person's behavior) rather than performance. The expanded task requirements are requirements for a *successful outcome.* Focal person might still be meeting the previous task requirements very well, but that may no longer suffice for task success.

The central theme here, then, is that we ought to conceptualize the focal person as having *a repertoire of potential responses*— represented as a distribution of probability (of response χ_i at time t_j), or of frequency (of responses $\chi_1, \chi_2, \chi_3, \ldots, \chi_i, \ldots, \chi_n$, during time interval T). Furthermore, we ought to be prepared to assess not just whether (and how well) he produces some special response, χ_i (which the investigator selects as the "right" response), but rather what array of responses $(\chi_1, \chi_2, \ldots, \chi_n)$ he *does* produce, and how well or at what intensity he produces them. *Then*, if we have some idea about *what he should do* in the situation (that is, what is the "best" response or pattern of responses to achieve some criterion outcome that *we* have in mind), we can impose that normative criterion in evaluating *whether or not he made the "right"* response selection. But we should not fool ourselves into believing that (under high stressor conditions, for example) the focal person "performed *the* task" (meaning response χ_i) poorly, when in fact what he did was *perform a different task.*

Let us also recognize that imposing a normative system about what the focal person *ought to do,* which is always necessary to establish a criterion of "effective performance," also always involves imposing a set of value judgments about what is best to do under the circumstances. Often, there is a potential conflict between what is "best" for the behavior system of which the focal person is a part (e.g., the work group or organization) and what is "best" for the focal person himself, as a human entity. Moreover, there are often multiple consequences ("pains and gains") of *any given* outcome, and the values associated with these consequences are likely to differ from person to person. Consequently, it is a strong assumption, indeed, for the investigator to suppose that he can anticipate *which* of the possible outcomes any given focal person is likely to attempt to achieve. And if the investigator does not know what goal the focal person is striving for, he is going to have grave difficulty deciding whether that person chose a means (i.e., a response) that is effective to reach *that* goal.

3. *Summary: Task, Stress, and Behavior:* This discussion highlights several important points. First, some aspects of tasks affect every portion of the stress cycle: appraisal, decision making, performance, and outcome. (This will also prove to be the case, later in this section, for roles, behavior settings, etc.) Second, consideration of tasks in relation to stress requires a relatively complex view of how a "task" fits into the schema of a person behaving in an organizational setting. There is more than one way a "task" can be related to a stress situation, and indeed there is often more than one "task" involved. Furthermore, the way we view the crucial second process link—decision making leading to response selection—is quite dependent on what the investigator defines as the "right" task for the focal person to be engaging in. Such normative choices by the investigator also affect the third performance link—and, indeed, such choices can determine the "shape" of

the relation between stress and performance. Thus, the links of the stress cycle are highly interdependent. Third, it is clear that our admittedly arbitrary specification of six sources of stress is far too "neat" for a sustained discussion. Our consideration of "tasks" has already spilled over into consideration of "roles" and "persons," and we will find ourselves covering some of the same ground, later in this section, under those headings.

Finally, it is clear that the concepts in our reformulated model of stress—perceived consequences, uncertainty, arousal, and so forth—represent processes which mediate the effects of tasks (and this will be true regarding roles, as well) in all four stages of the stress cycle. A summary of some of the key concepts connecting "tasks" with different portions of the stress cycle is presented in Figure 9.

B. Behavior Settings and Stress

A behavior setting is a time-place-thing milieu, with its attendant social "meanings."[7] The "things" in behavior settings are "behavior objects"—which are animate or inanimate entities (a desk, a person, a water cooler) toward which behavior is directed. Thus "tasks," in a narrow sense, could be construed as behavior objects; so could a role-relation. This is one of many areas of overlap. We find it more useful to consider a task as the *relation of a person* to some technological entities (goals and procedures), and a role as the *relation of a person* to some other person.

Barker holds that behavior settings "coerce" behavior, and vice versa, in a number of ways (Barker & Wright, 1955). Furthermore, he maintains that there is more uniformity or predictability in the behavior of a set of individuals within a specific behav-

---

[7] The concept of behavior setting is borrowed from the work of Barker (e.g., Barker, 1968; Barker & Wright, 1955). So is the term "behavior object." We shall draw upon the work of Barker and his colleagues throughout this section.

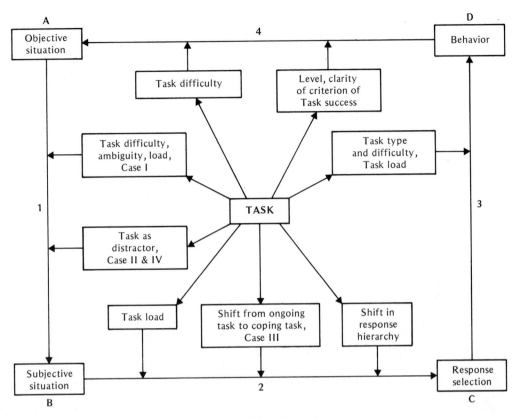

Figure 9. Some effects of task on various stages of the stress cycle.

ior setting than there is in the behavior of the same individual across varied behavior settings. While different people enter a setting with different purposes or ends in view, the "demands of the behavior setting" must be fulfilled and the behavior setting must "come off" if these are to be fulfilled. Hence, individuals are motivated to participate in, and behave appropriate to, the setting in order to achieve their own (potentially diverse) purposes.

Barker and his co-workers (Barker & Wright, 1955; Barker & Gump, 1964; Wicker, 1968, 1969) put great emphasis on the degree to which various behavior settings are overmanned or undermanned. Each setting is viewed as having an optimal number of occupants, and an optimal distribution of participation (roles). When an organization has a relatively large number

of behavior settings relative to available manpower, a condition of undermanning exists. Undermanned settings, they maintain, lead to: (a) increased pressures on the individual to participate, and to do so in relatively central roles (e.g., as active functionaries rather than as spectators), in more behavior settings, and in more varied behavior settings; (b) decreased barriers to entering and performing in settings, including lowered standards of ability/performance; and (c) increased satisfaction, increased feelings of involvement, and increased frequency of success experiences.

We can reconstrue these matters in terms of our four-stage, four-link stress cycle, and model of the stress process. Behavior settings represent a source of situational demands. The degree of "manning" of the setting affects the forces operating on the persons.

These should reasonably map to differences in perceived consequences, and in perceived task difficulty relative to "available resources." Hence, they should lead to differences in arousal. The more the person "cares about" the outcome of the behavior setting —whether it "comes off" or not, and how well—and the more the person sees the setting as posing performance demands which available resources may or may not be adequate to meet successfully, the greater the level of arousal.

But the behavior setting also places constraints on behavior—on what can be done and on what is "appropriate" to do in the setting. The constraints posed by the setting may restrict (and differentially weight) the available response alternatives which can be selected in the decision-making link. The behavior setting also may offer (or deny) "tools" which are more or less helpful in carrying out the behavior selected. Furthermore, the behavior setting is the locus of many of the situational factors which intervene between behavior (performance link three, doing what one decided to do) and the effect of that behavior on the situation

(outcome link four). Thus, factors in the behavior setting can play a part in each of the four stages of the stress cycle. (See Figure 10.)

Behavior settings, which are physical environments with associated social patterns, serve as *opportunities for,* and *place both demands and constraints on, behavior.* The key question for the first appraisal process link is: What is the "meaning" of the setting to the focal person? If the investigator thinks this is a case of setting X, does the focal person also think it's an "X" (i.e., does he read the meaning of the combined milieu-and-social-pattern in the same way as does the investigator)? If so, then he presumably knows what behavior is "appropriate." While this may resolve the appraisal question, it also may greatly constrain the response selection link. If he does *not* "read" the setting in the same way as the investigator, he may be "selecting" a response from a different array of alternatives—he may literally be behaving in a different situation— than that which the investigator has in mind.

Imagine that focal person comes into a formal conference, but he mistakes it for

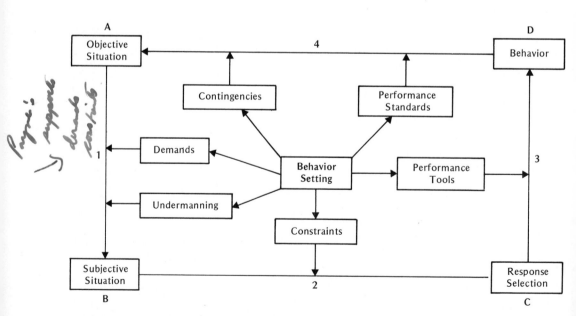

Figure 10.   Some effects of behavior setting on various stages of the stress cycle.

an informal coffee break. His behavior is likely to be "wrong," even weird, from the point of view of those who are defining the behavior setting "correctly" (that is, as a formal meeting). Obviously, we would expect the focal person to change his behavior very rapidly, and with embarrassment, as he detects his "error." But this presumes that there are cues, inherent in the situation or "sent" by the other persons, which focal person perceives, and which he uses to reappraise the "meaning" of the setting. Just what these cues are has not received very much research attention. (Indeed, many situation-comedy routines are built upon the occurrences and persistence of such misinterpretations of behavior settings.)

We can view behavior settings in a way analogous to "tasks." Behavior settings may give rise to stress through any of three parameters: (a) difficulty (demands); (b) ambiguity; and (c) load. A behavior setting may be too difficult if it places performance demands on the focal person(s) which exceed performance resources. A behavior setting may be ambiguous by not containing cues by which the focal person can accurately "read" the "meaning" of the setting. A behavior setting may be an overload by generating participation and performance demand on the focal person(s) beyond what he can handle, in the time allocation sense, though not necessarily involving any specific demand which could not be handled in the quality or level-of-performance sense. It is this latter condition, overload, that is involved in Barker's concept of "undermanning." The "difficulty" parameter is related to Barker's premise that standards for evaluating performance (i.e., criteria of task success) tend to be lowered when undermanning prevails and raised where there is overmanning. (Ambiguity of setting is a case not considered very much by Barker.)

Barker's thesis is that, as undermanning increases (that is, as the ratio of behavior settings to potential occupants increases), there is an increase of forces on occupants and potential occupants to enter and participate—so that the requirements of the setting will be fulfilled. When the number of persons in the setting is low, relative to the performance demands of the setting, we can reasonably view this as a condition of overload (or at least high load) on the participants.

Barker further postulates that, under such undermanning conditions, the standards for entrance and for evaluating performance tend to be lowered—presumably to make it more likely that additional members will enter and participate. These lowered standards of performance represent a reduction in "task difficulty," or an increase in probability of "successful" task outcome.

In the opposite case—conditions of overmanning, where there are many potential participants relative to the available behavior settings—there is a reduction of pressures to participate (load); indeed, there may be pressures not to participate. It follows, here, that standards for entrance and for performance tend to be raised (increased difficulty, decreased probability of success), so as to bring the actual number of participants more or less in line with the optimal number for the setting.

All of this seems to postulate an equilibrium which is brought about by an inverse compensation adjustment between load (tasks to be done relative to actual participants) and difficulty (standards for task success, or probability of task success).

We can consider this from the point of view of our stress model. In terms of perceived consequences, persons who participate when undermanning prevails must be those who value the consequences of the setting "coming off," relative to its failing to come off, sufficiently to assume the overload. Under conditions of overmanning, persons who "apply for" and enter the setting must value the consequences of their participating in the setting—presumably in terms of payoff from successful performance—if they are willing to strive for the high standards. Thus, the load-difficulty adjustment may serve to keep the motivation (i.e., perceived consequences) of actual participants high at all levels of the undermanning-overmanning continuum.

In terms of perceived difficulty and perceived ability—and their "match," leading to uncertainty—the situation is comparable. Variations in undermanning-overmanning supposedly lead to a similar compensatory adjustment between standards of entrance (i.e., ability) and standards for performance success (i.e., task difficulty). In the overmanned situation, it takes higher perceived ability to apply (and presumably higher actual ability to be admitted) for participation in the setting. At the same time, the standards for success are high. Thus, there is high uncertainty about success; that is, the perceived probability of success is in the vicinity of $p = .50$. In the undermanned setting, it takes less perceived ability to try to enter, less actual ability to enter, and standards for performance are lower. Thus, for many participants, there is *still* a close match between their (relatively low) perceived ability and (relatively low) perceived difficulty.

In terms of our stress model, then, the compensatory adjustments (of load and difficulty and of ability and performance standards) that are alleged to occur from overmanned to undermanned settings could serve to keep the level of arousal at a maximum (by keeping both perceived consequences and uncertainty high) *under all levels of undermanning and overmanning.* One can view the compensatory adjustments of load, difficulty, and ability standards as levels of "manning" change, as being responses by the "embedding system" (the broader system within which the behavior setting is embedded) to keep arousal at a high level and, therefore, to obtain effective performance. (Parenthetically, we should not permit ourselves to take seriously phrases which suggest that "behavior settings" or "embedding systems" made adjustments, or "have" social standards, or exhibit behaviors of various kinds. *People* behave; behavior

settings *are,* but they don't *do.* What we really mean in these instances is that "the people in charge of the setting" [or occasionally the people in it] make changes in standards, raise entrance requirements, and the like.)

So we can think of behavior settings as self-regulating systems which more or less effectively adjust standards and demands to: (a) compensate for over- or undermanning, while (b) keeping arousal at a maximum and, hence, getting effective performance. Where these adjustments are not made, the behavior setting becomes "ineffective." For example, if a setting which is grossly undermanned keeps its entrance and performance standards high, it is likely to go "out of business" from lack of participation. Conversely, if a setting which is grossly overmanned fails to raise entrance requirements, it is likely to be overpopulated with participants, many of whom do not have sufficient ability to achieve high performance standards.

E. Roles and Stress

Behavior in organizations is contingent not only upon the task activities that are being done and the behavioral settings in which these things are done, but also upon the patterns of interpersonal connectedness within which those behaviors take place. We will call such patterns of interpersonal connectedness "roles."[8]

In the framework presented in section II, we specified roles as the intersect of the "social environment" and the "person." That framework implies that roles are not tied to any specific milieu or setting, but rather transcend settings. (In an analogous sense,

---

[8] The term "role" has had a variety of usages in behavioral science. See Biddle and Thomas (1966) for a comprehensive treatment of the role concept and its variants. One of the most useful explications of roles and role behavior, in the context of organizations, is to be found in Kahn et al. (1964). This section will draw heavily on the Kahn et al. formulations and findings.

of course, tasks transcend social environments, and behavior settings transcend particular persons.)

It is possible to discuss behavior in organizations without reference to roles, but usually the same concepts are brought in under different labels. For example, Barker's behavior setting theory (cf., Barker & Wright, 1955) deals with the "position" or "office" aspect of roles under the term "behavior objects," and deals with the normative or role expectation aspects of role by referring to patterns of behavior which are "appropriate" to the setting. Discussions of organizational behavior which emphasize task activity often overlook effects of interpersonal relations, or treat them as disturbing complexities (error variance) to be minimized in job or organization design. The early time and motion work certainly took this stance; but the same is true of much more recent work, which has been done from an "operations research" emphasis.

But on the face of it, role relations (or some equivalent term), as expressed in organization charts, job titles, and the like, seem to be ubiquitous in organizational patterns. Who works for whom, who communicates with whom, who has influence on whom—these are questions as basic to one's orientation in "organizational space" as questions about the location of "north" are basic to one's orientation in geographical space.

Role connections are important because they represent "channels" through which flow the basic "stuff" of interpersonal behavior: "information," "influence," and "affect."[9] The crucial aspect of roles, for our

present purpose, is that they represent continuing relations between persons which transcend specific settings and transcend specific tasks, and which affect behavior (on tasks in settings). That is to say, a person's behavior on a given task, at a given time and place, is affected by his continuing relations with others involved in that task, with others present in that place, and indeed with others (e.g., his "boss") not necessarily present at all but "relevant" to the setting and/or the task. Such influence occurs, presumably, because the person carries "in his head" representations of the expectations that such "others" have about how he should behave on that task in that time and place.

These expectations are (to follow the Kahn et al. formulation) the results of (his "interpretation" of) communications sent to him in the past by these "others" (or members of the same class of others). Such communications, or role messages, or role demands, are not necessarily explicit communications labeled as addressed to him, the referent or focal person. Indeed, they are sometimes communicated quite indirectly and through subtle nonverbal cues. But they are also often given directly—in instructions, in job descriptions, in the expression of group or company "policy" or practices or norms.

Kahn et al. (1964) present a four-stage model of the role episode which has some similarities with the four-stage stress cycle presented here. They see role demands as coming from the "objective" situation (e.g., organizational or environmental factors). These, along with past history, are translated into "role expectations" held, for a given focal person, by members of his "role set" (that is, these persons with whom the focal person has continuing, patterned relations transcending any particular task and setting). These expectations are "sent"—in

---

[9] It is reasonable to consider that those three (the flow of information, of influence, and of affect) are the basic processes involved in interpersonal behavior, hence in role relations; and that descriptions of role structure or group structure represent descriptions of networks through which one or more of these "flow." See McGrath (1963) for a presentation of this view and of the connections between those three processes and concepts from other theorists such as Schutz (1958), Leary (1957), Osgood (1957), Hemphill (1950), and Cartwright and Zander (1960). For empirical work showing how these three processes fitted as dimensions of role relations, see Blackburn (1969) and Triandis (1964).

one way or another—as role demands on the focal person. They are received—more or less accurately—by the focal person. The perceived role expectations are translated into role behaviors, presumably intended to deal with the demands/expectations. Finally, the role behavior has effects on the situation and on the expectations of others in the role set.[10]

The "link" between "sent role" and "received role" is analogous to the appraisal link between stages A and B of the stress cycle in our formulation. The translation of received role into a behavior choice is like link two, the decision-making process. The acting out of that behavior choice is like link three (performance process). The feedback effects of that behavior on the situation and on the role senders reflect link four (outcome), although Kahn et al. do not explicitly distinguish between behavior and its consequences in their role episode model.

The "role episode" becomes a "stress cycle" when something goes awry in the match of role expectations, sent role demands, received role demands, and role behavior. Kahn et al. (1964) identified two general forms of role-based stress in organizations: role conflict and role ambiguity. One subform of role conflict is role overload. These, of course, are parallel to the forms of stress noted for tasks and for behavior settings.[11] Role conflict is related to "difficulty" in the task domain, and to the idea of "demands" or "requirements" or "constraints" imposed by behavior settings. Role ambiguity is akin to task ambiguity, and role overload is akin to task load as noted earlier in this section.

Role conflict can occur in any of several forms. First, different members (or subsets)

of the role set may hold different and conflicting expectations for focal person's role behavior. The classic case, here, is the first-line supervisor, the "man in the middle," for whom management and workers presumably hold contradictory expectations. To comply with the expectations of either is to spurn those of the other. Kahn et al. (1964) generalize this "man in the middle" idea, speaking of high incidence of role conflict for persons who spend a lot of their time and efforts crossing organizational (or sub-organizational) boundaries, as well as for those in subordinate-superordinate relationships.

A second form of role conflict can arise when the set of role demands, while agreed upon by all in the role set, contain internally contradictory expectations. For example, many readers can probably recall occasions when they have been asked to present some complex material "briefly but in detail." And many have probably experienced the pervasive dilemma of the parental role in our culture, the expectation to provide both love and discipline, often at the same time, within the same parent-child role relation.

A third form of role conflict, really person-role conflict, is when role expectations conflict with some attribute (trait, preference, value, or moral principle) of the focal person. There is a related case, perhaps more properly called role difficulty, where role expectations exceed the (perceived) performance capabilities of the focal person. At this point, of course, our consideration of role stress begins to overlap with our prior discussion of task stress.

Finally, there can be role-based conflict of a kind which Kahn et al. (1964) call inter-role conflict. One of the most frequent forms of this occurs as conflicting demands of job and family. This particular example is not a conflict about how to behave (on the job, or in the home), but rather a conflict about allocation of time (and attention) to job and family. Thus, it is more akin to problems of role overload (which Kahn et al. also treat as a kind of role conflict but which are treated separately here). But there are many situations of potential inter-role

---

[10] The Kahn et al. role episode formulation is a great deal more complicated and more sophisticated than can be expressed in the present brief treatment. See Kahn et al. (1964), Katz and Kahn (1966), and Kahn (1970) for more comprehensive presentations.

[11] This is no accident. The author acknowledges a considerable intellectual debt to the work of Kahn (1970; Kahn & French, 1970) in the role stress area, as well as to the work of Hackman (1970) in the task stress area, for the formulations presented in this chapter.

conflict between two or more work roles (such as the well-known political "conflicts of interest" cases in which members of regulatory panels or congressional committees have holdings or interests in enterprises which are regulated by those panels or committees). These are conflicts of expectation and not conflicts of allocation, and, therefore, belong in the role conflict category.

Kahn et al. found strikingly high frequencies of perceived role conflict in work organizations (cf., Kahn et al., 1964, pp. 55ff.). Fully five out of six men in the labor force (as reflected by a national sample) report some form of role-based tension. Nearly half of them are confronted with intersender conflict, in most cases with organizational superiors as one party to the conflict. Person-role conflicts—being required to do things against your better judgment—occur for 45 percent of the men in the sample; and 43 percent report having roles (or tasks) perceived as beyond their performance capabilities.

Kahn et al. found evidence of multiple effects of such role-based stress on the person. Those in high conflict roles tend to reduce trust, liking, and respect for the role senders from whom the conflict stems, attribute less power to them, and withdraw from or restrict communications with them. (That is, a reduction occurs in the "flow" of information, influence, and affect within the role set.) Those in high conflict roles experience more internal conflicts, reduced job satisfaction, decreased confidence in superiors and in the organization. Thus, role conflict has negative effects on the person's "relations" with himself, with others in his role set, and with the task and organizational setting.

Role ambiguity is apparently also pervasive in work organizations, and leads to stress. Kahn et al. (1964, pp. 71ff.) cite several major sources. Ambiguity arises because of size and complexity of modern organizations. Ambiguity also comes from high rates of change: (a) changes in technology and in the extra-organizational environment; (b) changes in associated social structures in

organization; and (c) changes in personnel who inhabit the organization. Thus, change comes from all three of the embedding systems. Ambiguity also arises because of restrictions on the flow of information within the organization—both the downward flow, as a more or less deliberate management policy, and the upward flow, as a counter-control technique.

Ambiguity can arise about the scope of one's responsibilities; about the limits of one's authority; about rules, sanctions, and their application; about which authorities are legitimate vis-à-vis which aspects of behavior; about job security and opportunities; and about evaluations of oneself by others. Ambiguity can also center around the connections of behaviors and (intended) goals—what leads to what.

Effects of role ambiguity parallel those of role conflict—intrapersonal tension, lowered job satisfaction, lowered self-esteem, reductions in positive affect for others in the role set. But ambiguity is likely to increase rather than decrease communication, at least initially.

Role overload is also widespread in work organizations. Almost half of all respondents, in the Kahn et al. study, reported role overload, but little is said there about the sources and effects of such perceived overload. One suspects that overload per se produces less stress, or at least less negative intrapersonal and interpersonal consequences, except when it leads to either of two possible secondary states: (a) a substantial reduction in quality of role performance on some of the role demands; and/or (b) a rejection of (and failure to perform at all) some of the role demands.

It is also probably the case that the appearance of role overload is sometimes used as a coping strategy.[12] Organizational members sometimes make use of real or alleged role overload as a legitimizing basis for re-

---

[12] It should also be noted that at least some forms of role ambiguity can be used as bases for coping with role demands; if others don't know what I'm doing, or what I'm supposed to do, they cannot discover that I'm doing it poorly.

jection of additional role demands. (All academics know the value of establishing visible membership on a supposedly demanding committee, as a basis for avoiding assignment to, or begging off from, membership on other less attractive committees.) Both Parkinson (1957) and Peter and Hull (1969) talk about the status value of adding subordinates to one's organizational unit, and of the importance of establishing work overload as a justification for such expansion. Apparent role overload can also be used to legitimize non-performance of especially difficult or unenjoyable role demands—because other demands of the role are so all-consuming. Thus, apparent role overload can serve to avoid those role demands which contain person-role conflicts of values or of competence.

The second process link, decision making, implies choice among alternatives. In the case of role conflict, the choice may be between honoring role demands from one source rather than from another. In the case of role overload, the choice may be between responding to one set of demands rather than another, or may involve the timing or sequencing of responses to different role demands. With role ambiguity, though, the "choice" is of a different sort. If I don't know what is expected, my "choice" of role behaviors can be regarded as a hypothesis about what might be expected.

As in our discussion of task-based stress, it is well to recognize that there often is a choice of what role demands to try to meet. If one measures the behavior exhibited (in a role episode or on a task), and expects to investigate the relationship between stress (e.g., role conflict) and performance, he must reckon with the question of *which* performance (that is, performance with respect to which subset of role demands) is to be assessed. For the investigator to decide to assess performance on one aspect of the role, when the focal person may well be attempting to perform other (equally legitimate) aspects of his role, is to confound the question of the effects of stress (arousal) on "per-

formance." As noted in the discussion of tasks earlier in this section, the investigator should be in a position to assess effectiveness of performance of a *spectrum* of role behaviors, not just on one selected behavior. Then he can ask how stress affects the distribution (or probability) of role responses, rather than how stress affects "the performance."

It is equally important here, as in our consideration of tasks, to distinguish between role behavior (focal person doing what he sets out to do) and the *impact* (effects, consequences, outcomes) of that behavior on the situation. Again, there are many factors *other than* focal person's behavior which play a part in determining the outcome or consequences of that behavior. Other persons, in or outside of the role set, may act in ways that offset focal person's intended effect—deliberately or unwittingly. "Chance," or extra-organizational events, may occur which modify the outcome. Furthermore, there may be a complex and probabilistic connection, or none at all, between the role behavior performed (however well executed) and the situational demand which it was intended to alleviate.

The degree of objective conflict in role demands on a given focal person, and of objective ambiguity, or lack of agreement among role senders, on those role demands, and of the objective sum total (i.e., load) of these role demands, are matters arising from the play of factors in the physical, technological, and organizational environment. The degree of *experienced stress* arising from role conflict, ambiguity, and load, is, of course, an interaction of person with those (objective) demands. We are calling that interaction the appraisal process, link one of the stress cycle. In considering link four—the outcome process—we are interested in the relation between focal person's role behavior and its effects on those objective role demands. Consequently, if the appraisal process goes awry—if focal person *misreads* the nature of the role demands—then even a "wise" response selection and an "effective" performance of that response will *not* serve to fulfill these objective role demands (even if actions of others, or chance factors, do not "intervene").

In this respect, role based stress in the form of ambiguity is likely to pose a special kind of problem for the individual. The problem is one of hypothesis-formation and test. Presumably, the individual will develop some hypotheses (guesses, if you like) about role expectations, will select a response to fit those hypotheses, and will then execute the response as effectively as he can. Presumably, if it "works"—that is, if his behavior produces a positively rewarding outcome— he will fix upon that hypothesis (i.e., reduce the ambiguity) and the associated response will become more probable on the next occasion. If, in the ambiguous role situation, positive feedback (successful outcome) should occur as a result of some factors *other* than focal person's role behavior (e.g., someone else's actions, or chance), the focal person may tend to become locked into a pattern of role behavior that really does not meet the situational demands.

In the case of role conflict, on the other hand, the demands are presumably clear, but contradictory. The decision-making process is crucial. Here, the focal person chooses to honor some demands and not others, or to compromise. At that stage, he has selected which situational demands he will try to fulfill, and which demands he will not be fulfilling. The decision-making process for role overload is similar to the role conflict case; focal person picks which role demands to try to meet and which to ignore, and expects his role behavior to fulfill the former but not the latter. Both role conflict and overload are more the case of choosing between relatively clear but incompatible alternatives, whereas role ambiguity requires the generation of probable alternatives.

Discussion of the role-based sources of stress, and of the Kahn et al. (1964) findings pertaining to such stress, points up several important features of the stress and behavior problem, and of our treatment of it in this chapter. First of all, there are a great many parallels between forms of stress arising from task aspects and forms of stress arising from interpersonal or role aspects of a situation. There are also similar parallels between these and stress arising from the behavior-setting. It is also clear that there is considerable redundancy involved in treating tasks, behavior settings, and roles separately.

At the same time, it is clear that role relations represent a major source of potential stress in organizations. The Kahn et al. findings show the pervasiveness of role-based stress, and indicate the multiple effects of such stress. While *some* of these forms of role stress overlap with those identified through consideration of tasks, and of behavior settings, some of them are distinctively tied to the continuing interpersonal connections, or role relations, which transcend both tasks and behavior settings.

Furthermore, the pervasive and diffuse effects of role-based stress, as reflected in the findings of Kahn et al. (1964; see also Kahn & French, 1970), make it apparent that effects of stress on performance is but one narrow segment of the potential effects of stress, and of behavior in response to that stress, in organizational settings. Indeed, role-based stress has an impact on the continuing pattern of interpersonal relations, and on the psychological and even physical (see, for example, Kahn & French, 1970) well-being of the focal person, as well as on his role performance. This raises some issues about the relatively narrow definition of "behavior" and "consequences" suggested in our model of the stress cycle.

Not only must we consider a repertoire of potential responses—some dealing with "the task," some coping with task-external stressors, some helping the individual avoid or escape the situation—in dealing with effectiveness of response selection and of tasks or role performance; we must also consider a spectrum of classes of "behaviors"—some related to tasks and role demands, some related to interpersonal conditions, some related to psychological conditions of the focal person. This adds another order of complexity to our consideration of the stress cycle.

F. The Three Embedding Systems as Sources of Stress

We now turn to consideration of the three embedding systems—physical and social environment and person system—as separate potential sources of stress. It is obvious that some further redundancy is involved here, since each of these systems contributes to two of the sources of stress already considered. Yet it is worth adding a few brief comments about each of the embedding systems, as such, because some of their properties, in extreme form, permeate *whole sets* of tasks, roles, and behavior settings and thus influence a large segment of behavior within that system.

Potential stressors in the physical environment include such noxious or dangerous conditions as extreme cold (or heat), hazards, and the like. As before, however, it is not the actual ("objective") danger, or potential hazard, that determines the experience of stress. Rather, it is the person's appraisal or interpretation of the environmental state. (Arctic researchers have written that it is not the cold that kills, it is the fear of the cold.) If there are truly hazardous conditions, but the person is not aware of them (e.g., high radiation levels) or is equipped to cope with them (e.g., controlled-atmosphere cabins in space or undersea craft), those conditions need not produce experienced stress. Conversely, the person may experience stress if he appraises a condition as portending undesirable consequences with which he cannot cope, whether or not those conditions actually are present and whether or not those conditions actually are dangerous. For example, if a person fears the effects of fluoride in the water he drinks, or toxic chemicals in his food, he may be undergoing "stress" from those conditions, whether or not such substances are present and whether or not they are truly dangerous.

The above example highlights two points.

One is that subjective stress from an environmental source implies an interpretation (appraisal) of that condition by the person—an interaction of person and environment. The second point is that the appraisal process, hence the stress cycle, is a function of the person's cumulative knowledge and understanding—his cognitive as well as his emotional state—and much of that cognitive state is in turn a function of the technological-cultural setting. For example, virtually no one was "stressed" by fear of mercury in his fish ten or twenty years ago, because virtually no one knew that it was there or that it was dangerous. Nor did Caesar fear germs, cancer, or radiation. On the other hand, most people in most contemporary industrialized cultures no longer fear ghosts or evil spirits (because we "know" "they" are not really there!). So the sociocultural system, through past effects on the person (i.e., his "learning"), influences the interpretation of physical-environmental conditions. Thus, stressor effects from the embedding systems seem to be mediated, through tasks, roles, and behavior settings, as our model suggests.

Historically, social-psychological research on organizations, and on stress, has had little to say about effects of physical environment. In a sense, that class of potential variables was abandoned after the famous Hawthorne studies, which seemed to show that certain physical-environmental variables (lighting conditions, work breaks, and the like) were of little consequence compared to certain social-environmental variables (cohesiveness, interpersonal compatibility, and the like). As the impact of the Hawthorne studies began to take hold, research began to concentrate on the "more interesting" social-psychological variables, and little attention was given to effects of physical environment. It is only quite recently that studies of effects of environment on behavior (and vice versa) have regained a place in the field. Some of the most interesting work in the relatively recent reawakening of interest in physical environment does not deal with stress in organizations, as such, but has major implications for that topic (e.g., Hall, 1966; Calhoun, 1962; Altman & Haythorn, 1965, 1967; Sommer, 1967; Sells, 1966). Sells, in particular, has championed the cause of environmental variables (Sells, 1962) and has developed a comprehensive taxonomy which represents a landmark for work in this area.

The social environment, on the other hand, has received a great deal of attention from behavioral scientists, especially sociologists and anthropologists. Much of the study of "organizations," of course, is the study of the social environment of persons in that organization. And insofar as features of that organizational environment place demands on the person (or constraints, or opportunities), or alter the impact of such demands, then those features represent potential sources of stress. But stress from the social environment does not act directly "on" the person. Its effects are mediated by the appraisal process. As with the physical environment, stressors are "there" (i.e., act as stressors) only if they (or their derivatives) are psychologically there. By and large, effects from the social environment occur in the form of effects on the "meanings" of behavior settings which the person inhabits, and/or on the nature of the role demands which he experiences.

Like the social environment, the person system also has received a lot of research attention from behavioral scientists, including those studying stress. There has been a virtual flood of research on stress as anxiety, viewed as a property of the "person system." There is a whole literature on both trait and state anxiety, and related concepts. (For good summaries and interpretations of portions of that literature, see Appley & Trumbull, 1967; Cofer & Appley, 1964; Lazarus, 1966; Murray, 1971; Weiss & Miller, 1971.) Many studies of stress have given major attention to personality factors underlying the stress experience (e.g., Haythorn, 1970; Kahn et al., 1964; Klausner, 1968; Lazarus, 1966). It would be impossible to attempt to deal with that extensive literature here.

One central feature of the investigation of stress-as-person-property has been the notion—derived from the inverted-U and from the individual differences themes—that there may be "stress resistant" persons. (The dichotomy of "repressers" and "sensitizers" is another form of the same concept.) The idea here is to locate a subset of persons who, because of some personality characteristics or pattern, can "resist" the negative effects of stress on performance so that their "inverted-U" curves don't start down until much higher levels of stress than is the case for other more "stress prone" individuals. This concept seems thoroughly embedded in the stress literature. Indeed, it is a compelling inference, given the premises about individual differences and the inverted-U. But this writer does not know of any solid, replicated findings which would support the idea that there are "stress resistant" persons, who are identifiable on the basis of some pattern of person-system properties, who show less experienced stress in the same objective situations (for a range of situations), and who simultaneously show better performance in those situations than some comparison (e.g., "stress prone") group. Indeed, results of the Lowe study discussed above, and the model derived from it, would suggest that if there were a subset of persons who consistently showed less experienced stress to a given class of situations, they would tend to show *poorer* performance in that situation. But it is by no means clear that such a special class of "less-stressable" persons exists, in some trans-situation sense, regardless of whether their performance would be better or poorer.

This is not to deny that people differ in their appraisal of, and reactions to, a given stressor condition. Of course they do, and the whole four-stage model of the stress cycle is based on that premise. But the question here is: (a) whether a given person is consistently more "stressed" (e.g., as measured by physiological reactions) by a given class of situations; (b) whether that person is identifiable by, say, some personality trait(s), *independent* of the measure indicating his degree of stress; (c) whether those conditions hold over various types of situations; and (d) whether they are associated with better, poorer, or average performance. The evidence, at this point, is not convincing.

It seems much more likely that experienced stress represents an *interaction* of the person with features of his environment—that is, that effects of the "person system" are mediated through "tasks" and "roles." It is the case, of course, that the same sets of person-properties—abilities as well as personality traits—will enter into and affect the whole array of tasks and roles in which that person participates. In the same sense, features of the physical environment have their effects through tasks and behavior settings—though the same environmental condition (e.g., extreme cold) may permeate *all* the tasks and *all* the settings of a given situation. An analogous state of affairs exists for effects of properties of the social environment; they have their effects via roles and behavior settings, but those effects may permeate the whole set of roles and the whole set of settings in a given case. Thus, we again find high redundancy; and we again reach the position that the three embedding systems have, mainly, indirect or second order effects on stress and behavior; and that those effects are mediated through tasks, roles, and behavior settings.

By the latter proposition, if stress arises from the physical environment, it will be manifested either as an effect on behavior settings (that is, the interaction of physical and social environment), or tasks (that is, the interaction of physical environment and person), or both. For example, an environmental hazard will shape the behavior settings in which the person behaves and/or the tasks which he executes. If stress arises from the social environment, it will be manifested either as an effect on behavior settings or on roles (that is, the interaction of the person with his social environment). For example, a conflict of cultural values will shape the "meanings" of behavior settings

within that culture and/or the patterns of role expectations for the person. If stress comes from the person setting, it will be manifested either as an effect on tasks or on roles. For example, a persistent personality characteristic (extroversion, anxiety, cognitive style, etc.) would shape the person's task performances and/or his enactment of roles.

But properties of the person system are a somewhat special case. After all, it is the person who executes the appraisal process, the decision-making process and the performance process. In other words, it is the person whose "behavior in organizations" we are examining. Properties of the person have profound influences on the appraisal process and on the decision-making process, as well as on the performance process. In principle, person-properties affect the understanding/interpretation/acceptance of tasks, and the selection of strategies to execute them, as well as task performance. And person-properties affect the perception of role demands, and the adjudication of conflicting or ambiguous role demands, as well as role performance.

It is only the outcome process—the effect of task or role performance on the behavior setting—which is more or less beyond the *direct* effects of the person and his "style," "traits," "skills," "repertoire," etc. That outcome process is a matter of the "real" connections—the reinforcement contingencies—that exist between specific behaviors of the person and features of the physical and social environments. Regardless of ability or personality, a thorough understanding of those outcome connections is necessary—but not sufficient—to allow the person to "deal" with potential stressors by means of accurate perception, rational choice, and effective coping behavior. In other words, to deal with stress, "you gotta know the territory"! And from the point of view of organizational planners, who seek to design the organization to obtain effective member performance with minimal negative side effects, it is crucial to examine these reinforcement contingencies—what behaviors actually lead to what consequences, with what probabilities—and to alter them to facilitate the intended consequences.

A Concluding Comment: Stress as a Value Term

The word "stress" is a pejorative term. Stress is a "bad" thing. Therefore, everyone "knows" that if a person is under "too much stress" he will perform poorly and suffer other negative consequences. It, therefore, becomes surprising, and a matter to be conjectured, when it turns out that a "little bit" of "stress" has some positive effects—as in the left-hand portion of the alleged inverted-U. From this point of view, though, it remains quite clear that, if stress is increased "enough," bad consequences will result—because "stress" is "bad."

The value-laden nature of a term like stress may well affect interpretation of evidence. What would have happened if the same set of variables and relationships had been studied under the label "challenge"? Would the inverted-U, then, not turn down? Indeed, research studies on what seem to be related problems, done under the rubric of "activation" rather than under the rubric of "stress," tend to find a monotonic relation between activation (arousal) and performance. The moral, here, is obvious: we must not build our research around value-laden concepts, lest our studies, our data, and especially our conclusions be caught in our own semantic trap.

The risk of error from use of value laden terms is present in all areas of the social sciences. Sherif's (1935) deviance and Asch's (1951) independence are operationally identical, though connotatively opposite. But the problem has particular force in the case of stress research. Lazarus has commented[13] that it is especially easy for students to conclude that reducing psychological threat is always a good thing—perhaps because of the

particular kinds of stimulus materials used to induce threat in his program (cf., Lazarus, 1966). He further points out that it is by no means necessarily a "good" thing for a person to be totally unresponsive to such materials (films of accidents, etc.). The point is that there are circumstances in which it would be dysfunctional for the person (or the organization) if he were *not* sensitive to the presence and potential impact of "stressor" conditions.

To expand this point further: it is also often the case that what is "good" for the organization and what is "good" for the member whose behavior we are examining are different, even mutually exclusive. In such a case which "good" will be taken as the criterion of performance that is to be maximized? And can we speak of the "relation" of "stress" to "performance," without presupposing that the "right" performance is to maximize one of these—the organization's "good" or the individual's "good" —at the expense of the other?

To investigate (empirically) what conditions lead to "more effective" performance, or to "goal attainment," or to "better" systems, or the like—all of these are decisions as to what criteria will be applied to define the "desirable" state of affairs. And choices of criteria are, necessarily, value choices. If the potential "objectives" embedded in a situation (e.g., individual gain, organization benefit, environmental damage, and the like) are mutually exclusive or otherwise conflicting, and if value-laden choices of criteria are necessary to decide what are the "good" consequences of states of affairs, then *those value choices will decide the direction and meaning of relationships* which are "found" in such empirical studies.

The intended message in all of the above includes, but is more than, the simple idea that if we name an area of study as a "bad" thing (e.g., "stress," or deviance), we will almost inevitably search for ways to reduce or eliminate "it." We don't make "stress" a good thing by renaming it "challenge." But by renaming "it" we may quit presuming

---

[13] Lazarus, personal communication.

"it" is a bad thing. Beyond the naming problem, we need to be sensitive to the general problem of value biases in all studies which take on a normative flavor—such as inquiring about "improving" performance or making conditions "better." Whenever conditions are such that the organization's "meat" is the organizational member's "poison," or vice versa (and they almost always are, to some extent, in any relatively complex system), then we must examine very carefully whose "good" we are talking about in our normative concepts—just whose ax we are about to grind and whose ox we are about to gore.

REFERENCES

Altman, I., & Haythorn, W. W. Interpersonal exchange in isolation. *Sociometry,* 1965, 28, 411–426.

Altman, I., & Haythorn, W. W. The ecology of isolated groups. *Behavioral Science,* 1967, 12, 169–182.

Appley, M. H., & Trumbull, R. *Psychological stress.* New York: Appleton-Century-Crofts, 1967.

Asch, S. E. Effects of group pressure upon the modification and distortion of judgments. In H. Guetzkow (Ed.), *Groups, leadership, and men.* New Brunswick, N.J.: Rutgers University Press, 1951, 171–190.

Barker, R. G. *Ecological psychology.* Stanford: Stanford University Press, 1968.

Barker, R. G., & Gump, P. *Big School, small school.* Stanford: Stanford University Press, 1964.

Barker, R. G., & Wright, H. F. *Midwest and its children.* New York: Harper and Row, 1955.

Biddle, B. J., & Thomas, E. J., Eds. *Role theory: Concepts and research.* New York: Wiley, 1966.

Blackburn, M. C. A paradigm for the analysis of role relationship patterns. Unpublished master's thesis, University of Illinois, Urbana, 1969.

Calhoun, J. B. Population density and social pathology. *Scientific American,* 1962, 206, 139–148.

Campbell, D. T., & Fiske, D. W. Convergent and discriminant validation by the multitrait-multimethod matrix. *Psychological Bulletin,* 1959, 56, 81–105.

Cartwright, D., & Zander, A., Eds. *Group dynamics.* (2nd ed.) New York: Row, Peterson, 1960.

Cofer, C. N., & Appley, M. H. *Motivation: Theory and research.* New York: Wiley, 1964.

Crider, A. Experimental studies of conflict-produced stress. In S. Levine & N. A. Scotch (Eds.), *Social stress.* Chicago: Aldine, 1970.

Hackman, J. R. Tasks and task performance in research on stress. In J. E. McGrath (Ed.), *Social and psychological factors in stress.* New York: Holt, Rinehart and Winston, 1970.

Hall, E. T. *The hidden dimension.* New York: Doubleday, 1966.

Haythorn, W. W. Interpersonal stress in isolated groups. In J. E. McGrath (Ed.), *Social and psychological factors in stress.* New York: Holt, Rinehart and Winston, 1970.

Hemphill, J. K., & Westie, C. M. The measurement of group dimensions. *Journal of Psychology,* 1950, 29, 325–342.

Kahn, R. L. Some propositions toward a researchable conceptualization of stress. In J. E. McGrath (Ed.), *Social and psychological factors in stress.* New York: Holt, Rinehart and Winston, 1970.

Kahn, R. L., & French, R. P. Jr. Status and conflict: Two themes in the study of stress. In J. E. McGrath (Ed.), *Social and psychological factors in stress.* New York: Holt, Rinehart and Winston, 1970.

Kahn, R. L., Wolfe, D. M., Snoek, J. E., & Rosenthal, R. A. *Organizational stress: Studies in role conflict and ambiguity.* New York: Wiley, 1964.

Katz, D., & Kahn, R. L. *The social psychology of organizations.* New York: Wiley, 1966.

Klausner, S. Z. The intermingling of pain and pleasure: The stress seeking personality in its social context. In S. Z. Klausner (Ed.), *Why man takes chances: Studies in stress seeking.* New York: Doubleday, 1968.

Lacey, J. I. Somatic response patterning and stress: Some revisions of activation theory. In M. H. Appley & R. Trumbull (Eds.), *Psychological stress.* New York: Appleton-Century-Crofts, 1967.

Lazarus, R. *Psychological stress and the coping process.* New York: McGraw-Hill, 1966.

Leary, T. *Interpersonal diagnosis of personality.* New York: Ronald Press, 1957.

Lowe, R. Stress, arousal, and task performance of little league baseball players. Unpublished doctoral dissertation, University of Illinois, Urbana, 1971.

Lowe, R., & McGrath, J. E. Stress, arousal, and performance: Some findings calling for a new theory. Project report, AF 1161-67, AFOSR, 1971.

McGrath, J. E. A descriptive model for the study of interpersonal relations in small groups. *Journal of Psychological Studies,* 1963, 14 (3), 89–116.

McGrath, J. E. Settings, measures, and themes: An integrative review of some research on social-psychological factors in stress. In J. E. McGrath (Ed.), *Social and psychological factors in stress.* New York: Holt, Rinehart and Winston, 1970. (a)

McGrath, J. E. Introduction. In J. E. McGrath (Ed.), *Social and psychological factors in stress.* New York: Holt, Rinehart and Winston, 1970, Chapter 1. (b)

McGrath, J. E. A conceptual formulation for research on stress. In J. E. McGrath (Ed.), *Social and psychological factors in stress.* New York: Holt, Rinehart and Winston, 1970, Chapter 2. (c)

McGrath, J. E. Major methodological issues. In J. E. McGrath (Ed.), *Social and psychological factors in stress.* New York: Holt, Rinehart and Winston, 1970. (d)

McGrath, J. E., Ed. *Social and psychological factors in stress.* New York: Holt, Rinehart and Winston, 1970. (e)

Murray, D. C. Talk, silence, and anxiety. *Psychological Bulletin,* 1971, 75 (4), 244–260.

Osgood, C. E., Suci, G. J., & Tannenbaum, P. H. *The measurement of meaning.* Urbana: University of Illinois Press, 1957.

Parkinson, C. N. *Parkinson's law.* Boston: Houghton Mifflin, 1957.

Peter, L. J., & Hull, R. *The Peter principle.* New York: William Morrow, 1969.

Roscoe, S. Enhancement of human effectiveness in Air Force system design, training, and operations. ARL-7001, March, 1970.

Schutz, W. C. *FIRO: A three-dimensional theory of interpersonal behavior.* New York: Holt, Rinehart and Winston, 1958.

Scott, W. E. Activation theory and task design. *Organizational Behavior and Human Performance,* 1966, 1, 3–30.

Sells, S. B., Ed. Dimensions of stimulus situations which account for behavior variance. Technical Report No. 5, April, 1962, Group Psychology Branch, Contract Nonr 3436(00) Office of Naval Research.

Sells, S. B. Ecology and the science of psychology. *Multivariate Behavioral Research,* 1966, 1, 131–144.

Sells, S. B. On the nature of stress. In J. E. McGrath (Ed.), *Social and psychological factors in stress.* New York: Holt, Rinehart and Winston, 1970.

Sherif, M. A study of some social factors in perception. *Archives de Psychologie,* New York, 1935, 27 (187).

Sommer, R. Small group ecology. *Psychological Bulletin,* 1967, 67 (2), 145–152.

Triandis, H. C. Exploratory factor analyses of the behavioral component of social attitudes. *Journal of Abnormal and Social Psychology,* 1964, 68 (4), 420–430.

Webb, E. J., Campbell, D. T., Schwartz, R. D., & Sechrest, L. *Unobtrusive measures: Nonreactive research in the social sciences.* Skokie, Ill.: Rand McNally, 1966.

Weiss, R. F., & Miller, F. G. The drive theory of social facilitation. *Psychological Review,* 1971, 78 (1), 44–57.

Weitz, J. Psychological research needs on the problems of human stress. In J. E. McGrath (Ed.), *Social and psychological factors in stress.* New York: Holt, Rinehart and Winston, 1970.

Wicker, A. Undermanning, performances, and students' subjective experience in behavior settings of large and small high schools. *Journal of Personality and Social Psychology,* 1968, 10, 255–261.

Wicker, A. Size of church membership and members' support of church behavior settings. *Journal of Personality and Social Psychology,* 1969, 13, 278–288.

Zajonc, R. B. Social facilitation. *Science,* 1965, 149, 269–274.

CHAPTER **32**

Decision Making and Problem Solving[1]

KENNETH R. MacCRIMMON
RONALD N. TAYLOR
University of British Columbia

THE INTENT OF THIS CHAPTER is to consolidate evidence from a variety of disciplines into a more unified view of decision making. The central sections of the chapter examine *strategies* available to the decision maker in dealing with environments characterized by *uncertainty, complexity,* and *conflict.* The more than seventy strategies identified are presented within each section in an order which reflects the extent of required interaction with the environment (e.g., modifying perceptions requires minimal interaction; structural changes require a high amount of interaction). In addition to these three core sections, there are sections on types of decision problems and on the characteristics of decision makers which influence the use of the various strategies.

Organizing studies of decision making and problem solving in the form of strategies rather than by the traditional format should help in applying the existing knowledge and also in indicating major needs for future studies.

SECTION 1. INTRODUCTION

In the behavioral sciences and in other disciplines, theorists and researchers have given considerable attention to decision making and problem solving, since these activities are crucial to the functioning of social systems. In a very real sense, our un-

derstanding of what makes a social system effective depends on our knowledge of how people make effective decisions.

1.1 Decision Making, Problem Solving, and Judgment

We shall not make any distinction in this chapter between the terms "decision making" and "problem solving," since the diverse literatures of decision making use these terms in many different ways. In some

---

[1] The authors wish to express their appreciation to J. Richard Hackman for his careful reading of an earlier draft of this chapter and his helpful suggestions.

cases, decision making is considered a sub-set of problem solving, with decision making dealing primarily with evaluation and choice from a set of alternatives, and problem solving dealing with the whole process of problem formation, alternative generation, and information processing which culminates in the choice. In other cases, problem solving is considered a subset of decision making, since problem solving deals primarily with simple situations that often have correct solutions, while decision making encompasses broader, more important contexts. Inseparable from decision making or problem solving is judgment. To the extent that judgment enters into decision making or problem solving processes, we will deal with it.

Decision making, problem solving, and judgment imply both thought and action (Miller et al., 1960). Indeed, they form a bridge between thought and action. Decision making can be defined as the processes of thought and action that culminate in choice behavior (MacCrimmon, 1973b).

1.2 Normative and Descriptive Theories

Descriptive and normative theories of decision making are both important since we need to know more about how people actually make decisions and how they can make better decisions. In this chapter, we utilize both types of studies. Our orientation in the central part of this chapter, Sections 3–5, is normative: the sections are organized in terms of strategies for managing uncertainty, complexity, and conflict in the decision environment. But since prescriptions must be founded in actual behavior, we also present the most relevant descriptive studies.

1.3 Focus on Decision Strategies

This chapter attempts to consolidate information from various disciplines into a more unified view of decision making. In organizing the literature by strategies instead of by the traditional paradigms, we hope to integrate the relevant theoretical and empirical developments from these various disciplines; we also hope to facilitate the exchange of theories, research findings, and operational strategies across disciplines, and to suggest fresh perspectives for understanding and applying the process of decision making.

To emphasize the strategy orientation, we have placed each sub-section heading in the core (Sections 3–5) of this chapter in the imperative mode. The reader should realize, however, that these strategies are not meant as universal principles but rather as guides to action that are appropriate under some conditions and inappropriate under others. We state some of these conditions, but are not as evaluative as we would like to be due to limitations of knowledge and space.

1.4 Organization of the Chapter

In the next section (Section 2), we examine some preconditions for decision problems and some basic concepts for characterizing decision situations. We consider well-structured problems in this section, since in the remainder of the chapter the emphasis is on ill-structured problems. Sections 3, 4, and 5 comprise the main part of the chapter in that they present and discuss strategies for coping with the main types of decision environments. Section 3 deals with decisions in uncertain environments, Section 4 with decisions in complex environments, and Section 5 with decisions in conflict environments. The classes of decision strategies presented in the sub-sections (e.g., 3.1) of Sections 3 through 5 are in order of action-oriented involvement of the decision maker in his environment from the very minimal involvement represented by strategies for modifying perceptual processes, to the somewhat greater involvement required in strategies for information seeking, and to the more extreme involvement required of strategies demanding structural modification of the decision environment.

While we naturally discuss in the earlier

sections characteristics of the decision maker that affect responses in these environments, we treat some of the decision maker's primary characteristics in more detail in Section 6. Even though, for convenience, we often speak of the "decision maker," we include, in both Section 6 and the earlier sections, the characteristics and strategies of multiple decision makers. Section 7 presents a brief summary.

SECTION 2. THE DECISION PROBLEM

The type of decision problem, the nature of the decision environment, and the current state of the decision maker dictate the strategy required for a solution. In this section, we will examine some of these preconditions which must be considered before initiating problem solving activity. The concept of problem structure includes the decision maker's extent of familiarity with the initial state, the desired terminal state, and the transformations appropriate for bridging the gap between these states. We will examine response strategies for well-structured problems in this section since these problems can generally be solved by using some type of standard algorithm and involve few of the strategies we shall consider throughout this chapter. Most of the strategies we discuss involve the more complex ill-structured problems.

2.1 Preconditions for Problem Solving

Reitman (1964) and other information processing theorists represent decision problems by a three component vector $(A, B, \rightarrow)$. The first component, A, represents the *initial* or *existing state;* the second component represents the *terminal* or *desired state;* while the third component, $\rightarrow$, represents *transformations* that may be applied to the states in order to move from one state to another. The initial state is the current state of the decision maker, or the resources that he has available; the terminal state is the target or goal that the decision maker is

trying to attain; and the transformations (also called *decision alternatives* or *operators*) are the processes or steps by which the decision maker can move from the initial state to the terminal state. In a chess game, for example, the initial state is the current position of your pieces and those of your opponent, while the terminal state (your goal) is to checkmate your opponent. The transformations are the sequences of legal chess moves you can make. In a personnel decision problem, the terminal state may be the complete staffing of a new department; the initial state is the current status of in-company availabilities, the condition of the employment market, etc.; and the transformations are the steps that can be taken to staff the department.

The existence of a *gap between the existing state and the desired state* is a necessary condition for the existence of a decision problem. Obviously, a decision problem does not exist if the initial state and the terminal state are identical.

Viewing decision problems in terms of existing and desired states implies that decision problems are subjective and relative to the decision maker we are considering. Thus, while one person may see a "gap" between the existing and desired states, another person may not. For instance, some people may believe that the current income distribution in this country is far from ideal and hence a decision problem exists; others, however, may find the income distribution completely satisfactory and may not consider it a decision problem.

Even though a *gap* is necessary for a decision problem to exist, there are several other conditions which determine whether you accept the situation as a decision problem for you to resolve. First, you must *be aware of the gap*. Perhaps the morale in your organization is low; however, if you are unaware of this fact, you do not have a decision problem to solve. In fact, it is not uncommon for some decision makers to deliberately avoid information that they know would raise some issue they would prefer to avoid. They do not expect the problem to go away, but if they refuse to confront it, at least they will not be involved.

Second, you must be motivated to resolve the problem. If you give a friend a chess problem of the form "white to mate in four moves," he may be aware that there is a gap between the terminal state (checkmate) and the initial state (the current board configuration), but if he does not care about reducing the gap, he would not view this as a decision problem. Clearly, there are many situations in the world in which you could be aware of a gap between an initial state and a terminal state, but for most of them you would not be motivated to try to reduce the gap. This suggests that if you are studying a particular gap (say, the pollution in Lake Erie) and particular decision makers (say, the governments of Ontario and Ohio), you should evaluate the possible self- and non-self-interests of the decision makers involved.

Finally, you need to have the *abilities* and *resources to resolve* the decision problem in order for it to be a meaningful decision problem for you. You may feel that certain international hostilities represent a gap that you would like to resolve, but unless you hold some major world policy making position, you do not have the ability to resolve the situation. Hence this is not a decision problem for you.

These conditions suggest that when we are considering a decision problem, we ask: (a) Is there a gap between the existing state and the desired state (for this decision maker)? (b) Is the decision maker aware of the gap? (c) Is the decision maker motivated to resolve the gap? (d) Does the decision maker have the resources to resolve the gap? (MacCrimmon, 1973a).

2.2 Problem Structure and the Decision Environment

A decision situation may seem well-structured or ill-structured, depending on the extent to which the decision maker feels he is familiar with the initial state, the terminal state, or the transformations necessary to get from one state to the other. If a decision maker is confronted with a decision problem in which he is familiar with the initial state, the desired state, and the transformations, then he is dealing with a well-structured (or well-defined, or programmed) problem. Suppose, for example, a decision maker wants to specify the wage rate for a new employee. This is a routine, repetitive situation for which the decision maker has standard operating procedures (SOPs): he uses the standard attributes to classify the employee and thus determines the wage rate. At the other extreme are situations in which the decision maker is unfamiliar with the existing state, the desired state, or the set of relevant transformations. In these situations, the decision maker is confronting ill-structured (or ill-defined, or unprogrammed) problems for which he will need innovative responses.

In between these extremes are situations in which the decision maker is familiar with only part of the decision problem. The extent of the decision maker's knowledge will generally determine how he goes about handling decision situations in this middle area. If, for example, he is very familiar with the initial state, but unfamiliar with the desired state or the necessary transformations, he may tend to make incremental moves out from his current location, testing to see if he is moving in the right direction.

If, on the other hand, he is familiar with the desired state, but unfamiliar with the initial state or the relevant set of transformations, he may tend to project backward from the familiar desired state to see if he can generate the set of transformations that will lead to his initial state; that is, he applies transformations in reverse.

If a decision maker is very familiar with a set of transformations that he has used in the past, he may try to specify the initial state and the desired state in such a way that he can apply these previously used transformations. Hence, a management consulting firm specializing in method X may tend to view most decision problems it confronts as ones requiring method X.

In each of these situations, then, the decision maker might apply his past experiences to the problem he currently confronts.

Responses to Well-Structured Problems

The responses appropriate for solving well-structured problems involve the application of standard transformations, such as the algorithms and heuristics found in program libraries. March and Simon (1958) have emphasized that routine responses can be viewed as programs comparable to computer programs. That is, when a situation arises for which a particular program seems appropriate, this program is called forth from the program library, applied to the situation, and returned to the program library to be called upon again when a similar situation arises. In organizations, the program library may exist only in the heads of the participants, or it may be written down in the form of individual memos, standard operating procedures, or organizational manuals. March and Simon (1958) and Cyert and March (1963) discuss the efficacy of these standard operating procedures in business and public organizations. Such programs serve to minimize the variability in organizational response by assuring that different participants in particular roles will carry out a standard series of operations (Cyert & MacCrimmon, 1968). An excellent description of how the U.S. Forest Service uses elaborate sets of programs as routine responses is given by Kaufman (1960).

Standard responses may take the form of algorithms or heuristics. An algorithm is a set of standard operations that *guarantees* a solution to a problem in a finite number of steps. Heuristics, which may be compared to rules of thumb, are procedures or outlines for seeking solutions. Although heuristics are relatively easy to use and have frequently proven effective in solving previous prob-

lems, they do *not guarantee* success. Nevertheless, even in programmed decisions where algorithms could conceivably be developed, it may be advantageous to develop heuristics that provide satisfactory solutions rather than spend the extra effort on generating and operating algorithms. In chess-playing programs, for example, reliance must be placed on heuristics such as "give priority to moves which leave the opponent with the least possible number of replies" (de Groot, 1965; Newell & Simon, 1972).

Heuristic programming can assist decision makers in a wide range of complex problems. Smith (1968), for example, has developed a simulation of the heuristics used in selecting and placing personnel. Because they are computationally simple and flexible with respect to parameters, heuristics have also proven useful in choosing warehouse locations. Using heuristics such as "locate regional warehouse near concentrations of demand," Kuehn and Hamburger (1963) developed a heuristic program that compared quite favorably to the linear programming solution to the problem. For an excellent overview of the use of heuristics, see Newell and Simon (1972).

Responses to Ill-Structured Problems

In organizations, most of the important decision problems are of the ill-structured variety. Ill-structured problems demand that the decision maker exert greater efforts to find effective strategies for solving them. Consequently, in this chapter our discussion of problem solving and decision making will deal mainly with ill-structured problems. We will examine the strategies appropriate for solving ill-structured problems under the three conditions of the decision environment which seem to contribute most strongly to ill-structuredness: uncertainty, complexity, and conflict. For a more complete discussion of environmental factors, see MacCrimmon (1970).

Decision making under uncertainty is represented by situations in which the decision maker (a) does not know which events affecting his outcomes will occur, (b) does not know the causal links in the environment, (c) has little control over the environment, or (d) is in an unstable environment. Most studies of decision making in uncertain environments are categorized under the heading of (statistical) decision theory. In Section 3 of this chapter, we shall draw upon Bayesian statistics and decision analysis, which deal with situation (a). We will also discuss other studies that suggest decision strategies for dealing with an uncertain environment.

Decision making under complexity is represented by situations in which the environment is (a) very large, (b) very heterogeneous, (c) very abstract, or (d) very interconnected. The areas of multi-attribute decision making, information processing theories, and group decision making have all provided useful studies of decision making in complex environments. In Section 4, we shall attempt to derive from these studies decision strategies for dealing with complex environments.

Decision making under conflict is represented by multi-person situations in which interaction is necessary among units having different (a) goals or (b) preferred resource allocations. Most studies of conflict are categorized under the heading of game theory or group dynamics. In Section 5, we shall formulate some decision strategies for dealing with conflict environments.

SECTION 3. UNCERTAINTY

Since uncertainty, by definition, exists in decision situations involving only partial knowledge of relevant variables, most practical management decision situations are characterized by considerable uncertainty. The decision maker may be uncertain about the nature of the problem, and when, or even whether, he should try to resolve it; he may be uncertain about the alternative actions he can take and whether he has the resources to carry them out; he may be uncertain about what exogenous events will occur and how they will affect the outcomes. In each of these cases, to say that uncertainty exists is analogous to saying that there is a lack of appropriate information.[2]

Such uncertainty may be analyzed in terms of the strategies that the decision maker can apply when he has only partial knowledge of the decision environment, and yet possesses the potential for reducing uncertainty in events due to determinant (non-chance) factors. It would be useful for the decision maker to distinguish between the elements which are within his control, those over which he could potentially acquire control, and those which are clearly uncontrollable. The partially controllable elements can be decomposed into their controllable and uncontrollable components (Howard, 1971). Since there is no uncertainty in the controllable factors, attempts to reduce uncertainty could focus on the factors which are not under the decision maker's complete control.

Control over uncertain elements is attained at a cost. Among the costs considered by Mack's (1971) "planning on uncertainty" approach are (1) uncertainty discounting costs (e.g., the differential price of person-to-person and station-to-station telephone calls), (2) costs incurred when the stress of facing uncertainty causes the decision maker's behavior to deteriorate, and (3) costs resulting from attempts to implement actions for reducing uncertainty.

The strategies we describe in this section can be viewed as attempts by the decision maker to reduce some aspect of uncertainty and, thereby, increase his control over the elements in the decision environment for a cost he is willing to pay.

The strategies for reducing uncertainty

---

[2] An early partitioning of uncertainty was into "measurable" uncertainty and "unmeasurable" uncertainty (Knight, 1920). This distinction has not proved fruitful and it is clear that management decisions involve use of experience, judgment, and available information to assign subjective probabilities under conditions of incomplete information (MacCrimmon, 1973b).

are discussed here in the general order of the degree of the decision maker's direct involvement with the decision situation. In this vein, they can be classified according to whether their intent is to reduce the decision maker's *perception* of uncertainty, model the uncertainty, reduce uncertainty by alternative generation and testing, reduce uncertainty by obtaining more complete information, or reduce uncertainty by changing adverse consequences. Uncertainty can also be reduced through such strategies as bargaining, negotiation, and collusion, but, since these strategies have more direct application in decision environments involving conflict, discussion of them is deferred until Section 5.

3.1 Strategies for Reducing Perceptions of Uncertainty

The strategies in this class represent conscious or unconscious attempts to ignore or bias decision makers' perceptions of uncertainty. These strategies do not reduce uncertainty by providing more complete information about the decision environment, nor do they necessitate gauging the magnitude of the uncertainty. Instead, the decision maker may (1) ignore or avoid uncertainty, (2) reduce the uncertainty to certainty, (3) delay, or (4) absorb the uncertainty. We shall examine each of these in turn.

Ignore or Avoid Uncertainty

Psychologists have studied people's aversion to ambiguity and uncertainty (Adorno et al., 1950; Rokeach, 1960). Results indicated that uncertainty beyond a particular level creates considerable anxiety. One way of obviating or reducing this anxiety is simply to ignore the more uncertain parts of the decision environment. Kates (1962) and White (1964), for example, describe how residents of flood plain areas disregard the threat of floods unless the floods occur so regularly that they cannot be ignored.

Cyert and March (1963) have reported a similar phenomenon: some business firms avoid uncertainty by neglecting to consider sources of uncertainty. To some extent this neglect may be due to an inability to consider all the potential sources of uncertainty, but when it occurs for major influences (e.g., wage-price controls) on the firm's decisions, then probably an avoidance strategy is being used.

Reduce to Certainty

It is uncommon for the decision maker to completely avoid important uncontrollable variables; however, it is not uncommon for the decision maker to act as if the uncertain events are more certain than they really are. Business firms, for example, may behave as though competitors' prices, interest rates, antitrust policy, etc. are going to be exactly the same in the future as they have been in the past, even though they may already have evidence to the contrary (Cournot, 1897; Cyert & DeGroot, 1970). This tendency has also been noted in a dynamic computer software firm (Carter, 1971).

Even though a decision maker may be willing to admit that occurrence of a particular event is uncertain, he may, after choosing an action, tend to convince himself that the event leading to more favorable outcomes for his chosen action will occur (Cyert & March, 1963).

A similar phenomenon was described by Festinger and his associates (1957, 1964) in their studies of post-decision dissonance reduction. They found that post-decision regret can change the desirability of the decision alternatives and can even result in a selective information search to strengthen these biases. Although this finding appears to have direct implications for managerial decisions, the results of the numerous studies investigating selective exposure to information within the cognitive dissonance framework should be interpreted with caution. In a review of these research efforts, Abelson (1968) has indicated a number of weaknesses that would limit the generalization of these findings to managerial decision making.

Delay

Strategies involving a delayed decision may sometimes be wise since some of the uncertainty may be resolved by waiting (Barnard, 1938); however, such strategies are appropriate only for very limited situations. Since delaying a choice of action while waiting for uncertainty to resolve itself also represents a decision alternative, the decision maker must be prepared to take any opportunity loss that results from not selecting a more adaptive alternative. Under most conditions, it seems a better strategy to base a decision upon the most complete information that can be feasibly obtained, keeping in mind that the course of action chosen may still involve monitoring the bothersome source of uncertainty.

Absorb Uncertainty

Still another way organizations may avoid perception of uncertainty is through "uncertainty absorption." As information is acquired, it is passed along to the various decision making units involved. During this transmittal process, the information tends to lose some of its uncertainty and become more precise—that is, a specious precision arises. Key decision making units further along the transmittal line often do not learn of the high degree of uncertainty that really exists. How this process operates in business firms is described by Woods (1966).

Knowledge of this phenomenon should alert the business manager to ways in which its effects could be detected and reduced. Although little is known about the specific causes of this distortion, it would appear to be a very pervasive tendency. Whenever information is transmitted from those who develop it to those who must use it as a basis for making decisions, this distortion may be likely to occur, and, when precise information is important, care should be exercised to ensure that the users are acquainted

with the degree of uncertainty residing in the information (e.g., the conditions under which it was obtained, the precision of the instruments or techniques used).

3.2 Strategies for Modeling the Uncertainty

A more direct response to uncertainty than the avoidance-type responses involves recognizing uncertainty and attempting to take account of it. This may range from trying solely to model the uncertain aspects of the environment to more action-oriented strategies such as generating alternatives, acquiring information, or actually trying to change possible adverse consequences.

Modeling the uncertain environment by identifying the uncertain variables, and systematizing any information that can lead to a better understanding of these variables, can provide assistance in coping with uncertainty. In modeling uncertainty, we may encounter two different situations. In the first, we are dealing with an uncertain variable that recurs over time—but we do not know what values it will take on. Levels of GNP, cost of living changes, and number of days lost per month due to strikes are examples of such variables. The common and useful approach involves a search for patterns and the application of models of varying sophistication to make projections. In the second situation we are dealing with unique events. Obviously we cannot discover patterns, but we can assign subjective probabilities to monitor the consistency of beliefs and to serve as inputs for later, more decision-oriented strategies.

Identify Patterns and Use Time-Series Forecasts

To cope with uncertain events, continued attempts are made to identify patterns and to fit occurrences into a simple model. Because the mind's processing capacity is limited, small numbers of concepts are used and instances are classified into a category, even though information suggesting an inappropriate classification may be suppressed (Bruner, Goodnow, & Austin, 1956). The extent of such classification depends on the cognitive complexity of the decision maker, as will be discussed in Section 6.

People tend to assign patterns even when they know they are dealing with a random process. Feldman (1963) has described the patterns that people insist they find in randomly generated sequences of binary digits. Some gamblers insist that sequences occur in spins of a roulette wheel, and the particular tendency to expect alternation (i.e., to think black is more likely if a sequence of reds has just appeared) is labeled as the "gambler's fallacy."

Even people willing to accept the concept of random processes are subject to biases in the patterns they expect. For example, to most people the order of births of boys and girls, GBBGBG, seems more likely to occur than the sequence BBBGGG, since it seems "more random." Similarly, in six tosses of a coin, only the sequence HTTHTH may appear really random. In distributing twenty marbles randomly, the distribution 4,4,5,4,3 may seem more likely than 4,4,4,4,4. Tversky and Kahneman (1974) provide an interesting discussion of these and other fallacies.

In modeling uncertain events, then, a decision maker should be wary of imputing a pattern to a random process. If it really is a random process, it is extremely unlikely to have a regular pattern, but on the other hand, it may not "look" random.

When we are dealing with a system in which we expect some regularities, though, it is reasonable to try to identify patterns. For example, yearly sales or unemployment rates change in systematic ways that can be discovered and utilized to reduce uncertainty.

A variety of techniques is available for dealing with time-series data. The most common is a moving average which weights a set of the most recent observations. Somewhat more sophisticated is the exponential smoothing method, which gives more weight to recent observations. Other more general methods are also available—see Chambers, Mullick, and Smith (1971) for a good discussion. Careful use of these techniques involves a separation of seasonal, cyclical, trend, and growth in trend effects. These methods are quite good for short-term forecasts but are poor for reducing uncertainty over the longer run. In the information acquisition sub-sections of this section and the next, we shall examine some strategies for longer run forecasting and the subsequent uncertainty reduction.

In dealing with manpower flows, using past transitions among jobs to build up a matrix of frequency of movement can be very useful in coping with uncertainty of future changes. Vroom and MacCrimmon (1968) describe the use of such a Markov chain model in an actual application.

Compute the Amount of Uncertainty

To determine how much information is needed to handle uncertainty, it is first necessary to try to identify how much uncertainty exists in the environment. If many possible events can occur and they all seem equally likely, then a high degree of uncertainty exists. On the other hand, if there are only a small number of possible events, or if one or two events are much more likely than any others, then, of course, less uncertainty exists. The amount of uncertainty existing is approximated by the number of yes/no answers that would be needed to remove all uncertainty (assuming a binary code). The expression giving the amount of uncertainty is: $H(x) = -\sum_i p(x_i) \log_2 p(x_i)$. For psychologically oriented discussions see Attneave (1959) and Garner (1962).

Assign Subjective Probabilities

In any situation involving uncertainty, the decision maker will have some beliefs about the events which may occur. With no extensive past history on which to make judgments of frequency of occurrence, he may only have a vague feeling about the events. Nevertheless, these beliefs will determine his choices, and, therefore, he should try to reflect upon these beliefs and examine them for consistency and correctness.

This externalization of beliefs may be done by attempting to assign subjective probabilities to events. For example, a subjective probability of 0.2 could be assigned to the event that a company's finances will necessitate cutting the work force next year. Since these numbers are probabilities, they have to obey the usual properties of probabilities. For example, from the above data the probability of conditions *not* requiring a cut in the work force must be 0.8.

Any set of consistent beliefs can be assigned subjective probabilities; however, to be assigned subjective probabilities, an event need not have an extensive record of frequencies, as in mortality tables. The very process of attempting to satisfy the consistency requirements of subjective probabilities can pinpoint inconsistent beliefs, and hence allow a decision maker an opportunity to make changes (de Finetti, 1964; Roberts, 1968; Savage, 1954).

Various biases have been found in the assignment of subjective probabilities. Often a decision maker is too confident in his beliefs and hence uses too narrow a distribution of values; for example, he may put too little probability in the tails for outlying values (Alpert & Raiffa, 1969). A decision maker often assigns too low a value to a high fractile of the distribution (for example, to what percentage increase in sales next year would you assign 9:1 odds of the actual sales being less than this figure), and hence inconsistencies can arise when going back and forth between the uncertain variables and the probability values (Tversky & Kahneman, 1971). Decision makers also tend to underestimate the probability of very likely events and overestimate the probability of rare events (Preston & Baratta, 1948). With these biases in mind, though, a person can monitor his subjective probabilities to assure that they are internally consistent and that they do reflect his true beliefs.

In any decision problem there will be many variables or events about which the decision maker is uncertain. Trying to assign subjective probabilities to each of them and then combine them would lead to a very complex model. The decision maker, then, has to exercise some judgment about which variables he treats as uncertain. This could be done by making some preliminary sensitivity analyses (Matheson, 1969).

Various methods exist for the assessment of subjective probabilities. The decision maker might directly assign a value. Alternatively, he might be assisted by associating the event with some partition of a random device—for example, tickets in a lottery, numbers, or sectors on a wheel (Pratt, Raiffa, & Schlaifer, 1965). In order to induce him to think about, and provide, his true beliefs, scoring rules have been suggested. These rules can be set up in repeatable processes which reward good estimates (or punish poor ones) by financial incentives. These rules use particular mathematical forms (e.g., quadratic or logarithmic forms) to determine the payoffs. For details, see Toda (1963) and Stäel von Holstein (1970). Interesting applications to weather forecasting and football pools are found in Roberts (1968), Winkler and Murphy (1968), and Winkler (1971).

3.3 Strategies for Reducing Uncertainty by Alternative Generation and Testing

When the decision maker is uncertain about the available courses of action, he requires strategies for developing appropriate alternatives. He often needs not only *more* alternatives, but also "creative"[3] alternatives.

---

[3] By creative alternatives we mean courses of action which, in addition to being *original* (statistically improbable or infrequent), meet the criteria of *relevance* and *practicality*. This distinction will be emphasized as we examine the products obtained by using the strategies for developing quality decision alternatives.

Strategies examined in this sub-section reduce uncertainty by helping to generate and to test high quality alternatives which will provide a sound basis for choice. Brainstorming and synectics are strategies which assist the decision maker in generating courses of action; simulating the results of these actions provides a preliminary test of their adequacy for solving the problem. It should be noted that in their emphasis on contiguity of remote ideas, morphology and relational algorithms bear similarities to the alternative generation strategies discussed in this sub-section. The former strategies are more appropriately included in our discussion of complex decision environments (Section 4) since their major value is for relating, in novel configurations, components of decision alternatives already known to the decision maker.

Brainstorm

Brainstorming, advanced by Osborn (1941), uses group participation to facilitate the generation of creative decision alternatives. In this strategy an unstructured group works together to develop a list of alternative solutions to a decision problem. To encourage free expression, the group works under three rules: (1) ideas are freely expressed without considering their quality, (2) group members are encouraged to modify and combine previously stated ideas, and (3) a moratorium is placed on the evaluation of ideas until all ideas have been stated.

It seems clear, however, that in producing both unique ideas and high quality ideas, the pooled efforts of individuals working in isolation are superior to the ideas of brainstorming groups (Dunnette et al., 1963; Taylor et al., 1958). With regard to the total number of ideas produced, the research evidence is mixed. Findings from a study by Cohen and his associates (1960) support Osborn's original assumption that the presence of other group members will stimulate the production of ideas in the brainstorming sessions. The studies by Taylor and others

(1958) and by Dunnette and others (1963), on the other hand, indicated that the pooled efforts of four individuals resulted in a greater number of ideas than did the actual brainstorming groups. A tentative resolution of these contradictory findings is suggested by Shaw (1971). He cites a study by Rosenbaum (1967) which provides evidence that the key may be the length of the work period; that is, with extended work periods, brainstorming groups tend to produce a greater number of ideas than do individuals. This led Shaw to conclude that groups tend to produce indefinitely, whereas individuals may "run dry." Vroom and Maier (1961), on the other hand, have suggested that group interaction in brainstorming may facilitate the process of evaluating alternatives more than it facilitates generating alternatives.

In addition to information about the productivity of individuals versus a group, some evidence has been obtained regarding the value of withholding evaluation of alternatives, changing the decision context, familiarity among group members, and deferring judgment. Instructing participants to "avoid criticism" and to "use your imagination" seems to increase the number of decision alternatives generated, but not their quality (Levy, 1968; Manski & Davis, 1968). Changing the decision context so that the subject must relate previously unrelated ideas (e.g., instructing subjects to list various ways an item can be used in a new situation) appears to be very effective in generating creative alternatives (Davis & Manski, 1966). Finally, forming cohesive groups appears to be more effective than using non-cohesive groups in generating alternatives (Cohen et al., 1960).

Use Synectics

In the synectics approach (Gordon, 1961; Prince, 1968), a carefully selected and trained group led by an experienced leader views the problem situation in various ways until they discover an innovative solution. Although the procedure incorporates a structure of eight "phases" from problem statement through solution, it is most useful in decision situations requiring creative decision alternatives. To generate such alternatives, the procedure forces participants to depart from the usual ways of thinking. By requiring the participants to use analogies, the procedure "makes the familiar strange." To free the participants from looking at the commonplace in a commonplace way, the procedure requires them to play the role of some element in the problem (e.g., a broken machine). In addition, they are asked to make direct analogies between the present problem and nature (e.g., the ability of chameleons and flounders to change color), to make symbolic analogies (e.g., mathematical models), and to make fantasy analogies (e.g., demons and elves).

In many respects, the synectics approach differs sharply from brainstorming. It is more structured, with a repeatable set of stages for both generating creative solutions through use of analogies and for choosing the most favorable alternative to recommend to management. As such, it requires evaluation of alternatives as they are generated. Moreover, it is not a do-it-yourself project for an organization. The selection interviews, the contrived situational tests, and the intensive training program would require most organizations to seek assistance. In both selection and training of group members, efforts must be made to form a cohesive unit. Cohesiveness is then increased by having members live together and work together, and finally, with the consent of other group members, a formal leader emerges from the group to coordinate intragroup efforts and to interact with management.

No formal study has determined whether, in fact, synectics is more effective than brainstorming in generating creative decision alternatives, nor would it seem to be a fruitful line of research. Selecting promising features of each technique, investigating their effectiveness, and combining them into an eclectic creative programming procedure would provide a stronger empirical base for recommending strategies.

Simulate Results

Although generating a large number of alternatives can help to reduce uncertainty, it cannot resolve the uncertainty about the effect of these alternatives. A very direct way to test the effect of the alternatives is to apply each alternative to a model of the uncertain situation. By conducting experiments on the model of the environment, the consequences can be anticipated, and the uncertainties can be more readily managed. Such simulations are necessarily crude approximations of what might happen, but they allow a large number of alternatives to be tried out—a procedure that is usually impractical in the real problem (Churchman, Ackoff, & Arnoff, 1957). Different values that the uncertain variables take on can be tried out and their effects on each alternative noted (Hertz, 1964, 1968). In these simulation models, then, the model of uncertain variables in the environment (Section 3.2) and the generated alternatives (from above) can come together to reduce uncertainty for the decision maker (Howard, 1968).

3.4 Strategies for Reducing Uncertainty by Information Acquisition

Uncertainty can be reduced by acquiring and processing more information. Under conditions of high uncertainty and problem importance, a decision maker may experience a state of conflict-induced arousal that activates quest for knowledge (e.g., Berlyne, 1962).[4] Behavioral scientists have generated

---

[4] According to Berlyne's theory of curiosity (1960), the strength of the acquisition response varies in an inverted U-shaped function with the degree of conflict produced by a choice situation. Conflict, in turn, is assumed to increase with both uncertainty and importance of the choice. The effect of uncertainty on information acquisition has generally been supported by research (e.g., Driscoll & Lanzetta, 1965; Lanzetta &

a sizable body of literature to describe the information acquisition behaviors of decision makers; a few of these studies are examined in Section 6 of this chapter. However, because this research is basically descriptive, it is of limited use in prescribing decision making strategies. Consequently, the strategies examined in the following subsection are derived from normative theories of information. They include using Bayesian probability revision, collecting information economically, and using economic team theory.

Use Bayesian Probability Revision

A strategy for prescribing the optimal impact that additional information should have on a decision maker's judgment of initially uncertain decision outcomes uses Bayes's theorem (Bayes, 1763). Basically, the strategy specifies that opinions should be represented as personal (subjective) probabilities and that Bayes's theorem should be used to determine optimal revision of opinions in the face of additional information. Bayes's theorem states that when two hypotheses are being considered, the posterior odds (i.e., the ratio of the two probabilities after the information) are proportional to the product of the prior odds and the likelihood ratio.

The extent to which actual information processing behavior departs systematically from the optimal Bayesian strategy has been investigated by psychological researchers. The most pervasive deviation of actual behavior from the optimal Bayesian revision is the decision maker's tendency toward "conservatism." When exposed to additional information, subjects typically revise their posterior probability estimates in the direction specified by the optimal strategy, but the revision is too small. The subjects act as though the data are less diagnostic than the

Kanareff, 1962; Long & Ziller, 1965), while evidence regarding the effect of problem importance has been mixed (e.g., Freedman & Sears, 1965; Hawkins & Lanzetta, 1965; Lanzetta & Driscoll, 1968).

Bayesian model would specify. In some studies (e.g., Peterson & Miller, 1965; Phillips & Edwards, 1966), the deviations were quite marked, sometimes requiring nine observations to revise judgments as much as the optimal strategy would specify for one observation.

The reason for conservatism on the part of decision makers has been hotly debated, with three alternative explanations being put forward by Edwards (1968): (1) misperception (failure to understand the basis for generating the data and its likelihood), (2) mis-aggregation (failure to put together the pieces of information into a single response), and (3) artifact or "response bias" (inability of subjects to adequately deal with responses outside the odds range from 1:10 to 10:1). Studies of the cause of the conservatism have not concluded that one of these three explanations is more valid. Rapoport and Wallsten (1972) suggest that the conservatism may be influenced as much by the measures that have been used (i.e., responses are not always systematically related to the Bayesian probabilities, since they do not vary monotonically with the physical characteristics of the stimuli) as by the decision maker's behavior. They suggest, therefore, that aspects of the system other than just Bayesian probabilities should be given closer attention.

Concern for conservatism and other inefficiencies in human information acquisition has led to the use of the Probabilistic Information Processing System (PIP) to assist decision makers in applying the Bayesian approach. The PIP, introduced by Edwards and his associates (1962, 1966, 1968), is a man-machine system in which the decision makers estimate likelihood ratios, and a computer aggregates these across data and across hypotheses according to Bayes's theorem. Edwards and Phillips (1964) advocated the PIP as a technique for improving both the speed and accuracy of diagnosis in traditional military and business command and control systems. Its advantages include the capacity to screen information for relevance, to filter out noise, to apply appropriate weight to each information element, and to specify an optimal procedure for extracting all the certainty available in the information. Moreover, it enables the decision maker and the computer to complement each other by appropriately using the talents of each.

The PIP system has generally been applied to military problems (e.g., Kaplan & Newman, 1966), but systems have been experimentally tested in realistically complex environments (Edwards et al., 1968; Phillips, 1966). The PIP has also been proposed for use in probation decisions (McEachern & Newman, 1969) and in medicine (Gustafson, 1969; Gustafson et al., 1969; Lusted, 1968). For excellent reviews of the Bayesian probability revision literature, see Slovic and Lichtenstein (1971) and Rapoport and Wallsten (1972).

Collect Information Economically

In a decision problem that is systematically organized into (1) events that may occur, and (2) actions that are available to the decision maker, it is possible to identify the best action to use for each possible event. If the values of these outcomes are then weighted by the probability of each of the possible events and added together, we obtain the expected value under certainty. The expected value of the best action represents the best we can do under the uncertain situation that exists. The difference between these two numbers gives "the expected value of perfect information" or thus serves as a completely accurate clairvoyant (Howard, 1966; Schlaifer, 1959). Even though the chance of acquiring such perfect information is rare, the concept is interesting because it represents an upper bound on what should be paid for any information.

In a personnel situation, for example, the number of people to be hired and trained may depend on which particular contracts are acquired over the next year. If the employer must make the hiring and training decision now, he could estimate the probabilities of acquiring various contracts and choose a policy which would attain the best expected or average benefit. This would be thought of as the best he could do under uncertainty (at the given information level). The "cost of uncertainty" (another name for the expected value of perfect information) could be estimated by taking all possible combinations of contracts in hand over the next year. For each of these situations, he could identify the best action to take under each contingency. The difference between each of these (absolute) best actions and the yield of his averaged best action when it is multiplied by the corresponding probabilities of those contingencies and the products are added together, gives the cost of uncertainty in not having more information about which contracts will be obtained. If this cost of uncertainty is very high, then perhaps by analysis or by overt information collection he can learn what is likely to occur and modify his hiring policy accordingly.

It is also possible to calculate the value of imperfect information, but the computation is much more difficult. The concept is simple, though, in that one still anticipates the best action (given the information) and weights this by a probability—in this case the probability is influenced by the diagnosticity of the information. By using these procedures, it is possible to calculate the optimal amount of information to collect to reduce uncertainty. In general, of course, it does not pay to keep collecting information, since at some point the net expected gain from having more information exceeds the cost of collecting it (Marschak, 1968). For some interesting marketing applications, see Newman (1971).

Use Optimal Team Communication

The economic theory of teams, developed primarily by Marschak (1955, 1959, 1968) and Radner (1959, 1961, 1962) and treated excellently in their book (Marschak & Radner, 1972), is a particularly well-developed normative theory of information flows in multiple-person situations in uncertain environments. It extends expected utility theory to a multiple-person situation in which no conflict of interest exists among participants. The theory focuses on three main problems: (1) how organizational members should make observations on the uncertain environment confronting the organization, (2) what communication channels and messages should be utilized to communicate this information to other members, and (3) what actions each member should take based on the information he receives. The first two issues are grouped together into the organization's "information structure," while the last one represents the organization's "decision rule."

At this point, the formal theory and algorithms are difficult to apply to real organizations, yet team theory is useful in specifying organizational communication strategy. It advocates communicating information only if the recipient will actually use the information—and not just use it, but use it to yield an increased payoff sufficient to justify the cost of the communication. Noting the decisions that follow from communication reveals that some seemingly paradoxical recommendations can arise; for example, one person may be advised not to take advantage of what seems to him a very favorable situation, since his involvement will reduce the payoff to the members considered as a whole (Marschak, 1959). In an experiment in which managers recommended optimal organizational designs for a hypothetical sugar plantation, MacCrimmon (1974) identified a variety of information processing heuristics and information-handling fallacies that occur in real situations. Such fallacies included collecting too much information, sending information that was not used, specifying communication when no provision was made for the proposed sender to acquire the information

in the first place, and having more information processors than is optimal—the "too many cooks" syndrome. The team theory framework of the experiment allowed these behaviors to be isolated and analyzed.

In simple situations, then, team theory offers the opportunity of computing optimal strategies for dealing with communications about uncertain environments; in more complex situations it offers a conceptual orientation toward monitoring behavior and avoiding information-communication fallacies.

3.5 Strategies for Reducing Uncertainty by Changing Adverse Consequences

Strategies of this class may help a decision maker cope with uncertainty by reducing the risk incurred in committing his resources. Essentially, these strategies operate through two mechanisms: (1) they diffuse the responsibility for the risky decision by reducing the potential loss (or gain) resulting from the decision, or (2) they build up a capacity to respond to the potentially adverse consequences.

Diffuse Responsibility

One approach to uncertainty is to try to affect the probabilities, either by increasing the probability of gain or by decreasing the probability of loss. Another approach is to attempt to affect the payoffs, either by increasing the size of the possible gains or by decreasing the size of the possible losses.

In investment decisions, for example, the main strategy for affecting the overall probabilities of gains and losses is through diversification. Investments are diversified by consolidating the various individual components into a portfolio which lacks the extreme probabilities of aggregate losses and gains. When companies hire employees with a wide range of talents, they are using diversification to make the consequences less disadvantageous in the face of uncertainty produced by unstable requirements for specific abilities.

For diversification to be effective, the components must be dissimilar; that is, they cannot be perfectly correlated. The most significant reduction of risk occurs when alternatives with high negative correlations can be matched (Borch, 1968; Markowitz, 1959).

The payoffs can also be affected through risk sharing agreements. No one decision maker may be willing to use an alternative which may possibly produce huge gains or huge losses, but if the losses (as well as the gains) can be broken into smaller amounts, then perhaps a group of decision makers (no one of which would have taken the alternative at the original scale) can be formed to share the risk (Raiffa, 1968). This type of risk sharing is particularly prevalent in reinsurance agreements (Borch, 1968). Risk sharing is also used by employer associations, which reduce risk from such potentially adverse outcomes as strike actions by employees of one firm.

Transfer Uncertainty

Uncertainty about future events may also be reduced by formal contractual arrangements (Cyert & March, 1963). Uncertainty about short-term fluctuations in prices and wage rates, for example, can be avoided by signing a longer-term contract with the suppliers of these resources. In commodities markets terms can be specified for the future purchase of goods even though the market price of those goods is highly uncertain. In most cases, though, the person attempting to avoid possible adverse consequences must pay a risk premium for the execution of these contracts. Life insurance, for instance, allows a person to avoid the adverse consequences of leaving his family with insufficient funds, but it also incurs a fairly high premium.

In most of these instances, uncertainty is transferred from one party to another. The one attempting to make his future environment more certain pays a fee (either directly or by offering more favorable contract terms) to the party willing to confront the uncertainty.

Adapt

Ackoff (1970) and Weick (1969) have discussed a strategy in which the decision maker ignores uncertainty in order to build up an adaptive capacity. Rather than devote resources to search and choice activities, the decision maker uses his resources to build up a capacity to respond quickly when action needs to be taken, no matter what values the uncertain variables take.

For example, when using an adaptive mode, you do not attempt to predict your competitor's prices and then choose an action, but rather you build up a flexible system and monitor his price movements so that you will be able to respond quickly when actions need to be taken. Similarly, an employer anticipating a possible labor dispute may prepare himself for the adverse consequences by building up an inventory. The strike may still occur, but the firm has reduced its adverse consequences. It should be noted that this strategy may also serve to strengthen the position of a decision maker in a high conflict environment.

SECTION 4. COMPLEXITY

The decision environments confronting managerial decision makers are typically quite complex in terms of both the sheer multiplicity of factors to be considered and the interconnections among the factors. Selection decisions, for example, may require identification and evaluation of a great many candidates, both within the organization and from outside. Each candidate must be considered in the light of a variety of capabilities, for example, mental ability, education, and physical skills, which are, as a rule, highly interrelated.

Experimental research in the laboratory and studies of ongoing organizations demonstrate that decision makers find complexity a major barrier to effective decision making. The use of simple strategies and devices which "prepackage" information (e.g., appeals to authority, expert opinion, rumors, common sense, stereotypes, or cultural biases) has been noted in decisions regarding governmental policy (Lindblom, 1965), military units (Wohlstetter, 1962), natural resource management (Kates, 1962), and business (Katona, 1951). The frequently observed tendency, however, of a decision maker to resort to overly simplistic strategies may reflect his limited capacity for information processing. The influence of cognitive limitations on decision strategies is examined in more detail in Section 6.

Complex decision environments require special strategies for specifying appropriate operators or decision alternatives. Such strategies are derived mainly from the cognitive process literature because the more formal literatures of decision making assume that the decision maker initially possesses an exhaustive list of feasible alternatives; thus, the latter approaches do not provide many useful concepts or techniques for specifying alternatives. In the majority of actual decisions, however, the alternative actions are far from obvious, and it takes great effort to generate alternatives that are feasible.

In discussing strategies for coping with complexity, we will continue to order the strategies in terms of the extent to which they actively involve the decision maker in reducing the complexity in the decision environment. Because modeling complexity (unlike modeling uncertainty) involves less of an action orientation than reducing perceptions of complexity, it will be discussed first. Other strategies, however, are discussed in an order which parallels that of Section 3. In addition to strategies for modeling complexity and reducing perceptions of complexity, we examine strategies for reducing complexity in diagnosing and specifying problems, in formulating decision alternatives, and in aggregating both information and preferences.

4.1 Strategies for Modeling Complexity

It is difficult to build meaningful models of complex environments because of their very nature. Because models are, of necessity, simplified representations, attempts to make them too complex defeat a major rationale for building them, namely, models can be manipulated more easily than the complex environment. For this reason, almost any model is a representation of something more complex than itself. There are, however, a few models that are specifically designed to deal with very complex systems. Input-output models and models attempting to exploit decomposable aspects of systems both use matrix representations and are designed to provide a better understanding of the interrelationships of very complex environments. Other models, especially those for aggregating preferences, are implicit in later sub-sections (4.6).

Develop Input-Output Models

Input-output models, developed by Leontief (1966) for macro-economic planning, systematically represent the interrelationships between the inputs and outputs of parts of a system (e.g., an economy or industry). Input-output formats have been presented as a convenient way to model complex environments in deterministic terms, but it should be noted that the model assumes a stable pattern of linear relationships between the various subsystems. Linearity facilitates manipulation of a large system of variables and equations, and the loss in accuracy which results from representation of nonlinear relationships through linear equations may be offset by the ability to enlarge and refine the model without surpassing the limits of computational feasibility. A major disadvantage of the input-output model is that a mistake in basic assumptions may void its usefulness for decision making, yet the degree of error is not readily discernable unless additional data, such as sensitivity of the model to assumptions, are provided.

In individual firms, input-output models have mainly been used to analyze production and sales patterns, but these models could be useful in other complex organizational processes, such as information flows.

Use Decomposable Matrices

Simon (1969) has suggested the use of decomposable matrices for modeling complexity in decision environments. In dealing with a complex structure, he advises decomposing it into semi-independent components corresponding to its many functional parts. This strategy is based on Simon's view of complex systems as being typically constructed as a hierarchy of levels in which the operation of the system at each level can be defined by describing its component functions.

Although the extremes of completely "decomposable" systems (i.e., no interactions among the mechanisms across functional components of a system) and completely "non-decomposable" systems (i.e., each variable is linked with almost equal strength to almost all other parts of the system) appear unlikely in social systems, a good many social systems would seem to be "nearly decomposable" (i.e., interactions among subsystems are weak but not negligible).

To reduce their complexity with comparatively little information loss, nearly decomposable systems can usually be represented as hierarchies. Since sub-parts belonging to different components of the system interact only weakly, the details of their interaction can be ignored. For example, it is not necessary to examine in detail the interaction of each member of one organization with each member of the second in order to study the interface of two organizations. The reduction in complexity attained by ignoring weakly related parts of a system's functional components brings the informational requirements of this task closer to the capabilities of human decision makers.

4.2 Strategies for Reducing Perceptions of Complexity

Strategies for reducing the decision maker's perceptions of environmental complexity recognize the human limitations involved in information processing. Because they were derived from observing the behaviors of decision makers attempting to cope with environmental complexity, these strategies (searching locally and applying disjointed incrementalism) make effective use of common tendencies observed among decision makers confronted with highly complex decision environments. In this sense, such strategies are descriptive rather than prescriptive.

Search Locally

Cyert and March (1963) have presented a strategy compatible with their view that both problem solving and searching for decision alternatives are "problem directed" since in problem solving the decision maker seeks immediate solutions in response to specific problems. The decision maker's search processes are usually directed toward simple models of causality and highly subjective perceptions of the decision situation; when he finds that the simple models fail to solve problems, then he is forced to turn to more complex models of causality.

Until learning modifies behavior, search for decision alternatives in organizations seems to be guided by two rules: (1) search in the neighborhood of problem symptoms (e.g., a department would first tend to look within its own activities to determine why it had failed to attain its goals) and (2) search in the neighborhood of the current alternative (e.g., begin by seeking similar policies to replace inadequate ones). These rules seem to imply that a decision maker looks for a cause near its effect and looks for a new solution near an old one.

Such an approach to problem solving represents an inappropriately simplistic perception of the typically complex decision environment of an organization, but Cyert and March point out that failure of local search can lead decision makers to more complex search strategies. In highly complex environments, the local search for decision alternatives seems inappropriately simple, and such a strategy is likely to fail. Although modification through trial and error learning may result in a more complex search strategy, this hit and miss procedure would possibly be a costly experience for an organization.

Apply Disjointed Incrementalism

The strategy of applying disjointed incrementalism (Braybrooke & Lindblom, 1963) may assist the decision maker in adapting to complex decision situations characterized by inadequately formulated values, strained cognitive capabilities, disorganized information base, and difficult cost analyses. The strategy does not attempt to examine the cognitive processes underlying decision making; instead, it attempts to reduce the demands made on decision makers in complex situations by prescribing a constructive approach for perceiving problems and for realistically restricting the number of decision alternatives and potential consequences of the alternatives to be considered.

The strategy does not require that the decision maker perceive the problem in terms of present states or desired states. Instead, the decision maker is advised to focus on increments or differences between consequences of the current policy or state and the relative consequences of the alternative actions or policies under consideration. The notion of "margin-dependent choice" implies that the decision maker need only be able to state how much of one value he is willing to sacrifice, at the margin existing in a given situation, to achieve an increment of another value (e.g., unemployment versus inflation). In this sense, the strategy of disjointed incrementalism is less demanding than more formal approaches which require ranking all alternative courses of action in order of preference. However, margin-dependent choice still requires that the major possible outcomes of many incrementally different decision alternatives be compared on a common scale.

The number of decision alternatives and consequences to be considered is reduced by retaining only those with detectable and incremental differences in their anticipated consequences. The number is also reduced in accordance with the decision maker's limited ability to generate alternatives, and on the basis of feasibility—that is, any alternative being considered must have the means for implementation. In practice, disjointed incrementalism involves a simultaneous development of means and ends and a long series of analyses and evaluations to incrementally modify policies as the decision environment changes.

This strategy represents a practical adaptation of decision making behavior to the complexities of social policy decisions. It accepts the fragmentation and disorder of highly complex decision environments and offers decision makers a cohesive assortment of practices for dealing with complexity due to (1) poor coordination among units analyzing and evaluating policy, (2) inability to clearly specify decision objectives, and (3) inability to consider an inordinate number of possible decision alternatives and their consequences.

4.3 Strategies for Reducing Complexity by Formulating Alternatives

Complexity in a decision environment hampers the ability of the decision maker to formulate decision alternatives. The multiplicity of elements (e.g., units, actions) with which he must contend creates the need for strategies offering systematic ways to recombine familiar elements into useful new solution alternatives. One promising approach is to use structured procedures for relating previously unrelated elements of the decision problem. Two strategies incorporating this feature, using morphology and the relational algorithm, are discussed in this section.

Use Morphology

Morphology (Wills et al., 1972; Zwicky & Wilson, 1965) provides a structured procedure for systematically relating combinations of factors to form new alternatives. It is based on the premise that the psychological set of decision makers makes them myopic in combining elements into unfamiliar solutions. Hence, decision makers are advised to follow a systematic program that will generate a large number of alternatives, most of which will be worthless but a few of which will hopefully be novel and important.

The morphological approach requires the decision maker to first identify the key dimensions of the solution. For example, if the problem involved developing an innovative program for recruiting college graduates, the decision maker may elect to examine all possible combinations of such elements as characteristics of potential recruits (e.g., degree level, degree program), recruiting media (advertising, visits to campus), assessment techniques (face-to-face interview, videotaped interview), interviewer (personnel department representative, operating manager, recent hiree), and interview location (in plant, on campus, both). For each of these dimensions, it is necessary to identify values, which are then taken in all possible combinations. In this case, one alternative may be to develop a college recruitment system which is focused on M.B.A.s and involves videotaped on-campus interviews conducted by a personnel department representative and viewed in the plant by the operating manager.

The advantage of using a systematic approach to relate elements of a complex decision environment is forced by this technique. Even with only a few attributes for each dimension, a very large number of combinations arises. By using this exhaustive strategy, the decision maker can formulate alternatives with little likelihood of neglecting important elements in the decision. For a discussion of more general aspects of morphological procedures, and some claims as to their applicability, see Zwicky (1969).

Use the Relational Algorithm

Another systematic procedure involving generation of combinations is the relational algorithm described by Crovitz (1970). To date, this approach has only been used for solving very simple laboratory problems (e.g., the two-string problem), but it seems to be applicable to at least some types of problems encountered outside the laboratory. It is based upon the observation that simple problems can often be solved by relating two objects (e.g., the pliers and the string). Relational words (e.g., "in," "on," "above," etc.) are used to specify an association between elements of solutions (e.g., "take object *A* on object *B*"). The different objects in the problem environment (e.g., the pliers and string) are inserted into the object word locations, and hopefully a good solution is generated. An example of this strategy is Dunker's X-ray problem (1944–1945), in which it is necessary by using X-rays to eliminate an inoperable stomach tumor without harming the healthy tissue. This problem contains two main words, "ray" and "stomach tumor," that can be related in searching for a solution. Crovitz applies the relational algorithm and shows how it generates several solutions, such as "take one ray *across* another ray" or "take the rays *around* the stomach tumor." For more details of the strategy and its uses, the reader is referred to Crovitz's book.

4.4 Strategies for Reducing Complexity in Problem Diagnosis and Specification

Highly complex decision environments challenge decision makers in their attempts to diagnose and specify problems. The many dimensions of existing and desired states typifying complex decision environments imply a multitude of possible gaps (e.g., multiple attribute decision problems) and interconnections (e.g., mutual influences among the factors). Yet the limited capacity of a decision maker clearly precludes his dealing with many different things at the same time (Miller, 1956; Simon, 1957a).

Cyert and March (1963) discuss a process for coping with multiple problems: the decision maker sequentially shifts his attention from one gap to another in an effort to identify problems, while permitting internal conflict to remain at an acceptable low level. As Drucker (1963) has noted, managing for results in complex decision environments requires that the decision maker set priorities for solving the problems facing him. He should allocate resources first to critical decision making activities, rather than waste them on low-potential activities.

As the decision maker attempts to cope with his cognitive limitations, he may become overly concerned with threats which may be thought of as the existing state changing while the desired state remains constant. Since the existing state is more apparent, threats are more readily perceived than opportunities (in which the desired state changes but the existing state remains the same). Decision strategies are then often characterized by avoidance, crisis management, and fire-fighting rather than by aggressive confrontation of problems.

Besides taxing the decision maker's cognitive abilities, complex decision environments also present special difficulties in diagnosing problems and in specifying appropriate actions to use in solving the problem. Clearly, the way a decision problem is defined can have considerable effect on the types of alternatives considered and the types of resources utilized. Maier (1931), for example, uses the two-string problem to demonstrate that the way the problem is defined (e.g., the string is too short, the string will not swing over, etc.) influences how the available resources (e.g., a pair of pliers) are likely to be used for solving the problem.

The decision strategies that have implications for problem analysis in complex environments include (1) determining the problem boundaries by focusing on what is or is not a part of the problem, (2) examining changes in the decision environment or decision maker which may have precipitated the problem, (3) factoring complex problems into subproblems, and (4) focusing upon the controllable components of a decision situation.

Focus on What Is or Is Not Part of the Problem

Kepner and Tregoe (1965) present a very practical approach for analyzing complex problems. The decision maker is advised to first attempt to determine the characteristics of the out-of-control part of the decision situation and the characteristics of the in-control part. Following such a determination, an attempt is made to find single causes that will explain the "is" part and discriminate it from the "is not" part. Using this approach, one may compare departments with low morale with high morale departments to find probable causes of the low morale. Factors common to all departments (e.g., work methods or pay plans) would be considered improbable causes of the morale problem and problem solving attention would focus upon factors which differ for high morale departments and low morale departments (e.g., nature of the immediate supervision).

Focus on Changes

In addition to determining what is or is not a part of the problem, Kepner and Tregoe advise that the many changes typically found in complex environments be systematically probed until the equilibrium-restoring action can be found. The rationale for this is that changes in desired or existing states must be the result of some other change in the decision situation; thus, a likely place to look for causes of a problem is in changes in procedures, materials, personnel, etc. In the previous example, an examination would be made of the changes that had occurred in the low morale departments prior to the time when morale first seemed to be deteriorating.

While Kepner and Tregoe do not limit the scope of their method to problems in which a system is temporarily out of equilibrium, it is difficult to see how it could be used more generally in problems which, for example, involve structural changes or which are open-ended (e.g., the problem of controlling inflation).

Factor Into Subproblems

Factoring the decision problem into subproblems, which in turn may be factored, is a strategy for resolving a wide range of complex decision problems. Simon (1960) has given an example of a watchmaker who, by arranging his assembly in terms of sub-parts, can be much more productive when interrupted than a watchmaker who tries to assemble whole clocks at one time (see also Koestler, 1967). Breaking up a problem into subproblems is only useful if there are not too many interrelationships among the subparts, otherwise the coordination problems would clearly outweigh the advantage of decomposition. Decomposition obviously permits the use of specialization and division of labor when the decision maker's subunits have differential capabilities. It also allows for additional parallelism in solving the decision problem, hence the decision maker's sequential processing limitations (Simon, 1969) can be overcome. Braybrooke and Lindblom (1963) have emphasized this common form of problem separation with their development of concepts of "disjointedness."

Apply Means-Ends Analysis

A useful strategy for coping with complexity in goal hierarchies or multiple goals is the means-end analysis of the factored problem. In this strategy, the desired sub-goal (the end) is compared with the present state of knowledge. The task is to find an operator (a means) that will reduce the gap. After the operator is applied, there may be a new gap to be reduced and new means may be considered. A computer program, the General Problem Solver, has been constructed to operate in this fashion (Newell, Shaw, & Simon, 1960).

Focus on Controllable Factors

A useful strategy is to classify the factors in a decision situation into those that are controllable and those that are uncontrollable. Ones that are partially controllable can be decomposed into their controllable and uncontrollable components (Howard, 1971). It is obviously not enough to be aware of the existence of a gap between desired and existing states: the decision maker must be able to take actions that will reduce the gap or there is little use in trying to solve the problem, for even if he were able to generate a solution, he would be unable to implement it.

Work Forward and Work Backward

One of the main problems in highly complex decision situations is finding the particular operators that will reduce the gap between the existing state and the desired state (Newell & Simon, 1961). A basic strategy for approaching a problem involves direction of search. In the terms we have used earlier, the decision maker may work (forward) from the existing state to see how it might be transformed into the desired state, or he may work (back) from the desired state to see if he can develop a means for arriving at the existing state (Feldman & Kanter, 1965; Miller, Galanter, & Pribram, 1960).

Although both approaches seem to be used in actual decision making, most problems do involve some type of forward search: one first tries out some method of attack and then decides if progress is being made. The information search progresses in simple, direct steps from start to finish. In working backward, on the other hand, one looks at the desired solution and asks what the previous step must have been to have arrived there. Then, from that step, the one just prior to it is determined, and so on, hopefully back to the starting point given in the original specification of the problem. Working backward is useful in some visual problems (e.g., reading a map to decide the route from one location to another) and in techniques such as dynamic programming (Bellman & Dreyfus, 1962). In some types of problem solving, a combination of working forward and working backward may be effective. In solving anagrams, for example, working forward helps generate letter sequences until a word is produced, and working backward helps produce words to compare with the anagram (Johnson, 1966).

4.5 Strategies for Reducing Complexity by Aggregating Information

Complex decision environments tend to place extreme demands upon the information processing capacity of a decision maker. The restricted capacity of the decision maker to process information places severe limits upon his ability to make a decision; hence, he must aggregate information into a form he can use efficiently in making a decision. Essentially, the problem is that, although the decision maker needs information which is both reliable and relevant to the decision, the complexity of the environment may require him to process information at a level that exceeds his cognitive abilities—thus producing a state of "overload" and declining efficiency in his ability to use information. We examine this phenomenon and the way in which it affects decision making under a variety of environmental conditions in Section 6. A similar phenomenon can be observed in the multiple-person decision problems that are typical of organizations (Ackoff, 1967).

The decision strategies discussed in this sub-section proceed from those appropriate for use by an individual decision maker to those involving multiple decision makers. Strategies of each class are discussed in the order of the decision maker's increasing involvement with the decision environment.

The strategies appropriate for an individual decision maker focus upon reducing the cognitive demands placed upon him by either providing him with a means of ordering information (chunking) or by arranging the information appropriately prior to his receiving it (level of aggregation). The multiple-person decision strategies for aggregating information are ordered in a similar manner. These strategies may involve sharing information with no face-to-face interaction among decision makers (Delphi), with some interaction among group members (communication nets), or with perhaps considerable interaction (participation of subordinates in decisions).

Chunk Information

Simon (1969) and others have prescribed a strategy of "chunking," which helps a decision maker to impose meaning upon a complex array of stimuli through effective organization of information. By grouping the information into categories ("chunks") and arranging them by order of importance, the decision maker may be able to considerably increase his information processing capacity. The operation of this strategy seems consistent with Posner's (1963) conclusion that the subject rarely stores a "pure representation" of the stimulus; rather, he is an active information handler who uses his understanding of the information to reduce his memory load. For example, our knowledge of a concept (e.g., animal) permits us to subsume many examples (e.g., horse, dog).

Use Optimal Level of Aggregation

Another strategy for efficient aggregation of information has been described by

Marschak (1964). He suggests that effective information partitioning must take into account the optimal "level of aggregation" for the decision at hand. In some cases the information might be too detailed (e.g., store-by-store sales), while in other cases it might be too aggregated (e.g., national sales). As a general rule, the more detailed information should be retained because, once the information is aggregated, it may be quite difficult to disaggregate for particular purposes.

Focus Gamble or Conservative Focus?

The strategies described by Bruner et al. (1956) for seeking information in concept attainment tasks approach the problem of reducing memory load by increasing the likelihood that instances encountered will contain appropriate information, by reducing strain of processing information, and by regulating risk. Four conjunctive strategies are described in their research—"simultaneous scanning" (testing many hypotheses at one time), "successive scanning" (testing one hypothesis at a time), "conservative focusing" (finding one positive instance and varying one attribute at a time), and "focus gambling" (varying more than one attribute at a time).

Of these strategies, the latter two seem to be of greatest interest for dealing with information load. If the individual has a hunch about the correct alternative, he can adopt a more risky strategy (focus gambling) to reach the solution more quickly and with less information processing. On the other hand, in the absence of information to make such hypotheses tenable, he would be more likely to take the safe strategy (conservative focusing).

A practical example of the application of these strategies occurs in new product introduction decisions. Potential products are conceptualized in terms of their characteristics or attributes, and marketers often think in terms of ideal levels for these attributes—that is, those levels most desired by consumers. It is these levels that the marketers wish to learn by test marketing. If they have a range of products and plan to test them sequentially, they can test products differing from preceding semi-successful ones by only a single attribute (conservative focusing) or differing on a number of attributes (focus gambling) in their attempt to find the ideal levels.

Use Reliable Information

Multiple sources of information in the decision environment also contribute to complexity and influence the way in which decision makers aggregate information. The value of the information depends heavily on its relevance to the decision and its reliability. In complex environments, a decision maker can reduce the amount of information he must process by selecting information from relevant and reliable sources and by ignoring information from other sources.

Berlyne (1964) theorized that individuals in a decision situation learn through "implicit trial and error" which sources or types of information can guide them to the optimal response by sequentially anticipating the outcomes of acting on each item. As Newell, Shaw, and Simon (1958) have shown, this procedure cannot be carried out profitably in a random order; information sources can, however, be tried out in an order that reflects how successful each source has been in the past. This type of order reflects individual bias towards information contributed by a source which has already proven itself reliable and relevant.

Support for this hypothesis can be drawn from studies of impression formation and from employment decisions. It has been repeatedly demonstrated (e.g., Hovland, 1954; Rosenbaum, 1967; Rosenbaum & Levin, 1968) that the impression formed from information about a person is a function of both the content of the information and the credence given to the source of the information. Similarly, studies of employment interviews have shown that information sources (e.g., application form, face-to-face interview, etc.) differentially influence hiring decisions (e.g., Carlson, 1967; Carlson & Mayfield, 1967; Springbett, 1958).

The implications of such source preferences for decision making seem rather direct. Sources perceived by the decision maker as conveying information which has led to successful decision making in the past should be sought, and sources seen as less profitable should be avoided. Resistance by the decision maker to new sources of information, or sources that have been previously supplying information perceived as of low quality would seem to be difficult to detect and overcome. If the bias is unfounded, it could have an undesirable effect on decision accuracy in many organizational contexts (e.g., employment interviewing, sales campaigns).

Collect Expertise Through Delphi

The Delphi technique (Dalkey & Helmer, 1963) employs interaction among decision makers, but attempts to prevent forceful group members from dominating the discussion and stifling contributions of other group members. This technique was developed at the RAND Corporation and used during the 1950s to estimate such things as the Soviet military capability ten to fifteen years in the future. In the Delphi procedure, the participants (experts in the area under consideration) are isolated from one another and are presented with a series of questionnaires in which their opinions and bases for these opinions are solicited. After each round of questionnaires is completed, information from the participants is consolidated and circulated anonymously to each member of the group. Depending on the requirements of the decision situation, variants of this method may be established. In one application (Turoff, 1971) communication among members of the group is facilitated by a time-shared computer-communication system. Such procedures are widely used in many contexts: in estimating the quality of life, in solving urban prob-

lems, and in changing governmental policies and capabilities (Cetron & Ralph, 1971).

Set up Appropriate Communication Networks

When multiple decision makers are involved, the arrangement of communication channels among group members has obvious implications for coping with complexity. Effective decision making by groups clearly depends upon accurate and efficient exchange of information among group members. As Shaw (1971) points out in his treatment of group process, research findings have seriously challenged the standard assumption of organizational planners that communication channels are most efficient when structured as a hierarchy.

Bavelas (1948, 1950) and Leavitt (1951) prompted a large number of studies of how different communication channel patterns affect the performance of a decision making group. A communication network is defined as a consistent pattern of information exchange during the course of decision making. Among the communication structures which have been studied are the wheel (only the member at the hub can communicate with other group members), the circle (each member is connected to two other members), the chain (a linear sequence), and the "comcon" (completely connected). Research has examined the degree to which imposed communication networks affect leadership emergence, member satisfaction, and group performance in decision making.

Evidence indicates that for the complex tasks, perhaps like those found outside the laboratory, decentralized networks are more efficient (Lawson, 1964; Mulder, 1960; Shaw, 1954), and they produce greater satisfaction among group members (Cohen, 1961; Lawson, 1965; Leavitt, 1951; Shaw, 1954). Complex tasks are defined as those for which information must be collected in one place and then processed before the solution can be known. Simple tasks, on the other hand, are those that require only the collection of information (e.g., color-, letter-, symbol-, and number-identification problems).

Leadership, however, is more likely to emerge in a centralized communication network than in a decentralized one. Leavitt (1951) found that a leader emerged more often in a wheel network than in a chain or Y network, and emerged least frequently in a circle network; that is, leadership emergence varied directly with the degree of network centrality. This finding has been substantiated by a number of subsequent studies (e.g., Hirota, 1953; Shaw, 1954; Shaw & Rothschild, 1956). For detailed reviews of the literature on experiments with communication networks, see Glanzer and Glaser (1961), Shaw (1964, 1971), and Collins and Raven (1969).

Allow Participation in Decisions

Participation of subordinates in decision making can be viewed as a strategy for achieving aggregations which reduce complexity in the decision environment. In this context, our concern is for the extent to which information bearing upon the decision should be sought from subordinates.

Relatively little is known about the manner in which subordinates contribute to managerial decisions (the decision processes involved in the participative meetings, content, interactions among group members, quality of the decision, etc.). Limited evidence indicates that the effectiveness of participation of subordinates in decision making depends on the nature of the decision and on the subordinates involved (e.g., Campbell et al., 1970; Vroom, 1960; Campion, 1968).

The desirability of having participation, and the manner in which information is collected from subordinates and used in management decisions (or the degree to which subordinates are actually involved in the decision process) seem to depend on such factors as the extent to which subordinates accept organizational goals, the quality of the decision necessary, and the

degree of acceptance necessary. Maier (1963), for example, has differentiated between problems which are quality-dominant and those which are acceptance-dominant. If the problem is one for which quality is much more important than acceptance, then a nonparticipative decision seems appropriate. If, however, acceptance of the decision is more important than quality, then a group decision seems desirable. Decisions that require both high quality and high acceptance are best handled by combined procedures.

Vroom in Chapter 34 of this *Handbook* considers these factors and presents a procedure by which decision urgency, resources of subordinates, and need for acceptance of the decision are analyzed through a "participation tree," to yield strategies that guide the manager in the degree to which he should consult with his subordinates and in the form the interaction should assume.

4.6 Strategies for Reducing Complexity by Aggregating Preferences

In evaluating alternative choices in a complex environment, the decision maker must often consider a large number of attributes or factors. Preferences can be assigned to each of these attributes, and the challenge for the decision maker is to effectively aggregate these preferences. The more successful strategies are those that recognize and account for the cognitive limitations of the decision maker. In this section, we shall consider some of the more useful strategies for aggregating preferences. For a more complete description, see MacCrimmon (1973c).

Bootstrap With a Linear Model

In situations where the decision maker makes a number of similar decisions, it is possible to build a simple model of his behavior. For example, in personnel selection,[5]

---

[5] For discussions of personnel selection decision strategies, see Guion (1965), Dunnette (1966), Cronbach (1970), Bray and Moses (1972).

the ratings given to job candidates can be the dependent variable, and the factors describing the candidates can be the independent variables. A linear regression can yield coefficients describing the decision maker's behavior. If the fit of the linear equation is good, then this equation can be used in place of the decision maker in routine situations (e.g., for preliminary screenings). In a large number of situations—from radiologists diagnosing X-rays to faculty members selecting graduate students, to judges deciding on workmen's compensation awards—a linear model has proven to be a good fit (Hoffman, Slovic, & Rorer, 1968; Dawes, 1971; Kort, 1968).

What is particularly intriguing about some of these studies is the finding that the linear model, once it has been determined, can do better than the decision maker for whose preferences it is a paramorphic representation. Application of the model "smooths out" the choices and avoids the unsystematic shifting of attention that sometimes misleads the human processor. Dawes (1971) interestingly develops this bootstrapping notion in the context of graduate admission decisions. Kunreuther (1969) discusses when one should rely on a simple model in production planning and when the decision maker should contravene. If some performance criterion is available, then clearly a regression should also be run against it, and it can be used as a supplement or substitute. For an excellent survey of this literature, with many applications, see Slovic and Lichtenstein (1971).

Apply a Subjective Weighting Model

The regression procedures, based on the actual choices or ratings of a decision maker, use statistical techniques to infer the preferences he was exhibiting. As an alternative, though, he could be asked directly for his preferences, and these figures could be used as coefficients in some model. In such cases, it is usual to separate the scaling of (intra-) attribute values from the (inter-) attribute weighting of importance. This allows for curvilinear relationships reflecting the worth of various attribute values to a decision maker (Miller, 1970).

The weighting of importance of attributes can be related to higher order objectives; that is, the instrumentality of attributes in reaching ends higher in some goal hierarchy determines the weighting (Sayeki & Vesper, 1971). In such models it is also possible to consider some quasi-additive models and to directly assess the coefficients of these multiplicative, and other, terms (Keeney, 1968a,b).

Direct assessment models are common to many areas of decision making and have a long history. In a letter to Joseph Priestly, for example, Benjamin Franklin (1772) described a method of "moral algebra": "...my way is to divide half a sheet of paper by a line into two columns; writing over the one *Pro,* and over the other *Con.* Then, during three or four days consideration, I put down under the different heads short hints of the different motives, that at different times occur to me, *for* or *against* the measure. When I have thus got them all together in one view, I endeavor to estimate their respective weights; and where I find two, one on each side, that seem equal, I strike them both out. If I find a reason *pro* equal to some two reasons *con,* I strike out the three. If I judge some two reasons *con,* equal to some three reasons *pro,* I strike out the five; and thus proceeding I find at length where the balance lies; and if, after a day or two of further consideration, nothing new that is of importance occurs on either side, I come to a determination accordingly."

Use Interactive Programming to Optimize

When the available alternatives can be defined by mathematical constraints and the decision problem has more of a "design" than a simple "choice" orientation, mathematical programming methods can be used. If a feasible alternative is first found, then these procedures obtain the local preferences of the decision maker in terms of his trade-offs for incremental changes in attribute values from this reference point. These trade-offs become part of an objective function in a mathematical programming problem, and a new solution (alternative) is obtained. The procedure continues in such an iterative fashion using the decision maker to make local trade-off inputs but leaving all calculations up to a computer algorithm. This procedure has been applied to scheduling an academic department (Feinberg, 1972; Geoffrion, Dyer, & Feinberg, 1972).

Set Constraints and Satisfice

For multiple attribute decision making, perhaps the least demanding procedure is for the decision maker to set preference constraints. For example, "a job applicant must have previous experience in the industry" would be one possible constraint. A number of such constraints could be set up to operate either conjunctively (all must be satisfied) or disjunctively (only one need be satisfied). For more details, see Dawes (1964) and Coombs (1964). The constraints may be set up sequentially and may depend on results of preceding tests. This approach is very common in cognitive process studies. (For applications to consumers, bank trust investment officers, MMPI analysts, and personnel specialists, see Bettman, 1971; Clarkson, 1962; Kleinmuntz, 1968; Smith & Greenlaw, 1967.)

The usual operating mode with these procedures is to search for an alternative that satisfies the constraints, without trying to determine whether a better alternative exists.

Use SPAN Voting

The procedures above that involve constraints are useful for multiple-person situations, since different people can impose different constraints; hence, their preferences can be reflected in a workable fashion without trying to aggregate them into a social choice function. A more explicit way of aggregating disjoint preferences in multi-person situations is through the development of voting procedures. In general, this can be viewed as a direct extension of the multi-person information exchange strategies discussed in the preceding section.

An interesting group voting strategy is the SPAN technique proposed by Mac-Kinnon and MacKinnon (1969). Each member is given a fixed number of votes which he may allocate directly to the alternatives being considered or to other voters. The underlying rationale is that he should allocate votes to other voters in situations when he has little knowledge and when he can identify those members with more expertise. This process is iterated until all the votes are distributed to alternatives.

It can be seen that the aggregation of preferences is across voters and not across attributes of alternatives. In both cases, though, the impetus is toward consolidating disjoint preferences. Other voting strategies, including having representatives, could be studied toward the same end, but we shall not discuss them further here. They are considered in the next section.

SECTION 5. CONFLICT

Conflict can arise in a decision situation when (a) there are multiple parties, (b) the actions of one person can affect the outcomes of others, (c) the parties have different preference orderings on the outcomes, and (d) the parties are aware of the situation. Each of these conditions is very common and so a decision maker will generally have to deal with a decision environment of considerable conflict potential.

Although each individual participating in an interdependent decision situation can be viewed as trying to better his position, the participants need not be unalterably opposed to each other; the decision makers may be able to better their positions simultaneously. Such mixed-motive situations, involving elements of both competition and cooperation, seem to provide the most valuable focus for our discussion of decision strategies under conflict because they most closely model real life interactions (Schelling, 1960). They encompass wars, strikes, negotiations, criminal defense, economic markets, and many other significant decision problems.

The usual formulation for deriving strategies to manage conflict has been the theory of games (Von Neumann & Morgenstern, 1944). Mixed-motive decision situations have, however, attracted a good deal of recent attention from behavioral scientists, and a body of descriptive, empirical literature dealing with what has generally been called "interpersonal accommodation" (e.g., Kelley, 1968) or "behavior exchange" (e.g., Gergen, 1969) is developing. The decision strategies appropriate to conditions of conflict which we discuss are drawn from literatures, such as mathematical game theory, conflict resolution, group processes, and persuasive communication.

In environments characterized by uncertainty and complexity, the decision maker will seek strategies for *reducing* these elements. Conflict, in contrast, has a potential advantage to offer to at least one of the involved parties. In order to include this possibility, we will generally refer to strategies for *managing* conflict, rather than *reducing* conflict.

The classes of decision strategies for managing conflict can be arranged according to the extent that they demand the decision maker's active involvement in the environment. Modeling conflict generally requires little interaction with the environment. Similarly, reducing the perception of conflict by avoiding the conflict or redirecting its focus usually involves only minimal efforts. Processing information to manage the level of conflict typically requires more interaction of the decision maker with his environment, while bargaining and achieving joint agreement require direct interaction among the conflicting parties. Structural mechanisms for resolving conflict require both a great deal of interaction among the parties and

involvement with the formal structures existing in the environment. The use of force, the most destructive of the strategies, demands the most involvement with the environment. Strategies representing each of these classes are discussed in this section.

5.1 Strategies for Modeling Conflict

Most of the representations of conflict and the accompanying models stem from the game theory literature. The type of representation chosen determines the concepts and variables emphasized and hence determines the way the conflict is handled: an extensive form representation is oriented toward the rules and information sets; a normal form representation is directed toward the available strategies; and a characteristic function form focuses on the coalition possibilities. For more detailed treatments, see Lucas (1972), Luce and Raiffa (1957), and Von Neumann and Morgenstern (1944). In contrast to these formal models, which are essentially languages, are the less formal but more interactive and more dynamic models of simulation and gaming.

Model in Extensive Form

Representing a conflict situation in extensive form helps to direct a decision maker's attention to the rules, the information, and particularly to the sequence of moves. One extensive form model is a game tree. In the game tree form, the branches extending from any given node represent the actions available to a player (decision maker) at some point in the game. Each player's set of nodes is partitioned into information sets which show the ambiguity of his position; that is, he does not know at which node he is because he does not know his opponent's preceding choices. The branches at the end of the tree represent the payoffs to each player. A player's sequence of actions at each of his choice nodes is called a strategy.

Model in Normal Form

While extensive forms can provide useful information, especially about the sequences of moves, they are often unwieldy representations. When the emphasis is on the strategies available to each player, a normal form representation is preferable. A normal form, the most common form used in behavior science studies, is essentially a (poly) matrix representation. In the usual two-person situation, the strategies of one player are shown as rows, while the strategies of the other player are shown as columns. The payoffs that each strategy would produce are entered into the cells. In a zero (or constant) sum game, one person wins what the other person loses—there can be no cooperative behavior. In the more common nonzero (or non-constant) sum games, however, the payoffs to one party are not necessarily gained at the expense of the other.

Model in Characteristic Function Form

The characteristic function, used in n-person situations in which coalitions may form, gives the total payoff to every (nonempty) subset of players. It does not give the distribution to each member since this is the heart of the coalition "problem." The implications of this representation are given by Rapoport (1970).

Model by Simulation and Gaming

By abstracting the key variables from a situation, a simpler representation can be built. This representation can be manipulated more easily than the real system and the decision maker can simulate the roles of the various participants in the system. This will allow him to obtain both a better understanding of the alternatives available to other participants and the significance of consequences to them. Even more important is the ability to trace through the implications of interdependent actions and hence to get greater insight into the dynamics of a conflict environment than the more formal, static models can provide. See Shubik (1971) for more details.

5.2 Strategies for Reducing the Perception of Conflict

As either a deliberate strategy or as an unconscious defense mechanism, a decision maker may tend to minimize his perception of conflict. His deliberate actions for reducing perceptions of conflict may be regarded as strategies, and indeed they may be effective in coping with a conflict, at least in the short run. Among the possible strategies a decision maker may use for reducing perceptions of conflict are to elect not to pursue his interests or to avoid admission of conflict. Strategies that are too passive, in particular those avoiding a recognition of the existence of conflict, may actually intensify the conflict in the environment.

Give up Conflicting Interests

Strategies such as withdrawal, yielding, and unilateral compromise may be useful when the decision maker does not currently possess sufficient resources to attain his desired outcomes in the conflict situation (Schelling, 1960). Although these strategies generally may be seen as admissions of defeat, they may also represent delaying moves which allow the decision maker to develop a more effective strategy for future use. Also, the balance of power may shift in his favor either through recouping or marshaling of resources or a weakening of the other parties to the conflict. It should be recognized that the terminal states implied by the strategies of this class may vary greatly in the degree to which they are binding; a unilateral compromise, for instance, may still leave the decision maker a chance to pursue his interests at decision points in the future.

Focus on Alternatives to Conflict

Strategies in which a decision maker avoids either recognizing or admitting that conflict exists in a decision environment include such actions as smoothing over or attending to goals compatible with those of the conflicting party. A strategy with a similar intent—to reduce the effect of conflicting interests—is the use of pleasant distractions in the decision situation. Experiments have indicated that a moderate level of pleasant distraction tends to increase the amount of influence produced by a persuasive appeal (e.g., Janis, Kaye, & Kirschner, 1965; Haaland & Venkateson, 1968). The frequently observed policy of conducting business in pleasant surroundings (e.g., over lunch or cocktails) may represent the use of this strategy.

5.3 Strategies for Managing Conflict Through Information Processing

If a decision maker is to manage conflict, he must be able to acquire and utilize information. These strategies help the decision maker to gain an advantage over parties with conflicting interests by accurately predicting their future behavior on the basis of information about their outcomes, response repertory, and contingent or constraining factors. Strategies for managing conflict through information processing include acquiring information about the outcomes and motives of the other party, using the maximin rules, preparing position papers, and using Hegelian inquiry to draw out conflicting opinions regarding the decision.

Acquire Information About Own and Other's Outcomes

A decision maker having complete information about the payoff matrices for his own and the other party's outcomes may use the information advantageously or disadvantageously. As Siegel and Fouraker (1960) have found in a series of bargaining experiments, whether or not the decision maker uses the information advantageously depends upon whether he is using a "fair" orientation (i.e., seeking equitable outcomes) or a "ruthless" orientation (i.e., trying to win).

Supposedly a "ruthless" decision maker would use his information to force his opponent to make concessions and thus reduce his opponent's level of aspiration. Instead, the experiments found that the decision maker having complete information about the other's profit table used the information disadvantageously; that is, the decision maker having complete information used a "fair" strategy, apparently aiming for a target price and quantity that would tend to equalize profits for both decision makers. While the decision maker with complete information stayed away from unreasonable levels of aspiration, the decision maker with incomplete information tended to set a high initial level of aspiration and often won out over the more informed decision maker.

The results of these experiments suggest that, in addition to knowledge about the opponent's outcomes, knowledge of the orientation being used by the opponent in a conflict situation would be extremely valuable to a decision maker. No matter whether the decision maker is using a "fair" or "ruthless" orientation, it would be to his advantage to know what he could expect from his opponent. Although subjects frequently adopt a highly competitive strategy in experiments, the extent to which similar orientations exist outside the laboratory is uncertain.

Identify and Utilize Social Motives

In social situations people may have a variety of motives for their actions. The usual assumption in economics and game theory is that people are motivated by self-interest (i.e., economic man). A variety of studies have identified other motives, including elements of altruism, hostility, and cooperation (Messick & McClintock, 1968; Tajfel, 1970).

In simple two-person situations in which a decision maker is faced with changing payoffs to himself and to his opponent, he may maximize or minimize (1) his own payoffs, (2) his opponent's payoffs, (3) the sum of his own and his opponent's payoffs, or (4) the difference between his and his opponent's payoffs. While other functions of payoffs could be identified, these eight types provide a good representation of the types of "pure" (used in a neutral sense) motives found in actual conflict situations.

In general, we would expect the complex combinations of motives employed to depend on such things as the social relation between the two parties and their relative status (Shubik, 1971). However, when the other party is getting much higher payoffs, we might expect most people to become somewhat aggressive (minimizing the difference). When the payoffs to both are in about the same range, they will probably become self-interested (maximizing their own payoffs) or cooperative (maximizing the joint payoffs), and when the other party is getting much lower payoffs, they will probably become altruistic (maximizing the other's payoffs) or equitable (minimizing the difference). An especially interesting way to represent complex social preferences such as these is in the form of indifference curves. For more details, see MacCrimmon and Messick (1974).

Identifying the social motives of various parties can be useful in several ways for resolving conflict. When, for instance, one of the conflicting parties holds a position of higher authority, knowing the motives of each party can indicate the ranges of payoffs which would be mutually satisfactory to all the parties involved, and attention can be more immediately directed to these areas. Similarly, understanding motives can be useful in selecting people who will be able to cooperate in joint activities. For the individual, identifying the other person's motives may indicate possibilities for either exploiting or cooperating effectively with the other party.

Maximin

The central result in two-person zero-sum games is that for each player there is a strategy which guarantees that one player will get at least a particular value of payoff, while the other player can hold the first to this value (Von Neumann & Morgenstern, 1944). This is done by identifying the minimum payoff that can result from the choice of any action and then choosing the action that maximizes this minimum payoff.

In general, this will be not a "pure" strategy but rather a "mixed" strategy that requires the player to choose one of the pure strategies subject to some probability distribution. Such randomization over strategies does not allow opponents to determine which strategy will be used. Some interesting implications and examples are given by Luce and Raiffa (1957).

Use Conflicting Opinions

Mason (1969) has suggested that encouraging conflict can improve the quality of the decision. Mason's two approaches, the devil's advocate and the dialectic, produce and capitalize upon conflicting opinions about the decision problem. In the devil's advocate approach, someone presents a side of the issue or an approach opposing the alternative favored by the decision maker. Hopefully, this technique will reveal any hidden biases or invalid assumptions in the preferred alternative, but it can result in destructive criticism of the original alternative. This technique assumes that truly sound decision alternatives can withstand all criticism. When the preferred alternative is found to be weak, however, this technique generally fails to present better alternatives to replace those criticized and may cause the decision maker to propose only "safe" alternatives which can withstand criticism.

As an alternative to the devil's advocate

approach, the Hegelian dialectic approach (Churchman, 1966; Hegel, 1964) offers several advantages. It is dialectic in that it requires one or more decision makers to examine a situation completely and logically from two opposing points of view. This approach begins by presenting a decision alternative and its underlying assumptions. Next, a search is made for a counter plan (e.g., another plausible alternative; perhaps one rejected earlier). During a structured debate, the case made for each alternative must attempt to interpret the entire data bank as supporting evidence. As a result of this process, the decision maker will be expected to develop a new decision alternative—a synthesis—which includes the best elements of the plan and counterplan.

Such an approach would ensure that evidence conflicting with the position to which a decision maker is already committed would be considered. Experimental evidence reviewed by Mills (1968) suggests that propensity toward exposing oneself to conflicting views depends on the degree of certainty about the correctness of the choice; that is, when decision makers are uncertain that their position is correct, they tend to seek supporting information. Mills has suggested a formulation to supplement dissonance theory. He asserts that decision makers want to be certain that the alternative they act upon is better than other alternatives and that dissonance is not solely a post-decisional phenomenon. Although it is clear that decision makers will collect information from the other side of an issue, the Hegelian dialectic approach should be useful to both individual and group decision makers as a strategy for selecting and interpreting evidence in a systematic and unbiased manner.

Prepare Position Papers

Preparing position papers is a widely used strategy for summarizing a decision maker's position and communicating this information (e.g., desired outcomes, capabilities, constraints, etc.) to both opponents and subordinate decision makers. As a technique for summarizing the position of a group, the position papers may clarify the group's position on the issues and solidify its goals, values, etc. into a united front. As communications media, position papers offer the decision maker a way to present information to others in a format carefully constructed to provide the desired influence. Position papers would seem to be especially appropriate as adjuncts to the more action-oriented strategies which we examine in the following sub-sections (e.g., persuasion, threats, voting, etc.).

5.4 Strategies for Managing Conflict Through Bargaining

Bargaining involves interaction among various participants, as well as interdependence of outcomes and information. To gain desired outcomes, the bargaining parties can exploit any advantage accruing from information they have about their party's or the other party's position (e.g., preferences, response capabilities, constraints). At the same time, the bargainer may try to conceal information that would give the other party an advantage, or he may even transmit information contrived to give the other party the impression he desires them to have about his position. While this may sound rather like espionage, the use of similar strategies has been shown by Schelling (1960) to occur in a variety of settings.

Bargaining fits the requirements of mixed-motive decision situations quite well in that the conflicting parties neither have to agree upon a formal rule for settling the conflict beforehand, nor do they have to completely agree on all desired outcomes at the conclusion of the bargaining. Although the parties may be diametrically opposed on certain preferences (e.g., wage rates or seniority provisions), they must share sufficient interests (e.g., continuance of the organization) to initiate and sustain the bargaining process.

Strategies for managing conflict by bargaining include interpersonal influence attempts, such as face-to-face discussion and persuasion, bluffing, threatening, conceding reluctantly, and tit-for-tat.

Discuss Face-to-Face

The face-to-face conference of leaders was studied by Sherif (1966) as a strategy for settling intergroup conflicts. The strategy seems to be widely used and to have merit for helping each group learn about the other and for building mutual trust in dealing with common problems. Yet, a limitation of the strategy noted in Sherif's series of experiments is its dependence upon the existence of some degree of cooperative interaction or common interests between the groups at the time it is to be used. It would appear, however, that this constraint would not be a serious problem in many practical applications of the strategy.

If such face-to-face interactions occur among members of groups which are cohesive, then there will be less conflict of interests to hamper mutual decision making. Studies investigating the effects of group cohesiveness (motivation of members to remain in the group) have found that cohesive groups tend to be more communicative and interactive (e.g., Lott & Lott, 1961), more cooperative and friendly (e.g., Shaw & Shaw, 1962), more influential over its members (Wyer, 1966), and more effective in achieving group goals (e.g., Shaw & Shaw, 1962). Cohesive decision making groups would provide less conflict to be managed in the process of reaching a mutual decision; but, unfortunately, it is difficult to specify conditions for developing group cohesiveness.

Persuade

In a bargaining situation, an individual attempting to influence another party may present only arguments that support his position, or he may admit that some arguments damaging to his position have validity. Studies in persuasive communication generally suggest that when the other party initially disagrees with your position or when the other party is likely to hear about weaknesses in your position from another source, then you can more effectively influence the other party by admitting that there are weaknesses in your position (e.g., McGinnies, 1966; Lumsdaine & Janis, 1953).

These studies also suggest that the most important aspects of a position be given either at the beginning or at the end of a presentation so that they will be remembered (e.g., Tannenbaum, 1954; Shaw, 1961). Whether it is best to present key arguments at the beginning or at the end has not been conclusively answered by the research evidence (e.g., Cromwell, 1950). It is clear, though, that arguments mentioned in the middle of a presentation tend to be forgotten most quickly and would seem less likely to sway the position of the other party. Karlins and Abelson (1970) provide a useful treatment of the research literature on persuasive communication that may suggest to the reader other strategies.

Bluff

The use of bluffing strategies has been viewed in the context of level of aspiration (e.g., Siegel & Fouraker, 1960). Studies of the initial positions the bargaining parties take in relation to the power inherent in their resources have an obvious application to actual bargaining practices. The amount of information the other party has about the motives, resources, and outcomes of the party attempting to bluff (5.3) does, of course, determine the effectiveness of bluffing. This strategy is related to the manner in which one makes concessions, to be discussed later in this sub-section.

Threaten and Promise

The use of threats and promises in strategies for decision making under conflict have been treated in some detail by Schelling (1960). The essential differences between a promise and a threat is that a promise offers the other party an outcome he desires (e.g., money) in exchange for an outcome desired by the promisor (e.g., services); a threat, on the other hand, offers an outcome undesired by the other party (e.g., bodily harm) if he fails to provide an outcome desired by the threatener (e.g., money). A promise, therefore, is costly when it succeeds, and a threat is costly when it fails—a successful threat is one that is not carried out.

Commitment and communication, two important elements in the use of promises and threats, have widespread strategic applications. If promises and threats are to be effective, the party using them as strategies must be committed to carrying them out or at least must make the other party think that they will be carried out. For example, a corporation's right to sue provides evidence that it has the potential to use a threat; its right to be sued provides evidence to other parties that it is committed to its promises. That an organization possesses the potential for using each of these techniques seems important to its ability to conduct its business. In addition to being committed to carrying out threats or promises, a party using these techniques effectively must be sure that the promises or threats are clearly communicated to the other party.

Studies of the effectiveness of fear appeals may be applied to the use of threats in bargaining. Such studies in the field of persuasive communication reveal that strong fear appeals seem effective in modifying behavior when presented by a highly credible source (Hewgill & Miller, 1965), and when they deal with issues that are relatively unfamiliar to the subject (e.g., Berkowitz & Cottingham, 1960; Insko et al., 1965; Kraus et al., 1966). However, if the fear appeals are to lead to changes in behaviors, the subjects must be told how the recommended behaviors are to be carried out (Leventhal et al., 1965, 1966), and they must be capable of taking action (Leventhal, 1967; Leventhal & Niles, 1965).

Concede Reluctantly

A bargainer may concede in ways which can in turn affect his opponent's demands and concessions. For example, a bargainer representing management can initially offer a relatively small wage increase but expect to make generous concessions. Or, he may take a position which is close to his maximum acceptable one. He may reciprocate a generous concession by his opponent, or he may stand his ground and exploit the apparent weakness of his opponent's position. The effect of different bargaining strategies on the final result has been studied by letting one subject of the bargaining pair be a stooge who uses a preplanned strategy. Komorita and Brenner (1968) found, for example, that a bargainer could get better results by conceding reluctantly rather than by matching his opponent's concessions. Pruitt and Drews (1969) found that high time-pressure on the negotiations decreased the initial demands, but not the rate with which demands changed over trials. Apparently, the basic mechanism of concession making is not appreciably influenced by decision urgency.

Respond Tit-for-Tat

The results of studies of cooperation in negotiation suggest that the most effective strategy is one called tit-for-tat (Sauermann, 1972). Essentially, the strategy involves reciprocating the cooperative or non-cooperative actions of the other party. Solomon (1960) compared strategies of "unconditional benevolence," "conditional benevolence," and "unconditional malevolence" to determine the extent of cooperation elicited by each from the other party in the prisoner's dilemma game. The conditional benevolence (i.e., rewards for cooperative actions and no rewards for uncooperative actions) was found to be most effective. Similarly, Deutsch et al. (1967) investigated three strategies: "turning the other cheek" (appealing to conscience), "non-punitiveness" (rewarding cooperation but not rewarding non-cooperation), and "deterrence" (rewarding cooperation, punishing non-cooperation). Turning the other cheek resulted in the most exploitation by the other party and deterrence gave the lowest joint outcomes. The non-punitive strategy yielded the highest joint outcomes, apparently because it encourages cooperative behavior but does not permit the other party to exploit the situation.

5.5 Managing Conflict Through Joint Agreements

Some strategies for facilitating decision making in conflict situations emphasize the development of joint agreements among the conflicting parties to reduce the disparity among their desired outcomes. The strategies for facilitating joint agreements that we will discuss in this sub-section operate through several mechanisms. The use of an impartial third party provides a sounding board for airing views before a rational and uncommitted individual. Mutual adjustment of ends and means provides a flexible format for considering the varied interests of the parties. The coalition involves the "joint use of resources" by two or more parties in their efforts to gain the outcomes they desire at the expense of other parties.[6] Collusion and cartels imply a relatively temporary arrangement to cooperate for mutual advantage, in order to gain a competitive advantage over other parties. Mergers involve a more complete pooling of resources for effective functioning, but they do not necessarily involve other parties who must suffer a loss as a result of the joint agreement.

Bring in a Disinterested Third Party

Bringing a disinterested third party into a conflict (Blake et al., 1964) may encourage

joint agreements even when the third party does not perform the role of a mediator or arbitrator. His presence seems to lend an objective viewpoint to the conflict situation and, perhaps, permits the conflicting parties to focus on the central issues, rather than on personalities or the emotional overtones of the issues.

Mutually Adjust

Lindblom (1965) has presented a strategy to assist parties with conflicting interests in moving toward mutually preferable points. This strategy, called "mutual adjustment," involves an open-minded, flexible approach for coping with decision environments characterized by multiplicity, fluidity, and conflict of values. Rather than requiring the involved parties to agree on preemptory rules which set absolute standards for evaluating alternative choices, this strategy explores alternatives for accomplishing broadly defined objectives. Because judgment is deferred, a wide variety of alternatives can be considered, and there is increased opportunity for reconciliation, compromise, and mutual agreement. The fluid approach is consistent with the broader strategy of "disjointed incrementalism" (Braybrooke & Lindblom, 1963), considered in Section 4, since it permits the mutual adjustment of the means and ends involved in the decision. By working back and forth between the themes and possible actions, the decision makers have more freedom to consider the parties' conflicting values and, hopefully, to focus upon the actions for attaining mutually agreeable objectives. Lindblom's discussion of this strategy emphasizes its use in governmental policy setting, but the potential applications would seem much broader.

Form Stable Coalition

A "grand coalition" which includes all the parties to the conflict tends to be stable

---

[6] We will attempt here only to describe strategies suggested by the extensive literature on coalition forma-

tion. For more on coalitions, see Gamson (1964) and Collins and Raven (1969).

since there are no parties outside the coalition to lure away coalition members by offers of more attractive outcomes. Frequently, however, coalitions of fewer than all the parties are advantageous, at least in some bargaining situations. A good deal of attention has been directed to this issue in game theory, and stable solutions have been suggested (e.g., the Von Neumann-Morgenstern imputations, the Shapley value, the core, the bargaining set). The minimum winning size coalition, discussed below, is one example of a stable coalition. Rapoport (1970) provides a good discussion of stable coalitions.

Form Minimum Winning Size Coalition

The most favorable stable coalition for the parties included in the coalition is the minimum winning size coalition (e.g., Gamson, 1961b, 1964). The minimum winning size coalition is the coalition which, out of all the possible winning coalitions, wins by the smallest margin. The reasons for its superiority have been explained on the basis of Gamson's (1961b) minimum resource theory. Since the outcomes will generally be divided among the winning coalition members in proportion to the resources brought to the coalition by its members, any coalition yielding more resources than are required to win would be less favorable for its members than the minimum winning size coalition. Moreover, the greater the excess resources produced by a coalition over those required to win, the less any given amount of resources is worth to a coalition member.

When Gamson (1961a) tested his theory in a make-believe convention, the theory had some success. In his experiment, five players controlled different numbers of votes, and the winning coalition members divided "jobs" among themselves. Payoff was positively related to resources, even when, according to game theory point of view, this was not necessary. To test this theory in a real-life situation, Gamson (1962)

analyzed the presidential nominating conventions since 1900. The theory appeared to have some success, though there are difficulties in applying the theory (e.g., the rewards are contingent on winning the election).

Collude or Merge

When two parties have conflicting interests arising from servicing a third party, they often find it advantageous to be mutually cooperative. Although the cooperation can be achieved implicitly by mutual adjustment described above, it will often be accomplished overtly. When a number of firms are bidding on a series of contracts, for example, they may find it mutually advantageous to agree on some alternating arrangement by which one firm gets the contract one time and another firm at another time, thus avoiding cutthroat pricing. The electrical manufacturers' scandals of the 1950s are examples of this behavior (Fuller, 1962).

To limit the extent to which collusion can take place, and thus protect the buyers of services, governments establish antitrust laws that cover not only firms which collude by remaining separate and forming joint agreements, but also those firms which collude by formally merging. Merger strategies can avoid the conflict by transferring resources among subunits of the merged organization as a subsidy for non-supply of services.

5.6 Managing Conflict Through Structural Mechanisms

Structures for assisting decision makers in conflict situations may take the form of providing or altering (1) rules, (2) procedures, or (3) environmental features. Strategies discussed here are ordered according to the extent to which they demand increasing active involvement of the decision maker with his environment as he attempts to construct mechanisms which help resolve conflict. Strategies involving the use of superordinate goals can be arranged without building an elaborate structure; they can be developed in response to specific conflict situations. Structural mechanisms represent intermediate levels of active involvement by the decision maker; they include market mechanisms, appeal to the legal system, use of sanctions and directives, and mediation and arbitration. Voting typically requires a great deal of active involvement with other decision makers to establish mutually agreed upon voting rules for future decisions.

Redefine Conflict Situation

A widely used strategy in organizations is to stress a shared allegiance to a higher level goal; for example, subordinating decisions regarding departmental budgets to higher-level goals of overall company financial position. Essentially, this strategy reflects the logic that if conflict results from mutually incompatible goals, common goals should promote cooperation. In a series of field experiments, Sherif (1966) found that conflict among groups of boys working toward incompatible goals could be reduced by having the groups work together toward a shared goal. He suggested that the cooperative efforts exerted to attain the superordinate goal reduced future hostilities between groups by increasing the familiarity among group members. It was found to be essential, however, that the groups working toward shared goals be recognized as groups, not as just a number of individuals. The superordinate goal principle is also found in Likert's (1961) formulation of organizational structure. Here members of an organization act as "linking pins" by holding membership in more than one group within the organization.

The "common enemy" effect, identified by the Sherif experiments (1966), provides the basis for redefining intragroup conflict as intergroup conflict. Basically, the experiments found that conflict between groups led to increased group cohesiveness, at least in the early stages of group development.

Although strategies of this general type appear widely used, it should be noted that this strategy simply widens the conflict and seems to provide only a temporary and unstable reduction in intragroup conflict.

Use Market Mechanisms

Recognizing that there are conflicting interests among different suppliers, different demanders, and between suppliers and demanders, we can see that under some very general conditions, market mechanisms serve to efficiently yield cooperative outcomes which make everyone better off (Koopmans, 1951; Buchanan & Tullock, 1962). Hence, in more micro-situations where conflict and cooperative tendencies are present, market mechanisms could be set up in an attempt to resolve the conflict. An additional feature of this approach, the impersonality of "letting the market decide," can lessen the overt antagonism among different parties.

Market mechanisms tend to break down (that is, tend not to yield Pareto-optimal outcomes) under four main conditions: (1) when there are increasing returns to scale, (2) when there are technological externalities, (3) when there are information gaps about production technologies and consumption possibilities, and (4) when there is monopoly power. For a further discussion of market mechanisms, the above conditions and possible solutions, see Davis and Kamien (1969).

Restructure the Environment

Strategies for managing conflict may focus upon restructuring elements of the decision environment to attain a more favorable level of conflict. Although a party may enhance his position by creating a higher level of conflict through environmental manipulation, the more valuable strategies for practical decision attempt to reduce the conflict.

Adding or removing communication channels linking the conflicting parties can effectively alter the level of conflict. Schelling (1960) has noted that communications are important in using decision strategies effectively in conflict situations. Manipulating communication channels by selectively opening or closing them, for example, can be effective as both a defense against threats and as a means for facilitating the use of threats. If a threat is not heard or understood, then the commitment to carry it out becomes meaningless (e.g., when the kidnapper is unable to deliver the ransom note).

Although widely used strategies for reducing conflict in organizations encourage the opening of communication channels among the conflicting parties, it should be recognized that not all situations are amenable to this approach. These strategies of increasing communication appear to be based on the assumption that interpersonal attraction will accompany greater proximity, contact, and interaction. As Shaw (1971) notes, however, increased interpersonal attraction is not due to interaction alone. For example, studies of the effects of increased proximity, through housing unit assignments (Festinger, 1953) and work assignments (Gundlach, 1956), indicate that increased communication enhances interpersonal attraction only when other conditions, such as physical attractiveness (e.g., Walster et al., 1966) or similarity in attitudes and personality (e.g., Byrne & Griffitt, 1966; Byrne et al., 1967) are present. When these conditions are present, opening communication channels should reduce conflict facing decision makers.

Whether, in fact, opening communication channels will increase cooperativeness depends upon the orientation of the parties to the conflict (e.g., Deutsch, 1960; Deutsch & Krauss, 1960). When communication is permitted in experimental studies, trusting parties (e.g., low on the F-Scale) seek a fair outcome and suspicious parties tend to exploit the situation. In other words, open-

ing communication channels permits the parties to employ a number of the strategies discussed earlier.

An alternate approach of reducing conflict by restructuring the environment is to provide buffers between conflicting parties, or even to isolate the parties (March & Simon, 1958). Mediation, discussed below, can be viewed as a means for opening communication channels between the disputants, but with the mediator providing a buffer. Another way to provide a buffer is to separate the parties in order to regulate the level of tension produced by the conflict of interests. For example, the duties delegated to managers competing for scarce resources or for advancement within an organization may be physically separated to reduce contact between them, and/or another individual may be designated to coordinate their functional areas.

Appeal to Legal System

The system of law and courts represents a device for resolving conflict by specifying outcomes for potential conflict situations. In effect, society (acting through the lawmakers, enforcement agencies, and the judicial branch) determines the acceptable outcomes for each party in an exhaustive set of standard conflict situations (e.g., libel suits, monopolistic behaviors in markets, automobile accidents, etc.). Since not all parties to conflict situations may accept the specified outcomes (e.g., a prison sentence), this system, unlike many of the others we discuss, must make provisions for enforcing the distribution of outcomes among the parties. Clearly, if mutually agreed upon sets of outcomes could be generated, the parties would not be likely to appeal to the courts.

Other strategies (e.g., mediation, arbitration, mergers, use of hostages, threats) represent subsets of the broad strategy involving appeal to the system of law and courts at various levels of government (local, national, international). For an extensive discussion of the use of the legal system as a conflict resolving strategy, with emphasis on decision processes, see Friedrich (1964) and Schubert (1963).

Issue Directives

When conflict exists among subunits over which a superordinate unit has some control, the conflict may be handled by directives. The higher level unit may prohibit the parties from engaging in any activities that would cause conflict. The government, for example, issues directives on auto pollution, cigarette advertising, etc. to resolve potential conflict situations (Davis & Kamien, 1969). The effectiveness of directives as a strategy obviously depends on the degree of control exercised by the higher authority and the sanctions available to it if the parties do not comply.

Mediate and Arbitrate

Mediation or conciliation is bargaining in the presence of an acceptable third party who assists the conflicting parties in resolving their differences. Strategies which facilitate the interaction of the conflicting parties through the efforts of an arbitrator or mediator have been widely used in labor disputes. When bargaining has failed, the mediator must use persuasion and compromise to bring the parties together. A skilled mediator may be able to obtain concessions from the parties by adroit maneuvering or he may find a basis for agreement between the parties by some other manner. The timing of the mediator's intervention is crucial; if he enters too early or too often, the parties may save concessions for mediation, and not bargain seriously prior to mediation. If the mediator enters too late, the positions may be too entrenched for concessions to occur. In practical applications, the value of mediation has been clearly demonstrated (e.g., Bloom & Northrup, 1965).

In contrast to mediation, compulsory arbitration vests the third party with power to force a settlement. Usually as a last resort, an unsettled dispute may be arbitrated to prevent serious consequences of non-settlement (e.g., a strike). Strikes or lockouts are forbidden, and the decision of the arbitrator is legally binding on the parties for the period of time stated in the arbitrator's decision. The binding nature of the decision makes it imperative that the parties be willing to accept the judgment of the arbitrator. For further details regarding actual experiences with mediation and arbitration strategies for resolving labor-management conflict, see Simkin (1971).

Vote

Voting involves the application of an external scheme for aggregating individual choice preferences, which must be agreed to by the parties beforehand. The most straightforward means of arriving at multiple-person choice is to use an aggregation rule that will directly transform the set of individual choices into the group choice. A variety of voting models can be used, each providing somewhat different ways of making this transformation. In their analytic study of voting, Buchanan and Tullock (1962) consider the degree of conjunctivity involved in various voting rules as central to the choice rule; that is, in choosing a voting rule, the participants must decide how many group members are required to commit the group. The most common of the voting rules are unanimity, plurality, and majority rule.

Buchanan and Tullock (1962) point out that political exchange is similar to economic exchange since mutual advantage results from the voluntary participation of individuals in the community effort. In Section 4 we discussed a very cooperative form of voting—the SPAN technique.

Different voting rules can apply at different levels. Although unanimity may apply at the constitutional level, less-than-unanimous decision rules may be accepted for carrying out operational decisions. In effect, the impact of the minority position may be felt in its ability to block the imposition of external costs (e.g., cost of a sewage system bond issue) on members of the minority, yet the minority would not have the ability to impose external costs on others.

Majority rule is a widely used voting method, yet it can lead to intransitivities within the voters' choices. Arrow (1951) has shown that only imposed or dictatorial social choices satisfy a reasonable set of axioms. One can, however, use voting methods that may violate one of the axioms at times. The simplest form of majority rule involves the standard referendum on a single issue. In this model, each voter indicates his preference, and the preference of the majority of the whole group is decisive. One defect in this rule is that it ignores the varying intensities of preferences among the voters (Pattanaik, 1971); a voter who is strongly opposed carries the same weight as one who is just mildly opposed to an issue.

Logroll

In sequences of decisions the practice of logrolling can allow for intensity of preferences and particularly for the strongly held views of a minority to be expressed. In this procedure, groups can trade off votes on issues they consider unimportant, but which other groups consider important, for future votes on issues which are important to them (Buchanan & Tullock, 1962; Coleman, 1966). By use of this method, even very weak groups can express some of their preferences.

5.7 Managing Conflict Through Force

A strategy involving the use of force by one or more of the parties in conflict is generally used as a last resort when all other strategies have failed. As Schelling (1960) notes, the party using force must expend resources that would not be necessary if other strategies (e.g., threatening) were used to accomplish the same end. Force would appear to be the admission by the parties to the conflict that their positions are irreconcilable by other means. Ordered by their increasing action orientation, strategies involving force range from gaining power, retaliating and taking hostages, to capturing or destroying the enemy.

Since the use of strategies involving force have limited application in most organizations, they will not be discussed in this chapter. See Boulding (1963) for a basic model of international conflict and Quade (1964) for numerous illustrations of attempts to develop systems for gaining power at the international level. Kaplan (1959) and Schelling (1960) discuss the implications of retaliation for deterring the use of force.

SECTION 6. THE DECISION MAKER

Attributes of *decision makers* that appear likely to mediate the effective use of decision strategies have been noted in discussing the various strategies earlier in this chapter. Taylor and Dunnette (1974) have empirically examined the relative influence of a number of psychological attributes on decision making behaviors. At least four such attributes—perceptual ability, information capacity, risk-taking propensity, and aspiration level—are sufficiently pervasive that they affect decision strategies applicable to each of the environmental conditions we have discussed. Hence, these attributes merit further examination here. The influence of decision maker attributes on the use of choice modes is also explored.

6.1 Perceptual Ability

The way in which a decision maker perceives a problem is a major determinant of the degree of uncertainty, complexity, and conflict he identifies and, hence, the strategies he considers using. His perceptions depend upon the premises he holds about the decision situation. Some of these premises may be explicitly stated while others are held implicitly by the decision maker, frequently through such psychological processes as transfer, set, and functional fixedness (Taylor, 1975). As Rokeach (1960) has noted, unjustified implicit premises may distort the perception of decision problems.

Transfer effects refer to the influence of a decision maker's previous experiences on the way he responds to a current problem. His prior experiences can either facilitate (i.e., positive transfer) or inhibit (i.e., negative transfer) the selection of an appropriate transformation. For example, a marketing approach used successfully with one product may also prove successful with another product. Conversely, the behavior of a businessman accustomed to a highly affiliative secretary may be offensive to her replacement.

The relationship between the previous problem and the current problem determines whether prior experience can successfully be transferred. Depending upon the extent of similarity perceived by the decision maker, transfer can involve specific responses, principles, or an entire class of problem solving behaviors (e.g., learning to learn). Associative learning theory suggests that the strength of a set increases with the number of times a particular solution is attempted in a given problem situation and the success attained by using it.

A problem solving set is a more restricted learned response than the notion of "learning to learn"; the set is usually specific to a single decision rule (punt on third down) or strategy (use participative management). Accordingly, it will aid in solving the kinds of problems for which it was developed but will hinder the solving of others. For example, the set "use participative management" would be an aid in situations where it was crucial that subordinates accept a decision, but would be a hindrance in situations where it was unimportant that subordinates accept a decision. Although problem solving set has been frequently regarded as undesirable in decision making, it should be emphasized that it has the potential to either help or hinder

the decision maker. In many instances, great efficiencies can be attained by identifying a problem as similar to another and using transformations developed previously. Specialized staff and programs in business firms are testimony to this.

Functional fixedness, on the other hand, is always inhibitory. It is the tendency to view as inapplicable a transformation that was previously used to solve another kind of problem (Dunker, 1944–1945). The common laboratory problem for studying this phenomenon is the "candle problem" in which it has been found that using a box to support candles is easier to solve if the box is empty (e.g., Adamson, 1952; Glucksberg, 1962). Functional fixedness occurs only when the transfer is from a familiar use of a transformation to an unfamiliar one; hence, it has considerable interest for the development of "originality" in responses. Maltzman (1960), for example, has presented a technique for prompting original behavior by overcoming functional fixedness.

6.2 Information Capacity

Information processing is generally regarded as a crucial ability of effective decision makers since it plays a major role in being able to utilize strategies under environmental conditions of uncertainty, complexity, and conflict. Almost all decision strategies require an information base, and many operate directly upon information processing capacity, compensating for the human decision maker's cognitive limitations in information search and aggregation.

Implicit assumptions about the information processing capacity of decision makers were made in discussing strategies for coping with informational demands in various situations. In this sub-section, we shall attempt to clarify some of these assumptions by considering individual differences among decision makers in ability to process information. Specifically, we will review the major research efforts directed toward relating psychological attributes of decision makers to information processing behaviors, emphasizing the implications of these relationships for decision making strategies.[7] The decision maker attributes examined here are conceptual structure, dogmatism, and post-decisional inflexibility.

Conceptual Structure

A decision maker's susceptibility to information overload also is mediated by his conceptual structure,[8] which is measured on a dimension of "abstractness" versus "concreteness." "Concreteness" is characterized by the use of few dimensions of information and a simple integrating schemata; "abstractness" is the tendency to process many dimensions of information and to use complex integrative schemata.

In accordance with Berlyne's (1962) theory of curiosity which is used to explain the relationship between conceptual structure and information processing behaviors, Schroeder, Driver, and Streufert (1965) proposed that "abstract" decision makers are more information oriented and would typically process more information in complex decision environments. "Concrete" decision makers, on the other hand, would be expected to reach an overloaded state at lower levels of environmental complexity, hence would tend to process less information than would the abstract decision maker. The research evidence has generally supported this position.

---

[7] Other attributes of decision makers which seem to influence information capacity, etc. are not discussed here because the research evidence demonstrating their influence is inconclusive (e.g., mental ability) or because effective decision making strategies would appear difficult to specify (e.g., age of the decision maker).

[8] The attribute of conceptual structure appears to be a modification of Bieri's (1955) dimension of cognitive complexity to investigate information processing and decision making in a context more general than the impression formation literature (Crockett, 1965) provided. See Schroeder and Suedfeld (1971) for a review of the conceptual structure literature.

In simple decision environments, the research findings suggest that "concrete" decision makers need more information to reach a decision than do "abstract" decision makers (e.g., Schroeder, Driver, & Streufert, 1965). The information seeking behaviors of groups of four "abstract" decision makers were less affected by changes in the amount of information presented to them as an information base than were the information seeking behaviors of groups of four "concrete" decision makers. Sieber and Lanzetta (1964) interpreted similar findings in terms of differential ability to reuse information by "abstract" and "concrete" decision makers. It was suggested that "concrete" individuals, who tend to relate one stimulus to one response, need more information under sub-optimal loads than do "abstract" individuals, who can reuse information for more complex integrations. The internal search processes, which do not appear to vary directly with information load, are hypothesized as the mechanism for generating more balanced search behavior for "abstract" decision makers.

The conceptual structure of a decision maker would appear to influence his effectiveness in a complex environment. Due to their ability to handle the cognitive demands for information search and integration, "abstract" decision makers would be better prepared to cope with uncertainty and disjointedness in the decision environment. Also, their more efficient utilization of information in decision making would seem to enable the "abstract" individuals to more effectively handle decision making under conditions of inadequate informational base.

Dogmatism

Research using the Rokeach Dogmatism Scale (Rokeach, 1960) supports the view that the dogmatic decision maker (i.e., one with a closed belief system) is characterized by rapid decisions based upon relatively little information, yet once made, those decisions are confidently and inflexibly held (e.g., Block & Petersen, 1955; Brengelmann, 1959). Accordingly, dogmatism has been interpreted by Long and Ziller (1965) as a defense mechanism that inhibits pre-decisional information processing. This conclusion has received further support from the positive association found between dogmatism and anxiety (Rokeach, 1960). Limited pre-decisional information search was hypothesized to serve as a defense; it closes the mind to new information and eliminates any need for the decision maker to reevaluate his self-concept. The dogmatic decision maker would, therefore, be expected to unduly restrict his information input. The resulting reduction in his information capacity would severely handicap his ability to apply strategies for coping with decision problems, especially those which appear to offer a personal threat to his self-concept.

Post-Decisional Inflexibility

In addition to differences in information processing abilities, effective use of decision strategies must consider the frequently observed tendency of decision makers to resist changing a decision once it is made (e.g., Gibson & Nicol, 1964; Pruitt, 1961). Pruitt, for example, when comparing the amount of information required to make a decision initially with the amount of information required to change a decision, found that considerably more information was required to change the decision than to make it initially. Gibson and Nicol (1964) confirmed Pruitt's conclusion and, furthermore, found that decisions based on more information were more resistant to change.

Evidence regarding the tendency of decision makers to seek supportive information following a decision (e.g., Mills et al., 1959; Rosen, 1961) has been seriously questioned in the Freedman and Sears review (1965). Although decision makers may attempt to justify their decisions during the post-decisional period, McGuire's (1968) discussion of the selective exposure research concluded that defensive avoidance seems to have only minor influence upon the selectivity noted in the post-decisional information search. The selectivity necessitated by the decision maker's limited information processing abilities would appear to exert a much more powerful influence upon the effective application of decision strategies.

6.3 Risk-Taking Propensity

Propensity for taking risks is another attribute of decision makers that pervasively influences decision strategies used to cope with a wide range of environmental characteristics. In a risky decision situation, the decision maker is uncertain about outcomes and about the possibility of losses (including opportunity losses) of resources. According to experimental findings from studies of gambling situations (Slovic & Lichtenstein, 1968), risk behavior is influenced more by the probabilities than by the payoffs.

Strategic Implications of Risk-Taking Propensity

A variety of approaches has been developed to represent risk-taking propensity: the utility function (Friedman & Savage, 1948), the mean-variance criterion (Markowitz, 1959), the measures developed in the psychological literature (e.g., Atkinson, 1957; Kogan & Wallach, 1964; Shure & Meeker, 1967).

Measuring risk-taking propensity can be useful to managers and co-workers seeking to obtain a better insight into their own and each other's attitudes toward risk. Grayson (1960) gives an example of how, when their utility functions were shown to them and the implications discussed, two co-owners (brothers) and a geologist in a small oil exploration firm obtained a better understanding of the risks each had been taking in the past and would take in the future.

Although Spetzler (1968) found a diversity of utility functions of the top managers within the same company, Swalm (1966) found that most managers in a large company had very risk-averse utility functions. Rather than using the more risk-neutral strategy that would be better for the company as a whole when small percentages of its resources were at stake, the managers seemed to be using their own very risk-averse utility. Having such knowledge provides the organization with a basis for changing the motivational arrangement so that managers at lower levels will be encouraged to take more risks.

An increasing number of theoretical and research articles have examined risk taking as a psychological trait and have attempted to relate it to problem solving ability (Bruner et al., 1956), creativity (McClelland, 1961), and vocational choice and entrepreneurship (McClelland, 1961; Ziller, 1957). They have discovered that risk-taking propensity can account for differences in behavior among decision makers within these spheres of activity. For an excellent summary of the implications of these factors, the reader is referred to Kogan and Wallach (1967).

Group Risk Taking

Knowing whether groups or individuals have greater risk-taking propensity may be helpful in determining appropriate situations for using decision making groups. Although early management literature suggested that groups tend to make less risky decisions than do individuals, within the past decade a number of experiments have indicated that groups make riskier decisions than do individuals (Kogan & Wallach, 1967).

Many of the experiments have used the choice dilemma problems in which individuals are asked to provide a minimum acceptable probability for a hypothetical choice situation. Then the individuals are formed into groups which discuss the problem until a consensus is reached. The groups usually recommend a probability higher than the average of the individual recom-

mendations, implying a shift toward risk. To account for this shift, various explanations have been advanced: (1) there is a diffusion of responsibility through the group, (2) there is a social value in being perceived as a risk taker, and (3) the leaders most influencing group discussions are likely to be more risk inclined. No one of these explanations seems to account for the risky shift in groups, but each has received some confirmation. Kelley and Thibaut (1969) suggest that riskier group decisions are produced by the mutual influence of (1) diffusion of responsibility and (2) our cultural acceptance of statements of risk. They conclude that it is the group discussion period, rather than the requirement of a decision, that produces the shift effect. Kogan and Wallach (1967) also provide a good review of this area, and Vinokur (1971) raises some provocative issues.

6.4 Aspiration Level

The decision maker's level of aspiration critically influences his effectiveness in applying decision strategies under a wide variety of environmental conditions. It strongly influences his effectiveness in identifying problems, evaluating alternative courses of action, and setting negotiation bids. Essentially, the aspiration level represents a threshold that the decision maker tries to attain (Lewin et al., 1944; Siegel, 1957) and according to some theorists, aspiration level represents the only vehicle for incorporating preferences into the decision (Simon, 1955).

Three conditions that affect aspiration level in decision tasks—prior experiences of success or failure, setting specific goals, and receiving knowledge of results—have been extensively researched.[9] Although these conditions may prove effective in a strategy for modifying the aspiration level of a decision

---

[9] For specific findings regarding conditions affecting aspiration level, see Solley and Stagner (1956), Feather (1966, 1967, 1968), Bryan and Locke (1967), and Brickman and Campbell (1971).

maker, the major efforts to empirically investigate the impact of aspiration level upon decision making have dealt with bargaining and are more appropriately reviewed in Section 5.

Helson's "hypothesis of par" states that individuals set a standard of excellence for themselves which is usually below their capabilities and that they try to meet, but not exceed, this standard. It is important that standards be set at an optimal level. Standards that are set too high lead to frustration since the decision maker continually fails to achieve them; aspiration levels that are set too low either do not serve as effective motivators of performance or do not provide appropriate standards for problem identification, since they can be readily achieved. Stedry (1960), using empirical results, develops the relationships between high and low aspiration levels and tight and loose budgets, and Ansoff (1965) and Hansberger (1969) discuss the uses of aspiration or goal level (e.g., achieving an increase of 20 percent in earnings per share) in corporate strategy decisions.

6.5 Influence of Decision Maker Attributes on Choice Modes

Effective use of choice modes is influenced by the attributes of the decision maker and by the attributes of the decision situation. The four decision maker attributes —perceptual ability, information processing capacity, aspiration level, and risk-taking propensity—appear to strongly influence the selection of an appropriate choice mode, since the choice modes—maximizing, satisficing, and incrementalizing—reflect different problem perceptions, require different information processing capacities, and imply different levels of aspiration and risk-taking propensity.

Maximizing

The maximizing mode typically involves a well-established set of alternatives and a clear specification of the ideal level of attainment. The alternative that comes closest to the ideal level is the one to be chosen. Maximizing modes place considerable information processing demands on the decision maker. In the extreme sense, he is expected to generate the complete set of alternatives, to specify all possible outcomes, and then to process the alternatives and compare them to the criterion. By maximizing, however, he will be better off—by definition. The only reason for not maximizing, then, would be that he is not able to do so.

The most general and well-developed maximizing theory of decision making involves the *maximization of expected utility*. The two main components of this theory, personal probabilities and utilities, are discussed at some length in Section 3 and earlier in this section. The theory first specifies the set of alternatives to choose among and identifies the set of payoff-relevant events. Personal probabilities are then assigned to the events, and utilities are assigned to the outcomes. The utility of an outcome is then mulitplied by the probability of the event leading to the outcome, and these products are then summed over all events to get an expected utility for a given action. The expected utilities for all the alternatives are compared, and the largest one is chosen (Fishburn, 1970; Ramsey, 1931; Savage, 1954).

The maximizing of expected utility is a normative theory in that it specifies what decision makers should do. Its prescriptive nature can be defended by pointing out that not to maximize expected utility would be to act contrary to the decision maker's own values and beliefs, since they are reflected in the expected utility. Perhaps more convincing is that, formally, the theorem prescribing maximization of expected utility is derived from some more simple axioms. If the decision maker wished to adopt all of these norms to guide his decision behavior, he should act so as to maximize expected utility. The axioms specify transitivity (i.e., circular judgments should not be made), independence of beliefs from tastes (i.e., wishful thinking should not be engaged in), dominance (i.e., an action that will always give at least as much as any other action is to be preferred), the irrelevance of identical outcomes (i.e., only outcomes that help to discriminate among alternatives are considered), and a few other structural properties (Marschak, 1964; Savage, 1954). MacCrimmon (1968a) has found that while business executives tend to violate one or more of these axioms in their actual choices, they would, upon reflection, generally accept them as good norms of behavior and would use them to guide future decisions; that is, they view violations of the axioms as mistakes that they would correct.

Satisficing

Given the high information processing demand, and the time and effort entailed in the maximizing methods, the decision maker may be willing to settle for something less than the maximum in his use of decision strategies. In a satisficing mode (Simon, 1957b), the decision maker sets up a feasible aspiration level, then searches for alternatives until he finds one that achieves this level. As soon as a satisfactory alternative is found, he terminates his search and chooses that alternative.

The theory is primarily descriptive, but to the extent that the decision maker cannot maximize, satisficing can be said to have some normative elements, too. Correspondence can be made between maximizing and satisficing at least at a formal level by noting that satisficing could be thought of as maximization with a two-valued (i.e., satisfactory and not satisfactory) utility function, or by explicitly taking into account the costs of search and by having an aspiration level that is based on costs and expectations in a direct utility assessment manner (Charnes & Cooper, 1963). Advocates of "satisficing man," however, would claim that the key element is that a decision maker cannot in fact make these determinations. Studies have found that satisficing is

commonly used, for example, by trust investment officers (Clarkson, 1962) and department store buyers (Cyert & March, 1963).

Incrementalizing

Successive limited comparisons, an approach described by Lindblom (1959) relates quite closely to satisficing. Under this strategy the decision maker will attempt to take only small steps or increments away from the existing state toward the desired state. Few objectives are considered, and the alternatives are generally ones that are familiar to the decision maker or that he can generate by local search. Possibly important outcomes, values, and alternatives are neglected. Agreement among the decision makers is sought instead of very high goal attainment. Lindblom has also called this approach "muddling through." Obviously, it is primarily a descriptive model of how decisions are made, rather than being prescriptive. Braybrooke and Lindblom's (1963) formulation of a strategy based on disjointed incrementalizing was discussed in Section 4.

SECTION 7. SUMMARY

Throughout this chapter, we have discussed the strategies a decision maker can use in dealing with an environment characterized by uncertainty, complexity, and conflict. The general classes of strategies we have examined are summarized in Table 1; again they are arranged in order of increasing active involvement with each type of environment.

Although organizing the material directly in terms of strategies, rules, or heuristics may be somewhat unusual, we hope that it will provide the decision maker with a set of responses he can actually employ in dealing with his environment. In some cases the strategies discussed are based on extensive descriptive studies: in other cases, the backing is very limited, but the degree to which the strategies are grounded in em-

TABLE 1
CLASSES OF STRATEGIES FOR MAKING DECISIONS UNDER UNCERTAINTY, COMPLEXITY,
AND CONFLICT REFERENCED BY SUB-SECTION NUMBER

Classes of Strategies	Attributes of Decision Environment		
	Section 3 Uncertainty	Section 4 Complexity	Section 5 Conflict
Perception	3.1	4.2	5.2
Models	3.2	4.1	5.1
Alternatives	3.3	4.3	5.4
Information processing	3.4	4.5	5.3
Adverse consequences	3.5		5.7
Problem diagnosis		4.4	
Aggregating preference		4.6	5.5
Structural			5.6

pirical research should be apparent from our discussion. In each area we have tried to provide key references to the more detailed studies.

We hope that organizing the decision making and problem solving studies in terms of their possible end use instead of traditional paradigms will provide the researcher with new perspectives that have a higher potential application. In addition, while it is a long way off, we hope that the different orientations will help to build toward general theories of decision making and problem solving.

REFERENCES

Abelson, R. P. A summary of hypotheses on modes of resolution. In R. P. Abelson, E. Aronson, W. J. McGuire, T. M. Newcomb, M. J. Rosenberg, & P. H. Tannenbaum (Eds.), *Theories of cognitive consistency: A sourcebook.* Chicago: Rand McNally, 1968.

Ackoff, R. L. Management misinformation systems. *Management Science,* 1967, 14, B147–B156.

Ackoff, R. L. *A concept of corporate planning.* New York: Wiley, 1970.

Adamson, R. E. Functional fixedness as related to problem solving: A repetition of three experiments. *Journal of Experimental Psychology,* 1952, 44, 288–291.

Adorno, T. W., Frenkel-Brunswik, E., Levinson, D. J., & Sanford, R. N. *The authoritarian personality.* New York: Harper and Row, 1950.

Alpert, M., & Raiffa, H. *A progress report on the training of probability assessors.* Unpublished manuscript, Harvard University, Cambridge, 1969.

Ansoff, H. I. *Corporate strategy.* New York: McGraw-Hill, 1965.

Arrow, K. J. *Social choice and individual values.* New York: Wiley, 1951.

Atkinson, J. W. Motivational determinants of risk-taking behavior. *Psychological Review,* 1957, 64, 359–372.

Attneave, F. *Applications of information theory to psychology.* New York: Holt, Rinehart and Winston, 1959.

Barnard, C. I. *The functions of the executive.* Cambridge: Harvard University Press, 1938.

Bavelas, A. A mathematical model for group structures. *Applied Anthropology,* 1948, 7, 16–30.

Bavelas, A. Communication patterns in task-oriented groups. *Journal of the Acoustical Society of America,* 1950, 22, 725–730.

Bayes, T. Essay towards solving a problem in the doctrine of chances. *Philosophical Transactions,* 1763, 53, 370–418.

Bellman, R. E., & Dreyfus, S. E. *Applied dynamic programming.* Santa Monica, Calif.: Rand Corporation, 1962.

Berkowitz, L., & Cottingham, D. The interest value and relevance of fear-arousing communications. *Journal of Abnormal and Social Psychology,* 1960, 60, 37–43.

Berlyne, D. E. *Conflict, arousal, and curiosity.* New York: McGraw-Hill, 1960.

Berlyne, D. E. Uncertainty and epistemic curiosity. *British Journal of Psychology,* 1962, 53, 27–34.

Berlyne, D. E. Attention, curiosity, and decision. In D. P. Hunt & D. L. Zink (Eds.), *Predecisional process in decision making,* AMRL-TDR-64-77, December, 1964, 101–115.

Bettman, J. R. The structure of consumer choice process. *Journal of Marketing Research,* 1971, VIII, 465–471.

Bieri, J. Cognitive complexity-simplicity and predictive behavior. *Journal of Abnormal Social Psychology,* 1955, 51, 263–268.

Blake, R. R., Shepard, H. A., & Mouton, J. S. *Managing intergroup conflict in industry.* Houston: Gulf, 1964.

Block, J., & Petersen, P. Some personality correlates of confidence, caution, and speed in a decision situation. *Journal of Abnormal Social Psychology,* 1955, 51, 34–41.

Bloom, G. F., & Northrup, H. R. *Economics of labor relations.* (5th ed.) Homewod, Ill.: Irwin, 1965.

Borch, K. H. *The economics of uncertainty.* Princeton: Princeton University Press, 1968.

Boulding, K. E. *Conflict and defense: A general theory.* New York: Harper and Row, 1963.

Bray, D. W., & Moses, J. L. Personnel selection. *Annual Review of Psychology,* 1972, 545–576.

Braybrooke, D., & Lindblom, C. E. *A strategy of decision.* New York: The Free Press, 1963.

Brengelmann, J. C. Abnormal and personality correlates of certainty. *Journal of Mental Science,* 1959, 105, 142–162.

Brickman, P., & Campbell, D. T. Hedonic relativism and planning the good society. In M. H. Appley (Ed.), *Adaptation-level theory: A symposium.* New York: Academic Press, 1971.

Bruner, J. S., Goodnow, J. J., & Austin, G. A. *A study of thinking.* New York: Wiley, 1956.

Bryan, J. F., & Locke, E. A. Goal setting as a means for increasing motivation. *Journal of Applied Psychology,* 1967, 53, 3, 274–277.

Buchanan, J. M., & Tullock, G. *The calculus of consent.* Ann Arbor: University of Michigan Press, 1962.

Byrne, D., & Griffitt, W. A developmental investigation of the law of attraction. *Journal of Personality and Social Psychology,* 1966, 4, 699–702.

Byrne, D., Griffitt, W., & Stefaniak, D. Attraction and similarity of personality characteristics. *Journal of Personality and Social Psychology,* 1967, 5, 82–90.

Campbell, J. P., Dunnette, M. D., Lawler, E. E. III, & Weick, K. E. Jr. *Managerial behavior, performance, and effectiveness.* New York: McGraw-Hill, 1970.

Campion, J. E. Jr. *Effects of managerial style on subordinates' attitudes and performance in a simulated organization setting.* Unpublished doctoral dissertation, University of Minnesota, Minneapolis, 1968.

Carlson, R. E. Selection interview decisions: The relative influence of appearance and factual written information on an interviewer's final rating. *Journal of Applied Psychology,* 1967, 51, 461–468.

Carlson, R. E., & Mayfield, E. C. Selection interview decisions: The effect of type of information on inter- and intra-interviewer agreement. *Personnel Psychology,* 1967, 20, 441–460.

Carter, E. E. The behavioral theory of the firm and top-level corporate decision. *Administrative Science Review,* 1971, 16, 413–429.

Cetron, M. J., & Ralph, C. A. *Industrial applications of technological forecasting.* New York: Wiley, 1971.

Chambers, J. C., Mullick, S. K., & Smith, D. D. How to choose the right forecasting technique. *Harvard Business Review,* 1971, 49, 45–74.

Charnes, A., & Cooper, W. W. Deterministic equivalents for optimizing and satisficing under chance constraints. *Operations Research,* 1963, 11, 18–39.

Churchman, C. W. *Hegelian inquiring systems: Space sciences: Lab social sciences project.* Working paper 49. Berkeley: University of California, 1966.

Churchman, C. W., Ackoff, R. L., & Arnoff, E. L. *Operations Research.* New York: Wiley, 1957.

Clarkson, G. P. E. *Portfolio selection: A simulation of trust investment.* Englewood Cliffs, N.J.: Prentice-Hall, 1962.

Cohen, A. M. Changing small group communication networks. *Journal of Communication,* 1961, 11, 116–124.

Cohen, D. J., Witmyre, J. W., & Funk, W. H. Effect of group cohesiveness and training upon group thinking. *Journal of Applied Psychology*, 1960, 44, 319–322.

Coleman, J. S. The possibility of a social welfare function. *The American Economic Review*, 1966, 56, 1105–1122.

Collins, B. E., & Raven, B. Group structure: Attraction, coalitions, communication, and power. In G. Lindzey & E. Aronson (Eds.), *The handbook of social psychology*. Reading, Mass.: Addison-Wesley, 1969.

Coombs, C. H. *A theory of data*. New York: Wiley, 1964.

Cournot, A. *Researches into the mathematical principles of the theory of wealth*. N. J. Bacon (trans.). New York: Macmillan, 1897.

Crockett, W. H. Cognitive complexity and impression formation. In S. A. Maher (Ed.), *Progress in experimental personality research*, Vol. 2. New York: Academic Press, 1965, 47–90.

Cromwell, H. The relative effect on audience attitude of the first versus the second argumentative speech of a series. *Speech Monographs*, 1950, 17, 105–122.

Cronbach, L. J. *Essentials of psychological testing*. (3rd ed.) New York: Harper and Row, 1970.

Crovitz, H. F. *Galton's walk*. New York: Harper and Row, 1970.

Cyert, R. M., & DeGroot, M. H. Multiperiod decisions models with alternating choice as a solution to the duopoly problem. *Quarterly Journal of Economics*, 1970, 84, 410–429.

Cyert, R. M., & MacCrimmon, K. R. Organizations. In G. Lindzey & E. Aronson (Eds.), *The handbook of social psychology*. Reading, Mass.: Addison-Wesley, 1968, Chapter 8.

Cyert, R. M., & March, J. G. *A behavioral theory of the firm*. Englewood Cliffs, N.J.: Prentice-Hall, 1963.

Dalkey, N., & Helmer, O. An experimental application of the Delphi method to the use of experts. *Management Science*, 1963, 9, 458–467.

Davis, D. A., & Kamien, M. I. Externalities, information and alternative collective action, analysis and evaluation of public expenditures: The PPB system. *Joint economic committee compendium, 91st Congress, 1st session*, 1969, 1, 67–86.

Davis, G. A., & Manski, M. E. An instructional

method for increasing originality. *Psychonomic Science*, 1966, 6, 73–74.

Dawes, R. Social selection based on multidimensional criteria. *Journal of Abnormal Psychology*, 1964, 23, 104–109.

Dawes, R. Graduate admissions: A case study. *The American Psychologist*, 1971, 26, 180–188.

de Finetti, D. Foresight: Its logical laws, its subjective sources. In H. E. Kyburg & H. E. Smokler (Eds.), *Studies in subjective probability*. New York: Wiley, 1964.

de Groot, A. D. *Thought and choice in chess*. The Hague: Moulton, 1965.

Deutsch, M. Trust trustworthiness, and the F-scale. *Journal of Abnormal and Social Psychology*, 1960, 61, 138–140.

Deutsch, M., & Krauss, R. M. The effect of threat upon interpersonal bargaining. *Journal of Abnormal and Social Psychology*, 1960, 61, 181–189.

Deutsch, M., Epstein, Y., Canavan, D., & Gumpert, P. Strategies of inducing cooperation: An experimental study. *Journal of Conflict Resolution*, 1967, 11, 345–360.

Driscoll, J., & Lanzetta, J. Effects of two sources of uncertainty in decision making. *Psychological Reports*, 1965, 17, 635–648.

Drucker, P. F. Managing for business effectiveness. *Harvard Business Review*, 1963, 41, 53–60.

Dunker, K. On problem solving. *Psychological Monographs*, 1944–1945, 58, 1–111.

Dunnette, M. D. *Personnel selection and placement*. Belmont, Calif.: Wadsworth Publishing, 1966.

Dunnette, M. D., Campbell, J. P., & Jaastad, K. The effect of group participation on brainstorming effectiveness for two industrial samples. *Journal of Applied Psychology*, 1963, 47, 30–37.

Edwards, W. Man and computers. In R. M. Gagné (Ed.), *Psychological principles in system development*. New York: Holt, Rinehart and Winston, 1962, 75–114.

Edwards, W. Introduction: Revision of opinions by men and man-machine systems. *IEEE Transactions*, 1966, HFE-7, 1–6.

Edwards, W. Conservatism in human information processing. In B. Kleinmuntz (Ed.), *Formal representation of human judgment*. New York: Wiley, 1968.

Edwards, W., & Phillips, L. Man as transducer for probabilities in Bayesian command and control systems. In M. W. Shelley & G. L. Bryan (Eds.), *Human judgments and optimality*. New York: Wiley, 1964, 360–404.

Edwards, W., Phillips, L. D., Hays, W. L., & Goodman, B. C. Probabilistic information processing systems: Design and evaluation. *IEEE Transactions on Systems, Science and Cybernetics*, 1968, SSC-4, 248–265.

Feather, N. T. Effects of prior success and failure on expectations of success and subsequent performance. *Journal of Personality and Social Psychology*, 1966, 3, 287–298.

Feather, N. T. Level of aspiration and performance variability. *Journal of Personality and Social Psychology*, 1967, 6, 1, 37–46.

Feather, N. T. Valence of success and failure in relation to task difficulty: Past research and recent progress. *Australian Journal of Psychology*, 1968, 20, 2, 111–122.

Feinberg, A. An experimental investigation of an interactive approach for multi-criterion optimization with an application to academic resource allocation. Unpublished doctoral dissertation, University of California at Los Angeles, 1972.

Feldman, J. Simulation of behaviour in the binary choice experiments. In E. A. Feigenbaum & J. Feldman (Eds.), *Computer and thought*. New York: McGraw-Hill, 1963, 329–346.

Feldman, J., & Kanter, H. E. Organizational decision making. In J. G. March (Ed.), *Handbook of organizations*. Chicago: Rand McNally, 1965.

Festinger, L. Group attraction and membership. In D. Cartwright & A. Zander (Eds.), *Group dynamics: Research and theory*. Evanston, Ill.: Row, Peterson, 1953, 92–101.

Festinger, L. *A theory of cognitive dissonance*. Evanston, Ill.: Row, Peterson, 1957.

Festinger, L. *Conflict, decision, and dissonance*. Stanford: Stanford University Press, 1964.

Fishburn, P. C. *Utility theory for decision making*. New York: Wiley, 1970.

Fouraker, L. E., & Siegel, S. *Bargaining behavior*. New York: McGraw-Hill, 1963.

Franklin, B. A letter to Joseph Priestley, 1772. Reprinted in B. Franklin, *The Benjamin Franklin sampler*. New York: Fawcett Publications, 1956.

Freedman, J. L., & Sears, D. O. In L. Berkowitz (Ed.), *Selective exposure: Advances in experimental social psychology*. New York: Academic Press, 1965.

Friedman, M., & Savage, L. J. The utility analysis of choices involving risk. *Journal of Political Economics*, 1948, 56, 279–304.

Friedrich, C. J., Ed. *Nomos VII: Rational decision*. New York: Atherton Press, 1964.

Fuller, J. G. *The gentlemen conspirators*. New York: Grove Press, 1962.

Gamson, W. A. An experimental test of a theory of coalition formation. *American Sociological Review*, 1961, 26, 565–573. (a)

Gamson, W. A. A theory of coalition formation. *American Sociological Review*, 1961, 26, 373–382. (b)

Gamson, W. A. Coalition formation at presidential nominating conventions. *American Journal of Sociology*, 1962, 68, 157–171.

Gamson, W. A. Experimental studies of coalition formation. In L. Berkowitz (Ed.), *Advances in experimental social psychology*, Vol. I. New York: Academic Press, 1964, 81–110.

Garner, W. R. *Uncertainty and structure as psychological concepts*. New York: Wiley, 1962.

Geoffrion, A. M., Dyer, J. S., & Feinberg, A. An interactive approach for multi-criterion optimization, with an application to the operation of an academic department. *Management Science*, 1972, 19, 357–368.

Gergen, K. J. *The psychology of behavior exchange*. Reading, Mass.: Addison-Wesley, 1969.

Gibson, R. S., & Nicol, E. H. *The modification of decisions made in a changing environment*. USAF-ESD-TR-No. 64-657, 1964.

Glanzer, M., & Glaser, R. Techniques for the study of group structure and behavior: II. Empirical studies of the effects of structure in small groups. *Psychological Bulletin*, 1961, 58, 1–27.

Glucksberg, S. The influence of strength of drive on functional fixedness and perceptual recognition. *Journal of Experimental Psychology*, 1962, 63, 36–51.

Gordon, W. J. J. *Synectics*. New York: Harper and Row, 1961.

Grayson, C. J. *Decisions under uncertainty*. Cambridge: Harvard University Press, 1960.

Guion, R. M. *Personnel testing*. New York: McGraw-Hill, 1965.

Gundlach, R. H. Effects of on-the-job experiences with Negroes upon racial attitudes of white workers in union shops. *Psychological Reports*, 1956, 2, 67–77.

Gustafson, D. H. Evaluation of probabilistic information processing in medical decision making. *Organizational Behavior and Human Performance*, 1969, 4, 20–34.

Gustafson, D. H. et al. *A decision-theory approach to measuring severity in illness.* Ann Arbor: Burn Research Center, University of Michigan, 1969.

Haaland, G., & Venkateson, M. Resistance to persuasive communications: An examination of the distraction hypotheses. *Journal of Personality and Social Psychology*, 1968, 9, 167–170.

Hansberger, R. V. Bob Hansberger shows how to grow without becoming a conglomerate. In J. McDonald, *Fortune*, October, 1969, 134ff.

Hawkins, C., & Lanzetta, J. Uncertainty, importance, and arousal as determinants of predecisional information search. *Psychological Reports*, 1965, 17, 791–800.

Hegel, G. W. F. *The phenomenology of mind.* (2nd ed.) London: George Allen and Unwin, 1964 (1820).

Hertz, D. B. Risk analysis in capital investment. *Harvard Business Review*, 1964, 42, 95.

Hertz, D. B. Investment policies that pay off. *Harvard Business Review*, 1968, 46, 96–108.

Hewgill, M., & Miller, G. Source credibility and response to fear-arousing communications. *Speech Monographs*, 1965, 32, 95–101.

Hirota, K. Group problem solving and communication. *Japanese Journal of Psychology*, 1953, 24, 176–178.

Hoffman, P. J., Slovic, P., & Rorer, L. G. An analysis-of-variance model for the assessment of configural cue utilization in clinical judgment. *Psychological Bulletin*, 1968, 68, 338–349.

Hovland, C. I. Effects of the mass media of communication. In G. Lindzey (Ed.), *Handbook of social psychology.* Reading, Mass.: Addison-Wesley, 1954.

Howard, R. A. Information value theory. *IEEE Transactions in Systems Sciences and Cybernetics*, 1966, SSC-2, 22–34.

Howard, R. A. The foundations of decision analysis. *IEEE Transactions in Systems Science and Cybernetics*, 1968, SSC-4, 1–9.

Howard, R. A. Proximal decision analysis. *Management Science*, 1971, 17, 507–541.

Insko, C., Arkoff, A., & Insko, V. Effects of high and low fear-arousing communications upon opinions toward smoking. *Journal of Experimental Social Psychology*, 1965, 1, 256–266.

Janis, I., Kaye, D., & Kirschner, P. Facilitating effects of "eating-while-reading" on responsiveness to persuasive communications. *Journal of Personality and Social Psychology*, 1965, 1, 181–186.

Johnson, D. M. Solution of anagrams. *Psychological Bulletin*, 1966, 66, 371–384.

Kaplan, M. A. The strategy of limited retaliation. *Policy memorandum 19 of the Center of International Study*, Princeton University, Princeton, 1959.

Kaplan, R. J., & Newman, J. R. Studies in probabilistic information processing. *IEEE Transaction*, 1966, HFE-7, 49–63.

Karlins, M., & Abelson, H. I. *Persuasion: How opinions and attitudes are changed.* New York: Springer, 1970.

Kates, R. W. *Hazard and choice perception in flood plain management.* Chicago: University of Chicago, Department of Geography, 1962.

Katona, G. *Psychological analysis of economic behavior.* New York: McGraw-Hill, 1951.

Kaufman, H. *The forest ranger.* Baltimore: Johns Hopkins University Press, 1960.

Keeney, R. L. Evaluating multidimensional situations using a quasi-separable utility function. *IEEE Transactions on Man-Machine Systems*, 1968, MMS-9, 25–28. (a)

Keeney, R. L. Quasi-separable utility functions. *Naval Research Logistics Quarterly*, 1968, 15, 551–565. (b)

Kelley, H. H. Interpersonal accommodation. *American Psychologist*, 1968, 23, 399–410.

Kelley, H. H., & Thibaut, J. W. Group problem solving. In G. Lindzey & E. Aronson (Eds.), *Handbook of social psychology*, Vol. 4. (2nd ed.) Reading, Mass.: Addison-Wesley, 1969.

Kepner, C. H., & Tregoe, B. B. *The rational manager.* New York: McGraw-Hill, 1965.

Kleinmuntz, B. The processing of clinical information by man and machine. In B. Kleinmuntz (Ed.), *Formal representation of human judgement.* New York: Wiley, 1968.

Knight, F. H. *Risk, uncertainty, and profit.* Clifton, N. J.: Kelley, 1920.

Koestler, A. *The ghost in the machine.* London: Hutchinson Publishing Group, 1967.

Kogan, N., & Wallach, M. A. *Risk taking: A study in cognition and personality.* New York: Holt, Rinehart and Winston, 1964.

Kogan, N., & Wallach, M. A. Risk taking as a function of the situation, the person, and the group. In G. Mandler (Ed.), *New directions of psychology, III.* New York: Holt, Rinehart and Winston, 1967.

Komorita, S. S., & Brenner, A. R. Bargaining and concession making under bilateral monopoly. *Journal of Personality and Social Psychology,* 1968, 9, 15–20.

Koopmans, T. C., Ed. *Activity analysis of production and allocation.* New York: Wiley, 1951.

Kort, F. A nonlinear model for the analysis of judicial decisions. *The American Political Science Review,* 1968, 62, 546–555.

Kraus, S., El-Assal, E., & De Fleur, M. Fear-threat appeals in mass communication: An apparent contradiction. *Speech Monographs,* 1966, 33, 23–29.

Kuehn, A. A., & Hamburger, H. J. A heuristic program for locating warehouses. *Management Science,* 1963, 9, 643–666.

Kunreuther, H. Extensions of Bowman's theory on managerial decision making. *Management Science,* 1969, 15, 415–439.

Lanzetta, J. T., & Driscoll, J. M. Effects of uncertainty and importance on information search in decision making. *Journal of Personality and Social Psychology,* 1968, 10, 479–486.

Lanzetta, J. T., & Kanareff, V. T. Information cost, amount of payoff, and level of aspiration as determinants of information seeking in decision making. *Behavioral Science,* 1962, 7, 459–473.

Lawson, E. D. Reinforced and non-reinforced four-man communication nets. *Psychological Reports,* 1964, 14, 287-296.

Lawson, E. D. Change in communication nets, performance, and morale. *Human Relations,* 1965, 18, 139–147.

Leavitt, H. J. Some effects of certain communication patterns on group performance. *Journal of Abnormal Social Psychology,* 1951, 46, 38–50.

Leontief, W. *Input-output economics.* Oxford, England: Oxford University Press, 1966.

Leventhal, H. Fear: For your health. *Psychology Today,* 1967, 1, 54–58.

Leventhal, H., & Niles, P. Persistence of influence for varying duration of exposure to threat stimuli. *Psychological Reports,* 1965, 16, 223–233.

Leventhal, H., Jones, S., & Trembly, G. Sex differences in attitude and behavior change under conditions of fear and specific instructions. *Journal of Experimental Social Psychology,* 1966, 2, 387–399.

Leventhal, H., Singer, R., & Jones, S. Effects of fear and specificity of recommendations upon attitudes and behavior. *Journal of Personality and Social Psychology,* 1965, 2, 20–29.

Levy, L. H. Originality as a role-defined behavior. *Journal of Personality and Social Psychology,* 1968, 9, 72–78.

Lewin, K., Dembo, L., Festinger, L., & Sears, P. Level of aspiration. In J. M. Hunt (Ed.), *Personality and behavior disorders.* New York: Ronald Press, 1944.

Likert, R. *New patterns of management.* New York: McGraw-Hill, 1961.

Lindblom, C. E. The science of muddling through. *Public Administration Review,* 1959, 19, 79–88.

Lindblom, C. E. *The intelligence of democracy: Decision making through mutual adjustment.* New York: The Free Press, 1965.

Long, B. H., & Ziller, R. C. Dogmatism and predecisional information search. *Journal of Applied Psychology,* 1965, 49, 376–378.

Lott, A. J., & Lott, B. E. Group cohesiveness, communication level, and conformity. *Journal of Abnormal and Social Psychology,* 1961, 62, 408–412.

Lucas, W. F. An overview of the mathematical theory of games. *Management Science,* January, 1972, 18, No. 5, Part 2, 3–19.

Luce, R. D., & Raiffa, H. *Games and decisions.* New York: Wiley, 1957.

Lumsdaine, A., & Janis, I. Resistance to "counter-propaganda" produced by a one-sided versus a two-sided "propaganda" presentation. *Public Opinion Quarterly,* 1953, 17, 311–318.

Lusted, L. B. *Introduction to medical decision making.* Springfield, Ill.: Thomas, 1968.

McClelland, D. C. *The achieving society.* Princeton: Van Nostrand, 1961.

MacCrimmon, K. R. Descriptive and normative implications of the decision theory postulates. In K. Borch & J. Mossin (Eds.), *Risk and uncertainty.* London: Macmillan, 1968. (a)

MacCrimmon, K. R. *Decision making among multiple attribute alternatives.* Santa Monica, Calif.: Rand Corporation, 1968. (b)

MacCrimmon, K. R. Elements of decision making. In W. Goldberg (Ed.), *Behavioral approaches to modern management,* Vol. 1. Gothenburg, Sweden: BAS, 1970, 15–44.

MacCrimmon, K. R. *Problem diagnosis for rational decision.* Unpublished book manuscript, 1973. (a)

MacCrimmon, K. R. Managerial decision making. In J. W. McGuire (Ed.), *Contemporary management: Issues and viewpoints.* Englewood Cliffs, N.J.: Prentice-Hall, 1973, Chapter 15. (b)

MacCrimmon, K. R. An overview of multiple objective decision making. In J. L. Cochrane & M. Zeleny (Eds.), *Multiple criteria decision making.* Columbia, S. C.: University of South Carolina Press, 1973, 18–44. (c)

MacCrimmon, K. R. Descriptive aspects of team theory. *Management Science,* 1974, 20, 1323–1334.

MacCrimmon, K. R., & Messick, D. *A framework for social motives.* Working paper number 288. Vancouver: University of British Columbia, 1974.

McEachern, A. W., & Newman, J. R. A system for computer-aided probation decision making. *Journal for Research on Crime and Delinquency,* July, 1969.

McGinnies, E. Studies in persuasion: III. Reactions of Japanese students to one-sided and two-sided communications. *The Journal of Social Psychology,* 1966, 70, 87–93.

McGuire, W. J. Selective exposure: A summing up. In R. P. Abelson, E. Aronson, W. J. McGuire, T. M. Newcomb, M. J. Rosenberg, & P. H. Tannenbaum (Eds.), *Theories of cognitive consistency: A sourcebook.* Chicago: Rand McNally, 1968.

Mack, R. P. *Planning on uncertainty.* New York: Wiley, 1971.

MacKinnon, W. J., & MacKinnon, M. J. Computers: The decisional design and cyclic computation of SPAN. *Behavioral Science,* 1969, 14.

Maier, N. R. F. Reasoning in humans: II. The solution of a problem and its appearance in consciousness. *Journal of Comparative Psychology,* 1931, 13, 181–194.

Maier, N. R. F. *Problem-solving discussions and conferences.* New York: McGraw-Hill, 1963.

Maltzman, I. On the training of originality. *Psychological Review,* 1960, 67, 229–242.

Manski, M. E., & Davis, G. A. Effects of simple instructional biases upon performance in the unusual uses test. *Journal of General Psychology,* 1968, 78, 25–33.

March, J. G., & Simon, H. A. *Organizations.* New York: Wiley, 1958.

Markowitz, H. *Portfolio selection.* New York: Wiley, 1959.

Marschak, J. Elements for a theory of teams. *Management Science,* 1955, 1, 127–137.

Marschak, J. Remarks on the economics of information. *Contributions to scientific research in management.* Los Angeles: W.D.P.C., 1959.

Marschak, J. Actual versus consistent decision behavior. *Behavioral Science,* 1964, 9, 103–110.

Marschak, J. Decision making: Economic aspects. *International Encyclopedia of the Social Sciences,* 1968, 4, 42–55.

Marschak, J., & Radner, R. *Economic theory of teams.* New Haven: Yale University Press, 1972.

Mason, R. O. A dialectical approach of strategic planning. *Management Science,* 1969, 15, B403–B414.

Matheson, J. Decision analysis practice: Examples and insights. In J. Lawrence (Ed.), *Proceedings of the fifth international conference on operational research.* London: Tavistock, 1969, 677–691.

Messick, D. M., & McClintock, C. G. Motivational bases of choice in experimental games. *Journal of Experimental Social Psychology,* January, 1968, 4, No. 1, 1–24.

Miller, G. A. The magical number seven, plus or minus two: Some limits on our capacity for processing information. *Psychological Review,* 1956, 63, 81–97.

Miller, G. A., Galanter, E., & Pribram, K. H. *Plans and the structure of behavior.* New York: Holt, Rinehart and Winston, 1960.

Miller, J. R. III. *Professional decision making.* New York: Praeger, 1970.

Mills, J. Interest in supporting and discrepant information. In R. P. Abelson, E. Aronson, W. J. McGuire, T. M. Newcomb, M. J. Rosenberg, & P. H. Tannenbaum (Eds.), *Theories of cognitive consistency: A sourcebook.* Chicago: Rand McNally, 1968, 771–776.

Mills, J., Aronson, E., & Robinson, H. Selectivity in exposure to information. *Journal of Abnormal Social Psychology,* 1959, 59, 250–253.

Mulder, M. Communication structure, decision structure, and group performance. *Sociometry,* 1960, 23, 1–14.

Newell, A., Shaw, J. C., & Simon, H. A. Elements of a theory of human problem solving. *Psychology Review,* 1958, 65, 151–166.

Newell, A., Shaw, J. C., & Simon, H. A. *Report on a general problem-solving program: Proceedings of the International Conference on Information Processing.* Paris: UNESCO, 1960.

Newell, A., & Simon, H. A. Computer simulation of human thinking. *Science,* 1961, 134, 2011.

Newell, A., & Simon, H. A. *Human problem solving.* Englewood Cliffs, N.J.: Prentice-Hall, 1972.

Newman, J. W. *Management applications of decision theory.* New York: Harper and Row, 1971.

Osborn, A. F. *Applied imagination: Principles and procedures of creative thinking.* New York: Scribner's, 1941.

Pattanaik, P. K. *Voting and collective choice: Some aspects of the theory of group decision making.* London, England: Cambridge University Press, 1971.

Peterson, C. R., & Miller, A. J. Sensitivity of subjective probability revision. *Journal of Experimental Psychology,* 1965, 70, 526–533.

Phillips, L. D. Some components of probabilistic inference. Technical report 1. Ann Arbor: University of Michigan Human Performance Center, 1966.

Phillips, L. D., & Edwards, W. Conservatism in a simple probability inference task. *Journal of Experimental Psychology,* 1966, 72, 3, 346–354.

Posner, M. I. Immediate memory in sequential task. *Psychological Bulletin,* 1963, 60, 333–349.

Pratt, J. W., Raiffa, H., & Schlaifer, R. *Introduction to statistical decision theory.* New York: McGraw-Hill, 1965.

Preston, M. G., & Baratta, P. An experimental study of the auction value of an uncertain outcome. *American Journal of Psychology,* 1948, 61, 183–193.

Prince, G. M. The operational mechanism of synectics. *The Journal of Creative Behavior,* 1968, 2, 1–13.

Pruitt, D. G. Informational requirements in making decisions. *American Journal of Psychology,* 1961, 74, 433–439.

Pruitt, D. G., & Drews, J. S. The effect of time pressure, time elapsed, and the opponent's concession rate on behavior in negotiation. *Journal of Experimental Social Psychology,* 1969, 5, 43–60.

Quade, E. S., Ed. *Analysis for military decisions.* Santa Monica, Calif.: Rand Corporation, 1964.

Radner, R. The application of linear programming to team decision problems. *Management Science,* January, 1959, 5, No. 2, 143–150.

Radner, R. The evaluation of information in organizations. *Proceedings of the fourth Berkeley symposium on probability and statistics,* 1961, 1, 491–530.

Radner, R. Team decision problems. *The Annals of Mathematical Statistics,* 1962, 33, 857–881.

Raiffa, H. *Decision analysis.* Reading, Mass.: Addison-Wesley, 1968.

Ramsey, F. P. *The foundations of mathematics.* London: Routledge & Kegan Paul, 1931.

Rapoport, A. *N-person game theory.* Ann Arbor: University of Michigan Press, 1970.

Rapoport, A., & Wallsten, T. S. Individual decision behavior. *Annual Review of Psychology,* 1972, 131–176.

Reitman, W. R. Heuristic decision procedures, open constraints, and the structure of ill-defined problems. In M. Shelley & G. Bryan (Eds.), *Human judgments and optimality.* New York: Wiley, 1964.

Roberts, H. V. On the meaning of the probability of rain. *Proceedings of the first National Conference of Statistical Meteorology,* Los Angeles, 1968, 133–141.

Rokeach, M. *The open and closed mind.* New York: Basic Books, 1960.

Rosen, S. Post-decision affinity for incompatible information. *Journal of Abnormal Social Psychology,* 1961, 63, 188–190.

Rosenbaum, M. E. The source of information in impression formation. *Psychological Science,* 1967, 8, 175–176.

Rosenbaum, M. E., & Levin, I. P. Impression formation as a function of source credibility and order of presentation of contradictory information. *Journal of Personality and Social Psychology,* 1968, 10, 167–174.

Sauermann, H., Ed. *Contributions to experimental economics,* Vol. 3. Germany: J. C. B. Mohr and Paul Siebeck, 1972.

Savage, L. J. *The foundations of statistics.* New York: Wiley, 1954.

Sayeki, Y., & Vesper, K. H. *Allocation of importance: Goal dependent utility.* Seattle: University of Washington, Department of Psychology, 1971, N. R. 151–313.

Schelling, T. C. *The strategy of conflict.* Cambridge: Harvard University Press, 1960.

Schlaifer, R. *Probability and statistics of business decisions.* New York: McGraw-Hill, 1959.

Schroeder, H. M., Driver, M. J., & Streufert, S. *Information processing systems in individuals and groups.* New York: Holt, Rinehart and Winston, 1965.

Schroeder, H. M., & Suedfeld, P. *Personality theory and information processing.* New York: Ronald Press, 1971.

Schubert, G., Ed. *Judicial decision making.* London: Collier-Macmillan, 1963.

Shaw, M. E. Some effects of problem complexity upon problem solution efficiency in different communication nets. *Journal of Experimental Psychology,* 1954, 48, 211–217.

Shaw, M. E. Some factors influencing the use of information in groups. *Psychological Reports,* 1961, 8, 187–198.

Shaw, M. E. Communication networks. In L. Berkowitz (Ed.), *Advances in experimental social psychology,* Vol. 1. New York: Academic Press, 1964, 111–147.

Shaw, M. E. *Group dynamics: The psychology of small group behavior.* New York: McGraw-Hill, 1971.

Shaw, M. E., & Rothschild, G. H. Some effects of prolonged experience in communication nets. *Journal of Applied Psychology,* 1956, 40, 281–286.

Shaw, M. E., & Shaw, L. M. Some effects of sociometric grouping upon learning in a second grade classroom. *Journal of Social Psychology,* 1962, 57, 453–458.

Sherif, M. *Group conflict and cooperation.* Boston: Houghton Mifflin, 1966.

Shubik, M. Games of status. *Behavioral Science,* March, 1971, 16, No. 2, 117–129.

Shure, G. H., & Meeker, R. J. A personality attitude schedule for use in experimental bargaining studies. *Journal of Psychology,* 1967, 65, 233–252.

Sieber, J. E., & Lanzetta, J. T. Conflict and conceptual structure as determinants of decision-making behavior. *Journal of Personality,* 1964, 32, 622–641.

Siegel, S. Level of aspiration and decision making. *Psychological Review,* 1957, 64, 253–262.

Siegel, S., & Fouraker, L. E. *Bargaining and group decision making: Experiments in bilateral monopoly.* New York: McGraw-Hill, 1960.

Simkin, W. E. *Mediation and the dynamics of collective bargaining.* Washington, D.C.: Bureau of National Affairs, 1971.

Simon, H. A. A behavioral model of rational choice. *Quarterly Journal of Economics,* 1955, 69, 99.

Simon, H. A. *Administrative behavior.* (2nd ed.) New York: Macmillan, 1957. (a)

Simon, H. A. *Models of man.* New York: Wiley, 1957. (b)

Simon, H. A. *The new science of management decision.* New York: New York University Press, 1960.

Simon, H. A. *The sciences of the artificial.* Cambridge, M.I.T. Press, 1969.

Slovic, P., & Lichtenstein, S. Comparison of Bayesian and regression approaches to the study of information processing in judgment. *Organizational Behavior and Human Performance,* 1971, 6, 649–749.

Slovic, P., & Lichtenstein, S. C. The relative importance of probabilities and payoffs in risk taking. *Journal of Experimental Psychology Monograph Supplement,* 1968, 78, No. 3, Part 2.

Smith, R. D. Heuristic simulation of psychological decision processes. *Journal of Applied Psychology,* 1968, 52, 4, 325–330.

Smith, R. D., & Greenlaw, P. S. Simulation of a psychological decision process in personnel selection. *Management Science,* 1967, 13, B409–B419.

Solley, C. M., & Stagner, R. Effects of magnitude of temporal barriers, type of goal, and perception of self. *Journal of Experimental Psychology,* 1956, 51, 62–70.

Solomon, L. The influence of some types of power relationships and game strategies upon the development of interpersonal trust. *Journal of Abnormal and Social Psychology,* 1960, 61, 223–230.

Spetzler, C. S. The development of a corporate risk policy for capital investment decisions. *IEEE Transactions on Systems Science and Cybernetics,* September, 1968, SSC-4, No. 3, 279–300.

Springbett, B. M. Factors affecting the final decision in the employment interview. *Canadian Journal Psychology,* 1958, 12, 13–22.

Stäel von Holstein, C-A. S. A family of strictly proper scoring rules which are sensitive to distance. *Journal of Applied Meteorology,* 1970, 9, 360–364.

Stedry, A. C. *Budget control and cost behavior.* Englewood Cliffs, N.J.: Prentice-Hall, 1960.

Swalm, R. O. Utility theory: Insights into risk taking. *Harvard Business Review,* 1966, 44, 123.

Tajfel, H. Experiments in intergroup discrimination. *Scientific American,* November, 1970, 96–102.

Tannenbaum, P. Effect of serial position on recall of radio news stories. *Journalism Quarterly,* 1954, 31, 319–323.

Taylor, D. W., Berry, P. C., & Block, C. H. Does group participation when using brainstorming facilitate or inhibit creative thinking? *Administrative Science Quarterly,* 1958, 3, 23–47.

Taylor, R. N. Perception of problem constraints. *Management Science,* 1975.

Taylor, R. N., & Dunnette, M. D. Relative contribution of decision maker attributes to decision processes. *Organizational Behavior and Human Performance,* 1974, 5, 632–643.

Toda, M. Measurement of subjective probability distribution. Report #3. Division of Mathematical Psychology, Institute for Research, Pennsylvania State University, State College, 1963.

Turoff, M. Delphi + computers + communications = ? In M. J. Cetron & C. A. Ralph (Eds.), *Industrial applications of technological forecasting.* New York: Wiley, 1971.

Tversky, A., & Kahneman, D. Judgement under uncertainty: Heuristics and biases. *Science,* 1974, 185, 1124–1131.

Vinokur, A. Review and theoretical analysis of the effects of group processes upon individual and group decisions involving risk. *Psychological Bulletin,* 1971, 74, 231–250.

Von Neumann, J., & Morgenstern, O. *Theory of games and economic behavior.* Princeton: Princeton University Press, 1944.

Vroom, V. H. *Some personality determinants of the effects of participation.* Englewood Cliffs, N.J.: Prentice-Hall, 1960.

Vroom, V. H., & MacCrimmon, K. Toward a stochastic model of managerial careers. *Administrative Science Quarterly,* June, 1968, 13, No. 1, 26–46.

Vroom, V. H., & Maier, N. R. F. Industrial social psychology. *Annual Review of Psychology,* 1961, 12, 413–446.

Walster, E., Aronson, V., Abrahams, D., & Rottman, L. Importance of physical attractiveness in dating behavior. *Journal of Personality and Social Psychology,* 1966, 4, 508–516.

Weick, K. *The social psychology of organizing.* Reading, Mass.: Addison-Wesley, 1969.

White, G. F. *Choice of adjustment to floods.* Chicago: University of Chicago, Department of Geography, 1964.

Wills, G., Wilson, R., Manning, N., & Hildebrandt, R. *Technological Forecasting.* Baltimore: Pelican, 1972.

Winkler, R. L. Probabilistic prediction: Some experimental results. *Journal of American Statistical Association,* 1971, 66, 675–684.

Winkler, R. L., & Murphy, A. H. "Good" probability assessors. *Journal of Applied Meteorology,* 1968, 7, 751–758.

Wohlstetter, R. *Pearl Harbor: Warning and decision.* Stanford: Stanford University Press, 1962.

Woods, D. H. Improving estimates that involve uncertainty. *Harvard Business Review,* 1966, 44, 91–98.

Wyer, R. S. Jr. Effects of incentive to perform well, group attraction, and group acceptance on conformity in a judgment task. *Journal of Personality and Social Psychology,* 1966, 4, 21–26.

Ziller, R. L. A measure of the gambling response set in objective tests. *Psychometrika,* 1957, 22, 289–292.

Zwicky, F. *Discovery, invention, research through the morphological approach.* New York: Macmillan, 1969.

Zwicky, F., & Wilson, A. *New methods of thought and procedure.* New York: Springer-Verlag, 1965.

CHAPTER 33

Group Influences on Individuals[1]

J. RICHARD HACKMAN
Yale University

THE EFFECTS OF GROUPS on individuals in organizations are reviewed. Special attention is given to (a) ways groups affect individual behavior indirectly by influencing the informational and the affective states of group members, and (b) direct group influences on individual behavior through the development and enforcement of group norms. Implications of these processes are drawn for (a) individual work effectiveness on various types of tasks or jobs, and (b) the health and effectiveness of the group as a whole.

INTRODUCTION

The other people with whom an individual interacts can affect profoundly how that person thinks, feels, and acts. In this chapter we will focus on the dynamics and consequences of such group-individual relationships in organizations. In addition, we will examine ways these relationships can be altered to improve both the effectiveness of organizational systems and the well-being of individual organization members.

There are numerous examples in the research literature which point up the substantial effects that a person's relations with his co-workers have on his own attitudes and behaviors at work. Probably the most widely known study of the impact of groups in organizational settings was performed at the Hawthorne plant of the Western Electric Company in the late 1920s (Roethlisberger & Dickson, 1939; summarized in Homans, 1950). This research program, which originally was intended to assess the impact of working conditions (e.g., lighting, rest pauses, etc.) on the productivity of employees, showed such conditions to be clearly less important in affecting the behavior of individual workers than various psychological and social conditions which developed. Of particular importance was the emergence of a group "identity" on the part of the workers who participated in the research. As a consequence, group norms were formed which specified what was and was not appropriate

[1] Preparation of this chapter was supported in part by the Office of Naval Research (Organizational Effectiveness Research Program, Contract No. N00014-67A-0097-0026, NR 170-744). The assistance of Judith D. Hackman and of G. Douglas Jenkins Jr. is gratefully acknowledged.

on-the-job behavior, and these norms strongly affected the behavior of individual workers—sometimes consistently with official company policy, sometimes not.

In another study, Coch and French (1948) found that workers were much more accepting of a change in work practices when they had participated (either directly or through representation) in the planning of the changes. Apparently participation facilitated the acceptance of the new procedures as a *group* goal, which was thereafter enforceable by the group. When participation was by representation, there was an initial fall-off of productivity, suggesting that it took longer for individual workers to understand and/or accept the new procedures when they personally were not involved. It is important to note, however, that in all three conditions (i.e., direct participation, participation by representation, and no participation) the changes led to a marked decrease in the amount of variation in the productivity of individuals in each group. Thus, the change itself seems to have led to an increase in the degree to which group productivity norms were enforced. In the participation condition, these norms were for higher production; in the no-participation condition, they were for lower production; and in the representation condition, they slowly moved toward higher production.

A case in which group norms had an especially strong effect on the quantity of work produced by an individual member is described by Newcomb (1954, cited by Golembiewski, 1962, pp. 223–224). The group under study had established a production norm of fifty units a day, but one particular worker wanted to produce more than that amount. Her attempts to do so were so successfully discouraged by her peers that her output finally dropped even below the fifty-unit norm. Subsequently, the work group was broken up so that the individual no longer worked with the employees who had established and enforced the fifty-unit norm. Her output soon

doubled—providing striking evidence of the effects group norms can have on individual behavior.

A final example, which shows how important group membership can be to individual organization members, is provided by the Tavistock studies of coal mining (Trist & Bamforth, 1951). Initially, coal miners in the Tavistock study worked together in small groups (usually from two to eight members) in which there was high interdependency—and high cohesiveness—among members both on and off the job. Partly because of the very real dangers involved in doing the work, there was a good deal of emotional closeness among group members. A technological change (i.e., shifting from a "shortwall" to a "longwall" method of removing coal) required that the existing groups be recomposed into larger work units of forty to fifty men. Members of these new groups worked under a single supervisor, but the workers often were widely separated from one another while working in the mines. Although a great deal of work interdependence was required (indeed, a mistake or poor performance by an individual worker could substantially decrease the productivity of the entire unit), existing interpersonal relationships on the job were severely disrupted. Productivity initially deteriorated following the change of procedures, with workers reporting heightened feelings of indifference and alienation from their work. Ultimately a norm of low productivity developed, apparently at least partly as a means of coping with the emotional and technological difficulties which had been encountered.

Such difficulties are not, of course, an unusual consequence of a major technological change. The negative impact of the change apparently was heightened in the Tavistock study, however, because exactly those social units which could have been most helpful in achieving personal readjustments by individual workers (i.e., the existing cohesive work groups) were themselves done away with as part of the change. The individual workers were, in effect, left without a social "anchor"—and a number of powerful negative consequences resulted both for the company and for the workers.

The Dynamics of Group Effects on Individuals

Why is it that groups seem to have such a pervasive and substantial impact on the behavior and attitudes of individuals in organizations? One way of approaching a general response to this question is to note that groups control many of the stimuli to which an individual is exposed in the course of his organizational activities. *Stimuli* are defined simply as those aspects of an individual's environment which potentially can be attended to by him, and which can affect his behavior. Thus, stimuli include people, verbal and overt behaviors emitted by other people, written materials, objects, aspects of the physical surround, money, and so on.

Our discussion of the impact of group-supplied stimuli on group members will be partitioned on two dimensions: (a) the circumstances under which the stimuli are available to group members; and (b) the type of impact the stimuli have on group members. These two distinctions, which are central to the organization of the chapter, are discussed immediately below and summarized in Table 1.

CONDITIONS OF STIMULUS AVAILABILITY. One's group memberships define, to a considerable extent, his "social universe." That is, being a member of some groups (and not being a member of others) restricts and specifies the set of stimuli which is available to the individual. Different groups deal with (and provide access to) different classes of stimuli, and, therefore, what stimuli are available to a person will depend in part upon what groups he belongs to. *Stimuli which potentially are available to all group members (that is, whose availability is contingent only upon group membership per se) will be called "ambient" stimuli.* Ambient stimuli pervade the group and/or its environment, and group members normally will be exposed to many of them as a regular part of their group-related activities. Indeed, each group member will have relatively little choice about being exposed to the ambient stimuli associated with his own group—and about *not* being exposed to the ambient stimuli associated with some other groups. Among the most important types of ambient stimuli are the other people in the group, materials in the task the group is working on, and aspects of the workplace of the

TABLE 1
THE AVAILABILITY AND IMPACT
OF GROUP-SUPPLIED STIMULI

IMPACT OF STIMULI

		Informational (i.e., on member beliefs and knowledge)	Affective (i.e., on member attitudes, values, and emotions)	Behavioral (i.e., directly on individual or social behavior in the group)
AVAILABILITY OF STIMULI	Ambient (pervades the group-setting)			
	Discretionary (availability at the discretion of other group members)			

group. The internal dynamics of a group are mostly irrelevant to understanding the impact of ambient stimuli on individual members; the point is merely that different groups trade in different kinds of coin, and how a member of a particular group behaves is affected to some degree by what that coin is.

Other stimuli are transmitted (or made available) to individual members of a given group differentially and selectively, at the discretion of the other group members. *Stimuli which can be transmitted selectively to individual group members at the discretion of their peers will be called "discretionary" stimuli.* Discretionary stimuli can include direct messages of approval or disapproval, physical objects, money, instructions about (or models of) appropriate behavior, and so on. Thus, the actual stimulus contents of ambient and discretionary stimuli can be the same; the difference is that for discretionary stimuli the group has direct and intentional control over the administration of the stimuli.

The internal dynamics of the group are, therefore, critical in understanding when discretionary stimuli will be administered to an individual group member by his peers, and what the impact of these stimuli will be on the individual. Which particular discretionary stimuli an individual will be exposed to depends jointly upon the attributes of the individual (including his behavior) and the characteristics of the group (including what the stimuli are over which it actually has discretionary control, and the intentions of group members about what member behaviors should be encouraged or discouraged). Obviously the behavior of individual group members can be significantly affected by the decisions his peers make about what discretionary stimuli to provide and withhold under various circumstances.

TYPES OF IMPACT OF GROUP-SUPPLIED STIMULI. The stimuli which an individual encounters in a group can affect (a) his informational state, (b) his affective state, and (c) his behavior. An individual's *informational* state includes both his current beliefs (e.g., about the organization or about himself) and his accumulated knowledge (e.g., about how to perform the activities required as part of his job). The work group can serve as a major source of information for its members—for example, about what behaviors "pay off" in the larger organization, about how the individual can behave so as to more effectively perform his organizational task, and so on.

An individual's *affective* state includes his attitudes (e.g., his likes and dislikes about the organization), his current level of psychological or emotional arousal, and his personal values (e.g., about what kinds of personal and organizational outcomes ultimately are desirable). The group can influence the affective state of a member by providing (or withholding) direct social satisfactions, by providing access to valued stimuli external to the group, or even by encouraging a member to explore (and possibly change) his basic values.

Stimuli encountered in the group-setting can affect *behavior* in two ways: (a) directly, as when the stimuli received by the individual serve to reward or punish certain of his behaviors, or (b) indirectly, through their effects on the member's informational and affective states—that is, what he thinks or believes, and what he likes or feels. Since in general individuals are quite limited in their capabilities to accept and process information, those stimuli provided by the immediate work group often have a pronounced impact on member attitudes, beliefs, and behaviors (cf., Weick, 1969, pp. 9–10). The bulk of this chapter is devoted to analyzing the dynamics and consequences of these effects.[2]

---

[2] Indeed, it can be argued that, taken together, the *groups* to which a person belongs and the *tasks* he performs probably provide more stimuli which directly impact actual work behavior than do any other aspects of the organizational environment. This suggests that the group- and task-environment of an individual may be among the primary proximal *causes* of vari-

Plan of the Chapter

The chapter is divided into four major sections:

1. *The impact of ambient stimuli on group members.* In this section, which follows immediately, the effects of those stimuli which pervade the group setting (and which are *not* under the discretionary control of the group) are examined. The effects of ambient stimuli on member informational and affective states are addressed separately.

2. *The impact of discretionary stimuli on group members.* This section begins with a discussion of why groups "send" discretionary stimuli to their members, and why individual members often seek out such stimuli. Then attention turns to the informational and affective effects of discretionary stimuli, and to their behavioral consequences.

3. *Group norms and their effects on member behavior.* One of the most efficient and powerful means a group has of directly influencing member behavior is through the creation and enforcement of behavioral norms. Norms specify the conditions under which discretionary stimuli are used by the group to reinforce desired behavior—and to inhibit behavior which is not desired. Considerable attention is given to how norms operate in groups in organizational settings, and to the consequences of member deviance from norms.

4. *Group influences on member performance effectiveness.* In this section, material in preceding sections of the chapter is brought together and focused on the question of individual work effectiveness. Particular emphasis is placed on the ways groups can facilitate the performance effectiveness of individual group members.

While issues relevant to the overall effectiveness of intact work groups are dealt with throughout the chapter, no attempt is made to provide a systematic treatment of the research literature on group problem solving or group decision making per se. For material on these topics, the reader is referred to Davis (1969), Kelley and Thibaut (1969), MacCrimmon and Taylor (1975), and Steiner (1972).

GROUPS AS DEFINING THE "SOCIAL UNIVERSE" OF THE INDIVIDUAL: THE IMPACT OF AMBIENT STIMULI

The particular groups to which an individual belongs are very important in identifying the "social universe" of that individual, and in defining his position within that universe. A person's set of group memberships can be viewed as defining his location in an organization in a way analogous to the way a person's spatial location defines his position in the physical universe. In both cases, one's location (i.e., his group memberships in the former case, his spatial location in the latter) strongly affects the quantity and substantive character of the stimuli to which he is exposed in the course of his day-to-day activities.

The analogy can be illustrated by the study of married student housing units at M.I.T. by Festinger, Schachter, and Back (1950). These authors hypothesized that an important basis of friendship formation was the occurrence of "passive contacts." These are brief contacts made as one goes about his normal business—in this case, walking about the neighborhood, going to or from one's own apartment, etc. Given some moderate frequency of occurrence (plus appropriate psychological conditions), passive contacts often develop into full-fledged friendships. Whom one "bumped into" frequently, then, was viewed as central

ation in individual behavior in organizations. If true, this view would imply that much of the impact of "organizational level" variables (e.g., organization size, number of hierarchical levels in an organization) may be through their effects on the way work groups typically are structured (and/or the ways tasks are designed) which, in turn, affect the kinds of stimuli to which individuals are exposed—and, ultimately, the direction of individual and organizational behavior. For a more detailed exposition of this point of view, see Porter, Lawler, and Hackman (1975).

in determining whom one would become friends with. And whom one "bumped into" was found to be strongly determined by one's physical location in the housing complex. Both physical distance among apartments and "functional distance" among them (e.g., the degree to which it is necessary to pass someone else's door to, say, empty the garbage—regardless of the actual physical distance involved) strongly predicted observed friendship patterns.

This research shows how a person's location in physical space affects what stimuli (in this case, social stimuli) one comes into contact with, and that such contacts can have long-term and important consequences for the individual. Similar findings have been reported relating physical location in an office to interaction and friendship development among clerical workers (Gullahorn, 1955), residential location to marriage choices (cf., Gouldner & Gouldner, 1963, pp. 328–355), and so on.

The analogy being drawn here suggests that the same general kinds of processes may operate vis-à-vis one's location in his social universe as operate in the physical universe. That is, simply by being a member of some particular groups in an organization (and not being a member of others), there are a goodly number of stimuli which will be excluded from an individual's experience —and others which literally will be forced to his attention. Such stimuli are what we are referring to as *ambient stimuli,* and they may vary strikingly from group to group.

Ambient stimuli may be associated with the physical place where the group regularly meets, with the external characteristics of the other people in the group, with the type of task the group usually deals with, etc. For example (and at a very general level), some groups deal much more with physical materials than with ideas and plans, and the reverse will be true for other groups. Members of some groups exchange stimuli which have high threat value, while members of other groups trade in more innocuous materials, and so on. The individual has relatively little choice about being exposed to ambient stimuli; he usually is required to encounter the stimulus materials that are being dealt with by the group, simply by virtue of his membership in the group.

The ambient stimuli present in a group-setting can have a great diversity of effects on group members. They are, after all, *stimuli*—and, therefore, they potentially can be linked to any response of which a person is capable. In this chapter, however, attention is restricted to those effects which are likely to be of significance for understanding behavior in organizations.

In the pages to follow, we first examine the impact of ambient stimuli on the *informational* states of group members, focusing on how such stimuli affect (a) members' awareness of what positive and negative outcomes are available in the organizational environment, and (b) members' perceptions of the behaviors which are expected to lead to the attainment or avoidance of these outcomes. Next, we turn to the effects of ambient stimuli on members' *affective* states, emphasizing how such stimuli influence (a) the motivational states which guide the behavior of individual group members, and (b) the overall positive versus negative affective character of the group for the individual. Finally (and something of a special case), we discuss how ambient stimuli can directly affect the *interpersonal relationships* among group members (i.e., the group interaction process)— and thereby indirectly affect member behavior, attitudes, and beliefs.

The Informational Impact of Ambient Stimuli

While it is clear that behavior is strongly affected by the information members have about the group and its environment, it is also true that the other group members often have a great deal of control over what information is made available to any given individual. Thus, the bulk of our discussion of member informational states is reserved for the section on discretionary stimuli. We focus here on how the ambient stimuli which pervade a group-setting can serve as "cues" which guide the behavior of individuals in the group and the organization.

Cueing Available Outcomes

As an example of how ambient stimuli can signal what kinds of outcomes are potentially available in a group-setting, consider a group in which some members have established close interpersonal relationships. A new member entering this group and observing what took place there would, at the least, see that the group provided the opportunity for gaining social or interpersonal satisfactions. If he valued such satisfactions, behavioral initiatives toward other group members might well develop as a consequence of this observation.

People spend enormous amounts of time in groups during their lives, and tend to become rather facile in differentiating among groups in terms of the kinds of satisfactions that can be obtained there. In just a moment or two of observation, for example, it is possible for most people to determine (usually with a good deal of accuracy) whether or not a given group offers the chance to develop strong friendship ties; whether the group is one in which a member could be psychologically emasculated if he did not watch his step; whether the group is one in which there is the possibility of sexual "action"; and so on.

It is suggested that the ambient stimuli associated with a given group are of central importance in making such identifications. The reason is simply that groups which offer the potential for certain kinds of satisfactions often are characterized by similar configurations of ambient stimuli—and that group members notice and respond to these similarities.

Cueing Behavior-Outcome Expectancies

While an individual's awareness of opportunities for satisfactions can be enhanced by the ambient stimuli he encounters in a group-setting, that is only half the story. When a member infers that the opportunity exists to attain certain personal satisfactions in a given group, the nature of his behavior in response to that observation also will depend upon his perceptions of "what leads to what" in that group-setting.

Merely knowing, for example, that a person believes he can obtain social satisfactions in a given group will not, by itself, allow prediction of his behavior. If, however, it also is known that the person believes that conforming to the attitudes of other members increases the likelihood of attaining social satisfactions in groups such as the present one, then specific behavioral predictions become a realistic possibility. In the present case, it would be reasonable to predict not only that the person would try to obtain social satisfactions from his group membership, but also that he would be likely to do this by agreeing with and reinforcing the opinions of other group members—rather than, for example, by being confronting and open about his own points of view.

The ambient stimuli which characterize a given group can strongly affect a group member's behavior-outcome expectancies (i.e., his perceptions of "what leads to what" for that group). Through a history of experiences in various kinds of groups, a person identifies certain cues (or configurations of cues) as reliable indicators of what specific behaviors are likely to lead to what outcomes. When these cues are present among the ambient stimuli in a new group, the previously learned contingencies between specific behaviors and their outcomes are reactivated (or made cognitively salient). At this point, then, the individual can be said to have a "behavior-outcome expectancy" for his present group.[3]

Unless there are discernable and reasonably regular associations between the presence (or absence) of certain ambient stimuli

---

[3] This perspective derives from the general expectancy theory of motivation, as originally formulated by Lewin (1938) and Tolman (1932), and applied to organizational settings by Vroom (1964) and others.

in group-settings and the existence of particular types of behavior-outcome contingencies, the mechanism posited here will not "work" (e.g., in the sense of helping an individual behave adaptively in a group-setting which is new to him). Fortunately, the work of Barker and his associates (e.g., Barker, 1968; Barker & Wright, 1955) as well as observations from everyday life suggest that groups with similar configurations of ambient stimuli also often are characterized by similar behavior-outcome contingencies. Consider, for example, the ambient stimuli which might characterize a traditional elementary school class: chairs lined up in rows and bolted to the floor, an older person standing behind a large desk at the front of the room, a large blackboard, communications routinely passing back-and-forth between the older person and the young people in the chairs (but not often among the younger people), and so on. These stimuli, by themselves, provide a new group member a good deal of information about the behavior-outcome contingencies which influence what takes place in that group. Based on his previous experiences in groups characterized by similar ambient stimuli, the new member forms (correct) expectancies that sitting quietly but attentively in a chair will result in no unpleasant interactions involving himself and the older person; that loud or frequent interaction with his peers while the older person is talking will lead to unpleasantries; and so on. No real experience in the group is necessary to arrive at these behavior-outcome expectancies; the ambient stimuli present in the group-setting, coupled with the individual's previous experience, are completely sufficient.

Consider one other example. A manager known to the author has a job which requires him to visit and work with a diversity of groups in organizational settings—some of which are characterized by free, open, and confronting exchanges of ideas and feelings, and others of which are typified more by high rationality and tact and

little expression of feelings or emotion. The interpersonal consequences of various behaviors are, according to the manager, quite different in the two types of groups. Further, the manager reports that he usually is able to tell within the first few minutes of observing a new group (and without speaking himself) which "type" the group is, based on his observations of the ways group members arrange themselves and address one another. For example, in one group previously unfamiliar to him, the manager noted that the group members situated themselves rather formally around a conference table, that all thoughts were expressed in intellectual and sometimes rather abstract terms, and that very little tentativeness or uncertainty was present in the contributions made by group members. On the basis of these observations, the manager concluded that a direct and confronting intervention by him about the directions being taken by the group (especially if said with feeling) would be resisted and negatively valued by the group members. When the opportunity for such an intervention arose, the manager made it and confirmed his prediction.

The point of this example is that the manager was able to generate predictions about the nature of the behavior-outcome contingencies in the group strictly on the basis of his observations of the ambient stimuli which characterized the group—and *without actually experiencing or observing these contingencies in operation in that specific group.* In other words, the ambient stimuli characterizing the group gave rise to a set of expectancies for the manager about what interpersonal behaviors would lead to what kinds of outcomes for that group. In this case, these expectancies turned out to be correct.

There will be other occasions when ambient stimuli prompt behavior-outcome expectancies which turn out to be partially or wholly incorrect. In such cases, the group member often is "reeducated" by others in the group through the selective application of discretionary stimuli. That is, an individual may engage in behavior X, based on an expectancy that (for groups such as the present one) behavior X will lead to desirable outcome Y. When he finds that the other group members have responded to his behavior with less-desirable outcome Z instead, he must begin to revise his behavior-outcome expectancies for that group. Indeed, it is through such application of discretionary stimuli that group members develop and enforce behavioral norms—about which more later.

For the present, suffice it to reemphasize that the ambient stimuli present in a group-setting can and do function as cues which signal group members about what behaviors are likely to lead to what outcomes. The impact of ambient stimuli in this regard may be especially powerful for new members who have not yet had a chance to experience and test for themselves the nature of the behavior-outcome contingencies which operate in that particular group.

The Affective Impact of Ambient Stimuli

Arousing Member Motive States

It was discussed earlier how ambient stimuli can "signal" group members about what positive and negative outcomes are available in a given group-setting. When such outcomes are of extremely high (positive or negative) value to individual group members, of course, one consequence of their presence will be to increase the level of psychological and physiological arousal (or "activation") experienced by members.

Moreover, the level of *desire* members have to seek out or avoid outcomes present in the group-setting also can be affected by the ambient stimuli which are present there. The mechanisms by which this takes place have been discussed in detail by McClelland (1951; McClelland et al., 1953), Atkinson (1954), and others. McClelland suggests that, if in an individual's previous history he has found that he experienced a good

deal of pleasure (or pain) in the presence of some particular set of stimuli, then that affective state can become conditioned (in the Pavlovian sense) to the stimuli which were present at the time he experienced it. In subsequent situations when those stimuli also are present, the prior affective state is fractionally reactivated. This reactivated affective state then can serve as an incentive for the individual to engage in behaviors which, based on previous experience, he believes will lead to the previously rewarding state of affairs (or avoid the previously punishing state of affairs). McClelland and his associates (see, for example, McClelland et al., 1953; Atkinson, 1958) have carried out a large number of experiments in which it has been shown that situational cues do arouse and depress needs from their normal levels, providing some support for the postulated theoretical mechanism. (For a skeptical review of some of this work and its conceptual underpinnings, however, see Klinger, 1966).

When most or all group members have similar patterns of previous experience, their need states can be simultaneously and similarly affected by the ambient stimuli present in a given group-setting—and the effect can be one of immediate and intense group activity oriented toward achievement of some particular satisfaction. This often happens, for example, at pot parties, at professional conventions, at singles bars, and at board-of-directors meetings. The nature of the ambient stimuli is quite different in each of these examples, as are the particular motive states likely to be aroused by them. But in each case the ambient stimuli serve simultaneously to heighten the motivation of individual members to achieve a particular class of outcomes, and to increase the degree to which these motivational orientations are shared among group members. The result, not surprisingly, is often a mutually reinforcing pattern of group behavior toward attainment of these outcomes.

In summary, the ambient stimuli which characterize a group-setting not only can provide cues to members about what kinds of satisfactions can be had there, but in addition can directly affect the strength of desire members have to achieve these satisfactions—virtually independently of the group interaction process itself.

Providing Direct Personal Satisfactions

The ambient stimuli which characterize a group-setting can contribute directly to the satisfaction (or dissatisfaction) of group members. For example, an individual who happens to be an airplane buff can derive important personal satisfactions from his membership in, say, a group of advertising writers assigned to an airline account—satisfactions which would not be present if that individual were assigned to the group working the aspirin account in the same advertising agency. Similarly, an individual who derives satisfaction from working with electronic equipment would find the stimulation received as a member of a repair crew in an electronics firm highly rewarding—but might be expected to become disenchanted when he was promoted to a management team in the same firm, in part because he could not get the same level of satisfaction from working with ideas, plans, and subordinates that he could from circuits, transistors, and ammeters.

Obviously, the affective value of the ambient stimuli a person encounters as a part of his group membership is a *joint* function of the stimuli themselves and his own personal need states. Only a masochist, perhaps, would be repelled by membership in a group which traded exclusively in love, status, and goodwill; the majority of the stimuli which are encountered in real-life groups, however, are open to quite different affective interpretations by different individuals.

In general, the degree of fit between the needs of individuals and the affective character of the ambient stimuli associated with a given group will bear significantly on the degree to which the individual is attracted

to the group and willing to become personally involved in it. This does not deny that the pattern of interaction which takes place in the group may in most cases be more potent than the ambient stimuli present in determining whether or not individuals maintain their personal investments in the group. The point is that, other things equal, ambient stimuli can contribute nontrivially to the motivation of individual members to gain and maintain group membership.

When, for example, a status-conscious person perceives the members of a certain group to be highly prestigious, he may be highly motivated toward membership—merely because he values association with highly prestigious people (cf., Lott & Lott, 1965). Whether or not social interaction with these people actually turns out to be rewarding to the individual (or whether such interaction even takes place) begs the present question: witness the "hangers on" who surround celebrities despite the fact that they are totally ignored by them. Similarly, when the stimuli associated with the task of the group are positively valued by an individual, his motivation to maintain group membership may be high—again, quite independently of whether or not the individual expects to gain other personal rewards from membership in the group (cf., Thibaut, 1950; Back, 1951).

When most or all of the members of some group find that the ambient stimuli associated with the group are rewarding, the development of high internal cohesiveness among group members will be facilitated. The reason is simply that group members share a perception of the group as a site where valued stimulation is received, and, therefore, have a shared stake in maintaining the existence and viability of the group.

This state of affairs may be especially characteristic of voluntary groups formed on the basis of shared special interests (e.g., the Vermillion Fishing Club). In such groups, the stimuli encountered in the group-setting often serve both as one of the main *reasons* for individual membership in the group, and as the "glue" which holds the group together. Such reliance on shared positive valuation of ambient stimuli for maintaining individual commitment to the group, however, is fraught with danger for the group over the long term.

Consider, for example, the history of the neighborhood Pornographic Flick Connoisseurs Club. During the early stages of the club's existence, internal cohesiveness was very high, since everyone in the group valued watching risqué motion pictures and desired to maintain the group in order to continue that activity. It turns out, however, that the half-life for interest in pornographic materials is very short. Therefore, *unless the group generated in its social interaction additional reasons for individuals to value group membership,* the cohesiveness of the group would be expected to drop sharply after a short period of time. The reason, of course, is that the ambient stimuli which originally had attracted people to the group and maintained their original commitment to it would have lost much of their value to the individuals involved—and in the absence of any other reasons for staying, people would withdraw and the group ultimately would dissolve.

Finally, it should be noted that the ambient stimuli an individual encounters as a group member may be experienced as negative rather than as positive. In the study of married student housing (described earlier) friendships among people who lived close to one another undoubtedly would *not* have developed if those individuals had experienced one another as highly unpleasant. Indeed, Festinger and Kelley (1951) describe a different housing project in which passive contact among residents (which occurred because of physical proximity) failed to lead to the development of friendships among residents. Many residents of this project had been forced to move there against their wishes because of an acute housing shortage at the time. Because the

project was government sponsored, residents often assumed that their neighbors were low-class people with whom it was undesirable to associate. As a consequence (and without really checking out their prior assumptions), a large proportion of the residents did not use the occurrence of passive contacts with their neighbors as occasions for initiating interaction and thereby developing friendships. Similarly, if the ambient stimuli a person encounters as a consequence of his membership in a group are perceived as generally noxious or unpleasant, the individual would be unlikely to develop a high level of attraction to the group—and, indeed, may elect to withdraw from it, unless there are other compensating advantages to group membership.

The Impact of Ambient Stimuli on the Group Interaction Process

The substantial effects of discretionary stimuli on the interpersonal exchanges which take place among group members are widely acknowledged and reasonably well-documented. For example, as group members selectively provide rewarding or punishing stimuli to others in the group, patterns of group interaction are gradually but powerfully shaped. The discretionary provision of information (or misinformation) to group members by their peers similarly can affect group process.

Less widely discussed are the effects of the ambient stimuli which pervade a group-setting on the group interaction which takes place there. But these stimuli, too, can influence the social process of a group in at least two ways: (a) as external cues which signal to individual members what types of social behavior are appropriate or desirable; and (b) as the "coin" of the social exchange process itself.

Ambient Stimuli as Social Cues

Earlier in this section we reviewed how ambient stimuli, working through an individual's previous experience, can affect both one's motivation to attain certain outcomes and his expectancies regarding the best ways to go about doing it. When the ambient stimuli present in a given group-setting have a similar effect on most or all of the group members, then group process may be strikingly affected. For example, if the ambient stimuli characterizing a given group-setting were affectively very potent as would be the case, say, for a demolition team defusing a bomb, little "loose" or casual interaction would be expected among group members. The reason is simply that the ambient stimuli would be likely to orient each group member strictly and intensely toward the task at hand—and the overall pattern of group interaction would be strongly determined as a consequence.

Of special interest in this regard are the ambient stimuli which are present in the physical setting of the group. The work of a number of scholars (e.g., Hall, 1966, Chap. 9; Sommer, 1966, 1967; Steele, 1968) suggests that the background characteristics of a meeting place can rather strongly affect what happens in a group. It appears that such effects may be due in large part to the impact of the ambient stimuli present in that place on the motivational and cognitive orientations of all members simultaneously —and thereby on the pattern of group interaction which emerges.

Ambient Stimuli as the Coin of Social Exchange

In the cases described above, the ambient stimuli which affect group interaction were external to the group process itself, and impinged upon it through the cognitive and motivational states of group members. Such external stimuli can include the stimulus characteristics of other persons present, the objective characteristics of the group task, the cues and rewards present in the group environment, and so on.

It also is true that the actual "materials" exchanged among group members are part of the universe of ambient stimuli present in any group-setting, and themselves can affect the nature of the group process. For example, there is good reason to believe that it makes a difference whether the "coin" of exchange among group members is predominantly ideas versus emotions versus physical materials, and so on. Although little systematic research has examined the impact of the coin of interpersonal exchange upon the nature of group process, there is some evidence to suggest that the effect may be a powerful one. Perhaps most relevant is the literature showing the relationship between the kind of task a group is working on and the characteristics of group interaction (e.g., Deutsch, 1951; Carter et al., 1951a, 1951b; Hare, 1962, Chap. 9; Talland, 1955; Morris, 1966). The group task often determines rather completely the kinds of "content" which are exchanged by group members— and part of the reason for the large effects of task differences on interaction may derive from such differences in stimulus contents. For example, Carter et al. (1951b) showed that the pattern of "leadership behaviors" exhibited in small groups depended in part upon whether the group was working on a reasoning task, a mechanical assembly task, or a discussion task—tasks which certainly require group members to deal with different types of content materials. Similarly, Talland (1955) showed that therapy groups differed significantly from laboratory task groups on Bales's (1950) interaction categories.

Unfortunately, studies of the relationship between types of tasks and group interaction process rarely have distinguished explicitly between the actual *task contents* group members must deal with (i.e., the stimulus materials in the task) and the *process demands* of the task which specify or imply what is to be done (Hackman, 1968). Therefore, attribution of obtained task effects on group process to the task contents must be done cautiously. Both Kent and McGrath (1969) and Hackman and Morris (1975) have shown, however, that task contents have a substantial impact on the *outcomes* of group interaction when differences in task-based demands have been completely controlled. It is, therefore, perhaps not too large a leap of inference to assume that task contents would have been found to affect process measures in these studies as well. Thus, although a definitive study relating task-specified stimulus contents to the dynamics of group interaction has yet to be done, there is good reason to believe that such relationships exist.

Additional support for the proposition that the content of the stimuli exchanged among group members affects the dynamics of that exchange is provided in the work of Foa (1971). Foa identified six different types of "resources" which can be exchanged among group members: love, status, information, money, goods, and services. Preliminary results have shown that the characteristics of the resource exchanged (i.e., the stimulus contents dealt with by the social unit) do have non-trivial effects on the patterns of social exchange which develop.

Conclusions and Implications: Ambient Stimuli

Ambient Stimuli versus Discretionary Stimuli

The mechanisms proposed in the preceding pages about how stimuli present in the group-setting affect behavior in groups are, by and large, very general ones. While the discussion has focused exclusively on ambient stimuli, the mechanisms postulated are relevant to understanding some of the effects of discretionary stimuli as well. For example, when an individual is presented with some discretionary stimulus (e.g., a friendly smile) by another group member, that stimulus can affect his motive states and/or cognitive expectancies by exactly the same mechanisms that have been proposed here to operate for ambient stimuli. Discretionary stimuli, of course, have a number

of additional types of effects on individual and social behavior in groups, which will be discussed in the next section of this chapter. But it should be kept in mind throughout that discretionary stimuli can and do affect behavior in groups through the same mechanisms as do ambient stimuli.

Indeed, at times it may be difficult to separate the effects of ambient and discretionary stimuli. Consider, for example, a case in which an organization member is promoted from an employee work group to membership in a supervisory group (as in the Lieberman, 1956, study). Such a change of work groups is likely to involve a simultaneous change of both the ambient and the discretionary stimuli which the individual encounters in his daily activities in the organization. If his attitudes, beliefs, and behaviors are observed to be different after the promotion, which set of stimuli is to be seen as causal?

Organizational psychologists typically have relied almost exclusively on discretionary stimuli for purposes of explanation. In the case given above, for example, it probably would be suggested that the employee ceased to be reinforced for pro-union statements and behavior (as he was before the promotion), and instead was rewarded by his new peers when he engaged in pro-management activities. While explanations such as this obviously should not be overlooked, it may well be that the ambient stimuli which pervade the new group-setting are significant in causing the observed changes as well.

The problem, of course, is that ambient stimuli have been all but forgotten in the general rush to collect data and generate theories about such topics as norm development and conformity—more glamorous concepts perhaps, but surely not deserving of all the attention of organizational social psychologists. As a result, so little is presently known about the impact of ambient stimuli in organizational settings that it is impossible to estimate the extent of their effects.

In the paragraphs to follow, a brief case

will be made for additional research and
conceptualizing which explicitly includes
the role of ambient stimuli in understanding
the effects of groups in organizations on
their members. In brief, it will be argued
that ambient stimuli contribute powerfully
to resistance to change in intact groups, and
that these stimuli sometimes can be used as
the basis for intervention activities with
intact groups—especially when it is difficult
or impossible to negotiate direct changes in
the ways discretionary stimuli are exchanged
among group members.

Ambient Stimuli and Social Inertia in Groups

There are at least three ways in which
ambient stimuli contribute to the "social
inertia" which so often characterizes intact
work groups in organizations:

1. *Ambient stimuli influence behavior in
groups—but only rarely are noticed.* By their
nature, ambient stimuli are part of the
"background" of group functioning. As a
consequence, group members frequently are
unaware of the continuing impact these
stimuli have on their attitudes and their behavior—just as the fish in the Hudson River
(if there *are* any fish in the Hudson River)
are unaware of the effects of their environment. The stimuli are just "there" and they
are always there, and as a result it is difficult to realize that they may be profoundly
influencing what is going on. It is not a coincidence, for example, that Hall (1966)
titles his book on the behavioral impact of
physical space "The *Hidden* Dimension."

Moreover, the operation of ambient
stimuli is largely covert. While discretionary
stimuli are exchanged and reacted to overtly
and visibly (albeit sometimes subtly) in the
interaction process of the group, ambient
stimuli often realize their effects by influencing the *implicit assumptions* individual group members have about what behaviors are appropriate or desirable. To the
extent that the effects of ambient stimuli are

in fact covert, the determinants of behavior
in groups often will not be readily observable by either group members or outside
observers. This will especially be the case
if one looks primarily to group member
"personality traits" or to the group interaction process to identify the reasons why
certain behaviors occur and others do not.

The implication of the above is that unless the private effects of ambient stimuli
can be brought to the attention of group
members and shared among them, existing
patterns of group behavior which are
prompted by these stimuli are likely to persist indefinitely, regardless of whether or
not these behaviors are functional for the
group over the long term.

2. *The diversity of ambient stimuli
which impinge on a group tends to become
narrowed and restricted over time.* In particular, as a group gains stability and develops a history, members tend to define
certain types of stimuli out of the domain
of consideration, and emphasize attention to
certain others. It is not unusual, for example,
for a group to find a place and time to meet
where "extraneous distractions" (i.e., ambient stimuli which are not relevant to the
immediate perceived purpose of the group)
are minimized.

Further, groups often develop rather
specific norms which effectively prevent
group members from encountering or dealing with certain kinds of stimuli. A managerial group, for example, might gradually
develop a norm which specified that, say,
topics having to do with the pay or promotional status of individual members are
not to be mentioned in the group; or that
emotional exchanges are out of bounds; or
that the group will focus on issues having
to do with day-to-day organizational functioning rather than with long-range planning or with organizational values, and so
on. Indeed, Goffman (1963, Chap. 11) has
described a very pervasive group norm
which requires members to ignore "extraneous" stimuli present in the environment,

and to *act* as if they are fully engrossed in the main task of the group—even when actually they are not.

When such norms are developed, they serve to restrict sharply the universe of stimuli to which group members are exposed. In many cases, the norms develop very gradually and group members may not be aware of the restriction or narrowing of focus which has taken place. As a consequence of this restriction, the predictability of the group may increase, and group members may develop a pleasant sense of being comfortable together. In addition, however, divergent and potentially unsettling stimuli from the environment may never be explicitly and overtly attended to or dealt with by group members. In some cases, this can have unintended and unfortunate implications for the effectiveness of the group (cf., Janis, 1972).

The above discussion is not meant to imply that groups should uncritically welcome all ambient stimuli which impinge from the external environment. Some such stimuli really can be distractive, disruptive, and generally dysfunctional to the effectiveness of the group. What is required instead is for group members to develop and maintain a "monitoring" stance vis-à-vis ambient stimuli which can provide the basis for deliberate choices about which stimuli should be attended to (and which ignored) by the group. Some thoughts on this issue are included in a subsequent section on ambient stimuli and behavior change in groups.

3. *Group members tend not to examine publicly the private inferences they generate from ambient stimuli.* It is tempting to conclude that the assumptions and expectancies which derive from ambient stimuli in the group-setting will have little impact on member behavior in well-established groups, since the validity of these assumptions can be checked directly in the group itself. In fact, however, only rarely do group members actually examine and discuss overtly the behavioral norms and implicit strategies which are guiding their behavior in the group (cf., Argyris, 1969; Shure et al., 1962; Weick, 1969, pp. 11–12). Therefore, unless a group member has direct personal experience in the group which contradicts his prior expectancies or assumptions about what behaviors are appropriate, revision of these assumptions is unlikely to occur.

Such direct confirmation (and disconfirmation) is much more likely to occur for those behaviors which are expected by a group member to lead to positive outcomes than for those which are expected to lead to negative outcomes. Thus, a group member may find to his surprise that, contrary to expectations, a friendly interpersonal overture does *not* lead to a friendly response in this particular group. He is quite *unlikely* to learn from direct experience that some behavior he expected to lead to a negative outcome instead leads to a positive one, simply because he is unlikely to try out such behavior in the group.

To the extent that a number of group members interpret the ambient stimuli present in a group-setting similarly (based on similar previous group experiences), it is possible for behaviors which would actually be functional for the group never to be exhibited—because each individual group member falsely fears that the behavior will lead to negative outcomes. Obviously, in such cases the expectancies initially prompted by the ambient stimuli never will be either confirmed or disconfirmed, and these expectancies will continue to guide the behavior of group members indefinitely.

The general tendency of group members not to explicitly discuss the ongoing process of the group is a good case in point. In many task-oriented groups in contemporary organizations, process observations are considered "bad form" and are negatively valued. As a result, many individuals have developed an expectancy that making such comments can, in a task-oriented group, lead to unpleasant or anxiety-arousing consequences. Hackman and Morris (1975) found, for example, that of 100 laboratory groups (each composed of three persons working on a fifteen-minute task), only 142 comments about the performance strategy being used by the group were made—less than two comments per group. Further, those comments about group strategy which were made virtually never reflected a deliberate and planned attack by the group on major strategic issues. Instead, such comments invariably occurred immediately after one member had behaved in a way noticeably inconsistent with the implicit norms which had been guiding group behavior.

In many groups in this study, the "deviant" act appeared to unfreeze the other group members from their previous unwillingness to discuss issues of strategy, and helped create conditions in which members could learn that comments about the group process do *not* necessarily lead to negative interpersonal outcomes. Indeed, it turned out that the process discussions may actually have facilitated group creativity: the judged creativity of group products in the Hackman-Morris study was found to be positively and significantly related to the number of comments about performance strategy which were made.

In summary, the ambient stimuli present in a group-setting often prompt fairly strong inferences by group members regarding what behaviors are likely to be appropriate and inappropriate in that group. The failure of most groups to discuss such inferences explicitly and overtly can serve to perpetuate shared and incorrect assumptions about the actual usefulness of various behaviors, create conditions of "social inertia," and thereby impair the effectiveness of the group as a whole.

Ambient Stimuli and
Behavior Change in Groups

The possibilities of using ambient stimuli (and member reactions to them) as a means of overcoming the social inertia which characterizes many intact groups in organizations are examined next.

EDUCATING GROUP MEMBERS. It may be difficult, at least in the short term, to change the learned responses of individual group members to the cues and rewards in their environment. That is, it is not likely that an individual will be able to break quickly or easily a cognitive or affective response to some particular stimulus which has been learned over an extensive history of group memberships. Nor will he readily stop experiencing certain events as rewarding and others as punishing. It often is possible, however, for group members to change some of the ambient stimuli they encounter as part of their group experience and thus provide all members with a *different* set of cues or rewards to which they must respond. If the learned responses of group members to these new stimuli are different from their responses to the old ones, then changes in behavior in the group would be expected. It should be relatively easy, for example, for many groups to change the physical surroundings where the group meets or, in some cases, to deal with different types of task materials in working toward group goals.

The implication is that educational programs which focus on the role that ambient stimuli play in guiding behavior in groups can be of considerable help in increasing the awareness of group members about what is going on in the group and why. Such heightened awareness should, in turn, increase the degree to which group members are genuinely able to control and change the directions that the group is taking. In particular, this type of educational program might usefully focus on helping group members learn how to effectively make explicit the perceptions, implicit assumptions, and motives which are guiding their behavior in the group; to identify when possible those ambient stimuli present in the group-setting which have prompted these motivational and cognitive orientations; and to share and discuss these new understandings with others in the group so as to facilitate general awareness of the "hidden" determinants of behavior in the group.

There is some evidence (as well as a good deal of folklore) that such educational programs ought to "work"—in the sense of increasing the effectiveness of a group in achieving its goals and in adapting to a changing external environment. Indeed, many T-group experiences explicitly are designed so as to increase member awareness of the hidden assumptions which guide interpersonal behavior in groups. Although the overall impact of such experiences is an unsettled question (see, for example, Campbell & Dunnette, 1968; House, 1967), the evidence suggests that heightened awareness of what is causing what within a group is, in fact, facilitative of group effectiveness in many cases.

The work of Steele (1969, 1973) on the physical surround of a group is a good case in point. Steele suggests that most people take their physical surroundings as immutable "givens"—even when these surroundings may be easily changeable. He uses the term "pseudo-fixed feature space" to refer to those physical features that are readily changeable or movable, but which are perceived and treated as if they were fixed—even when their arrangement is dysfunctional for what is being done.[4] Steele argues (and provides cases to demonstrate) that groups treat their surroundings (incorrectly and often inappropriately) as fixed a great deal of the time and that they tend to take a non-problem-solving stance toward their environments. When, however, group members come to view parts of their environment as under their control and, therefore, changeable, they often are able to devise new physical arrangements which are more facilitative of the attainment of group goals.

TASK AND SITUATIONAL DESIGN. Just as members of a group may themselves attempt to

change the ambient stimuli which impinge upon them (after they have become aware of the effects of these stimuli), so also can an external agent attempt to "engineer" these stimuli so as to affect group behavior in specified ways. There are three primary "sources" of ambient stimulation which are potentially manipulatable in this regard: (a) the particular people who compose the group, (b) the situation or environment in which the group functions, and (c) the task of the group.

While it is true that the stimulus characteristics of the individuals who compose a group are part of the universe of ambient stimuli to which group members are exposed, it is doubtful that merely changing such characteristics would lead to much of a change in behavior in most groups. The reason, as suggested by research on group composition (see, for example, the review by Haythorn, 1968), is that the *behaviors* of group members—which are highly variable and discretionary—are enormously more potent in affecting what happens in groups than are the stimulus characteristics of the particular people involved. The present discussion, therefore, will be limited to those ambient stimuli which have their source in the situation and the group task.

It often is possible to manipulate the stimulus characteristics of the task or situation so as to "highlight" the availability of certain rewards (or punishments), and to make particularly salient the relationships between various behaviors and these outcomes. Some of the literature on job design deals explicitly with how jobs can be arranged so as to make especially salient certain types of rewards, and signal employees about ways they can obtain them by work toward organizational goals. For example, Hackman and Lawler (1971) have specified a set of job characteristics which, when present, signal workers that they can achieve substantial intrinsic satisfactions (e.g., feelings of personal accomplishment, an increased sense of self-worth) when they work hard and effectively on their job. Results showed that people who valued such in-

---

[4] The term explicitly refers to the *psychological* character of the physical surrounds. It complements the notions of "fixed feature space" and "semi-fixed feature space" of Hall (1966), which refer, respectively, to the objective permanence versus movability of the physical surround.

trinsic rewards did in fact respond to these stimuli, and worked more effectively when their jobs had the characteristics specified. In the same vein, it may be possible to increase the motivation of group members to work together toward certain goals by manipulating the stimulus characteristics of group tasks—or of the situations in which groups work.

The task of a group can have another type of impact as well. It is the task which largely specifies the *content* of the group activities—that is, the nature of the materials that the group works with, and kinds of stimuli that are exchanged among group members. As was suggested earlier, the nature of such content can affect both the motivation of individual group members (e.g., how attracted they are to remain in the group and participate in its activities), and the pattern of interaction which takes place among group members (e.g., as suggested by the work of Foa, 1971, on the exchange of resources). Thus, the task or purpose of the group can have a very pronounced impact on group behavior on a number of fronts simultaneously—and careful attention to the design of group tasks would seem to be called for on the part of those wishing to influence behavior in groups.

In summary, it has been suggested that attempts to influence group behavior *which involve manipulation of the ambient stimuli which pervade the group-setting* should focus primarily upon:

1. Stimuli which themselves are expected to be rewarding or punishing to group members, and which, therefore, affect the attractiveness of the group and its activities.

2. Stimuli which are expected to serve as cues, signaling group members about (a) what rewards or punishments potentially are available in the group-setting, and/or (b) the conditions under which these outcomes become available.

3. Stimuli which are expected to have a direct impact upon the nature of the interaction or social exchange which takes place among group members.

These three statements are, obviously, very general. While they do suggest those classes of stimuli which should be of interest to a prospective group change-agent, they provide no hints about what *specific* aspects of the task or situation will have the effects intended. Unfortunately, present knowledge about the dynamics of the impact of ambient stimuli on group behavior does not permit much more than such general specifications. Little is known, for example, about what particular aspects of tasks and situations are likely to have high usefulness as cues for most individual group members; even less is known about the impact of the "content" of group activities on group processes. Further, virtually no data are available to suggest which ambient stimuli are likely to be perceived (and responded to) in similar ways by large numbers of individuals in this culture and which are more susceptible to idiosyncratic interpretation by individual group members based upon their particular prior experiences in groups and their personal needs and values.

In other words, before it becomes possible to effectively use ambient stimuli to effect changes in group behavior, much more needs to be known about the operating characteristics of these stimuli themselves. It is relatively easy to identify the potential *sources* of ambient stimuli in group-settings. It is much less clear how to tell what the impact of some set of stimuli will be on the motivation and cognitive orientations of group members—and, more importantly, to predict how these effects will be "assembled" in the group, especially when not all members are impacted in the same way by the same stimuli.

Conclusion

Many pages have been spent on ambient stimuli and their effects on group behavior. The reason is that the impact of such pervasive and generally unnoticed stimuli has received little attention from either researchers or group members. Yet ambient stimuli can be powerful determinants of what happens in groups and, at the same time, are generally easy to manipulate and change—whether by an external agent or by group members themselves. Additional attention to ambient stimuli and research on their effects on groups in organizations seems well-warranted.

THE GROUP AS A DISPENSER OF INFORMATION AND REWARDS: THE IMPACT OF DISCRETIONARY STIMULI

Up to this point, discussion has focused on the impact of ambient stimuli; that is, stimuli which pervade the group-setting and are encountered by anyone who is a member of a given group. Attention now turns to the ways group members are affected by discretionary stimuli. As was the case for ambient stimuli, discretionary stimuli may provide a group member with information, or they may have affective consequences for him, or both. To reemphasize the point of difference: discretionary stimuli are under the direct *control* of the group, and can be made available to specific group members on a strictly contingent basis—that is, depending upon the behavior a member exhibits or the opinions he expresses.

In the first part of this section, we discuss briefly the reasons groups send discretionary stimuli to their members, and the reasons individuals in groups seek such stimuli from their peers. Then we examine separately, and in some detail, the effects of discretionary stimuli on member informational states and on member affective states.

The Exchange of Discretionary Stimuli in Groups

Why Groups Initiate Discretionary Stimuli

TO EDUCATE AND SOCIALIZE. Influencing group member attitudes, beliefs, or behaviors is the primary purpose of some groups, such as religious study groups, political education groups, physical fitness clubs, and so on

(Cartwright & Zander, 1968, p. 141). In such cases, the group serves explicitly as a socializing agent for its members. Sometimes this is at the request of the member ("educate me") and sometimes it is not ("I'll put up with this religious nonsense because it's part of being a member of the Church Youth Fellowship, but that's sure not the main reason I'm here"). In either case, groups primarily oriented toward the education or socialization of their members rely heavily upon discretionary stimuli to bring about the desired changes. Such stimuli typically are dispensed quite selectively, contingent upon the current level of progress of each group member, and may provide the members with information, with rewards for "correct" ideas or behavior, or with punishment for being "incorrect."

TO PRODUCE UNIFORMITY. Even when member socialization is not a major purpose of a given group, however, there still are numerous occasions when groups take the initiative in meting out discretionary stimuli to their members. Group members often believe, for example, that a high level of uniformity among members is necessary or appropriate for group goal attainment (Festinger, 1950), and use their control of discretionary stimuli to achieve such uniformity. It often is functional for a work group to have uniform procedures for dealing with frequently encountered tasks, so that members can reliably predict the behavior of other members and thereby achieve a reasonable level of coordination and efficiency. Similarly, it may be useful for group members to hold similar beliefs about the external environment, especially if the group must respond as a unit to that environment. Finally, it sometimes is important for group members to have uniform and high levels of knowledge or skill for satisfactory performance effectiveness, for instance, among members of a musical ensemble or athletic team.

Groups may, however, seek uniformity for purely "maintenance" reasons; that is, keeping the group intact and functioning as a unit, independent of task-related activities (Cartwright & Zander, 1968, p. 142). Too much individualistic or idiosyncratic behavior on the part of a few members, for example, can threaten the very survival of a group. So can unresolved disputes among members regarding what the group should try to achieve and how it should proceed toward its goals. Perhaps reflective of a collective uneasiness about such dangers is the seeming ethic among members of intact groups to try to achieve consensus among all members on any matter of consequence, falling back on "majority rule" only as a second-best way of proceeding. (See Davis, 1973, and Davis et al., 1970, 1973, for a discussion of the antecedents and consequences of implicit decision rules used by groups.)

Yet despite the numerous apparent benefits of uniformity, and despite the substantial investment of time and energy by group members to achieve it, there are good reasons to believe that uniformity is dysfunctional for group effectiveness under some circumstances. Janis (1972) provides one striking example of the dysfunctional consequences of group-initiated pressures to uniformity in his discussion of the Bay of Pigs fiasco undertaken by President Kennedy and his advisors in 1961. Janis quotes Arthur Schlesinger explaining why he had not pressed more urgently his objections to the plan:

In the months after the Bay of Pigs I bitterly reproached myself for having kept so silent during those crucial discussions in the Cabinet Room, though my feelings of guilt were tempered by the knowledge that a course of objection would have accomplished little save to *gain me a name as a nuisance.* I can only explain my failure to do more than raise a few timid questions by reporting that one's impulse to blow the whistle on this nonsense was simply undone by the circumstances of the discussion. (Schlesinger, 1965, p. 255; italics added)

Had there been less pressure toward uniformity in the Kennedy group, Janis argues,

the strong reservations about the invasion plan held by Schlesinger (and others) might have been seriously considered, and the disaster averted.

Although the effectiveness of the Kennedy group in the Bay of Pigs case clearly was low, it may have been that the pressures to uniformity which pervaded the group did serve a "maintenance" function, by lessening the chance of severe interpersonal disruptions within the group. There are, in fact, many cases when pressures for uniformity are functional for the internal maintenance of the group *at the expense of* group task effectiveness or of contributions to the goals of the larger organization. The pressures toward uniformity of production in work groups are a case in point (cf., Roethlisberger & Dickson, 1939; Roy, 1952; Whyte, 1955). By establishing and enforcing a norm of uniform production among work group members, the group may achieve a heightened feeling of internal cohesiveness and simultaneously avoid dealing with a number of thorny interpersonal problems which would be likely to arise if each group member were allowed to select his own level of production (Mathewson, 1931). The cost to the larger organization in such cases can be substantial—except, of course, when the production norm selected by the group is very high, which is sometimes the case (Seashore, 1954; Lawler & Camman, 1972).

A more complete discussion of the process by which discretionary stimuli are used to establish group norms—and deal with member deviance from such norms—is provided later in the chapter.

To produce diversity. Apparently contrasting the pressures toward uniformity discussed above is the tendency for groups to use discretionary stimuli to help create and maintain *diversity* among members. In particular, a number of different member roles emerge in most groups, and these roles may become organized into a fairly complex and well-differentiated structure. As used here, the term "role" refers simply to expectations which are shared by group members regarding who is to carry out what types of activities under what circumstances (cf., Bates, 1956; Levinson, 1959; Thibaut & Kelley, 1959, Chap. 8).

In a new group, members initially create differentiations between those who will assume leadership roles versus those who will be followers, and between those who will specialize in task activities versus those who will perform maintenance functions (Slater, 1955; Bales & Slater, 1955; Thibaut & Kelley, 1959, Chap. 15; Gibb, 1969, esp. pp. 268–271).[5] As group members have further experience working together, additional role differentiation may take place. For example, a highly elaborated division of labor among members may emerge, complete with subleaders responsible for different classes of task activity (cf., Biddle & Thomas, 1966, Part VII; Guetzkow, 1960). Group maintenance functions may become highly differentiated as well. For example, one member (often the group wit) may be expected to reduce the level of interpersonal tension when it gets dangerously high, another may be responsible for providing encouragement and support when activities begin to drag, a third may provide social reinforcement to members who work especially hard or effectively on the group task, and so on. A perceptive description of the nature and consequences of role differentiation in a boys' street-corner gang is provided by Whyte (1943). Benne and Sheats (1948, pp. 42–45) and Thibaut and Kelley (1959, p. 276) provide summary lists of task and maintenance functions which may become part of the roles of group members.

As the group gains a history and its pattern of activity becomes more stable, the role assignments of individual members often become well-defined and resistant to change. When change is attempted by a

member, the group may use its control of discretionary stimuli to keep the existing role structure intact. It should be noted, however, that such resistance presupposes general satisfaction with the existing role structure by most group members; when consensus is low, a great deal of "jockeying" for position may ensue (cf., Heinicke & Bales, 1953).

The apparent need of group members for a well-defined role structure and for predictable behavior by role incumbents is sometimes strikingly illustrated in groups where some members have *formally* defined roles (i.e., roles assigned by the parent organization). Normally, the existence of formal roles should shortcut much of the process of role differentiation in a group. For example, in an organizational work group with an assigned supervisor or foreman, the leadership role is both defined (at least in part) and occupied on an a priori basis. But when an assigned leader refuses to fulfill his role according to the expectations of group members, serious disruption of the group process invariably takes place.

For example, Mills (1967, Chap. 6) describes the distress expressed by group members when the assigned leader of a "seminar on executive management" for military officers chose not to perform the "executive functions" expected of him, and instead asked the group members to organize their own learning experiences. Similar distress may be experienced initially by the subordinates of a manager who returns home from an off-premises T-group or executive development seminar with a new and unexpected way of enacting his formal leadership role (Argyris, 1962, Chap. 10). Finally, difficulties are experienced by group members when they and their formal leader agree on the *definition* of the leader's role— but group members feel that the leader is not performing the role in a satisfactory manner. In such cases, an informal or "shadow" organization often is formed within the group, which has its own set of differentiated roles—and which may

---

[5] The distinction between task and maintenance functions is quite similar to the distinctions made by Homans (1950) between "internal" and "external" systems and by Bales (1953) between "task" and "socioemotional" roles.

complement the formal role structure, or compete with it (Roethlisberger & Dickson, 1939).

In summary, it appears that group members have a strong tendency to create differences among themselves, and then to regularize and stabilize these differences over time. And research evidence (e.g., reviews by Sarbin & Allen, 1968b, pp. 503–504; Collins & Guetzkow, 1964) suggests that such internal organization, when it is task-appropriate and accompanied by high role clarity, can facilitate both group effectiveness and member satisfaction.

The issue may be even broader than that. Systems theorists (e.g., Allport, 1955, p. 475) have argued that *all* systems exhibit a basic tendency toward disorder and disorganization, which must be controlled if the system is to survive. Applied to groups, this principle suggests that *both* uniformity and structured diversity may be essential for maintaining the viability of the group as a social system. In this context, the striving of a group for *diversity* among members parallels its pressures toward *uniformity*: both processes, although superficially contradictory, reflect a tendency toward organization, order, and predictability. By judiciously controlling the discretionary stimuli at its command, a group should be able to move simultaneously towards uniformity and diversity, for example, by inculcating a common set of work values among members at the same time as generating a task-appropriate division of labor among them; or by creating a common set of beliefs about the external environment while spawning a number of different functional leadership roles.

Why Individuals Seek Out Discretionary Stimuli

In the section above, we examined the reasons groups dispense discretionary stimuli to individual group members. In such circumstances the individual must react in one way or another to those stimuli directed at him. In addition, however, individuals can and do *seek out* discretionary stimuli from the groups of which they are members. The view of the individual which characterizes our discussion, then, is one of a pro-active (as well as reactive) person, who often knows what he wants, seeks it out in his physical and social environment, and learns by observation and trial-and-error the most effective way to get it.

To obtain information. Groups are heavily used by individuals as sources of data about the nature of reality. According to Festinger (1950), the degree to which an individual turns to a group to validate an opinion or belief or to obtain a social "definition" of a situation is inversely proportional to the degree to which the relevant data are already available in physical reality. For example, while an individual may turn to the group to confirm his evaluation of the worth of a political candidate, he will not be as likely to use the group to test whether or not a surface is breakable; he can simply hit it with a hammer and find out for himself.

Individuals use the group for information not only about external reality, but for data about themselves as well. Indeed, socially obtained information has been central in many theories of how one's self-concept is developed and maintained. For example, Cooley's (1922) use of the term "looking glass self" highlights the importance of self-knowledge which is gained from the actions and reactions of others vis-à-vis oneself. Similarly, as Berkowitz (1969) notes, the original usage of the term "reference group" explicitly had to do with an individual seeking out data from others, which he could then use to obtain a more complete understanding of himself. Other research (some of which will be discussed in more detail later) has shown how individuals seek data from relevant others to ascertain their own level of ability and the validity of their opinions (e.g., Festinger, 1954); to test the appropriateness of their level of satisfaction with the rewards and costs they are experiencing (e.g., Merton & Kitt, 1950; Patchen, 1961); and even to appropriately label the emotions they are experiencing (e.g., Schachter, 1964).

It should be noted that group-controlled information—whether it be about external reality, about the self, or about specific behaviors and skills—can be sought by the individual for either (or both) of two reasons. First, the group member may derive *intrinsic* satisfaction merely from learning about or coming to "know" the proximal world. Festinger, for example, posited a drive for people to know about the accuracy of their beliefs and opinions about the world in his theory of social communication (1950); and an analogous drive to know about oneself in his theory of social comparison (1954). Similarly, White's (1959) notion of effectance motivation posits that individuals are driven to "master" their environment—to find out how the environment can be manipulated and what the consequences of such manipulations are. Thus, individuals would be expected for intrinsic reasons alone to seek out from other group members information about how to behave so as to manipulate aspects of the environment and skillfully handle the tasks they are expected to perform.

In addition to such intrinsic reasons for seeking information from the group, there often are some very good *instrumental* reasons for doing so. If an individual wishes to behave so as to achieve rewards which exist in the organizational environment, he must have a good understanding both of that environment (e.g., the behavior-outcome contingencies which operate there), and of himself (e.g., his own skill level relative to job requirements). The need for information in organizational environments is substantial; the degree to which a person can obtain it on his own is severely limited by his restricted time- and place-perspective; and a heavy reliance on other group members for assistance is pretty much inevitable as a consequence.

To OBTAIN GROUP-CONTROLLED REWARDS. In addition to controlling information needed by the individual in his pursuit of extrinsic rewards, groups also control stimuli which themselves are directly satisfying or dissatisfying to members. Some such stimuli can contribute directly to the psychological well-being of a member, for example, those which enhance his feelings of self-esteem and social acceptance, those which help a member adapt to high psychological stress from the external environment, and so on. Other stimuli may be more relevant to the member's physical or material well-being (e.g., physical safety and comfort, financial gain, and so on).

Since many rewarding stimuli originate within the group itself, they may be provided without any consideration of the environment outside the boundaries of the group. On the other hand, groups also often control *access* to rewarding stimuli which are located in the environment. A work group may, for example, select which of its members will be its representative to a conference on "new work techniques," thereby rewarding one of its members by giving him the opportunity to leave the group, get some rest, and maybe even gain some valuable learning.

The emphasis in either case is the fact that *control* over the positive stimuli resides with the group, and the individual who aspires to them must behave in such a way as to convince his fellow members that he is deserving. A similar process takes place when the group controls stimuli (or access to stimuli) which are likely to be experienced as unpleasant by group members. In both cases, the individual is highly dependent upon the group for the rewards he seeks, and because of this, the group can have a great deal of impact on his behavior and expressed attitudes.

Conclusion and a Caveat to the Reader

Group-individual relationships in organizations often are discussed simply as a process in which the individual "conforms" in some degree to group expectations in exchange for social acceptance from his peers. The main behavioral dilemma for the individual is seen as whether or not to conform; and the primary resources of the group are social acceptance and rejection.

Hopefully, the above discussion should make clear that group-individual relationships in organizations are considerably more complex than that. Groups send discretionary stimuli to their members for many different reasons, and have a diversity of resources (not just social acceptance) to offer. Similarly, members use their group memberships to serve a variety of personal needs, and are affected by group-supplied discretionary stimuli in many different ways —some of which have nothing whatever to do with behavioral conformity. The dynamics of these effects are examined in the sections to follow.

It should be noted at the outset, however, that in our discussion of the effects of discretionary stimuli we will talk of things that groups "do" vis-à-vis their members; for instance, "the groups sanction a member for exceeding his production quota." The implication of such statements is *not* that groups act as intact units, consciously and deliberately planning and executing behaviors in the same ways that individuals do. To take such a position would be reifying the group in a way that is not congruent with the way groups actually operate. Instead, we talk about "group behavior" vis-à-vis group members merely as a shorthand way of referring to the behavior of other people with whom individual organization members have meaningful and continuing contact. We could just as well refer to his "peers" or his "role set" in this regard; the term "group" is used because it is convenient, and because much of the research literature having to do with the effects of peers (or role partners) on organization members is conceptualized and discussed using "group" terminology. Or, as put by Moore (1969, p. 289):

Groups act through individuals, but it is equally true that individuals act *on behalf of groups*

[italics in original], or in conformity with other socially sanctioned expectations.... Neglect of the first part of the preceding statement can lead to a kind of social anthropomorphism, or the "group mind fallacy".... But neglect of the second part of the statement can lead to a kind of atomistic view of human behavior that is equally fallacious. One position is as inane as the other.

Effects of Discretionary Stimuli on Member Informational States

In this section, we examine the effects of group-supplied discretionary stimuli on (a) the beliefs a member holds about the group and its environment, (b) the beliefs a member holds about himself, and (c) the knowledge and skills a member has relevant to the activities required by his organizational role or job.

Shaping Beliefs About the Group and the Environment

Relying only upon their own senses and experiences, individuals in organizations can obtain neither a very complete nor, in many cases, a very accurate view of their environment. Individuals are, therefore, substantially dependent upon their work groups for information about that environment.

Many groups are only too happy to fill that need. To the extent that all group members have the same general perceptions of and beliefs about the environment, the likelihood of internal disagreements and dissension among members is somewhat lessened. Most groups are not very competent in handling overt disagreements among members. Indeed, group members often consider it a mark of their success as a group when they have done away with the appearances of internal disagreements and maintained instead a comfortable feeling of consensus and togetherness—even if that feeling was obtained by glossing over some very real differences among members.

As a result of this tendency to move

away from interpersonal discomfort, many groups tend to generate substantial pressure for uniformity of belief among members. The pressure is likely to be particularly evidenced (a) when there is turbulence in the environment of the group and members have a strong need for social reassurance, and (b) when new members join the group—since the perceptions and beliefs of these new members may turn out to be divergent from the existing shared views of veteran group members.

An example of how groups can use discretionary stimuli to maintain shared beliefs when all is not well in the environment is provided by Burns (1955). In the organization studied by Burns, cliques of older men met regularly to reassure each other about just how unfortunate things were in the organization. Various organizational features (e.g., the bonus system, formal communication procedures, and so on) invariably were discussed in deprecating terms. Groups of younger workers, on the other hand, had quite a different assessment of organizational reality. While they did not necessarily endorse the features deprecated by their older colleagues, they did tend more frequently to view them as challenges—as aspects of the system to be improved upon or to be overcome. In both cases, group members were actively involved in providing information about the organization to their fellows which served to preserve the protective "social reality" of their respective groups.

The pressure toward belief uniformity when new members join the group was evidenced in an exchange observed by the writer. In this case, a new group member was present during a conversation between two veteran members of the work group. The main topic of the conversation was the frustrations the veterans had experienced recently at the hands of management. The conversation ran its course without either participant appearing to notice the presence of the new employee. Questioned later, one of the veterans admitted that the conversation had been informally "staged," and that its main purpose was to help the newcomer learn that it was "useless to suggest any changes in how things are done here, because management never pays any attention"—which indeed represented the existing views of the work group. This interaction probably had a substantial impact on the beliefs of the new member, simply because his lack of personal experience in the organization made him heavily dependent upon his work group for information about the organization.

The pressure toward uniformity of belief in a group may sometimes be functional for the group. It does provide a kind of social reassurance regarding one's beliefs which many individuals desire, and it can provide the basis for effective concerted action in those task groups where unanimity of view is essential to carrying out the work of the group.

But such pressure almost certainly is dysfunctional when the beliefs shared about the environment have been obtained by stamping out genuinely different points of view among members. In such cases, perspectives which, if explored, could contribute importantly to the work of the group may never be considered at all (cf., Maier & Solem, 1952; Janis, 1972).

BELIEFS AND THE BEHAVIOR OF GROUP MEMBERS. Groups clearly cannot and do not attempt to provide members with information about all aspects of "reality." Those beliefs which are mostly irrelevant to the actual *behavior* of group members (and, therefore, unlikely to be disruptive to the group itself in any way), for example, are generally overlooked by the group. It is doubtful that a group would bother much with member beliefs about the total number of employees in the organization, with member perceptions of the color of the office walls, and so on. Instead, communication of information is likely to be focused rather intensely on two general issues (cf., the earlier discussion of the informational impact of ambient stimuli):

1. What rewards and costs are present in the environment, and who controls them; and

2. What behaviors by group members lead to these rewards (and avoid the costs).

Both of these aspects of reality are of immediate relevance to the behavior and outcomes of individual group members. Therefore, they are of considerable importance both to the individual (because he would like to maximize gain and minimize pain) and to the group (because if the individual goes off half-cocked on the basis of the "wrong" information, he may spoil things for everybody). Thus, it would be expected that the characteristics of the *supervisor* of the group would be the focus of a great deal of information-sharing by group members—since the boss is *both* a direct source of rewards and costs, and someone who can control the contingencies regarding what behaviors lead to what outcomes. Similarly, the pay and promotion system of the organization, the idiosyncrasies of machinery used on the job and, of course, the nature of the work group itself all would be the topic of communication which is intended to affect the belief states of individual group members.

When group members continually reinforce their common views on some matter (as, for example, in the groups of older men described by Burns), those views can become quite immune to change—even when they no longer accurately reflect objective reality. It is not uncommon, for example, for members of a work group to persist in believing that management will "lower the rate" if members produce over the standard in a piecework incentive system (e.g., at the Bank Wiring Room in the Hawthorne studies). Neither assurances from management nor objective guarantees to the contrary are likely to dent the beliefs (or change the behavior) of an individual in such a group, so long as group members continue to reinforce each other's views about the nature of the "system." Instead, it

would seem that before a management-introduced system could work in such a situation, the nature of social reality would have to change: the group would have to abandon beliefs such as "hard work only hurts the working man in the long run around here."

OBSERVATION AS A SOURCE OF BELIEFS. The above discussion has emphasized stimuli which are communicated directly from the group to individual members. It also should be noted that group members can use the group to obtain information about reality in another, more subtle, way: namely, by observing other group members in action, seeing the results of that action, and on the basis of these observations drawing inferences about the nature of the group and its environment. The group still has some control over such inferences (recall, for example, the description above of "acts" staged by groups precisely in order to get a message across to a new member). By and large, however, it is much more difficult for a group to "fake" its actual behavior than it is, say, to communicate a slightly distorted view of reality to a member verbally. This will be especially the case for information having to do with the sources of rewards and costs in the environment and the behaviors which lead to those outcomes. For such aspects of the environment (which, indeed, are those most likely to be attended to by the members), other group members can attempt to mislead the observer only at risk of negatively affecting their own outcomes.

There also are some traps, however, for a member who relies heavily on personal observations of the group as a strategy for learning about the environment. For example, what "works" for some group members (e.g., those with high status) may backfire when tried by a new member or one with low status. A member who bases his behavior on beliefs about reality gleaned solely from observational data, therefore, runs a high risk of behaving in a personally maladaptive way. In practice, most group members draw simultaneously upon several sources of information—including observations—to gain understanding of the environment. When there is consistency both across data sources and across time, a group member should be able to make attributions about reality with considerable confidence (Campbell, 1961; Heider, 1958), and safely base his behavior upon those attributions.

UNTANGLING NORMATIVE FROM INFORMATIONAL INFLUENCES ON MEMBER BELIEFS. The experimental research literature contains a great deal of material relevant to group influences upon member beliefs and opinions about the environment. Unfortunately, much of this literature is based on laboratory experiments which focus on beliefs or judgments about actual physical materials or items of factual information. It has been proposed here that member beliefs and perceptions *about the rewards, costs, and behavior-outcome contingencies which characterize the environment* are more powerful in controlling a group member's behavior in an organizational setting than are his other beliefs about the environment. To the extent that this is a valid assertion, then applications of findings from the experimental literature on conformity must be made with caution; the jump from a laboratory study in which group members estimate the magnitude of weights to a natural setting in which they must figure out the likely consequences of contemplated actions is a large jump indeed.

The experimental literature has been of considerable help, nonetheless, in differentiating between two major types of social influence: normative versus informational. Informational influence leads to a revision of one's own private belief states on the basis of group-supplied data which are accepted as valid by the individual. Normative influence, on the other hand, leads to changes in what one *says* his beliefs are—but not necessarily to what is privately believed. Or, as defined by Deutsch and Gerard (1955), informational social influence is "an influence to accept information obtained from another as *evidence* about reality," whereas normative social influence is "an influence to conform with the positive expectations of another" (p. 629, italics in original; see also Kelley, 1952).

The difference is an important one, because it bears directly on the pervasiveness and permanence of group influences on the individual. If a member is merely acting as if he holds a set of beliefs because of the normative expectations he has received (i.e., he is in a state of public compliance), then his behavior will tend to be consistent with those beliefs only when the presence of the group is salient in his mind. Further, he probably will experience difficulty adjusting to the group in the long run because of the conflict between the way he must act and his "real" beliefs. If, on the other hand, the group has genuinely affected his private beliefs, his behavior will be more pervasively affected, and the impact of the group will probably last for a longer time; that is, he is in a state of private acceptance (cf., Kiesler, 1969, Chap. 11; Allen, 1965, pp. 136–144).

It often is difficult to distinguish between the two influence processes, in part because messages exchanged in the real world frequently are "double-barreled." That is, ostensibly a group member may be given a helpful report of "the way things are" in the organization, as a matter of information —but behind the informational content is the additional message that the member is normatively *expected* by his peers to perceive things that way, and to behave accordingly.

The problems involved in separating normative from informational influence are well-illustrated in the classic experiments of Asch (1951) and Sherif (1936, 1965). In the Asch research, subjects were asked to match the length of a given line with one of three unequal lines. It was quite easy in each case to determine which of the comparison lines was the correct match. Subjects in groups of eight (seven confederates and one naive subject) were required to state their judgments aloud, and the naive subject, who answered last, was faced on critical trials with a unanimous majority of his peers giving what he perceived to be an incorrect response. About one-third of the responses given by the naive subjects on these trials were erroneous and in agreement with the stated answers of the confederates.

In the Sherif research, subjects were asked to estimate the amount of movement of a spot of light shown momentarily in an otherwise totally dark room. The light did not actually move, but did appear to do so (the autokinetic effect). When subjects were tested alone, each individual subjectively defined a reference point or standard against which, on subsequent trials, he was able to judge the amount the light "moved." When subjects were tested in groups, announcing their estimates of the amount of movement publicly, a *common* standard or reference point developed after a few trials, around which the estimates of all group members converged. Further, when subjects in the group condition were tested later on an individual basis, the group-defined standard continued to be the reference point for their judgments.

At first glance it might appear that the Asch subjects were conforming for strictly normative reasons (e.g., they feared being made fun of if they didn't go along with the group, even though they knew the group was incorrect); and that the Sherif subjects were using the group solely for informational purposes (e.g., in the absence of "hard" sense data, they used the subjective reports of other members as information). The situation is not, however, that straightforward. For example, Asch (1958, pp. 178–179) reports that interviews with subjects revealed three types of reactions among subjects who yielded to the incorrect group judgment, only one of which has an unambiguously normative flavor:

1. *Distortion of perception.* A few subjects were unaware that their estimates had been distorted by the majority, and believed that they were giving correct estimates throughout.

2. *Distortion of judgment.* Most subjects fell into this category, reporting that while they saw what they saw, their own perception must somehow have been incorrect, since everyone else saw it differently.

3. *Distortion of action.* These subjects were aware that they were correct, but deliberately chose to go along with the majority out of an "overmastering need not to appear different from or inferior to others ... (or) an inability to tolerate the appearance of defectiveness in the eyes of the group" (p. 179).

Likewise, when in the Sherif experiment there was a conflict between a subject's initial private judgment of the amount of movement (i.e., before any subjects gave their estimates) and the data provided by the other subjects, it is impossible to know the *reason* why the subjects moved toward the emerging group norm. It could be strictly because the subjects were using each other's data as information in a perceptually very ambiguous situation; but also it could be that subjects changed their initial private estimate after hearing the reports of others because of the fear of appearing foolish by saying aloud what they really thought they saw. There simply is no way to tell for sure.

Following the pioneering work of Asch and Sherif, a great deal of research effort has been expended to experimentally separate normative from informational social influences on group member beliefs and opinions about reality. This work is excellently summarized by Tajfel (1969, pp. 334–347). In general, the evidence suggests that substantial social influence remains even when group characteristics are manipulated so as to minimize normative forces on the individual to comply (e.g., by minimizing group cohesion or by creating conditions in which a "group" in any real sense does not even exist). Further, there is evidence that people are influenced by other group members when they believe that their own responses are anonymous, and when conditions are such that they are unaware that they actually have been influenced (as was the case for many subjects in the Sherif research). Despite such inferential evidence for the potency of informational influence, it probably is impossible to completely eliminate all traces of normative influence in any given social situation. Indeed, as Tajfel notes, "the experiential substratum of the yielding subject's response is perhaps, in the last analysis, an epistemological issue which can never be fully resolved on a purely empirical level" (1969, p. 348).

CONDITIONS FOR ACCEPTING GROUP-SUPPLIED INFORMATION ABOUT REALITY. The degree to which group members *accept* stimuli from the group in formulating their own views of the nature of reality varies considerably in different circumstances. Once again there is a vast literature in the conformity tradition regarding the conditions under which acceptance occurs; and once again it often is difficult to distinguish conditions which apply to normative influence processes versus those which apply to strictly informational influence. Sophisticated reviews of this material are provided by Allen (1965), Kiesler (1969, Chaps. 10 and 11), and Tajfel (1969, pp. 347–357).

In general, the evidence suggests that member acceptance of group-supplied data about reality is a function of the following three (and interrelated) factors:

1. *Characteristics of the Environment.* To the extent that the targets of a member's perceptions or beliefs are ambiguous or unclear, then his reliance on the group for information about those targets increases (e.g., Asch, 1951; Wiener, 1958). This suggests that in organizational settings individuals should be especially dependent upon group-supplied information for help in understanding the *social* environment (including sources of social rewards and behavior-outcome contingencies which are controlled by groups or by individuals), since the social environment characteristically is more ambiguous and obscure than is the physical environment.

2. *Characteristics of the Perceiver.* To the extent that an individual feels poorly qualified to assess the environment for himself, he will rely more heavily on the group for information about it (e.g., Kelley & Lamb, 1957; League & Jackson, 1964). Such

low personal confidence can be either a relatively enduring characteristic of a person, or a momentary state induced by recent failures to accurately perceive or assess the environment. The degree of influence of the group on member beliefs about the environment, then, should vary substantially from time to time as the situation changes and as the member's self-perceptions change.

3. *Characteristics of the Group.* Holding constant member self-confidence, a group member will tend to accept group-supplied data about reality to the extent he perceives the group as being a credible (competent, successful, trustworthy) source of information (cf., Rosenberg, 1961; Kelman, 1950). Again, such perceptions may be either relatively enduring ("This is an awfully competent group; I'd better listen to what they say") or a transitory ("They were right last time, so I guess I should hear them out this time"). Although the degree to which a group is seen as attractive by a member has been shown to affect acceptance of *normative* influence attempts, it is doubtful that attractiveness per se plays an important part in the acceptance of primarily informational materials from the group (Downing, 1958). Finally, it should be noted that the greater the unanimity of views of group members, the more an individual will accept information provided by the group (Allen & Levine, 1971a), probably at least in part because unanimity increases the perceived credibility of the group in the eyes of the member.

Shaping Beliefs About the Self

Just as the group significantly can affect a member's perceptions of the environment, so can it influence the beliefs he holds about himself. For example, Burke and Bennis (1961) show how—in the course of a three-week T-group experience—individual group members and their peers tended to converge in their perceptions of each individual on three global dimensions: friendliness-evaluation, dominance-potency, and participation-activity. The authors document that this phenomenon was due not merely to changes in others' perceptions of an individual (although such changes did take place), but to changes in the beliefs individuals came to hold about themselves as well. Unfortunately, since one goal of such group experiences is actual behavioral change by group members, it is impossible to tell from the study how much of the change in beliefs about the self was a function of the influx of trustworthy data about one's self from the other group members, and how much was a consequence of objective personal change.

Jones and Gerard (1967) make a useful distinction between "comparative appraisal" and "reflected appraisal" as means by which a group can affect the beliefs of an individual about himself. In *comparative appraisal,* the individual determines his relative standing vis-à-vis others on some attribute simply by observing the relevant others; no explicit action by them towards him is required. Thus, to assess one's relative skill on a task being performed simultaneously by group members, an individual might watch the performance of others even as he was working himself to see if he were doing better or worse than his peers. In his original statement of the theory of social comparison, Festinger (1954) focused solely on individuals' use of others to gain data about their abilities and the validity of their opinions. More recently, however, researchers have shown how comparative appraisal can yield information relevant to many different kinds of beliefs people hold about themselves—including their personality characteristics, their status in a given social system, and so on (Singer, 1966).[6] Further, although the original theory postulated that individuals tend to seek out persons *similar* to themselves for comparative purposes, recent

research (e.g., Thornton & Arrowood, 1966) has demonstrated that a person may seek out and utilize data from discrepant others as well—if circumstances are such that more or better information can be obtained from someone who is dissimilar.[7]

In *reflected appraisal,* an individual obtains information about himself by observing and interpreting the actual behaviors of other individuals toward him. Thus, following the notion of Cooley (1922) of the "looking glass self," an individual comes to gain self-understanding by inferring what he "must be like," given the way others behave towards him. As Jones and Gerard (1967, p. 322) note, individuals often arrange or "stage" situations in which it is especially likely that others will emit behaviors toward themselves that can be used to refine their self-perception.

In both comparative and reflective appraisal, the individual is actively seeking information about himself and/or using that information to make inferences and attributions about himself. It should be noted as well that groups often take direct action to influence the beliefs of a member about himself, by providing him with explicit personal evaluations or characterizations. When a group member is told, for example, to "stay out of the way while we do this task—you're no good at it," little inferential activity is required for the member to realize that his task-relevant abilities are not what they could be.

Such direct communications designed to affect a member can be facilitative of a group's efforts to achieve uniformity and regularity of member behavior (discussed earlier). If each member sees himself congruently with the way other members see him—that is, he "knows his place"—then he

---

[6] Indeed, some writers have postulated that one's experienced affective states (e.g., attitudes, emotions, motivational orientations) can best be understood when considered as "beliefs about the self" (cf., Bem, 1970, Chap. 5; Schachter, 1964). Despite the considerable elegance of this view, we will defer consideration of the impact of group-supplied stimuli on member attitudes, values, and the like until the next major section—which focuses explicitly on how discretionary stimuli affect member affective states.

[7] Additional data and commentary on factors affecting the choice of comparison others are provided by Wheeler et al. (1969), Arrowood and Friend (1969), and Latané (1966). The Latané reference is a special supplement to the *Journal of Experimental Social Psychology,* which contains reports of a number of diverse original investigations of the social comparison process, and includes a bibliography of relevant studies.

is likely to behave in a group-appropriate fashion with a minimum of fuss. For example, if a member genuinely believes that his skills and abilities are irrelevant to the group task, he is unlikely to try to assume a central role in the group task performance activities.

Sometimes a group will attempt to induce a member to believe things about himself which are objectively untrue. One way of dealing with a threatening new member who is obviously more task-competent than the current members, for example, is to convince the newcomer that he is not so capable as he might have thought. Alternatively, when a group faces an extremely difficult task, members may collude to convince one of their number that he is, in fact, quite able to handle the task—burying their own uncertainties in a burst of hopeful if somewhat unrealistic enthusiasm—and thereby building the confidence and motivation of the critical individual on whose shoulders the success or failure of the group rests.

It was noted earlier that a member will be more likely to accept group-supplied information about *external* reality when he is uncertain of his own ability to assess the nature of that reality for himself. Thus, if a group can appropriately manipulate the beliefs of a member about himself so that he comes to doubt his own perceptual or judgmental abilities, the dependence of that member upon the group for information about other matters should dramatically increase. Such a strategy—which would not seem that difficult to implement if all group members behaved so as to undermine the judgmental confidence of one of their number—could result in the group's having an extremely potent influence on the member's views of *external* reality.

Increasing Job-Relevant Knowledge and Skill

We turn now to a different type of informational impact which can derive from the exchange of discretionary stimuli in groups, namely, how such stimuli can be useful to group members in gaining the knowledge and skill needed to perform their jobs or fulfill their organizational roles. The distinction between this section and the two preceding ones parallels that of Ryle (1949) between "learning *that*" and "learning *how*." Ryle argues that acquiring information (learning *that*) can be directly imparted by others, whereas improving skills and response capabilities (learning *how*) can only be inculcated gradually, through coaching, practice, and example.

The group is of considerable importance in learning *how*, for several reasons. Personal trial-and-error in learning a new skill or behavior pattern is, in many cases, very inefficient. The help of other group members often permits an individual to "shortcut" his learning process and to lessen the personal risks involved in learning. Indeed, there are many skills and role-behaviors which probably are impossible to master without the active involvement of other people—for example, learning how to "manage" part of an organization, or learning how to operate a sophisticated piece of equipment. In his book *The Making of a Surgeon*, William Nolen describes numerous ways in which the fledgling surgeon is completely dependent upon other members of his medical team in developing the capability to execute surgical procedures with even minimal adequacy.

In general, the group can assist members in developing job-relevant knowledge and skills in three ways: (a) by direct instruction, (b) by providing feedback about behavior, and (c) by serving as "models" of correct or appropriate behavior.[8]

DIRECT INSTRUCTION. By itself, direct instruction is probably useful only for the most simple skills and behaviors. Simply being *told*, for example, how to drive a car or how to perform an appendectomy is not

---

[8] These three processes roughly parallel the functions of a coach for an actor learning a dramatic role. For a discussion of the dramaturgic model of complex role learning, see Goffman (1959) and Sarbin and Allen (1968b).

sufficient to master such skills. Nevertheless, the importance of direct instruction in skill- and role-learning should not be under-estimated, especially for new group or orga-nization members. If the group elects to withhold direct instruction from an indi-vidual, his adaptation can be severely im-paired: not knowing how to do something as simple as processing a request for paper clips through the bureaucracy can be highly stressful for a new organization member. Thus, while direct instruction is not *suffi-cient* for an individual to develop needed skills and behavior patterns, it often is a necessary part of such learning, and does represent an important resource held by the group which may be provided or withheld from an individual at the group's discretion.

FEEDBACK. Feedback from other group mem-bers can serve two major functions for a group member: it can provide him with information about what behaviors are "right" (or appropriate) and "wrong" (in-appropriate) in carrying out one's organiza-tional job or role; and it can provide re-inforcement, rewarding "right" behaviors and punishing "wrong" ones. Both func-tions, of course, can increase a member's job-relevant knowledge and skill.

Informational feedback (in the form of other members' responses to one's task ac-tivities) has been shown in laboratory in-vestigations to affect learning (Rhine, 1960), memory (Allen & Bragg, 1968a), and con-cept identification (Allen & Bragg, 1968b). Feedback which is primarily rewarding or punishing in impact also has been shown to affect skill-learning and role behavior (cf., Bandura, 1971; Berger & Lambert, 1968; Walters & Parke, 1964). Perhaps of special interest in this regard is research showing how it is possible to *change* the role of a given group member by selectively rein-forcing certain of his behaviors (e.g., Bavelas et al., 1965; Sarbin & Allen, 1968a). In the study by Sarbin and Allen, for ex-ample, reinforcing feedback from high status group members was shown to increase the level of participation of initially recalcitrant group members, and there was some tend-ency for negative feedback to decrease the participation of members who initially were highly verbal.

Unfortunately, very few studies of the role of feedback in skill or role-behavior learning have been conducted using groups of adults in the context of an on-going group or organization. One exception is a study by Smith and Kight (1959). Although plagued by methodological difficulties, this study demonstrates how group-generated feedback can facilitate role-learning by indi-vidual members, and that the overall effec-tiveness of the group may be enhanced in the process. The authors arranged for group members in the experimental condition to provide each other with "personalized feed-back" regarding their contributions to the leadership of the group—for example, whether they were talking too much or too little for the good of the group, and so on. It was found that such feedback increased both the problem solving efficiency of the experimental groups and, in some cases, the level of self-insight of group members.

MODELING. One of the most pervasive ways a group can be helpful to individual mem-bers in role and skill learning is through the provision of models. The need for models apparently is very great, especially for com-plex tasks and roles, some of which may be impossible to learn adequately in the absence of a concrete model (Kemper, 1968).

The earliest analyses of modeling and imitative learning (e.g., Miller & Dollard, 1941) focused on situations in which the learner simply "matched" the behavior of a model. It was shown, for example, that an observer who watched a model engage in some behavior and be rewarded for it would, if he also was motivated to obtain the reward, engage in the same behavior. If he was then rewarded, the new behavior would become established in his repertoire.

Although learning through "matching" clearly is one way people use others in developing skills, it is not the whole story. As the social learning theorists have pointed out, individuals can acquire robust *symbolic representations* of new activities by observing models—in addition to the simple stimulus-response associations required for "matching" behavior (Bandura, 1971). Thus, learning through modeling can occur without immediate reinforcement of the new behavior, and such learning can be "stored away" for use much later by the individual. Reinforcement is seen by the social learning theorists as a condition which may *facilitate* learning from models (because reinforcement—or anticipated reinforcement—can lead to increased attention to the model and retention of what the model does), but it is not viewed as a necessary condition for such learning. The social learning theorists agree with those of the stimulus-response persuasion, of course, that reinforcement controls when behaviors actually will be *performed* after they have been learned.

There is a large research literature on modeling (cf., Bandura, 1965, 1971; Berger, 1968; Berger & Lambert, 1969; Rosenbaum & Arenson, 1968; Walters, 1968). Once again, however, little or no research has focused on how members of groups in organizations use each other as models in increasing their job-relevant skills or their ability to adapt effectively to their roles in the organization.

SUMMARY. Although it is clear that individuals in organizations are substantially dependent upon members of their work groups for gaining the knowledge and skills they need to perform their jobs adequately, little controlled research has been carried out which illuminates how this process takes place in organizational settings.

The processes by which members use groups to increase their job-relevant knowledge may be of special interest in such settings, because of the *complexity* of the job- and role-behaviors required of many organization members. The more complex a job or role, the more likely an individual is to perform inadequately if left to his own devices—and also the more likely he is to need *all three* of the aids a group can provide to learn it well (i.e., direct instruction, feedback, and model-provision). This, of course, makes the individual heavily dependent upon the group in precisely those cases when the risk of failure for him is greatest. It would be expected, therefore, that the amount of power and influence a group has over an individual should be very great when the individual is attempting to obtain knowledge about how to perform a complex new job or role. In such circumstances, the capability of the group to influence that individual in *other* ways—such as obtaining behavioral or attitudinal conformity from him on matters not immediately relevant to the task at hand—also should be especially great.

Little attention has been given above to the use of the group as a site for increasing the job-relevant knowledge and skill of members *above* levels minimally required for adequate performance. The findings of Smith and Kight described earlier suggest that such a goal is not an unrealistic one. Moreover, many interpersonal "training groups" are explicitly designed so that group members can effectively use one another as resources in increasing their competence in interpersonal behavior (cf., Schein & Bennis, 1965; Bradford, Gibb, & Benne, 1964). Interestingly, it generally is assumed in the T-group movement that direct instruction can be of little help in learning new interpersonal skills; the focus instead is on the provision of information-full feedback and of models who demonstrate alternative ways of behaving. Apparently important to the success of such groups is the development of a climate within the group which is minimally threatening, thereby allowing and encouraging members to freely experiment with new interpersonal behavior.

To the extent that such a group climate is, in fact, necessary for the development of new interpersonal skills in a group, one would have to be substantially pessimistic about the usefulness of most existing groups in on-going organizations as sites in which group members could experiment with and learn radically new ways of behaving. Indeed, most groups in contemporary organizations seem instead to be characterized by very little experimenting, little risk-taking, and high interpersonal competitiveness (Argyris, 1969)—conditions which would not likely be conducive to members effectively using each other to learn genuinely innovative patterns of behavior.

Effects of Discretionary Stimuli on Member Affective States

We now turn from the informational states of group members to a discussion of how group-supplied discretionary stimuli can influence the level and character of the *affective* experiences of members. We examine separately the effects of discretionary stimuli on (a) member preferences, attitudes and values, and (b) the level of psychological arousal members experience in the group-setting.

Changing Member Preferences, Attitudes, and Values[9]

Numerous studies have documented that the groups of which a person is a member can have potent effects on his attitudes and values. For example, Lieberman (1956) reports a study of the attitudes of a number of unionized manufacturing workers over a period of almost three years, during which time the group membership of many of the

[9] As used here, a *preference* refers to a choice by an individual regarding which of a finite number of stimuli or alternatives he likes best; an *attitude* is simply the amount of positive or negative affect an individual has for some person, thing, or concept; and a *value* is the amount of positive or negative affect an individual holds regarding some abstract ideal or end-state. The three concepts are grouped here because they all reflect an individual's affect toward something; they differ mainly in generality and in the level of abstraction of the referent.

workers changed dramatically. During the first year of the study, twenty-three workers were promoted to foreman, and thirty-five workers were elected union stewards. Then, some time later, eight of the new foremen were returned to the worker role (because of cutbacks associated with an economic recession) and fourteen of the union stewards returned to the worker role (because they chose not to run again in union elections, or ran and were defeated).

Lieberman assessed the attitudes of the workers before any changes took place, after the initial round of changes, and again after some of the workers had reverted to their original roles. The focus of the research was on worker attitudes toward management, toward the union, and toward two different reward systems—one espoused by the union and one by management. In essence, the study was a naturally occurring field experiment, in which the groups of which the workers were members changed once—and then, for some of the subjects—changed back to the original state of affairs.

It was found that workers who became foremen became markedly more pro-management (and more critical of the union) after they had assumed their new role; and that when some of these workers subsequently were moved back to the worker role, their attitudes eventually reverted to those they previously had held. Foremen who remained in that role did not show this change. Results for workers who became union stewards were somewhat less clear. Following election to the union steward role there was some change in the pro-union, anti-management direction, but it was not so strong as for the workers who became foremen. Also, those who returned later to the worker role tended not to revert to their previously held attitudes.

The changes both for those who became foremen and those who became stewards in the Lieberman study involved shifts in the groups with whom the individuals were associated—and thus changes in the source and nature of the attitude-relevant stimuli to which the individuals were exposed. If it is assumed that groups of supervisory personnel tend to exchange stimuli (and encourage views) which are more pro-management and anti-union in orientation than do groups of workers, then the observed changes in attitudes for new foremen (and the reversion of these attitudes for those who reverted to the worker role) make good sense.[10] Further, it is reasonable that the observed changes were less strong for workers who became union stewards—simply because becoming a steward involves a much less significant change in group membership than does becoming a foreman. A union steward still tends to maintain close contact with the worker group, augmented by contact with other union stewards and some higher union officers. Thus, the Lieberman study would seem to provide good inferential data demonstrating how one's group memberships can affect his personal attitudes and values.

Yet there also is evidence available which suggests that *mere* membership in a given group is not sufficient for realizing affective changes—even if the individual is exposed to discretionary stimuli from that group on a more-or-less continuous basis. A well-known field study by Newcomb of Bennington College students in the 1930s is a good case in point (summarized by Newcomb, 1952).

Newcomb focused on the political attitudes of Bennington students during their four years at the college, and found that most students developed a more "liberal" stance as a result of their experiences at Bennington. Since a "liberal" point of view

was dominant among students and faculty at Bennington at that time, it can be argued that the group membership of the students somehow affected their own attitudes and values regarding political matters. Yet as Newcomb notes, there were some students for whom the modal changes did *not* take place; these students, it turned out, were ones who (for various reasons) had not accepted their membership group (i.e., other students and faculty at Bennington) as a positive point of reference for their own attitudes. In some cases, the Bennington group was actively rejected, and served as a *negative* point of reference (i.e., students tended to adopt values or attitudes in opposition to the dominant views at Bennington). In other cases, the Bennington group was merely not accepted, and college environment apparently had little impact on the political attitudes of these students one way or another. These latter students invariably had some other group of which they were a member (often the family) and which they maintained as the point of reference for their political attitudes.

Data consistent with the Newcomb findings are provided by Siegel and Siegel (1957), also in a college environment. A group of students expressed an interest in living in prestigious "row" houses (former sorority houses), and these students tended to score high on the Ethnocentrism-Fascism (E-F) scale, which reflects a decidedly "conservative" set of values. Only some of these students were able actually to move into row houses (because of logistic problems); the others were assigned to less prestigious dormitories. After one year, three groups had emerged: (a) row house occupants, for whom the row house group was both a membership and a reference group; (b) dormitory occupants who wanted to move to a row house—that is, for whom the "row" was a reference group but not a membership group; and (c) dormitory occupants who no longer wanted to move to a row house —that is, for whom the "row" was neither a

[10] It should be noted, however, that the nature of the *jobs* of the workers studied by Lieberman changed as well; it is likely that changes in job-supplied stimuli also were partly responsible for the attitude changes observed. In the particular setting where the research took place, the stimuli supplied in doing the new job probably reinforced those supplied by the new work group; this would not necessarily be true in other settings.

membership group nor a reference group. The E-F scale scores of the first group (membership *and* reference group) remained quite high; the scores of the second group (reference but not membership group) showed only a slight drop; and the scores of the last group (neither membership nor reference group) dropped very substantially.

These findings support the notion that the groups of which a person is a member can indeed have a powerful impact on one's attitudes and values—but only if that group is *accepted* as a relevant point of reference for those attitudes and values. Those in the Bennington study who remained conservatives during their four years at the college, according to Newcomb, never accepted Bennington as a valid reference group; and those subjects in the Siegel and Siegel study who ceased using the "row" as a point of reference (and presumably accepted instead the less conservative dormitory group as a reference group) changed their values to a less conservative orientation.

The above analysis may help explain why laboratory studies of group influences on member affective states have not, by and large, shown strong effects. Evidence was reviewed earlier in this chapter showing that group-supplied stimuli do often have a potent effect on group member *beliefs* (or opinions) about the environment. This is quite reasonable, given that research subjects may assume (often correctly) that other members have more or better knowledge of the "correct" state of the world than they themselves do. But, following the same line of reasoning, it would be expected that the effects of group-supplied stimuli on attitudes (and other affective states) should be less strong—simply because the subjects are less likely to accept at face value judgments of other subjects about how much they should *like or value* something. Subjects probably perceive their likes and dislikes as more personal and, therefore, "own" them more than they do many of their beliefs about the state of the world; thus, their affective states should be substantially immune to change

from stimuli supplied by a group of strangers whom they are not likely to see again.[11]

Consistent with this argument, Crutchfield (1955) found that conformity did not occur for preferences (among line drawings) as it did for more cognitive judgments; he concluded that preferences may indeed be immune from group pressure. Data counter to this claim recently have been reported by Allen and Levine (1971b). It is not clear, however, whether the Allen and Levine results reflect a genuine change in the level of affect subjects experienced for the stimuli provided, or merely public compliance with the choices they believed other subjects had made. If subjects were merely "going along" with the other subjects because of possible embarrassment (or for other extrinsic reasons), it would, of course, be inappropriate to conclude that their affective reactions to the stimuli had changed (cf., Kiesler, 1969, Chap. 11).

MECHANISMS FOR GROUP-GENERATED ATTITUDE CHANGE. In conclusion, three general mechanisms are suggested below by which groups can, over time, influence the affective states of their members. Each of the mechanisms, to be effective, requires that the target member *accept* the group (or stimuli provided by it), and each should be considerably more potent over an extended period of group membership than in the short term.

Mechanism One: Changing Behavior.

---

[11] An important exception would be a situation in which an individual was *unsure* whether or not he liked something (e.g., one's reaction to a concert of strange new music, in which the individual was aware of being "aroused" by the music, but not at all sure whether he liked or disliked it). In such cases, individuals often actively seek out cues from other people to use in interpreting their own ambiguous feelings (cf., Schachter, 1964; Nisbett & Valins, 1972). Only when the individual's reaction to the target stimulus is ambiguous, however, is he likely to use cues from other people for making self-attributions regarding his own affective state. In most organizational situations, individuals probably are fairly certain about their likes and dislikes regarding various aspects of the organizational environment.

with Affective Changes Following. As noted earlier, a group often is able directly to influence the behavior of selected members, simply by making group-controlled rewards contingent upon the members' engaging in the behavior deemed desirable by the group. As the individual finds himself exhibiting the behavior—and especially as the behavior tends to become habitual—his attitudes are likely to become more and more consistent with it. Consider, for example, a work group which subtly coerces one of its members to engage in dishonest behaviors aimed at subverting the attempt of the group's supervisor to increase the rate of production. It would not be surprising in this case to find the attitude of the worker toward the supervisor gradually changing in the negative direction. Over time, his attitude toward the supervisor would become increasingly consistent with the behaviors that he was exhibiting vis-à-vis the supervisor.

Two general explanations have been offered for the pervasive tendency for behavior and attitudes to become consistent over time: dissonance reduction (Festinger, 1957) and self-attribution (Bem, 1965). The former explanation, in brief, is that an individual experiences a state of tension or "dissonance" when he finds himself doing things that are inconsistent with his attitudes and beliefs; if he cannot conveniently rid himself of this tension by changing or terminating the behavior, he may change his attitudes or values to bring them into line with that behavior. The self-attribution hypothesis leads to nearly identical predictions, but from a different theoretical perspective. This hypothesis suggests that an individual observes himself engaging in a behavior and, in attempting to explain why he behaves as he does, he attributes to himself an attitude which would be an appropriate "reason" for the behavior. For example: "I seem to work very hard and very long hours—therefore, I must really like my work."

In each case, however, the more the group overtly coerces the individual to engage in the behavior by using very potent rewards or punishments, the *less* substantial the affective change of the individual. One feels little dissonance when he engages in a slightly aversive behavior for a large reward; nor does one have to look to his own attitudes to find a "reason" for that behavior— the extrinsic reward suffices, and attitude change is unlikely. This is probably part of the reason that the Chinese Communists' attempts to use group methods to "brainwash" prisoners were less than completely successful: the coercion to "confess and repent" was so strong that many prisoners were able to attribute their acquiescence to the demands of their captors to the group-supplied rewards and punishments rather than to any genuine change of their own values (cf., Schein, 1956).

When, however, a group is able to provide relatively subtle coercion to obtain the behavior (e.g., "Come on, everybody else is doing it, don't be a laggard!"), substantial affective changes may result. Yet it also should be kept in mind that unless the individual *values* the rewards controlled by the group, he is unlikely to "go along" with the group, and this mechanism for obtaining affective changes in group members will lose its power.

Mechanism Two: Changing Beliefs, with Affective Changes Following. As Fishbein (1967), Rosenberg (1956) and others have noted, attitudes tend to be based upon the *beliefs* individuals hold about the attitude object—and the affect an individual associates with that object may be changed by changing the beliefs he holds about it. A worker might, for example, have positive affect toward "labor unions" and base that affect on beliefs that unions lead to better pay for workers, keep managements from exploiting workers, and in general contribute to a healthy national economy. If (as in the Lieberman research) that worker became a member of management, he probably would be subjected to stimuli which would weaken the strength of his beliefs and, perhaps, introduce others in their place: for example, unions hinder industrial progress, union officials often are corrupt, and so on. To the extent that the worker's new group is effective in changing the content and/or the strength of the beliefs he holds about unions, his overall affect for labor unions is likely to change as well. Since (as discussed previously) groups often can powerfully affect the beliefs of their members, this mechanism probably is one very important means by which a person's group memberships affect his preferences, attitudes, and values.

For Mechanism Two to be effective, of course, it is essential that (a) the beliefs of the group member be open to change by group-supplied data, and (b) the group be valued by the individual and/or seen as a source of trustworthy data about the environment. Thus, Mechanism Two is likely to be much more potent in influencing the attitudes and values of new or low status group members than of those who are more experienced or more self-confident.

Mechanism Three: Direct Change of Affect. A substantial body of literature is available showing that attitudes (viewed as affective responses of the individual) can be classically conditioned in a manner identical to the conditioning of other individual responses (e.g., Lott, 1955; Staats & Staats, 1958). That is, if a target stimulus is paired with another stimulus which elicits positive affect in the individual, over time the target stimulus will come to elicit positive affect when presented alone. Further, the affective reactions will generalize from the target stimuli to other, new stimuli which are similar to it, following the principle of mediated generalization.

Thus, by judicious control of the positive or reinforcing stimuli which are at its command, a group should be able to condition the attitudes of group members regarding some person, object, or concept. In the Bennington study, for example, it was shown that the most popular students tended to be of a "liberal" persuasion. When other students were in the presence of these students, therefore, it is likely that they often were exposed simultaneously to social reinforcement (i.e., attention from someone who was admired) *and* to "liberal" political viewpoints. It is possible that such "conditioning" of student attitudes is part of the reason for the changes Newcomb observed at Bennington.

The process of affective change described above has some similarities to the process of "identification" postulated by Kelman (1958) —that is, the person adopts the attitude of another *because* that attitude is associated with a desirable or satisfying interpersonal relationship. Following Kelman's argument, the new attitude would be expected to persist only so long as the relationship itself was maintained and continued to be satisfying.

The literature on attitude conditioning would predict, however, that over time the new attitude would come to be internalized by the individual, even in the absence of the relationship from which it originated. Indeed, Thelen (1950, pp. 32–33) reports that the satisfaction of needs from one's group membership can, by itself, lead to the internalization of the values held by the group. To the extent that this finding has generality, it would appear that groups *which are experienced as satisfying by their members* can have a profound direct effect on the attitudes and values of their members—an effect which may persist well beyond the period of time that the individual is actually a member of the group.

Concluding Comment on the Three Mechanisms. Although the three mechanisms have been discussed separately, it is likely that most often they operate simultaneously. As mentioned previously, for each to be effective it is necessary for the individual to *value* what the group has to offer, and, in that sense, to be dependent upon the group for the satisfaction of his own needs. A group member who is very much his "own person" or who has plenty of alternative groups where he can satisfy his needs is not likely to find his preferences, attitudes, or values very much influenced by the group.

But when the group *is* of importance to the individual, the stimuli which are supplied by it can—and often do—have a great deal of impact on the person's likes and dislikes. Although the stimuli responsible for such effects are very much under the control of the group, it often is the case that substantial changes in attitudes or values may be realized without either the individual or his fellow group members being fully aware of what is happening or how it is happening. If a group were to deliberately set out to use its control over discretionary stimuli to change the attitudes of one or more members who were dependent upon the group for personal satisfactions, the amount of change realized could be very large indeed.

Changing the Level of Psychological Arousal of Members

There is a second and quite different type of impact that group-supplied discretionary stimuli can have on the affective states of group members—namely, raising or lowering the level of psychological arousal or "activation" that members experience in the group-setting. As will be seen below, member arousal can be affected simply by other group members "being there" and making their presence known to the target individual, or because of the specific content of discretionary stimuli supplied to the individual by the group.

Increasing arousal. Zajonc (1965), in an insightful untangling of previous research on social facilitation, proposed that the *mere presence* of other people can increase the level of arousal of individuals in performance-relevant situations. In reviewing research in support of this proposition, however, Zajonc noted that evidence was both "indirect and scant."

In recent years, a number of researchers have questioned whether it is the *mere* presence of others which increases arousal, or the presence of others who are in some specified relationship to the individual. The weight of the evidence seems to be that the mere presence of others is *not* itself arousal-producing—but the presence of others who are watching and potentially evaluating the performance activities of an individual does produce heightened arousal in the individual. For example, Cottrell et al. (1968) provide data which suggest that the *mere* presence of others (in this case, two blindfolded confederates presumably waiting in the experimental room and becoming visually "adapted" in preparation for a color-perception experiment) does not increase arousal. The presence of an *audience,* however (in this case, two confederates presumably waiting for a subsequent experiment who were not blindfolded and who were positioned so they could observe the subject), apparently does increase arousal. It should be noted, however, that arousal level was inferred in the Cottrell et al. experiment from differences in performance; no direct measures of arousal were obtained.

Henchy and Glass (1968) did attempt to obtain direct indicators of arousal, using both subject self-report and physiological measures (skin conductance and heart rate). These researchers included experimental conditions in which subjects (a) worked alone, (b) worked in the presence of two other persons (described to subjects as students in a community college who wanted to "watch a psychology experiment"), and (c) worked in the presence of two expert observers (described as staff members at Rockefeller University who were specialists in the study of "perceptual behavior and human learning"—areas directly related to the task of the subject). Results showed that while subjects reported more evaluation apprehension in the "expert" condition than in the other two, there was no significant difference in evaluation apprehension between the "alone" and "non-expert" conditions. Although the experimental conditions did not affect the physiological measures of arousal, observed differences in performance across conditions were consistent with predictions based on the Zajonc theory. In discussing their findings (p. 453), the authors raise the possibility that the measures of autonomic arousal used may not have been entirely appropriate for their experimental manipulations of arousal.

In summary, then, it appears that the presence of other people can increase the arousal of an individual—but only when the observer(s) are in an evaluative or potentially evaluative relationship vis-à-vis the individual. Thus, one would *not* expect that a worker's arousal would be much affected by being in a large room where a number of other people also were working, unless, as often happens, the worker had reason to believe that the other people might be assessing his rate or quality of output. If among the "other people" were members of management, who were responsible for *evaluating* the performance of the worker, his arousal could rise very high indeed.

Decreasing arousal and anxiety. Although at first glance it may seem contradictory to the material discussed immediately above, there also is good evidence available in the research literature showing that in some cases being in the presence of other people can *reduce* a person's level of anxiety and arousal. A number of researchers, following Schachter's (1959) pioneering work on the psychology of social affiliation, have shown that individuals who are highly aroused (especially when the arousal is due to fear) actively seek out others and prefer to spend their time in a group rather than alone.

For example, Gerard and Rabbie (1961) informed female subjects that they would receive a painful electric shock, and found that they preferred to spend the time waiting for the shock in the company of others rather than alone. In a subsequent study, Rabbie (1963) increased the uncertainty (and, presumably, the arousal) of some sub-

jects by telling them that only one out of each group of four subjects actually would receive the shock; others were told that all would receive the shock. Results showed that subjects in the "uncertain" condition wanted to await the shock in a group more strongly than did those in the "certain" condition.

Although Schachter (1959) suggests that fearful individuals want to be with others even if they cannot actually converse with them, Rabbie (1963) found that people have a *stronger* desire to be in a group where they can talk together than in one where conversation is not possible. There are, unfortunately, no data available which show explicitly how that conversation which does take place among people who are highly aroused helps (or hinders) the anxiety-reducing process. If, as the data suggest, the mere presence of others can be anxiety-reducing, then supportive or genuinely accepting social interaction should be dramatically helpful.

In general, the findings reviewed above fit well with those that show group members under external stress often seek out each other and develop new or heightened feelings of closeness or cohesiveness. When, for example, a natural disaster strikes or threatens a community, individuals show levels of mutual support, reassurance, and cooperation that previously were unknown. Similar phenomena often (but *not* always) occur when the survival of a work group (or even of an organization) is threatened from an external source—including threat from another group or organization (cf., Sherif, 1936; Klein, 1971).

Summary. Although research on the effects of group-supplied discretionary stimuli on the arousal of individual group members is scanty, some conclusions can be drawn. In general, it appears that in some circumstances being in a group can serve to *increase* one's level of arousal and anxiety, and in other cases, group membership can help decrease experienced upset. The research evidence suggests, in particular, that when the individual has reason to believe that other group members will provide negative or explicitly evaluative stimuli to him, his level of arousal increases; when he expects the stimuli to be positive (e.g., reassuring or fear-reducing), arousal decreases. These effects are based largely on research in which a subject is (or expects to be) merely in the presence of other people; as yet, few studies have examined what happens to a person's level of arousal as a function of actual social interaction in groups. It would be expected that the arousal-increasing and arousal-decreasing effects of the group should be considerably magnified when the other group members provide the member discretionary stimuli which confirm his expectations—whether those expectations have to do with the possibility of being socially evaluated, or with the possibility of being comforted and reassured. The effects of such changes in arousal level on individual performance effectiveness are discussed later in this chapter.

DIRECT EFFECTS OF GROUPS ON MEMBER BEHAVIOR: GROUP NORMS

In previous sections, we have examined how group-supplied discretionary stimuli can influence the informational and the affective states of group members. Change in the actual behavior of group members was viewed as a typical (but indirect) consequence of changes in member informational and affective states. It also is true, of course, that member behavior can be affected *directly* by the discretionary stimuli controlled by his fellows; indeed, one of the most general principles of psychology is that the behavior of a person can be shaped effectively by someone who is in control of stimuli which are valued (or disvalued) by the target person.

Since most groups do, in fact, have many resources which are valued by group members, member behavior can be directly affected by the rewards (and punishments) administered by the group contingent upon the actions of the individual. Such effects must, however, take place on a highly individualistic basis. That is, when other group members wish a particular person to engage in some behavior, they must use their control of discretionary stimuli in such a way that the individual comes to realize that it is in his personal best interest to comply with the behavioral demands of his peers.

Such a process, while powerful, can consume a great deal of the time and energy of group members, and, therefore, is not a very efficient means of coordinating the activities of group members—especially if the group is moderately large. Therefore, most of the "regulating" of group member behavior typically takes place through behavioral *norms* which are created and enforced by group members. Indeed, norms are so pervasive and powerful in groups that it has been suggested that "It is only in imagination that we can talk about a human group apart from norms" (Davis, 1950, p. 53).

This section focuses on the nature of group norms and their effects on member behavior. In particular, we will examine (a) the structural characteristics of norms, (b) what happens when someone deviates from a norm and the consequences of such deviation for the group as a whole, and (c) the conditions under which individuals are and are not likely to comply with group norms. In the paragraphs which follow immediately below, we specify several of the major characteristics of group norms which will guide the subsequent discussion.

1. *Norms are structural characteristics of groups which summarize and simplify group influence processes.* Although numerous definitions and conceptualizations of norms have been proposed, there is general agreement that a norm is a structural characteristic of a group which summarizes and highlights those processes within the group which are intended to regulate and regularize group member behavior (cf.,

Festinger, Schachter, & Back, 1950; Homans, 1950; Rommetveit, 1955; Bates & Cloyd, 1956; Thibaut & Kelley, 1959, Chap. 8; Golembiewski, 1962, Chap. 5). Thus, norms represent an important means of "short-cutting" the need to use discretionary stimuli on a continuous basis to control the behavior of individual group members.

2. *Norms apply only to behavior—not to private thoughts and feelings.* Although some writers speak of the effects of group norms on member attitudes and beliefs, norms are treated here as being exclusively relevant to the actual behavior of group members. This usage does include verbal behavior, so what a member *says* he believes or what he *says* his attitude is can be very much under the normative control of the group. It should be emphasized, however, that such behavioral compliance does not necessarily reflect the true private attitudes and beliefs of group members. As pointed out earlier in this chapter, group-supplied discretionary stimuli can indeed affect one's private attitudes and beliefs—but the process is considerably more complex and subtle than merely coercing a member to *say* he agrees with the stance of the group on some matter.

3. *Norms generally are developed only for behaviors which are viewed as important by most group members.* As Thibaut and Kelley (1959) note, norms generally develop only for behaviors which otherwise would have to be controlled by direct and continuous social influence. While this implies that only those behaviors viewed as most important in the eyes of group members will be brought under normative control, it does not imply that normatively controlled behaviors are necessarily *objectively* the most important to the group. Some businesses, for example, even today have a norm that one should wear a hat when one leaves the building; it is doubtful that hat-wearing behavior is objectively important to the group, but the fact that most members *believe* it to be important is sufficient cause for the norm to be developed and enforced.

4. *Norms usually develop gradually, but the process can be shortcutted if members want.* Norms about behavior typically develop gradually and informally as members learn what behaviors are, in fact, important for the group to control—and what discretionary stimuli seem most effective in regulating the occurrence of those behaviors. Indeed, Machotka (1964, Chap. 11) has noted that the process of norm formation and enforcement can be so gradual and covert as to be a mostly *unconscious* process. It is possible, nevertheless, for groups to consciously shortcut the process of norm development. If for some reason group members decide that a particular norm would be desirable or helpful, they may simply agree to institute such a norm suddenly by declaring that "from now on" the norm exists. Someone might say, for example, "We seem to interrupt each other a lot in this group; let's have a norm that nobody talks until the other person is finished." If the group as a whole agrees with this proposal, then one might observe marked differences in the social interaction within that group thereafter.

5. *Not all norms apply to everyone.* Finally, it should be noted that norms often do not apply uniformly to all group members. For example, high status members often have more "freedom" to deviate from the letter of the norm than do other people, as is discussed in detail later. Also, groups will at times form a norm which applies only to one person (or to a small subset of persons) within a group. In such cases, roughly following Thibaut and Kelley (1959, pp. 142–147), we may speak of the norms as representing the "roles" of the person(s) to whom the norms apply.

A Model of Group Behavioral Norms

An elegant conception of the structure of group norms has been proposed by Jackson (1960, 1965, 1966). The model, which focuses on the distribution of potential approval and disapproval others feel for various behaviors which might be exhibited in a given situation, can be represented in two-dimensional space: the ordinate is the amount of approval and disapproval felt, and the abscissa is the amount of the given behavior exhibited. A "return potential curve" can be drawn in this space, indicating the *pattern and intensity* of approval and disapproval associated with various possible behaviors. An example of a return potential curve is shown in Figure 1.

The Return Potential Model (RPM) can be used to describe any situation in which a group norm serves to regulate the behavior of group members. To apply the model, one would obtain from group members (or infer from observations of behavior in the group) the amount of approval or disapproval associated with various behaviors and, from these data, plot a return potential curve. The curve in Figure 1, for example, might reflect the norm of a group regarding the amount of talking an individual

member does during a group meeting. Both too little and too much talking, in this case, would be disapproved of, but the intensity of the disapproval is somewhat stronger for someone who talks too much than for someone who talks too little. (The units of behavior in the example in Figure 1 are arbitrary; in practice, the abscissa would be scaled using units appropriate to the behavior in question.)

A return potential curve can, theoretically, assume any shape. March (1954), in a formulation similar to that of Jackson, suggests three basic types of norms: the unattainable-ideal norm, the preferred-value norm, and the attainable-ideal norm. The unattainable-ideal and attainable-ideal norms are depicted in Figure 2; the preferred-value norm is of the general type shown in Figure 1. In essence, the unattainable-ideal norm connotes "the more the better"; thus, among a group of scholars, the more insightful one's contributions the better; or on a football team, the more tackles made the better. The preferred-value norm is often characteristic of the approval and disapproval felt by members of a work group regarding the productivity of individual members: too little output is disapproved—but so is too *much* output. March gives the following example of an attainable-ideal norm: A football team is in possession of the ball on the opponents' twenty-yard line. A halfback will earn increasing approval as he carries the ball increasing distances, but only up to twenty yards. After that, he will have made a touchdown and can gain no further approval; twenty-one yards is just as good as twenty-five. There are, of course, many other possible curves which would be descriptive of other types of group norms.

Much of the elegance of the RPM lies in its usefulness as a vehicle for generating quantitative measures of the characteristics of group norms. Jackson (1965, 1966), for example, suggests five specific characteristics of norms which can be measured using the RPM.

1. *The Point of Maximum Return:* the

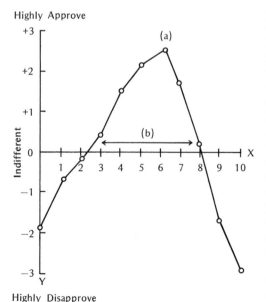

Figure 1. Schematic representation of the Return Potential Model (RPM) of normative structure. The ordinate is an axis of evaluation; the abscissa is an axis of behavior. (Adapted from Jackson, 1965, p. 303.)

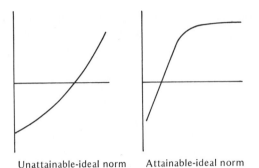

Unattainable-ideal norm   Attainable-ideal norm

Figure 2. Unattainable-ideal and attainable-ideal norms shown as Return Potential curves. (From March, 1954.)

point on the behavior dimension which generates the highest level of approval from others. (Point *a* in Figure 1.)

2. *The Range of Tolerable Behavior:* the segment of the behavior dimension which is *approved* by others. (Indicated by range *b* in Figure 1.)

3. *The Potential Return Difference:* the overall amount of approval or disapproval associated with norm-regulated behaviors. This index is computed by taking the algebraic sum of the ordinate values across all behaviors. The potential return difference, then, can be positive, neutral, or negative— and should reflect the relative emphasis a group places on rewards versus punishments in regulating member behavior.

4. *Intensity:* the overall strength of approval and disapproval associated with norm-regulated behaviors. This index is computed by summing the *absolute values* of the ordinates across all behaviors. Thus, intensity reflects the overall strength of affect associated with a norm, regardless of whether that affect is predominately positive or negative in direction. The measure would seem useful in comparing the amount of "normative regulation" characteristic of different groups or organizations; or in assessing the importance of different norms enforced by the *same* group or organization.

5. *Crystallization:* the degree of consensus among group members regarding the amount of approval or disapproval associ-

ated with each point on the behavior dimension. Crystallization of a norm may be estimated in terms of the variation of approval-disapproval among group members, across all points on the behavior dimension. (A more elegant means of computing an index of crystallization, involving profile similarity, is described briefly in Jackson, 1966.) The crystallization measure should reflect the potential of the group for effective behavioral control of its members; unless there is at least moderate agreement among members about the amount of approval or disapproval associated with each behavior, effective enforcement of norm-specified behavior will not be possible.

Jackson and his colleagues have used the RPM in research in a number of group and organizational settings, both for understanding the internal dynamics of ongoing groups and organizations and for making comparative studies of different social systems. This research is summarized in a forthcoming volume (Jackson, in press). It is unfortunate that the RPM (or variants of it) has not been more widely used in studies of groups and organizations. Among the advantages of the model (most of which remain unexploited) are:

1. The model offers a means of quantification which can be applied directly in field situations. The use of quantitative measures descriptive of norms generally has been lacking in previous research on group norms in organizations.

2. The model permits and encourages explicit comparisons between the norms which characterize a total group (e.g., operationalized as the mean return potential curve across all group members) and these same norms as *experienced* by individual members of the group. Such comparisons could provide considerable new insight into the dynamics of individual-group relationships.

3. The model can be used to compare norms which regulate different classes of behaviors within a given group, and even to study how the group may enforce a given

norm differentially for different group members, depending upon the current status of the members in the group.

4. Finally, the RPM seems to hold a great deal of potential for making general *diagnoses* of the normative state of affairs within a given group—as a first step in a change program involving diagnosis, feedback, and change. Through the model it should be possible to help group members see, objectively and in simple terms, what the group norms actually are and how they may be guiding behavior in ways that are unrealized or unintended. Raising implicit norms to the level of explicit awareness and discussion in this way should provide an excellent impetus for change.

Dealing With Deviance

Earlier in this chapter a quotation was presented from Arthur Schlesinger, in which he indicated that he had tempered the expression of his objections to the Bay of Pigs plans because he feared that vigorous protest would only "gain me a name as a nuisance." It is not difficult to see how Schlesinger might have come to hold that belief, given the following event:

At a large birthday party for his wife, Robert Kennedy, the Attorney General, who had been constantly informed about the Cuban invasion plan, took Schlesinger aside and asked him why he was opposed. The President's brother listened coldly and then said, "You may be right or you may be wrong, but the President has his mind made up. Don't push it any further. Now is the time for everyone to help him all they can." (Janis, 1972, pp. 41–42)

The "treatment" given Schlesinger illustrates how groups can use their control of discretionary stimuli to bring into line members who are behaving contrary to the group norm. A number of research studies document that when a group member expresses an opinion which deviates from that of the rest of the group, his fellow members do in fact increasingly direct communications

toward him (Schachter et al., 1951; Festinger & Thibaut, 1951; Emerson, 1954; Schachter et al., 1954; Berkowitz & Howard, 1959). The researchers interpret this communication as reflecting attempts to move the member into congruence with the group norm.[12] Sometimes the stimuli provided by group members may be material or physical rather than verbal: the practice of "binging" (i.e., hitting someone forcefully on the upper arm) has been described as an effective means used by work group members to correct the behavior of a worker who is violating group norms about production quantity (cf., Homans, 1950).

It may be recalled from earlier in the chapter that a *role* in a group can be described in terms of special behavioral norms which apply specifically to the role occupant(s). Thus, it is not surprising to find that a member who deviates from his role in the group (e.g., a leader who quits leading) encounters reactions which are similar to those observed when someone violates a general group norm. Unfortunately, experimental studies which focus on the reactions of groups to this type of deviance are scarce. The literature on role conflict (e.g., Gross, Mason, & McEachern, 1958; Kahn et al., 1964; Biddle & Thomas, 1966, Sections VIII and IX), however, offers some relevant insights. For example, research on inter-role conflict suggests that when a person deviates from his role (even if the reason is to fulfill another, equally legitimate role), discretionary stimuli may be applied swiftly by his peers to enforce the expectations associated with the first role. A similar process often ensues when an individual encounters inter-sender conflict—that is, when conflicting expectations are sent from different sources regarding appropriate behavior for the occupant of a single role. The essence

---

[12] This interpretation can be questioned, since the *content* of the communication generally has not been examined. See Berkowitz (1971) for a discussion of this and other interpretive issues having to do with the original Schachter experiment on communication with the deviant.

of role conflict (and the crux of the problem for the role occupant) in either case is that the individual is confronted with discretionary stimuli aimed at changing his behavior *regardless* of how he actually behaves. Because he cannot please all role-senders at once, the individual experiences conflict. (The effects of such conflict, and the ways individuals react to it, are discussed by Kahn et al., 1964, and by Sarbin & Allen, 1968b.)

Rejection of the Deviant

When a member persistently deviates from what is acceptable to his fellow group members, he becomes vulnerable to rejection by the group. In other words, the application of discretionary stimuli intended to persuade or "pressure" the deviant to change will persist only for so long, whereupon the other members may, in Festinger's (1950) terms, "change the composition of the psychological group." A number of studies provide moderate support for the hypothesis that a persistently deviant member tends to be rejected (e.g., Schachter, 1951; Schachter et al., 1954; Berkowitz & Howard, 1959).

It has not yet been satisfactorily demonstrated, however, that such rejection is accompanied or immediately preceded by a decline in communications to the deviant member, as would be expected. Schachter (1951) found a decline in communications to the deviant late in the group session by members who subsequently rejected him on sociometric measures. This happened, however, only in groups which were both highly cohesive and dealing with a topic directly relevant to the purpose of the group. Moreover, a replication of the Schachter study by Emerson (1954) failed to find evidence of a dropping off of communication to the deviant in any experimental condition.

A study by Sampson and Brandon (1964) suggests that groups will attempt to use their control over discretionary stimuli to change a deviant member when they can, and revert to rejection of the deviant only when change seems hopeless. Sampson and Brandon trained confederates to role-play along two different dimensions: (a) for the "role" manipulation, the confederates revealed themselves prior to the official start of the group discussion to be either racial bigots (role deviant) or liberals (role conformant); (b) for the "opinion" manipulation, the confederates either conformed to the modal position of the group on the discussion topic (opinion conformant), or disagreed substantially with that position (opinion deviant). Results showed that the opinion deviant received more communications than did the opinion conformant, as would be expected, but he was *not* rejected more than the opinion conformant. The role deviant, on the other hand, *was* rejected more than the role conformant, although more communications were addressed to the role conformant than the role deviant. These results suggest that group members may have been rejecting outright (and, therefore, not communicating at all with) a member whom they saw as having no hope for change (the bigot), but expending a great deal of communicative effort trying to "convert" the member who was at least potentially influenceable (i.e., the opinion deviant). Even at the end of the experimental session when the opinion deviant still had not changed, he was not rejected. These results suggest—and naive observations of groups in operation provide some confirmation—that rejection of a group member is viewed as a fairly serious step to take, and may be administered by a group only when all else has failed, or when the deviant is seen as completely incorrigible.[13]

---

[13] It may be significant that all three studies discussed above (i.e., those of Schachter, of Emerson, and of Sampson & Brandon) were laboratory investigations of fairly short duration (less than an hour). In that time period it is doubtful either that influence attempts addressed to the deviant would have ceased with any finality, or that the sociometric rejection of the deviant would have approached maximum severity. Indeed, the moderate reductions reported for the deviant on the

Yet there may be another reason why groups apparently are so hesitant to cease communicating with a deviant and reject him with finality. Dentler and Erikson (1959) argue that the group *needs* the deviant, and, therefore, cannot really afford to eliminate him completely. Group norms, for example, may become more explicit and more clearly understood by group members as a result of their observation of various "deviant" behaviors and the consequences which ensue. In addition, because deviants are observed to receive negative outcomes from the group, members are reminded of the *range* of outcomes which the group has under its control, and the incentive value of conformity may be enhanced as a result. Moreover, the process of dealing with deviant members may help the group clarify its own boundaries, and gain a better sense of what is distinctive about the group and central to its identity—and what is not. In a number of ways, then, deviant members can contribute positively to the stability of the group and to the maintenance of its identity. As a consequence, Dentler and Erikson argue, the role of the deviant often becomes institutionalized within the group, and group members will strongly resist any trend toward complete elimination of a deviant member (p. 102). While this particular perspective does not purport to handle all of the dynamics of a group's responses to deviance, it does suggest one important and frequently overlooked set of reasons why groups may be reluctant to respond to deviance by rejecting the member who deviates.

---

sociometric measures in the studies discussed do *not* suggest that the boundaries of the group have been redrawn to exclude the deviant. What seems needed, therefore, is a longitudinal investigation of deviation, communication, and rejection, which examines what happens to a deviant after his peers have tried virtually all the discretionary stimuli at their command to get him to change. In such circumstances, a sharper reduction of communication to the deviant and a more clear-cut rejection of him would not be surprising— despite the somewhat equivocal finding of short-term laboratory investigations of these same phenomena.

Deviance and Group Effectiveness

The experimental work on deviance described above depicts, in some ways, a fairly primitive type of group process. Caricatured a bit, the process operates as follows: Uniformity, conformity to norms, and adherence to one's role is the rule. When someone steps out of line, other members provide him with potent doses of discretionary stimuli designed to persuade or coerce him back to "normal." This pressure continues, until the would-be deviant (a) caves in and ceases expressing his deviant thoughts or exhibiting his deviant behavior; (b) is psychologically or bodily rejected by the group or becomes institutionalized by the group as the "house deviant"; or (c) finally convinces the other group members of the rightness of his thoughts or the appropriateness of his behavior.

The more the group has control of discretionary stimuli which are important to group members, the more it can realize alternative (a) above—that is, it can effectively eliminate most appearances of deviance on the part of its members. The members, in such circumstances, may faithfully behave in accord with their roles in the group, refrain from violating group norms, and express their endorsement of the "right" attitudes and beliefs. And from all visible indicators everything seems well with the group, at least in the short term.

It can be argued, however, that this pattern of dealing with deviance is highly dysfunctional for the *long-term* effectiveness of a group, for at least two reasons. First, if members comply primarily because of the application of "pressure" from the group (or the expected application of that pressure), the result may be public compliance *at the expense of* private acceptance and personal commitment to what is being done (cf., Kelman, 1961; Kiesler, 1969, pp. 279–295). And when a group is heavily populated by individuals who are saying and doing one thing, but thinking and feeling another, high effectiveness in the long haul is not very likely.

Secondly, to the extent a group uses its control of discretionary stimuli to swiftly extinguish any signs of deviance, the group loses the opportunity to explore the usefulness and ultimate validity of the very attitudes, beliefs, norms, and roles it is enforcing. For example, if compliance to a given behavioral norm is enforced so effectively that deviance from that norm virtually never occurs, the group will be unable to discover whether that norm is actually helpful or detrimental to the achievement of the goals of the group. In a nutshell, just as it is said that an unexamined life is not worth living, so it may also be true that an unexamined norm is not worth enforcing—at least if one aspires to high group effectiveness in the long run.

Despite these and other dysfunctions of excessive pressures against deviance, the research literature reviewed suggests that most groups have a strong tendency to stamp out (or at least sweep under the rug) behaviors which are not congruent with traditional standards of acceptability in the group. Apparently groups rarely attempt to work through the more basic problems of why people deviate from the group, what the consequences of that deviance are for the group, and how deviance can be most effectively dealt with for the good of both individual members and the group as a whole. This style of social behavior is consistent with the observation of Argyris (1969) that most groups in contemporary society operate according to what he calls Pattern A interpersonal rules. In a Pattern A world, conformity takes precedence over experimentation, intellective and cognitive matters drive out feelings and emotionality, and interpersonal behavior is characterized more by "diplomacy," mistrust, and caution than by interpersonal openness, trust, and risk-taking.

Consider, for example, the suggestion of Dentler and Erikson (1959, discussed earlier) that groups often "institutionalize" the role of the deviant, and resist attempts to explicitly reject deviant individuals. It is doubtful that this phenomenon reflects a conscious and deliberate decision by group members that the group would be best served by retaining the deviant in the group and using his behavior to help maintain the boundaries and equilibrium of the group. Instead, it is more likely that group members simply find themselves unable and unwilling to handle the emotional and interpersonal issues which invariably are involved in carrying off an overt rejection of one of their number. By gradually defining a "role" of deviance for the member in question, the problem of the deviant's behavior can be defused in the short term, without the necessity of surfacing issues which are "out of bounds" in a Pattern A world. The fact that there may be some functional payoffs for the group as a consequence of the deviant's membership in the group, then, is more a happy coincidence than the outcome of a conscious and deliberate decision by the group.

Despite some instances (such as that described above) in which Pattern A interpersonal behavior can lead to apparent solutions to problems which might be difficult for the group to deal with directly, Argyris argues that Pattern A behavior is *not* facilitative of group effectiveness in the long run. For generating short-term solutions to "easy" tasks and interpersonal problems (e.g., How can we get Member X to shut up so we can get back to work on the task), a Pattern A solution may be fine; but for more basic and more important problems (e.g., How can we more effectively deal with and learn from our individual and collective failures), it will be difficult or impossible for groups operating according to Pattern A rules to obtain valid interpersonal data and generate lasting solutions.

Even so, it is not difficult to understand why groups persist in handling deviance essentially according to Pattern A rules. The reason, in brief, is the same one proposed for why the groups discussed by Dentler and

Erikson developed institutionalized roles for deviants—namely, it is emotionally quite stressful and difficult for group members to deal openly with core questions of conformity, deviation, and interpersonal relationships in a group. Indeed, the work of both Argyris (1969) and Bion (1959) suggests that it may be impossible for a group to break out of traditional patterns of interpersonal behavior without outside professional assistance. Even with such assistance, as Bion points out, it may take a great deal of time and effort before a group can overcome the "basic assumptions" which guide its early behavior and develop into an effective and truly interdependent work group. When a group becomes able to make more open and conscious choices about the use of those discretionary stimuli under its control to deal with issues of conformity and deviance, the long-term effectiveness of the group should be greatly enhanced. The research of behavioral scientists to date, unfortunately, has provided only minimal insight into how to get there from here.

Some Determinants of Member Compliance With Group Norms

Group members tend to behave in accord with the norms of the group in two general cases:

Case I. When the norm-specified behaviors are congruent with the personal attitudes, beliefs, and prior behavioral dispositions of the group members. In this case, there is no conflict between the individual and the group; the member would tend to behave in norm-congruent ways, anyway. It should be noted, however, that the *reason* group members are predisposed toward compliance with the norm in such cases may be that the group has long ago done an effective job of inculcating in the individual attitudes and beliefs which are consistent with the norm.

Consider, for example, a work group that enforces a norm of not communicating very much or very openly with members of management. A member who has been in that group for some time may have come to genuinely believe that "managers can't be trusted—they'll use what you tell them to exploit you whenever they can." The group would not need to "pressure" this member into compliance with the norm; the more subtle and continuing influences of the group on his attitudes and beliefs over time would have rendered such direct pressure unnecessary.

Case II. It is frequently the case, however, that the behaviors specified by a group norm are *not* consistent with the personal attitudes or beliefs of one or more members. In the example described above, a recent college graduate just joining the work group might be quite unlikely to hold an "antimanagement" set of beliefs and attitudes, and, therefore, would not be likely to comply with the group norm if left entirely to his own devices. Whether or not the member does in fact comply with the group norm in such cases depends upon two conditions:

A. Pressures to comply must be sent from the group, and sent strongly enough to be experienced by the target individual.

B. The target individual must value the rewards (or devalue the sanctions) controlled by the group sufficiently that he is willing to be guided by the wishes of the group—rather than by his own predispositions or by the pressures he may experience from other groups.

In the paragraphs to follow, several factors are listed which affect the degree to which these two general conditions are met. In general, specific research findings in support of the summary propositions will not be discussed; excellent reviews of the relevant studies are provided by Allen (1965), Lott and Lott (1965), and Kiesler (1969).

A. *Noticeable pressures to comply must be sent by the group.* The degree to which discretionary stimuli will be sent to the target individual in form potent enough to attract his attention depends both upon (1) who the target individual is and what his role is in the group; and (2) the characteristics of the group and the nature of the deviant behavior in question.

1. Some members can "get away with" deviance more readily than others. Hollander (1958, 1964) has suggested that group members can earn "idiosyncratic credits" within a group. When held in sufficient number, these credits permit a member to exhibit some deviant behaviors without incurring the usual pressures or sanctions applied to members who violate a group norm. Group members generate idiosyncracy credits mainly by being "good group citizens"—that is, by generally conforming to the expectations of the group and by contributing effectively to the attainment of group goals (Hollander, 1960). Thus, new members should not have a balance of idiosyncracy credits to draw upon, and should not have much freedom to deviate early in their tenure. Consistent with this prediction Hughes (1946) found that new members of a work group were expected by their peers to conform more closely to group production norms than were other group members.

Members who have attained high status in the group would be expected to have a substantial balance of idiosyncracy credits (Hollander, 1961). And, as would be predicted, research evidence suggests that higher status members are able to be more resistive to conformity pressures than are their lower status peers (e.g., Harvey & Consalvi, 1960).

Yet even individuals with quite high status do not have unlimited freedom. For example, the findings of Wiggins, Dill, and Schwartz (1965) suggest that a high status person may be free to deviate only so long as his activities are not severely detrimental to group goal achievement. For moderate to low deviation in the Wiggins et al. study, a (simulated) high status member received fewer negative reactions than a moderate status member; but when the deviation of the high status member was clearly and seriously dysfunctional for task success, he received much *more* hostility from his peers than did a lower status member who was

equally deviant. Similarly, Alvarez (1968) showed that in successful (simulated) organizations, lower status members lost more esteem for deviant behavior than did higher status members, as would be expected from the idiosyncracy credit model. In organizations which were unsuccessful (by experimental manipulation), however, the relationship was reversed: higher status members who deviated showed sharper losses of esteem than did equally deviant members of lower status.

These findings suggest that the freedom to deviate is fairly fragile even for high status group members who have built up a nest egg of idiosyncracy credits. The low status member finds himself in even more severe straits: he has few idiosyncracy credits, so his group-given "freedom" to deviate without incurring sanctions is quite limited. Worse, if he does deviate, he may run an especially high risk of being rejected—precisely because his lower status in the group may also imply to other members that he is of little value to the group. For those low-status members who feel marginally involved in the group and who care only a little about its activities, there is not much at stake: they can behave pretty much as they wish, and if rejection comes, it doesn't hurt too badly. The low status member who *does* value his membership in the group, however, has a real problem: he has neither a great deal of latitude in how he can behave nor does he have a very substantial capability to improve things for himself other than by being "good" for a long period of time. A great deal of emotional distress among such members is not uncommon.

2. Some groups send more pressures to comply than do others, and even in the same group, some deviant behaviors will be sanctioned more severely than others. In general, one can infer from the literature that a group will tend to send more pressures to conform to group norms (a) when group members are motivated to achieve uniformity within the group—a condition frequently observed in highly cohesive groups

(Festinger, 1950); (b) when the norm is of high importance or relevance to the group; and (c) when a member's behavior is deviant from the norm to an especially noticeable extent.

Some support for these hypotheses is provided in the work of Festinger, Schachter, and Back (1950), Back (1951), Schachter (1951), Schachter et al. (1954), Emerson (1954), Berkowitz and Howard (1959), and Mudd (1968). The data are, in general, much stronger for sociometric measures (taken as indicators of rejection) than for frequency of communication (taken as indicators of pressure). For example, both Schachter (1951) and Emerson (1954) found that more communications were directed toward the deviant in low cohesive groups than in high cohesive groups, directly contrary to what would be predicted.

One explanation for the lack of clarity in previous research on pressures to comply to group norms may reside in the framing of the research question itself. Rather than focusing on the state of the group and the nature of the behavior involved, it might be more productive to examine directly the characteristics of the group norm in question. Using the Jackson formulation (described earlier), for example, it might be predicted that pressures to comply would be stronger:

(a) When the norm is of high intensity —that is, when group members hold strong feelings of approval or disapproval contingent upon norm-congruent behavior; and

(b) When the norm is highly crystallized—that is, there is substantial agreement among members about the amount of approval or disapproval associated with each possible behavior relevant to the norm.[14]

Both intensity and crystallization should be high when the group is highly cohesive,

and when the norm deals with behaviors which are of central importance to the purposes of the group. These expectations are, of course, congruent with the predictions made by Schachter, Festinger, and their colleagues in the 1950s. Using the Jackson formulation of norms, however, would make it possible to address separately the questions of (a) how group and situational factors affect the characteristics of norms themselves, and (b) how norm characteristics relate to group-generated pressures on members to comply. The answers to these questions might well clarify the conditions under which high cohesiveness (and/or "relevance") do and do not lead to an increase in compliance pressures—and thereby reduce some of the large uncertainties in this research area.

This approach to research on compliance to norms seems especially promising now that the Jackson formulation permits descriptions of norm characteristics in relatively clean, quantitative terms. It would not be difficult, for example, to measure the "magnitude of deviation" of a member's behavior in conjunction with (and on the same measurement scale as) norm intensity and norm crystallization. The amount of pressure to comply sent by the group at various levels of these variables could then be directly assessed and ultimately related back to the characteristics of the group and the situation.

B. *The stimuli used to enforce norms must be valued by the target member(s).* The second general condition which must be met for an initially recalcitrant member to comply with group norms is for the rewards of compliance (or sanctions for noncompliance) to be sufficiently valent (or disvalent) that the individual comes to *want* to change his behavior. Thus, the more a member personally needs or desires those resources over which the group has control, the more likely he is to "go along" with the group norms.

As noted earlier in the chapter, groups generally have control over many affectively

---

[14] High crystallization also would increase the likelihood that the member would experience the rest of the group as being unanimous (or nearly so) in support of the norm—a condition which has been shown strongly to affect norm conformity (e.g., Asch, 1955; Miller & Tiffany, 1963).

powerful stimuli. Therefore, a group typically has a variety of ways to add considerable "punch" to its sent pressures on members for compliance to group norms. It should be noted, however, that a group need not always actually *use* the stimuli under its control to obtain compliance of members; it often is quite sufficient merely for a member to know that the group has the *potential* to administer such stimuli. Or, one doesn't need to be struck down by a bolt of lightning to know the fear of God. It also is true, on the other hand, that when a group is not present in a given situation (or when responses of group members are made in private), behavioral compliance decreases—presumably in part because the capability of the group to apply rewarding or punishing stimuli to the members in such circumstances is lessened (cf., Kiesler, 1969, Chap. 11; Allen, 1965, pp. 145–146).

Previous research has focused on the use of *interpersonal* rewards and punishments as a means of gaining member compliance to group norms. Little attention has been given to the use of material rewards, to the provision of information as a reward, or to the provision of access to external rewards. The emphasis on interpersonal rewards and sanctions should not restrict the generality of research findings in the area very substantially, however, since interpersonal stimuli are probably the most widely used means of obtaining norm compliance in groups, and interpersonal rewards and punishments are highly potent for most people.

The not-surprising conclusion from such research is that, in general, the more an individual is attracted to a group (or the more he has a personal need for the social rewards controlled by the group), the more he conforms. Thus, as would be expected, compliance tends to be very high in highly cohesive groups (where members presumably care a great deal about being together and about continuing their mutually satisfying social interaction). Further, there is evidence that group members who do not much need or care about the social rewards

which can be provided by their fellows (e.g., very high status members or very low status members not committed to remaining in the group) often conform less than other group members. Literature relevant to these issues is reviewed in detail by Hare (1962), Allen (1965), Kiesler (1969), and Lott and Lott (1965).

It should be emphasized, however, that the relationship between a member's need for rewards controlled by a group and his conformity to a group assumes that "other things" are constant. Other things never are. Thus, Graham (1962) predicts that, if it *really mattered* to a subject to make a correct judgment in an Asch-type conformity situation, he would make it. And, by and large, it has been found that the higher an individual's personal stake in a performance situation (i.e., he has something else he may value as much or more than the potential rewards or punishments he may receive from the group), the less his conformity to the group (e.g., Vaughan & Mangan, 1963). Some of these "alternative values" may be reflected in more-or-less permanent differences among people; the role of individual differences (in personality as well as in what one values) in conformity to norms is reviewed by Hare (1962, pp. 32–35), by Marlowe and Gergen (1969), and by Mehrabian and Ksionzky (1970).

THE EFFECTS OF GROUPS ON INDIVIDUAL WORK EFFECTIVENESS: AN APPLICATION

Throughout this chapter we have examined in some detail how groups in organizations can affect their members, including members' affective states, their informational states, and their actual behaviors. We conclude by taking a more specific focus, namely, how work groups in organizations affect the actual work behavior of their members and especially how groups enhance or depress the *effectiveness* of individual work behavior.

Because of the multiple and complex influences of groups on their members, it is necessary to develop some means of summarizing the determinants of individual work behavior if any "gestalt" on the question is to be gained. It is proposed, therefore, that the major determinants of the actual work behavior of individuals in organizations can be summarized in terms of four classes of variables:

1. *The knowledge and skills of the individual.*

2. *The level of psychological arousal the individual experiences while working.*

3. *The approaches or "performance strategies" the individual uses in doing his work.*

4. *The level of effort the individual exerts in doing his work.*

The effects of these four classes of variables on work behavior are depicted in Figure 3 and discussed in some detail in the following pages. In general, it is proposed that most of the meaningful variation in work behavior is controlled by these four summary variables: knowledge and skill, arousal, performance strategy, and effort. To the extent the above assertion is true, then the effects of groups on individual work behavior can be conceptualized as operating *through* the four summary variables. By examining group effects in these terms, we may be able to achieve a considerably more parsimonious understanding of group effects on individual work behavior than would otherwise be possible.

CRITICAL TASK CONTINGENCIES. While understanding how a worker behaves, descriptively, is important and of interest, such understanding does not by itself imply much about the *effectiveness* of the person's behavior. The reason is simple: for different types of tasks or jobs, different behaviors are facilitative of work effectiveness. For example, on some tasks, how hard a person works may determine almost totally his measured work effectiveness; for other tasks, effort may be mostly irrelevant to effectiveness.

Thus, any attempt to analyze group influences on individual performance *effectiveness* must explicitly take account not only of the nature of the group influences themselves, but also of the contingencies in the task which specify what behaviors do and do not contribute to performance effectiveness for that task. Such contingencies

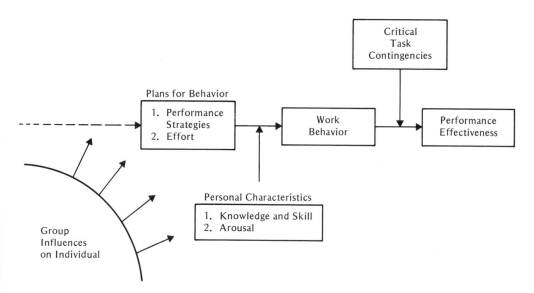

Figure 3.   Major determinants of group member behavior and performance effectiveness.

will be termed *Critical Task Contingencies* —that is, they specify what behaviors are critical to effective or successful performance for the task or job in question. The effect of these contingencies in moderating between actual work behavior and measured performance effectiveness is shown in Figure 3.

Depending upon what the Critical Task Contingencies are for a given task, one or more of the four classes of summary variables may not be relevant for understanding or changing performance effectiveness, and, therefore, can be safely dropped from consideration. On a routine and simple clerical job, for example, where the sole performance criterion of interest is quantity of acceptable output, only *effort* is likely to be of substantial importance in affecting work effectiveness. Therefore, in examining the effects of the work group on individual performance effectiveness, only the effects of the group on the level of effort expended by the worker are likely to be a worthwhile avenue for exploration. For other types of jobs, of course, strategy, ability, and/or arousal may be of particular importance.

The point is that which summary variables are important in determining performance effectiveness very much depends upon the Critical Task Contingencies. And, following the framework outlined in Figure 3, this means that when a researcher or a manager assesses the impact of the work group on an individual's performance effectiveness, he need deal only with those variables which can, in fact, have a significant impact on work effectiveness for the particular job in question. If effectiveness in a given situation is responsive to differences in *skill,* then the impact of the group on the ways worker skills are used must be examined; if the Critical Task Contingencies are such that different performance *strategies* can influence performance effectiveness, the impact of the group on the strategies used by workers must be assessed; and the same reasoning follows for effort.

In summary, it is proposed that a good deal of leverage can be brought to bear on the performance effectiveness of organization members by (a) assessing the Critical Task Contingencies for a given task or job, to determine which of the summary variables are likely to be most potent in influencing work effectiveness for that task, and then (b) examining the effects of work groups (as well as other "external" factors) on those summary variables. In the paragraphs below, this approach is used to analyze work group influences on individual performance effectiveness.

Ways Groups Influence Individual Work Effectiveness

By Affecting Member Knowledge and Skills

Performance on many tasks or jobs in organizations is strongly affected by the job-relevant knowledge and skill of the individuals who do the work. Thus, even if a worker has both high commitment to accomplish a particular piece of work and a well-formed strategy about how to go about doing it, the implementation of that plan can be constrained or terminated if he does not know how to carry it out, or if he knows how but is incapable of doing so (see Figure 3). While ability is relevant to the performance of jobs at all levels in an organization, its impact probably is somewhat reduced for lower-level jobs. The reason is that such jobs often are not at all demanding of high skill levels. Further, to the extent that organizational selection, placement, and promotion practices are adequate, *all* jobs should tend to be occupied by individuals who possess the skills requisite for adequate performance.

Discussion earlier in this chapter focused on how groups can improve the job-relevant knowledge and skills of an individual through direct instruction, feedback, and model-provision. For jobs in which knowledge and skill are important determiners of performance effectiveness, then, groups can be of help. Nevertheless, the impact of groups on member performance effectiveness by improving member knowledge and skill probably is one of the lesser influences groups can have—both because employees on many jobs tend already to have many or all of the skills needed to perform them effectively, and because there are other sources for improving skills which may be both more used and more potent than the work group, such as formal job training programs and self-study programs.

By Affecting Member Arousal Level

It was shown earlier in the chapter how a group can substantially influence the level of psychological "arousal" experienced by a member—both through the "mere presence" of the other group members, and by those others sending the individual messages which are directly arousal-enhancing or arousal-depressing. The conditions under which such group-prompted changes in arousal level will lead to increased performance *effectiveness,* however, very much depend upon the type of task being worked on (Zajonc, 1965).

In this case, the Critical Task Contingencies have to do with whether the initially *dominant task response* of the individual is likely to be correct or incorrect. Since the production of dominant responses is facilitated when a person is in an aroused state, arousal should facilitate performance effectiveness on well-learned tasks in which the dominant response is correct and needs merely to be executed by the performer (termed "performance" tasks by Zajonc). By the same token, arousal should impair effectiveness for new or unfamiliar tasks in which the dominant response is likely to be incorrect (termed "learning" tasks by Zajonc).

In his original statement of the above conceptualization, Zajonc (1965) argued that the *mere* presence of others should heighten the arousal of individuals sufficiently for the predicted performance effects to be obtained. As noted earlier in the chapter, however, it now seems that the *mere* presence of others

may not result in significant increases in arousal. Instead, only when the other group members are (or are seen as) in a potentially evaluative relationship vis-à-vis the performer are the predictions confirmed (cf., Zajonc & Sales, 1966; Cottrell et al., 1968; Henchy & Glass, 1968).

Groups can, of course, increase member arousal in ways other than taking an evaluative stance toward the individual. Strongly positive and encouraging statements also should increase arousal in some performance situations—for example, by helping the individual become personally highly committed to the group goal, and making sure he realizes that he is a very important part of the team responsible for reaching that goal. What must be kept in mind, of course, is that such devices represent a double-edged sword: while they may facilitate effective performance for well-learned tasks, they may have the opposite effect for new and unfamiliar tasks.

What, then, can be said about individual performance when the presence (and interaction) of other group members serves to *decrease* the level of arousal of the individual—as, for example, when people coalesce into groups under conditions of high stress? When the other members of the group are a source of support, comfort, or acceptance to the individual (and serve to decrease his arousal level), it would have to be predicted that performance effectiveness would follow a pattern exactly opposite that described above: the group would impair effectiveness for performance tasks (because arousal helps on these tasks, and arousal is being lowered), and facilitate effectiveness for learning tasks (because in this case arousal is harmful, and it is being lowered).

The relationships predicted above are summarized in Figure 4. As the group becomes increasingly threatening, evaluative, or strongly encouraging, effectiveness should increase for "performance" tasks and decrease for "learning" tasks. When the group is experienced as increasingly supportive, comforting, or unconditionally accepting,

effectiveness should decrease for "performance" tasks and increase for "learning" tasks.
And when no meaningful relationship at
all is experienced by the individual between
himself and the group, performance should
not be affected. While some of these predictions have been tested and confirmed (especially regarding the right-hand portion of
the horizontal axis, following Zajonc's conceptualization), others await research.[15]

Even that research which has been carried out on the relationship between group-
prompted arousal and individual performance effectiveness has not been designed or
conducted so as to illuminate how the phenomenon operates in actual organizational
situations. It is clear, however, that individuals in organizations do use their group
memberships as a means of achieving more
"comfortable" levels of arousal. Individuals

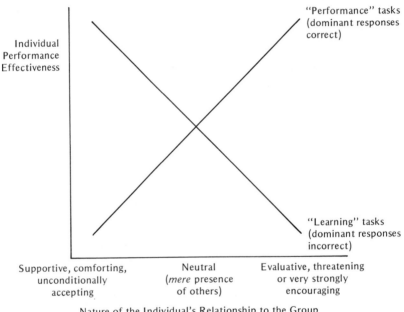

Figure 4.   Individual performance effectiveness as a function of type of task and
experienced relationship to the group.

---

[15] Perhaps of particular interest would be situations in
which group members provide the individual with extremely intense and explicitly evaluative or threatening
stimuli. In such cases, arousal level should become exceedingly high. Traditional wisdom in psychology is
that performance effectiveness (even on well-learned
tasks) should deteriorate under such circumstances
(cf., Cofer & Appley, 1964, pp. 392–398; Scott, 1966).
In a chapter in this volume, however, McGrath (1975)
argues that the predicted tail-off in effectiveness under
high arousal has not been satisfactorily demonstrated.
Further, McGrath argues (and provides field-experi-
mental evidence to support his position) that performance on well-learned tasks may be a positive linear

in high-pressure managerial jobs, for example, often find that they need to gather
around themselves a few trusted associates
who can and do provide reassurance and
continuing acceptance when the going gets
especially tough. This, presumably, should
help reduce the manager's level of arousal
and thereby increase the likelihood that he

function of arousal, even at very high levels of arousal
(other factors, such as task difficulty, held constant).
This prediction is, of course, consistent with the relationships suggested in Figure 4.

will be able to come up with *new or original* ways of perceiving and dealing with his immediate problem. If the theory is correct, however, this practice should not facilitate performance of the more "routine" (i.e., well-learned) parts of his job.

It is well known (cf., Scott, 1966) that overly routine jobs can decrease a worker's level of arousal to such an extent that his performance effectiveness is impaired. It seems quite possible to design the social environment of workers on such jobs so as to partially compensate for the "deadening" effects of the job itself and thereby lead to an increment in performance on well-learned tasks (e.g., routine monitoring or vigilance tasks). But, once again, research evidence on this possibility is presently scant.

In summary, there are a number of ways that the work group can affect the level of arousal of individual organizational members, but little systematic knowledge currently is available about how this phenomenon relates to the actual performance of people in organizational settings.

By Affecting Member Effort and Performance Strategies

The level of effort a person exerts in doing his work and the performance "strategy" or approach he follows are treated together because both variables, unlike arousal and skill level, are largely under the performer's voluntary control. The distinction between effort and strategy is a simple one: effort refers to the *intensity* of a person's work activities, and strategy refers to the *direction* of those activities. For example, a person's decision about whether to work hard or take it easy on the job is a decision about effort; his decision about whether to try to do high quality work or to produce large quantities of work instead is a decision about strategy.

DIRECT VERSUS INDIRECT INFLUENCES ON EFFORT AND STRATEGY. Throughout this chapter we have used a general "expectancy theory" approach to analyze those aspects of a person's behavior in organizations which are under his voluntary control. From this perspective, a person's choices about his effort and work strategy can be viewed as hinging largely upon his (a) *expectations* regarding the likely consequences of his behavioral choices, coupled with (b) the degree to which he *values* those expected consequences. Following this approach, it becomes clear that the group can have a direct and an indirect effect on the effort a group member exerts on his job, and on his choices about performance strategy.

The direct impact of the group on effort and strategy, of course, is simply the enforcement by the group of its own norms regarding what is an "appropriate" level of effort to expend on the job, and what is the "proper" performance strategy. We have discussed in some detail earlier in the chapter how groups use their control of discretionary stimuli to enforce group norms, and thereby affect such voluntary behaviors. Thus, if the group has established a norm about the level of member effort or the strategies members should use in going about their work, the group can control individual behavior merely by making sure that individual members realize that their receipt of valued group-controlled rewards is contingent upon their behaving in accord with the norm.

The indirect impact of the group on the effort and performance strategies of the individual involves the group's control of information regarding the state of the organizational environment outside the boundaries of the group. Regardless of any norms the group itself may have about effort or strategy, it can communicate to the group member "what leads to what" in the broader organization, and thereby affect the individual's *own* choices about his behavior.

For example, it may be the case in a given organization that hard work (i.e., high effort) tends to lead to quick promotions and higher pay; the group can influence the effort of the individual by helping him realize this objective state of affairs. Similarly, by providing individual members with information about what performance strategies "work" in the organization (in the sense of leading to outcomes valued by the person), the group can (indirectly) influence the work strategy of the individual.

Moreover, groups can, over time, affect the preferences and values of individual members, thereby affecting the level of *desire* (or "valence") individuals have for various outcomes available in the organizational setting. This long-term impact can increase even more the amount of influence the group has on member choices about effort and/or work strategy.

It should be noted, however, that such indirect influences on member effort and performance strategy will be most potent early in the individual's tenure in the organization, when he has not yet had a chance to develop through experience his own personal "map" of the organization. When the individual becomes less dependent upon the group for data about "what leads to what" and "what's good" in the organization, the group may have to revert to direct norm enforcement to maintain control of the work behavior of individual members.

In summary, the group can and does have a strong impact on both the level of effort exerted by its members and on the strategies members use in carrying out their work. This impact is realized both directly (i.e., by enforcement of group norms) and indirectly (i.e., by affecting the beliefs and values of the members). When the direct and indirect influences of a group are congruent, which is often the case, the potency of the group's effects on its members can be quite high. For example, if at the same time that a group is enforcing its *own* norm of, say, moderately low production, it also is providing a group member with data regarding the presumably *objective* negative consequences of hard work in the particular organization, the group member will experience two partially independent and mutually reinforcing influences aimed at keeping his rate of production down.

EFFORT, STRATEGY, AND PERFORMANCE EFFECTIVENESS. What, then, are the circumstances under which groups can improve the work *effectiveness* of their members through influences on individual choices about effort and strategy? Again, the answer depends upon the Critical Task Contingencies which operate in the particular work situation. Unless a job is structured so that effort or performance strategy actually can make an objective difference in work effectiveness, group influences on effort or strategy will be irrelevant to how well individual members perform.

Strategy. In general, groups should be able to facilitate member work effectiveness by influencing strategy choices more for complex jobs than for simple, straightforward, or routine ones. The reason is that on simple jobs, strategy choices usually cannot make much of a difference in effectiveness; instead, how well one does is determined almost entirely by how hard one works. On jobs characterized by high variety and autonomy, on the other hand, the work strategy used by the individual usually is of considerable importance in determining work effectiveness. By helping an individual develop and implement an appropriate work strategy, the group should be able to substantially facilitate his effectiveness.

Effort. In virtually all jobs in organizational settings, the Critical Task Contingencies are such that the harder one works, the more effective his performance is likely to be. Thus, group influences on the effort expended by members on their jobs are both a very pervasive and a very potent determiner of individual work effectiveness. There are, nevertheless, some exceptions to this generalization: the success of a complicated brain operation, for example, is less likely to depend upon effort expended than it is upon the strategies used and the job-relevant knowledge and skills of the surgeon.

When either effort or strategy (or both) are in fact important in determining performance effectiveness, then the individual will have substantial voluntary control over how well he does in his work. In such cases, the degree to which the group facilitates (rather than hinders) individual effectiveness will depend jointly upon (a) the degree to which the group has accurate information regarding the Critical Task Contingencies for that situation and makes that information available to the individual, and (b) the degree to which the norms of the group reinforce those contingencies.

PARTICIPATION. One management practice which should, it appears, contribute positively to meeting both of the above conditions is the use of "group participation" in making decisions about work practices. Participation has been widely advocated as a management technique, both on ideological grounds and as a direct means of increasing work effectiveness.[16] And, in fact, some studies have shown that participation can lead to higher work effectiveness (e.g., Coch & French, 1948; Lawler & Hackman, 1969). In the present framework, participation should contribute to increased work effectiveness in two different ways.

1. Participation can increase the amount and the accuracy of information workers have about work practices and the environmental contingencies associated with them. In the Lawler and Hackman study, for example, some groups themselves designed new reward systems keyed on coming to work regularly (a task clearly affected by employee *effort*—that is, trying to get to work every day). These groups responded both more quickly and more positively to the new pay plans than did other groups which had technically identical plans imposed on them by company management.

One reason suggested by the authors to account for this finding was that the participative groups simply may have understood their plans more accurately, and had fewer uncertainties and worries about what the rewards were (and were not) for coming to work regularly.

2. Participation can increase the degree to which group members feel they "own" their work practices, and, therefore, the likelihood that the group will develop a norm of support for those practices. In the participative groups studied by Lawler and Hackman, for example, the nature of the work-related communication among members changed from initial shared warnings about management and "things management proposes" to helping members (especially new members) come to understand and believe in "our plan." In other words, as group members come to experience the work or work practices *as under their own control or ownership,* it becomes likely that informal group norms supportive of effective behavior vis-à-vis those practices will develop. Such norms provide a striking contrast to the "group protective" norms which often emerge when control is perceived to be exclusively and unilaterally under management control.

In summary, group participative techniques can be quite facilitative of individual work effectiveness, but only under certain conditions:

1. When the topic of participation is relevant to the work itself. There is no reason to believe that participation involving task-irrelevant issues (e.g., preparing for the Red Cross Bloodmobile visit to the plant) will have facilitative effects on work productivity. While such participation may indeed help increase the cohesiveness of the work group, it clearly will not help group members gain information or develop norms which are facilitative of high work effectiveness. Indeed, such task-irrelevant participation may serve to direct the attention and motivation of group members *away*

---

[16] See Lowin (1968) and Vroom and Yetton (1973) for general reviews of participation as a management technique.

from work issues and thereby even lower productivity. The failure of the attempt by French, Israel, & As (1960) to replicate in Norway the classic finding of Coch and French was attributed by the researchers largely to the task-irrelevance of the participation in the replication study.

2. The objective task and environmental contingencies in the work setting must actually be supportive of more effective performance. That is, if through participation group members learn more about "what leads to what" in the organization, then it is increasingly important that there be real and meaningful positive outcomes which result from effective performance. If, for example, group members gain a quite complete and accurate impression through participation that "hard work around here pays off only in backaches," then increased effort as a consequence of participation is most unlikely. If, on the other hand, participation results in a new and better understanding that hard work can lead to increased pay, more chances for advancement, and the chance to feel a sense of personal and group accomplishment, then increased effort should be the result.

3. Finally, the Critical Task Contingencies must be such that increased effort (or a different and better work strategy) objectively can lead to higher work effectiveness. If it is true, as argued here, that the main benefits of group participation are (a) increased understanding of work practices and the organizational environment and (b) increased experienced "ownership" by the group of the work and work practices, then participation should increase productivity only when the *objective determinants of productivity are under the voluntary control of the worker*. There is no reason to believe, therefore, that participation should have a facilitative effect on productivity when work outcomes are mainly determined by worker skill and/or arousal level (rather than effort expended or work strategy used), or by objective factors in the environment over which the worker can have little or no control (e.g., the amount of work which arrives at the employee's station to be done).

Implications for Diagnosis and Change

This section has focused on ways that the group can affect the performance effectiveness of individual group members. While it has been maintained throughout that the group has a substantial impact on individual performance effectiveness, it has been emphasized that the nature and extent of this impact centrally depends upon the characteristics of the work being done.

To diagnose and change the direction or extent of social influences on performance in an organization, then, it should be important first to examine the task (including how effectiveness is measured on the task) to determine specifically what kinds of factors objectively can affect measured performance effectiveness for the task or job under consideration. Only by first determining "what really matters" in affecting work effectiveness, it is argued, can interventions be effectively designed. In particular, a diagnosis of social effects on performance might follow these steps:

1. Analysis of the Critical Task Contingencies to determine which of the four classes of variables (i.e., skills, arousal, strategies, effort) objectively affect measured performance effectiveness. This might be done simply by asking the question: "If skills (or arousal, or effort, or strategies) were brought to bear on the work differently than is presently the case, would a corresponding difference in work effectiveness be likely to be observed as a consequence?" By asking this question for each of the four classes of variables, it usually will become apparent which variables are objectively important to consider for that job. In many cases, of course, more than one class of variables will turn out to be of importance.

2. After one or more "target" classes of variables have been identified, the work group itself would be examined to unearth any ways in which the group was "block-

ing" effective individual performance. It might be determined, for example, that certain group norms were impeding the expression and use of various skills which individuals potentially could bring to bear on their work. Or it might turn out that the social environment of the workers created conditions which were excessively (or insufficiently) arousing for optimal performance on the task at hand. For effort and strategy, which are under the voluntary control of the worker, there are two major possibilities to examine: (a) that group norms are enforced in the group which coerce individuals to behave in ineffective ways; or (b) that the group provides information to the individual members about task and environmental contingencies in insufficient or distorted fashion, resulting in their making choices about their work behavior which impede task effectiveness.

The Return Potential Model of Jackson (discussed in a previous section) should be very useful in making such diagnoses. It provides a direct means of assessing group norms relevant to member effort and work strategy, and in addition, can be easily adapted for use in assessing worker perceptions of what the organizational "payoffs" are for various work behaviors.

3. Finally, the group and the broader social environment might usefully be assessed to determine if there are ways that the "people resources" in the situation could be more fully utilized in the interest of increased work effectiveness. That is, rather than focusing solely on ways the group may be blocking or impeding performance effectiveness, attention should be given as well to any unrealized *potential* which resides in the group. It might turn out, for example, that some group members could be of great help to others in increasing the level of individual task-relevant skills, but these individuals have never been asked for help. Alternatively, it might be that the group could be assisted in finding new and better ways of ensuring that each group member has available accurate and current informa-

tion about those task and environmental contingencies which determine the outcomes of various work behaviors.

The point is that the people who surround an individual at work can facilitate as well as impede his performance effectiveness, and that any serious attempt to diagnose the social environment in the interest of improving work performance should explicitly address unrealized possibilities for facilitating performance as well as issues for which remedial action may be required.

What particular organizational changes will be called for on the basis of such a diagnosis, or what techniques should be used to realize these changes, will, of course, largely depend upon the particular characteristics of the organization and of the resources which are available there. The major emphasis of this section is that there is *not* any single "universally useful" type of change or means of change, that instead, intervention should always be based on a thorough diagnosis of the existing social and task environment.

Conclusion: Cohesiveness, Conformity, and Group Effectiveness

The focus of this chapter has been on how groups (or, more broadly conceived, members of an individual's role set) affect individuals in organizations. While coverage has included group effects on a variety of different affective and informational states of the individual, the strong emphasis has been on those states which relate directly to individual work behavior and, ultimately, to work effectiveness.

In the last several pages, it was concluded that group influences on individual performance effectiveness may be especially potent in those circumstances where the individual has *voluntary control* over the behaviors which contribute to his work effectiveness. Or, more technically, group influences on individual effectiveness may be strongest when the Critical Task Contingencies are such that individual effort and/or performance strategies are powerful objective determinants of measured effectiveness. Yet omitted from our discussion was examination of how characteristics of the *group itself* moderate the extent and direction of social influence on the effort and performance strategies of group members. It is to this issue that we now turn in drawing the chapter to a close.

In general, as the cohesiveness of a work group increases, the conformity of members to the norms of the group also increases, for two different but mutually reinforcing reasons. First, as was shown in our earlier discussion of group norms, there tend to be stronger group-generated pressures toward uniformity and conformity in groups which are highly cohesive than in groups which are not. And secondly, group members are likely to value especially strongly the interpersonal rewards which are available in highly cohesive groups, precisely because of the strong positive feelings members have for one another in such groups. Therefore, group members are unlikely to risk losing those rewards by ignoring or defying pressures to conform to group norms. And, in fact, research evidence confirms that conformity is especially high in cohesive groups (cf., Tajfel, 1969, pp. 334–347; Lott & Lott, 1965, pp. 292–296; Schachter et al., 1951; Berkowitz, 1954).

The problem is that conformity to group norms which occurs in highly cohesive groups may *not* be functional for group or individual productivity, and indeed may be strongly dysfunctional for effectiveness in some performance situations, as is shown below.

DIRECTION OF NORMS. While highly cohesive groups are usually able to effectively control the behavior of their members so that behavior approximates the group norm, the *direction* of the group norm (i.e., toward high versus low productivity) has been found to be generally unrelated to how cohesive the group is (Schachter et al., 1951; Berkowitz, 1954; Seashore, 1954; French, 1951; Darley et al., 1952).[17]

For example, in the research by Schachter et al. and by Berkowitz, conditions of high versus low cohesiveness and high versus low productivity norms were created by experimental manipulation. It was found that member productivity was indeed closer to the group norms in the high than the low cohesiveness groups, for both high *and* low production norms. Similar findings are reported by Seashore (1954) using survey techniques. In a study of over 200 work groups in a machinery factory, Seashore found no correlation between cohesiveness and productivity, but, as would be expected, a negative relationship between cohesiveness and the amount of within-group variation in the productivity of group members.

GROUPTHINK. Recent research by Janis (1972) suggests that high cohesiveness can in some circumstances be actively dysfunctional for the effectiveness of the group as a whole. Janis suggests that as a group becomes excessively close-knit and develops a clubby feeling of "we-ness," it will become susceptible to a pattern of behavior he calls "groupthink." Among the several symptoms of groupthink is a marked decrease in the openness of group members to discrepant or unsettling information (from sources either inside or outside the group), and a simultaneous unwillingness to seriously examine and process such information when it is brought to the attention of the group. These interpersonal strategies, Janis argues, result in an increased likelihood that the group, in a spirit of goodwill and shared confidence, will develop and implement a course of action which is grossly inappropriate and in-

---

[17] Cohesiveness was operationalized in these studies in a diversity of ways. The Schachter et al. and Berkowitz studies employed an induction of "congeniality" to manipulate cohesiveness; the Seashore study used a questionnaire measure of group-supplied satisfactions; and the French and Darley et al. studies used a sociometrically based index of cohesiveness.

effective. Janis has shown how this phenomenon may have contributed substantially to a number of historical "fiascos" planned and executed by groups of government officials (e.g., the Bay of Pigs invasion, Britain's "appeasement" policy toward Hitler prior to World War II).

SHOULD COHESIVENESS BE AVOIDED? It might appear from the above that high cohesiveness of groups in organizations is something that should be avoided, to minimize the possibility of enforced low production norms in work settings or the likelihood that groupthink-like phenomena will develop among decision makers. Such a conclusion would be a very pessimistic one; low cohesiveness among members of work groups or decision-making groups would indeed lower the possibility of obtaining the negative outcomes mentioned, but also would require that the positive potential of cohesive groups be foregone as well, such as the increased capability of such groups to regulate behavior so as to increase the attainment of group and organizational goals.

The question, then, becomes how the nature or "direction" of the norms of highly cohesive groups can be changed. Unfortunately, very little presently is known about what factors affect whether a group will adopt a high or low production norm (Vroom, 1969, pp. 226–227). While broader organizational characteristics (e.g., the overall "climate" of the organization) undoubtedly have some influence on the direction of work group norms, it may be that the real crux of the matter has to do with the *basis* of the cohesiveness which exists in a group; that is, the reasons why group members have a strong desire to "stick together."

TASK VERSUS SOCIAL BASES FOR COHESIVENESS. In virtually all of the research cited above, cohesiveness was based upon the *interpersonal rewards* present or potentially present in the group. The "stake" of most group members in such situations, then, would be to refrain from behaviors that might disrupt the interpersonal satisfactions which are obtained from group membership. The control of the group over its members in such cases rests largely upon its capability to provide or withhold such valued social satisfactions. In the "groupthink" situation, such control results in interpersonal strategies characterized by lessened vigilance for new and potentially disruptive information, acceptance of the views of high status others as the doctrine of the group, and suppression of any interpersonal unpleasantries. Such a "group-maintenance" orientation can, as Janis notes, severely impair the work effectiveness of the group.

Were the basis for the cohesiveness a shared commitment to the *task* of the group (instead of a commitment to maintaining the interpersonal rewards received in the group), the picture might change radically. The criteria for when to accept information and direction from others in the group, for example, might change from something like "Will questioning what is being said by the leader risk my being rejected or ridiculed by the group?" to "Will such questioning contribute to our succeeding on the task?" Conformity, then, should remain high in such groups, but the norms to which conformity is enforced would focus on facilitating the group's task performance activities rather than on maintaining interpersonal "comfortableness." This change in orientation also would bear on the "direction" question raised by Vroom regarding the norms of individual production in work groups: if one of the major reasons for the cohesiveness of the group were a shared commitment to succeeding on the task, then that commitment should in most cases support the development of group norms toward high rather than low work effectiveness.

Data generally supportive of this view are provided by Back (1951) and by Thibaut and Strickland (1956). Back induced three "types" of cohesiveness into dyads: cohesiveness based (a) on personal attraction, (b) on the prestige of being a group member, and (c) on the task itself. The first two bases of cohesiveness are, of course, primarily interpersonal in nature, and led to predictable patterns of social interaction. In the "personal attraction" condition, for example, group members tended to make the interaction into a longish, pleasant conversation, and to resent any rejection of an influence attempt; in the "prestige" condition, members tended to engage in few interpersonal risks, and acted very cautiously, focusing more on their own behavior and its possible interpersonal impact than on the group task. In the "task" condition, however, group members tended to ignore interpersonal issues, and work rather intensely and efficiently to complete the task activity.

The problem in attempting to develop task-based cohesiveness in real-world work groups is two-fold. First, many tasks (and perhaps most production tasks) in organizations are not such as to generate genuine group commitment. Instead, the reverse may often be true: the task may be so uninteresting that the group accepts as an alternative a task of "getting management" or of "avoiding hard work." In such cases, the power resident in the group cohesiveness may be exceptionally dysfunctional for organizational goals. Secondly, it is quite difficult, even for objectively important tasks, for group members to overcome their orientation to interpersonal rewards and rejections. The Kennedy cabinet during the Bay of Pigs crisis, for example, certainly had an important task; but the heavy investment of each member toward remaining a member of the high-status, high-prestige group apparently was so strong that "not rocking the interpersonal boat" overwhelmed "doing the task well" as a behavioral criterion for most group members.

Thus, while there appears to be much to be said for the development of tasks which can provide a strong positive basis for group cohesiveness, few guidelines for designing such tasks currently exist. The crux of the problem, it seems, is to create conditions such that the rewards from genuinely shared task activities become as salient and as attractive to group members as are the skin-surface interpersonal satisfactions which, unfortunately, currently typify interpersonal relationships in most "cohesive" groups in organizations.

REFERENCES

Allen, V. L. Situational factors in conformity. In L. Berkowitz (Ed.), *Advances in experimental social psychology*, Vol. II. New York: Academic Press, 1965.

Allen, V. L., & Bragg, B. W. Effect of group pressure on memory. *The Journal of Psychology*, 1968, 69, 19–32. (a)

Allen, V. L., & Bragg, B. W. Effect of social pressure on concept identification. *Journal of Educational Psychology*, 1968, 59, 302–308. (b)

Allen, V. L., & Levine, J. M. Social support and conformity: The role of independent assessment of reality. *Journal of Experimental Social Psychology*, 1971, 7, 48–58. (a)

Allen, V. L., & Levine, J. M. Social pressure and personal preference. *Journal of Experimental Social Psychology*, 1971, 7, 122–124. (b)

Allport, F. H. *Theories of perception and the concept of structure.* New York: Wiley, 1955.

Alvarez, R. Informal reactions to deviance in simulated work organizations: A laboratory experiment. *American Sociological Review*, 1968, 33, 895–912.

Argyris, C. *Interpersonal competence and organizational effectiveness.* Homewood, Ill.: Irwin-Dorsey, 1962.

Argyris, C. The incompleteness of social psychological theory: Examples from small group, cognitive consistency, and attribution research. *American Psychologist*, 1969, 24, 893–908.

Arrowood, A. J., & Friend, R. Other factors determining the choice of a comparison other. *Journal of Experimental Social Psychology*, 1969, 5, 233–239.

Asch, S. E. Effects of group pressure upon the modification and distortion of judgments. In H. Guetzkow (Ed.), *Groups, leadership, and men.* New Brunswick, N.J.: Rutgers University Press, 1951.

Asch, S. E. Opinions and social pressure. *Scientific American,* November, 1955, 193, 31–35.

Asch, S. E. Effects of group pressure upon the modification and distortion of judgments. In E. E. Maccoby, T. M. Newcomb, & E. L. Hartley (Eds.), *Readings in social psychology.* (3rd ed.) New York: Holt, Rinehart and Winston, 1958, 174–183.

Atkinson, J. W. Explorations using imaginative thought to assess the strength of human motives. In M. R. Jones (Ed.), *Nebraska symposium on motivation: 1954.* Lincoln: University of Nebraska Press, 1954.

Atkinson, J. W. *Motives in fantasy, action, and society.* Princeton: Van Nostrand, 1958.

Back, K. W. Influence through social communication. *Journal of Abnormal and Social Psychology,* 1951, 46, 190–207.

Bales, R. F. *Interaction process analysis.* Reading, Mass.: Addison-Wesley, 1950.

Bales, R. F. The equilibrium problem in small groups. In T. Parsons, R. F. Bales, & E. A. Shils (Eds.), *Working papers in the theory of action.* New York: The Free Press, 1953.

Bales, R. F., & Slater, P. E. Role differentiation in small groups. In T. Parsons, R. F. Bales et al. (Eds.), *Family, socialization, and interaction process.* Glencoe, Ill.: The Free Press, 1955.

Bandura, A. Vicarious processes: A case of notrial learning. In L. Berkowitz (Ed.), *Advances in experimental social psychology,* Vol. II. New York: Academic Press, 1965.

Bandura, A. *Social learning theory.* New York: General Learning Press, 1971.

Barker, R. G. *Ecological psychology.* Stanford: Stanford University Press, 1968.

Barker, R. G., & Wright, H. F. *Midwest and its children.* New York: Harper and Row, 1955.

Bates, A. P., & Cloyd, J. S. Toward the development of operations for defining group norms and member roles. *Sociometry,* 1956, 19, 26–39.

Bates, F. L. Position, role, and status: A reformulation of concepts. *Social Forces,* 1956, 34, 313–321.

Bavelas, A., Hastorf, A. H., Gross, A. E., & Kite, W. R. Experiments on the alteration of group structure. *Journal of Experimental Social Psychology,* 1965, 1, 55–70.

Bem, D. J. An experimental analysis of self-persuasion. *Journal of Experimental Social Psychology,* 1965, 1, 199–218.

Bem, D. J. *Beliefs, attitudes, and human affairs.* Belmont, Calif.: Brooks/Cole, 1970.

Benne, K., & Sheats, P. Functional roles of group members. *Journal of Social Issues,* 1948, 4 (2), 41–49.

Berger, S. M. Vicarious aspects of matched-dependent behavior. In E. C. Simmel, R. A. Hoppe, & C. A. Milton (Eds.), *Social facilitation and imitative behavior.* Boston: Allyn and Bacon, 1968.

Berger, S. M., & Lambert, W. W. Stimulus-response theory in contemporary social psychology. In G. Lindzey & E. Aronson (Eds.), *The handbook of social psychology.* (2nd ed.) Reading, Mass.: Addison-Wesley, 1969.

Berkowitz, L. Group standards, cohesiveness, and productivity. *Human Relations,* 1954, 7, 509–519.

Berkowitz, L. Social motivation. In G. Lindzey & E. Aronson (Eds.), *The handbook of social psychology.* (2nd ed.) Reading, Mass.: Addison-Wesley, 1969.

Berkowitz, L. Reporting an experiment: A case study in leveling, sharpening, and assimilation. *Journal of Experimental Social Psychology,* 1971, 7, 237–243.

Berkowitz, L., & Howard, R. C. Reactions to opinion deviates as affected by affiliation need (*n*) and group member interdependence. *Sociometry,* 1959, 22, 81–91.

Biddle, B. J., & Thomas, E. J. *Role theory: Concepts and research.* New York: Wiley, 1966.

Bion, W. R. *Experiences in groups.* New York: Basic Books, 1959.

Bradford, L. P., Gibb, J., & Benne, K., Eds., *T-group theory and laboratory method.* New York: Wiley, 1964.

Burke, R. L., & Bennis, W. G. Changes in perception of self and others during human relations training. *Human Relations,* 1961, 14, 165–182.

Burns, T. The reference of conduct in small groups: Cliques and cabals in occupational milieux. *Human Relations,* 1955, 8, 467–486.

Campbell, D. T. Conformity in psychology's theories of acquired behavioral dispositions. In I. A. Berg & B. M. Bass (Eds.), *Conformity and deviation.* New York: Harper and Row, 1961.

Campbell, J. T., & Dunnette, M. D. Effectiveness of T-group experiences in managerial training and development. *Psychological Bulletin,* 1968, 70, 73–104.

Carter, L., Haythorn, W., Meirowitz, B., & Lanzetta, J. The relation of categorizations and ratings in the observation of group behavior. *Human Relations,* 1951, 4, 239–254. (a)

Carter, L. F., Haythorn, W., Shriver, B., & Lanzetta, J. The behavior of leaders and other group members. *Journal of Abnormal and Social Psychology,* 1951, 46, 589–595. (b)

Cartwright, D., & Zander, A. *Group dynamics: Research and theory.* (3rd ed.) New York: Harper and Row, 1968.

Coch, L., & French, J. R. P. Jr. Overcoming resistance to change. *Human Relations,* 1948, 1, 512–532.

Cofer, C. N., & Appley, M. H. *Motivation: Theory and research.* New York: Wiley, 1964.

Collins, B., & Guetzkow, H. *A social psychology of group processes for decision making.* New York: Wiley, 1964.

Cooley, C. H. *Human nature and the social order.* New York: Scribner's, 1922.

Cottrell, N. B., Wack, D. L., Sekerak, F. J., & Rittle, R. H. Social facilitation of dominant responses by the presence of an audience and the mere presence of others. *Journal of Personality and Social Psychology,* 1968, 9, 245–250.

Crutchfield, R. S. Conformity and character. *American Psychologist,* 1955, 10, 191–198.

Darley, J., Groos, N., & Martin, W. Studies of group behavior: Factors associated with the productivity of groups. *Journal of Applied Psychology,* 1952, 36, 396–403.

Davis, J. *Group performance.* Reading, Mass.: Addison-Wesley, 1969.

Davis, J. Group decision and social interaction: A theory of social decision schemes. *Psychological Review,* 1973, 80, 97–125.

Davis, J. H., Cohen, J. L., Hornik, J., & Rissman, A. K. Dyadic decision as a function of the frequency distributions describing the preferences of members' constituencies. *Journal of Personality and Social Psychology,* 1973, 26, 178–195.

Davis, J. H., Hornik, J. A., & Hornseth, J. P. Group decision schemes and strategy preferences in a sequential response task. *Journal of Personality and Social Psychology,* 1970, 15, 397–498.

Davis, K. *Human society.* New York: Macmillan, 1950.

Dentler, R. A., & Erikson, K. T. The functions of deviance in groups. *Social Problems,* 1959, 7, 98–107.

Deutsch, M. Task structure and group process. *American Psychologist,* 1951, 6, 324–325 (Abstract).

Deutsch, M., & Gerard, H. B. A study of normative and informational social influences upon individual judgment. *Journal of Abnormal and Social Psychology,* 1955, 51, 629–636.

Downing, J. Cohesiveness, perception, and values. *Human Relations,* 1958, 11, 157–166.

Emerson, R. M. Deviation and rejection: An experimental replication. *American Sociological Review,* 1954, 19, 688–693.

Festinger, L. Informal social communication. *Psychological Review,* 1950, 57, 271–282.

Festinger, L. A theory of social comparison processes. *Human Relations,* 1954, 7, 117–140.

Festinger, L. *A theory of cognitive dissonance.* Stanford: Stanford University Press, 1957.

Festinger, L., & Kelley, H. H. *Changing attitudes through social contact.* Ann Arbor: Research Center for Group Dynamics, 1951. (Summarized in: Festinger, L. Group attraction and membership. In D. Cartwright & A. Zander (Eds.), *Group dynamics: Research and theory.* Evanston, Ill.: Row, Peterson, 1953.)

Festinger, L., Schachter, S., & Back, K. *Social pressures in informal groups.* Stanford: Stanford University Press, 1950.

Festinger, L., & Thibaut, J. Interpersonal communication in small groups. *Journal of Abnormal and Social Psychology,* 1951, 46, 92–99.

Fishbein, M. A behavior theory approach to the relations between beliefs about an object and the attitude toward the object. In M. Fishbein (Ed.), *Readings in attitude theory and measurement.* New York: Wiley, 1967.

Foa, U. G. Interpersonal and economic resources. *Science,* January 29, 1971, 171, 345–351.

French, J. R. P., Israel, J., & As, D. An experiment on participation in a Norwegian factory. *Human Relations,* 1960, 13, 3–19.

French, R. L. Sociometric status and individual adjustment among naval recruits. *Journal of*

Abnormal and Social Psychology, 1951, 46, 64–71.

Gerard, H. B., & Rabbie, J. M. Fear and social comparison. *Journal of Abnormal and Social Psychology,* 1961, 62, 586–592.

Gibb, C. A. Leadership. In G. Lindzey & E. Aronson (Eds.), *The handbook of social psychology.* (2nd ed.) Reading, Mass.: Addison-Wesley, 1969.

Goffman, E. *The presentation of self in everyday life.* Garden City, N.Y.: Doubleday, 1959.

Goffman, E. *Behavior in public places.* New York: The Free Press of Glencoe, 1963.

Golembiewski, R. T. *The small group.* Chicago: University of Chicago Press, 1962.

Gouldner, A. W., & Gouldner, H. *Modern sociology: An introduction to the study of social interaction.* New York: Harcourt, Brace and World, 1963.

Graham, D. Experimental studies of social influence in simple judgment situations. *Journal of Social Psychology,* 1962, 56, 245–269.

Gross, N., Mason, W., & McEachern, A. *Explorations in role analysis.* New York: Wiley, 1958.

Guetzkow, H. Differentiation of roles in task-oriented groups. In D. Cartwright & A. Zander (Eds.), *Group dynamics: Research and theory.* (2nd ed.) Evanston, Ill.: Row, Peterson, 1960.

Gullahorn, J. Distance and friendship as factors in the gross interaction matrix. *Sociometry,* 1955, 15, 123–134.

Hackman, J. R. Effects of task characteristics on group products. *Journal of Experimental Social Psychology,* 1968, 4, 162–187.

Hackman, J. R., & Lawler, E. E. III. Employee reactions to job characteristics. *Journal of Applied Psychology Monograph,* 1971, 55, 259–286.

Hackman, J. R., & Morris, C. G. Group tasks, group interaction process, and group performance effectiveness: A review and proposed integration. In L. Berkowitz (Ed.), *Advances in experimental social psychology,* Vol. IX. New York: Academic Press, 1975.

Hall, E. T. *The hidden dimension.* Garden City, N.Y.: Doubleday, 1966.

Hare, A. P. *Handbook of small group research.* New York: The Free Press of Glencoe, 1962.

Harvey, O. J., & Consalvi, C. Status and conformity to pressures in informal groups.

Journal of Abnormal and Social Psychology, 1960, 60, 182–187.

Haythorn, W. W. The composition of groups: A review of the literature. *Acta Psychologica,* 1968, 28, 97–128.

Heider, F. *The psychology of interpersonal relations.* New York: Wiley, 1958.

Heinicke, C., & Bales, R. F. Developmental trends in the structure of small groups. *Sociometry,* 1953, 16, 7–38.

Henchy, T., & Glass, D. C. Evaluation apprehension and the social facilitation of dominant and subordinate responses. *Journal of Personality and Social Psychology,* 1968, 10, 446–454.

Hollander, E. P. Conformity, status, and idiosyncrasy credit. *Psychological Review,* 1958, 65, 117–127.

Hollander, E. P. Competence and conformity in the acceptance of influence. *Journal of Abnormal and Social Psychology,* 1960, 61, 361–365.

Hollander, E. P. Some effects of perceived status on responses to innovative behavior. *Journal of Abnormal and Social Psychology,* 1961, 63, 247–250.

Hollander, E. P. *Leaders, groups, and influence.* New York: Oxford University Press, 1964.

Homans, G. C. *The human group.* New York: Harcourt, Brace and World, 1950.

House, R. J. T-group education and leadership effectiveness: A review of the empirical literature and a critical evaluation. *Personnel Psychology,* 1967, 20, 1–32.

Hughes, E. C. The knitting of racial groups in industry. *American Sociological Review,* 1946, 11, 512–519.

Jackson, J. Structural characteristics of norms. In N. B. Henry (Ed.), *Dynamics of instructional groups.* The fifty-ninth yearbook of the National Society for the Study of Education. Chicago: University of Chicago Press, 1960.

Jackson, J. Structural characteristics of norms. In I. D. Steiner & M. Fishbein (Eds.), *Current studies in social psychology.* New York: Holt, Rinehart and Winston, 1965.

Jackson, J. A conceptual and measurement model for norms and roles. *Pacific Sociological Review,* 1966, 9, 35–47.

Jackson, J. *Norms and roles: Studies in systematic social psychology.* New York: Holt, Rinehart and Winston, in press.

Janis, I. L. *Victims of groupthink: A psychological study of foreign-policy decisions and fiascoes.* New York: Houghton Mifflin, 1972.

Jones, E. E., & Gerard, H. B. *Foundations of social psychology.* New York: Wiley, 1967.

Kahn, R. L., Wolfe, D. M., Quinn, R. P., & Snoek, J. D. *Organizational stress: Studies in role conflict and ambiguity.* New York: Wiley, 1964.

Kelley, H. H. Two functions of reference groups. In G. E. Swanson, T. M. Newcomb, & E. L. Hartley (Eds.), *Readings in social psychology.* New York: Holt, Rinehart and Winston, 1952.

Kelley, H. H., & Lamb, T. W. Certainty of judgment and resistance to social influences. *Journal of Abnormal and Social Psychology,* 1957, 55, 137–139.

Kelley, H. H., & Thibaut, J. W. Group problem solving. In G. Lindzey & E. Aronson (Eds.), *Handbook of social psychology.* (2nd ed.) Reading, Mass.: Addison-Wesley, 1969.

Kelman, H. C. Effects of success and failure on "suggestibility" in the autokinetic situation. *Journal of Abnormal and Social Psychology,* 1950, 45, 267–285.

Kelman, H. C. Compliance, identification, and internalization: Three processes of attitude change. *Journal of Conflict Resolution,* 1958, 2, 50–60.

Kelman, H. C. Processes of opinion change. *Public Opinion Quarterly,* 1961, 25, 57–78.

Kemper, T. D. Reference groups, socialization, and achievement. *American Sociological Review,* 1968, 33, 31–45.

Kent, R. N., & McGrath, J. E. Task and group characteristics as factors influencing group performance. *Journal of Experimental Social Psychology,* 1969, 5, 429–440.

Kiesler, C. A. Group pressure and conformity. In J. Mills (Ed.), *Experimental social psychology.* New York: Macmillan, 1969.

Klein, S. M. *Workers under stress: The impact of work pressure on group cohesion.* Lexington: University Press of Kentucky, 1971.

Klinger, E. Fantasy need achievement as a motivational construct. *Psychological Bulletin,* 1966, 66, 291–308.

Latané, B., Ed. Studies in social comparison. *Journal of Experimental Social Psychology,* Supplement 1, September, 1966.

Lawler, E. E., & Camman, C. What makes a work group successful? In A. J. Marrow (Ed.), *The failure of success.* New York: American Management, 1972.

Lawler, E. E., & Hackman, J. R. Impact of employee participation in the development of pay incentive plans: A field experiment. *Journal of Applied Psychology,* 1969, 53, 467–471.

League, B. J., & Jackson, D. N. Conformity, veridicality, and self-esteem. *Journal of Abnormal and Social Psychology,* 1964, 68, 113–115.

Levinson, D. J. Role, personality, and social structure in the organizational setting. *Journal of Abnormal and Social Psychology,* 1959, 58, 170–180.

Lewin, K. The conceptual representation and the measurement of psychological forces. *Contributions to Psychological Theory,* 1938, 1, No. 4.

Lieberman, S. The effects of changes in roles on the attitudes of role occupants. *Human Relations,* 1956, 9, 385–402.

Lott, B. E. Attitude formation: The development of a color-preference response through mediated generalization. *Journal of Abnormal and Social Psychology,* 1955, 50, 321–326.

Lott, A. J., & Lott, B. E. Group cohesiveness as interpersonal attraction: A review of relationships with antecedent and consequent variables. *Psychological Bulletin,* 1965, 64, 259–309.

Lowin, A. Participative decision making: A model, literature critique, and prescriptions for research. *Organizational Behavior and Human Performance,* 1968, 3, 68–106.

McClelland, D. C. *Personality.* New York Sloane, 1951.

McClelland, D. C., Atkinson, J. W., Clark, R. A., & Lowell, E. L. *The achievement motive.* New York: Appleton-Century-Crofts, 1953.

MacCrimmon, K. R., & Taylor, R. N. Decision making and problem solving. In M. D. Dunnette (Ed.), *Handbook of industrial and organizational psychology.* Chicago: Rand McNally, 1976.

McGrath, J. E. Stress and behavior in organizations. In M. D. Dunnette (Ed.), *Handbook of industrial and organizational psychology.* Chicago: Rand McNally, 1976.

Machotka, O. *The unconscious in social relations.* New York: Philosophical Library, 1964.

Maier, N. R. F., & Solem, A. R. The contribution of a discussion leader to the quality of group thinking. *Human Relations,* 1952, 5, 277–288.

March, J. G. Group norms and the active minority. *American Sociological Review,* 1954, 19, 733–741.

Marlowe, D., & Gergen, K. J. Personality and social interaction. In G. Lindzey & E. Aronson (Eds.), *The handbook of social psychology.* (2nd ed.) Reading, Mass.: Addison-Wesley, 1969.

Mathewson, S. B. *Restriction of output among unorganized workers.* New York: Viking Press, 1931.

Mehrabian, A., & Ksionzky, S. Models for affiliative and conformity behavior. *Psychological Bulletin,* 1970, 74, 110–126.

Merton, R. K., & Kitt, A. S. Contributions to the theory of reference group behavior. In R. K. Merton & P. F. Lazarsfeld (Eds.), *Continuities in social research: Studies in the scope and method of the American soldier.* Glencoe, Ill.: The Free Press, 1950.

Miller, G. R., & Tiffany, W. R. The effects of group pressure on judgments of speech sounds. *Journal of Speech and Hearing Research,* 1963, 6, 149–156.

Miller, N. E., & Dollard, J. *Social learning and imitation.* New Haven: Yale University Press, 1941.

Mills, T. M. *The sociology of small groups.* Englewood Cliffs, N.J.: Prentice-Hall, 1967.

Moore, W. E. Social structure and behavior. In G. Lindzey & E. Aronson (Eds.), *The handbook of social psychology.* (2nd ed.) Reading, Mass.: Addison-Wesley, 1969.

Morris, C. G. Task effects on group interaction. *Journal of Personality and Social Psychology,* 1966, 5, 545–554.

Mudd, S. A. Group sanction severity as a function of degree of behavior deviation and relevance of norm. *Journal of Personality and Social Psychology,* 1968, 8, 258–260.

Newcomb, T. M. Attitude development as a function of reference groups: The Bennington study. In C. G. Swanson, T. M. Newcomb, & E. L. Hartley (Eds.), *Readings in social psychology.* (Rev. ed.) New York: Holt, Rinehart and Winston, 1952.

Newcomb, T. M. *Social psychology.* New York: Dryden, 1954.

Nisbett, R. E., & Valins, S. Perceiving the causes of one's own behavior. In E. E. Jones, D. E. Kanouse, H. H. Kelley, R. E. Nisbett, S. Valins, & B. Weiner (Eds.), *Attribution: Perceiving the causes of behavior.* New York: General Learning Press, 1972.

Patchen, M. *The choice of wage comparison.* Englewood Cliffs, N.J.: Prentice-Hall, 1961.

Porter, L. W., Lawler, E. E. III, & Hackman, J. R. *Behavior in organizations.* New York: McGraw-Hill, 1975.

Rabbie, J. M. Differential preferences for companionship under threat. *Journal of Abnormal and Social Psychology,* 1963, 67, 643–648.

Rhine, J. The effects of peer group influence upon concept-attitude development and change. *Journal of Social Psychology,* 1960, 51, 173–179.

Roethlisberger, F. J., & Dickson, W. J. *Management and the worker.* Cambridge: Harvard University Press, 1939.

Rommetveit, R. *Social norms and roles.* Minneapolis: University of Minnesota Press, 1955.

Rosenbaum, M. E., & Arenson, S. J. Observational learning: Some theory, some variables, some findings. In E. C. Simmel, R. A. Hoppe, & C. A. Milton (Eds.), *Social facilitation and imitative behavior.* Boston: Allyn and Bacon, 1968.

Rosenberg, L. A. Group size, prior experience, and conformity. *Journal of Abnormal and Social Psychology,* 1961, 63, 436–437.

Rosenberg, M. J. Cognitive structure and attitudinal affect. *Journal of Abnormal and Social Psychology,* 1956, 53, 367–372.

Roy, D. Quota restriction and gold bricking in a machine shop. *American Journal of Sociology,* 1952, 57, 427–442.

Ryle, G. *The concept of mind.* London: Hutchinson, 1949.

Sampson, E. E., & Brandon, A. C. The effects of role and opinion deviation on small group behavior. *Sociometry,* 1964, 27, 261–281.

Sarbin, T. R., & Allen, V. L. Increasing participation in a natural group setting: A preliminary report. *The Psychological Record,* 1968, 18, 1–7. (a)

Sarbin, T. R., & Allen, V. L. Role theory. In G. Lindzey & E. Aronson (Eds.), *The handbook of social psychology.* (2nd ed.) Reading, Mass.: Addison-Wesley, 1968. (b)

Schachter, S. Deviation, rejection, and communication. *Journal of Abnormal and Social Psychology,* 1951, 46, 190–207.

Schachter, S. *The psychology of affiliation*. Stanford: Stanford University Press, 1959.

Schachter, S. The interaction of cognitive and physiological determinants of emotional state. In L. Berkowitz (Ed.), *Advances in experimental social psychology*, Vol. I. New York: Academic Press, 1964.

Schachter, S., Ellertson, N., McBride, D., & Gregory, D. An experimental study of cohesiveness and productivity. *Human Relations*, 1951, 4, 229–238.

Schachter, S., Nuttin, J., Demonchaux, C., Maucorps, P. H., Osmer, D., Duijker, H., Rommetviet, R., & Israel, J. Cross-cultural experiments on threat and rejection. *Human Relations*, 1954, 7, 403–439.

Schein, E. H. The Chinese indoctrination program for prisoners of war. *Psychiatry*, 1956, 19, 149–172.

Schein, E. H., & Bennis, W. *Personal and organizational change through group methods*. New York: Wiley, 1965.

Schlesinger, A. M. *1000 days*. Boston: Houghton Mifflin, 1965.

Scott, W. E. Activation theory and task design. *Organizational Behavior and Human Performance*, 1966, 1, 3–30.

Seashore, S. *Group cohesiveness in the industrial work group*. Ann Arbor: Institute for Social Research, University of Michigan, 1954.

Sherif, M. *The psychology of social norms*. New York: Harper, 1936.

Sherif, M. Formation of social norms: The experimental paradigm. In H. Proshansky & B. Seidenberg (Eds.), *Basic studies in social psychology*. New York: Holt, Rinehart and Winston, 1965.

Shure, G. H., Rogers, M. S., Larsen, I. M., & Tassone, J. Group planning and task effectiveness. *Sociometry*, 1962, 25, 263–282.

Siegel, A. E., & Siegel, S. Reference groups, membership groups, and attitude change. *Journal of Abnormal and Social Psychology*, 1957, 55, 360–364.

Singer, J. E. Social comparison—progress and issues. In B. Lantané (Ed.), *Studies in social comparison. Journal of Experimental Social Psychology*, Supplement 1, 1966.

Slater, P. E. Role differentiation in small groups. *American Sociological Review*, 1955, 20, 300–310.

Smith, E. E., & Kight, S. S. Effects of feedback on insight and problem-solving efficiency in training groups. *Journal of Applied Psychology*, 1959, 43, 209–211.

Sommer, R. Man's proximate environment. *Journal of Social Issues*, 1966, 22, 59–70.

Sommer, R. Small group ecology. *Psychological Bulletin*, 1967, 67, 145–152.

Staats, A. W., & Staats, C. K. Attitudes established by classical conditioning. *Journal of Abnormal and Social Psychology*, 1958, 57, 37–40.

Steele, F. The impact of the physical setting on the social climate at two comparable laboratory sessions. *Human Relations Training News*, 1968, 12, No. 4.

Steele, F. I. *Problem solving in the spatial environment*. (Mimeo.) New Haven: Department of Administrative Sciences, Yale University, 1969.

Steele, F. I. *Physical settings and organizational development*. Reading, Mass.: Addison-Wesley, 1973.

Steiner, I. D. *Group process and productivity*. New York: Academic Press, 1972.

Tajfel, H. Social and cultural factors in perception. In G. Lindzey & E. Aronson (Eds.), *The handbook of social psychology*. (2nd ed.) Reading, Mass.: Addison-Wesley, 1969.

Talland, G. A. Task and interaction process: Some characteristics of therapeutic group discussion. *Journal of Abnormal and Social Psychology*, 1955, 50, 105–109.

Thelen, H. A. Educational dynamics: Theory and research. *Journal of Social Issues*, 1950, 6, Whole No. 2.

Thibaut, J. W. An experimental study of the cohesiveness of under-privileged groups. *Human Relations*, 1950, 3, 251–278.

Thibaut, J. W., & Kelley, H. H. *The social psychology of groups*. New York: Wiley, 1959.

Thibaut, J., & Strickland, L. H. Psychological set and social conformity. *Journal of Personality*, 1956, 25, 115–129.

Thornton, D. A., & Arrowood, A. J. Self-evaluation, self-enhancement, and the locus of social comparison. In B. Lantané (Ed.), *Studies in social comparison. Journal of Experimental Social Psychology*, Supplement 1, 1966.

Tolman, E. C. *Purposive behavior in animals and men*. New York: Century, 1932.

Trist, E. L., & Bamforth, K. W. Some social and psychological consequences of the long-wall method of coal-getting. *Human Relations*, 1951, 4, 1–38.

Vaughan, G. M., & Mangan, G. L. Conformity to group pressure in relation to the value of the task material. *Journal of Abnormal and Social Psychology*, 1963, 66, 179–183.

Vroom, V. H. *Work and motivation.* New York: Wiley, 1964.

Vroom, V. H. Industrial social psychology. In G. Lindzey & E. Aronson (Eds.), *The handbook of social psychology.* (2nd ed.) Reading, Mass.: Addison-Wesley, 1969.

Vroom, V. H., & Yetton, P. W. *Leadership and decision making.* Pittsburgh: University of Pittsburgh Press, 1973.

Walters, R. H. Some conditions facilitative of the occurrence of imitative behavior. In E. C. Simmel, R. A. Hoppe, & C. A. Milton (Eds.), *Social facilitation and imitative behavior.* Boston: Allyn and Bacon, 1968.

Walters, R. H., & Parke, R. D. Social motivation, dependency, and susceptibility to social influence. In L. Berkowitz (Ed.), *Advances in experimental social psychology,* Vol. I. New York: Academic Press, 1964.

Weick, K. E. *The social psychology of organizing.* Reading, Mass.: Addison-Wesley, 1969.

Wheeler, L., Shaver, K. G., Jones, R. A., Goethals, F. G., Cooper, J., Robinson, J. E., Gruder, C. L., & Butzine, K. W. Factors determining choice of a comparison other. *Journal of Experimental Social Psychology,* 1969, 5, 219–232.

White, R. W. Motivation reconsidered: The concept of competence. *Psychological Review,* 1959, 66, 297–333.

Whyte, W. F. *Street corner society.* Chicago: University of Chicago Press, 1943.

Whyte, W. F. *Money and motivation.* New York: Harper and Row, 1955.

Wiener, M. Certainty of judgment as a variable in conformity behavior. *Journal of Social Psychology,* 1958, 48, 257–263.

Wiggins, J. A., Dill, F., & Schwartz, R. D. On "status-liability." *Sociometry,* 1965, 28, 197–209.

Zajonc, R. B. Social facilitation. *Science,* 1965, 149, 269–274.

Zajonc, R. B., & Sales, S. M. Social facilitation of dominant and subordinate responses. *Journal of Experimental Social Psychology,* 1966, 2, 160–168.

Leadership[1,2]

VICTOR H. VROOM
Yale University

THERE ARE FEW PROBLEMS of interest to behavioral scientists with as much apparent relevance to the problems of society as the study of leadership. This chapter recounts their efforts to shed light on the leadership process through empirical research. The author begins by describing the major approaches to the investigation of leadership, evaluating their theoretical underpinnings, and summarizing the principal empirical findings which bear on them. In the second half of the chapter, he attempts to sketch some new directions for the study of leadership—directions which build on evidence concerning the critical role of the situation in influencing how leaders behave and in determining the effectiveness of their actions. The nature of these new directions is then illustrated through a detailed examination of one facet of leadership—participation in decision making.

There are few problems of interest to behavioral scientists with as much apparent relevance to the problems of society as the study of leadership. The effective functioning of social systems from the local PTA to the United States of America is assumed to be dependent on the quality of their leadership. This assumption is reflected in our tendency to blame a football coach for a losing season or to credit a general for a military victory. While one can identify many factors influencing organizational effectiveness, some of which are outside the direct control of those in positions of leadership, the critical importance of executive functions and of those who carry them out to the survival and effectiveness of the organization cannot be denied. Any knowledge which the behavioral sciences can contribute to aid in the identification and enhancement of leadership in

[1] The author is grateful to Arthur Jago for his helpful suggestions on the final draft of this chapter.

[2] The research contained in this article was sponsored by the Organizational Effectiveness Research Program, Office of Naval Research (Code 452) under Contract to the author (No. N00014-67-A-0097-0027; NR 177-935). Reproduction in whole or in part is permitted for any purpose of the United States Government.

organized human endeavor would be of immense societal value.

This chapter recounts the efforts of social scientists to respond to this challenge. In the first half of the chapter the theoretical underpinnings of the major approaches are reviewed, the principal empirical findings summarized, and the practical implications of research on leadership examined. We have not sought, in this section of the chapter, to be exhaustive but have rather tried to put the major themes and issues in historical perspective. In the second half of the chapter, we attempt to sketch some new directions for the study of leadership— directions which build upon prior evidence concerning the critical role of the situation in leadership and which employ situational concepts in the analysis of both descriptive and normative issues involved in the study of leadership. The possible nature of these directions is illustrated through the detailed examination of one facet of leadership— participation in decision making.

LEADERSHIP AS A PERSONALITY TRAIT

One conception of leadership, which is still common in popular parlance and which has been the starting point for a considerable amount of research, views leadership as a unidimensional personality trait that is distributed in some fashion throughout the population. It is assumed that people vary in terms of the amount of this trait and that these differences are potentially measurable.

It is perhaps curious that those holding to this concept of leadership have not addressed themselves to the origin of these individual differences. There has been surprisingly little systematic work on the process by which individuals acquire this capacity for leadership. The empirical work stemming from the concept of leadership as a personality variable has been within the tradition of the psychology of individual differences and, as such, has been principally concerned with the nature and measurement of leadership.

If leadership were usefully conceived of as a unidimensional personality trait and if reliable and valid measures of this variable could be developed, the benefits to society could be tremendous. Most of our formal organizations are stratified hierarchically and are pyramidal in shape. People advance from lower level positions to less numerous higher ones based on highly subjective assessments of their ability to function effectively in the higher positions. If these subjective judgments could be replaced with a valid test of leadership, countless costly errors could be avoided. The test could be utilized to advantage in selecting students by institutions of higher learning whose objective is to train future leaders in the public and private sector; by industrial firms in screening the yearly supply of college undergraduates or in identification of the relative managerial potential of those in their employ. Even allowing for the typical errors which are inextricably involved in the process of psychological measurement, the net result would be a substantial improvement in our "batting average" in selecting leaders and result in improvements in the effectiveness of hospitals, industrial firms, universities, government, the military, and all other forms of organized human endeavor.

It should be reiterated that this technology for identifying those with leadership potential and for selecting leaders is a logical extension of the conception of leadership as a unidimensional personality variable and has not yet been developed. Its potential development in the future hinges on the soundness of the basic conception. Let us now turn to consideration of this question.

Empirical Studies

If leadership is a personality trait, then it is reasonable to assume that those who are presently functioning in higher level positions in organizations would, on the average, possess more of this attribute than those presently in lower level positions. For this to be true, it need not be the case that the "best man" is always chosen for the higher position but rather that the average person so chosen possesses more "leadership" than the average of those in the lower positions. Thus, Shartle and Stogdill (1952) assert that "persons who occupy positions which are commonly assumed to demand leadership ability are proper and likely subjects for the study of leadership" (p. 6).

Accordingly, the ingredients of the personality trait of leadership might be uncovered by a systematic study of differences between leaders and followers. A large number of studies have been conducted along these lines, including comparisons of bishops and clergymen, sales managers and salesmen, and railway presidents and station agents.

The results have been treated in detail elsewhere (Stogdill, 1948; Mann, 1959; Bass, 1960; Gibb, 1969), so will only be briefly summarized here. There appear to be a few traits which tend to distinguish leaders from non-leaders. In addition to being slightly superior on such physical attributes as height and weight, leaders tend to score slightly higher on tests of intelligence, extraversion, adjustment, dominance, and self-confidence than followers. The differences tend to be small in magnitude with large amounts of overlap between the distributions of scores of leaders and followers. It is not clear how much of the differences reflect the effects of occupancy of a leader position on test scores. Occupying the role of leader may contribute to better adjustment, self-confidence, or dominance rather than having those traits increasing one's chances of being selected as leader. Finally, and perhaps of greatest importance, there is considerable variance across situations in both the magnitude and even the direction of the relationship between most personality attributes and leadership status.

The small size of the differences between leaders and followers may be attributed to a number of factors, most notably errors in the leader selection process, errors of measurement in the tests, or failure to assess the most critical attributes. The reversals in direction of the relationships are more difficult to explain and pose more significant problems for the basic conception of leadership as a personality variable. These reversals suggest that those personal qualities which make for leadership capacity in one situation may be quite different from those which comprise leadership in another situation.

This conclusion is not altogether surprising. In fact, it would be surprising to find that the nature of the group or organization, its prevalent norms and values, and the critical problems it faces in its relations with its own environment have nothing to do with the kinds of people elevated to leader status. When situational demands are different from group to group, it is not possible to specify the personality traits which will be associated with accession to leadership without taking into consideration the nature of those demands.

A similar conclusion follows from studies which have sought to determine the relationship between personal traits of leaders and criteria of their effectiveness in carrying out their position. Fiedler (1967) has carried out what is undoubtedly the most extensive program of research using this approach in a set of studies of the relationship between the leaders' scores on a personality variable, which he calls LPC (least preferred coworker), and the measured effectiveness of his group or organization. Correlations have varied from strongly negative in some situations to strongly positive in others. Fiedler's contingency model, which will be discussed in a later section, purports to explain this variation by specifying the types of situations requiring leaders with high or low LPC scores.

The findings discussed in this section cast considerable doubt on the usefulness of a conception of leadership as a unidimensional personality trait. They do not imply that individual differences have nothing to do with leadership but rather that their significance must be evaluated in relation to the situation. Ultimately, it may be possible to identify classes or families of situations, each characterized by relatively invariant relations between leader personality and criteria of effectiveness. This could permit a resurrection of the trait conception of leadership in somewhat modified form. Instead of a general trait applicable to all situations, leadership might be expressed as a set of highly specific traits each of which would be applicable to clearly defined situations. One might look for one trait in selecting leaders for one situation and a different trait in selecting leaders for another situation. We will return to this idea in a later section.

To summarize, the conception of leadership as a "personality characteristic" proved to be oversimplified. The dream of a technology by which the relative amounts of leadership possessed by different people could be measured and the person with the largest amount of this trait selected as leader was unattainable since it rested on an erroneous foundation. The question, "Who will be the best leader?" is akin to asking, "Which will be the best fishing bait?" Neither question can be adequately answered as stated.

EFFECTIVE LEADER BEHAVIOR

If there appear to be no stable and situationally invariant personality characteristics which distinguish leaders from nonleaders, or effective leaders from less effective ones, it is still possible that there are methods or styles of leadership which are more effective than others. Instead of looking at the personality of the effective leader, it is possible we should be searching for behavioral correlates of effective leadership. Effective and ineffective leaders may not be distinguishable by a battery of psychological tests but may be distinguished by their characteristic behavior patterns in their work roles.

Stable and invariant relations between leader behavior and criteria of their effectiveness would have less obvious implications for leader selection but would have signifi-

cant import for leader development and training. Knowledge of the behavior patterns which characterize effective leaders would provide a rational basis for the design of programs to instill these behavior patterns in actual or potential leaders.

Interest in the behavior of leaders in their leadership roles was evident in two major research programs begun in the late 1940s and carried out at Ohio State University and at the University of Michigan.

The Ohio State Studies

These investigations began by attempting to identify, using factor analysis, the dimensions needed to characterize differences in the behavior of leaders. Originally four factors were identified but two of them, Consideration and Initiating Structure, accounted for the greatest portion of the variance and have subsequently been the subject of most research. Consideration includes supervisory behavior "indicative of friendship, mutual trust, respect, and warmth" while Initiating Structure includes behavior in which "the supervisor organizes and defines group activities and his relation to the group" (Halpin & Winer, 1957). The dimensions are conceptually similar to those labeled "task facilitative" and "socio-emotional" leadership by Bales (1949) in his research on leadership in small groups.

Two rather different methods have been developed for measuring these variables. The primary instrument is called the Leader Behavior Description Questionnaire (LBDQ) originally developed by Hemphill and Coons (1957) and subsequently modified for use in military and educational situations by Halpin and Winer (1957) and in industrial organizations by Fleishman (1957a). It is typically given to subordinates who are asked to describe the behavior of their supervisor. A related instrument called the Leadership Opinion Questionnaire (LOQ) has also been developed by Fleishman (1957b). It also provides scores on Consideration and Initiating Structure but is completed by supervisors who are asked to describe how they think they should behave.

It should be noted that both instruments yield scores on these two dimensions by aggregating over behaviors which are in some sense different (although correlated in the minds of respondents) and aggregating over time and situations. Thus, the statements, "He refuses to give in when people disagree with him" and "He demands more than we can do," contribute to low scores on consideration but are quite different forms of behavior. In addition, neither statement contains a referent of the situation in which the behavior is exhibited. Presumably the respondent's judgment is some aggregate estimate (perhaps influenced by primacy and recency) of its occurrence in all conceivable or remembered situations.

Aggregations over behavior and situations greatly simplify the measurement problem by permitting the reduction of all the subtleties of differences in leadership style to two-dimensional space. However, it could be expected to reduce correlations with criteria of effectiveness if the different behaviors have different consequences or the same behavior has different consequences in different situations.

A large number of investigations have been concerned with the relations between consideration and initiating structure scores and criteria of leadership effectiveness. Space limitations prevent a complete account of this work here. The major conclusions, however, can be summarized as follows:

1. Leaders who are high on consideration tend to have subordinates who are more satisfied with their leader than those who are low in consideration (Halpin & Winer, 1957; Halpin, 1957; Seeman, 1957; Fleishman, Harris, & Burtt, 1955). Their subordinates are also more likely to have fewer absences (Fleishman, Harris, & Burtt, 1955) and lower grievances rates (Fleishman & Harris, 1962).

2. The relationship between consideration and rated leader effectiveness varies substantially with the population. Negative correlations have been reported for air crew commanders in combat (Halpin & Winer, 1957) and production foremen (Fleishman, Harris, & Burtt, 1955), while positive correlations have been reported for nonproduction foremen (Fleishman, Harris, & Burtt, 1955), petrochemical supervisors (Bass, 1956), and both managers and office staff in a large industrial firm (Graen, Dansereau, & Minami, 1972).

3. Similarly, correlations between initiating structure and rated effectiveness while tending to be positive (Halpin, 1957; Halpin & Winer, 1957; Fleishman, Harris, & Burtt, 1955) also show considerable variability with a substantial number of reports of zero or negative relationships (Rambo, 1958; Fleishman, Harris, & Burtt, 1955; Bass, 1956, 1958).

4. There is an indication from one study (Fleishman & Harris, 1962) that consideration and initiating structure interact in determining both grievances and turnover rates. In general, low consideration and high initiating structure were found to be independently associated with high grievances and turnover. However, the positive relationship between initiating structure and turnover was more marked among those who were low in consideration than among those high in consideration. Similar results with respect to productivity have been reported by Cummins (1971).

The fact that there are few consistent findings that are both situation and population independent has recently led many scholars to the conclusion that attention must be given to the search for the situational variables which affect the relationship between Consideration and Initiating Structure and criteria of organizational effectiveness (Fleishman, 1973; House, 1973; Kerr, Schriesheim, Murphy, & Stogdill, 1974).

The Michigan Studies

The second set of studies to be considered was carried out by the Survey Research Center at the University of Michigan.

In many respects, the purpose behind these studies was similar to that of the Ohio State group. The investigators were interested in ascertaining behavioral differences between more and less effective leaders and did not begin with any theories about the leadership process. However, there were also some differences. The Michigan group did not exhibit much concern with the dimensionality of leader behavior. Their measures of leader behavior tended to be more casual and "ad hoc" and to vary somewhat from one study to another. However, this group does seem to have been somewhat more successful in obtaining objective criteria of leader effectiveness rather than relying on ratings of their superiors.

The earliest study (Katz, Maccoby, & Morse, 1950) carried out by this group illustrates the basic approach. It was carried out in the home office of a large insurance company. Twenty-four work groups were studied, half of which were high and half low in productivity as determined by prior work records. Each highly productive section was matched with another low in productivity as to type of work and number and kind of people. Differences in supervisory behavior between the high and low productivity sections were assessed by means of interviews with both supervisors and their subordinates. Three differences emerged from this analysis. Highly productive supervisors were more frequently employee-centered as opposed to production-centered, were more likely to exercise general rather than close supervision and were more likely to differentiate their roles from those of their subordinates in terms of duties performed.

Katz, Maccoby, Gurin, and Floor (1951) carried out a second investigation, similar in design but of railroad maintenance-of-way workers. As in the previous investigation, the more productive supervisors were found to be more employee-centered and to exercise more general supervision than those who were less productive. However, the difference in role differentiation found in the previous investigation was not found in this study.

Many field studies and experiments have since been conducted by the Michigan group. They are exceedingly difficult to summarize briefly due to the many different measures of leader behavior, populations, and research methods employed. The reader interested in a detailed review along with its managerial implications is referred to books by Likert (1961, 1967). There is in this work substantial evidence indicating that more effective leaders (1) tend to have relationships with their subordinates which are supportive and enhance the latter's sense of personal worth and importance, (2) use group rather than man-to-man methods of supervision and decision making, and (3) tend to set high performance goals. These concepts have been elaborated by Likert (1967) into a system of management which he calls System 4 or the participative-group system.

It may appear at first glance as though this program of research has uncovered a set of principles of leadership which are applicable regardless of the siuations in which they are exercised. On closer examination, it is apparent that situational differences are implicit in each of the principles. The three principles stated and other components of System 4 are outcomes both of leader behavior and other organizational conditions. The specific behaviors which result in these outcomes are not specified and likely in fact to vary markedly from one situation to another. To say that a leader should act in such a way as to enhance a subordinate's feelings of personal importance and self-worth is not to specify completely his behavior but rather to indicate a general direction for it. The leadership acts necessary to achieve this outcome are probably not specifiable without a detailed knowledge of the situation. It is in a sense a general blueprint for action rather than a detailed blueprint which would of necessity have to take situational factors into account. This distinction between broad principles and specific behaviors is recognized by Likert, who states:

Supervision is, therefore, always a relative process. To be effective and to communicate as intended, a leader must always adapt his behavior to take into account the expectations, values and interpersonal skills of those with whom he is interacting.... There can be no specific rules of supervision which will work well in all situations. Broad principles can be applied to the process of supervision and furnish valuable guides to behavior. These principles, however, must be applied always in a manner that takes fully into account the characteristics of the specific situation, and of the people involved. (Likert, 1961, p. 95)

Broad principles of leadership have the advantage of not having to deal in any precise way with the complexities of situational differences and their import for leader behavior. However, the more broadly stated the principle, the greater the risk that it will be empirically vacuous and prescriptively useless. It is possible to state principles of leadership in such a way that they are true by definition, incapable of empirical refutation and which elicit immediate acceptance by persons with drastically different leadership styles. To say that a leader should manage in such a way that personnel at all levels feel real responsibility for the attainment of the organization's goals (Likert, 1967) or alternatively that he should exhibit concern for both production and his employees (Blake & Mouton, 1964) is not saying a great deal about what he should do in particular situations or how to guide his responses to the concrete situations that he faces daily.

SITUATIONAL APPROACHES: PERSONALITY AND SITUATION

In the previous two sections, we have shown that an analysis of the situational demands was requisite to an understanding of the process of leadership. Attempts to determine the kinds of traits or leader behaviors which were characteristic of effective leaders continually encountered variability in the relationships obtained. The problem is apparently more complex. Empirically, it is necessary to ascertain the kinds of persons or behaviors which are effective in different situations. Theoretically, it is necessary to develop a set of concepts which are capable of dealing with differences in situations and a parallel set of concepts capable of dealing with differences among leaders or their styles.

Associated with this focus on situations is a new definition of leadership—not as a general personal trait or as a fixed pattern of behavior—but rather as a role to be performed, a job to be done, or a set of functions to be carried out. There are different ways of characterizing the leadership functions, but it is common practice to distinguish two basic types of group functions: (1) the achievement of goals external to the group and (2) the maintenance or strengthening of the group itself (Cartwright & Zander, 1968, Chap. 24). These functions may vary in importance as well as in their specific nature both between and within groups. Consequently, one would expect to find that the attributes of persons or of their behavior necessary for their successful execution would also vary.

One form of situational approach is an outgrowth of the focus on personal traits of leaders but seeks to reconcile this with differences in situational requirements. Undoubtedly, the leading exponent of this approach to the study of leadership is Fiedler (1967) who, along with his colleagues, has carried out over the last twenty years an extensive program of research on the way in which one of the leader's personality characteristics affects performance of his group or organization.

The variable used by Fiedler to characterize differences among leaders requires asking a leader to think of the person with whom he can work least well on a common task and to describe him by making a mark on an eight-point scale for each of a set of bipolar adjectives, such as pleasant-unpleasant, friendly-unfriendly. The variable is called Least Preferred Co-worker (LPC), and a high numerical score indicates that the respondent describes the person with whom he is least able to work on a common task in relatively favorable terms, while a low score would indicate that he describes the person in very unfavorable terms. LPC is a component of an earlier measure called Assumed Similarity between Opposites (ASO), which utilized the difference between descriptions of most and least preferred co-workers. These two variables (ASO and LPC) are very highly correlated (.80 to .90), and in recent work the simpler measure has been used exclusively.

The meaning of LPC scores is still a matter of some conjecture. From the nature of the measure itself, it is apparent that a person with a high LPC score tends to separate work performance and personality in the sense that he does not impute negative personal attributes to those with whom he cannot work effectively. On the other hand, one with a low LPC score sees his least preferred co-worker in negative terms, that is, as being unpleasant, unfriendly, cold, and boring. It is somewhat less clear what implications these personal dispositions have for the leader's personal leadership style. There is some evidence to support Fiedler's assumptions that high-LPC leaders derive their major satisfaction from successful interpersonal relationships, while low-LPC leaders derive their major satisfaction from task performance. However, the relationships between LPC scores and indicators of leader behavior tend to be weak with a sufficient number of reversals in direction to warrant substantial caution in characterizing leadership style on the basis of LPC score alone.

The essential purpose of the extensive program of research conducted by Fiedler was to determine the relationship between leader's LPC (or ASO) scores and objective criteria of group or organizational performance. A large variety of groups have been

studied, including high school basketball teams, student surveying parties, boards of directors of small corporations, army tank crews, gasoline service station managers, and crews in open hearth steel shops.

In each study coefficients of correlation were computed between the leader's LPC score and one or more criterion measures. These correlations varied over an extremely wide range (+.89 to −.81). This variation was initially quite difficult to understand. It was not obvious why open hearth crews should be more effective when their foremen have low LPC scores, whereas chairmen of successful boards of directors should perform better when they have high LPC scores.

In an attempt to understand these differences, Fiedler classified the groups employed in his studies into eight types or octants in accordance with their status (high or low) on three dimensions:

1. the degree of structure involved in the task (for example, open hearth steel crews were classified as highly structured and ad hoc student groups and boards of directors were classified as unstructured);

2. the amount of power given to the leader by virtue of his position (for example, informal leaders of high school basketball teams and surveying teams were classified as having low position power and ROTC groups with officially appointed leaders and managers of gas stations were classified as having high position power);

3. the quality of interpersonal relationships between the leader and members. (This variable was measured for each group by sociometric ratings or by other methods.)

This classification served to account for much of the variance in results. There proved to be substantial agreement in the correlations between leader LPC score and criteria of his group effectiveness within a given octant and wide variance between octants. Thus, for groups characterized as having structured tasks, strong position power, and good leader-member relations the median correlation was −.52, while for those groups having unstructured tasks, weak position power, and good leader-member relations the median correlation was .47.

But what is the nature of the process underlying these differences among octants? Fiedler reasoned that the three variables used in the classification of groups have a common element. They constitute indicators of the favorableness of the situation to the leader. Thus, the most favorable situation to a leader would be one in which the task is structured, he has high position power, and leader-member relations are good. The least favorable situation would be characterized by an unstructured task, low position power and poor leader-member relations. An additional assumption concerning the relative importance of these three dimensions in specifying "favorableness" permits a rank ordering of the octants from high to low on this underlying dimension. When this is done it becomes apparent (see Fiedler, 1967, p. 146) that the correlation between leader's LPC score and group effectiveness is highly related to the favorableness of the situation to the leader and that the shape of that relationship approximates an inverted *U*. In instances in which the situation is either highly favorable or highly unfavorable to the leader, the correlation is negative. However, in situations which are only moderately favorable or moderately unfavorable to the leader, the correlation between LPC and group effectiveness is positive.

Whenever a theory has been arrived at by inductive means, it is critical that it be validated by determining its ability to predict results other than those which entered into its formulation. Several validation studies have been conducted (Fiedler, 1966; Hunt, 1967; Hill, 1969; Mitchell, 1969). The degree to which the results are consistent with the predictions from the model is a matter of substantial disagreement. Fiedler (1967, p. 180) interprets the results as supporting the model, but Graen, Alvares, Orris, and Martella (1970) have reanalyzed the validational data and question this con-

clusion. Furthermore, a laboratory experiment specifically designed to test the interactions in the model (Graen, Orris, & Alvares, 1971) failed to find any support for the predictions. Recent reviews of the LPC research examine certain conceptual and methodological issues central to this current controversy in more detail than is appropriate here (Ashour, 1973; Fiedler, 1973; McMahon, 1972; Shiflett, 1973, 1974).

Fiedler has termed his theory of leadership effectiveness "The Contingency Model." In essence, it is a system for predicting which leaders will be effective in different situations. Its principal implications are for the processes of recruitment, selection, and placement of leaders. Fiedler outlines the general direction of such applications as follows:

If our theory is correct, then the recruitment and selection of leaders can be effective only when we can also specify the relevant components of the situation for which the leader is being recruited. There is no reason to believe that this cannot be done or that this should not be done in specific cases. Difficulties arise because leadership situations change over time. The organization must then be aware of the type of leadership situations into which the individual should be successively guided, but this is basically no different than seeing that an electrical engineer does not get assigned to bookkeeping duties. (Fiedler, 1967, p. 250)

A secondary potential application of this model is referred to by Fiedler as Organizational Engineering. It is predicated on the possibility of altering the situation to fit the personality characteristics of the leader. If a leader's LPC score is not suited to the demands of the position which he occupies, the contingency model provides an a priori rationale for making changes in the situation so as to improve his performance.

As was the case with its intellectual parent—the personality trait approach—Fiedler's model has no direct implications for leadership training or development. In his earlier writings, Fiedler specifically eschewed such efforts and was highly critical of the usefulness of existing programs designed to achieve this purpose. More recently (Fiedler & Chemers, 1974), he has extended his theory to deal with the possibility that training may indeed have an effect but not through changing the leader's style (which is fixed by his LPC score), but rather by changing the favorableness of his situation by giving him more control and influence. Leadership training may be either beneficial or detrimental to organizational performance depending on the leader's LPC score and the previous level of situation favorableness.

The possibility that some leaders may have flexible leadership styles or that people can be trained to adapt their behavior to the demands of the situation is rejected as unfeasible.

The alternative method would call for training the leader to develop a flexible leadership style and to adapt his leadership style to the particular situation. The author is highly pessimistic that this training approach would be successful. There may be some favored few who can be effective in any leadership situation, and some unfortunate few who would even find it difficult to lead a troop of hungry Girl Scouts to a hot-dog stand. However, our experience has not enabled us to identify these individuals. Nor have we found it possible to identify those who can switch their leadership style as the occasion demands. It would seem more promising at this time, therefore, to teach the individual to recognize the conditions under which he can perform best and to modify the situation to suit his leadership style. (Fiedler, 1967, pp. 254–255)

There are many questions still to be answered about the contingency model. Perhaps the foremost question concerns the behavioral or leadership style differences between high and low LPC leaders. Much more data are needed before Fiedler's assumption—that the former tend to derive satisfaction from relationships and the latter from task performance—can be accepted with confidence.

An even more basic question concerns the extent to which one can actually pre-dict leader behavior from a personality test like LPC or any other. Lewin's classic dictum (1951) that behavior is a function of both person and environment has been supported by a wide variety of studies which show that virtually all complex behaviors are influenced by both sets of variables in interaction with one another. Fiedler's model does not allow for the possibility that a leader's behavior may be influenced by the situation with which he is confronted or even that leaders have different rules for translating situational differences into actions on their part. Finally, it is not clear why leadership style should be as immutable as Fiedler implies. Presumably, leader behavior is learned and why then can it not be unlearned? Why should leaders be so resistant to the effects of educational or organizational environments intended to help them to recognize differences in situational demands and to make different but appropriate responses to each?

Fiedler's contingency model represents an ambitious and laudable effort to go beyond the obviously correct but vacuous statement that "leadership depends on the situation" and shows on what properties of the situation and of persons the phenomenon of leadership depends. To be sure the theory is crude in its present form and the practical implications are, at this point, matters of considerable uncertainty. Like most pioneering efforts it will undoubtedly be shown to be incorrect in detail if not in substance.

A NEW LOOK AT LEADERSHIP

In this section, we begin by postulating a number of necessary ingredients for a situational theory of leadership. These ingredients will be based on some of the things learned from the previous approaches that we have reviewed and from more general knowledge concerning both human behavior and the functioning of groups and organizations. We will then develop a model of one aspect of the leadership process to illustrate the approach.

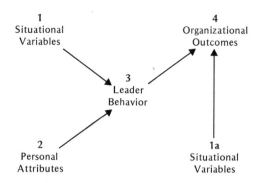

Figure 1. Schematic representation of variables used in leadership research.

Figure 1 shows a general road map to the terrain we will be examining. The key variable in this figure is labeled #3—the actions or behaviors exhibited by the leader in the course of carrying out his leadership role. One of the central objectives that one might set for a theory of leadership is the explanation of leader behavior itself. We need a descriptive model to explain the processes which govern the behavior of occupants of formal leadership positions. In research addressed to this issue, leader behavior becomes the dependent variable and properties of the situation (#1) and relatively stable properties of the person (#2) become the independent variables.

There is no reason to believe that the psychological processes which govern leader behavior are basically any different from those which govern complex behavior in other settings. Furthermore, there is strong a priori evidence that a theory which attempts to account for the behavior of a leader with only information concerning his personal attributes (such as his LPC score) or only of the situation he is confronting is automatically limited to explaining only a small portion of the variance.

Even in studies like those conducted at Ohio State there has been a strong temptation to think of a leader's score on the variables consideration and initiating structure as measured by the LBDQ as reflecting a property, trait, or style which *he possesses* rather

than as a result of the operation of both situational and individual difference variables. The potential risk of succumbing to this temptation is evident from the findings of Lowin and Craig (1968), who have shown that leaders exhibit less consideration, more initiating structure and much closer supervision toward subordinates who are low in performance than toward those who are high in performance.

So far we have examined only the first part of Figure 1—the part which is concerned with the explanation of leader behavior. If one starts with leader behavior but moves to the right across that figure, one gets into theoretical issues and empirical findings that are potentially normative in character. Leader behavior (#3) becomes the independent (rather than the dependent) variable and organizational outcomes (#4) become the dependent variables. The relevant processes are organizational rather than psychological. One is concerned here with understanding the nature of the actions which are required from the leader in guiding the system toward the achievement of its external objectives.

Evidence, presented earlier, to the effect that the relationship between leader behavior and group or organizational performance varied with the situation makes it necessary to include the situation in our schematic figure as a set of moderating variables which interact with leader behavior in determining organizational outcomes. The situation not only influences the patterns of leader behavior which will be exhibited but also influences the consequences of that behavior. In view of the potential differences between the specific situational variables which may be operating in the normative and descriptive analyses, we have chosen to use a different designation (#1a) to represent the former.

Using Figure 1, it is possible to depict the differences between the various approaches to the study of leadership that have been examined so far. The conception of leadership as a personality trait assumed that organizational outcomes (#4) were a function of personal attributes of the leader (#2); the search for effective leader behaviors assumed that organizational outcomes (#4) were a function of leader behavior (#3), and Fiedler's contingency model views organizational outcomes (#4) as a joint function of personal attributes (#2) and situational variables (#1a). In contrast, we are proposing the need for descriptive models in which leader behavior (#3) is treated as a joint function of situational variables (#1) and personal attributes (#2) and normative models in which organizational outcomes (#4) are a function of leader behavior (#3) and situational variables (#1a).

To illustrate the form that such models could take and the research methods that could be employed in their development, the remainder of this paper will deal with an example. For the last few years, the author has been interested in the determinants and consequences of participation in decision making. A major research program has been conducted which is consistent with the framework shown in Figure 1. The work is not intended to be an exhaustive treatment of leadership but does provide a concrete example of the directions which we believe to be important.

A NORMATIVE MODEL OF PARTICIPATION IN DECISION MAKING

One of the most persistent and controversial issues in the study of leadership concerns participation by subordinates in decision making. Many models of the leadership process have been autocratic in nature. The leader makes decisions within his area of freedom, issues orders or directives for his subordinates, and monitors their performance to ensure compliance with his directives. Most behavioral scientists, on the other hand, have argued for more opportunities for subordinates to participate in the decision-making process. Pointing to evidence

of restriction of output and lack of involvement under traditional leadership methods, they have argued for greater influence in decision making on the part of those who are held responsible for executing the decision. On matters affecting his entire unit the leader should not make decisions autocratically, but should instead meet with his subordinates as a group, share problems with them and encourage them to arrive at joint or consensual solutions to these problems. Such is the essence of Likert's System 4 (1967) and Maier's (1955, 1963) process of group decision.

The research evidence provides some but not overwhelming support for the efficacy of participative management. Comprehensive reviews of the literature appear elsewhere (Lowin, 1968; Vroom, 1970; Wood, 1973), so only a few of the more major studies will be cited here. On the positive side, field experiments by Coch and French (1948), Bavelas (reported in French, 1950), Strauss (reported in Whyte, 1955) and Marrow, Bower, and Seashore (1967) have shown that impressive increases in productivity can be brought about by giving employees a greater opportunity to participate in decision making. On the other hand, experiments by French, Israel, and As (1960) and Fleishman (1965) yielded no significant difference in production between workers who did and those who did not participate in decisions regarding the introduction of changes in work methods. To complicate the picture even further, Morse and Reimer (1956) found a significant increase in productivity following each of two experimental programs, one of which increased participation in decision making by rank and file workers while the other increased hierarchical control.

The conclusion appears inescapable that participation in decision making, like all of the other leader's behaviors and traits, has consequences which vary from one situation to another. Given its importance to the study of leadership, participation in decision making would appear to be an obvious candidate for the development of a normative model which would point to the kinds of situations in which various degrees of participation in decision making would be indicated by available research evidence. Such a model has been developed, and it, along with models of related aspects of the leadership process, are described in Vroom and Yetton (1973). A complete exposition of their normative model is beyond the scope of this chapter, and only the essential features will be presented here. We begin by examining the assumptions which guided the development of the model.

1. The normative model should be constructed in such a way as to be of potential value to managers or leaders in determining which leadership methods they should employ in each of the various situations that they encounter in carrying out their formal leadership roles. Consequently, it should be operational in that the behavior of the leader should be specified unambiguously.

2. No single leadership method is applicable to all situations; the function of a normative model should be to provide a framework for the analysis of situational requirements which can be translated into prescriptions of leadership styles.

3. The most appropriate unit for the analysis of the situation is the particular problem to be solved and the context in which the problem occurs.

4. The leadership method used in response to one situation should not constrain the method or style used in other situations.

5. There are a number of discrete social processes by which organizational problems can be translated into solutions, and these processes vary in terms of the potential amount of participation by subordinates in the problem-solving process. Choice among these processes can be made by the leader for all problems falling within his area of discretion or freedom.

6. The applicable processes or leadership methods vary with the number of the leader's subordinates who are affected by the decision. In particular, one should distinguish between individual problems (affecting only one of the subordinates reporting to the leader) and group problems (affecting all or a substantial subset of the leader's subordinates).

A discussion and elaboration of each of these assumptions may be found in Vroom and Yetton (1973) including examples of both group and individual problems. The model to be developed here deals exclusively with group problems. The taxonomy of leadership methods (or decision processes) deemed applicable to these problems is shown below:

AI: You solve problem or make decision yourself using information available to you at that time.

AII: You obtain necessary information from subordinates, then decide on solution to problem yourself. You may or may not tell subordinates what the problem is in getting the information from them. The role played by your subordinates in making the decision is clearly one of providing the necessary information to you, rather than generating or evaluating alternative solutions.

CI: You share the problem with relevant subordinates individually, getting their ideas and suggestions without bringing them together as a group. Then *you* make the decision, which may or may not reflect your subordinates' influence.

CII: You share the problem with your subordinates as a group, collectively obtaining their ideas and suggestions. Then you make the decision, which may or may not reflect your subordinates' influence.

GII: You share the problem with your subordinates as a group. Together you generate and evaluate alternatives and attempt to reach agreement (consensus) on a solution. Your role is much like that of chairman. You do not try to influence the group to adopt "your" solution and you are willing to accept and implement any solution which has the support of the entire group.

Conceptual and Empirical Basis of the Model

A model designed to regulate, in some rational way, choices among the leadership styles shown above should be based on sound empirical evidence concerning the likely consequences of the styles. The more complete the empirical base of knowledge, the greater the certainty with which one can develop the model and the greater will be its usefulness. To aid in this analysis of existing evidence, it is important to distinguish three classes of outcomes which bear on the ultimate effectiveness of decisions. These are:

1. The quality or rationality of the decision.

2. The acceptance or commitment on the part of subordinates to execute the decision effectively.

3. The amount of time required to make the decision.

The evidence regarding the effects of participation on each of these outcomes or consequences has been reviewed elsewhere (Vroom, 1970). He concluded that:

The results suggest that allocating problem-solving and decision-making tasks to entire groups as compared with the leader or manager in charge of the groups requires a greater investment of man hours but produces higher acceptance of decisions and a higher probability that the decisions will be executed efficiently. Differences between these two methods in quality of decisions and in elapsed time are inconclusive and probably highly variable. ... It would be naive to think that group decision making is always more "effective" than autocratic decision making, or *vice versa;* the relative effectiveness of these two extreme methods depends both on the weights attached to quality, acceptance, and time variables and on differences in amounts of these outcomes resulting from these methods, neither of which is invariant from one situation to another. The critics and proponents of participative manage-ment would do well to direct their efforts toward identifying the properties of situations in which different decision-making approaches are effective rather than wholesale condemnation or deification of one approach. (Vroom, 1970, pp. 239–240)

Stemming from this review, an attempt has been made to identify these properties of the situation or problem which will be the basic elements in the model. These problem attributes are of two types: (1) those which specify the importance for a particular problem of quality and acceptance considerations (see A and D below) and (2) those which, on the basis of available evidence, have a high probability of moderating the effects of participation on each of these considerations (see B, C, E, F, and G below). The following are the problem attributes used in the present form of the model. The reader interested in a more complete exposition of these attributes should see Vroom and Yetton (1973).

A. The importance of the quality of the decision.

B. The extent to which the leader possesses sufficient information/expertise to make a high quality decision by himself.

C. The extent to which the problem is structured.

D. The extent to which acceptance or commitment on the part of subordinates is critical to effective implementation of the decision.

E. The prior probability that the leader's autocratic decision will receive acceptance by subordinates.

F. The extent to which subordinates are motivated to attain organizational goals as represented in the objectives explicit in the statement of the problem.

G. The extent to which subordinates are likely to be in disagreement over preferred solutions.

Table 1 shows the same seven problem attributes expressed in the form of questions which might be used by a leader in diagnosing a particular problem prior to choosing a decision process. In phrasing the questions,

TABLE 1
PROBLEM ATTRIBUTES

Question A
Is there a quality requirement such that one solution is likely to be more rational than another?
Question B
Do I have sufficient information to make a high quality decision?
Question C
Is the problem structured?
Question D
Is acceptance of decision by subordinates critical to effective implementation?
Question E
If you were to make the decision by yourself, is it reasonably certain that it would be accepted by your subordinates?
Question F
Do subordinates share the organizational goals to be obtained in solving this problem?
Question G
Is conflict among subordinates likely in preferred solutions?

technical language has been held to a minimum. Furthermore, the questions have been phrased in Yes-No form, translating the continuous variables defined above into dichotomous variables. For example, instead of attempting to determine how important the decision quality is to the effectiveness of the decision (attribute A), the leader is asked in the first question to judge whether there is any quality component to the problem. Similarly, the difficult task of specifying exactly how much information the leader possesses that is relevant to the decision (attribute B) is reduced to a simple judgment by the leader concerning whether he has sufficient information to make a high quality decision.

Expressing what are obviously continuous variables in dichotomous form greatly simplifies the problem of developing a model incorporating these attributes which can be used by leaders. It sidesteps the problem of scaling each problem attribute and reduces the complexities of the judgments required of leaders.

It has been found that managers can diagnose a situation quite quickly and accurately by answering this set of seven questions concerning it. But how can such responses generate a prescription concerning the most effective leadership style or decision process? The judgments that one makes concerning the status of a given problem on each of the problem's attributes can be used to define a set of feasible alternatives. This occurs through a set of rules which eliminate decision processes from the feasible set under certain specifiable conditions.

The rules are intended to protect both the quality and acceptance of the decision. In the form of the model presented here, there are three rules which protect decision quality and four which protect acceptance. The seven rules are presented below:

1. *The Information Rule.* If the quality of the decision is important and if the leader does not possess enough information or expertise to solve the problem by himself, AI is eliminated from the feasible set. (Its use risks a low-quality decision.)

2. *The Goal Congruence Rule.* If the quality of the decision is important and if the subordinates do not share the organizational goals to be obtained in solving the problem, GII is eliminated from the feasible set. (Alternatives that eliminate the leader's final control over the decision reached may jeopardize the quality of the decision.)

3. *The Unstructured Problem Rule.* In decisions in which the quality of the decision is important, if the leader lacks the necessary information or expertise to solve the problem by himself, and if the problem is unstructured, that is, he does not know exactly what information is needed and where it is located, the method used must provide not only for him to collect the information but to do so in an efficient and effective manner. Methods that involve interaction among all subordinates with full knowledge of the problem are likely to be both more efficient and more likely to generate a high-quality solution to the problem. Under these conditions, AI, AII, and CI are eliminated from the feasible set. (AI does not provide for him to collect the necessary information, and AII and CI

represent more cumbersome, less effective, and less efficient means of bringing the necessary information to bear on the solution of the problem than methods that do permit those with the necessary information to interact.)

4. *The Acceptance Rule.* If the acceptance of the decision by subordinates is critical to effective implementation, and if it is not certain that an autocratic decision made by the leader would receive that acceptance, AI and AII are eliminated from the feasible set. (Neither provides an opportunity for subordinates to participate in the decision and both risk the necessary acceptance.)

5. *The Conflict Rule.* If the acceptance of the decision is critical, and an autocratic decision is not certain to be accepted, and subordinates are likely to be in conflict or disagreement over the appropriate solution, AI, AII, and CI are eliminated from the feasible set. (The method used in solving the problem should enable those in disagreement to resolve their differences with full knowledge of the problem. Accordingly, under these conditions, AI, AII, and CI, which involve no interaction or only "one-on-one" relationships and, therefore, provide no opportunity for those in conflict to resolve their differences, are eliminated from the feasible set. Their use runs the risk of leaving some of the subordinates with less than the necessary commitment to the final decision.)

6. *The Fairness Rule.* If the quality of decision is unimportant and if acceptance is critical and not certain to result from an autocratic decision, AI, AII, CI, and CII are eliminated from the feasible set. (The method used should maximize the probability of acceptance as this is the only relevant consideration in determining the effectiveness of the decision. Under these circumstances, AI, AII, CI, and CII, which create less acceptance or commitment than GII, are eliminated from the feasible set. To use them is to run the risk of getting less than the needed acceptance of the decision.)

7. *The Acceptance Priority Rule.* If acceptance is critical, not assured by an autocratic decision, and if subordinates share the organizational goals relevant to the problem, AI, AII, CI, and CII are eliminated from the feasible set. (Methods that provide equal partnership in the decision-making process can provide greater acceptance without risking decision quality. Use of any method other than GII results in an unnecessary risk that the decision will not be fully accepted or receive the necessary commitment on the part of subordinates.)

Application of these rules to a problem is aided by their pictorial representation in the form of a decision tree. Figure 2 shows a simple decision tree which serves this purpose. The problem attributes are shown at the top of the figure. To apply the rules to a particular problem one starts at the left-hand side and works toward the right, asking oneself the question pertaining to any box that is encountered. When a terminal node is reached, the number designates the problem type which in turn designates a set of methods which remains feasible after the rules have been applied. It can be seen that this method of representing the decision tree generates thirteen terminal nodes or problem types. Problem type is a nominal variable designating classes of problems generated by the paths which lead to the terminal nodes. Thus, all problems which have no quality requirements and in which acceptance is not critical are of Type 1; all problems which have no quality requirement, in which acceptance is critical, and the prior probability of acceptance of the leader's decision is low are defined as Type 2; and so on.[3]

The feasible set for each problem type is also shown in Figure 2. It can be seen that there are some problem types for which only one method remains in the feasible set, others for which two methods remain feasible, and still others for which

---

[3] For reasons too complex to be described here, problem Type 6 is divided into two sub-types (6a and 6b), each representing a different terminal node.

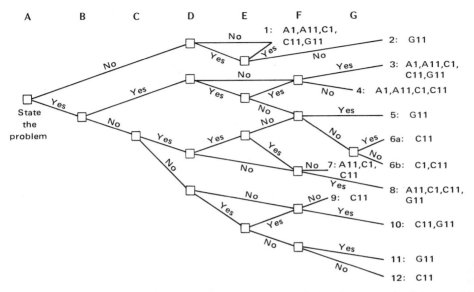

A. Is there a quality requirement such that one solution is likely to be more rational than another?
B. Do I have sufficient info to make a high quality decision?
C. Is the problem structured?
D. Is acceptance of decision by subordinates critical to effective implementation?
E. If I were to make the decision by myself, is it reasonably certain that it would be accepted by my subordinates?
F. Do subordinates share the organizational goals to be attained in solving this problem?
G. Is conflict among subordinates likely in preferred solutions?

Figure 2. Decision-process flow chart for group problems.

five methods remain feasible. It should be recalled that the feasible set is defined as the set of methods which remains after all those which violate rules designated to protect the quality and acceptance of the decision have been excluded.

Choosing Among Alternatives in the Feasible Set

When more than one method remains in the feasible set, there are a number of alternative decision rules which might dictate the choice among them. One, which will be examined in greatest depth, utilizes the number of man-hours used in solving the problem as the basis for choice. Given a set of methods with equal likelihood of meeting both quality and acceptance requirements for the decision, it chooses that method which requires the least investment in man-

hours. This is deemed to be the method furthest to the left (and most autocratic) within the feasible set. Thus, if AI, AII, CI, CII, and GII are all feasible as in problem Type 1, AI would be the method chosen.

This decision rule for choosing among alternatives in the feasible set results in the prescription of each of the five decision processes. AI is prescribed for three problem types (1, 3, and 4); AII is prescribed for two problem types (7 and 8); CI is prescribed for only one problem type (6b); CII is prescribed for four problem types (6a, 9, 10, and 12); and GII is prescribed for three problem types (2, 5, and 11). The relative frequency with which the five decision processes would be prescribed for any single leader would, of course, be dependent on the distribution of problem types he encounters in his role.

The "minimize man-hours" model seeks

to protect, if relevant, the quality of the decision, to create any necessary acceptance of the decision and to expend the least number of man-hours in the process. In view of its attention to conditions surrounding the making and implementation of a particular decision rather than any long-term considerations, it could be termed a short-term model.

However, it seems likely that leadership methods that may be optimal for short-term results may be different from those that would be optimal over a longer period of time. The manager who uses more participative methods could, in time, develop his or her subordinates, increasing not only the knowledge and talent that they could bring to bear on decisions but also their identification with organization goals. A promising approach to development of a long-term model is one that places less weight on man-hours as the basis for choice of method within the feasible set. With a long-term orientation, one would be interested in the development of subordinates rather than the conservation of time. If both time and development increase with participation, a model that places no weight on time and exclusive weight on development would choose the most participative process (i.e., the one farthest to the right) within the feasible set. The reader interested in examples of how the model can be applied to actual problem-solving or decision-making situations and in differences between short- and long-term solutions in these situations is referred to Vroom (1974) and Vroom and Yetton (1973) or Vroom and Jago (1974).

DESCRIPTIVE STUDIES OF PARTICIPATION IN DECISION MAKING

The model shown in Figure 2 purports to be normative, not descriptive. It consequently utilizes variables (#3, 4, and 1a) shown at the right-hand side of Figure 1. But how do leaders really behave? Do they employ a single leadership style or decision-making process independent of the nature of the situation which confronts them? If not, what factors do influence the degree to which they share their power with their subordinates? Are these factors similar to those used in the normative model?

These questions are a few of those that have been explored in a large-scale research program reported in detail in Vroom and Yetton (1973). In one of the principal research methods used, leaders have been asked to describe, in written form, a recent problem which they have had to solve in carrying out their leadership role. They have then been asked to specify the method (AI, AII, CI, CII, or GII) which came closest to the one which they actually used in dealing with that problem. Finally, to "diagnose" the problem they described, they were asked the set of questions shown in Table 1.

From these "recalled" problems several different sets of cases were selected to provide a second method of answering the questions posed above. These "standardized" sets ranged in size from thirty to fifty-four cases. They covered a wide range of organizational decisions including production scheduling, research and development, quality control, portfolio management, and personnel allocation. Each case depicted a leader (who might be a first line manager, a bank president, or a school principal) with a problem to solve or decision to make. The leader or manager is asked to read each case study and to specify the decision process he would employ if he were the leader confronted with the case. An important feature of this method of investigation stems from the fact that the selection of cases for inclusion is based on a multi-factorial experimental design in which each of the problem attributes is varied systematically. The nature of this design permits the determination of the effects of problem attributes on the degree to which a leader shares his decision-making power with his subordinates.

To date several thousand managers have

been studied using research methods incorporating either "recalled" or "standardized" problems. Perhaps the most striking contribution of this research program is the weakening of the widespread view that participativeness is a general trait that individual managers exhibit in different amounts. To be sure, there were differences *among* managers in their general tendencies to utilize participative methods as opposed to autocratic ones. On the standardized problems, these differences accounted for about 10 percent of the total variance in the decision processes observed. These differences in behavior between managers, however, were small in comparison with differences *within* managers. On the standardized problems, no manager has indicated that he would use the same decision process on all problems or decisions, and most use all five methods under some circumstances.

Some of this variance in behavior within managers can be attributed to widely shared tendencies to respond to some situations by sharing power and others by retaining it. It makes more sense to talk about participative and autocratic situations than it does to talk about participative and autocratic managers. In fact, on the standardized problems, the variance in behavior among problems or cases is about three times as large as the variance among managers!

What are the characteristics of an autocratic as opposed to a participative situation? An answer to this question would constitute a partial descriptive model of this aspect of the decision-making process and has been our goal in much of the research that we have conducted. From our observations of behavior on both recalled problems and on standardized problems, it is clear that the decision-making process employed by a typical manager is influenced by a large number of factors, many of which also show up in the normative model. Following are several conclusions empirically substantiated by our research: Managers use decision processes providing less opportunity for participation (1) when they possess all the necessary information than when they lack some of the needed information, (2) when the problem they face is well-structured rather than unstructured, (3) when their subordinates' acceptance of the decision is not critical for the effective implementation of the decision or when the prior probability of acceptance of an autocratic decision is high, and (4) when the personal goals of their subordinates are *not* congruent with the goals of the organization as manifested in the problem.

These general conclusions reflect relatively common or widely shared ways of dealing with organizational problems. Our results also strongly suggest that there are ways of "tailoring" one's approach to the situation that distinguish managers from one another. Theoretically, these can be thought of as differences among managers in decision rules that they employ about when to encourage participation. Statistically, they are represented as interactions between situational variables and personal characteristics.

Consider, for example, two managers who have identical distributions of the use of the five decision processes on a set of thirty cases. In a sense, they are equally participative (or autocratic). However, the situations in which they permit or encourage participation in decision making on the part of their subordinates may be very different. One may restrict the participation of his subordinates to decisions without a quality requirement, whereas the other may restrict their participation to problems with a quality requirement. The former would be more inclined to use participative decision processes (like GII) on such decisions as what color the walls should be painted or when the company picnic should be held. The latter would be more likely to encourage participation in decision making on decisions that have a clear and demonstrable impact on the organization's success in achieving its external goals.

Use of the standardized problem set permits the assessment of such differences in decision rules that govern choices among decision-making processes. Since the cases are selected in accordance with an experimental design, they can indicate differences in the behavior of managers attributable not only to the existence of a quality requirement in the problem but also in the effects of acceptance requirements, conflict, information requirements, and the like.

The research using both recalled and standardized problems has also enabled us to examine similarities and differences between the behavior of the normative model and the behavior of a typical manager. Such an analysis reveals, at the very least, what behavioral changes could be expected if managers began using the normative model as the basis for choosing their decision-making processes.

A typical manager says he would (or did) use exactly the same decision process as the "minimize man-hours" model in about 40 percent of the situations. In two-thirds of the situations, his behavior is consistent with the feasible set of methods proposed in the model. In other words, in about one-third of the situations his behavior violates at least one of the seven rules underlying the model.

The four rules designed to protect the acceptance or commitment of the decision have substantially higher probabilities of being violated than do the three rules designed to protect the quality or rationality of the decision. One of the acceptance rules, the Fairness Rule (Rule 6) is violated about three quarters of the time that it could have been violated. On the other hand, one of the quality rules, the Information Rule (Rule 1) is violated in only about 3 percent of occasions in which it is applicable. If we assume for the moment that these two sets of rules have equal validity, these findings strongly suggest that the decisions made by typical managers are more likely to prove ineffective due to deficiencies of acceptance by subordinates than due to deficiencies in decision quality.

Another striking difference between the behavior of the "minimize man-hours" model and of the typical manager lies in the fact that the former shows far greater variance with the situation. If a typical manager voluntarily used the model as the basis for choosing his methods of making decisions, he would become both more autocratic and more participative. He would employ autocratic methods more frequently in situations in which his subordinates were unaffected by the decision and participative methods more frequently when his subordinates' cooperation and support were critical and/or their information and expertise were required.

It should be noted that the typical manager to whom we have been referring is merely a statistical average of the several thousand who have been studied over the last three or four years. There is a great deal of variance around that average. As evidenced by their behavior on standardized problems, some managers are already behaving in a manner that is highly consistent with the model, while others' behavior is clearly at variance with it.

TECHNOLOGICAL IMPLICATIONS

Earlier in this chapter, we noted the potential contribution to society of methods which could aid in the processes of identification and enhancement of leadership in organized human endeavor. For each of the major approaches to the study of leadership-the relevant technologies were discussed. The research program just summarized was conducted in order to shed new light on the causes and consequences of decision-making processes used by leaders in formal organizations. In the course of the research, it became apparent that the data collection procedures, with appropriate additions and modifications, might also serve a useful function in leadership development. From this realization evolved an important by-product of the research activities—a new approach to leadership training based on the concepts in the normative model and the empirical methods of the descriptive research.

A detailed description of this training program and of initial attempts to evaluate its effectiveness is beyond the scope of this chapter but may be found in Vroom and Yetton (1973, Chap. 8). It is based on the premise that one critical skill required of all leaders is the ability to adapt their behavior to the demands of the situation and that a component of this skill involves selecting the appropriate decision-making process for each problem or decision he or she confronts. The purpose of the program is *not* to "train" managers to use the model in their everyday decision-making activities. Instead, the model serves as a device for encouraging managers to examine their leadership styles and for coming to a conscious realization of their own, often implicit, choices among decision processes, including their similarity and dissimilarity with the model. By helping managers to become aware of their present behavior and of alternatives to it, the training provides a basis for rethinking one's leadership style to be more consistent with goals and objectives. Succinctly, the training is intended to transform habits into choices rather than to program a leader with a particular method of making choices.

A fundamental part of the program in its present form is the use of a set of standardized cases previously described in connection with the descriptive phase of the research. Each participant specifies the decision process to be employed if he or she were the leader described in the case. Responses to the entire set of cases are processed by the computer, which generates a highly detailed analysis of the leadership style. The responses for all participants in a single course typically are processed simultaneously, permitting the calculation of differences between the person and others in the same program.

In its present form, a single computer printout for a person consists of three 15″ × 11″ pages, each filled with graphs and tables highlighting different features of behavior. Understanding the results requires a detailed knowledge of the concepts underlying the model, something already developed in one of the previous phases of the training program. The printout is accompanied by a manual that aids in explaining the results and provides suggested steps to be followed in extracting full meaning from the printout.

Following are a few of the questions that the printout answers:

• How autocratic or participative am I in my dealings with subordinates in comparison with other participants in the program?

• What decision processes do I use more or less frequently than the average?

• How close does my behavior come to that of the model? How frequently does my behavior agree with the feasible set? What evidence is there that my leadership style reflects the pressure of time as opposed to a concern with the development of my subordinates? How do I compare in these respects with other participants in the class?

• What rules do I violate most frequently and least frequently? On what cases did I violate these rules? Does my leadership style reflect more concern with getting decisions that are high in quality or with getting decisions that are accepted?

• What circumstances cause me to behave in an autocratic fashion; what circumstances cause me to behave participatively? In what respects is the way in which I attempt to vary my behavior with the demands of the situation similar to that of the model?

When a typical manager receives the printout, he or she immediately tries to understand what this means about himself or herself. After most of the major results are understood, this manager goes back to the set of cases to reread those in which he or she has violated rules. Typically, managers show an interest in discussing and comparing their results with others in the program, so groups of four to six persons gather to do this—a process which has been included as part of the program.

Recently, we have asked selected groups of managers to distribute problem sets to their immediate subordinates at the same time the manager himself responds to the cases (Jago & Vroom, 1974). The subordinates, assured of their anonymity, are asked to read the cases and decide how they think their superior would respond to each situation. Such data, in aggregate form, are then incorporated into the manager's individualized feedback. This procedure may prove an even more effective management development technique since frequent discrepancies between superior self-reports and subordinate descriptions can challenge the manager to examine more fully perceptual influences in his leader-member relationships.

It should be emphasized that this method of providing feedback on leadership style is just one part of the total training experience which encompasses from three to five successive days. To date, no long-term evaluations of its effectiveness have been undertaken, but initial results appear quite promising.

CONCLUSION

After describing the theoretical and empirical underpinnings of principal approaches to the study of leadership in organized human endeavor, a new approach to these issues was described. This approach was based on a clear-cut distinction between normative and descriptive models. The possible contribution of this research program to the technology of leadership development was also discussed.

The research reported in the second part of this paper deals with only one facet of leader behavior—the decision processes that should be and are used by the leader in resolving group problems, particularly the degree to which those processes provide opportunities for subordinate participation in the solution or decision reached. Further work reported in Vroom and Jago (1974) has extended the analyses, both normative and descriptive, to cover individual problems affecting only one of the leader's subordinates. A normative model has been developed to cover both kinds of problems and

descriptive research conducted on the determinants of power-sharing approaches to individual problems, including delegation. The results, too numerous to report here, reinforce the conclusions made, particularly with regard to the relative importance of situational factors and personal traits in the determination of leader behavior. It is believed that the basic framework presented in Figure 1 can also be useful in guiding investigation of other facets of the leadership process.

Some might argue that it is premature for social scientists to attempt to be prescriptive. Our knowledge is too little and the issues too complex to warrant explicit normative models dealing with matters such as leadership style. It is also true, however, that leaders are facing daily the task of diagnosing the critical elements in situations which they face and responding effectively to them. Is it likely that models which encourage them to deal analytically with the forces impinging upon them and which are consistent with an admittedly imperfect research base would produce less rational choices than those which they do make? The criterion for social utility is not perfection but improvement over present practice.

Social scientists are increasingly being prescriptive not only about issues of leadership style, but also on such matters as job design, training methods, and compensation systems. Too frequently, in the view of the present author, their prescriptions for actions, whether it be group decision making, job enrichment, sensitivity training, or piecerate methods of payments, are not based on a systematic analysis of the situation in a manner which would point to the costs and benefits of available alternatives.

Perhaps the most convincing argument for efforts to construct normative models is the fact that, in developing and using them, their weaknesses can be identified. Insofar as these weaknesses stem from a lack of basic knowledge, this deficiency can be remedied through further research. A strong case can be made for the continued interplay between the worlds of practice and social science on the basis of their mutual contributions to one another.

REFERENCES

Ashour, A. S. The contingency model of leadership effectiveness: An evaluation. *Organizational Behavior and Human Performance*, 1973, 9, 339–355.

Bales, R. F. *Interaction process analysis: A method for the study of small groups*. Reading, Mass.: Addison-Wesley, 1949.

Bass, B. M. Leadership opinions as forecasts of supervisory success. *Journal of Applied Psychology*, 1956, 40, 345–346.

Bass, B. M. Leadership opinions as forecasts of supervisory success: A replication. *Personnel Psychology*, 1958, 11, 515–518.

Bass, B. M. *Leadership, psychology, and organizational behavior*. New York: Harper and Row, 1960.

Blake, R., & Mouton, J. *The managerial grid: Key orientation for achieving production through people*. Houston: Gulf, 1964.

Cartwright, D., & Zander, A. *Group dynamics*. (3rd ed.) New York: Harper and Row, 1968.

Coch, L., & French, J. R. P. Jr. Overcoming resistance to change. *Human Relations*, 1948, 1, 512–532.

Cummins, R. C. Relationship of initiating structure and job performance as moderated by consideration. *Journal of Applied Psychology*, 1971, 55, 489–490.

Fiedler, F. E. The effect of leadership and cultural heterogeneity on group performance: A test of the contingency model. *Journal of Experimental Social Psychology*, 1966, 2, 237–264.

Fiedler, F. E. *A theory of leadership effectiveness*. New York: McGraw-Hill, 1967.

Fiedler, F. E. The contingency model—A reply to Ashour. *Organizational Behavior and Human Performance*, 1973, 9, 356–368.

Fiedler, F. E., & Chemers, M. *Leadership and effective management*. Glenview, Ill.: Scott, Foresman, 1974.

Fleishman, E. A. A leader behavior description for industry. In R. M. Stogdill & A. E. Coons (Eds.), *Leader behavior: Its description and measurement*. Columbus: Ohio State University, Bureau of Business Research, Research Monograph No. 88, 1957, 103–119. (a)

Fleishman, E. A. The leadership opinion questionnaire. In R. M. Stogdill & A. E. Coons (Eds.), *Leader behavior: Its description and measurement*. Columbus: Ohio State University, Bureau of Business Research, Research Monograph No. 88, 1957, 120–133. (b)

Fleishman, E. A. Attitude versus skill factors in work group productivity. *Personnel Psychology*, 1965, 18, 253–266.

Fleishman, E. A. Twenty years of consideration and structure. In E. A. Fleishman & J. G. Hunt (Eds.), *Current developments in the study of leadership*. Carbondale: Southern Illinois University Press, 1973.

Fleishman, E. A., & Harris, E. F. Patterns of leadership behavior related to employee grievances and turnover. *Personnel Psychology*, 1962, 15, 43–56.

Fleishman, E. A., Harris, E. F., & Burtt, H. E. *Leadership and supervision in industry*. Columbus: Ohio State University, Bureau of Educational Research, 1955.

French, J. R. P. Jr. Field experiments: Changing group productivity. In J. G. Miller (Ed.), *Experiments in social process: A symposium on social psychology*. New York: McGraw-Hill, 1950.

French, J. R. P. Jr., Israel, J., & Ås, D. An experiment on participation in a Norwegian factory. *Human Relations*, 1960, 13, 3–19.

Gibb, C. A. Leadership. In G. Lindzey & E. Aronson (Eds.), *Handbook of social psychology*. Reading, Mass.: Addison-Wesley, 1969, 4, 205–282.

Graen, G., Alvares, K., Orris, J. B., & Martella, J. A. Contingency model of leadership effectiveness: Antecedent and evidential results. *Psychological Bulletin*, 1970, 74, 285–296.

Graen, G., Dansereau, F., & Minami, T. Dysfunctional leadership styles. *Organizational Behavior and Human Performance*, 1972, 7, 216–236.

Graen, G., Orris, J. B., & Alvares, K. Contingency model of leadership effectiveness: Some experimental results. *Journal of Applied Psychology*, 1971, 55, 196–201.

Halpin, A. W. The leader behavior and effectiveness of aircraft commanders. In R. M. Stogdill & A. E. Coons (Eds.), *Leader behavior: Its description and measurement*. Columbus: Ohio State University, Bureau of

Business Research, Research Monograph No. 88, 1957, 52–64.

Halpin, A. W., & Winer, B. J. A factorial study of the leader behavior descriptions. In R. M. Stogdill & A. E. Coons (Eds.), *Leader behavior: Its description and measurement.* Columbus: Ohio State University, Bureau of Business Research, Research Monograph No. 88, 1957, 39–51.

Hemphill, J. K., & Coons, A. E. Development of the leader behavior description questionnaire. In R. M. Stogdill & A. E. Coons (Eds.), *Leader behavior: Its description and measurement.* Columbus: Ohio State University, Bureau of Business Research, Research Monograph No. 88, 1957, 6–38.

Hill, W. The validation and extension of Fiedler's theory of leadership effectiveness. *Academy of Management Journal,* 1969, 33–47.

House, R. J. A path-goal theory of leader effectiveness. In E. A. Fleishman & J. G. Hunt (Eds.), *Current developments in the study of leadership.* Carbondale: Southern Illinois University Press, 1973.

Hunt, J. G. A test of the leadership contingency model in three organizations. *Organizational Behavior and Human Performance,* 1967, 2, 290–308.

Jago, A. G., & Vroom, V. H. Perceptions of leadership style: Superior and subordinate descriptions of decision-making behavior. Unpublished report, School of Organization and Management, Yale University, New Haven, 1974.

Katz, D., Maccoby, N., Gurin, G., & Floor, L. G. *Productivity, supervision, and morale among railroad workers.* Ann Arbor: University of Michigan, Institute for Social Research, 1951.

Katz, D., Maccoby, N., & Morse, N. C. *Productivity, supervision, and morale in an office situation.* Ann Arbor: University of Michigan, Institute for Social Research, 1950.

Kerr, S., Schriesheim, C. A., Murphy, C. J., & Stogdill, R. M. Toward a contingency theory of leadership based upon the consideration and initiating structure literature. *Organizational Behavior and Human Performance,* 1974, 12, 62–82.

Lewin, K. *Field theory in social science.* D. Cartwright, Ed. New York: Harper and Row, 1951.

Likert, R. *New patterns of management.* New York: McGraw-Hill, 1961.

Likert, R. *The human organization.* New York: McGraw-Hill, 1967.

Lowin, A. Participative decision making: A model, literature, critique, and prescriptions for research. *Organizational Behavior and Human Performance,* 1968, 3, 68–106.

Lowin, A., & Craig, J. R. The influence of level of performance on managerial style: An experimental object-lesson in the ambiguity of correlational data. *Organizational Behavior and Human Performance,* 1968, 3, 440–458.

McMahon, T. The contingency theory: Logic and method revisited. *Personnel Psychology,* 1972, 25, 697–710.

Maier, N. R. F. *Psychology in industry.* (2nd ed.) Boston: Houghton Mifflin, 1955.

Maier, N. R. F. *Problem-solving discussions and conferences: Leadership methods and skills.* New York: McGraw-Hill, 1963.

Mann, R. D. A review of the relationship between personality and performance in small groups. *Psychological Bulletin,* 1959, 56, 241–270.

Marrow, A. J., Bowers, D. G., & Seashore, S. E. *Management by participation.* New York: Harper and Row, 1967.

Mitchell, T. R. Leader complexity, leadership style, and group performance. Unpublished doctoral dissertation, University of Illinois, Urbana, 1969.

Morse, N. C., & Reimer, E. The experimental change of a major organizational variable. *Journal of Abnormal and Social Psychology,* 1956, 52, 120–129.

Rambo, W. W. The construction and analysis of a leadership behavior rating form. *Journal of Applied Psychology,* 1958, 42, 409–415.

Seeman, M. A comparison of general and specific leader behavior descriptions. In R. M. Stogdill & A. E. Coons (Eds.), *Leader behavior: Its description and measurement.* Columbus: Ohio State University, Bureau of Business Research, Research Monograph No. 88, 1957, 86–102.

Shartle, C. L., & Stogdill, R. M. *Studies in naval leadership.* Columbus: Ohio State University, 1952.

Shiflett, S. C. The contingency model of leadership effectiveness: Some implications of its statistical and methodological properties. *Behavioral Science,* 1973, 18, 429–440.

Shiflett, S. C. Stereotyping and esteem for one's best preferred co-worker. *Journal of Social Psychology,* 1974, 93, 55–65.

Stogdill, R. M. Personal factors associated with leadership: A survey of the literature. *Journal of Psychology,* 1948, 25, 35–71.

Vroom, V. H. Industrial social psychology. In G. Lindzey & E. Aronson (Eds.), *Handbook of social psychology.* Reading, Mass.: Addison-Wesley, 1970, 5, 196–268.

Vroom, V. H. A new look at managerial decision making. *Organizational Dynamics,* 1974, 5, 66–80.

Vroom, V. H., & Jago, A. G. Decision making as a social process: Normative and descriptive models of leader behavior. *Decision Sciences,* 1974, 5, 743–769.

Vroom, V. H., & Yetton, P. W. *Leadership and decision making.* Pittsburgh: University of Pittsburgh Press, 1973.

Whyte, W. F. *Money and motivation: An analysis of incentives in industry.* New York: Harper and Row, 1955.

Wood, M. T. Power relationships and group decision making in organizations. *Psychological Bulletin,* 1973, 79, 280–293.

CHAPTER 35

Communication in Organizations[1]

LYMAN W. PORTER
University of California, Irvine

KARLENE H. ROBERTS
University of California, Berkeley

COMMUNICATION IS TREATED as an important, under-researched aspect of organizational functioning. The topic is first examined from an organizational theory perspective, followed by a critical review of recent relevant empirical investigations. These studies include those concerning interpersonal communication in organizations, and those pertaining to the organizational context of communication interactions. Methodological aspects of communication studies in the aggregate are discussed, with some suggestions offered concerning future research in this area.

Conclusions include: (1) no adequate theories exist to explain the nature of communication in organization; (2) considerable extrapolation of relevant research findings from other areas (i.e., attitude change) is required when these findings are applied to organizations; (3) available research findings are of limited usefulness in providing guidelines for effective ways to cope with communication problems in organizations; and (4) more varied and more innovative methodologies for studying organizational communication are necessary for future advances in knowledge in this area.

In his valuable review of the literature (published through 1963) on communication in organizations, Guetzkow (1965, p. 569) concluded with two questions: "Do we find in communications in organizations an area of study in which there is special richness in contingent, interactive effects? Or is it merely that a clarifying perspective— which would make the pieces fall more

[1] The preparation of this paper was supported by a grant from the Office of Naval Research, Contract No. N00014-69-A-0200-9001, NR 151-315, to the senior author. The authors wish to thank the following for their valuable assistance in the preparation of this chapter: Gene E. Bretton, Jerry Kaiwi, Charles A. O'Reilly III, and Richard M. Steers.

simply into the whole—remains hidden?" Our answer, some eight years later, is "yes" to both questions: it *is* an area rich in "contingent, interactive effects," and a "clarifying perspective" *does* remain hidden. There have been some advances in the last decade or so with respect to increasing our understanding of communication as it is found in the organizational context, but we are a long way from achieving adequate comprehension.

No one needs to belabor the point that communication is pervasive—and, therefore, important—in organizations. Indeed, as a number of writers suggest, the very extensiveness of communication in the social world in which we live is at the root of the problems involved in studying, analyzing, and understanding it. Since communication is everywhere in organizations, it is consequently very hard to find, in the sense of trying to separate it out as a phenomenon for investigation. It too easily merges into other topical areas such as leadership, interpersonal relations, and the like. And, as we will stress later, the relative paucity of research directly focused on communication in organizational settings suggests that it is the "water" that the organizational research "fish" seem to discover last.

The problems of trying to define "communication" are well illustrated in an article by Dance (1970). His review uncovered some ninety-five definitions of the concept of communication—many of them from articles written for the sole purpose of trying to provide "the" definition. By means of content analysis these definitions were reduced to no fewer than fifteen themes or "conceptual components," such as "interaction," "transfer," "understanding," "process," etc. Dance concluded that it is "difficult to determine whether communication is over-defined or under-defined but its definitions lead [scholars] in different and sometimes contradictory directions." This viewpoint characterizes much of the literature and also indicates the probable futility in attempting to generate a comprehensive

definition that will gain broad support. In everyday usage, the term seems to imply an attempt to share meaning via transmission of messages from senders to receivers.

More useful than trying to produce a universally agreed-upon definition of the term communication is to note a recent observation by Schramm (1971, p. 17): "Let us understand clearly one thing about it: Communication (*human* communication, at least) is *something people do*. It has no life of its own. There is no magic about it except what people in the communication relationship put into it. There is no meaning in a message except what the people put into it.... To understand human communication process one must understand how people relate to each other." [Italics Schramm's.]

In commenting on advances in developing useful models of communication, Schramm (1971, p. 6) draws the sober conclusion that "it would be pleasant to be able to report that [at least two decades] of ...broadening interest and effort [in developing a unified theory of human communication] have coalesced into a simpler, clearer model of communication. This is not the case." Thus, the search for a single overall conceptual scheme that will help clarify communication, especially as it relates to organizations, is likely to prove fruitless. Even the early promise of the information theory approach (Shannon & Weaver, 1949) seems not to have been highly useful for those interested in communication in social contexts. We tend to agree with Chapanis's rather strongly worded comments in this regard (1971, p. 952):

[The literature on communication/information theory] is essentially useless for our purposes. I have yet to find a single instance in which psychological research on communication theory has contributed to the solution of any practical psychological problem. For one thing, the bits, bytes, or chunks of communication theory are like mouthfuls of sawdust. They are as mindless as they are tasteless. Communication theory is concerned only with the randomness or, conversely, with the statistical organization of messages. It ignores completely their sense or content.

The picture with regard to progress in the empirical realm is, perhaps, not much better. It seems clear that the earlier hopes of Guetzkow (1965)—concerning the status of the research literature at the time of his review—have not been realized: "... with the dearth of studies about [communication in] organizations ... one can but join with others in speculation. Let us hope that the writer's foolhardiness [in making extrapolations from research in other settings] will serve to provoke the development of an abundance of insightful, empirical studies in the very near future" (p. 535). In point of fact, rather than increasing, the amount of research on communication in organizations seems to have fallen off considerably since the time of that review. The reasons for this decline are unclear, and it is likely that the phenomenon will prove to be relatively temporary.

There has, of course, been a certain amount of research since the time of Guetzkow's review, and it is that literature which forms the basis of this chapter. (Other past reviews that the reader might also find helpful are Thayer, 1967, on "communication and organization theory," and McLeod, 1967, on "the contribution of psychology to human communication theory.") Although studies published during the past ten years are emphasized, references are occasionally made to earlier work in order to develop the thread of research or conceptualization in a given area. Throughout the chapter the thrust is on *implications* of research and theory for *communication behavior in organizations*—particularly work organizations.

There are multiple ways to organize the rather diverse set of material dealing with communication, all of which have some merit. The sequence adopted for this chapter is the following: First, we examine what organization theorists have said about the role and place of communication. The next two sections review major portions of the relevant studies. One discusses the interpersonal literature germane to person-to-person communication in organizational settings. The other covers studies aimed more specifically at the organizational milieu. These sections are followed by a consideration of some methodological issues and by a set of basic conclusions derived from the review of the material dealt with in this chapter.

WHAT ORGANIZATIONAL THEORY SAYS

Organizational theory should be a good starting point to clarify our thinking about communication in organizations. Unfortunately, writers in this area often are unclear about what they mean by organizational communication. They do give high priority to other organizational phenomena, and we can discern from those priorities the elements of communication systems that they probably regard as worthy of more conceptual and empirical attention. For convenience, four categories of organizational writers (classical-structural, human relations, decision theorists, and process or systems views) are identified. Examples of only a few of the writers who might fall in each category are cited, but in each case we can ask "How might they direct our focus on organizational communication?"[2]

Classical Structuralists

The classical structuralist writers (Fayol, 1949; Gulick & Urwick, 1937; Mooney & Reiley, 1939; Taylor, 1911; Weber, 1947) described organizations as closed and static systems, stressing authority, span of control,

---

[2] A more extensive discussion of a number of points mentioned in the remainder of this section concerning the relationship between organizational theory and organizational communication can be found in Roberts, O'Reilly, Bretton, and Porter (1974), "Organizational Theory and Organizational Communication: A Communication Failure?"

and other internal structural relationships. Work efficiency is the most important outcome variable, and the nonhuman side of organizations is emphasized. For classical theorists, adequate job performance is assured through application of work routines or programs, rigidly followed by employees, and enforced through external controls. Communication is seldom specifically discussed by the classical writers, but researchers extending on their work would be primarily interested in describing formal communication channels and their content in organizations. Downward communication would be emphasized, as would the use of communication systems for authority, co-ordination, and control. One problem in applying the classical principles to organizational communication is that they are too broad and elusive to be of much help.

The Human Relationists

Reacting against the preoccupation of the classical structuralists with formal structure and hierarchy, another group of writers, labeled here the human relations theorists, focused on group interactions and informal communication systems in organizations. McGregor, Argyris, and Likert are illustrative of the human relations approaches to organizational communication. Strangely, McGregor (1960) ignores almost totally the role of communication in developing democratic, participative, theory Y (as opposed to autocratic theory X) management. The closest he came to detailing any aspect of communication appears to be in recognizing its importance as the means by which organizations exercise their power and through which members can develop mutual understanding of one another (McGregor, 1967).

Argyris (1957, 1960) appears to go no further than McGregor in speaking directly to aspects of organizational communication. In emphasizing the frustration which results from conflict between the needs of the mature individual and those of the formal organization, Argyris does note that it leads to a number of adaptive (from the viewpoint of the individual) processes including withdrawal (lack of communication) and the creation of informal interactions to sanction activities not encouraged or permitted by the formal organization. Under what circumstances such informal communication systems might be "disruptive" to ongoing organizational activities needs to be better understood and documented.

Argyris mentions only briefly the potentially dysfunctional aspects to organizations of informal interaction, while Likert (1961, 1967) specifically prescribes the use of informal networks in creating healthier organizations. His early book devotes an entire chapter to problems in organizational communication and highlights some variables, such as lack of trust, that may adversely affect interpersonal communication. In his later book, Likert discusses communication as an aspect of group decision making and of various management systems. He says "communication refers to a variety of kinds of activities" (1967, p. 143), but he is not specific about the composition of these activities. Increased communication within and across hierarchical levels is the key to effective management for Likert: "In system 4 organizations ... the principle of supportive relationships is applied and group methods of decision making are used in a multiple overlapping group structure. These two variables lead ... to intervening variables, such as ... excellent communication. ... These and similar intervening variables in turn lead to low absence and turnover ..." (1967, p. 138).

These theorists are not specific in identifying important components of communication, nor do they suggest testable hypotheses relating communication to other organizational variables. Some of the things they are concerned about, however, do provide potential directions for communication research in organizations. For example, their emphasis on participative leadership, group interaction, motivation, and job satisfaction leads to questions about the kinds of communication factors that may be correlated with various leadership styles and various motivators. More group interaction probably requires numerous communication links which may easily become overloaded. Attempts to develop mutual trust and confidence between superior and subordinate undoubtedly influence the information which is passed up and down inside organizations; the result may be reduced distortion but increased irrelevant information and overload. In contrast with the structural approach, the human relations approach forces us to look at interpersonal behavior inside the organization, and adds to our earlier, more simple view of organizational communication a richness missed by observing only formal communication systems.

Behavioral Decision Theorists

The behavioral decision theorists (not to be confused with the mathematical decision theorists) are considerably more complex in their views of organizations than are the classical structuralists, but they direct less attention to the broad range of human behavior than do the humanists. Those writers describe organizations as functionally specialized, goal-seeking, decision-making structures.

Simon (1945), March and Simon (1958), and Cyert and March (1963) are representative of theorists in this category. In their view, individuals in organizations find it difficult to make complex rational decisions without having limitations imposed upon them by organizations. These limitations include definition of member roles and sub-goals which guide decisions, formal rules, well-defined information channels, and training programs which narrow the range of alternatives considered in decision making. March and Simon (1958) state that the primary purpose of communication in

organizations is to transmit procedural information. They indicate that the information available in communication channels is always incomplete for decision making.

Organizations insure their own adequate functioning by establishing communication systems with specific information classification schemes built into them. "Uncertainty absorption," according to March and Simon, is the successive editing of information which occurs as it passes through these communication systems. This editing is greatest for information which fails to fit the extant classification schemes or for information entering already overloaded systems. Such data must be pushed, shoved, and altered until it fits the system. March and Simon's discussion draws the organizational communication researcher's attention to defining components of information distortion and gatekeeping (decisions to pass on or retain information) and describing how they occur. Neither they nor the structuralists stress the need to examine the influence of individual behavior on communication in organizations.

Process or Systems Theorists

Only a few of the writers who might be called process or systems theorists (Katz & Kahn, 1966; Thompson, 1967; Weick, 1969) have anything specific to say about organizational communication. Process or systems approaches orient us to multivariate views of organizational communication where the environments in which dynamic organizations live are important determinants of their behavior.

Weick (1969) provides an example of this kind of thinking in his extension of the March and Simon notion of uncertainty absorption. Weick states that organizations are information processing organisms existing in uncertain environments. Organizations are mechanisms for uncertainty absorption and must, to remain viable, process messages with the same degree of equivocality-unequivocality as in the message it-self. A testable proposition derived from Weick is that when organizations handle unequivocal information equivocally they lose opportunities, thus leading to atrophy.

In sum, organizational theorists offer surprisingly little *direct* help in our search for ways to view communication in organizations. They provide only a few diverse notions about explicating organizational communication as a variable. From the classical structuralists, we have the rather simplistic observation that communication might be related to organizational efficiency, but little is said to define precisely the relationship. The human relationists move us to consider the role of individual and group behavior in organizational systems, as well as informal (i.e., non-organizationally prescribed) patterns of communication. The decision theorists emphasize the relation of information to the decision-making process and how such information is distributed, altered, and absorbed. Finally, the systems theorists direct attention to forces outside the organization which influence internal communication, and to organizations as information processing mechanisms. Not only are specific discussions of communication relatively infrequent in the organizational theory literature, but also attempts to integrate the different approaches are generally lacking. Such integration is probably a necessary prerequisite to the development of viable theories concerned with organizational communication.

THE INTERPERSONAL MILIEU

Because there is such a large and relatively amorphous literature concerned with interpersonal communication, organizational researchers must ask if any of it is applicable to their interests. For the organizational behaviorist it is artificial to try to understand interpersonal communication without taking into account real life impingements on it. Yet, much of the conceptual and empirical literature on interpersonal communication fails to consider its organiza-

tional implications. The task here, then, is to estimate how definitions, theories, and research investigations, often devoid of the richness of everyday life, might generalize to communication in organizations.

What Is Interpersonal Communication?

Interpersonal communication can be defined as an interactive process which includes an individual's effort to attain meaning and to respond to it. It involves transmission and reception of verbal and nonverbal signs and symbols which come not only from another person, but also from the physical and cultural settings of both sender and receiver.

Models of Interpersonal Communication

The term model is used here loosely. The available frameworks create low fidelity road maps rather than rigorous formulations. Good models provide basic assumptions, identify crucial variables, postulate relationships, and explain and predict phenomena. Such sophisticated models have not yet been developed for interpersonal communication.

The most advanced theorizing about interpersonal communication comes from scholars primarily interested in attitude formation and change. They consequently focus on the antecedents of communication attempts rather than the process of communication. McGuire (1969), who offers a comprehensive and skilled review of the nature of attitudes and attitude change, states that "because of our stress on attitude change through communication from other people a large part [of the work in the area] could alternatively be titled 'social influence process'" (1969, p. 136). Unfortunately, social interaction theories coming from attitude research are not adequate to the task of describing, much less analyzing, the totality of interpersonal communication in organizations. Nor, for that matter, is any other available body of work.

Here we can only indicate some fragmentary conceptualizations which might be expanded and synthesized in future work on organizational communication. Individual researchers or teams generally have been concerned with only one aspect of communication. Some give primary attention to the *interactive process* to which other elements are bound. Some look at a single aspect such as the *meaning* attached to a message, or individual differences in communication behavior. Still others look at communication *effects*. In order to develop comprehensive theories of communication, however, these phenomena need to be simultaneously considered in future conceptual and empirical work.

Where in the interpersonal literature can the organizational researcher most profitably begin to study communication? It may be that he will initially learn the most by looking at those conceptualizations which concern the interaction process, because process is at the heart of the communication act. Other facets, such as meaning and effects, are attached to and ultimately derivable from the communication process.

INTERACTION PROCESS. Attention to the process of interpersonal communication begins with Shannon's (1948) work. His descriptive model identifies the information source, message, transmitter, receiver, and destination as components of the communication system.

While many process models of communication now exist (Thayer, 1967), the two mentioned here may be particularly useful to organizational researchers. Wiener's (1954) feedback principle is a critical aspect of the model proposed by Westley and MacLean (1957). In their model, person *A* abstracts and codes various elements from his environment. He transmits them to person *B*, whose environment may or may not include these elements. *B*'s response provides *A* with feedback about his own communication behavior. Westley and MacLean explain that messages may or may not be transmitted with the intention of modifying the behavior of others. The notion of intention is important in their model and in other

models of verbal communication (Carroll, 1953; Fearing, 1953).

Scholars who want to apply this model to communication in organizations will have to explicate aspects of the internal organizational environment which probably impinge on the communication process. Only after this is done can the degree to which *A* and *B* respond to similar external stimuli be estimated. Examining how feedback specifically modifies interaction is also crucial, particularly because of the frequent use of rewards and punishments in organizations. Even subtle and minimal changes in the behavior of *A* influence *B* if he thinks his rewards are contingent on responding to such subtleties.

Thayer (1967) presents another interaction systems approach to interpersonal communication which he discusses in the context of the complexity of phenomena involved in organizational communication. Four basic levels of analysis are involved in understanding organizational communication. They are the technological, sociological, psychological, and physiological levels. According to Thayer, in any two-person discussion between *A* and *B, A*'s world consists of his self-concept, his concept of *B*, and his concept of the purpose of their communication. *B*'s world contains his conception of these three things. The two persons interact, each processes data consistent with his own world and then behaves on the basis of these data. The behavior is potential data for the other person. Rather than emphasizing interaction as do Westley and MacLean (1957), Thayer focuses primarily on the psychological system of the individuals involved in communication, stating that "if the individual is viewed as a complex information processing system, research on human behavior in organizations could be based upon a view of the individual as the focal point of a set of information vectors that define that individual's functional role in that organization" (1967, p. 97).

One might extend this view to suggest that because of their functional activities, certain organizational units (and certain individuals in those units) act as magnets in communication networks. They attract specific information which is responded to, modified, sent on, or held back. It may be possible to uncover lawful regularities imbedded in such processes.

MEANING. Since message meaning is an underlying factor in any communication, it and communication effects are the two nonprocess conceptual aspects we consider here. Some writers believe that linguistic categorization determines perceptual response and ultimately influences social interactions. Anthropologists (Boas, 1940; Sapir, 1921, 1929) first noted that languages differ grammatically. Whorf (1941) argued that the syntax of a language determines a person's ideas. The various effects of language on an individual's perceptions and on his cognitive organization of the world have not been clearly differentiated. This and related problems in understanding the influence of language on the establishment of meaning are discussed by Tajfel (1969, pp. 71ff.), Carroll and Casagrande (1958), and others.

Osgood and his colleagues (Osgood, Suci, & Tannenbaum, 1957) were also interested in the meaning of verbal behavior. The basic assumption of their well-known semantic differential technique is that meaning can be mapped in semantic space. Applications of Osgood's technique have been made primarily in describing attitude objects. More relevant to the problem of establishing communication meaning, Triandis (1960a, 1960b) showed that individuals with a high degree of semantic similarity communicate more effectively than semantically dissimilar people. Runkel (1956), also interested in problems of categorization, extended verbal meaning to cover larger areas of semantic space. He found that people communicate more effectively the more similar they are in the way they dimensionalize cognitive space. Such similarity exists when people order the objects of their opinions along the same rather than different dimen-

sions. Using these concepts, researchers might assess the degree of effective communication in an organization in relation to the cognitive similarity of people at different levels or in different functional units. (See Triandis, 1959, for one approach to this problem.)

Mehrabian and his co-workers (Mehrabian, 1966; Wiener & Mehrabian, 1968) provide one innovative step in the study of meaning. They present a model for conceptualizing an aspect of verbal meaning they call "immediacy." Immediacy is the degree of psychological separation between a speaker and the object of his communication. For example, separation can be measured by the pronoun and verb tense used by the communicator. Statements which are more personal, subjective, and in the present, are more immediate. The statement "my subordinate and I might decide on this plan" is less immediate and means something different than does "we decided on this plan."

Wiener and Mehrabian suggest relationships of immediacy to other variables. A major hypothesis generated by the model and supported by considerable research is that non-immediacy reflects "increasing degrees of a communicator's negative affect, evaluation, or preference" (1968, p. 38). Perhaps individuals with little cognitive similarity express less immediacy about one another than do those of greater cognitive similarity. While the notion of immediacy appears useful in organizational research, it is unfortunate that a variety of similar constructs of verbal meaning are not available. From these we might be able to develop schemes for the integration of various components of message meaning.

To understand meaning more fully, simultaneous attention must be given both verbal and nonverbal cues. Behavioral researchers have been little concerned with this kind of integration. These two aspects of communication are primarily treated in the literature as independent entities, and one often comes away with the impression that they are mutually exclusive. Even worse, researchers of nonverbal phenomena are usually interested in one kind of cue or another (i.e., the meaning and use of space *or* the meaning of facial expressions), instead of considering how various nonverbal cues combine to provide meaning.

An example of one of the better attempts to integrate the nonverbal research is Argyle's work. Argyle and Kendon (1967) extend a model of sensorimotor performance (Broadbent, 1958; Welford, 1958) to cover social interaction. They say that a primary characteristic of interaction among people is that it is continually under the control of sensory input. Interacting individuals are engaged in skilled performances based on the performers' goals, perceptual input, translation, motor output, and on changes in the outside world which might act as feedback to the performers and determine how they modify their behavior. This model may interface Westley and MacLean's approach, previously discussed, and an interested researcher might work on the points of intersection.

Argyle and Kendon differentiate features of performance which are constant throughout an interaction (e.g., posture) and "set the stage" or provide a backdrop for that interaction, and the dynamic features which have a variety of functions depending on the encounter considered. They note that their analysis is sketchy, but attempts to understand the matrix of verbal and nonverbal cues to which meanings are attached by receivers in any situation seem a necessary step in developing models of interaction appropriate to organizations. Such models should explain how interactive cues combine with situational cues to determine the ultimate meaning to the actors and the responses they make to these meanings.

EFFECT MODELS. The rapidly growing area of attitude research has spawned a number of balance models which have made some con-tribution to communication research. Generally, these models focus on the consequence of making a person aware of conflicting cognitions. Heider (1946, 1958), who developed the first of the balance models, emphasized three elements (the person, another, and an impersonal entity) connected by sentiment or unit relationships such as liking or similarity. The sentiment relationships among the three elements can be consistent or inconsistent with one another.

Extending from Heider, Feather (Feather, 1965; Feather & Jeffries, 1967) presents a balance approach specific to communication effects, and evidence supporting his model. His is the only balance model which specifically discusses communication effects, but it is probably not as applicable to organizational communication as some other developments might be. The balance models generally focus on attitude change in individuals, rather than simultaneously considering the linkages among individuals in organized settings. Neither do balance models consider the simultaneous impact on individuals of messages coming from several others or the implication of various messages when the receiver knows the positions of the senders in the organization. Such models are not broad enough to consider the overall organizational expectations governing what individuals extract from a message and how they respond to it. Finally, balance models do not consider time as a facet of communication. Organizational life goes on and on, and the consequences of a message are probably different if viewed in the long rather than the short time perspective.

Empirical Investigations

The available empirical work on interpersonal communication was sometimes done to develop or support one or another communication model. However, there are also a number of studies not specifically addressed to any given model. Following the communication process from beginning to end, the research can be categorized under source, process, meaning, and effect headings.

SOURCE CHARACTERISTICS. Experimenters concerned with source characteristics have been interested primarily in communicator influence on attitude change, emphasizing the influence of communicator characteristics on communication results rather than on process. McGuire (1969, pp. 177–200) reviews the literature in the area to 1966, discussing different persuasive tactics favored by various (purported rather than actual) sources, methods for studying effects attributable to source variables, and components of source valence.

Source valence probably is the most thoroughly investigated characteristic, and current thinking is summed up in the postulate that the three components of source valence are credibility, attractiveness, and power (McGuire, 1969, p. 179). These characteristics may be particularly important mediators of how messages are received in work settings, but are not well researched there. A first step might be to differentiate personal and role characteristics of the source as they influence the communication process in organizations. For example, how do source importance (often related to job level and power in organizations) and personal attractiveness combine to determine the responses made to directives sent from the chief executive down to lower echelon personnel in organizations? Because so many researchers have been interested primarily in how sources influence attitude change, and because organizational researchers are often as interested in other outcomes, organizational research directed to source effects on message outcomes might be most productive if it is addressed to behavioral change.

COMMUNICATION PROCESS. A number of critical questions about the interpersonal process of sending and receiving messages in organizations have seldom been posed in research. Three of these might be considered first in organizational research. One problem is how information comes into organizations. A second is how information is internally generated in organizations, and a third concerns how information is transmitted, regardless of its origins.

The question of how information gets into organizations presents some difficult research problems. For example, it is not easy to disentangle the influences on information transmission of source and process. Several investigators, though, have attacked the problem. Allen and Cohen (1969), for instance, identify the kinds of external sources used by organizational gatekeepers for obtaining information in R&D laboratories. The classic studies of gatekeepers in newspaper organizations (Bass, 1969; Breed, 1955; White, 1969) also identify external sources, but concentrate more on the process of information transmission across organizational boundaries. Focusing on reporters as occupants of boundary roles in newspaper organizations, these studies show that the content of information accepted into the organization is often determined by its perceived importance, by the reporter's image of what readers want, by his perceptions of what his own reference group will accept and by the unwritten policy of his newspaper. These findings should be extended to other kinds of organizations. Researchers might attempt to specify the criteria used by people at organizational boundaries for assessing the importance of various kinds of information and for determining whether it will be accepted by the organization. They might then look at the influence of other boundary personnel (in one's own or in other organizations) on an individual's propensity to allow information to enter his organization. Finally, researchers might look at how importance, acceptability, and influence of one's reference group are weighted in determining what information enters organizations and how it is altered at the boundaries.

A second problem in considering organizational communication as a process concerns internal generation of information. We know of no empirical work which systematically compares internally and externally generated information. However, one might suppose that they are different in content and use, and perhaps travel along different routes inside organizations.

While nothing is known about differences in information attributable to point of origin, we do know that information is distorted as it goes from group to group (Allport & Postman, 1965; Caplow, 1947). We could apply to organizational transmission such Gestalt concepts as leveling and sharpening, and also assess in organizations the occurrence of systematic errors in communication (Campbell, 1958). In addition, such issues as how qualitative versus quantitative information is absorbed by groups and individuals as it moves from point to point in a system should be examined by organizational researchers. Some evidence shows that distrust influences information transmission and distortion in organizations. Mellinger (1956) reports, for instance, that in a government research organization where a communicator distrusts a recipient, the information he sends that person is distorted. Read (1962) provides similar findings in an industrial organization. The extent to which distrust is a barrier to communication is likely influenced by the perceived status of communicator and recipient and by the nature of the issue communicated.

The channels along which information travels appear to be important aspects of its processing. When written and oral channels are compared, we usually find that comprehension is greater when information is transmitted in written form, but opinion change is greater in face-to-face situations. Psychologists have been generally disinterested in media questions and the available comparative studies of media say almost nothing about the process of transmission (McGuire, 1969). It seems logical that multimedia transmission reduces information distortion, but the research findings relevant

to this are equivocal (Anderson, 1969; Hsia, 1968).

Once information reaches a group or individual who can act on it, the communication process is possibly different from that which accounts for getting information to appropriate places in the organization. If nothing else, face-to-face communication is more likely to predominate when information is acted upon in groups, with other modalities primarily used to transmit information across groups. The group task may determine the appropriate media for communicating about it. Where information transmission is necessary to problem solution, a number of factors should be examined. Researchers must at least be concerned with the influences on the group of the amount of information in the group, order of information presentation, and opportunity for feedback. In this connection, Shaw (1963) looked at the effects on the group of varying the amount of information possessed by any one member. He found that the amount of information an individual held was related to when he entered the discussion, how much task-oriented information he initiated, whether he was accepted by the group, perceived as helping them, and selected as a leader.

A great deal of attention has been devoted in the empirical literature to order of presentation of material because of the folk wisdom that material presented first has the greatest impact on the individual or the group. That work is adequately covered elsewhere (see Cohen, 1964; McGuire, 1969). A number of hypotheses exist to account for influences of order of presentation. However, most of the work has been done in the laboratory and probably is of limited usefulness to communication in organizations where there are continuing information exchanges and many opportunities for repetition.

MEANING. "I think you believe you understand what you think I said, but I am not sure you realize that what you heard is not what I meant." This statement reflects the problem of establishing communication meaning, a problem which has generated a great deal of research attention. As we indicated before, the meaning an individual attaches to a message results from a complex mix of personal, historical, and situational factors. Much of the important work on understanding meaning will eventually come from studies of perceptual phenomena. Issues such as those dealing with assimilation and contrast effects (Hovland, Harvey, & Sherif, 1957; Sherif, Sherif, & Nebergall, 1965) or the etiology of how perceptions are meshed into ongoing cognitive systems have generally not been extended to the communication literature. Yet, an understanding of these and related phenomena will substantially add to our knowledge of communication meaning.

There has been a considerable amount of research concerned with verbal meaning, but most of it is tangential to the concerns of the organizational researcher. One example of an aspect of verbal meaning that might be considered in organizational communication is the inherent factors in verbal messages which contribute to their meaning. McGuire (1969) discusses two factors: *pathos* and *logos*. "An argument is said to use *pathos* if it involves creating appropriate feelings in the receiver by appealing to his feelings, values, and emotions.... In *logos* appeals, the receiver is required to deduce the position being argued from a general principle which he accepts, or induce it from empirical evidence he accepts by means of logical argumentation" (p. 201). We do not know, at least with respect to organizational settings, the relative difference in meaning of appeals based on emotion versus those based on logic. Besides pathos or logos, other factors are also inherent in any specific appeal. The problems of identifying all of the meaning factors in messages, and of understanding their interrelationship and relationship to other behaviors, are enormous.

Man has a unique capacity for conveying meaning verbally, but like other organisms his silences and extra-linguistic manifestations also convey meaning. For example, combinations of laughter and silence sometimes (Olesen & Whittaker, 1966) express the strains of organizational life. Language is usually accompanied by additional meaning cues and verbal silence is often filled with such cues. In fact, nonverbal cues may have more impact than verbal ones on the meaning respondents infer (Argyle, Salter, Nicholson, Williams, & Burgess, 1970; Mehrabian & Ferris, 1967; Rosenberg & Langer, 1965), and it is to these that we now turn our attention.

Recently, more research useful to applied psychologists has dealt with nonverbal than with verbal meaning, but as previously stated, comprehensive communication models have yet to be developed from this work. Nonverbal research has focused on para-language, body, and spatial cues to meaning. Duncan (1969) reviewed this research covering six modalities: (1) body motion, (2) para-language, (3) proxemics, (4) olfaction, (5) skin sensitivity, and (6) use of artifacts. Of these, body motion, proxemics, and para-language have received the most empirical attention. Duncan indicates the research strategies used in the area and some of the questions which should be studied. Interested researchers should consult Duncan's (1969) and Mahl and Schulze's (1964) reviews of nonverbal phenomena. Two nonverbal modes of communication are probably of greatest interest to organizational researchers: the use of the face (particularly where its cues are inconsistent with verbal cues), and the way in which people at work use space to convey meaning.

The face seems to be the best of man's nonverbal communication devices, and the eyes the most expressive aspect of the face (Duncan, 1969). Davitz (1964) states that emotions can be expressed intentionally and can be recognized reliably regardless of the mode of expression. Nonverbal manifestations of affect can be accurately inferred from facial, postural, and distance cues (Mehrabian, 1968), and appear to be pan-cultural and innate (Ekman, Sorenson, & Friesen, 1969). Ekman and Friesen (1969) indicate that we evidently communicate nonverbally that part of a message we wish least to take responsibility for, and we are not good nonverbal liars. For example, a superior may tell a subordinate that things are going well in their work unit, when the expression in his eyes suggests something different to the subordinate. Organizational researchers might, based on findings such as those mentioned, design studies which simultaneously observe verbal and nonverbal facial behaviors, particularly since much nonverbal behavior may be more pervasive and less tied to socialization than we have heretofore thought, and since our everyday inferences about what people mean in inter-personal communication are primarily based on combinations of facial and verbal cues.

With desks, chairs, and offices serving as major nonhuman components of the work environment, the organizational psychologist might turn greater attention to understanding how people use space and furniture as communication devices. Hall (1963) defined as static aspects of interaction the physical distance between interactants, the presence or absence of physical contact, the form that physical contact takes, eye contact between interactants, and the use of thermal and olfactory cues. Later, he showed (1964) how these components combine to define different distance sets, and he provided (1966) some interesting notions about the meaning and use of these features by people in different cultures. More recent reviews of the literature concerned with proxemics are offered by Duncan (1969) and Sommer (1967). Sommer points out that "knowledge of how groups arrange themselves can assist in fostering or discouraging group relationships (1967, p. 150), and he gives examples of how spaces can be designed to enhance or discourage different kinds of group activity.

Even if we had adequate empirical evidence on verbal and nonverbal meaning, the question remains as to how it might be integrated. Scheflen (1968) describes the form of human behavior in terms of behavioral units which are combined in programs of activity. Participants in face to face communication perform and recognize standard, consistent behavioral units. When these units are combined into programs, interactants in specific programs infer from them similar meanings. If one could identify specific programs operable in various circumstances and learn how these programs are integrated with other programs as circumstances change, he could possibly develop theories useful to understanding organizational behavior.

COMMUNICATION EFFECTS. From the receiver's viewpoint, a communication may help him better understand the phenomena of his world, learn more, enjoy, dispose of, or decide upon some issue (Schramm, 1971, p. 19). All of the communication variables previously discussed constrain responses which might be made to them.

A loose cause-effect model underlies all research questions of communication effects. Effects are judged in terms of observable responses following in time some communication stimulus. We obviously choose to observe only some responses following a message and to infer an effect if the response is related to the concept and/or intent of the message. Undoubtedly, many consequences of communication are simply never noted, because we are at the mercy of the indicators of effect we choose to measure. "Regardless of which responses or behavior we choose to measure, most *observable* indicators of communication are, at minimum, one step removed from the fundamental locus of effect. Communications do not *directly* mediate overt behavior. Rather, they tend to affect the ways a receiver organizes his image of the environment, and this organization influences the way he behaves" (Roberts, 1971, p. 361).

Roberts's (1971) review of the literature

leads him to the following generalizations about how messages affect receivers:

1. People's interpretations of messages tend to follow the path of least resistance.

2. People are more open to messages consonant with their existing attitudes and beliefs.

3. Messages incongruent with beliefs engender more resistance than do congruent messages.

4. To the extent that individuals value need fulfillment, messages facilitating need fulfillment are more easily accepted than messages which do not.

5. As the environment changes, people become more susceptible to messages which help them restructure their environment.

An example of a question relevant to work organizations concerns what individuals do when they find themselves in disagreement with messages sent by those who have power over them. Little evidence exists about mechanisms for dealing with such situations, but Steiner, Anderson, and Hays (1967) show that in interpersonal disagreements, stress can be reduced by underestimating the degree of disagreement. One mechanism for doing this is illustrated in Burns's (1954) investigation, which points out that while superiors interpret certain of their comments to subordinates as instructions, subordinates view the same communication as helpful information. The consequent effects of communication are partially a function of the degree to which the recipient sees his attitude position as similar to that of the sender.

Summary

The theoretical and empirical work concerned with interpersonal communication is spotty at best. Most of the research findings are based on laboratory investigations, and their generalizability to real life organizational interactions is questionable. If nothing else, this brief review should indicate that a large number of unanswered questions about interpersonal communication in organizations are suggested by the existing literature.

Much of the theoretical work is associated with attitude change. "The concept of attitude, as presently interpreted, is not too useful for the study of information processing. The concept is non-situational. It is intended as an estimate of value for a single object across situations. Therefore, it does not tell us much of the value of an object in a given orientation situation" (Carter, 1965, p. 205). No adequate models, or even focused road maps, exist to direct the researcher who wants to test hypotheses concerned with how information is processed in organizations. Enterprising theorists might be able to extend the models of dyadic interpersonal communication to include all the structural, environmental, time frame, and other aspects of organizations which cannot be ignored. It is to the organizational setting and these variables that we now turn.

THE ORGANIZATIONAL MILIEU

In this section, we examine the organizational context of communication interactions. That is, we focus on organizational factors that affect the structure, process, and consequences of communication acts. Not all of the research we cover in this section has been carried out in "real life" organizations; however, much of it has, and the remainder has direct implications for the flow and content of communications in such settings. (Again, as in the previous section, primary concentration is on studies published in the last ten years.)

First, some of the fundamental characteristics of organizations, as they impinge upon communication, are briefly reviewed. The next part considers some general features of communication systems. This is followed by several sub-sections dealing with specific features of organization structure as they relate to communication: the total organizational configuration, the vertical or hierarchical dimension, the lateral or horizontal dimension, and group structure.

The Nature of Organizations as Related to Communication

If one examines the definitions of organizations provided by various theorists (such as Barnard, Etzioni, Schein, and Simon, among others), four or five characteristics emerge as fundamental (Porter, Lawler, & Hackman, 1975). Not every theorist includes all four or five, but most are mentioned by the majority. Each has relevance for communication.

SOCIAL COMPOSITION. A basic feature of complex organizations, and one that is a powerful determinant of the nature of communication within them, is that individuals do not work in isolation. Furthermore, they ordinarily are members of one or more formal or informal subunits within the organization. The implications for communication revolve around the fact that individuals frequently are not only representing themselves when they send a message, but they also are serving, in some degree, as agents of some social or organizational unit. Likewise, intended receivers usually are not just "independent" individuals, but rather are attached to groups or units that can be "reached" even when the apparent recipient is only one person. Additionally, of course, such reverberations occur beyond individual senders and receivers even when the communicator's intention is only to represent self or to communicate to a definite other person.

Since organizations are social entities and composed not just of individuals but also of groups of various types, this means that much of communication in organizations is of a group-to-group nature. Representatives from the personnel department meet with the production department; the finance committee reports to the board of directors; the X department provides data for the Y department; and so forth. While such group-to-group communication has not been studied to any extent compared to inter-individual communication, it never-theless is a prominent characteristic of organization life and constitutes an area needing more research attention.

GOAL ORIENTATION. A second basic feature of organizations is that they attempt to be goal oriented; that is, they are ordinarily considered to be purposeful in nature. The presumption of most people that formal organizations have objectives or goals has a decided impact in the communication behavior of the members in them (as well as on the communications that flow into and out of organizations in their relationships with their environments). It will influence the pattern of communication networks in terms of the frequency and direction of flow of messages. It will also regulate to a degree, but not completely determine, the content of organizationally relevant messages.

DIFFERENTIAL FUNCTIONS. If organizations have goals and objectives, however imprecisely and implicitly they may be stated and recognized, then they must embody means to attain them. One of these mechanisms is a third major characteristic of organizations: the differentiation of functions, or as commonly called, the division of labor.

The existence of differentiated functions in organizations directly affects communications by both making possible and limiting certain patterns of interactions, and by influencing the attitudes of individuals in different parts of organizations. The former kind of impact occurs because the parceling out of functions results in an increase in the frequency or likelihood of certain interactions and a decrease in the frequency or chance of other interactions. Thus, some communication patterns get firmly established with particular modes of operation that are difficult to disrupt even if individuals or organizations so desire. On the other hand, a particular implementation of differentiation will make it extremely difficult if not impossible for certain other patterns to originate, let alone continue. The second impact of differentiated functions—

on the attitudes of communicators and re-cipients—stems from the specific perspectives that individuals acquire because of the nature of the functions they are performing in the organization (e.g., Dearborn & Simon, 1958). This can facilitate communication among those performing similar functions and at the same time inhibit it across individuals from different functional areas.

SYSTEMS OF COORDINATION. The other major mechanism that organizations employ to facilitate goal achievement constitutes a fourth key characteristic of organizations: systems of attempted rational coordination. In considering the organization's attempts at rational coordination—for example, plans, regulations, role prescriptions, etc.—it is well to keep in mind that, as Schein (1970) stresses, it is *activities,* not people, that are coordinated. These activities cannot be co-ordinated without communication among the parts of the organization. Therefore, organizations not only encourage but seek out certain types and frequencies of com-munication so that such integration can be achieved.

CONTINUITY THROUGH TIME. One final char-acteristic of organizations has a strong influ-ence on communication: continuity through time. This feature of organizations is one of the key factors distinguishing them from other types of social entities, such as audiences, parties, or casual crowds. It crit-ically affects communication in organiza-tions because it gives individuals an aware-ness that their activities and interactions are likely to be repeated (though not precisely identically) in the future. Such an aware-ness can be presumed to affect greatly the types of communications that individuals or groups send and the interpretations put on them by receivers. Some messages will not be sent because of the anticipated future. Others will be sent precisely because the sender does anticipate a certain kind of future. Still others will be altered to take into account in some way the fact that the

organization is to continue. It is this feature of organizations—their tendency toward continuity—that makes it exceedingly dif-ficult and hazardous to extrapolate the re-sults of laboratory-type studies of communi-cation to actual, ongoing organizations. Such a feature is difficult to insert into the typical laboratory study, yet it is a pervasive part of the life of the typical organization that employs people.

The Nature of Communication Systems as They Relate to Organizations

STRUCTURAL ASPECTS. Whatever limitations laboratory studies of communication net-works in small groups may have for gener-alizing specific findings to real-life complex organizations, taken as a group they provide a source of ideas concerning the nature of the structural aspects of communication systems in organizations. These studies have been well summarized by Shaw (1964), and this source should be referred to for greater detail.

Basically, the network studies focus our attention on the dimension of centralization-decentralization in communication struc-tures. In the centralized structure, there is a high concentration of information-obtain-ing potential in one or a limited number of positions in the structure, with a correspond-ing low potential spread among the majority of positions. Positions with a high potential are said to have a high degree of com-munication "independence" (Leavitt, 1951; Shaw, 1954, 1964), while the other positions possess little or no such independence. In decentralized communication structures, the information-obtaining potential is more or less evenly spread among all of the positions, and thus the independence of each position is roughly equal. Findings from network studies generally indicate that centralized structures are more efficient when the prob-lems or issues to be dealt with are relatively simple and straightforward; however, such structures seem to be less efficient than decentralized ones for more complex problems and tasks, and in addition, they tend to generate lower morale and satisfaction (Shaw, 1964). (Other aspects and findings of some of the network studies are discussed later in this chapter.) Whether such generalizations concerning the structure of communication systems will be supported when we have data from ongoing, complex organizations rather than from small groups in laboratories remains to be seen. In any event, the centralization-decentralization dimension appears to be a key aspect of communication systems that must be considered in any analysis of the impact of organization structure.

Other structural features that will need to be subjected to empirical examination in a systematic fashion include the size of the structure, the heterogeneity/homogeneity of the types of positions within the structure, and the geographical and positional distances to be covered. (Some aspects of these structural factors are covered in more detail below to the extent that they are investigated in particular studies.)

Still another way to look at the structural features of communication systems in organizations is to consider the communication roles that various positions can perform. Essentially, these amount to four types: initiator, relayer, terminator, and isolator (Davis, 1953b; Sutton & Porter, 1968). That is, some positions typically initiate communications much more often than they either receive or pass on communications. This does not necessarily mean that they do it often, but only that they initiate relatively more than they receive or pass on. Other positions function as relays that seldom start or finish the communication process but rather receive and pass on messages. Positions with a different kind of reception pattern (e.g., many rank-and-file positions) are those which mostly receive but seldom relay information. And, finally, certain positions are relatively isolated from the normal communication channels and have a low frequency of either initiation or reception. While some studies have investi-

gated this way of looking at structural aspects of communication systems for informal or "grapevine" communications (Davis, 1953b; Sutton & Porter, 1968), relatively few applications have been made to formal organization communication networks. Yet, this categorization of communication roles should prove to be a useful set of structural distinctions to aid in the analysis.

INFORMATION-PROCESSING ASPECTS. A somewhat different way of viewing fundamental properties of communication systems as they relate to organizations is to focus on how information is processed by positions within the structure. Ference (1970), drawing upon the work of March and Simon (1958), developed a number of propositions that bear on this approach as it relates to decision making and problem solving in organizations. While most of his propositions are more pertinent to the problem-solving process per se, a number of them are directly relevant to the information-processing characteristics of communication systems and provide a fruitful basis for conceptualization. The following sample of these propositions is representative of this information-processing perspective (Ference, 1970, pp. B48-86):

...When information is evaluated and integrated at a position in a communications network, only the decision or inferences drawn from the information are transmitted; the information or evidence leading to the decision or inferences is not transmitted.

... When information is evaluated and integrated, the function of the person doing the processing will exert more influence than his personal motivation on the choice and interpretation of information. [Note the relevance of this proposition to our earlier discussion of the "differentiated functions" characteristic of organizations.]

... To the extent that problems are ill defined, information obtained through informal communication systems will be preferred to information obtained through formal communication systems.

Taken together, Ference's propositions emphasize the information evaluation and the information transmittal roles of positions in the structure. The propositions thus provide a potentially helpful basis for analyzing some of the diverse empirical findings that have been obtained from the actual communication behavior of participants in organizational settings.

The Total Organizational Configuration

The total configuration of an organization undoubtedly exerts a strong influence on the characteristics of communication within it. (Wilensky, 1967, for example, provides some interesting and illustrative case examples of such influence.) However, we have a considerable gap in our research knowledge about the possible impacts of major dimensions of the total organization. That is, most investigations have been devoted to more limited aspects of the organization, such as superior-subordinate relationships or properties of groups as they affect communication. Seldom have studies dealt with the effects on communication of the overall size or shape of the total organization, or the predominant technology utilized by the organization. Nevertheless, it may be useful to comment briefly on a few of the possible variables connected with the total organizational configuration:

1. *Institutional differences.* A fruitful but unexplored area for research is the comparative differences in communication patterns and practices across organizations operating in different institutional arenas. For example, are the communication problems encountered in public elementary schools similar to those found in governmental agencies? Is the relative rate of upward to downward communication in a manufacturing plant different from that of a comparable-sized hospital? Such questions will be difficult to answer because of the confounding effects of a number of uncontrolled variables, but even exploratory attempts to investigate comparative institutional commu-

nication patterns should contribute to basic organizational theory.

2. *Technological effects.* Recent research (e.g., Woodward, 1965; Lawrence & Lorsch, 1967) has demonstrated the influence of technology on various aspects of organizational behavior. However, with respect to communication we have relatively little sound information on the impact of technology. This is true even in the area of information technology, such as the introduction of electronic data processing. Despite the growing influence of such technological developments (Whisler, 1970a, 1970b), their effects on communication behavior have not as yet been documented in any systematic way.

One empirical study that did bear directly on technological influences on communication was carried out in a textile mill (Simpson, 1959). Although the study did not make comparisons of different types of technology, the findings from this setting led Simpson to believe that the degree of mechanization might have an effect on the rate of vertical communication. On the basis of his results, he hypothesized that, "Mechanization reduces the need for close supervision (vertical communication), since instead of the foreman the machines set the work pace of his subordinates; but automation (i.e., extreme mechanization) increases the need for vertical communication to deal with the frequent and serious machine breakdowns" (1959, p. 196). As yet, such a hypothesis remains to be tested, since, as noted, virtually no research has been carried out on the effects of different types and degrees of technology on the nature of organizational communication. As with the possible impact of different institutional realms, comparative research is needed in the area of technology.

3. *Size effects.* Outside of laboratory settings, where extremely small (and isolated) groups of three to six persons have been studied, the variable of size of organization has been relatively unresearched with respect to its relationships to organizational

communication. This is so even though most observers commonly believe that greater size has deleterious effects on the quality of communication. This is a presumption that has not yet been supported by carefully documented research. One unpublished study (Donald, 1959, cited in Guetzkow, 1965), dealing with units of the League of Women Voters organization, found that rates of communication upward from members to League officers decreased with increases in size of unit, but rates of communication among rank-and-file members were unaffected by size. This type of study remains to be replicated, and the results to be generalized, to other types of organizations and other ranges of unit and total organization size. In contrast to some other dimensions of the total organizational configuration, however, size should be one of the more easily researched variables.

4. *Shape.* Not only are the total sizes of organizations and units within them presumed to affect communications, but also their shape (tallness versus flatness). While no explicit research on shape has been carried out with respect to communication effects, other research (e.g., Porter & Lawler, 1964; Porter & Siegel, 1965) on shape indicates that it does have systematic relationships to other dependent variables such as job satisfaction. It might be hypothesized, for example, that tall organizations maximize communication difficulties across more than two organizational levels but minimize difficulties between two levels (because of the relatively small numbers of subordinates reporting to a given superior in a tall structure).

5. *Control (authority) structures.* Another crucial dimension that distinguishes different types of organizations is their patterns of formal authority and controls. Theorists have posited various categorization systems—for example, Etzioni's (1961) tripartite compliance relations scheme of normative, utilitarian, and coercive—with reference to the control features of organizations, and these are presumed to interact with the

quantity of communication. Although research evidence is again sketchy, Julian (1966) has provided data from five hospitals suggesting that more "blocks" to communication exist in normative-coercive hospitals than in purely normative ones. Furthermore, the blockages appear to affect both upward and downward communication. (The conclusions of this study must be regarded as tentative, because patients were the source both for classifying the hospitals and for describing the nature of the blockages.) In a rather intricate set of findings obtained on a sample of League of Women Voters units (the same sample as in Donald's study referred to previously), Smith and Brown (1964) indicate that the type of control structure—both the amount and the nature—interacts in complex ways with the prevailing communication patterns to determine organizational effectiveness and member loyalty. The study suggests that efficiency is related more to the nature of control patterns (determined by who makes the decisions), while level of member loyalty is related more to communication patterns. In any event, the findings from both the Julian and the Smith and Brown investigations are too tenuous to draw firm conclusions. The studies do, though, indicate the potential usefulness of researching the interrelationships of control and communication structures.

The Vertical Dimension (Hierarchical Effects)

THE ROLE OF STATUS AND POWER. Any analysis of the vertical dimension of communication in organizations must begin with a consideration of the variables that differentiate individuals holding higher positions from those holding lower positions. The theoretical and empirical literature has focused on two key variables in this respect: status (relative importance of a position) and power (relative ability to control or influence other people and events). In general, we can assume that individuals holding higher ranking positions in organizations will possess both greater status and greater power. However, there clearly can be exceptions to this generalization—particularly with respect to power—in specific organizational situations: sometimes high level positions have relatively little status attached to them (particularly when they are perceived as powerless), and frequently holders of high level positions will find themselves with relatively small amounts of legitimate power. So, although high rank, status, and formal power tend to be associated, there is no intrinsic reason for this to be so in all instances. The basic question is how status and power may act, either singly or in combination, to affect upward and downward communication in organizations.

A series of laboratory experiments by a variety of investigators, beginning with Kelley (1951) has attempted to isolate the impact of these two variables. One issue has concerned the effect of status and/or power on communications upward from low to high positions. Work by Cohen (1958) tended to show that status, when combined with power, affected upward communications considerably more than when power was absent. The amount of negative information sent upward was much less in the former condition than in the latter, emphasizing the impact of power. Subsequent experimental research (Jones et al., 1963; Watson, 1965; Watson & Bromberg, 1965) has attempted to clarify further the role of power. Findings confirm the influence that differential power can have on the nature of communications activity and the content of messages. All of the studies support the conclusion that individuals in low power positions, when sending messages upward, do screen out certain types of information (e.g., disagreements with the opinions of the high power person) that would tend to bring unfavorable reactions from the individual who has some potential control over them. However, research also shows that individuals in positions with high power can screen out in-

formation for the low power recipient (Jones et al., 1963).

The pervasive effects of both power and status differences are also demonstrated in field research. For example, Slobin, Miller, and Porter (1968) found that in a business organization individuals in middle level positions were much more willing to communicate self-disclosure information upward than they were to divulge it downward to subordinate levels. This was interpreted by the authors as attempts to establish greater "intimacy" with high status/power individuals so that there would be more equality between the two levels, while at the same time maintaining downward differences by avoiding self-disclosures that would signify close personal relationships. Here again, one finds evidence for screening in both upward and downward communication. The *content* of what is screened is, however, dependent on the direction of communications. The amount of information sent also appears to be affected by power and status differences. Barnlund and Harland (1963) and Allen and Cohen (1969) indicate that high status individuals communicate more with each other than with low status individuals, and that low status individuals are also more likely to attempt to communicate with high status persons than with other lower status persons.

Based upon the research—both field and laboratory—dealing with the effects of status and power on communication, it is obvious that these two variables interact to produce modifications in the communicative activities of participants and in the contents of their messages. It also appears that power accounts for more of the variance in communication behavior than does status. Differential power and status lead to substantial screening and shaping of information by both those who are low and those who are high in the hierarchy. The exact nature of the filtering depends on a number of specific aspects of a situation (see the research cited below on superior-subordinate interactions), but such behavior can be interpreted from a broadly instrumental perspective as attempts at self-protection, self-enhancement, and gratification.

COMMUNICATION ACROSS MORE THAN TWO ORGANIZATIONAL LEVELS. Most organizational studies of the hierarchical aspects of communication have focused on the nature of superior-subordinate interactions. However, a few investigations have examined vertical communication behavior across several different levels, and it may be worthwhile to look at these before turning to the interchanges between only two adjacent levels.

Davis (1953a) has developed a research method called "ecco analysis" that gathers information on where, from whom, and when an individual first received a piece of information and what he did with it. This approach has been used to investigate both informal or "grapevine" communication and formal organizational communication. Studies by Davis (1953b) and Sutton and Porter (1968) appear to show that the higher an individual's position is in the organizational hierarchy the more likely he is to know a specific piece of grapevine information; however, this finding is severely limited by the fact that in both studies the items of information selected for investigation were supplied by upper-level personnel. Both studies also showed that only a few individuals functioned as liaison links in receiving and passing on any given grapevine item. However, Davis found that different individuals served the liaison role from time to time, while Sutton and Porter found that the individuals were always the same. In addition, Sutton and Porter found that information tended to stay within a given department, while Davis found more interchange between departments. Since the Sutton and Porter respondents included a number of rank-and-file employees whereas the Davis sample was only managerial, this fact could account for the different results concerning this latter finding.

In a study of downward communication of formal information, carried out among managerial levels of two departments of a manufacturing company, Davis (1968) found extensive filtering of routine, non-task information by middle levels. On the other hand, task-type information was relatively well communicated from the top down to the lowest management levels.

Since so few studies have investigated communication across a number of hierarchical levels, generalizations concerning vertical communication must be made with caution. However, the available findings suggest that (1) the content of information influences individuals in deciding whether or not to pass it on—this is true for information by both formal and informal networks; (2) individuals differ in their propensities toward serving as key communication links, thus indicating that personality factors may play important roles in the quality and quantity of such communication activity; and (3) organizational structural factors—particularly the nature of groupings of individuals (such as into departments) that cut vertically across levels—help determine where and to whom information is communicated.

SUPERIOR-SUBORDINATE COMMUNICATION. As already noted, interactions of individuals in direct superior-subordinate relationships to each other have been the chief focus of research efforts investigating the vertical dimension of communication in organizational settings. Such research has provided data on the amount of this type of communication activity, the accuracy of this communication, and the nature of the reactions of individuals involved in the interactions.

Estimates of the amount of vertical communication activity of individuals in organizations have utilized both "percentage of time" and "percentage of interactions." Several studies (Dubin & Spray, 1964; Kelly, 1964; Lawler, Porter, & Tenenbaum, 1968) generally find that for managers, about two-thirds of their communication time is spent with superiors and subordinates, and about one-third is spent on lateral or horizontal communication. (An apparent exception to this general finding is provided by Wickesberg, 1968; his sample of managers reported spending only about one-third of their time in vertical communication, but another one-third of the total time was reported spent on "diagonal" interactions which can be assumed to have a vertical—though not superior-subordinate—component.) The available data indicate, therefore, that a majority of communication activity among managers in formal organizational settings is vertical, and that it is more prevalent than horizontal communication. However, if samples were limited strictly to rank-and-file employees rather than managers, the reverse proportions of vertical to horizontal might well be found. In any event, it appears that the attention that researchers have paid to superior-subordinate communication is well founded due to both its importance and its pervasiveness.

The perceived effectiveness or quality of communication between superiors and subordinates in relation to their degree of cognitive similarity about common objects in the environment was investigated in an early study by Triandis (1959). The findings, also replicated by him in a laboratory study (Triandis, 1960a), showed that such similarity in the thinking of superior-subordinate pairs—as measured by perceived similarities and differences among triads of concepts—was related to communication effectiveness. However, the study does not suggest how such cognitive similarity between individuals can be developed, whether it can be easily altered, and whether it has other possible positive or negative consequences in the work situation. (Perhaps, for example, too much similarity dampens tendencies toward creative solutions to problems.) Also, although the finding is intriguing, research related to it needs to be carried out under a broader set of field conditions before its generality can be confirmed.

The accuracy of communication between superiors and subordinates has been investigated in a series of studies by Maier and his associates (Maier, Hoffman, Hooven, & Read, 1961; Read, 1962; Maier, Hoffman, & Read, 1963). This research shows again that both the types of material being communicated and the characteristics of the communicators have a strong effect on accuracy. (Accuracy was measured in a somewhat limited fashion, namely, in terms of the degree of agreement between superiors and subordinates with respect to the importance of certain aspects of the subordinates' job.) One of the studies (Maier et al., 1961) found that accuracy was much higher for communications dealing with job duties than for those pertaining to job problems. Communications about job requirements and future job changes were intermediate in the degree of accuracy. These results indicate that the more tangible and the more objective the subject matter of the communication, the more likely it is that subordinates and their superiors will communicate accurately, whereas when the messages involve more subjective opinions and feelings there is less likelihood of accuracy. In his study of upward communication, Read (1962) found that the degree of agreement concerning the subordinate's problems was least when the subordinate held strong upward mobility aspirations and when he lacked trust in his superior. Even when trust was present, the existence of high subordinate aspirations tended to result in lack of boss-subordinate agreement, indicating the importance of this latter variable. (The findings concerning the effect of potential mobility in Read's study reinforce similar findings of Cohen's, 1958, earlier study carried out with a quite different methodology in a laboratory situation.) A potential modifying variable—greater knowledge of the subordinate's position by virtue of the superior having previously occupied it—was found not to affect the overall difficulty of superiors and subordinates in reaching agreement via communications about the nature of the subordinate's job problems (Maier, Hoffman, & Read, 1963).

Another aspect of accuracy relates to agreement between superiors and subordinates about the amount of communication activity between them. Intensive interview data collected by Webber (1970) on thirty-four pairs of superiors and subordinates show that in each role, whether superior or subordinate, a manager believes he initiates communications more often than the other person in his pair. However, this tendency is significantly greater in downward than in upward communication. In other words, bosses and subordinates differ substantially in their beliefs about how much the bosses communicate to the subordinates—superiors perceiving the amount to be much greater than their underlings. This difference, according to Webber, is heightened if the subordinate tends to have an "active personality" (as measured by behavior in a standardized mild stress interview), lending further support to the notion that problems of communication between two adjacent hierarchy levels are most likely to occur when the subordinate is forceful, aggressive, and has strong upward aspirations.

The quality and adequacy of communication between any pair of individuals not only involves questions of accuracy, but also the nature of feelings and reactions experienced by the recipient. Such attitudinal reactions to superior-subordinate interactions were investigated in a study of some 100 managers (about half of whom came from a manufacturing company and half from social service agencies) by Lawler, Porter, and Tenenbaum (1968). They utilized a modified version of a self-recording form developed by Burns (1954). In Burns's original study, the form asked the manager to supply factual information about each interaction episode, such as who initiated the interaction, how long it was, etc. (A sep-

arate form was completed for each episode.) Lawler et al. added five attitude scales to the form, asking the manager to record his reaction to each episode. Forms were completed by the 100 managers for five consecutive working days (with the average number of forms completed per manager across the five days being approximately forty). As might be expected, managers felt more positive about interactions *they* initiated than they did about those initiated by others. The most interesting aspect of the data, however, concerned the differential reactions a manager had to interactions that were upward toward the boss compared to those downward with a subordinate. "A significant majority of the managers reported more favorable attitudes toward the contacts they had with their superiors than the contacts they had with their subordinates. Overall, this tendency appears to hold for both samples and for all of the attitudes studied" (p. 437). The authors explain this finding by stating that "...a superior contact is relatively more 'unusual' than a subordinate contact. In addition, the superior has reward power over his subordinates. Thus, a superior-subordinate interaction is likely to be a more significant event for a subordinate than a superior" (p. 438). The implication of this, as the researchers pointed out, is that managers may not be placing high enough value on the communications they receive from subordinates, thereby creating conditions that can act to discourage effective upward communication.

The general pattern of findings reported above was replicated in a later study by Tenenbaum (1970), who focused on communications between specific superior-subordinate pairs of managers. Tenenbaum found subordinates evaluating their self-initiated interactions with superiors much more highly than did the superiors who "received" the subordinate communications; when superiors initiated a communication downward, both sender (superior) and receiver (subordinate) evaluated the episode about equally favorably. This pattern of results indicates again that subordinates feel they must take seriously the communication interactions they have with the boss, but the boss does not have to reciprocate the same degree of attentiveness and favorable reaction. Tenenbaum's study extended the earlier Lawler et al. findings by also investigating perceptions of the degree of attitude change that each party experienced and felt the other party experienced. His results showed clearly that subordinates report greater attitude change than do their superiors in mutual interactions. Furthermore, each party tends to overestimate the amount of opinion change actually reported by the other party. Overall, Tenenbaum's data again point up the inherent obstacles in achieving effective communication between managers at a given hierarchical level who have a certain amount of formal status and power—particularly reward power—and their subordinates who have less of these perquisites of rank.

The Lateral Dimension

The importance of the lateral or horizontal dimension in organizational communication has been emphasized by several writers (e.g., Simpson, 1959; Landsberger, 1961; Strauss, 1962; Dubin & Spray, 1964; Wickesberg, 1968; Hage, Aiken, & Marrett, 1971). The amount of time spent in lateral communication varies widely by the level and function of the individual, but evidence from several studies (those cited previously in estimating the time spent in vertical communication) indicates a mean (with a large standard deviation) of about 30 to 40 percent. While this is somewhat less than the proportion spent in vertical communication, it still represents a substantial volume of horizontal-type interactions.

As Porter (1974) has noted elsewhere, "the horizontal [communication] dimension is made up of at least several major types of communication interactions: (1) those occurring among peers within work groups,

(2) those occurring across major units within the organization, and (3) those occurring between line and staff types of positions." While all of these types share some features in common—for example, the general absence of formal status and power differences between communicators—each also has its own distinctive features.

Lateral communication among peers within work groups is undoubtedly the most prevalent type of horizontal communication —particularly informal communication— within organizations. In fact, the opportunity to engage in this type of interaction is often cited by operative employees as one of the chief (and in certain organizations almost the only) sources of satisfaction on the job. While relatively little research has been directed specifically at identifying factors that facilitate or inhibit this kind of communication, a considerable body of relevant research data on group size is available. In their review of studies of group size in industrial organizations, Porter and Lawler (1964) conclude that "the literature on subunit size shows that when blue-collar workers are considered, small size subunits are characterized by higher job satisfaction, lower absence rates, lower turnover rates, and fewer labor disputes" (p. 39). This cluster of findings points to an inference that satisfying (from the point of view of the participants) communication among peers in work groups might be facilitated by keeping the size of the groups relatively small. Of course, it must be noted that in some specific instances organizations may be desirous of holding down the volume of peer-peer communication in order to reduce "distractions." In such cases, large group size coupled with physical or geographical obstacles to easy contact might be advantageous from the organization's point of view. Whether it would be an advantage to have the peer-peer flow of communications reduced would depend, of course, upon what types of communications are hindered and what types will get through in any event. (Note: further aspects of communication within groups are discussed in the next sub-section.)

The second type of within-level communication in organizations involves inter-actions between members of different units. Recent research by Hage, Aiken, and Marrett (1971) suggests that the amount of such communication is affected by the structure of the organization, with a more differentiated and decentralized structure appearing to generate a higher volume of in-terdepartmental communication—as might be expected. Most of the research in this area of lateral communication has, however, focused on the problem of interdepart-mental conflicts and rivalries (e.g., Dalton, 1959; Landsberger, 1961; Strauss, 1962; Dut-ton & Walton, 1965). As Porter (1974) suggests, "the primary issue has been one of how the individual member of one department, who has loyalty to that depart-ment and whose immediate fate is bound in with its success or failure, is able to interact effectively with a member from another department who has similar loyal-ties and feelings toward his own work unit." Some investigators attribute much of the conflict that does arise to individual personality and motivational factors; others, such as Landsberger (1961), emphasize the inherent potential for conflict in the basic work flow with its differentiation of func-tions that creates a subunit orientation rather than an organizational perspective. Proposed remedies for dealing with this kind of con-flict are beyond the scope of this chapter, but it is clear that we need a good deal more in the way of systematic data collec-tion before we can pinpoint with any con-fidence the generalized communication characteristics of these types of interactions.

Line-staff interactions constitute the third major variety of lateral communication be-havior in organizations. Here again, as with cross-departmental communication, the po-tential for conflict is prevalent (Dalton, 1950). However, there is an additional ele-ment present in line-staff communication: the generally greater organizational and

geographical mobility of staff personnel. Several studies (Davis, 1953b; Burns, 1954; Zajonc & Wolfe, 1966) are in agreement that staff employees have, as Zajonc and Wolfe put it, "wider formal communication contacts than line employees" (p. 148). Members of the staff complement of or-ganizations appear to engage more often in communication activity and to have a better knowledge of events transpiring in the organization. Thus, while the formal power and even status of staff employees may be less than that of comparable level line members, their greater participation in communication provides them with a source of de facto power in dealing with the line.

The Group Dimension: Communication Within Subunits

It has already been noted that peer-peer communication appears to be strongly in-fluenced by the size of a group. We now turn to other structural aspects of groups as they affect communication, with par-ticular focus on the results and implications of laboratory studies of small group net-works. However, in viewing all of the communication network research in total we are forced to agree with Collins and Raven's (1969) assessment that "it is al-most impossible to make a single general-ization about any variable without finding at least one study to contradict the gen-eralization." (p. 147).

Research on communication under con-trolled conditions in small groups dates back to the pioneering work of Bavelas (Bavelas & Barrett, 1951) and Leavitt (1951). As mentioned previously, the focus was on the comparison of centralized (wheel) with decentralized (circle or com-pletely connected [comcon]) networks. The effects of these different structures have been studied with relation to group per-formance (usually "problem solving") and the satisfaction of various members of the group. The results from the early studies are summarized succinctly in the accompanying Table 1 from Shaw (1964, p. 123).

TABLE 1

NUMBER OF COMPARISONS SHOWING DIFFERENCES BETWEEN CENTRALIZED (WHEEL, CHAIN, Y) AND DECENTRALIZED (CIRCLE, COMCON) NETWORKS AS A FUNCTION OF TASK COMPLEXITY[a]

	Simple problems[b]	Complex problems[c]	Total
Time			
Centralized faster	14	0	14
Decentralized faster	4	18	22
Messages			
Centralized sent more	0	1	1
Decentralized sent more	18	17	35
Errors			
Centralized made more	0	6	6
Decentralized made more	9	1	10
No difference	1	3	4
Satisfaction			
Centralized higher	1	1	2
Decentralized higher	7	10	17

a. From Shaw (1964), Table I, p. 123.
b. Simple problems: symbol-, letter-, number-, and color-identification tasks.
c. Complex problems: arithmetic, word arrangement, sentence construction, and discussion problems.

The wheel or centralized networks were more likely to be faster and more error free with so-called "simple" problems, and the decentralized networks were faster and more accurate than the centralized ones on more complex problems. The average satisfaction of members was generally better in the decentralized circle and comcon networks regardless of the kind of problem.

Shaw utilizes two basic concepts to account for most of the observed effects. One factor is "independence," which refers to the "answer-getting potential" of positions in the network. Differences in relative independence-dependence between one person and others within groups can help to account for the differences in the satisfaction of various members. The other factor that

Shaw invokes for analysis is "saturation," which refers to the "total requirements placed upon an individual in a given position in the network." Such saturation varies with both communication demands —where there can be both channel overload and message overload—and task demands (e.g., problem solution responsibilities). This factor is presumed to account for the relative effectiveness of one or the other type of network in relation to the nature of the problem task faced by the group, with the efficiency of the centralized group decreasing as the tasks become more complex.

With one exception, research on small group networks since Shaw's (1964) review has not materially altered his basic conclusions. The subsequent research has, however, further refined some of the earlier conclusions. For example, Lawson (1964) and Burgess (1968, 1969) have shown that reinforcement contingencies can have an important effect on group performance via communication, especially for initially decentralized networks. It appears from their work and the previous work of Guetzkow (Guetzkow & Simon, 1955) that once decentralized groups proceed to organize themselves (often along the lines of a wheel network) they communicate in much the same manner as do centralized groups and with about as much speed. Burgess in particular argues that motivational impacts will not become apparent until a group is allowed to reach a steady state.

The major exception to the statement that research subsequent to Shaw's review has not altered the basic findings learned relatively early from network studies is provided by a study of small communication groups embedded in larger groups (Cohen, Robinson, & Edwards, 1969). These researchers rightly point out that almost all previous network investigations have been carried out on groups in isolation —that is, where they were not functioning as if they were also parts of larger groups, which would be a much more realistic set of conditions if one wishes to generalize to organizations. Cohen et al. set up a rather complex experimental design in which they formed eleven-member "organizations," with each such organization being composed of three five-man groups with overlapping membership. Within the various five-member subgroup combinations within the eleven-member organizations, different communication networks were prescribed to represent typical centralized and decentralized structures. The findings of the study showed that the embeddedness of groups within larger "organizations" had a decided impact on the communication behavior of members. For example, individuals in centralized wheel networks in their own groups tended to want to communicate much more with members of other groups than did members of decentralized groups, thereby "subverting" the internally oriented centralized system. Such behavior apparently contributed to the overall lower performance of organizations containing more centralized groups. Data on attitudes and feelings showed a more complex pattern than the typical network studies of isolated groups, indicating that such subjective responses are not only a function of one's position in his immediate group but also are a function of the individual's relationship to members of other groups within the same organization.

The study by Cohen et al. serves to illustrate the fact that many of the conclusions drawn to date about communication in small groups have been vastly oversimplified because such groups were not studied as parts of larger entities. It appears that the major thrust of future research on communication within small groups, particularly in controlled laboratory settings, should be in the direction of determining how these groups operate when part of larger structures. At the present point in time, we are only at the barest beginnings of this task. Perhaps the "embeddedness" direction of network studies will bring together both laboratory and field setting approaches to studying communication much more than

has been true to date. In the meantime, it would appear fair to conclude that the sum total of small group network studies carried out to date has contributed relatively little in the way of important insights or knowledge concerning communication in real life, complex organizations.

SOME METHODOLOGICAL CONSIDERATIONS

Crucial to the evaluation and utilization of the evidence derived from studies relating to communication in organizations—particularly field-type investigations—is a concern for the methods by which the data were obtained. Hence, in this section we examine some of the methodological directions for future studies. (See McGuire, 1969, for comments on many of the attitude change studies cited in our section on the interpersonal milieu, and Shaw, 1964, for an extended discussion of laboratory network investigations.)

We have summarized in Table 2 the basic features of twenty-two of the more important communication field studies. (The twenty-two studies represent the bulk of such research reported prior to 1972.) If one first looks at the type of organizations that have served as a locus for communication research, it can be seen that there is a great preponderance of manufacturing, industrial, and business firms. In only five studies (Hage et al., 1971; Jones et al., 1963; Julian, 1966; Smith & Brown, 1964; Sutton & Porter, 1968) are the majority of subjects from other types of organizations such as government agencies or hospitals. Clearly, only a quite limited variety of types of organizations has been sampled.

Roughly half of the studies drew samples of subjects from only a single organization. However, even among the remaining studies that drew samples from several organizations, the analyses often did not utilize comparisons across organizations. That is, such studies typically drew a few individuals from a number of different organi-

TABLE 2
SUMMARY OF METHODOLOGIES EMPLOYED IN
COMMUNICATION FIELD STUDIES

Investigator(s)	Problem(s) Investigated	Type of Organization	No. Organizations Studied		
			1	2	3+
Allen & Cohen (1969)	Influence of the organizational structure upon the communication network Technological gatekeepers	R & D Laboratories		X	
Burns (1954)	How executives spend their time	Large Business	X		
Davis (1953b)	Grapevine	Manufacturing Company	X		
Davis (1968)	Efficiency of chain-of-command Communication	Manufacturing Company	X		
Dubin & Spray (1964)	Executive activities	Savings & Loan banks; manufacturing firms			X
Hage, et al. (1971)	Relation of type of mechanism of coordination employed by organization and the volume and direction of communication	Health & welfare organizations			X
Jones, et al. (1963)	Status differences in task oriented groups	Naval ROTC Program	X		
Julian (1966)	Compliance patterns and communication blocks	Hospitals			X
Kelly (1964)	Executive behavior	Manufacturing Company	X		
Landsberger (1961)	Horizontal relations among managers	British engineering plants			X
Lawler, et al. (1968)	Managerial attitudes and behavior in communication episodes	Large mfg. plant, social service agencies			X
Maier, et al. (1963)	Effect of manager's previous position on superior-subordinate communication	Large industrial firm			X
Read (1962)	Motivational and attitudinal factors in upward communication	Large industrial firm			X
Simpson (1959)	Effect of mechanization on vertical and horizontal communication	Textile mill	X		
Slobin, et al. (1968)	Methods of address	Insurance firm	X		
Smith & Brown (1964)	Relative importance of communication structure and control structure	League of women voters			X
Sutton & Porter (1968)	Grapevine	State government office	X		
Tenenbaum (1970)	Managers' attitudes and perceptions of communication episodes	Large utility organization	X		
Triandis (1959)	Relation of cognitive similarity between superiors & subordinates & the effectiveness of interpersonal communications	Medium-sized firm	X		
Webber (1970)	Superior and subordinate perceptions of interactions	Railroad and electrical manufacturing firm		X	
Wickesberg (1968)	Characteristics of individual communication networks	Commercial, industrial & educational organizations			X
Zajonc & Wolfe (1966)	Relations between a person's position and his cognitions about his company	Industrial firm	X		

Footnotes: 1. Data was organized by amount of planning, etc. Results not broken down either by organization or subjects.
2. Includes observed hostility.

Data Analysis by Organization or Subject	Mgrs.; Professionals	Workers	Clerical	Misc.	N	Method of Data Collection	Attitudinal of Factual Data Collected	All Data From Same Source?	Hypothesis-Testing or Exploratory Research	Results Tested for Statistical Significance?
ORG.	X				58	Sociogram	A&F	Yes	H	Yes
—	X				4	Self-recording form	F	Yes	E	No
—	X				67	Ecco analysis	F	No	E	No
—	X				101	Ecco analysis	F	No	E	No
SUB.	X				8	Self-recording form	F	Yes	E	No
N/A[1]	X				N/A	Interviews	F	Yes	H	Yes
—				X	79	Self-ratings & partner ratings	A	No	E	Yes
ORG.				X	183	Interviews/Questionnaires	A	Yes	E	No
—	X				4	Activity Sampling	F	Yes	E	No
ORG.	X				N/A	Adaptation of Bales's Interaction Process Analysis	F[2]	Yes	E	No
SUB/ORG.	X				105	Self-recording forms	A&F	No	E	Yes
SUB.	X				80	Job ratings (interviews)	A[3]	No	E	Yes
SUB.	X				104	Interviews	A	No	E	Yes
—	X				8	Interviews	F	Yes	E	No
—	X		X		87	Interviews	A&F	Yes	E	No
ORG.[4]				X	Approx. 2847	Questionnaire	A&F	No	H	Yes
—	X		X		79	Ecco analysis	A&F	No	E	Yes
—	X	X	X		90	Self-recording form	A&F	No	H	Yes
—	X	X	X		155	Questionnaire	A	Yes	H	No
SUB.	X				54	Interviews	A&F	No	E	Yes
SUB.	X				91	Self-recording form	F	Yes	E	Yes
—	X	X	X		42	Employee descriptions of company	A&F	Yes	E	Yes

3. Perceptions of job duties, requirements, etc.
4. Organizations classified into large, medium, and small for analysis.

zations, but no attempt was made to analyze the data by types of organizations or characteristics of organizations. Thus, a reasonable conclusion is that the research to date that has been carried out in organizational settings has generally not contributed to our understanding of how the communication process functions in relation to specified organizational conditions. To take a simple example, we have little or no knowledge of whether communication in organizations that could be characterized as emphasizing participative-type management differs in fundamental ways—for example, utilization of different types of channels, structuring in distinctive patterns, etc.— from communication in more autocratically run organizations. Or, as another example, do organizations that contain many different functional specializations actually exhibit different communication characteristics from organizations that encompass (per a given size of unit) far fewer specializations?

An examination of the types of subjects involved in the field communication studies shows, again, a preponderance of only one type. In this case, it is managers or professional personnel (such as scientific researchers). Only three of the studies utilized rank and file workers and only four included clerical personnel. In contrast, nineteen of the twenty-two studies focused on, or included, managers and professionals. Quite obviously, communication researchers have concentrated their attention on the more verbally skilled and highly educated parts of the labor force, but have tended to ignore the vast bulk of employees in nonmanagerial and nonprofessional jobs. Given this state of affairs, extreme caution is urged in generalizing the findings of the studies considered as a whole. A further note of caution can also be found in the fact that most of the studies collected data from relatively small samples—only six of the studies involved more than 100 Ss. Or, to put this another way, with the exception of a single study (Smith & Brown, 1964) (utilizing a non-employee sample), our entire knowledge about how employees behave in terms of communicating in organizational settings is based on a total of fewer than 1,500 individuals! This contrasts sharply with the total number of subjects that have been involved in motivation, job satisfaction, or leadership/supervision studies over the years.

The situation with respect to the use of different types of data collection methods is somewhat better than might be expected. As is illustrated in Table 2, some six different methods for gathering data have been utilized in the twenty-two studies. Rather surprisingly—given their widespread use in many other areas of industrial/organizational psychology—typical attitude questionnaires have been the primary technique for data collection in only three of the investigations. More widely used have been interviews (eight studies) and self-recording forms (seven studies). Also used have been "ecco analysis" (see the discussion of Davis, 1953a, in the preceding section), observation, and sociometrics. Taken as a whole, the studies show a rather commendable use of a variety of methods for obtaining data concerning communication.

The type of data collected in each field study can be classified as either "factual" (e.g., "how many times a week do you communicate with your superior?") or "attitudinal" (e.g., "how do you feel about the frequency with which your superior communicates with you?"). Using this two-way breakdown, we see from Table 2 that some seventeen of the twenty-two studies collected at least some factual type of information about communication. Thus, the data base available from field studies is not wholly or even primarily "merely" attitudinal in character.

Somewhat more discouraging, however, is the fact that in approximately half of the studies all of the data collected came from the same source. That is, there were no checks or comparisons possible between two independent sources (i.e., sets of respondents) with respect to a given finding. Thus, many of the studies reported in the literature are subject to the possibility of contamination of the results due to the fact that only intra-subject variations contributed to any comparisons that were made.

Finally, with respect to the studies included in our survey of the more prominent field investigations, only five of them stated explicit hypotheses in advance of data collection. The others can be regarded primarily as "exploratory" studies. Such a state of affairs perhaps attests as much to the condition of our conceptual understanding of communication in organizations as it does to the methodological elegance (or lack thereof) of the studies. Furthermore, even granting the exploratory nature of most of the studies, only slightly more than half of the investigations proceeded to test their findings for statistical significance. This fact, coupled with the earlier observation that many of the studies focused on intra-subject rather than inter-subject comparisons, again argues for the rather modest state of our knowledge that has been obtained from studies of communication in organizations. Restated, the principle of caveat emptor surely applies for the potential consumer of the findings from such studies.

Let us now, however, turn to a consideration of methodological improvements that might be incorporated in future studies:

1. *More inclusive and representative samples from organizations:* So far, in most of the field studies, only quite limited samples of employees in organizations have provided data. Thus, for example, the typical field study in the past has involved only a scattering of one or two employees of several different units, or only the members of a single unit. Such samples obviously severely limit the generalizations that can be made, even about a single organization. They also prevent many useful and potentially significant inter-organization comparisons. Therefore, it seems then that future studies should include more complete and representative samples of organization members, so that conclusions about how *organizations* influence communication may be drawn.

2. *Simultaneous use of multiple methods of data collection:* We pointed out earlier that across some twenty-two studies at least six different types of data collection methods had been utilized. However, a closer look shows that in almost every study only a *single* method was used. Researchers in this area clearly need to heed the advice given some years ago by Campbell and Fiske (1959) to incorporate multiple methods into their studies. There is no reason, for example, why several methods of data collection—such as self-recording, observation, and interviews—could not be combined with an examination of several aspects of communication behavior, such as quality, quantity, initiation/reception ratio, preference for channel use, etc. In this way it might be possible to obtain more substantial findings that would lend themselves to valid generalizations. In any event, the continued use of only single methods of data collection in communication studies seems hazardous in that it may lead to some highly misleading conclusions.

3. *Longitudinal studies:* Most communication field studies have been cross-sectional in nature. However, several studies (e.g., Burns, 1954; Dubin & Spray, 1964; Lawler, Porter, & Tenenbaum, 1968) have collected data from a sample of subjects across a period of time, thus constituting a type of longitudinal study. Even in these studies, though, the time period has been short—usually only about two or three weeks. Also, data rarely have been analyzed in reference to changes across time. Instead, the several days or weeks of data collection have been used to build a more substantial and reliable data base for certain comparisons. Thus, in virtually none of the field studies has a true longitudinal research design been used to collect data relevant to communication. Consequently, it has not been possible to monitor changes in communication patterns across time, for example, or to determine the impact of specific kinds of organizational events on various aspects of communication behavior. While there are obvious inherent difficulties in col-

lecting communication data in organizations in a truly longitudinal research design, this type of study is clearly needed.

4. *Relation of communication variables to other types of variables:* Conspicuously missing in almost all of the research we have examined are data concerning relationships between communication patterns and behaviors and other organizational phenomena. The most glaring omissions so far are studies of how communication characteristics may relate to overall performance (individual or unit). At the simplest level, for example, we know nothing about how high performing employees differ in their communication behavior from low performers. Do they communicate more or less with their own superiors? Do they have a high rate of initiation? Do they tend to communicate about different things? Do they have quite different sets of linkages in the overall communication networks? Are they more likely to vary the channels they use? Could objective judges distinguish the quality of their communications from that of other employees? In a field such as industrial/organizational psychology, that places such heavy emphasis on performance, it is surprising to find so little about how communication behavior relates to performance indices.

5. *Interaction of field and laboratory studies:* Communication research has been more schizoid in separating "laboratory" from "field" studies than almost any other area of research. Even a hasty glance at the literature shows clearly how little impact laboratory network studies have had on field investigators and how little attention, in turn, laboratory researchers have paid to "real life" findings. In reviewing textbooks dealing with organizations and management, one seldom finds any real integration between the two types of studies. Continued separation of these two strands of research can only be injurious to further developments in this area.

6. *Field experiments:* Field experiments, used rather infrequently throughout indus-

trial/organizational psychology, have also been employed only rarely in communication research. It should not be too difficult to design such experiments, or at least quasi-experiments (Campbell & Stanley, 1963) in this area. For example, one can think of interjecting certain communication changes (e.g., change of channel use, more or less horizontal communications, etc.) in an experimental group and letting a control group continue in its normal communication patterns. Implementing the design for experimental field studies is always a problem, of course, but the potential benefits of pinpointing the effects of certain variables may make it worthwhile to attempt to overcome whatever difficulties are involved in setting up such a study. Designs of this type are, we predict, likely to become an important part of the communication research picture in the future.

CONCLUSIONS

Since we already have given summaries at various points, we limit our comments here to a few major conclusions:

1. No comprehensive nor fully adequate theories or conceptual systems exist for explaining the nature of communication in organizational settings. Neither theorists writing about communication, nor theorists writing about organizations have provided the sets of interrelated propositions that could give coherent impetus and direction to researchers. In this sense, communication clearly lags behind certain other areas of organizational phenomena, such as motivation and leadership.

2. The findings from social psychological research pertaining to interpersonal communication and attitude change are of only limited use to anyone concerned with organizational communication. Considerable extrapolation is required if one is to use such findings to analyze communication processes and patterns in organizations.

3. Laboratory "network" studies of communication seem largely to have run their

course, with little really new or exciting evolving from them in recent years. An exception, however, would be recent attempts to study networks embedded in other networks.

4. Research carried out to date on communication in actual organizational settings seems not to have penetrated to the heart of organizational communication problems; that is, such research does not appear to shed much light on providing effective ways to cope with such problems.

5. The need is great for more varied and more innovative methodological approaches to studying communication in organizations, if solid research advances are to be made in this area in the future. Otherwise, the area is in severe danger of becoming sterile and nonproductive.

6. Finally, we believe that communication represents such an under-theorized and under-researched area that it offers excellent opportunities for future contributions to the growing body of knowledge about behavior in organizations.

REFERENCES

Allen, T. J., & Cohen, S. I. Information flow in research and development laboratories. *Administrative Science Quarterly*, 1969, 14, 12–20.

Allport, G. W., & Postman, L. *The psychology of rumor*. New York: Russell and Russell, 1965.

Anderson, J. A. Single-channel and multi-channel messages: A comparison of connotative meaning. *Audio-Visual Communication Review*, 1969, 17, 428–434.

Argyle, M., & Kendon, A. The experimental analysis of social performance. *Advances in Experimental Social Psychology*, 1967, 3, 55–97.

Argyle, M., Salter, V., Nicholson, H., Williams, M., & Burgess, P. The communication of inferior and superior attitudes by verbal and nonverbal signals. *British Journal of Social Clinical Psychology*, 1970, 9, 222–231.

Argyris, C. *Personality and organization*. New York: Harper and Row, 1957.

Argyris, C. *Understanding organizational behavior*. Homewood, Ill.: Dorsey, 1960.

Barnlund, D. C., & Harland, C. Propinquity and prestige as determinants of communication networks. *Sociometry*, 1963, 26, 467–479.

Bass, A. Z. Refining the "gatekeeper" concept: A UN radio case study. *Journalism Quarterly*, 1969, 46, 69–72.

Bavelas, A., & Barrett, D. An experimental approach to organizational communication. *Personnel*, 1951, 27, 366–371.

Boas, F. *Race, language, and culture*. New York: Macmillan, 1940.

Breed, W. Social control in the newsroom: A descriptive study. *Social Forces*, 1955, 33, 326–335.

Broadbent, D. E. *Perception and communication*. New York: Macmillan (Pergamon), 1958.

Burgess, R. L. Communication networks: An experimental reevaluation. *Journal of Experimental Social Psychology*, 1968, 4, 324–337.

Burgess, R. L. Communication networks and behavioral consequences. *Human Relations*, 1969, 22, 137–160.

Burns, T. The directions of activity and communication in a departmental executive group. *Human Relations*, 1954, 7, 73–97.

Campbell, D. T. Systematic error on the part of human links in communication systems. *Information and Control*, 1958, 1, 334–369.

Campbell, D. T., & Fiske, D. Convergent and discriminant validation by the multitrait-multimethod matrix. *Psychological Bulletin*, 1959, 56, 81–104.

Campbell, D. T., & Stanley, J. *Experimental and quasi-experimental designs for research*. Chicago: Rand McNally, 1963.

Caplow, T. Rumors in war. *Social Forces*, 1947, 25, 298–302.

Carroll, J. *The study of language*. Cambridge: Harvard University Press, 1953.

Carroll, J. B., & Casagrande, J. B. The function of language classifications in behavior. In E. E. Maccoby, T. H. Newcomb, & E. L. Hartley (Eds.), *Readings in social psychology*. New York: Holt, Rinehart and Winston, 1958, 18–31.

Carter, R. F. Communications and affective relations. *Journalism Quarterly*, 1965, 42, 203–212.

Chapanis, A. Prelude to 2001: Explorations in human communications. *American Psychologist,* 1971, 26, 949–961.

Cohen, A. M., Robinson, E. L., & Edwards, J. L. Experiments in organizational embeddedness. *Administrative Science Quarterly,* 1969, 14, 208–221.

Cohen, A. R. Upward communication in experimentally created hierarchies. *Human Relations,* 1958, 11, 41–53.

Cohen, A. R. *Attitude change and social influence.* New York: Basic Books, 1964.

Collins, B., & Raven, B. Group structure: Attraction, coalitions, communication and power. In G. Lindzey & E. Aronson (Eds.), *Handbook of social psychology,* Vol. 4. Reading, Mass.: Addison-Wesley, 1969, 102–204.

Cyert, R., & March, J. *A behavioral theory of the firm.* Englewood Cliffs, N.J.: Prentice-Hall, 1963.

Dalton, M. Unofficial union-management relations. *American Sociological Review,* 1950, 15, 611–619.

Dalton, M. *Men who manage.* New York: Wiley, 1959.

Dance, F. E. X. The "concept" of communication. *The Journal of Communication,* 1970, 20, 201–210.

Davis, K. A method of studying communication patterns in organizations. *Personnel Psychology,* 1953, 6, 301–312. (a)

Davis, K. Management communication and the grapevine. *Harvard Business Review,* 1953, 31 (5), 43–49. (b)

Davis, K. Success of chain-of-command oral communication in a manufacturing management group. *Academy of Management Journal,* 1968, 11, 379–387.

Davitz, J. R., Ed. *The communication of emotional meaning.* New York: McGraw-Hill, 1964.

Dearborn, D., & Simon, H. Selective perception: A note on the departmental identifications of executives. *Sociometry,* 1958, 21, 140–144.

Donald, M. Some concomitants of varying patterns of communication in a large organization. Unpublished doctoral dissertation, University of Michigan, Ann Arbor, 1959.

Dubin, R., & Spray, S. Executive behavior and interaction. *Industrial Relations,* 1964, 3, 99–108.

Duncan, S. Nonverbal communication. *Psychological Bulletin,* 1969, 72, 118–137.

Dutton, J., & Walton, R. Interdepartmental conflict and cooperation: Two contrasting studies. *Human Organizations,* 1965, 25, 207–220.

Ekman, P., & Friesen, W. V. Nonverbal leakage and clues to deception. *Psychiatry,* 1969, 32 (1), 88–105.

Ekman, P., Sorenson, E. R., & Friesen, W. V. Pan-cultural elements in facial displays of emotion. *Science,* 1969, 164, 86–88.

Etzioni, A. *A comparative analysis of complex organizations.* New York: The Free Press, 1961.

Fayol, H. *General and industrial management.* London: Pitman and Sons, 1949.

Fearing, F. Toward a psychological theory of human communication. *Journal of Personality,* 1953, 22, 71–78.

Feather, N. T. A structural balance analysis of evaluative behavior. *Human Relations,* 1965, 18, 171–185.

Feather, N. T., & Jeffries, D. G. Balancing and extremity effects in reactions of receiver to source and content of communications. *Journal of Personality,* 1967, 35, 194–213.

Ference, T. P. Organizational communications systems and the decision process. *Management Science,* 1970, 17, B83–96.

Guetzkow, H. Communications in organizations. In J. G. March (Ed.), *Handbook of Organizations.* Chicago: Rand McNally, 1965, 534–573.

Guetzkow, H., & Simon, H. The impact of certain communication nets upon organization and performance in task-oriented groups. *Management Science,* 1955, 1, 233–250.

Gulick, L., & Urwick, L., Eds. *Papers on scientific administration.* New York: Columbia University, Institute of Public Administration, 1937.

Hage, J., Aiken, M., & Marrett, C. Organization structure and communications. *American Sociological Review,* 1971, 36, 860–871.

Hall, E. T. A system for the notation of proxemic behavior. *American Anthropologist,* 1963, 65, 1003–1026.

Hall, E. T. Silent assumptions in social communication. *Research Publication for the Association for Research in Nervous and Mental Disease,* 1964, 42, 41–55.

Hall, E. T. *The hidden dimension.* Garden City, N.Y.: Doubleday, 1966.

Heider, F. Attitudes and cognitive organization. *Journal of Psychology,* 1946, 21, 107–112.

Heider, F. *The psychology of interpersonal relations.* New York: Wiley, 1958.

Hovland, C. I., Harvey, O. J., & Sherif, M. Assimilation and contrast effects in communication and attitude change. *Journal of Abnormal and Social Psychology,* 1957, 55, 242–252.

Hsia, H. J. On channel effectiveness. *Audio-Visual Communication Review,* 1968, 16, 245–261.

Jones, E. E., Gergen, K. J., & Jones, R. C. Tactics of ingratiation among leaders and subordinates in a status hierarchy. *Psychological Monographs,* 1963, 77 (2, Whole No. 521).

Julian, J. Compliance patterns and communication blocks in complex organizations. *American Sociological Review,* 1966, 31, 382–389.

Katz, D., & Kahn, R. *The social psychology of organizations.* New York: Wiley, 1966.

Kelley, H. H. Communication in experimentally created hierarchies. *Human Relations,* 1951, 4, 39–56.

Kelly, J. The study of executive behavior by activity sampling. *Human Relations,* 1964, 17, 277–287.

Landsberger, H. The horizontal dimension in bureaucracy. *Administrative Science Quarterly,* 1961, 6, 299–332.

Lawler, E. E. III, Porter, L. W., & Tenenbaum, A. Managers' attitudes toward interaction episodes. *Journal of Applied Psychology,* 1968, 52, 432–439.

Lawrence, P., & Lorsch, J. *Organization and environment: Managing differentiation and integration.* Cambridge: Graduate School of Business Administration, Harvard University Press, 1967.

Lawson, E. D. Reinforced and non-reinforced four-man communication nets. *Psychological Reports,* 1964, 14, 287–296.

Leavitt, H. Some effects of certain communication patterns on group performance. *Journal of Abnormal and Social Psychology,* 1951, 46, 38–50.

Likert, R. *New patterns of management.* New York: McGraw-Hill, 1961.

Likert, R. *The human organization.* New York: McGraw-Hill, 1967.

McGregor, D. *The human side of enterprise.* New York: McGraw-Hill, 1960.

McGregor, D. *The professional manager.* New York: McGraw-Hill, 1967.

McGuire, W. J. The nature of attitudes and attitude change. In G. Lindzey & E. Aronson (Eds.), *Handbook of social psychology,* Vol. 3. Reading, Mass.: Addison-Wesley, 1969, 136–314.

McLeod, J. M. The contribution of psychology to human communication theory. In F. E. X. Dance (Ed.), *Human communication theory: Original essays.* New York: Holt, Rinehart and Winston, 1967, 202–234.

Mahl, G. F., & Schulze, G. Psychological research in the extralinguistic area. In T. A. Sebeok, A. S. Hayes, & M. C. Bateson (Eds.), *Approaches to semiotics.* The Hague: Mouton, 1964, 51–124.

Maier, N. R. F., Hoffman, L., Hooven, J., & Read, W. H. Superior-subordinate communications in management. *American Management Research Studies,* 1961, No. 52.

Maier, N. R. F., Hoffman, L., & Read, W. H. Superior-subordinate communication: The relative effectiveness of managers who held their subordinates' positions. *Personnel Psychology,* 1963, 16, 1–12.

March, J., & Simon, H. *Organizations.* New York: Wiley, 1958.

Mehrabian, A. Immediacy: An indicator of attitudes in linguistic communication. *Journal of Personality,* 1966, 34, 26–34.

Mehrabian, A. Inference of attitudes from the posture, orientation, and distance of communicator. *Journal of Consulting and Clinical Psychology,* 1968, 32, 296–308.

Mehrabian, A., & Ferris, S. R. Inference of attitudes from nonverbal communication in two channels. *Journal of Consulting Psychology,* 1967, 31, 248–252.

Mellinger, G. Interpersonal trust as a factor in communication. *Journal of Abnormal and Social Psychology,* 1956, 52, 304–309.

Mooney, J. D., & Reiley, A. C. *The principles of organization.* New York: Harper and Row, 1939.

Olesen, V. L., & Whittaker, E. W. Adjudication of student awareness in professional socialization: The language of laughter and silences. *Sociological Quarterly,* 1966, 7, 381–396.

Osgood, C. E., Suci, G. J., & Tannenbaum, P. H. *The measurement of meaning.* Urbana: University of Illinois Press, 1957.

Porter, L. W. Communication: Structure and process. In H. L. Fromkin & J. J. Sherwood (Eds.), *Integrating the organization.* New York: The Free Press, 1974.

Porter, L. W., & Lawler, E. E. III. The effects of "tall" versus "flat" organization structures on managerial job satisfaction. *Personnel Psychology,* 1964, 17, 135–148.

Porter, L. W., Lawler, E. E. III, & Hackman, J. R. *Behavior in organizations.* New York: McGraw-Hill, 1975.

Porter, L. W., & Siegel, J. Relationships of tall and flat organization structures to the satisfactions of foreign managers. *Personnel Psychology,* 1965, 18, 379–392.

Read, W. Upward communication in industrial hierarchies. *Human Relations,* 1962, 15, 3–16.

Roberts, D. F. The nature of human communication effects. In W. Schramm & D. F. Roberts (Eds.), *Process and effects of mass communication.* (Rev. ed.) Urbana: University of Illinois Press, 1971.

Roberts, K. H., O'Reilly, C. A., Bretton, G. E., & Porter, L. W. Organizational theory and organizational communication: A communication failure? *Human Relations,* 1974, 27, 501–524.

Rosenberg, B. G., & Langer, J. A study of postural-gestural communication. *Journal of Personality and Social Psychology,* 1965, 2, 593–597.

Runkel, P. J. Cognitive similarity in facilitating communication. *Sociometry,* 1956, 19, 178–191.

Sapir, E. *Language: An introduction to the study of speech.* New York: Harcourt, Brace, 1921.

Sapir, E. The status of linguistics as a science. *Language,* 1929, 5, 207–214.

Scheflen, A. E. Behavioral programs and their integration in interaction. *Behavioral Science,* 1968, 13, 44–55.

Schein, E. H. *Organizational psychology.* (2nd ed.) Englewood Cliffs, N.J.: Prentice-Hall, 1970.

Schramm, W. The nature of communication between humans. In W. Schramm & D. F. Roberts (Eds.), *The process and effects of mass communication.* Urbana: University of Illinois Press, 1971, 3–54.

Shannon, C. A mathematical theory of communication. *Bell System Technical Journal,* 1948, 27, 379–423, 623–656.

Shannon, C., & Weaver, W. *The mathematical theory of communication.* Urbana: University of Illinois Press, 1949.

Shaw, M. E. Some effects of problem complexity upon problem solution efficiency in different communication nets. *Journal of Experimental Psychology,* 1954, 48, 211–217.

Shaw, M. E. Some effects of varying amounts of information exclusively possessed by a group member upon his behavior in the group. *Journal of General Psychology,* 1963, 68, 71–79.

Shaw, M. E. Communication networks. In L. Berkowitz (Ed.), *Advances in experimental social psychology.* New York: Academic Press, 1964, 111–147.

Sherif, M., Sherif, C. W., & Nebergall, R. E. *Attitude and attitude change.* Philadelphia: Saunders, 1965.

Simon, H. *Administrative behavior.* New York: Macmillan, 1945.

Simpson, R. Vertical and horizontal communication in formal organizations. *Administrative Science Quarterly,* 1959, 4, 188–196.

Slobin, D., Miller, S., & Porter, L. W. Forms of address and social relations in a business organization. *Journal of Personality and Social Psychology,* 1968, 8, 289–293.

Smith, C., & Brown, M. Communication structure and control structure in a voluntary association. *Sociometry,* 1964, 27, 449–468.

Sommer, R. Small group ecology. *Psychological Bulletin,* 1967, 67, 145–152.

Steiner, I. D., Anderson, J., & Hays, R. Immediate and delayed reactions to interpersonal disagreements: Some effects of type of issue and order of response. *Journal of Experimental Social Psychology,* 1967, 3, 206–219.

Strauss, G. A. Tactics of lateral relationships: The purchasing agent. *Administrative Science Quarterly,* 1962, 7, 161–186.

Sutton, H., & Porter, L. W. A study of the grapevine in a governmental organization. *Personnel Psychology,* 1968, 21, 223–230.

Tajfel, H. Social and cultural factors in perception. In G. Lindzey & E. Aronson (Eds.), *Handbook of social psychology,* Vol. 3. (2nd ed.) Reading, Mass.: Addison-Wesley, 1969, 315–394.

Taylor, F. *Scientific management*. New York: Harper and Row, 1911.

Tenenbaum, A. Dyadic communications in industry. Unpublished doctoral dissertation, University of California, Berkeley, 1970.

Thayer, L. Communication and organization theory. In F. E. X. Dance (Ed.), *Human communication theory: Original essays*. New York: Holt, Rinehart and Winston, 1967, 70–115.

Thompson, J. *Organizations in action*. New York: McGraw-Hill, 1967.

Triandis, H. Cognitive similarity and interpersonal communication in industry. *Journal of Applied Psychology*, 1959, 43, 321–326.

Triandis, H. Cognitive similarity and communication in a dyad. *Human Relations*, 1960, 13, 175–183. (a)

Triandis, H. C. Some determinants of interpersonal communication. *Human Relations*, 1960, 13, 279–287. (b)

Watson, D. Effects of certain social power structures on communication in task-oriented groups. *Sociometry*, 1965, 28, 322–336.

Watson, D., & Bromberg, B. Power, communication, and position satisfaction in task-oriented groups. *Journal of Personality and Social Psychology*, 1965, 2, 859–864.

Webber, R. A. Perceptions of interactions between superiors and subordinates. *Human Relations*, 1970, 23, 235–248.

Weber, M. *The theory of social and economic organization*. Henderson and Parsons, trans. England: Oxford University Press, 1947.

Weick, K. E. *The social psychology of organizing*. Reading, Mass.: Addison-Wesley, 1969.

Welford, A. T. *Ageing and human skills*. London and New York: Oxford University Press, 1958.

Westley, B., & MacLean, M. A conceptual model for communication research. *Journalism Quarterly*, 1957, 34, 31–38.

Whisler, T. L. *Information technology and organizational change*. Belmont, Calif.: Wadsworth Publishing, 1970. (a)

Whisler, T. L. *The impact of computers on organizations*. New York: Praeger, 1970. (b)

White, W. J. An index for determining the relative importance of information sources. *Public Opinion Quarterly*, 1969, 33, 607–610.

Whorf, B. L. The relation of habitual thought and behavior to language. In L. Spier (Ed.), *Language, culture, and personality*. Menasha, Wis.: Sapir Memorial Publication Fund, 1941, 75–93.

Wickesberg, A. K. Communications networks in the business organization structure. *Academy of Management Journal*, 1968, 11, 253–262.

Wiener, M., & Mehrabian, A. *Language within language: Immediacy, a channel in verbal communication*. New York: Appleton-Century-Crofts, 1968.

Wiener, N. *The human use of human beings*. Boston: Houghton Mifflin, 1954.

Wilensky, H. L. *Organizational Intelligence*. New York: Basic Books, 1967.

Woodward, J. *Industrial organization: Theory and practice*. New York: Oxford University Press, 1965.

Zajonc, R., & Wolfe, D. Cognitive consequence of a person's position in a formal organization. *Human Relations*, 1966, 19, 139–150.

CHAPTER 36

Change Processes in Organizations[1]

CLAYTON P. ALDERFER
Yale University

Introduction	Changing States
Concepts and Propositions	Implications
Steady States	References

SOCIAL TECHNOLOGY is more advanced than theory building for applying behavioral science to organizations. In this chapter, boundary permeability and relationship mutuality, two concepts from open systems theory, are formulated to explain steady and changing states of individuals, groups, and organizations. Each level of human unit is examined from both internal and external perspectives; several cross-level hypotheses are proposed. Optimal boundary permeability occurs when mutual relationships are established among subsystems and between the system and its environment. Interpersonal and intergroup mutuality tend to be positively associated. Planned change programs in organizations are analyzed according to this "boundary-relationship" perspective. Organizations change in order to satisfy human needs more fully. Therefore, change programs introduced by applied behavioral scientists are fueled by the energy of human needs, but they vary according to the level of human unit they take as change target. The chapter closes by proposing a series of conceptually based guidelines for applying behavioral science to organizations.

INTRODUCTION

In the last twenty years, the use of behavioral science research in organizational settings has increased enormously (Bennis, 1966). Kurt Lewin provided much of the theory, methodology, and ideology on which applied behavioral science is based. When Lewin was writing, theory seemed ahead of practice. Now, the balance seems to have shifted; practice may be leading theory. Indeed, the technology for changing human systems has burgeoned.

The social technological orientation of many investigators is apparent. For example, in the important theoretical book *Social Psychology of Organizations* (1966), though

[1] The writer would like to thank Professors Chris Argyris, Dave Brown, Richard Hackman, Douglas Hall, Robert Kaplan, Roy Lewicki, Victor Vroom, Irving Janis, and Robert Neal for their helpful comments on an earlier version of this chapter and to acknowledge the support of the Office of Naval Research (Contract No. N00014-67-A-0097-0017).

Katz and Kahn discussed open systems theory, they placed more emphasis on technology than theory. They addressed the topic of organizational change primarily in terms of change methods: individual counseling, sensitivity training, group therapy, feedback, and the like. Similarly, Hornstein, Bunker, Burke, Hornstein, and Lewicki (1971) discussed theory, but emphasized social technology. They discussed strategies of social intervention—individual, technostructure, data-based, organizational development, violent and nonviolent.

In contrast, this chapter is theoretical and two of Kurt Lewin's ideas form the basis of this chapter. "There is nothing so practical as a good theory" (Marrow, 1969, p. ix) and "In order to gain insight into a process one must create a change and then observe its variable effects and new dynamics" (Marrow, 1969, p. 235). The present author suggests that, in addition, the study of change should extend beyond the immediate effect of the intervention. Moreover, theoretical concepts which help us understand change should also be relevant to steady states, and such concepts should be relevant not only to organizations but to individuals and groups. In an effort to understand change, steady states, organizations, groups, and individuals, a wide range of research is examined and reorganized.

The chapter is divided into four parts.

1. *Concepts and Propositions* identifies a number of ideas based on open systems theory which offer promise for understanding organizational change. The key terms, boundaries and relationships, are defined, and the major hypotheses relating these variables are stated. The propositions apply across levels of analysis: the individual, group, and organization.

2. *Steady States* examines the applicability of the theoretical assumptions for static conditions of individuals, groups, and organizations. Studies from various types of systems are compared. Research results are reinterpreted in light of the open systems concepts and propositions.

3. *Changing States* reports on numerous investigations of planned change in organizations. Attention is directed to changing individuals, groups, and organizations. In addition, concepts to explain the motivation or stimulation of change are introduced.

4. *Implications* addresses the future. This section spells out some of the possibilities for using theory in producing and studying change.

CONCEPTS AND PROPOSITIONS

The idea of using open systems concepts to study individuals, groups, and organizations is not new. At each level of analysis open systems reasoning is apparent. Allport (1960), for example, suggested using open systems theory in the study of personality. Menninger, Mayman, and Pruyser (1963) proposed a reorientation in psychiatric thinking by applying open systems concepts to psychopathology. Mills (1964) brought open systems thinking to the study of self-analytic groups, and in experimental social psychology, Ziller (1965) proposed a theory of open and closed groups. In organization psychology, while Rice (1969) and Katz and Kahn (1966) emphasized boundaries in organizational life, Argyris (1960), Bennis (1962), and Schein (1965) emphasized the relationships between the parts in organizations.

OPEN AND CLOSED SYSTEMS. A system is a set of units with relationships among them (Miller, 1965). The state of each unit is, therefore, at least partially dependent on the state of other units. Systems have a unity or whole which, as a result of the interaction among the parts, is *different* qualitatively and quantitatively from the sum of the parts. This difference may come about because the parts combine in ways that enable them to be *more* than the sum of the parts or because they undermine each other so that collectively they are *less* than the sum of the parts.

An open system is *not* totally separate from its environment. In contrast to a closed system, an open system engages its external environment through the exchange of matter, energy, and information. Living systems are open systems while nonliving systems are closed. Living systems depend on exchange with the environment for their survival. Not only does the system take in material, energy, and information, it also discharges material, energy, and information in the form of waste and product achievement.

Systems show disorder, disorganization, lack of pattern, and randomness; the second law of thermodynamics applies to systems. According to the second law of thermodynamics, thermodynamic degradation is irrevocable over time. Systems may move from a state of ordered arrangements to the more probable state of random disarray (Miller, 1965). Closed systems inevitably decay. Open systems, however, can counteract the entropy by absorbing inputs which have greater complexity than the systems outputs. This process is called increasing the negentropy (negative entropy) of a system. Through exchange with the external environment, an open system can forestall its death, guarantee its life, or even increase its vitality over time. Which of these tendencies predominates depends on the balance of entropy and negative entropy in the system. A relatively closed system, therefore, is a special case of an open system in which environmental exchange is minimal.

Persons, groups, and organizations may each be conceptualized as open systems. Individuals regularly exchange matter, energy, and information with their environments through such processes as ingestion, expulsion, and communication. Despite these processes, however, until recently one might still have viewed the person as partially a closed system because certain of its most important parts could not be rebuilt or replaced and, therefore ultimately decayed with age. But recent developments in medicine, such as artificial organ construction and transplantation, increase the inherent openness of the human body and offer the theoretical possibility of indefinite life for persons. Groups and organizations have the potential of indefinite life by recruitment of new people as senior members leave and through the restructuring of groups as new people enter the system and as new tasks are required of the unit.

BOUNDARIES. Whether a human system survives and flourishes depends not only on whether it is open to the external environment but also on how it regulates exchanges with the outside world. The external boundaries of a system regulate the flow of matter, energy, and information between a system and its environment, while the internal boundaries of a system regulate the input and output of subsystems of a unit. There tends to be more interaction among the set of parts which form a system than between this set of parts and any other set of parts in the external environment.

As a result of regulating the flow of inputs and outputs, the boundaries of a system play an important part in determining its organization. They hold the system together as an organized entity and thus help to distinguish what a system is from what it is not. In both systems and subsystems boundaries help define what is inside and what is outside the unit.

Boundaries may be identified operationally by two classes of indicators. First, there are physical, spatial, or temporal limits which can be readily observed. A person has his clothes and his skin. The membership of a group can be readily established by enumerating the persons who make up the unit. Such physical structures as fences. walls, gates, and so on frequently identify spatial boundaries. Individuals, groups, and organizations also can be defined by their time limits. The birth and death of persons is paralleled by the formation and disengagement of groups and organizations.

Subjective boundaries may also be identified for individuals, groups, and organizations. A substantial portion of psychoanalytic theory develops the concept of ego boundaries (Landis, 1970). "Specifically, the term *ego boundaries* [italics his] is a structural conception that refers to the boundaries that differentiate the phenomenal self in varying degrees . . ." (Landis, 1970, p. 1). Concepts such as a sense of cohesion, inclusion, involvement, and identification have been developed to characterize group and organizational boundaries (Cartwright & Zander, 1961; Schutz, 1958; Alderfer & Lodahl, 1971; Janis, 1963). That is, a group or organization in which the members feel highly cohesive, fully included, heavily involved, or strongly identified would also be one with well-established boundaries.

A number of investigations support the assertion that concrete and subjective boundaries tend to converge (Sommer, 1967). For example, Campbell, Kruskal, and Wallace (1966) found that the seating arrangements of Negroes and whites were associated with different ethnic attitudes. Mehrabian (1963) found that distance between pairs of people was strongly and inversely related to liking of people. Lett, Clark, and Altman (1969) reviewed a series of studies which supported the proposition that the more group members liked or knew each other, the closer was their interpersonal distance. Systems logic would argue that the causality of these associations is two-way. That is, when concrete boundaries are established, they tend to foster the formation of subjective boundaries, and subjective boundaries tend to promote the establishment of concrete boundaries.

The characteristic of boundaries with which we shall be most concerned in this chapter is their degree of permeability. Figure 1 shows a hypothetical relationship between system vitality—the tendency toward survival and growth—and boundary permeability. At one extreme, the permeability of the boundaries of a human system can approximate zero, making the system essentially closed. At this point, a potentially open system becomes closed and thereby subject to the second law of thermodynamics. A closed system will tend toward deterioration and eventually cease living. At the other extreme, fully permeable boundaries are not boundaries at all. Nothing can be kept in or out; there is no inside or outside to the system. The system with fully permeable boundaries cannot be distinguished from its environment: when there are no boundaries, there is no system. Thus, there is a close connection between the potential vitality of a system when its boundaries approximate zero permeability and when they are completely open; the life prospects of the system are quite low in both conditions. There is also a tendency for systems to vacillate rapidly between extreme closedness and extreme openness. A custodial prison, an example of a highly closed system, may have a rebellion in which many of its internal boundaries and some of its external boundaries are destroyed. A person suffering from severe mental disturbance, whose behavior is "out of control," is likely to be confined in some way so that he won't harm others or himself.

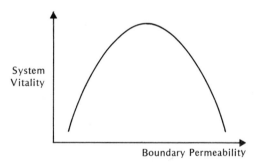

Figure 1. Hypothetical relationship between system vitality (the tendency toward survival and/or growth) and boundary permeability.

RELATIONSHIPS. Relationships among the parts of a system and between a system and its environment exist when there is regular exchange of matter, energy, or information. Relationships which are established within a system provide integration, coherence, and stability to the system and thereby strengthen its internal security. Relationships which are established across system boundaries facilitate the system's interaction with the environment; they provide an opportunity for the system to export waste and products and import nourishment and stimulation.

Both kinds of relationships are necessary for a system to survive and grow. Without internal relationships a system may be unable to utilize inputs from the environment. Without external relationships an open system becomes closed. However, if only internal relationships are formed, the system becomes closed and dies from lack of interaction with its environment. If only external relationships are formed, the boundary of the system disappears and the system disintegrates.

Relationships differ in their degree of *mutuality,* that is, in the extent that all relevant matter, energy, and information is both given and received by the parties in the relationship (Rogers, 1959; Argyris, 1962; Erikson, 1964).

In this chapter, we shall be primarily concerned with those relationships where the matters for exchange are ideas and feelings. The highest level of mutuality occurs when both agreements and disagreements about ideas are stated by one party and received by the others, and when both positive feelings (such as liking, support, and trust) and negative feelings (such as fear, anxiety, and mistrust) are expressed and accepted by the parties. Mutuality decreases to the extent that relevant ideas are excluded from an exchange, to the degree that relevant positive or negative feelings are systematically withheld or ignored, or to the extent that the exchange is one-way with one party only giving or only receiving.

The degree of mutuality in various relationships can be identified operationally by two classes of indicators: behavioral and subjective. Behavioral indicators of mutuality attempt to code or "score" the overt activities of parties who are relating to one another. A number of investigators have developed coding systems that give attention to one or more facets of mutuality as defined here. Argyris's (1965) measures of interpersonal competence include categories for coding the presence or absence of feelings

in an exchange and the degree of openness to one's self and to others. Mills (1964) has presented a coding system that emphasizes the distinction between positive and negative sentiments as group members interact with each other. Alderfer and Lodahl (1971) developed scales for "here-and-now" behavior, an indicator of the relevance of an exchange, and for the "openness" of actors' statements. The experimental literature also contains studies in which the independent variables have been manipulations of behavior which reflect more and less of certain features of mutuality. Maier and Solem (1952), for example, varied leader behavior in the degree to which the leader actively sought out the full range of member opinions during problem solving. Hoffman, Harburg, and Maier (1962) varied the degree to which low status members of a group expressed disagreement with high status group members. A new behavior coding system for measuring mutuality exactly as defined here has been developed by Alderfer, Kaplan, and Smith (1974).

Subjective measures of facets of mutuality include various personality scales for individuals and multiple perceptual indicators for interpersonal and group behavior. Gough's Chapter 13 in this *Handbook* provides an extensive review of personality measures, many of which tap intrapsychic emotional states. Argyris (1965), Bolman (1971), and Alderfer and Lodahl (1971) have developed subjective measures of interpersonal and group aspects of mutuality. There are a number of studies which demonstrate correlations between subjective and behavioral facets of mutuality (Argyris, 1965; Alderfer & Lodahl, 1971; Alderfer, Kaplan, & Smith, 1974).

BOUNDARIES AND RELATIONSHIPS. Relationships provide the links among different systems and among subsystems within a system. When a relationship provides positive feedback to a system, it becomes the vehicle whereby the system boundaries are nurtured and supported. In psychoanalytic writings, for example, theorists refer to the degree to which ego boundaries are cathected with libido—in the case of strong boundaries —or to the withdrawal of libido from ego boundaries—in the case of weakened boundaries (Landis, 1970, p. 9). Groups which succeed in their assigned tasks tend to receive positive feedback from the outside world, which supports their existing structures (Blake, Shepard, & Mouton, 1964). But there is also potential danger for a system that receives only positive feedback; there is no stimulation for adaptation or growth. There is the possibility that a system will become "fat and happy" and thus be vulnerable to an unanticipated catastrophe. But there are also dangers in negative feedback, if it is excessive. A system that receives extraordinarily high amounts of negative feedback will tend to close as a matter of self-preservation. If defense becomes habitual, the system loses its capacity to adapt and becomes more and more closed. In short, a relationship between boundary permeability and mutuality seems to exist. From this hypothesis a number of propositions can be derived, which in turn provide a viewpoint for understanding change processes in human systems.

Postulate: Optimal boundary permeability—that is, the degree of permeability at which system vitality is maximal—tends to be associated with high degrees of mutuality in system and subsystem relationships, while excessively closed or open boundaries tend to be associated with low degrees of mutuality among subsystems and among systems.

When a system has a closed external boundary, less opportunity is provided for input and output. Consequently, the parts of the system have less opportunity for external stimulation and for release of products and waste. On the other hand, when external boundaries are optimally permeable, the parts of the system are able to receive inputs from outside and discharge their own outputs. Internal boundaries also affect the state of external boundaries. For example, if the internal boundaries are permeable, the subsystem can stimulate the larger system to interact with the environment, thereby affecting the degree of permeability of the external boundaries. Thus, the degree of internal and external boundary permeability tends to be similar.

The degree of mutuality characterizing internal and external relationships also tends to be similar. For example, a system could not give to the external world what it was unable to get from within. Thus, when one detects departures from mutuality in external relations, it is likely that there will also be non-mutual relations internally.

Furthermore, the degree of permeability of the internal and external boundaries tends to match the degree of mutuality of the relationships of the system and subsystems. For example, a closed subsystem which has encapsulated an input is unlikely to engage in relationships that are mutual. There tends to be a parallelism between internal and external conditions such that: (1) External and internal boundaries tend to be congruent; that is, optimally permeable external boundaries tend to be associated with optimally permeable internal boundaries, while excessively closed or open external boundaries tend to be associated with excessively closed or open internal boundaries. (2) External and internal relationships tend to be congruent; that is, the degree of mutuality in external relations tends to parallel the degree of mutuality in internal relations.

SYSTEM CHANGE. The foregoing analysis shows that system change is a complex affair involving internal and external boundaries, internal and external relationships. Some theorists have proposed that the primary source of change is external to a system (e.g., Katz & Kahn, 1966, p. 448; Terreberry, 1968, p. 610), while the present position implies a very high interdependency between internal and external conditions. If the external world provides stimuli or opportunities for change which are not met by internal readiness, one would expect little movement. If internal sources identify needs for change which cannot be supported by external conditions, there is little reason to expect sustained change.

According to this theoretical position, there will be three primary system conditions:

Condition 1. When the system is excessively open and has relatively low levels of mutuality in internal and external relationships;

Condition 2. When the system is optimally open and has relatively high levels of mutuality in internal and external relationships; and

Condition 3. When the system is excessively closed and has relatively low levels of mutuality in internal and external relationships.

There is a sense in which system pathology is more severe in Condition 1 than in Condition 3 because when the boundaries of a system are threatened with dissolution, the very existence of the system is in question. In Condition 3, by comparison, the system boundaries are intact, although the system may be functioning very inefficiently. At the level of individual pathology, Condition 1 parallels that of psychosis in which internal and external ego boundaries are severely weakened (Landis, 1970), while Condition 3 parallels that of neurosis in which a person's relationships with others and himself are disturbed while his ego boundaries remain relatively intact (Horney, 1937). At the level of group pathology, Condition 1 exists when a group which should have formed has not, or when a group is breaking apart because of internal conflict or external stress. Condition 3 exists when a group has formed but is unable to communicate effectively internally or externally.

In changing Condition 1 toward Condition 2, the first priority for action is to aid in strengthening or establishing of system boundaries. As system boundaries form under high degrees of stress, it is likely that they will tend to be excessively closed. Thus, under Condition 1 if boundaries are formed, the system tends to move to Condition 3. Then movement to Condition 2 may be possible.

The three-system conditions represent quasi-stationary equilibria. Because of the interdependency of boundary and relationship conditions, each of the states tends to be self-reinforcing. Conditions 1 and 3, if they move at all, tend toward greater pathology, while Condition 2 tends to perpetuate adaptive openness. Perhaps when the pain is great enough a system will seek outside intervention, but it is more likely that a system experiencing mild departures from Condition 2 will seek help than a system in Condition 1 or 3. If a system is close to Condition 2, seeking outside relationships of mutuality is consistent with the equilibrium of Condition 2.

The constructs which were defined in the above section will be used in the following sections to understand and explain steady states and change processes in the individual, group, and organization.

STEADY STATES

Although systems change, they also establish and maintain steady states. If the previously discussed propositions are useful, they should apply to steady state conditions as well as to changing states. In this section, those general propositions form the framework for which research on individuals, groups, and organizations is discussed. The study of individuals and groups in this section is focused on the non-organization context; the emphasis is on individuals and groups per se. In the next section, devoted to changing states, the individual and the group in the organizational context are discussed. At each level of analysis—individual, group, and organization—both internal and external conditions are discussed.

Individuals

As Allport (1960) and Menninger et al. (1963) have shown, people can be conceptualized in terms of open systems theory. Persons have boundaries, both concrete and subjective, which separate them from their external environment. They form relationships with other persons and join groups and organizations. They rely on their environment as a source of both material and psychological support. They discharge solid waste and psychological refuse, the latter in the form of anger, frustration, or a sense of alienation. Within themselves, individuals vary in the degree to which their parts perform the necessary physiological functions; failure of a key organ to achieve the needed inputs and outputs threatens a person's life. Psychologically, individuals vary in the degree to which they are aware of and accept the potential and actual richness of their ideational and emotional lives.

Support for the preceding hypothesis is found in studies of authoritarian persons and creative persons. Initially, the authoritarian personality construct was described by, and such persons were identified by, a characteristic pattern of external relationships. Authoritarian persons tended to form non-mutual relations with large classes of significant others, namely parental figures and minority groups. In terms of boundary-relationship logic, those individuals relatively high in authoritarianism in contrast to those relatively low on this characteristic should show more closed external boundaries, more closed internal boundaries, relatively low internal mutuality, and relatively few signs of being able to adapt and change. Creative personalities were initially identified by their judged ability to produce novel and worthwhile products; their defining characteristic, therefore, was the tendency to stimulate adaptation and change. In terms of the boundary-relationship logic, those individuals relatively high in creativity in comparison to those relatively low in creativity should show more optimally permeable in-

ternal and external boundaries and higher mutuality in internal and external relationships.

INTERNAL CONDITIONS. One of the major characteristics of the more authoritarian male personality is his anti-intraceptiveness. He seems to be opposed to the subjective, the imaginative, or tender-minded (Adorno, Frenkel-Brunswik, Levinson, & Sanford, 1950; Brown, 1965). He is more inclined to recognize the positive trait in himself and to rationalize or deny the negative qualities. At the same time, however, the surface positive evaluation tends to be accompanied by an underlying contempt for the self. External forces outside his own control tend to be blamed for failures and difficulties. Masculine qualities in men (such as decisiveness and willpower) are exaggerated, and the more emotional qualities which could be considered feminine are minimized. An analogous pattern is observed for the more authoritarian female who tends to see herself as soft without admitting to masculine characteristics. Highly authoritarian persons tend to see themselves as highly controlled, and the occasional breakthroughs are either considered outside their influence or not understood. The authoritarian person also tends to abhor explanations of the self in terms of social and psychological conditions. The internal boundary conditions of the more authoritarian personalities, therefore, seem to show excessive closedness with an occasional sign of boundary weakness (the breakthroughs which could not be understood). The relationships among the parts of the personality can be characterized by non-mutuality because the more authoritarian types seem relatively unable to tolerate both desirable and undesirable traits in their awareness.

In contrast, the more creative personalities show a more rich and turbulent emotional life. Creative males show relatively high scores on femininity scales on personality tests, while creative females show relatively high masculine scores. Creative persons also tend to score high on such measures of pathology as depression, hypochondrias, hysteria, psychopathic deviation, and schizophrenia. But contrary to the usual pattern for other persons judged to be psychologically ill, the creative persons tend to have very high ego strength (Barron, 1965; Dellas & Gaier, 1970). The more creative personalities also show higher acceptance of both their desirable and undesirable characteristics than the less creative types. In terms of boundary and relationship language the more creative types tend to show more optimal permeability than the less creative types. They have greater permeability of the ego boundaries coupled with stronger boundaries. The relationships among the parts of their personalities are richer and more complex than the less creative persons.

EXTERNAL CONDITIONS. Authoritarians were originally identified because of their prejudice. Initially a particular type of ethnocentrism—namely, anti-Semitism—was the focus of attention, and later, the general trait of ethnocentrism was identified and measured (Adorno et al., 1950). Anti-Semitism includes negative opinions about Jews, hostile attitudes toward them, and a system of moral values to justify the views. Ethnocentrism is defined as an ideological system pertaining to groups and group relations. Ingroups, those groups with which the individual identifies himself, are the object of positive opinions and uncritically supportive attitudes, while outgroups, those groups to which an individual does not belong, are seen as antithetical to ingroups and are the object of negative opinions and hostile attitudes. General ethnocentrism has been found to be highly associated with authoritarianism. The final version of the authoritarianism scale (the F-scale) has an average correlation of .75 with ethnocentrism (Brown, 1965).

Authoritarianism as a personality construct includes more than non-mutual relationships with "outgroups." Authoritarians also tend to have characteristic responses

toward their parents and toward members of the opposite sex. Authoritarian persons tend to show an idealization of their parents; they tend to glorify their external features rather than the more psychological qualities. They are not likely to show much ability for a critical evaluation of their parents in psychological terms. Their discipline was harsh and threatening and relationships seem to have been based on roles of dominance and submission. Unconsciously, authoritarian persons seem to resent their parents. Occasionally, such attitudes break through into awareness. With regard to persons of the opposite sex, authoritarians tend to see persons of the opposite sex in terms of ways for obtaining status. They tend to separate affect and sex and do not tend to think of sex in personal terms. Often there is an underlying resentment against members of the opposite sex, and heterosexual interpersonal relations tend to have an exploitative-manipulative quality (Adorno et al., 1950).

Rokeach (1960), in his research growing out of the authoritarianism tradition, found that dogmatic persons reported having been influenced by a narrow range of people when they were growing up. He concluded that this indicated that authoritarian persons do not identify with broad human conditions.

The first investigators of the authoritarian personality hypothesized that socioeconomic class was an important variable contributing to the personality syndrome, and studies have consistently shown that authoritarianism is inversely correlated with social class. An investigation by MacKinnon and Centers (1956) confirmed the general hypothesis but also elaborated on it in an interesting way. These investigators asked each respondent to say in what social class he placed himself and to rate the strength of his sense of membership in that class. In both the working and middle classes, those persons who described themselves as borderline were the *least* authoritarian. Among the lower social classes, persons who identified in a broad rather than narrow way with a particular social class were less authoritarian.

In contrast, creative personality appears to have decidedly strong external ego boundaries. Compared to less creative colleagues in their own professions, the more creative persons appeared more self-confident, aggressive, independent, and poised (Dellas & Gaier, 1970).

Pelz and Andrews (1966) studied the nature of productive work climates and though they did not study creative persons per se, some of their findings seem relevant to a discussion of boundary permeability and relationship mutuality. They found a number of relational conditions associated with scientific effectiveness in university, government, and industrial settings. For example, the more sources a scientist reported influencing his goals, the more effective his performance was. Moreover, the more influence he felt he had over these sources, the more effective his performance was. The highest effectiveness came for those persons who had several sources of influence affecting them and at the same time could also influence these people. Mutual relationships, characterized by *both* giving and receiving influence, were associated with effective research performance. Moreover, the more effective scientists had more overall contact with their colleagues than the less effective researchers. They spent more time with more colleagues than the less effective scientists. The correlations between contact and performance were strongest when interaction was initiated by the scientist as compared to being started by the colleagues, the organization, or chance. Thus, a variety of relationship measures—none of which tapped mutuality as fully defined above, but each of which assessed some facet of it—are consistent with the proposition that the more creative producers tend to have both a history and a present pattern of greater mutuality in their relationships with others.

PROPENSITY TO CHANGE. For expository purposes, we have separated internal and external considerations. But this division cannot be maintained if one is to address questions of individual change. The foundation of open systems theory argues against it, and the propositions developed above propose an intimate connection between internal and external conditions. Probably one of the earliest writers to conceptualize the link was Anna Freud (1946, p. 100), who traced "a parallelism in the methods adopted by the ego for the avoidance of 'pain' from external and from internal sources." There are now a number of studies which support (sometimes causally) the connection between internal and external factors. Moreover, the data seem to suggest that individual change can be started or stopped at either place.

Most of the work on the authoritarian personality is correlational, prohibiting inferences of causality. However, there has been some experimental work bearing on the relationship between closedness to the external environment and the appearance of psychopathological symptoms. The research on sensory deprivation, or in boundary terminology closedness to the external environment, indicates that persons for whom sensory input is restricted tend to show various symptoms, one of which is hallucinations (Zubek, 1969). Initially, researchers were inclined to assume that the images reported by sensorily deprived subjects were identical to those shown by mental patients. Later research seemed to show that the sensations were not universally observed and only rarely had the complex, organized, and meaningful quality of pathological hallucinations. A still more advanced development in this research grew out of better measurement of the images and greater experimental control over the sensory deprivation conditions. These later results seem to indicate that the complexity of images tends to increase with the length and intensity of sensory deprivation (Zuckerman, 1969). These results suggest that the longer the human system remained closed to external stimulation, the more pathological the consequences seemed to become. Thus, for individuals, extreme system closedness seems to be causally related to pathology. Moreover, dogmatic or authoritarian persons do not seem to have positive mental health. Rokeach (1960) reported correlations in the range of .36 to .65 between dogmatism and anxiety for several American university samples, an English university sample, and an English worker sample. Rokeach also found that the prevalence of physical or psychosomatic symptoms in childhood was higher for the dogmatic persons than for the more open people. A more extensive review of the literature by Vacchiano, Strauss, and Hochman (1969) concluded that dogmatism appeared to be related to severity of psychological disorder, degree of impairment, length of hospitalization, and suitability for improvement.

A number of studies have been conducted relating dogmatism to performance in college courses. The studies have found an inverse correlation between dogmatism and grades in the social and behavioral sciences. Controls for IQ have tended to lower the strength of the observed relationship but not substantially. Despite the general pattern of positive findings, however, there has also been a spotiness observed among the results. Not every instance showed dogmatism inversely related to performance (Ehrlich & Lee, 1969). Costin (1968) developed two tests to measure learning in psychology, one a test of psychological principles and the other a test of conventional misconceptions about human behavior. Controlling for intelligence, he found no relationship between learning psychological principles and dogmatism, but he found a positive correlation ($r = .32$) between retention of misconceptions about human behavior and dogmatism.

If one may view sensory deprivation as a(n) (experimental) treatment destined to foster closedness in a person, one might also view psychotherapy as a (clinical) treatment designed to aid a person's becoming a more organized open system. Indeed, Barron (1963) has chosen to view psychotherapy as a "vitalizing relationship." But psychother-apy has long been a subject of controversy. Especially disputed has been the question of whether there is empirical evidence to support the efficacy of psychotherapy in helping those who have difficulties in living with others.

For some time Eysenck's (1952, 1965) arguments against the effectiveness of psychotherapy with neurotics have received wide acceptance. He marshalled empirical data to show that there was no convincing evidence that for *neurotics* psychotherapy was more effective than no treatment. However, Meltzoff and Kornreich (1970), after a review of 101 different studies, came to a different conclusion. Based on a thorough methodological analysis, they sorted these investigations into adequate and questionable categories. Among the adequate studies, 84 percent showed positive effects of psychotherapy, while 75 percent of the questionable studies reported significant benefits. The reviewers' conclusion was that "far more often than not, psychotherapy of a wide variety of types and with a broad range of disorders has been demonstrated under controlled conditions to be accompanied by positive changes in adjustment that significantly exceed those that can be accounted for by the passage of time alone" (Meltzoff & Kornreich, 1970, p. 175). Thus, planned intervention of a psychotherapeutic nature can change the individual system.

In summary, it is apparent that individual change for the better and for the worse is possible as a consequence of planned intervention based upon behavioral science concepts and technology. Some of the changes can be explained by the use of boundary and relationship concepts. For example, closing a person's external boundary can produce pathological symptoms, and psychotherapeutic relationships can lead to a reduction in pathology.

The proposition that, at the individual level, excessively closed systems tend to remain that way, despite intervention, while optimally open systems tend to be more responsive to outside intervention has also received support. For example, there is a positive correlation between level of ego strength and beneficial psychotherapeutic outcomes. While not all of the data are consistent, the predominant pattern is for ego strength—measured both by Barron's (1963) ego strength scale and by Klopfer's (1951) Rorschach Prognostic Rating Scale—to be predictive of success from psychotherapy (Meltzoff & Kornreich, 1970). Moreover, there is a tendency for authoritarian (or dogmatic) patients to benefit less from therapy and for those high in ego strength to benefit more.

This conclusion, arrived at by the collection and comparison of research results from diverse studies, was further supported by an investigation by Kelley and Stahelski (1970) in the area of prisoner's dilemma games. Their findings showed that competitive persons tended to assume that all other players were also competitive, while cooperative players had a wider range of expectations about others, which included competitiveness as well as cooperativeness. When competitors played a series of prisoner's dilemma games against cooperators, the cooperators tended to behave increasingly competitively. However, when their opponents became cooperative, the cooperators themselves changed to cooperative strategies. Competitors' strategies, therefore, were dominant, but the data showed that only the cooperators perceived this to be the case. Competitors not only misperceived the cooperators' intentions; they also misperceived the impact of their own behavior on provoking competitiveness. It appeared that a competitor's orientation created a self-fulfilling prophecy such that his initial incorrect perceptions eventually became reality because his own behavior (which he was not aware of) provoked cooperators to act in ways that he originally (then incorrectly) had expected. Cooperators, on the other hand, appeared more flexible and responsive to data about persons and the interaction in which they were engaged after interaction.

Groups

Groups as well as individuals can be studied with the use of open systems concepts. As systems by themselves, groups have boundaries separating the inside from the outside; subsystems (e.g., individuals, roles, subgroups, functions) separated by boundaries; relationships between the group and its external environment; and relationships among the parts within the group. The vast literature on group behavior has made relatively little use of open systems thinking, although more recently a number of authors have made some use of systems concepts for understanding group processes (Mills, 1964; Ziller, 1965). As a result the literature cited in this section will be of a broad range, most of which was not originally intended by the authors to be applied to open systems theory.

Research from a number of areas contributes to our understanding of groups. For example, data are available on groups which have been formed for learning about group processes. Depending on their particular orientation, these groups are called T-groups (for human relations training), self-study groups, or self-analytic groups. Interaction in these groups is more intensive than anyone's typical group experience. They provide an opportunity to examine the inner workings of small groups in ways that are not ordinarily available in either social psychological laboratories or in natural settings. However, their internal processes are not very amenable to experimental control.

Another area which has provided data about groups is the social psychology laboratory. Though experimental control is possible in the laboratory, the intense experiences are rare. Still another dimension on which group studies differ is whether groups were studied alone or in interaction with other groups. Investigations of this latter kind allow one to see not only what happens within but also among groups.

Intergroup studies also vary according to the purpose for which the groups were brought together for self-study or other purposes (Blake, Shepard, & Mouton, 1964; Higgin & Bridger, 1965; Sherif & Sherif, 1969; Johnson & Lewicki, 1969; Astrachan & Flynn, 1971).

INTERNAL CONDITIONS. Permeability of internal boundary conditions and mutuality of internal relationships differ within different groups. Argyris (1969) summarized coded behavioral data from a wide variety of field settings which showed some marked differences between the behavior typically found in executive decision-making sessions and that observed in the later phases of effective T-groups. In the T-groups, he found more evidence of overt expression of feelings and trust among group members than he did in more typical interpersonal settings. There was also more experimenting with new ideas and feelings in the T-groups than in the common decision-making sessions. Correlated with the nonemotional behavior in the decision-making groups were norms supporting the suppression of emotions and the exercise of directive leadership. Such norms might be interpreted as indicating closed psychological boundaries. T-group internal boundaries were less closed to emotions and, therefore, encouraged the direct expression of emotions through a facilitative model of leadership. The more open internal boundaries of a T-group, in contrast to normal decision-making groups, were consistent with the greater mutuality among members of that type of group.

Mills (1964) provided an extensive documentation of the development of a self-analytic group, which shows how the changing internal boundaries of the group are correlated with increasing mutuality among group members. He used a time series design for scoring the affect quality of the group's comments. References to events within and outside the group were coded separately. Key turning points in the group's

history were when the members "revolted" against the staff leader and when they confronted their peer relationships. After the revolt, the number of neutral comments (showing neither positive nor negative affect) decreased, and the number of positive comments increased. Less attention was given to matters external to the group and more comments were directed toward internal group dynamics. Then, after peer confrontation the expression of negative affect decreased. Each of the major developmental events involved increasing the permeability of a critical set of boundaries. In the first instance, the boundary separated the teacher from the students. In the second case, the boundaries separated members from each other.

Self-study group research is typically carried out without a measure of task performance. A study by Bruner (1962), however, was undertaken in an inventive group noted for its capacity to solve extremely difficult engineering problems. Although he was not seeking to connect his work to group dynamics theory, Bruner reported many qualities in his group of inventors which parallel those of internally open self-analytic groups. The relationships among the members were close and the individuals seemed psychologically minded. Indeed, all of the members had been psychoanalyzed or had had some contact with psychiatry. When a problem was brought to the group's attention by the leader, he gradually and generally and metaphorically introduced it for the group's consideration. When ideas were rejected, they were addressed directly and warmly. Nor did the group consider failure a sin. The leader was generous in his praise of members both before the group and in front of clients. Bruner observed that the group seemed to allow for the expression of more of each member's identities than normal circumstances did. Impulses relevant to problems were freely expressed, but personal problems were strenuously avoided. The internal openness of the group seemed to be of a different and significantly higher order than the usual task group.

The studies of group interaction from the social psychology laboratory seem to lead to similar conclusions about boundary permeability and relationship mutuality.

In a laboratory experiment, Maier and Solem (1952) used performance on the Horse Trading Problem (a problem which groups are frequently unable to solve) as a dependent measure to assess the impact of different styles of leadership. Two leader conditions were introduced. In one condition, an observer was appointed and was instructed to listen to the group but not offer his opinions. In the second condition, the leader was asked to encourage all members to express their opinions, to be receptive to them, and not to express his own views. The groups with the leader who sought others' opinions tended to avoid the trap in the problem more often than the groups with only an observing leader. This leader's behavior might be interpreted as increasing the mutuality among the group members.

In another experiment, Hoffman et al. (1962) structured the roles of some low status group members to oppose the suggestion of a high status group member. The solutions to the problems were more creative than when low status members agreed with the high status member's suggestion. In the disagreeing condition, the low status members might be viewed as making more mutual the relationship between themselves and the higher status person.

Still another approach to internal relationship management in a group is allowing persons to form their own working relationships. Van Zelst (1952) reported the results of recomposing building trades work groups based on sociometric choice. Union men had worked together with each other for an average period of five months prior to the experimental intervention. Each man was asked to nominate his first, second, and third choice as a work partner, and nearly

everyone was rematched on the basis of mutual choice. As a result of this change there was about a 5 percent savings in production costs and a significant reduction in turnover.

The results of both experimental and experiential studies of groups are consistent with the notion that groups which have more open internal boundaries tend to have more mutual relationships among members. Groups which have mutual relationships internally tend to be more adept at solving problems which require rare, unusual, or original responses, than groups which have less internal mutuality.

EXTERNAL CONDITIONS. Paralleling the research on sensory deprivation for individuals have been studies of small groups in confinement (Smith, 1969; Altman & Haythorn, 1967). Some of these studies have been done under carefully controlled experimental conditions, while others have been primarily descriptive. The range of settings has been widely varied: isolated laboratory groups, isolated duty stations in the Antarctic and Arctic, submarine habitability and selection studies, experiments with fallout shelters, space and aerospace assessments, manned space flight, and experiments on man-in-the-sea. While none of the group boundaries in these studies was completely closed, the general pattern was for the group members to be barred from human contact outside their immediate colleagues. In the laboratories the boundary would be maintained by the experimenters, while in the field settings the various missions typically had extensive geographic and communication barriers between the participants and the outside world.

In the field setting perhaps the most firmly established small-group-in-isolation finding was the presence of overt or covert interpersonal friction. Pronounced irritability, hostility, and personality conflicts were commonly reported. Smith (1969) reported twenty references supporting this assertion. Controlled laboratory studies yield the same result. Isolated groups had more interpersonal friction than control groups.

Closely related to the interpersonal conflict was the phenomenon of isolation. Group members in confinement tended to withdraw from one another, avoid the expression of personal or controversial subjects, and, not surprisingly, complain of loneliness within the group. Under these conditions outbreaks of "territoriality" were also noted. To preserve their privacy and escape from interaction with others, subjects claimed possession of certain geographic areas and highly personal objects. They reacted with hostility to those who might trespass their boundaries. These conditions could be interpreted as evidence for closed internal boundaries.

In addition, a number of studies reported evidence of hostility directed toward the outside world. Typically, these outbreaks would be directed toward the investigators for some partially reasonable complaint such as excessive demands for testing and the like. But the phenomenon was widespread enough across various studies for one to believe that it stemmed in part from confinement.

Overall the confined groups tended to show a decline in motivation and morale as time in isolation increased. Various psychological symptoms (sleeplessness, depression, compulsive behavior) and psychosomatic complaints (headaches, fatigue, and muscle soreness) appeared. In one study (Hammes, 1964) there was a remarkable reduction in symptomatology during the last five or six hours of a fourteen-day confinement period. Perhaps the mere anticipation of the end being in sight made the closed group more tolerable.

Physical confinement represents one kind of closedness of a group. Another kind stems from the lack of change in personnel. Wells and Pelz (1966) reported data from eighty-three research and development teams of varying group ages. They found that the scientific contribution of those groups declined with age. The communica-

tion frequency and duration with the group leader and with colleagues also declined as a function of group age.

External boundaries can also be manipulated by the exchange of group members. Torrance (1955) compared the functioning of permanent and temporary Air Force combat crews in solving a number of different kinds of problems. The permanent crews consisted of a pilot, navigator, and gunner who had been training together for several months, while the temporary crews were made up of men from the three different roles who had not trained together. For the three problems, the measure of influence was acceptance of a correct or incorrect answer. For each problem influence was associated with status. That is, the higher status members (pilots, then navigators, then gunners) were more likely to have both their correct and their incorrect answers accepted by their groups. The phenomenon of influence as a function of status was also present but diminished in potency for the temporary groups. In these groups lower status members with correct solutions were more likely to have their solutions accepted, and the higher status members with incorrect solutions were most likely to have their suggestions rejected.

Ziller, Behringer, and Goodchilds (1962) manipulated the conditions which they called open and closed groups. Open groups added, removed, or replaced members during their activities, while closed group membership remained fixed. The group task was to compose a caption for a *Saturday Evening Post* cartoon. Open groups showed higher ideational fluency and more originality than closed groups.

The parallels between the physically and geographically confined groups and the more permanent groups are marked. The confined groups exhibited interpersonal friction, isolation, territoriality, and external aggression while the older scientific groups showed decreased communication and secrecy. Moreover, groups which did alter their external boundary toward greater permeability by changing members tended to produce more novel and worthwhile products.

Being externally closed has deleterious effects on the internal functioning of a group. Groups with external boundaries that are relatively impermeable seem to develop internal boundaries of the same quality. It is as if the internal boundaries of a group mirror the external boundaries and vice versa. The failure of a living system to exchange with its environment prohibits stimulation from outside and discharge of waste from inside. The apparent hardening of internal boundaries as a consequence of external closedness seems to follow from the system's attempts to retain some modicum of organization. Increasing amounts of energy must be invested in holding hostility in check and are, therefore, less available for other kinds of work. Under such conditions firmer, less flexible internal boundaries must be developed in order for any organization to exist at all.

The degree of mutuality of internal and external relationships seems to be related to the degree of permeability of internal and external boundaries. Groups placed in win-lose competition are pushed toward having non-mutual relationships, and they tend to develop quite closed external boundaries in relation to one another. A number of social-psychological investigators have manipulated competition between groups and observed the consequences for both intergroup and intragroup relations (Sherif & Sherif, 1969; Blake, Shepard, & Mouton, 1964).

When groups face each other under conditions of win-lose competition, the relationships between the groups take on some highly predictable characteristics. In the Sherif and Sherif (1969) studies the boys' groups developed negative stereotypes of their adversaries. Name calling, physical encounters, and planned attacks among the groups expressed escalating feelings of hostility. Blake et al. (1964) found that the groups evaluated each other's products in similar ways.

The signs of weakness in one's own product were rationalized or denied while the shortcomings of one's competitor were downgraded. Contact between group representatives became a time to attack the other side and enhance or defend one's own position. Actual intellectual distortions occurred. In one study the impact of a tug-of-war was that *every* member of the winning team underestimated the duration of the contest, and *every* member of the losing team overestimated the length of the contest. Blake et al. (1964) found that comprehension of a group's own position was greater than understanding of a competitor's proposal. Prior to testing, group members were encouraged to examine the other side's position until they were certain they understood it. Upon testing, the groups tended to overlook commonalities between positions and credit only themselves with characteristics which were common to both contributions. Unique qualities of proposals were readily perceived with respect to one's own position but went unnoticed in the other side's position.

Intragroup relations also changed during competition. Groups tended to select as leaders or representatives persons whose personal characteristics seemed to be congruent with the intergroup relationship. In one of Sherifs' boys' groups a young man who had formerly been rejected as a bully became a group hero during intergroup competition. Another boy who did not take an antagonistic position in relationship to the outgroup was removed as leader. Blake et al. (1964) note that sometimes group takeovers occur by one or a few members. At the same time as power relationships become more solidified, tolerance for deviation or differences within the groups diminishes. Members who insist on differing with the group's position risk being cast out of the group. During intergroup competition the relationships within *and* between the groups has a decidedly non-mutual quality.

During intergroup competition the frequency of interaction between groups is low except to gain competitive advantage. The exchange between groups is strongly slanted to favor keeping all positive qualities associated with one's own group and all negative qualities connected with the other group. Meantime, within the groups, boundaries between the parts become less permeable as leadership functions are consolidated and individual differences are suppressed.

What happens to relations between groups when external boundaries become more permeable?

Answers to this question turn to a large degree on those few studies which have shown how hostile intergroup relations become more cooperative. One consistent finding is that mere contact between competing groups is not enough to change their relationships (Sherif & Sherif, 1969; Amir, 1969). However, if a superordinate goal is introduced by impersonal forces, identified with neither party, then a change in the relationship seems possible (Johnson & Lewicki, 1969). The goal has to be one that is naturally attractive to both parties and requires their cooperation in order to be achieved at all. The Sherifs' work with children showed that a *series* of superordinate goal exercises gradually changed the nature of a relationship between hostile groups. Eventually, friendship patterns crossed group lines. New—less derogatory, more friendly—names were made up for persons in the other group. The groups actually chose to carry out an activity together which could have been accomplished without cross-group collaboration.

External group relations seem to affect internal relations among members, and the permeability of external boundaries is associated with the permeability of internal boundaries. Moreover, as external boundaries close, external relationships become less mutual. As external relationships become less mutual, internal relationships also become more imbalanced, and internal boundaries become less permeable. The studies reviewed here pertained only to manipulations directed to external boundaries and relationships, but there are theoretical reasons to expect that the causality would operate from inside to outside as well as vice versa.

PROPENSITY TO CHANGE. As entities, groups change as a function of their boundary conditions. With individuals there is little doubt about when a person's external boundary is intact and holding the parts together. At the physical level being alive is usually enough, while at the psychological level being non-psychotic is the requisite condition (Menninger, Mayman, & Pruyser, 1963). However, with groups the question of boundaries is more problematic. An aggregate of individuals can exist without forming a group if no external boundary is formed around them to separate them from their external world.

Two kinds of studies in particular show that boundaries do change and the existence and operation of group boundaries can play a very important part for group members. In one, the investigators were able to study the establishment of group boundaries (Sherif & Sherif, 1969; Whyte, 1969). In another, the institution of a new technology was instrumental to the destruction of group boundaries, and the researchers were able to document the consequences (Trist & Bamforth, 1951).

The Sherifs (1969) brought together eleven-to-twelve-year-old boys and housed them together in a single large bunkhouse. Initially, they were completely free to select companions from the entire group for activities which were camp-wide. Within several days observers noted that small friendship clusters of two to four boys were beginning to form. At this time the entire camp was divided into two groups so that the friendship clusters were decomposed. The two new groups were formed so that two-thirds of the boys in each group were *not* with their best friends. Upon formation, the new groups went to live in separate cabins. Shortly thereafter each group also went on an overnight hike and camp-out. After this group formation process the boys were again asked to name their best friends. The friendship structure changed markedly. There was an increase of more than 50 percent of the friendship choices from *within* the new group.

In a sociological study Whyte (1969) observed change which was initiated by Peruvian peasants. He identified a pattern of group formation which greatly aided the peasants' obtaining a greater sense of control over their destiny. Prior to the formation of the peasant group, the peasants did not work together to effect their common fates. Instead, they were more or less at the mercy of large landholders who played one peasant family off against another. The landlords would provide differential rewards to the peasants according to their loyalty. The more loyal peasants would receive a greater proportion of the landlords' attention and favor. The peasants were also dependent upon the landlords for outside contacts with banks, the local government, politicians, and the market. However, after the peasants learned to group together for common purposes their internal and external relationships changed. Not only did they work together in dealing with the landlords, but they also established their own linkages with the outside world of government officials (both local and national), labor leaders, banks, and the market place. The formation of a group radically changed their lives.

Researchers from the Tavistock Institute in Great Britain studied the impact of new coal mining technology on the functioning of small autonomous work groups (Trist & Bamforth, 1951). Under the old system of coal mining, work teams ranged in size from two to eight members. These teams were highly autonomous in their activities and formation. Team leaders picked the members based upon mutual compatibility. Each group tended to set its own norms about work and the like, and the unit for payment was the entire group, not individuals. The advent of new coal-mining technology led the management to eliminate these small autonomous work groups and replace them with larger groups of forty to fifty persons (perhaps aggregates would be a better term), who were highly interdependent functionally. A number of undesirable consequences followed from this change. The miners actually undermined each others' activities. Absenteeism, sickness, and psychosomatic disorders were observed, and the expected increases in productivity failed to materialize. Apparently, the establishment or destruction of group boundaries is important.

Forming a group boundary changes an aggregate of individuals into a group, the members of which are affected in attitude and behavior by the existence of the group boundary. Eliminating a group boundary also has important effects. The mere presence or absence of a group boundary is important, for it defines the existence of a group whose members, under some circumstances, interact more with each other than with nonmembers. Equally important for groups—as for individuals—is the degree of openness of the boundaries and the nature of the internal and external relationships.

Organizations

Open systems theory has been applied more frequently to organizations than individuals or groups (Katz & Kahn, 1966; Miller & Rice, 1967). A growing area of research concerns the relationship of the organization to its external environment (Emery & Trist, 1965; Lawrence & Lorsch, 1967; Duncan, 1971). The findings from research on organizational environments show that for long-term viability an organization must remain sensitive to the state of its external world. Without some permeability of external boundaries, an organization cannot react to the outside world. Group boundaries become the primary area of attention when one focuses on the internal conditions of organizations.

To examine the boundary-relationship propositions at the organizational level, one turns to a comparison of systems that parallel those found at the individual level. Paralleling the authoritarian personality, research from organizations whose members are often heavily confined by the system will be discussed. Examples of such organizations include prisons, mental hospitals, and boarding schools. Similar to creative personalities are various innovative or research and development organizations. The proposition that differential boundary and relationship conditions are associated with varying outcomes will be examined.

INTERNAL CONDITIONS. The internal conditions of confinement institutions tend to consist of quite rigid boundaries and nonmutual relationships among individuals and groups. Goffman's (1961) analysis of "total institutions" is consistent with this proposition. He particularly identified the sharp boundary between staff and inmates, which helps to create many of the characteristics of an intergroup competition between parties of unequal power. Typically, the staff sees itself as righteous and superior, while the inmates see them as condescending, highhanded, and mean. The staff views the inmates as bitter, secretive, and untrustworthy while the inmates themselves feel inferior, weak, blame-worthy, and guilty. Much of the behavior of each party serves to support these stereotypes because each party tends to evoke self-fulfilling reactions from the opposite side.

While the institution (through the staff) tends to behave as if all inmates were alike, the social realities tend to be far different. In fact, pecking orders and other forms of differentiated roles develop among the inmates. Indeed, depending on the closedness of the system, the inmate roles may be as hazardous as anything the staff could do (Goffman, 1961; Sykes, 1958).

Alderfer and Brown (1975) obtained longitudinal attitude data on the sense of alienation felt by students at a boys' boarding school as the school year progressed. There was a general decline in involvement the longer the year went on. This decline was most for the first year students, next most for the second year students, and so on. At the start of the year, the freshmen were most involved, the sophomores next, the juniors next, and the seniors showed the least involvement. As the year progressed, each group became more alienated with life at the school. A small subset of students were not boarders but attended classes and participated in activities while living at home. These day students offered the possibility of a comparison group to see whether more time in the system produced more alienation. The day students did show a decline in involvement as the year progressed, but the sharpness of the decline was less than for the boarding students. It appeared that being in the closed system was a cause for increasing alienation, and being less in the system resulted in less of a decrease in involvement.

The literature on prisons and mental hospitals contains many references to the distinction between custodial and treatment orientations (Cressey, 1965; Perrow, 1965). Generally speaking, this difference pertains to goals: whether the institution addresses itself primarily to confinement or rehabilitation of inmates. One study reported by Street, Vinter, and Perrow (1966) compared the processes and outcomes of six institutions on a continuum of least-to-most treatment (or, conversely, most-to-least custodial). Many of the differences between the systems can be accounted for by open systems concepts.

The treatment oriented institutions had higher staff-to-inmate ratios, higher social service to inmate ratios, and more frequent inmate to social service contacts. In short, the boundary between the staff and inmates was more permeable in the treatment oriented institutions than in the custodial institutions.

Relationships among the inmates also differed between the different types of institutions. Having two or more friends in the system was positively related to having positive perspectives on the staff and institution in both kinds of organizations, but the measure of association was higher in treatment than in the custodial systems. Having friends was positively related to a positive self-image in both kinds of settings but the association was higher in the treatment than in the custodial settings. Overall, there seemed to be more mutuality among the treatment inmates than among the custodial inmates. The treatment inmates reported having more friends, hanging around with more boys, wanting to see more boys after release, being willing to discuss personal problems with other inmates, and being more loyal to the group than the custodial inmates. The boys selected as more influential by their peers had more positive attitudes toward the institution, the staff, and themselves than those not selected in the treatment institutions. No such relationship was observed in the custodial institutions.

Overall, the treatment oriented institutions turned out to have more open internal boundaries than the custodial institutions. Staff attitudes seemed more conducive to establishing and maintaining mutual relationships between themselves and the inmates. Inmates in the treatment institutions seemed to be less alienated from themselves and from the institution than in custodial institutions. Relationships among inmates in treatment institutions showed more mutuality than in the custodial settings. Regardless of institution, however, the more an inmate reported establishing friendships with other inmates, the less alienated from himself and his environmental setting he seemed to be.

Open systems theory would lead one to expect internally closed systems to experience strain as a result of their impermeable boundaries. How does one account for the continued viability of the highly closed organizations? One answer is that there are destructive explosions in the systems from time to time (Sykes, 1958; Stotland & Kohler, 1965). Another answer is that internally closed systems complement their overtly impermeable boundaries with covert

or latent openness. Some features of the covert openness are officially supported while others are decidedly illegal. However, certain features of the latent openness make it possible for members to deny that any openness exists.

Officially supported latent openness often takes the form of dramatic performances of some kind. Perhaps there is a newspaper written and edited by inmates which includes cartoons and editorials. Parties with skits where inmates act out their feelings toward staff members are another vehicle. On the surface events of this kind can be discredited as harmless, not real, exaggerated, and the like. In fact, they provide momentary episodes when the boundary between inmates and staff becomes more permeable (Goffman, 1961).

At the boys' school, Alderfer and Brown (1975) found that sarcasm was a very common element in interpersonal communication. Over 70 percent of the people in the school said that the prevalence of sarcasm was high or very high. A sarcastic communication gives two messages: one usually quite positive, the other quite negative. For example, "You're brilliant!" has multiple messages. The speaker gives and the listener receives mixed, often highly charged, messages. While both messages are communicated, the norms of sarcastic interaction legitimize the denial of part or all of the content. As a result, people live in ambiguity about their relations with each other. Sarcasm permits the discharge of many emotions (from very positive to very negative), but also reinforces the person's sense of isolation and alienation because he is often unsure about what is being said to him, and he cannot readily clarify the sarcastic exchange without encountering denial.

Another class of covert openness in closed systems is the highly illegal behaviors that often occur between lower ranking staff and inmates (Sykes, 1958). In order to carry out his duties at all, a guard must reach some kind of accommodation with inmates unless he has the capacity to resort entirely to force or fear. He is also a human being himself and cannot escape being touched by the prisoner's or patient's hardships. As a result he allows the rigid boundary between himself and the inmate to become more flexible. He may transmit illegal information to prisoners. He may fail to report certain rule infractions that occur. He may join the prisoners in criticizing the prison administration.

As a class of organizations, confinement-type systems are especially noted for the closedness of their internal boundaries and a low level of mutuality among individuals and groups within the systems. It seems as though the relatively closed external boundary is mirrored by relatively closed internal boundaries. Furthermore, when one is able to observe differing degrees of commitment to the primary goal of confinement—as in the Street et al. (1966) studies—the less confinement, more treatment oriented institutions show less closedness of the internal boundaries and greater mutuality among individuals and groups.

Innovative organizations also vary in their degree of internal openness. Burns and Stalker (1961) provided some very interesting case material from their studies of electronic firms in England and Scotland. Electronic firms were under pressure to be innovative. Some of the organizations seized upon and utilized the challenges offered by their turbulent environments while others failed. From their studies, the investigators coined the terms mechanistic and organic forms to characterize, respectively, those organizations which were unable to change and those which were able to change. The mechanistic versus organic distinction closely parallels the present distinction between internally open and internally closed organizations. Mechanistic systems tended to have more impermeable boundaries around tasks and groups than organic systems. Roles in mechanistic systems tended to be very precisely defined: rights, duties, obligations, and methods were carefully prescribed. Interaction tended to be primarily hierarchical.

Loyalty to the concern, local knowledge, and obedience to superiors tended to be emphasized. Organic systems tended to have more permeable boundaries around tasks and groups than mechanistic systems did. Roles tended to be defined by the nature of task demands and individual competencies and, therefore, were frequently redefined as new problems arose and complex interactions took place. Commitment tended to develop toward a whole concern rather than toward a narrow specialty. Interaction tended to go in both horizontal and vertical directions and to take the form of consultation rather than command. Authority was more situational than positional and based more on task competence than on organizational rank.

In one organic system, the actual composition of the top management group varied according to the dilemmas facing the system. Expansion of this group occurred when the firm seemed to be having difficulties of one kind or another (e.g., when there was a lot of overtime, when targets were not being met, and so on). These meetings began with the airing of complaints and criticisms; later, solutions were posed. When the problems became less, as a result of a series of such meetings, the size of the top management group became smaller again.

In the mechanistic system signs of internal isolationism were common. Typically, this resulted in intergroup conflict between research and manufacturing, and it placed an enormous strain on the head of the research division. In one case, the research group was doing no development work at all and instead was doing test work and consultation for manufacturing. In this case, the research manager was the most isolated member of the top management team. He was engaged in the smallest number of projects, communicated with the smallest number of other departments, spent the least amount of time with managers at his own level or above, and the most amount of time in his own office and department.

Lawrence and Lorsch (1967) studied the

differentiation and integration that firms faced with varying degrees of change in their external environments achieved. Although they found that systems facing rapid change in their markets and technology seemed to require greater differentiation, they also found that regardless of their degree of differentiation higher levels of integration among departments characterized the more effective firms. Regardless of degree of differentiation, the more that conflict was directly confronted and worked through rather than being smoothed over or forced, the more integrated key departments seemed to be. In addition, the more that influence was based on competence and expertise, the more effective collaboration seemed to be.

Duncan (1971) studied the responses of both manufacturing and research and development decision units to different degrees of uncertainty in their external environments. In general, he found that the decision units tended to "destructure" themselves when facing non-routine as compared to routine decisions. For non-routine decisions, the groups tended to use less hierarchical authority, more widely shared participation, fewer explicit rules and procedures, and a less sharply defined division of labor. The more effective decision units tended to have greater differences in the internal structure for routine and non-routine decisions. These results suggest that a group's capacity to make its internal boundaries more permeable, when the task demands it, is associated with greater effectiveness in making innovative decisions.

Data bearing on the internal workings of research groups also come from Smith (1970) and Gordon and Marquis (1966). Smith used a number of measures which can be taken as indices of the permeability of internal group boundaries. Horizontal and multidirectional consultation were both positively associated with the production of technical and unpublished papers. Reciprocal influence was also associated with the production of technical and unpublished papers.

Gordon and Marquis (1966) found that the most innovative medical sociology projects were produced when the researchers discussed their work with their administrative superiors but retained the freedom to determine their research procedures.

Data from both types of organizations, confining and innovative, seem to support the hypothesized correlation between degree of boundary permeability and degree of relationship mutuality. The data also seem to indicate that higher degrees of permeability and mutuality are associated with effectiveness. Impermeable boundaries were associated with non-mutual relationships, and permeable boundaries were associated with mutual relationships in both kinds of settings. Among the confinement organizations, the more internally open produced fewer deleterious and more constructive effects on inmates. Among the innovative systems, the more internally open showed greater effectiveness and survival. The literature on confinement organizations also contained evidence of latent openness among those systems that were very closed internally, suggesting that systems will move toward achieving some degree of openness even when they are tightly bounded.

EXTERNAL CONDITIONS. Confinement organizations are especially noted for having highly impermeable boundaries separating them from their external environments. Typically they have marked physical boundaries (walls, fences, locked doors, sharply defined and delimited entry places) which are congruent with their social and psychological boundaries.

Among the innovative organizations there was considerable evidence that the more effective systems had more permeable external boundaries. Hall and Lawler (1970) studied twenty-two applied research laboratories in Connecticut. They found that when the researchers had direct responsibility for customer contact, the organization was rated higher on technical and administrative performance. They also found that the more the researchers in an organization felt responsibility for obtaining financial support and keeping costs down, the higher the system was rated on technical and administrative performance. Both customer contact and financial responsibility increase the number and frequency of boundary crossing activities by members of the organization and thereby may be viewed as indices of external organizational openness. The more externally open organizations were more successful.

Smith (1970) examined the consultation processes in fifteen divisions of a large research laboratory in the midwest. He found that a number of variables which could be taken as indices of external openness were positively related to measures of performance. Extradivisional consultation, for example, was correlated with the production of technical papers and unpublished papers. Meetings with other divisions were positively correlated with the writing of unpublished and technical reports. The use of consultants, membership in professional societies, and other "contacts outside the company" were all positively correlated with the same two measures of scientific performance.

Gordon and Marquis (1966) investigated the innovativeness of 245 medical sociological studies produced in academic departments, health agencies, medical schools, and hospitals. Settings were grouped according to their marginality. In the more marginal settings the researchers had greater contact with the external environments they were studying. Innovativeness of projects produced in the more marginal settings was significantly higher than those produced in the less marginal settings.

Aiken and Hage (1968) studied the behavior of sixteen social welfare and health agencies in a large midwestern metropolis. They found that the number of joint programs between the agencies was strongly and positively correlated with the number of new programs which were not joint programs. To engage in a joint program an organization must increase the permeability of its external boundaries. Although the observed correlation does not demonstrate causality one can suggest that engaging in joint programs stimulates the system from outside and thereby aids its production of independent innovative programs.

The combined effect of the data bearing on external openness is consistent with the proposition that permeability of external boundaries is associated with effectiveness both for innovative organizations and for treatment oriented confinement organizations. When the results pertaining to internal conditions are combined with those pertaining to external conditions, both the confining and innovative organizations which had relatively permeable internal boundaries and relatively high mutuality among subsystems also tended to have relatively permeable external boundaries.

Conclusion

Steady states of individuals, groups, and organizations provide support for the major propositions derived from an analysis of the boundary and relationship conditions in open systems. At each level of analysis there was evidence that optimally permeable boundaries were associated with mutual relationships, while excessively closed boundaries were associated with non-mutual relationships. As predicted there was also a tendency for internal and external conditions to parallel each other. If a system had internal permeability and mutual relationships between the parts, it was likely to have similar external conditions, and vice versa. Systems with strong permeable boundaries and mutual relationships showed a greater tendency toward survival and health and were more likely to produce novel and worthwhile products than were systems with rigid boundaries and non-mutual relationships.

Individuals provide the primary internal unit in groups, and groups are the major unit in organizations. It follows from the parallelism of internal and external conditions that there can easily be disequilibrium set up between internal and external conditions if, for example, a relatively open person meets a relatively closed group. It also follows that change activities which address several levels simultaneously have a greater likelihood of producing movement than interventions that address only one level. In the following section, we shall examine organizational change programs according to the unit which they address.

CHANGING STATES

For a system—be it person, group, or organization—to change, it must move from one steady state to another. The preceding analysis suggests that one direction for movement is toward optimally permeable boundaries sustained by mutual relationships. Another direction is toward relatively closed boundaries with non-mutual relationships. Programs of planned change either directly or indirectly aim human systems toward being more optimally open. To this writer's knowledge, there have been no attempts in peacetime to use applied behavioral science intentionally to destroy system boundaries or to decrease the mutuality in human relationships. Not every planned change effort has directly addressed boundary and relationship conditions, but most attempts have dealt with these variables indirectly if they have not been the focal point of change activities.

The various approaches which have been used to change human systems can be classified according to the primary human needs which are aroused or need to be aroused in order to instigate change. Human needs may be conceptualized by a three-part system consisting of existence, relatedness, and growth (Alderfer, 1972). Existence needs refer to the wide range of material needs that people have, such as water, food, shelter, and the financial conditions permitting the attainment of these basic substances. Relatedness needs account for human beings'

needs for mutual relationships with significant other people. Failure to obtain adequate satisfaction of existence needs threatens the physical integrity of a person, while failure to obtain adequate satisfaction of relatedness needs threatens the psychological soundness of a person. Growth needs refer to a person's desires for challenge and stimulation, that is, for opportunities to use his capacities to the fullest and to be challenged to enlarge and enrich his potential.

Programs of planned change in organizational settings also vary in terms of the unit to which the change program is directed. Some take the individual as the primary unit for change; others address groups; and some attempt to proceed with the organization as a whole. Having classified change programs in terms of primary need categories and unit of analysis which they take as focal, we will proceed to examine how the relevant boundaries and relationships change when a system undergoes change.

Existence Need Studies

The use of financial incentives in industry has a long and controversial history. If men were rational, an argument goes, and they could obtain more money by working harder, their performances should be improved if an individual incentive system based on higher pay for better performance were instituted. The Lincoln Electric Company was able to show impressive results from individual pay incentives. They realized high profits while paying very high wages to their employees (Glover & Hower, 1957). At the other extreme, there are studies which show how workers can collude with each other to undermine the operation of a piece-rate system instituted by management. The employees set production quotas and enforce them harshly. People who attempt to break the group norms of not working at full capacity do so at considerable risk of becoming loners

(Whyte, 1955). These early reports suggest that financial incentives can be used effectively, but only under certain circumstances.

INDIVIDUAL LEVEL. Lawler and Hackman (1969) undertook a field experiment to compare a number of different ways of developing and introducing an individual incentive plan to reward job attendance. Nine work groups were involved in the study. Three groups designed their own incentive plans (the participative condition), two had incentive plans imposed on them, two talked with the researchers about attendance problems and the like, and two had no contact with the study at all. The investigators hypothesized that the pay incentive programs developed by the employees themselves would be more effective than those imposed by management.

The participative groups each greeted the experimenter with hostility and mistrust. His stance was to help the group develop a plan and inform them of effective incentive principles, but under no conditions impose or suggest a plan. Consistent with this approach, each of the participative groups developed a slightly different plan. Two groups wanted their bonuses to be paid weekly, while the other preferred a monthly program. There were differences in the size of bonuses requested and in the number of sick days permitted. The researchers presented the plans to management, who accepted them readily after adjustments were made so that the money available to the different groups was equivalent. Plans identical to those developed by the employees in the participative condition were imposed on two other groups. Time series data on attendance were collected twelve weeks before and sixteen weeks after the plans were implemented. It showed that there was a significant improvement in attendance for those groups who had developed their own plans but no improvement for those groups where the incentives were imposed by the management.

Approximately one year after the original study, Scheflen, Lawler, and Hackman (1971) returned to the organization to see what had happened to the various work groups. They found that management had discontinued two out of three of the participative plans. In the one participative group where the plan was still in effect, attendance remained approximately where it was at the end of the original study. In the two groups where the plan had been discontinued, attendance had decreased. The plans which had been imposed by management were still in effect. For those groups attendance had improved somewhat over the time immediately after the plans had been implemented but had not reached the same level as achieved by the participative group.

The company managers who dropped the participative plans did so with full knowledge that the experiment had worked and was resulting in higher attendance. When the plans were discontinued, the employees were given a higher hourly rate to compensate them for the lost attendance bonus and thereby maintain their goodwill. Obviously the plans were not dropped for financial reasons. Instead, the managers were primarily reacting to their own lack of participation in the development of the plans. They viewed the researchers' action in dealing with attendance problems as a sign that they were unable to solve those problems.

When the researchers used participative methods with the employees, they increased the permeability of the boundaries between the lowest and highest levels in the system and between the inside and outside of the system. Yet they did nothing about the intermediate levels; the boundary between the investigators and the middle managers did not become more open. Their relationship with these men was decidedly nonmutual. This oversight was a strategic error. The success and failure of this incentive system emphasizes not only the utility of making system boundaries more permeable but also the need to work on all the relevant boundaries if permanent change is to be achieved. In the Lawler-Hackman program, an individually based pay incentive system was successfully introduced through group methods, but two of the three programs were terminated because the next higher level in the system was excluded from a central role in its operation.

GROUP LEVEL. The Scanlon Plan was developed to enlist the cooperation of labor and management in improving organizational effectiveness (Lesieur, 1958). The program had basically two elements: (1) a social process for improving the flow of ideas on how to carry out the task more effectively, and (2) a labor cost savings formula for sharing the fruits of increased productivity (Whyte, 1955; Lesieur, 1958). This approach was not designed to reward individuals directly but rather to give incentives for cooperation within and among groups. Multiple and overlapping groups were involved in the plan: functional departments, staff groups, labor, and management.

Each department developed a production committee consisting of the foreman and a representative from labor who was *not* a grievance committee member. Sometimes other workers joined the duo to examine and discuss the ideas offered by members of the department. At the top of the organization there was a joint top management and labor group consisting of three persons from management and three from labor. This group was a court of appeal for the departmental committees and an integrating unit for changes that involved more than one department.

Labor cost savings were measured by the ratio of the total payroll to the sales value of what was produced by that payroll. A base period was used to establish standard operations for the company and any time the ratio went below the base level, the difference became the bonus pool. Usually

25 percent of the pool went to the company to provide some insurance against deficit months, and the rest was shared among *all* (labor and management) employees as a percentage of their payroll (Puckett, 1958).

A conference in which participants in the Scanlon Plan shared their experiences indicated organizations who successfully implemented the plan derived a number of beneficial outcomes. Productivity increases were commonly observed. Satisfaction with doing a good job, the development of healthier human relationships, and the establishment of more constructive attitudes toward the changing needs of the enterprise were frequently identified as benefits (Lesieur, 1958). Not all firms were successful, however, and some efforts were given to identifying the conditions which seemed to prevent successful implementation (Whyte, 1955; Shultz, 1958).

One reason was management's failure to "share its prerogatives," a situation that could be conceptualized as keeping a key boundary closed. Another cause was a union split by internal factions, another condition that could be understood as a subsystem being plagued by excessively closed boundaries. Although the plan seemed to work better in smaller units with good labor-management relations, exceptions could be found to both of these conditions. In general, the plan was set up to establish more open boundaries among all of the key groups in an organization for the attainment of more effective organizational performance. When key groups did not form, when their boundaries remained impermeable, or when the key relationships remained non-mutual, the plan did not work. The Scanlon Plan was an ingenious procedure for achieving cooperative intergroup relations, but it was not magical and certain internal boundary and relationship conditions could prevent its success.

ORGANIZATIONAL LEVEL. Beginning in 1952, a collaboration between Cornell University and the Peruvian Indians brought about a comprehensive change program in the public manor (large estate) of Vicos, Peru (Holmberg, 1965). Vicos covered an area of 40,000 acres and had a population of slightly over 1,700 Indians, who as serfs had been bound to the land since early colonial times. When the project began, Vicosinos were barely subsisting. The manor was run by several Mestizo (non-Indian) foremen, who supervised the Indian straw bosses and reported to the owner. The system was maintained by a combination of factors ranging from brute force to impounding of peasant property. Records showed that protest movements at Vicos had been squashed by a combination of the landlords, the clergy, and the police. Prior to intervention by the behavioral scientists, the principal means for gaining influence was to grow old, move upward in the politico-religious hierarchy, and obtain the wealth of one's elders as they died. The community had achieved a static equilibrium.

At the time of the intervention, Vicos was in many ways a closed system. The Cornell Peru Project intervened in the role of *patron* or owner. The industrial firm which was renting Vicos went bankrupt and the Project was able to sublease the property and serfs for a period of five years. Prior to the change in management, Mario Vazquez, a Peruvian anthropologist and member of the research team, had been living in and studying the manor as a social system. He had lived with an Indian family and was known and trusted by almost all of the community members (Vazquez, 1965).

The Project's intervention strategy turned first to where the system was facing the greatest pain—the economic area (Lasswell, 1965). Modern agricultural methods (e.g., use of fertilizer, good seed, pesticides, etc.) were successfully introduced. Profits from the Project's share were turned back to the community for additional agricultural improvements. Health care, educational organizations, and community administration were upgraded. While the old patron had obtained free labor from the serfs, the

Cornell Peru group paid people for their administrative, custodial, and agricultural services (Vazquez, 1965).

Initially, the academic patron worked with the straw bosses from the former administration. But these were older men, tied to static traditions. As economic success was achieved, it became possible to replace the retiring members by younger men who were more committed to the goals of modernization. As the age group for managing economic affairs changed toward younger men, a similar process was observed for the political process. Also, throughout the period of intervention the Project staff lived in equality among the Vicosinos, welcoming them at their tables and aiding them in the elimination of injustice inside and outside their community.

Vazquez (1965) reported striking changes in the amount and distribution of wealth at Vicos. Before the Cornell Peru Project his measurements indicated that about 52 percent of the population was poor; wealth in the form of livestock was concentrated in the hands of only 7.7 percent of the families. As of 1964, approximately 70 percent of the families no longer had to beg the wealthy to lend them money. In addition to their traditional sources of income, they also obtained funds from the cash sale of commercial agricultural products and from wages obtained in programs sponsored by their own community and the national government. Not everyone reached this level of material progress. A significant sector of the community still depended on the very rich for their economic welfare.

CONCLUSIONS. Persons from outside the system played an important role in most of the existence need change programs. But outsiders alone were not enough to effect lasting change. External input could be subverted by internal conditions which were inadequately prepared for change. Middle managers with whom Lawler and Hackman (1969) did not establish mutual relations undermined their change efforts, while divisiveness within a union or closedness on the part of management were reasons which prevented Scanlon Plans from being effective.

Each of the change programs—regardless of whether they were primarily concerned with individuals, groups, or the whole organization—dealt with more than one level of analysis. The most striking of the cases discussed was that by Lawler and Hackman (1969), who used group methods to change individual choices to attend work. In the Scanlon Plans and at Vicos, change agents worked with individual, group, and intergroup relations.

The various approaches also worked at more than one level in the organizational hierarchy. While the change agents did not work to decrease the power of those in command, they did tend to do things which had the effect of increasing the influence of more deprived sectors of the system. Lawler and Hackman (1969) aided employees in designing their own bonus system for attendance; the Scanlon Plans increased the technical influence of all parts of an organization; and at Vicos the peasant farmers gained some control over their own destinies. As these changes were taking place, however, the change agents—when they were successful—developed and maintained a mutual relationship with those who held formal power in the system.

Each of the sustained change programs brought about (and simultaneously required) more satisfying human relationships as well as more material gratification. Thus, even though the existence need programs utilized primarily material incentives, they seemed to bring about secondary gains in the area of improved human relationships. This additional (and qualitatively different) satisfaction probably provided even stronger bases for moving the systems to new steady states.

When change was achieved it included new boundary and relationship constellations. External and internal boundaries tended to become more permeable, and re-lationships moved toward greater mutuality. If these conditions could not be brought about, change efforts tended to die out. Moreover, all of the programs described in this section brought about changes in outcome as well as processes. The Lawler and Hackman (1969) project resulted in better attendance, the Scanlon Plans in labor cost savings, and the Vicos project in more wealth for the community.

Relatedness Need Studies

Perhaps more organizational change activity has been directed toward understanding and improving human relationships than any other single target. Perhaps one of the major reasons for this emphasis is the often two-fold payoff for systems when human relationships are changed for the better. There is the gratification that comes to each person when his own interactions with significant others are mutual. Also, in highly interdependent social systems, tasks are probably achieved more efficiently as less energy is lost in destructive conflicts among individuals and groups.

Attempts to develop more mutual human relationships in organizations have been directed toward the individual, group, and organization. Several different kinds of experiential learning programs now exist which deal with the various areas of learning (Alderfer, 1970). What level is the actual target for change depends on the level of the *intact* unit that participates in a change program. Most often it is individuals who participate, but whole groups and organizations have undertaken change programs to improve the quality of their human relationships.

INDIVIDUAL LEVEL. A number of investigations have examined the effects of such programs on relating and communicating with others (Miles, 1960; Bunker, 1965; Valiquet, 1968). Reviews of this literature have raised methodological questions about the research, but have also reached the general conclusion that individual behavior change can occur in laboratory education programs (Dunnette & Campbell, 1968; House, 1967). A key ingredient in most laboratory education programs is the unstructured small group. An educator, trainer, or consultant is present to help the group members to examine their group dynamics, their interpersonal relationships, and their individual roles in the group. The most extensively studied programs have been those conducted by the National Training Laboratories Institute for Applied Behavioral Science (Bradford, 1964). This organization has taken some of the major properties of open systems as values and practices to be taught to clients. Openness and mutuality in human relationships tend to be the focus of learning in most of the programs (Alderfer, 1970).

Frequently, research has indicated that participants in laboratory programs, upon returning to their work settings, are seen as changing their behavior in ways consistent with the stated values and goals of the program. Compared to controls who did not attend the programs, the trainees were more likely to be seen as receiving communication, establishing relationships, increasing their interdependence with others, and exerting self-control. Also in comparison to controls the trainees showed greater awareness of human behavior, sensitivity to group process, sensitivity to others, acceptance of others, comfort, and insight into the self and role behavior (Miles, 1960; Bunker, 1965; Valiquet, 1968).

A laboratory program usually takes place on some sort of "cultural island," such that the members are removed from their usual settings. Various elements in the laboratory design help to establish a boundary around the learning setting. Internal to the functioning of the learning community are efforts to make boundaries between persons and groups more permeable and relationships more mutual. The laboratory itself is a temporary system which tends to be externally closed and internally open

while functioning. Under normal circumstances this external isolation would probably result in destructive conflicts and eventually in internal isolation. But the role of the staff is to help participants work with rather than flee from the emotions that develop.

According to the theoretical argument advanced above, the use of closed external boundaries in laboratory education should increase the psychological hazards of the undertaking. A closely related theoretical position advanced by Rice (1969) and Astrachan (1970) views the group leader's role largely in terms of boundary management. Reasoning from such a position leads one to expect that the leader's behavior would have a strong impact on the likelihood of casualties arising from the group experience. A recent study by Yalom and Lieberman (1971) showed that a particular leader style tended to be associated with high casualty rates in encounter groups. This type of leader, termed the "aggressive stimulator" by the investigators, tended to precipitate casualties when he attacked group members or participated in a group attack on members. Such behavior might be conceptualized as excessive pushing for openness from members to the point of actually threatening the existence of their ego boundaries. Member casualties occurred in groups in which leaders used other styles—supporting the idea that the group itself can be dangerous—but it was only the aggressive stimulators who had excessively high casualty rates.

The theory of boundaries and relationships includes the proposition that steady states of systems, whether they be open or closed, tend to be self-reinforcing. Applied to the laboratory setting this would suggest that those persons who are already relatively open would find the least clash with laboratory methods. Harvey and Davis (1972) reported that participants in a 1963 Human Relations Laboratory were substantially below average in dogmatism. Steele (1968) employed the sensation-intuition scale of the Myers-Briggs Type Indicator in a study of processes and outcomes in laboratory education. (In studies of creative persons, this scale was found to discriminate between more and less creative people in the same professions. Creatives tended to be more intuitive than non-creatives.) Steele predicted that intuitives would endorse the laboratory values of shared control, trust, importance of feelings, and openness more than the sensors both before and after the laboratory. He also predicted that the intuitives would change more towards these values as a result of laboratory education than the sensors. In a general heterogeneous laboratory sample, he found support for the before and after predictions but no support for the change prediction. In a management laboratory, he found support for the change prediction but not for the before and after predictions.

In order to explain these outcomes more fully, Steele did a second study in which he obtained member and trainer behavioral ratings on each participant. He found that intuitives were rated significantly higher than sensors on engagement and involvement in the group processes but only slightly higher (not significantly) on change. It appears that intuition is a direct predictor of how one copes with a laboratory experience, but is only indirectly related to change.

GROUP LEVEL. The difference between programs that address group level changes and those that focus on the individual level is whether natural teams of work-mates who meet with the consultant or "strangers" come together only for training and later return to their different back-home organizations. When natural groups work together during the intervention period, the target for change is not only individual behavior, but also collective group behavior. As one might expect, the number of groups studied has been fewer than the number of individuals. The intervention strategies vary considerably. The unity among approaches

—if one may be permitted to claim that there is one—is that they all seem to converge on making the internal boundaries of the groups more permeable and relationships more mutual.

Argyris (1962) undertook and reported one of the earliest natural work group programs. Initially, he undertook a diagnosis of the work relations among several groups of top executives. After the diagnosis had been completed, one of the groups spent a week off-site with Argyris and an associate to examine their work relationships. Part of the time was devoted to "pure" T-group activities—examining the group's behavior as it happened in the program—while other activities were directed to the back-home problems. Argyris and Harrison, who independently evaluated the project, came to some similar conclusions about the effects of the program. Participants in the program felt that it had been a valuable learning experience for them and that there was some carry-over to back-home behavior and perceptions. The executives perceived more interpersonal components in their work and were able to adjust their behavior accordingly. The long-term effects of the diagnosis and training group activities were not positive, however. Returning home, the executives found that their increased openness did not transfer organization wide as easily as they might have expected. Subordinates had expectations about proper behavior of their superiors which did not change readily and perhaps could not without more direct involvement in diagnostic and training activities. The effects of the program were not sustained because the larger system did not support increased openness, and the program did not include activities with the larger system.

Friedlander (1967) reported the results of using organizational training laboratories with four of twelve natural work groups. These groups were part of one of the armed services' largest research and development stations. The eight groups which did not participate in training served as comparison groups for the four which did. The training groups met to identify work problems, find solutions to the problems, and plan their implementation. During the problem-solving sessions attention was also given to the various interpersonal and intergroup issues which arose while working on the problems. Friedlander's data indicated that the trained groups changed certain of their perceptions about group functioning in ways that differed from the comparison groups. Trained groups showed mutual influence among members, more personal involvement in meetings, and greater effectiveness in solving problems. There was no increase in feeling that the chairman was more approachable, that the group was more trustworthy, or that meetings were more worthwhile. However, among the groups who did not have training, there was a decrease in chairman approachability, and this decrease was not observed among the trained groups.

Sofer (1961) reported yet another approach—which he called sociotherapeutic—in which a consultant worked with key groups in different types of organizations. The cases he dealt with had sharply defined problems, and in this way differed from cases Argyris and Friedlander had. In the Argyris and Friedlander projects, group work focused more on the process employed to solve problems rather than on the problems themselves. For Sofer the content of the problems seemed to receive as much attention as the process.

A family run business was facing difficulties in providing for succession of managers to the board of directors. Top flight managerial talent outside the family was discouraged from entering the business because family members typically held the highest positions. In addition, some members of the family behaved ambivalently toward the idea of attracting talented managers because of doubts about their own abilities. Sofer aided the group in redesigning their selection and promotion processes and in making counseling facilities (through the Tavistock Institute) available to managers (both young and old) who wished help in thinking through their personal needs and abilities.

In another case he reported that the physician executives of a mental hospital were having difficulties in effectively combining research and clinical activities. In a third problem, the management department of a technical college was not satisfying itself or its clients with respect to the kind of education programs offered. At the mental hospital, Sofer helped the executives to clarify the degree to which their behavior perpetuated the clinical-research split and redesigned the duties of the research nurse to free her more fully for consultative work. At the technical college the consultant aided faculty members in achieving a more realistic assessment of their primary mission and assisted them in upgrading their technical skills so that they might more fully assist their clients.

Collecting and feeding back information about a group's functioning was an integral part of each of the foregoing studies. The data used in those settings were more qualitative than quantitative, although in some cases there was a mixture of both types of information. Other approaches use data which are more heavily quantitative.

Mann (1957) measures attitudes and opinions with a fixed alternative questionnaire format. In one study, Mann (1957) conducted a survey of opinions and attitudes of employees and managers throughout the firm. After top executives discussed the data, the supervisors of the natural work groups fed back the results of the survey to their work groups. The consultant assisted in the feedback sessions. Those departments that undertook more extended feedback meetings changed more significantly in the direction of having more favorable attitudes toward their supervisors and their work than those departments which did not do the extra feedback work.

Another systematic feedback approach was undertaken by Argyris (1965), who worked with a group of top research and development executives. Argyris began by making a quantitative diagnosis of the interpersonal competence of the group. He interviewed the executives and made behavioral observations. He reported his conclusions (which were not very positive) to the executives and agreed to meet with them again. The consultant's initial diagnosis of the group led him to think that a full blown laboratory education program for this particular group of executives might be harmful. Consequently, he suggested that the executives listen to tape recordings of their decision-making meetings. The group changed its behavior as a result of listening to the tapes. Their interpersonal competence scores increased and sustained the increase for fourteen months after the consultant left. At the conclusion of fourteen months behavioral observation stopped.

Brown (1971) administered an attitude questionnaire to the students at a boys' boarding school. Feedback sessions were conducted in which the research team shared their findings about the school with the students. Feedback meetings were undertaken so that the whole school received feedback over a period of three months, one third of the school at a time. Those groups receiving later feedback served as controls for the earlier groups. After each feedback session, natural living groups met to discuss the underlying reasons for some of the problems implied by the findings. They made efforts to understand and share the nature of their difficulties in living and proposed methods for improving things. A time series questionnaire was administered to both the feedback and control groups. The data indicated that feedback sessions could be credited with increasing students' sense of involvement in the school and increasing their perception of shared influence after they had participated in the research discussions. However, this "feedback effect" was short lived, disappearing two months after the feedback sessions had been undertaken. The positive changes on involvement and influence noted

in this study indicate that the feedback intervention may have served to increase the permeability of the boundaries among the students and between students and faculty. At the same time, however, it was apparent that a one-day session was not enough to permanently remove the forces pushing toward keeping the system closed.

If the results of new behavior tending toward greater system openness are to be sustained, it would appear that more is needed than single interventions. A number of studies support the proposition that sustained and regular contact with an external change agent-behavioral scientist greatly facilitates the likelihood of retention of newly achieved internal system openness. Alderfer and Ferriss (1972) compared the reactions to survey feedback when it was administered by an inside change agent working alone, to reactions to survey feedback when it was administered by an inside plus outside change-agent team. From these results it appeared that inside and outside members of the team made differential contributions to the feedback's impact. The joint team was associated with higher evaluation of the feedback and greater acceptance of the problems highlighted by the data. The "outside" expert seemed to add credibility and competence to the study's results, but it seemed to be the presence of an insider which provided hope that constructive changes might result from identifying and discussing group problems.

Friedlander (1968) in his work with an armed services research and development organization studied the effects of the extent, nature, and duration of consultants' contact with groups exposed to organization development. Friedlander indentified the groups which had benefited most and least from the organization development program. The most improved group changed positively on all six of his evaluation dimensions: group effectiveness, leader approachability, mutual influence, personal involvement, intragroup trust, and worth of meetings. Two other groups were identified as benefiting least on different subsets of the dimensions, and so both were compared with the group gaining most from the organizational development activities. The group which gained most from the development activities differed from the other groups most markedly in terms of the amount of pre- and post-work done by the external consultant. For the two least successful groups, the external consultant spent far less time in pre- and post-work on team development than for the most successful group. One of the less successful groups dealt with the consultant only during a four-day laboratory, and the other less successful group had contact with the consultant for six hours of pre-work and a three-day laboratory. On the other hand, the most successful group had ten days of pre-work, three-and-a-half days of laboratory, and five days of post-work with the external consultant. Moreover, contact between the external consultant and an internal consulting group was the most extensive for this group.

In a related series of case studies, Argyris (1971) found that open behavior among members of top management was "resilient." In the absence of an external consultant and faced with intragroup conflict, the executives tended to behave in ways that blocked open expression of feelings or experimenting with new ideas. This behavior occurred in spite of the men having participated in laboratory programs and being capable of behaving in a more open manner. The presence of a respected external consultant seemed to make it possible for the executives to express their feelings and experiment. It was not that the consultant taught them the new behavior but more that he enabled them to behave in ways that they already knew. His presence opened the group's external boundary and aided in their reaching greater internal openness.

The mutual interaction of boundaries and relationships in changing open systems calls attention not only to the way that an external boundary is opened by the entrance of an external consultant, but also to the initial internal conditions in a group. This theoretical orientation implies that open systems tend to stay open and closed systems tend to stay closed. Accordingly, the initial internal openness of a group should be in some measure predictive of their response to development sessions designed to facilitate further increases in internal openness. Friedlander's (1970) work is relevant to this point. He found that the work groups in which members expressed high trust in one another prior to training reached greater degrees of group effectiveness and had more worthwhile meetings after training than groups whose members felt competitive with one another. It seemed as though the initial conditions of trust multiplied with training to produce more effective groups. Friedlander's (1970) findings about the impact of initial conditions of groups on later reactions to training for increased openness roughly parallel those reported by Steele (1968) for individuals. At both the individual and group levels of analysis, initial internal openness tended to be positively associated with later internal openness.

ORGANIZATIONAL LEVEL. Surprisingly enough, a few well-documented case studies of planned change at the organizational level of analysis do exist. Three of these will be the focus of our attention in this section. They were selected because on the surface they might be viewed as representing quite different approaches, and in many specific details they did differ. Jaques (1952) studied Glacier Metals, an engineering-manufacturing firm in Great Britain. Whyte and Hamilton (1964) conducted action research with the Tremont, a midwestern hotel in the United States. Marrow, Bowers, and Seashore (1967) studied, reported, and changed the functioning of the Weldon clothing manufacturer in the eastern United States. Jaques's professional orientation grew out of the Tavistock Institute in Great Britain, where his perspectives had developed from social psychology, psychoanalytic theory, and medicine. Whyte and

Hamilton were applied industrial sociologists whose theoretical foundations were primarily concerned with activities, sentiments, and interactions. Marrow, Bowers, and Seashore were action oriented behavioral consultants who operated in an NTL (National Training Laboratories) mode with the research approach of the University of Michigan's Institute for Social Research. While the details of each project and the investigators differed markedly, in many ways they were similar.

Each of the consultants began their change processes at the top with the initiation and support of the key executives. Also present was some degree of prior contact between the highest ranking manager and some of the behavioral scientists who were researchers and change agents. At Glacier, the Managing Director had had contact with the Tavistock Institute before the project began (Brown, 1960). The chief operating officer at the Tremont Hotel had heard Whyte speak of his earlier studies of the restaurant industry. In addition to being the top executive officer at Weldon, Marrow was also a practicing applied behavioral scientist. Not surprisingly, the Weldon project made the most extensive and differentiated use of both behavioral and nonbehavioral consultants.

Each of the organizational change projects made use of a team of external change agents. Jaques headed a team of eight research people, six of whom were student trainees. Whyte and Hamilton operated with a team of three, themselves plus a third person who served as personnel manager during and after the change project. The Weldon project utilized several teams of external people. Some of the teams were subdivided. One group consisted of Survey Research Center people who undertook a primarily research and evaluation role in the project. Another group was made up of technical (engineering-management) consultants. Still a third team was the behavioral science trainers who were primarily responsible for changing the nature of the human relationships in the system. An external individual, or a pair, may be adequate to change a group or person, but these studies suggest that it takes a team to change an organization.

The consulting team may also be examined in terms of boundaries and relationships. The logic of open systems theory suggests that if the change team is not open to inputs from the organization (a very key element in *its* external environment), its own effectiveness would be severely limited. Moreover, one would also predict that the internal openness of the consulting team would affect its tendency to receive external input. This topic was not systematically addressed in the studies, but it was taken up in one way or another in each of the reports.

In the Glacier study, the eight-person team consisted of two senior men from the Institute and four research fellows. Jaques commented, in describing the background of the team members, that their previous work history probably facilitated the organization members' acceptance of them. Two research fellows were women economics graduates who had worked in the civil service. The four men consisted of a former coal miner, a fitter, a draftsman, and a skilled engineering worker. All four had formerly held trade union positions. In addition to the symbolic meaning which the former backgrounds of these people offered, their experience aided them in understanding and sensing key elements in the work lives of persons in the organization. At the same time, however, their past history might cause them to over-identify with the real or imagined plight of the organization members. The internal openness of the research team would be the natural corrective factor in this case. If the team did develop the requisite openness and tendencies to over-identify occurred, team members with different perspectives could confront those who were over-identifying. Little direct attention to this matter was given in the Jaques book, but various other corrective procedures were mentioned. For example, the team agreed to engage in no social contacts with their clients and their interventions were based on publicly observable "here-and-now" events in the sessions they attended.

Whyte and Hamilton (1964) explicitly discussed the roles and relationships among the team members in the Tremont project. Whyte spent the least total time with the organization, and, initially, exercised primary responsibility for dealing with the top executive in the system. A second member of the consultant team, Wiley, functioned as the personnel manager-change agent in the organization and worked primarily with middle and lower ranking personnel. Hamilton worked as a researcher, primarily at the lower levels of the system. Her primary commitment was to the university rather than to the hotel, and at two points in the project this factor was a source of strain for the change agent team. Moreover, Whyte was located at the university. One point came early in the project, when Hamilton's trips to the university to consult with Whyte had the unintended impact of leaving Wiley without adequate influence on issues directly affecting his internal change agent role. The team openly discussed the problem resulting in Wiley's also consulting with Whyte at the university. The second point came when Hamilton decided to return to full-time university work. Thus, a valuable resource became unavailable and this caused Wiley to consider leaving the system. Again, this issue was discussed among the team, and Wiley stayed on at the hotel. Without the open discussion, Wiley's sense of being abandoned might not have been worked through and he might have left the system immediately.

The Weldon project offered yet another constellation of boundaries and relationships among the consulting (external) team. In this case, the change agents consisted not only of different individuals but also of different groups. There were technological as well as behavioral consultants; among the behavioral consultants some had primarily research roles and others had primarily consultative roles. The report on this project gave explicit attention to these different roles and their respective contributions. Less attention was devoted to the relationships among the consulting groups, although clearly Marrow's position, as both a distinguished behavioral scientist and the top manager, provided a very crucial integrating function.

Change activities were multi-level in each project. Frequently, attention was directed toward individuals—key managers or executives. Attention was also directed toward the group level. Indeed, all of the organizational teams formed new and firmer boundaries around aggregates of individuals who had functional reasons to group, but had behaved without much coordination prior to interaction. Within the groups, efforts were made to identify and alter those factors which prevented the full and adequate exchange of relevant information. Anxiety and authority received special attention, although as theoretical concepts these terms played the biggest role in the Glacier project. Consultants worked to promote greater mutuality in interpersonal and intragroup relationships. They encouraged group members to stop avoiding difficult or tension-provoking issues.

Attention also focused on improving intergroup relations. Usually the consulting strategy involved bringing the warring groups together for a discussion of their mutual problems in the areas of both tasks and relationships. Labor-management issues were addressed in each setting; the common theme usually centered on job seniority and the relationship of pay to performance. Greater job security coupled with a reduction in turnover was achieved in each organization and both employees and company benefited from financial incentive systems at Glacier and Weldon. At Glacier, the consultants aided both the labor and management leaders in examining the feelings and behavior associated with their role performance.

Intergroup problems between different functional areas were also addressed. At the Tremont, the waitresses and the kitchen staff examined the task and human elements of their interdependence, and both groups benefited. Manufacturing and merchandising attempted similar work at Weldon, with mixed results. The role and personality of the various group leaders turned out to be quite crucial in the various intergroup problem-solving encounters. The unexpected receptivity of a chef at the Tremont speeded the improvement of waitress-kitchen relations in that setting. On the other hand, lack of openness on the part of the head of merchandising at Weldon turned out to be the first step leading toward the eventual loss of several merchandising managers in that organization, even after improvements had been achieved in the working relations between merchandising and manufacturing.

The reports of all three cases contained evidence that the intervention programs were credited with substantial improvements in organizational effectiveness. This evidence was most thoroughly documented at Weldon and least at Glacier. Indices ranged from profit and performance data through absenteeism and turnover to attitudes and morale. Surprisingly, at Weldon even though the organizational performance improved considerably, the attitude surveys did not indicate much individual attitude change. At Glacier and the Tremont, the more clear-cut changes dealt with subjective reactions, in part because the investigators attended more to these issues and thus probably gathered more complete data on these variables.

An additional unique feature about the Weldon study was that the investigators revisited the system after their last measures of the change process had been taken. In 1969, five years after the last measure of change, Seashore negotiated for another survey of employee and management attitudes toward their work experiences. He and Bowers reported, "The general picture is one of the maintenance of earlier gains in the favorability of employee attitudes or the further improvement in attitudes" (Seashore & Bowers, 1970, p. 229). Moreover, the investigator remarked on his own surprise about this outcome, having been prepared to find reversion to previous patterns rather than sustained change and continuing development. Although there was not heavy use of external resources, there was additional use of external consultants in ways that were considered normal and permanent. Thus, even after the period in which a large investment in developing greater openness of the external boundaries was observed, the new steady state contained provisions for continuing the use of external relationships to maintain and continue the change process.

Also consistent with the view that system states (whether tending toward openness or closedness) tend to reinforce themselves there was evidence in each organization that the leaders were moving toward greater openness prior to the behavioral science input, although the degree of sophistication and competence in this movement differed sharply among the systems. The top manager at the Tremont was searching for new approaches to personnel relations when he encountered Whyte. At Glacier, the Managing Director had been at work on developing a more open system for several years prior to the entry of Jaques's team. The system was having difficulty, however, and enlisted the Tavistock team to diagnose and improve their approach.

Despite a forward thrust in all three organizations, however, no program was without its flaws, incompleteness, and uncertainties. These, too, were reported in the studies.

CONCLUSIONS. At each level of analysis change programs that aimed for more mutual human relationships tended to be most effective when the unit was predisposed toward change before the program began. Steele (1968) found intuitives more ready than sensors. Friedlander (1970) learned that more trusting groups benefited more from group training than less trusting groups. The three organization studies each showed that the top leadership in the groups were actively searching for new ways to manage prior to the beginning of applied behavioral science. These findings support the argument that external stimulation alone is not enough to promote system change. Internal readiness should be coupled with external opportunities to increase the likelihood of sustained improvement in human relationships.

When more than the individual level of analysis was involved in the change effort, attention was given not only to the human relationships but also to the interaction between task activities and group relations. Intact groups who met with behavioral science consultants worked not only on their human relationships but also on the work problems faced by the group. At the organizational level of analysis, efforts were continually made to deal with how individual, group, and intergroup relations affected organizational performance.

There was no evidence to show that boundary and relationship changes had direct effects on hard performance measures at the individual or group levels of analysis. There was evidence to show that attitudes and behavior changed toward firmer, more permeable boundaries and more mutual relationships. But it was only the organization studies where hard performance measures showed positive change. Perhaps these measures were not available for groups, or perhaps a whole organization must be included in a change program addressed to human relationships if performance is to improve as a result.

There was both positive and negative data to show that sustained change requires more than short-term contact between consultants and the system they attempt to help. The group and organizational change programs that showed lasting changes all had

regular outside intervention. Short-term interventions typically had salutary effects but did not last.

Growth Need Studies

The primary reason for a person's being a member of a work organization—from the organization's point of view—is because he can, by virtue of utilizing more or less of his skills and talents, do something to benefit the goals of the system. How much an individual is called upon to use his abilities and how much he is required to learn more as he does his job determines in a large measure the degree to which he has a job which satisfies his growth needs. Excessive division of labor brought on by modern mass production technology has often required workers to perform the same narrowly defined activities again and again. Research over the years has shown the extraordinarily high human costs which have accrued to individuals who faced such tasks on a continuing basis (Walker & Guest, 1952; Argyris, 1964; Friedmann, 1961; Kornhauser, 1965). Some writers have even noticed the similarities between highly limited assembly-line jobs and the results of sensory deprivation experiments (Fiske & Maddi, 1961). The redesign and rotation of job assignments has provided a means by which some of these deleterious human costs of modern technology can be avoided. At the individual level of analysis, job enrichment has been a technique aimed at changing the job content of numerous lower level jobs. Groups have been formed, such that the combined tasks of the individuals within the group form a complete unit so that the individuals could see a meaningful unit of work completed. Changes in job design have come about both from efforts aimed directly at the work itself and from social and structural interventions.

INDIVIDUAL LEVEL. Friedmann (1961) reported findings pertaining to some of the earliest job enlargement experiments. Like many other efforts directed to organization change, the specific details of enlargement varied with the situation. At IBM's electric typewriter plant vocational training was introduced so that workers could better understand the whole production process to which they were contributing. Employees were asked to do more and different activities: sharpen tools, read blueprints, set up machines, calibrate, and inspect. A number of people were displaced by this change, but they were able to find work in other parts of the company, sometimes at increased rates of pay. The quality of work improved; the workers who performed the enlarged jobs were more satisfied; and costs of the products were reduced. Friedmann also noted that eliminating inspectors seemed to improve the quality of human relationships in the plant because the foremen began to discuss their problems directly with the workers.

Detroit Edison, a public utility, also undertook job enlargement experiments, but in their case, the effort was undertaken with white collar jobs. One example was the billing department, where prior to the changes work was highly subdivided among three machine work groups. To institute changes each employee was taught to work all of the machines. The supervisor was to assign work to each employee and permit job rotation. In actual practice, the employees learned to know where they were needed and distributed themselves among the jobs. At Detroit Edison job enlargement at the bottom led to a similar development in the duties of supervisors. The supervisors began hiring their own employees, preparing their own annual budget, making changes in budgetary procedures, and handling complaints and grievances. The results of this program produced a decrease in absenteeism and a rise in productivity.

More recently Lawler (1969) applied the logic of expectancy theory to job enrichment programs to argue that product quality was more likely to increase than product quantity. His literature search for reports of job enrichment identified ten studies, all of which had demonstrated work quality improvements from job enlargement. He found only four studies which resulted in quantity benefits from enlarging jobs. Paul, Robertson, and Herzberg (1969) recounted a number of British experiments in enrichment that dealt with higher ranking organizational positions. Experimental chemical engineers, sales representatives, design engineers, and foremen in different organizations all had their jobs enlarged. Results indicated that better performance and improved morale tended to follow from the job changes. Ford (1969) reported on a series of nineteen job enrichment studies undertaken in the American Telephone and Telegraph organization. Eighteen of these studies showed some beneficial effects on such measures as absenteeism, turnover, employee attitudes, performance rates, costs, managerial attitudes, and customer attitudes. Job enrichment, when properly undertaken and executed, must be considered a highly successful change strategy, benefiting both the individual and the organization.

When one moves upward in unit of analysis, however, programs of job enrichment become more problematic. Improved human relationships were outcomes in the earliest studies, but later investigations have paid less attention to interpersonal, group, and intergroup factors. Some researchers have even argued that improved job conditions can make human relations a matter of secondary importance (Guest, 1957; Herzberg, Mausner, & Snyderman, 1959; Davis, 1966). There is a growing body of evidence, however, which argues that job enlargement often cannot be conceptualized in solely individualistic terms, and failure to take into account more complex levels of analysis can undermine otherwise successful enlargement efforts.

GROUP LEVEL. One such study was reported by Alderfer (1967). He obtained attitudinal information related to the effects of a job enlargement program after the project had been completed. The advent of a new continuous process technology had provided a manufacturing firm with an opportunity to design new kinds of jobs for lower level employees. A training program was instituted, and the new jobs were designed to have a wider scope of responsibility and more challenge. When the study was undertaken, the job enlargement program was almost complete. Comparisons were made between the newly enlarged jobs and the older, more narrow positions. It was found that employees holding the new jobs were more satisfied with their pay and opportunities to use their skills and abilities than were employees on the older jobs. Another attitudinal difference between the jobs, however, was not part of the plan. In comparison to the older jobs, the new positions showed more unsatisfactory relationships between superiors and subordinates. The holders of the new machine operator jobs perceived significantly less respect from their superiors than the men in the older jobs.

Lawler, Hackman, and Kaufman (1973) obtained similar results. The directory assistance job of telephone operators was enlarged to increase autonomy and discretion in dealing with customers. The training period was shortened, and they were allowed certain liberties with customers and other employees which previously had been prohibited. In the follow-up study, the investigators found that the operators did perceive that the objective characteristics of their jobs had changed, but they did not react with the enthusiasm or commitment with which their supervisors did. Instead, they reported that they got along less well with other operators than before, and they were less satisfied with the opportunities to make and maintain friendships at work. In one aspect of the job, they reported less satisfaction with the amount of respect and fair treatment they received from their supervisors. In another part of the job, the operators indicated that they were more unhappy with the degree that supervisors were doing parts of the job which they thought they should be doing.

Job enlargement programs can also affect intergroup relations. Whyte (1955) studied women who were working on an incentive based assembly line. The women were given control over the speed of their line. As a result, their productivity, pay, and overall job satisfaction increased. These changes for the better, however, did not go unnoticed by other groups in the organization. The engineers who had developed specifications for the job were disturbed. The superintendent who managed several lines, including the one with the control over the speed of their line, was also upset. All of these external forces converged on the foreman of the women's group, who succumbed to the pressure and cancelled the experiment. Eventually, the foreman and six out of the eight girls who had participated in the experiment left the organization.

Each of the foregoing studies identified one or more key human relationships that was pushed in the direction of lower mutuality as a consequence of a job enrichment experiment that focused almost exclusively on the job itself without giving adequate attention to the relevant human relationships. The Alderfer (1967) study identified difficulties which arose in the superior-subordinate relationship; the Lawler, Hackman, and Kaufman (1973) study reported problems with both peer and superior-subordinate relationships; and the Whyte (1955) study showed evidence of strains in intergroup relations outside the unit where the experiment was undertaken. When these results are combined with the several earlier studies which reported inadvertent positive changes in human relationships as a result of job enlargement, one is led to the conclusion that it is probably the *rare* job enrichment experiment that does not imply relationship changes as well as job changes.

Still other reports underline the crucial role of human relationships when job changes are implemented. Trist, Higgin, Murray, and Pollack (1963), for example, studied the job of coal miners. New technology had led to the breaking up of small autonomous work groups and resulted in the establishment of large groups in which the miners were assigned to a narrowly defined set of duties. This conventional long-wall method was associated with poor production, absenteeism, and high accident rates. However, assigning highly specialized roles was not the only way to adapt to the modern technology. Groups of workers sharing responsibility for a complete cycle of tasks was another possible job design. The consultants introduced such a design and called it the composite longwall method, for it seemed to combine many of the features of the older (pre-technology) approach with new advantages of the more modern technology. The composite longwall method showed higher production, lower absenteeism, and lower accident rates than the conventional longwall method. Workers who used it experienced more stimulating and challenging task activities and more cooperative interpersonal and intergroup relations.

Rice (1958) undertook very similar changes in the calico mills of Ahmadabad, India. Upon arrival, the researchers found that the introduction of new technology in the mills had failed to produce the expected increases in quantity or quality of production. Contrary to the coal mining case, however, there did not seem to be morale problems or difficulties with interpersonal relationships. Workers had been assigned to twelve narrowly defined job roles. Their relationships with each other were generally confused, and no one, either by working alone or as a member of a group, was able to experience task completion. After thorough study, Rice proposed that groups of workers be given responsibility for groups of looms, under the direction of a group leader. In this way, a boundary would be drawn around sets of individuals whose relationships with each other had been previously unclear. Moreover, jobs which had been narrowly specialized before could be shared among members of a work team, thereby providing each person with an opportunity to use a wider range of his skills and abilities. These proposed changes were implemented by group discussions at successive levels of management. Generally, the suggestions were greeted with enthusiasm and the changes proved to be quite successful when introduced, even though there were periodic regressions to former levels of productivity after the changes had been made.

Spurred by Herzberg's (1966) theory of work motivation, AT&T has undertaken programs of job redesign directed toward making the "work itself" more rewarding, challenging, and meaningful to employees. Theoretically, to be successful such programs motivate growth needs. Ford's (1969) report makes a persuasive case for the success of these efforts. If one looks only at the independent variables included in his field experiments, individual growth needs are almost exclusively considered. However, looking only at the independent variables is misleading. Ford's (1969) reports of how to prepare for and implement changes in the work itself include many references to group and organizational considerations.

Frequently, a "work itself" program starts with an off-site workshop. At this setting, managers who might be affected by a job change or who know the job participate in a process called "green lighting" the job. Under a norm prohibiting criticism, they free associate aloud about changes in a job which might make it more stimulating and challenging. In addition, the managers set the goals and targets for the programs. Although Ford does not say so in these words, one could interpret the primary tasks of the workshops to be two-fold: to obtain information needed to redesign the jobs and to establish more open relationships with the managers affected so that they will support or (at a minimum) not undermine the job changes.

A similar theme appears when Ford addresses what he feels are the most important criticisms of the "work itself" effort. Many of the problems he cites can be conceptualized in terms of interpersonal or inter-group problems. Examples of problems are: union representatives not believing the purpose of the program is to make better jobs; in fact, sometimes job specifications are written into labor contracts. Or, the top management in a system may interfere with a program unintentionally. In short, it seems that the management of human relationships plays a key part in the successes and failures reached by "work itself" programs even though these variables have not played a central role in either Herzberg's theory or in the field experiments conducted in connection with work itself activities.

ORGANIZATIONAL LEVEL. In some ways, a patient in a mental hospital is analogous to persons holding assembly line jobs. In both roles the person has little influence over his life in the organization, has relatively little contact with the external world when he is in role, and is heavily confined by the system's technology. An important difference, however, is that the mental hospital's primary task is directed toward keeping the patient in custody and aiding his recovery, while the production system's primary mission is to manufacture large quantities of products. One result of this difference is that efforts to redesign the "job" of being a patient in a mental hospital tend to have broader implications for the total organization than activities that enrich the jobs of lower level employees.

Rubenstein and Lasswell (1966) reported on the processes and outcomes of an experimental effort to change the nature of patient roles in the Yale Psychiatric Institute (YPI), a small elite hospital for psychotics. The primary element in the innovation was the introduction of patient-staff meetings. At these sessions, the patients and staff were able to discuss matters of common concern. In particular, patients were able to raise questions about how decisions about their fate were made and, in some cases, influence the outcomes. Discussions and decisions which had formerly taken place privately

among staff members became more public and open. Prior to the introduction of the large group sessions, group therapy had been added to individual therapy as a treatment modality. As a result, the hospital had programs of treatment operating at the individual, group, and organizational levels of analysis.

A year after the patient-staff meetings had been introduced, the staff initiated a program of adult education which was intended to more fully utilize the facilities of Yale University and the city of New Haven. A patient-staff advisory group was also developed to deal explicitly with broad hospital policies. A systematic work program for patients was also begun after the large group intervention. As a result, patients worked from part to full time on jobs which allowed them to utilize more of their skills and abilities.

Rubenstein and Lasswell (1966) did not evaluate the outcomes of the extensive series of innovations in terms of recovery rates, recidivism, and the like, but they did report other consequences. They learned, for example, that even though there was an increase in power sharing throughout the system the director increased his power and was seen as authoritarian by some segments of the organization. The nurses were perhaps most displaced by the changes because some of the activities which they alone had done, like gathering information about the patients, were done during the patient-staff meetings. What happened to the nurses seems similar to what happens to those persons who have the most immediate and direct contact with the employees whose jobs are enriched. When the lowest level jobs are widened, the next level position is threatened unless efforts are made to take account of the interdependency among roles.

CONCLUSIONS. Appealing to incumbents' growth needs can be a highly successful change approach. However, for job enrichment programs to succeed they must address more than the individual level. When programs failed, interpersonal and intergroup relations played an important part in diminishing the benefits of the intervention. Indeed, in the more successful cases, interpersonal and intergroup factors were generally taken into account.

Some programs are specifically directed toward groups and the organization. Trist et al. (1963) and Rice (1958) showed that group formation around interdependent tasks resulted in job rotation, increased mutuality in relationships, and increased overall effectiveness. While the intention in these studies was to form and structure groups, a major outcome was more stimulating and meaningful tasks for the individuals to perform and, therefore, more satisfaction of growth needs. At the YPI, an organizational-level intervention, the patient-staff conference, resulted in patients developing and using their skills and abilities in educational and work programs.

Comparison Among Existence, Relatedness, and Growth Studies

Although it was possible to organize studies of planned change according to the type of need that was satisfied primarily, in many of the studies more than one type of need was satisfied. Greater satisfaction of relatedness needs was associated, at least indirectly, with all of the existence need programs which resulted in sustained change. Relatedness need satisfaction was also a key factor in each of the growth need programs. For example, when job enrichment programs were successful, interpersonal and intergroup issues were also typically addressed. The studies of coal getting by Trist et al. (1963) combined greater financial rewards with new organizational forms and thus touched all three types of human needs. The programs which gave primary attention to relatedness needs tended *not* to deal with the other needs. One might conclude that, regardless of the level of intervention, relatedness need satisfaction is a necessary, but not always a sufficient, condition for sus-

tained and constructive planned change. Whether the change is in task performance, attitudes, or interpersonal behavior seems to depend on the level at which the intervention is made. At the individual and group level, task performance does not seem to change; however, attitudes and interpersonal behavior do. At the organization level of intervention, marked changes in task performance were found in several studies. For the existence and growth studies, interventions at the individual and group level showed task performance changes.

The range of studies covered in this review, while not exhaustive, does point out that planned change efforts at each level of intervention can appeal to each type of human need. The predictions one would make based on boundary and relationship arguments say that system change is a multilevel phenomenon. Change at one level is closely related to the reactions at other levels. Moreover, one cannot understand, explain, or predict change without examining both the internal and external conditions at whatever level planned change is directed.

IMPLICATIONS

"Putting the theory to work" is the task of the applied behavioral scientist. The following guidelines are based upon boundary and relationship concepts and may be useful to the applied scientist.

1. *The primary tasks of applied behavioral scientists working with organizations involve identifying, understanding, and changing the nature of boundaries and relationships of individuals, groups, and the organization as a whole.*

2. *The primary goals of applied behavioral scientists working with organizations are to aid in the establishment of relevant boundaries, the opening of closed boundaries, and the movement of relationships from less to more mutuality.*

To identify and understand the important boundaries and relationships in a system, an applied behavioral scientist must first diagnose the problems. To get such information one must cross internal and external boundaries, and the quality of that information increases as relationships become more mutual. However, in the diagnostic phase, the purpose is to understand. The behavioral scientist gathers information so that he and the client can decide together what, if any, action should be taken.

In the action phase of an intervention, consultants work on both external and internal boundaries of systems. They address not only relationships between the parts of a subsystem but also the relationships between subsystems. Thus, intervention should be at all three levels. Individuals are the subsystems of groups; individuals and groups are subsystems of organizations, and all three levels need attention.

To establish a boundary where one formerly did not exist requires the development of relationships between those parts. To make a boundary more permeable means increasing the amount and kinds of material that flow in and out of the system or subsystem. Moving a relationship toward greater mutuality is a specific way of increasing the balanced flow of relevant information, energy, and matter between parts of a system or between whole systems.

3. *In deciding where to start and with whom to work, a consultant should keep in mind the tendency for both the openness and closedness of boundaries to be self-sustaining.*

4. *An optimal structure for changing organizations consists of establishing a team (or series of teams) including insiders and outsiders.*

5. *The team needs to have optimally open boundaries and relationships of mutuality among team members and between the team and the system.*

Boundary and relationship conditions tend toward being self-sustaining. Excessively closed or open systems tend toward staying that way as a consequence of establishing non-mutual relationships. Open systems tend toward staying open as a result of forming relationships of mutuality. There are now several studies which show that individuals or groups which move toward greater openness can regress toward closedness if the larger social system of which they are a part does not aid in sustaining the change (Fleishman, 1955; Harrison, 1962). At the same time there are also data to show that change can be maintained when there is pre- and post-work on the part of consultants (Friedlander, 1968; Seashore & Bowers, 1970; Argyris, 1971).

A consultant usually faces a dilemma in deciding where to invest his initial energies. If he starts where the system is most closed, he runs the risk of having a very short life in the organization. On the other hand, if he chooses to work only where the system is relatively open, he runs the risk of having his efforts contribute additional divisiveness to the organization. Those who support planned change may develop a competitive intergroup relationship with those who oppose it (Alderfer, 1971).

Establishment of insider-outsider teams provides a way of helping the organization to become more open to its external environment. Outsiders who have not been fully socialized by the host system provide fresh perspectives and stimulation. Insiders have the knowledge and empathy of the system which can be gained only through extensive experience with it.

If the change team is to facilitate greater organizational openness it, too, needs to be open. The team needs to be externally open to obtain valid information about the system it is seeking to change. It must be able to generate enough confidence and trust among members of the host system to be able to gain access to significant events and interactions. Moreover, the change team needs to be externally open so that the composition of the team can change depending upon the kinds of problems or tasks it addresses. New outside members might be added when they can contribute skills the team needs for a particular mission. New inside members might be added to enhance understanding of certain parts of the target system. For example, a job enrichment team might add members who are more expert in changing human relationships than they are. A team dealing with black-white relations in a system would ideally be comprised of both black and white staff members.

The team needs to be internally as well as externally open. A given orientation to a problem can provide insight, but it can also create blind spots. A team can benefit most from its differences if all relevant views can be identified, all relevant data shared, and alternative hypotheses tested against the shared information.

6. *Permanent change in systems (or subsystems) is most likely to be achieved and sustained if programmed through a series of cycles including diagnosis, action, and evaluation which are carried out by both insiders and outsiders.*

Initial diagnosis aids a system's unfreezing to prepare for change. Action strategies which employ both inside and outside personnel combine the perspectives of both sides. Evaluation of the various elements of a change program enables the team to learn from both mistakes and successes.

7. *Since knowledge depends on having access to information and closed systems restrict the flow of information, behavioral scientists can increase the quality of the results they obtain if they are able to change the systems they study toward having more optimally open boundaries with mutual relationships.*

A behavioral scientist will find more errors in his data in more closed systems. Moreover, there is reason to believe that the greater error in closed systems will not be random but systematic. Relatively closed systems are less likely to admit outside investigators than relatively open systems, and when entry is achieved the relationships that are established are less likely to be mutual. As a consequence data will be slanted either more positively or more negatively, depending on whether the respondents use the research as a chance to discharge some of their pent-up hostility or whether they see the research as a threat and withhold negative information.

A researcher, therefore, faces a dilemma which has no easy solution. In order to reduce error, he may attempt changes in order to obtain more valid data. But if he does this, the system about which he learns is different from the one he initially wished to study. On the other hand, he may join the system without attempting to change it. In doing this, he runs the risk of losing his perspective as a result of being heavily influenced by the system.

Changing organizational conditions can be extraordinarily useful in studying systems, but neither changing nor studying organizations is easy, and, unfortunately, more is uncertain and unchangeable in an excessively closed or open system than in an optimally bounded system.

REFERENCES

Adorno, T. W., Frenkel-Brunswik, E., Levinson, D. J., & Sanford, R. N. *The authoritarian personality.* New York: Harper and Brothers, 1950.

Aiken, M., & Hage, J. Organizational interdependence and intra-organizational structure. *American Sociological Review,* 1968, 33, 912–930.

Alderfer, C. P. An organizational syndrome. *Administrative Science Quarterly,* 1967, 12. 440, 460.

Alderfer, C. P. Understanding laboratory education: An overview. *Monthly Labor Review,* 1970, 93, 18–27.

Alderfer, C. P. Effect of individual, group, and intergroup relations on attitudes toward management development program. *Journal of Applied Psychology,* 1971, 55, 302–311.

Alderfer, C. P. *Existence, relatedness, and growth: Human needs in organizational settings.* New York: The Free Press, 1972.

Alderfer, C. P., & Brown, L. D. The human system of the boys' school. Manuscript, Yale University, Department of Administrative Sciences, New Haven, 1970.

Alderfer, C. P., & Brown, L. D. *Learning from changing: Organizational diagnosis and change,* in press.

Alderfer, C. P., & Ferriss, R. Understanding the impact of survey feedback. In H. Hornstein & W. Burke (Eds.), *The social technology of organizational development*. New York: Learning Resources Press, 1972.

Alderfer, C. P., Kaplan, R. E., & Smith, K. K. The effect of variations in relatedness need satisfaction on relatedness desires. *Administrative Science Quarterly*, 1974, 19, 507–532.

Alderfer, C. P., & Lodahl, T. M. A quasi-experiment on the use of experimental methods in the classroom. *Journal of Applied Behavioral Science*, 1971, 7, 43–69.

Allport, G. W. The open system in personality theory. *Journal of Abnormal and Social Psychology*, 1960, 61, 301–310.

Altman, I., & Haythorn, W. W. The ecology of isolated groups. *Behavioral Science*, 1967, 3, 169–182.

Amir, Y. Contact hypothesis in ethnic relations. *Psychological Bulletin*, 1969, 71, 319–342.

Argyris, C. *Understanding organizational behavior*. Homewood, Ill.: Dorsey Press, 1960.

Argyris, C. *Interpersonal competence and organizational effectiveness*. Homewood, Ill.: Irwin-Dorsey, 1962.

Argyris, C. *Integrating the individual and the organization*. New York: Wiley, 1964.

Argyris, C. *Organization and innovation*. Homewood, Ill.: Dorsey Press, 1965.

Argyris, C. The incompleteness of social-psychological theory: Examples from small group, cognitive consistency, and attribution research. *American Psychologist*, 1969, 10, 893–908.

Argyris, C. *Top management and organization development: The path from XA to YB*. New York: McGraw-Hill, 1971.

Astrachan, B. M. Towards a social systems model of therapeutic groups. *Social Psychiatry*, 1970, 5, 110–119.

Astrachan, B., & Flynn, H. The intergroup exercise: A paradigm for learning about the development of organizational structure. Manuscript, Yale University, Department of Psychiatry, New Haven, 1971.

Barron, F. *Creativity and psychological health*. Princeton: Van Nostrand, 1963.

Barron, F. The psychology of creativity. In T. M. Newcomb (Ed.), *New directions in psychology II*. New York: Holt, Rinehart and Winston, 1965, 1–134.

Bennis, W. G. Toward a "truly" scientific management: The concept of organizational health. *General Systems Yearbook*, 1962, 7, 269–282.

Bennis, W. G. *Changing organizations*. New York: McGraw-Hill, 1966.

Blake, R. R., Shepard, H. A., & Mouton, J. S. *Managing intergroup conflict in industry*. Houston, Tex.: Gulf, 1964.

Bolman, L. Some effects of trainers on their T-groups. *Journal of Applied Behavioral Science*, 1971, 7, 309–326.

Bradford, L. P. Membership and the learning process. In L. P. Bradford, J. P. Gibb, & K. D. Benne (Eds.), *T-Group theory and laboratory method*. New York: Wiley, 1964, 190–192.

Brown, L. D. Systems information processing and change: Response to feedback at three levels of analysis. Unpublished doctoral dissertation, Yale University, New Haven, 1971.

Brown, R. *Social psychology*. New York: The Free Press, 1965.

Brown, W. *Exploration in management*. New York: Wiley, 1960.

Bruner, J. S. The conditions of creativity. In H. E. Gruber, G. Terrell, & M. Wertheimer (Eds.), *Contemporary approaches to creative thinking*. New York: Atherton, 1962, 1–30.

Bunker, D. R. Individual applications of laboratory training. *Journal of Applied Behavioral Science*, 1965, 1, 131–148.

Burns, T., & Stalker, G. M. *The management of innovation*. London: Tavistock, 1961.

Campbell, D. T., Kruskal, W. H., & Wallace, W. Seating aggregation as an index of attitude. *Sociometry*, 1966, 29, 1–15.

Cartwright, D., & Zander, A. *Group dynamics: Research and theory*. (2nd ed.) London: Tavistock, 1961.

Costin, F. Dogmatism and the retention of psychological misconceptions. *Educational and Psychological Measurement*, 1968, 28, 529–534.

Cressey, D. R. Prison organizations. In J. G. March (Ed.), *Handbook of organizations*. Chicago: Rand McNally, 1965, 1023–1070.

Davis, L. E. The design of jobs. *Industrial Relations*, 1966, 6, 21–45.

Dellas, M., & Gaier, E. L. Identification of creativity: The individual. *Psychological Bulletin*, 1970, 73, 55–73.

Duncan, R. B. The effects of perceived environmental uncertainty on organizational decision unit structure. Unpublished doctoral dissertation, Yale University, New Haven, 1971.

Dunnette, M. D., & Campbell, J. P. Effectiveness of T-group experiences in managerial training and development. *Psychological Bulletin,* 1968, 70, 73–104.

Ehrlich, H. J., & Lee, D. Dogmatism, learning, and resistance to change: A review and a new paradigm. *Psychological Bulletin,* 1969, 71, 249–260.

Emery, F., & Trist, E. L. The causal texture of organizational environments. *Human Relations,* 1965, 18, 21–31.

Erikson, E. H. *Insight and responsibility.* New York: W. W. Norton, 1964.

Eysenck, H. J. The effects of psychotherapy: An evaluation. *Journal of Consulting Psychology,* 1952, 16, 319–324.

Eysenck, H. J. The effects of psychotherapy. *International Journal of Psychiatry,* 1965, 1, 99–142.

Fiske, D. W., & Maddi, S. R., Eds. *Functions of varied experience.* Homewood, Ill.: Dorsey Press, 1961.

Fleishman, E. A. Leadership climate, human relations training, and supervisory behavior. *Personnel Psychology,* 1955, 6, 205–222.

Ford, R. N. *Motivation through the work itself.* New York: American Management Association, 1969.

Freud, A. *The ego and the mechanisms of defense.* New York: International Universities Press, 1946.

Friedlander, F. The impact of organizational training laboratories upon the effectiveness and interaction of ongoing work groups. *Personnel Psychology,* 1967, 20, 289–308.

Friedlander, F. A comparative study of consulting processes and group development. *Journal of Applied Behavioral Science,* 1968, 4, 377–399.

Friedlander, F. The primacy of trust as a facilitator of further group accomplishment. *Journal of Applied Behavioral Science,* 1970, 6, 387–400.

Friedmann, G. *The anatomy of work.* Glencoe, Ill.: The Free Press, 1961.

Glover, J. D., & Hower, R. M. *The administrator.* Homewood, Ill.: Irwin, 1957.

Goffman, E. On the characteristics of total institutions. In E. Goffman (Ed.), *Asylums.* New York: Anchor, 1961, 1–124.

Gordon, G., & Marquis, S. Freedom, visibility of consequences, and scientific innovation. *American Journal of Sociology,* 1966, 72, 195–202.

Guest, R. H. Job enlargement: A revolution in job design. *Personnel Administration,* 1957, 20, 9–16.

Hall, D. T., & Lawler, E. E. Job characteristics and pressures and the organizational integration of professionals. *Administrative Science Quarterly,* 1970, 15, 271–281.

Hammes, J. A. Shelter occupancy studies at the University of Georgia. Final report, Civil Defense Research, Athens, 1964.

Harrison, R. Impact of the laboratory on perceptions of others by the experimental group. In C. Argyris (Ed.), *Interpersonal competence and organizatonal effectiveness.* Homewood, Ill.: Irwin-Dorsey, 1962, 261–271.

Harvey, J. B., & Davis, S. A. Some differences between laboratory and non-laboratory organizations. In W. G. Dyer (Ed.), *Modern theory and method in group training.* New York: Van Nostrand-Reinhold, 1972, 175–196.

Herzberg, F. *Work and the nature of man.* Cleveland: World Book, 1966.

Herzberg, F., Mausner, B., & Snyderman, B. B. *The motivation to work.* New York: Wiley, 1959.

Higgin, G., & Bridger, H. The psychodynamics of an intergroup experience. London: Tavistock, Pamphlet No. 10, 1965.

Hoffman, L. R., Harburg, E., & Maier, N. R. Differences and disagreements as factors in creative group problem solving. *Journal of Abnormal and Social Psychology,* 1962, 64, 206–214.

Holmberg, A. R. The changing values and institutions of Vicos in the context of national development. *American Behavioral Scientist,* March, 1965, 3–8.

Horney, K. *The neurotic personality in our time.* New York: W. W. Norton, 1937.

Hornstein, H. A., Bunker, B. A., Burke, W., Hornstein, M., & Lewicki, R. J. *Strategies of social intervention.* New York: The Free Press, 1971.

House, R. J. T-group education and leadership effectiveness: A review of the empiric literature and a critical evaluation. *Personnel Psychology,* 1967, 10, 1–32.

Jaques, E. *The changing culture of a factory.* London: Tavistock, 1952.

Janis, I. L. Group identification under conditions of external danger. *British Journal of Medical Psychology,* 1963, 36, 227–238.

Johnson, D. W., & Lewicki, R. J. The initiation of superordinate goals. *Journal of Applied Behavioral Science,* 1969, 5, 9–24.

Katz, D., & Kahn, R. L. *The social psychology of organizations.* New York: Wiley, 1966.

Kelley, H. H., & Stahelski, A. J. Social interaction basis of cooperators' and competitors' beliefs about others. *Journal of Personality and Social Psychology,* 1970, 16, 66–91.

Klopfer, B. Introduction: The development of a prognostic rating scale. *Journal of Projective Techniques,* 1951, 15, 421.

Kornhauser, A. *Mental health of the industrial worker.* New York: Wiley, 1965.

Landis, B. Ego boundaries. *Psychological Issues,* 1970, 6, Monograph 24.

Lasswell, H. G. The emerging policy sciences of development: The Vicos case. *American Behavioral Scientist,* March, 1965, 28–33.

Lawler, E. E. Job design and employee motivation. *Personnel Psychology,* 1969, 22, 426–435.

Lawler, E. E., & Hackman J. R. Impact of employee participation in the development of pay incentive plans: A field experiment. *Journal of Applied Psychology,* 1969, 53, 467–471.

Lawler, E. E., Hackman, J. R., & Kaufman, S. Effects of job redesign: A field experiment. *Journal of Applied Social Psychology,* 1973, 3, 49–62.

Lawrence, P. R., & Lorsch, J. W. *Organization and environment.* Cambridge: Division of Research Graduate School of Business Administration, Harvard University, 1967.

Lesieur, F. G., Ed. The Scanlon plan. Cambridge: M.I.T. Press, 1958.

Lett, E. E., Clark, W., & Altman, I. A propositional inventory of research on interpersonal distance. Bethesda, Md.: Naval Medical Research Institute, 1969.

MacKinnon, W. J., & Centers, R. Authoritarianism and urban stratification. *American Journal of Sociology,* 1956, 61, 610–620.

Maier, N. R. F., & Solem, A. R. The contribution of a discussion leader to the quality of group thinking. *Human Relations,* 1952, 5, 277–288.

Mann, F. C. Studying and creating change: A means to understanding social organization. In C. Arensberger et al. (Eds.), *Research in industrial human relations.* New York: Harper and Brothers, 1957, 157–167.

Marrow, A. J. *The practical theorist.* New York: Basic Books, 1969.

Marrow, A. J., Bowers, D. G., & Seashore, S. E. *Management by participation.* New York: Harper and Row, 1967.

Mehrabian, A. Relationship of attitude to seated posture, orientation, and distance. *Journal of Personality and Social Psychology,* 1968, 10, 26–30.

Meltzoff, J., & Kornreich, M. *Research in psychotherapy.* New York: Atherton, 1970.

Menninger, K., Mayman, M., & Pruyser, P. *The vital balance.* New York: Viking, 1963.

Miles, M. B. Human relations training: Processes and outcomes. *Journal of Counseling Psychology,* 1960, 7, 301–306.

Miller, E. J., & Rice, A. K. *Systems of organization.* London: Tavistock, 1967.

Miller, J. G. Living systems: Basic concepts, structure and process, cross-level hypotheses. *Behavioral Science,* 1965, 10, 193–237, 337–379, 380–411.

Mills, T. M. *Group transformation.* Englewood Cliffs, N.J.: Prentice-Hall, 1964.

Paul, W. J., Robertson, K. B., & Herzberg, F. Job enrichment pays off. *Harvard Business Review,* 1969, 47, 61–78.

Pelz, D. C., & Andrews, F. M. *Scientists in organizations.* New York: Wiley, 1966.

Perrow, C. Hospitals: Technology, structure, and goals. In J. G. March (Ed.), *Handbook of organizations.* Chicago: Rand McNally, 1965, 910–971.

Puckett, E. S. Measuring performance under the Scanlon plan. In F. G. Lesieur (Ed.), *The Scanlon plan.* Cambridge: M.I.T. Press, 1958, 65–79.

Rice, A. K. *Productivity and social organization: The Ahmadahad experiment.* London: Tavistock, 1958.

Rice, A. K. Individual, group, and intergroup processes. *Human Relations,* 1969, 22, 565–584.

Rogers, C. M. A theory of therapy, personality, and interpersonal relationships as developed in the client-centered framework. In S. Koch (Ed.), *Psychology: A study of a science,* Vol. 3. New York: McGraw-Hill, 1959, 184–256.

Rokeach, M. *The open and closed mind.* New York: Basic Books, 1960.

Rubenstein, R., & Lasswell, H. D. *The sharing of power in a psychiatric hospital*. New Haven: Yale University Press, 1966.

Scheflen, K. C., Lawler, E. E., & Hackman, J. R. Long-term impact of employee participation in the development of pay incentive plans. *Journal of Applied Psychology*, 1971, 55, 182–186.

Schein, E. H. *Organizational psychology*. Englewood Cliffs, N.J.: Prentice-Hall, 1965.

Schutz, W. C. *FIRO: A three dimensional theory of interpersonal behavior*. New York: Holt, Rinehart and Winston, 1958.

Seashore, S. F., & Bowers, D. G. Durability of organizational change. *American Psychologist*, 1970, 25, 227–233.

Sherif, M., & Sherif, C. *Social psychology*. New York: Harper and Row, 1969.

Shultz, G. P. Variations in the environment and the Scanlon plan. In F. G. Lesieur (Ed.), *The Scanlon plan*. Cambridge: M.I.T. Press, 1958, 100–108.

Smith, C. G. Consultation and decision processes in a research and development laboratory. *Administrative Science Quarterly*, 1970, 15, 203–215.

Smith, S. Studies of small groups in confinement. In J. P. Zubek (Ed.), *Sensory deprivation*. New York: Appleton-Century-Crofts, 1969, 374–403.

Sofer, C. *The organization from within*. London: Tavistock, 1961.

Sommer, R. Small group ecology. *Psychology Bulletin*, 1967, 67, 145–152.

Steele, F. I. Personality and the "laboratory style." *Journal of Applied Behavioral Science*, 1968, 4, 25–45.

Stotland, E., & Kohler, A. L. *Life and death of a dental hospital*. Seattle: University of Washington, 1965.

Street, D., Vinter, R. D., & Perrow, C. *Organization for treatment*. New York: The Free Press, 1966.

Sykes, G. M. *The society of captives*. New York: Atheneum, 1958.

Terreberry, S. The evolution of organizational environments. *Administrative Science Quarterly*, 1968, 12, 590–613.

Torrance, E. P. Some consequences of power differences on decision making in permanent and temporary three-man groups. In A. P. Hare, E. F. Borgatta, & R. F. Bales (Eds.), *Small groups*. New York: Knopf, 1955.

Trist, E., & Bamforth, K. Social and psychological consequences of the longwall method of coal getting. *Human Relations*, 1951, 4, 2–38.

Trist, E. L., Higgin, G. W., Murray, H., & Pollack, A. B. *Organizational choice*. London: Tavistock, 1963.

Vacchiano, R. B., Strauss, P. S., & Hochman, L. The open and closed mind: A review of dogmatism. *Psychological Bulletin*, 1969, 71, 261–273.

Valiquet, M. I. Individual change in a management development program. *Journal of Applied Behavioral Science*, 1968, 4, 313–325.

Van Zelst, R. H. Sociometrically selected work teams increase production. *Personnel Psychology*, 1952, 5, 175–185.

Vazquez, M. C. The interplay between power and wealth. *American Behavioral Scientist*, March, 1965, 9–12.

Walker, C. R., & Guest, R. H. *The man on the assembly line*. Cambridge: Harvard University Press, 1952.

Wells, W. P., & Pelz, D. C. Groups. In D. C. Pelz, & F. M. Andrews (Eds.), *Scientists in organizations*. New York: Wiley, 1966, 240–260.

Whyte, W. F. *Money and motivation*. New York: Harper and Row, 1955.

Whyte, W. F. *The myth of the passive peasant*. Ithaca, N.Y.: School of Industrial and Labor Relations, Cornell University, 1969.

Whyte, W. F., & Hamilton, E. L. *Action research for management*. Homewood, Ill.: Dorsey Press, 1964.

Yalom, I. D., & Lieberman, M. A. A study of encounter group casualties. *Archives of General Psychiatry*, 1971, 25, 16–30.

Ziller, R. C. Toward a theory of open and closed groups. *Psychological Bulletin*, 1965, 64, 164–182.

Ziller, R. C., Behringer, R. D., & Goodchilds, J. D. Group creativity under conditions of success or failure and variations in group stability. *Journal of Applied Psychology*, 1962, 46, 43–49.

Zubek, J. P., Ed. *Sensory deprivation: Fifteen years of research*. New York: Appleton-Century-Crofts, 1969.

Zuckerman, M. Hallucinations, reported sensations, and images. In J. P. Zubek (Ed.), *Sensory deprivation: Fifteen years of research*. New York: Appleton-Century-Crofts, 1969, 85–125.

CHAPTER 37

Cross-Cultural Issues in Industrial and Organizational Psychology[1]

GERALD V. BARRETT
University of Akron

BERNARD M. BASS
University of Rochester

THE RESEARCH LITERATURE was reviewed and integrated to provide an analysis of cross-cultural issues in industrial and organizational psychology. Four substantive areas were evaluated in terms of those aspects most sensitive to cross-cultural effects: motivation and attitudes, management and supervision, assessment, and training and development.

Cultural effects are clearly evident in the area of work motivation. A number of cultural, social, and economic factors which modify the structure of work relationships and motivation interact to shape the personality of members of a culture. Culture also has a moderating effect on job satisfaction, compensation models, managerial need satisfaction, and managerial goals.

Generalizations about management and supervision in the cross-cultural context are limited and confined by a number of methodological problems. Concepts and constructs (e.g., authoritarianism and participation) tend to shift in meaning as we move from one culture to another. Despite these conceptual problems, nations can be ordered on a dimension of preference for authoritarian supervision. In addition, countries can be clustered in terms of management and supervision styles.

Culture does play a role in the abilities and aptitudes developed by individuals. This is most dramatically illustrated in the area of cultural differences in perceptual processes. Despite the difficulties in adapting and using Westernized tests in other cultures, the evidence is remarkably clear that these tests can be used effectively for selection and prediction even in underdeveloped countries.

[1] Supported by ONR Contract #N00014-67-A-0398-0002, NR 171-029.

Limited empirical research is available in the area of cross-cultural training and development. Few training techniques have been empirically validated across or within cultures. The major research thrust has focused on training programs required to increase the effectiveness of managers working in a different culture. A training program, *The Culture Assimilator* (Fiedler, Mitchell, & Triandis, 1971), has been validated in both laboratory and field studies.

Cross-cultural investigations have considerable utility for industrial and organizational psychology. Research which is confined to one cultural context is constrained in both theory construction and practical applications. The wide range of cultural variations adds a necessary and essential dimension to the field. Future research effort should be directed toward the development of standardized instruments, the refinement of operational definitions of concepts, and the determination of basic cause and effect relations.

INTRODUCTION

In its most general sense, the cross-cultural study of men at work deals with the question of whether what is learned or developed in one culture can be transferred with or without modification for effective use in another. Can we generalize from one culture to another our understandings of why men work? Is there one best supervisory style? Are the valid assessment and relevant appraisal practices of one country equally valid or relevant anywhere else? What about the transferability of executives with experience and education in one country to another? Do decision-making practices vary in their potential applicability in different cultures? What about work patterns, work designs, safety procedures, and so on?

We will only touch here on some of these questions. In many instances, we will only be able to call attention to the issues.

Historical Background

These cross-cultural questions may seem of recent concern to the American industrial and organizational psychologist. Nevertheless, until the legislative reduction of immigration from a tide to a trickle in 1924, much of American industry was multinational, since immigrants constituted a large proportion of its industrial work force.

After 1890, language and cultural barriers caused increasing difficulties for immigrants, since these newer immigrants from southern and eastern Europe were less educated and skilled than the pre-1890 immigrants from northern and western Europe. In addition, the post-1890 immigrants spoke languages with less affinity to English and had customs, religions, and traditions further removed from the Anglo-American majority. Industrial psychologists recognized the problem and expressed concern about the proper technique for assimilating individuals from many nations, with different attitudes, values, and behavior into one organization (Frost, 1920). This concern was revealed from the period of 1919 to 1933 in six studies appearing in the *Journal of Applied Psychology* relating work curves to different nationalities, which resulted in the conclusion that no differences could be attributed to race or ethnic origin (Garth, Ikeda, & Gardner, 1933).

During the Commercial and much of the Industrial Revolution, international business was mainly a matter of arranging for the trading of goods supplied in one country and sought in another. Nevertheless, we sometimes forget that by the time of the Civil War, there was a great deal of direct investment by American firms in foreign countries (while the British and French were investing heavily in the United States at the same time). In 1852, Colt established its first branch factory abroad. Singer's activities abroad were spread far and wide by the 1860s. It probably was the first truly American international business. By 1867, Singer's international activities had grown so large, and the cost of domestic manufacturing was so high, that Singer decided to build foreign plants (Wilkins, 1970).

The United States increased investment abroad in the late nineteenth century, so that by 1914 the United States' direct foreign investment was 7 percent of its gross national product, the same percentage as in 1966 (Wilkins, 1970).

Nevertheless, what is new is that increasingly multinational firms are emerging with a total world outlook in *all* their activities. One of the best examples of this is IBM. Two of its ten models of the 360 computer were developed in Europe, and it now markets in over 100 countries (Lubar, 1969). Management of such firms is becoming multinational as well and although they were begun in America, top management is likely to include nationals of France, Venezuela, or Australia.

EXTENSIVITY. By the late 1960s, over 150 billion dollars had been invested abroad by United States firms and their foreign affiliates. Investment is not a one-way street, since many multinational firms originating abroad also invest in the United States. For example, Shell, Unilever, Sony, and Nestles are well-known companies whose parent firms come from outside the United States, but which have extensive investments in the United States—over 10 billion dollars in the late 1960s.

A spectre often raised, most prominently by Servan-Schreiber's (1969) book entitled *The American Challenge,* is that European business is being dominated by American companies. In fact, he lists the United States in Europe as one of the world's largest economies. It is true that the overseas subsidiaries of American firms have sales of about 200 billion dollars a year. But economic control does not necessarily mean management or labor dominance. For instance, in Europe, IBM employs some 65,000 people, but only 200 of these are Americans (Larsen, 1969).

Projected Japanese domination of the Asian economy has raised similar issues as has American business involvement in Europe (Kahn, 1970).

Available Behavioral Research

When considering the importance of multinational corporations for a long-time span in the major industrial countries of the world, and the accelerated growth and importance of such companies throughout the world since the Second World War, it is surprising that so little behavioral or organizational research has been done in the area. As recently as 1959, Harbison and Myers published *Management in the Industrial World,* the first effort of its kind in the study of comparative management. The Harbison and Myers work was based upon field studies in various countries; it was not until 1966 that Haire, Ghiselli, and Porter published the more quantitative *Managerial Thinking*—a survey comparison of managers in fourteen countries.

REVIEWS. During the late 1960s, a considerable output of cross-cultural comparisons in human performance appeared, making possible a number of reviews of various aspects of cross-cultural issues in industrial and organizational psychology. Nath (1969) treated the methodological issues in cross-cultural research, while Boddewyn and Nath (1970) assessed comparative management research focusing on studies dealing with business managers in two or more countries. Roberts (1970) took a broader perspective, categorizing over 500 organizational studies into some twenty-six areas of interest. Barrett and Bass (1970) reviewed comparative surveys of managers' attitudes and behavior.

Both Nath (1969) and Roberts (1970) were sharply critical of work in the field, Nath (1969) asserting that most of the investigations he could find had compared performance in only two selected countries. Further, most of the studies were based on one method—the interview. Finally, of twenty survey reports he reviewed, only three were based on samples of working managers rather than students.

In an even more critical survey of cross-cultural research related to organizations, Roberts (1970) concluded that little increment in knowledge of either a theoretical or practical nature resulted from such research. She did not feel they deserved the effort which had been expended on them. Roberts called for research directed toward understanding behavior in one culture before attempting further cross-cultural investigations.

The review by Barrett and Bass (1970) was more optimistic and was able to identify a sufficient number of consistencies and tentative generalizations to suggest that the field was viable. Nevertheless, it is evident that both serious methodological and theoretical problems remain in cross-cultural research on men in organizations, but some progress has been made during the short time that effort has been expended on the subject.

PROBLEMS IN METHODOLOGY. Those interested in cross-cultural behavioral issues in organizations come from a variety of disciplines —comparative management, sociology, political science, social psychology, economics, anthropology, industrial relations, and industrial and organizational psychology. Anthropologists were the first to be interested in both primitive and modern cultures on a cross-national basis. From the early anthropological studies and techniques have evolved a bewildering array of methods which often lack the necessary scientific controls. For this reason, there has been a great deal of debate concerning methodological and theoretical issues. The methodological questions in cross-cultural research have been discussed by individuals from

widely varying disciplines, each taking their own respective point of view (Holtzman, 1965; Naroll, 1968; Berry, 1969; Strodtbeck, 1964; Frijda & Jahoda, 1966). Perhaps the best general overall discussion has been by Triandis (1972), which has explored and discussed in detail the methodological issues in cross-cultural research. These methodological problems include equivalence of experimental manipulation, equivalence of measurement, sampling, familiarity with instruments, and interpretation of results.

Approach

A number of theoretical models for research have also been proposed by investigators from a variety of disciplines (Maslow & Honigmann, 1970; Estafen, 1970; Schollhammer, 1969; Perrow, 1967; Farmer & Richman, 1964). Since both the methodological and theoretical issues in cross-national research have been discussed in depth by many others, this chapter will not attempt to review that literature. Instead, we will concentrate on the empirical research findings which may contribute to understanding individual and organizational behavior using criterion questions suggested in part by Whiting (1968) as the basis for evaluating the contributions and including them in the present review. First, does the research allow us to generalize about human behavior and thereby extend understanding beyond one culture? Second, does discovery of an increased range of behavior add to understanding of the phenomenon in question? Third, can we determine if cross-cultural generalizations are valid at the level of intracultural individual differences?

We will attempt to show positive findings and point out the most serious shortcomings of the research, but our aim is not so much at critical analysis as at the integration of diverse pieces of the literature to show what has been accomplished and the possible new directions. We will deal with four substantive areas: motivation and attitudes, management and supervision, assessment, and training and development.

In examining each area we will obviously not be in a position to review all problems and practices culture-by-culture or across even two countries. For example, in considering personnel selection we could prepare a book merely on the methods, tests, measurements, techniques, and outcomes used in the United Kingdom in contrast to the United States. What we will be doing is focusing on those aspects of personnel selection which seem to be most sensitive to cross-national effects.

MOTIVATION TO WORK

We will start at the beginning, noting that what motivates us to work depends on what we will lack if we do not work. If we cannot survive without working, then our motivation to work will center on work to avoid starvation, a condition which is still commonplace in many parts of the world. In many nations, survival is still a prime motivation to work despite the disappearance of this motive as a significant factor in the more developed countries.

Once we move into more advanced regions where basic needs for food, clothing, and shelter are ordinarily met, then we will see that what *attracts* us to work will depend on what we value and what goals we have in life. Again, we will see national similarities and differences in what we value, and, therefore, in what will attract us to work.

Whether the work that attracted us lives up to our expectations will determine how satisfied we are at work. Again, we will see national differences of consequences relating to the extent our expectations are met through work. Thus, we may find the same need for self-actualization in many different countries. Nevertheless, generally, the extent this need is met through work varies from one country to another.

We will also note national differences in what objectives are set for the work force within an organization. Profit maximization is by no means a universal objective of industrial managers. Whether it should be is another question to be left to economic theorists. Related to what objectives are set is what ideology governs the reward systems pursued in the differing countries. And this in turn may affect national economic development as well as the efficiency of the average firm within a country.

From this examination, it will not be difficult to conclude that motivational factors play a particularly important role in the national differences observed in the work situation.

Motivation to Work for Survival and Security

A review of most commentary and research on the subject would give one the decided opinion that the motives that energize and direct men to work are universal in pattern and character. Cross-national analyses suggest otherwise. In developing nations where the struggle for food, clothing, and shelter is still of paramount importance, the motivation to work still centers on the lowest level of needs for survival and security. It is in more advanced countries that motivation to work depends primarily on satisfaction of higher level needs for affiliation, recognition, and self-actualization.

A more valid generalization is that *when the motivation to work is closely tied to basic survival, there is a restriction in the pattern and diversity of motives which induce people to work*. In the developed countries, the number of options a man has in deciding when and where to work are the greatest in the history of mankind. Nevertheless, the majority of the world's population still works for basic survival and security. Thus, the needs of IBM world trade personnel depend on the GNP per capita of the country in which they work. While nationals from rich countries working for IBM often express desires for more challenging work, autonomy, and departmental efficiency, those from poorer countries express a stronger need for job security (Greenwood, 1971).

In much of industrial society, work now has a positive connotation. Work itself can be a source of satisfaction for many, meeting their higher level needs for recognition, achievement, and self-actualization. When we examine underdeveloped nations, we are in a sense taking a step back in time from the perspective of the developed Western nations. The importance of this is evident when considering Maslow's (1954) theory of motivation, which suggests that before a higher level need can influence behavior, a lower level need must be satisfied. The lowest level needs are physiological. If the physiological needs such as thirst and hunger are satisfied, then the individual can be motivated by the next higher level in the hierarchy.

Unfortunately, where workers are at this lowest level of need, peculiar problems in productivity arise which were unrecognized by Maslow. In many underdeveloped countries a real limit upon the worker's productive capacity has been found, based upon the energy requirements of the job and the worker's intake of calories (Belli, 1971). But this is not to imply that malnutrition in a nation will necessarily result in slower economic growth of that country (Franke & Barrett, 1975).

In many underdeveloped countries the caloric intake of the typical worker is inadequate for him to provide the energy to produce anywhere close to the rate of workers in more developed countries. For example, because of their lower caloric intake, the estimated work capacity of employees in Nigeria is only one-quarter of that of workers from more developed countries (Kerkhoven, 1962).

The problem of the undernourished worker in the developing countries is complicated by the fact that while the worker will produce at a much slower rate, the slower rate may also be quite inefficient. In other words, there is an optimum work rate for most tasks, and a work rate which is considerably lower than optimum is usually quite inefficient (Corlett, 1970).

The usual solution in the underdeveloped nations has been to compensate for the reduced efficiency of the workers by using many more workers since labor is cheap. Another possible solution is to either raise the income level of the worker or provide nourishing meals in the plant itself to meet the energy requirements of the workers. The problem with the latter proposal is that there are often dietary customs and practices which are extremely hard to change even though these may be dysfunctional from a nutritional point of view.

An unusual solution suggested by Corlett (1970) would be to organize employees so that they worked only two hours per day, but at the work rate of employees from developed countries. This plan has several positive advantages in addition to reducing unemployment. First, the employer obtains the same productivity by using four times as many men for an eight-hour shift, assuming there is little warm-up time required. Second, the worker can perform his task at an optimum tempo and the total physiological cost to him is less than if he worked an eight-hour shift. Third, as the nutritional intake of workers is increased, and the developing countries become more affluent, workers will become used to a more realistic work rate. Pay increases will accrue from increasing hours of work. It is evident that for many workers in underdeveloped countries the physiological needs will be the most important and must be satisfied before security, the second level of needs, acts as a motivating force.

Factory workers in India perceive job security to be their most important need. Adequate earnings and adequate personal benefits come next in importance (Singh & Wherry, 1963). This is understandable in India, a country where mass unemployment is very common, and where a secure job paying adequate wages may be a matter of life and death. In the United States in the 1930s there was also considerable concern among factory workers for job security. But as economic conditions improved and the unemployment rate dropped, this factor became of less importance to the American workers. Another important consideration to the Indian employee is working conditions, which are still poor in much of India. This again is reminiscent of some of the unfavorable factory conditions found in the United States in the 1930s. Today, United States factory workers put comfortable working conditions near the bottom in importance.

As a further illustration of the extent to which the environment may place the heaviest importance on lower level needs, an attitude survey in Guatemala found that employees in a public bureaucracy stressed security. A very high percentage of the lower level employees such as clerical and service workers felt very insecure about their job status, due to lack of institutional safeguards (Weaver, 1970).

SITUATIONAL EFFECTS ILLUSTRATED. Maslow's theory of personality was the basis for an extensive cross-cultural study conducted by Aronoff (1967, 1970). The investigation began as a field study of an island in the British West Indies. It was designed to test a proposition that both personality and social-cultural structures are a result of three interacting factors: the environment, the past social-cultural institutions, and the basic psychological needs of the individuals involved. On the island, the investigator found two distinct groups of workers from the same village. These were the cane cutters and the fishermen; virtually all were descendants of Negro slaves. Nevertheless, the fishermen had a subculture and economic existence that were strikingly different from the cane cutters. The fishermen were, in effect, independent businessmen living more by their own personal effort, while the cane cutters were much more dependent on the

work from the sugar plantation. Moreover, the cane cutters had suffered a significantly greater loss of parents and siblings in their first twelve years of life than the fishermen had. Maslow's theory would suggest that those who have been deprived of safety gratification early in life will fixate at that level. The results confirmed the hypothesis. The cane cutters received higher scores derived from interview analyses on the physiological and safety levels. In contrast, the fishermen had low scores on these two need levels. But on the levels of affection and esteem needs, the reverse was found, with the fishermen scoring very high in these needs and the cane cutters scoring relatively low.

Even the economic work organization seemed to be oriented toward the individual needs of the two groups. The cane cutters were involved in a very authoritarian structure with little initiative expected or required of them. The pay schedule rewarded the group, not individual effort. In contrast, the fishermen had a more democratic organization. Their work roles required much more initiative and their pay system was strictly geared to their individual performance.

This study was conducted in the early sixties, and while interesting, does not give any indication of a cause and effect relationship. Fortunately, Aronoff (1970) was able to study the situation over a period of time and, in effect, was able to report upon a natural experiment.

In 1962, the cutters were under the supervision of a head cutter and were organized into gangs of about eleven men. The whole work effort was organized by the head cutter, and the very authoritarian nature of the position allowed him to take advantage of the men in terms of both the amount of work and payment for services. The pay was based upon the productivity of the whole gang, so the slowest worker was paid the same as the best.

Under a new pay system, in addition to weighing the cutting for each gang daily, a special "field man" estimated the exact tonnage each individual man reaped. In this manner, individual productivity was directly related to the wages received.

It was possible to move to this new plan because a new generation of cutters had arisen. The 1970 cane cutters were essentially a different work force. The needs of the new group of cane cutters did not focus upon the physiological and safety needs, but upon the affiliative and self-esteem needs. As was predicted by Maslow's theory, this new group of cane cutters had enjoyed a much more secure childhood during their first twelve years of life as compared with the older group of cutters.

It appears that in any social system there are a number of interacting forces which can shape both the personalities of the individuals in a culture and the structure of their work group. The pre-1962 group of cane cutters was raised in a time when the health problem was much worse than the younger, second sample of cane cutters. Over the period of time, the health conditions had dramatically improved in the West Indies so that these young laborers were not faced with a traumatic loss of a parent during their formative years.

Due to both the innovation in the pay scheme which allowed each cane cutter to receive a wage more directly proportional to his productivity, and the different personality makeup of the cane cutters, there was a definite change in the traditional form of work gangs. The old authoritarian structure of the cane gang was no longer tolerated by the new workers. These men, functioning at a higher motivational level, formed a cooperative work group which worked very effectively without the head cutter being able to play his old role.

This study illustrates how a number of social, medical, and cultural factors can interact to help shape the personality of members of a certain culture and, in turn, how various traditional structures of work relationships can be modified as a result of these interactions. It is important to realize

that the organization can make innovations in its traditional methods which may have beneficial effects, not only for the organization, but for the workers involved. If a manager is faced with a traditional authoritarian society where the need levels are still at the lowest level, perhaps then the more authoritarian structure is appropriate for both the requirements of production and the needs of the workers. What is more difficult is when the motivational patterns of younger workers are operating at a higher level at the time they enter this traditional work relationship. The traditional authority relationships may not be acceptable to these newer workers. In our discussion of need for achievement, we will see again motivation initially shaped by early childhood experiences confounded and moderated by subsequent organizational experiences.

Aronoff and Messe (1971) showed that the results obtained in the West Indies could be generalized for the United States. Screening twenty-five subjects with a combination of high safety needs and low esteem, and twenty-five with high esteem and low safety needs from 200 students, homogeneous five-man groups were formed. A standardized set of tasks was given to each group and the members' task-oriented behaviors were coded. As predicted, those groups made up of esteem-oriented persons were characterized by a desire to demonstrate competence both to themselves and to others, resulting in leadership functions being widely shared among members of the group. The safety-oriented groups had members who were reluctant to organize task activities because of their dependency and, as a result, leadership functions were concentrated in a few group members. Aronoff and Messe (1971) demonstrated that the prevailing needs of the homogeneous group does influence the social structure of the group. It is important to note that this experimental study grew out of the previous field investigations by Aronoff (1967, 1970). What was first found in a natural setting in groups with differences in background was subsequently reproduced in the laboratory and tested in a totally different culture. This lends more validity to the concepts and the importance of the needs being tested since results were replicated in two different cultures and in two different ways. These results stand in contrast to other research in organizations in the United States which have failed to substantiate Maslow's theory (Hall & Nougaim, 1968; Beer, 1968; Braun, 1969; Wofford, 1971), probably because it is difficult to find among the employed population many whose lower level needs are unsatisfied. Aronoff's studies illustrate two advantages of cross-cultural research—the possibility of having an extended range on an important variable and determining if generalizations are valid at the level of intra-cultural individual differences.

In addition, the studies demonstrate that motives appear to change over a relatively short period of time, and that different locations within a country may have quite different motivational patterns. This generalization has been demonstrated in other countries, such as Japan, where we see different values in what on the surface may appear to be a homogeneous culture.

Values and Orientation to Work

What is valued in differing cultures affects motivation to work: *particularism* or *universalism, traditionalism* or *modernity, white collar orientation, pragmatism* or *moralism, workplace* or *home,* and *intrinsic* or *extrinsic rewards.* What we shall see as we move from one culture to another is that wide divergences appear in these kinds of values concerning work and the workplace.

PARTICULARISM OR UNIVERSALISM. Parsons and Shils (1959) state that individuals will be influenced by a particularistic or universalistic value orientation. They further believe that these two contrasting value orientations will be culturally determined. The particularistic value orientation implies institutionalized obligations of friendship, while the universalistic value orientation stresses institutionalized obligations to society and puts less stress upon interpersonal considerations. Zurcher (1968) empirically tested and confirmed the proposition: that Mexican bank employees were more particularistic than Mexican-Americans, and Mexican-Americans were significantly more particularistic than the Anglo-Americans. This was true for both bank officers and for line employees. In addition, the officers were significantly more universalistic in their value orientation than the line employees.

As predicted, the employees' satisfaction with their positions and their plans to continue working in the bank were slightly related to a higher universalism score (Zurcher, Meadow, & Zurcher, 1965).

TRADITIONALISM OR MODERNITY. Dawson and his associates (Dawson, Law, Leung, & Whitney, 1971; Dawson, 1969a, 1969b; Dawson, 1967c) have developed an attitude change model which incorporates such factors as the degree of modern contact, nature of indigenous authority systems, nature of socialization system, and degree of culturally determined tolerance for cognitive inconsistency. A traditional-modern attitude scale has been developed for a number of cultures. The scaling of the items of the traditional-modern scale is always in terms of what is "modern" for that particular society, be it Chinese, African, or Australian. Dawson's well-developed model has been tested in a number of different cultures, both in survey conditions and in laboratory experiments. Contrary to what some might expect, it appears that those cultures which practice permissive socialization resist acceptance of modern attitudes, while those societies having very strict socialization practices appear to resolve the cognitive conflict by changing from the traditional to a modern attitude structure. Research has also indicated that as a culture group receives more education, they shift toward a modern attitude structure, but at a certain point there is a reversion by the most educated to a semitraditional point of view. This appears to be similar to what has occurred to the black culture movement in the United States.

In Hong Kong, Chinese traditional-modern concepts were related to Galvanic Skin Response (GSR) arousal. As predicted, those core Chinese concepts which were in conflict with the more modern viewpoints elicited the most GSR arousal. The most change in the value system was found for those Confucian concepts which were of peripheral importance. Dawson's research provided some important insights for those organizations operating in developing countries where social change is occurring.

The economic importance of the traditional-modern attitudes is underscored by Dawson's finding that a Western orientation was related to rated productivity even when educational achievement and intelligence were controlled. Adaptions of his scales in Nigeria have not been as successful, possibly for various methodological reasons (Wober, 1971).

WHITE COLLAR ORIENTATION. Like many other Latin American countries, Peru suffers from a small number of skilled workers and needs many more skilled technicians. Unfortunately, the cultural values present a barrier to recruiting more people into the ranks of skilled labor. In the United States, we often speak of blue and white collar workers. While there is a status difference between blue and white collar workers in the United States, it is extreme in Peru.

When high school boys in Peru were asked their preference, an overwhelming proportion chose to be an *empleado*—white collar employee—even if the salary is equal to that of an *obrero*—blue color employee. Only 13 percent of the boys actually being trained in an industrial arts high school for skilled workers chose *obrero*—blue collar employee. Over one-third of the boys said under no condition would they be an *obrero*. An additional one-third said they would be an *obrero* only if they received a salary which was close to being twice the

minimum wage for an *empleado*. This is indeed discouraging because these boys are being educated to be the skilled labor that Peru so badly needs, but only a very small minority actually plan to enter that occupation (Whyte, 1963). One suspects that similar results favoring white collar work are likely to appear even in countries where conscientious efforts have been made to glorify the blue collar worker. One probably could trace such attitudes back to ancient times, when white collar work was in the hands of educated priests, philosophers, or mandarins, and all blue collar work was done by slaves or serfs.

PRAGMATIC VALUES. One of the few programs of research to directly measure managerial values in several different countries was initiated by England (1967), using a Personal Values Questionnaire. The Values Questionnaire taps the relative importance of three values: the pragmatic, the affect, and the ethical-moral.

In one study, England (1970) compared value data from over 1,600 American, Japanese, and Korean managers. As might be expected, the managers in each country consistently favored a pragmatic orientation (England & Koike, 1970). The pervasiveness of the pragmatic orientation has also been found in an analysis of American and Indian managers' responses to the same Personal Values Questionnaire (Thiagarajan, 1968). The studies concur in showing that contrary to much popular opinion in the United States and abroad, American managers were less pragmatic than managers from other countries. The studies also show that managers from all countries surveyed were secondarily moralistically oriented and more like each other than like compatriots who are not managers. On the whole, managers' value orientations are quite similar across at least four countries, but these orientations are quite different from those of students and other occupational groups within the same countries. Cross-cultural effects in these areas may not be as powerful as occupational or educational differences within cultures. An illustration of its validity is revealed in finding that the pragmatic orientation is almost absent among theology students regardless of cultural background (England, 1970).

WORK VERSUS PERSONAL LIFE. The role demands of work and personal life may put unusual stress upon an individual in some cultures. For instance, in a comparison by Auclair (1968) of over 3,000 French Canadian and English Canadian managers, French Canadian managers placed a higher value on their role as the head of the family than did the English Canadian managers. As a result, the French Canadian manager perceived a great deal of stress placed upon him due to the conflicting role demands of family and business. In contrast, the English Canadian manager, placing less value upon his role in the family, experienced less conflict with role demands from his business organization.

Japanese workers also perceived the distinction between work and personal life differently from American workers. According to a questionnaire administered by Whitehill and Takezawa (1968) to approximately 2,000 Japanese workers, 57 percent thought of their company as "a part of my life at least equal in importance to my personal life," while only 22 percent of the United States workers endorsed that statement.

Since Abegglen's *The Japanese Factory* (1958), the one major difference often cited between the modernization process in the Western world and that of Japan, the fastest growing industrialized nation in the postwar period, has been the idea that the workers and the organization made a "lifetime commitment." This concept seemed to go against many ideas concerning the development and modernization of countries. With increased economic growth and increasing differentiation of the individual employees from out of the firm, there is usually increasing labor mobility—but this did not seem true for

Japan. Marsh and Mannari (1971) tended to confirm Abegglen's finding that within the larger firms which he studied, the company did have an obligation not to dismiss regular employees. For most workers, retirement is mandatory at fifty-five, but many are often kept on as temporary workers until there is an economic downturn. Furthermore, early retirement is a substitute for avoiding promotion into higher levels of an individual whose age and seniority would warrant it.

The larger firms studied by Abegglen do have a lower quit rate, but the obligation of employees is limited. The employee feels committed to give the organization his fullest potential only while he is working there, not for his entire lifetime. Quit rates indicate that there actually is a great deal of mobility among Japanese employees. For example, one-fourth of the Japanese manufacturing employees leave their place of employment annually. For over a ten-year period, at least two-thirds of these separations were for voluntary-personal reasons. Despite the facts, even Japanese managers and workers tend to believe that they have permanent employment, when the actual figures for an auto parts plant and a die cast plant showed separations of 17 and 23 percent, respectively (Cole, 1971). When Japanese speak of permanent employment, they appear to be talking more about limitations on the rights of the organization to fire, but not on the right of the worker to quit.

INTRINSIC VERSUS EXTRINSIC ORIENTATION. Herzberg's (1966) controversial theory of job attitudes and motivation is based upon the intrinsic and extrinsic aspects of the job. In Herzberg's conceptualization, the intrinsic aspects of the job are factors such as the work itself. He perceives this to be the motivating factor and the source of positive job satisfaction for a worker. The extrinsic aspects of the job, such as co-workers and the physical environment, are perceived to be less important for positive motivation or satisfaction. At most, the extrinsic aspects of a job are important in maintaining satisfaction, but not for providing any positive motivation. The technique for increasing both job satisfaction and worker motivation is to enrich each worker's job so that he has a task which is more satisfying to him. Herzberg (1965a, 1965b) reported that a job-attitude survey of both Finnish supervisors and 2,000 young workers in Russia supported his position. The actual results from the surveys were not presented, only the conclusions. In contrast, a well-designed investigation of approximately 342 employees from the foreign subsidiaries of a multinational American based electronics firm found strikingly different results (Simonetti & Weitz, 1972). Herzberg's contention of the generality of his theory across cultures was not supported in the three countries investigated. The intrinsic factor did contribute to overall satisfaction in all countries, but the contribution of extrinsic factors to satisfaction was a function of the country and occupational level.

Recently two investigators attempted to replicate Herzberg's original United States study in India. Both interviews and questionnaires were used to gather data from over 200 supervisors in twenty different textile mills. The results indicated that the factors that lead to satisfaction and dissatisfaction were stable over time. The results only partially confirmed Herzberg's original study. Perhaps of more importance was the fact that personality characteristics were related to factors leading to satisfaction or dissatisfaction. For example, interpersonal relationships of the superior were perceived by the extroverts as leading only to dissatisfaction. In the same vein, reported incidence of achievement on a job did not lead to increased satisfaction for those who scored low in achievement motivation. This study only reinforces the proposition that there are many factors, both cultural and personal, which lead to satisfaction or dissatisfaction on the job. It is doubtful that Herzberg's theory has universal application (Padaki & Dolke, 1970).

The Herzberg conceptualization is probably too simplified an explanation of behavior, especially in countries where the needs and motivational patterns may be markedly different from the highly developed Westernized countries, where job rationalization has resulted in reduction of job content.

It is clear that work and the work place mean quite different things to the Japanese, to the Mexican, and to the American today, just as it differed for the Inca, who saw it as a religious experience, and the Greek or Hebrew, who saw it as a burden.

LIFE GOALS. Individuals' assessments of their own life goals form an important part of their value structure and provide an interesting indicator of their aspirations and concerns.

In a study of over 2,000 middle managers from eight countries (Lazarus & Barrett, 1971), Exercise Life Goals (Bass, 1967b) was used to ascertain among managers the judged importance to themselves and others of eleven life goals. An identical procedure was used in all countries. First, each manager ranked the importance of the eleven life goals to himself. He then ranked the importance of each of the life goals to all the other managers in a small group with whom he had been working previously on other tasks. The validity of these rankings was revealed by demonstrating that the correlation of the agreement between raters and ratees increased directly with increases in the familiarity of raters with ratees (Filella, 1971).

There seems to be substantial consistency across nations at least in regard to the feeling that *self-realization* is an extremely important life goal. The one marked exception to this generalization is the Netherlands, where *expertness* is more highly valued than *self-realization*. At the other extreme, both prestige and wealth are perceived to be of little importance for managers from all eight countries (Lazarus & Barrett, 1971).

To a considerable degree, social desirability may be involved; however, the stated unimportance of wealth may be an accurate reading, particularly for lower levels of management. Managers at these levels tend to be less competitive, aggressive, and entrepreneural in interest.

In a more complex analysis of life goals' data, indices of assumed similarity, actual similarity, accuracy, and negation were calculated. (Negation is the tendency to judge as trivial that which others value as important and vice versa.) Assumed similarity was considerably higher than actual similarity. Accuracy suffered as a consequence. American and Indian managers were least accurate, with Americans, for instance, overestimating similarity with colleagues much more than most other national groups studied.

In terms of the tendency of managers to project their own values upon others, both the Indian and Spanish managers were least likely to do so. The Indian and Spanish managers were again clustered at one extreme with much higher negation scores.

Managers from both India and the United States revealed the least actual similarity in responses, possibly because of India's sixteen major language groups and the United States with its multiple melting pots of race, religion, and ethnic origins. The European countries with more homogeneous cultures, such as the United Kingdom, Norway, and Spain, exhibited much greater actual similarity in the managers' appraisals of their own life goals (Alexander, Barrett, Bass, & Ryterband, 1971).

Job Satisfaction

Inkeles (1960) reviewed studies that emphasize generalizations that can be made about job satisfaction across countries. In six countries, he found that proportions reporting job satisfaction increase as one goes up the occupational hierarchy. Across countries at the lower occupational levels, employees prefer job security to more pay. The reverse phenomenon is reported for those

employees at the more highly valued or esteemed occupations.

At the same time, there are consistent national differences in job satisfaction. Data collected in the 1950s and again in the late 1960s, for example, show Americans report greater job satisfaction than do Germans (Katona, Strumpel, & Zahn, 1971).

In one of the few studies which controlled for organizational structure and job task, Slocum (1971) found that blue collar workers in Mexico were significantly more satisfied than United States production workers. The two plants were similar in that they were from the same parent company, and engaged in the production of glass products. The production line contained identical machinery and used the same job classification system. Also, the formal structures of the plants were identical. This is the only cross-national comparison reviewed which controls these relevant variables. There are two immediate possibilities to explain Slocum's results, which are opposed to the usual findings that the United States managers and workers have the higher job satisfaction. First, working in the subsidiary of an American company in Mexico may be considered to be a job of relatively high prestige compared with the other available opportunities. Therefore, any comparison which the Mexican worker might make would serve to enhance his job satisfaction. Second, the plant in Mexico may be able to offer certain advantages over other Mexican concerns. This would tend to draw into it a higher quality of employee than is possible in the United States. Both of these factors may be interacting to produce results which are somewhat diverse from the usual cross-national findings.

Managerial Need Satisfaction

Approximately 3,600 managers from fourteen countries were surveyed by Haire, Ghiselli, and Porter (1966). The motivational aspect of their attitude questionnaire was based upon Maslow's (1954) concepts. An additional 500 managers from Yugoslavia were investigated with the identical questionnaire (Mozina, 1969) as were over 1,300 Australian managers (Clark & McCabe, 1970).

The higher level needs such as self-actualization and esteem were regarded as quite important by managers everywhere. But the degree to which these needs were satisfied did not live up to the managers' expectations. In contrast, the lower level needs were regarded by managers as being of relatively little importance to them, but were seen to be fairly well satisfied. The need for security, considered to be important, did not fall into either of the above two patterns, since it was relatively highly fulfilled and the fulfillment was in line with expectations.

Need satisfaction in this study was de-. fined as the difference between the perceived fulfillment of a need and the perceived expectation of fulfillment. In other words, if an individual expressed that a need was highly fulfilled and that he expected it to be fulfilled, his satisfaction score would be very high. Conversely, if an individual expressed the thought that he expected a need to be highly fulfilled but it was not, that is, there was a large discrepancy between the two, he would indicate low satisfaction. Based on this definition, the developing countries were the least satisfied by a fairly wide margin.

As an overall statement, the research indicated that there was a close relationship between the importance of a need to the managers and the degree to which it was perceived as unfulfilled. The developing countries as a group perceived all the needs to be more important to them than did managers from other countries who reported a greater sense of unfulfillment. At the other extreme, the Nordic-European countries tended to place the least importance on all the needs.

The data were also broken down in terms of the level of each manager in the organization. Managers at all job levels attached approximately equal importance to the needs, but the perception of degree of need fulfillment was a function of the level in the organization, particularly in Japan. There, the lower level managers consistently indicated greater dissatisfaction in all areas surveyed than the upper level managers. In general, in all countries surveyed, self-actualization was the least fulfilled need and regarded as the most important. This is consistent with managers' ranking of the importance of life goals in seven countries (Alexander, Barrett, Bass, & Ryterband, 1971).

Cross-National Aspects of Management Goals

Market research for a multinational corporation indicated that three new installations should be constructed, two in the United States and one in Western Europe, each costing five million dollars. A conflict occurred between the chief executive of the English subsidiary and the head of the French division. Each wanted the new European installation in his country. After negotiation, the problem was resolved by deciding to put an installation in both countries. It appeared in this case that five million dollars was the "side payment" to keep harmony in the organization. This appears to be a clear example of sub-optimization for this multinational organization as a whole, with profitability taking a back seat to harmonious relationships among the various divisions of the entire organization (Stagner, 1969). Of course, sub-optimization is not unique to multinational managements. A recent questionnaire study of over 200 vice presidents of large American corporations revealed the single corporate goal of profit maximization among respondents. The concept of a single utility was not borne out, but the idea of multiple utilities was supported by the data (Stagner, 1969).

Although it may be argued that management should be seeking a single ultimate goal of maximum profits, in fact, it has been shown repeatedly that managers actually seek a multiplicity of objectives which may or may not translate directly into ultimate profits. Classic economic theory assumes that the firm is a unit which acts to maximize profit in its operations and is completely informed about alternate courses of action and the effects upon profitability (Simon, 1959). Nevertheless, the assumption lacks validity. For instance, Simon (1960) points out that even if they wanted to maximize profits, managers are faced with the obvious fact that there are costs for information, that perfect information is a chimera, and that managers actually proceed on the basis of limited information.

To understand managers' decision processes requires an examination of their objectives. If these objectives systematically differ from country to country, then knowledge of them is useful in understanding cross-national managerial behavior.

ORGANIZATIONAL OBJECTIVES IN FIVE COUNTRIES. Exercise Objectives (Bass, 1967b) is a simulation which presents the participant manager with information concerning a hypothetical company. Information includes a profit and loss statement along with various details concerning employee turnover and absenteeism. Each participant individually studies five problems facing a manager of the hypothetical company. For each of the five problems, the manager chooses one of two alternate solutions. As part of the simulation, the managers also assess the importance of the six company objectives in making their personal decisions concerning the five problems.

Data from over a thousand managers from five countries who have taken part in this exercise were analyzed by Schaninger, Barrett, and Alexander (1973). The United States, Italy, Britain, the Netherlands, and Belgium all contributed over a hundred managers to this study. Budgeting decisions consistently varied from country to country,

although the managers as a whole seemed most likely to spend money on product improvement and least likely to be willing to spend money on cleaning up a stream pollution problem. Nevertheless, there were relatively wide national differences. For example, 65 percent of the United States managers were willing to spend money on stream pollution, but only 25 percent of the French-speaking Belgian managers were so inclined. Again, the Dutch managers were almost unanimous in seeing the need for product improvement, while such unanimity is expressed by the French-speaking Belgian managers only for expenditures for management development.

When we discuss national differences in company objectives, our problem is compounded by the fact that a large multinational firm may have a value system which obscures national differences. Looking at the two extremes, people working for the same organization could have the same organizational goals resulting in nearly identical decisions about problems. In contrast, people working for a large multinational corporation may not be influenced as much by some value system held by the total corporation as by the values of their own culture. Thus, data from Exercise Objectives suggest that in four national subsidiaries of a multinational company, managers respond quite differently in the importance they attach to various values.

In addition, data from American, Japanese, and Korean managers (England & Lee, 1972) have shown that organizational size moderates the emphasis placed on organizational goals and values.

As part of Exercise Objectives, the managers were also asked to rank the importance of six objectives which they had in mind when making their decisions. Profits were primary everywhere, except in Italy, where smooth operations were deemed more important. Beyond this, the English managers saw beating competition as being an important objective for their organization, while the French-speaking Belgians placed the least importance upon this objective (Schaninger, Barrett, & Alexander, 1973). It was evident that while the profit motive was expressed as a primary consideration to managers from all countries, there were other objectives which are also deemed important and which may influence decisions.

Attitudes Toward Compensation

What managers value becomes translated into what they feel is an equitable system of pay. National differences are likely to be particularly salient because pay is so directly tied to a variety of national, historical, political, and economic trends as well as national differences in employment opportunities, productivity, and so on. On the one hand, organizations tend to want uniform policies applicable to all employees, yet they must face the need to deal with national differences and demands. An American expects to earn more when transplanted to Paris; his French colleague does not appreciate the need for any differential payment. Multinational organizations must be sensitive to these issues. Using a simulation, Exercise Compensation (Bass, 1967b), which required managers to give merit increases to ten engineers, Barrett and Alexander (1973) found that recommended salary increases were the square of meritorious service; that is, a power function with an exponent of approximately two could fit the data in each of nine different countries. The power function provided a good fit across all countries for over 3,600 managers and more than 900 non-managers in associating recommended salary increases with announced merit. There were, however, sizable differences when managers from different countries gave salary increases to each of seven engineers who were at the 50th percentile in merit, but worked under different circumstances, such as hazardous or insecure conditions. It is evident that there are decided differences among countries in the perception of what are other legitimate reasons for awarding salary increases. For example, according to the managers in the sample, in Denmark dull work, unpleasant working conditions, and unfriendly co-workers should entitle a man at the 50th percentile in merit to be paid as if he were performing in the 78th percentile. Looking across countries, we see that managers from India and Zaire would not provide differential for a dull job, while managers from eighteen other countries are willing to give a salary differential for this job. In fact, Indian and most managers from Zaire are not willing to reward any of the seven non-merit cases above what would be expected on merit alone. All of the other eighteen national groups were willing to differentially reward at least one of the non-merit cases. While this study shows the differences and similarities among managers in their compensation decisions, more work needs to be done to specify the underlying psychological processes and organizational considerations which lead to these differential payments.

DIFFERING MODELS OF COMPENSATION. Consistent with a stark economic theory of man, but inconsistent with what one might expect in a country with socialistic ideals, the Soviet Union has developed one of the most comprehensive piece-rate systems of any country. The principle seems to be "to each according to his work" (Granick, 1960).

In the Soviet Union, the wage incentive system has been extended not only to managers, but also to skilled technicians, scientists, designers, and researchers in general. The program is designed to correct deficiencies in Soviet technology. In the past, the pay of technical personnel was almost entirely based upon the academic degree, and little consideration was given to actual performance. The new plan is designed to give monetary incentives of up to 30 percent above the base salary. As a unique part of the compensation plan, cuts in pay of 25 percent below base salary are permitted if performance is not up to expectations (Anon., 1970). This "reverse incentive" plan appears to be unique to the Soviet Union.

The manager of a plant typically earns five or six times as much as his average worker, both in the Soviet Union and the United States. The biggest difference in compensation between the United States and the Soviet Union is that typically a small part of an American executive's salary is from a bonus plan, while a large share of a Russian manager's compensation is tied to an incentive plan (Granick, 1960).

The value system plays an important role in individual expectations of organizational rewards (England & Koike, 1970). In the United States, the worker perceives that he receives his wages in exchange for services, but the model is quite different in Asia. In Japan, compensation is an obligation of the employer, who is responsible for the employee's welfare. It is often not directly related to the services performed, but is more directly related to the individual's needs or to his age or length of service. The whole concept of performance appraisal is often rejected in much of the Orient (Gellerman, 1967).

Secrecy about salaries varies from country to country. For example, in the Philippines, *Pakikisama* is a word which expresses all-encompassing friendship. This means that in many business organizations the *Pakikisama* system results in intense loyalty to one boss and the formulation of cliques. Since one of the characteristics of *Pakikisama* is to have no secrets from those with whom you share your friendship, the salaries of individuals are freely discussed. This means that in contrast to most western corporations, the compensation each employee receives is widely known. It appears that one of the reasons for this openness about salary is the fact that it enables each Filipino employee to monitor the fairness of management (Gellerman, 1967).

Motives and Economic Development

There have been a number of approaches and conceptual attempts to explain differences in economic growth of nations. Education (McClelland, 1966a), investments (Sommers & Suits, 1971), health and population growth (Frederiksen, 1969), malnutrition (Belli, 1971), influence of elites (Hagen, 1962), and environmental constraints (Farmer & Richman, 1965) have all been studied and related in one manner or another to the economic growth of nations.

The best known motivational research and most closely related to industrial and organizational psychology has been the work of McClelland (1961). McClelland, in research extending over twenty years, has related *n* Achievement to the overall economic development of nations. The model begins with childhood experience, where research has related the *n* Achievement motive to child rearing practices (Winterbottom, 1958; Moss & Kagan, 1961; Feld, 1967; Argyle & Robinson, 1962). There is positive evidence both in the American culture and separately in Turkey and Brazil that the early family relationship has a great deal to do with shaping the achievement patterns of sons in a culture. Common to both Brazil and Turkey, the authoritarian father dominates the family. In Brazil, in the usual father-dominated family, the sons are less likely to be self-reliant than sons in less authoritarian families. One of the most authoritarian family structures in the world can be found in Turkey. For example, in an interview situation, a man was asked if he had ever had any disagreements with his father. The man replied that he had never had any disagreements with his father since his father had died when he was very young. It later turned out that the father had died when the son was nineteen! This contrasts strongly with the typical family structure in the United States. In Turkey, it was found that as a group, Turkish junior executives had lower achievement scores than a comparable group of American junior executives. The achievement scores of the Turkish men were significantly higher, however, if they had not been dominated by their fathers, as a result of either living apart from the father or the father dying young (Bradburn, 1963).

The stability of *n* Achievement, *n*

Power, and *n* Affiliation has been shown over a twenty-year period (Skolnick, 1966; McClelland, 1966b). The *n* Achievement motive was related to the tendency to seek a job while unemployed (Sheppard & Belitsky, 1966), to entrepreneural occupations over a fourteen-year time span (McClelland, 1965), to occupational mobility, and to level in the class structure (Elder, 1968; Littig & Yeracaris, 1965; Crockett, 1962; Turner, 1970).

Other relevant behavior, such as the perception of time as having energized and dynamic meaning for those high in *n* Achievement, has also been demonstrated in various cultures (Knapp & Garbutt, 1958, 1965; Meade & Singh, 1970; Meade, 1966, 1971).

McClelland's conceptualization of the importance of the *n* Achievement motive was given support by several studies of managerial success in the United States (Meyer & Walker, 1961; Meyer, Walker, & Litwin, 1961). Cummin (1967) found that the more successful executives were higher both in *n* Achievement and in *n* Power. Consistent with this, Wainer and Rubin (1969) found that for fifty-one technical entrepreneurs who had founded and operated their own firms, each entrepreneur's need for achievement, power, and affiliation was related to the growth rate of their fifty-one companies. The highest performing companies were those which had an entrepreneur who was characterized by having high *n* Achievement and a moderate amount of *n* Power. A number of studies have been conducted in other countries, such as Turkey (Bradburn, 1963; Cansever, 1968), Nigeria (LeVine, 1966), Brazil (Angelini, 1966; Rosen, 1962, 1964), Iran (Tedeschi & Kian, 1962), South Africa (Morsbach, 1969), India (Singh, 1969, 1970), and Trinidad (Mischel, 1961), which also were generally supportive of the *n* Achievement conceptualization. Attempts to modify individual *n* Achievement levels have had limited success (McClelland & Winter, 1969).

Organizational variables interact with individual motive patterns to affect both performance of the men in the organization and organizational performance (Andrews, 1967; Lichtman, 1970). In particular, Andrews (1967) showed that the dominant style of an organization had an influence both upon the man's career progression and upon the success of the enterprise. Those executives who were high in *n* Achievement and also in an organization which fostered achievement were more successful than executives with high *n* Achievement in an organization which emphasized power.

To test the specific hypothesis that *n* Achievement was related to the economic growth of nations, McClelland (1961) sampled texts employed in public schools for twenty-five countries in 1925 and for forty-one countries in 1950. These were content analyzed, and achievement, affiliation, and power motives were derived. Through a cross-sectional correlation analysis, he showed an association between *n* Achievement in 1925 and growth in per capita electrical power production from 1928–1950. He also demonstrated the relationship with the growth of absolute electrical power production from 1950–1958 with the 1950 achievement motive. Longitudinal studies of Spain (Cortes, 1961), United States (deCharms & Moeller, 1962), and England (Bradburn & Berlew, 1961) also supported the proposition.

While the past research seems to have demonstrated that the *n* Achievement motive is acquired in childhood and is relatively stable, and that this motive can be related to a number of adult actions such as job seeking, career choice, and organizational success, there is a question of making the transition from the individual level to the aggregate level of analysis (Scheuch, 1966). An empirical link between individual behavior and the motives contained in the textbooks is provided by Lambert and Klineberg (1963). They obtained a .87 rank order correlation among nine countries between *n* Achievement as measured from the readers of the textbooks from that country, and the boys' occupational achievement aspirations.

Barrett and Franke (1971) posed three unresolved issues about McClelland's linking of *n* Achievement to national economic growth. First, is electrical power production a suitable measure of economic growth? Second, is it correct to consider countries of all sizes and levels of development as affected similarly by the level of achievement motivation, or is a cross-sectional examination more appropriate along dimensions such as those suggested by Sawyer (1967)? Third, research in United States firms had shown that high *n* Power and low *n* Affiliation were also important for the success of certain executives and were related to success of the firm. These motives were not considered by McClelland to be predictive of economic growth. In the reanalysis by Barrett and Franke (1971), a total of twelve indices of economic growth were used. For the total sample, McClelland's findings depend on the choice of the time period and economic measure chosen. In particular, growth in total energy consumption, gross domestic product, industrial production, and manufacturing production generally were unrelated across countries to previous need for achievement. In a finer breakdown of the findings, most *n* Achievement was related to economic growth only in smaller, already developed countries. The best single predictor of growth seemed to be an earlier record of low *n* Affiliation in children's readers, a finding similar to that in Finnish knitwear companies (Kock, 1965). High need for power was also found to be related to ten of the twelve measures of economic growth for the large developed countries and to a lesser extent, larger, less developed countries, but this did not correlate as well as low need for affiliation. The achievement motive did not forecast general economic growth across many measures and many different time spans. Low *n* Affiliation did the best job, and high *n* Power was second best. This would seem to fit some prior conceptualizations of Barry, Child, and

Bacon (1959) and some confirmed by Barry (1969) of a positive correlation between developed economic structures (measured in terms of relative accumulation of food resources) and patterns of authoritarian training. Berry (1967) confirmed the Barry, Child, and Bacon (1959) results at the individual level by using a modification of the Asch (1956) line matching technique. The low-food-accumulating Baffin Island Eskimos were significantly more independent than the high-food-accumulating Temne of Sierra Leone. This is an example of anthropological research on general cultural socialization practices being supported by an individual psychological technique. Just as an exhaustive analysis has been completed of what is being assessed by high *n* Achievement, so we need a comparable analysis of what is being assessed by low *n* Affiliation. When *n* Affiliation is high, perhaps it is impossible to break inefficient old patterns of behavior and introduce ways of dealing more efficiently with the environment.

The link from individual to nation is tenuous. For example, if we concentrate on the growth of currently developing nations, we need to be aware that "economic growth has begun only in agricultural societies or new societies created by migrants from agricultural or industrial societies...people who are nomadic or pastoral cannot accumulate..." (Hagen, 1962, p. 20). Motivational patterns are likely to be considerably different in agricultural as opposed to nomadic or pastoral societies. The correlation between predominant motives and growth may be due to this linkage.

The Effect of Values on Organizational Efficiency and Work Habits

Currently, the United States still has the lead in productivity over Europe; this cannot be accounted for solely on the basis of more capital equipment or other economic factors. The answer still appears to lie somewhere within the basic motivational patterns of the American work force and the effective management of its resources (Denison, 1967).

But this lead in productivity may diminish as American values shift away from task orientation. In the past decade, yearly productivity increases in the United States have been in the range of 2 to 3 percent, while in general they have been far higher in Japan and Europe.

Infrastructures such as roads, railroads, and electrical power have been repeatedly stressed as a precondition for rapid economic development of a nation. But as Heller (1969) has pointed out, less often has consideration been given to the importance of the values and habits of the nation. The values and habits which guide behavior in an organization can also be considered as important factors which may enhance or retard economic development of the nation.

Observational research by Heller (1969) in two South American countries illustrates the problems involved when values and habits antithetical to effective organizational operations exist. In fifty-nine out of sixty-eight business organizations studied, company board meetings were held without precirculated minutes and agendas. As a consequence, the board spent some 38 percent of its time going over subject matter which had been previously discussed, without adding any substance to previous remarks. Even more serious was the failure of definite board decisions to be carried out. In 56 percent of the cases where action had been taken by the board and decisions made to carry out certain specific instructions, six months later still no action had been taken.

The misuse of human resources can be seen by another example. In one South American country, secretaries are given extensive training in shorthand. Yet, when the work habits of all 260 managers in one organization were studied, only twelve managers, or less than 5 percent, were actually observed dictating reports or letters. When these same managers were interviewed, 95 percent of them reported that they wrote all or nearly all of their letters and reports in longhand. As a result, within a year or so after joining the company, the secretaries had lost most of their skill in shorthand, a skill acquired at considerable cost in time and money to both employee and employer. In addition, this skill was the basis for selection into the organization and the basis for their initial pay. (Actually, this pattern may be repeating itself in the United States and Western Europe; it has become much more efficient for managers to use transcription equipment, which obviates the need for personnel with shorthand skills.)

Heller (1969) also found important differences, which may reduce national efficiency, among managers from Argentina, Chile, and Uruguay as compared to American and British managers. The managers from the South American countries put a great deal of stress and importance upon the managerial skill, "making rapid decisions." This was seen somewhat less importantly by the Anglo-American manager, who more often prefers to "sleep on the problem" and to gather more information before making a decision. In contrast, the South American manager connects rapid decision making with power and authority. The concept is held that only the most senior managers with the most authority are able to make rapid decisions.

The case studies by Whyte and Williams (1968) in Peru also stress the misuse of resources in areas such as conspicuous consumption during fiesta time. Starbuck (1966), taking a methodological approach quite different from the observation and case studies of Heller (1969) and Whyte and Williams (1968), demonstrated differences in efficiency between British and American retail employees. Starbuck developed a model relating sales volumes per employee and store size. He then applied aggregate data on retail trade to the model, concluding, for example, that British clerk specialization results in retail organizations expending two or three times as much labor as an American organization to sell the same amount.

It is evident from this discussion that there are certain values and habit patterns more present in some cultures than others, which may be dysfunctional both for organization profits and for national economic growth. It is extremely difficult to make a convincing case for having a board meeting devoted to rehashing old business because minutes were not kept, or having the board make decisions which are never implemented.

The work of Heller (1969) illustrates one of the primary conflicts that a multinational firm must deal with. On the one hand, it wants to maintain satisfactory levels of efficiency in all its locations. Nevertheless, certain attitudes and beliefs peculiar to a culture in a particular location may be counter-productive for organizational efficiency. For an organization to compete effectively in the marketplace, it may be necessary for the organization to change practices which are counter-productive or initiate new practices to overcome inefficiencies. But these changes in turn may alienate members of the organization who believe previous practices to have special significance rooted in cultural values. Again, this is not a problem limited to operating in developing nations. Industrial effectiveness in many sections of the United States runs headlong into mass absenteeism each year at the opening of the hunting season.

MATCH BETWEEN ORGANIZATIONAL AND CULTURAL VALUES. When multinational companies move into a new country, some may find a favorable match between their company structure and cultural expectations. One of the best examples of this was the move of Sears Roebuck into Mexico. Sears Roebuck introduced modern merchandising methods, such as a fixed price for an article. This might have been thought to cause problems in the culture, but a deeper analysis revealed that this innovation was largely superficial. The general corporate structure of Sears Roebuck was consonant with Mexican cultural values. Moreover, a number of organizational values held by Sears made it acceptable for Mexican culture. For instance, the corporation has the policy of using local suppliers to provide a wide variety of merchandise for Sears. This fits well with the old *patron* tradition in Mexico, where there is a special relationship between an employer and an employee. Sears was able to build up a large number of small proprietors to supply merchandise on a continuing basis. In addition, the Mexican culture is oriented toward the concept that the employer provides a large number of benefits to the employee. This fitted in well with Sears' personnel policy, which can be best described as paternalistic—a policy of sharing profits, providing meals at less than cost, and providing extensive recreational facilities and other fringe benefits (Mann, 1965).

MANAGEMENT AND SUPERVISION

Is there one best way to supervise in all countries or does the best possible management style differ from one country to another? This is one question that has been addressed by numerous investigators. Also, if there are different styles required in different countries, are these clusters of countries similar? Some have looked at the two extremes in a given country: authoritarian direction versus democratic participation. Others have concentrated study on one particular style, say participation in several countries. Still others have looked at a variety of stylistic preferences and behaviors in different countries.

At least two kinds of problems face us as we try to make sense out of the cross-cultural differences we find. First, different methods and measurements do not uniformly reveal the same results. Evidence about supervisory-subordinate relations in different countries comes from several different sources: grid seminars, surveys of IBM personnel, questionnaire surveys of managers in training centers, and responses of managers to simulated supervisor-subordinate situations. Second, the concepts tend to shift in meaning as we move from one culture to another.

Managerial Styles

One method of data collection tends to reveal more similarity than differences across countries. Thus, self-reports of almost 2,500 middle and upper managers from eight cultural areas during grid seminars (United States, South Africa, Canada, Australia, Middle East, South America, and Japan) show a great deal of similarity. For the particular comparative analysis they reported, the general question asked of the participants was, "What is the best way for a company to operate?" A total of twenty questions, each presenting a variety of alternatives about organizational performance, were discussed in a group and a consensus reached. For each question, the participants could choose one of five alternatives ranging from "most sound" to "least sound." There was uniform agreement that the 9.9 management style (maximal concern with both production and people) is the ideal for the company (Mouton & Blake, 1970). The main difficulty with these findings is that all the results are based upon data obtained during and after the participant's indoctrination in a management development course. The results could be merely a reflection of the completeness of the indoctrination.

These uniform results are in contrast to how the managers viewed their own self-reported conduct at the end of the seminar. For instance, managers from Japan and South America were more concerned with production than with people.

Differences as well as similarities emerged in a large comparative survey of job goals and beliefs of 13,000 employees in forty-six countries, queried by IBM (Sirota, 1968). One of the questions dealt with the preferred and perceived leadership styles of their managers. The styles were based on the proposed model of Tannenbaum and Schmidt (1958). Four hypothetical managers were presented as follows: "tells," "sells," "consults," and "joins" (accepts majority decision).

Overall, although consultation and joint decision making were preferred, the directive managerial styles were perceived to occur more often. Consistency of some sort seemed preferable to erratic managerial behavior. The employee who said "my manager does not correspond at all closely to any of these four styles" was less satisfied with his job, company, and manager. This held true for all the countries surveyed and in particular all levels of two companies in the United Kingdom (Sadler, 1970).

The various managerial styles were also related to characteristic managerial behavior. In general, the manager who "consults" was viewed more favorably, while the manager who "tells" and especially the one with the "no style" were seen as least desirable. Interestingly, the manager who "joins" was not noted as a good counselor and many objected to the number of meetings he called.

The managers' conception of their own style did not match their employees' perception of their behavior. For one international group of 178 managers, 71 percent saw themselves as using a "consulting" leadership style, while only 29 percent of their employees perceived them as behaving in that way (Sadler & Hofstede, 1972).

The IBM studies contain a potentially rich fund of information. As yet, the results of this research have only been partially published (Sirota & Greenwood, 1971).

The inconsistencies of outcome, depending on what measurements were made, were illustrated in Haire, Ghiselli, and Porter's (1966) survey of approximately 3,600 managers in fourteen countries. They showed that there was a gap between the managers' beliefs concerning employees' capacity for initiative and leadership, and in the managers' beliefs about participative management. Most managers tended to believe in sharing information and encouraging subordinates to participate in the management decision process, but they also believed that the average individual preferred to be directed and wished to avoid responsibility. Clark and McCabe (1970) found somewhat similar results for an additional 1,300 managers in Australia as did Cummings and Schmidt (1972) for a small sample of Greek managers.

It is encouraging to note that two different studies using different methods can obtain similar results. For example, results from Exercise Communication (Bass, 1967b) showed that preference by country as a receiver of one-way communication correlated .82 with the Haire, Ghiselli, and Porter (1966) survey measure of propensity to share information and objectives (Barrett & Franke, 1969).

The Authoritarian Concept

Conceptual problems are illustrated by what happens to the meaning of *authoritarian* as we move from one culture to another. Turkey is often thought of as an authoritarian culture in contrast to the United States; yet Kagitcibasi (1970) showed that authoritarianism, as we tend to think of it, may not be a general syndrome in Turkey. In Turkey there are two strong values or norms which seem to contribute to attitude patterns. These are patriotism and respect for authority. In Turkey, a great deal of obligation is vested both in the nation and in the family, while in the United States the obligation seems to be more to the self. The Turkish family seems to be somewhat of a contradiction since it combines very high control with a great deal of warmth. In the United States, authoritarianism correlates with both family control and lack of affection, while in Turkey it correlates significantly only with control. This study raises the important point that we cannot naively assume that concepts that are widely held in the United States can be imposed upon the culture of other countries.

Despite conceptual problems, nations can be ordered on a dimension of preference for authoritarian supervision. Thus, preference by receivers in a given country for one-way communication in Exercise Communication correlates .89 with national differences in preference of subordinates for directive supervision in Exercise Supervise (Ryterband & Barrett, 1970).

The authoritarian dimension in preferred supervisory style helps explain other relevant findings. India often turns up authoritarian as compared with other countries, especially the United States, which is the least authoritarian among the countries sampled (Meade & Whittaker, 1967). For instance, an experimental replication of the classic Lippitt and White (1958) study of leadership in India by Meade (1967) demonstrated that both morale and productivity were higher under authoritarian than under nonauthoritarian leadership in India—a reversal of United States results.

After studying Israeli officers and crews, Foa (1957) concluded that authoritarian supervisors should be in charge of subordinates with authoritarian expectations. Therefore, it becomes critical to learn of national normative differences in such preferences.

INTERPERSONAL TRUST. An underlying dimension of importance appears to be the concept of interpersonal trust. Williams, Whyte, and Green (1966) demonstrated that Peruvian white collar workers had quite different preferences in supervisor-subordinate relationships than workers from the United States. For example, satisfied Peruvians preferred supervisors who emphasized production, but satisfied Americans preferred considerate supervisors. Previous work by Whyte (1963) had shown that the Peruvians tended to have a low level of faith in people. Williams, Whyte, and Green (1966) sorted the Peruvian workers into high, medium, and low trust groups using a "faith-in-people" questionnaire. Those workers high in interpersonal trust were very positive toward a leadership climate which was participative and democratic. In contrast, those low in interpersonal trust were satisfied with supervision that was more authoritarian. Only the Peruvian workers with high interpersonal trust were similar to the United States workers in terms of preferred supervisor-subordinate relationships. In the same way, Senner (1971) found that Brazilian bankers were more trusting than the Peruvian white collar workers, but the bankers were similar to American college students. The best single predictor of trust for the banker was the socioeconomic status of the individual in his organization. An organizational profile showed that banks with participative climates were perceived to be more effective than those with authoritarian climates by respondents both low and high in trust. Where trust and participative organizational climates prevailed, individuals felt more involved in work, more integrated with their work groups, and perceived that important motives could be satisfied by their job situations.

The level of trust managers have in their subordinates can even differentiate United States subsidiaries operating in India from local Indian companies, with the managers from United States subsidiaries having the expected higher trust (Negandhi & Prasad, 1971).

The Participation Concept

As the concept of authoritarianism varies in meaning across countries, the concept of participation varies also. First, there are wide formalized institutional differences from country to country, and second, participation may be a matter of in-company preference, again dictated by special programs, such as job enlargement or management-by-objectives. For example, in Yugoslavia workers are involved directly in many important decision-making processes. In other countries, such as the Federal Republic of Germany, workers of certain mining and steel firms may have representation on the supervisory board but actually participate very little. In still other countries, the workers' council or workers' committee has a small role to play and little influence upon the actual management of the firm (Schregle,

1970). In the United States, participation usually implies an informal involvement by workers in decisions of consequence to themselves. Worker representatives—the unions —ordinarily negotiate with management rather than participate in problem solving with management. In fact, formal methods of worker participation, not involving union negotiation, may reduce the average worker's influence on decisions of consequence to himself. Mulder (1971) found that when there are relatively large differences in the expert power of members in the system, an increase in participation will increase the power differences among the members. Laboratory research supported this proposition and is in accord with a large number of European surveys concerning the effectiveness of workers' councils. It is quite possible that this discrepancy between the workers' expectations of the amount of power they will have in the workers' council and their actual influence produces a certain degree of frustration which appears to reduce satisfaction with workers' councils in general (Obradovic, French, & Rodgers, 1970).

Obradovic (1970) studied twenty Yugoslav factories in order to relate participation with job satisfaction. He compared two main groups, the workers and members of workers' councils across three different technologies. Obradovic found greater job satisfaction among handicraft mechanized workers, but not among the automated workers who participated in the workers' council. Conversely, for all three occupational groups, those who participated in self-management were more alienated than the nonparticipants. In any case, the relationships were not particularly strong.

As Strauss and Rosenstein (1970) indicate, there are three major models of representative participation: the joint consultation model, the joint decision-making model, and workers' control model. All may actually allow the worker less true participation than where there is a strong independent union.

Clustering of Countries

Despite the methodological problems and despite the differences the same concepts may have in meaning as we go from one country to another, different investigators, using different methods, do tend to find the same clusterings of countries: Anglo-American, Latin or South European, North European, and Japanese. Moreover, developing and traditional countries tend to cluster together in managerial preferences and styles of behavior. In addition, the Anglo-Americans tend to be at one end of the dimension in preference for participation and equalitarian forms of behavior, while those from traditional countries like India tend to be at the other end of the dimension, favoring more directive, authoritarian approaches. Other culture clusters tend to lie in between, in general. Haire, Ghiselli, and Porter (1966) were able to cluster their fourteen countries into the above framework. Clark and McCabe (1970) found that Australians could be fit into the Anglo-American approach.

In all, there was a great deal of similarity between American, British, and Australian management attitudes. At the same time, however, Haire, Ghiselli, and Porter (1966) noted that Americans have a more favorable attitude toward the average person's capacity for leadership and initiative than do the British or the Australians (Clark & McCabe, 1970). For example, in comparison to American estimates, Heller (1971) found that British managers thought it would take twice as long for their subordinates to acquire the skill to take over their jobs. Again, Maier and Hoffman (1962) used a role-playing technique to compare American and British managers and found that the British seemed to be more attuned than the American managers to an authoritarian style in decision making.

On the other hand, illustrating the similarity of British and American managers, Heller and Porter (1966) asked managers to rank thirteen success traits in order of their importance. Both British and American managers agreed that intelligent, cooperative, and flexible managers were the best. Overall, a rank-order correlation (rho) of .87 was obtained between the rankings of the two groups. A related ranking of managerial requirements in terms of skill, function, and qualities resulted in almost identical agreement.

In Exercise Supervise (Bass, 1967b), managers are asked to choose five traits that they consider to be most and least important for the success of a middle manager in his job. The selection is made from a list of twenty-five traits. The same procedure is followed for rating important and unimportant traits for a top manager and the first-line foreman.

Definite differences were found among managers from eight different countries (Ryterband & Barrett, 1970). For example, 63 percent of the United Kingdom managers thought the trait *imaginative* was important for success as a top manager, while only 8 percent of the Danish managers held the same opinion. Similarly, one percent of the United Kingdom managers thought *logical* was a relatively unimportant trait for a top manager while 50 percent of the Indian managers were of the same opinion!

In another part of Exercise Supervise, managers were asked to participate in a role-playing situation. There were three managerial roles to play: the coercive (authoritarian) supervisor, the persuasive (tell-and-sell) supervisor, and the permissive (participative) supervisor. There were also three subordinate roles to play: the vitally interested subordinate, the marginally interested subordinate, and the uninterested subordinate. Each manager was assigned one of these roles. Each subordinate then met with each of the three supervisors for fifteen minutes. At the end of this time they indicated their satisfaction or dissatisfaction with the various roles. While 62 percent of the Dutch-Flemish cluster of managers were satisfied with the participative supervisor, only 22 percent of the Greek managers were satisfied with that managerial style. Fifty-six percent of the Greek managers preferred a passive subordinate while only twelve percent of the managers from the United States had that preference (Bass, 1968b). Thus, a hierarchy of countries exists in the degree to which their managers prefer involved, rather than passive, subordinates. Traditional countries like India and Greece are low in such interest while the United States and Great Britain are high. The Latin and Northern European countries are in between (Bass, 1968b; Thiagarajan & Deep, 1970).

Countries like Japan are more complex. We may see some evidence of authoritarianism and traditionalism. At the same time, there is heavy emphasis on participation and peer pressure to promote consensual decision making (Abegglen, 1958).

The supervisor has different relevance for the worker in Japan. He is likely to be more involved in the employee's off-the-job work life and accords the worker more status off the job. This is illustrated by a Japanese worker's response to the question, "If my immediate supervisor enters a crowded bus on which I am riding, I should (1) offer him my seat unless I am not feeling well or (2) remain seated and offer to hold any packages he may have": forty-four percent of the Japanese employees chose option one (compared to only two percent of United States respondents). Conversely, 65 percent of United States employees and 5 percent of the Japanese chose the second option (Whitehill & Takezawa, 1968).

Traditional attitudes are changing. Frager (1970) reported that over one-third of the Japanese college students studied actually exhibited anti-conformity in the Asch (1956) group-pressure situation. Anti-conformity occurred when the confederates unanimously gave the correct answer, but the subjects gave an incorrect answer; that is, the students did whatever they thought was the opposite of what was expected of them. This phenomenon has not been reported for American students, perhaps because the American samples were not studied recently enough or selected from among those who might be suspect as alienated students.

Hesseling and Konnen (1969) reported that during a simulated decision-making experience, Japanese managers were extremely critical of their peers compared to Dutch managers. The Japanese managers appeared to combine behaviors in this situation that to the Western observer may appear incompatible. For that reason the results of investigators, such as Misumi and Seki (1971), demonstrating that supervisory styles differentially affecting groups either high or low in n Achievement, may not be generalizable to Western managers.

Influence in Organizations

In contrast, we have evidence that there is considerable generalizability in the effects of distribution of control in an organization. Research by Rus (1970) with Yugoslavian organizations confirmed the findings of Tannenbaum (1968) in the United States that both American managers and workers have similar perceptions of the distribution of influence in an organization. Rus (1970) found that despite the fact that the Yugoslavian organizations have workers' councils which theoretically should bring about maximum participation and influence by the workers in the organization, both managers and workers see influence concentrated in top management in the same way as do American workers.

Consistent with much of modern management theory, Rus (1970) also found that both managers and workers in the more efficient organizations reported that each occupational group was perceived as having greater influence than its counterpart in the inefficient organization. In other words, the more total influence everyone has in the system, the greater the total system efficiency. This result was confirmed by Kavčič, Rus, and Tannenbaum (1971), who used two pairs of organizations that were similar in size and technology but different in productivity.

The more influence occurring, the more the organization can increase in effectiveness. Thus, the effectiveness of sixteen Brazilian development finance institutions depended upon the total control existing in each of the organizations and how evenly the control was distributed among these organizations (Farris, 1971). Contradicted was the often widely held assumption that in Latin American organizations, control is strictly authoritarian. Here, perceived control varied at different levels of the organization and in various stages of the decision-making process.

ASSESSMENT

Individuals differ reliably in their tested aptitudes for different kinds of work. Those with greater tested aptitude, say numerical aptitude, are more likely to succeed at jobs like engineering or accounting than those who lack this ability. Ethnic, racial, and national groups exhibit consistent differences in their mean test levels on this and other aptitudes.

The emotional question is whether the differences are due to nature and/or nurture. The more pragmatic questions that we will address here are (1) whether the tested differences reflect true differences in aptitude or are artifactual biases set up so that a test favors someone from one national group over another, (2) whether the tested differences are equally valid for forecasting success in a particular job regardless of culture, (3) whether and how processes of assessment are influenced by culture, and (4) what happens when the assessment takes place in one country and the job is to be performed in another.

At the turn of the century the selection problem was made simple in much of American industry by so-called "racial psychology." For example, the Croatians were thought to make the best miners and steel-workers, while the Dutch were considered best at furniture making and other crafts. Certain nationalities such as the French, Swiss, and Scandinavians were perceived to be easily assimilated into the American culture and organizations, while the Slovaks, Armenians, and Albanians were seen as clannish and more resistant to the adoption of new ways of living (Frost, 1920). Unfortunately, this simplistic reasoning was not only invalid for the most part, but was calculated to reduce the effectiveness and satisfaction of the utilization of these human resources in the United States. Moreover, it helped maintain the United States not as a "land of opportunity" but as a land of "differential opportunity." This kind of policy, however, was worldwide: Indians could only rise so high in the Raj; Africans had to maintain very limited horizons compared to their European colonial masters; much of the world remained at a level Diocletian had decreed at the end of the third century; one had to work in the same job as had one's father.

Culture-Free or Culture-Fair Testing?

No nationality has a monopoly on the intellectual and personality traits that make for success in an occupation. What is more likely is that the educational or cultural experience of those from certain nationalities may be markedly inferior to the educational advantages of those from more developed countries. Dominating much current thinking is the desire to assess aptitudes and capacities independently of race, ethnic origin, or national identity. The search, therefore, goes on for culture-free and culture-fair tests.

Even today we have stereotypes of nationalities that lead us to believe that individuals from a certain nationality are more suited to certain work than others. At the outset, we ought to say that there is some grain of truth in stereotypes but that scientific investigation is necessary. There is no doubt that culture does influence preferences for certain types of workers with occupations, skills, and emotional dispositions toward work and leisure. These can all be factors in the problem of selection.

When one considers the difficult selection problem in a cross-national setting, one hopes that tests will be culture-free. But reality frustrates such hope. So much of what is different among peoples in behavior tests are differences usually due to cultural and environmental factors. An extreme instance is seen in the spatial area. People from "non-carpentered" parts of the world seem unable to perceive certain geometric illusions, especially those involving three dimensions (Segall, Campbell, & Herskovits, 1963).

At times what may seem to be obvious to us may not be so for members of another culture. For example, when Navajos are asked to match one colored chip with an array of colored chips embedded in a display, they make a considerable number of errors; they have no name for certain colors in their language (Brown & Lenneberg, 1954). This illustrates the point that what may be reality for one culture, may not be for members of another culture. For the Navajos, not having a name for a color probably has no dysfunctional consequences, but the lack of certain perceptual qualities may present problems when new technology is introduced into a nation that does not have the basic aptitudes and abilities to support the new technology.

Certain perceptual processes in the underdeveloped countries are quite different from westernized countries. For example, in Africa two-dimensional perception of pictures is the usual mode, while three-dimensional perception is quite unusual (Hudson, 1967). The two-dimensional mode of perception has resulted in problems where pictorial material is used for projective tests and safety posters. The opposite connotation may be portrayed to the African worker because of failure to understand their domi-

nant perceptual mode. An important study by Dawson (1967a, 1967b), using a small experimental and control group of two-dimensional perceivers, showed that by appropriate training workers could be taught to perceive material in three dimensions. The most important fact is that this ability to learn to perceive material in three dimensions was highly related (.88) to the individual's prior perceptual style. Even within one country there are stable perceptual style differences among subcultures which are related to task performance even when intelligence is controlled (Preale, Amir, & Singer, 1970).

These variations among cultures should not blind us to the fact that tests can be successfully modified to compensate for differences in learned experiences. Often the most maligned tests are those used to measure intelligence. Nevertheless, empirical evidence from Africa and the West Indies shows intelligence tests (with their built-in biases from middle-class America or Europe) to be predictive of success in secondary schooling. What this may mean is that secondary schooling in developing countries requires the same kinds of abilities to work with words, numbers, and shapes as in North America and Europe. Since schooling in developing countries is often modeled after the developed countries, the criterion is as "contaminated" by culture as are the tests.

Indeed, a stronger case can be made for the use of testing in the underdeveloped countries than in the more developed ones (Vernon, 1969). This is so because for both schools and positions there are more applicants than there are openings. The selection ratio is more favorable. In addition, while we can often substitute previous educational success for testing as the basis for prediction in the developed world, in developing countries the quality of schools is so variable that achievement becomes an unreliable predictor. The evidence is remarkably clear that Western-type tests can be successfully used in a great number of cultures. In reviewing a number of validity studies with occupations ranging from manual workers to clerks in countries as diverse as New Guinea and Sierra Leone, Vernon (1969) found validity coefficients similar to those obtained in testwise western nations. It is true, however, that the content as well as the instructions for giving a test must be thoroughly worked out and adapted to the culture in which it is to be used (Schwarz, 1963). Schwarz and Schwarz (1961) have used aptitude tests in the developing nations of Africa and have developed a number of techniques to adapt tests to other cultures. In South Africa, Biesheuvel (1954) was also successful in administering tests through the medium of a sound motion picture. Tests have been validated in the African coal mining industry with the relationships often running above .6 for sizable numbers of subjects. Dawson (1963) found that West African miners with more traditional values were assessed as being poorer performers than those with more western concepts. There is evidence that there is a wide range of ability in underdeveloped countries, and western testing procedures can make a significant contribution in selecting those who would be most proficient in various categories of jobs. After reviewing the history of testing in underdeveloped countries, Irvine (1965) urged caution as to the constructs being measured by the tests. There is general agreement that the format of a test has its own built-in source of variance as does the method of presentation (Lovegrove, 1969). One source of variance unique to parts of Africa is an educational aptitude factor associated only with males (Irvine, 1969).

Vernon (1965) has argued that standardized western tests are useful for studying the effects of different environments on intellectual development. Wober's (1967) study comparing United States and African subjects illustrated the difference in cognitive style. Attributes that are closely related to United States subjects are unrelated to African subjects. The research results of Berry (1966) and the confirmation by MacArthur (1967) showing no sex differences in cognitive style for Eskimos, in contrast to sex differences found in the United States, lends support to women's groups which argue that the sex differences found in some western tests are largely a result of differential social experience. This conclusion is reinforced by ethnographic data (Barry, Bacon, & Child, 1957).

For the developing nation, the more critical question revolves around the introduction of new technological systems to a traditional culture. As Lee (1968) points out, the maintenance of a Boeing 707 or the programming of an IBM computer puts specific demands on the individual regardless of his origins. The western test which predicts proficiency in these endeavors, although not culture-free, is reasonably culture-fair.

Mathematically, one can show that culture may be irrelevant if we can assume it has constant effects on the individual's test performance within the culture. That is, if we find that everyone's test score in a particular culture is depressed by ten points, its correlation with job performance, for that group, remains unaffected. The true validity of a test is independent of a constant effect of culture on test performance. But if the mean test performance for a group is depressed by a constant, so the mean criterion performance for that group may also be depressed given a valid correlation between test and criterion. Lee (1968) gives a graphic example of some of the consequences of this in underdeveloped countries when complex systems are introduced. A procedure was devised to select African pilot trainees for an African airline. Since all the ground instruction, pilot training, and test materials were in the English language, it was decided to use American aptitude tests. Seven hundred applicants were tested and from these, sixteen African pilot trainees were selected. They averaged below 100 on an IQ test. The trainees required five times as much flight instruction as is normal to solo, and in the process suffered six accidents, including the demolishing of one aircraft. This process produced a total of six pilots. Lee believes that this difficulty was due to the educational and technological deprivation of the applicants.

What happened here may illustrate that culture influences aptitudes of importance to job success in a population. It cannot be ignored by consideration of culture-fairness or culture-freeness. Thus, airline pilots, engineers, and photo interpreters are much more field independent than the normal population (Cullen, Harper, & Kidera, 1969; Barrett & Thornton, 1967; Thornton, Barrett, & Davis, 1968). For many countries where field dependence is more the norm than field independence, the training of professional specialists such as pilots and engineers presents unusual difficulties (Witkin, 1967), as was found by Lee (1968) above.

Dawson (1967a, 1967b, 1969c) has clearly shown some of the bio-social considerations, such as malnutrition, which can result in wide divergences in perceptual style for different cultural groups.

Selection and Cultural Constraints

Cultural constraints may also play an important role in the total selection system. A most interesting study which indicates the extreme effect of culture upon selection comes from South Africa. There a bus company devised a series of tests to select African bus drivers. The testing procedure included an intelligence test among a variety of other aptitude tests. The testing program was very successful in predicting success in the training program. But, unfortunately, those who were successful in the training program were also found to have a very high subsequent accident rate as bus drivers (Shaw, 1965).

The problem seemed to be that the most intelligent Africans were chosen as bus drivers. However, South African racial discrimination policies prohibit further advancement for bus drivers. This resulted in an extreme degree of frustration among those who were the most intelligent in the applicant samples. Indeed, they should not have been bus drivers in the first place. African bus drivers who were less intelligent were better able to adapt to the frustrations of the total cultural system; they exhibited fewer emotional problems as well as fewer accidents on the job.

At the other end of the status hierarchy, a survey of chief executives in six European countries showed wide differences in personal characteristics, indicating implicit cultural selection constraints (Hall, deBettignies, & Amado-Fischgrund, 1969). These differences included age, social class, educational background, mobility, and the time required to reach top executive positions. In France, for example, almost all the chief executives were college graduates in contrast to Britain, where less than half had comparable educations.

On the other hand, often what appears to be most likely culture-bound turns out to be much freer of cultural constraints. Cassens (1966) studied the validity of the same biographical information blank for selecting executives from various nationalities. Nearly 400 were Latin Americans working in their native countries, and 200 were North American managers all working for Exxon.

The study was based upon the premise that successful executives have common biographical factors or common past histories regardless of the nationality or culture in which the executive was raised. The items covered one's life history and included areas such as home, family background, education, vocational planning, finance, leisure time activities, health history, and social and community relations.

A factor analysis revealed eight common factors labeled: Upward mobility through education; Role in society; Perception of personal ability and achievement; Attitudes toward family; Perceived role in social activities; Task orientation; Personal self-sufficiency; and Personal achievement.

The factor "attitudes toward the family"

was interesting in that, while the same factor appeared in the North American and Latin American samples, the content of the items making up the factor tended to be different for the two samples of managers. For the United States managers, the items in the factor tended to deal with the social class level of the parents' family. In contrast, for the Latin Americans, the items dealt more with the executives' general feeling about family relationships. Thus, while the factor structure of the executives' life histories may be the same, cultures differentially influenced how the behavior was expressed. This was demonstrated in Peru, Central America, and Colombia (Frye, 1967).

Chaney (1966) also concluded that biographical information used to predict British scientists' research performance involved the same variables as United States studies. However, there were differences in communication patterns, with more productive British scientists having less frequent communication with their superiors and colleagues, and with the opposite pattern found in the United States.

In a broader selection program, the biographical information as a whole predicted managerial success equally well in North America and Latin America. It formed part of a battery of tests, the Personnel Development Series. The battery consisted of four main parts. The first two parts were a biographical information blank previously discussed. The third part was a standardized personality test. The last part was a fifty-item multiple choice test of management judgment. This test presents the executive with typical problems faced on a job about which he is required to make appropriate decisions (Laurent, 1970).

This test battery was first validated in Exxon in the United States. The program was labeled the Early Identification of Management Potential and was found to be quite successful. Before the test battery is introduced to an affiliate of the company, a validation study is conducted to see if the battery is appropriate for the country involved. These tests were validated in Exxon Europe with affiliates in Norway, Denmark, and the Netherlands for 800 managers. The criterion of success was the Laurent Success Index. A score was obtained for each executive indicating his relative degree of success, adjusted for his age and organization salary structure. The tests were successful in predicting managerial success in all three European Exxon affiliates.

It is interesting to note that the two tests with the highest correlation were those dealing with the biographical information blank. On the surface, one might believe that questions dealing with an individual's early life might be culture bound. This appears not to be the case. The study presents fairly convincing evidence that the same traits and ability levels that are predictive of success of a United States manager are also predictive of success of managers in other countries *working in the same multinational corporation*. Several reasons may be involved. First, it may be that there are universal characteristics for effective managers. Second, Exxon may recruit and attract into its ranks "Americanized" Europeans and the Exxon organizational climate may impose uniformities in requirements that transcend cultures. There is some evidence that nationals differentially gravitate toward different multinational firms. Vansina and Taillieu (1970) reported that highly task-oriented Flemish business school graduates prefer to work for American or German companies, rather than their own nationally managed organizations. Elsewhere it has been shown that task-oriented managers tend to be more effective (Bass, 1967a). On the other hand, those who preferred to work only in a national company within their own nation were highest in self-orientation and authoritarianism.

Interpersonal Factors in Selection

In some countries, the government has institutionalized discrimination, as in Greece, where semi-public firms must hire Greek Orthodox citizens under 35 years of age (Triandis, 1963). There are also subtler influences upon selection decisions that reflect some of the underlying dimensions of the culture.

Triandis (Triandis, 1963; Triandis & Vassiliou, 1972) has systematically compared some of the factors influencing employee selection in the United States and Greece. Based upon knowledge of the Greek culture, particularly the importance and differential response to ingroup and outgroup members, a number of deductions were formulated and tested. Using a factorial design, Greeks and Americans completed a questionnaire describing sixteen hypothetical job applicants in which they rated willingness to hire the person described. The Greeks placed a great deal more importance upon recommendations of ingroup members than the Americans. Better knowledge of the Greeks' subjective culture might have avoided many of the problems encountered by Litton in its unsuccessful attempt to accelerate the economic development of the country (McGrew, 1972).

Prediction of Success in a Foreign Environment

It is estimated that currently over 35,000 United States citizens are in management positions overseas. Similar large numbers of Europeans and Japanese are serving outside their native countries. Despite the sizable population of these managers, little research has been completed about them. In response to a questionnaire survey, Baker and Ivancevich (1970, 1971; Ivancevich & Baker, 1970) found that only 20 percent of 127 companies used tests in selecting managers for overseas assignments. Of the firms using tests for selection, 77 percent reported that they did not validate their selection instruments—a reason why we were unable to find a single reported validation study on the performance of overseas managers employed by business concerns.

The task of predicting the performance of an individual in an overseas assignment is extremely difficult. There are a number of reasons for this, not the least of which is the fact that most overseas assignments tend to be unique, either as to task or country. Seldom is there a chance for an organization to fully evaluate by objective means the qualities that make for success or failure in an overseas assignment. Only the United States government in its Peace Corps Program has been able to send a large number of individuals on an overseas assignment to perform essentially the same task found in the designated countries.

A Peace Corps study by Ezekiel (1968) used as the principal instrument of prediction a fictional autobiography of the volunteer's personal future. These autobiographies were composed during the training session and were scored for three categories. The first category was termed "Differentiation" and was scored in terms of how complex and detailed a mapping of the future was presented. The second category was labeled "Demand" and was scored for the degree to which a personal future and pattern of life required long-term and continuing effort. The third category, "Agency," referred to the degree the respondent was the prime agent in determining the events of his future life.

These measures were specifically related to the performance of the Peace Corps volunteers in West Africa. There was a consistent relationship between all three of these attributes of fictional autobiography and performance during the second year. An overall autobiographical score resulted in a correlation of .41 for the second year. Some differences were found between males and females in the predictive power of the instrument, but religious background was even more differentiating. The prediction of Protestants' job performance was accurate—the correlation between the autobiography and the evaluation of performance was .64. In contrast, for the Catholic sample there was no relationship between the autobiography selection instrument and performance. Authoritarianism was not related to success (Smith, 1965). But in another study of Peace Corps teachers, authoritarianism was related to success (Mischel, 1965).

Other mainly negative Peace Corps findings were reported by Hare (1966) for 120 volunteers in the Philippines. Relationships are all low, with rated proficiency of training in the United States correlating .20 with success ratings.

LANGUAGE APTITUDE. Many executives have had successful business experiences in other countries despite the fact that they did not master the language of the host country, although the ability to master a second language undoubtedly would have helped. It is surprising that no published evidence is available on the relation between language fluency in a foreign country and performance as a manager in that country, particularly since learning the language often involves incidental learning about the culture of the country. The Modern Language Aptitude Test is a predictor of such aptitude (Carroll & Sapon, 1959). The wide variation in such aptitude was illustrated by a report on 700 U.S. Foreign Service officers (Anon., 1971).

CROSS-CULTURAL TRAINING AND DEVELOPMENT

Two somewhat unrelated issues need to be examined. First, is there one best way to train people regardless of their cultural background? Second, is there one best way of preparing people to work in a culture which is not their own? There is little published research on the first issue and only a modest amount of information on the second.

Method versus Culture

Visits to forty countries, and training experience in half of them, strongly suggest to the junior author that the utility of any given training method is strongly dependent on the cultural setting. It is our guess that in more traditional societies, more direct lecture approaches are expected and appear to be successful in the total training process, while in more advanced societies, particularly in the United States, participative approaches are most favored and accepted. The popularity of such participative approaches increased greatly after World War II, when American managers and schoolteachers with their expertise travelled to Europe on the heels of the American occupation forces. Similarly, English and French systems of education moved through their ex-colonies and affected industrial training practices in the respective countries. Industrial psychological evidence is sparse; nevertheless, particularly relevant is a preliminary unpublished study on the training of 120 colored immigrants and non-colored British trainee bus drivers by Smith and Pearn (1972). As tested performance shows below, for training in relatively simple matters, an interaction was obtained as one might expect between culture and the efficacy of the training method used: conventional lecture or participative discovery.

In the conventional method, trainees were told in advance what was to be learned. This method was more efficacious for the colored immigrants—recent arrivals from more traditional societies. On the other hand, discovery learning was better for white British driver trainees. Similar results were obtained with more difficult material as well.

Most immigrants came from rural, il-

	Conventional Learning	Discovery Learning	t	p
Immigrants	1.3	.8	2.3	< .01
Nonimmigrants	1.2	1.7	3.6	< .001

literate environments, where it seemed plausible that the conventional method which required rote learning and memorization was more useful with the immigrants; it was also preferred by them. We need a great deal more experimentation of this sort pointing to the utility of different approaches to training which may be required by different cultural groups.

This kind of outcome does not merely suggest that we adopt one way or another with particular culture groups. Rather, as Smith and Pearn (1972) state, perhaps we should concentrate on teaching those who favor rote-learned non-conceptual training methods how to learn general principles and how to use discovery methods before attempting to use those methods.

Preparing for Work in Another Culture

Here we will look at the problems of adjusting to work in other cultures and the ways that have been tried to prepare people for the adjustment.

ADJUSTMENT PATTERN TO A FOREIGN CULTURE. Ivancevich (1969) used a need satisfaction questionnaire (Porter, 1961) to collect data on 127 overseas United States managers. The results showed that middle managers in overseas jobs, as compared to domestic managers, perceived themselves to be less satisfied with their opportunities for friendships. The security needs of the overseas middle managers were reported to be unfulfilled compared to domestic managers. However, the overseas managers did perceive that their needs for esteem were more fulfilled than those of the domestic managers.

There seems to be a consistent pattern of adjustment and variation in attitude toward the host country by a foreign visitor. Lysgaard (1955) found a U-curve of adjustment, which has been replicated in other studies (Jacobson, Kumata, & Gullahorn, 1960). A consistent cycle seems to be followed. First is the "spectator" phase in which the visitor has extremely positive attitudes toward the

host country. After this phase, a certain amount of disillusionment sets in and the host culture is viewed in a perspective ranging from ambivalence to hostility. After this phase is resolved, he moves on to a more positive attitude, which allows him to see the host country in a more realistic manner. However, when he returns to his native country, a readjustment process seems to be called for and a similar adjustment cycle follows. Putting together the two U-curves yields a W-curve, which includes the return to the home country. The W-curve describes the total adjustment process (Gullahorn & Gullahorn, 1963, 1966), but a number of factors may interact to modify this curve (Brein & David, 1971).

As a consequence, apart from foreign language and customs education, special training efforts to prepare people for work abroad have centered on the adjustment processes. For instance, sensitivity training has been favored, particularly where participants are multinational. Thus, the International Institute for Organizational Development brings together senior managers from various European countries for sensitivity training programs. The effectiveness of these programs is not known.

It has often been speculated that the adjustment of the wife to a foreign culture is extremely important. Empirical support has been given to this proposition based on 300 American IBM employees where the wife's satisfaction was directly related to the employee's effectiveness (Purcer-Smith, 1970). While some organizations do provide training for the wife, most do not.

TRAINING APPROACHES. It is evident that mere contact with a different culture or ethnic group may result in unfavorable attitude changes (Amir, 1969). Most individuals enter a foreign culture with stereotypes which may not be functional (Brigham, 1971). Training programs are required to increase individual effectiveness while working in a different culture. Many approaches to preparing managers for work abroad

(Bass & Thiagarajan, 1968) are available but untested. Among the most promising are "contrast culture" simulations and cultural assimilators.

A modified form of role playing has been called "contrast culture" (Stewart & Pryle, 1966). In this technique, the modal values of the culture are identified. Then various situations and roles are created which will demonstrate the extreme contrast between various roles individuals from different cultures can play.

Among simulations available are those of Bass (1970), which consist of a program of exercises covering such areas as individual and group perceptions of company objectives, salary administration behavior, planning, risk taking, personal goals, and intergroup relationships. Through an international network of training and research organizations in North and South America, Europe, Africa, and Asia, training programs involving these exercises have been conducted in over forty countries with the data stored in a central bank (Barrett, 1969). Norms can be drawn from the data bank which allow managers from diverse nations and organizations to compare their attitudes, values, and behavior with others.

The Culture Assimilator is a programmed learning experience which requires approximately two to five hours of individual learning time. The 75 to 100 incidents contained in the typical culture assimilator are designed to expose a member of one culture to some basic concepts, attitudes, and values of another culture. Therefore, each culture assimilator is unique to one culture. Two techniques are used to select relevant information where misunderstanding might exist between the two cultures. First, the subjective culture can be analyzed; the subjective culture can be conceived as a characteristic way in which a cultural group responds to a social environment (Triandis, 1967, 1972). The second way is by gathering critical incident data from Americans and host nationals; they can be asked to describe some specific intercultural incident which made

a difference in their understanding of the culture.

The technique has been validated in both laboratory experiments and field studies. Culture assimilators developed for the Arab countries, Iran, Thailand, Central America, and Greece present information in a manner which can be used by Americans going into foreign cultures (Fiedler, Mitchell, & Triandis, 1971). For example, a feature of the Greek subjective culture is the differentiation between family roles and non-family roles (Triandis, Vassiliou, & Nassiakou, 1968). Such differentiation in the Greek culture can be learned by Americans trained with the assimilator. The results have not always been dramatic and more work needs to be done to fully understand what items are most effective. The culture assimilator helped teen-agers working in Central America to integrate the culture experience of those who had previously participated in the program (O'Brien, Fiedler, & Hewett, 1971).

One purpose of the culture assimilator is to be sure the individual makes the appropriate differentiations for the culture in which he is actively working. Inappropriate differentiations are likely to produce interpersonal tension. Incorrect differentiation with the critical incident approach was shown to result in unhappy endings for the members of the two cultures interacting.

As an additional sidelight, Indian and American graduate students were tested on a negotiation task. Beforehand, they received one of three kinds of training: culture assimilator, traditional training, and irrelevant training. Where Indians and Americans were trained with the culture assimilator, Indians judged the Americans more favorably than when the Americans were traditionally trained. The Americans' judgments about the group and negotiator did not show these differences, indicating that the Indians were more affected by the improved interpersonal knowledge than were the Americans (Nayer, Touzard, & Summers, 1968).

AN INTEGRATED APPROACH TO CROSS-CULTURAL ISSUES

It is commonplace to observe an employee stating a policy as if it were a universal one. Inquiry leads to the clarification that the employee is stating the policy of the firm to which he belongs. A strong determinant of his motivation, attitudes, beliefs, and behavior is his organizational affiliation. Some of this may be due to the selection of applicants who already share the organization's norms; more may be a consequence of socialization processes such as those described by Lieberman (1954). He showed that rank-and-file workers who are initially alike in attitudes gradually take on more pro-management attitudes after promotion to foreman, while those who become shop stewards gradually become more pro-union in outlook. When these foremen and stewards revert to the rank and file, their attitudes revert as well.

In the same way, we see that an individual worker's motivation, attitudes, beliefs, and behavior are associated with his cultural and national affiliation. Again, he may see his ideology as universal. Nevertheless, the pattern of his values, beliefs, and behavior may be particular to the culture and nation to which he belongs.

The boundaries of the culture may be coterminous with those of the nation, or the culture may spill over into other countries, or a single nation may contain several cultures. Whether an effect is due to nation or culture is secondary to the attempt to isolate what dimensions of each are of consequence.

Several efforts to develop unifying dimensions of national and cultural differences of consequence to individual performance have been suggested. The following economic variables are likely to be particularly significant to the world of work: wealth, growth rate, and unemployment rate.

In wealthy countries, managers can afford to be considerate, can afford expensive training efforts, but cannot afford to waste labor.

On the other hand, in rapidly growing countries managers need to be particularly alert to new opportunities, need to exhibit a readiness for risk, and cannot afford to settle for old sub-optimal ways of coping with the environment. In countries with endemic high unemployment rates, managers can be more directive, less concerned about replacement of workers, or the costs of labor intensive activities.

Societal variables of consequence are likely to include homogeneity in the culture of the nation and the age composition of the society. In a pluralistic society, there are likely to be multiple answers to the same question and greater conflict of ideologies. A society with a larger than average number of people outside the working years, either too young or too old, has obvious consequences for resource allocation in the country. Psychological variables will be of consequence. When norms favor individualism, more overt conflict may be seen among managers and workers than where norms stress cooperation.

Despite the multitude of studies from diverse disciplines and the fragmentary nature of much of the research investigations, as a whole the literature on cross-national variations about man at work is of considerable utility to industrial and organizational psychologists. In fact, a true integration of all areas of industrial and organizational psychology requires cross-national extension, for as we have shown, propositions about man at work are sensitive to the culture to which he belongs. A full understanding of industrial and organizational processes requires our knowledge of how much we can and cannot generalize across cultures.

Typically, the industrial and organizational psychologist looks at both practical problems and research and theoretical issues from a relatively narrow perspective. Those in one firm usually examine a problem from the limited perspectives of that one firm. Academicians are equally limited. One investigator may be oriented to the selection problem, another to training, a third to motivation and leadership. While we may occasionally talk about it (Bass, 1968a), seldom do we try to integrate the various factors of selection, motivation, and training into either our theoretical or our practical solutions with the problems. A mere inspection of industrial performance in cultural settings where selection techniques have been outlawed or where merit is less important than tribal ties should have some salutary influence on such restricted thinking.

Most research in industrial and organizational psychology is done within one cultural context. This context puts constraints upon both our theories and our practical solutions to the organizational problems. Since we are seldom faced with a range and variation of our variables which adequately reflect the possibilities of human behavior, we tend to take a limited view of the field. We sometimes forget that the socialization process in any one culture tends to prepare members of that culture to play a viable part in the established economic structure. There is usually no conflict between the socialization process and the dominant economic structure of a country unless the social goals of the country change. This is most evidenced in developing countries where there may be a transition from the semi-feudalistic agricultural society to an industrialized society. This is when the industrial and organizational psychologist may face both his most challenging problems and the point where he may have the opportunity to be more productive and to integrate his knowledge from all the areas of industrial and organizational psychology.

Both in terms of theoretical research and as a solution to practical problems, the industrial and organizational psychologist needs to understand the socialization process within the culture in which he is working. He should have some feeling for the dominant values and aptitudes of the individuals in that culture. Beyond that, he should have some appreciation for the prevailing authority structure within the culture and how new economic structures may influence or change

this perspective. Within a major culture, there are often minor ones of consequence to a large proportion of the work force. The North European psychologist is likely to be dealing with transient workers from Italy, Portugal, or Turkey; the white American with black American workers; and the Old Australian with New Australians. In many of the developed countries of the world, and the United States in particular, the whole educational process is geared to producing individuals who have the required values, aptitudes, and skills to be a functional part of the organization of that country. In the United States, society is willing to subsidize an individual for over eighteen years of school, so that he may enter an industrial organization with a graduate degree in business. When we remove ourselves from the one-culture perspective, we can better understand the interactions between individual variables and the cultural environment in which the individual is embedded.

Our concepts, structures, and models may shift from culture to culture. Thus, in the case of selection, there is evidence that while the same constructs may be appropriate for predicting success in the same organization in different countries, the actual pattern of responses may be somewhat different (Cassens, 1966). A dramatic example can be given by asking individuals in Turkey and in the West Indies the same basic question, "Is your father alive or dead and if dead, how old were you when he died?" In Turkey, if an individual replied that his father died when he was young, this will be an indication that he was removed from the authoritarian control exerted by the father and he would probably be significantly higher on the need for achievement than an individual who was reared in a Turkish family where the father lived throughout the individual's youth. In contrast, in the West Indies, if an individual told us that his father died when he was young, we could infer that this individual would be fixated at a level which demanded fulfillment of security needs and he would probably not be very independent or aggressive. So in two different cultures, the very same biographical information leads us to two opposite predictions concerning the individual's potential success as an independent, achieving junior executive.

The work of Shaw (1965) in South Africa, demonstrating that high aptitude African bus drivers are frustrated and, therefore, more accident prone than less academically capable drivers, allows us to predict some of the dysfunctional aspects of the selection program where the opportunity is very limited for certain subsets of the population. The South African study graphically shows the importance of integrating both selection and training considerations and dysfunctional consequences of validation using an intermediate criterion of proficiency. There are many other oppressed groups in other nations where the findings of Shaw (1965) would allow us to make similar predictions.

The contrasting value systems of Poland and Yugoslavia allow us to make some predictions concerning the effect of an elitist value structure in a society and its effect on participation. In Poland, the demise of the workers' council may be attributed to the elitist philosophy, while the continuance of the participatory workers' council in Yugoslavia may be traced to more equalitarian attitudes prevailing in that society (Rawin, 1970).

These examples illustrate the point that there is a wide range of individual variations on variables of interest to industrial and organizational psychologists.

We know that some countries have a wider range of variations in perceptual style, interpersonal trust, and other dimensions than do others. Beyond that, certain nations have predominant numbers of individuals who bunch at one end or the other of the continuum. There is also an extreme range of organizational practices ranging from workers' councils to one-man autocratic control procedures. There is a range of technology in various countries which varies

from the handicraft, through the mechanical or assembly line, to the very automated or process controlled industries. Some countries will have a great mixture of technology; other countries will be relatively homogeneous. Some countries will have a long tradition of industrialization, while in other countries it will be a relatively new phenomenon with few individuals in the nation having factory experience. In a sense, what we have cross-nationally is a number of national experiments with a range of variations on variables of interest and with interactions occurring which would never be true in any one country. This would seem to present a tremendous opportunity for both theory and application.

A full understanding of man at work must begin within a given country with an examination of the national socialization patterns. (The nation in question may be highly fragmented so that a number of socialization patterns are operating at the same time.) Next must follow attention to institutions peculiar to the country. For instance, education may concentrate on preparation of a technical elite or it may promote universal literacy but not much more.

Individual traits that distinguish a nation may be viewed next. Are the modal attitudes traditional or modern? What are the predominant motives and needs of the individuals in the culture? Values? Perceptual styles? Educational qualifications? Intellectual functioning? Other similar attributes?

Once consideration has been given to individual attributes, then attention can be focused on the predominant technology: handicraft or unit, batch or mechanized, automated or process (Obradovic, 1970; Harvey, 1968; Woodward, 1965). With this information, we should be able to gain some idea of what are the organizational objectives, the predominant compensation policies, and other considerations which have to do with management functioning and control of the viable organization.

Both the individual and the organization are operating in a larger environmental context. Political processes and the state of economic development of the country as a whole may have a bearing upon how the individual and the organization are integrated. There is only a limited amount of research on the influence of socioeconomic indicators on individual behavior and much of that is methodologically suspect (Ajiferuke & Boddewyn, 1970; Barrett & Franke, 1970; Greenwood, 1971).

More reports like the Ruedi and Lawrence (1970) investigation of German and American plastics firms are required which deal with the nature of the task, task effectiveness, individual needs, culture, and organizational climate in a contingent relationship.

In essence, we are advocating a very large contingency model which takes into account a number of disparate elements. At least in the developing countries, the industrial and organizational psychologist has much more latitude to match the individual with the organization. In most of the developing countries, there is a plethora of labor and a favorable selection ratio. Individuals can be selected and trained to meet the technological demands of the organization, or the control structure of the organization can be modified and changed within the limits of technology to accommodate the special attributes of the individual selected and trained.

Industrial and organizational psychology suffers from the fact that it has not properly or operationally defined constructs, such as participation, attitudes, needs, achievement, or values in a standardized manner (Barrett, 1972). Thus, while one investigator may talk about "modern" attitudes, his instrument and the construct he employs may have no relationship to the other investigator's assertion that he is also measuring the same construct. We now have enough single variable studies to know that certain constructs do appear to be useful in understanding behavior in a cross-national context. What is now required is the combination of these various constructs into one instrument which can be administered to individuals from various cultures. Standardized instruments should also be developed for systematically assessing the various aspects of the functions in the organizations in which the individuals are going to be employed. At the individual job level, it will be important to go beyond the standard job description and job specifications to include attributes which we tend to take for granted; that is, in the United States we assume that all individuals can see three-dimensionality in pictures. In the same way, a standardized scheme should be developed for rating the chief environmental constraints of the nation as a whole. These would include economic, social, and medical.

Once we have these three sets of information, we can make more intelligent decisions concerning the optimization of the goals in the organization in which we are working.

In some respects, the literature in the cross-national field takes two different perspectives. A small number of studies have a definite theoretical base, a definite hypothesis to be tested. By far the broader group of studies compares responses of subjects from two or more countries showing similarities or differences on some standardized instrument. The weak part of all of these studies is that if differences are found it is never clear what the cause of the differences or similarities might be. In some ways, this is reminiscent of studies in epidemiology where differences are found in two locations and attempts are made to try to find the cause of these differences. There have not been enough studies to follow up and determine first, if the differences are reliable, and second, the reasons for the differences.

These differences are likely to be of broad concern to anyone involved in the study of man at work. But for the organizational psychologist, there are more subtle considerations. First, the psychologist himself ordinarily sees the world in terms of his own single culture and its values. For the modal American psychologist, individual initiative is good, reward is more effective than punishment, and power equalization is to be encouraged. But for industrial psychologists in other areas of the world—Japan, Western Europe, the U.S.S.R., China, Latin America, Africa, and India—it is doubtful if more than one of the three propositions would be supported in each location. If so, it would probably be a different one of the three in each location.

REFERENCES

Abegglen, J. C. *The Japanese factory: Aspects of its social organization.* Glencoe, Ill.: The Free Press, 1958.

Ajiferuke, M., & Boddewyn, J. Socioeconomic indicators in comparative management. *Administrative Science Quarterly,* 1970, 15, 453–458.

Alexander, R. A., Barrett, G. V., Bass, B. M., & Ryterband, E. C. Empathy, projection, and negation in seven countries. In L. E. Abt & B. F. Riess (Eds.), *Clinical psychology in industrial organization.* New York: Grune and Stratton, 1971, 29–49.

Amir, Y. Contact hypothesis in ethnic relations. *Psychological Bulletin,* 1969, 71, 319–342.

Andrews, J. D. W. The achievement motive and advancement in two types of organizations. *Journal of Personality and Social Psychology,* 1967, 6, 163–168.

Angelini, A. L. Measuring the achievement motive in Brazil. *Journal of Social Psychology,* 1966, 68, 35–44.

Anon. Russia sets programs of wage incentives in scientific work. *The Wall Street Journal,* June 1, 1970, 12.

Anon. Notes for the corporate nomad: Learning languages. *Fortune,* March, 1971, 42.

Argyle, M., & Robinson, P. Two origins of achievement motivation. *British Journal of Social and Clinical Psychology,* 1962, 1, 107–120.

Aronoff, J. *Psychological needs and cultural systems.* Princeton: Van Nostrand, 1967.

Aronoff, J. Psychological needs as a determination in the formation of economic structures: A confirmation. *Human Relations,* 1970, 23, 123–138.

Aronoff, J., & Messe, L. A. Motivational determinants of small-group structure. *Journal of Personality and Social Psychology,* 1971, 17, 319–324.

Asch, S. E. Studies of independence and conformity: I. A minority of one against a unanimous majority. *Psychological Monographs,* 1956, 70, 1–70.

Auclair, G. Managerial role conflict: A cross-cultural comparison. Paper presented at 76th Annual Convention, American Psychological Association, San Francisco, September, 1968.

Baker, J. C., & Ivancevich, J. M. Multi-national management staffing with American expatriates. *Economic and Business Bulletin,* 1970, 23 (11), 35–39.

Baker, J. C., & Ivancevich, J. M. The assignment of American executives abroad: Systematic, haphazard, or chaotic. *California Management Review,* 1971, 13, 39–44.

Barrett, G. V. The international research groups on management information systems. In J. Blood Jr. (Ed.), *Management science in planning.* New York: TAPPI (Technical Association of the Pulp and Paper Industry), 1969, 271–287.

Barrett, G. V. New research models of the future for industrial and organizational psychology. *Personnel Psychology,* 1972, 25, 1–17.

Barrett, G. V., & Alexander, R. A. Estimates of equitable salary based upon merit and nonmerit consideration increases: A cross-national comparison. Technical Report 77, ONR Contract N00014-67(A), University of Rochester, Management Research Center, Rochester, N.Y., June, 1973.

Barrett, G. V., & Bass, B. M. Comparative surveys of managerial attitudes and behavior. In J. Boddewyn (Ed.), *Comparative management: Teaching, training, and research.* New York: Graduate School of Business Administration, New York University, 1970, 179–217.

Barrett, G. V., & Franke, R. H. Communication preference and performance: A cross-cultural comparison. *Proceedings, 77th Annual Convention, American Psychological Association,* 1969, 597–598.

Barrett, G. V., & Franke, R. H. "Psychogenic death": A reappraisal. *Science,* 1970, 167, 304–306.

Barrett, G. V., & Franke, R. H. Motives and national development. Unpublished paper,

Management Research Center, University of Rochester, Rochester, N.Y., 1971.

Barrett, G. V., & Thornton, C. L. Cognitive style differences between engineers and college students. *Perceptual and Motor Skills,* 1967, 25, 789–793.

Barry, H. Cross-cultural research with matched pairs of societies. *Journal of Social Psychology,* 1969, 79, 25–33.

Barry, H., Bacon, M. K., & Child, I. L. A cross-cultural survey of some sex differences in socialization. *Journal of Abnormal and Social Psychology,* 1957, 55, 327–332.

Barry, H., Child, I., & Bacon, M. K. Relation of child training to subsistence economy. *American Anthropologist,* 1959, 61, 51–63.

Bass, B. M. Social behavior and the orientation inventory: A review. *Psychological Bulletin,* 1967, 68, 260–292. (a)

Bass, B. M. Use of exercises for management and organizational psychology. *Training and Development Journal,* 1967, 21 (4), 2–7. (b)

Bass, B. M. The interface between personnel and organizational psychology. *Journal of Applied Psychology,* 1968, 52, 81–88. (a)

Bass, B. M. A preliminary report on manifest preferences in six cultures for participative management. Technical Report 21, ONR Contract N00014-67(A), University of Rochester, Management Research Center, Rochester, N.Y., June, 1968. (b)

Bass, B. M. When planning for others. *Journal of Applied Behavioral Science,* 1970, 6, 151–171.

Bass, B. M., & Thiagarajan, K. M. Differential preferences for long versus short term payoffs in India and the United States. Sixteenth International Congress of Applied Psychology, Amsterdam, Netherlands, August 18–22, 1968.

Beer, M. Needs and need satisfaction among clerical workers in complex and routine jobs. *Personnel Psychology,* 1968, 21, 209–222.

Belli, P. The economic implications of malnutrition: The dismal science revisited. *Economic Development and Cultural Change,* 1971, 20, 1–23.

Berry, J. W. Temne and Eskimo perceptual skills. *International Journal of Psychology,* 1966, 1, 207–229.

Berry, J. W. Independence and conformity in subsistence-level societies. *Journal of Personality and Social Psychology,* 1967, 7, 415–418.

Berry, J. W. On cross-cultural comparability. *International Journal of Psychology,* 1969, 4, 119–128.

Biesheuvel, S. The measurement of occupational aptitudes in a multi-racial society. *Occupational Psychology,* 1954, 28, 189–196.

Boddewyn, J., & Nath, R. Comparative management studies: An assessment. *Management International Review,* 1970, 10, 3–11.

Bradburn, N. M. *N* achievement and father dominance in Turkey. *Journal of Abnormal and Social Psychology,* 1963, 67, 464–468.

Bradburn, N. M., & Berlew, D. E. Need for achievement and English industrial growth. *Economic Development and Cultural Change,* 1961, 10, 8–20.

Braun, J. R. Search for correlates of self-actualization. *Perceptual and Motor Skills,* 1969, 28, 557–558.

Brein, M., & David, K. H. Intercultural communication and the adjustment of the sojourner. *Psychological Bulletin,* 1971, 76, 215–230.

Brigham, J. C. Ethnic stereotypes. *Psychological Bulletin,* 1971, 76, 15–38.

Brown, R. W., & Lenneberg, E. H. A study in language and cognition. *Journal of Abnormal and Social Psychology,* 1954, 49, 454–462.

Cansever, G. The achievement motive in Turkish adolescents. *Journal of Social Psychology,* 1968, 76, 269–270.

Carroll, J. B., & Sapon, S. M. *Modern language aptitude test manual.* New York: The Psychological Corporation, 1959.

Cassens, F. P. Cross-cultural dimensions of executive life history antecedents (biographical information). Dissertation published by the Creativity Research Institute of The Richardson Foundation, February, 1966.

Chaney, F. B. A cross-cultural study of industrial research performance. *Journal of Applied Psychology,* 1966, 50, 206–210.

Clark, A. W., & McCabe, S. Leadership beliefs of Australian managers. *Journal of Applied Psychology,* 1970, 54, 1–6.

Cole, R. E. *Japanese blue collar: The changing tradition.* Berkeley: University of California Press, 1971.

Corlett, E. N. Efficient labor utilization in a developing country. *Human Factors,* 1970, 12, 499–501.

Cortes, J. B. The achievement motive in the Spanish economy between the 13th and 18th centuries. *Economic Development and Cultural Change,* 1961, 9, 144–163.

Crockett, H. J. The achievement motive and differential occupational mobility in the United States. *American Sociological Review,* 1962, 27, 191–204.

Cullen, J. F., Harper, C. R., & Kidera, G. J. Perceptual style differences between airplane pilots and engineers. *Aerospace Medicine,* 1969, 4, 407–408.

Cummin, P. C. TAT correlates of executive performance. *Journal of Applied Psychology,* 1967, 51, 78–81.

Cummings, L. L., & Schmidt, S. M. Managerial attitudes of Greeks: The roles of culture and industrialization. *Administrative Science Quarterly,* 1972, 17, 265–272.

Dawson, J. L. M. Traditional values and work efficiency in a West African mine labor force. *Occupational Psychology,* 1963, 37, 209–218.

Dawson, J. L. M. Cultural and physiological influences upon spatial-perceptual processes in West Africa: Part I. *International Journal of Psychology,* 1967, 2, 115–128. (a)

Dawson, J. L. M. Cultural and physiological influences upon spatial-perceptual process in West Africa: Part II. *International Journal of Psychology,* 1967, 2, 171–185. (b)

Dawson, J. L. M. Traditional versus western attitudes in West Africa: The construction, validation, and application of a measuring device. *British Journal of Social and Clinical Psychology,* 1967, 6, 81–96. (c)

Dawson, J. L. M. Attitudinal consistency and conflict in West Africa. *International Journal of Psychology,* 1969, 4, 39–53. (a)

Dawson, J. L. M. Attitude change and conflict among Australian aborigines. *Australian Journal of Psychology,* 1969, 21, 101–116. (b)

Dawson, J. L. M. Theoretical and research bases of bio-social psychology. *University of Hong Kong Supplement to the Gazette,* 1969, 16 (3), 1–10. (c)

Dawson, J. L. M., Law, H., Leung, A., & Whitney, R. E. Scaling Chinese traditional-modern attitudes and the GSR measurement of "important" versus "unimportant" Chinese concepts. *Journal of Cross-Cultural Psychology,* 1971, 2, 1–27.

deCharms, R., & Moeller, G. H. Values expressed in American children's readers: 1800–1950. *Journal of Abnormal and Social Psychology,* 1962, 64, 136–142.

Denison, E. F. *Why growth rates differ: Postwar experience in nine western countries.* Washington: The Brookings Institution, 1967.

Elder, G. H. Achievement motivation and intelligence in occupational mobility: A longitudinal analysis. *Sociometry,* 1968, 31, 327–354.

England, G. W. Personal value systems of American managers. *Academy of Management Journal,* 1967, 10, 53–68.

England, G. W. Personal value system analysis as an aid to understanding organizational behavior: A comparative study in Japan, Korea, and the United States. Presented at Exchange Seminar on Comparative Organizations, Amsterdam, Netherlands, March 23–27, 1970.

England, G. W., & Koike, R. Personal value systems of Japanese managers. *Journal of Cross-Cultural Psychology,* 1970, 1, 21–40.

England, G. W., & Lee, R. Organization size as an influence on perceived organizational goals: A comparative study among American, Japanese, and Korean managers. Center for Comparative Studies in Technological Development and Social Change, 1972.

Estafen, B. D. System transfer characteristics: An experimental model for comparative management research. *Management International Review,* 1970, 10 (2–3), 21–34.

Ezekiel, S. The personal future and Peace Corps competence. *Journal of Personality and Social Psychology,* Monograph Supplement, 1968, 8, No. 2, Part 2, 1–26.

Farmer, R. N., & Richman, B. M. A model for research in comparative management. *California Management Review,* 1964, 1 (2), 55–68.

Farmer, R. N., & Richman, B. M. *Comparative management and economic progress.* Homewood, Ill.: Irwin, 1965.

Farris, G. F. The distribution of control in some Brazilian organizations. Paper presented at the 79th Annual Convention of the American Psychological Association, Washington, D.C., September, 1971.

Feld, S. C. Longitudinal study of the origins of achievement strivings. *Journal of Personality and Social Psychology,* 1967, 7, 408–414.

Fiedler, F. E., Mitchell, T., & Triandis, H. C. The culture assimilator: An approach to cross-cultural training. *Journal of Applied Psychology,* 1971, 55, 95–102.

Filella, J. F. Exercise life goals: Guess-work or interpersonal perception. *Experimental Publication System,* April, 1971, 11, No. 405–12.

Foa, U. G. Relation of workers' expectations to satisfaction with supervisor. *Personnel Psychology,* 1957, 10, 161–168.

Frager, R. Conformity and anti-conformity in Japan. *Journal of Personality and Social Psychology,* 1970, 15, 203–210.

Franke, R. H., & Barrett, G. V. The economic implications of malnutrition: Comment. *Economic Development and Cultural Change,* 1975, 23, 75–79.

Frederiksen, H. Feedbacks in economic and demographic transition. *Science,* 1969, 166, 837–847.

Frijda, N., & Jahoda, G. On the scope and methods of cross-cultural research. *International Journal of Psychology,* 1966, 1, 109–127.

Frost, E. What industry wants and does not want from the psychologist. *Journal of Applied Psychology,* 1920, 4, 18–24.

Frye, R. *Analysis of patterns of life history antecedents of executives from different countries.* Greensboro, N.C.: Creativity Research Institute of The Richardson Foundation, 1967.

Garth, T. R., Ikeda, K., & Gardner, D. A. Japanese work curves. *Journal of Applied Psychology,* 1933, 17, 331–336.

Gellerman, S. W. Passivity, paranoia, and "pakikisana." *Columbia Journal of World Business,* September-October, 1967, 59–66.

Granick, D. *The red executive.* Garden City, N.Y.: Doubleday, 1960.

Greenwood, J. M. Group attitudes and organizational performance. Paper presented at 78th Annual Convention of the American Psychological Association, Miami, September, 1971.

Gullahorn, J. E., & Gullahorn, J. T. American students abroad: Professional versus personal development. *The Annals,* 1966, 368, 43–59.

Gullahorn, J. T., & Gullahorn, J. E. An extension of the U-curve hypothesis. *The Journal of Social Issues,* 1963, 19, 33–47.

Hagen, E. E. *On the theory of social change.* Homewood, Ill.: Dorsey Press, 1962.

Haire, M., Ghiselli, E. E., & Porter, L. W. *Managerial thinking: An international study.* New York: Wiley, 1966.

Hall, D. J., deBettignies, H. C., & Amado-Fischgrund, G. The European business elite: An exclusive survey in six European countries. *European Business,* 1969, 23, 52–61.

Hall, D. T., & Nougaim, K. E. An examination of Maslow's need hierarchy in an organizational setting. *Organizational Behavior and Human Performance,* 1968, 3, 12–35.

Harbison, F., & Myers, C. *Management in the industrial world.* New York: McGraw-Hill, 1959.

Hare, A. P. Factors associated with Peace Corps volunteer success in Philippines. *Human Organization,* 1966, 25, 150–153.

Harvey, E. Technology and the structure of organizations. *American Sociological Review,* 1968, 33, 247–259.

Heller, F. A. The role of business management in relation to economic development. *International Journal of Comparative Sociology,* 1969, 10, 292–298.

Heller, F. A. Research on managerial skills and decision making: Phase II. Unpublished paper, 1971.

Heller, F. A., & Porter, L. W. Perceptions of managerial needs and skills in two national samples. *Occupational Psychology,* 1966, 40, 1–13.

Herzberg, F. Job attitudes in the Soviet Union. *Personnel Psychology,* 1965, 18, 245–252. (a)

Herzberg, F. The motivation to work among Finnish supervisors. *Personnel Psychology,* 1965, 18, 393–402. (b)

Herzberg, F. *Work and the nature of man.* Cleveland: World Publishing, 1966.

Hesseling, P., & Konnen, E. E. Culture and subculture in a decision-making exercise. *Human Relations,* 1969, 22, 31–51.

Holtzman, W. H. Cross-cultural research on personality development. *Human Development,* 1965, 8, 65–86.

Hudson, W. The study of the problem of pictorial perception among unacculturated groups. *International Journal of Psychology,* 1967, 2, 90–107.

Inkeles, A. Industrial man: The relation of status to experience, perception, and value. *The American Journal of Sociology,* 1960, 66, 1–31.

Irvine, S. H. Adapting tests to the cultural setting: A comment. *Occupational Psychology,* 1965, 39, 13–23.

Irvine, S. H. Factor analysis of African abilities

and attainments: Constructs across cultures. *Psychological Bulletin,* 1969, 71, 20–32.

Ivancevich, J. M. Perceived need satisfactions of domestic versus overseas managers. *Journal of Applied Psychology,* 1969, 53, 274–278.

Ivancevich, J. M., & Baker, J. C. A comparative study of the satisfaction of domestic United States managers and overseas United States managers. *Academy of Management Journal,* 1970, 13, 69–77.

Jacobson, E., Kumata, H., & Gullahorn, J. E. Cross-cultural contributions to attitude research. *Public Opinion Quarterly,* 1960, 24, 205–223.

Kagitcibasi, C. Social norms and authoritarianism: A Turkish-American comparison. *Journal of Personality and Social Psychology,* 1970, 16, 444–451.

Kahn, H. *The emerging Japanese superstate.* Englewood Cliffs, N.J.: Prentice-Hall, 1970.

Katona, G., Strumpel, B., & Zahn, E. *Aspirations and affluence.* New York: McGraw-Hill, 1971.

Kavčič, B., Rus, V., & Tannenbaum, A. J. Control, participation, and effectiveness in four Yugoslav industrial organizations. *Administrative Science Quarterly,* 1971, 16, 74–86.

Kerkhoven, C. L. M. The cost price of food calories for heavy work. *Ergonomics,* 1962, 5, 53–65.

Knapp, R. H., & Garbutt, J. T. Time imagery and the achievement motive. *Journal of Personality,* 1958, 26, 426–434.

Knapp, R. H., & Garbutt, J. T. Variation in time descriptions and need achievement. *The Journal of Social Psychology,* 1965, 67, 269–272.

Kock, S. E. *Foeretagsledgning och motivation (management and motivation).* Helsingfors: Affaersekonomisk Foerlagsfoerening, 1965.

Lambert, W. E., & Klineberg, O. Cultural comparisons of boys' occupational aspirations. *British Journal of Social and Clinical Psychology,* 1963, 3, 56–65.

Laurent, H. Cross-cultural, cross-validation of empirically validated tests. *Journal of Applied Psychology,* 1970, 54, 417–423.

Lazarus, S., & Barrett, G. V. National clusters of managers' life goals. Unpublished paper, University of Rochester, Management Research Center, Rochester, N.Y., 1971.

Lee, J. A. Developing managers in developing countries. *Harvard Business Review,* 1968, 46 (6), 55–65.

LeVine, R. *Dreams and deeds: Achievement motivation in Nigeria.* Chicago: University of Chicago Press, 1966.

Lichtman, C. M. Some intrapersonal response correlates of organizational rank. *Journal of Applied Psychology,* 1970, 54, 77–80.

Lieberman, S. The relationship between attitudes and roles: A natural field experiment. *American Psychologist,* 1954, 8, 418–419.

Lippitt, R., & White, R. K. An experimental study of leadership and group life. In E. E. Maccoby, T. M. Newcomb, & E. E. Hartley (Eds.), *Readings in social psychology.* (3rd ed.) New York: Holt, Rinehart and Winston, 1958, 496–510.

Littig, L. W., & Yeracaris, C. A. Achievement motivation and intergenerational occupational mobility. *Journal of Personality and Social Psychology,* 1965, 1, 386–389.

Lovegrove, M. N. Problems of educational selection and assessment in developing countries. *Proceedings of the Sixteenth International Congress of Applied Psychology.* Amsterdam: Swets and Zeitlinger, 1969, 782–787.

Lubar, R. The challenge of multinational business. *Fortune,* 1969, 80 (1), 73–74.

Lysgaard, S. Adjustment in a foreign society: Norwegian Fulbright grantees visiting the United States. *International Social Science Bulletin,* 1955, 7, 45–51.

MacArthur, R. Sex differences in field dependence for the Eskimo: Replication of Berry's findings. *International Journal of Psychology,* 1967, 2, 139–140.

McClelland, D. C. *The achieving society.* Princeton: Van Nostrand, 1961.

McClelland, D. C. *N* achievement and entrepreneurship: A longitudinal study. *Journal of Personality and Social Psychology,* 1965, 1, 389–392.

McClelland, D. C. Does education accelerate economic growth? *Economic Development and Cultural Change,* 1966, 14, 257–278. (a)

McClelland, D. C. Longitudinal trends in the relation of thought to action. *Journal of Consulting Psychology,* 1966, 30, 479–483. (b)

McClelland, D. C., & Winter, D. G. *Motivating economic achievement.* New York: The Free Press, 1969.

McGrew, W. W. Litton's "noble experiment."

Columbia Journal of World Business, 1972, 7 (1), 65–75.

Maier, N. R. F., & Hoffman, L. R. Group decision in England and the United States. *Personnel Psychology,* 1962, 15, 75–87.

Mann, C. K. Sears, Roebuck de Mexico: A cross-cultural analysis. *Social Science,* June, 1965, 149–157.

Marsh, R. M., & Mannari, H. Lifetime commitment in Japan: Roles, norms, and values. *American Journal of Sociology,* 1971, 76, 795–812.

Maslow, A. H. *Motivation and personality.* New York: Harper and Brothers, 1954.

Maslow, A. H., & Honigmann, J. J. Synergy: Some notes of Ruth Benedict. *American Anthropologist,* 1970, 72, 320–333.

Meade, R. D. Achievement: Achievement motivation and psychological time. *Journal of Personality and Social Psychology,* 1966, 4, 577–580.

Meade, R. D. An experimental study of leadership in India. *Journal of Social Psychology,* 1967, 72, 35–43.

Meade, R. D. Future time perspective of college students in America and in India. *Journal of Social Psychology,* 1971, 83, 175–182.

Meade, R. D., & Singh, L. Motivation and progress effects on psychological time in subcultures of India. *Journal of Social Psychology,* 1970, 80, 3–10.

Meade, R. D., & Whittaker, J. D. A cross-cultural study of authoritarianism. *Journal of Social Psychology,* 1967, 72, 3–7.

Meyer, H. H., & Walker, W. B. Need for achievement and risk preferences as they relate to attitudes toward reward systems and performance appraisal in an industrial setting. *Journal of Applied Psychology,* 1961, 45, 251–256.

Meyers, H. H., Walker, W. B., & Litwin, G. H. Motive patterns and risk preferences associated with entrepreneurship. *Journal of Abnormal and Social Psychology,* 1961, 63, 570–574.

Mischel, W. Delay of gratification, need for achievement, and acquiescence in another culture. *Journal of Abnormal and Social Psychology,* 1961, 62, 543–552.

Mischel, W. Predicting the success of Peace Corps volunteers in Nigeria. *Journal of Personality and Social Psychology,* 1965, 1, 510–517.

Misumi, J., & Seki, F. Effects of achievement motivation on the effectiveness of leadership patterns. *Administrative Science Quarterly,* 1971, 16, 51–59.

Morsbach, H. A cross-cultural study of achievement motivation and achievement values in two South African groups. *Journal of Social Psychology,* 1969, 79, 267–268.

Moss, H. A., & Kagan, J. The stability of achievement and recognition seeking behavior from childhood to adulthood. *Journal of Abnormal and Social Psychology,* 1961, 62, 504–513.

Mouton, J., & Blake, R. Issues in transnational organization development. In B. M. Bass, R. Cooper, & J. A. Haas (Eds.), *Managing for accomplishment.* Boston: D. C. Heath, 1970, 208–224.

Mozina, S. Management opinion on satisfaction and importance of psychosocial needs in their jobs. *Proceedings, Sixteenth International Congress of Applied Psychology.* Amsterdam: Swets and Zeitlinger, 1969, 788–794.

Mulder, M. Power equalization through participation? *Administrative Science Quarterly,* 1971, 16, 31–38.

Naroll, R. Some thoughts on comparative method in cultural anthropology. In H. M. Blalock & A. B. Blalock (Eds.), *Methodology in social research.* New York: McGraw-Hill, 1968, 236–277.

Nath, R. A methodological review of cross-cultural management research. In J. Boddewyn (Ed.), *Comparative management and marketing.* Glenview, Ill.: Scott, Foresman, 1969, 195–222.

Nayer, E. S. K., Touzard, H., & Summers, D. A. Training, tasks, and mediator orientation in heterocultural negotiations. *Human Relations,* 1968, 21, 283–294.

Negandhi, A. R., & Prasad, S. B. *Comparative management.* New York: Appleton-Century-Crofts, 1971.

Obradovic, J. Participation and work attitudes in Yugoslavia. *Industrial Relations,* 1970, 9, 161–169.

Obradovic, J., French, J. R. P., & Rodgers, W. L. Workers' councils in Yugoslavia. *Human Relations,* 1970, 23, 459–471.

O'Brien, G. E., Fiedler, E. F., & Hewett, T. T. The effects of programmed culture: Training upon the performance of volunteer medical teams in Central America. *Human Relations,* 1971, 24, 209–231.

Padaki, V., & Dolke, A. M. Two factors revisited. *Experimental Publication System,* October, 1970, 8, No. 272-2.

Parsons, T., & Shils, E. A., Eds. *Toward a general theory of action.* Cambridge: Harvard University Press, 1959.

Perrow, C. A framework for the comparative analysis of organizations. *American Sociological Review,* 1967, 32, 194–208.

Porter, L. W. A study of perceived need satisfactions in bottom and middle management jobs. *Journal of Applied Psychology,* 1961, 45, 1–10.

Preale, I., Amir, Y., & Singer, S. S. Perceptual articulation and task effectiveness in several Israel subcultures. *Journal of Personality and Social Psychology,* 1970, 15, 190–195.

Purcer-Smith, G. Studies of international mobility. Paper presented at the 78th Annual Convention of the American Psychological Association, Miami, September, 1970.

Rawin, S. J. Social values and the managerial structure: The case of Yugoslavia and Poland. *Journal of Comparative Administration,* 1970, 2, 131–159.

Roberts, K. H. On looking at an elephant: An evaluation of cross-cultural research related to organizations. *Psychological Bulletin,* 1970, 74, 327–350.

Rosen, B. C. Socialization and achievement motivation in Brazil. *American Sociological Review,* 1962, 27, 612–624.

Rosen, B. C. The achievement syndrome and economic growth in Brazil. *Social Forces,* 1964, 42, 341–354.

Ruedi, A., & Lawrence, P. R. Organizations in two cultures. In J. W. Lorsch & P. R. Lawrence (Eds.), *Studies in organizational design.* Homewood, Ill.: Irwin, 1970, 54–83.

Rus, V. Influence structure in Yugoslav enterprise. *Industrial Relations,* 1970, 9, 148–160.

Ryterband, E. C., & Barrett, G. V. Managers' values and their relationship to the management of tasks: A cross-cultural comparison. In B. M. Bass, R. Cooper, & J. A. Haas (Eds.), *Managing for accomplishment.* Lexington, Mass.: D. C. Heath, 1970, 226–261.

Sadler, P. J. Leadership style, confidence in management, and job satisfaction. *Journal of Applied Behavioral Science,* 1970, 6, 3–19.

Sadler, P. J., & Hofstede, G. H. Leadership styles, preferences, and perceptions of employees of an international company in different countries. *Mens En Onderneming,* 1972, 26, 43–63.

Sawyer, J. Dimensions of nations: Size, wealth, and politics. *American Journal of Sociology,* 1967, 73, 145–172.

Schaninger, M., Barrett, G. V., & Alexander, R. A. National, organizational, and individual correlates of simulated decision making. Technical Report 65, ONR Contract N00014-67 (A), University of Rochester, Management Research Center, Rochester, N.Y., 1973.

Scheuch, E. K. Cross-national comparisons using aggregate data: Some substantive and methodological problems. In R. L. Merritt & S. Rokkan (Eds.), *Comparing nations: The use of quantitative data in cross-national research.* New Haven: Yale University Press, 1966, 131–168.

Schollhammer, H. The comparative management theory jungle. *The Academy of Management Journal,* 1969, 12, 81–97.

Schregle, J. Forms of participation in management. *Industrial Relations,* 1970, 9, 117–122.

Schwarz, P. A. Adapting tests to the cultural setting. *Educational and Psychological Measurement,* 1963, 23, 673–686.

Schwarz, P. A., & Schwarz, J. M. Aptitude tests for the developing nations. American Institute for Research, Project C-34, Contract Nonr ICAc-1434, International Administration, August, 1961.

Segall, M. H., Campbell, D. T., & Herskovits, M. J. Cultural differences in the perception of geometric illusions. *Science,* 1963, 139, 769–771.

Senner, E. E. Trust as a measure of the impact of cultural differences on individual behavior in organizations. Paper presented at the 79th Annual Convention of the American Psychological Association, Washington, D.C., September, 1971.

Servan-Schreiber, J. J. *The American challenge.* New York: Atheneum, 1969.

Shaw, L. The practical use of projective personality tests as accident predictors. *Traffic Safety Research Review,* 1965, 9, 34–72.

Sheppard, H. L., & Belitsky, A. H. *The job hunt.* Baltimore, Md.: The Johns Hopkins Press, 1966.

Simon, H. A. Theories of decision making in economics and behavioral science. *American Economic Review,* 1959, 49, 253–283.

Simon, H. A. *The new science of management decision.* New York: Harper and Row, 1960.

Simonetti, S. H., & Weitz, J. Job satisfaction: Some cross-cultural effects. *Personnel Psychology*, 1972, 25, 107–118.

Singh, N. P. *n*/Ach among successful-unsuccessful and traditional-progressive agricultural entrepreneurs of Delhi. *Journal of Social Psychology*, 1969, 79, 271–272.

Singh, N. P. *n*/Ach among agricultural and business entrepreneurs of Delhi. *Journal of Social Psychology*, 1970, 81, 145–149.

Singh, N. P., & Wherry, R. J. Ranking of job factors by factory workers in India. *Personnel Psychology*, 1963, 16, 29–33.

Sirota, D. International survey of job goals and beliefs. Paper presented at 16th International Congress of Applied Psychology, Amsterdam, Netherlands, 1968.

Sirota, D., & Greenwood, J. M. Understand your overseas work force. *Harvard Business Review*, January-February, 1971, 53–60.

Skolnick, A. Motivational imagery and behavior over twenty years. *Journal of Consulting Psychology*, 1966, 30, 463–478.

Slocum, J. W. A comparative study of the satisfaction of American and Mexican operatives. *Academy of Management Journal*, 1971, 14, 89–97.

Smith, M. B. An analysis of two measures of "authoritarianism" among Peace Corps teachers. *Journal of Personality*, 1965, 33, 513–535.

Smith, M. C., & Pearn, M. A. The training of new commonwealth immigrants. A preliminary study, Industrial Training Research Unit, University College, London, unpublished manuscript, 1972.

Sommers, P. M., & Suits, D. B. A cross-section model of economic growth. *The Review of Economics and Statistics*, 1971, 80, 121–128.

Stagner, R. Corporate decision making: An empirical study. *Journal of Applied Psychology*, 1969, 53, 1–13.

Starbuck, W. H. The efficiency of British and American retail employees. *Administrative Science Quarterly*, 1966, 11, 345–385.

Stewart, E. C., & Pryle, J. B. Training for cross-cultural interaction. Paper presented at the annual meeting of the American Psychological Association, New York, September, 1966.

Strauss, G., & Rosenstein, E. Workers' participation: A critical view. *Industrial Relations*, 1970, 9, 197–214.

Strodtbeck, F. Considerations of meta-method in cross-cultural studies. *American Anthropologist*, 1964, 66, 223–229.

Tannenbaum, A. *Control in organizations*. New York: McGraw-Hill, 1968.

Tannenbaum, R., & Schmidt, W. H. How to choose a leadership pattern. *Harvard Business Review*, 1958, 36 (2), 95–101.

Tedeschi, J. T., & Kian, M. Cross-cultural study of the TAT assessment for achievement motivation: Americans and Persians. *Journal of Social Psychology*, 1962, 58, 227–234.

Thiagarajan, K. M. A cross-cultural study of the relationships between personal values and managerial behavior. Technical Report #23, University of Rochester, Management Research Center, Rochester, N.Y., 1968.

Thiagarajan, K. M., & Deep, S. D. A study of supervisor-subordinate influence and satisfaction in four cultures. *Journal of Social Psychology*, 1970, 82, 173–180.

Thornton, C. L., Barrett, G. V., & Davis, J. Field dependence and target identification. *Human Factors*, 1968, 10, 493–496.

Triandis, H. C. Factors affecting employee selection in two cultures. *Journal of Applied Psychology*, 1963, 47, 89–96.

Triandis, H. C. Interpersonal relations in international organizations. *Organizational Behavior and Human Performance*, 1967, 2, 26–55.

Triandis, H. C. *The analysis of subjective culture*. New York: Wiley-Interscience, 1972.

Triandis, H. C., & Vassiliou, V. Interpersonal influence and employee selection in two cultures. *Journal of Applied Psychology*, 1972, 56, 140–145.

Triandis, H. C., Vassiliou, V., & Nassiakou, M. Three cross-cultural studies of subjective culture. *Journal of Personality and Social Psychology Monograph Supplement*, 1968, 8 (4), Part 2.

Turner, J. H. Entrepreneurial environments and the emergency of achievement motivation in adolescent males. *Sociometry*, 1970, 33, 147–165.

Vansina, L. S., & Taillieu, T. Comparative study of the characteristics of Flemish graduates planning their careers in national or international organizations. In B. M. Bass, R. Cooper, & J. A. Haas (Eds.), *Managing for accomplishment*. Lexington, Mass.: D. C. Heath, 1970, 262–285.

Vernon, P. E. Ability factors and environmental influences. *American Psychologist,* 1965, 20, 723–733.

Vernon, P. E. *Intelligence and cultural environment.* London: Methuen, 1969.

Wainer, H. A., & Rubin, I. M. Motivation of research and development entrepreneurs: Determinants of company success. *Journal of Applied Psychology,* 1969, 53, 178–184.

Weaver, J. L. Value patterns of a Latin American bureaucracy. *Human Relations,* 1970, 23, 225–233.

Whitehill, A. M., & Takezawa, S. *The other worker.* Honolulu: East-West Center Press, 1968.

Whiting, J. W. M. Methods and problems in cross-cultural research. In G. Lindzey & E. Aronson (Eds.), *The handbook of social psychology,* Vol. 2. Reading, Mass.: Addison-Wesley, 1968, 693–728.

Whyte, W. F. Culture, industrial relations, and economic development: The case of Peru. *Industrial and Labor Relations Review,* 1963, 16, 583–593.

Whyte, W. F., & Williams, L. K. *Toward an integrated theory of development: Economic and noneconomic variables in rural development.* ILR Paperback No. 5, 1968.

Wilkins, M. *The emergence of multinational enterprises: American business abroad from the colonial era to 1914.* Cambridge: Harvard University Press, 1970.

Williams, L. K., Whyte, W. F., & Green, C. S. Do cultural differences affect workers' attitudes? *Industrial Relations,* 1966, 5, 110–117.

Winterbottom, M. R. The relation of need for achievement to learning experience in independence and mastery. In J. W. Atkinson (Ed.), *Motivation in fantasy, action, and society.* Princeton: Van Nostrand, 1958, 453–478.

Witkin, H. A. A cognitive-style approach to cross-cultural research. *International Journal of Psychology,* 1967, 2, 233–250.

Wober, M. Adapting Witkin's field independence theory to accommodate new information from Africa. *British Journal of Psychology,* 1967, 58, 29–38.

Wober, M. Adapting Dawson's traditional versus western attitudes scale and presenting some new information from Africa. *British Journal of Social and Clinical Psychology,* 1971, 10, 101–113.

Wofford, J. C. The motivational basis of job satisfaction and job performance. *Personnel Psychology,* 1971, 24, 501–518.

Woodward, J. *Industrial organization: Theory and practice.* London: Oxford University Press, 1965.

Zurcher, L. A. Particularism and organizational position: A cross-cultural analysis. *Journal of Applied Psychology,* 1968, 52, 139–144.

Zurcher, L. A., Meadow, A., & Zurcher, S. L. Value orientation, role conflict, and alienation from work: A cross-cultural study. *American Sociological Review,* 1965, 30, 539–548.

CREDITS AND ACKNOWLEDGMENTS

Acknowledgment is made to the following for their kind permission to reprint material from copyrighted sources:

Chapter 7

Figure 13: Her Majesty's Stationery Office (*A comparison of different shift systems in the glass trade,* by E. Farmer, in Report No. 24, Medical Research Council, Industrial Fatigue Research Board, 1924). Permission granted by Her Majesty's Stationery Office, London, England.

Figures 14 and 15: American Psychological Association ("Impact of employee participation in the development of pay incentive plans: A field experiment," by E. E. Lawler III and J. R. Hackman, in *Journal of Applied Psychology,* 1969). Copyright 1969 by the American Psychological Association. Reprinted by permission.

Figure 16: Sage Publications, Inc. (Modified from Figure 1 of "Determining the social effects of a legal reform: The British 'Breathalyser' crackdown of 1967," by H. L. Ross, D. T. Campbell, and G. V. Glass, in *American Behavioral Scientist,* Vol. 13, No. 4, March/April 1970, pp. 493–509). By permission of the Publisher, Sage Publications, Inc.

Figure 23: American Psychological Association ("Does intelligence cause achievement: A cross-lagged panel analysis," by W. D. Crano, D. A. Kenny, and D. T. Campbell, in *Journal of Educational Psychology,* 1972). Copyright 1972 by the American Psychological Association. Reprinted by permission.

Figure 25: American Psychological Association ("Does television violence cause aggression?" by L. D. Eron, L. R. Huesmann, M. M. Lefkowitz, and L. O. Walder, in *The American Psychologist,* 1972). Copyright 1972 by the American Psychological Association. Reprinted by permission.

Chapter 11

Table 9: American Psychological Association ("Work sampling for personnel selection," by J. E. Campion, in *Journal of Applied Psychology,* 1972). Copyright 1972 by the American Psychological Association. Reprinted by permission.

Key A: Harper & Row, Publishers, Inc. (*Essentials of psychological testing,* 3rd ed., by L. J. Cronbach, 1970). Permission granted by Harper & Row, Publishers, Inc.

Chapter 12

Table 1: John Wiley & Sons, Inc. (*The psychology of occupations,* by A. Roe, 1956). Permission granted by John Wiley & Sons, Inc.

Chapter 16

Figures 7, 8, and 20: International Communication Association ("Some relationships of mental aptitude, reading ability, and listening ability using normal and time compressed speech," by T. G. Sticht, in *Journal of Communication,* Vol. 18, 1968). Permission granted by the *Journal of Communication.*

Figure 9: McGraw-Hill Book Company (*Human engineering guide to equipment design,* by C. T. Morgan, J. S. Cook, A. Chapanis, and M. W. Lund, 1963). Copyright 1963 by McGraw-Hill Book Company. Used with permission of McGraw-Hill Book Company.

Figure 14: Johns Hopkins University Press ("Human engineering," by A. Chapanis, in C. D. Flagle, W. H. Higgins, and R. H. Roy, Eds., *Operations research and systems,* 1960). Permission granted by Johns Hopkins University Press.

Figures 17 and 18: John Wiley & Sons, Inc. (*Manual and automatic control,* by C. R. Kelley, 1968). Permission granted by John Wiley & Sons, Inc.

Table 4: American Psychological Association ("The effects of high intensity intermittent sound on performance, feeling, and physiology," by R. Plutchik, in *Psychological Bulletin,* 1959). Copyright 1959 by the American Psychological Association. Reprinted by permission.

Chapter 18

Figure 2: Macmillan Publishing Co., Inc. ("Personnel selection and job placement of the disadvantaged: Problems, issues, and suggestions," by M. D. Dunnette, in H. L. Fromkin, Ed., *Integrating the organization,* 1974). Copyright 1974 by Macmillan Publishing Co., Inc. Reprinted by permission.

Figure 3 and Table 1: John Wiley & Sons, Inc. (*The validity of occupational aptitude tests,* by E. E. Ghiselli, 1966). Permission granted by John Wiley & Sons, Inc.

Figure 5: American Psychological Association ("Methodological considerations relevant to discrimination in employment testing," by H. J. Einhorn and A. R. Bass, in *Psychological Bulletin,* 1971). Copyright 1971 by the American Psychological Association. Reprinted by permission.

Chapter 26

Figure 2: *Administrative Science Quarterly* ("The context of organization structures," by D. S. Pugh, D. J. Hickson, C. R. Hinings, and C. Turner, in *Administrative Science Quarterly,* 1969). Permission granted by *Administrative Science Quarterly.*

Figures 4 and 5: Plenum Publishing Corp. ("Organizational size and membership participation: Some empirical tests of alternative explanations," by B. P. Indik, in *Human Relations,* 1965). Permission granted by Plenum Publishing Corp.

Table 3: Basil Blackwell & Mott Ltd. ("A comparison of organization structure and managerial roles, Ohio, USA, and the Midlands, England," by J. H. Inkson, J. P. Schwitter, D. C. Pheysey, and D. J. Hickson, in *Journal of Management Studies,* 1970). Permission granted by Basil Blackwell & Mott Ltd.

Table 4: Plenum Publishing Corp. ("The Hemphill group dimensions description questionnaire: A British industrial application," by D. C. Pheysey and R. L. Payne, in *Human Relations,* 1970). Permission granted by Plenum Publishing Corp.

Table 5: Harvard University Press (*Motivation and organizational climate,* by G. H. Litwin and R. A. Stringer, 1968). Copyright © 1968 by the President and Fellows of Harvard College. Permission granted by Harvard University Press.

Table 8: Academic Press, Inc. ("Organizational climates and careers: The work lives of priests," by D. T. Hall and B. Schneider, in *Seminar Press,* 1973). Permission granted by Academic Press, Inc.

Table 9: John Wiley & Sons, Inc. (*People in context: Measuring person-environment congruence in education and industry,* by G. G. Stern, 1970). Permission granted by John Wiley & Sons, Inc.

Chapter 29

Figure 3: John Wiley & Sons, Inc. (*Organizations,* by J. G. March and H. A. Simon,

1958). Permission granted by John Wiley & Sons, Inc.

Figure 4 and Table 1: McGraw-Hill Book Company (*Pay and organizational effectiveness: A psychological view,* by E. E. Lawler, 1971). Copyright 1971 by McGraw-Hill Book Company. Used with permission of McGraw-Hill Book Company.

Chapter 30

Tables 1 and 2: American Psychological Association ("Satisfiers and dissatisfiers among white collar and blue collar employees," by E. A. Locke, in *Journal of Applied Psychology,* 1973). Copyright 1973 by the American Psychological Association. Reprinted by permission.

Table 3: *Organizational Behavior and Human Performance* ("A critique of Herzberg's incident classification system and a suggested revision," by J. Schneider and E. A. Locke, 1971). Permission granted by *Organizational Behavior and Human Performance.* American Psychological Association ("Satisfiers and dissatisfiers among white collar and blue collar employees," by E. A. Locke, in *Journal of Applied Psychology,* 1973). Copyright 1973 by the American Psychological Association. Reprinted by permission.

Table 6: Academic Press, Inc. ("Job satisfaction and job performance: A theoretical analysis," by E. A. Locke, in *Organizational Behavior and Human Performance,* 1970). Permission granted by Academic Press, Inc.

Chapter 33

Figure 2: The American Sociological Association ("Group norms and the active minority," by J. G. March, in *American Sociological Review,* 1954). Permission granted by the American Sociological Association.

Chapter 35

Table 1: Academic Press, Inc. ("Communication networks," by M. S. Shaw, in L. Berkowitz, Ed., *Advances in experimental social psychology,* 1964). Permission granted by Academic Press, Inc.

NAME INDEX

Abbott, P. S., 726
Abegglen, J. C., 1649, 1664
Abelson, H. I., 1430
Abelson, R. P., 420n, 424, 1403
Abrahams, N. M., 808
Acker, S. R., 766
Ackoff, R. L., 420, 1408, 1412, 1419
Adair, J. G., 440
Adams, J. S., 74, 105–106, 110, 169, 316, 449, 455, 1053, 1066, 1175–1198, 1321
Adams, R. N., 433n
Adamson, R. E., 1438
Adelberg, M., 1012, 1018
Adkins, W. R., 555
Adorno, T. W., 578, 593, 1403, 1598–1599
Aguilar, F. J., 1074n, 1081, 1095
Aiken, M., 1077, 1129, 1131, 1141, 1150, 1576–1577, 1613
Ajiferuke, M., 1677
Albert, R., 975
Albrecht, P. A., 874
Albrecht, R. E., 531, 586
Albright, D. W., 85, 91
Albright, L. E., 612, 619, 781, 797, 799
Alchian, A. A., 1105
Alderfer, C. P., 97–100, 156, 157n, 175, 177, 180–181, 945, 974–975, 1236, 1242, 1295, 1319, 1591–1634
Aldrich, H., 1139
Aleamoni, L. M., 382–383
Alexander, F., 592
Alexander, R. A., 1651–1654
Alf, E. F. Jr., 207, 805, 808
Alfred, T. M., 939, 971, 977
Alger, C. R., 421
Alland, A. Jr., 1105
Allen, T. J., 1562, 1572

Allen, V. L., 1476, 1481, 1483, 1485n, 1486, 1490, 1500–1501, 1503, 1506
Allport, F. H., 1476
Allport, G. W., 573, 576, 585, 609, 891, 896, 966, 1165, 1271, 1476, 1563, 1592, 1598
Alpert, M., 1406
Altman, H., 377
Altman, I., 488, 1391, 1594, 1604
Alutto, J. A., 383
Alvares, K. M., 453–454, 485, 1226, 1535
Alvarez, R., 1504
Amado-Fischgrund, G., 1668
Amir, Y., 440, 1607, 1666, 1672
Ammerman, H. L., 489, 670
Anastasi, A., 152–153, 471, 474–475, 478, 485, 488n, 511, 585, 618, 799, 816, 863, 1032
Anderson, B. B., 633
Anderson, C. W., 801
Anderson, H. E. Jr., 539
Anderson, H. H., 584
Anderson, J., 377
Anderson, J. A., 1563, 1566
Anderson, J. K., 997, 1009
Anderson, J. W., 972, 976
Anderson, L. R., 454, 1211, 1226
Anderson, L. S., 592
Anderson, T. H., 1130
Andretta, T., 872
Andrews, F. M., 288, 291, 1304, 1319, 1600
Andrews, I. R., 106–107
Andrews, J. D. W., 156, 1163, 1656
Angelini, A. L., 1656
Angel, J. L., 1010
Angell, D., 489
Angell, R. C., 400
Anglin, R. A., 1010
Angoff, W. H., 48

Porter, L. W., 1, 32, 78–80, 83, 85–87, 89, 92, 98–99, 111, 151, 442, 590, 754, 973–974, 1035, 1044, 1046, 1129–1130, 1158–1159, 1252, 1254, 1303, 1331n, 1332, 1335, 1459n, 1553–1585, 1641, 1651, 1660–1661, 1663, 1672

Posner, M. I., 1419

Posthuma, A. B., 534

Postman, L., 69, 1271, 1563

Poulton, E. C., 733

Powell, R. M., 997

Prange, A. J. Jr., 588

Prasad, S. B., 1662

Pratt, J., 268

Pratt, J. W., 1406, 1412, 1425, 1428

Preale, I., 1666

Prediger, D. J., 618

Premack, D., 72–73

Prentiss, R. J., 591

Presnall, L. P., 1016–1017

Pressey, S. L., 849, 1011

Preston, M. G., 1406

Pribram, K. H., 389, 1418

Price, J. L., 52, 367, 416

Price, L. A., 481

Price, P. S., 975

Prien, E. P., 487n, 748, 760, 1158

Primoff, E. S., 168, 690, 808

Prince, G. M., 1407

Pritchard, R. D., 15–16, 63–124, 316, 449, 455, 1053–1055, 1218, 1322

Pruitt, D. G., 914n, 1431, 1440

Pruyser, P., 1592, 1607

Pryle, J. B., 1673

Puckett, E. S., 921, 925, 977, 1616

Pugh, D. S., 154, 224, 1066, 1095, 1125–1169

Purcell, K., 396, 401

Purcell, T. V., 1013

Purcer-Smith, G., 1672

Pyle, W. C., 979, 1267

Quade, E. S., 1437

Qualls, D., 1105

Quarton, R. J., 269–271

Queen, S. A., 386, 392

Quinn, R. P., 102, 175, 958, 1008, 1140, 1205, 1319, 1328

Rabbie, J. M., 1494

Rabideau, G. F., 730

Rackham, J., 1249

Radhakrishnan, B. K., 359

Radloff, R., 616

Radlow, R., 1007

Radner, R., 1410–1411

Rahe, R. H., 592

Raiffa, H., 898n, 1406, 1412, 1425, 1428

Rajaratnam, N., 186, 188, 196, 198

Raju, N. S., 810

Ralph, C. A., 1421

Rambo, W. W., 763, 1531

Ramfalk, C. W., 800

Ramras, E. M., 654

Ramsey, F. P., 1442

Rand, A., 1303–1304, 1310, 1330, 1337

Rapoport, A., 42, 891, 905n, 908, 908n, 1180, 1409–1410, 1426, 1433

Rasch, G., 186

Rasch, P. J., 401

Ratner, H., 590

Raubenheimer, I., 808

Raush, H. L., 366

Raven, B. H., 445, 453, 903–904, 906–907, 913–914, 923, 1196, 1422, 1432n, 1577

Rawin, S. J., 1676

Rawls, D. J., 593, 621

Rawls, J. R., 593, 621

Ray, H. W., 314

Read, W. H., 1263, 1563, 1574–1575

Reavis, T. E., 967

Reed, L., 1302

Reed, L. E., 489

Rees, A., 268

Reeves, T. K., 1249

Regula, C. R., 435, 445, 451, 453

Rehmus, C., 911, 926

Reiley, A. C., 1555

Reimer, E., 256–257, 302, 319, 417, 1281

Reisberg, D. J., 763

Reisman, J. M., 401

Reisman, S. R., 435–436

Reitman, L. M., 378

Reitman, W. R., 1399

Reitz, H. J., 95

Remmers, H. H., 433n

Renner, K. E., 573

Resnick, L. G., 132, 137–138, 141, 145

Resnikoff, A., 522

Rest, S., 1302

Rettig, K., 400

Rezler, A. G., 550

Rhenman, E., 1085

Rhine, J., 1486

Rhode, J. G., 1267

Rice, A. K., 58, 939, 972, 974, 1180, 1592, 1608, 1619, 1630, 1632

SUBJECT INDEX